MURRAY ON CONTRACTS

MURRAY ON CONTRACTS

FIFTH EDITION

JOHN EDWARD MURRAY, JR.
Chancellor
Professor of Law
Duquesne University

Library of Congress Cataloging-in-Publication Data

Murray, John Edward.
   Murray on contracts / John Edward Murray, Jr. -- 5th ed.
     p. cm.
   Includes index.
   ISBN 978-1-4224-8155-4 (hardbound)
  1. Contracts--United States--Cases. I. Title.
   KF801.M87 2011
   346.7302--dc23

2011032246

This publication is designed to provide accurate and authoritative information in regard to the subject matter covered. It is sold with the understanding that the publisher is not engaged in rendering legal, accounting, or other professional services. If legal advice or other expert assistance is required, the services of a competent professional should be sought.

LexisNexis and the Knowledge Burst logo are registered trademarks and Michie is a trademark of Reed Elsevier Properties Inc., used under license. Matthew Bender and the Matthew Bender Flame Design are registered trademarks of Matthew Bender Properties Inc.

NOTE TO USERS

To ensure that you are using the latest materials available in this area, please be sure to periodically check the LexisNexis Law School web site for downloadable updates and supplements at www.lexisnexis.com/lawschool.

Editorial Offices
121 Chanlon Rd., New Providence, NJ 07974 (908) 464-6800
201 Mission St., San Francisco, CA 94105-1831 (415) 908-3200
www.lexisnexis.com

MATTHEW◆BENDER

(2011–Pub.3089)

PREFACE

Like the previous edition, the fifth edition of this treatise responds to numerous challenges. Thousands of new cases evidence the vitality in the law of contracts. Many of these cases are discussed or cited in this edition, not because they are new, but because they manifest emerging concepts of contract law. They may confirm or reject earlier trends or suggest new dimensions in the common law or the interpretation and construction of statutes that affect the social institution of contract. They must be examined and understood to assure a comprehension of twenty-first century contract law.

As the last edition was submitted for publication, the most recent draft of Article 2 of the Uniform Commercial Code which transformed classical contract law had appeared and was under discussion for possible enactment in state legislatures. Almost a decade later, it has become clear that neither a revised nor amended version of Article 2 will be enacted in the foreseeable future. While a few references to the amended draft appear in appropriate places as a matter of history or interest, other references have been removed to allow for other developments. The Uniform Computer Information Transactions Act (UCITA) suffered the same fate when controversy surrounding it made it clear that it would not be pursued beyond its initial enactments in Maryland and Virginia.

Contract law is anything but static. Both the common law of contracts and elaborations of the contract law of the Uniform Commercial Code continue to expand. The Restatement (Second) of Contracts continues to play a major role in contracts adjudication as courts weigh the Restatement analyses against other traditional and new analyses. The current applications, interpretations and constructions pervade the entire volume. Similarly, the Vienna Convention (CISG), which became U.S. law in 1988 has been adopted in more than seventy nations and constitutes the law governing the overwhelming majority of contracts for the international sale of goods. More than ever before, the law student, practitioner and judge must have a substantial awareness of this critical dimension of contract law which is found throughout this treatise. The UNIDROIT Principles that complement CISG, providing valuable insights in contract law as seen through an international lens, are found at appropriate points. Since the last edition, the Uniform Electronic Transactions Act (UETA) has been enacted in all but a handful of jurisdictions. UETA as the elaboration of its federal counterpart, the Electronic Signatures in Global and Network Commerce Act ("E-Sign"), must be understood as electronic contracts have become commonplace.

The treatise continues to pursue the rich history of innumerable contract doctrines from early common law to the present time without which the student of contract lacks a foundation to understand the current evolution of any part of contract doctrine. Absent an understanding of past mistakes and poor analyses, they could easily appear as superficial new doctrines without a hint of retrogression. The landmark cases continue to be found and others that are on the verge of becoming landmarks are also emphasized. The last third of the twentieth century presented a bevy of new contract theories and it is important for any comprehensive treatment of contract law to note their current status.

While the reporting of new case law and statutory developments is a critically important dimension of any comprehensive treatise, a critique of the evolving doctrine of contract as evidenced by these developments is equally important. Such a critique is impossible absent an immersion in batches of cases and related material to provide bases for any serious analysis. Every topic in this treatise is based on innumerable "immersions" in the cases and statues that have appeared since the last edition. The effort to meet the challenges in analyzing modern contract law have been arduous, fascinating and joyful. I dedicate this book to my students and my wife, Liz, without whom it would not have been possible.

John E. Murray, Jr.
Pittsburgh, Pennsylvania
2011

TABLE OF CONTENTS

TABLE OF CONTENTS

TABLE OF CONTENTS

TABLE OF CONTENTS

TABLE OF CONTENTS

TABLE OF CONTENTS

TABLE OF CONTENTS

TABLE OF CONTENTS

TABLE OF CONTENTS

TABLE OF CONTENTS

TABLE OF CONTENTS

TABLE OF CONTENTS

TABLE OF CONTENTS

TABLE OF CONTENTS

TABLE OF CONTENTS

TABLE OF CONTENTS

TABLE OF CONTENTS

TABLE OF CONTENTS

TABLE OF CONTENTS

TABLE OF CONTENTS

TABLE OF CONTENTS

TABLE OF CONTENTS

TABLE OF CONTENTS

TABLE OF CONTENTS

TABLE OF CONTENTS

TABLE OF CONTENTS

Chapter 1

INTRODUCTION

§ 1   THE CONCEPT OF "CONTRACT"

Historically and philosophically, the most fundamental concept of contract is that promises ought to be kept — *pacta sunt servanda*.[1] The concept is at least as old as the covenant between Jehovah and the people of Israel. The failure of the people to adhere to the covenant was a sin, but it was also a breach of contract.[2] Political philosophers who differ markedly in other respects seem compelled to adhere to a social contract theory, or government by the mutual consent of the governed.[3] The Lockian concept of social contract forms the basis of our constitutional philosophy,[4] and recent elaborations of the same view maintain the concept of social contract as the indispensable element of a just society.[5] Early American judicial thinking is clearly the product of a natural law tradition that regarded contract rights as emanating from immutable principles that preceded human law.[6]

In the late nineteenth century, Sir Henry Maine stated his famous aphorism, "The movement of the progressive societies has hitherto been a movement *from status to contract*."[7] In these "progressive" societies, the determination of the legal rights and duties of any member of that society no longer depends upon the status into which one was born. The

---

[1] "It is, therefore, a most sacred precept of natural law, and one that governs the grace, manner and reasonableness of all human life, that every man keep his given word, that is, carry out his promises and agreements." S. Pufendorf, De Jure Naturae Et Gentium, Bk. III, ch. IV, § 2. In the same section, Pufendorf quotes Aristotle, Rhetoric, Bk. I, ch. XV[22]: "If contracts are invalidated, the intercourse of men is abolished."

[2] "When the people of Israel in the wilderness worshiped at the feet of the golden calf, they were guilty of sin, but even worse — as my beloved friend and master, Edwin Patterson would have said — they were guilty of material breach of contract discharging Jehovah from performance of his side of the holy bargain." Jones, *The Jurisprudence of Contracts*, 44 U. Cinn. L. Rev. 43, 45 (1975).

[3] See, e.g., T. Hobbes, Leviathan XIV; J.J. Rousseau, The Social Contract; J. Locke, The Second Treatise of Government ch. VIII; I. Kant, The Foundations of the Metaphysics of Morals.

[4] J. Locke, The Second Treatise of Government ch. VIII, Of the Beginning of Political Societies.

[5] "My aim is to present a concept of justice which generalizes and carries to a higher level of abstraction the familiar theory of the social contract as found, say, in Locke, Rousseau, and Kant. In order to do this we are not to think of the original contract as one to enter a particular society or to set up a particular form of government. Rather, the guiding idea is that the principles of justice of the basic structure of society are the object of the original agreement. They are the principles that free and rational persons concerned to further their own interests would accept in an initial position of equality as defining the fundamental terms of their association. These principles are to regulate all further agreements; they specify the kinds of social cooperation that can be entered into and the forms of government that can be established. This way of regarding the principles of justice I shall call justice as fairness." J. Rawls, A Theory of Justice 11 (1971).

[6] "If, on tracing the right to contract, and the obligations created by contract, to their source, we find them to exist anterior to, and independent of society, we may reasonably conclude that those original and pre-existing principles are, like many other natural rights, brought with man into society; and, although they may be controlled, are not given by human legislation." Chief Justice Marshall in Ogden v. Saunders, 25 U.S. (12 Wheat.) 213, 345 (1827) (emphasis added).

[7] H. Maine, Ancient Law 141 (New Universal Library ed. 1905).

development described by Maine was inevitable because the status society did not reflect the felt needs and desires of its members. Human beings wish to make choices — they seek freedom to elect among alternatives. They have free will. Human beings are also aware of the future, and they are capable of projecting into the future. They wish to plan and to design their futures. They are capable of bringing the future plan into the present and contemplating that plan. They are capable of recognizing the geometric benefits available through reciprocal planning with others.[8] The basic problem of society has been described as that of "establishing, maintaining and perfecting the conditions necessary for community life to perform its role in the complete development of man."[9] If people cannot project their realistic needs, desires and aspirations into the future and be assured that they will be fulfilled, their creative energies will not be released. The social institution of contract is an indispensable condition, not only to economic freedom, but freedom, itself.

§ 2   MEANING OF THE WORD "CONTRACT"

We distinguish those promises that the law enforces from those that it does not enforce by calling the former "contracts." For practical purposes, a contract is a promise, or group of promises, that the law will enforce, or the performance of which it in some way recognizes as a duty.[10] This could hardly be called a definition, since it does not purport to set forth and delimit the constituent elements of the thing described. In fact, it is not practicable to state all the pertinent operative facts that are essential to create a contract, or all of the legal relationships that result from it, within the necessary limits of a definition. Such an elaboration must be left for detailed development in the sections that follow. At this point, it is important to keep in mind two elements of a contract that are critical: (1) It involves an undertaking or commitment (promise) that something shall or shall not be done in the future; and (2) the law sanctions such undertaking or commitment and puts its coercive machinery behind it.

Unfortunately, the use of the term "contract" as just described is not consistent. "Contract" may be used to refer to the document, the signed writing, that evidences a legally enforceable promise or group of promises. The writing, however, is not the contract; the words the parties speak manifesting their oral agreement is not the contract, nor is the conduct of the parties manifesting their intention to enter into a legally enforceable agreement the contract. All of these manifestations are mere *evidence* of the contract.

Where is the contract? One cannot touch, hear, smell, or feel the contract. The *evidence* of the contract is subject to sensory perception, but the contract is an abstract legal relationship between the parties. The legal relationship is composed of enforceable rights and correlative duties. If *A* and *B* enter into a contract for the purchase and sale of *A's* auto, they may reduce their understanding to writing. They may agree orally. It is even possible for them to agree without any words oral or written. *A* may be showing his car to a number of prospective

---

[8] Professor Ian Macneil identifies the "primal roots" of contract as society, specialization of labor and exchange, choice, and awareness of the future. I. MACNEIL, THE NEW SOCIAL CONTRACT 1–4 (1980).

[9] Snee, *Leviathan at the Bar of Justice*, in GOVERNMENT UNDER LAW (essays prepared for discussion at a conference on the occasion of the two hundredth anniversary of the birth of John Marshall, at the Harvard Law School, September 22–24 (1955)) 47, 52, *as cited in* H. HART, JR. & A. SACKS, THE LEGAL PROCESS: BASIC PROBLEMS IN THE MAKING AND APPLICATION OF LAW (tent. ed. 1958).

[10] *See* FIRST RESTATEMENT § 1 and RESTATEMENT 2d § 1. " 'Contract' means the total legal obligation which results from the parties' agreement as affected by this Act and any other applicable rules of law." UNIFORM COMMERCIAL CODE § 1-201(11). For a description of the UCC, see *infra* §§ 9–12.

purchasers. The sign on the car states the price at $10,000. *B*, a close friend of *A*, observes the display to potential buyers. *A* notices *B* standing nearby and *B* points to himself. *A* understands that *B* wants to buy the car at the stated price. *A* merely smiles and nods to *B* before telling the prospective purchasers that the car is sold. This may be called sign language, but it is not reduced to words, written or spoken. This manifestation of agreement, like the written or spoken words of agreement, is not the contract. It is merely evidence of the contract.

Sometimes the word "contract" is used to designate a transaction involving the exchange of goods or land for money. When money is exchanged for goods, this constitutes a sale. When money is exchanged for land, this constitutes a conveyance. Sales and conveyances result from previous contracts, but they are not contracts in themselves. They are performances of previous contracts. There is no undertaking or commitment to do or refrain from doing anything in the future.[11] This indispensable element of contract is missing. If *A* sells and delivers an automobile to *B* and is paid a price in exchange for the car, it is incorrect to suggest that a "contract" results from this sale.[12] Where there is a present transfer of property rights leaving nothing to be done in the future, the rights that are created by a sale of goods or conveyance of land are rights *in rem* or rights in the property itself.[13] There are no special rights *in personam* between the parties to the transaction. If *A* should deprive *B* of the automobile after selling and delivering it to him, *B* could not maintain an action for breach of contract but would be relegated to an action in tort for wrongful conversion of the auto. If a total stranger to the transaction, *C*, should deprive *B* of the auto, *B* would have the same right against *C* in tort. The legal relations created by the sale are relations *in rem* affecting not only the two parties involved in the transaction but all other members of society. If *A* had only *promised* to sell and deliver the auto to *B* in return for *B*'s promise to pay the agreed price, the legal relations created would be special *in personam* rights and correlative duties between *A* and *B*-contractual rights and duties. If either party refused to perform his promise, the other would have the exclusive *in personam* right to bring an action in contract for breach.

§ 3 THE ENFORCEMENT OF PROMISES — EARLY HISTORY — COVENANT, DETINUE, AND DEBT

One of the central questions of contract law is, which promises should be enforced? No legal system has attempted to enforce all promises. "Many of us indeed would shudder at the idea of being bound by every promise, no matter how foolish, without any chance of letting increased wisdom undo past foolishness."[14] It is important to distinguish what promises the law should enforce from the generic question, what kinds of promises should people keep?[15] The latter question involves moral philosophy. One might subscribe to the axiom *pacta sunt servanda* (promises must be kept) without simultaneously demanding that all promises be enforced by the legal system. Breach of a promise to make a gift that does not result in any

---

[11] Such a promise would be illusory, promising nothing at all. See Franconia Assocs. v. United States, 536 U.S. 129, 142 (2002) quoting an earlier edition of this book.

[12] A contract for the sale of goods involves at least an express warranty by description and, unless disclaimed, implied warranties that will continue after the sale is "executed" (after the goods are delivered and accepted by the purchaser). The warranties, however, do not result from the executed sale; they are part of the previous contract for sale which existed before any goods were tendered by the seller or accepted by the purchaser.

[13] See John E. Murray, Jr. Corbin on Contracts, Desk Edition § 47.04 (2009).

[14] Cohen, *The Basis of Contract*, 46 HARV. L. REV. 553, 573 (1933).

[15] Eisenberg, *Donative Promises*, 47 U. CHI. L. REV. 1 (1979).

measurable injury, though it may result in disappointment, is the kind of promise that a reasonable legal system such as ours may choose not to enforce. A social promise is another example of the kind of promise that a legal system will not enforce. The recipient of such a promise (the promisee) should not reasonably regard the promise as legally enforceable. The maker of a social promise does not assume a risk of legal liability. There are sound reasons for refusing to enforce a promise to attend a dinner, play golf or perform any other social promise.

It would be very difficult to measure the injury in terms of money (damages) incurred by the breach of such a promise. The legal system could be overburdened by any attempt to enforce social or gift promises. Moreover, social or moral sanctions for breaching such promises may be more effective than legal sanctions. An unexcused failure to appear at a dinner party may constitute a breach of promise resulting in a form of social ostracism that affects the promise-breaker in a more significant fashion than the payment of damages.[16]

Our system of contract law has developed principles for deciding which promises ought to be legally enforceable. These principle and related questions will be explored in a subsequent chapter dealing with the validation process.[17] The central question, *which promises ought to be enforced*, is at the heart of the history of the law of contracts. At this point, it is important to sketch that history as a foundation to a basic understanding of the modern law of contracts. Absent such a foundation, it will be impossible to understand how our law developed current devices for the separation of legally enforceable promises from other promises made by the members of society.

Since all promises will not be enforceable, it is not remarkable that Roman law developed categories of promises that would give rise to legal sanctions.[18] The common law, however, did not build upon the foundations of Roman contract law, though there is some evidence of Roman contract law traditions in England. Like Roman law, the common law evolved categories of enforceable promises. To be enforceable, a promise had to fit within one of the procedural categories that are known as common-law writs, i.e., forms of action that were the exclusive classifications providing remedies for claims.[19] No matter how meritorious the claim, if no writ

---

[16] *See The Invitation to Dinner Case*, in H. Hart, Jr. & A. Sacks, The Legal Process 477–78 (tent. ed. 1958). See C. Fried, Contract As Promise (1981) dealing with the inherent enforceability of promises.

[17] *See infra* Chapter 3.

[18] The Roman *stipulatio* was a promise made according to prescribed forms in a ceremony. It bound only one party (the promisor), i.e., it did not depend upon a reciprocal promise from the other party (the promisee). The "real" contract involved the conferring of a benefit under circumstances that bound the other party to perform, *e.g.*, a loan that bound the other party to repay once the loan was made. A "consensual" contract involved an exchange of promises — what would now be called an executory contract with performances promised but not yet performed on either side, which would be very modern indeed. However, such contracts were limited to partnership, mandate, sale and hire transactions. "Innominate" contracts were not limited to particular types of transactions and they depended upon an exchange, a *quid pro quo*. However, they were enforceable only when they were half completed, i.e., when one of the parties had fully performed one side of the contract. *See* F. Lawson, A Common Lawyer Looks at the Civil Law 113–37 (1955).

[19] "The medieval common law was a formulary system, whose content and basic structure were determined, to a very considerable extent, by the catalogue of original writs in the Register. In so far as it was possible to bring contractual actions in the common law courts, the possibility depended upon the existence of a suitable form of action. Inevitably the way in which medieval lawyers thought about contract law was very powerfully influenced by the formulary system with which they worked, and which provided them with their categories. We must not expect to find them thinking about their law of contract in the same way as we think of our law of contract." A. W. B. Simpson, A History of the Common Law of Contract 5 (1987).

or form of action existed for that claim, there was no relief at common law.[20]

While the early common-law courts were inhospitable to the enforcement of private agreements,[21] merchant courts developed as part of medieval fairs that were authorized by royal charters. These "piepowder" courts[22] dealt with the promises of merchants before juries composed of merchants in proceedings that were expeditious, due to the pragmatic necessity of adjudicating disputes between itinerant merchants.[23] Christian courts dealt with certain kinds of private agreements, such as promises to marry on a doctrinalized basis. Certainly, canon law was pervasive and breach of a promise was a serious or mortal sin according to those standards. Another source of relief beyond the common-law courts resided in the Chancellor, who, in equity and good conscience, had discretion to provide a remedy. Since private agreements (exchanges of promises) could be enforced elsewhere, the common-law courts ultimately decided to treat the enforcement of promises more seriously.[24] It must be said, however, that this was due, essentially, to the general desire of these courts to expand their jurisdiction rather than any perceived need to enforce promises. Having succeeded in wresting jurisdiction from merchant courts, church courts, and the Chancellor, it was necessary for the common-law courts to develop an effective methodology for distinguishing enforceable from unenforceable promises. The common-law writ system provided the basis for the development of this methodology.

Modern substantive classifications of the law, such as contract and tort, were unknown to the early common lawyer, who focused exclusively upon the availability of the proper writ that would fit each case. Absent such a writ, there was no cause of action at common law. There were, essentially, three forms of action or writs available to the early common lawyer: covenant, detinue, and debt.

Covenant was limited to enforcement of promises that adhered to a particular form — the promise under seal (a "specialty").[25] The seal was wax containing the insignia of the promisor.

---

[20] "The dependence of right upon remedy has a vivid illustration in the system of 'forms of action,' which embraces the occasions of remedy in the English common law. The question whether a man can bring this or that action, trespass, trover, assumpsit, etc., is the way the question of liability and substantive right presents itself. There ought indeed to be a remedy for every wrong (ubi jus, ibi remedium), yet the right of action at common law depends upon whether the case fits anywhere in a limited and arbitrary list of writs, within the scope and theory of which the facts may be brought. There are only so many rights of action, as there are forms of action. This system of forms of action persisted in actual use in English procedure for six centuries, from the time of Henry II and Edward I until the Judicature Acts (in force in 1875). Most states have abolished the necessity of choosing one of these specified theories in commencing suit. The forms of action we have buried. Yet, though we have buried them, says Professor Maitland [Maitland, Equity 296], 'they still rule us from their graves.'" B. SHIPMAN, HANDBOOK OF COMMON-LAW PLEADING 54 (3d ed. 1923).

[21] "[I]t is not the custom of the court of the lord king to protect private agreements, nor does it even concern itself with such contracts as can be considered to be like private agreements." *See* SIMPSON, *supra* note 19, at 4, quoting from Annulf Glanvill's *Tractatus de Legibus et Consuetudinibus Regni Anglie.*

[22] The name is derived from *pie poudre*, meaning "dusty foot," since the shoes of the merchant litigants were often dusty.

[23] The classic work in this area is Malnyes' LEX MERCATORIA, published initially in England in 1622. The author explains a system of law created by merchant custom quite separate from the common law.

[24] "[I]t is even possible that the decisive argument in favor of extending the action on the case to cover nonfeasance was that the Chancellor was going to annex the whole field of commercial law if the extension were not made." Barton, *The Early History of Consideration*, 85 LAW Q. REV. 372, 378 (1969).

[25] "It appears for a time as if the covenant might be of general use wherever there is an agreement (*conventio*), might become, in fact, a general action for breach of contract; but the practice of the thirteenth century decides that there must be a sealed writing." F. MAITLAND, THE FORMS OF ACTION AT COMMON LAW 52 (1909).

A written promise under seal provided evidence of the existence of the promise (the evidentiary function) and precluded unconsidered action (the cautionary function), since it would take time to heat the wax and deliberate action to place one's insignia on the wax. Modern scholars also recognize another function of the seal — it furnished a simple test of the enforceability of the promise (the channeling function).[26] Like the Roman *stipulatio*, the promise under seal was enforced exclusively because of the form of the promise. Though an attempt was made to make the writ available beyond formalistic promises under seal, by the fourteenth century it became clear that the only acceptable evidence for the use of the writ of covenant was the seal.[27]

Detinue was a form of action or writ used to recover chattels that were previously transferred to the defendant under a contract of *bailment*. If the defendant possessed goods owned by the plaintiff who had voluntarily surrendered possession of the goods to the defendant, a refusal by the defendant to surrender the goods to the plaintiff-owner permitted the action for detinue, which charged the defendant with unlawful detainer. Thus, the action of detinue would lie only for the recovery of specific chattels.[28] Great certainty was required in identifying the chattels to be recovered.[29]

One of the defects in this action was the conditional judgment against such a defendant, i.e., the defendant could choose either to surrender the goods or to retain the goods and pay for them. A much more serious defect attended detinue as well as other forms of action that antedated trial by jury. *"Wager of law"* permitted the defendant to make his oath that he did not detain the goods. If he could produce twelve oath helpers or compurgators to swear that they believed the defendant, the defendant prevailed.[30] This has been called a form of "licensed perjury"[31] since the oath of the defendant and the oaths of his twelve friends were conclusive. The limitation of detinue to the bailment situation and "wager of law" made detinue useless for those who attempted to enforce the typical executory, informal contract promise as we know it today.

Debt was the most common action for breach of contract at early common law. It was an action for a "sum certain" (liquidated amount) of money due for any reason. The plaintiff was held to a strict standard of proof of the exact amount alleged to be due. The essence of the debt action was the fact that the exchange between the parties was "half-completed," i.e., the contract had been performed on one side and a "sum certain" was owing to the promisee.[32] Thus, the defendant's liability depended upon his having received what he had sought in exchange for his promise, the quid pro quo. While the action of debt was originally available to plaintiffs who sought to recover either a specific chattel or money, detinue was later used for

---

[26] *See* Fuller, *Consideration and Form*, 41 Colum. L. Rev. 799, 800–01 (1941).

[27] *See* B. Shipman, Handbook of Common Law Pleading 141–43 (3d ed. 1923).

[28] Where a buyer of goods (chattels) paid for the goods but the seller retained them, the action was one of "debt" (discussed below) rather than "detinue." Here, the buyer is claiming that the goods became his only through the contract of sale. A party brining an action in detinue, however, is claiming the return of goods owned by him before he bailed the goods to the defendant.

[29] Shipman, *supra* note 27, at 114–19, 231–32.

[30] "Attempts have been made to rationalize and explain this fact. It has been said that debt and detinue were matters more particularly within the knowledge of the parties, and so on, but the simple explanation is that detinue and debt were older than trial by jury." F. Maitland, The Forms of Action at Common Law 51 (1909).

[31] *Id.* at 34.

[32] "As a rule the *quid pro quo* needed to support an action of Debt must be something actually given or done." Holdsworth, *Debt, Assumpsit, and Consideration*, 11 Mich. L. Rev. 347, 348 (1913).

chattels and debt was relegated to the recovery of money in the possession of the defendant. Debt was viewed in what modern lawyers would characterize as a tortious sense, and the recovery of the sum certain from the defendant may have been considered a form of restitution, except that the recovery was not limited to the value of the benefit conferred. Rather, it was the amount the defendant had promised to pay. Thus, the action of debt produced a specific performance recovery, i.e., "the recovery of a debt *eo nomine et in numero*, and not merely the recovery of damages."[33]

In covenant, detinue, and debt, the common-law courts afforded no mechanism for the enforcement of executory promises. Further imaginative extensions of the forms of action would be required to demonstrate an effective mechanism to make such promises enforceable.

§ 4 THE ENFORCEMENT OF PROMISES — ASSUMPSIT, COMMON COUNTS, *SLADE'S CASE*

The most significant extension of the common-law writs occurred in the extension to the action of assumpsit. At early common law, all civil injuries were divided into those with force or violence and those without force or violence. Thus, battery was an injury to the person involving force or violence, whereas slander was an injury not involving physical force or violence. There were two essential remedies for civil wrongs based upon the distinction. Violent wrongs were remedied through the action of trespass, while non-violent wrongs found remedies in actions of trespass on the case. Trespass on the case was developed through the statute of Westminster II, which provided clerks of the chancery with power to develop new writs or forms of action that were analogous (consimili casu) to existing writs. To permit what would be today called a tort recovery in a non-violent tort, i.e., one without force, the writ of trespass on the case (brevia de transgressione super casum) was created. Among the species of trespass on the case, the most important was *assumpsit.* As in other stages of the extension of common-law writs, the Court of King's Bench had begun to use this flexible generic writ of trespass on the case to generate more business for the Court. If someone undertook the performance of a service (e.g., to shoe a horse) and performed the undertaking badly, this *misfeasance* was the basis for an action of trespass on the case against the blacksmith.[34] The action was in that form of trespass on the case known as *special assumpsit* (he undertook or he promised). When the blacksmith performed badly or misfeased, there was a *detriment* to the promisee, the owner of the horse. As long as the emphasis was upon the *misfeasance* of the promisor, the action in special assumpsit sounded more in tort (*ex delicto*) than contract (*ex contractu*). To move to the goal of the enforcement of the purely executory exchange of promises, further development was essential.

If the promisor did not perform badly, i.e., he was not guilty of *misfeasance*, but simply failed to perform at all, would a remedy lie in special assumpsit not only for misfeasance but also for *nonfeasance*? If the defendant had performed no act at all, it was an action of trespass on the case and, therefore, special assumpsit was discovered by characterizing the nonfeasance as a form of deceit. Thus, where a defendant promised to sell a horse to plaintiff and, instead,

---

[33] *Id.* at 133; *see also* Ames, *Parol Contract Prior to Assumpsit*, 8 HARV. L. REV. 252, 260 (1894).

[34] "If on the other hand, one saw fit to authorize another to come into contact with his person or property, and damage ensued, there was, without more, no tort. The person injured took the risk of all injurious consequences, unless the other expressly assumed the risk himself, or unless the peculiar nature of one's calling, as in the case of the smith, imposed a customary duty to act with reasonable skill." Ames, *The History of Assumpsit*, 2 HARV. L. REV. 1, 3 (1888).

sold it to a third party, the allegation included deceit. Gradually, the emphasis was shifted from the "deceit" of the defendant to the failure to perform the promise. The emphasis in assumpsit was correspondingly shifted from the performance stage of the undertaking to the initial stage of the undertaking, i.e., to the formation stage. It is at this point that special assumpsit becomes an action *ex contractu*.[35]

At the end of the sixteenth century, it was recognized that a party who had made a promise in exchange for the promise of the other party had suffered a detriment since he was bound by his own promise. Notwithstanding the circularity of reasoning, this rationale permitted courts to enforce purely executory promises which had been exchanged for each other,[36] rather than merely half-completed exchanges (debt), promises under seal (covenant) or situations where goods were in the hands of a bailee (detinue).

Unfortunately, one problem still plagued parties who sought to bring actions in special assumpsit. If the old action of debt were available, one could not bring the action in assumpsit. This was devastating to some creditors since the action of debt was subject to the "licensed perjury" of "wager of law,"[37] whereas the more modern writ of assumpsit, developed after the trial by jury, was not subject to "wager of law." The common-law courts permitted assumpsit instead of debt where a party already indebted (indebitatus) undertook (assumpsit) to pay the "sum certain." This was known as indebitatus assumpsit or *general assumpsit* to distinguish it from *special assumpsit*, which would lie only for breach of an actual promise in an express contract. General assumpsit does not depend upon an actual promise or a real contract. It is based upon a promise implied in law where one party has already performed part of the contract (like debt, it depends upon some portion of the exchange being completed) or from some other debt resting upon the defendant. Since it was developed to provide an alternate to the cumbersome action of debt, it attempts to secure repayment of amounts owed though, unlike debt, it does not require a "sum certain." Quasi contract actions are actions to recover sums due from defendants who are unjustly enriched at the expense of the plaintiff. "Quasi" ("something like") modifies the term "contract" since they are not real contracts. There is neither express nor implied mutual assent or exchange of promises. Rather, there is a recognition that the defendant has money that belongs to the plaintiff that the plaintiff should

---

[35] "[I]f money was in fact paid for a promise to convey land, the breach of the promise by a conveyance to a stranger was certainly, as already seen, an actionable deceit by the time of Henry VII. This being so, it must, in the nature of things, be only a question of time when the breach of such a promise, by making no conveyance at all, would also be a cause of action. The mischief to the plaintiff was identical in both cases. The distinction between misfeasance and nonfeasance, in the case of promises given for money, was altogether too shadowy to be maintained. It was formally abandoned in 1504, as appears from the following extract from the opinion of Frowyk, C.J.: 'And so, if I sell you ten acres of land, parcel of my manor, and then make a feoffment of my manor, you shall have an action on the case against me, because I received your money, and in that case you have no other remedy against me. And so, if I sell you my land and covenant to enfeoff you and do not, you shall have a good action on the case, and this is adjudged. . . . And if I covenant with a carpenter to build a house and pay him £ 20 for the house to be built by a certain day, now I shall have a good action on my case because of payment of money, and still it sounds only in covenant and without payment of money in this case no remedy, and still if he builds it and misbuilds, action [on] the case lies. And also for nonfeasance, if money paid case lies.' " *Quoted in* Ames, *The History of Assumpsit*, 2 Harv. L. Rev. 1, 13 (1888) (citing Keilw. 77, pl. 25, which seems to be the same case as Y.B. 20 H. VII. 8, pl. 18. 21 H. VII. 41, pl. 66, per Fineux, C.J., *accord.* See also Brooke's allusion to an "action on the case upon an *assumpsit pro tali summa.*" Br. Ab. Disceit, pl. 29).

[36] *See* Strangborough v. Warner, 4 Leo. 3, 74 Eng. Rep. 686 (K.B. 1588).

[37] See the preceding section, which, inter alia, deals with the action of debt and "wager of law." But see Baker, *New Light on Slade's Case, Part II*, 29 Cambridge L.J. 213, 228–30 (1971), where the author concludes: "There is no clear evidence that wager of law did not work well."

recover to prevent the unjust enrichment of the defendant.

Common Counts-Quantum Meruit, Quantum Valebat. If the plaintiff had performed services for the defendant with the expectation of payment, he would typically plead his case under the common count of *quantum meruit* (work and labor done). To recover damages for goods sold and delivered, the common count of *quantum valebat* was used. If the defendant has received money that belonged to the plaintiff, the action would be for money had and received or money paid. While general assumpsit would lie for a partially executed express contract, it also provided a desirable alternative remedy where such an express promise could not be shown though the indebtedness from the defendant to the plaintiff was clear. Again, the action would be brought in general assumpsit using one of the "common counts" (quantum meruit, quantum valebat, money had and received, or money paid) to plead the cause of action. Pleading forms such as quantum meruit, however, should not be viewed as relegated to actions in quasi contract (contracts implied in law to achieve restitution). Indeed, quantum meruit is found in cases where the recovery is for contracts implied in fact.[38]

A debate raged for many years between the courts of Common Pleas and King's Bench concerning the use of the new form of assumpsit, general or indebitatus assumpsit, in place of debt. Common pleas urged a continuation of the conservative view that assumpsit would not lie where debt would lie since assumpsit was permitted to provide a remedy only where none was available. The King's Bench, however, was not concerned with a fastidious preservation of distinctions between forms of action. It simply permitted assumpsit to recover debts. A suggestion that this was another King's Bench effort to procure additional revenue through fees has been rejected.[39] "The debate seems rather to have been symptomatic of a more intellectual conflict, a final confrontation between the old learning and the new. It may perhaps be regarded as the last stand of Tudor legal conservatives against the legal renaissance of the sixteenth century, and the reformation of the old Year Book learning which this entailed."[40]

The resolution occurred in the most famous case of its era, *Slade's Case*, decided by all of the judges of the central courts of England in an argument won by Sir Edward Coke, then Attorney General, and lost by Sir Francis Bacon, his rival.[41] Much has been made of the statement of the words of Popham, C.J., "Every contract executory imports in itself an assumpsit."[42] One interpretation is that this statement is evidence of final recognition of the enforcement of mutual promises, but this interpretation can no longer stand.[43]

The more pervasive view of *Slade's Case* was that it disposed of the necessity of implying a fictional subsequent promise to pay the debt. Why was a subsequent promise necessary? One explanation suggests the importance of the deceit concept.[44] The main question in the case was

---

[38] See *Young v. Young*, 164 Wn. 2d 477, 485, 191 P. 3d 1258, 1262, n.5 (2008), where the court suggests that "quantum meruit" should be relegated to implied in fact contracts though the court recognizes that it has been applied to recoveries in both implied in fact and implied in law contracts, thereby "institutionalizing ambiguity."

[39] *See* Baker, *supra* note 37, at 215.

[40] *Id.* at 216.

[41] Slade's Case, 4 Co. Rep. 92b, 76 Eng. Rep. 1074 (1602).

[42] *Id.* at 94a, 1077.

[43] *See* Baker, *supra* note 37, at 226.

[44] "Why was the subsequent promise sufficient for that purpose? In the litigation between Tom and Dick, how was Tom's case notionally put? To say that by the middle of the sixteenth century *assumpsit* had become a purely contractual action, and that a debt precedent was accepted as a sufficient consideration, is an unsatisfying restatement;

whether the parties could be said to have undertaken a legally enforceable obligation though they failed to use express promissory language. Again, the more penetrating conflict raged between the court of Common Pleas and King's Bench concerning the availability of assumpsit to recover debts. Notwithstanding misinterpretations, it cannot be gainsaid that *Slade's Case* marked a critical passage in the common law of contract.[45] Indebitatus assumpsit (general assumpsit) became available in actions to recover debts, and the ineluctable movement toward the recognition and enforcement of executory promises continued. The term "consideration" was found in many of the lawyer's arguments of this time. In *Slade's Case* itself, Sir Francis Bacon used the term in arguing for the defendant.[46] "Consideration" was used to express vaguely the concept that there had to be some reason for enforcing a promise. Good and sufficient reasons for common lawyers were to be found in their old friends, the forms of action.

§ 5 CONTRACT LAW AND ECONOMICS — ECONOMIC ORGANIZATION — ANTITRUST LAWS

The last third of the twentieth century saw a heightened interest in scholarship concerning law and economics.[47] Any form of economic organization must be concerned with three basic issues: (1) *what* products shall be produced in what quantities; (2) *how* society shall produce

---

it also supposes that *assumpsit* had forgotten its parentage with unfilial alacrity. The likely answer is that here was another and more recondite application of the deceit ploy, and that Tom put his case like this: 'I had sold Dick goods and could have got my money from him by an action of debt; but because of his promise I did not do so, and have been kept out of my money for a time by his deceit.' Put in modern terms, the suggestion is that the subsequent promise really worked because [it was] made in consideration of forbearance of the debt. Expressed in terms of tortious deceit, it will be noticed that Tom was formally complaining of damage in being kept out of his money for a time rather than of the loss of the amount of the debt; and this explains the opening words of the fourth resolution in *Slade's Case*: 'that the Plaintiff in this Action on the Case in *Assumpsit* should not recover only Damages for the special Loss (if any be) which he had, but also for the whole Debt. . . .' If this is right, the allegations of deceit found in every *indebitatus* count were not mere abuse of the defendant for breaking his promise, but, in principle, the assertion of a definite wrong causing definite harm; and their original purpose was to express the matter as something other than mere non-payment of the debt for which the action of debt properly lay." *Quoted in* Milsom, *Not Doing Is No Trespass?: A View of the Boundaries of Case*, 1954 CAMBRIDGE L. REV. 105 (this applies to the question of why a second promise (on top of the original debt) was needed in the first place) (citing: RASTELL'S ENTREES, 1574 ed., f. 4 *sub. tit. Action sur le case in lieu de action de dett*; COKE'S ENTRIES, f. 1, *Action sur le case 1 (Pinchon's Case)* 4 Co. Rep. 91 at 94b).

[45] *See* Simpson, *The Place of Slade's Case in the History of Contracts*, 74 LAW Q. REV. 381 (1958).

[46] "And we put that a man, in consideration of certain corn delivered to him by the plaintiff will acknowledge himself to be indebted in 120. . . ." *See* Baker, *supra* note 37, at (Pt. I) 51, 61.

[47] The dominant scholarly figure in this effort is Professor and Judge Richard Posner. The most recent version of his seminal work, ECONOMIC ANALYSIS OF LAW, is now in its 7th edition (2007). For a discussion of the development of the discipline of law and economics, *see* Kitch, *The Fire of Truth: A Remembrance of Law and Economics at Chicago 1932-1970*, J. L. & ECON. 273 (1983). The economic analysis of law or EAL movement is often traced to articles by Ronald Coase, *The Problems of Social Cost*, 3 J. L. ECON. 1 (1960) (economic analysis of nuisance law) and Guido Calabresi, *Some Thoughts on Risk Distribution and the Law of Torts*, 70 YALE L.J. 499 (1961). Interdisciplinary efforts in law and economics were identified with the "Chicago School," i.e., the University of Chicago, though there were several other strands. For a comparison of these analyses, see NICHOLAS MERCURO AND STEVEN G. MEDEMA, ECONOMICS AND THE LAW (1997). The work of Posner and others associated with wealth maximization and specific theories, such as "efficient breach" of contract (*see* § 7 *infra*), spawned a vast literature, much of which was critical of "efficiency" as a return to a dangerous formalism, the largely discredited school of philosophical utilitarianism and a denial of libertarian values. With respect to formalism, see, e.g., Morton J. Horowitz, *Law and Economics: Science or Politics?*, 8 HOFSTRA L. REV. 905 (1980); Arthur Allen Leff, *Economic Analysis of Law: Some Realism About Nominalism*, 60 VA. L. REV. 451 (1974). As to the charge of utilitarianism, see, e.g., Jules L. Coleman, *Efficiency, Utility and Wealth Maximization*, 8 HOFSTRA L. REV. 509 (1980). Criticism based upon other "natural" values is suggested by, e.g., James

such products and how the scarce resources of society shall be allocated to such production; (3) *for whom* shall the products be produced, i.e., how shall societal production be distributed among the members of society.[48] These issues have been subject to three fundamentally different forms of economic organization. An early form was based on *status*, which answered the *what, how* and *for whom* questions through tradition. The manorial economic organization of feudal times or the more modern caste system of occupational choice in India are examples. Another approach is *centralized planning*, as evidenced by the decision of what to produce, how to produce, and how to distribute the production as found in the former Soviet Union. Either of these systems is unfamiliar to Americans. The economic organization of the United States is the *market* system.[49]

The market system depends upon atomistic decision making by innumerable consumers and producers instead of central planning. No single consumer or producer makes the decision as to what shall be produced, how it shall be produced, or how the production shall be distributed. These questions are answered by the market process, which involves utility maximization by millions of consumers and profit maximization by innumerable producers. The interface of supply and demand forces will not only determine which products will be made; it will also determine the *price* at which such products will be sold and the *quantity* that will be bought and sold. In their quest to maximize utility and profits, consumers and producers engage in *competition*, which is a form of economic organization, a process of selection, and an agency of social development.[50]

The form of economic organization that allocates resources through the invisible hand of the market place — the competitive model — evolved from the development of petty trade after the passage of the medieval regime of prelate and baron. Essentially, it consists of two pairs of institutions: property and contract; profit-making and freedom of trade. Private property determines who is to possess and control the resources of society. Contract determines how persons and resources are brought together in the productive and allocation processes. Property and contract together constitute the mechanism of competition. Profit and utility maximization compel firms and consumers to produce and to buy. Freedom of trade ensures that industry and markets will be open to those who seek to maximize their profits and utilities.

Economists construct models that range from the *perfectly competitive* to *monopoly* where one supplier exerts power and control over supply, demand and price. In the perfectly competitive model, the market is characterized by a large number of buyers and sellers, all of whom have perfect knowledge of prices and quantities of standardized products, and there is perfect mobility of resources into and out of an industry. The perfectly competitive model has never existed since one or more of the conditions of such a model will invariably be absent. Economists, however, project this model as an aspiration that might be approached. In such a perfectly competitive market, no single buyer or seller could affect the price. Buyers would be indifferent in their choice of sellers since the goods would always be standardized. It would be

---

M. Buchanan, *Good Economics-Bad Law*, 60 VA. L. REV. 483 (1974), and Richard A. Epstein, *The Next Generation of Legal Scholarship?*, 30 STAN. L. REV. 635 (1978). While Judge Posner has been resourceful in his defense of the efficiency theory of the common law and other insights provided by an analysis of law and economics (e.g., his articles, *The Economic Approach to Law*, 53 TEX. L. REV. 757 (1975), and *A Reply to Some Recent Criticisms of the Efficiency Theory of the Common Law*, 9 HOFSTRA L. REV. 775 (1981)), the scholarly debate continues.

[48] *See* F. SCHERER, INDUSTRIAL MARKET STRUCTURE AND ECONOMIC PERFORMANCE 11–12 (1970).

[49] *Id.*

[50] Hamilton, *Essay on Competition*, 4 ENCYCLOPEDIA OF THE SOCIAL SCIENCES 141 (1931).

irrational for any seller to charge higher prices since buyers would have perfect knowledge of prices and quantities, perfect mobility of resources would ensure the immediate shift of resources to any production that suggested a potential shortage, and buyers would always buy at the lowest price.

In the monopoly model, a single firm produces a product for which there are no substitutes. The industry and the firm are coextensive and the firm exercises complete control over price since the buyer has no alternative source of supply. The monopolist does not "take" a price as determined by the market; the monopolist is a price "maker." A comparison of the monopoly model with the perfectly competitive model clearly suggests that monopolists produce less at higher prices. The rational monopolist will restrict output when necessary to preserve monopolistic profits and thereby misallocate the resources of society. The income to purchasers found in the perfectly competitive model becomes profit to the monopolist. Since this comparison obviously suggests a preference for competition over monopoly, the United States has enacted antitrust laws, which are original legal products of the United States.[51] The antitrust laws seek to maintain competition and thereby preserve impersonal maintenance of the market. The objective is not perfect competition but some realistic form of imperfect competition, which is often called effective or workable competition.

§ 6   CONTRACT LAW AND ECONOMICS — "EXCHANGE" — "PROMISES" AND THE PURPOSE OF CONTRACTS

The social institution of contract is found in every society.[52] The law of contracts, like any other segment of law, can be pursued successfully only if its purpose is understood. Why is the institution of contract essential in society? There are phenomena in every society more fundamental than contract. A simple economic exchange — one person giving something of economic value to another in return for something of economic value — requires that the parties have control over the subject matter of the exchange. Ownership rights must be

---

[51] The Federal Antitrust Laws began with the Sherman Act, 15 U.S.C. §§ 1–11, first enacted in 1890. The basic provisions of the Sherman Act prohibit contracts, combinations or trusts (agreements) in restraint of trade (Section 1) and monopolizing in restraint of trade (Section 2). Two or more parties are required to violate Section 1 while one party or more than one party can violate Section 2. The Sherman Act contains criminal provisions. In 1974, fines were increased to $1,000,000 for corporations and $100,000 for other persons, and prison terms were increased from a maximum of one year to a maximum of three years in 1974. The Clayton Act of 1914, 15 U.S.C. §§ 12–27, was designed as a supplement to the Sherman Act. The Clayton Act proscribes exclusive dealing agreements (Section 3), price discrimination (Section 2, which was amended in 1936 by the Robinson-Patman Act) and mergers (Section 7, amended in 1950 by the Celler-Kefauver Amendment) which may substantially lessen competition. The Clayton Act contains no criminal provisions. Section 4 of the Clayton Act allows for the recovery of treble damages plus reasonable attorney's fees for any person injured by the violation of any antitrust law. The Federal Trade Commission Act (15 U.S.C. §§ 41–58), establishing the FTC, was also enacted in 1914 to further supplement the Sherman Act. Section 5 of the FTC Act proscribes unfair methods of competition. The Act does not contain criminal sanctions. The federal antitrust laws are enforced by the Antitrust Division of the Department of Justice and by the Federal Trade Commission though violations of Sections 1 and 2 of the Sherman Act are enforced exclusively by the Department of Justice because they contain criminal sanctions. Beyond the federal antitrust laws, states have enacted antitrust laws to supplement the federal statutes. It should be noted, however, that there has been a substantial decline in antitrust enforcement and litigation. *See* Gary Minda, *Symposium: Antitrust in the Twenty-First Century: Article: Antitrust at Century's End*, 48 SMU L. Rev. 1749 (1995).

[52] Farnsworth, *The Past of Promise: An Historical Introduction to Contract*, 60 Colum. L. Rev. 576, 578–82 (1969). "The attempt by the Soviet Union to administer the economy without the institution of contract failed." *See* Loeber, *Plan and Contract Performance in Soviet Law, in* Law in the Soviet Society 128–29 (La Fave ed., 1965).

recognized. Without a legal system, such control may be accomplished by force. With a legal system, the control occurs through recognition of rights in each person to control the subject matter of the exchange. Once it is recognized that the wheat possessed by one farmer belongs to him and the cow possessed by another farmer belongs to him, there is societal recognition of one of the basic requirements for a legally recognized system of exchange. This requirement is characterized as rights in property. The next step is the recognition that the holders of these rights (the owners of the property) may *exchange* their property. Both the recognition of property rights and the recognition of the right to exchange property can occur without the social institution of contract. The mere economic exchange of property rights, however, is an exchange of *existing* property, a system of *barter*.

In a barter system, myriad advantageous economic exchanges will simply not occur. The owner of the cow may be reluctant to surrender it in exchange for a mere *assurance* that he will receive wheat harvested months later by his neighboring farmer. The owner's family may be in need of clothing, utensils, or other commodities or services, but, again, he will be reluctant to surrender the cow for assurances that the economic goods he needs or desires will be delivered at some future time. To overcome this reluctance, the assurances offered to the owner of the cow must become binding assurances. If the legal system places its force behind the assurances to ascertain their fulfillment, the owner is no longer relegated to mere hope. He will have a legally recognized right creating a correlative duty in those who have provided the assurances. He will have the right to expect that assurances made to him in exchange for his present delivery of goods will be fulfilled.

Once a society moves from a primitive, bartering system of present economic exchange to a system of assured future exchange through promises, there is a new dimension of economic exchange creating geometric economic benefits. Innumerable advantageous economic exchanges become available to all members of society. They may engage in future exchanges as to property that does not yet exist. Parties may give assurances of property exchanges that they expect to acquire in exchange for property that does not yet exist. They commit themselves to future exchanges by their exchange of promises. The societal assurance that their promises will be enforced provides the essential incentive for each party to perform the promises. Such a system of assured future exchanges permits the parties to design their economic futures. Most important, it recognizes that the *promises* are valuable *in themselves*.[53] The wealth of any modern society is composed of such promises. The assurance that something will or will not happen in the future is nothing more than a promise. *A promise is a voluntary commitment or undertaking by the party making it (the promisor) addressed to the other party (the promisee) that the promisor will perform some action or refrain from some action in the future.*[54] A reliable system of assured future exchanges provides a basis for understanding the purpose of contract law: to ascertain the fulfillment of those expectations that have been induced in the promisee by the voluntary conduct of the promisor in making the promise.[55]

---

[53] R. POUND, AN INTRODUCTION TO THE PHILOSOPHY OF LAW 133 (rev. ed. 1954).

[54] RESTATEMENT OF CONTRACTS § 2(1) (hereinafter cited as FIRST RESTATEMENT); RESTATEMENT (SECOND) OF CONTRACTS § 2(1) (hereinafter cited as RESTATEMENT 2d). For an explanation of the original RESTATEMENT OF CONTRACTS and the RESTATEMENT 2d, *see infra* § 8.

[55] "[C]ontract law provided a framework of reasonably assured expectations within which men might plan and venture." J. HURST, LAW AND ECONOMIC GROWTH: THE LEGAL HISTORY OF THE LUMBER INDUSTRY IN WISCONSIN 1836–1915, at 297 (1964).

A complex industrial society cannot operate on the basis of barter. Sophisticated economic planning requires a comprehensive system of future exchange. By facilitating future exchanges, the institution of contract brings persons and resources together as a necessary condition to the operation of the market system. The enhancement of the resources of society and the maximizing of these resources to all members of society is illustrated by a simple example.

Suppose X owns goods which he values at $100,000 while the same property is worth $200,000 to Y. Since X has goods worth $100,000 and Y has cash valued at $200,000, the total wealth of X and Y is $300,000. If the legal system facilitates an exchange between these parties at a price of $150,000 for X's goods, X now has $150,000 and Y has goods worth $200,000 for a total of $350,000. Assuming no detrimental effects to non-parties and recognizing that the values to X and Y are values that they individually assume, the facilitation of this exchange has increased individual values *and* the value of the resources of the society of which X and Y are members. After the exchange, if X and Y each consider themselves at least no worse off than they were prior to the exchange, and if either party assumes that he is better off as a result of the exchange, economists would refer to this situation as a "Pareto-superior" outcome.[56] The psychology of exchange was long ago recognized by Adam Smith, who suggested that one cannot depend upon the benevolence of others. Rather, the appeal must be to the self-love of others rather than to one's own necessities.[57]

§ 7   CONTRACT LAW AND ECONOMICS — "EFFICIENT BREACH"

Among all of the promises made by the members of society, we have already recognized that no legal system will enforce all promises.[58] If a promise is within the scope of those the legal system deems enforceable, society will assure the performance of that promise by placing its legal machinery behind that promise. Yet, from an economic perspective, a refusal to perform a particular promise may not only be defensible but desirable. If X and Y exchange promises and X later discovers that the future exchange to which he has agreed will be detrimental rather than beneficial to him, X may breach the contract made by the exchange of promises. If X's refusal to perform his promise is accompanied by sufficient compensation to Y, the result may be economically efficient, whereas a legal insistence that X's promise be performed would be inefficient. "Efficiency" may be viewed as the utilization of economic resources in such a fashion that "value" — human satisfaction as measured by aggregate consumer willingness to pay for resources — is maximized.[59]

Normally, a refusal to perform a future exchange will result in loss to the non-breaching party that must be compensated to fulfill the expectations of that party.[60] Thus if X agrees to

---

[56] Pareto's view was that resources are not *optimally* employed if it is possible to make someone better off without making anyone worse off. V. PARETO, COURTS D'ECONOMIC POLITIQUE (1896–1897); MANUEL D'ECONOMIE POLITIQUE (2d ed. 1927).

[57] A. SMITH, AN INQUIRY INTO THE NATURE AND CAUSES OF THE WEALTH OF NATIONS 19 (1811 ed.).

[58] *See* § 3 *supra*.

[59] R. POSNER, ECONOMIC ANALYSIS OF LAW 10 (7th ed. 2007).

[60] "[I]f the promisor fails to perform as agreed, he has broken his contract even though the failure may have been beyond his power to prevent and therefore in no way blameworthy. The reason is that contracts often contain an insurance component. The promisor promises in effect either to perform or to compensate the promisee for the cost of nonperformance; and one who voluntarily assumes a risk will not be relieved of the consequences if the risk

supply 1,000 computers to *Y*, a refusal by *X* to perform will require *Y* to seek an alternative supplier of the computers. If *Y* must pay a higher price, the difference between the contract price and the higher (substitute purchase) price will make *Y* whole in terms of fulfilling *Y*'s reasonable expectations. Suppose, however, that *X* has agreed to deliver 1,000 BMI computers to Y at $2000 per unit. Before the future exchange is to be performed, *Z* informs X that Z requires 1,000 BMI computers. Neither X nor any other supplier has any more BMI computers because they are no longer being made. Neither *Y* nor other buyers has any interest in the brand name, BMI. *Y* can purchase substitute computers at $2100 per unit that will serve him as well as *X*'s BMI computers. No substitutes, however, would satisfy the unique needs of *Z*. *Z* is willing to pay *X* $2200 per unit. If *X* refuses to perform his promise to *Y*, *Y* may be compensated by a $100,000 payment from *X*, the difference between the price of X's BMI computers and the higher price of substitute computers. Having received $2200 per unit from Z, *X* receives $200,000 more than he would have received from *Y*. X fully compensates Y by paying X $100,000 while retaining an additional $100,000. Thus *Y* is made whole, *X* receives greater value, and Z is satisfied. Not only are the parties better off; the society in which the parties live is also better off in terms of efficiency or value maximization. This situation is often described as one of "efficient breach" of contract.[61] Under this theory, even a deliberate breach is not blameworthy. Contract law does not seek to punish the contract breaker. From an economic perspective, the protection of the aggrieved party's expectation interest provides an incentive for the other party to breach *only* if the gain from the breach (notwithstanding compensation to the injured party) is greater than the gain from contract performance. While there is limited juridical recognition of the desirability of an efficient breach,[62] the theory is not without its flaws. The payment of compensatory damages may appear to protect the aggrieved party's expectation interest, but the aggrieved party may encounter major obstacles in providing sufficient proof of contract damages to meet limiting doctrines such as foreseeability and reasonable certainty, discussed at length in a later chapter.[63] In addition, substantial transaction costs of litigation and negotiation are not recognized under the efficient breach theory.

§ 8   CONTRACT THEORIES — HISTORICAL AND MODERN — MULTIDISCIPLINARY

The fundamental principles of contract law developed at common law.[64] The principles evolved from innumerable decisions resolving countless disputes. It was, therefore, appropriate to think of contract law as a common-law subject with a few statutory modifications of the

---

materializes." Patton v. Mid-Continent Sys., Inc., 841 F.2d 742, 750 (7th Cir. 1988).

[61] *See* Birmingham, *Breach of Contract, Damage Measures, and Economic Efficiency*, 24 RUTGERS L. REV. 273 (1970). *But see* Macneil, *Efficient Breach of Contract: Circles in the Sky*, 68 VA. L. REV. 947 (1982), in which the author criticizes the "simple-efficient-breach" analysis on the footing that it assumes a world in which all relations between the parties can be conducted without transaction costs.

[62] *See Patton v. Mid-Continent Sys., supra* note 60 . The court, however, recognizes that some breaches are neither involuntary nor efficient, i.e., they may be "opportunistic" where the promisor seeks the benefit of the bargain without bearing the agreed-upon cost and exploits the inadequacies of compensatory remedies such as pre- and post-judgment interest rates that are below market levels and the fact that the party prevailing in the lawsuit will not recover its attorney's fees). For other cases approving the "efficient breach" analysis in contract law, see Allapattah Servs., Inc. v. Exxon Corp., 61 F. Supp. 2d 1326 (S.D. Fla. 1999), and cases cited therein.

[63] A detailed analysis of this purpose and contract remedies for breach appears in Chapter 9 *infra*.

[64] "Roman concepts of contract were known in England in the twelfth and thirteenth centuries. But although they

fundamental principles. Since the enactment of the Uniform Commercial Code in fifty-one jurisdictions, it is no longer possible to think of contract law exclusively as a common-law subject. Though the Code is technically applicable only to contracts for the sale of goods, it had a major impact on contract law generally. The RESTATEMENT (SECOND) OF CONTRACTS, a systematic and modern statement of the principles of contract law including comments and illustrations, incorporates most of the major Code changes for all contracts not otherwise covered by the Code.[65]

Restatement of Contracts. The original RESTATEMENT was published in 1932 by the American Law Institute for the guidance of the bench and bar. The Institute is a private organization that never intended the FIRST RESTATEMENT OF CONTRACTS or subsequent Restatements of the law in other areas to be viewed as statutory law. Restatements are designed to assist courts in the common law development of law. The Chief Reporter for the original RESTATEMENT OF CONTRACTS was Professor Samuel Williston, who was generally regarded as the leading contracts expert in America at that time. With the assistance of other luminaries, particularly Professor Arthur Linton Corbin, Professor Williston directed the effort to analyze the existing judicial decisions and to distill therefrom sound principles of contract law. Courts relied heavily on the RESTATEMENT to furnish guidance in the analysis of contracts questions, and the citations to the RESTATEMENT as sound authority in contracts cases are legion. With the enactment of the UCC throughout the country and with new conflicts among jurisdictions developing in various contracts cases, the American Law Institute undertook the compilation of a new RESTATEMENT OF CONTRACTS. The RESTATEMENT 2d was completed in 1979, and incorporated the major changes in contract law effected by the Uniform Commercial Code.

With only a few notable exceptions, Karl Llewellyn's "new" contract law in Article 2 of the Uniform Commercial Code was adopted as the contract law of the Second Restatement applicable to contracts not governed by the Code. Beyond this effort, the RESTATEMENT 2d performs the more traditional task of promoting sound resolutions of conflicting judicial decisions in contracts cases that have emerged since the publication of the FIRST RESTATEMENT. It has significantly influenced adjudications of contracts questions.

Williston and Corbin. In addition to the RESTATEMENT 2d, the production of scholarly contracts analyses in two treatises had an immense influence on the development of modern contract law. The treatise by Professor Williston (first published in 1920)[66] was almost exclusively relied upon by courts and lawyers seeking a discourse on any topic in the field. The later treatise of Professor Corbin (first published in 1950) tends to be regarded as the principal comprehensive work on the subject in the twentieth century.[67] It is difficult to overestimate the contribution of these two giants of contract law. There is, however, a substantial difference in their perspectives. The Williston view tends to be more rule-oriented than the Corbin view. Often characterized as a positivist view, the Williston analysis described a system of formal

---

inspired the comparable evolution of a general theory of contract in the civil law systems of the Continent, they exercised no significant influence on the common law. The common law was thus able to chart its own peculiar course in the direction of a general basis of the enforcement of promises." *See* Farnsworth, *supra* note 52, at 591.

[65] *See* Braucher, *Freedom of Contract and the Second Restatement*, 78 YALE L.J. 598 (1969).

[66] WILLISTON, CONTRACTS (1920) [hereinafter cited as WILLISTON]. Subsequently revised in 1936. The third edition, begun in 1957, was completed in 1979.

[67] The volumes of the treatise have been revised and remain current through biannual supplements. A Desk Edition providing a summary of all 89 chapter of the entire treatise appeared in 2009. JOHN E. MURRAY, JR., CORBIN ON CONTRACTS, DESK EDITION (2009).

rules or compartments into which any fact situation can be fit. The Williston position was criticized as mechanical and monistic.[68] On the other hand, Professor Corbin's work continues to enjoy wide approval. In the American "Legal Realist" tradition, the Corbin approach is more flexible in that it incorporates economic, social, moral, and ethical considerations. It recognizes the frailty of human institutions in judicial decisionmaking. It suggests that rules of law should be pliable and workable. It is willing to sacrifice some of the values of certainty and predictability in exchange for more relevant rationales and just results. The traditional criticism of the Corbin approach is its lack of certainty and predictability and its incorporation of extra-legal concepts into the "science" of law. For those who believe that certainty in the law can be an illusion,[69] the Corbin approach is the clear choice.

Llewellyn. Professor Karl Llewellyn was a Corbin disciple who significantly extended the realist tradition as the chief architect of the Uniform Commercial Code. The huge Llewellyn influence on contract law is displayed most prominently in Article 2 of the Uniform Commercial Code of which he was the principal draftsman.[70] Article 2 emphasizes the critical importance of the factual bargain of the parties.[71] The discovery of the factual bargain must be unfettered by "technical" constraints of classical contract law.[72] The objective is to discover, as closely as possible, the "true understanding" of the parties.[73] The Corbin/Llewellyn pursuit of workable principles and flexible rules of contract law that will more closely approximate the true agreement of the parties radically transformed classical contract law. In its modern context, it is often described as both realistic and "neoclassical." It is the dominant contract theory at this time.

Modern Contract Theories. Beyond the development of the economic analysis of law movement explored earlier,[74] the last third of the twentieth century saw the development of several theories critical of neoclassical contract law.[75] In 1974, a monograph by a highly reputable scholar under the dramatic title, *The Death of Contract*,[76] insisted that contract was destined to return to its roots in tort ("contort") and that the bargained-for-exchange theory of contract law was obsolete. Though generally regarded as historically and analytically

---

[68] *See* F. KESSLER & G. GILMORE, *Contract as a Principle of Order*, CONTRACTS, CASES AND MATERIALS (2d ed. 1970).

[69] 1 CORBIN § 1 (1963). "But certainty generally is illusion, and repose is not the destiny of man." Holmes, *The Path of the Law*, 10 HARV. L. REV. 457, 466 (1897).

[70] In general, see John E. Murray, Jr., *The Article 2 Prism: The Underlying Philosophy of Article 2 of the Uniform Commercial Code*, 21 WASHBURN L.J. 1 (1981).

[71] The definition of "agreement" in UCC 1-201(3) emphasizes the "the bargain of the parties *in fact* as found in their language, or by implication from other circumstances including course of dealing or usage of trade or course of performance."

[72] Numerous sections of Article 2 reflect this "anti-technical" purpose. For example, § 2-204(3) rejects the view that a contract will fail for indefiniteness simply because some terms are left open, so long as the parties intend to make a contract and there is a reasonable basis for affording a remedy. Comment 1 to § 2-206 expressly rejects "former technical rules." Section 2-207 significantly modifies the "mirror image" rule requiring the acceptance to exactly match the terms of the offer. Section 2-209(1) modifies the pre-existing duty rule by allowing a good faith modification of the contract absent consideration. These and other UCC concepts are explored in detail throughout this volume.

[73] UCC § 2-202 Comment 2. See also UCC § 2-207, Comment 2 that states, in part, "Under this Article, a proposed deal which in commercial understanding has in fact been closed is recognized as a contract."

[74] *See* §§ 5–7 *supra.*

[75] *See* John E. Murray, Jr., *Contract Theories and the Rise of Neoformalism*, 71 Fordham L. Rev. 869 (2002).

[76] GRANT GILMORE, THE DEATH OF CONTRACT (1974). Professor Gilmore participated in the creation of the Uniform Commercial Code.

unsound,[77] the reputation of the author, along with the wit and engaging style of his short book, created something of a sensation among contract scholars.[78] Together with the economic analysis of law movement, it provided a catalyst for contracts scholars to focus upon a wide range of contract theories.

Relational Contracts. Relational contract theory criticized neoclassical contract theory because of its focus on discrete or static transactions that failed to recognize sufficiently the on-going relationships created by the overwhelming majority of contracts.[79] While exposing important insights into the economics and sociology of contracting, there is a general consensus that relational theory provides a valuable emphasis in neoclassical theory, rather than constituting a separate theoretical foundation of contract law.[80]

Critical Legal Studies. The most provocative and controversial scholarly development during this period was the Critical Legal Studies (CLS) Movement.[81] This post-modern movement pursued an eclectic philosophy and obscure purposes supporting the radical deconstruction of any concept with an express intention of deliberately avoiding any substitute for existing systems except, perhaps, an ambiguous communitarian concept. As a variation on the philosophy of deconstructionism, the basic CLS theme insisted that any principle of law can be "deconstructed" to demonstrate its indeterminacy and logical incoherence. Neoclassical contract law was seen as "preach[ing] equality in distrust" which is "hostile to personal authority as a source of order."[82] The underlying philosophy of the movement was dominated by Marxist and nihilist themes that are antithetical to the market system and its facilitating machinery, contract law.[83] Though it inspired voluminous literature for two decades, as the twentieth century ended it became clear that the Critical Legal Studies movement had been deconstructed.[84]

Empirical Theories Versus Neoformalism. Empirical ("Law and Society") theorists extend relational theory in the search for comprehensive and contextual verification of the true

---

[77] *See, e.g.*, Richard E. Speidel, *An Essay on the Reported Death and Continued Vitality of Contract*, 27 Stan. L. Rev. 1161 (1975); Murray, *supra* note 75, at 871–73.

[78] *See* Robert A. Hillman, *Symposium: The Triumph of Gilmore's The Death of Contract*, 90 NW. U. L. Rev. 32 (1995).

[79] This theory is attributed to Professor Ian Macneil who wrote The New Social Contract (1980), as well as several important articles explicating the theory.

[80] *See* Melvin A. Eisenberg, *Relational Contract Theory: Unanswered Questions—A Symposium in Honor of Ian R. Macneil: Why There Is No Law of Relational Contracts*, 94 NW. U. L. Rev. 805 (2000); Murray, *supra* note 75, at 877–78.

[81] *See* Roberto Unger, *The Critical Legal Studies Movement*, 96 Harv. L. Rev. 563 (1983); Murray, *supra* note 75, at 873–77.

[82] *Id.* at 624.

[83] See Girardeau A. Spann, *A Critical Legal Studies Perspective on Contract Law and Practice*, 1988 Annual Survey of American Law, NYU School of Law 223 (1988), and the Commentary thereon by Judge Judith S. Kaye at 265 *et seq.*

[84] "During the late 1970s, and for a good part of the 1980s, critical legal studies played a leading role in the theoretical debates in American law schools. Hundreds attended annual conferences. Faculty appointments were made in some of the leading law schools. . . . Today, the situation is strikingly different. . . . The work of critical legal studies scholars is of virtually no interest in American philosophical circles. Many of its central tenets . . . have been renounced. . . . Critical legal studies is dead and all eyes have turned to feminism." Owen M. Fiss, *What is Feminism?*, 26 Ariz. St. L.J. 413, 424 (1994).

understanding of the parties.[85] The Corbin/Llewellyn realism is in general agreement with that goal. It insists that evidence of the parties factual agreement must include all surrounding circumstances such as trade usage, course of dealing and course of performance evidence as well as the words of the contract. While the empirical school finds that emphasis insufficient, the ultimate contextual analysis that empiricists desire is not only impractical, it is impossible. Even if it were affordable in terms of time and cost, the reconstruction of the original agreement process that would reveal all potentially relevant data could not be produced. While reconstructions of some well-known cases have provided valuable historical insights, a practical empirical judicial process has yet to be unveiled.

Neoformalism is stark reaction against relational and empirical theory as well as the realism of Corbin and Llewellyn.[86] Recognizing that empirical observations can never be complete, neoformalists emphasize the danger of relying on incomplete ("scattered") empirical observations. Casting serious doubt on the discovery of trade usage, course of dealing, course of performance or other common patterns of life, they eschew such "judicial speculation" and insist that courts respect only the static record of the agreement-the literal and explicit terms of the contract. While the Corbin/Llewellyn view manifested in the Uniform Commercial Code and Restatement (Second) of Contracts insists that the discovery of the "agreement" must consider the entire context as well as the written terms, neoformalists would limit the operative legal obligation to the express terms. While it is more than unlikely that the neoformalist theory will replace neoclassical theory, the judicial quest for certainty and predictability may augur a formalistic tendency. The notion that certainty can be achieved by limiting analysis to the express terms, however, is a dangerous illusion based on the fallacy that the express terms of an agreement are sufficiently clear, unambiguous and complete. A failure to appreciate the necessity for contextual analysis would inevitably lead to robotic decisionmaking and unjust results.

§ 9   THE UNIFORM COMMERCIAL CODE — HISTORY

The UCC is the product of two distinguished organizations. The National Conference of Commissioners on Uniform State Laws (NCCUSL) is composed of Commissioners from each of the states as well as the District of Columbia and Puerto Rico. Its principal purpose is the promotion of uniformity in state laws. The American Law Institute (ALI) is a voluntary organization composed of some 1500 judges, law professors, and leading practitioners. The Institute is concerned with the improvement and clarification of American law. It is widely known and respected for its production of Restatements of the law in various subjects, including contracts.

In 1938, the Merchants Association of New York City sponsored a proposal for a federal law to govern all interstate sales of goods. This proposal gave rise to an effort by NCCUSL to revise the Uniform Sales Act that had been promulgated by the National Conference in 1906 and was subsequently enacted in thirty-seven states. In 1940, the National Conference adopted a proposal to undertake the preparation of a uniform commercial code that would not only encompass the law of sales but other commercial problems such as negotiable instruments, bills of lading, warehouse receipts, and related problems. The following year, the American Law Institute (ALI) joined NCCUSL in this effort, and work on the enlarged product started

---

[85] See Murray, *supra* note 75, at 883–84.

[86] *See* Murray, *supra* note 75, at 891–902.

in 1945. Various advisory groups composed of judges, law professors, lawyers, and businessmen considered drafts that were submitted to the general memberships of NCCUSL and the ALI. The first complete draft of the new Code was promulgated in 1949. A final draft was completed in 1951 that was approved not only by NCCUSL and the ALI but also by the House of Delegates of the American Bar Association. A few amendments to the 1951 draft were made, leading to an "official" edition of the new Code in 1952. The 1952 draft was then submitted to various state legislatures for enactment.

The first state to enact the Code was Pennsylvania in 1953 (effective July 1, 1954). It was revised in 1958 to incorporate amendments recommended by the New York Law Revision Commission. Though fourteen states had enacted the Code prior to its enactment in New York, the 1962 enactment in that jurisdiction prompted enactment throughout the country. In 1961, the Code sponsors had established a Permanent Editorial Board to promote uniformity in state enactments and interpretation of the Code.[87] Various revisions and additions to the UCC have occurred since its inception.

§ 10 THE UNIFORM COMMERCIAL CODE — OVERVIEW

The Uniform Commercial Code is not a traditional, authentic code. A genuine code displaces any preexisting law. Section 1-103(b)[88] clearly states that preexisting principles of law that are not expressly displaced by the Code "supplement its provisions."[89] The Code is divided into thirteen articles. Article 10 is designed to set forth the effective date of the Code in the particular jurisdiction and to allow for transition from pre-Code law. Article 11 is also concerned with transition — the transition from an earlier version to allow for a revision of Article 9. The other eleven articles are substantive. A summary of each of these articles provides an overview of the entire Code.

Article 1. General Provisions. Article 1 sets forth the underlying purposes and policies of the Code in § 1-103(a): "(1) to simplify, clarify and modernize the law governing commercial transactions; (2) to permit the continued expansion of commercial practices through custom, usage and agreement of the parties; (3) to make uniform law among various jurisdictions." Section 1-302 expressly permits the parties the freedom to vary the provisions of the Code by their agreement unless such variation would be expressly or implicitly prohibited.[90] Section 1-201 contains forty-three definitions of terms used throughout the entire Code including the

---

[87] Schnader, *The Permanent Editorial Board for the Uniform Commercial Code: Can It Accomplish Its Object?*, 3 AM. BUS. L.J. 137 (1965).

[88] At the time of this writing, the revised Article 1 has already been enacted in 39 jurisdictions. References to this Article, therefore, will be to the revised version of Article 1.

[89] A genuine code directs courts to look at the statute afresh in each case, regardless of prior interpretations. The UCC must be read in the light of the precedents that have provided interpretations of the statutory language. It is clear that our courts, proceeding from the common-law tradition, continue the concept of *stare decisis* in their interpretations. One of the principal draftsmen and commentators on the UCC, Professor Grant Gilmore, suggests, "We shall do better to think of it as a big statute — or as a collection of statutes bound together in the same book — which goes as far as it goes and no further." Gilmore, *Article 9: What It Does for the Past*, 26 LA. L. REV. 285, 285–86 (1966).

[90] For example, Section 2-201 requires any contract for the sale of goods priced a t $500 or more to be evidenced by a sufficient writing or electronic record. An oral variation of this requirement would be prohibited since such a variation would emasculate this provision. Similarly, an express agreement to waive pervasive requirements such as unconscionability (§ 2-302) would not be enforceable.

critical definition of "agreement"that emphasizes the parties' "bargain of the parties in fact" found not only in their language, but inferred "from other circumstances including course of performance, course of dealing and usage or trade as provided in § 1-303,"[91] Section 1-305(a) emphasizes the purpose of contract law by requiring UCC remedies to be liberally administered so that "the aggrieved party may be put in as good a position as if the other party had fully performed. . . ." This principle is a codification of the purpose of contract law in protecting the expectation interests of the parties

Article 2. Sale of Goods. Article 2 deals with contracts for the sale of goods. It has been enacted in all United States jurisdictions except Louisiana which has enacted UCC Articles except Article 2 and 2A. Louisiana law is based on a civil law (Napoleonic Code) rather than English common law tradition.

Article 2 effects radical changes over its predecessor, the Uniform Sales Act (1906) that was based on a property orientation where the determination of which party had "title" to the goods was critical. Article 2 radically changes this property orientation to a contracts orientation, where questions of "title" are largely irrelevant. Article 2 is contract law, technically applicable only to contracts for the sale of goods. For the most part, the radical changes in Article 2 have been incorporated into the Restatement (Second) of Contracts. This is not surprising since the American Law Institute which is responsible for the Restatements of Law is half responsible for the UCC. These changes are the direct product of Professor Karl Llewellyn's criticism of classical contract law which, again, is not surprising in light of the influence of Professor Corbin on Llewellyn who viewed Corbin as his "father-in-law."

Numerous changes in classical contract law are wrought by Article 2. These changes may be viewed as more or less radical depending upon the particular aspect of classical contract law involved. Where the parties failed to include all of the terms of the contract, pre-Code courts would permit some terms to be implied, i.e., supplied by the court on a reasonable basis.[92] Article 2 liberalizes that view and permits virtually any term (with the exception of the quantity term) to be implied. Thus, if the parties intend to make a contract and there is a reasonable basis for a court to provide a remedy for the breach of that contract,[93] the failure to include terms such as price, time of delivery, place of delivery, or other details of the bargain will not constitute fatal indefiniteness. The precise time of contract formation need not be provable.[94] A party may accept an offer in any reasonable manner or medium.[95] The parties may have an enforceable contract even though there are additional or different terms in the acceptance of the offer.[96] This modification of the so-called "matching acceptance" or "mirror image" rule of classical contract law is one of the more radical changes in Article 2. Similarly, a court may refuse to enforce all or part of a contract if the court deems the whole or part to be "unconscionable."[97] The pre-Code Statute of Frauds requiring contracts for the sale of goods priced at $500 or more to be evidenced by a writing is modified in the Article 2 version.[98] These

---

[91] UCC § 1-201(b)(3).

[92] *See infra* § 91.

[93] UCC § 2-204(3).

[94] UCC § 2-204(2).

[95] UCC § 2-206(1)(a).

[96] UCC § 2-207.

[97] UCC § 2-302.

[98] UCC § 2-201 Between merchants, a writing signed by one party may be a sufficient memorandum of the contract

and other aspects of Article 2 will be considered in detail in the appropriate sections of this work. Again, it is important to understand the basic concern of Article 2, illuminated through the pre-Code scholarship of Karl Llewellyn, the principal draftsman of Article 2 and the chief architect of the entire Code. Llewellyn was concerned with the "bargain-in-fact" of the parties and believed that the identification of the factual bargain (the agreement) of the parties should not be fettered with technical rules of pre-Code classical contract law, because the application of these technical rules might well lead to a failure to recognize the true agreement or understanding of the parties.[99] Article 2 can be appreciated only with an understanding of this underlying philosophy. Similarly, the Article 2 concepts in the RESTATEMENT 2d which assures their application to contracts not governed by the UCC can only be appreciated by an awareness of this underlying philosophy.

Attempts to Revise or Amend Article 2. Amid considerable controversy throughout the entire decade of the 1990's, efforts were made to create a revision of Article 2. The ALI finally approved a draft of a revised version in 1999, but NCCUSL summarily rejected it. A new committee was then formed with a much more modest purpose of only amending rather than revising Article 2. The 2003 amended version, however, failed to be enacted in any jurisdiction and, at the time of this writing, there are no prospects for such enactment. The governing law, therefore, continues as the original 1958 "Official Text" though there are some variations in the state enactments of that version

Article 2A. Leases. In 1987, the ALI and NCCUSL approved this new Article dealing with the leasing of personal property. Leasing transactions account for billions of dollars annually. Leasing had been governed partly by the common law and partly by Articles 2 and 9 of the Code though neither were designed specifically for this purpose and the governance was spotty and confusing. Article 2A is the first comprehensive effort to deal with personal property leasing. While its provisions typically mimic its official Article 2 analogue, there are some marked differences between the two Articles.[100] Substantial amendments were made to the original (1987) version of 2A which have been enacted in all jurisdictions except Louisiana.

Articles 3, 4 and 4A. Article 3 deals with the rights and duties of parties in all forms of negotiable instruments, including checks, promissory notes, drafts, and certificates of deposit. Article 4 is concerned with issues involving bank deposits and collections as well as the relations between the bank and its customer. In 1989, Article 4A was added to provide a uniform law concerning the rights and duties of parties arising from *wire transfers* of funds that account for trillions of dollars in transactions. It has been adopted in all states. Articles 3 and 4 were revised in 1990 and amended in 2002.

Article 5. Letters of Credit. A letter of credit is a promise by a bank to pay a seller if and when certain specified conditions are met, i.e., the delivery of the goods ordered by the buyer and all necessary accompanying documentation. It assures the seller of payment through the credit of a party with impeccable credit standing (a bank) when the goods and documents are

---

binding the other party if that party does not object to the contract within 10 days of its receipt (§ 2-201(2)).

[99] *See generally* Llewellyn, *Why a Commercial Code?*, 22 TENN. L. REV. 779 (1953); K. LLEWELLYN, THE COMMON LAW TRADITION: DECIDING APPEALS 370 (1960). See also, John E. Murray, Jr., *The Article 2 Prism: The Underlying Philosophy of Article 2 of the Uniform Commercial Code*, 21 Washburn L. J. 1 (1981).

[100] For example, Article 2A contains no section dealing with the "battle of the forms" which is found in Article 2, § 2-207. The statute of frauds section in 2A, § 2A-201 differs from its counterpart, § 2-201 ($1000 instead of $500), the omission in 2A of a provision allowing a memorandum of contract sent by one merchant to another to suffice as found in § 2-201(2), and the omission of the § 2-201(3)(c) satisfaction of the statute's requirements by payment accepted.

properly delivered. In overseas or long-distance contracts for the sale of goods, many sellers insist upon the supporting credit of a bank through the letter of credit device that the buyer will have its bank issue before the goods are shipped. There is a rough similarity between letters of credit issued by a bank and credit cards (*e.g.*, Visa or MasterCard) issued by a bank that permit the seller to rely upon a presumably solvent party, the bank. This article of the Code is normally considered in courses that combine coverage of several Code articles. A 1995 revised version of Article 5 has been adopted in all states.

Article 6. Bulk Transfers. The original Article 6 of the Code was designed to complement other statutes (fraudulent conveyance and bankruptcy laws) in protecting unsecured creditors against sales of major parts of their debtors' inventories outside the ordinary course of business by placing notification requirements and other restrictions on such sales. Through technology and enhanced reporting services, however, today's creditor is in a much better position to make informed judgments about whether to extend credit. Moreover, Article 9 of the Code affords much better protection than pre-Code devices. As a result, in 1989 NCCUSL recommended the repeal of Article 6. Recognizing, however, that some states may be disinclined to repeal the bulk sales law, the Conference presented a revised version of Article 6 "designed to afford better protection to creditors while minimizing the impediments to good-faith transactions." Forty-three states have repealed Article 6 and four states have adopted the revised version.

Article 7. Documents of Title. Documents of title are receipts for goods, issued by public warehouses where the owner of the goods decides to store them (warehouse receipts) or by public carriers who issue documents of title called bills of lading when goods are placed with the carrier (railroad, trucking company, airline) for transportation. These documents of title take on great importance, particularly if they are negotiable, as they will control the disposition of the goods. Article 7 deals with the purchase and sale of these documents: the rights and duties of the issuer of the document and the holder of the document as well as the owner of the stored or transported goods. Article 7 replaced the Uniform Warehouse Receipts Act and the Uniform Bills of Lading Act and is considered in courses dealing with several articles of the Code. At the time of this writing, 31 states have adopted a 2003 revision of Article 7.

Article 8. Investment Securities. Article 8 is designed to govern transactions in securities (stocks, bonds, and other securities that serve as investment devices). It is not a regulatory statute. With some justification, it has been called a negotiable instruments law for investment securities. It replaces the Uniform Stock Transfer Act. Article 8 was revised in 1978 so as to permit it to deal with "uncertificated" or paperless securities. To further assure the free transferability of interests in investment securities and remove remaining ambiguities as to whether certain security transactions were within the coverage of Article 8, it was revised again in 1994. All states have adopted the revised version.

Article 9. Secured Transactions. Article 9 is often called the most significant contribution of the Code because it successfully replaced non-uniform and confusing state laws that pervaded commercial society. Prior to the Code, security interests in personal property were a curious assortment of conditional sales, factor's liens, chattel mortgages, and trust receipts. Each of these security devices was designed to accomplish the same purpose: to assure the repayment of outstanding indebtedness to the seller who sold the goods on *secured* credit, or the bank or other lending institution that lent the money with which the goods were purchased. Secured transactions reflect the way business is done in America.

The inventory in retail stores is typically purchased with funds borrowed from a commercial lender or on credit extended by the seller of those goods. The seller or lender takes a security interest in the goods and is repaid as those goods are resold. Security interests may be taken in the raw materials of manufacturing concerns to assure repayment when the goods are manufactured and sold. Commercial financing typically occurs through security interests in intangible property such as the accounts created when customer purchase products on credit. To secure the loan from the commercial lender, the retail store grants security interests or even sells the accounts to the lender.

If the outstanding loan is not repaid, the secured party may look to the collateral (the specific, identified tangible, or intangible property) in which the secured party has its security interest. The property will be repossessed (perhaps without any judicial proceeding), and the collateral will be sold to assure the repayment of the outstanding indebtedness. Article 9 of the Code deals with all aspects of secured transactions and is normally the subject of a separate law school course or a course covering several Code articles. The most recent revision of Article 9 was unveiled in 1999 and has been adopted in all states.

§ 11   UNIFORM COMMERCIAL CODE — SCOPE OF ARTICLE 2

Since Article 2 of the Code plays such a prominent role in the law of contracts, it is important to consider its scope. Section 2-102 refers to transactions in "goods" and the term "goods" is defined in § 2-105: "[A]ll things (including specially manufactured goods) which are moveable at the time of identification to the contract for sale other than money in which the price is to be paid, investment securities (Article 8) and other things in action. 'Goods' also includes the unborn young of animals, growing crops and other identified things attached to realty as described in the section on goods to be severed from realty (Section 2-107)."

Application of Article 2 by Analogy. While § 2-105 is helpful, it does not provide self-evident boundaries for Article 2. It emphasizes the inclusion of "moveable" goods, but some "moveables" such as investment securities are excluded because they are dealt with in Article 8. Security agreements in goods are covered by Article 9. Courts have often applied the provisions of Article 2 analogously to contracts not involving the sale of goods.[101] The warranty provisions of Article 2 have been applied to real property transactions though the name of the warranty may have been altered to reflect the nature of the transaction.[102] Prior to the enactment of Article 2A, Article 2 provisions were often applied in disputes over lease transactions.[103] An express invitation to apply a provision beyond its technical application is found in the comments to § 2-313 dealing with express warranties. While the section refers to "buyers" and "sellers," thereby limiting its technical operation to the sale of goods, the

---

[101] See, e.g., CBS, Inc. v. Ziff-Davis Pub. Co., 75 N.Y.2d 496, 553 N.E.2d 997 (1990), where the court relied heavily on UCC authorities in a case involving express warranties, though the facts involved the sale of a business rather than the sale of goods. In a case making analogous use of UCC Article 2 remedies, a court held that the Code was applicable by analogy to franchise agreements. Dunkin' Donuts of Am., Inc. v. Minerva, Inc., 956 F.2d 1566, 1579 (11th Cir. 1992). Other UCC provisions are also relied upon analogously as in United States v. Avila, 88 F.3d 229, 238 (3d Cir. 1996), where the court relied upon § 3-201, calling it "a persuasive analogy." The UCC definition of "course of dealing" in § 1-205 offered "guidance by analogy" in Galgay v. Gil-Pre Corp., 864 F.2d 1018, 1022 (3d Cir. 1988).

[102] *See infra* § 101.

[103] Baker v. City of Seattle, 79 Wash. 2d 198, 484 P.2d 405 (1971) (lease of a golf cart); Hertz Commercial Leasing Corp. v. Transportation Credit Clearing House, 59 Misc. 2d 226, 298 N.Y.S.2d 392 (Civ. Ct. 1969), *rev'd on other grounds*, 64 Misc. 2d 910, 316 N.Y.S.2d 585 (1970) (lease of equipment); Redfern Meats, Inc. v. Hertz Corp., 134 Ga. App. 381, 215 S.E.2d 10 (1975) (lease of truck). *See also* Daniel Murray, *Under the Spreading Analogy of Article 2 of the Uniform Commercial Code*, 39 FORDHAM L. REV. 447 (1971). *Contra* Bona v. Graefe, 264 Md. 69, 285 A.2d 607 (1972) (lease of golf cart not covered by UCC).

comment expressly recognizes "those lines of case law growth which have recognized that warranties need not be confined either to sales contracts or to the direct parties to such a contract. They may arise in other appropriate circumstances such as in the case of bailments for hire."[104]

Hybrid Transactions — Mixed Goods and Services. In mixed or hybrid transactions involving goods and services, "[w]hether a particular transaction is governed by the U.C.C., rather than the common law or other statutory law, hinges on the *predominant purpose of the transaction*, that is, whether the contract primarily concerns the furnishing of goods or the rendering of services."[105] When a wine glass broke in the hand of a diner, the restaurant was held liable under the warranty provisions of Article 2.[106] Where a customer of a beauty shop suffered injury from the application of a certain product as part of a permanent wave treatment, the court held the Code applicable though it recognized the hybrid nature of the transaction.[107] The spraying of crops has been held to be a sale of goods[108] as has the delivery of electricity[109] and natural gas.[110]

Other questions regarding the scope of Article 2 are dealt with more directly by specific sections within that Article. Thus, while crops that have already been planted and are growing are clearly goods, a contract requiring a farmer to sell all of the crops from a certain tract of land is within Article 2 even if they have not been planted at the time the contract is made.[111] Since the goods did not exist at the time of contract formation, the Code would characterize them as "future" goods that make the agreement a "contract to sell." However, a contract for the sale of minerals (including oil and gas) would be characterized as a contract for the sale of realty if the buyer was to sever such goods from the land.[112] If the contract provides for the seller to sever, the Code would characterize the contract as one for the sale of goods.[113] Under the 1962 version of the Code, timber was treated like minerals, i.e., whether it was a goods or land contract depended upon who was to sever the timber. However, under a revised (1972) version and currently, timber is treated as goods (like growing crops) regardless of which party severs.[114]

---

[104] UCC § 2-313 comment 2.

[105] Princess Cruises v. GE, 143 F.3d 828, 832–33 (4th Cir.), *cert. denied*, 525 U.S. 982, 119 S. Ct. 444, 142 L. Ed. 2d 399 (1998) (emphasis added) (repair of vessel was a contract for services rather than goods).

[106] Shaffer v. Victoria Station, Inc., 91 Wash. 2d 295, 588 P.2d 233 (1978) (§ 2-314(2)(e) applies the implied warranty of merchantability to the container or packaging of goods as well as the goods themselves).

[107] Newmark v. Gimbel's, Inc., 102 N.J. Super. 279, 246 A.2d 11 (1968), *aff'd*, 54 N.J. 585, 258 A.2d 697 (1969).

[108] Eichenberger v. Wilhelm, 244 N.W.2d 691 (N.D. 1976).

[109] Rochester Gas & Elec. Corp. v. Public Serv. Comm'n, 94 Misc. 2d 356, 404 N.Y.S.2d 801 (Sup. Ct. 1978), *rev'd*, 66 A.D.2d 509, 414 N.Y.S.2d 754 (1979), *aff'd*, 49 N.Y.2d 930, 428 N.Y.S.2d 675, 406 N.E.2d 490 (1980).

[110] University of Pittsburgh v. Equitable Gas Co., 5 Pa. D. & C.3d 303 (1978).

[111] UCC § 2-107(1).

[112] *Id.*

[113] *Id.* Coos Lumber Co. v. Builders Lumber & Supply Co., 104 N.H. 404, 188 A.2d 330 (1963) (sale of logs).

[114] UCC § 2-107(2).

§ 12   THE UNIFORM COMMERCIAL CODE — COMMENTS

Each section of the UCC is followed by "official comments" that elaborate the purpose and application of the section. They vary in length, clarity, and sophistication. It is important to recognize that these "official" comments are not part of the enacted law, i.e., the various legislatures enacted only the sections of the Code — not the comments. Moreover, the Permanent Editorial Board added comments after the Code had been enacted in various states. The comments, therefore, do not have the weight of "legislative history" in the interpretation of Code sections. An early version of the Code contained a section that stated that the comments "may be consulted in the construction and application of this Act."[115] However, that section was deleted in 1956, and no similar section was inserted in subsequent drafts. In theory, the comments may be ignored, but courts tend to rely on the comments in their construction and application of particular sections of the Code. Judicial adoption of the comments provides them with precedential force. The comments contain a wealth of material, but it must always be remembered that they are not legislation and, again, they are not exhaustive. One of the more useful aspects of the comments are their cross-references to statutory definitions found in other Code sections, but the cross-references are not always exhaustive. Since the comments are not part of the enacted law, should there be any conflict between the enacted section language and comment language, there is no question that the section language controls and the comment language must be rejected.

§ 13   INTERNATIONAL CONTRACTS FOR THE SALE OF GOODS (CISG) — UNIDROIT PRINCIPLES

Just as the UCC provides uniformity for *domestic* contracts for the sale of goods, the economic interdependence of countries throughout the world demonstrates a need for uniformity with respect to *international* contracts for the sale of goods. Even prior to 1930, efforts were made to construct such a code that would bind all of the major trading nations in the world.[116] The United States, however, did not participate in this effort until the eve of the 1964 Diplomatic Conference at the Hague which produced two conventions on international sales, the ULF (contract formation) and the ULIS (rights and duties under international contracts). Though these two conventions became effective in a few countries in Western Europe, the common law world, including the United States, did not participate. It is often suggested that the failure of the 1964 Hague Conventions was due to the lack of participation by the United States and other nations in the formulation of the Conventions which did not assimilate common law concepts.

Notwithstanding this failure, the expansion of international trade demanded an effective reaction in terms of a uniform sales law for international transactions. The reaction from the United Nations Commission on International Trade (UNCITRAL) overcame the fundamental defect of the Hague Conventions by ascertaining that its thirty-six members represented all parts of the world from the commencement of its efforts. UNCITRAL produced Arbitration Rules in 1976 which are used throughout the world. In 1985 it also produced a Model Arbitration Law which promises to be widely enacted. The most significant achievement of

---

[115] UCC § 1-102(3)(f) in the 1952 version.

[116] Commercial law experts throughout Western Europe were assembled under the auspices of the International Institute for the Unification of Private Law (UNIDROIT) with headquarters in Rome. *See* J. HONNOLD, UNIFORM LAW FOR INTERNATIONAL SALES UNDER THE 1980 SALES CONVENTION 49–56 (1982).

UNCITRAL, however, was the creation of a *Convention on Contracts for the International Sale of Goods* (hereinafter CISG).[117] A draft of this Convention was submitted to a Diplomatic Conference in Vienna in 1980 where sixty-two nations were represented as well as international organizations such as the European Economic Community (EEC). The Conference lasted for five weeks and resulted in unanimous approval. The slow ratification process then began.

What is often called the "Vienna Convention" was approved by the United States Senate on October 9, 1986, and the ratifications of ten other nations[118] were deposited on December 11, 1986. The Convention became effective in the United States on January 1, 1988. At the time of this writing, seventy-four nations, accounting for more than three quarters of all world trade, have become Contracting States.[119]

CISG applies to contracts for the sale of goods between parties whose places of business are in different Contracting States (i.e., they have ratified or approved CISG) or where only one of the States is a Contracting State and the rules of private international law lead to the application of the law of the Contracting State.[120] Rather than attempt to decide whether the goods would be shipped from one State to another, since the buyer typically does not care where the seller procured the goods and the seller does not care where the buyer will take the goods, the critical application question was deemed to be whether the contracting parties had their places of business in different States. Where the parties have their places of business in different States and both States are Contracting States, the general rule is that CISG preempts the internal contract law of either State. If a party has places of business in more than one State, the relevant State is the one with the closest relationship to the contract and its performance.[121] Where only one of the parties has a place of business in a Contracting State (again, a State that has ratified CISG), the application of CISG would depend upon normal rules of private international law that choose the appropriate law according to conflict-of-laws principles, e.g., the most significant contacts rule. If, therefore, the contract manifested the most significant contacts with the Contracting State, CISG would apply; otherwise, the law of the non-Contracting State would apply.[122]

---

[117] Among the other publications of the Convention, see U.N. Conference on Contracts for the International Sale of Goods, Final Act (Apr. 10, 1980), U.N. Doc. A/Conf. 97/18, *reprinted in* S. Treaty Doc. 98-9, 98th Cong., 1st Sess., 52 Fed. Reg.6262–6280 (Mar. 2, 1987), and 19 I.L.M. 668 (1980). The text of the Convention may also be found in the Uniform Commercial Code Reporting Service, Current Materials (Callaghan). Finally the text of CISG is reprinted in 8 J.L. & Com. 213–43 (1988) as part of a symposium on CISG in that issue of the Journal.

[118] Ratifications by ten nations were required to give effect to the Convention. This Convention enters into force, subject to the provisions of paragraph (6) of this article, on the first day of the month following the expiration of twelve months after the date of deposit of the tenth instrument of ratification. Art. 99(1).

[119] Albania, Argentina, Armeria, Australia, Austria, Belarus, Belgium, Bosnia-Herzegovina, Bulgaria, Burundi, Canada, Chile, China, Colombia, Croatia, Cuba, Cyprus, Czech Republic, Denmark, Ecuador, Egypt, El Salvador, Estonia, Finland, France, Gabon, Georgia, Germany, Greece, Guinea, Honduras, Hungary, Iceland, Iraq, Israel Italy, Japan, South Korea, Kyrgystan, Latvia, Lesotho, Liberia, Lithuania, Luxembourg, Macedonia, Mauritania, Mexico, Moldova, Mongolia, Netherlands, New Zealand, Norway, Paraguay, Peru, Poland, Romania, Russian Federation, St. Vincent & Grenadines, Serbia, Singapore, Slovakia, Slovenia, Spain, Sweden, Switzerland, Syria, Uganda, Ukraine, United States, Uruguay, Uzbekistan and Zambia.

[120] CISG Art. 1(1)(a) and (b).

[121] CISG Art. 10(a). If a party has no place of business, reference is to be made to his habitual residence under Art. 10(b).

[122] CISG Art. 1(b). Controversy over this principle led to the creation of Article 95, which permits any ratifying state to declare that it will not be bound by Art. 1(b). The United States made this declaration. *See* Senate Treaty Doc.

CISG applies only to contracts for the sale of goods, but it does not apply to every contract for the sale of goods. Goods to be manufactured[123] are covered by CISG unless the buyer agreed to supply a substantial part of the materials essential to manufacture or production.[124] The Convention does not apply where the preponderant performance of the seller is the supply of labor or other services.[125] Beyond these exclusions, there are a number of others which were designed to avoid not only endless discussion but the failure of the entire process. Article 2 of the Convention lists certain exclusions: (a) consumer goods;[126] (b) auction sales; (c) execution sales or other sales by authority of law; (d) stocks, shares, investment securities, negotiable instruments or money; (e) ships, vessels, hovercraft or aircraft; and, (f) electricity. Another important exclusion is the entire doctrine of products liability, which is not affected by the Convention.[127] Since the Convention deals only with the *formation* of sale-of-goods contracts and the rights and obligations of the parties to such contracts, it is expressly *not* concerned with the *validity* of the contract.[128] Thus, the Convention would not displace domestic law with respect to such issues as fraud, duress, illegality, mistake, or unconscionability.[129] Moreover, the Convention is not concerned with the effect of the contract on the "property in the goods sold," i.e., with issues of the rights of creditors in the goods or insolvency proceedings.[130]

The most important provision relating to exclusion is found in Article 6 of CISG. To foster freedom of the parties to make their own contracts and to avoid the dogmatic assertions of their predecessors under the Hague Conventions, the drafters of CISG included a provision permitting the parties to exclude the application of the Convention entirely, derogate from it, or vary the effect of any of its provisions.[131]

Differences Between CISG and the UCC. This freedom may be particularly important in negotiating and drafting the terms of a contract to which CISG would normally apply. The 101 Articles of CISG contain numerous differences with the Uniform Commercial Code contract law that will be noted throughout this volume.

UNIDROIT Principles. The UNIDROIT Principles of International Commercial Contracts ("Principles")[132] are a product of the International Institute for the Unification of Private Law

---

No. 98-9 at 21–22 where the Message of the President transmitting the Convention announces the rationale for this declaration.

[123] Such goods would be called "future" goods under the UCC. UCC § 2-105(2).

[124] CISG Art. 3(1).

[125] CISG Art. 3(2).

[126] These are defined in CISG as goods bought for personal, family, or household use. Art. 2(a) then adds phraseology that will undoubtedly cause interpretation questions: ". . . unless the seller, at any time before or at the conclusion of the contract, neither knew nor ought to have known that the goods were bought for any such use."

[127] CISG Art.5 states that the Convention does not apply to the liability of the seller for death or personal injury caused by the goods to any person.

[128] CISG Art. 4(a).

[129] *See* Peter Winship, *The Scope of the Vienna Convention on International Sales Contracts*, in International Sales: The United Nations Convention on Contracts for the International Sale of Goods § 1.02[6], at 1–37 (1984). Other examples of validity not governed by CISG would include a provision such as UCC § 2-718 refusing enforceability to penalty clauses. Whether UCC § 2-719(2) dealing with failure of essential purpose is a rule of validity is questionable since the circumstances giving rise to failure of essential purpose arise after the contract is formed.

[130] CISG Art. 4(b).

[131] CISG Art. 6.

[132] www.unidroit.org/english/principles/intro-1.htm.

(UNIDROIT) which inspired the United Nations Commission on International Trade Law (UNCITRAL) to create CISG. Principles are not designed to be enacted into the law of countries throughout the world. They are likened to an American Restatement of the law, to establish a balanced set of rules designed for use by courts and lawyers throughout the world with respect to international commercial contracts. The Articles of Principles are broader than CISG Articles, e.g., applying to questions of *validity* to which, as seen earlier, CISG does not apply. Like CISG, they do not apply to consumer transactions but the "lex mercatoria" concept that underlies Principles makes them applicable to the broadest variety of merchants.[133] Certain provisions of Principles are explored later in this volume.

§ 14   ELECTRONIC CONTRACTS — "E-SIGN" — UNIFORM ELECTRONIC TRANSACTIONS ACT (UETA)

As recently as 1996, only 3 million people, mostly Americans, used the Internet. Currently, worldwide Internet usage exceeds 1.7 billion people. History does not record any technological advance affecting so many people and enterprises in such a short time. Commercial contracts have been recorded on signed documents since time immemorial. Contracts for the sale of goods with a value of $500 or more are required to be evidenced by a signed writing.[134] Lease agreements with a total price of $1000 must be evidenced by a signed writing.[135] With billions in worldwide electronic commerce and conservative projections of continuing increases, the need to assure an effective legal reaction to this transformation in commercial practices became immediate and pervasive. A rush to enact state laws validating electronic signatures and electronic records produced statutes of varying scope and operative effect. The lack of uniformity in these embryonic legislative thrusts augured the possibility of a cure worse than the disease.

The overriding need for a uniform approach induced the National Conference of Commissioners on Uniform State Laws (NCCUSL) to sponsor the *Uniform Electronic Transactions Act* (UETA).[136] While the Congress of the United States is normally content to leave the enactment of commercial statutes to state legislatures, the dazzling speed with which electronic contracting was developing across the nation and the world induced Congress to create the *Electronic Signatures in Global & National Commerce Act* ("E-Sign") that was signed into law by the President of the United States on June 30, 2000 and became effective on October 1, 2000.[137] In the meantime, recognizing the need for uniformity, states began to choose the 1999 UETA as the state law facilitating electronic contracting. At the time of this writing, the UETA has been enacted in 48 states. Four states, including New York, have created their own electronic transactions law. Congress was eager to encourage state enactments of UETA since both statutes have the same essential purpose and use essentially identical language. If, therefore, a state has enacted UETA as approved by NCCUSL, E-Sign provides that the state law will govern.[138] If a state chooses to enact a modified version of

---

[133] A helpful analysis of Principles is found in the article by Joseph M. Perillo, *UNIDROIT Principles of International Commercial Contracts: The Black Letter Text and a Review*, 63 Fordham L. Rev. 281 (1994).

[134] UCC § 2-201.

[135] UCC § 2A-201.

[136] The text of UETA may be found at www.law.upenn.edu/bll/ulc/ulc_frame.htm.

[137] 15 USCS § 7001 (2000) (both houses of Congress approved S. 761).

[138] 15 USC § 7002[a][1]. With respect to the E-Sign preemption of the New York Electronic Signatures and Records

UETA, the federal statute may preempt the state law, depending upon the particular modification.

The essential purpose of both E-Sign and UETA is to facilitate the use of electronic transactions by removing barriers to electronic commerce.[139] Thus, a contract, record or signature will not be denied legal effect solely because it is in electronic form.[140] Where, for example, a statute requires a contract to be evidenced by a "signed" writing, an electronic record[141] and an "electronic signature"[142] will meet that requirement.[143] A Comment to UETA makes it clear that "[n]o specific technology need be used in order to create a valid signature. One's voice on an answering machine may suffice if the requisite intention is present. Similarly, including one's name as part of an electronic mail communication also may suffice, as may the firm name on a facsimile."[144]

E-Sign and UETA expressly state that they do not *require* any person to agree to use or accept electronic records or signatures.[145] Indeed, UETA insists that the parties must *agree* to conduct transactions by electronic means.[146] Beyond express agreements to use electronic means to conduct transactions, however, "agreement" or consent to the use of electronic means is construed broadly to include the parties' conduct. Thus, a business card or letterhead with an E-mail address may allow a reasonable inference that such party is willing to communicate electronically for business purposes.[147] E-Sign focuses heavily upon consent by consumers. Where a statute, regulation or other rule of law *requires* that information be made available in

---

Act (ESRA), see People v. McFarlan, 191 Mis. 2d 531, 744 N. Y. S. 2d 287 (2002).

[139] E-Sign, preamble: "An Act [t]o facilitate the use of electronic records and signatures in interstate or foreign commerce." UETA § 6(1): "This Act must be construed and applied to facilitate electronic transactions consistent with other law."

[140] E-Sign § 101; UETA § 7.

[141] UETA defines "record" in § 2(13) as "information that is inscribed on a tangible medium or that is stored in an electronic or other medium and is retrievable in perceivable form." The identical language is found in the E-Sign definition in § 106(9).

[142] UETA § 2(8) defines "electronic signature" as "an electronic sound, symbol or process attached to or logically associated with a record and executed or adopted by a person with the intent to sign the record." The identical language is found in the E-Sign definition in § 106(5).

[143] UETA § 7(c) and (d). It should be noted that the term "electronic" as used in UETA is defined as "relating to technology having electrical, digital, magnetic, wireless, optical, electromagnetic, or similar capabilities" (§ 2(5)). This broad definition was designed to allow for developing technologies to fulfill the purpose of the Act and, while the term "electronic" applies even to technologies that are not technically electronic, such as optical fiber technology, it was chosen as the most descriptive term for the majority of technologies. *See* UETA § 2 Comment 4.

[144] UETA § 2, Comment 7. UETA and E-Sign deliberately avoid specifying particular secure technologies as did some of the earlier state legislation with respect to the security of electronic signatures involving dual key encryption and third party certifiers, e.g., Utah Stat. Ann. § 46-3-101 *et seq.* Such requirements not only war against uniformity, they make the unwarranted assumption that such technology is static.

[145] E-Sign § 101(b)(2); UETA § 5(a).

[146] UETA § 5(b).

[147] See Comment 4 and example B. to UETA § 5. Other examples listed therein include a party with more than one E-mail address suggests that she is willing to pursue transactions within the scope of such addresses electronically. A party who orders goods from an online vendor suggests consent to electronic means of communication. In *Crestwood Shops, L.L.C. v. Hilkene*, 197 S.W.3d 641, 653 (Mo. Ct. App. 2006) the court noted that § 432.220.2 of the Missouri version of the Uniform Electronics Transactions Act "required the trial court to examine 'the context and surrounding circumstances, including the parties' conduct' in determining whether the parties agreed to conduct transactions by electronic means. It affirmed the trial court's determination that the parties course of performance manifested their intention to conduct business via email.

writing to a consumer, the statute allows the use of an electronic record to meet that requirement only if certain detailed procedures are followed to assure the consumer's assent to such use.[148]

The scope of UETA is limited "to electronic records and electronic signatures relating to a transaction."[149] Only business, commercial or governmental transactions as well as consumer transactions are covered under either statute.[150] Neither statute applies to wills, codicils or testamentary trusts[151] or to Uniform Commercial Code Articles 3 through 9 that deal with negotiable instruments, payment systems, letters of credit, investment securities or secured transactions and contain their own rules for electronic transactions.[152] Both statutes pursue a minimalist and procedural approach by deferring to state law with respect to substantive matters.[153]

While the statutes share the same essential purpose and even identical statutory language in some sections,[154] UETA is more comprehensive than E-Sign. Thus, UETA expressly allows the parties to vary its provisions by their agreement.[155] E-Sign contains no general provision concerning permissible variation and its mandatory consumer notice provisions may not be varied, regardless of state law.[156] E-Sign does not mention attribution, while UETA provides that where a signature appears on an electronic record, the named party is not bound unless she produced the signature, ratified it or is responsible for the agent who used the signature.[157] E-Sign does not address the effect of change or error in an electronic record while UETA sets

---

[148] E-Sign § 101(c). See UETA § 8(a), which allows electronic information to satisfy a legal requirement that a person must send or deliver information to another in writing if the recipient can retain the information, i.e., print and store the information. Where, however, a law requires a record to be posted or displayed in a certain manner or transmitted by a specific method or contain information formatted in a particular manner, these requirements must be met, albeit they may be met through electronic information. Thus, if information must be posted, a disc may be posted. The information thereon would have to meet any display and formatting requirements. *See* UETA § 8(b) and Comment 4.

[149] UETA § 3(a).

[150] See the UETA definition of "transaction" in § 2(16) and comments thereto. The § 106(13) E-Sign definition of "transaction" refers to business, consumer or commercial affairs and lists sales, leases, exchanges and licensing or other disposition of personal property (including intangibles and services) as well as transactions in real property.

[151] E-Sign § 103(a)(1); UETA § 3(b)(1).

[152] E-Sign § 103(a)(3); UETA § 3(b)(2). UETA § 3(b)(3) excludes coverage of the Uniform Computer Information Transactions Act since it contains its own provisions for electronic transactions involving computer information. E-Sign § 103(a)(2) contains an exception for state law concerning matters of adoption, divorce or other matters of family law. Here, UETA would allow the use of electronic agreements and records in relation to such matters as antenuptial agreements, property settlements and the like. E-Sign would neither validate nor bar such use. E-Sign § 103(b) also excludes court orders or notices, official court documents, any notice of cancellation or termination of utility services or health or life insurance benefits, notices of default, acceleration, repossession, foreclosure or eviction as well as product risk or recall notices or documents required to accompany any transportation or handling of hazardous or toxic materials. E-Sign § 104 states that the statute does not limit or supersede any federal or state regulatory requirement concerning the filing of records so as not to impose an obligation to immediately convert to electronic files.

[153] *See* UETA § 5(e) and *Draft Prefatory Notes*, § B. *See* E-Sign § 101(b).

[154] E.g., see certain definitions of terms in E-Sign § 106 and UETA § 2, which are identical, though each contains definitions that are not shared and UETA defines sixteen terms while E-Sign defines twelve terms. See also the language used in E-Sign § 103 and UETA § 3 concerning exceptions for wills, codicils, testamentary trusts and UCC Articles.

[155] UETA § 5(d).

[156] E-Sign § 101(c).

[157] UETA § 9.

forth specific rules for such situations.[158] UETA expressly provides that electronic records are not to be denied admissibility into evidence solely because they are in electronic form,[159] but there is no comparable provision in E-Sign. Nothing in E-Sign deals with the time and place of sending and receipt of electronic records, but UETA confronts these issues.[160]

Contracts between electronic agents[161] or between an individual and an electronic agent are recognized by both statutes.[162] The thought of two machines making a contract may seem unusual since there is no human intent to form a contract at the moment of formation. A moment's reflection, however, cures any concern since the programming and use of the respective machines provides the requisite intention.[163] Where an individual and an electronic agent interact, a contract will be formed when the individual performs actions that she is free to refuse to perform and which she knows or has reason to know will cause the electronic agent to complete the transaction or performance.[164] Thus, when the individual is advised that by clicking on an "agree" button she will form a contract, her clicking action will bind her to an enforceable agreement.

While E-Sign and UETA will not escape the furies of interpretation and construction in myriad applications, their stated purpose of facilitating electronic commerce through uniform applications should remove barriers and allow this new medium of commercial practice to flourish.

---

[158] UETA § 10. Where the parties have agreed upon a security procedure to detect changes or errors and one party has conformed to the procedure while the other has not, if the nonconforming party would have detected the change or error had he conformed, the conforming party may avoid the effect of the changed or erroneous record (§ 10(1)). In an "automated transaction" (§ 2(2)), a transaction conducted or performed in whole or in part by electronic means in which the acts or records of one or both parties are not reviewed by an individual) involving an individual, the individual may avoid the effect of his error in dealing with an "electronic agent" (§ 2(6)), a computer program or other automated means used independently to initiate an action or respond to electronic records or performances without review or action by an individual) if the agent did not provide an opportunity for prevention or correction of the error and, upon learning of the error, the individual promptly notifies the other party of the error and takes reasonable steps to return or destroy the consideration received and has not used or received any benefit or value. (§ 10(2)).

[159] UETA § 13.

[160] UETA § 15. The electronic record is *sent* when it is properly addressed to an information system designated by the recipient for the purpose of receiving the record, it is in a form capable of being processed by the recipient system, and enters an information processing system outside the control of the sender or of someone acting on his behalf, or enters a region of the information processing system designated by the recipient. An electronic record is *received* when the information enters a processing system designated for that purpose by the recipient and from which the recipient is able to retrieve the record and is in a form capable of being processed by that system. As to the *place* of sending or receipt, unless otherwise expressly provided, an electronic record is deemed to be sent from the sender's place of business and received at the recipient's place of business. If sender or recipient have more than one place of business, the place of business is the place having the closest relationship to the underlying transaction. If either party has no place of business, the place of business is the party's residence. An electronic record is received even if no individual is aware of its receipt. If either party is aware that an electronic record that was purportedly sent or received was not actually sent or received, the legal effect of sending or receipt is determined by other applicable law.

[161] See the definition of "electronic agent" in note 158, *supra.*

[162] E-Sign § 101(h); UETA § 14.

[163] *See* UETA § 14, Comment 1.

[164] UETA § 14(2).

§ 15   SOFTWARE TRANSACTIONS — LICENSES — UNIFORM COMPUTER INFORMATION TRANSACTIONS ACT (UCITA)

As the digital age became a pervasive reality, inevitable controversies were presented to courts concerning the agreement of the parties with respect to software transactions. Contracts to "buy" software are typically licenses for the use of copyrighted information. Computer programs pervade the products and services in 21st century society, but as even critical parts of otherwise predominant tangible moveable property, they are contracts for the sale of "goods." Whether Article 2 of the UCC applied to software per se, however, raised issues of whether the subject matter of the contract was "goods" as well as whether the transaction was a "sale" as contrasted with a license.

An early reaction was provided by the United States Court of Appeals for the Third Circuit which recognized software as copyrightable intellectual property, but also found software constituted "goods" under the UCC which certainly applies to "specially manufactured goods."[165] The court analogized the intangible intellectual property implanted in a medium to a compact disc recording of music which is not a "good," but when transferred to a readable medium becomes a merchantable commodity. Similarly, the original delivery of a professor's lecture is not a good, but when transcribed into a book or other record, it becomes a good.[166] The fact that software is typically licensed rather than sold was met by the scope of Article 2 which "applies to *transactions* in goods.[167] The broader term, "transactions," encompasses both sales and licenses. Though there was a split of authority, courts generally recognized that computer software licensing qualified as a transaction in "goods"to which the UCC applied.[168]

Courts would certainly view a transaction in "off the rack" software as a transaction in goods. If the contract predominantly involves intellectual property rights to the software, however, Article 2 would not apply.[169] The dichotomy between goods and services often arises in software transactions raising the issue of whether "goods" or "services" predominate.[170] Software is often modified for a given party. Such customization, however, does not undermine the nature of the transaction as one in "specially manufactured goods" to which Article 2 applies.[171] Typical services accompanying software transactions including installation, training and technical support do not convert the transaction to one for services rather than goods. The allocated dollar value of materials and labor are factors to be considered, but they are not dispositive.[172]

UCITA. The concern for the special character of software contracts led to attempts to revise UCC Article 2 by inserting provisions for computer information transactions. The configuration included a "hub" of general principles that would apply to sales of goods and information

---

[165] Advent Systems Ltd. v. Unisys Corp., 925 F.2d 670, 675 (3d Cir. 1991). UCC § 2-105 includes "specially manufactured goods" within the definition of "goods."

[166] *Id.*

[167] UCC § 2-102. See Colonial Life Ins. Co. v. Electronic Data Systems Corp., 817 F. Supp. 235, 239 (D. N. H. 1993).

[168] See Dealer Mgmt. Sys. v. Design Auto. Group, Inc., 355 Ill. App. 3d 416, 822 N.E.2d 556 (2005), and cases cited therein.

[169] Archetronics, Inc. v. Control Systems, Inc., 935 F. Supp. 425, 432 (S.D.N.Y. 1996).

[170] See § 11, *supra*, dealing with mixed (hybrid) transactions.

[171] Micro Data Base Systems, Inc. v. Dharma Systems, Inc., 148 F.3d 649, 654–55 (7th Cir. 1998).

[172] *Dealer Mgt. Systems, supra* note 168, 822 N. E. 2d at 562 quoting *Advent Systems, supra* note 165, 925 F.2d at 676.

transactions followed by chapters or "spokes" of the hub to address specific issues in each type of transaction.[173] This design was rejected and gave way to an effort to produce a separate and extensive Article of the UCC, Article 2B. This initiative was also rejected as part of the UCC, but the Article 2B draft was almost immediately resurrected as the Uniform Computer Information Transactions Act (UCITA), approved only by the National Conference of Commissioners on Uniform State Laws (NCCUSL) in 1999. UCITA was quickly enacted, but only in only two states, Maryland and Virginia.[174] Beyond the question of whether an entire statute of this magnitude was necessary to govern computer information transactions, UCITA has engendered great controversy and has not been enacted elsewhere. After rejection by the American Bar Association House of Delegates, in 2003, the Executive Committee of NCCUSL announced that it "would not expend any additional Conference energy or resources in having UCITA enacted" though it was "not abandoning [its] interest in the subject matter."[175]

§ 16   CONTRACTS CLASSIFIED

Contracts are classified in various ways. In relation to formation, they are classified as formal or informal. With respect to the time of formation, classical contract law characterized them as unilateral or bilateral. In terms of the legal sanctions involved, contracts are enforceable, voidable, or unenforceable. An understanding of the meaning of these terms will avoid confusion and facilitate later discussion of more specific issues.

§ 17   FORMAL AND INFORMAL CONTRACTS

In general, our law recognizes two ways in which a promise may become legally obligatory. The formal method makes a promise enforceable simply because certain prescribed formalities were observed in the making of the promise. The informal method depends upon the presence in the transaction of certain elements such as the intended exchange of rights that normally indicate that the promises were made with binding intent.

The formal method of making a contract is historically the older. In the early stages of our law, a promise had no binding force unless its making was accompanied by the observance of certain set formalities.[176] Of the formal contracts known to the early law, four are of importance to the present day lawyer. These are: (1) the contract under seal;[177] (2) the recognizance;[178] (3) the negotiable instrument and document;[179] and (4) the letter of credit.[180]

---

[173] *See* Marion W. Benfield & Peter A. Alces, *Symposium: The Revision of Article 2 of the Uniform Commercial Code: Reinventing the Wheel*, 35 WM. & MARY L. REV. 1405 (1994); Raymond T. Nimmer, *Symposium: The Revision of Article 2 of the Uniform Commercial Code: Intangible Contracts: Thoughts of Hubs, Spokes and Reinvigorating Article 2*, 35 WM. & MARY L. REV. 1337 (1994).

[174] Va. Code Ann. § 59.1-501.1, effective July 1, 2001. Md. Code Ann., Com. Law § 22-101, effective October 1, 2000.

[175] August 1, 2003 letter from K. King Burnett, President of NCCUSL.

[176] *See* Hazeltine, *The Formal Contract of Early English Law*, 10 COLUM. L. REV. 806 (1910), SELECTED READINGS ON CONTRACTS 1 (1931); Pollock, *Contracts in Early English Law*, 6 HARV. L. REV. 389 (1892), SELECTED READINGS ON CONTRACTS 10 (1931).

[177] The contract under seal was enforced under the writ of "covenant" at common law as discussed earlier in this chapter in § 3.

[178] The simple form of the recognizance brought a debtor to court voluntarily to acknowledge (*recognoscere*) that he owed a certain sum of money to the creditor. The acknowledgment was then enrolled on the record of the court and

The antithesis of the formal contract is the informal contract, which is sometimes also called a simple contract or bargain.[181] It is not informal because it is casual. It is "informal" because it does not derive is legally recognized status from any external sign such as the seal or certain words of phrases that will make a promise enforceable. Rather, the informal contract is an agreement that manifests the parties' mutual assent to a bargained for exchange where each promise not only induces a detriment but was induced by a detriment. This is the validation device known as "consideration." Mutual assent and consideration (as well as other validation devices) will be examined in detail when we come to consider the question as to how an informal contract is created.[182] The informal contract may exist either with or without a writing or any other formality unless statutes have changed the common-law rules. Statutes called Statutes of Frauds require certain kinds of informal contracts to be evidenced by a writing or electronic record to be enforceable.[183] These statutes do not convert informal to formal contracts. Where a particular type of contract is required by statute to be evidenced by a writing or electronic record, the writing requirement does not form the contract. The contract results from the parties bargained-for-exchange as in any other informal contract such as a promise to purchase land or goods in exchange for a price. The contract is formed by that exchange though there may be no writing at that moment. If the contract is oral, however, this otherwise valid contract is not enforceable because the statute is designed to prevent claims to such a contract without sufficient evidence. If a signed writing was executed after the contract was orally formed, the contract that existed from the moment it was formed would then become an enforceable, valid contract.

The informal contract is the typical contract familiar in society. The formal contract, such as the contract under seal, is rare, since, as will be seen, the seal no longer serves as an effective validation device in many situations.

§ 18   UNILATERAL AND BILATERAL CONTRACTS

Classical contract law emphasized the distinction between contracts involving two promises, said to be bilateral, and contracts involving only one promise, called unilateral contracts.[184] While this distinction will be discussed in subsequent chapters, neither the UCC nor the RESTATEMENT 2d continues this classification of contracts because of serious doubt as to its utility as well as the confusion it is capable of producing.[185] Nonetheless, the traditional

---

was essentially a judgment that avoided the creditor's bringing an action in covenant or in debt. *See* A. W. B. SIMPSON, A HISTORY OF THE COMMON LAW OF CONTRACT 126–28 (1987).

[179] Negotiable instruments and documents take on a special character because of the form in which they are written. The ordinary printed check contains the "words of negotiability"-"Pay to the order of. . . ." Other instruments may be "payable to bearer." Such formalities make such instruments freely transferable when transferred to a "holder in due course" who takes the instrument free of most defenses if certain conditions are met.

[180] See RESTATEMENT 2d § 6 comments c, d, e, and f.

[181] See RESTATEMENT 2d § 6 comment a (1973), indicating that the "formal" and "informal" usage is avoided. For historical background, see Ames, *Parol Contracts Prior to Assumpsit*, 8 HARV. L. REV. 252 (1894), SELECTED READINGS ON CONTRACTS 23 (1931); Ames, *The History of Assumpsit*, 2 HARV. L. REV. 1, 53 (1888), SELECTED READINGS ON CONTRACTS 33 (1931).

[182] *See infra* Chapters 2 and 3.

[183] *See infra* Chapter 4.

[184] FIRST RESTATEMENT § 12.

[185] *See* RESTATEMENT 2d, reporter's note at 17.

classification continues to appear in the case law.[186] The student must be aware of the traditional analysis as well as modifications of that analysis explored in later sections dealing with the acceptance of the offer.[187]

If the parties to a contract exchange promises, the contract is formed as soon as the promises are exchanged. At that point, there are two outstanding obligations since both promises remain to be performed or, as it is sometimes put, the contract is *executory* on both sides. When there are two outstanding obligations resulting from an exchange of promises, the contract is said to be bilateral or two-sided. There are two rights and two duties in such a contract since each of the parties has a right against the other and each has a duty of performance to the other. Another characteristic of a bilateral contract is that there are two promisors and two promisees. Since each party has made a promise to the other, each has given and received a promise.

A simple example of the bilateral contract is a promise by A to sell his auto to B for $10,000 in exchange for B's promise to buy A's car for $10,000. As soon as the promises are exchanged, a bilateral contract exists. A is a promisor whose duty is to deliver the car to B. A is also a promisee since he has received B's promise to pay the price. As a promisee, A has the right to collect $10,000 from B. B is a promisor whose duty is to pay the price to A. B is also a promisee since he has received A's promise to deliver the car. As a promisee, B has the right to the auto. Thus, both A and B are promisors and promisees. Both have rights and duties. When the contract was formed upon the exchange of promises, there were two rights and two duties.

In a unilateral or one-sided contract, there is only one promise. Therefore, there is only one promisor and one promisee.[188] The promisor manifests his intention that he does not seek a promise in exchange for his promise. Rather, he desires an act, a completed performance to form the contract. The classic illustration of the unilateral contract finds A saying to B, "If you will walk across the Brooklyn Bridge I will pay you $100." A does not seek B's *promise* to walk across the bridge. He requires B's act (*performance*) of walking across the bridge. The contract will be *formed* when B successfully traverses the bridge. At that point, A will have already received that which he wanted in exchange for his promise. B will have already performed the act requested by A at the moment the contract is formed. Therefore, at the time the unilateral

---

[186] For a modern illustration, see Dahl v. HEM Pharmaceuticals Corp., 7 F.3d 1399 (9th Cir. 1993).

[187] *See* Restatement 2d, reporter's note at 17; John E. Murray, Jr., *Contracts: A New Design for the Agreement Process*, 53 Cornell L. Rev. 785 (1968).

[188] *See* First Restatement § 12; 1 Corbin § 21 (1963). The distinction between a unilateral and a bilateral contract is sometimes inaccurately, expressed by saying that a unilateral contract is one in which the requested consideration for the promise is some act or forbearance other than the making of a promise, whereas a bilateral contract is one in which the consideration consists of a return promise. Thus in Brackenbury v. Hodgkin, 116 Me. 399, 401, 102 A. 106, 107 (1917), it is said, "The offer was the basis, not of a bilateral contract, requiring a reciprocal promise, a promise for a promise, but of a unilateral contract requiring an act for a promise." *See also* Port Huron Mach. Co. v. Wohlers, 207 Iowa 826, 221 N.W. 843 (1928); Petterson v. Pattberg, 248 N.Y. 86, 161 N.E. 428 (1928). In the older cases, the term "unilateral contract" was frequently used to refer to a promise that had no consideration to support it and therefore was not legally enforceable, unless it had been put in the form of a formal contract. *See* Great N. Ry. v. Witham, L.R. 9 C.P. 16 (1873); Perfection Mattress & Spring Co. v. Dupree, 216 Ala. 303, 113 So. 74 (1927); Edwards v. Roberts, 209 S.W. 247, 250 (Tex. Civ. App. 1918); Cal Hirsch & Sons Iron & Rail Co. v. Paragould & M. R. Co., 148 Mo. App. 173, 127 S.W. 623 (1910). Where there is no legal obligation, the transaction may properly be called a "unilateral promise" or an "offer looking to the formation of a unilateral contract" but it is hardly accurate to call it "unilateral contract." See High Wheel Auto Parts Co. v. Journal Co. of Troy, 50 Ind. App. 396, 98 N.E. 442 (1912), where the court said of the term "unilateral contract" when so used that it is a "legal solecism."

contract is formed, there is only one right in B to collect $100 because B has already performed and has no further duty. There is only one correlative duty. Since A has already received what he bargained for (B's performance), A has no right. He has the only duty to pay B $100.

In *Dahl v. HEM Pharmaceuticals Corp.*,[189] the defendant promised plaintiffs who were suffering from chronic fatigue syndrome that, if they completed a certain experimental program to test the effects of a new drug, Ampligen, they would receive free Ampligen for a full year thereafter. The plaintiffs were free to withdraw at any time. When the plaintiffs completed the program, the defendant refused to supply free Ampligen, arguing that there was no contract since the plaintiffs could have withdrawn at any time. The court disagreed, stating that, "the category of unilateral contracts seems to have escaped HEM's notice." Since the defendant-offeror did not seek a promise but actual performance, at the moment the plaintiffs completed their performance to test the effects of the drug, a unilateral contract was formed.

The unilateral/bilateral distinction will be further explored later in this volume.

§ 19   VOID AND VOIDABLE CONTRACTS

In certain types of contracts, one or more of the parties may have the legal power to put an end to the contract simply by manifesting an election to do so. This is known as a "voidable" contract since it can be avoided by one or more of the parties. Until the party who has the power of avoidance elects to exercise it, the contract remains intact. Moreover, even though one of the parties has the power of avoidance, he may extinguish that power by ratification of the contract.[190]

Illustrations of voidable contracts include those where one party is an infant (minor)[191] (i.e., one who has not attained the age (typically 18) providing full capacity to enter into contracts) or contracts induced by fraud, mistake, or duress. If a sixteen-year-old infant enters into a contract with an adult, both the adult and the infant are bound to the contract, but the infant has the legal power to avoid the contract. The power of avoidance is conferred by the law to protect the interests of parties such as minors against their own improvidence in entering contracts. This power continues in the infant until she reaches the age of full capacity, at which time she will either affirm (ratify) the contract or disaffirm it, thereby avoiding any obligations thereunder. If the infant does not disaffirm within a reasonable time after reaching maturity, her silence will operate as an affirmance of the contract.

If a party is induced to enter into a contract by fraud, there is a contract, but the fraudulent representations of the other party give the defrauded party a power of avoidance (also called a power of disaffirmance). On the other hand, the defrauded party may wish the contract to be performed because, notwithstanding the fraud, he believes the contract to be beneficial to him. In that situation, he simply does not exercise the power of avoidance; instead, he affirms or ratifies the contract. The identical analysis would apply to a contract induced by mistake or duress. The policy reasons underlying various types of voidable contracts will be discussed in subsequent sections.

---

[189] 7 F.3d 1399 (9th Cir. 1993).

[190] United States v. Baird, 218 F.3d 221, 230–31 (3d Cir.2000) quoting an earlier edition of this book. See also RESTATEMENT 2d § 7.

[191] *See infra* § 25.

"Void Contract." The phrase "void contract" is a misnomer. Unlike a voidable contract that is a contract until avoided, a "void contract" never was a contract since there was never any legal obligation. It was void from the inception *(void ab initio)*.[192] The phrase is a contradiction and any promise under a void contract that is breached will not give rise to any remedy nor will the law recognize any duty of performance by the promisor. Sometimes "void contracts" are referred to as "illegal contracts." While public policy may dictate that a particular bargain that has all the earmarks of a contract receive no legal sanction whatsoever because the bargain, if performed, would result in an illegal act, the phrase "illegal contract" as a substitute for "void contract" is inaccurate. While certain illegal bargains are clearly "void" in the sense that there is no legal sanction attached to them, there are certain kinds of "illegal contracts" that are merely voidable bargains.

§ 20 ENFORCEABLE AND UNENFORCEABLE CONTRACTS

Courts may recognize the existence of a contract but refuse to enforce it when it is breached. Here, the contract is said to be "unenforceable."[193] Since the court will not enforce the contract, no remedy will be available. However, the court still recognizes, in some fashion, that a duty of performance has been created.[194] An illustration of this situation occurs in relation to certain types of contracts that are not enforceable unless there is a signed writing (or electronic record) to evidence the contract.[195] Contracts for the sale of land or contracts for the sale of goods priced at $500, among others, must be evidenced by a writing. Thus, an oral contract for the sale of land or an oral contract for the sale of goods at $500 or more that fulfills all of the requirements of a contract will still not be enforceable unless there is some writing or record to evidence it. If either the seller or the buyer breaches and the other party seeks damages or (in the land contract) specific performance, the breaching party may simply raise what is known as the Statute of Frauds as a defense. The policy reasons underlying the Statute of Frauds will be explored in a later chapter. At this point, the student should regard this

---

[192] See More Light Investments v. Morgan Stanley, DW, Inc., 2009 U.S. Dist. Lexis 112927 (D. Ariz. 2009) (In a transaction involving the sale of Cuban bonds prohibited by Federal regulations, the court awarded restitution of the purchase price to avoid unjust enrichment. The plaintiff also sought attorney fees under an Arizona statute allowing judicial discretion to award attorney fees in disputes arising out of contracts. Even assuming Arizona law applied, the court was not persuaded that this dispute arose out of a contract. The court's order referred to a "voided contract" leading the court to explain that a "void contract" is not a contract.) See also the concurring opinion by Mr. Justice Breyer, joined by Justice O'Connor, in Oubre v. Entergy Operations, Inc., 522 U.S. 422, 430–32, 118 S. Ct. 838, 139 L. Ed. 2d 849 (1998), where an employee signed a release that did not comply with the requirements of the Older Workers Benefit Protection Act (OWBPA), 29 U.S.C.S. § 626, which allows an individual to waive claims under the Age Discrimination Employment Act (ADEA), 29 U.S.C.S. § 621 *et seq.* , only if certain requirements designed to insure a knowing and voluntary waiver are met. The employee had received payments under the invalid release. Defendant claimed that the employee had ratified the release by failing to return or offering to return the payments. Mr. Justice Breyer emphasized the important distinction between void and voidable promises, concluding that the employee's promise herein was voidable. If it were deemed void, the employer could refuse to perform its obligation even if the employee chose not to sue under ADEA. If, however, the promise is voidable, the employer must continue payments and medical benefits. If the employee then disaffirms by bringing an ADEA action, the employer may recover the amount of payments made under the defective release.

[193] *See, e.g., infra* Chapter 12. Such agreements are sometimes called "agreements of imperfect obligation." *See* Pollock, Contracts 682 (8th ed. 1921). *See also* First Restatement § 14; Restatement 2d § 8.

[194] "An unenforceable contract is one for the breach of which neither the remedy of damages nor the remedy of specific performance is available, but which is recognized in some other way as creating a duty of performance, though there has been no ratification." Restatement 2d § 8.

[195] The recent statutory changes discussed in §§ 14–15, *supra*, allow electronic records to evidence such contracts.

discussion as simply an illustration of an unenforceable contract. Again, it is important to emphasize the fact that courts refusing to enforce such oral contracts are not deciding that the contracts do not exist. They simply hold that even if the contracts do exist, they are unenforceable because of an overriding policy that requires such contract to be evidenced by writings or electronic records. It is important to distinguish "unenforceable" contracts from "voidable" contracts. As suggested in the preceding section,[196] a voidable contract is one that allows one of the parties to the contract to avoid it. The party with the power of avoidance may elect to either avoid the contract or affirm it. An unenforceable contract is one in which the duty of performance does not depend solely on the election of one party. If A, an infant, enters into an oral contract with B, an adult, whereby B agrees to sell and A agrees to buy a tract of land, A's promise is voidable because of his infancy. B's promise to sell the land is also unenforceable because of the Statute of Frauds, but it is not voidable since B is an adult. Assume that B delivers to A a signed writing stating the terms of the contract. At this point, the contract is enforceable since the Statute of Frauds writing requirement has been satisfied; but the contract is still voidable by A. A may choose to avoid the contract or to ratify it. If he chooses the former, the contract is enforceable but avoided since A has elected to exercise his power of avoidance. If A chooses to affirm or ratify the contract, however, the enforceable contract is no longer subject to the power of avoidance since that power has been extinguished by A's affirmance or ratification.

§ 21   EXPRESS AND IMPLIED CONTRACTS

Contracts are sometimes classified as being either express or implied. Implied contracts are in turn classified as implied in fact or implied in law.

A contract is said to be "express" when it has been stated in oral or written words, as distinguished from an "implied-in-fact" contract in which the undertaking is inferred from conduct other than the speaking or writing of words. "Whether a contract is styled express or implied involves no difference in legal effect, but lies merely in the mode of manifesting assent."[197] This classification is of no practical value and may mislead. All true contracts are necessarily express contracts, in that they must arise out of an expressed intention. The undertaking that the law sanctions and calls a contract does not have to be manifested in language but may be evidenced by conduct, but this does not militate against the conclusion that the undertaking in all cases is one that has been expressed. To speak of it as "implied in fact," when it has been expressed in ways other than through the use of language, is simply to confuse the real issue, which is whether an intention to assume the alleged undertaking has been manifested in some discernible fashion.[198]

A party entering a taxi is impliedly promising to pay a reasonable fare to be transported to the address he announces. Millions of transactions occur daily in self-service stores selling food, books, clothing, or just about any other desired product. The transaction never includes

---

[196] See § 19, supra.

[197] Janusauskas v. Fichman, 264 Conn. 796, 804, 826 A. 2d 1066, 1072 (2003).

[198] Kennedy v. Forest, 129 Idaho 584, 587, 930 P.2d 1026, 1029 (1997): "A contract implied-in-fact is a true contract whose existence and terms are inferred from the conduct of the parties." In Francis v. St. Louis County Water Co., 322 S.W.2d 724, 726 (Mo. 1959), the court states, "And as a matter of fact there is no difference in legal effect between an express contract and an implied contract; if there was a contract it was of course an express contract whether the agreement was in writing, verbal, or an inference from the acts and conduct of the parties. The distinction lies in the manner of manifesting mutual assent."

a buyer's statement offering to purchase the products or the seller's statement accepting the offer. Simply placing the chosen products at the checkout counter manifests the intention to purchase the products. No words are spoken or written and, therefore, the traditional characterization would be a contract "implied in fact." However, the outward manifestations of the parties clearly expressed the consensual elements necessary for a genuine contract. The parties expressed themselves through their conduct just as effectively as they would have expressed themselves through language.

The "implied contract" term can be misleading because it can refer to an "implied-in-law" contract that is even more unfortunate.[199] Where one party will be unjustly enriched at the expense of another party, a court may remedy this injustice by granting restitution in the amount of such enrichment to the party who conferred the benefit. There are situations where no contract exists but one party, reasonably expecting to be compensated, confers a benefit upon another. To avoid unjust enrichment, the law permits the party who has conferred the benefit to recover the reasonable value of the benefit. Through this action, he is restored to *status quo ante*, i.e., he is placed in the position he would have been in if there had been no unjust enrichment. At common law, this restitutionary action was brought in the form of a contract action (assumpsit) with a fictitious promise "implied in law" to permit the recovery. There is no real promise and none of the other elements of a real contract.[200] The exclusive connection between this kind of action and a real contract is the historic accident of the form of action that was used to accomplish restitution. Since there is no true contract involved, the enforceable obligation came to be known as a "contract implied in law" or "quasi-contract,"[201] i.e., "something like" a contract, but not a real contract. Though the common-law forms of action have been abolished, this anomaly continues at the present time and is traditionally dealt with in courses and books dealing with contract law. The purpose of a quasi-contract remedy is to accomplish restitution, i.e., to return the parties to status quo as if no unjust enrichment had occurred. The purpose of a remedy for breach of a real contract is not to return the aggrieved promisee to the position she was in before the real contract was made. Rather, it is to place the aggrieved party in the *future* position she expected to be in had the contract been performed.

Quasi-contracts can arise in myriad situations. The student is cautioned against viewing a single example as the only kind of situation in which this restitutionary device can be used.[202] A statute in Ohio provided that a county board of education had a duty to provide transportation to schoolchildren within the county who resided more than four miles from the appropriate school. The family resided more than four miles from the appropriate school. The county board refused to perform its statutory duty of providing transportation for the children. Their father transported the children to school during the academic year and then presented his bill to the board which refused to pay. The court held that the father conferred a benefit upon the board by performing the board's statutory duty to transport the children. The board

---

[199] Vertex, Inc. v. Waterbury, 278 Conn. 557, 573–74, 898 A. 2d 178, 190 (2006).

[200] Hercules Inc. v. United States, 516 U.S. 417, 424, 116 S. Ct. 981, 134 L. Ed. 2d 47 (1996): "[A]n agreement implied in law is a fiction of the law where a promise is imputed to perform a legal duty, as to repay money obtained by fraud or duress." Continental Forest Prods. v. Chandler Supply Co., 95 Idaho 739, 518 P.2d 1201, 1205 (1974): "[A] contract implied in law is not a contract at all, but an obligation imposed by law for the purpose of bringing about justice and equity without reference to the intent or the agreement of the parties and, in some cases, in spite of an agreement between the parties."

[201] *See* F. WOODWARD, THE LAW OF QUASI-CONTRACTS § 4 (1913).

[202] *See infra* § 127[B][1].

was, therefore, unjustly enriched at the expense of the father who was a proper person to perform the duty, i.e., he was not "officious" (an intermeddler) since he was the father and a taxpayer in the county who had no intention of making a gift to the board. He reasonably expected to be compensated and was entitled to recover the reasonable value of the benefit conferred.[203] There was no contract since the board never agreed to compensate the father for transporting his children. The board was, however, unjustly enriched at the father's expense and was liable for the reasonable value of the service provided.

§ 22 PARTIES TO CONTRACTS

At least two persons, either natural or artificial (one a promisor and the other a promisee), are necessary to the making of a contract, although any number greater than two may participate.[204] When there is more than one promisor or more than one promisee, the promisors or the promisees may act together as a unit, they may act separately as individuals, or they may act together and separately. Traditionally the obligation is said to be either "joint," "several," or "joint and several," depending upon the circumstances.[205] The RESTATEMENT 2d avoids the terminology "joint," "several," and "joint and several" because of their obsolete connotations.[206] The RESTATEMENT 2d substitutes "multiple promisors and promisees."[207]

§ 23 REQUIREMENT OF CAPACITY TO CONTRACT

Persons who make contracts differ markedly as to their intelligence, background, experience, judgment, and maturity. In general, it is impracticable for the law to consider these differences. If there is a clear impairment of the ability to participate in the contracting process, however, the law will consider such impairment and find a lack of capacity to make a contract.[208]

The basic requirement of any contract is an objective manifestation of intention to be bound to a bargain. An objective manifestation of assent may be impossible if physical or mental impairment is so extreme that the person cannot form the necessary intent. In such cases, there is a *total* lack of capacity and no contract is formed. Sometimes the effect of finding a total lack of capacity is characterized as a "void contract." This usage should be avoided because the

---

[203] Sommers v. Putnam County Bd. of Educ., 113 Ohio St. 177, 148 N.E. 682 (1925).

[204] RESTATEMENT 2d § 9. "It is a first principle, that in whatever different capacities a person may act, he never can contract with himself nor maintain an action against himself. He can in no form be both obligor and obligee." Eastman v. Wright, 23 Mass. (6 Pick.) 316, 320 (1828). *Accord* People's Bank of Butler v. Allen, 344 Mo. 207, 125 S.W.2d 829 (1939); Dotson v. Skaggs, 77 W. Va. 372, 87 S.E. 460 (1915); Gorham's Adm'r v. Meacham's Adm'r, 63 Vt. 231, 22 A. 572 (1891). *But see* Breedlove v. Freudenstein, 89 F.2d 324 (5th Cir.), *cert. denied*, 302 U.S. 701, 58 S. Ct. 20, 82 L. Ed. 541 (1937), *commented on*, 51 HARV. L. REV. 351 (1937), in which it was held that a national bank that was authorized by statute to act as executor of an estate could make a binding contract for the borrowing of money in its capacity as executor with itself as a bank. So, also, it apparently was not possible, in the earlier law, for one member of an unincorporated group to contract with the group as a whole. There was no such thing as group entity at the common law. *See* Faulkner v. Lowe, 2 Exch. 593, 154 Reprint 628 (1848); Napier v. Williams, 1 Ch. 361 (1911); Ellis v. Kerr, 1 Ch. 529 (1910).

[205] *See* RESTATEMENT 2d §§ 288–289.

[206] RESTATEMENT 2d § 10, reporter's note at 26.

[207] RESTATEMENT 2d § 10.

[208] RESTATEMENT 2d § 12.

phrase, "void contract," is a contradiction.[209] A total lack of capacity will preclude the formation of any contract.

If the lack of capacity is merely *partial*, a contract will be formed but it is properly characterized as "voidable" since the party who suffers from some impairment of capacity will have a legal power of avoidance or, as it is often called, a power of disaffirmance. Where the capacity impairment is partial, the power of disaffirmance will be available to the impaired party in certain transactions, but not in others. Under certain circumstances, the power of disaffirmance will be limited or unavailable. It is essential that the student of contract law become aware of how the law has dealt with impairment of the capacity to contract. To facilitate that understanding, we will consider the types of persons whose capacity to contract has been questioned by the courts. The traditional classification of such persons includes (1) married women; (2) artificial persons (e.g., corporations); (3) infants (minors); (4) mentally ill persons; (5) persons whose capacity is affected by alcohol or drugs; and (6) persons under legal guardianship.

§ 24 MARRIED WOMEN AND ARTIFICIAL PERSONS

There are no longer limitations concerning the capacity of married women and artificial persons to make contracts. At common law, a married woman had no capacity to bind herself by contract during the life of her husband.[210] Her promises were regarded as totally ineffectual. Courts of equity, however, recognized a limited capacity in a married woman to contract with reference to property conveyed to her separate use (her equitable separate estate). The enactment of Married Women's Acts provided women with full power to contract though some restrictions such as interspousal immunity for contract or tort actions predicated upon the "unity" of married persons remained. These common law throwbacks have been eroded through new interpretations of the original legislation, judicial recognition of the modern status of women, equal rights amendments, and equal protection arguments.[211] It is now clear that *any* restriction on the capacity of a married woman to contract is unconstitutional.[212]

Artificial persons such as corporations and government agencies were traditionally limited to such powers as were conferred upon them by the sovereign that created them. Their power to make contracts, therefore, had to be within the limits of those conferred powers. If they

---

[209] *See* § 19, *supra*.

[210] "At common law, when a woman married, she lost her separate legal identity. It became merged in the husband during coverture. Husband and wife were but one person in the law." 2 COKE ON LITTLETON § 187a; 2 BLACKSTONE COMMENTARIES 182. *See also* Currie, *Married Women's Contracts*, 25 U. CHI. L. REV. 227 (1958).

[211] See, e. g., the Michigan statute, MCLS 557.21 quoted and discussed in Canjar v. Cole, 283 Mich. App. 723, 729, 770 N.W.2d 449, 453 (2009). "Legal disabilities imposed on married women by the common law have been removed." Bartrom v. Adjustment Bureau, Inc., 600 N.E.2d 1369, 1371 (Ind. Ct. App. 1992). For cases discussing this erosion of any remaining limitations upon the rights of married women, see Burns v. Burns, 518 So. 2d 1205 (Miss. 1988); Garrity v. Garrity, 399 Mass. 367, 371, 504 N.E.2d 617, 620 (1987) (note 12 of this opinion lists states with statutes similar to Massachusetts which have interpreted such statutes as granting married women the broad, unimpeded right to contract); Boblitz v. Boblitz, 296 Md. 242, 462 A.2d 506 (1983); Memorial Hospital v. Hahaj, 430 N.E.2d 412 (Ind. Ct. App. 1982).

[212] *See, e.g.*, Cleveland Bd. of Educ. v. La Fleur, 414 U.S. 632, 94 S. Ct. 791, 39 L. Ed. 2d 52 (1974) (irrebuttable presumption); Reed v. Reed, 404 U.S. 71, 92 S. Ct. 251, 30 L. Ed. 2d 225 (1971) (irrational classification). *See also* Craig v. Boren, 429 U.S. 190, 97 S. Ct. 451, 50 L. Ed. 2d 397 (1976), and Frontiero v. Richardson, 411 U.S. 677, 93 S. Ct. 1764, 36 L. Ed. 2d 583 (1973).

attempted to contract, they were said to be operating *ultra vires*, i.e., beyond their conferred powers, and any such attempt would be unlawful. Modern legislation, however, has significantly restricted the *ultra vires* limitation to provide, in effect, full capacity to such persons.[213] Other forms of business organization, such as partnerships or unincorporated associations may be limited in making contracts in certain situations. Where this is so, their attempted contracts may bind their individual members.[214]

§ 25 INFANTS (MINORS)

At common law, a person was an infant (minor) until he reached the age of twenty-one.[215] Virtually all states have lowered the age to eighteen.[216] At common law, the capacity of an infant or minor to make a contract was considered impaired. The older common law view was that infants' contracts were void, voidable, or invalid.[217] The modern view, however, clearly makes such contracts voidable, i.e., the infant has a power of disaffirmance.[218]

A thirteen-year-old plaintiff was seriously injured in the defendant's snow tubing facility. The defendant sought summary judgment on the basis of a release of defendant's liability which the plaintiff and his mother had signed. The court held the release was voidable even though it was not only signed by the minor but by his mother. Parental relationship does not provide the parent with authority to release the claims of a minor child.[219] To suggest that a person who has yet to reach the statutory age of majority is necessarily impaired in his judgment or maturity and, therefore, must be protected against his own improvidence, is necessarily arbitrary. A certain seventeen-year-old may possess greater maturity, judgment, and even business acumen than most adults. The costs and uncertainties of distinguishing the capacities of minors, however, preclude any rule except an arbitrary one. The law, therefore, indulges what amounts to a conclusive presumption concerning the capacity of minors. A minor may disaffirm a contract he has made even though he is experienced and knowledgeable, successful in business, emancipated by his parents, or married.

---

[213] MODEL BUSINESS CORPORATION ACT § 3.02 (1984). Even in the absence of legislation, the defense of *ultra vires* is not favored by the courts. *See, e.g.*, Stadium Realty Corp. v. Dill, 233 Ind. 378, 119 N.E.2d 893 (1954); Valley Stream Teachers Fed. Credit Union v. Commissioner of Banks, 376 Mass. 845, 384 N.E.2d 200 (1978).

[214] *See* RESTATEMENT 2D AGENCY § 20, and RESTATEMENT 2d TRUSTS §§ 97 and 98.

[215] RESTATEMENT 2d § 14.

[216] The twenty-sixth amendment to the U.S. Constitution lowered the voting age to 18. This prompted almost all of the states to enact statutes reducing the age of majority for contracting to 18. *See, e.g.*, 23 PA. CONS. STAT. § 5101 (2009). Majority age in Alabama, however, is nineteen. Code of Ala. § 26-1-1 (2009). A representative list of other statutes may be found in RESTATEMENT 2d § 14 in the Reporter's Note. Such statutes do not affect preexisting rights, Prinze v. Jonas, 38 N.Y.2d 570, 381 N.Y.S.2d 824, 345 N.E.2d 295 (1976).

[217] As early as the fifteenth century, there were decisions holding an infant's contract to be voidable. 2 WILLISTON § 223 (3d ed. 1959).

[218] RESTATEMENT 2d § 14 comment b. Many states have enacted statutes recognizing the power of disaffirmance in infants.

[219] Mavreshko v. Resorts USA, Inc., 2005 U.S. Dist. LEXIS 45191 (M.D. Pa., May 31, 2005). Similar results are found in other cases involving for-profit defendants which can insure themselves. Where, however, a parent signs a release for her child in connection with school, community or volunteer-run activities courts have upheld the release See the discussion of these cases in Global Travel Mktg., Inc. v. Shea, 908 So. 2d 392, 400 (Fla. 2005).

Exceptions. Statutes may provide that majority is reached upon marriage,[220] or that the infant is bound by his contract if the other party had good reason to believe that the infant had reached majority because the infant was engaged in business as an adult.[221] If a minor engaged in business fails to post a sign conspicuously at the place of business and publish a notice of his status as an infant, he will lose his power of disaffirmance under a Virginia statute.[222] A Georgia statute holds infants to their contracts if the minor is operating in a profession, trade or business as an adult through the permission of his parents.[223] Where a seventeen-year-old sued his employer under an employment contract containing an arbitration clause, the court granted the employer's motion to compel arbitration. On appeal, the infant claimed the power to disaffirm the contract including the arbitration clause. The Supreme Court of Hawaii noted that Hawaii had long recognized that contracts entered into by infants were voidable, but there were legislative exceptions including the right of sixteen and seventeen year olds to be employed. Such child labor legislation eliminated the infant's power of avoidance but contained other protections for minors. The court held that the plaintiff was not entitled to disaffirm the contract. While an otherwise enforceable arbitration provision would have been enforceable against the infant plaintiff, the requirements for an enforceable provision were not met in this case.[224]

Surrendering the Power of Disaffirmance. Infants cannot surrender the power of disaffirmance during their minority since the surrender itself would be subject to the power of disaffirmance. In the eyes of the law, the infant must be protected against his own improvidence. Any adult who deals with an infant, therefore, must assume the risk that the infant may decide to disaffirm the contract. Consequently, the very power of disaffirmance conferred by the law creates a limitation on the capacity of the infant since the infant, again, is incapable of forming a contract absent the power of disaffirmance.[225] The infant may disaffirm before or after he attains majority except in real estate conveyances.[226] Any such disaffirmance is irrevocable.[227] There are no formal requirements for disaffirmance; any manifestation of intention not to be bound to the contract is sufficient. Disaffirmance may be oral or in writing[228] and it may be manifested by conduct.[229] A minor may not disaffirm burdensome portions of a contract and affirm beneficial portions.[230] If the infant chooses to

---

[220] See, e. g., ALASKA STAT. § 25.20.020 (2009).

[221] E. g., KAN. STAT. ANN. § 38-103 (2008).

[222] VA. CODE § 8.01-278 (2009).

[223] GA. CODE ANN. § 13-3-21 (2009).

[224] Douglass v. Pflueger Haw., Inc., 110 Haw. 520, 135 P.3d 129 (2006).

[225] Bancredit, Inc. v. Bethea, 65 N.J. Super. 538, 168 A.2d 250 (1961).

[226] "Any disaffirmance (which necessarily would have to be by the execution of another deed) made by the infant alone before reaching his majority would be of the same voidable nature, and for that reason the courts generally hold that such attempted disaffirmances are not effectual for that purpose." New Domain Oil & Gas Co. v. McKinney, 188 Ky. 183, 189, 221 S.W. 245, 249 (1920).

[227] Smith v. Wade, 169 Neb. 710, 100 N.W.2d 770 (1960). Michigan takes the unusual position that no disaffirmance can occur until majority. Poli v. National Bank of Detroit, 355 Mich. 17, 93 N.W.2d 925 (1959).

[228] For an illustration of an effective oral disaffirmance, see Tracey v. Brown, 265 Mass. 163, 163 N.E. 885 (1928).

[229] A minor injured by defendant's truck signed a discharge of all claims and received payment for medical expenses and a small payment. Nonetheless, the minor brought a negligence action against defendant and the court treated his conduct in bringing the action as a disaffirmance of the contract discharging all claims. Tharpe v. Cudahy Packing Co., 60 Ga. App. 449, 4 S.E.2d 49 (1939).

[230] "This is not a case in which a minor seeks to disaffirm a contract. He may, of course, do so. . . . Such a course,

surrender the power of disaffirmance, he may *ratify* the contract. Unlike the power of disaffirmance, any attempt to ratify, i.e., to surrender the power of disaffirmance prior to majority, will be ineffective since such an act of ratification would, itself, be voidable. There are no formal requirements for ratification. Any manifestation of intention to be bound to the voidable contract will be sufficient. Absent a statutory requirement that such ratification be evidenced by a writing,[231] the ratification may be oral. Generally, however, a promise to perform rather than a mere acknowledgment of the contractual obligation is required.[232] Since a ratification is, essentially, a promise to perform a voidable duty, like other such promises,[233] it needs no consideration or other validation device to support it. Beyond an express ratification whereby the infant, after attaining majority, expressly promises to perform, ratification may be implied from the infant's conduct.[234] For example, if the infant reaches majority and then retains and enjoys the use of property received under the contract, ratification will have occurred absent his express promise to perform.[235] If the infant has not received and enjoyed the property but partly performs (e.g., part payment), this alone will not constitute ratification.[236]

The question arises, if ratification can occur through the conduct of the infant, does such "conduct" include inaction, i.e., will the infant be said to have ratified the contract by failing to disaffirm the contract within a reasonable time after reaching majority? It is not difficult to find statements in the case law to the effect that the infant has only a "reasonable time" to disaffirm upon attaining majority.[237] Otherwise, he will be said to have ratified. Such statements must be carefully applied to particular fact situations since an absence of benefit to the infant and lack of prejudice to the adult may lead a court to permit disaffirmance a number of years after the infant has attained majority.[238] If the contract has been completely performed (executed) and the infant has received a benefit that he has retained after reaching majority, he will have to be prompt in disaffirming. However, if the contract is wholly executory or has been performed

---

however, would leave plaintiff with *no* insurance. What he seeks here, by whatever name it is called, is to retain the benefits of the policy but to avoid the one provision which has become burdensome. . . . Disaffirmance, if asserted, goes to the whole contract." Langstraat v. Midwest Mut. Ins. Co., 217 N.W.2d 570, 571 (Iowa 1974).

[231] *See, e.g.*, MISS. CODE ANN. § 15-3-11 (2009). *See also* RESTATEMENT 2d § 89 comment b.

[232] "In general, a mere partial payment by a person, after coming of age, on a contract made by him during infancy, without an express promise or intention to ratify, does not constitute a ratification of the contract." Bronx Sav. Bank v. Conduff, 78 N.M. 216, 217, 430 P.2d 374, 375 (1967). *See also* Estate of Derouen v. General Motors Acceptance Corp., 245 La. 615, 159 So. 2d 695 (1964).

[233] RESTATEMENT 2d § 85.

[234] NBA basketball star Kobe Bryant entered into a marketing contract when he was seventeen years old. Upon reaching majority (eighteen), he received payments under this contract and also performed duties thereunder. The court held that he had ratified the contract. *In re* Score Bd., Inc., 238 B.R. 585, 592 (D.N.J. 1999).

[235] "Affirmance is not merely a matter of intent. It may be determined by the actions of a minor who accepts the benefits of a contract after reaching the age of majority, or who is silent or acquiesces in the contract for a considerable length of time. What act constitutes ratification or disaffirmance is ordinarily a question of law to be determined by the trial court. . . . We agree that what constitutes a reasonable time for affirmance or disaffirmance is ordinarily a question of fact to be determined by the facts in a particular case." Jones v. Dressel, 623 P.2d 370, 374 (Colo. 1981). *See also* Bobby Floars Toyota, Inc. v. Smith, 48 N.C. App. 580, 269 S.E.2d 320 (1980), *and* Cassella v. Tiberio, 150 Ohio St. 27, 80 N.E.2d 426, 5 A.L.R.2d 1 (1948).

[236] *See also* Lee v. Thompson, 124 Fla. 494, 168 So. 848 (1936).

[237] What is a "reasonable time" is a question of fact. Jones v. Dressel, 623 P.2d 370, 374 (Colo. 1981).

[238] See, e. g., Madrid v. Rodriguez, 133 N. M. 553, 66 P. 3d 326 (2003), though more than 60 years had passed since the formation of the voidable contract, since the infant obtained no benefit under the contract the court held there was no reason to bar the infant from disaffirming.

only by the infant, there is no reason to insist upon prompt disaffirmance when the infant reaches majority. The preferable view considers the effect on the adult caused by the inaction of the infant under all of the circumstances rather than a mechanical test of whether the contract has been executed.[239] Reliance by the adult for some period after the infant has attained majority may result in the infant's loss of the power of disaffirmance.[240]

§ 26   INFANTS' LIABILITY FOR NECESSARIES AND RESTITUTION

An infant is liable for necessaries furnished to him, but he is not liable on the contract. He is liable for the reasonable value of the necessaries in a quasi contract action rather than for the contract price.[241] "Necessary" is a relative term that depends upon the particular situation of the infant, including his social position.[242] It is a question of fact, though it is clear that food, clothing, and shelter are necessaries.[243] It is the quality of these items in relation to the infant's particular status that must be considered.[244]

If an infant purchases goods on credit and refuses to pay for them, an action by the adult seller is subject to the infant's power of avoidance. However, if the infant still possesses the goods, he must return them.[245] If the infant no longer has the goods, he is under no liability,

---

[239] *See* Walker v. Stokes Bros. & Co., 262 S.W. 158 (Tex. Civ. App. 1924).

[240] See Jones v. Godwin, 187 S.C. 510, 198 S.E. 36 (1938) in which a mortgagee made loans for many years after a mortgagor attained majority and the mortgagor remained silent. See also Martin v. Elkhorn Coal Corp., 227 Ky. 623, 13 S.W.2d 780 (1929), where an adult incurred considerable expense installing a mine operation for eight years after the minor attained majority.

[241] *See* University of Cincinnati Hosp. v. Cohen, 57 Ohio App. 3d 30, 566 N.E.2d 187, 189 (1989) (medical expenses); Fellows v. Cantrell, 143 Colo. 126, 352 P.2d 289 (1960); Doenges-Long Motors, Inc. v. Gillen, 138 Colo. 31, 328 P.2d 1077 (1958) (damages); Dixon Nat'l Bank v. Neal, 5 Ill. 2d 328, 125 N.E.2d 463 (1955); Gastonia Personnel Corp. v. Rogers, 276 N.C. 279, 172 S.E.2d 19 (1970) (contract for services of employment agency).

[242] See Zelnick v. Adams, 263 Va. 601, 561 S. E. 2d 711 (2002) (contract for legal services may constitute a "necessary.").

[243] See, however, Webster Street Partnership, Ltd. v. Sheridan, 220 Neb. 9, 368 N.W.2d 439 (1985), in which the court held that an apartment was not a necessary for two infants who had voluntarily chosen to leave home and could return whenever they wished. On the other hand, in Rose v. Sheehan Buick, Inc., 204 So. 2d 903 (Fla. Dist. Ct. App. 1967), where a minor used an automobile for school, social, and business activities, the court found the car to be a necessary. In Valencia v. White, 134 Ariz. 139, 654 P.2d 287 (Ct. App. 1982), the repair of a truck was not a necessary for the minor's trucking business since board, room, clothing, medical needs, and education were provided for him and it was not necessary that he engage in business.

[244] "While the work, labor and professional services alleged in the complaint do not fall within the generally accepted notion of what constitutes necessaries, and might not be for a minor of *average* talents, the infant defendant, according to the complaint, is no ordinary child. The educational opportunities and training which should be afforded to a child whose gift holds promise of success in the entertainment world might, in part, well be of a type radically different from those educational opportunities and the kind of training which should be afforded to a child whose talents are directed along more traditional lines." Siegel & Hodges v. Hodges, 20 Misc. 2d 243, 245, 191 N.Y.S.2d 984, 987–88 (1959). "What constitutes necessaries is a relative, somewhat flexible term, depending upon social position, the infant's fortune and situation in life." Daubert v. Mosley, 487 P.2d 353, 356 (Okla. 1971). *See also* Robertson v. King, 225 Ark. 276, 280 S.W.2d 402, 52 A.L.R.2d 1108 (1955); Fisher v. Cattani, 53 Misc. 2d 221, 223, 278 N.Y.S.2d 420, 422 (1966): "An infant may not, however, disaffirm contracts for necessaries. Even here, the phrase necessaries, does not possess a fixed interpretation, but must be measured against both the infants [sic] standard of living, and the ability and willingness of his guardian, if he has one, to supply the needed services or articles." (Citations omitted.).

[245] Though the infant should restore any value that he has received if he still possesses it, that may not be a condition precedent to the exercise of his power of avoidance. Weathers v. Owen, 78 Ga. App. 505, 51 S.E.2d 584 (1949).

according to the prevailing view, even though he has negligently destroyed or wasted them.[246] The infant may have paid for the goods in advance and, upon disaffirmance, he may seek to recover that payment in a restitutionary action. Here, the infant is a plaintiff and to many courts the traditional view should prevail, i.e., the infant need only account for any goods or other value he retains after disaffirmance and therefore is entitled to the return of the prior payment.[247]

This view has been seriously questioned and a sizeable number of courts are willing to take a different position when the infant is a plaintiff, i.e., suing to recover prior payments.[248] If an infant purchases an automobile for $3000 and pays the purchase price at the time of delivery, many courts hold that, upon his disaffirmance, his recovery of the purchase price will be offset by either the depreciation in the value of the car, the value of the use of the auto to the infant, or both.[249] It may seem anomalous to suggest a different result when the infant is a defendant being sued by a seller to enforce the contract from the result that an increasing number of courts are willing to take when the infant is a plaintiff (attempting to recover prior payments). Yet, there are decisions that clearly recognize this distinction and, from the standpoint of risk allocation, it may suggest considerable merit.[250] Some sellers would not extend credit to infants because of the infancy but would sell to an infant for cash. Those courts that recognize a distinction between the infant as plaintiff and the infant as defendant are protecting the infant

---

[246] Taylor v. Grant, 220 Or. 114, 349 P.2d 282 (1960); Russell v. Buck, 116 Vt. 40, 68 A.2d 691 (1949); Kiefer v. Fred Howe Motors, Inc., 39 Wis. 2d 20, 158 N.W.2d 288 (1968) (discussion of issues and policy questions involved in infancy cases). Kiefer (20 years old) bought a car that had a cracked block. Subsequently, he disaffirmed the contract and sued for the purchase price. Held, he could disaffirm despite the fact that he was married and had a child.

In Halbman v. Lemke, 99 Wis. 2d 241, 298 N.W.2d 562 (1980), the plaintiff (infant) bought a car from the defendant for $1200. After paying substantially the full amount, plaintiff had car trouble, which cost $700 to repair. Plaintiff did not pay for repairs but disaffirmed the contract and demanded his money back. The court followed RESTATEMENT 2d § 15 — minor may disaffirm but he must return property to vendor. However, plaintiff was entitled to the return of his money, and did not have to make "restitution" for value of depreciation of the vehicle. "[W]e believe that to require a disaffirming minor to make restitution is, in effect, to bind the minor to a part of the obligation which by law he is privileged to avoid." *Id.* at 567. *Accord* Weisbrook v. Clyde C. Netzley, Inc., 58 Ill. App. 3d 862, 374 N.E.2d 1102 (1978); Boudreaux v. State Farm Mut. Auto. Ins. Co., 385 So. 2d 480 (La. Ct. App. 1980).

[247] Loomis v. Imperial Motors, Inc., 88 Idaho 74, 396 P.2d 467, 12 A.L.R.3d 1166 (1964). *See* Annot., *Infant's Liability for use or depreciation of subject matter, in action to recover purchase price upon his disaffirmance of contract to purchase goods*, 12 A.L.R.3d 1174 (1967). An Arkansas statute (ARK. STAT. ANN. § 9-26-101 (2000), formerly § 68-1601) requires infants to make "full restitution" upon disaffirmance. "Full restitution of property means that the property must be returned in substantially the same condition as received. If this cannot be done, there must be returned the property plus a sum of money which equals the difference between the fair market value of the property at the time the . . . contract was made and its fair market value at the time of the rescission." *See* Wheeless v. Eudora Bank, 256 Ark. 644, 509 S.W.2d 532 (1974). In New York, a married infant may not avoid contracts for real property or hospital care. There are also restrictions on infants who are veterans, professional athletes, or performing artists as to the exercise of their powers of avoidance. N.Y. GEN. OBLIG. LAW § 3-105 (repealed-1983). *See also* NY CLS ART & CULT. AFFR. § 35.03.

[248] Boyce v. Doyle, 113 N.J. Super. 240, 273 A.2d 408 (1971); Keser v. Chagnon, 159 Colo. 209, 410 P.2d 637 (1966); Porter v. Wilson, 106 N.H. 270, 209 A.2d 730, 13 A.L.R.3d 1247 (1965).

[249] The cases are unclear as to whether both depreciation and the use value may be recovered or, if only one of the measures is recoverable, which one is preferable. One problem is that courts often equate the two measures. Another problem is that the allowance of either measure normally exhausts the amount paid by the infant. For further discussion, see Annot., *Infant's liability for use or depreciation of subject matter, in action to recover purchase price upon his disaffirmance of contract to purchase goods*, 12 A.L.R.3d 1174, 1187 et seq. (1967).

[250] Rodriguez v. Northern Auto Auction, Inc., 35 Misc. 2d 395, 225 N.Y.S.2d 107 (1962); Pettit v. Liston, 97 Or. 464, 191 P. 660 (1920).

from improvident commitments but not from equally improvident expenditures. An extrapolation of this position, often called the New Hampshire view (where it was pioneered), would allow a recovery in restitution for the value of any benefits conferred upon the infant, whether or not the benefit conferred constitutes necessaries.[251]

The courts have been troubled by the situation in which the infant intentionally misrepresents his age and the other party reasonably and in good faith relies upon that misrepresentation, thereby suffering a substantial loss. Notwithstanding the fraud of the infant, some courts have continued to permit the infant to disaffirm the contract whether the plaintiff has brought an action at law or suit in equity.[252] Other courts have expressly or impliedly followed the view of Lord Mansfield that the power of disaffirmance is a shield and not a sword and should never be permitted to be used as an offensive weapon of fraud or injustice.[253] Thus, where an infant misrepresented his age in purchasing an automobile and was no longer in possession of it, the infant was estopped from pleading the defense of infancy since the seller acted in good faith and would have suffered a substantial loss because the infant could not return the auto. To permit the defense of infancy in such a case would place the court in the position of providing a "weapon of injustice."[254] The case law suggests that modern courts are more receptive to the Mansfield view of disallowing the power of avoidance where the elements of conscious misrepresentation by the infant and reasonable and good faith reliance causing substantial detriment to the other party are present.[255]

§ 27   MENTALLY ILL AND MENTALLY DEFECTIVE PERSONS

The older cases suggest that contracts as well as executed transactions of mentally incompetent parties are void rather than voidable.[256] However, as in the case of infants, the prevailing view today is that such contracts are merely voidable.[257] There are other similarities between infants' contracts and contracts involving the mentally incompetent. The incompetent is liable in a quasi-contract action for necessaries furnished to him or his family.[258] Like an infant, the mental incompetent has a power of avoidance, but the other party to the contract (the competent party) does not. If the incompetent recovers from his illness or defect, he may ratify the contract. Only the recovered incompetent, his heirs, or his personal representative after death may exercise the power of avoidance or ratification.[259]

---

[251] Porter v. Wilson, 106 N.H. 270, 209 A.2d 730, 13 A.L.R.2d 1247 (1965). *See also* Pankas v. Bell, 413 Pa. 494, 198 A.2d 312 (1964).

[252] *See* Gillis v. Whitley's Discount Auto Sales, Inc., 70 N.C. App. 270, 319 S.E.2d 661 (1984).

[253] Zouch *ex dem.* Abbot & Hallet v. Parsons, 3 Burr 1794, 97 Eng. Rep. 1103 (1765).

[254] Haydocy Pontiac, Inc. v. Lee, 19 Ohio App. 2d 217, 221, 250 N.E.2d 898, 901 (1969). *See also* Johnson v. McAdory, 88 So. 2d 106 (Miss. 1956).

[255] *See* Annot., *Infant's misrepresentation as to his age as estopping him from disaffirming his voidable transaction*, 29 A.L.R.3d 1270 (1970).

[256] *See Mental Illness and the Law of Contracts*, 57 MICH. L. REV. 1020 (1959).

[257] RESTATEMENT 2d § 15. See *Palmer v. Salazar*, 324 Fed. Appx. 729, 733 (10th Cir. 2009), citing this section of the Second Restatement. The trial court failed to address the issue of mental incompetency concerning the waiver of an ADEA complaint and the court of appeals remanded for a consideration of whether the waiver was valid in light of the allegation of mental incompetency.

[258] *See* RESTATEMENT 2d § 12 comment f.

[259] RESTATEMENT 2d § 15 comment d.

The test of contractual mental competency has been the subject of some judicial dispute. The traditional test, still generally applied, is known as the *cognitive* test, i.e., did the party understand the nature and consequences of the transaction? The RESTATEMENT 2d adopts the traditional cognitive test,[260] but criticism of that test as "nineteenth century psychology" induced it to also recognize the uncontrolled manner of acting ("motivational" or "affective") test: Though a party may have a complete understanding of the transaction, if he lacks the ability to control his acts in a reasonable manner because of mental illness, the contract is voidable if the other party has reason to know of this condition.[261] A jurisdiction may determine incompetency if either Restatement (Second) of Contracts standard is met.[262]

The contract standard of mental incompetency applied today recognizes a wide range of mental illnesses or defects including congenital deficiencies in intelligence, brain damage caused by organic disease or accident, deterioration caused by old age, and various mental illnesses giving rise to symptoms such as hallucinations, delusions, confusion, or depression. It is important to emphasize that there is complete capacity to contract unless the mental illness or deficiency has affected the particular contract.[263] Certain persons may be able to contract normally in relation to simple or even complicated transactions. Their mental incompetency may be activated only in relation to certain types of transactions, and it is only these contracts that are voidable.[264] Unless there has been a prior adjudication of incompetency, the party asserting the incompetency has the burden of proving it.[265]

When a mentally incompetent person enters into a contract, the other party to the contract may be unaware that the first party suffers from such illness or deficiency. Under an objective standard that is generally applied in contract law, it is the manifestation of assent rather than subjective assent that is operative. Therefore, if the competent party is unaware of the deficiency of the other and makes a fair contract with the incompetent, the policy of protecting reasonable expectations and the security of transactions should prevail and the contract should,

[260] § 15(1)(a). For a recent application of this test, see Brent Belcher & Olon Belcher Props., Ltd. v. Queen, 2009 Ala. LEXIS 220 where the Supreme Court of Alabama relied on precedent recognizing the "correct test" as whether a party was able to understand what he was doing at the time he signed the contract.

[261] § 15(1)(b) and Illustration 1 to this section induced by Ortelere v. Teachers' Retirement Bd., 25 N.Y.2d 196, 303 N.Y.S.2d 362, 250 N.E.2d 460 (1969). For an elaboration of the *Ortele* re analysis, see Blatt v. Manhattan Medical Group, P. C., 519 N. Y. S. 2d 973, 975–76 (App. Div. 1987). See also Krasner v. Berk, 366 Mass. 464, 319 N.E.2d 897 (1974), that recognizes the uncontrolled manner of acting test, expressly following RESTATEMENT 2d § 15(1)(b).

[262] Estate of Marquis, 822 A.2d 1153, 1157 (Me. 2003) (quoting § 15 and confirming it as Maine law). See also *Dickson v. Long*, 2009 Tenn. App. LEXIS 295 at *8, citing Rawlings v. John Hancock Mut. Life Ins. Co., 78 S.W.3d 291, 297 (Tenn. Ct. App. 2001), where the court held that incompetency may be determined from either standard as set forth in the Restatement (Second) of Contracts, § 15. An Oregon court of appeals stated that, although Oregon courts may have applied certain aspects of the "affective" test, the trial court did not err in applying the cognitive test that "appears to be the law of [Oregon], and we are bound to follow it." Davis & Davis, 193 Ore. App. 279, 280, 89 P. 3d 1206, 1207 (Ore. App. 2004).

[263] "The test of contractual capacity is whether a person is able to understand the nature of his action and apprehend its consequences. . . . This capacity is measured at the time of the execution of the contract. . . . Even where there are substantial indications of mental incompetence, it is possible that a person may have 'lucid intervals' during which he possesses the requisite capacity." Uribe v. Olson, 42 Or. App. 647, 651, 601 P.2d 818, 820 (1979). In Van Wagoner v. Van Wagoner, 131 Mich. App. 204, 346 N.W.2d 77 (1983), the court applied the "cognitive" or "understanding" test and held that emotional disorders, alone, will not invalidate a contract.

[264] RESTATEMENT 2d § 15 comment b.

[265] RESTATEMENT 2d § 15. *See* Butler v. Harrison, 578 A.2d 1098 (D. C. 1990); Barrows v. Bowen, 1994 Del. Ch. LEXIS 63 (Del. Ch. May 10, 1994).

therefore, be enforced.[266] On the other hand, a mentally ill or defective person may have to be protected against his own improvidence (similar to an infant) because of deficiencies in his judgment in relation to the particular transaction. The evolving case law has attempted to reconcile these policies.[267]

When the incompetent regains full capacity, he may either affirm (ratify) or disaffirm (exercise the power of avoidance) the contract. The reconciliation of the policies just set forth has resulted in a compromise in the case law. Where the contract is executory (not performed), the result is exactly the same as the infant contract, i.e., it is voidable. However, if the contract has been executed in whole or in part, the power of avoidance may be exercised only on equitable terms. If the competent party was unaware of the mental illness or deficiency and did not take unfair advantage of the incompetent, the contract is voidable only if the incompetent can restore the other party to status quo.[268] For example, in a contract for the sale of land where the buyer was incompetent, the seller did not know of the incompetency and the price was fair. The incompetent died shortly after title to the land was transferred. The personal representative of the incompetent could recover the part payment made by the incompetent only upon reconveyance of the land to the seller. Since the reconveyance was possible in this case, the contract was voidable.[269] Where the exercise of the power of avoidance would be inequitable, however, the contract will not be voidable. For example, an incompetent and her husband mortgaged land on fair terms to a bank. With the acquiescence of the incompetent, the money was paid to her and her husband. When the money was substantially squandered by the husband, the court held the contract was not voidable.[270] This is to be contrasted with situations where the competent party knows or reasonably should know of the other's incompetency at the time of contracting or takes unfair advantage of the incompetent. In such cases, any value received by the incompetent that he has dissipated need not be restored.[271]

§ 28   PERSONS UNDER THE INFLUENCE OF ALCOHOL OR DRUGS — GUARDIANSHIP

There have been numerous contracts cases dealing with the effects of alcoholism or drug addiction on one of the parties to the contract. The concepts developed in relation to mental illness, mental deficiency, and intoxication will be applied to the capacity of the drug user.[272]

If compulsive alcoholism or drug addiction qualifies as a type of mental illness, the same concepts apply as those set forth in the previous section. It would be possible to consider any voluntary intoxication or drug use as a form of mental illness, but the courts have not yet done so, apparently on the ground that the one who voluntarily becomes drunk (or uses drugs) has

---

[266] "[T]he majority of jurisdictions [hold] that absent fraud or knowledge of the incapacity by the other contracting party, the contractual act of an incompetent is voidable by the incompetent only if avoidance accords with equitable principles." Hauer v. Union State Bank, 532 N. W. 2d 456, 462 (Ct. App. Wis. 1995).

[267] See RESTATEMENT 2d § 15, comment a.

[268] *See* Pappert v. Sargent, 847 P.2d 66 (Alaska 1993).

[269] Verstandig v. Schlaffer, 296 N.Y. 62, 70 N.E.2d 15 (1946).

[270] Sparrowhawk v. Erwin, 30 Ariz. 238, 246 P. 541, 46 A.L.R. 413 (1926).

[271] Brandt v. Phipps, 398 Ill. 296, 75 N.E.2d 757 (1947); Spence v. Spence, 239 Ala. 480, 195 So. 717 (1940); Fecht v. Freeman, 251 Ill. 84, 95 N.E. 1043 (1911).

[272] See Reid v. IBM, 1997 U.S. Dist. LEXIS 8905, at *23 (S.D.N.Y. June 24, 1997).

less reason to be excused than the party who is mentally ill or mentally defective.[273] Therefore, courts take the position that the contract will be enforceable (including even executory contracts) if the other party to the contract had no reason to know of the intoxication.[274] This situation tends to be rare because of the standard established as to the degree of intoxication that must occur in any event to avoid a contract. The intoxicated party must not be able to understand the nature and consequences of the transaction.[275] Normally, the other party to the contract will be aware of such a degree of intoxication. However, if the competent party is not reasonably aware of the intoxication, the contract is enforceable. An intoxicated party has a power of avoidance only if he is sufficiently intoxicated and the competent party has reason to know of the intoxication. Situations do arise in which the competent party induces the intoxication before the drunken party signs the contract or, in some fashion, exploits the afflicted party's need for alcohol or drugs. These cases are really not decided on grounds of lack of capacity; they may speak of mistake or a species of fraud on the part of the competent party.[276] In any such case, the intoxicated party may avoid the contract since his intoxicated condition has been consciously induced by the other party to the contract. When the intoxicated person does have the power of avoidance, the normal rules as to ratification or avoidance of the contract are applied. Upon regaining a sober condition, the afflicted party must act promptly to disaffirm, and he must offer to restore any value received. However, if the value has been squandered or otherwise dissipated during the period of intoxication, the afflicted party may not have to offer the return of any value received.[277]

The cases involving the exploitation of alcoholics or drug users are quite similar to cases involving parties suffering from other kinds of infirmity, such as the aged and bedridden, as well as those suffering other infirmities that may indicate that they are in a state of shock or great pain. The trend is clear that some infirmity coupled with overreaching on the part of the competent party will provide the court with a sufficient base to avoid the enforcement of the contract. The fact situations are myriad and the case may ultimately be captioned under a heading such as "fraud," "unconscionability," "intoxication," or some form of mental infirmity.[278] Regardless of the caption, the courts have little difficulty in avoiding the contract if the two elements of infirmity and overreaching are present.

Guardianship.

If a party suffering from mental illness or defect or a party who is an habitual drunkard, a drug addict, a spendthrift, or an aged person is adjudicated incompetent and a guardian is

---

[273] "Drunkenness may be insanity, but it is voluntary. If it is no excuse from the consequences of a crime, why should it be against those acts affecting property? Sound policy requires that it should not, unless brought about by the other party, or unless it was so total as to be palpable evidence of fraud in the person entering into a contract with one so intoxicated." Burroughs v. Richman, 13 N.J. (1 Green) 233, 23 Am. Dec. 717 (1832). *See also* Cook v. Bagnell Timber Co., 78 Ark. 47, 94 S.W. 695 (1906).

[274] RESTATEMENT 2d § 16. See Reid v. IBM, 1997 U.S. Dist. LEXIS 8905 (S.D.N.Y. June 24, 1997); Ervin v. Hosanna Ministry, 1995 Conn. Super. LEXIS 3138 (Conn. Super. Ct. Nov. 8, 1995). *See also* Scherer v. Scherer, 405 N.E.2d 40, 47 (Ind. Ct. App. 1980) (dicta). Husband who signs divorce papers while drunk and under influence of valium is estopped from raising this defense of incapacity if he later acts (prior to bringing suit) inconsistent with his objections. "Tacit encouragement test."

[275] Williamson v. Matthews, 379 So. 2d 1245 (Ala. 1980); Olsen v. Hawkins, 90 Idaho 28, 408 P.2d 462 (1965).

[276] *See, e.g.*, Stacey v. Mikolowski, 367 Mich. 550, 116 N.W.2d 757 (1962).

[277] RESTATEMENT 2d § 16 comment c.

[278] *See* Virtue, *Restitution From the Mentally Infirm* (Pts 1–2), 26 N.Y.U. L. Rev. 132, 191 (1951).

appointed, any contracts made by such a person are void since he has absolutely no capacity to incur contractual duties.[279] The purpose of guardianship is to protect the property from being squandered or in some other fashion improvidently used. The adjudication of guardianship is public notice of the incapacity of the ward. Therefore, even though the other party to the contract may be unaware of the guardianship, there is no contract with the ward.[280] The ward's property is under the control of the guardian subject to the supervision of the court. Until the guardianship is either judicially terminated or otherwise abandoned, the ward is totally incapable of contracting.[281] His contracts are not merely voidable; they are void, which suggests that there never was a contract to either avoid or to ratify. Under certain circumstances, property under guardianship may be available to satisfy quasi-contractual obligations of the ward.[282] If, however, the ward has received any value, an innocent party who has contracted with the ward may reclaim any value received by the ward if it is still available.[283] In the case of necessaries, the competent party may recover the fair value of the consideration received to avoid the unjust enrichment of the ward. It must be emphasized that simply committing a person to an asylum or hospital where no guardian has been appointed does not make the contracts of the afflicted person void. In such cases, the contracts are voidable.[284] Another classification is the appointment of a guardian of the person as contrasted with the guardian of the property. Unless there has been an adjudication that a party has been named as guardian of the afflicted person's property, the principles set forth in this section do not apply.[285]

---

[279] Kenai Chryselr Ctr., Inc. v. Denison, 167 P. 3d 1240 (Alaska 2007); *see also* RESTATEMENT 2d § 13.

[280] Restatement (Second) of Contracts, § 13, comment a.

[281] When the ward recovers from his infirmity, the guardianship should be terminated by decree of a court. However, the guardianship may be abandoned informally, i.e., absent any adjudication. If the ward resumes control over the property without interference, or if the guardian dies and a successor is not appointed, the incapacity may terminate.

[282] *See* RESTATEMENT 2d § 13, comment b, and § 18 comment f.

[283] Reeves v. Hunter, 185 Iowa 958, 171 N.W. 567 (1919).

[284] Lorelli v. Lorelli, 2009 U.S. Dist. LEXIS 38505 at *15–16 (D. Conn. 2009).

[285] See Gallagher v. Comprehensive Personal Care Servs., Inc., 742 So. 2d 268, 270 (Fla. App. 1997), noting, "The distinctions between guardian of one's person and guardian of one's property are often blurred."

Chapter 2

THE AGREEMENT PROCESS

§ 29   THE ESSENTIAL ELEMENTS OF CONTRACT FORMATION

There are six essential elements to the formation of a contract: (1) mutual assent;[1] (2) consideration or another validation device;[2] (3) two or more contracting parties;[3] (4) an agreement that is sufficiently definite;[4] (5) parties that have legal capacity to make a contract;[5] (6) no legal prohibition precluding the formation of a contract.[6] In this Chapter, the concept of mutual assent and the requirement that the agreement be sufficiently definite will be explored. The other elements have either been explored in Chapter 1 or will be analyzed in subsequent chapters.

---

[1] *See infra* § 30.

[2] Consideration and other validation devices are explored in Chapter 3.

[3] A party may not contract with himself. See United States v. Alaska S.S. Co., 491 F.2d 1147 (9th Cir. 1974), and RESTATEMENT 2d § 9.

[4] *See infra* § 39.

[5] *See* Chapter 1, §§ 22–28.

[6] *See* Chapter 1, §§ 19–20.

§ 30   MUTUAL ASSENT — AGREEMENT — BARGAIN — PROMISE — OFFER — ACCEPTANCE

When parties make commitments to each other to act or refrain from acting in a certain way in the future, they have expressed their *mutual assent* concerning such actions or inactions. Mutual assent may be seen very simply as an expression of *agreement* between or among parties. Parties often display mutual assent expressing agreements that are not contracts. They may agree on matters of fact or opinion. None of these agreements are contracts. A contract is a species of the wider concept of agreement. A contract is an agreement that involves a bargain which is a future economic exchange of promises or an exchange of a promise for a future performance.[7] While certain promises are enforceable without a bargain, the typical contract requires a manifestation of mutual assent to a bargained-for-exchange.[8]

In a society of free economic exchange, each party decides whether to make a commitment to do or not to do some act at some future time. If that commitment was induced by a commitment from another party, the elements of a bargained-for-exchange are present. Where Ames commits herself to sell her used automobile to Barnes in exchange for Barnes' commitment to pay $10,000 to Ames, the parties have manifested a mutual commitment to a future economic exchange.

A basic question of contract law is whether two or more parties arrived at an agreement to perform a future economic exchange. The anatomy of the agreement process has been developed through innumerable judicial decisions over centuries. Central to the agreement process is the concept of *promise*. A promise may be defined as "a manifestation of intention to act or refrain from acting in a specified way, so made as to justify a promisee in understanding that a commitment has been made."[9]

When parties desire a future economic exchange, the period of negotiation will typically depend on the nature of the exchange. In ordinary consumer transactions for food and other necessities, negotiation would be rare. In commercial exchanges such as involving an acquisition of one company by another, the period of negotiation is typically very long. If the negotiations culminate in a contract, at some point they evidence a party's *promise* to act or refrain from acting in a certain way in exchange for an act, inaction or promise from the other party. Expressions of agreement or mutual assent typically are evidenced in the spoken or written language of the parties but may also be found in other conduct.[10] Ames' promise to sell her car to Barnes was induced by Barnes' promise to pay Ames $10,000. The parties exchanged promises that committed them to future action. If Ames promises to pay Barnes $50 if he will cut her lawn and Barnes proceeds to cut the lawn without promising to do so, his conduct alone manifests his agreement to perform in accordance with Ames' wishes. Ames received the desired performance from Barnes and her promise should be enforced. If Barnes owned

---

[7] RESTATEMENT 2d § 3.

[8] Mason Agency Ltd. v. Eastwood Hellas SA, 2009 U. S. Dist. LEXIS 89927 at *10 (S. D. N. Y. 2009) quoting Mizuna Ltd. v. Crossland Fed. Sav. Bank, 90 F. 3d 650, 658 (2d Cir. 1996) citing Restatement 2d of Contracts, § 17.

[9] RESTATEMENT 2d § 2.

[10] The UCC defines "Agreement" as "the bargain of the parties in fact as found in their language or by implication from other circumstances including course of dealing or usage of trade or course of performance." UCC § 1-201(3). "Agreement" has a wider meaning than "contract." Parties may enter an "agreement" without the legal protections of a "contract." Landers-Scelfo v. Corporate Office Systems, Inc., 356 Ill. App. 3d 1060, 1068–69, 827 N. E. 2d 1051, 1059 (2005).

property adjacent to the residence of Ames and Ames discovered that Barnes intended to remove certain trees on his property that Ames found useful for her privacy, the parties may agree that Ames would pay Barnes a certain sum in exchange for his promise to forebear cutting his trees, i.e., Barnes would perform his promise by *inaction*. His inaction would be the performance of his promise not to do something which he had a legal right to do, often called *forbearance*.

Offer. The agreement process is initiated by the discovery of an *offer*.[11] Almost invariably, an offer is created by a promise, i.e., the initial promise is the offer and the party making that promise is both a promisor and an offeror.[12] The party to whom the promise/offer is made is both a promisee and an offeree. When the offeree performs in the manner required by the offer by performing an act, forebearing from acting, or promising to perform in accordance with the offer, the offeree has *accepted* the offer. The parties have expressed their mutual assent by making an agreement that is a bargain or deal. If the other elements necessary for the formation of a contract are present,[13] the parties have formed a legally enforceable agreement — a contract. Thus, the mutual assent which the law requires for the formation of an informal contract is an agreement found in the usual bargain of the parties, normally expressed through an offer by one and an acceptance by the other.[14]

It is possible to discover a manifestation of mutual assent though neither the offer nor the acceptance can be identified as such, and the precise moment of contract formation cannot be determined.[15] In the typical case, however, the offer and acceptance as well as the moment of contract formation can be identified and the acceptance invariably follows the offer.[16] Since

---

[11] "An offer is the manifestation of willingness to enter into a bargain, so made as to justify another person in understanding that his assent to that bargain is invited and will conclude it" (quoting RESTATEMENT 2d § 24 in Fletcher-Harlee Corp. v. Pote Concrete Contrs., Inc., 482 F. 3d 247, 250 (3d Cir. 2007). The concepts of offer and acceptance will be fully explored in subsequent sections.

[12] A rare situation suggests the possibility that the offer is not a promise. For example, if Ames had lent a book to Barnes and, while the book was still in Barnes' possession, Ames said, "Promise to pay me $50 and the book is yours," the promise by Barnes would form a contract. It is suggested that the offer is one of performance in exchange for a promise and ownership of the book is transferred immediately upon the promise by Barnes. This type of agreement is also called a "reverse unilateral contract" since the normal unilateral contract involves a promise by the offeror requiring an acceptance by performance, whereas this agreement involves performance by the offeror and a promissory acceptance by the offeree. RESTATEMENT 2d § 55; *see also* § 24 comment a. Yet the transaction may be viewed as a promise by Ames to transfer ownership of the book (which happens to be in the possession of Barnes) to Barnes in exchange for Barnes' promise to pay $50 to Ames. Williston refers to such an offer as a promise though it is "self-operating."

[13] *See supra* § 29.

[14] Section 3 of the RESTATEMENT 2d defines "agreement" as a manifestation of mutual assent on the part of two or more persons. It defines "bargain" as an agreement to exchange promises or to exchange a promise for a performance or to exchange performances. The "mode of assent" ordinarily takes the form of an offer or proposal by one party, followed by an acceptance by the other party or parties. RESTATEMENT 2d § 22. *See* Dantz v. Amer. Apple Group, LLC, 123 Fed. Appx. 702, 707 (6th Cir. 2005); Bourque v. FDIC, 42 F.3d 704, 708 (1st Cir. 1994); I.M.A., Inc. v. Rocky Mountain Airways, Inc., 713 P.2d 882 (Colo. 1986); Kristerin Dev. Co. v. Granson Inv., 394 N.W.2d 325 (Iowa 1986).

[15] Quoting § 1.12 of Corbin on Contract, the court in Accela, Inc. v. Sarasota County, 993 So. 2d 1035, 1044 (Fla. App. 2008) recognizes that there are many cases at common law where it is clear that a contract was formed but the offer and acceptance process cannot be specifically reconstructed. Section 2-204(2) of the UCC states, "An agreement sufficient to constitute a contract for sale may be found even though the moment of its making is undetermined." A comment to this section indicates that exchanged correspondence may not disclose the exact point at which the deal was closed, but the actions of the parties may be sufficient evidence that a binding obligation was undertaken.

[16] Professor Corbin suggests the hypothetical of a document expressing agreement between *A* and *B*, prepared in

virtually all negotiations leading to contract formation can be analyzed in terms of offer and acceptance, they have become the traditional analytical tools used by courts in formation questions. Before proceeding to an exploration of offer and acceptance, however, certain preliminary matters must be understood to avoid unnecessary confusion in subsequent sections.

§ 31   OBJECTIVE VERSUS SUBJECTIVE ASSENT — "MEETING OF THE MINDS"

The requirement of mutual assent explored in the previous section is complicated by the question of *when* that mutual assent must occur which leads to the critical question of when the *necessary evidence* of mutual assent existed. Older common law cases contained statements suggesting that mutual assent must be simultaneous: "Now, whatever in abstract discussion may be said as to the legal notion of its being necessary, in order to the effecting of a valid and binding contract, that the minds of the parties should be brought together at one and the same moment, that notion is practically the foundation of English law upon the subject of the formation of contracts."[17] It was typically expressed as requiring a "meeting of the minds," a phrase that continues to be popular.[18]

Notwithstanding its popularity, the phrase is misleading. If understood literally, "meeting of the minds" and simultaneous mutual assent suggest that mutual assent must be *actual* (subjective) mutual assent, i.e., the thought processes of the parties must be identical with respect to their bargain at the same moment in time. It is not uncommon to discover statements suggesting that, until the mid-nineteenth century, courts generally accepted the view that a subjective "meeting of the minds" as well as an expression of mutual assent was essential to the consummation of a contract. A more accurate view, however, suggests that "objective approaches have predominated in the common law of contracts since time immemorial."[19] A moment's reflection suggests the folly of a subjective approach. If A makes an offer to sell his house to B who manifests his assent to this transaction, may A later say, "I'm sorry, but we have no contract since, without notifying you, I changed my mind before your acceptance"? The hardship to B whose reasonable expectations were induced by what appeared to be a serious promise by A would be intolerable if those expectations could be

---

advance by a third party, C. After reading the document, A and B stand in each other's presence and, in unison, say, "We mutually agree in accordance with the terms prepared for us by C." Corbin can find no recorded instance of such a case, but concludes that a contract would be formed. He then suggests that, "Offer followed by acceptance is the substantially universal method." 1 CORBIN ON CONTRACTS § 1.12.

   [17] Thesiger, L.J., in Household Fire Ins. Co. v. Grant, 4 Ex. D. 216, 220 (1879).

   [18] The phrase, "meeting of the minds," appeared in more than 1100 cases in 2009. Judges, however, understand that they are using the phrase in the sense of an objective manifestation of mutual assent. This thought was communicated most effectively by Judge Posner who wrote, "So a literal meeting of the minds is not required for an enforceable contract, which is fortunate, since courts are not renowned as mind readers." Colfax Envelope Corp. v. Local No. 458-3M, Chicago Graphic Communications Int'l Union, 20 F.3d 750, 752 (7th Cir. 1994). See also 216 Jamaica Ave., LLC v. S & R Playhouse Realty, 540 F. 3d 433, 440 (6th Cir. 2008). The Restatement of Contracts, § 17, comment c, places the phrase in quotes and explains that any mental reservation of a party does not impair his obligation under the contract. While little harm may be perceived from the use of the phrase on the assumption that it is being used without the intention of asserting the necessity of subjective intention, it is unnecessary and misleading absent explanation.

   [19] Joseph M. Perillo, *The Origins of the Objective Theory of Contract Formation and Interpretation*, 69 Fordham L. Rev. 427, 428 (2000). The author adds, "The account is not seamless; there was brief but almost inconsequential flirtation with subjective approaches in the mid nineteenth century. . . . Subjective approaches did, however, transform the availability or relief for mistake, duress, and other grounds of avoidance."

destroyed by a belated announcement of an undisclosed subjective intention. No workable system of contract law is possible under a subjective test since it would be impossible to prove the subjective intention of either party at any time. The demise of the romantic notion of two minds subjectively agreeing to certain contract terms at the same moment in time was, however, only grudgingly accepted by some.[20]

American pragmatism prevailed. Undisclosed intention could not be the basis for making or accepting an offer to form a contract. A mere undisclosed thought of making an offer is not an offer just as the thought of accepting a communicated offer absent a manifestation of that acceptance does not create a contract. Any other rule would be absurd. If, however, a party appeared to manifest assent to a bargain and later claimed, quite honestly, that he intended only a joke or did not intend to be bound for other reasons, the other party has a right to rely on the other's *apparent* manifestation of intention, regardless of that party's *subjective* state of mind. In countries pursuing Anglo-American contract law, the *expression* or *manifestation* of assent, rather than actual assent, will evidence contractual obligation.[21]

---

[20] In his famous concurring opinion in Ricketts v. Pennsylvania R. Co., 153 F.2d 757, 760–62 (2d Cir. 1946), Judge Jerome Frank agreed that the actual intent theory of the "subjectivists" had been carried too far, but he also felt that those who supported only the manifested (expressed) intent of the parties (the "objectivists") also went too far by excluding any evidence of the actual intention of the parties. He accused the objectivists of importing "that stubborn anti-subjectivist, the 'reasonable man' " from the law of torts apparently because they desired "legal symmetry." A more recent judicial analysis of the objective/subjective controversy is found in Newman v. Schiff, 778 F.2d 460 (8th Cir. 1985).

[21] "[T]he subjective intent of the parties is generally irrelevant. . . ." Steveson v. United Subcontractors, Inc., 2009 U.S. App. LEXIS 27046, *2 (9th Cir. 2009)"[W]e are not concerned what was going through the heads of the parties. . . . Rather, we are talking about objective principles of contract law." Kay-R Elec. Corp. v. Stone & Webster Constr. Co., 23 F.3d 55, 57 (2d Cir. 1994), (citing Restatement 2d § 21). The determination of "intent does not invite a tour through [the plaintiff's] cranium." Skycom Corp. v. Telstar Corp., 813 F. 2d 810, 814 (7th Cir. 1987). One of the classic expressions of this view is that of Judge Learned Hand: "A contract has, strictly speaking, nothing to do with the personal, or individual, intent of the parties. A contract is an obligation attached by the mere force of law to certain acts of the parties, usually words, which ordinarily accompany and represent a known intent. If, however, it were proved by twenty bishops that either party, when he used the words, intended something else than the usual meaning which the law imposes upon them, he would still be held, unless there were some mutual mistake, or something else of the sort. Of course, if it appears by other words, or acts, of the parties, that they attribute a peculiar meaning to such words as they use in their contract, that meaning will prevail, but only by virtue of the words, and not because of their unexpressed intent." Hotchkiss v. National City Bank, 200 F. 287, 293 (D.N.Y. 1911), aff'd, 201 F. 664 (2d Cir. 1912), aff'd, 231 U.S. 50, 34 S. Ct. 20, 58 L. Ed. 115 (1913). Almost two decades later, Judge Hand wrote "It is quite true that contracts depend upon the meaning which the law imputes to the utterances, not what the parties actually intended; but, in ascertaining what meaning to impute, the circumstances in which the words are used is always relevant and usually indispensable. The standard is what a normally constituted person would have understood them to mean, when used in their actual setting." New York Trust Co. v. Island Oil & Transp. Corp., 34 F.2d 655, 656 (2d Cir. 1929). Innumerable opinions contain similar statements. "The law of contracts is not concerned with the parties' undisclosed intents and ideas. It gives heed only to their communications and overt acts." Kitzke v. Turnidge, 209 Or. 563, 307 P.2d 522 (1957). "[M]utual assent is, however, unimportant except as it is manifested by one party to the other, generally by a communicated offer and acceptance. . . . So, the obligations depend not on the so-called real intent of a party, but on that expressed. . . . The phrase 'meeting of the minds' can properly mean only the agreement reached by the parties as expressed, i.e., their manifested intention. . . . Frequently ['meeting of the minds'] is misapplied seemingly to impose the requisite that there is no contract unless both parties understood the terms alike, regardless of the expressions they manifested. . . . The mere fact that each had a different subjective idea of what the term included did not prevent a binding agreement on this objective basis." Leitner v. Braen, 51 N.J. Super. 31, 143 A.2d 256, 260 (1958). "If a party's words or acts, judged by a reasonable standard, manifest an intention to agree to the matter in question, that agreement is established, and it is immaterial what may be the real but unexpressed state of the party's mind on the subject." Wesco Realty, Inc. v. Drewry, 9 Wash. App. 734, 735, 515 P.2d 513, 515 (1973). The most comprehensive judicial analysis is found in Newman v. Schiff, 778 F.2d 460 (8th Cir. 1985).

The only major nation in the world where the objective theory is not dominant is France, but the French Civil Code influences legal systems in various parts of the world. While the objective test attaches binding force to the *appearance* of assent, the French doctrine focuses on the subjective will, suggesting a real "meeting of the minds" view. There are, however, mitigating doctrines leading scholars to conclude that the subjective and objective doctrines throughout the world function in ways that are "strikingly close to each other but through a labyrinthine maze of theoretically varied routes."[22]

§ 32 INTENTION OF LEGAL CONSEQUENCES

It is commonly asserted that, even though all of the elements of a contract are present, there is no contract unless the parties also intend their agreement to be legally binding. Like other general statements, however, this statement is unreliable absent qualification.[23] Parties do not typically consider, much less express, any intention concerning legal consequences at the time of contract formation. There is no requirement that parties either intend or understand the legal consequences of their actions.[24] As the contract is formed, the typical party is contemplating the performance he expects in return for his performance and does not consciously advert to the legal consequences of the agreement. In analyzing the so-called requirement that legal consequences must be intended by the parties as a prerequisite to any contract, four general situations should be considered:

(A) the parties express their intention to be legally bound; (B) the parties express their intention *not* to be legally bound; (C) the expressions of the parties are properly *interpreted* as either intending or not intending legal consequences; (D) the parties manifest no intention whatsoever in relation to legal consequences. Each of these situations will now be considered.

[A] The Parties Express Their Intention to Be Legally Bound

Since parties to a typical contract do not consciously consider the legal consequences of their agreement, it will be rare to discover a statement that they intend their agreement to be legally binding. Should they include such a statement, however, the parties have eliminated any question as to their intention of legal consequences if all of the other elements of an enforceable contract are in place. A court should enforce the manifested intention of the parties, but an agreement that would not be enforceable as a contract does not become enforceable simply because it includes a statement that they intend legal consequences to attach to that agreement. Certainly, an agreement against public policy would still be unenforceable notwithstanding a provision that the parties intended legal consequences to attach.[25]

---

[22] Pavix Owsia, *Formation of Contract: A Comparative Study Under English, French, Islamic and Iranian Law* at 569, quoted in Wayne Barnes, *The French Subjective Theory of Contract: Separating Rhetoric From Reality*, 83 Tul. L. Rev. 359, 393 (2008).

[23] See the criticism of this statement in 1 CORBIN ON CONTRACTS § 2.13.

[24] Acton v. Fullmer, 323 B. R. 287, 295 (D. Nev. 2005).

[25] An obvious example would be an agreement between parties whereby one promised to murder the spouse of the other. Such an agreement would be void and no statement concerning the intention of legal consequences would be sufficient to convert that void understanding into an enforceable contract. A less obvious example would be an agreement between married persons that would be considered unenforceable because it would change an essential element of the marriage relationship. *See* RESTATEMENT 2d § 190.

[B]   The Parties Express Their Intention Not to Be Legally Bound — Letters of Intent — Employee Benefits

On the surface, the second situation appears as free from doubt as the first, i.e., if the parties clearly state their intention not to be legally bound, again, the courts have no need to discover their intention. The intention of the parties should be effectuated since courts ought to respect the manifested intention of the parties even though the bargain they have made appears to be the kind that is normally enforced at law. In general, the courts have adopted this position.[26]

Letters of Intent. Courts recognize that, "[o]ne of the most difficult areas of contract law concerns the enforceability of letters of intent and other preliminary arrangements."[27] Where parties are negotiating major transactions such as mergers, acquisitions, an initial public offering of stock or long term transactions, they often find it useful to maintain a record of their complex negotiations. Such a record will facilitate negotiations by recording matters of preliminary agreement that will avoid duplication and misunderstandings. Such letters provide assurance of continuing good faith negotiations and the pursuit of due diligence in the analysis of confidential information.[28] The typical "letter of intent" or "agreement in principle" will evidence agreement on many terms though it will also include a statement such as, "no liability or obligation of any nature whatsoever is intended to be created" by the letter of intent.[29] Moreover, it will often state that the obligations of the parties are subject to the preparation of a final, definitive agreement that is approved by the board of directors.[30] Notwithstanding such statements, the parties may proceed to reach agreement on all material matters and even publicize their agreement though the "definitive" and final memorial of the agreement has yet to be executed. Simply because a document is captioned "letter of intent" does not preclude a court from finding that the document evidences a contract.[31] The question is difficult because it is one of intention.[32]

An analysis by a district court judge in such cases has proven to be helpful to subsequent courts. In *Teacher's Insurance and Annuity Association of America v. Tribune Co.*,[33] Judge Leval distinguished two types of preliminary agreements that are binding. A Type I "fully binding preliminary agreement"exists where the parties have reached a complete agreement, including an agreement to be bound, on all issues perceived to require negotiation. The agreement is "preliminary" only in the sense that the parties *desire* but do not require a final, formalized statement of their existing binding agreement.[34]

---

[26] The classic exposition of this principle is found in Rose & Frank Co. v. J.B. Crompton Bros., [1923] 2 K.B. 261 (C.A.) where the parties clearly expressed an intention not to be legally bound and the court found that such a "gentleman's agreement" was not binding.

[27] Venture Associates Corp. v. Zenith Data Systems, 96 F. 3d 275, 276 (7th Cir. 1996), Posner J.

[28] See Feldman v. Allegheny International, Inc. 850 F. 2d 1217, 1221 (7th Cir. 1988) discussing the significant amount of time, effort, research and expense attending a complex business transaction.

[29] Dunhill Sec. Corp. v. Microthermal Applications, Inc., 308 F. Supp. 195, 197 (S.D.N.Y. 1969).

[30] Arnold Palmer Golf Co. v. Fuqua Industries, 541 F. 2d 684 (6th Cir. 1976).

[31] Garner v. Boyd, 330 F. Supp. 22 (N.D. Tex. 1970), *aff'd per curiam*, 447 F.2d 1373 (5th Cir. 1971), which held that a document was evidence of a contract notwithstanding its caption of "letter of intent."

[32] See the related discussion of "agreements to agree" at § 33, *infra*.

[33] 670 F. Supp. 491, 498 (S.D.N.Y. 1987) (Judge Pierre N. Leval), *appeal dismissed*, 816 F.2d 670 (2d Cir. 1987).

[34] In Hunneman Real Estate v. Norwood, 54 Mass. App. Ct. 416, 765 N. E. 2d 800 (2002), the court noted that a

A Type II "binding preliminary agreement" does not commit the parties to their ultimate contractual objective. It does, however, commit the parties to negotiate open issues in good faith and fair dealing in an attempt to reach the contractual objective within the agreed framework. A Type II agreement bars a party from renouncing the deal, abandoning the negotiations or otherwise insisting on conditions that do not conform to the preliminary agreement.[35] The two types of preliminary agreements that are generally not binding are agreement where the parties agree to be bound by some terms but leave other material terms open, or where they simply agree to agree at a later time.[36]

Fairness-Employee Benefit Plans. Considerations of fairness may also limit the application of a clause negating legal obligation. Thus, if an agreement containing a "not legally binding" clause has been performed by one of the parties and a refusal to enforce it against the other party would result in manifest unfairness, as in some employee benefit cases, courts will enforce the agreement notwithstanding the clause.[37] Benefits plans are typically analyzed as unilateral contracts where an employee is entitled to the promised benefits by completing performance for the required number of years as set forth in the plan.[38] One view would treat the employer's promise as illusory since an unfettered power to amend the plan promises nothing. A second view is to ignore the employer's power to amend the plan and enforce the promises in the plan to any employee who fully performs. A third view would also vest the benefits of the plan in any employee who has fully performed, unless a clause in the plan explicitly reserves the right of the employer to amend the plan retroactively even after the employee's performance.[39] Legislation has been enacted to overcome the unfairness of "not legally binding" clauses in pension plans. The Employee Retirement Income Security Act

---

signed letter of intent twice expressly stated the parties intention to be bound in prominent parts of the letter and held that any missing terms could be supplied.

[35] See Venture Assocs. Corp. v. Zenith Data Sys. Corp., 96 F.3d 275 (2d Cir. 1996). *See also* Channel Home Ctrs., Div. of Grace Retail Corp. v. Grossman, 795 F.2d 291 (3d Cir. 1986).

[36] See Cochran v. Norkunas, 398 Md. 1, 13, 919 A.2d 700, 707-08 (2007), where the court repeats the Leval analysis while adding the two additional categories of unenforceable preliminary agreements, all four of which are capture in the Corbin analysis at § 2.9 of the Corbin treatise quoted by the court. Other cases in which the Leval analysis has been used include Burbach Broadcasting Co. of Del. v. Elkins Radio Corp., 278 F. 3d 401 (4th Cir. 2002); Arcadian Phosphates, Inc. v. Arcadian Corp., 884 F. 2d 69 (2d Cir. 1989).

[37] RESTATEMENT 2d § 21 comment b, suggests that parties are free to include "not legally binding" clauses which are normally enforced. However, they may raise difficult questions of interpretation, misrepresentation, mistake, or overreaching, i.e., unconscionability. In Tilbert v. Eagle Lock Co., 116 Conn. 357, 165 A. 205 (1933), an employee received a "certificate of benefit" stating that his beneficiary would receive a certain sum upon his death if he should die while an employee of the company. The certificate stated that it was not a contract and conferred no legal rights on the employee. When the company decided to withdraw the benefit some eight years later, it posted notices of withdrawal. However, the employee died at 2 A.M. on the day such notices were posted and the court held the notices of withdrawal ineffective until the end of the day on which they were posted.

[38] Hoefel v. Atlas Tack Corp., 581 F.2d 1, 3–5 (1st Cir. 1978), *cert. denied*, 440 U.S. 913, 99 S. Ct. 1227, 59 L. Ed. 2d 462 (1979). The employer's announcement of the plan was an offer that was accepted by the performance of the employees. Where, however, the plan includes a clause reserving to the employer a right to amend or discontinue it at any time and the employer subsequently terminates the plan, there is a split of authority as to whether employees are entitled to the benefits of that plan. See the collection of cases dealing with this issue in McGrath v. Rhode Island Retirement Bd., 88 F.3d 12, 16–17 (1st Cir. 1996). The court adds the caveat that there may be a difference in the treatment of public sector retirement plans based on the necessity for governmental flexibility concerning retirement benefits the state offers to public employees.

[39] See *Abbott v. Schnader Harrison Segal & Lewis LLP*, 50 Pa. D. & C. 4th 225 (2001), *aff'd*, 805 A. 2d 547 (Pa. Super. 2002), adopting the third view as set forth in *Kemmerer v. ICI Americas, Inc.*, 70 F.3d 281 (3d Cir. 1995).

(ERISA) contains an "anti-cutback" provision that prevents amendments from decreasing the accrued benefits of a participant in a plan.[40]

[C]   The Expressions of the Parties Are Interpreted as Intending or Not Intending Legal Consequences — Jest, Physicians' Statements

Where the parties have not clearly indicated their intention concerning legal consequences, courts are faced with the usual task of interpreting their manifestations of intention under all of the circumstances to determine whether they intended to be legally bound. There are two kinds of cases, in particular, that raise this question. In the first type, one of the parties to an agreement insists that he was only joking or bragging and should not have been taken seriously, i.e., he intended no legal consequences. When confronted with the defense that the defendant was only joking or bragging and should not have been taken seriously, courts have considered all of the relevant circumstances and applied the following test: should the party's expressions have been reasonably understood as expressing himself in that fashion so that the other party would be unreasonable in assuming that he had the power to form a binding agreement?

In what has become a popular illustration of this principle occurred in *Leonard v. Pepsico, Inc.*, where[41], a teenager saw a television commercial that offered certain merchandise in exchange for "Pepsi points" available on the offeror's product or by purchasing "points" at ten cents each. The commercial displayed a teen operating a Harrier jet aircraft with a subtitle stating its cost at 7 million points. With the teen flying the jet, it landed at his school, blowing the clothing off a teacher as his classmates watched. The Jet prize did not appear with other "Pepsi points" items in the printed Pepsi catalogue. The plaintiff accumulated $700,000 and sent it to the defendant, demanding the Harrier jet though the plane was estimated to cost some $23 million. The defendant claimed that the Harrier jet part of the commercial was "fanciful," and was "included to create a humorous and entertaining ad."

The court emphasized that it must not consider either the plaintiff's or defendant's subjective intent. Rather, the test is "what an objective, reasonable person would have understood the commercial to convey."[42] Thus, if a party is reasonable in assuming that the other party was serious, i.e., not joking or bragging, a contract will have been formed regardless of the secret, undisclosed intention of the other party.

The Zehmers owned a farm and discussed its sale with Lucy in a bar. Lucy insisted on a writing evidencing the transaction which Mr. Zehmer signed. At Lucy's demand, the writing was amended to include t he signature of Mrs. Zehmer. The defendants claimed that the entire discussion was a joke. Mr. Lucy testified that he whispered the fact that it was a joke to Mrs. Zehmer and he also insisted that the parties were simply "drunk." The court found that the evidence did not support Zehmer's claim of intoxication and, otherwise, there was no basis

---

[40]   29 U.S.C. § 1054(g). See Anderson v. Suburban Teamsters of N. Ill. Pension Plan, 2009 U. S. App. LEXIS 26107 at *17 (9th Cir. 2009).

[41]   88 F. Supp. 2d 116 (S.D.N.Y. 1999), *aff'd*, 210 F.3d 88 (2d Cir. 2000).

[42]   88 F. Supp. 2d at 127. The court also quotes Corbin at § 1.11 stating that the "kind of [act] that creates a power of acceptance" "must be an act that leads the offeree reasonably to conclude that a power to create a contract is conferred."

for Lucy to assume that the owners were not serious in agreeing in writing to sell the farm.[43]

Promises by Physicians. The second type of case that has proven difficult under this third classification involves statements by physicians to patients. It is certainly possible for a surgeon to make an enforceable promise to perform an operation. Performance by another surgeon without the informed consent of the patient will constitute a battery and the original surgeon may be sued in contract or tort.[44] Most of the cases involving physician's promises, however, concern alleged promises to cure a particular malady or related matters, such as the duration of a hospital stay. The physician may suggest a surgical procedure to cure the condition and may respond to questions concerning the period of recovery with some assurances that the period will not exceed a certain time. Whether these statement are contractual promises to the patient or are professional opinions or judgment is a question of fact. Courts, however, require clear evidence of an express promise to cure as contrasted with professional assurances that are not promises to cure.[45]

Even if the physician has used promissory language, courts typically hold that the patient should not have understood the physician as undertaking a legal obligation in the same sense that a merchant makes a legally binding promise in a commercial transaction. Rather, the patient should have understood the physician's statements as suggesting what is likely to occur notwithstanding language that, in other contexts, may be interpreted as promissory. A therapeutic reassurance should not be understood as a contractual promise.[46] Courts are reluctant to cast contractual liability upon physicians because they recognize that physicians necessarily make judgmental and predictive statements to their patients. Courts also recognize the special relationship of doctor and patient that may permit a physician to refrain from discussing all of the dangers that may be present even in a relatively simple surgical procedure since excessive candor may create a psychic reaction that would seriously impair the success of the treatment.[47]

---

[43] Lucy v. Zehmer, 196 Va. 493, 84 S.E.2d 516 (1954). Cases involving "bragging" include Newman v. Schiff, 778 F.2d 460 (8th Cir. 1985), in which Schiff, a "tax rebel," appeared on a television news program and offered to pay $100,000 to anyone who could disprove his theory that the Internal Revenue Code contained no provision making the payment of taxes mandatory. The court held that the statement, albeit a bragging one, was an offer. The segment of that program containing the offer was rebroadcast on a news program by the same network (CBS) where Newman saw it. Newman attempted to accept the offer because he had become aware of it on the rebroadcast. The court held the rebroadcast was not a renewal of the offer but only a news report of the original offer that terminated at the end of the "call-in" program. In Barnes v. Treece, 15 Wash. App. 437, 549 P.2d 1152 (1976), the court found a statement made by a promoter of punch boards that he would pay a certain sum if anyone could prove that such devices were "crooked" to be an effective offer which was accepted.

[44] For an interesting analysis of such cases, see Dingle v. Belin, 358 Md.354, 749 A. 2d 157 (Ct. App. 2000).

[45] *See* Sullivan v. O'Connor, 363 Mass. 579, 296 N.E.2d 183 (1973). *See also* Burns v. Wannamaker, 281 S.C. 352, 355, 315 S.E.2d 179, 181 (Ct. App. 1984) (while some courts hold that liability against a physician or dentist based upon breach of an express warranty must be evidenced by a separate consideration, this court required no separate consideration, did require proof of the existence of the alleged warranty by clear and convincing evidence).

[46] See *Sullivan*, 296 N.E.2d at 186. If contract actions can be readily maintained against physicians, they may be frightened into practicing "defensive medicine."

[47] Gault v. Sideman, 42 Ill. App. 2d 96, 191 N.E.2d 436 (1963). *See Annot., Recovery against physician on basis of breach of contract to achieve particular result or cure*, 43 A.L.R.3d 1221 (2008).

While medical malpractice claims are generally governed by tort principles,[48] the relationship underlying the duty of care that gives rise to a physician's liability is contractual in nature. Where a physician undertakes to treat a patient, he expressly or impliedly contracts to exercise reasonable care and diligence in treating the patient. The doctor/patient relationship forms the contractual base from which a tort obligation may arise.[49] Notwithstanding the reluctance of courts to find a breach of promise by a physician, if the promise is abundantly clear, courts recognize that a physician is capable of making an enforceable promise to effect a cure or result to which legal consequences will attach.[50]

The celebrated case is *Hawkins v. McGee*[51] where a boy suffered a severe scar on his hand resulting from a burn. The physician attempted to persuade the parents for several years to permit an operation to remove the scar although skin specialists had advised against surgery. The parents resisted these efforts, but when the boy turned eighteen, he agreed to the surgery. The physician stated that the operation would be simple, quick, and effective and said, "I will guarantee to make the hand a hundred percent perfect hand." He also told the father that the boy would be hospitalized no more than four days. After the operation, the patient bled badly for several days, the hand was partially closed and the scar worsened. Moreover, the hand was densely covered with hair. Other specialists stated that nothing could be done to remedy the problem. The physician claimed that his statements were mere opinions or predictions rather than promises. With respect to the statement that the hand would be "a hundred percent perfect hand," the court disagreed since the physician was so persistent and had clearly gone beyond statements of opinion or prediction. With respect to the duration of the hospital stay, the court held that statement to be prediction rather than promise. The jury awarded the plaintiff $3000, but the case was settled for $1400.

Six decades later, the same court considered a surgeon's promise that the "operation could" provide "a knee that was stronger than . . . before," and the plaintiff would be able to play ball again. The court distinguished *Hawkins v. McGee* on the footing that this surgeon did not solicit or request that he be allowed to perform the plaintiff's surgery. Indeed he informed the plaintiff that he could have another surgeon perform the operation and the plaintiff did consult another surgeon before agreeing to the surgery. The court concluded that the statements were only statements of opinion or predictions of the probable duration of the treatment and outcome of the surgery.[52]

---

[48] *See* Note, *Contractual Liability in Medical Malpractice* — Sullivan v. O'Connor, 24 DE PAUL L. REV. 212, 214 (1974); Note, *Physicians and Surgeons* — Sullivan v. O'Connor: *A Liberal View of the Contractual Liability of Physicians and Surgeons*, 54 N.C. L. REV. 885, 887 (1976).

[49] Greenberg v. Perkins, 845 P.2d 530, 534 (Colo. 1993).

[50] *See* Sullivan v. O'Connor, 363 Mass. 579, 296 N.E.2d 183 (1973) (promise to make patient more beautiful), and Stewart v. Rudner, 349 Mich. 459, 84 N.W.2d 816 (1957) (promise to perform Caesarian section).

[51] 84 N.H. 114, 146 A. 641 (1929).

[52] Anglin v. Kleeman, 140 N. H. 257, 260, 665 A. 2d 747, 750 (1995).

[D]   The Parties Manifest No Intention About Legal Consequences — Social Agreements, Agreements Between Married Persons and Unmarried Cohabitants

If the parties have not manifested any intention concerning legal consequences so that courts may not legitimately find such an intention through interpretation of the parties' expressions, courts have generally concluded that legal consequences should attach. Since the typical agreement involves no thought about legal consequences, courts are faced with the necessity of deciding what reasonable parties would have intended had they considered the matter at all. The judicial assumption that the parties would have intended legal consequences had they thought about it may be said to lead to the conclusion that no genuine intent concerning legal consequences is essential. This apparent conundrum is overcome through the practical necessity of attaching legal consequences to the overwhelming majority of agreements in which the parties do not manifest any such intention. Absent the presumption, the majority of agreements would not be contracts. Thus, the simplistic statement that the parties must intend legal consequences to attach before any contract can be recognized has been replaced with the modern view: "Neither real nor apparent intention that a promise be legally binding is essential to the formation of a contract, but a manifestation of intention that a promise shall not affect legal relations may prevent the formation of a contract."[53] Thus, the general rule is that legal sanctions attach unless the parties manifest their intention that they shall not attach. Like any general rule, however, this rule is subject to exceptions.

If parties agree to a social engagement, no legal obligation attaches. If *A* invites *B* to dinner or another social engagement and *B* accepts the invitation, there is no manifestation of intention regarding legal consequences. Under the general rule that legal obligation attaches absent express negation by the parties, legal obligation would attach. But that result is contrary to the reasonable expectation of parties to the typical social engagement. The law recognizes the normal understanding of parties in such circumstances, i.e., had they thought about the matter at all, they would have regarded such an engagement as binding only in honor.[54] In effect, the law substitutes the normal understanding of parties in social engagements for an expression manifesting their intention that legal consequences should not attach.

A similar conclusion is found in domestic arrangements. Where a husband and wife are living in harmony, the normal understanding is that agreements between spouses are ordinarily not intended to be legally binding.[55] Even where the family relationship is not as close as the husband and wife relationship, the normal understanding is that such agreements are binding only in honor. If, however, members of the same family were to enter into a

---

[53] RESTATEMENT 2d § 21.

[54] "There are agreements between parties which do not result in contract within the meaning of that term in our law. The ordinary example is where two parties agree to take a walk together, or where there is an offer and an acceptance of hospitality. Nobody would suggest in ordinary circumstances that those agreements result in what we know as a contract." Balfour v. Balfour, 2 K.B. 571 (1919). *See also* Mitzel v. Hauck, 78 S.D. 543, 105 N.W.2d 378 (1960) (promise to go duck hunting was not a contractual promise — it was a social engagement). Nor is a politician liable for campaign promises: O'Reilly v. Mitchel, 85 Misc. 176, 148 N.Y.S. 88 (Sup. Ct. 1914).

[55] Balfour v. Balfour, 2 K.B. 571 [1919]. *See also In re* Weide's Estate, 73 S.D. 448, 44 N.W.2d 208 (1950) (wife, a registered nurse, presented a bill to the estate for caring for husband-decedent; *held*: the services were presumed to be gratuitous).

business arrangement, the result could change if the inference was unwarranted.[56]

A number of cases involve agreements between unmarried cohabitants. The leading case involved actor Lee Marvin, who lived with Michelle Marvin for seven years. Title to all property was held by Lee Marvin. Michelle alleged an oral contract that they would share equally any property accumulated while cohabiting. She further alleged the parties had agreed to represent themselves as a married couple, and that her contribution was that of companion, homemaker, housekeeper and cook. This and similar cases focus on the question of whether such agreements violate public policy or even criminal statutes proscribing fornication or adultery. In *Marvin*, the court held that a relationship that appears conventional and does not flout public standards should not be characterized as contrary to public policy on the ground that it is meretricious unless the contract is explicitly founded on payment for sexual services.[57] Another court held that the contract may contemplate sexual intercourse as part of cohabitation and is still enforceable if the sole or dominant consideration is not sexual intercourse.[58] The overwhelming majority of courts are in agreement.[59]

Since the great majority of courts hold that legal consequences should attach to agreements between unmarried cohabitants, they may be said to have returned to the general rule that legal consequences attach in the absence of a contrary manifestation. This shift, however, is predicated upon the assumption that, had the parties thought about the matter at all, they would have intended legal consequences. In contrast, the agreement between married persons living in harmony suggests the contrary assumption, i.e., that the agreement is binding only in honor. The indefinite duration of relationships between unmarried cohabitants and the lack of legal sanctions attending such relationships suggests that the parties would have contemplated legally binding effects had the parties consciously considered the matter.

§ 33　"AGREEMENT TO AGREE" — MISSING TERMS — FINAL WRITING CONTEMPLATED

If parties enter into an agreement to later agree, will a court recognize such an agreement as a contract to make a contract? The traditional judicial reaction was to find no contract on the ground that an "agreement to agree" is a contradiction in terms since parties cannot be contractually bound until they arrive at a final agreement:

---

[56]　*See* Boston v. Boston, 1 K.B. 124 [1904].

[57]　Marvin v. Marvin, 134 Cal. Rptr. 815, 557 P.2d 106 (1976). The court also recognized the trend toward trial relationships.

[58]　Latham v. Latham, 274 Or. 421, 547 P.2d 144 (1976).

[59]　See Salzman v. Bachrach, 996 P.2d 1263 (Colo. 2000); Wilcox v. Trautz, 427 Mass. 326, 693 N.E.2d 141 (1998), and Boland v. Catalano, 202 Conn. 333, 521 A.2d 142 (1987), which list numerous cases in general conformity with the *Marvin* rationale throughout the country. *Wilcox*, however, disagrees with *Marvin* and other cases which grant property rights to a nonmarital partner in the absence of an express contract. A minority view is found in Hewitt v. Hewitt, 77 Ill. 2d 49, 62, 394 N.E.2d 1204, 1209 (1979): "We cannot confidently say that judicial recognition of property rights between unmarried cohabitants will not make that alternative to marriage more attractive by allowing parties to engage in such relationships with greater security [than the marriage relationship]. . . . In thus potentially enhancing the attractiveness of a private arrangement over marriage, we believe that the appellate court decision in this case contravenes the [legislative] policy of strengthening and preserving the integrity of marriage." Other minority views are found in Long v. Marino, 212 Ga. App. 113, 441 S.E.2d 475 (1994); *In re* Estate of Alexander, 445 So. 2d 836 (Miss. 1984). Schwegmann v. Schwegmann, 441 So. 2d 316 (La. Ct. App. 5th Cir. 1983), *cert. denied*, 467 U.S. 1206, 104 S. Ct. 2389, 81 L. Ed. 2d 347 (1984).

"[A]n agreement that [the parties] will in the future make such a contract as they may then agree upon amounts to nothing. An agreement to enter into negotiations, and agree upon the terms of a contract, if they can, cannot be made the basis of a cause of action. There would be no way by which the court could determine what sort of a contract the negotiations would result in; no rule by which the court could ascertain whether any, or, if so, what damages might follow a refusal to enter into such future contract. So, to be enforceable, a contract to enter into a future contract must specify all its material and essential terms, and leave none to be agreed upon as the result of future negotiations."[60]

Missing Terms Not Fatal. Such a strict position is not in accordance with modern contract law where many contracts may be found to exist though some terms, even some material terms, are left for future agreement between the parties. The general formation of contracts section of the Uniform Commercial Code states the modern view: "Even though one or more terms are left open a contract for sale does not fail for indefiniteness if the parties have intended to make a contract and there is a reasonably certain basis for giving an appropriate remedy."[61] A contract may be found though numerous terms, even the price term, may be missing.[62] The departure from classical contract law, however, is considerably less radical than it may appear upon first blush.

To find a contract notwithstanding missing terms, the two critical conditions expressed in the UCC and replicated in the Second Restatement of Contracts must be satisfied: there must be evidence that the parties intended to make a contract notwithstanding the missing terms, *and* the court must have a reasonably certain basis for giving an appropriate remedy. These are the same factors underlying the flat rejection of "agreements to agree" in the earlier cases. The difference between the modern and older view, therefore, is one of degree rather than kind. The modern view is that even a material missing term does not, *per se*, preclude a court from finding a contract. As explorations in later sections will reveal, the modern view is more liberal in allowing courts to imply terms that will recognize a contract if that appears to be the parties' intention. The more liberal implication process, however, will not permit a court to imply all terms, and even terms that a court would normally imply will not be implied where there is evidence that the implied term may differ from the term the parties intended.

Final Writing Contemplated. If the question is whether parties who have reached an agreement but also contemplate a final writing can be bound whether the final writing is ever executed, the modern view replicates the older case law view. As in cases involving letters of intent, the answer depends on whether they intended to be bound before executing the writing. If their expressions of agreement and other surrounding circumstances indicate that they understood themselves to be bound as soon as they agreed on essential terms, their contract was formed as soon as they reached that agreement though a final writing is never created.[63]

---

[60] Shepard v. Carpenter, 54 Minn. 153, 155, 55 N.W. 906, 906 (1893), *quoted with approval in* St. Louis & S. F. R. v. Gorman, 79 Kan. 643, 100 P. 647 (1909). The concept can be found at least as early as Ridgway v. Wharton, 6 Clark's H.L. Cases 238, 306 (1857), in which the court states the strict view that "[a]n agreement to enter into an agreement upon terms to be afterward settled between the parties is a contradiction in terms."

[61] § 2-204(3). *See also* RESTATEMENT 2d §§ 33 and 54.

[62] UCC § 2-305. The implication of missing terms will be explored in later sections.

[63] In Kazanjian v. New England Petroleum Corp., 332 Pa. Super. 1, 8, 480 A.2d 1153, 1157 (1984), the court stated: "[I]f the parties orally agree to all of the terms of a contract between them and mutually expect the imminent drafting of a written contract reflecting their previous understanding, the oral contract may be enforceable." *See also* Courtin

In such a case, the final writing is intended as nothing more than a mere memorial of their existing contract. If, however, their expressions and surrounding circumstances indicate that they mutually understood no binding obligation to exist until the writing was executed, the law will give effect to that intention. In that situation, what occurred prior to the writing would be viewed as mere preliminary negotiations. The classic statement is found in *Mississippi & Dominion S.S. Co. v. Swift*:

> If the party sought to be charged intended to close a contract prior to the formal signing of a written draft, or if he signified such an intention to the other party, he will be bound by the contract actually made, though the signing of the written draft be omitted. If, on the other hand, such party neither had nor signified such an intention to close the contract until it was fully expressed in a written instrument and attested by signatures, then he will not be bound until the signatures are affixed. . . . If the written draft is viewed by the parties merely as a convenient memorial or record of their previous contract, its absence does not affect the binding force of the contract. If, however, it is viewed as the consummation of the negotiation, there is no contract until the written draft is finally signed.[64]

> Where the parties express neither intention, courts confront the same question of fact, the question of fact that arises in numerous cases letters of intent cases explored earlier.[65]

The most important of the factors that courts view as significant in this determination is whether the parties have reached agreement on all essential terms prior to the consummation of the formal document evidencing their agreement.[66] Courts will also consider the nature of the transaction and the circumstances surrounding it since they may be sufficient to convince the fact finder of the parties' intention. In *Arnold Palmer Golf Co. v. Fuqua Industries, Inc.*,[67] the parties prepared an extensive memorandum of intent containing all of the essential terms of the transaction but also stating that the parties would proceed to prepare a "definitive agreement" as a condition to their respective obligations. The defendant issued a press release indicating that the transaction was completed but later withdrew from the transaction. The

---

v. Sharp, 280 F.2d 345 (5th Cir. 1960), *cert. denied*, 365 U.S. 814, 81 S. Ct. 693, 5 L. Ed. 2d 692 (1961); Smith v. Onyx Oil & Chem. Co., 218 F.2d 104 (3d Cir. 1955). *See* RESTATEMENT 2d § 27.

[64] 86 Me. 248, 258, 29 A. 1063, 1066 (1894). *See also* Ferranti Int'l, PLC v. Jasin, 2000 U.S. Dist. LEXIS 6663 (E.D. Pa. May 3, 2000), holding that a written manifestation of mutual assent was a condition to contract formation. *Accord* Barry v. James, 74 Ill. App. 3d 975, 394 N.E.2d 55 (3d Dist. 1979) (a written memorial was a condition precedent to contract formation).

[65] See § 32[B], *supra*, concerning letters of intent. While the parties' intention to execute a final document justifies a strong inference that they do not intend to be bound until the writing is executed, if all of the material terms had been agreed upon, it may be inferred that the writing to be drafted is a mere memorial of the contract. There may be sufficient evidence for a jury to reach either inference. Situation Mgmt. Sys. v. Malouf, Inc., 430 Mass. 875, 724 N.E.2d 699 (2000). *See also* Burkett v. Morales, 128 Ariz. 417, 626 P.2d 147 (Ct. App. 1981) (parties executed a memorandum which was to be followed by a formal document to be drafted by the lawyer of one of the parties; the court held that whether the parties intended to be bound only after the execution of the formal document was a question of fact).

[66] If the writing is to contain a material term upon which agreement has not been reached previously, courts typically regard the parties as intending no legal consequences until the writing is executed. *See* Scholnick's Importers—Clothiers, Inc. v. Lent, 130 Mich. App. 104, 343 N.W.2d 249 (1983). It should be noted, however, that the parties may have manifested their intention to be bound prior to a formal writing even though they have left a material term for future agreement. See UCC § 2-305, which permits parties to conclude a contract for sale even though the price is not settled. The critical language is in subsection (1): "if they [the parties] so intend. . . ."

[67] 541 F.2d 584 (6th Cir. 1976).

court held that these were sufficient facts to overrule the lower court's summary judgment to allow a trial concerning the parties' intention to be bound or not bound absent a final writing.

In *Lambert Corp. v. Evans*,[68] the defendant had exchanged correspondence with the plaintiff concerning the acquisition of a particular line of products owned by the plaintiff. The defendant's vice-president visited the plaintiff for an entire day and discussed the proposed acquisition. This was followed by further correspondence and later by a telephone exchange during which the parties agreed to execute a formal document and also congratulated each other on having reached agreement. Defendant argued that the parties were not bound at that point since a more extensive review of the product line and related matters by engineers, accountants, and lawyers would be appropriate in such an acquisition. The court rejected this argument on the ground that a sensible businessman would not engage in such a costly review for an acquisition valued at only $20,000. Moreover, this was not the procedure defendant itself had followed in small acquisitions.[69] On the other hand, sensible parties are unlikely to enter major transaction on the basis of a handshake.[70]

Beyond the aforementioned guides, courts will consider the complexity of the transaction and apply a common sense guideline: the more detailed the transaction, the less likely is the parties' intention to be bound prior to the execution of the formal document they contemplated.[71] Another guide is found in the partial performance of the parties. If the parties contemplate a writing but, prior to its execution, they begin to perform, their course of performance may indicate that they either intended the contract to be formed prior to the final writing, or they have modified their agreement to dispense with the final writing as a necessary condition to contract formation.[72]

Where neither the expression of the parties nor the surrounding circumstances provide any convincing evidence of the parties' intention to be bound or not to be bound until a final document has been executed, some courts have taken the position that the mere contemplation of a writing by the parties is sufficient evidence of their intention not to be bound until the

---

[68] 575 F.2d 132 (7th Cir. 1978).

[69] *See* Jolley Elevator Co. v. Schwegmann Bros. Giant Super Markets, 230 So. 2d 640 (La. Ct. App. 4th Cir. 1970) (size of transaction was $12,376 and court found a contract when parties shook hands and said they had a deal).

[70] See Perles v. Kagy, 473 F. 3d 1244, 1251 (D. C. Cir. 2007) ("It strains credulity to suggest that Perles and Kagy, both of whom are attorneys, intended a single, undocumented telephone conversation to give rise to a mutually binding agreement giving a junior attorney the potential right to millions of dollars in compensation for her work.")*See also* Ryan v. Schott, 109 Ohio App. 317, 159 N.E. 2d 907 (1959) (in a contract for the purchase of stock which would provide the buyer with a large office building, court held no contract upon a hand shake and statement that a deal had been made).

[71] See Rosenbluth v. Prudential Securities, Inc., 134 Fed. Appx. 124, 125–26 (9th Cir. 2005). See also RESTATEMENT 2d § 27, in particular comment c, which contains a sound statement of the various circumstances a court should consider in determining whether a contract has been concluded prior to the execution of the final writing. The writing itself may be so cursory, omitting essential elements, that a court may not be convinced that the parties intended such a writing as evidence of an enforceable agreement. *See* Hill v. McGregor Mfg. Corp., 23 Mich. App. 342, 178 N.W.2d 553 (1970). A court may, however, find that the parties have concluded a contract notwithstanding a statement in a "confirmation" or "letter agreement" that they intended an even more formal, and final, writing. In Field v. Golden Triangle Broadcasting, Inc., 451 Pa. 410, 305 A.2d 689 (1973), *cert. denied*, 414 U.S. 1158, 94 S. Ct. 916, 39 L. Ed. 2d 110 (1974), a letter agreement was subject to a final agreement, but the letter agreement was so complete in its terms and executed with such extraordinary care and finality that the court held the parties intended to be bound at the time they executed it, i.e., prior to the "final" agreement.

[72] *See* Dunkel Oil Corp. v. Independent Oil & Gas Co., 70 F.2d 967 (7th Cir. 1934).

writing is executed.[73] Thus, no contract would exist prior to the writing unless the inference drawn could be overcome by some other affirmative evidence. Such an inference or presumption is unwarranted. The isolated fact that the parties contemplated a writing sheds little or no light on the question of their intention as to when legal obligation shall attach. It is just as likely that the parties desired the writing as a mere memorial of their agreement, i.e., as satisfactory evidence of a contract already consummated. In the preceding section, we discovered that parties need not consciously intend legal consequences to attach to an agreement in order that a contract be said to exist. It follows that, in cases where the parties merely indicate that a writing is contemplated and the circumstances do not allow for the application of the guides suggested earlier in this section, a contract is formed as soon as agreement on all essential terms has been reached even though the contemplated final document is yet to be executed. While the problem has not always been analyzed in this fashion, this view accords with the results reached in most of the decided cases.[74]

Again, it must be remembered that this analysis proceeds on the assumption that the parties have reached agreement upon all essential matters intended to be agreed upon prior to the execution of the formal document.[75] The analysis also assumes the absence of any statute that superimposes the requirement of a signed writing regardless of finding the parties' intention to be bound by an agreement absent such a writing.[76]

The consequences of determining that a contract existed prior to the execution of a formal document were dramatically illustrated in the much publicized dispute between the Texaco Corp. and the Pennzoil Co. Pennzoil made several attempts to take control of the Getty Oil Corp. and its final attempt resulted in what was characterized as "an agreement in principle" for the merger of Getty Oil and a newly formed entity to be owned jointly by Pennzoil and Gordon P. Getty as trustee of a family trust and a charitable trust. While lawyers worked on the implementation of that plan, Getty's representatives were considering the possibility of a better arrangement and began discussions with Texaco. Shortly thereafter, it was announced that Getty would be acquired by Texaco. After unsuccessful attempts to enjoin this merger, Pennzoil brought an action in a district court in Texas on a theory of tortious interference with Pennzoil's rights under its contract with Getty. The critical question in the case was whether

---

[73] Some cases suggest that the contemplation of a writing, by itself, is "some evidence" of the intention not to be bound until the writing is executed. Berman v. Rosenberg, 115 Me. 19, 97 A. 6 (1916). Other courts suggest that "strong evidence" is necessary to overcome the "presumption" that no final contract has been formed until the writing is executed. Atlantic Coast Realty Co. v. Robertson's Ex'r, 135 Va. 247, 116 S.E. 476 (1923). *See also* Blair v. Dickinson, 54 S.E.2d 828 (W. Va. 1949).

[74] Recognizing the scholarship of Professor Williston and Professor Corbin in this area, the United States Court of Appeals for the Third Circuit suggests: "The emphasis of these two eminent writers is, it seems to us, inclined toward finding the formation of a contract prior to the signing of the document unless the parties pretty clearly show that such signing is a condition precedent to legal obligation. And since contract law has passed the formalism of elaborate doctrines pertaining to sealed instruments, it seems to us such emphasis is quite natural and quite correct." Smith v. Onyx Oil & Chem. Corp., 218 F.2d 104, 108 (3d Cir. 1955). *See also* Barton Chem. Co. v. Penwalt Corp., 79 Ill. App. 3d 829, 399 N.E.2d 288 (1st Dist. 1979); Western Bank v. Morrill, 245 Or. 47, 420 P.2d 119 (1966); Dohrman v. Sullivan, 310 Ky. 463, 220 S.W.2d 973 (1949).

[75] In County of Jackson v. Nichols, 175 N. C. App. 196, 623 S. E. 2d 277 (2005), the court held that a separation agreement was not binding because the parties did not intend to be bound until a right of first refusal agreement was executed.

[76] See O'Neil v. Bunge Corp., 365 F. 3d 820 (9th Cir. 2004), where the Longshoremen and Harbor Workers' Compensation Act (33 U. S. C. § 908(i)) precluded an unsigned agreement evidencing all material terms as enforceable because the Act contained a "bright line" requirement of a signed writing.

the "agreement in principle" was a binding agreement before all of the details to implement the arrangement were effectuated. The jury awarded Pennzoil $7.53 billion in actual damages and $3 billion in punitive damages, the largest civil judgment in history to that time. Reducing the punitive damages $1 billion, a Texas appellate court upheld the award.[77]

§ 34 THE EFFECT OF OFFERS — POWER OF ACCEPTANCE

To this point, we have explored the requirement of mutual assent and concluded that the parties must manifest mutual assent by arriving at an agreement to form a contract. We explored the fundamental requirements of an agreement and the traditional fashion in which courts discover an agreement — the existence of offer and acceptance. The determination of whether an offer exists can be complex, and the two sections which follow will explore this question in detail. Before considering the ways in which courts determine whether an offer exists, however, it is important to understand the legal effect of an offer.

The general definition of an offer has been widely accepted: "[T]he manifestation of willingness to enter a bargain, so made as to justify another person in understanding that his assent to that bargain is invited and will conclude it."[78] An offer is the first manifestation of assent to a bargain. The expression of assent may be oral or written; no particular form is required. By far, the typical manifestation of assent is by promise. As suggested earlier, a promise is a commitment or undertaking to act or refrain from acting in a particular fashion.[79]

Conferring a Power on the Offeree. If Ames makes a promise to Barnes to sell Ames' automobile to Barnes for $10,000, Ames is an *offeror* and Barnes is an *offeree.* Before making the promise to sell her car to Barnes, Ames may have discussed the possibility of the sale with Barnes; she may have negotiated with Barnes who may have originally suggested an unwillingness to pay more than $9000 for the automobile. At a particular point in these negotiations, if Ames said, "I will sell my car to you for $10,000," or a similar expression with the same meaning, Ames has made the first *legally operative* statement in the negotiations. A statement is operative when it creates a legal effect. Ames' statement is operative because she has made an offer which *creates a power of acceptance* in the offeree, Barnes. The preliminary discussion, negotiation, or higgling and haggling over price or other terms prior to the offer created did not have legal effect with respect to the formation of a contract. Once an offer is made, however, the offeree, Barnes, now has something which he did not have prior to the offer. He has a legal *power,* a power of acceptance. Barnes now has a choice: he may or may not choose to *exercise* his power of acceptance. If he chooses to exercise the power conferred on him by Ames with a statement such as, "I will buy your car for $10,000," or an expression with the same meaning, a contract is formed.

It is important to emphasize that a contract is formed at this point even though Ames may have changed her mind about the price, other terms or even the basic decision to sell the car to Barnes or to anyone. She may have decided to withdraw (revoke) her offer to sell at that

---

[77] Texaco, Inc. v. Pennzoil Co., 729 S. W. 2d 768 (Tex. Ct. App. 1987). Texaco later settled with Pennzoil for $5 billion which allowed Texaco to emerge from bankruptcy.

[78] RESTATEMENT 2d § 24. Article 14(1) of the United Nations Convention on Contracts for the International Sale of Goods (CISG) defines an offer: "A proposal for concluding a contract addressed to one or more specific persons constitutes an offer if it is sufficiently definite and indicates the intention of the offeror to be bound in case of acceptance."

[79] *See* RESTATEMENT 2d § 2.

price. Before Barnes said, "I will buy your car for $10,000," Ames may have intended to revoke her offer, but Barnes would not be aware of Ames' subjective intention in exercising his power of acceptance and forming a contract. After Barnes communicates his acceptance, a statement by Ames that she had decided to revoke the offer before the acceptance was communicated would be to no avail. Like any offeror, Ames could have revoked her offer, but once the offer is accepted, a contract is formed. An offeror cannot revoke a contract. There is no offer to revoke. Indeed, there is no longer an offeror or offeree. The former offer and acceptance are merged into a contract creating legal rights and duties which did not exist prior to the formation of the contract.

By creating a power of acceptance in Barnes, Ames made herself *susceptible* to Barnes with respect to her car. By exercising his power of acceptance, Barnes made the second *operative* statement in the transaction. His acceptance has the legal effect of forming a contract. By the exchange of their expressions of offer and acceptance, the parties have created a legal relationship between them. Prior to Barnes' exercise of the power of acceptance, there was a power-susceptibility relationship between Ames and Barnes. Through Ames' offer, Barnes had a power and Ames was susceptible to that power since Barnes could form a contract so long as Ames had not revoked the offer which would eliminate Barnes' power of acceptance. As soon as the contract was formed through the exercise of Barnes' power, however, a new legal relationship was created between the parties. Both parties acquired legal rights and duties. Barnes had the right to become the owner of Ames' auto and he had the duty to pay Ames $10,000. Ames had the right to Barnes' $10,000 and she had the duty to transfer ownership of her automobile to Barnes. The relationship between the parties became a relationship of correlative rights and duties which were created by the contract they formed.[80] The cases are now legion in which the legal effect of an offer is characterized as the creation of a "power of acceptance."[81]

---

[80] These relationships were described by Professor Wesley Hohfeld in FUNDAMENTAL LEGAL CONCEPTS AS APPLIED IN JUDICIAL REASONING (1919). Hohfeld suggested that fundamental legal relations are *sui generis*, i.e., unique of their own kind and class. Therefore, he felt that attempts at formal definition are unsatisfactory and probably useless. Rather than definitions, Hohfeld provided an analysis of all of the various legal relations in terms of "jural opposites" and "jural correlatives": Jural opposites: right/no-right; privilege/duty; power/disability; immunity/liability. Jural correlatives: right/duty; privilege/no-right; power/liability; immunity/disability.

The Hohfeld analysis provides an explanation of each "opposite" and "correlative." As to "power," he suggests that the party whose volitional control is paramount may be said to have the (legal) power to effect the particular change of legal relations involved in the problem. When an offer is made, the offeror has created a power of acceptance in the offeree and the correlative of "power" is "liability" in the offeror. It may, however, be more precise to refer to the status of the offeror as one of "susceptibility" as suggested earlier, since the offeree may exercise the power and form a contract even though, at the moment of contract formation, the offeror is contemplating the revocation of the offer. (Revocations of offers will be explored in a subsequent section.) Once a contract is formed, the parties then have a right-duty correlative relationship.

[81] "Under common law contract principles, the offeror, by extending an offer, creates a power of acceptance in the offeree that continues until terminated through acceptance by the offeree, rejection by the offeree (either expressly or by making a counteroffer), or revocation by the offeror." Ellison v. Premier Salons Int'l, Inc., 164 F.3d 1111, 1114 n.3 (8th Cir. 1999)."For an agreement to be enforced as a contract, there must be mutual assent; one party must accept the other party's offer. An offer creates a power of acceptance in the offeree and may be revoked at the will of the offeror at any point before acceptance." Safeco Ins. Co. of Am. v. City of White House, 36 F.3d 540, 546 (6th Cir. 1994). *See also* Contempo Constr. Co. v. Mountain States Tel. & Tel. Co., 736 P.2d 13 (Ariz. Ct. App. 1987); Eakins v. New England Mut. Life Ins. Co., 130 Ill. App. 3d 65, 473 N.E.2d 439 (1984); Foremost Pro Color, Inc. v. Eastman Kodak Co., 703 F.2d 534 (9th Cir. 1983), *cert. denied*, 465 U.S. 1038, 104 S. Ct. 1315, 79 L. Ed. 2d 712 (1984) (no power of acceptance created). The classic analysis is found in Corbin, *Offer and Acceptance and Some of the Resulting Legal Relations*, 26 YALE L.J. 169, particularly at 199–200 (1917).

§ 35 TESTS TO DETERMINE WHETHER AN OFFER HAS BEEN MADE — CISG

The scores of cases that have sought to determine whether, in a given set of facts, an offer has been made are notoriously deficient in suggesting clear guidelines. A glance at modern cases may even reveal a statement of virtual despair such as, "It is impossible to formulate a general principle or criterion for its determination."[82] Courts recognize that whether an offer has been made can only be determined by considering the objective manifestations of the parties and circumstances under which those manifestations occurred. It is a question of fact.[83] The only guide suggested by the RESTATEMENT 2d is of limited assistance, i.e., whether a purported offeree was justified in understanding a manifestation of intention as creating a power of acceptance.[84] Notwithstanding the legitimate insistence that the question is one of manifested intention, i.e., one of fact, and the assertion that no general principle can be stated, there are discernible guidelines in the case law that will now be examined.

[A] Present Intention Versus Promises — Preliminary Negotiations — Advertisements — Definiteness — Identifiable Offerees

A basic distinction is made between *statements of present intention* on the one hand and *commitments or promises* on the other. If A says to B, "I intend to sell my car for $10,000," and B replies, "I will buy it for $10,000," there is no contract if these statements are taken at face value. A's statement involves no promise, commitment or undertaking; it is merely a statement of present intention. That statement, alone, does not justify B in understanding that he has the power to conclude a contract with A. On its face, A's statement cannot reasonably be interpreted to mean, "I will sell this car to you, B, for a price of $10,000." Rather, A's statement may indicate A's intention either to make an offer at some future time, or to receive an offer at $10,000 to sell his car. Neither manifestation of intention is, itself, an offer. This analysis is found in myriad cases involving advertising appearing in newspapers, catalogs, trade circulars and the like, or with respect to goods displayed in stores.[85] Such advertising or display of goods is generally construed to constitute mere solicitation of offers rather than offers.[86]

---

[82] See Rich Products Corp. v. Kemutec, Inc., 66 F. Supp. 2d 937, 956 (E.D. Wis. 1999); R. E. Crummer & Co. v. Nuveen, 147 F.2d 3, 5 (7th Cir. 1945), *quoted in* Maryland Supreme Corp. v. Blake Co., 279 Md. 531, 369 A.2d 1017 (1977), *and* Interstate Indus., Inc. v. Barclay Indus., Inc., 540 F.2d 868 (7th Cir. 1976).

[83] The determination of whether a question is one of fact or law is a topic dealt with in procedure texts. The law/fact dichotomy may be seen as false when questions are characterized as questions of law rather than questions of fact on the basis of who is to decide the questions. The shibboleth is that questions of fact are decided at the trial level by juries or judges sitting without juries. Questions of law, on the other hand, are decided by judges, and appellate courts deal only with "law" questions while questions of fact are not reviewable absent an abuse of discretion by the fact finder. Yet, in many situations, factual questions will be resolved by judges, although such questions will be called questions of law because the judge decides them and they are reviewable by appellate courts. The interpretation of a writing susceptible to different interpretations raises questions normally reserved to judges. The question "What happened?" is one of fact that should be decided exclusively by the trier of fact and should not be susceptible to judicial review, again, absent a manifest abuse of discretion.

[84] "An offer is the manifestation of willingness to enter into a bargain, so made as to justify another person in understanding that his assent to that bargain is invited and will conclude it." RESTATEMENT 2d § 24.

[85] *See* Ford Motor Credit Co. v. Russell, 519 N.W.2d 460 (Minn. Ct. App. 1994) (newspaper advertisement setting forth a certain annual percentage rate was not an offer).

[86] *See* Zanakis-Pico v. Cutter Dodge, Inc., 47 P.3d 1222 (Haw. 2002) (newspaper advertisement for various vehicles

In a narrow range of advertisement cases, however, courts have found offers by suggesting that the advertisement was sufficiently clear, definite and explicit, but this is a misleading rationale. Much advertising contains considerable detail concerning the advertised goods and states a definite price. Where an advertisement is sufficiently clear, definite and explicit, it is still not an offer. For an advertisement or any other statement to constitute an offer, the critical manifestation of intention is a statement of promise, i.e., that the party issuing the statement will perform or refrain from performing an act in the future.

Where a store advertised sufficiently described items at a definite price with the commitment "First Come First Served," the court found that offers had been made.[87] While the court's conclusion was correct, it failed to provide an effective analysis. A reasonable interpretation of language in the advertisement provides the critical ingredient missing in the typical advertisement. Instead of a mere announcement of described items for sale at stated prices, "First Come First Served" is a promise, a commitment by the advertiser, to sell the described goods to the first buyers who present the advertised price for the goods. The store is promising to sell valuable goods at a price far below market value. A prospective buyer, therefore, reasonably understands that the first customer to present the necessary payment for such an advertised item has the power of acceptance to form the contract. Similarly, where an advertisement calls for performance of a specific act and leaves nothing for further negotiation, it can constitute an offer which is accepted by performance of the act.[88]

Since store advertising of specific goods at specific prices is addressed to the public at large rather than specific parties, it is sometimes suggested that the risk to the store would be unreasonably large if advertisements were construed as offers. This view is based upon two concerns: (1) the offerees are not identified, which suggests that the advertisement was not designed as an offer, and (2) the number of offerees is left uncertain, which creates an unreasonable risk for the purported offeror-shopkeeper.[89] With respect to the first concern, there is no indefiniteness if the offeree is *identifiable.* In the "First Come First Served" advertisement, the offerees will be the customers who first present themselves as prospective buyers of the goods, conditioned only upon their tendering the advertised prices. Similarly, where rewards are made to the public, the lack of identity of the offeree at the time the offer is made is no bar to finding a contract. One of the most famous cases in the law of contracts is illustrative.

---

at certain prices were not offers since they did not invite acceptance without further negotiations.). Foremost Pro Color, Inc. v. Eastman Kodak Co., 703 F.2d 534 (9th Cir. 1983), *cert. denied,* 465 U.S. 1038, 104 S. Ct. 1315, 79 L. Ed. 2d 712 (1984) (information circular, like other trade circulars, catalogs, and advertisements, which are uniformly regarded as mere preliminary negotiations creating no power of acceptance in the recipient, was not an offer). Steinberg v. Chicago Med. Sch., 69 Ill. 2d 320, 330, 371 N.E.2d 634, 639 (1977) (brochure did not evidence an offer but an invitation to make an offer).

[87] *See* Lefkowitz v. Great Minneapolis Surplus Store, Inc., 251 Minn. 188, 86 N.W.2d 689 (1957).

[88] Harris v. Time, Inc., 191 Cal. App. 3d 449, 455, 237 Cal. Rptr. 584, 587 (1st Dist. 1987) (junk mail advertisement stating that if the recipient would simply open the envelope he would receive a new watch was an offer which was accepted by the opening of the envelope).

[89] The classic statement is found in Crawley v. Rex (1909) Transvaal 1105 (S. Africa): "It would lead to most extraordinary results if that were the correct view of the case. Because then supposing a shopkeeper were sold out of a particular class of goods, thousands of members of the public might crowd into the shop and demand to be served, and each one would have a right of action against the proprietor for not performing his contract." In Ford Motor Credit Co. v. Russell, 519 N.W.2d 460, 463 (Minn. Ct. App. 1994), the court stated, "Because . . . Monticello Ford does not have an unlimited number of Ford Escorts to sell, it was unreasonable for appellants to believe that the advertisement was an offer binding the advertiser."

In *Carlill v. Carbolic Smoke Ball Co.*,[90] the advertisement read:

> £100 reward will be paid by the Carbolic Smoke Ball Company to any person who contracts the increasing epidemic influenza, colds or any disease caused by taking cold after having used the ball three times daily for two weeks according to the printed directions supplied with each ball. £1000 is deposited with the Alliance Bank, Regent Street, shewing our sincerity in the matter.

The court did not question whether the language of the advertisement was promissory since the language clearly evidenced a commitment by the advertiser — the "reward will be paid." The opinion carefully considered the deposit with the Alliance Bank as a manifestation of sincerity — the advertisement was not mere "puff." Moreover, there was no question concerning the proper interpretation of this advertisement as an offer notwithstanding the lack of identified offerees at the time the offer was made.

Since the act required by the offer was the use of the product (the smoke ball) in accordance with directions for the period stipulated, all members of the public were potential offerees and those who used the product accordingly were offerees who accepted the offer. The proper use of the product formed a contract between the company and all such users. The company thereby had a duty to pay the reward to any such user, but the company's duty was conditioned on the involuntary act of contracting influenza, i.e., contracting influenza was a condition precedent to the activation of the defendant's duty.

The case is also instructive with respect to the second concern: the risk assumed by the manufacturer of the product arising from the potentially large number of offerees. The risk of a large number of offerees who met the condition of contracting influenza was clearly assumed by the offeror. While the typical shopkeeper may not be said to have assumed the risk of an unlimited number of offerees, such an offeror could place a reasonable limitation on the number of advertised items. In the absence of an express limitation, the shopkeeper should not be confronted with the risk of having an unlimited number of such items available for an unexpected number of customers, because the number of available items would be subject to a reasonable limitation under the circumstances.[91]

The advertisement cases dealing with statements to an indefinite number of prospective parties may be seen as containing a negative implication that a statement addressed to a

---

[90] 1 Q.B. 256 [1893].

[91] Where a party has only one item for sale, *e.g.*, a tract of land, it is possible for that party to make offers to innumerable offerees, none of whom are aware of the other offers. If more than one offeree accepts, the offeror has contracts with all of the offerees. He can perform only one of the contracts and must breach the others. The question remains, did the owner of the land make an offer to anyone? In Lonergan v. Scolnick, 129 Cal. App. 2d 179, 276 P.2d 8 (1954), the owner placed an ad in a newspaper describing the land. The ad prompted an inquiry from the plaintiff to which the owner responded with directions to the land, a "rock-bottom price," and the following statement: "This is a form letter." Plaintiff responded with further questions concerning the topography and a particular bank as escrow agent. The owner replied with further information concerning the land and indicated that the named bank would be a satisfactory escrow agent. This letter ended with "If you are really interested, you will have to decide fast, as I expect to have a buyer in the next week or so." The court held that the owner had made no offer to the plaintiff. The owner's first letter ending with "This is a form letter" clearly indicated that the owner made no commitment to the plaintiff. The second letter from the owner made it clear that the owner reserved the right to sell the land to another buyer, i.e., the buyer who first tendered the "rock-bottom" price, who was, necessarily, unidentified but identifiable. The owner's statements were, in effect, treated by the court as a "first come, first served" expression which would constitute an offer to any such offeree. Since the land was sold to another prior to the receipt of any tender from the plaintiff, the owner was free to sell to the party who became an offeree by being the first to tender the price.

definite party should necessarily be construed as an offer. This is an unreliable suggestion. Even where parties are dealing exclusively with each other, what may appear to be an offer may, upon careful examination, be a mere invitation of an offer.[92]

CISG. Under the CISG, however, "A proposal, other than one addressed to one or more specific persons, is to be considered merely an invitation to make offers, unless the contrary is clearly indicated."[93] This is a confusing directive. Many advertisements, trade circulars and the like are addressed to specific persons and are not offers. Because of this language, where CISG is the governing law, it is desirable to express the intention of the proposing party to assure that it is interpreted in accordance with the proposer's intention to either solicit an offer or create an offer.

Conclusion-Searching for a "Promise." The unpersuasive rationales found in numerous cases involving the question of whether an offer exists and the insistence that no general principle can be stated, because the question is one of fact, do not deter the judicial search for a promise or commitment to future action. Thus, in a case suggesting the futility of discovering a general principle, the court quotes from an earlier opinion:

> In order to hold that the parties entered into a contract to buy and sell at the [quoted] prices, there must be evidence of an offer. . . . Such an offer must have manifested a present intention of a promise to sell. . . .[94]

The requirement of a promise — a commitment — is the pervasive element in the entire body of case law distinguishing offers from preliminary negotiations. If a general contractor desires to place a bid for a particular construction project, his invitation to various subcontractors to bid on various parts of the project is seen as his invitation for offers, i.e., he is asking subcontractors to promise that they will supply certain goods or services at definite prices to enable him to bid on the project. He is not committing himself to the lowest bidder.[95]

[B]   Opinions and Predictions — Express Warranties Distinguished

If a party makes a statement of *prediction* or *opinion*, it is not a promise and the party making the statement is not an offeror. In a well-known case, a tenant farmer worried about the water supply before making a decision concerning the purchase of cattle. His landlord said, "Never mind the water, John, I will see that there will be plenty of water because it never failed in Minnesota yet." The farmer purchased more than 100 cattle and later suffered a loss when the water supply failed. In an action against the landlord, the court found the landlord's statement to be mere prediction and the farmer was not justified in relying upon it.[96] If the landlord had said, "Don't worry, John. If you suffer any loss as a result of a water shortage, I

---

[92] See Rhen Marshall, Inc. v. Purolator Filter Div., Purolator, Inc., 211 Neb. 306, 318 N.W.2d 284 (1982), relying upon the classic case of Nebraska Seed Co. v. Harsh, 98 Neb. 89, 152 N.W. 310 (1915), in which the defendant sent a letter to the plaintiff which stated, in pertinent part, "I want $ 2.25 per cwt. for this seed f. o. b. Lowell." The attempted acceptance by the plaintiff was ineffective since the plaintiff had no power of acceptance. The defendant's letter was a mere invitation to plaintiff to make an offer at the stated price. *See also Lonergan v. Scolnick, supra* note 91.

[93] Article 14(2).

[94] Thos. J. Sheehan Co. v. Crane Co., 418 F.2d 642, 644 (8th Cir. 1969), *as quoted in* Interstate Indus., Inc. v. Barclay Indus., Inc., 540 F.2d 868, 871–72 (7th Cir. 1976) (emphasis supplied).

[95] Milone & Tucci, Inc. v. Bona Fide Builders, Inc., 49 Wash. 2d 363, 301 P.2d 759 (1956); Anderson v. Board, etc., of Pub. Schs., 122 Mo. 61, 27 S.W. 610 (1894).

[96] Anderson v. Backlund, 159 Minn. 423, 199 N.W. 90 (1924).

will reimburse you" (or words to that effect), this would have been a promise upon which the farmer could justifiably rely. Earlier in this chapter, cases involving alleged promises by physicians concerning the recovery time or chance of recovery by patients were explored.[97] Those cases typically involve the question of whether a physician is merely stating an opinion or prediction concerning a cure or period of recovery rather than a promise. As the prior discussion indicates, such statements by a physician will be viewed as statements of opinion or prediction absent clear and convincing evidence that the physician's statement constituted a promise. In a related situation, the UCC requires statements of *fact* as contrasted with statements of opinion or commendation by the seller to constitute an express warranty.[98] If a seller of goods informed a prospective buyer of how "wonderful" the goods are, or how extremely valuable they are, such statements would be statements of the seller's opinion or commendation. Earlier courts would refer to such statements as mere "puff," i.e., statements with no legal effect. If, however, the seller provides statements of fact, descriptions,[99] specifications, blueprints, samples or models[100] which become part of the basis of the bargain, they are factual assertions by the seller and, as such, constitute express warranties under the UCC.

[C]   Summary of Guidelines — Application — *Harvey v. Facey*

The effort to discover criteria or guides to be applied to myriad fact situations that are effective in distinguishing offers from preliminary negotiations is not in vain. A summary of the guides developed to this point is in order.[101] It is fashionable to begin with the basic test found in the RESTATEMENT 2d: Is there a manifestation of willingness to enter into a bargain that would justify the party to whom it is made in understanding that his assent to that bargain is invited and will conclude it?[102] We have seen that this definition of an offer is almost a tautology, i.e., the manifestation will be an offer if a reasonable party would have understood it as an offer. But, what is the basis for such a reasonable understanding? Since modern contract law tolerates considerable indefiniteness in contract formation,[103] one of the guides found in numerous cases is not particularly helpful, i.e., the more definite the statement, the more likely that the statement is an offer.[104] In light of innumerable advertisements and other

---

[97] *See supra* § 32[C].

[98] *See* UCC § 2-313(2). It should be noted that express warranties may be created not only by promises relating to the quality of the goods that become part of the basis of the bargain, but also by affirmations of fact relating to the goods that become part of the basis of the bargain, § 2-313(1)(a). For a discussion of the elusive concept of "basis of the bargain," see Murray, *Basis of the Bargain: Transcending Classical Concepts*, 66 U. MINN. L. REV. 283 (1982).

[99] UCC § 2-313(1)(b).

[100] UCC § 2-313(1)(c).

[101] Southworth v. Oliver, 284 Or. 361, 587 P.2d 994 (1978), expressly relies on these guidelines as found in an earlier edition of this work (2d ed. at 37–40).

[102] RESTATEMENT 2d § 24. In Barnum v. Review Bd. of Indiana Employment Sec. Div., 478 N.E.2d 1243 (Ind. Ct. App. 1985), the RESTATEMENT 2d definition was applied and the court found no offer because the party to whom the statement was addressed would not have been reasonable in understanding that his assent would conclude a contract. *See also* Contempo Constr. Co. v. Mountain States Tel. & Tel. Co., 736 P.2d 13 (Ariz. Ct. App. 1987).

[103] UCC § 2-204(3) expressly permits such indefiniteness. When one or more terms are left open, a contract will be formed if (1) the parties intended to make a contract, and (2) there is a reasonably certain basis for giving an appropriate remedy. The same concept is found in RESTATEMENT 2d § 33(2). The concept of indefiniteness will be explored in detail in later sections.

[104] In Chasan v. Village Dist. of Eastman, 128 N.H. 807, 523 A.2d 16 (1986), the court's finding of no offer relies

preliminary statements that often provide more detail than any reasonable potential buyer desires to know, it is misleading to suggest that the likelihood of an offer depends upon the definiteness of the statement. While offers must be sufficiently definite, an advertisement or other solicitation of an offer will not be construed as an offer on the basis of definiteness alone since many ads are filled with information about the product. Another guide suggests that the more definite the party or parties to whom the statement is addressed, the more likely it is that an offer will be found. Yet, the reward cases and other cases involving advertisement offers to the public make that guide usable only if the offeree is not *identifiable*, i.e., the fact that the party to whom the expression is addressed is not identified at the moment the expression occurs does not suggest that the manifestation cannot be an offer.

There is only one, constant, unexcepted criterion that can be stated: the expression must be a promise. From this base, the following guide can be constructed: If a statement is sufficiently definite and there is a manifestation of commitment, a promise designed to induce action or forbearance which the promisor desires,[105] an offer exists because the party to whom such a statement is addressed reasonably understands that his assent will form a contract. No test should be viewed algebraically. It is not a litmus test, since the discipline is law and not science. The question is one of manifested intention, a question of fact,[106] and courts will decide this question of fact. There is no mathematical formula that promises a certain and just result in all cases. "Since two cases are never identical in the exact words used, in the existing relations and history of the parties, in the circumstances surrounding the communication, the decision made in one of them can never be regarded as a conclusive precedent for the other. Nevertheless, it may be suggestive and enlightening precedent."[107]

One of the classic cases in contract law, *Harvey v. Facey*, demonstrates this difficulty.[108] Facey owned certain property known as Bumper Hall Pen. He had been negotiating with the town council for the sale of the property. Harvey and another were interested in the property and telegraphed Facey as follows: "Will you sell us Bumper Hall Pen? Telegraph lowest cash price — answer paid." Facey replied by telegram: "Lowest cash price for Bumper Hall Pen £900." Harvey assumed this was an offer by Facey — a commitment to sell the property to Harvey justifying him in assuming that his assent would form a contract for the property. He replied, "We agree to buy Bumper Hall Pen for the sum of nine hundred pounds asked by you." Facey refused to convey the property and Harvey sued. Was Facey's telegram to Harvey an offer? The court analyzed the first telegram from Harvey as containing two questions: (1) would Facey sell the property to Harvey, and (2) what was the lowest price Facey would accept? Since Facey answered only the second question ("Lowest cash price for Bumper Hall Pen £900"), the court found that Facey had made no offer; he had merely quoted the price. Facey had not, for example, started his telegraphic answer with, "Yes, I will sell Bumper Hall Pen to you." Absent that kind of statement or, at least, the word "Yes" before announcing the price, the court found no offer.

---

almost entirely upon the lack of definiteness of the language. Numerous cases, however, do not find a missing term fatal in their quest to discover an offer. See, e.g., Wilcom v. Wilcom, 66 Md. App. 84, 502 A.2d 1076 (1986), where the failure to identify the price or the number of shares of stock to be sold did not deter the court from discovering an offer where the necessary information was ascertainable from facts beyond the writing.

[105]   A promise that induces action or forbearance desired by the promisor is a partial statement of the requirement of consideration, to be discussed in the next chapter dealing with the validation process.

[106]   *See supra* note 65.

[107]   1 CORBIN § 2.2.

[108]   62 L.J., P.C. 127, A.C. 552 [1893].

The court's analysis may be criticized as rigid because it failed to consider the medium used — telegrams — which promote relatively cryptic messages since every additional word adds to the cost, regardless of which party is paying the fee. Even parties who are not concerned about cost may feel compelled to sound cryptic in telegraph or mailgram messages, as that is the accepted style of communicating in that medium. The 21st century features "texting" with its own shorthand language. On the other hand, the subject matter of the transaction was land which is among the more serious transactions typically evidenced by writings stating comprehensive terms and may not reasonably be understood as completing a contract by the mere exchange or preliminary telegrams. There was also public knowledge that the defendant had offered the property to the City the day before the plaintiffs sent their telegram. Plaintiffs' knowledge of this fact could lead to the conclusion that they should not have viewed the defendant's telegram response as an offer if they knew that defendant had already made an offer to the City. The court, however, does not indicate whether plaintiffs had knowledge of the offer to the City nor does it present its analysis on the basis of these additional facts.

The question remains, would a reasonable party in Harvey's position understand that he had a power of acceptance? The factual patterns illustrating this kind of borderline or "gray area" case are myriad, and the judicial task is essentially the same in each: to approximate, as closely as possible, the manifested intentions of the parties, which are more often than not imperfectly expressed. The use of the guide suggested in this section should prove helpful to courts in their performance of this task. Again, it is no more than a guide, since, as Aristotle and others remind us, we should not expect as much certainty in our law as we expect in our physics.

§ 36   THE EFFECT OF CAPTIONS AND HEADINGS — "QUOTATION," PURCHASE ORDER, ETC

A prospective buyer of goods or services may solicit a price quotation ("quote") from one or more vendors. The solicitation is not an offer. It is an invitation to negotiate or, in antiquated usage, "an invitation to treat." In response to the solicitation, the vendor may send a document captioned "quotation." As recently suggested, "Courts have found it difficult to determine when a price quotation constitutes a definite offer and when it is merely a preliminary step in negotiations leading to an offer."[109] There are many cases suggesting that a typical "price quotation" is not an offer,[110] while a typical "purchase order" is an offer.[111] A "quotation," however, may be construed to be an offer if it is sufficiently detailed and it reasonably appears

---

[109] Verasun Fort Dodge, LLC v. Industrial Air Technology Corp., 2008 U. S. Dist. LEXIS 99292 at *42–43, citing cases (N. D. Iowa 2008).

[110] *See, e.g.*, White Consol. Indus., Inc. v. McGill Mfg. Co., 165 F.3d 1185, 1190 (8th Cir. 1999) (citing Litton Microwave Cooking Prods. v. Leviton Mfg. Co., 15 F.3d 790, 794 (8th Cir. 1994)); Interstate Indus., Inc. v. Barclay Indus., Inc., 540 F.2d 868 (7th Cir. 1976). When a court has concluded that a price quotation is not an offer in a given case, it almost invariably refers to such a price quotation as a "mere" price quotation: "[W]e find no reason to disturb the district court's conclusion that the . . . letter . . . was not an offer but merely a quotation of prices." Pro Spice, Inc. v. Omni Trade Group, Inc., 128 Fed. Appx. 836, 838 (3d Cir. 2005). On its face, a "quote" or quotation may appear to solicit an offer. *See* RESTATEMENT 2d § 26 comment c. It is not intended to be binding when the purchaser reacts by sending its order in response to the quotation.

[111] *See, e.g.*, Kraft Foods N. Am. v. Banner Eng'g & Sales, Inc., 446 F. Supp. 2d 551,568–69 (E.D. Va. 2006); Master Palletizer Sys., Inc. v. T.S. Ragsdale Co., 725 F. Supp. 1525, 1531 (D. Colo. 1989), *aff'd*, 937 F.2d 616 (10th Cir. 1991); J. B. Moore Electrical Contractor, Inc. v. Westinghouse Elec. Supply Co., 221 Va. 745, 273 S.E.2d 553 (1981).

"that assent to that quotation is all that is needed to ripen the offer into a contract."[112] "Factors relevant in determining whether a price quotation is an offer include the extent of prior inquiry, the completeness of the terms of the suggested bargain, and the number of persons to whom the price quotation is communicated."[113]

A "purchase order" that is typically viewed as an offer will be construed to be an acceptance if it was intended to be used as an acceptance.[114] Similarly, documents with other captions may or may not be offers.[115]

Contextual Interpretation and Construction. Whether a price quotation, purchase order or documents with other captions are offers, "mere" preliminary negotiations or even acceptances of offers requires a careful analysis of the language in the documents, any trade usage, course of dealing or course of performance evidence and all of the other surrounding circumstances to allow an interpretation and construction in *context.*[116] In a classic case, the phrase, "for immediate acceptance" at the end of what otherwise appeared to be a price quotation converted the preliminary negotiation into an offer. A response to a price solicitation provided a series of prices on various sizes of jars in carload lots, but ended with "for immediate acceptance." These three words were sufficient for the court to conclude that the seller had made an offer since they indicated the seller's promise or commitment to sell.[117] In another case, a document captioned "quotation" was construed to be an offer because the parties

---

[112] Quaker State Mushroom Co. v. Dominick's Finer Foods, Inc., 635 F. Supp. 1281, 1284 (N.D. Ill. 1986). If a document referred to a price quotation as a manifested binding intention upon submission of the buyer's order through the typical purchase order, such a quotation would be an offer. McCarty v. Verson Allsteel Press Co., 89 Ill. App. 3d 498, 411 N.E.2d 936 (1st Dist. 1980). See also Memphis-Shelby County Airport Auth. v. Illinois Paving Co., 2006 U. S. Dist. LEXIS 79970 (W. D. Tenn. 2006) (quotation-bid was an offer); Maryland Supreme Corp. v. Blake Co., 279 Md. 531, 369 A.2d 1017 (1977), where the "quotation" for the supply of concrete for the construction of a building which stated, "[T]he price will be guaranteed to hold throughout the job" was construed to be an offer.

[113] Nordyne, Inc. v. International Controls & Measurements Corp., 262 F. 3d 843, 846 (8th Cir. 2001) citing RESTATEMENT 2d § 28, comment c.

[114] *See, e.g.,* Memphis-Shelby County Airport Auth. v. Illinois Paving Co., 2006 U. S. Dist. LEXIS 79970 (W. D. Tenn. 2006) (purchase order was an acceptance responding to quotation bid). See also Island Creek Coal Co. v. Lake Shore, Inc., 636 F. Supp. 285 (W.D. Va. 1986); Daitom, Inc. v. Pennwalt Corp., 741 F.2d 1569 (10th Cir. 1984); Mead Corp. v. McNally-Pittsburgh Mfg. Corp., 654 F.2d 1197 (6th Cir. 1981); Idaho Power Co. v. Westinghouse Elec. Corp., 596 F.2d 924 (9th Cir. 1979); Earl M. Jorgensen Co. v. Mark Constr., 56 Hawaii 466, 540 P.2d 978 (1975). In particular, see Phillips Petroleum Co. v. Bucyrus-Erie Co., 125 Wis. 2d 418, 373 N.W.2d 65 (Ct. App. 1985), *rev'd on other grounds,* 131 Wis. 2d 21, 388 N.W.2d 584 (1986).

[115] *See, e.g.,* Paloukos v. Intermountain Chevrolet Co., 99 Idaho 740, 588 P.2d 939 (1978) ("worksheet" construed as evidence of contract rather than mere preliminary negotiations); Empire Mach. Co. v. Litton Bus. Tel. Sys., 115 Ariz. 568, 566 P.2d 1044 (Ct. App. 1977) ("Equipment Sales Agreement" signed by the purchaser was an offer because it required seller's authorized signature to become legally binding); J. B. Moore Electrical Contractor, Inc. v. Westinghouse Elec. Supply Co., 221 Va. 745, 273 S.E.2d 553 (1981) (purchase order form supplied by seller construed to be an offer rather than an invitation to the buyer to make an offer because it did not contain a purchaser's signature line).

[116] *See* the discussion and cases cited in Verasun Fort Dodge, L.L.C. v. Industrial Air Technology Corp., 2008 U. S. Dist. LEXIS 99292 at *43–45 (N. D. Iowa 2008) See also, Dyno Constr. Co. v. McWane, Inc., 198 F.3d 567 (6th Cir. 1999).

[117] Fairmount Glass Works v. Grunden-Martin Woodenware Co., 106 Ky. 659, 51 S.W. 196 (1899). RESTATEMENT 2d § 26 ill. 3 suggests that a letter from *A* to *B*, stating, "I can quote you flour at $5 per barrel in carload lots" would not, itself, be an offer in view of the word "quote" and incompleteness of the terms. However, the same letter in response to an inquiry specifying detailed terms "would probably" convert the letter into an offer. Moreover, if *A* had added, "for immediate acceptance," the RESTATEMENT 2d suggests that an intention to make an offer would then be "unmistakable."

manifested their intention that it operate as an offer.[118] Even the term "offer" may not be sufficient to create a power of acceptance if the statement otherwise suggests that it sought to induce offers.[119]

While captions and other characterizing terms within a statement are not conclusive of the legal effect to be accorded a statement, it would be foolhardy to characterize a statement as a "quotation" if an offer were intended, or to characterize it as an "offer" if a preliminary negotiation were intended. In an otherwise close case, the use of a term normally associated with offers or non-offers can be persuasive.[120] In summary, whether a particular manifestation of intention is an offer as contrasted with a preliminary negotiation will depend upon the proper interpretation of the entire statement under the surrounding circumstances as one which is sufficiently definite to permit a remedy to be fashioned and, in particular, whether the statement is promissory.[121]

§ 37 AUCTION SALES AND SELF-SERVICE TRANSACTIONS

[A] Auction Sales

The determination of who makes the offer at the typical auction sale was the subject of considerable controversy at one time. When the auctioneer places goods up for sale, is he making an offer to sell to the highest bidder, or is he merely inviting bidders to make offers? An early case took the view that the typical auction sale is one in which the auctioneer merely invites offers, i.e., the auctioneer is saying, "What am I bid?"[122] Under this view, if the auctioneer is dissatisfied with the level of bidding, he need not accept any bid and can withdraw the item.

The early interpretation of the typical auction sale as one where the bidder is the offeror and the acceptance of the offer does not occur until the auctioneer brings down the hammer or in some other customary manner manifests that acceptance has been uniformly accepted.[123] Section 2-328(2) of the UCC indicates that the typical auction sale "is complete when the auctioneer so announces by the fall of the hammer or in other customary manner." In *Bradshaw v. Thompson*,[124] the court applied this section of the Code pursuant to the sale catalogue in a horse auction which, in boldface, indicated that the horse could be withdrawn even after the fall of the hammer so long as the horse had not been taken from the sale ring. Where the seller has reserved the right to reject any bids, the customary means of acceptance is not the fall of the hammer but some other objective manifestation of acceptance.[125] In

---

[118] *See* Earl M. Jorgensen Co. v. Mark Constr., Inc., 56 Haw. 466, 540 P.2d 978 (1975).

[119] *See supra* § 35.

[120] For example, in Interstate Indus., Inc. v. Barclay Indus., Inc., 540 F.2d 868 (7th Cir. 1976), the reference to the contents of a letter as a "price quotation" was one of four factors leading a court to conclude that the statement was not an offer. In Chasan v. Village Dist. of Eastman, 523 A.2d 16 (N.H. 1986), the court points to the fact that the document did not purport to be an offer and, while not dispositive, the court was somewhat persuaded by that fact.

[121] *See supra* § 35.

[122] Payne v. Cave, 3 Term. Rep. 148 (1789).

[123] See Pyles v. Goller, 109 Md. App. 71, 674 A.2d 35 (1996).

[124] 454 F.2d 75 (6th Cir.), *cert. denied*, 409 U.S. 878, 93 S. Ct. 130, 34 L. Ed. 2d 131 (1972).

[125] Rosin v. First Bank of Oak Park, 126 Ill. App. 3d 230, 466 N.E.2d 1245, 1250 (1st Dist. 1984).

Atlantic Orient Corp. v. AOC Energy, LLC,[126] the court held that, even without an express agreement, the parties understanding that the sale was not complete until delivery of the balance of the purchase price and bill of sale changed the normal rule in § 2-328(2) making sales "complete" at the fall of the hammer.

Since the bidder is the offeror in the typical auction sale, he may revoke his offer prior to its acceptance, i.e., he may withdraw his bid at any time prior to the fall of the hammer or the completion of the sale in other customary manner. It is important to emphasize that the typical auction sale is treated as a sale "with reserve," i.e., the auctioneer is not compelled to sell anything to anyone. Auction sales are presumed to be "with reserve" unless they are expressly announced to be "without reserve."[127] Bids are merely offers at a "with reserve" sale and any offer may be rejected by the auctioneer. This view was adopted by the old Uniform Sales Act[128] and has been recodified in its successor, the UCC.[129]

In auctions expressly announced to be "without reserve" or sufficiently similar language, the offer-acceptance analysis changes dramatically. In "with reserve" sales, the auctioneer is saying, "What am I bid," but in "without reserve" sales, the auctioneer is saying, "I will sell to the highest bidder." The offeree is not identified until he makes a bid, but he is identifiable as the highest bidder.[130] Thus, in "without reserve" sales, the auctioneer is making an offer, i.e., creating a power of acceptance, in any prospective bidder. When the auctioneer calls for bids in a "without reserve" sale, the offer is open for a reasonable time and the item may not be withdrawn from sale unless no bid is made within a reasonable time.[131] The first bidder at such a sale is, necessarily, the highest bidder since it is possible that no other bids may be made. There is, therefore, a contract with the first bidder who has exercised his power of acceptance. If no other bid is made, that contract is completed. If one or more higher bids are made, there is a contract with each subsequent higher bidder. The contract formed by the previous bid is discharged as soon as the higher bid is made.[132] Thus, a contract formed by the making of the current highest bid at a "without reserve" sale is conditioned upon no higher bid

---

[126] 2003 Bankr. LEXIS 206 (N. H. 2003).

[127] UCC § 2-328(3). *See* Dreding v. Alabama Diesel, Inc., 741 So. 2d 1096 (Ct. Civ. App. Ala. 1999); Love v. Basque Cartel, 873 F. Supp. 563 (D. Wyo. 1995).

[128] Uniform Sales Act § 21.

[129] UCC § 2-328(2). *See also* Restatement 2d § 28(1)(a).

[130] See Sly v. First Nat'l Bank of Scottsboro, 387 So. 2d 199 (Ala. 1980), where the public notice stated that the sale was to be "at public outcry to the highest, best and last bidder." The court held this notice to be insufficient notice of a "without reserve" sale; therefore, the sale was automatically "with reserve." The court appeared to insist upon the literal phrase, "without reserve," in the notice to constitute such a sale, i.e., no substitute phrase would accomplish this result. However, in Dublin Livestock & Com. Co. v. Day, 178 Ga. App. 50, 341 S.E.2d 913 (1986), an announcement that the auction would be "absolute" and that everything would be sold for the highest dollar bid was construed to be an announcement of an auction sale "without reserve." Courts will generally accept clear language in substitution for the literal phrase, "without reserve." *See* Chevalier v. Sanford, 475 A.2d 1148, 1149 (Me. 1984): "The advertisement in the present case did not expressly state that the forthcoming sale was without reserve nor did it contain any language subject to the interpretation that the right to reject any and all bids was not reserved."

[131] UCC § 2-328(3). *See* Dublin Livestock & Com. Co. v. Day, 178 Ga. App. 50, 341 S.E.2d 913 (1986).

[132] "[I]n an absolute auction, or an auction held without reserve, mutual contingent assent is achieved when an offer is made. Each bid made is a mutual assent between the seller and the respective bidder, contingent only on no higher bid being received. As each high bid is made, the previous contract is extinguished and a new contract based on mutual contingent assent comes into being. At the point when no further bids are made, the contingency in the last bid made is extinguished and a final contract in the series of contingent contract is established." Pyles v. Goller, 109 Md. App. 71, 82, 674 A.2d 35, 40 (1996).

being made before the bidding ends upon the fall of the hammer or other customary method.

If the highest bid in a "without reserve" sale is disappointing to the seller, the sale is, nonetheless, complete and the bidder can enforce the contract. The seller has assumed the risk of selling to the highest bidder in such a sale. If the bidding in a "with reserve" sale is disappointing, however, the auctioneer can withdraw the item from sale since, again, he is merely inviting offers and can reject any offer. To avoid negative public relations, the auctioneer may resort to employing a seller's agent or "shill" to enhance the bidding. If the agent does not succeed in elevating the bidding to a level satisfactory to the auctioneer, the auctioneer may then pretend to sell the item to the agent who becomes a fictitious highest bidder. Where this practice was employed in a "with reserve" sale of real estate and the second highest (good faith) bidder claimed a contract, an old case decided that while this action was not a straightforward method of withdrawing the item from sale, it had the same effect, i.e., the offer had been withdrawn with respect to the second-highest good faith bidder.[133] The UCC pervasive requirement of good faith, however, requires a different result.[134] Even with respect to auction sales not governed by the UCC, a court may apply the UCC concept analogously to preclude such a bad faith practice.[135] *A fortiori*, in sales "without reserve," neither the seller nor his agent may bid on the property since the seller could out-bid a competitor, thereby rejecting the highest bidder's acceptance of the offer made by the auctioneer. An owner bidding on his own property would thereby transform an auction held 'without reserve' into one held 'with reserve.'[136]

In terms of contract theory, the application of the traditional offer-acceptance analysis to "with reserve" auction sales needs no accommodation since the bidder is the offeror who may withdraw (revoke) his bid/offer at any time before the manifestation of acceptance by the auctioneer. The making of a bid creates a power of acceptance in the auctioneer/offeree which he need not exercise if he is dissatisfied with the level of bids. In "without reserve" sales, however, the accommodation to traditional offer-acceptance analysis is strained.

If a contract is formed upon the making of the first and any subsequent higher bid, it should be impossible for either party, highest bidder or auctioneer, to withdraw from that contract. This was conceptually essential in classical contract law since a contract is formed upon the acceptance of an offer and the bid is the acceptance in a "without reserve" sale. Basic contract law would preclude either party from unilaterally withdrawing from the contract. Yet, the Sales Act permitted the bidder to withdraw his bid so long as the auctioneer had not announced the sale to have been completed.[137] Under this theory, the auctioneer (offeror) is bound as soon as the bid is made, but the bidder (the offeree who accepted the offer by making the bid) is free to retract the bid until completion of the sale. Thus, the auctioneer is bound to a contract but the bidder may withdraw. An early version of the UCC prohibited *both* the auctioneer and the bidder from withdrawing.[138] The purification of "without reserve" rules to

---

[133] *See* Freeman v. Poole, 37 R.I. 489, 93 A. 786 (1915).

[134] *See* UCC § 2-328(4): "If the auctioneer knowingly receives a bid on the seller's behalf or the seller makes or procures such a bid, and notice has not been given that liberty for such bidding is reserved, the buyer may at his option avoid the sale or take the goods at the price of the last good faith bid prior to the completion of the sale."

[135] *See* Forbes v. Wells Beach Casino, Inc., 307 A.2d 210, 219 (Me. 1973).

[136] *See* note 134, *supra*.

[137] Uniform Sales Act § 21.

[138] UCC § 2-328(3) (Final Draft No. 1, 1944).

coincide with traditional contract theory was, however, of short duration. The Code was subsequently revised to conform to the theoretical anomaly of the old Sales Act and the current version retains that anomaly. A bidder may withdraw before completion of the sale in either a "with reserve" or "without reserve" sale and the retraction of a bid does not revive any previous bid.[139] The violation of basic contract theory may be explained since the "without reserve" auction sale seeks to induce more prospective bidders to the sale by promising to sell to the highest bidder. If a bidder at such a sale were precluded from withdrawing a bid before the sale closed, however, the inducement factor of "without reserve" sales may be undermined. A similar theoretical issue occurs in *self-service transactions*.

[B]   Self-Service Transactions

Several cases have confronted the question of who makes the offer in a self-service transaction. These cases are often concerned with the application of warranty protection for buyers under the UCC. If a shopper in a supermarket takes a carton of cola from the shelves and one or more of the bottles explode, injuring the shopper before he has presented the cola and other items in the shopping cart to the checker for payment, questions of contract formation become highly relevant. The UCC provides an implied warranty of merchantability for purchasers of such goods if a contract for the sale of the goods has been made.[140] Though such buyers may also be able to resort to tort remedies,[141] an action under the UCC may be a desirable alternative in certain situations.[142]

When courts have been confronted with the necessity of applying the offer-acceptance analysis to the self-service situation, they have suggested two views, both analytically flawed. In a decision by Queen's Bench,[143] the defendant operated a self-service chemists' shop where shelves contained drugs found on the Poisons List of the British Pharmacy and Poisons Act which had to be sold under the supervision of a registered pharmacist. The pharmacist was at the check-out counter. If the shop was making an offer by placing the goods on the shelves and the customer was accepting the offer by taking the goods off the shelves, the contract for sale was not made under the supervision of a registered pharmacist and would violate the Poisons Act. If, however, the customer made no contract until she offered to pay for the goods at the check-out counter where the shop accepted that offer, the contract was made under appropriate supervision and no violation of the statute occurred. The court held that the contract was made at the check-out counter. This view also satisfies contract theory in allowing customers in self-service stores to change their minds by replacing goods on shelves since no contract was made. Theoretically, however, the customer would have no right to purchase the goods from the store at the checkout counter, i.e., the customer could only offer to purchase

---

[139] UCC § 2-328(3).

[140] UCC § 2-314(1). One of the requirements of the section is that a contract for the sale of goods has been formed.

[141] In addition to a tort theory based upon negligence (which may be difficult to prove), the injured party in such a situation may be able to resort to the strict liability theory, of the RESTATEMENT 2D OF TORTS § 402A (1977), which has been adopted throughout the country as part of the products liability revolution.

[142] For example, in some jurisdictions, a plaintiff in such an action who waits beyond the torts statute of limitations (e. g., two years for personal injury) may still be able to take advantage of the UCC where § 2-725 provides a statute of limitations of four years from the time the goods are delivered. *See* Williams v. West Penn Power Co., 313 Pa. Super. 461, 460 A.2d 278 (1983). Depending upon the jurisdiction, however, warranty theory may limit the buyer to an action against the buyer's immediate seller rather than a remote manufacturer of the product with whom the buyer is not in "privity." There is no privity issue under the typical action for products liability in tort.

[143] Pharmaceutical Soc'y of Great Britain v. Boots Cash Chemists (Southern) Ltd., [1953] 1 Q.B. 401.

and the store could reject the offer. Moreover, the customer would have no right to the goods in her possession while shopping. Theoretically, store officials or, perhaps, other customers, could take a scarce good from a customer's basket. American courts have analyzed the situation differently.

American courts have found a contract when the buyer takes the goods from the shelves. The display of the goods is said to be an offer and the customer's act of taking the goods from the shelves constitutes an acceptance of the offer with the implication of a promise to pay for the goods at the check-out counter.[144] This theory supports recovery by plaintiffs pursuant to the implied warranty of merchantability under the UCC by finding a contract for sale when the customer reduces the goods to possession and is injured by them before presenting them at the check-out counter.[145] Whatever may be said for the desirability of protecting such customers, the analysis is flawed. If a contract is formed as soon as a customer takes goods from the shelves of a self-service store, the customer may be said to have breached that contract by changing her mind and returning the goods to the shelves. Yet, the custom and usage is clear that innumerable customers change their minds and return goods to shelves under the reasonable assumption that they may do so without liability. American courts find an implied power of termination for the purchaser in the contract to justify replacement of goods without breaching the contract.[146]

[C]   A Suggested Analysis in Self-Service and "Without Reserve" Contracts

In self-service contracts, the customer could be said to have an irrevocable power of acceptance, i.e., an "option contract," for a reasonable time upon taking possession of goods from a shelf. The store would be seen as making an irrevocable offer for a reasonable (shopper's) time in exchange for the customer shopping at its store rather than other stores. If the customer changed her mind and replaced the goods, it would simply be a decision not to exercise her irrevocable power of acceptance. The "option" contract could also satisfy the requirement of the implied warranty of merchantability under the UCC.[147] Moreover, the bizarre possibility of others taking the goods from the customer's possession would be eliminated since the customer would have the exclusive right to complete the purchase of the goods for a reasonable time. This analysis reflects the reasonable understanding of self-service stores and their customers.

The same theory may prove useful in "without reserve" auction sales. By characterizing the "without reserve" sale bid as providing the bidder with an irrevocable power of acceptance to purchase the item subject to no higher bid being made, the bidder could, consistent with

---

[144] *See, e.g.*, Barker v. Allied Supermarket, 596 P.2d 870 (Okla. 1979). *See also* Sheeskin v. Giant Food, Inc., 20 Md. App. 611, 318 A.2d 874 (1974).

[145] UCC § 2-314(1) implies a warranty of merchantability only where a contract has been made and the seller is a merchant with respect to goods of that kind.

[146] *See Barker*, note 144, *supra*. The power of termination is defined in UCC § 2-106(3): "Termination occurs when either party pursuant to a power created by agreement or law puts an end to the contract otherwise than for its breach. . . ." It is distinguished from "cancellation" in § 2-106(4) which applies where either party puts an end to the contract for breach by the other party. The effect is the same as "termination," but the cancelling party retains remedies for breach of contract.

[147] Finding an option contract for the sale of goods to satisfy the UCC § 2-314(1) requirement of a contract for the sale of goods is supported by the general UCC directive that the Code should be "liberally construed." UCC § 1-102(1).

contract theory, withdraw the bid prior to the completion of the sale, but the auctioneer could not withdraw. The same option contract analysis would apply to create an irrevocable power of acceptance in the bidder. By attending the sale "without reserve," the bidder has provided the consideration sought by the seller who sought to induce the bidder to attend. The seller would not only be promising to sell without reserve to the highest bidder; he would also be promising not to revoke his offer for a reasonable time after the item is placed up for sale as well as permitting the then highest bidder to announce that he would not exercise his irrevocable power of acceptance and, thereby, withdraw from the transaction. If the bidder failed to withdraw prior to the completion of the sale, he would be said to have impliedly exercised his power of acceptance and would be bound to purchase the item at the bid price.[148]

§ 38 ASSENT THROUGH CONDUCT

The normal exchange of offer and acceptance is by language, oral or written. The parties typically exchange promises, but such verbal exchanges do not constitute the exclusive mode of expressing mutual assent.[149] Acts or conduct may evidence mutual assent. Such contracts are often said to be "implied-in-fact."[150] A contract implied-in-fact from the conduct of the parties "is as binding as one that is express."[151] Indeed, all contracts are "express" contracts though the parties' mutual assent may be expressed by conduct or words.[152] Where an express contract expires by its terms, but the parties continue to perform, courts may infer that the parties conduct manifests their implied agreement to continue to perform under an implied-in-fact contract that includes the terms of their previously expired express agreement.[153]

Bunting was an acting branch manager of a bank who was fired for notarizing a customer's signature without having observed the customer signing the document. Bunting, however, had pursued similar acts in the past pursuant to the direction of supervisors, a widespread practice at the bank. The court denied the bank's motion for summary judgment since a jury could find breach of an implied-in-fact contract modifying Bunting's at-will employment contract that she would not be fired by following the bank's policy on such notarizations.[154]

Shoppers in self-service stores typically present items to a cashier with nary a spoken word concerning their contract, but there is no doubt that in these and myriad other situations manifesting mutual assent by conduct, a contract has been created. Assume neighbors discussed the possibility of the erection of a party wall between their properties that will provide mutual benefit, and both neighbors have reason to know that the cost of such a wall will

---

[148] While the Corbin treatise refers to the foregoing theory as "intellectually satisfying," Corbin on Contracts, § 2.7, note 6, it has yet to be adopted in any jurisdiction.

[149] RESTATEMENT 2d § 19.

[150] See § 21 *supra*, which distinguished "implied-in-fact" and "implied-in-law" contracts, recognizing that the latter are not contracts but restitutionary devices. This topic will be further explored later in this chapter in § 52[B].

[151] Leibowitz v. Cornell University, 584 F. 3d 487, 507 (2d Cir. 2009). In a contract for the sale of goods, the UCC expressly recognizes contracts by conduct. UCC § 2-204(1).

[152] In re Estate of Roccomante, 346 N. J. Super. 107, 118, 787 A. 2d 198, 206 (2001); Morgan Truck Body LLC v. Integrated Logistics Solutions, 2008 U. S. Dist. LEXIS 21962 at *11 (E. D. Pa. 2008) citing comment a, § 4 of the Restatement (Second) of Contracts, noting only a difference in the mode of manifesting assent but no difference in legal effect between express and implied-in-fact contracts.

[153] Sanford Housing Authority v. Perkins Propane, Inc., 2004 Me. Super. LEXIS 203.

[154] Bunting v. Citizens Financial Group, Inc., 2006 Del. Super. LEXIS 118.

be shared.[155] Assume they have reached no contract through their discussions, i.e., there is no commitment by either party concerning this project; it is a mere possibility. Later, one of the parties begins to construct the wall with the full knowledge of the other party who does not object. Under these circumstances, an agreement for sharing the costs for the party wall can be found through their conduct.[156] The neighbor's conduct in commencing work on the wall could be viewed as offering to build it in exchange for one-half of its cost. The knowing silence of the other neighbor could be viewed as an acceptance of the offer,[157] just as the display of goods on shelves in a supermarket or other self-service store could be viewed as an offer.

The Test. Whether particular conduct expresses an offer and acceptance must be determined on the basis of what a reasonable person in the position of the parties would be led to understand by such conduct under all of the surrounding circumstances.[158] In keeping with this standard, a party will be responsible for creating the appearance of an offer whether done so intentionally or negligently. Assume that Ames writes a letter to Barnes containing an offer. She encloses the letter in a properly addressed and stamped envelope, but decides not to mail it. By mistake, she includes the letter in a group of other letters she does intend to mail. Barnes receives the mistakenly mailed letter and accepts the offer by return mail. Unless Barnes knows or has reason to know of Ames' mistake, a contract results because Ames is responsible for negligently creating the appearance of an offer.[159] This analysis is consistent with the objective theory of contract law since the undisclosed intention of Ames is irrelevant; her manifested intention to make an offer created a reasonable understanding in Barnes that his assent would conclude a contract.[160]

---

[155] RESTATEMENT 2d § 19, comment b, suggests that a person has "reason to know" a fact, present or future, if he has information from which a person of ordinary intelligence would infer that the fact in question does or will exist. Moreover, if the inference would be that there is such a substantial chance of the existence of the fact that, if exercising reasonable care with reference to the matter in question, the person would predicate his action upon the assumption of its possible existence.

[156] *See* Day v. Caton, 119 Mass. 513, 20 Am. Rep. 347 (1876). *See also* Earhart v. William Low Co., 25 Cal. 3d 503, 600 P.2d 1344 (1979). Contracts inferred from benefits received are discussed in § 52[B], *infra.* The contract between the parties will often be characterized as an "implied-in-fact" contract which simply means that the manifestation of mutual assent was not in language, oral or written. One must be careful, however, to distinguish so-called implied-in-fact contracts from "implied-in-law" contracts which are not contracts in any sense but are judicial constructions to avoid unjust enrichment. *See* § 21, *supra.*

[157] The question of silence as acceptance requires separate exploration. A conduct acceptance may be found where goods are shipped to a party who exercises dominion and control over them. *See* Preston Farm & Ranch Supply, Inc. v. Bio-Zyme Enters., 625 S.W.2d 295 (Tex. 1981). This situation is explored in § 52,*infra.*

[158] Quoted in *Woods v. ERA Med LLC,* 2009 U. S. Dist. LEXIS 3965 at *12 (E.D. Pa. 2009) as previously quoted from an earlier edition of this book in *Temple University Hospital, Inc. v. Healthcare Mgmt. Alternatives,* 764 A.2d 587 (Pa. Super. Ct. 2000).

[159] *See* RESTATEMENT 2d § 19 ill. 3.

[160] *See supra* § 31.

§ 39   REASONABLE CERTAINTY — INDEFINITENESS

[A]   General Requirement of Definiteness

It is commonly suggested that, although parties intend to form a contract, if the terms of their agreement are not sufficiently definite or reasonably certain, no contract will be said to exist.[161] As noted in a recent opinion, "It is not enough to allege, in a conclusory fashion, that the facts demonstrate a breach of contract. Rather, it is 'essential to state with substantial certainty the facts showing the existence of the contract and legal effect thereof.' "[162] These and similar general statements, however, offer only limited assistance absent an elaboration of the modifying terms, "sufficient." and "reasonably." If the terms of the contract need not be absolutely certain or definite but only "reasonably" certain or "sufficiently" definite, courts will enforce contracts containing terms that lack clarity and courts will also enforce contracts that do not contain all of the terms of the agreement. A court, however, cannot enforce a contract if it cannot ascertain its terms. At some point, the terms of the agreement may be so unclear, or the agreement may be silent on such important terms or so many terms that courts will not be able to determine whether any breach occurred and it will be impossible for a court to fashion an appropriate remedy.[163] Many older cases found indefiniteness to be fatal,[164] but the applied standards were so vague that the older case law may appear contradictory.[165]

Modern courts are much less willing than their predecessors to regard indefiniteness as fatal. Where parties had not agreed on the fixtures and finishes for their new house, the defendant claimed the contract lacked sufficient certainty to be enforced. The court held that the parties' ovrriding intention to purchase the house should not be frustrated by the

---

[161] *See, e.g.*, Miller v. Rose, 138 N.C. App. 582, 532 S.E.2d 228, 232 (2000); Zurcher v. Herveat, 238 Mich. App. 267, 605 N.W.2d 329, 336 (1999); Ault v. Pakulski, 520 A.2d 703 (Me. 1987); Bishop v. Hendrickson, 215 Mont. 158, 695 P.2d 1313 (1985); North Coast Cookies, Inc. v. Sweet Temptations, Inc., 16 Ohio App. 3d 342, 476 N.E.2d 388 (1984); Arrowhead Constr. Co. v. Essex Corp., 233 Kan. 241, 662 P.2d 1195 (1983); Almeida v. Almeida, 4 Haw. App. 513, 669 P.2d 174 (1983); Porter v. Porter, 637 S.W.2d 396 (Mo. Ct. App. 1982). The definition of an offer in CISG Art. 14(1) requires a proposal to be "sufficiently definite" to constitute an offer. See § 35, note 93, *supra.*

[162] Vieira v. First Am. Title Ins. Co., 668 F. Supp. 2d 282, 288–89 (D. Mass. 2009) quoting Doyle v. Hasbro, Inc., 103 F. 3d, 186, 194–95 (1st Cir. 1996).

[163] Lake Michigan Contractors v. Manitowoc Co., 2002 U. S. Dist. LEXIS 9547 at *21(W. D. Mich. 2002). Restatement 2d § 33(2) suggests, "The terms of a contract are reasonably certain if they provide a basis for determining the existence of a breach and for giving an appropriate remedy." Section 2-204(3) of the UCC provides: "Even though one or more terms is left open, a contract for sale does not fail for indefiniteness if the parties have intended to make a contract and there is a reasonably certain basis for giving an appropriate remedy."

[164] *See, e.g.*, Klimek v. Perisich, 231 Or. 71, 371 P.2d 956 (1962) (vague agreement to remodel house at cost not exceeding $10,000 with prices of certain items to be agreed upon at most reasonable price available); Smith v. Chickamauga Cedar Co., 263 Ala. 245, 247, 82 So. 2d 200 (1955) (agreement to furnish logs in quantities deemed "feasible and economical" by lumberman); Hardman v. Polino, 113 W. Va. 404, 168 S.E. 384 (1933) (agreement to loan money to develop farms to their highest efficiency); Varney v. Ditmars, 217 N.Y. 223, 111 N.E. 822 (1916) (promise to pay "a fair share of my profits").

[165] An agreement to erect a structure in accordance "with plans to be approved by your company" and to conform "to the most recent stores" was fatally indefinite in Peoples Drug Stores, Inc. v. Fenton Realty Corp., 191 Md. 489, 62 A.2d 273 (1948). Similarly, an agreement to erect "a permanent and first-class hotel" was fatally indefinite in Hart v. Georgia R. Co., 101 Ga. 188, 28 S.E. 637 (1897). Yet, a promise to erect "a First-class Theatre" was sufficiently definite to be enforced because "First-class Theatre" could refer to a similar theatre owned by the promisor and local building codes could be used to establish construction standards. Bettancourt v. Gilroy Theatre Co., 120 Cal. App. 2d 364, 366, 261 P.2d 351 (1953).

necessity of making a choice between conflicting meanings and the filling of some gaps the parties left to be determined.[166] A failure of the parties to specify the location of an easement in their contract was not fatally indefinite. The court held that this gap could be filled by allowing the landowner to select the location of the easement, such authority to be limited by the landowner's duty to effect the stated purpose of the easement.[167]

This is not to suggest that modern courts will always err on the side of discovering sufficient certainty. Where two documents captioned "Agreement in Principle" contained numerous "proposals" to develop broad-based entertainment projects with no definition of such projects, budget projections or numerous other details, the court concluded that there was no enforceable agreement, not because of vagueness of terms, but because the parties had not agreed on any terms.[168]

Uniform Commercial Code-Definiteness-Missing Terms. The willingness of modern courts to find enforceable agreements notwithstanding some uncertainty is largely attributable to the general and specific directives concerning indefiniteness in the UCC. Section 2-204(3) establishes the general principle:

> Even though one or more terms are left open a contract for sale does not fail for indefiniteness if the parties have intended to make a contract and there is a reasonably certain basis for giving an appropriate remedy.

This general prescription is elaborated by numerous sections providing for the implementation of terms as "gap-fillers" conditioned on the critical requirements of the parties' manifested intention to be bound and sufficient certainty to allow the court to fashion a remedy.[169]

The general requirement that a court should find an enforceable agreement if it discovers an intention to be bound and a reasonable basis to afford a remedy served as a catalyst to chart a new, anti-technical course away from fatal indefiniteness to promote the enforcement of the factual bargain of the parties in accordance with the underlying philosophy of Article 2 of the Code.[170] The influence of this initiative, aided and abetted by the Second Restatement of

---

[166] Warren v. Sharabi, 2002 Cal. App. Unpub. LEXIS 3342 (Cal. Ct. App. 2002).

[167] Evans v. Board of County Commissioners, 2005 Ut. 74, 123 P.3d 432 (2005). The current view suggests that "the law leans against the destruction of contracts for uncertainty" and "courts favor the determination that an agreement is sufficiently definite." *In re* Sing Chong Co., 1 Haw. App. 236, 239, 617 P.2d 578, 581 (1980).

[168] Portman v. Zoetrope Corp., 2005 Cal. Unpub. LEXIS 4093 (2005). In Bishop v. Hendrickson, 215 Mont. 158, 695 P.2d 1313, 1314 (1985), though it applied § 33 of the Restatement 2d provision concerning reasonable certainty, the court could not discover sufficient certainty to enforce an agreement between partners in a law firm that, "in the event any of their children ever became lawyers and wanted to practice law with the firm that there would be a place for such child or children in the law firm."

[169] Part 3 of Article 2 of the Code contains numerous gap-filling terms. The fact that terms such as price (§ 2-305), place of delivery (§ 2-308), and time of delivery (§ 2-309) are missing will not cause the agreement to fail for indefiniteness where the two critical conditions of § 2-204(3) are present. Output and requirements contracts (§ 2-306) that preclude a certain quantity term at the time of formation though the quantity will be ascertained at the conclusion of the contract are "not too indefinite" (comment 2 to § 2-306). If the parties leave particulars of performance to be specified by one of the parties, the contract does not fail for indefiniteness under § 2-311. For an examination of these and other Article 2 changes, see Murray, *The Article 2 Prism: The Underlying Philosophy of Article 2 of the Uniform Commercial Code* , 21 Washburn L.J. 1 (1982).

[170] See Nebraska Builders Prods. Co. v. Industrial Erectors, Inc., 239 Neb. 744, 478 N.W.2d 257 (1992), where the Supreme Court of Nebraska relies on UCC § 2-204 and related sections in reversing the trial court, which the Supreme Court read as relying on common law principles with insufficient awareness of the liberalized standards of the UCC. Section 2-204(3) is one of several sections illustrating the purposeful, anti-technical nature of Article 2 of the UCC.

Contracts, is clearly seen in non-sale of goods contracts.[171]

The initiative recognizes that parties often and, perhaps, typically, do not express themselves precisely or comprehensively when they make an agreement. Rather than focusing on what parties failed to say, the Code and RESTATEMENT 2d focus upon the overriding question of whether the parties manifestly intended to make a binding arrangement. If that manifestation is present, the only remaining concern is whether the terms are definite enough to permit courts to afford an appropriate remedy. The second requirement assists courts to determine the degree of permissible indefiniteness. If an appropriate remedy cannot be fashioned, that, alone, may be sufficient to indicate that the parties have not manifested their intentions adequately and, therefore, it is impossible for a court to discover the agreement or "deal" which the parties may have intended as binding. As usual, Professor Corbin provides the cryptic but penetrating analysis: "A court cannot enforce a contract unless it can determine what it is."[172] Since determinations of sufficient definiteness necessarily require interpretations of language and the surrounding circumstances, it is important to consider certain clusters of cases that have focused on these questions.

[B]   Agreements to Agree — Indefiniteness

We have already explored two situations that are often listed under the caption, "agreements to agree."[173] Where neither of these situations are present, the question arises, may a court discover an enforceable agreement if the parties fail to include certain terms

[1]   Missing Immaterial Terms

Courts have never experienced much difficulty enforcing agreements where all of the material terms, such as subject matter, quantity, and price, have been agreed upon, though the parties have, either inadvertently or purposely, left relatively insignificant matters for future determination.[174]

Subsequent sections of this book will explore other anti-technical sections, including § 2-206, which expressly warns against formal technical rules as to offer and acceptance (comment 1 to § 2-206) and § 2-209(1), which expressly eschews "the technicalities which presently hamper" modifications of contracts without consideration (comment 1 to § 2-209).

[171] RESTATEMENT 2d § 33(2) and comment b which is a paraphrase of UCC § 2-204(3). See Arbitron, Inc. v. Trayllyn Broad, Inc., 400 F. 3d 130, 137–38 (2d Cir. 2004) quoting UCC § 2-204(3) though it was "not clear whether, under New York law, a license agreement of the sort at issue in this case [radio ratings and data] constitutes a contract for the sale of goods."

[172] CORBIN CONTRACTS § 4.1.

[173] In § 32[B], *supra*, we considered letters of intent, which are preliminary understandings facilitating continuing negotiations in anticipation of a contract. In § 33, we explored situations in which parties arrived at agreement on the essential terms of the contract but manifest an intention that the complete contract will be evidenced by a final document.

[174] "Even if the contract were indefinite as to some items, it must appear that such items were so essential to the contract that it would be unfair to enforce the remainder." Palmer v. Aeolian Co., 46 F.2d 746, 753 (8th Cir.), *cert. denied*, 283 U.S. 851, 51 S. Ct. 560, 75 L. Ed. 1458 (1931). In Shann v. Dunk, 84 F.3d 73,78 (2d Cir. 1996), the court suggests a possible distinction between "material" terms and "essential" terms, i.e., "material" terms bear upon the subject matter of the contract, "essential" terms are prerequisites to the formation of a contract (citing *In re* Windsor Plumbing Supply Co., 170 B.R. 503, 523 n.5 (Bankr. E.D.N.Y. 1994)).

[2]   Missing Material Terms

Where the parties fail to express one or more *material* terms of their contract in words and there is no trade usage, course of dealing or course of performance evidence to assist a court in supplying such a term, the parties appear to have left such terms for future negotiation. The cases are legion in which courts have held that such an "agreement to agree" upon a *material* term is not enforceable.[175] Since the "agreement" of the parties consists of more than expressed words, even with respect to material terms, the indefiniteness of an agreement may be cured by trade usage, course of dealing or the parties' performance that permits courts to supply the term.[176] Similarly, if one party is willing to eliminate the risk of indefiniteness by undertaking to expand his obligation, indefiniteness would be cured. Thus, where one party held an option to purchase land and the parties had left the terms of payment for future agreement, the indefiniteness was cured when the option holder agreed to pay cash or to make payments on terms imposed by the seller.[177]

It is important to emphasize the underlying assumption of the traditional view, i.e., since the parties may subsequently fail to agree on the postponed material term, the court would have no basis for supplying the missing term and enforcing the contract.[178] If the parties had clearly manifested their intention to be bound, but had simply *forgotten* to include the term, a modern

---

[175] Association Benefit Services, Inc. v. Caremark RX, Inc., 493 F.3d 841, 850 (7th Cir. 2007) (stating that if "essential" terms are missing, there is no contract); Copeland v. Merrill Lynch & Co., 47 F.3d 1415, 1425 (5th Cir. 1995) ([T]he record demonstrates that there was only an 'agreement to agree'. . . upon substantial additional negotiation. Such agreements to agree, particularly absent material terms . . . are unenforceable under Texas law."). *See also* Tractebel Energy Marketing, Inc. v. AEP Power Marketing, 487 F. 3d 89, 95 (2d Cir. 2007) (quoting Martin Delicatessen, Inc. v. Schumacher, 436 N.Y.S.2d 247, 249, 417 N.E.2d 541 (1981); Belitz v. Riebe, 495 So. 2d 775 (Fla. Dist. Ct. App. 1986); Gregory v. Perdue, Inc., 47 N.C. App. 655, 267 S.E.2d 584 (1980); Burgess v. Rodom, 121 Cal. App. 2d 71, 262 P.2d 335 (1953).

[176] Custom and usage in the building industry allowed a court to cure the indefiniteness of a missing term in a building contract in *Denver D. Darling, Inc. v. Controlled Environments Constr. Co.*, 89 Cal. App. 4th 1221, 108 Cal. Rptr. 2d 213 (2001). "Indefiniteness may be fleshed out by the course of performance by the parties after the agreement." Linton v. E. C. Gates Agency, Inc., 113 P. 3d 26, 30 (Wy. 2005). "The courts should be extremely hesitant in holding a contract void for indefiniteness, particularly where one party has performed under the contract and allowed the other party to obtain the benefit of his performance." Blackhawk Heating & Plumbing Co. v. Data Lease Fin. Corp., 302 So. 2d 404, 408 (Fla. 1974). See Florida Fruit & Vegetable Self-Insurers Fund v. Rolling Meadow Ranch, Inc., 424 So. 2d 195 (Fla. Dist. Ct. App. 1983), in which the indefinite term in an agreement concerning workmen's compensation was the term "premium." However, premium payments were made and submitted claims were paid. Thus, the court was willing to interpret the indefinite term in accordance with the parties' course of performance. If trade usage or prior course of dealing evidence were sufficient to make a superficially indefinite term sufficiently definite, there would be no indefiniteness problem from the inception since parties are assumed to have used any contract term in accordance with such trade usage or prior course of dealing unless the contract expressly negates such evidence. *See* Columbia Nitrogen Corp. v. Royster Co., 451 F.2d 3 (4th Cir. 1971).

[177] Morris v. Ballard, 56 U.S. App. D.C. 383, 16 F.2d 175 (1926). *See also* Shull v. Sexton, 154 Colo. 311, 390 P.2d 313 (1964). Where, however, an earnest money agreement for the sale of land indicated that the parties intended to agree upon material terms at a later date, the court refused to grant specific performance of the contract. Snyder v. Miniver, 6 P.3d 835 (Idaho Ct. App. 2000).

[178] In Lo Cascio v. James V. Aquavella, M.D., P.C., 206 A.D.2d 96, 99, 619 N.Y.S. 2d 430, 432 (4th Dep't 1994), the court states, "[W]ithout [definiteness as to material matters], a court could not intervene without imposing its own conception of what the parties should or might have undertaken, rather than confining itself to a bargain to which they have mutually committed themselves" (citing Bernstein v. Felske, 143 A.D.2d 863, 864–65, 533 N.Y.S.2d 538 (2d Dep't 1988)). Similarly, in Ablett v. Clauson, 43 Cal. 2d 280, 285, 272 P.2d 753, 755 (1954), the court stated, "Since either party by the terms of the promise may refuse to agree to anything to which the other party will agree, it is impossible for the law to affix any obligation to such a promise."

court may supply the missing term, e.g., by implying a reasonable term, without violating the intentions of the parties. The reasonable term could be supplied on the assumption that it is probably the term the parties would have inserted had they thought about the matter at all. Where, however, the parties manifest *their* intention to agree later on a material term, they *have* thought about the matter. Where parties manifest their intention to be bound immediately and to later agree upon a price reflecting prevailing industry standards or market price, by supplying that term the court is simply reflecting the manifested intention of the parties.[179] Where, however, the parties contemplated agreeing upon a specific process for determining the price, i.e., *their* future agreement as to the price, and have not expressed their intention as to the status of their otherwise binding agreement if they fail to agree on a price, a court should not imply a 'reasonable price' since the parties have insisted upon a particular process for determining a material term. A court should not imply a price that contradicts the express intention of the parties.[180]

The former president of a corporation alleged a contract under which he would receive 25% of the "fair market valuation" of the corporation minus $5 million, the market value when the plaintiff became president. The court recognized that a "fair market value" standard may be sufficiently definite, but where even the plaintiff realized that the parties had to agree on a method to determine fair market value, leaving such a major unresolved element of the contract for future negotiations made the contract unenforceably indefinite as a matter of law.[181]

[3]   Future Agreements Concerning Rental Payments

A cluster of conflicting cases deal with a lessee's option to renew the lease for a certain period at a rental to be agreed upon. Courts that have adopted the view that the indefiniteness cannot be cured by the implication of a reasonable rental term are concerned that the court would be imposing its own concept of what the parties should have inserted as the rental term.[182] Such a rationale, however, not only ignores the reliance and expectation interests of the lessee; it also ignores the completed performance by the lessee and the lessee's restitution interest. The lessor has already received an indivisible part of the lessee's rental payment in exchange for the lessee's right to choose renewal of the lease. To allow the lessor to retain that benefit for nothing in return would unjustly enrich the lessor at the expense of the lessee whose payments for the option would be forfeited.

Where the lease contains a methodology for determining the new rental by reference to fair rental values of similar properties, the appraisal or experts or arbitration, courts have no difficulty in discovering the rental term based on the methodology the parties have expressed in their lease agreement.[183]

---

[179] Cobble Hill Nursing Home, Inc. v. Henry & Warren Corp., 74 N.Y.2d 475, 548 N.Y.S.2d 920, 923, 548 N.E.2d 203 (1989), *cert. denied*, 498 U.S. 816, 111 S. Ct. 58, 112 L. Ed. 2d 33 (1990).

[180] See Transazct Techs., Ltd. v. Evergeen Partners, Ltd., 2001 U. S. Dist. LEXIS 14043 (N. D. Ill. 2001).

[181] Playoff Corporation v. Blackwell, 2009 Tex. App. LEXIS 8382 (Ct. App. Tex. 2009).

[182] Joseph Martin, Jr., Delicatessen, Inc. v. Schumacher, 52 N.Y.2d 105, 436 N.Y.S.2d 247, 417 N.E.2d 541 (1981). See also Centreville Veterinary Hospital, Inc. v. Butler-Baird, 2007 Del. Ch. LEXIS 116 at *23 (Ct. Ch. 2007) noting the "hopeless conflict"in the case law concerning this issue.

[183] Etco Corp. v. Hauer, 161 Cal. App. 3d 1154, 208 Cal. Rptr. 118 (1st Dist. 1984); Joseph Martin, Jr. Delicatessen, Inc. v. Schumacher, 52 N.Y.2d 105, 110, 436 N.Y.S.2d 247, 417 N.E.2d 541 (1981) (recognizing this possibility but finding no such methodology "within the four corners of the lease").

Other courts, however, will enforce the lease contract even though it contains no method or guideline for determining the new rental when the parties fail to agree. These courts imply a reasonable rental payment without regret that they are making a contract for the parties.[184] This in the view of the Uniform Commercial Code in contracts for the sale of goods, replicated in the Restatement (Second) of Contracts that facilitates its application to other contracts.[185]

[4]   Agreements to Agree Under the Uniform Commercial Code — Implying Reasonable Price

The Code provision for a missing price term is § 2-305.[186] A comment to that section confirms the Code departure from the traditional view: "This Article [2] rejects in these instances the formula that 'an agreement to agree is unenforceable' if the case falls within subsection (1)" [the parties intend to conclude a contract].[187] Section 2-305 was designed to deal not only with the relatively simple situation of a missing price term where the parties said nothing about price;[188] it also deals with agreements to agree upon a future price,[189] agreements to have the price established by an objective standard when that objective standard fails,[190] and agreements where the price is to be fixed by the seller or the buyer.[191] The requirement of finding that the parties intended to conclude a contract though the price was not settled is repeated, emphatically, in the last subsection of § 2-305.[192]

Section 2-305 is not radical in permitting courts to imply a reasonable price when the parties have omitted the price term where the price can be established by prior course of dealing or trade usage since such a price term would necessarily be a term of the contract.[193] Prior to the

---

[184] See Kenai v. Ferguson, 732 P.2d 184 (Alaska 1987); Cassinari v. Mapes, 91 Nev. 778, 542 P.2d 1069 (1975); Playmate Club, Inc. v. Country Clubs, Inc., 62 Tenn. App. 383, 462 S.W.2d 890, 58 A.L.R.3d 494 (1970); Chaney v. Schneider, 92 Cal. App. 2d 88, 206 P.2d 669 (1949); Moss v. Olson, 148 Ohio St. 625, 76 N.E.2d 875 (1947).

[185] See Moolenaar v. Co-Build Cos., 354 F. Supp. 980 (1973) (analogizing to § 2-305 of the UCC) and Restatement 2d of Contracts, § 33, comment e.

[186] See RESTATEMENT 2d § 33, comment e. See Echols v. Pelullo, 377 F. 3d 272, 277 and note 3 (3d Cir. 2004) (noting the Restatement recognition of § 2-305 in comment e concerning the uncertain price term.).

[187] § 2-305, comment 1. (Emphasis supplied.).

[188] § 2-305(1)(a).

[189] § 2-305(1)(b).

[190] § 2-305(1)(c).

[191] § 2-305(2) which requires the buyer or seller to set the price in good faith.

[192] § 2-305(4). Where the parties intend *not* to be bound unless they have agreed upon the price and they have not agreed, no contract exists. In such a case, the buyer must return any goods received. If unable to do so, the buyer must pay the reasonable value of the goods received.

[193] Under the definition of "agreement." UCC §§ 1-201(b)(3), course of dealing and trade usage (defined in § 1-303(a) and (b)) are necessarily terms of the agreement and ensuing "contract" (§ 1-201(12)) unless carefully negated by the parties (see § 2-202, comment 2). **CISG** would also allow a price to be determined by prior course of dealing or trade usage, CISG Art. 8(3). Unlike the UCC, however, CISG may not otherwise provide for judicial insertion of a reasonable price. Article 55 of CISG states that, where the parties have formed a contract without expressly or implicitly stating a price, absent a contrary intention, they will be deemed to have impliedly referenced generally charged at the time of formation for the kind of goods sold under comparable circumstance. This language suggests that a market price may be implied, but another interpretation suggests that Article 55 is designed for use only where a Contracting State declared under Article 92(1) that it will not be bound by part II of CISG (dealing with formation of contract). If the non-CISG law of that State found a contract to be validly concluded, but litigation occurred to which Part III of CISG applied, only then would Article 55 permit a court to insert the "price generally charged" in such a "validly concluded" contract. The controversy is explored in John E. Murray, Jr., *Buyer Obligations*

Code, price and other terms could be supplied in accordance with standards of fairness.[194] Nor was Section 2-305 viewed as particularly progressive in permitting the parties to agree that the price will be established by some objective standard and then permitting a court to establish the price under that standard. Pre-Code law, however, would excuse the parties from performance if the external standard failed.[195] In that situation, the parties did not intend to fix the price by their own subsequent agreement. They had agreed upon an objective standard that failed. By allowing courts to imply a reasonable price in that situation, the Code cuts deeply against the tradition precluding so-called agreements to agree for a very good reason. If the parties manifest their intention to be bound to a contract though they postpone the time for agreement upon the price, the protection of reliance interests and fairness to both parties suggests that such an agreement should not fail for indefiniteness simply because the parties may later fail to agree upon the price. Such a failure may be caused by the refusal of the other party to bargain in good faith concerning the price term[196] or simply because one party seeks to avoid his contractual obligation though the other party is suggesting reasonable terms in good faith.[197]

The courts have demonstrated little difficulty in the application of § 2-305 where the parties have failed to agree upon a price term for their previously formed contract, or where they have simply omitted the price term,[198] or left it to be determined by an external standard that subsequently failed.[199] At the same time, courts have adhered to the Code directive that the

---

Under the CISG, 440, 444–448 in The Draft UNCITRAL Digest (Ferrari, Flechtner & Brand, eds. 2005).

[194] In his analysis of certain sections of UCC Article 2 for the New York Law Revision Commission that was charged with the responsibility of studying the Code when it was considered for enactment in New York, Professor Edwin Patterson of Columbia Law School concluded that the implication of a price term under § 2-305(1)(a) where nothing is said as to price — "is supported by respectable authority [in New York]. . . ." 1 Study of the Uniform Commercial Code, State of New York, Law Revision Commission 329 (1955).

[195] Interstate Plywood Sales Co. v. Interstate Container Corp., 331 F.2d 449 (9th Cir. 1964) (decided under pre-Code law), held that a pricing formula was intended as the only binding method of determining price and, when it failed, the contract was unenforceable. Thus, there was a contract when the parties fixed the pricing formula, but the contract became unenforceable upon failure of the external standard. It is important to recognize the critical importance of intention in this regard. Even the UCC continues to permit the parties to be bound only by a price set by a particular third person's judgment, *if the parties so intend*. If they intend that person as the only person in the world to establish the price, no reasonable substitute is available when that party is not available. The distinction is one between choosing a barometer or index of a fair price as contrasted with the particular, subjective judgment of a named third party. An example of the latter is rare, under the Code, as in the case of the determination of the value of a painting by a known and trusted expert. UCC § 2-305 comment 4.

[196] *See* Wagner Excello Foods, Inc. v. Fearn Int'l, Inc., 235 Ill. App. 3d 224, 601 N.E.2d 956 (1st Dist. 1992) (construing 2-305(1) and (4) and concluding that in both subsections, the intent of the parties is the dispositive factor). See also Schmieder v. Standard Oil Co., 69 Wis. 2d 419, 230 N.W.2d 732 (1975), which provided Standard with an option to purchase certain equipment of Schmeider on a price to be mutually agreed upon. Schmeider submitted a price that was filled with discrepancies and Standard sought to withdraw from the arrangement because the parties could not agree upon a price. The court held that § 2-305(1)(b) supplies a reasonable price in such circumstances.

[197] *See* D.R. Curtis Co. v. Mathews, 103 Idaho 776, 653 P.2d 1188 (Ct. App. 1982).

[198] *See, e.g.*, Robinson v. Stevens Indus., Inc., 162 Ga. App. 132, 290 S.E.2d 336 (1982).

[199] 2-305(1)(c). *See* North Cent. Airlines, Inc. v. Continental Oil Co., 574 F.2d 582, 187 U.S. App. D.C. 371 (1978) (parties intended the price of aviation fuel under a long term contract to be determined by an objective index based on posted crude oil prices; when that price index was replaced by a two-tiered pricing system, the court substituted a reasonable price). See also Oglebay Norton Co. v. Armco, Inc., 52 Ohio St. 3d 232, 556 N.E.2d 515 (1990), a transportation contract, where a pricing mechanism upon which the parties had relied failed and the court discerned a reasonable price between the extremes of "reasonable" prices proved at trial. Since the contract was one for services

parties must intend to be bound, notwithstanding a missing price term, if § 2-305 is to apply.[200]

If the parties agree that the price is to be fixed by the seller or the buyer, the price must be fixed "in good faith."[201] In determining whether this good faith standard of honesty-in-fact and reasonable commercial dealing in the trade has occurred, a comment states that, in the "normal case," a "posted price" or a future buyer or seller's "given price" or "price in effect" or "market price" would satisfy the good faith requirement. This presumption was designed as a "safe-harbor" approach to alleviate the burden of the price setter to demonstrate good faith. The majority of courts accept the presumption as conclusive where the price set is within the normal range of commercially reasonable prices if it is applied in a non-discriminatory fashion.[202]

[5]   Uniform Commercial Code: Missing Performance Terms — Additional "Gap Fillers"

The UCC makes provision for numerous "gap-filling" terms beyond the price term where the parties have omitted such terms and still intend to be bound to their agreement.[203] For example, where the contract is silent concerning delivery in single lots or installments,[204] the place for delivery,[205] or the time for shipment or delivery which inserts a reasonable time where the parties have not otherwise specified the time,[206] the contract does not fail for

---

and thus not governed by the UCC, the court relied on § 33, and comment e of the Restatement 2d of Contracts which incorporates the standard of UCC § 2-305(1)(c).

[200] *See In re* Glover Constr. Co., 49 B.R. 581 (Bankr. W.D. Ky. 1985); Billings Cottonseed, Inc. v. Albany Oil Mill, Inc., 173 Ga. App. 825, 328 S.E.2d 426 (1985).

[201] § 2-305(2).

[202] See the discussion in Autry Petroleum Co. v. BP Prods. North America, Inc., 334 Fed. Appx. 982, 985–86 (11 Cir. 2009).

[203] See Nebraska Builders Prods. Co. v. Industrial Erectors, Inc., 239 Neb. 744, 755, 478 N.W.2d 257, 266 (1992). See also RESTATEMENT 2d § 204 comment d, dealing with supplying an omitted term and referring to UCC sections which supply missing terms such as § 2-309, a "reasonable" time implication, and § 2-305, "reasonable" price implication. See also UCC § 2-306, setting forth criteria in output and requirements contracts where there is no stated estimate, § 2-307, dealing with the number of deliveries and payment for such deliveries where the agreement is silent, § 2-308, providing for the place of delivery where the agreement is silent, § 2-310(a), providing for the time when and place where payment is due where the agreement is silent, and § 2-311, providing for particulars of performance to be specified by one of the parties. One could also include such "default" terms (UCC norms that apply absent the express intention of the parties to the contrary) such as the warranty of title (§ 2-312) which is not captioned, "implied" because it contains its own requirements for disclaimer in § 2-312(2) but is, nonetheless, an implied warranty, as well as the implied warranty of merchantability (§ 2-314) and the implied warranty of fitness for a particular purpose (§ 2-315). Much of Part 3 of Article 2 can, therefore, be characterized as containing Code "gap-fillers" where the parties have failed to manifest their agreement. Other gap-fillers or default terms are derivable from other sections or comments to the Code. For example, where the parties have not expressed an FOB term which, under the Code will determine risk of loss, comment 5 to § 2-503 indicates that "the 'shipment' contract is regarded as the normal one and the 'destination' contract as the variant type." Thus, absent the parties' expression to the contrary, the FOB term will be the "FOB shipment" contract which, pursuant to § 2-509(1)(a), places the risk of loss on the buyer when the goods are duly delivered to the independent carrier. *See* Ninth Street East, Ltd. v. Harrison, 5 Conn. Cir. Ct. 597, 259 A.2d 772 (1968). The implication of various terms where the parties have omitted such terms but otherwise intend to form a contract will be explored later in this volume.

[204] UCC § 2-307. *See* Luedtke Eng'g Co. v. Indiana Limestone Co., 740 F.2d 598 (7th Cir. 1984).

[205] UCC § 2-308. *See* Dura-Wood Treating Co. v. Century Forest Indus., 675 F.2d 745 (5th Cir.), *cert. denied*, 459 U.S. 865, 103 S. Ct. 144, 74 L. Ed. 2d 122 (1982).

[206] UCC § 2-309. *See* Southern Utils., Inc. v. Jerry Mandel Mach. Corp., 71 N.C. App. 188, 321 S.E.2d 508 (1984).

indefiniteness. These Code provisions manifest little or no change from pre-Code law, whether or not the contract was one for the sale of goods.[207] The Code has also resolved situations where the pre-Code case law was split. A contract for the sale of definite quantities of certain brands of motor oil specified prices that depended upon the weight (viscosity) of the oil to be chosen by the purchaser, i.e., the higher the weight, the higher the price. When the seller telephoned the buyer to determine the buyer's selection, the buyer refused to select and canceled the contract. The court held the contract to be fatally indefinite with regard to buyer's choice of weights.[208] The buyer was permitted to withdraw from the bargain simply by refusing to cooperate in choosing the weights of the motor oil. Other common law courts saw no difficulty with indefiniteness in holding sellers to such arrangements where the buyer notified the seller of the selection.[209] The difficulty in affording a remedy where the buyer refuses to exercise the right to select should not be seen as insuperable. One solution would afford the seller the least profit the seller would have received.[210] The UCC, however, permits the aggrieved party to perform in any reasonable manner which would, presumably, permit the selection to be made by the aggrieved seller in substitution for the buyer's selection. If the buyer refuses to accept the goods as selected by the seller, all of the seller's UCC remedies are available.[211] The seller would proceed to recover based upon a commercially reasonable selection which necessarily includes good faith rather than the selection that would have netted the "lowest profit."[212] This analysis is more in keeping with the protection of the seller's reasonable expectations.[213]

---

[207] *See, e.g.*, Orlowski v. Moore, 198 Pa. Super. 360, 181 A.2d 692 (1962) (lease providing lessee with first refusal had to be exercised within a reasonable time under all of the circumstances); Marsh v. Brown-Crummer Inv. Co., 138 Kan. 123, 23 P.2d 465 (1933) (agreement to repurchase bonds on demand, no time being fixed within which demand was to be made); Cameron Coal & Mercantile Co. v. Universal Metal Co., 26 Okla. 615, 110 P. 720 (1910) (contract for sale of goods). The presumption of a "reasonable time" where the parties had not otherwise specified was a continuation of the presumptions throughout the Uniform Sales Act: §§ 19, 43(2), 47(1), 48, 49 and 69(3). The presumption concerning the *place* of delivery under § 2-308 of the Code was a continuation of § 43(1) of the Uniform Sales Act and pre-Code case law. The presumption concerning delivery in single lots in § 2-307 was, essentially, a continuation of § 45(1) of the Uniform Sales Act and interpretations thereof.

[208] *See* Willhelm Lubrication Co. v. Brattrud, 197 Minn. 626, 268 N.W. 634 (1936).

[209] See Fairmount Glass Works v. Grunden-Martin Woodenware Co., 106 Ky. 659, 51 S.W. 196 (1899), where the buyer brought an action for the buyer's selection of glass containers in a case that otherwise focused upon whether the seller's quotation was an offer.

[210] *See, e.g.*, Dolly Parker Motors, Inc. v. Stinson, 220 Ark. 28, 245 S.W.2d 820 (1952).

[211] The remedies of the seller are listed in UCC § 2-703. Sections 2-704 through 2-710 adumbrate the generic list in § 2-703.

[212] Where a contact permitted a buyer of onions to specify the fields from which onions were delivered, the buyer's refusal to take onions from other fields was not a breach of the buyer's duty of good faith under UCC § 2-311. Panike & Sons Farms, Inc. v. Smith, 212 P. 3d 992, 998 (Idaho 2009). *See* UCC § 2-103(1)(b): " 'Good faith' in the case of a merchant means honesty in fact and the observance of reasonable commercial standards of fair dealing in the trade." An unrevised version of the Article 1 definition of good faith applicable to non-merchants was limited to "honesty in fact in the conduct or transaction concerned." Section 1-201(20) of the revised Article 1, however, defines good faith as requiring both honesty in fact and the observance of reasonable commercial standards except for Article 5 which retains the subjective "honesty in fact" standard.

[213] The general policy of the Code concerning remedies for breach of contract is found in revised § 1-305, "Remedies to be Liberally Administered." "(1) The remedies provided by this Act must be liberally administered to the end that the aggrieved party may be put in as good a position as if the other party had fully performed. . . ."

[6]   Employment Contracts Terminable-at-Will

[a]   The Common Law Approach

The general willingness of courts to imply a reasonable time in contracts where the parties have not manifested their intention concerning the duration of the contract is subject to a stark exception. By the end of the nineteenth century, most American courts adopted the following principle: If an employee is hired, absent language or circumstances identifying the duration of that employment, the employment is terminable at the will of either party.[214] This view is traceable to the unwarranted utterances of a text book writer[215] and the laissez-faire philosophy of the period which reserved absolute power to the employer to dismiss the employee because it was essential to preserve the autonomy of managerial discretion, as well as the freedom of the parties to make their own contract.[216] As early as 1562, an English statute prohibited the discharge of an employee except for reasonable and sufficient cause[217] and, even after that statute was repealed, English courts presumed that an employment contract of indefinite duration continued for one year.[218] Notwithstanding this precedent, American courts adhered to the flat rule that such contracts are terminable at will "for good cause, for no cause or even for cause morally wrong."[219] An at-will contract is created by an offer that is accepted by the performance of the prospective employee. It is an at-will contract only because it has no duration. A unilateral contract is formed by the employee's performance, but the duration of that unilateral contract is within the sole discretion of each of the parties. There is no employer obligation to allow the employment to continue just as there is no obligation on the employee to continue to work.

[b]   "Permanent" or "Lifetime" Employment

Even a promise for "permanent" or "lifetime" employment will typically be insufficient to overcome the presumption of at-will employment absent a clear manifestation of intention to do so.[220]

The usual rationale regards "permanent" or "lifetime" employment as referring to the

---

[214] See Magnan v. Anaconda Indus., Inc., 193 Conn. 558, 479 A.2d 781 (1984), and Toussaint v. Blue Cross & Blue Shield of Mich., 408 Mich. 579, 292 N.W.2d 880 (1980), which trace the history of the "terminable at will" concept.

[215] H.G. WOOD, MASTER AND SERVANT § 134 (1877): "With us the rule is inflexible, that a general or indefinite hiring is *prima facie* a hiring at will, and if the servant seeks to make it out a yearly hiring, the burden of proof is upon him to establish it by proof."

[216] Coppage v. Kansas, 236 U.S. 1, 10, 35 S. Ct. 240, 59 L. Ed. 441 (1915).

[217] Statute of Labourers, 5 Eliz. C. 4 (1562), found in Pickering's Statutes 159–60 (1763).

[218] The rule was premised "upon a principle of natural equity, that the servant shall serve, and master maintain him, throughout all the natural revolutions of the respective seasons, as well when there is work to be done, as when there is not. . . ." 1 BLACKSTONE'S COMMENTARIES 335 (1832). *See* The King v. Inhabitants of Hampreston, 5 TR 205, 101 Eng. Rep. 116 (1793).

[219] Payne v. Western & Atl. R.R. Co., 81 Tenn. 507, 519–20 (1884), *overruled on other grounds*, Hutton v. Watters, 132 Tenn. 527, 179 S.W. 134 (1915).

[220] Grose v. P&G Paper Products, 866 A. 2d 437, 441 (Pa. Super. 2005). See Newfield v. Insurance Co. of West, 156 Cal. App. 3d 440, 203 Cal. Rptr. 9 (2d Dist. 1984); Fisher v. Jackson, 142 Conn. 734, 118 A.2d 316 (1955). See also Page v. Carolina Coach Co., 667 F.2d 1156 (4th Cir. 1982) (statements of employer could not reasonably be interpreted as promise of lifetime appointment; rather, they were words of encouragement); Brown v. Safeway Stores, Inc., 190 F. Supp. 295, 297 (E.D.N.Y. 1960) (employer said he needed district managers to stay with them and there would always be a job for them, and said to plaintiff, "You will always be one of us"; held, not a promise for lifetime employment since

position as permanent, rather than the tenure of the employee as permanent. Evidence of the parties' communications and other circumstances, however, may suggest an interpretation of "permanent" as a position with a duration as long as the employer continues in business with work for the employee to perform and as long as the employee performs in a satisfactory fashion.[221] Where the employee is to be paid for services on a daily, weekly, monthly or yearly basis, whether the parties intended the employment to last for at least one pay period is a question of interpretation. The strong terminable-at-will presumption has convinced many courts that such a contract could still be terminated by the employer at any time, but there is conflicting authority.[222]

Restrictions and Exceptions. The terminable-at-will presumption has eroded over the years. There are numerous statutory and judicial restrictions protecting employees from arbitrary discharge[223] or from discharge for reasons against public policy.[224]

[c]   Consideration Exception

Courts generally recognize that the terminable-at-will presumption may be overcome where additional consideration is provided by the employee.[225] An employee will sometimes argue that he left his former position to take the new job and that detriment should be viewed as consideration. As will be seen in the sections dealing with consideration in the next chapter, the detriment suffered in such cases by the employee is simply a necessary condition to accepting the new position since the employee is typically incapable of maintaining two employments simultaneously. Such a detriment is not "bargained-for" and does not constitute consideration. If, however, an employee already has a lifetime or permanent position that he is induced to leave by the clear promise of a new permanent position, consideration may be

---

the language was not sufficiently clear and unequivocal to create a lifetime contract which is unusual and extraordinary).

[221] Boothby v. Texon, Inc., 414 Mass. 468, 608 N. E. 2d 1028 (1993). The court found that the employer's agent had the authority to make such a contract and there was evidence of considerable discussion concerning the employee's reliance on the promise and surrendering other desirable employment.

[222] *See* Boatright v. Steinite Radio Corp., 46 F.2d 385, 390 (10th Cir. 1931). *Contra* Southwell v. Parker Plow Co., 234 Mich. 292, 207 N.W. 872 (1926), and RESTATEMENT 2d § 33 ill. 6.

[223] With respect to civil service employees, see, e.g., 5 U.S.C. § 7513, which requires a showing of "such cause as will promote the efficiency of the service" to dismiss a civil servant.

[224] Among the various possibilities of public policy violations, whether in statutory or case law form, the following are merely illustrative. Discharge for reasons of race, color, religion, sex, or national origin is prohibited by 42 U.S.C. §§ 2000(e)–(2)(a)(1). *See* Pipkins v. City of Temple Terrace, 267 F. 3d 1197 (11th Cir. 2001). *See also* Spriggs v. Diamond Auto Glass, 165 F.3d 1015 (4th Cir. 1999), where the plaintiff succeeded in its action under 42 U.S.C. § 1981, based on the Civil Rights Acts of 1866 and 1870 (pursuant to the thirteenth amendment to the U.S. Constitution), guaranteeing all persons the right to make and enforce contracts "as is enjoyed by white citizens." The court held that the plaintiff's terminable-at-will contract was a "contract" under this statute. Discharge for reasons of age is prohibited by 29 U.S.C.A. § 623(a)(1) *See* Munoz v. Oceanside Resorts, Inc., 223 F. 3d 1340 (11th Cir. 2000). A discharge because an employee served on a jury or filed an unemployment compensation claim, or refused to submit to a polygraph test is against public policy. Weaver v. Harpster, 975 A. 2d 555, 563–564 (Pa. 2009). A discharge because of union activities will be prohibited. *See* 29 U.S.C.A. § 158(a)(3).

[225] Holt v. United Airlines, Inc., 8 Fed. Appx. 804 ((9th Cir. 2001) (A contract for "permanent" or "steady" employment is terminable only for just cause if the employee gives consideration in addition to contemplated services). Mursch v. Van Dorn Co., 851 F. 2d 990 (7th Cir. 1988). There is a basis for enforcing a promise of "permanent" or "lifetime" employment that overcomes the terminable-at-will presumption where the employee provides consideration additional to the services incident to the employment.

found.[226]

[d]   Illusory Promise?

As an incentive to retain the services of the original eight at-will employees of a company formed in 1996, an employer promised them that if they remained with the company, they would receive 5% of the value of any merger or sale of the company. Seven of the eight were employees of the company when it was acquired in 2001. Their action for their share of the proceeds was met by a motion for summary judgment which the trial court granted and the court of appeals affirmed on the footing that the employer's promise was illusory since the at-will employees could have been fired at any time prior to the merger of the company. Though it agreed that the employees could have been fired, the Supreme Court of Texas stated, "But whether the promise was illusory at the time it was made is irrelevant; what matters is whether the promise became enforceable by the time of the breach."[227]

The court explained that virtually all unilateral contracts begin with an illusory promise which is an offer that can only be accepted by the performance of the offeree. If an employer promises to pay a certain hourly wage to a prospective at-will employee, the employee could be fired after working only one hour. Whether the employee works for one hour or thousands of hours, however, the promise to pay the promised hourly rate becomes enforceable when the work is performed.[228]

[e]   Promissory Estoppel

Since an employment at-will can be terminated a moment after the employee commences work, can it be terminated prior to commencement of work? Where an employer promises employment at will, the promisee may rely to her detriment on the promise by surrendering or forbearing other opportunities. If the promisor can be said to reasonably expect such reliance but terminates the promise before the employment was to begin, the promisee may seek to recover damages suffered as a result of her reliance on the basis of the doctrine of promissory estoppel.[229] There is a split of authority concerning the application of promissory estoppel to at-will employment contracts. Because the promisee could have been discharged immediately after commencing work, some courts assert that it would be illogical to expose an

---

[226] Such cases often involve conflicting evidence. *See* Jasmin v. New England Plasma, 2006 Conn. Super. LEXIS 3691 at *11–17 (Nov. 20, 2006).

[227] Vanegas v. Amer. Energy Servs., 302 S.W.3d 299, 303 (Tx. 2009).

[228] *Id.* at *12 where the court quotes from § 1.17 of the 2009 Supplement to Corbin on Contract by John E. Murray, Jr. and Timothy P. Murray, criticizing the court of appeals decision. The court notes that the court of appeals decision would potentially jeopardize all pension plans, vacation leaves and other forms of compensation based on a particular term of service made to at-will employees. It attributes the court of appeals confusion to the failure to distinguish unilateral and bilateral contracts. Where parties exchange promises to form a bilateral contract, if one of the promises is illusory because it promises nothing (e. g., "I will sell my car to you for $10,000 unless I change my mind"), the counter promise ("I will pay you $10,000 for your car") would not be enforceable since nothing was promised in exchange for that promise. An offer that promises pay a certain amount for a performance as the exclusive manner of acceptance, does not seek a return promise. It does not require the offeree/promisee to perform. If she chooses to perform, however, she is entitled to enforce the promise as made.

[229] Promissory estoppel is one of the principal bases for making a promise enforceable. A promise which the promisor should reasonably expect the promisee to rely upon may be enforceable if promisee suffers a detriment by reasonable reliance and injustice can only be avoided by enforcing the promise. See § 90 of the Restatement 2d of Contracts which is explored in detail in the Chapter 3, Section 67.

employer to liability invoking its right terminate an at-will contract before the employment was scheduled to begin, but absolve the employer from liability if the termination occurs immediately after the employee reports to work.[230] While recognizing the illogical appearance, other courts note a distinction between a promise to employ which may induce reasonable detrimental reliance by the prospective employee before the employment is scheduled to begin, and actual employment which may be terminated as soon as the employment begins.[231]

Where the employer's promise induces a detriment suffered by the promisee in forbearing other opportunities that the employer should have expected the promisee to surrender before the employment begins, the promisee has detrimentally relied on the employer's promise. If that reliance was reasonable, injustice can be avoided only by enforcement of the promise, but only to the extent of the promisee's reliance since her reliance is the only reason the promise will be enforced at all.

Reliance damages are provable out-of-pocket (reliance) losses as contrasted with damages based on the promisee's expectation interest which would place the promisee in the position she would have been in had the contract been performed. The expectation interest cannot be recovered because the employer could have terminated the employment immediately after it began. Expectation damages would not be recoverable because they are speculative (uncertain). Courts allowing a reliance recovery analogize to cases involving pre-contractual promises to grant franchises. Where the franchise is not granted, the relying party may recover reliance losses sustained in preparing to become a franchisee.[232]

[f]   Employee Manuals, Unilateral Contracts

Considerable litigation has addressed the question of the effect of statements in employee handbooks, manuals or policy statements from the employer which may preclude discharge of an employee except for cause. The purpose of this "exception" to the terminable-at-will rule based upon employer's statements of personnel policy "is to protect the legitimate expectations of employees who have justifiably relied on manual provisions precluding job termination except for cause."[233] The overwhelming majority of the courts addressing this question have concluded that such statements may give rise to contractual obligations of the employer, thereby substantially modifying the terminable-at-will rule.[234]

Where the employer distributes a handbook stating that the employee will not be discharged except for cause or that certain procedures must precede any discharge, the employee's performance of starting or continuing work after receiving the handbook is

---

[230] Slate v. Saxon, Marquis, Betroni & Todd, 166 Ore. App.1, 999 P. 2d 1152 (2000).

[231] Goldstein v. Unilever, 2004 Conn. Super. LEXIS 1126 (2004) relying on Bower v. AT& T Technologies, Inc., 852 F. 2d 361, 363–64 ((8th Cir. 1998).

[232] See, e. g., Pop's Cones, Inc. v. Resorts Int'l Hotel, Inc., 307 N. J. Super. 461, 704 A. 2d 3221 (App. Div. 1998) discussed along with other franchise cases in Chapter 3, § 67, *infra.*

[233] Castiglione v. Johns Hopkins Hosp., 69 Md. App. 325, 341, 517 A.2d 786, 793 (1986).

[234] *See, e.g.,* Anderson v. Douglas & Lomason Co., 540 N.W.2d 277 (Iowa 1995); Duldulao v. St. Mary of Nazareth Hosp. Ctr., 115 Ill. 2d 482, 505 N.E.2d 314 (1987); Finley v. Aetna Life & Casualty Co., 5 Conn. App. 394, 499 A.2d 64 (1985); Woolley v. Hoffmann-La Roche, Inc., 99 N.J. 284, 491 A.2d 1257 (1985); Pine River State Bank v. Mettille, 333 N.W.2d 622 (Minn. 1983); Toussaint v. Blue Cross & Blue Shield of Mich., 408 Mich. 579, 292 N.W.2d 880 (1980). Cases taking a contrary position include White v. Chelsea Indus., 425 So. 2d 1090 (Ala. 1983); Heideck v. Kent Gen. Hosp., Inc., 446 A.2d 1095 (Del. 1982); Johnson v. National Beef Packing Co., 220 Kan. 52, 551 P.2d 779 (1976).

construed to be an acceptance of the offer forming a unilateral contract. The employee has the burden of proving the creation of such a contract. Whether the handbook or manual is sufficiently definite to create a contract as contrasted with merely setting forth company policies is a question of fact. Mere statements of the employer's policies are insufficient. "[T]he promises in the employee manual must be in definite terms" and "if the alleged promises are nothing more than vague assurances the issue can be decided as a matter of law."[235] If an employee handbook contains a disclaimer stating that the handbook is not intended to create any contractual rights, courts recognize such statements of intention as binding though they typically require the disclaimers to be clear and/or conspicuous. Whether a disclaimer is "conspicuous" will depend upon its placement in the handbook as well as the print in which it appears (boldface, capital letters, etc.).[236]

Where an employee did not sign a receipt slip for an employee handbook and claimed that she had not received much less read the handbook which contained an arbitration clause, a court held that the employer's repeated notifications followed by the employee's continued employment bound her to the terms of the arbitration policy in the handbook notwithstanding the absence of her signature or her inability to recall receiving the handbook.[237] Analogizing the distribution of such a handbook to all employees as a standardized agreement between the employer and a class of employees as contrasted with an individually negotiated agreement, courts have held that the handbook offer had been accepted by the employee's continuing work thereby binding both the employee and employer to the terms of the handbook though the employee had not read the terms.[238]

---

[235] Selfridge v. Dollar Gen. Corp., 9 P.3d 695, 698 (Okla. Civ. App. 2000). Grose v. P&G Paper Products, Inc., 866 A. 2d 437, 441 (Pa. Super. 2005) requires a clear express in the handbook of the employer's intent to overcome the at-will presumption. *See also* Boulay v. Impell Corp., 939 F.2d 480, 482 (7th Cir. 1991); Bell v. South Cent. Bell, 564 So. 2d 46 (Ala. 1990); Johnson v. McDonnell Douglas Corp., 745 S.W.2d 661, 662 (Mo. 1988).

[236] In Greene v. Quest Diagnostics Clinical Labs, Inc., 2006 U. S. Dist. LEXIS 75956 at *30–31 (D. S. C. 2006) the court describes a conspicuous disclaimer:

> Here, Quest's manual gives the employees a guide regarding their employment without altering the at-will status. The manual contained a conspicuous disclaimer . . . in the front of the handbook. The document entitled 'Employment Relationship' in large bold letters states that the manual "is not a legal document or contract of employment." The document goes on to state "Quest Diagnostics" is an at-will employer. This means that you or the company may terminate the employment relationship at any time and for any reason, with or without cause."

See also Chambers v. Valley Nat'l Bank, 721 F. Supp. 1128, 1131 (D. Ariz. 1988) (bold print in introductory paragraph); Butler v. Westinghouse Elec. Corp., 690 F. Supp. 424, 429 (D. Md. 1987) (bold print at front of handbook); Hanson v. New Tech., Inc., 594 So. 2d 96, 99 (Ala. 1992) (disclaimer on first page of handbook). Cf. UCC § 1-201(1), defining "conspicuous" as a clause that is "so written that a reasonable person against whom it is to operate ought to have noticed it," suggesting examples or larger or contrasting type or color. These and other cases involving the clear and conspicuous requirement are reviewed in Anderson v. Douglas & Lomason Co., 540 N.W.2d 277, 287–88 (Iowa 1995), concluding that such a requirement does not apply under Iowa law, which only requires that a reasonable employee would understand the disclaimer to mean that the employer has not assented to be bound by the handbook's provisions. ("This Employee Handbook is not intended to create any contractual rights in favor of you or the Company. The Company reserves the right to change the terms of the handbook at any time." Though this statement appeared on the last page (53) of the handbook, the court found it constituted an effective disclaimer.).

[237] Brown v. St. Paul Travelers Co., 331 Fed. Appx. 68 (2d Cir. 2009).

[238] Anderson v. Douglas & Lomason Co., 540 N.W.2d 277, 284 (Iowa 1995), relying on Kinoshita v. Canadian Pac. Airlines, Ltd., 68 Haw. 594, 604, 724 P.2d 110, 116–17 (1986), which, in turn, relied upon RESTATEMENT 2d § 211(2): "A standardized agreement 'is interpreted wherever reasonable as treating alike all those similarly situated, without regard to their knowledge or understanding of the standard terms of the writing.' " Section 211 of the RESTATEMENT 2d is explored in detail at § 98, *infra*.

Notwithstanding the exceptions and limitations placed on the at-will rule, it continues to be the general rule primarily because of the great reluctance of courts to thrust an unwanted employee upon an employer.[239]

§ 40 TO WHOM AN OFFER IS ADDRESSED — WHO IS THE OFFEREE?

As the master of the offer, the offeror creates a power of acceptance exclusively in the party or parties to whom the offer is addressed. The offer is addressed to the party who will provide the exchange demanded by the offeror.[240] While the general principle may appear to be self-evident, there are problems in the identification of the offeree. In our prior discussion of guides to distinguish preliminary negotiations from offers,[241] we suggested that courts have often considered whether the proposal was addressed to a specified person or persons on the assumption that, the more definite the addressee of the proposal, the more likely the proposal would constitute an offer. That guide was not conclusive since a proposal to an indefinite party or parties could be an offer to one or all such parties. In cases of reward offers or the unusual advertisement constituting an offer, where the power of acceptance is restricted to one or several *identifiable* parties, such proposals to the public may constitute offers.[242] It is also possible to create powers of acceptance in an unlimited number of persons and the exercise of that power by one person may or may not have an effect on the continuation of the power in the others. Thus, where a reward offer is made, any party who knows of the offer[243] and is not disabled from accepting[244] may accept the offer. The language or circumstances of such an offer typically indicate that the offeror will pay only once. If Ames offers $10,000 for information leading to the arrest and conviction of the murderer of Ames' brother, the first person providing that information would be viewed as an offeree and the exercise of that power would terminate the powers in other offerees, i.e., members of the public who had become aware of the offer.[245] On the other hand, if a manufacturer of a cold remedy promised to pay $100 to any party contracting a cold after using the remedy in accordance with directions, the

---

[239] For a defense of the terminable-at-will rule, see the opinion of Judge Cirillo in Greene v. Oliver Realty, Inc., 363 Pa. Super. 534, 526 A.2d 1192 (1987), citing sections of an earlier edition of this book with respect to unilateral contracts and the terminable-at-will rule.

[240] *See* RESTATEMENT 2d § 52. Ill. 3 to this section is based upon the well known case, Boston Ice Co. v. Potter, 123 Mass. 28 (1877). The illustration states, "A promises B that A will sell and deliver a set of books to B if B's father C will promise to pay $150 for the set. B is the promisee of A's promise; C is the offeree of A's offer. Only C can accept the offer by making the return promise invited by A."

[241] *See supra* § 35[A].

[242] Thus, in a "First Come, First Served" advertisement, the identifiable parties would be offerees. *See* Lefkowitz v. Great Minneapolis Surplus Store, Inc., 251 Minn. 188, 86 N.W.2d 689 (1957). We discovered an offer via advertisement in the famous case of Carlill v. Carbolic Smoke Ball Co., 1 Q.B. 256 (1893).

[243] *See* RESTATEMENT 2d § 23. One cannot accept an offer unless one is aware of it, since no mutual assent would be possible, otherwise. This concept will be further explored in this chapter.

[244] For example, a police officer who has the duty to discover an alleged murderer would not be able to accept an offer for the capture of that party because he has a pre-existing duty to perform the act in any event. *See* RESTATEMENT 2d § 73 ill. 1.

[245] *See* RESTATEMENT 2d § 29 ill. 1. Where the offeror contemplates the payment of one sum to one identifiable party, e.g., the first person to provide information leading to the arrest and conviction of the murderer, where several offerees collectively provide the information sought by the offeror, how is the duty of the offeror to be performed? The problem has rarely come before the courts, so that there is no dispositive case law. Professor Corbin recommends a pro rata distribution among the claimants to the extent of the information provided. CORBIN ON CONTRACTS § 3.10.

offer is made to an unlimited number of parties. If one or thousands use the preparation in accordance with directions, they are offerees who have exercised their powers of acceptance.[246]

Perhaps the most difficult problem concerning the person or persons entitled to exercise a power of acceptance occurs when the offer is made to an impersonal entity, e.g., a business whether or not it is incorporated. In a well-known case, the plaintiff had been the foreman and manager for a manufacturer with whom defendants had dealt. The plaintiff bought the business and, thereafter, defendants ordered goods from the manufacturer without knowledge that the business had been sold. The plaintiff struck the name of his former employer and inserted his own on the order as he supplied the goods. The court held that the plaintiff was not entitled to accept the offer, though the judges were split on the preferable rationale for the result and none suggested a desirable rationale.[247]

Unintended Offerors. The determination of who has a power of acceptance must be found in the manifested intention of the offeror since the offeror is the master of the offer and may create a power of acceptance in any person or persons he chooses.[248] In accordance with the overriding objective test,[249] the offeror is also responsible for creating the appearance of an offer, i.e., if he knows or has reason to know that he is creating the appearance of having made an offer to a particular person or persons, he is bound by that outward manifestation of appearance.[250]

A golfer arrived at a particular hole and saw a new automobile with a sign stating that whoever scores a hole-in-one wins the car. Upon firing a hole-in-one, the golfer demanded the car which the owner refused to deliver because the prize offer had been designed for a charity golf tournament that was completed two days before the plaintiff scored the hole-in-one. The owner had failed to remove the auto and the sign. The court held for the golfer on the usual footing that it is the *manifested* intention of the offeror that determines the person or persons in whom a power of acceptance is created.[251]

Where a publishing company intended to offer a prize only to subscribers to a magazine, the plaintiff was a subscriber though her name was mistakenly listed under another name. She received the card allowing participation in the contest though it was addressed to the mistaken name. She corrected the name on the card and inserted her own. Her card was chosen to win

---

[246] *See* RESTATEMENT 2d § 29 ill. 3. While each user of the remedy has exercised his or her power of acceptance and has, therefore, formed a contract with the manufacturer, a condition to the manufacturers' contractual duty must occur before that duty is activated, i.e., the user must catch a cold. The illustration is based on the famous *Carbolic Smoke Ball* case, *supra* § 35[A]. For another offer to the public with unlimited offerees, consider Rosenthal v. Al Packer Ford, Inc., 36 Md. App. 349, 374 A.2d 377 (1977) (offer of $20,000 to anyone who could prove it was not "absolutely true" that cars were being sold for $89 over the invoice price). *See also* Newman v. Schiff, 778 F.2d 460 (8th Cir. 1985) (offer to pay anyone $100,000 if they could disprove offeror's theory that the Internal Revenue Code contained no provision making the payment of taxes mandatory.).

[247] Boulton v. Jones, 2 H. & N. 564 (Ex. 1857). One judge took the straightforward view that the defendants had intended to deal with the plaintiff's predecessor, thus precluding a power of acceptance in the plaintiff. Another judge discussed setoffs and concluded that the identity of the offeree was material to the defendants. A third judge thought that the plaintiff should have notified the defendants of the change in ownership prior to shipment of the goods.

[248] *See* RESTATEMENT 2d § 29(1) and comment a.

[249] *See supra* § 31.

[250] RESTATEMENT 2d § 29, comment a.

[251] Cobaugh v. Klick-Lewis, Inc., 385 Pa. Super. 587, 561 A.2d 1248 (1989), Citing Restatement 2d § 29.

$150,000. The court held that plaintiff was an intended offeree.[252]

Focusing on the Party With the Power of Acceptance. The determination of which party is the offeror and which party is the offeree is not always obvious. A common illustration of a party becoming an offeror without knowing it results from the use of standardized printed forms containing "boilerplate" clauses that are rarely read or understood. For example, a seller of tires signed the telephone company's printed application for an advertisement to appear in the yellow pages of the telephone directory. One of the standard clauses in the application stated, "It is mutually understood and agreed that publication of the advertising in the Telephone Directory shall constitute an acceptance of this application. . . . Otherwise, this application is not binding on either of the parties."

When the advertisement did not appear due to the admitted fault of the telephone company, the plaintiff's claim for lost business was summarily dismissed since no contract had been formed. Whether the tire seller knew it or not, the document it signed was an offer because the document stated that the only act that could create a binding contract was the publication of the advertisement-an act that could be performed only by the telephone company. The offer dictates the mode of acceptance. Thus, the telephone company was the offeree and, by signing the telephone company's form, the tire seller was making an offer that was never accepted because the acceptance-the publication of the advertisement-never occurred.[253]

Similar printed forms are used by sellers of various goods and services stating that no contract is formed until it is approved at the seller's home office. Where a sales representative presents the seller's form containing all of the material terms of the transaction and the form is signed by the buyer, the buyer may or may not be aware that he is making an offer since the form he signed contains the standard clause stating that the final act necessary to form a contract is the seller's authorization at the corporate headquarters. Thus, the power of acceptance resides exclusively in the seller who is necessarily the offeree. The buyer, perhaps unwittingly, has demanded that the contract exist only upon such a seller's signature.[254]

§ 41   OFFERS PROPOSING ONE CONTRACT VERSUS A SERIES OF CONTRACTS

The typical offer contemplates a single acceptance forming one contract. It is, however, possible that the offer contemplates a series of acceptances forming a series of contracts. Thus, where the seller of goods offered to pay a 5% commission on all orders obtained by the offeree, it was held that a separate and distinct unilateral contract was made every time he sent an order for goods.[255]

---

[252] Lucas v. Godfrey, 161 Wis. 2d 51, 467 N.W.2d 180 (Ct. App. 1990). *See also* Restatement 2d §§ 52 and 53 comment g. The issue of mistake in relation to who may accept an offer will be explored later in this volume.

[253] BC Tire Corp. v. GTE Directories Corp., 730 P. 2d 726 (Wash. Ct. App. 1986).

[254] See, e. g., Empire Machinery Co. v. Litton Business Systems, 566 P.2d 1044 (Ariz. Ct. App. 1977). Other factors in this case which resulted in a contract are discussed later in this chapter. The essential rationale for the approval requirement is the seller's desire to avoid being bound by contracts made by sales representatives who, in their zeal to make a sale, may vary the standard terms which the seller deems indispensable absent a modification by an authorized official at the home office. See also Antonucci v. Stevens Dodge, Inc., 73 Misc. 2d 173, 340 N. Y. S. 2d 979 (1973).

[255] Strang v. Witkowski, 138 Conn. 94, 82 A.2d 624 (1951). *See* Restatement 2d § 31.

An insurance company sent pricing letters to auto glass suppliers announcing the prices it would pay for the supply of replacement auto glass to its insureds. The letters constituted offers that could be accepted by supplying the glass *and* submitting invoices consistent with the amounts in the pricing letters that would form a series of unilateral contracts. When the suppliers provided the glass to the insureds but submitted invoices inconsistent with the amounts in the pricing letters, the court held that there had been no acceptance of the insurance company offers.[256]

Several cases arose concerning the discharge of credit card debts under the Federal Bankruptcy Act. The issue required a determination of contract formation in the use of credit cards. The majority of courts have concluded that the issuance of a credit card is an offer which is accepted each time the cardholder uses the card. The offeror (issuer of the cards) contemplates a series of unilateral contracts. Such contracts are made whenever the cardholder uses the card to pay for goods or services.[257] Whether the proposal embodies only one offer or a series of offers is a problem of interpretation that is solved under the usual test of what a reasonable person in the position of the offeree would understand.[258] A continuing guaranty contemplates a series of transactions whereas a restricted guaranty is limited to either a single transaction or to a number of specific transactions and each successive loan was a separate acceptance creating a unilateral contract. Since guaranty proposals constitute offers, they are, like other offers, revocable. A continuing guaranty is an offer that may be revoked at any time by the guarantor upon notice to the obligee.[259] Where the chief executive officer and substantial owner of a furniture company executed a personal guaranty to the company's creditor for the company's debts, the chief executive made an offer that was accepted serially by each extension of credit to the company. Each of these unilateral contracts made the chief executive a surety on each new debt.[260] While the continuing guaranty stated that it could only be revoked by notice to the creditor, the creditor became aware that the debtor had become insolvent. Months before, the surety had sold his interest in the corporation and the creditor knew that the surety was unaware of this substantial increase in risk. Without notifying the surety of this substantial change in risk, the creditor extended further credit to the debtor. Notwithstanding the surety's failure to revoke the guaranty by notifying the creditor, the court found that the surety has no liability for this extension of credit under these changed circumstances.[261]

As will be seen in subsequent sections, questions of notice of acceptance arise when an offer is accepted by performance rather than by promise and an offer of guaranty can be accepted by performance. In a classic case, the defendant in Nova Scotia wrote to the plaintiff in Illinois,

---

[256] Auto Glass Express, Inc. v. Hanover Ins. Co., 293 Conn. 218, 975 A. 2d 1266 (2009).

[257] Bank of America v. Jarcyzk, 268 B. R. 17 (W. D. N. Y. 2001). See also, Unifund CCR Assignee of Providian v. Ayhan, 2008 Wash. App. LEXIS 1922 (2008).

[258] McCullough v. Cashmere Sch. Dist. 222 of Chelan Cty., 115 Wash. App. 730, 551 P.2d 1046, 1049 ((1976): "Whether an offer contemplates more than one acceptance depends upon the intent of the parties to be discovered by reading the document as a whole, together with surrounding facts and circumstances, if necessary." (Two teachers were offered reemployment contracts including their traditional curricular positions but adding extracurricular duties. The teachers deleted the extracurricular duties and signed the contracts. Held: Though the assignments offered could have been handled as separate contracts, i.e., offers contemplating two acceptances, that was not the intention of the parties.).

[259] Phelps Dodge Corp v. Schumacher Elec. Corp., 415 F. 3d 665 (7th Cir. 2005).

[260] Georgia-Pacific Corp., Williams Furniture Div. v. Levitz, 149 Ariz. 120, 122, 716 P.2d 1057, 1059 (Ct. App. 1986).

[261] *Id.*

"If Harry [the defendant's brother] needs more money, let him have it, or assist him to get it, and I will see that it is paid." Shortly thereafter, relying on the defendant's letter, the defendant became a surety to assist Harry to obtain a loan. He sent a properly addressed letter to the defendant, notifying him of his undertaking for Harry. The defendant claimed he never received the letter. The court analyzed the contract as follows:

> It was an offer to be bound in consideration of an act to be done, and in such a case the doing of the act constitutes the acceptance of the offer. . . . Ordinarily there is no occasion to notify the offerer of the acceptance of such an offer, for the doing of the act is a sufficient acceptance, and the promisor knows that he is bound when he sees that action has been taken on the faith of his offer. But if the act is of such a kind that knowledge of it will not quickly come to the promisor, the promisee is bound to give him notice of his acceptance within a reasonable time after doing that which constitutes the acceptance.[262]

§ 42 DURATION OF POWER OF ACCEPTANCE

[A] The Early Law

Since an offer creates a power of acceptance, how long does that power continue? The early law viewed this issue on a notion of the parties' subjective assent, i.e., an actual "meeting of the minds." As such, it was unwilling to admit the possibility that an offer could create a continuing power of acceptance in the offeree. Even if the offeror had stated that the offer would continue and could be accepted during a specified period and manifested no change of intention in the meantime, early courts felt conceptually barred from treating the offer as remaining open during that period if the offeror subjectively changed his mind.[263] Thus, an offer had to be accepted practically on the spot if any contract was to result from it since a subjective theory of mutual assent presumes that an offer indicates the offeror's true state of mind only at the moment it is made. This mode of dealing with the problem is impracticable because a subjective theory of contract is and has always been impracticable.[264] The impracticability of this notion was recognized early with respect to contracts by correspondence.

A period of time must elapse between the sending of an offer by mail and its receipt by the offeree. Subjectively, the offeror could change his mind a moment after posting the offer. Certainly he could change his mind prior to any acceptance by the offeree. There was a grudging recognition that the acceptance may occur though the offeror had changed his mind prior to the acceptance. To reconcile this practicable and necessary result with the subjective theory, one court indulged the fiction that the offeror, in such a situation, "must be considered in law as making, during every instant of the time [his] letter is traveling, the same identical offer."[265] The statement is fundamentally flawed since the addressee of an offer must receive it before she can possibly have any power of acceptance. Apparently, the court meant to suggest that it must be conclusively presumed that the offeror is still willing to contract at the

---

[262] Bishop v. Eaton, 161 Mass. 496, 499, 37 N.E. 665, 667 (1894).

[263] Head v. Diggon, 3 M. & R. 97 (1828); Cooke v. Oxley, 3 Term. Rep. 653 (1790).

[264] *See supra* § 31.

[265] Adams v. Lindsell, 1 Barn. & Ald. 681 (1818).

time his proposal reaches the offeree, regardless of the actual state of mind of the offeror at that moment. While the court's attempt to accommodate practicability and the subjective theory is awkward, it was inevitable that courts would recognize a continuing power of acceptance.[266]

[B] Offers With a Specified Time Limit — Offeror as "Master of the Offer"

General rule. One of the traditional statements about the agreement process is as true today as it ever was: *The offeror is the master of the offer.*[267] The offeror may, therefore, make any offer she pleases and may place whatever time limitation upon it that seems desirable to her.[268] If Ames offers to sell Blackacre to Barnes for a certain price, the offer to be open for one hour, Barnes' power of acceptance is limited to one hour. A late acceptance would be ineffective as an acceptance since the power of acceptance expired at the end of the hour. If the offeree attempts to accept after the time prescribed in the offer, there is no acceptance since the offeree lacks the power to accept. Such an ineffective attempt at acceptance, however, may constitute a new offer, which could be accepted through a manifestation of assent by the original offeror. Courts may refer to new offers as "counter offers" though there is nothing "counter" about them.[269] Since Ames creates the power of acceptance, she is entitled to decide its duration. Any suggestion that the duration seems unreasonable under the circumstances ignores the fact that Ames was under no obligation to create any power of acceptance. Moreover, even though the power of acceptance will terminate after the time stated in the offer, absent other circumstances, we will see that the offeror may revoke the offer prior to the end of the time stated.[270]

---

[266] RESTATEMENT 2d § 35(1).

[267] Auto Glass Express, Inc. v. Hanover Ins. Co., 293 Conn. 218, 227, 975 A.2d 1266, 1273 (2009). *See also* RESTATEMENT 2d § 29 comment a. The statement may be even more true today than heretofore. See the discussion of the manner of acceptance, *infra* § 46.

[268] *See* Cain v. Noel, 268 S.C. 583, 235 S.E.2d 292 (1977). *See also* RESTATEMENT 2d § 41 comment a.

[269] *See* United States v. Graham, 278 Fed. Appx. 538, 546 (6th Cir. 2008) (plea agreements are interpreted according to the principles of contract law and an attempt to accept a government offer of a plea after its expiration is considered to be a counter offer, citing Houston Dairy, Inc. v. John Hancock Mut. Life Ins. Co., 643 F.2d 1185 (5th Cir. 1981); *see also*, Childs v. Adams, 322 Ark. 424, 432, 909 S.W.2d 641, 645 (1995) (characterizing the late acceptance as a counter offer). RESTATEMENT 2D § 70, comment b, refers to the late acceptance as an "offer." It rejects the view that the offeror can regard the late acceptance as an effective acceptance by "waiving" the requirement that the acceptance occur within the time prescribed by the offer and remaining silent. Generally, acceptances must be communicated. *See* Ellefson v. Megadeth, Inc., 2005 U.S. Dist. LEXIS 545, n9 (S.D.N.Y., Jan. 13, 2005) (recognizing that California "employs a variant on the counter offer approach-a "waiver" doctrine in its analysis of defective acceptances." The court found "no genuine substantive difference between the waiver approach as applied in California and the counter offer approach" which the court applied in this case where the acceptance was late.) Another problem addressed in § 70 of the RESTATEMENT 2D involves an offeree who "erroneously but plausibly" believes he has accepted within the time prescribed by the offer, § 70 comment a. Here, the RESTATEMENT 2D places a duty upon the offeror to speak. The reference to § 20 dealing with the effect of misunderstanding suggests that the duty is predicated upon the offeror knowing or having reason to know that the offeree has made a mistake and should be informed of that mistake. Thus, the offeror could not remain silent in the face of an understanding by the offeree that a contract had been formed.

[270] *See* RESTATEMENT 2d § 42 and the discussion of termination of offers, *infra* § 43. As will be seen later, however, there are several ways in which an offer may become irrevocable for a stated period of time or a reasonable time. The classic way to make an offer irrevocable is the option contract where the offeror receives consideration in exchange for the surrender of the power of revocation of the offer.

Interpreting Duration. The common problem in the application of this rule is one of interpretation. The offer may specify a time limit in ambiguous or indefinite fashion. If, for example, the offer states that it must be accepted "by return mail," should that phrase be taken to mean that the offeree must immediately write a letter of acceptance and hurry to the mailbox? Or, could "by return mail" permit the offeree to consider the offer in the morning and send a letter of acceptance by afternoon mail? Since the offeree is mailing the letter on the same day he received the offer, though he misses the first possible return mail, there is a basis for concluding that the offeree has met the basic requirement of "by return mail," in the absence of other circumstances.[271] Again, the test can only be the understanding of a reasonable person in the position of the offeree under all of the surrounding circumstances, including any trade usage, prior course of dealing, and the like. What the offeror in fact actually intended is, as usual, irrelevant since it is his manifestation of intention as reasonably understood by the offeree that must control.[272] Even where the offeror attempts to be more definite, ambiguity may intrude. Where the offer stated that the offeree had "eight days in which to accept the offer," did the offeror mean (a) eight days from the date of the letter, (b) eight days from the time the letter was received, (c) eight days in which to decide whether to accept and then to notify the offeror on the ninth day, (d) that the letter of acceptance had to be posted on the eighth day from either (i) the date of the offer or (ii) the date the offer was received, (e) that the letter of acceptance had to be received by the offeror on the eighth day from either (i) the date of the offer, or (ii) the date the offer was received or, (f) none of the above? Thus, even in an expression as superficially innocent as, "eight days in which to accept the offer," the ambiguities may become exponential. The court interpreted the phrase as permitting the offeree eight days from the time the offer was received on the footing that the power of acceptance did not exist in the offeree until the offeree received the offer.[273]

CISG. A different interpretation of the same phrase would be required under the Convention on Contracts for the International Sale of Goods. CISG would measure the eight days in a telegram or letter from the moment the telegram is handed in for dispatch or from the date shown on the letter or, absent a date on the letter, from the date shown on the envelope. If, however, the message is by telephone, telex or other means of instantaneous communication (e.g., E-mail), the period begins to run from the moment the offer reaches the offeree.[274]

Other ambiguities arise in relation to the computation of the period of acceptance. Where the offer states that it "expires July 1," does the offeree have until midnight of July 1 to accept, i.e., is the day of acceptance counted in its entirety? Courts generally hold that the

---

[271] RESTATEMENT 2d § 41 comment e suggests the "normal understanding that mail is promptly answered if a reply is mailed at any time on the date of receipt."

[272] *See* L. & E. Wertheimer, Inc. v. Wehle-Hartford Co., 126 Conn. 30, 9 A.2d 279 (1939) (offer requiring "immediate confirmation"); Chesebrough v. Western Union Tel. Co., 76 Misc. 516, 135 N.Y.S. 583 (1912), *aff'd*, 157 A.D. 914, 142 N.Y.S. 1112 (1913) (offer calling for "immediate reply by wire" delayed in transmission without offeree's knowledge; acceptance on receipt held to be on time). Maclay v. Harvey, 90 Ill. 525, 32 Am. Rep. 35 (1878) ("return mail"); Palmer v. Phoenix Mut. Life Ins. Co., 84 N.Y. 63 (1881) ("return mail"). *See* RESTATEMENT 2d § 41 comment e, *id.*, and RESTATEMENT 2d § 60 comment a, ill. 1, which suggests that a reasonable interpretation of, "I must receive your acceptance by return mail" would include other means of communication which reaches the offeror as soon as a letter sent by return mail would normally arrive because a fair interpretation of the offer requires only acceptance within the time required rather than the method suggested.

[273] Caldwell v. Cline, 109 W. Va. 553, 156 S.E. 55 (1930).

[274] CISG Art.20(1).

first day of the period is excluded and the last day is included in its entirety.[275]

The rule is somewhat arbitrary and should give way to other manifestations of intention. Where a buyer's signed offer to buy a ranch stated a deadline of 5 P. M. on July 21, it stated that "buyer and seller each acknowledge that this agreement when signed becomes a legally binding contract." It also required all notices and communications to be in writing, delivered in person or by registered mail. The seller signed at 4:53 P. M. and his agent left a voice message for the buyer at 5:12 P. M. The court interpreted the contract as requiring only that the agreement be signed by 5 P. M. to form the contract. Thus, the seller's acceptance was held to be timely. The court found the provision for written communication applied only to notices after the contract was formed and not to the acceptance of the offer. The court, however, also noted that its interpretation was heavily influenced by the parties' course of performance after July 21 since they clearly acted in a manner consistent with a binding contract between them until December 5 when the seller notified the buyer that it would not sell the ranch to him.[276]

Still another problem arises in relation to an offer with a specified time that is delayed in transmission. If an offer is delayed and the offeree knows or has reason to know it has been delayed, the power of acceptance is not extended, i.e., the offeree has only the same time to accept as if the offer had not been delayed.[277] Thus, if an offer dated January 3 states that the power of acceptance must be exercised within 10 days from the date of the letter and the letter is not received until January 20, the offeree has no power of acceptance upon learning of the offer. Moreover, the same analysis applies even though the delay in transmission is exclusively the fault of the offeror. If, however, the offeree neither knows nor has reason to know of the delay in transmission, his power of acceptance lasts for as long as it would normally last, except that the period is measured from the time it *appears* to have been sent rather than from the time it was actually sent.[278] This analysis is in strict conformity with the preferable test, i.e., the reasonable understanding of the offeree.

[C]   Offers Without a Specified Time Limit

If an offer contains no specified duration of the power of acceptance, it might be supposed that the offer continues indefinitely unless revoked by the offeror. Such a rule would lead to manifestly unjust results. After a period of time has elapsed, if the offeror has heard nothing from the offeree, the offeror is usually reasonable in assuming that the offeree is not interested in the proposed deal, and further assuming that it is unnecessary to notify the offeree that the offer has expired. Under these circumstances, it would be grossly unfair to permit the offeree to bind the offeror by a purported acceptance of the offer. To avoid such an unfair result, the cases are legion which hold that a power of acceptance created by an offer without a specified time limit continues only for a reasonable time.[279]

---

[275] Thus, in an offer that became effective on January 5, if the offeree had to accept on the tenth day, the count would begin with January 6 and the power of acceptance could be exercised until midnight on January 15. *See* Dobson & Johnson, Inc. v. Waldron, 47 Tenn. App. 121, 336 S.W.2d 313 (1960); Housing Auth. of Lake Arthur v. T. Miller & Sons, 239 La. 966, 120 So. 2d 494 (1960). See also Clements v. Pasadena Fin. Co., 376 F.2d 1005 (9th Cir. 1967) applying Section 10 of the CAL. CIV. CODE to the same effect.

[276] Keller v. Bones, 260 Neb. 202, 211–12, 615 N.W.2d 883,889 (2000).

[277] RESTATEMENT 2d § 49.

[278] *Id.*

[279] *See, e.g.,* Stern v. Wesner, 395 N.W.2d 585 (S.D. 1986); Miller v. Campello Co-operative Bank, 344 Mass. 76, 181

While providing a result in keeping with the presumable intention of the parties had they consciously adverted to the question, the difficulty comes in determining what constitutes a reasonable time in a given case. A court must consider a wide range of circumstances in making this determination, including the nature of the proposed contract and the purposes of the parties, as well as any trade usage or prior course of dealing between the parties. Again, the general test is, how much time for acceptance would a reasonable person in the position of the offeree assume he had under all of the circumstances?[280] Where the parties are bargaining face-to-face or by the telephone, the general rule is that the time for acceptance does not extend beyond the end of the conversation[281] unless there is a manifestation of intention to the contrary.[282] A reasonable time in one case may be only a few moments, whereas in another case it may be several days or even years.[283]

The importance of ascertaining the purpose of the offeror in determining reasonable time is illustrated by cases involving the settlement of claims. Where the offeree tendered her acceptance of an offer to settle a claim after the statute of limitations had lapsed on the claim, the court rejected the trial court's finding that the acceptance was within a reasonable time as a matter of law. The court deemed the fact that the statute of limitations had run as "unquestionably relevant" to a determination of a reasonable time since the purpose of such agreements is to settle claims.[284]

N.E.2d 345 (1962); Fortin v. Wilensky, 142 Me. 372, 53 A.2d 266 (1947); RESTATEMENT 2d § 41(1).

[280] *See* Restatement 2d § 41, cmt. b; Sherrod v. Kidd, 138 Wn. App. 73, 76, 155 P.3d 876, 977 (2007); *see also* Jennings v. Hatfield, 2005 Tex. App. LEXIS 8730 at *7–8 (2005) ("What constitutes a reasonable time depends on the circumstances in each case, including the nature and character of the thing to be done and the difficulties surrounding and attending its accomplishment." citing RESTATEMENT 2d § 41(2)).

[281] RESTATEMENT 2d § 41 comment d and ill. 4. Under CISG, an oral offer must be accepted immediately unless the circumstances indicate otherwise. Art. 18(2).

[282] *See* Yaros v. Trustees of the Univ. of Pa., 742 A.2d 1118 (Pa. Super. Ct. 1999) (settlement offer did not expire at the end of a face-to-face discussion where the parties manifested an intention that the offer would continue beyond that time).

[283] *See* Textron, Inc. v. Froelich, 223 Pa. Super. 506, 302 A.2d 426 (1973). Seller offered steel at certain prices in a telephone conversation. Buyer replied that he wanted time to check with his customers. Five weeks later, buyer attempted to accept and seller responded, "Fine, thank you." Court held that while telephone offers may generally end with the completion of the conversation, the facts suggest that a jury could have found the offer still open at the time of buyer's acceptance. In any event, since buyer and seller manifested mutual assent five weeks later, there was a contract. In Orlowski v. Moore, 198 Pa. Super. 360, 181 A.2d 692 (1962), the lessee of property had an option to purchase in the form of a right of first refusal, i.e., the lessee had to be informed of the availability of another purchaser willing to buy at a certain price and then given a reasonable time (in the absence of a stated time) to exercise his power of acceptance to purchase the property. In mid-January, the owners notified the lessee that they had a willing purchaser at a certain price and the lessee should decide whether to exercise his right to purchase. The lessee had been unable to pay the modest monthly rental for the months of December and January on time. He finally paid the overdue rent in early February, at which time the owners, again, informed him of the willing purchaser. At that time, he told the owners that his attempt to secure a loan from the bank was unsuccessful but that he would continue his effort to obtain a loan. On February 10, the owners, believing that the lessee could not obtain a loan, agreed to sell the house to the other purchaser. Before title was conveyed, the lessee informed the owners that he had secured a loan and sought to exercise his right of first refusal. In determining whether the lessee had been given a reasonable time to exercise his right of first refusal, the court considered all of these facts and concluded that the lessee had been given a reasonable time though the total time involved was less than one month. If the lessee had evidence greater financial stability, a court may have decided that the time provided was not reasonable.

[284] In Vaskie v. West American Ins. Co., 556 A.2d 436 (Pa. Super. Ct. 1989). See also Brzezinek v. Covenant Ins. Co., 810 A.2d 306 (Conn. App. Ct. 2002). In offers to the public such as reward offers, an offer of reward for information leading to the arrest and conviction of the party guilty of a crime may last only as long as the statute of limitations for that crime, but the duration could be shorter or longer.

If a municipality has been experiencing a series of arson crimes and the city officials post a reward for information leading to the arrest and conviction of the arsonist, if no arson occurs for several years, the offer may have lapsed before an attempted exercise of the power of acceptance because the apparent purpose of the offeror was to deal with a particular problem at a particular time.[285]

Where the subject matter of the transaction involves great and rapid fluctuations in price, such as securities or goods on a commodities exchange, the reasonable time for acceptance will be very short, perhaps instantaneous through an appropriate means of telecommunication. The duration of the power of acceptance will be much greater with respect to subject matter that does not fluctuate rapidly in value.[286] Such common sense guides reflect the overriding test of what a reasonable offeree should assume with respect to a time for acceptance. The offeree should not, for example, expect to enjoy a period of time to speculate at the expense of the offeror.[287]

[1]   Acceptance Beyond a Reasonable Time That Is Effective — Cross-Offers Distinguished

Having seen that an offer without a specified duration is open for a reasonable time, it is clear that the offeror may either extend or decrease that duration. As the master of the offer, the offeror may extend the duration of the offer, whether the offer contained a specified time for acceptance or was subject to the substituted reasonable time where no time was specified.[288] Similarly, since an offeror may revoke the typical offer at any time after it is made, even if it contained a specified duration or the revocation occurred long before what would have been a reasonable time for acceptance, the offeror may shorten the time for acceptance by communicating that intention to the offeree.[289] The more difficult question is whether the life of the offer may be extended or shortened through the manifested but uncommunicated intention of the offeror. In the well-known case of *Mactier's Administrators v. Frith*,[290] an offer had been before the offeree for a period of two and one-half months before he purported to accept it. In the light of the surrounding circumstances and the nature of the offer involved, more than a reasonable time for acceptance had passed. In the meantime, however, the offeror

---

[285] *See* Loring v. Boston, 48 Mass. 409 (1844). RESTATEMENT 2d § 41 ill. 2. If, however, the apparent purpose of the offeror is to deal with a continuing problem over a long period of time, such as an offer by a group of banks concerning bank robbery, the reasonable duration of the power of acceptance could be much longer. *See* Carr v. Mahaska County Bankers Ass'n, 222 Iowa 411, 269 N.W. 494 (1936) and RESTATEMENT 2d § 41 ill. 3.

[286] RESTATEMENT 2d § 41 comment f.

[287] Illustration 8 to RESTATEMENT 2d § 41 concerns an offer by mail to buy, at a fixed price, stock not listed on an exchange. The offeree waits for two days before sending a telegraphic acceptance, which was sent only after the offeree learned of a significant increase in the price, bid over-the-counter. The illustration suggests that the acceptance may be too late even though it arrives before a prompt acceptance by mail would have arrived. Comment f explains that where an offeree uses the allowed time to accept for speculative purposes, there may be a lack of good faith and the acceptance may not be timely though it arrives within the time contemplated by the offeror.

[288] See Continental-Wirt Electronics Corp. v. Sprague Electric Co., 329 F. Supp. 959, 964 (E.D. Pa. 1971), where the court recognizes that the conduct of the parties may indicate an intention to extend the duration of the offer. Even if an offer lapses, it has long been recognized that the offeror may recreate the offer though it would be preferable, in such a case, to regard the recreation as a new offer creating a new power of acceptance. *See* Averill v. Hedge, 12 Conn. 424 (1838); Tinn v. Hoffman, 29 L. T. 271 [1873].

[289] *See* RESTATEMENT 2d § 42 ill. 1.

[290] 6 Wend. 103, 21 Am. Dec. 262 (N.Y. 1830).

had written indicating his intention that the offer was still open. Had this communication reached the offeree, there would have been no question that the duration of the power of acceptance had been extended. The communication, however, had not reached the offeree. Thus, there was a manifestation of intention on the part of the offeror of which the offeree was unaware. The court, nevertheless, held that the acceptance was timely.[291] At first blush, the result may appear to support the outmoded subjective theory of mutual assent, but a careful analysis belies that conclusion. There was an objective manifestation from the offeror to extend the duration of the power of acceptance, but it was not communicated to the offeree prior to his otherwise untimely exercise of the power of acceptance. As will be seen subsequently, normally an offer cannot be accepted unless the offeree is aware of the offer since mutual assent requires each party to manifest assent with reference to the manifestation of the other.[292] The classic illustration involves a party who provides information leading to the arrest and conviction of a murderer without knowledge of the reward offer.[293] It is quite another matter, however, to know of an offer and to attempt to accept it beyond what may be a reasonable time where there has been a manifestation of extension of that period though the manifestation was not communicated to the offeree. As suggested earlier, in the absence of a specified duration of the offer, the obvious purpose of the reasonable time limitation is to protect the offeror, since a reasonable offeror would assume that the offeree chose not to accept the offer after a reasonable time. If, however, the offeror has manifested his intention to extend the normal reasonable time duration of the offer, the purpose of protecting the offeror by the original reasonable time limitation is unnecessary, even though the offeree has not become aware of the extension. Where the reason for the rule stops, so should the rule. There is, therefore, no unfairness in permitting the acceptance to be effective under such circumstances.[294] If, however, the offeror had manifested his intention to shorten the reasonable time for acceptance and the offeree had not received that communication, that manifestation should not be effective because there is another purpose behind the rule permitting a reasonable time for acceptance. The rule protects not only the offeror; it protects the offeree who is entitled to assume a reasonable time for acceptance. If the offeree manifests acceptance within a reasonable time, the expectation and possible reliance of the offeree should not be frustrated when a manifestation of a shortening of the duration of the offer that had not been received prior to acceptance is later discovered.

---

[291] The opinion stated, "Then we are to determine, as a matter of fact, whether Frith's offer was held out for Mactier's acceptance until the thirty-first of March, if Frith intended it should stand so, and he viewed himself as tendering it to Mactier down to that time, we are bound to regard it as standing, unless his intention was the result of the fraudulent conduct of Mactier. The acts of Frith after the death of Mactier, could do nothing towards completing an unfinished contract; but I think they may be fairly adverted to for the purpose of ascertaining his intentions in relation to the continuance of his offer." Marcy, J., *id.* at 274. *Accord* RESTATEMENT 2d § 13 comment d and ill. 6.

[292] RESTATEMENT 2d § 23.

[293] *See* Glover v. Jewish War Veterans of United States, Post No. 58, 68 A.2d 233 (Mun. Ct. App. D.C. 1949). This situation will be analyzed later in this chapter.

[294] *CISG.* The Convention on Contracts for the International Sale of Goods requires an acceptance to reach the offeror within the time fixed in the offer or, absent a fixed time, within a reasonable time. Art. 18(2). If, however, the acceptance is late due to the fault of the offeree, the offeror may still treat the acceptance as effective by orally informing the offeree or dispatching a notice to that effect. Art. 21(1). If the delay in the arrival of the acceptance is due to transmission problems, i.e., absent such problems the acceptance would have been timely, the late acceptance is effective unless the offeror orally informs the offeree or dispatches a notice to the offeree that he considers the offer as having lapsed. Art. 21(2).

This situation should not be confused with the rare problem of cross-offers, i.e., identical offers crossing in the mails. If Ames sends a letter to Barnes offering to sell Ames' auto for $10,000 and Barnes, without knowledge of the Ames offer, sends a letter to Ames offering to purchase Ames' auto for $10,000, two powers of acceptance have been created, but there is no contract because the mutual assent of each party was not manifested with reference to the mutual assent of the other.[295] The parties have not made a bargain[296] and promises must be bargained for.[297] In the situation involving an otherwise late acceptance after an uncommunicated manifestation of extending the duration of the offer, however, there clearly is a bargained-for exchange.

§ 43   TERMINATION OF THE POWER OF ACCEPTANCE

[A]   Introduction — Methods of Termination

The power of acceptance created by an offer may be terminated in numerous ways. If an offer is not accepted within the time stated in the offer, or, where no time is stated, within a reasonable time, the offer lapses. An offer may be rejected by the offeree or revoked by the offeror. The offeree may make a counter offer that normally rejects the offer and death terminates the power of acceptance.[298] As the master of the offer,[299] the offeror may revoke the offer at any time, even if a time for acceptance has been previously specified.[300] The power of acceptance will come to an end if it is rejected by the offeree either by a manifestation not to accept (a rejection),[301] or by the submission of a different bargain, i.e., a counter-offer.[302] Death or incapacity of either the offeror or offeree will terminate the power of acceptance.[303] The power of acceptance in a given situation may be subject to a supervening event that operates to terminate the power.[304] Each of these methods of terminating the power of

[295] *See* Restatement 2d § 23 comment d and ill. 4. *See also* Tinn v. Hoffman, 29 L. T. 271 [1873].

[296] "Bargain" is defined as an agreement to exchange promises or to exchange a promise for a performance or to exchange performances. Restatement 2d § 3.

[297] As will be seen in the next chapter dealing with the Validation Process, one of the requirements for an enforceable agreement, i.e., a contract, is the requirement of consideration though there are additional validation devices under certain circumstances. *See* Restatement 2d § 71.

[298] Restatement 2d § 36(1). See First Home Sav. Bank, FSB v. Nernberg, 436 Pa. Super. 377, 388, 648 A.2d 9, 15 (1994).

[299] *See* Restatement 2d § 29 comment a.

[300] Restatement 2d § 42 comment a. See Farley v. Champs Fine Foods, Inc., 404 N.W.2d 493, 494 (N.D. 1987), where the court states, "Even though a definite time in which acceptance may be made is named in a proposal, the proposer may revoke his proposal within that time unless it was given for consideration." Note, however, that while *CISG* Art. 16(1) states that an offer can be revoked if the revocation reaches the offeree before he has dispatched an acceptance, where the offer states a fixed time for acceptance, Art. 16(2)(a) makes the offer irrevocable. Under the common law, if the offer states the duration of the power of acceptance, absent an option contract or other exceptions, the offer remains revocable.

[301] Restatement 2d § 38. See Chaplin v. Consolidated Edison Co., 537 F. Supp. 1224 (S.D.N.Y. 1982), where an offer was limited to the precise terms of the offer and those terms were rejected.

[302] Restatement 2d § 39. See Ardente v. Horan, 117 R.I. 254, 366 A.2d 162 (1976), where a response to an offer sought to impose additional terms and add limitations. The court found that the response was a counter offer rejecting the original offer.

[303] Restatement 2d § 48. *See* Beall v. Beall, 291 Md. 224, 434 A.2d 1015 (1981).

[304] We have already seen examples in auctions without reserve where the power of acceptance is subject to no

acceptance will be explored. As this exploration proceeds, it must be remembered that an offer can be made irrevocable in various ways, which will be analyzed in the next section.

[B]   The Power of Revocation — Direct and "Indirect"

A manifestation by the offeror to withdraw the offer prior to the moment of acceptance terminates the offeree's power of acceptance.[305] The common law rationale is one of fairness to the offeror, i.e., if offers were irrevocable, the offeror would be bound but the offeree would not be bound, thus violating the common law principle of "mutuality of obligation" that is commonly stated as, "Either both parties are bound or neither are bound."[306]

"Direct Revocation." To be effective, a revocation must be received by the offeree.[307] Without knowledge of a revocation, an offeree may accept the offer and reasonably assume there is a binding agreement. To protect reasonable expectations and possible reliance, the revocation of the offer must, therefore, be received by the offeree to be effective. An oral notice of revocation is received when the offeree or his agent learns of it or has reason to know it exists.[308] A written revocation is received when it comes into the possession of the offeree or his agent, or when it is deposited in an authorized place.[309]

Interpretation questions may arise as to whether the offer has been revoked. Terms such as "revocation" or "withdrawal" are clear, but they are not prerequisites to effecting a revocation of an offer. If the offeror manifests an intention sufficient to indicate to a reasonable offeree that the offeror no longer intends to form the contract, the offer is revoked though the statement may be somewhat indefinite. In the leading case of *Hoover Motor Express Co. v.*

---

higher bid being made, *supra* § 37, and reward offers which contemplate the exercise of the power of acceptance only by the first party to exercise it, *supra* § 40.

[305] *See* GMH Assocs. v. Prudential Realty Group, 752 A.2d 889, 899 (Pa. Super. Ct. 2000): "It is hornbook law that an offeree's power to accept an offer is terminated by a revocation of the offer." *See also* Pribil v. Ruther, 200 Neb. 161, 262 N.W.2d 460 (1978) (indicating that a revocation communicated prior to the deposit of the acceptance in the mail would be effective); Restatement 2d § 42. The civil law does not share this common law view. 1 Formation of Contracts: A Study of The Common Core of Legal Systems 780–83 (R. Schlesinger ed. 1968). CISG is influenced by this view. *See* note 285 *supra.*

[306] The doctrine of "mutuality of obligation" is discussed in the next chapter proving that the "doctrine", is nothing more than a statement of the requirement of consideration to make a promise binding.

[307] The classic case is Byrne & Co. v. Leon Van Tienhoven & Co., L.R. 5 C.P.D. 344 (1880) (letter of acceptance mailed before letter of revocation was received). See also L. & E. Wertheimer v. Wehle-Hartford Co., 126 Conn. 30, 9 A.2d 279 (1939), Annot., 125 A.L.R. 985 (1940), and the modern confirmation of that view in Town of N. Branford v. Aais, 1995 Conn. Super. LEXIS 363, at *2–3 (Conn. Super. Ct. Feb. 6, 1995). In Etablissement Asamar Ltd. v. Lone Eagle Shipping Ltd., 882 F. Supp. 1409, 1411 (S.D.N.Y. 1995), the court states that a revocation by mail or electronic means is not effective until it is received. *See* Restatement 2d § 42 comment b. Under the influence of the "Field Code," which was drafted pursuant to the subjective theory, some western states have adopted legislation making revocations effective when they are put in the course of transmission to the offeree. *See, e.g.,* Cal. Civ. Code §§ 1583, 1587; Mont. Code Ann. §§ 28-2-502, 28-2-512.

[308] *See* UCC § 1-202 (a): "A person has 'notice' of a fact when (c) from all the facts and circumstances known to him at the time in question he has reason to know that it exists. . . ."

[309] *See* Restatement 2d § 68 and Night Commander Lighting Co. v. Brown, 213 Mich. 214, 181 N.W. 979 (1921) (revocation effective when received by agent who took order for his company). *See also* UCC § 1-202(e) to the effect that a person has notice when "he has received a notice or notification,"or when . . . it is duly delivered at the place of business through which the contract was made, or at another location held out by that person as the place for receipt of such communications."

Clements Paper Co.,[310] the court found that a statement by the offeror that it "didn't think they were going through with the proposal" was sufficient to indicate to the offeree that the offer was revoked. Lesser statements, however, may not be sufficient to constitute a revocation.[311] Where an offer of reinstatement of employment was followed by statements such as, "You don't want to come back to work here" and "[a] lot of accidents happen around here," there was a clear unwillingness to contract which amounted to a revocation of the offer.[312] Where an offer that had not been accepted was followed by a new offer with a new price term, the new offer manifested the offeror's intention to revoke the original offer.[313]

"Indirect Revocation." Courts may refer to such revocations as "indirect," but they are "indirect" only in the sense that the offeror has not stated that "the offer is revoked." Other statements or actions amounting to revocations are still emanating directly from the offeror to offeree. The phrase "indirect revocation" is often relegated to situations where the notification of revocation comes not from the offeror, but from a third party, as in the well-known case of *Dickinson v. Dodds.*[314]

The owner of land created a power of acceptance with a specified time limit. Before the offer had expired according to its terms, the offeree's agent told the offeree that the offeror "had been offering or agreeing to sell the property" to another. The court interpreted the communication as making the offeree aware that the offeror no longer intended to sell the property to the offeree and this knowledge constituted an *indirect* revocation of the offer. If the owner had told the offeree that he had agreed to sell the property to another, the revocation would be abundantly clear and direct.

Where the same knowledge is communicated by a third person, the offeree has been informed that the offeror has taken action inconsistent with the continuation of the offeree's power of acceptance which should constitute a revocation of the offer as effectively as direct communication from the offeror. Where, for example, an offeree is informed by a reliable source that the land he had an offer to buy had been sold to another, his power of acceptance was terminated.[315] What, however, constitutes *knowledge* on the part of the offeree? Must the offeree investigate every rumor about actions on the part of the offeror? The question scarcely survives its statement.

A reasonable offeree need not be concerned about statements by third parties who would not be viewed as *reliable* sources. The town gossip who is known for making statements without sufficient foundation need not be relied upon, even if the information he conveys turns out to be true on this occasion. Even where the source is someone who normally would be viewed as trusted and reliable as in *Dickinson v. Dodds* where the source was the agent of the offeree, there is still no effective revocation if the information is erroneous though it was submitted in good faith. Such an indirect revocation requires both a reliable source and correct information. Moreover, even if the information is correct and the source reliable, the

---

[310] 193 Tenn. 6, 11, 241 S.W.2d 851, 853 (1951).

[311] *See* Restatement 2d § 42, cmt. d. Illustration 5 to this section is based on the *Hoover* case as noted by the court in *Monsour's Inc. v. Menu Maker's Foods, Inc.*, 2007 U.S. Dist. LEXIS 39870 at *6 (D. Kan., May 31, 2007), that follows *Hoover.*

[312] NLRB v. Browne, 890 F.2d 605, 609 (2d Cir. 1989).

[313] Norca Corp. v. Tokheim Corp., 643 N.Y.S.2d 139, 140 (2d Dep't 1996).

[314] 2 Ch. D. 463 (1876).

[315] Berryman v. Kmoch, 221 Kan. 304, 559 P.2d 790 (1977). *See* Restatement 2d § 43.

information must amount to a sufficiently definite manifestation of intention by the offeror that he no longer intends to form a contract with the offeree. An offer or even a contract with another may turn out to be consistent with the original offer. For example, the contract made with another may be expressly conditioned on the originally offeree's failure to exercise the power of acceptance within the time stated in the original offer. Absent this qualification of information relayed by a reliable third party, the information would be incorrect because it is incomplete and a timely exercise of the power of acceptance by the original offeree would still be effective.[316] With these qualifications in mind, the *indirect revocation* principle is firmly ensconced and applies beyond the narrow range of contracts for the sale of land to which the First RESTATEMENT had limited it.[317]

While offers may be indirectly revoked, they may not be indirectly created by reliable third parties without authority. Thus, if A tells B of A's intention to offer A's auto to C for a certain price but does not empower B to communicate such an offer to C, if B informs C of A's intention, C does not have a power of acceptance since A has not made an offer to C.

Revocations of Offers to the Public. If an offer is made to the world at large such as a reward offer, an obvious difficulty is encountered in the revocation of such an offer. It would be absurd to require communication to each member of the public. The pragmatic solution requires the offeror to promulgate the intention to revoke to the same extent and through the same media through which the original offer was published since no better means of notification is available.[318] Where a bank was robbed in 1935, the plaintiff furnished information leading to the arrest and conviction of the bank robbers and claimed a reward that had been posted in the bank sometime prior to 1930. The poster, however, had been removed and discarded several years earlier. The bank argued that the removal of the poster constituted a revocation of the reward offer but the court disagreed, citing the *Shuey* case and holding that the revocation should have been posted in the same manner as the reward offer was posted. Simply removing the poster was insufficient.[319]

Where it is practicable to notify a number of offerees individually, i.e., the number is not so great as to make individual notification prohibitively difficult, a general publication of revocation would be ineffective.[320] Finally, if a general notice of revocation would otherwise be acceptable but the medium used to announce the offer is not available, the same pragmatism would suggest an alternate medium of similar scope as an effective device to communicate the revocation.[321]

---

[316] *See* RESTATEMENT 2d § 43 comment d and CALAMARI & PERILLO, CONTRACTS 98 (3d ed. 1987) (citing the prior edition of this book). *A fortiori*, mere negotiations with another potential purchaser of the property would not constitute sufficient information of an intention to revoke the offer.

[317] *See* FIRST RESTATEMENT § 43 and RESTATEMENT 2d § 43 comment c.

[318] *See* Shuey v. United States, 92 U.S. (2 Otto) 73 (1876) (ineffective attempt to accept reward offered for apprehension of accomplice of John Wilkes Booth), and FIRST RESTATEMENT § 43.

[319] Carr v. Mahaska County Bankers Ass'n, 222 Iowa 411, 269 N.W. 494 (1936).

[320] *See* Long v. Chronicle Pub. Co., 68 Cal. App. 171, 228 P. 873 (1924).

[321] An offer made through a national publication might be effectively revoked through a similar, national publication when the first publication either ceased to exist or was unavailable for a period of time.

[C]   Rejection Terminating the Power of Acceptance

Normal Effect of Rejection. An offeree has a power of acceptance, but the power does not have to be exercised. If an intention not to exercise the power of acceptance is manifested by the offeree, the offeree has rejected it and the power of acceptance is terminated.[322] Any other rule would subject the offeror to undue risk. An offer may be rejected by words or conduct.[323]

When the offeree informs the offeror by words or conduct that the offeree is not interested in the proposal, the offeror may change plans in reliance on the rejection without bothering to revoke the rejected offer. Revocation by the offeror in such a case would be a useless gesture. The reliance of the offeror on the rejection may be difficult to prove. If the offeree were then permitted to change his mind and exercise a power of acceptance after putting the offeror off guard, obvious injustice could result. Thus, the firm principle has been established that rejection of an offer terminates it, and the principle is not affected by the inclusion of a definite time for acceptance in the offer if the rejection occurs before that time has expired.[324]

Normal Effect of Rejection Changed by Offeror or Offeree. There are, however, two situations that must be distinguished. The first involves a manifestation that the offer will not be terminated for a definite time notwithstanding earlier rejections by the offeree. Thus, if *A* offers to sell *A'*s auto to *B* for $10,000 and also states, "This offer will expire 90 days from its date regardless of any statement of rejection on the part of *B*," would a rejection by *B* on the 45th day terminate *B'*s power of acceptance? The answer must be, no. We return to the general principle that the offeror, *A*, is master of the offer and may create a power of acceptance which includes abnormal risks for the offeror. As suggested earlier, the rule that rejection terminates an offer is designed to protect the offeror. The offeror is free to create a power of acceptance that eliminates that protection.[325]

A similar effect occurs where an offeree responds to an ordinary offer by stating, "I reject it for the time being, but will reconsider it later." Assuming the power of acceptance would not have lapsed at the time of reconsideration by the offeree, the power of acceptance is not terminated by such a statement.[326] In this situation, it is unfortunate to characterize the offeree's response as a rejection even though the term "rejection" is used. A proper interpretation of the response would be, "I am not rejecting your offer but I cannot accept at

---

[322] *See* Lamb v. Decatur Fed. Sav. & Loan Ass'n, 201 Ga. App. 583, 585 411 S.E.2d 527, 529 (1991): "An offer, when once rejected, loses its legal force and cannot be accepted thereafter so as to create a binding agreement unless it is renewed after the rejection by the original offeror. No revocation of the offer is, therefore, necessary to prevent its subsequent acceptance after it has been once rejected." *See also* Chaplin v. Consolidated Edison Co. of N.Y., 537 F. Supp. 1224 (S.D.N.Y. 1982) (offer of settlement stated that, if not satisfactory, all offers would be withdrawn; reply that attorney could not get clients to agree constituted rejection); Nabob Oil Co. v. Bay State Oil & Gas Co., 208 Okla. 296, 298, 255 P.2d 513, 515 (1953) ("It is elementary that plaintiff could not revive the offer by orally accepting it . . . after its rejection. . . ."); Restatement 2d § 38. Normal rejection rules are overcome by the policies of the National Labor Relations Act governing collective bargaining between employers and labor unions. *See* Pepsi-Cola Bottling Co. v. NLRB, 659 F.2d 87 (8th Cir. 1981).

[323] See, e. g., Jones v. Hirschfeld, 348 F. Supp. 2d 50, 61, note 8 (S. D. N. Y. 2004): "Jones' unambiguous conduct . . . clearly manifests an intention to reject Hirschfeld's money and justified Hirschfeld in inferring that Jones no longer intended to accept his offer" of $1,000,000 to abandon her lawsuit against President Clinton.

[324] See Banc One Fin. Servs. v. Advanta Mortg. Corp., USA, 2002 U. S. Dist. LEXIS 960 at *25–26 (N. D. Ill. 2002) citing Restatement 2d § 38, comment a.

[325] Restatement 2d § 38 comment b.

[326] Paris v. Ford Motor Co., 2007 U. S. Dist. LEXIS 96631 at*7 (D. N. M. 2007) quoting comment b to Restatement 2d § 38(2).

this time. I would like to consider accepting at a later time." The effect is the same as an offeree responding that he will take the offer under advisement which does not reject the offer.[327]

In either of these distinguishable situations, i.e., the offeror eliminating the protection normally enjoyed through a rejection, or the offeree indicating the possibility of acceptance at a subsequent time, the offeror may not justifiably rely upon the offeree's response as a termination of the power of acceptance. Since the reason for the rule is absent, the rule should not apply. It should be noted, however, that the offeror has not surrendered the power to *revoke* the offer in either situation. Only the effect of rejection on the power of acceptance has been abrogated.[328]

[D] Counter Offer Terminating Power of Acceptance — "Grumbling Acceptance"

Upon receiving an offer, an offeree may choose to propose a different bargain to the offeror relating to the same subject matter. If *A* offers to sell her auto to *B* for $10,000, *B* may choose to reply, "Your price is too high. I will give you $8000 for the car." *B*'s reply is a counter offer which normally has the same effect as an rejection, i.e., it terminates *B*'s power of acceptance because it manifests *B*'s intention not to accept *A*'s offer.[329] Yet, *B*'s response is different from an outright rejection in that the counter offer is, itself, an offer that creates a power of acceptance in the original offeror.[330] counter offers manifest an intention to continue negotiations rather than to break them off.[331]

"Qualified" ("Conditional") Acceptances vs. Unqualified Acceptances Including Requests or Suggestions. The counter offer may indicate an acceptance of the offer, but only with qualifications. For example, the offeree manifests its assent to most but not to all of the terms and insists upon some modification of the offer. Such a "qualified acceptance" is not an acceptance. It is a counter offer that operates as a rejection of the original offer notwithstanding language of "acceptance." It is important to determine whether a response to an offer insists on new or modified terms or whether it constitutes an unequivocal acceptance of the terms of the offer together with mere requests or suggestions.

Where the sellers of property presented a document offering to sell their real estate, the buyers' attorney returned the document signed by his clients with a cover letter stating that the clients were "concerned" that specific furniture and fixtures "remain with the real estate" and they "would appreciate your confirming that these items are a part of the transaction."

---

[327] Scoular Co. v. Denny, 151 P. 3d 615, 619 (Colo. App. 2006), citing Restatement 2d § 38.

[328] This statement assumes that the offer stating the duration of the power of acceptance at 90 days is not a "firm offer" that is statutorily irrevocable or irrevocable on another basis. The "irrevocable offer" concept is explored in § 44, *infra.*

[329] *See* Dataserv Equip., Inc. v. Technology Fin. Leasing Corp., 364 N.W.2d 838 (Minn. Ct. App. 1985); Normile v. Miller, 313 N.C. 98, 326 S.E.2d 11 (1985); Glende Motor Co. v. Superior Court, 159 Cal. App. 3d 389, 205 Cal. Rptr. 682 (1984); Duval & Co. v. Malcom, 233 Ga. 784, 214 S.E.2d 356 (1975), and Ebline v. Campbell, 209 Md. 584, 121 A.2d 828 (1956), all of which involve purported acceptances adding qualifications or otherwise changing the terms of the offer. In these and similar cases, courts hold the response to be a counter offer which has the effect of terminating the power of acceptance. *See* Restatement 2d § 39.

[330] *See* Hall v. Add-Ventures, 695 P.2d 1081 (Alaska 1985); Steele v. Harrison, 220 Kan. 422, 552 P.2d 957 (1976).

[331] Restatement 2d § 39 comment a.

The sellers treated the buyer's response as a counter offer which the sellers refused to accept. The buyers insisted that they intended to accept the offer. The court noted that an acceptance of an offer may include mere requests or suggestions that are not conditions to acceptance, but a response to an offer that conditions an acceptance on different or additional terms is a counter offer that rejects the offer. The court recognized that whether such a response is an acceptance or a counter offer is a question of interpretation that is not always easy to answer. It concluded that the buyer's response in the case before it was not a mere request for additional property but a counter offer that rejected the original offer.[332]

A mere request that identified furniture to be included in a transaction will not make the acceptance conditional.[333] Where an offer does not deal with a method of payment, the unconditional nature of an acceptance is not marred by a suggestion concerning a normal method of payment.[334] Even a suggested change in a material term such as price will not affect an unconditional acceptance if the offeree clearly indicates agreement to the original prices. Thus, if A offers to sell A's auto to B for \$10,000 and B replies, "I will pay your very high price and we have a deal though I would be much happier if you would let me have it for \$8000," there is an acceptance which may be viewed as a "grumbling acceptance" with a suggestion or request for a discount.[335] If the offer or acceptance expresses a term that is implied in the other manifestation of assent, there is no difference in terms so that no question of a counter offer or other failure of mutual assent occurs.[336]

Non-Rejecting Counter Offers. While a counter offer normally rejects the original offer, it need not do so. Just as an offer can state that it will remain open for a period of time notwithstanding earlier rejections, an offeror can manifest an intention to continue the power of acceptance for the time stated in the offer notwithstanding counter offers. An employer's December, 2002 offer for continued work by at-will employees included a new dispute resolution program including arbitration of any disputes. The offer expressly stated that employees were not required to accept immediately, but they had until March 1, 2003 to decide, after which participation would be mandatory. The plaintiff-employee stated that she would not participate in the new dispute resolution program but would continue to work. Early in 2003, the employer posted a reminder of the program and its mandatory nature after March 1. The plaintiff did not renew her objection but continued to work after March 1. While noting that the earlier counter offer made by the employee typically rejects an offer, the court held that it does not have that effect where the offer, as in this case, states a contrary intention which was confirmed by the continuous posting of the offer even after the plaintiff's counter offer By continuing to work after March 1, the plaintiff manifested acceptance of the offer.

---

[332]   Ardente v. Horan, 117 R.I. 254, 366 A.2d 162 (1976). *See also* the cases *supra* note 329, and, in particular, the *Glende Motor Co.* case therein. *See also* RESTATEMENT 2d § 39 comment b.

[333]   *See* McAfee v. Brewer, 214 Va. 579, 580, 203 S.E.2d 129, 130 (1974) (acceptance of terms specified in offer plus a request that "the red secretary" be included). *See* RESTATEMENT 2d § 61, ill. 2.

[334]   *See, e.g.,* Kodiak Island Borough v. Large, 622 P.2d 440, 448 (Alaska 1981) ("The fact that the assent was accompanied by a suggestion as to terms of payment, a detail not inconsistent with the . . . offer, did not convert it into a counter offer."). *See* Martindell v. Fiduciary Counsel, Inc., 131 N.J. Eq. 523, 26 A.2d 171, aff'd, 133 N.J. Eq. 408, 30 A.2d 281 (1943), and Rucker v. Sanders, 182 N.C. 607, 109 S.E. 857 (1921), both of which involve a sale of stock where buyer suggested method of payment. *See also* RESTATEMENT 2d § 61.

[335]   *See* Massachusetts Hous. Fin. Agency v. Whitney House Assocs., 37 Mass. App. Ct. 238, 638 N.E.2d 1378, 1380 (1994); Brangier v. Rosenthal, 337 F.2d 952 (9th Cir. 1964).

[336]   *See* United States v. National Optical Stores Co., 407 F.2d 759 (7th Cir. 1969); Burkhead v. Farlow, 266 N.C. 595, 146 S.E.2d 802 (1966); RESTATEMENT 2d § 59 and, particularly, ill. 3.

Her claim against the employer had to be adjudicated in arbitration pursuant to the new dispute resolution program.[337]

The second situation involves an offeree proposing a counter offer without rejecting the original offer. *A* offers to sell her auto to *B* for $10,000 and *B* responds, "I am interested in your offer and will take it under advisement. In the meantime, I am willing to pay $8000 for your car right now." B has not rejected A's offer though he has made a counter offer.[338] Each party now has a power of acceptance, i.e., *A* to accept *B'* s counter offer at $8000, and *B* to accept *A'* s original offer at $10,000. In either of these situations, i.e., a contrary intention expressed by either the offeror or offeree concerning the normal operation of counter offers as rejections of the original offers, the parties have clearly manifested their intention that the counter offer should not be understood as a rejection of the original offer. They have, therefore, overcome the normal understanding that, by making a counter offer, the offeree intends to reject the original offer and the offeror will reasonably understand the counter offer is not rejecting the original offer.

[E]   Termination of Power of Acceptance by Death or Incapacity

It has generally been held that death[339] or incapacity[340] terminates the power of acceptance. As an original question, there is grave doubt whether this rule is desirable. It is a product of the outmoded subjective theory of mutual assent[341] and a logical application of that theory. Long ago, Professor Corbin provided the telling criticism: while one cannot contract with a dead man, there is no obstacle in creating legal relations with the personal representative who will be responsible for paying the debts of the estate.[342] Professor Williston would have preferred a different rule in the FIRST RESTATEMENT[343] but, remarkably, failed to convince the Council of the American Law Institute.[344] The RESTATEMENT 2d retains the rule but identifies it as a "relic of the obsolete view that a contract requires a 'meeting of the minds.' "[345] The effect of the rule may be particularly egregious where the offeree accepts by performance, unaware of the offeree's death or incapacity prior to such performance. Notwithstanding universal criticism, the rule remains intact except for isolated statutory changes.[346]

---

[337] Hardin v. First Cash Fin. Servs., 465 F. 3d 470 (10th Cir. 2006). *See* RESTATEMENT 2d § 39(2) and comment c.

[338] See Restatement 2d § 39(2), illustration 3.

[339] O'Neil v. Bunge, 365 F. 3d 820, 826 (9 th Cir. 2004); Lewis v. Motorists Ins. Co., 96 Ohio App. 3d 575, 584, 645 N.E.2d 784, 790 (1994); Beall v. Beall, 291 Md. 224, 434 A.2d 1015 (1981); Jordan v. Dobbins, 122 Mass. 168 (1877). RESTATEMENT 2d § 48.

[340] Capacity to contract is explored *supra* §§ 21–28, Chapter 1. *See* Union Trust & Sav. Bank v. State Bank, 188 N.W.2d 300 (Iowa 1971) (before acceptance of guaranty offer, a conservator of the guarantor was appointed; held: appointment of conservator for guarantor with plaintiff's knowledge served to revoke the then unaccepted guaranty offer). In Swift & Co. v. Smigel, 115 N.J. Super. 391, 279 A.2d 895 (1971), aff'd, 60 N.J. 348, 289 A.2d 793 (1972), however, the court held that while guarantor was incompetent at the time the guaranty offer was accepted, there was an acceptance unless plaintiff should have been aware of guarantor's incompetency. *See* RESTATEMENT 2d § 48.

[341] *See supra* § 31.

[342] Corbin, *Offer and Acceptance and Some of the Resulting Legal Relations*, 26 YALE L.J. 169, 198 (1917).

[343] AM. L. INST. PROC. 198 (1925).

[344] The authority of Professor Williston was rarely questioned with respect to the FIRST RESTATEMENT.

[345] RESTATEMENT 2d § 48 comment a.

[346] *See, e.g.,* UCC § 4-405(a) concerning the authority of a bank to pay a properly drawn check presented for

§ 44   IRREVOCABLE POWER OF ACCEPTANCE

[A]   Need and Methods

Under the common law system, offers are revocable even if they contain a specified period for acceptance and the offeror promises not to revoke during that period.[347] Just because an offer states the duration of the power of acceptance, the offeror is not bound by this promise since he received no consideration, i. e., something of value in exchange for surrendering the power to revoke the offer regardless of the stated duration.[348] A promise not to revoke the offer for a stated time is necessarily unenforceable if it is not supported by consideration.[349]

Notwithstanding the common law insistence upon revocable offers, the need for an irrevocable power of acceptance in myriad situations was clear. The offeree may be very interested in a proposal but require time to make a final decision as to whether to accept it. She may require time to determine whether necessary funds can be raised, or may have to await the occurrence or nonoccurrence of other events before deciding to accept. While in the process of deciding, the offeree does not want to assume the risk that the offer may be revoked. To provide the offeree with a dependable basis for decision, it was inevitable that devices would be developed to ascertain that the power of acceptance would be irrevocable.

The original common law device which allowed for the desired result was the *option contract*. We will explore option contracts in this section followed by an exploration of other methods to achieve an irrevocable power of acceptance including statutes making the offer irrevocable such as the *firm offer, irrevocability through part performance*, and *irrevocability through reliance*. As will be seen, these devices are predicated essentially on protection of the offeree in situations where revocation of the power of acceptance would lead to manifestly unjust results.

[B]   Option Contracts

If *A* offers to sell Blackacre to *B* for $100,000, *B* may be quite interested in the offer but may require time to make a final acceptance decision. The offer, however, may be voluntarily revoked by the offeror, or revocation may occur through the death or incapacity of the offeror. To assure retention of the power of acceptance, *B* may offer to pay *A* a certain sum, often a relatively small amount, in exchange for *A'* s promise not to revoke the offer for a stated period, e.g., 30 days. If *A* accepts *B'* s offer, the parties have formed a separate *option contract*.[350] An option contract has only one purpose: to create an irrevocable power of

---

payment: "Neither death nor incompetence of a customer revokes such authority to accept, pay, collect or account until the bank knows of the fact of death or of an adjudication of incompetence and has reasonable opportunity to act on it." *See also* with respect to incompetency, *Swift & Co. v. Smigel*, discussed *supra* note 340.

[347] *See* RESTATEMENT 2d § 42 comment a: ". . . [T]he ordinary offer is revocable even though it expressly states the contrary. . . ."

[348] Consideration and other validation devices will be explored in Chapter 3.

[349] *See, e.g.*, Crowley v. Bass, 445 So. 2d 902 (Ala. 1984); Beall v. Beall, 291 Md. 224, 235, 434 A.2d 1015, 1021–22 (1981).

[350] "One method by which an offer is rendered irrevocable is by the acceptance of consideration by the offeror in exchange for his promise to keep the offer open." Northwestern Bell Tel. Co. v. Cowger, 303 N.W.2d 791, 794 (N.D. 1981).

acceptance in the offeree with respect to the main offer,[351] i.e., *A'*s offer to sell Blackacre to *B* for $100,000 for thirty days. "An option is nothing but an enforceable promise that limits an offeror's power to revoke."[352]

An early theoretical argument threatened the effectiveness of this device: It was asserted that the option contract only created a *duty* in the offeror not to revoke the offer. By exercising the power to revoke, he was only breaching the duty not to revoke for which he can be sued and would have to pay whatever damages the optionee could prove. The offer, however, would not be terminated by the revocation since the *power* to revoke was not surrendered by the option contract. This view was based on the notion that an "irrevocable offer" is contrary to the legal conception of an offer, i.e., it is a legal impossibility because of the old subjective theory that an acceptance is impossible where one of the parties is expressing unwillingness to contract.[353] The argument has long been put to rest. As suggested in a concurring opinion more than a century ago,

> While it may seem at first blush a legal paradox that a contract for the sale of land, mutual and enforceable, can be made when at the time it is claimed to have been made one party to it is openly protesting that he will make no such contract, and while reasons may be advanced to support the proposition that the option holder should be in such a case remitted to an action for damages for refusal to hold the offer open for the stipulated time, there is reason and precedent for holding that the offer to sell, if paid for, may not be withdrawn during the stipulated time, being, in law, a continuing offer to sell.[354]

Effect of Option Contract. It is clear that, by entering into an option contract, the offeror has made a promise that creates not only a *duty* not to revoke his offer, but the surrender of the *power* to revoke, thereby creating an irrevocable power of acceptance in the offeree. Not only is such an irrevocable power of acceptance not terminated by the offeror's attempted revocation; neither is it terminated by rejection, counter offer or the death or incapacity of the offeror.[355] Though death revokes the typical offer, death does not revoke an irrevocable power of acceptance created by an option contract.[356] To hold that a counter offer by an optionee during the option period invalidates the option "would seriously undermine the value" of the option.[357] The offeror's duty under the option, however, may be discharged. For example, to permit the offeror to convey land to another, if the offeree informed the offeror that he did not intend to exercise his irrevocable power of acceptance, the offeror is justified in relying on the

---

[351] "An option contract has two elements: 1) the underlying contract which is not binding until accepted; and 2) the agreement to hold open to the optionee the opportunity to accept." Plantation Key Developers, Inc. v. Colonial Mortg. Co., 589 F.2d 164, 168 (5th Cir. 1979).

[352] Driscoll v. Norprop, Inc., 129 Ohio App. 3d 757, 764, 719 N.E.2d 48, 52 (1998). The RESTATEMENT 2d § 25: "An option contract . . . limits the promisor's power to revoke an offer." Presumably, this language is designed to ascertain that while the power of acceptance cannot be terminated through the offeror's revocation, it can be terminated in any way in which any contractual duty can be terminated. However, comment d to this section suggests that, "A revocation by the offeror is not of itself effective, and the offer is properly referred to as an irrevocable offer."

[353] This suggestion is primarily attributable to C. LANGDELL, SUMMARY OF THE LAW OF CONTRACTS § 178 (1880).

[354] Solomon Mier Co. v. Hadden, 148 Mich. 488, 111 N.W. 1040, 1043 (1907) (concurring opinion).

[355] RESTATEMENT 2d § 37.

[356] *See, e.g.*, Crowley v. S.E. Bass, 445 So. 2d 902 (Ala. 1984).

[357] Kidd v. Early, 289 N.C. 343, 360, 222 S.E.2d 392, 404 (1976). See also Roazen v. A.P. S., Inc., 1991 Me. Super. LEXIS 141 at *6 (1991).

offeree's rejection of the offer in selling the land to another. The offeree's power of acceptance is terminated.[358]

Right of First Refusal. The paradigmatic illustration of a right of first refusal arises in lease contracts which provide the lessee with a right to purchase the property by matching an offer to purchase the property made by a third party to the owner-lessor. Where a lease includes a right of first refusal, in exchange for lease payments the lessee receives not only the use of the premises, but the right to purchase the property whenever the owner notifies the lessee that the owner has found a prospective buyer to whom the owner is willing to sell at a certain price. This is a condition to activating the lessee's "right of first refusal" to purchase the property at a matching price. The lessee has a right to be notified of the third party offer and provided with the time stated in the lease or a reasonable time to exercise his right of first refusal. At this point, the lessee has what amounts to an option, an irrevocable power of acceptance to purchase the property at the price offered by the third party.[359]

Different terms may be used to characterize this right such as "first option to buy," "first right to purchase," "preemptive option" or other captions. A statement in an equipment lease that a party was "willing to consider renegotiation," was not a right of first refusal.[360]

Recital Clauses. The consideration for an option contract is often found in what are called "recital clauses" in documents typically reciting a small or nominal consideration in exchange for granting an option, e. g., "In consideration of one dollar in hand paid." The "one dollar" is hardly bargained for. If the court concludes that it was intended only as "sham" consideration or if the recited amount of more than nominal consideration, was not, in fact, paid, serious questions arise as to the enforceability of the option contract.[361] Different judicial reactions to recital clauses in the attempted creation of option contracts are explored in the analysis of consideration later in this volume.[362]

Strict Construction of Offers. Courts are generally quite insistent that the exercise of an irrevocable power of acceptance conform precisely to the terms of the main offer that created the option.[363] Court also insist that the option be exercised in timely fashion.[364] As will be seen

---

[358] *See* RESTATEMENT 2d § 37 ill. 2.

[359] See Park-Lake Car Wash, Inc. v. Springer, 352 N.W.2d 409 (Minn. 1984), where the court distinguished the right of first refusal provision in a lease by suggesting that such a right requires a condition precedent before it may be exercised, i.e., the owner must have received a bona fide offer from a third party which he or she is willing to accept. Except for this distinction, the court indicates that such a right of first refusal is like any other option. See, however, CORBIN at § 11.3 distinguishing a number of situations under the generic caption, "right of first refusal," which are not option contracts.

[360] Bristol-Meyers Squibb Co. v. Ikon Office Solutions, Inc. 295 F. 3d 680, 686 (7th Cir. 2002).

[361] *See, e.g.*, Hamilton Bancshares, Inc. v. Leroy, 131 Ill. App. 3d 907, 911, 476 N.E.2d 788, 791 (4th Dist. 1985) ("If a consideration of 'one dollar' or some other consideration is stated but which has, in fact, not been paid, . . . [t]he document will amount only to an offer which may be withdrawn at any time before acceptance.").

[362] *See infra* § 62.

[363] See, e.g., Westinghouse Broadcasting Co. v. New England Patriots Football Club, Inc., 10 Mass. App. 70, 406 N.E.2d 399, 491 (1980), in which the court stated, "Generally, conditions for the exercise of an option require a more strict degree of adherence than may be the case in provisions of a bilateral contract. . . . The rationale for the lesser inclination of courts to inquire into the materiality of a breach of an option condition is that an optionee has a unilateral right. . . . He may choose to compel or not to compel the optionor to a course of performance which intervening facts (*e.g.*, an increase in the value of the optioned rights) may have been made unpalatable to the latter. In the circumstances it may not be too much to ask that a person seeking to keep alive and to exercise option rights turn his corners squarely."

later in this chapter, the so-called "dispatch" or "mailbox" rule makes acceptance of an ordinary revocable offer effective upon dispatch or mailing in contracts by correspondence unless the offer otherwise indicates.[365] The "dispatch" rule, however does not apply to an irrevocable power of acceptance created by an option contract. To be effective, courts generally require such an acceptance to be received to be effective.[366]

[C]   Statutes Making Offers Irrevocable — Firm Offers — Public Policy

[1]   UCC — "Firm Offer"

The common law requirement that an offer without a separate option contract could be revoked though the offeror promised it would be irrevocable for a certain time could result in manifest injustice. The offeree may have in good faith reasonably relied upon the promise of irrevocability, but the offer was still revocable. The best-known statutory response is found in the UCC which is limited to contracts for the sale of goods.

If a merchant[367] makes an offer in a signed[368] writing[369] which, by its terms, gives assurance that it will be held open, the offer will be irrevocable for the time stated in the writing or for a reasonable time, but in no event to exceed three months.[370]

---

[364] *See* Trueman-Aspen Co. v. North Mill Inv. Corp., 728 P.2d 343 (Colo. Ct. App. 1986).

[365] *See infra* § 48.

[366] *See* Santos v. Dean, 96 Wn. App. 849, 855, 982 P. 2d 632, 635 (1999). See RESTATEMENT 2d § 63, comment f, which suggests that acceptances under option contracts must be received because the offeree may not speculate at the expense of the offeror since the offeror has already assumed the risk of such speculation by providing an irrevocable power of acceptance for the time stated in the offer. The *Santos* court notes contrary holdings, e. g., Palo Alto Town & Country Village, Inc. v. BBTC Co., 11 Cal. 3d 494, 113 Cal. Rptr. 705, 521 P.2d 1097 (1974) where the issue is governed by statute.

[367] "Merchant" is defined in § 2-104 of the Code. For most of the sections of Article 2, including the "firm offer" section (2-205), the definition of merchant is so broad that it includes virtually anyone in business. With respect to the implied warranty of merchantability in § 2-314, however, the merchant must be one who regularly deals in goods of that kind. *See* comment 2 to § 2-104.

[368] See UCC § 1-201(37), which includes a very broad definition of "signed," i.e., "any symbol executed or adopted by a party with present intention to adopt or accept a writing." Comment 37 indicates that this would include a printed, stamped or written signature, initials or thumbprint, and in appropriate cases may be satisfied by the printed billhead or letterhead of the purported signer. The comment emphasizes that it is not presenting an exhaustive list of possible ways in which the "signed" requirement may be met since the question is always whether a party had a present intention to adopt or accept the writing.

[369] See UCC § 1-201(43), defining "written" or "writing" as including printing, typewriting or any other intentional reduction to tangible form.

[370] UCC § 2-205. See Taft-Peirce Mfg. Co. v. Seagate Tech., Inc., 789 F. Supp. 1220, 1223 (D.R.I. 1992) (offer assuring irrevocability for 30 days was a firm offer under UCC § 2-205).In New York, a written and signed offer stating that it will be irrevocable for a stated period will be irrevocable for the period stated or, if no time is stated, for a reasonable time, without any limitation to three months or otherwise. N.Y. GEN. OBLIG. LAW § 5-1109. *See* Coastal Aviation v. Commander Aircraft Co., 937 F. Supp. 1051, 1061 (S.D.N.Y. 1996), *aff'd per curiam*, 108 F.3d 1369 (2d Cir. 1997). The statute, however, expressly excepts offers by merchants in contracts for the sale of goods under the UCC since New York, like all other states in the United States except Louisiana, has adopted Article 2 of the Code and § 2-205, therefore, applies exclusively to such offers.

[2]   Three Month Limitation

A UCC firm offer will become revocable at the end of three months regardless of whether it stated a term of irrevocability longer than three months, or whether, in the absence of a stated period, a reasonable time under the circumstances would exceed three months.[371] The section was not designed for long term options[372] and the three month period is considered an absolute limitation. If the offer is "firm" until the occurrence of a contingency that will occur within three months, the offer will remain irrevocable until that time.[373] Thereafter, if the offer has not lapsed, it is revocable.

[3]   Inadvertent Firm Offers

Since merchants sometimes make offers by signing printed forms supplied by the other party, such a form may contain a "firm offer" provision to which the merchant/offeror may not consciously advert. To protect such a party from making an inadvertent firm offer, § 2-205 requires that "any such term of assurance on a form supplied by the offeree must be separately signed by the offeror."[374]

The purpose of the firm offer provision is to effectuate the deliberate intention of a merchant to make an offer binding for a specified time or a reasonable time since the common law rule that offers assuring irrevocability are still revocable is deemed contrary to modern business practices evidenced by the reasonable understanding of merchants.[375] To determine whether a merchant has made a "firm offer" courts search for a manifestation of deliberate intention to keep an offer open. Absent such a manifestation, the offer will be revocable.[376]

[4]   Distinguishing Mere Statements of Duration of an Offer

If an offer from a merchant in a signed writing merely states the time when the offer will lapse, the offer does not contain the necessary assurance that it will be held open and is, therefore, revocable. Otherwise, offerors who intend to make revocable offers of limited duration would be surprised to discover they had made irrevocable offers simply by stating the period after which the offer will lapse. This was not the intention of the drafters of § 2-205. Whether a statement meets the level of assurance to constitute a firm offer will often be left

---

[371] *See* Mid-South Packers, Inc. v. Shoney's, Inc., 761 F.2d 1117 (5th Cir. 1985).

[372] *See* comment 3 to UCC § 2-205.

[373] *Id.*

[374] See UCC § 2-205 and particularly comment 4 to that section. Under the broad definition of "signed" discussed above, the offeror may meet this requirement by the normal device of inserting initials in the space adjacent to the firm offer provision in the printed form supplied by the offeree. This is the normal practice though other forms of separate signing would be acceptable. The separate signing requirement is one of several safeguards found in Article 2 of the Code. A similar requirement is found in § 2-209(2) where a "no oral modification" clause on a form supplied by a merchant must be separately signed by a non-merchant. Still another safeguard is found in § 2-316(2), requiring a written disclaimer of the implied warranty of merchantability to be "conspicuous" as defined in § 1-201(10). These and other safeguards are in keeping with the underlying philosophy of Article 2 to identify, more precisely and fairly, their "agreement," defined in § 1-201((b)(3) as "the bargain of the parties in fact as found in their language or inferred from other circumstances, including course of performance, course of dealing or usage of trade as provided in Section 1-303."

[375] *See* comment 2 to UCC § 2-205 and E. A. Coronis Assocs. v. M. Gordon Constr. Co., 90 N.J. Super. 69, 216 A.2d 246 (1966).

[376] *See* Janke Constr. Co. v. Vulcan Materials Co., 386 F. Supp. 687 (W.D. Wis. 1974), *aff'd*, 527 F.2d 772 (7th Cir. 1976).

to the trier of fact.[377] It is clear, however, that the *assurance* of irrevocability must be expressly stated; it will not be implied.[378]

[5]   CISG and "Firm Offers"

The firm offer concept takes on a significantly different character with respect to international contracts for the sale of goods governed by CISG. While CISG states a general rule that an offer may be revoked at any time before the offeree has dispatched an acceptance of the offer,[379] it is subject to a major qualification: "However, an offer cannot be revoked: (a) if it indicates, whether by stating a fixed time for acceptance or otherwise, that it is irrevocable."[380] Thus, a CISG offer that merely states the duration of the power of acceptance will have the same effect as a UCC firm offer in making the offer irrevocable. Moreover, such a CISG irrevocable offer has no time limitation, i.e., it could be irrevocable for more than three months. This striking difference between CISG and the UCC suggests the necessity of clearly stating the purpose of an offer containing a duration for the exercise of the power of acceptance. If the offeror intends a typical revocable offer with a limited duration to buy or sell goods under a CISG contract, it is essential that the offer state its derogation from Article 16(2)(a) and the retention of the power of revocation. While such a clear qualification may not appear necessary under UCC § 2-205 standards, even here care should be taken to ascertain that a mere statement of duration in the offer is not susceptible to converting the revocable offer to a firm offer.

[6]   Rule 68 Firm Offers

The Federal Rules of Civil Procedure provide that, at least 14 days before the date set for trial, the defendant may serve on the plaintiff an offer to allow judgment on specified terms with costs then accrued. If the offer is not accepted and the judgment the offeree obtains is not more favorable than the unaccepted offer, the offeree must pay the costs incurred after the offer was made.[381] While the rule does not expressly state that such offers are irrevocable, they are typically treated as irrevocable since the rule is designed to put pressure on the plaintiff who will suffer the consequences of not accepting the offer if the litigation result is not more favorable than the terms of the offer. To allow such an offer to be revoked would permit tactical pressuring by the defendant.[382]

---

[377] *See* City Univ. of New York v. Finalco, Inc., 93 A.D.2d 792, 461 N.Y.S.2d 830 (1st Dep't 1983).

[378] Ivey's Plumbing & Elec. Co. v. Petrochem Maintenance, Inc., 463 F. Supp. 543 (N.D. Miss. 1978). If the offer states that the offeree has "the non-exclusive right to purchase . . . for a period of thirty (30) days," it is not a firm offer since it expressly provided that it was non-exclusive. Friedman v. Sommer, 63 N.Y.2d 788, 788, 471 N.E.2d 139, 139 (1984). It is noteworthy that the court in this case applied § 2-205 to a sale of a cooperative apartment which was, according to the court, in reality a sale of securities in a cooperative corporation. The court relied upon Weiss v. Karch, 62 N.Y.2d 849, 477 N.Y.S.2d 615, 466 N.E.2d 155 (1984).

[379] CISG Art. 16(1). It should be noted that CISG does not follow the dispatch or "mailbox" rule of the common law in allowing an acceptance to be effective upon dispatch (reviewed in § 48, *infra*). Under CISG, Art. 18(2), an acceptance does not become effective until it reaches the offeror. When the acceptance is dispatched, however, the offer becomes irrevocable under CISG Art. 16(1).

[380] CISG Art. 16(2)(a).

[381] Fed. R. Civ. Proc. 68 (2009). The 2009 revision changed the former ten-day requirement to 14 days.

[382] See *Pope v. Lil Abner's Corp.*, 92 F. Supp. 1327, 1328 (S.D. Fla. 2000), where the court applied Restatement 2d § 37 in concluding that a counter offer does not terminate such an irrevocable offer See, however, Cesar v. Rubie's Costume Co., 219 F. R. D. 257, 259 (E. D. N. Y. 2004), where the court discusses conflicts among the Circuits concerning

[7]   Are Statutory Firm Offers Options?

UCC Section 2-205 and other "statutory firm offers"[383] may be viewed as option contracts in terms of their effect.[384] These statutes simply remove the consideration requirement of classical option contracts. Again, it must be emphasized that the particular firm offer statute may be limited in ways similar to the UCC with respect to the type of contract involved, qualifications of the offeror ("merchant"), formal requirements of a writing that must be signed, and time limitations. Different statutes will have different limitations.[385] Whether the device is the classical option contract, a statutory firm offer, or one of the devices yet to be discussed in this section, the purpose is the same: to protect the justifiable reliance and expectations of the offeree.

[D]   Irrevocability Through Part Performance — Section 45 of the Restatement 2d

As master of the offer, an offeror may require the offer to be accepted only by promising or only by performing.[386] An offer that expressly prescribes an exclusive manner of acceptance, however, is unusual. The typical offer is the indifferent offer, i. e., the offeror is indifferent as to whether the offer is accepted by promise or by performance.[387] With respect to the typical indifferent offer, the power of acceptance may be exercised in any reasonable manner,[388] but where an offer prescribes an exclusive manner of acceptance, acceptance can occur only in that fashion.[389] Even where there is no express limitation in the offer, the nature of the offer may dictate the manner of acceptance. The obvious example is an offer to the public, such as a reward offer, which does not contemplate a promissory acceptance. Where the offer can only be accepted by performance, the contract will be formed when performance is completed. At that time, a *unilateral* contract will be formed with one right in the former offeree, and one

---

the irrevocability of Rule 68 offers. State rules analogous to Federal Rule 68 may also treat such offers of judgment as irrevocable. Shelton v. Sloan, 127 N. M. 92, 97–98, 977 P.2d 1012,1017–18 (1999).

[383] See *supra* note 370, which contains an analysis of the statutory firm offer in New York.

[384] Restatement 2d § 87(2).

[385] In an auction without reserve, the offer is irrevocable for the reasonable time of the bidding. UCC § 2-328(3). For an analysis of auctions without reserve, *see supra* § 37[A]. Under statutes authorizing or requiring government units to award contracts on the basis of competitive bidding, the public officials may refuse to permit the withdrawal of a bid after it is opened. See Restatement 2d § 87 comment d.

[386] *See* UCC § 2-206(1) ("Unless otherwise unambiguously indicated by the language or the circumstances. . . .") and Restatement 2d § 30(2) ("Unless otherwise indicated by the language or the circumstances. . . .").

[387] This is one of the major changes induced by the UCC and confirmed by the Restatement (Second) of Contracts. *See* John E. Murray, Jr., *Contracts: A New Design for the Agreement Process*, 53 Cornell L. Rev. 785 (1968) and § 46[C], *infra*. Restatement 2d § 60, indicates that the offer may prescribe the place, time or manner of acceptance, all of which must be complied with if the power of acceptance is to be exercised. If the offeror merely *suggests* a permitted place, time or manner of acceptance, however, other methods of acceptance are not precluded. See § 30, comment a. *See* Overman v. Brown, 220 Neb. 788, 372 N.W.2d 102 (1985). *See also* Panhandle E. Pipe Line Co. v. Smith, 637 P.2d 1020 (Wyo. 1981) (where there is a dispute concerning the mode of acceptance, the offer itself must clearly and definitely express an exclusive mode of acceptance).

[388] UCC 2-206(1)(a) and Restatement 2d § 30(2) both allow the typical indifferent offer to be accepted in any reasonable manner.

[389] *See, e.g.*, BC Tire Corp. v. GTE Directories Corp., 46 Wash. App. 351, 730 P.2d 726 (1986) discussed *supra* at note 253.

correlative duty in the former offeror.[390] An attempt by the offeree to accept such an offer by promising would be ineffective. To accept the offer, the offeree must perform the act required by the offeror in exchange for the offeror's promise. There is only one promisor and one promisee in such a contract. On the basis of this analysis, and remembering the common law obsession that offers are revocable absent an option contract, a problem arises. Its classic exposition is found in the following hypothetical created by Professor Wormser.

> A offers to pay B $100 if B will walk across the Brooklyn bridge and B can accept only by performing, i.e., walking across the bridge. B wants to accept the offer and begins walking across the bridge. When B is halfway across, A shouts, "I revoke the offer." At this point, there is no contract since A did not offer to pay B in exchange for B's walking partway across the bridge. B must complete the act to accept the offer and form the contract. A's duty and B's correlative right to payment, therefore, do not arise until B completes the walk across the bridge.[391]

The example was reiterated most recently by the court in *Dahl v. HEM Pharmaceuticals Corporation.*[392]

Classical contract theory requires A's revocation to be effective since the offer was revocable. Yet, the result is harsh to B who has begun to perform in the only manner possible to accept the offer only to have his attempt to complete performance and accept the offer revoked. The revocation was effective since the offeree, B, had not promised to walk across the bridge that would have created a duty to complete the walk across the bridge. Moreover, B's promise would have be ineffective to exercise the power of acceptance of an offer that required an acceptance by performance. Since B was not bound to complete the walk, the logic of offer and acceptance rules dictated that A should not be bound prior to the completion of the walk by B. Otherwise, one party would be bound and the other party would not be bound.

While such an offeree has no duty to complete the act, however, by starting to perform, he evidences a present intention to complete performance in reliance on the offer with a reasonable expectation that there will be an opportunity to complete performance. If X offered Y $1,000 to paint X's house and insisted that the offer could only be accepted by performance, a revocation of the offer after the house was half-painted would not form a contract, but it would allow the offeree to recover the reasonable value of the benefit conferred on the offeror.[393] There is, however, no measurable benefit to A in by B walking half way across the bridge. Indeed, there is no measurable benefit to A if B had completed the walk across the bridge. A restitutionary remedy is, therefore, precluded. Yet, the offeree has suffered the detriment of expending time and effort in performing the act that was requested by the offeror

---

[390] A description of unilateral vs. bilateral contracts is found in § 18 *supra.*

[391] This famous example is found in Wormser, *The True Conception of Unilateral Contracts*, 26 Yale L. J. 136 (1916).

[392] 7 F. 3d 1399 (9th Cir. 1999). Eighteen people participated in a "double blind" experiment of a drug in exchange for the promise to provide a year's supply of the drug at no cost to the participants who completed the experiment. The defendant refused to perform its promise on the footing that the participants were free to withdraw at any time. The court reminded the defendant of the "category of unilateral contracts," citing the Brooklyn Bridge illustration and held that, upon completing the experiment, the participants had accepted the offer and a binding contract was formed.

[393] In such a case, no contract would exist since the act was not completed. However, when one party confers a requested benefit on another and there is a contemplation that the performing party expects to be compensated, an action in quasi contract may lie to prevent the unjust enrichment of the offeror at the expense of the offeree. The restitution interest of the offeree is thereby protected. An analysis of the restitution interest later in this volume.

up to the point of revocation.[394] The manifest injustice resulting from permitting the offeror to revoke as the offeree is attempting to complete performance had to be overcome. The only issue was the theory that would be devised to support the inevitable solution.

The "Bilateral" Theory. One of the earliest theories solved the problem very simply: When the offeree begins performance, the contract takes on a bilateral character, i.e., we will treat the beginning of performance as the offeree's promise to complete performance.[395] There is, however, considerable difficulty in discovering how an offer for a unilateral contract takes on a bilateral character through the offeree's part performance.[396] Moreover, if the offeree, who has not promised to complete performance decides, after part performance, to stop performing, the offeree would be said to have breached the contract formed by the part performance. It was important to develop another theory that did not contain these analytical and practical impediments.

First Restatement § 45 — Conditional Contract. The FIRST RESTATEMENT announced its theory in what became one of the more familiar sections of that work, Section 45.[397] Under this theory, a contract is formed upon part performance, but the offeror's duty under that contract is conditioned upon his receiving the completed performance requested in the offer within the time stated in the offer or, in the absence of a stated time, within a reasonable time. A case which antedated the original § 45 disclosed an offer to the offeror's son-in-law which stated that if he would move from Missouri to Maine and care for the offeror for the remainder of her life, he would have the offeror's farm upon her death. The court held that the contract was complete when the offeree moved from Missouri to Maine, but the offeree would not be entitled to the farm unless he performed the condition to the offeror's duty, i.e., caring for her until her death.[398] While this theory is superior to the "bilateral" theory, it does not reflect the manifested intention of the offeror who did not want part performance as an acceptance, but full performance. In the offer to the son-in-law, full performance could not possibly occur until the death of the offeror. By placing a duty on the offeror when the offeree performed in part, however, the theory manages to avoid revocation of the offer, thereby protecting the offeree against harsh results. At the same time, by implying a condition to the constructed duty of the offeror upon part performance that the remainder of performance must occur before the duty is activated, the original § 45 achieves the necessary result and still permits the offeree to refuse to complete performance with impunity. Though the result is just, instead of resorting to several fictions, a straightforward theory is set forth in the comment to the original § 45: " 'The main offer includes as a subsidiary promise, necessarily implied, that if part of the

---

[394] There is no requirement that a discernible benefit be found a promisor. There is "consideration" to support the promise if there is a detriment to the promisee as seen in Chapter 3.

[395] *See* Los Angeles Traction Co. v. Wilshire, 135 Cal. 654, 67 P. 1086 (1902).

[396] "This is a remarkable instance of confusion of thought. By what magic the offer had been turned into a 'contract' does not appear." Ashley, *Offers Calling for a Consideration Other Than a Counter Promise*, 23 HARV. L. REV. 159, 164 (1910).

[397] § 45 of the FIRST RESTATEMENT reads as follows: "If an offer for a unilateral contract is made, and part of the consideration requested in the offer is given or tendered by the offeree in response thereto, the offeror is bound by a contract, the duty of immediate performance of which is conditioned on full consideration being given or tendered within the time stated in the offer, or, if no time is stated, within a reasonable time."

[398] Brackenbury v. Hodgkin, 116 Me. 399, 102 A. 106 (1917). *See also* Winslow v. White, 163 N.C. 29, 79 S.E. 258 (1913). Holland v. Earl G. Graves Publ'g Co., 46 F. Supp. 2d 681, 687 (E.D. Mich. 1998), records Illustration 6 to RESTATEMENT 2d § 45, suggesting an identical situation but a different "option contract" theory discussed below.

requested performance is given, the offeror will not revoke his offer, and that if tender is made it will be accepted."[399]

While this theory implies a promise, it is a more than plausible implication and arrives at the desired result without the necessity of any further implication or fiction. Moreover, it preserves the intention of the offeror and the reasonable understanding of the offeree that no contract is formed until performance is completed. It was the forerunner to new theory in the Second Restatement.

Second Restatement § 45 — "Option Contract." The RESTATEMENT 2d § 45 also implies a subsidiary promise not to revoke the offer. The only difference is that the implied subsidiary promise is accepted by part performance, forming an option contract.[400]

Section 45, in its original FIRST RESTATEMENT form or in the option contract mode of the RESTATEMENT 2d, can be applied to any offer requiring a performance acceptance where the question of revocability of the offer occurs. It has been applied in a cluster of cases involving services by employees pursuant to retirement plans or other employee benefits.[401] It also appears in cases involving performance by real estate brokers under exclusive agency or exclusive right to sell arrangements[402] and sundry other applications. Where a father promised to devise property to each of his three sons in equal shares in exchange for the completion of certain improvements to the property, the father died after the sons had begun performance which they completed after the father's death. While death normally revokes an offer, under § 45, the court held that the sons' part performance made the offer irrevocable and allowed the sons to complete the performance after the offeror's death.[403] There is no question that the concept is universally accepted.[404]

---

[399] FIRST RESTATEMENT § 45 comment b.

[400] RESTATEMENT 2d § 45 states: "(1) Where an offeror invites an offeree to accept by rendering a performance and does not invite a promissory acceptance, an option contract is created when the offeree begins the invited performance or tenders part of it. (2) The offeror's duty of performance under any option contract so created is conditional on completion or tender of the invited performance in accordance with the terms of the offer."

[401] The application of the unilateral contract theory in employee terminable-at-will situations has been explored in § 39[B][6], *supra*. In DeMasse v. ITT Corp., 194 Ariz. 500, 506, 984 P.2d 1138, 1144 note 3 (1999), the court cited RESTATEMENT 2d § 45 in stating, "In the unilateral or at-will context, once the offer is accepted by commencement of performance, the terms cannot be change. Thus, if an employer offers a day's pay for a day's work, the employer cannot, after employee performance, reduce the offer of pay that induced the performance." *See also* Marvel v. Dannemann, 490 F. Supp. 170 (D. Del. 1980); Dangott v. ASG Indus., Inc., 558 P.2d 379 (Okla. 1976); Taylor v. Multnomah County Deputy Sheriff's Retirement Bd., 265 Or. 445, 510 P.2d 339 (1973); Sylvestre v. State, 298 Minn. 142, 214 N.W.2d 658 (1973).

[402] Under an "exclusive agency," the owner may still sell the property himself. Under an "exclusive right to sell," he may not do so. Cases applying § 45 in situations involving performance by real estate brokers include Ranier Fund v. Blomfield Real Estate Co., 717 P.2d 850 (Alaska 1986); Ladd v. Teichman, 359 Mich. 587, 103 N.W.2d 338 (1960); Hutchinson v. Dobson-Brainbridge Realty Co., 31 Tenn. App. 490, 217 S.W.2d 6 (1946). It has also been applied to a real estate broker's situation involving a non-exclusive agency: Marchiondo v. Scheck, 78 N.M. 440, 432 P.2d 405 (1967).

[403] Eaton v. Eaton, 2005 Del. Ch. LEXIS 202 (Ct. Ch. 2005).

[404] Professor Wormser, who created the famous Brooklyn bridge hypothetical, recanted more than three decades later: "[N]ow, clad in sackcloth, I state frankly, that my point of view has changed. I agree, at this time, with the rule set forth in the Restatement. . . ." Book Review, 3 J. LEGAL EDUC. 145, 146 (1950).

[1]   Starting Performance Versus Preparation

For an offer to become irrevocable under § 45, what is tendered or performed must be part of the actual performance required by the offer to preclude revocation of the offer. Beginning preparations, no matter how necessary, are insufficient.[405] The line between performance and mere preparation, in a given case, may not be very bright. It can be particularly difficult when the act requested by the offer is one that can be performed almost instantaneously. The classic example is found in the well-known case of *Petterson v. Pattberg*.[406] The holder of a mortgage (the mortgagee) offered to accept a discount from the full amount due on the mortgage debt in exchange for the payment of the lesser amount in advance of the original maturity date. The offeree (mortgagor) proceeded to raise the money which he brought to the residence of the offeror and, after identifying himself said, "I have come to pay off the mortgage." The offeror answered, "I have sold the mortgage," which was a revocation of the offer. If performance had begun, the offer could not be revoked. What was the performance required by the offer? The court held that the required performance was the act of "payment" which required the cooperation of the offeror, i.e., the act of payment requires a tender of the payment (by the offeree) *and* the acceptance of that payment by the offeror. By presenting himself at the door of the offeror and announcing that he had come to pay off the mortgage, the court held that the offeree had not tendered payment but had merely taken the necessary preparatory step to make a tender. Since the entire act of tender is completed in a moment, it is difficult to apply a § 45 analysis to this type of act though it is theoretically possible to do so.

If the offeree had simply knocked at the door and, upon the offeror opening the door, the offeree extended his hand containing the full payment of cash, a tender would have been completed making the offer irrevocable before the offeror attempted to revoke by saying "I have sold the mortgage." Absent an actual tender, the offer had not become irrevocable and the court so decided. The author of the majority opinion, however, stated his individual view that the result would not have changed even if the offeree had made a tender of payment.[407] Such an analysis is fundamentally flawed. The court treats the mortgagor as an offeree with a power of acceptance to pay off the mortgage at a discount price by paying early. The only way he could exercise that power of acceptance was by tendering the payment before the offeror revoked the offer. If the offeror refused to cooperate in accepting the money, the offeree was powerless to insist that it be taken. Thus, if a tender of payment had occurred in this case, the offeree would have done more than begin performance by such a tender; he would have *completed* performance by that tender since he could perform no additional act to accept the offer. The RESTATEMENT 2d deals effectively with this situation by finding an acceptance upon tender.[408] It is also clear that where an "offeror" reserves a power to revoke even after the offeree has begun performance, there is no offer since the offeree has no power of acceptance.[409]

---

[405] RESTATEMENT 2d § 45, comment f.

[406] 248 N.Y. 86, 161 N.E. 428 (1928).

[407] Justice Kellogg stated his "individual view" at 248 N. Y. At 90, 161 N. E. at 430.

[408] *See* RESTATEMENT 2d § 45(1), ". . . an option contract is created when the offeree *tenders* or begins performance" (emphasis added), and comment c. Nine years after the *Petterson* case, New York enacted a statute precluding revocation of a signed offer after tender, N.Y. GEN. OBLIG. LAW § 15-503.

[409] See Transport Workers Union, Local 290 v. SEPTA, 145 F.3d 619, 624 (3d Cir. 1998) (quoting RESTATEMENT 2d § 45, comment b: "A reservation of power to revoke after performance has begun means that as yet there is no promise and no offer.").

Again, the offeree in *Petterson* did not begin performance. Rather, he prepared to perform. Another well-known case provides assistance in drawing the line between preparation and performance In *White v. Corlies*,[410] the offeror desired the remodeling of his office and received specifications from the offeree. Satisfied with the specifications, the offeror stated, "You may begin at once." The offeree purchased lumber and began to work on the lumber prior to the revocation. The work he performed, however, was suitable for many other applications, i.e., it was not specifically referable to the performance required by the offer. The court, therefore, held that performance had not begun. The RESTATEMENT 2d adopts this case as a basis for an illustration[411] and suggests that the distinction between preparing for performance and beginning performance may turn on, *inter alia*, "the extent to which the offeree's conduct is clearly referable to the offer."[412]

[2]   Reconciling the Mitigation Principle

A final problem is raised in reconciling the § 45 theory with the general principle of contract law concerning the mitigation of damages. Where *A* and *B* have formed a bilateral contract and before the performance by *B* is complete, *A* informs *B* that *A* will not perform his duty under the contract, *A* has committed a total breach—a repudiation of the contract. The mitigation of damages principle precludes the aggrieved party, *B*, from recovering any damages he could have avoided without undue difficulty or expense if he had stopped performing at the time *A* announced that he would not perform.[413] If *A*'s offer demanded a performance acceptance, the contract would not be formed until B completed performance. If the condition to *A*'s duty is the completion of performance by *B*, under § 45 *B* would face the dilemma of either completing performance and violating the mitigation principle, or ceasing performance and not fulfilling the condition to *A*'s duty. The problem is solved by *excusing* the condition to the activation of *A*'s duty if the offeror prevents performance or repudiates the contract.[414]

In such a case, normal recovery would be measured by the contract price promised by *A*, less any amount B saved by not having to perform the remainder of the contract. A full recovery, however, is possible in such a case. In *Harwood v. Avaya, Inc.*[415] the plaintiffs were offered retention bonuses if they would continue to work for the defendant corporation until March 31, 2005, but they were discharged prior to that date. The court recognized that § 45(2) of the RESTATEMENT 2d conditioned the employer's duty to pay the bonuses only upon completion of the performances to March 31, 2005. Under comment e to § 45, however, the court explained that completion of performance is excused where the offeror prevents that performance as in this case. Since the plaintiffs had not completed performance, the defendant argued that the plaintiffs were entitled to only a pro rata share of the bonuses to the time they were discharged. The court disagreed. Treating the early discharge as the defendant's repudiation of the contract, the court held that the plaintiffs were entitled to their expectations

---

[410] 46 N.Y. 467 (1871).

[411] *See* RESTATEMENT 2d § 62 ill. 1.

[412] RESTATEMENT 2d § 45 comment f.

[413] There is no "duty" on the part of the innocent party, *B*, to mitigate (avoid) damages by acting reasonably after the breach. *B*, however, may not recover damages he could have avoided after that time. The mitigation principle is fully explored in § 123, *infra*.

[414] *See* RESTATEMENT 2d § 45 comment e. Complete performance by the offeree may also be waived by the offeror.

[415] 2007 U. S. Dist. LEXIS 61899 (S. D. Ohio 2007).

and awarded them the full measure of the promised bonuses which could be proved with sufficient certainty in this case.[416]

[E]   Irrevocability Through Reliance — General Contractor and Subcontractors

One of the major validation devices that will be explored in the next chapter dealing with the validation process is detrimental reliance, popularly known as "promissory estoppel." In essence, that device makes a promise enforceable if the promisee justifiably suffers a detriment by changing his position in reliance on the promise where the promisor should reasonably expect his promise to induce such reliance.[417] The question arises, may an *offer* become irrevocable if the offeree has relied on that offer? It would be a simple matter for any offeree to rely upon any offer and thereby attempt to make an otherwise revocable offer irrevocable. Absent one or more of the devices explored in this section, the common law principle that offers are revocable remains steadfast. If the X Corporation offers to sell steel to the Y Corporation, Y may pursue activity with the expectation of accepting the X offer. It may prepare to receive steel from X; it may reject an offer from another potential supplier because it intends to accept X's offer; Y may even change its production plans in anticipation of receiving the steel from X. Absent other circumstances, this type of reliance on a typical offer is not justifiable. Y may engage in any number of preparatory steps which, we have seen, will not make the offer irrevocable since performance has not begun. Whatever activity Y may pursue in anticipation of a contract with X, it is commercially unreasonable to pursue such action before exercising its power of acceptance in response to X's offer. X has no reason to assume that its offer has induced Y to change its position in reliance on the offer. X reasonably expects that Y will either accept or reject the offer, but not change its position in reliance on the offer before accepting the offer. Thus, regardless of Y's activity, X may revoke the offer. There are, however, situations where reliance on an offer may be justifiable.

The paradigm case involves an offer by a subcontractor to a general contractor who intends to submit a bid (offer) on a particular building project. General contractors must assemble their bids from a series of subcontractors' bids — the plumbing, electrical, carpentry, masonry and other necessary parts of a building project. Having assembled all of the sub bids, the general contractor submits its complete bid/offer on the entire project. Typically, the general's bid/offer will be irrevocable.[418] Each subcontractor submitting a bid to the general contractor knows or has reason to know that the general's bid is irrevocable. The general contractor, however, is in no position to accept the bids of the subcontractors used in making the general bid because it may not be awarded the contract and would have no use for the labor and materials to be supplied by the subcontractors. If, however, the general is the winner of the competitive bidding contest, it is contractually bound to complete the entire project at the bid price, the price predicated on the various bids of subcontractors the general has used in computing the total bid. Though it has been awarded the contract, however, the general has

---

[416] 2007 U. S. Dist. LEXIS 61899 at*26–28.

[417] *See* RESTATEMENT 2d § 90.

[418] "[W]hen statutes authorize or require that government work be awarded to contractors on the basis of competitive bidding, it may be fairly implied that the public officials in charge may protect the integrity of the competition by refusing to allow a bid to be withdrawn after bids are opened." RESTATEMENT 2d § 87 comment d. General contractors submit a bid bond issued by a bonding company to assure the performance of the building contract according to the bid price if the general is awarded the contract and fails to perform.

yet to accept the offers of the subcontractors who provided the necessary sub bids (offers). May one or more of the subcontractors be able to revoke their offers before the general has an opportunity to accept the very offers used in computing his bid?

This was the issue in two cases with differing opinions authored by two of the judicial giants of the twentieth century, Judge Learned Hand of the United States Court of Appeals for the Second Circuit, and Justice Roger Traynor of the Supreme Court of California. The more specific issue was whether detrimental reliance (promissory estoppel)[419] which had been applied to unbargained-for promises[420] should now be applied to a commercial transaction in a bargained-for exchange context. In *James Baird Company v. Gimbel Brothers, Inc.*, Judge Hand wrote:

> Offers are ordinarily made in exchange for consideration, either a counter-promise or some other act which the promisor wishes to secure. In such cases they propose bargains; they presuppose that each promise or performance is an inducement to the other. . . . But a man may make a promise without expecting an equivalent; a donative promise, conditional or absolute. The common law provided for such by sealed instruments, and it is unfortunate that these are no longer generally available. The doctrine of 'promissory estoppel' is to avoid the harsh results of allowing the promisor in such a case to repudiate when the promisee has acted in reliance upon the promise. . . . But an offer for an exchange is not meant to become a promise until a consideration has been received, either a counter-promise or whatever else is stipulated. To extend it would be to hold the offeror regardless of the stipulated condition of his offer. . . . There is no room in such a situation for the doctrine of 'promissory estoppel.'[421]

Justice Traynor did not agree:

> When plaintiff [general contractor] used defendant's [subcontractor's] offer in computing his own bid, he bound himself to perform in reliance on defendant's terms. Though defendant did not bargain for this use of its bid neither did defendant make it idly, indifferent to whether it would be used or not. On the contrary, it is reasonable to suppose that defendant submitted its bid to obtain the subcontract. It was bound to realize the substantial possibility that its bid would be the lowest, and that it would be included by plaintiff in his bid. It was to its own interest that the contractor be awarded the general contract; the lower the subcontract bid, the lower the general contractor's bid was likely to be and the greater its chance of acceptance and hence the greater the defendant's chance of getting the . . . subcontract. Defendant had reason not only to expect plaintiff to rely on its bid but to want him to. Clearly defendant had a stake in plaintiff's reliance on its bid. Given this interest and the fact that plaintiff is bound by his own bid, it is only fair that plaintiff should have at least an opportunity to accept defendant's bid after the general contract has been awarded to him.[422]

---

[419] As will be seen, the antecedents of promissory estoppel are very old, even older than the traditional validation device, consideration.

[420] The typical case was a gift promise with reliance, such as a charitable subscription promise. See the most famous exposition of this doctrine in such a context in the opinion by Benjamin Cardozo in Allegheny College v. National Chautauqua County Bank, 246 N.Y. 369, 159 N.E. 173 (1927).

[421] James Baird Co. v. Gimbel Bros., Inc., 64 F.2d 344, 346 (2d Cir. 1933).

[422] Drennan v. Star Paving Co., 51 Cal. 2d 409, 333 P.2d 757, 760 (1958).

Justice Traynor analogized the situation to one under RESTATEMENT § 45 making the offer irrevocable upon part performance, and specifically relied upon a Comment to § 45 in the original RESTATEMENT: "[M]erely acting in justifiable reliance on an offer may in some cases serve as sufficient reason for making a promise binding (*see* § 90)."[423] That concept is now reflected in a separate section of the RESTATEMENT 2d.[424] Traynor discovered an implied subsidiary promise on the part of the subcontractor not to revoke the offer since the subcontractor must have foreseen the reasonable change of position in reliance upon its offer by the general contractor, whose expected course of performance was to include the subcontractor's bid in the general bid. Having implied the subsidiary promise, the detrimental reliance of the general contractor was sufficient to make the subcontractor's offer irrevocable for a reasonable time. In effect, an option contract was created through detrimental reliance rather than part performance, providing the offeree/general contractor with an irrevocable power of acceptance for a reasonable time after being awarded the general contract.

Both solutions to the subcontractor/general contractor problem suggest potentially negative ramifications. Under the Hand approach, the general contractor will have no legal remedy where the subcontractor revokes before the general accepts the sub's offer, though the general's bid has been accepted. Under the Traynor approach, the general need not accept the bid of the subcontractor after being awarded the contract since the general made no promise to the subcontractor.[425] This creates the unfortunate situation of one party being bound while the other (general) is not bound. Some general contractors may use the lowest subcontractors' bids in order to get the job and then make contracts with other subcontractors with whom they intended to contract from the inception. This practice and others favoring the general contractor, who often has superior bargaining power in any event, wars against the application of the Traynor position.[426] Justice Traynor sought to overcome some of the potential inequities in his analysis by insisting that a general contractor is not free to delay acceptance after being awarded the contract, nor can the general reopen bargaining with the subcontractor and still claim an irrevocable power of acceptance with respect to the original offer, i.e., delays in acceptance or attempts to "chisel" the price with the subcontractor will result in the loss of the irrevocable power of acceptance.[427] Statutory protection of subcontractors is also afforded in some jurisdictions by requiring that the general list the names of the subcontractors in his bids[428] and that such named subcontractors may not be changed by the general contractor without the consent of the owner.[429] A subcontractor may also negate any reasonable reliance

---

[423] FIRST RESTATEMENT § 45 comment b.

[424] RESTATEMENT 2d § 87(2).

[425] Milone & Tucci, Inc. v. Bona Fide Builders, Inc., 49 Wash. 2d 363, 301 P.2d 759 (1956); Williams v. Favret, 161 F.2d 822 (5th Cir. 1947).

[426] See Schultz, *The Firm Offer Puzzle: A Study of Business Practice in the Construction Industry*, 19 U. Chi. L. Rev. 237 (1952), *cited in* Pavel Enters., Inc. v. A. S. Johnson Co., Inc., 342 Md. 143, 674 A.2d 521 (1996), where the court indicates that the substantial and detrimental reliance required to make the subcontractor's offer irrevocable can dissipate where the general contractor engages in actions that belie such reliance such as bid shopping, "bid chopping," "bid peddling" or delay in accepting the subcontractor's offer after being awarded the contract on the entire project. *See also* Note, *Another Look at Construction Bidding and Contracts at Formation*, 53 VA. L. REV. 1720 (1967).

[427] Drennan v. Star Paving Co., 51 Cal. 2d 409, 333 P.2d 757, 760 (1958).

[428] *See*, e. g., MASS. ANN. LAWS ch. 149, §§ 44A-44I and particularly § 44F (1980).

[429] *See* Subletting and Subcontracting Fair Practices Act, CAL. GOV'T CODE § 4100 *et seq.*, particularly § 4107 proscribing the substitution by the prime contractor of a subcontractor listed in the original bid. *See* Coast Pump Assocs. v. Stephen Tyler Corp., 62 Cal. App. 3d 421, 133 Cal. Rptr. 88 (1st Dist. 1976).

by a general contractor by expressly stating that its bid should not be relied on. Where a general contractor sent a bid form to subcontractors stating that the bid had to be held open for a minimum of 60 days, a subcontractor submitted a bid expressly stating that its bid was for informational purposes only, did not constitute a "firm" offer, and should not be relied on. Nonetheless the general contractor used the bid in the total bid on the project. When the general was awarded the contract, the subcontractor insisted on a higher price. The court found that the subcontractor's bid did not even amount to a counter offer because it expressly disclaimed an intention to be bound. It held that, while the subcontractor may have exhausted any goodwill it had "by bucking industry custom," the language of the disclaimer in its bid was so plain that it had to be enforced.[430]

Where the subcontractor simply presents a bid to the general contractor, the overwhelming majority of courts considering this question have adopted the Traynor position.[431] It is also supported by the RESTATEMENT 2d which characterizes an offer by a subcontractor made irrevocable by detrimental reliance as another form of option contract.[432] In keeping with its general concept of detrimental reliance to be explored later in this volume, the RESTATEMENT 2d limits the option contract protection "to the extent necessary to avoid injustice."[433] Presumably, any nefarious activity on the part of the general contractor after being awarded the general contract by, for example, unnecessarily delaying the acceptance of the subcontractor's offer or attempting to renegotiate with the subcontractor for a lower price, would eliminate the protection of an irrevocable offer enjoyed by the general contractor under this RESTATEMENT provision.

CISG: Irrevocability of Offers Through Reliance. Our exploration of promissory estoppel in the ensuing chapter will recognize the availability of the concept of detrimental reliance to protect reliance interests in pre-formation situations other than the subcontractor-general contractor model, even where there may be no offer.[434] Yet, as we have already indicated, the common law view that offers are revocable wars against making offers irrevocable on the basis of detrimental reliance.[435] The subcontractor/general contractor situation explored above is a rare exception because of the subcontractor's clear expectation that the general contractor will rely on the sub's offer. In typical bargaining situations, offerors do not reasonably expect the offeree to rely on the offer. International sale of goods contracts to which CISG applies,

---

[430] Fletcher-Harlee Corp. v. Pote Concrete Contractors, Inc., 482 F. 3d 247 (3d Cir. 2007).

[431] For a cogent analysis of the Hand/Traynor positions, see Pavel Enters., Inc. v. A. S. Johnson Co., Inc., 342 Md. 143, 674 A.2d 521 (1996). Other courts adopting the Traynor analysis include Arango Constr. Co. v. Success Roofing, Inc., 46 Wash. App. 314, 730 P.2d 720 (1986); Powers Constr. Co. v. Salem Carpets, Inc., 283 S.C. 302, 322 S.E.2d 30 (Ct. App. 1984); Illinois Valley Asphalt, Inc. v. J. F. Edwards Constr. Co., 90 Ill. App. 3d 768, 413 N.E.2d 209 (3d Dist. 1980); Montgomery Indus. Int'l, Inc. v. Thomas Constr. Co., 620 F.2d 91 (5th Cir. 1980) (Texas law); Janke Constr. Co. v. Vulcan Materials Co., 386 F. Supp. 687 (W.D. Wis. 1974); James King & Son, Inc. v. De Santis Constr. No. 2 Corp., 97 Misc. 2d 1063, 413 N.Y.S.2d 78 (Sup. Ct. 1977); Constructors Supply Co. v. Bostrom Sheet Metal Works, Inc., 291 Minn. 113, 190 N.W.2d 71 (1971); N. Litterio & Co. v. Glassman Constr. Co., 115 U.S. App. D.C. 335, 319 F.2d 736 (1963). But see Home Elec. Co. v. Hall & Underdown Heating & Air Conditioning Co., 86 N.C. App. 540, 358 S.E.2d 539 (1987), which rejects the promissory estoppel application in the subcontractor/contractor situation.

[432] RESTATEMENT 2d § 87(2) and comment e.

[433] *Id.*

[434] *See* Pop's Cones v. Resorts Int'l Hotel, Inc., 307 N.J. Super. 461, 704 A.2d 1321 (App. Div. 1998); Hoffman v. Red Owl Stores, Inc., 26 Wis. 2d 683, 133 N.W.2d 267 (1965); Wheeler v. White, 398 S.W.2d 93 (Tex. 1965); Goodman v. Dicker, 169 F.2d 684, 83 U.S. App. D.C. 353 (1948).

[435] See text after note 402 *supra.*

however, may suggest a different view. CISG permits an offer to become irrevocable "if it was reasonable for the offeree to rely on the offer as being irrevocable and the offeree has acted in reliance on the offer."[436] While this broad language, alone, may suggest no necessary conflict with American law, there is some additional evidence that CISG would take a broader view. For example, while domestic law would not regard mere preparation to accept an offer as sufficient reliance to make an offer irrevocable, certain CISG commentary that may be viewed as legislative history suggests that "[e]xtensive *investigation* to determine whether [one] should accept and offer" may constitute justifiable reliance to make the offer irrevocable.[437] Such a difference would not be remarkable in light of the civil law influence that pervades CISG and the propensity of the civil law to make offers irrevocable.

§ 45 ACCEPTANCE OF OFFER TO FORM A CONTRACT

[A] The Essence of Acceptance

An acceptance is a manifestation of assent made by the offeree in a manner invited or required by the offer.[438] We have already seen that an offer confers upon the offeree a power of acceptance that causes a contract to come into being where the offeree provides the act, forbearance or promise required or invited by the offer that manifests assent to the offer.[439] It is important to emphasize the dual nature of the act of acceptance. Normally, when the offeree makes the promise or performs the act required or invited by the offer, the promise or act, itself, manifests assent to the offer. There are, however, cases where this is not so as will appear from the exploration that follows.

[B] Can an Offer Be Accepted Without Knowledge of Its Existence?

It is possible for a person to perform an act required to accept an offer without knowledge that the offer exists. A person may, for example, bring about the arrest and conviction of a criminal not knowing that a reward has been offered for the act which has been performed. Does a contract come into being under these circumstances? The typical reward offer contemplates a bargain, i.e., it seeks to induce action on the part of any member of the public capable of such action. If a person acted without knowledge of the reward, he was not induced to act by the reward offer and had no expectation of receiving payment under the reward offer when he completed the act. He had, therefore, no power of acceptance; he was not an offeree. The case law is clear that no contract can come into existence unless the offeree knew of the offer when he or she performed the act required by the offer.[440] Governmental bodies may

---

[436] CISG, Art. 16(2)(b).

[437] The United Nations Conference on Contracts for the International Sale of Goods-Official Records, U. N. Doc. A/Conf. 97/19 at 22 (1981) (emphasis added).

[438] Fosson v. Palace (Waterland), Ltd., 78 F.3d 1448, 1453 (9th Cir. 1996) (quoting RESTATEMENT 2d § 50).

[439] *See* Contempo Constr. Co. v. Mountain States Tel. & Tel. Co., 153 Ariz. 279, 736 P.2d 13 (Ct. App. 1987), RESTATEMENT 2d § 50 and *supra* § 34.

[440] *See* Drown v. Howlett, 1999 U.S. Dist. LEXIS 19834, at *5 (D. Neb. Dec. 21, 1999); Alexander v. Russo, 1 Kan. App. 2d 546, 571 P.2d 350 (1977); Sumerel v. Pinder, 83 So. 2d 692 (Fla. 1955); Glover v. Jewish War Veterans, 68 A.2d 233 (Mun. Ct. App. D.C. 1949); Broadnax v. Ledbetter, 100 Tex. 375, 99 S.W. 1111 (1907). *Accord* RESTATEMENT 2d § 23 comment c and RESTATEMENT 2d § 51 comment a. See, however, Anderson v. Douglas & Lomason Co., 540 N.W.2d 277 (Iowa 1995), involving a purported offer in an employee handbook distributed to all employees where the court

provide standing reward offers to create an atmosphere in which people do certain acts with the hope of earning unknown rewards and the performance of the required act without knowledge of the reward may, in such "public" reward cases, give rise to recovery of the offered amount.[441] The preferable governmental award analysis is that the reward is paid for policy reasons, e.g., creating an atmosphere of assistance in the minds of the citizenry in assisting governmental authorities to bring criminals to justice, beyond a contractual analysis.[442]

It may be desirable to treat reward offers, private or governmental, as payable to parties who perform the desired act regardless of knowledge, i.e., to treat all reward cases beyond the traditional categories of offer and acceptance. A party who performs the requested act, albeit without knowledge of the reward, may reasonably expect to receive the reward for his services when he subsequently learns of it. The case law denying such recoveries is based on the offer/acceptance analysis which appears sound only because it is the traditional analysis which suggests a procrustean quality. It has made reward offers fit the bed of contracts analysis without regard for the reasonable disappointment it may engender. Perhaps it is time to recognize that such an analysis need not be mandated in the reward offer situation.[443]

Since an offer cannot be accepted without knowledge of its existence, the Restatement 2d states that offers which cross each other in the mail do not create a contract though they happen to contain identical terms.[444] If, however, one party creates a reasonable understanding in the other that an offer or acceptance exists, that reasonable understanding will be protected. If *A* sends what appears to be an offer to *B*, even though the writing sent by *A* was drafted by a third party and *A* was unaware of its contents, *B* has a power of acceptance. Similarly, if *A* intentionally sends an offer in a letter to *B* who decides to manifest acceptance without reading the letter, there is a contract though *B* literally did not know of the offer.[445] This is in keeping with the necessary objectivity of regarding the manifestations of the parties as controlling[446] and permitting manifestations of assent to be operative in accordance with the intention of the party who neither knew nor had reason to know of the other party's lack of intention to assent.[447]

---

emphasized that it was not an individually negotiated transaction, but a standardized agreement between the employer and a class of employees. The employee had not read the portions of the handbook upon which he was pursuing his claim, but the court held it was unnecessary since standardized agreements should treat alike all of those similarly situated. The court, however, also emphasized that its holding was a "narrow divergence" from the usual rule that it is impossible to become an offeree without knowledge of the offer. In pursuance of the "narrowness" of the holding, it has been more recently relegated to the unilateral contract situation illustrated by employee handbook cases. Thus, it would have no application to a bilateral contract. See Owen v. MBPXLI Corp., 173 F. Supp. 2d 905 (N. D. Iowa 2001). *See* also § 39[B][6]. *supra.*

[441] *See* California Teachers Ass'n v. Cory, 155 Cal App. 3d 494, 508, 202 Cal. Rptr. 611, 619 (3d Dist. 1984). *See also* State v. Malm, 143 Conn. 462, 123 A.2d 276 (1956).

[442] *See* Restatement 2d § 23 comment c.

[443] Under a contracts analysis, a civic-minded person with no knowledge of the reward offer will not be entitled to it upon providing information leading to the arrest and conviction of the party who committed the crime. A mercenary will provide such information only when induced to do so by a reward offer.

[444] *See* Restatement 2d § 23 comment d and illustration 4. *supra* § 31.

[445] Restatement 2d § 23 comment b. In Scwartz v. Comcast Corp., 256 Fed. Appx. 515 (3d Cir. 2007, the court quoted this comment to the effect that where an offer is contained in a writing, the offeree may, without reading it, manifest assent to it, binding himself to its terms.

[446] *See supra* § 31.

[447] *See* Restatement 2d § 20(2): " "The manifestations of the parties are operative in accordance with the meaning

A final problem in this area is whether an act that is begun without knowledge of the offer, but completed with knowledge of the offer, constitutes acceptance. Assume that *A* offers a reward for information leading to the arrest and conviction of a murderer. *B*, without knowledge of the reward offer, is in the process of providing the information when he learns of the reward offer. He then provides the remainder of the information which, in total, leads to the arrest and conviction. Has *B* accepted the offer? The FIRST RESTATEMENT answered "no," since assent to the entire proposal was lacking.[448] Professor Corbin criticized this view on the footing that the normal person who learns of the reward after beginning performance will proceed with that performance, relying upon the offer with expectation of receiving the reward.[449] The RESTATEMENT 2d adopts the Corbin view with the suggestion that knowledge of the offer after part performance can induce the offeree to complete performance and, since part performance is valueless to the offeror, there is a reasonable inference that the offeror intends to create a power of acceptance in a party who has yet to complete the performance required by the offer.[450]

[C]   Intention to Exercise Power of Acceptance — Motivation

It is often suggested that an offeree must demonstrate an intention to accept the offer.[451] In promissory acceptances, the promise, itself, is an objective manifestation of this intention. The problem arises in performance acceptances. With knowledge of an offer, the offeree may perform the required act but may do so for reasons apart from the offer. At the moment the offeree performs the act, notwithstanding his knowledge of the offer, he may not be consciously adverting to the offer but may be performing the act for other reasons. An employee who knew of his employer's reward offer of $5000 in exchange for information leading to the arrest and conviction of persons stealing from the employer did not rely upon the offer at the time he gathered the information. As a supervisor, he may have gathered the information in any event. The court, nonetheless, followed the generally accepted view that, in rendering the performance requested in the offer, "it is not necessary that the *sole* motive of the offeree shall be his desire for the offered reward."[452] Similarly, where a prize was offered to anyone who caught a particular, tagged fish, a fisherman who caught the fish need not have been consciously adverting to the offer at that moment if he had been aware of the offer but had gone fishing for pleasure.[453] The offeror or the offeree may have many different reasons or motives for creating or exercising a power of acceptance and the motivation to enter into a contract may be quite subsidiary to other motivations.[454] Prizes in golf or tennis tournaments

---

attached to them by one of the parties if: (a) that party does not know of any different meaning attached by the other, and the other party knows the meaning attached by the first party; or (b) that party has no reason to know of any different meaning attached by the other, and the other has reason to know the meaning attached by the first party.' "

[448] *See* FIRST RESTATEMENT § 53.

[449] 1 CORBIN § 3.6.

[450] RESTATEMENT 2d § 51 comment b. *See* Sharp Elecs. Corp v. Deutsche Fin. Servs. Corp. 216 F. 3d 388, 397 (4th Cir. 2000) where the court held that § 51 resolved the case at hand since, even if one party was unaware of the offer when it began to perform, it completed performance after gaining knowledge of the offer. See also Miller v. Dictaphone Corp., 334 F. Supp. 840 (D. Or. 1971).

[451] *See* FIRST RESTATEMENT § 55. *See also* Braun v. Northeast Stations & Servs., Inc., 93 A.D.2d 994, 461 N.Y.S.2d 623, 624 (4th Dep't 1983).

[452] Consolidated Freightways Corp. v. Williams, 139 Ga. App. 302, 305, 228 S.E.2d 230, 233 (1976).

[453] *See* Simmons v. United States, 308 F.2d 160 (4th Cir. 1962).

[454] *See Consolidated Freightways Corp., supra* note 452.

may be offered and accepted though the offerors and offerees may be much more concerned about support for a given charity that will benefit from a given tournament, or the prestige connected with sponsoring or winning the tournament. Star athletes may be primarily motivated to win another championship rather than the financial rewards for such an effort. The fact that an act is performed with numerous motivations, some or all of which are superior to a motivation to accept the offer, should not preclude an effective exercise of the power of acceptance. On this basis, it is often suggested that the motivation of a party who performs the requested act with knowledge of the offer is irrelevant.[455] There are, however, cases to the contrary. In *Vitty v. Eley*,[456] the plaintiff was aware of a reward offer but was afraid to provide the information to the police for fear of retaliation. When threatened with arrest, the plaintiff provided the information. The court denied a recovery of the offered reward on the footing that the plaintiff had not provided the information voluntarily, i.e., it had been "corkscrewed out of him." The court also stated its disagreement with a well-known English case where motivation had been deemed irrelevant.[457] The RESTATEMENT 2d utilizes the facts of both cases as the bases for illustrations.[458] It is possible to read the illustration based on the *Vitty* case as a modification of the actual facts in *Vitty*. A comparison of the actual facts of the two cases, however, reveals an irreconcilability that the RESTATEMENT illustrations cannot overcome. It would have been highly preferable for the RESTATEMENT 2d to emphasize the language in § 53(3):

> "Where an offer of a promise invites acceptance by performance . . . , the rendering of the invited performance does not constitute an acceptance if before the offeror performs his promise, the offeree manifests *an intention not to accept*.[459]

This language is a major shift from the FIRST RESTATEMENT requirement that the offeree manifest an intention to accept to a rebuttable presumption of acceptance arising from performance by the offeree.[460] Notwithstanding its somewhat confusing illustrations, the RESTATEMENT 2d properly focuses on the virtual impossibility of finding no intention to accept absent an explicit disclaimer by the purported offeree to the effect that he has no intention of accepting the offer by rendering the performance requested in the offer.[461] If, therefore, the act requested in the offer is performed by a party who has knowledge of the offer, the

---

[455] *See* RESTATEMENT 2d § 53 comment c: "[I]nquiry into his motives is unnecessary." *See also* Hamilton v. Oakland Sch. Dist., 219 Cal. 322, 26 P.2d 296 (1933), and *Braun v. Northeast Stations & Servs., Inc., supra* note 451, 461 N.Y.S.2d at 624: "It is well settled, however, that 'motivation of a person performing the acts required by an offer of a reward is immaterial, but consent to the offer is vital' " (citing Reynolds v. Eagle Pencil Co., 285 N.Y. 448, 35 N.E.2d 35 (1941)).

[456] 51 A.D. 44, 64 N.Y.S. 397 (1900).

[457] Williams v. Cawardine, 4 B. & Ad. 621 [1833].

[458] Illustration 1 is said to be based on the facts of *Williams v. Cawardine*, and ill. 2 is said to be based on the facts of *Vitty v. Eley*.

[459] Emphasis added.

[460] "[T]he favored rule shifts the emphasis away from a manifestation of intent to accept to a manifestation of intent not to accept; thereby establishing, it would appear, a rebuttable presumption of acceptance arising from performance when the offer invites acceptance by performance." Industrial Am., Inc. v. Fulton Indus., 285 A.2d 412, 416 (Del. 1971), quoted with apparent approval in Reporter's Note to RESTATEMENT 2d § 53. *See* FIRST RESTATEMENT § 55.

[461] *See* comment c. and ill. 3 to RESTATEMENT 2d § 53. In Whitewood v. Robert Bosch Tool Co., 323 Fed. Appx. 397, 405 (6th Cir. 2009) the trial court had omitted an instruction that quoted Restatement 2d § 53(3) The court noted that the party seeking such an instruction had to first establish that it was a correct statement of the law. The court held that it was a correct statement of the law.

presumption is very strong that he or she acted with some reference to the offer though perhaps having had one or more superior motivations for performance of the requested act. Absent a clear manifestation of an intention not to accept the offer, the performance evidences acceptance of the offer.[462]

[D] Who May Accept the Offer?

Earlier we considered to whom an offer is addressed and that analysis explored certain problems in identifying the party with a power of acceptance.[463] There, we suggested that since the offeror is master of the offer, it is the offeror's manifestation of intention that determines the person or persons in whom a power of acceptance is created.[464] It is, therefore, clear that only such a person or persons may exercise the power of acceptance and that power is not assignable by the offeree to another.[465] The earlier analysis should be reconsidered at this point since it necessarily deals with the problems relating to the identification of the person or persons holding a power of acceptance. One of the points emphasized in that analysis bears repetition: whether a particular party has the power of acceptance will often be a question of interpretation of the language of the offer under all of the surrounding circumstances. Thus, where a reward offer was made by an employer to pay $5000 to the person providing information leading to the arrest and conviction of the party or parties stealing from the employer, and the reward notice ended with the statement, "Contact your supervisor," the question before the court was, did the plaintiff who was a supervisor have a power of acceptance? In holding that the plaintiff had a power of acceptance, the court applied generally accepted guides to interpretation.[466]

Other questions concerning the power of acceptance where the offeror has made a mistake of identity will be considered in the sections dealing with mistake in the agreement process.[467]

§ 46 THE MANNER AND MEDIUM OF ACCEPTANCE

[A] Introduction: Manner Versus Medium

The *manner* of acceptance refers to the way in which an offer may be accepted, i.e., by *promising* to perform or actually *performing* the act requested in the offer. The *medium* of acceptance refers to the means used to communicate acceptance. As master of the offer, the

[462] See Drown v. Howlett, 1999 U. S. Dist. LEXIS 19834, at *5 (D. Neb. Dec. 21, 1999).

[463] *See supra* § 40.

[464] *See* RESTATEMENT 2d § 29.

[465] RESTATEMENT 2d § 52. *See* Baker v. Goldman Sachs & Co., 2009 U. S. Dist. LEXIS 84416 at *15 (D. Mass. 2009); Von Hillman v. Colonial Penn Ins. Co., 19 Kan. App. 2d 375, 377, 869 P.2d 248, 249 (1994). With respect to the non-assignability of the power of acceptance, see Deutsche Credit Corp. v. Chesapeake Yacht Sales, 1996 U.S. App. LEXIS 20221, at *12 (4th Cir. Aug. 12, 1996); Ott v. Home Sav. & Loan Ass'n, 265 F.2d 643 (9th Cir. 1958). Agents may accept offers for their principals, see RESTATEMENT 2d AGENCY § 292. If an agent does not have agency authority in a given case, the principal/offeree may ratify the acceptance. RESTATEMENT 2d AGENCY §§ 82-104.

[466] Consolidated Freightways Corp. v. Williams, 139 Ga. App. 302, 228 S.E.2d 230 (1976), where the court applied the following generally accepted interpretation guides: the writing (the reward notice) must be construed against the party drafting it; a construction should be given that will enhance the beneficial purpose of the contract; the promise must be construed in light of the substantial purpose which influenced the parties to enter the contract.

[467] *See infra* § 92[F].

offeror may specify the manner and/or medium of acceptance. Absent such a requirement in the offer, however, questions arise concerning both. Currently, there is little difficulty concerning the medium of acceptance. Starting with the general proposition that any reasonable medium of acceptance will be effective,[468] the case law supports common sense guidelines in the determination of what is reasonable. If, for example, the offeror uses the mail to make an offer, it would be reasonable for the offeree to adopt the mail as a reasonable medium of acceptance. An electronic communication may constitute a reasonable medium of acceptance, particularly where the subject matter of the contract may require a faster medium than the post.[469] A private but reliable service that is customarily used in commercial dealings would also be a reasonable medium.[470] The use of a particular medium, however, may be induced by another question, i.e., what is a reasonable time for acceptance in the absence of a specified time in the offer? If an offeree waits beyond the reasonable time to exercise the power of acceptance, the use of faster medium will not remedy a lapsed power of acceptance.[471]

While the question of a reasonable medium of acceptance is not terribly difficult under modern case law, there are a number of questions surrounding the proper *manner* of acceptance. The UCC, which governs contracts for the sale of goods, brought significant changes in the common law structure of the agreement process with respect to the *manner* of acceptance.[472]

[B]   Manner of Acceptance — First Restatement — "Bilateral" — "Unilateral"

If the offer does not specify a particular manner of acceptance, i.e., it requires neither a promise nor performance but is silent as to the manner of acceptance, it would seem a relatively simple matter to generate a workable rule to be used in such cases. The traditional common law view set forth in the First Restatement, however, assumed that the great majority of offers could be separated into (a) those which requested a promise to exercise the power of acceptance to form a *bilateral* contract, and (b) those which requested the ultimate performance sought by the offeror as the acceptance, thereby forming a *unilateral* contract.[473] The bilateral/unilateral dichotomy was clear. In a bilateral contract, the contract was formed by a promissory acceptance and the resulting contract manifested two rights and two correlative duties, as well as two promisors and two promisees. In a unilateral contract, as we have seen in earlier analyses, the acceptance occurred upon complete performance of the

---

[468] Restatement 2d § 30(2); UCC § 2-206(1)(a).

[469] An exploration of the recognition of electronic contracts and signatures as effective is found in §§ 14–15, *supra.*

[470] Restatement 2d § 65 comment b suggests a less than exhaustive list of circumstances relating to the reasonableness of a particular medium: speed, reliability of the medium, prior course of dealing between the parties, and usage of trade. The Restatement recognizes the likelihood that new media will develop, or that existing media will become more reliable or faster.

[471] Restatement 2d § 41, ill. 8 suggests that the acceptance may be too late even though it arrives before a prompt acceptance by mail would have arrived. Comment *f* explains, "If the offeree makes use for speculative purposes of time allowed for communication there may be a lack of good faith, and an acceptance may not be timely even though it arrives with the time contemplated by the offeror."

[472] These changes are essentially replicated in the Restatement 2d. For an exploration of these changes and their effects, see Murray, *Contracts: A New Design for the Agreement Process,* 53 Cornell L. Rev. 785 (1968).

[473] First Restatement § 52.

requested act (though the offer became irrevocable upon part performance),[474] and a contract was formed with one right in the former offeree and one correlative duty in the former offeror. In such contracts, there was only one promisor (the offeror) and one promisee (the offeree).[475]

If the offeror as master of the offer specified the particular manner of acceptance, no contract would exist until the acceptance was exercised in the specified manner. If, however, the offer did not specify the manner of acceptance, a workable rule as to the proper manner of acceptance was essential. Such an offer was characterized as ambiguous or "doubtful" with respect to the manner of acceptance. The doubt was resolved by presuming that the offer invited a promissory acceptance because a promissory acceptance immediately and fully protects both parties to the contract.[476] Where the offer was doubtful but, instead of promising to accept, the offeree simply performed the act requested in the offer, the presumption that a doubtful offer requires a promissory acceptance would suggest that there was no acceptance of the offer. This required common law courts to create an exception to the presumption. By receiving the performance without a prior promise, the offeror was said to have received something better than the promise he presumably requested, i.e., the actual performance underlying the promise which was, after all, the ultimate desideratum of the offeror.[477] The exception applied even where the offer required a promissory acceptance, i.e., it applied beyond doubtful offers. This, in turn, raised a theoretical difficulty: if the offeror is the master of the offer, and the master requires a promise as the exclusive manner of acceptance, how can a non-promissory acceptance be effective? This objection was ignored in light of the rationale that the offeror should be pleased to receive the actual performance desired, and the fact that no promise was made should be irrelevant. Other difficulties such as the offeror not hearing from the offeree (who was in the process of performing) and proceeding to contract with another[478] were also dismissed. The theoretical and practical problems, however, remained.[479]

---

[474] *See supra* § 44.

[475] If there is a "non-promissory" offer, a unilateral contract may be formed where the promisor is the offeree and the promisee of the offeror. Thus, if *A* owns a book that is in *B*'s possession and *A* offers to sell the book to *B* by saying, "If you promise to pay me $10 for that book which you now possess, the book is yours," upon *B*'s promise to pay the $10, a contract is formed. There is one right in the offeror/promisee to receive the $10, and one duty in the offeree/promisor to pay the $10. Since there is one right and one correlative duty as well as one promisor and one promisee, the contract is "unilateral." However, since the normal unilateral situation has the right in the offeree/promisee and duty in the offeror/promisor, the reversing of the parties has led to the characterization of this type of contract as a "reverse unilateral." *See* RESTATEMENT 2d § 55 comment a.

[476] FIRST RESTATEMENT § 31. For an illustration of the operation of the First Restatement analysis, see Davis v. Jacoby, 1 Cal. 2d 370, 34 P.2d 1026 (1934).

[477] FIRST RESTATEMENT § 63.

[478] See Goble, *Is an Offer a Promise?*, 22 ILL. L. REV. 567 (1928) and the reply by Professor Williston in 22 ILL. L. REV. 788 (1928).

[479] Courts managed to achieve just results in most cases without a consistent theoretical base. There was a lack of law settlement with courts only sometimes using various sections of the FIRST RESTATEMENT in accordance with their stated purposes. *See* Murray, *supra* note 472, at 792.

[C]   Manner of Acceptance — Uniform Commercial Code — RESTATEMENT 2d — Indifferent Offers

[1]   The Fundamental Change

The fundamental change effected by the UCC, incorporated in the Restatement 2d, is a major change in assumption concerning the "doubtful" offer. Unlike their predecessors, the Code and RESTATEMENT 2d proceed on the assumption that the doubtful offer, i.e., the offer not requiring a particular manner of acceptance, is the normal or typical offer rather than the relatively rare offer assumed by the FIRST RESTATEMENT. The new assumption is that, in the overwhelming majority of cases, offerors are *indifferent* as to the manner of acceptance. Based on this assumption, the fundamental policy change is set forth: "Unless otherwise unambiguously indicated by the language or circumstances an offer to make a contract shall be construed as inviting acceptance in any manner and by any medium reasonable in the circumstances."[480]

A court expressed the modern view of the manner of acceptance where a security agreement assuring repayment of a loan was not signed, thereby failing to evidence a promise, but the bank lent the money:

> Acceptance can be effectuated by performance as well as by a signature. *Restatement (Second) of Contracts* § 30(2) (1981); . . . see also UCC § 2-206(1)(a) . . . And while parties can specify that performance shall not be effective as acceptance, *Restatement, supra*, § 30, comment a, this would be an implausible interpretation of the acceptance clause. ... It would amount to saying that if the parties had been asked, "if the bank fails to sign the agreement, will the agreement be void even if the parties behave in a way that shows they thought it was in effect?" they would have said "yes." Or that if they had been asked, "does the bank's failure to sign mean that the debtor could repudiate the agreement at any time?" they would have said "yes." What they really would have said would have been, "don't be silly; it was just an oversight, of no significance. . . ."[481]

Having restructured the basic concept of the manner of acceptance, other specific changes were essential. Thus, the former presumption of a promissory acceptance of a "doubtful" offer had to be changed since such a typical offer where the offeror is indifferent as to the manner of acceptance, could now be accepted by the offeree choosing either to promise to perform or to perform.[482] If the offeror is not indifferent as to the particular manner of acceptance required, the offeror became the absolute master of the offer, i.e., there are no exceptions to the requirement that the exclusive manner of acceptance is that required by the offeror.[483]

---

[480] UCC § 2-206(1)(a). The RESTATEMENT 2d formulation in § 30(2) is almost identical: " 'Unless otherwise indicated by the language or the circumstances, an offer invites acceptance in any manner and by any medium reasonable in the circumstances." RESTATEMENT 2d § 32 elaborates the basic principle in terms of the new assumption concerning doubtful (indifferent) offers: "In case of doubt an offer is interpreted as inviting the offeree to accept either by promising or by rendering the performance as the offeree chooses." In the Reporter's Note to § 32, the following appears: "This Section is derived from former § 31 [First Restatement], but replaces that Section's presumption that an offer invited a bilateral contract with the present formulation."

[481] Falconbridge U. S., Inc. v. Bank One, Ill., N. A., 227 F. 3d 928, 932–33 (citations omitted) (7th Cir. 2000), Posner, J.

[482] RESTATEMENT 2d § 32; UCC § 2-206(1)(b).

[483] The following statement appears in the Reporter's Note to RESTATEMENT 2d § 62: "This Section [62] is modified

[2] "Bilateral" Contract Formed Upon Beginning Performance

Under the new structure of the agreement process, if the offer is indifferent as to the manner of acceptance and the offeree chooses to promise to perform, the contract is formed by a promissory acceptance. Under traditional labels which neither the Code nor the RESTATEMENT 2d continue but still appear in the case law, the contract would be a bilateral contract with two rights, two correlative duties, two promisors and two promisees. If, however, the offeree chooses to accept such an indifferent offer by performance, the question arises, when is the contract formed? The RESTATEMENT 2d clearly indicates that such a contract is formed upon the beginning of the requested performance or a tender of performance[484] and such an acceptance (the beginning of performance or tender of performance) operates as a promise to render complete performance,[485] thereby creating, in traditional terms, a *bilateral* contract.

It is important to emphasize a basic distinction between this situation, i.e., beginning performance in response to an indifferent offer, and beginning performance in response to an offer requiring performance as the exclusive manner of acceptance. In the first situation, the offeree may either promise to perform or start to perform. Since the offeree has this choice, an implication that such beginning performance constitutes a promise to complete performance is warranted. In the second situation where the offeree must complete performance to form a *unilateral* contract, there is no choice as to the manner of acceptance. The offeror has relegated acceptance to one, exclusive manner, i.e., complete performance. The beginning of performance cannot be acceptance of such an offer, even if the offeree desired it to be so. To imply a promise by the offeree under such circumstances, therefore, thrusts an unwarranted risk on the offeree and has no effect in the formation of a contract. As discussed earlier, such an offer becomes irrevocable upon part performance to protect the offeree from an unwarranted revocation by the offeror before the offeree has an opportunity to accept by completing performance.[486]

The UCC was primarily responsible for this change since it preceded the RESTATEMENT 2d, which replicated most of the substantial changes in classical contract law effected by Article 2 of the Code. Under the Code, where the offer is indifferent as to the manner of acceptance, the offeree may choose to promise or to perform, and the beginning of performance will form the contract.[487] A comment to this section, however, suggests, "Such a beginning of performance must unambiguously express the offeree's intention to engage himself."[488] Such a beginning of performance would be tested according to the reasonable understanding of the offeror, i.e., if

---

from former [First Restatement] § 63. That Section stated that performance is an effective acceptance even if the offer requires acceptance by promise. Thus the rule was made an exception to former [First Restatement] §§ 52 and 59. Those exceptions mitigated the effect of former [First Restatement] § 31, which stated a presumption that an offer invites acceptance by promise. Section 32 of the present [Second] Restatement states that in case of doubt an offer invites either acceptance by promise or acceptance by performance as the offeree chooses. This change makes unnecessary these departures from the basic principle that the offeror is master of his offer."

[484] RESTATEMENT 2d § 62(1).

[485] RESTATEMENT 2d § 62(2).

[486] *See* § 44[D], *supra.* It should be recalled that an early theory to protect the offeree against revocation before the offeree completed performance by treating the party part performance as an implied promise creating a bilateral contract was justifiably criticized and is not followed. *See supra* § 44[D]. The beginning of performance in response to an offer demanding performance as the exclusive manner of acceptance cannot form a contract and the implication of a promise from such part performance is unwarranted.

[487] UCC § 2-206(2).

[488] *See* comment 3 to UCC § 2-206.

such an offeror would regard the start of performance as an expression of the offeree's intention to complete the performance, the beginning of performance would constitute an implied promise to complete and, in the traditional usage, a bilateral contract would be formed at that time.[489] If the offeree expressly indicated that performance was not to be construed as an acceptance, his manifested intention would be respected. If the offeror knew or had reason to know that the offeree was not engaging upon the start of performance, no contract would be formed until performance was complete. Thus, if the offeree indicated some doubt as to whether he could complete performance, his beginning of performance would not be an engagement constituting an implied promise to complete performance.

The Code drafters were very much aware of this situation in the shipment of goods as an acceptance of an offer: an order or other offer to purchase goods for prompt or current shipment may be accepted either by a prompt promise to ship or by prompt or current shipment.[490] This is simply a specific application of the general rule that indifferent offers may be accepted by promising or by performing. But the Code provision adds an important element: if the offeree chooses to accept by the prompt shipment of goods rather than by promising to ship, he accepts the offer by the prompt shipment of conforming *or nonconforming* goods.[491]

[D]   Shipment of Nonconforming Goods — Acceptance or Counter Offer?

Under pre-Code law, if a seller shipped nonconforming goods, i.e., goods that were different from the goods required by the offer, the seller was not accepting the offer; he was making a counter offer, and if the buyer accepted the nonconforming goods, the buyer was accepting the seller's counter offer. Under the Code, however, when the seller ships even nonconforming goods in response to the buyer's offer, such a shipment is normally understood "to close the bargain."[492] The ramifications of this change over pre-Code law are radical. Assume, for example, that the buyer offers to purchase model X-35 widgits and, in response to this order, the seller ships X-47 widgits which do not conform to the good desired by the offeror. A court applying the Code provision would find that a contract has been formed for the X-35 widgits and that contract has been, simultaneously, breached by the shipment of the nonconforming goods.[493] The buyer may reject the nonconforming goods,[494] but the seller typically has the right to "cure" the defect[495] if that can be accomplished prior to the time conforming goods

---

[489] *See* Nasco, Inc. v. Dahltron Corp., 74 Ill. App. 3d 302, 392 N.E.2d 1110 (2d Dist. 1979) (on the assumption that there was merely an offer to purchase goods, the contract came into being when the seller began to execute the buyer's order). See also American Bronze v. Steamway Products, 456 N. E. 2d 1295, 1300 (Ohio App. 1982); Besk Oil v. Brown, 1989 Del Super. LEXIS 14 at *5–6 (1989).

[490] UCC § 2-206(1)(b). Comment 2 explains that "shipment" is to be understood in the same sense as it si found in § 2-504 where the seller is authorized to ship the goods by an independent carrier. Thus, "shipment" would not include the beginning of delivery by the seller's own truck.

[491] *Id.*

[492] UCC § 2-206 comment 4. *See* Corinthian Pharmaceutical Sys., Inc. v. Lederle Labs., 724 F. Supp. 605 (S.D. Ind. 1989).

[493] Comment 4 to UCC § 2-206 suggests: "Such a non-conforming shipment is normally to be understood as intended to close the bargain, even though it proves to have been at the same time a breach."

[494] UCC § 2-601.

[495] UCC § 2-508.

should have been shipped.[496]

[1]   Shipment of Nonconforming Goods — Counter Offer

The seller can also avoid the effect of forming a contract in shipping nonconforming goods by notifying the buyer that the shipment of nonconforming goods is sent as an accommodation to the buyer.[497] A seasonable[498] notification to the buyer that the shipment of nonconforming goods was intended to accommodate the buyer constitutes a counter offer by the seller. The buyer need not accept such nonconforming goods, but if he does so, he has accepted the seller's counter offer. The same analysis will be applied even where the seller ships conforming goods in quantities or prices that do not conform to the offer.[499] Thus, the more expansive application would apply not simply to nonconforming goods, but to nonconforming shipments of goods.

It is, of course, still possible for an offeror to require performance as the exclusive manner of acceptance. We have already explored the analysis of part performance in response to such offers under § 45 of the RESTATEMENT 2d.[500] Should such an offer be made in a contract for the sale of goods, it is clear that the same analysis would apply under the Code.[501] It is unusual for an offeror to require performance as the exclusive manner of acceptance.[502] More often, the nature of the offer will suggest that a promissory acceptance would be worthless to the offeror as in the case of reward offers or other offers to the public, such as prizes in a contest requiring the performance of certain acts[503] or offers of guaranty.[504] Though the term "unilateral" contract is not mentioned in the UCC and has been intentionally omitted from the RESTATE-MENT 2d,[505] numerous cases involving terminable-at-will employment contracts and other

---

[496] The UCC "cure" section, 2-508(1), allows cure only "within the contract time." If, however, the seller had reasonable grounds to believe that the tender would have been acceptable, the seller, upon notification to the buyer, will have a "further reasonable time" to cure. § 2-508(2).

[497] UCC § 2-206(1)(b) and comment 4. See *Corinthian Pharmaceutical Sys.*, note 492 *supra*.

[498] Under the Code, an action is taken "seasonably" when it is taken at or within the time agreed, or if no time is agreed, within a reasonable time. § 1-204.

[499] In *Corinthian, supra*, note 492, the buyer offered to purchase 1000 vials of DTP vaccine at $64.32 each. The seller shipped 50 vials at $64.32 each and notified the buyer that the balance of the order would be priced at $171.00 each. The notice to the buyer stated that the seller was sending the 50 vials at the lower price as an exception to its general policy and that buyer could reject the proposal to ship the remaining 9,950 vials at the higher price. The court found the notice sufficient to characterize the shipment as an "accommodation shipment" constituting a counter offer.

[500] *See supra* § 44[D].

[501] The UCC does not change any law that it does not expressly replace. UCC § 1-103(b). Moreover, § 2-206 comment 3 indicates: "Nothing in this section however bars the possibility that under the common law performance begun may have an intermediate effect of temporarily barring revocation of the offer. . . ."

[502] See, e.g., BC Tire Corp. v. GTE Directories Corp., 46 Wash. App. 351, 730 P.2d 726 (1986), where the plaintiff signed defendant's standard form to have an advertisement for its business in the telephone directory. The form stated that the publication of the advertising requested in the form "shall constitute an acceptance of this application. . . . Otherwise, this application is not binding on either of the parties." Another standard clause stated that the defendant would not be liable for any errors or omissions or failure to include such advertising. The defendant negligently failed to include the plaintiff's ad. The court held that the application signed by the plaintiff was an offer of a unilateral contract. Since publication was the required manner of acceptance, there was no contract when publication did not occur.

[503] *See* RESTATEMENT 2d § 32 comment b. *See also* Rosenthal v. Al Packer Ford, Inc., 36 Md. App. 349, 374 A.2d 377 (1977); Grove v. Charbonneau Buick-Pontiac, 240 N.W.2d 853 (N.D. 1976).

[504] *See, e.g.*, King v. Industrial Bank of Wash., 474 A.2d 151 (D.C. 1984).

[505] See Reporter's Note to comment f of RESTATEMENT 2d § 1, which indicates that the "unilateral"/"bilateral"

contracts involving a performance acceptance explored earlier utilize a theory of unilateral contract.[506]

§ 47 NOTICE OF ACCEPTANCE

[A] General Principles in Bilateral Versus Unilateral Contracts

As the master of the offer, the offeror may insist that the offeree's assent be communicated before a contract can exist. To exercise the power of acceptance, the offeree must comply with this requirement and any other requirements concerning the notice of acceptance stated in the offer.[507] This is simply an expression of the general principle that the offeree must comply with the place, time, manner or medium of acceptance mandated by the offer.[508] Often, however, the offer does not expressly indicate that notice of acceptance is necessary. In that situation, must the offeree notify the offeror of the acceptance? There is confusion in this area resulting from an antiquated view that notice of acceptance is always required.[509] This "rule," however, is emasculated where the offer requires a performance acceptance. In such a contract, the performance, itself, is the consideration for the offeror's promise and it is also the offeree's manifestation of assent.[510] Notice of assent in such cases should, therefore, be required only where the offeror would not be aware of the performance.[511] Where the offer requires or allows for a promissory acceptance, however, notice of acceptance is usually required.[512] A promise may be inferred by conduct. The typical promise, however, involves communication in language and it is, therefore, generally understood that acceptance requires communication of the offeree's manifestation of assent to the offeror. Yet, we will later explore situations where the offeree has pursued reasonably diligent efforts to communicate acceptance to the offeror but, through no fault of the offeree, such efforts have failed.[513] The acceptance will be said to be effective in those situations. The RESTATEMENT 2d formulation of the guiding principle, therefore, seems preferable, i.e., acceptance by promise requires either a reasonably diligent effort to notify the offeror, or the offeror's receipt of the notice of acceptance within the time stated in the offer (or a reasonable time).[514]

---

definitions of the FIRST RESTATEMENT have not been "carried forward because of doubt as to the utility of the distinction, often treated as fundamental, between the two types." *See* Sharp Elecs. Corp. v. Deutsche Fin. Servs. Corp., 216 F.3d 388, 393 (4th Cir. 2000), *cert. denied*, 121 S. Ct. 763, 148 L. Ed. 2d 664 (2001). While not using these captions, the RESTATEMENT 2d clearly recognizes that an offer may require an exclusive manner of acceptance by promise, or an exclusive manner of acceptance by performance as well as being indifferent to the manner of acceptance as suggested in the analysis of the UCC and RESTATEMENT 2d modifications of traditional contract theory.

[506] *See supra* § 39[B][6].

[507] *See* Dempsey v. King, 662 S.W.2d 725 (Tex. App. 1983); Crockett v. Lowther, 549 P.2d 303 (Wyo. 1976).

[508] *See* RESTATEMENT 2d §§ 58 and 60.

[509] *See* the opinion by Bramwell, J., in Household Fire Ins. Co. v. Grant, 4 Ex. D. 216, 233 [1879].

[510] Hauk v. First Nat'l Bank of St. Charles, 680 S.W.2d 771 (Mo. Ct. App. 1984).

[511] See subsection C of this section for an exploration of this concept.

[512] *See* Normile v. Miller, 313 N.C. 98, 326 S.E.2d 11 (1985); Hauk v. First Nat'l Bank of St. Charles, 680 S.W.2d 771 (Mo. Ct. App. 1984); Mintzberg v. Golestaneh, 390 So. 2d 759 (Fla. Dist. Ct. App. 1980).

[513] For example, where the offer is by post and the offeree deposits his letter of acceptance in the mailbox but the letter is lost in the mails.

[514] RESTATEMENT 2d § 56.

The difference between acceptance by promise and acceptance by performance caused some courts to state different notice requirements depending upon whether the contract was "bilateral" or "unilateral." Since it is now clear that a "bilateral" contract can be formed by the *performance* of the offeree where the offeror is indifferent as to how it is accepted,[515] that distinction is no longer viable. A modern restatement of the rule should eschew "bilateral" or "unilateral" characterizations. It might be stated as follows: Where acceptance occurs through performance, notice of acceptance is usually not required; where acceptance occurs through promising, notice to the offeror or a reasonably diligent effort to notify the offeror is required.

[B] May the Offeror Dispense With the Necessity of Notice of Acceptance?

As master of the offer, the offeror may dispense with any notice of acceptance. If the offeror manifests a willingness to be bound without any communication or manifestation of acceptance by the offeree, the law takes him at his word.[516] Unfortunately, the situation often involves an unwitting waiver of the notice requirement by the offeror.

"Home Office Approval" Clauses. A seller of goods or services presents the seller's printed form to the prospective buyer. The buyer signs the form and typically assumes she has formed a contract with the seller. Had she read all of the provisions of the form carefully, however, the buyer would have discovered a clause stating that the agreement evidenced by this document does not become a contract until it is approved or signed by an officer of the seller at its home office. The buyer is an unwitting offeror who has not only created a power of acceptance in the seller/offeree, but has unknowingly dispensed with any requirement of notice of acceptance. The acceptance is effective when the seller, through one of its officers, signs the document at the home office, even though, at the moment of formation, the buyer (offeror) is unaware of that signing and consequent exercise of the power of acceptance. Notification to the buyer is unnecessary simply because the offer made by the buyer dispenses with such notification.[517]

Waiver. If it is later determined that the seller did not sign the document, the failure to adhere to the terms of the offer would normally preclude the formation of a contract. Part performance, however, may be sufficient to manifest a waiver of this otherwise mandatory manner of acceptance. Where a contract for burglary alarm services included an exculpatory clause, the plaintiff claimed that the defendant could not rely upon the clause since the contract also contained a requirement that it had to be signed by an authorized representative of the seller and was never signed. While recognizing the absence of such a "home office approval" signature as otherwise fatal to the formation of the contract, the court noted that such clauses are designed for the protection of the seller by allowing upper level officials to

---

[515] *See supra* § 46[C].

[516] *See* Restatement 2d § 54(2)(c) and § 56 comment a.

[517] The classic case is International Filter Co. v. Conroe Gin, Ice & Light Co., 277 S.W. 631 (Tex. Comm'n App. 1925). There are many other illustrations in the case law. *See, e.g.,* Pacific Photocopy, Inc. v. Canon U. S. A., Inc., 57 Or. App. 752, 646 P.2d 647, *rev. denied,* 293 Or. 634, 652 P.2d 810 (1982); Three-Seventy Leasing Corp. v. Ampex Corp., 528 F.2d 993 (5th Cir. 1976); Antonucci v. Stevens Dodge, Inc., 73 Misc. 2d 173, 340 N.Y.S.2d 979 (1973). See also J.B. Moore Elec. Contractor, Inc. v. Westinghouse Elec. Supply Co., 221 Va. 745, 748, 273 S.E.2d 553, 555 (1981), where, in a curious analysis of a printed form supplied by the seller containing the provision, "This Order is subject to the Company's acceptance at its office . . . ," the court distinguished similar cases on the footing that this form contained no signature line for the seller, whereas other cases holding such forms to be offers when signed by the buyer contained such lines for the seller's signature.

review and approve contracts before the company is bound. Thus, the seller can waive the home office approval requirement and the best evidence of such waiver is the seller's performance though its printed document was not signed by an "authorized representative."[518]

[C] Notice Where Offers are Accepted by Performance — RESTATEMENT 2d and Uniform Commercial Code

As suggested earlier, the general rule is that notice is not required in a performance acceptance.[519] Where an offer requires or permits acceptance by performance, it is the performance, itself, that manifests the offeree's assent and the contract should be said to be formed without notice of acceptance.[520] There are, however, situations in which the offeree knew or reasonably should have known that the offeror would not learn of the offeree's performance with reasonable promptness or certainty. For example, if the offeree knows that the offeror is located at a considerable distance when the performance occurs and will not, therefore, be aware of the offeree's performance/acceptance, should notice be required in such a case? Some cases took the position that, even in that situation, notice was not essential since the offeror could have insisted upon notice and chose not to do so.[521] Other cases went so far as to hold that no contract was formed until notice was communicated.[522] Under this view, if the offeree performed the act required by the offeror, there would be no contract until notice of performance had been communicated to the offeror. A third view, though announced even earlier, presented a sound analysis. In the well-known case of *Bishop v. Eaton*,[523] the court rejected an all-or-nothing approach in suggesting that, ordinarily, there is no necessity to notify an offeror that the act requested in the offer has been performed because the offeror is bound when he or she sees the act performed. If, however, the act is of such a kind that knowledge of its performance will not reach the offeror promptly, the offeree must provide notice. The court further insisted that the doing of the act, the performance, was the acceptance of the offer, i.e., a contract is formed at that point, even though the situation is one requiring notice within a reasonable time. This analysis withstood the test of time and has become the prevailing view.[524] It is important to recognize the significance of treating the performance as the acceptance forming the contract even though the situation calls for notice to the offeror. If *A* tells *B*, "I am going away for a few months during which time my brother, Harry, may need money. If he needs it, let him have it and, if he does not repay you with interest, I will." Assume that *B* lends money to Harry while *A* is away. *B* is about to send notice to *A* that he has lent the money when he receives a note from *A* revoking the offer. If

---

[518] Synnex Corp. v. ADT Services, Inc., 394 N. J. Super.577, 586, 928 A. 2d 37, 42 (2007) citing, *inter alia*, Empire Mach. Co. v. Litton Bus. Tel. Sys., 115 Ariz. 568, 566 P.2d 1044 (Ct. App. 1977).

[519] *See supra* subsection A.

[520] *See* Compton v. Shopko Stores, Inc., 93 Wis. 2d 613, 287 N.W.2d 720 (1980). *See also* RESTATEMENT 2d § 54(1).

[521] *See* Midland Nat'l Bank v. Security Elevator Co., 161 Minn. 30, 200 N.W. 851 (1924); City Nat'l Bank v. Phelps, 86 N.Y. 484 (1881).

[522] *See* Kresge Dep't Stores v. Young, 37 A.2d 448 (Mun. Ct. App. D.C. 1944); German Sav. Bank v. Drake Roofing Co., 112 Iowa 184, 83 N.W. 960 (1900).

[523] 161 Mass. 496, 37 N.E. 665 (1894).

[524] *See* RESTATEMENT 2d § 54, particularly, ills. 5 and 6. The situation arose often in guaranty cases, i.e., where the offeree becomes a guarantor or surety for a principal debtor. In Miller v. Walter, 165 Mont. 221, 527 P.2d 240, 244 (1974), the court provides the analysis of Professor Corbin at the predecessor section of § 3.14 of CORBIN ON CONTRACTS in describing the notice requirement in such cases.

the acceptance was not effective until notice was either sent or received by *A*, the revocation could be said to be effective unless the act of lending was seen as partial performance making *A'* s offer irrevocable so that *B* would have a reasonable time to complete performance by sending the notice. Even if § 45 of the RESTATEMENT 2d or other irrevocable offer theory[525] applied to a situation where the offer could be accepted only by performance, however, such theories do not apply to a performance acceptance of an indifferent offer, i.e., one that could be accepted either by promising or performing.

Under the UCC and RESTATEMENT 2d, the typical, indifferent offer may be accepted by a promise or by performance.[526] If an offeree chooses to accept such an offer by performance, the question of notice should be analyzed in precisely the same fashion as if the offer could be accepted exclusively by performance, i.e., the *Bishop v. Eaton* analysis applies to *any* performance acceptance whether it is an acceptance of an indifferent offer, or an acceptance of an offer that can be accepted exclusively by performance.[527]

The Meaning of "Notice." Notice is not part of the acceptance since the acceptance was completed upon performance. If notice is not part of the acceptance, what is it? Section 2-206(2) of the UCC states: "Where the beginning of a requested performance is a reasonable mode of acceptance, an offeror who is not notified of acceptance within a reasonable time may treat the offer as having lapsed before acceptance." Yet, if beginning performance constitutes acceptance, there is no longer any offer to lapse. Both the offer and acceptance have merged into a contract. To suggest, therefore, that an offer is accepted by performance but, because the former offeree failed to provide the notice that should have been provided, the "offer lapses," is theoretically impossible. The situation is worsened by a comment to this section of the Code.[528] Again, the offeror does not seek notice; he or she does not bargain for notice where the acceptance is by performance. If the offer is indifferent as to the manner of acceptance and the offeree chooses to accept by performance, notification will not be essential unless the offeror would not learn of the performance/acceptance with reasonable promptness. The contract is formed upon the start of performance in that situation as both the UCC and

---

[525] *See supra* § 44[D].

[526] *See supra* § 46[C].

[527] RESTATEMENT 2d § 54 comment b appears to support this view. However, it suggests that a performance acceptance dispensing with notification would be rare because a performance acceptance of an indifferent offer "often carries with it a return commitment" pursuant to § 62. Subsection (2) of § 62 indicates that a performance acceptance of an indifferent offer "operates as a promise to render complete performance." To provide such performance with the operative effect of a promise merely binds the offeree to complete performance. Comment b requires further elaboration. By starting to perform in response to an offer that can be accepted exclusively by performance, an offeree may manifest the same intention of completing performance as does an offeree who begins to perform in response to an indifferent offer. Yet, no contract will be formed by such part performance in the first situation (though the offer will become irrevocable), while a contract will be formed in the second. The essential difference is that the offeree who decides to accept by performance in response to an indifferent offer could have chosen to promise performance to form the contract. An implication of promise from part performance in response to such an offer is, therefore, warranted. Where the offer requires performance as the exclusive manner of acceptance and the offeree, therefore, cannot possibly accept prior to completing performance, an implication of promise from the start of performance is not warranted. Notwithstanding the language in comment b to § 54 of the RESTATEMENT 2d, there is no question that it supports the view that the notice requirement analysis is the same whether the performance acceptance refers to an indifferent offer or an offer requiring only a performance acceptance.

[528] Comment 3 to UCC § 2-206 states: "The beginning of performance by an offeree can be effective as acceptance so as to bind the offeror only if followed within a reasonable time by notice to the offeror. Such a beginning of performance must unambiguously express the offeree's intention to engage himself. For the protection of both parties it is essential that notice follow in due course to *constitute acceptance*." (emphasis added).

the RESTATEMENT 2d indicate.[529] Where notice is necessary because the offeror would not become aware of the acceptance promptly, notice is not part of the acceptance; it is a *condition precedent* to the duty of the former offeror. That duty of the former offeror was created when the performance occurred, forming the contract. A contract existed at that moment in time, else there would be no contractual duty. The analysis indicating that notice is a condition precedent to the former offeror's duty is the primary analysis in the RESTATEMENT 2d[530] though it nods in an illustration by resorting to the intellectually untidy, "lapsed offer" notion of its half-brother, the UCC.[531]

Perhaps a more important problem in the Code formulation is Comment language that may be read to suggest that notice of performance by an offeree who chooses to accept in that manner is always essential.[532] The RESTATEMENT 2d does not attempt to deal with this Code defect. It insists that notice is essential as a condition after a performance acceptance *only* where the former offeror will not learn of the performance/acceptance promptly and with reasonable certainty.[533] Fortunately, the Code comment is not part of the enacted law. It should be ignored since it is analytically unsound.[534] If courts choose to consider it, it could be interpreted as not requiring notice in all performance acceptance situations. At least courts should be persuaded by the sound analysis of the RESTATEMENT 2d even if they read the Code comment to insist upon notice as part of the acceptance in all performance acceptance situations.[535] It is important to consider the case law under the Code to this time.

---

[529] UCC § 2-206(2) and RESTATEMENT 2d § 62.

[530] "If an offeree who accepts by rendering a performance has reason to know that the offeror has no adequate means of learning of the performance with reasonable promptness and certainty, the *contractual duty* of the offeror is charged. . . ." RESTATEMENT 2d § 54(2).

[531] *See* ill. 1 to § 54 which indicates that the absence of notice discharges the contractual duty, but then, sadly, it adds, ". . . and he [the former offeror] may treat the offer as having lapsed before acceptance unless within a reasonable time [the former offeree] sends notification of acceptance. . . ." It is clear that the drafters of the RESTATEMENT 2d felt considerable pressure to create a new Restatement reconcilable with the UCC wherever possible. Since the Code is the controlling statute in contracts for the sale of goods, it was obviously desirable to present as much uniformity for all contracts as possible. Moreover, Article 2 of the Code generally presents a highly desirable movement toward a more effective system of modern contract law. *See* RESTATEMENT 2d, *Legislation*, in Introduction, at page 2. On occasion, however, another motivation may have moved the RESTATEMENT 2d drafters to the Code view, to wit, the fact that the American Law Institute is fully responsible for the RESTATEMENTS and it was also partly responsible for the UCC.

[532] *See* comment 3 to § 2-206 of the Code quoted *supra* note 528.

[533] RESTATEMENT 2d § 54(2).

[534] Karl Llewellyn, the chief architect of the Code and the principal draftsman of Article 2, did not intend notice to be part of the acceptance so as to permit revocation by the offeror after part performance. In the earliest draft of Article 2 which is regarded as the work of Llewellyn exclusively, a comment to then § 3-F suggests his thinking: "The giving of such notice, however, is a matter which has no need at all to coincide with the moment at which revocation is barred. And it repeatedly happens that the seller's reasonably invited action, even before time for reply or for sending notice has expired, is both a material disarrangement of *his* affairs and an unambiguous expression of intention to perform. In such case, the seller needs protection, *even though* a communication of notice may still be due the buyer, and may be due promptly. . . . The matter of notification is here treated as one of completing acceptance, rather than as one of breach, because it deals with the effective creation of the offeror's expectations, and because it commonly comes within the time for promissory acceptance." NATIONAL CONFERENCE OF COMMISSIONERS ON UNIFORM STATE LAWS, REPORT ON AND SECOND DRAFT OF A REVISED UNIFORM SALES ACT 77–78 (1941). Section 3-F, itself, envisioned making the offer irrevocable upon part performance by the offeree, and the "perfection" of that part performance "acceptance" by notifying the offeror of such acceptance. It is therefore clear that, once performance had begun, Llewellyn would not permit a revocation of the offer.

[535] *See* Murray, *Contracts: A New Design for the Agreement Process*, 53 CORNELL L. REV. 785, 796–800 (1968).

[D]   Notice in "Shipment" Contracts

If a buyer offers to purchase goods to be manufactured and indicates that manufacturing should begin, the start of manufacturing will be viewed as an acceptance because beginning performance in response to such an offer will be considered a "reasonable mode" of acceptance under the Code.[536] Since the typical, indifferent offer can be accepted in any reasonable manner under the Code and the "prompt shipment" of goods is expressly regarded as a reasonable manner of acceptance, where the seller promptly ships in response to a purchase order (offer), shipment constitutes acceptance.[537]

If a seller chooses to accept an indifferent offer by shipping the goods, it is important to recognize "shipment" as complete performance when the goods are delivered by the seller to an independent carrier at the seller's place of business. This is the normal transportation contract under the Code.[538] The act of "shipment" under these circumstances is not simply the beginning of performance as it would be where, for example, the seller is required to deliver the goods to the buyer and begins loading the goods on his own truck for delivery to the buyer.[539] Section 2-206(2) only applies to situations "[w]here the beginning of performance is a reasonable mode of acceptance of an offer" where notice of such a beginning of performance must occur within a reasonable time. The fact that this section applies only to notice after "the beginning of a requested performance" and not to a performance acceptance which is complete is sometime ignored.[540] The question remains, if the seller completes his performance by "shipment," must he then notify the buyer of such shipment? A comment suggests that "shipment" is used in § 2-206(1)(b) in the same fashion as it is used in another section of Article 2 dealing with the duties of the seller in the normal FOB "shipment"

---

[536] § 2-206(2). *See* American Bronze Corp. v. Streamway Prods., 8 Ohio App. 3d 223, 456 N.E.2d 1295 (1982).

[537] *See* Home Lumber Co. v. Appalachian Reg'l Hosps., Inc., 722 S.W.2d 912 (Ky. Ct. App. 1987); Rangen, Inc. v. Valley Trout Farms, 104 Idaho 284, 658 P.2d 955 (1983) (separate contracts formed through sending of purchase order by buyer and shipment seller).

[538] "[T]he 'shipment' contract is regarded as the normal one and the 'destination' contract as the variant type. § 2-503, comment 5.

[539] Under an FOB "shipment" contract (the normal contract when goods are to be shipped through an independent carrier to the buyer), the seller's performance is complete when he delivers the goods to the carrier at the seller's place of business at which time the risk of loss passes to the buyer. *See* UCC §§ 2-504 and 2-509(1)(a). If, however, the seller is to deliver to the buyer by his own truck, the risk of loss will not pass to the buyer until the buyer receives the goods and the seller will be obligated to make a reasonable tender of the goods to the buyer. *See* §§ 2-503 and 2-509(3). *See also* comment 2 to § 2-206.

[540] In the middle of February, the J. I. Case Credit Corporation offered to sell a repossessed tractor located in the woods near Morton, Washington, on an "as is, where is" to Thompson. Thompson picked up the tractor on March 1, but hearing nothing from Thompson by March 12, Case agreed to sell the tractor to Petersen. On the assumption that Case had simply offered the tractor to Thompson who could accept by taking possession of it, the court held that the question of reasonable notice of Thompson's acceptance arose under UCC § 2-206(2). Thompson's notice to Case occurred either two or four weeks after he picked up the tractor. Since a delay of four weeks may have been beyond a reasonable time, the court remanded the judgment to try that issue. Petersen v. Thompson, 506 P.2d 697 (1973). Again, however, § 2-206(2) applies only "[w]here the beginning of a requested performance is a reasonable mode of acceptance . . . ." Thompson's performance was completed when he picked up the tractor. It would be possible to require notice from Thompson as soon as he began the process of loading the tractor on his vehicle for transportation ("beginning performance"), but § 2-206(2) was apparently designed to protect an offeree who began to perform from revocation of the offer. Where the performance acceptance is complete,§ 2-206(2) does not easily apply, but the common law concept of notice to a former offeror who would not have become aware of acceptance by complete performance in *Bishop v. Eaton* (discussed in note 523, *supra)* could be applied to this contract for the sale of goods on the footing that the Code has not displaced that common law concept (§ 1-103(b)).

contract.[541] That section requires the seller to *promptly notify the buyer of the [completed] shipment*. If, however, the seller fails to do so, the buyer may reject the goods "only if material delay or loss ensues."[542] Moreover, the failure to notify promptly must *cause* the material loss or delay.[543]

The RESTATEMENT 2d suggests that, in the normal situation of "shipment" of goods as an acceptance of the offer, notice is not necessary because the acceptance (shipment) "will come to the offeror's attention in normal course."[544] Since the UCC is a statute and will govern in cases of contracts for the sale of goods, the notice requirement cannot be ignored and a court may find that a failure of prompt notice of shipment permits the buyer to reject the goods, thereby shifting the risk of loss to the seller when the goods suffer casualty in transit.[545]

The discrepancies between the Code and RESTATEMENT 2d concerning notice and the awkward notice language of § 2-206 of the UCC have yet to appears as controversies in the case law. They should not undermine the significance of the fundamental change in traditional contract law effected by the UCC and replicated in the RESTATEMENT 2d. Treating the indifferent (doubtful) offer as the typical offer that may be accepted in any reasonable manner while emphasizing the absolute mastery of the offer constitute desirable modifications of classical contract law.

§ 48 ACCEPTANCE IN CONTRACTS BY MAIL AND OTHER MEDIA — THE "MAILBOX" OR "DISPATCH" RULE

[A] The Problem and Original Solutions — The Risk of Transmission

The offeror as master of the offer may insist that acceptance be communicated through a particular medium such as the mail.[546] Where the offeror does not specify such a medium, the power of acceptance may be exercised through any medium reasonable under the circumstances.[547] Normally, notice of acceptance must be communicated in contracts

---

[541] § 2-206, comment 2.

[542] UCC § 2-504 (c).

[543] *See* Monte Carlo Shirt, Inc. v. Daewoo Int'l (Am.) Corp., 707 F.2d 1054 (9th Cir. 1983).

[544] RESTATEMENT 2d § 62 comment b.

[545] *See* Rheinberg-Kellerei GMBH v. Vineyard Wine Co., 53 N.C. App. 560, 281 S.E.2d 425 (1981). If the buyer has the right to reject because the seller has failed to comply with § 2-504 of the Code, even under an FOB shipment contract, the buyer may treat the risk of loss as remaining on the seller until cure or acceptance under § 2-510(1). See the analysis if John E. Murray, Jr., *The Revision of Article 2: Romancing the Prism*, 35 Wm. & Mary L. Rev. 1447, 1459–1464 (1994).

[546] See RESTATEMENT 2d § 60 and UCC § 2-206 and the earlier discussion *supra* § 45[A].

[547] If the offer may be fairly interpreted as merely suggesting a particular medium of acceptance, another medium of equal reliability and speed will suffice. Thus, if an offer states that the offeror must receive acceptance by return mail, the offer may be interpreted as referring to the speed of acceptance rather than the particular medium. In such a case, an electronic, fax or Federal Express response would be sufficient if sent within the time the return mail would arrive. If, however, an offer by mail to sell a commodity which fluctuates in price such as securities is received and the offeree waits two days and then, after learning of a sharp rise in the price of the securities, sends an email acceptance, the acceptance will be too late though it arrives in the same time as a prompt acceptance by mail would have arrived. The offeree should not be permitted to speculate at the offeror's expense. *See* RESTATEMENT 2d § 41 ill. 8. See

requiring or permitting a promissory acceptance.[548] If, therefore, the offeror does not require a particular medium of promissory acceptance, the offer is made by mail, and notice of acceptance is required because the acceptance is promissory, how shall that acceptance requirement be fulfilled? Absent contrary requirements in the offer, an acceptance by mail should be effective where the offer came by mail since the mail would certainly be a reasonable medium of acceptance. It is reasonable to assume that the offeror has impliedly authorized the mail as a reasonable medium of acceptance by using the mail to make the offer.[549] Yet, a problem remains.

The Risk of Transmission. If the mail or other medium is a reasonable medium of acceptance, suppose the offeree uses such a medium but the letter or other communication does not reach the offeror, e.g., it is lost in the mail. In contracts by correspondence, there is a risk of transmission and the question arises, who bears that risk? Is an acceptance dispatched through a reasonable medium effective when dispatched, e.g., when a letter of acceptance is placed in the mailbox, or is it not effective until it is received by the offeror?

If the acceptance is effective when posted or dispatched, certain ramifications are clear. When a letter of acceptance is lost in the mail, the offeror is unaware that the offer has been accepted, and on the assumption that the offeree is not interested in the proposal, the offeror may make a contract with another. The offeree, however, may reasonably assume that a contract has been formed and may proceed to rely on that assumption. There is also the problem of revocation of offers. If the offeror has not yet received the acceptance by mail, he or she may send a letter to the offeree revoking the offer. Revocations, however, must be received to be effective.[550] If the offeree has already accepted by posting the letter of acceptance, the revocation comes too late, i.e., the offer has already been accepted and there is, therefore, no offer to revoke.[551]

Certainly the opposite rule could be chosen, i.e., making an acceptance effective only upon receipt by the offeror,[552] but this rule is also problematic. Such a rule places the risk of transmission on the offeree. If an offeree mailed a letter of acceptance, he or she could not rely upon having any contractual right until the letter was received by the offeror. Moreover, absent a qualification of such a rule, the offeree would be subject to having its power of acceptance revoked at any time prior to the receipt of acceptance.[553]

The Adoption of the "Mailbox" Rule. Another problem occurs in determining whether the offeror had received the letter of acceptance. If the offeror was required to notify the offeree,

---

RESTATEMENT 2d §§ 30 and 65, and UCC § 2-206(1)(a) and discussion of this topic *supra* § 45[A].

[548] *See supra* § 47[B]. and text accompanying note 500.

[549] *See, e.g.,* Farley v. Champs Fine Foods, 404 N.W.2d 493 (N.D. 1987).

[550] *See supra* § 43[B]. Similarly, rejections of offers, including rejecting counter offers, must be received to become effective.

[551] *See Farley v. Champs Fine Foods, supra* note 549, where the revocation was effective before the acceptance was mailed.

[552] International contracts for the sale of goods governed by CISG adopts this rule. Art. 18(2) requires the acceptance to "reach" the offeror within the time stated in the offer to become effective. If no time is "fixed" in the offer, the acceptance must reach the offeror within a reasonable time. While CISG adheres to the civil law tradition in requiring the acceptance to be received, once the acceptance is dispatched, the offer becomes irrevocable for the period of time stated in the offer. Art. 16(1).

[553] This problem is addressed under CISG by making the offer irrevocable once the acceptance is dispatched though the acceptance is not effective until received by the offeror within the time required by the offer. *Id.*

this notice of receipt of acceptance may be lost in the mail and the offeree would not learn that the letter of acceptance was received. Assuming the notice from the offeror was received by the offeree, how would the offeror learn that the offeree had received such notice? Another notice would be in order. Again, any of these notices could be lost in transmission. The *ad nauseam* replication of notice upon notice was recognized very early in the landmark case of *Adams v. Lindsell*.[554] That case was decided when the subjective theory of mutual assent was still influential making it doubtful whether an offer could ever be said to create a continuing power of acceptance in the offeree. That view would have made it practically impossible to consummate a contract by correspondence. A compromise was inevitable. The court held that the offer would be operative until the offeree had an opportunity to manifest acceptance by an unequivocal overt act, but the power of acceptance would not last beyond that moment. Thus, once the offeree had performed the overt act of placing the acceptance letter in the post, the contract was formed. Three decades later, the House of Lords reaffirmed the rule[555] and it has never been doubted in England since that time. A few attempts to overcome the rule in the United States[556] were unsuccessful. The rule has been accepted throughout the country.[557]

There is difficulty in suggesting that the offeree has manifested assent to an offeror by the posting of a letter which may never be received by the offeror. In an ineffective attempt to harmonize the dispatch rule with the requirements of mutual assent, arguments were advanced that the postal service is the "agent" of the offeree or the mutual agent of both parties, or that mutual assent is manifested upon the "loss of control" of the letter of acceptance once it is mailed.[558] The RESTATEMENT 2d does not attempt a significant rationale. It merely suggests that "the offeree needs a dependable basis for his decision whether to accept."[559] There is, however, a rationale for the rule beyond certainty and stability.

[B]   Rationale for the "Dispatch" Rule

A contract by correspondence involves two innocent parties. The risk that the communication of acceptance through a reasonable medium will be lost or delayed on its journey to the offeror must be allocated to one of the parties. Forced to choose one of two innocent parties, there is some justification for allocating the risk to the offeror. As master of the offer, the offeror can insist that no acceptance will be effective until it is received.[560] If he

---

[554] 1 B. & Ald. 681 [1818].

[555] *See* Dunlop v. Higgins, 1 H.L. Cas. 381 [1848].

[556] Rhode Island Tool Co. v. United States, 128 F. Supp. 417, 130 Ct. Cl. 698 (1955); Guardian Nat'l Bank v. Huntington County State Bank, 206 Ind. 185, 187 N.E. 388 (1933). Both cases were based on the ability to recall a letter after it was mailed by following postal regulations for such recall. This rationale has been rejected by other courts and commentators as well as the RESTATEMENT 2d. *See* RESTATEMENT 2d § 63 comment a. For a suggestion that the postal acceptance exception to the normal rule requiring communication of promissory acceptances is unwarranted, see Samek, *A Reassessment of the Present Rule Relating to Postal Acceptance*, 35 AUSTL. L.J. 38 (1961). For a more flexible approach, see Macneil, *Time of Acceptance: Too Many Problems for a Single Rule*, 112 U. PA. L. REV. 947 (1964).

[557] See Norkunas v. Cochran, 168 Md. App. 192, 203, 895 A. 2d 1101, 1107 (2006). See also *Farley v. Champs Fine Foods, supra* note 549 and Morrison v. Thoelke, 155 So. 2d 889 (Fla. Dist. Ct. App. 1963) and RESTATEMENT 2d § 63. The mailbox rule has been codified in several Western states.

[558] See Morrison v. Thoelke, *Id.*, for an analysis of these and other earlier theories. The "loss of control" theory was overcome by postal regulations permitting the offeree to withdraw the letter of acceptance from the mail.

[559] *See* RESTATEMENT 2d § 63 comment a.

[560] See Zimmerman v. American States Ins. Co., 763 F. Supp. 228, 231 (S.D. Ohio 1990) (quoting Professor Corbin).

chooses not to require receipt of acceptance, he should bear the risk of transmission since, as between the offeror and offeree, only the offeror had the power to control that risk.[561]

Mailbox Rule Inapplicable to Other Situations. It is important to recognize that, for almost all other purposes other than acceptance of an offer, mailing a letter is insufficient to make an action legally operative.[562] In particular, there is a superficial inconsistency between the acceptance-upon-dispatch rule and the rules that a revocation of an offer must be received. This alleged inconsistency disappears, however, when we remember that an offeror invites acceptance by post or other reasonable medium if the offer is made in that fashion, but an offeree does not invite a revocation. Similarly, a rejection of an offer must be received since an offeror does not invite a rejection any more than the offeree invites a revocation.[563]

[C]   Instantaneous Media — "Presence" Versus "Distance"

If the offeror and offeree are in the *presence* of each other rather than at some *distance*, there is virtually no risk in the transmission of the acceptance. Where the parties form their contract face-to-face, the acceptance will be effective when *heard* by the offeror rather than when it was *spoken* by the offeree.[564] If the offeror will receive the communication of acceptance instantaneously through the use of a telephone, telegram, fax message, E-mail or other electronic transmission, is the acceptance effective when spoken or sent (the "distance" rule), or is it effective only when heard or received (the "presence" rule)?

Courts have consistently applied the "distance" (dispatch) rule to media other than the post. The dispatch rule would be applied even where a private messenger is used by the offeree if the messenger was independent and maintained accurate records of its activities.[565] For the entire twentieth century and even earlier, telegrams and mailgrams have been viewed like the post, i.e., reasonable media to which the dispatch rule should apply.[566] A modern court may see no essential difference between acceptance by telegram and an acceptance by a facsimile message.[567] If the "presence" rule were to be applied to any medium, contracts by telephone present the most instantaneous medium. Yet, where parties located in different jurisdictions make a contract by telephone and there is an issue as to which law applies, the

---

[561] This analysis proceeds from the analysis by Professor Corbin, who indicates that we can place the risk on either the offeror or offeree, but we must choose one in the interest of certainty and stability. Corbin supports the choice of the mailbox rule because it closes the deal more quickly and enables performance to proceed more promptly. Moreover, he suggests that communications of acceptance through reasonable media are rarely lost or delayed. 1 CORBIN § 3.24.

[562] See, e. g., the mailbox rule did not apply to satisfy the notice requirements of an alleged violation of Title VI of the Civil Rights Act, DT v. Somers Cent. School Dist., 588 F. Supp. 2d 485, 495 (S. D. N. Y. 2008). The mailing of a letter is insufficient notice to quit a tenancy, it is not the actual payment of money enclosed in the letter, not sufficient to transfer title to a negotiable instrument, and not sufficient notice required as a condition precedent to a contractual duty. CORBIN ON CONTRACTS, 3.26.

[563] RESTATEMENT 2d § 68.

[564] RESTATEMENT 2d § 64 comment a. If, however, the offeree knows or has reason to know that his spoken words have not been heard or understood by the offeror, there is no acceptance.

[565] See RESTATEMENT 2d § 63 comment e and ill. 11, however, suggests that an acceptance sent through the offeree's own employee would not permit the application of the dispatch rule. In such a situation, the acceptance would not be effective until received.

[566] *See, e.g.,* Western Union Tel. Co. v. Wheeler, 114 Okla. 161, 245 P. 39 (1926); L. & E. Wertheimer, Inc. v. Wehle-Hartford Co., 126 Conn. 30, 9 A.2d 279 (1939), Restatement 2d § 63, comment a.

[567] Trinity Homes, L.L.C. v. Fang, 63 Va. Cir. 409, 2003 Va. Cir. LEXIS 349 (2003) citing and discussing Osprey L.L.C. v. Kelly-Moore Paint Co., 984 P.2d 194, 200 (Okla. 1999).

extant case law holds that the contract is formed where the acceptance is spoken rather than where it is heard, notwithstanding some recognition that the "presence" rule may be theoretically preferable.[568] The accelerating movement toward electronic contracting in a digitalized society will raise the same issue.[569]

Neither the Uniform Electronic Transactions Act nor the Electronic Signatures in National and Global Commerce Act ("E-Sign") address the issue of whether the mailbox rule applies to electronic acceptances such as email.[570] While it can be an important issue in a given situation, it pales by comparison to the panoply of issues involving media defects or breakdowns in the communication process, whether a given E-mail or other electronic communication should be attributed to a particular person, whether a party has complied with the requirements of a secure network, changes or errors in electronic contracts, and issues arising from contracts made between an individual and an electronic agent (a computer program) or between two electronic agents.[571]

Where there is a break in communication by telephone or other reasonable electronic medium, the RESTATEMENT 2d applies familiar principles. If an offer is made through the use of such a device and the offeree speaks or sends an acceptance but knows or has reason to know that the acceptance has not been heard or received, the acceptance is not effective when spoken or dispatched. Where the offeror knows that a reply has been transmitted but not received and the offeree is unaware of this problem, the offeror bears the risk of transmission.[572] If the offeror and offeree are equally innocent or equally at fault in not pursuing further communication after a break in transmission, there is no contract.[573] This is in keeping with the usual rule that misunderstanding between parties where neither or both parties are at fault precludes the formation of a contract.[574]

---

[568] Though it recognized the "presence" rule that would make the acceptance effective upon receipt as theoretically sound, the court in Linn v. Employers Reinsurance Corp., 392 Pa. 58, 139 A.2d 638 (1958), followed the line of cases applying the dispatch rule to telephone acceptances, thus holding that the place of contracting was where the acceptance was spoken, rather than where it was heard. See also Pierce v. Foley Bros., Inc., 283 Minn. 360, 168 N.W.2d 346 (1969), and RESTATEMENT 2d § 64. Where the acceptance is posted, courts have no difficulty holding that the contract was formed at the place of the posting. See Snow Techs., Inc., v. Sho-Deen, Inc., 1993 U.S. Dist. LEXIS 18770 (E.D. Mich. 1993).

[569] In Madaus v. November Hill Farm, Inc., 630 F. Supp. 1246 (W.D. Va. 1986), the court held that a contract was formed when the acceptance was sent by telex. However, in Centre-Point Merchant Bank Ltd. v. American Express Bank Ltd., 2000 U.S. Dist. LEXIS 17296, note 7 (S.D.N.Y. 2000), the court states, "[T]he issue of whether the 'mailbox rule' applies to contracts created through telex [is] apparently still unresolved" (quoting Metropolitan Air Serv., Inc. v. Penberthy Aircraft Leasing Co., 648 F. Supp. 1153, 1156 (S.D.N.Y. 1986)).

[570] For an analysis of statutory recognition of electronic contracts, records and signatures under the federal "E-Sign" law and the more detailed Uniform Electronic Transactions Act (UETA), see § 14 supra.

[571] UETA, which is more comprehensive than "E-Sign," addresses some of these issues in a fundamental fashion. See § 14 supra.

[572] See RESTATEMENT 2d § 64 ills. 1 and 2.

[573] RESTATEMENT 2d § 64 comment b.

[574] RESTATEMENT 2d § 20. This concept will be explored later in this volume.

[D]   Application in Option Contracts

Under the prevailing view, the dispatch rule does not apply to an irrevocable power of acceptance created by an option contract.[575] The option holder has a firm and reliable basis for making a decision to accept the offer without concern that the offer will be revoked. He can confidently rely upon the contract that only he has the power to create.[576] The parties may, of course, manifest a different intention and that manifestation will control.[577] Moreover, a statute codifying the "mailbox" rule may be interpreted to apply the rule to option contracts.[578]

[E]   Proper Address and Payment of Charges

The reasonableness of the particular medium of acceptance chosen by the offeree would depend in large part on its reliability and speed as well as any prior dealings with the offeror or usage of trade.[579] Assuming the choice of a reasonable medium, it is essential that the offeree properly address the communication and pay any charges so that it will be delivered in due course.[580] If, for example, a letter of acceptance is delayed because of insufficient postage or because it is misaddressed, the offeror does not assume the risk of such defects in the communication and the dispatch rule would not apply.[581] It should be noted, however, that the failure to use a reasonable medium of acceptance or the defective use of a reasonable medium by, e.g., misdirecting the letter or telegram or failure to pay necessary charges, will still be operative upon dispatch if it is received when a properly dispatched acceptance would have been received.[582]

---

[575] RESTATEMENT 2d § 63(b).

[576] This is the analysis in Romain v. A. Howard Wholesale Co., 506 N.E.2d 1124, 1128 (Ind. Ct. App. 1987) (citing a previous edition of this book). See Santos v. Dean, 96 Wn. App. 849, 855, 982 P. 2d 632. 635 (1999). Comment f to RESTATEMENT 2d § 63 suggests that an option contract provides a dependable basis for the decision whether to exercise the power of acceptance and removes the primary reason for the dispatch rule.

[577] See Smith v. Hevro Realty Corp., 199 Conn. 330, 337, 507 A. 2d 980, 984 (1986).

[578] See APC Operating Partnership v. Mackey, 841 F.2d 1031, 1034 (10th Cir. 1988), applying Oklahoma law — Worms v. Burgess, 620 P.2d 455, 458–59 (Okla. Ct. App. 1980) — and referring to a similar holding in California, Palo Alto Town & Country Village, Inc. v. BBTC Co., 11 Cal. 3d 494, 521 P.2d 1097 (1974).

[579] RESTATEMENT 2d § 65 comment b.

[580] For a discussion of this requirement, see University Emergency Med. Found. v. Rapier Invs., Ltd., 197 F.3d 18, 23 (1st Cir. 1999).

[581] If the offeree misdirects the letter of acceptance or fails to place proper postage thereon, RESTATEMENT 2d § 66 indicates that the dispatch ("mailbox") rule is inoperative.

[582] RESTATEMENT 2d § 67. If the misaddressed letter of acceptance manages to arrive when it would have arrived if properly addressed, the dispatch rule would be applicable. This rule is designed to avoid the possibility of the offeree's "disavowal" of acceptance upon mailing. (Comment a to § 67). Thus, if a letter with insufficient postage or the incorrect address were mailed on Monday and arrived when it would have arrived with proper address and postage, e.g., on Wednesday, the FIRST RESTATEMENT, § 67, would make the acceptance effective only upon receipt because the offeree failed to accept properly and, therefore, should lose the advantage of the "mailbox" rule. Suppose, however, that on Tuesday the offeree changed her mind and sent a telegram rejecting the offer. Such a result permits the offeree to speculate at the offeror's expense only because the offeree has misaddressed the letter of acceptance or failed to provide proper postage. The RESTATEMENT 2d avoids that possibility in new § 67. The identical analysis applies if the offeree used an uninvited medium of acceptance.

[F] Proving the Acceptance Dispatched Acceptance was Received — Mail — Fax

There is a rebuttable presumption that a mailed or otherwise dispatched item has been received. "Courts uniformly presume that an addressee receives a properly mailed item when the sender presents proof that it was properly addressed, stamped and deposited in the mail."[583] That presumption is not rebutted by the offeror's testimony denying receipt of the item.[584] In a business setting, evidence that a letter was written and signed in the ordinary course of business and placed in the usual place for mailing is receivable as evidence that the item was duly mailed.[585]

Fax. Several courts have recognized the same rebuttable presumption based on a fax confirmation generated by the sender's fax machine while other courts stop short of the presumption and regard the fax confirmation as strong evidence of receipt.[586]

[G] Interference With Normal Operation of the Dispatch Rule — Overtaking Rejections, Etc.

There is a pervasive concept of fault at work in contract law. If A knows or has reason to know that B is laboring under a mistake but chooses not to inform B of any misunderstanding, A will not be permitted to enforce a contract on A's terms but may be subject to a contractual duty on B's terms.[587] Similarly, if an offeree chooses to interfere with the normal and reasonable operation of the dispatch rule, her acceptance may not be effective on dispatch.

Reclaiming the Acceptance. If an offeree decides to post a letter manifesting her acceptance of an offer and then changes her mind, the acceptance is effective even though the offeree meets the requirements of the U. S. Postal Service or other medium of acceptance in reclaiming her letter of acceptance. The offeree may not speculate at the expense of the offeror. Therefore, if the offeror can prove that an acceptance was mailed, a contract was formed regardless of legal reclamation of the letter by the offeree.[588]

Rejection Sent Before Acceptance. Suppose an offeree decides to reject an offer and sends a notice of rejection to the offeror. The offeree then changes her mind and decides to accept. Rejections must be received to be effective while acceptances are effective upon dispatch. If these rules are applied mechanically, an acceptance would be effective if it were dispatched before the rejection was received. The obvious injustice arises if the offeror receives the rejection not knowing the acceptance has been mailed and relies upon the rejection by

---

[583] Stephenson v. El-Batrawi, 524 F. 3d 907, 913 (8th Cir. 2008).

[584] *See* Berkowitz v. Mayflower Secs., Inc., 455 Pa. 531, 317 A.2d 584 (1974).

[585] *See* Christie v. Open Pantry Food Marts, Inc., 237 Pa. Super. 243, 246, 352 A.2d 165, 1166–67 (1975) (relying upon McCormick, Evidence § 195, at 464 (2d ed. 1972)). A letter or notice of acceptance is not "sent," however, until it has been posted with the United States Post Office as contrasted with an internal mailing process. *See In re* Hilsen, 119 B.R. 435, 442 (S.D.N.Y. 1990).

[586] The cases are analyzed in Laouini v. CLM Freight Lines, Inc., 586 F. 3d 473 (7th Cir. 2009). The court notes that the few cases cited by the defendant that, at first blush, appear to lend support to the view that such a confirmation does not prove receipt were of little help to the defendant.

[587] *See* § 20 of the Restatement 2d. This concept will be explored thoroughly in subsequent sections dealing with mistake.

[588] Restatement 2d § 63 comment c.

forming a contract for the same subject matter with another party. Had the acceptance been received before the rejection, the offeror would assume a contract has been formed with the offeree. To avoid harm to the innocent offeror under these circumstances, the dispatch rule is modified. An acceptance started *after* the sending of an outright rejection or a counter offer rejection is, itself, a counter offer unless the acceptance is received by the offeror before receipt of the rejection or counter offer.[589] Since the offeree first sent a rejection before sending an acceptance, the dispatch rule does not apply to her acceptance. The acceptance will have to be received to be effective and it will not be effective unless it is received before the rejection is received.[590]

Overtaking Acceptance With a Rejection. If the offeree mails a letter of acceptance but changes her mind and overtakes her letter of acceptance with a faster medium, such as a fax message or email stating that the offer is rejected, a contract has been formed at the moment the offeree posted the acceptance. Again, however, it is necessary to protect an offeror who has justifiably relied upon the fax stating that the offer has been rejected. While a contract was formed when the acceptance letter was dispatched, the offeree will be estopped from enforcing the contract against an innocent offeror who has relied on the offeree's overtaking rejection.[591] By holding the offeree to the bargain she made by dispatching the letter of acceptance while precluding her from enforcing that bargain where the innocent offeror relied upon the overtaking rejection, the bargain and protection of the offeror are preserved. Absent reliance by the offeror, the contract that was formed when the acceptance was mailed is effective.

Repudiation or Rescission. The offeree's attempt to revoke the acceptance of the offer could be interpreted as a repudiation of her duties under the contract, i.e., the contract created upon posting the letter of acceptance. Alternatively, the fax or email rejecting the offer could be seen as a proposal by the offeree that the parties surrender their mutual rights and duties that were created when the offeree mailed her acceptance, i.e., an offer to rescind the recently formed contract. If the offer of rescission is accepted, the contract is discharged.[592]

Importance of Purpose. In any permutation of the dispatch rule, the *purpose* of the rule must be kept in mind, i.e., the risk of transmission is normally allocated to the offeror, not because the offeror is at fault in any real sense, but only because the offeror could have controlled the risk of transmission and chose not to do so. The risk of transmission allocated to the offeror should not go beyond loss or delay in a properly addressed and stamped letter or other medium where the dispatch by the offeree was proper.[593] Like any other workable rule of contract law, the dispatch rule is not sacred. When its purpose is not being served, the rule will not apply or, at the very least, it will be modified to avoid injustice to innocent parties.

---

[589] RESTATEMENT 2d § 40.

[590] *Id.*, comment b.

[591] *See* RESTATEMENT 2d § 63 comment c.

[592] *See* RESTATEMENT 2d § 63 comment c, which, without elaboration, suggests the possibility of an overtaking communication of revocation operating either as a repudiation of the contract or an offer to rescind it.

[593] RESTATEMENT 2d § 66.

§ 49   "MIRROR IMAGE" — "MATCHING ACCEPTANCE" — QUALIFIED OR CONDITIONAL ACCEPTANCE — EQUIVOCAL ACCEPTANCE — ACCEPTANCE REQUESTING ADDITIONAL TERMS — "GRUMBLING ACCEPTANCE"

[A]   The "Mirror Image" Rule

Since the offeror is the master of the offer,[594] the offeree may exercise the power of acceptance created by the offer only by complying with the requirements of the offer. Any attempt by the offeree to change the terms of the offer and, simultaneously, exercise the power of acceptance is theoretically impossible. The offeror has assumed a risk of a certain scope by making the offer. It would seem impossible for the offeree to enlarge the scope of that risk by varying the terms of the offer in attempting to accept it because the only power conferred upon the offeree by the offeror is the power to accept the offer created by the offeror. This is the inexorable logic underlying the so-called "mirror image" (matching acceptance) rule: the acceptance must be the "mirror image" of the offer, i.e., it must exactly match the terms of the offer.[595]

The rule, however, is often easier to state than to apply. The express terms of any offer may be subject to interpretation. The offer may be silent with respect to certain terms and the offeree may indicate his intention to proceed according to reasonable terms not mentioned in the offer. The offeree may manifest an intention to accept the offer while indicating his displeasure with the offer or suggesting additional arrangements between the parties. Moreover, the manifestation of acceptance may be anything but clear. It is important to distinguish among *qualified* or *conditional* acceptances, *equivocal* acceptances, acceptances which suggest additional or different terms and "grumbling acceptances." Some of these responses to offers are operative acceptances and others are not.

[B]   Qualified or Conditional Acceptance

We have already explored the situation involving a purported acceptance that adds terms or changes terms in the offer and manifests the offeree's intention to be bound only on the condition that new or different terms will be part of the contract. We concluded that such a purported acceptance is not an acceptance. Since it is not an acceptance, the common law requires it to be placed in another category. It is a counter offer that typically rejects the original offer and creates a new power of acceptance.[596] To constitute a qualified or conditional

---

[594] Restatement 2d § 29.

[595] "Unless an acceptance mirrors the offeror's terms, neither omitting nor adding terms, it has no legal effect as an acceptance and operates as a rejection and a counter offer." Safeco Ins. Co. of Am. v. City of White House, Tennessee, 36 F.3d 540, 546 (6th Cir. 1994). What has become the classic case illustrating this rule is Poel v. Brunswick-Balke-Collender Co., 216 N.Y. 310, 110 N.E. 619 (1915), in which the purported acceptance contained a printed clause requiring acknowledgment by the other party. Since a literal application of this requirement would place the power of acceptance in that party, the purported acceptance was a conditional acceptance and, therefore, a counter offer. In § 58 of the Restatement 2d, the requirement is stated as follows: "An acceptance must comply with the requirements of the offer as to the promise to be made or the performance to be rendered." Then, in § 59, "A reply to an offer which purports to accept it but is conditional on the offeror's assent to terms additional to or different from those offered is not an acceptance but is a counter offer." For a narrative of the "ribbon matching" or "mirror" rule of common law, see Dorton v. Collins & Aikman Corp., 453 F.2d 1161 (6th Cir. 1972).

[596] *See* Restatement 2d § 39 comment b and § 59 comment a. *See also* Davis v. Satrom, 383 N.W.2d 831 (N.D. 1986);

"acceptance" (counter offer), the response to the offer must expressly condition the offeree's assent to the variant terms in the offeree's response. Such a response, however, must be carefully distinguished from other types of responses.

[C]   Equivocal Acceptance

Where the offer requires or permits an acceptance by promise, thereby necessitating notice of acceptance,[597] it is often suggested that the acceptance must be unequivocal, i.e., that the offeror is entitled to a clear manifestation of acceptance by the offeree before the offeror will be said to be bound to a contract.[598] The offeror is not required to guess or draw inferences of assent from the offeree's response to the offer. If the offeror receives a response in the form of an acknowledgment merely stating that the offer has been received, such a response is equivocal and does not bind the offeror. Thus, simply logging a purchase order as received does not manifest acceptance of the offer.[599] If, however, the offeror reasonably relies on certain manifestations of the offeree that indicate acceptance of the offer, the offeror will be protected. A court will find a contract formed though the manifestation of acceptance is ambiguous.[600] The concept is based upon fairness to an offeror who neither knows nor should know the meaning attached by the offeree to the offeree's equivocal response to the offer.[601] If, therefore, the offeror may justifiably infer assent to his offer from the offeree's response and he acts on that justifiable inference, a contract will be formed to protect the offeror. He need not, however, infer assent from an equivocal response, but may reasonably assume his offer has not been accepted. The test to be applied is the reasonable understanding of the offeror.[602]

[D]   Acceptance Merely Suggesting Variant Terms

If an acceptance is stated in clear, unequivocal terms but merely suggests or requests terms different from the offer as contrasted with conditioning or qualifying the response on the offeror's assent to the different terms, the acceptance is effective and the suggested or requested terms are mere proposals for addition to the contract.[603] A clear illustration is an

---

Dataserv Equip., Inc. v. Technology Fin. Leasing Corp., 364 N.W.2d 838 (Minn. Ct. App. 1985); Normile v. Miller, 313 N.C. 98, 326 S.E.2d 11 (1985); Glende Motor Co. v. Superior Court of Sutter Cty., 159 Cal. App. 3d 389, 205 Cal. Rptr. 682 (3d Dist. 1984); Duval & Co. v. H. A. Malcom, 233 Ga. 784, 214 S.E.2d 356 (1975); Ebline v. Campbell, 209 Md. 584, 121 A.2d 828 (1956).

[597] See supra § 47.

[598] "[P]laintiff's October 16, 2009 email did not constitute an unequivocal and unambiguous acceptance, demonstrating a meeting of the minds. Indeed, plaintiff's October 16, 2009 email conceded to one of defendant's demands and then deleted a provision regarding partial payments." Deval Denizilik Ve Ticaret A. S. v. Schenker Italiana, 2009 U. S. Dist. LEXIS 120947 at *5 (S. D. N. Y. 2009). See also Kutsmeda v. Informed Escrow, Inc., 2006 U. S. Dist. LEXIS 42081 (E. D. Va. 2006) and RESTATEMENT 2d § 57.

[599] Foremost Pro Color, Inc. v. Eastman Kodak Co., 703 F.2d 534, 539 (9th Cir. 1983), cert. denied, 465 U.S. 1038, 104 S. Ct. 1315, 79 L. Ed. 2d 712 (1984). RESTATEMENT 2d § 57, ill.1.

[600] See Empire Mach. Co. v. Litton Bus. Tel. Sys., 115 Ariz. 568, 566 P.2d 1044 (Ct. App. 1977), and RESTATEMENT 2d § 57 comment b.

[601] See RESTATEMENT 2d § 20.

[602] See Murray, The Standardized Agreement Phenomena in the Restatement (Second) of Contracts, 67 CORNELL L. REV. 735, 756–58 (1982).

[603] A request for an addendum to a contract did not constitute a counter offer. Merely requesting such an addition or modification does not affect the power of acceptance. Abbevill Offshore Quarters, Inc. v. Taylor Energy Co., 286 Fed. Appx. 124, 127 (5th Cir. 2008) citing RESTATEMENT 2d § 61.

offer that does not contain any terms relating to a method of payment and a response that unequivocally accepts the offer but adds a suggested method of payment.[604] If a buyer unequivocally accepts a seller's offer to sell goods but adds a desire to purchase other goods not mentioned in the original offer, there is an acceptance of the original offer and a new offer to purchase the other goods.[605] Whether the offeree's response unequivocally accepts the offer and merely suggests or requests additional or different terms as contrasted with conditioning the "acceptance" on the offeror's assent to the variant terms is a question of the fair interpretation of the response according to the reasonable understanding of the offeror.[606] Finally, a response to an offer that suggests terms consistent with trade usage[607] or prior course of dealing[608] is an operative acceptance since such terms become part of the contract absent any contrary expression in the offer.[609]

[E]   "Grumbling Acceptance"

If the response to an offer indicates dissatisfaction or displeasure with the offer but still manifests an unequivocal and unconditional acceptance, it operates as an acceptance notwithstanding the "grumbling" statements of the offeree. An offeree need not be pleased with an offer; he need not like the offer and may even harbor ill feelings toward the offeror. Nonetheless, he has a power of acceptance and may exercise it though adding an expression of discontent in an otherwise clear manifestation of acceptance. Thus, where an employee responded to a renewal of his contract for another term by suggesting, in effect, "I don't like your offer, I don't think it's right or fair, but I accept it," the court rejected the employer's claim that this response was a qualified or conditional acceptance amounting to a counter offer. Rather, these expressions of dissatisfaction constituted a "grumbling acceptance" but an acceptance, nonetheless.[610]

§ 50   THE "BATTLE OF THE FORMS" PROBLEM

[A]   Non-Matching Terms — "Dickered" and "Non-Dickered"

The last section emphasized that the common law principle that a conditional or qualified "acceptance" was not an acceptance because it did not match the terms of the offer. Such an "acceptance" is a counter offer. It is abundantly clear that, if *A* offers to sell 1000 units of X35

---

[604] *See* Kodiak Island Borough v. Large, 622 P.2d 440 (Alaska 1981); Martindell v. Fiduciary Counsel, Inc., 131 N.J. Eq. 523, 26 A.2d 171, *aff'd*, 133 N.J. Eq. 408, 30 A.2d 281 (1943); Rucker v. Sanders, 182 N.C. 607, 109 S.E. 857 (1921).

[605] *See* McAfee v. Brewer, 214 Va. 579, 203 S.E.2d 129 (1974). Even though this case involved an analysis of UCC § 2-207, to be explored in the next section of this volume, the analysis presented in this section would be effective dehors the Code section.

[606] *See* Murray, *supra* note 602, at 758 and RESTATEMENT 2d § 61 comment a.

[607] See UCC § 1-205(2), which defines "usage of trade" as "any practice or method of dealing having such regularity of observance in a place, vocation or trade as to justify an expectation that it will be observed with respect to the transaction in question."

[608] UCC § 1-205(1) defines "course of dealing" as "a sequence of previous conduct between the parties to a particular transaction which is fairly to be regarded as establishing a common basis of understanding for interpreting their expressions and other conduct."

[609] See Columbia Nitrogen Corp. v. Royster Co., 451 F.2d 3 (4th Cir. 1971), suggesting that such terms automatically become part of the contract unless they are expressly negated. See UCC § 2-202, comment 2.

[610] Price v. Oklahoma College of Osteopathic Med. & Surgery, 733 P.2d 1357 (Okla. Ct. App. 1986).

plastic to *B* at $10 per unit for a total price of $10,000, a purported acceptance by *B* which states that he "accepts" the offer but will take only 500 units at $10 per unit, or 1000 units at $9 per unit, or 1000 units of R43 plastic at $10 per unit, none of the responses could possibly be an acceptance of *A'* s offer because each seeks to create a contract the offeror never intended. Terms such as the identification of the goods, price or quantity are consciously intended as terms that circumscribe the power of acceptance. To suggest that *B*'s power of acceptance could create such new or different risks that *A* never assumed is absurd. Cases raising this issue are clear in holding that no such power of acceptance exits.[611]

"Standardized" (Prefabricated) Contract Forms. There is, however, a pervasive problem affecting millions of daily transactions evidenced by standardized, printed forms where the response *appears* to manifest the offeree's acceptance of the offer though it also contains prefabricated terms that vary the terms of the offer. The records of the overwhelming majority of contracts in our society are standardized forms.[612] The use of prefabricated forms promote high levels of efficiency. It would not be possible to create the millions of contracts made hourly in a modern market economy if every clause had to be repeatedly read, reconsidered and renegotiated. Efficiency demanded "standard" clauses that would be generally ignored while the parties focused upon their bargained-for terms where they consciously considered the subject matter, the quantity, the price and, perhaps, a delivery term. Questions of warranties, remedies and adjudication of disputes are not consciously adverted to in the typical transaction. Efficiency in the use of printed forms, however, can lead to unintended and unjust results in some situations.

Standardized "Boilerplate" Terms. Instead of consciously considered terms, the fine print clauses, often called "boilerplate," contain legal language in fine print that disinvites reasonable parties from reading them. Consumers or merchants are convinced that they would not understand such clauses even if they took the time to read them. Moreover, they recognize that they are typically nonnegotiable for any buyer with inferior bargaining power. Among the typical clauses on sellers' forms are attempts to disclaim or exclude implied warranties that would otherwise automatically attach under the UCC.[613] They also seek to limit the buyer's normal remedies, exclude consequential damages,[614] reduce the period of the statute of limitations,[615] and require any disputes to be resolved through arbitration, thereby replacing resolution of disputes in court as assumed by the Code. Choice-of-law and choice-of-forum clauses are also common. Reasonable parties, including merchants in commercial transactions, do not read the fine print "boilerplate" on the forms received in response to their

---

[611] *See, e. g.*, United Foods v. Hadley-Peoples Mfg. Co., 1994 Tenn. App. LEXIS 277 (Tenn. Ct. App. May 20, 1994) (citing Howard Constr. Co. v. Jeff-Cole Quarries, Inc., 669 S.W.2d 221, 229 (Mo. Ct. App. 1983)). *See also* Koehring Co. v. Glowacki, 77 Wis. 2d 497, 253 N.W.2d 64 (1977) (purported acceptance in a telegram adds a condition to the terms of the offer changing the terms of the offer); Duval & Co. v. Malcom, 233 Ga. 784, 214 S.E.2d 356 (1975) (purported acceptance contained a material alteration in the quantity term).

[612] Professor W. David Slawson suggested that standard forms are probably the written evidence of the contract in up to 99% of all contracts. Slawson, *Standard Form Contracts and Democratic Control of Lawmaking Power*, 84 HARV. L. REV. 529 (1971).

[613] The implied warranty of merchantability in § 2-314, the warranty of fitness for a particular purpose under § 2-315.

[614] The buyer's remedies for a seller's breach are listed in UCC § 2-711 and consequential damage are defined in § 2-715. Consequential damages may be excluded unless the exclusion is unconscionable (§ 2-719(3).

[615] UCC § 2-725 provides a four-year statute of limitations commencing upon tender of delivery.

proposals.[616]

The paradigm transaction. The common problem is illustrated by an offer in the form of a purchase order sent to a seller who responds with an acknowledgment form manifesting acceptance[617] of the negotiated terms of the offer, i.e., the subject matter, the quantity, the price and, perhaps, certain delivery terms. These are the terms of either form which have been consciously considered by the offeror-buyer and the offeree-seller. They are often called negotiated or "dickered" terms.[618] The seller's acknowledgment form clearly indicates that the seller will ship the goods at the price and on the delivery terms found in that purchase order. A comparison of the "dickered" terms of both forms, i.e., the terms that were typewritten or word processed in the blank spaces of the paper forms and, more recently, inserted in the boxes on computer screens, clearly manifests a "matching acceptance" of an offer. The seller's acknowledgment form, however, contains the standard, prefabricated boilerplate terms that were present on the form before the buyer made the offer. Upon receiving this acknowledgment, the typical buyer ignores prefabricated terms. Moreover, it is just as likely that the seller neither read nor understood such printed terms albeit they appear on his own form. The printed terms are drafted by lawyers in their attempts to protect their clients against any contingency.[619] Should the buyer be bound by material, risk-shifting provisions on the seller's form that a reasonable buyer would not have read or understood? It is important to understand the common law reaction to a simpler situation before continuing with our discussion of what came to be known as the "battle of the forms."

[B]   Duty to Read Non-Dickered Terms in a Single Document

If only *one* document containing printed clauses was signed by both parties and represented the exclusive written evidence of the contract, the common law treated the document as binding the parties to its "dickered" *and* printed clauses though there may have

---

[616] "Judges are skeptical that even businesspeople read boilerplate, so they are reluctant, rightly or wrongly, to make a contract fail on the basis of a printed condition in a form contract." Northrop Corp. v. Litronic Indus., 29 F.3d 1173, 1178 (7th Cir. 1994). *See also* Murray, *supra* note 602, at 778–79 n.207.

[617] A response that merely acknowledges receipt of the order (offer) is not an acceptance. *See* § 49.C., text accompanying note 602.

[618] The chief architect of the UCC and principal draftsman of Article 2, Professor Karl Llewellyn, suggested that "dickered" terms were the terms to which the parties consciously adverted: "The answer, I suggest, is this: Instead of thinking about 'assent' to boiler plate clauses, we can recognize that so far as concerns the specific, there is no assent at all. What has in fact been assented to, specifically, are the few dickered terms, and the broad type of the transaction, and but one thing more. That one thing more is a blanket assent (not a specific assent) to any not unreasonable or indecent terms the seller may have on his form, which do not alter or eviscerate the reasonable meaning of the dickered terms. The fine print which has not been read has no business to cut under the reasonable meaning of those dickered terms which constitute the dominant and only real expression of agreement, but much of it commonly belongs in." K. LLEWELLYN, THE COMMON LAW TRADITION: DECIDING APPEALS 370 (1960).

[619] "[T]he form document is not the direct product of the businessman's knowledge. Rather, it is the product of the draftsman's art. Between the drafting party and the actual draftsman, much knowledge, and much of the sense of fairness, may be lost. More importantly, the professional draftsman's goal is to protect his client as fully as possible from legally enforceable obligations, including some relating to risks that the businessman might be willing to accept. In this process, the temptation, and indeed the art, is to draft up to the limit allowed by law, rather than to change only those features of the background law that must be altered for the trade reasonably to proceed." Rakoff, *Contract of Adhesion: An Essay in Reconstruction*, 96 HARV. L. REV. 1173, 1205 (1983). This is an elaboration of the insight of Karl Llewellyn, "Business lawyers tend to draft to the edge of the possible." Statement of K. Llewellyn in 1 STATE OF NEW YORK LAW REVISION COMMISSION HEARINGS ON THE UNIFORM COMMERCIAL CODE 113 (1954). Further support is found in Murray, *The Chaos of the "Battle of the Forms": Solutions*, 39 VAND. L. REV. 1307, 1350–51 (1986).

been good reason to believe that one of the parties, *e.g.*, a consumer, would not have read or understood one or more clauses that shifted a material risk to that party. This result was predicated upon the logic of the common law rule that one is bound by what he signs:

> It will not do for a man to enter into a contract and, when called upon to respond to its obligations, to say that he did not read it when he signed it, or did not know what it contained. If this were permitted, contracts would not be worth the paper on which they are written. But such is not the law. A contractor must stand by the words of his contract; and, if he will not read what he signs, he alone is responsible for his omission.[620]

A modern restatement of the same rule would invariably emphasize exceptions for fraud,[621] duress[622] or unconscionability.[623] Beyond these exceptions, a modern court may decide that a particular printed clause should not be binding on the party against whom it was designed to operate simply because such a party cannot be fairly said to have manifested assent to a particular clause.[624] While the general rule remains that one is bound by to terms in a document to which he has manifested assent, modern courts have become more concerned about the abuse of the bargaining process, including the operative effect of standardized terms. As will be seen in a later discussion of these issues, however, the pristine analysis has proven to be elusive.[625]

[C]   Winning the "Battle of the Forms" at Common Law — The Last Shot Principle

If a buyer receives a seller's acknowledgment that repeats the "dickered" terms of the buyer's purchase order, such a response appears to be a definite expression of acceptance. If, however, the same acknowledgment contains non-dickered, standardized clauses of warranty disclaimers, exclusions of consequential damages, arbitration mandates or other terms that vary from normal implied terms, should such "boilerplate" terms that are typically ignored by

---

[620] Upton v. Tribilcock, 91 U.S. 45, 50, 23 L. Ed. 203 (1875).

[621] *See* Pioneer Credit Co. v. Medalen, 326 N.W.2d 717, 719 (N.D. 1982): "Failure to read a document before signing it does not excuse ignorance of its contents unless the party shows that 'he was prevented from reading it by fraud, artifice or design by the other party or his authorized representative' " (citing Oliver-Mercer Elec. Coop. v. Fisher, 146 N.W.2d 346, 357 (N.D. 1966)).

[622] Colburn v. Mid-State Homes, Inc., 289 Ala. 255, 266 So. 2d 865, 868 (1972): "If no duress or fraud has been exercised, . . . he is . . . presumed to know what it was that he signed."

[623] *See* Richardson Greenshields Secs., Inc. v. Metz, 566 F. Supp. 131, 133 (S.D.N.Y. 1983): The failure to discuss or negotiate the terms of an agreement and the fact that no one explained the agreement to the signer does not make the agreement unenforceable unless it rises "to the level of fraud, overreaching or unconscionability." The concept of unconscionability permits a court to declare a part or all of a contract inoperative if it would result in "unfair surprise" or if it would be "oppressive" to the signer. It is an elusive concept that is explored in detail later in this volume. See UCC § 2-302 and the comments thereto.

[624] See Parton v. Mark Pirtle Oldsmobile-Cadillac-Isuzu, Inc., 730 S.W.2d 634, 637–38 (Tenn. Ct. App. 1987), holding that a clause exculpating a dealer from any loss or damage to a vehicle was not enforceable. Though recognizing that its fomulation may appear to be based on the doctrine of unconscionability, the court emphasized that it did not intend to predicate its holding on that doctrine in this case. Rather, "[I]t is simply a matter of ascertaining the agreement of the parties in light of modern notions of fair play: a matter of finding the elusive 'circle of assent' which contains the agreement of the parties." The "circle of assent" analysis quoted in part by the court at 637 of its opinion is taken from the second edition of this book at §§ 352–353.

[625] *See* § 98, *infra.*

reasonable buyers preclude a court from characterizing the acknowledgment as an acceptance of an offer? The common law reaction was clear: such an acknowledgment could not possibly constitute an acceptance since it violated the "matching acceptance" or "mirror image" rule that the acceptance had to match the terms of the offer.

If the response to an offer did not match and, therefore, did not constitute an acceptance, the response had to be something other than an acceptance. The only remaining common law compartment was the counter offer. A non-matching acceptance had to be a counter offer because it appeared to be a qualified or conditional acceptance which is, necessarily, a counter offer.[626] The typical counter offer rejects the original offer and creates a new power of acceptance.[627]

Reasonable buyers and seller were generally unaware of these manufactured legal effects. Both parties assumed they had made a contract by their exchange of the purchase order and acknowledgment forms because the "dickered" terms of both forms — the terms to which such parties would consciously advert — were identical. Thus, after the seller sent its acknowledgment, it shipped the goods and the buyer received and accepted the goods. Millions of such transactions occur daily without difficulty. It would have been more than rare to discover a buyer or seller who realized or cared that their exchange of forms did not create a contract since the seller's acknowledgment containing the different or additional boilerplate terms was a counter offer. If, however, the buyer later discovered a defect in the goods and the seller refused to cure the defect or compensate the buyer for any losses, the dispute would focus on the hitherto ignored terms of the contract.

If the buyer claimed a breach of the implied warranty of merchantability,[628] the seller's lawyer would rely upon the printed acknowledgment clause disclaiming the implied warranty of merchantability. The warranty term in the buyer's form and the disclaimer of warranty in the seller's form clashed — the paradigmatic "battle of the forms" problem. The seller would not argue that his form was superior to the buyer's purchase order. Rather, the seller would pursue the inexorable logic of the common law, i.e., the seller's acknowledgment did not match the terms of the offer. It was, therefore, a counter offer which had the effect of rejecting the buyer's offer. The counter offer created a new power of acceptance in the former offeror. The buyer was now an offeree and could exercise that power of acceptance in any reasonable manner, i.e., by promising to purchase the goods on the terms of the seller's acknowledgment, or simply by accepting the goods since an acceptance by conduct is an effective acceptance.[629] By accepting the goods shipped by the seller, the buyer had accepted the seller's counter offer to ship on the terms of the seller's acknowledgment. Since the terms of that counter offer acknowledgment disclaimed the implied warranty of merchantability, the contract contained no such warranty and the buyer's effort to recover for breach of that warranty was in vain. *The seller "won" the "battle of the forms" simply because it fired the last shot in the battle.*

The Logical but Defective Common Law Analysis. The traditional common law analysis was based on unassailable logic of common law offer and acceptance rules, but it ignored the agreement that the parties thought they had made when they exchanged their forms, i.e., it

---

[626] *See supra* § 49[B].

[627] *See supra* § 43[D].

[628] The implied warranty of merchantability is currently set forth in UCC § 2-314.

[629] *See* RESTATEMENT 2d § 19. *See also supra* § 46.

ignored the parties factual bargain[630] or "true understanding"[631] or "genuine assent"[632] of the parties. The analysis compelled a result based upon technical constraints of the common law.[633] By regarding the unread, printed clauses of the acknowledgment form as operative, the common law discovered a "conditional" or "qualified" acceptance, i.e., a counter offer, but the offeror did not understand the acknowledgment as a counter offer. He assumed it was an acceptance and that the deal was closed. Moreover, the seller was typically operating under the same assumption at the moment the forms were exchanged. No reasonable merchant would have discovered a condition to the seller's acceptance of the buyer's purchase order in such printed clauses that were ignored by both parties when the forms were exchanged.[634] The possible manifest injustice to buyers in the typical situation was equally applicable to sellers where the buyer is the offeree. In a classic illustration of the injustice of the common law analysis of the battle of the forms, a buyer escaped a contract that the buyer and seller thought they had made. As an afterthought, the buyer discovered a printed clause on the purchase order form it had intended as an acceptance of the seller's offer. The clause required an acknowledgment of the buyer's order because the form was typically used as an offer seeking an acknowledgment to confirm acceptance of the offer. Notwithstanding compelling evidence that neither party regarded the printed clause in the purchase order as operative, the court held that it was, necessarily, a counter offer. No contract was formed and the buyer escaped the closed deal that both parties had assumed.[635]

In the typical situation involving a buyer's offer and a seller's acknowledgment that is construed as a counter offer, no contract results from the exchange of forms. The seller's shipment and buyer's acceptance of the goods formed a contract by conduct. Though surprising to the buyer and only belatedly discovered by the seller, the terms of that contract were the terms of the seller's counter offer, the "*last shot*" fired in the battle of the forms. The "*last shot*" principle was firmly embedded in the very common situation of exchanged forms where the "dickered" terms were identical but the printed clauses did not match. It was abundantly clear to Professor Karl Llewellyn, who was to become the chief architect of the UCC and the principal draftsman of Article 2 of the Code, that a party should not win the "battle of the forms" simply because he fired the last shot in that battle.[636] Moreover,

---

[630] See the definition of "agreement" in § 1-201(3) of the UCC, i.e., "the bargain of the parties in fact." *See also* Murray, *The Article 2 Prism: The Underlying Philosophy of* Article 2 of the Uniform Commercial Code, 21 WASHBURN L.J. 1 (1981), and Murray, *The Standardized Agreement Phenomenon in the Restatement (Second) of Contracts*, 67 CORNELL L. REV. 735 (1982).

[631] See comment 2 to UCC § 2-202, which states the objective as arriving at the "true understanding" of the parties' agreement.

[632] See Parton v. Mark Pirtle Oldsmobile-Cadillac-Isuzu, Inc., 730 S.W.2d 634, 637 (Tenn. Ct. App. 1987), relying upon §§ 352–353 of the second edition of this book in which the concept of "genuine" assent is distinguished from "apparent assent."

[633] For several illustrations of the attempt to overcome the technical constraints of the common law of contracts which interfere with the effectuation of the factual bargain or "true understanding" or "genuine assent" of the parties, see Murray, *Chaos, supra* note 619, at 1312 n.18.

[634] In dealing with this problem with respect to the then new UCC, Professor Karl Llewellyn stated, "Those unhappy cases which find a condition where no businessman would find one are carefully disapproved." 1 STATE OF NEW YORK LAW REVISION COMMISSION HEARINGS ON THE UNIFORM COMMERCIAL CODE 55 (1954).

[635] Poel v. Brunswick-Balke-Collender Co., 216 N.Y. 310, 110 N.E. 619 (1916). The case is analyzed in Murray, *Chaos, supra* note 619, at 1315–18.

[636] Professor Grant Gilmore, who is best known for his scholarship with respect to security interests in personal property, was one of Professor Llewellyn's co-workers in creating the UCC. With respect to the "battle of the forms"

Llewellyn recognized the total lack of assent to any bargain other than the bargain which the parties thought they had made. He was eager to change the procrustean rules of common law to recognize the bargain the parties reasonably thought they had made — the factual bargain. He knew that this effort would require a radical transformation of classical contract law with respect to the "matching acceptance" rule.[637]

[D] Non-Dickered Terms in a Confirmation

It is not uncommon to see a statement that the "battle of the forms" involves two forms.[638] On its face, this appears eminently sensible since a "battle" involving only one form is reminiscent of the Zen riddle of "the sound one hand clapping." While the paradigm situation involves two forms, a purchase order and a seller's acknowledgment containing additional or different terms, a not uncommon situation involves only one form.

Where the parties have arrived at an oral agreement in person or by telephone, one or both of the parties will typically dispatch a confirmation of the agreement. If there are two confirmations with conflicting terms, the "battle of the confirmations" is certainly a worthy battle of the forms. If, however, only one party sends a confirmation which contains terms different from or additional to the terms of the oral agreement, there is a "battle" between the terms of the original oral contract and the different or additional terms in the confirmation to determine whether the confirmation terms become part of the contract.[639] Thus, the popular characterization, "battle of the forms," is misleading since it is inaccurate to suggest that the "battle" must involve two exchanged forms. Situations involving either one or two confirmations are discussed in the next section.[640]

---

problem, he commented that it was a problem that Professor Llewellyn "dearly loved." *See* Coogan, Dunn, Farnsworth, Gilmore, Hogan, Kripke, Leary & Sachse, *Advanced ALI-ABA Course of Study on Banking and Secured Transactions Under the Uniform Commercial Code*, Transcript at 108 (1968).

[637] Professor Llewellyn was disturbed by suggestions that the changes he contemplated in Article 2 and sales law in general were misunderstood as merely changing the law in "a few particulars." He made it clear that the Code would "remake" sales law *vigorously and over the whole field* in order that the law may be made to conform to commercial practice, and may be read and make sense. . . . The changes are, in fact, deep, wide, vital. And they are utterly needed in order to produce intelligent and workable commercial law. Professor Mentschikoff's comments in your final session are peculiarly on point: The present law 'works' by being *ignored* by the *decent* business man." 1 State of New York Law Revision Commission Hearings on the Uniform Commercial Code 49 (1954) (emphasis in original). [Professor Soia Mentschikoff is well-known for her major contributions to the UCC while working with her husband, Karl Llewellyn.].

[638] See, e.g., ProCD v. Zeidenberg, 86 F.3d 1447 (7th Cir. 1996), where the court unsuccessfully distinguishes its fact situation from another case, Step-Saver Data Sys., Inc. v. Wyse Tech., 939 F.2d 91 (3d Cir. 1991), on the footing that *Step-Saver* involved two forms. As will be seen later in this chapter, in effect, *Step-Saver* involved only one form and it was, nonetheless, a "battle of the forms" case.

[639] For a well-known "battle of the forms" case where the court recognizes a situation involving only one confirmation of an oral agreement, see Dorton v. Collins & Aikman Corp., 453 F.2d 1161 (6th Cir. 1972).

[640] § 51[G], *infra*.

§ 51   "BATTLE OF THE FORMS": SOLUTIONS — SECTION 2-207 OF THE UNIFORM COMMERCIAL CODE

[A]   The Essential Purpose of Section 2-207 — Overcoming the "Last Shot" Principle

We have just explored the common law insistence that responses to offers containing variant terms, even ignored boilerplate clauses, convert such responses to counter offers. Where a seller sends an acknowledgment containing dickered terms identical to the offer, it is likely unaware that its variant boilerplate precludes it from constituting an acceptance. Similarly, a reasonable buyer may view such an acknowledgment as an acceptance. Notwithstanding the absence of any contract via the exchange of forms, reasonable sellers may mistakenly assume that shipment of the goods is a necessary duty required under an existing contract, and the buyer similarly assumes that it has a contractual duty to accept the shipped goods. If disputes arise, however, the buyer will be surprised to learn that he is bound by the seller's terms. UCC Section 207 was designed to remedy the possible injustice in the application of the "last shot rule."[641]

It is important to focus on the language of the "celebrated" or "infamous" Section 2-207.

Section 2-207 — Additional Terms in Acceptance or Confirmation.

(1) A definite and seasonable expression of acceptance or a written confirmation which is sent within a reasonable time operates as an acceptance even though it states terms additional to or different from those offered or agreed upon, unless acceptance is expressly made conditional on assent to any different or additional terms.

(2) The additional terms are to be construed as proposals for additions to the contract. Between merchants, such terms become part of the contract unless:

(a) the offer expressly limits acceptance to the terms of the offer;

(b) they materially alter it; or

(c) notification of objection to them has already been given or is given within a reasonable time after notice of them is received.

(3) Conduct by both parties which recognizes the existence of a contract is sufficient to establish a contract for sale although the writings of the parties do not otherwise

---

[641] A number of courts expressly recognize this essential purpose of 2-207. *See, e.g.,* v. Union Carbide Industrial Gases, Inc., 347 N. J. Super. 524, 534, 790 A 2d 962, 968 (2002) (Section 2-207 "was enacted to reform the common law mirror-image rule and reject the last shot doctrine which accorded undue advantage to the order in which forms were sent"). Brewster of Lynchburg v. Dial Corp., 33 F.3d 355, 362 (4th Cir. 1994) ("This code section displaces the common law's 'last shot rule' ") Step-Saver Data Sys., Inc. v. Wyse Technology, 939 F.2d 91, 99 (3d Cir. 1991) ("The reasons that led to the rejection of the last shot rule, and the adoption of section 2-207, apply fully in this case"); Diamond Fruit Growers, Inc. v. Krack Corp., 794 F.2d 1440, 1444 (9th Cir. 1986) ("Section 2-207 accomplishes this result in part by doing away with the common law's 'last shot' rule); Frank M. Booth, Inc. v. Reynolds Metals Co., 754 F. Supp. 1441, 1447 (E.D. Cal. 1991) ("At common law, the offeree/counter offeror gets all of its terms simply because it fired the last shot in the exchange of forms. Section [2-207] does away with this result"); Transwestern Pipeline Co. v. Monsanto Co., 46 Cal. App. 4th 502, 513, 53 Cal. Rptr. 2d 887, 893 (2d Dist. 1996) (2-207 was intended to abolish the "last shot rule"); Uniroyal, Inc. v. Chambers Gasket & Mfg. Co., 177 Ind. App. 508, 517, 380 N.E.2d 571, 582 note 2 (1978) ("[T]he objective of 2-207 . . . is to eradicate the last-shot technique available to an offeree under the common law mirror image rule").

establish a contract. In such case, the terms of the particular contract consist of those terms on which the writings of the parties agree, together with any supplementary terms incorporated under any other provision of this Act.[642]

[B]   "A Definite and Seasonable Expression of Acceptance" Instead of a Counter Offer

The opening phrase of § 2-207(1) states a threshold requirement of "[a] definite and seasonable expression of acceptance." The millions of words expended on explaining this controversial section of the UCC, however, often ignore this critical requirement. To suggest the existence of a "definite expression of acceptance" that also includes different or additional terms is counterintuitive, at least to the common lawyer who regards the "mirror image" rule as sacred. It is not uncommon for courts to state, "As a general rule, under section 2-207 the common law counter offer becomes an acceptance if it contains a 'definite and seasonable expression of acceptance.' "[643] The quintessential question, remains: what is a "definite expression of acceptance" that includes terms that do not appear in the offer or are different from terms that are implied in the offer? A comment suggests the "frequent example" of "the exchange of printed purchase order and acceptance (sometimes called 'acknowledgment') forms:"

> Because the forms are oriented to the thinking of the respective drafting parties [translation: the respective lawyers of the buyer and seller, particularly the seller's lawyer, seek to load the forms with protective boilerplate, as Karl Llewellyn suggests, "drafting to the edge of the possible"], the terms contained in them often do not correspond. Often the seller's form contains terms different from or additional to those set forth in the buyer's form [translation: the seller's boilerplate terms seek to remove the protection afforded to buyers under the UCC such as implied warranties that last for up to four years, a panoply of remedies including consequential damages, the implication that adjudications will occur in a court of law rather than arbitration, and a statute of limitations lasting four years]. Nevertheless, the parties proceed with the transaction.[644]

Having exchanged the forms containing different or additional terms, why do the parties "nevertheless proceed with the transaction"? The answer is critical: because "parties usually assume they have a binding contract and act accordingly."[645] Is such an assumption reasonable? It would not be reasonable to assume a binding contract with different or additional terms if one party objected to such terms in the other's printed form or insisted that it makes contracts only on the basis of its own printed form.[646] It would not be reasonable to assume a "definite expression of acceptance" if the variant term in the response to the offer is

---

[642] This is the current version of § 2-207 of the UCC. For an analysis of earlier drafts of § 2-207, see Murray, *Chaos*, *supra* note 619, at 1319–30.

[643] Transwestern Pipeline Co. v. Monsanto Co., 46 Cal App. 4th 502, 514, 53 Cal Rtr. 2d 887, 893 (1996). *See also* Idaho Power Co. v. Westinghouse Elec. Corp., 596 F.2d 924, 926 (9th Cir. 1979).

[644] Comment 1 as amended in 1966.

[645] Verasun Fort Dodge, L. L. C. v. Industrial Air Technology Corp., 2008 U. S. Dist. LEXIS 99292 at *53 (N. D. Iowa 2008), quoting J. White & R. Summers, HANDBOOK OF THE LAW UNDER THE UNIFORM COMMERCIAL CODE § 1-3.

[646] South Central Steel, Inc. v. McKnight Construction Co., Inc., 263 Fed. Appx. 806 (11th Cir. 2008); Crossley Constr. Corp. v. NCI Building Systems, Inc., 123 Fed. Appx. 687, 690 (6th Cir. 2005).

a "dickered" terms such as a different price or product or quantity or another term which differed from a term in the offer that should have been reasonably understood as important to the offeror.[647]

Test. Thus, to determine whether response to the offer is a definite expression of acceptance rather than a counter offer, the essential test must be whether, in light of the express terms of the response to the offer as well as any trade usage, course of dealing and course of performance under all of the surrounding circumstances, a reasonable offeror would understand the response to the offer as a definite expression of acceptance notwithstanding different or additional nondickered terms.

[C]   The Effect of Variant Terms in Acceptance Under § 2-207

If no definite expression of acceptance is found, § 2-207(1) does not apply. If a definite expression of acceptance notwithstanding different or additional terms is found, it is necessary to determine the fate of such terms under § 2-207(2) which applies only if a court decides that the response to the offer qualifies as a definite and seasonable expression of acceptance under 2-207(1). If the response is interpreted as a counter offer, 2-207(2) has no application. Where the parties fail to form a contract through the exchange of their respective forms but proceed to perform as if they had formed a contract, the terms of such a contract by conduct are determined under Section 2-207(3).

This simple summary of the operation of 2-207, however, belies what has become the most complex and controversial section of the entire Uniform Commercial Code. While the statutory language has been the subject of legitimate criticism,[648] these defects have been multiplied through judicially manufactured complexity and confusion that pervades 2-207.

[1]   Issues Generated by 2-207 and Related Norms

The 2-207 case law manifests a spectrum of issues: What is the precise effect of 2-207 on the common law "mirror image" rule?[649] If a response contains a term that materially alters the terms of the offer, may such a response constitute an acceptance? Does 2-207 apply to merchants and non-merchants? What is the test for determining whether an altering term is "material"? What is the effect of trade usage or prior course of dealing in determining materiality? Section 2-207(1) contemplates definite expressions of acceptance containing "different" or "additional" terms, but Section 2-207(2) mysteriously refers only to "additional"

---

[647] See the cases cited in note 611, *supra.*

[648] The most colorful aspersion is from Reaction Modling Technologies v. General Elec. Co., 585 F. Supp. 1097, 1104 (E. D. Pa. 1984): "§ 2-207 is a defiant lurking demon patiently waiting to condemn its interpreters to the depths of despair." The statute is a "murky bit of prose," Southwest Eng'g Co. v. Martin Tractor Co., 205 Kan. 684, 694, 473 P.2d 18, 25 (1970); "The statute is not too happily drafted," Roto-Lith, Ltd. v. F. P. Bartlett & Co., 297 F.2d 497, 500 (1st Cir. 1962). Section 2-207 is "one of the most important, subtle and difficult in the entire Code, and well it may be said that the product as it finally reads is not altogether satisfactory." R. DEUSENBERG & L. KING, 3 SALES AND BULK TRANSFERS § 3.02 (1986); "The 1952 version of 2-207 was bad enough . . . but the addition of subsection (3)without the slightest explanation of how it was supposed to mesh with (1) and (2) turned the section into a complete disaster," Professor Grant Gilmore (who worked with Karl Llewellyn) in a letter to Professor Robert Summers of the Cornell Law School, *quoted in* R. SPEIDEL, R. SUMMERS & J. WHITE, COMMERCIAL AND CONSUMER LAW 54–55 (3d ed. 1981).

[649] The common law rule is also accurately called the "matching acceptance" rule, i.e., to be an acceptance, the response must exactly match the terms of the offer. The phrase "mirror image" is not inherently preferable, but it is very popular in judicial opinions.

terms. How are "different" terms in responses to offers treated under 2-207? How are confirmations containing variant terms analyzed under 2-207? Since 2-207 was designed to preclude definite expressions of acceptance from being converted to counter offers, how are counter offers made under 2-207?

Beyond these complexities, it is also necessary to examine recent case law suggesting that 2-207 has no application to post-purchase terms that a buyer has an opportunity to review only after the goods are delivered. The United Nations Convention on Contracts for the Sale of Goods (CISG) presents an approach to these issues that is more than reminiscent of the common law last shot principle. UNIDROIT Principles provide still another dimension.

[2]   Effect on the "Mirror Image" Rule-Rejection or Modification?

It is often suggested that § 2-207 strikes at the very heart of the common law rule that requires an acceptance to be the mirror image of the offer. Indeed, the conventional wisdom insists that the fundamental change of the Section is the *rejection* of the "mirror image" rule of classical contract law.[650] Section 2-207(1), however, does *not* reject the mirror image rule. Only a response to an offer to buy or sell goods that meets the § 2-207(1) requirement of "a definite and seasonable expression of acceptance" will such a response "operate as an acceptance" though it also contains terms that are "different from or additional to" the terms of the offer. No court would fail to continue to recognize the mirror image rule with respect to "dickered terms" such as subject matter, price and quantity.[651]

Where a response to an offer changes the description of the goods, the price, the quantity or any other dickered term in the offer, courts insist on applying the traditional mirror image rule. They hold that such a response to an offer is a common law counter offer, clearly indicating that Section 2-207 has no application to such facts.[652] Thus, 2-207 does not *destroy* the "mirror image" rule; it *modifies* its technical application to prevent what is reasonably understood as an acceptance from operating as a counter offer simply because undickered variant terms appear, typically in the boilerplate language in the response to the offer. The mirror image rule properly precludes the imposition of additional or different dickered terms on the offeror. It departs from reality and becomes a technical construct, however, where it precludes the recognition of a contract that both parties reasonably assume they have made simply because there are some *ignored* terms in the fine print of a form that do not match the terms of the offer.[653] Section 2-207, therefore, is one of several UCC sections designed to

---

[650] *See, e. g.*, Deere & Co. v. Ohio Gear, 462 F. 3d 70, 707 (7th Cir. 2006): "Specifically, UCC § 2-207(1) rejects the common law 'mirror image' rule. . . ." *See also Idaho Power*, note 643 *supra* ; Gardner Zemke Co. v. Dunham Bush, Inc., 115 N.M. 260, 850 P.2d 319, 322 (1993); Diamond Fruit Growers, Inc. v. Krack Corp., 794 F.2d 1440 (9th Cir. 1986); C. Itoh & Co. v. Jordan Int'l Co., 552 F.2d 1228 (7th Cir. 1977); Hohenberg Bros. Co. v. Killebrew, 505 F.2d 643 (5th Cir. 1974); Uniroyal, Inc. v. Chambers Gasket & Mfg. Co., 177 Ind. App. 508, 380 N.E.2d 571 (1978); Steiner v. Mobil Oil Corp., 20 Cal. 3d 90, 141 Cal. Rptr. 157, 569 P.2d 751 (1977); Dorton v. Collins & Aikman Corp., 453 F.2d 1161 (10th Cir. 1972).

[651] Moreover, courts will also recognize a counter offer with respect to standardized (boilerplate) terms if the response to the offer clearly insists upon such terms. See the "Counter Offer Riddle," § 51[H],*infra.*

[652] *See, e.g.*, United Foods, Inc. v. Hadley-Peoples Mfg. Co., 1994 Tenn. App. LEXIS 277, at *14 (Tenn. Ct. App. May 20, 1994) (citing Howard Constr. Co. v. Jeff-Cole Quarries, Inc., 669 S.W.2d 221, 229 (Mo. Ct. App. 1983)). *See also* Koehring Co. v. Glowacki, 77 Wis. 2d 497, 253 N.W.2d 64 (1977); Duval & Co. v. Malcom, 233 Ga. 784, 214 S.E.2d 356 (1975).

[653] For an elaboration of this concept, see Murray, *Section 2-207 of the Uniform Commercial Code: Another Word About Incipient Unconscionability*, 39 U. Pitt. L. Rev. 597, 601 *et seq.* (1978). Comments to § 2-207 clearly support

eliminate technical common law constraints that would interfere with the recognition of the parties' factual bargain.[654]

[D]   Section 2-207(2) — "Merchant" vs. "Non-Merchant"

If a response to an offer containing variant terms operates as an acceptance, it is necessary to determine the disposition of the varying terms. Section 2-207(2) was designed to meet this challenge. If read out of context, the first sentence of 2-207(2) suggests that additional terms in an otherwise definite expression of acceptance are mere proposals that may be accepted or rejected by the offeror. The next sentence, however, limits the "proposal" concept to contracts in which a non-merchant is a party. In contracts "between merchants"[655] to which 2-207 is principally directed, variant terms *become* part of the contract *unless* any one of three exceptions apply. It is important to recognize the 2-207(2) distinction between merchants and non-merchants. While it applies to both, as described by one court, "Section 2-207(2) . . . states the general rule that additional terms are construed as 'proposals for addition to the contract' *except in the case of contracts between merchants where certain additional terms may become part of the contract.*"[656]

[1]   The Disposition of Variant Terms "Between Merchants"

Article 2 of the UCC emphatically adopts the common law view that the offeror is the master of the offer.[657] In keeping with this principle, Section 2-207(2)(a) becomes extremely important for offerors. If the offeror expressly limits acceptance to the terms of the offer, *any* additional

---

this analysis. Comment 1 recognizes the commercial reality that, "Because the [printed] forms are oriented to the thinking of the respective drafting parties, the terms contained in them often do not correspond. Often the seller's form contains terms different from or additional to those set forth in the buyer's form. Nevertheless, the parties proceed with the transaction." UCC § 2-207 comment 1. The implication is clear: § 2-207 recognizes the commercial reality that parties, including merchants, do not read or understand such non-matching, printed, clauses and that this conduct is not unreasonable. Comment 2 supports the underlying philosophy of Article 2, "Under this Article a proposed deal which in commercial understanding has in fact been closed is recognized as a contract." UCC § 2-207 comment 2. *See also* Murray, *The Article 2 Prism: The Underlying Philosophy of Article 2 of the Uniform Commercial Code* , 21 WASHBURN L.J. 1 (1981).

[654] Illustrations of the anti-technical design include Section 1-102(1): "This act shall be liberally construed and applied to promote its underlying purposes and policies"; § 1-106, "Remedies to be Liberally Administered," is designed "to negate unduly narrow or technical interpretation of some remedial provisions of prior legislation." (Comment 1, *id.*) Examples of the anti-technical nature of Article 2 include § 2-204 (a contract may be made in any manner, it does not fail because the moment of its making cannot be determined nor because one or more terms is missing); § 2-206, Comment 1 ("Former technical rules as to acceptance . . . are rejected"); § 2-205 recognizing "firm offers" and § 2-209(1) (an agreement modifying a contract needs no consideration to be binding). *See* Murray, *The Article 2 Prism: The Underlying Philosophy of Article 2 of the Uniform Commercial Code* , 21 WASHBURN L.J. 1 (1981).

[655] UCC § 2-104(3) defines the phrase "between merchants" as "any transaction in which both parties are chargeable with the knowledge and skill of merchants." "Merchant" is defined in UCC Section 2-104(1). As Comment 2 to this section suggests, for most of the sections of Article 2, "merchant" has a broad meaning referring to virtually anyone in business. Other sections, e.g., 2-314, the implied warranty of merchantability, apply a narrow definition to "merchant," i.e., a party who regularly deals in goods of that kind. For a case involving the definition of "merchant" with respect to 2-207, see Providence & W.R. Co. v. Sargent & Greenleaf, 802 F. Supp. 680, 685, note 2 (D.R.I. 1992).

[656] Lucien Bourque, Inc. v. Raymond E. Conkrite, 557 A.2d 196 (Me. 1989) (emphasis supplied). *See also* Lemmer v. IDS Properties, Inc., 304 N.W.2d 864, 870 (Minn. 1980): "Under 2-207(2), such additional terms are construed as proposals for additions to the contract. Where the transaction is not between merchants, the proposals do not become a part of the contract unless they are agreed to by the affected party."

[657] *See* § 46[C], *supra.*

term, material or immaterial, cannot become part of the contract. If the response to the offer constitutes a definite and seasonable expression of acceptance, the different or additional terms will not be recognized as operative terms of the contract.[658] Similarly, where an offeror objects to any additional term in the response to the offer, either through an anticipatory objection in the offer itself, or by objecting within a reasonable time after the acceptance is received, Section 2-207(2)(c) precludes *any* additional term from becoming part of the contract.[659] Where there is neither an express limitation to the terms of the offer or notification of objection to additional terms in the response, Section 2-207(2)(b) states that additional terms "become part of the contract unless . . . they *materially* alter it."[660] Whether an additional term is a material or immaterial alteration of the offer has become a complex issue.

[E]   Variant Terms in the Response — "Material" vs. "Immaterial"

[1]   Purpose and Test

It is clear that Karl Llewellyn was particularly concerned that the offeror not be burdened with any substantial or material additions to the risks contemplated by the offer.[661] The primary purpose of § 2-207 is the avoidance of unfair surprise and hardship[662] and the materiality of additional terms will be determined according to this test.[663] Actual (subjective) hardship is insufficient. The test is objective, i. e., whether a reasonable party would be unfairly

---

[658] UCC § 2-207(2)(a). It is irrelevant whether the additional terms are material or immaterial. Stemcor USA, Inc v. Trident Steel Corp., 471 F. Supp. 2d 362, 369–70 (S.D.N.Y. 2006).

[659] UCC § 2-207(2)(c). See Crossley Constr. Corp. v. NCI Bldg. Sys., L. P., 123 Fed. Appx. 687, 691 (6th Cir. 2005).

[660] UCC § 2-207(2)(b) (emphasis supplied).

[661] "In a word, the existing law is confused and uncertain. Some improvement is to be hoped from the provision of § 2-207(2) which allows minor additional terms to enter the contract without the express consent which (more frequently than not) never occurs. What terms will be construed as *'materially'* altering the contract is indeed a question for the courts' determination; but at least the Code focuses the question." Statement of Karl Llewellyn, 1 New York Law Revision Commission Hearings on the Uniform Commercial Code 56 (1954). The comments to § 2-207 contain illustrations of material versus immaterial alterations. A prime example of a material alteration is a disclaimer of warranty clause and another is a cancellation clause (comment 4). If an additional term merely specified a reasonable time for part of the performance within customary time limits, it would be an immaterial addition and would not be subject to excision under § 2-207(2)(b) comment 5.

[662] Comment 4 to § 2-207 indicates that the test for a material alteration is "whether the variant term in the acceptance would result in surprise or hardship if incorporated without express awareness by the other party. . . ." Comment 5, dealing with immaterial alterations, suggests the converse, i.e., "clauses which involve no element of unreasonable surprise and which therefore are to be incorporated in the contract unless notice of objection is seasonably given. . . ."

[663] See Bayway Ref. Co. v. Oxygenated Mktg. & Trading A.G., 215 F.3d 219, 223 (2d Cir. 2000), and cases cited therein. *See also* JOM, Inc. v. Adell Plastics, Inc., 193 F.3d 47 (1st Cir. 1999); *In re* Chateaugay, 162 B.R. 949 (Bankr. S.D.N.Y. 1994); Maxon Corp. v. Tyler Pipe Indus., Inc., 497 N.E.2d 570, 576 (Ind. Ct. App. 1986); Trans-Aire Int'l, Inc. v. Northern Adhesive Co., 882 F.2d 1254 (7th Cir. 1989); Dale R. Horning Co. v. Falconer Glass Indus., Inc., 730 F. Supp. 962 (S.D. Ind. 1990). The principle of avoiding oppression and unfair surprise also underlies the UCC concept of unconscionability in UCC § 2-302. There is considerable overlap between §§ 2-207 and 2-302. The essential difference may be seen as avoiding unfair surprise and hardship as a threshold matter by precluding certain terms from becoming operative terms of the contract *ab initio* under § 2-207, while § 2-302, allows courts to excise terms from an existing contract if their operation would cause unfair surprise or hardship to the party against whom they are designed to operate. See comment 1 to § 2-302, suggesting that the principle of unconscionability "is one of the prevention of oppression and unfair surprise. . . ." For an analysis of the sections in terms of the identity of underlying principle, see Murray, *Section 2-207 of the Uniform Commercial Code: Another Word About Incipient Unconscionability*, 39 U. Pitt. L. Rev. 597, 606–08 (1978).

surprised.[664] While "hardship" has often been viewed as substantial economic hardship[665] and treated as independent from "surprise,"[666] there is a growing recognition that such an analysis may be flawed. Simply because a contract requires performance that may be characterized as a hardship, it may still be an operative term of the contract if it is an "expected" term,[667] i.e., it is not objectively surprising. "Hardship is a consequence [of material alteration], not a criterion."[668]

[2]   Trade Usage and Prior Course of Dealing Terms Are Not "Additional" Terms

It is important to recognize that what may appear as a material alteration is not an alteration, material or immaterial, if the term merely confirms established trade usage or prior course of dealing. Where an arbitration clause appeared in the sellers' form confirming a textile contract, the trial court noted that such a term would constitute a material alteration of the offer in that jurisdiction and, as such, would not become part of the contract. On appeal, the sellers argued that disputes in the textile industry had been adjudicated through arbitration for more than fifty years. The court recognized arbitration as the standard in the textile industry. As such, it constituted trade usage which is necessarily a part of every agreement entered into between parties in that trade. As defined in the UCC, "agreement" expressly includes such terms.[669] Unless they are "carefully negated," such terms are "taken for granted" as terms of the contract from its inception.[670] Thus, the court explained that such an arbitration term in this trade could not be an alteration of the offer, material or immaterial, since it was not an additional term. It was part of the contract from its inception and 2-207, therefore, did not apply.[671]

[3]   Repeated Sending of Printed Forms as Course of Dealing

It may be argued that the mere repeated sending of the same ignored boilerplate containing variant terms will constitute a course of dealing that will insert such terms in subsequent contracts.[672] Courts have generally rejected this faulty analysis.[673] Even assuming an offeror

---

[664] See, in particular, *Bayway* and *In re Chateaugay, id.*

[665] See, in particular, *Trans-Aire* at 1262 and *Horning* at 967, *id.* note 639.

[666] UCC 2-207, Comment 4 refers to surprise *or* hardship.

[667] See Union Carbide Corp. v. Oscar Mayer Foods Corp., 947 F.2d 1333, 1336 (7th Cir. 1991), where the court suggests the following "gloss": "An alteration is material if consent to it cannot be presumed." The court explains that this is equivalent to "unreasonable surprise" since what is expected is unsurprising, but what is unexpected is surprising.

[668] *Bayway*, note 663, *supra*, at 225, quoting Union Carbide, *id.*, at 1336 and citing Suzy Phillips Originals, Inc. v. Coville, Inc., 939 F. Supp. 1012, 1017–18 (E.D.N.Y. 1996), and *In re Chateaugay*, note 663, *id.* at 957.

[669] UCC § 1-201(3) defines "agreement" as including course or dealing or usage of trade along with course of performance as these terms are defined in UCC §§ 1-205 and 2-208.

[670] UCC § 2-202, Comment 2.

[671] Atlantic Textiles v. Avondale, Inc., 505 F. 3d 274 (4th Cir. 2007).

[672] *See* Schulze & Burch Biscuit Co. v. Tree Top, Inc., 831 F.2d 709, 714–15 (7th Cir. 1987). But see Trans-Aire Int'l v. Northern Adhesive Co., 882 F.2d at 1262–63 note 9 (7th Cir. 1989), which refuses to follow *Schulze.*

[673] *See, e.g.*, Step-Saver Data Sys., Inc. v. Wyse Technology, 939 F.2d 91, 104 (3d Cir. 1991). *Accord In re* CLFC, Inc., 166 F.3d 1012, 1017 (9th Cir. 1999); PCS Nitrogen Fertilizer, L.P. v. Christy Refractories, L.L.C., 2000 U.S. App. LEXIS 23314, at *21 (8th Cir. 2000).;

would not be surprised to discover such a term in a seller's boilerplate response that had been sent many times in the past, the offeror would be surprised to discover that it was bound by a term *that was never acted upon, discussed or negotiated* in any past transaction between the parties, but was simply included among other boilerplate terms in the seller's acknowledgment.[674] "Course of dealing" requires a previous sequence of *conduct between the parties.*[675] The passive conduct of sending and receiving the same boilerplate should not be said to establish a course of dealing.

[4]   Burden of Proof

The burden of proving that an additional term materially alters the offer is on the offeror since the offeror is the party opposing the term.[676] Having assigned this burden of proof, it is not uncommon for a court to then suggest that the other party has the burden of proving a trade usage or prior course of dealing to establish the otherwise altering term as a term of the agreement, thereby refuting the claim that it is an additional term.[677] Sufficient proof that the term is part of the agreement through trade usage or prior course of dealing necessarily means that it never was a variant term and questions of materiality disappear.

[5]   Illustrations — Material vs. Immaterial

The leading UCC illustration of a term that would *materially alter* the terms of the contract is a term that negates such "standard warranties" as the implied warranty of merchantability or the implied warranty of fitness for a particular purpose.[678] Courts currently treat warranty disclaimers as alterations that are material *per se*, i.e., they are conclusively presumed to manifest surprise or hardship.[679] Such holdings, however, should be seen as a prima facie establishment of the surprise and hardship elements. The other party is not precluded from proving that the term was part of the original agreement through trade usage or prior course of dealing. The same analysis should apply to variant indemnification terms in the response to an offer which courts view in the same fashion as warranty disclaimers, i.e., material *per se*, because they shift material risks.[680]

Arbitration clauses. Whether an arbitration clause would be unfairly surprising creating undue hardship had been the source of considerable litigation. Currently, such clauses are not

---

[674] *Step-Saver, id. See also* Welsh v. Tex-Mach, Inc., (D. Mass. 2009).

[675] UCC § 1-205(1).

[676] See Bayway Ref. Co. v. Oxygenated Mktg. & Trading A.G., 215 F.3d 219, 223 (2d Cir. 2000), and cases cited therein.

[677] *Id.* at 225 note 4. Here, the court suggests the fairness of not imposing the burden of proving a negative on the party claiming surprise.

[678] UCC § 2-207, Comment 4. Other examples of "material" alterations in this Comment include a clause requiring a guaranty of performance exceeding the trade usage; a clause reserving to the seller a power to cancel the contract upon the buyer's failure to meet any invoice when due; and a clause requiring that complaints be made in a time materially shorter than customary or reasonable.

[679] *See* Glyptal, Inc. v. Engelhard Corp., 801 F. Supp. 887, 894–95 (D. Mass. 1992); Tuck Indus., Inc. v. Reinhold Chems., Inc. 542 N.Y.S.2d 676, 678 (App. Div. 2d Dep't 1989). Both cases are cited approvingly for the proposition that "Warranty disclaimers are universally viewed as material alterations under UCC Section 2-207(2)(b), and do not become part of the parties' contract." *In re* Chateaugay, 162 B.R. 949, 958 note 8 (Bankr. S.D.N.Y. 1994).

[680] *See* Trans-Aire Int'l, Inc. v. Northern Adhesive Co., 882 F.2d 1254 (7th Cir. 1989); Maxon Corp. v. Tyler Pipe Indus., Inc., 497 N.E.2d 570, 576 (Ind. Ct. App. 1986).

generally viewed as *per se* material alterations.[681] Even in a jurisdiction that held arbitration clauses to constitute *per se* material alterations, the court allowed evidence of trade usage and prior course of dealing to determine whether arbitration should be viewed as a term of the agreement.[682] "To carry its burden [of sufficient surprise and hardship], the nonassenting party must establish that, under the circumstances, it cannot be presumed that a reasonable merchant would have consented to the additional term."[683]

Forum Selection — Waiver of Jury. A California buyer order goods via telephone from a New York seller whose invoice contained a clause stating that disputes would be litigated in New York law and the buyer waived trial by jury. The court viewed the clause as a material alteration of the parties oral contract.[684]

Immaterial Terms. Comment 5 to 2-207 suggests examples of *immaterial* terms that would become part of the contract between merchants.[685] Where a seller supplied insulation products to a buyer at price of $871,000, the seller's invoice stated, "net 45 days from date of invoice; 1.25% per month finance charge on late payments." The court relied upon Comment 5 in finding that such clauses are not considered material alterations and, therefore, become contract terms.[686] The examples suggest no significant issues except for a final example in Comment 5 that has provoked controversy.

Remedy Modifications. UCC Section 2-719 allows the parties to agree to modify or limit Article 2 remedies. For example, the parties may agree to an exclusive buyer's remedy of repayment of the price while eliminating other traditional remedies such as "cover" in Section 2-712, recovery of the contract price/market price differential in 2-713, as well as the exclusion of consequential damages for economic loss as defined in Section 2-715. Boilerplate provisions in sellers' standardized forms commonly limit remedies in this fashion. The last example of an *immaterial* alteration in Comment 5 refers to Section 2-719 and suggests that a limitation of remedy "in a reasonable manner" is an example of an immaterial alteration. A number of courts have ignored this language and concluded that such a limitation of remedy clause is a *per se* material alteration because of its essential nature in shifting substantial risks to a buyer.[687]

---

[681] *See* Avedon Eng'g, Inc. v. Seatex, 126 F.3d 1279 (10th Cir. 1997).

[682] Marlene Indus. Corp. v. Carnac Textiles, Inc., 45 N.Y.2d 327, 380 N.E.2d 239, 242 (1978). In Aceros Prefabricados, S. A. V. Trade-Arbed, Inc., 282 F. 3d 92 (2d Cir. 2002), the court noted the United States Supreme Court's construction of the Federal Arbitration Act (Perry v. Thomas, 482 U. S. 483 (1987)) precluding disparate treatment of arbitration clauses previously found in New York where more than a preponderance of the evidence was necessary to find an enforceable agreement to arbitrate disputes. The court applied the usual test of surprise and hardship which it held the party opposing the clause failed to sustain.

[683] *Aceros Prefabricados, id.* at 100, quoted in Standard Bent Glass Corp. v. Glassrobots Oy, 333 F. 3d 440, 448 (3d Cir. 2003).

[684] Hugo Boss Fashions, Inc. v. Sam's European Tailoring, 293 A. D. 2d 296, 742 N. Y. S. 2d 1 (2002). Accord, Metropolitan Alloys Corp. v. State Metals Industries, Inc., 416 F. Supp. 2d 561 (E. D. Mich. 2006).

[685] UCC § 2-207, Comment 5. Examples include a clause slightly enlarging the otherwise statutorily accepted excuses for non-performance beyond the seller's control or a clause setting forth a reasonable proration formula where the seller is justifiably excused from full performance. Clauses fixing a reasonable time for issuing complaints within customary limits or providing for inspection by a sub-purchaser are immaterial alterations as are clauses providing for interest on overdue invoices, fixing the seller's standard credit terms when they are within the range of trade practice, or clauses limiting the right of rejection for defects that fall within customary trade tolerances.

[686] Inspec. Foams, Inc. v. Claremont Sales Corp., 2002 U. S. Dist. LEXIS 13932 (N. D. Ill. 2002).

[687] *See, e.g.*, Altronics of Bethlehem, Inc. v. Repco, Inc., 957 F.2d 1102, 1107–08 (3d Cir. 1992); National Controls, Inc. v. Commodore Business Machines, Inc., 163 Cal. App. 3d 688, 209 Cal. Rptr. 636 (1st Dist. 1985), that relies on Air

Other courts, however, read Comment 5 as referring exclusively to Section 2-719 to determine the materiality of a clause excluding consequential damages, i.e., if such an exclusion is reasonable under 2-719, it is an immaterial term that becomes part of the contract between merchants.[688] This view, however, converts the surprise and hardship test of 2-207 into a reasonableness test under 2-719. The overriding issues of surprise and hardship should dominate the 2-207 inquiry into materiality rather than a reasonableness standard under 2-719. Reasonableness is only one aspect of the material alteration analysis.[689]

Again, it important to remember that an offeror may avoid encounters with materiality issues by expressly limiting acceptance of the offer to the terms of the offer, or notifying the offeree of objection to such terms.[690] Either of these methods will preclude *any* additional term, material or immaterial, from becoming part of the contract.

[F]   "Different" vs. "Additional" Terms

Section 2-207(2) was designed to determine the operative effect of variant terms in an otherwise definite and seasonable expression of acceptance. The language of that subsection, however, immediately presents a dilemma. While Subsection (1) recognizes an acceptance with different *or* additional terms, Subsection (2) refers only to *additional* terms. Moreover, there is no other statutory language dealing with *different* terms. In the absence of such statutory guidance or dispositive legislative history, courts have been forced to determine whether "different" should be included within subsection (2).[691]

In favor of limiting subsection (2) to "additional" terms, it has been suggested that, had the drafters of Article 2 intended to include "different," they could have easily done so.[692] It is, however, equally plausible to assume that the drafters did not deliberately intend to create confusion. If they deliberately intended to exclude "different" terms, they could just as easily have emphasized this intention in the statutory language or, at least, in the Comments. Instead, Comment 3 clearly contemplates both kinds of terms:

Prods. & Chems., Inc. v. Fairbanks Morse, Inc. 58 Wis. 2d 193, 206 N.W.2d 414 (1973). *See also* Glyptal, Inc. v. Engelhard Corp., 801 F. Supp. 887 (D. Mass. 1992).

[688] *See* Hydraform Prods. Corp. v. American Steel & Aluminum Corp. 127 N.H. 187, 498 A.2d 339 (1985). In Kathenes v. Quick Food Stores, 596 F. Supp. 713, 716 note 3 (D.N.J. 1984), the court states, "If it is reasonable under 2-719, then it is not a material alteration under 2-207 and hence becomes part of the contract." *Accord*: Intrastate Piping & Controls v. Robert-James Sales, Inc., 733 N.E.2d 718 (Ill. App. Ct. 2000), where the court disagrees with an earlier Illinois holding that an exclusion of consequential damages is a *per se* material alteration; Album Graphics, Inc. v. Beatrice Foods Co., 87 Ill. App. 3d 338, 408 N.E.2d 1041 (1st Dist. 1980), on the footing that the *Album Graphics* opinion relied upon Comment 4 to 2-207 while ignoring Comment 5.

[689] Dale R. Horning Co. v. Falconer Glass Indus., Inc., 730 F. Supp. 962, 965 (S.D. Ind. 1990). For an exploration of differing views, see *In re* Chateaugay Corp., 162 B.R. 949 (S.D.N.Y. 1994).

[690] UCC § 2-207(2)(a) and (2)(c).

[691] "The Code does not explain, however, what happens if the offeree's response contains different terms (rather than additional ones) within the meaning of Section 2-207(1). There is no consensus on that question. See James J. White & Robert S. Summers, Uniform Commercial Code 33–36 (3d. ed. 1988); John E. Murray, Jr., *The Chaos of the "Battle of the Forms": Solutions*, 39 Vand. L. Rev. 1307, 1354–65 (1986)." Northrop Corp. v. Litronic Indus., 29 F.3d 1173, 1175 (7th Cir. 1994).

[692] *See* James White and Robert Summers, Uniform Commercial Code 32 (5th ed. 2000) (hereinafter White & Summers).

"Whether or not additional *or different* terms will become part of the agreement depends upon the provisions of subsection (2)."[693]

In the statutory language itself, Subsection 2(b) directs the excision of any additional term that would "materially alter" the terms of the contract.[694] Beyond the normal understanding of the term "alter" ("to differ in some particular") there is strong evidence that the essential concern of Karl Llewellyn was to avoid oppressing unsuspecting parties through material alterations that would enlarge the risks they reasonably assumed they undertook when the contract was formed.[695] There is a plausible analysis concluding that the absence of "different" was an inadvertent drafting error.[696] Most important, however, is the compelling argument that all additional terms are different and all different terms are additional, i.e., any attempt to distinguish "different" from "additional" has been described as "hair-splitting" or "metaphysical."[697]

Notwithstanding such cogent arguments that 2-207(2) should be read to include "different" as well as "additional," only a few recorded decisions construe 2-207(2) to include "different."[698] The prevailing view construes § 2-207(2) literally to apply only to "additional" and not "different" terms.[699]

[1]   Problematic Application — The "Knockout" View

Where a definite expression of acceptance contains an *express* term that contradicts an *express* term in the offer, if 2-207(2)(b) is limited to "additional" terms, it would not apply to such "different" terms. For example, where an offer states that any dispute must be submitted to arbitration and the acceptance expressly rejects arbitration, how is this dispute resolved with no statutory guidance? If 2-207(2) applies only to additional terms, a plausible argument can be made that the expressly conflicting term converts the "acceptance" into a counter offer, but this would contradict 2-207(1) that recognizes acceptances with "different" terms. The prevailing analysis, therefore, eliminates both clauses under a "knockout" view that leaves the gap to be filled by UCC terms.[700] Since the UCC contains no "gap-filler" favoring arbitration, the net result is a contract under which disputes are resolved in traditional fashion in court since the UCC assumes that standard. This analysis requires the rejection of Comment 3 that

---

[693] Comment 3 to 2-207 (emphasis supplied).

[694] "Between merchants, such terms become part of the contract unless: . . . (2) they materially alter it." § 2-207(2)(b).

[695] *See* Murray, note 663 *supra*.

[696] John L. Utz, *More on the Battle of the Forms: the Treatment of 'Different" Terms Under the Uniform Commercial Code*, 16 UCC L.J. 103, 110–12 (1983).

[697] *Northrop*, 29 F.3d at 1175 (citing Douglas G. Baird & Robert Weisberg, *Rules, Standards and the Battle of the Forms: A Reassessment of Section 2-207*, 68 VA. L. REV. 1217, 1246 (1982)).

[698] *See* Westinghouse Elec. Corp. v. Nielsons, Inc., 647 F. Supp. 896, 900 n.3 (D. Colo. 1986); Lockheed Elecs. Co. v. Keronix, Inc., 114 Cal. App. 3d 304, 170 Cal. Rptr. 591, 595 (2d Dist. 1981); Steiner v. Mobil Oil Corp., 20 Cal. 3d 90, 569 P.2d 751 (1977); Air Prods. & Chems., Inc. v. Fairbanks Morse, Inc., 58 Wis. 2d 193, 206 N.W.2d 414, 423 (1973).

[699] The leading case is Daitom, Inc. v. Pennwalt Corp., 741 F.2d 1569 (10th Cir. 1984), which cites supporting cases. More recent support for this position is found in Flender Corp. v. Tippins International, Inc. 830 A. 2d 1279, 1286 (Pa. Super. 2003) citing cases. Indeed, the majority view is so strong that a Federal Court of Appeals assumed that Illinois state courts would follow that view and therefore applied it notwithstanding its "own preferred view that assimilates 'different' to 'additional.' " *Northrop*, note 691 *supra*.

[700] *Id.*

expressly includes "different" terms.[701] The prevailing "knockout" rule relies on Comment 6 though that Comment deals with "confirmations" of existing contracts.[702] Moreover, by eliminating an arbitration clause from the offer, the analysis rejects the general proposition that the offeror is the master of the offer, a view otherwise emphasized in UCC Article 2.[703]

Applications of the "knockout" rule reveal profound effects on offers. A seller's offer to supply cable in an airport project included a disclaimer of warranties and an exclusion of liability for consequential damages. The buyer's acceptance included warranty and indemnity clauses that were nearly the opposite of the seller's terms. Since the acceptance was not expressly conditioned on the seller's assent to the buyer's terms, the response was an acceptance rather than a counter offer. The court deemed the seller's terms as "different" terms to which § 2-207(2) did not apply. Under the "knockout" view, the court held the expressly different terms in the exchanged forms cancelled each other, leaving gaps to be filled by the relevant provisions of the UCC. Thus, the resulting contract included all UCC warranties and remedies that allow consequential damages. The terms of the seller's offer were negated.[704]

Where a seller's offer limited warranty protection to 90 days and the buyer's otherwise definite expression of acceptance contained a standardized clause requiring a warranty of unlimited duration, the court recognized the buyer's term as "different." It reluctantly accepted the prevailing "knockout" view that "different" terms are not within 2-207(2) and, therefore, cancel each other, leaving a gap.[705] The court supplied a "neutral" UCC term which, in this case, was deemed to be a warranty of "reasonable duration" to fill the gap.[706] An offeror may

---

[701] Comment 3 is said to "go beyond the text" except as it applies to confirmations.

[702] UCC § 2-207 Comment 6 reads, in part, "Where clauses on confirming forms sent by both parties conflict each party must be assumed to object to a clause of the other conflicting with one on the confirmation sent by himself. As a result the requirement that there be notice of objection which is found in subsection (2) [2-207(2)(c)] is satisfied and the conflicting terms do not become part of the contract."

[703] In the book, THE UNIFORM COMMERCIAL CODE at § 1-3, Professor Robert Summers disagrees with his co-author, Professor James White who was responsible for the "knockout view." Professor Summers suggests that the arbitration term in the offer must control. Under this view, the "no arbitration" provision in the acceptance simply "falls out" (the "fallout" view which has not been adopted by the courts). A much more direct criticism of the "knockout" view is suggested by Professor Farnsworth: "There is, however, little reason to suppose that the drafters of the Code intended such a startling departure from the notion that the offeror is the master of the offer." E. ALLAN FARNSWORTH, CONTRACTS at 170 (3d ed. 1999). Professor White recognizes that, while the Code does not expressly authorize this result, "it does not bar it either." The new contract law of Article 2 of the UCC not only reaffirms the common law position that the offeror is master of the offer, but eliminates common law exceptions to that principle that were generated because of the faulty common law analyses of the agreement process. See § 46[C], supra. A clear illustration of the UCC insistence that the offeror is master of the offer is Section 2-206(1)(a) that allows an offeror to control absolutely, with no exceptions, the manner and medium of acceptance of an offer.

[704] Memphis-Shelby County Airport Auth. v. Illinois Valley Paving Co., 2006 U. S. Dist. LEXIS 79970 (W. D. Tenn. 2006).

[705] Northrop Corp. v. Litronic Indus., 29 F.3d 1173 (7th Cir. 1994). The court expressed its preference for the "minority" view that would read "different" into 2-207(2), because it "substitutes a manageable inquiry into materiality" (citing John E. Murray, Jr., *The Chaos of the Battle of the Forms: Solutions*, 39 VAND. L. REV. 1307, 1355 (1986)). As a federal court, however, it felt compelled to adopt the "majority" view that it assumed would be adopted in the relevant state, Illinois.

[706] This result was achieved by the magistrate judge who based her construction of a warranty of reasonable duration on UCC § 2-309(1): "The time for shipment or delivery or any other action under a contract if not provided in this Article or agreed upon shall be a reasonable time." Section 2-601 also allows a reasonable time to reject the goods. The buyer (offeree) in this case rejected the goods within six months which the magistrate judge held to be a

be surprised learn that the power of acceptance and limitations of risk in its offer have been materially changed without his assent through the application of the "knockout" rule. The cases are not unique. An identical analysis had the same effect in the leading exposition of the "knockout" view.[707]

[2]   Knockout Rule Inapplicable to Implied Terms — "Different" Becomes "Additional"

It is important to compare this analysis with the prevailing view where an acceptance includes an express term in conflict with an *implied* Code term in an offer. Where, for example, a purchase order is silent concerning warranties and the acknowledgment contains an express disclaimer of implied warranties, which term prevails in the "battle"? Comment 4 insists that the implied warranty of merchantability and the implied warranty of fitness for a particular purpose are "standard warranties" that "normally" attach to contracts for the sale of goods and any attempt to disclaim such warranties would "materially alter" the terms of the offer.[708] Section 2-207(2)(b) obviously contemplates acceptances containing materially altering terms. Where the materially altering term is a disclaimer of warranty, it would certainly appear to be a "different" term since it is an attempted negation of the implied warranty of merchantability which attends any offer to purchase goods from a merchant dealing in goods of that kind. If, however, 2-207(2) is limited to "additional" terms, 2-207(2)(b) ("materially alters") would not apply. Yet, this necessary conclusion is ignored as the disclaimer of warranty is characterized as an "additional" rather than a "different" term and, therefore, excised under 2-207(2)(b). The disclaimer should be excised, but not because it is an "additional" term. It is a "different" term that should be excised under 2-207(2) which should be interpreted as applying to "different" as well as "additional" terms.[709]

---

reasonable time within the period of the gap-filling warranty of reasonable duration since the product (printed wire boards) required complex testing.

[707] The classic illustration is found in the case cited by the author of the "knockout" view as the leading authority supporting that view. Daitom, Inc. v. Pennwalt Corp., 741 F.2d 1569 (10th Cir. 1984), expressly adopts Professor White's position at 1579. The court construed the seller's proposal as an offer, which limited the statute of limitations to one-year as expressly permitted by § 2-725(1) instead of the normal four years provided in this section. The buyer's purchase order was construed to be an acceptance. It contained a general statement reserving all rights and remedies available at law. The court held that this express clause was "different" from the seller's offer since it inferentially included the normal UCC statute of limitations of four years under 2-725. The court stated that 2-207(2) does not apply to "different" terms. Thus, the conflicting express clauses were "knocked out," leaving a gap filled by the normal period of four years. Faithful to Professor White's view, the court relied upon Comment 6. While there was some dispute over when the cause of action in this case accrued, the court admitted that its refusal to recognize the offeror's express one-year limitation as an operative term would allow the buyer to prevail. The court also rejected an inference from the lower court's opinion that the proper interpretation would treat the buyer's term as a material alteration of the offer under 2-207(2)(b), which would have excised it from the resulting contract, leaving the one-year limitation in the offer intact and changing the result in this case.

[708] § 2-207, Comment 4.

[709] White & Summers claim that Comment 4 of 2-207 supports the characterization of warranty disclaimers as "additional" rather than "different" terms. If anything, the opposite is clearly suggested by the language. Comment 4 should be read in context with Comment 3 which begins, "Whether or not additional *or different* terms will become part of the agreement depends upon the provisions of subsection (2). If they are such as materially to alter the original bargain they will not be included unless expressly agreed to by the other party. . . ." (Emphasis supplied). Comment 4 begins, "Examples of typical clause which would normally 'materially alter' the contract and so result in surprise or hardship if incorporated without express awareness by the other party are. . . ." Thus, Comment 4 is designed merely to *illustrate* material alterations as an elaboration of Comment 3 which refers to both additional and different terms. Comment 5 follows to provide illustrations of *immaterial* terms. Not only does Comment 4 lack language of support

In summary, under the current construction of 2-207(2), (i) *express* terms in an offer negating UCC implied terms and *express* terms reserving such terms in the acceptance will be construed as "different" terms to which 2-207(2) does not apply. These terms will cancel each other (the "knockout" view) leaving gaps filled by UCC implied terms. The term in the offer will not be operative. In this situation, the offeror is *not* the master of the offer, e.g., a disclaimer of warranty in the offer will be knocked out by an *express* reservation of that warranty in the acceptance.

(ii) An *express* term such as a disclaimer of warranty or an exclusion of consequential damages in the offer, however, will *not* be "knocked out" by a contrary *implied* UCC term in the acceptance.[710] Here, the offeror *is* recognized as the master of the offer. The contrary implied term in the acceptance is viewed as an "additional" term, though it is a "different" term. Since 2-207 applies, § 2-207(2)(b) excises such an implied term as a material alteration of the offer. The singular notion that a purchase order includes all UCC implied terms when it is construed as an offer, but the same purchase order does *not* include such implied terms when it is construed to be an acceptance, should be rejected.[711]

(iii) Where the offer contains the *implied* UCC terms, such as the implied warranty of merchantability, an *express* disclaimer of that warranty in the *acceptance* will not become part of the contract.[712] Here, the contrary express term in the acceptance is incredibly characterized as an "additional" rather than "different" term, thereby activating 2-207(2)(b) that excises such a term in a contract between merchants because it materially alters the terms of the offer.[713] In this situation, the offeror is deemed to be the master of the offer via the implied term in the offer.[714]

---

for the elimination of "different," it refers to "a clause *negating* such standard warranties as that of merchantability or fitness for a particular purpose. . . ." (Emphasis supplied). Construing "negating" to mean "additional" is beyond the pale. The statutory language, itself, deals with terms that materially *alter* the terms of the contract. Not only are terms such as "alter" and "negating" deemed insufficient to suggest "different" terms, the terms are magically transformed into "additional" terms, again, ignoring Comment 3 that expressly states the inclusion of additional or different terms.

[710] *See* Idaho Power Co. v. Westinghouse Elec. Corp., 596 F.2d 924 (9th Cir. 1979), as approved in White & Summers at 36–37. *See also* Polyclad Laminates, Inc. v. VITS Maschinenbau GmbH, 749 F. Supp. 342 (D.N.H. 1990).

[711] Phillips Petroleum Co. v. Bucyrus-Erie Co., 125 Wis. 2d 418, 373 N.W.2d 65 (Ct. App. 1985), rev'd on other grounds, 131 Wis. 2d 21, 388 N.W.2d 584 (1986). In reversing the intermediate appellate court, the Supreme Court of Wisconsin expressly avoided 2-207 issues, stating, " '[W]hatever Byzantine complexities the original exchange of contract documents might pose, . . . a rather straight-forward modified contract arose during the course of negotiations. . . .' *Id.* at 590. In light of the fact that typical reasonable parties pay no attention to which form constitutes the offer or acceptance, it is difficult to justify the view that UCC implied terms will or will not be recognized in the same form depending upon its accidental use.

[712] The opposite result was reached in the severely criticized *Roto-Lith* case which has been overruled. *See* note 648 *supra.*

[713] White & Summers (§ 1-3 at note 22) insist that the implied term in the acceptance is an "additional (not 'different') term," on the footing that Comment 4 to 2-207 supports this view. This conclusion, however, is based on their *a priori* view that 2-207(2) does not apply to "different" terms which emanates from their anti-contextual construction of Comment 4 that fails to consider Comment 3 (see note 709, *supra*).

[714] JOM, Inc. v. Adell Plastics, Inc., 193 F.3d 47 (1st Cir. 1999), involved a purchase order/offer that was "silent" concerning UCC implied terms, while the acceptance contained a clause excluding consequential damages. The buyer argued that because its offer impliedly contained the UCC standard allowing consequential damages, it operated as notice to the seller of buyer's objections to any additional terms in the acceptance pursuant to 2-207(2)(c) that allows an offeror to nullify additional terms in an acceptance by notifying the offeree to that effect. The court, however, held that such notifications of objection must be expressly stated and the implied UCC default terms or gap-fillers are not

This confusion and attendant complexity is attributable to the refusal to recognize that "different" as well as "additional" terms in otherwise definite expressions of acceptance should be governed by Section 2-207(2). The popularity of this position is predicated on the premise that a recognition of "different" terms in 2-207(2) would result in the offeror always prevailing since a "different" term is, of necessity, a material alteration of the offer that would be excised from the terms of the contract under 2-207(2)(b).[715] While there is a legitimate concern that 2-207 may overcome the "last shot" rule only to unwittingly foster a "first shot" rule,[716] it is even more difficult to justify the augmentation of the risk the offeror expressly assumed by the terms of the offer which may result whenever the acceptance contains an express term that conflicts with the offeror's manifested intention and "knocks out" the express term in the offer. Moreover, since the "knockout" view applies only to conflicting express terms, it provides no solution where one of the conflicting terms is implied.[717]

[G]   Confirmation Operating as an Acceptance — Statute of Frauds Distinguished

Having seen the basic operation of § 2-207(1) and (2) where the response to the offer is characterized as an acceptance though it contains variant terms, it is important to consider another situation which is one of the principal concerns of § 2-207.[718] Contracts are often formed orally, i.e., in person or by telephone. As will be seen later in this volume, certain kinds of contracts must be evidenced by a writing to be enforceable pursuant to the Statute of Frauds, which began in Seventeenth Century England and was adopted in this country as part of our English legal heritage.[719] Contracts for the sale of goods with a price of $500 or more must be evidenced by a writing.[720] The written evidence of the contract, however, need not exist at the moment of contract formation. A memorandum of a prior oral contract will be sufficient to satisfy the Statute of Frauds. Where parties form their contract orally, therefore, it is common practice for one or both parties to send a confirmation of the oral contract to provide reliable written evidence of that contract.[721]

A *confirmation* is necessarily subsequent to the formation of the oral contract. Section 2-207 applies to confirmations in a situation that occurs with great frequency. *A* and *B* have a meeting in person or a telephone discussion during which *A* agrees to sell 1000 units of X-35 plastic to *B* at a price of $100 per unit for a total price of $100,000. The parties have evidenced

---

sufficient to constitute such notice. This holding necessarily raised the issue of whether the buyer could prove that the additional remedy limitation clause constituted a *material* alteration that would be excised under 2-207(2)(b). If immaterial, the remedy limitation *becomes* a term of the contract between merchants in accordance with the second sentence in 2-207(2).

[715] Daitom, Inc. v. Pennwalt Corp., 741 F.2d 1569, 1580 (10th Cir. 1984).

[716] See the discussion of this criticism of 2-207 in subsection H *infra*.

[717] *Id.*

[718] UCC § 2-207, Comment 1 states that the section was designed to deal with two typical situations: "[O]ne is the written confirmation, where an agreement has been reached either orally or by informal correspondence between the parties and is followed by one or both parties sending formal memoranda embodying the terms so far as agreed upon and adding terms not discussed."

[719] The Statute of Frauds is explored in Chapter 4.

[720] UCC § 2-201.

[721] While the legal requirement of a writing evidencing the contract may be a motivating factor inducing recorded confirmations of the transaction, such a record would undoubtedly be a standard business practice even if there were no legal requirement of a writing to make a contract enforceable.

their mutual assent to this arrangement in their oral discussion of the subject matter, the quantity and the price. They may have also discussed certain delivery terms. Typically, however, they will not discuss warranty terms or terms concerning remedies for breach or arbitration of disputes. Having formed their oral contract, either one or both send a confirmation to the other confirming the oral contract. They typically use their printed purchase order and acknowledgment forms for this purpose.[722] Absent a prior oral agreement, these forms would evidence the typical "battle of the forms"-the purchase order (offer) and the acknowledgment (acceptance) — a definite expression of acceptance containing different or additional boilerplate terms. In this use of the forms, as we have seen, the variant terms would be subject to § 2-207(2). Where there has been a prior oral agreement, the exchange of the same purchase order and acknowledgment forms constitute an exchange of confirmations of a prior oral contract since the offer and acceptance already occurred at the time of the oral agreement. The confirmations contain the terms that were discussed, the identical "dickered" terms, as well as the undiscussed boilerplate terms in the seller's acknowledgment. Section 2-207(1) recognizes "A definite and seasonable expression of acceptance *or a written confirmation . . . operates as an acceptance* even though it states terms additional to or different from those offered *or agreed upon. . . .*"[723]

How can a written confirmation of a contract *operate as an acceptance*? The contract has already been formed and the written confirmation, therefore, must be confirming a *contract*. Professor Llewellyn was particularly eager to deal with this issue which he viewed as "hopelessly confused" under pre-Code law.[724] The only *factual bargain* was the oral agreement. Any different or additional terms in one or more confirmations of that oral contract were not consciously considered. Section 2-207(1) treats a confirmation *as if it were an acceptance* so that any different or additional terms are subject to § 2-207(2) like any other definite expression of acceptance. Any materially altering terms in a confirmation are excised under § 2-207(2)(b). Conflicting terms in exchanged confirmations may be seen as mutual notices of objection to each other's terms, i.e., having the same effect as a notice of objection clause pursuant to § 2-207(2)(c).[725] The result is to effectuate the purpose of § 2-207 in finding a contract according to the factual bargain of the parties rather than one including variant terms to which the parties had not consciously adverted when they made their oral contract.

---

[722] The confirmation of such contracts through electronic messages has become a common practice.

[723] UCC § 2-207(1) (emphasis added).

[724] *See* statement of Professor Llewellyn at 1 STATE OF NEW YORK LAW REVISION COMMISSION HEARINGS ON THE UNIFORM COMMERCIAL CODE 55–56 (1954).

[725] Comment 6 to § 2-207 begins with the enigmatic statement, "If no answer is received within a reasonable time after additional terms are proposed, it is both fair and commercially sound to assume that their inclusion has been assented to." This initial statement is not designed to deal with written confirmations of an existing oral contract. Rather, it seems to suggest that silence by the offeror will manifest assent to additional terms in the offeree's expression of acceptance. As one commentator observed, this is not true except as to immaterial additional terms and even those terms may be made inoperative by the offeror's limitation of acceptance to the terms of the offer or notice of objection to such additional terms. After this initial statement, Comment 6 then attempts to deal with written confirmations of oral contracts where the confirmations contain additional or different terms: "Where clauses on confirming forms sent by both parties conflict each party must be assumed to object to a clause of the other conflicting with one on the confirmation sent by himself. As a result the requirement that there be notice of objection which is found in subsection (2) is satisfied and the conflicting terms do not become part of the contract. The contract then consists of the terms originally expressly agreed to, terms on which the confirmations agree, and terms supplied by this Act. . . ." See Duesenberg, *Contract Creation: The Continuing Struggle with Additional and Different Terms Under Uniform Commercial Code Section 2-207* , 34 BUS. LAW. 1477, 1485 (1979).

[1]   Distinguishing the Statute of Frauds

Some courts fail to distinguish the "battle of the forms" under § 2-207 from the distinct requirement under UCC § 2-201 that an oral contract for the sale of goods priced at $500 or more must be evidenced by a writing sufficient to show that the parties intended to be bound by such an agreement. The Statute of Frauds requires a sufficient memorandum evidencing a contract for the sale of goods that identifies the parties, the subject matter, the quantity and is properly signed.[726] If such a memorandum is present, the party attempting to persuade the court that a contract was made has met the threshold requirement of a sufficient writing. This, however, is not a § 2-207 issue. For example, an acknowledgment form that confirms the contract may be sufficient to satisfy the Statute of Frauds though it also contain terms additional to or different from the terms the parties discussed while forming their oral contract.[727] The challenge concerning the variant terms is a "battle of the forms" problem exclusively. There is no longer any Statute of Frauds issue though some courts became hopelessly confused in this area.[728]

If only one record is sent in confirmation of the contract, 2-207 will still apply to deal with alleged variant terms in a single confirmation.[729] If the only confirmation is a purchase order, however, a Statute of Frauds problem can arise if a court determines that such a purchase order only evidences an *offer* while the Statute of Frauds requires a record evidencing a *contract*.[730] Again, however, if the single confirmation is an acknowledgment from the seller, it will typically evidence a contract between the parties that satisfies the Statute of Frauds.[731] Such a document will be an effective confirmation for Statute of Frauds purposes though it contains terms that vary from the prior oral agreement. If such varying terms are material alterations of the oral agreement, they will not become part of the contract.[732]

---

[726] UCC § 2-201, comment 1. As will be seen in the exploration of the Statute of Frauds in Chapter 4, a single confirmation between merchants to which the other party does not object within ten days from receipt will satisfy the Statute against the non-signing party. UCC § 2-201(2).

[727] UCC § 2-201(2) allows a confirmation sent by one merchant to another merchant to satisfy the statute if the receiving merchant does not object to it within ten days after it is received. As will be seen in the discussion of this topic in Chapter 4, this provision overcomes pre-Code unfairness where only one party sent a confirmation which allowed the contract to be enforced against that party while the other party could raise the defense of the Statute of Frauds since he had not signed a document evidencing the contract.

[728] See, e.g., *Marlene Indus. Corp. v. Carnac Textiles, Inc.*, 59 A.D.2d 359, 399 N.Y.S.2d 229 (1st Dep't 1977), which was, fortunately, reversed by a court that understood the distinction: 45 N.Y.2d 327, 408 N.Y.S.2d 410, 380 N.E.2d 239 (1978). Another illustration of confusion is found in Campanelli v. Conservas Altamira, S.A., 86 Nev. 838, 477 P.2d 870 (1970).

[729] *See, e.g.,* Dorton v. Collins & Aikman Corp. 453 F.2d 1161 (6th Cir. 1972). See, however, ProCD v. Zeidenberg, 86 F.3d 1447 (7th Cir. 1996).

[730] See a discussion of this distinction in Harry Rubin & Sons v. Consolidated Pipe Co., 396 Pa. 506, 153 A.2d 472 (1959).

[731] A single confirmation evidencing a contract between merchants may be sufficient to satisfy the Statute of Frauds.

[732] American Parts Co. (Detroit Body Prods. Co. Div.) v. American Arbitration Ass'n, 8 Mich. App. 156, 154 N.W.2d 5, 12 (1967).

[H]   The Counter Offer Riddle — Contract by Conduct Under § 2-207(3)

To understand the operation of counter offers under 2-207, it is important to remember that § 2-207 was not designed to modify the matching acceptance (mirror image) rule with respect to dickered terms such as price, quantity and subject matter to which the parties consciously advert. Rather, it was to treat response to offers that matched the dickered terms of the offer and otherwise appeared to constitute a definite expression of acceptance as an acceptance, notwithstanding different or additional boilerplate terms. Thus, the mirror image rule is modified only to this extent.[733] Though undickered boilerplate terms in an otherwise definite expression of acceptance will no longer create a counter offer, § 2-207 *does* permit a party to make a counter offer with respect to such terms.

[1]   The § 2-207 Formula Counter Offer — Manufactured Complexity

If the response to an offer contains matching dickered terms in what appears to be a definite expression of acceptance, UCC § 2-207(1) states that a definite expression of acceptance operates as an acceptance though it contains different or additional terms "unless acceptance is expressly made conditional on assent to the additional or different terms." It is clear that Professor Llewellyn and his associates intended this proviso to permit an offeree to make a counter offer: "We are attempting to say, whether we got it said or not, that a document which said, 'This is an acceptance only if the additional terms we state are taken by you' is not a definite and seasonable expression of acceptance but is an expression of a counter-offer."[734]

This straightforward explanation, however, has been unwittingly converted into needless complexity through tortured judicial analyses. Where an acknowledgment stated that the "acceptance is subject to the terms and conditions contained on the front or reverse side" of the acknowledgment form, the court found such language conditional "to some extent" but insufficiently similar to the statutory proviso language because it was not *expressly* conditional on the offeror's *assent* to such terms.[735] This analysis heralded a string of cases that focused on whether language in various responses to offers was *sufficiently similar* to the proviso language to be called a "conditional acceptance," i.e., a counter offer. The holdings are difficult to reconcile.[736] Faced with this uncertainty and still desirous of making a counter offer, it

---

[733] See § 50, text at note 594 *supra.*

[734] Statement of Karl Llewellyn, 1 NEW YORK LAW REVISION COMMISSION HEARINGS ON THE UNIFORM COMMERCIAL CODE 117 (1954). For an exploration of the history of this proviso, see Murray, *Chaos, supra* note 691, at 1322–30.

[735] See the acknowledgment as quoted in Dorton v. Collins & Aikman Corp., 453 F.2d 1161 (6th Cir. 1972).

[736] In Boese-Hilburn Co. v. Dean Mach. Co., 616 S.W.2d 520, 525 (Mo. Ct. App. 1981), the court recognized that "[j]udicial interpretation of the language 'expressly made conditional' in 207(1) ranges across a broad spectrum." In Challenge Mach. Co. v. Mattison Mach. Works, 138 Mich. App. 15, 359 N.W.2d 232 (1984), the court held that the following statement did not create a conditional acceptance (counter offer): [B]uyer expressly limits acceptance to the terms hereof and no different or additional terms proposed by seller shall become part of the contract." In Idaho Power Co. v. Westinghouse Elec. Corp., 596 F.2d 924 (9th Cir. 1979), the following language was insufficient to meet the "expressly conditional" standard: "[A]cceptance of this order shall be deemed to constitute an agreement . . . to the conditions named hereon and supercedes all previous agreements." On the other hand, the following clause in capital letters was sufficient to create a counter offer: "The terms set forth on the reverse side are the only ones upon which we will accept orders; these terms supersede all prior written understandings, assurances and offers. Your attention is especially directed to the provisions concerning warranty and liability of supplier and claims procedure. In any event,

became clear to lawyers drafting such language that the safe harbor was the replication of Code language. Thus, where an acknowledgment states, "Seller's acceptance is . . . expressly conditioned on Buyer's assent to the additional or different terms and conditions set forth below and printed on the reverse side," it mimics the statutory proviso of 2-207(1) and courts suffer no doubt in treating such language as evidencing a counter offer.[737]

The proviso language in 2-207(1), however, is anything but clear. An "acceptance" that is expressly conditional on the offeror's assent is *not* an acceptance. Courts recognize that language tracking the proviso is *ambiguous*.[738] Notwithstanding its ambiguity, the use of the statutory language is conclusive evidence of a counter offer. If other language was used, the only question was whether it was sufficiently similar to the statutory language.[739]

It is important to recall an important weapon in the "battle of the forms." Where a purchase order states that the acceptance is expressly limited to the terms of the purchase order, any different or additional terms, material or immaterial, in the seller's otherwise definite expression of acceptance are eliminated from the resulting contract.[740] Where, however, the purchase order containing such an express limitation is used as an acceptance, is the "acceptance" converted to a counter offer? The language of 2-207(2)(a), alone, suggests that it was designed to permit the master of the offer, the offeror, to limit the power of acceptance.[741] Two courts concluded that such a provision does not constitute a counter offer because it is not the equivalent of language expressly conditioning the acceptance on the seller's assent to the terms of the purchase order.[742] A recent case, however, reported the following language in a purchase order used as an acceptance: "This purchase order is buyer's offer to seller and acceptance is expressly limited to the terms of the offer." Though it replicates the critical language of 2-207(2)(a) designed to limit acceptance to the terms of an offer and does not expressly condition assent on the other party's assent to the terms of the purchase order as required by the proviso of 2-207(1), the court found that it converted the purchase order

---

these terms shall become binding on both parties upon you acceptance of our first delivery of any goods specified herein, or upon commencement of manufacturing operations. Advise us immediately if anything in the acknowledgment is incorrect or is otherwise unacceptable." Ralph Shrader, Inc. v. Diamond Int'l Corp., 833 F.2d 1210, 1213 (6th Cir. 1987). "Our acceptance of the order is conditional on buyer's acceptance of the conditions of sale printed on the reverse side hereof" was also sufficient. Uniroyal, Inc. v. Chambers Gasket & Mfg. Co., 177 Ind. App. 508, 380 N.E.2d 571 (1978). In PCS Nitrogen Fertilizer, L.P. v. Christy Refractories, L.L.C., 2000 U.S. App. LEXIS 23314 (8th Cir. 2000), "Seller's acceptance of any offer by Purchaser to purchase the Products is expressly conditional upon the Purchaser's assent to all the terms and conditions herein, including any terms additional to or different from those contained in the offer to purchase" was sufficient to meet the expressly conditional language. In Verasun Fort Dodge, L. L. C. v. Industrial Air Technology, 2008 U. S. Dist. LEXIS 99292 (N. D. Iowa 2008), the buyer's purchase order stated, "This purchase order is buyer's offer to seller and acceptance is expressly limited to the terms of the offer." The purchase order responded to the seller's quotation which the court found detailed enough to constitute an offer. Beyond the absence of any express language conditioning the "acceptance" on the seller's assent to the terms of the purchase order, it is obvious that the quoted language was designed to take advantage of a § 2-207(2)(a) clause expressly limiting acceptance to the terms of the *offer.*

[737] C. Itoh & Co. v. Jordan Int'l Co., 552 F.2d 1228 (7th Cir. 1977) is the leading case exposing this analysis.

[738] "[T]he seller injected *ambiguity* into the transaction by inserting the 'expressly conditional' clause in his form. . . ." (emphasis supplied). *Id.* At 1238.

[739] Note 737, *supra.*

[740] Section 2-207(2)(a). See the text at notes 657–58, *supra.*

[741] "[T]he offer expressly limits acceptance to the terms of the offer . . ."

[742] Polytop Corp. v. Chipsco, Inc., 8265 A.2d 945 (R.I. 2003); Phillips Petroleum Co. v. Bucyrus-Erie Co., 125 Wis. 2d 418, 373 N.W.2d 65 (Ct. App. 1985), *rev'd on other grounds,* 131 Wis. 2d 21, 388 N. W. 2d 584 (1986).

"acceptance" to a counter offer.[743]

[2]   Accepting a § 2-207(1) Counter Offer

Like other counter offers, a § 2-207(1) counter offer will reject the offer and create a new power of acceptance in the original offeror. Where such a counter offer by a seller is followed by the shipment of the goods which the buyer accepts, however, echoes of the "last shot" principle had to be repressed. Having recognized that the formula response replicating the proviso language is *ambiguous*, a reasonable offeror may not understand such ambiguous language as a counter offer. The offeror could reasonably view an offeree's response as an acceptance forming a contract. Thus, to hold that the offeror accepted the formula counter offer and its variant terms merely by the act of accepting the goods would unfairly surprise and oppress the offeror. Moreover, it would undermine the whole purpose of § 2-207 by allowing a seller-offeree to rejuvenate the "last shot" principle simply by inserting an ambiguous clause in the response to a buyer's purchase order offer. Thus, while a 2-§ 207(1) formula counter offer does not form a contract, the buyer's mere acceptance of the goods is not an acceptance of the counter offer and its terms. Unless the buyer expressly assents to the terms of the counter offer by signing the seller's counter offer or otherwise expressly manifesting assent, the counter offer is not accepted.[744] While this analysis accomplished a just result with respect to formula counter offers, courts have not distinguished such "ambiguous" counter offers from those that are clear and unequivocal.

[3]   Clear (Unambiguous) Counter Offers

Where a clause in a form responding to an offer stated, "The terms set forth on the reverse side are the only ones upon which we will accept orders: These terms supersede all prior written understandings, assurances and offers," the court properly held that this language constituted (A) counter offer notwithstanding its dissimilarity to the 2-207(1) proviso language.[745] The court insisted that this language "can be no clearer in conditioning acceptance." It expressly rejected any requirement that only a mimic of the 2-207(1) proviso could be a counter offer.[746] If language is abundantly clear in stating that the offeree will deal only on its terms, the creator of 2-207 would emphatically agree that it constitutes a counter offer.[747] The only remaining issue is whether such a clear and unambiguous counter offer may be accepted by conduct, e.g., a buyer/offeror's acceptance of the goods.

Rejecting a conduct acceptance of a *formula* counter offer is necessary to avoid unfair surprise to the offeror who may not understand such an ambiguous response to constitute a counter offer. Where, however, the offeree's response clearly and emphatically states that the

---

[743] Verasun Fort Dodge L.L.C. v. Industrial Air. Technology, 2008 U. S. Dist. LEXIS 99292 (N. D. Iowa 2008).

[744] Deere & Co. v. Ohio Gear, 462 F.3d 701, 707 (7th Cir. 2006). In *Costal & Native Plant Specialties, Inc. v. Engineered Textile Products, Inc.*, 139 F. Supp. 2d 1326 (N.D. Fla. 2001), the seller's invoice stated that it was "subject to an expressly conditioned on" the buyer's assent to the seller's terms, the court held that only the buyer's express assent would bind the buyer to the seller's terms. This conclusion was not affected by a provision in the seller's form stating, "Buyer shall be deemed to have assented to the provisions hereof in all respects by its acceptance of any goods shipped or by failure to give Seller written notice of objection within five business days of Buyer's receipt of this invoice."

[745] Ralph Shrader, Inc. v. Diamond Int'l Corp., 833 F.2d 1210, 1213, n.4 (6th Cir. 1987).

[746] *Id.* at 1215.

[747] See the statement by Karl Llewellyn in the text at note 734 *supra*.

offeree is unwilling to be bound by any terms other than its own terms, there can be no unfair surprise to the original offeror. Yet, the case law insists that even a counter offer that suffers from no ambiguity can be accepted only by the express assent of the offeror.[748] As authority for this conclusion, however, courts rely on cases where the response to the offer is a formula counter offer,[749] oblivious to the sole rationale for precluding a conduct acceptance of a formula counter offer, i.e., such counter offers are *ambiguous*. Where there is no ambiguity in a counter offer, the rationale disappears. Under current interpretations of 2-207, however, even a counter offer expressed in the most clear and convincing terms would apparently require express assent by the offeror.

[4]   Terms of the "Contract by Conduct" — § 2-207(3)

Where the parties exchange of writings do not create a contract because the response to the offer is a counter offer but the parties proceed to perform as if a contract had been formed, they have formed a contract by conduct. Section 2-207(3) sets forth the terms of such a contract. Where, for example, a purchase order is an offer to buy goods and the response states that the "acceptance" is expressly conditioned on buyer's assent to any variant terms in the response, the formula counter offer will prevent the formation of a contract. When the seller ships the goods and the buyer accepts them, the buyer/offeror is not accepting the terms of the counter offer. It is, however, clear that the parties have formed a contract by their conduct. Section 2-207(3) sets for the terms of such a contract: "In such case the terms of the particular contract consist of those terms on which the writings of the parties agree, together with any supplementary terms incorporated under any provisions of this Act."[750]

Section 2-207(3) applies only where the parties have exchanged "writings," i.e., one writing will not be sufficient.[751] Though failing to form a contract, the writings of the parties are the best evidence of their intention concerning dickered terms or other terms on which the writings match. Non-matching terms are discarded and the remaining "gaps" are filled with UCC terms. The effect favors buyers. Consider, for example, the typical purchase order that

---

[748] See PCS Nitrogen Fertilizer, L.P. v. Christy Refractories, L.L.C., 225 F. 3d 974, 980 (8th Cir. 2000).

[749] Thus, *PCS Nitrogen, id.*, cites, among others, C. Itoh & Co. v. Jordan Int'l Co., 552 F.2d 1228, 1235 (7th Cir. 1977), which is the classic formula counter offer case. Another formula counter offer case upon which the court relies is particularly disarming. In Diamond Fruit Growers, Inc. v. Krack Corp., 794 F.2d 1440 (9th Cir. 1986) an acknowledgment form contained the "expressly conditional" language of § 2-207(1) as well as an exclusion of consequential damages. The parties were in a continuous relationship and the buyer negotiated with the seller to have the seller remove the exclusion of consequential damages clause from the seller's form. The seller refused. The parties then continued to deal with each other using the same forms. When consequential damages occurred, the seller insisted that his clause should be enforced as a term of the contract since the parties had consciously negotiated with respect to this clause and the buyer clearly understood that the clause was a term of the contract and continued to deal with the seller with such actual knowledge. The court, however, held that a conduct acceptance was ineffective. Since the buyer had never expressly assented to the terms of the seller's counter offer, the counter offer was never accepted.

[750] UCC § 2-207(3). See Deere & Co. v. Ohio Gear, 462 F. 3d 701, 707–708 ((7th Cir. 2006). See also Comment 7, added in 1966, stating that, in such a case, it is not necessary to determine which party was the offeror or offeree.

[751] *See* Album Graphics, Inc. v. Beatrice Foods Co., 87 Ill. App. 3d 338, 408 N.E.2d 1041, 1047 (1st Dist. 1980). A single writing evidencing an earlier contract would be a confirmation. If it contained different or additional terms, the terms would be subject to 2-207(2) as discussed earlier. Section 2-207(3), however, assumes the exchange of forms that failed to create a contract followed by conduct manifesting the parties intent to form a contract. It should also be remembered that Section 2-207 has no application to a response to an offer with different or dickered terms such as price or quantity. Such a response is a common law counter offer and the subsequent shipment and acceptance of the goods would create a contract on the terms in the seller's form.

includes the implied warranty of merchantability. A response disclaiming the warranty also includes the formula counter offer language. There is no contract. Either party may "walk away" from the transaction.[752] After shipment and acceptance of the goods, however, there is a contract by conduct. The non-matching terms concerning the warranty are excised. They cancel each other.[753] The gap is then filled by the UCC "supplementary" implied warranty of merchantability. The effect, therefore, is that the buyer wins the battle of the forms, not because its form is preferred over the seller's form, but because the gap-filling terms of the Code favor the buyer.

A question has arisen concerning the proper interpretation of the language in 2-207(3), "supplementary terms incorporated under any other provision of this Act." Should this language be limited to "supplementary terms," such as implied warranties, or should it be read more expansively to include *any* provision of the Code, e.g., trade usage or prior course of dealing? Though the case law is scant, the current interpretation favors an expansive reading of this language.[754] The more expansive interpretation accords with the general Code directive that it should be "liberally construed."[755]

[I]   The Offeror Prevails — "First Shot" Instead of "Last Shot"

While the principal purpose of section 2-207 was to preclude a party's terms from becoming the operative terms of the contract simply because it fired the "last shot" (counter offer) in the battle of the forms, 2-207 may be criticized on the footing that it creates a similar injustice by insisting that the party who fired the "first shot" (the offeror) prevails in the battle. Consider the following examples.

(1) A seller sends a "quotation" to the buyer which is construed as a mere preliminary negotiation, not an offer. Buyer responds with a purchase order that is an offer. It is silent concerning warranties but, as an offer, will contain the implied warranty of merchantability. The response is an acknowledgment that is a definite expression of acceptance containing the identical "dickered" terms found in the offer, but also containing a disclaimer of the implied

---

[752] C. Itoh & Co. v. Jordan Int'l Co., 552 F.2d 1228, 1238 (7th Cir. 1977).

[753] Such mutual cancellation of terms has the same effect as the "knockout" rule which applies where there are expressly conflicting ("different") terms in the exchange forms. The "knockout" rule, however, is a judicial creation based on the assumption that 2-207(2) does not apply to "different" terms. See subsection [F], *supra*.

[754] Where an offer that expressly limited acceptance to the terms of the offer included a fifteen month warranty and the reply not only limited the warranty to twelve months but also stated a formula counter offer in the language of the 2-207(1) proviso, the parties then performed creating a contract by conduct. Under 2-207(3), the warranties terms were excised. The offeror sought to have its warranty included in the terms of the contract by conduct under 2-207(3) on the footing that course of dealing, trade usage or prior course of dealing as defined in UCC 2-208 and 1-205 are terms or "provisions" which 2-207(3) should be said to include since the language refers to *any* other provisions of the Code. The seller sought a narrow reading of the language that would limit it to "supplementary" terms such as implied warranties. The court chose the more expansive interpretation. Dresser Indus., Inc., Waukesha Engine Div. v. Gradall Co., 965 F.2d 1442 (7th Cir. 1992), notwithstanding its earlier opinion in *C. Itoh & Co. v. Jordan Int'l Co., id.* The *Dresser* court attempted to distinguish *Itoh* on the footing that the court was not directly confronted with the same question. The *Itoh* opinion, however, states that "supplementary terms" under 2-207(3) "are limited to those supplied by the standardized 'gap-filler' provisions of Article Two." 552 F.2d at 1237. Moreover, *Itoh* expressly adopted the narrow interpretation favored by Professors White & Summers in their 1972 edition at 29 while the *Dresser* court (1451) rejects the White & Summers interpretation (3d ed. 1988, at 45), choosing instead the expansive interpretation of Professor William Hawkland, Uniform Commercial Code Series 2-207:04, at 109–10 (1990). *Dresser* expressly adopts the expansive interpretation in Daitom, Inc. v. Pennwalt Corp., 741 F.2d 1569, 1579 (10th Cir. 1984).

[755] UCC § 1-105(1).

warranty of merchantability. The acknowledgment does not contain any counter offer language. This is a typical case where there is a contract on the express and implied terms of the offer; the additional or different term in the acknowledgment (the warranty disclaimer) will not become part of the contract under § 2-207(2).

(2) The seller sends a quotation identical to the quotation in (1) except that it contains language that makes it an offer. The buyer sends the same purchase order as in (1). The seller's quotation contains the same clause disclaiming warranties found in the seller's acknowledgment in (1). Since the quotation is now an offer, the purchase order is construed to be an acceptance of the offer.[756] If the purchase order (acceptance) is construed as containing the implied warranty of merchantability, such a term would vary the term of the offer that contains the warranty disclaimer. The variant term in the purchase order (acceptance) is the implied warranty of merchantability that will be excised under subsection (2)(b) because it materially alters the quotation/offer. As an acceptance, the purchase order may even be said not to contain implied terms. Thus, a court has held that the usual UCC terms are implied in a purchase order as an offer, but the same terms are not implied in a purchase order when it is construed to be an acceptance.[757] The characterization of a purchase order as an offer or acceptance, however, is a judicial afterthought typically unrelated to the parties' conscious use of their forms. The net effect is to permit the offeror, whether buyer or seller, to prevail though the parties may have paid no attention to which of them happened to be the offeror.[758] Instead of the party firing the "last shot," the party firing the "first shot" wins the battle.

Courts and scholars favoring the "knockout" view sometimes urge it as a solution to the potential injustice that allows an offeror, even an unwitting offeror, to prevail in the "battle" simply because he happens to be the offeror.[759] As the earlier discussion noted, however, the "knockout" view may result in enlarging the risk of an offeror well beyond the expressed terms of the offer.[760] Moreover, since the "knockout" rule applies only to *express* conflicting terms in exchanged forms, it has no effect on an express term in an offer prevailing over an implied term in an acceptance.

---

[756] Though a purchase order may appear to be an offer on its face, it will be construed as an acceptance if the parties "intended" that effect. *See, e.g.*, Daitom, Inc. v. Pennwalt Corp., 741 F.2d 1569 (10th Cir. 1984); Mead Corp. v. McNally-Pittsburgh Mfg. Corp., 654 F.2d 1197 (6th Cir. 1981); Idaho Power Co. v. Westinghouse Elec. Corp., 596 F.2d 924 (9th Cir. 1979); Earl M. Jorgensen Co. v. Mark Constr., 56 Haw. 466, 540 P.2d 978 (1975). In particular, see Phillips Petr. Co., Norway v. Bucyrus-Erie Co., 125 Wis. 2d 418, 373 N.W.2d 65 (Ct. App. 1985), *rev'd on other grounds*, 131 Wis. 21, 388 N.W.2d 584 (1986).

[757] See Phillips Petroleum Co. v. Bucyrus-Erie Co., 125 Wis. 2d 418, 373 N.W.2d 65 (Ct. App. 1985), *rev'd on other grounds*, 131 Wis. 2d 21, 388 N.W.2d 584 (1986).

[758] See Southern Idaho Pipe & Steel Co. v. Cal-Cut Pipe & Supply, Inc., 98 Idaho 495, 567 P.2d 1246, 1253–54 (1977), *cert. denied*, 434 U.S. 1056, 98 S. Ct. 1225, 55 L. Ed. 2d 757 (1978), where the court comments: "Cal-Cut makes the argument that since its document was the offer, Southern Idaho's expression of acceptance was an acceptance of all the terms on this form. . . . Under this argument, the first party to a sales transaction will always get his own terms. In most commercial transactions, which party processes its form first is purely fortuitous. To allow the contents of a contract to be determined on this basis runs contrary to the underlying purposes of the Uniform Commercial Code of modernizing the law governing commercial transactions. . . . We cannot accept such an arbitrary solution." *See also* McCarty v. Verson Allsteel Press Co., 89 Ill. App. 3d 498, 411 N.E.2d 936 (1st Dist. 1980). For an analysis supporting the view that the printed form of one party should not control simply because that party is the offeror, *see* Murray, *Chaos, supra* note 691, at 1366–72.

[759] See the text at subsection [F][1], note 699 *supra* , which recognizes this view in Daitom, Inc. v. Pennwalt Corp., 741 F.2d 1569, 1580 (10th Cir. 1984).

[760] *See* subsection [F][1] at note 699, *supra.*

[J]   Post-Purchase Terms — "Rolling" ("Accept or Return") Contracts — "Shrinkwrapped" Licenses

After a contract has been formed, numerous cases have rejected attempts by sellers to impose post-formation terms that would limit the rights the buyer enjoyed at the time of formation.[761] In *Step-Saver Data Systems, Inc. v. Wyse Technology*,[762] after a contract for the license of software had been formed, the software was delivered in a box containing license terms that disclaimed warranties, limited remedies and stated that "Opening this package indicates your acceptance of these terms and conditions." The court viewed these "box top license" terms as additional terms in a confirmation that materially altered the parties' agreement and, therefore, did not become part of the contract under Section 2-207(2)(b). The only other possible basis for recognizing changed terms was a good faith modification under the UCC that needs no consideration but must manifest an agreement.[763] Five years later, however, a radically different analysis appeared. In *ProCD, Inc. v. Zeidenberg*,[764] a buyer purchased software on compact disks offered to the general public at a price of $150. The disks contained more than 95 million residential and commercial telephone numbers as well as zip codes and industrial codes, organized to facilitate searches. The database could not be copyrighted since the information was simply telephone numbers taken from some 3000 telephone directories. The database, however, required millions to compile and keep current. The plaintiff sold two versions of the software, one to businesses at higher prices than the version sold to the general public through retail computer stores. The product was contained in a "shrinkwrapped" box[765] with a statement in small print at the bottom of the package that users were subject to license terms inside the box.[766] Inside the box, the printed license terms revealed a "single-user license," prohibiting any sub licenses of the information. The license was also encoded on the disks, alerting the user to its terms when the program was "run." The license included the right to the return of the purchase price to a user who rejected the license terms. The defendant copied the non-copyrightable material and created his own business in competition with the plaintiff. When plaintiff sought to enjoin such use as a violation of the license terms, the defendant claimed he was not bound by the terms inside the box that were

---

[761] In Razor v. Hyundai Motor America, 222 Ill. 2d 75, 854 N. E. 2d 607 (2006), the court held that a limitation of remedy clause in a new car warranty that was not made available to the buyer at the time the contract was formed was unconscionable and, therefore, unenforceable. Bowdoin v. Showell Growers, Inc., 817 F.2d 1543 (11th Cir. 1987) (two weeks after purchase of equipment, instruction manual accompanied delivery of equipment, including a disclaimer of warranty); Gold Kist, Inc. v. Citizens & S. Nat'l Bank, 286 S. C. 272, 333 S.E.2d 67, 70 (Ct. App. 1985): "[A] disclaimer printed on a label or other document and given to the buyer at the time of delivery of the goods is ineffective if a bargain has already arisen." *See also* Pennington Grain and Seed, Inc. v. Tuten, 422 So. 2d 948 (Fla. Dist Ct. App. 1982); Midland Supply Co. v. Ehret Plumbing & Heating Co., 108 Ill. App. 3d 1120, 440 N.E.2d 153 (5th Dist. 1982); Hartwig Farms, Inc. v. Pacific Gamble Robinson Co., 28 Wash. App. 539, 625 P.2d 171 (1981).

[762] 939 F.2d 91 (3d Cir. 1991).

[763] In a contract for the sale of goods, a good faith modification of the contract needs no consideration to be binding. § 2-209(1).

[764] 86 F.3d 1447 (7th Cir. 1996).

[765] The term, "shrinkwrap license," refers to the tight plastic wrapping on boxes that may have license terms printed on the box, unlike the facts of this case.

[766] The Seventh Circuit opinion does not offer this description of the notice on the box. The opinion states, "Every box containing its [ProCD's] consumer product *declares* that the software comes with restrictions stated in the enclosed license." 86 F.3d at 1450 (emphasis supplied). The reality of the "small print at the bottom of the package" description is discoverable only in the lower court's opinion at 908 F. Supp. at 654. The ordinary definition of "declare" is "to make known clearly." The notice on the box does not approach that definition.

undisclosed at the time of purchase. The lower court refused to bind the defendant to the terms. The Seventh Circuit agreed that a buyer should not be bound by hidden terms, but pointed to the notice on the box incorporating the license terms inside the box, and concluded,

"Notice on the outside, terms on the inside, and a right to return the software for a refund if the terms are unacceptable . . . may be a means of doing business valuable to buyers and sellers alike."[767]

Heralding the efficiency of standardized terms, the court referred to transactions where the exchange of money precedes the communication of detailed terms as "common," using examples of insurance contracts, purchases of airline tickets, a forum selection clause on a cruise line ticket and a case involving a complicated interpretation of a statute involving bills of lading. It fails to note the severe limitations on the enforceability of typically unread clauses in insurance policies[768] and the regulations of terms in the boilerplate of airline tickets. It avoids mentioning the fact that the majority of the United States Supreme Court upholding the forum selection clause insisted on assuming that the parties were aware of the clause at the time the contract was formed,[769] or that the bill of lading case involved a technical interpretation of a Federal Statute,[770] hardly an apposite precedent.

The court insisted that its opinion was based on the common law of contracts and contract formation sections of the Uniform Commercial Code, but it avoids any reference to the numerous cases that have refused to enforce post-formation limitations on buyers' rights.[771] Rather, the court relies on the general formation section of the UCC, Section 2-204(1), that allows a contract to be made in any reasonable manner, including conduct by the parties. It states the truism that, "A vendor, as master of the offer, may invite acceptance by conduct, and may propose limitations on the kind of conduct that constitutes acceptance."[772] Recognizing that a contract can be, and often is, formed by paying the price and walking out of the store, the court insists that the UCC recognition of contract formation in any reasonable manner must include a formation process where the buyer becomes aware of post-purchase terms only upon delivery of such terms with the goods. She can either accept such terms by failing to object to them within the time frame prescribed by the terms "inside the box," or reject the terms and have the purchase price returned.[773]

---

[767] 86 F.3d at 1451.

[768] The boilerplate on insurance contracts has been subject to intense scrutiny under a "reasonable expectations" test, i.e., would the insured "reasonably expect" such a clause as part of the policy. For a recent analysis of this test, see Max True Plastering Co. v. United States Fidelity & Guar. Co., 912 P.2d 861 (Okla. 1996).

[769] See Carnival Cruise Lines v. Shute, 499 U.S. 585, 589, 111 S. Ct. 1522, 113 L. Ed. 2d 622 (1991), where the majority opinion upheld the forum selection clause on the back of a cruise line ticket only after insisting that its decision rested upon the assumption that the "respondents had sufficient notice of the forum clause before entering the contract."

[770] Vimar Seguros y Reaseguros, S.A. v. M/V Sky Reefer, 515 U.S. 528, 115 S. Ct. 2322, 132 L. Ed. 2d 462 (1995) (interpretation of Section 3(8) of the Carriage of goods by Sea Act (COGSA), 46 U.S.C. § 1303(8)).

[771] See note 761, *supra*.

[772] 86 F.3d at 1452.

[773] *Id.* Here, the court adds the rather curious analysis of a situation in which the terms inside the box state, "You owe us an extra $10,0000," suggesting that, "Any buyer finding such a demand can prevent formation of the contract by returning the package, as can any consumer who concludes that the terms of the license make the software worth less than the purchase price." Suppose the buyer does not return the package. Does he then owe the extra $10,000, or is this a case in which the seller's attempt to add a material term to the contract should be excised under 2-207(2)(b)?

The court attempts to distinguish *Step-Saver Data Systems*[774] first, by the curious suggestion that the defendant was a consumer and 2-207 does not apply to transactions involving non-merchants. Such a construction, however, would eliminate the first sentence of Section 2-207(2) which applies to non-merchants and reject considerable case law to the contrary.[775] Moreover, as will be seen below, the same court later rejected a claim that this precedent was limited to consumer transactions. The second basis for distinguishing *Step-Saver* is astonishing, i.e., where the transaction involves only one form, "§ 2-207 is irrelevant."[776] Thus, on the assumption that *Step-Saver* involved two forms while *ProCD* involved only one form (the seller's terms), it held that 2-207 did not apply.[777] Beyond the fact that 2-207(1) refers to "a confirmation," the court ignores cases such as *Dorton v. Collins & Aikman Corp.*,[778] an oft-cited case in discussions of 2-207, involving a single confirmation containing different or additional terms to which the court applied 2-207. Most important, the court ignores the essential rationale for the inclusion of confirmations in 2-207 as the first of its two principal targets: "The one is the written confirmation, where an agreement has been reached either orally or by informal correspondence between the parties and is followed *by one or both* of the parties sending formal memoranda embodying the terms so far as agreed upon and adding terms not discussed."[779] Section 2-207(1) clearly applies to a single confirmation of an existing contract where the confirmation contains different or additional terms.[780]

Still another departure from precedent is the court's notion that the buyer's silence in not objecting to terms delivered with the goods necessarily constitutes acceptance. Where a post purchase standardized form suggested various types of assent to the terms in the form, a court emphatically rejected any notion of a UCC change in the common law negation of silence or inaction as a mode of acceptance.[781] Section 2-207 may be said to allow the inclusion of an additional term by silence in a certain context. Comment 6 suggests that the failure to object to an additional term may be fairly regarded as the equivalent of assent to such a term under 2-207(2)(c) that precludes additional terms upon the objection of the offeor. This possibility, however, not only fails to support the *ProCD* analysis but further refutes it. It would apply only to immaterial additional terms since any material alteration would be excised under 2-207(2)(b).

Apart from these failed attempts to distinguish prior cases and other distortions of UCC contract formation sections, it may have been possible to treat *ProCD* as a justified aberration

---

[774] 939 F.2d 91 (3d Cir. 1991).

[775] See the discussion of § 2-207(2) *supra.*

[776] 86 F. 3d at 1452.

[777] The court fails to note that the parties in *Step-Saver* had exchanged matching forms prior to the submission of the container with the box-top license which became the single non-matching form.

[778] 453 F.2d 1161 (6th Cir. 1972).

[779] UCC 2-207, Comment 1 (emphasis supplied).

[780] *See* Klocek v. Gateway, Inc., 104 F. Supp. 2d 1332 (D. Kan. 2000), where the court recognizes the application of Section 2-207 to confirmations and concludes that Kansas and Missouri courts would not follow *ProCD* or other cases adopting that analysis. Scholars are in agreement that the Court was "wrong" in holding that 2-207 applies only where there are two forms. *See, e.g.*, Robert A. Hillman, *Rolling Contracts*, 71 Fordham L. Rev. 743, 753 (2002); James J. White, *Default Rules in Sales and the Myth of Contracting Out*, 48 Loy. L. Rev. 53, 81 (2002); John E. Murray, Jr., *Contract Theories and the Rise of Neoformalism*, 71 Fordham L. Rev. 860, 905, n.193 (2002).

[781] *Dorton*, note 778 *supra.* Exceptions to the general rule that silence does not constitute acceptance are discussed in § 52, *infra.* The "rolling formation of contract" analysis creates a new exception.

since the defendant could not have been unfairly surprised or oppressed to discover a single-user limitation of mass marketed software. Beyond the slim reed of a small print notice on the outside of the box of terms inside, the defendant could hardly justify using the work product of the plaintiff to establish a new business in competition with the plaintiff in exchange for a $150 retail purchase price. The single-user limitation could have been enforced as an implied term in any software license that any licensee should contemplate as part of the contract. Any hope for such a narrow but justifiable precedent was quickly dashed, however, by another Seventh Circuit offering six months later that would clearly revolutionize the law of "accept or return" contracts and leave several sections of the Uniform Commercial Code lying in its wake.

In *Hill v. Gateway 2000, Inc.*,[782] the Hills purchased a computer by telephone, providing their credit card number for payment. No statement, in small print or otherwise, appeared on the outside of the box containing the computer other than "fragile," and "This side up." Terms inside the box, however, required any dispute between the parties to be submitted to arbitration and bound the buyers to such terms unless they objected within 30 days, again ignoring the fundamental common law principle that silence may not constitute acceptance.[783] If the buyers had objected to the post-purchase terms, their sole remedy would be the return of the purchase price. The buyers did not object to the terms within 30 days. Subsequently, they discovered defects in the product and sought to enforce certain express warranty terms provided by the seller. The defendant insisted on arbitration. The lower court refused to enforce the arbitration clause on the footing that there was insufficient notice of the clause. Refusing to limit the *ProCD* analysis to software, the Seventh Circuit reversed, stating that the buyers accepted the post-purchase terms by their silence. The court emphasized the impracticability of a seller's agent, such as a cashier in a store or a telephone agent reading boring boilerplate terms to a buyer during the formation process.[784]

Curiously equating the post-purchase terms that subtract protection with post-formation express warranties that have been recognized since the inception of the UCC,[785] the court completed its creation of what has been christened a *"rolling contract"* theory. The theory insists that, when a buyer pays for an item at a store or agrees to purchase it by telephone or through the Internet and pays for the product via credit card, the formation process is not completed under this theory.

The court begins its analysis of the formation process by stating that the "vendor" is the master of the offer.[786] The court simply assumes that the vendor was the offeror,[787] though the

---

[782] 105 F.3d 1147 (7th Cir. 1997).

[783] *See* § 52, *infra.*

[784] The court creates the scenario of such a person droning through a page of boilerplate that would be incomprehensible to the buyer. There is, however, limited difficulty in a telephone operator stating, "Please read the important binding contract terms enclosed with the product. If you do not agree with these terms, return the product and you will not be charged." Such a statement, however, may not be conducive to the most successful marketing practices.

[785] See UCC § 2-313, Comment 7. There is no corresponding suggestion in the entire UCC dealing with an enforceable post-formation disclaimer of warranties or other material, risk-shifting term absent the express assent of the party opposing such a term. Moreover, Comment 7 assumes a modification in good faith, enforceable under UCC Section 2-209(1). Such a modification must manifest the assent of the parties. *See* Arizona Retail Sys., Inc. v. Software Link, Inc., 831 F. Supp. 759 (D. Ariz. 1993).

[786] 83 F.3d at 1452. The *ProCD* case involved a self-service transaction where the buyer (Zeidenberg) took the box

purchaser in such transaction is normally considered to be the offeror.[788] Unless the vendor is the offeror, however, the "rolling contract" theory evaporates. The theory is said to be applicable to merchants and non-merchants. If a merchant buyer places a telephone order for goods, such a buyer would be subject to the vendor's terms inside the carton containing the shipped goods. Though he may be surprised that his telephone order was not an offer, this unsound construction is essential to the success of the "rolling" theory. If the telephone order was the offer, the seller's shipment of the goods would constitute acceptance under § 2-206 of the UCC which recognizes a contract formed by promising to ship or by shipment and any additional terms inside the container would be viewed as post-formation terms. The Seventh Circuit studiously ignores § 2-206 which is the specific offer and acceptance section of UCC Article 2. Rather, the court relies exclusive on the generic "formation" section for its "rolling contract" theory.

Rather than telephoning its order, if the same buyer-merchant had submitted its purchase order, the Seventh Circuit would insist that it was an offer and any different or additional terms in the vendor's acknowledgment would be subject to 2-207. If the merchant-buyer had telephoned the offer and sent a confirmation, any conflicting terms on a seller's confirmation would be subject to 2-207. If only one merchant sent a confirmation, however, the Seventh Circuit's ukase that 2-207 requires two forms would be a clear contradiction of the statutory language as well as the first comment to the section.[789] This quiet revolution by the Seventh Circuit is predicated on the concept of efficiency that is at the heart of the law and economics movement. A recent iteration by the same court in an opinion written by the same Judge (Easterbrook) is a brief but clear manifestation of the underlying rationale:

Ever since *Carnival Cruise Lines, Inc. v. Shute*, 499 U.S. 585, 111 S. Ct. 1522, 113 L. Ed. 2d 622 (1991), enforced a forum-selection clause printed in tiny type on the back of a cruise-ship ticket, it has been hard to find decisions holding terms invalid on the ground that something is wrong with non-negotiable terms in form contracts. . . . As long as the market is competitive, sellers must adopt terms that buyers find acceptable; onerous terms just lead to lower prices. See, e.g., *Hill v. Gateway 2000, Inc.*, 105 F.3d 1147 (7th Cir. 1997); *ProCD, Inc. v. Zeidenberg*, 86 F.3d 1447 (7th Cir. 1996).[790]

---

of disks from the shelf. American case law views the vendor as the offeror in such transactions allow contract formation at the moment the purchaser takes possession of the goods, subject to a power of termination if the buyer decided to return the goods to the shelf. English case law suggests that the buyer makes the offer at the checkout counter. *See* § 37[B], *supra*. This does not resolve the question of which party is the offeror in a telephone or Internet transaction. Presumably, it is the buyer who is responding to the vendor's advertising invitations to make an offer in accordance with basic common law principles.

[787] The court suggests that "the Hills knew before they ordered the computer that the carton would include *some* important terms and they did not seek to discover these in advance. Gateway's ads state that their products come with limited warranties and lifetime support." 143 F. 3d at 1150.

[788] See Klocek v. Gateway, Inc., 104 F. Supp. 2d 1332, 1340 (D. Kan. 2000).

[789] 2-207(1) begins, "A definite and seasonable expression of acceptance or *a confirmation* which is sent with a reasonable time operates as an acceptance . . ." (Emphasis supplied). Comment 1 describes the "typical" situations to which 2-207 applies. The first "is the written confirmation where an agreement has been reached either orally or by informal correspondence between the parties and is followed by *one* or both of the parties sending formal memoranda . . . adding terms not discussed." (emphasis supplied). The "rolling contract" theory may be said to avoid this criticism since it does not treat the vendor's terms inside the box as a "confirmation," but that excuse requires the critic to ignore the notion that the vendor is the offeror. Like discovering the magician placing the bunny in the hat, the court's insistence on identifying the vendor as the offeror destroys the illusion.

[790] IFC Credit Corp v. United Business & Industrial Fed. Credit Union, 512 F. 3d 989 992, 93 (7th Cir.2008).

Economists, however, recognize that situation-specific monopolies created after parties of unequal bargaining power agree on a price are particularly likely to suggest inefficient terms. Noting that in the "landmark" cases of *Zeidenberg* and *Hill* cases, the Seventh Circuit upheld the vendor's terms included inside the packaging on the ground that the buyers could have returned the products if they did not wish to be bound by such adhesive terms, a scholar suggests the irony of such holdings:

> After the purchase, however, the buyers had already invested in the particular products, and returning them would have required expending additional time and effort. Although the sellers were not monopolists at the time of sale, they enjoyed a situation-specific monopoly vis-a-vis customers who had already purchased their merchandise. Of course, they could not have taken advantage of this by charging a higher price, because the price term had already been agreed upon (and paid). Unable to renegotiate price, the sellers had an incentive to try to capture benefits of their monopoly position by providing low-quality terms.[791]

[1]   The "Rolling Contracts" Progeny

Most of the courts reacting to the theory have manifested their approval of it though there are contrary views and the scope of courts approving the analysis is not always clear.[792] In *Wachter Management Co. v. Dexter & Chaney, Inc.*,[793] the Supreme Court of Kansas provides its review of the extant case law in which it distinguished the case before it from *ProCD* and *Hill v. Gateway* but strongly disagreed with the analysis by the majority of the court in *M. A. Mortensen v. Timberline Software Group*[794] where a Washington court adopted the Seventh Circuit analysis. The extent of that adoption, however, became particularly uncertain after another bout by the Washington Court of Appeals with the "demon" § 2-207.[795] In *De Fontes v. Dell, Inc.*,[796] the Supreme Court of Rhode Island pursued an extensive review of the current case law referring the cases following the Seventh Circuit as the majority view, concluding that

> The *ProCD* line of cases is better reasoned and more consistent with contemporary consumer transactions. It is simply unreasonable to expect a seller to apprise a consumer of every term and condition at the moment he or she makes a purchase. A modern consumer neither expects nor desires to wade through such minutia,

---

[791] Russell Korobkin, *Bounded Rationality, Standard Form Contracts, and Unconscionability*, 70 U Chi. L. Rev. 1203, 1265 (2003).

[792] *See, e.g.*, Brower v. Gateway 2000, Inc., 246 A.D.2d 246, 676 N.Y.S.2d 569 (1st Dep't 1998) (adopting the *ProCD/Hill* analysis but recognizing the substantive unconscionability of a very expensive arbitration process); M.A. Mortensen Co. v. Timberline Software Group, 93 Wash. App. 819, 970 P.2d 803 (1999). *Contra* Rogers v. Dell Computer Corp., 138 P. 3d 826 (Ok. 2005) Novell, Inc. v. Network Trade Ctr., 25 F. Supp. 2d 1218 (D. Utah 1997). Particularly insightful criticisms appear in Klocek v. Gateway, Inc., 104 F. Supp. 2d 1332 (2000), which rejected the rolling contract analysis. See also Step-Saver Data Sys., Inc. v. Wyse Tech., 939 F.2d 91 (3d Cir. 1991), which, as the text suggests, *ProCD* seeks to distinguish with dubious success. *ProCD* also distinguishes Arizona Retail Sys., Inc. v. Software Link, Inc., 831 F. Supp. 759 (D. Ariz. 1993), failing to mention that *Arizona* clearly adopts the *Step-Saver* analysis.

[793] 282 Kan. 365, 144 P. 3d 747 (2006).

[794] 93 Wash. App. 819, 970 P. 2d 803 (1999).

[795] Tacoma Fixture Co. v. Rudd Co., Inc., 174 P. 3d 721 (Ct. App. Wash. 2008). The court referred to 2-207 as a "defiant lurking demon patiently waiting to condemn its interpreters to the depths of despair," quoting Reaction Molding Technologies, Inc. v. General Electric Co., 585 F. Supp.1097, 1104 (E. D. Pa. 1984). *See also* Murray, John E., *Layered Contracts Encounter the Battle of the Forms and Confusion Abounds*, LEXIS Expert Commentary (2008).

[796] 984 A.2d 1061 (R.I. 2009).

particularly when making a purchase over the phone, where full disclosure of the terms would border on the sadistic. Nor do we believe that, after placing a telephone order for a computer, a reasonable consumer would believe that he or she has entered into a fully consummated agreement. . . . Rather, he or she is aware that with delivery comes a multitude of standard terms attendant to nearly every consumer transaction.[797]

The limitation in the holding and rationale of the court to *consumer* transactions leaves the question of whether it would apply the same analysis to a transaction between merchants. The Seventh Circuit leaves no doubt:

The question in *ProCD* was not whether the terms were added to a contract after formation-but how and when the contract was formed-in particular whether a vendor may propose that a contract of sale be formed, not in the store (or over the phone) with a payment of money or a general 'send me the product,' but after the customer has had a chance to inspect both the item and the terms. *ProCD* answers 'yes' for merchants and consumers alike.[798]

[2]　The Antidote

In a jurisdiction applying the "rolling contract" formation theory, instead of rejecting the goods, assume the buyer rejects some or all of the printed terms that appear for the first time inside the package containing the goods. Within the time stated in the seller's terms, the buyer notifies the seller that the buyer will retain the goods and pay the full purchase price, but not be subject to a term such as arbitration. Moreover, the buyer's counter offer states that, unless the seller objects to the counter offer within a time frame (providing the seller with the same period that the seller's terms provided), the seller's silence indicates assent to the counter offer. Such an effort should succeed in the same fashion as the effort of the Rebars who contracted with Cook's Pest Control. The agreement contained an arbitration provision. When time arrived for the agreement to be renewed, Cook's requested that the Rebars renew the agreement by their payment of the annual fee. The Rebars' payment included an "addendum" which notified Cook's of a change in the agreement that required Cook's to propose arbitration but expressly precluded the Rebars from any obligation to arbitrate future disputes. Cook's accepted and negotiated the Rebar's check. In a subsequent dispute, the Rebars opposed Cook's motion to compel arbitration and the court agreed that arbitration was no longer part of the agreement.[799]

Nothing in the rolling contract analysis would prevent the offeree from making such a counter offer. While the offer instructs the offeree to accept or reject the offer, the offeree may still choose to make a counter offer which the other party may reject or accept absent another judicial revolution in contract law.

---

[797] *Id.* at 1071. The court added that the "crucial question" is whether the defendants reasonably invited acceptance by clearly stating that, by accepting the defendant's product, the plaintiff was accepting the terms, and the consumer could reject the terms and conditions by returning the product.

[798] Hill v. Gateway 2000, Inc., 105 F. 3d at 1150.

[799] Cook's Pest Control v. Rebar, 852 So. 2d 730 (Ala. 2002).

[K]   Uniform Computer Information Transactions Act (UCITA) and the "Battle of the Forms"

Contracts to "buy" software are often licenses for the use of copyrighted information. The attempt to revise Article 2 of the Uniform Commercial Code in the decade of the 1990's included an effort to provide separate treatment for computer information transactions. A new design for Article 2 would have created a separate "chapter" for such transactions. That idea was replaced with the concept of a new "Article 2B" for computer information transactions that turned out to be as elaborate and complex as Article 2.[800] When the American Law Institute did not agree with the inclusion of the new Article 2B in the Code, its partner, the National Conference of Commissioners on Uniform State Laws, sponsored it as a new uniform law under a new name, the Uniform Computer Information Transaction Act (UCITA). UCITA was enacted in Maryland and Virginia,[801] but claims that it was drafted to protect software companies made it highly controversial. After its rejection by the American Bar Association, it was no longer supported for enactment in other jurisdictions.

UCITA dramatically changes the Article 2 concept of the "battle of the forms." The essential change is found in the opening UCITA language:

> "[A] definite and seasonable expression of acceptance operates as an acceptance, *unless the acceptance materially alters the offer.*"[802]

Thus, it is impossible for a response to constitute an acceptance if it contains *any* material alteration. Though a comment suggests that it conforms to Section 2-207(1) of Article 2,[803] there is no basis for this suggestion. By characterizing any "acceptance" containing a materially different term as a counter offer, UCITA suggests a return to a version of the pre-UCC "last shot" principle and an analysis that is highly reminiscent of a severely criticized and rejected early interpretation of 2-207.[804] If the acceptance contains *immaterial* additional

---

[800] The logic was based on the existence of Article 2A that had been added to deal with leases or goods which are not sales of goods to which Article 2 is technically limited. Article 2B was envisioned as a similar effort which would relieve any dispute over the application of Article 2 to sales of software.

[801] Va. Code Ann. § 59.1-501.1 (effective July 1, 2001). Md. Com. Law Code Ann. § 22-101 (effective October 1, 2000).

[802] UCITA § 204(b). Section 204(a) states that "an acceptance materially alters an offer if it contains terms that materially conflict with or vary the terms of the offer or that add material terms not contained in the offer." Comment 3 describes a "material change" as "one that would result in surprise, hardship or fundamental change if incorporated without express agreement by the other party, or one that would significantly alter the bargain proposed by the offeror."

[803] UCITA § 2-204, comment 2: "[A] response is not an acceptance if it materially alters the offer. One does not accept by proposing materially different terms."

[804] In one of the earliest interpretations of § 2-207, Roto-Lith, Ltd. v. F. P. Bartlett & Co., 297 F.2d 497 (1st Cir. 1962), the response to the offer (an acknowledgment form) appeared to manifest acceptance but contained a clause disclaiming the implied warranty of merchantability. The offeror argued that the response was a definite expression of acceptance under 2-207 notwithstanding the different warranty term that should not become a part of the contract since it constituted a material alteration of the terms of the offer. The court was so imbued with the mirror image rule that it could not assimilate the radical change effected by § 2-207. It insisted that § 2-207 should not be interpreted to allow a response containing a *materially* altering term to operate as an acceptance. Such a response had to be a counter offer in the eyes of this court. The holding frustrates the essential purpose of § 2-207. Section 2-207(2)(b) expressly recognizes that an acceptance may contain a materially altering term such as a disclaimer of warranty. *Roto-Lith* was the subject of considerable criticism in other jurisdictions. *See, e.g.,* C. Itoh & Co. v. Jordan Int'l Co., 552 F.2d 1228 (7th Cir. 1977); Dorton v. Collins & Aikman Corp., 453 F.2d 1161, 1168 (6th Cir. 1972); Ebasco Servs. v. Pennsylvania Power & Light co., 402 F. Supp. 421, 437–38 (E.D. Pa. 1975); Steiner v. Mobil Oil Corp., 20 Cal. 3d 90,

terms, UCITA treats them as proposals for addition to the contract unless the transaction is between merchants where such terms become part of the contract, absent notice of objection by the offeror.[805] Where a material alteration in response to an offer precludes contract formation, the parties may proceed to form a contract by conduct, the terms of which will be the terms of the offer to which the other party manifested assent.[806] If an offer or acceptance is conditioned on agreement by the other party to the terms of the offer or acceptance, no contract is formed unless the other party agrees to such terms.[807] Where such an offer or acceptance is conditioned on acceptance of terms in standard forms, but a party proceeds to perform notwithstanding a lack of assent to its standard terms, such a party adopts the terms of the offer except for any terms in the offer that conflict with any expressly agreed terms on price or quantity.[808]

Another conspicuous difference between the UCITA and the Article 2 version of the "battle of the forms" is the absence of any mention of *confirmations* in the UCITA version. This is quite deliberate since UCITA includes the "rolling contract" concept. The final formation will not occur until after a party has an opportunity to review different or additional "license" terms. By postponing the time of formation until after the previously unrevealed terms have been divulged, the terms cannot be characterized as additional or different terms since there is no existing contract to which terms could be added or with which such belated terms could possibly differ. Similarly, there can be no confirmation of such a "contract" since there never was any contract to confirm. Thus, what used to be characterized as a "confirmation" is not a confirmation. Silent acquiescence in such terms constitutes the final phase of acceptance of the offer forming a completed contract.

[1]   The World Without UCITA

In the absence of UCITA or other statutory addition, courts have generally applied Article 2 of the UCC by viewing software contracts as contracts for the sale of "goods."[809] "Off-the-rack" software is typically treated as a contract for the sale of goods, while a contract transferring intellectual property rights to software would be outside the scope of Article 2. Creating new software would be viewed as "predominantly" a contract for services rather than goods,[810] but a customization of existing software may be viewed as a contract for the sale of

---

107, 569 P.2d 751, 764 (1977); Uniroyal, Inc. v. Chambers Gasket & Mfg. Co. 177 Ind. App. 508, 517–18, 380 N.E.2d 571, 578 (1978). It was eventually overruled in Ionics, Inc. v. Elmwood Sensors, Ins., 110 F.3d 184 (1st Cir. 1997). *See also* JOM, Inc. v. Adell Plastics, Inc., 193 F.3d 47 (1st Cir. 1999). The UCITA analysis is also very similar to the CISG analysis explored in the next section that clearly favors the pre-UCC "mirror image" rule.

[805] UCITA § 204(d).

[806] UCITA § 204(c).

[807] UCITA § 205(b).

[808] UCITA § 205(c).

[809] See Dealer Mgt. Systems v. Design Automotive Group, Inc., 355 Ill App. 3d 416, 822 N. E. 2d 556 (2005) which cites, *inter alia*, Micro Data Base Systems, Inc. v. Dharma Systems, Inc., 148 F. 3d 649. 654 (7th Cir. 1998) (New Hampshire law), Advent Systems Ltd. v. Unisys Corp., 925 F. 2d 670, 675–76 (3d Cir. 1991), (Pa. Law), ePresence, Inc. v. Evolve Software, Inc., 190 F. Supp. 2d 159, 163 (D. Mass. 2002), Olcott International & Co. v. Micro Data Base Systems, Inc., 693 N. 2d 1063, 1071 (Ind. App. 2003), and Architectronics, Inc. v. Control Systems, Inc., 935 F. Supp. 425, 432 (S. D. N. Y. 1996) (N. Y. law).

[810] In mixed contracts for goods and services, courts apply the "predominance" test. See, e. g, Princess Cruises v. General Electric Co., 143 F. 3d 828 (4th Cir. 1998).

"specially manufactured goods" to which Article 2 applies.[811] Licensing a party to use software will also be characterized as a sale of goods under the Code if the copy of the software provides the buyer with an unlimited period of possession.[812]

[L]   CISG and the "Battle of the Forms" — UNIDROIT Principles

In light of the confusion and complexity surrounding UCC Section 2-207, the framers of CISG chose not to follow it.[813] By treating a reply to an offer containing additions, limitations or other modifications as a counter offer that rejects the offer,[814] a court states that CISG "reflects the common law's 'mirror image' rule"[815] and the attendant "last shot" principle. The statement, however, is not entirely accurate. A response *will* operate as an acceptance if it merely contains different or additional terms that do not *materially* alter the offer unless the offeror objects to the immaterial term.[816] This apparent relaxation of the "mirror image" is significantly narrowed, however, by a broad list of different or additional "material" terms which includes, "among other things," the price, payment, quality, and quantity of the goods, place and time of delivery, extent of liability or the settlement of disputes.[817] Since there are no comments in CISG, one can only wonder what might be included under "other things."[818] Assuming a court would deem a different or additional term "immaterial," the offeror may nullify it by objecting to it. Absent such an objection, the immaterial term would become part of the contract.[819]

The UNIDROIT Principles ("Principles") are a product of the International Institute for the Unification of Private Law (UNIDROIT) which inspired the United Nations Commission on International Trade Law (UNCITRAL) to create CISG. Principles are not designed to be enacted into the law of countries throughout the world. They are likened to an American Restatement of the law, to establish a balanced set of rules designed for use by courts throughout the world. They are broader than CISG Articles, applying to questions of "validity" to which CISG does not apply. They are not designed to apply to consumer transactions, but the "lex mercatoria" concept that underlies Principles makes them applicable to the broadest variety of merchants.[820] Principles include an Article replicating the

---

[811]   § 2-103(1)(k) includes "specially manufactured goods" within the general definition of "goods" ("things that are moveable at the time of identification to a contract for sale. . . .").

[812]   Softman Products Co., LLC v. Adobe Sys., Inc., 171 F. Supp. 2d 1076, 1085–86 (C.D. Cal. 2001).

[813]   The United Nations Convention on Contracts for the International Sale of Goods. See J. HONNOLD, UNIFORM LAW FOR INTERNATIONAL SALES UNDER THE 1980 SALES CONVENTION 193 (1982), where the author suggest that the framers were well advised not to follow 2-207.

[814]   CISG, Art. 19(1).

[815]   Magellan Int'l Corp. v. Salzgitter Handel GmbH, 76 F. Supp. 2d 919, 925 (N.D. Ill. 1999). The court admits, in note 14, that its use of the term "reflects" is an intended pun.

[816]   CISG, Art. 19(2).

[817]   CISG, Art. 19(3).

[818]   Professor Farnsworth found it difficult "to imagine variations that would not be material." Alan Farnsworth, FORMATION OF CONTRACT IN INTERNATIONAL SALES: THE UNITED NATIONS CONVENTION ON CONTRACTS FOR THE INTERNATIONAL SALE OF GOODS § 3.04, at 3–17.

[819]   CISG Art.19(2). Unlike the common law, there is no "dispatch" ("mailbox") rule under CISG, (Art. 18(2) requires the acceptance to "reach the offeror" to be effective, but dispatching the acceptance does have the effect of making the offer irrevocable (Art. 16(1)).

[820]   UNIDROIT Principles of International Commercial Contracts (1994) ("Principles"), http://www.unidroit.org/

CISG treatment,[821] but a recognition of the unfairness of the "last shot" rule induced special treatment of the "battle of the forms." Principles define "standard terms" as provisions prepared in advance for general and repeated use without negotiation.[822] Unlike the UCC, Principles first deals with standard terms in a single form presented by one party and accepted by the other, i.e., where there is no "battle of the forms." Though recognizing the concept that a party should be bound by standard terms that she has accepted regardless of knowledge of their contents, Principles includes an "important exception" to this rule by relieving the party of the effect of standard terms which she should not "reasonably have expected" to be included in the standardized form.[823] The purpose is to avoid unfair surprise to a reasonable party who may not, under the surrounding circumstances, expect such a term.[824]

Turning to the "battle of the forms," Principles recognizes that such boilerplate terms are ignored on such standardized forms as purchase orders and acknowledgments,[825] i.e., these terms may conflict with each other, notwithstanding agreement on negotiated terms that Karl Llewellyn would call "dickered" terms. Where, therefore, the negotiated terms match but the standard terms conflict, Principles finds a contract on the matching dickered terms as well as matching standard terms while excising any non-matching standard terms. If, however, a party *clearly* informs the other party either in advance or later, without undue delay, that it does not intend to be bound except on its standard terms, such a manifestation of intention will preclude the formation of a contract except on its terms.[826] This Article rejects the "last shot" rule[827] unless a party clearly expresses its unwillingness to contract except on its standard as well as negotiated terms. A statement expressing such unwillingness in the standard (boilerplate) terms will not be sufficient. It must appear in the "non-standard" terms where it would be more likely to be noticed.[828] Thus, Principles suggests that the kind of formula counter offer as a standard term recognized by the UCC would not be effective.

---

english/principles/intro-1.htm. A helpful analysis as well as the text of Principles is found in Joseph M. Perillo, *UNIDROIT Principles of International Commercial Contracts: The Black Letter Text and a Review*, 63 FORDHAM L. REV. 281 (1994).

[821] Principles, Art. 2.11.

[822] Principles, Art. 2.19.

[823] Principles, Art. 2.20.

[824] Principles, Art. 2.20. Comment 2 suggests that a term excluding or limiting contractual liability may or may not be surprising in a particular case. If they are common in the trade or consistent with the way in which the parties negotiated the deal, they would not be surprising. In other contexts, they would be surprising. Where a travel agency offers package tours for business trips and the advertisement suggests that the agency takes full responsibility for various services comprising the package, a term in the standard form that states the agency is acting only as an agent for the hotel or innkeeper, thereby denying liability, would be excised as an unexpected term. Illustration 1 to Comment 2. Comment 3 suggests that terms may be surprising because of their language or presentation, i.e., the terms are found in obscure or minute print. A foreign language may not provide the full implications of the terms to a party who otherwise appears to accept the terms. Thus, a Hamburg commodity dealer may use the term "Hamburg-Freundschaftliche Arbitrage" which, in local circles, means that disputes are to be submitted to a special arbitration under local rules. In contracts with foreign customers who otherwise accept all of the dealer's standard terms, such a standard term may be ineffective because foreign customers would not understand its implications. *Cf.* RESTATEMENT 2d § 211, particularly Comment *f*; John E. Murray, Jr., *The Standardized Agreement Phenomena in the Restatement (Second) of Contracts*, 67 Cornell L. Rev. 735 (1982).

[825] Principles, Art. 2.22, Comment 3.

[826] Principles, Art. 2.22.

[827] Principles, Art. 2.22, Comment 2.

[828] Principles, Art. 2.22, Comment 3, illustration 2.

Assuming matching non-standard terms and no clear statement of unwillingness to contract except on one's standard terms, Principles expressly adopts the "knockout doctrine" to deal with conflicting standard terms.[829]

[M]   Comparing § 2-207, CISG and "Principles"

A comparison of the "battle of the forms" in § 2-207, CISG and Principles suggests the following:

(1) The offer insists on its standard terms and the response contains a variant standard term. Section 2-207(2)(a) will prevent the variant term, material or immaterial, from becoming part of the contract. Under CISG, if the term is material, the response will be a counter offer.[830] Principles requires that a statement insisting on one's terms be included in non-standard terms to assure that it is "clear." Assuming such a clear statement, any variant standard term in the response will be excised and the contract will be formed in accordance with the terms of the offer.[831]

(2) Where the *response* to the offer insists on the standard terms of the response, under 2-207, assuming the statement meets the requirements of a 2-207 counter offer (formula or very clear counter offer), no contract is formed via the exchange of forms. Subsequent acceptance of the goods does not accept the terms of the counter offer. Rather, 2-207(3) applies.[832] Under CISG, the response would be a counter offer and subsequent acceptance of the goods would result in a contract on the terms of the counter offer (the "last shot" principle). Principles would recognize the statement in the response as a counter offer only if it appeared in non-standard terms. If it is such a clear counter offer, it will reject the offer and subsequent acceptance of the goods will accept the terms of the counter offer.

(3) The non-standard terms match, but the response contains a materially altering term. Section 2-207 will recognize a contract without the term under 2-207(2)(b). CISG will characterize the response as a counter offer, i.e., the "last shot" principle will apply. Principles will recognize a contract without the materially altering term. If the non-standard term in the response is *immaterial*, it will become part of the contract under 2-207, absent a 2-207(2)(a) or (2)(c) reservation by the offeror. Similarly, CISG would recognize an acceptance unless the offeror objects to the immaterial variant term. Principles would find a contract without the variant standard term, material or immaterial.

(4) The offer contains an express standard (boilerplate) term that is expressly contradicted by a standard term in the acceptance. The clearly prevailing 2-207 view is the "knockout" view. There is a contract without the contradictory terms that cancel each other. The resulting "gap" is filled with a UCC term. Under CISG, the response is a counter offer and subsequent acceptance of the goods would result in a contract on the terms of the counter offer — again, the "last shot" principle would apply. Principles would apply the "knockout" view, excising the

---

[829] Principles, Art. 2.22, Comment 3.

[830] If the term is one of the rare immaterial terms under CISG, it would become part of the acceptance unless the offeror objected to it. Unlike the UCC, such an objection would destroy the acceptance. CISG, Art. 19(2). UCC § 2-207(2)(c).

[831] See Principles, Art. 2.22, Comment 3, illustration 3.

[832] Section 2-207(3) includes the matching terms of the exchanged forms and excises non-matching terms. Gaps are filled with supplementary UCC terms, such as the normal warranties and remedies of the Code.

conflicting standard terms and recognizing a contract on the non-standard terms and standard terms that are common in substance.[833]

(5) The offer contains the same boilerplate term as in (4), but the standard terms in the response are silent with respect to this term. Section 2-207 would assume that the offer has been accepted according to its terms. Under CISG, the same result would follow since the response would not be viewed as containing any variant term. Principles, however, would view the standard term in the offer as not "common in substance" with the standard terms in the response and excise the term in the offer, recognizing a contract without that term.[834]

§ 52 SILENCE, INACTION, RETENTION OF BENEFITS AND EXERCISE OF DOMINION AS ACCEPTANCE — UNSOLICITED GOODS

[A] Silence

It has often been asserted that, as a general rule, silence may not constitute acceptance of an offer.[835] Exceptions to this general rule, however, augur a more cautious statement found in numerous cases that silence will not constitute acceptance of an offer unless there is a duty to speak.[836] When does an offeree have a duty to inform the offeror that the offeree does not intend to accept the offer?

If A offers to sell an automobile to B at a certain price and concludes the offer with the following statement, "If I do not hear from you within 10 days from the date you receive this letter, I will assume you have accepted my offer," should B's silence indicate assent so that he will be said to have accepted the offer? Just because a party makes such an offer, the offeree cannot be bound to expressly reject the offer to avoid being bound to a contract.[837] But, neither can B's silence be viewed as a rejection of the offer. The offeree's silence, by itself, is ambiguous because it does not indicate the offeree's state of mind. His silence may indicate that he is ignoring the offer or that he desires to reject it. It may, however, indicate that he intends to accept the offer and he is silent because he is following the command of the offeror in exercising the power of acceptance. While the offeror may not infer assent to the offer from

---

[833] Principles, Art. 2.22, Comment 3, illustration 1.

[834] The language of Principles Art. 2.22 states that, "Where both parties use standard terms and reach an agreement on those terms, a contract is concluded on the basis of the agreed [non-standard] terms *and of any standard terms which are common in substance. . . .*" (Emphasis supplied). Since the standard terms of the offer contain a term not contained in the standard terms of the acceptance, the contract did not include the "uncommon" term in the offer. For a helpful analysis concerning the differences among 2-207, CISG and principles, see Maria del Pilar Perales Viscasillas, *"Battle of the Forms" Under the 1980 United Nations Convention on Contracts for the International Sale of Goods: A Comparison with Section 2-207 and the UNIDROIT Principles*, 10 Pace Int'l L. Rev. 97 (1998).

[835] *See, e.g.*, Vogt v. Madden, 110 Idaho 6, 713 P. 2d 442 (Ct. App. 1985); Bestor v. American Nat'l Stores, Inc., 691 S.W.2d 384 (Mo. Ct. App. 1985); Rosin v. First Bank of Oak Park, 126 Ill. App. 3d 230, 466 N.E.2d 1245 (1st Dist. 1984).

[836] *See, e.g.*, Chorba v. Davlisa Enters., Inc., 303 Pa. Super. 497, 450 A.2d 36 (1982).

[837] See E & A Northeast Ltd. Partnership v. Music City Record Distributors, Inc., 2007 Tenn App. LEXIS 145 (Ct. App. 2007) quoting § 3.19 of Corbin on Contracts: "[A]n offeror has no power to cause silence of the offeree to operate as an acceptance when the offeree does not intend it to do so."

the offeree's silence,[838] the offeree has a power of acceptance created by the offer which may be exercised through silence though he does not manifest his intention in any other objective fashion.[839] In such a case, the evidence of *B*'s exercise of his power of acceptance is the ambiguous act of silence and B's subsequent claim that he intended to accept through such silence. The offeror, however, will not be heard to complain that an unambiguous manifestation of acceptance is lacking since the offeror, as master of the offer, created the ambiguity. If an offeror decides to create a power of acceptance that can be exercised by silence or any other ambiguous action or inaction, the power can be exercised by the offeree in that fashion, but he will not be bound unless he intends to be bound, and such intention can be adduced in this situation only by the subsequent statement of the offeree.[840]

The ambiguity surrounding silence or inaction on the part of the offeree may be removed in certain situations. The classic case involves a prior course of dealing between the parties. Where a seller of goods solicited offers from a merchant and, on repeated occasions, the seller had shipped the ordered goods within a certain period absent any notification other than the bill accompanying shipment, the merchant was justified in relying upon the silence of the seller as acceptance of the latest order. Such silence will constitute acceptance because the parties' prior relationship creates a reasonable obligation on the offeree to speak, i.e., to notify the offeror, if he does not intend to accept.[841]

A similar analysis is found in cases where an insurance company fails to respond to an application for an unreasonable length of time. The applicant may be justified in understanding that he is insured, particularly where a premium has been paid and retained by the insurance company.[842] Silence may also constitute acceptance where the parties enter into a contract and, as part of that contract, agree that a subsequent offer to modify their contract will be accepted by silence.[843] As in the previous situation, here silence can operate as

---

[838] See, however, the discussion of *ProCD v. Zeidenberg* and related cases at § 51[J], *supra*.

[839] *See* RESTATEMENT 2d § 69(1)(b) and comment c. *See* Smarttext Corp. v. Interland, Inc., 296 F. Supp. 2d 1257, 1265 (D. Kan. 2003); Golden Eagle Ins. Co. v. Foremost Ins. Co., 20 Cal. App. 4th 1372, 1387, 25 Cal. Rptr. 2d 242, 251 (21993). See also Sollenbarger v. Mountain States Tel. & Tel. Co., 121 F.R.D. 417, 428-29 (D. N. M. 1988) noting the adoption of the same view from the First or Second Restatement in several jurisdictions.

[840] If an offeror insists that the only way in which his offer can be accepted is by the offeree's eating or not eating breakfast on a given day, the action or inaction required by the offer is an ambiguous act. If performed, a contract will be formed if the offeree intended to accept by such action or inaction, but it will not be formed absent such intention.

[841] *See* Ammons v. Wilson & Co., 176 Miss. 645, 170 So. 227 (1936); RESTATEMENT 2d § 69(1)(c) and comment d; Richard A. Berjian, D.O., Inc. v. Ohio Bell Tel., 54 Ohio St. 2d 147, 375 N.E.2d 410 (1978). *See also* Laredo Nat'l Bank v. Gordon, 61 F.2d 906, 907 (5th Cir. 1932), *cert. denied*, 289 U.S. 726, 53 S. Ct. 524, 77 L. Ed. 1476 (1933): "It is true that, generally speaking, an offeree has a right to make no reply to offers, and hence that his silence is not to be construed as an acceptance. But where the relation between the parties is such that the offeror is justified in expecting a reply, or the offeree is under a duty to reply, the latter's silence will be regarded as an acceptance." Trade usage could also serve as a basis for a justifiable assumption that silence constitutes acceptance. Section 1-205(2) of the UCC defines trade usage as "any practice or method of dealing having such regularity of observance in a place, vocation or trade as to justify an expectation that it will be observed with respect to the transaction in question."

[842] *See* American Life Ins. Co. v. Hutcheson, 109 F.2d 424 (6th Cir.), *cert. denied*, 310 U.S. 625, 60 S. Ct. 898, 84 L. Ed. 1397 (1940). *See also* RESTATEMENT 2d § 69 comment d: "In many states by statute or decision an insurance company is under a duty to act without unreasonable delay on insurance applications solicited by its agents. . . ." *See* Annot., 32 A.L.R.2d 487 (1953).

[843] *See* Fineman v. Citicorp USA, Inc., 137 Ill. App. 3d 1035, 1037, 485 N.E.2d 591, 592 (1st Dist. 1985). Credit card contract contained amendment provision concerning finance charges and annual percentage rate that required cardholder to notify issuer of card of objection to any changes. Absent notification, the provision indicated that the issuer "will understand that you agree to the changes in the notice." *Held:* silence was effective as a matter of contract

acceptance because the parties have a existing contractual relationship which manifests their intention that silence will constitute acceptance.

[B] Retention of Benefits — "Implied-in-Fact" vs. "Implied-in-Law"

The ambiguity of silence was removed where a teacher had been employed for many years under a contract stating that she could be removed without cause. The teacher signed and returned the contract with a notation that took an exception to this statement. The notation stated that she expected a showing of just cause for a non-renewal of her contract. The school did not respond to the teacher's notation but employed her for that year. When she was not offered a contract for the following year, the court held that the silence of the school constituted acceptance of the teacher's counter offer because of their prior dealings with the teacher and because the school took the benefits of her services with knowledge of her counter offer.[844]

Even where the parties have no prior relationship, silence or inaction in conjunction with acceptance of valuable goods or services will evidence an agreement between the parties.[845]

In a well-known case,[846] a court inferred a promise to pay on the part of the recipient of valuable services who had an opportunity to reject them, but accepted them knowing or having reason to know that the other party expected to receive compensation. The silence or inaction of the recipient of such benefits is not ambiguous since he knows or has reason to know he is receiving benefits and could, without difficulty or expense, inform the other party that he rejects them. Failing to speak and the retention of benefits in such circumstances manifests an acceptance of the offer.[847]

It is important to distinguish this situation from one allowing restitutionary relief for unjust enrichment. If a court implies a promise to pay for services rendered because the recipient had an opportunity to reject the services but chose not to do so with knowledge or reason to know that the other party expected to be paid, the court is discovering a genuine contract — a contract by conduct. It is often called an "implied-in-fact" contract because the acceptance is not expressed in language; it is expressed by the action or, in this case, the inaction of the offeree where he should manifest an objection if he does not intend to accept.[848] Where facts do not permit such an inference but benefits are knowingly received at the expense of a party conferring such benefits who is neither officious nor should have been understood to be conferring such benefits gratuitously, an action in restitution will normally lie. Such an action is not an action for breach of contract. Rather, it is an action to prevent the unjust enrichment

---

law and there was no violation of the Illinois consumer protection law, ILL. REV. STAT. 1981, ch. 12, paras. 261 et seq. and 311 et seq.

[844] Shively v. Santa Fe Preparatory School, 21 Fed. Appx. 875, 2001 U.S. App. LEXIS 24578 (10th Cir. 2001). Restatement 2d § 69, comment a, suggests the exceptional cases holding silence constitutes acceptance fall into two main classes: where the offeree silently takes offered benefits, and where one party relies on the other party's manifestation of intention that silence will constitute acceptance.

[845] See Bump v. Robbins, 24 Mass. App. Ct. 296, 509 N.E.2d 12 (1987) (finding that, notwithstanding the possibility of discovering an agreement through silent retention of services, such a finding was not justified in a situation involving a brokerage commission since brokerage agreements involve a high risk of noncompensation).

[846] Day v. Caton, 119 Mass. 513, 20 Am. Rep. 347 (1876).

[847] See RESTATEMENT 2d § 69(1)(a) and comment b. See also Laurel Race Course, Inc. v. Regal Constr. Co., 274 Md. 142, 333 A.2d 319 (1975).

[848] See, e.g., Ganley v. G & W Ltd. Partnership, 44 Md. App. 568, 409 A.2d 761 (1980).

of the party who has received the benefits. The action is often referred to as one in *quasi contract*, a so-called implied-in-law contract constructed by the court, again, to prevent unjust enrichment.[849]

The recovery under quasi contract will be measured by the reasonable value of the benefits conferred rather than a contract price since there is no contract. If, however, a court finds an offer that has been accepted though it discovers that acceptance inferentially from the conduct of the parties and the surrounding circumstances rather than the oral or written expressions of the offeree, a true acceptance has occurred forming a genuine contract albeit one implied from conduct.[850] The duty of the offeree under such a contract is not merely to pay the reasonable or fair value of the benefits conferred; it is a duty to pay the price set forth in the offer that has been accepted.[851]

[C]   Unsolicited Goods — "Unordered Merchandise"

If a seller ships goods to a buyer who has not offered to buy them, the mere receipt of the goods is not a manifestation of acceptance of the seller's offer since the buyer must have an opportunity to discover that he has received unordered goods.[852]

Once the buyer knows or should know that he has received unordered goods, he may, of course, reject them though, while they are in his possession, he will have certain duties with respect to such goods.[853] If the buyer does not reject unordered goods but chooses to use them or otherwise exercise dominion or control over them in a way inconsistent with the seller's ownership, the buyer will be said to have accepted the seller's offer to sell the unordered goods.[854] If the offer to sell the unordered goods states a price, the use of the goods will constitute an acceptance of the offer at the price stated in the offer, i.e., the offeree may not use the goods and simultaneously pay a price he deems fair if that price is less than the

---

[849] See Weichert Co. Realtors v. Ryan, 128 N.J. 427, 608 A.2d 280 (1992). *See also supra* § 21.

[850] See the exploration of the distinction between implied-in-fact contracts and implied-in-law (quasi) contracts in § 21, Chapter 1. See also Chapter 9, *infra*, dealing with contract remedies, including the protection of the restitution interest. In a given fact situation, the line between a genuine contract, albeit one implied-in-fact, and a quasi contract (which is not a contract but goes under the name of contract only because relief for unjust enrichment was brought under a common law form of action which was used for true contracts, i.e., assumpsit) is extremely difficult to draw. The RESTATEMENT 2d suggests that, in certain cases, the line is "often indistinct." *See* RESTATEMENT 2d § 4 comment b and § 19 comment a.

[851] *See* RESTATEMENT 2d § 69 comment b.

[852] Even where the parties had a prior contract to buy and sell goods, the buyer's receipt of the goods does not amount to acceptance *of the goods*. The buyer is normally entitled to inspect the goods before he will be said to have accepted them. *See* UCC §§ 2-513(1) and 2-606(1)(a) and (1)(b). Acceptance of the goods pursuant to a prior contract of sale must be distinguished from acceptance of unordered goods. Where the buyer accepts unordered goods, he is accepting the seller's offer made through the seller's conduct of tendering unordered goods to the buyer and, simultaneously, he is accepting the goods, themselves, which precludes a right of rejection that must occur within a reasonable time after delivery or tender of the goods. UCC § 2-602(1). If the buyer has accepted the goods, he may not reject them but may, under appropriate circumstances, revoke his acceptance of the goods under UCC § 2-608.

[853] *See* UCC §§ 2-603 and 2-604 which place certain duties on a buyer who rejects concerning perishable goods or goods that are not perishable but threaten to decline in value speedily. Where the seller has no place or business or agent at the buyer's location, the rejecting buyer must follow any reasonable instructions from the seller and, in the absence of such instructions, may have to dispose of the goods for the seller's account. Typically, the buyer may either store the goods, reship them, or resell them as commercial reasonableness requires.

[854] *See* Pace v. Sagebrush Sales Co., 114 Ariz. 271, 560 P.2d 789 (1977); European Import Co. v. Lone Star Co., 596 S.W.2d 287 (Tex. Civ. App. 1980).

price at which the goods were offered.[855] In such a situation, the offeror has the choice of treating the recipient as a tort-feasor who has converted the goods or an offeree who has exercised his power of acceptance by accepting the goods. If the offeror chooses to treat the offeree as having contracted to purchase the goods, the offeree is bound to pay the price stated in the offer.[856]

Where a party not only receives but uses unordered goods, at common law the use is viewed as an acceptance of the seller's unsolicited offer.[857] Sellers may, however, attempt to thrust their products on an unsuspecting party who uses the goods without awareness that she is subjecting herself to contract liability. A number of statutory modifications to protect the public against contract liability for unsolicited goods have modified the common law rule. A federal statute permits a party receiving unordered merchandise *through the mail* to retain, use or dispose of the merchandise without obligation.[858] There are also state statutes that relieve the recipient of the obligation to pay for unsolicited goods when the goods have been received through the mail or otherwise.[859]

---

[855] *See* RESTATEMENT 2d § 69 ill. 9.

[856] *Id.*

[857] See Austin v. Burge, 156 Mo. App. 286, 137 S.W. 618 (1911), where the recipient of a newspaper continuously complained that he had not ordered it. Since he read it, however, he was said to have accepted the offer. Simply inspecting or storing goods, however, will not amount to acceptance of the offer.

[858] 39 U.S.C. § 3009. The delivery of unordered merchandise through the postal system (except conspicuously marked "free" samples or merchandise mailed by a charitable organization soliciting contributions) is an unfair method of competition in violation of the Federal Trade Commission Act. For an interpretation of this statute, see Kipperman v. Academy Life Ins. Co., 554 F.2d 377 (9th Cir. 1977), where the court decided that a private action for declaratory relief would lie though an injunction would not lie. The subject matter of this case was unsolicited insurance (an intangible) that is not "merchandise" within the meaning of the statute. Moreover, the court held that the communication by the insurance company in this case was a mere offer to sell. Thus, even if insurance were construed to be "merchandise," like an offer to sell kitchen appliances, it would not fall within the scope of the statute which assumes the delivery of unordered merchandise through the mail that the recipient may treat as a gift.

[859] *See, e. g.*, NEB. REV. STAT. § 63-101 (2009) (newspapers, magazines or other periodicals); 73 PA. STAT. § 2001 (2009) (goods-by mail, gift); N.Y. GEN. OBLIG. LAW § 5-332 (2010) (goods, wares, merchandise-unconditional gift).

Chapter 3

THE VALIDATION PROCESS

217

§ 53   THE ENFORCEABILITY OF PROMISES — "PACTA SUNT SERVANDA"

[A]   The Enforcement of Promises — The Validation Process

In a society devoted to the ideal concept, "pacta sunt servanda" (all promises must be kept), the only question would be whether a member of that society made a promise. With sufficient evidence of a promise, the promise would be enforced. A moment's reflection, however, suggests myriad complications. If the promise was made under duress or induced by fraud or mistake, should the promise be enforced at law?[1] If the promisor did not intend to be bound until a more formal agreement was executed, should his promise be enforced prior to that formal agreement?[2] If the promise was made in jest and would have been reasonably understood as a joke, should that promise be enforced?[3] If the promise was made to a member of the promisor's family or to his friend and dealt with ordinary domestic or social matters, should the legal system enforce that kind of promise?[4] And, what of promises to make gifts? A promisor may have every intention of performing a donative promise before encountering unforeseen difficulties which prohibit performance of that promise. Should the promisor be subject to a legal proceeding for nonperformance even though the promisee has lost nothing as a result of the donative promise?[5] These and other questions support the view that, "No

---

[1]   *See infra* Chapter 6.

[2]   On the question of intention to be legally bound before a final writing is executed, see *supra* § 32.

[3]   *See supra* § 32[C].

[4]   *See supra* § 32[D].

[5]   For an analysis of why donative promises should not be enforceable, see Eisenberg, *Donative Promises*, 47 U. CHI. L. REV. 1 (1979). Professor Eisenberg suggests that the legal system may fairly take the position that its compulsory processes will be invoked only to remedy injuries of a certain intensity, *e.g.*, the prevention of unjust enrichment or the promotion of a social policy, such as the promotion of the economy and the injury to the donative promisee is typically slight, involving defeated expectations in the form of disappointment. Typically there will be no unjust enrichment of

legal system does or can attempt to enforce all promises."[6]

If a basic principle of any legal system is that it cannot enforce all promises, one of the most important questions in contract law must be confronted: Of all the promises made in a given society, which promises should be enforced at law? What criteria are to be used to separate those promises which the law will enforce from those that it will not recognize in terms of legal sanctions? In common law fashion, the criteria have evolved over centuries. The decisions in which this evolution has occurred evidence an admixture of rationality, pragmatism and historic accident. Something more than mutual assent, as manifested in an offer and acceptance, has always been necessary to create an informal contract, i.e., the typical contract involving a bargained-for-exchange.[7]

Long before the simple or informal contract was known to the common law, however, the process for making a promise enforceable was formal or ritualistic.[8] It did not focus upon any bargained-for-exchange between the parties where each party is receiving something he values in exchange for surrendering something the other party values. Rather, the question was whether certain prescribed formalities had been met. At any given time in the history of our legal system, it has been possible to identify the recognized criteria used in that system to answer the fundamental question: which promises ought to be enforced? At this time, therefore, we find certain devices that are currently used in our system to validate promises, i.e., to make them legally enforceable. We group these devices under the caption, "The Validation Process," because that process explores all of the current devices used to make promises enforceable. The validation process is not static. Certain promises that were not enforceable in the past are now enforceable. In this chapter, we will explore the current validation devices.

the promisor and, while the author would not go so far as to suggest that a gift is a sterile transmission from an economic perspective because they do have a wealth redistribution effect, the enforcement of gratuitous promises would have a relatively insignificant effect in achieving wealth redistribution as a goal of contract law. While his thesis suggests that our legal system is correct in withholding legal enforcement from gratuitous promises, Professor Eisenberg emphasizes the distinction between the questions, what promises should the *law* enforce, and what promises should people keep? There are myriad extra-legal sanctions for breaking a promise that is not legally enforceable, *e.g.*, loss of business, loss of friends, loss of self-respect, and other, difficult-to-measure, losses. In a given situation, one of these sanctions may be a more effective deterrent to promise-breaking than the mere payment of money damages, which is the typical legal sanction for failure to perform one's legally enforceable promise.

[6] *See* Cohen, *The Basis of Contract*, 46 Harv. L. Rev. 553 (1933).

[7] The cases are legion which repeat the elements of a contract as "offer, acceptance and consideration." *See, e.g.*, Trustmark Life Ins. Co. v. University of Chicago Hosps., 207 F.3d 876, 882 (7th Cir. 2000); Dyno Constr. Co. v. McWane, Inc., 198 F.3d 567 (6th Cir. 1999); Harvard Univ. v. Goldstein, 2000 Mass. Super. LEXIS 42, at *4 (Mass. Super. Ct. Feb. 11, 2000); Steiger v. Huntsville City Bd. of Educ., 653 So. 2d 975, 978 (Ala. 1995); Crane v. Crane, 986 P.2d 881 (Alaska 1999); Koltis v. North Carolina Dep't of Human Resources, Div. of Facility Servs., 125 N.C. App. 268, 271, 480 S.E.2d 702, 704 (1997); Straub v. B. M. T. by Todd, 645 N.E.2d 597, 598 (Ind. 1994). As will be seen, however, the shibboleth that a contract requires offer, acceptance and consideration is not entirely accurate since consideration is only one of the mutually exclusive devices that make promises enforceable.

[8] For the basic distinction between formal and informal contracts, see § 17 *supra*.

[B]   Current Validation Devices

[1]   The Seal and Other Formalistic Devices

If a promise is to be enforced simply because it adheres to certain formalities such as a writing that contains certain language or symbols, the mere presence of such formalistic validation devices make the promises enforceable. The oldest formalistic validation device is the seal which will be examined in the next section. We will also examine modern formalistic validation devices that became necessary after the seal was either abolished or severely restricted in scope.

[2]   Consideration

Consideration is the best-known validation device. It does not rest on any prescribed formalities. Since no particular words or symbols are necessary, the result is an "informal" contract rather than a "formal" contract. The informal contract is the kind of contract made billions of times each day. The focus is not on form but substance. The evidence must display an agreement between two or more parties evidencing a bargained-for-exchange of value between the parties. The consideration validation device is so well-known that it is often found in general statements that make it appear as the only validation device.[9] Yet, long prior to the development of the consideration concept, promises were enforced on other bases. Because consideration does not depend upon certain words or symbols, courts must consider whether something of value has been bargained-for to make either party's promise enforceable. Such inquires produce innumerable cases and the determination of whether consideration exists in a given situation can be problematic. The fact that the determination of whether consideration exists in various situations, however, should not mislead the student of contract law into believing that consideration is a superior or more important validation device than the others.

[3]   Promissory Estoppel (Detrimental Reliance)

Like consideration, the validation device popularly known as "promissory estoppel" does not depend upon adherence to any prescribed formalities. It requires a promise, in no particular form, inducing the promisee to rely to his or her detriment where the promisor should have contemplated such reliance. Though there is no bargained-for-exchange, a promise upon which a promisee reasonably relies may be enforceable. While promissory estoppel is sometimes viewed as a more recent addition to recognized validation devices, the reliance concept to make promises enforceable antedates the doctrine of consideration.

[4]   Moral Obligation

It is commonly stated that circumstances giving rise to a moral as contrasted with a legal obligation will not make a promise enforceable. Later in this chapter, however, we will identify narrow clusters of cases where courts enforce promises exclusively on the basis of moral obligation. Though moral obligation as a validation device is extremely limited in scope, it is entitled to be listed among currently recognized validation devices.

---

[9] *See* note 7, *supra*. Courts making such statements would, however, be quick to agree that there are other validation devices.

§ 54 CONTRACTS UNDER SEAL — FORMALISTIC VALIDATION DEVICES

[A]   The Functions of Formalistic Validation Devices

The classic exposition of the functions of formalities was supplied by Professor Lon L. Fuller who suggested three functions that are performed by formalistic devices: (1) the evidentiary function, (2) the cautionary function, and (3) the channeling function.[10] The *evidentiary* function is the obvious function of a legal formality. In the event of controversy, a writing, attestation or some official certification provides reliable evidence of a contract and its terms. The original record does not change. Unlike human memory, it is not subject to the favorable or unfavorable recollection of witnesses. In place of a writing, certain ceremonies or rituals may be pursued to assure human memory. For example, Professor Fuller mentions the Roman *stipulatio* which required the oral statement of the promise in a significant ceremony.[11]

The second function of formalities, the *cautionary* function, is described by Fuller in terms of deterrence against inconsiderate or impulsive action. The early affixing of the seal, for example, required the heating of wax, placing the wax on the writing and impressing it with one's seal, which may have been inscribed on a ring worn by the promisor containing his unique inscription.[12] This or a similar act required time and allowed the promisor to carefully consider the action.[13] Fuller believed that the affixing and impressing of a wax wafer was a splendid device for creating that circumspective frame of mind to guard against pledging the promisor's future performance without some contemplation of the potentially serious consequences. One of the reasons for the demise of the seal was the elimination of the impressed wax and the substitution of pre-printed forms with the word "seal" or simply the initials "l.s." (locus sigilli — the place of the seal). Signing such a printed form was devoid of the cautionary function of the original ceremony of the seal.

The third function, the *channeling* function, is one that Professor Fuller accurately noted as essentially overlooked in earlier discussions of legal formalities. The channeling function permits one to simply observe compliance with prescribed formalities in order to recognize the document as containing an enforceable promise.[14]

---

[10] Fuller, *Consideration and Form*, 41 COLUM. L. REV. 799 (1941).

[11] A conveyance of land would include the handing of soil from the land to the grantee with a young witness who was likely to be alive in the event of controversy illustrates ceremonial conduct serving an evidentiary function. Religious ceremonies, such as the conferring of the Sacrament of Confirmation in the Roman Catholic religion or the Jewish bar or bat mitzvah currently manifest functions similar to those suggested by Professor Fuller.

[12] The term "signet" ring is a modern manifestation of the instrument used by often illiterate promisors to impress the wax with their "seals."

[13] Wedding ceremonies involve the most serious exchange of promises. The length of the ceremony may be said to allow for the cautionary function.

[14] The channeling function is found in the formal requisites of a negotiable instrument such as the ordinary check. The formal requisites are set forth in § 3-104 of the UCC: (a) signed by the maker or drawer; (b) containing an unconditional promise or order to pay a sum certain in money and no other promise, order, obligation or power given by the maker or drawer except as authorized by this Article; (c) payable on demand or at a definite time; and (d) payable to order or bearer. Students unfamiliar with negotiable instruments law will still recall that their checks contain the "words of negotiability," "Pay to the order of. . . ." This and the other formal requisites present the necessary test to determine whether a particular writing is negotiable so that a party who is asked to purchase such

In summary, Fuller suggests that a formalistic validation device such as the seal "not only insures a satisfactory memorial of the promise [evidentiary] and induces deliberation in making the promise [cautionary]. It also serves to mark or signalize the enforceable promise; it furnishes a simple and external test of enforceability [channeling]."[15]

[B]   The Essential Formalities of the Contract Under Seal

The essence of a contract under seal was a promise, in writing, evidencing certain prescribed formalities. The contract under seal was frequently called a deed, specialty or covenant. At early common law, if all of the formalities were met, the promise was enforceable even in light of evidence that the seal was lost or stolen and affixed by another, or induced by fraud.[16] If one or more of the required formalities was not observed, however, the early law refused legal enforcement of the sealed promise. It is important to examine the essential formalities of a contract under seal: (1) the writing, (2) sealing, and (3) delivery.

[1]   What Is a Sufficient Writing?

Blackstone's Commentaries states that a contract under seal had to be written on paper or parchment.[17] The writing had to be complete in itself, i.e., it must contain a sufficiently definite promise and must identify the promisor and promisee.[18] A signature, however, is not required because one of the original functions of the seal was to authenticate a document without the signature of an illiterate promisor who found the seal to be an effective substitute for his inability to sign his name. Thus, while modern contracts under seal are invariably signed, a signature is not required.[19] Rather than a signature, authentication of the writing was supplied by other formalities which we will explore, i.e., sealing and delivery.

---

an instrument can know that if he or she purchases it for value, in good faith, and without notice of any claims or defenses, he or she can become a holder in due course (§ 3-302) and take the instrument free of most of the typical claims and defenses of prior parties to such instruments (§ 3-305). If the instrument is not a negotiable instrument, the purchaser would be subject to such claims as a mere transferee or assignee of the instrument. Therefore, whether he or she will purchase it may very well depend upon its negotiability, and whether it is negotiable will depend upon its external manifestation of compliance with the formal requisites set forth above.

[15] Fuller, *supra* note 10, at 801.

[16] *See, e.g.,* Mason v. Ditchbourne, 1 Mo. & R. 460, 174 Eng. Rep. 158 [1835], and Wright v. Campbell, 1 F. & F. 393, 175 Eng. Rep. 1111 (1861), holding that fraud is not a defense to a sealed instrument. *See generally* J. Ames, Lectures on Legal History 98 (1913).

[17] 2 Blackstone's Commentaries 297 (1765) suggest that a "deed must be written, or I presume printed, for it may be in any character or any language; but it must be upon paper or parchment. For if it be written on stone, board, linen, leather, or the like, it is no deed."

[18] See Restatement 2d §§ 95(1)(c) and 108, which indicate that the promisor and promisee must be named in the document or so described as to be capable of identification when the document is delivered. See also Green v. Horne, 1 Salk 197 [1965], where the deed contained a promise but did not name or describe the promisee. Held: the obligation was not enforceable as a deed. Comment a to § 108 of the Restatement 2d refers to the Restatement 2d Agency §§ 151, 191 and 296, which indicate that a principal is not a party to a sealed instrument unless he appears in the instrument as a party.

[19] *See* Restatement 2d § 95 comment c.

[2]   Sealing — Nature of the Seal

The original seal was composed of wax attached to the writing and an impression upon the wax.[20] That ancient form, however, was relaxed no later than the nineteenth century:

"Anciently a seal was defined to be an impression on wax; but it has long been held, that a seal by a wafer, or other tenacious substance, upon which an impression is or may be made is a valid seal."[21] The evolution of the seal allowed an impression on the writing, itself, rather than something attached to the writing.[22] The final extension of the early common law rule is manifested by writings containing a scrawl or scroll or other mark or symbol, made with pen or pencil, or printed on the document with the apparent intention that such mark or symbol constitute a seal. Earlier cases tended to view such marks as insufficient,[23] but later cases generally held them adequate to constitute seals when used or adopted for that purpose.[24] The word "seal" has been held sufficient[25] and, by judicial decision or statute, the term "seal," "locus sigilli" (the place of the seal), its abbreviation, "L.S.," "scroll" or "scrawl" may be sufficient.[26] Even if the word "seal" or a substitute such as "L.S." is printed on a standardized form, it will often be sufficient.[27]

The modern relaxation of the form of the seal has substantially affected its significance. It is commonplace for pre-printed forms containing "seal" to be signed without the reflection required under the ancient form of the wax impression. The functions of formalistic validation devices are compromised by permitting the seal to be affixed in this fashion. The cautionary function is destroyed when documents containing the preprinted word, "seal," are signed without reflection on the significance of that term. It is difficult to treat such a form of sealed instrument as manifesting anything like conclusive evidence that the writing was intended by the signer to have any special significance. Thus, the channeling function is severely mitigated, if not destroyed. Even the evidentiary function is made ineffective through such unconscious adoption of the writing as a sealed instrument, i.e., just because it contains a printed term such as "seal" or "L.S." that the typical signer does not understand. Such "sealing," unlike the

---

[20] Sealed instruments (called "specialties") were necessary in action of debt *sur obligation* in the early law of contract. "The essentials were the use of parchment or paper, sealing by the obligor, and delivery as a deed, normally witnessed and attested. Sealing was no great chore; . . . although it could be a grand affair, a blob of wax with some sort of impress on it sufficed. Loss of the seal, or any material erasure or alteration of the bond [obligation] rendered the bond invalid, as did any suspicious circumstance such as the fact that the bond had been smoked or the seal glued back on to the label; the courts were prudently suspicious of any signs of monkey business." A. W. B. SIMPSON, A HISTORY OF THE LAW OF CONTRACT 90 (1987).

[21] Tasker v. Bartlett, 59 Mass. (5 Cush.) 359 (1850). *Accord* Maddocks v. Keene, 114 Me. 469, 96 A. 785 (1916).

[22] Hendee v. Pinkerton, 96 Mass. (14 Allen) 381 (1867); Hastings v. Vaughn, 5 Cal. 315 (1855); Allen v. Sullivan R.R., 32 N.H. 446 (1855). See also Seals, 1 AM. L. REV. 638 (1866), in which it is sought to be established that the essential characteristic of the early seal was the impression, rather than the substance on which the impression was made.

[23] *See, e.g.,* McLaughlin v. Randall, 66 Me. 226 (1877); Bates v. Boston & N.Y.C.R. Co., 92 Mass. (10 Allen) 251 (1865); Warren v. Lynch, 5 Johns. 239 (N.Y. 1810).

[24] *See, e.g.,* Appeal of Hacker, 121 Pa. 192, 15 A. 500 (1888) (dash one-eighth of an inch long following signature); Pitts v. Pitchford, 201 So. 2d 563 (Fla. Dist. Ct. App. 1967) (L.S. — abbreviation for *locus sigilli* — the place of the seal, scrawl or scroll would be sufficient).

[25] *See, e.g.,* Avery v. Kane Gas Light & Heating Co., 403 F. Supp. 14 (W.D. Pa. 1975).

[26] A list of statutory modifications of the *form* of the seal is found in RESTATEMENT 2d § 94 as part of the "statutory note" to that section.

[27] *See* Warfield v. Baltimore Gas & Elec. Co., 307 Md. 142, 512 A.2d 1044 (1986); Biggers v. Evangelist, 71 N.C. App. 35, 321 S.E.2d 524 (1984).

affixing of the wax impression, can no longer be considered conclusive evidence that the signer intended the sealed instrument to contain an enforceable promise just because it is sealed. For the most part, signers appear to pay no attention to such printed terms on the documents they are signing. It was inevitable that courts and legislatures would begin to recognize this reality. The focus shifted from the mere form of the document which could no longer be relied upon as evidence of the signer's intention to adopt the writing as a sealed instrument, to other evidence of the promisor's intention. Intention became the crucial factor since it could no longer be presumed conclusively from the form of the writing.

[3]   Reciting the Fact that the Writing Is Sealed

When the wax impression was the exclusive manner of sealing, it would have been superfluous for the writing to contain a statement that the promisor intended the writing to be sealed. Whether a writing was sealed had to be determined from an inspection of the document itself; extrinsic evidence was not admissible to prove the fact of sealing.[28] The strict rule was totally compatible with the channeling function of such a formalistic validation device, i.e., if a writing had the wax impression containing the insignia of the promisor, it was conclusively presumed to evidence an enforceable obligation. With the relaxation of the form of the seal and the consequent shift to focusing upon the intention of the promisor, courts sought other evidence of that intention. Once it became permissible to make use of virtually any mark or device as a seal, the question of intention became much more difficult to determine. The mere presence of a scrawl or scroll or, in particular, the printed term "seal" or a substituted printed term was very little evidence that the mark was intended as a seal. In search of other evidence that the writing was intended to be a sealed instrument, some courts demanded a statement in the writing manifesting the intention of the promisor that the writing should be considered sealed.[29] Other courts, however, did not view the recital as either necessary or conclusive, i.e., they did not require recitals to hold promises binding under seal,[30] and where the writing recited that it was sealed, they did not view the recital as conclusive evidence that the promise was under seal since recitals can be false.[31] A recital of sealing alone, however, may be the equivalent of a seal according to some statutes or case law.[32]

The movement away from a mere inspection of the document to determine its validity to the admissibility of extrinsic evidence to determine the intention of the promisor is clear from numerous cases permitting such evidence under myriad circumstances.[33]

---

[28] *See* Jacksonville, Mayport, Pablo Ry. & Nav. Co. v. Hooper, 160 U.S. 514 (1899); Corlies v. Vannote, 16 N.J.L. 324 (1838). The strict position was that extrinsic evidence was not admissible even to show that the instrument was voidable for fraud. RESTATEMENT 2d § 108 comment a.

[29] *See, e.g.*, McCalla v. Stuckey, 233 Ga. App. 397, 504 S.E.2d 269 (1998) (both recital and seal are required); Aronow Roofing Co. v. Gilbane Bldg. Co., 902 F.2d 1127, 1129 (3d Cir. 1990) (with the exception of mortgages which are normally expected to be sealed, Delaware law requires a recital and extrinsic evidence manifesting the parties' intent to conclude a sealed contract).

[30] See Warfield v. Baltimore Gas & Elec. Co., 307 Md. 142, 512 A.2d 1044 (1986), and cases cited therein.

[31] RESTATEMENT 2d § 100. But see Mobil Oil Corp. v. Wolfe, 297 N.C. 36, 252 S.E.2d 809 (1979), holding that a recital is conclusive evidence that the promise is under seal.

[32] *See* RESTATEMENT 2d § 100 comment b. *See* ALA. CODE § 35-4-22; MASS. GEN. LAWS ANN. ch. 4, § 9A; *see also In re* Leary, 241 B.R. 266, 271 n.7 (Bankr. D. Mass. 1999).

[33] For example, see Garrison v. Blakeney, 37 N.C. App. 73, 246 S.E.2d 144, *cert. denied*, 295 N.C. 646, 248 S.E.2d 151 (1978), denying summary judgment with respect to the issue of the promisor's intent to adopt the term "sign" as his seal. *See also* Transbel Inv. Co. v. Venetos, 279 N.Y. 207, 18 N.E.2d 129 (1938) (admitting extrinsic evidence);

[4]   What Constitutes Sealing? — Adoption of a Seal — Corporate Seals Distinguished

It has long been held that an obligor need not place the seal on the document — he may adopt as his own a seal already on the writing.[34] Moreover, the fact of adoption may be shown by extrinsic evidence.[35] Where several persons execute the instrument, a separate seal for each obligor is not necessary; one seal will serve for any number of persons.[36] If the previously attached or printed seal appears to refer to the signature of the obligor, there is an inference that the signer has adopted it.[37] In the case of multiple obligors with only one seal or, at least, fewer seals than the number of obligors, the inference of adoption may be found if a seal follows the signature of the first signer so that all those signing after him or her would be presumed to have adopted it.[38] Since the question of adoption is one of intention, a recital of sealing by all signers would remove any doubt that each signer intended to adopt the seal.[39]

Corporate Seals. The seal of a corporation is typically not intended to perform the function of a seal as a validation device. A corporate seal will identify a document as an official document of the corporation whose seal is printed thereon. Neither the corporation nor a party signing a document containing the corporate seal normally intends to adopt such a seal as validating any obligation evidenced by that writing.[40]

[5]   Delivery

We have considered the first and second elements necessary to make a promise binding under the formalistic validation device traditionally called the sealed contract: (1) a sufficient writing, and (2) the fact of sealing. The third and final element is the requirement of delivery. The delivery of the sealed writing is the final act required to consummate a contract under seal.[41] The early law merely required the obligor voluntarily to hand over the writing, i.e., to part with physical possession of it. It quickly became apparent, however, that the document may have been handed over merely for inspection. Consequently, it soon became the rule that delivery involved two elements: (a) surrendering physical possession of the writing accompanied by (b) the apparent intention that the writing should evidence an immediately binding

---

Graybill v. Juniata County Sch. Dist., 21 Pa. Commw. Ct. 630, 347 A.2d 524 (1975) (dicta).

[34] For example, in Loraw v. Nissley, 156 Pa. 329, 27 A. 242 (1893), the printed word "seal" after the signature was held valid by adoption. *See also* Warfield v. Baltimore Gas & Elec. Co., 307 Md. 142, 512 A.2d 1044 (1986); Van Domelen v. Westinghouse Elec. Corp., 382 F.2d 385 (9th Cir. 1967).

[35] *See* Transbel Inv. Co. v. Venetos, 279 N.Y. 207, 18 N.E.2d 129 (1938), and Pickens v. Rymer, 90 N.C. 282, 47 Am. Rep. 521 (1884). *See also* RESTATEMENT 2d § 98.

[36] Gilderhorn v. Columbia Real Estate Title Ins. Co., 271 Md. 387, 317 A.2d 836 (1974); McNulty v. Medical Serv. of D.C., Inc., 176 A.2d 783 (Mun. Ct. App. D.C. 1962). *See also* RESTATEMENT 2d § 99.

[37] RESTATEMENT 2d § 98.

[38] *See* RESTATEMENT 2d § 98 ill. 2. See, however, Eames v. Preston, 20 Ill. 389 (1858) (*semble*), suggesting that, if the seal appears after the name of one of the signers, it will be presumed that all whose signatures follow his have adopted the seal, whereas those whose names come before his are not presumed to have adopted it.

[39] *See* RESTATEMENT 2d § 99 ill. 1.

[40] *See, e.g.,* Square D Co. v. C.J. Kern Contractors, Inc., 314 N.C. 423, 334 S.E.2d 63 (1985); Georgetown College v. Madden, 505 F. Supp. 557 (D. Md. 1980) (corporate seal alone is insufficient — the body of the contract must indicate that the parties intended to establish an agreement under seal); Federalsburg v. Allied Contractors, Inc., 275 Md. 151, 338 A.2d 275, *cert. denied*, 423 U.S. 1017, 96 S. Ct. 452, 46 L. Ed. 2d 389 (1975).

[41] *See* RESTATEMENT 2d § 95(1)(b).

obligation.[42] The second of these two elements has become, by far, the more important. For some time, English courts have taken the position that the second element is the only essential element, i.e., evidence of the obligor's intention that the instrument shall be presently binding consummates the contract under seal even though the instrument is not physically transferred. Thus, where the officers of an insurance company executed a burglary policy and left it with the secretary for delivery, it was held to be a binding contract although the policy at all times remained in the hands of the secretary.[43] There is substantial support for this view in American case law.[44] The RESTATEMENT 2d, however, clings to the requirement that the promisor put the writing out of his possession.[45] Professor Corbin insisted upon the view supported by English and some American case law, i.e., an overt manifestation of the obligor's intention to make the sealed document immediately operative should be effective even without a manual transfer of the document. Thus, "delivery" may be evidenced by a manifestation of intention other than physical transfer of the writing. As is almost always the case, the Corbin view appears preferable.

[6]   Conditional Delivery — Escrow Delivery

If a promisor signs a sealed writing and delivers it to the obligee with the understanding that the obligation is irrevocable but that it will not be activated until a certain event occurs, delivery of the sealed writing is effective even though it is conditional upon the occurrence of the particular event.[46] Such a *conditional delivery* is effective since the obligor is irrevocably bound unless the condition does not occur.[47] If the condition does not occur, the duty of the obligor is discharged by the failure of a condition over which he or she had no control, i.e., it is not discharged by any act of the obligor.[48] A typical situation would be the handing over of a sealed promise to sell or buy land if the other party pays a certain sum or transfers a deed to the land within a certain time.[49] Such a promise under seal (where the seal is still effective) would create an option contract, i.e., it would provide the other party with an irrevocable power

---

[42] RESTATEMENT 2d § 102.

[43] Roberts v. Security Co., 1 Q.B. 111 [1897]. *See also* Xenos v. Wickham, L.R. 2 H.L. 2296 [1866].

[44] See, e.g., Twining v. National Mortg. Corp., 268 Md. 549, 302 A.2d 604 (1973), where the sealed writing was not handed over manually, but the court relied heavily upon the scholarship of Professor Corbin whose treatise (§ 10.6) suggests that, while "delivery" is usually a manual delivery of the writing, "the operative fact is overt action by the obligor expressing an intention to make the sealed document at once operative and justifying the obligee in relying upon it." Thus, courts "do not abandon the word ['delivery'] when they hold that another mode of expression is effective; instead, they merely stretch the word 'delivery' so as to include facts other than a manual transfer of possession." In La Fleur v. All Am. Ins. Co., 157 So. 2d 254 (La. Ct. App. 1963), an insurance policy in the hands of insurance company's general agent was in force though the insured died before physical delivery could be accomplished. *See also* McMahon v. Dorsey, 353 Mich. 623, 91 N.W.2d 893 (1958); Gurley v. Life & Casualty Ins. Co., 132 F. Supp. 289 (D.N.C. 1955), *aff'd*, 229 F.2d 326 (4th Cir. 1956) (constructive delivery).

[45] RESTATEMENT 2d § 102 comment b.

[46] *See* RESTATEMENT 2d § 103(2).

[47] *See* Hudson v. Hudson, 287 Ill. 286, 122 N.E. 497 (1919).

[48] If the "condition" required the obligor to manifest assent to the obligation at some later time, the obligation would simply be a revocable promise by the obligor and delivery would not have occurred. *See* RESTATEMENT 2d § 103 comment c.

[49] Conditional delivery of a sealed promise is irrevocable for the time stated by the promisor or, if no time is specified, for a reasonable time. RESTATEMENT 2d § 103(4). The performance of the condition on time may be waived by the promisor, thus extending the time for its occurrence. *See* Sunset Beach Amusement Corp. v. Belk, 31 N.J. 445, 158 A.2d 35 (1960).

of acceptance during the time stated in the writing. Thus, the obligor manifests a willingness to provide a binding assurance but insists that he will not be liable until he receives a particular value from the obligee in exchange for his commitment. The obligee is assured that if she relies upon the promise and provides the necessary exchange, she will receive what is promised in the writing with no concern that the obligor will revoke the power of acceptance during the time stated. When the conditions attached to the sealed promise have been fulfilled, the sealed writing becomes effective without any further act or delivery by anyone.[50]

A virtually identical analysis applies to a ***delivery in escrow.*** "Escrow" is derived from the Norman-French term for a writing,[51] but the term has come to be understood as describing the delivery of property or a writing intended to benefit the obligee to a third party who holds the property or writing until a conditioning event has occurred or failed to occur. If the condition occurs, the title to the property held by the third party passes to the grantee. If the third party is holding a sealed writing, the document takes effect according to its terms when the condition occurs. Lawyers often refer to the property held by the third party as "the escrow," while the delivery of the writing or property is characterized as a delivery "in escrow." Thus, a sealed promise delivered "in escrow" is delivered to a third party, i.e., a party other than the promisee. As in the conditional delivery to the promisee, the sealed promise is not revocable by the promisor[52] and there is an intention manifested that it is to become effective upon the occurrence of a certain condition. Such a delivery "in escrow" is an effective delivery.[53] Since the same operative effects flow from either a conditional delivery to the promisee or a delivery "in escrow," it is possible to discover a court mischaracterizing a conditional delivery as an escrow delivery.[54] The RESTATEMENT 2d, however, properly insists upon the foregoing distinction between the two forms of delivery.[55]

The only difficulty that arises in relation to the foregoing analysis is the possible inconsistency with a rule concerning the admissibility of evidence that would change or vary the terms of the writing. The "parol evidence rule" might be said to preclude the admission of evidence of an oral condition since the writing is absolute on its face.[56] The complexities of the parol evidence rule will be explored later in this volume.[57] At this time, it is sufficient to report that, with respect to conditional delivery or escrow delivery of a sealed promise, the views of Professor Corbin have prevailed, i.e., evidence of such a condition will be admissible because to deny it would be to frustrate the intentions of the parties in too many cases.[58]

---

[50] *See* Gardiner v. Gardiner, 36 Idaho 664, 214 P. 219 (1923); Craddock v. Barnes, 142 N.C. 89, 54 S.E. 1003 (1906).

[51] The terms "scroll" or "scrawl" are similarly derived. RESTATEMENT 2d § 103 comment a.

[52] If the promisor had reserved a power of revocation, the third party would operate as the *agent* of the promisor. *See* RESTATEMENT 2d AGENCY § 14D.

[53] RESTATEMENT 2d § 103(1).

[54] *See, e.g.*, Whitaker & Fowle v. Lane, 128 Va. 317, 104 S.E. 252, 11 A.L.R. 1157 (1920).

[55] RESTATEMENT 2d § 103 comment d.

[56] *See, e.g.*, Hume v. Kirkwood, 216 Ala. 534, 113 So. 613 (1927).

[57] *See infra* §§ 83–85.

[58] *See* CORBIN, *Conditional Delivery of Written Contracts*, 36 YALE L.J. 443 (1926). *See also* RESTATEMENT 2d § 217 comments a and b.

[7]   Acceptance by the Promisee

The earliest recorded cases involving sealed promises made it clear that acceptance of the promise or assent by the promisee has never been essential to the consummation of a contract under seal.[59] Some American courts, apparently pursuing the requirement of mutual assent in informal (unsealed) contracts, required assent by the promisee but quickly nullified the effect of that requirement by holding that, in the absence of a disclaimer by the promisee, acceptance would be presumed.[60] It is, however, more accurate to state that acceptance is simply unnecessary.[61] Just as an offer can be rejected by an offeree, a promisee may disclaim the benefit of the obligation created by the sealed promise. Unless the promisee disclaims within a reasonable time after learning of the existence and terms of the promise, however, the promise is enforceable without any manifestation of assent by the promisee.[62] The only situation requiring a communication of acceptance by the promisee is one which contemplates a return promise. Thus, if the sealed promise is one providing the promisee with thirty days to accept an offer to purchase the promisee's land for $50,000, the sealed promise creates an option contract making the promise irrevocable for thirty days *and* the sealed promise manifests the contemplation of an acceptance of the irrevocable offer if the promisee chooses to accept. In such a situation, acceptance by the promisee would be essential.[63] Where the sealed promise does not require acceptance, the promisee may still manifest acceptance. Whether or not acceptance is required, once it is manifested, a disclaimer would, thereafter, be ineffective. Similarly, if the promisee disclaims the benefit contained in a sealed promise, the disclaimer is irrevocable.[64]

[8]   "Consideration" in Sealed Contracts — "Want" vs. "Failure" of Consideration — Equitable Relief

Since contracts under seal long antedated the doctrine of consideration, it is absurd to suggest that the seal "imports consideration" or that the seal is the "real consideration" for a particular contract.[65] Since a sealed contract is binding absent consideration,[66] there is no need to mention consideration in holding that the sealed promise is binding. Apparently, some courts have "imported" or "presumed" consideration in sealed promises either because they have momentarily forgotten the independence of the seal as a validation device, or because they wish to harmonize that validation device with the mutually exclusive validation device called consideration. These unfortunate utterances should are historically and analytically unsound. The defense of want of consideration is may not be raised when the instrument is under seal, but want of consideration must be distinguished from failure of consideration.

---

[59] See *Butler v. Baker's Case*, 3 Coke 25a, 26b [1591], in which delivery of the instrument to a third person, without the knowledge of the obligee, was held effective to bind the obligor unless and until the obligee disclaimed. *See also* Malott v. Wilson, 2 Ch. 494 [1903].

[60] The American cases so holding involve conveyances. There is, however, no reason to suppose that a different rule would have been said to apply in the case of a contract. The cases are collected in 4 TIFFANY, REAL PROPERTY § 1057 (3d ed. 1939).

[61] *See* RESTATEMENT 2d § 104 comment a.

[62] RESTATEMENT 2d § 104.

[63] RESTATEMENT 2d § 105.

[64] RESTATEMENT 2d § 104(3).

[65] See County Commissioners v. Forty West Builders, Inc., 178 Md. 328, 385, 941 A.2d 1181, 1214 (2008).

[66] RESTATEMENT 2d § 95(1).

Where the parties have a bargained-for-exchange of promises and one of the parties cannot or will not perform his side of the bargain, just because the document evidencing the agreement is under seal will not make the other party's promise enforceable. The distinction is between want of consideration where no consideration was intended to pass and the seal makes the promise enforceable, and failure of consideration where consideration was contemplated and the seal is irrelevant.[67]

Another situation that may appear as an exception to the rule that sealed promises (where the seal is still effective) are enforceable without consideration. If an aggrieved party is not seeking ordinary relief in the form of money (damages), but is seeking equitable relief in the form of specific performance or an injunction, the remedy may not be granted unless there is consideration for the sealed promise, some prior benefit to the promisor or detriment to the promisee, or evidence of a substantial change of position by the promisee in reliance on the sealed promise.[68]

[9]   Parties with Rights and Duties Under a Sealed Contract — Agent's Authority

Before one can be held on a contract under seal, he must make a promise in writing in his own name and seal and deliver the instrument.[69] Therefore, if the contract is "bilateral" in operation, i.e., it is intended to contain reciprocal promises, then both parties must seal and deliver the writing.[70] If both parties have sealed and delivered their written promises, they are both bound by the formalities of the sealed instrument.[71] If, however, the promise is unilateral in its operation, only the promisor need seal and deliver it because the promisee/obligee need

---

[67] See Interdigital Communs. Corp v. Fed. Ins. Co., 403 F. Supp. 2d 391, 392 (E. D. Pa. 2005) quoting In re Commonwealth Trust Co. of Pittsburgh, 54 A. 2d 649, 652 (Pa. 1947): "In the absence of any evidence to the contrary, the seal imports consideration. When, however, the agreement itself reveals the insufficiency or lack of consideration, the rule will not be applied to the detriment of the promisor."

[68] See Russ v. Barnes, 23 Md. App. 691, 329 A.2d 767 (1974); Community Sports, Inc. v. Denver Ringsby Rockets, Inc., 429 Pa. 565, 240 A.2d 832 (1968) (holding that even a "past" consideration would not be effective for a sealed promise when the relief sought is specific performance). RESTATEMENT 2d § 364 comment b suggests, "A contract, other than an option contract on fair terms . . . that is binding solely because of a nominal payment or by reason of some formality such as a seal . . . will not ordinarily be enforced by specific performance or an injunction." See, however, Marine Contractors Co. v. Hurley, 365 Mass. 280, 310 N.E.2d 915, 919 (1974), where the defendant urged that a contract under seal should not be specifically enforced, relying upon § 366 of the FIRST RESTATEMENT and citing Professor Corbin's treatise, the predecessor section to § 10.14. The court replied, "The short answer to this argument . . . is that the rule of the Restatement is not the law of Massachusetts."

[69] Therefore, a principal cannot be held on a contract under seal executed by his agent in the agent's own name. See RESTATEMENT 2d AGENCY §§ 151, 191 and 296 where a principal is not a party to a sealed instrument unless he appears in the instrument as a party. See, however, Nalbandian v. Hanson Restaurant & Lounge, Inc., 369 Mass. 150, 338 N.E.2d 335 (1975), in which the Supreme Judicial Court of Massachusetts overruled prior law and held that, upon proof of its identity, an undisclosed principal could be held liable on a sealed contract to the same extent that it could be held on an unsealed contract.

[70] Such an instrument is often referred to as an *indenture* to distinguish it from an instrument executed only by one party, which is called a *deed poll*. The term, "indenture" comes from the early practice followed when two parties executed a deed. Two copies of the deed were usually written on the same piece of parchment and then cut apart in a waving or serrated line. The "deed poll," which involved a sealed promise by only one party, was cut evenly.

[71] If an obligee is supposed to make a reciprocal promise and does so without sealing and delivery, he may still be liable on his *informal* promise, i.e., if it is supported by a validation device other than the seal. However, he is not liable on the sealed contract, alone, i.e., he would not be liable in the common law action called "covenant."

not execute the instrument to have rights under it.[72] Since the early common law viewed the sealed instrument as *the* contract, a party not named in the instrument could not have rights under it.[73] Some of the earlier authorities extended this rule. If a deed, bilateral in form, stated on its face that it was made between certain persons, these authorities held that only those persons (between whom the deed was stated to have been made) could have any rights under it. Thus, even a promisee named in the deed would have no rights under it if he was not one of the persons between whom the contract was stated to have been made.[74] Modern courts may permit even an unnamed party to bring an action on a sealed contract[75] and, in light of the widespread changes in the effects of the seal, an application of the strict rules would be difficult to discover in modern case law.

While the common law required no formality for the appointment of an agent to make an informal contract on behalf of the principal, authority to execute a sealed contract for a principal could be conferred only by an instrument under seal.[76] Where the seal retains its common law effect, this rule obtains, except in the case of an agent executing a sealed contract on behalf of a corporation.[77]

[10] Effect of the Seal — Statutes of Limitations

As we have seen, the principal effect of the seal, where still effective, is to make a promise enforceable simply because it conforms to the form of the seal. In the next subsection we will examine statutory changes that have either abolished this effect or reduced it to a presumption of consideration. Modern cases dealing with the seal in jurisdictions in which it retains its effectiveness are typically concerned with the applicable statute of limitations. Actions on a contract under seal at common law are not subject to any statute of limitations though a presumption of payment will arise after a lengthy period, such as twenty years.[78] Since a writing under seal provides a permanent and, presumably, careful manifestation of a promise that the promisor intends to be enforceable, it has often been asserted that an action on a written contract under seal should enjoy a long statute of limitations.[79] Contracts under seal

---

[72] RESTATEMENT 2d § 109.

[73] Exchange Realty Co. v. Bines, 302 Mass. 93, 18 N.E.2d 425 (1939); Case v. Case, 203 N.Y. 263, 96 N.E. 440 (1911); Harvey v. Maine Condensed-Milk Co., 92 Me. 115, 42 A. 342 (1898); Newberry Land Co. v. Newberry, 95 Va. 119, 27 S.E. 899 (1897). *Accord* RESTATEMENT 2d § 108.

[74] Scudamore v. Vandenstone, 2 COKE'S INSTITUTES 673 [1587]; Chesterfield & Midland Silkstone Colliery Co. v. Hawkins, 3 H. & C. 677 [1865].

[75] *See, e.g.*, Philipsborn v. 17th & Chestnut Streets Holding Corp., 111 Pa. Super. 9, 169 A. 473 (1933). *See also* Annot., 170 A.L.R. 1299 (1947). While the RESTATEMENT 2d clings to the strict rule requiring all parties to be named, it admits that the rule is a remnant of medieval strictures. RESTATEMENT 2d § 108 comment a.

[76] RESTATEMENT 2d AGENCY § 28(1).

[77] RESTATEMENT 2d AGENCY § 28(2)(b). It should also be noted that where the agent acts in the presence of his principal, he can bind the principal on a sealed contract even without sealed authority. Here, the theory is that the agent is the mere mechanical instrument through which the principal himself executes the sealed instrument. RESTATEMENT 2d AGENCY § 28(2)(a).

[78] Kirkwood Kin Corp. v. Dunkin' Donuts, 1995 Del. Super. LEXIS 297 (Del. Super. Ct. June 30, 1995) (presumption of payment after twenty years). See also Transbel Inv. Co. v. Scott, 344 Pa. 544, 546, 26 A.2d 205, 207 (1942) (presumption of payment after 21 years); but see 42 Pa. Cons. Stat. § 5529, which imposes a twenty-year statute of limitations on sealed contracts.

[79] *See* Solomon v. Birger, 19 Mass. App. 634, 477 N.E.2d 137 (1985) (quoting 118 WILLISTON, CONTRACTS § 2020, at 678).

are clearly recognized in the statutes of limitations of at least twenty jurisdictions and in five other states where there is no special limitations period governing contracts under seal.[80] In these jurisdictions, a case may turn on whether the promise is under seal, thereby activating a much longer limitations period.[81]

[11] Statutory Modification and Substitutes for the Seal

At the beginning of our discussion of formalistic validation devices, we explored the functions of these formalities. When the ritual attending the affixation of the seal evolved from the reflective effort of heating wax and imprinting it to the modern, pre-printed form containing the word "seal" or a substitute, we saw the erosion of the evidentiary, cautionary and channeling functions since printed forms were typically signed with little or no thought given to the nature of the seal or its effect. This evolution caused numerous modifications, typically statutory, of the effect of the seal. Some statutes modified the form of the seal, i.e., permitting various kinds of marks, such as the word "seal," the abbreviation for *locus sigilli* or statements in the writing that it was intended to be under seal to be effective.[82] Many other changes have attended the erosion of the sealed contract doctrine.[83] Some twenty-five states and the Virgin Islands have abolished the seal or, as it is often put, they have abolished any distinction between sealed and unsealed instruments.[84]

The most significant statutory abolition of the seal is found in the UCC which makes "seals inoperative", i.e., affixing a seal to a writing evidencing a contract for the sale of goods or to an offer to buy or sell goods does not make the writing a sealed instrument and the law of sealed instruments does not apply to such a contract or offer.[85] Since all American jurisdictions except Louisiana have enacted Article 2 of the Code, and Louisiana never adopted the seal, the seal is abolished with respect to contracts for the sale of goods (or offers to buy or sell goods) throughout the United States. Some statutes have reduced the seal to "presumptive evidence of consideration,"[86] while others have abolished the seal but presume consideration with respect to written promises.[87] The statutes are not always drafted in clear and precise terms,

---

[80] RESTATEMENT 2d § 94, *Statutory Note*. This Note contains a list of jurisdictions setting forth periods of limitation ranging from 5 to 20 years. The RESTATEMENT 2d indicates that there is no specified statute of limitations on sealed contracts in Delaware, but there is a common law presumption of payment after 20 years. *See* Di Biase v. A & D, Inc., 351 A.2d 865 (Del. Super. Ct. 1976).

[81] *See, e.g.*, McCalla v. Stuckey, 233 Ga. App. 397, 504 S.E.2d 269 (1998); *In re* Leary, 241 B.R. 266 (Bankr. D. Mass. 1999); Warfield v. Baltimore Gas & Elec. Co., 307 Md. 142, 512 A.2d 1044 (1986) (12 years); Biggers v. Evangelist, 71 N.C. App. 35, 321 S.E.2d 524 (1984) (10 years); Telefair Fin. Co. v. Williams, 172 Ga. App. 489, 323 S.E.2d 689 (1984) (20 years).

[82] See the list of modified forms in RESTATEMENT 2d § 94, *Statutory Note*.

[83] "Despite its lengthy pedigree, however, the sealed contract doctrine has been under heavy assault at least since the days of the Industrial Revolution." Knott v. Racicot, 442 Mass.314, 320, 812 N. E. 2d 1207, 1212–13 (2004) (prospectively overruling the enforceability of option agreements under seal).

[84] *See* Eric Mills Holmes, *Status of a Promise Under Seal as a Legal Formality*, 29 Willamette L. Rev. 617 (1993).

[85] UCC § 2-203. *See* Osguthorpe v. Anschutz Land & Livestock Co., 456 F.2d 996 (10th Cir. 1972); Associates Discount Corp. v. Palmer, 47 N.J. 183, 219 A.2d 858 (1966). See, however, North Carolina Nat'l Bank v. Holshouer, 38 N.C. App. 165, 247 S.E.2d 645 (1978), refusing to apply the four-year statute of limitations under § 2-725 of the UCC to an Article 9 security agreement under seal to which the court applied the North Carolina 10-year statute of limitation, expressly rejecting the holding and rationale in *Associates Disct. Corp.*

[86] RESTATEMENT 2d § 94 *Statutory Note*.

[87] *Id.*

so their effects are not always certain.

Substitutes for the Seal. Notwithstanding the abolition or diminishing effects of the seal in many jurisdictions, the need for formalistic validation devices remains. Though the UCC made seals inoperative, we have already seen the inclusion of a formalistic validation device in the UCC to permit offers to become irrevocable (the "firm offer")[88] and we will explore another UCC device to permit subsequent modifications of a contract to be enforceable without consideration.[89] Still another UCC section allows a waiver or renunciation of any claim or right arising out of an alleged breach to be effective if it is signed and delivered by the aggrieved party.[90] Other state statutes permit "firm offers" without consideration.[91] A statute may direct that any contract in writing "shall import consideration in the same manner and as fully as sealed instruments have heretofore done."[92] These are clear illustrations of a statutory reaction to the felt need for formalistic validation devices to replace the seal.

The most ambitious substitute was presented prior to the general abolition or weakening of the seal. A legislative innovation originally captioned the Uniform Written Obligations Act was produced by the National Conference of Commissioners on Uniform State Laws. Designed for enactment throughout the country, Pennsylvania enacted it in 1927 and is currently the only state where the Act is effective. Its title has been changed to the Model Written Obligations Act.[93] It permits a written release or promise, signed by the releasing or promising party, to be enforceable without consideration if it contains an express statement, in any form of language, that the signer intends to be legally bound.[94] It is an effective substitute for the seal. The failure of many jurisdictions to enact it appears to be due, in large measure, to legislative inertia. There is a need for formalistic validation devices, but the need has been addressed to specific kinds of promises, such as firm offers, rather than a general requirement for an effective and modern formalistic device.

§ 55   CONSIDERATION — ORIGINS

Although consideration is only one of the validation devices recognized to make a promise enforceable, it is the dominant validation device for the overwhelming majority of contracts. Consideration is an historic accident. It cannot be understood absent an understanding of its origins. In Chapter 1, we sketched the development of the common law writ system that permitted the enforcement of promises under writs called covenant, debt, and detinue, which did not facilitate the enforcement of informal executory promises.[95] The need for a flexible writ or form of action to permit the enforcement of informal promises was clear. The Court of King's Bench expanded the writ of *trespass on the case* to permit the development of the action in *special assumpsit* which involved an *undertaking* (assumpsit — he undertook) by a party who

---

[88] UCC § 2-205. *See supra* § 44[C].

[89] UCC § 2-209.

[90] UCC § 1-107.

[91] *See, e.g.,* N.Y. Gen. Oblig. Law § 5-1109.

[92] N.M. Stat. Ann. § 38-7-2. It is unfortunate that this New Mexico statute suggests that the seal "imported consideration" since, as suggested at the commencement of our exploration of the seal, the seal antedates consideration. While the enactment is historically untidy, the point is clear.

[93] Utah had enacted the "Uniform" Act but quickly repealed it.

[94] Pa. Stat. Ann. tit. 33, § 6.

[95] *See* § 3, *supra.*

performed the undertaking badly, i.e., he committed *misfeasance*. The blacksmith, for example, undertook to shoe a horse and he performed badly, injuring the horse. The "undertaking" coupled with the blacksmith's misfeasance permitted the action in special assumpsit. Because he had performed badly, there was a *detriment* to the promisee, the owner of the horse. Thus, the origins of special assumpsit were what modern lawyers would call tort (*ex delicto*) since the emphasis was upon the *misfeasance* of the promisor.

If the party who undertook to perform did not misfease but simply failed to perform at all ("nonfeased"), there was no apparent connection to the basic concept of trespass — even an expansion of trespass on the case in the form of special assumpsit — because there would be no deviant conduct. Some connection had to be found. The connection was created by finding that a defendant who simply failed to perform a promise at all was guilty of *deceit*. In a simple case involving a promise to sell a house, if the defendant breached the promise by selling the house to a third party, there was an allegation that this constituted deceit to the plaintiff. Gradually, the emphasis shifted from the performance stage where the defendant was guilty of deceit to the initial stage of the undertaking (promise) itself moving assumpsit toward an action *ex contractu* rather than *ex delicto*.

Slade's Case. The Court of King's Bench was eager to continue the development of assumpsit because it derived fees from the litigating parties. In 1602, *Slade's Case*[96] provided a quantum leap in this development. If a chattel was purchased from the plaintiff and the defendant breached the agreement to pay for it, unless the promise of the defendant was under seal, the only action that would lie was the action in *debt*. *Covenant* would not lie for an unsealed promise, and *detinue* was unavailable absent an unjust detainer of the goods. If, however, the defendant subsequently *promised* to pay a second time, the second promise would permit an action in *indebitatus assumpsit* (being indebted, he undertook). In *Slade's Case*, the court held that the second promise need only be alleged and not proved, thus permitting the writ of assumpsit in actions where debt alone had previously been available. Assumpsit became the popular remedy for breach of contract since it could be brought without confronting the notorious "wager of law" that attended the writ of *debt*.[97] "Slade's case virtually abolished wager [of law] as an institution."[98]

The new action created significant problems. Would assumpsit lie for breach of *any* promise, or would there be limitations? The term "consideration" was first used in pleadings suggesting

---

[96] 4 Coke 92b [1602].

[97] "Wager of law" or "compurgation" is aptly described in A. W. B. Simpson, A History of the Common Law of Contract 137–40 (1987). In what the author suggests would appear "slightly ridiculous" to the modern lawyer, the defendant would plead to the action brought against him and offer to "wage his law," i.e., to guarantee that he would successfully exculpate himself by an oath that he owed nothing. The court would set the day on which the defendant and eleven "compurgators" (oath-helpers) would appear. The defendant would swear an oath with hand on the Bible and kiss the book. Each of the compurgators would do the same. If he and the compurgators committed perjury, the penalty was punishment for mortal sin rather than judicial sanction. Notwithstanding the availability of this method of defense that appears absurd to the modern lawyer, the author reports (at 139) that a considerable portion of reported cases suggest that "wager of law" was not used. Rather, the defendant opted for a trial by jury that may suggest the difficulty of discovering eleven helping perjurers in the sixteenth century.

[98] *Id.* at 298. Here, the author makes the telling point that, while "wager of law" made it too easy for debtors to evade payment of just debts, plaintiffs in such actions were not above discovering witnesses who would testify that the defendant owed the debt. Some compurgators who lost their profession found another in testifying for the plaintiff to juries not known for their impartiality. To protect defendants from false claims, Parliament passed the Statute of Frauds in 1677, requiring certain kinds of contracts to be evidenced by a signed writing. We will explore the original Statute of Frauds and its modern manifestations in the next chapter.

different contents. For example, the pleadings might state, "In consideration that the buyer had paid &100 pound, the seller promised to deliver his horse and car to the buyer." The term was used to express vaguely the concept that there had to be some reason for enforcing the promise and this required an inquiry into why the promise was made, i.e., what induced or motivated the promise?[99] What were good and sufficient reasons for enforcing a promise? A popular notion is that common lawyers resorted to their familiar forms of action. They recognized that assumpsit had been applied to situations where the action of debt had been applied, i.e., situations involving an exchange, a *quid pro quo*, where the defendant had already received a *benefit* — the half-completed exchange.[100] They also recognized that assumpsit had been applied to the misfeasance situations where the promise or undertaking by the defendant had been performed badly resulting in a *detriment* to the promisee. Thus, if there was an *exchange* resulting in *either* a *benefit* to the promisor or a *detriment* to the promisee, there was reason for enforcing the promise. The characterization that developed from this formula was *consideration*. What has become the traditional formula for consideration — bargained for exchange plus either a benefit to the promisor or a detriment to the promisee — was not easily developed, nor was it the product of a grand design.

A related theory of the origins of consideration emanates from the reflection of Holmes who argued that the "quid pro quo" requirement fulfilled an evidentiary function.[101] Since witnesses could testify only to facts within their personal knowledge, they could testify that the performance on one side was in exchange for performance on the other in an action for *debt*. The evidentiary function in actions on a sealed instrument under the writ called *covenant* was fulfilled by the prescribed form of the promise. Still another theory emanates from the Roman law concept of "causa." Though quite distinct from consideration, "causa" is another suggested basis for the eventual development of consideration on the footing that "causa" found its way into canon law and, from there, to the consciousness of English chancellors who influenced English common law.[102] There are, however, important assertions that consideration is not traceable to either debt or causa.[103] There is an amusing view that the bargain theory of consideration can be traced only as far back as 1881, i.e., to the alleged creator of this revolutionary concept, O. W. Holmes, Jr.[104] The evidence, however, is compelling that at least as early as the sixteenth century, English courts had discovered the central device for determining which promises were enforceable: "[E]ach party had in fact desired some act or abstention of the other in return for which he had agreed to perform his own."[105]

In the eighteenth century, the great Lord Mansfield, Chief Justice of King's Bench from 1756 to 1788, was almost solely responsible for the erosion of the doctrine of consideration for

---

[99] *Id.* at 321.

[100] But see *id.* at 424, where the author expresses considerable doubt concerning this analysis.

[101] O. HOLMES, THE COMMON LAW 254–59 (1923).

[102] J. SALMOND, JURISPRUDENCE AND LEGAL HISTORY ch. iv, 27 (London: Stevens & Haynes 1891).

[103] INTRODUCTION TO THE REPORTS OF SIR JOHN SPELMAN 292–97 (Selden Society, J. H. Baker, ed. 1978).

[104] GILMORE, THE DEATH OF CONTRACT 19–21 (1974), in which the author relies essentially upon two sentences from HOLMES' COMMON LAW at 230 (Howe ed. 1963).

[105] J. DAWSON, GIFTS AND PROMISES 203 (1980). Another scholar suggests that the concept of "bargain" is found in fourteenth and fifteenth century English cases, K. SUTTON, CONSIDERATION RECONSIDERED 6, 13–18 (1974). For another view contrary to the assertion of Gilmore, see Speidel, *An Essay on the Reported Death and Continued Vitality of Contract*, 27 STAN. L. REV. 1161 (1975). Note also that there are American cases prior to 1881 suggesting the necessity of a bargain theory of consideration: Hardesty v. Smith, 3 Ind. 39 (1851).

a period of approximately thirteen years. In 1765, Mansfield suggested that a promise should be enforced simply because it was in writing. Consideration only afforded evidence of the contract. Since a writing provided sufficient evidence, consideration was unnecessary.[106] This view, however, was rejected in 1778 when the House of Lords emphatically reinstated the requirement of consideration.[107] In its 1937 Report, the British Law Revision Committee was highly critical of consideration and recommended significant limitations, though many members of the Committee would have preferred the abolition of the doctrine.[108] The recommendations included making agreements in writing enforceable without consideration, as well as other substantial incursions. The recommendations were not adopted.

There have been vigorous debates over the origins of consideration for many years.[109] Notwithstanding different views, it is clear that consideration was not a well-planned, rationally conceived device for deciding which promises are enforceable. Yet, it remains the principal device for determining which promises are enforceable in the eyes of the law. A thorough understanding of the doctrine of consideration can be achieved only through an exploration of the doctrine in operation.

§ 56 THE ELEMENTS OF CONSIDERATION

The classic formula of consideration requires a "bargained-for-exchange" of something which, in the eyes of the law, is of some value: "[A] performance or a return promise must be bargained for."[110] The cases are legion in which courts describe consideration in terms of a benefit to the promisor or detriment to the promisee, i.e., the concentration is on the "legal value" element of consideration.[111] Other courts remember to add the other critical element, bargained-for-exchange, as part of the formula.[112] There is no doubt that all courts would consider the bargained-for-exchange element essential.

---

[106] Pillans & Rose v. Van Mierop & Hopkins, 3 Burr. 1663, 97 Eng. Rep. 1035 (K.B. 1765).

[107] Rann v. Huges, 7 T.R. 350, 101 Eng. Rep. 1014 (1778).

[108] LAW REVISION COMMISSION (GREAT BRITAIN) SIXTH INTERIM REPORT (1937).

[109] *See* Dawson, *supra* note 105, particularly at 199–221. See also Patterson, *An Apology for Consideration*, 58 COLUM. L. REV. 929 (1958); Sharp, *Pacta Sunt Servanda*, 41 COLUM. L. REV. 783 (1941); Llewellyn, *Common Law Reform of Consideration: Are There Measures?*, 41 COLUM. L. REV. 863 (1941); Wright, *Ought the Doctrine of Consideration To Be Abolished*, 49 HARV. L. REV. 1225 (1936), and the sources cited earlier in the notes to this section.

[110] RESTATEMENT 2d § 71(1). Section 71 is quoted in Chemical Realty Corp. v. Home Fed. Sav. & Loan Ass'n of Hollywood, 84 N.C. App. 27, 30, 351 S.E.2d 786, 788 (1987): (1) To constitute consideration, a performance or a return promise must be bargained for. (2) A performance or return promise is bargained for if it is sought by the promisor in exchange for his promise and is given in exchange for that promise. (3) The performance may consist of (a) an act other than a promise, or (b) a forbearance, or (c) the creation, modification, or destructions of a legal relation. (4) The performance of a return promise may be given to the promisor or to some other person. It may be given by the promisee or some other person.

[111] Examples of cases suggesting this traditional formula include USLife Title Co. v. Gutkin, 152 Ariz. 349, 732 P.2d 579 (Ct. App. 1986); Vogelhut v. Kandel, 308 Md. 183, 517 A.2d 1092 (1986); Chasan v. Village Dist. of Eastman, 128 N.H. 807, 523 A.2d 16 (1986); Cook v. Heck's, Inc., 176 W. Va. 368, 342 S.E.2d 453 (1986); Nordwick v. Berg, 223 Mont. 337, 725 P.2d 1195 (1986); Artoe v. Cap, 140 Ill. App. 3d 980, 489 N.E.2d 420 (1st Dist. 1986); Hyde v. Shapiro, 216 Neb. 785, 346 N.W.2d 241 (1984); W.E. Koehler Constr. Co. v. Medical Ctr. of Blue Springs, 670 S.W.2d 558 (Mo. Ct. App. 1984); *In re* Windle, 653 F.2d 328 (8th Cir. 1981).

[112] *See, e.g.*, Federal Sign v. Texas S. Univ., 951 S.W.2d 401, 408 (Tex. 1997); Miles Homes Div. of Insilco Corp. v. First State Bank, 782 S.W.2d 798, 800 (Mo. Ct. App. 1990); Twin City Fire Ins. Co. v. Philadelphia Life Ins. Co., 795 F.2d 1417 (9th Cir. 1986).

There is significant difficulty in discovering definitional terminology sufficient to encompass all that is meant by "consideration." As usual, definitions in the study of law are of highly limited assistance. The consensus is clear that the two elements are essential, but they can be understood only by examining them in operation, i.e., as applied by courts in myriad circumstances.

§ 57   THE FIRST ELEMENT: LEGAL VALUE — "BENEFIT" OR "DETRIMENT"

[A]   Generally

The classic description of the legal value element of consideration is found in *Currie v. Misa*,[113] where the Court of Exchequer stated, "A valuable consideration, in the sense of the law, may consist either in some right, interest, profit or benefit accruing to the one party, or some forbearance, detriment, loss or responsibility, given, suffered, or undertaken by the other."[114] While the formula for this element is stated in the alternative, benefit to the promisor or detriment to the promisee, the typical contract will manifest *both* benefits and detriments.

Which Promisor? If Ames agrees to purchase Barnes' car at a price of $10,000, there are benefits and detriments to both parties. The benefit to Ames is the receipt of Barnes' car. The benefit to Barnes is the receipt of Ames' $10,000. The detriment to Ames is the surrender of $10,000, and the detriment to Barnes is the surrender of his car. Where there are two promisors and two promisees, it is helpful to focus upon which of the two promisors is meant in the formula statement requiring "a benefit to *the* promisor or detriment to *the* promisee." Very simply, the promisor refers to the party whose promise is sought to be enforced. If Ames refused to perform the promise to pay $10,000 and Barnes sued Ames, Barnes would have to prove consideration for Ames' promise, i.e., what is the benefit to *the* promisor, Ames, or the corresponding detriment to promisee Barnes. If Barnes breached the promise to deliver the car and Ames sued, Ames would have to prove the benefit to promisor Barnes or the detriment to promisee Ames. Thus, *the* promisor is the party against whom an action is brought to enforce the promise.

---

[113] L.R. 10 Ex. 153, 162 [1875].

[114] Identical statements can be found in modern cases. *See, e.g.*, Hunts Point Coop. Mkt. Inc. v. Madison Fin. LLC, 2009 U. S. App. LEXIS 19382 at*22 (3d Cir. 2009); Source Assocs. v. Valero Energy Corp., 273 Fed. Appx. 425, 427 (6th Cir. 2008); Chaganti & Assocs., PC v Nowotny, 470 F.3d 1215, 1221 (8th Cir. 2006). *See also* Cook v. Heck's, Inc., 176 W. Va. 368, 373, 342 S.E.2d 453, 458 (1986) ("some right, interest, profit, or benefit accruing to one party, or some forbearance, detriment, loss, or responsibility given, suffered or undertaken by another"); Artoe v. Cap, 140 Ill. App. 3d 980, 985, 489 N.E.2d 420, 423 (1st Dist. 1986) ("some right, interest, profit or benefit accruing to one party or some forbearance, disadvantage, detriment, loss or responsibility given, suffered or undertaken by the other"). Other statements of the "legal value" element are often truncated. *See, e.g.*, United States v. Meadors, 753 F.2d 590, 595 (7th Cir. 1985) ("[T]he one who made the promise receives consideration if he gets something, or if the one to whom he makes the promise gives something up. Either alternative will do."); Hyde v. Shapiro, 216 Neb. 785, 785, 346 N.W.2d 241, 241 (1984) ("there is a consideration if the promisee does anything legal which he is not bound to do or refrains from doing anything which he has a right to do. . . .").

[B]   Either Benefit or Detriment — "Legal" Detriment

[1]   The Absence of Benefit

While the typical contract provides benefits and exacts detriments from both parties, benefit *and* detriment are not essential, i.e., if either is present, the "value" element of consideration is present. It is not difficult to suggest examples where there is no discernible "benefit" to the promisor, but where the "detriment" to the promisee is clear. The classic case is *Hamer v. Sidway*,[115] where an uncle promised his nephew $5000 on his twenty-first birthday in consideration of the nephew's refraining from drinking, smoking, swearing and gambling until he reached that age. The benefit to the uncle (promisor) is not discernible. We can only speculate on his motivation. He may have been concerned about his nephew's health and welfare or he may have been interested in preserving his reputation by inducing his nephew of the same name to avoid notorious behavior. The fact that the benefit to the promisor is not discernible does not affect finding consideration. Whatever the benefit to the promisor-uncle, if any, there was a detriment to the promisee since the nephew surrendered his legally recognized right to pursue behavior that the uncle induced him to avoid by the promise to pay $5000.[116] It is clear that courts will not require a showing of any discernible benefit to the promisor if the promisee has suffered a detriment induced by the other party's promise.[117]

[2]   "Legal" Detriment Distinguished

It may appear unusual to characterize refraining from alcohol, smoking and other arguably unhealthy pursuits as a detriment to the nephew. To constitute consideration, a detriment need not constitute any economic or physical loss. From the standpoint of health or finances, the nephew received a benefit. Yet, by abstaining from those substances and practices as required by the promisor, the promisee-nephew surrendered his right, protected by law, to use those substances and engage in the practices his uncle induced him to avoid.[118] The suggestion that

---

[115]   124 N.Y. 538, 27 N.E. 256 (1891).

[116]   Another example is found where Ames seeks to borrow money. Her credit rating is poor and the bank will not make a loan to Ames on Ames' credit alone. Ames may call her brother-in-law, Barnes, and request that Barnes become secondarily liable on Ames' debt to the bank. If Barnes agrees to repay the loan if Ames does not repay (i.e., to become a surety on Ames' obligation) and, on the basis of that promise, the bank lends the money to Ames, there is no discernible benefit to the promisor, Barnes. He may have become surety for Ames only because he is related to Ames, and may have undertaken this secondary obligation to the bank grudgingly. Though the benefit to Barnes is speculative, there is no question about the detriment to the bank. The bank would not have lent the money to Ames on her credit alone. Barnes agreement to pay the bank if Ames failed to pay induced the bank to make the loan to Ames. The detriment suffered by the bank can be described as parting with its money in exchange for two promises: the promise of Ames to repay the debt with interest, and the promise of Barnes to pay the same amount if Ames fails to perform her promise to repay the loan. Again, however, Barnes has received no discernible benefit for his promise — there is no "benefit to the promisor." It is plausible to consider various motivations of promisors who appear to receive no discernible benefit. In one sense, if the promisor induces the promisee to suffer a detriment, the promisor receives the benefit of that detriment, i.e., why the promisor sought the particular detriment is her own affair. In such situations, therefore, it is desirable to suggest that there is no "discernible" benefit to the promisor, i.e., whatever benefit the promisor may have received from the detriment suffered by the promisee is speculative.

[117]   In Citibank, N.A. v. Bearcat Tire, A.G., 550 F. Supp. 148, 152 (N.D. Ill. 1982), the court states, "First year law school principles teach us that consideration, ample to support contract liability, may stem from *detriment* to the *promisee* rather than benefit to the promisor."

[118]   "A benefit to the promisor or a detriment to the promisee is a sufficient consideration for a contract. The detriment need not be real; it need not involve actual loss to the promisee. The word, as used in the definition, means

we must distinguish economic, health or other detriments from "legal" detriments, since only the latter constitute the value element of consideration, has been criticized on the ground that consideration may be found absent any actual loss to the promisee.[119] While the descriptive adjective, "legal," does not provide any insight into this question, it is no worse a label than that provided for other legal concepts which cannot be understood simply by the description attached to them.

The concept of "legal" detriment as contrasted with what one court has termed, "detriment in fact,"[120] can be described as follows: if the promisee has done or forborne something, or promised to do or to forbear doing something, the doing or forbearing of which involves the surrender of a legal right or the circumscribing of his liberty of action, the legal value element of consideration is present. Thus, there is an "actual loss" or a promise of "actual loss" in every contract.[121] Thus, the nephew-promisee surrendered a legal right to drink, smoke, swear and gamble. In surrendering that right, he suffered a loss — a loss of his freedom of action or a circumscription of his liberty. In this sense, he has suffered a "detriment" which is recognized as the kind of detriment a promisee must suffer if the legal value element of consideration is to be found.

[3]   Absence of Detriment

It is impossible to conceive of a situation where consideration would exist based only on a benefit to the promisor with no detriment to the promisee. If Ames tells Barnes, "I will pay you $100 if you will refrain from driving my (Ames') car tomorrow," there is no detriment to the promisee, Barnes, if he has no pre-existing right to drive Ames' car absent Ames' permission. Thus, he surrenders no right in forbearing from driving Ames' car. Neither is there a benefit to Ames since she received nothing in exchange for her promise to pay $100 to which she was not previously entitled. Unlike the situation described above where there is a clear detriment to the promisee and no discernible benefit to the promisor, it is not possible to meet the legal value element of consideration absent a detriment to the promisee. Consequently, while the formula for this element of consideration is typically stated as a benefit to the promisor or detriment to the promisee, the emphasis is upon the detriment to the promisee since there will

---

legal detriment as distinguished from detriment in fact. It is the giving up by the promisee of a legal right; the refraining from doing what he has a legal right to do, or the doing of what he has the legal right not to do." Phillips, J., in Petroleum Refractionating Corp. v. Kendrick Oil Co., 65 F.2d 997, 998 (10th Cir. 1933). In Harris v. Time, Inc., 191 Cal. App. 3d 449, 453, 237 Cal. Rptr. 584, 586 (1st Dist. 1987), the three-year-old son of a prominent attorney received mail addressed to him containing a statement clearly visible from the unopened envelop that the sender would give to the addressee a "NEW CALCULATOR WATCH FREE Just for Opening this Envelope. . . ." The boy's mother opened the envelope for her son. The contents revealed that a magazine subscription would have to be purchased to receive the watch. This requirement was not visible simply by reading the terms of the offer on the envelope. One of the issues in the case was whether the act of opening the envelope would constitute consideration for the promise to supply the watch. The court held that even though the opening of the envelope may have been relatively insignificant to the promisee, it was, nonetheless, an act or forbearance sought by the promisor and did constitute consideration. The action had been brought, inter alia, for punitive damages of $15 million. Notwithstanding its holding concerning consideration, the court held for the defendant on the footing that "the law disregards trifles" (de minimis non curat lex).

[119] Restatement 2d § 79, comment b concludes, "It is more realistic to say that there is no requirement of detriment."

[120] Harrington v. Harrington, 365 N.W.2d 552, 555 (N.D. 1985).

[121] In *Harrington, id.,* the court describes "legal detriment" as "giving up something which the promisee was privileged to retain, or doing or refraining from doing something which he was privileged not to do, or not to refrain from doing."

be no benefit to the promisor absent a detriment to the promisee. Again, however, the student should recall that the typical contract involves benefits and detriments to both parties.

[4]   Benefit to the Promisee or Detriment to the Promisor

When the traditional formula of benefit to the promisor or detriment to the promisee is under analysis, students sometimes wonder why the formula cannot be reversed, i.e., why is there no consideration where there is a benefit to the promisee or a detriment to the promisor? If Ames promises to give $10,000 to Barnes and Barnes accepts by saying, "Thank you, very much," there is no consideration for Ames' promise. Ames has made a gratuitous promise which is not enforceable.[122] There is a detriment to the promisor, Ames, and a benefit to the promisee, Barnes. Thus, when the traditional formula for legal value is reversed, it describes an unenforceable gift promise.

[5]   Benefits or Detriments to or From Third Parties

In the typical situation, the consideration moves between the promisor and promisee. Thus, where Ames promises to sell her car to Barnes in exchange for Barnes' promise to pay Ames $10,000, we have seen that both parties are promisors and promisees and, as such, both receive benefits and suffer detriments in their capacities of promisor and promisee. From the standpoint of Barnes as promisor, he is receiving the benefit of the car. As a promisee, Barnes is surrendering his $10,000. Promisor Ames receives the $10,000 and promisee Ames surrenders the car. There is a benefit to each promisor and a detriment to each promisee with the legal value moving to the promisor and from promisee. While this is the typical situation, it is possible for the consideration to move *to* a party other than the promisor or *from* a party other than the promisee. Nonetheless, the promise is enforceable because it is supported by consideration regardless of the party to whom it moves.

If Barnes promises to pay Ames $10,000 if Ames will deliver her car to Barnes' daughter, Ames' performance in delivering the car to the daughter is consideration for Barnes' promise even though the consideration moved *from* the promisee, Ames, to a third party, the daughter. Assuming that the daughter now has the car, if Ames promises to pay $10,000 to Barnes if Barnes' daughter will deliver the car to Ames, there is consideration for Ames' promise even though it is not moving from the promisee to the promisor, but from a third party to the promisor. The English courts quite consistently held that the consideration must move from the person who seeks to enforce the promise (the promisee) and that no one, be he promisee or beneficiary, who did not furnish at least some part of the consideration for the promise can have any rights under it.[123] Thus, English courts would not recognize a right in a third party beneficiary such as Barnes' daughter. As the exploration of third party beneficiary law will reveal, that stubborn view overcome only by a 1999 Act of Parliament.[124] While there was some early support for that view in this country,[125] it was rejected. It is clear that, "It matters not from whom the consideration moves or to whom it goes."[126]

---

[122] For an analysis of donative promises and the bases for the refusal to enforce such promises in our legal system, see Eisenberg, *Donative Promises*, 47 U. Chi. L. Rev. 1 (1979).

[123] *See* Dunlap Pneumatic Tire Co. v. Selfridge & Co., A.C. 847 [1915].

[124] Chapter 10, *infra*.

[125] *See, e.g.*, Cottage Street Methodist Episcopal Church v. Kendall, 121 Mass. 528, 531, 23 Am. Rep. 286 (1877).

[126] Restatement 2d § 71(4), comment e. See Marine Contractors Co. v. Hurley, 365 Mass. 280, 310 N.E.2d 915, 919

[6] Detriment in Contracts Involving Mutual Promises

Where the parties form their contract through a mutual exchange of promises, the consideration for either promise is the promise received from the other party to form what is traditionally known as a bilateral contract.[127] This raises the question, is *any* promise sufficient to support a counter-promise? If the response to a promise (offer) is the performance of the act requested by the promisor, the necessary detriment to the promisee is found in the performance of the act as the exchange for the promise.[128] In a bilateral contract, however, a promise is given in exchange for a counter-promise. Since no one is bound to make a promise, it could be argued that it is the making of the promise itself that supplies the necessary detriment to the promisee to evidence consideration.[129] An examination of this proposition, however, immediately suggests that it is unsound. If, for example, Ames promises Barnes $100 in exchange for Barnes' promise to forbear from driving Ames' automobile for twenty-four hours, if Barnes had no prior right to drive Ames' car, Ames is receiving nothing for her promise *except the promise of Barnes*. It is conceivable that Ames simply wanted Barnes to articulate a promise-to say the words. Since Barnes had no preexisting duty to speak the words, saying them would constitute a detriment even though the words were a promise to forbear from an act which Barnes had a legal duty to forbear. Absent such a weird detriment of merely articulating the words of a promise, it is clear that a party to a contract does not seek a promise of performance alone, but seeks both the promise of performance as well as the performance itself.[130] While courts often speak in terms of a promise exchanged for a counter-promise as consideration, they are quick to qualify that general statement by insisting that the promise must signify an act or forbearance that would, without a promise, constitute a bargained-for detriment to the promisee.[131] A theory suggesting that the detriment to the promisee is to be found in the legal obligation which the promisee's promise imposes upon him[132] has long been discredited as circular reasoning. Consideration is necessary because without it (or another validation device), a promise is not legally binding. To find the required

---

(1974), where the consideration moved to the promisor from a party other than the promisee and the court quoted from Palmer Sav. Bank v. Insurance Co. of N. Am., 166 Mass. 189, 196, 44 N.E. 211, 213 (1896): "[I]t is not in all cases necessary that the consideration should move from the promisee to promisor." *See also* Panasonic Communication Systems Co. v. State, 1996 Me. Super. LEXIS 55 (1996).

[127] Ebling v. Gove's Cove, Inc., 34 Wash. App. 495, 499, 663 P.2d 132, 134 (1983) ("A bilateral contract is one in which there are reciprocal promises. The promise by one party is consideration for the promise by the other."); Pick Kwik Food Stores, Inc. v. Tenser, 407 So. 2d 216, 218 (Fla. Dist. Ct. App. 1981) ("In a bilateral contract, the promise of one party constitutes the sole consideration for the promise of the other.").

[128] RESTATEMENT 2d § 72.

[129] *See* Ames, *Two Theories of Consideration*, 12 HARV. L. REV. 515 (1898), 13 HARV. L. REV. 29 (1899).

[130] *See* 1 CORBIN § 5.25.

[131] "The general rule is that an executory agreement, by which the plaintiff agrees to do something on the terms that the defendant agrees to do something else, may be enforced, if what the plaintiff has agreed to do is 'either for the benefit of the defendant or to the trouble or prejudice of the plaintiff.'" Bolton v. Maddan, L.R. 9 Q.B. 55, 56 [1873]. "If one party has the unrestricted right to terminate the contract at any time, that party makes no promise at all and there is not sufficient consideration for the promise of the other." Pick Kwik Food Stores, Inc. v. Tenser, 407 So. 2d 216, 218 (Fla. Dist. Ct. App. 1981). "The Defendant asks this Court to recognize the 'agreement' as an enforceable bilateral contract, where the necessary consideration is the parties' promise of performance. . . . Generally, the Defendant's promise to forbear from engaging in an activity that she had the legal right to engage in, can provide her necessary consideration for the Plaintiff's return promise. . . . [A]lthough the Defendant's promise to forbear could constitute consideration, it cannot if it was not sought after by the Plaintiff, and motivated by his request. . . ." Whitten v. Greeley-Shaw, 520 A.2d 1307, 1309-10 (Me. 1987).

[132] *See* Langdell, *Mutual Promises as a Consideration for Each Other*, 14 HARV. L. REV. 496 (1900).

detriment that creates consideration in the legal obligation which results from the presence of consideration is circular reasoning. Rather, the detriment is found in what has, in fact, been undertaken — if the doing of what has been undertaken by the promisee is a legal detriment to the promisee, the promisee's promise is sufficient.[133]

§ 58 ILLUSORY PROMISES

[A] Basic Concept — Conditional Promises Where Promisor Does Not Control Condition

If Ames promises to purchase a car from Barnes unless Ames changes her mind, the promise of Ames is illusory because Ames has not committed herself to any future action or inaction. As one court suggests, "An illusory contract may be defined as an expression cloaked in promissory terms, but which, upon closer examination, reveals that the promisor has not committed himself in any manner. In other words, an illusory promise is a promise that is not a promise. The promise is an illusion."[134] One should not, however, easily arrive at the conclusion that a particular promise is illusory. A promise that may first appear to leave the promisor wholly unconstrained may, upon reflection, reveal a detriment.

If Ames' promise to purchase Barnes' car for $10,000 is conditioned on her receipt of a $10,000 bequest from her recently deceased uncle's estate in exchange for Barnes' promise to sell the car on these terms, Ames' promise may appear to leave Ames without detriment since the conditioning event, the receipt of the bequest, may not occur. Unless Ames is aware that the condition cannot occur at the time she makes the agreement with Barnes, however, she has made a commitment which circumscribes her liberty of action.[135] If the conditioning event does not occur, Ames' duty will never be activated and she will have no liability to Barnes. The duty, however, existed from the moment the agreement with Barnes was made. The objection may be that this is circular reasoning in that the duty exists only if a contract is made, and a contract exists only if a duty exists. At the moment of the agreement, however, Ames circumscribed her liberty of action in promising to purchase the car from Barnes if an event over which she had no control occurred. Her commitment was, therefore, detrimental and constituted consideration to support Barnes' counter promise even though the failure of the condition to occur would prevent the activation of Ames' duty.[136]

---

[133] See Williston, *Consideration in Bilateral Contracts*, 27 Harv. L. Rev. 503 (1913).

[134] Harrington v. Harrington, 365 N.W.2d 552, 555 (N.D. 1985). *See also* Board of Educ. v. James Hamilton Constr. Co., 119 N.M. 415, 420, 891 P.2d 556, 561 (1994); Krebs v. Strange, 419 So. 2d 178 (Miss. 1982), and Restatement 2d § 77 comment a.

[135] If Ames knew that she would receive nothing from her uncle's estate when she made the agreement with Barnes, she would be promising nothing. Restatement 2d § 76(1).

[136] See Doughty v. Idaho Frozen Foods Corp., 112 Idaho 791, 736 P.2d 460 (Ct. App. 1987) (if less than 10 percent of potatoes were of a desired size, buyer need not accept them — held, not illusory though seller did not have coextensive right to cancel); Charles Hester Enters., Inc. v. Illinois Founders Ins. Co., 114 Ill. 2d 278, 499 N.E.2d 1319 (1986) (dram shop statute limited liability of insured to $15,000; insurer's promise to pay amounts exceeding statutory limit if statute was amended was detrimental); Hoffman v. Garden State Farms, Inc., 76 N.J. Super. 189, 184 A.2d 4 (1962) (promise to give refunds to milk consumers when state milk control law is repealed or changed; though the law may never be repealed or changed so as to activate the duty to give refunds, the promise was still detrimental); Rosenberg v. Garfinkel, 294 Mass. 196, 200 N.E. 907 (1936) (promise to guarantee payment of all debts of a corporation though the corporation was solvent and eventually paid all of its debts).

Millions of contracts evidence agreements to purchase a house conditioned on the ability of the buyer to secure adequate financing through a mortgage loan. The fact that the buyer may be unsuccessful in an attempt to procure the loan does not make the promise to purchase illusory, though the commitment to buy is conditional. If the condition does not occur, the buyer will be discharged from the duty under the contract.[137] The contract, however, existed from the moment the parties exchanged their promises. The buyer could not refuse to make application for the loan since that action would prevent the occurrence of the condition.[138] The seller could not treat the buyer's promise as non-detrimental and proceed to sell the house to another before Ames had an opportunity to seek the loan. Innumerable transactions of this nature occur daily, binding the parties to an exchange of promises though one or both promises are conditioned upon an event beyond the control of either party.

[B]   Condition Within Control of Promisor — Policy Favors Finding Consideration

If the conditioning event is *within* the control of the promisor, such a promise may appear to be illusory beyond question. Again, however, further reflection suggests that even this type of promise may be supported by consideration. The classic illustration is found in a case where the defendant, who was contemplating the purchase of a ship, promised to charter the ship to the plaintiff if the defendant purchased the ship. The defendant had not promised to purchase the ship and could, therefore, refrain from purchasing it without violating any duty. His promise was to charter the ship only if he decided, in his sole discretion, to purchase it. To understand why the defendant's promise was not found to be illusory,[139] it is important to consider his status before and after making the promise to charter the ship conditioned upon his purchase of the ship. Before making the promise, the defendant could decide to purchase or not purchase the ship without any restriction upon his subsequent freedom of action. After making the promise, however, while he was still free to purchase or not to purchase the ship, that decision could no longer be made in an unfettered fashion. After making the promise, if he purchased the ship, his duty to charter it to the plaintiff would be activated. That duty could be discharged only if defendant decided against purchasing the ship. The analysis of such cases is often put in terms of alternative performances, i.e., the promisor has a choice of alternative performances. If one of the alternatives is not detrimental, there is no consideration.[140]

---

[137] *See* Lach v. Cahill, 138 Conn. 418, 85 A.2d 481 (1951) (buyer is entitled to recover any deposit when he was unable to obtain the mortgage loan since seller's retention of the deposit would unjustly enrich the seller). In Di Benedetto v. Di Rocco, 372 Pa. 302, 93 A.2d 474 (1953), the condition was that if buyer "cannot" make the settlement, he may cancel the agreement. The court held that "cannot" does not mean "will not," i.e., the condition went to the buyer's objective ability to make the settlement rather than his unfettered discretion. The promise was, therefore, detrimental. See, however, Paul v. Rosen, 3 Ill. App. 2d 423, 122 N.E.2d 603 (1st Dist. 1954), where the agreement was conditioned upon the buyer obtaining a new lease from the owner for a period of five years from a certain date under a contract to purchase a retail liquor business. The seller refused to perform and the court held for the seller, indicating that the conditional promise of the buyer was non-detrimental. This decision and rationale are unsound.

[138] Ames would be said to have impliedly promised to make good faith efforts to obtain a suitable mortgage loan.

[139] Scott v. Moragues Lumber Co., 202 Ala. 312, 80 So. 394 (1918).

[140] The RESTATEMENT 2d § 77 states that a promise or apparent promise is not consideration if the promisor reserves a choice of alternatives unless each of the alternatives would have been consideration if it, alone, had been bargained for, or if one of the alternative performances would have been consideration and there is a substantial possibility that before the promisor exercises a choice with respect to an alternative that would not have been consideration, events may have eliminated that alternative. See Heuser v. Kephart, 215 F.3d 1186, 1191 (10th Cir. 2000), applying this section

Again, if Ames agrees to purchase Barnes' car for $10,000 unless Ames changes her mind, the alternative of not purchasing the car at the whim or caprice of Ames is non-detrimental. If, however, Ames promises to sell the car only to Barnes for $10,000 if she sells it to anyone within a certain period, she has circumscribed her liberty of action just as the promisor in the ship illustration. She must either sell the car to Barnes, which is detrimental, or not sell the car to anyone, which is also detrimental.[141]

Policies Favoring Finding Consideration. Other promises that may appear to suggest that a particular performance is within the sole discretion of the promisor and, therefore, illusory, may be construed by modern courts to contain limitations making such promises detrimental. Thus, even though a state official had the discretion to set rates for medical and dental services, a court held that the discretion was not uncontrolled; it had to reflect the "usual charges" for such services.[142] Even the phrase "sole discretion" may, by implication, impose the duty of good faith and fair dealing upon the promisor in the exercise of that discretion and, thereby, so limit it as to make it detrimental.[143] Courts are not eager to find promises to be illusory. If they have a choice between a construction that makes the contract illusory and enforceable, they will adopt the construction that makes the contract enforceable.[144] The limitation of good faith in requirements and output contracts for the sale of goods eliminates any suggestion that such contracts are illusory. The questions surrounding such contracts necessitate a comprehensive exploration, which is found in the next section.[145]

[C]   Notice as a Detrimental Alternative — Termination

If Ames promises to purchase Barnes' auto for $10,000 and the promise is terminable at will, the promise is illusory. If, however, Ames must notify Barnes that she will not purchase it, the alternative performance of notification is detrimental to Ames and is generally held to

---

of the Restatement 2d and holding that, where a party has unfettered choice of alternatives and one alternative would not have been consideration if separately bargained for, the promise in the alternative is not consideration. *See also* Dwyer v. Graham, 99 Ill. 2d 205, 457 N.E.2d 1239 (1983) (use of premises as long as desired was non-detrimental); Mastaw v. Naiukow, 105 Mich. App. 25, 306 N.W.2d 378 (1981) (unfettered discretion of counsel to approve or not approve settlement agreement).

[141] The same analysis would apply even if the conditioning event were fortuitous, thereby making the promise an "aleatory" promise. An aleatory promise is one under which the duty of the promisor to perform is conditioned upon a purely fortuitous event. RESTATEMENT 2d § 232 comment c. The classic example is a casualty insurance contract under which the insurer-promisor agrees to pay if the casualty (fire, flood or the like) occurs. If the casualty never occurs, the promisor's duty is never activated. Aleatory promises are not illusory since they are detrimental. *See* RESTATEMENT 2d § 76 comment c.

[142] California Med. Ass'n v. Lackner, 117 Cal. App. 3d 552, 172 Cal. Rptr. 815 (3d Dist. 1981).

[143] GMC v. Dept. of Treasury, 466 Mich. 231, 240, 644 N. W. 2d 734, 738–39 (2002); Omni Group, Inc. v. Seattle-First Nat'l Bank, 32 Wash. App. 22, 645 P.2d 727 (1982). *See also* Wyss v. Inskeep, 73 Or. App. 661, 699 P.2d 1161 (1985) (discretion to fix amounts employees were to receive from bonus plan was not unlimited; it had to be exercised in good faith); California Med. Ass'n v. Lackner, 117 Cal. App. 3d 552, 172 Cal. Rptr. 815 (1st Dist. 1981) (fact that one of the parties has the power to fix the price or other performance does not make his promise illusory if the power is subject to prescribed or implied limitations — with respect to discretion to set prices in contracts for the sale of goods, see UCC § 2-305); Ledford v. Wheeler, 620 P.2d 903, 906 (Okla. Ct. App. 1979) ("Buyer gave an enforceable promise to buy [real property] unless, in good faith, he determined the title was unsatisfactory. This limitation on Buyer's freedom is sufficient detriment to supply the needed consideration. . . .").

[144] *See, e.g.*, Peirce v. Peirce, 994 P.2d 193, 199 (Utah 2000); K G Dev., Inc. v. City of Waukesha, 163 Wis. 2d 527, 472 N.W.2d 249 (Ct. App. 1991).

[145] *See infra* § 59.

constitute consideration.[146] It is clear that the alternative performances are both detrimental. Consequently, it may seem that there is no question that consideration is present. Giving notice is not much of a detriment, but courts should not inquire into the adequacy of consideration.[147] Consideration, however, requires more than a detriment to the promisee. As will be seen in later sections of this chapter, the detriment to the promisee must be "bargained-for" if consideration is to be found. If Ames may either pay $10,000 to Barnes for his auto, or simply notify Barnes that she will not purchase it, it is at least questionable whether Barnes "bargained for" Ames' promise to give notice. Courts that have dealt with this situation have concluded that notice is a detrimental alternative constituting consideration and they have not focused upon the lack of the bargained-for element.[148] If there is a unilateral right to cancel the contract and there is no requirement that notice of cancellation be given, there is no discernible detriment to the promisee in cancelling.[149] Again, however, it is possible to construe such a right to cancel as requiring the giving of notice, thereby discovering a detrimental alternative to performance of the contract.[150] While the RESTATEMENT 2d is in accord with this analysis,[151] it suggests an interesting illustration.[152] A orders goods from B for shipment within three months, reserving the right to cancel the order prior to shipment. B has the goods in stock and accepts the offer. The RESTATEMENT 2d concludes, "A's promise to pay for the goods is consideration for B's promise to ship, since B can prevent cancellation by shipping immediately."[153] Notwithstanding doubt over whether the alternative performance of notice of cancellation was bargained for, the illustration suggests that a contract was formed and will be subject to cancellation upon notice from the buyer, so long as notice occurs prior to shipment by the seller.

---

[146] BCD LLC v. BMW Mfg. Co., LLC, 2010 U. S. App,. LEXIS 400 at *13, note 2 (4th Cir. 2010) where the court notes that such an illusory promise is converted by a promise supported by consideration when the notice requirement is added, citing Restatement 2d § 77, cmt. a.

[147] *See infra* § 60.

[148] The best known case is Sylvan Crest Sand & Gravel Co. v. United States, 150 F.2d 642 (2d Cir. 1945), where the court interpreted a clause in the contract, "cancellation may be effected at any time," as requiring the government to either take and pay for the trap rock to be used in an airport project, or to notify the supplier of cancellation. *See also* Johnson Lakes Dev., Inc. v. Central Neb. Pub. Power & Irrigation Dist., 254 Neb. 418, 435, 576 N.W.2d 806, 817 (1998): "A requirement that advance notice be given is sufficient to prevent a unilateral right of termination from being regarded as illusory in nature." Wilson v. Gifford-Hill & Co., 570 P.2d 624, 626 (Okla. Ct. App. 1977): "[W]here notice of cancellation is required the promisor is bound sufficiently so that his promise to buy or give notice of cancellation meets the requirement of consideration." *See also* Lauren, Inc. v. Marc & Melfa, Inc., 446 So. 2d 1138, 1139 (Fla. Dist. Ct. App. 1984).

[149] *See Wilson, id.*

[150] *See Sylvan Crest, supra* note 148.

[151] *See* RESTATEMENT 2d § 77.

[152] Ill. 7 to § 77.

[153] *Id.*

[D]   Notice of Termination and Good Faith

[1]   Section 2-309 of the Uniform Commercial Code

If a contract contains no stated duration, it is terminable at will.[154] If the parties agree that one party will supply another with goods but the agreement is indefinite in duration, the UCC prescribes that such a contract is valid for a reasonable time, but, unless otherwise agreed between the parties, either party may terminate the contract at any time.[155] The power to terminate such a contract, however, is circumscribed under the Code. Termination becomes effective only upon the receipt of reasonable notification of such termination, and if the parties' agreement provides that notification is unnecessary, that provision will be deemed invalid if its enforcement would be unconscionable.[156] The requirement of notification under this Code section is designed to effectuate good faith and commercially reasonable practices. Thus, if a seller has been supplying goods to a buyer under a terminable at will contract, notification of the seller's intention to terminate the agreement should permit the buyer to discover a substitute supplier[157] and the buyer should have a reasonable time to discover the substitute supplier. What is a "reasonable time" will depend upon the particular circumstances — it is a question of fact.[158] No particular form of notice is required,[159] but notice is a requirement for an effective termination and, like the exercise of the power of termination, it must demonstrate good faith.[160] While the parties may provide that notice of termination will not be necessary, such a provision will be a nullity if it is deemed unconscionable.[161] Unconscionability is a concept that will be explored fully later in this volume. It may be summarily described as providing courts with the power to nullify contractual provisions or entire contracts on the ground of unfair surprise or oppression created by a party with superior bargaining power.[162] Finally, it should be emphasized that a *breach* of a terminable at will contract will justify *cancellation* of the contract without any notice[163] since the breach discharges the duty of the aggrieved party.

---

[154] *See, e.g.*, Brownsboro Rd. Restaurant, Inc. v. Jerrico, Inc., 674 S.W.2d 40 (Ky. Ct. App. 1984).

[155] UCC § 2-309(2). *See* Jespersen v. 3M, 183 Ill. 2d 290, 295, 700 N.E.2d 1014, 1017 (1998).

[156] UCC § 2-309(3). *See* Delta Servs. & Equip., Inc. v. Ryko Mfg. Co., 908 F.2d 7, 12 (5th Cir.'1990).

[157] UCC § 2-309 comment 8.

[158] *See* Best Distrib. Co. v. Seyfert Foods, 714 N.E.2d 1196, 1206 (Ind. Ct. App. 1999); Monarch Beverage Co. v. Tyfield Importers, Inc., 823 F.2d 1187, 1189 (7th Cir. 1987); Zeidel Explorations, Inc. v. Conval Int'l, Ltd., 719 F.2d 1465 (9th Cir. 1983); Leibel v. Raynor Mfg. Co., 571 S.W.2d 640 (Ky. Ct. App. 1978); Superior Foods, Inc. v. Harris-Teeter Super Markets, Inc., 288 N.C. 213, 217 S.E.2d 566 (1975); McGinnis Piano & Organ Co. v. Yamaha Int'l Corp., 480 F.2d 474 (8th Cir. 1973).

[159] *See* Circo v. Spanish Gardens Food Mfg. Co., 643 F. Supp. 51 (W.D. Mo. 1985).

[160] The "good faith" requirement for merchants under the UCC combines honesty-in-fact and commercial reasonableness under § 2-103(1)(b). Non-merchants need only meet the honesty-in-fact standard, § 1-201(19).

[161] UCC § 2-309(3).

[162] The unconscionability provision of the Code is found in § 2-302. *See also* RESTATEMENT 2d § 208. Cases dealing with the alleged unconscionability of clauses making notice of termination unnecessary include Zapatha v. Dairy Mart, Inc., 381 Mass. 284, 408 N.E.2d 1370 (1980), and Sinkoff Beverage Co. v. Joseph Schlitz Brewing Co., 51 Misc. 2d 446, 273 N.Y.S.2d 364 (1966).

[163] *See* International Therapeutics, Inc. v. McGraw-Edison, 721 F.2d 488 (5th Cir. 1983). *See also* comment 9 to UCC § 2-309, and UCC § 2-703(f).

[2]   Franchise Contracts

The common law notion that contracts without a stated duration are terminable at will could have a devastating effect upon a distributor of a manufacturer's products or a franchisee operating a business under the nationally-recognized name of a franchisor. The distributor or franchisee could invest considerable time, effort and money in the development of the business only to be terminated at the will of the manufacturer or franchisor.[164] As seen above, § 2-309 of the UCC can apply to a contract for the resale of the manufacturer's products and require reasonable notice of termination to provide the distributor with a reasonable time to seek a substitute arrangement.[165] The Code will not apply to numerous franchise agreements, however. The franchisee does not purchase goods from the franchisor. Rather, the franchisee is licensed to operate a business under the trademark name of the franchisor and must adhere to the requirements set forth in the licensing agreement. To avoid injury to franchisees who devote considerable time and effort to the development of the business but are subject to termination at the whim of the franchisor, statutes may prohibit cancellation or nonrenewal of franchise agreements except for good cause.[166] These efforts may be seen as part of the general judicial or statutory developments to avoid unfairness resulting from terminable at will contracts evidenced in employment contracts with no stated duration.[167]

§ 59   REQUIREMENTS AND OUTPUT CONTRACTS — § 2-306 OF THE UNIFORM COMMERCIAL CODE

If a buyer promises to purchase from a particular seller all of a particular product that the buyer "requires," or if a seller promises to sell his entire output of a particular product to a particular buyer, are such "requirements" or "output" agreements enforceable? If either type of promise is properly construed as a commitment to deal exclusively with the other party, i.e., if the buyer may not purchase certain goods from any other supplier or if the seller may not sell his products to any other buyer, there can be no question that the promisor suffers a detriment. Therefore, the promise is not illusory. If, however, the promisor may choose to deal with others, there is no restriction upon his freedom of action — the lack of *exclusivity* makes the promise illusory.[168] A contract need not explicitly state that it is exclusive, i.e., extrinsic

---

[164] *See* Brownsboro Rd. Restaurant, Inc. v. Jerrico, 674 S.W.2d 40 (Ky. Ct. App. 1984); Plaskitt v. Black Diamond Trailer Co., 209 Va. 460, 164 S.E.2d 645 (1968).

[165] *See* City Builders Supply Co. v. National Gypsum Co., 39 U.C.C. Rep. Serv. (CBC) 826 (D. Mass. 1984).

[166] In Dunkin' Donuts of Am., Inc. v. Middletown Donut Corp., 100 N.J. 166, 495 A.2d 66 (1985), the Supreme Court of New Jersey analyzes the New Jersey Franchise Practices Act, N.J. Stat. Ann. §§ 56:10-1 to 10-15, as well as a number of other statutes with similar purposes though the scope and details of the statutes differ. The opinion represents desirable analysis of the current application of these statutes. The best known federal legislation of this type is the 1956 Congressional legislation designed to protect automobile dealers from arbitrary termination by the manufacturer. The Automobile Dealer Franchise Act (15 U.S.C. §§ 1221–1225) (sometimes called the "Auto Dealer's Day in Court Act") imposes a "good faith" standard on the manufacturer who seeks to terminate, cancel, or refuse to renew a franchise.

[167] The extensive judicial development concerning the protection of employees in terminable-at-will employment contracts was explored in *supra* § 39 B[6], Chapter 2.

[168] *See* Brooklyn Bagel Boys, Inc. v. Earthgrains Refrigerated Dough Prods., 212 F.3d 373, 379 (7th Cir. 2000): "An essential elements of a requirements contract is the promise by the buyer to purchase all of its requirements, or at least a minimum quantity, from the seller." *See also* Orchard Group v. Konica Med. Corp., 135 F.3d 421, 429 (6th Cir. 1998); Torres v. City of Chicago, 261 Ill. App. 3d 499, 632 N. E. 2d 54 (1994); Mid-South Packers v. Shoney's, Inc., 761 F.2d 1117, 1120–21 (5th Cir. 1985).

evidence may be admitted to show that it was intended.[169] This analysis, however, may be difficult to apply if there is no maximum or minimum limitation on the quantity of goods which the seller must produce or the buyer must purchase. If, for example, a buyer enters into a requirements contract on a speculative basis, i.e., while promising to purchase all the widgets he requires from a particular seller, the buyer is a middleman who will purchase large quantities of widgets if the market price exceeds the price in his contract with the supplier. If the market price is below the contract price, however, he will purchase no widgets. Such a buyer (or a seller in a comparable output contract) appears to be virtually unfettered in his freedom of action, leading some older cases to characterize his promise as illusory.[170] Yet, in terms of a detriment to the promisee, the buyer suffers a detriment in that he is precluded from contracting with any other supplier of widgets, even at a price below the market price, to purchase widgets for resale. Though it is more than unlikely that he will do so should not detract from discovering the necessary detriment to support a counter promise. The problem is not one of discovering a detriment; the judicial problem is one of discovering appropriate terms to be implied where there are no stated estimates, much less "ceiling" or "floor" quantities in the agreement.

Where, for example, the buyer has no established business and there are, therefore, no prior requirements upon which to base an estimate of his needs, courts may not discern any detriment to support a counter promise.[171] In another well-known case,[172] however, the buyer agreed to purchase all of the sand that the buyer could resell outside the City of Tulsa, Oklahoma. Though the buyer was an experienced sand salesman, he had no established business. The court found consideration supporting the promise of the buyer since he could either not sell any sand outside Tulsa, or sell sand anywhere in that vast universe outside Tulsa only if he purchased the sand from the defendant.[173] A number of older cases supported this

---

[169] Essco Geometric v. Harvard Indus., 46 F.3d 718, 728 (8th Cir. 1995). The written evidence of the contract, however, may preclude the implication of an exclusive dealing intention. *See* United Servs. Auto Ass'n v. Schlang, 111 Nev. 486, 493, 894 P.2d 967, 971 (1995).

[170] *See, e.g.*, Crane v. C. Crane & Co., 105 F. 869 (7th Cir. 1901).

[171] See Pessin v. Fox Head Waukesha Corp., 230 Wis. 277, 282 N.W. 582 (1939), where the defendant agreed to supply the plaintiff with as much beer as plaintiff would require in becoming the sole distributor of defendant's beer in a certain territory. The court held that in the absence of an established business or known enterprise, there was no measurable obligation on the part of the plaintiff which could constitute a detriment, i.e., the contract lacked "mutuality of obligation." In G. Loewus & Co. v. Vischia, 2 N.J. 54, 65 A.2d 604 (1949), the plaintiff was assured of an ample supply of wine from the defendant. In return, however, plaintiff was required to purchase such wines from defendant that plaintiff might require under labels bearing its brand or trade names, i.e., names owned exclusively by the plaintiff. The trial court found that neither party was in a position to make a reasonable estimate of the wines the plaintiff might require. Since the plaintiff was not required to purchase any wine from the defendant except that which plaintiff would resell in bottles bearing its brand or trade names, the court found no consideration, i.e., a lack of mutuality of obligation, in that plaintiff was not circumscribed in its liberty of action or, perhaps, that it was not sufficiently limited as to its future action. The court, however, appeared to confuse the requirement of consideration with the requirement of sufficient definiteness.

[172] McMichael v. Price, 177 Okla. 186, 58 P.2d 549 (1936).

[173] The court was not as clear and decisive in its rationale as it could have been. Though finding consideration, the court countered the argument that plaintiff could escape liability by going out of the sand business with the statement that, "[I]t was the intent of the parties to enter into a contract which would be mutually binding." *Id.*, 177 Okla. at 190, 58 P.2d at 553. Regardless of the intention of the parties to be mutually bound, if the liberty of one party is not circumscribed, he suffers no detriment and the promise of the other party is not supported by consideration. This is sometimes described by suggesting that there is a lack of "mutuality of obligation," i.e., both parties must be bound

analysis,[174] but there were occasional statements of a contrary view that was often the product of confusing the requirement of consideration with the requirement of sufficient definiteness of the terms of the agreement. If the parties agree to a requirements or output agreement without any specification of minimum or maximum levels and there is no prior business history established to which the court can look for guidance as to the terms of the contract or, even with such a history, drastic changes in requirements or output occur, courts may feel hard-pressed to discover sufficiently definite terms. Even then, however, courts should not conclude that the agreement is unenforceable because there is no consideration which is a separate question from the question of sufficient definiteness.

Since requirements and output contracts are desirable planning instruments, assuring a continuous source of supply at predictable prices or a single customer bound to purchase all that the seller produces at agreed upon prices, many courts were astute to avoid the argument that such contracts were too indefinite to enforce if they could discover some plausible basis for estimating a reasonable quantity. The apparent desirability of output and requirements contracts made it clear that their use would not only continue but increase.

[A]   UCC § 2-306 — The "Good Faith" Standard

The UCC makes a valiant effort to react to this felt commercial need. In § 2-306(1), the Code deals with the problems of consideration and sufficient definiteness.[175] The consideration problem is met by requiring the party who will determine quantity (the seller by output and the purchaser by requirements) "to operate his plant or conduct his business in good faith and according to commercial standards of fair dealing in the trade so that his output or requirements will approximate a reasonably foreseeable figure."[176] The challenge of sufficient definiteness is met by defining the quantity under such contracts as the actual good faith output or requirements of the particular party.[177] The general thrust of the Code provision directed courts to favor the enforceability of requirements and output contracts and to eschew notions of any lack of "mutuality of obligation" (i.e., consideration) or sufficient definiteness unless that were impossible.[178] These issues were dealt with through the implication of good faith,[179] a rather amorphous standard that required case law elaboration.

---

or neither is bound. This unfortunate phrase will be explored and, it is hoped, emasculated, later in the discussion of consideration.

[174] *See, e.g.*, T. W. Jenkins & Co. v. Anaheim Sugar Co., 247 F. 958 (9th Cir. 1918) (promise to buy requirements of sugar); Minnesota Lumber Co. v. Whitebreast Coal Co., 160 Ill. 85, 43 N.E. 774 (1895) (promise to buy requirements of anthracite).

[175] "A term which measures the quantity by the output of the seller or the requirements of the buyer means such actual output or requirements as may occur in good faith, except that no quantity unreasonably disproportionate to any stated estimate or in the absence of a stated estimate to any normal or otherwise comparable prior output or requirements may be tendered or demanded." UCC § 2-306(1).

[176] UCC § 2-306 comment 2. See GMC v. Paramount Metal Products Co., 90 F. Supp. 2d 861, 873 (E. D. Mich. 2000) quoting the predecessor section of Corbin on Contracts, § 6.5: "The promise to buy of another person or company all or some of the commodity or service that the promisor may thereafter need or require in his business is not an illusory promise and such a promise is a sufficient consideration for a return promise.

[177] 2-306(1) (comment 2)

[178] *See* Stacks v. F & S Petroleum Co., 6 Ark. App. 327, 641 S.W.2d 726 (1982).

[179] The UCC definitions of "good faith" are found in § 1-201(19) ("honesty in fact in the conduct of the transaction concerned"), which is generally applicable, and the Article 2 "merchant" standard of good faith in § 2-103(1)(b) (" 'Good faith' in the case of a merchant means honesty in fact and the observance of reasonable commercial standards of fair

"Good faith" cannot be used as a substitute for consideration, i.e., if a buyer is free to purchase his requirements from others, there is no consideration to support the promise of the seller to supply all that the buyer desires to purchase from that seller.[180] With respect to the measurement of quantity, while a comment to § 2-306 indicates that output or requirements contracts will not fail for indefiniteness since the measurement of quantity will be based upon "actual good faith output or requirements of the particular party,"[181] the language of § 2-306(1) refers to "stated estimates" or, in the absence of stated estimates, "to any normal or otherwise comparable prior output or requirements." It is theoretically possible for a court to confront a situation that is bereft of any "normal" standard to which the court may resort to ascertain the quantity term in such a contract and where one party is subject to an enormous risk while the other party risks very little.[182] The implication of "good faith" in such an agreement may be insufficient to meet the requirement of sufficient definiteness.

While the standard of "actual output or requirements as may occur in good faith" sets a reasonably workable standard, it is qualified: "except that no quantity unreasonably disproportionate to any stated estimate or in the absence of stated estimate to any normal or otherwise comparable prior output or requirements may be tendered or demanded."[183] Since a demand for or tender of any "unreasonably disproportionate quantity" suggests bad faith, this "exception" may appear to be nothing more than an explication of the more general good faith standard. It is, however, problematic for *underdemanding* buyers.

Where a buyer increases its demand some sixty-three percent above a contract estimate for a given year in order to pursue new lines of business that were not the basis for the original estimate so as to profit from a fixed price when market prices were increasing rapidly, the increase is obviously in bad faith.[184] Such a buyer is demanding a quantity "unreasonably disproportionate to the stated estimate" which the statute forbids. Thus, this language in 2-306 clearly applies to the *overdemanding* buyer. There are situations, however, where a buyer may, in good faith, have severe reductions in requirements and even no requirements. Where a contractor no longer had any requirements for concrete in the building of a state hospital when the state terminated the project, the contractor's reduction of requirements to zero was held to be a good faith reduction.[185] The question arises, should the "unreasonably disproportionate" concept apply to an *underdemanding* buyer? If a buyer may reduce its

---

dealing in the trade."). The Article 1 definition, not applicable to merchants, may be somewhat facetiously described as the "pure heart/empty head" type of good faith, i.e., the assumption is that one can be honest but unreasonable. Merchants, however, must be both honest in fact and commercially reasonable. *See* Summers, *"Good Faith" in General Contract Law and the Sales Provisions of the Uniform Commercial Code*, 54 Va. L. Rev. 195 (1968).

[180] In Harvey v. Fearless Farris Wholesale, Inc., 589 F.2d 451 (9th Cir. 1979), the court found no consideration where the buyer could purchase from others if their prices were lower. It should be noted, however, that even in such a case, a detriment to the buyer can be shown, i.e., he must purchase from the seller unless he can purchase the same goods at lower prices from others.

[181] UCC § 2-306 comment 2.

[182] For example, where a middleman may choose to purchase nothing or a very large quantity on the basis of market price, it is conceivable that a court may find such an agreement to be fatally indefinite even under the liberal standards of § 2-306 of the UCC.

[183] UCC § 2-306(1).

[184] Orange & Rockland Utils., Inc. v. Amerada Hess Corp., 59 A.D.2d 110, 397 N.Y.S.2d 814 (2d Dep't 1977) (sale of power to a power pool which had not been considered at the time of the original estimate and which permitted plaintiff to profit from its contract to purchase oil at fixed prices when oil and other energy prices were increasing rapidly).

[185] Wilsonville Concrete Prods. v. Todd Bldg. Co., 281 Or. 345, 574 P.2d 1112 (1978).

requirements to zero, the underdemanding buyer should be treated differently from the overdemanding buyer.[186] Again, however, any allowable disproportionate reduction must be evidenced by good faith.[187] While a seller will have the burden of proving that a buyer who eliminated its requirements acted in bad faith, a buyer's failure to produce evidence justifying such action will be presumed to operate in bad faith.[188] A loss of profit or even no profit on a particular item will not justify a shut down by a seller under an output contract or a buyer under a requirements contract. In *Vulcan Materials Co. v. Atofina Chemicals, Inc.*,[189] Atofina operated two chemical plants. Vulcan supplied Atofina's "entire requirements" for choloform used to make R-22, at Atofina's Wichita plant. Atofina closed its Wichita plant and ceased purchases from Vulcan. The court concluded that Atofina's decision was simply a reflection of its dissatisfaction with the bargain it had made with Vulcan. It continued to sell roughly the same amount of R-22 it had previously sold, except that it freed itself of the contract with Vulcan. Atofina was not privileged to go out of business in Wichita in this fashion to escape what it viewed as a burdensome contract.[190]

If a buyer under a requirements contract decides to stockpile or otherwise purchase unneeded goods because the fixed price under the contract is beneficial, such an increase in demand is not in good faith because it is not generated by the purchaser's actual requirements.[191] On the other hand, a seller's tender of a lesser quantity unreasonably disproportionate to a stated estimate or prior output will violate § 2-306.[192] A stated estimate provides a median or center from which variations can be measured to determine whether the output or requirements are unreasonably disproportionate.[193] Absent any estimate, prior output or requirements furnishes a similar basis for determining unreasonably disproportionate increases or decreases.[194] In general, courts have found § 2-306 to be a

---

[186] Empire Gas Corp. v. American Bakeries Co., 840 F.2d 1333, 1337 (7th Cir. 1988). *See also* G.D. Searle & Co. v. Fisons Corp., 1993 U.S. Dist. LEXIS 2445, at *9 (N.D. Ill. Feb. 26, 1993).

[187] R. A. Weaver & Assocs., Inc. v. Asphalt Constr., Inc., 587 F.2d 1315, 190 U.S. App. D.C. 418 (1978); Miami Packaging, Inc. v. Processing Sys., Inc., 792 F. Supp. 560, 563 (S.D. Ohio 1991).

[188] See *Empire Gas*, note 186 *supra*.

[189] 355 F. Supp. 2d 1214 (D. Kan. 2005).

[190] Comment 2 to UCC § 2-306: "A shutdown by a requirements buyer for lack of orders might be permissible when a shut-down merely to curtail losses would not."

[191] *See* Homestake Mining Co. v. Washington Public Power Supply Sys., 476 F. Supp. 1162 (N.D. Cal. 1979), *aff'd*, 652 F.2d 28 (9th Cir. 1981); Massachusetts Gas & Elec. Light Supply Corp. v. V-M Corp., 387 F.2d 605 (1st Cir. 1967). *See also Amerada Hess*, *supra* note 184.

[192] *See* Harry Thuresson, Inc. v. United States, 453 F.2d 1278, 197 Ct. Cl. 88 (1972) (tendered quantity of 1.7% of estimated quantity was "unreasonably disproportionate" in an output contract).

[193] *See* comment 3 to UCC § 2-306: "If an estimate of output or requirements is included in the agreement, no quantity unreasonably disproportionate to it may be tendered or demanded. Any minimum or maximum set by the agreement shows a clear limit on the intended elasticity. In similar fashion, the agreed estimate is to be regarded as a center around which the parties intend the variation to occur." See also Shea-Kaiser-Lockheed-Healy v. Department of Water & Power of City of Los Angeles, 73 Cal. App. 3d 679, 686, 140 Cal. Rptr. 884, 888 (2d Dist. 1977), which applies this "median" standard.

[194] In Duval & Co. v. Malcom, 233 Ga. 784, 214 S.E.2d 356 (1975), the seller offered to supply its entire output of cotton from certain acreage to the buyer as it had in the past. In two prior crop years, the acreage had produced 756 bales and 380 bales, respectively. When the buyer received the written offer, he added an estimate of 875 bales. The court held that this estimate was a material alteration of the offer since, under § 2-306, the estimate of 875 bales added by the purchaser was unreasonably disproportionate to prior output.

workable statutory guide in their efforts to determine appropriate quantity standards in output and requirements contracts.

[B] Exclusive Dealing Contracts — "Best Efforts" — UCC § 2-306(2)

In the celebrated case of *Wood v. Lucy, Lady Duff-Gordon*,[195] the plaintiff was an agent who was to have the exclusive right to place the indorsement of the defendant on the designs of others. In exchange, the defendant was to receive one-half of all profits and revenues derived from any contract made for such products by the plaintiff. The contract was to last for a year with annual renewals unless terminated upon 90 days' notice. When the defendant allowed her name to be used on products through others, plaintiff brought his action to which the defendant replied that no contract existed because the statement evidencing the alleged contract did not expressly state that the plaintiff would use his efforts to place the defendant's indorsements. In a famous opinion by Judge Benjamin Nathan Cardozo, the court reacts to this argument:

> We think, however, that such a promise is fairly to be implied. The law has outgrown its primitive stage of formalism when the precise word was the sovereign talisman, and every slip was fatal. It takes a broader view today. A promise may be lacking, and yet the whole writing may be 'instinct with an obligation,' imperfectly expressed. . . . If that is so, there is a contract.[196]

The "best efforts" doctrine may be seen as necessary protection of a party who is at the mercy of the other party in an exclusive dealing contract.[197] Absent a contrary agreement, the Uniform Commercial Code construes exclusive dealing agreements as imposing an obligation by the seller to use best efforts to supply the goods and by the buyer to use best efforts to promote their sale.[198]

[1] Meaning of "Best Efforts"

The "best efforts" standard is vague.[199] While § 306(2) implies a "best efforts" standard in exclusive dealing contracts for both sellers and buyers, there is confusion as to how that standard differs materially from a seller's ordinary good faith standard. As contrasted with the buyer, merely obligating the seller to use best efforts to supply the goods may appear to suggest an obligation less burdensome than the seller's duty under a requirements to supply the buyers' requirements. A comment, however, incorporates all of the duties under subsection

---

[195] 222 N.Y. 88, 118 N.E. 214 (1917).

[196] *Id.* at 91, 118 N.E. at 214. A recent version of this analysis is found in B. Lewis Productions, Inc. v. Angelou, 2005 U. S. Dist. LEXIS 9032 (S. D. N. Y. 2005).

[197] Aventis Environmental Science USA LP v. Scotts Co., 383 F. Supp. 2d 488, 505 (S. D. N. Y. 2005).

[198] § 306(2). *See also* RESTATEMENT 2d § 77, illustration 9.

[199] In their article, *Principles of Relational Contracts*, 67 VA. L. REV. 1089, 1111 (1981), Professors Goetz & Scott suggest that, "[T]he precise legal meaning to be attached to a best efforts requirement is not at all clear, either from a consideration of the case law or from theoretical discussions in standard legal scholarship." They proceed to suggest (1111-26) an analysis of "best efforts" on the basis of an economic model and suggest that best efforts cases "hinge on two factors, strategic adaptation to the conflict of interest between the parties and the problem of managerial incompetence."

(1) of 2-306 and requires the seller to refrain from supplying any other dealer or agent within an exclusive territory.[200]

If the supplier may not supply others within the buyer (dealer's) territory, the supplier has agreed to supply its dealer exclusively within that territory. Output is irrelevant in such an arrangement. Rather, the requirements of the buyer in its effort to expand the market for the seller's product within a given territory are relevant. In such a situation, a "best efforts" obligation may be imposed upon the supplier to ascertain that it provides the dealer with a sufficient and expeditious supply of the product to allow the dealer to use its best efforts in promoting the sale of the product.[201] Unlike the seller, the implied obligation of "best efforts" is obvious in its application to the dealer who must use all of his capabilities to foster the marketing of the seller's product.[202]

As to the "best efforts" standard for buyers, the same Code comment explains that buyers operating as exclusive dealers must "use reasonable effort and due diligence in the expansion of the market or the promotion of the product." Noting the judicial confusion between the "good faith" and "best efforts" standards, a court suggests that the core of "good faith" is a standard of honesty and fairness, while the essence of "best efforts" is diligence.[203] Again, however, there is no UCC or other satisfactory definition or description of "best efforts." Courts recognize that the phrase cannot be defined in terms of a fixed formula but will vary under the circumstances.[204] The parties may choose to include their own definition of "best efforts" in their contract,[205] just as they may chose to negate any "best efforts" obligation.[206] A "best efforts" clause does not, of itself, impose a duty of exclusive dealing, nor does it prohibit, per se, the promotion of a competing product.[207] The issue of whether a distributor used best efforts will often arise, however, where the distributor decides to sell another product in competition with the original supplier's product. Whether the sale of a competing product will violate an obligation to use best efforts will depend upon the particular circumstances in

---

[200] 2-306, comment 5. *See* Sally Beauty Co. v. Nexxus Prods. Co., 801 F.2d 1001 (7th Cir. 1986). In Flynn v. Gold Kist, Inc., 181 Ga. App. 637, 353 S.E.2d 537 (1987), the court casually suggests that, regardless of whether the good faith requirement of § 2-306(1) or the best efforts requirement of § 2-306(2) applies, the good faith standard applies.

[201] See Famous Brands, Inc. v. David Sherman Corp., 814 F.2d 517, 521 (8th Cir. 1987), where, after discovering an implied promise by the distributor to promote the products of the supplier, the court indicates that the arrangement could also be regarded as a requirements contract. *See also* Sally Beauty Co. v. Nexxus Prods. Co., 801 F.2d 1001 (7th Cir. 1986).

[202] Bloor v. Falstaff Brewing Corp., 454 F. Supp. 258 (S.D.N.Y. 1978), *aff'd*, 601 F.2d 609 (2d Cir. 1979).

[203] First Union National Bank v. Steele Software Systems Corp., 154 Md. App. 97, 139, 838 A. 2d 404, 429 (2003), quoting E. Allan Farnsworth, *To Keep One's Promises: The Duty of Best Efforts in Contract Law*, 46 U. Pitt L. Rev. 1, 7–8 (1984).

[204] *First Union Bank, id.*, 838 A. 2d at 428; NCNB Nat'l Bank v. Bridgewater Steam Power Co., 740 F. Supp. 1140 (W.D.N.C. 1990) (quoting Triple-A Baseball Club Assocs. v. Northeastern Baseball, Inc., 832 F.2d 214, 224 (1st Cir. 1987), *cert. denied*, 485 U.S. 935, 108 S. Ct. 1111, 99 L. Ed. 2d 272 (1988)). In Joyce Beverages of N.Y., Inc. v. Royal Crown Cola, 555 F. Supp. 271, 277 (S.D.N.Y. 1983), the court indicates that an express best efforts clause should be read in the light of trade practice and usage.

[205] Pinnacle Books, Inc. v. Harlequin Enters., Ltd., 519 F. Supp. 118, 121 (S.D.N.Y. 1981).

[206] Aventis Environmental Science USA LLP v. Scotts Co., 2005 U. S. Dist. LEXIS 419 (S. D. N. Y. 2005) ("take or pay" provision precluded the implication of a "best efforts" obligation). *See also* Flight Concepts Ltd. Partnership v. The Boeing Co., 819 F. Supp. 1535, 1552 (D. Kan. 1993) (expressly stating that there was no duty to promote the product), *aff'd*, 38 F.3d 1152 (10th Cir. 1994).

[207] *First Union Bank*, note 203, *supra*, 838 A.2d at 429.

each case.[208]

Though "best efforts" must always be viewed in the particular circumstances of each case, it should be clear that the phrase imports some positive and drive beyond the good faith standard of honesty in fact and commercial reasonableness.[209] The essential obligation of diligence imposed by a best efforts obligation suggests a level of industry and creativity that would not be appropriate in describing the good faith obligation.

§ 60   EQUIVALENCE IN VALUE — "ADEQUACY" OF CONSIDERATION — "SUFFICIENT" CONSIDERATION — "PEPPERCORN" THEORY

[A]   Actions at Law for Damages

Contracts are made by private parties who are free to place whatever value they wish upon that which they seek in exchange for a promise or performance. "Generally, a court will not inquire into the adequacy of consideration for a contract, inasmuch as consideration based on value of property or performance of a promise is a matter of personal judgment by parties to a contract."[210] Legions of cases, therefore, assert that courts will not generally inquire into the adequacy of consideration, i.e., the relative values exchanged.[211] It is not possible for courts to police the bargain of the parties in terms of their estimates of value. A dissatisfied party could always complain that he or she did not receive "adequate" or "sufficient" consideration, thereby necessitating the impracticable task of judicial policing of value. Courts have, therefore, studiously avoided questions of the relative values exchanged by the parties except where fraud or similar overreaching can be shown or when a court is asked to decree an equitable remedy.[212] If a promise has some value, that is, if it involves a detriment which the

---

[208] In *Joyce, id.*, note 204, the court concluded that the sale of a competing cola would violate the best efforts obligation, basing that decision upon trade practice and usage. In HML Corp. v. General Foods Corp., 365 F.2d 77 (3d Cir. 1966), the court interpreted the "Supply Agreement" to ascertain primarily that the distributor had a ready source of supply rather than an agreement requiring promotion on the part of the distributor. In Parev Prods. Co. v. I. Rokeach & Sons, Inc., 124 F.2d 147 (2d Cir. 1941), the court candidly recognized that the parties had not contemplated certain market changes concerning competing products from other suppliers which required the court to decide the case absent any such intention by the parties. The court permitted the distributor to market a new product, competing with the old product, until the plaintiff could demonstrate that the sale of the new product reduced royalty payments beyond reductions that would have occurred through sales of other manufacturers' products even if the new product had not been marketed.

[209] UCC § 2-103(1)(b).

[210] Melcher v. Bank of Madison, 248 Neb. 793, 802, 539 N.W.2d 837, 844 (1995). *See also* Keith v. Day, 81 N.C. App. 185, 343 S.E.2d 562 (1986); Buckingham v. Wray, 219 Neb. 807, 366 N.W.2d 753 (1985).

[211] Recent cases attest to the continuing strength of this statement. *See, e.g.*, Christian v. Gouldin, 72 Conn. App. 14, 804 A. 2d 865 (2002); Graley v. Yellow Freight Sys., 2000 U.S. App. LEXIS 14085 (6th Cir. June 14, 2000); Tanton v. Grochow, 707 N.E.2d 1010, 1012 (Ind. Ct. App. 1999); Wagner v. Nutrasweet Co., 95 F.3d 527, 532 (7th Cir. 1996); Caisse Nationale De Credit Agricole-CNCA v. Valcorp, Inc., 28 F.3d 259, 265 (2d Cir. 1994). *See also* Carroll v. Lee, 148 Ariz. 10, 712 P.2d 923 (1986); Kristerin Dev. Co. v. Granson Inv., 394 N.W.2d 325 (Iowa 1986); Vogelhut v. Kandel, 308 Md. 183, 517 A.2d 1092 (1986); Haretuer v. Klocke, 709 S.W.2d 138 (Mo. Ct. App. 1986); C & D Inv. v. Beaudoin, 364 N.W.2d 850 (Minn. Ct. App. 1985). *See also* RESTATEMENT 2d § 79 comment c.

[212] *See* Bayshore Royal Co. v. Doran Jason Co., 480 So. 2d 651 (Fla. Dist. Ct. App. 1985); Harwood v. Randolph Harwood, Inc., 124 Mich. App. 137, 333 N.W.2d 609 (1983). The question of adequacy of consideration where a party seeks an equitable remedy such as specific performance is explored in part B of this section.

law recognizes, the promise will be binding. The value need not be significant and it need not involve any economic detriment or actual loss. In the sense of a real economic detriment rather than a "legal" detriment, the RESTATEMENT 2d suggests that, "[T]here is no requirement of detriment."[213] Perhaps the best-known statement of the virtual worthlessness of the detriment is the suggestion that even a "peppercorn" will be sufficient.[214]

In *Haigh v. Brooks*,[215] the plaintiff surrendered a document which the parties thought to be a binding guaranty. However, it was claimed that the document was a worthless scrap of paper. The court held that the surrender of this scrap of paper, even if it were worthless, was consideration for a promise to guarantee the payment of $110,000 under the circumstances.[216] A modern example of a trivial detriment is seen in a case involving an offer contained in an envelope addressed to a three-year old containing a statement on the face of the envelope, "I'll give you this versatile new calculator watch free Just for Opening this Envelope Before Feb. 15, 1985." The mother of the child opened the envelope for her son and discovered that it was necessary to subscribe to a magazine in order to procure the watch. The defendant argued that, "the mere act of opening the envelope was valueless and therefore did not constitute adequate consideration" which the court found to be "technically . . . incorrect" because "any bargained-for act or forbearance will constitute adequate consideration."[217]

Money Exchanged for Money. It is sometimes suggested that there is an exception to the general proposition that courts of law will not inquire into the relative values exchanged where the exchange consists of one sum of money for a different sum. Thus, a promise to pay $200 in exchange for one cent was held not supported by consideration.[218] The refusal of courts to view such promises as supported by consideration, however, is not a reflection on the inadequacy of the value of one cent compared to two hundred dollars. Rather, such an exchange is what the RESTATEMENT 2d calls a "pretended exchange."[219] The promise was made to carry out the intentions of the promisor's beloved wife who had manifested her intention of leaving certain individuals each $200 in her will. Since she had no separate estate, the payments could not be made. The husband made formal promises of $200 payments in exchange for one cent from each of the promisees. While the payment of "one cent" is a detriment, it must not be forgotten that consideration requires more than a detriment to the

---

[213] RESTATEMENT 2d § 79 comment b.

[214] See Whitney v. Stearns, 16 Me. 394, 397 (1839), which can be traced as far as Lord Coke's discussion where, in a rent apportionment situation, he suggested that a "pepper corn" would be sufficient. E. COKE ON LITTLETON 222 (1628). *See also* Hyde v. Shapiro, 216 Neb. 785, 785, 346 N.W.2d 241, 243 (1984): "[E]ven 'a peppercorn' may be sufficient."

[215] 10 A. & E. 309 [1839].

[216] See, however, Newman & Snell's State Bank v. Hunter, 243 Mich. 331, 220 N.W. 665 (1928), where a widow promised (through her own note) to pay the indebtedness of her husband to the bank which surrendered the husband's note. The court found no consideration because the note was a worthless piece of paper. Yet, the widow may have valued what to others was a worthless piece of paper. She may have desired the note to satisfy her husband's obligation. If, however, she mistakenly assumed her own liability, the promise should not be enforced. As suggested in *Hyde v. Shapiro*, *supra* note 214, at 243–44, "A valuable consideration to support a contract need not be one translatable into dollars and cents; it is sufficient if it consists of the performance, or promise thereof, *which the promisor treats and considers a value to him*" (quoting Asmus v. Longenecker, 131 Neb. 608, 611, 269 N.W. 117, 119 (1936) (emphasis added)).

[217] Harris v. Time, Inc., 191 Cal. App. 3d 449, 456, 237 Cal. Rptr. 584, 587 (1st Dist. 1987).

[218] Schnell v. Nell, 17 Ind. 29, 79 Am. Dec. 453 (1861). *See also* T.P. Shepard & Co. v. Rhodes, 7 R.I. 470, 84 Am. Dec. 573 (1863).

[219] RESTATEMENT 2d § 79 comment d.

promisee. The detriment must be bargained-for, i.e., the promise must induce the detriment *and* the detriment must induce the promise. It should be noted, however, that if the one cent were a rare or sentimental coin, it is could be bargained-for and consideration would be found in such a transaction. Similarly, where parties are buying and selling money as a commodity, i.e., purchasing and selling foreign currency, such a transaction clearly evidences detriments which are the subject of a bargained-for exchange.[220]

"Sufficiency." The confusion surrounding the phrase "adequacy of consideration" is exacerbated by the use of the term "sufficiency of consideration" which has appeared in tens of thousands of cases and continues to be used.[221] To the extent that "sufficiency" is an inquiry into "adequacy," it is generally irrelevant. "Sufficiency," however, is often used as a redundant qualification of the existence of consideration. Yet, consideration either exists or it does not exist, i.e., one cannot find "insufficient" consideration and still have "some" consideration. The RESTATEMENT 2d, therefore, properly rejects the usage of "sufficient consideration" as redundant.[222] The Restatement's desirable effort to correct the usage, however, has been a conspicuous failure at the time of this writing.

The view that courts should not inquire into the adequacy of consideration, absent a showing of fraud, mistake or overreaching, is the only sensible view that can be supported. There is no standard for measuring the values of detriments exchanged between the parties. Economic values are so variable as to defy equivalence even if courts attempted to discover equivalence. If the promisor is content to make a particular bargain, there is no reason for refusing enforcement of that bargain, again, in the absence of fraud, mistake or overreaching.[223] If, however, inadequacy of consideration is accompanied by evidence of fraud, mistake or overreaching, or if it is so "gross" as to give rise to an inference of fraud,[224] relief may be obtained in an equitable action of rescission or cancellation.[225]

[B] Inadequacy of Consideration in Equity — Equitable Unconscionability

Mere inadequacy of consideration will not prevent a court, sitting as a court of equity, from decreeing specific performance of a contract.[226] If, however, the consideration is grossly inadequate, or the enforcement of the contract will cause unreasonable hardship or loss to the defendant or third persons or, finally, if the contract was induced by some sharp practice, misrepresentation or mistake, a court may refuse the discretionary remedy of specific performance.[227] The elements just described may appear in varying combinations and the fact

---

[220] The "bargained-for-exchange" element of consideration will be explored in subsequent sections.

[221] See, e.g., Hinkel v. Sataria Distributing & Packaging, Inc., 2010 Ind. App. LEXIS 93 at *10 (2010).

[222] *See* RESTATEMENT 2d § 17 comment d.

[223] *Cf.* Note, *The Peppercorn Theory of Consideration and the Doctrine of Fair Exchange in Contract Law*, 35 COLUM. L. REV. 1090 (1935).

[224] *See, e.g.*, Dreyer v. Dreyer, 48 Or. App. 801, 617 P.2d 955 (1980).

[225] RESTATEMENT 2d § 79 comment e. See Kenda Corp. v. Pot O' Gold Money Leagues, Inc., 329 F.3d 216, 228–29 (1st Cir. 2003). *See also* Ryan v. Weiner, 610 A.2d 1377 (Del. Ch. 1992).

[226] *See* Seier v. Peek, 456 So. 2d 1079 (Ala. 1984). *See also* RESTATEMENT 2d § 208 comment c.

[227] *See* Patterson v. Goldsmith, 292 S.C. 619, 358 S.E.2d 163 (Ct. App. 1987); Phil Bramsen Distributor v. Mastroni, 151 Ariz. 194, 726 P.2d 610 (Ct. App. 1986); Patterson v. Merchants Truck Line, Inc., 448 So. 2d 288 (Miss. 1984). *See also* RESTATEMENT 2d § 364. Where a tax sale of three parcels of property each valued at $5000 were each sold for

situation must, as usual, be considered in context. Thus, a slight inadequacy which, alone, would not prevent the equitable remedy may be sufficient to prevent it in combination with some sharp practice, some severe hardship or other factor.[228] Courts must, however, be careful to focus on the adequacy of consideration at the time the contract is formed, rather than some later time such as the time of trial when the values exchanged may appear grossly disproportionate.[229]

In the absence of fraud, duress, mistake or misrepresentation, the fact that a contract could be characterized as harsh, oppressive or "unconscionable" was insufficient to make such a contract unenforceable, void or voidable at common law.[230] Yet, the discretionary remedy of specific performance was often denied in such cases.[231] When the remedy is denied, it may be asserted that the plaintiff is not deprived of all remedies but is merely relegated to his action at law for damages. Yet, the denial of the equitable remedy may be a complete denial of remedy in the typical specific performance case, i.e., where the remedy at law is either inadequate or useless.

[1] Unconscionability in Equity vs. Uniform Commercial Code and RESTATEMENT 2d

The use of the amorphous term, "unconscionable," in cases denying the equitable remedy has been part of equity jurisprudence since time immemorial. Its current use in equity, however, may cause some confusion in relation to the doctrine of unconscionability that appeared in the mid-twentieth century in the Uniform Commercial Code and was later replicated in the Restatement 2d of Contracts.[232] The Code and Restatement 2d concepts of unconscionability were designed to permit courts to police against the enforcement of contracts or portions of contracts which evidenced certain unexpected and harsh risk-shifting terms from becoming operative against parties of inferior bargaining power. This use of "unconscionability" is explored later in this volume.[233] The material, risk-shifting term would often be inconspicuously printed and contain language that only lawyers could begin to appreciate.[234]

---

amounts under $290, the court stated, "A court of equity cannot set aside a tax sale because of mere inadequate consideration (citing cases). Rather, the consideration must be so grossly inadequate that it amounts to constructive fraud or confiscation, shocking the court's conscience." In re Mgr. of the Div. of Fin. of Jackson County v. La-Sha Consulting, Inc., 224 S. W. 3d 605, 606 (Ct. App. Mo. 2006).

[228] *See* FIRST RESTATEMENT § 367 comment c.

[229] *See* Pitts Truck Air, Inc. v. Mack Trucks, Inc., 173 Ga. App. 801, 328 S.E.2d 416 (1985).

[230] *See* 5A CORBIN § 1164.

[231] *See, e.g.,* Payne v. Simmons, 232 Va. 379, 350 S.E.2d 637 (1986); Pascarella v. Bruck, 190 N.J. Super. 118, 462 A.2d 186 (1983); Smith v. Harrison, 325 N.W.2d 92 (Iowa 1982); Lenawee County Bd. of Health v. Messerly, 98 Mich. App. 478, 295 N.W.2d 903 (1980), *rev'd*, 417 Mich. 17, 331 N.W.2d 203 (1982). See also Ryan v. Weiner, 610 A.2d 1377, 1382 (Del. Ch. 1992), listing cases in various jurisdictions where courts refused to enforce conveyances because of price unfairness or inequitable or oppressive conduct.

[232] UCC § 2-302; Restatement 2d § 208. In denying specific performance due to a combination of inadequacy of consideration and other circumstances, a court may resort to the use of "unconscionable." *See, e.g.,* McKinnon v. Benedict, 38 Wis. 2d 607, 157 N.W.2d 665 (1968).

[233] Chapter 6, *infra*. For a case antedating the UCC concept of unconscionability but containing the elements just described, see Cutler Corp. v. Latshaw, 374 Pa. 1, 97 A.2d 234 (1953) (confession of judgment clauses printed on reverse sides of standardized forms, the reverse sides deliberately ignored by the plaintiff though fewer sheets could have been used to set forth the specifications).

[234] The classic example is found in Williams v. Walker-Thomas Furniture Co., 350 F.2d 445, 121 U.S. App. D.C. 315

Moreover, even if the disfavored party was totally aware of the ramifications of the clause, he was often unable to seek another bargain since he required the goods or services contracted for and would not be able to obtain them elsewhere on less oppressive terms. In this "take-it-or-leave-it,"[235] *contract of adhesion* posture,[236] the signature of the disfavored party on the document did not represent his *genuine* assent to the terms of the contract though it displayed his *apparent* assent.[237] The UCC or Restatement 2d concepts of unconscionability permit courts to refuse enforcement of provisions apparently assented to under such circumstances, whether the court is asked to grant legal or equitable relief. This development will be explored in a later section.[238]

Because the principles of unconscionability as found in the UCC appeared to some to be as amorphous as earlier equitable statements of unconscionability, it was tempting to suggest that the Code had simply incorporated the earlier concepts. Scholarly explorations, however, have revealed clear differences between the old equity notion of unconscionability and the new concept under the UCC.[239] Beyond the fact that there is no reliance on the old equity concept in the new Code formulation, the equity concept applied to overreaching in individualized bargaining transactions while the Code concept applies to situations involving mass transactions in which the standardized, printed ("pad") contract form is used. The equity doctrine was applied to situations involving inadequacy of consideration or "gross overall imbalance," while the Code and Restatement 2d concepts typically apply to separate, unconscionable clauses though an entire contract manifesting gross overall imbalance may be deemed unconscionable. The Code and Restatement 2d concepts also focus on a party's ability and opportunity to review the terms of a proposed contract. Questions such as whether a particular clause was printed in such a fashion as to be readily readable and understandable and whether a party had any reasonable choice in apparently agreeing to a harsh or oppressive provision are common.[240] While equitable unconscionability often involves one or more of these elements, it may also be used when they are absent but when the *result* of the deal is harsh or oppressive. For all of these reasons, the student of contract law must distinguish the equitable concept of unconscionability — often mentioned in connection with an inquiry into the relative values exchanged (adequacy of consideration) — and the UCC and Restatement 2d concepts

---

(1965) (an "add-on" clause was part of a "maze" of fine print and subjected the purchaser of an inexpensive stereo set to the loss of all the furniture she had ever purchased from the seller and paid for prior to the purchase).

[235] See Henningsen v. Bloomfield Motors, Inc., 32 N.J. 358, 161 A.2d 69 (1960), the landmark case suggesting the unconscionability analysis before the UCC.

[236] The phrase, "contract of adhesion," referring to the absence of any meaningful choice, is usually attributed to Professor Patterson in his article, *The Delivery of a Life Insurance Policy*, 33 Harv. L. Rev. 198, 222 (1919). However, the development of the concept is principally attributable to Professor Eherenzweig, *Adhesion Contracts in the Conflict of Laws*, 53 Colum. L. Rev. 1072, 1088–89 (1953), and Professor Kessler, *Contract of Adhesion—Some Thoughts About Freedom of Contract*, 43 Colum. L. Rev. 629 (1943).

[237] In Parton v. Mark Pirtle Oldsmobile-Cadillac-Isuzu, Inc., 730 S.W.2d 634 (Tenn. Ct. App. 1987), the court adopts the "genuine assent/apparent assent" analysis, citing the third edition of this book. This analysis will be explored in detail later in this volume with respect to the modern concept of unconscionability. See, however, Cubic Corp. v. Marty, 185 Cal. App. 3d 438, 229 Cal. Rptr. 828 (4th Dist. 1986), indicating that a contract of adhesion may be enforced unless the terms are oppressive.

[238] *See infra* § 97.

[239] See the important article by Professor Leff, *Unconscionability and the Code — The Emperor's New Clause*, 115 U. Pa. L. Rev. 485, 528–41 (1967).

[240] For a listing of unconscionability factors, see Doughty v. Idaho Frozen Foods Corp., 112 Idaho 791, 736 P.2d 460 (Ct. App. 1987) (one-sided, superior bargaining power).

(considered in Chapter 6) which deal with assent to allegedly oppressive or unfairly surprising terms typically found in printed provisions of standardized (form) contracts.

§ 61   BARGAINED-FOR-EXCHANGE — CONDITION OF A GRATUITOUS PROMISE DISTINGUISHED

[A]   The Basic Concept

The fundamental concept that underlies the informal contract is that of bargain or exchange. It is not enough that the promisee suffers a detriment even if that detriment is induced by the making of a promise. As we have seen, detriment is one of the two necessary elements of consideration. The detriment, however, must be bargained-for and it is not bargained for simply because it was induced by the making of a promise. The most famous judicial description of bargained-for-exchange is that of Justice O. W. Holmes, Jr.:

> " '[T]he promise and the detriment are the conventional inducements each for the other. No matter what the actual motive may have been, by the express or implied terms of the supposed contract, the promise and the consideration must purport to be the motive each for the other, in whole or at least in part. It is not enough that the promise induces the detriment or that the detriment induces the promise if the other half is wanting."[241]

The term "motive" as used by Holmes, however, must be understood to mean the result the promisor seeks rather than a mere state of mind. Consideration for a promise is the action or forbearance the promisor is seeking in exchange for his promise. To paraphrase the Holmes' description, the promise must induce the detriment *and* the detriment must induce the promise. The RESTATEMENT 2d provides further assistance in describing the "bargained-for-exchange" element: "A performance or return promise is bargained for if it is *sought* by the promisor in exchange for his promise and is *given* by the promisee in exchange for that promise."[242]

These descriptions, while accurate and helpful, can be assimilated only through their application. It is important to consider illustrative cases.

[B]   Determining Whether the Detriment Was Bargained-For — Illustrations

The typical contract for the purchase and sale of goods or services presents no obstacle in identifying the bargained-for-exchange. If Ames agrees to sell her car to Barnes for $10,000 in exchange for Barnes' promise to purchase the car at that price, Ames' promise induces Barnes' detriment of parting with $10,000 and the payment of $10,000 is clearly what Ames wants in exchange for her promise. Barnes' promise to pay the $10,000 induces Ames' detriment to

---

[241] Wisconsin & M. R. Co. v. Powers, 191 U.S. 379, 386, 24 S. Ct. 107, 108, 48 L. Ed. 229, 231 (1903).

[242] RESTATEMENT 2d § 71(2). Another description of "bargained-for-exchange" provided by Justice Holmes is "reciprocal conventional inducement," as suggested in his famous work, THE COMMON LAW 230 ([1881] Howe ed. 1963). For a suggestion that Holmes created this bargain theory of consideration from whole cloth, see G. GILMORE, The Death of Contract 17–21 (1974). For a balanced view in disagreement with Professor Gilmore, see Richard Speidel, *An Essay on the Reported Death and Continued Vitality of Contract*, 27 STAN. L. REV. 1161, 1167–71 (1975).

transfer ownership of the car and that detriment is clearly sought by Barnes in exchange for his promise to pay $10,000.

Where the facts are not that clear with respect to a bargained-for-exchange, the analysis can be assisted by focusing upon the *purpose* of the promisor, i.e., in making the promise, was it the purpose of the promisor to induce the detriment? Did the promisor make the promise because she wanted the promisee to do something which the promisee had a legal right to forbear, or forbear an action that the promisee had the legal right to perform? If the promisor made the promise for the purpose of inducing the detriment, the detriment induced the promise. If, however, the promisor made the promise with no particular interest in the detriment that the promisee had to suffer to take advantage of a promised benefit, the detriment was incidental or conditional to the promisee's receipt of the benefit.

Janice loaned $90,000 to relatives secured by a mortgage on property they owned. A bank also held a mortgage on the property that was subordinate to Janice's mortgage. When the relatives required additional financing, the bank required Janice to subordinate her interest to the bank's mortgage on the property. Janice signed the subordination agreement and the loan was made. When Janice later claimed that there was no consideration for her promise to the bank, the court recited the formula that the promise must induce the detriment *and* the detriment must induce the promise for a bargained-for-exchange to exist. It must appear ("express or implied") that the detriment was suffered at the request of the promisor. The court held that, by signing the subordination agreement, Janice impliedly requested the bank to make the additional loan to her relatives. Thus, her promise induced the bank's detriment and the bank's detriment induced her promise.[243]

Where, however, a husband claimed that he left his tire business to assist his wife in her franchised business in exchange for his wife's promise to share her business with him, the court held that the husband's purpose in coming to the aid of his ill wife was to aid his wife pursuant to the normal presumption of gratuitous services of husband to wife rather than in exchange for a share of her business.[244] Consider a modern version of a classic illustration provided by Professor Williston.

Ames is a benevolent woman who sees Barnes, a homeless person, shivering in the winter cold on a city street. Ames tells Barnes that if he will go to a clothing store a half mile away, Barnes may charge a warm coat to her account. If Barnes walks to the store, he has suffered a detriment induced by Ames' promise. The detriment of walking to the store, however, did not induce Ames' promise, i.e., in the phrase of Justice Holmes, the "other half is wanting." Ames was not induced to make her promise to see Barnes walk to the store. She did not seek Barnes' act of walking to the store in exchange for her promise. Neither did Barnes walk to the store in exchange for Ames' promise. Ames made a gift promise to Barnes. Walking to the store was a necessary condition to accept the gift. Ames' promise, therefore, was not supported by consideration. On any reasonable construction, while Ames' promise induced the

---

[243] Meincke v. Northwest Bank & Trust Co., 756 N. W. 2d 223 (Iowa 2008).

[244] Penley v. Penley, 65 N.C. App. 711, 310 S.E.2d 360 (1984). See also Baehr v. Penn-O-Tex Oil Corp., 258 Minn. 533, 104 N.W.2d 661, 665 (1960), where forbearance in instituting a suit, albeit a detriment, was not bargained-for. The opinion states, "Consideration, as essential evidence of the parties' intent to create a legal obligation, must be something adopted and regarded by the parties as such. Thus, the same thing may be consideration or not, as it is dealt with by the parties."

detriment, the detriment did not induce the promise.[245] Whether a promisee's action or inaction was sought in exchange for a promise, i.e., whether it was bargained-for, or whether it was a mere condition to the acceptance of a gift is a question of interpretation dependent upon all of the outward manifestations of the parties and the surrounding circumstances.

In a famous old case,[246] a brother-in-law promised to provide a residence for his widow sister-in-law and her family. The promisee surrendered her residence in a dangerous neighborhood some 60 miles away and moved to the brother-in-law's property, where she was placed in "comfortable houses" and given land to cultivate. Two years later, she was notified to move to a less comfortable house. Thereafter, she was told to leave even that house. She brought an action claiming breach of contract to which the court replied that the promise to her was "a mere gratuity" and no action would lie thereon. She was induced to suffer a detriment in surrendering her original abode and moving to the promisor's property, thereby fulfilling one-half of the bargained-for-exchange requirement that the promise induce the detriment, but the other half of the formula was wanting, i.e., her detriment did not induce the bother-in-law's promise. He did not seek the detriment as the price of his promise. Rather, it was a necessary condition to the fulfillment of his gratuitous promise. Consequently, the court found no consideration because of the lack of a bargained-for-exchange. Modern courts would also find no consideration in such facts, but would enforce on the basis of another validation device to be discussed later in this chapter, i.e., the device known popularly as promissory estoppel.[247]

Consider a father who has enjoyed a close and loving relationship with his son who has just been graduated from college. The father invites the son to lunch at a restaurant near a jeweler where the father promises to purchase an expensive watch for the son. By forbearing other choices and traveling to the luncheon meeting, the son could be viewed as suffering a detriment induced by the father's promise. The detriment, however, did not induce the father's promise which was gratuitous. There is no consideration.

Assume, however, that the father and son were estranged. The father has attempted to meet the son several times but the son has refused to meet. The father promises to purchase the expensive watch for the son if the son will join him for lunch. Here, the father's promise, again, induced the detriment, but, unlike the previous illustration, the son's detriment induced the father's promise to purchase the watch for the son. Both halves of the bargained-for-exchange requirement are met and there is consideration for the father's promise. Recall that the value of the son's detriment is irrelevant, i.e., courts will not inquire into the adequacy of consideration.

Finally, a comparison of two well-known cases is helpful. Where a newspaper advertised a "permanent" position for a reporter and the plaintiff surrendered his job in a bakery to take the position, it was clear that the promise of the employer induced the plaintiff to suffer the detriment of surrendering his position at the bakery, i.e., the promise induced the detriment. The promisor, however, evidenced no particular interest in the detriment suffered by the plaintiff. Though the plaintiff could not work at the newspaper and the bakery simultaneously,

[245] This is a paraphrase of the famous Willison "tramp" illustration. 1 WILLISTON § 112 (3d ed. 1957).

[246] Kirksey v. Kirksey, 8 Ala. 131 (1845).

[247] See, e.g., Miles Homes Div. of Insilco Corp. v. First State Bank, 782 S.W.2d 798 (Mo. Ct. App. 1990), where the court finds no consideration because of the lack of a bargained-for-exchange, but recognizes the promise as enforceable on the basis of the validation device called promissory estoppel to be discussed later in this chapter.

the promisor was disinterested in the detriment, i.e., the surrender the bakery position was simply a necessary condition to his performance at the newspaper. The newspaper did not attempt to entice him away from the bakery. Thus, the court held that there was no bargained-for-exchange that would have converted the contract from one terminable-at-will to a lifetime duration because the detriment did not induce the promise though the promise had induced the detriment.[248]

For a detriment to induce a promise, the promisor must desire that detriment, i.e., he or she must want the promisee to suffer that detriment as the price of the promisor's promise. If, for example, engineering firm X was desirous of employing an engineer from competing engineering firm Y though the engineer was pleased to be at Y, X could entice the engineer to leave Y and to join X for "permanent" or "lifetime" employment. In such a situation, the promise induces the detriment *and* Y's detriment in surrendering his employment induces the promise because X desire that detriment as the necessary price of its promise. The engineer's surrender of the position at Y would not be a mere incident of accepting the position at X as it was in the case of the employee who surrendered his job at the bakery to become a reporter. Rather, it would be a bargained-for detriment.[249] While firm X seeks the ultimate benefit of having the engineer work for X, it must first entice him away from Y. The newspaper did not seek to entice the plaintiff from his bakery position. Therefore, we may view the engineer's detriment of his departure from Y as a detriment that X sought in exchange for its promise since the suffering of that detriment was essential to the ultimate benefit to X of having Y employed by X rather than his former employer.

In the other well-known case,[250] the defendant was eager to attract potential buyers to an auction of certain residential lots. The advertisement for the sale contained an offer to give potential buyers a chance to win a new Ford automobile. In response to the offer, the plaintiff attended the sale, received her chance and won the contest. The defendant refused to provide the prize and defended its action on the ground that there was no consideration to support its promise. The court found consideration since the object of the defendant was to attract persons to the sale and the plaintiff, among others, suffered the detriment sought by the defendant, i.e., the detriment induced the promise. Since the promise also induced the detriment of the plaintiff, surrendering other choices to attend the auction, the detriment was bargained-for. The ultimate desire of the defendant was to sell lots to those in attendance. To achieve that goal, the defendant had to attract potential buyers to the sale and offered a chance at winning a new automobile in exchange for the detriment suffered by those who were induced to attend by the promise of an opportunity to win the car.

[C] Aids in Determining the Purpose of the Promisor — Other Favored Policies

In determining whether a purpose of the promisor is to have the promisee suffer the detriment or whether the detriment is a mere incident to the completion of a gift or other benefit to the promisee, courts may consider whether there was any discernible benefit to the

---

[248] Fisher v. Jackson, 142 Conn. 734, 118 A.2d 316 (1955).

[249] See Collins v. Parsons College, 203 N.W.2d 594 (Iowa 1973), where the court held that the surrender of a tenured position at one school was consideration for a promise of tenure at another school where the employment surrendered was permanent (tenured) and the new employer was aware of the facts.

[250] Maughs v. Porter, 157 Va. 415, 161 S.E. 242 (1931).

promisor as well as the extent of the detriment to the promisee.[251] The purpose of the promise is also an important factor, i.e., if the purpose of the promise is favored in the eyes of the law, it will be much easier to satisfy a court that the promise was bargained-for even though doubt exists as to whether the promisor sought the detriment in exchange for the promise.[252] Similarly, courts may discover a bargained-for-exchange in highly doubtful circumstances if they are eager to modify outmoded or mistaken contract doctrines that may be said to perpetuate injustice. Thus, to modify the traditional "terminable-at-will" doctrine governing employment contracts with no stated duration, a number of courts have discovered a bargained-for-exchange from statements in a employee manual, handbook or stated policy issued by the employer subsequent to the employment contract which allegedly contain promises by the employer with a purpose of having the employee suffer the detriment of continuing his or her employment, thereby forming a unilateral contract by the employee's continued performance.[253] As will be seen in the remainder of our exploration of the concept of consideration, there are other situations in which courts find consideration with little or no discussion of the bargained-for-exchange element. In some of these cases, there is little doubt that courts have unwittingly ignored that element. In others, there is little doubt that courts have deliberately ignored it to achieve what they perceive to be just and desirable results.[254]

---

[251] See, e.g., Davies v. Rhonda Dist. Urban Council 87 L. J. (K.B.) (n.s.) 166 [1917] (defendant promised to continue the salary of any teacher who enlisted in the army); Miller v. Bank of Holly Springs, 131 Miss. 55, 95 So. 129, 31 A.L.R. 698 (1922) (bank promised to keep customer's savings stamps in its regular vaults if he could continue to leave them in its care; the bank failed to perform its promise and the stamps were stolen).

[252] The classic example is the celebrated opinion by Judge Cardozo in De Cicco v. Schweizer, 221 N.Y. 431, 117 N.E. 807, 810 (1917), where consideration was found to support a promise of a father to his prospective son-in-law to pay an annuity to his daughter after the marriage even though the parties were affianced at the time of the father's promise. The opinion ends with the admission that marriage settlements are enforced "where consideration, if present at all, has been dependent upon doubtful inference. . . . It strains, if need be, to the uttermost interpretation of equivocal words and conduct in the effort to hold men to the honorable fulfillment of engagements designed to influence in their deepest relations the lives of others." The opinion is fully explored in § 65[C], infra. A similar Cardozo effort is found in another celebrated opinion, Allegheny College v. National Chautauqua County Bank, 246 N.Y. 369, 159 N.E. 173 (1927), where Judge Cardozo discovers a bargained-for-exchange supporting a charitable subscription promise. Such promises are looked upon with great favor by the courts as will be seen in § 62, infra. See RESTATEMENT § 90(2) which makes charitable subscription or marriage settlement promises binding without proof of any bargained-for exchange.

[253] See the analysis and cases in § 46[C], supra. See also Matlock v. Data Processing Sec., Inc., 607 S.W.2d 946 (Tex. Civ. App. Forth Worth 1980), holding that a promise not to compete after severance from the employer was supported by the employer's forbearance from discontinuing the employment relationship, even though the promise was made after the employment contract was formed. See, however, George W. Kistler, Inc. v. O'Brien, 464 Pa. 475, 347 A.2d 311 (1975), holding that such covenants not to compete made after the employment relationship is already established requires new consideration which is not found in the continuation of the employment relationship despite the fact that the employment contract was terminable at will.

[254] When courts "discover"a bargained-for-exchange in a situation where it apparently does not exist, the result they seek to achieve is often desirable. In such cases, it would be preferable for courts to dispense with the fiction that bargained-for-exchange and, therefore, consideration exists, and to arrive at the desired result on the basis of sound policy reasons. Such an approach would promote law settlement, i.e., predictability and consistency which are, indeed, high values in any legal system.

§ 62   NOMINAL, FORMAL, AND "SHAM" CONSIDERATION — MUST THE DETRIMENT BE A REAL INDUCEMENT OR MOTIVE?

[A]   Nominal Consideration — First RESTATEMENT and RESTATEMENT 2d Distinguished

If Ames wants to make a legally enforceable gratuitous promise, i.e., a promise to give Barnes, her nephew, land worth $100,000, absent the availability of the seal or a more modern formalistic validation device, Ames confronts a significant problem. She may attempt to make her promise to Barnes enforceable by the creation of a document evidencing a promise to convey the land to Barnes in exchange for one dollar which Barnes promises to pay. If the parties sign this document and Barnes then pays one dollar to Ames, should Ames' promise be binding? It is patently clear that the payment of one dollar, albeit a technical detriment to Barnes, did not motivate or induce Ames to promise to convey the valuable land.[255] The statement or "recital" of consideration in such a document is a mere formality often called "nominal" consideration and it is so understood by the parties. It is consideration in name only. Since there is no bargained-for-exchange involved in such a transaction, it is impossible to characterize the promise by Ames as supported by consideration. If, however, a court merely requires a formal exchange to constitute what it calls "consideration" without any bargained-for-exchange, the promise will be enforceable. Some decisions cannot easily be explained on any other basis. The best known example is Thomas v. Thomas, in which the brothers of the deceased, in order to carry out his wishes, promised to convey a life estate in certain property in exchange for a promise to pay £1 per year and to keep the premises in good repair. The court found that the promise to pay £1 annually clearly established consideration.[256] There is little question that the brothers were not induced to make their promise to convey the life estate in exchange for the nominal payment or even the promise of good repair, i.e., there was no bargained-for-exchange. The court seems disposed to enforce the promise to carry out the deathbed wishes of the husband and to regard the payment of £1 annually as consideration because it was a detriment to the promisee, notwithstanding the lack of bargained-for-exchange.

The FIRST RESTATEMENT supports this view[257] The RESTATEMENT 2d, however, finds no consideration where there is "a mere pretense of bargain . . . as where there is a false recital of consideration or where the purported consideration is merely nominal."[258] While the

---

[255] Consideration must not be confounded with motive. Thus, in Clayman v. Bibler, 210 Iowa 497, 500, 231 N.W. 334, 336 (1930), the court distinguishes these concepts: " 'Motive' and 'consideration' are not identical. The expectation of a definite result is often the motive which prompts the execution of a contract. Such expectation is not, however, binding. Ordinarily, 'consideration' is the price paid for the undertaking of the promisor." While it is undoubtedly true that a promise is not binding simply because it was made as the result of a worthwhile motive, as Justice Holmes suggests, "[I]t is of the essence of consideration, that by the terms of the agreement, it is given and accepted as the motive or inducement of the promise." O. W. HOLMES, THE COMMON LAW 293 (1881).

[256] 2 Q.B. 852, 114 Eng. Rep. 330 [1842].

[257] In § 84 ill. 1, it suggests that a promise by A to convey land worth $5000 to B in exchange for one dollar is supported by "sufficient" consideration.

[258] RESTATEMENT 2d § 71 comment b. In ill. 5 to this section of the RESTATEMENT 2d, A desires to make a binding promise to give $1000 to B. Recognizing the unenforceability of gratuitous promises, A offers to purchase a book worth less than $1 from B for a price of $1000. It concludes, "There is no consideration for A's promise to pay $1000." Among

RESTATEMENT 2d insists that mere pretense of a bargain where even the nominal amount stated is not paid ("sham consideration") is not consideration, that situation must be distinguished from situations involving a combination of bargain and gift in which the dominant motivation of the promisor may be gratuitous.

[B]   Recital of "Nominal" & "Sham" Consideration — Option and Guaranty Contracts

Two types of contracts where the fiction of consideration is most prominent are option contracts and guaranty (surety) contracts.

[1]   Option Contracts

The purpose of an option contract is to keep another offer — the main offer — irrevocable for the time stated in the option contract or, if no time is stated, for a reasonable time.[259] Such options may be evidenced by a recital clause. The paradigm is an offer by Ames to sell her land to Barnes for $1 million that also contains a "recital": "In consideration of ten dollars in hand paid, receipt of which is hereby acknowledged, this offer shall remain open for 30 days." The recital is a record of an option contract since it attests the receipt of value ($10) that was paid in exchange for the surrender of the power to revoke the main offer to sell the land for $1 million. The payment of the $10 is "nominal" consideration — consideration in name only — which typically evidences a nominal sum such as $10.

It would be absurd to suggest Ames had agreed to take her land off the market and surrender her power to sell it to any other party for 30 days in exchange for $10. It is clear beyond peradventure that the $10 was not bargained for and, therefore, constitutes "nominal" consideration which is not consideration. Numerous cases, however, involving recited consideration of one, five or ten dollars, where the question of whether that nominal amount was bargained for is ignored.[260]

It is not a sufficient answer to suggest that courts do not inquire into the adequacy (relative values) of consideration. While the RESTATEMENT 2d suggests the difficulty of determining the worth of the irrevocability of offers, it clearly admits that gross disproportion between the amount paid by the option holder and the value of the option typically indicates that there was no bargained-for-exchange.[261]

---

the cases supporting this view, see Fischer v. Union Trust Co., 138 Mich. 612, 101 N.W. 852 (1904); T.P. Shepard & Co. v. Rhodes, 7 R.I. 470, 84 Am. Dec. 573 (1863). The RESTATEMENT 2d position, however, should be carefully distinguished from its position with respect to recital clauses in guaranty or option contracts discussed later in subsection B. of this section.

[259] See the discussion of option contracts at § 44[B], *supra*.

[260] For example, in Solomon Mier Co. v. Hadden, 148 Mich. 488, 11 N.W. 1040 (1907), the option contract provided the offeree with an irrevocable offer from June, 1906 to November 1, 1906 for a payment of one dollar. There was no discussion of whether the one dollar was bargained-for. A recital clause in a release of liability is often said to "import consideration." *See, e.g.*, Buddy "L", Inc. v. General Trailer Co., 672 S.W.2d 541 (Tex. App. Dallas 1984).

[261] RESTATEMENT 2d § 87 comment b. *See* Ganser v. Schwartz, 216 Wis. 2d 385, 1998 Wis. App. LEXIS 69, at *16 (Ct. App. 1998).

[2]   Surety Contracts

A suretyship (or guaranty) contract is one in which the surety promises to pay the debt of another (the principal obligor) if the principal fails to pay. A bank or other lender of money or credit may not be willing to suffer the detriment of lending money in exchange for the promise of a principal debtor with an insufficient credit rating. If, however, the principal arranges for a surety to promise to pay if the principal fails to pay, the creditor is willing to assume the risk. If a party becomes a surety at the time the credit is extended, there is consideration since the loan or credit extended is a detriment inducing the promise of the principal debtor and the guarantor and the detriment to the creditor induced both promises.[262] If, however, the creditor and principal debtor have contracted prior to the promise of the surety, the surety's promise must be supported by consideration or another validation device.[263] A recital of nominal consideration to support such a promise suffers the same absence of bargained-for-exchange found in recitals supporting option contracts.

[3]   "Sham" Consideration — Consideration Not Paid

Any scintilla of doubt as to whether the consideration was bargained for is removed when such a measly sum is not even paid. The recital clause is exposed as a total lie manifesting "sham" consideration. Yet, most courts hold that, upon proof that the recited amount has not been paid, the promise fails for want of consideration.[264]

Since the typical recital clause does not evidence genuine consideration even if the nominal amount recited was paid, to suggest that evidence revealing the falsity of the recital converts a promise supported by consideration into one not supported by consideration is emphatically unsound. If a court deludes itself into believing that the typical recital clause evidences genuine consideration, i.e., that the one dollar or other nominal sum was bargained for, evidence that the sum was not paid should result in a finding of a *failure* of consideration, i.e., a breach by the party who was to pay the consideration, rather than the notion that the failure to pay converts the option or guaranty promise into one not supported by consideration at the time the promise was made. Even where the recited amount is not paid, however, courts pursued fictions to save the option or guaranty contract.

In the well-known case of *Lawrence v. McCalmont*,[265] Mr. Justice Story dealt with a clause reciting the payment of one dollar to a guarantor who had not, in fact, received the dollar:

> The guarantor acknowledged the receipt of the one dollar and is now estopped to deny it. If she has not received it, she would now be entitled to recover it. A valuable consideration, however small or nominal, if given or stipulated for in good faith, is, in the absence of fraud, sufficient to support an action on any parol contract.

---

[262] *See, e.g.*, Days Inn of Am., Inc. v. Regency Manor Ltd., 94 F. Supp. 2d 1200, 1203 (D. Kan. 2000). A guaranty promise may also be binding because of the reliance of the creditor, RESTATEMENT 2d § 88(c) and comment d. It may also be statutorily binding, *e.g.*, UCC §§ 3-113 and 3-408 and RESTATEMENT 2d § 88(b). If there is a failure of consideration in the contract between the principal debtor and the creditor, the guarantor may assert that defense when called upon to pay the debt. Jones v. Dixie O'Brien Div., O'Brien Corp., 174 Ga. App. 67, 329 S.E.2d 256 (1985).

[263] *See* City Nat'l Bank v. Russell, 246 Ill. App. 3d 302, 307, 615 N. E. 2d 1308, 1311 (4th Dist. 1993).

[264] See Lewis v. Fletcher, 101 Idaho 530, 617 P.2d 834 (1980), and cases cited therein.

[265] 43 U.S. (2 How.) 426, 452, 11 L. Ed. 326, 335–36 (1844).

The "estoppel" view, however, has attracted an extremely limited following.[266] Another narrow minority view, also suggested in Justice Story's pronouncement, treats the failure to pay as an implied promise to pay the nominal consideration, thereby making the promise enforceable.[267]

[4]   The RESTATEMENT 2d Solution — A Formalistic Validation Device

Notwithstanding the lack of consideration, the RESTATEMENT 2d suggests that a recital of nominal consideration which is a fiction, is "sufficient to support a short-time option proposing an exchange on fair terms."[268] The rationale is important: "The fact that the option is an appropriate preliminary step in the conclusion of a socially useful transaction provides sufficient substantive basis for enforcement, and a signed writing taking a form appropriate to a bargain satisfied the desiderata of form."[269] The operative term in this rationale is *form*. The part of the RESTATEMENT 2d in which this rationale appears collects thirteen sections under the caption, "Contracts Without Consideration."[270] It is clear that the RESTATEMENT 2d suggests that recital clauses in option or guaranty contracts have been and should continue to be regarded as formalistic validation devices which have nothing to do with consideration. Yet, the particular *form* of these validation devices should be a "signed writing taking a form appropriate to a bargain. . . ."[271] By reciting the payment of nominal consideration in a signed writing, therefore, a promise to keep an offer open is made enforceable even though it is clear that there is no consideration in terms of any bargained-for-exchange. The recital of consideration takes on a life of its own, i.e., it has the same effect as the seal (prior to its abolishment or severe modification). The Supreme Judicial Court of Massachusetts (where the seal remained effective) prospectively overruled its long-term adherence to the seal as an effective validating device for option contracts. The court concluded that the seal has "lost all practical utility" in this role. Thus, it held that,

> the giving of consideration, a necessary element of ordinary (simple or informal) contracts, should be required for option contracts that happen to be impressed with a seal or to recite a talismanic formula importing a seal.

Having concluded that option contracts will henceforth require "the giving of consideration," the court immediately contradicts that statement:

> We henceforth adopt the Restatement (Second) of Contracts § 87(1) . . . 'An offer is binding as an option contract if it (a) is in writing and signed by the offeror, recites a

---

[266]   Real Estate Co. of Pittsburgh v. Rudolph, 301 Pa. 502, 153 A. 438 (1930), which expressly relies upon *Lawrence v. McCalmont.*

[267]   *See* Jones v. Smith, 206 Ga. 162, 56 S.E.2d 462 (1949); Smith v. Wheeler, 233 Ga. 166, 210 S.E.2d 702 (1974); Baumer v. United States, 580 F.2d 863, *reh'g denied*, 585 F.2d 520 (5th Cir. 1978) (applying Georgia law). The RESTATEMENT 2d § 87 comment c properly rejects this view on the basis that the recited consideration was not bargained for whether it was paid, impliedly promised to be paid, or not paid.

[268]   RESTATEMENT 2d § 87 comment b. *See* First Nat'l Bankshares v. Geisel, 853 F. Supp. 1344, 1353 n.6 (D. Kan. 1994).

[269]   *Id.*

[270]   This is "Topic 2" of the RESTATEMENT 2d which includes §§ 82–94.

[271]   RESTATEMENT 2d § 87 comment b, (option contracts), Restatement 2d § 88, comment be (guaranty contracts).

purported consideration for the making of the offer, and proposes an exchange on fair terms within a reasonable time. . . .[272]

Thus, in Massachusetts, the recital of a seal will no longer create an option contract to make an offer irrevocable, but a recital of a "purported consideration" will make the offer irrevocable under an enforceable option contract. The court has simply traded the old fashioned seal for its newly created formal validation device.

There is, however, no reason why a formalistic validation device cannot be judicially created. The sole difficulty has been the reluctance of courts to admit what they were doing. The RESTATEMENT 2d openly confesses the lack of any consideration and the "socially useful" desirability of recital clauses to make promises enforceable under option contracts. It properly qualifies the strength of this device by insisting that the terms of the main contract be fair. What may appear to be a second qualification, however, may be questioned. The RESTATEMENT 2d may be read to suggest that a recital device will be effective only for "short-term" options, but it is questionable as to whether the RESTATEMENT 2d would insist upon this "short-term" qualification.

One of its illustration suggests the payment of twenty-five cents for a 120-day option on a tract of land priced at $100,000.[273] It concludes that, since the terms of the exchange of land for a price of $100,000 are fair, the option is effective making the offer irrevocable for four months.[274] The notion that only "short term" options are made effective through the formalistic recital device is made even more dubious by another illustration in which a ten-year option to take phosphate from land is supported by the payment of one dollar. The terms of the main contract require the taker to pay a royalty of twenty-five cents per ton on phosphate taken from the land. The taker knows that the prevailing royalty exceeds one dollar per ton. The terms of the main exchange, therefore, are not fair and the RESTATEMENT 2d concludes that the offer is not made irrevocable by the one dollar payment for the option.[275] Presumably, had the royalty payment been set at prevailing market rates, the ten-year option in exchange for one dollar would be effective. Consequently, the statement in the RESTATEMENT 2d that a nominal, unbargained-for, consideration recorded in a recital clause "is regularly held sufficient to support a *short-term* option proposing an exchange on fair terms,"[276] simply represents holdings in a number of cases. The RESTATEMENT 2d will insist only that the main exchange is on fair terms.

The RESTATEMENT 2d expressly adopts the view that a clause reciting nominal consideration in either a guaranty or an option contract should operate as a formalistic validation device, supporting the promise in either type of contract, regardless of the fact that the recited amount was never paid:[277]

> 'The signed writing has vital significance as a formality while the ceremonial manual delivery of a dollar or peppercorn is an inconsequential formality. In view of the dangers of permitting a solemn written agreement to be invalidated by oral testimony

---

[272] Knott v. Racicot, 442 Mass. 314, 322–323, 812 N. E. 2d 1207, 1214 (2004).

[273] RESTATEMENT 2d § 87 ill. 1.

[274] The illustration is based on Marsh v. Lott, 8 Cal. App. 384, 97 P. 1163 (1908).

[275] RESTATEMENT 2d § 87 ill. 2. based on Killebrew v. Murray, 151 Ky. 345, 151 S.W. 662 (1912).

[276] RESTATEMENT 2d § 87 comment b (emphasis added).

[277] RESTATEMENT 2d § 87 comment c and § 88 comment b.

which is easily fabricated, therefore, the option [or guaranty] agreement is not invalidated by proof that the recited consideration was not in fact given.[278]

The RESTATEMENT 2d position maintains total consistency with its view that a recital clause should be treated as a formalistic validation device. The guaranty or option contract promise supported by such a device is made enforceable exclusively because of the form of the written promise. A formalistic validation device is effective exclusively because it signals the enforceability of a promise by the appearance of the promise, i.e., on its face, it is recognized as an enforceable promise because of the particular form of the promise. There is no consideration in the typical recital clause since the amount recited therein is not bargained for. Under these circumstances, it is irrelevant whether the recited amount has or has not been paid since the payment of a nominal sum is not the inducement for the promise. Though the Restatement 2d view continues as the "minority position," more modern courts have begun to recognize its desirability.[279]

[C]   Bargain and Gift Motivations Combined — Mixed Motivations

If Ames has a house for sale which has a reasonable market value of $100,000, is her agreement to sell that house to her only child for $25,000 supported by consideration? The situation differs markedly from one in which the promisor is willing to part with property worth $100,000 for one dollar since $25,000 is, on its face, more than nominal consideration. Ames would not sell the house for $25,000 to anyone in the world except her only child. Clearly, she is motivated to make a gift to her child. Yet, Ames' promise is supported by consideration.[280] Beyond the fact that $25,000 is clearly more than nominal in this example,[281] courts should find consideration for several reasons. As seen earlier in this chapter,[282] courts will not normally inquire into the adequacy of consideration, i.e., the relative values exchanged by the parties. That rationale, however, misses the mark since the question remains, was the detriment bargained for? Even though Ames clearly appears to be motivated by a desire to make a gift to her child, she also wants the payment of $25,000 from her child, i.e., the detriment to the promisee-child is something Ames desires in exchange for her promise. Numerous reasons may be hypothesized for this desire. She may not be able to afford a complete gift of the property, or, perhaps Ames is very wealthy and wants the child to pay $25,000 only for the purpose of ascertaining that the child develop a sense of responsibility in financial matters. Whatever her motivation, the fact that she insists upon the detriment from the child in exchange for the property indicates that the detriment is bargained-for.[283]

---

[278] RESTATEMENT 2d § 87 comment c. The parol evidence rule would not bar evidence that a fact recited in an integrated agreement is untrue. RESTATEMENT 2d § 218.

[279] The Texas Supreme Court adopted § 87(1) in 1464-Eight, Ltd. v. Joppich, 154 S. W. 3d 101 (2004) quoting from this treatise as well as others and noting that the authors of national treatises have generally endorsed ths approach.

[280] See Pasant v. Jackson Nat'l Life Ins. Co., 52 F.3d 94, 98 (5th Cir. 1995).

[281] It is conceivable that $25,000 could be nominal consideration to a multi-billionaire with a millionaire child in the sale of property worth millions of dollars.

[282] See supra § 60.

[283] See RESTATEMENT 2d § 71 comment c: "Even where both parties know that a transaction is in part a bargain and in part a gift, the element of bargain may nevertheless furnish consideration for the entire transaction." See Fritz v. Fritz, 2009 Iowa App. LEXIS 204 (2009) where parents conveyed property to a child under a contract that expressly included consideration and a gift. After citing this section and comment to Restatement 2d, the court states, "An altruistic motive may coexist with a valid legal contract, supported by consideration." (at *12).

The fact that the dominant motivation of Ames is gratuitous is also irrelevant. A promise may be induced by a number of motivations, including the motivation to make a gift. The principal desire of Ames may be to give the property to her child. If, however, she also wants the $25,000 payment in exchange for her promise, her promise is supported by consideration. As the RESTATEMENT 2d suggests, "Unless both parties know that the purported consideration is mere pretense, it is immaterial that the promisor's desire for the consideration is incidental to other objectives and even that the other party knows this to be so."[284] The motivations other than a desire for the detriment may be of an almost endless variety, i.e., they need not be gratuitous. At this point, one should recall the analogous situation involving the question of the motivation of an offeree who, with knowledge of an offer, performs the act requested in the offer. In the earlier exploration of that concept, we saw that such an offeree accepts the offer by performing the act, notwithstanding evidence that his motivation for performing it was dominantly for reasons other than his desire to accept the offer, so long as he still apparently intended to accept the offer by his performance.[285] Just as mixed motivation does not prevent acceptance of an offer, mixed motivation does not preclude a finding of bargained-for-exchange. Again, however, the detriment must, to some extent, induce the promise if consideration is to be found in support of the promise.

§ 63   CONSIDERATION IN CHARITABLE SUBSCRIPTION AGREEMENTS

When a promise is made to a charitable institution, e.g., a church, hospital, educational institution or similar institution, is such a promise supported by consideration? In most cases, it is clear that the typical promise to a charity is intended to be gratuitous, i.e., it is motivated, not by the desire to receive something in exchange, but rather by motives of generosity, moral duty, the hope of heavenly reward or some other aspiration which the promisee could not possibly provide.[286] It is, of course, possible that the promisor seeks recognition from his promise of a gift. In a famous opinion, Judge Cardozo reminds us that, "The longing for posthumous remembrance is an emotion not so weak as to justify us in saying that its gratification is a negligible good."[287] A particular promisor may, for example, combine a gratuitous motivation with a genuine desire to have a university building, a university chair or a hospital wing dedicated in his name. It is even possible that a promisor may make a subscription promise with no gratuitous motivation whatsoever, i.e., he or she would be exclusively concerned with a named memorial. If a charity or school promised to name something in exchange for the promise, a detriment is clearly present, and if it is bargained-for, even where there is an accompanying donative intention, there is consideration.[288] Courts look upon charities, schools and the like as institutions that perform useful public service.[289] It is, therefore, not remarkable that courts favor the discovery of a validation device to make the promise of the subscriber enforceable. While English courts took the strictly logical view that

---

[284] RESTATEMENT 2d § 81 comment b.

[285] *See supra* § 45[C].

[286] "[I]n the nature of charitable subscriptions, it is presupposed the promise is made as a gift and not in return for consideration." Salsbury v. Northwestern Bell Tel. Co., 221 N.W.2d 609, 612 (Iowa 1974).

[287] Allegheny College v. National Chautauqua County Bank, 246 N.Y. 369, 377, 159 N.E. 173, 176 (1927).

[288] The more liberal view of the Restatement 2d § 90(2), comment f, disregards mixed motives in enforcing charitable subscription promises.

[289] See *Salsbury*, note 286 *supra*, at 612.

such promises are gratuitous and, therefore, unenforceable in the normal case,[290] our courts have managed to discover one or another validation device to make such promises enforceable.[291] In seeking consideration, some courts have stretched to find an implied promise on the part of the charity to continue its humanitarian work[292] or to perpetuate the name of the donor in connection with a memorial fund she promised to establish.[293] Often, a subscription fund drive will identify the purpose of the drive, leading some courts to discover an implied promise by the charity to use the funds in accordance with the terms of the subscription.[294] Another imaginative effort may discover consideration in the mutual promises of subscribers, i.e., *A* subscribes in consideration of *B*'s promise which is consideration for *C*'s subscription and the like with the charity receiving the benefit as a donee beneficiary of the contract.[295] Beyond the fact that the typical subscriber is not bargaining for the promises of others, he is not making his promise to other subscribers. He is making his promise to the charity, which is a promisee, and not a third party beneficiary, of the mutual promises of others.[296]

Still another judicial initiative is found in those cases which enforce charitable subscription promises on the basis of promissory estoppel, i.e., the charity has relied on the promise(s) to its substantial detriment.[297] Whatever the merits of this theory generally, in a given situation it may be difficult to discover a substantial change of position on the part of the charity in reliance on one or more subscription promises.[298]

---

[290] *See* Governors of Dalhousie College v. Boutilier, 3 D.L.R. 593 [1934]; *In re* Hudson, 54 L.J. Ch. 811 [1885].

[291] "There can be no denying that the strong desire on the part of the American courts to favor charitable institutions has established a doctrine which once would have been looked upon as legal heresy. Doubtless this judicial attitude is largely responsible for the massive machinery of benevolence to be observed on every side. The reasons announced in justification of these holdings, however, have not always been technically satisfying." Danby v. Osteopathic Hosp. Ass'n of Del., 34 Del. Ch. 427, 104 A.2d 903, 907 (1954).

[292] I. & I. Holding Corp. v. Gainsburg, 276 N.Y. 427, 12 N.E.2d 532 (1938).

[293] *Allegheny College, supra* note 287.

[294] *In re* Estate of Couch, 170 Neb. 518, 103 N.W.2d 274 (1960); Central Maine Gen. Hosp. v. Carter, 125 Me. 191, 132 A. 417, 44 A.L.R. 1333 (1926).

[295] *See* Congregation B'Nai Sholom v. Martin, 382 Mich. 659, 173 N.W.2d 504 (1969). However, in Jordan v. Mount Sinai Hosp., 276 So. 2d 102 (Fla. Dist. Ct. App. 1973), *aff'd*, 290 So. 2d 484 (Fla. 1974), a recital that the promise was in consideration of the subscriptions of others was held ineffective. The consideration-among-subscribers theory may also be pursued in the "bellweather" situation of a promise by a major contributor whose promise is conditioned upon other subscribers matching the amount promised or reaching some other goal.

[296] Third party beneficiary contracts will be fully explored in a later chapter.

[297] Promissory estoppel, including the enforcement of charitable subscription promises based on promissory estoppel, is explored in § 67, *infra*.

[298] See *Salsbury*, note 286, *supra*, at 612. In the famous *Allegheny College* opinion, *supra* note 287, which undoubtedly prompted subsequent courts to use the detrimental reliance device to support charitable subscription promises, Judge Cardozo provides a *tour de force* of the application of detrimental reliance to such promises. He then finds, however, that there is no need to resort to the detrimental reliance device since the facts can be fitted within the traditional mold of consideration by finding an implied promise on the part of the College to forever promulgate the memorial fund in the name of the donor, Mary Yates Johnson. There is more than a suspicion that Judge Cardozo recognized a problem in the application of the detrimental reliance device to the facts of the case, i.e., that no particular reliance by the College could be shown. This may have induced him to find consideration which he discovers in typical Cardozo fashion, by creatively circumventing any lack of bargained-for-exchange and discovering an implied promise. The modern view suggested in § 90(2) of the Restatement 2d takes the position that the probability of reliance is sufficient. There is no requirement of demonstrating actual reliance (comment f). Whatever criticisms may be made of this opinion, its pursuit of the concepts of consideration, detrimental reliance, and other actual and possible validation devices constitute a premier pedagogical effort.

For many years, it has been an open secret that courts will typically discover means to enforce promises which they favor whether they are charitable subscription promises or marriage settlement promises.[299] Instead of resorting to myriad fictions, no matter how creative or entertaining, the high values of predictability and certainty long ago suggested the desirability of a candid recognition that such promises, though typically gratuitous, should be enforceable simply because institutions such as charities, schools and the institution of marriage are socially useful and desirable and that promises made to benefit and help perpetuate them should be enforced. The RESTATEMENT 2d has adopted this candid approach by recognizing charitable subscription or marriage settlement promises to be enforceable though there is no evidence that they induced any action or forbearance (much less bargained-for action or forbearance) on the part of the promisee.[300] They are enforced simply because it is desirable, as a matter of public policy, to enforce them. Some courts, however, reject this view and insist upon a finding of consideration or detrimental reliance to support a charitable subscription promise:

> Courts should act with restraint in respect to the public policy arguments endeavoring to sustain a mere charitable subscription. To ascribe consideration where there is none, or to adopt any other theory which affords charities a different legal rationale than other entities, is to approve fiction.[301]

§ 64   FORBEARANCE FROM SUIT AS CONSIDERATION — THE INVALID CLAIM

If bargained for, a promise to forbear suit on a valid claim is a detriment that clearly constitutes consideration for a counter-promise. If, however, the claim which is surrendered is groundless or invalid, the immediate tendency is to suggest that it cannot constitute consideration because it is a surrender of nothing of value in the eyes of the law. On the other hand, a promise to forego a lawsuit may be viewed as the surrender of a legal right since there are no impediments to the bringing of an action. Yet, examples leap to mind that suggest the folly of this notion. If Ames, knowing that she has no claim whatsoever against Barnes, promises to forego suing Barnes in exchange for Barnes' promise to pay Ames $1000, Barnes may be justifiably concerned that he will be forced to defend against even a groundless claim and may choose to promise Ames $1000. If such promises were enforceable, the knaves of any era would quickly discover and pursue such a form of legal extortion. A party may have the power to do something which he has no legal right to pursue simply because there is no effective method of prevention. It would hardly be sound policy to give effect to such an action

---

[299] See the estimable effort by Judge Cardozo in De Cicco v. Schweizer, 221 N.Y. 431, 117 N.E. 807 (1917), where he converts a promisee into a third party beneficiary, finds that the created promisee impliedly agreed with the real promisee not to rescind their agreement to marry, and discovers that detriment as having induced a marriage settlement promise by the father of the bride to pay an annuity to his married daughter notwithstanding clear evidence of the donative intent of the father-promisor. In the end, however, Judge Cardozo freely admits that he has developed the whole analysis to ascertain the enforcement of marriage settlement promises which the law clearly favors.

[300] RESTATEMENT 2d § 90, comment f: Where recovery is rested on reliance in such cases, a probability of reliance is enough. . . ." This approach has been expressly followed in Salsbury v. Northwestern Bell Tel. Co., 221 N.W.2d 609 (Iowa 1974). In Milligan v. Mueller, 2006 Iowa App. LEXIS 1056 (2006), while recognizing that Slasbury involved written pledges, the court held that enforcement of the promise is not relegated to written promises unless it is the type of promise that is required to be evidenced by a writing under the statute of frauds.

[301] Jordan v. Mt. Sinai Hosp. of Greater Miami, Inc., 276 So. 2d 102, 108 (Fla. Dist. Ct. App. 1974), quoted and followed in King v. Trustees of Boston University, 420 Mass. 52, 57, 647 N. E. 2d 1196, 1200 (1995).

when the party bringing it knows that her claim is groundless. If, however, the claimant honestly believes that her claim is valid, it is at least arguable that she has a right, rather than a mere power, to bring the action, whatever the merits of his case may later prove to be.

One of the principal reason courts exist is the necessity of having tribunals with power to determine the justice of claims honestly made. On this view of the matter, it can be persuasively argued that one who honestly believes he has a claim has a legal right to prosecute it and, if he bargains to surrenders that right, he suffers a legal detriment that will support a promise to pay for the surrender of that right. In light of this analysis, the evolution of the judicial reaction to promises to forbear suit on an invalid claim was not remarkable. There are three discernible stages of that development at common law. In the first stage, courts held that the surrender of a groundless claim could not be consideration under any circumstances.[302] Later, English courts began to hold that, if the surrendered claim was in fact doubtful, i.e., if either the facts or the law were in doubt, then refraining from suit would be consideration for a promise even though it should ultimately appear that the claim was groundless.[303] The third stage evolved in the latter part of the nineteenth century: one who surrenders a claim which he honestly believes he may enforce will constitute a bargained-for detriment.[304] Each of these stages in the evolution of the law in England is reflected in American decisions. A few American cases take the view that the surrender of a groundless claim, regardless of honest belief in the assertion of the claim, cannot constitute consideration.[305] The dominant view, however, is reflected in the FIRST RESTATEMENT OF CONTRACTS: forbearance to assert an invalid claim would constitute consideration only if the party asserting the claim had *both* an honest *and* reasonable belief in the possible validity of the claim and this view was widely followed.[306]

In what is sometimes regarded as the high water mark of the invalid claim cases, the plaintiff promised to forbear a bastardy prosecution in exchange for defendant's promise to pay the expenses of the birth and to provide for the support of a child plaintiff alleged the defendant fathered. After making some payments, the defendant refused to perform the remainder of his

---

[302] *See* Johnes v. Ashburnham, 4 East 455 [1804]; Loyd v. Lee, 1 Str. 94 [1718]; Barnard v. Simons, 1 Rolle's Abr. 26, pl. 39 [1616].

[303] Longridge v. Dorville, 5 B. & Ald. 117 [1821].

[304] *See* Miles v. New Zealand Alford Estate Co., 32 Ch. D. 266 [1886].

[305] See State *ex rel.* Ludwick v. Bryant, 237 Kan. 47, 697 P.2d 858 (1985), suggesting that the issue was not the validity of the debt but the possibility of enforcing it. If there is no possibility of enforcing a claim, both the claim and forbearance to press it are valueless and cannot constitute consideration. The court quotes Professor Corbin at 1 CORBIN § 140, at 600–01 for this view (1963 ed.). The Corbin statement, however, is merely descriptive of the position taken by some courts and is followed by, "Some of these decisions seem not in harmony with generally prevailing decisions. . . ." (601). Another well-known but much earlier opinion from the Supreme Court of Kansas, Ralston v. Mathew, 173 Kan. 550, 250 P.2d 841 (1952), relies upon earlier Kansas precedent in suggesting that forbearance to assert a claim that is reasonably doubtful and not obviously invalid, worthless, or frivolous constitutes consideration. Such a reasonably doubtful but ultimately invalid claim would constitute consideration. In the *Ludwick* case, however, even if a claim were valid, if it were not enforceable, forbearance to assert it could not be consideration. In Orange County Found. v. Irvine Co., 139 Cal. App. 3d 195, 188 Cal. Rptr. 552, 555 (1983), the court states, "Compromise of a wholly invalid claim is inadequate consideration to support a contract." The case, however, dealt with the appropriateness of a summary judgment where the pleadings alleged bad faith. Renney v. Kimberly, 211 Ga. 396, 86 S.E.2d 217 (1955), is the only recent American case clearly holding that forbearance to sue on a groundless claim cannot constitute consideration.

[306] FIRST RESTATEMENT § 76(b). This view finds wide support in the case law. *See, e.g.,* Union v. Terrible Herbst, Inc., 331 F.3d 735 (9th Cir. 2003); Wickman v. Kane, 136 Md. App. 554, 766 A. 2d 241 (2001); Agristor Credit Corp. v. Unruh, 1977 OK 215, 571 P.2d 1220 (1977); Intermodal Transp. Sys., Inc. v. Hucks Piggyback Serv., Inc., 30 N.C. App. 289, 226 S.E.2d 859 (1976).

promise because blood tests revealed that he could not have been the father. The plaintiff instituted bastardy proceedings and the defendant was acquitted because of the blood tests. The plaintiff then sought to enforce the defendant's promise and the court held the promise was supported by consideration since the forborne claim had been honestly asserted and was not frivolous, baseless, or vexatious.[307] While there was no question concerning the requirement of good faith, courts encountered considerable difficulty in articulating the objective standard of merit the claim had to meet. Instead of clinging to the requirement that the claim be "reasonable," courts resorted to negative characterizations such as "not obviously unfounded,"[308] or not "utterly groundless"[309] or not "wholly baseless or utterly unfounded."[310] The most candid judicial recognition of this difficulty is found in an opinion from a Missouri appellate court:

> It is difficult to reconcile the antinomous rules and statements which are applied to the 'doubtful claims' and to find the words which will exactly draw the line between the compromise . . . of an honestly disputed claim which has some fair element of doubt and is therefore to be regarded as consideration and . . . a claim, though honestly made, which is so lacking in substance and virility as to be entirely baseless. . . . We think we had best leave definitions alone, confident that, as applied to each individual case, the facts will make the thing apparent. But if we should make further effort to distinguish, we would say that if the claimant, *in good faith*, makes a mountain out of a mole hill the claim is 'doubtful.' But if there is no discernible mole hill in the beginning, then the claim has no substance.[311]

Though the statute of limitations had expired on a claim when the settlement agreement was made, the court held the settlement enforceable since forbearance to assert a claim constitutes consideration for a return promise if the claim is in fact doubtful because of uncertainty as to the facts or the law.[312] Even where a trial court has already determined a claim to be without merit at the time the parties agree upon a settlement of the claim, forbearance to appeal such a judgment constitutes consideration for the settlement.[313]

The RESTATEMENT 2d no longer requires a combination of good faith and some objective merit in the claim. Rather, if the claim (or defense) is doubtful in fact or law, *or* if the forbearing or surrendering party believes that the claim or defense may be valid, there is consideration.[314] If the claim was doubtful in fact or in law, there is no need to inquire into the subjective honesty of the forbearing party. If the invalidity of the claim should have been clear at the time it is

---

[307] Fiege v. Boehm, 210 Md. 352, 123 A.2d 316 (1956). This case is criticized, however, in Jordan v. Knafel, 378 Ill. App. 3d 219, 880 N. E. 2d 1061 (Ill. Ct. App. 2007) After proving that he was not the father of the child, Jordan sought rescission of his alleged promise to pay $5 million to Knafel in exchange for her promise to forbear a paternity action. The court noted that Knafel's failure to disclose her relations with another man constituted a misrepresentation or mistake which was a basic assumption on which the contract was made would be a basis for rescission of a contract with the plaintiff.

[308] Bullard v. Curry-Cloonan, 367 A.2d 127, 131 (D.C. 1976).

[309] Frasier v. Carter, 92 Idaho 79, 81, 437 P.2d 32, 34 (1968).

[310] Agristor Credit Corp. v. Unruh, 1977 OK 215, 571 P.2d 1220, 1224 (1977).

[311] Duncan v. Black, 324 S. W.2d 483, 486 (Mo. Ct. App. 1959).

[312] Union Oil Co. v. Terrible Herbst, Inc., 331 F.3d 735 (9th Cir.2003).

[313] Kalis v. Colgate-Palmolive Co., 272 Ill. Dec.367, 787 N. E. 2d 182 (Ill. Ct. App. 2003).

[314] RESTATEMENT 2d § 74(1)(a) and (b).

forborne or surrendered, an honest belief in the claim is still sufficient.[315] Courts have considered the reasonableness of the claim as a significant though not conclusive factor in determining the underlying requirement of good faith.[316] The RESTATEMENT 2d indicates that where the invalidity of the claim is obvious, such evidence may indicate that the party surrendering or forbearing suit on the claim knew that it was invalid and could not, therefore, honestly assert it.[317] Again, however, the significant change in the RESTATEMENT 2d is finding consideration for *either* an objectively (fact or law) doubtful claim *or* an honest belief that it may be determined to be valid without any objective validity in the claim. This view is a recognition of the natural evolution in the case law. Courts appear to focus on the honesty of the claimant while minimizing the requirement of an objective validity test with respect to the claim itself as manifested by their difficulty in attempting to articulate the standard to be applied to that requirement.[318] The RESTATEMENT 2d test suggests a heightened awareness of the strong policy in favor of compromise and settlement. A requirement that the forborne claim manifest some objective validity wars against that policy by permitting litigation of the compromise.[319]

It should be noted that some earlier cases took the position that actual forbearance, as contrasted with a promise to forbear, could not constitute consideration for a promise, i.e., it was not possible to have a "unilateral" contract in which the consideration consists of the forbearance itself.[320] The reason for this position is not entirely clear. It probably resulted from a misapprehension as to what, in fact, had been decided in certain cases — where the actual forbearance was, for other reasons, not consideration. If, for example, the promisor requests a promise to forbear as the exchange for his promise, it is clear that nothing short of a promise will consummate a contract.[321] Another type of case in which it is suggested that actual forbearance is not consideration occurs where the promisor hopes for forbearance but does not request it in exchange for his promise.[322] In this type of case, no contract results, not because actual forbearance cannot constitute consideration, but because, in this instance, the promise was, in fact, gratuitous. The RESTATEMENT 2d recognizes this difficulty in suggesting that, where the forbearance is temporary and it is contemplated that the claim will be asserted later, there may be a question of whether the forbearance was bargained for.[323] In general, however, there is no reason to question actual forbearance, if bargained for, any more than a promise to

---

[315] RESTATEMENT 2d § 74 comment b. See Denburg v. Parker Chapin Flattau & Klimpl, 82 N.Y.2d 375, 383, 624 N.E.2d 995, 1000 (1993).

[316] *See, e.g.*, Dick v. Dick, 167 Conn. 210, 355 A.2d 110 (1974).

[317] RESTATEMENT 2d § 74 comment b.

[318] Church of Bible Understanding v. Bill Swad Leasing Co., 2 Ohio App. 3d 382, 442 N.E.2d 78 (Ohio Ct. App. 1981).

[319] Dyer v. National By-Products, Inc., 380 N.W.2d 732, 735 (Iowa 1986) (adopting the RESTATEMENT 2d position and overruling contrary holdings). See also Matrix Fin. Services v. Dean, 288 Ga. App. 666, 655 S. E. 2d 290 (2007).

[320] *See, e.g*, Cowan v. Browne, 63 Mont. 82, 206 P. 432 (1922); Saunders v. Bank of Mecklenburg, 112 Va. 443, 71 S.E. 714 (1911); Smith v. Bibber, 82 Me. 34, 19 A. 89 (1889).

[321] *See, e.g.*, Lewis v. Siegman, 135 Or. 660, 296 P. 51 (1931); Sellars v. Jones, 164 Ky. 458, 175 S.W. 1002 (1915); Strong v. Sheffield, 144 N.Y. 392, 39 N.E. 330 (1895); Miles v. New Zealand Alford Estate Co., 32 Ch. D. 266 [1886].

[322] "Forbearance, at request, is a valid consideration. Not so in the absence of both request and promise to forbear." Shaw v. Philbrick, 129 Me. 259, 262, 151 A. 423, 424 (1930) (citation omitted). *See also* Schroyer v. Thompson, 262 Pa. 282, 105 A. 274, 2 A.L.R. 1567 (1918); J. H. Queal & Co. v. Peterson, 138 Iowa 514, 116 N.W. 593 (1908).

[323] RESTATEMENT 2d § 74 comment d.

forbear as consideration.[324] Finally, in later sections of this chapter we will examine the validation device popularly known as promissory estoppel where promises are enforced because they induce detrimental reliance on the part of the promisee though the reliance does not induce the promise, i.e., there is no consideration because the promise was not bargained for. Even though forbearance is not bargained for in a given situation, a promise inducing such forbearance may be enforceable on the basis of promissory estoppel.[325]

§ 65   THE PRE-EXISTING DUTY RULE

[A]   The Basic Doctrine

A promise to perform a duty under an existing contract cannot be consideration for a return promise because the promisor is already bound to perform that promise. He has a pre-existing duty to do what he is promising to do.[326] If, for example, an employee refuses to perform his contractual duty unless he receives additional compensation or if a seller of goods refuses to deliver the goods unless it receives a higher price, a promise to pay the additional amount lacks all of the traditional elements of consideration. There is no benefit to the promisor who is already entitled to the counter performance and there is no detriment to the promisee who is already under a pre-existing duty to perform. There can be no bargained-for-exchange since there is nothing to exchange.[327] There may be an economic benefit to the promisor in avoiding the trouble and expense of litigation. Yet, there can be no recognized benefit to the promisor or detriment to the promisee. Otherwise, anyone who knows that the other party to the contract would face economic and other difficulties if the promisor refused to perform absent additional consideration would be able to exact an enforceable promise to pay additional consideration before performing his contractual duty. The pre-existing duty rule, therefore, provides an effective defense against such extorted promises.

The best-known case involving the refusal of employees to perform their contractual duties absent additional compensation is *Alaska Packers Ass'n v. Domenico*, where employees were hired to fish for salmon in Alaska. Upon arrival, they refused to perform and threatened to leave unless their wages were doubled. The employees knew the employer could not find

---

[324] Thus, in *In re* All Star Feature Corp., 232 F. 1004 (D.N.Y. 1916), it is said, "Forbearance, even without an agreement to forbear, will serve as a consideration, if it be completed." *See also* Veilleux v. Merrill Lynch Relocation Mgmt., Inc., 226 Va. 440, 309 S.E.2d 595 (1983); Ruegg v. Fairfield Sec. Corp., 308 N.Y. 313, 125 N.E.2d 585 (1955); McDonald Bros. Co. v. Koltes, 155 Minn. 24, 192 N.W. 109 (1923); Dillon v. Lineker, 266 F. 688 (9th Cir. 1920); Fullerton v. Provincial Bank of Ireland, A.C. 309 [1903]. RESTATEMENT 2d § 74 comment d.

[325] RESTATEMENT 2d § 74 comment d.

[326] Contempo Design, Inc. v. Chicago & Northeast Ill. Dist. Council of Carpenters, 226 F.3d 535, 550 (7th Cir. 2000), *cert. denied*, 121 S. Ct. 776, 148 L. Ed. 2d 674 (2001).

[327] A classic exposition of this analysis occurred in a case where an architect (Jungenfeld) refused to proceed with work under his contract unless the owner of the property (Wainwright) paid additional compensation. Faced with the necessity of completing the work, Wainwright acceded to Jungenfeld's demands. The court states, "It is urged upon us . . . that this was a new contract. New in what? Jungenfeld was bound by his contract to design and supervise this building. Under the new promise he was not to do anything more or anything different. What benefit was to accrue to Wainwright. He was to receive the same service from Jungenfeld under the new that Jungenfeld was bound to tender under the original contract. What loss, trouble or inconvenience could result to Jungenfeld that he had not already assumed? No amount of metaphysical reasoning can change the plain fact that Jungenfeld took advantage of Wainwright's necessities, and extorted the promise of [additional compensation]." Lingenfelder v. Wainwright Brewery Co., 103 Mo. 578, 592, 15 S.W. 844, 848 (1891).

substitutes in time for the salmon fishing season. Faced with this adhesive choice, the employer agreed to the fishermen's demands but subsequently refused to perform that promise. Recognizing the coercion in such a transaction, the court relied upon the pre-existing duty rule in finding no consideration to support the promise to pay additional compensation.[328] The result can also be justified on the basis of duress which removes volition from the promisor.[329] The pre-existing duty rule also protects employers or the public against failures of performance absent additional incentives. Thus, employees of a bank[330] or a police department[331] who provide information requested in a reward offer are performing their pre-existing duties rather than providing consideration for the reward promise.[332] Where a party promises to forbear the assertion of a claim that has no basis in fact or in law, there can be no question that such a promise lacks consideration to support a counter-promise.[333] Similarly, a promise to perform ordinary marital obligations will not constitute consideration for a counter-promise.[334]

[1]   Criticism of the Pre-Existing Duty Rule

Notwithstanding the continued use of the pre-existing duty rule in such cases, it has been severely criticized for many years as "one of the relics of antique law which should have been discarded long ago."[335] It is important to compare the effect of the rule as a bar to unfair pressure as contrasted with the operation of the rule as a technical constraint to the fulfillment of reasonable expectations. If a builder threatens to stop construction unless the owner agrees to pay additional compensation, the owner's promise to pay the additional amount will not be enforced and the rationale supporting the holding will be a classic pre-existing duty rule analysis, i.e., the builder is only promising to do what he had a pre-existing duty to perform. The owner is receiving nothing for his promise, but makes the promise because of the practical problems of delay and litigation he would face in pursuing his legal rights against the builder. The application of the pre-existing duty rule in such a case suggests a desirable purpose, again, the prevention of extorted promises. If, however, the facts are changed to place the builder in a reasonable, good faith posture, the application of the rule is not easily justified. Suppose, for example, the builder encounters what has come to be called an unanticipated difficulty, e.g., an

---

[328] 117 F. 99 (9th Cir. 1902). *See Contempo Design*, note 326 at 549–550, relying on *Alaska Packers* and citing additional cases in support. *See also* Argeros & Co. v. Commonwealth, Dep't of Transp., 67 Pa. Commw. 531, 447 A.2d 1065 (1982) (alleged promise to pay painter additional compensation for painting bridge); Palmer v. Safe Auto Sales, Inc., 114 Misc. 2d 964, 452 N.Y.S.2d 995 (Civ. Ct. 1982) (promise to pay additional consideration for a new car was not supported by consideration); Garrett v. Mathews, 474 F. Supp. 594 (N.D. Ala. 1979) (promise of college teacher to do only what he was previously bound to do under his contract was not consideration), *aff'd*, 625 F.2d 658 (5th Cir. 1980).

[329] *See* Rissman v. Rissman, 213 F.3d 381, 387 (7th Cir. 2000).

[330] *See* Denney v. Reppert, 432 S.W.2d 647 (Ky. 1968).

[331] *See* Slattery v. Wells Fargo Armored Serv. Corp., 366 So. 2d 157 (Fla. Dist. Ct. App. 1979).

[332] A law enforcement officer out of his jurisdiction, however, has no pre-existing duty in another jurisdiction. His performance, therefore, constitutes consideration for the promise. *See Denney v. Reppert, supra* note 330.

[333] Agristor Credit Corp. v. Unruh, 571 P.2d 1220 (Okla. 1977) (promise to forego disruption of a foreclosure sale where promisors had no claim doubtful in fact or in law). RESTATEMENT 2d § 73.

[334] Earp v. Earp, 57 N.C. App. 194, 290 S.E.2d 739 (1982). *See also* Altman v. Munns, 82 N.C. App. 102, 345 S.E.2d 419 (1986) (separation agreement required defendant to pay for his children's college expenses and no distinction was made between private and public college; therefore, promise to pay private college tuition was not consideration for modification of separation agreement).

[335] Rye v. Phillips, 203 Minn. 567, 569, 282 N.W. 459, 460, 119 A.L.R. 1120 (1938).

unanticipated subsoil condition will make it impossible for the builder to complete the job without considerable financial hardship. Not only will the builder fail to make a profit on the job; he will lose a considerable sum and the situation does not permit him to be legally excused.[336] If the owner promises to pay additional compensation to the builder under these circumstances and, upon completion of the work, the owner refuses to make that payment, should that promise be enforced? There is no consideration for the subsequent promise of the owner. He is receiving no more than he should have received under the pre-existing contract since the risk of the subsoil condition was on the builder. Yet, when compared with the illustration involving an extorted promise, there is more than a plausible argument that the pre-existing duty rule should not bar enforcement of the owner's promise to pay the additional amount to the builder. There is no unfair pressure or coercion in the second illustration and the objectively demonstrable reason for the owner's promise to pay constitutes a fair and equitable basis for enforcement notwithstanding the lack of consideration.[337] A strict application of the pre-existing duty rule would preclude the enforcement of the promise. Later in this section we will consider how the rule may be avoided in this situation.

Other situations make the application of the pre-existing duty rule questionable. For example, if merchants agree upon a modification of their contract in good faith and the modification lacks consideration, the refusal to enforce the modification may be viewed as an unnecessary technical bar to an otherwise desirable modification.[338] Another situation involves a promise by a stranger to a pre-existing contract. If, for example, Ames promises to pay $1000 to Barnes if Barnes will perform an act which Barnes is already bound to perform under a contract with Smith, the pre-existing duty rule will prevent the enforcement of Ames' promise since Barnes had a pre-existing duty to perform, albeit that duty was owed to Smith. Yet, there is little probability of coercion or other unfair pressure on the promisor, Ames, in such a case. The application of the rule in these circumstances may also be avoided.[339] The pre-existing duty rule will also prevent the enforcement of a promise by a creditor to permit her debtor to pay a matured debt over a period of time or to pay a lesser sum than the amount owed since the creditor is receiving nothing for her promise.

Dissatisfaction with the application of the rule in these and other circumstances, however, has led courts to search for some additional detriment, *no matter how slight*, to discover consideration to enforce the promise.[340] The fact that the additional detriment was not bargained-for is of little concern to a court seeking to circumvent the pre-existing duty rule to enforce a promise that it believes should be enforced.[341] Other fictions have been employed to circumvent the rule. One of the methods of discharging a contract is a contract of rescission where the parties to an executory contract surrender their rights against each other. Some

---

[336] Mere unanticipated difficulty does not excuse a party's performance of his contractual duty. *See* Ramco Roofing & Supply Co. v. Kaminsky, 156 Ga. App. 708, 275 S.E.2d 764 (1980); Codell Constr. Co. v. Commonwealth of Ky., 566 S.W.2d 161 (Ky. Ct. App. 1977). The doctrines of impossibility of performance or commercial impracticability which can excuse performance will be discussed in a subsequent chapter.

[337] *See* Restatement 2d § 89 comment b.

[338] UCC § 2-209 comment 1.

[339] Restatement 2d § 73 comment d.

[340] *See* West India Indus., Inc. v. Tradex, Tradex Petr. Servs., 664 F.2d 946, 950 (5th Cir. 1981); Howarth v. First Nat'l Bank of Anchorage, 596 P.2d 1164 (Alaska 1979).

[341] One of the recognized exceptions to the pre-existing duty rule "is for the promisee to undertake to do something in addition to what he already is obliged to do." Contempo Design, Inc. v. Chicago & Northeast Ill. Dist. Council of Carpenters, 226 F.3d 535, 550 (7th Cir. 2000), *cert. denied*, 121 S. Ct. 776, 148 L. Ed. 2d 674 (2001).

courts have avoided the pre-existing duty rule by finding a simultaneous rescission and modification of the original contract which, as will be seen, is an analytical impossibility.

It is important to consider these and other direct and indirect attacks on the pre-existing duty rule.

[B]   Payment of Debt as Consideration — Disputed (Unliquidated) Claims and the Application of Uniform Commercial Code § 1-207

[1]   Liquidated (Undisputed) Debts

At a very early time, it was said that payment of a lesser sum in satisfaction of a greater sum cannot satisfy the entire debt owed.[342] Ever since that time it has been quite uniformly held that if Ames owes Barnes $1000 which is payable at a stated time and, at the time the debt is mature, Barnes agrees to accept $500 in full satisfaction of the undisputed debt of $1000, there is no consideration to support Barnes' promise.[343] This is popularly known as the doctrine of *Foakes v. Beer*.[344] Whatever criticism that doctrine has engendered,[345] an agreement to discharge a debt is, like any other agreement, in need of a validation device and there is no consideration in such an agreement. Even though it may be necessary to resort to the trouble and expense of litigation to enforce the payment of a debt, it can hardly be admitted that the debtor suffers any detriment that should be recognized as consideration in paying what she already owes, or that the creditor gets any benefit that could be recognized as consideration in being spared the expense and trouble of a lawsuit. While the debtor can, in fact, refuse payment, she has no right to do so and the purported surrender of such an illusory right is a surrender of nothing. There is no benefit to the creditor and no detriment to the debtor.

Notwithstanding the lack of consideration in such agreements, dissatisfaction with the pre-existing duty rule has made courts astute in discovering some additional detriment, no matter how insignificant,[346] beyond that which the debtor was already bound to perform, and

---

[342] In *Pinnel's Case*, 5 Coke Rep. 117a, 77 Eng. Rep. 237 [1600], the statement appeared ". . . that payment of a lesser sum on the day in satisfaction of a greater, cannot be any satisfaction for the whole, because it appears to the judges that by no possibility a lesser sum can be a satisfaction to the plaintiff for a greater sum." It may be doubted, however, whether Pinnel's case intended to raise or decide any question of consideration, although it has generally been so interpreted by later authorities. *See* Gold, *The Present Status of the Rule in Pinnel's Case*, 30 KY. L.J. 72 and 187 (1941).

[343] In Claybrook v. SOL Building Materials Corp., 2004 Bankr. LEXIS 520 (D. Del.2004), the court rejected the bankrupt's claim that it had given "new value" when it paid an undisputed debt with 90 days of bankruptcy which made the payment a preferential transfer under the bankruptcy act. As used in the Act, "new value" was intended to codify the usual rules of consideration and payment of an antecedent debt does not constitute consideration.

[344] 9 App. Cas. 605 [1884].

[345] *See, e.g.*, Ferson, The Rule in Foakes v. Beer, 31 YALE L.J. 15 (1921). A few cases repudiate the doctrine. *See* Winter Wolff & Co. v. Co-op. Lead & Chem. Co., 261 Minn. 199, 111 N.W.2d 461, 465–67 (1961) (influenced by the dictum in Rye v. Phillips, 203 Minn. 567, 569, 282 N.W. 459, 460, 119 A.L.R. 1120 (1938)). *See also* Watkins & Son v. Carrig, 91 N.H. 459, 21 A.2d 591, 138 A.L.R. 131 (1941).

[346] This circumvention of the pre-existing duty rule has been an open secret for many years. For example, in Levine v. Blumenthal, 117 N.J.L. 23, 186 A. 457 (N.J. Super. Ct. 1936), the court notes that any consideration for the promise, however insignificant, satisfies the pre-existing duty rule. For example, a promise to pay part of a debt before maturity, to pay the debt at a different place than required by the original contract, to pay in some form of property other than money as required by the original contract, or similar change in the original duty of the promisee would be sufficient.

to treat that detriment as consideration. If, for example, a debtor pays the debt before it is due,[347] or at a place other than that in which it is in terms payable,[348] or pays in a different medium or provides some insignificant additional performance in addition to the payment of the amount already owed,[349] consideration is usually found to exist. While a "legal" detriment can be found in such cases, it is often inserted not as a bargained-for exchange but as a formality designed to make the promise binding.[350] If the new performance is bargained-for, consideration is clearly present.[351]

[2]   Unliquidated (Disputed) Claims

Where the debt is unliquidated, i.e., where the amount involved has not been agreed upon or where it cannot be precisely determined, or where the debt is disputed in good faith by the debtor, a different analysis is required. Consideration can be found in these cases in the payment of part or all that is claimed by the creditor. Where an honest dispute exists in regard

---

The RESTATEMENT 2d § 73 comment c admits that, "Slight variations of circumstance are commonly held to take a case out of the rule, particularly where the parties have made an equitable adjustment in the course of performance of a continuing contract. . . ." Other cases indicating that even slight, additional consideration is sufficient to avoid the pre-existing duty rule include Betterton v. First Interstate Bank, N.A., 800 F.2d 732 (8th Cir. 1986) (withholding payment from pay check was new consideration though the amount was unchanged); Leone v. Precision Plumbing & Heating, 121 Ariz. 514, 515, 591 P.2d 1002, 1003 (Ct. App. 1979) (any new obligation, "even if the new obligation involves almost the same performance as the pre-existing duty," is sufficient).

[347] Codner v. Siegel, 246 Ga. 368, 271 S.E.2d 465 (1980); Princeton Coal Co. v. Dorth, 191 Ind. 615, 133 N.E. 386 (1921); Sonnenberg v. Riedel, 16 Minn. 83 (1870).

[348] Jones v. Perkins, 29 Miss. 139, 64 Am. Dec. 136 (1855); Harper v. Graham, 20 Ohio 105 (1851). See, however, *Foster County State Bank v. Lammers*, 117 Minn. 94, 134 N.W. 501 (1912), where the court held that if a debt is not paid at maturity, the creditor has a legal right to collect it wherever he can find the debtor regardless of the place stipulated for payment in the contract. See also Vanbergen v. St. Edmonds Properties Ltd., 2 K.B. 223 [1933], holding that payment at a different place was merely a favor, i.e., the different place of payment had not been bargained-for as the price of the promise and did not, therefore, constitute consideration.

[349] Betterton v. First Interstate Bank, N.A., 800 F.2d 732 (8th Cir. 1986) (payments deducted from pay check was enough to support the promise); Raedeke v. Gibraltar Sav. & Loan Ass'n, 10 Cal. 3d 665, 111 Cal. Rptr. 693, 698, 517 P.2d 1157, 1162 (1974) (promise to find suitable buyer). In a number of cases, the debtor has given a check or note for part of the debt. In American Seeding Mach. Co. v. Baker, 55 Ind. App. 625, 104 N.E. 524 (1914), and Goddard v. O'Brien, 9 Q.B.D. 37 [1882], giving a check for part of the debt was held to be consideration. However, in Shanley v. Koehler, 80 A.D. 566, 80 N.Y.S. 679 (1st Dep't 1903), *aff'd*, 178 N.Y. 556, 70 N.E. 1109 (1904), the debtor's note for part of the debt was not consideration. In Vaughn v. Robbins, 254 Mass. 35, 149 N.E. 677, 41 A.L.R. 1488 (1925), the debtor gave the check of a firm of which he was a member for part of the debt which the court upheld as consideration. In Jaffray v. Davis, 124 N.Y. 164, 26 N.E. 351 (1891), the giving of a note and chattel mortgage as security for part of the debt was upheld as consideration. UCC § 3-408 indicates that ". . . no consideration is necessary for an instrument or obligation thereon given in payment or as security for an antecedent obligation of any kind."

[350] The RESTATEMENT 2d would characterize such arrangements as "pretense" since they are not bargained-for (§ 71 comment b). It later suggests that "Any payment . . . at an earlier time, or in a different medium from that required by the duty, is consideration . . . if the difference in performance is part of what is requested and given in exchange for the promise." *See* § 73 comment c ill. 7. Statements in the case law to the effect that anything new, no matter how slight, will operate as consideration, seem to ignore the bargained-for element.

[351] Where additional loans to a financially distressed company are conditioned upon modification of the original contract, the promise is supported by consideration. American Hosp. Supply Corp. v. Hospital Prods., Ltd., 780 F.2d 589 (7th Cir. 1986). If the creditor agrees to extend the maturity of the debt with the understanding that interest will continue during the extension, consideration is present since the creditor bargains for the additional interest that he would not have received had the debt been paid at the original maturity date. *See* Adamson v. Bosick, 82 Colo. 309, 259 P. 513 (1927).

to the amount owed,[352] the liability itself,[353] or even the method of payment,[354] no legal duty arises until the question of amount, liability or method has been determined. If, for example, services have been performed or goods have been delivered with no prior agreement as to price and the parties have an honest dispute over the amount owed, if the debtor pays a definite amount, she is surrendering her right to pay a lesser amount if the matter had been adjudicated. The creditor may be receiving more than he would have received after adjudication. Whether either party actually received more or less than he or she would have received had the matter been adjudicated will never be known. The mutual surrender of rights to receive more or pay less, however, are detriments which constitute consideration for the mutual promises of the parties to pay and receive the "settled" amount.[355]

[3]   "Payment in Full": Accord and Satisfaction — Uniform Commercial Code Section 1-207 — Uncashed Check

Debtors often attempt to settle good faith, disputed claims by tendering a check in an amount the debtor believes he owes, marking the check "payment in full" or similar phrase. Such a tender constitutes an offer by the debtor to settle the disputed claim with the intention of putting the creditor to the choice of returning, destroying or cashing the check. If the creditor cashes the check, the common law treated this act as an acceptance of the debtor's offer. The resulting contract is called an "accord and satisfaction," which is a contract under which an obligee agrees to accept a stated performance in satisfaction of the obligor's existing duty.[356] An agreement to settle a prior unliquidated or disputed obligation is an accord. The "satisfaction" is the performance of the accord. When the creditor cashes a check marked "payment in full" tendered by a debtor where the obligation is unliquidated or honestly disputed, the accord and satisfaction occur simultaneously and the duty of the debtor is discharged.[357] Consideration is found in the debtor's payment of a sum which may or may not be owed and the creditor's surrender of a claim which may be greater than the debt. As we have seen earlier, if the amount owed is neither unliquidated nor honestly disputed, there could be no consideration for the payment of a lesser sum than the definite amount owed. Thus, if the creditor cashed a check for an amount less than a liquidated, undisputed debt, though the

---

[352] *See* Nowicki Constr. Co. v. Panar Corp., N.V., 342 Pa. Super. 8, 492 A.2d 36 (1985); Air Power, Inc. v. Omega Equip. Corp., 54 Md. App. 534, 459 A.2d 1120 (1983); Ruble Forest Prods., Inc. v. Lancer Mobile Homes of Or., Inc., 269 Or. 315, 524 P.2d 1204 (1974).

[353] *See* Koedding v. N.B. West Contracting Co., 596 S.W.2d 744 (Mo. Ct. App. 1980).

[354] Gottlieb v. Charles Scribner's Sons, 232 Ala. 33, 166 So. 685 (1936).

[355] *See* RESTATEMENT 2d § 74 comment c. Where part of a claim is undisputed and the other part is disputed, payment by the debtor of the undisputed part is generally held to be consideration for the creditor's promise to release the debtor as to the balance. *See* RESTATEMENT 2d § 74 ill. 6. Where there are two distinct claims, although both arise from a single contract and one is liquidated, its payment is not consideration to support a discharge of the other, unliquidated claim. Lippard v. Dupont Garage Co., 63 U.S. App. D.C. 229, 71 F.2d 350 (1934); Jefferson Standard Life Ins. Co. v. Lightsey, 49 F.2d 586 (4th Cir. 1931); Commercial Union Assurance Co. v. Creek Cotton Oil Co., 96 Okla. 189, 221 P. 499 (1923). The RESTATEMENT 2d is in accord with this position, but adds that where there are no circumstances of unfair pressure or economic coercion and the disputed item is closely related to an undisputed item, the two should be treated as constituting a single, unliquidated claim permitting payment of the amount admittedly due to constitute consideration for a promise to surrender the entire claim. RESTATEMENT 2d § 74 comment c.

[356] RESTATEMENT 2d § 281(1). *See* Cook & Franke, S.C. v. Meilman, 136 Wis. 2d 434, 402 N.W.2d 361 (Ct. App. 1987); Dyke Indus., Inc. v. Waldrop, 16 Ark. App. 125, 697 S.W.2d 936 (1985); Charleston Urban Renewal Auth. v. Stanley, 176 W. Va. 591, 346 S.E.2d 740 (1985).

[357] *See* RESTATEMENT 2d § 281 ill. 6.

check was marked "payment in full," the debtor's duty to pay the remainder of the liquidated or undisputed obligation would not be discharged.

Creditors are rarely pleased to receive a check in an amount less than that which they believe they are owed marked "payment in full." Their desire to receive the proceeds of the check is strong, but they also wish to preserve what they perceive to be their right to collect the full amount of the claim as they perceive it. To avoid the Hobson's choice of not cashing the check or taking less than the creditor believes it is owed, a creditor may resort to such tactics as deleting the phrase, "payment in full," or similar phrase. The erasure or deletion of the phrase, however, will not affect the legal characterization of the transaction, i.e., the cashing of the check after the deletion of the phrase will still constitute an accord and satisfaction — the underlying obligation will be discharged.[358]

In their quest to discover a way to receive the proceeds of the check without surrendering the remainder of the disputed claim, creditors discovered a section of the Uniform Commercial Code that arguably allowed them to achieve this result by inserting a phrase such as "without prejudice" or "under protest."[359] Courts were forced to confront the issue of whether Section 1-207 of the UCC was designed to change the common law of accord and satisfaction with respect to checks marked "payment in full."

While most of the courts addressing this issue found that Section 1-207 was not intended to have this effect,[360] there was a contrary view.[361] The issue was resolved through a 1990 amendment to 1-207 that added a subsection stating that the section did not apply to an accord and satisfaction.[362] The amendment was necessary to assure consistency with revised UCC Section 3-311 which governs an accord and satisfaction through the use of a negotiable instrument, such as a check. Thus, subject to certain exceptions, where a party in *good faith*[363] tenders a negotiable instrument *conspicuously*,[364] stating that it is tendered in full satisfaction of an *unliquidated* claim[365] or a *bona fide dispute*,[366] and the claimant obtains payment of the instrument, the claim is discharged.[367]

---

[358] *See* Wong v. Paisner, 14 Mass. App. Ct. 923, 436 N.E.2d 990 (1982).

[359] The original version of UCC § 1-207 read as follows: A party who with explicit reservation of rights performs or promises performance or assents to performance in a manner demanded or offered by the other party does not thereby prejudice the rights reserved. Such words as "without prejudice," "under protest" or the like are sufficient.

[360] The opinion by Chief Justice Peters of the Connecticut Supreme Court provides a comprehensive analysis in County Fire Door Corp. v. C. F. Wooding Co., 202 Conn. 277, 520 A.2d 1028 (1987).

[361] See Horn Waterproofing Corp. v. Bushwick Iron & Steel Co., 66 N.Y.2d 321, 488 N.E.2d 56 (1985).

[362] The original § 1-207 is now subsection (1) while subsection (2) makes it inapplicable to an accord and satisfaction.

[363] "Good faith" in relation to negotiable instruments requires not only honesty in fact, but the observance of reasonable commercial standards of fair dealing. UCC § 3-103 (a)(4). Where the good faith element was absent, the court found that there was no accord and satisfaction. Commonwealth of Virginia v. Wills, 1995 Va. Cir. LEXIS 1450, 27 U.C.C. Rep. Serv. 2d (CBC) 926 (Va. Cir. Ct. 1995).

[364] See New Hampshire Boring, Inc. v. Adirondack Environmental Assocs., Inc., 762 A.2d 1036 (N.H. 2000), which repeats the test for "conspicuous" as whether attention can be reasonably be expected to be called to certain language as stated in UCC § 1-201(10) comment 10, and holds that a letter stating that an enclosed check was tendered in full satisfaction met the "conspicuous" requirement. Typically, "full satisfaction" statements are placed on the check, itself.

[365] Where the claim is liquidated, i.e., not subject to an honest dispute, there can be no accord and satisfaction. See Employers Workers' Compensation Ass'n v. W.P. Indus., 925 P.2d 1225, 1229 (Okla. Ct. App. 1996).

[366] McMahon Food Corp. v. Burger Dairy Co., 103 F.3d 1307, 1313 (7th Cir. 1996): "[T]here can be no accord and satisfaction unless there was an 'honest dispute.' . . ."

[367] UCC §§ 3-311(a) and (b).

To avoid an inadvertent accord and satisfaction, if an organization proves that within a reasonable time prior to the tender of the instrument the organization sent a conspicuous statement to the debtor requiring any such instrument in full satisfaction to be sent to a designated person, office or place and the instrument was not received by that person or at that location, the debt would not be discharged.[368] Similarly, even where the creditor has not designated a person, office or place to which such instruments are to be sent, if the claimant tenders repayment of the amount of the check within 90 days after payment of the instrument, the claim is not discharged.[369] Neither of these exceptions applies, however, where the claimant or its agent had actual knowledge that the instrument was tendered in full satisfaction of the claim and, with such knowledge, obtained payment of the instrument.[370] If an accord and satisfaction is not pursued through the use of a negotiable instrument, the law of contract applies. Regardless of whether § 3-311 applies, however, § 1-207 has no application to an accord and satisfaction.[371]

Uncashed Check. Where a check "in full satisfaction" is received by the creditor but not cashed, if the check is held for an inordinate time without notifying the debtor that the creditor finds the amount unacceptable, a court may find that the debt was discharged. The key factor, however, is not the length of time the uncashed check is held, but the length of time it is held before notifying the debtor that the creditor does not accept the check in satisfaction of the claim.[372]

[C]   Rescission — Two Parties and Three Parties

If an employee provides highly valuable service in a particular job at a particular time, his threat to breach may induce the promise of additional compensation by the employer. The employer may have weighed the advantages and disadvantages of this commitment. The employee may have been underpaid and the additional compensation may equal fair compensation for the employee's valuable services. The employer may perceive the continuation of the employment as an efficient use of resources. Regardless of these justifications, there is no consideration to support the employer's new promise. The inescapable fact remains that the new promise is not induced by any new consideration, i.e., there is no benefit to the promisor (employer) nor any detriment to the promisee (employee) that could possibly be called the surrender of a legal right because the law must regard the employee's continued performance of his contract, even if undersalaried in terms of the market value of his service, as a duty. The employee has no more "right" to breach that duty than he does to commit a tort. The promise to perform his duty is the quintessential

---

[368] UCC § 3-311(c)(1).

[369] UCC § 3-311(c)(2). Comment 6 to this section explains that organizations are sometimes reluctant to notify a debtor of a particular person, office or place to which such instruments should be sent because it may result in confusion and consequent loss of the benefit of rapid processing of checks. Thus, an organization may prevent an inadvertent accord and satisfaction by tendering repayment of the amount of the check that had been tendered in full satisfaction of the claim.

[370] UCC § 3-311(d).

[371] UCC § 1-207 comment 3.

[372] Wagner v. Foremost Bldgs., Inc., 2009 Wisc. App. LEXIS 913 (Ct. App. 2009) (holding the uncashed check for more than ten months would not support a summary judgment that the debt was discharged. where there was evidence of the creditor's notification that the check was unacceptable within weeks of its receipt.).

illustration of the promise to perform a pre-existing duty.[373] We have explored efforts to circumvent the pre-existing duty rule in other contexts and the effort to circumvent it in this context is no exception.

To permit the enforcement of the agreement modifying the salary of the employee without any modification of his duties, it may be suggested that it is possible to view the pre-existing duty as consideration for the new agreement so as to encourage the enforcement of modifications.[374] It would have been preferable if these courts had simply found the modifying promise enforceable without consideration. The fiction is absurd.

Another method is much more imaginative but equally flawed. Before this device can be seen for what it is, it is important to understand the concept of rescission. *Rescission* is a term that is so widely used that it is subject to considerable ambiguity. Ideally, it should be relegated to its essential purpose. *Rescission* is a contract between parties already bound to an executory contract who agree to surrender their rights against each other with the purpose of discharging their unperformed obligations under the existing contract. A rescission is like any other contract, i.e., it must be supported by a validation device. If *A* and *B* have an unperformed (executory) contract and decide that it would be in their mutual interest to discharge that contract, by surrendering their rights against each other, they each suffer a detriment and each receive a benefit that is bargained for in their release of each other from the remaining duties under their contract.[375]

If the parties agree to rescind their original contract, they are free from any obligations to each other and may enter into another contract on any terms they choose. This scenario includes three separate contracts — the first contract that is still executory, the second contract of rescission that discharges the first contract,[376] and the third contract allowing for new (additional) compensation. If Barnes has agreed to work for Ames at $1000 per week and is grumbling about his salary, the parties could enter into a contract of rescission under which Ames releases Barnes from his duties and Barnes does the same for Ames. At that point, the parties are entirely free from any legal duties toward each other. Since Barnes's former legal duty to work for Ames has been extinguished, Ames' promise to pay Barnes $2000 per week under a new contract is supported by consideration. Similarly, Ames could offer Barnes $500 per week and, if Barnes accepted, the new (third) contract would evidence consideration. While there is nothing in these arrangements violating any prescript of consideration, another arrangement that may superficially appear to be identical is fatally flawed.

If Ames and Barnes conclude a rescission contract and *simultaneously* enter into the new contract on terms different from the terms of the first (original) contract of employment, it is impossible to discover consideration to support Ames' promise to pay more ($2000 per week)

---

[373] Herremans v. Carrera Designs, 157 F.3d 1118, 1122 (7th Cir. 1998).

[374] This is sometimes called the "Wisconsin fiction." *See* Mid-Century, Ltd. v. United Cigar-Whelan Stores Corp., 109 F. Supp. 433 (D.D.C. 1953); Holly v. First Nat'l Bank, 218 Wis. 259, 260 N.W. 429 (1935). See criticism of this position in Note, 39 CORNELL L.Q. 114 (1953).

[375] For a general discussion of contracts of rescission, see Lemlich v. Board of Trustees, 282 Md. 495, 385 A.2d 1185 (1978). A contract of rescission has only one purpose, i.e., to discharge a prior executory contract. When the rescission contract is formed, it not only discharges the original contract but discharges itself, i.e., it is completely performed and, in this sense, it self-destructs. The concept of rescission will be discussed further in the last chapter of this volume dealing with discharge.

[376] A contract of rescission not only discharges the original contract, but discharges itself upon formation. Upon formation, it is self-destructive and destroys the original contract simultaneously.

or Barnes' promise to accept less ($500 per week). Cases validating simultaneous rescissions and new agreements modifying the original agreement ignore the consideration requirement.[377] In the simultaneous rescission of the old agreement and formation of the new agreement, Ames was never free of her duty to Barnes and Barnes was never free of his duty to Ames. There was no consideration for the new promises. There must be some period of time, perhaps only a moment, between the formation of the rescission contract and the formation of the third contract.[378] If there never was a mutual release of duties, the parties were never free to enter into a new contract since they were still bound by the original contract. There would be no third contract in this situation. The second contract of rescission and simultaneous modification would lack consideration. Contrary reasoning is necessarily circular and is seen as such by other courts.[379]

Three Parties. If the promise of additional consideration is not made by one of the parties to the contract but by a third party stranger to the contract, the situation becomes more complex. A well-known case involved a driver who had a contractual duty with the owner of a horse to drive in a particular trotting race. A stranger to the contract promised the driver $1000 if he won the race. The driver "won" the race.[380] The stranger was particularly desirous that the horse being driven would win since he owned the dam of the entered horse and stood to benefit if the driven horse was victorious. Since the driver had a pre-existing duty to use his best efforts to win the race under his contract with the owner of the horse, the question arose, was the promise of the stranger supported by consideration? The court accepted the traditional view that there was no consideration to support the promise since there was no detriment to the promisee-driver.[381]

Both RESTATEMENTS, however, take a contrary position.[382] It is possible to construct consideration by finding a benefit to the third party. Even though the driver owed a pre-existing duty to the owner, he owed no duty to the stranger. Thus, when the driver performs the act requested by the stranger, the stranger receives a benefit. Though there is no detriment to the promisee-driver, the classic consideration formula is satisfied, i.e., there must be *either* a benefit to the promisor *or* a detriment to the promisee.[383] This theory collapses, however, when applied to the facts of the driving case because the argument is circular. One

---

[377] The classic illustration is Schwartzreich v. Bauman-Basch, Inc., 231 N.Y. 196, 131 N.E. 887 (1921). As early as 1895, another court concluded that such an analysis indulges the worst kind of fiction since it invites parties to repudiate their contractual obligations whenever they perceive a gain thereby. King v. Duluth, M. & N. R. Co., 61 Minn. 482, 63 N.W. 1105, 1106 (1895).

[378] McCallum Highlands v. Washington Capital Dus, 66 F.3d 89, 94 (5th Cir. 1995): [W]here an alleged rescission is coupled with a simultaneous re-entry into a new contract and the terms of the new contract are more favorable to one of the parties, doubt is created as to the mutuality of the agreement to rescind the original contract," *quoted in* Contempo Design, Inc. v. Chicago & Northeast Ill. Dist. Council of Carpenters, 226 F.3d 535, 550 (7th Cir. 2000), *cert. denied*, 121 S. Ct. 776, 148 L. Ed. 2d 674 (2001).

[379] *See* Recker v. Gustafson, 279 N.W.2d 744, 758 (Iowa 1979). RESTATEMENT 2d § 89 comment b rejects the simultaneous rescission and new agreement concept as "fictitious."

[380] One should not forget the efforts of the horse.

[381] McDevitt v. Stokes, 174 Ky. 515, 192 S.W. 681 (1917).

[382] First RESTATEMENT § 84(d); RESTATEMENT 2d § 73 comment d.

[383] *See* Briskin v. Packard Motor Car Co., 269 Mass. 394, 169 N.E. 148 (1929); Shadwell v. Shadwell, 30 L. J. C. P. 145, 9 C. B. (n. s.) 159 [1860]. *See also* Morgan, *Benefit to the Promisor as Consideration for a Second Promise for the Same Act*, 1 MINN. L. REV. 383 (1915); SELECTED READINGS ON CONTRACTS 491 (1931); FIRST RESTATEMENT § 84(d), *approved in* Willard v. Hobby, 134 F. Supp. 66 (D. Pa. 1955).

can be entitled to a performance by another only if the other has a legal duty to perform and that duty must rest upon some contractual theory. If there is a contract, there is a duty on the part of the promisee-driver to the stranger. In order to find this contractual duty, however, consideration must exist. Though the driver may have felt an extra incentive because of the stranger's promise, under his pre-existing duty to the owner he was still required to use his best efforts to win the race. No greater effort could be judicially recognized. Thus, the driver could not be induced to win the race by the stranger's promise. The theory suggesting that a benefit to the stranger suffices necessarily eliminates the requirement that the detriment induce the promise, i.e., that the promise of the stranger must be bargained for. The stranger's promise could not be induced by the detriment since the driver, necessarily, suffered no detriment. Notwithstanding this analysis, both RESTATEMENTS insist that the promise is enforceable. The RESTATEMENT 2d appears to recognize that such promises by third parties are not enforceable on the basis of consideration. Rather, they are enforceable because "there is less likelihood of economic coercion or other unfair pressure" in making a promise by a stranger enforceable than there would be if the promise had been made by one of the parties to the original contract.[384] Unfortunately, the analysis proceeds to suggest that, "the tendency of the law has been simply to hold that performance of contractual duty can be consideration if the duty is not owed to the promisor."[385] Here, "consideration" appears to be used as a conclusion for suggesting that the promise is enforceable rather than any strong assertion that the technical requirements of consideration are present.[386]

De Cicco v. Schweizer. Another circumvention device is suggested by one of the best-known cases in the literature of contract law.[387] Blance and the Count were engaged to be married at a time when the engagement contract could be enforced. The father of the prospective bride promised the Count that he would pay an annuity to the bride during her lifetime. Since the couple had previously agreed to marry, there was no readily observable detriment to the promisee (Count) in proceeding with the marriage. In an imaginative opinion by Judge Cardozo, however, the court held that the father's promise induced the parties to refrain from rescinding their marriage contract and the forbearance from rescission induced the father's promise. To accomplish this feat, Judge Cardozo had to characterize the daughter

---

[384] RESTATEMENT 2d § 73 comment d. Cases supporting the First Restatement view include Perry M. Alexander Constr. Co. v. Burbank, 83 N.C. App. 503, 350 S.E.2d 877 (1986) (promise to third party to perform demolition where the demolition duty was already owed to another — applying FIRST RESTATEMENT § 84(d)); Burton v. Kenyon, 46 N.C. App. 309, 264 S.E.2d 808 (1980) (applying FIRST RESTATEMENT § 84(d)), and Morrison Flying Serv. v. Deming Nat'l Bank, 404 F.2d 856 (10th Cir. 1968), *cert. denied*, 393 U.S. 1020, 89 S. Ct. 628, 21 L. Ed. 2d 565 (1969) (applying FIRST RESTATEMENT § 84(d)). The position is also supported by Professor Corbin in 1 CORBIN ON CONTRACTS § 176 (1950). Cases supporting the RESTATEMENT 2d view (§ 73) include Patterson v. Katt, 791 S.W.2d 466 (Mo. Ct. App. 1990); Scherer v. Laborers' Int'l Union, 746 F. Supp. 73 (N.D. Fla. 1988); USLife Title Co. v. Gutkin, 152 Ariz. 349, 732 P. 2d 579 (Ct. App. 1986).

[385] *Id.* Ill. 12 to § 73 is based upon the race horse case and concludes that the driving of the race is consideration for the promise of the stranger. Under agency law principles, however, the illustration suggests that, while the stranger owes the promised amount to the driver, the owner of the horse may be entitled to that amount (citing RESTATEMENT 2d AGENCY §§ 313, 388).

[386] In comment b to § 73, the RESTATEMENT 2d finds no consideration in a promise to a public official to perform his public duty. The policy reasons for this result are sound, i.e., public officials may threaten to withhold the performance of their duties which threaten public and private interests. Yet, from the standpoint of consideration, if there is consideration in the promise of a stranger to a driver of a trotting horse, a third-party promise to a public official such as a police officer might also admit of consideration. Again, the determination of whether such promises by strangers should be enforced is properly placed on policy grounds rather than a technical consideration construct.

[387] 221 N.Y. 431, 117 N.E. 807 (1917).

as a promisee as well as the Count though the promise was made exclusively to the Count. Cardozo creates that fact by assuming that the daughter had learned of the promise prior to the marriage though the record was devoid of supporting evidence to this effect. Having transformed the daughter from a third party (donee) beneficiary to a promisee, the stage was set to discover another implied fact, i.e., that the Count and daughter refrained from rescinding their agreement in exchange for the father's promise. Judge Cardozo was faced with precedent indicating that a promise to one party to a contract seeking forbearance from rescission was valueless since it takes two to rescind. Absent that precedent, it is possible to discover consideration by the forbearance of one party *offering* a rescission to the other party. This would be particularly true in a marriage agreement where emotions play a greater role than commercial contracts. Thus, if it could be demonstrated that the father promised an annuity to the daughter *in exchange* for the Count's promise to forbear offering a rescission of the marriage contract to the daughter, there would be consideration for the father's promise. The facts of the case, however, show little justification for any bargained-for exchange or forbearance from rescission. Notwithstanding the use of the term "consideration" in the father's written promise, there is no evidence that it was anything other than a gift promise conditioned only upon the occurrence of the marriage. After this remarkable effort in discovering consideration, Judge Cardozo admits the influence of a strong policy of the law in favor of marriage settlements and the willingness of courts to construct consideration, if need be, to make such promises enforceable. While the RESTATEMENT 2d mentions the possibility of discovering a mutual forbearance to rescind or the forbearance of an offer to rescind as consideration for a third-party promise, it appears to dismiss that rationale as less than persuasive.[388]

[D]   Modifications Without Consideration Enforced Because of Unanticipated Difficulties

Where a promisee begins to perform his contractual duty and encounters unanticipated difficulties, he may not abandon his contract because of such difficulties.[389] If, however, the promisor agrees to pay additional compensation because of the unanticipated difficulties, there is authority for holding the modification enforceable absent any consideration for the new promise.[390] The RESTATEMENT 2d adopts this position with no suggestion that it amounts to consideration.[391] A modification based upon unanticipated difficulty is typically devoid of

---

[388] RESTATEMENT 2d § 73 comment d.

[389] *See, e.g.,* Ramco Roofing & Supply Co. v. Kaminsky, 156 Ga. App. 708, 275 S.E.2d 764 (1980); Codell Constr. Co. v. Commonwealth of Ky., 566 S.W.2d 161 (Ky. Ct. App. 1977). If, however, the promisee relied upon an estimate of the promisor as to the amount of work to be done, the promisee is free to abandon the remainder of the work absent assurances of additional compensation and, as to any additional work already performed, he may recover in quantum meruit for the reasonable value of the additional work, i.e., a restitutionary recovery to prevent the unjust enrichment of the promisor. *See* Murdock-Bryant Constr. v. Pearson, 146 Ariz. 57, 703 P.2d 1206 (Ct. App. 1984).

[390] *See, e.g.,* Angel v. Murray, 113 R.I.482, 322 A.2d 630 (1974) (city promised to pay trash collector $10,000 per year more on contract to collect all trash because of unanticipated increase of dwelling units within city); Pittsburgh Testing Lab. v. Farnsworth & Chambers Co., 251 F.2d 77 (10th Cir. 1958) (supporting this concept though holding that a promise to pay additional compensation was based on settlement of a bona fide dispute); *see also Lichtenstein v. Watt,* 221 U.S. App. D.C. 435, 684 F.2d 957 (D.C. Cir. 1982) (discussing the unanticipated difficulty concept and Watkins & Son v. Carrig, 91 N.H. 459, 21 A.2d 591, 138 A.L.R. 131 (1941)).

[391] RESTATEMENT 2d § 89(a). This is one of the sections in Topic 2 of the RESTATEMENT 2d (§§ 82–94) captioned, "Contracts Without Consideration." See United States v. Sears, Roebuck & Co., 778 F.2d 810, 816, 250 U.S. App. D.C. 189 (1985).

unfair pressure or economic coercion which may be said to justify the continuation of the pre-existing duty rule where a promisee demands additional payment only because he is in a position to place unfair pressure upon the promisor.[392]

It is important to distinguish "unanticipated" difficulty which may be remotely foreseeable from "unforeseeable" contingencies that materially change the nature of the bargain and may be sufficient to excuse the promisee from performing.[393] The modification must be fair and equitable under circumstances that were not anticipated at the time of contract formation.[394] It is important to consider any evidence of pressure or imposition on the promisor which would suggest a rejuvenation of the pre-existing duty analysis. Among other circumstances, the relative bargaining power of the parties and the extent of performance under the new promise should be considered. Absent bad faith on the part of the promisee and assuming a voluntary commitment by the promisor, the modification should be enforced with a candid recognition that the basis for enforcement is the effectuation of good faith adjustments in on-going transactions rather than any fictitious notion of consideration or another validation device.

[E]   Modifications Without Consideration — Uniform Commercial Code

[1]   UCC § 2-209(1): Changing the Pre-Existing Duty Rule

The Uniform Commercial Code governs contracts for the sale of goods. Under the Code, good faith modifications of such contracts need no consideration to be binding.[395] "Under the UCC, the common law pre-existing duty rule is largely abrogated, requiring no additional consideration for contract modifications."[396] In light of prolonged criticism of the pre-existing duty rule prior to Code, it is not remarkable that the Code would include a section dispensing with the need for consideration or any other validation device. While the earlier criticism facilitated the inclusion of this concept, it is at least arguable that it would have been included absent that criticism. The "father" of the Code and principal draftsman of Article 2, Professor Karl Llewellyn, was more than insistent that technical barriers to good faith and commercially reasonable practices be removed.[397] Permitting the parties to a contract for the sale of goods to make modifications without the technical constraint of consideration is a clear illustration of

---

[392] RESTATEMENT 2d § 89 comment b.

[393] Impossibility of performance, impracticability of performance and frustration of purpose permit the promisee to be legally excused from performing. RESTATEMENT 2d §§ 261–272 and UCC §§ 2-614 and 2-615. Unanticipated difficulty does not excuse the promisee. *See* RESTATEMENT 2d § 89 comment b.

[394] RESTATEMENT 2d § 89(a). See Roussalis v. Wyoming Med. Ctr., Inc., 4 P.3d 209, 240 (Wyo. 2000); McCallum Highlands v. Washington Capital Dus, 66 F.3d 89, 94 (5th Cir. 1995).

[395] "An agreement modifying a contract with this Article needs no consideration to be binding." UCC § 2-209(1).

[396] Sara Lee Corp. v. Quality Mfg., Inc., 201 F. Supp. 2d 608, 613 (M. D. N. C. 2002) (modification to increase prices was enforceable without consideration).

[397] Comment 1 to UCC § 2-209 illustrates the anti-technical nature of Article 2 with respect to modifications: "This section seeks to protect and make effective all necessary and desirable modifications of sales contracts without regard to the technicalities which at present hamper such adjustments." Other illustrations of the anti-technical nature of Article 2 include § 2-204(3) (contract does not fail for indefiniteness notwithstanding absence of one or more terms, if parties intended to form a contract and there is a basis for an appropriate remedy); § 2-206 comment 1 ("[f]ormer technical rules as to acceptance . . . are rejected"). In Columbia Nitrogen Corp. v. Royster Co., 451 F.2d 3, 10 (4th Cir. 1971), the court speaks of "the overly legalistic interpretations which the Code seeks to abolish."

the underlying philosophy of Article 2 of the Code, which seeks to identify the factual bargain of the parties.[398]

Section 2-209(1) may be criticized because it does not expressly require modifications to be made in good faith.[399] The good faith standard, however, is implied in any contract and a comment clearly limits enforceable modifications without consideration to those made in good faith.[400] The same comment suggests the possibility that such modifications require a "legitimate commercial reason" or "an objectively demonstrable reason" for seeking modification.[401] Unforeseen difficulty that would provide a legal excuse[402] is not necessary. If, however, the requirements of § 2-209(1) were compared to the "unanticipated difficulty" concept of the RESTATEMENT 2d discussed *supra*,[403] there is no such requirement in § 2-209(1) though the existence of such a difficulty or other sound commercial reason for the modification would provide evidence of the essential requirement of good faith.

A contract required delivery of goods by a certain date under a "time of the essence" clause. As an express FOB "destination" contract, the seller was obliged to pay shipping charges.[404] Because of the seller's delay in production and shipping, it was necessary to deliver the goods by air freight which the seller claimed the buyer agreed to pay under a modification of the contract. Recognizing that the good faith modification standard requires a legitimate commercial reason outside of the control of the party seeking the modification, the court held that no such legitimate reason outside of this seller's control existed. Even though the buyer did not object to the seller's demand that the buyer pay the air freight, since the modification was sought in bad faith, it was not enforceable.[405] Where, however, the plaintiff informed the defendant that the job of printing a magazine would cost more than the original price quotation and the defendant did not object at that time nor after receiving a confirming letter to that effect and an invoice reflecting the price increase. Only after receiving the entire shipment did defendant object. The court applied § 2-209(1), enforcing the modification.[406] A defendant purchased two used trucks without warranties, but the plaintiff later agreed to perform major

---

[398] The factual bargain analysis is predicated upon the definition of "contract" in UCC § 1-201(11), which defines contract in terms of effect, i.e., "the total legal obligation which results from the parties' agreement. . . ." "Agreement" is defined in § 1-201(3) as "the bargain of the parties in fact as found in their language or by implication from other circumstances including course of dealing or usage or trade or course of performance. . . ." For a more complete statement of the factual bargain analysis, see Murray, *The Article 2 Prism: The Underlying Philosophy of* Article 2 of the Uniform Commercial Code, 21 WASHBURN L.J. 1 (1981). *See also* Murray, *The Chaos of the "Battle of the Forms": Solutions*, 39 VAND. L. REV. 1307 (1986).

[399] Section 2-103(1)(b) defines good faith in the case of a merchant as "honesty in fact and the observance of reasonable commercial standards of fair dealing in the trade." This standard had differed from the original general (non-merchant) definition of good faith found in unrevised § 1-201(19): "honesty in fact in the conduct or transaction concerned." The revised version in § 1-201(20), however, imports both "honesty in fact and the observance of reasonable commercial standards of fair dealing."A comment explains that the limited "honesty in fact" standard applied throughout the Code except in Article 2 which included the commercial reasonableness standard as applied to merchants. As other Articles of the Code broadened their definitions of "good faith," only Article 5 was left with the standard of subjective honesty. The new Article 1 definition, therefore, excepts Article 5.

[400] Comment 2 to § 2-209.

[401] *Id.*

[402] *See* UCC §§ 2-614 and 2-615.

[403] RESTATEMENT 2d § 89(a).

[404] UCC § 2-503.

[405] T & S Brass and Bronze Works, Inc. v. Pic-Air, Inc., 790 F.2d 1098 (4th Cir. 1986).

[406] Gross Valentino Printing Co. v. Clarke, 120 Ill. App. 3d 907, 458 N.E.2d 1027 (1st Dist. 1983).

engine repairs without charge. The court held the subsequent modification enforceable without consideration under § 2-209(1).[407] One of the better-known cases construing § 2-209(1) is *Skinner v. Tober Foreign Motors, Inc.*,[408] where the buyer of an airplane agreed to pay the purchase price in installments, both parties contemplating that the installment payments would be made out of future earnings. When the engine developed problems not covered by the warranty, the buyer could not afford to maintain the monthly payments and pay for the repairs. He sought to return the plane in exchange for a release. The parties agreed to modify the contract to permit the buyer to make reduced payments and to extend the obligation. The modification was viewed as one made in good faith and was upheld notwithstanding the lack of consideration.

Courts have experienced very few problems in the application of § 2-209(1), the UCC exception to the pre-existing duty rule. Problems have arisen, however, with respect to the remaining four subsections of § 2-209. Before considering these problems, we explore the international dimension.

[2]   CISG and UNIDROIT Principles — Consideration and Modifications

Neither the Convention on Contracts for the International Sale of Goods (CISG) nor UNIDROIT Principles[409] contain any mention of consideration. It is, therefore, not surprising to discover a CISG provision that permits parties to modify or terminate their contract by "mere agreement"[410] or a provision in *Principles* allowing a contract to be concluded "by the mere agreement of the parties without any further requirement."[411] Since CISG does not govern the "validity" of any contract within its provisions,[412] it is theoretically possible that consideration is a validity issue that is not displaced by CISG. With respect to modifications, however, there is some evidence that CISG is designed to adhere to the Civil Law tradition of enforcing agreements where there is sufficient *cause* regardless of consideration.[413]

[3]   No Oral Modification (NOM) Clauses — Common Law and UCC § 2-209(2)

Common Law. The parties to a written contract may decide that any modification or rescission of their contract will not be enforceable unless it is evidenced by writing. These "no oral modification" (NOM) clauses were not favored at common law because of the principle that parties to a contract should not be deterred from changing their minds.[414] In the colorful

---

[407] Bone Int'l, Inc. v. Johnson, 74 N.C. App. 703, 329 S.E.2d 714 (1985).

[408] 345 Mass. 429, 187 N.E.2d 669 (1963).

[409] For an overview of CISG and UNIDROIT Principles, see § 13 *supra*.

[410] CISG Art. 29(2).

[411] *Principles* § 3.2.

[412] CISG Art. 4(a).

[413] See the United Nations Conference on Contracts for the International Sale of Goods-Official Records, U. N. Doc. A/Conf. 97/19, n 31, at 28 (1981).

[414] Professor Corbin suggests, "Any written contract . . . can be rescinded or varied at will by the oral agreement of the parties; and this is held to be true, except as otherwise provided by statute, even of a written agreement that the contract shall not be orally varied or rescinded." CORBIN, 6 CORBIN ON CONTRACTS § 1295, at 206 and n.32. Judge Cardozo states, "Those who make a contract may unmake it. The clause which forbids a change, may be changed like

language of Justice Musmanno of the Supreme Court of Pennsylvania, "The most ironclad written contract can always be cut into by the acetylene torch of parol modification supported by adequate proof. . . . Even where the contract specifically states that no non-written modification will be recognized, the parties may yet alter their agreement by parol negotiation. The hand that pens a writing may not gag the mouths of the assenting parties. The pen may be more precise in permanently recording what is to be done, but it may not still the tongues which bespeak an improvement in or modification of what has been written."[415] Absent a statutory exception, such as Section 2-209(1) of the Uniform Commercial Code discussed above, however, such a modification must be evidenced by consideration or an alternate validation device such as promissory estoppel.[416]

Statutory Requirements. A New York statute made such clauses enforceable and, to avoid circumvention of the statute through oral discharges, it was amended to prohibit terminations as well as modifications.[417] Section 2-209(2) of the UCC is fashioned after the New York statute. It makes clauses excluding modifications or rescissions except by a signed writing enforceable and adds a safeguard to protect non-merchants against such clauses on forms supplied by merchants by requiring the clause to be separately signed by the non-merchant:

> A signed agreement which excludes modification or rescission except by a signed writing cannot be otherwise modified or rescinded, but except as between merchants such a requirement on a form supplied by the merchant must be separately signed by the other party.[418]

When parties include such an NOM clause in their original contract, it is sometimes referred to as a "private" statute of frauds clause, as contrasted with the "public" statute of frauds which we will now explore.

[4]   Section 2-209(3) The Contract as Modified — Statute of Frauds

An understanding of Section 2-209(3) of the UCC requires a preview of the Statute of Frauds that will be explored in the next chapter.[419] To prevent false allegations that particular parties had made promises or contracts, a statute of frauds was enacted in England in 1677 to prevent fraud and perjury. Under this statute, certain types of contracts were required to be evidenced by a writing to be enforceable. Promises by sureties, executors or administrators to answer for the debt of another, contracts for the sale of land, contracts in consideration of marriage, contracts not to be performed within one year from their making, and contracts for

---

any other." Beatty v. Guggenheim Exploration Co., 225 N.Y. 380, 387, 122 N.E. 378, 381 (1919). *See also* RESTATEMENT 2d § 148.

[415] Wagner v. Graziano Constr. Co., 390 Pa. 445, 448, 136 A.2d 83, 83–84 (1957). Numerous cases support this view. *See, e. g.*, Rule Sales & Serv. v. U.S. Bank Nat'l Ass'n, 133 Idaho 669, 675, 991 P.2d 857, 863 (Ct. App. 1999) (citing Canizaro v. Mobile Communications Corp. of Am., 655 So. 2d 25, 29 (Miss. 1995), and Autotrol Corp. v. Continental Water Sys. Corp., 918 F.2d 689, 692 (7th Cir. 1990), among other cases).

[416] See *Rule Sales & Service, id*, 991 P.2d at 862.

[417] N.Y. GEN. OBLIG. LAW § 15-301. For a statement of the history of the New York statute, see the analysis of Professor Edwin Patterson of the Columbia Law School, 1 N.Y. Law Rev. Comm'n, STUDY OF THE UNIFORM COMMERCIAL CODE 307–08 (1955).

[418] UCC § 2-209(2).

[419] Chapter 4, §§ 69–81.

the sale of goods were within the original statute of frauds.[420] The requirement of a writing to evidence certain kinds of contracts continues in the 21st century including contracts for the sale of goods priced at $500 or more.[421] In this section we address the application of this requirement to modifications of contracts for the sale of goods. A modification agreement involves two analytically distinct operative effects: (1) the termination or rescission of the original contract, and (2) the creation of a new contract. The typical modification incorporates both effects simultaneously in an entire (indivisible) contract so that the resulting (second) contract contains part of the terms of the original contract and the new terms.[422] There has never been any question that "the new contract is viewed as a whole,"[423] i.e., "the contract as modified."[424]

Since UCC § 2-201 requires a contract for the sale of goods priced at $500 or more to be evidenced by a writing, it necessarily applies to any modified contract for the sale of goods priced at $500 or more. Since the effect of modifying the original is to end that contract leaving only the contract as modified, that remaining contract must satisfy the statute. If the original contract involved a price less than $500, no writing (record) would be necessary. If the parties modified that contract to increase the price to $500 or more, a writing would be necessary to make the contract as modified enforceable. The essential question is, eliminating all thought of the original contract which no longer exits, is there a sufficient writing to satisfy the statute of frauds for the only extant contract-the modified contract?

It was not necessary to include another UCC section to restate the writing requirement for the contract as modified. Nonetheless, the Code restates the obvious:

> The requirements of the statute of frauds section of this Article (Section 2-201) must be satisfied if the contract as modified is within its provisions.[425]

A comment leaves no doubt about the purpose of this subsection: "The Statute of Frauds provisions of this Article are expressly applied to modifications by subsection (3)."[426] Thus, 2-209(3) is simply a reminder that 2-201 must be satisfied to assure the enforceability of the contract as modified. To apply the requirements of 2-201 to modified contracts, therefore, it is essential to be aware of the requirements for a "sufficient" writing (record). The writing need not contain all of the material terms of the contract. The essential requirement is that "the

---

[420] Stat. 29 Car. II, c. 3 (1677).

[421] § 2-201 of the UCC. The statute will now be satisfied by a record ("writing") in either traditional writing or electronic form. See the summary of the Uniform Electronic Transactions Act (UETA) and the Electronic Signatures in Global and Network Commerce Act ("E-Sign") in § 14 *supra*. The more expansive term, "record," defined in UETA § 13, includes both traditional writings and electronic records as evidence of a contract and may be used to refer to the evidence of the contract.

[422] *See* Restatement 2d § 149 and Murray, *The Modification Mystery:* Section 2-209 of the Uniform Commercial Code, 32 Vill. L. Rev. 1, 21 (1987).

[423] Restatement 2d § 149 comment a.

[424] Corbin on Contracts § 13.3 suggests: "The second agreement is within the statute if these two parts, taken together, make a contract that would be within the statute if it had been the only executory contract that the parties had made, otherwise not." Although the contract as modified contains some terms from the original contract and some terms from the modification, the new contract is viewed independently as a whole for the purposes of the statute of frauds. See Restatement 2d § 149, comment a.

[425] § 2-209(3).

[426] Comment 3 to 2-209, 2nd paragraph.

writing afford a basis for believing that the offered oral evidence rests on a real transaction."[427] Because some pre-Code courts insisted that the price term be included in such a writing, the comment emphasizes that the price term need not be stated.[428]Indeed,

> [o]nly three definite and invariable requirements as to the memorandum [writing] are made by the subsection. First it must evidence a contract for the sale of goods, second it must "signed," a word which includes any authentication which describes the party to be charged [a word processed, typewritten, or printed signature (even on a letterhead) will do, include the name of a sender on an email-comment 37 to § 1-201(37)and third, it must specify a quantity.[429]

Thus, terms such as "[t]he price, time and place of payment or delivery, the general quality of the goods, or any particular warranties may be omitted."[430] On the basis of these Code directives, consider the following: A signed writing evidences a signed contract for the sale of goods sufficiently identifying the goods and the parties to the transaction. It also contains a definite quantity term, but says nothing about price, time or place of delivery, warranty or other terms. The requirements of 2-201 are clearly met. If the parties had agreed upon the price, that evidence would be admissible. If they intended to be bound and had not agreed upon the price, a reasonable price would be implied.[431] Before the time for performance of the contract, assume the parties changed the price term, the place or time of delivery term or other term that was not required to be in the original writing to satisfy the statute of frauds. Would the modified contract require a new writing to satisfy the statute? The question scarcely survives its statement since 2-209(3) only requires a writing that would satisfy the contract as modified. The original writing was sufficient though it stated no price or time or place of delivery. The original writing should be clearly sufficient, *but the prevailing view requires a new writing.*

If terms such as quantity or sufficient identification of one or both parties or subject matter were changed in the modified contract, clearly a new writing evidencing such terms would be essential. If a quantity term of 10,000 units were changed in a modification to 20,000 units but the writing was not changed, the only enforceable contract would remain one for 10,000 units.[432] There is, however, no basis whatsoever for a court requiring a term to be evidenced by a writing under 2-209(3) which is not required under 2-201 since, again, the exclusive purpose of 2-209(3) is a reminder that 2-201 requirements must be met in the contract as modified. The scholars are in unanimous agreement with this analysis, but, with rare exception, the courts insist that *the modification of any term requires a writing to satisfy 2-209(3).*[433] It

---

[427] 2-201, comment 1.

[428] *Id.*

[429] *Id.*, 3rd paragraph. See American Iron & Metal Co. v. U. S. Ferrous Trad. Div., 2007 U. S. Dist. LEXIS 27847 at *15 (D. Conn. 2007) which also notes the parties need not be identified in the writing as buyer or seller so long as they are otherwise sufficiently identified.

[430] *Id.*, 1st paragraph.

[431] § 2-305(1)(a). If the parties had otherwise agreed on delivery and other terms, parol evidence of such terms would be admissible. The writing would not be insufficient because it did not contain t hose terms. If the parties had not agreed on delivery or other missing terms, they would be implied. See §§ 2-306-2-311.

[432] 2-201(1): "A writing is not insufficient because it omits or incorrectly states a terms agreed upon, but the contract is not enforceable beyond the quantity of goods shown in such writing."

[433] *See* Zemco Mfg., Inc. v. Navistar Int'l Transp. Corp., 186 F.3d 815 (7th Cir. 1999) where the court notes the unanimous view of the scholars but, via Erie R.R. v. Tompkins, 304 U.S. 64, 58 S. Ct. 817, 82 L. Ed. 1188 (1938), was

is even more distressing that the prevailing view is not predicated on any comprehensible basis. As the Seventh Circuit notes, there is "little analysis" in these opinions concerning this issue which leaves the impression that courts simply assume that 2-209(3) refers to *any* modification without adequate concern for the language or purpose of that provision.[434] The failure of courts to understand the extremely limited purpose of § 2-209(3) as a mere reminder has created confusion in the application of that provision as well as the remaining subsections of § 2-209.[435] Finally, a construction requiring "any" modification of a contract for the sale of goods to be evidenced by a writing emasculates 2-209(2) that commands the express enforcement of clauses prohibiting oral modifications. There is no need for such a clause if any modification must be evidenced by a writing under 2-209(3). The protection of non-merchants in 2-209(2) requiring their separate signing of NOM clauses in forms supplied by the merchant becomes particularly absurd under a construction of 2-209(3) requiring any modification to be evidenced by a writing.

[5]   Sections 2-209(4) and (5): Waivers and Retractions

Section 2-209(4) suggests that an attempt at modification that does not satisfy subsection (2) (NOM clauses) or (3) (§ 2-201 as applied to the contract as modified) "can operate as a waiver."[436] Like other parts of § 2-209, this subsection is an effort to codify pre-Code law.[437] The term, "waiver," has always been troublesome because it is used to describe a variety of events.[438] The most common definition is "a voluntary and intentional relinquishment of a known right,"[439] but this definition is misleading. It is possible to relinquish a known right voluntarily without waiving it.[440] A gratuitous assignment terminates a right, but it is not a

---

compelled to assume that Indiana would follow the prevailing view that *any* modification had to meet the requirements of 2-201. That opinion lists the following cases representing the prevailing view: Van Den Broeke v. Bellanca Aircraft Corp., 576 F.2d 582, 584 (5th Cir. 1978) (orally modified warranty); Cooley v. Big Horn Harvestore Sys., Inc., 767 P.2d 740, 744 (Colo. 1988), *rev'd on other grounds*, 813 P.2d 736 (Colo. 1991) (orally modified warranty); Green Constr. Co. v. First Indem. of Am. Ins. Co., 735 F. Supp. 1254, 1261 (D.N.J. 1990) (orally modified delivery term); Leasing Serv. Corp. v. Diamond Timber, Inc., 559 F. Supp. 972, 976–77 (S.D.N.Y.) (orally modified delivery terms), *aff'd*, 729 F.2d 1442 (2d Cir. 1983). Costco Wholesale Corp. v. World Wide Licensing Corp., 78 Wash. App. 637, 644, 898 P.2d 347, 351 (1995) (quoting Murray, *The Modification Mystery*: Section 2-209 of the Uniform Commercial Code, 32 VILL. L. REV. 1, 15 (1987)) suggests the opposing view. *Cotsco* was more recently followed in Welt v. Amerisourcebergen Drug Corp., 2009 U. S. Dist. LEXIS 75315 at *18 (S. D. Fla. 2009).

[434] "Although these courts have provided little analysis, they essentially interpret § 2-209(3) to mean that, if the post-modification terms fits within the terms of § 2-201 (i.e., it is a sale of goods for more than $500), then any modification of it must be in writing." *Zemco, id.*, 186 F.3d at 819.

[435] See Thorn's Diesel Serv. v Houston Ship Repair, 233 F. Supp. 2d 1332, 1342, note 12 (M. D. Ala. 2002) for a review of different constructions of 2-209(3).

[436] UCC § 2-209(4).

[437] For an exploration of the pre-UCC history of §§ 2-209(4) and (5), see Murray, *The Modification Mystery*: Section 2-209 of the Uniform Commercial Code, 32 VILL. L. REV. 1, 33–44 (1987).

[438] Meanings of the term were the subject of study in the early part of the century. *See* J. EWART, WAIVER DISTRIBUTED AMONG THE DEPARTMENTS: ELECTION, ESTOPPEL, CONTRACT, RELEASE (1917). The term "has been given various definitions and is used under many varying circumstances." CORBIN ON CONTRACTS § 4.1.

[439] *See, e.g.*, Van Den Broeke v. Bellanca Aircraft Corp., 576 F.2d 582, 584 (5th Cir. 1978); Farmers Elevator Co. of Reserve v. Anderson, 170 Mont. 175, 552 P.2d 63 (1976); Clark v. West, 193 N.Y. 349, 86 N.E. 1 (1908).

[440] Rubin v. Los Angeles Fed. Sav. & Loan Ass'n, 159 Cal. App. 3d 292, 298, 205 Cal. Rptr. 455, 459 (4th Dist. 1984): "Although waiver is frequently said to be the intentional relinquishment of a known right, waiver may also result from conduct 'which, according to its natural import, is so inconsistent with the intent to enforce the right in question as to induce a reasonable belief that such right has been relinquished.' "

waiver. Moreover, the requirement of a "known" right suggests that the waiving party must "know" the legal effect of his promise, as contrasted with simply knowing the essential facts.[441]

If a seller was not to deliver goods until a pre-payment was made by the prospective buyer, the failure of the buyer to make the payment would be a breach of his contractual duty — a failure of a constructive condition to the duty of the seller. The seller, however, could choose to perform notwithstanding the failure of pre-payment that would evidence a waiver of the constructive condition. Similarly, the seller could expressly waive the pre-payment duty before it was due by informing the buyer that he need not make the pre-payment as required under the contract. If this announcement caused the buyer to change his position by relying on the seller's statement, the seller should be precluded from asserting this failure to defend a refusal to deliver the goods. Such a seller may be said to be "estopped" from asserting the failure of the condition or that the condition has been "waived." "Estoppel" and "waiver," however, are mere conclusions. If the buyer has not relied, the condition can be reinstated if the seller notified the buyer within a reasonable time to make the pre-payment. The UCC replicates this analysis in 2-209(4) and (5). Subsection (4) states that an attempt at modification that does not satisfy 2-209(2) or (3) can operate as a waiver followed by 2-209(5):

> A party who has made a waiver affecting an executory portion of the contract may retract the waiver by reasonable notification received by the other party that strict performance will be required of any term waived, unless the retraction would be unjust in view of a material change of position in reliance on the waiver.

In a well-known case,[442] the Seventh Circuit addressed a contract for the sale of goods containing a clause prohibiting oral modifications, which prohibition was enforceable under 2-209(2). The issue was whether the attempted oral modification could be a waiver. Writing for the majority, Judge Posner stated that if an oral modification that was unenforceable under 2-209(2) could become enforceable as a waiver under 2-209(4), subsection (2) would be superfluous. The majority found the difference between modification and waiver by stating that a waiver under 2-209(4) must be supported by reliance. It distinguished 2-209(5) by applying it to express, written waivers while 2-209(4) was said to apply to oral waivers. A dissent by Judge Easterbrook, however, explained that this construction nullifies 2-209(5) which states that a waiver may be retracted unless the other party has relied on the waiver. The majority would treat 2-209(4) waivers as a subset of 2-209(5). Judge Easterbrook emphasized that "Things are the other way around. Subsection (4) says that an attempt at modification may be a 'waiver,' and subsection (5) qualifies the effectiveness of 'waivers' in the absence of reliance."[443] As to the majority's notion that 2-209(5) applied to express written and signed waivers, the dissent noted that they would not be waivers; they would be written modifications meeting the requirements of either 2-209(2) or (3).

The Eleventh Circuit subsequently agreed with Judge Easterbrook:

> Judge Posner, however, ignores a fundamental difference between modifications and waivers: while a party that has agreed to a contract modification cannot cancel the modification without giving consideration for the cancellation, a party may unilaterally

---

[441] *See* RESTATEMENT 2d § 84 comment b. Courts may suggest that a party must have "actual or constructive knowledge" of the right to be waived. Dooley v. Weil, 672 F.2d 1340, 1347 (11th Cir. 1982).

[442] Wisconsin Knife Works v. National Metal Crafters, 781 F.2d 1280 (7th Cir. 1986).

[443] *Id.* at 1291. Here, the dissent cites comment 4 to 2-209 which includes the statement that the section was not designed to limit, in other respects, the legal effect of the parties' later conduct.

retract is waiver of a contract term provided it gives reasonable notice. The fact that waivers may unilaterally be retracted provides the difference between subsections (2) and (4) that allows both to have meaning.[444]

An unenforceable oral modification does not become enforceable simply by calling it a "waiver." A simple illustration clarifies the point. Under the prevailing (albeit highly questionable) construction of 2-209(3), *supra,* "any" modification of a contract for the sale of goods must be evidenced by a writing. Assume the contract in this illustration also contains an NOM clause. Thus, either by the "public" statute of frauds (2-209(3)) or the "private" statute of frauds (2-209(2)), any modification of this contract requires a writing (record). Sometime prior to shipment of the goods, the buyer orally requests a three week delay in the shipment because the buyer is experiencing storage problems at its location. The seller orally agrees. Three weeks after the original scheduled delivery date, the seller ships the goods and, upon their arrival, the buyer rejects the shipment as arriving too late. The attempted oral modification changing the delivery date violated both 2-209(2) and (3). Such an "attempted modification," however, can operate as a waiver and, in this situation, courts would deem that it has operated as a waiver. Since it is impossible to deliver the goods at the originally scheduled date, there has been clear reliance by the seller which made the waiver irrevocable since allowing retraction would be "unjust" under the statute.[445] If, shortly after making the oral modification, the buyer's space problem had been alleviated and the buyer telephoned the seller instructing delivery at the originally scheduled time, such a retraction of the waiver is expressly recognized as effective absent a showing that it would be unjust in light of a material change of position by the seller.[446]

It is important to emphasize the very narrow application of §§ 2-209(4) and (5) of the UCC. These provisions become operative only if the oral modification fails to meet the requirements of the "public" (§ 2-201) or "private" (§ 2-209(2)) statute of frauds. There are other ways in which the statute of frauds can be satisfied such as making a substantial beginning on the manufacture of specially manufactured goods the seller would not sell in its ordinary course of business,[447] admitting in court that the contract was made,[448] or through the buyer's acceptance of any part of the goods or the seller's acceptance of any part of the payment for the goods.[449] Moreover, where one merchant sends a written confirmation of an oral contract for the sale of goods to another merchant who does not object to its contents within 10 days from its receipt, the confirmation satisfies the statute of frauds requirement against the receiving merchant who neither wrote nor signed anything.[450] Any of these "exceptions" which

---

[444] BMC Industries v. Barth Industries, 160 F.3d 1322, 1334 (11th Cir. 1998). See also, Dynamic' Machine Works, Inc. v. Machine & Elec. Consultants, Inc., 444 Mass. 768, 771–72, 831 N. E. 2d 875, 878–79 (2005): The UCC does not define "waiver" or "modification," but they are distinct concepts. . . . .While a waiver may be effectuated by one party, a modification is the result of the bilateral action of both parties to the sales transaction. . . . By the plain terms of 2-209(5), a waiver is retractable in the absence of reliance. . . . A modification, in contrast, cannot be retracted unilaterally."

[445] See Gold Kist, Inc. v. Pillow, 582 S.W.2d 77 (Tenn. Ct. App. 1979).

[446] 2-209(5).

[447] 2-201(3)(a). This subsection also recognizes reliance by a seller who does not manufacture the goods but makes commitments for the procurement of specially manufactured goods to make the oral contract enforceable.

[448] 2-201(3)(b) — admission in pleadings, testimony or otherwise in court.

[449] 2-201(3) Such part performance makes the contract enforceable to the extent of the part performance without any writing.

[450] 2-201(2). These exceptions and other aspects of the Statute of Frauds are explored in Chapter 4.

expressly satisfy 2-201 should certainly satisfy 2-209(3). Moreover, by analogy they should also satisfy the requirements of 2-209(2) since a failure to recognize them with respect to no oral modification clauses would subvert the purposes and underlying philosophy of Article 2 of the UCC.

§ 66 MUTUALITY OF OBLIGATION

It seems simple enough to state that it is impossible to discover consideration if both parties are not bound by their agreement. Many years ago, this truism was elevated to the so-called "doctrine" of mutuality of obligation. The "doctrine" is generally said to have originated in the early case of *Harrison v. Cage* involving an exchange of promises to marry. In response to the argument that the man's promise was not consideration for the woman's promise, but the woman's promise was consideration for the man's promise, the court suggested that either both promises are binding or neither is binding: "[E]ither all is a nudum pactum, or else one promise is as good as the other."[451] This dictum has been repeated in scores of cases.[452] The dictum, like the "doctrine," is devoid of any substance. It is meaningless and confusing. If the statement means that a promise that is not legally binding cannot constitute consideration, it is a tautology.

Earlier in this chapter, we recognized that an illusory promise promises nothing, *e.g.*, "I promise to sell you my car unless I choose not to sell you my car." Such a promise cannot support a counter promise to purchase the car for a certain sum because the buyer-promisor is receiving nothing for his promise. There is no consideration for the buyer's promise. To suggest that such an agreement lacks "mutuality of obligation" adds absolutely nothing to the analysis. A number of courts have recognized the superfluousness of this "doctrine." Quoting this treatise, the Ninth Circuit Court of Appeals stated, "Mutuality of obligation is simply a conclusory phrase stating the requirements of consideration."[453]

One of the classic cases dealing with so-called "mutuality of obligation" is *Hay v. Fortier*.[454] The defendant became surety on a bond and when the principal debtor did not pay, as surety

---

[451] 5 Mod. 411 [1698].

[452] For example, De Witt County Public Bldg. Comm'n v. County of De Witt, 128 Ill. App. 3d 11, 18, 469 N.E.2d 689, 695 (4th Dist. 1984): "In its most elemental sense, the doctrine of mutuality of obligation means that unless both parties to a contract are bound by its terms, neither is bound."

[453] Melton v. Phillip Morris, Inc. 71 Fed. Appx. 701, 703 (9th Cir. 2003). In Zamore v. Whitten, 395 A.2d 435, 443 n.3 (Me. 1978), the court states: "The phrase 'mutuality of obligation' has caused much confusion to courts and commentators over the years. . . . In fact, mutuality embodies a particularized application of the consideration doctrine in the context of formation of a bilateral contract. In a bilateral contract, one promise is good consideration for another. If the promisee fails to give the required return promise, mutual obligations are not, in fact, created. It is less confusing, and equally accurate, however, to conclude that no contract exists due to the promisee's failure to give legally sufficient consideration." In Riedman Corp. v. Jarosh, 289 S.C. 191, 345 S.E.2d 732 (Ct. App.), *aff'd*, 290 S.C. 252, 349 S.E.2d 404 (1986), the court notes that "consideration" and "mutuality of obligation" are sometimes confused. Consideration is essential; mutuality of obligation is not. The doctrine of mutuality of obligation is simply a statement of the rule that mutual promises constitute considerations for each other. The RESTATEMENT 2d in § 79 comment f criticizes the doctrine: " 'Both parties must be bound or neither is bound.' That statement is obviously erroneous as applied to an exchange of promise for performance; [It is generally suggested that the 'doctrine' does not apply to unilateral contracts since there is no unilateral contract until the promisee completely performs the act required by the offeror. it is equally inapplicable to contracts governed by §§ 82–94 and to contracts enforceable by virtue or their formal characteristics under § 6."

[454] 116 Me. 455, 102 A. 294 (1917).

she was called upon to perform her promise to pay. She sought an extension of time by promising to pay the entire amount then due in installment payments over a stated period of time. She promised nothing more than the amount already due, i.e., she did not promise to pay additional interest on the debt during the extension period or provide any other new consideration. In exchange for this promise to do nothing beyond her present duty, she sought forbearance from suit on the principal obligation (the bond) by the creditor. The creditor's promise to forbear was not, therefore, supported by consideration because he received nothing in exchange for his promise. If, immediately after promising, the creditor had brought an action on the bond, he would have breached no contract since his promise to extend the time for payment was not supported by consideration. While this situation appears to be a perfect manifestation of the requirement that either both parties are bound by their promises or neither is bound, to clutter the analysis with conclusory labels such as a lack of "mutuality of obligation" adds nothing to the analysis. Again, the creditor's promise is not binding because it is not supported by consideration. Notwithstanding the lack of consideration to support the plaintiff's promise to forbear, the plaintiff did, in fact, forbear for a period exceeding the promised duration of forbearance. The defendant-surety failed to perform her subsequent promise to pay the debt in installments and the creditor brought an action on the subsequent promise rather than the original debt evidenced by the bond.[455]

The defendant argued that there was no consideration for her promise since the plaintiff's promise was unenforceable because it was not supported by consideration. There should be no confusion about this analysis. If the transaction is viewed at the moment the promises were exchanged, there was no consideration. Defendant could not enforce the plaintiff's promise because there was no consideration for that promise. Since the defendant could not enforce that promise, she received nothing for her promise. Thus, there was no consideration to support her promise. When, however, the plaintiff performed its otherwise unenforceable promise, the defendant received the forbearance for which she had bargained. Thus, when viewed at the moment the promises were exchanged, the agreement lacked consideration. However, once the plaintiff performed the act sought by the defendant, the court held the defendant's promise enforceable:

> "Having enjoyed the forbearance of the plaintiff from bringing the action against her on the bond for the full period agreed upon, the defendant is now estopped from refusing performance on her part on the ground that the contract was not originally binding on the plaintiff, who did, nevertheless, perform it and she received the benefit thereof."[456]

It is unfortunate that the court resorted to the conclusory label of estoppel. Precisely why was the defendant estopped from refusing the performance or her promise to pay in installments? The simple but sound analysis is that, upon completion of the forbearance by the plaintiff, a unilateral contract was formed with one right in the plaintiff who had already suffered a detriment in performing the requested act, and one correlative duty in the defendant who had received the benefit of the performance. The act of forbearance by the plaintiff was completed when the plaintiff did not pursue the defendant's obligation during the period of extension she had requested. Thus, while there was no executory bilateral contract because the exchange of promises lacked consideration, there was a unilateral contract in which the

---

[455] The plaintiff had brought an action on the bond but that action was "discontinued without costs and without prejudice."

[456] 102 A. at 295.

defendant's promise was supported by consideration.[457]

The FIRST RESTATEMENT refused to adopt this or any other analysis that would make the defendant's promise enforceable.[458] The RESTATEMENT 2d, however, finds the promise enforceable conditioned on the performance of the act, i.e., the plaintiff's forbearance.[459] The formulation in the RESTATEMENT 2d, however, is devoid of any useful rationale.[460] The unilateral contract analysis is highly preferable. In any case, the "doctrine" of mutuality of obligation provides no assistance in the pursuit of a sound analysis.

[A]   "Mutuality of Remedy" and Other "Doctrines" Distinguished

The "doctrine" of mutuality of obligation is capable of creating confusion in a number of ways. It is often confused with an equitable doctrine often called "mutuality of remedy," suggesting that the remedy of specific performance cannot be had of the defendant's promise unless the contract is one which could have been specifically enforced against the plaintiff.[461] While mutuality of obligation is simply a conclusory phrase stating the requirement of consideration, "mutuality of remedy" deals with the specific enforcement of mutual promises.[462] The confusion surrounding their use is attributable to the fact that both doctrines are devoid of substance. As one court suggests, "both doctrines are largely dead letters."[463] Courts are, therefore, confronted with the necessity of clarifying their respective purposes and operative effects, if any.[464] The so called "doctrine" of "mutuality of remedy" doctrine is

---

[457] A similar analysis is found in First Wis. Nat'l Bank of Milwaukee v. Oby, 52 Wis. 2d 1, 9, 188 N.W.2d 454, 458–59 (1971): "Though at its inception the agreement lacked mutuality of obligations since plaintiff was not bound to make any loans whatsoever, the real question is whether at the time this action was brought the plaintiff had fully or partially executed the act which formed the basis for defendant's promise. Clearly it had. . . . It is sufficient that something of value flows from the promisee, or that it performed any act or suffered any inconvenience which it was not obligated to, and that it relied upon the strength of the promise as the inducement for such act. Therefore, to the extent that plaintiff's promise no longer remained executory and illusory, but was executed, sufficient consideration . . . was given in reliance upon the promises of defendant and her husband to support her promise, and to allow enforcement of the contract against defendant."

[458] FIRST RESTATEMENT § 78 ill. 4.

[459] RESTATEMENT 2d § 75 ill. 4. See Ward v. Goodrich, 34 Colo. 369, 372, 82 P. 701 (1905): "While it is settled that the promising to do, or the doing of, that which the promisor is already legally bound to do, does not, as a rule, constitute consideration for a reciprocal promise, or support a reciprocal undertaking given by the promisee, it by no means follows that such promise may not be enforced against such promisor by the promisee, although its enforcement compels the performance of that which was already a legal obligation."

[460] Illustration 4 to § 75 is based on the facts, but not the rationale, of *Hay v. Fortier.* "*A* promises to forbear suit against *B* in exchange for *B*'s promise to pay a liquidated and undisputed debt to *A*. *A*'s promise is not binding because *B*'s promise is not consideration . . . but *A*'s promise is nevertheless consideration for *B*'s. . . . *B*'s promise is conditional on *A*'s forbearance and can be enforced only if the condition is met." Having suggested that *A*'s promise is not binding because *B*'s promise is not consideration, it is difficult to understand how "*A*'s *promise* is nevertheless consideration for *B*'s" promise. It is submitted that *A*'s promise is never consideration for *B*'s *promise.* Rather, *A*'s promise becomes enforceable in exchange for *B*'s act of forbearance.

[461] See Ames, *Mutuality in Specific Performances,* 3 COLUM. L. REV. 1 (1903); Stone, *The Mutuality Rule in New York,* 16 COLUM. L. REV. 443 (1916). For a case that mentions both types of mutuality and refers to both as necessary in a suit for specific performance, see Madaio v. McCarthy, 199 N.J. Super. 430, 489 A.2d 1197 (1985).

[462] "Mutuality of Remedy" is analyzed in § 128[B][2][c], *infra.*

[463] Doctor's Assocs., Inc. v. Distajo, 66 F.3d 438, 451 (2d Cir. 1995), *cert. denied,* 517 U.S. 1120, 116 S. Ct. 1352, 134 L. Ed. 2d 520 (1996). Design Benefit Plans v. Enright, 940 F. Supp. 200, 205 (N.D. Ill. 1996), refers to RESTATEMENT 2d 363 comment c that rejects the doctrine of mutuality of remedy.

[464] *See, e.g., Doctor's Assocs., id.;* Lackey v. Green Tree Fin. Corp., 330 S.C. 388, 400, 498 S.E.2d 898, 904 (Ct. App.

analyzed in a subsequent section.[465]

Mutuality of obligation may also be confused with "adequacy of consideration," i.e., the relative values promised by each party.[466] Still another source of confusion occurs with respect to promises that may become unenforceable that nonetheless constitute consideration. A promise voidable because of the infancy or insanity of the promisor, or because of fraud, duress or illegality, is still consideration that makes a counter-promise enforceable by a party who has no power of avoidance or disaffirmance because of such lack of capacity.[467] Voidable promises are enforceable until the party with the power of avoidance chooses to disaffirm. Thus, there is consideration even though one party is given a power to disaffirm because of incapacity. A promise that is unenforceable only because it does not satisfy the statute of frauds will constitute consideration.[468] The statute of frauds imposes an evidentiary requirement on an otherwise enforceable promise, i.e., it has nothing to do with the general requirement that promises must be supported by consideration or another validation device.

§ 67   DETRIMENTAL RELIANCE — "PROMISSORY ESTOPPEL"

[A]   The Doctrine and Its Antecedents — The Lack of Bargained-For-Exchange

In our exploration of the doctrine of consideration, we emphasized the requirement of bargained-for-exchange. Where the promise induces the detriment but the detriment does not induce the promise, there is no bargained-for-exchange and no consideration exists to support the promise. Where, however, promisor expects a promisee to rely on the promise and the promisee does rely to its substantial detriment, it would be unjust to refuse to enforce the promise which may be enforced under the doctrine of promissory estoppel.[469] It is important to understand the origins of this mutually exclusive validation device.

The purpose of contract law is often stated as the fulfillment of those expectations induced by the making of a promise.[470] The expectations are fulfilled by placing a party aggrieved by the other party's breach in the position the innocent party would have occupied had there been no breach. While the expectation interest has been recognized as the normal interest

---

1998); Federal Sign v. Texas S. Univ., 951 S. W. 2d 401, 409 (Tex. 1997); Reed v. Citizens Ins. Co., 198 Mich. App. 443, 449, 499 N.W.2d 22, 25 (1993).

[465] *See* § 128, *infra.*

[466] The "adequacy of consideration" doctrine was explored in § 60, *supra.* For a case in which this confusion is discussed, see Hillsman v. Sutter Community Hosps., 153 Cal. App. 3d 743, 200 Cal. Rptr. 605 (3d Dist. 1984). *See also* Zamore v. Whitten, 395 A.2d 435, 443 n.3 (Me. 1978), where the court mentions Professor Corbin's criticism of the expression, "mutuality of obligation," for its tendency to connote a need for obligations equivalent in terms of detriment and value.

[467] RESTATEMENT 2d § 78 comment b.

[468] RESTATEMENT 2d § 78 comment c.

[469] This fundamental distinction is effectively recognized in Miles Home Division v. First State Bank of Joplin 782 S.W.2d 798 (Mo. Ct. App. 1990).

[470] CORBIN ON CONTRACTS § 1. "[C]ontract law provided a framework of reasonably assured expectations with which men might plan and venture." J. HURST, LAW AND ECONOMIC GROWTH: THE LEGAL HISTORY OF THE LUMBER INDUSTRY IN WISCONSIN 1836–1915, at 297 (1964). *See also* Straup v. Times Herald, 283 Pa. Super. 58, 70, 423 A.2d 713, 719 (1980): "The purpose of contract law may be stated as the fulfillment of expectations induced by the making of a promise" (citing the second edition of this treatise.).

protected by contract law, the reliance interest may be seen as presenting a greater claim to protection.[471] If a party has reasonably relied to his detriment on the promise of another, he has suffered a loss which is properly characterized as an out-of-pocket or minus quantity.[472] If an executory bilateral contract is breached before any performance has occurred, neither party has suffered any minus quantity. The non-breaching party will be entitled to recover damages for his defeated expectations, his disappointment. If a promisee relies on a promise and suffers a detriment, however, he is more obviously injured since he has already suffered a measurable loss when the promisor refuses to perform. The injured promisee presents a compelling argument to be compensated, at least to the extent of restoring him to *status quo ante*, i.e., the position he was in before he justifiably relied, by permitting him to recover the amount of his out-of-pocket (minus quantity) loss.

There is reason to believe that the original enforcement of informal contracts was based on the reasonable reliance of the promisee rather than his disappointed expectations.[473] The concept of reliance certainly antedates the concept of protected expectations.[474] With the development of consideration, however, there was a tendency to ignore the protection of the reliance interest. Where a promise induces reliance, the promisee has suffered a detriment. Yet, as we have seen in the exploration of the bargained-for-exchange element of consideration, if the detriment did not induce the promise, consideration is lacking. For those who viewed consideration as the apotheosis of validating promises, a promise that merely induced a detriment where the detriment did not also induce the promise was unenforceable. There was a great fear that reliance would make gratuitous promises enforceable and the doctrine of consideration would be emasculated.[475] That fear has been overcome because of the manifest injustice in refusing to recognize that certain promises induce a substantial change of position in reasonable promisees and should, therefore, be enforced.[476]

Unfortunately, general recognition of detrimental reliance as a validation device is a product of twentieth-century contract law. It was given limited recognition in Section 90 of the FIRST RESTATEMENT, and that recognition has been augmented substantially in Section 90 of the RESTATEMENT 2d. Notwithstanding its more recent discovery as a general validation device, the doctrine has clearly identifiable antecedents. Family promises, gratuitous promises to convey land, gratuitous bailments and charitable subscription promises clearly recognized the vitality of detrimental reliance before its recognition as a general validation device.[477] It is important to consider these antecedents.

---

[471] Fuller & Perdue, *The Reliance Interest in Contract Damages (pts. 1 & 2)*, 46 YALE L.J. 52, 373 (1936).

[472] See discussion of the reliance interest as well as the expectation and restitution interests, *infra* Chapter 9.

[473] Fuller & Perdue, *supra* note 471, at 68.

[474] See Loranger Constr. Corp. v. E. F. Hauserman Co., 376 Mass. 757, 384 N.E.2d 176, 179 (1978), where Justice Braucher, former Reporter of the RESTATEMENT 2d so states relying, in part, on RESTATEMENT 2d § 90 comment a.

[475] "It would cut up the doctrine of consideration by the roots, if a promisee could make a gratuitous promise binding by subsequently acting in reliance on it." O. W. Holmes, Jr. in Commonwealth by Commissioners of Sav. Banks v. Scituate Sav. Bank, 137 Mass. 301, 302 (1884).

[476] *See* Minor v. Sully Buttes Sch. Dist. No. 58-2, 345 N.W.2d 48 (S.D. 1984) (citing the 2d edition of this book at § 91).

[477] *See* Pavel Enters. v. A. S. Johnson Co., Inc., 342 Md. 143, 164, 674 A.2d 521, 531 (1996). *See also* Overlock v. Central Vt. Pub. Serv. Corp., 126 Vt. 549, 237 A.2d 356 (1967).

[1]   Family Promises — Equitable Estoppel to "Promissory Estoppel"

A promise made by one member of a family to another member was enforceable even without consideration if the promisee reasonably relied upon the promise. Some courts would find consideration to support such promises notwithstanding the lack of a bargained-for-exchange.[478] Other courts candidly recognized the lack of consideration but found the promise enforceable because of detrimental reliance. The best known case is *Ricketts v. Scothorn*,[479] where a grandfather delivered a written promise in the form of a note in the amount of $2000 with interest to his granddaughter to permit her to leave her employment. The granddaughter left the employment. At the time of his death, the grandfather had not paid the note, though he had paid some of the interest thereon. The granddaughter brought an action against the executor of the estate to recover the total amount due. The court recognized that there was no consideration to support the promise since the grandfather did not require the granddaughter to suffer the detriment of leaving her employment. There was no bargained-for-exchange. The evidence indicated that his purpose was to permit her to be independent, i.e., to either work or remain idle, but to require nothing from her. Yet, she suffered a detriment and, though her detriment had not induced her grandfather's promise, his promise had induced her detriment. Moreover, the grandfather certainly contemplated that she would rely on his promise by suffering the detriment of surrendering her employment.

The court found an "equitable estoppel" which precluded the defendant from showing that the note lacked one of the essential elements of a contract, i.e., consideration. The application of an equitable estoppel theory to the facts of the case, however, is misleading. Normally, equitable estoppel occurs where a party makes a false representation to, or knowingly conceals material facts from, another party with the intention that the innocent party should act upon the false representation or concealment.[480] Liability attached if the innocent party so acted to his detriment. There was no false representation in the *Ricketts* case. Rather, the grandfather made a *promise*, apparently in good faith. The notion that the promise is enforceable notwithstanding the lack of consideration because the promisor is *estopped* to deny consideration is nothing more than a conclusion. The promise was enforceable because the promisee changed her position to her detriment in the reasonable belief that the promise would be performed. The court's use of equitable estoppel to make the promise enforceable because of

---

[478] See, e.g., Devecmon v. Shaw, 69 Md. 199, 14 A. 464 (1888), where an uncle promised to reimburse a nephew for his expenses if he would take a trip to Europe. The court found the promise to be enforceable as supported by consideration, though the facts and the rationale of the court clearly indicate that the basis for enforcing the promise was detrimental reliance notwithstanding the lack of any bargained-for-exchange.

[479] 57 Neb. 51, 77 N.W. 365 (1898). Modern courts regard this case as a "classic illustration" of promissory estoppel. Arasimowicz v. Bestfoods, Inc., 2000 U.S. Dist. LEXIS 17818, at *25 (S.D.N.Y. Nov. 27, 2000). *See also* D & G Stout, Inc. v. Bacardi Imports, Inc., 805 F. Supp. 1434, 1446 (N.D. Ind. 1992) ("seminal case").

[480] This statement appeared in § 91 of the second edition of this book and is quoted by the court in Valley Bank v. Dowdy, 337 N.W.2d 164, 165 (S.D. 1983). Equitable estoppel, or estoppel *in pais*, is frequently defined as, "The species of estoppel which equity puts upon a person who has made a false representation or a concealment of material facts, with knowledge of the facts, to a party ignorant of the truth of the matter, with the intention that the other party should act upon it, and with the result that such party is actually induced to act upon it to his damage." Henderson, *Promissory Estoppel and Traditional Contract Doctrine*, 78 YALE L.J. 343, 376 n.182 (1969). For an analysis and comparison of equitable estoppel and promissory estoppel, see Cottle Enters., Inc. v. Town of Farmington, 693 A.2d 330, 330–35, 336 n.6 (1997). *See also* Cohn v. Checker Motors Corp., 233 Ill. App. 3d 839, 845, 599 N.E.2d 1112, 1117 (1st Dist. 1992).

reliance may be laid to the felt necessity of the court to discover an extant doctrine in support of the result the court sought to reach.

Subsequently, it became clear that *equitable estoppel* was too narrow a ground to support the enforcement of promises which had induced reasonable detrimental reliance. Though not inevitable, it was predictable that, instead of rejecting the estoppel notion and developing the doctrine in accordance with its substantive basis, detrimental reliance, courts and scholars would permit the doctrinal antecedents to persist in modified fashion. The modern doctrine, therefore, is known as "promissory estoppel."[481]

The fact that "estoppel" has nothing to do with the enforcement of the promise and that the continuation of that term can be misleading has not deterred the use of the label, "promissory estoppel."[482] The student, however, should remember that the essence of the doctrine is justifiable detrimental reliance which makes the promise enforceable or, in the language of its caption, "estops" the promisor from denying the enforcement of the promise. A recent opinion suggests that both "promissory estoppel" and "equitable estoppel" are equitable judicial doctrines based on detrimental reliance. Promissory estoppel is a cause of action and equitable estoppel is a defensive doctrine used to bar opposing parties from asserting a claim or defense. Promissory estoppel permits the enforcement of a promise that would otherwise be unenforceable. The court concludes by quoting a 9th Circuit opinion, "Promissory estoppel is a sword, and equitable estoppel is a shield."[483]

[2]   Gratuitous Promises to Convey Land

Like other gratuitous promises, a gratuitous promise to convey land is unenforceable because it lacks consideration. If, however, the promisee takes possession of the land and makes valuable improvements, the promisee will succeed in a suit for specific performance of the promise to convey the land.[484] A gratuitous license to use the land has been held to be specifically enforceable where the licensee has incurred substantial outlays in reliance on the promise.[485] While some courts felt compelled to discover "consideration" in such cases because

---

[481]   The label, "promissory estoppel," is attributed to Professor Williston at 1 WILLISTON ON CONTRACTS § 139 (1st ed. 1920), in Boyer, *Promissory Estoppel: Requirements and Limitations of the Doctrine*, 98 U. PA. L. REV. 459 (1950). In Valley Bank v. Dowdy, 337 N.W.2d 164, 165 (S.D. 1983), the court cites § 91 of the second edition of this book in explaining, "When cases first appeared involving agreements lacking the element of consideration and the promisee reasonably relied upon a promise to his detriment, courts held the detrimental reliance substituted for the consideration and enforced the contract under equitable estoppel. . . . Courts then subsequently developed the broader theory of detrimental reliance, which is usually referred to as the doctrine of promissory estoppel."

[482]   See Loranger Constr. Corp. v. E. F. Hauserman Co., 376 Mass. 757, 761, 384 N.E.2d 176, 179 (1978), where the opinion by Justice Braucher suggests that "the expression, 'promissory estoppel' tends to confusion rather than clarity." Prior to his judicial career, Justice Braucher was a member of the Harvard Law Faculty and served as Reporter for the RESTATEMENT 2d. When he joined the Supreme Judicial Court of Massachusetts, he was replaced as Reporter by Professor Alan Farnsworth of the Columbia University School of Law. In light of Justice Braucher's criticism of the label "promissory estoppel," it is not remarkable that the RESTATEMENT 2d does not employ that terminology though it is mentioned in comment a to § 90. The Chief Reporter of the FIRST RESTATEMENT, Professor Williston, avoided the use of the phrase in the original § 90.

[483]   In Peters v. Gilead Sciences., Inc., 533 F.3d 594, 598, n. 5 (7th Cir. 2008), quoting Jablon v. United States, 657 F.2d 1064, 1068 (9th Cir. 1981).

[484]   Seavey v. Drake, 62 N.H. 393 (1882). *See also* Miller v. Lawlor, 245 Iowa 1144, 66 N.W.2d 267, 48 A.L.R.2d 1058 (1954).

[485]   Lembke v. Lembke, 196 Iowa 136, 194 N.W. 367 (1923).

of the reliance of the promisee,[486] it is clear that the overwhelming majority of decisions in this area are based upon detrimental reliance.[487]

[3]   Gratuitous Bailments — Gratuitous Agency — Insurance

Perhaps the oldest antecedents of the modern doctrine of detrimental reliance (promissory estoppel) are those involving gratuitous bailments. From a very early day it has been held that a promise by a gratuitous bailee made before the goods were delivered to him was enforceable if it was relied upon by a bailor who suffered a serious loss because the bailee failed to perform his promise. Where, for example, prior to the delivery of goods, a gratuitous bailee promised that he would have them insured but failed to do so after they were delivered to him, he was held liable for the loss when the goods were destroyed. It was held that the delivery of the goods to the bailee was the "consideration" for the promise to insure.[488] This is patently unsound since it is clear that the parties had not bargained for anything in this situation. The promise of the bailee to procure insurance was gratuitous and the bailor-promisee relied on that promise by not procuring insurance. It seems clear that the bailee should be liable for his dereliction, but it is impossible to discover a basis for that liability on any theory of consideration. The basis of liability in this type of case can be traced to the earliest notions of assumpsit as an action sounding in tort (*ex delicto*), i.e., when one who undertook to do something performed *badly*, he *misfeased* and was liable under the writ of assumpsit.[489] In a gratuitous bailment, if a party promises to become a bailee but does not enter upon the performance of the bailment, the promisor will be guilty of *nonfeasance* and no liability is imposed when the promisor fails to perform the bailment at all. If, however, the promisor begins to perform as a bailee and then breaches his promise, he is guilty of *misfeasance* and is liable.[490]

The distinction between misfeasance and nonfeasance was evident in other older cases. Thus, while an unperformed promise to procure insurance was not enforceable (nonfeasance),[491] a promisor was liable if he procured insurance and the insurance was

---

[486] *See, e.g.*, Lindell v. Lindell, 135 Minn. 368, 160 N.W. 1031 (1917).

[487] Greiner v. Greiner, 131 Kan. 760, 293 P. 759 (1930), upon which ill. 16 to RESTATEMENT 2d § 90 is based: *A* orally promises to give her son *B* a tract of land to live on. As *A* intended, *B* gives up a homestead elsewhere, takes possession of the land, lives there for a year and makes substantial improvements. *A*'s promise is binding. While enforcement of a promise based upon detrimental reliance should certainly protect at least the reliance interest, at first blush there would seem to be little possibility of protecting the restitution interest which requires a showing of benefit to the promisor, i.e., an unjust enrichment, while the essence of detrimental reliance is a minus quantity, i.e., an out-of-pocket loss to the promisee. Where a promise induces the promisee to make valuable improvements to land, however, if the promise is not specifically enforceable, the restitution interest of the relying promisee may be protected through a judicial declaration that the promisor holds the land as a constructive trustee for the relying promisee. A constructive trust is a trust created by the court to prevent unjust enrichment, i.e., to protect the restitution interest. The best-known case of this type is Monarco v. Lo Greco, in an opinion by Justice Traynor, at 35 Cal. 2d 621, 220 P.2d 737 (1950).

[488] Siegel v. Spear & Co., 234 N.Y. 479, 138 N.E. 414 (1923). See comments on this case in 22 MICH. L. REV. 64 (1923), 23 COLUM. L. REV. 573 (1923), 32 YALE L.J. 609 (1923). The classic case is Coggs v. Bernard, 92 Eng. Rep. 107 (K.B. 1703).

[489] *See* 3 HOLDSWORTH, HISTORY OF ENGLISH LAW 336 (1909).

[490] *See* Tomko v. Sharp, 87 N.J.L. 385, 94 A. 793 (Super. Ct. 1915). *See also* Coggs v. Bernard, 92 Eng. Rep. 107, 114 (K.B. 1703).

[491] Thorne v. Deas, 4 Johns 84 (N.Y. 1809). *See also* Comfort v. McCorkle, 149 Misc. 826, 268 N.Y.S. 192 (Sup. Ct. 1933).

ineffective (misfeasance).[492] These cases involved gratuitous agencies and modern courts no longer permit liability to depend upon misfeasance versus nonfeasance in such cases. Rather, they recognize an agent's promise as one that may cause justifiable detrimental reliance whether or not the agent has begun to perform.[493] Where a mortgagee fails to perform a gratuitous promise to obtain insurance for a homeowner who is obligated under the mortgage to maintain insurance on the property, the weight of authority allows the enforcement of the promise on the basis of promissory estoppel.[494]

The promise may involve liability that is quite substantial, particularly with respect to gratuitous promises to procure insurance. In light of the risk allocated to the promisor in such cases, evidence of the fact of reliance and the justifiable nature of the reliance under the circumstances should be clear.[495] While the misfeasance/nonfeasance distinction is emasculated in gratuitous agency situations, it remains in the gratuitous bailment cases though the justification for the distinction in such cases is purely historical.

[4]   Charitable Subscriptions

We have already explored the proclivity of courts to discover one or more validation devices to make promises to charities enforceable.[496] The use of the detrimental reliance device in charitable subscription cases long antedated the recognition of detrimental reliance as a general validation device. One jurisdiction, for example, has traced its use to a case in the

---

[492] In Barile v. Wright, 256 N.Y. 1, 175 N.E. 351 (1931), the defendant promised to obtain insurance and did so. However, the policy he procured contained a clause to the effect that the insurer would not be liable if there was any other policy covering the insured property. There was such a policy as the defendant well knew. By failing to obtain a waiver or consent concerning the clause, the defendant failed to exercise reasonable diligence and was held liable to the mortgagor for the face amount of the policy. *See also* Elam v. Smithdeal Realty & Ins. Co., 182 N.C. 599, 109 S.E. 632 (1921).

[493] *See, e.g.,* Verschoor v. Mountain W. Farm Bureau Mut. Ins. Co., 907 P.2d 1293, 1297–1301 (Wyo. 1995); Franklin Inv. Co. v. Huffman, 393 A.2d 119 (D.C. App. 1978); Estes v. Lloyd Hammerstad, Inc., 8 Wash. App. 22, 503 P.2d 1149 (1972); Spiegel v. Metropolitan Life Ins. Co., 6 N.Y.2d 91, 188 N.Y.S.2d 486, 160 N.E.2d 40 (1959); Graddon v. Knight, 138 Cal. App. 2d 577, 292 P.2d 632 (1st Dist. 1956); East Providence Credit Union v. Geremia, 103 R.I. 597, 239 A.2d 725 (1968). See RESTATEMENT 2d AGENCY § 378, which is an application of the detrimental reliance concept to gratuitous promises by agents. See also RESTATEMENT 2d TORTS § 323, which makes one who undertakes, gratuitously or for consideration, to render services to another which the promisor should recognize as necessary for the protection of the other person or things, liable for failure to exercise reasonable care if such failure increases the risk of harm or the harm is suffered due to the other's reliance upon the undertaking. See also Wangerin, *Damages for Reliance Across the Spectrum of Law: Of Blind Men and Legal Elephants*, 72 IOWA L. REV. 47 (1986), in which the author traces the reliance concept to five different areas, i.e., contracts, agency, torts, insurance, and constructive trusts (restitution), concluding that legal scholars have failed to expose overlaps among these areas concerning the reliance interest and the possibilities of different remedies depending upon which substantive analysis is chosen as the vehicle to protect the relying promisee.

[494] See Shoemaker v. Commonwealth Bank, 700 A.2d 1003, 1007 (Pa. Super. Ct. 1997), and cases cited therein.

[495] RESTATEMENT 2d § 90 comment e: "The appropriate remedy for breach of such a promise makes the promisor an insurer, and thus may result in liability which is very large in relation to the value of the promised service. Often the promise is properly to be construed merely as a promise to use reasonable efforts to procure the insurance and reliance by the promisee may be unjustified or may be justified only for a very short time. Or it may be doubtful whether he did in fact rely. Such difficulties may be removed if the proof of the promise and the reliance are clear, or if the promise is made with some formality, or if part performance or a commercial setting or a potential benefit to the promisor provide a substitute for formality." See McCarthy v. Louisville Cartage Co., 796 S.W.2d 10, 12–13 (Ky. Ct. App. 1990).

[496] *See supra* § 63.

middle of the nineteenth century.[497] Later, in the famous opinion by Judge Cardozo in *Allegheny College v. National Chautauqua County Bank*, we are told that, "[T]here has grown up of recent days a doctrine that a substitute for consideration or an exception to its ordinary requirements can be found in what is styled 'a promissory estoppel,' "[498] which could be applied to charitable subscriptions. Judge Cardozo, however, found consideration to support a promise to the charity and there is reason to believe he did so because it would have been difficult for the charity to prove a critical element of promissory estoppel, i.e., that the charity had actually relied upon the promise.[499] More recent cases suggest the same infirmity.[500]

The RESTATEMENT 2d sought to meet this challenge. Emphasizing the fact that our courts have shown high favor for charitable subscriptions and marriage settlements, the RESTATEMENT 2d allows such promises to be binding "without proof that the promise induced action or forbearance."[501] A comment candidly recognizes that the judicial discovery of consideration in some cases ignored the element of bargained-for-exchange. It further recognizes that when recovery is rested upon reliance in promises to charities, "a probability of reliance is enough. . . ."[502] This view has yet to be generally accepted as courts continue to insist upon a definite showing of reliance by charities.[503]

[B]   Section 90 of the First and RESTATEMENT 2d

The inclusion of the detrimental reliance device in the FIRST RESTATEMENT promulgated in 1933 was grudgingly accepted since consideration was the dominant validation device.[504] A new version of § 90 appears in the RESTATEMENT 2d and it is important to compare it with its predecessor. The First Restatement version reads as follows:

§ 90. Promises Reasonably Inducing Definite and Substantial Action.

---

[497] In Maryland Nat'l Bank v. United Jewish Appeal Federation, Inc., 286 Md. 274, 407 A.2d 1130 (1979), the court finds the detrimental reliance concept as a validation device for promises to charities espoused in Gittings v. Mayhew, 6 Md. 113 (1854). Though the statement of the law in *Gittings* was dictum, there is no question that the court was stating what it believed to be a principle that should be generally recognized. At pp. 131–132 of the *Gittings* opinion, the court makes this point with unquestioned clarity: "In whatever uncertainty the law concerning voluntary subscriptions of this character may be at this time, in consequence of the numerous decisions pronounced upon the subject, it appears to be settled, that where advances have been made, or expenses or liabilities incurred by others, in consequence of such subscriptions, before notice of withdrawal, this should, on general principles, be deemed sufficient to make them obligatory, provided the advances were authorized by a fair and reasonable dependence on the subscription. . . . The doctrine is not only reasonable and just, but consistent with the analogies of the law."

[498] 246 N.Y. 369, 159 N.E. 173, 175 (1927).

[499] *See* § 63 *supra*. For a current view of promissory estoppel as applied in New York, see Cyberchron Corp. v. Calldata Sys. Dev., 47 F.3d 39, 44–46 (2d Cir. 1995).

[500] *See* Maryland Nat'l Bank v. United Jewish Appeal Federation, Inc., 286 Md. 274, 407 A.2d 1130 (1979); Mt. Sinai Hosp., Inc. v. Jordan, 290 So. 2d 484 (Fla. 1974).

[501] RESTATEMENT 2d § 90(2). *See* P.H.C.C.C., Inc. v. Johnston, 340 N.W.2d 774, 776 (Iowa 1983).

[502] RESTATEMENT 2d § 90 comment f.

[503] King v. Trustees of Boston Univ., 420 Mass. 52, 57, 647 N.E.2d 1196, 1200 (1995); Arrowsmith v. Mercantile-Safe Deposit & Trust Co., 313 Md. 334, 353–54, 545 A.2d 674, 683–84 (1988).

[504] "Only the scholarly counterattack by Professor Corbin prevented the complete ascendancy of consideration by confronting the *Restatement* drafters with a multitude of reliance decisions. Corbin succeeded in carving out a place for promissory estoppel as an instance of the *Restatement's* residual category of 'Informal Contracts Without Assent or Consideration.' " Feinman, *Promissory Estoppel and Judicial Method*, 97 HARV. L. REV. 678–80 (1984) (citing G. GILMORE, THE DEATH OF CONTRACT 62–64 (1974)).

A promise which the promisor should reasonably expect to induce action or forbearance of a definite and substantial character on the part of the promisee and which does
induce such action or forbearance is binding if injustice can be avoided only by
enforcement of the promise.

The RESTATEMENT 2d version of § 90 contains two subsections. We have just explored § 90(2)
dealing with charitable subscription promises. Section 90(1) is the modified version of original
§ 90. In the following quotation, the language deleted from the FIRST RESTATEMENT is in
brackets, while the new language added by the RESTATEMENT 2d is italicized.

§ 90. Promise Reasonably Inducing [Definite and Substantial] Action or Forbearance.

(1) A promise which the promisor should reasonably expect to induce action or
forbearance [of a definite and substantial character] on the part of the promisee *or a
third person* and which does induce such action or forbearance is binding only if
injustice can be avoided by enforcement of the promise. *The remedy granted for breach
may be limited as justice requires.*

Among the distinctions between the two versions, the reference to "forbearance" in the caption
to the RESTATEMENT 2d version is merely stylistic. Since the FIRST RESTATEMENT contemplated
forbearance as well as action, the addition of "forbearance" suggests no substantive difference.
There are, however, three significant changes in the RESTATEMENT 2d version: (1) the deletion
of the requirement that reliance be "of a definite and substantial character," (2) the addition
permitting protection of "a third person" who relies upon the promise, and (3) the addition of
a flexible remedy standard, i.e., the remedy "may be limited as justice requires."[505] It is
important to explore the similarities and differences in the two iterations.

[1]   Requirement of a "Promise"

Under both versions, there must be a "promise" that courts typically require to be "clear
and definite."[506] " 'A mere expression of intention, hope, desire or opinion which shows no real
commitment cannot be expected to induce reliance' and, therefore is not sufficiently promissory."[507] Where the plaintiff alleged contributions of time and money to the Democratic
National Committee and his reliance on its promises in the election of President Obama, the
court held that such "promises" were statements of principle and intent and were not
enforceable promises under contract law to allow the application of promissory estoppel.[508] The
promise need not meet the requirements of an offer which manifests a commitment to enter

---

[505] See Valley Bank v. Dowdy, 337 N.W.2d 164, 165 (S.D. 1983), suggesting the differences between the two versions
of § 90 and citing the second edition of this treatise at § 91.

[506] *See, e.g.*, Leila Hosp. & Health Ctr. v. Xonics Med. Sys., Inc., 948 F.2d 271, 275 (6th Cir. 1991); Willis v. New
World Van Lines, Inc., 123 F. Supp. 2d 380 (E.D. Mich. 2000); Lohse v. Atlantic Richfield Co., 389 N.W.2d 352 (N.D.
1986); See, however, Pop's Cones, Inc. v. Resorts Int'l Hotel, 307 N.J. Super. 461, 471, 704 A.2d 1321, 1326 (App. Div.
1998): "As we read the Restatement [2d § 90], the strict adherence to proof of a 'clear and definite' promise . . . is being
eroded by a more equitable analysis to avoid injustice." See also Mt. Carmel Mercy Hosp. v. Allstate Ins. Co., 194 Mich.
App. 580, 487 N.W.2d 849 (1992), holding that an unequivocal promise not to assert the statute of limitations is not
necessary if conduct induced definite and substantial reliance. For an extensive discussion of the meaning of "promise"
as applied in promissory estoppel cases, see State Bank of Standish v. Curry, 442 Mich. 76, 500 N.W.2d 104 (1993).

[507] William St. Paul v. Easter Seals Goodwill Indus. 2004 Conn. Super. LEXIS 912 at 18 (2004), quoting Corbin on
Contracts, § 8.9.

[508] Berg v. Obama, 574 F. Supp. 2d 509, 529 (E. D. Pa. 2008).

into a contract. Offers are promises, but all promises are not offers.[509]

The promise must also be sufficiently definite. In a discussion concerning possible employment in a new organizational structure, the plaintiff stated that he had an offer from his prior employer of $2.45 million to which the defendant replied, "We can match that. That's not a problem." The plaintiff allowed the offer from the previous employer to expire and proceeded with serious discussions with the defendant who allegedly reiterated the statement of matching the $2.45 million. The parties agreed upon a salary of $400,000, but some eight months after beginning work, the plaintiff was terminated and sought to recover $2.45 million on a promissory estoppel theory. While noting that a promise need not constitute an offer, the court held that the defendant's statement of matching the offer from the previous employer lacked sufficient definiteness to sustain a promissory estoppel claim. When the first statement was made, there were no specifics concerning the nature of the employment and no indication what the long-term compensation would be. In the alleged second iteration of the statement, there was no discussion of what "matching" $2.45 million would constitute in terms of salary, bonuses, stock options or other possibilities. Neither did the plaintiff seek clarification of how the $2.45 million might be matched. Moreover, as to the alleged second statement, the plaintiff could not have detrimentally relied since he had allowed the offer from the previous employer to expire before that discussion.[510]

[2]   Reliance Must Be Foreseeable

The promisor must reasonably expect to induce reliance, i.e., reliance by the promisee must be foreseeable at the time the promise is made. Where a court found the other requisites for the application of promissory estoppel, it found that the promisee failed to establish that his reliance on the promise by extending a personal loan to a corporation was foreseeable by the defendant.[511]

[3]   Reliance of a "Definite and Substantial Character"

The promisee (or third party under the RESTATEMENT 2d version) must actually rely, and it is common for courts to state that the reliance must be "definite and substantial."[512] Since this requirement is embedded in the case law, why has the "definite and substantial" language been deleted from the RESTATEMENT 2d version of § 90? The rationale is found in the flexible remedy.

---

[509] Stewart v. Cendant Mobility Servs. Corp., 267 Conn. 96, 105, 837 A. 2d 736,742 (2003) citing Corbin's explanation that the prerequisite for the application of promissory estoppel is a clear and definite promise, while an offer is a necessary prerequisite to a bargained-for-exchange.

[510] Brooks v. Aon Corp., 404 F. Supp. 2d 567 (S. D. N. Y. 2005).

[511] Henneberry v. Sumitomo Corp. of America, 2005 U. S. Dist. LEXIS 7475 (S. D. N. Y. 2005). *See also* Leonardi v. City of Hollywood, 715 So. 2d 1007, 1009 (Fla. Dist. Ct. App. 1998); Onorato Constr. v. Eastman Constr. Co., 312 N.J. Super. 565, 572, 711 A.2d 1363, 1366 (App. Div. 1998). *See also* Gerson Elec. Constr. Co. v. Honeywell, Inc., 117 Ill. App. 3d 309, 453 N.E.2d 726, 728 (1st Dist. 1983); Farm Crop Energy, Inc. v. Old Nat'l Bank, 38 Wash. App. 50, 685 P.2d 1097 (1984), *rev'd on other grounds, en banc*, 109 Wash. 2d 923, 750 P.2d 231 (1988); Berryman v. Kmoch, 221 Kan. 304, 559 P.2d 790 (1977).

[512] *See, e.g.*, Brown v. Branch, 733 N.E.2d 17, 24 (Ind. Ct. App. 2000); Arasimowicz v. Bestfoods, Inc., 2000 U.S. Dist. LEXIS 17818 (S.D.N.Y. Nov. 27, 2000); Landess v. Borden, Inc., 667 F.2d 628 (7th Cir. 1981). However, see Farber & Matheson, *Beyond Promissory Estoppel: Contract Law and the "Invisible Handshake,"* 52 U. CHI. L. REV. 903 (1985), in which the authors deal with cases applying promissory estoppel where the actual reliance is at least doubtful, *e.g.*, Vastoler v. American Can Co., 700 F.2d 916 (3d Cir. 1983), and Oates v. Teamster Affiliates Pension Plan, 482 F. Supp. 481 (D.D.C. 1979).

If the remedy may be limited as justice requires, a court may decide upon partial enforcement of the promise rather than refusing to enforce the promise at all because the requirement of reliance of a definite and substantial character has not been met in a particular case.[513] Under the FIRST RESTATEMENT version of § 90, controversy arose as to whether the substantial change of position on the part of the promisee had to result in serious economic loss.[514] The deletion of the "definite and substantial" requirement seeks to alleviate that concern. The new Section 90 is not suggesting that a promise should be enforced without sufficient reason. It continues to condition the enforceability of the promise on the avoidance of injustice. If the reliance is neither definite nor substantial, a court would be hard pressed to discover sufficient injustice to meet that requirement. Moreover, comment b to the new § 90 indicates that one of the factors to be considered in determining whether injustice can be avoided is "the definite and substantial character" of the reliance.[515] At this time, courts are paying preciously little attention to the reduction of this standard to comment status. They continue to insist upon "measurable" reliance as a critical element of promissory estoppel.[516]

[4] Detrimental Reliance by Third Persons

"Or a third person. . . ." The RESTATEMENT 2d change providing protection to a relying third person as well as the promisee is abundantly clear with respect to "intended beneficiaries." Where there is consideration for a promise, if Barnes agrees to pay Ames in exchange for Ames' promise to provide goods or services to a third party, Carr, it is clear that Carr is an intended beneficiary who may bring an action against the promisor, Ames, if Ames fails to perform. If, however, Ames makes the same promise but it is not supported by consideration, there would be no recovery under classical contract law even though the third party, Carr, justifiably relied upon the promise to his detriment.[517] To permit a promisee to recover on the basis of detrimental reliance, but to preclude a recovery for a third party who is equally justified in relying upon the promise, is unsound. Reliance by such an intended beneficiary should, therefore, provide a basis for recovery.[518] This change, alone, would be extremely

---

[513] *See* Reporter's Note to RESTATEMENT 2d § 90.

[514] In the earliest major article on the original § 90, Dean Benjamin Boyer suggested that there was no reason to insist upon relegating the loss to those of an economic nature. Boyer, *Promissory Estoppel: Requirements and Limitations of the Doctrine*, 98 U. PA. L. REV. 459, 478 (1950). *See also* Boyer, *Promissory Estoppel: Principle From Precedents*, 50 MICH. L. REV. 639, 873 (1952).

[515] The splendid analysis of Dean Knapp recognizes this problem and further suggests that the deletion of the "definite and substantial" test may be traceable to an earlier draft that attempted to deal with charitable subscriptions cases only in a comment. With the addition of subsection (2) to the new § 90, however, it is clear that the "definite and substantial" test would not apply to such cases since subsection (2) removes any requirement that the promise induced the action or forbearance. Knapp, *Reliance in the Revised Restatement: The Proliferation of Promissory Estoppel*, 81 COLUM. L. REV. 52, 59 (1981). Dean Knapp is supported in this analysis by language in the final version of comment b to § 90: "[R]eliance need not be of substantial character in charitable subscription cases, but must in cases of firm offers and guaranties. . . . §§ 87, 88." Sections 87 and 88 are special cases of reliance-supported promises that will be discussed later in this section. Dean Knapp refers to these and two other reliance sections of the RESTATEMENT 2d (§§ 89 and 150) as "satellite promissory estoppel sections." *Id.* at 59.

[516] For example, in Gray v. First State Financial, Inc., 2009 Ky. App. LEXIS 175 at *10 (2009), the court rejected the plaintiff's assertion that the elimination of "definite and substantial character" from the First Restatement version of § 90 meant that it was no longer necessary to prove measurable loss. The court explained the new iteration that "[t]he remedy for breach may be limited as justice requires" as follows: "In other words, if no measurable injustice has occurred, no remedy is warranted."

[517] Third party beneficiaries are explored fully in Chapter 10, *infra.*

[518] RESTATEMENT 2d § 90 comment c.

modest in light of the general acceptance of promissory estoppel as a validation device. The RESTATEMENT 2d version of § 90, however, extends recovery to justifiably relying third parties who are *not* intended beneficiaries, though it recognizes that justifiable reliance by a third party who is not an intended beneficiary is less likely.[519] Even this extension is not radical in light of earlier case law allowing third parties to recover on a promissory estoppel theory.[520]

In what has become the classic illustration of recovery by such a third party, a husband and wife relied on representations by the defendant's agents who encouraged them to pursue numerous actions in preparation for becoming a franchised owner of a supermarket chain store. With respect to losses incurred on property owned by the plaintiffs in joint tenancy, the defendant argued that it should be liable for only one half of that loss, the husband's half, since defendant had no dealings with the wife and only the husband, therefore, was a promisee. The court responded,

> Ordinarily only the promisee and not third persons are entitled to enforce the remedy of promissory estoppel against the promisor. However, if the promisor actually foresees, or has reason to foresee, action by a third person in reliance on the promise, it may be quite unjust to refuse to perform the promise [citing the predecessor section of § 8.9 of Corbin on Contracts expressing this concern]. Here, not only did defendants foresee that it would be necessary for Mrs. Hoffman to sell her joint interest in the bakery building, but defendants actually requested that this be done.[521]

While the extension to third parties has been recognized either before or after the appearance of the modified § 90 of the RESTATEMENT 2d,[522] some courts have rejected the extension or indicated the importance of proceeding cautiously in its application.[523]

---

[519] *Id.*

[520] See Chesus v. Watts, 967 S.W.2d 97, 107 (Mo. Ct. App. 1998), and cases cited therein.

[521] *See* Hoffman v. Red Owl Stores, Inc., 26 Wis. 2d 683, 699, 133 N.W.2d 267, 275 (1965). In Ruud v. Great Plains Supply, Inc., 526 N.W.2d 369, 372 n.4 (Minn. 1995), the court distinguished *Hoffman* in finding that the promisor had not specifically requested the third party to act in reliance on the promise.

[522] *See Chesus v. Watts*, note 520 *supra*.

[523] See Lee v. Paragon Group Contractors, Inc., 78 N.C. App. 334, 337 S.E.2d 132 (1985), which refused to apply the doctrine to a third party beneficiary. *See also* Bolden v. General Acc., Fire & Life Assurance Corp., 119 Ill. App. 3d 263, 456 N.E.2d 306, 309 (1st Dist. 1983), where the court refused to apply the RESTATEMENT 2d protection to third persons because it was not clear whether an agreement existed between the parties and the plaintiffs failed to adequately allege the requisite detriment, i.e., a definite and substantial action or forbearance. Thus, this case "would not provide the best vehicle for effectuating a change in Illinois law, *even if desirable*. . . ." (emphasis added). In C. R. Fedrick, Inc. v. Sterling-Salem Corp., 507 F.2d 319 (9th Cir. 1974), the plaintiff was denied recovery where defendant quoted a price to its customer who was plaintiff's supplier. The price was different from the price quoted by the supplier to plaintiff. Plaintiff claimed reliance upon defendant's price and the court found that the defendant did not reasonably expect the plaintiff (third party) to rely upon the price defendant quoted to its customer. The court, however, also expressed reservations about the application of new § 90 to protect third parties. At the very least, these cases suggest the necessity of clear, justifiable, reliance by the third party. Such caution, however, not inconsistent with language in comment c to new § 90 which suggests that, "Justifiable reliance by third persons who are not intended beneficiaries is less likely. . . ."

[5]   Preventing Manifest Injustice

Both versions of § 90 suggest a condition to the enforcement of the promise if all elements are met, i.e., that *injustice* can be avoided only by enforcing the promise. There is very little discussion of this requirement in the case law. In *Cohen v. Cowles Media Co.*,[524] the plaintiff who worked for a gubernatorial candidate claimed reliance on promise by newspapers to keep his identity confidential, but the newspaper revealed his identity when it published a controversial story about an opposing candidate based on the plaintiff's information. The negative effect on the plaintiff's candidate caused the plaintiff to be fired. The newspaper argued that it was not unjust for it to publish the truth, but the court held that the substantial detriment to the plaintiff who lost his job required a remedy to avoid injustice.

RESTATEMENT 2d § 90 comment b describes the elements to be considered in satisfying the "injustice" requirement:

> the reasonableness of the promisee's reliance on its definite and substantial character in relation to the remedy sought, on the formality with which the promise is made, on the extent to which the evidentiary cautionary deterrent and channeling functions of form are met by the commercial setting or otherwise, and on the extent to which such other policies as the enforcement of bargains and the prevention of unjust enrichment are relevant.

The requirement appears conclusory once it is shown that a party justifiably relied on a promise and the promisor reasonably expected such reliance. One court has suggested that the "injustice" requirement is a matter of "law," while the other elements constitute questions of fact.[525]

[6]   Flexible Remedy of New Section 90 — Partial Enforcement

The third change in new § 90, the creation of a flexible remedy that would permit either full or partial enforcement of the promise, was clearly designed as the principal change.[526] The change was fostered by the scholarship of Professor Corbin, who emphasized the origin of the action in assumpsit where damages were measured by the extent of reliance injury rather than by the value of the promised performance[527] and by the well-known Fuller and Perdue article.[528] The classic illustration was one of the highlights in the discussion of the original § 90 in 1926. The Chief Reporter, Professor Williston, was presented with a hypothetical of an uncle promising $1000 to a nephew who reasonably relied upon the promise by purchasing an automobile for $500. Under the original § 90, Professor Williston was asked, is the uncle liable

---

[524]   479 N.W.2d 387 (Minn. 1992).

[525]   R. S. Bennett & Co. v. Economy Mech. Indus., Inc., 606 F.2d 182 (7th Cir. 1979). In Hoffman v. Red Owl Stores, Inc., 26 Wis. 2d 683, 698, 133 N.W.2d 267, 275 (1965). the court suggests that the "injustice" requirement "involves a policy decision by the court" that "embraces an element of discretion." It may be suggested that insubstantial reliance need not be remedied since the requirement that injustice be avoided is not met in such a case. Yet, any requirement concerning the extent of reliance is dealt with by the "substantial" requirement in the original § 90, while the new § 90 permits partial enforcement to alleviate the difficulty of determining whether particular reliance was substantial. This distinction between the two versions of § 90 is explored *infra*.

[526]   *See* Reporter's Note to RESTATEMENT 2d § 90.

[527]   CORBIN ON CONTRACTS § 8.8.

[528]   Fuller & Perdue, *The Reliance Interest in Contract Damages:* 46 YALE L.J. 52, 63–65 (1935); *id.*: 46 YALE L.J. 373, 401–06 (1937).

for $500 or $1000? Professor Williston left no doubt about the clear answer: the uncle would be liable for $1000. "Either the promise is binding or it is not. If the promise is binding it has to be enforced as it is made."[529]

The RESTATEMENT 2d does not embrace this all-or-nothing approach. It provides courts with discretion to determine the remedy "as justice requires."[530] Since "justice" is a fine aspiration but a Delphic guide, users of the RESTATEMENT 2d may rush to the relevant comment to § 90. The comment, however, does not provide substantial assistance: "The same factors which bear on whether any relief should be granted also bear on the character and extent of the remedy."[531] The factors suggested to determine whether any relief should be granted begin with the well-known requirement that the promisor must foresee the reliance and enforcement must be necessary to avoid injustice.[532] More specific factors are the reasonableness of the promisee's reliance, its definite and substantial character in relation to the remedy sought, the formality with which the promise was made, whether evidentiary, cautionary, deterrent and channeling functions are met in the context in which the promise was made, and whether the enforcement of bargains and the prevention of unjust enrichment have any bearing on the enforcement of the promise.[533]

The illustrations supporting this analysis begin with one based upon a well-known case where the plaintiff was induced to incur expenses based on the representations of the defendant that plaintiff would secure a franchise to sell a certain brand of radios. The court allowed a recovery for the plaintiff's cash outlays (out-of-pocket expenses protecting the reliance interest), but refused any expectation interest for lost profits.[534] The second illustration merely changes the promise to a misrepresentation where, because of the bad faith of the promisor, the promise is enforced completely, i.e., the promisee recovers his lost profits or expectation interest.[535] The notion that the remedy is normally limited to the reliance interest is undermined by another comment preceding these illustrations suggesting that "full-scale enforcement by normal remedies is often appropriate."[536]

The next illustration is based on the *Hoffman v. Red Owl* case discussed earlier with respect to a promissory estoppel recovery by a third party.[537] The case is also well-known for its

---

[529] 4 ALI Proceedings, Appendix at 103–04 (1926).

[530] RESTATEMENT 2d § 90(1).

[531] RESTATEMENT 2d § 90 comment d.

[532] RESTATEMENT 2d § 90 comment b.

[533] *Id.*

[534] Illustration 8 to RESTATEMENT 2d § 90 is based upon Goodman v. Dicker, 169 F.2d 684, 83 U.S. App. D.C. 353 (1948). Professor Wangerin suggests that Goodman v. Dicker "had nothing to do with the idea of flexible damages in contract law reliance situations. Rather, *Goodman* represented nothing more than routine application of a somewhat obscure principle in the common law of agency, a principle named the 'Missouri Rule,'" which, the author traces to Beebe v. Columbia Axle Co., 233 Mo. App. 212, 117 S.W.2d 624 (1938), where a distributorship was terminated and the court held the distributor could not collect lost profits but was awarded out-of-pocket expenditures. Wangerin, *Damages for Reliance Across the Spectrum of Law: Of Blind Men and Legal Elephants*, 72 IOWA L. REV. 47, 55 (1986). Professor Wangerin relies, in part, on the scholarship of Professor Gellhorn, *Limitations on Contract Termination Rights — Franchise Cancellations*, 1967 DUKE L.J. 465, 479–80.

[535] Illustration 9 to RESTATEMENT 2d § 90 is based on Chrysler Corp. v. Quimby, 51 Del. 264, 144 A.2d 123, 885 (1958). For a discussion of reliance recovery through tort misrepresentation theories, *see* Wangerin, *infra* note 555, at 58–69.

[536] RESTATEMENT 2d comment d.

[537] See text at note 521 *supra*.

remedial aspects. Induced by various assurances from the defendant, a franchisor of supermarkets, to understand that he could enter the grocery business for a limited sum, the plaintiff followed the defendant's advice by selling his bakery business and purchasing a small grocery to gain experience. The defendant's assurances induced other reliance in selling the grocery and other actions. Subsequently, the defendant informed the plaintiff that the original sum required to become a franchisee of defendant's supermarket chain would have to be increased substantially. At this point, the negotiations collapsed and the plaintiff brought an action based on promissory estoppel. The court limited the plaintiff's recovery to his actual losses, i.e., the reliance interest.[538] The RESTATEMENT 2d illustration adopts that conclusion because "the proposed agreement was never made."[539]

If this rationale were based upon the lack of certainty or foreseeability of the damages to a party such as the plaintiff, it would be understandable since certainty and foreseeability limit the recovery of damages even where an agreement is complete and the defendant's promise is supported by consideration.[540] Absent further explanation, however, the RESTATEMENT 2d illustration could be interpreted as requiring only reliance damages whenever the agreement is incomplete regardless of the foreseeability or certainty of expectation damages.[541] Again, however, the suggestion that "full-scale enforcement by normal remedies is often appropriate"[542] belies this analysis.

The uncertainties suggested by the flexible remedy in the new § 90 have not been addressed by the overwhelming majority of courts.[543] The typical reaction among those that have addressed the issue is to eschew a "mechanical" approach to damages in order to fashion a "discretionary"[544] or "equitable"[545] remedy. Whether particular courts have or have not confronted the flexible remedy issue, there is evidence that typical recovery protects the

---

[538] Hoffman v. Red Owl Stores, Inc., 26 Wis. 2d 683, 133 N.W.2d 267 (1965). *Accord* Mooney v. Craddock, 35 Colo. App. 20, 26, 530 P.2d 1302, 1305 (1974).

[539] RESTATEMENT 2d § 90 ill. 10.

[540] See Royal Am. Dev., Inc. v. City of Jacksonville, 508 So. 2d 528 (Fla. Dist. Ct. App. 1987), where the court permitted recovery of preconstruction expenditures on assurances of municipality and did not discuss any possibility of expectation recovery. The certainty and foreseeability limitations as well as other limitations on contract damages will be fully explored in a subsequent chapter dealing with contract remedies.

[541] Jarboe v. Landmark Community Newspapers, 644 N.E.2d 118 (Ind. 1994), relied upon D & G Stout, Inc. v. Bacardi Imports, Inc., 923 F.2d 566, 569 (7th Cir. 1991), where the court distinguished expectation and reliance damages in an employment-at-will contract, holding that the employee had only an expectation of income in future wages that promissory estoppel will not support. On the other hand, with respect to wages foregone in order to prepare to move as well as moving expenses, the employee surrendered a presently determinate sum for the purpose of relocating. These opportunity costs are reliance costs and not expectancy damages. See § 39[B][6][e], *supra*, for analysis of the application of promissory estoppel to contracts terminable-at-will.

[542] RESTATEMENT 2d § 90 comment d.

[543] Professor Wangerin suggests that over forty jurisdictions, virtually all of which readily accept the general concept of detrimental reliance, "have avoided the issue of flexibility." Wangerin, *Damages for Reliance Across the Spectrum of Law: Of Blind Men and Legal Elephants*, 72 IOWA L. REV. 47, 94 (1986). Another study identified 222 cases over the decade 1975-1985 which applied either version of § 90 of the RESTATEMENTS. Only 72 of these cases addressed the issue of the extent of recovery. Farber & Matheson, *Beyond Promissory Estoppel: Contract Law and the "Invisible Handshake,"* 52 U. CHI. L. REV. 903 n.14, 907, 909 n.24 (1985).

[544] *See* Gerson Elec. Constr. Co. v. Honeywell, Inc., 117 Ill. App. 3d 309, 453 N.E.2d 726 (1st Dist. 1983) (lost profits allowed).

[545] *See* Farm Crop Energy, Inc. v. Old Nat'l Bank of Wash., 38 Wash. App. 50, 685 P.2d 1097 (1984) (lost profits allowed).

expectation interest, i.e., full enforcement of the promise, rather than partial enforcement by protecting the reliance interest.[546]

If the promise is enforceable through detrimental reliance, undoubtedly some courts will protect the interest they have always protected regardless of the validation device, i.e., the expectation interest. If the plaintiff cannot prove expectation damages with reasonable certainty or, if they were unforeseeable at the time of the promise, a court could not award expectation damages any more than it could do so if the promise had been supported by consideration. In such a situation, the reliance interest — the minus quantity or out-of-pocket loss — should be awarded to restore the relying promisee to *status quo ante*. In discussions concerning possibility of relocating the plaintiff's franchise on casino property, the defendant urged the plaintiff to forego renewal of a lease in the original location because of the virtual certainty of a new arrangement with the casino. The plaintiff relied but the casino withdrew from further negotiations. The trial court granted judgment for the defendant as a matter of law. On appeal, the court noted the trial court's error in assuming the plaintiff was seeking enforcement of a lease that had yet to be negotiated much less made. If the only possible remedy was the plaintiff's expectation the court would have agreed with the trial court. The plaintiff, however, was seeking its reliance interest — its out-of-pocket losses induced by the casino's assurances which, the court held, were recoverable under promissory estoppel.[547] If the expectation damages can be shown and there is doubt concerning the proper measurement of reliance damages, "injustice" may be avoided only by enforcing the promise to fulfill the relying party's expectations. If the expectation interest is protected, the reliance interest is normally protected and it is preferable to enforce the promisee's expectation to ascertain protection of the reliance interest.

If reliance and expectation damages are each provable with mathematical certainty, which interest should be protected? It is certainly appropriate for the remedy to be co-extensive with the validation device. If the sole reason for enforcing the promise is the detrimental reliance of the promisee and justice requires that reliance to be compensated, there may appear to be little reason for awarding expectation damages such as lost profits. There may be other losses, however. Lost opportunities, albeit impossible to prove with reasonable certainty, may be present. The RESTATEMENT 2d also suggests the possibility of a deterrence factor with respect to the bad faith of the promisor that could not be shown with the required certainty. The presence of such factors may suggest the protection of the expectation interest in a given case which is feasible with the flexible remedy in § 90 of the Restatement 2d.

[C] Application and Expansion of Detrimental Reliance

As suggested earlier, there was great concern about the use of a new validation device that might interfere with the purity of consideration in all of its bargained-for-exchange glory.[548] Many saw its application restricted to gratuitous promises in family situations or charitable subscriptions. None other than the legendary Judge Learned Hand insisted that "There is no

---

[546] *See supra* note 543. *But see* Robert Hillman, *Questioning the "New Consensus" on Promissory Estoppel: An Empirical and Theoretical Study*, 98 COLUM. L. REV. 580, 609–10 (1998) (while the evidence is inconclusive, a study of cases during 1994–96 shows that courts take seriously the admonition of the RESTATEMENT 2d to award damages as justice requires).

[547] Pop's Cone's v. Resorts Int'l Hotel, Inc. 704 A.2d 1321 (N.J. 1998).

[548] *See supra* § 67[A]. note 492.

room in such a [commercial] situation for the doctrine of 'promissory estoppel.' "[549] Today, however, there is no question concerning the broad application of the doctrine to myriad situations including those that contemplate a bargained-for-exchange.

While it is still possible to discover a judicial utterance of the notion that detrimental reliance is a "substitute for consideration,"[550] courts now recognize detrimental reliance for what it is, i.e., an independent validation device that should not be pursued only after a court concludes that an agreement lacks consideration.[551] The device will not be limited to particular fact situations though the typical offer is revocable and does not engender justifiable reliance to make it irrevocable. Promissory estoppel can be found in myriad cases such as promises by employers,[552] franchisors[553] and subcontractors[554] as well as cases involving leases,[555] stock acquisitions[556] and sundry other matters.[557] The most controversial applications, however, have occurred in cases where it may be said that no "offer" occurred, or where the promise was not clear and definite, or where the terms of the arrangement were so indefinite that there would have been no enforceable agreement had consideration been present, i.e., there would have been a mere "agreement to agree."

[549] James Baird Co. v. Gimbel Bros., Inc., 64 F.2d 344, 346 (2d Cir. 1933). This is the famous case explored earlier in this volume at Chapter 2, § 44[E], *supra*, involving the promise (bid) by a subcontractor to a general contractor to allow the latter to bid on the entire project. The subcontractor-promisor reasonably expects the general contractor to rely on the sub's bid. If the general does rely by using the sub's bid and is then awarded the contract, the issue was whether promissory estoppel will prevent the sub from revoking its bid upon which the general has relied. Judge Hand answered no because he could not conceive of the doctrine applying in a bargained-for-exchange transaction. In Drennan v. Star Paving Co., 51 Cal. 2d 409, 414, 333 P.2d 757, 760 (1958), another judicial giant, Justice Roger Traynor, disagreed and held the offer to be irrevocable based on comment b to § 45 in the First Restatement, which refers to § 90: "[M]erely acting in justifiable reliance on an offer may in some cases serve as sufficient reason for making a promise binding." (*See* § 90.) As suggested in the earlier exploration of these issues, the Traynor view prevailed.

[550] *See, e.g.*, Middle East Banking Co. v. State St. Bank Int'l, 821 F.2d 897, 907 (2d Cir. 1987). The court cites the opinion by Judge Cardozo in Allegheny College v. National Chautauqua County Bank, 246 N.Y. 369, 373, 159 N.E. 173, 175 (1927), which, indeed, did contain the phrase "substitute for consideration." The continuation of the error a half century later, however, hardly seems necessary.

[551] *See* Metzger & Phillips, *The Emergence of Promissory Estoppel as an Independent Theory of Recovery*, 35 Rutgers L. Rev. 472 (1983). *See also* Farber & Matheson, *supra* note 543, at 908 and, in particular, n.19.

[552] *See, e.g.*, D'Ulisse-Cupo v. Board of Dirs. of Notre Dame High School, 6 Conn. App. 153, 503 A.2d 1192 (1986); Mers v. Dispatch Printing Co., 19 Ohio St. 3d 100, 483 N.E.2d 150 (1985); Perlin v. Board of Educ., 86 Ill. App. 3d 108, 407 N.E.2d 792 (1st Dist. 1980). *See also* Feinberg v. Pfeiffer Co., 322 S.W.2d 163 (Mo. Ct. App. 1959) (promise to pay pension to long-time employee whenever she decided to retire).

[553] *See, e.g.*, Hoffman v. Red Owl Stores, Inc., 26 Wis. 2d 683, 133 N.W.2d 267 (1965); Pop's Cones, Inc. v. Resorts Int'l Hotel, Inc., 307 N.J. Super. 461, 704 A.2d 1321 (App. Div. 1998).

[554] Pavel Enters., Inc. v. A. S. Johnson Co., Inc., 342 Md. 143, 674 A.2d 521 (1996). .

[555] Kramer v. Alpine Valley Resort, Inc., 108 Wis. 2d 417, 321 N.W.2d 293 (1982) (lease terms not a defense to promissory estoppel claim).

[556] *See, e.g.*, Gruen Indus., Inc. v. Biller, 608 F.2d 274 (7th Cir. 1979) (promissory estoppel rejected not because the doctrine was inapplicable but because the reliance was unreasonable).

[557] *See, e.g.*, Hoo Siong Chow v. Transworld Airlines, 544 N.E.2d 548 (Ind. Ct. App. 1989) (airline assurances that passenger would arrive in time for a connecting flight); Reeve v. Georgia-Pacific Corp., 510 N.E.2d 1378 (Ind. Ct. App. 1987) (workmen's compensation benefits via equitable estoppel or promissory estoppel); Mesa Petroleum Co. v. Coniglio, 629 F.2d 1022 (5th Cir. 1980) (promissory estoppel theory permitted recovery on a promissory note).

[1]   Precontractual Reliance — Indefiniteness — Absence of Offer

Where there is reliance upon assurances in contemplation of a bargained-for-exchange, the parties understand that no contract has yet been formed and a number of terms have yet to be agreed upon. In such cases, there is not only no contract, there is no offer. To permit a reliance recovery in such cases on the basis of promissory estoppel immediately confronts the repeated standard that the promise relied upon must be "clear and definite."[558] In *Hoffman v. Red Owl Stores, Inc.*[559] discussed earlier, the negotiations were in a bargain context but no bargain was made. There were several assurances by authorized agents of the defendant that the plaintiffs, husband and wife, had relied upon. The contract to which these preliminary, relied-upon assurances was supposed to lead, however, was never formed. A later court referred to the *Hoffman* case as the classic case of a promisor "stringing along" a promisee.[560] The *Hoffman* court was not dissuaded by the fact that the parties ultimately envisioned a bargain but never achieved one, or because the preliminary negotiations had not achieved an adequate level of definiteness to constitute an offer, much less a contract. The court saw the need to avoid manifest injustice caused by detrimental reliance which the promisors not only foresaw but urged upon the promisees.

In another well-known case, *Wheeler v. White*,[561] the defendant promised to procure construction financing for the plaintiff's shopping center and, failing that, to furnish such financing himself. In justifiable reliance upon that promise, the plaintiff proceeded to reconstruct the site for the new center by, *inter alia*, tearing down existing structures. When the defendant did not perform, the plaintiff sought damages on the basis of the agreement evidenced by a writing which an intermediate appellate court found too indefinite to enforce. The Supreme Court of Texas held the agreement to be fatally indefinite as a traditional contract, but felt compelled to protect the reliance interest of the plaintiff who had justifiably relied on the defendant's assurances. The court explained its holding that damages should be limited to the reliance interest by placing "partial" responsibility on the plaintiff who failed to bind the promisor to a legally sufficient contract. With respect to such a plaintiff, the court concluded that justice required only that the plaintiff be placed in the position he would have been in had he not acted in reliance on the promise.

A case following *Hoffman* suggests a relaxation of strict adherence to the requirement of a "clear and definite" promise, particularly where the plaintiff seeks to enforce a contract not fully negotiated, but is seeking damages from assurances or promises made during preliminary negotiations.[562] The court read RESTATEMENT 2d § 90 as not requiring "strict adherence to proof of a 'clear and definite promise' [which] is being eroded by a more equitable analysis designed to avoid injustice."[563] Several courts hold that the promise necessary to activate promissory estoppel need not amount to an offer or otherwise include all of the elements of a contract.[564]

---

[558] *See* § 67[B], *supra*.

[559] 26 Wis. 2d 683, 133 N.W.2d 267 (1965).

[560] *See* Pappas Industrial Parks, Inc. v. Psarros, 24 Mass. App. Ct. 596, 511 N.E.2d 621 (1987).

[561] 398 S.W.2d 93 (Tex. 1965).

[562] Pop's Cones, Inc. v. Resorts Int'l Hotel, Inc., 307 N.J. Super. 461, 469–70, 704 A.2d 1321, 1325 (App. Div. 1998). Precontractual assurances that lease would be granted where defendant advised plaintiff to surrender its present location.

[563] *Id.* at 471, 704 A.2d at 1326.

[564] *See, e.g.*, Rosnick v. Dinsmore, 235 Neb. 738, 749, 457 N.W.2d 793 (1990); Quake Constr., Inc. v. American

Other courts, however, insist that all essential elements of the contract are necessary to invoke promissory estoppel.[565]

[D]   RESTATEMENT 2d "Satellite" Sections — Detrimental Reliance

The detrimental reliance concept is not relegated to § 90 of the RESTATEMENT 2d. With respect to reliance by a general contractor on a bid from a subcontractor discussed earlier, the RESTATEMENT 2d deals with offers made irrevocable through reliance in a separate section.[566] Similarly, any offer which the offeror expects to induce and does induce substantial[567] reliance is made irrevocable through such reliance. Thus, an option contract for the purchase and sale of land may be binding because of detrimental reliance.[568] Another RESTATEMENT 2d section applies the detrimental reliance analysis to promises by sureties which induce reliance of a substantial character.[569] A third section applies the § 90 analysis to promises modifying duties under executory contracts. Such promises are made enforceable where the promisee changes his position materially in reliance on the promise.[570] A RESTATEMENT 2d section addresses problems of reliance on oral promises which are unenforceable because of the statute of frauds.[571] Still another section concentrates on problems of reliance on oral modifications, i.e., the "waiver" of the statute of frauds and the irrevocability of such waivers because of reliance.[572] This section attempts to set forth the analysis found in §§ 2-209(4) and (5) of the Uniform Commercial Code, which was explored earlier in this chapter.[573]

While Section 90 of the RESTATEMENT 2d could be applied in each of these and other situations,[574] the drafters of the RESTATEMENT 2d felt compelled to devote separate sections to these particular situations to complement § 90 and to emphasize the wide application of the reliance concept by leaving no doubt that courts should continue to apply it in particular situations.

Airlines, Inc., 141 Ill. 2d 281, 310, 565 N.E.2d 990 (1990); Bixler v. First Nat'l Bank, 49 Or. App. 195, 199–200, 619 P.2d 895 (1980).

[565]   See Owasso Dev. Co. v. Associated Wholesale Grocers, 19 Kan. App. 2d 549, 550–51, 873 P.2d 212, 213 (1994), and cases cited therein.

[566]   See RESTATEMENT 2d § 87(2). See Pavel Enters., Inc. v. A. S. Johnson Co., Inc., 342 Md. 143, 674 A.2d 521 (1996).

[567]   The "satellite" sections of RESTATEMENT 2d § 90, i.e., §§ 87(2), 88(c), 89(c), and 150, require either a reliance of substantial character, or a material change of position in reliance on the promise.

[568]   See Berryman v. Kmoch, 221 Kan.304, 559 P.2d 790 (1977), where the court discusses the elements of promissory estoppel in such a case but concludes that the elements are not found in the case before the court. See RESTATEMENT 2d § 87, ill. 4.

[569]   RESTATEMENT 2d § 88(c). See Fred Hutchinson Cancer Research Ctr. v. United of Omaha Life Ins. Co., 821 F. Supp. 644 (D. Or. 1993) (court states that either §§ 88(c) or 90 could be applied to make the promise enforceable). Suretyship contracts will be considered in the next chapter, the Statute of Frauds, where oral promises by sureties will be examined.

[570]   RESTATEMENT 2d § 89(c). See Wachovia Bank & Trust Co., N.A. v. Rubish, 306 N.C. 417, 293 S.E.2d 749 (1982). See also § 2-209 of the UCC, which is explored in detail supra § 65.

[571]   See RESTATEMENT 2d § 139. See Alaska Democratic Party v. Rice, 934 P.2d 1313 (Alaska 1997) (citing cases adopting and rejecting the RESTATEMENT 2d approach). This concept will be explored more fully in the next chapter dealing with the Statute of Frauds.

[572]   RESTATEMENT 2d § 150. See Jafari v. Wally Findlay Galleries, 1989 U.S. Dist. LEXIS 11299 (S.D.N.Y. Sept. 25, 1989).

[573]   See supra § 65[E][5].

[574]   See Fred Hutchinson Cancer Research Ctr., note 569 supra.

[E]   Detrimental Reliance in the Twenty-First Century

Scholarship concerning the importance and vitality of detrimental reliance was catalyzed by the little book called *Death of Contract* by Professor Grant Gilmore in 1974 which eschewed the bargain theory of consideration as a creation of O. W. Holmes. Though history and analysis were not on his side, Gilmore's elegant and whimsical style made his book popular in presenting the apotheosis of promissory estoppel to replace bargain theory with such notions as "contort." Though amused by Gilmore's views, other scholars disagreed in suggesting other dubious notions including the suggestion that actual reliance was no longer important in promissory estoppel. Only the "promise" mattered.[575] Other efforts relegated promissory estoppel to a marginal status,[576] but rejected the view that detrimental reliance was no longer essential for promissory estoppel in terms of successful use of the doctrine in litigation. An empirical study based on cases won versus cases lost, however, may not reveal the pervasive spirit of the detrimental reliance concept in twenty-first century contract law.[577] It is difficult to quarrel with the vision of Dean Charles Knapp who suggests that promissory estoppel is not an "aberrational displacement of an otherwise orderly pattern of contract law, but an integral part of that pattern-not a hole where the carpet has worn through, but recurrent motif, woven into the fabric itself."[578]

§ 68   PROMISES ENFORCEABLE THROUGH MORAL OBLIGATION

[A]   Past Acts and Precedent Debts as "Consideration"

Promises not supported by consideration, detrimental reliance or a formalistic validation device are generally unenforceable in our law, but there are exceptions to this general rule. Certain types of promises have been enforced without any evidence of traditional validation devices simply because of a conviction that such promises should be enforced. Three common law concepts must be explored to understand the bases of these exceptions: (1) the idea that a past act done at request should operate as consideration for a subsequent promise; (2) the doctrine that a precedent debt is consideration for a promise to pay that debt; and (3) the doctrine that a moral obligation is consideration for a promise to perform that obligation.

[1]   Past Acts as Consideration

A "past consideration" — some act or forbearance done or suffered in the past — cannot support a later promise. If certain work is performed and the beneficiary later promises to pay for the completed work, there is no benefit to the promisor since he received the benefit prior to making his promise, and there is no detriment to the promisee since he suffered the detriment before he became a promisee. There was no bargained-for-exchange since the

---

[575] *See, e.g.,* Farber & Matheson, note 543, *supra*; Edward Yorio & Steve Thel, *The Promissory Basis of Section 90*, 101 Yale L. J. 111 (1991).

[576] *See, e.g.,* Robert A. Hillman, *Questioning the "New Consensus" on Promissory Estoppel: An Empirical and Theoretical Study*, 98 Colum. L. Rev. 580, 586 (1990).

[577] *See* Juliet P. Krotristky, *The Rise and Fall of Promissory Estoppel Or Is Promissory Estoppel as Unsuccessful as Scholars Say It Is: A New Look At The Data*, 37 Wake Forest L. Rev. 531 (2002).

[578] Charles L. Knapp, *Rescuing Reliance: The Perils of Promissory Estoppel*, 49 Hasting L. J. 1191, 1331 (1998).

promise induced no detriment and the detriment induced no promise. Consequently, "past consideration" is "no consideration."

Notwithstanding this unassailable logic, at the end of the sixteenth century, where a past act was done at the request of the promisor, it was held that a later promise was made enforceable by the doing of the past act.[579] At the time these cases were decided, the action was brought in assumpsit and assumpsit would lie only upon a promise expressed in language.[580] Under modern contract law, if one requests another to perform valuable services, an inference of an enforceable promise to pay for them is drawn without difficulty. The early limitations on the action of assumpsit precluded such an obvious inference. To overcome this injustice, courts decided to enforce a promise expressed after receipt of the services by carrying over the prior services to support the later promise. These holdings were later broadened to permit the enforcement of a subsequent promise for a past act that was originally requested as a favor.[581]

By the nineteenth century, we find English courts repudiating the broad doctrine of the earlier cases and holding that a past act, though done at request, will not support a subsequent promise.[582] There were American cases taking the modern English view,[583] but a number of older cases applied the old rule quite broadly.[584] Whether or not such cases have been expressly overruled, they would not be followed today. Except for the isolated situations that follow, moral obligation is not an accepted validation device.[585]

[2] Precedent Debt as "Consideration"

Another well-settled rule of sixteenth century common law was that a precedent debt was consideration for a subsequent promise to pay that debt.[586] At early common law, if the writ of *debt* would lie, the action of assumpsit could not be employed to enforce the obligation. Earlier in this volume, the severe limitations on the action of debt were explored.[587] Inasmuch as assumpsit was a much more advantageous remedy than debt, it was inevitable that courts

---

[579] *See, e.g.*, Riggs v. Bullingham, Cro. Eliz. 715, 78 Eng. Rep. 949 [1599]; Hunt v. Bate, 3 Dyer, 272 (a), 73 Eng. Rep. 605 [1568].

[580] *See* Ames, *The History of Assumpsit*, 2 HARV. L. REV. 1, 53 (1888).

[581] *See* Bosden v. Thinne, Yelv. 40, 80 Eng. Rep. 29 [1603].

[582] "In *Lampleigh v. Braithwait* (Hobard, 105), it was assumed that the journeys which the plaintiff performed at the request of the defendant, and the other services he rendered, would have been sufficient to make any promise binding if it had been connected therewith in one contract; the peculiarity of the decision lies in connecting a subsequent promise with a prior consideration after it had been executed. Probably at the present day, such service on such request would have raised a promise by implication to pay what it was worth; and the subsequent promise of a sum certain would have been evidence for the jury to fix the amount." Kennedy v. Broun, 13 Q.B. (n.s.) 677, 740 [1863]. *See also* Roscorla v. Thomas, 3 Q.B. 234 [1842].

[583] *See, e.g.*, Conant v. Evans, 202 Mass. 34, 88 N.E. 438 (1909).

[584] *See, e.g.*, Friedman v. Suttle, 10 Ariz. 57, 85 P. 726 (1906); Montgomery v. Downey, 116 Iowa 632, 88 N.W. 810 (1902); Stuht v. Sweesy, 48 Neb. 767, 67 N.W. 748 (1896).

[585] See Passante v. McWilliam, 53 Cal. App. 4th 1240, 1247, 62 Cal. Rptr. 2d 298, 301 (4th Dist. 1997), suggesting the "universal rule throughout the United states that past consideration will not support a promise which is in excess of the promisor's existing debt or duty." See also Davis v. Davis, 2007 Mass. App. Div. 123, 124 (2007), 2007 Mass. App. Div. LEXIS 45 at *4 (2007) ("Massachusetts courts have long held that satisfaction of a moral obligation is not valid consideration for a legally enforceable contract"); Estate of Graham v. Morrison, 168 N. C. App. 63, 69, 607 S. E. 2d 295, 300 (2005) ("Past consideration or moral obligation is not adequate consideration to support a contract.").

[586] Ames, *The History of Assumpsit*, 2 HARV. L. REV. 53 (1888).

[587] *See* Chapter 1, § 3 *supra*.

would eventually discover a way to circumvent the limitations required by the action in debt. That effort culminated in *Slade's Case*,[588] after which the writ of assumpsit became the dominant cause of action for the enforcement of informal promises.

[3]　Moral Obligation

The doctrine that a moral obligation is a sufficient reason to make a promise enforceable was a product of Lord Mansfield, Chief Justice of King's Bench in England from 1756 to 1788. The Chief Justice was trained in the civil law, which made him impatient with some of the more technical rules of the common law, in particular, the requirement of consideration. In 1782, he authored an opinion involving a promise by an executrix to pay a legacy which promise was not supported by consideration where he stated that moral obligation constitutes consideration.[589] The same ground was relied upon to uphold a promise by an overseer of the poor to pay an apothecary who had, in an emergency, rendered medical aid to a pauper without first consulting the overseer.[590] A debtor's promise to pay the lawful part of a usurious debt[591] and a widow's promise to repay money loaned at her request[592] were enforced absent consideration. While these cases illustrate the moral obligation doctrine, the promises were not gratuitous, but were unenforceable because of existing procedural requirements, the choice of the wrong court, or because of a technical rule of law such as that which made it impossible for a married woman to bind herself by contract.

Since each case clearly demonstrated a duty to perform that which had been promised, there was a strong urge to brush aside technical problems to make the promises enforceable. While the doctrine of moral obligation survived for some time after Lord Mansfield's death, it was accepted by the courts with some misgivings.[593] Finally, in 1840, it was repudiated in England.[594] The rationale for the repudiation of the doctrine is the same rationale found in modern cases that reject moral obligation as a general validation device. The court could discover no satisfactory limits to the notion that a moral obligation is sufficient to make a promise enforceable. To do so would emasculate the doctrine of consideration since the mere fact that a promise has been made creates a moral obligation to perform it. The identical objection can be found in modern cases. In 1961, an American court expressed its objection to moral obligation as a general validation device in the following terms:

> "The difficulty we see with the doctrine is that if a mere moral, as distinguished from a legal, obligation were recognized as a valid consideration for a contract, that would practically erode to the vanishing point the necessity for finding a consideration. This is so, first because in nearly all circumstances where a promise is made there is some moral aspect of the situation which provides the motivation for making the promise

---

[588]　4 Coke 92(b) [1602].

[589]　"Where a man is under a moral obligation which no Court of Law or Equity can enforce, and promises, the honesty and rectitude of the thing is a consideration." Hawkes v. Saunders, 1 Cowper 289, 290, 98 Eng. Rep. 1091 [K.B. 1782]. *See also* Atkins v. Hill, Cowper 284 [1775].

[590]　Watson v. Turner, Buller's N.B. 129 [1767].

[591]　Barnes v. Hedley, 2 Taunt. 184 [1809].

[592]　Lee v. Muggeridge, 5 Taunt. 36 [1813].

[593]　See Littlefield v. Shee, 2 B. & Ad. 811 [1831], where Lord Tenderten said, "I must also observe that the doctrine that a moral obligation is a sufficient consideration for a subsequent promise is one which should be received with some limitation."

[594]　Eastwood v. Kenyon, 11 A. & E. 438 [1840].

even if it is to make an outright gift. And second, if we are dealing with the moral concepts, the making of a promise itself creates a moral obligation to perform it. It seems obvious that if a contract to be legally enforceable need be anything other than a naked promise, something more than mere moral consideration is necessary. The principle that in order for a contract to be valid and binding, each party must be bound to give some legal consideration to the other by conferring a benefit upon him or suffering a legal detriment at his request is firmly implanted in the roots of our law.[595]

The statement suggests two major problems in the recognition of moral obligation as a validation device. The first problem is one of uncertainty, i.e., if moral obligation is recognized, would every promise then become enforceable on the footing that there is a moral obligation to perform one's promises (*pacta sunt servanda* — promises must be kept)? If not, which moral obligations would be sufficient to support a promise? A classic response to this concern, however, is provided by Professor Fuller who stated that the threat to certainty suggested by the recognition of moral obligation is not solved by simply rejecting the doctrine out of hand. Rather, the solution lies in "taming it" through the process of judicial inclusion and exclusion which is certainly not foreign to the common law methodology.[596]

The second concern in the quoted statement rejecting moral obligation is that consideration is threatened and that consideration is the only sound validation device. We have already seen other validation devices, particularly detrimental reliance, that can operate as effectively as consideration. Indeed, many scholars believe that consideration is so riddled with exceptions and has been modified by statute and the courts in so many ways that it has proven to be "a rather awkward tool."[597]

[B] Contract Without Consideration or Detrimental Reliance in Modern Contract Law — Moral Obligation

Modern courts enforce certain promises though they evidence no consideration, detrimental reliance or formalistic validation device because courts have decided there is sufficient reason for enforcing them without these devices. It is difficult to categorize these promises. Some are widely enforced while others have very limited judicial support. Essentially, there are three classifications of promises that come within the ambit of promises enforceable without consideration, detrimental reliance or an otherwise operative formalistic device: (1) situations in which a legal duty created by a promise is subject to an absolute defense because of a more or less arbitrary rule and a new promise is made to perform that duty; (2) cases in which the promisor had promised to perform but his duty was voidable under a rule designed to protect him and he makes a new promise to perform; (3) cases in which the promisor has received substantial economic benefits for which he should make restitution although the law furnishes no remedy to compel him to do so and he promises to pay for those benefits.

[595] Manwill v. Oyler, 11 Utah 2d 433, 361 P.2d 177, 178 (1961).

[596] Fuller, *Consideration and Form*, 41 Colum. L. Rev. 799, 821–22 (1941).

[597] C. Fried, Contract as Promise 39 (1981) (Professor Fried is here paraphrasing some of the views of Professor Fuller).

[1]   Promise to Perform a Prior Legal Duty Discharged by Operation of Law — Statute of Limitations and Bankruptcy Discharges

[a]   Statute of Limitations

A promise to pay a debt barred by the statute of limitations is enforceable without consideration or detrimental reliance. Moral obligation is sufficient to sustain the new promise.[598] While courts are adamant in refusing to recognize moral obligation as a general validation device,[599] they are in agreement that moral obligation will support a promise to perform a duty which had been enforceable but became unenforceable because of the statute of limitations.[600]

There are any number of situations that may be said to create moral obligations of greater significance than ordinary debts barred by the statute of limitations. For example, where a neighbor intervened to save a husband from an axe-wielding wife, the neighbor was seriously injured and the husband promised to pay her damages. After paying a small sum, he refused to complete payment. The court held his promise unenforceable because it lacked consideration, notwithstanding the fact, recognized by the court, that the defendant should have been impelled by common gratitude to alleviate the plaintiff's misfortune.[601] Why, then, do courts choose to refuse enforcement of this kind of promise while enforcing promises to pay debts barred by the statute of limitations? The essential reason is "certainty," i.e., enforcing an otherwise legally enforceable promise barred only by the statute of limitations is an exception that courts can abide because it avoids the necessity of making distinctions among myriad moral obligations that would be required if moral obligation were a generally recognized validation device.

A promise to pay a debt barred by the statute of limitations may be inferred from a mere acknowledgment admitting the present existence of the antecedent debt.[602] A promise or acknowledgment of the debt will restart the limitations period anew.[603] A promise not to plead the statute of limitations will amount to a promise to pay an antecedent debt.[604] Even a part

---

[598] "The remedy to enforce the payment of debt is gone, but the moral obligation to pay it still remains and is good consideration for a new promise." San Diego Mun. Credit Union v. Smith, 176 Cal. App. 3d 919, 924, 222 Cal. Rptr. 467, 469 (4th Dist. 1986). *See also* Young v. Pileggi, 309 Pa. Super. 565, 455 A.2d 1228 (1983); Kopp v. Fink, 204 Okla. 570, 232 P.2d 161 (1951). RESTATEMENT 2d § 82.

[599] Schoenfeld v. Ochsenhaut, 114 Misc. 2d 585, 452 N.Y.S.2d 173, 174–75 (Civ. Ct. 1982).

[600] *See* Stone v. Lynch, 68 N.C. App. 441, 315 S.E.2d 350, 354 (1984), *aff'd*, 312 N.C. 739, 325 S.E.2d 230 (1985); International Aircraft Sales, Inc. v. Betancourt, 582 S.W.2d 632, 636 (Tex. Civ. App. Corpus Christi 1979).

[601] *See, e.g.*, Harrington v. Taylor, 225 N.C. 690, 36 S.E.2d 227 (1945).

[602] RESTATEMENT 2d § 82(2)(a). See Sheffield Capital Corp. v. Konen, 1995 Tex. App. LEXIS 632 (Tex. App. Mar. 23, 1995), which also provides a cogent statement of the legal history of acknowledgments.

[603] Fleet National Bank v. Laquidara, Inc., 736 N. Y. S. 2d 813 (App. Div. 2002).

[604] RESTATEMENT 2d § 82(2)(c). It is generally held that a promise to "waive" or not to plead the statute of limitations as part of the original promise is invalid. If the promise is made after the maturity of the debt, however, it can be treated as a new promise or acknowledgment of the debt and will be valid. If, however, it is properly interpreted as a new promise not to plead the statute of limitations but to retain all other possible defenses, a new consideration will be required to support that promise. *See* RESTATEMENT 2d § 82 comment f and ill. 16. Section 2-725(1) of the UCC permits the parties to reduce the period of limitation to not less than one year in their original agreement. The parties may not, however, extend the period of limitation, which is four years, commencing from the time of delivery of the

payment of the old debt amounts to a promise to pay it and renews the limitations period if the part payment recognizes the entire debt and manifests an intention to pay it.[605] Where there are multiple debts, however, and the debtor makes a payment after the limitations period has run on all of the debts, unless the debtor specifies the debt to which the payment is directed, the payment does not prove that the debtor recognized a particular debt.[606] If a part payment is made on a *single* debt *before* the statute of limitations has expired, the partial payment restarts the statute of limitations because the payment is a sufficient acknowledgment of the debt to imply a promise to pay the remainder.[607] If an undesignated payment is made on *multiple* debts *before* the statute has run, the creditor has the discretion of applying that payment tolling the statute of limitations on any debt on which the statute of limitations has not yet run.[608]

In many states, an express or implied promise or acknowledgment of an antecedent debt must be evidenced by a writing.[609] Statutes requiring a writing, however, do not apply to promises implied from part payment of the debt.[610] It must be emphasized that the prior indebtedness must be either contractual or quasi contractual. A promise to perform an obligation arising from a tort that has become barred by the statute of limitations is not enforceable absent new consideration or detrimental reliance.[611]

[b]   Debts Discharged in Bankruptcy — Bankruptcy Reform Act Changes

The United States Constitution permits Congress to enact laws discharging debtors who would otherwise be unable to begin their financial lives anew with a "fresh start."[612] Congress has facilitated the "fresh start" concept by enacting and amending a federal bankruptcy code for many years.[613] Prior to the Bankruptcy Reform Act of 1978,[614] the analysis of promises to

---

goods, regardless of the aggrieved party's lack of knowledge of the breach at time of delivery. The purpose of this four-year statute of limitations for contracts for the sale of goods was to eliminate jurisdictional variations which had hampered interstate sellers prior to the UCC.

[605] Yeiter v. Knights of St. Casimir Aid Society, 607 N. W. 2d 68 (Mich. 2000). See also First Hawaiian Bank v. Zukerkorn, 633 P.2d 550 (Haw. Ct. App. 1981); RESTATEMENT 2d § 82(2)(b).

[606] Drake v. Tyner, 914 P.2d 519, 522 (Colo. Ct. App. 1996).

[607] See White v. Sikes, Kelly, Edwards & Bryant, P.C., 410 So. 2d 66 (Ala. Civ. App. 1982); Wells v. Barefoot, 55 N.C. App. 562, 286 S.E.2d 625 (1982).

[608] Anderson v. Stanley, 753 S.W.2d 98 (Mo. Ct. App. 1988).

[609] RESTATEMENT 2d § 82 comment a. Acknowledgments may also have to be evidenced by a writing. *See, e.g.*, Tex. Civ. Prac. & Rem. Code Ann. § 16.065. This requirement is traceable to Lord Tenderten's Act, Geo. 4, c. 14 (1828), which is now the Limitation Act, 2 & 3 Geo. 6 c. 21, § 24 (1939), in England. The purpose of the original Act was to avoid disputes as to whether a subsequent promise was made.

[610] RESTATEMENT 2d § 110(4).

[611] *See* RESTATEMENT 2d § 82 comment b. If a tortfeasor promises to settle a tort claim or not to plead the statute of limitations, reliance on such a promise may make it enforceable. See Eddings v. Sears Roebuck & Co., 2002 Tenn. App. LEXIS 514 (2002).

[612] U.S. CONSTITUTION, art. 1, § 8, cl. 4.

[613] The first three Bankruptcy Acts had brief lives. The Act of 1800 was repealed in 1803; the Act of 1841 was repealed after only 18 months; the Act of 1867 was repealed in 1878. The fourth Bankruptcy Act of 1898 lasted 81 years, though it was substantially amended and subject to much judicial interpretation over its lifetime. It was replaced by the current Bankruptcy Reform Act of 1978 that was amended in 1984 and in 1994.

[614] The Bankruptcy Reform Act is found in Title 11 of the U.S.C.

pay debts barred by the statute of limitations which we have just explored was essentially the same analysis applied to promises to pay debts discharged in bankruptcy. Courts had no difficulty in discovering a moral obligation as a validation device for such promises since the debt had been legally enforceable and was now barred only by a discharge in bankruptcy.[615] There were, however, some differences between the two analyses. We saw that an acknowledgment or part payment could operate as a promise to pay a debt barred by the statute of limitations. With respect to a debt discharged in bankruptcy, however, an express promise to pay that debt was essential.[616] While an express or implied promise to pay a debt barred by the statute of limitations was typically subject to a statutory writing requirement, promises to pay debts discharged in bankruptcy were required to be in writing in only a few states.[617] A promise to pay a debt discharged by a voluntary composition among creditors was enforceable without a new validation device if the composition occurred pursuant to the Bankruptcy Act. A promise to pay a debt discharged outside of bankruptcy through a voluntary composition of creditors, however, required a new validation device.[618]

While the adjudicated bankrupt need not make a new promise to pay the discharged debt, creditors were often highly persuasive in encouraging such "reaffirmation" promises. As suggested by one scholar," "The promisor, burdened with the guilt accompanying financial failure and intoxicated at the promise of a future free of debt, fails to understand the consequences of reaffirmation. Therefore, these reckless commitments rarely produce reasonably equivalent benefits for the promisor."[619]

A new federal Bankruptcy Code[620] sought to address serious abuses of debtors discharged in bankruptcy by their creditors who applied undue pressure to have unsophisticated debtors sign reaffirmation agreements promising to pay debts discharged in bankruptcy. If the discharged debtor signed a reaffirmation agreement without full knowledge of his rights under the bankruptcy discharge or without awareness of the significance of the reaffirmation agreement, he could be placed back on the road to bankruptcy shortly after his "fresh start" was supposed to begin.[621] The 1978 version of the new Code, therefore, placed significant

---

[615] *See* Hageman/Fritz, Byrne, Head & Harrison, L. L. P. v. Luth, 150 S. W. 3d 617, 626 (Ct. App. Tex. 2004) ("It is not well settled that a moral obligation is a sufficient consideration for a subsequent promise of a debtor to pay in the case where the original debt is barred by limitations or the bankruptcy or insolvency laws."). See also, Minnesota Mut. Life Ins. Co. v. Anderson, 1992 Minn App. LEXIS 443, at *9 (Minn. Ct. App. Apr. 29, 1992); Super Chief Credit Union v. McCoy, 3 Kan. App. 2d 25, 595 P.2d 346 (1978); Stanek v. White, 172 Minn. 390, 215 N.W. 784 (1927); Herrington v. Davitt, 220 N.Y. 162, 115 N.E. 476 (1917). *See also* RESTATEMENT 2d § 83.

[616] See, e.g., Windman v. American Book-Stratford Press, Inc., 1989 U.S. Dist. LEXIS 10924 (S.D.N.Y. Sept. 14, 1989), holding that part payment is insufficient to revive a debt discharged in bankruptcy. RESTATEMENT 2d § 83.

[617] RESTATEMENT 2d § 83 comment a. An example of a statute that *does* require such promises to be evidenced by a writing is N.Y. GEN. OBLIG. LAW § 5-701(a)(5).

[618] *See* RESTATEMENT 2d § 83 comment b.

[619] Douglas Boshkoff, *Fresh Start, False Start, or Head Start?*, 70 IND. L.J. 549, 558 (1995).

[620] Most of the Bankruptcy Reform Act (Title 11 U.S.C.) became effective on October 1, 1979.

[621] To avoid undermining the "fresh start" policy, some legislators sought to place a blanket prohibition on *all* reaffirmation agreements. That position was rejected, however, in favor of the compromise in Section 524(c) which permitted the enforcement of such promises under court supervision if they meet the tests set forth in that section. *In re* Farmer, 13 B.R. 319 (Bankr. M.D. Fla. 1981). A 1984 amendment of the Bankruptcy Act, however, replaced the supervision of the bankruptcy judge with a mere affidavit filed by the debtor's attorney stating that the new promise is fully informed and voluntary and does not impose an undue hardship on the debtor. 11 U. S. C. § 524(c)(3). This changed has invoked some harsh criticism: "[T]he rule's creditor sponsors were extraordinarily clever. Instead of trying to eliminate the approval requirement, a difficult task, they opted for a change in the person whose approval was

restraints on the enforceability of reaffirmation agreements. Under § 524(c), an agreement between a holder of a claim and the debtor, "the consideration for which, in whole or in part, is based on a debt" dischargeable in bankruptcy, is enforceable only if certain conditions are met: (1) the agreement was made *before* the granting of the discharge in bankruptcy; (2) the agreement contains a clear and conspicuous statement advising the debtor that the agreement may be rescinded at any time prior to discharge or within sixty days after such agreement is filed with the court — whichever occurs later — through notice of rescission to the holder of the claim; (3) the agreement has been filed with the court and is accompanied by a declaration or affidavit of the debtor's attorney stating that the agreement (a) represents a fully informed and voluntary agreement of the debtor, and (b) does not impose undue hardship on the debtor or a dependent of the debtor; (4) the debtor has not rescinded the agreement within the sixty-day period of condition (2) above; (5) any hearing required by subsection (d) of § 524 has been complied with; (6) where an individual was not represented by an attorney while the agreement was negotiated, the court must approve the agreement as not imposing undue hardship on the debtor or a dependent of the debtor, and as one which is in the best interest of the debtor.[622]

The typical promise to pay a debt already discharged in bankruptcy will not be enforceable under this preempting federal statute if the "consideration" for such a promise is "in whole or in part" based on the debt discharged in bankruptcy. Prior to 1984, the agreement would be enforceable if the court discerned that it was either a good faith settlement *or* was in the best interest of the debtor and would not cause undue hardship.[623] Under the 1984 amendment to § 524(c), however, the good faith settlement alternative was deleted. The reaffirmation agreement must now be in the best interest of the debtor and not cause the debtor undue hardship. A creditor's demonstration that the agreement was a good faith settlement is irrelevant.[624]

The denouement is that it is still possible to make an enforceable promise to pay a debt discharged in bankruptcy, but only by complying with the statutory safeguards of the bankruptcy law.

[2]   Promise to Perform Previous Undertaking Subject to Defenses

Certain executory promises are said to be voidable at the election of the promisor because of a rule of law designed to protect the promisor. We have, for example, explored promises made by infants and other incapacitated parties[625] who are given a power of avoidance or disaffirmance because the law seeks to protect such persons against their own improvidence. Similarly, promises induced by fraud or duress provide the promisor with a power of avoidance. If the promisor freely makes a new promise to perform his previously voidable promise, he ratifies the original undertaking and the new promise is binding without consideration or any other validation device,[626] assuming the new promise is not subject to the same defense which

---

needed. They replaced the independent bankruptcy judge with an attorney decision-maker who will often find it difficult to oppose his client's wishes." Boshkoff, note 619 *supra*, at 559.

[622] 11 U.S.C. § 524(c). See Close v. Edison, 2003 Bankr. LEXIS 1507 (E. D. Pa. 2003).

[623] *See* former 11 U.S.C. § 524(c)(4)(B) (1982).

[624] *In re* Hirte, 71 B.R. 249 (Bankr. D. Or. 1986).

[625] *See* Chapter 1, *supra*, § 25 *et seq.*

[626] RESTATEMENT 2d § 85.

made the original promise voidable. Some courts have held a promise to perform an undertaking that is void rather than merely voidable to be enforceable. Other courts, however, reached contrary conclusions on the ground that a subsequent promise is effective without consideration only when the original undertaking was voidable as distinguished from void.[627] Since a power of ratification applies to a voidable contract,[628] a new promise to perform a voidable duty may be viewed as an exercise of that power or conversely as a waiver of a defense, such as infancy, fraud or the like. This analysis presents no conflict with the doctrine of consideration. Where, however, the original undertaking was void, the only basis for the new obligation is the new promise which appears to require consideration or another effective validation device. Notwithstanding this analytical distinction, where the rule of law that relieves the obligor from performing is more or less arbitrary, there is good reason for holding that a subsequent promise should be enforceable since that promise is made at a time when the circumstances which made the rule of law operative no longer exist.

[3] Promise to Pay for Benefits Previously Received — "Material Benefit" Rule

Where one person confers benefits upon another under circumstances negating a gratuitous intention, the recipient of those benefits may be under no legal duty to pay for them. In a classic case, the plaintiff cared for the adult son of the defendant for several weeks when the son became ill. Though the father had no obligation to pay for this care, he promised to reimburse the plaintiff for his expenses but later refused to perform the promise. The court held for the defendant, distinguishing promises to pay for debts barred by the statute of limitation or discharged in bankruptcy on the footing that such promises simply remove an impediment created by law to debts honestly due.[629] If the benefits have been conferred because of a mistake or in an emergency, quasi contractual relief may be available to prevent unjust enrichment.[630] If the recipient of the benefits requested them and should have expected to pay for them, a real contract can be discovered though it may be characterized as an "implied-in-fact" contract.[631] If, however, benefits are conferred voluntarily without prior request, mistake or emergency, neither contractual nor quasi contractual relief may be available. Under these circumstances, the recipient of the benefits who had no legal duty to pay for them may decide to promise payment for the past benefits received. A few courts have enforced the promise because ". . . the moral obligation to make recompense for benefits received will sustain a subsequent promise to pay for the benefits."[632] The prevailing view,

---

[627] *See, e.g.*, Stout v. Humphrey, 69 N.J.L. 436, 55 A. 281 (1903); Holloway's Assignee v. Rudy, 60 S.W. 650, 22 Ky. L. Rptr. 1406 (1901).

[628] Restatement 2d § 85 comment a.

[629] Mills v. Wyman, 20 Mass. (3 Pick.) 207 (1826).

[630] The concept of the restitution interest for which the quasi contract device is used will be discussed subsequently in this volume.

[631] A so-called "implied-in-fact" contract is one where the manifested intention of the parties to be bound to each other is found in their conduct rather than language. In the sense of expressing mutual assent, it is as much an express contract as one manifested in the words, written or spoken, of the parties.

[632] Holland v. Martinson, 119 Kan. 43, 43, 237 P. 902, 902 (1925). *See also* Kaiser v. Fadem, 280 P.2d 728 (Okla. 1955) (subsequent promise to pay commission to finder of property desired by promisor); Edson v. Poppe, 24 S.D. 466, 124 N.W. 441 (1910) (tenant dug well on landlord's property without the knowledge of the landlord, who later promised to pay). See also cases discussed later in this section.

however, is clearly contrary.[633]

Notwithstanding the prevailing case law, the RESTATEMENT 2d adopts the view that a promise made in recognition of received benefits from the promisee should be enforceable to the extent necessary to prevent injustice.[634] Among the illustrations in this section, two are based upon well-known cases which apply what is often called the "material benefit" rule.

Where a rescuer suffered permanent disability in saving the life of his employer who subsequently promised to pay the rescuer $15.00 every two weeks for the rest of his life, the court enforced the promise even though the benefit was conferred without the request of the promisor. The court reasoned that the emergency nature of the rescue precluded the possibility of a request from the employer, but such a request would have occurred had there been time. The court concluded that a moral obligation is "a sufficient consideration" to support a subsequent promise even though the promise was not one to pay for a voidable or barred legal obligation. Rather, since the employer received a "material benefit," moral obligation was sufficient to support the promise.[635]

The RESTATEMENT 2d indicates that a promise for benefits previously received is not binding if the promisee had conferred the benefit as a gift *or* if the promisor had not been unjustly enriched for other reasons. There would be no cause of action in quasi contract (i.e., for unjust enrichment) by the rescuer. His emergency action would be presumed to be gratuitous. Yet, the RESTATEMENT 2d suggests that the subsequent promise "may remove doubt as to the reality of the benefit and as to its value, and may negate any danger of imposition of a false claim. A positive showing that payment was expected is not then required. An intention to make a gift must be shown to defeat restitution."[636] Thus, because the recipient of the benefit has made a promise to pay for the benefit, the RESTATEMENT 2d removes the normal requirement of the rescuer's expectation of payment and places the burden of establishing a gratuitous intention on the promisor.

The second illustration is based upon *In re Hatten's Estate*,[637] where a wealthy bachelor was provided with innumerable meals, companionship and other services, including transportation by the promisee and her son over a number of years. The bachelor subsequently promised to pay an amount that was greater than the value of the services received. The promise was contained in a negotiable instrument, which provided the court with a traditional basis for enforcing the promise, i.e., there is a presumption of consideration in negotiable instruments. The court, however, chose to add another rationale, i.e., the Wisconsin "liberal" view that moral obligation is an effective validation device when the promisor has received an actual benefit sufficient to arouse a moral, as contrasted with a legal, "consideration." The fact that the value of the bachelor's promise was disproportionate to the benefit he received would appear to make the promise unenforceable under the RESTATEMENT 2d view, which suggests that such a promise

---

[633] *See, e.g.,* Stone v. Lynch, 68 N.C. App. 441, 315 S.E.2d 350 (1984), *aff'd,* 312 N.C. 739, 325 S.E.2d 230 (1985); Miller v. Miller, 664 P.2d 39 (Wyo. 1983); Schoenfeld v. Ochsenhaut, 114 Misc. 2d 585, 452 N.Y.S.2d 173 (Civ. Ct. 1982); International Aircraft Sales, Inc. v. Betancourt, 582 S.W.2d 632 (Tex. Civ. App. Corpus Christi 1979).

[634] RESTATEMENT 2d § 86(1).

[635] Webb v. McGowin, 27 Ala. App. 82, 168 So. 196 (1935). Illustration 7 to RESTATEMENT 2d § 86 is based on the facts of Webb v. McGowin. *Contra* Harrington v. Taylor, 225 N.C. 690, 36 S.E.2d 227 (1945).

[636] RESTATEMENT 2d § 86 comment d.

[637] 233 Wis. 199, 288 N.W. 278 (1940). Illustration 12 to RESTATEMENT 2d § 86 is based on the facts of this case.

is not binding "to the extent that its value is disproportionate to the benefit."[638] Yet, the illustration based on these facts concludes that a promise to pay $25,000 for a benefit valued at no more than $6,000 is binding.[639] The next illustration is based on the same facts except that the bachelor makes an oral promise to leave his *entire estate* to the promisee.[640] The illustration concludes that the promise is binding only to the extent of the reasonable value of the benefit conferred, i.e., the restitution interest. One of the differences between the illustrations is that one promise is in writing and the other is oral. Presumably, a written promise is sufficient to ward off the dangers of false claims,[641] whereas an oral promise may not be sufficient. The major difference, however, appears to be the gross disproportion between a $6,000 benefit and the entire estate valued in the millions as contrasted with a promise to pay $25,000 for a $6,000 benefit. Notwithstanding this explanation, the comment language is still difficult to reconcile with the illustration.[642] As the Reporter for this section indicated, however, the section "bristles with nonspecific concepts."[643] It will continue to present a significant challenge to courts.

The "material benefit" rule, supported by the RESTATEMENT 2d though not yet generally accepted by our courts,[644] has much to commend it. As the RESTATEMENT 2d insists, there is little danger of false claims since benefits have been received and the subsequent promise to pay for the benefits fulfills an evidentiary function.[645] There may, however, be a problem in the lack of what Professor Fuller would call the "cautionary" function, i.e., the immediate and overwhelming sense of gratitude on the part of the recipient of the benefit, particularly in extreme situations that could induce an impulsive promise. Notwithstanding this danger, if the promise is not excessive in relation to the benefit received, there would appear to be little risk in enforcing it where the benefit received is substantial. The usual arguments against enforcing such promises on the ground of uncertainty should not prevail. Modern courts opposing the "material benefit rule" or more general notions of moral obligation suggest little more than the fact that contract law has not enforced such promises in the past.[646] Surely this is an insufficient basis for opposing an otherwise desirable extension of the validation concept.

---

[638] RESTATEMENT 2d § 86(2)(b).

[639] Illustration 12 to RESTATEMENT 2d § 86.

[640] RESTATEMENT 2d § 86 ill. 13.

[641] This is the rationale stated in support of ill. 7 involving the promise to pay the disabled rescuer. RESTATEMENT 2d § 86, however, does not require the promise to be evidenced by a writing.

[642] "Where the value of the benefit is uncertain, a promise to pay the value is binding and a promise to pay a liquidated sum may serve to fix the amount due if in all the circumstances it is not disproportionate to the benefit." RESTATEMENT 2d § 86 comment i.

[643] *See* 42 ALI Proceedings 274 (1965). *See also* Braucher, *Freedom of Contract and the Second Restatement*, 78 YALE L.J. 598, 605 (1969). The nonspecific concepts include "injustice," "unjust enrichment," and "gift."

[644] See, however, Worner Agency, Inc. v. Doyle, 133 Ill. App. 3d 850, 479 N.E.2d 468 (4th Dist. 1985) (past material benefit conferred was sufficient to support promise to pay a finder's fee). In First National Bankshares v. Geisel, 853 F. Supp.1344, 1356–57 (D. Kan. 1994), the court discussed the Restatement 2d version of the material benefit rule but found that it did not apply because the promise was more than called for under the pre-existing duty.

[645] A New York statute makes promises for past benefits binding if the promise is in a signed writing, is proved to have been given or performed and would have been a valid consideration except for the time it was given. N.Y. GEN. OBLIG. LAW § 5-1105. *See also* CAL. CIV. CODE § 1606 and Henderson, *Promises Grounded in the Past: The Idea of Unjust Enrichment and the Law of Contracts*, 57 VA. L. REV. 1115 (1971).

[646] *See, e.g.*, Manwill v. Oyler, 11 Utah 2d 433, 361 P.2d 177 (1961).

Chapter 4

THE STATUTE OF FRAUDS

§ 69   ORIGIN OF THE STATUTE OF FRAUDS — REPEAL OF THE ENGLISH STATUTE

Except for contracts under seal, the common law does not require contracts to be evidenced by a writing. A promise is legally binding though expressed orally or by conduct if the other essentials for contract formation exist. Any requirement that a contract be evidenced by a writing is a statutory requirement. In practically every state, certain types of contracts are required to be evidenced by a writing as a matter of enforceability, proof, or validity. These statutes emulate certain sections of the Statute of Frauds which was enacted by Parliament during the reign of Charles II in 1677, and they are commonly indexed under that caption in the statute books.[1] The original Statute of Frauds contained twenty-five sections. Only two are important for our purposes, Sections 4 and 17, though Section 4 contains six subsections designating five types of contracts that must be evidenced by a writing:

Sec. 4. And be it further enacted by the authority aforesaid. That from and after the said four and twentieth day of June no action shall be brought (1) whereby to charge

---

[1] In New Mexico, the English Statute of Frauds was adopted as part of New Mexico common law. *See* Whelan v. New Mexico Western Oil & Gas Co., 226 F.2d 156, 160 (10th Cir. 1955). In Maryland, the statute is in effect as part of the Maryland Declaration of Rights, Md. Const. art. 5. All other states except Louisiana have statutes similar to the original English Statute of Frauds of 1677.

any executor or administrator upon any special promise, to answer damages out of his own estate; (2) or whereby to charge the defendant upon any special promise to answer for the debt, default, or miscarriages of another person; (3) or to charge any person upon any agreement made upon consideration of marriage; (4) or upon any contract or sale of lands, tenements, or hereditaments, or any interest in or concerning them; (5) or one year from the making thereof; (6) unless the agreement upon which such action shall be brought, or some memorandum or note thereof, shall be in writing, and signed by the party to be charged therewith, or some other person thereunto by him lawfully authorized.

Sec. 17. And be it further enacted by the authority aforesaid. That from and after the said four and twentieth day of June no contract for the sale of any goods, wares and merchandises, for the price of ten pounds sterling or upwards, shall be allowed to be good, except the buyer shall accept part of the goods so sold, and actually receive the same, or give something in earnest to bind the bargain, or in part of payment, or that some note of memorandum in writing of the said bargain be made and signed by the parties to be charged by such contract, or their agents thereunto lawfully authorized.

In 1677, the essentially medieval trial by jury left much to be desired. Not only was there little or no control over jury verdicts, but the jurors were free to decide the facts on their own knowledge, disregarding the evidence. The parties to the contract were precluded from testifying on their own behalf, and the general history of the period lent itself to "fraudulent practices which are commonly endeavored to be upheld by perjury and subornation."[2] One of the puzzling aspects of the Statute was the choice of six types of contracts made subject to its requirements. There is little doubt that an earlier draft covered all contracts with certain exceptions.[3] Historians have discovered earlier parallels on the Continent which lend support to the notion that the reasons behind the Statute were much broader than fear of perjury and subornation.[4]

American versions of the English Statute reveal minor differences in terminology among the different states to which attention will be directed as this exploration proceeds. Modern versions of the statute will often include types of contracts not covered by the original Statute.[5] Thus, promises to pay a commission to a real estate broker or contracts to leave property by will are often included.[6] The student of contract law should also recall that a promise to pay a debt barred by the statute of limitations is typically required to be evidenced by a writing

---

[2] This is the preamble to the bill that was finally enacted. Lord Keeper Finch (later Lord Nottingham and Chancellor under Charles II from 1673 to 1682) is generally regarded as the principal instigator of the Statute of Frauds as enacted in 1677.

[3] A 1673 draft attributed to Lord Nottingham stated that in all actions of assumpsit or debt on promises or agreements by parole there would be a limit on recoverable damages absent written evidence. It would not, however, apply to sales of goods, loans or money, *quantum meruit*, or other promises arising by operation of law. There was no specified amount for the limitations of damages in the draft which proceeded to a first reading in Parliament. The bill was sent to committee where it died. It was reintroduced in 1675 but, again, sent to committee which now included Sir Francis North, Chief Justice of Common Pleas, who is credited with the creation of what became Section 4 of the Statute. The Lord Nottingham approach was rejected in favor of "amendments" created by the committee (including the new Section 4 model) which, after some modifications, became the 1677 Statute of Frauds as we know it. *See* A. W. B. SIMPSON, A HISTORY OF THE COMMON LAW OF CONTRACT 601–02 (1987).

[4] *See* Rabel, *The Statute of Frauds and Comparative Legal History*, 63 LAW Q. REV. 174 (1947).

[5] *See* RESTATEMENT 2d Ch. 5, Statutory Note, "Other Similar Statutes."

[6] *Id.*

though this requirement emanates from a nineteenth century English statute.[7] The modern version of Section 17 of the original Statute dealing with contracts for the sale of goods is now found in the Uniform Commercial Code.[8] The UCC, however, requires other types of promises to be evidenced by a writing.[9]

The main features of the original Statute of Frauds have been copied with remarkable unanimity.[10] Having spawned the Statute of Frauds, England repealed it, except for two sections, by the Law Reform Act of 1954.[11] This action was based on a report of the English Law Revision Committee in 1937.[12] After indicating that contemporary opinion was almost unanimous in condemning the statute and favoring its amendment or repeal, the report suggests that the conditions which gave rise to the statute had long passed away. At a time when the parties themselves could not give evidence and the jury was entitled to act on its own knowledge of the facts in dispute, there may have been some reason for the statute. There can be no quarrel with the report in this regard, i.e., these conditions no longer exist. The report further suggests that the statute promotes more fraud than it prevents. While it shuts out perjury, it also more frequently shuts out the truth since it strikes impartially at the perjurer and the honest man who has omitted a precaution, "sealing the lips of both." The classes of contracts covered by the statute appear to have been arbitrarily selected and to exhibit no common quality.[13] The report insists that the statute operates in a partial manner. Thus, when A and B contract and A has signed a sufficient memorandum and B has not, B can enforce the contract against A, but A cannot enforce the contract against B who has signed no writing. (Later, we will see how the UCC remedies this situation in contracts for the sale of goods priced at $500 or more.) The report also suggests that the statute is obscure and ill-drafted, making it the subject of considerable litigation.

---

[7] Lord Tenderten's Act, 9 Geo. IV, c. 14, sometimes referred to as the Statute of Frauds Amendment Act, enacted in England in 1828. *See* RESTATEMENT 2d Ch. 5, Statutory Note which quotes this Act.

[8] UCC § 2-201.

[9] *See* § 2-205 (firm offer must be in writing); § 2-209(2) (enforcing no oral modification clauses which require any modifications to be in writing); § 9-203 (b)(3)(a) (security agreement). The 1978 version of Article 8 of the Code required a writing to evidence a sale of securities (§ 8-319), but a 1994 amended version of Article 8 now includes § 8-113 that dispenses with any writing requirement on the footing that the increasing use of electronic communication makes the "statute of frauds unsuited to the realities of the securities business." The same section also eliminates the one-year provision of the statute of frauds for securities contracts. Former § 1-206 provided a statute of frauds for "kinds of personal property not otherwise covered" which included intangible property rights in patents, trademarks and copyrights. That concept has been deleted (revised § 1-206 defines the term "presumption" as used in the Code). The "Legislative Note" accompanying that change states that the deletion of the former section should not be viewed as a recommendation against requiring such general intangibles to be subject to the statute of frauds. Rather, it simply indicates that there is no need for the UCC to determine that issue.

[10] *See* RESTATEMENT 2d, Statutory Note at the beginning of Chapter 5.

[11] Act, 1954, 2 & 3 Eliz. 2, ch. 34. The two exceptions are contracts to answer for the debt of another (the suretyship provision) and contracts for the sale of land. For comments on the Acts of 1954, see Note, 70 LAW Q. REV. 441 (1954), and 17 MOD. L. REV. 451 (1954).

[12] English Law Revision Committee (Sixth Interim Report) (1937), the full text of which can be found in 15 CAN. B. REV. 585 (1937).

[13] See, however, the suggestion by A. W. B Simpson in A HISTORY OF THE COMMON LAW OF CONTRACT at 610 (1987), where the author points out that the types of contract listed in Section 4 of the 1677 Statute of Frauds were not recognized at all at common law under the pre-assumpsit older remedies unless they were formalized by a sealed instrument. Thus, with respect to these types of contracts, he suggests the possibility that, "The Statute of Frauds put the clock back, substituting only the signature for the seal."

A number of American scholars have been critical of the statute. One of the giants of American contract law, Arthur Linton Corbin, suggests that, if the statute were repealed in the United States, he would suffer only to the extent that one volume of his treatise would no longer be sold.[14] Professor Corbin, however, expressed grave doubt that the statute would be repealed in the United States since, unlike England, each of our states would have to repeal the statute.

Another giant of American law, Karl Llewellyn, best known as the chief architect of the UCC, was one of the rare defenders of the statute:

> That statute is an amazing product. In it de Leon might have found his secret of perpetual youth. After two and one half centuries the statute stands, in essence better adapted to our needs than when it first was passed. By 1676 literacy (which need imply no great consistency in spelling) may well have been expected in England of such classes as would be concerned in the transactions covered by the statute's terms. Certainly, however, we had our period here in which that would hardly hold — we counted our men of affairs who signed by mark in plenty. But schooling has done its work. The idea, which must in good part derive from the statute, that contracts at large will do well to be in writing, is fairly well established in the land. 'His word is as good as his bond' contains a biting innuendo preaching caution. Meantime the modern developments of business-large units, requiring internal written records if files are to be kept straight, and officers informed, and departments coordinated, and the work of shifting personnel kept track of; the practice of confirming oral deals in writing; the use of typewriters, of forms-all these confirm the policy of the statute; all these reduce the price in disappointments exacted for its benefits.[15]

Notwithstanding Llewellyn's defense of the statute, as will be seen later in this chapter, his version of the statute in relation to contracts for the sale of goods in the UCC contains a number of modifications designed to overcome justified criticism of the treatment of such contracts in the original Statute and its progeny. There is little question that current versions of the statute are often applied narrowly by our courts because of its irrationality in certain situations.[16] As we will see, the one-year provision of the Statute is a prime example that has engendered particularly harsh criticism.[17] We will also see the judicial recognition of reliance in lieu of a writing as a method or device to satisfy the statute which indicates further erosion of the statute, at least in its original form.

The student of contract law must be aware of judicial trends in the application of the statute. They can be understood, however, only if three basic questions are thoroughly pursued: (1) What contracts are embraced within the terms of the statute? (2) What are the requirements of the statute in relation to contracts within its scope? (3) What is the effect of failing to fulfill

---

[14] 2 CORBIN ON CONTRACTS § 275 now revised in § 12.1.

[15] Llewellyn, *What Price Contract? ? An Essay in Perspective*, 40 YALE L.J. 704, 747 (1931).

[16] See In re Marriage of Takusagawa, 38 Kan. App. 2d 401, 408, 166 P. 3d 440, 446 (Kan. 2007) noting the narrowing interpretation of the statute of frauds, citing this section.

[17] Thus, Article 8 of the UCC (investment securities) has not only dispensed with the Statute of Frauds (§ 8-113) but has also repealed the one-year provision. Earlier drafts of a revised Article 2 of the UCC in the 1990's would have repealed the statute and also eliminated the one-year provision with respect to contracts for the sale of goods. Later drafts, however, reinstated a Statute of Frauds, raising the threshold to a price of $5000 instead of the extant $500 threshold, evidencing inflation since the original Statute became effective in 1954 in Pennsylvania. Efforts to revise or amend Article 2, however, have failed. *See* § 10, *supra*.

the requirements of the statute? Before proceeding with this exploration, however, it is important to note the absence of a writing requirement in contract for the international sale of goods.

[A]   International Contracts — CISG and UNIDROIT Principles

The Vienna Convention on international contracts for the sale of goods manifests pervasive Civil Law influences including Article 11: "A contract of sale need not be concluded in or evidenced by writing and is not subject to any other requirement as to form."[18] Beyond the continental law influence, such a provision is certainly not remarkable in light of the repeal of the Statute in the land of its birth and the continuous criticism of the Statute in the United States. Where CISG applies, it displaces the domestic law of "contracting states" such as the United States and seventy-three other nations. The UNIDROIT Principles are in accord.[19] There are, however, two other Articles that have an important bearing on the general CISG provision. Article 12 emphasizes the power of contracting states whose legislation requires a contract of sale to be evidenced by a writing to utilize Article 96 which permits that state, at any time, to make a declaration that any provision of CISG that permits contracts, modifications, terminations or any other event to be operative without a writing does not apply where any party has a place of business in that contracting state.[20]

§ 70 SURETYSHIP PROMISES — CONTRACTS OF EXECUTORS AND ADMINISTRATORS

[A]   The Basic Concept of Suretyship — Types of Suretyship Promises

Suretyship involves three parties, the *principal debtor or obligor* (D) who is obligated to a *creditor or obligee* (C) and a *surety*, S, who promises to pay C if D fails to pay. If, for example, D seeks goods, services or a loan from C, C may be unwilling to extend credit to D because D has a poor credit rating. C may agree to D's request only if D and a third party, S, agree to repay C. If the agreement contemplates that S will pay only if D fails to pay, and if C either knows or has reason to know of this relation, the promise of S is a suretyship promise *within* the statute of frauds, i.e., S's promise must be evidenced by a writing.[21] D and S are both liable for the full amount of the obligation though C is entitled to only one satisfaction. As between D and S, D should perform because D is the principal debtor and S is surety who has undertaken to pay C only if D does not pay. S is *promising to answer for the debt of another,*

---

[18] The Convention on International Contracts for the Sale of Goods (CISG or the Vienna Convention) and UNIDROIT Principles are described in § 13 *supra.*

[19] UNIDROIT Principles, Art. 1.2: "Nothing in these Principles requires a contract to be concluded in or evidenced by a writing."

[20] Article 96 declarations have been taken by Argentina, Armenia, Belarus, Chile, China, Estonia, Hungary, Latvia, Lithuania, Paraguay, Russian Federation and Ukraine. The United States has not taken this reservation. See Zhejiang Shaoxing Yongli Printing & Dyeing Co., Ltd. v. Microflock Tex. Group Corp., 2008 U. S. Dist. LEXIS 40418 (S. D. Fla. 2008).

[21] A promise *within* the statute of frauds is one that is covered by the statute of frauds and must be evidenced by a writing. A promise *without* (outside) the statute of frauds does not require a writing and may be enforced as an oral promise.

i.e., *S*'s promise is "collateral" to the promise of the principal debtor. Therefore, *S*'s promise is within the statute of frauds. It is important to emphasize that the relation between the two obligors (*D* and *S*) as one of principal and surety *must be known to the Creditor, C*. If goods are delivered or services are rendered to *D* with the understanding that they are to be charged to *S alone*, i.e., *C* is not extending any credit to *D* but is relying solely upon *S* to pay, *S*'s promise is not that of a surety, i.e., it is not a "collateral" promise. Rather, it is an "original" or "primary" promise that is *without* the statute of frauds and, therefore, need not be evidenced by a writing.

The inclusion of suretyship promises within the statute of frauds is clearly designed to serve the same function as that served by requiring other types of promises to be in writing, i.e., an evidentiary function.[22] The original Statute of Frauds was captioned, "An Act for the Prevention of Frauds and Perjuries."[23] Suretyship promises were included because they appeared to be particularly inviting targets for inspiring false allegations. If a principal debtor fails to pay and is judgment proof, the creditor may be inclined to seek another source of payment. Requiring written evidence of an alleged surety's promise provides a threshold safeguard against such false allegations. In addition to the evidentiary function, the requirement of a writing for promises of suretyship also serves a cautionary function, i.e., "guarding the promisor against ill-considered action."[24]

The first and second clauses of the original Statute of Frauds are directed at suretyship promises. It is important to consider each clause to determine the relationship between them.

[1]   Contracts of Executors and Administrators

The language used in the first clause of the original Statute of Frauds concerning promises of executors or administrators is clearly limited to contracts made in relation to the affairs of the deceased *only* when the contract requires a performance by the executor or administrator in his personal, rather than his representative, capacity. The statute has no application to a contract by an executor or administrator concerning his personal affairs, nor does it apply to a contract to be performed only out of the assets of the estate.[25] If there was no debt chargeable to the estate at the time of the promise of the executor or administrator, the promise is obviously not one to pay a debt of the estate from the personal assets of the executor or administrator.[26]

The question arises, what is the difference between the "special promise" of an executor or administrator in the first clause of the statute, and the "special promise" of any other promisor to answer for the debt of another in the second clause of the statute? The answer is found in the apparent purpose of Parliament to single out the executor or administrator for special mention. Courts have taken the position that the promise of an executor or administrator to answer for the debts of the estate is merely a species of the general requirement that the

---

[22] "In general the primary purpose of the Statute of Frauds is assumed to be evidentiary." RESTATEMENT 2d § 112 comment a.

[23] 29 Car. II, ch. 3.

[24] RESTATEMENT 2d § 112 comment a.

[25] *See* Perlberg v. Jahn, 773 S.W.2d 925, 927 (Tenn. Ct. App. 1989).

[26] *See, e.g.*, Schneider v. Bytner, 105 A.D.2d 498, 481 N.Y.S.2d 777 (3d Dep't 1984).

promise of any surety be evidenced by a writing.[27] The classic exposition of this explanation is found in *Bellows v. Sowles*:[28]

> The promise must be 'to answer damages out of his own estate.' This phraseology clearly implies an obligation, duty, or liability on the part of the testator's estate, for which the executor promises to pay damages out of his own estate. The statute was enacted to prevent executors or administrators from being fraudulently held for the debts or liabilities of the estates upon which they were called to administer. In this view of the case this clause of the statute is closely allied, if not identical, in principle, with the following clause: 'No action, etc., upon a special promise to answer for the debt, default or misdoings of another.' And so Judge Royce, in delivering the opinion of the court in Harrington v. Rich, 6 Vt. 666, declares these two classes of undertaking to be 'very nearly allied,' and considers them together. This seems to us to be the true idea of this clause of the statute — that the undertaking contemplated by it, like that contemplated by the next clause, is in the manner of a guaranty; and that the reasoning applicable to the latter is equally applicable to the former.

In light of this rationale which has been generally accepted, it is appropriate to proceed with the discussion of the requirement that any suretyship promise, including that of an executor or administrator, must be evidenced by a writing.

[2]   Promises to Answer for the Debt of Another — Determining Whether the Surety's Promise Is Within or Without the Statute of Frauds

At the beginning of this section we explored the basic concept of suretyship and the application of the statute of frauds to promises of sureties. We emphasized the fact that there must be a relationship between the two obligors (*S* and *D*) whereby *D*, the principal debtor, should pay and *S*, the surety, should pay only if *D* does not pay. We also emphasized the requirement that the creditor, *C*, must be aware of this relationship. We distinguished *original* from *collateral* promises, i.e., if the understanding is that the promisor is solely liable, the promise is *original*. If, however, the promisor is to pay only if the principal debtor does not pay, the promise is *collateral*. These labels, however, are mere conclusions that depend upon an analysis of the facts under which the promises are made. A number of problems arise in making this determination.

[a]   Was the Promise *Original* or *Collateral*?

Whether a promise is a suretyship (collateral) promise or an original (sometimes called "primary" or "direct") promise is a question of interpretation. The foreman of a construction company had been obtaining meals on credit from a café and his account was in arrears. The owner of the construction company paid the full amount of the debt. When the foreman was again in arrears, the company owner told the café to "Go ahead and let him continue to have meals and I will pay for it if he doesn't." The café continued to supply meals to the foreman. The owner of the café testified, "I would not have advanced that line of credit if Mr. Johnson

---

[27] *See* RESTATEMENT 2d § 111 comment a. Both types of promises may be found in the same paragraph of a state Statute of Frauds. *See* 33 PA. CONS. STAT. ANN. § 3.

[28] 57 Vt. 164, 52 Am. Rep. 118, 119 (1884).

[the owner of the company] had not promised to pay it." Johnson's promise was clearly *within* the suretyship provision of the statute of frauds.[29]

A more difficult interpretation involved a promise by a daughter to a physician who answered an emergency call to provide services to her father. The father was unconscious and the daughter directed the physician to "do everything under the sun to see this man is taken care of." A witness testified that the daughter also said, "I want my father taken care of, and give him the best care you can give him, and what the charges are . . . I will pay for it." The court viewed the daughter's promise as *original* in *form*, i.e., on its face, it was not a promise to answer for the debt of another. Rather, it appeared to be a primary, direct or, again, *original* promise which would make only the daughter liable. Thus, on the basis of the *form* of the promise, it was not within the statute of frauds. The court, however, properly considered how the promisee (the plaintiff-physician) apparently understood the daughter's statement. The plaintiff sought to recover from the estate of the injured party. When payment was not forthcoming from the estate, the plaintiff sent bills to the injured party's widow. Only after failing to collect the amount due from these other sources did the plaintiff finally seek recovery from the daughter. Thus, the conduct of the plaintiff raised an inference that he understood the daughter's promise as a suretyship promise, notwithstanding its form. While the plaintiff's earlier attempts to collect from others were not conclusive evidence of his understanding of the daughter's promise, he offered no explanation to rebut the inference that he regarded the daughter's promise as a suretyship (collateral) promise. The court, therefore, found the daughter's promise to be a suretyship promise which is *within* the statute of frauds and unenforceable because it was not evidenced by a writing.[30] To determine the proper characterization of the promise, it is not enough to consider merely the form of the promise. As in other questions of interpretation, all of the relevant circumstances must be considered.[31]

[b]   Joint Obligors

If two parties make oral promises for the same consideration, a question of suretyship may arise. The Restatement 2d of Contracts notes that a promise to answer for the debt of another is not within the statute of frauds unless the promisee is an obligee of the other's duty, the promisor is a surety for the other and the promisee knows or has reason to know of the suretyship relationship.[32] Thus, if D and S both orally promise to pay for goods from C, S's promise will be a suretyship promise *only* on the following conditions: (1) as between S and D, the parties understand that S will be a surety; (2) the promisee, C, knows or has reason to know that the goods will be delivered and used exclusively by D, i.e., no benefit will inure to S, and (3) the promises are joint and do not create *several* duties or *joint and several* duties.[33] With respect to the first element, if there is no suretyship relation between the parties, S

---

[29] Johnson Co. v. City Café, 100 S.W.2d 740, 741 (Tex. Civ. App. 1936).

[30] Lawrence v. Anderson, 108 Vt. 176, 184 A. 689 (1936).

[31] Where an auto insurance company promised orally to pay a claim but later refused to perform its promise, the court rejected the company's Statute of Frauds defense because the company did not agree to pay the claim only if its insured became legally responsible. Rather, it was settling its own possible obligation and its own duty to defend the insured. Thus, the company had assumed primary responsibility for the debt. Carter v. Allstate Ins. Co., 962 S.W.2d 268 (Tex. App. Houston 1st Dist. 1998). *See also* UCSF-Stanford Health Care v. Hawaii Mgmt. Alliance Benefits & Servs., Inc., 58 F. Supp. 2d 1162 (D. Haw. 1999).

[32] § 112. See Harriott v. Tronvold, 671 N. W. 2d 417, 422 (Iowa 2003).

[33] *See* Doodlesack v. Superfine Coal & Ice Corp., 292 Mass. 424, 198 N.E. 773 (1935). With respect to all three elements, see RESTATEMENT 2d § 113.

cannot be said to have made a suretyship promise. As to the second element, it is not enough that S and D intended only D to benefit from C's performance. There is the general requirement that C, the creditor, know or have reason to know that S is promising as a surety. To understand the third element requires a basic understanding of the distinction between joint liability as contrasted with several or joint and several liability.

Joint promisors were historically viewed as a unit, i.e., the obligation of one of the joint promisors could not be viewed as that of "another" for the purposes of the suretyship provision of the statute of frauds because there was only one obligation owed by both promisors and that obligation must, therefore, be *original* rather than *collateral*. If the promisors were under joint liability, the promisee could not bring an action against one of the joint promisors without joining all other living joint promisors. If, however, the promisors undertook "joint and several" or simply "several" liability, the promisee avoided this disadvantage. Joint and several liability or just several liability involves more than one obligation.[34] Therefore, a joint and several or several promise could be a promise to answer for the debt of "another". The archaic rules of multiple promisors have been changed by statutes indicating that, although the express terms of the contract provide for joint liability, the duties of the parties are treated as joint and several.[35] Thus, a joint promise would typically create joint and several liability and the suretyship provision of the statute of frauds would apply.

[c] Primary Obligation Must Exist at Time "Special" Promise Is Performed

While the suretyship provision requires a promise to answer for the *debt* of *another*, it is not necessary for the debt of the other to be in existence at the time the suretyship *contract is formed*.[36] It is, however, universally agreed that the primary obligation of a third party (D) must be in existence at the time the "special" *promise is to be performed*.[37] Thus, if the third person, for whose supposed debt the promisor has agreed to be answerable, is not liable, either because he never actually made an undertaking,[38] or because he lacked even voidable capacity to bind himself,[39] or for any other reason, the statute is not applicable.[40]

---

[34] The terms "joint" and "several" do not refer to whether the promises call for the same performance or separate performances. These terms are employed with respect to the *same* performance. Rather, the terms "joint" and "several" refer to whether the *promises* of the same performance have been as a *unit* or whether the promises of the same performance have been made *separately*.

[35] Courts often find joint and several liability where a promise signed by two parties is phrased in the singular. See Carriage House Condominiums, GP v. DeRaimos, 2008 U. S. Dist. LEXIS 4653 (E. D. Pa. 2008) citing Restatement 2d § 289, comment c.

[36] See Rosewood Care Ctr. v. Caterpillar, Inc., 226 Ill. 2d 559, 577 N. E.2d 1091 (2007), clarifying Illinois interpretation of 19th century cases.

[37] "It is essential that a primary obligation of some kind be incurred in order to bring the case within the statute. . . . A promise is not within this clause of the statute unless there is an obligation of some third person to the promisee. The third person must at some time be under a legal duty of performance to the promisee, a duty that will be discharged by the performance of the new promisor. . . ." General Elec. Co. v. Hans, 242 Miss. 119, 124, 133 So. 2d 275, 276 (1961).

[38] *See, e.g.*, Duca v. Lord, 331 Mass. 51, 117 N.E.2d 145 (1954) (decedent promised orally to pay for repairs to property if trustees did not pay; the oral promise was not within the statute because there was no obligation on the part of the trustee to which decedent's promise could be secondary); Mease v. Wagner, 1 McCord 395 (S.C. 1821) (promise to pay for goods furnished for a friend of the promisor if the nephew of the deceased did not pay; the nephew had made no promise and later refused to pay).

[39] If the claim asserted against the principal debtor is *void, e.g.*, a claim against a party suffering from mental illness

[d] Novation

A novation is a tripartite arrangement whereby a creditor releases the debtor in exchange for a new debtor in substitution for the original debtor. By agreement of all three parties to a contract, a novation discharges one of the original parties to the contract and substitutes a new one. Since the debt of the original obligor is discharged as soon as the contract is made between the substitute debtor and the creditor, there is no "debt of another" in existence as of the moment the new promise is made and the new promise cannot be a suretyship promise within the statute of frauds.[41] The original debtor need not know that the debt is discharged at the moment the contract between the creditor and substitute debtor is formed.[42] If the original debtor is not released at the time the new debtor's promise is made, the new promise is within the suretyship provision because the original obligation would then be in existence after the new promise is made.

[e] Promise Made to the Debtor Rather than the Creditor

The purpose of the suretyship provision was to preclude false claims by creditors who, not having been paid by their debtors, might be inclined to allege that a promise to pay the debt had been made by another. It is unlikely that a debtor would claim that a party made a promise to the debtor to pay the debt to a third party creditor absent consideration moving to such a promisor. There is therefore, universal agreement among our courts that the promise to answer for the debt of "another" should be interpreted as a promise to the creditor of the "other," rather than to the debtor, since the debtor is the "other."[43]

---

or other incapacity who has been adjudicated incompetent and a guardian has been appointed, a promise by a purported surety would not be within the statute because there is no debt of *another*. If, however, there is an obligation of another, albeit a *voidable* or *unenforceable* obligation, the promise of the surety is within the statute of frauds. Thus, a promise to answer for the debt of an infant is within the statute of frauds even though the infant's obligation is voidable. Similarly, a promise to pay the debt of another who may avoid enforcement of the debt on the grounds of fraud or duress is also a promise within the statute of frauds. If the debtor's obligation, itself, is within the statute of frauds, a promise to pay that debt if the debtor fails to pay is within the statute of frauds even though the principal obligation may be said to be unenforceable because of the statute of frauds.

[40] If the performance of a promise involves only the performance of a duty which the promisor is bound to perform because of a duty other than that imposed by the promisee (*e.g.*, a trust relationship), the promise is not within the suretyship provision. Whenever a promisor, albeit a surety, promises to answer for his own obligation as well as that of another, his promise is not within the suretyship provision. *See* RESTATEMENT 2d § 114.

[41] *See* Healy v. Brotman, 96 Misc. 2d 386, 409 N.Y.S.2d 72, 73 (1978). *See also* Klag v. Home Ins. Co., 116 Ga. App. 678, 158 S.E.2d 444 (1967); Blaylock v. Stephens, 36 Tenn. App. 464, 258 S.W.2d 779 (1953); La Duke v. John T. Barbee & Co., 198 Ala. 234, 73 So. 472 (1916); Wilhelm v. Voss, 118 Mich. 106, 76 N.W. 308 (1898). RESTATEMENT 2d § 115.

[42] While concurrence by the original debtor is normal, there are decisions holding that concurrence is not necessary. The "consent" of the original debtor is usually not stressed. Some courts suggest a presumption of such consent though the original debtor would have the right to disclaim the benefit of having his obligation satisfied. *See* Greenwood Leflore Hosp. Comm'n v. Turner, 213 Miss. 200, 56 So. 2d 496 (1952).

[43] "A promise, as here, to the debtor to pay the debtor's debts — in contrast to a promise to the creditor to pay debts owed by another — is not contemplated by the statute of frauds." Brad Ragan, Inc. v. Callicutt Enters., Inc., 73 N.C. App. 134, 137, 326 S.E.2d 62, 64 (1985). *See also* Allen v. Rosen, 526 So. 2d 1050, 1051 (Fla. Dist. Ct. App. 1988); Brownlee-Kesterson, Inc. v. Continental Cas. Co., 1985 Tenn. App. LEXIS 3364, at *12 (Tenn. Ct. App. Dec. 6, 1985); Farmers State Bank v. Conrardy, 215 Kan. 334, 524 P.2d 690 (1974); Danby v. Osteopathic Hosp. Ass'n, 34 Del. Ch. 427, 104 A.2d 903 (1954); Eastwood v. Kenyon, 11 A. & E. 438 [1840].

[f]   The Four-Party Indemnity Situation

The word "indemnity" is often misused.[44] It should be relegated to those situations where a promise is made to a debtor or obligor to save him harmless from loss or liability. If, therefore, *A* promises to save *B* from loss if *B* will purchase goods from *C*, the promise is made to a debtor and, as we have just seen, *A*'s promise is *without* the statute of frauds. Another situation involving four parties, however, creates additional questions.

Suppose that *A* says to *B*, "If you (*B*) will become a surety on *C*'s loan to *D*, I (*A*) will save you harmless from loss." Is *A*'s promise to indemnify a surety within the statute of frauds? The judicial analysis of this question focuses upon the proper characterization of the promisee (*B*). *B* may be characterized as an obligor (debtor) because, in relation to *C*, he will be liable as a surety on *C*'s loan to *D*. *B*, however, may also be characterized as a creditor because, in relation to *D*, *B* will be entitled to reimbursement or exoneration from *D*, the principal debtor, if *B* must pay *C* after *D* fails to pay. The prevailing view is to treat *B* as a debtor whose promise is, therefore, without the statute of frauds.[45] The justification for the prevailing view is best suggested by Professor Corbin who believes there is no harm in distinguishing this type of situation from ordinary suretyship cases that fall within the statute of frauds.[46] Moreover, when confronted with a situation that may or may not require the statute to be applied, modern courts are inclined to avoid the statute if only technical purity rather than necessary protection of a promisor is served by its application.

[g]   The "Main Purpose" or "Leading Object" Rule — Assignors and *Del Credere* Agents — The New York View

Certain types of transactions, though falling within the literal language of the suretyship provision, are excluded from its operation because they do not present the dangers the statute sought to avoid. Where, for example, a party promises to answer for the debt of another out of the debtor's funds that were deposited with the promisor for that purpose or where the debtor has consented to the payment, the form of the promise is one to answer for the debt of another. The suretyship provision, however, was designed to protect promisors from false assertions that would make them personally liable. Thus, the *purpose* of the suretyship provision is not served by including such a promise within the statute of frauds.[47] Focusing upon the purpose of the provision has enabled courts to discover other clusters of promises that are outside the scope of the suretyship provision.

---

[44] Sometimes the word "indemnity" is used to mean guaranty or surety. Generally, indemnity contracts are those in which the promisee is a debtor (obligor), whereas in suretyship or guaranty contracts, the promisee is an obligee (creditor). The Restatement 2d distinguishes "non-surety" indemnitors from surety indemnitors. *See* Restatement 2d § 118 comments a and b.

[45] *See* Feiler v. Rosenbloom, 46 Md. App. 297, 416 A.2d 1345 (1980), *rev'd* on other grounds, 290 Md. 598, 431 A.2d 102 (1981); Biestek v. Varricchio, 34 Conn. Supp. 620, 380 A.2d 1351 (Conn. Super. Ct. 1977); Thomas v. Williams, 173 Okla. 601, 49 P.2d 557 (1935); Newbern v. Fisher, 198 N.C. 385, 151 S.E. 875 (1930); Tighe v. Morrison, 116 N.Y. 263, 22 N.E. 164 (1889). *Accord* Restatement 2d § 118 (differing from the First Restatement § 186). Cases holding that the promise of an indemnitor to a surety is a promise to a creditor and, therefore, within the statute of frauds include Wilder v. Clark, 263 Ala. 55, 81 So. 2d 273 (1955), and Nugent v. Wolfe, 111 Pa. 471, 4 A. 15, 56 Am. Rep. 291 (1886).

[46] 2 Corbin on Contracts § 16.17.

[47] This is sometimes called the "debtor's fund" exception to the suretyship provision of the statute. *See* CBA Collection Servs. v. Roeberg & Assocs., P.A., 1996 Del. Super. LEXIS 330, at *4 (Del. Super. Ct. Aug. 14, 1996), *aff'd*, 1997 Del. LEXIS 40 (Del. Feb. 5, 1997).

One of the better statements of the purpose of the suretyship provision is found in the opinion of Justice Brewer in the leading case of *Davis v. Patrick*:[48] There is . . . a temptation for a promisee, in a case where the real debtor has proved insolvent or unable to pay, to enlarge the scope of the promise, or to torture mere words of encouragement and confidence into an absolute promise; and it is so obviously just that a promisor receiving no benefits should be bound only by the exact terms of his promise, that this statute requiring a memorandum in writing was enacted. Therefore, whenever the alleged promisor is an absolute stranger to the transaction, and without interest in it, courts strictly uphold the obligations of this statute. But cases sometimes arise in which, though a third party is the original obligor, the primary debtor, the promisor, has a personal, immediate and pecuniary interest in the transaction and is therefore himself a party to be benefitted by the performance of the promisee. In such cases the reason which underlies and prompted this statutory provision fails, and the courts will give effect to the promise.

The portion of this quotation suggesting that, if a promisor has an immediate pecuniary interest either in the creation or payment of the third person's debt, the promise is outside the statute, is often called the *main purpose* or *leading object* rule.[49] The purpose of the rule is to recognize a distinction between promises which are made principally for the promisor's benefit and promises made for the benefit of another. Innumerable cases have taken promises out of the suretyship provision of the statute on this basis though, superficially, the promise appears to be within the provision.[50] The difficult question has been, and continues to be, what is the test for determining when the promisor's purpose is basically or essentially to benefit himself, rather than to benefit and accommodate another?

The formulations found in the case law are invariably insufficient.[51] Where, for example, the promise is characterized as *original* rather than *collateral*, the courts are stating conclusions rather than supplying workable tests.[52] The description of the "main purpose" doctrine may suggest a similar infirmity. Thus, it may be described as requiring three elements: (1) the promisor intended to become primarily liable for the debt, in effect, making it his original obligation, rather than to become a surety for another; (2) there was consideration for the promise; and (3) receipt of the consideration was the promisor's main purpose or leading object in making the promise.[53] If element (1) can be shown, however, there is little left to be decided. The question, however, is one of fact where the challenge in formulating a workable test relates to the purpose, motive, object or desire of the promisor.[54] Evidence of the benefit

[48] 141 U.S. 479, 487–88, 12 S. Ct. 58, 35 L. Ed. 826 (1891).

[49] For a general discussion of the main purpose or leading object rule, see Rosewood Care Ctr., Inc. v. Caterpillar, Inc., 226 Ill.2d. 559, 572, 877 N.E. 2d 1091,1098 (2007). *See also* Power Entertainment v. NFL Properties, Inc., 151 F. 3d 247 (5th Cir. 1998); Contractor's Crane Serv. v. Vermont Whey Abatement Auth., 147 Vt. 441, 519 A.2d 1166 (1986). Morrison-Knudsen Co. v. Hite Crane & Rigging, Inc., 36 Wash. App. 860, 678 P.2d 346 (1984). RESTATEMENT 2d § 116.

[50] Statutes in several western states set forth a "main purpose" exception to the statute of frauds. *See, e.g.,* CAL. CIV. CODE § 2794; MONT. CODE ANN. tit. 30, § 105; N.D. CENT. CODE § 22-01-05; UTAH CODE ANN. § 25-5-6.

[51] *See* Contractor's Crane Serv. v. Vermont Whey Abatement Auth., 147 Vt. 441, 519 A.2d 1166 (1986).

[52] See Henry C. Beck Co. v. Ft. Wayne Structural Steel Co., 701 F.2d 1221 (7th Cir. 1983), which cites an earlier edition of this treatise for this criticism.

[53] *In re* Fairchild Aircraft Corp. (Butler Aviation Int'l v. Whyte), 6 F.3d 1119, 1127 (5th Cir. 1993).

[54] Quoted from an earlier edition in Webb Mfg. Co. v. Sinoff, 449 Pa. Super. 534, 540, 674 A.2d 723, 726 (1996), relying upon Thomas A. Armbruster, Inc. v. Barron, 341 Pa. Super. 409, 491 A.2d 882 (1985). See also First Nat'l Bank in Clarksville v. Moore, 628 S.W.2d 488 (Tex. App. Texarkana 1982), holding that promisee's failure to secure a jury

to the promisor must be clear,[55] but the mere discovery of consideration to support such a promise should not lead a court to conclude that the *main* purpose or *leading* object of the promisor was necessarily to benefit himself rather than the principal debtor. Some judicial opinions display this confusion.[56] Even though the promisor received an economic benefit for his promise, his promise may still be a promise within the suretyship provision.[57] A benefit to the promisor of substantial pecuniary value, however, will be strong evidence that his promise, though in the form of a suretyship promise, was the main purpose of the promisor and should, therefore, be taken out of the suretyship provision of the statute. The substantial benefit received by the promisor provides an evidentiary substitute for written evidence of the promise.[58]

The difficulties encountered in discovering a sufficient articulation of the "main purpose" or "leading object" rule suggest a brief consideration of certain clusters of cases that illustrate its use. In certain cases, the evidence may be abundantly clear that the promise was made exclusively for the benefit of the promisor. Where, for example, the defendant had granted an exclusive license to market football cards and the licensee declared bankruptcy, owing defendant $800,000 in unpaid royalties, plaintiff's promise to pay the amount of this debt in exchange for becoming the new licensee was hardly intended to benefit "another."[59] Where a subcontractor refused to continue supplying labor and materials because the general contractor failed to pay, the owner orally promised to pay the subcontractor to induce the completion of performance. Clearly, the owner's promise is, in form, a suretyship promise within the statute. Yet, it is equally clear that the owner's leading object is to benefit himself substantially. He has no particular interest in benefitting the general contractor for whom he may even feel some hostility, but he has an overriding desire to see the completion of the building and he makes the promise to pay the subcontractor to serve that main purpose. Such a promise is taken out of the suretyship provision of the statute even though the promise is to pay the debt of another.[60]

---

finding that the main purpose of the promisor was to obtain a benefit to himself resulted in the promise remaining within the suretyship provision of the statute of frauds.

[55] See Westwind Seafood Int'l, Inc. v. Anchor Frozen Foods, 1992 U.S. App. LEXIS 18418 (9th Cir. July 24, 1992), where the court found the evidence of alleged benefit to the promisor to be speculative.

[56] In 1811, Chancellor Kent suggested that a promise to pay the debt of another arising from some new and original consideration takes the promise out of the suretyship provision. Leonard v. Vredenburgh, 8 Johns. 29, 5 Am. Dec. 317 (N.Y. 1811). For a modern manifestation of this confusion of thought, see *Gulf Liquid Fertilizer Co. v. Titus*, 163 Tex. 260, 354 S.W.2d 378 (1962). These opinions overlook the fact that any promise needs consideration or an alternate validation device to support it. Thus, to say that the promise is supported by consideration does not, in itself, provide any assistance in the determination of whether the promisor made the promise essentially to benefit himself. As suggested in *Webb Mfg. Co. v. Sinoff*, 449 Pa. Super. 534, 541, 674 A.2d 723, 726 (1996), the statute is not rendered inapplicable merely because a party "may indirectly receive some gain when he promises to pay the debt. . . ."

[57] *See* First Nat'l Bank in Clarksville v. Moore, 628 S.W.2d 488 (Tex. App. Texarkana 1982); Colpitts v. L. C. Fisher Co., 289 Mass. 232, 193 N.E. 833 (1935); Knight v. Kiser, 271 F. 869 (4th Cir. 1921); Wells & Morris v. Brown, 67 Wash. 351, 121 P. 828 (1912); Templeton v. Bascom, 33 Vt. 132 (1860).

[58] *See* RESTATEMENT 2d § 116 comments a and b.

[59] The court reversed the lower court's grant of a motion to dismiss on the footing that plaintiff could prove the "main purpose" exception. Power Entertainment, Inc. v. NFL Props., Inc., 151 F.3d 247 (5th Cir. 1998).

[60] Fairview Lumber Co. v. Makos, 44 Wash. 2d 131, 265 P.2d 837 (1954) (house builder was in arrears to a materials supplier and the land owner promised to pay the past debt and future charges if the promisee would continue to supply materials). This is, essentially, the fact situation of ill. 3 of RESTATEMENT 2d § 116. In Morrison-Knudsen Co. v. Hite Crane & Rigging, 36 Wash. App. 860, 678 P.2d 346 (1984), a general contractor promised to pay the debt of a subcontractor to a supplier of crane services and the court held that the promise was made to assure the completion

Another group of cases applying the main purpose rule are those where the promisor has an interest in certain property on which the promisee either has a lien or has the power to create a lien as security for a debt of another. If the promisor agrees to discharge the debt of another in exchange for the promisee's forbearance to enforce the lien or to create one, courts have found the main purpose of the promisor was to avoid the lien on his property rather than to benefit the debtor.[61]

Promises by stockholders of corporations to pay corporate bills if promisees continue to supply goods or services to the corporation may appear to suggest another application of the main purpose or leading object rule since the promises are often motivated by the stockholder's own interests and their leading object may be seen as an effort to protect the value of their stock. Yet, such promises are usually held to remain within the suretyship provision of the statute unless the benefit to the promisor can be shown to be *special, direct and/or immediate*.[62] A stockholder's promise to answer for the debt of the corporation normally provides no more than a remote and indirect benefit to the promisor.[63] A promise made merely to protect the value of one's shares does not activate the main purpose rule.[64] If the promisor seeks to protect his personal financial interests beyond the value of his shares, however, a special, direct or immediate benefit may be shown as sufficient to apply the main purpose rule.[65]

Where the holder of a contract right assigns that right, the assignor may promise that the obligor (the party who has the correlative duty) will perform his duty. Though the promise may appear to be within the suretyship provision, it is typically made for the benefit of the assignor who is eager to effectuate the assignment. It falls, therefore, within the rationale of the "main purpose" exception.[66] A *del credere* agent is one who takes possession of the creditor's goods and earns a commission in reselling them. A promise by the agent to the creditor that guarantees the accounts of customers who purchase the goods is not within the

of the contract on schedule. See also Wilson Floors Co. v. Sciota Park, Ltd., 54 Ohio St. 2d 451, 377 N.E.2d 514 (1978), where a bank's promise to a subcontractor to ascertain continuation of payments was held to be for the interest of the bank in reducing the costs of completing the project.

[61] *See* Grammar v. Builders Brick & Stone Co., 277 S.W.2d 185 (Tex. Civ. App. San Antonio 1955); Miller v. Hanna-Logan, Inc., 95 Colo. 464, 37 P.2d 393 (1934).

[62] See Thomas A. Armbruster, Inc. v. Barron, 341 Pa. Super. 409, 491 A.2d 882, 886 (1985), which quotes this portion of the second edition of this treatise.

[63] Martin Roofing, Inc. v. Goldstein, 60 N.Y.2d 262, 469 N.Y.S.2d 595, 457 N.E.2d 700, 702 (1983), *cert. denied*, 466 U.S. 905, 104 S. Ct. 1681, 80 L. Ed. 2d 156 (1984).

[64] *See* 2 CORBIN ON CONTRACTS § 16.7.

[65] *See Thomas A. Armbruster, Inc. v. Barron, supra* note 54, where the promise was held to go beyond the purpose of protecting the value of shares, i.e., it was made to insure the financial success of a new enterprise. In Merdes v. Underwood, 742 P.2d 245 (Alaska 1987), the promise was held to be outside the statute because it was made to serve the promisor's own business advantage in forestalling litigation against a corporation in which the promisor initially had an 80% interest and later a 100% interest. The promise also served to benefit his credit reputation. *See also* Mid-Atlantic Appliances, Inc. v. Morgan, 194 Va. 324, 73 S.E.2d 385, 35 A.L.R.2d 899 (1952). Cf. Contractor's Crane Serv. v. Vermont Whey Abatement Auth., 147 Vt. 441, 519 A.2d 1166 (1986), where the court held that a group of producers of cheese who formed a joint venture to dispose of liquid whey, a by-product of cheese, were liable on their promise to pay for the debt of the joint venture concerning the hauling of the whey because their main purpose was to enable them, as cheese producers, to continue disposing of their whey. Contracts of guaranty insurance are excluded from the "main purpose" exception regardless of whether the promisor is in the regular business of providing such insurance. RESTATEMENT 2d § 116 comment c.

[66] RESTATEMENT 2d § 121(1).

suretyship provision of the statute because, typically, the agent seeks only to advance his own interest and falls within the rationale of the "main purpose" exception.[67]

New York View. Any criticism of the "main purpose" rule is drowned in the sea of cases that have found it useful in removing certain promises from the suretyship provision. With the exception of New York, the "main purpose" rule is recognized throughout the country.[68]

[h]   Contract to Purchase the Creditor's Right

A party in the business of debt collection may promise the creditor to purchase the right of the creditor against the debtor. If the right is assigned at the moment the promise is made, there is a mere substitution of a new creditor for the original creditor and the suretyship provision of the statute of frauds is not involved. If, however, the creditor agrees to assign the right sometime after the promise to pay the creditor consideration (typically less than the amount of the debt because there may be some obstacles in collecting the debt), it is possible to stretch the language of the suretyship provision to bring this situation within its scope. Such a promise is not, however, within the suretyship provision of the statute of frauds for the obvious reason that no suretyship was intended.[69]

§ 71   AGREEMENTS MADE IN CONSIDERATION OF MARRIAGE

The language of the original Statute of Frauds provides that "[N]o action shall be brought to charge any person upon any agreement made in consideration of marriage." The all-inclusive phrase "any agreement" would, if read literally, include even mutual promises to marry. There is reason to believe that even the drafters of the original Statute, however, did not intend it to apply to such promises.[70] Early decisions made it clear that courts would not apply this provision of the Statute to mutual promises to marry which are typically exchanged in an ambience suggesting the inappropriateness of a writing requirement.[71] Modern courts continue this policy though, in a number of jurisdictions, judicial exclusion became unnecessary

---

[67] Restatement 2d § 121(2).

[68] The New York approach is traceable to nineteenth century cases. In Rintoul v. White, 108 N.Y. 222, 15 N.E. 318 (1888), the court dealt with the main purpose rule in accordance with its understanding of New York precedent. It suggested three necessary elements: (a) there must be consideration to support the promise of the surety; (b) the consideration must benefit the promisor; (c) the promisor must come under an independent duty of payment regardless of the liability of the principal debtor. The third element has been more recently interpreted as to require a manifested intention by the parties that the promisor become a principal debtor, primarily liable. Martin Roofing v. Goldstein, 60 N.Y.2d 262, 469 N.Y.S.2d 595, 457 N.E.2d 700 (1983), *cert. denied,* 466 U.S. 905, 104 S. Ct. 1681, 80 L. Ed. 2d 156 (1984). Unless the third element is satisfied, the court may not treat the promise as having been taken out of the suretyship provision. Thus, a suretyship promise that would be removed from the statute in other jurisdictions will remain subject to the statute in New York. *See* Capital Knitting Mills, Inc. v. Duofold, Inc., 131 A.D.2d 87, 519 N.Y.S.2d 968 (1st Dep't 1987). This opinion contains a splendid analysis of the treatment of the main purpose rule in New York, as well as a suggestion that the New York Court of Appeals might be receptive to reconsidering the unique New York approach so as to have New York recognize the main purpose concept in accordance with other jurisdictions. For a recent application of the New York view, see GBJ Corp. v. Eastern Ohio Paving Co., 139 F.3d 1080, 1085–86 (6th Cir. 1998) (applying New York law).

[69] Restatement 2d § 122.

[70] Restatement 2d § 124 comment a.

[71] *See, e.g.,* Short v. Stotts, 58 Ind. 29 (1877); Withers v. Richardson, 21 Ky. 94, 17 Am. Dec. 44 (1827). It was also early held, however, that mutual promises to marry can be within the provision of the statute requiring promises not to be performed within one year from the making. *See* Derby v. Phelps, 2 N.H. 515 (1822).

where mutual promises to marry are excluded from the marriage provisions.[72] Moreover, actions for breach of promise to marry have been legislatively proscribed in a number of jurisdictions.[73]

The marriage provision applies to a promise to surrender any property right in consideration of marriage.[74] Thus, an antenuptial agreement concerning the disposition of property is within the marriage provision of the statute.[75] A promise by a third party, X, to pay a sum to Y, if she will marry Z, is within the marriage provision.[76] Agreements to adopt children[77] or to permit a spouse's parent to live with the couple[78] have been held to be within the marriage provision of the statute. If, however, the marriage is merely the occasion for making the contract or if the contract is made merely in contemplation of marriage where the promises are supported by other consideration, the contract is not within the statute.[79] Similarly, if the marriage is merely a condition of a promise which is supported wholly by some other consideration, the contract is not within the statute.[80] Courts are often astute to find that a contract is outside the operation of the statute for one or another of these reasons. It is, however, generally held that the occurrence of the marriage in reliance upon an oral agreement within the marriage provision is not sufficient part performance to take the contract out of the statute.[81]

Elsewhere in this volume, we explore the problem of contracts between unmarried cohabitants. Contracts between the cohabitants may not be reduced to written form.[82] While the possibility of fraudulent claims may suggest a greater need for the application of the

---

[72] See Tice v. Tice, 672 P.2d 1168, 1170 (Okla. 1983), which mentions OKLA. STAT. § 136(3). See also HAW. REV. STAT. § 656-1(3).

[73] These statutes are often called "heart balm" (or "anti heart balm") statutes because they permit the former lovers' heartaches to heal without resort to the courts. This description as well as a listing of jurisdictions that have enacted such statutes is found in Wildey v. Springs, 840 F. Supp. 1259, 1261 (N.D. Ill. 1994). See also Miller v. Ratner, 114 Md. App. 18, 688 A.2d 976 (1997).

[74] See, e.g., Byers v. Byers, 618 P.2d 930 (Okla. 1980), where the court held that the situation of a wife who promised to marry only because her husband agreed to support a child fathered by another prior to the marriage was within the statute of frauds. See also Stevens v. Niblack's Adm'r, 256 Ky. 255, 75 S.W.2d 770 (1934), where a promise of the father, made to the mother of a child born out of wedlock, to leave the father's estate to the child in consideration of the mother's promise to marry was within the statute of frauds. If the agreement is not made in contemplation of marriage, however, the statute does not apply. See In re Marriage of Lemoine-Hoffman, 827 P. 587, 590 (Colo. Ct. App. 1992).

[75] See, e.g., Dewberrty v. George, 62 P. Ed 525 (Ct. App. Wa. 2003) (oral antenuptial separate property agreement was subject to the marriage provision of the statute of frauds, but satisfied statute through complete performance); Rossiter v. Rossiter, 4 Haw. App. 333, 666 P.2d 617 (1983) (alleged oral antenuptial agreement that wife would never force the sale of marital residence). A postnuptial agreement, however, may be prohibited regardless of a writing unless it is accompanied by a separation agreement. See King v. King, 2000 Ohio App. LEXIS 1190 (Ohio Ct. App. Mar. 20, 2000).

[76] RESTATEMENT 2d § 124 ill. 4.

[77] Maddox v. Maddox, 224 Ga. 313, 161 S.E.2d 870 (1968).

[78] Koch v. Koch, 95 N.J. Super. 546, 232 A.2d 157 (1967).

[79] Riley v. Riley, 25 Conn. 154 (1856) (promise to prospective bridegroom that note held by fianceé should be paid out of his estate, made in consideration of forbearance, on the eve of marriage).

[80] Bader v. Hiscox, 188 Iowa 986, 174 N.W. 565, 10 A.L.R. 316 (1919) (promise of father to convey land to woman seduced by his son, if she would drop civil and criminal bastardy proceedings).

[81] Rossiter v. Rossiter, 4 Haw. App. 333, 666 P.2d 617 (1983). RESTATEMENT 2d § 124 comment d.

[82] The alleged contract may not even have been expressed orally and the action is based on an implied-in-fact contract. See Marvin v. Marvin, 18 Cal. 3d 660, 134 Cal. Rptr. 815, 557 P.2d 106 (1976).

marriage provision of the statute of frauds to these contracts, the marriage provision has been held inapplicable to them.[83] To discourage such "palimony" suits, some jurisdictions have amended their respective marriage provisions of the statute of frauds to require written evidence of agreements in consideration of nonmarried conjugal cohabitation.[84] Though the unamended marriage provision does not apply to such contracts, other provisions of the statute of frauds such as those applicable to a contract to transfer an interest in real estate, or a contract that cannot be performed within one year from the making thereof, will apply to such contracts if the contract activates such provisions.[85]

§ 72   CONTRACTS FOR THE SALE OF LAND

[A]   History — Distinguishing Contracts and Conveyances

One of the types of contracts covered by the original Statute of Frauds was a contract for the conveyance of an interest in land. The purpose of the land contract provision is the same as the purpose underlying the other provisions of the Statute dealing with other types of contracts, i.e., to protect an owner or purchaser of real estate from fraudulent claims that he or his agent have agreed to sell or buy an interest in real estate.[86]

It is important to distinguish the section of the statute of frauds requiring written evidence of an executory contract to transfer an interest in land from another section of the statute dealing with the conveyance or present transfer of an interest in land. A conveyance is an executed transaction and the requirements for its validity are commonly prescribed by separate statutes beyond the scope of this book. The situation is made somewhat confusing by the fact that the English version of the land contract clause of the Statute of Frauds uses the language, "contract or sale," which would appear to cover both a contract to convey as well as the conveyance itself. In view of the fact, however, that other sections of the original Statute cover the subject of conveyances more directly and comprehensively,[87] the land contract clause of the fourth section has commonly been viewed as if it only contained the words "contract for the sale." Most of the American versions of the land contract clause are worded in this fashion.

While there is no doubt that the statute applies to any promise to transfer an interest in land, there has been some question as to whether a promise to *buy* an interest in land is also within the statute. The prevailing view is that such promises are covered by the statute[88] and

---

[83] *See* Morone v. Morone, 50 N.Y.2d 481, 429 N.Y.S.2d 592, 413 N.E.2d 1154 (1980). See, however, Posik v. Layton, 695 So. 2d 759, 762 (Fla. Dist. Ct. App. 1997), suggesting that the marriage provision should apply to "non-marital, nuptial-like agreements."

[84] This is the phraseology of TEX. BUS. & COM. CODE ANN. § 26.01(b)(3). *See* Zaremba v. Cliburn, 949 S.W.2d 822, 872 (Tex. App. Fort Worth 1997). *See also* Hollom v. Carey, 343 N.W.2d 701, 703 (Minn. Ct. App. 1984) (applying MINN. STAT. §§ 513.075 and 513.076).

[85] See, e.g., Baron v. Jeffer, 131 A.D.2d 411, 515 N.Y.S.2d 857 (2d Dep't 1987), where the contract between unmarried cohabitants did not require a writing because of the marriage provision, but did require a writing because of the one year provision (*see infra* § 73) and the provision concerning contracts for the sale of land (*see infra* § 71).

[86] Wiggins v. Barrett & Assocs., 295 Or. 679, 669 P.2d 1132 (1983).

[87] *See* 29 Car. 2, ch. 3, § 1. *See also* RESTATEMENT OF PROPERTY §§ 467, 522.

[88] RESTATEMENT 2d § 125 comment d.

even payment of the price, itself, will not satisfy the statute.[89] If the owner of the land tenders a deed to the buyer who accepts the deed, however, the buyer's oral promise to pay is taken out of the statute and becomes enforceable unless the "price" which the buyer promised to pay was, in whole or in part, itself an interest in land.[90] Presumably, the evidentiary formalities of the statute are satisfied by an executed conveyance, but they are not satisfied by performance of a promise to pay.

[B]　What Is an "Interest in Land"?

One of the fundamental questions concerning this section of the statute is, what is an interest in land? In general, the section encompasses any contract the performance of which involves the transfer or creation of what, historically, is known as a property interest in real estate.[91] The real estate interest promised may be legal or equitable.[92] The statute, therefore, applies not only to a promise to transfer a legal estate in lands,[93] or to create or transfer an easement,[94] or profit,[95] or rent,[96] or other similar legal property interest, but also an agreement to rescind,[97] or to assign,[98] a land contract, or to create or assign a beneficiary's

---

[89] RESTATEMENT 2d § 129.

[90] RESTATEMENT 2d § 125(3) and comment e thereto.

[91] The words "lands, tenements and hereditaments" of the original Statute have not been accorded individual meanings. It has been assumed that they are synonymous with the phrase "real estate." See RESTATEMENT 2d § 127. In re Tavern Motor Inn, Inc., 80 B.R. 659, 661 (D. Vt. 1987), quotes Blackstone's definition of an "incorporeal hereditament" as "a right issuing out of a thing corporate (whether real or personal). . . ." Rents are listed among ten principal incorporeal hereditaments.

[92] See Shalimar Ass'n v. D.O.C. Enters., 142 Ariz. 36, 688 P.2d 682 (Ct. App. 1984) (implied restriction limiting use of property to a golf course was an equitable restriction generally considered to be an interest in land within the statute of frauds).

[93] See, e.g., Starnes v. Premier Trust Servs., 1995 U.S. App. LEXIS 9157 (7th Cir. Apr. 17, 1995) (transfer of beneficial interest in land trust); Carley v. Carley, 705 S.W.2d 371 (Tex. App. San Antonio 1986) (life estate is an interest in land within the statute). See also Moloney v. Weingarten, 118 A.D.2d 836, 500 N.Y.S.2d 320 (2d Dep't 1986) (statute applicable to a contract purporting to create or convey an interest in a cooperative apartment); Del Rio Land, Inc. v. Haumont, 118 Ariz. 1, 574 P.2d 469 (Ct. App. 1977) (sale of real property at auction is within the statute). If the price for the land is something other than money, the statute applies: Sealock v. Krug-Robinson Auto Co., 110 Kan. 302, 203 P. 728 (1922) (promise to convey land in exchange for automobiles); Baxter v. Kitch, 37 Ind. 554 (1871) (promise to convey land for services rendered); Purcell v. Miner, 71 U.S. (4 Wall.) 513 (1867) (agreement to exchange lands). A unilateral contract to purchase land at the owner's option is within the statute: Alamoe Realty Co. v. Mutual Trust Life Ins. Co., 202 Minn. 457, 278 N.W. 902 (1938). A contract to convey or purchase land owned by a third person is within the statute, Wright v. Green, 67 Ind. App. 433, 119 N.E. 379 (1918). Most courts hold an agreement conferring an "option" on lands to be within the land contract clause of the statute, Rooney v. Dayton-Hudson Corp., 310 Minn. 256, 246 N.W.2d 170 (1976); but see DiPietro v. Boynton, 628 A.2d 1019, 1023 (Me. 1993), holding that the *assignment* of an option contract for the purchase of land is not within the statute.

[94] C/R TV, Inc. v. Shannondale, Inc., 27 F.3d 104 (4th Cir. 1994); Bob Daniels & Sons v. Weaver, 106 Idaho 535, 681 P.2d 1010 (Ct. App. 1984) (easement); Wiggins v. Barrett & Assocs., 295 Or. 679, 669 P.2d 1132 (1983) (easement); Estabrook v. Wilcox, 226 Mass. 156, 115 N.E. 233 (1917) (right of way). See also Silva v. McGuinness, 189 Mont. 252, 615 P.2d 879 (1980) (agreement to change exit of road involves an interest in land subject to the statute of frauds).

[95] Riddle v. Brown, 20 Ala. 412, 56 Am. Dec. 202 (1852) (promise to give the right to dig and carry away ore).

[96] An assignment of rents already due is an assignment of a mere chose in action and would not be within the statute of frauds. An assignment of the right to rent payments as they become due, however, is a transfer of an interest in land that is within the statute. In re Tavern Motor Inn, Inc., 80 B.R. 659 (D. Vt. 1987).

[97] See Annot., 38 A.L.R. 294 (1925). Cf. Nicholson v. Nicholson, 199 N.J. Super. 525, 489 A.2d 1247 (1985), where the parties entered into a reconciliation agreement in which the wife agreed to resume cohabitation with the husband and to abandon her plan to divorce him on ground of adultery in exchange for husband's promise to convey his interest in

interest in land held in trust,[99] or an equitable lien by mortgage,[100] or restriction on land.[101]

Under the English Statute, leases (which are both contracts and conveyances) were excepted from the Statute if they did not exceed three years "from the making thereof." Today, most of the American statutes make an exception for short term leases for a term up to one year,[102] and the year is typically not measured from the time the contract is made.[103] It is equally well settled that the statute does not affect a contract merely because the performance of it relates to land or the use of land, so long as the transfer of what is known as a "property interest" or "right in rem," as distinguished from a "contract right" or "right in personam," is not involved. Consequently, a promise to construct a building on land,[104] or to do work on land,[105] or give another a mere license to go on land for some purpose[106] is not within the land provision of the statute. Moreover, if an actual conveyance as contrasted with a promise to convey has occurred, a promise to pay the agreed price in consideration of the actual conveyance of an estate or interest in land is not within the land contract provision of the statute.[107] A majority of courts hold that a contract creating a partnership is not within the statute though the transaction includes an understanding that the partnership shall own lands or deal in lands to be held in the name of one or less than all of the partners.[108]

---

the marital home. The court held that, since the agreement involved real estate, compliance with the statute of frauds was essential.

[98] *See* Hyman Freightways v. Carolina Freight Carriers Corp., 942 F.2d 500 (8th Cir. 1991) (assignment of lease). *See also* Esslinger v. Pascoe, 129 Iowa 86, 105 N.W. 362 (1905).

[99] Holmes v. Holmes, 86 N.C. 205 (1882).

[100] *See, e.g.*, Quintana v. First Nat'l Bank, 1995 U.S. App. LEXIS 22567 (10th Cir. Aug. 16, 1995); Phoenix Four Grantor Trust #1 v. 642 Broad St. Assocs., 2000 U.S. Dist. LEXIS 9149 (E.D. Pa. June 29, 2000); Lambert v. Home Fed. Sav. & Loan Ass'n, 481 S.W.2d 770 (Tenn. 1972). *See, however,* Martyn v. First Fed. Sav. & Loan Ass'n, 257 So. 2d 576 (Fla. Dist. Ct. App. 1971), *cert. denied*, 262 So. 2d 446 (Fla. 1972) (limiting land contract provision to transfers of *title* and holding a mortgage is not within the statute if state law treats it only as a lien). See Douglas Co. v. Gatts, 8 Ohio App. 3d 186, 456 N.E.2d 841 (1982), holding that an oral agreement to release or discharge a mortgage is within the land contract provision of the statute because a mortgage is an interest in land.

[101] Ham v. Massasoit Real Estate Co., 42 R.I. 293, 107 A. 205 (1919). *Contra* Thornton v. Schobe, 79 Colo. 25, 243 P. 617 (1925), *noted*, 24 MICH. L. REV. 854 (1926). No attempt has been made to catalog the myriad kinds of rights in relation to land that are classified as property interests.

[102] Hyman Freightways v. Carolina Freight Carriers Corp., 942 F.2d 500 (8th Cir. 1991) (assignment of lease of more than one year is within the statute of frauds).

[103] The short term lease is excepted from both the land contract and one year provisions of the statute of frauds. RESTATEMENT 2d § 125(4). As will be seen in the exploration of the one year clause in the next section, the measurement of one year begins with the making of the contract. A literal application of that clause of the statute to a one year lease would measure the year from the time the oral contract of lease was made. If the lease term is not to commence until some time after the making of the contract, the contract would be within the one year provision. The typical exception in American statutes for short term leases, however, does not measure the year from the time of contract formation. Thus, whether a short term lease contract is within the one year provision depends upon the duration of the lease itself, regardless of the time the lease contract was formed.

[104] Smith v. Hudson, 48 N.C. App. 347, 269 S.E.2d 172 (1980); Scales v. Wiley, 68 Vt. 39, 33 A. 771 (1895).

[105] Plunkett v. Meredith, 72 Ark. 3, 77 S.W. 600 (1903); Haight v. Conners, 149 Pa. 297, 24 A. 302 (1892).

[106] *See* Moon v. Central Builders, Inc., 65 N.C. App. 793, 310 S.E.2d 390 (1984) (promise to permit use of road during construction work); Burgess v. Swetnam, 257 Ky. 64, 77 S.W.2d 385 (1934) (promise to permit neighbor to use gas from well on property); Johnson v. Wilkinson, 139 Mass. 3, 29 N.E. 62 (1885) (promise to permit use of hall for entertainment purposes). *Accord* RESTATEMENT 2d § 127 comment b. *See also* RESTATEMENT OF PROPERTY § 514.

[107] Pettett v. Cooper, 62 Ohio App. 377, 24 N.E.2d 299 (1939).

[108] Potter v. Homestead Preservation Ass'n, 330 N.C. 569, 412 S.E.2d 1 (1992). *See also* Dobbs v. Vornado, Inc., 576

Similarly, an agreement to divide profits on the intended sale of real property is not within the statute.[109]

[C]   Purchases and Sales by Agents

A number of jurisdictions have added a provision to their statutes of frauds requiring a contract to pay a commission to a real estate broker to be evidenced by a writing.[110] In the absence of such a statutory provision, however, a contract defining the terms under which an agent undertakes merely to negotiate on behalf of his principal for the purchase or sale of land is not within the land contract provision of the statute.[111] If the agent agrees, however, to purchase the land in his own name and later to convey it to the principal, or if the agent, though he is to take title in the name of the principal, is to pay for the land out of his own pocket in the first instance so that he becomes the beneficiary of a resulting trust,[112] or if he contracts to cause the land to be conveyed to his principal,[113] the contract is within the statute.[114]

F. Supp. 1072, 1077 (E.D.N.Y. 1983) ("But suppose two persons, by parol agreement, enter into a partnership to speculate in lands, how do they come in conflict with the statute of frauds? No estate or interest in land has been granted, assigned or declared. When the agreement is made no lands are owned by the firm, and neither party attempts to convey or assign any to the other.") See, however, Barrett v. Poag & McEwen Lifestyle Ctrs. — Deer Park Town Ctr., LLC, 1999 U.S. Dist. LEXIS 13594 (N.D. Ill. Aug. 23, 1999), where the court agrees with the general rule that joint ventures and partnerships formed for the development of real estate are generally exempt from the statute of frauds, but a joint venture formed for the purpose of transferring land from one joint venturer to another is not exempt.

[109] Jacobs v. Thomas, 26 Conn. App. 305, 600 A.2d 1378 (1991); Bowart v. Bowart, 128 Ariz. 331, 625 P.2d 920 (Ct. App. 1980).

[110] See, Argent Real Estate Services, LLC v. Kaminski, 2007 Minn App. Unpub. LEXIS 1044 (2007) applying Minn. Stat. § 82.18, subd. 2). See also, Cal. Civ. Code § 1624(d), as discussed in Phillippe v. Shapell Indus., 43 Cal. 3d 1247, 241 Cal. Rptr. 22, 743 P.2d 1279 (1987), cert. denied, 486 U.S. 1011, 108 S. Ct. 1742, 100 L. Ed. 2d 205 (1988); N.J. Stat. Ann. § 25:1-9, as discussed in Joseph Hilton & Assocs. v. Evans, 201 N.J. Super. 156, 492 A.2d 1062 (1985); Ind. Code § 32-2-2-1, as discussed in Shrum v. Dalton, 442 N.E.2d 366 (Ind. Ct. App. 1982). See also Mont. Code Ann. § 37-51-401 and Wash. Rev. Code § 19.36.010(5).

[111] In Reich v. Kimnach, 216 Va. 109, 216 S.E.2d 58 (1975), the court held that the statute of frauds did not apply to an oral listing agreement between a seller and a broker because it was a contract for services, and not a contract for the sale of real estate. In 1976, however, Virginia added a brokerage provision to its statute of frauds, currently Va. Code Ann. § 11-2(7), which brought such contracts within the statute. See Murphy v. Nolte & Co., 226 Va. 76, 307 S.E.2d 242 (1983); Lindsay v. McEnearney Assocs., 260 Va. 48, 531 S.E.2d 573 (2000). Even without a provision dealing with brokerage commissions, however, where the consideration for the broker's services is, itself, an interest in real estate, the contract is within the statute. See Smith v. Gilbraltar Oil Co., 254 F.2d 518 (10th Cir. 1958).

[112] McDonald v. Conway, 254 Mass. 429, 150 N.E. 200 (1926); Houston v. Farley, 146 Ga. 822, 92 S.E. 635 (1917).

[113] Allen v. Richard, 83 Mo. 55 (1884).

[114] Where a conveyance of land is signed by one purporting to act as agent for another, the agent must be expressly authorized to so act and the authorizing principal must be identified as such in the conveyance or in the form of a signature of acknowledgment. Thus, where husbands signed a conveyance, but their joint-owner wives did not sign the document, a court will not recognize an implied agency between the spouses to convey their jointly owned property. Golf Resorts, Inc. v. Peshak, 1993 U.S. App. LEXIS 8438 (7th Cir. Apr. 13, 1993).

[D]   Minerals, Timber, and Growing Crops — Uniform Commercial Code

Prior to the UCC, courts were confronted with the proper characterization of minerals such as coal, timber, growing crops and other products attached to the land. Should such products of the land be characterized as "land," so as to bring a contract for their sale within the land contract provision of the statute of frauds, or should they be characterized as goods, placing contracts for their sale outside the land contract provision and within sale of goods provision? As will be seen, there are significant differences in the satisfaction of the land contract provision versus the provision dealing with contracts for the sale of goods.

There was little disconcertion about growing crops, i.e., annual crops such as wheat and corn grown with human assistance and known as *fructus industriales*. Growing crops were considered chattels, i.e., goods, even if the contract to sell such crops was formed prior to their severance. Thus, the land contract provision did not apply to such "goods" even prior to the UCC.[115] Contracts for the purchase and sale of minerals, coal, oil and the like, i.e., products which developed without human intervention, created considerable confusion among the courts as to whether they were within the land contract provision of the statute. Some courts adopted the rule that the proper characterization depended on how the parties to the contract dealt with the subject matter as land or chattels.[116] Other courts held that the proper characterization of the products depended upon whether the thing agreed to be sold was to be removed promptly, i.e., if it was to be left as part of the land for a considerable time, the contract was for an interest in land to which the land contract provision applied. If the products were to be severed promptly, however, the contract was one for the sale of chattels.[117] Still other courts adopted a more persuasive analysis. They suggested that if the buyer was to become the owner before the product was severed from the land, he would then acquire title while it was still land and the contract was one for the transfer of an interest in land. If, however, the buyer was not to become the owner of the timber, coal or other minerals until after it was severed from the land, he was agreeing to purchase goods. In that situation, the only right the buyer would receive in relation to the land would be a license to enter and to sever the product. We have already seen that a license is not regarded as an interest in land within the meaning of the statute.[118] Several courts adopted this analysis.[119]

Under the 1962 version of the UCC, the problem was resolved by adopting a similar analysis. As to standing timber, minerals, structures attached to the land or the like, the contract was for the sale of *goods* if the contract required or authorized the seller to sever them, i.e., the seller would be selling severed products (tangible and moveable products) which are "goods." If the understanding was that the buyer was to sever such products, however, the contract was characterized as one for the sale of an interest in land.[120] A contract for the sale

---

[115] *See* Shedaker v. James, 107 N.J.L. 400, 154 A. 394 (1931); Marshall v. Ferguson, 23 Cal. 65 (1863).

[116] *See, e.g.,* Home Owners' Loan Corp. v. Gotwals, 67 S.D. 579, 297 N.W. 36 (1941); Leonard v. Medford, 85 Md. 666, 37 A. 365 (1897); Long v. White, 42 Ohio St. 59 (1884).

[117] *See, e.g.,* Marshall v. Green, L.R. 1 C.P.D. 35 [1875].

[118] *See supra* note 103 and accompanying text.

[119] *See* Baird v. Elliott, 63 N.D. 738, 249 N.W. 894 (1933); Rosenstein v. Gottfried, 145 Minn. 243, 176 N.W. 844 (1920); Wetkopsky v. New Haven Gas Light Co., 88 Conn. 1, 90 A. 30 (1914).

[120] UCC § 2-107(1), 1962 Official Text: "A contract for the sale of timber, minerals or the like or a structure or its materials to be removed from realty is a contract for the sale of goods within this Article if they are to be severed by

of growing crops or other things attached to realty and capable of severance without material harm to the realty continued to be characterized as a contract for the sale of goods under the Code, regardless of which party was to sever them.[121]

The 1972 version of the UCC modified the earlier version by placing timber in the same classification as growing crops, i.e., a contract for the sale of timber would thereafter be regarded as a contract for the sale of goods regardless of which party is to sever the timber.[122] This change was designed to reflect the same change that had been effected earlier in several timber-growing states. The change was, therefore, in keeping with the basic UCC philosophy of reflecting commercial practices in accordance with the normal intention of parties engaged in making particular types of contracts.[123] With respect to the classification of minerals or the like, the 1972 version further clarified the earlier version by expressly including oil and gas as products that would be characterized as land if they were to be severed by the purchaser.[124]

§ 73   CONTRACT NOT PERFORMABLE WITHIN ONE YEAR FROM FORMATION

[A]   Origins — Narrow Application — Possibility of Performance — Measurement of One Year

The fifth section of the original Statute of Frauds required written evidence of "an agreement that is not to be performed within the space of one year from the making thereof." While critics of the statute of frauds find desirable targets in any of its provisions, the "one-year" provision is the most heavily criticized on the footing that it admits of no redeeming virtue since it defies rationality.[125] The origins of this provision remain mysterious.[126] If the

---

the seller but until severance a purported present sale thereof which is not effective as a transfer of an interest in land is effective only as a contract to sell."

[121] UCC § 2-107(2).

[122] UCC § 2-107(2) (1972 Official Text). In Fordham v. Eason, 351 N. C. 151, 157, 521 S.E.2d 701, 705 (1999), the court rejected the argument that a party with a contract right to timber required a deed to evidence the transaction since timber had been reclassified as "goods" and a much less formal writing will suffice to satisfy the statute of frauds in a contract for the sale of goods under the UCC. The contract provided the buyer with constructive possession of the timber, thereby satisfying a requirement for its action of trespass to chattels. Even under the new version treating timber as goods, however, the buyer may not acquire a property interest in the timber until "identification" occurs, UCC § 2-501. If a buyer agrees to purchase an entire stand of timber, identification would occur when the contract is formed. If, however, the intention of the parties is that the buyer will pay only for the timber cut and payment is due after severance, the parties may be said to have intended that the buyer would have a property interest only in cut timber. In one case, this distinction led to a devisee rather than residuary legatees taking the proceeds of a timber contract. See Fisher v. Elmore, 610 F. Supp. 123 (E.D.N.C. 1985).

[123] UCC § 1-102(2)(b).

[124] UCC § 2-107(1) (1972 Official Text).

[125] See C. R. Klewin, Inc. v. Flagship Properties, Inc. 220 Conn. 569, 575, 600 A.2d 772, 775 (1991) ("the one-year provision . . . has caused the greatest puzzlement among commentators"); Goldstick v. ICM Realty, 788 F.2d 456, 464 (7th Cir. 1986) ("Courts tend to take the concept of 'capable of full performance quite literally. . . . They do this because they find the one year limitation irksome."); Farmer v. Arabian American Oil Co., 277 F.2d 46, 51 (2d Cir.), cert. denied, 364 U.S. 824, 81 S. Ct. 60, 5 L. Ed. 2d 53 (1960) ("[W]e are not disposed to expand [the] destructive force [of the one-year provision]."). See Restatement 2d § 130, comment a. The one-year provision is not part of the Pennsylvania or North Carolina statutes of frauds. Article 8 of the UCC (investment securities) included a special statute of frauds in the 1978 version (§ 8-319) which was expressly excluded in § 8-113 the 1994 revision which also took it upon excludes the one-year provision for contracts within the scope of Article 8. Early drafts of the attempted

one-year provision was designed to avoid trusting the memory of witnesses for more than one year, it fails to achieve this essential purpose. The provision includes only those contracts whose terms are such that performance cannot be completed within a year *from the time they are made.* Thus, an oral contract of employment for one year will be within this provision of the statute if performance is to begin the day after it is made and breached immediately.[127] The one year duration commences on the date of formation, i.e., with the acceptance of the offer, and ends on midnight of the anniversary of the day on which the contract was formed.[128] The rationale concerning the memory of witnesses is further eroded by the fact that a typical contracts statute of limitations may allow an action to ensue up to six years after the cause of action accrues. Recognizing the infirmities in the provision, courts have accorded it the narrowest of constructions.[129]

[B]   "Possible" Performance — "Lifetime" and "Permanent"

Unless the contract cannot *possibly* be performed within one year from its making, it will be not be subject to the one year provision.[130] Thus, where the *express terms* of the contract preclude its performance within one year from its making, it is clearly within the one-year provision. On the other hand, where the contract states no duration, it will be construed as performable within one year though such a holding under the circumstances may tax credulity.[131] Thus, most courts view an agreement to work for, employ, or to support another for life is not within the one year provision of the statute.[132] Since the term of the contract is "life," it is completely performable within one year from the making.[133] A "lifetime" or "permanent" employment contract may be completely performed within one year from its

---

revision of Article 2 replicated this view, though subsequent drafts restored a statute of frauds with certain modifications. Revised and amended versions of Article 2, however, have not been enacted.

[126] See A. W. B. Simpson, A History of the Common Law of Contract 612 (1987), where the author refers to this provision as "curious." After suggesting the possibility that it was borrowed from seventeenth century Scotland where contracts of service of more than one year required proof by writ, the author recognizes Smith v. Westhall, I Ld. Raym. 316 [1697] where Lord Holt stated that the design of the statute was not to trust to the memory of witnesses for a longer time than one year.

[127] See Farmer v. Arabian American Oil, note 125 supra ("The limitation is apparently founded on a concern with the tendency of evidence to go stale with the passage of time, but the foundation is weak because the limitation applies even if the promise is broken the day after it is made and suit on it is brought immediately.") See also Kass v. Ronnie Jewelry, 118 R.I. 100, 371 A.2d 1060 (1977), where a one year employment contract was held to be within the statute since the employee would not begin performance until four days after contract formation.

[128] Fractions of a day are disregarded. See Restatement 2d § 130 comment c.

[129] Assuming the one year provision was designed to avoid trusting the memory of witnesses for longer than one year, the language was not effective to ascertain that purpose. The courts have, therefore, narrowed its application. See Restatement 2d § 130 comment a.

[130] Louros v. Cyr, 175 F. Supp. 2d 497, 512 (S. D. N. Y. 2001).

[131] C. R. Klewin, Inc. v. Flagship Proper ties, Inc., 600 A.2d 772 (Conn. 1991).

[132] See Hesston Corp. v. Roche, 599 So. 2d 148, 152 (Fla. Dist. Ct. App. 1992); Thurston v. Nutter, 125 Me. 411, 134 A. 506 (1926) (agreement to support for life); Pierson v. Kingman Milling Co., 91 Kan. 775, 139 P. 394 (1914) (agreement to employ for life). In City of New York v. Heller, 127 Misc. 2d 814, 487 N.Y.S.2d 288, 290 (Civ. Ct. 1985), the court held that an oral agreement for a tenancy measured by the life of the tenant was not within the one year provision since a "lifetime can be shorter than a year."

[133] Some states have added a "lifetime" provision to their statutes of frauds. Such a provision brings the lifetime contract within the statute. See N.Y. Gen. Oblig. Law § 5-701(1); Cal. Civ. Code § 1624(6).

making since the employee may die within that time.[134] Some Illinois cases, however, viewed the possibility of death within one year not as *performance* of the contract, but as excusable nonperformance.[135] While unpersuaded by this distinction, the Supreme Court of Illinois concluded that a "lifetime" employment contract is essentially a "permanent" employment contract that inherently anticipates a long-term duration extending beyond one year. As such, the court departed from the prevailing view by treating such a contract as within the one-year provision.[136]

Where the contract is one of indefinite duration, it has been held that the *possibility* of performance within one year from its making removes it from the one-year provision although the parties may have intended its operation to extend through a much longer period.[137] This is so even though actual performance has extended beyond the year,[138] and even though this likelihood was contemplated when the contract was formed. Thus, a leading case held that a contract to furnish a right-of-way "so long as the promisee needed it" was not within the one year provision because it was possible that the contract would be completed within one year, although, at the time the contract was formed, it was assumed that performance would continue for 20 or 30 years, and it had, in fact, continued for 13 years prior to the alleged breach.[139] In a $120 million contract for the construction of twenty industrial buildings, a 280 room hotel and housing for 592 graduate students and professors, the trial court concluded that there was no possibility of performance within one year. Beyond the scope of the project which implied a duration exceeding one year, the plaintiff admitted that the contemplated time for completion of the entire project was at least three and as many as ten years. The Supreme Court of Connecticut, however, reversed because the *express* terms of the contract did not require performance within one year.[140] Absent a stated time for performance, however, other courts will determine whether the contract is performable within a reasonable time and the

---

[134] *See* Bussard v. College of St. Thomas, Inc., 294 Minn. 215, 200 N.W.2d 155 (1972). In Wior v. Anchor Indus., Inc., 669 N.E.2d 172 (Ind. 1996), the court recognized that the contingency of death in a lifetime employment contract may serve as "performance" of the contract. In this case, however, the employer's offer stated that the employee could work until retirement age, thus assuring "20 plus" years with company. In this situation, the parties have bargained for a period of years greater than one. Like a two-year employment contract, death will not serve as performance if it occurs within a year.

[135] See, e. g., Sinclair v. Sullivan Chevrolet Co., 45 Il. App. 2d 10, 15, 195 N. E. 2d 250.252 (1964).

[136] McInerney v. Charter Golf, Inc., 176 Ill. 2d 482, 680 N.E.2d 1347 (1997).

[137] *See* Griffith v. One Inv. Plaza Assocs., 62 Md. App. 1, 488 A.2d 182, 184 (1985). In Jakovich v. Hill, Stonestreet & Co., (N. D. Ohio 2005), the plaintiff sold his accounting practice to the defendant in 2002 in exchange for compensation including payments from his former clients through 2008. "[L]iberally construing the principle of possible performance within one year or that there would be no work to be billed within one year," the court enforced the defendant's promise that was otherwise unenforceable because the agreement was unsigned.

[138] City of Clewiston v. B & B Cash Grocery Stores, Inc., 445 So. 2d 1038 (Fla. Dist. Ct. App. 1984). In Aldape v. State, 98 Idaho 912, 575 P.2d 891 (1978), a lease terminable at will was held not to be within the one year provision since it was possible that the contract would be performed within one year. In Nickerson v. President & Fellows of Harvard College, 298 Mass. 484, 11 N.E.2d 444, 114 A.L.R. 414 (1937), an agreement to work for one year, the employment to begin whenever the employer should elect, was held outside the statute since it was possible that the employment could begin on the date of formation. The fact that the employment contract is not performed within one year is irrelevant since it was *possible* that it would be performed within a year from the time of formation.

[139] Warner v. Texas & P. R. Co., 164 U.S. 418, 17 S. Ct. 147, 41 L. Ed. 495 (1896). *See also* Freedman v. Chemical Constr. Corp., 43 N.Y.2d 260, 401 N.Y.S.2d 176, 372 N.E.2d 12 (1977) (agreement to procure a contract and to construct a chemical plant in Saudi Arabia which required three years to procure the contract and six years to construct the plant; held: contract was still performable within one year from the making).

[140] *See C. R. Klewin*, note 125 *supra*.

factual determination will indicate whether the reasonable time exceeds one year from formation, thus bringing the contract within the one year provision.[141]

[C]   Alternative Performances — Excuse — Termination — Renewal

If the parties agree that performance will be completed upon the performance of either of two acts, only one of which is capable of being performed within a year from formation, the contract is not within the one year provision since the contract may be completely performed within a year if that alternative is chosen.[142] When applied to certain situations, however, this principle becomes murky. Where, for example, the contract contains a promise not to compete for a period exceeding one year, some courts have held that the promise is not within the one year provision because the implied alternative of death of the promisor within a year from formation would assure the completion of performance since competition after death is impossible.[143] Other courts view the possibility of the promisor's death within a year as excusable nonperformance or justifiable termination of the contract, i.e., death is not an alternative performance.[144]

Perhaps the best known case in which the question was raised is *Hopper v. Lennen & Mitchell, Inc.*,[145] where the plaintiff agreed to perform radio programs for the defendant for a total period of five years divided into twenty-six week segments. This unusually detailed verbal agreement specified an increase in the plaintiff's salary for each segment after the first twenty-six weeks and defendant's power to terminate the agreement by giving notice one month before the end of any segment. If the agreement was interpreted to permit alternative performances, one of which could be completed within twenty-six weeks from formation, the contract was not within the statute. If, however, the contract was construed to allow either *performance* requiring more than a year (five years) or *termination* by the defendant within a year, the contract would be within the statute of frauds because only *performance* could not be completed within a year, i.e., *termination* is not an alternative mode of *performance*. The *Hopper* court, relying in part on a New York case,[146] applied California law and held that the

---

[141] *See* Mercer v. C. A. Roberts Co., 570 F.2d 1232 (5th Cir. 1978); Apache Trailer Sales, Inc. v. Redman Indus., 117 Ariz. 504, 573 P.2d 904 (Ct. App. 1977).

[142] North Shore Bottling Co. v. C. Schmidt & Sons, Inc., 22 N.Y.2d 171, 292 N.Y.S.2d 86, 239 N.E.2d 189 (1968) (defendant orally agreed to make plaintiff the exclusive wholesale distributor of defendant's beer in Queens County as long as defendant sold beer in the New York metropolitan area. The court held that the distributorship could have continued (1) indefinitely, or (2) until defendant stopped selling beer in the New York metropolitan area. Since the second alternative permitted the possibility of performance within one year, the contract was not within the statute. In D & N Boening, Inc. v. Kirsch Beverages, Inc., 99 A.D.2d 522, 471 N.Y.S.2d 299 (2d Dep't 1984), the court recognized the distinction in *North Shore*, but distinguished it from the case before it, which provided that a distributorship would continue so long as plaintiff satisfactorily distributed the product. If the distributor had not performed satisfactorily during the first year of the contract, the unsatisfactory performance would not have constituted a contemplated alternative mode of performance. Rather, it would have been a breach of the agreement. If fulfillment of an alternative is not contemplated except in the case of a breach of the main promise, the contingency is not a true alternative but, rather, a breach of the agreement.

[143] The leading case is Doyle v. Dixon, 97 Mass. 208 (1867). *Accord* Decker v. West, 273 Ill. App. 532 (1934); Sauser v. Kearney, 147 Iowa 335, 126 N.W. 322 (1910); Erwin v. Hayden, 43 S.W. 610 (Tex. Civ. App. 1897). The RESTATEMENT 2d § 130 takes this position.

[144] *See, e.g.*, Collection & Investigation Bureau, Inc. v. Linsley, 37 Md. App. 66, 375 A.2d 47 (1977); Higgins v. Gager, 65 Ark. 604, 47 S.W. 848 (1898).

[145] 146 F.2d 364 (9th Cir. 1944).

[146] Blake v. Voight, 134 N.Y. 69, 31 N.E. 256 (1892). This case was the progenitor of what is now viewed as the "New

defendant's promise was outside the one year provision of the statute.[147] Other courts, however, would place the promise within the one year provision because the exercise of a power of termination is not *performance*.[148]

Where a party who fails to perform a contract requiring more than one year to perform is legally excused from completing performance, the promise is within the statute. If, for example, *A* orally promises to work for *B* for a period of five years, *A* may die within a year of formation. *A*'s death, however, is not an alternative performance; it is excusable nonperformance. To complete the *performance* of this promise would require a period of five years and that is impossible if *A* is dead. *A*'s promise, therefore, is within the one year provision.[149] Even if the contract expressly states that it will be terminated upon the death of the employee, the same result should follow.[150] On the other hand, where *A* orally promises to work for *B* for a period of five years if *A* lives that long, courts may be willing to view that promise as providing alternative performances, one of which is, in effect, a promise to work for life, not exceeding five years, which could be performed within a year.[151]

The different views on performance versus termination or excusable nonperformance were not confined to case law. The two giants of contract law, Professor Williston and Professor Corbin, disagreed.[152] The more traditional view was Williston's, i.e., a contract with a stated duration exceeding one year which provided one or both parties with a power of termination is within the one year provision because such a contract cannot be *performed* within one year. Professor Corbin championed the view that such a contract should fall within the rules of conditional promises and alternative performances, i.e., the party with the power and privilege to terminate has a choice between performing for the entire duration (beyond one year), or for less than one year. The duty to work for the entire period is expressly conditioned upon the absence of termination before that time. With the split in the case law and the differences between the giants of contract law, the stage was set for a resolution of the problem in the RESTATEMENT 2d.

A comment to the RESTATEMENT 2d suggests, "This distinction between performance and excuse for nonperformance is sometimes tenuous; it depends on the terms and the circumstances, particularly on whether the essential purposes of the parties will be

---

York" view that, "where the parties explicitly are given the option to terminate the agreement within one year, the Statute of Frauds will not apply." Finch, Pruyn & Co., Inc. v. Niagara Paper Co., 228 A.D.2d 834, 643 N.Y.S.2d 773, 775 (3d Dep't 1996) (citing *D & N Boening*, note 142 *supra*).

[147] The California position has extended this analysis by treating the alternative "performance" of "termination" to include a clause allowing termination for good cause. *See* Abeyta v. Jolene Co., Inc., 17 Cal. App. 4th 1037, 21 Cal Rptr. 2d 680, 686 (2d Dist. 1993) (relying on Foley v. Interactive Data Corp., 47 Cal. 3d 654, 765 P.2d 373 (1988)). New York, however, rejects this possibility. *See* Celi v. Canadian Occidental Petroleum Ltd., 804 F. Supp. 465 (E.D.N.Y. 1992).

[148] Deevy v. Porter, 11 N.J. 594, 95 A.2d 596 (1953); Blue Valley Creamery Co. v. Consolidated Prods. Co., 81 F.2d 182 (8th Cir. 1936); Hanau v. Ehrlich, 37 A.C. 39 [1911].

[149] *See e.g.*, Adams v. Greenbrier Olds/GMC/Volkswagen, (4th Cir. Jan. 28, 1999); Rath v. Selection Research, Inc., 246 Neb. 340, 345, 519 N. W. 2d 503, 507 (1994) (the court refers to death as "termination" which is not "performance.") Dickens v. Tennessee Elec. Power Co., 175 Tenn. 654, 137 S.W.2d 273 (1940).

[150] See Gilliam v. Kouchoucos, 161 Tex. 299, 340 S.W.2d 27 (1960), where the court held that an express termination upon death provision did not alter the analysis.

[151] *See* Silverman v. Bernot, 218 Va. 650, 239 S.E.2d 118 (1977).

[152] 3 WILLISTON §§ 498A, 498B; 2 CORBIN § 449.

attained."[153] A more recent case adheres to this standard. The defendant agreed to sponsor events conducted by the plaintiff for two seasons, but the agreement provided the defendant with an election that allowed it to terminate its sponsorship upon the conclusion of only one season. Notwithstanding the characterization of a two season agreement with an option to terminate, the court held that the purpose was not to provide the defendant with an option to terminate at will or upon the occurrence of an event. Rather, it provided the defendant with two alternative ways of satisfying its obligations as contemplated by the agreement. It contemplated an alternative performance of one season, capable of completion within less than one year. Where an agreement can be so interpreted, the court held that it is not within the statute of frauds.[154]

Another situation with a similar split of authority occurs where the parties form an oral contract that can be performed within a year from formation but which includes an option for renewal or extension.[155] Still another is found where the contract cannot be performed in the manner contemplated by the parties, but can be performed within a year in some other fashion, without violating the literal terms of the contract.[156]

[D]   Performance on One Side — Unilateral Contracts

An oral contract which is *executory* on both sides is within the one year provision unless *both* promises can be performed within a year from the making of the contract.[157] Yet, an overwhelming majority of the decided cases have held that the provision is not applicable if the contract is one that can be, and in fact has been, completely performed *on one side*, without regard to the time required for the other party's performance.[158] This concept, which

---

[153] RESTATEMENT 2d § 130 comment b. Illustrations 6 and 7 following this directive confirms the tenuous distinction. They each suggest an oral employment contract with a stated term of five years. Illustration 6 assumes the contract permits either party to terminate by giving 30 days notice at any time. This is said to be an agreement of uncertain duration that is not within the one-year provision. Illustration 7 permits one of the parties to quit at any time which is within the one-year provision.

[154] Professional Bull Riders, Inc. v. Autozone, Inc., 113 P. 3d 757 (Colo. 2005).

[155] *See* Hand v. Osgood, 107 Mich. 55, 64 N.W. 867 (1895) (within the statute), and Ward v. Hasbrouck, 169 N.Y. 407, 62 N.E. 434 (1902) (without the statute). See also Conger Life Ins. Co. v. Deimel, 441 So. 2d 1116 (Fla. Dist. Ct. App. 1983), holding an oral renewal of a one year oral contract of employment, performance of which was to commence on the day the renewal was entered into, is not within the one year provision of the statute. Professor Corbin suggests that, since the option may never be exercised, complete performance could occur within one year. 2 CORBIN ON CONTRACTS § 19.7.

[156] Cumberland & M. R. Co. v. Posey, 196 Ky. 379, 244 S.W. 770 (1922) (promise to pay a bonus upon completion of a railroad), and White v. Fitts, 102 Me. 240, 66 A. 533 (1906) (contract to log a tract of land as fast as timber was needed by the owner's mill), hold such contracts to be within the statute. *Contra* McClanahan v. Otto-Marmet Coal & Mining Co., 74 W. Va. 543, 82 S.E. 752 (1914) (agreement to cut and deliver all the mine props on a large tract of land).

[157] RESTATEMENT 2d § 130(2).

[158] *See* Urda v. Sahl, 2003 Conn. Super. LEXIS 1151 (2003); Tomson v. Stephan, 1988 U.S. Dist. LEXIS 3027 (D. Kan. Mar. 9, 1988); Lambousis v. Johnston, 657 P.2d 358 (Wyo. 1983); Glass v. Minnesota Protective Life Ins. Co., 314 N.W.2d 393 (Iowa 1982); Nesson v. Moes, 215 Cal. App. 2d 655, 30 Cal. Rptr. 428 (1963). A notable exception is New York which requires full performance on *both* sides to take a contract out of the one year provision. *See* Montgomery v. Futuristic Foods, Inc., 66 A.D.2d 64, 411 N.Y.S.2d 371 (2d Dep't 1978). *See also* Ordon v. Johnson, 346 Mich. 38, 77 N.W.2d 377 (1956); *In re* Hippe's Estate, 200 Wis. 373, 228 N.W. 522 (1930). Some jurisdictions adopting the majority view qualify it be requiring the full performance on one side to be completed within one year from the time of formation.

is a departure from the plain language of the statute,[159] first appeared in an early English case[160] which simply stated a conclusion that the statute should not apply in such a case. Presumably, the court considered the unfairness of permitting a defendant who had received full performance from the other party to rely on the statute as a defense.[161] If full performance on one side should satisfy the evidentiary function of the statute's one year provision, there would seem to be little reason for refusing to enforce the other (executory) promise. If, for example, an employee had fully performed his contract and the only remaining executory duty was the employer's payment of money, the statute of frauds should not bar enforcement of that duty.[162] Moreover, it should make no difference whether the executed promise was performed within a year, or whether its performance required more than a year.[163] The same rationale precludes the application of the one year provision to unilateral contracts. A unilateral contract is not formed until there is complete performance by the promisee; it is necessarily fully performed within one year of its "making" since it is fully performed on one side at the moment of its making.

[E]   Application of One Year Provision Where Other Provisions Apply

Unlike the other provisions of the statute of frauds that are limited to specific types of contracts, the one year provision cuts across the whole field of contracts, regardless of their subject matter or whether they are included within another clause of the statute. Thus, a contract to provide services not within another provision of the statute would still be subject to the one year provision. Absent statutory modification, a promise of suretyship, a promise in consideration of marriage, a promise to buy or sell land[164] or a promise within any other section of the statute must meet the requirements of those sections and, if it is also a promise not to be performed within one year from the making thereof, it is subject to the one year provision. Focusing on the satisfaction of another section of the statute may result in the failure to recognize the requirement of the one year provision. Thus, if an oral suretyship promise was taken out of the suretyship provision through the "main purpose" exception, but the same promise was not performable within a year of formation, the promise would remain unenforceable because it failed to meet the requirement for the one year provision though the suretyship provision had been satisfied. The same caveat applies to contracts in consideration of marriage or contracts for the sale of land or goods.[165]

---

[159] See 2 CORBIN ON CONTRACTS § 19.14. The Corbin treatise, however, supports the majority rule.

[160] Donnellan v. Read, 3 B & Ad. 899 [1832], followed in Cherry v. Heming, 4 Exch. 631 [1849].

[161] The court suggested, "[A]nd surely the law would not sanction a defense on that ground, when the buyer had the full benefit of the goods on his part."

[162] See Mapes v. Kalva Corp., 68 Ill. App. 3d 362, 386 N.E.2d 148 (2d Dist. 1979).

[163] This is the position of the RESTATEMENT 2d § 130 comment d.

[164] In most jurisdictions, statutes except from the one year provision leases of land for one year, though the lease term will not begin until a future date. The one year provision will also not prevent specific performance of a contract to transfer an interest in land if there has been sufficient reliance on the contract as suggested in RESTATEMENT 2d § 129.

[165] RESTATEMENT 2d § 110 comment b.

§ 74 CONTRACTS FOR THE SALE OF GOODS — UNIFORM COMMERCIAL CODE

[A]   History — "Price" Versus "Value" — "Future" Sales

Section 17 of the original Statute of Frauds required any contract for the sale of goods for the *price* of ten pounds sterling or more to be evidenced by a writing. Section 4 of the Uniform Sales Act, widely enacted in the United States, required any contract for the sale of goods with a *value* of $500 or more be evidenced by a writing. The current statute of frauds provision for sale-of-goods contracts is § 2-201 of the UCC,[166] which generally requires any contract for the sale of goods with a *price* of $500 or more to be evidenced by a writing.[167] The return to a *price* minimum in the Code rather than a *value* minimum is desirable to avoid inevitable controversies over the proper value of goods. If, however, the parties agree to exchange goods for other goods, it is necessary to ascertain the value of the exchange to determine whether the $500 threshold has been met.[168] The modest return to price instead of value is only one of many changes in the statute of frauds effected by the UCC. As will be seen, the other changes are much more significant. They must be explored in terms of their purposes as well as their current interpretation.

An issue under the original statute was whether the sale of goods section should include a contract to transfer ownership of goods in the future as well as a contract to effect a present

---

[166] The only U.S. jurisdiction that has not enacted Article 2 of the UCC is Louisiana which has enacted other UCC Articles.

[167] UCC § 2-201 provides:

(1) Except as otherwise provided in this section a contract for the sale of goods for the price of $500 or more is not enforceable by way of action or defense unless there is some writing sufficient to indicate that a contract for sale has been made between the parties and signed by the party against whom enforcement is sought or by his authorized agent or broker. A writing is not insufficient because it omits or incorrectly states a term agreed upon but the contract is not enforceable under this paragraph beyond the quantity of goods shown in such writing.

(2) Between merchants if within a reasonable time a writing in confirmation of the contract and sufficient against the sender is received and the party receiving it has reason to know its contents, it satisfies the requirements of subsection (1) against such party unless written notice of objection to its contents is given within ten days after it is received.

(3) A contract which does not satisfy the requirements of subsection (1) but which is valid in other respects is enforceable:

(a) if the goods are to be specially manufactured for the buyer and are not suitable for sale to others in the ordinary course of the seller's business and the seller, before notice of repudiation is received and under circumstances which reasonably indicate that the goods are for the buyer has made either a substantial beginning of their manufacture or commitments for their procurement; or

(b) if the party against whom enforcement is sought admits in his pleading, testimony or otherwise in court that a contract for sale was made, but the contract is not enforceable under this provision beyond the quantity of goods admitted; or

(c) with respect to goods for which payment has been made and accepted or which have been received and accepted (Sec. 2-606)."

[168] Section 2-304(1) of the UCC permits the "price" to be payable either in money "or otherwise." When the price is payable in goods, each party is a "seller" with respect to the goods he is to transfer. Thus, when a purchaser of a new car pays for the car in part with a trade of his old car, he is a "seller" of the old car. *See* Martin v. Melland's, Inc., 283 N.W.2d 76 (N.D. 1979) (purchase of truck and haystack mover for a total price of $35,389, with purchaser being allowed $17,389 on his old unit as a trade-in allowance; buyer was a "seller" of his old unit and, therefore, the risk of loss had not passed to the "buyer"(dealer) of the old unit when it was destroyed while still in the possession of the original owner).

transfer of ownership. Prior to the UCC, it had become well settled that both kinds of transactions were covered[169] and the UCC now expressly provides for "both a present sale of goods and a contract to sell goods at a future time."[170]

[B]   Modifications Effected by the Uniform Commercial Code

Modifications of the Statute of Frauds provision for the sale of goods effected by the UCC are substantial. In summary, they include permitting a memorandum signed by a merchant to be effective against another merchant who signed nothing if the recipient does not object within ten days of its receipt,[171] enforcing oral contracts for specially manufactured goods unsuitable for sale to others in the ordinary course of the seller's business if their manufacture has begun or commitments for their procurement have been made,[172] permitting enforcement of an oral contract to the extent that it is admitted by the party to be charged in his or her pleadings, testimony or other evidence in court,[173] and permitting enforcement of an oral contract for the sale of goods to the extent of receipt and acceptance of the goods or receipt and acceptance of payment for the goods.[174] Each of these modifications of pre-Code law will be explored in appropriate sections throughout this chapter.

[C]   Goods — Alternate UCC Statutes of Frauds — Mixed Transactions — Specially Manufactured Goods — Leases — Computer Transactions

"Goods" are defined in the UCC as "all things (including specially manufactured goods) which are moveable at the time of identification to the contract for sale other than money in which the price is to be paid, investment securities (Article 8) and things in action." The UCC contains other statutes of frauds where the property involved does not meet this definition of "goods." We have already explored some of the issues generated by the proper characterization of a contract for the sale of land versus a contract for the sale of goods and the UCC solution to those problems.[175] Where, however, the contract requires a transfer of both real estate and goods in exchange for money and there is no sound basis for allocating the consideration between the real and personal property, the land contract provision of the statute of frauds will apply.[176] If the monetary consideration can be allocated between the real estate and the goods intended to be transferred, the "goods" portion of the transaction can be made subject to the provisions of the Code.[177] If the real estate portion of the transaction is

---

[169] *See, e.g.*, Russell v. Bettes, 107 Ark. 629, 156 S.W. 457 (1913).

[170] UCC § 2-106(1). See also UCC § 2-102, where Article 2 of the Code is said to apply to "transactions in goods" whether it is a "contract to sell or present sale."

[171] UCC § 2-201(2).

[172] UCC § 2-201(3)(a).

[173] UCC § 2-201(3)(b).

[174] UCC § 2-201(3)(c).

[175] *See supra* § 72[D]. Where the parties agree that part of the "price" will be paid by transferring an interest in land in exchange for goods, the transfer of the goods and the seller's obligations concerning the goods are governed by Article 2 of the UCC, but the Code does not apply to the transfer of the interest in realty or the transferor's obligations in connection with that transfer. UCC 2-304(2).

[176] *See* Beaulieu of Am., Inc. v. Coronet Indus., Inc., 173 Ga. App. 556, 327 S.E.2d 508 (1985).

[177] *See* Foster v. Colorado Radio Corp., 381 F.2d 222 (10th Cir. 1967).

relatively minor in relation to the goods component, the contract may be viewed as dominantly one for the sale of goods and the UCC may apply exclusively.[178]

It is not uncommon for the subject matter of the contract to be a hybrid mixture of services and goods.[179] Prior to the Code, a contract to furnish labor and materials in the erection of a building or other fixture on land, or to repair an automobile, in the absence of a manifested intention to transfer ownership of the materials prior to annexation, was typically held to be outside the statute, although the value of the material to be furnished exceeded the statutory minimum amount. [180]

Courts facing similar problems under the Code have settled upon the analysis already suggested with respect to contracts involving land and goods, i.e., if the predominant or primary purpose of the contract is the sale of goods, the contract will be subject to § 2–201 of the Code.[181]

[1]   Specially Manufactured Goods

An oral contract for the purchase and sale of specially manufactured goods not suitable for sale to other buyers in the ordinary course of the seller's business is not subject to the goods provision of the statute of frauds.[182] The traditional justification for this "exception"[183] is "the assurance that, by virtue of the unique nature of the goods, the manufacturer would not have produced such unique goods absent an agreement with the alleged buyer."[184] The more modern justification also recognizes that the buyer's breach of such a contract will cause more serious injury to the manufacturer because it will be unable to resell goods suitable for sale only to the breaching buyer.[185] Like its predecessor, the Uniform Sales Act, the UCC recognizes the production of special goods as performing an evidentiary function in lieu of a writing

---

[178] *See* Dehahn v. Innes, 356 A.2d 711 (Me. 1976).

[179] Newmark v. Gimbel's, Inc., 54 N.J. 585, 258 A.2d 697 (1969).

[180] *See, e.g.*, Frederick Raff Co. v. Murphy, 110 Conn. 234 147 A. 709 (1929) (contract to supply and install plumbing fixtures); Underfeed Stoker Co. v. Detroit Salt Co., 135 Mich. 431, 97 N.W. 959 (1904) (contract to furnish and install stoker); Scales v. Wiley, 68 Vt. 39, 33 A. 771 (1895) (contract to furnish labor and materials in erecting a building on land)..

[181] *See, e.g.*, Princess Cruises v. General Electric co., 143 F. 3d 828 (4th Cir. 1998). *See also* Colorado Carpet Installation, Inc. v. Palermo, 668 P.2d 1384, 45 A.L.R.4th 1113 (Colo. 1983) (suggesting that factors to be considered are whether the contract included an overall price for goods and labor as contrasted with separate billings for each, the ratio of the cost of goods to the total contract price, and whether a reasonable buyer would be particularly interested in acquiring a property interest in the goods). It should be noted that numerous consequences beyond the application of the UCC statute of frauds provision (§ 2-201) attend a determination of whether the contract is one for goods, services, or land. Thus, whether the warranty protection of the UCC is available will depend upon whether the contract is one for goods or one for services. A well-known case confronting this issue is *Newmark v. Gimbel's, Inc.* where the New Jersey Supreme Court held the UCC applicable where the plaintiff received a permanent wave and suffered severe hair loss and scalp problems allegedly due to a product used by the provider of the wave, even though the price for the product was not separated from the total price of the wave. The court described the transaction as a hybrid involving incidents of sale and service, but applied the UCC on the basis that there is no sound reason for restricting implied warranties such as found in of the UCC to "conventional sales of goods."

[182] UCC § 2-201(3)(c).

[183] It has become common to view the specially manufactured goods section of the UCC statute of frauds, § 2-201(3)(a), as one of several "exceptions" to the normal requirements of a writing to evidence a contract for the sale of goods.

[184] Webcor Packaging Corp. v. Autozone, Inc., 158 F.3d 354, 356 (6th Cir. 1998).

[185] *Id.* (quoting William D. Hawkland, Uniform Commercial Code Series § 2-201:03 (1984)).

requirement.[186] Under the predecessor to the UCC, the Uniform Sales Act,[187] the exception applied only where the seller was the manufacturer of the specially manufactured goods. Under the UCC, however, there is no requirement that the seller, itself, must be the manufacturer of the goods. The language of the Code permits the exception to apply where the seller "has made . . . commitments for their procurement" from another manufacturer.

In their construction of this UCC provision, courts have insisted on certain requirements: (1) the goods must be specially manufactured for the buyer; (2) the goods must not be suitable for sale to others in the ordinary course of business; (3) the seller must have either made a substantial beginning of the manufacture of the goods or commitments for their procurement; (4) the seller's manufacturing or commitments must reasonably indicate that the goods are for the buyer; (5) the seller's manufacturing or commitments must occur before the seller received notice of repudiation from the buyer.[188] Each of these requirements requires further elaboration.

It has been suggested that the first and second requirements appear redundant. If the goods must be specially manufactured for the buyer, they are necessarily not suitable for sale to other buyers.[189] The circumstances surrounding the transaction must be such as to reasonably indicate that the goods are for the buyer.[190] Where, however, there are multiple buyers, a court has held that the exception does not apply.[191]

The second element is the central focus. The goods must not be suitable for sale to others in the seller's ordinary course of business. If the manufacturer can, with only "slight alterations" as contrasted with "essential changes," resell the goods to another buyer, they do not meet the "specially manufactured" requirement.[192] Simply because the seller normally

---

[186] UCC § 2-201(3)(c). Impossible Electronics Techniques, Inc. v. Wackenhut Protective Sys., Inc., 669 F.2d 1026 (5th Cir. 1982), elaborates this position. Where a seller has commenced or completed manufacture of goods conforming to the special needs of a particular buyer, thereby rendering the goods unsuitable for sale to others, the nature of the goods provides an alternative evidentiary function. The likelihood of a perjured claim of a contract is diminished and denying enforcement of such a contract would impose a substantial hardship on the seller.

[187] Uniform Sales Act § 4.

[188] Contours, Inc. v. Lee, 10 Haw. App. 368, 375–76, 874 P. 2d 1100, 1104–05 (1994).

[189] In *Webcor, supra* note 184, at 357, the court suggests this "tautological construction."

[190] An obvious application of this requirement is found in Flowers Baking Co. of Lynchburg v. R-P Packaging, Inc., 229 Va. 370, 329 S.E.2d 462 (1985), where cellophane wrapping material was manufactured to the size required by the buyer's containers and was imprinted with the buyer's name and unique artwork.

[191] *Id.* The defendant sold prepackaged automotive parts purchased from multiple vendors under defendant's brand name. The defendant recommended plaintiff as the supplier of the packaging carrying defendant's brand name though the vendors were free to purchase packaging elsewhere. To assure the supply of packaging, plaintiff extended its inventory and alleged that defendant orally promised to indemnify plaintiff should the packaging containing the defendant's brand become obsolete. When defendant chose to discontinue the brand name, plaintiff's inventory of packaging with the defendant's brand name was obviously unsuitable for sale to others. In plaintiff's action, the defendant raised the statute of frauds and plaintiff claimed a "specially manufactured" goods exception. The trial court held that the exception applied only where the goods were specially manufactured for a single buyer, rejecting plaintiff's argument that the defendant was the "ultimate" purchaser. Though critical of the "single buyer" interpretation that may ignore modern transactions involving multiple buyers, the appellate court concluded that the transaction was too attenuated to apply the specially manufactured goods exception.

[192] AGA Shareholders, LLC v. CSK Auto, Inc. 589 F. Supp. 2d 1175, 1186 (D. Ariz. 2008). Impossible Electronics Techniques, Inc. v. Wackenhut Protective Sys., Inc., 669 F.2d 1026, 1037 (5th Cir. 1982). Breaking the product into component parts for resale would constitute "essential changes." R.M. Schultz & Assocs. v. NYNEX Computer Servs. Co., 1994 U.S. Dist. LEXIS 4509, at *15 (N.D. Ill. Apr. 8, 1994).

manufactures custom-made goods for sale in the ordinary course of its business does not preclude such goods from being characterized as "specially manufactured goods." Again, the critical inquiry is whether the goods can be sold to others in the ordinary course of business.

The third and fourth elements require the seller either to have made a substantial beginning of the manufacture of the special goods or commitments for their procurement indicating that the goods are for the buyer.[193] The "substantial beginning of manufacture element has been narrowly construed.[194] While the jury decides fact questions, whether undisputed facts satisfy the specially manufactured goods section of the statute of frauds is a question of law decided by the court.[195]

The fifth element requiring substantial part performance by a seller prior to receiving notice of repudiation from the buyer is not always listed as a requirement since the seller would not be justified in commencing *any* performance after receiving such notification. What otherwise appears as a truism, however, suggests the essential rationale for the entire "specially manufactured goods" exception, i.e., the *reliance* of a seller which is remediable only by enforcing the oral contract with the buyer since there is no possibility of reselling the goods to others. This is the only express indication of a reliance satisfaction device in all of UCC Section 2-201 and it is a very narrow exception indeed, relating only to "specially manufactured goods." Relegating reliance as an alternate satisfaction device to these narrow confines is relevant to whether courts are justified in judicially engrafting a general reliance alternate satisfaction device on the express terms of Section 2-201 as we will see later in this chapter.[196]

[2]   Leases of Goods and the Statute of Frauds

While both sales and leases of goods involve a transfer of rights in personal property, a lease is not a sale. A lease of goods merely allows a party other than the owner to possess and use the goods for a certain time. A considerable body of case law addressed the question of the applicability of Article 2 of the Uniform Commercial Code to leases of goods. A number of courts applied Article 2 to lease transactions on the basis of any one of three rationales if not all three: (1) Article 2 applies to "transactions in goods" which is sufficiently broad to include lease transactions; (2) Article 2 applies where the lease transaction is the functional equivalent of a sale of goods; (3) Article 2 applies by analogy to lease transactions.[197] Other justifications included reliance on the UCC direction to liberally construe its underlying purposes and policies which include facilitating the continued expansion of commercial practices and making

---

[193] *See, e.g.*, Frank Adams & Co. v. Baker, 1 Ohio App. 3d 137, 439 N.E.2d 953 (Hamilton County 1981); LTV Aerospace Corp. v. Bateman, 492 S.W.2d 703 (Tex. Civ. App. Tyler 1973). As to what constitutes a "substantial beginning of performance," *see* Perlmuter Printing Co. v. Strome, Inc., 436 F. Supp. 409 (N.D. Ohio 1976) (contract for advertising flyers where 62 percent of the 17,000,000 flyers ordered were printed which was considerably more than a "substantial beginning"); Epprecht v. IBM Corp., 36 U.C.C. Rep. Serv. (CBC) 391 (E.D. Pa. 1983) (production of 7000 parts fell within the "specially manufactured" goods exception, but there was no evidence to suggest that this production was a "substantial beginning" of an alleged remaining 43,000 parts).

[194] Chambers Steel Engraving Corp. v. Tambrands, Inc., 895 F. 2d 858 (1st Cir. 1990) (the creation of a prototype was not viewed as a "substantial beginning of manufacture").

[195] *Id.* at 860.

[196] *See* § 79[C], *infra.*

[197] *See* Matka Corp. v. Tolland County Times, 1993 Conn. Super. LEXIS 671, at *3 (Conn. Super. Ct. Mar. 22, 1993). See also Glenn Dick Equip. Co. v. Galey Constr., 97 Idaho 216, 220, 541 P.2d 1184, 1188 (1975), and cases cited therein.

commercial law uniform among the various jurisdictions.[198] An invitation to apply certain sections of the Code analogously could also urge its application.[199] Notwithstanding such arguments, courts were not easily convinced to apply Article 2 provisions to leases.[200] Even where courts were willing to apply some provisions of Article 2 under one or more of the rationales, they balked at applying all Article 2 provisions. Thus, courts have refused to apply the Article 2 statute of frauds to lease transactions because the Article 2 section expressly limits its application to contracts "for the sale of goods."[201]

Article 2A governing leases was added to the Uniform Commercial Code in 1987 and amended three years later. It has been enacted in all jurisdictions except Louisiana. Article 2A contains a statute of frauds provision modeled on the Article 2 section,[202] but there are significant differences in the 2A version. The threshold amount required to activate the 2A statute of frauds is $1000 rather than $500 in Article 2.[203] Later we will explore a modification of the statute in Article 2 allowing a memorandum signed by one merchant to bind the other merchant unless the second merchant objects within ten days of receipt.[204] This provision is excluded in the 2A version because the number of such transactions in leases as contrasted with sales of goods was deemed to be modest.[205] Another provision in the Article 2 statute of frauds allows an oral contract to be enforced to the extent payment has been made and accepted by the seller.[206] Since lessees do not tender payment in full for the goods but make partial payments for one or more months, part payment was deemed an insufficient substitute for the required memorandum to satisfy the lease statute of frauds.[207] The Article 2A version does, however, replicates the Article 2 exceptions for partial receipt and acceptance of goods, "specially manufactured goods" and for admissions by the party sought to be charged that a lease contract was made.[208]

---

[198] UCC § 1-102. All-States Leasing Co. v. Bass, 96 Idaho 873, 878, 538 P.2d 1177, 1182 (1975).

[199] *Id.*, quoting Comment 2 to UCC § 2-313, recognizing case law growth in the application of warranties beyond the technical confines of the statutory language.

[200] See, e. g., Sellers v. Frank Griffin AMC Jeep, Inc., 526 So. 2d 147 (Fla. Dist. Cy. App. 1988), where the court considered ten criteria in deciding not to extend Article 2 to the lease transaction before the court. In Cucchi v. Rollins Protective Servs. Co., 524 Pa. 514, 574 A.2d 565 (1990), the Supreme Court of Pennsylvania handed down a split decision concerning the application of Article 2 to leases. In American Warehouse & Moving Serv., Inc. v. Floyd's Diesel Serv., Inc., 164 Ga. App. 106, 296 S.E.2d 64 (1982), the court recognized the application of Article 2 in warranty cases in other jurisdictions but concluded that the express language of the UCC referring to sales contracts requires a different conclusion.

[201] Walter E. Heller & Co. v. Convalescent Home of First Church of Deliverance, 49 Ill. App. 3d 213, 365 N.E.2d 1285 (1st Dist. 1977). *See also* George F. Mueller & Sons, Inc. v. Northern Illinois Gas Co., 12 Ill. App. 3d 362, 299 N.E.2d 601 (1st Dist. 1973).

[202] UCC § 2A-201, modeled on § 2-201.

[203] UCC § 2A-201(1)(a). The amount represents "total payments to be made under the lease contract excluding payments for options to renew or buy.

[204] UCC § 2-201(2) explored in § 75[D], *infra.*

[205] UCC § 2A-201, Comment ("Purposes").

[206] UCC § 2-201(3)(c).

[207] UCC § 2A-201, Comment ("Purposes").

[208] UCC § 2A-201(4)(a) & (b). The "admissions" exception in Article 2 is discussed at § 76[A], *infra.*

[3]   Computer Transactions and the Statute of Frauds — UCITA

The application of the sale-of-goods statute of frauds under the UCC to software transactions depends upon the characterization of the transaction as explored in some detail earlier.[209]

As that exploration revealed, software transactions are generally viewed as transactions in goods to which the UCC applies. Thus, such transactions must satisfy the requirements of 2-201 of the UCC. As also noted in that exploration, only Maryland and Virginia adopted the controversial Uniform Computer Information Transactions Act (UCITA). Under UCITA, a license contract requiring payment of $5000 or more (as contrasted with the mere possibility of reaching that amount in other ways such as through royalties or options) with a duration of one year or more must be evidenced by a sufficient "record."[210] No particular formalities are required under UCITA. If the record indicates that a contract was formed and reasonably identifies the copy of the information, it will be sufficient though it omits or incorrectly states a term. The contract, however, is not enforceable beyond the number of copies or subject matter shown in the record. Exceptions to the record requirement include full performance of the contract, an admission in court that the contract was made, or a confirming record not objected to within ten days of its receipt. The parties may also agree in an authenticated record to conduct future business without additional authenticated records.

§ 75   SATISFACTION OF THE STATUTE — SUFFICIENT MEMORANDUM OR "RECORD"

A signed writing is the specified, traditional mode for satisfying the requirements of the statute of frauds with respect to any type of contract within its provisions. The essential questions concerning the writing (memorandum) deal with its *form*, its *content*, the requirement that it be *signed*, and questions concerning the *time of its making* and the effect of *destruction* of a satisfactory memorandum. Recent statutes that recognize electronic records as sufficient to satisfy the "writing" requirement add additional dimensions. These questions will now be explored.

[A]   Form of Memorandum or Record

The typical American statute of frauds does not require the writing evidencing the contract to be intended by the parties as their complete or final statement of the contract. A *memorandum* of the contract will be sufficient.[211] It is important to emphasize the requirement that the writing evidence a *contract* rather than a mere offer or preliminary

---

[209] § 15, *supra.*

[210] See the discussion of electronic contracts, *supra* § 14, where the broader term "record" is used rather than "writing" to accommodate electronic records. The Uniform Electronic Transactions Act (UETA) defines "record" in § 2(13) as "information that is inscribed on a tangible medium or that is stored in an electronic or other medium and is retrievable in perceivable form." The identical definition is found in the federal Electronic Signatures in Global and National Commerce Act ("E-Sign") in § 106(9) — also discussed in § 14, *supra.* Further discussion of electronic records to satisfy the statute of frauds is found in § 75[A], *infra.*

[211] RESTATEMENT 2d § 131. If, however, a particular statute of frauds requires the "contract" to be in writing, a mere memorandum may not be sufficient. *See* comment a.

negotiation.[212] It is clear that a writing evidencing a contract will satisfy the statute even though it was not dealt with by the parties as the final embodiment of the terms of their agreement.[213]

No particular form of writing or record is required. A record of the contract in emails will suffice.[214] Where a buyer issued a check payable to the seller containing a statement that it was a deposit on identified real property, the seller endorsed the check and cashed it. The court held the check to be a sufficient memorandum of the contract.[215] A writing satisfying the statute of frauds may appear in an invoice,[216] in corporate minutes,[217] in a pencilled note on a scratch pad,[218] a diary entry,[219] a petition filed in a court proceeding relating to some other transaction,[220] a contract with another party,[221] or even a will.[222] Under recent statutes facilitating electronic contracting, even voice mail may be sufficient.[223] It is of utmost importance, however, to recognize the distinction between the satisfaction of the statute of frauds and the burden on the plaintiff to establish that a contract has been made. A memorandum that would be sufficient to satisfy the statute does not, in itself, establish that a contract was made.[224]

---

[212] *See* Central Illinois Light Co. v. Consolidation Coal Co., 349 F. 3d 488, 490 (7th Cir. 2003); Easy Way, Inc. v. Transp. Int'l Pool, Inc., 67 Fed. Appx. 863, 867 (6th Cir. 2003); E. I. DuPont de Nemours & Co., 42 Fed. Appx. 605, 607 (4th Cir. 2002).

[213] As will be seen in the next chapter, if the parties intend their writing to be the final embodiment of their contract, evidence of prior understandings will not be admissible under the "parol evidence rule." The curiosity is that, where the parties evidence their contract by a mere memorandum which is not intended to be final and/or complete (fully or partially "integrated"), extrinsic evidence of their oral agreement is admissible. If the admissible evidence contradicts a term of the writing, the writing may be destroyed as evidence of the contract sufficient to satisfy the statute of frauds. A recognition of the distinction between the parol evidence rule and the statute of frauds is found in Wemhoff v. Investors Mgmt. Corp. of Am., 528 A.2d 1205 (D.C. 1987), *cert. denied*, 491 U.S. 906, 109 S. Ct. 3189, 105 L. Ed. 2d 698 (1989), where, after suggesting the different purposes of the parol evidence rule and the statute of frauds, the court concludes that the statute of frauds does not require an exhaustive, integrated statement of the agreement, but only a sufficient writing to establish that there was an agreement to which the party to be charged should be bound.

[214] See Crestwood Shops, L.L.C. v. Hilkene, 197 S. W. 3d 641, 651 (Mo. App. 2006). See also Adani Exports, Ltd. v. Amci Exp. Corp., 2007 U. S. Dist. LEXIS 88969 at *32 (W. D. Pa. 2007) referring to various jurisdictions recognizing emails as sufficient records to satisfy the statute of frauds. See subsection [1], *infra*.

[215] *See* A. B. C. Auto Parts, Inc. v. Moran, 359 Mass. 327, 268 N.E.2d 844 (1971).

[216] Bicknell v. Joyce Sportswear Co., 173 Ga. App. 897, 328 S.E.2d 564 (1985).

[217] *See, e.g.*, Prodromos v. Howard Sav. Bank, 295 Ill. App. 3d 470, 692 N.E.2d 707 (1st Dist. 1998) (requiring all of the terms of the contract and approval of the minutes by the board of directors).

[218] UCC § 2-201 comment 1.

[219] *See* RESTATEMENT 2d § 133 comment b.

[220] McCall v. Lee, 182 N.C. 114, 108 S.E. 390 (1921).

[221] *See* Morris Cohon & Co. v. Russell, 23 N.Y.2d 569, 245 N.E.2d 712 (1969).

[222] See Newman v. Huff, 632 N.E.2d 799, 804 (Ind. Ct. App. 1994).

[223] See The Uniform Electronic Transactions Act (UETA) suggests that a voice mail may suffice as a "signature." UETA § 2, comment 7.

[224] *See* Lorenz Supply Co. v. American Std., Inc., 419 Mich. 610, 358 N.W.2d 845 (1984); C. Itoh & Co. v. Jordan Int'l Co., 552 F.2d 1228 (7th Cir. 1977), chiding certain courts for their fundamental misconception of the purpose and effect of the statute of frauds, relying upon comment 3 to § 2-201 of the UCC: "The only effect is to take away . . . the defense of the statute of frauds; the burden of persuading the trier of fact that a contract was in fact made orally prior to the [writing] is unaffected." *See also* Spinnerin Yarn Co. v. Apparel Retail Corp., 614 F. Supp. 1174 (S.D.N.Y. 1985).

The fact that the writing was made for some other purpose, or that it also contains extraneous matter not related to the contract, is not material.[225] A memorandum intended as a repudiation of an oral contract will be a sufficient writing to satisfy the statute of frauds, provided it contains the necessary terms.[226] The requirement may be satisfied by a writing even though it is undelivered and never intended to be delivered to the other contracting party.[227] The writing may be in the form of a letter though it is addressed to a third person.[228]

[1] Electronic Records — "E-Sign" and UETA

Even prior to the enactment of uniform statutes stating that a contract, record or signature will not be denied effect simply because it is in electronic form,[229] a few courts recognized the use of electronic media to satisfy the statute of frauds. Though recognizing that the Electronic Signatures in Global and National Commerce Act was not designed to be retroactive, the Seventh Circuit Court of Appeals concluded that, without relying on the statute, a sender's name on an email satisfied the signature requirement of the statute of frauds.[230] In light of the sudden and pervasive development of electronic commerce, it would have been possible for courts to accept an expansive definition of "writing" or "memorandum" by including electronic forms. In relation to contracts for the sale of goods, such an expansion would effectuate the express UCC directive of liberally construing the underlying purpose of permitting the continued expansion of commercial practices.[231] Even assuming courts would have eventually recognized the necessity of such an expansion, a case-by-case development of this reaction to a felt need of society would have required years to develop. Such a cumbersome effort would

---

[225] See Bicknell v. Joyce Sportswear Co., 173 Ga. App. 897, 328 S.E.2d 564 (1985), where invoices were held to be sufficient writings between merchant parties. See also Azevedo v. Minister, 86 Nev. 576, 471 P.2d 661 (1970), where periodic accountings were held sufficient confirmations of the oral agreement between the merchant parties. See RESTATEMENT 2d § 133. An exception is made, however, with respect to contracts in consideration of marriage since the marriage provision performs a cautionary as well as an evidentiary function. See RESTATEMENT 2d § 124 comment d and RESTATEMENT 2d § 133 comment a.

[226] RESTATEMENT 2d § 133 comment c. In Atlas Road Constr. Co. v. Commercial Stone Co., 33 Pa. D. & C.3d 477, 41 U.C.C. Rep. Serv. (CBC) 1186 (1984), the court held that a letter sent by plaintiff's attorney containing the terms of an oral agreement alleging a breach thereof constituted a sufficient memorandum to satisfy the statute of frauds.

[227] See, e.g., Smith v. McClam, 289 S.C. 452, 346 S.E.2d 720 (1986), where the court found a memorandum to be sufficient even though it was not delivered to the other contracting party, nor intended for, nor known to him, if it otherwise evidences the contract of the parties and its contents are disclosed for that purpose. See UCC § 2-201 comment 6: "It is not necessary that the writing be delivered to anybody."

[228] See, e.g., Boswell v. Rio De Oro Uranium Mines, Inc., 68 N.M. 457, 362 P.2d 991 (1961); Dennison v. Hildt, 180 Okla. 399, 70 P.2d 56 (1937).

[229] E-Sign § 101, UETA § 7. For an introduction to these statutes, see § 14, supra.

[230] Cloud Corp. v. Hasbro, Inc., 314 F. 3d 289, 295–96 (7th Cir. 2002). A few courts were willing to recognize that tape recordings satisfied the statute. In Ellis Canning Co. v. Bernstein, 348 F. Supp. 1212 (D. Colo. 1972), the court held that a tape recording which the parties had agreed to would satisfy the requirement of former UCC § 8-319, i.e., the UCC statute of frauds relating to the sale of securities which has since been repealed (see § 8-113 of the 1994 revision). The court relied upon the broad definition of a "writing" in UCC § 1-201(46) which includes "any intentional reduction to tangible form." In Londono v. City of Gainesville, 768 F.2d 1223 (11th Cir. 1985), the court held that a tape recording satisfied the provision of the Florida Statute of Frauds dealing with contracts for the sale of land. However, in Swink & Co. v. Carroll McEntee & McGinley, Inc., 266 Ark. 279, 584 S.W.2d 393 (1979), the court stated that, even assuming the tape recording can be characterized as a "writing," it fails because it was not "signed." In Sonders v. Roosevelt, 64 N.Y.2d 869, 487 N.Y.S.2d 551, 476 N.E.2d 996 (1985), the New York Court of Appeals held that a tape recording is not a memorandum in writing subscribed by the defendant as required by N.Y. GEN. OBLIG. LAW § 5-701(a).

[231] UCC § 1-102(2)(b). Comment 1 to this section emphasizes the flexible and "semi-permanent" nature of the UCC.

have retarded the development of "E-Business" in a world committed to this new form of contracting. A quick and decisive response was essential.

Initial state legislative attempts to react to this felt need were often hurried and anything but uniform in scope or application. They augured mass confusion. A uniform statute that recognized accelerating changes in technology that would not constrain the development of unborn methods of creating electronic records or securing electronic signatures was essential. The *Uniform Electronic Transactions Act* (UETA) succeeds in this minimalist approach simply by removing any bar to the recognition of electronic records and electronic signatures which are reasonable under the circumstances. The Congressional desire to inspire uniform recognition of this basic concept in the *Electronic Signatures in Gloal and Network Commerce Act* (E-Sign), which validates UETA, further assures the removal of barriers to electronic contracting. Having explored these recent statutes earlier,[232] we need only summarize their application with respect to the statute of frauds.

By the simple proposition that a contract, record or signature will not be denied legal effect solely because it is in electronic form,[233] both statutes validate records in electronic form. Where, for example, the statute of frauds requires a contract to be evidenced by a "signed writing," an electronic record[234] and an "electronic signature"[235] will suffice. There is no attempt to specify the particular technology necessary for an effective electronic record or signature.[236] The electronic sound, symbol or process, however, must be executed or adopted with an intent to sign the record. Thus, where a party's voice was surreptitiously recorded, the sound which could identify his voice was procured without his knowledge or intent to "sign" the record.[237] Both statutes emphasize that parties are not *required* to use electronic means to make their contracts, and UETA insists that the parties *agree* to conduct transactions electronically and whether they agreed is determined from the context and surrounding circumstances including their conduct.[238] Such agreement or consent, however, is broadly defined. Thus, a business card or letterhead with an E-mail address may allow a reasonable

---

[232] For an overview of UETA and E-Sign, see § 14, *supra*.

[233] E-sign § 101; UETA § 7.

[234] UETA defines "record" in § 2(13) as "information that is inscribed on a tangible medium or that is stored in an electronic or other medium and is retrievable in perceivable form." The identical language is found in the E-Sign definition in § 106(9).

[235] UETA § 2(8) defines "electronic signature" as "an electronic sound, symbol or process attached to or logically associated with a record and executed or adopted by a person with the intent to sign the record." The same definition appears in E-Sign § 106(5).

[236] UETA and E-Sign deliberately avoid specifying particularly secure technologies as did some earlier state legislation concerning electronic signatures. UETA § 2, comment 7 is emphatic in stating that, "No specific technology need be used in order to create a valid signature. One's voice on an answering machine may suffice if the requisite intention is present. Similarly, including one's name as part of an electronic mail communication may also suffice, as may the firm name on a facsimile."

[237] Sawyer v. Mills, 295 S. W. 3d 79 (Ky.2009) where the court notes that a signature procured through trick without intent on the party to execute a record may be viewed as a forgery.

[238] UETA § 5(b). In Audi AG v. D'Amato, 381 F. Supp. 2d 644 (E. D. Mich. 2005), the court found no evidence that the parties intended a legally binding contract by their exchange of emails. In Alliance Laundry Systems, LLC v. Thyssenkrupp Materials, N A, 570 F. Supp. 2d 1061, 1067, n. 3 (E. D. Wis. 2008), the court noted that the defendant's argument that parties may not form a contract electronically unless they first agree to do so was not technically correct. The UETA does not provide the substantive law that determines whether the parties made a contract. The purpose of the UETA was simply to remove barriers to electronic commerce by effectuating electronic records and signatures.

inference of consent to communicate electronically for business purposes. A party who orders goods from an online vendor also manifests consent.[239]

UETA is limited to "electronic records and electronic signatures relating to a transaction."[240] It applies to business, commercial, governmental and consumer transactions, but neither UETA nor E-Sign apply to wills, codicils, testamentary trusts, or transactions governed by UCC Articles 3 through 9, such as negotiable instruments, payment systems, letters of credit, investment securities or secured transactions which contain their own rules for electronic transactions.[241] Again, both statutes reflect a procedural and minimalist approach by deferring to state law concerning substantive matters.[242] UETA is more detailed than E-Sign by allowing parties to vary its provisions by agreement.[243] It sets forth standards concerning attribution[244] as well as changes or errors in electronic records.[245] UETA does not, however, pretend to establish comprehensive and highly specific rules for all of the issues that may arise with respect to electronic media in the formation of contracts. Such an attempt would have been presumptuous and counterproductive at this embryonic stage of development in the use of this technology.

[B]   The Memorandum Must Be Signed

[1]   Form of Signature — Electronic Signature

The usual requirement of the statute of frauds is that the memorandum be signed "by the party to be charged or his agent." As early as 1814, Lord Ellenborough removed any doubt that "signed" as used in the original statute did not require a handwritten signature.[246] No particular form or kind of signature is essential.[247] It may be printed or typewritten,[248]

---

[239] UETA § 5, comment 4, example B. There are, however, special concerns about consumers. Where a statute, regulation or other rule of law requires that information be made available to a consumer, electronic communication of such information must be capable of being printed and stored. If the information is required to be posted or displayed in a certain manner or transmitted by a specific method or formatted in a particular manner, these requirements must be met in any electronic communication. UETA § 8(a). See also E-Sign § 101(c).

[240] UETA § 3(a).

[241] E-Sign § 103(a)(3); UETA § 3(b)(2). Where the issue was whether personal appearance of the affiant before a notary was necessary to meet the statutory requirement of an affidavit, the court rejected the claim that the UETA would permit en electronic transmission since the "transaction" did not relate to the conduct of business, commercial, governmental or consumer transactions and was not, therefore, within the scope of UETA. Hepfinger v. White, 2005 Mich. App. LEXIS 2192 (Ct. App. Mich. 2005).

[242] UETA § 5(e) and *Draft Prefatory Notes*, subsection [B]. *See also* E-Sign § 101(b).

[243] UETA § 5(d).

[244] UETA § 9. *See* § 14, *supra*, text at note 157.

[245] UETA § 10. *See* § 14, *supra*, note 158.

[246] Schneider & Another v. Norris, 2 M. & S. 286, 105 Eng. Rep. 388 [1814].

[247] RESTATEMENT 2d § 134. "[T]he principle that any mark, when coupled with an intent by the maker that it be a signature, will satisfy the statute of frauds is so well settled that citations to the legions of cases so holding are unnecessary." Pierce v. Foreign Mission Bd. of the Southern Baptist Convention, 28 Va. Cir. 168, 172, 1992 Va. Cir. LEXIS 264, at *7 (1992). UCC § 1-201(b)(37) defines "signed" as any symbol executed or adopted with present intention to adopt or accept a writing." See R. M. Schultz & Assocs., Inc. v. Nynex Computer Serv. Co., 1994 U. S. Dist. LEXIS 4509 (N. D. Ill. 1994).

[248] Hansen v. Hill, 215 Neb. 573, 340 N.W.2d 8 (1983) (printed); Vess Beverages, Inc. v. Paddington Corp., 941 F.2d

stamped,[249] or made with a pencil[250] as well as with pen and ink. An existing symbol on paper may be adopted by the party as his signature as in the case of a billhead or letterhead.[251] Initials, a mark, or even a thumbprint may be sufficient.[252]

We have already explored the recent statutory changes stating that a contract, record or signature will not be denied legal effect solely because they are in electronic form.[253] An electronic signature may be "an electronic sound, symbol or process attached to or logically associated with a record and executed or adopted by a person with the intent to sign a record."[254] An email signature does not require a typed name at the bottom. The header of the email containing the name of the sender and "hitting the send button" manifests an intention to presently authenticate and adopt the content of the email as well as the signature.[255]

The essential question has little to do with the particular symbol used or adopted. Rather, the question is, *did the party execute or adopt the symbol with a present intention, actual or apparent, to authenticate the writing as the signer of the writing?*[256] Whether such intention is manifested is a question of fact.[257] Where a sender's name was automatically imprinted by a fax machine on each page transmitted, the court held that "the act of identifying and sending a document to a particular destination does not, by itself, constitute a signing authenticating the document for Statute of Frauds purposes. . . ."[258] Electronic messages are presumably attributed to senders, but where an 8-K form was filed electronically with the SEC by mistake,

---

651, 654 (8th Cir. 1991) (typewritten); Jerry Harmon Motors v. First Nat'l Bank & Trust Co., 472 N.W.2d 748, 753 (N.D. 1991) (typewritten).

[249] *See* Kocinski v. Home Ins. Co., 147 Wis. 2d 728, 734, 433 N.W.2d 654, 657 (Wis. Ct. App. 1988) (attorney's stamped signature was sufficient).

[250] Kleine v. Kleine, 281 Mo. 317, 219 S.W. 610 (1920).

[251] *See, e.g.*, Monetti v. Anchor Hocking Corp., 931 F.2d 1178, 1185 (7th Cir. 1991); Cox Eng'g, Inc. v. Funston Mach. & Supply Co., 749 S.W.2d 508, 511 (Tex. App. Fort Worth 1988). UCC § 1-201 (b)(37) comment 37 suggests that the signature may be discovered in a billhead or letterhead.

[252] In Barber & Ross Co. v. Lifetime Doors, Inc., 810 F.2d 1276, 1280 (th Cir. 1987), the court found a brochure with defendant's trademark to be sufficient. *See also* Stephens v. Perkins, 209 Ky. 651, 273 S.W. 545 (1925) (mark); Salmon Falls Mfg. Co. v. Goddard, 55 U.S. (14 How.) 446 (1852) (initials). UCC § 1-201(39) comment 39 (thumbprint or initials).

[253] *See* § 74[A][1], *supra*.

[254] UETA § 2(8); E-Sign § 106(5).

[255] International Casings Group, Inc. v. Premium Standard Farms, Inc., 358 F. Supp. 2d 863, 873 (W. D. Mo. 2005). Under UETA, the signature must be attributable to the person whose name appears on the email.

[256] RESTATEMENT 2d § 134 and UCC § 1-201(39). An oral settlement agreement that was read into court was "probably . . . the legal equivalent of a written signature for purposes of the statute of frauds. The record does not disclose the type of equipment used by the court reporter, but it would be quite rare today for a court reporter's equipment not to at least require electricity. The UETA deems records generated by electronic means . . . to be electronic records." In re Marriage of Takusagawa, 38 Kan. App. 2d 401, 410, 166 P. 3d 440, 447 (2007).

[257] "The sufficiency of a memorandum to constitute a contract meeting the requirements of the statute of frauds is a question of law. . . . [T]he determination of whether or not the party intended to authenticate the document by the typewritten 'signature' is a question of fact." Jerry Harmon Motors v. First Nat'l Bank & Trust Co., 472 N.W.2d 748, 753–54 (N.D. 1991)." Here, if not the actual intention, it was certainly the apparent intention . . . to use the letterhead to authenticate the writing. . . ." Jeshiva v. United States Mattress Corp., 1994 U.S. Dist. LEXIS 6592, at *4 (D.N.J. Jan. 10, 1994).

[258] Parma Tile Mosaic & Marble Co., Inc., v. Short, 87 N.Y.2d 524, 527, 663 N.E.2d 633, 634 (1996). It should also be noted that the statute in this case required the signature to be "subscribed," an issue addressed in the next subsection.

the court held that the signature could be disavowed under the UETA.[259] Similarly, while a printed signature with intent to authenticate will be sufficient, where a printed document stated that it is not valid unless signed and accepted by an officer of the company, an officer's printed signature was insufficient.[260]

[2]   Placement of Signature

The original Statute of Frauds did not require the signature to be at a particular place on the writing, e.g., it did not require signing at the end of the document. Some statutes, however, are drafted with the term "subscribed," which can mean at the end or foot though it can also be viewed as a loose synonym for "signed."[261] Whether a court construing a statute using "subscribed" will require the document to be signed at the end or will accept a signature elsewhere on the document will depend upon the court's construction of "subscribed."[262] The difficult issue concerning the placement of the signature where more than one writing is necessary to satisfy the statute and the signature appears on less than all of the writings is explored later in this section.[263]

[3]   Who Must Sign the Memorandum?

The 1677 version of the Statute of Frauds requires the writing "signed by the party to be charged therewith, or some other person thereunto by him lawfully authorized" and, with rare exception,[264] this requirement continues in modern versions of the statute. Since only the "party to be charged" or his agent must sign, the non-signing party is placed in a superior position. If only one of the parties has signed a memorandum evidencing a contract, that party can be charged while the other, non-signing party cannot be charged. For example, the defendant's agent sent a written offer to the plaintiff who signed the offer and mailed it to the agent enclosing a $5000 check as a down payment, which the agent returned with a letter stating that defendant had rejected the offer. Since the writing had not been signed by the defendant, the "party to be charged," the statute of frauds was not satisfied.[265] The apparent inequity is solved by some courts who suggest that, when the non-signing party brings suit on the contract, he binds himself to the contract, thereby rendering it mutual.[266] This is not a complete solution, however, since the signing party cannot enforce the contract against the

---

[259] Berger v. Newhouse, 83 Fed. Appx. 19 (5th Cir. 2003).

[260] Toppings v. Rainbow Homes, Inc., 200 W. Va. 728, 490 S.E.2d 817 (1997).

[261] RESTATEMENT 2d § 134 comment b.

[262] "The word 'subscribed,' as used in the statute of frauds, means a signature of the person to be charged placed immediately at the end of a printed or written instrument." Alaska Continental, Inc. v. Trickey, 933 P.2d 528, 533 note 5 (Alaska 1997). See Commercial Credit Corp. v. Marden, 155 Or. 29, 62 P.2d 573 (1936), where the Oregon court construed "subscribed" as interchangeable with "signed" and did not, therefore, require the writing to be signed at the end thereof. See *Parma Tile Mosaic*, note 258, *supra*, interpreting N.Y. GEN. OBLIG. LAW § 5-701 requiring the writing to be "subscribed."

[263] *See* § 75[B][5], *infra.*

[264] The Pennsylvania Statute of Frauds pertaining to leases requires both the landlord and tenant to sign. 68 PA. STAT. ANN. § 250.202. *See* Flight Sys., Inc. v. Electronic Data Corp., 112 F.3d 124, 128 (3d Cir. 1997).

[265] Flannery v. Marathon Oil Co., 75 Ill. App. 3d 690, 394 N. E. 2d 706 (1st Dist. 1975).

[266] Cottom v. Kennedy, 140 Ill. App. 3d 290, 488 N.E.2d 682 (1986). That this analysis does not provide a complete solution to the problem will become apparent in the discussion of the UCC change in the statute concerning confirmations between merchants which is explored in the next subsection.

non-signing party who raises the statute of frauds as an affirmative defense. As we will see in the next subsection, the Uniform Commercial Code, § 2-201(2), addresses this issue in contracts between merchants.[267]

With respect to contracts for the sale of land, a given statute of frauds may not include the phrase, "signed by the party to be charged" and be interpreted to require only the grantor's signature regardless of whether he is the party to be charged.[268] This view creates a problem for unwitting vendees. If a vendor decides to sue a vendee on a land contract, the vendor has the power to sign a memorandum evidencing an alleged contract with the non-signing vendee just before the vendor brings his action. To defeat this possibility, most courts will require the memorandum signed by the vendor to be delivered to and accepted by the vendee, i.e., the vendee's signature is not necessary, but his act of accepting the memorandum signed by the vendor is essential to remove the statute of frauds bar to enforcement of the contract.[269]

A party may appoint an agent to sign and the agent's signature will have the same effect as if the party (principal) himself had signed.[270] Only a small minority of states have statutes generally requiring a writing to evidence the conferral of agency authority to sign for a principal. Many more, however, require such written authority with respect to land contracts.[271]

[4] Multiple Writings

If a writing is incomplete, the issue arises of whether other writings relating to the same transaction may be considered in overcoming the deficiency. There is no doubt that the memorandum required to satisfy the statute of frauds may be found in more than one writing.[272] A signed offer and a signed acceptance will constitute a sufficient memorandum if they contain the essential terms of the agreement and manifestly refer to each other.[273] Any number of separate pieces of paper may be joined to constitute a sufficient memorandum so long as one of the writings is signed and they manifestly relate to the same transaction.[274] If the writings are physically attached and, together, constitute a sufficient memorandum, the statute of frauds is satisfied.[275]

---

[267] *See* § 75[D], *infra.*

[268] Cases are collected in Palmer v. Wheeler, 258 Or. 41, 481 P.2d 68 (1971) (applying California law).

[269] Schwinn v. Griffith, 303 N.W.2d 258 (Minn. 1981); Simpson v. Dyer, 268 Mich. 328, 256 N.W. 341 (1934); National Bank of Ky. v. Louisville Trust Co., 67 F.2d 97 (6th Cir. 1933), *cert. denied*, 291 U.S. 665, 54 S. Ct. 440, 78 L. Ed. 1056 (1934).

[270] The agent must be expressly or impliedly authorized to sign. *See* Doehla v. Wathne Ltd., 1999 U.S. Dist. LEXIS 11787 (S.D.N.Y. Aug. 2, 1999).

[271] RESTATEMENT 2d § 135 comment b.

[272] Evco Distrib., Inc. v. Commercial Credit Equip. Corp., 6 Kan. App. 2d 205, 627 P.2d 374 (1981); Alaska Indep. Fishermen's Mktg. Ass'n v. New England Fish Co., 15 Wash. App. 154, 548 P.2d 348 (1976); Marks v. Cowdin, 226 N.Y. 138, 123 N.E. 139 (1919).

[273] *See* Huntington Beach Union High Sch. Dist. v. Continental Information Sys. Corp., 621 F.2d 353 (9th Cir. 1980).

[274] Pentax Corp. v. Boyd, 111 Nev. 1296, 1300, 904 P.2d 1024 (1995) (some nexus between the writings must be shown but they need not be express cross-references if the memoranda refer to the same transaction). *But see* Beggin v. Ft. Worth Mortg. Co., 93 Ohio App. 3d 333, 338, 638 N.E.2d 604, 607 (1994) (the reference must be sufficiently specific).

[275] The RESTATEMENT 2d suggests that if the party to be charged physically attaches the writings or places them in

[5]   Some Writings Not Signed

The problem with a memorandum evidenced by several writings relates to the signature requirement where not all of the writings are signed. The issue is whether the signed writing must expressly refer to the unsigned writings, or is it enough that there is clear evidence that the unsigned writings refer implicitly to the same agreement between the parties? Some courts insist upon an explicit reference in the signed writing to the unsigned writing.[276] They seem particularly concerned that the writings satisfy the statute without the aid of parol evidence: "If the writing in question refers to other writings which can be identified by this reference without the aid of parol evidence, then the two writings can constitute compliance with the statute."[277] A well-known case took the position that the signed writing need not expressly refer to the unsigned writings where the writings all referred to the same transaction. Oral evidence was admissible to demonstrate the connection among the writings.[278] The RESTATEMENT 2d adopts this view: "It is sufficient that the signed writing refers to the unsigned writing explicitly or by implication."[279] If the unsigned writing is stapled or otherwise physically attached to the signed writing[280] or enclosed in the same envelope,[281] there is an implicit manifestation of reference to the signed writing. There is, however, no requirement of any such physical attachment. As a recent case suggests,

> That the single factor separating what this court can and cannot consider in evaluating the validity of the [agreements] is what was held together by a staple at the moment they were signed, is, in the opinion of the court, an impractical and absurd application of a rule that is based on practical concerns.[282]

There is no escape from the critical question of whether the parties intended to incorporate the unsigned writing as part of their contract.

[C]   Content of Memorandum — Relaxation of Requirements Under the Uniform Commercial Code

We will see that the Uniform Commercial Code has relaxed the requirements for a sufficient memorandum to satisfy the statute of frauds in a contract for the sale of goods. Before exploring the UCC approach, however, it is important to consider the requirements of

---

the same envelope, the writings may be considered together in determining the sufficiency of the memorandum. RESTATEMENT 2d § 132 comment c.

[276] *See, e.g.,* Bower v. Jones, 978 F.2d 1004, 1008 (7th Cir. 1992). *See also* Hoffman v. S V Co., 102 Idaho 187, 190, 628 P.2d 218, 221 (1981): "[A]n unsigned writing may be considered as part of the memorandum only where express reference is made to it in a signed writing.": Alaska Indep. Fishermen's Mktg. Ass'n v. New England Fish Co., 15 Wash. App. 154, 159, 548 P.2d 348, 351–52 (1976): "[T]he signed writing [must] expressly refer to the unsigned writing."

[277] Module Mobile, Inc. v. Fulton Nat'l Bank, 150 Ga. App. 808, 258 S.E.2d 614, 616 (1979).

[278] Crabtree v. Elizabeth Arden Sales Corp., 305 N.Y. 48, 110 N.E.2d 551 (1953). *See also* Wells Fargo Home Mortgage, Inc. v. Spaulding, 930 A.2d 1025 (Me. 2007); Kelly-Stehney & Assocs. v McDonald's Indus. Prods., 265 Mich. App. 105, 113, 399. 693 N. W. 2d 394, 399 (2005); Simplex Supplies, Inc. v. Abhe & Svoboda, Inc., 586 N.W.2d 797 (Minn. Ct. App. 1998).

[279] RESTATEMENT 2d § 132 comment c. See PayoutOne v. Coral Mortgage Bankers, 602 F. Supp. 2d 1219, 1225 (D. Colo. 2009).

[280] See National Union Fire Ins. Co. v. Lumberman's Mut. Casualty Co., 385 F. 3d 47, 54–55 (1st Cir. 2004).

[281] Restatement 2d § 132, comment c.

[282] Preston Exploration Co. v. Chesapeake Energy Corp., 2010 U. S. Dist. LEXIS 12915 at *17 (S. D. Tex. 2010).

a sufficient memorandum to satisfy other provisions of the statute. In general, the memorandum must reasonably identify the subject matter of the contract, indicate that a contract with respect to that subject matter has been made between certain parties, and set forth the essential terms of the contract with reasonable certainty.[283] If the memorandum contains an unambiguous statement of all of the terms agreed upon by the parties in relation to their bargain, including the consideration for any promise made, so that one can determine from an inspection of the document what obligations were assumed and by whom they were assumed, the memorandum will be sufficient even though it also contains extraneous matter. A contract for the sale of land will require an adequate description of the land.[284] The only questions of doubt are raised in determining what, if anything less than this, will satisfy the statutory requirements.

[1]   Must the Consideration Be Expressed in the Writing?

An early English case emphasized the term "agreement" in the original statute[285] and held that everything agreed upon by the parties that is material to the transaction, including the consideration, must be expressly stated in the writing.[286] The case, however, involved a suretyship promise where the writing failed to state the consideration which had been completely executed. Most of our courts distinguish executory contracts from those which have been executed on one side. If the contract is executory, our courts will insist that the memorandum state conditions which qualify the defendant's undertaking.[287] Thus, in the case of an executory bilateral contract, the memorandum must evidence the agreed exchange for the defendant's performance. If, however, the contract is executed on one side, the memorandum need not express the consideration that has already been performed. Thus, in a contract for the sale of land, if the price has already been paid, the memorandum need not contain the price. If the price has not been paid, however, the memorandum must contain the price to be a sufficient memorandum under this provision of the statute.[288]

The question of the expression of consideration may, of course, be controlled by statute. Some statutes of frauds require the consideration to be expressed in the memorandum[289] or a court may interpret a particular statute as requiring the consideration to be expressed in the writing.[290] There are also statutes that expressly negate any requirement of stating the

---

[283] *See* North Coast Cookies, Inc. v. Sweet Temptations, 16 Ohio App. 3d 342, 476 N.E.2d 388 (1984); Brechman v. Adamar of N.J., Inc., 182 N.J. Super. 259, 440 A.2d 480 (1981). *See* RESTATEMENT 2d § 131.

[284] Lawler v. Dixtor Int'l, Inc., 1999 Tex. App. LEXIS 5829 (Tex. App. Dallas Aug. 6, 1999).

[285] The original Statute also contains the term "promise" and the term "contract."

[286] Wain v. Warlters, 5 East 10 [1804], followed in Saunders v. Wakefield, 4 B. & Ald. 595 [1821]. This view was changed in England by the Mercantile Law Amendment Act, 19 & 20 Vict. c. 97, § 3 [1856].

[287] *See, e.g.*, Standard Oil Co. v. Koch, 260 N.Y. 150, 183 N.E. 278 (1932); Reid v. Diamond Plate-Glass Co., 85 F. 193 (6th Cir. 1898). *Contra* Ruzicka v. Hotovy, 72 Neb. 589, 101 N.W. 328 (1904); Hayes v. Jackson, 159 Mass. 451, 34 N.E. 683 (1893).

[288] RESTATEMENT 2d § 131 comment h, cited in Wells-Reit II-80 Park Plaza LLC v. Director Division of Taxation, 24 N J. Tax 98, 104 (2008). See also Baldwin County v. Purcell Corp., 971 F.2d 1558, 1565 (11th Cir. 1992).

[289] *See, e.g.*, MINN. STAT. § 513.01 and Triple B & G v. Fairmont, 494 N.W.2d 49 (Minn. Ct. App. 1992); N.Y. GEN. OBLIG. LAW § 5-703 and HPSC, Inc. v. Matthews, 179 A.D.2d 974, 579 N.Y.S.2d 474 (3d Dep't 1992); OR. REV. STAT. § 41.580 and Barman v. Union Oil Co. Of Cal., 1999 U.S. Dist. LEXIS 13973 (D. Or. Aug. 13, 1999).

[290] See, e.g., the interpretation of § 9-505 of the Idaho Code in Hoffman v. S V Co., 102 Idaho 187, 190, 628 P.2d 218, 221 (1981).

consideration in the memorandum.[291]

[2]   Resort to Oral Evidence to Overcome Deficiencies in the Memorandum

Questions concerning the use of oral or parol evidence to supply deficiencies in the memorandum have created some disconcertion among the courts. The general rule is that the memorandum must contain, within itself, all of the contract terms.[292] Earlier in this section, however, we recognized that the writing need not be intended as a complete statement of the parties' agreement or as a writing to satisfy the statute. Any writing must be *interpreted*. In a well-known opinion by Judge Cardozo,[293] an employment contract formed orally in January was evidenced by a memorandum signed the following December. The memorandum described a continuing employment but failed to describe the position. The plaintiff had been performing the services of sales manager and the defendant attempted to change the plaintiff's duties materially. Plaintiff claimed that he was entitled to continue in his sales manager position. The court admitted evidence to identify the position described in the writing and described the process as one of turning signs and symbols into their equivalent realities, a process which must always occur regardless of the number of identifying tokens in the writing. Earlier signed writings described the role of the plaintiff and the court adopted the accepted view that more than one writing can be used to create the memorandum.[294] It insisted, however, that the writings, considered together, must contain all of the material terms of the agreement, and held: "We exclude the writing that refers us to spoken words of promise. We admit the one that bids us ascertain a place or a relation by comparison of the description with some 'manifest, external and continuing fact.' "[295] The plaintiff did not require one spoken word of promise to identify his position. The identification emanated exclusively from the writings.

The most extensive recent analysis of the confusion in this area is found in an opinion from the Supreme Court of California which disapproved of "statement in California cases barring consideration of extrinsic evidence to determine the sufficiency of a memorandum under the statute of frauds."[296] The court held,

> [I]f a memorandum includes the essential terms of the parties' agreement, but the meaning of those terms is unclear, the memorandum is sufficient under the statute of frauds if extrinsic evidence clarifies the terms with reasonable certainty and the evidence as a whole demonstrates that the parties intended to be bound.[297]

The holding is an expression of the general rule that permits oral or parol evidence to be used for the purpose of making the indefinite definite, i.e., interpreting or translating the words or

---

[291] See, e.g., the Virginia Statute of Frauds, § 11-2, concerning the sale of real estate where the statute states, ". . . but the consideration need not be set forth or expressed in writing . . . ," as applied in Drake v. Livesay, 231 Va. 117, 120, 341 S.E.2d 186, 188 (1986). *See also* KY. REV. STAT. § 371.010.

[292] "Consideration of parol evidence in assessing the adequacy of a writing for statute of frauds purposes would otherwise undermine the very reason for the statute itself." Bazak International Corp. v. Mast Industries, Inc., 538 N. Y. S. 2d 503, 505, 535 N. E. 2d 633, 635 (Ct. App. 1989).

[293] Marks v. Cowdin, 226 N.Y. 138, 123 N.E. 139 (1919).

[294] *See supra* subsection [B][5].

[295] 226 N.Y. 138, 144, 123 N.E. 139, 141 (1919).

[296] Sterling v. Taylor, 40 Cal. 4th 757, 770, 152 P.3d 410, 427 (2007).

[297] *Id.*, 40 Cal. 4th at 771, 152 P. 3d at 428.

symbols in the writing without, under any circumstances, enlarging the obligations manifested by the writing.[298]

[3]   Uniform Commercial Code Relaxation of Memorandum Requirements Concerning Content

The UCC effected a major change to the contents of the memorandum necessary to satisfy the requirement of a writing in a contract for the sale of goods. The language of the statute itself is quite instructive since it only requires "some writing sufficient to indicate that a contract for sale has been made between the parties and signed. . . ."[299] A sufficient writing or record may certainly be created after an oral contract is formed as in the case of a confirmation expressly recognized by the statute.[300] Even a memorandum made *before* the contract is formed may, in appropriate cases, be sufficient.[301] To suggest, therefore, that the UCC statute of frauds provision requires a contract for the sale of goods with a price of $500 or more to be "in writing" is imprecise. Rather, an oral contract for the sale of goods with a price of $500 or more will be enforceable if *some* signed writing or electronic record indicating a contract for the sale of goods between the parties can be produced.[302] The general principle of the UCC memorandum requirement is that "the writing afford a basis for believing that the offered oral evidence rests on a real transaction."[303] The buyer and seller must be identified though the record need not identify them as buyer or seller.[304] "The price, time and place of payment or delivery, the general quality of the goods, or any particular warranties may all be omitted."[305] Thus, the goods must be sufficiently identified though their quality need not be mentioned in the writing. There is a tendency to overstate the frugality of terms required to satisfy the UCC statute of frauds. Indeed, based upon comment language, courts often suggest that the only indispensable term in the writing is the *quantity* term.[306] This assertion, however, assumes that there is a memorandum or record evidencing that a contract has been made that is signed by the party to be charged.[307]

---

[298] Where, however, an agent uses her own name in the writing, courts will permit parol evidence that the name was used as a pseudonym for the name of the principal. The memorandum, therefore, would be sufficient to make the principal a party to the contract, though she is not identified in the writing by her own name or by any other form of description peculiarly appropriate to the purpose. Looman Realty Corp. v. Broad Street Nat'l Bank, 32 N.J. 461, 161 A.2d 247, 253 (1960) (while the case involved signatures by the agents who informed the seller that they were acting for an unnamed company that they owned, the case suggests that parol evidence would have been admissible had the agents not mentioned the existence of an unnamed principal).

[299] UCC § 2-201(1).

[300] UCC § 2-201(2), recognizing a confirmation between merchants that need not be signed by the party to whom the confirmation is sent.

[301] See Monetti, S.P.A. v. Anchor Hocking Corp., 931 F.2d 1178, 1183 (7th Cir. 1991).

[302] *See* Impossible Electronics Techniques, Inc. v. Wackenhut Protective Sys., Inc., 669 F.2d 1026 (5th Cir. 1982).

[303] UCC § 2-201, comment 1.

[304] *Id.* See American Iron & Metal Co. v. U. S. Ferrous Trad. Div. Tube City Div., 2007 U. S. Dist. LEXIS 27847 at *14 (D. Conn. 2007).

[305] *Id.*

[306] "The only term which must appear is the quantity term which need not be accurately stated but recovery is limited to the amount stated." UCC § 2-201 comment 1. *See, e.g.*, Rosenfeld v. Basquiat, 78 F.3d 84, 93 (2d Cir. 1996); Omega Eng'g v. Eastman Kodak Co., 908 F. Supp. 1084, 1090 (D. Conn. 1995).

[307] In addition to the cases in the previous note, see Coastal Aviation v. Commander Aircraft Co., 937 F. Supp. 1051, 1061 (S.D.N.Y. 1996).

It is often forgotten that the quantity term requirement is a reflection of the general contract formation section of the UCC that allows one or more terms to be left open if the parties intended to make a contract but insist that "there is a reasonably certain basis for giving an appropriate remedy."[308] Absent a quantity term, the contract will fail for indefiniteness, but courts may find that a statement of a general range to satisfy the requirement of a sufficiently certain quantity term. Where a quantity term was stated as "projections" of "½ to 1 million cases," the court found that the requirement of a quantity term had been met, relying on a comment to § 2-201 stating that "the quantity term need not be accurately stated but is limited to the amount stated."[309] The court concluded that, "This language suggests that description in quantity in terms of a range satisfies the Statute of Frauds but that the plaintiff may be limited in its recovery to the lower end of the range."[310] A range of quantity differs from a quantity term in a requirements or output contract. Such a term is necessarily undetermined at the moment of formation, but it is *determinable* and will be determined at the conclusion of the contract term when all of the buyer's requirements or seller's output have been ascertained.[311] Just as these contracts are not fatally indefinite in terms of contract formation,[312] neither do they lack an identifiable quantity term. The notion that there is an "exception" to the memorandum requirement in relation to output and requirements contracts is a misconception.[313]

While the UCC substantially relaxes the requirements for a sufficient memorandum, the requirement that the writing evidence a *contract* rather than a mere offer or preliminary negotiation is maintained.[314] It is also clear that a sufficient writing merely satisfies the statute of frauds under the Code, i.e., it does not, in itself, prove the terms of the contract.[315] Neither does the Code affect the case law concerning a memorandum composed of more than one writing, i.e., a court is just as likely to require the signed writing to refer expressly to the unsigned writings as it would if the contract had been within another provision of the statute of frauds rather than the sale-of-goods provision of the UCC.[316] The UCC modification of the memorandum requirements relate exclusively to content, i.e., "The required writing need not

---

[308] UCC § 2-204(3).

[309] UCC § 2-201, comment 1.

[310] Nora Beverages, Inc. v. Perrier Group of Am. Inc., 164 F. 3d 736, 749 (2d Cir. 1998). See also Am. Iron & Metal Co. v. U. S. Ferrous Trad. Div. Tube City Div., 2007 U. S. Dist. LEXIS 27847 (D. Conn. 2007) ("about 30–35,000 MT total" was held to be a sufficient quantity term).

[311] In Syrovy v. Alpine Resources, Inc., 68 Wash. App. 35, 39, 841 P.2d 1279, 1282 (1992), where the writing evidenced a contract for all of the timber growing on described land that could be harvested within two years, the court held that this was a sufficient quantity term.

[312] UCC §§ 2-306 and 2-204(3).

[313] See Mega Tech Int'l Corp v. Miller Elec. Mfg. Co., 1997 U.S. Dist. LEXIS 20426, at *8 (S.D.N.Y. Dec. 22, 1997), where the court refers to the "exception" to the quantity rule concerning output and requirements contracts.

[314] *See, e.g.*, R. S. Bennett & Co. v. Economy Mech. Indus., 606 F.2d 182 (7th Cir. 1979) (writings evidence offer rather than contract); Conaway v. 20th Century Corp., 491 Pa. 189, 420 A.2d 405 (1980) (suggesting that the relaxation of the memorandum requirements of § 2-201 does not evidence an intention to relax the requirement that the writing must indicate that a contract for sale has been made); Derden v. Morris, 247 So. 2d 838 (Miss. 1971) (letter indicated parties were still negotiating); Arcuri v. Weiss, 198 Pa. Super. 506, 507, 184 A.2d 24, 25 (1962) (check with notation "[t]entative deposit on tentative purchase" did not evidence parties' intention to close a contract).

[315] See Advent Systems, Ltd. v. Unisys Corp., 925 F. 2d 670, 677 (3d Cir. 1991), quoting an earlier edition of this book to this effect. *See also* Lorenz Supply Co. v. American Std., Inc., 419 Mich. 610, 358 N.W.2d 845 (1984).

[316] *See, e.g.*, Alaska Indep. Fishermen's Mktg. Ass'n v. New England Fish Co., 15 Wash. App. 154, 548 P.2d 348 (1976).

contain all the material terms of the contract and such material terms as are stated need not be precisely stated. All that is required is that the writing afford a basis for believing that the offered oral evidence rests on a real transaction."[317] This is completely consistent with the underlying philosophy of contract law under the Code, i.e., the effectuation of the factual bargain of the parties[318] and the pervasive anti-technical nature of Article 2 of the Code.[319] Other changes in the statute of frauds for the sale of goods under the Code will be explored in the following sections.

[D]   Uniform Commercial Code — Confirmation Writing Between Merchants

[1]   An Overview of Uniform Commercial Code Section 2-201(2) — "Merchants"

Under the old Uniform Sales Act and prior versions of the statute of frauds provision for contracts for the sale of goods, a typical business transaction could result in manifest unfairness to one of the parties. If Ames and Barnes formed an oral contract, it was and is common practice for one or both parties to send written confirmations of the already formed contract. Where parties sent accurate and matching confirmations, or one party sent an accurate confirmation that the other signed and returned, there was no potential unfairness. If, however, Ames sent a confirmation to Barnes who received it but did not sign and return that confirmation or send his own to Ames, Barnes could speculate at the expense of Ames. Since Barnes had signed no memorandum, he could raise the statute of frauds as an effective bar to any action by Ames. If Barnes chose to enforce the contract against Ames, however, Ames' signed confirmation deprived Ames of the same defense. At the time the contract was to be performed, if Barnes decided that the contract was beneficial to him, he could enforce the contract. If, however, the contract was beneficial to Ames and not to Barnes, Barnes could preclude the enforcement of the contract. The UCC includes an innovative provision to avoid such manifest injustice.

If both parties are "merchants" as defined in the UCC,[320] a written confirmation sent within a reasonable time by one merchant to the other satisfies the statute with respect to the

---

[317] UCC § 2-201 comment 1.

[318] "Contract" is defined in the UCC as "the total legal obligation which results from the parties' agreement as affected by this Act and any other applicable rules of law. (Compare "Agreement"). UCC § 1-201(11). The more fundamental definition is that of "Agreement": ". . . the bargain of the parties *in fact* as found in their language or by implication from other circumstances including course of dealing or usage of trade or course of performance. . . ." UCC § 1-201(3). For an elaboration of the "factual bargain" concept, see Murray, *The Article 2 Prism: The Underlying Philosophy of Article 2 of the Uniform Commercial Code*, 21 WASHBURN L.J. 1 (1981).

[319] See, e.g., § 2-204(3) of the UCC, which precludes the necessity for completeness of terms if the parties intended to make a contract and there is a reasonable basis for affording a remedy. Other Article 2 sections of the Code which manifest this anti-technical nature include § 2-206 which, as comment 1 to this section indicates, rejects formal "technical" rules of contract formation; § 2-209(1) comment 1, suggests that this section makes good faith modifications enforceable "without regard to the technicalities which at present hamper such adjustments." *See also* §§ 2-305 and 2-202 and their comments.

[320] See the definition of "merchant" in UCC § 2-104(1). While the statutory definition is helpful, it is important to consider comment 2 to this section which identifies three types of merchants. In general, however, there are two types of merchants which may be generally characterized as "broad" or "narrow" merchants. Certain sections of Article 2 apply to the broad definition of merchant who is anyone in business. Thus, a bank purchasing crystal which it intends

non-signing recipient of that confirmation. The confirmation must be "sufficient against the sender," the recipient have reason to know its contents, and the recipient must not have given notice of objection to the sender within ten days from receipt of the confirmation.[321] The provision appears radical since a non-signing party can be bound by the writing signed by the other party. Again, however, the non-signing recipient can avoid this possibility by simply sending timely notice of objection. Such a notice of objection effectively destroys the confirmation as a memorandum in satisfaction of the statute.[322]

[2]   Recipients of Memorandum

While this UCC provision appears to provide a solution to the evil it sought to eradicate, it is not without its challenges. If a confirmation of a fictitious contract is received by a merchant, he may no longer ignore it with impunity. If he fails to object to the confirmation within ten days from receipt, he loses the statute of frauds as a defense.[323] Though the other merchant would still have the burden of proving the contract, it would not have to overcome the threshold defense of the statute of frauds. Thus, the merchant-recipient of a confirmation should be advised to send timely notice of objection to any confirmation evidencing a contract the recipient has not made.

---

to provide to its customers as incentives to open accounts would be a merchant. A University purchasing necessary supplies would be a merchant. Section 2-201 of the Code (the statute of frauds) applies to such merchants as do §§ 2-205, 2-207 and 2-209. A "narrow" merchant, however, is a merchant with respect to goods of that kind. Thus, a merchant who regularly sells appliances or other goods would sell such goods with an implied warranty of merchantability (§ 2-314) attached to them because he is a merchant who regularly sells goods of that kind. A bank providing crystal as a "premium" to entice customers to open accounts would not be engaged in selling such goods on a regular basis. Similarly, if a corporation found that it had purchased an excess number of personal computers and sold some to another company, the seller would not be a narrow merchant because it does not regularly sell such goods. Thus, such casual sales would not include the implied warranty of merchantability. 2-104(3) defines "between merchants" as a transaction to which both parties are chargeable with the knowledge and skill of merchants. The determination of whether a particular party is a "merchant" for the purposes of § 2-201(2) can be troublesome. While there is a split of authority, the majority view is that farmers may be viewed as "merchants" under § 2-201(2) in certain instances. A merchant with a pervasive knowledge and years of experience in a particular industry may very well be characterized as a "merchant" under this provision. *See, e.g.*, Smith v. General Mills, Inc., 291 Mont. 426, 431–32, 968 P.2d 723, 726 (1998). *See also* Sebasty v. Perschke, 404 N.E.2d 1200 (Ind. Ct. App. 1980) (farmer was a merchant in a grain transaction); Currituck Grain, Inc. v. Powell, 38 N.C. App. 7, 246 S.E.2d 853 (1978) (farmer raising corn and soybeans was a merchant). Other circumstances may suggest that a particular farmer should not be characterized as a merchant in a given transaction. *See, e.g.*, Terminal Grain Corp. v. Freeman, 270 N.W.2d 806 (S.D. 1978) (the farmer had no experience with respect to future commodity contracts); Loeb & Co. v. Schreiner, 294 Ala. 722, 321 So. 2d 199 (1975) (cotton farmer who allegedly promised to sell cotton to a corporation engaged in the business of selling cotton was not a merchant).

[321] UCC § 2-201(2). For an extensive discussion of this provision, see Conagra, Inc. v. Nierenberg, 7 P.3d 369 (Mont. 2000).

[322] Section 2-201(2) requires the recipient to "give notice." Section 1-202(d) indicates that such a recipient would "give" notice "by taking such steps as may be reasonably required to inform the other in ordinary course whether or not such other actually comes to know of it." Thus, if the recipient simply mails a notice of objection within ten days from the date he receives the confirmation, such notice is effectively "given."

[323] C.I.F. Productions, Inc. v. Burlington Coat Factory Warehouse Corp., 881 F. Supp. 104 (S.D.N.Y. 1995), provides an example of a recipient losing the statute of frauds defense under UCC § 2-201(2) by failing to object to a confirmation within ten days of its receipt.

[3]   Sending Memorandum — Within a Reasonable Time

While the Code specifies ten days from receipt to object to a confirmation, there is no specified time to send the confirmation. Rather, it must be sent "within a reasonable time."[324] The determination of a "reasonable time" depends upon "the nature, purpose, and circumstances of the transaction."[325] Courts are generally agreed that this phrase is not very helpful since it raises a question of fact. They have been less than clear in deciding whether a particular period between the formation of the oral contract and the sending of the confirmation is reasonable. As one court noted, "There are a host of cases from other jurisdictions which have considered the question of what constitutes a reasonable time under the written confirmation exception to the Uniform Commercial Code."[326] Trade usage, course of dealing, volatile marketing conditions and a large sale price would certainly have a bearing on what constitutes a reasonable time.[327] Cases reveal situations where delays of several months may be reasonable while a delay in sending a confirmation in less than one month was unreasonable.[328]

[4]   Sufficient Against Sender — Purchase Orders

The confirming writing sent by one merchant to the other must be sufficient against the sender, i.e., it must be a writing that would be effective to satisfy the statute if an action were brought by the non-signing merchant against the merchant who sent it.[329] There is, therefore, no particular form required of this writing any more than there would be if the writing was not a confirmation but one that had been executed prior to or contemporaneously with the formation of the contract. While the term "confirmation" need not be used,[330] the writing must evidence a contract between the parties rather than a mere offer or other preliminary negotiation. Thus, a purchase order, without more, may appear to be a mere offer rather than a confirmation of a contract.[331] Even if the writing is captioned "letter of confirmation," but its contents indicate that the other party must submit a written acceptance of such a "letter," the

---

[324] UCC § 2-201(2).

[325] UCC § 1-205(a).

[326] St. Ansgar Mills v. Streit, 613 N. W. 2d 289, 295 (Iowa 2000), (citing cases from other jurisdictions.).

[327] *Id.*

[328] Serna, Inc. v. Harman, 742 F.2d 186 (5th Cir. 1984) (3 and ½ months was not unreasonable where the parties were in communication with each other and the price of the goods did not fluctuate during this period); Cargill, Inc. v. Stafford, 553 F. 2d 1222, 1224 (10th Cir. 1977) (less than one month unreasonable); Azevedo v. Minister, 86 Nev. 576, 471 P.2d 661 (1970) (ten weeks was not unreasonable as a matter of law).

[329] *See* R. S. Bennett & Co. v. Economy Mechanical Indus., Inc., 606 F.2d 182 (7th Cir. 1979).

[330] Bazak Int'l Corp. v. Mast Indus., Inc., 73 N.Y.2d 113, 535 N.E.2d 633 (1989); Perdue Farms, Inc. v. Motts, Inc. of Miss., 459 F. Supp. 7 (N.D. Miss. 1978).

[331] In *Bazak Int'l Corp., id.,* while the majority found purchase orders with handwritten notes to constitute a sufficient memorandum under § 2-201(1) which, therefore, met the requirements of a writing "sufficient against the sender" under § 2-201(2), a dissenting opinion emphasized that the purchase orders described themselves as offers and did not otherwise evidence the existence of a completed agreement. See Audio Visual Assocs., Inc. v. Sharp Elecs. Corp., 210 F.3d 254, 261 (4th Cir. 2000) ("In sending its purchase order, in this case, however, Audio Visual sought to form a contract, rather than confirm one"); Trilco Terminal v. Prebilt Corp., 167 N.J. Super. 449, 400 A.2d 1237 (1979) (purchase orders did not refer to any previous contract). See also Harry Rubin & Sons, Inc. v. Consolidated Pipe Co., 396 Pa. 506, 153 A.2d 472 (1959), where the court indicated doubt that the purchase order, alone, would constitute a confirmation of the contract. However, when combined with a letter, the writings were sufficient to evidence a confirmation. See also Dura-Wood Treating Co. v. Century Forest Indus., 675 F.2d 745 (5th Cir.), *cert. denied*, 459 U.S. 865, 103 S. Ct. 144, 74 L. Ed. 2d 122 (1982), where the court recognized that an order for goods, alone, often evidences only an offer but can, in a given case, constitute sufficient evidence of confirmation of a contract.

writing will fail as a confirmation of the contract.[332] As usual, the caption atop the document does not provide a conclusive characterization.

Where court deemed writings to be insufficient to meet the requirements of the statute of frauds, it also addressed the plaintiff's claim that the writing it received from the defendant was a sufficient memorandum between merchants to meet the requirements of § 2-201(2). The court explained that, even if the writings received by the plaintiff from the defendant constituted a sufficient memorandum, § 2-201(2) would be inapplicable since it was designed to allow the *sender* of a sufficient memorandum to satisfy the statute of frauds if the recipient did not object within ten days of receipt. Thus, a *recipient* of an otherwise sufficient writing would not be eligible to enforce the contract under § 2-201(2).[333] The court, however, did not address the implication of its statement. If such a writing were a sufficient memorandum, the recipient would not be in need of the § 2-201(2) exception since the writing would be sufficient under § 2-201(1) to enforce the contract against the sender-the "party against whom enforcement is sought" — absent the unwarranted assumption that the statute of frauds also requires a sufficient memorandum signed by the party who is seeking enforcement.

[5] Recipient Must Have Reason to Know Contents of Confirmation

The requirement that the recipient of the confirmation have "reason to know its contents" may raise a question concerning the recipient of a confirmation who never made a contract with the sender. In such a situation, does the recipient have reason to know the contents of the memorandum? There is a dearth of case law concerning this question. It has been suggested that a confirmation should have been anticipated, i.e., it is the result of actual negotiations.[334] If the parties have dealt with each other in the past, a confirmation may be anticipated.[335] Another question concerns the addressee of the confirmation. Where the oral contract was made through a specific agent of a corporation, but the confirmation was not addressed to that particular individual but to the company, the court held the confirmation effective, i.e., it construed the language of § 2-201(2) that the recipient have reason to know the contents of the confirmation as not requiring the confirmation to be received by any particular person.[336] The case law applying this language of § 2-201(2) typically deals with questions of *receipt* of the confirmation. Thus, the sender is entitled to the presumption that a properly addressed, stamped and mailed writing was received.[337]

---

[332] Great Western Sugar Co. v. Lone Star Donut Co., 721 F.2d 510 (5th Cir. 1983).

[333] Siesta Sol, LLC v. Brooks Pharmacy, Inc., 617 F. Supp. 2d 38, 45–46 (D.R.I. 2007).

[334] "The receipt of a spurious document would not burden the recipient with a risk of losing the [Statute of Frauds] defense." *Perdue Farms, Inc. v. Motts, supra* note 330, at 20. *Accord*, Thomson Printing Machinery Co. v. B.F. Goodrich Co., 714 F.2d 744, 747-48 (7th Cir. 1983).

[335] See Hatzlachh Supply v. Moishe's Elecs., 828 F. Supp. 178 (S.D.N.Y. 1993), where the parties had pursued a process of an oral contract followed by a confirmation in 42 transactions over a period of two years for a total dollar amount of $1.85 million. The court held that the buyer should have had reason to know the contents of a subsequent confirmation.

[336] Thompson Printing Mach. Co. v. B.F. Goodrich Co., *supra* note 334.

[337] Sebasty v. Perschke, 404 N.E.2d 1200 (Ind. Ct. App. 1980); Tabor & Co. v. Gorenz, 43 Ill. App. 3d 124, 356 N.E.2d 1150 (2d Dist. 1976); Perdue Farms, Inc. v. Motts, Inc. of Miss., 459 F. Supp. 7 (N.D. Miss. 1978). See also Pillsbury Co. v. Buchanan, 37 Ill. App. 3d 876, 346 N.E.2d 386 (4th Dist. 1976), where the confirmation was improperly addressed, thereby negating the presumption. However, the trial court's finding of receipt was supported by evidence that the

[E]   Time of Making and Destruction of Memorandum

[1]   Time of Making

Statutes of frauds, as they are commonly worded, do not purport to fix the time when the memorandum must be made with relation to the time the contract was formed. Neither does the English version of the fourth section of the Statute, which has often been copied literally in this country, purport to invalidate the contract if no memorandum is made. Rather, it provides that "no action shall be brought" on the contract, unless a memorandum is made.[338] The traditional view, therefore, is that the statute is satisfied if the memorandum evidencing the contract comes into existence at any time before the action in which it is sought to be used, regardless of when the contract came into being.[339] The RESTATEMENT 2d, however, goes further in also permitting the memorandum to be made even after the action is begun.[340] It is conceivable that a written pleading would be a sufficient memorandum.[341] Neither the statutory language nor the history of the statute suggest that the memorandum exist prior to the filing of a lawsuit in which it would be used. Moreover, as will be seen in the next section, if a party admits in her pleadings, testimony or otherwise in court that she made the contract, she may not use the statute as a shield. If an admission in court will be sufficient to satisfy the statute, a memorandum created after the action has begun, whether or not in the form of a court document, should be admitted as written evidence of the contract.

[2]   Destruction of Memorandum

It is quite clear that the loss or destruction of the memorandum is not fatal to the party who seeks to enforce a contract within the statute of frauds.[342] The statute of frauds is not a rule of evidence, though its purpose is evidentiary. If, therefore, the writing does not exist at the time the action is brought, the plaintiff is entitled to prove by parol or circumstantial evidence that the writing did in fact exist and oral evidence of its contents is admissible.[343]

§ 76   ADMISSIONS — UNIFORM COMMERCIAL CODE

Should a party who admits in his pleading, testimony or otherwise in court that he made the contract, nonetheless, be permitted to use the statute of frauds as an effective bar to the enforcement of a contract which he has admittedly made? If the question were one of first

---

letter had not been returned and by defendant's admission that he was known in the small town to which the letter had been sent.

[338] The statute of frauds section of the predecessor of the UCC, the Uniform Sales Act, uses the language, "shall not be enforceable by action," which is deemed to be the equivalent of the original fourth section of the English Statute. UCC § 2-201 states, ". . . a contract . . . is not enforceable by way of defense unless there is some writing. . . ."

[339] See Watson v. McCabe, 527 F.2d 286 (6th Cir. 1975); Gaines v. McAdam, 79 Ill. App. 201 (1898). This was the view set forth in the FIRST RESTATEMENT § 215.

[340] RESTATEMENT 2d § 136 comment b. See Lincoln Benefit Life Co. v. Edwards, 45 F. Supp. 2d 722, 734, n. 7 (D. Neb. 1999).

[341] See RESTATEMENT 2d § 133 comment d.

[342] Gipson v. Mattox, 2006 U. S. Dist. LEXIS 86207 (S. D. Ala. 2006); Connecticut Bank & Trust Co. v. Wilcox, 201 Conn. 570, 574, 518 A.2d 928, 931 (1986) (citing RESTATEMENT 2d § 137).

[343] See id., Connecticut Bank (preponderance of the evidence). See also Love v. Spector, 215 A.D.2d 733, 627 N.Y.S.2d 87, 88 (2d Dep't 1995); Combs v. Lufkin, 123 Ariz. 210, 598 P.2d 1029, 1032–33 (Ct. App. 1979).

impression, it would seem that it scarcely survives its statement. If a defendant admits that he made the contract upon which the action against him is brought, there is no possibility that the plaintiff is asserting a false claim. Any requirement of a sufficient writing to evidence the admitted contract becomes superfluous after such an admission. Indeed, "[F]or more than one hundred years after the passage of the [original] Statute of Frauds, there continued to be expressions of belief in the principle that the statute was not intended to be used to defeat performance of an admitted oral agreement."[344]

By the close of the eighteenth century, however, this view was reversed for reasons which now appear fatally flawed. The rationale may be stated as follows: If a defendant who made an oral contract were forced to admit or deny that he made the alleged oral contract, he has two choices: (a) to admit he made the contract thereby losing the statute of frauds as a defense, or (b) to commit perjury by denying he made the contract. The inducement to make a perjured denial is a great temptation. To remove that temptation, the defendant was allowed to admit he made the contract while still raising the statute of frauds as an effective bar to the enforcement of the contract. The modern reaction to this "rationale" is effectively suggested by the statement, "[A]part from creating obvious ethical problems, this approach is in obvious contradiction to the rationale of other recognized exceptions to the Statute."[345]

Notwithstanding the absurdity of this rationale, American courts adopted it so that the prevailing view in this country permitted an admission of the contract and an effective use of the statute of frauds. In the first half of this century, only a few American courts came to insist upon the sound analysis that had prevailed in England for a century after the passage of the original Statute.[346] We will explore more recent developments in American jurisdictions. First, however, it is important to consider the significant change concerning judicial admissions effected by the UCC.

[A]   The Uniform Commercial Code Admissions Exception

As one of several alternate devices to satisfy the statute of frauds in the absences of a sufficient writing, the UCC provides that "if a party admits in his pleadings, testimony or otherwise in court that a contract for sale has been made," the admitted contract is enforceable to the extent of the quantity of goods admitted.[347] It is clear that a contract made enforceable by an admission rather than a writing is enforceable only to the extent of the

---

[344] Stevens, *Ethics and the Statute of Frauds*, 37 CORNELL L.Q. 355, 367 (1952). The Stevens article is the seminal piece concerning the use of the statute of frauds by a defendant who admits the making of the oral contract. Professor Stevens points to Child v. Godolphin, 1 Dickens 39 (Ch. 1723) as the leading, early case from which he provides the following quotation (at 42): "His Lordship said, the plea insisting on the statute was proper, but then the defendant ought by answer to deny the agreement; for if she confessed the agreement, the Court would decree a performance notwithstanding the statute, for such confession would not be looked upon as perjury, *or intended to be prevented by the statute.*" (emphasis added).

[345] Wolf v. Crosby, 377 A.2d 22, 26 (Del. Ch. 1977).

[346] *See* Shedd, *Statute of Frauds: Judicial Admission Exception? Where Has It Gone? Is It Coming Back?*, 6 WHITTIER L. REV. 1 (1984). Professor Shedd cites Hagedorn v. Hagedorn, 194 Iowa 172, 188 N.W. 980 (1922), Degheri v. Carobine, 100 N.J. Eq. 493, 135 A. 518 (N.J. Ch. 1927), and Trossbach v. Trossbach, 185 Md. 47, 42 A.2d 905 (1945), as important early cases in this century recognizing the judicial admission exception as precluding the effective use of the statute of frauds.

[347] UCC § 2-201(3)(b).

admission.[348] It is not necessary that a party expressly admits making the contract. It is sufficient if his admitted words or conduct lead to that conclusion.[349] Courts have generally concluded that involuntary admissions made by a party as an adverse witness under direct examination constitute admissions within the contemplation of the statute.[350] The statute provides that the admission must be made by the party against whom enforcement is sought. While an agent of the party can make such an admission,[351] it has been held that an admission by a former agent or employee of the party to be charged cannot bind the former employer without authorization from the employer.[352] Where, however, a manager of a company on cross examination was asked whether he had any doubt that a former employee with agency authority had ordered goods which had been delivered, the manager's answer, "Yes, I believe he did," constituted an admission by the company that the contract was made.[353]

The reaction to this statutory exception to the UCC statute of frauds was not unanimously acclaimed. The language was deemed to be so "imprecise" in California that the legislature originally chose to delete it from the California version of UCC § 2-201. Questions were raised concerning its application to discovery procedures or testimony in other cases.[354] The phrase, "otherwise in court," requires elaboration. A comment refers to stipulations or oral statements before the court and concludes, "Under this section it is no longer possible to admit the contract in court and still treat the statute as a defense."[355] The admissions exception has been held inapplicable to letters and memoranda produced during discovery that allegedly admit a contract since they are not viewed as admissions "otherwise made in court."[356] Admissions in depositions, however, have generally been held to fall within the statutory requirement of admissions made in pleadings, testimony or "otherwise in court" whether such admissions are voluntary or involuntary.[357]

---

[348] *See* Barton v. Tra-Mo, Inc., 73 Or. App. 804, 699 P.2d 1182 (1985).

[349] St. Francis Mercantile Equity Exch. v. Newton, 27 Kan. App. 2d 18, 996 P.2d 365, 370 (2000); *see also* Nebraska Builders Prods. Co. v. Industrial Erectors, Inc., 239 Neb. 744, 759, 478 N.W.2d 257, 268 (1992) (citing Lewis v. Hughes, 276 Md. 247, 346 A.2d 231 (1975) (involuntary admission of existence of contract during cross-examination satisfies UCC § 2-201(3)(b)).

[350] *See* Bahnsen v. Rabe, 276 N.W.2d 413 (Iowa 1979).

[351] *See, e.g.,* Roth Steel Prods. v. Sharon Steel Corp., 705 F.2d 134 (6th Cir. 1983); Oskey Gasoline & Oil Co. v. Continental Oil Co., 534 F.2d 1281 (8th Cir. 1976).

[352] Miller v. Sirloin Stockade, 224 Kan. 32, 578 P.2d 247 (1978).

[353] Saga Solutions, LLC v. Sherwin-Williams Co., 2002 Conn. Super. LEXIS 1571 (2002).

[354] *See* Isaac v. A & B Loan Co., 201 Cal. App. 3d 307, 247 Cal. Rptr. 104 (2d Dist. 1988). Section 2-201(3)(b), however, was restored to the California version of § 2-201 by a 1988 amendment. There is a question as to whether the amendment would have changed the result in the case which dealt with the defendant's declaration in another case that allegedly constituted an admission of an agreement with the defendant.

[355] UCC § 2-201 comment 7.

[356] Precise-Marketing Corp. v. Simpson Paper Co., 1999 U. S. Dist. LEXIS 6325 (S. D. N. Y. 1999).

[357] *See* Babst v. FMC Corp., 661 F. Supp. 82 (S.D. Miss. 1986); Roth Steel Prods. v. Sharon Steel Corp., 705 F.2d 134 (6th Cir. 1983); URSA Farmers Coop. Co. v. Trent, 58 Ill. App. 3d 930, 374 N.E.2d 1123 (4th Dist. 1978). See, however, Precise-Marketing Corp. v. Simpson Paper Co., 1999 U.S. Dist. LEXIS 6325, at *32 (S.D.N.Y. 1999), where the court suggests that documents produced during the discovery phase of the litigation do not constitute pleadings, testimony or an admission otherwise made in court and, consequently, UCC § 2-201(3)(b) is inapplicable. Under the proposed amendments to Article 2 of the UCC which have yet to be enacted in any jurisdiction, the phrase, "otherwise in court" is changed to "or otherwise under oath" to remove doubt concerning admissions in depositions or affidavits though not made "in court."

The overriding question left unanswered was whether the party seeking to enforce the oral agreement could compel the other party to admit or deny the making of the contract.[358] It has been held that acceptance of the factual allegations in the complaint as true for the purposes of summary judgment, a motion to dismiss or demurrer will not constitute an "admission" under the UCC admissions exception.[359] Thus, if the defense may be raised through such a pleading device thereby avoiding the necessity to either admit or deny the making of the contract, the effect will be to emasculate the admissions exception under § 2-201(3)(b). Some courts confronting this question have concluded that permitting the statute to be raised in this manner would effectively negate the Code provision. In these jurisdictions, the statute may not be raised in this manner. Rather, the defendant is forced to admit or deny the making of the contract in a responsive pleading, pre-trial discovery or during the trial.[360] Other jurisdictions continue to permit the use of a motion to dismiss or the like to establish the statute of frauds as a bar to the enforcement of the alleged oral contract.[361]

One solution to this dilemma is to permit the plaintiff to depose the defendant. If the deposition does not evidence the making of a contract as alleged, a motion for summary judgment could then be granted. Yet, forcing a continuation of proceedings in terms of a trial with respect to a defendant who has not, in fact, made a contract, however, may be said to permit judicial harassment of the defendant and to ignore the value of judicial economy.[362] The insightful analysis is suggested by Judge Posner:

> When there is a bare motion to dismiss, or an answer, with no evidentiary materials, the possibility remains a live one that, if asked under oath whether a contract had been made, the defendant would admit it had been. The only way to test the proposition is for the plaintiff to take the defendant's deposition, or, if there is no discovery, to call the defendant as an adverse witness at trial. But where as in this case the defendant swears in an affidavit that there was no contract, we see no point in keeping the lawsuit

---

[358] "The Comment does not indicate that such was intended, but it is not clearly foreclosed by the language of the section." 1 Re Port of N.Y. Law Revision Comm'n, Study of the Uniform Commercial Code 372 (1955).

[359] See, e.g., R. M. Schultz & Assoc. Inc. v. Nynex Computer Servs. Co., 1994 U.S. Dist. LEXIS 4509 (N.D. Ill. Apr. 8, 1994) (summary judgment) (citing Triangle Mktg., Inc. v. Action Indus., 630 F. Supp. 1578 (N.D. Ill. 1986), holding that a Rule 12(b)(6) motion to dismiss and a Rule 12(c) motion for judgment on the pleadings admits the complaint's allegations only in a technical sense inadequate to meet the UCC § 2-201(3)(b) admission requirement). Anthony v. Tidwell, 560 S.W.2d 908, 910 (Tenn. 1977) (motion to dismiss was granted and upheld where the complaint alleged an oral contract for the sale of goods within the UCC statute of frauds and the court stated that "technical admissions of this nature, made solely in connection with a motion to dismiss, do not necessarily constitute admissions chargeable to the party for the purposes of the litigation as a whole"); Beter v. Helman, 7 W.J.L. Vol. XLI (Pa. C. P. Westmoreland Cty. 1958), held that demurrer was not the type of "admission" referred to in § 2-201(3)(b) of the UCC.

[360] See M & W Farm Serv. Co. v. Callison, 285 N.W.2d 271 (Iowa 1979); Duffee v. Judson, 251 Pa. Super. 406, 380 A.2d 843 (1977); Garrison v. Piatt, 113 Ga. App. 94, 147 S.E.2d 374 (1966).

[361] In Rinderknecht v. Luck, 965 P.2d 564, 566 note 4 (Utah Ct. App. 1998), the court states, "The gist of the argument is that disposing of such cases on summary judgment, early on in a lawsuit, denies a plaintiff the opportunity to ever elicit an admission from a defendant through deposition testimony, cross examination or the like. While this may be true to some extent . . . , Utah courts have not hesitated to grant summary judgment based on the Statute of Frauds." See also Boylan v. G. L. Morrow Co., 63 N.Y.2d 616, 623, 479 N.Y.S.2d 499, 503, 468 N.E.2d 681 (1984) (two judges vigorously dissented, concluding, "If a prepleading motion to dismiss is permitted to defeat a cause of action on an oral sales contract before plaintiff has had an opportunity to elicit from defendant a statement in court of any kind, only malpractice by defendant's attorney would subject the defendant to the statute's ameliorative purpose." 468 N.E. at 682); International Plastics Dev., Inc. v. Monsanto Co., 433 S.W.2d 291 (Mo. 1968); Anthony v. Tidwell, supra note 359.

[362] See Weiskopf, In-Court Admissions of Sales Contracts and the Statute of Frauds, 19 UCC L.J. 195, 217 (1987).

alive. Of course the defendant may blurt out an admission in a deposition, but this is hardly likely. . . . [R]emote possibilities do not warrant subjecting the parties and the judiciary to proceedings almost certain to be futile.[363]

[B]   Extension of Judicial Admission Exception Beyond the Uniform Commercial Code

The satisfaction of the statute of frauds through judicial admissions for contracts other than UCC sale-of-goods contracts can be found in numerous jurisdictions. In 2002, in reviewing the judicial admissions exception throughout the country, a court stated, "[V]irtually every court that has addressed the issue during the last twenty-five years has held that judicial admissions are an exception to the statute of frauds."[364] The applicable statute of frauds may contain such an exception.[365] Without any statutory change, some courts have returned to the basic view of the English courts in the first century after the enactment of the original Statute, i.e., the purpose of the statute is to prevent fraud, not to perpetuate fraud- often called the "judicial admissions" exception.[366] Other courts have recognized that fundamental concept and they have also been influenced by the Uniform Commercial Code provision in engrafting the admissions exception on all contracts within the statute of frauds.[367] In addition to the merit of the admissions exception, there is something to be said for uniformity and consistency in the treatment of all provisions of the statute of frauds to the extent permissible under the statutory language. Absent a negation of the admissions exception by the legislature, courts should not feel precluded from recognizing this exception with respect to any provision of their statutes of fraud. The only possible preclusion is found in antiquated and flawed precedent that should not be followed.[368]

---

[363] DF Activities Corp. v. Brown, 851 F.2d 920, 922 (7th Cir. 1988).

[364] Gibson v. Arnold, 288 F. 3d 1242, 1246–47 (10th Cir. 2002), citing cases from numerous jurisdictions, of which only two (Washington and Alabama) had declined to adopt a judicial admissions exception. North Carolina has also declined. See note 362, *infra*.

[365] *See* Iowa Code Ann. § 622.34; Alaska Stat. § 09.25.020.

[366] *See, e.g.*, Flight Sys., Inc. v. Electronic Data Sys. Corp., 112 F.3d 124, 128 (3d Cir. 1997); Sea-Van Invs. Assocs. v. Hamilton, 71 Wash. App. 537, 546, 861 P.2d 485, 491 (1993); Timberlake v. Heflin, 180 W. Va. 644, 647, 379 S.E.2d 149, 152 (1989).

[367] *See, e.g.*, Hackney v. Morelite Constr., 418 A.2d 1062, 1066–67 (D.C. 1980).

[368] In Pierce v. Gaddy, 42 N.C. App. 622, 257 S.E.2d 459, 462 (1979), the court rejects the admissions exception out of hand, citing two nineteenth century North Carolina cases. In Durham v. Harbin, 530 So. 2d 208, 212 note 5 (Ala. 1988), the court stated, "We are not wholly deaf to the strong arguments by the commentators favoring a judicial admission exception to the Statute, and, in a proper case, might be inclined to consider whether the legislative intent behind the Statute of Frauds favors such a construction."

§ 77 PERFORMANCE SATISFYING THE STATUTE OF FRAUDS

[A]   Effect of Part Performance in General

Parties to a contract within one or more provision of the statute of frauds may, of course, perform their contract and, once fully performed, it is an executed contract to which the statute of frauds has no application.[369] If, however, the contract is not fully performed, the issue arises of whether part performance will remove the contract from the enforcement bar of the statute of frauds. Only three types of contracts within the statute of frauds admit of a part performance satisfaction: (i) contracts that cannot be performed within one year from their making; (ii) contracts for the sale of land; (iii) contracts for the sale of goods. Otherwise, it is the general rule that part performance will not make a contract enforceable where it would otherwise be unenforceable. We have already examined the part performance exception with respect to contracts that cannot be performed within one year from formation.[370] We will now examine the cases allowing part performance in the other two classifications.

[B]   "Part Performance" — Reliance — Contracts for the Sale of Land

Soon after the original Statute of Frauds was enacted, English courts of equity permitted what was called part performance of a land contract, such as payment of the purchase price or the transfer of possession of the land to the grantee,[371] to satisfy the statute of frauds notwithstanding contrary language in the statute. Today, it is clear that once a transfer of an interest in land has been completed, the promise to pay the price will be enforceable notwithstanding the lack of any writing to evidence the contract unless the price, itself, is wholly or partially an interest in land.[372] If, however, only the price has been paid by the prospective buyer, it is well established that the buyer may not obtain specific performance of the contract since he may be restored to status quo through the remedy of restitution.[373] Some performance beyond payment of the price will be required to allow a buyer to avoid the application of the statute. It is often suggested that whatever the performance, it must be *unequivocally referable* to the alleged oral agreement.[374] It has been held that where the buyer pays all or part of the purchase price and the seller gives possession of the land to the buyer, the oral contract will be enforced.[375] Other courts have found satisfaction of the statute

---

[369] *See* Frost Nat'l Bank v. Burge, 29 S.W.3d 580 (Tex. App. Houston 2000); Alexander v. Holmberg, 410 N.W.2d 900 (Minn. Ct. App. 1987).

[370] *See supra* § 73.

[371] *See* Butcher v. Stapley, 1 Vern. 363, 23 Eng. Rep. 524 (Ch. 1685).

[372] RESTATEMENT 2d § 125(3).

[373] *See, e. g.*, Perkins v. Owens, 721 N. E. 2d 289, 292 (Ct. App. Ind. 1999); Pugh v. Gilbreath, 571 P.2d 1241 (Okla. Ct. App. 1977). *Contra* Hamilton v. Traub, 29 Del. Ch. 475, 51 A.2d 581 (1947).

[374] The famous statement of this requirement is found in the opinion by Judge Cardozo in Burns v. McCormick, 233 N.Y. 230, 232, 135 N.E. 273, 273 (1922), which emphasizes that the performance "must itself supply the key to what is promised. It is not enough that what is promised may give significance to what is done." The performance, therefore, must be the dominant manifestation of intention since such conduct will be the evidentiary substitute for the writing. To permit the alleged oral promise to be the dominant evidence contradicts the purpose of the land contract provision of the statute of frauds.

[375] *See* Darby v. Johnson, 477 So. 2d 322 (Ala. 1985); Smith v. Cox, 247 Ga. 563, 277 S.E.2d 512 (1981); Shaughnessy v. Eidsmo, 222 Minn. 141, 23 N.W.2d 362 (1946).

in possession plus the making of valuable improvements to the land.[376] Certainly, if the buyer pays all or part of the purchase price, takes possession of the land and makes valuable improvements thereon, the contract will be removed from the Statute.[377]

Reliance — The Underlying Rationale. Since oral contracts for the sale of land do not include terms dealing with the taking of possession and making improvements, however, such acts are not genuine "part performance" though they are often so labeled. They constitute *detrimental reliance* which is the accurate rationale which the Restatement 2d of Contracts recognizes as the essential[378] Payment of the purchase price *is* part performance but, again, it is not sufficient to remove the contract from the Statute. In such cases, restitution of such payment is the appropriate remedy.[379] Similarly, where the relief sought is damages, the exception is inapplicable because the exception is based on allowing the party who has taken possession and made valuable improvements to seek equitable relief, i.e., specific performance of the contract.[380] The making of valuable improvements is often viewed as having special significance in terms of part performance.[381]

The reliance of a party in taking possession of the land and making valuable improvements serves the evidentiary function of the statute of frauds. Such reliance should not go unremedied.[382] Detrimental reliance sufficient to remove a contract from the statute of frauds may also be discovered in acts other than the taking of possession and the making of valuable improvements to the land.[383] There can be no doubt that courts are primarily concerned with the protection of promisees who justifiably rely upon oral promises, though they may resort to a less than precise "part performance" characterization, rather than a direct application of detrimental reliance.[384] More recent cases may focus on reliance, alone. Where an owner orally extended an option to purchase property to allow the tenant to complete improvements

---

[376] Amato v. United States, 94 F. Supp. 2d 1081, 1085 (D. Idaho 1999); Weston v. Donnelly, 927 F.2d 369, 372 (8th Cir. 1991). The classic case is Seavey v. Drake, 62 N.H. 393 (1882), generally viewed as an antecedent of the modern doctrine of detrimental reliance (promissory estoppel). Detrimental reliance is not only an effective validation device. It may also be an effective device to satisfy the statute of frauds.

[377] Cain v. Cross, 293 Ill. App. 3d 255, 687 N. E. 2d 1141 (5th Dist. 1997).

[378] RESTATEMENT 2d § 129 comment a which "restates what is widely known as the 'part performance doctrine' " into a reliance doctrine which is more precise since acts such as taking possession and making valuable improvements when the contract does not provide for such conduct is not "part performance." See Owens v. M. E. Schepp Partnership, 218 Ariz. 222, 226, 182 P. 3d 664, 668 (2008). Thus, *reliance* is a more accurate rationale for these holdings. Section 129 is a particular application of the generic Section 139 of the RESTATEMENT 2d that recognizes a promissory estoppel (detrimental reliance) analysis to satisfy any provision of the statute of frauds. We will explore § 139 later in this chapter. For a case discussing the application of §§ 129 and 139 to a contract for the sale of land involving reliance, see Town of Rutland v. City of Rutland, 743 A.2d 585, 591 note 2 (Vt. 1999).

[379] *See* Zipper v. Health Midwest, 978 S.W.2d 398 (Mo. Ct. App. 1998) (refusing to find an application of promissory estoppel because the requirement that injustice can be avoided only by enforcing the promise is absent where a down payment can be restored through a remedy in restitution).

[380] *See Cain v. Cross*, note 371 *supra.* RESTATEMENT 2d § 129, comment c.

[381] *See* Breen v. Phelps, 186 Conn. 86, 439 A.2d 1066, 1073 (1982).

[382] RESTATEMENT 2d § 129 comment b. See Pendleton v. King, 55 Ill. App. 3d 1, 4, 370 N.E.2d 590, 592 (5th Dist. 1977), recognizing that when a party makes improvements on the land or changes the property in some way, he does so in reliance on the oral agreement.

[383] See Chapman v. Bomann, 381 A.2d 1123 (Me. 1978), where the court held that a promise to make a memorandum sufficient to satisfy the land contract provision of the statute of frauds may, if relied upon, create a promissory estoppel to bar the assertion of the statute.

[384] *See* RESTATEMENT 2d § 129, comment a. See also Dunham v. Dunham, 204 Conn. 303, 528 A.2d 1123, 1130 (1987),

on a part of the property to be leased so that the tenant could purchase the property and make monthly payments, the court held that the tenant's reliance required specific performance notwithstanding the statute of frauds.[385]

[C]   Part Performance of Contracts for the Sale of Goods — Uniform Commercial Code

Section 17 of the original Statute of Frauds required contracts for the sale of goods for the price of ten pounds sterling or more to be evidenced by a writing *unless* the buyer received and accepted *part* of the goods or gave "something in earnest to bind the bargain, or in *part* of payment. . . ."[386] Thus, part performance in terms of receipt and acceptance of the goods or in the form of part payment or giving something in earnest would allow a court to enforce an oral contract for the sale of goods. As to the latter exception, Professor Corbin emphasizes the difference between giving "something in earnest to bind the bargain" and "part of payment," i.e., the former is not part of the purchase price as is the latter. Rather, giving something in earnest to bind the bargain may refer to the payment of a token sum, apart from the purchase price, or the delivery of a chattel of some value, either of which would serve an evidentiary function so as to permit a court or jury to find that an alleged oral contract was made.[387] Whether the payment of money in a given situation was intended as giving something in earnest or payment of part of the purchase price would be determined by oral testimony. The Uniform Sales Act, which was widely enacted throughout the United States, continued the part performance exceptions to the writing requirement for a sale-of-goods contract.[388] They have been substantially modified, however, under the UCC.[389]

The most significant UCC modification is the change from enforcement of the entire contract through part performance to enforcement of the oral contract only to the extent of part performance.[390] The Code views receipt and acceptance of the goods or the price of the goods as "unambiguous overt admission[s] by both parties that a contract actually exists."[391] But, '[p]artial performance' as a substitute for the required memorandum can validate the contract only for the goods which have been accepted or for which payment has been made and accepted."[392] While the Code has generally liberalized the statute of frauds, the part performance exception has been tightened to reflect consistency with other provisions throughout § 2-201. Thus, if there is a writing evidencing the parties' contract for the sale of

---

where the court deals with the "part performance" exception and emphasizes the RESTATEMENT 2d § 129 requirement of "reasonable reliance *on the contract.*"

[385] See, e. g., Sytchov v. Eon, 2006 Mass. Super. LEXIS 555 (2006).

[386] 29 Car. II, ch. 3 [1677] (emphasis added).

[387] "The legislature did not mean to require great formality in the sale transactions of everyday business; it meant only to require some objective evidential factor to supplement oral testimony. . . ." 2 CORBIN § 494, at 662–63.

[388] Uniform Sales Act § 4.

[389] *See In re* Augustin Bros. Co., 460 F.2d 376 (8th Cir. 1972); Cohn v. Fisher, 118 N.J. Super. 286, 287 A.2d 222 (1972).

[390] UCC § 2-201(3)(c).

[391] UCC § 2-201 comment 2. *See* Allied Wire Prods., Inc. v. Marketing Techniques, Inc., 99 Ill. App. 3d 29, 424 N.E.2d 1288 (1st Dist. 1981).

[392] *Id. See* Del Hayes & Sons v. Mitchell, 304 Minn. 275, 230 N.W.2d 588 (1975), and Bagby Land & Cattle Co. v. California Livestock Com. Co., 439 F.2d 315 (5th Cir. 1971) (enforceability only with respect to goods received and accepted); *In re* Augustin Bros. Co., 460 F.2d 376 (8th Cir. 1972) (enforcement only to the extent of part payment).

goods, the necessary quantity "need not be accurately stated but recovery is limited to the amount stated."[393] Similarly, if there is no writing but the party sought to be charged admits in his pleading, testimony or otherwise in court that he made the contract alleged by the plaintiff, the contract is enforceable only to the extent of the admission.[394] There is simply no evidentiary basis for enforcing an oral agreement beyond the quantity admitted, or stated in the memorandum, or received and accepted, or the quantity for which payment has been made and accepted. Unlike part performance of a contract for the sale of land, however, there is no requirement that the performance be "unequivocally referable" to the oral agreement.[395] An understanding of this part performance concept under the UCC is aided by separate exploration of receipt and acceptance of goods followed by an exploration of receipt and acceptance of *payment.*

[1]   Receipt and Acceptance of Goods

Prior to the UCC, it was generally agreed that "receipt" dealt with possession of the goods, whereas "acceptance" related to title to the goods.[396] While the concept of "receipt" has remained virtually unchanged under the UCC, one of the radical changes effected by the Code was the emasculation of "title" as an analytical tool.[397] Thus, the concept of "acceptance" under the Code has undergone a marked change and is no longer related to "title." We begin our exploration with the concept of "receipt."

Courts have dealt with the concept of "receipt" in essentially the same fashion before and after the enactment of the UCC. The goods must have been "actually received" in the sense that actual possession, or the immediate right to possession, of part or all of the goods, with the seller's consent, must have occurred.[398] Moreover, the buyer need not have received the goods

---

[393] UCC § 2-201 comment 1.

[394] UCC § 2-201(3)(b) states that, in the case of such an admission, "the contract is not enforceable . . . beyond the quantity of goods admitted. . . ." *See* § 76 *supra.*

[395] *See* Hofmann v. Stoller, 320 N.W.2d 786 (N.D. 1982); West Cent. Packing, Inc. v. A. F. Murch Co., 109 Mich. App. 493, 311 N.W.2d 404 (1981).

[396] *See* United States Rubber Co. v. Bercher's Royal Tire Serv., Inc., 205 F. Supp. 368 (W.D. Ark. 1962); Gordy v. Leonard, 113 Conn. 760, 155 A. 67 (1931).

[397] Sales law under the UCC is essentially contract law, rather than property law that relies heavily upon the title concept. A cogent example is the allocation of risk of loss for goods to be delivered by an independent carrier lost or damaged during transit. UCC § 2-509(1)(a) and (b) allocate the risk between buyer and seller on the basis of the contract term, i.e., either an FOB "shipment" or "destination" contract. The UCC philosophy with respect to the title concept is best expressed in a comment to § 2-101: "The arrangement of the present Article [2] is in terms of *contract for sale* and the various steps of its performance. The legal consequences are stated as following directly *from the contract* and action taken under it without resorting to the idea of when property or title passed or was to pass as being the determining factor. The purpose is to avoid making practical issues between practical men turn upon the location of an intangible something, the passing of which no man can prove by evidence and to substitute for such abstractions proof of words and actions of a tangible character" (emphasis supplied). See also Martin v. Melland's, Inc., 283 N.W.2d 76 (N.D. 1979), where the court indicates that the risk of loss is determined not by title but by contract. The court also refers to § 2-401 of the Code which does provide rules for the passage of title. That section is not designed as an analytical tool for Article 2 of the Code, however. Rather, it was inserted to deal with extra-Code issues involving criminal law, taxation, and public regulation, as well as questions of "ownership" which may arise beyond the Code in such matters as liability insurance coverage.

[398] In Hofmann v. Stoller, 320 N.W.2d 786 (N.D. 1982), the court suggests that "receipt" requires the goods to change possession, while "acceptance" contemplates unilateral action on the part of the buyer. *See* the discussion of "acceptance" later in this subsection. UCC § 2-103(1)(c) defines "receipt" of goods as taking physical possession of them.

himself, i.e., if they have been delivered to a third party at the direction of the buyer, the buyer will be said to have received them.[399] Receipt alone, however, without acceptance is insufficient.[400]

Acceptance. There are three ways in which goods will be said to have been accepted under the UCC.[401] The obvious method of acceptance under the UCC is the buyer's conduct with respect to the goods, i.e., treating the goods in a fashion inconsistent with the seller's ownership.[402] If a buyer has received the goods and begins to use them, the statute of frauds will be satisfied with respect to the goods which the buyer has, in effect, treated as his own since he will be said to have accepted such goods.[403] The least obvious method occurs where the buyer receives the goods and, after a reasonable opportunity to inspect, "signifies" to the seller either that the goods are conforming or that the buyer will retain them despite their nonconformity; this manifestation of the buyer's intention constitutes acceptance.[404] The third method of acceptance occurs through inaction and silence by a purchaser who is in possession of the seller's goods.[405] With certain exceptions,[406] a buyer may reject goods for *any* nonconformity of the goods or their tender.[407] The buyer, however, must have a reasonable opportunity to inspect the goods before deciding upon acceptance or rejection.[408] If the buyer

---

[399] Pre-Code cases include Houghton & Dutton Co. v. Journal Engraving Co., 241 Mass. 541, 135 N.E. 688 (1922); Cuask v. Robinson, 1 B. & S. 209 [1861]. UCC cases include Allied Wire Prods., Inc. v. Marketing Techniques, Inc., 99 Ill. App. 3d 29, 424 N.E.2d 1288 (1st Dist. 1981); Jim & Slim's Tool Supply, Inc. v. Metro Communities Corp., 328 So. 2d 213 (Fla. Dist. Ct. App. 1976); Double R Enters. v. Sappie, 11 Pa. D. & C.3d 56 (1978). Under the pre-Code law, courts would not recognize the "receipt and acceptance" exception to the normal requirement of a writing if the seller retained a lien on the goods. *See, e.g.*, E.A. Clark & Co. v. D. & C. E. Scribner Co., 122 Me. 418, 120 A. 609 (1923). This was so even though legal title to the goods had already vested in the buyer. Rodgers v. Jones, 129 Mass. 420 (1880). Under the UCC, however, there is no preclusion of the "receipt and acceptance" exception of § 2-201(3)(c) simply because the seller or another has retained a security interest in the goods under Article 9 of the Code. It is conceivable that a seller would have an attached security interest in goods which, except for possessory security interests, requires a written security agreement, § 9-203(1)(a), that would not satisfy the memorandum requirement of § 2-201 because, e.g., it failed to state a quantity term. Thus, an Article 2 statute of frauds issue could be raised. If all or a portion of the goods were received and accepted by the purchaser or a third party at his direction, however, § 2-201(3)(c) would remove the statute of frauds as a bar to enforcement to the extent of the goods received and accepted.

[400] *In re* Estate of Nelsen, 209 Neb. 730, 311 N.W.2d 508 (1981).

[401] UCC § 2-606.

[402] UCC § 2-606(1)(c).

[403] *See, e.g.*, Johnson v. Holdrege Coop. Equity Exch., 206 Neb. 568, 293 N.W.2d 863 (1980) (commingling seller's goods with buyer's own goods).

[404] UCC § 2-606(1)(a). It is important to note comment 3 to § 2-606, which emphasizes that the act of "payment" after tender of the goods is "one circumstance tending to signify acceptance of the goods but in itself can never be more than one circumstance and is not conclusive. Also, a conditional communication of acceptance always remains subject to its expressed conditions."

[405] For a brief discussion of UCC § 2-606(1)(a) and (b), see Plateq Corp. of North Haven v. Machlett Labs., 189 Conn. 433, 456 A.2d 786, 789 (1983).

[406] UCC § 2-601 excludes contrary agreements by the parties or installment contracts (UCC § 2-612). The right to reject or, as it sometimes called, the "perfect tender" rule is also subject to the seller's right to "cure," i.e., make a perfect tender within the time permitted under the contract (§ 2-508) as well as the pervasive requirement of good faith.

[407] UCC § 2-601.

[408] The buyer's right to inspection is found in UCC § 2-513(1), which states, in pertinent part, ". . . the buyer has a right before payment or acceptance to inspect them. . . ." Even this right is subject to contrary agreement because the subsection begins, "Unless otherwise agreed. . . ." One of the examples of parties agreeing that the buyer will pay the price before acceptance is the "C. O. D." (cash on delivery) contract recognized expressly in § 2-513(3)(a).

chooses to ignore the right to inspect and simply permits the goods to remain in his possession beyond the reasonable time for inspection, the buyer will be said to have accepted the goods.[409] If the buyer's attempt at rejection is ineffective, it will be treated in the same fashion, i.e., as if he had made no rejection with the reasonable time permitted for rejection.[410] Thus, failure to make an effective rejection constitutes acceptance and, together with the prior receipt of the goods, will serve to satisfy the statute of frauds with respect to the goods received and accepted.[411]

If the buyer has not only received and accepted goods shipped by the seller but has also paid the seller who has accepted the payment, the conduct of the parties has provided ample evidence of the contract and no writing is needed to make it enforceable.[412]

[2]   Receipt and Acceptance of Payment — the Indivisible Unit

Prior to the UCC, questions as to what constituted part payment to satisfy the statute of frauds as it related to a contract for the sale of goods were not particularly troublesome. The payment need not have been made in money, i.e., the delivery of anything of value as part of the agreed price or exchange for the goods would suffice. Thus, in a contract for the sale of corn, the buyer's delivery and seller's acceptance of sacks in which the corn was to be put and which the parties had agreed would constitute part of the price was held to be sufficient to satisfy the statute if the allegation could be established by the evidence.[413] Where the buyer of hay baled the hay at his own expense pursuant to the agreement with the seller, the buyer's work was considered to be part payment which satisfied the statute of frauds to make the agreement for the purchase and sale of hay enforceable.[414] It must be remembered that part performance under the pre-UCC statute of frauds took the entire contract out of the statute, rather than making the contract enforceable only to the extent of the part performance, as the UCC directs for reasons explored earlier in this section. Pre-Code cases also required the actual transfer of something of value-a benefit-to the seller. Thus, a surrender of a job, though a bargained-for detriment, was insufficient part performance to make the contract enforceable.[415]

Other questions concerning part performance by payment were troublesome to pre-Code courts. Thus, whether the taking of a check before it was cashed[416] or whether the buyer's

---

[409] UCC § 2-606(1)(b).

[410] UCC § 2-606(1)(b). Typically, a rejection is ineffective because it fails to meet the requirements of § 2-602, requiring the rejection to be within a reasonable time and also requiring the buyer to "seasonably notify" the seller. Since the buyer is only required to notify the seller, i.e., there is no requirement that the seller receive the notice, pursuant to the definition of "notifies" in § 1-201(26), the notice need only be sent through a proper medium for which the proper fee (e.g., postage) is paid, and the correct address should appear. The risk of transmission is on the seller with respect to the rejection notice.

[411] See, e.g., Alarm Device Mfg. Co. v. Arnold Indus., Inc., 65 Ohio App. 2d 256, 417 N.E.2d 1284 (1979).

[412] See TCP Indus., Inc. v. Uniroyal, Inc., 661 F.2d 542 (6th Cir. 1981); Alabama Great S. Ry. Co. v. McVay, 381 So. 2d 607 (Miss. 1980).

[413] Weir v. Hudnut, 115 Ind. 525, 18 N.E. 24 (1888).

[414] Conway v. Marachowsky, 262 Wis. 540, 55 N.W.2d 909 (1952). See also Driggs v. Bush, 152 Mich. 53, 115 N.W. 985 (1908).

[415] Patterson v. Beard, 227 Iowa 401, 288 N.W. 414 (1939). Annot., 125 A.L.R. 399 (1940).

[416] Some courts suggested that, if the check were accepted as a present discharge of the seller's claim for the price of the goods or some part thereof, the statute was satisfied. See, e.g., Dutton v. Bennett, 256 Mass. 397, 152 N.E. 621

agreement to accept goods in complete or partial satisfaction of an existing obligation owed by the seller to the buyer constituted "payment" were troublesome. An older English case, obiter, said that if the buyer had accepted the promise to deliver goods as a present discharge of the pre-existing obligation (an accord and satisfaction), it constituted "payment."[417] There was support for this view in some American courts,[418] though others concluded that such evidence was precisely the kind of "say-so" evidence of the parties that the statute was designed to prevent.[419] Another problem was the timing of the part payment, i.e., was it sufficient if the payment was received and accepted at any time prior to the commencement of litigation as some courts held,[420] or did the statute specify that the payment must be made at the time of the formation of the oral contract? Some statutes were so drafted prior to the adoption of the predecessor to the Code, the Uniform Sales Act, and, under such statutes, payment at a time later than the time of contract formation would not suffice.[421]

Against this background, the major UCC change is, again, the limitation of enforceability to the extent of the part payment[422] which immediately suggests the problem of the *indivisible* unit. A comment suggests that with respect to receipt and acceptance of goods or receipt and acceptance of payment for goods, a court must be able to make a just apportionment of the agreed price of any good actually delivered or "an apportionable part of the goods" with respect to the part payment made and accepted.[423] If part payment is to make a contract enforceable only to the extent of an apportionable part of the goods, what is to be done in the case of an indivisible item, such as an automobile, for which the buyer has made and seller has accepted a part payment? A strict reading of the Code section precludes enforcement of the contract to any extent and an early trial court so concluded: "The Code . . . makes an important change by denying the enforcement of the contract where in the case of a single object the payment made is less than the full amount."[424] There is no longer any doubt that this initial interpretation was unduly restrictive as evidenced by the holdings of numerous courts that the oversight by the Code drafters would be resolved in favor of a liberal interpretation where the goods could not be apportioned as, again, in the example of the automobile.[425] If apportionment

---

(1926); Coffman v. Fleming, 301 Mo. 313, 256 S.W. 731 (1923); Summers v. Wood, 131 Ark. 345, 198 S.W. 692 (1917). If, however, there was no affirmative evidence to establish such an understanding, the usual presumption applied, i.e., that the claim for the price was not discharged until the check had been cashed. Thus, a number of courts provided the logical and technically correct position, i.e., that "payment" had not occurred. *See, e.g.*, Gay v. Sundquist, 42 S.D. 327, 175 N.W. 190 (1919); Bates v. Dwinell, 101 Neb. 712, 164 N.W. 722 (1917). A few courts, however, took the position that the statute should be satisfied by giving a check. *See, e.g.*, Logan v. Carroll, 72 Mo. App. 613 (1897); McLure v. Sherman, 70 F. 190 (C.C.D. Mont. 1895).

[417] Walker v. Nussey, 16 M. & W. 302 [1847].

[418] *See, e.g.*, Roberts v. Williams, 6 Wash. 2d 599, 108 P.2d 334 (1940) (buyer's deposit of money with seller in connection with an offer later withdrawn constituted payment and acceptance with respect to a new agreement where the parties understood the money in seller's possession to apply to the purchase price). *See also* Dow v. Worthen, 37 Vt. 108 (1864).

[419] *See* Scott v. Mundy & Scott, 193 Iowa 1360, 188 N.W. 972 (1922).

[420] *See, e.g.*, United States Rubber Co. v. Bercher's Royal Tire Serv., Inc., 205 F. Supp. 368 (W.D. Ark. 1962); Dean v. W.S. Given Co., 123 Me. 90, 121 A. 644 (1923).

[421] *See, e.g.*, Jackson v. Tupper, 101 N.Y. 515, 5 N.E. 65 (1886).

[422] UCC § 2-201(3)(c).

[423] UCC § 2-201 comment 2.

[424] Williamson v. Martz, 11 Pa. D. & C.2d 33, 35 (1956).

[425] *See, e.g.*, The Press, Inc. v. Fins & Feathers Pub. Co., 361 N.W.2d 171 (Minn. Ct. App. 1985); Morris v. Perkins Chevrolet, Inc., 663 S.W.2d 785 (Mo. Ct. App. 1984); Sedmak v. Charlie's Chevrolet, Inc., 622 S.W.2d 694 (Mo. Ct. App.

is possible, however, the part payment continues to take the contract out of the statute of frauds only to the extent of the part payment.[426]

The part payment must not only be made, it must be accepted.[427] In the case of payment by check, however, the UCC provision has fared no better that its common law ancestors. The case law is sparse on this issue, with some courts suggesting that the check must be cashed,[428] while others find that a check, albeit conditional payment which is subject to defeat if dishonored,[429] still constitutes payment.[430] Certainly, if the check has been negotiated or presented to the drawee for payment, the payment has been accepted even where the drawee refuses to pay the instrument by honoring a stop payment order. In such a case, the seller has still manifested its intention to accept the payment by presenting the check for payment.[431] The fact that the check has been dishonored is irrelevant since the instrument and the underlying obligation it represents can be enforced. The requirement that the payment be "accepted" certainly does not mean that the *drawee* (third party) of the check must have accepted payment upon presentment of the instrument. If a seller received payment via check and had every intention of cashing it but lost it, he nonetheless should be said to have "accepted" the check as payment. If the recipient of the check treats it as his own, he should be said to have accepted it.

Where payment is in the form of goods or services, it has been held that the goods or services must not only be received but accepted to satisfy the statute of frauds.[432] Where funds are deposited with a third party escrow agent, it has been held that payment has not been made and accepted.[433]

1981); Paloukos v. Intermountain Chevrolet Co., 99 Idaho 740, 588 P.2d 939 (1978); Thomaier v. Hoffman Chevrolet, Inc., 64 A.D.2d 492, 410 N.Y.S.2d 645 (2d Dep't 1978); Lockwood v. Smigel, 18 Cal. App. 3d 800, 96 Cal. Rptr. 289 (2d Dist. 1971).

[426] *See, e.g.*, Seven Seas Trading co. v. Nan Hong Farm, 1997 U.S. Dist. LEXIS 9290 (S.D.N.Y. June 27, 1997); *In re* Augustin Bros. Co., 460 F.2d 376 (8th Cir. 1972).

[427] UCC § 2-201 comment 2.

[428] *See* Integrity Material Handling Sys., Inc. v. Deluxe Corp., 317 N.J. Super. 406, 417, 722 A.2d 552, 557 (App. Div. 1999), where the court found insufficient evidence that a down payment was "accepted" since the check was never cashed nor submitted for negotiation. *See also* Nelson v. Hy-Grade Constr. & Materials, Inc., 215 Kan. 631, 527 P.2d 1059 (1974).

[429] UCC § 2-511(3).

[430] See Kaufman v. Solomon, 524 F.2d 501 (3d Cir. 1975), where a check was held for 30 days without being cashed or negotiated and the court recognized that it may have been "accepted." *Inter alia*, the court recognized that a check was considered payment under the Uniform Sales Act (citing cases) and UCC § 2-511(2) states that tender of payment is sufficient if made in any manner current in the ordinary course of business. *See also* Uni-Products, Inc. v. Bearse, 153 B. R. 774, 772 (Bankr. E.D. Mich. 1993).

[431] *See* Miller v. Wooters, 131 Ill. App. 3d 682, 476 N.E.2d 11 (5th Dist. 1985).

[432] UCC § 2-201 comment 2.

[433] Brenner v. Glosser, 29 Ill. App. 3d 395, 327 N.E.2d 87 (1975).

§ 78 ENFORCEMENT OF PART OF THE CONTRACT — MULTIPLE PROMISES

Where the contract contains one or more promises within the statute of frauds and one or more without the statute and the statute has not been satisfied, it has generally been held that the whole contract is unenforceable under the statute.[434] While there is nothing in the statute requiring this conclusion, any other result would be unjust in the normal case. The parties formed the contract on the assumption that all promises would be performed. It would, therefore, be unfair to enforce some of the promises if others are unenforceable since there is always the possibility that the promises that are outside the statute would not have been made if the parties understood that the remainder of the contract would not be enforced. The same analysis applies even though the contract is divisible, i.e., portions of the performances on each side are the agreed equivalents of performances on the other side,[435] and divisible portions of the performance on both sides are outside the statute.[436] Some courts have enforced divisible portions of contracts within the one year provision of the statute, however, though their analyses contain no suggestion that they could not be extended to other types of contracts within the statute.[437] It is at least plausible to suggest that these courts see no distinction between a contract that is divisible into agreed equivalents and separate contracts. If the parties have, in fact, made separate contracts, the statute of frauds does not prevent a court from enforcing the contracts that are outside the statute while refusing to enforce those within the statute. Whether the parties have, in a given situation, made one divisible contract or separate contracts, however, can be a difficult question of interpretation.[438]

Another distinction must be made with respect to a contract that permits alternative performances. If, for example, a promisor may completely fulfill his contractual duty by either conveying real property or paying a sum of money, the promise to pay money is enforceable since it is outside the statute and, if performed, will discharge the duty of the promisor.[439] This distinction should be viewed in the context of a broader principle recognized by the RESTATEMENT 2d, i.e., where part of a contract within the statute of frauds is exclusively beneficial to the party seeking enforcement, he may enforce that part if he agrees to forego the

---

[434] *See* RESTATEMENT 2d § 147(3). *See also* Paley v. Ogus, 1994 U.S. App. LEXIS 36461 (D.C. Cir. Dec. 22, 1994); Fuller v. Apco Mfg. Co., 51 R.I. 378, 155 A. 351 (1931).

[435] *See* § 77 *supra.*

[436] *See* Hornady v. Plaza Realty Co., 437 So. 2d 591 (Ala. Civ. App. 1983).

[437] *See* Vanston v. Connecticut Gen. Life Ins. Co., 482 F.2d 337, 342 (5th Cir. 1973): "If the contract is severable-that is, susceptible of division and apportionment, having two or more parts not necessarily dependent on each other-the fact that one obligation is unenforceable does not prevent a recovery as to the other." *See also* Dickenson v. Dickenson Agency, Inc., 127 A.D.2d 983, 512 N.Y.S.2d 952 (4th Dep't 1987); Buttorf v. United Elec. Labs., 459 S.W.2d 581 (Ky. 1970); and Blue Valley Creamery Co. v. Consolidated Prods. Co., 81 F.2d 182 (8th Cir. 1936).

[438] The RESTATEMENT 2d suggests the following guide: "Whether an agreement creates a single contract or more than one for the present purpose, depends primarily on the terms of the agreement, the interdependence of its parts, and the possibility of apportioning the consideration on one side among several promises on the other without doing violence to the expectation of the parties." RESTATEMENT 2d § 147 comment c. It is interesting to compare this statement with the quotation from the *Vanston* case in the preceding note. The consideration in a divisible contract must be capable of being apportioned without doing violence to the expectation of the parties. Unlike separate contracts, however, an assumption that the parts of a divisible contract are not interdependent is typically unwarranted.

[439] *See* Chandler v. Doran Co., 44 Wash. 2d 396, 267 P.2d 907 (1954); Ward v. Ward, 94 Colo. 275, 30 P.2d 853 (1934); Welsh v. Welsh's Estate, 148 Minn. 235, 181 N.W. 356 (1921).

remainder of the contract.[440] Thus, a party may insist upon an alternative performance without the statute of frauds if he foregoes the alternative performance within the statute. Even where the performances are not alternative, however, the party seeking enforcement exclusively beneficial to himself may enforce the part without the statute while foregoing the part within the statute.[441]

Finally, if the promises within the statute of frauds have become enforceable or are discharged because they have been completely performed or legally excused, there is no harm in enforcing any unperformed promises outside the statute of frauds, i.e., they may be treated as if they were separate contracts.[442]

§ 79   RELIANCE TO AVOID THE STATUTE OF FRAUDS — ESTOPPEL

[A]   Equitable Estoppel

It has long been recognized that a party may be estopped from relying on the statute of frauds as a defense if the other party has reasonably and substantially relied on a misrepresentation or concealment of material facts. A so-called equitable estoppel arises where one party misrepresents or conceals material facts with the knowledge that her representations are untrue and where the other party is unaware of the misrepresentation or concealment and relies thereon to his detriment.[443] Thus, if a party misrepresents that she has signed a satisfactory memorandum evidencing an oral contract within the statute, she will be estopped to assert the statute as a defense.[444] Similarly, if a party misrepresents his intention to sign a memorandum satisfying the statute of frauds, he will be estopped from asserting the statute.[445] Absent evidence of such misrepresentation, however, the doctrine of equitable estoppel would not apply, regardless of substantial detrimental reliance by a promisee.[446] The application of the doctrine almost invariably compels a court to inveigh against the use of the statute of frauds to protect a fraud rather than prevent a fraud or similar exhortation.[447] As we noted in our exploration of "promissory estoppel," however,[448]

---

[440] RESTATEMENT 2d § 147(1). This subsection is expressly inapplicable to contracts for the transfer of property on the promisor's death on the footing that it would be contrary to the Statute of Wills and because of the availability of the remedy of restitution.

[441] In ill. 2 to § 147, the RESTATEMENT 2d suggests a promise by *A* to insure a shipment of *B*'s goods against casualty and to answer for certain defaults of the carrier. *B* pays a single premium in exchange for *A*'s promises. When the goods are damaged by fire, *B* may enforce the insurance coverage promise. The illustration is based on Mobile Marine Dock & Marine Ins. Co. v. McMillan & Son, 31 Ala. 711 (1858).

[442] RESTATEMENT 2d § 147(2). *See* Holt v. Katsanevas, 854 P.2d 575, 580 (Utah Ct. App. 1993).

[443] *See* Frantz v. Parke, 111 Idaho 1005, 729 P.2d 1068, 1073 (Ct. App. 1986). *See also* Ozier v. Haines, 411 Ill. 160, 103 N.E.2d 485 (1952) (suggesting that deceit on the part of the defendant must be shown).

[444] *See* FIRST RESTATEMENT § 178 comment f.

[445] Seymour v. Oelrichs, 156 Cal. 782, 106 P. 88 (1909).

[446] Ozier v. Haines, 411 Ill. 160, 103 N.E.2d 485 (1952).

[447] See, e.g., Lunning v. Land O'Lakes, 303 N.W.2d 452, 457 (1980), "Where an application of the Statute will protect, rather than prevent, a fraud, equity requires that the doctrine of equitable estoppel be applied." The most familiar suggestion is, "The purpose and intent of the Statute of Frauds is to prevent fraud, and not to aid in its perpetration." Dean v. Myers, 466 So. 2d 952, 955 (Ala. 1985) (quoting 73 Am. Jur. 2d *Statute of Frauds* § 562 (1974)).

[448] *See supra* § 67.

the suggestion that a party is "estopped" is hopelessly conclusory. The reason that one party is estopped is justifiable reliance by the other party. Just as the restrictions of equitable estoppel were removed to allow promissory estoppel to operate as a validation device in lieu of consideration, the development of promissory estoppel as a device to satisfy the statute of frauds proceeds apace. It is not difficult to discover a modern case treating equitable and promissory estoppel interchangeably to avoid the statute of frauds.[449] It is, however, more than premature to suggest the general acceptance of promissory estoppel as an alternate device to satisfy the statute.[450] As in other developing areas of our law, it is important to trace this development to the present time.

[B]   The Shift to Promissory Estoppel — RESTATEMENT 2d § 139

A landmark opinion written by Justice Roger Traynor for the Supreme Court of California provided the catalyst for the current development of reliance as a judicially engrafted device to satisfy the statute of frauds. In *Monarco v. Lo Greco*,[451] eighteen-year old Christie Lo Greco decided to leave the home of his mother and stepfather in quest of an independent living. They persuaded him to remain and participate in the family farm enterprise which was then valued at $4,000. They orally promised Christie that, if he stayed and worked, they would keep the property in joint tenancy so that it would pass to the survivor who would then leave it to Christie by will. Christie remained and worked diligently in the family venture, surrendering any opportunity for further education or other opportunity to accumulate his own property. He received only lodging and spending money. When he married, his mother told him that his wife should move in with the family. Mother then repeated the original promise that Christie would receive the property when she and her husband died. Two decades after the original promise to Christie, the value of the farm had increased to $100,000. Shortly before the stepfather died, he arranged conveyances to terminate the joint tenancy and executed a will leaving all his property to a grandson who received the property after probate and brought an action for partition, relying on the statute of frauds to defeat the oral promise on which Christie had relied for twenty years. Since no assurance had been made to Christie that he would be protected from the statute of frauds, the plaintiff argued that the doctrine of equitable estoppel should not apply. Writing for the Court, Justice Traynor emphasized precedent which applied the doctrine of estoppel to prevent fraud that would result from the refusal to enforce oral contracts in circumstances involving unconscionable injury to a relying promisee or unjust enrichment of the promisor. The opinion departed from the concept that estoppel can be based only on representations by a party that he will not rely upon the statute of frauds as a defense, or that he will execute a writing to satisfy the statute, or that a writing is not necessary. The opinion focused on unconscionable injury or unjust enrichment where the remedy of restitution would not be adequate, as in Christie's situation.[452] Where such injury and consequent unjust enrichment exists, Traynor suggested

---

[449] *See, e.g.*, Nygard v. Nygard, 156 Mich. App. 94, 401 N.W.2d 323 (1986).

[450] *See, e.g.*, Florida Power & Light Co. v. American Ltd. Corp., 511 So. 2d 1103 (Fla. Dist. Ct. App. 1987) (stating that promissory estoppel is not a valid bar to the statute of frauds).

[451] 35 Cal. 2d 621, 220 P.2d 737 (1950).

[452] There is considerable difficulty in measuring the benefit conferred by a member of the family who has devoted himself to an enterprise over a long period such as two decades. Recognizing that the work performed by someone in the position of Christie LoGreco was not in exchange for any wage but was, rather, a lifetime commitment to an enterprise he assumed he would own, the impossibility of adequately compensating such a person by way of restitutionary damages becomes clear.

that the representation requirements are ignored. Rather, courts should focus on the promise and the substantial reliance on that promise by the other party. Though the *Monarco* opinion clearly invited the application of a reliance device without the shackles of the traditional representation requirements of equitable estoppel, its emphasis upon unconscionable injury or unjust enrichment which could not be adequately remedied through restitution continues to operate as an effective deterrent to a general application of reliance as a satisfaction device.[453]

Another judicial opportunity appeared four years after *Monarco*. In *Alaska Airlines v. Stephenson*,[454] the plaintiff was permitted to take a leave of absence from his employment at Western Airlines without prejudice to his tenure to become general manager of the defendant, a new airline. When the six month leave was about to expire, the parties orally agreed that plaintiff would have a two year contract and that defendant would execute a writing evidencing the contract as soon as it obtained a certificate to operate the airline between Seattle and Alaska. Plaintiff had moved his family to Alaska and had relied by surrendering his tenure at Western. Though it obtained the certificate, defendant discharged the plaintiff. In holding the oral promise to be enforceable, the court was heavily influenced by a comment in the FIRST RESTATEMENT: ". . . [A] promise to make a memorandum, if similarly relied on, may give rise to an effective promissory estoppel if the Statute would otherwise operate to defraud."[455] Thus, the combination of a traditional element of equitable estoppel — an unperformed promise to make a memorandum — and the elements of promissory estoppel permitted enforcement of a contract violating the one-year provision of the statute of frauds.

These cases augured the application of a virtually unfettered promissory estoppel concept as a statute of frauds satisfaction device. The RESTATEMENT 2d confirmed that prophecy in a section that is virtually identical to the promissory estoppel section, § 90, except that it makes promises "enforceable notwithstanding the Statute of Frauds" rather than simply making them "binding" in the absence of other validation devices.[456] There is no requirement of unconscionable injury, unjust enrichment or an unperformed promise to execute a writing to satisfy the statute of frauds. There is, however, a separate subsection listing five "circumstances" that are "significant" in deciding whether injustice can be avoided only by

---

[453] *See, e.g.*, Phillippe v. Shapell Indus., 43 Cal. 3d 1247, 241 Cal. Rptr. 22, 743 P.2d 1279 (1987), *cert. denied*, 486 U.S. 1011, 108 S. Ct. 1742, 100 L. Ed. 2d 205 (1988). In Classic Cheesecake Co. v. JPMorgan Chase Bank, N. A., 546 F. 3d 839 (7th Cir.2008), the court rehearses Justice Traynor's *Monarco* analysis and compares it with requirements of "unjust and unconscionable injury and loss" required under Indiana law to avoid the statute of frauds.

[454] 217 F.2d 295 (9th Cir. 1954).

[455] FIRST RESTATEMENT § 178 comment f.

[456] RESTATEMENT 2d § 139(1) substitutes "enforceable notwithstanding the Statute of Frauds" for "binding" in § 90. The only other change is in the last sentence of both sections. Section 90 reads, "The remedy granted for breach *may be* limited as justice requires," while § 139(1) reads, "The remedy granted for breach *is to be* limited as justice requires." (emphasis added). The difference may appear to permit judicial discretion in § 90 as to an expectation or reliance interest remedy while § 139(1), on its face, may suggest that courts should be more willing to limit relief to the reliance interest. Comment d to § 139, however, belies this notion by suggesting, "In some cases, it may be appropriate to measure relief by the extent of the promisee's reliance rather than by the terms of the promise. *See* § 90 comment e and illustrations." Since comment e to § 90 deals with gratuitous promises to procure insurance, the § 139 comment reference is undoubtedly to comment d of § 90, which deals with partial enforcement. It should also be recalled that RESTATEMENT 2d § 129 provides for specific performance of an oral contract for the sale of land on a reliance basis. *See* § 77[B], *supra*. This is the modern form of the "part performance" doctrine discussed earlier in § 77[B]. See also RESTATEMENT 2d § 128, involving "part performance" in boundary and partition agreements. Comment a to § 139 suggests that §§ 128 and 129 are particular applications of the reliance principle to land contracts.

enforcing the oral promise notwithstanding the statute.[457]

While this creation of the RESTATEMENT 2d found support even in tentative draft form,[458] it has not been an unbridled success.[459] It is also possible to discover an analysis adhering to the views of Justice Traynor almost three decades ago.[460] Thus, a court refused to adopt the RESTATEMENT 2d position and, instead, adhered to the requirement of "an unjust and unconscionable injury and loss."[461] Other courts continue to be wary of taking a contract out of the statute of frauds through reliance absent some additional element of fraud or misrepresentation suggesting equitable estoppel.[462]

Though there is no general reliance exception to the UCC statute of frauds, it has not escaped this tendency which we now explore.

[C]   Reliance Satisfying the Uniform Commercial Code Statute of Frauds

A search for reliance as a method for satisfying the UCC Statute of Frauds begins with the "specially manufactured goods" subsection which we have already explored.[463] Where goods are not suitable for sale to others in the ordinary course of the seller's business and the seller, before notice of repudiation, has made either a substantial beginning of their manufacture or commitments for their procurement, such reliance will overcome the bar of the Statute of Frauds.[464] The question is whether a court should enlarge this very narrow reliance exception for specially manufactured goods to allow a general reliance exception for any kind of goods-

---

[457] RESTATEMENT 2d § 139(2) lists "(a) the availability and adequacy of other remedies, particularly cancellation and restitution; (b) the definite and substantial character of the action or forbearance in relation to the remedy sought; (c) the extent to which the action or forbearance corroborates evidence of the making and terms of the promise, or the making and terms are otherwise established by clear and convincing evidence; (d) the reasonableness of the action or forbearance; (e) the extent to which the action or forbearance was foreseeable by the promisor."

[458] *See, e.g.*, Warder & Lee Elevator, Inc. v. Britten, 274 N.W.2d 339 (Iowa 1979); Walker v. Ireton, 221 Kan. 314, 559 P.2d 340 (1977); McIntosh v. Murphy, 52 Haw. 29, 469 P.2d 177 (1970). But see Tanenbaum v. Biscayne Osteopathic Hosp., Inc., 190 So. 2d 777 (Fla. 1966), for an early rejection of this view.

[459] A case adopting RESTATEMENT 2d § 139 lists a few cases that have also adopted § 139 together with numerous cases that have implicitly and explicitly rejected it. *See* Alaska Democratic Party v. Rice, 934 P.2d 1313, 1316 note 2 (Alaska 1997) where the court adopted § 139, joining in New Mexico and Hawaii. Other jurisdictions, however, have also adopted § 139. See Kolkman v. Roth, 656 N. W. 2d 148 (Iowa 2003); Roussalis v. Wyoming Med. Ctr., Inc., 4 P.3d 209, 243 (Wyo. 2000), Cooper v. RE-MAX Wyandotte Cty. Real Estate, Inc., 241 Kan. 281, 736 P.2d 900 (1987) and Kiely v. St. Germain, 670 P. 2d 764 (Colo. 1983).See the discussion in Classic Cheesecake Co., Inc. v. JPMorgan Chase Bank N. A., 546 F. 3d 839 (7th Cir. 2008) where the court notes the express declination of § 139 by Indiana courts where an "estoppel" precluding the statute of frauds would be justified only through the infliction of unjust and unconscionable injury and loss.

[460] Where a contractor relied on the oral bid of subcontractor, the defendant was permitted to plead the statute of frauds since he was not unjustly enriched. *See* C. R. Fedrick, Inc. v. Borg-Warner Corp., 552 F.2d 852 (9th Cir. 1977).

[461] Whiteco Indus., Inc. v. Kopani, 514 N.E.2d 840, 845 (Ind. Ct. App. 1987).

[462] In Sawyer v. Mills, 295 S. W. 3d 79 (Ky. 2009), determining whether reliance could defeat the statute of frauds, the Supreme Court of Kentucky noted a statement in *Rivermont Inn, Inc. v. Bass Hotels & Resorts, Inc.*, 113 S. W. 3d 636, 642 (Ky. 2003), stating that promissory estoppel, alone, is insufficient to defeat the statute of frauds. Actual fraud must be proven. It also noted that the statement in *United Parcel Service Co. v. Rickert*, 996 S. W. 2d 464, 471 (Ky. 1999) that "the statute of frauds is not a bar to a fraud or promissory estoppel claim based on an oral promise of indefinite employment" was "dicta" since the decision turned on equitable estoppel involving fraud.

[463] *See* § 74[C][1], *supra*.

[464] UCC § 2-201(3)(a).

an exception akin to RESTATEMENT 2d § 139, discussed above.

As a matter of statutory construction, there are two substantial arguments opposing such a judicial enlargement. The Code drafters were certainly aware of the use of reliance as a device to satisfy the statute of frauds in lieu of a writing. The appearance of reliance exclusively in the specially manufactured goods context, suggests that reliance was to be limited to that narrow exception in contracts for the sale of goods. The intention to restrict it is expressly supported by the opening phrase of § 2-201 of the Code, "Except as otherwise provided in this section. . . ." In light of the Code's liberalization of the statute of frauds[465] and the normal constraints of statutory construction, restricting the exceptions to those stated in § 2-201 seems neither harsh nor unduly conservative. Some courts, however, have judicially engrafted a general reliance exception under § 2-201 on the basis of the UCC directive that principles of law not displaced by particular provisions of the Code shall supplement its provisions.[466] A substantial number of cases can be found on either side of this divide.[467] The courts refusing to add a general reliance exception typically emphasize the statutory construction arguments addressed above.[468] The courts accepting general reliance as an additional satisfaction device are not persuaded by the arguments of statutory construction and also seem to be heavily influenced by the need to recognize a promissory estoppel theory to satisfy the statute of frauds.[469]

Acceptance of a general reliance theory would make the narrow reliance exception concerning specially manufactured goods superfluous. Thus, if a seller has relied to his substantial detriment in manufacturing ordinary goods that it would not have otherwise made, a court accepting the general reliance device would hold the contract to be enforceable even though the goods are still suitable for sale to others in the seller's ordinary course of business. Similarly, if a general reliance device is judicially added to § 2-201, the concept of irrevocable waivers through oral modifications under UCC §§ 2-209(4) and 2-209(5) may also be superfluous.[470]

---

[465] The relaxation of pre-Code requirements include (1) the recognition of a frugal writing that only has to evidence an intention to make a contract, identify the parties (and not as buyer and seller), the goods, and the quantity term, (2) the effectiveness of a confirmation against a non-signing party in a deal between merchants, and (3) the admissions exception, which makes a contract enforceable to the extent of an admission made in pleadings, testimony, or otherwise in court. UCC §§ 2-201(1), (2), and (3)(b). As suggested earlier in this subsection, the specially manufactured goods exception has been enlarged to include non-manufacturer sellers, but tightened to require reliance in § 2-201(3)(a), and the part performance exception in § 2-201(3)(c) has been limited to make the contract enforceable only to the extent of the part performance.

[466] UCC § 1-103(b). The illustrative list of acceptable supplementary principles expressly mentions "estoppel."

[467] See Columbus Trade Exch., Inc. v. AMCA Int'l Corp., 763 F. Supp. 946 (S. D. Ohio 1991), listing cases taking either position.

[468] See, e.g., McDabco, Inc. v. Chet Adams Co., 548 F. Supp. 456 (D.S.C. 1982); Ivey's Plumbing & Elec. Co. v. Petrochem Maintenance, Inc., 463 F. Supp. 543 (N.D. Miss. 1978); Cox v. Cox, 292 Ala. 106, 289 So. 2d 609 (1974).

[469] See, e. g., Potter v. Hatter Farms, Inc., 56 Or. App. 254, 641 P.2d 628 (1982); Warder & Lee Elevator, Inc. v. Britten, 274 N.W.2d 339 (Iowa 1979); R. S. Bennett & Co. v. Economy Mech. Indus., Inc., 606 F.2d 182 (7th Cir. 1979); Robert Johnson Grain Co. v. Chemical Interchange Co., 541 F.2d 207 (8th Cir. 1976).

[470] See Murray, *The Modification Mystery: Section 2-209 of the Uniform Commercial Code*, 32 VILL. L. REV. 1, 42 (1987): "Thus, assuming the addition of a general reliance satisfaction device to § 2-201, the possibility of waiver under § 2-209(4) and (5) becomes academic." This thesis is based on the assumption that § 2-201 satisfaction devices would be effective in satisfying the requirements of § 2-209(2) involving no oral modification (NOM) clauses. See *supra* § 65[E][3].

[D]   The Future of the Statute of Frauds and Reliance

Any analysis concerning the future of a general reliance exception to the statute of frauds must be pursued in the context of the pervasive criticism of the statute in general by courts and commentators. As we have seen, the one-year provision is despised and the remaining provisions are anything but favored. There is a persistent reminder that, except for the land and suretyship provisions, the statute was repealed almost a half century ago in the country of its birth. Article 8 of the UCC dealing with investment securities has repealed the statute for transactions within its ambit as well as any one-year provision that might otherwise apply to such transactions. Early drafts of the proposed revision of Article 2 also repealed the statute and the one-year provision but, with some reluctance, a modified version of the statute was restored in a 1997 draft that included a general reliance exception. While that exception disappeared in later drafts, there is no doubt that considerable opposition to the continuation of the statute remains.

Notwithstanding the reservations of courts which currently reject the reliance concept as an alternate satisfaction device because the statutory language does not easily admit such judicial enlargement, the developments traced in this section augur a continuous evolution of detrimental reliance as a device that will avoid the statute of frauds. In the garb of "part performance" and "equitable estoppel," reliance has always been recognized as a significant basis for refusing to permit the statute to bar the enforcement of an oral contract. The recognition of promissory estoppel as a validation device at least equal to consideration suggested the strong concern for the protection of relying promisees. If such reliance can overcome technical constraints of classical contract law with respect to the validation of a promise, it should not seem remarkable that the same concept would be viewed as equally deserving of protection to overcome the infinitely more technical constraint called the statute of frauds.

§ 80   EFFECT OF FAILING TO COMPLY WITH THE STATUTE OF FRAUDS

[A]   Legal Operation of Statute — Language of the Statute — "Void," "Voidable," and "Unenforceable"

If an oral agreement is within one of the provisions of the statute of frauds, what effect does the statute have on that agreement? Does the statute preclude the agreement from recognition as a contract? If it is a contract, is it "void," "invalid," "voidable" or "unenforceable"? These and related questions have been confronted since the original Statute of Frauds was enacted. The fourth section of the original Statute states that no action shall be brought against the promisor absent a signed memorandum. Does this mean that any attempt to bring such an action will be regarded as a nullity? The seventeenth section (sale of goods) of the original Statute uses the words, "no contract shall be allowed to be good. . . ." Does this language suggest that there is or was a contract but it will be prevented from being valid or enforceable? Some statutes specify that a contract must fulfill the requirements of the statute to be "valid," i.e., if it fails to meet those requirements, it is "invalid." Still others prescribe that contracts failing to meet the statutory requirements "shall be void" or "are void." UCC § 2-201(1) states that a contract failing to comply with the statute of frauds provision "is not enforceable by way of action or defense." It is possible to discover different effect language attached to different provisions of a single statute of frauds.

It is important to recognize the significant differences that could flow from particular language in the statute. A so-called "void contract" is a contradiction. It was void *ab initio* and never had any legal effect. If a contract is "voidable," one party has a legal power — a power of avoidance or disaffirmance.[471] Where only one party to an oral contract has signed a sufficient memorandum that makes the contract enforceable against her, though she cannot enforce the contract against the non-signing party, it is less than accurate to suggest that the other non-signing party has a power of avoidance or disaffirmance. The non-signer need not bring an action on the contract, but if he does bring an action against the signer of the memorandum, the signer may raise any available defense on the contract though she could not have enforced the contract.[472] This is only one of many illustrations of the operative effect of a contract that will not be enforced because it is within the statute of frauds. Thus, even where a contract is unenforceable between the parties to it, a third party who allegedly induced one of the parties to breach the unenforceable contract may still be held liable by either party to the contract for tortious interference with that contract.[473] Where benefits have been conferred through the performance of one party to a contract within the statute of frauds, though the contract is unenforceable, it may be admitted as evidence of the understanding that the party conferring the benefit expected compensation as well as evidence of the value of the services.[474] There is considerable doubt that the drafters of the various statutes of fraud were interested in suggesting effects different from the original Statute. Apparently, they were attempting to duplicate the original Statute. The divergences in language have typically been glossed over and minimized by the courts.[475]

If, for example, a particular statute states that a contract failing to comply with its requirements will be "void," courts have generally displayed little difficulty in reading "void" as "unenforceable"[476] or at least "voidable."[477] Numerous cases insist that contracts failing to comply with the statute of frauds are "voidable" and not "void."[478] There is little precision among courts and lawyers in using the precise statutory term. In particular, the terms "void"

---

[471] *See supra* § 19.

[472] *See* Johnston v. Holiday Inns, Inc., 565 F.2d 790 (1st Cir. 1977). *See also* RESTATEMENT 2d § 140. There are a few decisions that would prevent the non-signer from successfully bringing an action against the signer on the footing that the signer received nothing in exchange for his signed promise, i.e., there would be no "mutuality of obligation." *See* Burg v. Betty Gay of Washington, Inc., 423 Pa. 485, 225 A.2d 85 (1966). This view is not generally accepted, however. Another court has held that an agreement to forego one's rights under an oral contract within the statute does not constitute consideration to support a counter promise. Fuller v. Apco Mfg. Co., 51 R.I. 378, 155 A. 351 (1931). This view is unsound since even forbearance to sue on an invalid claim constitutes consideration.

[473] Daugherty v. Kessler, 264 Md. 281, 286 A.2d 95 (1972). *See also* RESTATEMENT 2d § 144. Section 142 of the RESTATEMENT 2d illustrates how an unenforceable contract may include authority or consent to perform acts which would otherwise be tortious. Thus, an oral contract for the sale of land may include an understanding that the buyer would have an immediate license to enter the land. If the buyer went on the land, the contract would remain unenforceable, but the buyer would have a defense to the seller's action for trespass.

[474] *See* Rice v. Insurance & Bonds, Inc., 366 So. 2d 85 (Fla. Dist. Ct. App. 1979). RESTATEMENT 2d § 143.

[475] *See* Svoboda v. De Wald, 159 Neb. 594, 68 N.W.2d 178 (1955); Herring v. Volume Merchandise, Inc., 249 N.C. 221, 106 S.E.2d 197 (1958).

[476] *See, e.g.,* Country Corner Food & Drug, Inc. v. Reiss, 22 Ark. App. 222, 737 S.W.2d 672 (1987) (equating "void" with "unenforceable"). *See also* Montanaro Bros. Builders, Inc. v. Snow, 4 Conn. App. 46, 492 A.2d 233 (1985).

[477] Korff v. Pica Graphics, Inc., 121 A.D.2d 511, 504 N.Y.S.2d 17 (2d Dep't 1986).

[478] See, e. g., Countrywide Home Loans, Inc. v. Brown, 223 Fed. Appx. 13 (2d Cir. 2007); Cain v. Cross, 293 Ill. App. 3d 255, 258, 687 N. E. 2d 1141, 1143 (1997).

and "unenforceable" are often used interchangeably.[479] The Second Restatement of Contracts suggests that statutes of frauds are generally interpreted to mean that a contract failing to comply with its provisions is "unenforceable."[480] Under this interpretation, it is clear that a contract which can be effective for many other purposes exists, though it cannot be enforced by one or both parties to the contract.[481]

[B]   Pleading the Statute as a Defense

If the statute of frauds is viewed as a defense to an otherwise enforceable contract and the defendant does not raise the statute as a defense, a contract that is otherwise established by the plaintiff should be enforceable. Thus, the statute must be pleaded as an affirmative defense[482] and failure to do so will constitute a waiver of the defense.[483] Such pleading is required even where the applicable statutory language indicates that a contract failing to comply with the statute shall be "void" since courts do not view contracts that fail to meet the statutory requirements as void. Again, such contracts are unenforceable. Older cases that permitted the statute to be raised by a general denial were simply reflecting the outmoded view that a failure to meet the requirements of the statute compels the holding that no contract ever existed, i.e., the so-called contract was void *ab initio*.[484] Since the statute is an affirmative defense, it will not be permitted to be raised for the first time on appeal.[485]

Current issues concerning how the statute is pleaded concern the "admission" exception, i.e., whether the statute can be raised via a demurrer, motion to dismiss or summary judgment without admitting or denying that the contract was made. These issues have been explored in a previous section.[486]

---

[479] In Capital Dev. Co. v. Port of Astoria, 109 F.3d 516, 518 (9th Cir. 1997), the court states, "The district court held that the lease therefore did not comport with the requirements of the Oregon Statute of Frauds, and was thus void or voidable and unenforceable."

[480] RESTATEMENT 2d § 138.

[481] *See* Pike v. SEC, 1995 U.S. App. LEXIS 8924, at *6 (D.C. Cir. Apr. 4, 1995): "Even contracts that fall within a statute of frauds create legal obligations; they are not void or even voidable but only unenforceable in most circumstances."

[482] The cases are legion that characterize the statute of frauds as an affirmative defense. *See, e.g.*, Parker v. Shecut, 340 S.C. 460, 531 S.E.2d 546, 561 (Ct. App. 2000) ("Affirmative defenses, such as the statute of frauds, must be set forth in a responsive pleading."). *See also* Gerstacker v. Blum Consulting Eng'rs, Inc. 884 S.W.2d 845, 849 (Tex. App. Dallas. 1994).

[483] *See, e.g.*, Woolridge v. Newman, 2000 Ohio App. LEXIS 2733, at *4 (Ohio Ct. App. June 8, 2000) ("the failure to plead the statute of frauds as an affirmative defense constitutes a waiver of that defense.") *See also* AM Cosmetics, Inc. v. Solomon, 67 F. Supp. 2d 312, 319 (S.D.N.Y. 1999); Majewski v. Cantrell, 293 Ark. 360, 737 S.W.2d 649 (1987); Hubbard v. Peairs, 24 Mass. App. Ct. 372, 509 N.E.2d 41 (1987); Brown v. Brown, 744 P.2d 333 (Utah Ct. App. 1987); Good v. Hansen, 110 Idaho 953, 719 P.2d 1213 (Ct. App. 1986); McCracken v. Olson Cos., 149 Ill. App. 3d 104, 500 N.E.2d 487 (1st Dist. 1986); Marcoux v. Marcoux, 123 A.D.2d 844, 507 N.Y.S.2d 458 (2d Dep't 1986); Altomare v. Altomare, 355 Pa. Super. 391, 513 A.2d 486 (1986); Baudanza v. Mood, 496 A.2d 310 (Me. 1985).

[484] *See, e.g.*, Bruder v. Wolpert, 178 Minn. 330, 227 N.W. 46 (1929); Jordan v. Greensboro Furnace Co., 126 N.C. 143, 35 S.E. 247 (1900).

[485] See cases cited *supra* note 475.

[486] *See* § 76 *supra*.

§ 81   RESTITUTION IN UNENFORCEABLE CONTRACTS

[A]   The Concept of Restitution — Applied to Part Performance Under a Contract Unenforceable Because of the Statute of Frauds

The interest normally protected in the law of contracts is the expectation interest, so as to place the injured party in the position he would have been in had the contract been performed. Two other interests are also recognized: the reliance interest to compensate the injured party for his loss or minus quantity suffered in reliance on a promise, and the restitution interest which compensates the injured party for losses sustained through the unjust enrichment of another. Both restitution and reliance differ from the expectation interest in that they seek to restore the injured party to *status quo ante*, i.e., the position he was in before the reliance or unjust enrichment as contrasted with placing the injured party in the *future* position he would have been in had his expectation been fulfilled. Restitution differs from reliance in that the former is concerned with a plus quantity (the unjust enrichment or benefit conferred upon the other party) at the expense of the party conferring the benefit (the minus quantity), whereas reliance is concerned only with the minus quantity, i.e., the loss suffered by the relying party. Each of these interests are explored in a subsequent chapter dealing with contract remedies[487] and we have already explored the reliance interest in connection with promissory estoppel in a prior chapter.[488] As will be seen in the exploration of remedies, the restitution interest may be protected in lieu of the expectation or reliance interest where the defendant has breached the contract.[489] The restitution interest, however, may also be protected where no enforceable contract exists, i.e., the plaintiff may recover the amount of the unjust enrichment in quasi contract.[490] It is not remarkable that our courts would look quite favorably upon the avoidance of unjust enrichment since it suggests a stronger claim to protection than either the expectation or reliance interest.[491]

With this brief background, it is appropriate to consider the plight of a party who has conferred a benefit upon another party by performing part of a contract that turns out to be unenforceable under the statute of frauds. On the assumption that the contract is not enforceable even to the extent of part performance,[492] the tension is between allowing a party to be unjustly enriched at the expense of another and undermining the statute of frauds. In an action to recover the reasonable value of the benefit conferred where the statute precluded

---

[487] *See infra* Chapter 9.

[488] *See supra* § 78.

[489] *See, e.g.*, Bausch & Lomb v. Bressler, 977 F.2d 720 (2d Cir. 1992) (plaintiff may elect to recover restitutionary damages for breach of contract). This concept will be explored *infra* in Chapter 9.

[490] See, e.g., Anderson v. Schwegel, 118 Idaho 362, 796 P.2d 1035 (Ct. App. 1990), where, in the absence of a contract, the court allowed a quasi contract recovery. This concept will be explored *infra* in Chapter 9.

[491] The expectation interest may be protected absent any out-of-pocket loss by the plaintiff. While the reliance interest protects such a loss, the restitution interest protects against a loss to the plaintiff and a commensurate gain to the unjustly enriched party. For a complete analysis of the three interests and the greater claim suggested by the restitution interest, see the classic article by Fuller and Perdue, *The Reliance Interest in Contract Damages*, 46 YALE L.J. 52, 373 (1936).

[492] If an oral contract for the sale of goods is partly performed through receipt and acceptance of part of the goods, or receipt and acceptance of part payment which can be related to a portion of the goods, the contract becomes enforceable to that extent. UCC § 2-201(3)(c). See *supra* § 76[C], for a discussion of this concept.

enforcement of the contract, a trial court dismissed the claim, stating that one who fails to produce a writing to comply with the statute cannot "come in the back door." The appellate court, however, stated,

> It is true that a plaintiff may not escape the Statute of Frauds by simply affixing the label 'quantum meruit'[493] to the very contract claim that is barred. A cause of action does exist, however, where the plaintiff merely seeks to recover for the value of the work performed. This is because the cause of action does not depend upon an unenforceable promise.[494]

Thus, where services are rendered in exchange for a promise that is unenforceable under the statute, the party who has rendered the services may recover their reasonable value in a quasi contract action to protect her restitution interest.[495] If parties have made an oral contract for the purchase and sale of land and the buyer has made a down payment, the unenforceability of the contract will not prevent the buyer's recovery of a down payment so as to avoid the unjust enrichment of the owner.[496] Indeed, a refusal to return such a down payment would amount to its conversion.[497] Thus, our courts have taken the position that the statute of frauds is clearly not undermined by permitting restitution of the benefits conferred under a contract that cannot be enforced because of the statute of frauds.[498]

[B]   The Measure of Restitutionary Recovery

There is no difficulty in measuring the restitution interest where money has been paid in part performance of an unenforceable contract. The recipient of the money is unjustly enriched to the extent of the payment and by returning that amount to the other party, the injured party is restored to status quo.[499] Where the benefit is in the form of services rendered, the recovery is normally the reasonable value of the services.[500] While it is traditional to characterize the measure of restitutionary recovery as the amount of the "benefit conferred" on the unjustly enriched party, it is possible for a party to perform services pursuant to an unenforceable contract that confers no benefit upon the other party in terms of enhancing that party's economic position. If, however, the performance has been received in accordance with the unenforceable contract, it will be viewed as a benefit, notwithstanding the lack of any discernible economic benefit to the recipient.[501] If the plaintiff's acts are merely preparatory to performing the contract, however, it is usually

---

[493] "Quantum meruit" is an old common law pleading seeking to recover the reasonable value of "work and labor done" to protect the restitution interest.

[494] Grappo v. Alitalia Linee Aeree Italiane, 56 F.3d 427, 433 (2d Cir. 1995) (citations omitted).

[495] See, e.g., Peters v. Morse, 96 A.D.2d 662, 466 N.Y.S.2d 504 (3d Dep't 1983) (nurse renders medical services to an elderly couple in exchange for the couple's unenforceable oral promises to convey their farm to the nurse upon their death).

[496] See, e.g., Jay v. A & A Ventures, LLC, 2008 Conn. Super. LEXIS 493 (2008); Gilton v. Chapman, 217 Ark. 390, 230 S.W.2d 37 (1950).

[497] See Jones v. Wide World of Cars, Inc., 820 F. Supp. 132 (S. D. N. Y. 1993).

[498] RESTATEMENT 2d § 375.

[499] See RESTATEMENT 2d § 375 ill. 2.

[500] See RESTATEMENT 2d § 375 ill. 1.

[501] See Farash v. Sykes Datatronics, Inc., 59 N.Y.2d 500, 452 N.E.2d 1245 (1983).

suggested that no action in restitution will lie since no performance has been received.[502] In such a situation, the plaintiff would be relegated to an attempt to recover the reliance interest.[503] In jurisdictions recognizing promissory estoppel as a method of satisfying the statute of frauds, the plaintiff's reliance interest would be protected notwithstanding the fact that the contract is within the statute of frauds.[504]

[C]   Limitations on Restitutionary Recovery

While restitutionary recovery is not generally seen as undermining the statute of frauds because it only prevents the unjust enrichment of another, a particular statute of frauds could expressly preclude such recovery and a court would have no discretion in granting it in such a situation. Even where the statute does not expressly prevent such recovery, a court may perceive the purpose of a particular provision of the statute of frauds as preventing such recovery, i.e., unjust enrichment would be tolerated to effectuate an overriding statute of frauds purpose. Statutes of frauds in numerous jurisdictions preclude the recovery of a real estate broker's commission unless there is a written memorandum of the contract.[505] Real estate brokers are subject to statutory licensing requirements and are typically licensed only after having demonstrated their knowledge of laws relating to real estate transactions, including the statute of frauds with respect to their commissions. Where such a broker fails to meet a requirement that a contract for a commission must be evidenced by a writing, to permit such a licensed broker to recover in restitution would frustrate the purpose of the statute.[506] Curiously, however, another jurisdiction exempts real estate brokers from statute of frauds requirements for the very reason that they are otherwise licensed and regulated by the state.[507]

If a party seeking restitution for performance under an unenforceable contract is himself in breach of the contract, the old view that there could be no recovery by such a contract breaker has bowed to the view that a defaulting plaintiff should recover that amount over and above the loss to the defendant caused by the plaintiff's breach.[508] If, therefore, such a recovery were permissible in general, it should be permitted where the contract is unenforceable under the statute of frauds.

---

[502] RESTATEMENT 2d § 370.

[503] RESTATEMENT 2d § 349.

[504] *See* RESTATEMENT 2d § 139. This concept is explored *supra* § 79[B].

[505] *See, e.g.*, CONN. GEN. STAT. § 20-325(a).

[506] See Phillippe v. Shapell Indus., 43 Cal. 3d 1247, 241 Cal. Rptr. 22, 743 P.2d 1279 (1987), *cert. denied*, 486 U.S. 1011, 108 S. Ct. 1742, 100 L. Ed. 2d 205 (1988), where the court provides the policy rationale for a rigorous application of the statute of frauds to *licensed* real estate brokers and holds that even equitable estoppel will not apply to such brokers except where the real estate broker cancelled a contract with the sellers of the property in reliance on the buyer's oral promise to pay the commission, or where the broker's principal represented to the broker that his authorization was in writing when in fact it was not. The same analysis was later used to prevent a recovery in a fee-sharing arrangement between attorneys where the writing requirement of the rules of professional conduct was not met. Margolin v. Shemaria, 85 Cal. App. 4th 891, 102 Cal. Rptr. 2d 502 (2d Dist. 2000). *See also* Louisville Trust Co. v. Monsky, 444 S.W.2d 120 (Ky. 1969), and RESTATEMENT 2d § 375 ill. 3.

[507] N.Y. GEN. OBLIG. LAW § 5-701(a)(10). *See, e.g.*, R. B. Ventures, Ltd. v. Shane, 112 F. 3d 54, 58 (2d Cir. 1997).

[508] The classic case, albeit not a statute of frauds case, is Britton v. Turner, 6 N.H. 481 (1834). *See also* RESTATEMENT 2d § 374. This concept will be explored thoroughly *infra* Chapter 6.

The RESTATEMENT 2d takes the position that specific restitution or, in the older terminology, restitution *in specie*, is also permitted (though not for a breaching plaintiff) where monetary restitution is permitted if, in the court's discretion, such a remedy would not unduly interfere with the certainty of title to land or otherwise cause injustice.[509] This view is considerably more liberal than older views which restricted such relief to cases involving fiduciary relationships[510] or to the creation of constructive trusts which required a showing of fraud, mistake, misrepresentation, duress or undue influence, or a fiduciary relationship.[511] One of the interesting carry-overs from the FIRST RESTATEMENT[512] appears at this point. If the plaintiff claims restitutionary damages and the defendant tenders what has been received, i.e., the defendant provides specific restitution, the RESTATEMENT 2d adheres to its predecessor's view that the defendant can discharge his duty by tendering such restitution, with or without a sum of money in addition to the particular benefit tendered, if the plaintiff will be placed in substantially the same position he would have been in through restitution in money.[513]

---

[509] RESTATEMENT 2d § 372(1).

[510] *See* RESTATEMENT OF RESTITUTION § 182.

[511] A constructive trust could also be created where the transfer of land was made exclusively as security. *See* Straight v. Hill, 622 P.2d 425 (Alaska 1981).

[512] FIRST RESTATEMENT § 355.

[513] RESTATEMENT 2d § 372(3).

Chapter 5

OPERATIVE EXPRESSIONS OF ASSENT
(Parol Evidence, Interpretation, and Mistake)

§ 82 INTRODUCTION — DEFINING THE AGREEMENT OF THE PARTIES

Where parties apparently intend to conclude an agreement, the parameters of their agreement must be established. Evidence of their agreement is found in their language, conduct and the totality of relevant surrounding circumstances including trade usage, prior course of dealing and course of performance.[1] Manifestations of assent must be viewed objectively, i.e., courts cannot read minds and can only determine their agreement from

---

[1] See the definition of "agreement" in UCC § 1-201(3).

outward manifestations. A subjective approach is unworkable.[2] We also know that some outward manifestations will be denied operative effect. In the last Chapter, we recognized that certain oral expressions of the parties will be denied such effect under the statute of frauds.[3] In the next Chapter, we will see that certain expressions, oral or written, will be also denied operative effect because the bargaining process has been abused or because the bargain is opposed to public policy. In the present Chapter, we will explore how courts *define the agreement of the parties* by confronting issues involving the parol evidence rule, interpretation and mistake. The *parol evidence rule* is invoked where the parties take the time and trouble to reduce their agreement to writing, but one of the parties later claims that their agreement should be said to include prior or contemporaneous understandings that either contradict or add to the terms of the writing. Should the writing be treated as their sole and exclusive manifestation of agreement, i.e., should evidence of alleged understandings prior to the writing be denied operative effect? The *parol evidence rule* may preclude the admission of such evidence. The essential question is whether the parties intended their writing to be the final or complete expression of their agreement.[4] Though such a question of intention is a question of *fact*, it will be decided by a court rather than a jury because jurors may not give the unchanged and more reliable written record of the parties' agreement the greater weight it deserves as compared to the less reliable recollection of the witnesses memories of that intention at the time the contract was formed.

By addressing parol evidence issues, a court has merely defined the parameters of the agreement. It must then turn its attention to the preferred *meaning* of all of the manifestations of assent within those parameters through the process of *interpretation*. The language and conduct manifesting agreement is typically imprecise. Language or conduct may superficially appear to be so clear and unambiguous that it requires no interpretation. Professor Corbin, however, provides the consummate rejection of this view:

> It is sometimes said, in a case in which the written words seem plain and clear and unambiguous, that the words are not subject to interpretation or construction. One who makes this statement has of necessity already given the words an interpretation- the one that is to him plain and clear; and in making the statement he is asserting that any different interpretation is "perverted"and untrue.[5]

Where a defendant agreed to harvest a crop grown by the plaintiff, a clause in the contract excused the defendant from harvesting under "adverse weather conditions." Unusually good weather conditions prevailed, causing the crops to mature simultaneously, precluding the harvesting of all of the crops. The court was confronted with the proper interpretation of the phrase, "adverse weather conditions," which may appear to have been contemplated as an excuse for poor weather conditions. The court, however, held that unusually good weather conditions that caused loss could be included within the phrase.[6] Trade usage may dictate an

---

[2] *See supra* Chapter 2, § 30.

[3] *See supra* Chapter 4.

[4] This statement is quoted in Woolridge v. World Champion Sports Network, 2009 U.S. Dist. LEXIS 85057 (D. Md. 2009).

[5] Corbin, *The Interpretation of Words and the Parol Evidence Rule*, 50 Cornell L.Q. 161, 171–72 (1965). *See also* Farnsworth, *"Meaning" in the Law of Contracts*, 76 Yale L.J. 939 (1967).

[6] Stender v. Twin City Foods, Inc., 82 Wash. 2d 250, 510 P.2d 221 (1973). While the parties may not have consciously adverted to the possibility of unusually good weather conditions, if their purpose was to permit additional time if the harvesting process was delayed because of weather conditions, the fact that the conditions were unusually good rather

interpretation that differs from the dictionary definition of a term in the agreement. Thus, "fifty percent" may be shown to mean less than fifty percent to the members of a particular trade.[7] The expression of the parties may also be affected by their prior course of dealing, in effect, a private trade usage, which should be viewed as more important evidence of the meaning of their expressions than the general usage of trade.[8] If the parties have begun to perform their contract, their course of performance will constitute the strongest evidence of the meaning of their written expression or of a modification of their express terms.[9] There may be inconsistencies or contradictions between or among different manifestations of agreement and the courts will have to choose that which they believe best effectuates the intention of the parties-again, deciding which of the expressions should be accorded operative effect. Statutory[10] and common law guidelines[11] aid courts in this process and their use must be explored.

If the parties have not manifested any intention concerning an unforeseeable event that changes their agreement, courts may be faced with a problem that can hardly be called one of interpretation since there is nothing to interpret. Courts are not supposed to "make a contract for the parties," but this situation may require courts to create terms that appear fair under the changed circumstances.[12]

If questions of parol evidence and interpretation are answered, other facts may reveal that the parties have made a contract which one or both may later seek to avoid on the ground of *mistake.* There are mutual mistakes and various types of one-sided or *unilateral* mistake that must be explored. Where both parties make a basic assumption at the time of contract formation that is not in accord with the facts, relief may be available under the doctrine of *mutual* mistake. Another challenge arises where the parties have a mutual misunderstanding caused by a *latent ambiguity* inducing each party to attach a different meaning to a term of their contract. Still another issue arises where neither party has made a mistake, but the intermediary chosen to deliver a message may have mistakenly transmitted it or otherwise caused a reasonable recipient to believe something other than that intended by a reasonable sender.

---

than unusually bad should not deter a court from applying the clause in terms of its underlying purpose.

[7] Hurst v. W.J. Lake & Co., 141 Or. 306, 16 P.2d 627, 89 A.L.R. 1222 (1932).

[8] UCC §§ 1-205(1) and (3). *See also* Columbia Nitrogen Corp. v. Royster Co., 451 F.2d 3 (4th Cir. 1971).

[9] UCC § 2-208(3).

[10] *See, e.g.,* UCC §§ 1-205(4) and 2-208(3). A similar problem occurs where there is a conflict of warranties, i.e., express warranties (§ 2-313), the implied warranty of merchantability (§ 2-314) and the implied warranty of fitness for a particular purpose (§ 2-315), which is dealt with in § 2-317.

[11] Courts often use maxims (or canons) of construction or interpretation which are nothing more than common sense guidelines to assist in these matters. The maxims are criticized because there is, arguably, a counter-maxim for every maxim. *See* Llewellyn, *Remarks on the Theory of Appellate Decision and the Rules or Canons About How Statutes Are to Be Construed,* 3 VAND. L. REV. 395 (1950). While the canons, rules, or maxims are discussed in the context of statutory interpretation, they are also applied to the interpretation of contracts.

[12] *See* Parev Prods. Co. v. I. Rokeach & Sons, Inc., 124 F.2d 147 (2d Cir. 1941).

§ 83   THE PAROL EVIDENCE RULE

[A]   Scope of the Parol Evidence Rule: Subsequent Agreement

In his 1898 treatise on evidence law, James Bradley Thayer begins his discussion of the parol evidence rule as follows: "Few things are darker than this or fuller of subtle difficulties."[13] To avoid needless confusion and mystery, a precise understanding of the *scope* of the parol evidence rule is critical. If parties express agreement but change their minds by expressing a subsequent agreement that they intend to prevail over their earlier agreement, their final expression will prevail. This is *not* a statement of the parol evidence rule because "the rule does not prohibit the subsequent modification of written contract terms, even if done orally."[14] It is a much broader statement because it is accurate in the following situations:

(a)   Both expressions of agreement are oral;

(b)   the first expression is written and the second is oral;

(c)   both expressions are written;

(d)   the first expression is oral and the second is written.

The parol evidence rule may become operative only in situations (c) and (d) where the second expression is evidenced by a *writing*. Yet, the general principle that the subsequent expression prevails over the antecedent expression is true in all of the foregoing situations where the parties intend the second expression to be their only operative expression of assent.[15] Where the second agreement is evidenced by a writing, the parol evidence process *may* become operative whether the prior agreement was oral or written. If one of the parties alleges that the subsequent written agreement was intended to be the final or complete and exclusive expression of the parties' agreement, thereby discharging any prior agreement, the parol evidence process is activated. It then becomes necessary to decide a question of intention, i.e., whether the parties intended their written expression of agreement to become their final or complete and exclusive expression,[16] or, whether they intended to be bound by their prior (oral or written) agreement as well as the agreement manifested in their last

---

[13] James Bradley Thayer, Preliminary Treatise on Evidence at the Common Law (1898). As quoted in Lano Equip., Inc. v. Clark Equip. Co., 399 N.W.2d 694, 699 (Minn. Ct. App. 1987), the statement continues: "[A]nd this condition of the law all members of the profession will concede. The so-called parol evidence rule is attended with confusion and obscurity which make it the most discouraging subject in the whole field of evidence."

[14] Woodland Harvesting, Inc. v. Ga. Pac. Corp., 2010 U.S. Dist. LEXIS 2893 at *8 (E. D. Mich. January 14, 2010). See also, New England Sav. Bank v. Quarry Trail Dev. Corp., 1992 Conn. Super. LEXIS 1661, at *10 (Conn. Super. Ct. June 4, 1992) (stating that the parol evidence rule does not apply to subsequent agreements).

[15] Professor Corbin insists that a written integration of the parties intention into a writing should have no greater effect upon antecedent agreements than a "parol integration" since, in both cases, the later agreement discharges the antecedent ones in so far as it contradicts or is inconsistent with the earlier ones. 3 CORBIN ON CONTRACTS § 573, at 369 (1963 ed.).

[16] In Restatement 2d of Contracts terminology, a "final" expression would be deemed a "partial integration" of the parties' agreement into their writing, while a "complete and exclusive" expression would be a "full integration." The UCC version of the parol evidence rule avoids the use of the term, "integration" by focusing on whether the parties viewed their written expression of agreement as "final" or "complete and exclusive" with respect to any alleged (prior) extrinsic agreement.

writing. *This is the only situation that will invoke the parol evidence rule.*[17]

If the parties disagree as to the *meaning* of their manifestations of intention, the parol evidence rule will not resolve that question since it is interpretation issue. The parol evidence rule "is not a rule of interpretation, but rather it defines the subject matter of interpretation."[18] If a party alleges a condition precedent to the *formation* of the contract, there is no parol evidence issue. If one of the parties alleges that the writing does not state the true intention of the parties, the remedy of reformation may be granted on clear and convincing evidence of the mistake in the writing. Again, the parol evidence rule is not involved. An understanding of the parol evidence rule is enhanced by clearly distinguishing situations to which it does not apply. Each of these and related matters will be explored.

[B] The Parol Evidence Rationale — Substantive Rule of Contract Law Rather than a Rule of Evidence — Preference for Written Evidence

Why has the relatively simple matter, the determination of the intention of the parties with respect to the finality or completeness of their last written manifestation of agreement, been described as a legal concept whose mysteries are familiar to many but fathomed by few?[19]

Substantive Rule of Law-Not a Rule of Evidence. The "parol evidence rule" is a misnomer. It is neither limited to dealing with "parol" (oral) evidence, nor is it a rule of evidence law concerned with the probative reliability of proffered oral evidence. What is called the "parol evidence rule" is a substantive rule of contract law. Professor Corbin has amply demonstrated fundamental flaws in the rationale for the parol evidence rule.

> Any contract can be discharged by a subsequent agreement of the parties, whether the subsequent agreement is oral or written. In his refreshing and illuminating fashion, Professor Corbin states the proposition very simply: "Today may control the effect of what happened yesterday; but what happened yesterday cannot change the effect of what happened today. This, it is believed, is the substance of what has been unfortunately called the 'parol evidence rule.' "[20]

Where the subsequent agreement is oral, the question is simply whether the parties intended the subsequent expression to control the earlier expression of agreement. Courts have no difficulty analyzing that question in the usual fashion of whether the subsequent agreement was so intended by the parties. They do so without mentioning the parol evidence

---

[17] See Murray, *The Parol Evidence Rule: A Clarification*, 4 Duq. L. Rev. 337 (1966), as cited in the leading case of Masterson v. Sine, 68 Cal. 2d 222, 436 P.2d 561 (1968).

[18] Wachovia Bank, N. A. v. Dresdner, 2009 Bankr. LEXIS 3241, 52 Bankr. Ct. Dec. 72, n. 5 (E. D. Va. 2009) quoting Restatement 2d § 213 comment a. *See also* Expeditors Int'l of Wash., Inc. v. Crowley Am. Transp., Inc., 117 F. Supp. 2d 663, 670 (S.D. Ohio 2000). This concept appears to suggest that the parol evidence application must precede the process of interpretation. If, however, a party claims that certain evidence of agreement prior to the final writing contradicts that writing, it will be necessary to interpret the writing before deciding the parol evidence question since, "No parol evidence that is offered can be said to *contradict* a writing until, by process of interpretation, it is determined what the writing means." Tigg Corp. v. Dow Corning Corp., 822 F.2d 358, 362 (3d Cir. 1987), *cert. dismissed*, 506 U.S. 1042, 113 S. Ct. 834, 122 L. Ed. 2d 111 (1993).

[19] This phrase is quoted from the first edition of this book in Astor v. Boulos Co., 451 A.2d 903 (Me. 1982).

[20] 3 Corbin on Contracts § 574, at 372 (1963 ed.).

rule. An oral subsequent agreement may constitute a final and complete expression of the parties' intended agreement.[21]

Special Protection for Writings. It is only where the last expression of agreement is written, however, that the parol evidence is invoked, based on the traditional policy of affording special protection to written evidence of agreements.[22] Since memories of oral understandings are fallible and subject to favorable or unfavorable (conscious or unconscious) recollection,[23] the recorded evidence of the parties' intention as a permanent record of their intention not subject to the vagaries of memory should prevail. Here again, however, the rationale is flawed since the parol evidence rule is said to apply to prior oral or written evidence. To provide the final written evidence with the strength that courts felt it deserved, they created a rule which sounded very much like a rule of evidence. Legions of cases have repeated the incantation that denies admissibility of evidence that would "vary or contradict the terms of the writing."[24] Like all such phrases, this conclusion is of preciously little assistance in analyzing parol evidence issues.

Professor Corbin applauds the basic justification for the "rule" that would fulfill the intention of parties who seek to be bound only by their final and/or complete expression of agreement. He convincingly asserts, however, that the purpose of the parol evidence rule can and should be attained without regard to whether the final expression is written or oral-a rule of rudimentary contract law dispensing with any discussion of "parol" or "evidence." Notwithstanding his monumental contributions to twentieth century contract law, Corbin's parol evidence analysis has not been accepted by courts or the RESTATEMENT 2d though the RESTATEMENT 2d was certainly influenced by his views.

Question of Fact Becomes Question of "Law." Because judges assumed that juries would lack the necessary sophistication to provide the written evidence of the contract with the preference such evidence deserved over the relatively unreliable prior oral expressions, the judges reserved to themselves the determination of the admissibility of the prior evidence as a "question of law." They did so even though the question was clearly one of fact,[25] i.e., was

---

[21] RESTATEMENT 2d § 209, comment b., states, "Indeed, the parties to an oral agreement may choose their words with such explicit precision and completeness that the same legal consequences follow as whether there is a completely integrated agreement."

[22] *See* Poelker v. Jamison, 4 S.W.3d 611, 613 (Mo. Ct. App. 1999). In Gangahar v. Gangahar, 2000 Minn. App. LEXIS 405, at *8 (Minn. Ct. App. Apr. 25, 2000), the court states that the parol evidence rule does not prevent all evidence that contradicts a writing. Rather, it precludes certain evidence that contradicts or varies the terms of a *written contract.* The writing in this case was an affidavit.

[23] *See* Luria Bros. & Co. v. Pielet Bros. Scrap Iron, 600 F.2d 103, 110 n.5 (7th Cir. 1979).

[24] See the cases in note 20 *supra. See also* Long v. Beach, 529 S.E.2d 901, 902 (Ga. Ct. App. 2000); North Atl. Instrums., Inc. v. Haber, 188 F.3d 38, 48 (2d Cir. 1999); Federal Deposit Ins. Corp. v. First Mortg. Inv., 76 Wis. 2d 151, 250 N.W.2d 362 (1977). Kruse Classic Auction v. Aetna Cas. & Sur., 511 N.E.2d 326, 329 (Ind. Ct. App. 1987): "Parol or extrinsic evidence is inadmissible to expand, vary, or explain the instrument unless there has been a showing of fraud, ambiguity, illegality, duress or undue influence." The court in MacLeod v. Chalet Susse Int'l, Inc., 401 A.2d 205, 208 (N.H. 1979), suggests the illusory character of such statements: "Nevertheless the apparent neatness of the stated rule is misleading; for whether extrinsic evidence is offered to 'interpret' rather than to 'vary' the terms of the writing, or whether the writing is indeed the 'complete and accurate integration' of the agreement rather than a partial or incomplete integration are, in many cases, questions not easily answered."

[25] Courts characterize the question as one of fact. *See* Eie v. St. Benedict's Hosp., 638 P.2d 1190, 1194 (Utah 1981) (where a party seeks the application of the parol evidence rule, "the court must determine as a question of fact whether the parties did in fact adopt a particular writing or writings as the final and complete expression of their bargain"). *See also* Morgan v. Stokely-Van Camp, Inc., 34 Wash. App. 801, 663 P.2d 1384 (1983).

there an oral agreement and, if so, did the parties intend to abandon that agreement when they expressed themselves in writing?

The writing may be incomplete overall, but final with respect to certain matters of agreement, i.e., it may be "partially integrated." Again, the prior agreement may be written or oral. Thus, a more comprehensive statement of the parol evidence rule is required:

If a transaction is embodied in whole or in part in a single memorial such as a writing or writings, and if the parties regard that memorial as the exclusive expression of their intention as a whole, or of a part thereof, then all other prior or contemporaneous utterances by the parties in connection with that transaction, whether oral or written, are inoperative for the purpose of ascertaining the terms of their contract, or at least so much of it as it embodied in the memorial.[26]

The fact that this rule is one of substantive law rather than a rule of evidence has been amply demonstrated for many years.[27] Thus, even if a party failed at trial to object to the admission of evidence violating the rule, the evidence would not be considered operative on appeal.[28] Similarly, a federal court required to apply state law under the familiar doctrine of *Erie R.R. v. Tompkins*[29] would apply the state parol evidence rule because it is a rule of substantive law, rather than a rule of evidence.[30] The purpose of the rule is much broader than one of keeping oral evidence from juries who might give such evidence undue significance when comparing it with a later written statement of the parties' agreement.

[C]   Form of Writing

The written expression of the parties need not be in any particular form. It may be in one document, or it may appear in more than one writing.[31] While it is theoretically possible that an ordinary check could be intended as a final and complete statement of the agreement, it is

---

[26] This statement is quoted, in the slightly different form in which it appeared in the second edition of this book, in Friestad v. Travelers Indem. Co., 260 Pa. Super. 178, 393 A.2d 1212 (1978). In Corn Exch. Nat'l Bank & Trust Co. v. Taubel, 113 N.J.L. 605, 175 A. 55, 58 (1934), the court states, "[W]here, as here, the parties have made a memorial of their bargain, or a writing is required by law, their actual intent unless expressed in some way in the writing is ineffective, except when it may, in accordance with established principles, afford the basis for a reformation of the writing. While the intention of the parties is sought, it can be found only in their expression in the writing. In effect, it is not the real intent but the intent expressed or apparent in the writing that controls. . . . Otherwise, there would be a disregard of the well-settled rule forbidding the introduction of parol evidence to contradict the terms of the written contract."

[27] *See* Academic Imaging, LLC v. Soterion Corp., 2009 U.S. App. LEXIS 25027 at *13 (6th Cir., Nov. 13, 2009); HLO Land Ownership Assocs., Ltd. Partnership v. City of Hartford, 248 Conn. 350, 727 A.2d 1260, 1265 (1999); Lower Kuskokwim Sch. Dist. v. Alaska Diversified Contractors, 734 P.2d 62 (Alaska 1987), *cert. denied*, 493 U.S. 1022, 110 S. Ct. 725, 107 L. Ed. 2d 744 (1990); Franklin v. White, 493 N.E.2d 161 (Ind. 1986).

[28] *See Lower Kuskokwim Sch. Dist.*, *id.* at note 1; Davison v. FastComm, Inc., 46 Va. Cir. 25, 1998 Va. Cir. LEXIS 264, at *12 (1998); Tuttle v. Simpson, 735 S.W.2d 539 (Tex. App. Texarkana 1987); First Tennessee Bank Nat'l Ass'n v. Wilson, 713 S.W.2d 907 (Tenn. Ct. App. 1985). *But see* Top of Iowa Coop. v. Sime Farms, Inc., 608 N.W.2d 454, 470 (Iowa 2000).

[29] 304 U.S. 64, 58 S. Ct. 817, 82 L. Ed. 1188 (1938).

[30] *See* Ungerleider v. Gordon, 214 F.3d 1279, 1282 (11th Cir. 2000); Beta Labs., Inc. v. Hines, 647 F.2d 402 (3d Cir. 1981).

[31] RESTATEMENT 2d § 209 comment b. A question arose concerning the UCC statement of the parol evidence rule which refers to "confirmatory memoranda" in § 2-202. In the second edition of this book, it was suggested that the UCC version would permit either a single confirmatory memorandum or more than one writing to operate as an

unlikely.[32] A mere acknowledgment of receipt will not constitute a final and complete integration since it is statement of fact, rather than a term of the agreement.[33] On the other hand, an invoice may qualify as a final and complete writing if it manifests all of the essential terms of the agreement.[34] As will be seen later, however, the mere *appearance* of the writing should not be deemed a conclusive test of the parties' intention that it is their final and complete or exclusive statement of their contract.[35]

§ 84 THE PAROL EVIDENCE RULE — "INCONSISTENT" AND "CONTRADICTORY" — FORM OF WRITING — THE MEANING OF "INTEGRATION"

[A] The Possible Intention of the Parties — Three Possibilities

The parties to a contract may express their assent in oral or written language or by their conduct. The terms of their agreement may be discovered in any combination of such manifestations of assent. When the parties take the time and trouble to express their agreement in writing, three possibilities arise:

(1) they do not intend their written expression to preclude evidence of other expressions of agreement;

(2) they intend their writing to be final as to any matters contained in the writing, but they also intend to be bound to other manifestations of agreement not contained in the writing; or

(3) they not only intend their writing to be the final expression of their agreement with respect to the matters set forth in the writing; they also intend their writing to be the complete and exclusive manifestation of their agreement, i.e., they do not intend any other manifestation of their agreement prior to the writing to be operative.

In the last section, we saw the question of intention as one of fact, though it will be decided by judges rather than jurors. If the parties clearly express their intention as to whether their writing is final, complete, or neither, there will be no question as to the effect of their written expression of agreement since they have consciously adverted to the question and directed that their writing have one or another effect. A common method for achieving a manifestation of intention in the writing that the writing is complete and final is a clause that is often called a *merger* clause, which simply expresses the parties' intention that their writing was intended to

---

"integration" because § 2-202 also refers to "a writing." *See* CALAMARI & PERILLO, CONTRACTS at 151–52 (1986): "Another interesting question is whether it is possible under the Code to have a total integration based upon a single confirmatory memorandum. It has been argued that this result may no longer obtain because of the use of the words 'confirmatory memoranda.' [citing Album Graphics, Inc. v. Beatrice Foods Co., 87 Ill. App. 3d 338, 42 Ill. Dec. 332, 408 N.E.2d 1041 (1st Dist. 1980).] Professor Murray disagrees and argues that a single confirmatory memorandum may still operate as [a] total integration under the Code and Professor Farnsworth agrees with him."

[32] *See* Rogen v. Scheer, 1991 U.S. Dist. LEXIS 2715 (S.D.N.Y. Feb. 22, 1991).

[33] *See* Bremer v. Schroeder, 144 Or. App. 358, 927 P.2d 144, 145 (1996). *See also* Jake C. Byers, Inc. v. J.B.C. Invs., 834 S.W.2d 806 (Mo. Ct. App. 1992).

[34] See Calzaturificio Claudia s.n.c. v. Olivieri Footwear Ltd., 1998 U.S. Dist. LEXIS 4586, at *16 (S.D.N.Y. Apr. 6, 1998), and cases cited therein.

[35] *See* § 84[C][1] *infra*.

be complete and final.[36] The same clause may also be called an "integration" clause or even a "zipper" clause as discussed in a subsequent section.[37] If the parties do not expressly indicate their intention concerning their writing, i.e., final, complete, both or neither, a court will then decide which of the possibilities is more likely under all of the relevant circumstances.

[B]   The Unlikely Possibility

Absent countervailing evidence, the first possibility-that the parties did not intend their writing to eclipse any prior manifestations of agreement-is unlikely. If the parties have taken the time and trouble to express themselves in writing, certainly evidence of prior *contradictory* agreements pales in comparison to their subsequent written agreement. Assuming the prior agreement was made, if the parties later executed a written agreement containing contradictory terms, the later expression of agreement should prevail on the rudimentary principle of contract law that the parties may always agree today to rescind or modify their agreement of yesterday. Thus, where there is a final writing, an extrinsic term (prior to the writing) which is *inconsistent* with the terms of the writing, in the sense that it contradicts or negates a written term,[38] will not be operative since this is the apparent intention of the parties.

[C]   The Second and Third Possibilities — The RESTATEMENT 2d and "Integration"

Having decided that prior inconsistent statements of the parties will be inoperative, a court will likely decide that the second possibility is the appropriate interpretation of the parties' intention, i.e., that the parties intended their writing to be final as to any matters set forth in the writing. The parties, however, may have also intended their writing to be not only final as to the matters set forth therein; they may have intended the writing to be their complete and exclusive manifestation of agreement, i.e., the third possibility. In this situation, evidence of *any* prior agreement between the parties-even consistent (non-contradictory) agreements — would be excluded since the parties intended to be bound only by the terms of the writing

---

[36] A clause stating the parties' intention that the writing supersede all prior agreements and that it constitute the entire contract of the parties helps to resolve the question of the parties' intent concerning the effect of their written expression of agreement. It does not, however, conclusively establish the parties' intention, i.e., the extrinsic matter must still be examined to determine whether the parties intended it to be a part of their operative bargain. *See* Gerdlund v. Electronic Dispensers Int'l, 190 Cal. App. 3d 263, 235 Cal. Rptr. 279 (6th Dist. 1987).

[37] *See* § 84[C][2]. *infra*.

[38] The prior term may be characterized as "inconsistent" with the terms of the subsequent writing. In Hatley v. Stafford, 284 Or. 523, 588 P.2d 603 (1978), the court quotes Hunt Foods & Indus., Inc. v. Doliner, 26 A.D.2d 41, 43, 270 N.Y.S.2d 937, 940 (1st Dep't 1966), as follows: "In a sense any oral provision which would prevent the ripening of the obligations of a writing is inconsistent with the writing. But that obviously is not the sense in which the word is used. . . . To be inconsistent the term must contradict or negate a term of the writing." In § 213 comment b, the RESTATEMENT 2d suggests, "Whether a binding agreement is completely integrated or partially integrated, it supersedes inconsistent terms of prior agreements." (The distinction between "partially integrated" and "fully integrated" is explored later in this section.) Again, in comment b to § 215, the RESTATEMENT 2d suggests, "Whether there is a contradiction depends, as is stated in § 213, on whether the two are consistent or inconsistent." Thus, the RESTATEMENT 2d may be said to equate "inconsistent" with "contradictory." In Michigan Nat'l Bank v. Holland-Dozier-Holland Sound Studios, 73 Mich. App. 12, 250 N.W.2d 532 (1976), the court adopted this construction, citing Murray, *The Parol Evidence Process and Standardized Agreements Under the* Restatement (Second) of Contracts, 123 U. PA. L. REV. 1342, 1362 (1975). "Inconsistent" and "contradictory" are used interchangeably in Best v. City of Findlay, 1997 Ohio App. LEXIS 5479 (Ohio Ct. App., Dec. 5, 1997).

which they viewed as the *exclusive* repository of their agreement. Whether the writing is merely final or complete and exclusive, evidence of an alleged prior agreement that contradicts the terms of the writing will be excluded with little difficulty. The more difficult questions arise where the extrinsic evidence is not inconsistent with the terms of the writing and courts must decide whether the parties intended their writing to be complete and exclusive as well as final We will explore various tests used by courts in dealing with this question of intention. At this point, it is critically important to focus on the threshold question in the application of the parol evidence rule: *Did the parties intend their writing to be final at least as to the matters expressed therein, or did they intend their writing to be not only final but complete and exclusive so that no prior expression of agreement of any kind will be operative?*

[D]　The Meaning of "Integrated" — "Fully" or "Partially" Integrated

If a court determines that the parties intended their writing to be *final and complete*, i.e., an expression of their *entire* agreement, the writing is said to be "fully integrated." If, however, the parties intended their writing to be only *final* as to the matters expressed therein but not complete as to any consistent extrinsic matter, the writing is said to be "partially integrated." "If a writing is only partially integrated, evidence of prior or contemporaneous agreements is admissible to supplement its terms though not to contradict it."[39] Unfortunately, considerable emphasis has been placed on the term "integrated" as if it were an effective analytical tool. The RESTATEMENT 2d uses the phrase "parol evidence rule" in connection with a section captioned, "Effect of Integrated Agreement on Prior Agreements."[40] Subsections (1) and (2) of this section are truisms: (1) a binding integrated agreement has the effect of discharging prior agreements to the extent that they are inconsistent with the "integrated" writing;[41] (2) a binding *completely* integrated agreement discharges prior agreements to the extent that they are within the scope of the completed integrated writing.[42]

---

[39] Merk v. Jewel Food Stores Div. of Jewel Cos., 945 F.2d 889, 893 (7th Cir. 1991), *cert. denied*, 504 U.S. 914, 112 S. Ct. 1951, 118 L. Ed. 2d 555 (1992). The UCC parol evidence rule in § 2-202 does not use the phrases "partially integrated" or "fully integrated." Rather, it uses the terms, "final expression" and "complete and exclusive statement," which are the respective counterparts to "partially integrated" and "fully integrated." *See* Intercorp, Inc. v. Pennzoil Co., 877 F.2d 1524, 1528 (11th Cir. 1989).

[40] RESTATEMENT 2d § 213.

[41] The RESTATEMENT 2d uses the phrase "integrated agreement," rather than the phrase "integrated writing." This phraseology is confusing because it does present an important distinction between the two terms. Any written expression of the agreement is nothing more than the manifestation of agreement. It is not the agreement. "Two forms of intention must be distinguished if any attempt to understand the parol evidence process is to be successful. In order to have any binding agreement, the parties must intend to be bound to certain obligations they have voluntarily undertaken. . . . The parol evidence process, on the other hand, is concerned with a different intention, the intention to be bound exclusively to those undertakings evidenced by a writing or writings." Murray, *The Parol Evidence Process and Standardized Agreements Under the* Restatement (Second) of Contracts, 125 U. PA. L. REV. 1342, 1353–54 (1975).

[42] *Id.* Courts are not always precise in their use of the terms "partially integrated" or "fully" or "completely" integrated. For example, in South Side Plumbing Co. v. Tigges, 525 S.W.2d 583, 588 (Mo. Ct. App. 1975), the court suggests that prior or contemporaneous agreements which vary or contradict the terms of a written instrument are not admissible if the instrument "is a complete integration of the parties' agreement. . . ." Later, the court suggests that, "Testimony concerning a prior or contemporaneous agreement, if consistent with the writing, may supplement a writing incomplete on its face, but should not, in any case, be permitted to vary or contradict the writing." If, however, the writing is "a complete integration," even consistent prior terms should not be admissible. If by the phrase "incomplete on its face" the court meant to suggest that the writing would not be a "complete integration" but would

Though recognizing that the term "integrated" is not very useful, the RESTATEMENT 2d Reporter could discover no better term.[43] Again, the term "integrated" states a conclusion rather than a test. Only a comment to this RESTATEMENT 2d section begins to reveal the underlying problem:

> Whether a binding agreement is completely integrated or partially integrated, it supersedes inconsistent terms of prior agreements. To apply this rule, the court must make preliminary determinations that there is an integrated agreement and that it is inconsistent with the term in question.[44]

The trial court will make "preliminary determinations" as to whether the writing is "partially integrated" (final, but not complete), "fully integrated" (complete and exclusive) or not integrated at all. The trial court may receive extrinsic evidence bearing only on the single issue of "integration."[45] If the court determines that the writing is partially integrated, extrinsic evidence contradicting terms in the writing will be inadmissible, though consistent additional terms may be admitted. If the court determines that the writing was intended by the parties to be fully integrated (complete, exclusive and entire), neither contradictory nor consistent additional terms will be admitted. *The critical question is, how does a court go about making the preliminary determination of whether the parties intended their written expression to be "partially" or "fully" "integrated"?* There are many facets to this question and several accepted guides which courts use in their efforts to arrive at the conclusion of partial or complete integration. It is, therefore, more accurate to view this judicial effort as a process, rather than the application of a mechanical rule.

§ 85   THE PAROL EVIDENCE PROCESS — TESTS

Once it is recognized that the critical question in the parol evidence process is how a judge determines whether the writing is partially (finally) or fully (completely) integrated, a significant amount of the mystery surrounding the parol evidence rule is removed. The response to the critical question is, however, controversial. At first glance, the question appears quite simple, i.e., did the parties intend the writing to be their final and/or complete statement of agreement? In determining precisely how the judge proceeds to deal with that question, however, the courts and scholars have devised various tests and the UCC has added its own. The RESTATEMENT 2d has attempted to incorporate all of the tests including the conflicting views of Professors Williston and Corbin. Unfortunately, the result exacerbates the confusion surrounding the parol evidence rule. This section provides a critical analysis of each of the tests. To avoid unnecessary confusion, certain preliminary questions will be examined before each of the tests is explored.

---

only be a "partial integration," its statement is reconcilable with generally accepted distinctions between "partial" and "complete" integrations. Since the court was dealing with what it viewed as a "complete integration" because of a "merger" or "integration" clause in the writing, however, it is difficult to assure such a reconciliation.

[43] 68 ALI Proceedings 446 (1971).

[44] RESTATEMENT 2d § 213 comment b. *See also* McGuire v. Schneider, Inc., 368 Pa. Super. 344, 534 A.2d 115 (1987); Costello v. Watson, 111 Idaho 68, 720 P.2d 1033 (Ct. App. 1986); Shain Inv. Co. v. Cohen, 15 Mass. App. Ct. 4, 443 N.E.2d 126 (1982).

[45] Intercorp, Inc. v. Pennzoil Co., 877 F.2d 1524, 1529 (11th Cir. 1989).

[A]   "Prior," "Contemporaneous" and "Subsequent" Statements

The parol evidence rule was designed to preclude evidence of *prior* agreements that would contradict or add to the terms of the writing the parties intended to be the final or complete "integration" of their agreement. It was not designed to preclude parties from changing their minds and forming a new contract. Thus, innumerable cases support the principle that the parol evidence rule has no application to *subsequent* agreements or modifications.[46] Where the evidence sought to be introduced is characterized as "contemporaneous" rather than either prior or subsequent, should such evidence be barred by the parol evidence rule?[47]

The FIRST RESTATEMENT made any oral or written agreements prior to a written integration inoperative, and it also made "all contemporaneous oral agreements relating to the same subject matter" inoperative.[48] If the contemporaneous agreement was in writing, however, it became part of the integration.[49] The rationale for the exclusion of oral agreements contemporaneous with an integration was based on the definition of "integration." "An integration by definition contains what the parties agreed upon as a complete statement of their promises."[50] If, therefore, the parties have agreed that their writing contains a complete statement of their undertakings, they do not intend to be bound by any contemporaneous oral agreements. Professor Corbin found error in this view. If "contemporaneous" meant "simultaneous," Corbin could not understand how the parties could have assented to a complete and final writing and, at the same time, assented to the oral addition evidenced by the contemporaneous oral agreement. If the parties had assented to both the terms of the writing and a contemporaneous (simultaneous) oral agreement, unassailable logic compelled the conclusion that the writing was not a complete integration because "One cannot express simultaneous assent to two things and at the same instant agree that one of them supplants the other."[51] Once the parties are found to have assented to a complete integration, Corbin suggested that there is no simultaneous oral addition.[52] If "contemporaneous" does not mean "simultaneous," the oral agreement was either before or after the integration. The parol evidence rule would apply to such an agreement made before a valid integration, and would have no applicability to an agreement made after the integration since the rule does not affect subsequent modifications.[53] Whether to use "contemporaneous" along with "prior" in

---

[46] Quoted in Butcher v. Dravo Corp., 2009 U.S. Dist. LEXIS 24128, n. 60 (W.D. Pa. 2009). *See also* Wayman v. Amoco Oil Co., 923 F. Supp. 1322, 1340 (D. Kan. 1996); South Atl. Prod. Credit Ass'n v. Gibbs, 257 Ga. 521, 361 S.E.2d 167, 169 (1987); Wilson v. Landstrom, 281 S.C. 260, 315 S.E.2d 130, 134 (Ct. App. 1984).

[47] In Heider v. Glasstech, Inc., 1999 Ohio App. LEXIS 3331, *20 note 2 (Ohio Ct. App., Wood County July 16, 1999), the court quotes a dictionary definition of "contemporaneous": "existing, occurring, or originating during the same time." For a case dealing with "contemporaneous" evidence, see Webb v. National Union Fire Ins. Co., 207 F.3d 579 (9th Cir. 2000) ("contemporaneous" extrinsic evidence would prove that the parties intended a policy to provide sole coverage).

[48] FIRST RESTATEMENT § 237.

[49] FIRST RESTATEMENT § 237 comment a. See McDonald's Corp. v. Butler Co., 158 Ill. App. 3d 902, 110 Ill. Dec. 735, 511 N.E.2d 912 (2d Dist. 1987), in which the court states that the parol evidence rule does not bar contemporaneous written documents from being admitted.

[50] FIRST RESTATEMENT § 237 comment b.

[51] 3 CORBIN § 577, at 401 (1963 ed.).

[52] *Id.*

[53] See cases cited at note 45 *supra. See also* Michigan Nat'l Bank v. Holland-Dozier-Holland Sound Studios, 73 Mich. App. 12, 14, 250 N.W.2d 532, 533 (1976): "The swath of the parol evidence rule is not so broad as to prevent a showing of subsequent oral modifications."

statements of the parol evidence rule provides one of several clear illustrations of the RESTATEMENT 2d effort to be all things to all persons, in this instance, to reconcile the Williston/ FIRST RESTATEMENT analysis of the rule with the perceptions of Professor Corbin. In one of the critical sections of the parol evidence analysis, the RESTATEMENT 2d conspicuously avoids the use of "contemporaneous,"[54] but adds the term in the next section.[55] The Reporter admits that he was torn between the logic of Corbin and the pull of tradition.[56] The logic of the Corbin position has had no effect on judicial statements of the parol evidence rule that universally continues to bar the introduction of prior or *contemporaneous* written or oral agreements that contradict or vary the terms of an integrated writing.[57] The UCC version of the parol evidence rule also precludes "contemporaneous" as well as prior agreements.[58]

[B]   Admissibility of Evidence Concerning Intention to Integrate

We have already emphasized that the critical "preliminary determination" for a court rather than a jury is to determine whether the parties intended their writing to be a final or final and complete ("integrated") statement of the terms of their contract.[59] As one court suggests, "The antecedent question, therefore, is always whether the writing is the full agreement of the parties."[60] This preliminary determination permits admission of all relevant evidence, i.e., there is no question of exclusion of evidence until it is determined that the parol evidence rule is operative, and the rule becomes operative only after it is determined that the parties intended to adopt their writing as a final (partially integrated) or complete and exclusive (fully integrated) writing.[61] Thus, courts generally determine the issue of integration at the summary judgment stage since "[t]he factors that weigh in determining whether a contract is integrated are necessarily fact based and not appropriate for determination on a motion to dismiss."[62] It is a "fact-specific analysis" in which the court analysis will include

---

[54] RESTATEMENT 2d § 213.

[55] RESTATEMENT 2d § 214.

[56] The Reporter included "contemporaneous" in the subsequent section (§ 214) at the suggestion of an unidentified member of the American Law Institute, explaining the omission in § 213 as follows: "I left out the 'or contemporaneous' partly because Professor Corbin was so opposed to the idea, and partly because I don't know that anything is ever contemporaneous with anything else really, it either comes before or after. But it can be relatively contemporaneous, and I think what we say here is that evidence of prior or contemporaneous agreements or negotiations is not admissible in evidence to contradict the term of the writing, that is to say, show a different agreement from the one that the writing would show." 48 ALI Proceedings 449 (1971).

[57] Illustrations include Lund v. Jevne, 2009 U.S. App. LEXIS 26788 at *2 (9th Cir. 2009); Partner & Partner, Inc. v. Exxonmobil Oil Corp., 2009 U.S. App. LEXIS 9708 at *8 (6th Cir. 2009); BNX Sys. Corp. v. Worldwide Investigations & Research, Inc., 2009 U.S. App. LEXIS 2097 at *4 (4th Cir. 2009); Berezin v. Regency Sav. Bank, 234 F.3d 68 (1st Cir. 2000) (quoting Kobayashi v. Orion Ventures, 42 Mass. App. Ct. 492, 678 N.E.2d 180, 184 (1997)); Ungerleider v. Gordon, 214 F.3d 1279, 1282 (11th Cir. 2000).

[58] UCC § 2-202. *See* International Mktg., Ltd. v. Archer-Daniels-Midland Co., 192 F.3d 724, 729 (7th Cir. 1999).

[59] *See* § 83[D], *supra*.

[60] Wulfing v. Kansas City Southern Indus., Inc., 842 S.W.2d 133, 147 (Mo. Ct. App. 1992).

[61] Among the cases supporting this proposition, see McMahon Food Corp. v. Burger Dairy Co., 103 F. 3d 1307, 1314 (7th Cir. 1996); Hunter v. Board of Trustees of Broadlawns Med. Ctr., 481 N.W.2d 510, 514 (Iowa 1992); Shultz v. Delta-Rail Corp., 156 Ill. App. 3d 1, 508 N.E.2d 1143, 108 Ill. Dec. 566 (2d Dist. 1987); Marani v. Jackson, 183 Cal. App. 3d 695, 228 Cal. Rptr. 518 (1st Dist. 1986); Union Bank v. Swenson, 707 P.2d 663 (Utah 1985); Burge v. Frey, 545 F. Supp. 1160 (D. Kan. 1982); *See also* RESTATEMENT 2d § 209(2) and comment c.

[62] All R's Consulting, Inc. v. Pilgrims Pride Corp., 2008 U.S. Dist. LEXIS 30626 at *35, note 7 (S. D. N. Y. 2008).

evidence of the parties' negotiations.[63] Thus, for a court to determine whether the agreement is integrated, it will have to receive (provisionally) the same extrinsic evidence that the parol evidence rule will bar if the court determines that the writing is integrated.[64]

[C]   Tests Used in the Application of the Parol Evidence Rule

The parol evidence process begins with the trial judge who must decide whether to admit or exclude evidence of agreements or negotiations occurring prior to (or contemporaneously with) the writing. In a jury trial, the judge must ascertain that the jury is unaware of the evidence extrinsic to the writing unless and until he decides to admit it. In a nonjury trial, the judge finds the facts and also applies the law. In that situation, as will be seen, he may consider extrinsic evidence for the purpose of determining its admissibility and later decide that it should be excluded. Then, as the fact finder, he must not consider evidence which he earlier excluded. It is important to have a precise understanding of the various tests that have been created by courts to guide the trial judge in these determinations.

[1]   The "Appearance" Test

The question before the court is one of intention, i.e., did the parties intend their writing(s) to be the final (partially integrated) or complete and exclusive (fully integrated) memorial of their agreement? The first step in this process is for the judge to examine the writing. It is possible to discover cases holding that the entire parol evidence process is contained in this examination. Thus, if the judge simply examines the writing and, from its appearance alone, indulges a *conclusive* presumption that it is "complete," the writing becomes the sole criterion of its own completeness.[65] As Dean Wigmore suggested long ago, however, "The conception of a writing as wholly and intrinsically self-determinative of the parties' intent to make it a sole memorial of one or seven or twenty-seven subjects of negotiation is an impossible one."[66] The critical question is whether the writing was intended to cover certain subjects of negotiation, and that cannot be known until the writing is *compared* with the extrinsic matter. The judge admits the evidence provisionally, out of the earshot of the jury in a jury trial, to determine whether he will subsequently admit or exclude the proffered evidence.[67] Cases adopting the "appearance" test almost invariably allow for this approach.[68] As one court suggests,

> Protection against judicial enforcement of writings that *appear* to be binding integrations but in fact are not lies in the provision that all relevant evidence is

---

[63] Sterling International, Inc. v. Virtools Can., Inc., 2006 U.S. Dist. LEXIS 52749 at *11 (E. D. Wash. 2006). See also Mytee Prods. v. H. D. Prods., 2006 U.S. Dist. LEXIS 96385 at *17 (S. D. Cal. 2006).

[64] *See* Cananwill, Inc. v. Emar Group, Inc., 250 B.R. 533, 548 n. 12 (M.D.N.C. 1999).

[65] In Jake C. Byers, Inc. v. J.B.C. Inv., 834 S.W.2d 806, 812 (Mo. Ct. App. 1992), the court states, "In Missouri, consistent with our desire to preserve the sanctity of written contracts, we look to the written document first. If it appears to be a complete agreement on its face, it is, in effect, conclusively presumed to be the final as well as the complete agreement between the parties." The court also notes that its view is more consistent with a Williston "four corners" approach than with a Corbin approach that the court identifies with the RESTATEMENT 2d in § 209(3).

[66] 9 WIGMORE, EVIDENCE § 2431, at 103 (3d ed. 1940). In support of the Wigmore concept, see Hurst v. Nichols Research Corp., 621 So. 2d 964, 967 (Ala. 1993).

[67] *Id.*, § 2430(2), at 98.

[68] In the famous case of Masterson v. Sine, 68 Cal. 2d 222, 226, 436 P.2d 561, 563 (1968), Justice Traynor writes, "Even under the rule that the writing alone is to be consulted, it was found necessary to examine the alleged collateral agreement before concluding that proof of it was precluded by the writing alone."

admissible on the threshold issue of whether the writing was adopted by the parties as an integration of their agreement.[69]

The "appearance" test is likely to be stated in relatively obvious cases. The prerequisite is a writing that appears to state all of the terms of the transaction clearly and specifically. Absent credible evidence that such an expression is not the final writing of the parties, the trial court may easily determine that the writing is integrated.[70] The defendant will have the burden of showing that a writing that appears to be complete was not intended to be a final expression of agreement.[71] The writing, itself, may provide even more assistance to help the trial judge resolve the issue. For example, the writing may contain a clause stating the parties' intention that it is a fully integrated expression of their agreement (a "merger" clause which we will next explore).[72] Another use of the "appearance" test may be suggested where the comparison of the writing and the proffered evidence clearly indicates that the extrinsic matter contradicts a term in the writing. Such a determination would certainly facilitate a finding that the writing is at least "final" with respect to that matter.[73]

The RESTATEMENT 2d suggests that a writing that appears to be complete and specific may be deemed fully integrated absent other evidence that rejects such a finding.[74] This statement may be said to create a *rebuttable* presumption that the writing is a complete integration.[75] This provision, however, is immediately and emphatically qualified to reflect the Wigmore analysis by insisting that a writing cannot prove its own completeness and "wide latitude must be allowed for inquiry into circumstances bearing on the intention of the parties."[76] The RESTATEMENT 2d clearly eschews the outmoded notion of permitting a writing to be the sole source of proving its own completeness. Since the appearance test is typically relegated to obvious cases, it will not serve as an effective test in the more difficult cases.

[2]   Merger Clause Test

If the central question in determining the completeness of the writing is one of the intention of the parties, should a clear statement of that intention in the parties' writing conclusively establish the writing as a complete and exclusive statement of their intention so as to require

---

[69] Union Bank v. Swenson, 707 P.2d 663, 665 (Utah 1985) (emphasis supplied).

[70] *See, e.g.*, Bailey-Allen Co. v. Kurzet, 945 P.2d 180, 191 (Utah Ct. App. 1997); People's Heritage Sav. Bank v. Recoll Mgmt., Inc., 814 F. Supp. 159, 163 (D. Me. 1993).

[71] *See, e.g.*, Maryland Nat'l Bank v. Traenkle, 933 F. Supp. 1280, 1284 (D. Md. 1996).

[72] Even here, however, relevant evidence would still be admissible to show that the parties did not intend the expression to be fully integrated. *See Union Bank v. Swenson, supra* note 69.

[73] Fleet Bank of Me. v. Prawer, 1993 U.S. App. LEXIS 7500, at *14 (1st Cir. Apr. 7, 1993).

[74] "Where the parties reduce an agreement to a writing which in view of its completeness and specificity reasonably appears to be a complete agreement, it is taken to be an integrated agreement unless it is established by other evidence that the writing did not constitute a final expression." RESTATEMENT 2d § 209(3). This section is relied upon in United Artists Communications, Inc. v. Corporate Prop. Invs., 410 N.W.2d 39 (Minn. Ct. App. 1987).

[75] STMicroelectronics, Inc. Pension Restoration Plan v. Santoni, 2008 U.S. App. LEXIS 26147 (9th Cir., Oct. 23 2008) ("ST fails to rebut the presumption that the written plan is integrated" (citing Restatement 2d § 209(3)).

[76] "A document in the form of a written contract, signed by both parties and apparently complete on its face, may be decisive of the issue [of the intention of the parties to adopt the writing as a completely integrated agreement] in the absence of credible contrary evidence. *But a writing cannot of itself prove its own completeness, and wide latitude must be allowed for inquiry into circumstances bearing on the intention of the parties.*" RESTATEMENT 2d § 210 comment b (emphasis added).

a court to refuse to admit any evidence of prior understandings, simply because of the statement in the writing? The parties may include such a "merger" ("integration" or "zipper") clause in their writing, stating that the writing constitutes the sole and exclusive repository of the parties' agreement and somewhat redundantly adding that they do not intend to be bound by any other agreement, understanding or negotiation of whatsoever kind or nature.[77]

Professors Corbin and Williston suggest that such a merger clause should have conclusive effect in determining an integration unless the writing was obviously incomplete, the clause was inserted as a result of fraud or mistake, or there are grounds to set aside the contract.[78] Corbin is careful to point out that such a clause does not prove that the writing itself was ever assented to or became operative as a contract.[79] The RESTATEMENT 2d suggests that a merger clause "if agreed to" is likely to conclude the issue whether the agreement is "completely integrated."[80] The phrase, "if agreed to," is later amplified with the Corbin influence, "But such a clause does not control the question whether the writing was assented to as an integrated agreement. . . ."[81]

Another possible interpretation of "if agreed to" and the attendant requirement of "assent" may suggest a distinction between a printed merger clause in a standard form and a negotiated merger clause which the parties have apparently consciously considered. One of the more frustrating challenges of contract law that will be explored in the next chapter is how do deal with printed ("boilerplate") clauses in standardized agreements. It cannot be gainsaid that there is a pervasive practice of not reading printed clauses, even among merchants. Serious questions attend the enforceability of printed merger clauses. Absent rare evidence that the parties have consciously considered and assented to such a clause, it certainly should not be afforded conclusive effect with respect to the question of integration.[82]

The RESTATEMENT 2d refuses to give conclusive effect to a merger clause. Though admitting that such a clause "is likely to conclude" the question of integration,[83] it insists that "such a declaration may not be conclusive."[84] Several cases have also shown reluctance in affording

---

[77] In Betz Labs. v. Hines, 647 F.2d 402, 403 (3d Cir. 1981), the following merger clause appeared in the writing: "This agreement contains the whole agreement between the Seller and Buyer and there are no other terms, obligations, covenants, representations, statements or conditions, oral or otherwise, of any kind whatsoever."

[78] 4 WILLISTON § 633; 3 CORBIN § 578 (1963 ed.).

[79] *See* CORBIN § 578, at 405 (1963 ed.).

[80] RESTATEMENT 2d § 216 comment e (emphasis added). *See* Tallmadge Bros. v. Iroquois Gas Transmission Sys., L.P., 252 Conn. 479, 746 A.2d 1277, 1291 (2000).

[81] *Id.* See I. G. L. Racquet Club v. Midstates Builders, Inc., 323 N.W.2d 214, 215 (Iowa 1982).

[82] In Eberhardt v. Comerica Bank, 171 B.R. 239, 243 (E.D. Mich. 1994), the court states, "The presence of an integration clause, while often taken as strong evidence of the parties' intent, is not conclusive in all cases, particularly when the contract is a pre-printed form drawn by a sophisticated seller." *See also* Sierra Diesel Injection Serv. v. Burroughs Corp., 874 F.2d 653, 656 (9th Cir. 1989). In Levien Leasing Co. v. Dickey Co., 380 N.W.2d 748 (Iowa Ct. App. 1985), the court distinguishes a prior holding involving a negotiated ("handcrafted") contract in Montgomery Props. Corp. v. Economy Forms Corp., 305 N.W.2d 470 (Iowa 1981), from the "boilerplate motor vehicle lease" containing a printed merger clause which did not convince the court that the parties intended the lease to be a complete expression of the parties' agreement. In Zinn v. Walker, 87 N.C. App. 325, 361 S.E.2d 314 (1987), the court refused to give effect to a preprinted merger clause where the parties manifested their intention to include collateral agreements in their contract.

[83] RESTATEMENT 2d § 216 comment e. See Mary Karen Erbe v. 2010 U.S. Dist. LEXIS 21916 at *26 (W. D. Pa. Feb.17, 2010) citing this treatise.

[84] RESTATEMENT 2d § 209 comment b.

conclusive effect to such clauses, i.e., a judge may not ignore the collateral evidence simply because the writing contains a merger clause.[85] A number of other courts, however, follow the path created by Williston[86] in holding such clauses conclusive absent fraud, mistake, or another reason for setting aside the contract.[87] There can be no question that evidence of fraud, mistake or other invalidating causes cannot be precluded by a merger clause.[88]

In the absence of such invalidating causes, if the parties have assented to a negotiated merger clause, why should a court even consider extrinsic evidence of a prior agreement? One possible answer is found in a case where a writing containing a merger clause did not mention the principal inducement for the plaintiff's execution of the writing. The court held that the merger clause stating that the writing contained the entire agreement "means that the writing contains the entire agreement as to its limited subject matter alone."[89] An agreement may be "partially integrated" and the writing evidencing that agreement will not contain evidence of other, non-contradictory agreements between the parties. If, therefore, the parties intended to be bound only by the terms of the writing with respect to the subject matter of the writing, such evidence may be admissible even in the face of a merger clause in the partially integrated agreement. A carefully drafted merger clause, however, could avoid such a holding if it was assented to and there was no evidence of fraud or the like.

[3] The Natural Omission Test — Williston/Corbin — *Gianni v. Russel* — *Mitchill v. Lath* — *Masterson v. Sine*

If the writing of the parties appears to be complete though it contains no merger clause and the extrinsic evidence does not contradict the terms of the record, the integration issue becomes more difficult. If the question of whether the extrinsic (prior) agreement is to be

---

[85] *See, e.g.*, Gerdlund v. Electronic Dispensers Int'l, 190 Cal. App. 3d 263, 235 Cal. Rptr. 279, 282 (6th Dist. 1987). "Our Supreme Court held in Masterson v. Sine that such a clause, while it certainly helps to resolve the issue, does not of itself establish an integration; the collateral agreement itself must be examined in order to determine whether the parties intended it to be part of their bargain." To the same effect, see Matthews v. Drew Chem. Corp., 475 F.2d 146 (5th Cir. 1973), and Anderson & Nafziger v. G. T. Newcomb, Inc., 100 Idaho 175, 595 P.2d 709 (1979).

[86] *See supra* text at note 74.

[87] New Jersey is said to be particularly rigid in giving "unequivocal integration" clauses conclusive effect. *See* Telecom Int'l Am., Ltd. v. AT&T Corp., 67 F. Supp. 2d 189, 202 (S.D.N.Y. 1999). In Smith v. Central Soya of Athens, Inc., 604 F. Supp. 518, 526 (E.D.N.C. 1985), the court states that a merger clause "clearly precludes a court from admitting extrinsic evidence on a theory that the writing was not a final expression. It further creates a rebuttable presumption that the writing is a complete and exclusive statement of the contract terms. In order to rebut the presumption and, in effect, invalidate the merger clause, a party must offer evidence to establish the existence of fraud, bad faith, unconscionability, negligent omission or mistake in fact." *See also* Colafrancesco v. Crown Pontiac-GMC, Inc., 485 So. 2d 1131 (Ala. 1986).

[88] This statement is quoted in Kronenberg v. Katz, 872 A. 2d 568, 592, n.45 (Del. Ch. 2004). Betz Labs. v. Hines, 647 F.2d 402 (3d Cir. 1981), relies upon the second edition of this book as authority for the proposition that an "integration" (merger) clause is part of the contract and if fraud taints the relationship between the parties, the integration clause is, itself, struck down. RESTATEMENT 2d § 214(d) lists evidence of illegality, fraud, duress, mistake, lack of consideration, or other invalidating causes as not being barred by the parol evidence rule even in the face of a merger clause. *See* GTE Automatic Elec., Inc. v. Martin's, Inc., 127 A.D.2d 545, 512 N.Y.S.2d 107 (1st Dep't 1987) (evidence of fraudulent misrepresentations are not barred by the parol evidence rule); Franklin v. White, 493 N.E.2d 161 (Ind. 1986) (parol evidence rule does not bar evidence of mistake); City of Warwick v. Boeng Corp., 472 A.2d 1214 (R.I. 1984) (parol evidence rule does not bar evidence of lack of consideration). A contrary view which should be rejected is found in Danann Realty Corp. v. Harris, 5 N.Y.2d 317, 157 N.E.2d 597 (1959).

[89] Gem Corrugated Box Corp. v. National Kraft Container Corp., 427 F.2d 499, 503 (2d Cir. 1970) (principal inducement for plaintiff to purchase its requirements of boxes was stock purchase plan not mentioned in the writing).

operative is determined on the basis of the intention of the parties, Professor Williston was concerned that the parol evidence rule would be destroyed.[90] Consider, for example, a well-known case.[91]

Gianni leased space in an office building conducting a business which included selling tobacco, fruit, candy and soft drinks. Russel acquired the property and negotiated a new lease with Gianni which contained a provision that the lessee would thereafter sell only fruit, candy, soda water and the like, but that he would not sell tobacco in any form. The lease was carefully read to Gianni. Shortly after this lease was signed, Russel leased the adjoining room in the building to a pharmacy that began to sell soda water and soft drinks. Gianni claimed that two days before signing the lease, he had been assured that he had the exclusive right to sell these products and that he had surrendered his right to sell tobacco in exchange for the exclusive right. The court held this evidence inadmissible because the writing was "integrated."

Professor Williston was concerned that if someone such as Mr. Gianni could prove by a mere preponderance of the evidence that the oral agreement concerning Gianni's exclusive right to sell soda water and soft drinks had actually been made, and if this proof would be sufficient to make the extrinsic agreement operative as part of the overall agreement, there would be no need for the parol evidence rule, and the special status afforded final written evidence of an agreement would be emasculated. Williston believed that the test had to focus *not* on whether the extrinsic agreement had, in fact, been made, but *whether reasonable parties, situated as were the parties to this contract, would have naturally and normally included the extrinsic matter in the writing*. If parties might naturally form a separate agreement as to such extrinsic matter, the writing would not be integrated as to that matter.

Professor Corbin was not persuaded by this test. He insisted on a test that would have the trial judge (in most cases) consider the extrinsic evidence for two purposes: (a) to determine whether there existed "respectable" evidence to show that the antecedent agreement was made, and (b) to determine whether such an antecedent agreement had been discharged by the subsequent writing which one of the parties relied upon as the sole repository of the agreement.[92] The Corbin position is simple: Either the parties assented to the writing as an integrated agreement or they did not, and all "respectable" evidence should be considered to determine this critical question. This position is consistent with the basic Corbin view that courts must determine whether the parties have agreed today to nullify their agreement of yesterday and that there is no need to call upon some "parol evidence rule" to prove that intention.[93] It is generally assumed that the Corbin position would virtually emasculate the parol evidence rule.[94]

In terms of the recorded American cases, it is clear that the Williston test which was, not remarkably, replicated in the FIRST RESTATEMENT,[95] became the dominant, common law[96] test in American case law. Even though other "tests" are often mentioned, the Williston analysis is often the basis for the court's decision. Thus, in the *Gianni* case, though the court mentions

---

[90] 4 WILLISTON § 633.

[91] Gianni v. R. Russell & Co., 281 Pa. 320, 126 A. 791 (1924).

[92] 3 CORBIN § 582 (1963 ed.).

[93] *Id.* at 457.

[94] *See* ALI Proceedings at 442 (1971).

[95] FIRST RESTATEMENT § 240(1)(b). Professor Williston was the Reporter for the FIRST RESTATEMENT.

[96] The UCC test which will be considered later modifies the Williston test.

other tests, it states that the extrinsic (oral) agreement between Gianni and Russel had to be compared with the written lease to determine "whether parties situated as were the ones to the contract would naturally and normally include the one in the other *if it were made.*"[97] The court is not to determine whether the alleged extrinsic agreement was, in fact, made. Rather, on the assumption that it was made, was it the kind of agreement, in light of the subject matter of the writing when compared to the subject matter of the extrinsic agreement, that would ordinarily (naturally and normally) be executed at the same time and placed in the writing? The question is for the court and, in this case, the court encountered no difficulty in holding that the extrinsic agreement, concerning the *exclusive* right to sell soda water and soft drinks, was clearly the kind of agreement that reasonable parties would naturally and normally include in a writing which was a lease of premises to be used for the purpose of selling such products as well as others.

Mitchill v. Lath[98] involved the sale of a farm. The sellers also owned an unsightly icehouse on land owned by another across from the farm. Prior to the execution of the writing for the sale of the farm, the parties allegedly agreed that the sellers would remove the unsightly icehouse. When they failed to perform, the buyer brought an action and sought to introduce evidence of the icehouse removal agreement. While it suggested other tests that will be discussed later in this section, the majority of the court applied the Williston test, i.e., whether the extrinsic agreement concerning the icehouse was the kind of agreement that the parties would not ordinarily be expected to be embodied in a writing such as the one before the court for the purchase and sale of the farm.[99] The majority refused to admit the evidence, though it could have been established by the overwhelming weight of the evidence. A dissenting opinion quarreled not with the test used but with its application.[100]

Four decades later, Justice Traynor wrote the opinion for the court in *Masterson v. Sine*,[101] where a grant deed reserved an option in the grantors to repurchase the property for the same consideration as that received by the grantors with a depreciation allowance. The property was a ranch owned by the brother of one of the grantees. Upon the bankruptcy of the grantor, the trustee in bankruptcy sought to enforce the option. The defendants sought to introduce evidence that the parties intended the option to be exercised only by a member of the family because the parties wanted the property kept in the family though there was no such provision in the writing. In a pedagogical opinion, Justice Traynor relied upon the Williston test, i.e., was

---

[97] *Gianni*, 281 Pa. at 323, 126 A. at 792 (emphasis added). For a more recent application of the same test, see Hinkel v. Sataria Distrib. & Packaging, Inc.,920 N. E. 2d 766 (Ct. App. Ind. 2010), where the plaintiff claimed that, prior to signing an employment contract, he was promised a year's salary and insurance benefits if he were involuntarily terminated. The written contract specified Hinkel's compensation, title, location, start date and the date on which insurance coverage would begin. It said nothing about any severance benefit. Quoting Williston on Contracts § 33. 25, the court concluded that a lucrative severance provision would "naturally and normally" be included in an employment contract. The court held that the written contract superceded any alleged prior promises.

[98] 247 N.Y. 377, 160 N.E. 646, 68 A.L.R. 239 (1928).

[99] The court stated that the extrinsic agreement "must be one that parties would not ordinarily be expected to embody in the writing; or put in another way . . . *it must not be so clearly connected with the principal transaction as to be part and parcel of it.*" 247 N.Y. at 381, 160 N. E. at 647. The italicized portion of the test is stated in Western Intermodal Servs. v. Singamas Container Indus. Co., 2000 U.S. Dist LEXIS 3909, at *6 (S.D.N.Y. Mar. 31, 2000).

[100] Judge Lehman's dissent clearly reveals his disagreement based on his view that parties such as the parties in this case would naturally and normally omit an agreement to remove the icehouse from the kind of writing involved. The writing was for the conveyance of land and the promise to remove the icehouse was not related to that subject matter.

[101] 68 Cal. 2d 222, 65 Cal. Rptr. 545, 436 P.2d 561 (1968).

the extrinsic agreement the kind of agreement that might naturally be made as a separate agreement by parties situated as were the parties to the written contract? The opinion focuses upon these parties, i.e., the parties to this contract, and concludes that there was nothing in the record to indicate that these parties to this *family* transaction, inexperienced in land transactions, had any awareness of the disadvantages of failing to include the entire agreement in this kind of writing-a deed. Thus, parties *situated as were these parties* would not naturally include a provision restricting the exercise of the option to a family member in the deed. The evidence was admissible.[102]

In each of these well-known cases, there was no merger clause expressing the parties' intention concerning integration. The extrinsic agreements did not contradict the terms of the subsequent writing. Yet, the writings were extensive though they did not mention the alleged extrinsic matter. Such cases are the more difficult cases to which the parol evidence rule must be applied. Conclusory statements that the extrinsic agreement is or is not "collateral" or that the writing is or is not "integrated" are useless. They are excuses for avoiding the critical question of the presumable intention of the parties concerning the finality and completeness of the writing. In such cases, the Williston test has withstood the test of time,[103] except where it is statutorily modified by the UCC in contracts for the sale of goods, and it appears to be well ensconced for future application.

[4]   The Wigmore Aid and the "Collateral Agreement" Test

[a]   Wigmore

Dean Wigmore early on suggested a cogent analysis of the parol evidence process which was designed to overcome any reliance on the "appearance" test. As suggested earlier,[104] Wigmore thought it impossible to determine what the writing of the parties was intended to cover until it is known what there was to cover. Thus, he insisted that the extrinsic matter be received provisionally by the judge to be compared to the writing so as to permit the judge to determine whether the writing was intended to cover the extrinsic matter.[105] The Wigmore test, however, is admittedly quite modest:

> In deciding upon this intent, the chief and most satisfactory index for the judge is found in the circumstance whether or not the particular element of the alleged extrinsic negotiation is dealt with at all in the writing. If it is mentioned, covered, or dealt with in the writing, then presumably the writing was meant to represent all of

---

[102] In Hanson v. McCaw Cellular Communications, 881 F. Supp. 911, 916 (S.D.N.Y. 1995), *aff'd*, 77 F.3d 663 (2d Cir. 1996), the court distinguishes the facts of *Masterson*: "Unlike the situation in Masterson, this was not a contract among family members, and the supposed parol agreement was not the sort of understanding that naturally might have been left out of the formal documentation. This was an arm's length transaction involving millions of dollars among sophisticated business people." Justice Traynor's statement of the "natural omission" test quoted the language from § 240(1)(b) of the First Restatement. A more recent statement of the same language relying upon *Masterson* appears in Bank of Beverly Hills v. Catain, 128 Cal. App. 3d 28, 35, 180 Cal. Rptr. 67, 71 (2d Dist. 1982).

[103] In addition to the cases previously cited applying the "natural omission" test, see Steinke v. Sungard Fin. Sys., 121 F.3d 763, 770 (1st Cir. 1997); M.T. McBrian v. Liebert Corp., 1998 U.S. Dist. LEXIS 1512, at *20 (N.D. Ill. Feb. 6, 1998); Lanning Constr. v. Rozell, 320 N.W.2d 522, 524 (S.D. 1982).

[104] See the discussion of the "Appearance" test in § 84[C][1], *supra*.

[105] 9 Wigmore on Evidence § 2430 (3d ed.).

the transaction on that element; if it is not, then probably the writing was not intended to embody that element.[106]

As such, this test could preclude evidence of consistent additional terms simply because the writing mentioned the subject matter of such extrinsic terms. If the extrinsic terms *contradicted* the terms of the subsequent writing, the evidence would be excluded under any test, including the Wigmore test. As stated, however, the test suggests an intention to have a complete and exclusive writing with respect to any matter mentioned or dealt with at all in the writing since it would, again, preclude evidence of consistent (non-contradictory) terms dealing with that subject matter. It may also be interpreted to permit evidence of extrinsic agreements which would normally be included in the writing simply because the writing does not mention the particular extrinsic matter. Since Wigmore did not suggest the test as anything more than an aid to a judge, he apparently recognized that its utility was limited. The test appears, along with others, in various cases when it can serve as a bulwark to a decision reached on the basis of other tests, usually the Williston ("natural omission") test.[107] It is not viewed as a dispositive test in the extant case law.[108]

[b]   The "Collateral Agreement" Test

The well-known case of *Mitchill v. Lath*[109] was explored earlier[110] as an illustration of the "natural omission" test created by Professor Williston. Like many other cases confronting a parol evidence issue, that opinion suggested other "tests," though both the majority and dissenting opinions appeared to rely on the "natural omission" test for their opposed results. The majority opinion suggested that, before any evidence of a prior oral agreement which is not supported by a separate consideration could be admitted, three conditions had to be met: (1) the agreement must in form be a collateral one, (2) the extrinsic evidence must not contradict express or implied provisions of the "written contract," and (3) it must be one which the parties would not ordinarily (naturally) be expected to embody in the writing. The third condition is clearly the Williston test and, again, it appeared to be the basic analysis leading the court to hold that the extrinsic evidence was not admissible. The second condition is a truism and would apply even if the writing were "final" ("partially integrated") rather than complete. The first condition-that the agreement must appear to be a "collateral" one — provides no analytical basis for a court to decide the question of admissibility. The *Mitchill* majority concluded, "Were such an agreement [the extrinsic agreement concerning removal of an icehouse] made it would seem most natural that the inquirer should find it in the contract [for the purchase and sale of the farm]."[111] Having concluded that parties situated as were the

---

[106] *Id.*, § 2430(3), at 98.

[107] *See, e.g.,* Traudt v. Nebraska Pub. Power Dist., 197 Neb. 765, 251 N.W.2d 148 (1977); Gianni v. R. Russell & Co., 281 Pa. 320, 126 A.2d 791 (1924).

[108] Dean Wigmore's work is cited in modern case law for the basic proposition that the parol evidence rule is a rule of substantive law. His denunciation of the "appearance" test may also be found in modern cases. *See* § 84[C][1], *supra.* His "test," however, is generally not discoverable in modern cases.

[109] 247 N.Y. 377, 160 N.E. 646, 68 A.L.R. 239 (1928).

[110] *See supra* text following note 95.

[111] 247 N.Y. at 382, 160 N.E. at 647. This is the "natural omission" test of Williston which, again, was the basis for the decision. The RESTATEMENT 2d mentions the case only with respect to the natural omission test, i.e., "[P]rior oral agreement discharged if parties would 'ordinarily be expected to embody' it in the writing." RESTATEMENT 2d § 213, Reporter's Note to comment c.

parties to this contract would have naturally included the extrinsic matter in the writing, it is superfluous to suggest that the agreement concerning the icehouse removal is not admissible because it is not a "collateral" agreement. If the evidence were admissible because parties would not have included such extrinsic matter in the writing, it is equally superfluous to suggest that the extrinsic agreement *was* "collateral." Another application of the *Mitchill v. Lath* analysis reveals the conclusory nature of the "collateral agreement" requirement.

The plaintiffs contended that an insurance agent had agreed to supply a homeowner's policy and a workmen's compensation policy to cover casualty to a home which was to be constructed and liability coverage for any workman injured on the premises during the construction. The writing dealt exclusively with homeowner's coverage and the plaintiffs sought to introduce evidence concerning the negotiations for the workmen's compensation coverage. The trial court admitted the evidence over defendant's objections that it violated the parol evidence rule. On appeal, the Supreme Court of Alabama followed *Mitchill v. Lath*, concluding that, "any agreement to provide workmen's compensation coverage would have been collateral to the agreement to issue a homeowner's policy." Finding no contradiction between the extrinsic evidence and the writing, it proceeded to the condition under *Mitchill*: "A reasonable person would not ordinarily expect workmen's compensation coverage to be included in the same writing as homeowner's coverage."[112] The essential rationale is clear: to determine whether a particular extrinsic agreement was a collateral agreement, it is necessary to determine whether the parties would ordinarily (naturally and normally) include such coverage in the particular writing expressing their agreement. If they would have naturally included it in this type of writing, the extrinsic agreement is not called "collateral" and the evidence is excluded. If, however, they would not have naturally included such a matter in the writing, the extrinsic agreement is called "collateral" and the evidence is admitted. Again, however, the question of admissibility is determined by the "natural omission" test and not by the label attached to the extrinsic agreement.

A more recent illustration of the vacuousness of the "collateral" label regards the "collateral agreement" rule as an exception to the parol evidence rule. Quoting from an earlier opinion, the court hastens to add,

> However, under this exception, "any such collateral agreement must not contradict the terms of the written agreement and the agreement must be one that would naturally be omitted from the written instrument."[113]

The so-called "collateral agreement" test is not a test; it is a superfluous conclusory label attached after the critical natural omission test has been applied and the court has already determined whether the evidence should be admitted.

---

[112] Alabama Farm Bureau Mut. Casualty Ins. Co. v. Haynes, 497 So. 2d 82, 85 (Ala. 1986).

[113] Patrick v. Ressler, 2005 Ohio App. LEXIS 4971 at *20 (2005) quoting Pingue v. Durante, 1996 Ohio App. LEXIS 1857.

[5] The RESTATEMENT 2d Analysis: "Natural Omission," "Separate Consideration," and "Scope" Tests

The RESTATEMENT 2d includes the Williston test, among others,[114] calling it the "natural omission" test: "An agreement is not completely integrated if the writing omits a consistent additional agreed term which is . . . such a term as in the circumstances might naturally be omitted from the writing."[115] What may appear to be another RESTATEMENT 2d test is a carry-over from the FIRST RESTATEMENT.[116]

If the extrinsic agreement is one that has been made for a "separate consideration," evidence of that agreement is admissible. Certainly, if the parties made separate contracts supported by separate considerations, the last contract does not supersede the earlier contract. Even if the parties have made only one contract, however, evidence of a consistent additional (prior) term supported by a separate consideration is not excluded under this test. As the RESTATEMENT 2d admits, however, the "separate consideration" test is nothing more than "a particular application or species of the rule of Subsection 2(b)" which allows evidence of "a term as in the circumstances might naturally be omitted from the writing."[117] The illustration supporting the "separate consideration" test clearly supports this conclusion. Where A and B have signed an integrated writing for the purchase and sale of an automobile and, as part of their transaction, the parties have orally agreed that B may keep the auto in A's garage for one year for $15 per month, evidence of the oral agreement is admissible.[118] The fact that the parties have agreed upon a separate consideration for the garage rental simply reinforces their manifestation of intention that the garage rental agreement was not intended to be merged into their writing concerning the purchase and sale of the car.

Another discernible test in the RESTATEMENT 2d may be called the "scope" test, the description of which becomes complicated. Because the RESTATEMENT 2d is obsessed with the notion of "integration," it places this test in a section captioned, "Effect of Integrated Agreement on Prior Agreements (Parol Evidence Rule)."[119] This caption focuses upon integration and suggests that when the integration question is resolved, the application of the parol evidence rule will follow without difficulty. As suggested throughout the foregoing analysis of the parol evidence rule, the critical question is whether the parties intended their writing to be a final or both final and complete statement of their agreement. *How* a court goes

---

[114] RESTATEMENT 2d § 216 is quoted in O'Meara v. Pritchett, 97 Or. App. 329, 335, 776 P.2d 866, 869 (1989): "(1) Evidence of a consistent additional term is admissible to supplement an integrated agreement unless the court finds that the agreement was completely integrated. (2) An agreement is not completely integrated if the writing omits a consistent additional term which is (a) agreed to for a separate consideration, or (b) such a term as in the circumstances might naturally be omitted from the writing."

[115] RESTATEMENT 2d § 216(2)(b). Comment d to this section suggests that this test would be particularly applicable to contracts evidenced by standard, printed forms which often do not allow space for additional terms. The comment is careful to emphasize that these examples are not exclusive. *See* Denny's Restaurants, Inc. v. Security Union Title Ins. Co., 71 Wash. App. 194, 859 P.2d 619, 624 n.8 (1993). For other applications of the RESTATEMENT 2d "natural omission" test, see Felco, Inc. v. Doug's North Hills Bottle Shop, 579 N.W.2d 576, 581 (N.D. 1998); Abercrombie v. Hayden Corp., 320 Or. 279, 883 P.2d 845, 851 (1994); 1010 Potomac Assocs. v. Grocery Mfrs. of Am., Inc., 485 A.2d 199, 206 (D.C. 1984).

[116] *See* FIRST RESTATEMENT § 240(1)(a).

[117] RESTATEMENT 2d § 216 comment c. *See* GCIU Employer Retirement Fund v. Chicago Tribune Co., 66 F.3d 862, 865 (7th Cir. 1995); Brennan v. Carvel Corp., 929 F.2d 801, 807 (1st Cir. 1991).

[118] RESTATEMENT 2d § 216 ill. 3.

[119] RESTATEMENT 2d § 213.

about answering that question in a given situation is the heart of the parol evidence process, i.e., what tests or guidelines do courts utilize in that effort. Unfortunately, the Restatement 2d "scope" test does not facilitate that analysis. Its conclusion that, "A binding integrated agreement discharges prior agreements to the extent that it is inconsistent with them," does not facilitate any analysis.[120] The critical question is whether there is a "binding integrated agreement" and, more particularly, how does a court decide that question. The next subsection adds to the confusion: "A binding completely integrated agreement discharges prior agreements to the extent that they are within its scope."[121] In a prior section, the RESTATEMENT 2d defines "a completely integrated agreement" as "an integrated agreement adopted by the parties as a complete and exclusive statement of the terms of the agreement."[122] A comment to that section distinguishes partially integrated from completely integrated agreements. A partially integrated agreement is one which the parties intend to be final on some matters but does not evidence an intention to preclude consistent additional terms. A fully integrated agreement, however, is intended to be the complete statement of the terms of agreement between the parties. If that was the intention, "evidence of the alleged making of consistent additional terms must be kept from the trier of fact."[123] This is a clear and effective statement of the effect of a completely integrated agreement which is restated in a separate section.[124] In yet another section, however, we are told that such a completely integrated agreement discharges prior agreements only "to the extent that they are within its scope."[125] The inevitable question arises, if an agreement is completely integrated, what kind of prior agreements are not within its scope?

The two RESTATEMENT 2d illustrations following this analysis are anything but helpful. In the first, the parties orally agree on repair services to certain property to be completed by October 1. They then execute a memorandum of their agreement which is complete in all respects except that it is silent on the time for performance. The conclusion is hardly satisfying: "If the memorandum is a binding completely integrated agreement, the agreement to finish by October 1 is discharged, and the repairs are to be finished within a reasonable time."[126] There is a question as to whether a memorandum that is silent on the time for performance is a completely integrated agreement. Professor Corbin suggests that judicial gap-fillers, such as "a reasonable time," do not constitute any part of the "integration" that is protected by the parol evidence rule. Moreover, he suggests that his view is supported by the weight of authority.[127] Thus, the writing in the illustration may be said to have been only partially integrated. If it *had* been completely integrated, just as night follows day, the effect would be to exclude evidence of the prior agreement that the repairs would be finished by October 1. The RESTATEMENT 2d fails to address the question of how such an agreement could be said to be completely integrated.

---

[120] RESTATEMENT 2d § 213(1).

[121] RESTATEMENT 2d § 213(2).

[122] RESTATEMENT 2d § 210(1).

[123] RESTATEMENT 2d § 210 comment a.

[124] RESTATEMENT 2d § 216(1).

[125] RESTATEMENT 2d § 213(2).

[126] RESTATEMENT 2d § 213 ill. 3. The illustration is based on Hayden v. Hoadley, 94 Vt. 345, 111 A. 343 (1920).

[127] 3 CORBIN § 593, at 556–57 (1963 ed.).

The second and last illustration of the "scope" test is even more curious. The parties made an agreement for the purchase and sale of land with a hotel thereon together with the hotel furniture. They employed a lawyer to draft the writing evidencing the contract and the writing contained no mention of the furniture. The inescapable conclusion is, "The agreement as to furniture is discharged if there is a binding completely integrated agreement covering the entire transaction, but not if only the part of the agreement relating to real property is integrated."[128] The case upon which this illustration is based relied upon Dean Wigmore's analysis of the parol evidence process and found that the agreement was not completely integrated, thereby admitting the evidence as to the furniture.[129] Like the previous illustration, this illustration suggests that *if* the agreement is completely integrated, the extrinsic evidence is not admissible; if it is not completely integrated, the evidence is admissible. Unfortunately, the scope test amounts to nothing more than this, i.e., the scope test is a snare and a delusion since it leaves the question of how a court decides whether a writing is partially or fully integrated unanswered. The only test in the RESTATEMENT 2d which assists courts in that process is the "natural omission" (Williston) test explored earlier.

The inescapable conclusion is that the RESTATEMENT 2d speaks of four tests and contains only one. The "appearance" test in the RESTATEMENT 2d self destructs.[130] The "separate consideration" test is an admitted species of the "natural omission" test, and the "scope" test is a truism that requires the support of the only viable test in the RESTATEMENT 2d to determine whether a writing is completely integrated, again, the "natural omission" test. In a number of areas, the RESTATEMENT 2d makes many valuable contributions to the analysis of contract law. Unfortunately, its treatment of the parol evidence process is not among them.[131]

[6]   The Uniform Commercial Code Parol Evidence Rule

Unlike the RESTATEMENT 2d analysis of the parol evidence rule, the UCC provides a significant improvement over prior attempts to restate the concept. In one tightly drafted section and valuable Comments, the UCC version manages to overcome much of the confusion of the past and provides a highly effective guide to courts confronted with a parol evidence issue in a contract for the sale of goods.[132] Section 2-202 of the Code avoids a basic flaw found in the RESTATEMENT 2d by captioning its parol evidence section, "Final Written *Expression:* Parol or Extrinsic Evidence," instead of "Agreement," thereby distinguishing "agreement" from the writing expressing the agreement. The UCC also avoids the unfortunate, conclusory term, "integration," and the necessity of distinguishing between a "partial" and "full" or "complete" integration. Rather, it characterizes writings as either "final" (comparable to

---

[128] RESTATEMENT 2d § 213 ill. 4.

[129] Brown v. Oliver, 123 Kan. 711, 256 P. 1008 (1927).

[130] *See* § 84[C][1], *supra.*

[131] For an analysis of the RESTATEMENT 2d parol evidence rule analysis, see Murray, *The Parol Evidence Process and Standardized Agreements Under the Restatement (Second) of Contracts,* 123 U. PA. L. REV. 1342 (1975).

[132] UCC § 2-202: Final Written Expression: Parol or Extrinsic Evidence.

Terms with respect to which the confirmatory memoranda of the parties agree or which are otherwise set forth in a writing intended by the parties as a final expression of their agreement with respect to such terms as are included therein may not be contradicted by evidence of any prior agreement or a contemporaneous oral agreement but may be explained or supplemented

(a) by course of dealing or usage of trade (Section 1-205) or by course of performance (Section 2-208); and

(b) by evidence of consistent additional terms unless the court finds the writing to have been intended also as a complete and exclusive statement of the terms of the agreement.

"partial integration") or "complete and exclusive" (comparable to "full" or "complete" integrations). In a dozen lines, it sets forth the following principles: (1) If the parties intend their written expression of agreement to be merely *final*, the terms of that final agreement may not be *contradicted* by any prior or contemporaneous oral agreement.[133] (2) Such terms in a final writing may, however, be explained or supplemented by evidence of consistent additional terms or by evidence of course of dealing, usage of trade or course of performance. (3) If the parties intended their writing to be not merely *final* but also a *complete and exclusive* statement of the terms of their agreement, evidence of consistent additional terms is excluded, but even with respect to such a complete and exclusive expression of agreement, evidence of trade usage, course of dealing, and course of performance is admissible.[134]

The UCC parol evidence rule unequivocally rejects concepts that had traditionally been employed. It rejects any presumption that a written contract sets forth the entire contract of the parties, i.e., it "looks beyond the four corners of the document to the circumstances surrounding the transaction."[135] As one court insightfully states,

> Perhaps one of the fundamental departures of the Code from prior contract law is found in the parol evidence rule and the definition of an agreement between two parties. Under the UCC, an agreement goes beyond the written words on a piece of paper. 'Agreement' means the bargain of the parties in fact as found in their language or by implication from other circumstances including course of dealing or usage of trade or course of performance [§ 1-201(b)(3)]. . . . Express terms, then, do not constitute the entire agreement, which must be sought also in evidence of usages, dealings and performance of the contract itself.' "[136]

Thus, the UCC rejects the familiar rule that, absent an ambiguity, the intent of the parties is to be determined from the face of the contract without resort to extrinsic evidence.[137] To determine whether the parties intended their writing to be final and/or complete, the Code provision adds a third level to a traditional two level inquiry. Instead of merely determining whether the express terms of the writing are ambiguous on their face and, if they are, pursuing their meaning, even where the language appears unambiguous on its face, the Code directs courts to consider evidence of course of dealing, usage of trade and course of performance as a separate test of ambiguity.[138] Instead of a presumption that the writing is the complete and exclusive expression of the parties' agreement, the opposite is assumed, i.e., the writing will not be viewed as complete and exclusive unless the court finds that the parties intended it to be

---

[133] American Industrial Technologies, Inc. v. Aero Tec Laboratories Inc., 1994 U.S. Dist. LEXIS 6233 at *61 (D. Del. 1994) citing this treatise.

[134] An earlier version of this statement in the third edition of this treatise is quoted in Middletown Concrete Products, Inc. v. Black Clawson Co., 802 F. Supp. 1135, 1144–45 (D. Del. 1992).

[135] Betaco, Inc. v. Cessna Aircraft Co., 32 F.3d 1126, 1132 (7th Cir. 1994). *See* UCC § 2-202, Comment 1.

[136] Nanakuli Paving & Rock Co. v. Shell Oil Co., 664 F.2d 772, 794 (9th Cir. 1981). In Mylan Pharmaceuticals v. American Cyanamid Co., 1995 U.S. App. LEXIS 4197, at *21 (4th Cir. Mar. 3, 1995), the court states, "the U.C.C. modified the common law parol evidence rule by giving special weight to evidence of trade usage and commercial practices. In effect, trade usage becomes part of the contract: '[Contracts] are to be read on the assumption that the course of prior dealings between the parties and the usages of trade were taken for granted when the document was phrased. Unless carefully negated, they have become an element of the meaning of the words used.' " UCC § 2-202, comment 2.

[137] See *Betaco, supra* note 135, and Comment 1(b) to UCC § 2-202.

[138] Bloom v. Hearst Entertainment, 33 F.3d 518, 522 (5th Cir. 1994). *See also* Allapattah Servs. v. Exxon Corp., 61 F. Supp. 2d 1308, 1315 (S.D. Fla. 1999).

complete and exclusive by considering extrinsic evidence as well as the language of the writing.[139]

There is an emphatic recognition that trade usage and course of dealing are automatic terms of the contract, i.e., the writings evidencing the contract "are to be read on the assumption that the course of dealings between the parties and the usages of trade were taken for granted when the document was phrased."[140] Moreover, even a complete written expression of agreement may be *explained or supplemented* by such terms.[141] It must be remembered that interpretation is essential regardless of the completeness of the writing since the *parol evidence rule merely defines the subject matter of that interpretation.* While merger (integration) clauses are effective to manifest the intention of the parties that their written expression is complete,[142] evidence of trade usage, course of dealing and course of performance will be admissible even if the writing contains a merger clause indicating that the parties intended their writing to be the complete and sole repository of their agreement,[143] whether the merger clause is a printed clause ("boilerplate")[144] or a negotiated clause.[145] The only route to the excision of such automatic contract terms is through their express negation, and a merger clause will be insufficient for that purpose.[146]

UCC Modified Natural Omission Test. If there is a flaw in the UCC version of the parol evidence rule, it is the failure to state *in the language of the section* the test to be used to determine whether the writing is complete and exclusive (in the vernacular of the older cases and RESTATEMENT 2d, "completely integrated"). The test is found, however, in a comment: "If the additional terms are such that, if agreed upon, they *would certainly* have been included in the document in the view of the court, then evidence of their alleged making must be kept from the trier of fact."[147] This is a modified Williston test. Under the Williston test ("natural omission"), if parties situated as were the parties to the contract would have naturally (normally or ordinarily) included the alleged extrinsic matter in the kind of writing they executed, the evidence is excluded. Under the UCC test, only if such parties *would certainly* have included such extrinsic terms in their writing is the evidence excluded. Thus, more evidence is admissible under the UCC test since a court will exclude it only if parties *would certainly* have included such extrinsic matter in the writing as contrasted with naturally or

---

[139] *See* Killion v. Buran Equip. Co., 27 U.C.C. Rep. Serv. (CBC) 970, 972 (Cal. App. 1979).

[140] UCC 2-202, comment 2.

[141] *See* UCC §§ 1-205 and 2-208. *See also* Kaiser Aero. & Elecs. Corp. v. Alliant Techsystems, 1997 U.S. App. LEXIS 35509, at *14 (4th Cir. Dec. 17, 1997), and Trans World Metals, Inc. v. Southwire Co., 769 F.2d 902 (2d Cir. 1985), permitting trade usage to explain or supplement the contract terms.

[142] *See* Earman Oil Co. v. Burroughs Corp., 625 F.2d 1291 (5th Cir. 1980).

[143] A & A Mech. v. Thermal Equip. Sales, 998 S. W. 2d 505, 510–511 (Ct. App. Ky. 1999).

[144] *See* Nanakuli Paving & Rock Co. v. Shell Oil Co., 664 F.2d 772 (9th Cir. 1981).

[145] *See* Columbia Nitrogen Corp. v. Royster Co., 451 F.2d 3 (4th Cir. 1971).

[146] Allapattah Servs. v. Exxon Corp., *supra* note 138. UCC § 2-202 comment 2, requires "careful negation" of trade usage and prior course of dealing. As to course of performance, such evidence is typically subsequent to the writing and, as the strongest source of interpretation of the writing among the three aids to interpretation (UCC § 2-208(2)) and a *subsequent* manifestation, it could operate as a modification of the express terms of the writing (§§ 2-208(3) and 2-209(1)). As such, it would not be affected by the parol evidence rule because the rule applies only to prior or contemporaneous agreements. *See* § 84[A], *supra.*

[147] UCC § 2-202 comment 3 (emphasis added).

ordinarily including it.[148]

The UCC parol evidence concept, like other UCC sections, does not replace all of the common law that preceded it. Unless displaced by the provisions of the Code, the principles of the common law are operative.[149] Therefore, parol evidence concepts developed at common law remain effective unless they are displaced by the UCC section on parol evidence.[150] Parol evidence may be introduced to show fraud[151] even in the face of a merger clause.[152] As in other applications of the parol evidence rule, the court decides the question of the intention of the parties to have a final or complete expression of agreement.[153] Even if the UCC is not technically applicable to a particular transaction, some courts have applied the Code parol evidence provision by analogy.[154] In sum, the UCC version of the parol evidence rule is a significant improvement over its predecessors. The RESTATEMENT 2d recognizes the UCC version in its effort to restate the concept, but any Code influence was lost in the maze of language attempting to support various views of the rule. It is unfortunate that the RESTATEMENT 2d did not simply replicate the UCC version as the basic model which could have been elaborated into a highly effective analysis.

[7]   International Transactions — CISG — Parol Evidence Rule Inapplicable — Merger Clauses — Unidroit Principles

As noted in our discussion of the Statute of Frauds in an earlier chapter, contracts for the sale of goods within the United Nations Convention on Contracts for the International Sale of Goods (CISG) need not be evidenced by a writing.[155] It should not, therefore, seem remarkable that where the parties *choose* to evidence their CISG contracts in writing, evidence of prior negotiations will be admissible.[156] Though CISG now displaces domestic law in contracts for the sale of goods in the United States (the UCC) and some fifty-seven other nations, United

---

[148] The earliest judicial manifestation of this distinction is found in the opinion of Justice Traynor in Masterson v. Sine, 68 Cal. 2d 222, 228, 65 Cal. Rptr. 545, 547, 436 P.2d 561, 563 (1968): "The draftsmen of the Uniform Commercial Code would exclude the evidence in still fewer instances. . . ." This is only one illustration of Justice Traynor's precocious awareness of the changes effected by UCC Article 2. It is possible that his insights were fueled as a student of Professor Karl Llewellyn, the chief architect of the UCC and draftsman of Article 2. *See also* Cosmopolitan Fin. Corp. v. Runnels, 2 Haw. App. 33, 625 P.2d 390 (1981). See also Aero Consulting Corp. v. Cessna Aircraft Co., 867 F. Supp. 1480, 1490–91 (D. Kan. 1994), where the court concludes that, under all of the circumstances (an extensive writing including a merger clause evidencing a half-million dollar contract), the alleged extrinsic evidence "would certainly" have been included in the writing.

[149] UCC § 1-103.

[150] *See* Glenn Dick Equip. Co. v. Galey Constr., 97 Idaho 216, 541 P.2d 1184 (1975).

[151] Cone Mills Corp. v. A. G. Estes, Inc., 377 F. Supp. 222 (N.D. Ga. 1974). See also Universal Drilling Co. v. Camay Drilling Co., 737 F.2d 869 (10th Cir. 1984), where fraud in the inducement could not be proven but court would allow such evidence notwithstanding the parol evidence rule.

[152] City Dodge, Inc. v. Gardner, 232 Ga. 766, 208 So. 2d 794 (1974).

[153] Peoria Harbor Marina v. McGlasson, 105 Ill. App. 3d 723, 61 Ill. Dec. 431, 434 N.E.2d 786 (3d Dist. 1982).

[154] *See* Interstate Indus. Uniform Rental Serv., Inc. v. F. R. Lepage Bakery, Inc., 413 A.2d 516 (Me. 1980) (uniform rentals) (the article 2A (leases) provision is also § 202 and is identical to § 2-202); Conran v. Yager, 263 S.C. 417, 211 S.E.2d 228 (1975) (sale of real estate).

[155] CISG, Art. 11. Under Article 12, however, a "Contracting State" may, pursuant to Art. 96, declare that Art. 11 does not apply. The United States has not taken such a reservation. Thus, contracts governed by CISG between a United States party and a party in another of the many CISG countries need not be evidenced by a writing unless that "Contracting State" has taken an Art. 96 reservation. For an overview of CISG, see § 13 *supra*, in Chapter 1.

[156] CISG, Art. 8(3).

States case law interpreting CISG is scant. With respect to the parol evidence rule, however, case law clearly confirms the absence of the parol evidence rule under CISG.[157] When compared to the UCC parol evidence rule analysis, "[T]he standard UCC inquiry regarding whether a writing is fully or partially integrated has little meaning under the CISG."[158] The CISG provision allowing evidence of prior negotiations is part of Article 8 dealing with interpretation. The first provision of that Article has been interpreted to allow evidence of "subjective" intent" where the other party knew or certainly should have known of that intent.[159] To preclude the admission of such evidence, therefore, would emasculate the first guide to interpretation set forth under CISG.

Though the parol evidence rule is not part of CISG, it should be recalled that parties may agree to exclude the application of the Convention or derogate from any of its provisions.[160] Thus, parties may agree to derogate from Article 8(3) of CISG (which allows the admission of parol evidence) with the expressed intention of being bound exclusively by the terms of the writing, in effect creating a "private" parol evidence rule. A "merger" ("integration") clause in the record of the contract *may* accomplish this result.[161] To assure this result, however, it is wise to add an express statement to such a clause that the parties have agreed to derogate from Article 8(3) and intend their contract to preclude any prior or contemporaneous evidence that either adds to or is inconsistent with the terms of the final and complete record of their agreement. In general, whenever parties choose to exclude all of CISG or derogate from any of its provisions, such exclusion or derogation should leave no doubt concerning the intention of the parties. Otherwise, the parties are trusting to an interpretation of their language to arrive at the result they seek. The Article enabling such exclusion of derogation may not allow such intention to be implied.[162]

---

[157] MCC-Marble Ceramic Ctr. v. Ceramica Nuova D'Agostino, S.P.A., 144 F.3d 1384, 1389 (11th Cir. 1998), *cert. denied*, 526 U.S. 1087, 119 S. Ct. 1496, 143 L. Ed. 2d 650 (1999). *See also* Mitchell Aircraft Spares v. European Aircraft Serv. AB, 23 F. Supp. 2d 915 (N.D. Ill. 1998); Calzaturificio Claudia, s.n.c. v. Olivieri Footwear, 1998 U.S. Dist. LEXIS 4586 (S.D.N.Y. Apr. 6, 1998).

[158] *Calzaturificio, id.* at 19.

[159] Art. 8(1): "For the purposes of this Convention statements made by and other conduct of a party are to be interpreted according to his intent where the other party knew or could not have been unaware what that intent was." The MCC-Marble court interpreted this provision as requiring a court to consider evidence of such "subjective intent." 144 F.3d at 1388.

[160] CISG, Art. 6.

[161] *See* J. Honnold, Uniform Law for International Sales Under the 1980 Sales Convention 142 (1982). While the UNIDROIT Principles (described in § 13 *supra*) do not address the parol evidence rule, unlike CISG, they clearly state that where the parties include a merger clause, the writing may not be "contradicted or supplemented by evidence of prior statements or agreements." Art. 2.17. Thus, to the extent that "Principles" are recognized as elaborations of CISG, a merger clause would be effective.

[162] CISG, Art. 6.

§ 86   SITUATIONS TO WHICH THE PAROL EVIDENCE RULE DOES NOT APPLY

[A]   Integration, Interpretation, Invalidating Causes — Consideration

The most significant test of one's understanding of the parol evidence process may be the ability to distinguish it from situations to which it does not apply. Some of these distinctions have already been suggested. Thus, we have seen that the parol evidence rule does not preclude evidence to determine the preliminary question of integration, i.e., whether the parties intended their writing to be the final (partially integrated) or complete and exclusive (fully or completely integrated) statement of their agreement.[163] Another critical process that must be distinguished from the parol evidence process is interpretation, which will be explored in sections to follow. Throughout our prior discussion of the parol evidence concept, we have distinguished the interpretation process[164] and emphasized the admissibility of trade usage, course of dealing, and course of performance evidence regardless of how complete the final writing of the parties.[165] We have also recognized the admissibility of evidence that would lead a court to hold a contract void, voidable, or unenforceable regardless of the parol evidence process. Thus, evidence of fraud, misrepresentation, duress, mistake, or other invalidating cause, such as the lack of consideration, is admissible.[166] The parties may have included a clause reciting that consideration has been received by one of the parties who later attempts to introduce evidence to show that the recital is false. The RESTATEMENT 2d indicates that such

---

[163] *See supra* § 84[B]. In addition to these authorities, see Clarke v. Di Pietro, 525 A.2d 623 (Me. 1987); Burge v. Frey, 545 F. Supp. 1160 (D. Kan. 1982).

[164] *See, e.g.,* § 82 *supra,* particularly the text at note 15.

[165] *See supra* § 84. *See also* Phillips Oil Co. v. OKC Corp., 812 F.2d 265 (5th Cir.), *cert. denied,* 484 U.S. 851, 108 S. Ct. 152, 98 L. Ed. 2d 107 (1987) (testimony of accounting experts did not violate parol evidence rule).

[166] In addition to references in earlier discussions, see National Bldg. Leasing, Inc. v. Byler, 252 Pa. Super. 370, 374, 381 A.2d 963, 965 (1977), citing the second edition of this book for the following proposition: "If the bargain between the parties is illegal or induced by fraud or duress, or if there is no validation device, evidence of these and other invalidating causes is admissible with no concern for the parol evidence rule." See Galmish v. Cicchini, 90 Ohio St. 3d 22, 27, 734 N.E.2d 782, 788 (2000). *See also* RESTATEMENT 2d § 214(d). If a promise is made with a preconceived intention of not performing it, the fraud or misrepresentation is called "promissory fraud." *See* Scott v. Minuteman Press Int'l, 1995 U.S. App. LEXIS 30130, at *6 (9th Cir. Oct. 13, 1995). While fraud and misrepresentation evidence may be introduced without violating the parol evidence rule, there is a split of authority concerning evidence of "promissory fraud." *See* Parker v. Columbia Bank, 91 Md. App. 346, 362, 604 A.2d 521, 529 (1992). Some courts insist that the promissory fraud exception applies only where the false promise is independent of and not inconsistent with the terms of the written agreement. *See Scott v. Minuteman, supra.* Other courts, however, treat promissory fraud as any other type of fraud, evidence of which does not violate the parol evidence rule. It is important to distinguish this situation from proper applications of UCC § 2-316(1), which clearly indicates that evidence of express warranties made by oral or written statements prior to the execution of an integrated writing will be inadmissible because of the § 2-202 parol evidence rule. It is not uncommon for salespersons to make statements about goods which amount to express warranties prior to the execution of a writing which may be final or complete and exclusive. Should the parol evidence be inadmissible under proper application of the § 2-202 standard, the statement will not be operative. The UCC is silent with respect to evidence of fraud in such matters. Pre-Code standards pursuant to § 1-103 are then applied. *See* Associated Hardware Supply Co. v. Big Wheel Distrib. Co., 355 F.2d 114 (3d Cir. 1965). If the proponent of the evidence could establish that the seller had no intention of warranting the goods when the statement was made, promissory fraud could be shown and the evidence may be admissible regardless of § 2-202. As to the minority of courts holding that evidence of promissory fraud may be barred by the parol evidence rule, see the criticism of these cases in Sweet, *Promissory Fraud and the Parol Evidence Rule,* 49 CAL. L. REV. 877 (1961).

evidence is admissible.[167] This view, however, should be considered in the context of the analysis explored earlier as to the effect of recital clauses in the discussion of consideration.[168]

Beyond these situations to which the parol evidence process does not apply, two others are worthy of separate consideration: (1) the admissibility of evidence that the *writing* of the parties is mistaken, i.e., that it fails to state the true intention of the parties, and one of the parties is seeking *reformation* of the writing, and (2) the admissibility of evidence that the parties did not intend their writing, which may appear to evidence a contract between them, to operate as such evidence until a certain event has occurred, i.e., the parties did not intend to be bound to *any* contract until a *condition precedent to contract formation* occurred. We will now explore these situations.

[B]   Reformation and the Parol Evidence Rule — Mistake in Expression

The parties may have entered into an agreement about which they are not mistaken, i.e., they may have a clear understanding of all of the terms of their agreement. The written expression of that agreement, however, may be mistaken in any one of several ways: (1) the expression may contain terms which the parties never intended; (2) it may fail to express terms to which the parties actually agreed; (3) the written expression may contain the terms the parties intended, but the legal effect of those terms may be inconsistent with the actual intention of the parties. In each of these cases, there is a mistake in *expression*, i.e., the parties agreement-their contract-is not mistaken; their expression of that agreement in the writing is mistaken because it does not evidence their true intention of the parties. It is important to contrast a mistake in *expression* from the mutual mistake of the parties themselves. In any agreement, the parties make certain basic, factual assumptions. A buyer of timber, for example, may agree to purchase a tract of land. At the moment of contracting, unknown to either party, a fire has destroyed the timber.[169] In such cases, there has been a material effect on the agreed exchange of the parties because of their mistake of fact, which was a basic assumption of their agreement, and the buyer of the timber can avoid the contract.[170] There was, however, no mistake in expression.

Contrast that situation with an agreement to buy and sell a tract of land which the parties understand to be "Blueacre." When their agreement is reduced to writing by a third party, the land is mistakenly identified as "Greenacre" which, coincidentally, is a separate tract owned by the same seller. Here, the parties made no mistake in their actual agreement. The mistake was in the *expression* of the agreement-known at the early common law as a "scrivener's error."[171] The actual intention of the parties (as objectively manifested apart from the writing) was to purchase and sell Blueacre. Under proper evidentiary safeguards, a court, sitting as a court of equity, may *reform* the writing to state the true intention of the parties.[172] To do so, a court must receive the prior evidence of the parties intention, and such evidence will be

---

[167] Restatement 2d § 218(1).

[168] *See supra* Chapter 3, § 61[C].

[169] *See* Restatement 2d § 152 ill. 1.

[170] Restatement 2d § 152. This type of mistake as well as other types will be discussed later in this chapter.

[171] *See, e.g.*, Olds v. Jamison, 195 Neb. 388, 238 N.W.2d 459 (1976) ("lessor" should have read "lessee").

[172] *See* Davenport v. Beck, 576 P.2d 1199 (Okla. Ct. App. 1977). *See also* Restatement 2d § 155.

admissible notwithstanding the parol evidence rule.[173] If parol evidence were not admissible in such a case, the rule would become an instrument of the very fraud it was designed to prevent.[174] On the other hand, where there is no mistake in expression but the parties, themselves, made a mutual mistake, the equitable remedy of reformation is not available because there is no true intention to which the written expression can be reformed. The contract may be avoided, but reformation will not lie. Thus, where the parties agreed to buy and sell the tract containing timber, their written expression was precisely in accordance with their actual agreement. The mistaken basic assumption (that the timber continued to exist at the time of the agreement) occurred prior to their actual agreement. Therefore, where the parties are mutually mistaken, the mistake is *antecedent* to the actual agreement, while in reformation cases, the mistake occurs *after* the actual agreement, i.e., it occurs in the reduction of the actual agreement to written form where the mistake in expression is made.[175]

Reformation in mutual mistake cases is appropriate because the parties have a real agreement and later find themselves signatories to a writing that does not accurately reflect their agreement. Where only one party is mistaken, there is a unilateral mistake as to the agreement itself and reformation is not an appropriate remedy.[176] If, however, the other party knows or should know that the first party is mistaken, reformation will be granted to state the true intention of the mistaken party.[177] Courts will allow parol evidence and grant reformation where a party is induced by fraud or misrepresentation to sign a writing that, to the knowledge of the other party, does not represent the true intention of the signer.[178] Reformation is also available where there is an omission in the writing,[179] as well as a mistake as to the legal effect of the expression of agreement.[180] In a fascinating case, a plaintiff sought a particular interpretation of a clause in a contract, which a court rejected. Accepting that court's interpretation, the plaintiff sought reformation of the clause, alleging a mistake in

---

[173] Weil Bros.-Cotton, Inc. v. T. E. A., Inc., 181 Ga. App. 122, 351 S.E.2d 670 (1986). *See also* Chimart Assocs. v. Paul, 66 N.Y.2d 570, 498 N.Y.S.2d 344, 489 N.E.2d 231 (1986).

[174] "The rationale . . . is that the very nature of a reformation action is such that it is outside the field of operation of the parol evidence rule. Parol or extrinsic evidence is not received for the purpose of varying the contract of the parties but to show what their contract really was. The thing being reformed is the writing, not the contract." Duenke v. Brummett, 801 S.W.2d 759, 766 (Mo. Ct. App. 1991). *See also* Alabama Farm Bureau Ins. Co. v. Hunt, 525 So. 2d 415 (Ala. 1987).

[175] Though it was raised in the context of a plea agreement, the analysis is clearly set forth in United States v. Williams, 198 F.3d 988, 994 (7th Cir. 1999): "Both voidance and reformation are appropriate remedies where a contract is infected by mutual mistake of fact. . . . Reformation is the appropriate remedy when the mistake 'is one as to expression-one that relates to the contents or effect of the writing that is intended to express [an] agreement.' Restatement (Second) of Contracts § 55 cmt. a. Voidance is the proper remedy 'where a mistake of both parties at the time a contract was made as to a basic assumption on which the contract was made has a material effect on the agreed exchange of performances.' Restatement (Second) of Contracts § 152(1)."

[176] Benderson Dev. Co. v. United States Postal Serv., 1996 U.S. Dist. LEXIS 16919, at *15 (W.D.N.Y. Oct. 30, 1996).

[177] *See* River-Pennington v. CRSS Capital, 1995 Del. Ch. LEXIS 22 (Del. Ch. Mar. 6, 1995).

[178] *See* Hermelink v. Dynamic Operations East, Inc., 109 F. Supp. 2d 1299, 1305 (D. Kan. 2000).

[179] *See, e.g.,* Parrish v. City of Carbondale, 61 Ill. App. 3d 500, 378 N.E.2d 243, 181 Ill. Dec. 779 (5th Dist. 1978) (omission of rights of plaintiffs to use city water and sanitary facilities at the same rates as users within the city limits); Bollinger v. Central Pa. Quarry Stripping & Constr. Co., 425 Pa. 430, 229 A.2d 741 (1967). Omission of understanding that defendant would remove topsoil and place refuse between topsoil and bare earth. The facts of this case may also suggest that the parties had modified their written expression through course of performance, or such course of performance may have been strong evidence of the proper interpretation of the writing. Neither of these views, however, is found in the opinion.

[180] Rolph v. McGowan, 20 Wash. App. 251, 579 P.2d 1011 (1978) (legal effect of "subject to").

expression because the clause was mistaken. It failed to state the true intention of the parties. The court granted reformation.[181]

Courts insist that reformation will not be granted unless the plaintiff can prove the actual agreement of the parties by more than a preponderance of the evidence. The usual statement is that, for reformation purposes, the evidence must be "clear and convincing,"[182] but a number of other phrases may be found in the case law from the nebulous "heavy"[183] to "clear, cogent and convincing,"[184] a "high order" of evidence required to overcome the presumption that the deliberately prepared writing manifests the true intention of the parties,[185] or various other phrases similar to "clear and convincing."[186] It is important to emphasize that the remedy of reformation, like other equitable remedies, will depend heavily upon the facts of the case and, in particular, the inherent credibility of the evidence.[187]

[1]   Negligence — Failure to Read Mistaken Document

Where a party seeking reformation has not read the document which allegedly fails to state the true intention of the parties, the defendant often argues that reformation should be denied because of the negligence of the plaintiff in failing to read. Some older cases accepted this view, particularly in cases of reformation because of mistake rather than fraud, though some refused the remedy even where fraud was shown.[188] Other older cases, however, recognized that the failure to read amounts to a bar to the remedy of reformation only if the negligence was "gross."[189] More recent cases either agree that ordinary negligence should not bar reformation[190] or that only "reasonable diligence" is required, and the innocent failure to read the formal document is not a departure from that standard.[191]

Finally, it should be noted that reformation may be granted at the request of any party to the contract, including a third party beneficiary, or the right of a successor in interest. It may be granted to a party whose performance would have been unenforceable or voidable absent reformation.[192]

---

[181] *See* Sadowski v. General Discount Corp., 295 Mich. 340, 294 N.W. 703 (1940), and General Discount Corp. v. Sadowski, 183 F.2d 542, 546–47 (6th Cir. 1950).

[182] *See Parrish v. City of Carbondale, supra* note 179. *See also* Accenture LLP v. Meridian Partnership Mgt., Inc., 2006 Wash. App. LEXIS 263 (2006); Taylor v. McCollom, 153 Or. App. 670, 958 P.2d 207, 214 (1997).

[183] *See* Manley v. AmBase Corp., 126 F. Supp. 2d 743 (S.D.N.Y. 2001); A.J. Cameron Sod Farms v. Continental Ins. Co., 142 N.H. 275, 700 A.2d 290, 295 (1997).

[184] Union Am. Ins. Co. v. Atlas Constr. Co., 2000 Conn. Super. LEXIS 1527, at *9 (Conn. Super. Ct. May 12, 2000).

[185] *Chimart Assocs. v. Paul, supra* note 173.

[186] See Rentenbach Eng'g Co., Constr. Div. v. General Realty, Ltd., 707 S.W.2d 524 (Tenn. Ct. App. 1985), where the court rehearses numerous phrases similar to "clear and convincing" used by prior Tennessee courts.

[187] Restatement 2d § 155 comment c.

[188] *See, e.g.,* Knight & Bostwick v. Moore, 203 Wis. 540, 234 N.W. 902 (1930).

[189] *See, e.g.,* Kroschel v. Martineau Hotels, Inc., 142 Or. 31, 18 P.2d 818, 823 (1933).

[190] "[M]ere negligence is not a bar to reformation." Young v. Verizon's Bell Atl. Cash Bal. Plan, 2009 U.S. Dist. LEXIS 102349 (N.D. Ill. 2009). "In mutual mistake cases, the failure by one party (or both parties) to read the written contract before signing it is irrelevant. . . . [T]hat has been the law in New York for more than one hundred years." *Benderson Development, supra* note 176. *In re* Schick, 232 B.R. 589, 598 (Bankr. S.D.N.Y. 1999) (stating that the negligent failure to read the agreement before signing it generally does not bar relief).

[191] *See* Akkerman v. Gersema, 260 Iowa 432, 149 N.W.2d 856 (1967).

[192] Restatement 2d § 155 comment e.

[C]   Condition Precedent to Formation — RESTATEMENT 2d Analysis

The parol evidence rule does not affect questions concerning the formation, validity or enforceability of a contract. If, therefore, the parties do not intend their contract to come into existence until a certain event occurs, evidence of such intention does not vary, add to, or contradict the terms of their writing. Rather, such evidence relates exclusively to whether there is any contract at all. Innumerable cases have held such evidence admissible, notwithstanding the parol evidence rule.[193] As will be seen in a subsequent chapter dealing with conditions, however, the typical condition is one that merely postpones the activation of a duty, i.e., the contract is formed and the existing duty of one or both parties remains in a state of quiescence until a particular event has occurred. If, therefore, one of the parties attempts to introduce evidence of a typical condition to an existing duty under a formed contract where the writing evidencing that contract is integrated and does not mention the condition, the parol evidence rule is applicable and such evidence will be subjected to the usual tests of admissibility.[194]

Though the case law is clear that there is no reason to apply the parol evidence rule where the question is whether any enforceable agreement exists, the RESTATEMENT 2d rejects this analysis. It suggests that, where the written agreement is subject to the occurrence of a stated condition, the agreement is not *integrated* with respect to the oral condition.[195] A

---

[193] *See* Smith v. Rosenthal Toyota, Inc., 83 Md. App. 55, 573 A.2d 418 (1990) (husband signed contract to purchase a truck on the oral condition that his wife would agree, the court held that, even assuming an integration clause applied to the document, the agreement is not integrated with respect to the oral condition-citing RESTATEMENT 2d § 217); Palatine Nat'l Bank v. Olson, 366 N.W.2d 726, 730 (Minn. Ct. App. 1985) (written release indicated no condition and letter stated that party was discharged from loan, but testimony was admissible parol evidence that the release was subject to the condition precedent of bringing the loans to a successful conclusion) (quoting Jansen v. Herman, 304 Minn. 572, 575–76, 230 N.W.2d 460, 463–64 (1975): "In every instance where the parol evidence rule is sought to be applied, however, a threshold question must be asked: Is the contract valid and operative? If the contract was to be binding only upon performance of an agreed-upon condition precedent, then the contract goes into force only upon the performance of that condition. Thus, parol evidence may be admissible to show that, notwithstanding the existence of a written contract, it was the intention of the parties that the contract should not become operative except upon the happening of some future event. . . . In Minnesota we have repeatedly held that parol evidence is admissible to show that, notwithstanding the delivery of an instrument, the intention of the parties was that it should not become operative as a binding contract except upon the happening of a future contingent event. . . . Whether or not a certain oral agreement constituted a condition precedent for a subsequent contract is a factual determination to be decided by the trier of fact."). *See also In re Prior Bros., Inc.*, 29 Wash. App. 905, 632 P.2d 522 (1981) (§ 2-202 of the UCC does not address this matter and, therefore, pre-Code law must apply); Hunt Foods & Indus., Inc. v. Doliner, 26 A.D.2d 41, 270 N.Y.S.2d 937 (1st Dep't 1966) (condition to formation was "consistent" and, therefore, not barred by § 2-202 of the UCC), *aff'd*, 26 A.D.2d 623, 272 N.Y.S.2d 686 (1st Dep't 1966); White Showers, Inc. v. Fischer, 278 Mich. 32, 270 N.W. 205 (1936) (evidence admissible that contract for irrigation system was not to become effective until prior contract was canceled); Hicks v. Bush, 10 N.Y.2d 488, 225 N.Y.S.2d 34, 180 N.E.2d 425, 427 (1962): "Parol testimony is admissible to prove a condition precedent to the legal effectiveness of a written agreement. . . ."; Blackstad Mercantile Co. v. Parker & Glover, 163 N.C. 275, 79 S.E. 606 (1913) (sales order containing merger clause did not prevent evidence that the signed order was not to be "sent in" until defendant gave a further direction to that effect). *See also* Brummet v. Pope, 685 S.W.2d 238 (Mo. Ct. App. 1985); Rincones v. Windberg, 705 S.W.2d 846 (Tex. App. Austin 1986); The classic case is Pym v. Campbell, 6 El. & Bl. 370 (Q.B. 1856) (buyer of invention permitted to show that his purchase was conditioned on approval of invention by a particular engineer).

[194] See Hong Kong Deposit & Guaranty Co. v. Hibdon, 611 F. Supp. 224 (S.D.N.Y. 1985), and Schacht v. Beacon Ins. Co., 742 F.2d 386 (7th Cir. 1984), where the courts refused to apply the condition precedent to formation exception to the parol evidence rule because the conditions sought to be proven were "subsequent", i.e., they were attached to existing contractual duties.

[195] RESTATEMENT 2d § 217.

comment explains, "If the parties orally agreed that performance of the written agreement was subject to a condition, either the writing is not an integrated agreement or the agreement is only partially integrated until the condition occurs."[196] Even a merger clause which explicitly negates oral terms does not control the question of whether the agreement is integrated.[197]

Certainly, a writing may appear to be a complete and exclusive statement of the parties' intention and it may contain a well-drafted merger clause to strengthen that effect. Yet, the most complete and exclusive statement of agreement may not be intended as legally binding until a conditioning event has occurred. In addition to the obsession of the RESTATEMENT 2d with the notion of "integration" in its treatment of the parol evidence process, an explanation may be found in a Reporter's note to this section which refers the user to a comment in another section defining conditions.[198] That comment and the Reporter's note explaining it are critical of the use of the term "condition" to describe an event upon which the *existence* of a contract is dependent. The definition of "condition" in the RESTATEMENT 2d is relegated to an event upon which the *performance* of a duty under an existing contract is dependent, i.e., the typical use of the term "condition" as described above. Yet, the RESTATEMENT 2d explanation suggests, "[T]here is no great substantive disparity between the terminology used in this [Restatement Second] Comment and descriptions of such events as conditions to the existence of a contract."[199] Notwithstanding the lack of "great substantive disparity," the RESTATEMENT 2d appears to reject the generally accepted rationale of conditions precedent to the *existence* of a contract only because of its preferred (narrower) definition of "condition." Yet, ambiguity in the use of the term "condition" can be avoided by identifying that to which the condition is attached, again, to the *existence* of a contract or to a *duty* under an existing contract. Indeed, as will be seen in the later discussion of conditions, when conditions are described as either "precedent" or "subsequent," ambiguity in the use of these descriptive terms (which are no longer used in the RESTATEMENT 2d) can be avoided by identifying the referent point, i.e., "precedent" or "subsequent" to what? The case law permitting evidence of a condition to the existence of a contract almost invariably identifies the condition as "precedent" to such *existence*. The RESTATEMENT 2d rejection of the case law and its substitution of a puzzling, alternative rationale lacks any apparent justification.

§ 87   INTERPRETATION, CONSTRUCTION AND "PLAIN MEANING"

[A]   The Process of Interpretation — Who Decides? — Construction

The parties to a contract may have manifested their agreement by words (oral or written), or by conduct. Whatever the expression of agreement, the *meaning* of that expression must be ascertained, and the process of ascertaining *meaning* is the process of *interpretation*.[200] Who shall decide the meaning of the parties' expression of agreement, i.e., shall it be the judge or

---

[196] RESTATEMENT 2d § 217 comment b.

[197] *Id.*

[198] RESTATEMENT 2d § 224 comment c.

[199] RESTATEMENT 2d § 224 Reporter's Note.

[200] *See* RESTATEMENT 2d § 200: "Interpretation of a promise or agreement or a term thereof is the ascertainment of its meaning."

jury? Is it a question of *law* the judge will decide, or a question of *fact* that the jury should decide?

The notion that questions of fact are for the jury while questions of law are for the judge is a tautology. It is an open secret that certain questions of fact are decided by the court and characterized as questions of "law" because the court chooses to decide them.[201] Since interpretation deals with the meaning of language, it is clearly a question of fact.[202] Earlier courts, however, distrusted jurors, some of whom were illiterate, and even modern courts recognize the desirability of characterizing certain questions of interpretation as questions of law to preserve judicial review that would be lost if the question were characterized as one of fact.[203] Where the evidence is so clear that reasonable parties would not disagree on the meaning of certain manifestations of intention, the question of interpretation is for the court though it is a question of fact.[204] If, however, the interpretation depends upon extrinsic evidence or a choice among reasonable inferences to be drawn from that evidence, the trier of fact (jury or judge sitting without a jury) should perform that task.[205] An important dimension of this question, however, is whether extrinsic evidence of alternate reasonable meanings will be admitted, i.e., whether the court merely inspects the parties expression of agreement for facial ambiguity based solely on the linguistic experience of the judge.[206] This question is pursued in the next section [B].

If the question is one of the *legal effect* of the parties' expression rather than their meaning, this process should be understood as *construction* rather than interpretation.[207] The process of interpretation-the determination of meaning — must precede the process of construction-the determination of legal effect. Though this distinction is sound, the untidy fashion in which courts sometimes use the term "construction" to mean "interpretation" affects the utility of the distinction.[208]

---

[201] For a superb analysis of the "law"/"fact" dichotomy, *see* HART & SACKS, THE LEGAL PROCESS: BASIC PROBLEMS IN THE MAKING AND APPLICATION OF LAW 369 *et seq.* (Cambridge, tentative ed. 1958).

[202] Chief Justice Traynor candidly recognized the question of interpretation as a question of fact, but still insisted that interpretation "is essentially a judicial function to be exercised according to the generally accepted canons of interpretation." Parsons v. Bristol Dev. Co., 62 Cal. 2d 861, 865, 402 P.2d 839, 842 (1965).

[203] See RESTATEMENT 2d § 212 comment d, which suggests that appellate review of such questions may contribute to stability and predictability, particularly in cases involving standardized printed forms. See also the opinion by Traynor in *Parsons v. Bristol Dev. Co., id.*, where it is suggested that appellate courts are not bound by a construction of the contract based solely by the terms of the writing.

[204] See American Med. Int'l v. Scheller, 462 So. 2d 1, 7 (Fla. Dist. Ct. App. 1984), where the court held that the trial court had improperly shifted to the jury the burden of initially construing the contract.

[205] RESTATEMENT 2d § 212 comment e; C & J Fertilizer, Inc. v. Allied Mut. Ins. Co., 227 N.W.2d 169 (Iowa 1975); Meyers v. Selznick Co., 373 F.2d 218 (2d Cir. 1966).

[206] See SMS Aktiengesellschaft v. Material Science Corp., 2005 U.S. LEXIS 22643 at *4 (S. D. Ill. 2005).

[207] *See* 3 CORBIN ON CONTRACTS § 24.30. RESTATEMENT 2d § 201 comment c. "[C]ontract interpretation is a question of fact, and review is according to the clearly erroneous standard. . . . In contrast, contract construction, that is, the legal operation of the contract, is a question of law mandating plenary review." Welch & Forbes, Inc. v. Cendant Corp. (*In re* Cendant Corp. Prides Litig.), 233 F.3d 188, 193 (3d Cir. 2000) (referring to the extensive analysis of the distinction between "interpretation" and "construction" in Ram Constr. Co. v. American States Ins. Co., 749 F.2d 1049, 1052–53 (3d Cir. 1984)).

[208] See American Med. Int'l v. Scheller, 462 So. 2d 1, 7 (Fla. Dist. Ct. App. 1984), where the court uses the term "construction" meaning "interpretation."

[B]   Whose Meaning Should Prevail? — "Plain Meaning" Standard

Once the issue of *who* is to decide is resolved, the next question is, *whose meaning should prevail?* This is a complicated question to be explored in this and following sections. The test or standard of interpretation is critical in dealing with this question. The meaning which a reasonable (hypothetical) third party may attach to certain expressions of intention may be different from the meaning which one or both parties attach. If the standard is that of the reasonable third party and a court refuses to consider evidence of particular meanings attached by the contracting parties, the court may discover a contract that neither party intended. If the parties have attached different individual meanings, which of these meanings should prevail? Should there be a contract at all if neither party knew of the other's meaning, or if both knew of the other's meaning? Issues of ambiguity (double meanings or equivocal meanings) or vagueness (a spectrum of meanings) arise. Indeed, it is questionable whether a word exists which may be accurately described as having an ideal meaning, apart from any particular usage. There is a "plain meaning" school of interpretation that would ascribe a singular meaning to any word. Professor Corbin exquisitely emasculates this view:

> It is sometimes said, in a case in which the written words seem plain and clear and unambiguous, that the words are not subject to interpretation or construction. One who makes this statement has of necessity already given the words an interpretation-the one that is to him plain and clear; and in making the statement he is asserting that any different interpretation is "perverted" and untrue.[209]

The view that words do have an ideal meaning and that parties would be held to that meaning regardless of how far it may differ from their intention is traceable to an earlier period in our law. Fortunately, we have seen much progress in this area. "The history of the law of interpretation is the history of a progress from a stiff and superstitious formalism to a flexible rationalism."[210] The earlier point of view is frequently expressed in the supposed rule that you cannot depart from "the strict, plain, common meaning of the words themselves."[211] That such a rule is unsound is amply demonstrated by Wigmore:

> The fallacy consists in assuming there is or ever can be *some one real* or absolute meaning. Certainly, it should be made prohibitively difficult for an unscrupulous party to establish a meaning foreign to what was in fact understood by the parties at the time of contract formation. However, this result can be accomplished without the aid of an inflexible rule. The so-called rule should be viewed "not so much as a canon of construction as a counsel of caution."[212]

---

[209] Corbin, *The Interpretation of Words and the Parol Evidence Rule*, 50 Cornell L.Q. 161, 171–72 (1965).

[210] 9 Wigmore, Evidence § 2461 (3d ed. 1940).

[211] "[T]he general rule I take to be, that where the words of any written instrument are free from ambiguity in themselves, and where external circumstances do not create any doubt or difficulty as to the proper application of those words to claimants under the instrument, or the subject matter to which the instrument relates, such instrument is always to be construed according to the strict, plain, common meaning of the words themselves; and that, in such case, evidence dehors the instrument, for the purpose of explaining it according to the surmised or alleged intention of the parties to the instrument, is utterly inadmissible." Tindal, C.J., in Attorney-General v. Shore, 11 Sim. 592, 615 [1833–34]. *See also* Young v. Hornbrook, Inc., 153 Me. 412, 140 A.2d 493 (1958); Goode v. Riley, 153 Mass. 585, 28 N.E. 228 (1891).

[212] 9 Wigmore, Evidence § 2462 (3d ed. 1940).

While the interpretation process should begin with the usual and ordinary meaning of the words in a contract, courts should be willing to admit evidence that would supercede the usual meaning, e.g., evidence of trade usage,[213] or other evidence of the parties' understanding of the words used.[214] A famous remark by O. W. Holmes, Jr. rejects the "plain meaning" standard: "A word is not a crystal, transparent and unchanged, it is the skin of a living thought and may vary greatly in color and content according to the circumstances and the time in which it is used."[215] Holmes, however, balked at the use of private conventions or codes between the parties. Thus, "five hundred feet . . . should not mean one hundred inches."[216]

Modern courts which reject the view that a judge may determine whether a writing is ambiguous by simply reading it (the "plain meaning" or "four corners" approach) and insist that the court must allow the parties to present evidence to determine whether the terms are susceptible to different meanings, may still refuse to permit the objective trade meaning of a term to be overcome by evidence of a private agreement between the parties.[217] While courts would permit evidence that "ten dollars" meant "ten Canadian dollars," they may not permit the parties to show that "ten dollars" meant "twenty dollars." If, however, there is sufficient evidence that the parties shared such a peculiar meaning, there is no justification for a different interpretation that would enforce a contract that the parties never made. Extrinsic evidence is admissible to show that certain fictitious names were intended to designate a specific name.[218]

[1] Is Facial Ambiguity Required?

Must words must appear to be ambiguous on their face before any evidence may be admitted to explain their meaning. The question should scarcely survive its statement. In a well-known case, the Third Circuit explained,

> If a judge simply applied his own linguistic background and experience to the words of a contract, contracting parties would live in a most uncertain environment. . . . A court must have a reference point to determine if words may reasonably admit of different meanings. Under a 'four corners' approach, a judge sits in chambers and

[213] See, e.g., Fryar v. Currin, 280 S.C. 241, 312 S.E.2d 16 (Ct. App. 1984), which quotes the second edition of this book to this effect.

[214] See Pacific Gas & Elec. Co. v. G. W. Thomas Drayage & Rigging Co., 69 Cal. 2d 33, 39, 442 P.2d 641, 645 (1968), where Justice Traynor, writing for the court, states that the extrinsic evidence should not be limited to a meaning derived from trade usage. The interpretation should be open to other evidence as to the parties' understanding of the words used whenever they differ from the judge's understanding.

[215] Towne v. Eisner, 245 U.S. 418, 425, 38 S. Ct. 158, 159, 62 L. Ed. 372, 376 (1918).

[216] Holmes, *The Theory of Legal Interpretation*, 12 HARV. L. REV. 417, 420 (1899), based upon his famous opinion in Goode v. Riley, 153 Mass. 585, 586, 28 N.E. 228 (1891).

[217] In Mellon Bank, N.A. v. Aetna Bus. Credit, Inc., 619 F.2d 1001 (3d Cir. 1980), the court recognizes that certain terms may appear unambiguous, but prior dealings or trade usage may reveal that the terms are more than susceptible to a meaning which differs from the uninformed interpretation of the judge. Thus, where parties contract for 100 ounces of platinum at a price of $100,000, there may be a consistent course of dealing in Canadian dollars and a trade usage measuring platinum in troy ounce (12 rather than 16 ounces to the pound). A "pound of caviar" is fourteen ounces. When one goes to a lumber yard and asks for a "two by four," he does not receive wood two inches thick and four inches wide. In fact, if he did receive wood measuring two by four, he would not have received what he bargained for.

[218] As one modern court suggested, if the parties "wish the symbols 'one Caterpillar D9G tractor' to mean '500 railroad cars full of watermelons,' that's fine — provided parties share this weird meaning." *TKO Equip. Co. v. C & G Coal Co.*, 863 F.2d 541 (7th 1988).

determines from his point of view whether the words before him are ambiguous. An alternative approach is for the judge to hear the proffer of the parties and determine if there is objective indicia that, from the linguistic reference point of the parties, the terms of the contract are susceptible of different meanings. We believe the latter approach to be the correct approach. . . . If a *reasonable* alternative interpretation is suggested, even though it may be alien to the judge's linguistic experience, objective evidence in support of that interpretation should be considered by the fact finder.[219]

The Uniform Commercial Code "definitely rejects" any "requirement that a condition precedent to the admissibility of" trade usage, course of dealing or course of performance evidence "is an original determination by the court that the language is ambiguous."[220]

Notwithstanding the progress made in rejecting the "plain meaning" rule, the decisions are often ambiguous. Twenty-one years after its careful explanation (quoted above) of why the "four corners" view should not be said to apply in Pennsylvania, the court admitted

[W]hen a court is faced with a contract containing facially unambiguous language, it seems that Pennsylvania law both requires that the court interpret the language without using extrinsic evidence, and allows the court to bring in extrinsic evidence to prove latent ambiguity.[221]

It is still possible to discover modern cases supporting this flawed view.[222] Judge Posner

---

[219] Mellon Bank, N.A. v. Aetna Bus. Credit, Inc., 619 F.2d 1001, 1010, 1011 (3d Cir. 1980). See also *Pacific Gas & Electric, supra* note 214, where the trial court refused to admit extrinsic evidence because the contract had a "plain meaning." The court reversed, stating, *inter alia,* "When a court interprets a contract on this basis, it determines the meaning of the instrument in accordance with the 'extrinsic evidence of the judge's own linguistic education and experience' (quoting 3 Corbin on Contracts § 579). . . . This belief is a remnant of a primitive faith in the inherent potency and inherent meaning of words." 442 P.2d at 643–44. See also Sawyer v. Arum, 690 F.2d 590 (6th Cir. 1982), holding that Michigan law rejects any requirement that facial ambiguity must be discovered to permit the consideration of interpretation evidence.

[220] UCC § 2-202 comment 1(c). See Walk-In Medical Centers, Inc. v. Breuer Capital Corp., 818 F. 2d 260, 264 (2d Cir. 1987), (UCC § 2-202 "authorizes the use of [trade usage] evidence to explain a contract term whether or note the terms has been found to be ambiguous.") That opinion is quoted and followed in Constellation Power Source, Inc. v. Select Energy, Inc., 467 F. Supp. 2d 187, 209 (D. Conn. 2006). For a case that totally misreads this UCC comment, see Corporate Commun. Servs. of Dayton, LLC v. MCI Commun. Servs., 2009 U.S. Dist. LEXIS 105045 at *36 (S. D. Ohio 2009) where the court states the comment without the critical opening phrase, "This section definitely rejects," and, therefore, concludes that a finding of ambiguity is a necessary condition precedent to the admission of trade usage or course of dealing evidence.

[221] Bohler-Uddeholm Am., Inc. v. Ellwood Group, Inc., 247 F.3d 79, 94 (3d Cir. 2001).The Pennsylvania Supreme Court, however, has stated, "Contractual language is ambiguous if it is reasonably susceptible of different constructions and capable of being understood in more than one sense. This is not a question to be resolved in a vacuum. Rather, contractual terms are ambiguous if they are subject to more than one reasonable interpretation when applied to a particular set of facts. We will not, however, distort the meaning of the language or resort to a strained contrivance in order to find an ambiguity.

[222] See, e.g., Trident Ctr. v. Connecticut Gen. Life Ins. Co., 847 F.2d 564 (9th Cir. 1988), where the court is extremely critical of the holding and rationale in *Pacific Gas & Elec., supra* note 214, where the opinion by Justice Traynor stated, "If words had absolute and constant referents, it might be possible to discover contractual intention in the words themselves and in the manner in which they were arranged. Words, however, do not have absolute and constant referents." The *Trident* court, though compelled to follow this view of California law, nonetheless stated, "Pacific Gas casts a long shadow of uncertainty over all transactions negotiated and executed under the law of California. . . . [E]ven when the transaction is very sizeable, even if it involves only sophisticated parties, even if it was negotiated with the aid of counsel, even if it results in contract language that is devoid of ambiguity, costly and protracted litigation cannot be avoided if one party has a strong enough motive for challenging the contract. While this

focuses on the distinction between objective and subjective evidence to prove a seemingly clear contract to be ambiguous. Trade usage is an illustration of objective evidence which should be permitted, while the self-serving subjective testimony of one of the parties should be permitted only if the contract seems ambiguous.[223] There is, however, a general consensus rejecting the myth that language can have a singular, unalterable meaning. It can only be discerned in the context of all the surrounding circumstances.[224]

§ 88 STANDARDS OF INTERPRETATION — MUTUAL MISUNDERSTANDING — MISTAKE IN EXPRESSION

[A]   FIRST RESTATEMENT — Williston/Corbin

The FIRST RESTATEMENT listed six possible "standards"[225] of interpretation:[226]

(1) General Usage: what the hypothetical average person in the community or nation as a whole would understand the expression to mean. This is sometimes called the "popular" standard.

(2) Limited Usage: This is a constriction of (1), differing only in degree. Here, the test is the meaning which would be given to the expression in a particular locality, trade or profession.

(3) Mutual Standard: The meaning that conforms to the intention of the parties to the contract, even if such meaning violates common and other usages.

(4) Individual Standard: The meaning intended by the expressing party *or* the understanding of the party to whom the expression was directed.

(5) Reasonable Expectation: The meaning which the expressing party should reasonably expect the expression would convey to the other party.

(6) Reasonable Understanding: The meaning which the party to whom the manifestations are addressed would reasonably give to such expressions.

The FIRST RESTATEMENT characterized standards (1), (2), (5), and (6) as *objective*, and (3) and (4) as *subjective* since (3) and (4) are based upon the actual intention of the parties.[227] The test in (3) and (4), therefore, would not be based on the standard of the hypothetical reasonable person, but on the actual intention of the parties. This recognition of the subjective

---

rule [allowing extrinsic evidence that apparently unambiguous terms may have a different meaning according to the intention of the parties] creates much business for lawyers and an occasional windfall to some clients, it leads only to frustration and delay for most litigants and clogs already overburdened courts." 847 F.2d at 569. *See also* First Union Real Estate Equity & Mortg. Ins. v. Crown Am. Corp., 639 F. Supp. 838 (M.D. Pa. 1986).

[223] Cole Taylor Bank v. Truck Ins. Exch., 51 F. 3d 736, 737 (7th Cir. 1995).

[224] UCC § 2-202 comment 1(b); RESTATEMENT 2d § 212 comment b. *See* SMS Demag Aktiengesellschaft, v. Material Sciences Corp.,2005 U.S. Dist. LEXIS 22643 at *3–4 (S. D. Ill. 2005); Still v. Cunningham, 94 P. 3d 1104, 1109–10 (Alas. 2004); Friedman v. Donenfeld, 2004 Conn. Super. LEXIS 907 (April 2, 2004); Columbia Nitrogen Corp. v. Royster Co., 451 F.2d 3 (4th Cir. 1971); Hurst v. W.J. Lake & Co., 141 Or. 306, 12 P.2d 627 (1932).

[225] Professor Corbin disliked the term "standard" and suggested that, if it is to be used at all, he preferred to say that "standards are the evidential tests by which to determine whether a man's mode of expression and understanding have been prudent and reasonable." 3 CORBIN § 560, at n.22 (1963 ed.).

[226] FIRST RESTATEMENT § 227 comment a.

[227] FIRST RESTATEMENT § 227 comment b.

standard, however, was qualified by *integration*, i.e., whether the parties adopted a writing as the final and complete expression of agreement.[228] The standard of interpretation applied to an integrated agreement was the second, i.e., limited usage, as viewed by an objective third (reasonable) person. Thus, the test was the meaning to be attached by a reasonably intelligent person acquainted with all operative usages and knowing all of the circumstances prior to and contemporaneous with the integration, *other than statements by the parties of what they actually intended the final and complete writing to mean.*[229] There is considerable case law support for this test.[230]

The exclusion of statements by the parties as to their actual intention is important. A comment emphasizes the exclusion of "oral statements by the parties of what they intended the written language to mean . . . though these statements might show the parties gave their words a meaning that would not otherwise be apparent. Such a common understanding may justify reformation, but cannot be the basis of interpretation of an integration."[231] A justification is found in the next comment,[232] which suggests that, where parties contract without an integrated writing, they are not focusing upon the symbols of their agreement, i.e., their oral or written expressions. Rather, they are concentrating on the things for which the symbols stand. Where, however, they reduce their agreement to an integrated writing, they are deemed to be concentrating on the symbols themselves.[233] Thus, where the agreement is evidenced by an integrated writing, "the terms of the writing are conclusive, and a contract may have a meaning different from that which either party supposed it to have."[234]

Professor Corbin "flatly disapproved" of this view.[235] He vigorously asserted that, "No contract should ever be interpreted and enforced with a meaning that neither party gave it."[236] He suggests an example of *A* intending to sell Blackacre and *B* intending to purchase Whiteacre. The final writing of the parties, however, evidences a contract between them (interpreted according to the understanding of a reasonable third party) as one for the purchase and sale of Greenacre. Corbin believed that enforcement of a contract for the purchase and sale of Greenacre under these circumstances would be "to hold justice up to ridicule."[237]

It is important to emphasize a limitation on the FIRST RESTATEMENT (Williston) position. If an integration is interpreted according to the FIRST RESTATEMENT test described above, but that interpretation produces an uncertain or ambiguous result, a different "standard" applies,

---

[228] FIRST RESTATEMENT § 228.

[229] FIRST RESTATEMENT § 230.

[230] *See, e.g.,* Smith v. Liberty Mut. Ins. Co., 130 N.H. 117, 536 A.2d 164 (1987); State Auto. Ins. Ass'n v. Anderson, 365 Pa. Super. 85, 528 A.2d 1374 (1987); Soliva v. Shand, Morahan & Co., 176 W. Va. 430, 345 S.E.2d 33 (1986); Sherman v. Ward, 68 Md. App. 212, 511 A.2d 64 (1986); Roth v. Farmers Mut. Ins. Co., 220 Neb. 612, 371 N.W.2d 289 (1985); Howard Univ. v. Best, 484 A.2d 958 (D.C. 1984).

[231] FIRST RESTATEMENT § 230 comment a.

[232] FIRST RESTATEMENT § 230 comment b.

[233] *Id.* Williston, of course, agrees in 4 WILLISTON § 606, at 84.

[234] FIRST RESTATEMENT § 230 comment b (emphasis added).

[235] 3 CORBIN § 539, at n.61.5 (1963 ed.).

[236] 3 Corbin § 572 B (1971 Supp.).

[237] 3 CORBIN § 539, at 81 (1963 ed.).

i.e., the test applicable to unintegrated agreements.[238] The test applicable to unintegrated agreements is standard (5), i.e., the standard of the reasonable expectation of the party manifesting assent of the meaning his words or other manifestations would convey to the other party.[239] An illustration suggests that A and B have agreed that in any future stock transactions, the term "abracadabra" shall mean "Northern Pacific." This "code" term is used to conceal the nature of the dealings. Subsequently, a writing evidences a contract for the purchase of 100 shares of "abracadabra." If the writing was integrated, the application of standard (2) would produce an uncertain result since the meaning of "abracadabra" is uncertain. Thus, the oral understanding of the parties as to the meaning of "abracadabra" can be shown in this situation.[240]

Another illustration has a seller agreeing to sell "my horse" though he owns two horses. "My horse" is, therefore, ambiguous.[241] If, however, the evidence discloses the actual intention of the parties relates to the same horse, such evidence would be admissible to show that "my horse" meant the same horse to both parties.[242]

A third illustration is more troublesome. A and B wish to buy and sell stock but they also wish to conceal the nature of the dealing. They orally agree that, in any future deals, the word "buy" shall mean "sell" and "sell" shall mean "buy." Assuming a subsequent integrated writing evidences an offer from A to "sell" stock to B, the evidence of their private understanding (the "subjective" third standard, the "mutual standard" of interpretation) would not be admissible to make "sell" mean "buy."[243] This conclusion is consistent with the view that the application of the normal standard to integrated writings (the reasonable person standard) will not be changed unless that process produces uncertain or ambiguous results. Unlike the "abracadabra" illustration, if the term "sell" is interpreted by an objective third person who is not acquainted with the actual intention of the parties, "sell" is neither uncertain nor ambiguous and will not, therefore, permit a different test (standard) of interpretation. The illustration goes on to suggest, however, that B can recover through reformation, assuming the clear and convincing evidence standard is met. Professor Corbin is particularly critical of this illustration.

First, Corbin wonders whether the analysis would change if the private understanding of the parties was written rather than oral. Second, he suggests that if the parties had agreed that a word such as "run" would be understood as "buy" rather than "sell" meaning "buy," presumably the application of the normal standard applied to an integrated writing would not have produced a certain or unambiguous result. Thus, the standard for unintegrated writings would be applied permitting evidence of the mutual understanding that "run" means "buy." Yet, just as "sell" does not mean "buy" according to the dictionary, neither does "run" mean "buy" in the dictionary. The third Corbin criticism is the most devastating. Recall that the illustration suggested that one of the parties may be able to secure a decree for reformation,

---

[238] FIRST RESTATEMENT § 231.

[239] FIRST RESTATEMENT § 227 comment a.

[240] FIRST RESTATEMENT § 231 ill. 1.

[241] The situation creates a latent ambiguity requiring extrinsic evidence for interpretation between two possible meanings. *See* Crown Mgmt. Corp. v. Goodman, 452 So. 2d 49 (Fla. Dist. Ct. App. 1984); Hamada v. Valley Nat'l Bank, 27 Ariz. App. 433, 555 P.2d 1121 (1976).

[242] FIRST RESTATEMENT § 231 ill. 3.

[243] FIRST RESTATEMENT § 231 ill. 2.

thereby giving effect to the private understanding of the parties. Yet, there is no antecedent agreement to buy or sell anything, i.e., the FIRST RESTATEMENT view does not admit of a "true intention" of the parties to which the writing may be reformed. The prior agreement of the parties dealt exclusively with their understanding of a certain word and its meaning. Earlier we saw that reformation is granted on the basis of fraud or mistake. There is neither fraud nor mistake in the illustration. The writing is not mistaken. It is an accurate expression of the parties' intention as to the symbols they sought to use. Reformation, therefore, should not be an available remedy and *B* can only recover if a court permits an interpretation of the parties' symbols in accordance with the "mutual standard" or *actual* intention of the parties.[244]

The RESTATEMENT 2d which we will now explore has been influenced by the Corbin analysis.

[B]   RESTATEMENT 2d Analysis — Parties Attach Materially Different Meanings to Their Expressions — "Chicken" and "Peerless"

The leading exponent of the view that contract language should be interpreted according to a standard of reasonableness without regard for the meaning of the language attached by the parties at the time of contract formation was Judge Learned Hand.[245] Such a total objectivist view, however, was criticized:

> If . . . contract law is viewed as a functional instrument whose purpose is to effectuate the objectives of the parties to a promissory transaction if appropriate conditions are satisfied and subject to appropriate constraints, then the principles of interpretation should be responsive, where appropriate, to subjective intentions. Accordingly, under modern contract law subjective elements have an important place in interpretation.[246]

When the parties dispute the meaning of the terms of their agreement, they are attaching different meanings to those terms. Courts must attempt to determine the meaning attached by the parties at the time of formation since they obviously disagree on the proper interpretation of their mutual manifestations at the time of trial.[247] The parties, however, may have given little or no thought to the particular language which they assumed was an accurate reflection of their intentions. There are many reformation cases where an unread or barely considered writing

---

[244] See this analysis in 3 CORBIN § 540, at 93–94 (1963 ed.).

[245] Judge Learned Hand made several statements to the effect that the actual intention of the parties is irrelevant. *See, e.g.*, Eustis Mining Co. v. Beer, Sondheimer & Co., 239 F. 976, 985 (D.N.Y. 1917): "[I]f both parties severally declared that their meaning had been other than the natural meaning, and each declaration was similar, it would be irrelevant, saving some mutual agreement between them to that effect." In New York Trust Co. v. Island Oil & Transp. Corp., 34 F.2d 655, 656 (2d Cir. 1929), he wrote, "[C]ontracts depend upon the meaning which the law imputes to the utterances, not upon what the parties actually intended. . . ." In Hotchkiss v. National City Bank, 200 F. 287, 293 (D.N.Y. 1911), he suggested, "A contract has, strictly speaking, nothing to do with the personal, or individual, intent of the parties." Later, however, he added, "Of course, if it appear by other words, or acts, of the parties, that they attribute a peculiar meaning to such words as they use in the contract, that meaning will prevail, but only by virtue of the other words, and not because of their unexpressed intent." Judge Hand is usually regarded as one of the leading spokespersons of the objectivists who reject a standard of mutual understanding of the language of an agreement if that understanding differs from the understanding of a reasonable person. As can be seen from these quotations, however, even Judge Hand would permit evidence of a mutual understanding of unusual meaning to attach to certain expressions of agreement if such understanding was manifested and the parties had agreed to that understanding.

[246] Melvin Eisenberg, *Symposium of the Law in the Twentieth Century: The Emergence of Dynamic Contract Law*, 88 CAL. L. REV. 1743, 1757 (2000).

[247] *See* McConocha v. Blue Cross & Blue Shield Mut. of Ohio, 930 F. Supp. 1182, 1186 (N.D. Ohio 1996) (quoting this text).

fails to reflect the true intention of the parties. An even more compelling example of this phenomena occurs in the massive use of standardized, printed forms which evidence most of the contracts in our society.[248] It is an open secret that parties to such contracts do not read, understand or otherwise consciously advert to much of the "boilerplate" language in such forms. Similarly, where parties enter into a long term contract, though it is evidenced by a negotiated writing, their lack of omniscience will become clear with respect to situations that were unanticipated at the time of contract formation. While it is common for courts to continue to speak in terms of the "intention of the parties" in such cases, judicial candor may require recognition of the fact that there may be no discoverable intention of the parties under the circumstances.[249] As will be seen in a later section, in such cases a court must supply a term which is reasonable in the circumstances.[250]

There are numerous rules which are more aptly described as common sense guides to interpretation available to courts in their quest for the meaning of the expressions or manifestations of the parties, viewing the parties as reasonable parties under all of the circumstances. We will discuss these rules in the next section. For now, it is important to emphasize how courts must *begin* their search for the meaning of the outward manifestations of the parties. Evidence of particular meanings attached by one or both parties to the contract may not be ignored. Following a Corbin approach, the RESTATEMENT 2d begins its treatment of interpretation by making it clear "that the primary search is for a common meaning of the parties, not a meaning imposed on them by law."[251] Thus, the caption of this primary section on interpretation in the RESTATEMENT 2d is "Whose Meaning Prevails."[252] It is useful to consider classic cases dealing with vague, equivocal or ambiguous terms.

[1] Vague and Equivocal Terms-The Meaning of "Chicken"

A celebrated case confronted the issue, "What is chicken"?[253] The buyer argued that "chicken" meant only "young" chicken suitable for broiling or frying as contrasted with stewing chicken or fowl. The seller argued that "chicken" includes stewing chicken and, therefore, when it shipped such chicken, plaintiff had no basis for damages as to the chicken it had accepted. Nothing in the written expressions of the parties mentioned types of chicken. The parties had used the same word to describe the subject matter of the contract, i.e., "chicken." They apparently operated in good faith in later asserting their different interpretations of that term. The parties had both "said" the same word but they assumed that "chicken" communicated different thoughts to the other, i.e., they each *meant* different things.[254] Each party presented

---

[248] *See* Murray, *The Standardized Agreement Phenomena in the Restatement (Second) of Contracts*, 67 CORNELL L. REV. 735 (1982); Slawson, *Standard Form Contracts and Democratic Control of Lawmaking Power*, 84 HARV. L. REV. 529 (1971).

[249] The classic illustration of judicial candor is found in the opinion by Judge Clark in Parev Prods. Co. v. I. Rokeach & Sons, 124 F.2d 147 (2d Cir. 1941).

[250] *See* RESTATEMENT 2d § 204.

[251] RESTATEMENT 2d § 201 comment c. In Klair v. Reese, 531 A.2d 219, 223 (Del. 1987), the court expressly adopts this position.

[252] RESTATEMENT 2d § 201.

[253] Frigaliment Importing Co. v. B.N.S. International Sales Corp. 190 F. Supp. 116 (S.D.N.Y. 1960).

[254] See the Corbin criticism of the court's acceptance of the famous remark by O. W. Holmes, Jr. (THE PATH OF THE LAW, COLLECTED LEGAL PAPERS at 178): "[T]he making of a contract depends not on the agreement of two sets of external signs — not on the parties having meant the same thing but on their having *said* the same thing." 3 CORBIN § 543 B

evidence of the trade usage in the business of buying and selling chickens as to what members of the trade would understand from the term, "chicken." The buyer's evidence from experts in the trade was, however, unpersuasive.[255] When the buyer argued that the contract price was closer to the market price of "young" chicken than stewing chicken, the court found that the argument failed to recognize the necessity for the seller to make a profit on the transaction. References to dictionary definitions and U.S. Department of Agriculture definitions of "chicken" were inconclusive.

In his cogent analysis of this case, Professor Corbin argued that "chicken" has more than one *objective* meaning and the problem before the court was how the term was used in this context by the parties. Since the buyer sued for damages, the buyer had the burden of showing that the seller either knew or had reason to know that the buyer intended to purchase only broilers or fryers rather than fowl. It failed to sustain that burden and this is why the buyer lost the case, i.e., the buyer did not lose because it failed to show that *an* objective meaning of the term "chicken" was limited to young chicken.[256]

The RESTATEMENT 2d bases one of its illustrations on this case but changes the facts by having the buyer reject the shipment of chicken. Each party then seeks damages from the other. Both parties acted in good faith, and neither had reason to know of the difference in the meaning of "chicken" attributed by the other. Under these facts, the RESTATEMENT 2d suggests that both claims fail.[257] The analysis presumes that, had the seller brought the action for the buyer's refusal to accept the chicken, the seller may not have been able to show that the buyer had reason to know of the meaning attributed by the seller. Such a conclusion is too facile. Based on the evidence reported by the court, "Chicken" should be viewed in a generic sense as comprising both types of chicken. Absent sufficient evidence of prior course of dealing, trade usage or other specification of "young" chicken by the purchaser, the seller's shipment of stewing chicken is justified as performance within the range of meaning embraced by the term, "chicken."[258]

(3d ed.). For further criticism of the Holmes view, see the text at note 261 *infra*.

[255] Thus, when one witness testified that he would understand "chicken" to mean young chicken, i.e., in accordance with the plaintiff-buyer's position, he also testified that in his own transactions he was careful to distinguish types of chicken. This led the court to recall the remark of Lord Mansfield in Edie v. East India Co., 2 Burr. 1216, 1222 (1761), that no credit should be given "witnesses to usage, who could not adduce instances in verification."

[256] 3 CORBIN § 543 B (1971 Supp.).

[257] RESTATEMENT 2d § 201 ill. 4.

[258] See Young, *Equivocation in the Making of Agreements*, 64 COLUM. L. REV. 619, 629 (1964), where the author analyzes a case involving "egg coal," Indiana Fuel Supply Co. v. Indianapolis Basket Co., 41 Ind. App. 658, 84 N.E. 776 (1908). The seller tendered "steam egg coal" and the buyer asserted a right to the more expensive "domestic egg coal." The buyer prevailed because of evidence of prior dealings. Professor Young suggests that, absent such evidence, the seller should have prevailed for the reasons set forth in the text. See also Mellon Bank, N.A. v. Aetna Bus. Credit, Inc., 619 F.2d 1001 (3d Cir. 1980), which permitted evidence that the parties had used the term "insolvency" in a narrower sense than its usual meaning as a legal term of art, but held that the evidence was insufficient to persuade the court that the parties had understood the term to be used in the narrower sense.

[2]   "Peerless" — *Raffles v. Wichelhaus*[259]

The term "chicken" may be viewed as vague, i.e., as one having a "spectrum of applications."[260] Vagueness may be remedied, at least sufficiently for judicial applications, by defining a term more precisely.[261] Had the parties precisely defined the type of "chicken" they intended to buy and sell, any vagueness in their contract term would have been cured. "Chicken" could also be viewed as an equivocal term, i.e., one with a double meaning, if it may be treated as meaning one type of chicken ("young") or the other ("fowl").[262] The classic case of equivocation is *Raffles v. Wichelhaus*,[263] which is often characterized as a case involving "latent ambiguity" rather than equivocation.[264]

The parties agreed upon the purchase and sale of cotton from a ship named *Peerless* which was to depart from Bombay. Subsequent evidence revealed two ships named *Peerless*, both of which departed from Bombay albeit, at different times, i.e., one in October and the other in December. The buyer claimed that the contract should be interpreted to mean the October *Peerless*, while the seller claimed that it should be interpreted to mean the December *Peerless*. The seller alleged that he had tendered the cotton from the December *Peerless* but the buyer had refused the tender. The buyer did not deny these allegations, but proceeded to urge its interpretation of the contract language. The facts of the case do not reveal how the buyer may have been affected by a delivery from the December *Peerless* rather than the October *Peerless*. Presumably, the buyer's concern for delivery from the October *Peerless* was based on the precipitous decline in the price of cotton.[265] The court simply treated the contract as one in which the particular ship carrying the cotton was of material importance to the parties. Thus, if the buyer "meant" the October *Peerless* while the seller "meant" the December *Peerless*, there was no *consensus ad idem* and no binding contract.[266] The only evidence before the court was the statement of each party's intention *at the time of dispute*. These statements disagreed,

---

[259] 2 Hurl. & C. 906, 159 Eng. Rep. 375 (Ex. 1864).

[260] *See* Young, *supra* note 258, at 627.

[261] *See, e.g.*, WAISMANN, VERIFIABILITY, IN LOGIC AND LANGUAGE 117, 120 (1st ser. Flew ed. 1951).

[262] Dean Wigmore viewed equivocation as "a term which, upon application to external objects, is found to fit two or more of them equally." 9 WIGMORE EVIDENCE § 2472 (3d ed. 1940). In the example of "egg coal," *supra* note 258, Professor Young describes the term as "equivocal" in the sense that the coal must have been one ("steam") or the other ("domestic"). He argues, however, that contract rules dealing with ambiguous (equivocal) manifestations of agreement should not apply to this case. *See* Young, *supra* note 258, at 626.

[263] 2 Hurl. & C. 906, 159 Eng. Rep. 375 (Ex. 1864).

[264] For a criticism of the term "ambiguity" as applied to this case, see Young, *supra* note 258, at 626. Recent cases suggesting that "latent ambiguity" refers to a situation where the language employed by the parties is clear and suggests a single meaning, but extraneous evidence creates the necessity for choosing among two or more possible meanings, include Crown Mgmt. Corp. v. Goodman, 452 So. 2d 49 (Fla. Dist. Ct. App. 1984), and Hamada v. Valley Nat'l Bank, 27 Ariz. App. 433, 555 P.2d 1121 (1976).

[265] Professor Gilmore suggests that after the contract had been formed, the Union army had captured the port of New Orleans, a critical cotton port which the Union had previously blockaded, and the price of cotton was declining steeply. G. GILMORE, THE DEATH OF CONTRACT at 37, n.87 (1974).

[266] "The straightforward point is that the two parties, though they seemed to have agreed, had not agreed in fact. . . . There is just no agreement as to what is or turns out to be an important aspect of the arrangement. In *Raffles* there was agreement to purchase cotton from India on a ship named *Peerless*. As it turned out, there was no agreement at all on the crucial issue of which ship *Peerless*. . . . The one basis on which these cases cannot be resolved is on the basis of the agreement-that is, contract as promise. The court cannot enforce the will of the parties because there are no concordant wills. Judgment must therefore be based on principles external to the will of the parties." C. FRIED, CONTRACT AS PROMISE 59–60 (1981).

not as to what the parties *said*, but by what each party *meant* by the term *Peerless* in their agreement.[267] There was no evidence of any prior understanding, prior course of dealing or trade usage available to assist the court in making a determination that, for example, a reasonable person in the position of one or both parties would have understood the agreement to refer to the earlier or later *Peerless*. In the absence of such evidence, there is no *objective* basis to prefer one interpretation over another. The case, therefore, is viewed as one of an innocent, mutual misunderstanding of a term which is not ambiguous on its face, and the buyer's asserted interpretation is equal to the asserted interpretation of the seller. "If neither party can be assigned the greater blame for the misunderstanding, there is no nonarbitrary basis for deciding which party's understanding to enforce, so the parties are allowed to abandon the contract without liability."[268]

If the language is ambiguous on its face, i.e., if it is *patent* rather than *latent*, the parties each assume the risk that the other's interpretation will be preferred by the tribunal to which the dispute is submitted.[269]

[3] The Analyses of the RESTATEMENT — The Effect of Misunderstanding on Mutual Assent and Interpretation Compared — Ramifications

Both the FIRST RESTATEMENT and RESTATEMENT 2d provide an analysis of the *Peerless* situation.[270] The following analysis is based on the RESTATEMENT 2d version. There are essentially three categories to be considered in a purported contract between parties who attach materially different meanings to their manifestations of agreement.

(1) If neither party knows nor has reason to know the meaning attached by the other, there is no mutual assent and no contract. Both parties are blameless.

---

[267] "To preserve the classical school program, Holmes argued that the result in the Peerless case could be explained by objective theory. 'The true ground of the decision was not that each party meant a different thing from the other . . . but that each said a different thing. The plaintiff offered one thing, the defendant expressed his assent to another.' But if both parties subjectively meant the December Peerless, Buyer should have been deemed in breach; and Seller should have been deemed in breach if both parties subjectively meant the October Peerless. Holmes had it backwards: the result in Peerless is correct because they *meant* different things, not because they said different things." Melvin Eisenberg, *The Emergence of Dynamic Contract Law*, 88 CAL. L. REV. 1743, 1759 (2000).

[268] Colfax Envelope Corp. v. Local No. 458-3M, Chicago Graphic Communications International Union, 20 F.3d 750, 753 (7th Cir. 1994). The court also refers to "an American Raffles-like case," Oswald v. Allen, 417 F.2d 43, 45 (2d Cir. 1969), where a buyer who did not speak English understood a seller of a Swiss Coin collection to be referring to the coins in that collection as well as other rare Swiss coins in a separate collection, whereas the seller understood the agreement as restricted to the coins in the Swiss coin collection. The court found "no sensible basis for choosing between conflicting understandings." *See also* Hill-Shafer Partnership v. Chilson Family Trust, 799 P.2d 810 (Ariz. 1990). In Griffith v. Clear Lakes Trout Co., 143 Idaho 733, 152 P. 3d 604 (2007), the court held that the alleged latent ambiguity attached to the contract term "market size" was cured by the parties' course of performance of the contract over a three-year period which revealed a sufficiently mutual interpretation. That objective evidence distinguished the case from *Raffles v. Whchelhaus*.

[269] *Colfax, id.* at 754: "It is common for contracting parties to agree-that is, to signify agreement-to a term to which each party attaches a different meaning. It is just a gamble on a favorable interpretation by the authorized tribunal should a dispute arise." See also Bourke v. The Dun & Bradstreet Corp., 159 F.3d 1032, 1036 (7th Cir. 1998), distinguishing the *Peerless* case situation involving what the court labels "extrinsic" (latent) ambiguity from cases involving "intrinsic" (patent) ambiguity.

[270] FIRST RESTATEMENT § 71; RESTATEMENT 2d § 20.

(2) If both parties know or have reason to know the meaning attached by the other, there is no mutual assent and no contract. Both parties are at fault.

(3) If one party knows or has reason to know the meaning attached by the other who neither knows nor has reason to know of any different meaning, there is a contract according to the intention of the party who does not know of the different meaning. One party is at fault and the other is innocent.

This section of the RESTATEMENT 2d (§ 20) is found in the chapter dealing with formation of contracts as it relates to mutual assent and the *effect* of misunderstanding on mutual assent and formation. Since the SECOND RESTATEMENT is committed to the view that the primary concern in interpretation is the search for the common meaning of the parties rather than the meaning imposed on the parties by law,[271] the first substantive section of the topic of interpretation is the section captioned, "Whose Meaning Prevails."[272] That section is drafted in accordance with the underlying concept and terminology of § 20. Thus, (1) if the parties have attached the same meaning to the terms of their contract, that meaning will prevail, regardless of whether it would have been the meaning attached by the hypothetical reasonable person; (2) if the parties have attached different meanings and one party either knows or has reason to know of any different meaning attached by the other, the meaning attached by the party who neither knows nor has reason to know (the innocent party) will prevail; (3) if neither party knows nor has reason to know the meaning attached by the other, and each party has attached a different meaning to the expression, neither is bound by the meaning attached by the other, notwithstanding a failure of mutual assent.[273] It is important to consider the ramifications of this approach.

If the parties to a contract attach the same meaning to their expression, it should prevail over the meaning which a hypothetical reasonable party would attach.[274] Returning to the famous case involving the meaning of "chicken," if the buyer and seller attached the meaning of "young chicken" to the word "chicken" as used in their manifestation of agreement, a court should provide an interpretation in accordance with the meaning of both parties even if a reasonable interpretation by an objective third party would lead to a different meaning of "chicken."[275] If both parties in the *Peerless* case had intended the December *Peerless*, that meaning should prevail even in the face of trade usage or other objective evidence that such parties would have normally attached an October meaning to the term *Peerless*.[276] If one party in either the "chicken" or *Peerless* situation either knew or had reason to know of a meaning attached by the other party, the meaning attached by the innocent party should prevail and there is a contract according to that interpretation.[277]

---

[271] *See* RESTATEMENT 2d § 201 comment c.

[272] RESTATEMENT 2d § 201.

[273] *See* Merced County Sheriff's Employees Ass'n v. County of Merced, 188 Cal. App. 3d 662, 233 Cal. Rptr. 519 (5th Dist. 1987) (suggesting that the basic principle governing material misunderstanding is that no contract is formed if neither party is at fault or if both parties are equally at fault and citing RESTATEMENT 2d § 20. See Blue Cross & Blue Shield United v. United States, 117 Fed. Appx. 89, 95 (Fed. Cir. 2004).

[274] This statement is quoted in Farmington Police Officers Assn. Commun. Workers, Local 7911 v. City of Farmington, 139 N. M. 750, 757, 137 P. 3d 1204, 1211 (2006).

[275] *See* Sunbury Textile Mills, Inc. v. Commissioner of Internal Revenue, 585 F.2d 1190 (3d Cir. 1978) (conclusive meaning given to the words as both parties intended them).

[276] *See* note 261 *supra.*

[277] In relation to actual knowledge, see, e.g., Hamann v. Crouch, 211 Kan. 852, 508 P.2d 968 (1973); Jet Forwarding,

There are two important dimensions to this analysis. The obvious dimension is the *fault* concept: if one party knows the meaning attached by the other (innocent) party, the first party may be guilty of misrepresentation which would provide the innocent party a power of avoidance.[278] Whether that power is exercised, as in the situation involving mere reason to know rather than actual knowledge, the contract expression will be construed against the party at fault and in favor of the innocent party.[279] In the *Peerless* case, there was no evidence that either party knew or had reason to know the meaning of the term attached by the other. In the "chicken" case, however, had the action been brought by the seller instead of the buyer, a court may have found that the buyer had reason to know that a reasonable seller of chicken might attach the meaning of stewing chicken to the contract term "chicken," notwithstanding the truth of the buyer's assertion that he attached the narrower meaning of "young" chicken to the contract expression. Thus, where the parties attach different meanings to one or more words in their agreement, one should not easily conclude that there is no contract for lack of mutual assent. If one of the meanings is more reasonable under the circumstances, the parties will be bound in accordance with the more reasonable meaning.[280] If, however, both parties know or have reason to know the different meaning attached by the other, neither party is bound to the meaning attached by the other[281] since both parties are at fault, and no contract is formed.[282]

The second and less obvious dimension of the analysis is the pervasive recognition of a *subjective* standard. It is commonly known that the subjective standard becomes acceptable in the *Peerless* case only because of the rare absence of any objective evidence that would allow a court to choose one ship over another. Thus, we are left with one party stating its intention and the other party stating an opposite intention. The pure objectivist would regard such post-formation statements of intention by the parties as irrelevant. They are allowed in this rare situation, however, because there is no relevant evidence except their statements. The subjective standard, however, by no means ends with the facts of *Peerless*. As we have seen, if there was evidence that both parties intended the same ship, that subjective intention would prevail over objective evidence that the other ship was intended. If both parties know of the ambiguity, evidence of their different subjective interpretations will preclude the finding of a contract. If one party knows or should know of the ambiguity while the other neither knows nor should know, the subjective intention of the innocent party will prevail over contrary objective evidence. It is, therefore, clear that the purpose of interpretation is to discern what the parties meant (their intention) rather than what they said (their words or other expressions of agreement.).[283]

Inc. v. United States, 437 F.2d 987, 194 Ct. Cl. 343 (1971). In relation to "reason to know," see, e.g., United States *ex rel.* Union Bldg. Materials Corp. v. Haas & Haynie Corp., 577 F.2d 568 (9th Cir. 1978); Emor Inc. v. Cyprus Mines Corp., 467 F.2d 770 (3d Cir. 1972).

[278] *See* RESTATEMENT 2d § 164. For a case in which a buyer was misled by a seller's advertisement where the court applied the analysis of discovering a contract according to the intention of the innocent party, see Izadi v. Machado (Gus) Ford, Inc., 550 So. 2d 1135 (Fla. Dist. Ct. App. 1989).

[279] RESTATEMENT 2d § 20 comment d.

[280] See, e.g., Sunshine v. M. R. Mansfield Realty, Inc., 195 Colo. 95, 575 P.2d 847 (1978), where the court upheld the "reasonable" meaning after finding that the parties had ascribed different meanings to a clause in their agreement.

[281] RESTATEMENT 2d § 201(3).

[282] RESTATEMENT 2d § 20 comment d. In this situation as in the case where both parties are equally innocent (*Peerless*), there is no basis for deciding which party's understanding to enforce, so the parties are allowed to abandon the contract. *See Colfax, supra* note 268.

[283] "Illinois has largely rejected the traditional rule, sometimes called the 'four corners rule,' which holds that if a

[C]   CISG — Unidroit Principles — A Subjective Standard

The leading guide to contract interpretation under Article 8 of the Vienna Convention[284] bristles with subjectivity: "For the purposes of this Convention statements made by and other conduct of a party are to be interpreted according to his intent where the other party knew or could not have been unaware what that intent was."[285] Only if this rule is not applicable does CISG allow for a "reasonable person" (objective) test.[286] Where a Florida corporation agreed to purchase ceramic tiles from an Italian corporation, representatives of both parties arrived at an oral agreement on the crucial terms of price, quality, quantity, delivery and payment. The agreement was then recorded on the seller's standard, pre-printed order forms which the buyer signed. A clause on the reverse side of the form, 6(b), allowed the seller to suspend or cancel the contract if the buyer was in default or delayed payments. The seller refused to satisfy the buyer's later orders for tile on the footing that the buyer had violated clause 6(b). The buyer brought an action for breach of this contract for the sale of goods governed by CISG since both parties had their places of business in CISG "contracting states."

The buyer claimed that it was not bound by the terms of the seller's form because the parties never intended the terms and conditions on the reverse side of the seller's form to apply to their agreements. In support of that claim, the buyer sought to introduce affidavits from its own representative as well as two of the seller's representatives, all three affiants stating that the parties *subjectively* intended not to be bound by the terms on the reverse side of the form, despite a provision directly below the signature line stating that the buyer is aware of the conditions stated on the reverse side and that he expressly approves of them with special reference to certain expressly numbered clauses, including clause 6. The district court granted the seller's motion for summary judgment but the court of appeals reversed and remanded the case.[287]

The court construed CISG Article 8(1) as allowing an inquiry into the subjective intent of the parties, "[c]ontrary to what is familiar practice in United States courts." Quoting Justice Holmes' "forceful terms" that United States domestic contract law "has nothing to do with the actual state of the parties' minds,"[288] the court found the elements of Article 8(1) were satisfied in the affidavits that not only attested to the subjective intention of the parties but also acknowledged that the seller's representatives were aware of the buyer's subjective intent

---

contract is clear 'on its face,' no other evidence may be introduced to contradict its terms. . . . Thus, Illinois courts may look to extrinsic evidence in hope of discovering the principals' genuine intent, and parties can no longer be certain that they will be stuck with the language of the agreements they sign, no matter their actual intent." R.T. Hepworth Co. v. Dependable Ins. Co., Inc., 997 F.2d 315 (7th Cir. 1993).

[284] The United Nations Convention on Contract for the International Sale of Goods (CISG). *See* Chapter 1, § 13 *supra.*

[285] CISG, Art. 8(1).

[286] "If the preceding paragraph is not applicable, statements made by and other conduct of a party are to be interpreted according to the understanding that a reasonable person of the same kind as the other party would have had in the circumstances." CISG, Art. 8(2).

[287] MCC-Marble Ceramic Ctr., Inc. v. Ceramica Nuova D'Agostino, S.P.A., 144 F.3d 1384 (11th Cir. 1998), *cert. denied,* 526 U.S. 1087, 119 S. Ct. 1496, 143 L. Ed. 2d 650 (1999). The court recognized that the affidavits were relatively conclusory and unsupported by facts that would objectively establish the buyer's intent not to be bound by the form terms. Yet, while they were not conclusive proof of what the parties intended, they raised an issue of material fact regarding the parties' intent that should not have been dismissed out of hand.

[288] OLIVER W. HOLMES, THE COMMON LAW 242 (Howe ed. 1963).

with respect to the inoperative effect of the terms on the seller's form.[289] The parol evidence rule was not a bar to this evidence since CISG expressly permits evidence of the prior negotiations of the parties.[290]

The court suggests that the CISG rule of interpretation is diametrically opposed to the common law view. The court's emphasis upon Justice Holmes' insistence on an objective theory, however, suggests a view that is not in accord with our earlier analysis, i.e., the essential purpose of interpretation is to ascertain the parties intention in terms of what they meant rather than what they said. If, therefore, *both* parties attest not only to their individual intention that the form terms would not be operative, but to their awareness that such intention was mutual, why would a court under a common law interpretation, much less a CISG interpretation, insist on enforcing a contract that neither party intended to be made? Indeed, Article 8(1) of CISG can be reconciled with the essential purpose of interpretation as stated in the Corbinized Restatement 2d "that the primary search is for a common meaning of the parties, not a meaning imposed on them by law."[291] Analogously, there is a pervasive common law principle discussed in later sections that where a purported offeree is aware of the offer's mistake, such an offeree cannot snap up the offer. Such awareness will be as rare under Article 8(1) as it is under the common law. Thus, the 8(1) standard will be the exception while the dominant standard of interpretation under CISG will be the reasonable person standard, albeit appearing in Article 8(2). UNIDROIT Principles[292] of interpretation parallel CISG provisions. They begin with a general directive that "[a] contract shall be interpreted according to the common intention of the parties"[293] and only if that intention cannot be established does a "reasonable person" standard apply.[294] A more specific provision then replicates the language of CISG,[295] followed by a provision listing "relevant circumstances" to be considered when applying the "subjective" test. These "circumstances" begin with "preliminary negotiations between the parties," thereby following CISG in rejecting the parol evidence rule.[296] Other "circumstances" include prior course of dealing, course of performance, the nature and purpose of the contract, the meaning commonly given to terms, as well as expressions in the trade and trade usages.[297]

[D]   Mistake in Expression

A mistake in expression suggests a misunderstanding between the parties. The FIRST RESTATEMENT and RESTATEMENT 2d include the same illustration but reach different conclusions.

---

[289] Article 8(1) requires that the other party (here, the seller) knew or could not have been unaware of the intent of the first party (here, the buyer).

[290] CISG, Art. 8(3). See the discussion of CISG and the parol evidence rule at § 84[C][7], *supra.*

[291] RESTATEMENT 2d § 201, comment c.

[292] *See* Chapter 1, § 13, *supra.*

[293] Principles, Art. 4.1(1).

[294] Principles, Art. 4.1(2).

[295] Principles, Art. 4.2 "which corresponds almost literally to Art. 8(1) and (2) of CISG." Comment 1.

[296] Principles, Art. 4.3(a). Here, it should be recalled that Principles allows for merger clauses that will cause the writing or record of the parties to be viewed as final and complete. Article 2.17. Such extrinsic evidence, however, will still be allowed for the purpose of interpretation. This view accords with the UCC position in UCC § 2-202.

[297] Principles, Art 4.3(b) through (f).

"*A* says to *B*, 'I offer to sell you my horse for \$100.' *B* knowing that *A* intends to offer to sell his cow for that price, not his horse, and that the word 'horse' is a slip of the tongue, replies, 'I accept.' "

The FIRST RESTATEMENT found no contract for the sale of the horse or the cow.[298] The RESTATEMENT 2d finds no contract for the sale of the horse, but finds a contract for the sale of the cow.[299] As to the sale of the horse, there is no question that the offeree, *B*, may not "snap up the offer" because he knew or had reason to know of the mistake by *A*.[300] The problem arises with respect to the contract for the sale of the cow. The RESTATEMENT 2d result is consistent with the principle that there is a contract for the sale of the cow because the innocent party, *A*, had the cow in mind and *B* knew that *A* intended to offer to sell the cow. No explanation is offered in the FIRST RESTATEMENT for its conclusion that there is no contract for the sale of the cow. A critic of the RESTATEMENT 2d view, however, provides the rationale: "When the words are unambiguous neither of the generally accepted bases of contract formation is present. There has been neither actual agreement nor expression of agreement for the sale of the cow."[301] The criticism is that suggested earlier concerning the "mutual" standard of interpretation to integrated agreements.[302]

In the illustration, if *B* knows that *A* intends to offer to sell his cow for \$100 notwithstanding *A*'s use of the term "horse," there must be objective evidence to support a finding that *B* knows. The evidence that *B* knows of *A*'s mistake in expression and of *A*'s intent to offer the cow for sale is sufficient in both RESTATEMENTS to preclude a contract for the sale of the horse. If the standard of interpretation applied were exclusively that of an objective third person with no knowledge of prior dealings or other evidence to support *B*'s knowledge, there should be a contract for the sale of the horse. If *B* knew that *A* did not intend to sell the horse, but did not know that *A* *did* intend to sell the cow, there should be no contract for the sale of the cow. The illustration, however, indicates that *B* knew both, i.e., that *A* did not intend to sell the horse but did intend to sell the cow. If *A* and *B* had a prior understanding that a code term, "gork," meant "cow," even under the FIRST RESTATEMENT, the evidence of their mutual understanding of the term "gork" would be admissible to assist a court to discover a contract for the cow. Critics of the RESTATEMENT 2d would admit such evidence because the term "gork" is ambiguous or uncertain. Their criticism of the RESTATEMENT 2d change in result in the horse/cow illustration is, therefore, predicated upon the use of an *unambiguous* term, i.e., "horse," which, to them, simply cannot mean "cow." Yet, no word is totally certain or unambiguous. The contextual evidence of a transaction can certainly lead to an irrefutable finding that parties meant "cow" when they said "horse," or "buy" when they meant "sell," or "black" when they meant "white."

There are, however, certain ramifications that could lead to unjust results. Critics point to the possibility that *A*'s offer to sell the cow may have been for \$600 where the cow is worth only \$300 and the horse is worth \$1000. To hold *B* to the cow contract at a price that is double

---

[298] FIRST RESTATEMENT § 71 ill. 2.

[299] RESTATEMENT 2d § 20 ill. 5.

[300] *See* RESTATEMENT 2d § 153. Tyra v. Cheney, 129 Minn. 428, 430, 152 N.W. 835 (1915): "One cannot snap up an offer knowing that it was made in mistake." Speckel v. Perkins, 364 N.W.2d 890, 893 (Minn. App. 1985). For a "reason to know" example, see Geremia v. Boyarsky, 107 Conn. 387, 140 A. 749 (1928).

[301] Palmer, *The Effect of Misunderstanding on Contract Formation and Reformation under the* Restatement of Contracts, Second, 65 MICH. L. REV. 33, 48 (1965).

[302] *See supra* subsection A.

the value of the cow would, according to the criticism, inflict "a punishment on *B* that does not fit the wrong."[303] The RESTATEMENT 2d avoids this problem in the illustration by adding a fact not contained in the original illustration, i.e., that $100 is a fair price for either the horse or cow.[304] In apparent reaction to the criticism and the possibility that the price of the cow would be excessive, the Reporter's Note to this section suggests that, in such a case, the court may refuse to enforce the contract against *B* ($600 for the cow worth only $300) "on grounds analogous to those applicable in a suit for reformation."[305] The "analogous" application of reformation concepts would allow a court to use discretion in recognizing or refusing to recognize a contract for the cow.

§ 89   RULES OF INTERPRETATION

A number of rules or guides to interpretation have been developed by courts over the years. It should be emphasized that they are mere aids, developed in a common sense fashion for determining the meaning to be attributed to the expressions of the parties to the contract and are not to be applied with conclusive effect.

[A]   Surrounding Circumstances — Context

When all contracts were in writing and under seal, the tendency of the early common law authorities was to suggest that the document must "speak" for itself, and all aids to a determination of the sense of the expressions had to be found within that document.[306] This arbitrary view has long since been abandoned. If a court seeks to determine the meaning attributed by the parties to their expressions of agreement, it is important for the court to place itself in the position of the parties at the time the contract was made.[307] It must take into account all of the surrounding circumstances prior to and contemporaneous with the making of the contract so as to more precisely identify the sense of the expressions in questions as apparently understood by the parties.[308] The meaning of words manifesting the parties intent depends upon the context in which they are stated.[309]

---

[303] *See* Palmer, *supra* note 301, at 49.

[304] RESTATEMENT 2d § 20 ill. 5.

[305] *See* RESTATEMENT 2d § 20 Reporter's Note, referring to § 166 comment a.

[306] *See* 9 WIGMORE, EVIDENCE § 2470 (3d ed. 1940).

[307] RESTATEMENT 2d § 202 comment b. *See* Farragut Mortg. Co. v. Arthur Andersen LLP, 1999 Mass. Super. LEXIS 284, *28, 10 Mass. L. Rep. 285 (Mass. Super. Ct. 1999). *See also* McConocha v. Blue Cross & Blue Shield Mut., 930 F. Supp. 1182, 1186 (N.D. Ohio 1996) (quoting the third edition of this book in support of this principle).

[308] Recent judicial expressions of this guide to interpretation include American Medical Centers v. Rowley, 2006 Text. App. 2648 at *14 (Ct. App. Tex. 2006) ("This interpretation considers the entire contract and surrounding circumstances. . . ."). *See also*, Hunger United States Special Hydraulics Cylinders Corp. v. Hardie-Tynes Mfg. Co., 2000 U.S. App. LEXIS 1520, at *22 (10th Cir. Feb. 4, 2000); Lupien v. Citizens Utils. Co., 159 F.3d 102, 104–05 (2d Cir. 1998); Jack Rowe Assocs., Inc. v. Fisher Corp., 833 F.2d 177, 181 (9th Cir. 1987); Merdes v. Underwood, 742 P.2d 245 (Alaska 1987); Koontz v. Lee, 737 S.W.2d 766 (Mo. Ct. App. 1987).

[309] *See* Stanford Ranch v. Maryland Casualty Co., 89 F.3d 618, 626 (9th Cir. 1996). *See also* Estate of Johnson v. Carr, 288 Ark. 461, 706 S.W.2d 388 (1986). RESTATEMENT 2d § 202 comment b.

[B]　The General and Specific Purpose of the Parties — Preambles (Recitals) ("Whereas" Clauses)

The expressions of the parties are typically words written on paper or recorded on hard drives or discs though the parties may also manifest their intention by conduct. To make sense of these expressions, one of the more helpful guides to interpretation is to discover the apparent *purpose* of the parties. "The parties manifest purpose controls the interpretation of the contract provisions."[310] Courts will often suggest that the parties' expression should give effect to their "general purpose." This rule, guide, or aid to interpretation, however, is invariably couched in terms of the next guide to be discussed, i.e., the requirement that the expression of the parties be read as a whole.[311]

The determination of the purpose of particular language in the contract can be significant where the language is vague or ambiguous. Where a clause excused a party from complete harvesting of crops because of "adverse weather conditions," the purpose of the parties was particularly helpful in deciding whether unusually good weather that caused the crops to mature simultaneously was contemplated within that clause.[312] Similarly, where a contract permitted an extension of time for performance "in the event of high water" and the purchaser was to sever the timber, the court viewed the purpose of the clause as providing additional time if the purchaser was prevented from exercising his rights rather than the incidental occurrence of high water at some point during the original severance period.[313] Where a party feigned suicide, left his wife and "married" another woman, the court considered his purpose in determining the meaning of "wife" in an insurance policy he had procured before his actual death.[314] While courts invariably seek the intention of the parties, they are essentially seeking the purpose of the parties in making the contract. If the principal purpose of the parties is ascertainable, it is given great weight by the courts and further interpretation of the contract is guided by it.[315]

Parties sometimes seek to emphasize their purpose by inserting a *preamble* ("recital" or "whereas") clause in the written expression of their agreement which typically appears at the inception of the writing. It is an introductory statement explaining the purpose of the document. These clauses are viewed as persuasive but not controlling in determining the intention or purpose of the parties.[316] Where there is ambiguity or inconsistency between the preamble and the remainder of the writing, the following construction has been accepted: (a) where the preamble (recital or whereas clause) is clear and the remainder of the writing is ambiguous, the preamble will control; (b) where the preamble is ambiguous and the remainder

---

[310] Misano Di Navigazione. SpA v. United States, 968 F. 2d 273, 275 (2d Cir. 1992). *See also* Bourke v. Dun & Bradstreet Corp., 159 F.3d 1032, 1039 (7th Cir. 1998) ("purpose" is given great weight). *See also* Fort Meyer Constr. Co. v. United States, 2000 U.S. App. LEXIS 853, at *5 (Fed. Cir. Jan. 24, 2000).

[311] *See, e.g.*, Rosebud Sioux Tribe v. A & P Steel, Inc., 733 F.2d 509 (8th Cir.), *cert. denied*, 469 U.S. 1072, 105 S. Ct. 565, 83 L. Ed. 2d 506 (1984).

[312] Stender v. Twin City Foods, Inc., 82 Wash. 2d 250, 510 P.2d 221 (1973).

[313] Lawson v. Martin Timber Co., 238 La. 467, 115 So. 2d 821 (1959).

[314] *In re* Soper's Estate, 196 Minn. 60, 246 N.W. 427 (1936).

[315] Alvin, Ltd. v. United States Postal Serv., 816 F.2d 1562 (Fed. Cir. 1987); Crestview Bowl, Inc. v. Womer Constr. Co., 225 Kan. 335, 592 P.2d 74 (1979); Hanson v. Stern, 102 Ga. App. 341, 116 S.E. 2d 237, 239 (1960). Restatement 2d § 202 comment c.

[316] This statement is quoted from an earlier edition of this treatise in Creamer v. AIM Telephones, Inc., 159 B. R. 440, 444, n. 4 (E. D. Pa. 1993). *See also* Cain Restaurant Co. v. Carrols Corp., 273 Fed. Appx. 430, 434 (6th Cir. 2008).

clear, the remainder will control; (c) where the preamble and remainder are both clear but inconsistent with each other, the remainder of the writing will control.[317] These are common sense directives essentially stating that a particular manifestation will control a general expression, or a more recent or more detailed manifestation of the parties' intention should prevail over earlier inconsistent or more general statements. These aids will be further considered later in this section.

[C]   The Transaction Must Be Viewed as a Whole

Numerous cases indicate that all of the different parts of an agreement must be viewed together, i.e., as a whole, and each part interpreted in the light of all of the other parts.[318] As suggested earlier,[319] this guide is often found in statements suggesting that courts must be concerned about the "general purpose" of the parties to the contract and that purpose can be discovered only by interpretation of the whole agreement of the parties. Similarly, the requirement that interpretation occur in *context* is another illustration of this guide since only by a contextual determination is the general purpose of the parties discernible and, again, that purpose is discernible only by considering the entire expression of the parties. As the RESTATEMENT 2d suggests, "A word changes meaning when it becomes part of a sentence, the sentence when it becomes part of a paragraph."[320] Thus, an interpretation which gives meaning to every part of the expression will be preferred to one that gives no effect to one or more parts.[321] If this is not reasonably possible, the expression should be interpreted to give effect to the apparent principal purpose of the parties.[322]

A corollary to the rule that the contract should be interpreted as a whole is that all of the different writings relating to the same transaction should be interpreted together, whether or not they form a single contract.[323]

[D]   A Reasonable, Lawful, or Effective Interpretation Is Preferred

It is a general rule of interpretation that a reasonable interpretation of an expression is preferred to one that is literal, unusual, absurd, or of no effect.[324] Thus, it has been held that an interpretation permitting a professional guide not only to be a contestant in a bass fishing

---

[317] *See* Stech v. Panel Mart, Inc., 434 N.E.2d 97 (Ind. Ct. App. 1982) (relying on Maddux & Sons v. Trustees of Ariz. Laborers, 125 Ariz. 475, 478–79, 610 P.2d 477, 480–81 (Ct. App. 1980), which quotes Williams v. Barkley, 165 N.Y. 48, 57, 58 N.E. 765, 767 (1900)). Both of the cases relied upon quote the originator of this concept, i.e., Lord Esher in Ex parte Dawes, 17 Q.B.D. 275, 286 (1886).

[318] *See* Lindsay v. Safeco Ins. Co. of Amer., 447 F. 3d 615 (8th Cir. 2006); Stetzer v. Dunkin' Donuts, Inc., 87 F. Supp. 2d 104, 110 (D. Conn. 2000); Elliott Leases Cars v. Quigley, 118 R.I. 321, 373 A.2d 810 (1977); Pritchard v. Wick, 406 Pa. 598, 178 A.2d 725 (1962) (also stating other guides to interpretation). RESTATEMENT 2d § 202(2) and comment d.

[319] *See supra* text at note 304.

[320] RESTATEMENT 2d § 202 comment d.

[321] Intertherm, Inc. v. Coronet Imperial Corp., 558 S.W.2d 344, 351–52 (Mo. Ct. App. 1977); Central Ga. Elec. Membership Corp. v. Georgia Power Co., 217 Ga. 171, 121 S.E.2d 644, 646 (1961). RESTATEMENT 2d § 203(a) and comment a.

[322] *See supra* subsection B.

[323] *See* Paisner v. Renaud, 102 N.H. 27, 149 A.2d 867 (1959), and RESTATEMENT 2d § 202(2).

[324] Williamson v. Kay (*In re* Villa West Assocs.), 146 F.3d 798, 803 (10th Cir. 1998) (a reasonable interpretation is favored and result that vitiates purpose or leads to absurd result should be avoided). *See also* Soliva v. Shand, Morahan & Co., 176 W. Va. 430, 345 S.E.2d 33 (1986); Harper v. Gibson, 284 S.C. 274, 325 S.E.2d 586 (Ct. App. 1985); Rosebud

tournament but allowing him to fish the tournament waters prior to the tournament would be an absurd interpretation which is not permitted.[325] Similarly, an interpretation that would allow a $7,000 forfeit for an uncompleted repair costing $50 was rejected as absurd.[326] An interpretation that will make the transaction a lawful and effective contract is preferred to one that will make it illegal. Where a car rental contract provided that the renter agreed to assume all responsibility for damages while the car is in his possession, the state no-fault act prohibited contractual assignment of collision damages. Since it is presumed that parties intend their agreements to be valid and lawful, a lawful interpretation is preferred. The court found that the rental contract was valid, but the assignment provision was unenforceable.[327] It is presumed that parties intend every portion of the contract to be effective. Where, a clause allowing environmental costs was separately negotiated and included in the contract, the court rejected an interpretation that would largely eviscerate the purpose of the clause as applied in a given context.[328] Similarly, where a provision in a settlement agreement concerning access to a military reservation required consultation with the other parties, the court rejected the Army's "limit first, consult later" interpretation of the agreement since it virtually eliminated the concept of consultation.[329] A clause in a real estate contract required any dispute to be first submitted to mediation but added that nothing in the clause prohibited the buyer from seeking specific performance. The buyer pursued specific performance and thereafter made an offer for mediation. The court granted the seller's motion to dismiss since allowing the buyer's action would render the mediation requirement ineffective.[330]

[E]   Public Interest Favored

If the transaction in question affects the public interest, an interpretation will be preferred that is most favorable to the public interest.[331] This rule is one of "construction" rather than interpretation, i.e., the theory is not that it aids in determining the intention of the parties; rather, it is based on the policy that it is desirable to favor the public interest where there is doubt as to the intended meaning. It finds its most frequent applications in contracts made by public utilities[332] or in contracts where one of the parties is a governmental unit.[333] It will

---

Sioux Tribe v. A & P Steel, Inc., 733 F.2d 509 (8th Cir.), *cert. denied*, 469 U.S. 1072, 105 S. Ct. 565, 83 L. Ed. 2d 506 (1984); City of Baltimore v. Industrial Elecs., Inc., 230 Md. 224, 186 A.2d 469 (1962). RESTATEMENT 2d § 203(a).

[325] Newmac/Bud Light Team Bass Circuit, Inc. v. Swint, 486 So. 2d 255 (La. Ct. App. 1986).

[326] Brown v. Hotard, 428 So. 2d 505 (Ct. App.), *cert. denied*, 433 So. 2d 182 (La. 1983).

[327] Universal Underwriters Ins. Co. v. Kneeland, 628 N. W. 2d 491 (Mich. 2001). See RESTATEMENT 2d § 203(a) and comment c.

[328] Abraham v. Rockwell International Corp., 326 F. 3d 1242, 1254 (Fed Cir. 2003).

[329] Malama Makua v. Gates, 2008 U.S. Dist. LEXIS 19201 at *30 (D. Haw. 2008).

[330] Miller Family Real Estate, LLC v. Hajizadeh, 2008 Utah App. LEXIS 477 (2008).

[331] "[A] sound public policy favors the free and unrestricted use of land by the legal holder, and therefore alleged restrictive covenants should be construed strictly against the establishment and effect of such covenants, and liberally in support of the free use of the land." Ferguson v. Beth-Mary Steel Corp., 166 Md. 666, 672, 172 A. 238, 240 (1934); Seman v. First State Bank of Eden Prarie, 394 N.W.2d 557 (Minn. App. 1986) (public interest in preserving integrity of cashier's checks); *see also* Houk v. Ross, 34 Ohio St. 2d 77, 63 Ohio Op. 2d 119, 296 N.E.2d 266 (1973); De Long Corp. v. Lucas, 176 F. Supp. 104 (D.N.Y. 1959), *aff'd*, 278 F.2d 804 (2d Cir. 1960), *cert. denied*, 364 U.S. 833, 81 S. Ct. 71, 5 L. Ed. 2d 58 (1960). *See also* RESTATEMENT 2d § 207.

[332] In a contract between two utilities, however, the public utilities commission will not intervene unless the contract is adverse to the public interest. *See* Lemhi Tel. Co. v. Mountain States Tel. & Tel. Co., 98 Idaho 692, 571 P.2d 753 (1977).

apply, however, to any type of contract. Where an arbitration agreement that would have otherwise allowed punitive damages included a choice-of-law clause naming New York that allows only courts and not arbitrators to award punitive damages, the court viewed the choice-of-law clause as inserting ambiguity into the contract. Recognizing the strong public policy of the Federal Arbitration Act in favor of resolving disputes through arbitration, the court concluded that the choice-of law provision applied only to the state substantive law but not its rules limiting arbitrators' awards damages.[334]

[F] Subsequent Conduct of the Parties (Course of Performance) as an Interpretation Aid

If the parties to a contract have started to perform the contract and their performance illustrates the parties' common understanding of their prior expression of agreement, this evidence will be given great weight in determining the meaning attributed to their expressions.[335] As will be seen in the next section dealing with trade usage, course of dealing, and course of performance under the UCC, course of performance evidence is the strongest evidence of the parties' intention beyond their express terms, and even their express terms can be overcome by course of performance evidence that constitutes a subsequent modification of their prior expression of agreement.[336] It is not remarkable that course of performance evidence has been elevated to this premier position since it is the most recent and most specific manifestation by the parties themselves as to the meaning of their contract.

[G] Construction Against Drafter — Contra Proferentem

It is a general rule of interpretation that an expression is to be interpreted against the party responsible for its drafting.[337] The rule is particularly applicable if it has been embodied in a writing prepared by the skilled adviser of one of the parties, or if the person who drew it had special competence in such matters. The rule finds frequent application in cases dealing with insurance contracts or other contracts containing standardized (printed) terms.[338] The common sense basis for the rule is that, where the language may be reasonably interpreted in a way that favors the drafter or in a way that favors the non-drafter, the latter interpretation will be preferred since the drafter had control over the language and may even have left the language less than clear so as not to alert the other party to certain troublesome possibilities

---

[333] *See* Codell Constr. Co. v. Commonwealth of Ky., 566 S.W.2d 161 (Ct. App. 1977) (rule in construing contracts to which government is a party is to resolve ambiguities in its favor because an interpretation is preferred which favors the public).

[334] Mastrobuono v. Shearson Lehman Hutton, 514 U.S. 52 (1995).

[335] Berg v. Hudesman, 115 Wash. 2d 657, 801 P.2d 222, 234 (1990); EEOC v. Outrigger Restaurant, Inc., 2000 U.S. Dist. LEXIS 330, at *11 (S.D. Ala. Jan. 10, 2000); RESTATEMENT 2d § 202(4) and comment g.

[336] See. Bayer Chemical Corporation v. Albermarle Corporation, 2006 U.S. App. LEXIS 6994 (3d Cir. 2006).

[337] *See* Hulda Schoening Family Trust v. Powertel/Ky., Inc., 265 F. Supp. 2d 781, 785 (W. D. Ky. 2003) (citing the third edition of this treatise; Z.R.L. Corp. v. Great Cent. Ins. Co., 156 Ill. App. 3d 856, 109 Ill. Dec. 481, 510 N.E.2d 102 (1st Dist. 1987) (citing the second edition of this treatise). *See also*; Quality Asphalt Paving v. State, 71 P. 3d 865 (Alas. 2003); Pappas v. Bever, 219 N.W.2d 720 (Iowa 1974).

[338] Kunin v. Benefit Trust Life Ins. Co., 910 F.2d 534, 538–39 (9th Cir.), *cert. denied*, 498 U.S. 1013, 111 S. Ct. 581, 112 L. Ed. 2d 587 (1990) (the rule of contra proferentem is the most familiar expression in the reports of insurance cases).

of which the drafter now seeks a favorable interpretation.[339] Since the drafter is responsible for the unclear language, it should be interpreted against him even if he intended no advantage to himself in drafting it.

The *contra proferentem* rule may be seen as a rule of construction rather than a rule of interpretation.[340] If the sound interpretation remains in doubt after all of the relevant evidence has been considered and other common sense guides have been applied, the court may choose a construction against the drafter applied as a "tie breaker."[341] Courts, however, may not limit *contra proferentem* to a tie-breaking role where the drafter is an insurance company, the paradigm drafter inspiring the rule. When three horseback riders were injured while engaging in practicing horse racing, the insurer for the defendant racing association claimed that the policy covered injuries sustained in horse racing, not practicing horse racing. The trial court applied *contra proferentem*, construing the language against the insurance company. On appeal, the defendant pointed to Delaware precedent in claiming that this rule of construction should only be used as a last resort, again, a tie-breaker. The court, however, held that the defendant's argument ignored parts of the precedent stating that *contra proferentem* is particularly appropriate where the provisions drafted by the defendant could easily have been made clear.[342]

[H]   Noscitur a Sociis

Noscitur a Sociis is typically translated as "known by the company it keeps," or "known by its neighbors." Thus, the meaning of an unclear term in a contract may be clarified by referring to other associated words in the contract.[343] It is, however, a relatively weak guide that is only capable of demonstrating that associated terms are related but not synonymous.[344] Where a lease placed the duty of repair of the premises on the lessee except for damages resulting from "fire, the elements, floods, tornadoes or other acts of God," the court held that the term "elements" referred to the same type of sudden and unexpected causes of damage as the associated words in the lease. Thus, damage caused by normal weather conditions did not fall within the exception.[345]

[I]   Expressio Unius Est Exclusio Alterius — The Enumeration of Some Excludes Others

Parties to a contract may specify certain items in detail in their contract. This invokes a rule of interpretation that the specification of such items impliedly excludes other items relating to the same general matter, i.e., the expression in the contract of one or more things of a class implies exclusion of all not expressed, or, *expressio unius est exclusio alterius*.[346] An

---

[339] RESTATEMENT 2d § 206 and comment a.

[340] *Id.*

[341] Calogero v. Horizon/CMS Healthcare Corp., 2003 U.S. Dist. LEXIS 6989 at *14–15 (N. D. Ill. 2003).

[342] Twin City Fire Ins. Co. v. Del. Racing Assn., 840 A. 2d 624 (Del.2003).

[343] See SMI Mgt. Corp. v. Underwriters at Lloyd's, 179 S. W. 3d 619, 625, n. 2 (Ct. App. Tex. 2005).

[344] Schenkel & Schultz, Inc. v. Homestead Ins. Co., 119 F. 3d 548, 551 (7th Cir. 1997).

[345] Sky Harbor Air Service v. Airport Auth. of Omaha, 174 Neb.243, 117 N. W. 2d 383 (1962).

[346] *See* Smart v. Gillette Co. Long-Term Disability Plan, 70 F.3d 173, 179 (1st Cir. 1995) (where parties listed specific benefits, any other benefit not so listed is thought to be excluded). *See also* Eden Music Corp. v. Times Square

agreement to acquire a 49 percent interest in another corporation included a power of termination, subject to certain conditions. The chairman and controlling stockholder of the buyer's board later voted against the agreement. The power of termination was exercised on the ground there had been no stockholder approval, but stockholder approval was not one of the conditions listed in the agreement to trigger the power of termination. The court applied the *expressio unius* guide in holding that stockholder approval was not intended as a condition to terminating the agreement.[347] Where a stock bonus plan was not listed in a settlement agreement which listed similar items, the court applied the *exclusio unius* guide in holding that the plan was not part of the agreement.[348] Like other guides to interpretation, this rule is not conclusive[349] and may give way to superior rules of interpretation.[350]

[J]   Ejusdem Generis

Where the language of a contract is uncertain, another canon of construction or interpretation to which courts sometimes resort is the rule of *ejusdem generis* which applies where general language in the contract is followed by enumerated specific terms relating to the same subject matter. The meaning of the general language is said to be limited to matters similar in kind or classification to the enumerated specific terms.[351] Where a lease contract could be terminated "for good cause" and this general language was followed by enumerated items such as nonpayment of rent, serious or repeated damage to the premises, or the creation of physical hazards, the general phrase, "for good cause," did not include other violations of the lease, such as maintaining a dog.[352] The rule of *ejusdem generis* may be avoided by including language indicating that the general language includes but is *not limited to* the specific, enumerated items following it.[353]

Music Publications Co., 127 A.D.2d 161, 514 N.Y.S.2d 3 (1st Dep't 1987); Sonneman v. Blue Cross & Blue Shield, 403 N.W.2d 701 (Minn. Ct. App. 1987); United States v. First Nat'l Bank of Crestview, 513 So. 2d 179 (Fla. Dist. Ct. App. 1987).

[347] Kansas City Southern v. Grupo TMM, S. A., 2003 Del Ch. LEXIS 116 (2003).

[348] Gorman v. Gorman, 883 A. 2d 732 (R. I. 2005).

[349] CKB & Assoc., Inc. v. Moore McCormack Petroleum, Inc., 734 S.W.2d 653 (Tex. 1987). *See also* RAD-Razorback Ltd. Partnership v. B.G. Coney Co., 289 Ark. 550, 713 S.W.2d 462 (1986) (rule is not dispositive).

[350] National Ins. Underwriters v. Carter, 17 Cal. 3d 380, 131 Cal. Rptr. 42, 551 P.2d 362 (1976) (the "expressio unius" maxim cannot defeat the rule of "contra proferentem" in insurance contracts which rests on basic considerations of policy).

[351] *See* Liberty Mut. Ins. Co. v. East Cent. Okla. Elec. Coop., 97 F.3d 383, 390 (10th Cir. 1996) (when interpreting a general word that follows a series of specific words, the specific words restrict the meaning of the general-encompassing only action of the same general type). *See also* SMI Realty Mgt. Corp. v. Underwriters at Lloyd's, 179 S. W. 3d 619 (Ct. App. Tex. 2005); General Elec. Credit Corp. v. Larson, 387 N.W.2d 734 (N.D. 1986); Propis v. Fireman's Fund Ins. Co., 112 A.D.2d 734, 492 N.Y.S.2d 228 (4th Dep't 1985); United Cal. Bank v. Prudential Ins. Co., 140 Ariz. 238, 681 P.2d 390 (Ct. App. 1984).

[352] Housing Auth. of Mansfield v. Rovig, 676 S.W.2d 314 (Mo. Ct. App. 1984).

[353] *See* Cooper Distrib. Co. v. Amana Refrigeration, Inc., 63 F.3d 262, 280 (3d Cir. 1995). *See also* Eastern Air Lines, Inc. v. McDonnell Douglas Corp., 532 F.2d 957 (5th Cir. 1976) (delays in performance due to causes beyond seller's control, including but not limited to, enumerated events).

[K]   Presumptions About Interpretation — Ordinary Meaning, Technical Meaning, Legal Meaning, and Trade Usage

As we have seen, no single standard of interpretation is necessarily applied in determining the meaning of the contracting parties' expressions. Certain presumptions, however, reappear in the case law and should be considered.

1. The ordinary or popular sense of words as used throughout the country is preferred in the absence of circumstances indicating a contrary understanding.[354]

2. Technical terms and words of art are to be given their technical meaning unless the circumstances indicate a contrary understanding.[355]

3. Where words have come to have an established meaning in the law, that meaning will be adopted, in the absence of competent affirmative evidence of a contrary understanding.[356] If mutual understanding is overcome by statute or administrative regulation, the obligation results from the governmental regulation rather than interpretation.

4. The usage of a trade, locality, profession or the like will supersede the ordinary or popular sense of words where the situation justifies the assumption that these usages would more nearly approximate the understanding of the parties.[357] Whether it is the meaning of "publish" in a contract between the hardcover and softcover publishers of a book,[358] "program" in the television programming industry,[359] "delinquency" in the credit card industry,[360] the meaning of "sudden and accidental" in an insurance policy covering pollution,[361] or any other contract terms, evidence of trade and local usage is admitted to discern their meaning since it is expected that the parties observed that practice when they made their contract.[362] If the usage is, in fact, the settled habit of expression of the group in question and not merely the expression of a few persons, and if the parties to the contract are members of the group, the special usage will always prevail in the absence of competent

---

[354] *See* Williamson v. J.C. Penney Life Ins. Co., 226 F.3d 408, 409 (5th Cir. 2000). *See also* Fryar v. Currin, 280 S.C. 241, 312 S.E.2d 16 (Ct. App. 1984) (citing the second edition of this book for this proposition); Scott v. East Alabama Educ. Found., Inc., 417 So. 2d 572 (Ala. 1982); RESTATEMENT 2d § 202(3)(a).

[355] *See* Bandak v. Eli Lilly & Co. Ret. Plan, 2009 U.S. App. LEXIS 25369 at *3 (7th Cir. 2009) ("The term 'qualified defined benefit plan' is an American legal term that means a plan approved by the Internal Revenue Service for favorable federal tax treatment. . . . The presumption in interpreting a contract is that the meaning of a technical term is its technical meaning (citing cases) and thus, if it a technical legal term, its technical legal meaning." The court cited RESTATEMENT 2d of Contracts 202(3)(b).

[356] *See, e.g.*, Mellon Bank, N.A. v. Aetna Bus. Credit Inc., 619 F.2d 1001 (3d Cir. 1980) (legal term of art, "insolvent," interpreted in accordance with technical meaning where defendant failed to sustain burden of showing different meaning attached by the parties). Where, however, legal terms are pieced together by a lay person, they are not particularly helpful in determining the parties' intention. Atalla v. Abdul-Baki, 976 F.2d 189, 194 (4th Cir. 1992).

[357] *See* Stewart v. Brennan, 7 Haw. App. 136, 748 P.2d 816 (1988); Bischoff v. Quong-Watkins Props., 113 Idaho 826, 748 P.2d 410 (Ct. App. 1987); Hurst v. W. J. Lake & Co., 141 Or. 306, 16 P.2d 627 (1932). *See* RESTATEMENT 2d § 202(5).

[358] U.S. Naval Institute v. Charter Communications, 875 F. 2d 1044 (2d Cir. 1989).

[359] Employment Television Enterprises v. Barocas, 100 P. 3d 37 (Colo. Ct. App. 2004).

[360] Capital Funding VI, LP v. Chase Manhattan Bank, USA, 191 Fed. Appx. 92 (3d Cir. 2006).

[361] Sunbeam Corp. v. Liberty Mut. Ins. Co., 566 Pa. 494, 781 A. 2d 1189 (2001).

[362] UCC § 1-303(c) defines "usage of trade" as "any practice or method of dealing having such regularity of observance in a place, vocation or trade as to *justify an expectation* that it will be observed with respect to the transaction in question." (Emphasis supplied).

evidence that the parties understood that some other meaning was to be attributed to the language in question. The UCC has emphasized the importance of trade usage, course of dealing, and course of performance as evidence of the factual bargain of the parties.[363]

[L]   Interpretation of Inconsistent Expressions

Generally accepted rules are found in the case law to avoid apparent inconsistencies in the parties' expression of their contract.

1. Specific terms will usually be held to qualify general terms since parties are more likely to advert consciously to specific rather than general terms and the specific terms, therefore, normally suggest a more precise identification of the parties' intentions. Where a disability insurance policy offset benefits received by the insured under any "government plan," the court held that this specific term controlled the more general provisions in the policy where the teacher had received disability payments from a teachers fund that was a "government plan."[364] Where the lease of a supermarket tenant in a shopping mall permitted the use of banking machines, the defendant withheld permission for the tenant to sublease space for the operation of a bank. The court held that the specific contract language that limited the premises to banking machines precluded general banking.[365]

2. A word or phrase used more than once is to be interpreted in the same sense throughout the contract absent a clear indication of contrary intention.[366]

3. Obvious mistakes of grammar or punctuation will usually be corrected or they will be disregarded to the extent that they conflict with a clear intention expressed in the contract.[367]

4. Where there is a conflict between printed and written provisions, the preferred interpretation will give effect to the written provisions as superior evidence of the parties' intentions.[368] Similarly, separately negotiated terms will be preferred over standardized printed terms which have not been separately negotiated.[369]

5. Where one clause of the contract suggests one intention and another clause of the same contract suggests an inconsistent intention, the intention manifested in the principal or more important clause should be preferred.[370]

---

[363]   See the definitions in UCC § 1-303.

[364]   Fortis Benefits Ins. Co. v. Hauer, 636 N. W. 2d 200 (N. D. 2001). *See also* RESTATEMENT 2d § 203(c).

[365]   Norville v. Carr-Gottstein Foods, Inc., 84 P. 3d 996 (Alas. 2004).

[366]   Jordan v. Smith, 596 F. Supp. 1295 (N.D. Ga. 1984).

[367]   Ultimate Computer Servs. v. Biltmore Realty Co., 183 N.J. Super. 144, 443 A.2d 723 (1982).

[368]   Zygar v. Johnson, 169 Or. App. 638, 643–44, 10 P.3d 326, 329 (2000); Wood River Pipeline Co. v. Willbros Energy Servs. Co., 241 Kan. 580, 738 P.2d 866 (1987); Tuzman v. Leventhal, 174 Ga. App. 297, 329 S.E.2d 610 (1985). Cf. UCC § 3-114 with respect to negotiable instruments, such as checks: handwritten terms control typewritten and printed terms, and typewritten control printed; words control figures except that if the words are ambiguous, figures control.

[369]   RESTATEMENT 2d § 203(d).

[370]   Joseph Cumacho Assocs., Inc. v. Millard, 169 Ga. App. 937, 315 S.E.2d 478 (1984).

[M]   Inconsistent Warranties — Uniform Commercial Code

The UCC requires courts to strive to construe express and implied warranties as consistent with each other.[371] Where such construction is unreasonable, however, the UCC includes rules of construction consistent with common law guidelines that more particular or detailed statements of warranty are preferred over more general warranty statements, and the parties' expressions prevail over any warranties implied by law. Thus, exact or technical specifications which constitute express warranties are preferred over more general express warranties, such as those created by sample, model or general language of description.[372] A warranty created by taking a sample from an existing bulk of goods displaces inconsistent general language of description,[373] and express warranties prevail over inconsistent implied warranties of merchantability,[374] but not over implied warranties of fitness for a particular purpose,[375] since the latter are created through the buyer's reasonable reliance on the seller's exercise of skill or judgment.[376]

Like other rules or aids to interpretation, the UCC rules "are designed to ascertain the intention of the parties by reference to the factor which probably claimed the attention of the parties in the first instance."[377] They are not, however, absolute rules[378] and may be varied if the circumstances indicate that their application would preclude the effectuation of the dominant intention of the parties.[379]

---

[371] "Warranties whether express or implied shall be construed as consistent with each other and as cumulative, but if such construction is unreasonable the intention of the parties shall determine which warranty is dominant. . . ." UCC § 2-317. It should be noted that the UCC § 2-312 warranty of title is not a technical "implied warranty" for the purposes of § 2-317. In Quality Components Corp. v. Kel-Keef Enters., 316 Ill. App. 3d 998, 250 Ill. Dec. 308, 738 N.E.2d 524 (1st Dist. 2000), the court noted that while the warranty of title under UCC § 2-312 functions like an implied warranty, it is not called an implied warranty because the disclaimer of implied warranty provisions of § 2-316 were designed to apply only to the implied warranty of merchantability and the implied warranty of fitness for a particular purpose (§§ 2-314 and 2-315, respectively). When, therefore, § 2-317 states that an express warranty may displace an "implied" warranty, it is not referring to the warranty of title under the UCC.

[372] UCC § 2-317(a).

[373] UCC § 2-317(b). See Lithuanian Commerce Corp. v. Sara Lee Hosiery, 179 F.R.D. 450, 479 (D.N.J. 1998), aff'd, in part, rev'd, in part, 2000 U.S. App. LEXIS 31996 (3d Cir. Nov. 13, 2000).

[374] In Commonwealth v. Johnson Insulation, 425 Mass. 650, 682 N.E.2d 1323, 1327 (1997), the Commonwealth sought damages for products supplied that contained asbestos. Defendant claimed that plaintiff specified the product it supplied, i.e., an express warranty displacing the implied warranty of merchantability. Held: the specifications were not sufficiently detailed and precise to exclude the implied warrant of merchantability. In Dickerson v. Mountain View Equip. Co., 109 Idaho 711, 710 P.2d 621, 625 (Ct. App. 1985), a 90-day express warranty did not displace an implied warranty of merchantability. Such an express warranty is not inconsistent with an implied warranty. UCC § 2-316 sets forth methods for disclaiming the implied warranty of merchantability.

[375] The implied warranty of fitness for a particular purpose is found in UCC § 2-315.

[376] UCC § 2-317(c). See Singer Co. v. E. I. Du Pont de Nemours & Co., 579 F.2d 433 (8th Cir. 1978), and Morrison v. Devore Trucking, Inc., 68 Ohio App. 2d 140, 428 N.E.2d 438 (1980) (dealing with the conflict between express warranties and the implied warranty of fitness for a particular purpose).

[377] UCC § 2-317 comment 3.

[378] Id.

[379] See, e.g., Stewart-Decatur Sec. Sys., Inc. v. Von Weise Gear Co., 517 F.2d 1136 (8th Cir. 1975), where an exact or technical specification was inconsistent with a model, but the evidence clearly indicated that the parties intended to contract with reference to the model, rather than the specification. Thus, the rule of interpretation in UCC § 2-317(a) that exact or technical specifications displace inconsistent express warranties by sample or model was inapplicable.

§ 90   CUSTOM AS A STANDARD — TRADE USAGE, COURSE OF DEALING, COURSE OF PERFORMANCE — UNIFORM COMMERCIAL CODE

[A]   Custom as Standard — Definitions

In a given trade, profession, or calling, parties may adhere to certain practices to such an extent that the practices may appear to be the "standard" within that industry or vocation. There may be a temptation to treat the customary practices as the legal standard. Judge Learned Hand reminded us some time ago, however, that the determination of the legal standard of reasonable conduct still lies with courts, regardless of how well-established a particular practice may be.[380] If, however, a court is attempting to discern the intention of the parties to a contract, in the absence of express terms to the contrary, it is reasonable to assume that the parties have contracted in the context of any applicable trade usage.[381] *Trade usage* is defined in the UCC as "any practice or method of dealing having such regularity of observance in a place, vocation or trade as to justify an expectation that it will be observed with respect to the transaction in question."[382] Parties may have dealt with each other in the past. If their prior *course of dealing* constituted "a sequence of previous conduct . . . which is fairly to be regarded as establishing a common basis of understanding for interpreting their expressions and other conduct,"[383] it would be foolhardy for a court to ignore such course of dealing in determining the intention of the parties in a given transaction. After forming a contract, the parties may have begun to perform it. If their *course of performance* involved "repeated occasions for performance . . . with knowledge of the nature of the performance and opportunity for objection to it by the other, any course of performance accepted or acquiesced in without objection [should] be relevant to determine the meaning of the agreement."[384]

[B]   Hierarchy — Modifications Through Course of Performance

Among the three concepts of trade usage, course of dealing, and course of performance, trade usage is the most general since it covers all who deal in a particular trade. Course of dealing is much more specific since it relates only to prior transactions between the parties to the current contract. Course of performance is not only equally specific as course of dealing, it is a present manifestation of the parties' intentions under the very contract at issue. Where it is not possible to treat the three concepts as consistent with each other in a given situation,

---

[380] The T. J. Hooper v. Northern Barge Co., 60 F.2d 737 (2d Cir. 1932).

[381] RESTATEMENT 2d § 220(1) suggests that an agreement is to be interpreted in accordance with a relevant usage if each party either knew or had reason to know of the usage, and neither knew nor had reason to know that the meaning attached by the other was inconsistent with the usage.

[382] UCC § 1-205(2). *Accord* RESTATEMENT 2d § 222. *See* Capital Funding VI LP v. Chase Manhattan Bank, USA, 191 Fed. Appx. 92, 97 (3d Cir. 2006) ("delinquency" not defined in the agreement was defined in accordance with the meaning commonly understood in the credit card industry).

[383] UCC § 1-205(1). *Accord* RESTATEMENT 2d § 223. See Ward v. National Geographic Society, 284 Fed. Appx. 822 (2d Cir. 2008) (the plaintiff's conclusory interpretation of the contract was contradicted by a consistent course of dealings between the parties).

[384] UCC § 2-208(1). *Accord* RESTATEMENT 2d § 202(4). See Metro Area Transit, Inc. v. Nicholson, 463 F. 3d 1256 (Fed. Cir. 2006) (course of performance for three years manifested the parties understanding that "handicapped transportation" included wheelchair patient transportation but not "taxi and litter" patients).

therefore, course of performance will control course of dealing, and course of dealing will control trade usage.[385] While express terms of the parties' agreement are typically viewed as dominant over all three,[386] since course of performance is subsequent to the express terms of the contract, it may demonstrate a modification of the contract or waiver of one or more of its terms by conduct. In this sense, course of performance will be superior to even the express terms of the contract.[387]

[C]   Custom Versus Trade Usage — Existence, Scope, and Meaning of Trade Usage

The UCC is very clear in its departure from common law notions of "custom." Common law tests which required custom to be "ancient," "immemorial," "universal," "notorious" or the like have been abandoned by the Code.[388] New and current usages observed by the great majority of dealers in the trade will be observed.[389] Moreover, there is no requirement that trade usage be certain or precise in the sense that "custom" had to be certain or precise.[390]

The existence and scope of trade usage are questions of fact,[391] but if the trade usage is found in a written code or similar document, the interpretation of the document is a question for the court and, as such, it is a question of "law."[392] There may be a specific usage of trade in a locality to which the parties are bound that differs from the general usage of trade.[393] Industry standards may be explained by trade usage.[394] Parties who are engaged in a trade

---

[385] UCC § 1-303(e) (formerly §§ 1-205 and 2-208(2)). *Accord* RESTATEMENT 2d § 203(b). *See* CA, Inc. v. Ingres Corp., 2009 Del. Ch. LEXIS 204 at *75 (2009) (analysis under N. Y. Law). See also Delano Growers' Coop. Winery v. Supreme Wine Co., 393 Mass. 666, 473 N.E.2d 1066 (1985) (course of dealing controls usage of trade); R. G. Le Tourneau, Inc. v. Quinn Equip. Co., 131 Ill. App. 2d 295, 266 N.E.2d 151 (1st Dist. 1970) (course of performance controls course of dealing and usage of trade).

[386] *See* Affiliated FM Ins. Co. v. Constitution Reinsurance Corp., 416 Mass. 839, 626 N.E.2d 878, 892 (1994).

[387] UCC § 2-208(3), referring to UCC § 2-209 dealing with modifications, which, it should be recalled, require no consideration to be binding if made in good faith. *See* Employers Reinsurance Co. v. Superior Court, 161 Cal. App. 4th 906, 921, 74 Cal. Rptr. 3d 733, 745 (2008) (course of performance may supplement the terms of the agreement); Mulberry-Fairplains Water Ass'n v. Town of North Wilkesboro, 105 N.C. App. 258, 412 S.E.2d 910, 916 (1992) (years of performance modified contract); Jannus Group, Inc. v. Independent Container, Inc., 1999 U.S. Dist. LEXIS 6791 (S.D.N.Y. May 10, 1999) (wavier). *See also* T. J. Stevenson & Co. v. 81,193 Bags of Flour, 629 F.2d 338 (5th Cir. 1980) (failure to object to buyer's failure to comply with contract provisions concerning notice of breach constituted a modification of the notice requirement).

[388] UCC § 1-205 comment 5. *See also* Threadgill v. Peabody Coal Co., 34 Colo. App. 203, 526 P.2d 676 (1974).

[389] RESTATEMENT 2d § 222 comment b, concurs.

[390] *See* Nanakuli Paving & Rock Co. v. Shell Oil Co., 664 F.2d 772 (9th Cir. 1981). *See* Levie, *Trade Usage and Custom under the Common Law and the Uniform Commercial Code*, 40 NYU L. REV. 1101 (1965).

[391] UCC § 1-205(2). *See* Atlantic Textiles v. Avondale, Inc., 505 F. 3d 274, 281, n.4 (4th Cir. 2007) (arbitration as trade usage in textile industry); Voest-Alpine Trading USA Corp. v. Bank of China, 288 F. 3d 262 (5th Cir. 2002) (whether a letter of credit complied with usage of trade was a question of fact).

[392] RESTATEMENT 2d § 222(2). See *supra* § 86, where the tautology of questions of "fact" versus questions of "law" was explored.

[393] *See* Nanakuli Paving & Rock Co. v. Shell Oil Co., *supra* note 366.

[394] Craig Food Indus. v. Weihing, 746 P.2d 279 (Utah Ct. App. 1987). In Action Time Carpets, Inc. v. Midwest Carpet Brokers, Inc., 271 N.W.2d 36 (Minn. 1978), evidence that "at once" as used in a purchase order was understood in the carpet industry to mean "as soon as possible." See also Hurst v. W.J. Lake & Co., 141 Or. 306, 16 P.2d 627, 89 A.L.R. 1222 (1932), where the question of the meaning of "minimum 50 per cent protein" was explained as permitting a protein content of not less than 49.5 percent. *Inter alia*, the court also suggests the following industry or trade

are subject to the trade usage even if they are newcomers to the trade.[395] In general, courts have applied the standard of trade usage to parties who either know or have reason to know the usage.[396] There is no requirement that the trade usage be consistent with the meaning of the agreement apart from trade usage nor that the agreement be ambiguous before evidence of trade usage will be admitted.[397]

As will be seen later in this section, trade usage may be used by courts to interpret the expression of the parties, or it may be seen as supplying terms in the agreement of the parties.

[D]   Existence, Scope, and Meaning of "Course of Dealing"

If parties have engaged in prior dealings, their actions with respect to a specific term or clause in such dealings may justify an inference that they have incorporated the understanding into their subsequent contract.[398] Both the RESTATEMENT 2d and UCC describe "course of dealing" as a *sequence of previous conduct between the parties* establishing *a common basis of understanding for interpreting their expressions or other conduct.*[399] A *sequence of previous conduct* is not defined in terms of the number of transactions that must occur before a course of dealing may be said to be established. A *sequence* would suggest a number of prior transactions. Yet, the number of transactions alone would not necessarily determine the existence of a course of dealing. Parties may have dealt with each other on several occasions in the past, but their prior dealings could be insufficiently similar to a current transaction. The Code adds the requirement that the "sequence of previous conduct" must be "fairly to be regarded as establishing a common basis of understanding for interpreting their expressions and other conduct." One, relatively small, bank transaction did not constitute course of dealing for a larger transaction.[400] Even where a single prior

---

standards: in the bricklaying trade, a contract fixing the bricklayer's compensation at "$5.25 per thousand" does not contemplate that he will lay 1000 bricks but that he will build a wall of a certain size; in the lumber industry, a contract requiring the delivery of 4000 shingles will be fulfilled by the delivery of only 2500 because the trade usage regards two packs of a certain size as 1,000 shingles and delivery of eight packs fulfills the contract though they actually contain only 2500.

[395] UCC § 1-205(3). There is no requirement of actual knowledge. *See* Den norske Bank AS v. First Nat'l Bank of Boston, 75 F.3d 49, 57 n.9 (1st Cir. 1996). *See also* United States *ex rel.* Union Bldg. Materials Corp. v. Haas & Haynie Corp., 577 F.2d 568 (9th Cir. 1978).

[396] RESTATEMENT 2d § 222(3). Harris Bank Naperville v. Morse Shoe, Inc., 716 F. Supp. 1109, 1121 (N.D. Ill. 1988). *See also* Mieske v. Bartell Drug Co., 92 Wash. 2d 40, 593 P.2d 1308 (1979) (consumer who supplied home movies for splicing on large reels was not bound by trade usage concerning exclusionary clause though film processors would be bound by such usage). L. F. Pace & Sons, Inc. v. Travelers Indem. Co., 9 Conn. App. 30, 38–39, 514 A.2d 766, 771 (1986) ("In its instructions, the court also cautioned the jury that custom and usage would not be the basis for the defendant's obligation if the plaintiff knew or had reason to know that the defendant had an intention inconsistent with such usage. The trial court's instructions were correct in law. . . .").

[397] RESTATEMENT 2d § 222 comment b. *See* Merchants Envt'l Indus. v. SLT Realty, 314 Ill. App. 3d 848, 731 N.E.2d 394, 246 Ill. Dec. 866 (1st Dist. 2000). *See also* American Mach. & Tool Co. v. Strite-Anderson Mfg. Co., 353 N.W.2d 592 (Minn. Ct. App. 1984), and Camargo Cadillac Co. v. Garfield Enters., Inc., 3 Ohio App. 3d 435, 438, 445 N.E.2d 1141, 1145 (1982) (a showing of ambiguity need not be made before evidence of trade usage may be introduced).

[398] *See* New Moon Shipping Co. v. Man B&W Diesel AG, 121 F.3d 24 (2d Cir. 1997).

[399] RESTATEMENT 2d § 223; UCC § 1-205(1).

[400] Atlanta Corp. v. Ohio Valley Provision Co., 489 Pa. 389, 395, 414 A.2d 123, 126 (1980). See MAFCO Elec. Contractors, Inc. v. Turner Constr. Co., 2009 U.S. App. LEXIS 27941 (2d Cir. 2009) (agreement to settle one batch of claims does not constitute "a continual course of business dealings").

transaction is identical or sufficiently similar to the present transaction, it hardly constitutes a sequence of prior events necessary to establish a course of dealing between the parties.[401] On the other hand, a continuous relationship for the purchase and sale of goods in a consistent fashion over a period of five years obviously establishes a course of dealing between the parties.[402]

As in the case of trade usage, there is no necessity to establish ambiguity in the contract before evidence of course of dealing is admissible,[403] and the course of dealing evidence may be inconsistent with the meaning of the agreement apart from the course of dealing.[404] Again, as in the case of trade usage, course of dealing evidence may be used to interpret the parties' expression of agreement, or it may be used to evidence a term of the agreement as will be seen later in this section.

[E]   Existence, Scope, and Meaning of "Course of Performance"

Course of performance relates to conduct after the formation of the contract, i.e., the parties conduct in performing the previously made contract. The UCC does not parrot the language used to define course of dealing (prior to formation conduct), i.e., a sequence of conduct. Rather, course of performance requires "repeated *occasions* for performance . . . with knowledge of the nature of the performance and opportunity for objection to it by the other [party]" that would indicate acceptance of or acquiescence in such performance.[405] While one instance of performance could not qualify as "repeated occasions" constituting a course of performance,[406] as few as two instances could qualify where there were only two possible occasions to demonstrate adherence to a particular mode of performance.[407] Where there are "repeated occasions" for performance by one party with knowledge and opportunity for objection by the other party who does not object, there is little question that a course of performance has been established.[408] Like trade usage and course of dealing, course of performance evidence is admissible to interpret the expressions of the parties.[409] Moreover, it is the strongest evidence of that meaning.[410] While the express terms of the contract are said

---

[401] International Therapeutics, Inc. v. McGraw-Edison Co., 721 F.2d 488 (5th Cir. 1983).

[402] Delano Growers' Coop. Winery v. Supreme Wine Co., 393 Mass. 666, 473 N.E.2d 1066 (1985).

[403] Senior Exec. Benefit Plan Participants v. New Valley Corp. (*In re* New Valley Corp.), 89 F.3d 143, 150 (3d Cir. 1996), *cert. denied*, 519 U.S. 1110, 117 S. Ct. 947, 136 L. Ed. 2d 835 (1997). See also Columbia Nitrogen Corp. v. Royster Co., 451 F.2d 3 (4th Cir. 1971), that is explored in detail in the next subsection.

[404] Restatement 2d § 223 comment b.

[405] UCC § 2-208(1) (emphasis added).

[406] Prewitt v. Numismatic Funding Corp., 745 F.2d 1175 (8th Cir. 1984).

[407] Nanakuli Paving & Rock Co. v. Shell Oil Co., 664 F.2d 772 (9th Cir. 1981).

[408] Blue Rock Indus. v. Raymond Int'l, Inc., 325 A.2d 66 (Me. 1974); Oskey Gasoline & Oil Co. v. OKC Ref. Inc., 364 F. Supp. 1137 (D. Minn. 1973).

[409] *See, e.g.*, Bayer Chems. Corp. v. Albemarle Corp., 171 Fed. Appx. 392, 400 (3d Cir. 2006) (quoting UCC § 1-303(d): "course of performance evidence may give particular meaning to specific terms of the agreement and may supplement or qualify the terms of the agreement."); Wagner Excello Foods, Inc. v. Fearn Int'l, Inc., 235 Ill. App. 3d 224, 601 N.E.2d 956, 962. 176 Ill. Dec. 258 (1st Dist. 1992).

[410] Restatement (2d) of Contracts, § 202, comment g. See also United States ex. rel. Pioneer Constr. Co. v. Pride Enterprises, Inc., 2009 U.S. Dist. LEXIS 110935 at *17 (M. D. Pa. 2009); Nanakuli Paving & Rock Co. v. Shell Oil Co., 664 F.2d 772 (9th Cir. 1981).

to be superior to course of performance evidence concerning the meaning of the agreement,[411] course of performance which is inconsistent with the express terms of the contract and, therefore, not admissible as interpretation evidence, may constitute a modification of the contract.[412] If the parties have knowingly engaged in repeated occasions of performance which are inconsistent with the express terms of the contract, they have manifested their intention to modify their contract.[413] It is difficult to conceive of a court refusing to regard such conduct as a subsequent modification of the contract. In this sense, course of performance becomes superior to the express terms of the contract. Thus, as will be seen below, just as trade usage and course of dealing may *supply* terms to the original contract which precede express terms (as well as providing assistance in determining the meaning of terms expressed in the contract), course of performance may provide *new* terms, i.e., terms that modify the prior, express terms of the contract.

Unlike the definitions of trade usage and course of dealing which appeared in the original Article 1 of the UCC and thereby applied to all commercial contracts including, but not limited to, contracts for the sale of goods, the definition of course of performance appeared in original Article 2 which is relegated to contracts for the sale of goods. This placement caused some courts to insist that the operation of course of performance was limited to contracts for the sale of goods as contrasted, for example, with security agreements governed by Article 9 of the UCC.[414] Other courts disagreed since the UCC definition of "agreement" in the original Article 1 included course of performance.[415] The revised Article 1 which has been widely enacted includes the essentially unchanged definition of course of performance in a section that also defines course of dealing and usage of trade.[416]

[F]   Supplying Contract Terms Through Trade Usage, Course of Dealing, and Course of Performance

It is important to recall the changes effected by the Uniform Commercial Code in the parol evidence rule.[417] In summary, where the parties intend their written expression of the agreement to be *final*, the terms of that writing may not be *contradicted* by evidence of any prior agreement or contemporaneous agreement. If, however, the writing was intended to be not only final but "complete and exclusive" ("fully integrated"), evidence of even *consistent* additional terms is inadmissible. Evidence of usage of trade, course of dealing or course of

---

[411] UCC § 2-208(2).

[412] *See supra* note 363.

[413] *See* Westinghouse Credit Corp. v. Shelton, 645 F.2d 869, 870 (10th Cir. 1981). Course of performance was sufficient not only to waive express term requiring installment payments when due, but was also sufficient to waive express "anti-waiver" clause which read, "The waiver or indulgence of any default by the Buyer of any provision of this Agreement or any promissory note which it secures shall not operate as a waiver of any subsequent default by the Buyer of such provision or as a waiver of any of the other rights of (Westinghouse) herein. Time shall be deemed the essence of this Agreement." *See also* Oregon Bank v. Nautilus Crane & Equip. Corp., 68 Or. App. 131, 683 P.2d 95 (1984) (which suggests that not only anti-waiver clauses may be waived by course of performance, but, pursuant to UCC § 2-316(3)(c), implied warranties may be excluded or modified by either trade usage or course of performance).

[414] *See, e. g.*, Cox v. Bancoklahoma Agri-Service Corp., 641 S.W.2d 400 (Tex. App. Amarillo 1982).

[415] § 1-201(3). *See* Westinghouse Credit Corp. v. Shelton, *supra* note 389; National Livestock Credit Corp. v. Schultz, 653 P.2d 1243 (Okla. Ct. App. 1982).

[416] § 1-303. At the time of this writing, the revised Article 1 has been enacted in thirty-seven states and the U.S. Virgin Islands.

[417] *See* § 84[C][6] *supra*.

performance, however, is always admissible to *explain or supplement* (but not "contradict") the terms of the writing.[418] Such evidence is admissible regardless of a determination that the writing was intended to be the complete and exclusive record of the parties' agreement. Indeed, even a well-drafted merger clause would not, by itself, exclude such evidence.[419] The UCC provision is not remarkable at all with respect to course of performance evidence since the parol evidence rule has no application to agreements made after the writing is executed. Allowing trade usage and course of dealing evidence in the teeth of a complete and exclusive writing, however, appeared radical.[420] Precisely why does the UCC parol evidence rule insist that consistent additional terms are precluded, but trade usage, prior course of dealing and course of performance evidence is admissible, notwithstanding the parties' intention that their writing is complete and exclusive ("fully integrated")?

The explanation lies essentially in the concept of *agreement* as found in the UCC, which emphasizes that the parties' agreement, their "bargain-in-fact," is to be discovered not only from the language of their agreement, but from all surrounding circumstances, expressly including trade usage, prior course of dealing and course of performance.[421] Since the agreement of the parties is not limited to their words, trade usage and course of dealing are not *added* to the agreement of the parties; rather, they pre-exist the agreement of the parties. The writings of the parties, albeit complete and final, "are to be read on the assumption that the course of prior dealings between the parties and the usages of trade were taken for granted when the document was phrased."[422] Thus, course of dealing and usage of trade evidence do not "supplement" the terms of the agreement as if added judicially after the writing existed. Rather, such evidence, though judicially discovered after the writing, *preceded* the writing, no matter how final and complete, and must be viewed as the background against which the written terms are interpreted. If prior course of dealing or trade usage evidence does not *contradict* the express terms of the writing, there is no question concerning its admissibility since such terms are as much a part of the contract as are the written terms.[423] Evidence of consistent terms other than trade usage and course of dealing may be admitted to explain or supplement the terms of the writing if the writing is only a "final expression" of the parties agreement. Unlike trade usage or course of dealing, these terms would constitute genuine supplements to the agreement.[424] If the writing is deemed not merely final but "complete and exclusive," however, additional (supplementary) consistent terms will not be admissible.[425]

---

[418] § 2-202 prefaces subsections (a) and (b) with the proviso, "but may be explained or supplemented. . . ."

[419] See § 84(C)(6), *supra.*

[420] *See, e.g.,* Carter Baron Drilling v. Badger Oil Corp., 581 F. Supp. 592, 595 (D. Colo. 1984) ("Before the adoption of the Uniform Commercial Code in Colorado, the Colorado courts took the position that evidence of custom and usage was not admissible to vary the terms of an unambiguous contract. . . . However, since its adoption, parol evidence of usage of trade, course of dealings and course of performance can be introduced to explain or supplement a contract.").

[421] UCC § 1-201(b)(3).

[422] UCC § 2-202 comment 2.

[423] *See, e.g.,* Budget Sys., Inc. v. Seifert Pontiac, Inc., 40 Colo. App. 406, 579 P.2d 87 (1978) (course of dealing concerning mileage limitation admissible where such evidence did not contradict language of writing).

[424] UCC § 2-202(a).

[425] *Id.* Such a writing would be fully integrated.

[1]   The "Consistency" Mystery — *Columbia Nitrogen*, et al.

The most significant judicial exploration of the concept of "agreement" under the UCC is found in a well-known case, *Columbia Nitrogen Corp. v. Royster Co.*[426] Royster had been a major purchaser of products from Columbia for a number of years. After constructing a phosphate producing facility, however, Royster had excess phosphate and agreed to sell large quantities to Columbia over a three year term. The contract was evidenced by what appeared to be a complete writing, which included a price escalation clause. Soon after the contract was formed, the market price of phosphate plunged precipitously and Columbia ordered only part of the annual scheduled tonnage of 31,000 tons it was required to purchase from Royster. When Columbia refused delivery at the contract price, Royster resold the unaccepted phosphate at prices substantially below market prices. Columbia attempted to introduce evidence of trade usage to the effect that uncertain crop and weather conditions, farming practices and government agricultural programs created an understanding of all dealers in the trade that contracts for products, such as phosphate in the mixed fertilizer industries, were not viewed as legally binding arrangements, i.e., they were mere projections to be adjusted according to market forces. Columbia also sought to introduce prior course of dealing evidence of its long relationship with Royster, demonstrating a pattern of repeated and substantial deviation from contract prices and four instances where Royster (then a buyer rather than a seller) had taken none of the goods contracted for, resulting in a total variance of a half million dollars in reduced sales to Columbia. The trial court refused to admit the evidence on the ground that it contradicted the plain language of the contract. In a sophisticated opinion that was precocious for its time, the United States Court of Appeals for the Fourth Circuit reversed.

Relying heavily on the UCC parol evidence section, the court focused upon the critical question of whether the trade usage and course of dealing evidence was inconsistent with the express terms of the writing since UCC § 1-205(4) states the hierarchy mentioned earlier, i.e., express terms control course of dealing and trade usage.[427] The court found no inconsistency in the express terms of the contract, which were silent concerning price adjustments to reflect *declining* markets.[428] Moreover, the court emphasized the UCC directive that course of dealing and usage of trade would "supplement" the written terms unless they were "carefully negated."[429] In *Nanakuli Paving & Rock Co. v. Shell Oil Co.*,[430] the contract stated that Nanakuli would purchase asphalt material from Shell at "Shell's posted price." Dramatic price increases occurred in 1973-74 as a result of the oil crisis. Nanakuli claimed that trade usage

---

[426] 451 F.2d 3 (4th Cir. 1971).

[427] It will be recalled that course of performance is preferred over course of dealing and course of dealing controls trade usage, but express terms are superior to all three as a matter of interpretation. UCC § 1-303(e).

[428] As suggested in Carter Baron Drilling v. Badger Oil Corp., 581 F. Supp. 592 (D. Colo. 1984), there is some dispute among the courts as to what constitutes "consistent" trade usage or course of performance. The court points to *Columbia Nitrogen Corp.*, *supra* note 426, Chase Manhattan Bank v. First Marion Bank, 437 F.2d 1040 (5th Cir. 1971), and Nanakuli Paving & Rock Co. v. Shell Oil Co., 664 F.2d 772 (9th Cir. 1981), as suggesting liberal interpretations of "consistent," while other courts, such as Southern Concrete Servs., Inc. v. Mableton Contractors, Inc., 407 F. Supp. 581 (N.D. Ga. 1975), *aff'd per curiam*, 569 F.2d 1154 (5th Cir. 1978), and Luria Bros. & Co. v. Pielet Bros. Scrap Iron & Metal, Inc., 600 F.2d 103 (7th Cir. 1979), "are less generous" in their interpretations of "consistent." The *Carter Baron* court decided to adopt the liberal position on the footing that this was the result desired by the drafters of the UCC and admission of such evidence does pose the risks against which the parol evidence rule was designed.

[429] UCC § 2-202 comment 2.

[430] 664 F.2d 772 (9th Cir. 1981).

required Shell to maintain the old price on projects that were already committed. The court rejected the view that inconsistency between an express term and trade usage ends the inquiry. When such inconsistency appears, the parties' intention is unclear. Recognizing that *Columbia Nitrogen* was criticized because the evidence of usage may not have been sufficiently established, the court found the evidence of usage before it to be overwhelming. While the court stopped short of holding that trade usage may *contradict* the express terms of the writing, it held that such usage may *qualify* ("cut down") express terms: " 'Here, the express price term was 'Shell's posted price at time of delivery.' A total negation of that term would be that the buyer was to set the price. It is a less than complete negation of the term that an unstated exception exists at times of price increases, at which times the old price is to be charged, for a certain period or for a specified tonnage, on work already committed at the lower price on nonescalating contracts."[431]

Thus, the court concluded that trade usage need not be entirely consistent with the express terms of the contract in order to be admissible. Under the facts of the case, however, this analysis may not have been necessary. If the trade usage or course of dealing evidence can be reasonably construed as consistent with the express terms, it may be used to explain or supplement the express terms.[432] An explanation of the express term, "Shell's Posted Price," could admit of an interpretation that the price would not apply retroactively where the trade usage was as clear and convincing as it was in the Nanakuli case.[433] Other cases, though not all, have announced "liberal" views of trade usage evidence where the express terms may be viewed as literally inconsistent.[434]

The parties may choose to overcome trade usage or prior course of dealing by the express terms of their agreement. Trade usage or course of dealing evidence which the parties intend to be overcome by the *negotiated* express terms of their contract should be inadmissible on the footing that the parties have expressly addressed the particular matter which would otherwise be controlled by trade usage or course of dealing and intended their express terms to control.[435] Clear expressions of intent constitute a "careful negation" of such evidence.[436] Parties may always change their prior agreement manifested by either language on the one hand or trade usage or course of dealing on the other. For example, if the trade usage or prior course of dealing indicated that the time for performance should be thirty days, a negotiated

---

[431]   *Nanakuli*, 664 F.2d at 805.

[432]   *See* Wayman v. Amoco Oil Co., 923 F. Supp. 1322, 1339 (D. Kan. 1996).

[433]   See White & Summers, UNIFORM COMMERCIAL CODE, § 2-10 suggesting that the court could have rested on the language of former § 1-205(1) that the usage established "a common basis of understanding for interpreting" the language, "Shell's Posted Price." Section 1-205(1), however, defines "course of dealing" rather than "usage of trade." Since § 2-202 allows trade usage to "explain or supplement" the language of the contract, it is simpler to allow Shell's Posted Price" to be *explained* (interpreted) so as not to apply retroactively.

[434]   See, e.g., Carter Baron Drilling v. Badger Oil Corp., 581 F. Supp. 592 (D. Colo. 1984), reviewing *Columbia Nitrogen, Nanakuli* and other cases suggesting a "liberal view," while recognizing that other courts have been "less generous" in their interpretations of "consistency," such as Southern Concrete Servs., Inc. v. Mableton Contractors, Inc., 407 F. Supp. 581 (N.D. Ga. 1975), and Luria Bros. & Co. v. Pielet Bros. Scrap Iron & Metal, Inc., 600 F.2d 103 (7th Cir. 1979). *Carton Baron* adopts the "liberal view." *See also* Ralph's Distrib. Co. v. AMF, Inc., 667 F.2d 670 (8th Cir. 1981); Heggblade-Marguleas-Tenneco, Inc. v. Sunshine Biscuit, Inc., 59 Cal. App. 3d 948, 131 Cal. Rptr. 183 (5th Dist. 1976).

[435]   See, e.g., CS First Boston Ltd. v. Behar, 1995 U.S. Dist. LEXIS 21036, at *4 (S.D.N.Y. June 4, 1995), where the agreement stated that the express terms control and supersede any course of performance, course of dealing or usage of trade. *See also* State *ex rel.* Nichols v. Safeco Ins. Co., 100 N.M. 440, 671 P.2d 1151 (Ct. App. 1983).

[436]   *See* UCC § 2-202, comment 2.

express term requiring performance in a shorter time or allowing a greater time for performance should control if that is the intention of the parties. In such a situation, the course of dealing could be viewed as having been "carefully negated." If, however, the parties have used standardized (printed) forms in the past that set forth a time for performance or other term which the parties have contradicted by their course of performance on repeated occasions, such course of performance evidence as to past transactions could be viewed as a course of dealing with respect to a new, identical transaction that is inconsistent with one or more express terms of the printed form evidencing their agreement. In this situation, the course of dealing indicates that the parties have ignored the relevant printed terms of the documents evidencing their past transactions and have substituted a different understanding of such terms.[437] The objective is to discover the "true understanding of the parties" —[438] their "bargain in fact."[439] Courts must be careful, however, to admit trade usage or course of dealing evidence to make such determinations because they are questions of fact. Thus, where the express terms of the writing required shipment of limestone at 1500 tons per day, course of dealing evidence clearly indicated that the 1500 ton figure was a goal rather than a requirement, and the buyer did not reasonably expect the seller to meet that goal under the circumstances.[440]

[2]   Warranty Disclaimer and Other Limitations

The UCC implies certain warranties of quality in contracts for the sale of goods, i.e., the implied warranty of merchantability[441] and the implied warranty of fitness for a particular purpose.[442] Another Code section sets forth the ways in which such warranties may be disclaimed.[443] One of the methods of disclaiming such warranties is through trade usage, course of dealing and course of performance,[444] and courts have properly adhered to this provision in finding such warranties disclaimed.[445] Another method of disclaimer of the implied warranty of merchantability authorized by the UCC is effective if the language mentions the term, "merchantability," and, if the disclaimer is written, the language is "conspicuous."[446] If a seller attempts to disclaim the implied warranty of merchantability in this fashion, but fails to mention "merchantability" or fails to insert the written disclaimer in conspicuous fashion, he

---

[437] See *Nanakuli*, note 430, *supra*, at 804, where the court states: "Because the stock printed forms cannot always reflect the changing methods of business, members of the trade may do business with a standard clause in the forms that they ignore in practice. If the trade consistently ignores obsolete clauses at variance with actual trade practices, a litigant can maintain that it is reasonable that the courts also ignore these clauses."

[438] *See* UCC § 2-202 comment 2.

[439] UCC § 1-201(b)(3).

[440] Luedtke Eng'g Co. v. Indiana Limestone Co., 740 F.2d 598 (7th Cir. 1984).

[441] UCC § 2-314.

[442] UCC § 2-315. This warranty, however, is implied only where the seller has reason to know of the buyer's particular purpose and the buyer has relied on the seller's skill and judgment in choosing a product fit for that particular purpose.

[443] UCC § 2-316.

[444] UCC § 2-316(3)(c).

[445] *See, e.g.*, Kincheloe v. Geldmeier, 619 S.W.2d 272 (Tex. Civ. App. Tyler 1981) (trade usage); Agricultural Servs. Ass'n v. Ferry-Morse Seed Co., 551 F.2d 1057 (6th Cir. 1977) (course of dealing); Gulash v. Stylarama, Inc., 33 Conn. Supp. 108, 364 A.2d 1221 (Super. Ct. 1975) (course of performance).

[446] UCC § 2-316(2). "Conspicuous" is defined as "so written that a reasonable person against whom it is to operate ought to have notice of it." UCC § 1-201(10).

may still prove an effective disclaimer through the mutually exclusive method of trade usage, course of dealing or course of performance.[447] The normal remedies set forth in the UCC may also be limited through the agreement of the parties.[448] Since the definition of "agreement" includes trade usage, course of dealing and course of performance, courts have held that such remedies may be limited through these non-language manifestations of agreement.[449] Other limitations through trade usage, course of dealing or course of performance include the necessity of notice under certain circumstances[450] or the necessity to seek a particular remedy within a certain time.[451]

§ 91 OMITTED TERMS

In an earlier chapter,[452] the implication of various terms where parties failed to mention them, such as a reasonable time for performance, a reasonable price and many other "gap-filling" terms, was explored. The parties may fail to include a term because they did not foresee a particular situation which later causes a dispute between them; they may have failed to manifest their intention with respect to a foreseeable situation; or they may have deliberately avoided manifesting any intention with respect to a foreseeable situation because it could have hampered negotiations or simply because they considered the matter not worth mentioning.[453] Two classic examples are instructive.

"Listerine." After devising a secret formula for an antiseptic liquid compound called "Listerine," in 1881 Dr. Lawrence formed a contract with the predecessor of the Warner-Lambert Company, whereby Lawrence and his heirs, executors, and assigns would receive royalty payments on the sale of the product. No later than 1949, the trade secret formula was known to the public as it was published in medical and pharmacy journals. The royalty payments had risen to $1.5 million annually. Warner-Lambert sought a declaratory judgment that it was no longer liable to pay royalties to the heirs of Dr. Lawrence on the ground that a term should be implied in the contract that royalty payments could be terminated when the secret formula became public knowledge. The court refused to imply the term, clinging to what it saw as the "plain and unambiguous"[454] agreement of the parties that the royalties would be paid "as long as this preparation is manufactured and sold by Lambert and his successors"[455] regardless of the disclosure of the secret formula.[456]

---

[447] *See, e.g.,* South Carolina Elec. & Gas Co. v. Combustion Eng'g, Inc., 283 S.C. 182, 322 S.E.2d 453 (Ct. App. 1984); Basic Adhesives, Inc. v. Robert Matzkin Co., 101 Misc. 2d 283, 420 N.Y.S.2d 983 (1979).

[448] UCC § 2-719.

[449] *See, e.g.,* Transamerica Oil Corp. v. Lynes, Inc., 723 F.2d 758 (10th Cir. 1983); Kunststoffwerk Alfred Huber v. R. J. Dick, Inc., 621 F.2d 560 (3d Cir. 1980).

[450] *See* Provident Tradesmens Bank & Trust Co. v. Pemberton, 196 Pa. Super. 180, 173 A.2d 780 (1961).

[451] *See* Valley Nat'l Bank v. Babylon Chrysler-Plymouth, Inc., 53 Misc. 2d 1029, 280 N.Y.S.2d 786 (Sup. Ct.), *aff'd,* 28 A.D.2d 284, 284 N.Y.S.2d 849 (2d Dep't 1967).

[452] Chapter 2, *supra* § 38.

[453] Restatement 2d § 204 comment b. *See* National Educ. Ass'n-Coffeyville v. Unified Sch. Dist. No. 445, 268 Kan. 384, 996 P.2d 821, 829 (2000); Boatmen's Bank of Mid-Missouri v. Crossroads W. Shopping Ctr., 907 S.W.2d 800, 803 (Mo. Ct. App. 1995).

[454] Warner-Lambert Pharmaceutical Co. v. John J. Reynolds, Inc., 178 F. Supp. 655, 660 (D.N.Y. 1959).

[455] *Id.*

[456] Warner-Lambert Pharmaceutical Co. v. John J. Reynolds, Inc., 178 F. Supp. 655 (D.N.Y. 1959), *aff'd,* 280 F.2d 197 (2d Cir. 1960).

Parev Products. Rokeach obtained the exclusive use of a secret formula for the manufacture and sale of a kosher cooking oil (Nyafat) from Parev, who was to receive royalties from the sale of the oil for a term of twenty-five years with an option to renew for twenty-five years. For the first fifteen years, royalties of some $135,000 were paid to Parev. Rokeach then began marketing another kosher cooking oil under a different formula (Kea) to compete with new products-Crisco and Spry-which had begun to cut into the Nyafat market. Kea competed with Nyafat but Rokeach argued that it required a product that could compete more effectively with Crisco and Spry. Parev claimed that Rokeach sought to reduce its royalty obligation on Nyafat sales through the marketing of Kea and sought an injunction against further sales of Kea through the implication of a negative covenant in the contract that defendant would not compete with sales of Nyafat. The court candidly stated that the contract simply did not deal with an unforeseen situation, i.e., there was no intention of the parties to be judicially discovered as to this development fifteen years into the contract. It proceeded to recognize the reasonable protection required by Parev, i.e., the continuation of Nyafat sales without interference by Kea so as to insure maximum royalties. On the other hand, Rokeach had to compete effectively with the new products that had not been contemplated fifteen years earlier. The court unveiled the equitable solution of permitting Rokeach to continue to sell Kea so long as it did not invade the Nyafat market, a point which the court felt was susceptible to proof. While refusing to grant an injunction that would be vague and meaningless, it invited the plaintiff, Parev, to return with proof that sales of Nyafat had been lost to sales of Kea rather than to sales of the competing products, Crisco and Spry.[457]

When an omitted term is supplied by a court, it is not *interpreting* the contract, i.e., it is not discovering such a term by discerning the meaning of the parties' expression of agreement.[458] The process is one of judicial construction,[459] in which courts supply an omitted term which is fair and reasonable under the circumstances.[460] Before a court may supply such an omitted term, it must first interpret the expression of agreement to determine whether such implication is necessary.[461] If the manifestations of the parties provide such a term, the court may not overcome that manifested intention. If, however, there is a dispute over the proper interpretation of a contract and neither party's suggested interpretation is acceptable, the court must then supply the omitted term.[462] Where the manifestations of the parties evidence no intention concerning a term that is necessary to effectuate a contract, the search for any such intention is fruitless. A court must then supply a reasonable term based on a logical deduction from the agreed terms or, where that is not possible, on standards of fairness

---

[457] Parev Prods. Co. v. I. Rokeach & Sons, Inc., 124 F.2d 147 (2d Cir. 1941).

[458] *See* Lerner v. Lerner Corp., 132 Md. App. 32, 750 A.2d 709, 715 (2000).

[459] See Reynolds v. Alabama DOT, 1998 U.S. Dist. LEXIS 4834, at *28 (M.D. Ala. Jan. 13, 1998).

[460] *See, e.g.*, Harmony Antique Cars, Inc. v. LSH, Inc., 238 Wis. 2d 447, 617 N.W.2d 907 (2000).

[461] *See* Banks Eng'g Co. v. Polons, 561 Pa. 638, 752 A.2d 883, 886 (2000) (citing the third edition of this book).

[462] *See* Costello v. Cook, 852 P.2d 1330 (Colo. Ct. App. 1993) (amount of payment of contingent fee for cases pending when plaintiff left the law firm). *See also* Haines v. City of New York, 41 N.Y.2d 769, 364 N.E.2d 820 (1977). City agreed to construct, operate, and maintain a sewage system for two communities so as to prevent untreated sewage from entering a stream feeding the city's water supply. Years later, a state environmental control law prohibited the discharge of untreated sewage into the stream and, after a half century when the system reached full capacity, the city refused to expand the disposal plant or otherwise meet the demand of the communities. The city argued that the contract should be interpreted to be "terminable at will," while the communities argued that it should be interpreted to bind the city in perpetuity. The court rejected both suggested interpretations.

policy.[463]

Parties to a contract have an obligation to cooperate with each other. Indeed, the obligation of good faith and fair dealing implied in all contracts is a manifestation of the implied duty of cooperation. Where a buyer promised to purchase $10 million of snack products from the plaintiff, the contract contained a formula for pricing the products on a cost plus basis. The issue was whether the plaintiff had the obligation to first provide a product and price list to the buyer, or whether the buyer was required to first provide the seller with ordering information so that the seller could quote a price on the products. Since the question was not answered by the express terms of the contract, the court felt compelled to supply the missing term as noted in § 204 of the Restatement 2d which the court cited. The court noted Section 2-311 of the UCC where a buyer has the choice of assorted products. Where the buyer's choice will dictate the price, the buyer has the initial obligation to notify the seller of its choice. The buyer may not escape its contractual obligation by refusing to choose.[464]

[A]   "Good Faith"

The cases are legion which imply what courts often call a "covenant" of *good faith* in every contract.[465] The UCC mandates a general "obligation of good faith" in the performance and enforcement of every contract[466] as well as a definition: "Good faith means honesty in fact and the observance of reasonable commercial standards of fair dealing."[467] While insisting that they are independent, the lines separating fraud, duress, undue influence, misrepresentation, unconscionability and good faith are wavering and blurred, as we will see in the next chapter. *Good faith* is a standard connoting decency, fairness or reasonableness.[468] It is applied in a variety of contractual contexts which emphasize "faithfulness to an agreed common purpose and consistency with the justified expectations of the other party."[469] It is, however,

---

[463] See Dobson v. Hartford Fin. Servs. Group, 389 F. 3d 386 (2d Cir. 2004) (Whether the plaintiff was entitled to interest payments on overdue disability benefits was not addressed in the contract. The court quoted comment b, § 204 of the Restatement 2d of Contracts to imply a provision "indispensable in effectuating the intention of the parties."). In Cottrell v. Cottrell, 332 Ark. 352, 965 S.W.2d 129 (1998), the court held that it would not supply a duration term in an employment contract because it would violate the policy that contracts without such a term are terminable at will. *Accord* Bisbee v. Grogan Chrysler-Plymouth, Inc., 1992 Ohio App. LEXIS 3599, at *9 (Ohio Ct. App. July 10, 1992).

[464] Family Snacks of N. C. v. Prepared Products Co., Inc., 295 F. 3d 864 (8th Cir. 2002).

[465] *See, e.g.*, AT&T Communications of Cal., Inc. v. Pacific Bell, 2000 U.S. App. LEXIS 23215, at *5 (9th Cir. Sept. 8, 2000); GMAC v. Baymon, 732 So. 2d 262, 269 (Miss. 1999); Sons of Thunder v. Borden, Inc., 148 N.J. 396, 690 A.2d 575, 587 (1997); Acetylene Gas Co. v. Oliver, 939 S.W.2d 404, 410 (Mo. Ct. App. 1996). RESTATEMENT 2d § 205.

[466] UCC § 1-304 and the comment thereto.

[467] See UCC § 1-201(b)(20). The former Article 1 definition of good faith in unrevised § 1-201(19) required only "honesty in fact" while Article 2 (§ 2-103(1)(b)) applied the standard of "honesty in fact and the observance of reasonable commercial standards of fair dealing in the trade" to merchants. Thus, in Zapatha v. Dairy Mart, Inc., 381 Mass. 284, 408 N.E.2d 1370 (1980), the court noted that the Article 2 definition applicable to merchants included a higher standard of conduct through the addition of the observance of reasonable commercial standards of fair dealing in the trade. In Martin Marietta Corp. v. New Jersey Nat'l Bank, 612 F.2d 745 (3d Cir. 1979), the court distinguished the Article 1 standard as "subjective" and the Article 2 standard as "objective." The Article 2 definition with both honesty (subjective) and reasonableness (objective) standards remains unchanged. The comment (20) to the new Article 1 section that incorporates both standards is the product of amendments to other UCC Articles incorporating both standards for "good faith," with the exception of Article 5 which retains the "honesty" (subjective) standard.

[468] RESTATEMENT 2d § 205, comment a.

[469] Black Horse Lane Assoc., L.P. v. Dow Chem. Corp., 228 F.3d 275, 288 (3d Cir. 2000) (quoting RESTATEMENT 2d § 205, comment a).

particularly important to recognize that the obligation of good faith, alone, does not provide an independent cause of action.

> Rather, this section means that a failure to perform or enforce, in good faith, a specific duty or obligation under the contract, constitutes a breach of that contract or makes unavailable, under particular circumstances a remedial right or power.[470]

Thus, the implied obligation of good faith has no existence separate from the underlying contract to which it is attached. It requires each party to the contract to perform contractual duties and to exercise discretion in a fashion that promotes the fulfillment of the reasonable expectations of the other party. It is essential to focus on the purpose of the agreement and the consequent reasonable expectations of the parties to determine whether each party is operating in good faith.[471]"Conduct prohibited by the covenant of good faith is circumscribed by the purposes and express terms of the contract."[472] Preventing a party from performing a contract in accordance with the spirit of the contract, interfering with his performance or denying him the expected benefit of the contract is a denial of good faith.[473] It cannot be used to vary the express terms of the contract.[474] Parties are not prevented from protecting their respective economic interests.[475] On the other hand, where a party has contractual discretion to promote its own interest, the good faith requirement precludes action that would contravene the reasonable expectations of the other party.[476] Thus, where the defendant had a duty to merchandise the plaintiff's products, the use of inexperienced personnel, mistiming the merchandising campaign and waiving guarantees under licensing agreements violated the implied covenant of good faith.[477]

While the common law duty of good faith applies to the performance of a contract, it has been held not to apply to the formation of a contract.[478] The RESTATEMENT 2d would enlarge the application of the good faith standard to the "assertion, settlement and litigation of contract claims and defense,"[479] but courts may find such an extension to interfere with zealous advocacy within the bounds of professional ethics.[480]

---

[470] UCC § 1-304, comment 1.

[471] Gilson v. Rainin Instrument, LLC, 2005 U.S. Dist. LEXIS 16825 (W. D. Wis. 2005). "[C]onduct prohibited by the covenant of good faith is circumscribed by the purposes and express terms of the contract."

[472] also *AT&T Communications*, note 465 *supra*, at *5.

[473] Mahan v. Avera St. Luke's, 621 N.W.2d 150, 160 (S.D. 2001); Countrywide Servs. Corp. v. SIA Ins. Co., 235 F.3d 390 (8th Cir. 2000).

[474] City of Riviera Beach v. John's Towing, 691 So. 2d 519, 521 (Fla. Dist. Ct. App. 1997).

[475] This statement is quoted in Wisconsin Elec. Power Co. v. Union Pac. R.R. Co., 557 F. 3d 504, 510 (7th Cir. 2009). See also *GMAC*, *supra* note 465.

[476] Cox v. CSX Intermodal, Inc., 732 So. 2d 1092, 1097 (Fla. Dist. Ct. App. 1999).

[477] Marsu, B.V. v. Walt Disney Co., 185 F.3d 932, 937 (9th Cir. 1999).

[478] S.E.A., Inc. v. Southside Leasing Co., 2000 Tenn. App. LEXIS 649 (Tenn. Ct. App. Sept. 29, 2000) (citing RESTATEMENT 2d § 205, cmt. c).

[479] RESTATEMENT 2d § 205, cmt. e.

[480] Roussalis v. Wyoming Med. Ctr., 4 P.3d 209, 256 (Wyo. 2000).

[1]   Good Faith — CISG and UNIDROIT Principles

The Vienna Convention stops short of imposing a good faith obligation in contracts for the sale of goods.[481] The lack of certainty in such a general requirement was a sufficient concern to preclude its imposition as a duty, but it does appear as a guide to interpretation: "In the interpretation of this Convention, regard is to be had to . . . the observance of good faith in international trade."[482] While the statement is deliberately timid, its placement at the inception of "General Provisions" in the company of other foundational statements of "regard" as to the international character of the Convention and the need to promote uniformity is reminiscent of the "underlying purposes and policies" of the Uniform Commercial Code, though there is no doubt that the UCC principles obligate courts in the construction and application of its provisions.[483] The same CISG Article also contains a directive that matters not expressly settled in its provisions "are to be settled in conformity with the general principles on which it is based."[484] Presumably, one of those "general principles" appears in the preceding subsection, i.e., the "regard" for good faith. Further support for characterizing "good faith" as a principle underlying CISG may be found in the UNIDROIT Principles that impose a duty to act in good faith and fair dealing *in international trade*.[485] This principle is so fundamental that the parties may not eliminate it by their contract. The standard, however, is not a domestic standard. It is to be applied as an international standard. Unlike United States domestic law that does not apply the good faith standard to negotiations, *Principles* makes a party liable for bad faith in negotiations, i.e., by misrepresenting facts or by negotiating without an intention to form a contract.[486]

§ 92   MISTAKE

[A]   Definition — Poor Judgment and Prediction Distinguished — Mistake of "Law" Versus "Fact"

The FIRST RESTATEMENT defined "mistake" as "a state of mind that is not in accord with the facts."[487] The RESTATEMENT 2d definition is similar: "A mistake is a belief that is not in accord with the facts,"[488] i.e., "an erroneous belief."[489] The RESTATEMENT 2d is careful to restrict its use of "mistake" to facts existing at the time of contract formation, i.e., it is not used to refer to an "improvident act" such as assuming a risk that the facts will remain as they are at the time of contract formation.[490] Moreover, "mistake" does not refer to a prediction or exercise of

---

[481] *See* JOHN HONNOLD, UNIFORM LAW FOR INTERNATIONAL SALES UNDER THE 1980 UNITED NATIONS CONVENTION 147 (2d ed. 1991).

[482] CISG Art. 7(1).

[483] UCC § 1-103(a) states that the Code "shall be liberally construed and applied to promote is underlying purposes and policies" which are then set forth.

[484] CISG, Art. 7(2).

[485] Principles, Art. 1.7(1).

[486] Principles, Art. 2.15.

[487] FIRST RESTATEMENT § 500.

[488] RESTATEMENT 2d § 151.

[489] *Id.* at comment a.

[490] Illustration 1 to § 151 defining "mistake" deals with the facts of Wills v. Shockley, 52 Del. 295, 157 A.2d 252

judgment that a particular situation will exist in the future.[491] Thus, in the sale of a business, both buyer and seller may believe that the business will earn a certain amount in the ensuing year and that judgment may be the basis for a reasonable prediction. If, however, the economy or other events do not permit that prediction to prove true, neither party has made a "mistake" as defined in the RESTATEMENT 2d, i.e., an erroneous belief of fact existing at the time the contract is formed. It was a mistake of judgment.[492] The erroneous belief of a fact existing at the moment of contract formation may be articulated or unarticulated, and it may be a mistake as to the contents or the legal effect of an expression of agreement i.e., a so-called mistake of law is, itself, a *fact* which can be the basis for an erroneous belief.[493]

[B]   Types of Mistake and Related Matters to Be Explored

We have already explored some of the kinds of mistake and its effects in the law of contracts. Thus, we have considered *mistakes in expression* such as a slip of the tongue.[494] We have explored the problems surrounding *mutual misunderstanding* as suggested in the famous case involving two ships named *Peerless*,[495] where mistake and equivocal meanings, particularly those involving latent ambiguity, overlap. We have analyzed the problems of a mistake in the writing where, for example, a scrivener fails to set forth the true intention of the parties in the document evidencing their contract giving rise to the possible remedy of reformation.[496] We now explore the other types of mistake.

In this section we will consider *mistake of identity*, i.e., where a party has an erroneous belief as to the party with whom he is dealing, *mistake of subject matter*, where one or both parties entertain erroneous beliefs concerning the subject matter of the contract, *computation mistake* where one of the parties has made what amounts to a clerical error, *mistake of value* where the parties may have entertained an erroneous belief as to the value of the subject matter *at the time of contract formation* as contrasted with the predicted value,[497] *mistake by the intermediary* where neither party to the contract has made any mistake but the intermediary responsible for communication between or among the parties has made a mistake and, finally, *releases* of claims where, *e.g.*, a personal injury claimant who has signed a release of her claim may later seek to attack it on the ground that she was, at the time of the release, unaware of the full extent of her injury.

(1960), where *A* contracted to raise and float *B*'s boat which had run aground. *A* believed that the sea would remain calm until the work was completed, but a sudden storm caused the boat to fall into deep water making it much more difficult to raise. The RESTATEMENT suggests that *A*'s poor judgment was not a "mistake" as it defines the term.

[491] *See* Hansen v. Little Bear Inn Co., 9 P.3d 960, 964 (Wyo. 2000) (relying on RESTATEMENT 2d § 151, cmt. a).

[492] See RESTATEMENT 2d § 151 ill. 2, based on Leasco Corp. v. Taussig, 473 F.2d 777 (2d Cir. 1972), where the buyer of a business argued that the parties assumed that they were dealing with a corporation that would earn $200,000 in a given year and the company lost $12,000 instead. The court viewed the assumption as nothing more than a poor prediction, rather than a mistake that would have permitted the buyer to avoid the contract.

[493] The RESTATEMENT 2d suggests the possibility of mistake based on an assumption of a party who is unaware of alternatives. It also rejects earlier distinctions between mistakes of "fact" versus mistakes of "law" since the law existing at the time of contract formation is a fact at that time. An erroneous belief as to the law, regardless of its basis in a statute, judicial decision, or otherwise, is, therefore, a mistake of fact. RESTATEMENT 2d § 151 comment a. *See* Scott v. Petett, 63 Wash. App. 50, 816 P.2d 1229, 1231 (1991).

[494] *See supra* § 87[D].

[495] *See supra* § 87[B][2], [3], [C].

[496] *See supra* § 85[B].

[497] *See supra* text at note 307.

It will be necessary to consider the difference between unilateral and mutual mistake and their legal effects as well as other factors which will govern the legal effect of mistake including: (a) the importance of the mistake, (b) the actual or presumed knowledge of the mistake by either or both parties, (c) the negligence of the mistaken party, (d) the reliance by the nonmistaken party, (e) any manifestation of risk assumption by either party and (f) the possible remedies a court may grant to balance the conflicting interests under all of the circumstances, including the circumstance of mistake, itself.

Before considering the various types of mistake and their legal effects, certain preliminary questions will now be explored to avoid later confusion.

[C]   Offeree's Knowledge of Mistake — Failure to Read — Misrepresentation

In an earlier analysis of mistake of expression,[498] we saw that an offeree cannot "snap up an offer"[499] if he knows[500] or reasonably should know[501] that the offeror is making a mistake. That concept is applicable to any type of mistake, i.e., a mistake in identity of the other party to the contract, a mistake in subject matter, an error in computation or any other type of mistake to be considered later in this section. Where, however, an offeree appears to assent to an offer, e.g., by signing a writing containing the terms of the proposed contract, he will be bound to the terms of that contract even though he failed to read it or understand it, providing the offeror was not aware of the offeree's misconception[502] and provided that the contract is otherwise not susceptible to claims of unconscionability[503] or other grounds of avoidance.[504]

---

[498] See supra § 87[D].

[499] See Tyra v. Cheney, 129 Minn. 428, 152 N.W. 835 (1915). A more recent statement of the same concept is found in Howell v. Waters, 82 N.C. App. 481, 347 S.E.2d 65, 69 (1986), and Fisher v. Stolaruk Corp., 110 F.R.D. 74 (E.D. Mich. 1986) (rescission is justified where offeree who snaps up an offer refuses to permit the mistake to be corrected when discovered by the offeror). See also Speckel v. Perkins, 364 N.W.2d 890 (Minn. Ct. App. 1985) (offer to settle lawsuit stated that the case was not worth the policy limits of $50,000 but proceeded to offer $50,000 instead of $15,000; held, the letter was internally inconsistent and imposed a duty on the recipient to inquire).

[500] Where one party has actual knowledge of a mistake by the other as to a basic assumption on which the other is making the contract, and the first party deliberately fails to disclose that information, such non-disclosure amounts to an assertion that the fact does not exist. See Restatement 2d § 161.

[501] Where one party makes a mistake and the other party had reason to know of the mistake, the contract is voidable under § 153(b) of the Restatement 2d.

[502] See, e.g., Quinn v. Briggs, 172 Mont. 468, 565 P.2d 297 (1977).

[503] Unconscionability and related concepts will be explored in the next chapter.

[504] See Betaco, Inc. v. Cessna Aircraft Co., 32 F.3d 1126, 1136 (7th Cir. 1994); G & R Trie Distribs., Inc. v. Allstate Ins. Co., 177 Conn. 58, 61, 411 A.2d 31, 34 (1979). The following charge by the trial court was not erroneous: "[t]he general rule is that where a person of mature years who can read and write signs or accepts a formal written contract affecting his pecuniary interests, it is his duty to read it, and notice of its contents will be imputed to him if he negligently fails to do so; but this rule is subject to qualifications including the intervention of fraud or artifice, or mistake not due to negligence, and applies only if nothing has been said or done to mislead the person sought to be charged or to put a man of reasonable business prudence off his guard in this matter." A "bad bargain" does not provide any basis for relief for a party who has signed a release without reading it. Sanger v. Yellow Cab Co., 486 S.W.2d 477 (Mo. 1972). See also § 3-305(a)(1)(iii) of the UCC, which permits a defense by a party to a negotiable instrument where there is "fraud that has induced the obligor to sign the instrument with neither knowledge nor reasonable opportunity to learn of its character or its essential terms. . . ." Comment 1 to this section suggests that this type of misrepresentation is sometimes called "real" or "essential" fraud or "fraud in the factum" involving trick or artifice in having someone sign a negotiable instrument in the belief that it is merely a receipt or some other document. If a party

Such a rule is obviously proper since one who has negligently induced an offeror to believe that the offer has been accepted is hardly in a position to demand relief because he, the offeree, did not take the time or trouble to inform himself of the contents of the writing he signed.[505] This logical rule, however, is subject to an exception in mistake cases. If a mistaken party is held to a standard of "reasonable care," the mistake could be avoided in the great majority of cases by the exercise of such care and the mistaken party would be without remedy. Thus, a party's failure to read a particular contract document or to discover facts before making a contract, notwithstanding a lack of diligence which some courts may choose to call negligence, will not preclude the remedy of avoidance or the equitable remedy of reformation unless the mistaken party fails to act in good faith and in accordance with reasonable standards of fair dealing.[506]

Where the offeror has misrepresented the contents of the writing and the offeree relies upon the misrepresentation without reading the document before signing it, courts are confronted with the fraud of one party versus the negligence of the other. While some older cases held the negligent offeree to the bargain notwithstanding the fraud of the offeror,[507] the better view was effectively suggested by an early Kentucky decision: "Is it better to encourage negligence in the foolish, or fraud in the deceitful? Either course has most obvious dangers. But judicial experience exemplifies that the former is the least objectionable, and least hampers the administration of pure justice."[508]

Courts must balance the conflicting policies of deterring fraud on the one hand and discouraging inattention to the obligations in a written instrument on the other. They should, however, be reluctant to deny relief on the footing that, had one party been more attentive and

---

cannot read or understand a document, he must seek assistance in having the writing read or explained to him. Absent fraud, he will not be able to avoid his obligation under the instrument simply because he failed to understand it. The effect of fraud in the factum is to render the transaction void, while fraud in the inducement merely renders it voidable. For a recent statement of the distinction, see Gulfstream Dev. Group, LLC. v. Schwartz, 2009 U.S. Dist. LEXIS 33387 at *22 (M. D. Fla. 2009).

[505] "[I]n the absence of fraud or misrepresentation, a party is charged with knowing the legal effect of a contract voluntarily made. . . . To state the rule differently, absent fraud, a party to a contract who has access to the full information of its contents cannot avoid it on the ground of his own neglect in failing to read it." Reynolds-Penland Co. v. Hexter & Lobello, 567 S.W.2d 237, 240 (Tex. Civ. App. Dallas 1978). *See also* RESTATEMENT 2d § 157 comment b.

[506] *See, e.g.*, Ollie v. Plano Indep. School Dist., 323 Fed. Appx. 295, 298 (5th Cir. 2009) ("A mistaken party's fault in failing to know or discover the facts before making the contract does not bar him from avoidance or reformation . . . unless his fault amounts to a failure to act in good faith and in accordance with reasonable standards of fair dealing" (citing RESTATEMENT 2d § 157)); Wehner v. Schroeder, 354 N.W.2d 674 (N.D. 1984) (the negligent failure of a party to read an instrument before signing it does not, in itself, bar reformation) (citing RESTATEMENT 2d § 157 comment b). *Accord* Northwestern Bank v. Roseman, 81 N.C. App. 228, 344 S.E.2d 120 (1986), *aff'd*, 319 N.C. 394, 354 S.E.2d 238 (1987). *See also* Floral Consultants, Ltd. v. Hanover Ins. Co., 128 Ill. App. 3d 173, 473 N.E.2d 527, 83 Ill. Dec. 401 (1st Dist. 1984) (while insured's failure to read policy may amount to contributory negligence, it does not operate as a bar to relief as a matter of law); Precision Castparts Corp. v. Johnson & Higgins, Inc., 44 Or. App. 739, 607 P.2d 763 (1980) (failure to read insurance policy does not excuse defendant upon whom plaintiff was entitled to rely in securing the appropriate policy); Brewer v. Vanguard Ins. Co., 614 S.W.2d 360 (Tenn. Ct. App. 1981) (failure to read insurance policy, especially a renewal policy, is not such negligence as will defeat insured's right to reform the policy).

[507] *See, e.g.*, Mutual Benefit Health & Accident Ass'n v. Ferrell, 42 Ariz. 477, 27 P.2d 519 (1933); Crum v. McCollum, 211 Iowa 319, 233 N.W. 678 (1930); J. B. Colt Co. v. Thompson, 114 Okla. 61, 242 P. 1030 (1926).

[508] Western Mfg. Co. v. Cotton & Long, 126 Ky. 749, 757, 104 S.W. 758, 760 (1907). So also in the law of torts, it is generally held that the negligence of the plaintiff is not a defense to an action based upon the defendant's intentional misrepresentation. W. PROSSER & R. KEETON, TORTS 750 (5th ed. 1984).

carefully read the document, the fraud of the other would have been ineffective.[509] Whether the party who failed to read the document was reasonable in relying on the misrepresentation by the other party is a question of fact.[510]

[D]   Mistake in Formation, Integration, or Performance — The Anatomy of Mistake — "Basic Assumption," "Material Effect," and Risk Allocation

Before considering different types of mistakes such as those relating to identity, subject matter, value, or the like, it is important to recognize that the parties to a contract can make mistakes at different stages of the contract. They can hold an erroneous belief as to the facts at the time of formation, i.e., they assume a past or existing fact and their belief is erroneous at the time the contract is made. If the parties make no mistake at the time of formation, they may fail to insert an agreed term in the writing memorializing their agreement, i.e., a mistake in integration. Assuming no mistake at formation or integration, the parties may make a mistake in the performance of the contract where, for example, one party overpays or underpays the other.[511] A mistake as to integration may activate the parol evidence rule. Where the omission in the writing causes the writing to state an intention different from the true intention of the parties, the equitable remedy of reformation may be appropriate. Where a party underpays the other during the performance stage of the contract, the other has a claim for full payment. A party who overpays will have a claim for restitution to avoid the unjust enrichment of the other.[512] If a party seeks to *avoid* the contract, however, the only type of mistake that will permit avoidance is the first type of mistake, i.e., a mistake in the *formation* stage of the contract.

A mistake in the formation stage must be *foundational* to the contract — "the mistake must be of an existing or past fact which is material; it must be as to a fact which enters into and forms the basis of the contract, or in other words it must be of the essence of the agreement, the *sine qua non*, or, as is sometimes said, the efficient cause of the agreement, and must be such that it animates and controls the conduct of the parties."[513] The mistake must relate to a past or existing fact which is material where the risk of mistake should not be allocated to one of the parties. In the language of the RESTATEMENT 2d, the mistake must constitute a *basic assumption* on which the contract was made, it must have a material effect on the agreed exchange of performances, and the otherwise adversely affected party must not bear the risk of the mistake.[514]

---

[509] Northwestern Bank v. Roseman, 81 N.C. App. 228, 344 S.E.2d 120, 124 (1986), *aff'd*, 319 N.C. 394, 354 S.E.2d 238 (1987).

[510] *Id.*

[511] *See* Pathology Consultants v. Gratton, 343 N.W.2d 428, 437 (Iowa 1984).

[512] *See* Sharp v. Bowling, 511 So. 2d 363 (Fla. Dist. Ct. App. 1987). *See also* RESTATEMENT OF RESTITUTION § 20.

[513] Howell v. Waters, 82 N.C. App. 481, 486, 347 S.E.2d 65, 69 (1986) quoting MacKay v. McIntosh, 270 N.C. 69, 73–74, 153 S.E.2d 800, 804 (1967)).

[514] RESTATEMENT 2d §§ 152(1) and 153, comment b.

[1]   "Basic Assumption" on Which Contract Was Made

The phrase, "basic assumption," is found in the UCC and the Restatement 2d of Contracts in a different context.[515] There is, however, no UCC or RESTATEMENT definition of "basic assumption," though the phrase suggests that for an assumption to be "basic," it must be foundational to the contract or, in the earlier quoted language of one court, the *sine qua non* or *efficient cause* of the contract.[516] The basic assumption need not be expressly stated.[517] If the parties merely disagreed as to the interpretation of their contract, they are not mistaken as to an existing material fact.[518] If one of the parties suffers disappointed expectations concerning the value or profit from the contract, there is no mistake as to basic assumptions.[519] As suggested earlier,[520] that situation is one of poor judgment or prediction. Neither party is justified in assuming that market conditions or its own financial situation may not change,[521] i.e., the opposite prediction is more reasonable. If, however, the parties have attempted to limit future risks in market changes and have employed a particular formula for that purpose, their basic assumption concerning the formula may be mistaken at the time of contract formation. If that mistake has a material effect on the agreed exchange, the contract may be avoided.[522]

[2]   Material Effect on Agreed Exchange

The RESTATEMENT 2d suggests a stark illustration of a mistake as to a basic assumption which has a material effect on the agreed exchange. *A* purchases an annuity from *B*, an insurance company, on the life of *C*. Both *A* and *B* believe at the time of contract formation that *C* is alive but their beliefs are erroneous since *C* is dead. Thus, there was a mistake as to a basic assumption at the time of contract formation which had a material effect upon the agreed exchange. The contract is voidable by the purchaser.[523] Where parties entered a contract on the basic assumption that they were buying and selling rental income property and later learned that the property had no value because it has been condemned as unfit for human habitation, their erroneous belief with respect to the basic assumption had a material effect upon their agreed exchange.[524]

---

[515] This phrase is used in the UCC section dealing with commercial impracticability, § 2-615, and is used in that connection by the RESTATEMENT 2d (§§ 261 and 266(1)) as well as in the section dealing with the related doctrine of frustration of purpose (§§ 265 and 266(2)).

[516] *See Howell v. Waters, supra* note 513, quoted at 489.

[517] Hillside Associates of Hollis, Inc. v. Maine Bonding & Cas. Co., 135 N.H. 325, 605 A.2d 1026, 1030 (1992).

[518] Creative Communications Consultants, Inc. v. Gaylord, 403 N.W.2d 654 (Minn. Ct. App. 1987).

[519] *See* Diedrich v. Northern Ill. Pub. Co., 39 Ill. App. 3d 851, 350 N.E.2d 857, 862 (2d Dist. 1976).

[520] *See supra* text at note 408.

[521] RESTATEMENT 2d § 152 comment b.

[522] *See* Aluminum Co. of Am. v. Essex Group, Inc., 499 F. Supp. 53 (W.D. Pa. 1980) (price formula in long term aluminum conversion contract held mistaken from the moment of contract formation—"a present actuarial error"—and the court reformed the contract to its interpretation of the true intention of the parties, though it curiously suggests that reformation was not an available remedy). *See also* Phil Bramsen Distributor v. Mastroni, 151 Ariz. 194, 198, 726 P.2d 610, 614 (Ct. App. 1986). Parties agreed on an escalation clause based on the rate of inflation and the attorney (scrivener) inserted a term, "cost of living index for the City of Phoenix prepared by the Bureau of Labor Statistics." No such cost of living index existed. The parties mistakenly believed they had a workable formula at the time of contract formation.

[523] *See* RESTATEMENT 2d § 152 ill. 6. The same illustration is mentioned in comment b to this section.

[524] *See* Lenawee County Bd. of Health v. Messerly, 417 Mich. 17, 331 N.W.2d 203 (1982) (material effect on agreed

To emphasize how material, essential and foundation a mistake must be to allow relief for the mistaken party, it is not uncommon for a court to suggest it must be convinced that, "but for the mistake the complainant would not have assumed the obligation from which he seeks to be relieved."[525] In a given situation, however, that showing may be insufficient. Though a party establishes a shared mistake as to a basic assumption that was the efficient cause for his entering the contract, unless he can also demonstrate that the effect on the agreed exchange is such that he should not be called upon to perform, he has not established the critical element of material effect upon the agreed exchange. Where the defendant leased property to use as a distribution center that would allow for the parking of cars and trucks, fleet shops for maintenance and repair of autos and other uses, both parties mistakenly assumed the applicable zoning laws would permit such use. When the mistake was discovered, the defendant sought to avoid the contract since it would not be permitted to conduct auto repairs on the premises. The defendant had acknowledged that it could outsource the fleet shop work though it would be more costly. Unlike an earlier case where the parties mistakenly assumed that a nonprofit tennis and swim club could be operated,[526] the court found that the fleet shops did not constitute the "very basis" of this contract. They were not listed among the permissible uses in the lease. Though the defendant may not have entered into the contract had it known it could not operate the fleet shops on that property, such an effect on the agreed exchange was not sufficiently foundational Quoting the Restatement 2d of Contracts,[527] the court noted that, "It is not enough for [a party] to prove that he would not have made the contract had it not been for the mistake. He must show that the resulting imbalance in the agreed exchange is so severe that he cannot be fairly required to carry it out."[528]

If the discovered mistake reveals an exchange that is not only substantially less desirable for one party, but substantially more desirable for the other, a court will be more amenable to granting relief than if there is merely a loss to one party without a corresponding gain to the other.[529] A combination of gain to one party and a corresponding loss to the other party-the protection of the restitution interest or prevention of unjust enrichment-was long ago identified as more deserving of legal protection than other, commonly protected interests in contract law, i.e., the expectation or reliance interests.[530] The standard of materiality is the usual standard,

---

exchange but contract allocated risk to purchasers). *See also* Winter v. Skoglund, 404 N.W.2d 786 (Minn. 1987) (mistake about a basic assumption that there was no risk that certain trusts were not bound affecting Minnesota Vikings football team that had material effect upon agreed exchange); Dover Pool & Racquet Club, Inc. v. Brooking, 366 Mass. 629, 322 N.E.2d 168 (1975) (erroneous basic assumption at the time of formation concerning zoning laws which had a material effect upon the operation of a pool and racquet club; as suggested earlier, mistakes of "law" are erroneous factual assumptions).

[525] *See* Knudsen v. Jensen, 521 N.W.2d 415, 418 (S.D. 1994).

[526] Dover Pool & Racquet Club, Inc. v. Brooking, *supra* note 524.

[527] § 152, comment c.

[528] Shawmut-Canton LLC v. Great Springs Waters of America, Inc., 62 Mass. Ct. App. 330, 338, 816 N. E. 2d 545, 551, n. 10 (2004).

[529] See *Hillside Associates, supra* note 517. In *Aluminum Co. of Am. v. Essex Group, supra* note 522, for example, the projected loss to Alcoa was $60 million with a substantial gain to Essex.

[530] "The 'restitution interest,' involving a combination of unjust impoverishment with unjust gain, presents the strongest case for relief. If, following Aristotle, we regard the purpose of justice as the maintenance of an equilibrium of goods among members of society, the restitution interest presents twice as strong a claim to judicial intervention as the reliance interest, since if *A* not only causes *B* to lose one unit but appropriates that unit to himself, the resulting discrepancy between *A* and *B* is not one unit but two." Fuller & Perdue, *The Reliance Interest in Contract Damages*, 46 Yale L.J. 52, 56 (1936), *quoted in* United States v. Algernon Blair, Inc., 479 F.2d 638, 641 (4th Cir. 1973).

i.e., one that must be considered in light of all the circumstances. If the mistake does not relate to a material aspect of the bargain but only to a collateral matter, there is no material effect upon the agreed exchange and no relief for such a mistake is available.[531]

[3]   Risk Allocation

If the parties have allocated the risk of mistake by their agreement, the party to whom the risk has been allocated is precluded from later alleging the mistake as a ground for avoidance.[532] Thus, if the parties contemplated and assumed certain risks, neither party could later raise such risks as the basis of either avoidance or reformation.[533] Where the parties have not expressly agreed to allocate certain risks, they may have contracted with complete awareness of their lack of knowledge concerning potential risks. Where, for example, a settlement agreement was formed while the parties thought that a motion for summary judgment was merely pending though it had been granted, the court held that such a risk was assumed.[534]

The *conscious ignorance* of a party who has contracted with knowledge that he is unaware of certain facts or has only limited knowledge of certain facts is the basis for allocating the risk to him.[535] If the evidence is clear that a party formed an agreement on certain terms with knowledge that he was unaware of certain critical facts, to suggest that such party has not agreed to bear potential risks relating to consciously unknown facts misconceives the concept of agreement. Where, for example, an agreement required a party to obtain life insurance and the parties failed to consider the eventuality that the party would be uninsurable, the court held that the failure to adequately predict this result was not a mistake of the parties allowing avoidance of the contract, but merely a poor prognostication.[536]

"Conscious ignorance" will not be found where a party is reasonably diligent in pursuing the relevant facts. Thus, where a defect in the foundation of a house was "latent and hidden," the trial court's finding that the buyer should have been "more cautious" in conducting an investigation was reversed on the footing that a reasonably diligent investigation would not have revealed the defect.[537]

Where the parties have not allocated the risk by their agreement or it has not been allocated to a party with limited knowledge of facts to which the mistake relates, the RESTATEMENT 2d suggests that a court may decide to allocate the risk of a mistake to one of the parties because

---

[531] *See* Horner v. Bourland, 724 F.2d 1142, 1145 (5th Cir. 1984) (mistaken assumption that FHA loan could be recast was not material); Interstate Industrial Uniform Rental Serv., Inc. v. Couri Pontiac, Inc., 355 A.2d 913, 918 (Me. 1976) (mistake related to collateral issue of wisdom of entering into bargain and did not touch the subject matter of the bargain). *See also* Perry v. Stewart Title Co., 756 F.2d 1197, 1205–06 (5th Cir. 1985) (alleged mistake concerning land survey did not relate to a material aspect of the bargain but merely to a collateral matter).

[532] *See* RESTATEMENT 2d § 154(a) and particularly comment b.

[533] *See* Beecher v. Able, 575 F.2d 1010 (2d Cir. 1978). *See also* RESTATEMENT OF RESTITUTION § 11(1) comment d.

[534] Sheng v. Starkey Lab., 117 F.3d 1081 (8th Cir. 1997).

[535] RESTATEMENT 2d § 154(b): Where a party "is aware at the time the contract is made, that he has only limited knowledge with respect to the facts to which the mistake relates but treats his limited knowledge as sufficient," that party bears the risk of the mistake. See also comment c and Public Util. Dist. No. 1 v. Washington Public Power Supply Sys., 104 Wash. 2d 353, 705 P.2d 1195 (1985), *corrected by*, 713 P.2d 1109 (Wash. 1986).

[536] Hansen v. Little Bear Inn Co., 9 P.3d 960, 965 (Wyo. 2000).

[537] Knudsen v. Jensen, 521 N.W.2d 415, 419 (S.D. 1994).

it is reasonable to do so.[538] The common illustration is a seller of farm land seeking to avoid the contract on the ground that valuable mineral rights have been newly found on the land. The court will allocate that risk to the seller.[539] The seller may not be said to have been "consciously ignorant" of the value of the land. In a well-known case,[540] the plaintiff found a stone and, not knowing what it was, offered it to the defendant who was also unaware of its identity or value. The defendant offered one dollar for the stone and the plaintiff chose not to sell it. At a later time, still ignorant of its identity or value, the plaintiff agreed to sell the stone to the defendant who was equally unaware of the stone's value. Subsequently, the value of the stone was established at $700 and the defendant sought its return by tendering $1.10 (the original price plus interest). The plaintiff refused the tender and the court held that the risk of value had been assumed by the plaintiff-seller. Clearly, the seller had assumed the risk that the value of the stone would be much greater than the amount received from the buyer since the seller chose to sell the stone with full consciousness that she was unaware of its value. Moreover, the seller had *agreed* to assume that risk by committing to sell the stone with such consciousness, i.e., the seller said, in effect, I hereby part with my ownership of this "thing," regardless of its worth, for one dollar, and I assume all risks of value in relation to this transaction. To require the parties to express a specific agreement concerning risk allocation in such a setting in order to find that they had agreed upon such allocation is excessively formalistic. The factual bargain of the parties clearly manifests that both parties assumed all risks of value.

Like the seller of the stone, the seller of the farm land may have never consciously considered the possibility that valuable minerals were part of the land. Yet, when one is parting with the ownership of any property, real or personal, it would be unreasonable for that seller to assume that he or she reserves the right to reclaim it should it prove to be more valuable. In such cases, courts are faced with the necessity of supplying an omitted term.[541] That process requires a determination of whether the parties have manifested an intention as to allocate risks. If a court cannot discover such a manifestation, it must proceed to a consideration of the apparent purposes of the parties in making the contract and the court's empathy for the parties in that position.[542]

[E]   Unilateral Versus Mutual Mistake — Remedies

The preceding analysis has not distinguished *unilateral* from *mutual* mistakes. A *unilateral* mistake occurs where only one of the parties has an erroneous belief at the time of formation as to a basic assumption on which he made the contract which will have a material effect on the agreed exchange that is adverse to him.[543] A *mutual* mistake is found where both parties have an erroneous belief as to a basic assumption of the contract at the time of formation which will have a material effect on the agreed exchange as to either party.[544] There

[538] Restatement 2d § 154(c) and particularly comment d. *See* Chemical Bank v. Washington Public Power Supply Sys., 102 Wash. 2d 874, 691 P.2d 524 (1984), *cert. denied*, 471 U.S. 1075, 105 S. Ct. 2154, 85 L. Ed. 2d 510 (1985).

[539] *See* Restatement 2d § 154 comments a and d.

[540] Wood v. Boynton, 64 Wis. 265, 25 N.W. 42 (1885).

[541] *See supra* § 90.

[542] The Restatement 2d suggests this concept in somewhat different language: "[T]he court will consider the purposes of the parties and will have recourse to its own general knowledge of human behavior in bargain transactions. . . ." Restatement 2d § 154 comment d.

[543] Restatement 2d § 154.

[544] Restatement 2d § 152.

is, however, a significant problem in permitting a contract to be avoided on the ground of unilateral as contrasted with mutual mistake. If only one party is mistaken, unless the other party knows or should know of the mistake, the other party is innocent and has a legitimate claim to the protection of her expectations under the contract.[545] It is, therefore, not uncommon to find a court stating, "[A] unilateral mistake by a contract party, as distinct from a mutual mistake, is not a generally recognized excuse for failing to comply with the contract's terms."[546] Modern courts, however, admit that "the qualification in 'generally' is critical."[547] There are several types of unilateral mistake for which relief will be granted.

As suggested earlier, there has never been any doubt that an offeree who knows or should know that the offeror is making a mistake may not "snap up the offer." That situation, however, borders on misrepresentation or deceit that has always been subject to relief for the mistaken party including the remedy of reformation.[548] Absent knowledge of mistake by the non-mistaken party or some other form of misrepresentation or fraud inducing the mistake, we will examine cases allowing relief for unilateral mistakes involving excusable negligence found in clerical errors by bidders in construction contracts.[549] A possibility of relief for unilateral mistake occurs in other types of cases. Where the purchasers of a house discovered that the house was not suitable for year-round living, the court granted rescission of the contract where the buyers were neither negligent nor imprudent, the mistake had such a material effect upon the agreed exchange that the consequences would work an unconscionable hardship on the buyers, and the seller could be restored to *status quo*.[550] The RESTATEMENT 2d recognizes this possibility, but there should be no illusion that it creates an easy path to relief. A unilaterally mistaken party must not only show a mistake as to a basic assumption that has a material effect on the agreed exchange adverse to him, he must also show that he did not bear the risk of the mistake,[551] the effect of the mistake is to make enforcement of the contract unconscionable or that the other party had reason to know of the mistake or his fault caused the mistake.[552]

---

[545] *See* A. J. Concrete Pumping, Inc. v. Richard O'Brien Equip. Sales, Inc., 256 Ga. 795, 353 S.E.2d 496 (1987) (denying reformation for unilateral mistake).

[546] In re UAL Corp., 411 F. 3d 818, 823 (7th Cir. 2009). See also Mutual of Enumclaw Ins. Co. v. Wood By-Products, 107 Idaho 1024, 695 P.2d 409 (Ct. App. 1984) where the court suggests that unilateral mistake is "not ordinarily" a basis for relief.

[547] UAL Corp., *id.* See the discussion of Colorado law in City of Raton v. Ark. River Power Authority, 2009 U.S. Dist. LEXIS 49794 (D.N.M. 2009) where the court quotes a statement from the Colorado Supreme Court stating that avoidance of the contract on the ground of mistake requires a mutual mistake, but discovers other Colorado case law recognizing unilateral mistake in certain cases.

[548] "As for reformation, the Court of Chancery observed that such relief is granted in the absence of fraud or misrepresentation only where it is demonstrated that there was a mutual mistake, or a unilateral mistake coupled with a knowing silence. . . ." Bank of Delaware v. Claymont Fire Co. No. 1, 528 A.2d 1196, 1198 (Del. 1987).

[549] These cases will be discussed in subsection [H],*infra.*

[550] Cummings v. Dusenbury, 129 Ill. App. 3d 338, 84 Ill. Dec. 615, 472 N.E.2d 575 (2d Dist. 1984). Courts have suggested relief for unilateral mistake in other types of contracts. See, e.g., Gamewell Mfg., Inc. v. HVAC Supply, Inc., 715 F.2d 112 (4th Cir. 1983) (settlement agreement).

[551] RESTATEMENT 2d § 154.

[552] RESTATEMENT 2d § 153. See Contempo Design, Inc. v. Chicago & Northeast Ill. Dist. Council of Carpenters, 226 F.3d 535 (7th Cir. 2000), cert. denied, 121 S. Ct. 776, 148 L. Ed. 2d 674 (2001) (quoting RESTATEMENT 2d § 153). See also Lanci v. Metropolitan Ins. Co., 388 Pa. Super. 1, 564 A.2d 972 (1989) (the other party had reason to know that plaintiff's lawyer was operating under the erroneous belief that the policy limits were $15,000 in agreeing to a release when, in fact, the limits were $250,000; RESTATEMENT 2d § 153(b)).

If the relief sought is not contract avoidance but reformation, absent fraud or clearly inequitable conduct, that remedy is only available where both parties share a mistake with respect to the written expression of agreement.[553] Whether the mistake is mutual or unilateral, however, a court may, in addition to permitting avoidance of the contract, provide additional relief in the form of restitution (to prevent unjust enrichment where it is not possible to return benefits conferred) or it may protect the reliance interest where avoidance of the contract fails to protect that interest sufficiently.[554]

[F] Mistake of Identity

Mistakes of identity of the other party are unilateral mistakes. A mistake of identity provides a significant illustration of why relief for unilateral mistake should be granted only to avoid an unconscionable result. Assume that Ames offers to sell goods to Barnes thinking Barnes is a particular Barnes with whom Ames would like to develop a continuous contractual relationship. Barnes, however, is a different Barnes who does nothing to induce Ames to make the mistake and has no reason to assume that Ames is making a mistake. Barnes accepts the offer and, when Ames discovers her mistake, she seeks to avoid the contract. There is every reason to enforce this contract against Ames in favor of Barnes who is totally innocent and should not be deprived of his expectation interest.[555] The only escape from this analysis may be found in situations where compelling Ames to perform would be unconscionable as in situations where Barnes would be an insolvent buyer and where Ames is likely to lose the goods shipped to such a buyer.[556] The RESTATEMENT 2d would permit relief for Ames where unconscionability is shown.[557] If, however, a buyer is insolvent, query, does such a buyer have reason to believe that a party agreeing to sell to such a buyer on credit is mistaken as to the buyer's ability to pay? There is, at least, a plausible argument to this effect and it may provide relief for a seller such as Ames on the usual footing that buyer Barnes, having reason to know of such a mistake, may not "snap up the offer." If, therefore, this situation can be fitted into that generally accepted analysis, the possibility of relief for a unilateral mistake of identity where the buyer neither knows nor has reason to know of any mistake appears even more remote.

---

[553] See, e.g., Air Line Pilots Ass'n v. Shuttle, Inc., 55 F. Supp. 2d 47, 54–55 (D.D.C. 1999). See also A. J. Concrete Pumping, Inc. v. Richard O'Brien Equip. Sales, Inc., 256 Ga. 795, 353 S.E.2d 496 (1987). RESTATEMENT 2d § 155 comment b.

[554] See RESTATEMENT 2d § 158.

[555] In a well-known case, the court adopts this analysis on the basis of § 503 of the FIRST RESTATEMENT (ill. 2), but then finds a "solvent," i.e., that an offer can be accepted only by the party to whom it is made. See Nutmeg State Mach. Corp. v. Shuford, 129 Conn. 659, 30 A.2d 911 (1943). While it cannot be gainsaid that an offer can be accepted only by the party to whom it is made (because the offeror creates a power of acceptance only in the offeree), if offeror Ames reasonably appears to make an offer to offeree Barnes, Barnes has a power of acceptance, i.e., he would not have such a power only if he knew or had reason to know that he was not an offeree. See RESTATEMENT 2d § 52 comment b. See Boulton v. Jones, 2 H. & N. 564 (Ex. 1857), and In re Gendron, 13 F.2d 263 (D. Mass. 1926). See also Williams, Mistake as to Party in the Law of Contracts, (Pt. II), 23 CAN. B. REV. 380, 383–97 (1945).

[556] As to the seller's difficulty of an action in reclamation in such a case, see In re Samuels & Co., 510 F.2d 139, rev'd en banc, 526 F.2d 1238 (5th Cir. 1976), cert. denied, 429 U.S. 834, 97 S. Ct. 98, 50 L. Ed. 2d 99 (1976).

[557] RESTATEMENT 2d § 153.

[G]   Mistake of Subject Matter

Among the numerous cases involving a mistake of subject matter are those in which the buyer makes a unilateral mistake and the seller neither knows nor has reason to know of the mistake. Thus, where a buyer sent its agent to inspect a used dredge and then decided to purchase it, the buyer could not avoid the contract when it later determined that the dredge was not suited to its needs.[558] Since law students and some lawyers may have difficulty envisioning the operation of a dredge, a simple illustration may be even more compelling. If a buyer tells a store clerk that the buyer wishes to purchase a displayed item, the clerk will typically provide the purchaser with the same item in a sealed container rather than the sample on display. If the purchaser returns within a few days announcing that the product "doesn't work," and responds to the clerk's inquiry of the nature of the defect with, "I plug it in, press the buttons and talk into it but it doesn't record," the buyer may be startled to hear the clerk's retort: "That's because it's a word processor." If the reasonable buyer should have known that the displayed item was a word processor and not a tape recorder because it had all of the normal appearance of a word processor, he has made a unilateral mistake of subject matter for which relief should not be granted.[559] Similarly, where the seller thought it was selling 21 or 22 acres of land but agreed upon the insertion of a clause as to another tract of land as part of the sale and later learned that the contract required the conveyance of some thirty-five acres, relief on the basis of unilateral mistake of the subject matter was denied because the mistake was not sufficiently grave as to cause an unconscionable result.[560]

If the mistake as to subject matter is mutual, courts are willing to grant relief since the mistake, albeit as to a basic assumption made at the time of contract formation, need only have a material effect upon the agreed exchange, i.e., an unconscionable effect absent relief need not be shown where the mistake is mutual. Thus, as suggested earlier, where the parties agreed to buy and sell property which they later discover cannot be used for the purpose both intended because of a mutual mistake as to a basic assumption at the time of contract formation which has a material effect upon the agreed exchange, the contract is voidable.

[H]   Computation Mistakes — Erroneous Bids

In making an offer to supply a number of items or different services, a party may make a mistake in the computation of the total price or in omitting an item that should have been included in the computation. If the offeree neither knows nor has reason to know that the total price is predicated upon a faulty computation and accepts at the stated price, should the offeror be bound to a contract at that price, notwithstanding the relatively innocent computation error? There is not mistake in the offer in such situations. The offeror *intended* to make the offer at the price stated, i.e., his mistake was not one of expressing a price he did not intend. Rather, his mistake was antecedent to the making of the offer. Unless the offeree is or should have been aware of the mistake, the acceptance of the offer manifests the mutual assent to form a contract. The only question is whether relief will be granted because of the

---

[558] Anderson Bros. Corp. v. O'Meara, 306 F.2d 672 (5th Cir. 1962).

[559] There is nothing unconscionable about compelling the buyer to pay for the word processor. On the other hand, a store may have a policy of returning the purchase price in such a transaction notwithstanding no legal compulsion to do so. Of course, if the policy creates a course of dealing, the store may be legally compelled to return the purchase price regardless of the lack of any defect in the product sold.

[560] Montgomery v. Strickland, 384 So. 2d 1085 (Ala. 1980).

unilateral mistake of the offeror in miscomputing or omitting an item in totaling the offer before it was made.

The situation typically arises in submitting bids in construction contracts. A bidder on such a project is typically required to submit a bid bond which promises to pay the difference between its bid and the next higher bid should the bidder refuse to perform the contract with the owner. Since the mistake involved in such cases is unilateral, relief will be granted only if (a) the mistake is material, (b) enforcement of the contract pursuant to the erroneous bid would be unconscionable, (c) the mistake was the type of mistake that a reasonable person would make rather than "culpable negligence," (d) the non-mistaken party will not be prejudiced by granting relief, and (e) prompt notice of the mistake is given. If these requirements are met, there are a substantial number of cases granting relief for such a computational (clerical) mistake which does not rise to the level of "culpable negligence."[561] As in other questions concerning the element of materiality, there is no specific number or percentage that can be provided as a litmus test. Cases dealing with this question have found the computation or omission mistake to be material where the percentage of total bid affected by the mistake is as low as three and one-half percent.[562] Normally, however, the percentage has to be considerably higher.[563] A relatively small percentage of a very large total bid may still result in the a substantial loss for the bidder.[564] The amount to be lost by the bidder is relevant concerning the element of unconscionability. Thus, if a bidder omits a $25,000 item in a $100,000 bid, it may appear to be a material mistake. If, however, the bid included a $50,000 profit the only hardship on the bidder would be a reduction in its profit to $25,000 and there would be no unconscionability in the enforcement of the contract.[565] Assuming a material effect upon the agreed exchange that would cause an unconscionable result, the mistake will still not serve as the basis for contract avoidance if the bidder is clearly careless in his creation of the bid. On the other hand, where the bidder may operates within the zone of reasonableness of reasonable businesses which, on occasion, suffer computation mistakes, such a computational error will not be fatal.[566] Even where the foregoing elements are met, there is concern for the possible hardship to the other party to the contract. If the only complaint from the owner is that it will not gain the advantage of what appears to be a bargain that would be clearly inequitable to the bidder, the contract may be avoided by the bidder.[567]

---

[561] See Boise Junior College Dist. v. Mattefs Constr. Co., 92 Idaho 757, 450 P.2d 604 (1969). *Accord* First Baptist Church v. Barber Contracting Co., 189 Ga. App. 804, 377 S.E.2d 717 (1989); National Fire Ins. Co. of Hartford v. Brown & Martin Co., Inc., 726 F. Supp. 1036 (D.S.C. 1989), *aff'd per curiam*, 907 P.2d 1139 (4th Cir. 1990); Alaska Int'l Constr. v. Earth Movers, 697 P.2d 626 (Alaska 1985).

[562] *See* Smith & Lowe Constr. Co. v. Herrera, 79 N.M. 239, 442 P.2d 197 (1968).

[563] *See Alaska Int'l Constr., Inc.*, *supra* note 561, where the court held that two and one-half percent of the total bid was insufficient to meet the materiality requirement, setting forth (note 8) a comprehensive list of cases where the percentages were deemed material.

[564] Devils Lake v. St. Paul Fire & Marine Ins. Co., 497 F. Supp. 595 (D.N.D. 1980) (4 ½% error where bidder would lose a considerable sum was deemed material).

[565] This is the example suggested in the *Boise* case, *supra* note 561. *See also* RESTATEMENT 2d § 153 ills. 1 and 2.

[566] *See* M. F. Kemper Constr. Co. v. City of Los Angeles, 37 Cal. 2d 696, 235 P.2d 7 (1951). See also Regional Sch. Dist. No. 4 v. United Pac. Ins., 4 Conn. App. 175, 493 A.2d 895, 897 (1985), where the court rejects the suggestion that there must be an absence of negligence in order to permit rescission of the contract due to the bidder's error. Rather, the court suggests that the true criterion is the achievement of equity under all of the circumstances.

[567] *See* Florsheim Co. v. Miller, 575 F. Supp. 84, 85 (E.D. Tex. 1983) (suggesting that rescission of the contract will be granted if the parties can be returned to *status quo ante*, i.e., defendant will not be prejudiced except by loss of its bargain — applying Texas law).

If, on the other hand, the owner has justifiably and substantially relied on the mistaken bid and will suffer a significant loss if the contract is not performed at the mistaken price, as between the mistaken bidder and the innocent owner, the owner should prevail. To guard against such reliance, courts add a requirement of prompt notification of the mistake to the owner. This, however, is not a separate requirement since prompt notice is a factor with respect to the fourth criterion of damage to the offeree-owner.[568] The question of prompt notice, however, may be seen as a manifestation of diligence by the bidder to overcome the effect of his mistake at the earliest opportunity.[569]

Though the case law suggests relief for a bidder when all of the elements are met, there are a number of older cases enforcing such contracts against the mistaken bidder. There can be no question that a contract between the mistaken bidder and the owner exists and should be enforced where the elements for the mistaken bidder's relief are not present. The case law, therefore, must be carefully considered to determine whether those elements exist. If all of the elements for relief exists, it is likely that a modern court will grant that relief.

[I]   Mistake of Value — Rose 2d of Aberlone

A purchaser of stock may hope that the value of the security will increase. If it does, she reaps the benefits of her wise purchase; if it decreases, she has assumed the risk of devaluation and suffers the loss. A seller of land may be distressed to learn that the new owner has discovered valuable mineral deposits. A buyer of goods agrees to pay what appears to be a low price until the buyer discovers that the market price has fallen. Any number of other illustrations could be provided to support the generally accepted view that, in the absence of fraud, misrepresentation or actual or presumed knowledge of the mistake on the part of the non-mistaken party, or contrary agreement between the parties, including any course of dealing or trade usage, *risks of value are normally assumed by the parties to the contract.* Any other rule would be entirely unworkable. Courts would be besieged by petitions for relief from contracts that proved less valuable than the prediction of one of the parties. One of the fundamental precepts of contract law is that courts will not inquire into the "adequacy of consideration," i.e., the relative values exchanged. We saw that predictions are necessarily fraught with peril and our law takes the position that contracting parties ought to be aware of that peril and the genuine possibility of a change in circumstances that will reduce the value of their bargains. We also saw that courts will allocate the risk of a mistake to a party who should have assumed that risk, as in the case involving the purchase and sale of a stone, the value of which was consciously unknown by either party.[570]

The best known case dealing with mistake of value involves a contract for the sale of a cow named Rose 2d of Aberlone.[571] Walker was a breeder of cattle and sold Rose 2d of Aberlone to Sherwood, a banker. The court found that both parties believed that Rose was sterile and the purchase price of $80 reflected that belief. When Walker discovered that Rose was fertile, he refused to deliver her because she was worth some $750. Sherwood brought an action to replevy Rose and the court held for Walker on the curious ground that Rose was not in fact

---

[568] *See Boise, supra* note 561.

[569] *See Regional Sch. Dist. No. 4 v. United Pac. Ins., supra* note 566.

[570] See text at note 511 *supra.*

[571] Sherwood v. Walker, 66 Mich. 568, 33 N.W. 919 (1887). Professor Brainerd Currie created a ballad concerning Rose of Aberlone which appeared in the Harvard Law School Record, March 4, 1954.

the animal, or the kind of animal, that Walker intended to sell or Sherwood intended to buy since a breeding cow is a substantially different creature from a barren cow. Such a metaphysical explanation fails as a reliable analysis.

The RESTATEMENT 2d provides little additional assistance. It mentions the famous case involving Rose as an analogy relating to an illustration where A agrees to assign to B for $100 a $10,000 debt owed to A by C who is insolvent. A and B believe the debt to be unsecured and, therefore, worthless. In fact it is secured by stock worth some $5000. The illustration concludes that the contract is voidable by A.[572] It is difficult to understand why the contract should be voidable by A in this illustration any more than the holding that Walker need not surrender Rose. Rose was the same cow that the parties had in mind. The mistake was as to a quality of the cow.[573] In the case involving the sale of a stone that turned out to be an uncut diamond, the same analysis may appear to apply.[574] In the stone case, however, there was a conscious assumption of the risk of value, i.e., both parties expressed their ignorance as to the value of the stone. Thus, whatever its real value, the risks to each party were consciously assumed. In the case of Rose, the parties believed that the value was exclusively the value of a barren cow. The result in that case may, therefore, be justified on the basis that the parties either manifested an intention to bear no risk beyond the risk that the value of the cow would be that of a barren cow, or, in the absence of such manifested intention, the circumstances made it reasonable for a court to conclude that the seller should not bear that risk. Professor Corbin reminds us that the court's judgment is a judgment on a matter of fact, not a judgment of law. Thus, "No rule of thumb should be constructed for cases of this kind."[575]

A modern illustration appears in *Estate of Nelson v. Rice*[576] where two paintings were sold at an estate sale for $60. Though the buyer dabbled in art, he was not an "educated purchaser." The representatives of the estate had hired an appraiser for the sale, but the appraiser had informed them that she did not appraise fine art and, if she saw any, they would need to hire an additional appraiser. Since the appraiser did not report any fine art, they proceeded with the sale absent further expert advice. The paintings were discovered to be the product of artist Martin Johnson Heade which were sold for the buyer at a Christie's auction for over a million dollars. The court held that the Estate bore the risk of the mistake in value under § 154(b) of the Restatement 2d since the representatives of the Estate were aware at the time the contract was made that they had only limited knowledge concerning the facts to which the mistake related. Their appraiser confessed to know nothing about fine art, but they nonetheless relied on her to discover fine art that would have to be appraised by another qualified appraiser. Thus, the representatives consciously ignored the possibility that the Estate assets might include fine art. By proceeding with the sale with such conscious ignorance, they bore the risk of the mistake. The court also noted § 154(c) in recognizing that a court may allocate the risk to a party on the ground that such an allocation is reasonable. Since the Estate had ample opportunity to discover the value of what it was selling, the Estate

---

[572] RESTATEMENT 2d § 152 ill. 5. The other relevant RESTATEMENT 2d concept is that which has already been explored, i.e., the necessity for courts on occasion to allocate the risk of mistake in a manner reasonable under the circumstances. *See* RESTATEMENT 2d § 154(c) discussed at text, *supra* note 513 *et seq.*

[573] *See* Hecht v. Batcheller, 147 Mass. 335, 17 N.E. 651 (1888) (parties made no mistake as to subject matter but rather its quality).

[574] *See* Wood v. Boynton, 64 Wis. 265, 25 N.W. 42 (1885), discussed at text, *supra* note 511.

[575] 3 CORBIN § 605, at 643 (1963 ed.).

[576] 12 P. 3d 238 (Ariz. Ct. App. 2000).

was a "victim of its own folly," thereby making the allocation risk to the Estate reasonable.

[J]   Mistake by an Intermediary

Where an offer is transmitted through an intermediary such as the telegraph and the message received by the offeree is not the message sent, but the offeree has no reason to believe a mistake has occurred and purports to accept the offer, is a contract formed? If the offer is sent at $10 million but transmitted at $9 million, which the offeree may assume is a reasonable and not mistaken amount, if a court finds a contract between the parties, what is the critical price term, $9 million or $10 million? The case law is neither voluminous nor recent but does suggest several views.

First, there is a fictitious agency view that binds the offeror because its agent, the telegraph company, made the mistake in transmission and the principal is liable for the mistakes of its agent.[577] An even worse fiction is that the telegraph company is a special agent which has exceeded its authority in transmitting an incorrect message and the offeree deals with a special agent at the offeree's peril.[578] A third view, represented by the best-known case in this area,[579] is much more sensible. It recognizes the innocence of both offeror and offeree and does not resort to the absurdity of treating the telegraph or other intermediary as an agent. As between these two innocent parties, the court chooses the party who selected the telegraph as the means of communication as the party to bear the loss.[580] Yet, even this analysis limps considerably. The party who chose the means of transmission may have done so casually and reasonably. Moreover, though the court uses the term "first proposer" to characterize the party who will bear the risk of transmission,[581] it is not clear that the court necessarily means "offeror" by "proposer." Suppose one party (a future offeree) chooses the telegraph medium to inquire as to price or other information concerning a potential contract. The response is an offer which is incorrectly transmitted but innocently accepted by the offeree. Is the offeree the "proposer" since he happened to select the telegram as the medium of communication, or is the offeror the "proposer" since only offers create legal powers and the offer was the first incorrectly transmitted message?

The notion that the party who chooses the medium must bear the risk is a slender reed. As between the two innocent parties, it makes much more sense to recognize that there is a complete albeit innocent absence of mutual assent. If an offeror seeks to contract at a price ($10 million) which the offeree may or may not have found acceptable, the offeree has not assented to that price if he can demonstrate conclusively that he agreed to purchase only at $9 million. It is preferable to find no contract in these circumstances.[582] Another famous case, albeit not involving the telegraph, supports this analysis.

---

[577] *See* Des Arc Oil Mill, Inc. v. Western Union Tel. Co., 132 Ark. 335, 201 S.W. 273, 6 A.L.R. 1081 (1918). The same analysis has been applied for a mistake by an interpreter, Bonelli v. Burton, 61 Or. 429, 123 P. 37 (1912).

[578] *See* Postal Tel. Cable Co. v. Schaefer, 110 Ky. 907, 62 S.W. 1119 (1901); Henkel v. Pape, L.R. 6 Ex. 7 [1870].

[579] Ayer v. Western Union Tel. Co., 79 Me. 493, 10 A. 495 (1887).

[580] "The first proposer can select one of many modes of communication, both for the proposal and the answer. The receiver has no such choice, except as to his answer. If he cannot safely act upon the message, he receives through the agency selected by the proposer, business must be seriously hampered and delayed." *Id.* at 497.

[581] *Id.*

[582] *See, e.g.*, Murray Oil Prods. Co. v. Poons Co., 190 Misc. 110, 74 N.Y.S.2d 814 (City Ct. 1947), *aff'd*, 191 Misc. 1005, 80 N.Y.S.2d 28 (App. Term 1948); Holtz v. Western Union Tel Co., 294 Mass. 543, 3 N.E.2d 180 (1936).

A landowner and building contractor signed what they innocently believed were duplicate copies of a contract for the construction of a Turkish bath house. The architect provided the copies to each party and fraudulently stated the amount on the owner's copy at $23,000 and $34,000 on the contractor's copy. The court held that there was no mutual assent since both parties assumed they were contracting at the respective amounts they intended. Since the price differential was not discovered until the building was substantially completed, the court allowed the builder to recover its restitution interest in quasi contract measured by the reasonable value of the benefit conferred upon the owner, which turned out to be close to the amount the contractor expected to receive under the non-existing contract.[583] While this case involved fraud by the intermediary and the telegraph cases involve only negligence by the intermediary, in either situation there is a total lack of mutual assent which precludes the finding of any contract between the parties. The demise of the telegram as a medium of communication has left the cupboard barren of recent cases dealing with mistakes by an intermediary.[584]

[K]   Releases — "Unknown Injury" Rule

If a party has a claim against another party, he may agree to release that claim in exchange for certain consideration. In an earlier chapter concerning the validation process, we noted how strongly our courts have favored settlements of such claims, even to the point of treating forbearance to sue on an invalid claim as consideration to support the promise received in exchange for such forbearance.[585] In agreeing to such a settlement, the claimant often signs a *release* designed to protect the other party from any and all claims which might have otherwise been asserted against him by the claimant. Subsequently, the former claimant may discover a claim that was unknown at the time he signed the release, or he may discover that the nature or extent of his claim was unknown at the time he signed the release. He may, therefore, seek rescission or avoidance of the release agreement on the basis of mistake. While the problems in this area may involve any kind of claim, they are particularly significant with respect to personal injury claims and the courts have not been consistent in their approach to these problems.

If a claimant signs a release at a time when he assumes that he suffers from a particular injury and later discovers that the nature or extent of the same injury is greater than he had originally assumed, most of our courts will not permit him to avoid the release on the basis of his mistake.[586] If, however, a different injury discovered after the execution of the release was unknown as contrasted with the discovery of unknown consequences of injuries known at the

---

[583] Vickery v. Ritchie, 202 Mass. 247, 88 N. E. 835 (1909).

[584] In Donovan v. RRL Corporation., 109 Cal. Rptr. 2d 807, 27 P. 3d 702 (2001) an automobile dealer's advertisement in a local newspaper listed a 1995 Jaguar automobile for sale at the mistaken price $25,995 rather than $37,995. The newspaper had made the mistake in assembling the advertisement. Under a vehicle code regulating licensed auto dealers, the advertisement was viewed as an offer. The plaintiff tendered the advertised price, but the dealer refused to accept it. The California Supreme Court found that a contract had been formed but could be rescinded on the basis of unilateral mistake. Though the mistake was made by the newspaper, the court treated it as a mistake by the dealer and proceeded to a unilateral mistake analysis under the Restatement 2d of Contracts, § 153 finding all of the elements in the facts before it to allow a rescission of the contract.

[585] See Restatement 2d § 74 and the treatment of this concept *supra* Chapter 3.

[586] *See, e.g.*, Dustin v. Union Pac. R.R., 109 Idaho 361, 707 P.2d 472 (Ct. App. 1985). *See also* CONRAIL v. Portlight, Inc., 188 F.3d 93, 97 (3d Cir. 1999) ("[A] party who underestimates the future severity of her injuries will not be permitted to avoid the consequences of a settlement agreement based on mutual mistake. This is entirely consistent

time of the release, the overwhelming majority of our courts apply what has become known as the "unknown injury" rule, which permits avoidance of the release on the basis of this kind of mistake.[587] The form of the release signed by the claimant will have an effect on this analysis. Thus, some courts will refuse to permit a release agreement to be avoided or rescinded if the release document clearly and explicitly discharges liability for both known and unknown injuries.[588] Other courts have held that such clear and explicit language does not necessarily preclude avoidance of a release because such all-inclusive language is often standardized and may not be consciously adverted to by the claimant.[589] This is another manifestation of courts disregarding certain printed form (boilerplate) language in agreements as conclusive. One court has declined to follow either of these approaches and adopted the view that it must consider the intent of the parties to be inferred from all of the circumstances of the agreement, including, but not limited to, the language of the release.[590]

There is no parol evidence bar to the admission of such evidence.[591] If a claimant signed a release when he was consciously ignorant of his injuries, the risk of exacerbation of those injuries or even unknown injuries (where the release contemplated unknown injuries) will be allocated to the claimant.[592] The RESTATEMENT 2d focuses upon the basic assumptions of the parties at the time of the release and, in particular, suggests that the following circumstances be considered: the fair amount required to compensate the claimant for his known injuries, the probability that the other party would be liable on such a claim, the amount actually received by the claimant under the release, and the relationship between the known and unknown injuries.[593]

The RESTATEMENT 2d properly suggests that express provisions in releases that are all inclusive concerning known and unknown injuries may be judicially disregarded as

---

with the more general principle of mutual mistake doctrine that erroneous predictions of future events do not qualify as a mistake") (citing RESTATEMENT 2d § 151, cmt. a).

[587] See La Fleur v. C.C. Pierce Co., 398 Mass. 254, 496 N.E.2d 827 (1986), and cases cited therein.

[588] See, e.g., Hybarger v. American States Ins. Co., 498 N.E.2d 1015 (Ind. Ct. App. 1986) (holding agreement not voidable where the release document was captioned, "FULL AND FINAL RELEASE," and by its terms released the defendant from all claims and causes of action and all other loss and damage of every kind and nature caused by or resulted or hereafter resulting to the claimant from a particular accident, even though the release did not specify "unknown" or "unforeseen" injuries). See also Gecy v. Prudential Ins. Co., 273 S.C. 437, 257 S.E.2d 709, 712 (1979) (release included subsequently discovered unknown injuries). But see Wicker v. CONRAIL, 142 F.3d 690 (3d Cir.), cert. denied, 525 U.S. 1012, 119 S. Ct. 530, 142 L. Ed. 2d 440 (1998) (contrasting releases governed by the FELA and non-FELA releases).

[589] See, e.g., Mangini v. McClurg, 24 N.Y.2d 556, 564, 249 N.E.2d 386 (1969).

[590] See La Fleur v. C.C. Pierce Co., supra note 587. Wild v. Minntech Corp., 1999 U.S. App. LEXIS 19292, at *7(8th Cir. Aug. 13, 1999), Minnesota courts consider the following factors to determine the validity of a release: (a) the length of period between the injury and the settlement; (b) the amount of time elapsed between the settlement and the attempt to avoid the settlement; (c) the presence or absence of independent medical advice of plaintiff's own choice before and at the time of the settlement; (d) the presence or absence of legal counsel of plaintiff's own choice before and at the time of the settlement; (e) the language of the release itself; (f) the adequacy of the consideration; (g) the competence of the releasor; and (h) whether the injury complained of by the releasor was an unknown injury at the time of the signing of the release or merely a consequence flowing from a known injury.

[591] For this proposition, the court in LaFleur cites Mickelson v. Barnet, 390 Mass. 786, 792, 460 N.E.2d 566 (1984).

[592] See Hoggatt v. Jorgensen, 43 Wash. App. 782, 719 P.2d 602 (1986), aff'd, en banc, 108 Wash. 2d 386, 739 P.2d 648 (1987).

[593] RESTATEMENT 2d § 152 comment f.

unconscionable if that language appears inconsistent with the basic assumption of the parties at the time of the release.[594]

---

[594] *Id.*

Chapter 6

ABUSE OF BARGAIN, UNCONSCIONABILITY, GOOD FAITH, AND ILLEGALITY

§ 93   INTRODUCTION — RELATION AMONG CONCEPTS EVIDENCING AN ABUSE OF THE BARGAINING PROCESS

In the last two chapters, we distinguished expressions of assent that were operative from those that were inoperative, i.e., having no legal effects. We saw expressions of assent deemed inoperative because of the statute of frauds, the parol evidence rule, the interpretation process or because of a mutual or unilateral mistake. Concepts to be explored in this chapter could also be grouped under the same caption, "operative expressions of assent," since we will analyze how courts decide that certain expressions of agreement will or will not be legally recognized. The focus, however, will be on *abuses* of the bargaining process that may have the effect of rendering certain apparent manifestations of agreement inoperative.

We will consider these abuses from the egregious to the subtle. The compelling example of the most egregious abuse of the bargaining process is a manifestation of assent induced by physical compulsion, such as a writing signed by a party at the point of a gun or other physical force. The circumstances under which such a writing is signed belies the apparent manifestation of assent by the victim of the *duress*. It is the antithesis of volition and assent. Courts have no difficulty in treating such cases as involving no contract at all, i.e., there is no need for the abused party to exercise a power of avoidance or disaffirmance to avoid the contract. An agreement induced by duress never was a contract. Lesser forms of duress involve improper threats that are sufficiently grave to induce assent by the victim of the threat. Here, courts will view the agreement as a contract that is voidable by the victim. In a rare situation, the victim may choose to have the contract enforced against the party committing duress.

In the absence of duress, one party may induce the assent of another by misleading the other. Such *misrepresentation* permits the other party to avoid the contract, again making the apparent manifestation of agreement inoperative. Where neither duress nor misrepresentation can be shown, one party may be in a position to exert *undue influence* upon another, thereby inducing assent to an unfair transaction where the adversely affected party falls victim to the improper persuasion of the other. Again, the victim may avoid the contract. Where duress, misrepresentation or undue influence cannot be established, if a court deems a contract or particular terms thereof to be *unconscionable*, it will refuse operative effect to that contract or certain terms of the contract. The concept of unconscionability is amorphous. It has all of the qualities of the even broader concept of "justice." It is often suggested that "justice" does not admit of anything resembling a precise definition.[1] On the other hand, manifest injustice can often be discerned quite easily. Similarly, unconscionability may be detected in a given situation though the court may be hard pressed to suggest the parameters of the concept.[2] A similarly elusive concept is the pervasive concept of *good faith* which is implied in all contracts.[3] Where there is no duress, misrepresentation, undue influence or unconscionability, the absence of good faith will permit a court to refuse to enforce all or part of a contract, i.e., a court will deem the parties' expression of agreement to be inoperative because one of the parties has not performed in good faith. Finally, even where there is no lack of good faith and no evidence of duress, misrepresentation, undue influence, or unconscionability, certain agreements of the parties may be deemed unenforceable because they violate what is, perhaps, the most elusive standard called "*public policy.*" The nebulous nature of "public policy" has long been recognized.[4] Yet, courts have confronted the necessity of deciding whether a particular agreement exceeds the bounds of public policy where, for example, enforcement of a contract would violate a statutory or common law standard.

A court may refuse to enforce the entire bargain between the parties, or it may decide that the agreement may be enforced after surgically removing the portion of the agreement that violates a pervasive standard in society. In either event, the court is, again, deciding which manifestations of agreement shall or shall not be operative. These and related problems will be explored in the portion of this chapter dealing with "*illegal bargains.*"

---

[1] A classic definition is the product of Ulpian, a second century Roman jurist, who suggested that justice means to render to each his due. Such a cryptic description is not unlike many other tautological efforts.

[2] See, e.g., Jones v. Star Credit Corp., 59 Misc. 2d 189, 298 N.Y.S.2d 264 (1969), where the court suggests that deciding that unconscionability exists in a given situation is substantially easier than explaining it.

[3] For a courageous effort to analyze the concept of good faith, see Summers, "*Good Faith" in General Contract Law and the Sales Provisions of the Uniform Commercial Code*, 54 VA. L. REV. 195 (1968).

[4] "I, for one, protest . . . against arguing too strongly upon public policy: — it is a very unruly horse, and when once you get astride it you never know where it will carry you. It may lead you from the sound law. It is never argued at all but when other points fail." Justice Burrough in Richardson v. Mellish, 2 Bing. 229, 252 (C.P. 1824). On the general subject, see Percy H. Winfield, *Public Policy in the English Common Law*, 42 HARV. L. REV. 76 (1928).

§ 94 DURESS

[A] Duress — Types — Threats — Physical Compulsion — "Void" vs. "Voidable"

Courts generally recognize two types of duress. Where a party is physically compelled to manifest assent to an agreement, the agreement is not a contract because the agreement is rendered *void* by such action.[5] If there is no physical compulsion but improper threats are made that leaves the victim no reasonable alternative but to sign a contract, the contract is *voidable*.[6] "Improper threats" include threats of a crime or tort, criminal prosecution, the threat of civil process made in bad faith, or a threat constituting a breach of the duty of good faith and fair dealing.[7]

If a party is compelled to manifest assent by physical force where, for example, his hand is physically forced to sign a document or where he signs at gunpoint or another physical threat, it is clear that the signature does not manifest assent since the signer had no intention of performing the act. The phrase often quoted is that the compelled party is "a mere mechanical instrument"[8] operating as a robot controlled by physical means. Since such a signature is not an effective manifestation of assent, there is no assent and there is no contract. Such physical compulsion creates a *void* contract rather than a *voidable* contract. A *void* contract is a contradiction since there is no assent and no contract ever existed. A *voidable* contract, however, is perfectly valid though the party with the power of avoidance or disaffirmance may exercise that power to avoid it. If a check is signed at gunpoint, the check is void, i.e., the party signing the check (the drawer) will have a defense even against a subsequent party who takes the check in good faith, for value and without notice of any defenses to the instrument.[9] If, however, the duress is lesser in degree as where an instrument is signed under a threat to prosecute a relative of the signer for theft, the instrument may be merely voidable.[10]

Whether duress by physical compulsion is exercised by the other party to the purported contract or by a third person, the effect is the same, i.e., there can be no contract since the agreement is void.[11] A party who appears to manifest assent will not be held to have manifested an operative (legally effective) assent if such a manifestation has been induced by sufficient control over his consciousness. Thus, one who is hypnotized or under the influence of a mind controlling drug may not be responsible for a manifestation of assent, i.e., though his

---

[5] Restatement 2d § 174. The phrase "void ab initio" (void from the inception) is redundant but continues to appear. During the twelve months prior to the completion of this treatise, it appeared 600 times in the case law.

[6] Restatement 2d § 175. See Resolution Trust Corp. v. A.W. Assocs., Inc., 869 F. Supp. 1503, 1511 (D. Kan. 1994), where the court makes this distinction.

[7] *See* Shufford v. Integon Indem. Corp., 73 F. Supp. 2d 1293, 1298 (M.D. Ala. 1999) (quoting Restatement 2d § 176).

[8] *See* Restatement 2d § 174 comment a.

[9] UCC § 3-305(a)(1)(ii). The defense is often characterized as a "real" defense which is available even against a holder in due course, defined in the UCC at § 3-302(a).

[10] See UCC § 3-305 comment 1, which suggests this example and concludes that, if the instrument is merely voidable, the defense would not be available against the holder in due course described in the preceding note.

[11] Restatement 2d § 174 comment b. See, however, United States use of Trane Co. v. Bond, 322 Md. 170, 182, 586 A.2d 734, 740 (1991), where the court suggests that the Restatement 2d § 174 test of "physical compulsion" may be too narrow. The court suggests that a contract may be deemed void where "in addition to physical compulsion, a threat of imminent physical violence is exerted upon the victim of such magnitude as to cause a reasonable person, in the circumstances, to fear loss of life, or serious physical injury, or actual imprisonment for refusal to sign the document."

conduct appears to suggest assent, he does not voluntarily create that impression of assent.[12]

[B]   Duress by Threat — Improper Threat in General

A threat is an expression of intention to injure another.[13] The expression may be by words or conduct. If one person commits a battery against another or imprisons another, the victim's fear of further blows or imprisonment will constitute duress.[14] Promises induced by threats of violence must be unenforceable so as to discourage such threats.[15] On the other hand, if Ames is desirous of purchasing an automobile from Barnes and Barnes will not sell unless Ames pays what Ames views as an excessive price, Ames may characterize Barnes' demand as a threat. Any offer could be viewed as a threat not to make a contract unless the offeree acquiesces in the terms of the offer.[16] "Driving a hard bargain" is commonplace in numerous negotiations.[17] On the day prior to the wedding, insisting that the bride sign a prenuptial agreement as a condition to marriage was held to be neither a threat nor unlawful.[18] Where, however, three days before her visa expired, a Ukranian plaintiff whose English was very poor was told by her future husband that marriage was conditioned on her signing a prenuptial agreement or being sent back to her country. As the husband knew, she was pregnant with his child, had no means of support and would have been forced to return to the Ukraine. The court found the prenuptial agreement had been signed under duress.[19] Even if a demand could be called a "threat," it does not necessarily amount to duress.[20] As is so often the case, the question becomes, at what point does a party step over the line separating the legitimate, though perhaps harsh, demand from the demand which should be viewed as illegitimate? The line is not bright; it is wavering and blurred. The ancient common law view relegated the type of threat necessary to show duress to loss of life, loss of a member, mayhem or imprisonment.[21] The modern position has greatly enlarged the categories of threats that may cause duress. The difficulty of providing an appropriate characterization of the type of threat that modern courts regard as a *sine qua non* to a finding of duress is implicit in the current

---

[12] See RESTATEMENT 2d § 19(2) and comment c thereto, suggesting that a manifestation of assent is not the mere appearance of assent if the party is not responsible for that appearance. "There must be conduct and a conscious will to engage in that conduct."

[13] *In re* Zardies B., 64 Cal. App. 3d 11, 14, 134 Cal. Rptr. 181, 182 (4th Dist. 1976), the court repeated a definition of "threat" as found in WEBSTER'S THIRD NEW INTERNATIONAL DICTIONARY: "expression of an intention to inflict evil, injury or damage on another, usually as retribution or punishment" and an "expression of intention to inflict loss or harm on another by illegal means and especially by means involving coercion or duress of the person threatened."

[14] *See* RESTATEMENT 2d § 175 comment a. See also Polito v. Polito, 121 A.D.2d 614, 503 N.Y.S.2d 867 (2d Dep't 1986), where a former wife had been battered by her former husband on many occasions and was in fear of further physical abuse when she succumbed and signed a release.

[15] *See* Selmer Co. v. Blakeslee-Midwest Co., 704 F.2d 924, 927 (7th Cir. 1983).

[16] RESTATEMENT 2d § 176 comment a.

[17] "Hard bargaining . . . [is] acceptable . . . in our economic system." Rich & Whillock, Inc. v. Ashton Dev., Inc., 157 Cal. App. 3d 1154, 1159, 204 Cal. Rptr. 86, 89 (4th Dist. 1984).

[18] Miller v. Miller, 2002 Iowa App. LEXIS 1103 (Iowa App. Oct. 15, 2002).

[19] Holler v. Holler, 612 S. E. 2d 469 (S. C. Ct. App. 2005).

[20] Coca-Cola Bottling Co. v. Coca-Cola Co., 769 F. Supp. 671, 738–39 (D. Del. 1991), *cert. denied*, 510 U.S. 908, 114 S. Ct. 289, 126 L. Ed. 2d 239 (1993).

[21] *See* E. COKE, SECOND INSTITUTE 482–83 (1642). *See also* Rubenstein v. Rubenstein, 20 N.J. 359, 120 A.2d 11, 14 (1956).

characterization that the threat must be *improper*.[22] The First Restatement test required the victim to be precluded from the exercise of free will and judgment.[23] The Second Restatement, however, states that a contract is voidable by a victim whose manifestation of assent has been induced by an improper threat if the victim has no reasonable alternative.[24] If only improper threats are sufficient to cause duress, it is essential to distinguish between proper and improper threats. Those who seek a litmus test to distinguish proper from improper threats will be disappointed since no such test exists. As usual, we must examine clusters of cases to determine how courts have made the distinction.

[C]   Improper Threats Not Causing Duress

If the threatened act would be a crime or a tort, the threat is improper. Thus, threats of gangster violence and arsenic poisoning are improper threats.[25] It should be emphasized that, even if the threat is a technical crime or tort and is, therefore, improper, there may be no duress because other elements of duress are absent. Thus, if the improper threat failed to induce the assent of the victim or if the victim of the threat had a reasonable alternative to succumbing to the threat, duress will not be found notwithstanding the improper threat. The plaintiff worked in a hospital where her husband, with whom she had serious marital difficulties, was the chief executive officer. The husband was involved in an affair with another employee. He presented the plaintiff with an employment separation agreement (release) allegedly threatening her with financial ruin and stating that he would "destroy her life" if she refused to sign it. She signed the release and received approximately $70,000 but claimed she had signed under duress. Citing the Restatement 2d of Contracts, § 175, comment b, the court noted that even an improper threat does not amount to duress if the victim has a reasonable alternative. Notwithstanding her emotional distress, the plaintiff testified that she knew she had two choices to either sign the agreement or to sue. "The choice of doing nothing never came up." The court held the release was valid.[26]

[D]   Threatened Act Is Proper But Threat Is Improper

The threatened act may not be wrongful, but the threat, itself, may be wrongful. Thus, where a wife claimed that she signed a settlement agreement with her husband because she feared that he might carry out his threat to inform the Internal Revenue Service of her failure to report income from her business, the court found duress.[27] The court recognized the right of the husband to turn his wife in to the IRS. His *threat* to do so for his own pecuniary advantage, however, constituted extortion under the law of that state.[28]

---

[22] A similar characterization is "wrongful." *See, e.g.*, Jones v. Jones, 276 Or. 1125, 557 P.2d 239 (1976).

[23] FIRST RESTATEMENT § 429(b).

[24] RESTATEMENT 2d § 175(1). See Gilbert v. Baltimore County, 2000 U.S. App. LEXIS 23951 (4th Cir. Aug. 15, 2000) comparing the First and Second Restatement tests. See also Barton v. Brassring, Inc., 2006 Mass. Super. LEXIS 549 at *12 (Oct. 26, 2006) where the court states the standard requiring the victim to demonstrate that he was "under the influence of such fear as precludes him from exercising free will and judgment," followed by the statement that "the availability of a reasonable alternative . . . will defeat a claim for duress" (citing Restatement 2d § 175, comment b).

[25] *See Rubenstein v. Rubenstein, supra* note 21.

[26] Gascho v. Scheurer Hospital, 2009 U.S. Dist. LEXIS 63246 (E. D. Mich. 2009).

[27] Berger v. Berger, 466 So. 2d 1149 (Fla. Dist. Ct. App. 1985).

[28] FLA. STAT. § 836.05.

[E]   Threat to Do That Which One Has Legal Right to Do — Threat of Criminal Prosecution

A threat may be neither tortious nor criminal. One of the axiomatic statements found in numerous cases is that it is never duress to threaten to do that which one has a legal right to do.[29] Like so many maxims in our law, however, this one can be misleading. Thus, a threat of criminal prosecution, whether against the other party to the agreement or a third person, is an improper threat even if the party making the threat honestly believes the threatened party to be guilty of a crime, and even if such party is guilty of the crime.[30] The honest belief (good faith) of the party making the threat is irrelevant since he is misusing, for personal gain, a power designed for other proper ends. Where a wife was told to sign two judgment notes, by the representative of her husband's former employer, one of the notes was for a definite amount while the other was a document the wife did not understand and contained no amount though the amount would later be inserted by the employer. The wife understood that signing the note would prevent her embezzler husband from going to jail. When the second judgment note was later completed by the employer and entered in judgment, the wife petitioned to open the judgment. The court found the note was signed under duress. The guilt or innocence of the person whose prosecution is threatened is irrelevant. Indeed, where the person is guilty, it may be easier to demonstrate duress. The critical issue is whether the promisor (wife) had any reasonable alternative. The court found she had no reasonable alternative and her petition to open the confessed judgment was granted.[31] Modern courts have, therefore, modified the maxim that it is never improper to threaten to do that which one has a legal right to do, by carefully excepting threats of criminal prosecution and even suggesting the possibility of other exceptions.[32]

[F]   Threat of Civil Process

It is difficult to characterize a threat to institute a civil action as improper in our legal system which prides itself on free access to that system. Recall that even the assertion of claims that turn out to be invalid constitute consideration to support a promise if the assertion was made in good faith.[33] The emphasis, however, is upon the good faith assertion of such claims. Thus, if a threat is made to institute a civil action in bad faith, i.e., the party making the assertion did not believe that he had a reasonable foundation to assert the claim, the threat would be improper.[34] Similarly, if the threat to institute legal proceedings is done with an

---

[29] *See, e.g.,* Kelso v. McGowan, 604 So. 2d 726, 732 (Miss. 1992).

[30] RESTATEMENT 2d § 176 comment c. Moreover, as suggested in *Berger v. Berger, supra* note 27, the threat, itself, may constitute a crime.

[31] Germantown Mfg. Co. v. Rawlinson, 341 Pa. 42, 491 A.2d 138 (1985). Relief was available to the wife on several other grounds including fraud in the inducement since she had no basis for understanding that she was signing two judgment notes for two different (large) amounts, rather than one. See, however, Cox v. Griffin, 2006 U.S. Dist. LEXIS 26887 (W. D. Ark. 2006) where a wife claimed that a trustee in bankruptcy had induced her to surrender an emerald ring and automobile under duress since another attorney had informed her that contesting that proceeding would put her husband "at stake" in a criminal proceeding. The court noted that duress must be proven by clear, cogent and convincing evidence and there was no evidence that the trustee had made such a statement to the wife.

[32] *See, e.g.,* Internet Mgmt. Info. Sys. v. Hanes Morgan & Co., Inc., 2000 U.S. Dist. LEXIS 1509, at *10 (S.D.N.Y. Feb. 16, 2000). See also *Shufford,* note 7 *supra.*

[33] See discussion of the assertion of such invalid claims *supra* § 64, Chapter 3.

[34] *See, e.g.,* Leeper v. Beltrami, 53 Cal. 2d 195, 1 Cal. Rptr. 12, 347 P.2d 12 (1959) (extortion of funds through

intent to coerce a grossly unfair contract not related to the proceedings, the threat is improper.[35] Again, even if the threat to institute civil proceedings is improper, it will often not amount to duress because the recipient of the threat will have the reasonable alternative of defending in the threatened action.[36] The alternative of defending the threatened action, however, may not be a reasonable alternative as will be seen later in this section.

[G]　Economic Duress — Business Compulsion — Threat to Breach a Contract — Modifications Induced by Threat — Uniform Commercial Code

A party to a contract may threaten to breach it unless it is modified. In response to a claim asserted by one party, the other may threaten to pay nothing unless the first party agrees to accept only half or less of the claimed amount in settlement of the claim. Freedom of contract is favored in our society as is the desirability of settling disputes without litigation. These values have traditionally made courts reluctant to interfere with modifications or settlements and releases of claims, even those induced by a threatened breach.[37] Suing for an admittedly due debt was considered a reasonable alternative even if the plaintiff was in financial difficulty and could not practically await judicial relief.[38] Modern courts, however, recognize that there is no freedom of contract between bargaining unequals. They are much more reluctant to enforce agreements made under economically coercive circumstances.[39] For a number of years, courts have recognized a form of duress that is not dependent upon showing that the threat is tortious or criminal. A party may not avoid a contract simply because he can demonstrate that he agreed to a modification or a settlement and release because his financial situation was necessitous.[40] If, however, the financial distress was caused by the other party's conduct, duress may be shown.[41] Even where the financial distress was not caused by the other party, duress may be shown under certain circumstances. If Ames knows that she owes Barnes $157,000 and she also knows that unless Barnes receives at least $5,000 immediately, Barnes will lose certain valuable property through foreclosure proceedings, Ames knows that

---

mortgage foreclosure). In Texas, however, "the threat to institute a civil suit or even the actual institution of a suit does not, as a matter of law, constitute duress." McMahan v. Greenwood, 108 S. W. 3d 467, 483 (Tex. App. 2003).

[35] *See* Link v. Link, 278 N.C. 181, 179 S.E.2d 697 (1971) (wife confessed adultery and husband threatened to take children away unless wife transferred valuable stocks to him). The RESTATEMENT 2d would characterize such a demand as "exorbitant" and would call the threat improper because it was made in bad faith. RESTATEMENT 2d § 176 comment d.

[36] *See* RESTATEMENT 2d § 175 comment b and ill. 1.

[37] See the well-known case of Hackley v. Headley, 45 Mich. 569, 8 N.W. 511 (1881), where the defendant knew he owed the plaintiff $4,260 but also knew that the plaintiff would face financial ruin if he did not receive payment quickly. The defendant offered the plaintiff $4,000 on a take-it-or-leave-it basis and the plaintiff signed the release required by the defendant. The plaintiff then sought to avoid the release on the basis of duress and the court held that no duress had been shown.

[38] If the contract was with the government, it was early recognized that there may be no remedy since the government could raise the sovereign immunity defense. That defense, however, has been in a state of decline for a number of years. Courts also recognized that contracts with public utilities or common carriers were one-sided in that the utilities and carriers had a lawful monopoly. Thus, if a utility or a carrier induced an oppressive bargain, the other party had no reasonable alternative but to succumb.

[39] *See* Totem Marine Tug & Barge v. Alyeska Pipeline Serv. Co., 584 P.2d 15, 21 (Alaska 1978).

[40] *See* Selmer Co. v. Blakeslee-Midwest Co., 704 F.2d 924, 928 (7th Cir. 1983).

[41] "The mere stress of business conditions will not constitute duress where the defendant was not responsible for the conditions." Johnson, Drake & Piper, Inc. v. United States, 531 F.2d 1037, 1042, 209 Ct. Cl. 313, 322 (1976).

she has Barnes "over a barrel." Barnes cannot afford to await a judicial remedy to recover the acknowledged amount due. Thus, Ames offers Barnes $5,000 and demands an immediate release with the threat to pay Barnes nothing and force him to sue unless he signs the release. Barnes' signature on such a release is the antithesis of freedom of contract. The agreement is inherently coercive because Barnes was forced to accept a sum grossly disproportionate to the amount owed. There was no honest dispute about the amount owed. The debtor simply took advantage of the immediate financial necessity of the creditor. It is not remarkable that courts find duress in such cases.[42] This type of duress is not physical compulsion nor is the threat involved a tort or a crime. Yet, it is viewed as duress and often characterized as *economic duress* or *business compulsion.* "Business compulsion" should not be viewed as distinct from economic duress.[43] It is often suggested that a threat to breach a contract is not, in itself, improper.[44] Yet, if such a threat constitutes a breach of the duty of good faith and fair dealing which every contract imposes, it is improper and can, therefore, constitute the basis of avoidance for duress.[45] The classic illustration of such a breach occurred in the well-known case, *Alaska Packers' Ass'n v. Domenico,*[46] where sailors and fishermen had agreed to work for the defendant at a stated compensation in distant waters during a short fishing season. The plaintiffs knew that the defendant had a significant investment in the operation and, upon arrival at the distant location, they refused to perform their contract unless the defendant agreed to a modification through which they would receive additional compensation. The defendant agreed to the modification but refused to perform it. When plaintiffs sued for breach of the modified contract, the court held for the defendant on the basis of a lack of consideration, i.e., the pre-existing duty rule provided a technical basis for refusing to enforce the modification. There is, however, no question that the court was concerned about the coercive nature of the modification. As one court suggests:

> *Alaska Packers Ass'n* shows that because the legal remedies for breach of contract are not always adequate, a refusal to honor a contract may force the other party to the contract to surrender his rights. . . . It undermines the institution of contract to allow a contract party to use the threat of breach to get the contract modified in his favor not because anything has happened to require modification in the mutual interest of the parties but simply because the other party, unless he knuckles under to the threat, will incur costs for which he will have no adequate remedy.'[47]

As we have seen earlier in this volume, the UCC permits contract modifications without consideration if such modifications are made in good faith.[48] A comment to this section makes clear that extortionate "modifications" to escape performance of the original contract are

---

[42] The figures and other circumstances in the example are identical to those found in Capps v. Georgia-Pacific Corp., 253 Or. 248, 453 P.2d 935 (1969), where the court found duress and permitted the release to be avoided. For a similar fact situation and holding, see Rich & Whillock, Inc. v. Ashton Dev., Inc., 157 Cal. App. 3d 1154, 204 Cal. Rptr. 86 (4th Dist. 1984) ($72,286.45 admittedly due and debtor insisted that creditor sign a release in exchange for $50,000 knowing that creditor was in dire need of funds). *See also Totem Marine Tug & Barge v. Alyeska Pipeline, supra* note 39.

[43] *See* Dalzell, *Duress by Economic Pressure, I, II,* 20 N.C. L. Rev. 237, 341 (1942).

[44] *See* Restatement 2d § 176 comment e.

[45] Restatement 2d § 176(1)(d). *See* Eulrich v. Snap-On Tools Corp., 121 Or. App. 25, 853 P.2d 1350, 1354 (1993), *vacated, remanded,* 512 U.S. 1231, 114 S. Ct. 2731, 129 L. Ed. 2d 854 (1994).

[46] 117 F. 99 (9th Cir. 1902).

[47] Opinion by Posner, J., in Selmer Co. v. Blakeslee-Midwest Co., 704 F.2d 924, 927 (7th Cir. 1983).

[48] UCC § 2-209(1). *See supra* § 65[E], Chapter 3.

barred since they are, necessarily, bad faith modifications. Moreover, even a technical consideration will not support a bad faith modification.[49] To draw the line between good faith and bad faith modifications, one court suggests two distinct inquiries: (1) whether the party inducing the modification has acted in accordance with reasonable commercial standards and fair dealing in the trade, and (2) whether the parties were in fact motivated to seek modification by an honest desire to compensate for commercial exigencies.[50] The first inquiry requires that the party asserting the modification demonstrate that the decision to seek a modification was the result of a factor (e.g., increased costs) which would cause an ordinary merchant to seek a modification. The second inquiry is less clear since it requires the party asserting the modification to demonstrate that he was, in fact, motivated by a sound commercial reason and that he did not offer such a reason as mere pretext to induce additional compensation. The court adds that, "[T]he trier of fact must determine whether the means used to obtain the modification are an impermissable [sic] attempt to obtain a modification by extortion or overreaching."[51]

The RESTATEMENT 2d provides a striking illustration of the difficulty in drawing the distinction between a modification induced by bad faith and one induced by good faith. *A* contracts to excavate *B*'s cellar for a stated price and encounters solid rock during the excavation. He threatens not to complete performance unless *B* agrees to a modification which will increase the price nine times the original price. *B* has no reasonable alternative and agrees to the modification, induced by *A*'s threat. The new price is reasonable in light of the unanticipated difficulty. The RESTATEMENT 2d concludes that there is no duress because *A* is not violating his duty of good faith and fair dealing.[52] The illustration is similar to that found in another RESTATEMENT 2d section dealing with fair and equitable modifications in light of unanticipated circumstances[53] except for the presence of a "threat" by *A*. If *A*'s "threat" is based upon *A*'s good faith, but erroneous, belief that he is excused from performing because of the unanticipated solid rock, it is difficult to discover any duress.[54] If, however, *A* is fully aware of his contractual responsibility but threatens to breach because he knows of *B*'s critical need to have the work performed without delay, the situation appears quite similar to cases discussed earlier involving coerced settlements.[55] Certainly, the threat in such a case is not made in good faith and, as such, it should be deemed improper.[56] The only consistent conclusion, therefore, is that the RESTATEMENT 2d illustration assumes *A*'s good faith in "threatening" to cease his performance.

---

[49] UCC § 2-209 comment 2.

[50] Roth Steel Prods. v. Sharon Steel Corp., 705 F.2d 134, 146 (6th Cir. 1983).

[51] *Id.* As the court suggests in a footnote to this sentence (note 24), this question might be more properly analyzed in terms of procedural unconscionability, which will be discussed in a subsequent section.

[52] RESTATEMENT 2d § 176 ill. 8.

[53] *See* RESTATEMENT 2d § 89(a) and ill. 1 thereto.

[54] Cf. Pittsburgh Testing Lab. v. Farnsworth & Chambers Co., 251 F.2d 77 (10th Cir. 1958), where the court focused upon the question of consideration and discovered a solution through the settlement of a bona fide dispute and further suggested the possibility of using the doctrine of good faith modifications in light of unanticipated circumstances.

[55] For example, where the threatening party knows that the other party needs cash immediately and offers a lesser amount than the liquidated debt which is not honestly disputed.

[56] RESTATEMENT 2d § 176(1)(d).

[H]   Threats Resulting in Unfair Exchanges — RESTATEMENT 2d

The RESTATEMENT 2d divides improper threats into two categories. The first category includes the kinds of threats already discussed, i.e., threats amounting to crimes or torts, threats of criminal prosecutions, threats to use the civil process in bad faith, and threats amounting to breaches of the duties of good faith and fair dealing.[57] The second category deals with threats that become improper if the resulting exchange is not on fair terms.[58] Thus, if a former employer threatens to prevent a former employee from obtaining other employment unless the employee agrees to a release of his claim against the employer, the threatened act would harm the employee but would not benefit the employer, i.e., the act would be malicious or vindictive. The resulting exchange is unfair and is voidable by the employee.[59] Similarly, while a threat to refuse to deal with a particular buyer is normally not improper, if a supplier of goods induces a customer to believe that he will supply such goods in the future causing the buyer to rely upon that assurance until the goods are unavailable elsewhere, the supplier's subsequent threat to refuse to deal with that buyer except at an extortionate price is improper.[60] A threat to breach a contract, itself not improper, can become improper because of prior unfair dealing by the threatening party, which places the recipient of the threat in a position of having no reasonable alternative but to succumb to the threat. An agreement inducing the victim to appear to assent under these circumstances should be voidable because of duress.[61] A threat to use a power for illegitimate ends resulting in an unfair exchange is also an improper threat. Thus, if a party threatens to refuse delivery of goods unless another party pays an amount owed to the threatening party by a third party, a court could conclude that this constitutes use of a power for illegitimate ends.[62]

Again, the line between hard bargaining and illegitimate use of power resulting in an unfair exchange may be very difficult to draw in a given situation. It is important for the student of contract law to recognize the willingness of modern courts to find duress where that line has been crossed.

---

[57] RESTATEMENT 2d § 176(1).

[58] RESTATEMENT 2d § 176(2). See *Eulrich*, note 45 *supra.*

[59] *See* Perkins Oil Co. v. Fitzgerald, 197 Ark. 14, 121 S.W.2d 877 (1938). *See also* RESTATEMENT 2d § 176(2)(a).

[60] *See* Hochman v. Zigler's, Inc., 139 N.J. Eq. 139, 50 A.2d 97 (Super. Ct. 1946).

[61] *See, e.g.*, Litten v. Jonathan Logan, Inc., 220 Pa. Super. 274, 286 A.2d 913 (1971). Pursuant to an oral agreement, plaintiffs transferred all of the stock of two corporations to defendant in exchange for defendant's promise to pay corporate loans, pay the excess to plaintiffs, employ plaintiffs for one year, and give one of the plaintiffs an option to purchase stock. Defendant failed to perform even the first promise of paying creditors and, when plaintiffs were threatened with bankruptcy proceedings, defendant presented plaintiffs with a written agreement which was different from the oral agreement, but which defendant insisted plaintiff sign the same day with the threat that the creditors would not be paid unless plaintiff signed. After resisting, plaintiff signed with manifestations of protest. *See also* RESTATEMENT 2d § 176(2)(b).

[62] See the discussion of ill. 15 of the FIRST RESTATEMENT § 318(2) (which illustration is repeated as ill. 15 in RESTATEMENT 2d § 176) in Eckstein v. Eckstein, 38 Md. App. 506, 379 A.2d 757, 762 (1978). *See also* RESTATEMENT 2d § 176(2)(c).

[I]   Causation — Overcoming the Will of a Person of Ordinary Firmness — Depriving a Party of Free Will — No Reasonable Alternative — Objective Versus Subjective

We have seen that the threat inducing action or forbearance by the recipient of the threat must be *improper* in order for the contract to be avoided. It is important to emphasize the requirement that the threat *cause* or *induce* a manifestation of assent by the recipient.[63] Causation must be a fact question requiring an analysis of all of the surrounding circumstances to determine whether the threat, in fact, induced or caused apparent assent. The causation element has not been very troublesome with respect to duress. Courts, however, have spent considerable energy dealing with a related question, i.e., what is the test to determine whether the recipient of the threat was justified in succumbing to the threat?

The early judicial standard used to deal with this question shifted from an objective standard employed at early common law requiring evidence that a "resolute" person or person of "ordinary firmness" would have bowed to the threat under the circumstances[64] to a subjective standard that the recipient was deprived of free will, a standard still found in modern cases.[65] The RESTATEMENT 2d rejects both the "ordinary firmness" and deprivation of "free will" tests because of their "vagueness and impracticability" and substitutes a test that requires the victim to show that he had "no reasonable alternative" to manifesting assent to the improper threat.[66] Earlier we saw that a threat to institute a civil action is ordinarily not duress because the aggrieved party typically has the reasonable alternative of asserting his rights in that action. Yet, the circumstances may suggest that such an alternative may not be reasonable under the circumstances. For example, where Ames leaves a piece of equipment for repair with Barnes and, though Ames has paid for the repairs, Barnes refuses to deliver the equipment unless Ames either pays an additional amount or agrees to have Barnes do additional work. While Ames has a cause of action in replevin for her equipment, her immediate need for the equipment may cause the remedy to be inadequate.[67] Similarly, where a party threatens to breach a contract unless the victim manifests assent to a modification, the circumstances may suggest that an exercise of the victim's right to bring an action for breach may prove inadequate, thereby leaving him no reasonable alternative but to succumb to the

---

[63] There is no special rule for causation of duress found in the RESTATEMENT 2d. Rather, it is suggested that the same standard be used as found in the section dealing with the causation of misrepresentation, i.e., § 167, which suggests that "[a] misrepresentation induces a party's manifestation of assent if it substantially contributes to his decision to manifest assent." See also Wilson v. Wilson, 642 S.W.2d 132 (Mo. Ct. App. 1982), where the court found no duress because the demand for the agreement to which Mr. Wilson agreed was not made by Mrs. Wilson. Rather, the idea was Mr. Wilson's, who apparently felt a need to motivate Mrs. Wilson to alter her behavior.

[64] *See* 2 H. BRACTON, ON THE LAW AND CUSTOMS OF ENGLAND 65 (Thorne Tr. 1968).

[65] *See, e.g.,* Peter Matthews, Ltd. v. Robert Mabey, Inc., 117 A.D.2d 943, 499 N.Y.S.2d 254, 255 (3d Dep't 1986); Raymundo v. Hammond Clinic Ass'n, 449 N.E.2d 276, 283 (Ind. 1983); Food Fair Stores, Inc. v. Joy, 283 Md. 205, 389 A.2d 874 (1978) (mentioning different RESTATEMENT 2d test — discussed, *infra,* this subsection, and suggested that application of the new RESTATEMENT test would only serve to attenuate the claim of duress in this case).

[66] RESTATEMENT 2d § 175(1) and, particularly, comment b thereto. *See* Jenks v. Jenks, 232 Conn. 750, 657 A.2d 1107 (1995); Andreini v. Hultgren, 860 P.2d 916, 921 (Utah 1993); Penn v. Transportation Lease Haw., 2 Haw. App. 272, 275, 630 P.2d 646, 649 (1981), and *In re* Marriage of Hitchcock, 265 N.W.2d 599 (Iowa 1978), which adopts this test.

[67] *See* S. P. Dunham & Co. v. Kudra, 44 N.J. Super. 565, 131 A.2d 306 (1957), and Murphy v. Brilliant Co., 323 Mass. 526, 83 N.E.2d 166 (1948). The earlier common law version of this type of duress was characterized as "duress of goods." *See* Astley v. Reynolds, 2 Strange 915, 93 Eng. Rep. (K.B. 1732) (where pawned goods were threatened to be detained absent payment of excessive interest).

threat by manifesting assent to the modification.[68]

The RESTATEMENT 2d standard may create confusion as to whether it is objective or subjective because it requires two elements: (1) the victim's manifestation of assent must be induced by an improper threat and (2) the induced assent must leave the victim no reasonable alternative to manifesting assent to the threat.[69] As to the first element, the RESTATEMENT 2d clearly intends a subjective standard which would consider age, background and the relationship between the parties.[70] The focus is upon *causation*, i.e., if the threat *in fact* caused the manifestation of assent because the victim was an infant, timid, or otherwise easily frightened, where the same threat would have been ignored by a reasonable person, duress is shown.[71] The second element, i.e., whether the victim had a reasonable alternative, is irrelevant in such a case since such a victim would not consider any reasonable alternative, having been induced by a threat which, itself, would not induce a reasonable person to manifest assent. The maker of the threat to such a victim should not escape a finding of duress on the ground that the victim was unreasonable in taking the threat seriously. The requirement that there be no reasonable alternative, by its very characterization, suggests an objective standard and is imposed only upon a reasonable person. Such a person may have been reasonable in taking the threat seriously. If, however, he had a reasonable alternative to manifesting assent induced by the threat, he would not be able to establish duress.

[J]   Remedies for Duress — Ratification of Voidable Contracts

As we have seen, an agreement induced by physical compulsion is not a contract, though it is sometimes inartfully called a "void contract."[72] Early in our discussion of duress, we saw that it made no difference whether such "real" duress was caused by the other party to the contract or by a third person since there never was any contract. The parties had a *void* agreement.[73] Where the duress is of the "improper threat" variety, making the contract only voidable, the victim has a power of avoidance which can be exercised, again, whether the duress was caused by the other party or by a third person.[74] Where a party chooses to accept the benefits flowing from the contract, or remains silent or otherwise acquiesces in the contract for a considerable time after the threat has ceased, the power of avoidance is relinquished. The former victim will be said to have ratified or affirmed the contract.[75] If a third party causes duress that would normally allow the victim to avoid the contract, but the

---

[68] See the discussion of the classic case of Alaska Packers' Ass'n v. Domenico, 117 F. 99 (9th Cir. 1902), in Selmer Co. v. Blakeslee-Midwest Co., 704 F.2d 924, 927 (7th Cir. 1983).

[69] RESTATEMENT 2d § 175(1).

[70] RESTATEMENT 2d § 175 comment c. See Ohio Casualty Ins. Co. v. Todd, 813 P.2d 508, 515 (Okla. 1991).

[71] *See* ills. 8 and 9 to RESTATEMENT 2d § 175.

[72] See *supra* subsection A. of this section.

[73] See text at note 11 *supra*.

[74] See Dorale v. Dorale, 2009 Iowa App. LEXIS 352 (May 6, 2009) where a divorced wife signed an agreement to sell property to her former husband when she encountered her angry husband at her father's home. The father was eager to have the husband leave, but he would not leave. The father (third person) urged his daughter to sign because he wanted to bring the argument to an end to avoid someone getting hurt. The wife's agreement, therefore, was induced by her concern for her father who was, in turn, induced to apply that pressure to have the daughter sign by the husband's behavior.

[75] Wright v. Foreign Service Grievance Board, 503 F. Supp. 2d 163, 174 (D. D. C. 2007); Seal v. Riverside Fed. Sav. Bank, 825 F. Supp. 686, 696 (E.D. Pa. 1993). *See also* Restatement 2d § 174, comment b.

other party to the contract, without knowledge of the duress, gives value or materially relies on the victim's assent to the contract, the contract is not voidable.[76] If an agreement is *void ab initio* or if the victim has exercised the power of avoidance with respect to a voidable contract, the victim is entitled to have restitution of any benefit the victim had conferred upon the threatening party to avoid unjust enrichment. Similarly, the victim must return any benefit received under the avoided (rescinded) contract. The relief is designed to restore the parties to *status quo ante*. If specific restitution can occur, it will be ordered. If a sum of money is paid under duress, an action in quasi contract will lie to provide restitution to the victim.[77] Often, the benefits cannot be returned and an action in quasi contract for the reasonable value of goods or services supplied under a voidable contract will be appropriate.[78] If the benefit conferred has enhanced the property of the defendant, the victim may be able to have a constructive trust or equitable lien decreed which, again, protects the restitution interest.[79]

§ 95   UNDUE INFLUENCE

Whereas duress involves an improper threat, undue influence involves improper or *unfair persuasion*.[80] Unfair persuasion may result from the domination of the party exercising the persuasion resulting from a confidential relationship between the parties where the party reposing the trust is not on guard, i.e., he is exposed and relies on the other because he is justified in assuming that the other will act in a manner consistent with his welfare.[81] "A confidential relationship exists between two persons when one has gained the confidence of the other and purports to act or advise with the other's interests in mind."[82]

Judicial and scholarly discussions of undue influence invariably assume a confidential relationship, though its assertion without such a relationship is theoretically possible. In a rare case where there was no pre-existing confidential relationship, a teacher was arrested on charges (later dismissed) of homosexual activity. When he was released on bail after forty hours without sleep, school officials persuaded him to resign. The teacher argued that his resignation occurred under duress. In reviewing the plaintiff's complaint which had been dismissed on a demurrer, the appellate court described undue influence as the use of excessive pressure by a dominant subject to a subservient object who is unduly susceptible to such pressure. The plaintiff claimed that he was particularly susceptible to the pressure created by school officials at the time he was persuaded to make the decision to resign. While recognizing that undue influence cannot be used to escape a bad bargain, the critical question is whether overpersuasion took place. It occurred in this case when the school officials took advantage of his weak position by telling him that, if he did no resign immediately, the school district would

---

[76] Travelers Indemnity Co. v. Claywell Electric Co., 2008 Conn. Super. LEXIS 1057 at *9–10 (April 23, 2008). See also Employers Ins. of Wausau v. Bond, 1991 U.S. Dist. LEXIS 951 (D. Md. Jan. 25, 1991); RESTATEMENT 2d § 175, comment e.

[77] *See, e.g.*, Stroop v. Rutherford County, 567 S.W.2d 753 (Tenn. 1978).

[78] *See, e.g.*, Jurgensmeyer v. Boone Hosp. Ctr., 727 S.W.2d 441 (Mo. Ct. App. 1987); First Nat'l Bank of Cincinnati v. Pepper, 454 F.2d 626 (2d Cir. 1972).

[79] *See, e.g.*, Balish v. Farnham, 92 Nev. 133, 546 P.2d 1297 (1976) (discussing constructive trust remedy for duress); Worley v. Ehret, 36 Ill. App. 3d 48, 343 N.E.2d 237 (5th Dist. 1976) (discussing equitable lien remedy for duress).

[80] *See* Kazaras v. Manufacturers Trust Co., 4 A.D.2d 227, 164 N.Y.S.2d 211 (1st Dep't 1957), *aff'd*, 4 N.Y.2d 930, 151 N.E.2d 356 (1958).

[81] *See* Smith v. Ellison, 171 Or. App. 289, 294, 15 P.3d 67, 69 (2000) (citing RESTATEMENT 2d § 177).

[82] *Id.* at 294, 15 P.3d at 70.

dismiss him from his position and publicize the proceedings. If, however, he did resign, the incident would not be publicized and his opportunity for a teaching position elsewhere would not be jeopardized.[83] A confidential relationship shifts the burden of proof to the party seeking to uphold the validity of the transaction to establish that the transaction was fair and voluntarily concluded by the other.[84] Thus, one who has the advantage of such a relationship and who profits at the expense of the other may not claim an arm's length transaction, i.e., the transaction is presumptively voidable.[85]

The relationship is often one between spouses, parent and child, physician and patient, or clergyman and parishioner.[86] Numerous other relationships may be confidential as well. Thus, a bank and its depositor/debtor[87] may manifest such a relationship. The dominant party must have used unfair persuasion over the servient person.[88] The determination of whether the persuasion was "unfair" is, as usual, a fact question.[89] As suggested earlier, the test has been stated as overcoming the will of the servient person,[90] or "the exercise of an improper influence over the mind and will of another to such an extent that the action is not that of a free agent,"[91] or whether the victim has been deprived of "the free and competent exercise of judgment."[92] In determining whether the victim has been deprived of the free and competent exercise of his judgment, courts will consider whether he had independent advice or whether the other party urged him to act immediately without such advice.[93] Courts will also consider the unfairness of the bargain struck by the influenced party and his susceptibility to persuasion under the circumstances.[94] The alleged victim's age, mental condition and health are also factors to be

---

[83] Odorizzi v. Bloomfield School District, 246 Cal. App. 2d 123, 54 Cal. Rptr. 533 (1966). In Barber v. Pound (*In re* Estate of Strozzi), 120 N.M. 541, 544, 903 P.2d 852, 854–55 (Ct. App. 1995), the court recognized the theoretical but unusual possibility that undue influence outside a confidential relationship can be exerted, but it proceeded to assume, without deciding, that a confidential relationship is a necessary element of undue influence. See, however, Berdel, Inc. v. Pennsylvania Real Estate Inv. Trust, 1997 Del. Ch. LEXIS 177, at *16 (Del. Ch. Dec. 15, 1997), where the court suggests the possibility of undue influence without a confidential relationship.

[84] *Berdel, id.*, suggests that, absent a confidential relationship, the burden of proving undue influence falls upon the party who asserts that defense. That burden includes four elements: (1) a person who is subject to influence; (2) an opportunity to exact under influence; (3) a disposition to exert undue influence; (4) a result indicating the presence of undue influence.

[85] Peoples Bank & Trust Co. v. Lala, 392 N.W.2d 179 (Iowa Ct. App. 1986).

[86] *See* RESTATEMENT 2d § 177 comment a.

[87] *See* Peoples Bank & Trust Co. v. Lala, 392 N.W.2d 179 (Iowa Ct. App. 1986).

[88] *See* Dent v. Wright, 322 Ark. 256, 909 S.W.2d 302, 305 (1995). *See also In re* Cheryl E., 161 Cal. App. 3d 587, 601, 207 Cal. Rptr. 728, 737 (2d Dist. 1984). "Undue influence consists in the use of excessive pressure by a dominant person over a servient person. . . ."

[89] Goldman v. Bequai, 19 F.3d 666, 675, 305 U.S. App. D.C. 227 (1994).

[90] "Excessive pressure . . . resulting in the apparent will of the servient person being in fact the will of the dominant person." *Matter of Cheryl*, note 88 *supra.*

[91] *See* Curl v. Key, 311 N.C. 259, 265, 316 S.E.2d 272, 276 (1984).

[92] RESTATEMENT 2d § 177 comment b. *See* Rich v. Fuller, 666 A.2d 71, 76 (Me. 1995); Fisher v. Estate of Welch (*In re* Estate of Welch), 534 N.W.2d 109, 112 (Iowa Ct. App. 1995).

[93] See, *Odorizzi supra* note 83, where the principal and school district superintendent urged the victim to resign immediately because he did not have time to consult an attorney.

[94] RESTATEMENT 2d § 177 comment b. *See* Dolloff v. Dolloff, 593 A.2d 1044, 1046 (Me. 1991). Unfairness of the bargain, however, is not controlling. North Am. Rayon Corp. v. Commissioner of Internal Revenue, 12 F.3d 583, 590 (6th Cir. 1993).

considered, though mental incompetency is not dispositive of the undue influence issue.[95]

A contract induced by undue influence is voidable by the victim.[96] If the undue influence emanates from a third party, the victim may still avoid the contract unless the other party to the contract had no reason to know of the undue influence and, in good faith, gave value or relied materially on the contract.[97]

§ 96 MISREPRESENTATION

[A] Definition — Concealment and Non-Disclosure Distinguished

Misrepresentation is typically defined as "an assertion that is not in accord with the facts."[98] Such an assertion is usually spoken or written, but it may be inferred from conduct. *Concealment* does not involve language, but it is an affirmative act designed to prevent another from learning the fact. Thus, where a builder knew of a defect in the floor of a basement and covered the defect with tile to conceal it, this was a conduct assertion not in accordance with the facts.[99] There is an element of non-disclosure in such a case. Concealment, however, involves an affirmative act to prevent the other party from learning the facts. *Non-disclosure*, on the other hand, involves no affirmative act. The notion that one party has a duty to disclose relevant information to the other party who has equal access to such information was antithetical to courts holding traditional views of individuality and bargaining. The great Chief Justice John Marshall could find no duty to disclose where a party purchased a large quantity of tobacco with private knowledge that the Treaty of Ghent had been signed, ending the War of 1812, resulting in a more than substantial increase in the price of tobacco through the removal of the British blockade of New Orleans.[100]

A modern court finds no duty to disclose knowledge to the seller of valuable coal or gas deposits on land unless the information was obtained by improper means, such as by trespass.[101] Modern courts do, however, recognize that non-disclosure may have the same effect as misrepresentation. In *Mitsubishi Power Systems Americas, Inc. v. Babcock & Brown Infrastructure Group*, the court noted,

> The duty to speak does not typically arise when parties sit at opposite ends of the bargaining table negotiating a contract at arm's length. The ancient rule of *caveat emptor* remains alive and well in New York. A party generally has a duty to speak in three situations: (1) where disclosure is necessary to complete or clarify the party's

---

[95] See *Goldman, supra* at note 89.

[96] RESTATEMENT 2d § 177(2). Like duress, undue influence is generally not, itself, an actionable tort. The victim is usually limited to avoidance of the contract and does not have an affirmative action for damages. Glenfed Fin. Corp., Commercial Fin. Div. v. Penick Corp., 276 N.J. Super. 163, 174–75, 647 A.2d 852, 857 (App. Div. 1994).

[97] RESTATEMENT 2d § 177(3). *See also* First Wisconsin Trust Co. v. Midatlantic Home Mortg. Co., 439 Pa. Super. 192, 202, 653 A.2d 688, 693 (1995).

[98] RESTATEMENT 2d § 159.

[99] Jenkins v. McCormick, 184 Kan. 842, 339 P.2d 8 (1959). *See also* Sage v. Broadcasting Publications, Inc., 997 F. Supp. 49 (D.D.C. 1998) (concealment of certain material facts in a corporate merger). *See* RESTATEMENT 2d § 160.

[100] *See* Laidlaw v. Organ, 15 U.S. (2 Wheat.) 178, 4 L. Ed. 214 (1817).

[101] See Mallon Oil Co. v. Bowen/Edwards Assocs., Inc., 965 P.2d 105, 111 (Colo. 1998).

prior disclosure; (2) where the party with superior knowledge knows the other party is operating on the basis of mistaken belief; and (3) when the parties stand in a fiduciary or confidential relationship.[102]

A failure to respond truthfully to a buyer's question may result in fraudulent nondisclosure. Where a seller of property failed to disclose a flooding incident when asked a relevant question about a sump hole, the court held that the seller had a duty to speak when asked that question, and its failure to meet that duty was fraudulent nondisclosure.[103] Similarly, where a buyer asked about a water conditioner in the basement and the seller answered that it was simply a device to soften the water-failing to disclose that the well water on the property was so laden with sulfur that even more expensive treatment would make the water barely drinkable-the court allowed rescission of the contract.[104] Even the failure to disclose that a house was widely reputed to be haunted, thereby arguably lowering its economic value, was sufficient for a divided court to allow rescission of the contract.[105]

A number of cases deal with the sale of a residence infested with termites, known to the seller, who fails to disclose that fact to the buyer. Courts hold that the vendor has a duty to disclose such a material fact.[106]

The fact situations requiring disclosure of a material fact are myriad. Thus, if a party knows that the drawer of a check is stopping payment on a check, but arranges to have the check cashed, he knows that the other party would not cash the check if the information concerning the stop payment process were disclosed. This failure to act in good faith to correct the mistake of the other as to an assumption that is basic to the transaction is the equivalent of an assertion not in accordance with the facts.[107] Similarly, a half-truth will operate as a misrepresentation unless the party to whom it is made does not believe it or rely upon it.[108] Even where the statement was completely true when made, if subsequent conditions make the statement false and the maker fails to disclose the change to the other party who is assuming the truth of the original statement, this failure to correct the original statement can amount to a misrepresentation.[109] If one party knows that a writing evidencing a contract does not contain a term which the other party thinks it contains, non-disclosure of the second party's mistake, notwithstanding his failure to read, may amount to a misrepresentation under the circum-

---

[102] 2010 Del Ch. LEXIS 11 at *43 (2010). The court found no evidence of (1) or (3). As to superior knowledge, the court held that Mitsubishi had no duty to disclose mechanical issues with the same product in earlier transactions, but its earlier email together with contradictory specifications made an intentionally vague and misleading partial disclosure constituting half truths to prevent the buyer from learning the facts which is an assertion that such facts did not exist. See Restatement 2d § 160.

[103] Marchand v. Presutti, 7 Conn. App. 643, 509 A.2d 1092 (1986).

[104] Cushman v. Kirby, 148 Vt. 571, 536 A.2d 550 (1987).

[105] Stambovsky v. Ackley, 169 A.D.2d 254, 572 N.Y.S.2d 672 (1st Dep't 1991).

[106] See, e.g., Ensminger v. Terminix Int'l Co., 102 F.3d 1571 (10th Cir. 1996); Johnson v. Davis, 480 So. 2d 625 (Fla. 1985); Mercer v. Woodard, 166 Ga. App. 119, 303 S.E.2d 475 (1983); Lynn v. Taylor, 7 Kan. App. 2d 369, 642 P.2d 131 (1982).

[107] Bossuyt v. Osage Farmers Nat'l Bank, 360 N.W.2d 769 (Iowa 1985). See also Allstate Redevelopment Corp. v. Summit Assocs., Inc., 206 N.J. Super. 318, 502 A.2d 1137 (1985) (question of disclosure of state's riparian claim prior to execution of lease), and RESTATEMENT 2d § 161, cited in both cases.

[108] See Nader v. Allegheny Airlines, Inc., 626 F.2d 1031, 200 U.S. App. D.C. 167 (1980).

[109] RESTATEMENT 2d § 161(b). See also Bursey v. Clement, 118 N.H. 412, 387 A.2d 346 (1978) (failure to correct original statement concerning certain legislation).

stances.[110] The relationship between the parties, even though it does not rise to a technical fiduciary relationship, may be one of such trust and confidence as to create an expectation of disclosure.[111]

[B]   Fraudulent or Material

A statement not in accord with the facts may amount to a misrepresentation even though it is not fraudulent.[112] "A contract is voidable if a party's assent is induced by either a fraudulent or material misrepresentation by the other party, and is an assertion on which the recipient is justified in relying."[113] A misrepresentation is *fraudulent* where the maker knows or believes the assertion to be false and intends to mislead the other party. This type of misrepresentation involves *scienter*, i.e., the maker knows or believes what he is asserting is untrue. Even if the maker does not know or believe his assertion is untrue, if he makes the assertion with apparent confidence, though he does not have such confidence, his statement is reckless. Here, the maker is lying about the basis for his assertion and the assertion is a fraudulent misrepresentation. Similarly, where he implies certain knowledge in the assertion, though he does not have a basis for the assertion, the making of the assertion in this fashion with the intention of inducing assent is a fraudulent misrepresentation.[114]

A misrepresentation is *material* if it would be likely to induce a *reasonable* party to manifest assent,[115] or if the maker knows that, because of special reasons, it would be likely to induce a *particular* party to assent, though it would not induce such assent by a reasonable party.[116] If the misrepresentation is nonfraudulent, it must be material to be actionable.[117] The interesting question is, why should an immaterial but fraudulent misrepresentation

---

[110] *See* Restatement 2d § 161(c). In Skagit State Bank v. Rasmussen, 43 Wash. App. 178, 716 P.2d 314 (1986), the court held that where a party was asked to sign a document while he was busy and spoke only briefly with the party presenting the document, signing under these circumstances was not negligent. On appeal, however, the court reversed, holding that nothing precluded the signer from an opportunity to review the document. 109 Wash. 2d 377, 745 P.2d 37 (1987).

[111] See Shaffer v. Terrydale Mgmt. Corp., 648 S.W.2d 595, 607 n.8 (Mo. Ct. App. 1983), where the court suggests that even the rule that one able to read and understand is bound by his signature regardless of whether he read the document "is tempered where the relation of trust and confidence subsists between the drafter and signatory" (citing Restatement 2d § 161(d) and comment f thereto). *See also* Nie v. Galena State Bank & Trust Co., 387 N.W.2d 373 (Iowa Ct. App. 1986).

[112] That the doctrine of "innocent misrepresentation," first enunciated in Michigan in 1866 in Converse v. Blumrich, 14 Mich. 109, 123, 90 Am. Dec. 230 (1866), still prevails in Michigan is the holding of United States Fidelity & Guar. Co. v. Black, 412 Mich. 99, 313 N.W.2d 77, 83 (1981).

[113] Carpenter v. Vreeman, 409 N.W.2d 258, 260–61 (Minn. Ct. App. 1987) (citing Restatement 2d § 164(1) in support).

[114] In general, see *Carpenter v. Vreeman, id. See also* Restatement 2d § 162(1).

[115] *Id. See Skagit State Bank, supra* note 110, at 317. *See also* Parlak v Holder, 578 F. 3d 457, 465 "a natural tendency to influence the decisions of the" affected party. (6th Cir. 2009). Cousineau v. Walker, 613 P.2d 608, 613 (Alaska 1980) (was the assertion one to which a reasonable person might be expected to attach importance in making a choice of action). *See* Hampton v. Sabin, 49 Or. App. 1041, 1049, 621 P.2d 1202, 1207 (1980) (a representation is material if "it would be likely to affect the conduct of a reasonable man with reference to a transaction with another person") (quoting Millikin v. Green, 283 Or. 283, 285, 583 P.2d 548 (1978)).

[116] *See* Restatement 2d § 162(2) and comment c. A maker may know of particular idiosyncrasies of the recipient and, while the assertion may not induce a reasonable person to assent, the maker may know that the assertion is likely to induce this person. *See* Restatement of Torts 2d § 526(2)(b).

[117] *See* Hendren v. Allstate Ins. Co., 100 N.M. 506, 672 P.2d 1137, 1140 (Ct. App. 1983) (if misrepresentations are

create a power of avoidance or disaffirmance in the recipient?

If a misrepresentation is *not* likely to induce a reasonable party to manifest assent, or if the maker does *not* know of any special reasons making it likely to induce assent by a particular person where a reasonable person would not be induced by the assertion, it is still possible for an assertion to induce assent in an unwise or foolish person. If such an assertion is fraudulent, the recipient should have a power of avoidance notwithstanding the immateriality of the assertion because it did, in fact, induce assent. The dearth of case law involving fraudulent albeit immaterial assertions does not detract from the universal view that a misrepresentation can be the basis for avoidance of the resulting agreement if it is *either* fraudulent or material.[118]

[C]   Inducement — Fraud in the Inducement Versus Fraud in the Execution or Factum

The misrepresentation need not be the sole or dominant factor influencing the conduct of the other party. It is sufficient if the assertion substantially contributed to that conduct.[119] Normally, misrepresentation only *induces* the conduct or assent of the other party, who may then exercise a power of avoidance or disaffirmance. It is possible, however, for the misrepresentation to go to the *execution* or *factum*, thereby creating a different legal effect. Suppose, for example, Ames returns from a visit to the ophthalmologist and cannot read a document presented by Barnes, her confidant. Barnes falsely tells Ames that the document is a rent receipt which Ames should sign. Ames signs, not knowing that the document is a contract which will have an unfair effect upon Ames. Here, Ames was unaware of the true character of the document she signed and was induced to sign by the misrepresentation of a party in whom Ames legitimately reposed trust and confidence. The misrepresentation or "fraud" is so foundational in this case as to go to the very *execution* of the writing and results in no contract being formed or, as some courts unfortunately suggest, a "void contract" as contrasted with a voidable contract.[120] The principal significance of the distinction between fraud in the *execution* or *factum*, which precludes the formation of any contract, and fraud in the *inducement*, which creates a contract that is voidable by the victim of the fraud, relates to the rights of third parties.

Where a party is tricked into signing a negotiable instrument because it was represented as a mere receipt, the signature is ineffective since he did not intend to sign such an instrument at all.[121] This is a classic illustration of "fraud that induced the party to sign the instrument with neither knowledge nor reasonable opportunity to learn of its character or its essential

---

material, it makes no difference whether the maker acted fraudulently, negligently, or innocently). *See also* Guardian Life Ins. Co. v. Tillinghast, 512 A.2d 855 (R.I. 1986).

[118]   See also RESTATEMENT 2d § 161 comment b: "[t]here is . . . no requirement of materiality if it can be shown that the non-disclosure was actually fraudulent."

[119]   RESTATEMENT 2d § 167 and, in particular, comment a.

[120]   *See* RESTATEMENT 2d § 163. For an analysis of this concept and its application to various cases, see Hetchkop v. Woodlawn at Grassmere, Inc., 116 F.3d 28, 31–32 (2d Cir. 1997). *See also* Huene v. Commissioner of IRS, 1991 U.S. App. LEXIS 14816, at *7 (9th Cir. July 2, 1991) (parties reach an understanding concerning the contract which they will execute, but one of the parties intentionally substitutes a writing containing essential terms different from those agreed upon).

[121]   UCC § 3-305 comment 1.

terms. . . ."[122] This type of fraud in the execution or factum will be an effective defense even against a holder in due course, i.e., a party who takes the check from the misrepresenting party for value, in good faith, and without notice that it is overdue or has been dishonored or of any other defense against it.[123] If, however, the misrepresentation simply *induces* a party to make a note or draw a check and the maker or drawer knows what he or she is signing, such misrepresentation will not be a defense against a holder in due course.[124] Similarly, if a party signs an arbitration agreement with knowledge of what he or she is signing, a misrepresentation as to the legal effect of the agreement, absent a confidential relationship or other special circumstances, is not fraud in the execution or factum leading to a determination that the agreement is void. Rather, it is fraud in the inducement that allows the victim to avoid the contract.[125] Analogously, if a party procures goods through misrepresentation, that party has *voidable* title and a good faith purchaser from such a party will prevail over the true owner.[126] On the other hand, if goods are stolen, the thief has no power to transfer ownership to even a good faith purchaser for value since no "transaction of purchase" has occurred.[127]

[D] Reliance by the Induced Party — Disclaimer of Reliance

To this point, we have analyzed the elements necessary to permit a contract to be avoided for misrepresentation, save one. We have defined misrepresentation and insisted that it be either fraudulent or material. We then added the causation element, i.e., the victim's manifestation of assent must have been "induced" by that assertion. The final element is the requirement that the victim must be justified in relying on the misrepresentation.[128] This element may be viewed as simply another perspective of the "inducement" element, i.e., a misrepresentation cannot be a substantial factor in the victim's manifestation of assent unless the victim relied on the misrepresentation.[129] This fact is emphasized by a Texas court's comment on a clause expressly disclaiming reliance which "can defeat claims for fraud, fraudulent inducement and negligent misrepresentation *because reliance is a necessary element of each of these claims.*"[130]

---

[122] UCC § 3-305(a)(1)(iii). *See* United Bank & Trust Co. of Md. v. Schaeffer, 280 Md. 10, 370 A.2d 1138 (1977) (signer who was unable to read was told he was signing a character reference). *See also* First Nat'l Bank v. Fazzari, 10 N.Y.2d 394, 223 N.Y.S.2d 483, 179 N.E.2d 493 (1961) (party unable to read or write English was induced to sign a promissory note upon the misrepresentation that it was a statement of wages).

[123] UCC § 3-302.

[124] *See* Standard Fin. Co. v. Ellis, 3 Haw. App. 614, 657 P.2d 1056 (1983). It should be noted that the misrepresentation in such a case would allow the maker or drawer to avoid the underlying obligation against the original party to the contract. Again, however, it would not be a defense against a holder in due course of the instrument, i.e., a third party who has, in good faith and without notice of any defenses to the instrument, exchanged value for the instrument.

[125] Harold Allen's Mobile Home Factory Outlet v. Early, 2000 Ala. LEXIS 275, at *11 (Ala. June 30, 2000).

[126] UCC § 2-403(1).

[127] UCC § 2-403(1) requires a "transaction of purchase" to create voidable title in a party who has, *e.g.*, misrepresented his identity or otherwise procured goods through misrepresentation. "Purchase" is defined in UCC § 1-201(32), which lists various methods of "taking" goods, all of which are "voluntary transactions creating an interest in property." There is no such voluntary transaction where goods are stolen.

[128] *See* RESTATEMENT 2d § 164(1).

[129] RESTATEMENT 2d § 167 comment a. *See* Barrer v. Women's Nat'l Bank, 761 F.2d 752, 759, 245 U.S. App. D.C. 349 (D.C. Cir. 1985) ("Inducement, as comment a explains, is shown through actual reliance.").

[130] Garza v. C. T. X. Mortgage Co., L. L. C., 285 S. W. 3d 919, 927 (Tex. App. 2009), (emphasis supplied). Nightingale

Absent a "no reliance" clause, whether a party is justified in relying upon certain representations is a question of fact to be determined by the trial court.[131] There are a number of issues surrounding the general question, what constitutes justifiable reliance?

[1]   Victim's Failure to Investigate or Read

If the relying party is at fault in failing to make a reasonable investigation which would have exposed the misrepresentation, that party's reliance upon a misrepresentation (fraudulent or innocent) will still be justifiable unless the fault amounts to a failure to act in good faith or in accordance with reasonable standards of fair dealing.[132] As suggested by one court, "[T]he purchaser of business property is entitled to rely on the truth of the seller's representations even though the falsity could have been ascertained had the buyer made an investigation — unless the latter *knew* the representations to be false, or the falsity was *obvious* to him — if the seller, as owner of the property, had *superior knowledge* of its size, condition and income."[133] Any duty to investigate will be absolved where deliberate misrepresentations have lulled the recipient into a false sense of security.[134] Courts are more than reluctant to permit the maker of a misrepresentation to escape the victim's power of avoidance on the footing that the victim was negligent or credulous.[135] While the failure to read a legible document that need not be signed immediately is not consonant with justifiable reliance,[136] we have seen that other circumstances such as a relation of trust and confidence between the parties will overcome even this kind of "fault" by the victim.

Home Healthcare, Inc. v. Anodyne Therapy, LLC, 589 F.3d 881, 885 (7th Cir. 2009), provides an insight into disclaimer-of-reliance clauses:

> It is true that many courts will enforce a "no reliance" or "disclaimer of reliance" clause, at least against a sophisticated party. Such "clauses serve a legitimate purpose in closing a loophole in contract law" by heading off a suit for fraud used as "a device for trying to get around the limitations that the parol evidence rule and contract integration clauses place on efforts to vary a written contract on the basis of oral statements made in the negotiation phase," *Extra Equipamentos E Exportacao Ltda. v. Case Corp.*, 541 F.3d 719, 724 (7th Cir. 2008) — which is what Nightingale is trying to do.
>
> "[N]o-reliance clauses are called 'big boy' clauses (as in 'we're big boys and can look after ourselves')," and hence in some states are not enforced without "an inquiry into the circumstances of its negotiation, to make sure that the signatory knew what he was doing." *Id.*

[131] *See* Carpenter v. Vreeman, 409 N.W.2d 258, 261 (Minn. Ct. App. 1987).

[132] *See Barrer v. Women's Nat'l Bank, supra* note 129. *See also* First Nat'l Bank & Trust Co. v. Notte, 97 Wis. 2d 207, 293 N.W.2d 530 (1980), and RESTATEMENT 2d § 172.

[133] See Yost v. Rieve Enters., Inc., 461 So. 2d 178, 182 (Fla. Dist. Ct. App. 1984), which relies upon this quotation for its holding. *See* Hennig v. Ahearn, 230 Wis. 2d 149, 174, 601 N.W.2d 14, 26 (Ct. App. 1999); Exceptional Subs v. Fazzone, 1998 Conn. Super. LEXIS 1971, at *12 (Conn. Super. Ct. July 8, 1998); Colon v. Gremer Dev. Co., 28 V.I. 83 (Terr. Ct. 1993). In Bodenhamer v. Patterson, 278 Or. 367, 370, 563 P.2d 1212, 1216 (1977), the court suggests, "[A] purchaser who has, in fact, been induced to enter a contract by an intentional misrepresentation may rescind the contract even though his reliance may have been negligent."

[134] *See* Marino v. United Bank of Ill., N.A., 137 Ill. App. 3d 523, 92 Ill. Dec. 204, 484 N.E.2d 935, 938 (2d Dist. 1985). *See also* West v. Western Cas. & Sur. Co., 846 F.2d 387 (7th Cir. 1988).

[135] *See* Negyessy v. Strong, 136 Vt. 193, 388 A.2d 383 (1978). *See also* James & Gray, *Misrepresentation — Part II*, 37 MD. L. REV. 488, 511 (1978). Part I of this article appears at 37 MD. L. REV. 286 (1977).

[136] *See, e.g.*, Maw v. McAlister, 252 S.C. 280, 166 S.E.2d 203 (1969) (failure to read release).

[2] Opinion — Fact Versus Knowledge — Reliance on Opinion — Value, Quality, Quantity, Price — Matters of Law

A distinction is often suggested between statements of fact which may induce justifiable reliance and statements of opinion which should not induce such reliance.[137] The distinction has been criticized on the footing that statements of opinion are, themselves, statements of fact, i.e., if a person states an opinion, he is stating his particular state of mind which is a fact.[138] Such statements imply that the person making the statement does not have sufficient knowledge to assert the statement as fact as contrasted with belief. At most, it suggests that he is unaware of facts that are incompatible with his belief. The true distinction, therefore, should be between assertions of *knowledge* (rather than facts) and assertions of opinion.[139] If a person says, "This computer is compatible with an IBM personal computer," he asserts his *knowledge.* If, on the other hand, he says, "I believe this computer is compatible with an IBM personal computer, but I can't be sure," he is clearly stating an opinion. Normally, reliance on statements of opinion is not justified for the obvious reason that the statement is couched in terms that suggest the party making the statement may be wrong.[140] Under certain circumstances, however, the recipient may be justified in relying on a statement of opinion.

One court states the test as whether, "under the circumstances surrounding the statement, the representation was intended and understood as one of fact as distinguished from one of opinion."[141] Thus, where a builder asserted there was "nothing wrong" with a house, it could have been reasonably understood to be an assertion based on sufficient information to justify the builder's opinion and, as such, reliance on such a statement could be justifiable.[142] Where there is a relationship of trust and confidence between the parties, the recipient may be reasonable in relying upon a statement of opinion.[143] If the recipient is reasonable in believing that the person making the statement of opinion has particular skill or judgment with respect to the subject matter of the statement, the recipient may be justified in relying thereon. This is particularly true in cases involving statements about artistic ability or talent. Thus, if a violin teacher would inform a prospective pupil or the parent of the pupil that the pupil has great potential as a violinist, even though the teacher knows that the pupil demonstrates little or no aptitude as a violinist and is making the statement merely to encourage payment for lessons,

---

[137] For example, in Woodling v. Garrett Corp., 813 F.2d 543, 552 (2d Cir. 1987), the court suggests that to constitute a misrepresentation, a statement must falsely assert fact rather than opinion. In West v. Western Cas. & Sur. Co., 846 F.2d 387 (7th Cir. 1988), the court suggests that a statement merely expressing an opinion or relating to future or contingent events rather than past or present facts does not constitute an actionable misrepresentation. In Barnes v. Barnes, 207 Va. 114, 148 S.E.2d 789, 795 (1966), the court suggests that, for a statement to amount to fraud, it must be a positive statement of fact and not a mere expression of opinion.

[138] RESTATEMENT 2d § 168 comment a.

[139] *Id.*

[140] The famous statement of Chancellor Kent is worth remembering: "Every person reposes at his peril in the opinion of others, when he has equal opportunity to form and exercise his own judgment." J. KENT, COMMENTARIES ON AMERICAN LAW 381 (1st ed. 1827).

[141] Crowther v. Guidone, 183 Conn. 464, 468, 441 A.2d 11, 13 (1981).

[142] Johnson v. Healy, 176 Conn. 97, 101, 405 A.2d 54, 57 (1978).

[143] *See* Goldman v. Bequai, 19 F.3d 666, 674, 305 U.S. App. D.C. 227 (D.C. Cir. 1994); DSK Enters., Inc. v. United Jersey Bank, 189 N.J. Super. 242, 459 A.2d 1201 (1983). *See also* RESTATEMENT 2d § 169(a) and RESTATEMENT 2D OF TORTS § 542.

reliance on the teacher's statement is justified and the contract would be voidable.[144] The recipient of the statement of opinion may be particularly gullible through lack of intelligence, immaturity or similar reasons. Reliance on the statement of opinion by such a person may also be justifiable.[145]

Statements of value or quality are typically statements of opinion because reasonable parties should expect different opinions on such matters and seller's "puff" as to value or quality is part of common experience.[146] Statements of quantity, however, or statements of the price which something had previously brought, are not statements of opinion.[147] General statements regarding legal conclusions are viewed as mere expressions of opinion,[148] but such assertions are treated like other assertions. If, for example, there is an assertion that a particular statute has been enacted or repealed or a certain court has rendered a decision, it is an assertion that may induce justifiable reliance.[149] As suggested earlier, a party may justifiably rely upon an assertion of opinion if the statement is made by one with special knowledge. Thus, an opinion by a lawyer may permit justifiable reliance,[150] though a statement by a lawyer concerning the possible outcome of litigation or how a court might rule on a particular issue would typically be viewed as a statement of opinion.[151] If the maker of the statement is not a lawyer but has other special competence, her statement may be viewed as an opinion upon which the other party may justifiably rely.[152]

[E]   Effects of Misrepresentation — Remedies for Misrepresentation

Except for those rare situations where misrepresentation goes to the execution of a document and no contract results,[153] misrepresentation which *induces* a contract makes the contract *voidable*.[154] Thus, the victim may exercise a power of avoidance or disaffirmance,[155] though courts often characterize this effect as providing the victim with a ground for

---

[144] *See* Vokes v. Arthur Murray, Inc., 212 So. 2d 906 (Fla. Dist. Ct. App. 1968) (dance lessons). *See also* RESTATEMENT 2d § 169(b).

[145] *See DSK Enters., supra* note 143. *See also* RESTATEMENT 2d § 169(c).

[146] *See* Page Inv. Co. v. Staley, 105 Ariz. 562, 468 P.2d 589 (1970) (statement that land worth only $4000 per acre was worth $7500 per acre was mere opinion). *See also* RESTATEMENT 2d § 168 comment c. Compare the distinction between mere statements of value or commendation versus express warranties under the UCC. Section 2-313(2) of the Code suggests, "but an affirmation merely of the value of the goods or a statement purporting to be merely the seller's opinion or commendation of the goods does not create a warranty." *See, e.g.*, In re Ford Motor Co. E-350 Van Products Liability Litigation (No. II), 2008 U.S. Dist. LEXIS 73690 (D. N. J. 2008).

[147] RESTATEMENT 2d § 168 comment c.

[148] *See* Pennsylvania Life Ins. Co. v. Bumbrey, 665 F. Supp. 1190, 1201 (E.D. Va. 1987) ("Generally, statements regarding legal conclusions have been held to be mere expressions of opinion.").

[149] RESTATEMENT 2d § 170 comment a.

[150] Woodling v. Garrett Corp., 813 F.2d 543, 553 (2d Cir. 1987). RESTATEMENT 2d § 170 comment b.

[151] *See* Piedmont Trust Bank v. Aetna Casualty & Sur. Co., 210 Va. 396, 171 S.E.2d 264, 267 (1969). *See also* RESTATEMENT 2d § 170 comment b.

[152] *See, e.g.*, Hendren v. Allstate Ins. Co., 100 N.M. 506, 672 P.2d 1137 (Ct. App. 1983) (statement of insurance claims adjuster concerning uninsured motorist coverage).

[153] *See supra* § 96[C].

[154] *See* RESTATEMENT 2d § 164(1). *See* Addisu v. Fred Meyer, Inc. 198 F.3d 1130, 1137 (9th Cir. 2000).

[155] *See, e.g.*, Carpenter v. Vreeman, 409 N.W.2d 258, 260 (Minn. Ct. App. 1987) ("A contract is voidable if a party's assent is induced by either a fraudulent or a material misrepresentation by the other party, and is an assertion on which the recipient is justified in relying.") (citing RESTATEMENT 2d § 164(1)).

rescission of the contract.[156] The victim may lose his power of avoidance by affirming the contract. Such affirmance occurs through a manifestation of his intention to affirm, or acts inconsistent with disaffirmance, after the circumstances permitting avoidance have stopped, or after the victim has reason to know of a non-fraudulent misrepresentation or knows of a fraudulent misrepresentation.[157] The victim should not be permitted to disaffirm "beyond a reasonable" time after he discovers or should have discovered the misrepresentation, or use the property of the other party (except for preservation) and inconsistently exercise the power of disaffirmance.[158] Further, if the misrepresentation is "cured" before the victim exercises his power of disaffirmance and the victim has suffered no injury, the contract should no longer be voidable.[159] It should be emphasized, however, that a misrepresentation may estop the maker from asserting the bar of the statute of limitations if the victim relied upon such misrepresentation to his detriment.[160] Moreover, a victim should not be precluded from bringing a tort action for deceit (if the elements of that tort are established) and avoiding the contract, so long as the circumstances do not render such remedies incompatible.[161] Unless the contract is divisible, however, the contract cannot be avoided only in part.[162]

Where the power of avoidance is effectively exercised, courts seek to restore the parties to *status quo ante*, i.e., the position they were in before the voidable contract was made. Thus, courts seek to protect the restitution interest. The victim who seeks restitution must return or offer to return any benefit he has received under the contract.[163] Where, however, the product

---

[156] *See, e.g.*, Held v. Trafford Realty Co., 414 So. 2d 631, 632 (Fla. Dist. Ct. App. 1982) ("Whether made innocently or knowingly, misrepresentation of a material fact acted on by the other party to his detriment is a ground for rescission of a contract.").

[157] Restatement 2d § 380(1) and (2). *See* Schoenwald v. ARCO Alaska, Inc., 1999 U.S. App. LEXIS 20955, at *3 (9th Cir. Aug. 30, 1999).

[158] *See, e.g.*, Hampton v. Sabin, 49 Or. App. 1041, 1052, 621 P.2d 1202, 1208 (1980) ("The law is well settled that upon discovery of fraud one who desires to rescind a contract must act promptly. . . . The question, however, is whether they should be held to constructive notice of fraud sooner. If they are, rescission would be barred by their delay and their actions which were inconsistent with their intent to rescind, such as continuing to operate the business and putting the property up for sale."). Cf., under the UCC, a buyer must revoke acceptance of goods within a reasonable time after he discovers or should have discovered the basis for such revocation. UCC § 2-608(2). UCC § 2-606(1)(c) states that any act inconsistent with the seller's ownership constitutes acceptance of the goods, thereby depriving the buyer of his right to reject under § 2-601.

[159] *See* Restatement 2d § 165.

[160] *See, e.g.*, Bryant v. Doe, 50 Ohio App. 3d 19, 552 N.E.2d 671 (1988). The expression is often stated as misrepresentation "tolling" the statute of limitations.

[161] If, for example, the victim sues in tort for deceit but is precluded from recovery in that action because the statute of limitations has run, he is not precluded from subsequently avoiding the contract. *See* Schenck v. State Line Tel. Co., 238 N.Y. 308, 144 N.E. 592 (1924). *Accord* UCC § 2-721 and Restatement 2d § 380 ill. 4. The contrary view is predicated on an antiquated "election of remedies" notion, which suggests that a party injured by fraud may elect to accept the situation and recover damages or repudiate the transaction and seek restoration of the status quo, but he cannot do both. Albin v. Isotron Corp., 421 S.W.2d 739, 744 (Tex. Civ. App. Texarkana 1967). This opinion is expressly rejected by the Restatement 2d: *see* Reporter's Notes to § 380.

[162] Restatement 2d § 383. A party may not, for example, affirm a desirable part of the contract while disaffirming the undesirable part. *See* GE Capital Mortgage Servs., Inc. v. Pinnacle Mortgage Inv. Corp., 897 F. Supp. 854, 864 (E.D. Pa. 1995). If, however, the contract is divisible (severable), and the victim discovers the misrepresentation after performing a divisible portion thereof, he may avoid the remainder of the contract. This is equitable in that the portion of the contract already performed consisted of agreed equivalents, so that the portion remaining to be performed is, by definition, not the undesirable portion of the contract.

[163] See Borsheim v. O & J Properties, 481 N.W.2d 590, 594 (N.D. 1992), relying on Restatement 2d § 384. An earlier distinction between law and equity concerning the victim's offer to return any benefit received saw courts, sitting as

the victim has received is expected to be consumed, this requirement is relaxed.[164] Where the property is not expected to be consumed but cannot be returned, courts will achieve a return to *status quo* through an award of damages.[165] If the property restored to the victim has been improved, the victim will be liable for any increase in value.[166] Equitable remedies protecting the restitution interest, such as a constructive trust or an equitable lien, are also available to the victim. Under the UCC, the victim has a security interest in goods in his possession for any payments made on their price, as well as any expenses incurred in receiving or possessing such goods.[167]

§ 97   UNCONSCIONABILITY — "GOOD FAITH"

[A]   Freedom of Contract — Unconscionability in Equity

The indispensable tool in the operation of a free enterprise society is contract. The essence of contract is volition, that free exercise of will by parties who are on a relatively equal economic footing and who are brought together in the dynamic market place by their needs and desires.[168] This natural process through which each individual pursues his own, perhaps selfish, interests was deeply imbedded in the thinking of Americans in the late 18th and 19th centuries. The dominant belief was that a *laissez faire* system would permit the greatest possible individual contributions that would combine automatically to achieve the best interests of the community. "Freedom of contract" was an oft-repeated phrase of that time. There was a strong belief that the free enterprise system itself was automatically regulated through competition, the mechanics of which were supplied by the social institution of contract. In the great growth period of American law, the 19th Century, competition, like contract, was considered a natural self-regulating mechanism. Competition continuously accommodated the production of goods to the changing demand for them.

Absent fraud or the like, common law courts would not refuse to enforce a contract merely because it was oppressive or contained harsh provisions. Courts of equity, however, have traditionally refused to grant injunctions where the hardships clearly outweigh the benefits, and they have refused to grant specific performance where enforcement would be oppressive

---

courts of law, insisting upon an offer to return such benefits as a condition to an action for rescission of the contract. Courts of equity, however, did not require such an offer because the equitable decree could be conditioned on such an offer. The merger of law and equity has made this distinction untenable. Therefore, the RESTATEMENT 2d takes the position that a party will be granted restitution either upon his offer to return any interest in property received or upon the court's assurance of such return. § 384(1)(a) and (b).

[164] *See* Consumer Protection Div. Office of Attorney Gen. v. Consumer Pub. Co., 304 Md. 731, 501 A.2d 48, 72 (1985) (misrepresentation concerning diet pills which were consumed).

[165] *See* Neidermeyer v. Latimer, 79 Or. App. 116, 717 P.2d 1265, 1267 (1986) (dry rot discovered in cabin, causing buyer to hire contractor whose efforts resulted in making cabin uninhabitable), *aff'd*, 307 Or. 473, 769 P.2d 771 (1989).

[166] *See* Walker v. Galt, 171 F.2d 613 (5th Cir. 1948), *cert. denied*, 336 U.S. 925, 69 S. Ct. 656, 93 L. Ed. 1086 (1949).

[167] UCC § 2-711(3). This remedy applies to any buyer who rightfully rejects or justifiably revokes acceptance of the goods, whether or not a misrepresentation has induced the contract. The buyer may resell such goods as if he is an aggrieved seller under § 2-706.

[168] This statement is quoted from the second edition of this book in Brokers Title Co. v. St. Paul Fire & Marine Ins. Co., 610 F.2d 1174, 1179 (3d Cir. 1979). The basis for many of the thoughts suggested in this section is found in the classic introduction, *Contract as a Principle of Order*, in F. KESSLER & M. SHARP, CASES AND MATERIALS ON CONTRACTS (1953).

or cause disproportionate hardship to the defendant.[169]

In a well-known case, a farmer agreed to supply carrots to a canner under a contract containing provisions that were obviously harsh to the farmer. When the type of carrots to be supplied were in short supply, causing a more than substantial increase in the market price, the farmer began selling them elsewhere. The canner sought to enjoin such sales as well as specific performance of the contract. The lower court circumvented the issue of the harsh provisions by holding that the subject matter of the contract was not unique, thereby precluding the remedy sought by the canner.[170] The appellate court affirmed, but on the forthright ground that the provisions of the contract were so harsh or oppressive to the farmer that they were unconscionable, concluding, "That equity does not enforce unconscionable bargains is too well established to require elaborate citation."[171]

The document evidencing the contract in this case was a standardized printed form contract. The growth of a complex, industrialized society included the inevitable development of such printed forms for the sake of efficiency. They are used by the large enterprise in all of its repeated transactions and the printed provisions ("boilerplate") of such form contracts are typically duplicated in the form contracts used by competitors of the large enterprise. Standardized forms have clearly enhanced efficiency in contracting, but the costs of such efficiency include risk-exclusion or risk-limitation provisions for the benefit of the large firm with immensely greater bargaining power. The provisions are not negotiable. The weaker party to the contract must *adhere* to the dictated terms of the printed form if he wants the goods or services at all. There is no point in choosing a competitor of the large firm where the competitor uses a printed form containing clauses indistinguishable from the clauses in the form contract of the original, large enterprise.

[1]   Precocious Views of Unconscionability — Contracts of Adhesion — No Choice — Economic Theory

These standardized contracts are called contracts of *adhesion*.[172] They are "drafted unilaterally by a business enterprise and forced upon an unwilling and often unknowing public for services that cannot readily be obtained elsewhere. . . . An adhesion contract is generally not bargained for but is imposed on the public for a necessary service on a take or leave it basis."[173] They may contain oppressive provisions which are imposed on the individual who may not even be cognizant of their existence. An early illustration of the contract of adhesion occurred in a well-known case where the buyer contracted to purchase a new automobile. The contract contained an express warranty from the manufacturer for the replacement of

---

[169] See McKinnon v. Benedict, 38 Wis. 2d 607, 157 N.W.2d 665 (1968), relying on the First Restatement § 367(b), and refusing to grant specific performance of a contract involving harsh restrictions on the use of land in exchange for a $5000 interest-free loan, where the interest would have amounted to only $145.

[170] Campbell Soup Co. v. Wentz, 75 F. Supp. 952 (D. Pa.), *aff'd*, 172 F.2d 80 (3d Cir. 1948).

[171] *Id.* at 83 (3d Cir. 1948) (citing (in n.12) Pomeroy, Equity Jurisprudence § 1405a (5th ed. 1941), and 5 S. Williston, Contracts § 1425 (rev. ed. 1937)).

[172] The phrase, "contract of adhesion," is usually attributed to Professor Patterson, *The Delivery of a Life Insurance Policy*, 33 Harv. L. Rev. 198, 222 (1919). The development of the concept, however, is principally attributable to Professor Ehrenzweig, *Adhesion Contracts in the Conflict of Laws*, 53 Colum. L. Rev. 1072, 1088–89 (1953), and Professor Kessler, *Contracts of Adhesion — Some Thoughts About Freedom of Contract*, 43 Colum. L. Rev. 629 (1943).

[173] Jones v. Dressel, 623 P.2d 370, 374 (Colo. 1981). A comprehensive discussion of contracts of adhesion is found in Rakoff, *Contracts of Adhesion: An Essay in Reconstruction*, 96 Harv. L. Rev. 1173 (1983).

defective parts but it also included a standardized disclaimer of all other warranties, express or implied. The buyer brought an action for breach of the implied warranty of merchantability and the seller defended on the basis of the disclaimer in the contract signed by the buyer, i.e., the buyer should be bound by what he signs, whether or not he read the terms of the document he signed. The court agreed that the defendant had stated a general rule which it normally followed, but quickly added that such general rules should not be applied on a "strict, doctrinal basis."[174] The court recognized the development of contracts of adhesion and proceeded to illuminate this development:

> The warranty before us is a standardized form designed for mass use. It is imposed upon the automobile consumer. He takes it or leaves it, and he must take it to buy an automobile. No bargaining is engaged in with respect to it. . . . The form warranty is not only standard with Chrysler but . . . it is the uniform warranty of the Automobile Manufacturers Association. . . . [Here, the court noted that the membership of the Association included virtually all American manufacturers.] The gross inequality of bargaining position occupied by the consumer in the automobile industry is thus apparent. There is no competition among the car makers in the area of express warranty. Where can the buyer go to negotiate for better protection? Such control and limitation of his remedies are inimical to the public welfare, and, at the very least, call for great care by the courts to avoid injustice through the application of strict common-law principles of freedom of contract.[175]

In this portion of the opinion, the court focused upon the lack of any meaningful choice by the typical automobile buyer who had to choose between signing a contract taking away fundamental protection accompanying the purchase of any product[176] or not receiving a product that was material to his economic well-being. Thus, such a buyer has no reasonable choice.[177] The typical buyer of an automobile or innumerable other products or services is unaware of such risk-shifting provisions in the fine print clauses of the form he signs. Such a buyer does not read such provisions and, even for the rare buyer who does read them, there is more than considerable doubt that he understands what he read. The buyer who is thoroughly aware of such material, risk-shifting provisions over which he has no bargaining power is extremely rare, but it is not unreasonable for even that buyer to ignore such fine print since the terms are not negotiable. The sad reality is that the typical consumer does not have the foggiest notion of such provisions, but signs what the salesperson refers to as the "standard form," though the salesperson is equally ignorant of the import of the boilerplate provisions.[178] Moreover, any notion that a merchant buyer is any more aware of the import of a powerful seller's printed terms than a consumer buyer is not supportable.[179]

---

[174] Henningsen v. Bloomfield Motors, Inc., 32 N.J. 358, 161 A.2d 69, 84 (1960).

[175] *Id.* at 87.

[176] There is no more fundamental protection than that afforded by the implied warranty of merchantability found in UCC § 2-314. Such protection, *inter alia*, assures goods that are fit for ordinary purposes, § 2-314(2)(c).

[177] If the product is not necessary to the physical or economic well-being of the buyer, arguably he does not require or need the product and, therefore, the seller may impose otherwise harsh provisions on the buyer. This argument, however, suggests a difficult and often nebulous distinction, i.e., the distinction between goods that are "necessaries" and those that are not, a distinction that has not proven analytically effective in other contexts. *See* John E. Murray, Jr., *Unconscionability: Unconscionability*, 31 U. Pitt. L. Rev. 1, 29–30 (1969).

[178] "[C]an it be said that an ordinary layman would realize what he was relinquishing?" Henningsen v. Bloomfield Motors, 32 N.J. 358, 399, 161 A.2d 69, 92 (1960).

[179] The author's experience in working with numerous purchasing departments of national and multi-national

Standard law and economic theory suggests that concerns over the fairness of the superior bargaining party's nonnegotiable terms are clearly overdrawn since the market will induce sellers to include only efficient terms in their boilerplate. When a market functions effectively, the theory suggests that buyers and sellers will prefer the same rational contract terms. If so, the theory suggests that the seller's boilerplate should be enforced even where negotiation of different terms is not possible. The standard theory, however, assumes that buyers are fully informed, rational decision-makers; but that is an illusion. As noted by a prominent law and economic scholar, buyers focus on certain elements of a bargain. Sellers have an incentive to make such "salient" terms competitive, but they also have an incentive to make other terms — the non-salient terms of which buyers are typically oblivious — favorable to themselves.[180] The tension is between the necessity to insure the stability of contracts through the requirement that one must be bound by what he signs, whether or not he reads or understands it, and the reality that consumer buyers and even merchant buyers are unwittingly manifesting assent to clauses disclaiming basic warranties and excluding fundamental remedies without awareness of choice. It was inevitable that courts would confront this paradox by searching for devices to avoid injustice to the unknowing buyer, while paying lip service to the preservation of the citadel of stability that one is bound by what he signs, regardless of his failure to read or understand it.

[2] Non-Contractual Documents — Precocious Views of Unconscionability — Covert Tools

It is one thing to suggest that a party is not excused from the terms of a writing on the footing that he neither read nor understood it,[181] but quite another to bind a party to a contract when the writing allegedly representing that contract is not reasonably identified as evidence of a contract. Where a package is left in a parcel room and the owner is handed a small, cardboard check, is he unreasonable if he views that pasteboard merely as a means of identifying his parcel at the time of retrieval rather than evidence of a special contract limiting the liability of the parcel room? A number of courts have said no, i.e., the owner is not bound by unread material on such a claim check because, as a reasonable person, he would not have understood the check as evidence of a contract and did not therefore, agree to be bound by its terms.[182] In *Magliozzi v. P & T Container Serv. Co.*,[183] an indemnity clause on pickup ticket issued by trash collector was not enforceable because the other party neither knew nor had

---

international corporations for more than two decades emphatically revealed a pervasive ignorance of their suppliers' boilerplate as well as a resignation that such terms were not subject to negotiation. Where, however, the merchant buyer has superior bargaining power, the seller's terms become negotiable.

[180] Russell Korobkin in *Bounded Rationality, Standard Form Contracts, and Unconscionability*, 70 U Chi. L. Rev. 1203, 1206 (2003).

[181] *See* Independent Directory Corp. v. Vandenbrock, 43 Ohio Op. 229, 94 N.E.2d 228, 230 (Ct. App. 1950): "It is somewhat unusual that a court at this late day should have to repeat, that one who signs a contract without first making a reasonable effort to learn what is in it may not in the absence of fraud, or mutual mistake, avoid the effect of such a contract. . . . 'It will not do for a man to enter into a contract and, when called upon to respond to its obligations, to say that he did not read it when he signed it, or did not know what it contained. If this were permitted, contracts would not be worth the paper on which they are written; but such is not the law. A contractor must stand by the words of his contract; and, if he will not read what he signs, he alone is responsible for his omission. . . .'"

[182] *See* Klar v. H. & M. Parcel Room, Inc., 270 A.D. 538, 61 N.Y.S.2d 285 (1946), *aff'd*, 296 N.Y. 1044, 73 N.E.2d 912 (1947).

[183] 34 Mass. App. Ct. 591, 614 N.E.2d 690 (1993).

reason to know that the ticket purported to be a contract.[184]

Where the writing evidenced a contract containing material, risk-shifting clauses appearing inconspicuously in barely readable print, other courts did not shirk from holding such provisions inoperative. Where a particularly oppressive provision was printed on the reverse side of a writing calling for the buyer's signature on the face of the writing, the clause was held unenforceable because the clause was not even remotely contemplated.[185]

These devices and others[186] designed to avoid oppression of the party against whom they are designed to operate, however, could be subsequently overcome by redrafting of the document. For example, placing the nefarious provision on the side of the document where the signature appears may make it enforceable.[187] Yet, the physical placement of such a clause hardly insures its cognizance by its victim.[188] The drafter has often taken the document "to the absolute limit of what the law can conceivably bear."[189] Even if the language is excruciatingly clear, courts were willing to suggest that such "unbelievable" provisions could have been made clearer.[190] Thus, courts used "covert tools" to achieve just ends, giving rise to the famous dictum of Karl Llewellyn, "Covert tools are never reliable tools."[191] What was needed was a principle that would bring this judicial process "out into the open," i.e., a principle that would permit courts to say what they were doing — that in essence would have courts state, "[W]hen it gets too stiff to make sense, then the court may knock it over."[192] The principle appeared in § 2-302 of the UCC, the section on unconscionability.

---

[184] *See also* Lachs v. Fidelity & Casualty Co., 306 N.Y. 357, 117 N.E.2d 555 (1954) where the decedent procured airline insurance from a vending machine at the airport and a clause in the policy restricted coverage to scheduled airline flight. The majority of the court held the clause inoperative because it provided insufficient notice.

[185] Cutler Corp. v. Latshaw, 374 Pa. 1, 6, 97 A.2d 234, 237 (1953), where Justice Musmanno, in typically florid language, suggested, "One of the most hateful acts of the ill-famed Roman tyrant Caligula was that of having the laws inscribed upon pillars so high that the people could not read them. Although the warrant of attorney in the numerous sheets of the contract at bar was within the vision of the defendant, it was so placed [on the reverse side where her signature was not required] as to be completely beyond her contemplation of its purport. An inconspicuously printed legend on a contract form or letterhead which is obviously fortuitous, irrelevant, or superfluous is no more part of the agreement entered into than the advertisements on the walls of the room in which the contract is signed."

[186] Still another device to avoid oppressive clauses is the strict construction of clauses against the drafter, *e.g.*, Galligan v. Arovitch, 421 Pa. 301, 219 A.2d 463 (1966) (construing clause exculpating the lessor from liability strictly as not involving "lawns," where clause mentioned sidewalks and other places of injury).

[187] See L. B. Foster Co. v. Tri-W Constr. Co., 409 Pa. 318, 186 A.2d 18 (1962), which can be read to suggest that confession of judgment clauses become enforceable if they appear on the same side of the document as the signature.

[188] For an early recognition that extremely complicated, fine-print clauses of casualty insurance policies were virtually impossible for the insured to understand, *see* De Lancey v. Insurance Co., 52 N.H. 581 (1873).

[189] Statement of Karl Llewellyn in 1 STATE OF NEW YORK 1954 LAW REVISION COMMISSION REPORT, HEARINGS ON THE UNIFORM COMMERCIAL CODE at 113.

[190] "The clause is perfectly clear and the court said, 'Had it been desired to provide such an unbelievable thing, surely language could have been made clearer.' Then counsel redrafts, and they not only say it twice as well, but they wind up saying, 'And we really mean it,' and the court looks at it a second time and says, 'Had it been the kind of thing really intended to go into an agreement, surely language could have been found. . . .'" K. Llewellyn, *id.* at 114.

[191] "The net effect is unnecessary confusion and unpredictability, together with inadequate remedy, and evil persisting that calls for remedy. Covert tools are never reliable tools." Llewellyn, *Book Review*, 52 HARV. L. REV. 700, 703 (1939) (reviewing O. PRAUSNITZ, THE STANDARDIZATION OF COMMERCIAL CONTRACTS IN ENGLISH AND CONTINENTAL LAW (1937)).

[192] K. Llewellyn, *supra* note 189, at 114.

[B]   The Meaning of Unconscionability

[1]   Vague Definitions — Uniform Commercial Code — Llewellyn's Purpose — RESTATEMENT 2d

It is almost mandatory to begin an exploration of the meaning of unconscionability with the quotation from an eighteenth century English case, i.e., an unconscionable agreement is one "such as no man in his senses and not under delusion would make on the one hand, and as no honest and fair man would accept on the other."[193] This statement has no more utility than those found in many opinions by courts of equity which pervasively foster "conscionable" conduct by frowning on "unconscionable" conduct. Unfortunately, it cannot be said that the Llewellyn solution in the UCC fares any better: "If the court as a matter of law finds the contract or any clause of the contract to have been unconscionable at the time it was made the court may refuse to enforce the contract, or it may enforce the remainder of the contract without the unconscionable clause as to avoid any unconscionable result."[194]

Courts have expressly recognize that the UCC does not attempt to define unconscionability.[195] The harshest criticism of the § 2-302 UCC statement of unconscionability which is replicated in § 208 of the Restatement 2d of Contracts is that it amounts to no more than "an emotionally satisfying incantation" which clearly indicates that "it is easy to say nothing with words."[196] Yet, Professor Llewellyn regarded this section "as perhaps the most valuable section

---

[193] Hume v. United States, 132 U.S. 406, 10 S. Ct. 134, 33 L. Ed. 393 (1889) (quoting Earl of Chesterfield v. Janssen, 2 Ves. Sen. 125, 155, 28 Eng. Rep. 82, 100 (Ch. 1750)).

[194] UCC § 2-302(1).

[195] *See, e.g.,* Lucier v. Williams, 366 N.J. Super.485, 492, 841 A.2d 907, 911 (2004) ("There is no hard and fast definition of unconscionability. As the Supreme Court explained in Kugler v. Romain, 58 N J. 522, 543 279 A.2d 640 (1971), unconscionability is "an amorphous concept obviously designed to establish a broad business ethic.' "). United Cos. Lending Corp. v. Sargeant, 20 F. Supp. 2d 192, 205 (D. Mass. 1998) (unconscionability requires a case-specific assessment; there is no clear, all-purpose definition of unconscionability); NEC Techs., Inc v. Nelson, 267 Ga. 390, 478 S.E.2d 769, 771 (1996) (determination of unconscionability is to be made on the basis of a variety of factors not unifiable into a formula); Goodwin v. Ford Motor Credit Co., 970 F. Supp. 1007, 1013 (M.D. Ala. 1997) (Alabama law provides no implicit standard of unconscionability; each case must be decided on its own facts). In Bishop v. Washington, 331 Pa. Super. 387, 399, 480 A.2d 1088, 1094 (1984), the court suggests, "It is impossible to formulate a precise definition of the unconscionability concept."

[196] Arthur Leff, *Unconscionability and the Code — The Emperor's New Clause,* 115 U. PA. L. REV. 485, 558–59 (1967). Professor Leff's article was the first major analysis of the concept, to be followed by a plethora of law review articles on the subject. Professor Leff describes his work as "a study in statutory pathology, an examination in some depth of the misdrafting of one section of a massive, codifying statute and the misinterpretations which came to surround it." *Id.* at 485. Another analysis, critical of the Leff approach, is John Murray, *Unconscionability: Unconscionability,* 31 U. PITT. L. REV. 1 (1969). This article was submitted to three scholars for their comments and reactions which appeared in a subsequent issue of U. PITT. L. REV.: Braucher, *The Unconscionable Contract or Term,* 31 U. PITT. L. REV. 337 (1970); Speidel, *Unconscionability, Assent and Consumer Protection,* 31 U. PITT. L. REV. 359 (1970); Leff, *Unconscionability and the Crowd — Consumers and the Common Law Tradition,* 31 U. PITT. L. REV. 349 (1970). In commenting on all of these articles, one text writer suggested that the academic effort to afford meaning to the concept of unconscionability has become embroiled in concepts that might be justly called elusive, though the debaters are about as elusive as the concepts. D. DOBBS, HANDBOOK ON THE LAW OF REMEDIES 708 n.12 (1973). Among the numerous additional articles, the following deserve mention: Ellinghaus, *In Defense of Unconscionability,* 78 YALE L.J. 757 (1969); Spanogle, *Analyzing Unconscionability Problems,* 117 U. PA. L. REV. 931 (1969); Epstein, *Unconsciona-bility: A Critical Reappraisal,* 18 J.L. & ECON. 293 (1975); Schwartz, *A Reexamination of Nonsubstantive Unconscionability,* 63 VA. L. REV. 1053 (1977); Hillman, *Debunking Some Myths About Unconscionability: A New Framework for UCC § 2-302 ,* 67 CORNELL L. REV. 1 (1981).

in the entire Code."[197] He certainly did not believe that the section itself would provide the necessary certainty, stability, and predictability that "covert tools" failed to provide. Rather, courts had to confront questions of unfairness in the bargaining process without the aid of covert tools. The statute, itself, would not be effective because "an approach by statute [is] dubious, uncertain and likely to be both awkward in manner and deficient and spotty in scope."[198] The first part of § 2-302, therefore, simply directs *courts* to confront these questions which are necessarily fact questions, though they will be decided exclusively by courts.[199] Llewellyn's intended result of these confrontations would be "precedent." To restrain "the untutored imagination of courts,"[200] the second part of the section permits "all kinds of [business] background to be presented to instruct the court."[201] He envisioned the overall effect of the section to "greatly advance certainty in a . . . most baffling, most troubling, and almost unreckonable situation."[202] Thus, Llewellyn unequivocally presented the challenge of adumbrating the concept of unconscionability to the courts.

The lack of guidance in the language of § 2-302 invites the use of the comments to the section. In keeping with the purpose of Llewellyn, the first comment unequivocally indicates the intention of the drafters to permit courts "to police explicitly against the contracts or clauses which they find to be unconscionable . . . ," and to avoid past judicial efforts to accomplish this effect through such "covert tools" as "adverse construction of language, manipulation of the rules of offer and acceptance or by determinations that the clause is contrary to public policy or to the dominant purpose of the contract."[203] The comment provides the test to be applied:

> The basic test is whether, in the light of the general commercial background and the commercial needs of the particular trade or case, the clauses involved are so one-sided as to be unconscionable under the circumstances existing at the time of the making of

---

[197] K. Llewellyn, *supra* note 189, at 57.

[198] K. LLEWELLYN, THE COMMON LAW TRADITION: DECIDING APPEALS 370 (1960).

[199] Section 2-302(1) restricts questions of unconscionability to courts rather than juries. Northwest Acceptance Corp. v. Almont Gravel, Inc., 162 Mich. App. 294, 412 N.W.2d 719 (1987); Frank's Maintenance & Eng'g, Inc. v. C. A. Roberts Co., 86 Ill. App. 3d 980, 42 Ill. Dec. 25, 408 N.E.2d 403 (1st Dist. 1980); Industralease Automated & Scientific Equip. Corp. v. R.M.E. Enters., Inc., 58 A.D.2d 482, 396 N.Y.S.2d 427 (2d Dep't 1977). In Mullan v. Quickie Aircraft Corp., 797 F.2d 845 (10th Cir. 1986), the court suggests that, while a finding of unconscionability is a question of law, when such a finding is made upon the presentation of evidence, the finding becomes a mixed question of law and fact. If what must be decided in the mixed question involves primarily a consideration of legal principles, the appellate court reviews *de novo* (citing *In re* Tri-State Equip., Inc., 792 F.2d 967 (10th Cir. 1986)).

[200] K. Llewellyn, *supra* note 189.

[201] *Id.* UCC § 2-302(2): "When it is claimed or appears to the court that the contract or any clause thereof may be unconscionable the parties shall be afforded a reasonable opportunity to present evidence as to its commercial setting, purpose and effect to aid the court in making the determination." *See* Carlson v. General Motors Corp., 883 F. 2d 287, 292 (4th Cir. 1989) ("[U]nconscionability claims should rarely be determined on the bare bones pleading — that is, with no opportunity to present relevant evidence of the circumstances surrounding the original consummation of their contractual relationship."). *See also.* Capital Assocs. v. Hudgens, 455 So. 2d 651, 653 (Fla. Dist. Ct. App. 1984); Luick v. Graybar Elec. Co., 473 F.2d 1360 (8th Cir. 1973); Beckman v. Vassall-Dillworth Lincoln-Mercury, Inc., 321 Pa. Super. 428, 468 A.2d 784 (1983) (full evidentiary hearing not required as long as no issue of material fact exists). *See also* Lindemann v. Eli Lilly & Co., 816 F.2d 199 (5th Cir. 1987) (district court raised issue of unconscionability *sua sponte* — held: trial court's procedure fundamentally disadvantaged appellant and deprived it of defense since the court must have evidence of unconscionability before it can support any finding on that issue and a defendant is entitled to fair notice that a portion of its contract will be challenged for unconscionability).

[202] K. Llewellyn, *supra* note 189.

[203] UCC § 2-302 comment 1.

the contract. . . . The principle is one of the prevention of oppression and unfair surprise . . . and not of disturbance of the allocation of risks because of superior bargaining power.

"Oppression" was seen as the element of leaving no reasonable choice for the weaker party to negotiate different terms, while "unfair surprise" resulted from the insertion of the allegedly unconscionable clause, drafted in prolix language, in a maze of fine print. The last portion of the quoted comment, i.e., that risks should not be disturbed simply because of the appearance of superior bargaining power, is generally viewed as regarding the mere existence of superior bargaining power as insufficient to declare a contract or term unconscionable. Rather, it is the oppressive use of such power that should alert courts to strike down an offensive contract or clause.[204]

Sixteen years after the UCC version of unconscionability appeared,[205] the RESTATEMENT 2d version of the concept replicated the Code statement. Like its older sibling, it made no attempt to set forth a workable statement of unconscionability, but merely indicated what a court may do once it finds that a contract or clause of a contract is unconscionable.[206] The accompanying comment suggests that unconscionability must be determined in the light of its setting, and "[r]elevant factors include weaknesses in the contracting process."[207] Echoes of historic equitable unconscionability attend another comment. While inadequacy of consideration, itself, would not signal unconscionability, "gross disparity in the values exchanged [overall imbalance] may be an important factor in a determination that a contract is unconscionable. . . ."[208]

It is abundantly clear that both the UCC and RESTATEMENT 2d direct courts to adumbrate the concept of unconscionability on a case-by-case basis. The Restatement notes that, "This section is new; it follows Uniform Commercial Code § 2-302."[209] Modern cases, however, often cite the Restatement with no mention of its UCC twin. The Restatement 2d version may be referred to as "common law" unconscionability in a context suggesting an unwarranted inference that it is simply a continuation of the ancient concept of unconscionability in equity.[210] Like the replicated language of unconscionability in the Restatement 2d, however, the judicial analyses accompanying § 208 are the mirror image of the analyses of UCC § 2-302.

---

[204] See Anderson v. Ashby, 873 So. 2d 168, 194 (Ala. 2003) and cases cited therein.

[205] The first jurisdiction to enact the Code was Pennsylvania, where it became effective in 1954. The preliminary draft of the RESTATEMENT 2d section on unconscionability appeared in 1970.

[206] "If a contract or term thereof is unconscionable at the time the contract is made, a court may refuse to enforce the contract, or may enforce the remainder of the contract without the unconscionable term, or may so limit the application of any unconscionable term as to avoid any unconscionable result." RESTATEMENT 2d § 208. Courts recognize that this is not an "attempt to define unconscionability in a black letter rule of law." Steinhardt v. Rudolph, 422 So. 2d 884, 890 (Fla. Dist. Ct. App. 1982).

[207] RESTATEMENT 2d § 208 comment a.

[208] RESTATEMENT 2d § 208 comment c.

[209] RESTATEMENT 2d § 208, Reporter's Notes.

[210] See, e. g., Doe v. SexSearch.com, 551 F. 3d 412, 419–20 (6th Cir. 2008).

[2]   The Meaning of Unconscionability in the Courts

[a]   Scope

While the UCC is a statutory prescription requiring courts sitting as courts of law to police contracts for unconscionability, even apart from the Restatement 2d version, the use of the doctrine was not relegated to contracts for the sale of goods though the Code is technically applicable only to such contracts. "Many courts have applied the UCC approach to cases not strictly governed by the Code."[211] Thus, the doctrine has been held applicable to cases involving oil and gas royalty rights,[212] an equipment lease,[213] a ground lease of condominium property,[214] rental agreements for mobile home lots,[215] a judgment note,[216] a mortgage loan,[217] an employment dispute,[218] failure to list the plaintiff's business in a telephone directory,[219] a bank signature card,[220] a contract to promote a concert tour,[221] and numerous other cases not involving a sale-of-goods contract. California originally did not enact Section 2-302 of the UCC but, in 1979, it enacted a statute with identical language that is not limited to contracts for the sale of goods.[222] With the incorporation of the concept in the RESTATEMENT 2d[223] and the inclusion of similar concepts in various consumer protection statutes,[224] there is no doubt that the doctrine may be applied to any type of contract whether through use of the RESTATEMENT 2d provision, a specialized statute, or through analogous application of the UCC provision where the Code does not otherwise apply.

---

[211] Resource Mgmt. Co. v. Weston Ranch & Livestock Co., 706 P.2d 1028 (Utah 1985).

[212] *Id.*

[213] John Deere Leasing Co. v. Blubaugh, 636 F. Supp. 1569 (D. Kan. 1986). See UCC Article 2A (promulgated in 1987), § 108, which applies the unconscionability concept to personal property leases.

[214] Steinhardt v. Rudolph, 422 So. 2d 884 (Fla. Dist. Ct. App. 1982).

[215] Garrett v. Janiewski, 480 So. 2d 1324 (Fla. Dist. Ct. App. 1985).

[216] Germantown Mfg. Co. v. Rawlinson, 341 Pa. Super. 42, 491 A.2d 138 (1985).

[217] United Cos. Lending Corp. v. Sargeant, 20 F. Supp. 2d 192 (D. Mass. 1998).

[218] Kinney v. United HealthCare Servs., Inc., 70 Cal. App. 4th 1322, 83 Cal. Rptr. 2d 348 (4th Dist. 1999).

[219] Rozeboom v. Northwestern Bell Tel. Co., 358 N.W.2d 241 (S.D. 1984).

[220] Perdue v. Crocker Nat'l Bank, 141 Cal. App. 3d 200, 190 Cal. Rptr. 205 (1st Dist. 1983), *superseded*, 38 Cal. 3d 913, 216 Cal. Rptr. 345, 702 P.2d 503 (1985).

[221] Graham v. Scissor-Tail, Inc., 28 Cal. 3d 807, 623 P.2d 165 (1981).

[222] See CAL. CIV. CODE § 1670.5.

[223] RESTATEMENT 2d § 208.

[224] See, e.g., John Deere Leasing Co. v. Blubaugh, 636 F. Supp. 1569, 1572 (D. Kan. 1986), where the court states that unconscionability came into the law of Kansas through the UCC along with the Consumer Credit Code (KAN. STAT. ANN. § 16a-5-108), the Consumer Protection Act (KAN. STAT. ANN. § 50-627) and the Residential Landlord and Tenant Act (KAN. STAT. ANN. § 58-2544). See also Uniform Consumer Sales Practices Act of 1970 and Uniform Consumer Credit Code of 1974, which contain provisions dealing with unconscionability though neither has been enacted in a large number of jurisdictions as of the date of this writing. UCC § 2A-108(2) is modeled on the Uniform Consumer Credit Code, § 5.108, 7A U.L.A. 167–69 (1974).

[b]   Tests of Unconscionability in the Courts — "Procedural — Substantive" et al.

Notwithstanding the plethora of case law dealing with the concept of unconscionability, as suggested earlier,[225] there is no single description of the concept to which all courts subscribe. Courts emphasize the "flexibility" of the concept depending upon the facts.[226] The time for determining whether a contract or clause thereof is unconscionable is the time the contract was made.[227] Numerous cases contain the historic definition of unconscionability as a contract or clause that no person in his right senses would make.[228] They will also include quotations or paraphrases from the UCC comments, i.e., "The principle is one of the prevention of oppression and unfair surprise."[229] The leading expression attempting to define the concept is the statement from a well-known opinion by Judge J. Skelly Wright: "Unconscionability has generally been recognized to include an absence of meaningful choice on the part of one of the parties together with contract terms which are unreasonably favorable to the other party."[230]

"Oppression" and "unfair surprise" and Skelly Wright's "absence of meaningful choice" and "unreasonably favorable terms" blossomed into an analysis that would pervade discussions of unconscionability thereafter. Notwithstanding his disdain for the language of 2-302 which he characterized as an "emotionally satisfying incantation proving that it is easy to say nothing with words,"[231] Professor Arthur Leff provided a new diction that would become the conventional wisdom: "procedural" and "substantive" unconscionability.

Procedural Unconscionability. Leff viewed defects in the bargaining process as *procedural* unconscionability ("bargaining naughtiness"), i.e., the manner in which the contract was negotiated under the circumstances. One court has suggested the following indices of *procedural* unconscionability:

> The use of printed form or boilerplate contract drawn skillfully by the party in the strongest economic position' generally offered on a take-it-or-leave-it basis, . . . phrasing contractual terms 'in language that is incomprehensible to a layman or that

---

[225] See note 195, *supra.*

[226] *See, e.g.,* Perdue v. Crocker Nat'l Bank, 141 Cal. App. 3d 200, 190 Cal. Rptr. 205, 209 (1st Dist. 1983), *superseded,* 38 Cal. 3d 913, 216 Cal. Rptr. 345, 702 P.2d 503 (1985); A & M Produce Co. v. FMC Corp., 135 Cal. App. 3d 473, 486, 186 Cal. Rptr. 114, 121 (4th Dist. 1982).

[227] Doctor's Associates v. Jabush, 89 F. 3d 109, 113 (2d Cir. 1996). *See also* Resource Mgmt. Co. v. Weston Ranch & Livestock Co., 706 P.2d 1028, 1043 (Utah 1985): "Generally, the critical juncture for determining whether a contract is unconscionable is the moment when it is entered into by both parties. . . . To judge the substantive fairness of contracts at a date subsequent to their making could nullify many contracts entailing a speculative element." *See also* Zapatha v. Dairy Mart, Inc., 381 Mass. 284, 408 N.E.2d 1370 (1980).

[228] See the full text of the quote at text, *supra* note 200.

[229] UCC § 2-302 comment 1. Concepts of oppression and unfair surprise as found in this comment are mentioned in numerous unconscionability cases. *See, e.g.,* Deutsche Bank National Trust Co. v. Pevarski, 2010 Ohio App. LEXIS 655 at *17 (March 1, 2010); North Water LLC v. North Water St. Tarragon, LLC, 2009 Conn Super. LEXIS 2696 at *53 (Oct. 13, 2009); Resource Mgmt. Co. v. Weston Ranch & Livestock Co., 706 P.2d 1028, 1041 (Utah 1985); A & M Produce Co. v. FMC Corp., 135 Cal. App. 3d 473, 486, 186 Cal. Rptr. 114, 121–22 (4th Dist. 1982); Kerr-McGee Corp. v. Northern Utils., 673 F.2d 323 (10th Cir.), *cert. denied,* 459 U.S. 989, 103 S. Ct. 344, 74 L. Ed. 2d 385 (1982).

[230] Williams v. Walker-Thomas Furniture Co., 350 F.2d 445, 449, 121 U.S. App. D.C. 315 (1965), which is introduced in Snyder v. Rogers, 346 Pa. Super. 505, 499 A.2d 369, 1371 (1985), with the statement, "As other courts have done, . . . we turn to Judge Skelly Wright's definition. . . ." *See also* Municipality of Anchorage v. Locker, 723 P.2d 1261 (Alaska 1986); A & M Produce Co. v. FMC Corp., 135 Cal. App. 3d 473, 486, 186 Cal. Rptr. 114 (4th Dist. 1982).

[231] Leff, *supra* note 196, at 558–59.

divert[s] his attention from the problems raised by them or the rights given up through them,' . . . concealing key contractual provisions in a maze of fine print, . . . or in an inconspicuous part of the document, . . . minimizing key contractual provisions by deceptive sales practices, . . . 'lack of opportunity for meaningful negotiation,' . . . whether the aggrieved party was compelled to accept the terms, . . . an 'exploitation of the underprivileged, unsophisticated and illiterate. . . .'[232]

Substantive unconscionability, on the other hand, is concerned with whether the obligations assumed are unreasonably favorable to one of the parties, i.e., whether a term of the contract itself is overly harsh, particularly one-sided or lopsided, or manifests an outrageous degree of unfairness.[233] The use of these new labels, however, was not always symmetrical. One court suggests that "Substantive unconscionability is indicated by 'contract terms so one-sided as to oppress or unfairly surprise an innocent party,' "[234] while another court suggests that the *procedural* element encompasses the two factors of oppression and surprise.[235] Still another court suggests that clauses of an oppressive character suggest *substantive* unconscionability, while *procedural* unconscionability is either (1) lack of knowledge ("unfair surprise") or (2) lack of voluntariness (*e.g.*, a contract of adhesion).[236] The lack of precision in the use of these labels raises doubts as to whether it is the "oppression" and "unfair surprise" notions, the *procedural* and *substantive* labels, or both, that lack utility. Regardless of their usefulness, it would be extremely rare to find any significant discussion of unconscionability in the current case law without reference to procedural and substantive unconscionability.

[c]   Are Both Procedural and Substantive Unconscionability Necessary? Contracts of Adhesion Are No Longer Evil

The inutility of the "procedural" and "substantive" labels is emphasized by the judicial reaction to whether there must be sufficient evidence of both procedural and substantive unconscionability to refuse enforcement of a contract or term. Many courts suggest that it is necessary to show both procedural and substantive unconscionability,[237] but that conventional wisdom displays serious erosion. Considerable confusion concerning this issue may exist in the case law of a given jurisdiction.

A Florida district court held that Florida law required the plaintiff to show both procedural and substantive unconscionability to establish that a class action waiver in an arbitration

---

[232] Resource Mgmt. Co. v. Weston Ranch & Livestock Co., 706 P.2d 1028, 1042 (Utah 1985).

[233] See Pendergast v. Sprint Nextel Corp., 592 F. 3d 1119, 1139 (11th Cir. 2010). See also Garrett v. Janiewski, 480 So. 2d 1324, 1326 (Fla. Dist. Ct. App. 1985): "Substantive unconscionability requires proving that the terms of the contract are unreasonable and unfair. . . . [I]t requires a showing of commercial unreasonableness. . . . [T]he terms must be unreasonably favorable to one party."

[234] Resource Mgmt. Co. v. Weston Ranch & Livestock Co., 706 P.2d 1028, 1041 (Utah 1985) (relying on Bekins Bar V Ranch v. Huth, 664 P.2d 455, 462 (Utah 1983)).

[235] Sanchez v. Western Pizza Enterprises, Inc., 172 Cal. App. 4th 154, 171, 832, 90 Cal. Rptr. 3d 818, 832 (2009), citing A & M Produce Co. v. FMC Corp., 135 Cal. App. 3d 473, 486, 186 Cal. Rptr. 114, 121 (4th Dist. 1982) (emphasis added).

[236] Bank of Indiana, N.A. v. Holyfield, 476 F. Supp. 104, 109 (S.D. Miss. 1979).

[237] See, e. g., Lynn v. McKinley Ground Transport, LLC, 2009 Ohio App. LEXIS 5098 at *17 (Nov. 16, 2009); Clark v. DaimlerChrysler Corp., 268 Mich. App. 138, 143, 706 N. W. 2d 471, 474 (2005); Armendariz v. Foundation Health Psychcare Services, Inc., 24 Cal. 4th 83, 114, 6 P. 3d 660, 690 (2000); Harris v. Green Tree Financial Corp., 183 F. 3d 173, 181 (3d Cir. 1999) (Pennsylvania).

agreement was unenforceable. Finding that the waiver was not procedurally unconscionable, the court enforced it without addressing substantive unconscionability. On appeal, the Eleventh Circuit had no difficulty finding Florida precedent confirming the district court's holding, but it also found precedent that appeared to reject the requirement that both procedural and substantive unconscionability had to be shown. Statements suggesting that the procedural/substantive analysis is only a "general approach" and not a "rule of law" were found along with "balancing" or "sliding scale" approaches. In a previous opinion, the court had recognized that Florida had rejected the procedural-substantive analysis as a rule of law but also noted that "it is generally helpful." The confusion required the court to certify the question of the proper analytical method to be used in the application of the procedural-substantive approach to the Florida Supreme Court.[238]

Under the "sliding scale" approach, the two types of unconscionability need not be present to the same degree. Thus, the more substantively oppressive the term of the contract, the less evidence of procedural unconscionability would be necessary to avoid the term and vice versa.[239] Several cases, however, suggest that substantive unconscionability alone will be sufficient to rid a contract of egregious terms. As suggested by one court, "While determinations of unconscionability are ordinarily based on a conclusion that both the procedural and substantive elements are present, there have been exceptional cases where a provision of the contract is so egregious as to warrant holding it unenforceable on the ground of substantive unconscionability alone."[240]

While other jurisdictions suggest that *either* procedural or substantive unconscionability can be sufficient,[241] procedural unconscionability, alone, is problematic. There is considerable caution in the statement, "While it is conceivable that a contract might be unconscionable on the theory of unfair surprise without any substantive imbalance in the obligations of the parties to the contract, that would be rare."[242] It is important to remember the paradigm of procedural unconscionably, the contract of adhesion. "Procedural unconscionability generally takes the form of a contract of adhesion, that is, a contract drafted by the party of superior bargaining strength and imposed on the other, without opportunity to negotiate the terms."[243] Though the contract of adhesion clearly illustrates the "absence of meaningful choice," that concept has eroded as the standardized form contract with non-negotiable terms has gained

---

[238] Pendergast v. Sprint Nextel Corp., 592 F. 3d 1119 (11th Cir. 2010).

[239] Shroyer v. New Cingular Wireless Servs., 498 F. 3d 976, 981–82 (9th Cir. 2007) indicating that California applies the "sliding scale" approach as does New York, see Ford Motor Credit Co. v. Meehan, 2008 U.S. Dist. LEXIS 25474 at *11 (E. D. N. Y. 2008) and Missouri, see Pleasants v. Amer. Exp. Co., 2007 U.S. Dist. LEXIS 60747 at *12 (E. D. Mo. 2007).

[240] Gillman v. Chase Manhattan Bank, N. A., 73 N Y. 2d 1, 12, 534 N. E. 2d 824, 829 (1988), quoted in Ragone v. Atlantic Video, 2010 U.S. App. LEXIS 3018 at *17 (Feb. 17, 2010) and followed in Brower v. Gateway 2000, Inc., 246 A. D. 2d 246, 676 N. Y. S. 2d 569 (1998). In Dallas Aero., Inc. v. CIS Air Corp., 352 F.3d 775, 787 (2d Cir. 2003), however, the court emphasizes that the *Gillman* analysis would only apply to the "exceptional" case. No such limitation is found in Adler v. Fred Lind Manor, 103 P. 3d 773, 783 (Wn. App. 2004). In Maxwell v. Fidelity Financial Services, 184 Ariz. 82, 90, 907 P.2d 51, 59 (1995) the court noted that substantive unconscionability alone is sufficient, "especially in cases involving either price-cost disparity or limitation of remedies."

[241] See, e. g., Kelly v. Whitehaven Settlement Funding, LLC, 2010 U.S. Dist. LEXIS 17490 (S. D. Ill. Feb. 26, 2010); Fryar v. Sav-Amil, LLC, 2009 U.S. Dist. LEXIS 121981 (N. D. Miss. Dec. 10, 2009); L. A. Fitness International LLC v. Harding, 2009 U.S. Dist. LEXIS 110585 (W. D. Wash. Nov. 25, 2009).

[242] Resource Mgmt. Co. v. Weston Ranch & Livestock Co., 706 P.2d 1028, 1043 (Utah 1985).

[243] Laster v. AT& T Mobility LLC, 584 F. 3d 849, 853 (9th Cir. 2009). Contracts of adhesion are fully discussed in the text at note 172 *et. seq., supra.*

acceptance. Courts now view contracts of adhesion as quite ordinary and, at worst, a factor to be considered in the unconscionability analysis. Indeed, in the eyes of some courts, there is nothing at all wrong with a contract of adhesion since standardized contract terms are essential for the efficient operation of the social institution of contract.[244] Something beyond the contract of adhesion is necessary. In the words of the New Jersey Supreme Court, "[A]dhesive consumer contracts, which are ordinarily enforceable, may rise to the level of unconscionability when substantive contractual terms and conditions impact 'public interests' adversely."[245] Courts have also been reluctant to determine whether procedural unconscionability, alone, is sufficient.[246] The rare exception, however, occurred where a pre-printed clause in a contract to purchase an automobile excluded consequential damages. The contract appeared in an owner's manual deposited in the glove box of the auto delivered to the buyer after the contract was formed. The buyer had no opportunity to see the clause when she signed the contract. While recognizing that cases typically involve both procedural and substantive unconscionability, the court explained that a contract "may be voidable without substantive unconscionability if the procedural unconscionability is sufficiently severe." Thus, the Supreme Court of Illinois found the clause to be unconscionable on the basis of procedural unconscionability alone.[247] The court's rationale included the fact that the buyer was a consumer who had no hand in drafting the clause and no power to bargain for different terms. These factors, however, only caused the court to "disfavor" the clause; they were not dispositive with respect to unconscionability. The additional fact that "tipped the balance in the plaintiff's favor" was the fact that the contract terms were not made available to the plaintiff at or before the time she signed the contract.[248] In a subsequent case involving a class action waiver, the court found the insufficiency of information provided in the agreement to allow a finding of a "degree" of procedural unconscionability, but it would be insufficient to make the clause unenforceable absent a finding of substantive unconscionability.[249]

The confusion over "procedural" and "substantive" unconscionability labels prompts a return to Professor Leff's critique of the UCC version of unconscionability in § 2-302 as nothing more than an "emotionally satisfying incantation proving that it is easy to say nothing with words." The labels, "procedural" and "substantive," however, might constitute more emotionally satisfying incantations.

[d]   Alternate Analysis — "Circle of Assent"

An alternate analysis of unconscionability is derived from Karl Llewellyn's concept of "blanket" versus genuine assent. The fundamental concept of contract law is the concept of assent. The basic idea that parties exercise their volition by committing themselves to future action and that the law provides their *circle of assent* with the status of a private law is fundamental to any discussion of contracts.[250] As for those boilerplate, printed terms that go

---

[244]   Carbajal v. H&R Block Tax Services 372 F. 3d 903, 906 (7th Cir. 2004).

[245]   Muhammad v. County Bank of Rehoboth Beach, 189 N. J. 1., 19, 912 A.2d 88, 99 (2006).

[246]   Adler v. Fred Lind Manor, 153 Wn. 2d 331, 347, 103 P. 3d 773, 782 (2004) recognized substantive unconscionability as sufficient, but left the question of whether procedural unconscionability would be sufficient for another day.

[247]   Razor v. Hyundai Motor America, 222 Ill. 2d 75, 100, 854 N. E. 2d 607, 622 (2006).

[248]   *Id.*, 854 N. E. 2d at 623.

[249]   Kinkel v. Cingular Wireless, LLC, 857 N E. 2d 250, 266 (Ill. 2006).

[250]   Quoted with approval from the second edition of this treatise in A & M Produce Co. v. FMC Corp., 135 Cal. App.

unread, the parties should be said to have assented to those which are reasonable, fair, expected, or, to use the term chosen by Professor Llewellyn, "not indecent."[251] Whether a term is reasonable, fair, expected or not indecent must depend upon the particular circumstances. Certainly, a clause simply repeating the automatic warranty protection a buyer would receive under the UCC would be a decent or reasonable, as well as expected, term. On the other hand, a more realistic scenario finds a disclaimer of basic warranty protection, e.g., a disclaimer of the implied warranty of merchantability or a limitation of its duration, in a printed form.[252] This is a deviation from the standard term of a contract for the sale of goods.[253] Similarly, it is normal for a buyer to expect to be compensated for consequential damages caused by a seller's breach.[254] A typical printed form will exclude such damages. Apart from its unconscionability provision, the UCC places threshold safeguards on the disclaimer of implied warranties. Thus, where the implied warranty of merchantability is disclaimed in writing and no trade expressions are used,[255] to help insure at least *apparent* assent by the purchaser to such a disclaimer, the Code requires the written disclaimer to be *conspicuous*[256] *and to mention the term "merchantability."*[257] While no similar requirement is expressly set forth to exclude consequential damages,[258] a court may require such an exclusionary clause to be conspicuous.[259] Requirements such as conspicuousness, however, are

---

3d 473, 186 Cal. Rptr. 114, 122 n.11 (4th Dist. 1982), and Perdue v. Crocker Nat'l Bank, 141 Cal. App. 3d 200, 190 Cal. Rptr. 204 (1st Dist. 1983), *superseded*, 38 Cal. 3d 913, 216 Cal. Rptr. 345, 702 P.2d 503 (1985).

[251] "Instead of thinking about 'assent' to boilerplate clauses, we can recognize that so far as concerns the specific, there is no assent at all. What has in fact been assented to, specifically, are the few dickered terms, and the broad type of the transaction, and but one more. That one more is a blanket assent (not a specific assent) to any not unreasonable or indecent terms the seller may have on his form, which do not alter or eviscerate the reasonable meaning of the dickered terms. The fine print which has not been read has no business to cut under the reasonable meaning of those dickered terms which constitute the dominant and only real expression of agreement, but much of it commonly belongs in." K. LLEWELLYN, THE COMMON LAW TRADITION: DECIDING APPEALS 370 (1960).

[252] The UCC permits implied warranties to be disclaimed under § 2-316(2) and (3), subject to certain safeguards. These safeguards will be discussed *infra*. The Magnuson-Moss Warranty Act, 15 U.S.C. §§ 2308(a) and (b) (§§ 108(a) and (b)), precludes the disclaimer of implied warranties in relation to *consumer* goods, but permits the warranty to be *limited in duration*.

[253] See Rakoff, *Contracts of Adhesion: An Essay in Reconstruction*, 96 HARV. L. REV. 1173, 1182 (1983), who suggests that Article 2 of the Code "is in large part a catalogue of the implied terms of contracts of sale," i.e., the standardized terms of sales, and any deviation from such terms are deviations from the parties' normal expectations and are frowned upon. There is no need for clauses of a contract to deal with warranties at all since they are implied under §§ 2-314 and 2-315 of the Code, or expressed through descriptions, affirmations of fact, promises, samples, or models pursuant to UCC § 2-313. Thus, when parties deal with warranties in one or more printed clauses, they are engaging in an exercise of "specifying deviation from the standardized plan rather than in defining the obligation *ab initio." Id. See also* Hartwig Farms, Inc. v. Pacific Gamble Robinson Co., 28 Wash. App. 539, 544, 625 P.2d 171, 174 (1981): "The code does not imply disclaimers; in fact, disclaimers are not favored in the law."

[254] Consequential damages are defined in UCC § 2-715 and are recoverable by the purchaser in proper circumstances along with the buyer's direct damages, such as contract price/market price differential (§ 2-713) or the remedy of "cover," § 2-712.

[255] UCC § 2-316(3)(a) permits implied warranties to be disclaimed by trade expressions like "as is" or "with all faults."

[256] UCC § 1-201(10) sets forth the test for conspicuousness: "[W]hen it is so written that a reasonable person against whom it is to operate ought to have noticed it."

[257] UCC § 2-316(2).

[258] *See* UCC § 2-719(3).

[259] *See, e.g.*, Insurance Co. of N. Am. v. Automatic Sprinkler Corp., 67 Ohio St. 2d 91, 423 N.E.2d 151 (1981). The prevailing view, however, is otherwise.

physical requirements, e.g., placing the clause on the front of a printed form in larger or darker print. Most buyers, consumers and merchants alike, are, however, unaware of the drastic nature of such a disclaimer or exclusionary clause. Thus, while a physically conspicuous clause may assure apparent assent, it does not assure *genuine or substantive assent*. If, therefore, the clause is physically conspicuous but incomprehensible to a reasonable buyer regardless of its print size or placement on the printed form, should the disclaimer be effective?

An even more compelling argument can be found in the situation of one who reads and understands a clause that would shift a material risk to him. Understanding the legal effect of a particular clause and signing the form containing that clause may still not manifest assent to the clause if the clause is presented as a contract of adhesion, i.e., a take-it-or-leave-it contract. Again, such an arrangement is the antithesis of volition and factual agreement of the parties — there is no bargain-in-fact in such a case. While the signing of such a document may, again, manifest *apparent* assent, it does not manifest *genuine* or *real* assent. The parties are certainly free to reallocate normal risks in their agreement and, if both *apparent* and *genuine* assent are present, such a reallocation is within their circle of assent.[260] Yet, a party should not be bound to a material, risk-shifting, inconspicuous provision in a standard form.[261] At a minimum, the reallocation must be physically conspicuous and it should be substantively conspicuous, i.e., understandable to a reasonable buyer. Moreover, the party against whom it is designed to operate should have had a reasonable choice in relation to such reallocation of normal risks at the time the contract was formed.[262]

On the basis of the foregoing, unconscionability may be seen as falling within either of two categories involving material, risk-shifting terms: (a) where such terms are unexpected by the party against whom they will operate, or (b) where such terms, though known and, therefore, not unexpected, are dictated by the party with superior bargaining power since the other party has no reasonable choice. "Unexpected" unconscionability is equivalent to "unfair surprise," i.e., the terms are such that they are not expected by the party who is asked to assent to them. Such a clause often appears in the "boilerplate" of a seller's form. It is not, however, unconscionable simply because it appears in the fine print. The clause must be a material, risk-shifting clause that the party would not expect to find therein.[263] The other type of unconscionability which may be captioned, "no choice," is equivalent to "oppression" since it

---

[260] Even here, if the reallocation of risks eventually leaves the buyer remediless because, *e.g.*, there is an express warranty of repair or replacement and that warranty is breached, the remedy in the contract "fails of its essential purpose" and the buyer is entitled to normal remedies under the Code notwithstanding the document that excludes such remedies. UCC § 2-719(2).

[261] "The most detailed and specific commentaries serve that a contract is largely an allocation of risks between the parties, and therefore that a contractual term is substantially suspect if it reallocates the risks of the bargain in an objectively unreasonable or unexpected manner." Perdue v. Crocker Nat'l Bank, 141 Cal. App. 3d 200, 190 Cal. Rptr. 204, 210 (1983) (relying on Murray, *Unconscionability: Unconscionability*, 31 U. PITT. L. REV. 1, 12–23 (1969)), *superseded*, 38 Cal. 3d 913, 216 Cal. Rptr. 345, 702 P.2d 503 (1985).

[262] The "circle of assent" analysis is adopted in Parton v. Mark Pirtle Oldsmobile-Cadillac-Isuzu, Inc., 730 S.W.2d 634, 637 (Tenn. Ct. App. 1987) (quoting from the 2d edition of this book, and followed in Board of Dirs. of Harriman Sch. Dist. v. Southwestern Petroleum Corp., 757 S.W.2d 669 (Tenn. Ct. App. 1988)). One Stop Supply v. Ransdell, 1996 Tenn. App. LEXIS 228 (Tenn. Ct. App. Apr. 19, 1996), continues to recognize this analysis, though it is inapplicable to the facts of this case. See also Germantown Mfg. Co. v. Rawlinson, 341 Pa. Super. 42, 491 A.2d 138, 146 (1985), which also adopts this analysis.

[263] This "expectation" test is particularly well-developed with respect to clauses in insurance contracts. *See, e.g.*, Darner Motor Sales v. Universal Underwriters Ins. Co., 140 Ariz. 383, 682 P.2d 388 (1984).

involves a party who requires certain goods or services that are necessary for her physical or economic well-being and who signs the dictated terms of the seller's form because she has no reasonable alternative. This is the classic contract of adhesion.

In a recent application of this analysis, the issue was whether a disclaimer of warranties in a rental agreement was within the "circle of assent." The district court upheld the disclaimer clause. On appeal, the Ninth Circuit agreed that the disclaimer was "conspicuous" as defined by the UCC as enacted in Tennessee and there was no violation of Tennessee public policy. Nonetheless, the court reversed the decision below since the "circle of assent" analysis allows the reallocation of risks in a bargain only if there is both apparent and genuine assent to it. Such a reallocation will be effective only if (1) it is physically conspicuous, (2) it is manifested in a fashion comprehensible to the party against whom it is sought to be enforced, and (3) that party had a reasonable choice in relation to such a reallocation.[264]

[e]   The Case Law of Unconscionability — Merchants — Affirmative Defense — Applications

The bedrock definition of unconscionability in *Williams v. Walker-Thomas Furniture Co.* antedated the enactment of the UCC in the District of Columbia: "Unconscionability has generally been recognized as the absence of meaningful choice on the part of one of the parties together with contract terms which are unreasonably favorable to the other party."[265] As authority for its description of unconscionability, the court cites the foundational opinion in *Henningsen v. Bloomfield Motors, Inc.*,[266] which provided the two central themes for the doctrine of unconscionability though it did not use the term, "unconscionability." In *Williams*, the concept was applied to a poor consumer purchaser of a stereo set who signed a form contract containing an "add-on" clause that permitted the seller, upon the buyer's default, to repossess all items which the buyer had purchased from that seller over a five year period, though she had paid for the prior items except for a relatively small balance. The clause was oppressive as well as obscure.[267] The application of the unconscionability concept was clear:

> Ordinarily, one who signs an agreement without full knowledge of its terms might be held to assume the risk that he has entered a one-sided bargain. But when a party of little bargaining power, and hence little real choice, signs a commercially unreasonable contract with little or no knowledge of its terms, it is hardly likely that his consent, or even an objective manifestation of his consent, was ever given to all the terms. In such a case the usual rule that the terms of the agreement are not to be questioned should

---

[264] Curtis v. Ryder TRS, Inc., 43 Fed. Appx. 103, 106, 2002 U.S. App LEXIS 16134 (9th Cir. 2002) (noting the analysis which first appeared in 2d edition of this treatise as adopted in *Parton v. Mark Pirtle Oldsmobile* at note 262, *supra*).

[265] 350 F.2d 445, 449 (D. C. Cir.1965). Though this litigation antedated the enactment of the UCC in the District of Columbia, the court decided the case as if § 2-302 of the Code applied by suggesting that the pre-Code common law of unconscionability in the district was essentially identical to that set forth in the Code section.

[266] 32 N. J. 358, 161 A.2d 69 (1960).

[267] The court states, "The effect of this rather obscure provision was to keep a balance due on every item purchased until the balance due on all items, whenever purchased, was liquidated. As a result, the debt incurred at the time of purchase of each item was secured by the right to repossess all the items previously purchased by the same purchaser, and each new item purchased automatically became subject to a security interest arising out of previous dealings." 350 F.2d at 448.

be abandoned and the court should consider whether the terms of the contract are so unfair that enforcement should be withheld.[268]

Thus, a party with no choice who is reasonably unaware of a material provision which attempts to allocate an unexpected risk to that party is not bound by such a provision. In determining the lack of apparent assent, the particular circumstances of the buyer must be considered. The court emphasized the buyer's general lack of education as well as her failure to read or understand the fine print provision.[269] The inability of the buyer to speak English is also a manifestation of the lack of apparent assent, i.e., such a person could easily be "unfairly surprised" at what he had signed. Where a Spanish-speaking buyer had agreed to pay over $1100 for a freezer which had a wholesale cost of less than $350, the court was influenced by the buyer's apparent lack of understanding of the transaction that was aggravated by the salesman's representation that the freezer would cost nothing since the buyer would receive a $25 commission on every sale made to friends.[270] A premarital agreement provided that, in the event of divorce, each party waived their interest in the other party's property. The wife would receive $100,000 if the parties continued to be married upon the death of the husband. The wife had arrived from Morocco in 1996. She spoke Arabic and broken English though she also relied on translators. She surrendered her employment in Morocco to marry the defendant and had no employment in the United States. The defendant had brought her to his lawyer's office to sign a "marriage paper." She did not receive an advance copy of the agreement nor did she receive a copy after signing it. She did not read the agreement and was not represented by counsel. The husband's net worth was approximately $20 million. The court noted that gross disparity in the value exchanged is a significant factor in determining whether oppressive influences affected the agreement to such an extent that it was unconscionable. The court held that the trial court had erred in determining that the wife failed to establish a prima facie case that the premarital agreement was unconscionable.[271]

Even where the buyer is capable of understanding the writing, if the risk-shifting provision is in light-colored print, buried in the fine print or indecipherable, the buyer may be said to lack even apparent assent to such a clause.[272] It cannot be gainsaid that such a clause is unexpected. A clause that is highly legible and understandable, on the other hand, cannot be characterized as unexpected. If, however, the clause shifts a material risk to the buyer and the seller has a monopoly on an important product or service, or if all sellers use essentially the same printed form containing such a clause, the buyer literally has no choice but to sign the contract containing the oppressive provision and, for that reason alone, the oppressive clause should be deemed unconscionable.[273]

---

[268] *Id.* at 449–50.

[269] *Id.* Other cases considering a party's lack of education include Wille v. Southwestern Bell Tel. Co., 219 Kan. 755, 549 P.2d 903 (1976); Johnson v. Mobil Oil Corp., 415 F. Supp. 264 (E.D. Mich. 1976); Weaver v. American Oil Co., 257 Ind. 458, 276 N.E.2d 144 (1971).

[270] Frostifresh Corp. v. Reynoso, 52 Misc. 2d 26, 274 N.Y.S.2d 757 (1966), *rev'd*, 54 Misc. 2d 119, 281 N.Y.S.2d 964 (App. Term 1967).

[271] Chaplain v. Chaplain, 54 Va. App. 762, 682 S. E. 2d 108 (2009).

[272] In John Deere Leasing Co. v. Blubaugh, 636 F. Supp. 1569 (D. Kan. 1986), the lease agreement contained a default provision making the lessee liable for the purchase price. The clause was on the back of the form and written in such fine, light print as to be nearly illegible. Neither party was able to obtain a photocopy because the print was so light. Thus, the court did not read the lease until it received the original and then had to use a magnifying glass to read the reverse side.

[273] *See* Rozeboom v. Northwestern Bell Tel. Co., 358 N.W.2d 241 (S.D. 1984) (contract between telephone company

Price Disparity. Courts have traditionally avoided any inquiry into the so-called "adequacy of consideration"-the relative values exchanged-except where they sit as courts of equity and the values are grossly disproportionate. As a practical matter, courts cannot afford to deal with the plethora of claims that would be assessed because of an alleged unfair bargain, and the problems of determining whether a particular price was "excessive" may appear overwhelming. Sharp increases in price, alone, will not permit a court to condemn a contract or clause as unconscionable since these risks are obviously assumed at the time the contract is formed.[274] While gross disproportion between price and value, alone, will be insufficient, if the the buyer is at a bargaining disadvantage because of illiteracy, unfamiliarity with the language or sharp practices by the seller's representative, courts have found such contracts unconscionable.[275] Where a wife argued that gross disparity in a marital settlement agreement made the agreement unconscionable, the court held that the agreement must not only evidence gross disparity in the division of assets alone; there must also be sufficient evidence of overreaching or oppressive influences.[276]

Merchants — Commercial Entities. The successful use of unconscionability to strike down a contract or clause typically involves a consumer buyer. With respect to merchants, it is more than difficult to establish the lack of apparent assent, i.e., the element of "unfair surprise." Where sophisticated corporate entities negotiate a contract over several months, there is virtually no possibility of a successful use of unconscionability.[277] It would be rare to find a court declaring a clause unconscionable in a contract between businesses.[278] Though there may be and often are differences in the relative bargaining strengths in merchant transactions, that factor alone, will not make the contract unconscionable.[279] Even if the buyer is relatively small, if he is knowledgeable about business and the law, courts will be loathe to find any unfair surprise. A company providing temporary labor argued that the plaintiff was a large, sophisticated corporation that used its superior bargaining power to command an indemnity

---

and merchant containing clause exculpating the telephone company for any liability beyond the amount of advertising charges for failure to publish the plaintiff's business in the yellow pages of the new directory).

[274] *See* Kerr-McGee Corp. v. Northern Utils., 673 F.2d 323 (10th Cir.), *cert. denied*, 459 U.S. 989, 103 S. Ct. 344, 74 L. Ed. 2d 385 (1982).

[275] *See* Maxwell v. Fidelity Fin. Servs., 187 Ariz. 82, 907 P.2d 51 (1995) ($6500 price for a water heater in a modest home with a total time-payment price of $14,860.43 with a security interest not only in the homeowner's water heater but on his home); *Frostifresh Corp. v. Reynoso, supra* note 270; Kugler v. Romain, 58 N.J. 522, 279 A.2d 640 (1971); American Home Improvement, Inc. v. MacIver, 105 N.H. 435, 201 A.2d 886 (1964); Jones v. Star Credit Corp., 59 Misc. 2d 189, 298 N.Y.S.2d 264 (1969); Central Budget Corp. v. Sanchez, 53 Misc. 2d 620, 279 N.Y.S.2d 391 (1967); Toker v. Westerman, 113 N.J. Super. 452, 274 A.2d 78 (1970).

[276] Galloway v. Galloway, 47 Va. App. 83, 622 S. E. 2d 267 (2005).

[277] Cleveland Ins. Agency, Inc. v. Redshaw, Inc., 524 So. 2d 367, 369 (Ala. Civ. App. 1987).

[278] Imaging Fin. Servs. v. Graphic Arts Servs., Inc., 172 F.R.D. 322,327 (N.D. Ill. 1997). See, also, Bowlin's, Inc. v. Ramsey Oil Co., Inc., 662 P.2d 661, 669 (1983).

[279] In *De Valk Lincoln Mercury, Inc v. Ford Motor Co.*, 811 F. 2d 326, 333 (7th Cir. 1987), the court quoted § 208, comment d of the Restatement 2d of Contracts which suggests that a bargain is not unconscionable just because the parties are in unequal bargaining positions. Gross inequality and grossly unfavorable terms, however, may confirm the absence of any meaningful choice. Simply considering the size of the respective parties may also be deceptive. In Salt River Project Agric. Improvement & Power Dist. v. Westinghouse Elec. Corp., 143 Ariz. 368, 384, 694 P.2d 198, 214 (1984), the court explained, "There is no doubt that SRP and Westinghouse are both commercial 'giants' and bargained for the LMC in a commercial setting. However, comparability of size among corporations does not mean, as a matter of law, that in a particular transaction a corporation has bargaining strength relatively equal to all other corporations of similar size. Much depends on the nature of the transaction, the nature of the product, the relative knowledge of the parties concerning the product and the availability of other products to fit the needs of the purchaser."

clause be placed in the contract. The court was not persuaded that the defendant was a tiny, unsophisticated business in light of its 20 accounts of which the plaintiff was not the largest. The court found no evidence of unconscionability.[280] Where, however, the buyer is a technical merchant because he is in business, but his business and educational background is no greater than that of a consumer and the seller knows or reasonably should be aware of that fact, courts treat such a buyer as having no more awareness or bargaining power than a consumer.[281] In a few merchant cases involving franchisees, courts have been willing to discover unconscionability on the footing that the dealer has no choice but to sign a renewal contract containing an unfair clause.[282] Courts have emphasized the inherent unfairness of such clauses and the obvious lack of any bargaining power on the part of the dealer. Where a buyer is a substantial corporation, however, it is difficult for courts to believe that such a buyer is in a substantially inferior bargaining position.[283]

For such a buyer to establish that it had no choice but to assent to a material, risk shifting clause, it would have to demonstrate that it could not purchase the product elsewhere absent such a clause or that the seller was the sole supplier of such a product. Moreover, the buyer would have to produce evidence that it made significant efforts to have the clause removed from the writing before it was executed. With such evidence, it is conceivable that a court would find the provision unconscionable. Corporate buyers, however, may see no point in such negotiations or attempts to purchase the product elsewhere without such a clause because such efforts may appear to be useless gestures.[284] It would require considerable foresight and care to pursue such negotiations. Yet, the possibility exists that courts would consider such evidence as sufficient to discover no choice unconscionability if the evidence were clear and convincing.

Affirmative Defense. Unconscionability does not provide the basis for a lawsuit. It is viewed as an affirmative defense to the enforcement of one or more terms or the entire contract.[285] The affirmative defense of unconscionability has arisen in myriad situations beyond contracts for the sale of goods under the UCC.[286] By far, however, the last two decades have seen an

---

[280] Allied Waste North America, Inc. v. ITS Enterprises, Inc., 2009 U.S. Dist. LEXIS 25367 (D. Ariz. March 25, 2009).

[281] *See, e.g.*, Johnson v. Mobil Oil Corp., 415 F. Supp. 264 (E.D. Mich. 1976); Weaver v. American Oil Co., 257 Ind. 458, 276 N.E.2d 144 (1971).

[282] *See, e.g.*, Shell Oil Co. v. Marinello, 63 N.J. 402, 307 A.2d 598 (1973), *cert. denied*, 415 U.S. 920, 94 S. Ct. 1421, 39 L. Ed. 2d 475 (1974) (clause giving Shell absolute right to terminate on ten days notice was unenforceable). *Accord* Ashland Oil v. Donahue, 159 W. Va. 463, 223 S.E.2d 433 (1976). Other courts, however, have been unsympathetic to this view. *See, e.g.*, Zapatha v. Dairy Mart, Inc., 381 Mass. 284, 408 N.E.2d 1370 (1980); Corenswet, Inc. v. Amana Refrigeration, Inc., 594 F.2d 129 (5th Cir.), *cert. denied*, 444 U.S. 938, 100 S. Ct. 288, 62 L. Ed. 2d 198 (1979).

[283] See, however, the quotation from the *Salt River Project* case, *supra* note 279.

[284] In Potomac Elec. Power Co. v. Westinghouse Elec. Corp., 385 F. Supp. 572, 579 (D.D.C. 1974), the court states that the buyer failed to show that it was precluded from contracting with a competing domestic manufacturer or a foreign manufacturer. Nor did the buyer show that it was a reluctant or unwilling purchaser forced to yield to the seller's allegedly onerous terms. If such a buyer had made efforts to have one or more clauses removed from the seller's draft and had also attempted to contract with other manufacturers whose documents contained similar or identical clauses, the court appears to suggest that it would consider such evidence as evidence of the lack of genuine assent, i.e., no choice unconscionability.

[285] *But see* In Ricotta v. Finance America LLC, 2007 U.S. Dist. LEXIS 24387 at *10–11 (D. Colo 2007) where the court noted that a claim for unconscionability is typically an affirmative defense and, therefore, inappropriate as a basis for a direct claim. In this case, however, a liberal construction of the amended complaint "could reasonably deem" the unconscionability defense as a claim seeking a declaration that the contract is invalid on the basis of unconscionability.

[286] For example, see Repair Masters Construction, Inc. v. Gary, 277 S. W. 3d 854 (Mo. App. 2009) (liquidated

explosion of cases claiming that arbitration clauses in employment, consumer and other contracts are unconscionable. These cases deserve special attention.

[f] Arbitration and Unconscionability

The Supreme Court of the United States has made it very clear that the Federal Arbitration Act[287] should be regarded as a national policy favoring arbitration.[288] Nonetheless, the Act itself states that a written arbitration provision is enforceable "save upon such grounds as exist at law or in equity for the revocation of any contract."[289] Thus, whether an arbitration provision is unconscionable is governed by state contract law.[290] The case law evidences certain provisions of arbitration agreements with which the courts have struggled.

One of the pervasive issues is whether an arbitration clause that binds one party to arbitrate any dispute while the other party may pursue judicial remedies is sufficient to doom the agreement as unconscionable. Where an arbitration permitted the mortgagee to pursue foreclosure proceedings in court, the court recognized that it may be burdensome for the mortgagor to litigate substantively similar claims in two courts, but the burden was not sufficient to deem the arbitration provision unconscionable.[291] The same issue may arise under the rubric, "mutuality of obligation," a generally rejected "doctrine" that is nothing more than a synonym for consideration. Just because only one party has an additional or different duty from the other party does not signal any absence of consideration, nor does it signal unconscionability.[292] Where, however, an arbitration agreement requires the employee to arbitrate any dispute with the employer but the employer was not so limited in claims against the employee, absent a justification based on "business realties" as may be found in allowing a creditor to foreclose in a judicial proceeding, the Supreme Court of California found such a one-sided term to be unconscionable.[293] The Alabama Supreme Court, however, saw no evil in a provision giving the employer the right to alter, amend or revoke the arbitration policy at any time with or without notice. A majority of the court concluded that there is nothing inherently unconscionable about arbitration, nor is it a remedy. Thus, absent other bases, the

---

damages clause); Giacalone v. Helen Ellis Mem. Hosp. Foundation, 8 so. 3d 1232 (Fla. App. 2009) (hospital bill); Vintage Health Res. Inc. v Guiangan, 2009 Tenn. App. LEXIS 567 (employment agreement); Lawrence v. Miller, 853 N. Y. S. 2d 1 (N. Y. App. Div. 2007) (contingent fee agreement); Poff v. Brown, 288 S. W. 3d 620 (Ark.2008) (sale of mineral rights); Agfa Photo United States Corp. v. Parham, 2007 U.S. Dist. LEXIS 40980 (E. D. Tenn. 2007) (lease agreement); Kriedler v. Taylor, 2007 U.S. Dist. LEXIS 39262 (D. Ore. 2007); (agreement to avoid foreclosure on real property); Echostar Satellite L. L. C. v. Persian Broadcasting Co., 2006 U.S. Dist. LEXIS 8955 (D. Colo. 2006) (programming agreement).

[287] 9 U.S. C. § 1 *et. seq.*

[288] See, e. g., Southland Corp. v. Keating, 465 U.S. 1 (1984).

[289] 9 U.S. C. § 2.

[290] Olmstead v. Dell, Inc., 2010 U.S. App. LEXIS 2499 at *9 (9th Cir. 2010).

[291] Delta Funding Corp. v. Harris, 189 N. J. 28, 48, 912 A.2d 104, 116 (2006). The Pennsylvania Supreme Court found this opinion helpful in holding that the mere fact that an arbitration provision reserved additional remedies associated with foreclosure did not create a presumption of unconscionability. Salley v. Option One Mtge. Corp., 925 A.2d 115 (Pa. 2007).

[292] See Reno v. Bethel Village Condominium Assn., Inc., 2008 Ohio App. LEXIS 3772 (Ohio Ct. App. 2008) where the court held that requiring the owner of a condominium unit to arbitrate all disputes while allowing the association to pursue additional remedies did not make the agreement unconscionable. *See also* the discussion and cases cited in Torrance v. Aames Funding Corp., 242 F. Supp. 2d 862 (D. Ore. 2002). The court, however, found unconscionability on other grounds.

[293] Armendariz v. Foundation Health Psychcare Services, Inc, 24 Cal. 4th 83, 118, 6 P. 3d 669 692 (2000).

court held that the arbitration agreement did not become unconscionable because of the employer's power of termination.[294]

Another issue deals with arbitration provisions waiving class actions. Where the damages to a large number of consumers is so small that no individual consumer is likely to bring an action, the class action is the obvious remedial device. An arbitration clause that waives the right to participate in a class action, however, would preclude the only practical remedy. Courts have generally not permitted class actions to proceed in arbitration. In *Green Tree Financial Corporation v. Bazzle*,[295] there was a dispute as to whether the contract precluded class arbitration. Four members of the United States Supreme Court concluded that whether the arbitration agreement authorizes class arbitration is to be determined by the arbitration agreement. Thus, the implication was that a provision in an arbitration agreement precluding class arbitration would be enforceable which induced numerous entities to include such provisions. Claims that such provisions are unconscionable inevitably followed.

In *Discover Bank v. Superior Court of Los Angeles*,[296] the California Supreme Court concluded that class action waivers in arbitration agreements are unconscionable where the agreement is a contract of adhesion, the disputes are likely to involve small amounts of money, and where it is alleged that the party with superior bargaining power has schemed to cheat large groups of consumers out of their individual small amounts.[297] While rejecting any suggestion that class-action waivers in arbitration are *per se* unenforceable, the New Jersey Supreme Court suggested a fact-sensitive analysis to determine what kinds of damages and attorney's fees would be available for individual claims and why such individual actions would be insufficient.[298] The Third Circuit assumes a similar analysis in Pennsylvania law where class action waivers are not unconscionable *per se* but would be unenforceable if the waiver immunized a party from wrongdoing. In the case before the court, it held that the waiver was not unconscionable since the consumer could recover damages, costs and attorney's fees under his individual claim.[299] The Illinois reaction to class action waivers was closer to the California position with, perhaps, even less leeway for a result upholding the waiver.[300] Where an arbitration provision was silent concerning class arbitration, the Supreme Court held that arbitration was a matter of contract and an arbitration panel's decision to permit class arbitration violated the terms of the arbitration agreement.[301] While *Stolt-Nielsen* held that a party cannot be forced to engage in class arbitration unless he has agreed to do so, the Court did not hold that a clause barring class arbitration is enforceable *per se*.[302]

A case approaching that issue, however, was already in process.[303] A cellular telephone contract between AT&T and the Concepcions allowed customers to initiate dispute proceedings by filing a one-page form that would activate AT&T's right to offer a settlement.

---

[294] Ex Parte McNaughton, 728 So. 2d 592, 597 (1998).

[295] 539 U.S. 444 (2003).

[296] 36 Cal. 4th 148, 30 Cal. Rptr. 3d 76 (2005).

[297] *Accord* Olmstead v. Dell, 2010 U.S. App. LEXIS at *12, n3 (9th Cir. Feb. 5, 2010).

[298] Muhammad v. County Bank of Rehoboth Beach, Delaware, 912 A.2d 88, 100, n.5 (N.J. 2006).

[299] Cronin v. Citifinancial Services, Inc., 2009 U.S. App. LEXIS 20113 (3d Cir., Sept. 9. 2009).

[300] Kinkel v. Cingular Wireless, LLC, 828 N.E.2d 812 (Ill. Ct. App. 2005).

[301] Stolt-Nielsen S. A. v. AnimalFeeds Int'l Corp., 130 S. Ct. 1758 (2010).

[302] National Supermarkets Assn. v. Am. Exp. Travel Related Servs. Co., 634 F.3d 187, 193 (2d Cir. 2011).

[303] Laster v. T-Mobile USA, Inc., 2008 U.S. Dist. LEXIS 103712 (S.D. Cal. 2008).

Absent such an offer, or, if no settlement was reached within 30 days, the customer could initiate arbitration in the county of the customer. AT&T would pay all costs for nonfrivolous claims. For claims under $10,000, the customer could choose arbitration in person, by telephone or by submissions. The arbitration award could provide any form of relief including injunctions and punitive damages. Either party could proceed in a small claims court in lieu of arbitration. If a customer received an arbitration award greater than AT&T's offer of settlement, AT&T was required to pay a minimum $7,500 recovery and twice the amount of the claimant's attorney's fees. Under no circumstances was AT&T entitled to reimbursement for attorney's fees. Arbitration, however, was limited to claims brought by parties in their individual capacities and not as a class member in any purported class or representative proceeding.

The Concepcions entered into a contract with AT&T pursuant to an advertisement for "free phones." While they were not charged for the phones, they were charged $30.22 in sales tax based on the retail value of the phones. The plaintiffs claimed fraud and false advertising by AT&T by charging sales tax on phones advertised as free. AT&T moved to compel arbitration which the Concepcions opposed as unconscionable under California law since it disallowed classwide procedures.

While the District Court described the AT&T arbitration process contract as "quick," "easy to use," and likely to prompt full or even excess payment to the customer without the need to arbitrate or litigate, it held that the waiver of class actions made the clause unconscionable since the California *Discover Bank* holding equated arbitration agreements with class action waivers in contracts barring class action litigation in courts or arbitration. The Ninth Circuit agreed, holding that the *Discover Bank* rule was not preempted by the Federal Arbitration Act (FAA) since the rule was only a refinement of the unconscionability analysis applicable to contracts generally in California.[304]

In a 5-4 decision, *AT&T Mobility, LLC v. Concepcion*,[305] the Supreme Court reversed the Ninth Circuit and held that California's *Discover Bank* rule was preempted by the FAA because it would stand as an obstacle to the execution and accomplishment of the full purposes and objectives of Congress. The Court restated the purpose of the FAA as a "liberal federal policy favoring arbitration" placing arbitration agreements on a par with other contracts that should be enforced according to their terms. The savings clause in § 2 of the FAA ("save upon such grounds as exist in law or equity for the revocation of any contract") allows arbitration agreements to be invalidated by generally applicable contract defenses such as fraud, illegality and unconscionability, but it does not recognize defenses that apply only to arbitration or derive their meaning from the fact that an agreement to arbitrate is at issue.

The Court stated the issue as whether § 2 preempts the *Discover Bank* rule classifying most collective-arbitration waivers in consumer contracts as unconscionable. It found that the *Discover Bank* rule interferes with arbitration since a switch from bilateral to class arbitration sacrifices the principal advantage of arbitration — informality — thereby making the process slower, more costly and more likely to generate procedural morass. Class arbitration requires procedural formality as manifested in the American Arbitration Association rules governing class arbitrations that mimic the Federal Rules of Civil Procedure for Class Litigation. Class arbitration greatly increases the risks to the defendants who are

---

[304] Laster v. AT&T Mobility LLC, 584 F.3d 849, 857 (9th Cir. 2009).

[305] 131 S. Ct. 1740 (2011).

willing to accept the costs of errors in the relatively informal arbitration proceeding because the risk is limited to the individual dispute. Potential damages to thousands of claimants, however, may make the risk of such errors unacceptable. Arbitration is poorly suited to high stakes litigation.

While the *Discover Bank* opinion stated that its holding was limited to consumer adhesion contracts under some circumstances, the court found those limitations insufficient to guard against interference with the purposes of the FAA. The court was not impressed by the limitation to consumer adhesion contracts since "the times in which consumer contracts were anything other than adhesive are long past." The *Discover Bank* rule was also limited to damages that are sufficiently small and it required the consumer to allege a scheme to cheat consumers. The court, however, viewed the limitation of damages as toothless and malleable, citing a case where a court found $4,000 sufficiently small.[306] As to the required allegation to cheat consumers, it found no limiting effect at all in a mere allegation.

Other issues that affect the determination of whether an arbitration clause is unconscionable in employment contracts include cost-splitting provisions[307] as well as limitations on time to assert a claim,[308] allowing the arbitrator to allocate all fees to an employee who did not succeed in her claim (a "loser pays" provision),[309] or forcing a waiver of substantive rights and remedies under various statutes.[310]

The language of an arbitration provision, the opportunity to review it, the clarity of the language, and whether the surrender of important rights such as the right to trial by jury which necessarily attends an agreement to arbitrate, are conspicuous are factors affecting a determination of whether the provision is unconscionable.

[g] Unconscionability Notwithstanding Adherence to Uniform Commercial Code Formulas

One of the questions that had caused controversy among scholars and courts is whether a clause that meets the requirements of the UCC to disclaim warranties or limit or exclude certain remedies may still be declared unconscionable. The Code insists upon certain safeguards as prerequisites to an effective disclaimer of implied warranties. Thus, a written disclaimer must be conspicuous and, with respect to the implied warranty of merchantability, must include the term "merchantability,"[311] or use trade language like "as is" or "with all

---

[306] Oestricher v. Alienware Corp., 322 Fed. Appx. 489, 492 (2009) (unpublished).

[307] See, e. g., Ingle v. Circuit City Stores, 328 F. 3d 1165 (9th Cir. 2003) finding such provisions unconscionable, but see Motsinger v. Lithia-Rose-Ft., Inc., 156 P. 3d 156 (Ore. 2007) where the agreement was silent concerning the costs of arbitration. The court relied on Green Tree Financial v. Rudolph, 531 U.S. 71, 91 (2000) which held that the claim of being saddled with prohibitive costs of arbitration in such a case is speculative. An arbitration provision is not unconscionable simply because the employee confronted undetermined costs if she were to lose.

[308] Thirty day limitation to assert a claim is substantive unconscionable. Parillla v. IAP Worldwide Services, VI, Inc., 368 F. 3d 269 (3d Cir. 2004).

[309] A provision requiring the losing party to bear the arbitrator's cost and expenses. Alexander v. Anthony International, L. P., 341 F. 3d 256 (3d Cir.2003).

[310] See, e. g., Coady v. Cross Country Bank, Inc., 2007 Wis. App. LEXIS 47 where the court found substantive unconscionability because the arbitration clause prevented the plaintiffs from relief under the Wisconsin Consumer Act, thereby forcing the waiver of rights and remedies under that statute.

[311] UCC § 2-316(2).

faults" to communicate the disclaimer.[312] If a seller's clause adheres to these Code prescriptions, can such a disclaimer still be attacked on the ground of unconscionability? The debate considers the language of the UCC disclaimer of warranty section and other sections, as well as comments and cross-references to the unconscionability section. The prevailing scholarly view is that a disclaimer that meets UCC requirements may still be unconscionable[313] and case law supports this view.[314] To strip a contract of the basic protection provided by the implied warranty of merchantability, which essentially requires only that the goods be fit for the ordinary purposes of such goods,[315] is a major deviation from the presumed factual bargain of the parties. Thus, the drafters of the section disclaiming such warranties were eager to assure threshold safeguards of a formalistic nature. If these safeguards are not met, it might safely be suggested that the disclaimer is unconscionable *per se* because it does not allow for minimal apparent assent. A comment to the UCC disclaimer section suggests its purpose:

> "It seeks to protect a buyer from unexpected and unbargained language by denying effect to such language . . . and permitting the exclusion of implied warranties only by conspicuous language or other circumstances which protect the buyer from surprise.[316]

The purpose is clearly one of preserving apparent assent. If the buyer is aware of disclaimer language at the time he manifests assent, he may not claim *procedural* unconscionability. He may, however, still have no choice but to agree to this language. Thus, to preclude the possibility of finding such a clause unconscionable simply because it meets formalistic safeguards would remove the possibility of discovering substantive unconscionability, i.e., the contract of adhesion or no choice unconscionability precluding genuine assent. Moreover, there is still the question of whether a reasonable consumer buyer would have understood the import of a clause disclaiming implied warranties even though the clause met the threshold safeguards of the Code. Thus, it is conceivable that even apparent assent may be absent, notwithstanding compliance with the safeguards, and a finding of procedural unconscionability is theoretically possible.

Unconscionable Limitations of Consequential Damages. The UCC permits the parties to

---

[312] UCC § 2-316(3)(a). Implied warranties may also be disclaimed through pre-contract inspections of the product or refusals to inspect under § 2-316(3)(b), and trade usage or prior course of dealing under § 2-316(3)(c).

[313] Professor Leff was the principal advocate for the view that a disclaimer meeting UCC requirements could not be attacked on the footing that it was unconscionable. Leff, *Unconscionability and the Code: The Emperor's New Clause*, 115 U. PA. L. REV. 485, 523–24 (1967). In response, see Murray, *Unconscionability: Unconscionability*, 31 U. PITT. L. REV. 1, 45–49 (1969), suggesting the contrary view. In general, other scholars reach the same conclusion as Murray. *See, e.g.,* Ellinghaus, *In Defense of Unconscionability*, 78 YALE L.J. 757, 798–803 (1969); R. DUESENBERG & L. KING, SALES AND BULK TRANSFERS UNDER THE U.C.C. § 7.03[2] (1980). In their well-known treatise, THE UNIFORM COMMERCIAL CODE § 12–11 (2d ed. 1980), Professors White & Summers disagree. Professor White believes that a disclaimer clause adhering to UCC requirements should not be susceptible to a finding of unconscionability, while Professor Summers takes the opposite view. Professor Farnsworth concludes that the view permitting an unconscionability attack on a clause meeting UCC requirements is "sounder." E.A. FARNSWORTH, CONTRACTS § 4.29 (1982).

[314] *See, e.g.,* Martin v. Joseph Harris Co., 767 F.2d 296 (6th Cir. 1985); Barco Auto Leasing Corp. v. PSI Cosmetics, Inc., 125 Misc. 2d 68, 478 N.Y.S.2d 505 (Civ. Ct. 1984); A & M Produce Co. v. FMC Corp., 135 Cal. App. 3d 473, 186 Cal. Rptr. 114 (4th Dist. 1982); Hahn v. Ford Motor Co., 434 N.E.2d 943 (Ind. Ct. App. 1982). *See also* Schroeder v. Fageol Motors, Inc., 80 Wash. 2d 256, 544 P.2d 20 (1975).

[315] UCC § 2-314(2)(c), which is one of six descriptive criteria of the implied warranty of merchantability though it is often viewed as the fundamental criterion.

[316] UCC § 2-316 comment 1.

agree that the seller will not be liable for consequential damages in the event of a breach. This section, however, expressly precludes enforcement of such clauses if they are unconscionable and, with respect to consequential damages for personal injury, such a clause is prima facie unconscionable.[317] There is no express requirement that such clauses be conspicuous and most courts have read the statute literally.[318] Conspicuousness, however, may be a factor in determining whether an exclusionary clause is unconscionable.[319] There is also no question that such clauses are necessarily subject to the overriding requirement that they be conscionable,[320] and unconscionability may be found even though the loss suffered is not a bodily injury.[321]

[h]   Remedy Limitations — Failure of Essential Purpose — Consequential Damages

The UCC expressly permits parties to limit remedies normally available under their contract for the sale of goods to a lesser remedy, such as return of the goods and repayment of the price or repair and replacement of nonconforming goods or parts.[322] Unless such a limited remedy is expressly agreed to be the exclusive remedy it is not the sole remedy available to the buyer. The buyer's usual default remedies remain available.[323] The limited remedy may also exclude consequential damages unless the exclusion is deemed to be unconscionable.[324] If the exclusion is not unconscionable at the time of contract formation, it is enforceable. Subsequent events, however, may leave the buyer remediless. Thus, if the seller fails to perform its warranty of repair or replacement,[325] or fails to perform within a reasonable time,[326] or will not or cannot repair the product,[327] a limited repair and replacement remedy that was supposed to substitute for the buyer's normal UCC remedies is worthless. In this situation, the UCC provides, "Where circumstances cause an exclusive or limited remedy to *fail of its essential purpose*, remedy may be had as provided in this Act."[328] Thus, when the exclusive limited remedy fails of its essential purpose, the buyer returns to the buyer's remedies under the Code and chooses a remedy that would have been available absent the limitation of remedy clause. Thus, the buyer could pursue damages for breach of

---

[317] UCC § 2-719(3).

[318] Cases holding that no conspicuous requirement be read into UCC § 2-719 include Xerox Corp. v. Hawkes, 124 N.H. 610, 475 A.2d 7, 11 (1984); Flintkote Co. v. W. W. Wilkinson, Inc., 220 Va. 564, 260 S.E.2d 229 (1979); Collins Radio Co. v. Bell, 623 P.2d 1039 (Okla. Ct. App. 1980). For a contrary view, see Avenell v. Westinghouse Elec. Corp., 41 Ohio App. 2d 150, 324 N.E.2d 583 (Cuyahoga County 1974).

[319] *See* Schroeder v. Faegol Motors, Inc., 86 Wash. 2d 256, 544 P.2d 20, 23–24 (1975).

[320] *See, e.g.,* A & M Produce Co. v. FMC Corp., 135 Cal. App. 3d 473, 186 Cal. Rptr. 114 (4th Dist. 1982).

[321] Gladden v. Cadillac Motor Car Div., General Motors Corp., 83 N.J. 320, 416 A.2d 394 (1980).

[322] UCC § 2-719(1)(a).

[323] § 2-719(1)(b).

[324] UCC § 2-719(3).

[325] *See* Waters v. Massey-Ferguson, Inc., 775 F.2d 587 (4th Cir. 1985); Adams v. J. I. Case Co., 125 Ill. App. 2d 388, 261 N.E.2d 1 (4th Dist. 1970).

[326] *See* Jones & McKnight Corp. v. Birdsboro Corp., 320 F. Supp. 39 (N.D. Ill. 1970).

[327] *See* Clark v. International Harvester Co., 99 Idaho 326, 581 P.2d 784 (1978); S. M. Wilson & Co. v. Smith Int'l, Inc., 587 F.2d 1363 (9th Cir. 1978).

[328] UCC § 2-719(2) (emphasis supplied).

warranty,[329] cover,[330] or the difference between the contract price and market price at the time the buyer learned of the breach.[331] Each of these remedies, however, also permits the recovery of consequential damages. Viewing § 2-719(2) in isolation which allows "remedy . . . as provided in this Act," it would appear that failure of the limited remedy would allow the buyer to recover any provable consequential damages along with the direct damages allowed under one of the buyer's remedies. Neither contract nor statutory provisions, however, may be interpreted and construed in isolation. § 2-719(3) states, "Consequential damages may be limited or excluded *unless the limitation or exclusion is unconscionable.*" Thus, the issue is whether an exclusion of consequential damages provision is independently governed by § 2–719(3), regardless of whether a limited remedy fails of its essential purpose.

If an exclusion of consequential damages clause was not only conditioned on whether it is unconscionable but also on whether a limited remedy to which it is appended fails of its essential purpose, §§ 2-719(2) and (3) are dependent. Yet, where failure of essential purpose of a limited remedy is found and the clause excluding consequential damages is unconscionable, it did not become unconscionable because the exclusive remedy failed. It was unconscionable at the time the contract was formed and should not be enforced, regardless of the failure of the exclusive remedy. Moreover, clauses excluding consequential damages need not be appended to other remedy limitations. Thus, where the exclusive remedy fails but the exclusion of consequential damages is not unconscionable, most courts will treat the two subsections as setting forth independent standards. The buyer may choose an appropriate UCC remedy, but the exclusion of consequential damages will be enforced.[332] A court may place emphasis upon the particular language of the exclusion of consequential damages in a substitute remedy clause. If, for example, the parties express their intention that consequential damages will be excluded even if the limited remedy clause fails, a court should normally honor that intention.[333]

[C]   The "Good Faith" Requirement

Beyond the doctrines of fraud, duress, misrepresentation, wrongful nondisclosure and unconscionability, there is a generally recognized requirement that every contract imposes a duty of *good faith* upon the parties to a contract. The Restatement 2d imposes a standard of good faith and fair dealing in all contracts. The Uniform Commercial Code states, "Every contract or duty within this Act imposes an obligation of good faith in its performance or

---

[329] See UCC § 2-714, which measures the damages by the difference in the value of the goods received and the value they should have had if they had been as warranted.

[330] UCC § 2-712, i.e., the difference between the contract price and the price of identical or reasonable substitute goods from another supplier.

[331] UCC § 2-713. This is the basic expectation interest remedy which provides damages measured by the difference between the contract and relevant market price at the time the buyer learned of the breach.

[332] *See* Rheem Mfg. Co. v. Phelps Heating & Air Conditioning, Inc., 746 N. E. 2d 941 (Ind. 2001) (holding that the independent construction "harmonizes the language in § 2-719(2) . . . with the unconscionability test imposed by § 2-719(3)"). *See also* Chatlos Sys., Inc. v. National Cash Register Corp. (NCR Corp.), 635 F. 2d 1081, 1086 (3d Cir. 1980), *cert. dismissed*, 457 U.S. 1112, 102 S. Ct. 2918, 73 L. Ed. 2d 1323 (1982) ("It appears to us that the better reasoned approach is to treat the consequential damage disclaimer as an independent provision, valid unless unconscionable. This poses no logical difficulties. A contract may well contain no limitation on breach of warranty damages but specifically exclude consequential damages.").

[333] *See* Cooley v. Big Horn Harvestore Sys., Inc., 813 P.2d 736 (Colo. 1991).

enforcement."[334] In the earlier, unrevised Article 1 of the UCC, "good faith" was defined as "honesty in fact in the conduct or transaction concerned," a subjective standard recognizing the possibility of a good heart but empty head.[335] Article 2, however, applied, and continues to apply, a standard to "merchants" that combined honesty in fact with "the observance of reasonable commercial standards of fair dealing in the trade."[336] The revised Article 1 also combines the "honesty" and objective "commercially reasonable" standards in the general definition of good faith for all UCC articles since amendments to other UCC Articles had broadened the definition, leaving only Article 5 (Letters of Credit) with a subjective definition of good faith.[337] Like other definitions, these statements can hardly be characterized as comprehensive since it is impossible to consider the myriad contexts of good faith within the confines of a definition.[338] Indeed, like attempted definitions of "justice," it is much easier to determine its absence, i.e., "bad faith," than it is to set forth a meaningful definition of "good faith."[339]

[1] Obligation of Good Faith Does Not Support an Independent Cause of Action

In 1994, an explanatory comment was added to the UCC section stating the obligation of good faith in every contract. That comment now appears in the revised Article 1:

> This section does not support an independent cause of action for failure to perform or enforce in good faith. Rather, this section means that a failure to perform or enforce, in good faith, a specific duty or obligation under the contract, constitutes a breach of that contract or makes unavailable, under the particular circumstances, a remedial right or power. This distinction makes it clear that the doctrine of good faith merely directs a court toward interpreting contracts within the commercial context in which they are created, performed and enforced, and does not create a separate duty of fairness and reasonableness which can be independently breached.[340]

---

[334] RESTATEMENT 2d § 205. UCC § 1-304. There are numerous illustrations of the good faith standard applied throughout contract law. We have already considered the application of the standard to output and requirements contracts under UCC § 2-306. See § 59 supra. The Code also requires that the power to terminate a contract be exercised in good faith. UCC § 2-309. We have also reviewed the implication of the good faith standard in franchise agreements where a franchisee invests considerable time, effort and money in the development of a business only to be terminated capriciously by the franchisor, a number of states have enacted legislation requiring adherence to a good faith standard. § 58[D][2]. supra and Dunkin' Donuts of Am., Inc. v. Middletown Donut Corp., 100 N.J. 166, 495 A.2d 66 (1985), where the court analyzes several of these statutes.

[335] UCC § 1-201(19).

[336] UCC § 2-103(1)(b).

[337] UCC § 1-201(20) and comment 20. Only a few states retain Article 6 on Bulk Sales. Article 6 has no definition of good faith, but comment 2 to revised § 6-102 states that the Article incorporates the Article 1 definition of good faith.

[338] RESTATEMENT 2d § 205 comment a suggests, "The phrase 'good faith' is used in a variety of contexts and its meaning varies somewhat with the context." See also Robert Summers, "Good Faith" in General Contract Law and the Sales Provisions of the Uniform Commercial Code, 54 VA. L. REV. 195, 201 (1968), where the author suggests that "good faith" takes on specific meaning in a particular context.

[339] Id. Comment d to RESTATEMENT 2d § 231, for example, suggests that subterfuge and evasion would demonstrate the absence of good faith.

[340] UCC § 1-304, comment 1.

There is no independent cause of action for breach of the duty of good faith. Rather, the implied duty of good faith is infused into the provisions of the contract itself.[341] The rights and duties are created by the contract. The implied covenant of good faith and fair dealing requires those duties to be performed and enforced in accordance with the reasonable expectations of the parties. The good faith imposition requires each party to avoid hindering the performance of the other party and cooperation in the fulfillment of those expectations. The duty of good faith, however, "cannot give parties rights which are inconsistent with those set out in the contract."[342] Where a contract stated that a dealership could not be assigned without the prior approval of the manufacturer, the court found no violation of the duty of good faith in the refusal to approve the assignment. The implied covenant could not override the express terms and there was no evidence that the manufacturer failed to exercise "honesty in fact."[343]

[2]   Good Faith in Negotiations Versus Performance — Contractual Relationships and Good Faith

It is clear that the obligation of good faith extends only to the performance of the contract and not to its formation.[344] It is important to understand the pre-contractual relationship of the parties and contrast that with their relationship after the contract is formed. What has become the leading case in this area, *Market Street Associates v. Frey*,[345] provides a cohesive analysis that is well-worth pursuing in detail.

Where a long-term (twenty-year-old) lease provided that the lessee had the right to request financing of improvements by the lessor, the lessee made such a request but did not mention an important provision of the lease (paragraph 34): If the lessor did not give reasonable consideration to a request for financing improvements, paragraph 34 gave the lessee the opportunity to purchase the property at the original price plus an annual increase of 6 percent. Under this provision, the purchase price would be less than the market value of the property. The district judge granted summary judgment for the lessor on the footing that the lessee had operated in bad faith by failing to remind the lessor of paragraph 34. The court held that this was a violation of the duty of good faith that is read into every contract. The judge found that the lessee hoped the lessor would reject the request for financing without noticing the provision since that would allow the lessee to purchase the property at a very low price instead of its higher market value. The judge found support for this finding in the deposition of a general partner (Orenstein) of the lessee who was representing the lessee in the transaction. Orenstein stated that it had occurred to him that the representative of the lessor (Erb) might not know of paragraph 34 though Orenstein thought that was unlikely. On appeal, the lessor claimed that either as a matter of interpretation or the imposition of good faith, a provision requiring the

---

[341] See, e. g., Tribal Consortium v. Pierson, 2009 U.S. Dist. LEXIS 120482 at *34 (W. D. Okla. 2009): "The implied covenant of good faith modifies, and becomes part of, the provisions of the contract itself. As such, the covenant is not independent of the contract." Northview Motors, Inc. v. Chrysler Motors Corp., 227 F.3d 78, 91 (3d Cir. 2000): "Courts have utilized the good faith duty as an interpretive tool to determine the parties' justifiable expectations in the context of a breach of contract action, but that duty is not divorced from the specific clauses of the contract and cannot be used to override an express contractual term."

[342] Barn-Chestnut, Inc. v. CFM Development Corp., 457 S. E. 2d 502, 509 (1995).

[343] Taylor Equip. v. John Deere Co., 98 F.3d 1028 (8th Cir. 1996), *cert. denied*, 520 U.S. 1197, 117 S. Ct. 1553, 137 L. Ed. 2d 702 (1997).

[344] *See, e.g.*, El Paso Natural Gas Co. v. Minco Oil & Gas, 8 S.W.3d 309, 313 (Tex. 1999) (UCC); Wallace v. National Bank of Commerce, 938 S.W.2d 684, 687 (Tenn. 1996); Tolbert v. First Nat'l Bank, 312 Or. 485, 823 P.2d 965, 969 (1991).

[345] 941 F. 2d 588 (7th Cir. 1991), opinion by Posner, J.

lessee to remind the lessor of paragraph 34 should be read into the lease.

The court noted that the "moral overtones" of the caption, "good faith," may suggest a fiduciary relationship between the parties, but that view is unsound. A contract signatory is not his "brother's keeper," particularly where the other party is an immense and sophisticated party as was the lessor. While a party may make a binding contract to buy something he knows the seller undervalues, that statement applies to formation of the contract rather than its performance. Good faith is minimized at the precontractual stage where negotiating parties are wary of each other. During the performance stage, however, the parties enter a cooperative venture where the duty of good faith forbids taking opportunistic advantage of the other party. There is an implied condition of cooperation in every contract that could substitute for the good faith concept. If a fiduciary is to treat the other party as the fiduciary would treat herself, there is no fiduciary duty at the precontractual stage. Neither is there a full fiduciary duty at the performance or enforcement stages of the contract. The court suggests that the good faith standard applicable to parties at those stages is halfway between no fiduciary duty and full fiduciary duty. The court concluded that there were two possible scenarios concerning that standard in this case. One was the district judge's assumption that Orenstein tricked lessor into selling at the bargain price under paragraph 34. That recital, however, construed the facts as favorably to the lessor as the record permitted which was not the correct standard for summary judgment. The other scenario would view the lessee as being entitled to assume that a large, sophisticated entity like the lessor would be aware of paragraph 34 and otherwise manifest no bad faith. The essential question is what Orenstein believed which required the reversal of the summary judgment and remand to assess believability.

Modern descriptions of "good faith" often refer to "opportunistic behavior" or taking "opportunistic advantage." Thus, the implied obligation of good faith suggests "an implied undertaking not to take opportunistic advantage in a way that could not have been contemplated at the time of drafting, and which therefore was not resolved explicitly by the parties."[346] Obvious examples of opportunistic behavior include taking advantage of a necessitous party who has made a sizeable investment in a project as where a movie star sulks in the hope of being offered more compensation when production of a film is virtually complete,[347] or in the classic case of workers, knowing that substitutes are unavailable, refusing to perform their contracts unless they receive additional wages.[348]

Where a contractual duty is expressly conditional, the prevention or hindrance of the condition will constitute a violation of the good faith duty. The "prevention" doctrine is subsumed under the good faith obligation in the RESTATEMENT 2d.[349] Here, the duty of good faith has both positive and negative functions. As suggested by one court, "The implied covenant of good faith and fair dealing requires a promisor to reasonably facilitate the occurrence of a condition precedent by either refraining from conduct which would prevent or hinder the occurrence of the condition, or by taking positive action to cause its occurrence."[350] If, for example, a party signs a contract to purchase a home conditioned upon his ability to

---

[346] Savedoff v. Access Group, Inc., 524 F. 3d 754, 764 (6th Cir. 2008) quoting Kham & Nate's Shoes No. 2, Inc. v. First Bank of Whiting, 908 F.2d 1351, 1357 (7th Cir. 1990).

[347] Industrial Representatives v. CP Clare Corp., 74 F.3d 128 (7th Cir. 1996).

[348] Alaska Packers' Ass'n v. Domenico, 117 F. 99 (9th Cir. 1902).

[349] RESTATEMENT 2d § 230, as relied upon in Mendoza v. COMSAT Corp., 201 F.3d 626, 631 (5th Cir. 2000).

[350] Cauff, Lippman & Co. v. Apogee Fin. Group, Inc., 807 F. Supp. 1007, 1022 (S.D.N.Y. 1992).

obtain mortgage financing, there is a positive obligation to seek such financing and the deliberate failure to do so would not only excuse the condition but constitute a violation of the good faith obligation.[351] Where a contract provided an option to a party to present evidence that a second test score was the product of his work rather than another, the deliberate failure of the defendant to consider the evidence was a violation of the implied duty of good faith.[352]

As we saw earlier, the typical contract does not create a fiduciary relationship between the parties. Where, however, such a relationship exists and the breach is egregious, such extreme bad faith may amount to a tort of bad faith breach allowing punitive damages. After a number of cases involving insurance contracts allowed such actions, a celebrated case extended the possibility of a tort action beyond the insurance cases.[353] Subsequently, however, it was restricted to its facts[354] and later overruled.[355]

§ 98   STANDARDIZED AGREEMENTS (PRINTED FORMS)

[A]   The Basic Problem and RESTATEMENT 2d Approach

One of the constant themes in the discussion of unconscionability is the enforceability of boilerplate terms in standardized forms. No challenge in modern contract law has been more perplexing than those associated with the massive use of standardized, printed forms to evidence the contract.[356] The overwhelming majority of all contracts are evidenced by standard forms.[357]

The essential challenge may be stated rather simply: Since virtually no one (consumer or merchant) bothers to read the printed clauses of forms in regular use, is the non-drafting party bound by all of the terms contained in the form?[358] One response to this question is predicated on the stability and security of transactions, i.e., one is bound by the terms of the form whether he reads it or not. There have always been exceptions to the prescription that one is bound to a particular document whether he reads it or not. We have already considered obvious exceptions, such as documents that cannot reasonably be viewed as contractual, *e.g.*, receipts, parcel checks, invoices, and the like.[359] Another exception occurs when the printed

---

[351] See the discussion of such cases in § 111 *infra*.

[352] Dalton v. Educational Testing Serv., 87 N.Y.2d 384, 639 N.Y.S.2d 977, 663 N.E.2d 289 (1995).

[353] Seaman's Direct Buying Serv., Inc. v. Standard Oil Co., 36 Cal. 3d 752, 686 P.2d 1158 (1984).

[354] Foley v. Interactive Data Corp., 47 Cal. 3d 654, 254 Cal. Rptr. 211, 765 P.2d 373 (1988) (refusal to extend the concept to employment contract).

[355] Freeman & Mills, Inc. v. Belcher Oil Co., 11 Cal. 4th 85, 900 P.2d 669 (1995).

[356] See J. Murray, *The Standardized Agreement Phenomena in the Restatement (Second) of Contracts*, 67 CORNELL L. REV. 735 (1982).

[357] Slawson, *Standard Form Contracts and Democratic Control of Lawmaking Power*, 84 HARV. L. REV. 529 (1971).

[358] In all probability, standardized clauses on computer screens engender clicking "next" buttons as parties pay scant attention to the standardized clauses that flash on the screens.

[359] Magliozzi v. P & T Container Serv. Co., 34 Mass. App. Ct. 591, 614 N.E.2d 690 (1993) (indemnity term on pickup ticket did not become part of the contract); Culbreth v. Simone, 511 F. Supp. 906 (E.D. Pa. 1981) (condition on money order did not become part of the contract); Birmingham Television Corp. v. Water Works, 292 Ala. 147, 290 So. 2d 636 (1974) (term on back of warehouse receipt not part of contract); Iowa-Missouri Walnut Co. v. Grahl, 237 Mo. App. 1093, 170 S.W.2d 437 (1943) (term on back of check did not become part of contract); Charles v. Charles, 478 S.W.2d 133 (Tex. Civ. App. Dallas 1972) (written statement on back of promissory note not part of contract); Green's Ex'rs v. Smith, 146

form is signed by a party under duress or misrepresentation as discussed in previous sections.[360] We then saw numerous cases holding printed clauses unconscionable.[361] There are so many unconscionability cases involving printed forms that some courts mistakenly list the printed form as a prerequisite to a finding of unconscionability.[362]

There can be no doubt over the substantial intersection between the problem of whether one is bound by particular printed clauses and the concept of unconscionability. Much earlier in this volume we explored the maze of problems connected with the exchange of printed forms that do not match, the "battle of the forms."[363] The fundamental tenet of that radical UCC solution is that merchants do not read or understand their own printed forms, much less those received from the other party.[364] Certain provisions in such forms are not binding because they would result in "surprise or hardship" to the party against whom they are designed to operate.[365] The critical comment to the unconscionability section of the Code speaks in terms of avoiding "oppression" and "unfair surprise."[366] The relationship between these sections may be seen as the "battle of the forms" section, 2-207, precluding certain printed provisions from becoming operative *ab initio*, while the unconscionability section, 2-302, is designed to permit courts to excise certain terms that manifest apparent assent. Thus, § 2-207 may be seen as a form of unconscionability, i.e., an "incipient unconscionability."[367]

If there is no exchange of forms and, therefore, no "battle of the forms" because only one form is signed or adopted as evidence of the contract by both parties, the problem of the enforceability of unread, printed provisions remains. The UCC did not address this problem directly. The FIRST RESTATEMENT ignored it,[368] but the RESTATEMENT 2d confronted it. Unfortunately, the results of that confrontation are unclear. The new section on Standardized Agreements is disconcertingly included in that part of the RESTATEMENT 2d captioned, "Effects of Adopting a Writing,"[369] dealing with integrated agreements and other parol evidence rule issues. The first part of the new section is faithful to the FIRST RESTATEMENT view that one is bound by what he signs or adopts as evidence of the contract:

> "Except as stated in Subsection (3), where a party to an agreement signs or otherwise manifests assent to a writing and has reason to believe that like writings are regularly

---

Va. 442, 131 S.E. 846 (1926) (terms on circulars enclosed with monthly bills under the contract did not become part of contract).

[360] *See, e.g.*, United States v. 1,557. 28 Acres of Land, 486 F.2d 445 (10th Cir. 1973); Laemmar v. J. Walter Thompson Co., 435 F.2d 680 (7th Cir. 1970); College Watercolor Group, Inc. v. William H. Newbauer, Inc., 468 Pa. 103, 360 A.2d 200 (1976); Allen-Parker Co. v. Lollis, 257 S.C. 266, 185 S.E.2d 739 (1971).

[361] *See supra* § 97.

[362] *See* § 97[B][2][b] *supra*, note 228.

[363] See the discussion of the "Battle of the Forms" *supra*, Chapter 2, §§ 50 and 51.

[364] *See* Murray, *The Chaos of the "Battle of the Forms": Solutions*, 39 VAND. L. REV. 1307, 1317 at note 47. *See also Standardized Agreement, supra* note 356, at 778–79, n.207.

[365] *See* UCC § 2-207 comment 4.

[366] UCC § 2-302 comment 1.

[367] *See* Murray, *Section 2-207 of the Uniform Commercial Code: Another Word About Incipient Unconscionability*, 39 U. PITT. L. REV. 597 (1978).

[368] The FIRST RESTATEMENT § 70 took the uncompromising position that, absent fraud, duress, or mistake, one is bound by what he signs or adopts as the written evidence of the contract although he is ignorant of the terms of the writing or the proper interpretation of those terms.

[369] Chapter 9, Topic 3 of the RESTATEMENT 2d.

used to embody terms of agreements of the same type, he adopts the writing as an integrated agreement with respect to the terms included in the writing.[370]

This subsection was designed to do nothing more than restate the obvious.[371] If the intention was to bind a party to the terms of a standardized writing to which he assented but did not read, that intention is faithful to the same concept in the FIRST RESTATEMENT[372] which did not refer to "integration." The new section need not have referred to integration since the central problem is not whether a standardized document is the final or complete ("integrated") manifestation of agreement. The problem is whether all of the printed terms contained in such a document are operative and, if not, what is the test to determine whether one or more printed terms shall be inoperative? Since § 211(1) is expressly subject to subsection (3), it is important to consider that subsection: "Where the other party has *reason to believe* that the party manifesting such assent would not do so if he knew that the writing contained a particular term, the term is not part of the agreement."[373]

When should a party have "reason to believe" that the other party would not have manifested assent if he knew that the writing contained a particular term? A comment to the section states that "reason to believe" may be inferred from the fact that a particular term in the writing is "bizarre or oppressive, from the fact that it eviscerates the non-standard terms explicitly agreed to, or from the fact that it eliminates the dominant purpose of the transaction."[374] If the term is illegible or otherwise hidden, or if the "adhering party" had no opportunity to read the term, the inference is reinforced.[375] The language is more than reminiscent of an unconscionability analysis. Under this RESTATEMENT 2d section, a party should not be bound by a term in a printed form that "unfairly surprises" him. A "bizarre" or oppressive term would be unexpected. The drafters, however, insisted on maintaining loyalty to the fundamental tenet that one is bound by what he signs. Thus, if a term is perfectly legible, it cannot be unexpected. If that legible term is allegedly oppressive in some way, the drafters suggest that the question is not within § 211. Rather, it must be considered under the unconscionability section, § 208.[376] Though recognizing a significant relationship between the unconscionability section and the standardized agreement section, the drafters intended to limit the scope of the latter to terms that were not only oppressive but were also hidden. The distinction, however, is anything but clear. This ambiguity is attended by the confusion created by § 211(2) which states that a standardized writing "is interpreted wherever reasonable as treating alike all those similarly situated, without regard to their knowledge or understanding of the standard terms of the writing."[377] While these deficiencies do not augur an effective

---

[370] RESTATEMENT 2d § 211(1).

[371] "I stated first a rather reactionary proposition, which is subsection (1); that is, that when you agree to a standard agreement, you agree to it, and that means everything that's in it, subject, of course, to qualifying terms." This statement of the original Reporter of the RESTATEMENT 2d, Robert Braucher, is found in 47 ALI Proceedings 524 (1970).

[372] FIRST RESTATEMENT § 70.

[373] RESTATEMENT 2d § 211(3) (emphasis supplied).

[374] RESTATEMENT 2d § 211 comment f.

[375] *Id.*

[376] *See Standardized Agreement, supra* note 356, at 766–67.

[377] The standard is explained as treating the party who signs or otherwise assents to the printed document as "the average member of the community who is likely to use this kind of agreement." 47 ALI Proceedings 524–25 (1970). As suggested in *Standardized Agreement, supra* note 356, at 774: "This immediately raises the question: Should one's

judicial analysis of the enforceability of boilerplate terms in standardized agreements, the *seeds* of an effective analysis are discoverable in the new section.

[B]   The "Reasonable Expectation" Test — The Insurance Cases

The "reason to believe" test suggests a focus on the "belief" of the party who will not be adversely affected by the clause, i.e., the drafter or the party for whom the draft was created. If that party has "reason to believe" that the other would not have assented to a term in the standardized document, "the term is not an operative term of the agreement."[378] A comment to the section, however, suggests a different focus: "Although customers typically adhere to standardized agreements and are bound by them without even appearing to know the standard terms in detail, they are not bound to unknown terms which are beyond the range of *reasonable expectation.*"[379] Here, we see a focus on the belief or assumption of the assenting party, rather than an exclusive focus on the belief of the drafter. Thus, if a party signs a standardized agreement, may she subsequently insist that she did not assume or reasonably believe that she would be bound to a term beyond her reasonable expectations? This issue was raised in the formulation of the section and concluded with an agreement that the section should cover both the drafter's "reason to believe" and the assumption or belief of the assenting party.[380] The language of the comment suggests the "reasonable expectation" test which had its origins in a line of insurance cases.

---

education, experience, or particular knowledge of the printed form be a factor in determining the operative effect of one or more printed terms? In dealing with the meaning of 'reason to believe' in subsection (3), the Reporter emphasized that it is an objective standard requiring the exercise of reasonable judgment in light of the facts available to the party whose 'reason to believe' is at issue. If a seller submits a printed form to a customer who is knowledgeable and sophisticated regarding such forms, the seller may very well have reason to believe that such a customer is aware of certain clauses in the form. If that customer assents with presumed knowledge of these clauses, the seller would then have reason to believe that the buyer intended to assent to them. Yet, the comment attempting to explain section 211(2) states: '[C]ourts in construing and applying a standardized contract seek to effectuate the reasonable expectations of the average member of the public who accepts it. The result may be to give the advantage of a restrictive reading to some sophisticated customers who contracted with knowledge of the ambiguity or dispute.' " [§ 211, comment e.] In *Anderson v. Douglas & Lomason Co.*, 540 N. W. 2d 277, 284 (Iowa 1995), the court relied on this concept in holding the standardized terms of an employee handbook distributed to all employees were binding on the employer, though the employees had not read the terms. The court concluded that this constituted an exception to the familiar rule that an offeree must be aware of an offer before he can accept it. Menagerie Productions v. Citysearch, 2009 U.S. Dist. LEXIS 108768 (C. D. Cal. 2009) was a class action where the defendant argued that it would be necessary to consider individual members' understanding of a standardized agreement, but the plaintiff resisted on the basis of the provision of § 211 that all signers of the agreement should be treated alike.

[378]   RESTATEMENT 2d § 211(3).

[379]   RESTATEMENT 2d § 211 comment f (emphasis added).

[380]   In the discussion of RESTATEMENT 2d § 211 by members of the American Law Institute, this concept is developed in the following colloquy:

> Judge Conford [N.J.]: I'm not sure whether the formulation by Mr. Willard [who was one of the principals involved in formulating the language of § 211] would cover both the situations of the signing party or the assenting party assuming that a provision was in as well as an assumption that the assenting party assumed that a provision was out. In other words, would it cover both? I think it should cover both."

> "Professor Braucher: I think I need Mr. Willard's help on this. I think we mean to cover both, but I think the language does not quite cover both."

> "Mr. Willard: I think that's correct, Mr. Reporter, and if a form of words can be found to say it both ways, that seems to me to be appropriate." 47 ALI Proceedings 526 (1970).

Since the judicial notion of a "contract of adhesion" first arose in cases involving insurance contracts which may be viewed as the quintessence of "take-it-or-leave-it" contracts,[381] it is anything but remarkable that the "reasonable expectation" concept would appear in such cases.[382] The dominant application of this concept in an insurance contract context was announced by the Supreme Court of Arizona, relying upon the older reasonable expectation test as well as the new RESTATEMENT section.[383] Numerous courts in other jurisdictions have adopted the test in relation to insurance contracts.[384] Arizona courts have also extended the test beyond insurance contracts. For example, in *Broemmer v. Abortion Services of Phoenix, Ltd.*,[385] the plaintiff signed a standardized form stating that she agreed to arbitrate any dispute. The court found that the agreement was an adhesion contract since it was offered on a "take it or leave it" basis. The weaker party has no realistic choice in assenting to its terms since the services would not be performed absent her apparent assent to the arbitration requirement. Thus, the party with superior bargaining power dictated the terms that controlled the risks assumed under the contract. While insisting that the adhesive nature of the contract alone is not determinative of its enforceability, the court suggests that where the terms are beyond the reasonable expectations of the adhering party or where they are unconscionable, they will not be enforced.[386]

The Arizona decisions have been criticized on the footing that they "look directly at the state of the mind of the 'party manifesting assent,' not at the belief of the drafter about what a hypothetical signer might think."[387] If a party's subjective assertion that she did not expect the term and had no knowledge of it is believed, the term would not be enforceable if her expectation was reasonable.[388] The criticism assumes that even though a party is reasonable

---

[381] *See* Patterson, *The Delivery of a Life Insurance Policy*, 33 HARV. L. REV. 198, 222 (1919).

[382] *See* Keeton, *Insurance Law Rights at Variance with Policy Provisions*, 83 HARV. L. REV. 961 (1970). In his treatise on insurance law, the same author suggests that the doctrine of reasonable expectations finds courts refusing to enforce insurance policies to the extent that they conflict with the reasonable expectations of the insured unless such conflicting terms are clear and conspicuous. *See* KEETON, BASIC TEXT ON INSURANCE LAW 350–61 (1971).

[383] Darner Motor Sales v. Universal Underwriters Ins. Co., 140 Ariz. 383, 682 P.2d 388 (1984) (policy limited coverage to $15,000 on an auto liability claim though insurer had created reasonable expectations of coverage of $100,000). For a more recent application of the concept in Arizona, see Harrington v. Pulte Home Corp., 119 P.3d 1044 (Ariz. Ct. App. 2005).

[384] See Max True Plastering Co. v. United States Fidelity & Guar. Co., 912 P.2d 861 (Okla. 1996), where the court adopts the test, suggesting that, of thirty-six jurisdictions addressing the reasonable expectations doctrine with respect to insurance contracts, only four courts have rejected it. The court also suggests that the test conforms to RESTATEMENT 2d § 211 (quoting Comment f (note 379 *supra*)).

[385] 173 Ariz. 148, 840 P.2d 1013 (1992).

[386] The court expressly relied on the analysis in Graham v. Scissor-Tail, Inc., 28 Cal. 3d 807, 171 Cal. Rptr. 604, 611, 623 P.2d 165, 172 (1981). In *The New Meaning of Contract: The Transformation of Contracts Law by Standard Forms*, 46 U. PITT. L. REV. 21 (1984), Professor David Slawson discussed the application of the "reasonable expectation" test to contracts other than insurance contracts in other jurisdictions.

[387] James J. White, *Consumer Protection and the Uniform Commercial Code: Form Contracts Under Revised Article 2*, 75 WASH. U.L.Q. 315, 346 (1997). Professor White analyzes the Arizona cases applying the "reasonable expectations" test and the differences between the test as interpreted and applied in those cases and RESTATEMENT 2d § 211. The article also criticizes a similar effort on the part of the drafters of the revision of UCC Article 2, which had included a section applying a reasonable expectations test to consumers signing standardized contracts. The section was deleted in subsequent drafts.

[388] Professor White suggests that where a consumer is willing to testify that he did not expect the particular term and did not have knowledge of it, "[i]f one believes this *subjective* assertion, the consumer is not bound by the contract, *at least if the consumer's expectation was 'reasonable.'*" *Id.* at 319 (emphasis supplied).

in *not* expecting a particular term to be part of the boilerplate, the drafter may still have no "reason to believe" that she would not have manifested assent had she been aware of it. The assumption may be unwarranted. Moreover, courts relying on § 211 RESTATEMENT 2d appear to accept the comment that suggests a reasonable expectation test as a guide to the meaning of the drafter's "reason to believe."[389]

An even more direct application of the "reasonable expectation" test is found in the UNIDROIT Principles that are designed to supplement the United Nations Convention on Contracts for the International Sale of Goods (CISG):[390] "No term contained in standard terms which is of such a character that the other party could not reasonably have expected it is effective unless it has been expressly accepted by the other party."[391]

A reasonable expectation test may be viewed as a logical extension of the underlying philosophy of the UCC which insists on an identification of the "bargain-in-fact" of the parties.[392] The operative agreement should include unread boilerplate, whether it is unread in printed documents or on computer screens, but only if such terms are in accordance with the reasonable expectations of the parties. Such terms should become the terms of the contract because they are reasonably expected, not because they are part of the unread boilerplate. A reasonable expectation test may be criticized on the same basis as other doctrines such as unconscionability, i.e., their necessary open-ended texture or vagueness. Myriad failures to state a more precise rule, however, should recognize the inevitable frustration of attempting to create anything resembling a litmus test. There is no escape from an analysis of all of the circumstances surrounding the apparent assent to a standardized agreement. Focusing on the reasonable expectations of the assenting party under myriad circumstances may promise a workable solution, as it has in cases involving insurance contracts. While insurance contracts are the paradigm standard form contracts of adhesion, their characteristics are replicated in other standardized agreements.

§ 99 CONTRACTS AGAINST PUBLIC POLICY — "ILLEGAL BARGAINS"

[A] General Principles

Like any other freedom, freedom of contract is circumscribed by overriding policies. If a statute or other governmental regulation prohibits the enforcement of an agreement, courts will not enforce it, notwithstanding the presence of all the other requirements of an enforceable agreement. Even if a statutory policy or judicially created policy is silent with respect to agreements violating that policy, courts will refuse to lend aid to their enforcement. If a court discovers an overriding interest of society that is incongruous with the enforcement

---

[389] *See, e.g., Max True Plastering Co.*, note 384 *supra. See also* Lauvetz v. Alaska Sales & Serv., 828 P.2d 162, 164 (Alaska 1991).

[390] For a description of CISG and the UNIDROIT Principles, see § 13 in Chapter 1 *supra.*

[391] UNIDROIT Principles, § 2.20(1). Section 2.20(2) states that, in determining whether a term is of such a character, regard shall be had to its content, language and presentation. Professor White's article at note 387 *supra*, at 320, indicates that the drafters of Revised UCC Article 2 had inserted a section copied from this provision of the UNIDROIT Principles to protect consumer against unexpected terms. The section was deleted in subsequent drafts.

[392] "Agreement" is defined in terms of the factual bargain of the parties in § 1-201(3) of the UCC. For an elaboration of this view, see *Standardized Agreement, supra* note 356, at 741–44.

of an agreement, it will refuse to enforce it. There are two fundamental reasons for such court action: (a) deterrence of undesirable conduct and (b) the great reluctance of courts to become involved in suggesting any justification for an unsavory transaction.[393]

If an agreement is prohibited by statute, there is considerable certainty as to the policy reason for refusing its enforcement. Considerable uncertainty, however, may attend a decision to refuse enforcement because the agreement is contrary to "public policy." The "unruly horse" called "public policy" is difficult to describe, much less define.[394] Certain types of conduct are so outrageous that they may be viewed as contrary to public policy *per se*. Thus, an agreement to commit a crime[395] or a tort,[396] as well as a promise to breach a fiduciary duty,[397] has no redeeming virtue and is obviously contrary to public policy. Where, however, the agreement does not involve a commitment to pursue such outrageous conduct, the lines become wavering and blurred. This is because the very idea of "public policy" is predicated upon a "community common sense and common conscience . . . applied . . . to matters of public morals, public health, public safety, public welfare, and the like. It is that general and well-settled public opinion relating to man's plain, palpable duty to his fellow men, having due regard to all the circumstances of each particular relation and situation."[398] In an era of relativism where any notion of objective moral standards is often viewed with disdain, it may be particularly difficult for a court to provide a satisfactory basis for deciding that a certain agreement is contrary to "public morals" or that it is in accordance with "well-settled public opinion," which is often anything but well-settled. We have also known for a considerable time that these standards are not only difficult to identify in general, but change over time.[399] Moreover, such changes often occur at a highly accelerated pace. Judges of the past would undoubtedly be surprised, if not shocked, by decisions explored later in this section. Thus, we will see decisions upholding agreements between unmarried cohabitants, decisions enforcing wagering contracts, decisions upholding clauses exculpating a party from his own negligence and numerous other changes in precedent that are said to reflect the changing mores of our society.

Complete volumes can be devoted to the wide spectrum of problems found in agreements allegedly violating one or more standards of public policy. We focus on those clusters of cases that have addressed particular problems in this area over many years — problems that continue to inspire litigation. An exploration of these cases will not only provide necessary

---

[393] *See* RESTATEMENT 2d, Introductory Note to Chapter 8, Unenforceability on Grounds of Public Policy, §§ 178–199.

[394] See the famous dictum of Judge Burrough in Richardson v. Mellish, 2 Bing. 229, 252, 130 Eng. Rep. 294, 303 (1824), where the opinion suggests that public policy is "a very unruly horse, and when once you get astride it you never know where it will carry you. It may lead you from the sound law. It is never argued at all but when other points fail."

[395] *See, e.g.*, State v. Grimes, 85 Or. App. 159, 735 P.2d 1277, 1278 (1987) (Or. Rev. Stat. § 167.007(1)(a) makes it a Class A misdemeanor to engage in sexual conduct for a fee; an agreement to do so would on its face be an illegal contract and would, therefore, be unenforceable). An agreement immunizing a party from criminal prosecution in exchange for cooperation with authorities, is, however, enforceable. *See, e.g.*, Zani v. State, 701 S.W.2d 249 (Tex. Crim. App. 1985).

[396] *See* RESTATEMENT 2d § 192. "It is axiomatic that one may not contract to commit a tort." Fisher v. Halliburton, 2010 U.S. Dist. LEXIS 10497 (S. D. Tex. 2010) citing § 192.

[397] *See* RESTATEMENT 2d § 193.

[398] McCardie, J. in Naylor, Benzon & Co. v. Krainische Industrie Gesellschaft, 1 K.B. 331 [1881].

[399] "The standard of such policy is not absolutely invariable or fixed, since contracts which at one stage of our civilization may seem to conflict with public interests, at a more advanced stage are treated as legal and binding." Brown, J., in Pope Mfg. Co. v. Gormully, 144 U.S. 224, 233, 12 S. Ct. 632, 636, 36 L. Ed. 414, 418 (1892).

comprehension of these developed areas; it will also provide a sense of how courts attempt to deal with the necessary flexibility of an amorphous concept.

It has become common to characterize the problems in this area as "illegal bargains." While a particular bargain or agreement may be illegal, in large measure the kinds of agreements dealt with by courts under the rubric "illegal bargains" are not "illegal," i.e., courts will simply refuse to enforce them because they violate one or more standards of public policy, rather than any statute with criminal sanctions. For the most part, therefore, we will avoid the use of the phrase "illegal bargain," except when it is accurately used, for example, as in a conspiracy under a criminal statute that would be an illegal bargain.

[B]   Agreements Exculpating a Party From Tort Liability — Indemnity — Strict Liability

Standards of conduct requiring all members of society to avoid creation of unreasonable risks are imposed under the law of torts. Agreements to exempt a party from creating such a risk, i.e., to exempt him from tort liability, are not enforceable for intentional or reckless torts or gross negligence.[400] If, however, the tort liability arises from negligence, absent statutory prohibitions,[401] the modern view suggests that a clause exempting the tortfeasor from such liability will be enforceable unless its purpose is to exempt an employer from liability to an employee, or to exculpate one charged with a public service duty. Courts consider certain criteria for determining whether a party is performing a public service duty:

(1) whether the enterprise is a business of a type generally thought suitable for public regulation; (2) whether the service is of great importance to the public and which is often a matter of practical necessity for some members of the public; (3) whether the party performing the service holds itself out as willing to perform it for any member of the public who seeks it or, at least, for any member of the public within certain established standards; (4) whether the nature of the service and the economic setting give the provider a decisive advantage of bargaining strength against any member of the public who might seek the service; (5) whether the provider exercises its superior bargaining power through a standardized adhesion contract of exculpation and makes no provision to allow a purchaser to pay additional fees to obtain protection against negligence; (6) whether those who seek the service must be placed under the control of the provider, thereby becoming subject to the risk of carelessness on the part of the provider.[402]

A common carrier,[403] innkeeper,[404] hospital,[405] house inspection service[406] or even an automobile repair garage[407] may constitute a public service duty that does not admit of

---

[400] *See* New London County Mutual Insurance v. Nissan North America, Inc., 2007 Conn. Super. LEXIS 950; Murphy v. North Am. River Runners, 186 W. Va. 310, 412 S.E.2d 504, 510 (1991). *See also* RESTATEMENT 2d § 195(1).

[401] In Tassinari v. Key West Water Tours, L.C., 2007 U.S. Dist. LEXIS 46490 (S. D. Fla. 2007), the court recognized that provisions limiting liability from ordinary negligence are generally enforceable, where a statute imposes a standard of conduct, a court may find that exemption from that standard is unenforceable. The court cited Restatement 2d of Contracts, § 195, comment a.

[402] These criteria are found in Tunkl v. Regents of University of Cal., 60 Cal. 2d 92, 32 Cal. Rptr. 33, 383 P.2d 441 (1963). They are repeated in Chauvlier v. Booth Creek Ski Holdings, Inc., 109 Wn. App. 334, 35 P.3d 383 (2001) and Gardner v. Downtown Porsche Audi, 180 Cal. App. 3d 713, 225 Cal. Rptr. 757 (2d Dist. 1986). *See also* Szczotka v. Snowridge, Inc., 869 F. Supp. 247, 250 (D. Vt. 1994), and RESTATEMENT 2d § 195(2).

[403] *See* Lohman v. Morris, 146 Ill. App. 3d 457, 100 Ill. Dec. 263, 497 N.E.2d 143 (3d Dist. 1986) (suggesting the

exculpation, while a ski resort[408] or a service providing recreational boats[409] does not meet the criteria.

A related issue concerns indemnity clauses ("hold harmless" clauses) which seek to indemnify a tortfeasor against his own negligence.[410] A majority of courts have rejected the older view that such contracts violate public policy.[411] The widespread use of insurance against such risks is largely responsible for the rejection of the older view.[412] Again, however, the general rule is subject to the exception that the indemnity clause must not promote a breach of a public duty[413] or breach of a statutory proscription.[414] As in the case of exculpatory clauses generally, an indemnification agreement purporting to indemnify the tortfeasor against intentional torts is against public policy since it can be effective only with respect to unintentional torts and when the agreement is made without any unlawful design.[415] Courts are particularly insistent that any exculpatory clause be clearly stated. Some cases insist that the clause expressly mention "negligence" to release a party from liability for its own negligence.[416] While other courts will not insist on the use of the term, "negligence," they will

---

general rule that such exculpatory contracts are valid as long as they do not involve a unique relationship, such as those between common carrier and passenger or those between employers and employees). While exculpatory clauses will not be enforceable in contracts involving common carriers or public utilities, they may be able to limit their liability. For example, see the Carmack Amendment, 49 U.S.C. § 20(11), permitting common carriers to limit their liability.

[404] Yang v. Voyagaire Houseboats, Inc., 701 N. W. 2d 783 (Minn. 2005). The defendant claimed that renting houseboats provided a recreational activity. Noting that the defendant described its houseboats as "floating homes," it was offering services as an "innkeeper" which falls into the category of services subject to public regulation which also includes common carriers, hospitals, public utilities, public warehouses, and services involving extra-hazardous activities. Such an innkeeper may not require guests to sign an agreement releasing the innkeeper from liability.

[405] See *Tunkl*, note 402 *supra.*

[406] See Mattegat v. Klopfenstein, 50 Conn. App. 97, 717 A.2d 276 (1998).

[407] Under CAL. CIV. CODE § 1668, an automobile repair garage may not exempt itself from liability, even for ordinary negligence, if it provides a service involving the public interest.

[408] See *Szczotka*, note 402 *supra* and Berry v. Greater Park City Co., 171 P. 3d 442 (Utah 2007).

[409] Waggoner v. Nags Head Water Sports, 1998 U.S. App. LEXIS 6792, at *18 (4th Cir. 1998): "North Carolina courts will enforce an exculpatory clause unless it is violative of a statute, gained through inequality of bargaining power, or contrary to a substantial public interest." Plaintiff could not fit the exculpatory clause in this case within any of these categories.

[410] An indemnity clause generally creates an obligation by one party to pay for loss or damage another party has incurred. An illustration is found in Morton Thiokol, Inc. v. Metal Bldg. Alteration Co., 193 Cal. App. 3d 1025, 238 Cal. Rptr. 722 (1st Dist. 1987): "Metal Building . . . agrees to indemnify and hold harmless the Owner and its agents and employees from any and all liability, loss, damage, cost and expense (including attorney's fees) sustained by reason of Contractor's breach of warranty, breach of contract, misrepresentation or false certification, or failure to exercise due care." *See also* Cunningham v. Goettl Air Conditioning, Inc., 194 Ariz. 236, 980 P.2d 489 (1999).

[411] *See* Kuhn v. State of Alaska, 692 P.2d 261 (Alaska 1984).

[412] Manson-Osberg Co. v. State, 552 P.2d 654 (Alaska 1976).

[413] *See, e.g.*, Northwest Airlines, Inc. v. Alaska Airlines, Inc., 351 F.2d 253 (9th Cir. 1965), *cert. denied*, 383 U.S. 936, 86 S. Ct. 1068, 15 L. Ed. 2d 853 (1966).

[414] See, e.g., GA. CODE ANN. § 13-8-2(b), proscribing indemnification of the promisee against his own negligence in a construction contract as against public policy.

[415] Jacksonville State Bank v. Barnwell, 481 So. 2d 863 (Ala. 1985). *See also* RESTATEMENT 2d § 192 comment.

[416] See Powell v. American Heal Fitness Center, 694 N. E. 2d 757 (Ind. App. 1998); Ethyl Corp. v. Daniel Constr. Co., 725 S.W.2d 705 (Tex. 1987), setting forth an express negligence test to be applied to an indemnity provision which seeks to absolve the indemnitee from its own negligence.

strictly construe such clauses "since they are not favorites of the law."[417] A provision simply exculpating a party from any future damages is unenforceable because such language would include exemption from intentional torts.[418]

Strict liability in tort is imposed on sellers of products for defects causing personal injury or economic loss to other property without personal injury.[419] Before this theory saw the light of day, warranty theory was used to provide a strict liability basis for recovery.[420] The case law is scant as to whether parties may agree to exempt the seller of a defective product for such strict liability. There are cases precluding the enforcement of such exculpatory clauses on the ground that strict liability causes of action are independent of the contract.[421] Other cases, however, distinguish disclaimers of strict liability in consumer contracts and contracts between commercial parties. A court reviewed the rationale for refusing to enforce such exculpatory clauses in consumer contracts which included the public concern for human life and health, advertising to the public representing the safety of the product, and the justice of imposing the loss on the party creating the risk and reaping the profit by placing the product in the stream of commerce. The court concluded that this these policies would not apply to a commercial party with equal bargaining power.[422] The RESTATEMENT 2d treats such exemption clauses as generally unenforceable, but would permit an exception in the case of a contract between business entities if there were no taint of unconscionability in such an agreement.[423]

---

[417] *See also* Osgood v. Medical, Inc., 415 N.W.2d 896 (Minn. Ct. App. 1987) (while "negligence" need not be mentioned in an indemnity provision exculpating the indemnitee from his own negligence, the language must otherwise be sufficiently clear to permit that interpretation). In Morton Thiokol, Inc. v. Metal Bldg. Alteration Co., 193 Cal. App. 3d 1025, 238 Cal. Rptr. 722 (1st Dist. 1987), the court distinguished "general" indemnity clauses which do not address themselves to the indemnitee's own negligence, and those that provide for such indemnity which must be "clear and explicit."

[418] All Business Solutions, Inc. v. NationsLine, Inc., 629 F. Supp. 2d 553 (W. D. Va. 2009).

[419] *See* RESTATEMENT 2D OF TORTS § 402A.

[420] See the warranties of quality under UCC §§ 2-313, 2-314 and 2-315, the allowance for third party recovery in § 2-318 and the recognition of consequential damage recovery for injury to person or property in § 2-715(2)(b). See the classic exposition of products liability in Seely v. White Motor Co., 63 Cal. 2d 9, 45 Cal. Rptr. 17, 403 P.2d 145 (1965).

[421] See Ruzzo v LaRose Enterprises, 748 A.2d 261, 268 (R. I. 2000), *See also* Superior Leasing, LLC v. Kaman Aero Corp., 2006 U.S. Dist. LEXIS 92426 at *48–49 (D. Ore. 2006); Sterner Aero AB v. Page Airmotive, 499 F.2d 709, 713 (10th Cir. 1974) ("We construe [Oklahoma law] as precluding the defendants from asserting the existence of a contractual disclaimer provision as a valid defense to liability," quoting comment m to § 402A of the RESTATEMENT 2D OF TORTS. The court proceeds, however, to suggest that it would be possible for the parties to agree that the seller would be exempt from negligence liability, though an effective disclaimer of warranty liability under the UCC would not be sufficient for this purpose.

[422] Chicago Steel Rule & Die Fabricators Co. v. ADT Security Systems, Inc., 327 Ill. App. 3d 642, 763 N. E. 2d 839 (2002). *See* Island Creek Coal Co. v. Lake Shore, Inc., 692 F. Supp. 629, 634 (W.D. Va. 1988). Keystone Aeronautics Corp. v. R. J. Enstrom Corp., 499 F.2d 146 (3d Cir. 1974) construes comment m to § 402A of the RESTATEMENT 2D OF TORTS as relegated to the typical consumer situation, since the comment is concerned with consumer buyers. The opinion, however, finds the clause in question unenforceable because it merely disclaimed warranties as provided by the UCC. Since such an effective warranty disclaimer would not be an effective clause exempting negligence liability, it was not effective to exempt the seller from strict liability under § 402A. See also Delta Air Lines, Inc. v. McDonnell Douglas Corp., 503 F.2d 239 (5th Cir. 1974), *cert. denied*, 421 U.S. 965, 95 S. Ct. 1953, 44 L. Ed. 2d 451 (1975), which upholds a clause that is broad enough to exempt the seller from negligence liability or strict liability with no reference to § 402A or its comments.

[423] *See* Kellar v. Lloyd, 180 Wis. 2d 162, 509 N.W.2d 87, 94 (Ct. App. 1993). See also RESTATEMENT 2d § 195(3) and comment c, which further suggest that the exempting clause would not affect the rights of third parties. The exception is expressly predicated upon *Keystone Aeronautics Corp.*, 499 F. 2d 146 (3d Cir. 1974).

[C]   Contracts in Restraint of Trade

In a very broad sense, every contract concerning trade is a contract in restraint of trade since the parties to the contract necessarily restrict themselves from future dealings with other parties with respect to the subject matter of the contract.[424] It would, therefore, be absurd to suggest that Anglo-American law ever recognized a principle that *all* contracts in restraint of trade, in the literal sense, were illegal bargains. In the early, immobile society of the guilds, however, contracts which adversely affected the opportunity of a person to earn a livelihood or engage in a trade or business were viewed with deep suspicion. When a promisor undertook to refrain from engaging in a particular occupation, trade or business, the contract was viewed as inimical to the public interest and was, therefore, illegal because it was a contract in restraint of trade. Yet, other types of promises or covenants in restraint of trade would be enforced.

[1]   Covenants Not to Compete — Sale of a Business

If a person had established a trade or business and was desirous of selling it so as to benefit from the good will his work and labor had developed over a period of time, a prospective buyer would be wary of buying the business if the seller were not prohibited from establishing a competing business in the same territory. The protection required by such a purchaser would necessarily prevent the seller from establishing the competing business and, thus, deprive the buyer of the patronage for which he had paid. The only suitable protection was a promise by the seller that he would not engage in that business within the relevant geographic market of the buyer, at least for a period of time that permitted the buyer to cement the relationships with customers that he had gained by purchasing the good will. To protect such buyers and to permit sellers to dispose of their good will for a fair consideration, it was necessary for courts to distinguish enforceable and unenforceable covenants in restraint of trade. Courts began to develop these distinctions between covenants in restraint of trade that were subsidiary (ancillary or indirect) to a legitimate purpose, such as the sale of a business, and those that were naked covenants not to compete (direct or non-ancillary restraints), whose purpose was to permit monopolistic control of a trade or business in a given territory.[425] Thus, the classic example of a direct, non-ancillary contract in restraint of trade that has no redeeming virtue is an agreement among competitors to fix prices or to divide markets. While there is considerable diversity of opinion as to how non-ancillary restraints were viewed at common law,[426] the better view is that most American courts treated them as illegal *per se*.[427] Again, however, ancillary restraints were upheld if they were partial rather than general.

If a hair stylist wishes to sell his or her business, often the only valuable asset is the good will of the business, i.e., "an established business at a given place with the patronage that

---

[424] See the classic exposition of this concept by Justice Brandeis in Chicago Bd. of Trade v. United States, 246 U.S. 231, 38 S. Ct. 242, 62 L. Ed. 683 (1918).

[425] The distinction between ancillary and non-ancillary restraints is found in the classic exposition by Justice Taft in United States v. Addyston Pipe & Steel Co., 85 F. 271 (6th Cir. 1898).

[426] *See* Dewey, *The Common Law Background of Antitrust Policy*, 41 Va. L. Rev. 759 (1955); Letwin, *The English Common Law Concerning Monopolies*, 21 U. Chi. L. Rev. 355 (1954); Peppin, *Price Fixing Agreements Under the Sherman Antitrust Law*, 28 Cal. L. Rev. 297 (1940).

[427] *See* M. Handler, A Study of the Construction and Enforcement of the Federal Antitrust Laws (4–5 TNEC Monograph No. 38, 1941).

attaches to the name and the location."[428] The premises and equipment may be leased and even the incidental sales of products may be on a consignment basis. The good will, however, may be valuable and may constitute the only asset of significant value that the efforts of the stylist have created at that site over a period of time. To facilitate the legitimate purpose of the stylist to sell that good will, courts must be willing to enforce a promise by the stylist that she will not compete with the buyer in the same territory, at least for a period necessary to permit the new owner to reestablish relationships with the customers of that business. By allowing restrictive covenants in such cases, courts add to the value of the business.[429] Absent such willingness on the part of courts, the stylist will not be able to sell her only valuable asset. The resulting restraint of trade is ancillary to a legitimate purpose and is, therefore, enforceable if it is reasonable.[430]

Courts have developed certain guidelines to provide some predictability in the application of the test. Thus, it is generally agreed that the restraint of trade is unreasonable if it is greater than required for the protection of the party for whose benefit it is imposed.[431] Other factors include the degree of hardship imposed upon the restricted party, possible injury to the public, and the tendency of the restraint to create a monopoly or to unreasonably restrict the alienation of property.[432] If the restraint is not ancillary to a contract for the sale of a business or other legitimate purpose, it will be viewed as unreasonable absent statutory authorization or overriding social or economic justification.[433] The Kroger Co. signed a long-term lease for space in a shopping center to operate a grocery store. The lease contained a restrictive covenant precluding the lease of space to another grocery store in the shopping center. Kroger decided to close all of its stores in the region and assigned this lease to another supermarket grocery chain (Pay Less) which subleased the space to an appliance store. Pay Less conceded that it had no intention of operating a grocery store in the center in place of the Kroger operation. Rather, since it operated two other supermarkets grocery stores within two miles of the center, the restrictive covenant would preclude the center from leasing to a competing

---

[428] Sagarino v. SCI State Funeral Servs., Inc., 2000 Conn. Super. LEXIS 1384 at 10 (Conn. Super. Ct. May 22, 2000).

[429] *Id.*

[430] *See* Mattis v. Lally, 138 Conn. 51, 82 A.2d 1155 (1951) (sale of barbering business, where seller agreed not to engage in the barbering business in the city where the business was located for a period of five years, was not against public policy). *See also* RESTATEMENT 2d § 188(2)(a). In the well-known case of Mitchell v. Reynolds, 1 P. Williams 181, 24 Eng. Rep. 347 (1711), a lease of a messuage and bakehouse was assigned to the plaintiff. An ancillary covenant to this assignment made the defendant liable to the plaintiff in the sum of fifty pounds if the defendant exercised his trade as a baker in a certain area during a five-year period. The ancillary covenant in restraint of trade was upheld because it was reasonably limited in time and geographical area. The opinion, however, suggested that all general restraints, i.e., those unlimited in time or space, were invalid *per se.* This view was changed by the middle of the 19th Century [*see* Hitchcock v. Coker, 6 A. & E. 438, 112 Eng. Rep. 167 [1837] — covenant not to carry on the trade of chemist or druggist within the town of Taunton, in the county of Somerset, or within three miles thereof, unlimited as to time]. By the end of that century, the House of Lords stated the broad test to be one of reasonableness as suggested in the opinion by Lord M'Naghten in Nordenfelt v. Maxim Nordenfelt Guns & Ammunition Co., A.C. 535, 565 [1894]: "It is a sufficient justification, and indeed it is the only justification, if the restriction is reasonable — reasonable, that is, in reference to the interests of the public so framed and so guarded as to afford adequate protection to the party in whose favour it is imposed, while at the same time it is in no way injurious to the public." The "reasonableness" test prevails at this time. *See* RESTATEMENT 2d §§ 186–188.

[431] *See* RESTATEMENT 2d § 188(1)(a).

[432] *See* RESTATEMENT 2d 188(1)(b). For an application of §§ 188(a) and (b), see Hopper v. All Pet Animal Clinic, 861 P.2d 531 (Wyo. 1993).

[433] *See* RESTATEMENT 2d § 187.

grocery store. The Kroger use of the restrictive covenant promoted the shopping center while encouraging investment and diversity in serving the public. The Pay Less use of the covenant was not ancillary to a legitimate purpose. It was being used as a direct restraint of trade in that region and, as such, it was clearly unenforceable.[434]

[D]   The Protection of Good Will and Employer's Rights — Postemployment Restraints

There is a tendency to place all types of restraints of trade into one category and then to focus upon the problem of distinguishing reasonable and unreasonable restraints. It is, however, important to consider the purpose of the restraint in each situation since purposes will differ from one situation to another, and the determination of purpose will assist courts to analyze each situation more effectively.

We have seen that the good will of a business in the hands of the new buyer must be protected since the essential value of many businesses is found only in their good will. The purpose of another type of ancillary restraint, however, is quite different. Employers often require new employees to agree that they will not compete with their employer's business when the employee leaves the job. The purpose of these types of post-employment restraints is typically to protect the employer against the use of certain information (*e.g.*, trade secrets, secret processes, and customer lists) which the employee has acquired during employment. The sale of a business where good will is the dominant part of the agreed exchange requires protection against the seller's competition so that the very consideration moving to the buyer will not be diminished in value. In postemployment restraints, however, the employee who has rendered full services during the term of employment is not providing the essential consideration for his or her wages when refraining from using certain information or from soliciting certain customers after the employment is completed. The main purpose of the employment was fulfilled through the services rendered during that term. It has, therefore, been aptly suggested that, "courts properly should, and do, look more critically to the circumstances of the origin of post-employment restraints than to circumstances of other classes of restraint."[435]

[1]   Consideration

Where a reasonable postemployment restraint is part of the original contract of employment, there is no need for separate consideration to support such a promise since the original consideration supports both the present employment and the restrictive covenant. Where, however, the restrictive covenant is not made until after the original contract is formed, courts are not uniform in requiring or not requiring separate consideration. Where an employee worked for a company for a year before signing a noncompetition agreement, the issue was whether the agreement was supported by consideration. The court noted that many courts hold that continued employment alone is sufficient consideration to support a covenant not to compete entered into after the commencement of an at-will employment contract. Other courts

---

[434] Tippecanoe Assocs. II, LLC v. Kimco Lafayette 671, Inc., 829 N.E.2d 512 (Ind. 2005).

[435] *See* Amex Distrib. Co. v. Mascari, 150 Ariz. 510, 724 P.2d 596, 600, 604 (Ct. App. 1986) (restrictive covenants tending to prevent employee from pursuing a similar vocation after termination of employment are disfavored and where such a noncompetition covenant seeks to eliminate competition *per se* and has no valid interest in protecting the employer is unenforceable). *See also* Restatement 2d of Contracts, § 188, comment b.

question whether there is an real bargain involved in such agreements. These courts are more comfortable with some manifestation of consideration related directly to the covenant not to compete. The instant court, however, recited the most compelling argument for finding consideration to support the covenant not to compete.

The same consideration analysis applies to such agreements at the commencement of the contract or after the contract is formed. A promise to employ can ask for both the employee's services and a noncompete agreement. Starting to work would constitute acceptance of such an offer and clear consideration for the employee's noncompete agreement. If the at-will employee has already begun to work and is told that continuation of that employment will require the additional promise not to compete, the at-will employee has no right to the continuation of that employment and the employer's willingness to allow the employment to continue on the new basis constitutes ample consideration. The court affirmed the decision of the trial court to enforce the noncompetition agreement.[436] It is important to remember that there is no pre-existing duty to the employee or the employer. Either party may walk away with impunity. Just as such an employer can announce a change in the employee's duties or even a decrease in compensation, or the employee can announce his requirement of different duties or increased compensation, the parties can agree to a noncompete clause — or not. Dissatisfactions with this analysis are not genuine disputes over consideration. Rather, they may emanate from general dissatisfaction with the employment-at-will concept or they may find the terms of a particular noncompetition clause to be unreasonable for other reasons. A quarrel with the reasonableness of a postemployment restraint or whether the nature of the employer's business necessitated any such restraint with a particular employee at all may be very legitimate quarrels since such restraints should be, and typically are, disfavored. Such underlying concerns, however, should not be contested under the consideration rubric. As the inimitable Karl Llewellyn suggested, "Covert tools are unreliable tools."

[2]   The Elements of "Reasonableness" of Noncompetition Clauses

With respect to the sale of a business or postemployment restraints, courts generally agree that restrictive covenants must be (a) necessary to protect the legitimate interest of the buyer of the business or interests of the employer, (b) reasonable with respect to territory and time, (c) not unduly harsh or oppressive on the seller or employee, and (d) not injurious to the public.[437] Although the requirement that the restraint must not be unduly harsh or oppressive to the seller may be stated separately,[438] it actually relates to the relative degree of restraint necessary to protect the buyer. If the restraint is necessary to protect the buyer, presumably it is not oppressive to the seller. As to the requirement that the restraint not be injurious to the public, this element is typically explored in cases involving post-employment restraints, such as professional practices in which a young physician is employed by a doctor with an established practice or a partnership arrangement between the old and new physicians. Thus, in one case,

---

[436] Summits 7, Inc. v. Kelly, 886 A.2d 365. (Vt. 2005). See Lake Land Employment Group of Akron, LLC v. Columber, 101 Ohio St. 3d 242, 804 N. E. 2d 27 (2004) (noting the split of authority, but holding that continued employment of an at-will employee constitutes consideration).

[437] See Fine Foods v. Dahlin, 147 Vt. 599, 523 A.2d 1228 (1986) (sale of business); Compton v. Joseph Lepak, DDS, PC, 154 Mich. App. 360, 397 N.W.2d 311 (1986) (post-employment); Boisen v. Petersen Flying Serv., Inc., 222 Neb. 239, 383 N.W.2d 29 (1986) (post-employment); Knight Vale & Gregory v. McDaniel, 37 Wash. App. 366, 680 P.2d 448 (1984) (post-employment); Jewel Box Stores Corp. v. Morrow, 272 N.C. 659, 158 S.E.2d 840 (1968) (sale of business); Montgomery v. Getty, 284 S.W.2d 313 (Mo. Ct. App. 1955) (sale of business). See also RESTATEMENT 2d § 188.

[438] See, e.g., McCook Window Co. v. Hardwood Door Corp., 52 Ill. App. 2d 278, 202 N.E.2d 36 (1st Dist. 1964).

the question was whether the reduction of 70 doctors by one in the territory would cause such injury to the public as to justify the court in refusing to enforce the restrictive covenant.[439] While courts will be concerned about the duration and territorial extent of restraints, neither is conclusive.[440] Courts may not be concerned if the covenant fails to limit a post-employment restraint in time since a reasonable time can be implied.[441] The absence of a geographical limitation may be insignificant to protect trade secrets or customer contacts.[442] Many cases, however, regard the duration of the restraint and the reasonableness of the territorial limitation as vitally important.[443]

In light of the different purpose normally associated with post-employment restraints and the consequent refusal of courts to limit the former employee's activity beyond the point of necessary protection of the former employer,[444] courts must carefully explore all of the circumstances surrounding such restraints.[445]

Since the protection of the employer's customer relationships is typically involved in such restraints, it is important to consider certain critical factors in relation to that purpose. These factors include (1) the number of contracts between the employee and customers; (2) the exclusiveness of such contracts, i.e., whether these are the only contracts between the business and the customer; (3) the place of the contracts, i.e., either at the situs of the business or at the customer's home or place of business; (4) the kind of functions performed by the employee, i.e., routine and mechanical functions versus functions requiring a high degree of skill which may make the customer more conscious of the efforts of the particular employee.[446] Postemployment restraints designed to prevent the divulging of confidential information (as contrasted with preserving customer relationships) must also be explored critically. The two basic

---

[439] *See* Bauer v. Sawyer, 8 Ill. 2d 351, 134 N.E.2d 329 (1956) (finding that restraint would not injure the public).

[440] See Dunning v. Chemical Waste Mgmt., Inc., 1993 U.S. Dist. LEXIS 10620, at *15 (N.D. Ill. July 29, 1993).

[441] *See Compton v. Joseph Lepak, DDS, PC, supra* note 437; Karpinski v. Ingrasci, 28 N.Y.2d 45, 320 N.Y.S.2d 1, 268 N.E.2d 751 (1971).

[442] *See, e.g.*, Lawter Int'l, Inc. v. Carroll, 116 Ill. App. 3d 717, 451 N.E.2d 1338, 1345 (1st Dist. 1983).

[443] *See, e.g.*, Briggs v. R. R. Donnelley & Sons Co., 589 F.2d 39 (1st Cir. 1978) (suggesting that the temporal duration and geographical extent of the commitment not to compete are two important factors in determining the enforceability of the covenant). *See also* Fidelity Union Life Ins. Co. v. Protective Life Ins. Co., 356 F. Supp. 1199 (N.D. Tex. 1972), *aff'd per curiam*, 477 F.2d 594 (5th Cir. 1973).

[444] *See, e.g.*, Howard Schultz & Assocs., Inc. v. Broniec, 239 Ga. 181, 182, 236 S.E.2d 265, 267 (1977) (employee's covenant not to accept employment "in any capacity" imposed a greater limitation upon the employee than was necessary to protect the employer).

[445] See, e.g., Philip G. Johnson & Co. v. Salmen, 211 Neb. 123, 317 N.W.2d 900, 904 (1982), where the court suggested the following factors: the degree of inequality of bargaining power, the risk of the employer losing customers, the extent of respective participation by the parties in securing and retaining customers, the good faith of the employer, the existence of sources or general knowledge pertaining to the identity of customers; the nature and extent of the business position held by the employee, the employee's training, health, and education and needs of his family, the current conditions of employment, the necessity of the employee changing his calling or residence, and the correspondence of the restraint with the need for protecting the legitimate interest of the employer. The covenant in this case was too broad since it sought to prohibit the employee from earning fees from clients or former clients of the accounting firm, or from such clients' officers and agents, no matter where they may be.

[446] In BDO Seidman v. Hirshberg, 93 N.Y.2d 382, 690 N.Y.S.2d 854, 712 N.E.2d 1220, 1223 (1999), the court states, "With agreements not to compete between professionals, however, we have given greater weight to the interest of the employer in restricting competition within a confined geographical area. . . . The rationale for the different application of the common-law rule of reasonableness expressed in our decisions was that professionals are deemed to provide 'unique or extraordinary services.'"

inquiries will center around the nature of the confidential information and the efforts of the employer to protect the confidentiality of the information.[447] A trade secret which is clearly valuable in the industry is entitled to substantial protection, particularly if it is the result of the employer's investment of time, money and effort. Thus, where a restraint was not ancillary to the sale of a business or employment, but ancillary to an agreement to grant a nonexclusive, nontransferable license to analyze, examine, modify and otherwise use certain software to develop joint software, the court recognized such a restraint as reasonable.[448]

[E]   The Severance Rule — "Blue Pencil" Rule

If the restrictive covenant attached to the sale of a business or former employment is too broad in geography or too long in duration, courts are often asked to enforce the covenant in terms of a lesser area or shorter duration if such a modification would make the restraint reasonable. While there appears to be little reason for precluding a court from such judicial modification, the concept of "divisibility" or "severance" created problems as early as 1843. In *Mallan v. May*,[449] the court created what came to be known as the "blue pencil" rule. If the restrictive covenant was drafted so that certain portions could be deleted leaving the remaining portion intact and enforceable as a reasonable restraint, the covenant, so modified, became enforceable. Thus, if a seller of the good will of a business promised not to compete for a certain duration "in Los Angeles or elsewhere in California," it would be possible to "blue pencil" the phrase "or elsewhere in California." If the restraint would be reasonable if confined to Los Angeles, it could be enforced since the court merely had to delete a phrase and did not have to otherwise modify the covenant. This approach, however, was mechanical and could be used only where the parties happened to include an overly broad clause in a form that was subject to such deletion or blue pencilling. If, therefore, the covenant precluded competition in California, a court could not "blue pencil" its way to a reasonable restriction. In a recent case, the court noted the difficulty in using North Carolina's version of the "blue pencil" rule:

> North Carolina's blue pencil rule, however, is narrow and its employment by the courts is discretionary. When the language of a non-compete is overly broad, North Carolina's 'blue pencil rule' severely limits what the court may do to alter the covenant. A court at most may choose not to enforce a distinctly separable part of a covenant in order to render the provision reasonable. The court may not otherwise revise or rewrite the covenant.[450]

Many courts, however, have rejected the mechanical "blue pencil" approach by enforcing restrictive covenants for smaller areas or shorter durations, though no mechanical division of the language was possible, if the enforceable portion has been obtained in good faith and in accordance with standards of fair dealing.[451] Where a covenant not to compete contained a "reimbursement clause" requiring an accountant to compensate the former employer for lost

---

[447] *Id.* at 671–74.

[448] ProtoComm Corp. v. Fluent, Inc., 1995 U.S. Dist. LEXIS 40 (E.D. Pa. Jan. 3, 1995), *aff'd per curiam*, 1997 U.S. App. LEXIS 33441 (3d Cir. Oct. 29, 1997).

[449] 11 M. & W. 653 [1843].

[450] Technology Partners v. Hart, 298 Fed. Appx. 238, 243 (4th Cir. 2008).

[451] *See* Cintas Corp. v. Perry, 517 F. 3d 459 (7th Cir. 2008), where the court describes the transition in Ohio Courts from the mechanical blue pencil rule to a discretionary judicial authority to modify unreasonable non-compete provisions. See also A.N. Deringer, Inc. v. Strough, 103 F.3d 243 (2d Cir. 1996). The RESTATEMENT 2d § 184 rejects the "blue pencil" approach.

patronage of clients with whom he never acquired a relationship through his former employment or clients who came to his former employer solely because of his independent recruitment efforts, the court found that the former employer had no legitimate interest in preventing the defendant from competing for their patronage. The court adopted the more flexible position of enforcing the covenant absent the reimbursement clause.[452]

Again, however, it should not be assumed that the "blue pencil," mechanical approach has been totally abandoned in modern courts. In addition to North Carolina, other courts cling to the original, mechanical approach.[453] Moreover, Georgia courts have refused to accept the blue pencil rule in any form.[454] The severability concept, whether in its rule of reason or mechanical "blue pencil" form, can be criticized on the footing that it may induce the drafting of overly broad clauses which, even if successfully attacked, will still be enforced in modified form. To mitigate this inducement, courts, again, will insist that the enforceable portion have been obtained in good faith and in accordance with standards of fair dealing.[455]

[F]   Antitrust Statutes — Non-Ancillary Restraints — Naked Covenants Against Competition

As a practical matter, much of the law dealing with non-ancillary restraints is now governed by statute. On the federal level, the antitrust laws began with the "charter of economic freedom" known as the Sherman Act of 1890.[456] Major additions occurred in 1914 with the enactment of the Clayton[457] and Federal Trade Commission Acts,[458] in 1936 with the Robinson-Patman amendment to the Clayton Act concerning price discrimination,[459] and in 1950 with the Celler-Kefauver amendment[460] to the Clayton Act in relation to mergers. The states have also enacted laws against naked contracts in restraint of trade and monopolizing which often contain proscriptions similar to the federal statutes.[461] While the statutes now

---

[452] BDO Seidman v. Hirshberg, 93 N.Y.2d 382, 690 N.Y.S.2d 854, 712 N.E.2d 1220, 1226 (1999).

[453] See Valley Med. Specialists v. Farber, 194 Ariz. 363, 982 P.2d 1277, 1285 (1999) ("eliminating grammatically severable unreasonable provisions"). See also Industrial Techs. v. Paumi, 1997 Conn. Super. LEXIS 1499 (Conn. Super. Ct. May 28, 1997), discussing differences between the Connecticut and Massachusetts views; CAE Vanguard, Inc. v. Newman, 246 Neb. 334, 518 N.W.2d 652, 655 (1994); Fowler v. Printers II, Inc., 89 Md. App. 448, 598 A.2d 794, 802 (1991).

[454] Advance Technology Consultants, Inc. v. Roadtrac LLC, 250 Ga. App. 317, 320, 551 S. E. 2d 735, 737 (Ct. App. 2001).

[455] RESTATEMENT 2d § 184(2). See BDO Seidman, note 452 supra: "[I]f the employer demonstrates an absence of overreaching, coercive use of dominant bargaining power, or other anti-competitive misconduct, but has in good faith sought to protect a legitimate business interest, consistent with reasonable standards of fair dealing, partial enforcement may be justified." See also Laidlaw, Inc. v. Student Transp. of Am., Inc., 20 F. Supp. 2d 727 (D.N.J. 1998) (bad faith). Comment b to § 184 emphasizes the fact that the power of a court to enforce part of such a restrictive covenant is not a power of reformation, i.e., the court will not increase the scope of the term in any fashion.

[456] 15 U.S.C. §§ 1–7.

[457] 15 U.S.C. §§ 12–27.

[458] 15 U.S.C. §§ 41–45.

[459] 15 U.S.C. § 13.

[460] 15 U.S.C. § 18.

[461] See, e.g., section 2 of the Michigan Antitrust Reform Act (MARA), MICH. COMP. LAWS § 445.772; MICH. STAT. ANN. § 28.70(2), which is identical to the same provision in the Uniform State Antitrust Act (USAA) promulgated by the National Conference on Uniform State Laws in 1973: "A contract, combination or conspiracy between 2 or more persons in restraint of trade, or to monopolize trade or commerce in a relevant market is unlawful." The language is

govern, antitrust law requires extensive judicial elaboration because the statutes are typically drafted in broad language designed to permit courts to cope with myriad types of anticompetitive behavior. Under the basic federal statute, the Sherman Act, with the exception of certain blatant manifestations of anticompetitive behavior which suggest no redeeming virtue and are, therefore, viewed as *per se* illegal,[462] courts apply a "rule of reason," requiring a definite factual showing of illegality to determine whether the conduct in question has the actual or probable effect of injuring competition.[463]

Section 1 of the Sherman Act requires a contract, combination or conspiracy, i.e., some manifestation of agreement to restrain trade. Section 2 proscribes monopolizing, i.e., some positive drive, apart from sheer competitive skills, to control a relevant market.[464] Later antitrust statutes such as the Clayton Act and Robinson-Patman amendment to the Clayton Act require a showing of actual or probable substantial lessening of competition. The statutory language is, at best, only a point of departure in such an inquiry, with the overwhelming effort devoted to a study of the precedent and its application to the actual or probable economic effect in the case *sub judice*. Further exploration of antitrust law must be left for courses in that area and the extensive antitrust literature.

[G]   Wagers and Gambling Contracts — Aleatory Contracts — "Futures" — "Changing Mores"

There was no policy condemning wagers and gaming contracts in English common law. Such agreements were regarded as illegal only if the subject matter of the particular transaction was deemed to be inconsistent with the public welfare. As time went on, however, English judges became astute in finding reasons for refusing to sanction such agreements,[465] and in 1845 a statute was enacted which made all wagering and gambling contracts unenforceable.[466] American courts, however, clung to the view that such bargains were *per se* contrary to public policy because of their tendency to induce shiftlessness, poverty, and immorality.[467] Eventually, statutes were enacted in practically every jurisdiction prohibiting lotteries as well as all other gaming and wagering transactions. As will be seen below, the mores of our society have changed dramatically with respect to wagers, lotteries, and gaming

---

similar to §§ 1 and 2 of the Sherman Antitrust Law of 1890 as amended.

[462] See, e.g., Arizona v. Maricopa County Med. Soc'y, 457 U.S. 332, 102 S. Ct. 2466, 73 L. Ed. 2d 48 (1982), where the majority opinion by Justice Stevens deals with the classic *per se* categories of price fixing, division of markets, group boycotts (collective refusals to deal) and tying arrangements (citing Northern Pac. R.R. v. United States, 356 U.S. 1 (1958)), and suggests the rationale for *per se* illegality, i.e., the elaborate inquiry into the reasonableness of such a restraint is costly and the litigation of the effect or purpose of the restraint is often excessive, complex, and often wholly fruitless. Moreover, even though it is conceivable that cases not fitting the generalization of *per se* illegality may arise, they are not sufficiently common or significant to justify the time and expense necessary to identify them. United States v. Topco Assocs., Inc., 405 U.S. 596, 92 S. Ct. 1126, 31 L. Ed. 2d 515 (1972).

[463] The "rule of reason" approach requiring an inquiry into the purpose of the restraint, the market power of the parties involved, and the actual or probable effects of the restraint was created in the opinion by Justice Brandeis in Chicago Bd. of Trade v. United States, 246 U.S. 231, 38 S. Ct. 242, 62 L. Ed. 683 (1918).

[464] The most celebrated case involving Section 2 of the Sherman Act at the time of this writing is United States v. Microsoft Corp., 87 F. Supp. 2d 30 (D.D.C. 2000), which also involved a violation of Section 1.

[465] *See* Thackoorseydass v. Dhondmull, 6 Moore, P.C. 300, 13 Eng. Rep. 699 [1848].

[466] 8 & 9 VICT., c. 109, § 18. *See* Hampden v. Walsh, 1 Q.B.D. 189 [1876]. For a brief summary of the history of wagering contracts in English law, see PATTERSON, CASES ON INSURANCE 103–06 (1932).

[467] The early American cases are collected in 37 AM. ST. REP. 697 (1894).

contracts. The casino industry has spread to several jurisdictions. Like other changes in society, this change has given rise to new controversies. Before we consider these changes, however, it is important to understand the common law reaction to wagering contracts.

Aleatory Contracts. Among the problems courts have confronted with such contracts is the necessity of determining the kind of transaction falling within the ban. Certain contracts may be called "aleatory," i.e., an aleatory promise is conditional on the happening of a fortuitous event, i.e., an event of chance.[468] The fortuitous event may never occur. The classic example is the fire insurance contract where the insurance company agrees to indemnify the owner against loss of property in exchange for the payment of a premium by the owner. Casualty to the property is a fortuitous event that the insured hopes will not occur. The insurance company assumes the risk of such an event in exchange for a premium payment. Such contracts promote public policy. They are not wagering contracts because the owner has an interest in the contingency (the property loss) prior to the formation of the contract. Wagering contracts are aleatory contracts because the promises are conditioned on fortuitous events that may never occur and there is no agreed equivalent exchange. They are against public policy, however, because the only risk in such contracts is the risk created by the wagering contract itself. Thus, if a party insures a particular house against fire in which the insured has *no* interest, the promise is a wager and unenforceable since the only interest that either party has in the contingency (the fire) is to determine whether the insurer must pay the amount of the policy. The only risk assumed was created by such a wagering contract. Similarly, in any game of chance in which a party promises to pay a certain sum with the hope of receiving some multiple of that sum which the other party has promised to pay upon a chance event, such as a drawing of a lottery ticket, neither party has an interest in the occurrence of the contingency other than as a determinant of the enforceability of the promise to pay. Such a bargain is not an enforceable aleatory promise. It is a wagering bargain and, therefore, unenforceable.

It is generally agreed that a bargain is a wager if the promisor is required to pay upon the happening of an uncertain event and will not have received anything of commensurate value with the payment he makes, and the promisee will have suffered no detriment commensurate with the promisor's payment.[469] The mere fact that a promisee has a conditional right to receive a benefit upon the occurrence of a fortuitous event, however, does not necessarily make the transaction objectionable. Where, for example, a purchaser of land upon which cotton was grown agreed to pay a higher or a lower price for the land depending upon the future price of cotton, it was held that the contract was lawful since the price of cotton had a direct relation to the value of the land, i.e., the buyer's interest in the land was directly affected by the fortuitous market value of cotton.[470]

The determination of whether a contract dependent upon a fortuitous event is enforceable is typically involved in contests with money or valuable prizes held out as awards to the winner. If the cash or other valuable prize is to be awarded on the basis of mere chance and each of the contestants has paid to enter the contest, the transaction amounts to a lottery and

---

[468] *See* In re Tex. Assn. of School Boards, Inc., 169 S. W. 3d 653, 658 (Tex. 2005) quoting this treatise. *See also,* RESTATEMENT 2d § 379 comment a. "Aleatory" is derived from the Latin, "alea," meaning dice.

[469] *See* Chenard v. Marcel Motors, 387 A.2d 596, 600 (Me. 1978). *See also* FIRST RESTATEMENT § 520.

[470] Ferguson v. Coleman, 3 Rich. 99, 45 Am. Dec. 761 (S.C. 1846).

is illegal on that ground.[471] If mental or physical prowess or other skill is involved, however, the agreement is not illegal, provided the prize is not furnished as a result of the contributions of one or more of the contestants.[472] Even if the contestants are required to pay an entry fee, the transaction is not invalidated unless the collected fees are the sole or primary source of the prize.[473] A modern, complex, and insidious version of a prize from the contestants' entry fees may be seen in various kinds of "chain letter" and "pyramiding" schemes involving multi-level membership recruitments, with the payment of finder's fees for membership recruitment and advancement within the various levels of such a plan. Notwithstanding their complexity, courts will penetrate the veneer of legitimacy and discover an illegal lottery.[474] Even though a lottery is an illegal activity, however, the voluntary delivery of a prize awarded in such a lottery is not prohibited. A plaintiff won a new car as a prize in a lottery and delivered the winning ticket to the defendant, who agreed to pick up the car for the benefit of the plaintiff. The defendant subsequently refused to return the car to the plaintiff on the footing that the car had been received through an illegal lottery. The court held that the plaintiff was entitled to the car since the only party who could successfully assert the defense of an illegal lottery was the conductor of the lottery, i.e., that defense is available only as between the immediate parties to the contract.[475]

[1]   Future Deliveries That Never Occur

Another common transaction in which it is difficult to distinguish between lawful agreements and unlawful wagers involves an agreement for the sale of goods for future delivery. It is clear that such a transaction is not *per se* unenforceable. Yet, such a transaction may be nothing more than a mere cover for a wager relating to the future price of the goods involved. When this is the true character of the arrangement, it is unenforceable. If the parties to the agreement contemplate that the goods agreed to be sold are not to be received or delivered, but the transaction will be liquidated by the payment of the difference between the market price of the goods and the contract price, it is generally held that such an agreement is a wager and unenforceable.[476] While it is usually suggested that the wrongful intent must be shared by both parties to the transaction to make the contract unenforceable,[477] it has been held that if one party alone harbors such an intent, he will not be permitted to enforce the contract, although

---

[471] See Youngblood v. Bailey, 459 So. 2d 855 (Ala. 1984), suggesting three elements are required to constitute a lottery violative of Article IV, § 65 of the Alabama Constitution: (a) a prize, (b) awarded by chance, (c) for a consideration.

[472] *See* Brenard Mfg. Co. v. Jessup & Barrett Co., 186 Iowa 872, 173 N.W. 101 (1919).

[473] *See* Chenard v. Marcel Motors, 387 A.2d 596 (Me. 1978) (prize of new car for any golfer who shot a hole in one was not violative of gambling and lottery laws where the payment of entrance fees do not make up the purse). *See also* Toomey v. Penwell, 76 Mont. 166, 245 P. 943 (1926).

[474] *See* Frye v. Taylor, 263 So. 2d 835 (Fla. Dist. Ct. App. 1972).

[475] Matta v. Katsoulas, 192 Wis. 212, 212 N.W. 261 (1927). Even if the taint of illegality has been removed from a particular activity, however, an agreement between the operator of the activity and a contestant may not be enforceable. For example, in Kennedy v. Annandale Boys Club, Inc., 221 Va. 504, 272 S.E.2d 38 (1980), the court refused to enforce an agreement by the winner of $6000 in a bingo game, even though the legislature had legalized bingo in the sense of precluding criminal prosecutions for those conducting or playing the game. In removing the criminal sanctions, the legislature did not render valid and enforceable agreements between the operators of the game and those who play. Such agreements under Virginia law are "utterly void."

[476] *See, e.g.*, Rohrer v. Traina, 35 Ill. App. 3d 770, 342 N.E.2d 390 (2d Dist. 1976).

[477] *See* Browne v. Thorn, 260 U.S. 137, 43 S. Ct. 36, 67 L. Ed. 171 (1922); Benson-Stabeck Co. v. Reservation Farmers' Grain Co., 62 Mont. 254, 205 P. 651 (1922).

the other party, having no such intent, could successfully bring an action upon it.[478] If both parties intend at the time of formation that delivery of the goods shall be made and received, but later agree that there will be a settlement of their difference rather than a delivery, the transaction is unobjectionable.[479] A related problem dealing with off-setting contracts must be distinguished.

[2]   Commodity Exchange "Futures"

Under the mechanism of a commodity exchange involving "futures" contracts, it is possible to avoid taking delivery of goods purchased by making off-setting contracts. Such transactions appear to be indistinguishable from gaming contracts since no delivery of the commodities is contemplated. Rather, the parties appear to be wagering on the future of the price of certain commodities, i.e., as the price of the commodity changes, offsetting contracts will be made since the parties are dealing simply for a margin. Even though the parties intended to settle on the margin and intended no delivery of the goods, if they have effected a bona fide buy and sell transaction on a recognized board of trade or commodity exchange, the transaction will be lawful and "delivery" can be accomplished by offset.[480] It is important to note that statutes governing dealing in futures have been enacted in virtually every state, as well as by the Congress of the United States, and such statutes should be consulted.[481]

[3]   Changing Mores — Public Policy

At the beginning of this discussion concerning wagering and gaming contracts, it was suggested that the mores of society have changed rather dramatically concerning such agreements in recent years due, in some measure, to legislation condoning or inviting various forms of wagering. It is, therefore, sometimes difficult for courts to assess the strength of precedent decided prior to these legislative developments. Thus, as one court suggests:

> A significant difference, however, is that when [certain cases] were decided there were no exceptions to the lottery and gambling laws. Subsequent to these opinions, the Legislature has legalized pari-mutuel betting at harness and running horse race-tracks, licensed bingo games and gambling conducted by nonprofit organizations, and a state-operated lottery. These exceptions have riddled the gambling and lottery statutes to the point where it can no longer be said that it is 'the intention of the legislature to prohibit every pecuniary transaction in which pure chance has any place.' [482]

If a state legislature has authorized various forms of gambling and is, itself, conducting a statewide lottery which it solicits citizens to pursue, it is impossible to suggest that the public policy of that state is contrary to gambling. Casino gambling is no longer relegated to one or

---

[478] Nash-Wright Co. v. Wright, 156 Ill. App. 243 (1910); Higgins v. McCrea, 116 U.S. 671, 65 S. Ct. 557, 29 L. Ed. 764 (1886) (*semble*).

[479] *See* T. Barbour Brown & Co. v. Canty, 115 Conn. 226, 161 A. 91 (1932); Gettys v. Newburger, 272 F. 209 (8th Cir.), *cert. denied*, 257 U.S. 649, 42 S. Ct. 56, 66 L. Ed. 416 (1921).

[480] *See* Merrill Lynch, Pierce, Fenner & Smith, Inc. v. Schriver, 541 S.W.2d 799 (Tenn. Ct. App. 1976).

[481] See, e.g., TENN. CODE ANN. § 39-2028, which withdraws from all gaming and wagering laws all transactions executed up and in accordance with the rules and regulations of a legitimate produce, stock, or cotton exchange or board of trade.

[482] Chenard v. Marcel Motors, 387 A.2d 596, 600 (Me. 1978).

two states. Whatever the merits or faults of such a determination by a given jurisdiction, the older public policy against wagering or gaming and its attendant evils is significantly modified. While a private wager on a sporting event between two or more individuals is still an illegal bargain in these jurisdictions, the moral force of the arguments against gambling which had been available to support such holdings is significantly diminished since the state can no longer be said to take a policy position against gambling. Rather, it merely requires gambling to be conducted in various ways authorized by the state. The state may justify its position by pointing to the regulation of gambling and consequent fairness to the participants through these authorized means. Yet, the dominant motivation for legalization is more than clear, i.e., the raising of additional revenue.

Among the issues spawned by the proliferation of state lotteries, casinos and the like, questions arise concerning the recognition of wagering contracts, lawful in the state of their formation, by a state that continues to view such contracts as contrary to its public policy. Where parties in a state with no legalized lottery agreed to purchase state-sponsored lottery tickets in another jurisdiction and divide any winnings, the first jurisdiction found no violation of its own policy against wagering in such agreements.[483] A Virginia resident asserted that she had accepted offers of free accommodations and limousines by a New Jersey casino, which induced her to gamble at the casino and lose substantial sums. In an action to recover her losses, she claimed that the contracts to induce her to gamble were made in Virginia (her acceptance of the offer was the last act necessary to complete the alleged inducement contracts). She sought recovery of her losses under Virginia law, which viewed wagering agreements as void. The defendant argued that the contracts were formed in New Jersey where plaintiff's gambling occurred. The court agreed, but added that, even if Virginia law had applied, gambling contracts are illegal or immoral contracts in Virginia that will not lend its aid to enforce or rescind such agreements.[484]

[4]   Distinguishing Gambling on Credit

Where a California resident wrote checks in exchange for chips and proceeded to lose $22,000 in a Nevada casino, he stopped payment on the checks. Checks evidencing gambling debts were enforceable in Nevada, but not in California. The casino did not seek a judgment in Nevada on the gambler's debts. It assigned its claim to a collection agency that brought an action in California to recover the amount owed. The California court recognized that a forum state must give full faith and credit to a sister state *judgment* regardless of the forum state's public policy on the underlying claim.[485] The forum state, however, may refuse to entertain a lawsuit on a sister state *cause of action* if its enforcement is contrary to the strong public policy of the forum state. The court was very clear in recognizing that Californians cannot afford to be "too pious about the matter of gambling" in light of California's state lottery, pari-mutuel betting and other forms of legalized gambling. Nonetheless, the court emphasized its historic and continuing strong public policy against judicial enforcement of gambling debts. Gambling on credit underlies pathological gambling, a mental disorder. The court concluded that

---

[483] In Talley v. Mathis, 265 Pa. 179, 453 S.E.2d 704 (1995), the court upheld the agreement stating that there is nothing illegal about Georgia residents purchasing lottery tickets in a sister state where such purchases are legal, and that the public policy of Georgia does not preclude a contract to divide any winnings.

[484] Rahmani v. Resorts Int'l Hotel, Inc., 20 F. Supp. 2d 932 (E.D. Va. 1998), *aff'd*, 182 F.3d 909 (4th Cir. 1999).

[485] The United States Constitution, Art. IV, § 1, affords full faith and credit to the public acts, records and judicial proceedings of sister states.

California's strong public policy against the enforcement of gambling debts should continue.[486]

[H]   Contracts Adversely Affecting the Administration of Justice, Champerty, and Maintenance — Arbitration

Common law courts viewed with disfavor any contract which had a tendency to promote unnecessary litigation or to interfere with the proper administration of justice. Where rights of action were transferred to influential persons to obtain their support and favor, the early law took a particularly severe view of such "maintenance" and "champerty."[487] In simple terms, maintenance is helping another prosecute a lawsuit and champerty is maintaining a lawsuit in return for a financial interest in the outcome.[488] It constitutes intermeddling by an officious party who has no interest in the original dispute. Today, however, it is generally agreed that a contract to assist another in litigation is lawful if it is actuated by charitable motives or by an intention to secure a decision on a question affecting the interest of a party, and not merely by a desire to promote litigation for ulterior purposes.[489] Thus, where a sister responded to a request by her brother to lend funds to allow him to continue litigation in which she had no interest other than assisting her brother, the agreement was not champertous.[490] Earlier rules against lawyers shouldering the cost of litigation are now described as relics of old English rules against champerty, maintenance and barratry.[491] It is ordinary practice for a law firm to pay some of the costs of its clients.[492] Rules of professional conduct allow lawyers to defray the costs of litigation if the lawsuit is unsuccessful.[493] In some jurisdictions, additional expenses may also be defrayed to guard against a party in financial need accepting a low settlement offer.[494] Contingent fee arrangements, however, continue to be carefully scrutinized.

An attorney in a criminal[495] or divorce[496] proceeding may not recover on a contingent fee agreement.[497] Contingent fees for alimony and child support are also unenforceable.[498] Public policy also condemns the payment of contingent fees for legal services in criminal cases.[499]

---

[486] Metropolitan Creditors Serv. v. Sadri, 15 Cal. App. 4th 1821, 19 Cal. Rptr. 2d 646 (1st Dist. 1993).

[487] *See* Winfield, *The History of Maintenance and Champerty*, 35 L.Q. Rev. 50 (1919).

[488] See Elliott Assocs., L.P. v. Banco De La Nacion, 194 F.3d 363, 372 (2d Cir. 1999) (quoting *In re* Primus, 436 U.S. 412, 424 n.15, 98 S. Ct. 1893, 56 L. Ed. 2d 417 (1978)).

[489] *See* Reed v. Chase, 238 Mass. 83, 130 N.E. 257 (1921); Johnson v. Great N. R. Co., 128 Minn. 365, 151 N.W. 125 (1915).

[490] Kraft v. Mason, 668 So. 2d 679, 683 (Fla. Dist. Ct. App. 1996).

[491] Rand v. Monsanto Co., 926 F.2d 596, 600 (7th Cir. 1991). "Barratry" is a continuing practice of maintenance or champerty.

[492] Boccardo v. Commissioner of Internal Revenue, 56 F.3d 1016, 1018 (9th Cir. 1995).

[493] *See* ABA Model Rules of Professional Conduct, Rule 1.8(e).

[494] *See Rand*, note 491 *supra*.

[495] *See* O'Donnell v. Bane, 385 Mass. 114, 431 N.E.2d 190 (1982). *See* First Restatement § 502. See, in general, Restatement 2d § 178.

[496] *See* Shanks v. Kilgore, 589 S.W.2d 318 (Mo. Ct. App. 1979).

[497] Bonus fees in the nature of contingent fees are also unenforceable. King v. Young, Berkman, Berman & Karpf, P. A., 709 So. 2d 572 (Fla. Dist. Ct. App. 1998).

[498] Williams v. Garrison, 105 N.C. App. 79, 411 S.E.2d 633 (1992).

[499] *See* Fogarty v. State, 270 Ga. 609, 513 S.E.2d 493, 496, *cert. denied*, 528 U.S. 852, 120 S. Ct. 131, 145 L. Ed. 2d

Even more important is the possible conflict of interest for a lawyer who may be influenced to advise against a favorable plea bargain.[500] Similarly, in divorce proceedings, if the lawyer will receive payment on the contingency that the divorce is decreed, such an attorney may be influenced to avoid a reconciliation between the spouses, and the law favors reconciliation.[501] Even if an agreement is champertous as, for example, where an attorney agrees to be paid contingent on the successful outcome of a criminal proceeding, the contingent fee agreement is unenforceable, but a court may permit an attorney to recover in quasi contract for the reasonable value of services rendered.[502] There is some authority for the view that a contract for a contingent fee that would otherwise be lawful is unenforceable if it contains a provision that the client shall not compromise or settle his claim since the law favors settlements.[503]

Notwithstanding the decline of maintenance and champerty, an agreement that has an undue tendency to promote litigation for the benefit of the promoter rather than the litigant, or which is oppressive to the litigant, or which involves an abuse of legal proceedings, is more than likely to be deemed unenforceable.[504]

Similarly, any agreement that tends to interfere with the proper functioning of the judicial machinery is unenforceable. The following agreements have been held unenforceable on this ground: a contract to pay another a contingent fee for procuring evidence to be used in a lawsuit,[505] a contract to pay a physician for treatment and testimony in a personal injury action with an understanding that part of the physician's fee would emanate from the personal injury recovery,[506] an agreement to pay a witness who is amenable to process a fee, contingent or fixed, in addition to that which he is entitled to by law,[507] an agreement to pay a witness for testimony, the content of which is specified in the bargain,[508] a contract having for its purpose

---

111 (1999) (where, however, the lawyer's compensation was stated as a retainer of $25,000, of which only $10,000 would be payable if the case were dismissed without a trial, the agreement merely attempted to relate the amount of the fee to the service provided and was not an improper contingent fee contract).

[500] See Winkler v. Keane, 7 F.3d 304, 307 (2d Cir. 1993), *cert. denied*, 511 U.S. 1022, 114 S. Ct. 1407, 128 L. Ed. 2d 79 (1994).

[501] *See* Thompson v. Thompson, 70 N.C. App. 147, 319 S.E.2d 315 (1984). An appeal did not raise the question of whether contingency fees should be permitted in divorce proceedings, but whether the lawyer may recover in quasi contract. The court held that the lower court erred in allowing intervention for such recovery. 313 N.C. 313, 328 S.E.2d 288 (1985). Burns v. Stewart, 290 Minn. 289, 188 N.W.2d 760 (1971).

[502] *See* Genins v. Geiger, 144 Ga. App. 244, 240 S.E.2d 745 (1977), *cert. denied*, 444 U.S. 991, 100 S. Ct. 521, 62 L. Ed. 2d 420 (1979) (contract providing for payment of $25,000 contingent on a disposition of criminal charge is against public policy, but did not preclude recovery on a quantum meruit (quasi contract) basis). *See also* Ownby v. Prisock, 243 Miss. 203, 138 So. 2d 279 (1962); Application of Kamerman, 278 F.2d 411 (2d Cir. 1960).

[503] *See* Davy v. Fidelity & Casualty Ins. Co., 78 Ohio St. 256, 85 N.E. 504, *aff'd*, 78 Ohio St. 433, 85 N.E. 1120 (1908).

[504] *See, e.g.*, Ellis v. Frawley, 165 Wis. 381, 161 N.W. 364 (1917) (agreement between lawyers to discover persons having claims against a power company and to induce them to permit the lawyers to prosecute the claims on a contingent fee basis); Gammons v. Johnson, 76 Minn. 76, 78 N.W. 1035 (1899) (scheme of attorney to employ a layman to hunt up claims against a railroad to be prosecuted by the attorney for a share of the proceeds).

[505] Duteau v. Dresbach, 113 Wash. 545, 194 P. 547 (1920).

[506] Weinberg v. Magid, 285 Mass. 237, 189 N.E. 110 (1934).

[507] Dodge v. Stiles, 26 Conn. 463 (1857). If, however, the witness is rendering an expert opinion, particularly where he will have to inform himself of the facts prior to trial, the witness may be paid an additional fee. *See* Lincoln Mountain Gold Mining Co. v. Williams, 37 Colo. 193, 85 P. 844 (1906).

[508] Griffith v. Harris, 17 Wis. 2d 255, 116 N.W.2d 133 (1962), *cert. denied*, 373 U.S. 927, 83 S. Ct. 1530, 10 L. Ed. 2d 425 (1963).

the concealment or compounding of a crime or suspicion of crime,[509] an agreement calling for the use of personal influence to induce a court or prosecuting officer to discharge or to be lenient with a criminal,[510] an agreement by a law enforcement official not to disclose relevant and pertinent information to a judge,[511] an agreement prescribing certain rules of evidence to be applied if a lawsuit should arise out of the contract[512] or providing that a statutory presumption shall not apply,[513] an agreement involving a lawyer who was incorporated to practice law and conducted another business in the same office,[514] and an agreement containing an unreasonable limitation on the time permitted to commence an action or extending the period of time beyond that permitted by the relevant statute of limitations.[515] Under the Social Security Act, any endeavor by an attorney to gain more than the statutory fee or to charge the claimant a non contingent fee is a criminal offense.[516]

Courts are jealous of their jurisdiction and have, therefore, been inclined to condemn as illegal any agreement tending to oust them from it. Earlier decisions held that an agreement to arbitrate a dispute,[517] whether in the form of a promise or a condition, was unenforceable, particularly if the agreement contemplated arbitration of all matters, including the existence of a cause of action and not merely a fact question.[518] That view has undergone a sea change.[519] In an increasingly litigious society, the need for alternatives to traditional judicial resolution or disputes became abundantly clear. Arbitration is the paradigm alternative

---

[509] *See* Good Hope State Bank v. Kline, 303 Ill. App. 381, 25 N.E.2d 425 (1940); Farmers' Nat'l Bank v. Tartar, 256 Ky. 70, 75 S.W.2d 758 (1934); Union Exch. Nat'l Bank v. Joseph, 231 N.Y. 250, 131 N.E. 905 (1921). A party injured by the commission of a crime may agree to settle his claim for his injury, and such an agreement is enforceable unless part of the consideration consists of an express or implied promise to refrain from instituting criminal proceedings. The mere fact that a criminal prosecution does not occur is not, of itself, material. *See* Wilhelm v. King Auto Fin. Co., 259 Mich. 463, 244 N.W. 130 (1932); Blair Milling Co. v. Fruitager, 113 Kan. 432, 215 P. 286 (1923). See also O'Neil v. Dux, 257 Minn. 383, 101 N.W.2d 588 (1960), where the injured party agreed not to present the matter to the county attorney. The court enforced the agreement because no prosecution had been threatened.

[510] Liberty Mut. Ins. Co. v. Gilreath, 191 S.C.244, 4 S.E.2d 126 (1939); Aycock v. Gill, 183 N.C. 271, 111 S.E. 342 (1922).

[511] Grant v. State, 73 Wis. 2d 441, 243 N.W.2d 186 (1976).

[512] Fidelity & Deposit Co. v. Davis, 129 Kan. 790, 284 P. 430 (1930) (provision in indemnity contract that certain prescribed evidence shall be conclusive of the liability of the principal obligor).

[513] Modern Woodmen of Am. v. Michelin, 101 Okla. 217, 225 P. 163 (1924) (agreement that the statutory presumption of death arising from seven years of absence shall not apply).

[514] Marvin N. Benn & Assocs., Ltd. v. Nelsen Steel & Wire, Inc., 107 Ill. App. 3d 442, 63 Ill. Dec. 251, 437 N.E.2d 900 (1st Dist. 1982) (the conduct of another business in the same office from which the attorney conducts his legal practice is a form of solicitation or recommendation which violates the code of professional responsibility).

[515] *See* Page County v. Fidelity & Deposit Co., 205 Iowa 798, 216 N.W. 957 (1927) (agreement limiting the time to 90 days after default); Burlew v. Fidelity & Casualty Co., 276 Ky. 132, 122 S.W.2d 990 (1938) (agreement extending time for bringing suit). UCC § 2-725 establishes a four year statute of limitations in contracts for the sale of goods, the four years to commence from the time of delivery of the goods, regardless of the aggrieved party's knowledge of the breach. Section 2-725(1) permits the parties to agree to reduce the period to not less than one year, but precludes any agreement to extend the period.

[516] Brandenburg v. Astrue, 2009 U.S. Dist. LEXIS 35406 at *3 (D. Ore. 2009).

[517] Parties agree to submit their dispute to neutral third parties chosen by the parties or a neutral entity, such as the American Arbitration Association, to resolve the dispute by announcing a binding decision.

[518] *See* W. H. Blodgett Co. v. Bebe Co., 190 Cal. 665, 214 P. 38 (1923).

[519] *See* Pettinaro Constr. Co. v. Harry C. Partridge, Jr. & Sons, Inc., 408 A.2d 957, 961 (Del. Ch. 1979): "It is no longer of any consequence that a court, otherwise competent to hear the dispute, is ousted of its jurisdiction by the arbitration process."

dispute resolution process designed to provide expeditious resolutions at lower costs. Facilitated by the Federal Arbitration Act[520] and the Uniform Arbitration Act,[521] arbitration is now viewed as a highly desirable method of resolving disputes.

[I]   Contracts Tending to Corrupt or Cause a Neglect of Duty — Lobbying

A contract that has a tendency to corrupt a public official or cause neglect of duty is contrary to public policy and, therefore, unenforceable. Bribes of public officials or witnesses are criminal acts.[522] Blatant forms of this activity, such as bribing a public officer, are such obvious violations that the dearth of case law illustrating actions brought to recover unpaid bribes is not remarkable. Almost as obvious is a bargain contemplating personal influence or other improper means used to induce a public official.[523] It is, however, perfectly lawful for one person to employ another for a consideration to present the merits of a particular proposition to a public official though courts are astute in scrutinizing such agreements to ascertain that the use of personal influence is not contemplated before a contract will be upheld. Nevertheless, where a lawyer was hired to represent a trucking company and it was clear that the only reason for this contract was the lawyer's personal relation with the President of the United States, the court upheld the contract on the footing that one may employ an agent or attorney to use his influence to gain access to a public official as long as the case is presented on its merits after access is gained.[524] A statute, however, may preclude payment under a contract to a person whose exclusive use is one of influence to public officials.[525] This entire area of agreements to assist in bringing about desired action by one or more public officials are well-known under the caption, "lobbying contract," and there are numerous federal and state statutes, executive orders and administrative regulations in this area which go well beyond the scope of this section or volume.[526]

Since the earlier cases in particular tended to frown on contingent fee contracts, it is not remarkable that some courts took the position that any agreement based on the contingency

---

[520] 9 U.S.C. § 1 (2000). *See* David P. Pierce, *Comment: The Federal Arbitration Act: Conflicting Interpretations of Its Scope*, 61 U. Cin. L. Rev. 623 (1992).

[521] The Uniform Arbitration Act is a product of the National Conference of Commissioners on Uniform State Laws (NCCUSL), which unveiled the Act in 1955. It was adopted in 49 jurisdictions. The popularity of arbitration induced a revision of the Act in 2000 to further the arbitration process and clarify the relationship between state arbitration law and the federal statute, *id.*

[522] See 18 U.S. C. § 201.

[523] *See, e.g.,* Ewing v. National Airport Corp., 115 F.2d 859 (4th Cir. 1940), *cert. denied*, 312 U.S. 705, 61 S. Ct. 828, 85 L. Ed. 1138 (1941).

[524] Troutman v. Southern R. Co., 441 F.2d 586 (5th Cir.), *cert. denied*, 404 U.S. 871, 92 S. Ct. 81, 30 L. Ed. 2d 115 (1971). The court suggested that decisions in these cases will necessarily depend largely on the particular facts in each case. The burden of proving illegality is upon the party asserting it.

[525] See, e.g., Samuel J. Plumeri Realty Co. v. Capital Place Urban Renewal Assocs., Inc., 101 N.J. 13, 499 A.2d 1356 (1985), construing New Jersey statute proscribing retaining persons on a commission basis to obtain state contracts, unless such persons are bona fide employees or bona fide established commercial or selling agencies maintained by the contractor for the purpose of securing business. Since the broker in this case could not demonstrate continuity in the relationship with the contractor, the contract violated this statute, N.J. Stat. Ann. § 52:34-15.

[526] *See* 2 USCS §§ 1601 *et seq. See also* Taylor Thieman & Aitken v. Hayes, 23 Va. Cir. 464, 1991 Va. Cir. LEXIS 75 (1991) failure to register under lobbying act prohibited recovery of fees for services prohibited by the Act absent appropriate registration.

that an agent would succeed in persuading a public official to a particular action or vote was illegal *per se*.[527] While a lobbying contract for a contingent fee is not invalid *per se*,[528] more often than not it will be unlawful.[529] If a person hires a lawyer to prosecute a claim against the government and the only feasible remedy to compensate that person is private legislation, a contingent fee contract in such circumstances would be upheld.[530] There can be no doubt, however, that a contingent fee contract in relation to securing a particular result from one or more public officials will be viewed with initial suspicion.

It is not only agreements which tend to corrupt public officials or to induce violations of their duties that are illegal; any bargain that has a tendency to cause a person who is subject to a private duty to violate that duty is equally obnoxious in the eyes of the law, whether he is an agent, trustee, corporate stockholder, officer or director, or one who has assumed to act on another's behalf.[531]

[J] Contracts Concerning Marriage — Changing Mores — Cohabitation Agreements

Our courts have always viewed the marriage relationship as the foundation stone of the social order. It is, therefore, not difficult to discover numerous cases suggesting that any agreement which tends to prevent marriage or to disrupt a marriage already consummated has been traditionally viewed with disfavor.[532] Older cases pursued this position to its logical extension in holding that *any* bargain that had a tendency to prevent or restrain a first marriage, even though the restraint would be operative for only a limited time, was illegal.[533] Subsequent cases were not as rigid. They applied a "rule of reason" approach not unlike the reasonableness test of a contract in restraint of trade. One of the earliest manifestations of flexibility came from a Texas court:" "[T]he term 'general restraint' as used in the rule should be construed to mean restraint which binds a competent person not to marry any one at any time, and that the validity of a contract, where the restraint it imposes is only against

---

[527] *See, e.g.*, Trist v. Child, 88 U.S. (21 Wall.) 441, 22 L. Ed. 623 (1875). *See also* Chambers v. Coates, 176 Okla. 416, 55 P.2d 986 (1936); Noonan v. Gilbert, 63 U.S. App. D.C. 30, 68 F.2d 775 (1934); *In re* Crooks' Estate, 316 Pa. 285, 175 A. 410 (1934).

[528] "The payment of contingent fees in public contracts is not illegal *per se*." State by Kugler v. Arnold Constable Corp., 138 N.J. Super. 551, 351 A.2d 771, 778 (1976).

[529] For example, in Oklahoma, "most contingent fee lobbying contracts are unlawful." Sholer v. State ex. rel. Dept. of Pub. Safety, 149 P. 3d 1040, 1046 (Okl. 2006) citing 21 O.S. 2001 § 334.

[530] *See* Gesellschaft Fur Drahtlose Telegraphie M. B. H. v. Brown, 64 U.S. App. D.C. 357, 78 F.2d 410, 413–14, *cert. denied*, 296 U.S. 618, 56 S. Ct. 139, 80 L. Ed. 439 (1935).

[531] *See, e.g.*, McQuade v. Stoneham, 263 N.Y. 323, 189 N.E. 234 (1934) (agreement between stockholders to elect themselves as directors and then to elect particular individuals as officers at named salaries); Y. & M. V. R. Co. v. Whittington, 191 Miss. 776, 4 So. 2d 343 (1941) (father who was operating as guardian of his child received certain payments for agreeing to approve a settlement of the child's personal injury claim); King v. Raleigh & P. S. R. Co., 147 N.C. 263, 60 S.E. 1133 (1908) (railroad's payment to newspaper editor for favorable editorials); Pike v. Pike, 266 Mass. 186, 165 N.E. 5 (1929) (agreement to make payment in return for advising another to refrain from making a certain will).

[532] *See, e. g.*, "The State is an interested party in divorce proceedings because t he rights of the plaintiff and defendant are not isolated from the general interest of society in preserving the marriage relation as the foundation of the home and the state." Vandervort v. Vandervort, 134 P. 3d 892, 895 (Okla Civ. App. 2005).

[533] *See* McCoy v. Flynn, 169 Iowa 622, 151 N.W. 465 (1915) (promise to pay $3000 if promisee should be unmarried after three years — promise made in connection with an agreement to settle a claim for breach of promise to marry); Sterling v. Sinnickson, 5 N.J.L. 756 (1820) (promise to pay $1000 if promisee should remain unmarried for six months).

marrying a particular person, or a person of a particular class, or within a specified limited time, should be determined with reference to the reasonableness of such restraint under the circumstances of the particular case."[534]

If, therefore, the restraint is "general" (unlimited), it manifests no redeeming virtue and should be unenforceable. If, however, a father agreed to pay a daughter a certain sum if she would forebear marriage and take care of her mother until death or five years, the restraint would be reasonable. Some courts, however, have upheld contracts restraining second marriages, particularly where there are children of the first marriage, or if the other spouse has made financial provision for the promisor.[535] Promises to marry made while the promisor is already married are unenforceable even though the promisor has separated from the other spouse and is in the process of securing a divorce.[536] Courts have traditionally held that any contract tending to encourage or facilitate separation or divorce, or to diminish the reciprocal rights and duties which the law attaches to the marital relationship, is unenforceable.[537]

At common law, where a husband and wife agreed, either before or during marriage, that the husband will not have to support the wife as provided by law either during or after marriage, such agreements were unenforceable.[538] Only after the parties separated or, contemporaneously with a separation, agreed upon a property settlement, were such agreements enforceable, and then only if adequate provision was made for the support of the wife.[539] Where the agreement dealt with the custody of any children, the disposition of custody was consistent with the best interests of the children.[540] The modern view is that a premarital agreement that limits the duty of support may be enforceable.[541] Courts, however, insist that such agreements must be procedurally and substantively fair. Thus, as described by one court, the parties must have entered the agreement voluntarily, each spouse must have made a fair and reasonable disclosure of his or her financial status to the other, and the substantive provisions dividing the property upon divorce are fair.[542] Under the *Uniform Premarital Agreement Act*, parties may conclude an enforceable premarital agreement that may modify or even eliminate spousal support and other rights and duties that are not opposed to public policy.[543] An important case development argues for the elimination of any

---

[534] Barnes v. Hobson, 250 S.W. 238, 242–43 (Tex. Civ. App. 1923) (promise of 16-year-old girl to her uncle upon whom she was dependent that she would not marry until she was 22 years old). *See also* RESTATEMENT 2d § 189: "A promise is unenforceable on grounds of public policy if it is unreasonably in restraint of marriage."

[535] *See* In re Marriage of Dodge, 501 N. E. 2d 1354,1358 (App. Ct. Ill. 1986) citing Cowan v. Cowan, 247 Iowa 729, 75 N.W.2d 920 (1956).

[536] Norton v. Hoyt, 278 F. Supp. 2d 214, (D. R. I. 2003); Beach v. Arblaster, 194 Cal. App. 2d 145, 14 Cal. Rptr. 854 (2d Dist. 1961).

[537] *See* RESTATEMENT 2d § 190.

[538] *See* Cord v. Neuhoff, 94 Nev. 21, 573 P.2d 1170 (1978) (agreement limiting the husband's duty to support wife during marriage and after any termination thereof); Werlein v. Werlein, 27 Wis. 2d 237, 133 N.W.2d 820 (1965) (antenuptial agreement limiting husband's liability to wife in the event of separation or divorce).

[539] Gallemore v. Gallemore, 94 Fla. 516, 114 So. 371 (1927).

[540] *See In re* Custody of Neal, 260 Pa. Super. 151, 393 A.2d 1057 (1978). *See also* RESTATEMENT 2d § 191.

[541] *In re* Marriage of DiFatta, 306 Ill. App. 3d 656, 239 Ill. Dec. 795, 714 N.E.2d 1092 (2d Dist. 1999) (waiver of maintenance agreement in premarital agreement upheld).

[542] Coulbourn v. Lambert, 1996 Del. Fam. Ct. LEXIS 128 (Del. Fam. Ct. Dec. 19, 1996).

[543] Uniform Premarital Agreement Act (UPAA) § 3. The Act was first promulgated in 1983. Currently, 27 states have adopted the UPAA and it is regularly introduced in other state legislatures. Section 1(1) defines a premarital agreement as "an agreement between spouses made in contemplation of marriage and effective upon marriage." The

special dimension of fairness in such agreements:

> 'There is no longer validity in the implicit assumption . . . [of] earlier decisions . . . that spouses are of unequal status and that women are not knowledgeable to understand the nature of the contracts they enter. Society has advanced, however, to the point where women are no longer regarded as the 'weaker' party in marriage, or in society generally. Indeed, the stereotype that women serve as homemakers while men work as breadwinners is no longer viable. Quite often today both spouses are income earners. Nor is their viability in the presumption that women are uninformed, uneducated, and readily subjected to unfair advantage in marital agreements. * * * Paternalistic presumptions and protections that arose to shelter women from the inferiorities and incapacities which they were perceived as having at earlier times have, appropriately, been discarded.[544]

Other courts demonstrate a "gradual minimization" of the extent to which a special emphasis on substantive fairness should attend premarital agreements.[545] Such cases suggest that premarital agreements should be interpreted and construed like any other contract.

Cohabitation. The most significant development in this area deals with cohabitation agreements, i.e., express or implied agreements between unmarried cohabitants who choose to live together in a fashion identical or very similar to husband and wife though they do not marry. In *Marvin v. Marvin*,[546] the plaintiff averred that she and the well-known actor, Lee Marvin, orally agreed that, while living together, they would combine their efforts and earnings and would share equally all accumulated property. Plaintiff agreed to render her services as companion, homemaker, housekeeper, and cook to the defendant. Plaintiff surrendered "her lucrative career as an entertainer" to devote herself full time to the defendant. The defendant argued that the alleged contract was of an "immoral" character and, therefore, violative of public policy. The court recognized "radical" changes in the mores of society regarding marriage, though it reiterated the long-held belief that societal structure depends largely on the institution of marriage. Yet, the court felt that it could not ignore the increasing number of nonmarital relationships and concluded that unmarried cohabitants could enter into an enforceable contract, unless their contract was explicitly based upon "the immoral and illicit consideration of meretricious sexual services." This approach has spawned considerable litigation. It is now clear, however, that it is generally accepted in other jurisdictions.[547]

Act requires such agreements to be evidenced by a writing and signed by both parties, setting forth a fair and reasonable disclosure of property and financial obligations. The agreement must be voluntary. For illustrative applications of the Act, see *In re* Marriage of Pownall, 197 Ariz. 577, 5 P.3d 911 (Ct. App. 2000); Huntley v. Huntley, 538 S.E.2d 239 (N.C. Ct. App. 2000).

[544] Simeone v. Simeone, 525 Pa. 392, 581 A.2d 162, 165 (1990). See also Stoner v. Stoner, 572 Pa. 665, 819 A.2d. 529 (2003).

[545] *In re* Marriage of Spiegel, 553 N.W.2d 309, 315 (Iowa 1996).

[546] 18 Cal. 3d 660, 134 Cal. Rptr. 815, 557 P.2d 106 (1976).

[547] See Wilcox v. Trautz, 427 Mass. 326, 693 N.E.2d 141 (1998), and cases cited therein; Boland v. Catalano, 202 Conn. 333, 521 A.2d 142 (1987), which cites cases from seventeen other jurisdictions adopting the *Marvin* rationale. See also Carroll v. Lee, 148 Ariz. 10, 712 P.2d 923 (1986), which suggests agreement with the *Marvin* approach in a case involving the partition of property where the title was in the names of unmarried cohabitants. *See* Perry, *Dissolution Planning in Family Law: A Critique of Current Analyses and a Look Toward the Future*, 24 Fam. L.Q. 77 (1990). See, however, Hewitt v. Hewitt, 77 Ill. 2d 49, 394 N.E.2d 1024, 1209, 31 Ill. Dec. 827 (1979): "We cannot confidently say that judicial recognition of property rights between unmarried cohabitants will not make that alternative to marriage more attractive by allowing the parties to engage in such relationships with greater security [than the marriage

Courts allowing the enforcement of cohabitation agreements have sought to avoid any misconceptions concerning the holding in *Marvin* by emphasizing the narrowness of that holding, i.e., it simply established the right of unmarried cohabitants to enter into a valid contractual obligation of support to the extent that the agreement does not rest upon illicit meretricious consideration.[548] An agreement based on the performance of sexual acts is obviously unenforceable.[549] If, however, "homemaking" and other legal purposes can be severed from a meretricious relationship, the agreement can be enforceable.[550] Where fornication or cohabitation are still criminal offenses, such statutes have not persuaded courts to view cohabitation agreements as unenforceable if the relationship resembles a normal family relationship.[551] On the other hand, actions based upon the *Marvin* rationale are generally relegated to express or implied contracts between the parties, though a court may insist upon an express agreement.[552] The unmarried partners are not protected by legislation designed for the marital relationship.[553] Thus, an unmarried cohabitant may have no cause of action for the equitable distribution of property[554] or loss of consortium which would be available to a married spouse.[555] Where an unmarried same-sex couple agreed to have a child and the plaintiff gave birth to a child, the defendant stated that she desired no further relationship with the plaintiff or the child. The court concluded that a contract of parenthood was against public policy and not enforceable. Moreover, any implied promise the defendant allegedly made concerning child support was inextricably connected to her promise to co-parent the child and was, therefore, equally unenforceable.[556] Since unmarried cohabitants are relegated to protection via their contract, they are well-advised to set forth their agreement in a detailed writing so as to avoid problems of proving the existence and terms of their contract.

[K] Contracts Facilitating an Illegal Purpose

A contract that appears to be perfectly legal may be held illegal because it facilitates an illegal purpose. Where the effect of the parties' agreement was to conceal a financial interest from the effects of a federal tax lien, the court held the agreement unenforceable.[557] A

---

relationship]. . . . In thus potentially enhancing the attractiveness of a private arrangement over marriage, we believe that the appellate court decision in this case contravenes the [legislative] policy of strengthening and preserving the integrity of marriage." Other courts reflect similar concerns: Rehak v. Mathis, 239 Ga. 541, 238 S.E.2d 81 (1977); Schwegmann v. Schwegmann, 441 So. 2d 316 (La. Ct. App. 1983), *cert. denied*, 467 U.S. 1206, 104 S. Ct. 2389, 81 L. Ed. 2d 347 (1984). Other courts have mentioned the *Hewitt* rationale favorably: Grishman v. Grishman, 407 A.2d 9, 12 (Me. 1979); Merrill v. Davis, 100 N.M. 552, 673 P.2d 1285, 1287 (1983). Another court suggests that cohabitation agreements would contravene the public policy in favor of de jure marriage. Slocum v. Hammond, 346 N.W.2d 485, 491 (Iowa 1984).

[548] Norman v. Unemployment Ins. Appeals Bd., 34 Cal. 3d 1, 192 Cal. Rptr. 134, 663 P.2d 904 (1983).

[549] *See* State v. Grimes, 85 Or. App. 159, 735 P.2d 1277 (1987); Hill v. Estate of Westbrook, 95 Cal. App. 2d 599, 213 P.2d 727 (1950).

[550] Carroll v. Lee, 148 Ariz. 10, 712 P.2d 923 (1986).

[551] *See In re* Estate of Steffes, 95 Wis. 2d 490, 290 N.W.2d 697 (1980); Tyranski v. Piggins, 44 Mich. App. 570, 205 N.W.2d 595 (1973).

[552] Wilcox v. Trautz, 427 Mass. 326, 693 N.E.2d 141 (1998).

[553] *See* Schafer v. Superior Ct. of San Diego County, 180 Cal. App. 3d 305, 225 Cal. Rptr. 513 (4th Dist. 1986).

[554] *See Wilcox v. Trautz*, note 552 *supra.*

[555] *Id.*

[556] T.F. v. B.L., 442 Mass. 522, 813 N.E.2d 1244 (2004).

[557] Culwell v. Huff, 50 Va. Cir. 180 (1999), relying on RESTATEMENT 2d § 182. If both parties knew of and facilitated an illegal purpose or knew that the purpose involved serious moral turpitude, the contract is void and unenforceable.

promissory note was unenforceable because it was signed as part of a plan to deceive liquor control authorities.[558] Whether a contract will be unenforceable because one of the parties has an illegal purpose depends upon the gravity of the violation of public policy and the awareness of such violation by the otherwise innocent party. Thus, while a contract for the purchase and sale of a gun is not illegal absent statutory restrictions, if the seller knows that the buyer intends to use the gun to commit homicide, such an agreement would be unenforceable since the harm to society is so grievous. On the other hand, where the social harm is not so grievous, mere knowledge that the other party may use the property for some illegal purpose does not make the contract unenforceable where the seller is indifferent to the buyer's use of the property.[559] If the seller made the contract with the purpose and intent of enabling the other party to carry out his wrongful purpose, however, such a seller is not simply indifferent to the use of the property by the purchaser and may not enforce the contract.[560] Again, if the contemplated wrongful act involves the commission of a serious crime, a seller should not be able to claim indifference as to the buyer's use of the property.[561]

[L] Statutory Prohibitions on Contracting — Sunday, Usury, Licensing, and Other Statutes

Where a statute expressly or by implication prohibits the making of a certain kind of contract, it is clear that any agreement in violation of that statute is unenforceable. It is, however, important to consider legislative intention because that intention may suggest that a contract in contravention of the statute is voidable and not void, thereby permitting an action in restitution to avoid a forfeiture.[562]

[1] Sunday Statutes ("Blue Laws") — Usury

Among the common illustrations of statutes that expressly or impliedly prohibit the making of certain kinds of contracts are Sunday ("Sabbath-breaking") laws which prohibit the making of certain types of contracts on Sunday (often called "Blue laws"). Only a few jurisdictions retain these provisions and there is considerable variation among those that remain.[563]

---

[558] Zenon v. R. E. Yeagher Mgmt. Corp., 57 Conn. App. 316, 748 A.2d 900 (2000).

[559] *See* Potomac Leasing Co. v. Vitality Ctrs., Inc., 290 Ark. 265, 718 S.W.2d 928 (1986) (otherwise lawful lease of equipment that lessee intended to use for an unlawful purpose); Carroll v. Beardon, 142 Mont. 40, 381 P.2d 295 (1963) (sale of real property to be used as house of prostitution); Graves v. Johnson, 179 Mass. 53, 60 N.E. 383 (1901) (sale of liquor to be resold in another jurisdiction contrary to its laws).

[560] Blossom Farm Prods. Co. v. Kasson Cheese Co., 133 Wis. 2d 386, 395 N.W.2d 619 (Ct. App. 1986) (use of illegal ingredient in cheese product); Advance Whip & Novelty Co. v. Benevolent Protective Order of Elks, 106 Vt. 72, 170 A. 95 (1934) (contract to supply merchandise and games of chance to be used for gambling purposes); *See also* RESTATEMENT 2d § 182(a).

[561] *See* Hanauer v. Doane, 79 U.S. (12 Wall.) 342, 20 L. Ed. 439 (1871) (consequence of seller's acts are too serious and enormous to permit the seller to plead that, although he knew of the buyer's purpose, he did not sell the goods for that purpose). *See also* Tracy v. Talmage, 14 N.Y. 162 (1856), and RESTATEMENT 2d § 182(b).

[562] Yank v. Juhrend, 151 Ariz. 587, 729 P.2d 941 (Ct. App. 1986) (permitting restitution in accordance with RESTATEMENT 2d § 197 comment b).

[563] There is considerable variation in the types of transactions prohibited by such statutes. *See* Denton v. Winner Communications, Inc., 726 P.2d 911 (Okla. Ct. App. 1986) (Sunday statute prohibited only public selling or offering or exposing for sale certain commodities; therefore, contract for stallion's stud services was not within the scope of the statute). *See also* Sauls v. Stone, 286 Ala. 461, 241 So. 2d 836 (1970) (agreement for sale of business violated Sunday statute). There is no common law restriction on making contracts on Sunday. Rodman v. Robinson, 134 N.C. 503, 47

Where a Sunday law prohibits doing work or carrying on a business on Sunday, a contract requiring performance on a Sunday, though made on a weekday, the agreement is unenforceable. A court will not aid either party seeking redress for such a contract.[564] Where, however, the performance is not required on Sunday, it is generally held that performance is acceptable on the next business day.[565]

Usury. Though there is no common law restriction on the rate of interest charged for the loan of money, usury statutes prohibit the lender of money from charging more than a specified maximum rate of interest.[566] The scope of a usury statute must be carefully considered since certain types of loans may not violate the statute. The typical usury statute only applies to the loan of money as contrasted with a sale of property on credit. Thus, even though the credit price in such a transaction exceeds the cash price by more than the amount of interest permitted under the applicable usury statute, there is no violation of the statute.[567] If the contract provides for acceleration of the loan upon default of the debtor, i.e., the entire principal and interest becomes due upon such default, such clauses are not violative of usury statutes.[568] Such statutes typically do not apply to lease contracts.[569] Courts will, however, will not always focus on the form rather than the substance of a transaction in discovering a usurious contract.[570] When an agreement is held to violate the applicable usury statute, different effects are discernible: the contract may be void and unenforceable in its entirety,[571] or it may even give rise to a penalty recoverable by the injured party.[572] Typically, however, the usurious contract will be deemed only voidable as to the interest specified beyond the lawful rate.[573]

S.E. 19 (1904); Ward v. Ward, 75 Minn. 269, 77 N.W. 965 (1899); Richmond v. Moore, 107 Ill. 429, 47 Am. Rep. 445 (1883). Therefore, absent a statutory proscription, contracts made on Sunday are enforceable.

[564] *See Sauls v. Stone*, note 563, *supra.*

[565] See, e. g., Logan v. Linden Props., 2001 Mass. Super. LEXIS 6, at *4 (Mass. Super. Ct. 2001).

[566] *See, e.g.,* Metro Hauling, Inc. v. Daffern, 44 Wash. App. 719, 723 P.2d 32 (1986).

[567] *See, e.g.,* Servpro Indus., Inc. v. Pizzillo, 2001 Tenn. App. LEXIS 87 (Tenn. Ct. App. Feb. 14, 2001). Defendant did not borrow money from plaintiff, but purchased tangible and intangible property and gave his note in exchange for the property. This was, therefore, a time-price differential transaction that is not usurious under the statute. In Transmedia Restaurant Co. v. 33 East 61st St. Restaurant Corp., 184 Misc. 2d 706, 710 N.Y.S.2d 756 (Sup. Ct. 2000), plaintiff made a cash advance to defendant restaurant in exchange for credits for plaintiff's members as discounts on food and beverages. The loan would not be repaid. Only the credits could be used. The court held that this transaction did not come within the usury statute.

[568] *See, e.g.,* Campbell v. Werner, 232 So. 2d 252 (Fla. Dist. Ct. App. 1970).

[569] *See, e.g.,* T.F. James Co. v. Vakoch, 604 N.W.2d 459 (N.D. 2000).

[570] *See* Cashback Catalog Sales, Inc. v. Price, 102 F. Supp. 2d 1375 (S.D. Ga. 2000) (check cashing service with ersatz catalog goods met the requirements to establish a usurious claim: (1) a loan or forbearance of money; (2) an understanding that the principal must be repaid; (3) an agreement to pay in return for the loan or forbearance a greater profit than is authorized by law; (4) the contract was made with an intent to violate the law).

[571] *See* Beneficial Fin. Co. v. Administrator of Loan Laws, 260 Md. 430, 272 A.2d 649 (1971). *See also* Yakutsk v. Alfino, 43 A.D.2d 552, 349 N.Y.S.2d 718 (1st Dep't 1973).

[572] *See* Cerasoli v. Schneider, 311 A.2d 880 (Del. Super. Ct. 1973); White v. Seitzman, 230 Cal. App. 2d 756, 761, 41 Cal. Rptr. 359, 362 (2d Dist. 1964) (treble damage recovery under usury statute not recoverable where plaintiff had not only knowingly initiated and consented to the transaction, but had been the "guiding hand" and "had originated the scheme or device to evade the Usury Law").

[573] *See* Thomas Lakes Owners Ass'n v. Riley, 9 Neb. Ct. App. 359, 612 N.W.2d 529 (2000); Duggan v. Marshall, 7 S.W.3d 888 (Tex. App. Houston 1999).

[2]   Licensing — Regulatory or Revenue Purpose

There are numerous statutes prohibiting a party from engaging in a particular line of business or a profession without a license. Thus, statutes require real estate brokers, milk dealers, pawn brokers, lawyers, dentists, physicians, and many others to secure a license to conduct their businesses or practice their professions. Whether contracts made in pursuance of such businesses or professions without a license are unenforceable is a question of sound public policy since these statutes often do not expressly deal with that question. The purpose of the statute must be the decisive judicial guide in such cases.

Where the licensing statute has a *regulatory* purpose designed for the protection of third parties or the public in general, it is generally held that a contract made in violation thereof is unenforceable by the person who has violated the statute. An electrician who could not continue on a project because he had no license promised to pay a licensed electrician for obtaining a permit, The licensed electrician performed no work on the project. The court held that the promise by the unlicensed electrician was unenforceable.[574] Where a nursing agency failed to obtain a license before entering into a contract to provide nurses to a hospital, the court held the contract unenforceable because the statute served a regulatory purpose in protecting the public and was not simply a revenue measure.[575] Where, however, the dominant purpose of the statute is not regulatory but clearly one designed to raise revenue, a contract made by an unlicensed party should not be unenforceable because the penalties which the statute imposes are deemed adequate to insure its observance.[576] Even if the statute has a regulatory purpose, a technical violation where the purpose of the statute has been met does not preclude enforcement of the contract unless the court deems the public policy manifested by the statute to be so emphatic that it admits of no exception.[577] A renal transplant center performing competent services had not obtained a permit under a state statute requiring such permits for the purpose of avoiding the creation of unnecessary health facilities. The court held that this violation of the statute could be distinguished from a license requirement to protect the public against incompetent practitioners.[578] Moreover, if a party has performed a contract and "denial or relief is wholly out of proportion to the requirements of public policy or appropriate individual punishment," the contract will be enforced despite the violation of the statute.[579] In such cases, courts must balance the regulatory purpose of the statute and the public policy supporting it against the forfeiture to the performing party and the consequent unjust enrichment of the other party.[580] It is, however, important to note that courts will tolerate forfeiture where the statutory mandate is clear and the act involves moral turpitude. Thus, where a buyer received goods pursuant to a contract obtained by bribing the store's agent, the

---

[574] In Rice v. James, 844 S.W.2d 64 (Mo. Ct. App. 1992).

[575] U.S. Nursing Corp. v. Saint Joseph Med. Ctr., 39 F.3d 790 (7th Cir. 1994). *See also* RESTATEMENT 2d § 181.

[576] *See, e.g.*, Howard v. Lebby, 197 Ky. 324, 246 S.W. 328 (1923).

[577] *See* H. O. Meyer Drilling Co. v. Alton V. Phillips Co., 2 Wash. App. 600, 468 P.2d 1008 (1970), *aff'd*, 79 Wash. 2d 431, 486 P.2d 1071 (1971) (failure to obtain renewal certificate and pay $20 fee for contractor registration deprived no class of beneficiaries of the protection intended by the statute). Where however, a home improvement contractor met all licensing requirements for which it had applied, but formed a contract a month prior to receiving the license, a divided court held that the contract violated the regulatory purpose of protecting homeowners against unscrupulous contractors. Cevern, Inc. v. Ferbish, 666 A.2d 17 (D.C. Ct. App. 1995).

[578] Rush-Presbyterian-St. Luke's Med. Ctr. v. Hellenic Republic, 980 F.2d 449 (7th Cir. 1992).

[579] John E. Rosasco Creameries v. Cohen, 276 N.Y. 274, 11 N.E.2d 908 (1937).

[580] RESTATEMENT 2d § 181(b).

court refused to enforce the promise to pay for the goods.[581]

[M]   Effect of Agreements Contravening Public Policy

The manner in which common law courts have dealt with agreements contravening public policy has often left something to be desired. While it is frequently asserted that such a bargain is "void," as if no contract had been made, this is not the effect in many cases. Unless otherwise prescribed by a statute, common law courts have generally taken the position that the judicial machinery is not available to one who has participated in a transaction violating public policy, i.e., "No court will lend its aid to a man who founds his cause of action upon an immoral or an illegal act."[582] The parties to an illegal transaction are left where they find themselves, not because the court seeks to protect the defendant, but because it will not lend its aid to the plaintiff.[583] No aid will be extended to a party to enforce an illegal bargain which he has made, or to restore what he has parted with in performing, unless the result of refusing aid would be to defeat the purpose sought to be accomplished in condemning the transaction.

If a statute or administrative regulation is designed to protect one of the parties, the party who is supposed to be protected may enforce the contract. Thus, where an innocent party deals with an unlicensed architect or contractor who fails to perform in a reasonable fashion, the innocent party who was unaware of the license deficiency may bring an action on the contract.[584] Where, however, the court takes the usual path and refuses to aid either party, the result may be that one wrongdoer is enriched at the expense of another. No doubt the theory supporting this conclusion is that the refusal to aid has a deterrent effect. Where, for example, a provider of home improvement services failed to meet statutory requirements of a written contract, a divided court refused a quasi contract recovery on the footing that any unjust enrichment of the defendant must be tolerated to effect the purpose of the statute.[585]

For many years, courts took the position that illegality need not be pleaded by the defendant, i.e., a court will, on its own motion, deny relief to a plaintiff whose cause of action appears from his own presentation to emanate from an illegal bargain.[586] One should not, however, rely on the older cases, particularly where the contravention of public policy does not involve moral turpitude. Unless the evidence shows a contract which is inherently wrongful, such as a contingent fee arrangement with an attorney in a criminal matter, a claim of illegality not presented on the pleadings will not be considered).[587]

---

[581] *See* Sirkin v. Fourteenth St. Store, 124 A.D. 384, 108 N.Y.S. 830 (1st Dep't 1908). *See also* McConnell v. Commonwealth Pictures Corp., 7 N.Y.2d 465, 166 N.E.2d 494 (1960).

[582] Lord Mansfield in Holman v. Johnson, 1 Cowper 341 [1875].

[583] *Id. See also* Golberg v. Sanglier, 96 Wash. 2d 874, 639 P.2d 1347 (1982).

[584] *See* Hedla v. McCool, 476 F.2d 1223 (9th Cir. 1973) (architect); Cohen v. Mayflower Corp., 196 Va. 1153, 86 S.E.2d 860 (1955) (contractor).

[585] Barrett Builders v. Miller, 215 Conn. 316, 325, 576 A.2d 455, 459 (1990): "[I]f recovery is permitted despite the fact that the underlying home improvement contract is invalid, a contractor could unilaterally expand the scope of the project beyond the contemplation of the invalid agreement, without the homeowner's consent, and recover for the unwanted work." Allowing a quasi contract recover in such cases would "thwart" the purpose and clear intent of the statute since the end result would provide the contractor with a recovery for the work performed.

[586] *See* Oscanyan v. Arms Co., 103 U.S. (13 Otto) 261, 26 L. Ed. 539 (1881).

[587] O'Donnell v. Bane, 385 Mass. 114, 431 N.E.2d 190 (1982).

•

If illegality is treated as an affirmative defense, like other such defenses, the failure to plead it would normally result in its waiver.[588] While insisting that illegality is an affirmative defense, however, a number of courts have recognized an exception for this defense because the invalidity of a contract offensive to public policy cannot be waived.[589] Thus, a court may raise the defense *sua sponte.*

[N]   Effect of Partial Contravention of Public Policy — Divisibility

Where a contract only partially contravenes public policy, a court may enforce the other part of the contract if that part is not an essential part of the agreed exchange and if the party seeking enforcement of that part operated in good faith and fairly and did not engage in serious misconduct.[590] We have already explored clear illustrations of a judicial willingness to sever an unreasonable provision from a covenant not to complete.[591] If there is a serious contravention of public policy so that a considerable degree of moral turpitude attaches to it, courts generally refuse to enforce any part of the agreement.[592] If, however, the violation of public policy is not of so serious a character, the contract may be divisible in the technical sense of certain performances being the agreed equivalents of counter performances. If such divisible parts, standing alone, would not contravene public policy, they may be enforced, while the other parts of the contract would remain unenforceable.[593] Notwithstanding a willingness to apply this principle, courts are precluded from applying it where the contract is simply not divisible.[594] Even where the contract is technically entire, however, if the lawful part of the defendant's promise is separable and the entire consideration furnished by the plaintiff is

---

[588] FED. R. CIV. P. 8(c).

[589] *See* Kidder, Peabody & Co. v. IAG Int'l Acceptance Group, N.V., 1999 U.S. Dist. LEXIS 132, at *35 (S.D.N.Y. Jan. 12, 1999), and cases cited therein.

[590] RESTATEMENT 2d § 184. Unenforceable exclusionary clauses in insurance policies are clear illustrations. *See, e.g.,* Leibrand v. National Farmers Union Prop. & Cas. Co., 272 Mont. 1, 898 P.2d 1220, 1226 (1995), and Canal Ins. So. v. Benner, 980 F.2d 23, 26 (1st Cir. 1992). *See also* Schoepf v. Rudy, 1993 U.S. App. LEXIS 15003, at *9 (10th Cir. June 15, 1993) (failure to obtain license). The "good faith" of the party seeking enforcement of the clause is an important element. See, e.g., Technical Aid Corp. v. Allen, 134 N.H. 1, 591 A.2d 262 (1991), where the court found an absence of good faith.

[591] *See* § 99[E]. *supra.* There we explored the "blue pencil" rule and the more flexible approach of RESTATEMENT 2d § 184. A cogent illustration as discussed in that section appears in BDO Seidman v. Hirshberg, 93 N.Y.2d 382, 690 N.Y.S.2d 854, 712 N.E.2d 1220, 1226 (1999). *See also* A.N. Deringer, Inc. v. Strough, 103 F.3d 243, 247 (2d Cir. 1996).

[592] See, e.g., People v. Hare, 315 Ill. App. 3d 606, 734 N.E.2d 515, 518, 248 Ill. Dec. 587 (2d Dist. 2000), where a court dealt with a plea agreement that violated sentencing standards. Recognizing that plea agreements are subject to contract law principles so long as they are consistent with constitutional due process, the court held that where an unenforceable aspect of an agreement is an essential part of the agreed exchange (here, the concession of the State was a major element of the consideration for defendant's guilty plea), the entire clause is unenforceable. See also cases involving bribery, such as McConnell v. Commonwealth Pictures Corp., 7 N.Y.2d 465, 199 N.Y.S.2d 483, 166 N.E.2d 494 (1960), and Sirkin v. Fourteenth St. Store, 124 A.D. 384, 108 N.Y.S. 830 (1st Dep't 1908). *See also* Smilansky v. Mandel Bros., 254 Mich. 575, 236 N.W. 866 (1931) (original contract against public policy where foreign corporation was unauthorized to do business taints new promise to perform the same contract pursuant to settlement of litigation).

[593] *See* Jones v. Brantley, 121 Miss. 721, 83 So. 802 (1920) (part of contract performable on Sunday).

[594] *See, e.g.,* Starr v. Robinson, 181 Ga. App. 9, 351 S.E.2d 238 (1986) (attorney sued to recover lump sum fee in exchange for handling all matters connected with sale, including services as a real estate broker, and attorney was not licensed as broker; the fee was not apportioned with respect to different services and the court, therefore, could not enforce any part of the contract); Slusher v. Greenfield, 488 So. 2d 579 (Fla. Dist. Ct. App. 1986) (physicians who were junior shareholders of professional corporation could not prevent voiding of entire contract where illegal provisions for senior shareholders were indivisible).

lawful and he is prepared to perform the whole of it, the promise will be enforced.[595] On the other hand, if any part of the consideration offends public policy, no part of the defendant's promises will be enforced, though all of his promises are, in themselves, in accordance with public policy.[596]

The decisions concerning partial "illegality" often appear to be technical or arbitrary, though there is an underlying manifestation of judicial effort to avoid forfeitures where the violation of public policy is not sufficiently serious to justify a penalty.

[O]   Mitigating Doctrines — Pari Delicto and Locus Poenitentiae — Restitution

The maxim, *In pari delicto, potior est conditio defendentis* (in case of equal fault, the condition of the party defending is the stronger), is found in many cases involving contracts violating public policy. The maxim is generally understood to mean that neither party will be aided by a court, neither to enforce it or set it aside.[597] Where a Syrian national, Kardoh, obtained four alien registration cards from an undercover agent posing as a corrupt immigration official to whom Kardoh paid $40,000, Kardoh was arrested and deported. He then sought to recover the $40,000. The district court held that he could recover the payment since he had not been convicted of any crime. On appeal, the court noted the settled rule that property delivered under an illegal contract cannot be recovered by any party in pari delicto. The pari delicto principle was used originally in the context of criminal activity to bar the return of funds used to bribe a public official. The pari delicto doctrine, however, was extended to other illegal transactions. While the government would be expected to pursue criminal prosecutions in cases such as this case, the court held that the failure to prosecute does not automatically mean that a claimant's motion for return of property should be granted. The fact that the government chose to deport Kardoh rather than prosecute him did not make his payment to the undercover officer less guilty. The court reversed the decision below.[598] If, however, a party to a bargain violating public policy has conferred a benefit upon the other party and then seeks restitution, he may be successful if he is not in pari delicto, i.e., "not equally in the wrong" with the other.[599] Moreover, even if he was in pari delicto, he may have "repented" and chosen to withdraw from the agreement prior to the attainment of its "unlawful" purpose.[600] If his withdrawal is timely, he is said to have done so within his "locus poenitentiae," literally a place for repentance, though it is used to mean simply an opportunity for withdrawal prior to the fulfillment of the improper purpose.[601] It is important to recognize the two requirements for the application of the *locus poenitentiae* concept: (1) the improper

---

[595] *See* Illinois Bankers Life Assurance Co. v. Brydia, 180 Okla. 436, 70 P.2d 73 (1937); Poultry Producers of Southern Cal., Inc. v. Barlow, 189 Cal. 278, 208 P. 93 (1922); McCall Co. v. Hughes, 102 Miss. 375, 59 So. 794 (1912).

[596] Kukla v. Perry, 361 Mich. 311, 105 N.W.2d 176 (1960); Johnson v. McMillion, 178 Ky. 707, 199 S.W. 1070 (1918). See also Schara v. Thiede, 58 Wis. 2d 489, 206 N.W.2d 129 (1973), where a one-year lease was expressly conditioned upon the faithful performance of an illegal agreement and the court held that the contract was so permeated by illegality that it left the parties where it found them.

[597] United States v. Farrell, 606 f. 2d 1341, 1348, n. 21 (1979).

[598] Kardoh v. United States, 572 F. 3d 697 (9th Cir. 2009).

[599] *See* RESTATEMENT 2d § 198(b).

[600] Actual repentance is unnecessary, i.e., it is enough that the party withdrew. *See* Aikman v. City of Wheeling, 120 W. Va. 46, 195 S.E. 667 (1938).

[601] Where a party has a right to avoid the contract and seek restitution but continues to proceed with the contract,

("illegal") purpose has not been attained and restitution will avoid such attainment;[602] (2) the illegality did not involve "moral turpitude"[603] or, as the RESTATEMENT 2d suggests, the party claiming restitution "did not engage in serious misconduct."[604]

Another exception to the illegality doctrine may allow recovery by a guilty party who would otherwise be in pari delicto where the other party is guilty of fraud. The Treeses were general contractors who lost their public works license and bonding capacity. They entered into a joint venture with the Kerseys, licensed general contractors, who would bid on projects in their name, procure the bond, insurance and pay the bills while the Treeses would be responsible for everything else including the function of general contractor on the projects. They agreed to split the profits, fifty-fifty. The joint venture performed numerous projects, but the Kerseys defrauded the Treeses. The district court awarded the Treeses $332, 049.66 in actual damages and $150,000 in punitive damages. On appeal, the Kerseys argued that the court should not aid either party who were in pari delicto. The court, however, noted an exception to the doctrine where both parties are not equally at fault because one party commits fraud, or there is duress, oppression or undue influence over the other party. The district court found many instances of fraud by the Kerseys, independent of harm to the public, of which the Treeses were unaware. While under the law of Idaho, punitive damages may be allowed for fraud or oppressive conduct, the Tresses knew that their agreement with the Kerseys was illegal. The court vacated the award of punitive damages, but affirmed the award of actual damages for the Treeses.[605]

There are numerous statements in the case law to the effect that a party who was not in pari delicto may recover the value of any performance he has rendered if he was not, in the language of the FIRST RESTATEMENT, guilty of serious moral turpitude.[606] The RESTATEMENT 2d prefers more neutral language in suggesting that such a party need only be "not equally in the wrong with the promisor."[607] One of the better-known cases involved the delivery of $28,000 worth of jewelry to the defendant in exchange for defendant's promise to obtain visas for the plaintiff and his family by bribing a public official. The defendant absconded with the jewelry and did not perform his promise. When the plaintiff much later sought restitution of his money, the court recognized plaintiff's actions as attempting to save himself and his family from the Nazi army and held that the plaintiff was not in pari delicto with the defendant.[608] Though bribing a public official would normally be characterized as a serious wrong or, in the older usage, "serious moral turpitude," the circumstances of this case clearly precluded that characterization.

---

any such withdrawal is not timely and a party may be said to have waived it right to rescission. *See* Bagel Enters., Inc. v. Baskin & Sears, 467 A.2d 533 (Md. App. 1983).

[602] *See* Woel v. Griffith, 253 Md. 451, 253 A.2d 353 (1969), and RESTATEMENT 2d § 199(b).

[603] *See* Williams v. Brown, 362 S.W.2d 177, 179 (Tex. Civ. App. Dallas 1962). *But see* Town of Meredith v. Fullerton, 83 N.H. 124, 139 A. 359, 365 (1927).

[604] RESTATEMENT 2d § 199.

[605] Trees v. Kersey, 138 Idaho 3, 56 P. 3d 765 (Ida. 2002). The court also noted two other exception in Idaho: (1) where the agreement involves an innocent plaintiff and is not declared void by statute, and (2) where the unenforceability of a void insurance policy may defeat the purpose for which a statute has been acted.

[606] FIRST RESTATEMENT § 604. *See also* Wade, *Restitution of Benefits Acquired Through Illegal Transactions*, 95 U. PA. L. REV. 261 (1947).

[607] RESTATEMENT 2d § 198(b).

[608] Liebman v. Rosenthal, 185 Misc. 837, 57 N.Y.S.2d 875 (Sup. Ct.), *aff'd*, 269 A.D. 1062, 59 N.Y.S.2d 148 (1945).

Where the parties are not in pari delicto, the plaintiff may be a member of a class designed to be protected by the public policy standard. Thus, if a party were prevented from recovering usurious interest, the purpose of the usury statute would be defeated because the aggrieved party has typically acquiesced in the terms of the contract because of his inferior bargaining power.[609] Courts do not deem contracts made with an unlicensed party void. Since the innocent party is one of the persons the licensing statute is designed to protect, he is not in pari delicto with the unlicensed party.[610] The purpose of a particular statute is a critical determinant in these cases. Thus, where a plaintiff sought treble damages under an antitrust statute for a violation of the antitrust laws, the defense argued that the plaintiff had enjoyed the benefits of the unlawful agreements and should be precluded from recovery because he was in pari delicto. The United States Supreme Court refused to recognize the "complex" defense of pari delicto in such an action, though it suggested that complete and voluntary participation in an antitrust offense could bar a plaintiff's recovery.[611] Similarly, where a court finds that a gambling statute is designed to curb organized gambling, a party to a wager is not in pari delicto with a professional bookmaker.[612]

Where a party incurred a gambling debt and pledged a bond with a market value more than double the debt as security, the pledgee confessed that he had sold the bond when the pledgor tendered the amount of the bet. In an action by the pledgor for the market value of the bond, the court recognized the doctrine of pari delicto which would leave these parties where they were, but it superimposed the concept that one has a right to withdraw from such an improper agreement either to retain or recover his property or money before it goes into the hands of the winner. Thus, where money or property is placed with a third party (stakeholder) from which it can be withdrawn, the loser can recover from the stakeholder. Even though the bond in this case had been delivered to the winner, it had been delivered as security for the debt and ownership of the bond remained in the loser. Therefore, it could be recovered.[613]

[P]   Mitigating Doctrines — Justifiable Ignorance of Facts

Sometimes a bargain that is proper on its face is contrary to public policy because of extrinsic facts known only to one of the parties. Courts generally permit the innocent party who is justifiably ignorant to recover damages as if the contract were proper if the facts or legislation violated are of a relatively minor character.[614] If a party is excusably ignorant of certain facts, he may also be entitled to restitution.[615] These principles may be viewed as a species of the general concept protecting a party not in equal fault (in pari delicto) with the other party.

---

[609] *See* Glyco v. Schultz, 62 Ohio Op. 2d 459, 289 N.E.2d 919 (Misc. Ct. 1972).

[610] *See* Southern States Life Ins. Co. v. McCauley, 81 N.M. 114, 464 P.2d 404 (1970); Cohen v. Mayflower Corp., 196 Va. 1153, 86 S.E.2d 860 (1955).

[611] Perma Life Mufflers v. International Parts Corp., 392 U.S. 134, 88 S. Ct. 1981, 20 L. Ed.2d 982 (1968).

[612] Watts v. Malatesta, 262 N.Y. 80, 186 N.E. 210 (1933).

[613] Gehres v. Ater, 148 Ohio St. 89, 73 N.E.2d 513 (1947). *See also* RESTATEMENT 2d § 199(a).

[614] See Advanced Cell Technology v. Infigen, Inc., 2002 Mass. Super. LEXIS 377 at *25 (2002). *See also,* RESTATEMENT 2d § 180.

[615] RESTATEMENT 2d § 198(a). Where, however, neither party was excusably ignorant of zoning laws that precluded the lease of certain premises for a printing business, restitution was denied. Central States Health & Life Co. v. Miracle Hills Ltd. Partnership, 235 Neb. 592, 456 N.W.2d 474 (1990).

[Q]   Effect of Substituted Contract in Discharge of Bargain

It is often suggested that a transaction growing out of an "illegal" bargain is, itself, unenforceable though it may be intrinsically "lawful."[616] Some courts, however, have taken a different view where the impropriety is not particularly serious. They have held that when the illegal contract has been discharged by an unperformed substituted contract, which is not in and of itself unlawful in character, the latter contract may be enforced. Thus, where a lottery resulting in an accounting showing money due the plaintiff which defendant promised to pay, the court held that the plaintiff could enforce the promise. Though it recognized that other courts would refuse to enforce such a promise where the original bargain was tainted with illegality, this court suggested:

> [T]his court long ago committed itself to a contrary doctrine, and has established the rule that, where an illegal contract has been fully performed, the illegality is no defense to an action brought upon a subsequent promise to pay over the balance in the hands of one of the parties to the original contract.[617]

Where a promise to pay a previous usurious loan includes the usurious interest, the subsequent promise is as unenforceable as the first promise, though interest on the debt from the time of the second promise was not usurious. If, however, a new promise is made to pay the original debt with legal interest from the inception of that debt, the new promise is enforceable.[618]

[R]   Effect of Change in Law

It is generally held that a contract that is contrary to public policy when made does not become enforceable if the law is changed to validate such agreements before an action on the agreement is brought.[619] The rule is sometimes justified on the ground that the contract was originally void and therefore could gain no validity from the subsequent change in the law.[620] This view is, however, less than persuasive since contracts violating public policy are not void absent an express statutory directive to that effect.[621] If the contract is unenforceable at the time of formation because of *facts* of which both parties were unaware, a change of those facts

---

[616] In Smilansky v. Mandel Bros., 254 Mich. 575, 236 N.W. 866, 867 (1931), the court quotes from an early American case, Comstock v. Draper, 1 Mich. 481, 53 Am. Dec. 78 (1850): "It is a well settled doctrine in the English and American books, that an illegal transaction cannot constitute a good consideration for a promise. If the connection between the original illegal transaction and the new promise can be traced, if the latter is connected with and grows out of the former, no matter how many times and in how may different forms it may be renewed, it cannot form the basis of a recovery, for repeating a void promise cannot give it validity." Here, the court held that settlement of litigation, though normally sufficient consideration for a new promise, is insufficient consideration where it will have the effect of enforcing an illegal promise.

[617] Central Labor Council v. Young, 136 Wash. 550, 240 P. 919, 920 (1925). *Accord In re* Lowe's Estate, 104 Neb. 147, 175 N.W. 1015 (1920).

[618] Restatement 2d § 86 comment h.

[619] *See* Interinsurance Exch. of Auto. Club v. Ohio Cas. Ins. Co., 58 Cal. 2d 142, 23 Cal. Rptr. 592, 373 P.2d 640, 642 (1962): "Whether it be the rule in this state that an unlawful contract is void . . . or only unenforceable, . . . the law here is, and should be, that a contract or provision in a contract which contravenes public policy when made is not validated by a later statutory change in that public policy."

[620] *See* McLain v. Oklahoma Cotton Growers' Ass'n, 125 Okla. 264, 258 P. 269 (1927).

[621] *See* American Sav. Life Ins. Co. v. Financial Affairs Mgmt. Co., 20 Ariz. App. 479, 513 P.2d 1362 (1973).

should make the contract enforceable.[622] The only justification for the rule involving a change in law validating such transactions is that parties who made the contract when it violated a statute or other legal standard cannot be absolved from their wrongdoing simply because the law has changed. Yet, if legislation is changed because the legislature decides that the underlying rationale of the statute was originally misguided or no longer appropriate, there would seem to be little reason for refusing to enforce the contract that was invalid when originally made. Thus, some cases suggesting a different analysis have begun to appear.

A change of law may make an illegal bargain legal where the legislature manifests an intention to validate such bargains.[623] Absent such a manifested legislative intention, a new statute is normally applied prospectively rather than retroactively to make former unenforceable contracts enforceable. Even where the legislative intention is neither expressed nor clear, however, a court may deduce a sufficient legislative desire to change the public policy so as to validate prior agreements. Thus, where a common law prohibition concerning contracts to transfer ground water was removed by a statutory change, even in the absence of a legislative mandate to apply the statute retroactively, the court concluded that such a result was in keeping with its reading of the new public policy.[624] Where a contract violated a statutory prohibition against relieving a husband from the common law duty to support his wife when the contract was formed, the statute had been changed to allow such contracts to be enforceable at the time the defense of illegality was raised. While recognizing the general rule that the validity of a contract will depend upon the law that existed at the time the contract was made, the court nonetheless held a contract may be affected by subsequent legislation announcing a new public policy. Since the new public policy abrogated the gender-based unconstitutional distinction of its predecessor, the court held that the law on the date the action was commenced was applicable, thus removing the former prohibition from earlier agreements.[625]

Other manifestations of the relaxation of the rigid common law rule may be seen in cases where the illegal bargain is ratified after the law is changed to make such bargains enforceable. The common law rule was clear that such a ratification would not validate an agreement that was against public policy.[626] While declining to reach the issue of whether a mere change in the law would automatically ratify a previously illegal agreement, a modern court held that "the express ratification of a previously illegal agreement subsequent to a change in the law that removes the illegality of the agreement validates the original agreement," even where the prior law deemed such agreements to be "void."[627]

---

[622] *See* First Restatement § 609.

[623] First Restatement § 609(b).

[624] Springer v. Kuhns, 6 Neb. Ct. App. 115, 571 N.W.2d 323 (1997).

[625] Goldfarb v. Goldfarb, 86 A.D.2d 459, 450 N.Y.S.2d 212 (2d Dep't 1982). This analysis was expressly followed in Propp v. Propp, 112 A.D.2d 868, 493 N.Y.S.2d 147 (1st Dep't 1985). The statutory changes reflect the fair and reasonable safeguards normally surrounding such agreement as explored in § 99[J]. *supra.*

[626] *See, e.g.*, Handy v. St. Paul Globe Publishing Co., 41 Minn. 188, 42 N.W. 872 (1889).

[627] TCA Bldg. Co. v. Northwestern Resources Co., 922 S.W.2d 629, 635 (Tex. App. Waco 1996).

[S]   Enforcement of "Illegal" Bargains That Are "Legal" Where Made

A contract may be enforceable under the public policy of the jurisdiction where it was made or performed but not under the public policy of the jurisdiction where enforcement is sought. One of the repeated maxims of contract law is that a contract valid under its governing law is valid everywhere.[628] Courts hasten to add, however, that there is an exception to this general rule in that where the enforcement would violate the fixed, settled, or strong public policy of the state in which the action is brought, it will not be enforced.[629] Cogent examples of these issues were seen earlier in the exploration of wagering contracts.[630] Where the winner of a gambling debt enforceable in one jurisdiction seeks to enforce it in a jurisdiction where such an agreement contravened public policy, a court will enforce the agreement if it does not contravene the strong public policy of its jurisdiction.[631] Similarly, where a restrictive covenant is enforceable in one jurisdiction, another jurisdiction will refuse to enforce it if it violates the strong public policy of the second jurisdiction.[632]

---

[628] *See* Continental Mortg. Invs. v. Sailboat Key, Inc., 354 So. 2d 67, 71 (Fla. Dist. Ct. App. 1977).

[629] *Id.*

[630] *See* § 99[G]. *supra.*

[631] Intercontinental Hotels Corp. v. Golden, 15 N.Y.2d 9, 203 N.E.2d 210 (1964) (gambling agreement did not contravene the law of Puerto Rico and court held that such arrangements did not contravene the strong public policy of New York, which had by that time legalized pari-mutuel betting and the operation of bingo games and were considering off-track betting). See, however, Metropolitan Creditors Serv. v. Sadri, 15 Cal. App. 4th 1821, 19 Cal. Rptr. 2d 646 (1st Dist. 1993), where the court refused to enforce a claim for a gambling debt incurred in Nevada for which the defendant had issued checks in exchange for gambling chips and later stopped payment of the checks. This case is discussed in § 99[G]. *supra.*

[632] *See* Hollingsworth Solderless Terminal Co. v. Turley, 622 F.2d 1324 (9th Cir. 1980).

Chapter 7

PERFORMANCE, CONDITIONS, AND BREACH

§ 100   MEANING AND NATURE OF CONDITION

[A]   Common Usage

A common dictionary definition of "condition" suggests that some event — any event — must occur before something is completed or effective, i.e., some operative fact must happen before a subsequent situation can exist. Used in this broad fashion, a conditioning event may be *any* event. For example, before a contract may be said to exist, an offer must occur as a condition to a power of acceptance, and the power of acceptance must be exercised as a "condition" to the formation of a contract. In such a broad use of the term, it may be suggested that when Ames promises to pay Barnes $1000 thirty days from the date of the promise (in exchange for something of value), the mere lapse of thirty days or whatever period of time the parties establish in their agreement is a condition to Ames' promise to pay $1000. Innumerable other examples of the broad use of the term "condition" may be found. The caption, "terms and conditions" often appears above boilerplate clauses on standardized purchase order and acknowledgment forms without any indication of which clause contains a "term" and which contains a "condition." Such usage is a paradigm of the kind of "slovenly thinking" that so annoyed Professor Corbin in his efforts to explain the meaning of "condition."[1] All of these and other layperson uses of the term "condition" must be rejected if the concept of condition as used technically in the law of contracts is to be understood.

---

[1] Corbin, *Conditions in the Law of Contracts*, 28 Yale L.J. 739, 743 (1919).

[B]   "Condition" as Used in Contract Law

In contract law, "condition" is an event, other than the mere lapse of time, that is not certain to occur but must occur to *activate* an existing contractual duty, unless the condition is excused.[2] The fact or event properly called a condition occurs during the *performance* stage of a contract, i.e., after the contract is formed and prior to its discharge.[3] When the essential requisites for contract formation have been fulfilled, i.e., offer, acceptance, and validation devices between or among parties with capacity to contract, there is a contractual relationship between the parties. The parties are bound by their duties and each of the duties has correlative rights. These rights and duties, however, may not be immediately active duties or immediately enforceable rights. They are often subject to some conditioning fact or event that must occur to activate the duties thereby making the rights immediately enforceable.

Insurance contracts invariably contain conditions, such as a fire or other casualty loss, which must occur to activate the duty of the insurer to pay the amount of the policy. In one of the more common transactions occurring innumerable times each day, parties agree upon the purchase and sale of real estate where the agreement recites the requirement that a certain fact or event occur before the buyer's duty to pay the purchase price becomes activated and the seller's correlative right to receive the purchase price becomes enforceable. Typically, that fact or event is the buyer's success in obtaining suitable financing secured through a real estate mortgage to pay a large portion of the purchase price. The buyer's duty to pay the purchase price is, therefore, *conditioned* on the occurrence of that fact or event. It is sometimes forgotten that the parties are bound to each other at the moment their real estate contract is formed, i.e., before the occurrence of the conditioning event. At the moment the contract is formed, the seller may not agree to sell the property to another and the buyer may not refuse to perform his obligation by, for example, failing to make a reasonable effort to obtain financing. The contract obligation is created at the moment of formation.[4] The performance of that obligation is subject to the occurrence of the condition of financing. If the financing cannot be obtained through reasonable efforts, the condition has not occurred, and the buyer's duty is not activated and the seller's right is not enforceable.[5] Once it is clear that the condition will not occur, since the duty to which it attached will never become activated, the duty is discharged and the correlative right can never be enforced. Only at that time are the parties free from each other. Contract obligation must not be confused with contract performance.[6]

---

[2] This description of a condition is similar to the Restatement 2d definition in § 224: "A condition is an event, not certain to occur, which must occur, unless its non-occurrence is excused, before performance under a contract becomes due." Numerous cases have adopted this definition. *See, e.g.*, Cedyco Corp. v. Petroquest Energy, LLC, 497 F.3d 485, 489, n. 3 (5th Cir. 2007); Nebraska Pub. Power Dist. v. MidAmerican Energy Co., 234 F.3d 1032, 1045 (8th Cir. 2000); Sharp Elecs. Corp. v. Deutsche Fin. Servs. Corp., 216 F.3d 388, 394 (4th Cir. 2000), *cert. denied*, 121 S. Ct. 763, 148 L. Ed. 2d 664 (2001); Washington Props. v. Chin, Inc., 760 A.2d 546, 549 (D.C. App. 2000).

[3] While the parties may have agreed that a certain event (condition) must occur before a contract is formed (*see* § 86[C], *supra*), the use of the term does not refer to the formation stage of the contract (offer, acceptance, consideration or another validation device). Rather, it assumes an existing contract with existing rights and duties which are not *performable* until a certain event (condition) occurs. *See* American Multi-Cinema, Inc. v. Southroads, LLC, 115 F. Supp. 2d 1257, 1262 n.4 (D. Kan. 2000).

[4] *See* Brigdon v. Lamb, 929 P.2d 1274, 1277 (Alaska 1997) (citing this section).

[5] *See* Preferred Realty v. Weber, 201 Wis. 2d 816, 549 N.W.2d 287 (Ct. App. 1996).

[6] For a clear exposition of this analysis in a real estate contract setting, see Highland Inns Corp. v. American Landmark Corp., 650 S.W.2d 667 (Mo. Ct. App. 1983).

Students of contract law will recall another illustration found in the classic *Carbolic Smoke Ball*[7] case discussed earlier in relation to the agreement process.[8] The advertisement offered £100 to any person using the smoke ball in accordance with directions who thereafter contracted influenza, presumably within the "flu season." The acceptance of that offer occurred through the use of the smoke ball in accordance with directions. At that moment, a contract between the defendant company and any such user was formed. It was a contract involving only one right and one duty, in traditional contract law terms, a "unilateral" contract, since the user had performed the act of acceptance required by the offer of using the ball in accordance with directions, thereby creating a right in the user and a correlative duty in the manufacturer of the ball. Thousands of these contracts were formed, but the duty of the Smoke Ball Company to pay £100 pounds was conditioned upon the user contracting influenza. The occurrence of that operative fact or event would activate the *existing* duty of the manufacturer.[9] As will be seen in the pages that follow, the typical contract containing a condition may be analyzed in this fashion. It is important to consider what kind of fact or event may constitute a condition.

[C]   Nature of the Fact or Event Constituting a Condition

Virtually any act or event may constitute a condition.[10] The event may be an act to be performed or forborne by one of the parties to the contract, an act to be performed or forborne by a third party, or some fact or event over which neither party, or any other party, has any control.[11] Moreover, the event constituting the condition need not be a significant or material event, i.e., the parties may agree upon an event that does not appear to be either important or reasonable even where a forfeiture would result where the condition does not occur. Yet, modern courts are loathe to permit the nonoccurrence of an insignificant condition to result in a forfeiture. Thus, as will be seen later in this section, courts will resort to interpretation[12] or other devices and, on rare occasion, simply refuse to give effect to the condition where manifest injustice would otherwise result.[13]

If the contract requires a particular event to occur and no party to that contract has *promised* that it will occur, the occurrence of the event can only be construed as a condition that qualifies one or more duties of the parties. If, however, one of the parties has *promised* that a particular event will occur while the other party's duty is qualified by the identical event, the event is a promise by one party creating a duty in that party and the same event is a condition that must occur to activate the duty of the other party. Thus, where a seller of goods promises to ship the goods to a destination named by the buyer conditioned upon the

---

[7] Carlill v. Carbolic Smoke Ball Co., 1 Q.B. 256 [1893].

[8] *See supra* Chapter 2.

[9] In the analysis of conditions, much of the terminology employed is suggested by the classic analysis of Professor Corbin in his article, *Conditions in the Law of Contract*, 28 YALE L.J. 739 (1919).

[10] *See* K & K Pharmacy, Inc. v. Barta, 222 Neb. 215, 382 N.W.2d 363 (1986) (conditioning event was the ability of buyer to obtain a new lease satisfactory to buyer).

[11] Rezendes v. Barrows, 1998 Mass. Super. LEXIS 427, at *29 (Mass. Super. Ct. 1998): "A duty may be conditioned upon the failure of something to happen rather than upon some event occurring."

[12] *See, e.g.*, United Plate Glass Co. Div. of Chromalloy American Corp. v. Metal Trims Indus., 106 Pa. Commw. 22, 525 A.2d 468 (1987). *See also* RESTATEMENT 2d § 227(1).

[13] *See* Jackson v. Richards 5 & 10, Inc., 289 Pa. Super. 445, 433 A.2d 888 (1981) (refusal to effectuate immaterial conditions where forfeiture would otherwise result).

buyer's providing notice of that destination by a certain date, and the buyer also promises to provide that notice by a certain date, the giving of notice is a promised duty of the buyer while the same event is a condition to the seller's duty to perform.[14] Where the same event is both a promise and a condition, it has been labeled a *promissory condition*.[15]

Events constituting conditions are typically events that will or will not occur in the future.[16] This tends to obscure the fact that such events may be past, present, or future. A policy of marine insurance may be issued after the loss has occurred without the knowledge of the parties, i.e., the effect of a promise must be judged on the basis of what the parties themselves apparently know. If the parties are unaware of a past or present fact as to these parties, it is an uncertain fact and may operate as a condition.[17] If, however, one or both parties are aware of the occurrence of a particular event, the promise cannot be characterized as conditional, i.e., it is either an absolute promise or a nullity.

[D]   Differences Between a Promise and a Condition

The concept of condition is illuminated through a comparison of the legal effects of a promise, versus a condition, as suggested in the classic analysis of Professor Corbin where he presents four essential differences:[18]

(1) a promise is always made by one of the parties to the contract, whereas an event operates as a condition only where the parties agree that it shall operate as such, except where conditions are created by the court;

(2) a promise creates a duty in the promisor, whereas the purpose of a condition is to postpone a duty in the promisor;

(3) when a promise is performed, the duty is discharged, but where a condition occurs, the quiescent duty is activated;

(4) where a promise is not performed, a breach of contract occurs and the promisee has a remedial right to damages or other relief.

The failure of a condition to occur, however, breaches no duty. It leaves the duty in its dormant state, i.e., it is simply not activated and, unless the condition is excused, the duty will be discharged when there is no longer any possibility of its activation.[19]

---

[14] *See* Internatio-Rotterdam, Inc. v. River Brand Rice Mills, Inc., 259 F.2d 137 (2d Cir. 1958), *cert. denied*, 358 U.S. 946, 79 S. Ct. 352, 3 L. Ed. 2d 352 (1959).

[15] *See* Popovich v. Sommer Elec. Co., 1993 U.S. App. LEXIS 33861, at *9 (7th Cir. Dec. 28, 1993).

[16] Heidelberg Harris, Inc. v. Loebach, 145 F.3d 1454, 1459 (Fed. Cir. 1998) ("[T]he mere passage of time as to which there is no uncertainty is not a condition.").

[17] *See* Restatement 2d § 224 comment b. *See also* Seward & Scales v. Mitchell, 41 Tenn. (1 Cold.) 87 (1860); Ollive v. Booker, 1 Ex. 416 [1847].

[18] *See* Corbin, *Conditions in the Law of Contracts*, 28 Yale L.J. 739, 745 (1919).

[19] *See* Restatement 2d § 225. *See* Shovel Transfer & Storage, Inc. v. Pennsylvania Liquor Control Bd., 559 Pa. 56, 739 A.2d 133, 139 (1999) (citing this section) and Oregon Homes. Inc. v. Murray, 214 P. 3d 835, 848, n. 12 (Ore. App. 2009) (citing this analysis in an earlier edition of the treatise). *See also* Indiana State Highway Comm'n v. Curtis, 704 N.E.2d 1015, 1018 (Ind. 1998).

In the previous section, we explored the possibility that the same event is a promised duty of one party and a condition to the duty of the other party, i.e., a promissory condition.[20] When characterized as a promise, the failure of that event to occur would constitute a breach of duty created by the promise that it would occur. The non-occurrence of the event, however, would leave the other party's duty dormant and, if the condition could not occur, the duty would die in its sleep since only the occurrence of the condition could awaken it. It is important to appreciate the significance of the same event constituting a promise and a condition. If, for example, one party promises to give notice by a certain time and fails to do so, he has breached his promise. If that failure is not a material breach (materiality of breach will be explored later in this chapter), the duty of the aggrieved party is not discharged though he will have a cause of action for any loss caused by the immaterial breach. If the same event — giving notice — is also a condition to the other party's duty to perform, however, the non-occurrence of the condition has the effect of leaving the other party's duty in a state of quiescence, i.e., unactivated, and that duty will be discharged if the condition can never occur. Thus, the non-occurrence of a condition can have a drastic effect on the rights and duties of the parties whereas a breach may have a much less significant effect.

§ 101 CONDITIONS DISTINGUISHED FROM WARRANTIES — UNIFORM COMMERCIAL CODE

[A] The Concept of "Warranty" — "Title" and "Quality"

The term "warranty" has been used in several distinct senses over the years. Article 2 of the UCC contains four different warranties in relation to a contract for the sale of goods. Beyond a warranty of title or ownership of the goods,[21] there are three warranties of quality that will be explored: express warranties,[22] the implied warranty of merchantability,[23] and the implied warranty of fitness for a particular purpose.[24] We will see that even as used in the

---

[20] *See supra* text at note 14.

[21] See UCC §§ 2-312(1)(a) and (b), which contain the basic warranty of the seller that the title conveyed by him is good and its transfer rightful and that the goods shall be delivered free from any security interest or other lien or encumbrance of which the buyer at the time of contracting has no knowledge. Also, under this section, in § 2-312(3), a seller who is a merchant with respect to goods of the kind sold also warrants that the goods will be delivered free from the rightful claim of any third party by way of patent infringement or the like, though it places a duty on the buyer who furnishes specifications to indemnify the seller against any claim arising out of the buyer's specifications. While the "warranty of title" in this section is not expressly referred to as an "implied" warranty, it *is* implied since no expression of this warranty is necessary for it to exist in a given sale of goods. The reason this warranty is not captioned "implied" is that it contains its own method of disclaimer in § 2-312(2), which requires extremely clear language or other circumstances to evidence the intention of the parties that they contracted without this fundamental warranty. *See* Quality Components Corp. v. Kel-Keef Enters., 738 N.E.2d 524, 535-36 (Ill. App. 2000), Other UCC warranties dealing with the quality of goods, i.e., the implied warranty of merchantability in § 2-314 and the implied warranty of fitness for a particular purpose in § 2-315, both of which are discussed later in this section, are captioned "implied" and they must be disclaimed according to the formulas in § 2-316(2) of the Code. To avoid the application of § 2-316(2) to warranties of title, the warranty of title section is not designated as an "implied" warranty though, again, it is certainly "implied." *See* comment 6 to § 2-312. In one sense *more* implied than the other implied warranties since it is more difficult to disclaim than the other implied warranties. Again, this is the essential reason for ascertaining that the more liberal disclaimer provisions of § 2-316(2) do not apply to "implied" warranties of title.

[22] UCC § 2-313.

[23] UCC § 2-314.

[24] UCC § 2-315.

UCC, the concept of "warranty" is subject to considerable confusion.

The principal draftsman of Article 2, Karl Llewellyn, was anything but fond of the term "warranty" or the confusing set of ideas it suggested.[25] Llewellyn and others encountered difficulty in determining whether a warranty is a promise, a condition, or both. For example, in a simple contract to buy and sell a new lawnmower, if the seller tells the buyer that the mower will operate effectively in cutting a normal, flat lawn, the seller's promise may be viewed as a promise of indemnification, i.e., a promise by the seller to hold the buyer harmless if the mower does not operate effectively. If the mower does not operate effectively, the seller will perform his promise of indemnity by taking the mower back and replacing it with one that works, or by returning the purchase price, or, if the purchase price has not yet been paid, by cancelling the debt. If, however, the statement by the seller is not a promise but only a representation of fact, if that representation turns out to be false, it may be said that a condition precedent to the buyer's duty to pay for the mower has not occurred. The buyer's duty, therefore, would not be activated and the duty is discharged.[26]

The characterization of warranties as promises or conditions, however, is no longer significant. They have taken on a life of their own. The warranties of quality that we will examine in this section raise three distinct questions: (1) does the seller in a given sales transaction have any obligation as to the quality of the goods? (2) if the seller does have an obligation as to quality, what kind of goods must he deliver to meet that obligation? (3) if the seller fails to meet his obligation as to quality, what are the buyer's remedies? We will explore the first and second questions in this section and leave the third question for exploration in a later chapter under the topic of remedies for breach of contract.[27]

[B]   Express Warranties — "Basis of the Bargain"

The UCC recognizes the creation of express warranties by (a) statements of fact or promises by the seller relating to the goods which become *part of the basis of the bargain;* (b) descriptions of the goods which become *part of the basis of the bargain;* (c) samples or models of the goods which are made part of the *basis of the bargain.*[28] As will be seen, the phrase, "basis of the bargain," has given rise to considerable consternation.

No particular form of language is necessary to create an express warranty, e.g., the term "warranty" or "guarantee" need not be used, but the statement must be a statement of *fact* as contrasted with a statement of the seller's opinion or commendation of the goods.[29] Where a seller referred to an automobile as "excellent," "unusual," in "mint" and "very good" condition, a court found that the statements were mere statement of value, i.e., "puffing" or "seller's

---

[25] "To say 'warranty' is to say nothing definite as to legal effect. . . . [T]he sane course is to discard the word from one's thinking." K. LLEWELLYN, CASES AND MATERIALS ON THE LAW OF SALES 210 (1930). As to why Professor Llewellyn agreed to retain the term "warranty" in the UCC, its retention was simply one of innumerable compromises he made to ascertain the enactment of the new Code throughout the country. A new commercial code dehors the traditional term "warranty" would have appeared radical, indeed.

[26] As it appeared in the second edition of this book, this analysis is cited in Langley v. FDIC, 484 U.S. 86, 108 S. Ct. 396, 98 L. Ed. 2d 340 (1987).

[27] *See infra* Chapter 9.

[28] UCC § 2-313(1)(a), (b), and (c).

[29] UCC § 2-313(2).

talk" that did not create express warranties.[30] If, however, a seller indicates that the car has not been driven more than 200 miles or that the brake linings have been replaced within the last fifty miles or other statement of fact, an express warranty has been created. Whether a particular statement is one of commendation or opinion as contrasted with a statement of fact is, itself, a question of fact.[31] Since a statement, description, model, or sample will not become an express warranty under the Code unless it becomes part of the *basis of the bargain*, it is important to consider this requirement.[32]

Pre-Code tests to determine the existence of an express warranty generally did not require buyers to demonstrate that they actually relied upon a seller's statement as to the quality of the goods. Rather, courts adhered to the Williston view that the buyer need only show that the seller's statements were of a kind which would naturally induce a buyer to purchase the goods and that the buyer actually purchased the goods.[33] Controversy under the Code has centered on whether the "basis of the bargain" requirement is simply a restatement of the pre-Code "natural inducement" test. UCC comments to the express warranty section suggest that the old test has been rejected since they expressly reject any requirement of a showing of "particular reliance" and presume that any statement of fact by the seller constitutes an express warranty.[34] Another comment suggests the possibility of a post-formation warranty, i.e., an express warranty created for the first time after the contract for the sale of the goods was formed if it amounts to a subsequent modification.[35] The drafting history and language of the comments in particular may suggest that Professor Llewellyn and his colleagues were not thinking in terms of the classical "bargained-for-exchange" in using the phrase "basis of the bargain." Rather, they may have been pursuing a bargain continuum-a bargaining process extending beyond the moment in time when the contract of sale was made.[36]

---

[30] Web Press Servs. Corp. v. New London Motors, Inc., 203 Conn. 342, 351, 525 A.2d 57, 62 (1987).

[31] *See* Artistic Carton Co. v. Thelamco, Inc., 2009 U. S. Dist. LEXIS 86994 at &*13 (N. D. Ind. 2009) (the decisive test is whether a given expression representation is an express warranty is whether the seller asserts a fact or merely states an opinion or judgment); In re Ford Motor Co. E-350 Van Products Liability Litigation (No. II), 2008 U. S. Dist. LEXIS 73690 (D. N. J. 2008) (determining whether the phrase, "15 passenger van" constitutes an express warranty"). See also Ewers v. Eisenzopf, 88 Wis. 2d 482, 276 N.W.2d 802 (1979), where the buyer of certain sea shells, a piece of coral, and a driftwood branch asked a clerk in a store selling such items among sundry items whether these particular goods were "suitable for placement in a salt water aquarium," to which the clerk responded that they had come from salt water and were suitable for salt water aquariums if they were rinsed. Though the buyer rinsed the items in a normal fashion, his fish died. Experts testified that the items would have been suitable if they had been subjected to a week-long cleansing process consisting of soaking the items in boiling water. The majority held that an express warranty had been created by the clerk's statement and that warranty had been breached.

[32] *See* J. Murray, *"Basis of the Bargain": Transcending Classical Concepts*, 66 MINN. L. REV. 283 (1982).

[33] *See* Uniform Sales Act § 12 and 1 WILLISTON ON CONTRACTS § 206.

[34] See Murray, *supra* note 32, at 287–91, analyzing these comments and related sections of the UCC.

[35] Comment 7 to § 2-313 states, "The precise time when words of description or affirmation are made or samples are shown is not material. The sole question is whether the language or samples or models are to be regarded as part of the contract. If language is used after the closing of the deal (as when the buyer when taking delivery asks and receives an additional assurance) the warranty becomes a modification and need not be supported by consideration if it is otherwise reasonable and in order (§ 2-209)."

[36] See R. NORDSTROM, LAW OF SALES 206 (1970), which is a basic concept found in the Murray analysis, *supra* note 32. Comment 7 to § 2-313 of the UCC states: "The precise time when words of description or affirmation are made or samples are shown is not material. The sole question is whether the language or samples or models are to be regarded as part of the contract."

The case law in this area reflects confusion. Some courts suggest that reliance is necessary and proceed to suggest that it can be presumed, though they also suggest that it must actually induce the purchase.[37] A few courts seem to suggest that the UCC test did not change the pre-Code test.[38] Other courts appear to reject a reliance test, but proceed to suggest that "lack of reliance" is the test.[39] With only rare exception,[40] courts have been particularly reluctant to find an express warranty simply on the basis of the seller's statements or representations if the buyer was unaware of them at the time the contract was formed. The current conventional wisdom is manifested by *Cipollone v. Liggett Group, Inc.*,[41] holding that, where a buyer proves she was aware of the affirmation of fact or promise, it becomes an express warranty absent clear proof by the defendant that the buyer knew the statement was untrue.

[1]   Express Warranty — Leases — CISG

UCC Article 2A governing leases contains an express warranty section that replicates the Article 2 section on sales of goods, except for the substitution of leasing terminology.[42] While CISG does not use the term "warranty," it does require the seller to "deliver goods which are the quantity, quality and description required by the contract and which are contained or packaged in the manner required by the contract."[43] A separate section of CISG requires that goods conform to any sample or model.[44]

[C]   Implied Warranty of Merchantability

The basic warranty protection afforded by the UCC is provided through the implied warranty of merchantability.[45] In any contract for the sale of goods[46] by a seller who deals in goods of that kind,[47] a warranty that the goods "are fit for the ordinary purposes for which

---

[37] *See, e.g.*, Sessa v. Riegle, 427 F. Supp. 760 (E.D. Pa. 1977), *aff'd per curiam*, 568 F.2d 770 (3d Cir. 1978).

[38] *See, e.g.*, Milbank Mut. Ins. Co. v. Proksch, 309 Minn. 106, 244 N.W.2d 105 (1976); General Supply & Equip. Co. v. Phillips, 490 S.W.2d 913 (Tex. Civ. App. Tyler 1973); Hagenbuch v. Snap-On Tools Corp., 339 F. Supp. 676 (D.N.H. 1972).

[39] *See, e.g.*, Indust-Ri-Chem Lab., Inc. v. Par-Pak Co., 602 S.W.2d 282 (Tex. Civ. App. Dallas 1980).

[40] *See* Martin v. American Med. Sys., 116 F.3d 102, 105 (4th Cir. 1997) (relying on Daughtrey v. Ashe, 243 Va. 73, 413 S.E.2d 336 (1992) (citing Murray, *"Basis of the Bargain": Transcending Classical Concepts*, 66 MINN. L. REV. 283 (1982); Heckman, *"Reliance" or "Common Honesty Speech": The History and Interpretation of Section 2-313 of the Uniform Commercial Code*, 38 CASE W. RES. L. REV. 1 (1987)).

[41] 893 F.2d 541 (3d Cir. 1990).

[42] UCC § 2A-210.

[43] CISG, Art. 35(1). CISG governs contracts for the sale of goods between parties with principal places of business in CISG nations.

[44] CISG, Art. 35(2)(c).

[45] UCC § 2-314.

[46] There must be a contract for the sale of goods for the implied warranty of merchantability to attach, § 2-314(1). This requirement has given rise to questions of contract formation in self-service store situations. *See* Barker v. Allied Supermarket, 596 P.2d 870 (Okla. 1979), and Sheeskin v. Giant Food, Inc., 20 Md. App. 611, 318 A.2d 874 (1974), *aff'd*, 273 Md. 592, 332 A.2d 1 (1975), holding that a contract for the sale of goods occurs prior to a customer presenting the goods for purchase at the checkout area in a supermarket, thereby permitting the court to find an implied warranty of merchantability in "exploding bottle" cases.

[47] The implied warranty of merchantability does not attach to goods sold by a seller who normally does not deal

such goods are used"[48] is implied. Under this warranty, the buyer is entitled to receive non-defective goods, goods which are of fair or average quality, and goods that perform in accordance with reasonable standards of performance — not the highest quality of such goods, but of reasonable quality.[49] If trade usage or prior course of dealing suggest a certain margin of allowable imperfection, such as a certain percentage of defective goods in a total shipment, and if the percentage of defective goods does not exceed that percentage, the buyer has received merchantable goods.[50] The standard of "fair, average quality" or "fitness for ordinary purposes," like other legal standards, cannot be applied in algebraic fashion. As usual, the question is one of fact. For example, in a contract for commercial steel, the buyer was entitled to steel that did not crack when welded on to railroad cars.[51] No breach of the implied warranty of merchantability was found where a twenty-month old automobile, subjected to at least the wear and tear of a car of that vintage, developed rust around the tail lights.[52] On the other hand, where linoleum yellowed shortly after installation, the court had no difficulty in finding such a product unmerchantable.[53] While no automobile is accident-proof, any new automobile must meet an ordinary standard of "crashworthiness" or reasonable safety.[54] Whether food served in a restaurant is merchantable had earlier been determined by a "natural/normal" test that would find a breach of the implied warranty of merchantability whenever any food contained an unnatural ingredient. That test has given way to a "reasonable expectation" test, which would find a breach even where a natural but unexpected ingredient caused injury.[55]

It is not only the product, itself, which must be merchantable; the container, package, or label must also be adequate. Thus, selling a quart of milk in a paper bag is ridiculous. A seller

---

in such goods. Therefore, a casual sale by a party who has ordered too many computers, for example, would not carry the implied warranty of merchantability because the seller is not a merchant with respect to goods of that kind. *See* UCC § 2-314(1) and § 2-104 comment 2.

[48] Section 2-314(2)(c). This description is usually considered the most essential of six descriptions of the implied warranty of merchantability in subsection (2) of § 2-314. The others are: "(a) pass without objection in the trade under the contract description; and (b) in the case of fungible goods, are of fair average quality within the description; and . . . (d) run within the variations permitted by the agreement, of even kind, quality and quantity within each unit and among all units involved; and (e) are adequately contained, packaged and labeled as the agreement may require; and (f) conform to the promises or affirmations of fact made on the container or label if any."

[49] American Suzuki Motor Corp. v. Superior Court of Los Angeles Cty., 37 Cal. App. 4th 1291, 1295, 44 Cal. Rptr. 2d 526 (2d Dist. 1995) (implied warranty of merchantability arises by operation of law (as contrasted with express warranties) and assure minimum quality).

[50] *See, e.g.*, Agoos Kid Co. v. Blumenthal Import Corp., 282 Mass. 1, 184 N.E. 279 (1932) (certain percentage of rotted goat skins allowable according to trade usage). The UCC continues this position through §§ 2-314(2)(a) (pass without objection in the trade under the contract description) and 2-314(2)(d) (run, within the variations permitted by the *agreement*), and "agreement" is defined in § 1-201(3) as including prior course of dealing and usage of trade.

[51] *See* Ambassador Steel Co. v. Ewald Steel Co., 33 Mich. App. 495, 190 N.W.2d 275 (1971).

[52] *See* Taterka v. Ford Motor Co., 86 Wis. 2d 140, 271 N.W.2d 653 (1978).

[53] Mindell v. Raleigh Rug Co., 14 U.C.C. Rep. Serv. (CBC) 1124 (Mass. 1974).

[54] *See* Smith v. Fiat-Roosevelt Motors, Inc., 556 F.2d 728 (5th Cir. 1977); Frericks v. General Motors Corp., 274 Md. 288, 336 A.2d 118 (1975).

[55] *See* Phillips v. Town of West Springfield, 540 N. E. 2d 1331 (Mass. 1989). *See also* Hochberg v. O'Donnell's Restaurant, Inc., 272 A.2d 846 (D.C. App. 1971) (apparently pitted olive in martini contained an olive pit causing plaintiff to break a tooth). The last sentence of UCC § 2-314(1) deals specifically with the problem of whether food served in a restaurant is a sale of goods rather than a service. The section resolves the problem by calling food or drink served a sale of goods whether it is consumed on the seller's premises or elsewhere. *See* Koster v. Scotch Assocs., 273 N.J. Super. 102, 640 A.2d 1225, 1227 (Law Div. 1993).

of drinks is also liable when the glass containing the otherwise merchantable beverage breaks in the hand of a patron who is using the glass in a normal fashion.[56]

An overlap with express warranties is found in that portion of the implied warranty of merchantability description which requires the product to conform to any promises or affirmations of fact made on the container or label such as the statement on a golfing game, "Completely Safe. Ball Will Not Hit Player."[57] It is important to remember the existence of an express warranty in such a case since, as we will see later in this section, implied warranties may be disclaimed but express warranties may not be disclaimed. Overlaps between express warranties and another implied warranty, the implied warranty of fitness for a particular purpose, are also not uncommon.

[1] Products Liability — Warranty vs. Tort Standard

One of the more interesting questions concerning the merchantability standard is its comparison with the tort standard of a defective product in a products liability case. While warranty theory was popular when a tort action had to be based on negligence, with the widespread adoption of a strict liability standard in RESTATEMENT 2D OF TORTS Section 402A, the future of warranty theory in such cases was placed in some doubt. While there are several differences between warranty and tort theory,[58] one of the more difficult issues is whether the concept of "defect" in torts is coextensive with the warranty standard of "unmerchantability." Some courts have insisted that the standards are different, thereby suggesting that a jury could discover no violation of the tort standard based upon a "risk/utility" analysis while finding a violation of the warranty standard of reasonable consumer expectations.[59]

[2] Merchantability — Leases — CISG

There is an implied warranty for leases of goods that replicates the UCC warranty for sales of goods.[60] The merchantability warranty, however, does not apply to "finance leases" where the only role of the lessor is to provide financing for the product desired and selected by the lessee.[61] For international sales of goods, CISG requires goods to be "fit for the purposes for which goods of the same description would ordinarily be used,"[62] which is very similar to the central UCC standard.[63]

---

[56] *See* Shaffer v. Victoria Station, Inc., 91 Wash. 2d 295, 588 P.2d 233 (1978) (wine glass broke in plaintiff's hand).

[57] Hauter v. Zogarts, 14 Cal. 3d 104, 109, 120 Cal. Rptr. 681, 683, 534 P.2d 377, 379 (1975), where the court found a breach of the implied warranty of merchantability, *inter alia*, via § 2-314(2)(f) dealing with statements on the container or label.

[58] For example, there are "privity" limitations in warranty theory that are not uniform among the states. See Hyundai Motor America, Inc. v. Goodin, 822 N. E. 2d 947 (Ind. 2005). The typical statute of limitations for a tort action will run from the time of the injury, though it is much shorter in duration, while the warranty statute of limitations under UCC § 2-725 is four years from the time the goods are delivered, regardless of the aggrieved party's lack of knowledge of the breach. There are notice provisions under the UCC (§ 2-607(3)) that do not apply to tort actions.

[59] *See* Castro v. QVC Network, 139 F.3d 114 (2d Cir. 1998), and Denny v. Fort Motor Co., 87 N.Y.2d 248, 662 N.E.2d 730, 639 N.Y.S.2d 250 (1995).

[60] UCC § 2A-212 that is identical to UCC § 2-314, except for changes to reflect leasing terminology.

[61] *See* Dudley v. Business Express, 882 F. Supp. 199 (D.N.H. 1994).

[62] CISG Art. 35(2)(a).

[63] UCC § 2-314(2)(c).

[D]   Implied Warranty of Fitness for a Particular Purpose — Inconsistent Warranties

If goods are merchantable and all express warranties are fulfilled, the seller may still be liable for breach of the third warranty of quality, the implied warranty of fitness for a particular purpose.[64] A product may be suitable for ordinary purposes but unsuitable for the special or particular purpose of the buyer. If the seller is unaware of the special or particular purpose for which the buyer seeks to use the goods, it would be absurd to hold a seller to a quality standard higher than merchantability. If, however, the seller is aware of the particular purpose of the buyer *and* the seller is aware that the buyer *relies* on the seller's skill and judgment in choosing a product for that purpose, the reliance of the buyer justifies the imposition of a higher quality standard. Where, for example, an operator of a mill purchased hydraulic equipment and asked his regular supplier of lubricants for a proper lubricant to be used in this equipment, the seller knew or had reason to know the particular purpose of the buyer. The seller also knew that the buyer was relying on the seller's skill and judgment in choosing the product that would suit the particular purpose of the buyer. The buyer then purchased the product recommended by the seller, which was a lubricant containing a detergent. Serious loss occurred when the equipment malfunctioned and much of it had to be replaced. The problem was eventually traced to the lubricant recommended by the seller. When a non-detergent lubricant was substituted, the equipment problems disappeared. There is no reason to doubt that the recommended lubricant was merchantable, i.e., fit for *ordinary* purposes. There is no reason to question the fulfillment of any express warranty with respect to statements on the container or other express warranties concerning the original lubricant. Notwithstanding the lack of any breach of express or merchantability warranties, the case is a classic illustration of the breach of the implied warranty of fitness for a particular purpose.[65]

Where a manufacturer encountered difficulty in painting the chassis of its products, it relied upon the skill and judgment of a supplier of paint to provide the paint and process necessary to correct the problem. When the process failed to produce the results sought by the purchaser, there was no breach of the implied warranty of merchantability or any express warranties. In fact, the seller argued that its compliance with all express warranties made any action for breach of warranty impossible because express warranties should displace any inconsistent implied warranties. Yet, the UCC is clear that express warranties displace inconsistent implied warranties of merchantability, but they do not displace implied warranties of fitness for a particular purpose.[66] There is no inconsistency between such

---

[64] UCC § 2-315.

[65] Lewis v. Mobil Oil Corp., 438 F.2d 500 (8th Cir. 1971).

[66] UCC § 2-317(c). This section sets forth a hierarchy of rules to deal with inconsistent manifestations of warranty. Thus, in § 2-317(a), exact or technical specifications displace inconsistent samples or models or general language of description (which is nothing more than the usual rule of construction that the particular normally controls the general). Section 2-317(b) is another illustration of the same concept, i.e., a sample from an existing bulk displaces inconsistent language of description. Then subsection (c) has express warranties displacing inconsistent implied warranties, but not the implied warranty of fitness for a particular purpose. It is, however, important to note that this section is "designed to ascertain the intention of the parties by reference to the factor which *probably* claimed the attention of the parties in the first instance." Comment 3 to § 2-317 (emphasis added). The comment then emphasizes the fact that such rules are only rules of construction, i.e., they are not absolute, and "may be changed" by showing that the construction called for by the rules is unreasonable. For a splendid example, see Stewart-Decatur Sec. Sys., Inc. v. Von Weise Gear Co., 517 F.2d 1136 (8th Cir. 1975), where the defendant seller submitted a prototype geared motor which the buyer tested. Satisfied with the test, the buyer ordered 1560 motors by purchase order, which

warranties since a product may meet all express warranties and still not be fit for the particular purpose for which it was purchased. The court found the elements of seller's knowledge of the buyer's particular purpose, seller's awareness that the buyer was relying on the seller to choose the product and process involved, and the actual reliance on the seller through the purchase of the products and process. There was an implied warranty of fitness for a particular purpose which the seller breached even though its products met all express warranty standards and, again, presumably, the goods were suitable for ordinary purposes, thus satisfying the merchantability standard.[67]

Courts do not always clearly identify which warranty may exist or has been breached. For example, in a case involving an eye injury cased by the shattering of the lens of sunglasses that were advertised as "baseball" sunglasses, fit for any number of different athletic activities not limited to baseball, the court found a breach of the implied warranty of fitness for a particular purpose, rather than breach of the implied warranty of merchantability.[68] Yet, baseball sunglasses are *ordinarily* used in playing baseball with all of the attendant risks. Consider a buyer of ordinary shoes or boots. Such a buyer is not entitled to shoes or boots suitable for mountain climbing. If, however, boots are described as designed for mountain climbing, they must meet the ordinary purposes of such goods. Thus, a claim against the manufacturer of mountain climbing boots for defects in the product should be brought on the basis of the implied warranty of merchantability rather than fitness for a particular purpose, just as a buyer of baseball sunglasses should be able to demonstrate a breach of the implied warranty of merchantability when the baseball sunglasses shatter when hit by a baseball.[69]

Since the buyer must demonstrate actual reliance on the seller's skill or judgment to establish the implied warranty of fitness for a particular purpose, the drafters of the Code clearly understood how to insert an express reliance element into a particular warranty section of the UCC. Because they deliberately chose to do so with respect to this warranty while deliberately avoiding the insertion of a similar or identical requirement in the express warranty section,[70] we see another reason why the earlier argument against requiring any showing of reliance with respect to express warranties appears sound.[71]

---

provided that the motors were to be as "per prototype" and to have input speeds of 1590 r.p.m. The seller delivered motors precisely in conformity with the prototype, but with input speeds of 3200 r.p.m. Section 2-317(a) suggests that exact or technical specifications displace an inconsistent model. Yet, the court recognized that § 2-317 is nothing more that a list of guides to assist courts to ascertain the probable intention of the parties. When, as here, the parties clearly intended to buy and sell motors of the prototype, that dominant intention should prevail and the court so held.

[67] Singer Co. v. E. I. Du Pont de Nemours & Co., 579 F.2d 433 (8th Cir. 1978).

[68] *See* Filler v. Rayex Corp., 435 F.2d 336 (7th Cir. 1970).

[69] See McHugh v. Carlton, 369 F. Supp. 1271 (D.S.C. 1974), where the court held that an action based on the implied warranty of fitness for a particular purpose did not state a claim upon which relief could be granted.

[70] UCC § 2-313.

[71] *See supra* subsection B.

[E] Warranty Disclaimers and Remedy Limitations Under the Uniform Commercial Code

[1] Warranty Disclaimers — May Express Warranties Be Disclaimed?

While the warranty of title may be disclaimed, we saw earlier that such a disclaimer must meet an extraordinarily high standard of clarity in the disclaimer language.[72] A separate section of Article 2 of the Code is devoted to safeguards against warranty disclaimers in relation to the implied warranty of merchantability and the implied warranty of fitness for a particular purpose. Before considering Code requirements for the disclaimer of such warranties, it is important to consider the question of whether express warranties may be disclaimed. In the section of the UCC captioned "Exclusion or Modification of Warranties," the first subsection[73] suggests that contract language or conduct creating express warranties and language or conduct negating or limiting such warranties is inoperative unless it is reasonable to construe such language or conduct as consistent. A buyer of goods should not be held to "unexpected and unbargained language of disclaimer."[74] It would, for example, be ludicrous to honor a clause generally disclaiming all express warranties. If given literal effect, such a clause would effectively disclaim even the express warranty arising from a description of the goods. In a contract for the sale of an automobile, the seller could tender a cardboard box without breaching an express warranty. If, therefore, an express warranty is found to exist, it may not be *disclaimed*. The UCC, however, carefully distinguishes the impossibility of disclaiming express warranties from the loss of such warranties pursuant to the parol evidence rule.[75] A statement amounting to an express warranty will be inadmissible if the writing of the parties is so final and complete that reasonable parties would certainly include such a statement of fact about the goods in such a writing.[76]

While express warranties may not be disclaimed, implied warranties are subject to disclaimer. The typical disclaimer of implied warranties is often contained in what may appear to be protection for the buyer through an express warranty. Thus, the garden variety clause will warrant goods against defects in materials and workmanship for some relatively short period, *e.g.*, 90 days. This express warranty would be superfluous except for the typical statement following it which may be phrased in any number of ways, but invariably looks something like the following: "SELLER MAKES NO [OTHER] WARRANTIES INCLUDING ANY WARRANTIES AS TO MERCHANTABILITY OR FITNESS EITHER EXPRESS OR IMPLIED WITH RESPECT TO THE PROPERTY."[77] This disclaimer illustrates *one* method of effectively disclaiming the implied warranties under the UCC[78] absent a showing of unconscionability.[79] Where the parties agree that such implied warranties will be

---

[72] See the explanation *supra* note 21, in subsection A. *supra*.

[73] UCC § 2-316(1).

[74] UCC § 2-316 comment 1.

[75] In § 2-316(1), the Code carefully conditions its directive: "but subject to the provisions of the Article on parol or extrinsic evidence (Section 2-202). . . ."

[76] This is the essential UCC parol evidence rule test as found in comment 3 to § 2-202.

[77] This disclaimer is essentially that found in Hunt v. Perkins Mach. Co., 352 Mass. 535, 226 N.E.2d 228 (1967).

[78] UCC § 2-316(2).

[79] In the discussion of unconscionability, *supra* § 97, we saw that the fulfillment of the UCC formula for a warranty

disclaimed in writing under this methodology, there are safeguards built into such disclaimers: written disclaimers of either type of implied warranty must be "conspicuous"[80] and, for the implied warranty of merchantability, the term "merchantability" must be stated.[81] Thus, disclaimer language is often found in print that is large, boldface, italicized, or some combination of these, and it invariably includes the term "merchantability."

Three additional methods of disclaiming implied warranties are also recognized in the Code. The use of "language which, in common understanding, calls the buyer's attention to the exclusion of warranties and makes plain that there is no implied warranty" is illustrated in the Code by the phrases "as is" or "with all faults."[82] While other phrases may be adequate substitutes, it is folly to use them instead of "as is" or "with all faults," which constitute officially approved UCC language.[83] There is no express requirement that such phrases be written or conspicuous, though the section language indicating that the purpose is to call the buyer's attention to the warranty exclusions and to "make plain" the fact that no implied warranties exist may easily suggest the requirement of conspicuousness.[84] The "as is" or "with all faults" method of disclaiming implied warranties may be seen as similar to another method, i.e., the disclaimer of implied warranties by usage of trade, course of dealing, or course of performance.[85] It is important to emphasize the concepts of usage of trade,[86] course of dealing,[87] and course of performance,[88] which were discussed in a prior chapter dealing with interpretation.[89] If any of these concepts is established as constituting a term of the agreement disclaiming implied warranties, there is no reason why such disclaimers should not be effective through this method since it is the very agreement of the parties that establishes the disclaimer.[90] In fact,

---

disclaimer would not preclude an overriding determination that such a clause was unconscionable, *e.g.*, a contract of adhesion or "no choice" unconscionability.

[80] UCC § 1-201(10), which defines "conspicuous" as requiring a clause to be so written that a reasonable person against whom it is to operate ought to have noticed it.

[81] UCC § 2-316(2).

[82] *See* UCC § 2-316(3)(a).

[83] Other language may be interpreted to be sufficient to disclaim implied warranties under this section. For example, "I accept the above described car in its present condition" was the equivalent of an "as is" disclaimer in Joseph Charles Parrish, Inc. v. Hill, 173 Ga. App. 97, 98, 325 S.E.2d 595, 597 (1984). Whether different language equates to UCC language, however, is a question of interpretation which can be avoided by the use of "as is" or "with all faults."

[84] *See* Woodruff v. Clark County Farm Bur. Coop. Ass'n, 153 Ind. App. 31, 286 N.E.2d 188 (1972): "The close interrelation of these two subsections [§ 2-316(2) and (3)] is manifested by their like intent to call the buyer's attention to the exclusion of implied warranties and it would do violence to their stated purpose to do otherwise than imply that excluding expressions like 'as is' must be conspicuous. This interpretation harmonizes with the basic purpose of the UCC which is designed to protect purchasers from surprise." *Accord* White v. First Fed. Sav. & Loan Ass'n of Atlanta, 158 Ga. App. 373, 280 S.E.2d 398 (1981); Fairchild Indus. v. Maritime Air Serv., Ltd., 274 Md. 181, 333 A.2d 313 (1975). Osborne v. Genevie, 289 So. 2d 21 (Fla. Dist. Ct. App. 1974). See, however, Gilliam v. Indiana Nat'l Bank, 337 So. 2d 352 (Ala. Civ. App. 1976), holding that such disclaimers need not be conspicuous.

[85] UCC § 2-316(3)(c) and comment 7 suggesting the relationship between this subsection and § 2-316(3)(a).

[86] UCC § 1-205(2).

[87] UCC § 1-205(1).

[88] UCC § 2-208(1).

[89] *See supra* Chapter 5.

[90] *See* Standard Structural Steel Co. v. Bethlehem Steel Corp., 597 F. Supp. 164 (D. Conn. 1984) (course of dealing for 62 years effectively disclaimed implied warranties); Oregon Bank v. Nautilus Crane & Equip. Corp., 68 Or. App. 131, 683 P.2d 95 (1984) (course of performance may effectively disclaim implied warranties); R. D. Lowrance, Inc. v.

this method is less likely to permit unconscionability or other overreaching.

The final method recognized by the Code for effectively disclaiming implied warranties is essentially a risk allocation based upon the fault of the buyer. If a buyer examines goods before purchasing them, he should have seen whatever defects were observable by a reasonable party in his position. No action for breach of implied warranty will lie with respect to non-conformities which the buyer ought to have observed.[91] In one sense, it is not accurate to speak of non-conformities under these circumstances since the buyer has, presumably, decided to purchase with an actual or presumed awareness of what he is purchasing. Thus, there is no non-conformity except one later alleged by the purchaser. The same analysis applies where the buyer has refused the seller's demand that he examine the goods prior to purchasing them. Here, the buyer has consciously assumed the risk of what would otherwise be one or more breaches of the implied warranty by refusing to examine the goods. He, therefore, assumes the risks of any defects which such an examination would have revealed to a reasonable buyer.[92] If a risk has been assumed, there is no warranty as to that risk. To suggest, therefore, that a warranty has been disclaimed through assumption of risk may be seen as inaccurate because the warranty never arose concerning that risk. Nonetheless, it is common to characterize such risk assumption as another method of "disclaiming" or "excluding" implied warranties.

[2] Disclaimers in Leases — CISG

The UCC allows warranties in leases to be disclaimed in a manner similar to disclaimers in contracts for the sale of goods.[93] Unlike its counterpart, however, the lease disclaimer section does not admit of an oral disclaimer and requires "trade talk" disclaimers, "as is" and "with all faults," to be evidenced by a conspicuous writing.

CISG deals with disclaimers in international sales of goods in an extremely frugal fashion. There are no writing or "conspicuous" requirements, no separate rules for different types of warranty (CISG does not create categories of warranties like the UCC), and no "safe harbor" clauses or other directives to use specified language. The basic CISG disclaimer concept is found in the simple proviso introducing the warranty standards, "Except where the parties have otherwise agreed. . . ."[94] The only supplement protects the seller from defects that a "buyer knew or could not have been unaware of" at the time the contract was formed,[95] which is similar to the UCC disclaimer by inspection, trade usage or prior course of dealing.[96]

Peterson, 185 Neb. 679, 178 N.W.2d 277 (1970) (implied warranties may be disclaimed by trade usage).

[91] UCC § 2-316(3)(b). *See* Hall Truck Sales, Inc. v. Wilder Mobile Homes, Inc., 402 So. 2d 1299 (Fla. Dist. Ct. App. 1981). Implied warranties, however, are not disclaimed if the defect could be revealed only by unreasonably stringent tests. *See* Henry Heide, Inc. v. WRH Prods. Co., 766 F.2d 105 (3d Cir. 1985). It should also be noted that the successful use of this method of disclaiming implied warranties has typically occurred with respect to used goods.

[92] *See* Richards v. Goerg Boat & Motors, Inc., 179 Ind. App. 102, 384 N.E.2d 1084 (1979).

[93] UCC § 2A-214.

[94] CISG Art. 35(2). See Norfolk S. Ry. Co. v. Power Source Supply, Inc., 2008 U. S. Dist. LEXIS 56942 at *14 (W. D. Pa. 2008) citing this treatise.

[95] CISG Art. 35(3).

[96] UCC § 2-316(3)(c).

[3]   Limitation of Remedies

Even if the buyer retains all warranties under a contract for the sale of goods, they will be of little use if the parties have agreed to limit the buyer's remedies where the buyer's damages suffered by a breach of warranty far exceed the limitation in the contract. The UCC, for example, permits the parties to agree to limit the buyer's remedies to a return of the goods and repayment of the price, or to the replacement of nonconforming goods and parts.[97] Moreover, the Code permits the limitation or exclusion of consequential damages unless the limitation or exclusion is unconscionable,[98] or if exclusive remedies in substitution of normal Code remedies "fail of their essential purpose."[99] These matters have already been considered in the earlier exploration of unconscionability.[100]

§ 102   CLASSIFICATION OF CONDITIONS

[A]   Overview

Conditions in contract law are classified in various ways. As to the effect of their operation, they are said to be either *precedent* or *subsequent*, though this traditional classification is rejected in the RESTATEMENT 2d of Contracts[101] We will explore the case law in this area and the RESTATEMENT 2d analysis. As to how conditions are created, they are often classified as either *express, implied,* or *constructive.* We will explore each of these concepts in this section.

[B]   Conditions Precedent Distinguished From Conditions Subsequent

[1]   The Fallacy of the Distinction — Form Over Substance

There has been considerable confusion created by the classification of conditions into those which are "precedent," as contrasted with those which are "subsequent." The typical description of a condition is that which has been stated earlier in this section, i.e., a condition is an event that must occur in order to activate the contractual duty to which it is attached. In this sense, all conditions are *precedent* to the critical activation of the duty since they must occur *before* the duty is activated. When stating a condition to a duty under their contract,

---

[97] UCC § 2-719(1)(a). *See* Asp v. Toshiba Am. Consumer Prods., LLC, 616 F. Supp. 2d 721 (S. D. Ohio 2008); Frick Forest Prods., Inc. v. International Hardwoods, Inc., 161 Ga. App. 359, 288 S.E.2d 625 (1982); Mostek Corp. v. Chemetron Corp., 642 S.W.2d 20 (Tex. App. Dallas 1982); Potomac Elec. Power Co. v. Westinghouse Elec. Corp., 385 F. Supp. 572 (D.D.C. 1974), *rev'd per curiam,* 174 U.S. App. D.C. 70, 527 F.2d 853 (1975).

[98] UCC § 2-719(3). Limitation of consequential damages for personal injury is deemed prima facie unconscionable under this section. As suggested in the earlier section dealing with unconscionability, *supra* § 97, unconscionability in this context will typically fail where the parties are commercially sophisticated. *See* AMF, Inc. v. Computer Automation, Inc., 573 F. Supp. 924 (S.D. Ohio 1983). If, however, there is a non-negotiable, material, risk-shifting term on a printed form supplied by a large corporate seller to a small, inexperienced buyer, unconscionability may be an effective deterrent to the enforceability of a clause excluding remedies. *See* A & M Produce Co. v. FMC Corp., 135 Cal. App. 3d 473, 186 Cal. Rptr. 114 (4th Dist. 1982).

[99] UCC § 2-719(2). See also Perry v. Gulf Stream Coach, Inc., 814 N. E. 2d 634 (Ct. App. Ind. 2004).

[100] See, in particular, *supra* § 97[B][2][e].

[101] RESTATEMENT 2d § 224 comment e; § 227 comment e.

however, parties may choose language that creates the faulty impression that the condition is "subsequent."

In the well-known case of *Gray v. Gardner*,[102] as part of their agreement to buy and sell a quantity of whale oil, the parties executed two written promises evidencing the buyer's agreement to pay for the oil. One promise stated the price at eighty-five cents per gallon but added a condition stating that, if a greater quantity of oil should arrive at a certain destination between certain periods of time than arrived at that destination between such periods during the previous year, "this obligation to be void." The other promise provided an absolute obligation to pay for the oil at sixty cents per gallon. The purpose of the parties was clear, i.e., the price of the oil would depend upon the amount of supply available since the greater the supply, the lower the price. The seller sought to enforce the first promise at the higher price. The condition in this promise was the non-occurrence of an event, i.e., a greater quantity had not arrived by a certain time. If there is no difficulty in proving the occurrence or non-occurrence of a condition, either party can sustain the burden of proof. In this case, however, it was difficult to prove whether a greater quantity had arrived since it depended upon whether a particular ship, the Lady Adams, had moored by a certain time. The court allocated the burden of proof to the defendant simply because the parties happened to state the condition in the form of a condition "subsequent," i.e., the parties had written the condition as if it defeated an already activated duty. The writing containing the promise to pay eighty-five cents per gallon was a simple promise to pay that amount *followed* by the statement that if a certain event occurred (more oil arriving than the previous year), the promise was void. The parties could have just as easily structured the writing by placing the condition *before* the duty, *e.g.*, "If a greater quantity of oil does *not* arrive than the amount that arrived in the same time frame the previous year, the buyer will pay eighty-five cents per gallon." If their writing had been in this *form*, the condition would be *precedent* in form and the court would have allocated the burden of proving the occurrence of the conditioning event (a greater quantity not arriving) on the seller.

Any condition may be stated either in the *form* of a condition precedent or condition subsequent.[103] Thus, in the purchase and sale of real property, the condition of obtaining the mortgage loan may be stated as (1) "If the buyer obtains financing of eighty percent of the purchase price no later than March 1, 2001, the buyer promises to purchase the described property for the purchase price of $100,000" (precedent); (2) "The buyer promises to pay $100,000 as the full purchase price for the described property. If, however, the buyer is unable to secure mortgage financing for eighty percent of the purchase price no later than March 1, 2001, this promise shall be null and void" (subsequent). The *form* of the condition depends upon the stage of the transaction to which it is related. *The question must always be asked, precedent or subsequent to what?* There must be a reference point in the transaction to which the condition is related.[104] Since a condition can be stated in either form, it is of critical importance to determine the status of a condition as a matter of *substance*. If an existing contractual duty cannot possibly be activated unless a condition has occurred, the condition, as a matter of *substance*, must be *precedent*.[105] In the case of the purchase and sale of the oil, the

---

[102] 17 Mass. 188 (1821).

[103] See In re Michener, 342 B. R. 428, 434 (D. Del. 2006), quoting this treatise.

[104] *See* Harnett & Thornton, *The Insurance Condition Subsequent: A Needle in a Semantic Haystack*, 7 FORDHAM L. REV. 220 (1948).

[105] See City of Haverhill v. George Brox, Inc., 47 Mass. App. Ct. 717, 716 N.E.2d 138, 143 (1999), where the court

duty of the buyer to pay the higher price of eighty-five cents per gallon could not possibly be activated until it was determined whether a greater quantity of oil arrived by the deadline established in the contract. If a greater quantity did not arrive by that time, the condition had occurred and the duty was activated because the substantive effect of the condition was to activate the duty to pay the higher price only if a greater quantity did not arrive in time. If it did arrive by that time, the condition did not occur and the duty was not and never could be activated so that the duty to pay eighty-five cents per gallon was discharged, leaving only the other obligation intact, i.e., the absolute duty to pay sixty cents per gallon. In the example of the mortgage loan, the identical analysis applies, i.e., the duty of the buyer to pay the purchase price could not possibly be activated until after March 1, 2001 if the mortgage loan for eighty percent of the purchase price had been arranged. Thus, *regardless of the form of the conditions, both conditions are, in substance, conditions precedent.*[106]

[2]   Burden of Pleading and Proof

It has been suggested that the distinction between conditions precedent and subsequent "has little substantive meaning" since the only effect of one characterization over another will be to allocate the burden or pleading and proof.[107] If there is no difficulty in sustaining the burden of proving the occurrence or non-occurrence of a condition, neither party should suffer by the characterization of the condition as precedent or subsequent in form. In the rare case where such a burden cannot be sustained by either party, however, the party upon whom that burden is cast will necessarily lose. To allocate the burden of proving the occurrence or non-occurrence of a condition on the accidental basis of its form as precedent or subsequent has never made any sense. Yet, courts continue this absurdity.[108] Thus, where a duty was conditioned upon the obtaining of a new lease satisfactory to the defendant, the court mechanically allocated the burden of proving the defendant's satisfaction to the plaintiff simply because the condition was in the form of a condition precedent.[109] It cannot be gainsaid that a

---

makes this point in correcting the lower court determination that the condition was subsequent when it had to be precedent to activate the duty.

[106] *See* RESTATEMENT 2d § 227 comment e: "Circumstances may show that the parties intended to make an event a condition of an obligor's duty even though their language appears to make the non-occurrence of the event a ground for discharge of his duty after performance has become due. . . . The language, in spite of its form, is interpreted so that the failure of that thing to happen is a condition of the obligor's duty. Unless that condition occurs, no performance is due." In addition to Gray v. Gardner, however, other cases have found substantive conditions precedent to be subsequent because of the form of expression used: Horn v. Brand, 133 Ark. 567, 203 S.W. 5 (1918); Root v. Childs, 68 Minn. 142, 70 N.W. 1087 (1897). *See also* FIRST RESTATEMENT § 259 comment b.

[107] Simeone v. First Bank Nat'l Ass'n, 971 F.2d 103, 106 (8th Cir. 1992).

[108] *See, e.g.*, Lerner v. Gudelsky Co., 230 Va. 124, 334 S.E.2d 579, 584 (1985); Schmidt v. J.C. Robinson Seed Co., 220 Neb. 344, 370 N.W.2d 103 (1985) (using RESTATEMENT 2d analysis but clinging to the precedent/subsequent distinction); Smith v. Government Employees Ins. Co., 558 P.2d 1160 (Okla. 1976). The determination of a condition as "precedent" is almost always substantively correct. The mechanical allocation of the burden of pleading and proof on this basis alone, however, is unsound. See also Stephens v. Fire Ass'n of Philadelphia, 139 Mo. App. 369, 123 S.W. 63 (1909), where a fire insurance policy exempted the insurer from liability for damage caused by an explosion which was not preceded by a fire. *Held:* the fact of the explosion preceding the fire was a condition subsequent and since the fact was uncertain, the insurer could not sustain the burden of proving the condition and was liable for the loss. See, however, Harris-Teeter Supermarkets, Inc. v. Hampton, 76 N.C. App. 649, 652, 334 S.E.2d 81, 83 (1985): "[W]hether conditions are conditions precedent or conditions subsequent depends entirely upon the intention of the parties shown by the contract, as construed in the light of the circumstances of the case, the nature of the contract, the relation of the parties thereto, and other evidence admissible to aid the court in determining the intention of the parties."

[109] K & K Pharmacy, Inc. v. Barta, 222 Neb. 215, 382 N.W.2d 363 (1986).

party is in a much better position to prove a lack of his own satisfaction. While the burden of pleading has been alleviated by permitting a general averment that conditions have been performed,[110] the burden of proof should be allocated on the rational basis of which party is in a better position to sustain the burden.

[3]   A "True" Condition Subsequent

A true substantive condition subsequent may exist in a rare case. The typical example is a fire insurance policy which, like all such policies, is necessarily conditioned on the occurrence of a fire damaging the insured premises. The fire and consequent loss is a condition precedent to the duty of the insurance company to pay for the loss. Such a policy, however, may contain a clause stating that no action of any kind may be brought against the insurer unless such action shall be commenced within twelve months after the loss.[111] Upon the occurrence of the fire, the condition precedent to the duty of the insurer to pay has occurred, activating that duty. When the insurer refuses to perform that activated duty, the insured's cause of action is said to be conditioned upon bringing that action within twelve months from the time of the loss. The failure of that condition to occur discharges the previously activated duty of the insurer and, in that sense, it may be termed a condition subsequent.

Even the discovery of a "true" condition subsequent provides no justification for the typical case which characterizes conditions precedent as subsequent simply because of the form in which they are stated.[112] Again, the allocation of the burden of pleading and proving the occurrence of the condition should not automatically follow from the characterization of conditions as precedent or subsequent.

[4]   RESTATEMENT 2d Analysis — Event That Terminates a Duty

The RESTATEMENT 2d seeks to avoid these characterization problems by dispensing with the "precedent" and "subsequent" labels.[113] It insists that the only true condition is a condition precedent and since all conditions are precedent, it eliminates the characterization by simply calling them "conditions," all of which must occur (unless excused) before performance under a contract becomes due, i.e., before the duty to which the condition is attached is activated. If the parties provide that the occurrence of an event will extinguish an activated duty (using the example above of the failure to commence an action within a prescribed time), the RESTATEMENT 2d rejects the appellation, "condition subsequent," since such an event is not a condition at all;

---

[110] *See* Trevino v. Allstate Ins. Co., 651 S.W.2d 8 (Tex. App. Dallas 1983) (where plaintiff avers generally that all conditions have been performed, he is then required to prove the performance of only those conditions specifically denied by the defendant; thus, the rule operates to shift the burden of pleading to the defendant, but not the burden of proof). *See also* FED. R. CIV. P. 19.

[111] *See, e.g.,* Northwestern Nat'l Life Ins. Co. v. Ward, 56 Okla. 188, 155 P. 524 (1916).

[112] See also Rutherford v. John O'Lexey's Boat & Yacht Ins., 118 Ariz. 380, 382, 576 P.2d 1380, 1382 (Ct. App. 1978), where an insurer promised temporary coverage on condition that the insured submit a completed application by a certain date and the court construed the condition as a condition subsequent because "completion of the application by Monday was a condition that had to be performed before [the insurer] had any duty to perform." Presumably, the court was suggesting that the condition had to occur before the duty of the insurer was activated. It clearly appears that the duty of the insurer under an existing contract of insurance was conditioned on the submission of a completed application. Therefore, it was a condition precedent and the court's own language suggests the legal effect of a condition precedent. Yet, it characterizes the condition as a condition subsequent, citing the FIRST RESTATEMENT § 250.

[113] *See* RESTATEMENT 2d § 224 comment e.

rather, it is *an event that terminates a duty.*[114] If the event occurs, the formerly activated duty is discharged. The rule, however, is subject to certain exceptions. Thus, if the event occurs because the obligor breached his general obligation of good faith or fair dealing, or if the event could not have been prevented because of impracticability and the obligor is not subjected to a materially increased burden because of the continuance of the duty,[115] or, finally, if the obligor promises to perform his duty even if the event occurs and does not revoke that promise before the obligee materially changes his position in reliance on the promise,[116] the duty of the obligor is not discharged even though the event occurs.

In an early application of the new RESTATEMENT analysis,[117] a homeowner signed a contract with an aluminum siding contractor promising to pay for the new siding subject to the following condition: "This contract null and void if customer cannot get disability and death and sickness insurance." The homeowner was recuperating at home and anticipating a return to work when the contract was signed. Shortly after it was signed, the contractor arrived to perform the work but was told by the homeowner not to commence the work. The contractor reappeared to commence the work and the homeowner again refused to permit the work to begin. Conversations then occurred between the contractor's workmen and the agent who had procured the contract, as well as an insurance agent, resulting in the homeowner permitting the work to be done. The homeowner returned to his job but became disabled again after only ten days. He then discovered that he was unable to procure disability insurance. The work had been completed and the contractor sought payment. The homeowner claimed that his inability to procure disability insurance discharged his obligation under the contract. Notwithstanding its scrupulous effort to apply the RESTATEMENT 2d analysis, the court concluded that the disability insurance clause that had been inserted by the homeowner was a condition because it referred to an event not certain to occur.[118] Yet, the event set forth in the clause was characterized as a "negative condition," i.e., "an Event that Terminates a Duty, formerly a 'Condition Subsequent.' "[119] The court found that no waiver of the condition had occurred. The contractor had performed with full knowledge of the clause, it was not impracticable to await performance until the determination of the procuring of disability insurance could be made, the homeowner operated in good faith, and the obligor never promised to pay if he did not receive the insurance. Therefore, the event (not procuring the insurance) had occurred. Thus, the duty of the homeowner to pay was terminated. Such a characterization, however, is unsound. There was a positive event — a condition — that had to occur before the homeowner's duty to pay was activated. That condition — procuring disability insurance — did not occur and the duty never was or could be activated after the death of the homeowner. Thus, the duty was discharged. The court's analysis arrives at this conclusion in holding that the contractor simply made a "poor" bargain and was not even entitled to quasi-contractual relief. Since there was no difficulty in proving the occurrence of the event, burden of pleading and proof issues were not raised in this case, but the confusion between conditions "precedent" and "subsequent" continues. Confusion in this terminology was more recently recognized in Texas law where the two types of conditions are "lumped together," inducing the court to suggest the best approach is found in

---

[114] RESTATEMENT 2d § 230.

[115] RESTATEMENT 2d § 230(2).

[116] RESTATEMENT 2d § 230(3).

[117] Cambria Sav. & Loan Ass'n v. Estate of Gross, 294 Pa. Super. 351, 439 A.2d 1236 (1982).

[118] 249 Pa. Super. at 357, 439 A.2d at 1239 (citing RESTATEMENT 2d § 224).

[119] *Id.*

the Restatement 2d relegation of "condition" to substantive conditions precedent.[120] The RESTATEMENT 2d analysis, however, has been called "semantic" by one court,[121] and others appear to pay lip service to the new characterization while continuing to use the "condition subsequent" terminology.[122] If, however, the RESTATEMENT 2d fails in its effort to rid contract law of the "condition subsequent" terminology, no perceptible societal change will occur. It would have been helpful for the RESTATEMENT 2d to deal clearly with the only significant question in the "precedent"/"subsequent" dilemma, i.e., the procedural question of the burden of pleading and proof. In fairness to the RESTATEMENT drafters, however, they are constrained by some existing law that can be "restated." Here, they had no desirable law-not even an extreme minority view-upon which they could fashion an effective RESTATEMENT principle concerning that issue.

[C]   Express, Implied, and Constructive Conditions Distinguished

A condition is created by either of two methods: (1) the parties have manifested an intention (by words or conduct) that the duty to render a promised performance shall be subject to the occurrence of some fact or event other than a mere lapse of time; (2) a court, in the interests of equity and justice, determines that a contractual duty should be subject to a condition even though the parties have manifested no such intention. Where a condition is created by the first method, the manifested intention of the parties, it is an *express* condition.[123] It is a "real" condition established by the agreement of the parties as manifested by their words or conduct. Where the intention is discovered in their conduct, the condition may be said to be "implied in fact." Where a condition is created under the second method, i.e., by a court reading conditions into a contract for reasons of its own notwithstanding the lack of any manifested words or conduct of the parties, such a condition is called a *constructive* condition (sometimes referred to as an "implied in law" condition).[124]

This classification has not been uniformly accepted. Some courts and writers insist on a classification including express conditions, by which they mean conditions created by the *words* of the parties, implied-in-fact conditions, meaning conditions created by the manifested *conduct* of the parties, and implied-in-law conditions, meaning conditions created by courts to achieve just results.[125] Such a classification may lead to confusion in distinguishing so-called implied-in-fact from implied-in-law conditions. Moreover, there is no utility in distinguishing express and implied-in-fact conditions since both have their basis in the manifested intention of the parties, the only difference growing out of the manner in which that manifestation

---

[120] Cedyco Corp. v. Petroquest Energy, LLC, 497 F.3d 485, 489, note 3 (5th Cir. 2007).

[121] Redux v. Commercial Union Ins. Co., 1995 U.S. Dist. LEXIS 2545, at *10 (D. Kan. Feb. 7, 1995).

[122] For example, Chromium Indus. v. Milwaukee Boiler Mfg. Co., 204 Wis. 2d 110, 552 N.W.2d 898, 1996 Wisc. App. LEXIS 963, at *6 (Wis. Ct. App. 1996):"[L]iability may be avoided by the satisfaction of a condition subsequent . . . or, in the terminology of the Restatement (Second) of Contracts § 230, an event that terminates a duty." *See also* McGrath v. Rhode Island Retirement Bd., 906 F. Supp. 749, 761 (D.R.I. 1995), *aff'd*, 88 F.3d 12 (1st Cir. 1996): "In contract terms, Cranston's continued involvement in the Retirement System functioned as an implied condition subsequent; Cranston's withdrawal would have excused the state's contractual obligations to McGrath. See Restatement (Second) of Contracts, § 230 ('Event That Terminates a Duty')."

[123] *See* RESTATEMENT 2d § 226 comment a.

[124] *See* RESTATEMENT 2d § 226 comment c. *See also* Holloway v. Jackson, 412 So. 2d 774, 777 (Ala. 1982) (quoting the FIRST RESTATEMENT § 253: "[A] 'constructive condition' is a condition that is such because of a rule of law, and is not based on interpretation of a promise or agreement.").

[125] *See* G. COSTIGAN, THE PERFORMANCE OF CONTRACTS 7 (2d ed. 1927).

occurs. Whether expressed in words or through other conduct, the condition can properly be called "express." The only significant distinction, therefore, is the distinction between those conditions that are manifested by words or conduct and those which are added by the court. Thus, the distinction set forth in the text between express and constructive conditions is not only more simple, it is more accurate and clear.[126]

Since express conditions result from a manifestation of intention, it is clear that the only difficulty likely to arise in determining their existence and operation is one of interpretation. On the other hand, the problem of determining the existence of a constructive condition is wholly different. It is not a question of interpretation; rather, it is a question of whether the court should construct a condition in order to achieve equity and justice in a situation not foreseen by the parties. While these two kinds of conditions are distinct in theory, in practice it is not always easy to distinguish them. First, the manifestations of intention in a particular case are frequently so uncertain that it is difficult to determine whether a court may justifiably find that the parties intended a condition though it may be clear that finding a condition would be desirable regardless of their manifested intention. In this situation, the discovery of a condition can be justified on either of two theories (express or constructive) and the court is likely to ignore the distinction in discovering a condition. Second, earlier courts were not willing to admit that they could "make a contract" for the parties though they frequently did so, disguising their operation under the fiction of interpretation. Modern courts, however, are much more willing to admit that conditions may be found to exist, notwithstanding the manifested intention of the parties.[127] Yet, it is still not always clear whether the court has discovered a condition from the intention of the parties or from the necessity of a just and equitable result.

A franchise agreement provided that the agreement could be terminated if the franchisee was in breach, but it was silent as to whether it could be terminated by the franchisee where the franchisor had breached. The franchisor had committed many breaches, but the franchisee could not establish damages. The court held that the failures of the franchisor to perform were not only breaches of its duties, but failures of conditions precedent to the activation of the franchisee's duties. Otherwise, the franchisee would be left remediless.[128] This judicial effort suggests a combination of discovering a condition which may have been part of the contemplation of the parties at the time of contract formation and establishing the condition to avoid manifest injustice to the franchisee.

§ 103   INTERPRETATION — PROMISE VERSUS CONDITION

To determine whether a particular provision in a contract is an express condition, i.e., one intended by the parties to qualify a duty rather than a promise to create a duty, it is necessary to interpret the expression of the parties, and the usual guides to interpretation prevail.[129]

---

[126] For a case adopting this analysis as it appeared in the second edition of this book, see Dorn v. Stanhope Steel, Inc., 368 Pa. Super. 557, 534 A.2d 798 (1987).

[127] *See, e.g.*, Seman v. First State Bank of Eden Prairie, 394 N.W.2d 557 (Minn. Ct. App. 1986) (court found bank's duty to stop payment on a cashier's check subject to condition implied by the court that the purchaser provide a legally sufficient reason to the bank for stopping payment because of the nature of a cashier's check, i.e., it is viewed as more trustworthy than a personal check).

[128] United Campgrounds, U. S. A. v. Stevenson, 175 Mont. 17, 571 P.2d 1161 (1977).

[129] *See supra* Chapter 5, §§ 87–91.

Where, for example, the Internal Revenue Service agreed to pay an informant a certain percentage of an award "on the same day" the information was provided, the court applied the usual rule of interpretation that all parts of the agreement had to be considered and the repeated reference to "collection" throughout the agreement created a condition of collection of the defaulting taxpayer's liability that had to occur to activate the duty to pay the informant.[130] Beyond the usual rules of interpretation, there are certain policy considerations that influence the interpretation of the parties' expressions which have given rise to what the RESTATEMENT 2d calls "Standards of Preference with Regard to Conditions."[131] It is important to consider clusters of cases which illustrate the judicial effort to interpret expressions as conditions or promises with regard to these preferences.

[A]   The Avoidance of Forfeiture

One of the maxims often repeated in contract law is that the law abhors forfeitures.[132] Forfeiture suggests a penalty and contract law is not interested in penalizing any party; it is concerned with compensating aggrieved parties. Conditions may be viewed as drastic devices because their non-occurrence may result in a forfeiture of a right a party has earned by reliance or performance. Thus, where a contractor completed performance, the owner's duty to pay for the work was not activated because of a failure of condition.[133] Parties are free to make that kind of conditional contract within broad limits, and such agreements will be enforced regardless of forfeiture.[134] Yet, the abhorrence of forfeitures creates a proclivity in courts to avoid them through interpretation of the parties' expressions or, as will be seen in a subsequent section, by excusing conditions under certain circumstances. If the expression of the parties is phrased in unmistakable language of condition, courts will not be able to circumvent the operative effect of the condition through interpretation. There are, however, myriad cases where the language of the parties does not rise to that level of clarity. While courts approach the interpretation process in these cases under the traditional rubric of ascertaining the intention of the parties,[135] the overriding concern for the avoidance of

---

[130] Confidential Informant 92-95-932x v. United States, 2000 U.S. Claims LEXIS 201 (Fed. Cl. 2000). *See also* Certain Underwriters at Lloyd's London v. Clark, 1998 U.S. Dist. LEXIS 10458, at *12 (E.D. Pa. July 15, 1998).

[131] RESTATEMENT 2d § 227.

[132] *See, e.g.,* Stevenson v. Parker, 25 Wash. App. 639, 608 P.2d 1263, 1267–68 (1980): "This court has held the general doctrine that forfeitures are not favored in the law, and that courts should promptly seize upon any circumstance arising out of the contract or relations of the parties that would indicate an election or an agreement to waive the harsh, and at times unjust, remedy of forfeiture, a remedy which is oftentimes too freely granted by those who have taken no account of the misfortunes and disappointments which conditions, unforeseen and beyond a party's control, have raised as a bar to performance, however honest may be his intent. . . ." (quoting Spedden v. Sykes, 51 Wash. 267, 272, 98 P. 752, 754 (1908)).

[133] *See* Cambria Sav. & Loan Ass'n v. Estate of Gross, 294 Pa. Super. 351, 439 A.2d 1236 (1982), discussed *infra* § 102[B][4], text at notes 117 and 118.

[134] See A.A. Conte, Inc. v. Campbell-Lowrie-Lautermilch Corp., 132 Ill. App. 3d 325, 87 Ill. Dec. 429, 477 N.E.2d 30, 33 (1st Dist. 1985), where the court found language in a contract between a general contractor and subcontractor making the general's duty to pay contingent upon the general receiving payment unambiguous and, though recognizing that "courts will not construe stipulations to be a condition precedent when such a construction would result in forfeiture, . . . plain, unambiguous language contained in the contract binds the parties to a condition precedent." *See also* RESTATEMENT 2d § 227 comment b and § 229 comment a.

[135] "The parties to a contract are at liberty to agree upon a condition precedent upon which liability shall depend. Whether the doing of an act is a condition precedent depends, not on any hard and fast rule, but on the intention of the parties as deduced from the whole instrument." Partlow v. Mathews, 43 Wash. 2d 398, 406, 261 P.2d 394, 398 (1953).

forfeitures is invariably present.[136] In the exploration that follows, it is important to remember this overriding concern.

[B] Form of Expression — Favors and Frowns to Avoid Forfeiture — Preference for Promise

There is no particular form of expression required to create a condition, but the form of the parties' expression remains a significant factor in determining whether they intended to create a condition or a promise. Certainly, an expression such as "The parties hereby agree that the duty is subject to the following express condition precedent . . . ," though redundant, would create an insuperable obstacle for a court seeking to avoid construing such language as a condition. Again, however, even where parties intend to create a condition, their language may lack clarity. One court suggests that terms or phrases used to signify conditions include "on condition," "provided that," "when," "so that," "while," "as soon as," and "after."[137] Another court was convinced that a condition was present where the phrase used was "subject to."[138] It would, however, be foolish to seek a particular word or phrase as conclusive evidence of the parties' intention to create a condition.[139] Thus, if several clauses of a document begin with the phrase "provided that" or "provided further," which may be viewed typically as language of condition, but some of these clauses reflect the parties' intention to create duties and, therefore, suggest that the language should be construed as language of promise, the overuse of conditional phraseology will cause a court to reject the conditional characterization.[140]

Such drafting provides the court with a basis for doubt in interpreting the language. With some doubt established, a court may proceed to a rule of construction, i.e., *where it is doubtful whether language creates a promise or a condition, the language will be construed as creating a promise.*[141] This "rule" is simply a species of the general abhorrence of forfeitures.[142] If the language is construed as a condition, the failure of the condition to occur may cause a forfeiture. If, however, it is construed as a promise and the promise is breached, the promisor is liable in damages but will not suffer a forfeiture. A corollary of the "rule" that a construction

---

"Whether a provision in a contract is a condition, the nonfulfillment of which excuses performance, depends upon the intent of the parties, to be ascertained from a fair and reasonable construction of the language used in the light of all the surrounding circumstances." Ross v. Harding, 64 Wash. 2d 231, 391 P.2d 526, 531 (1964).

[136] *See, e.g.,* United Plate Glass Co. Div. of Chromalloy American Corp. v. Metal Trims Indus., 106 Pa. Commw. 22, 525 A.2d 468, 470 (1987); Rohauer v. Little, 736 P.2d 403, 409 (Colo. 1987); Wemhoff v. Investors Mgmt. Corp. of Am., 528 A.2d 1205, 1209 (D.C. App. 1987), *cert. denied,* 491 U.S. 906, 109 S. Ct. 3189, 105 L. Ed. 2d 698 (1989); Jones Assocs., Inc. v. Eastside Props., Inc., 41 Wash. App. 462, 704 P.2d 681, 686 (1985).

[137] *See* Vogt v. Hovander, 27 Wash. App. 168, 616 P.2d 660 (1979).

[138] Ross v. Harding, 64 Wash. 2d 231, 391 P.2d 526 (1964). *See* Shared Imaging v. Campbell Clinic, 994 F. Supp. 919, 924 (W.D. Tenn 1998), *aff'd per curiam,* 173 F.3d 856 (6th Cir. 1999), *reported in full at* 1999 U.S. App. LEXIS 6356 (6th Cir. Apr. 2, 1999) (the phrase "subject to" usually indicates a condition).

[139] As will be seen in the next subsection, terms or phrases such as "when" or "as soon as" are typically construed not to create conditions.

[140] *See* Southern Surety Co. v. MacMillan Co., 58 F.2d 541 (10th Cir.), *cert. denied,* 287 U.S. 617, 53 S. Ct. 18, 77 L. Ed. 536 (1932).

[141] *See, e.g.,* United States *ex rel.* Virginia Beach Mech. Servs., Inc. v. Samco Constr. Co., 39 F. Supp. 2d 661, 673 (E.D. Va. 1999); Howard v. Federal Crop Ins. Corp., 540 F.2d 695 (4th Cir. 1976).

[142] *See* Rohauer v. Little, 736 P.2d 403, 409 (Colo. 1987) ("Where, however, there is doubt as to whether a contractual provision is intended as a promise or a condition, it is preferable to construe the provision as a promise, thereby avoiding the potentially harsh effects of a forfeiture that can result in some cases by a contrary construction.").

resulting in a promise rather than a condition will be preferred is another "well settled rule of contract interpretation that conditions are disfavored and will not be found in the absence of unambiguous language indicating the intention to create a conditional obligation"[143] — another species of the policy against forfeitures. It is clear beyond peradventure that courts frown upon the construction of language as conditional and favor the construction of the same language as promissory to avoid forfeitures.

In keeping with this strong preference, courts are quick to seize upon promissory language. Thus, where the expression states that certain documents "shall be furnished the purchaser,"[144] or that certain parties "will furnish evidence" of a certain fact,[145] or that title to certain equipment "shall pass to lessor upon installation,"[146] courts are pleased to announce their interpretation of such language as promissory.

[C]   Performance Due After an Event Has Occurred — "Pay-When-Paid" Clauses

A number of cases have dealt with the construction of language where performance is said to be due only at a time after a particular event has occurred. Terms such as "when," "as soon as," "after," or the like are often used to indicate *when* performance (typically payment) is due. The language appears to be conditional. Yet, a contextual interpretation may reveal that the parties intended nothing more than to measure the time for performance, i.e., they did not intend to suggest that if a certain event never occurred, the promisor's duty would not be activated. Thus, where a party received valuable services for which he promised to pay "as soon as the crop can be sold or the money raised from any other source," the court held the money was payable within a reasonable time from the date of the promise though neither of the events in the promise had occurred.[147] This interpretation was made much more certain by the last phrase, "or the money raised from any other source," which manifested the promisor's intent to make an absolute promise to pay, merely postponing the time for performance to a later or more convenient time, without any intention to make the duty to pay conditional upon the occurrence of either event.

The RESTATEMENT 2d emphasizes forfeiture avoidance, i.e., where the event will occur *before* either party has relied, the obligee risks only the loss of his expectation interest and the language may be construed as an express condition. Where, however, the event will occur only *after* the obligee has performed or relied by preparing to perform, he risks forfeiture and is likely to have assumed that risk only if the event is within his control. Under those circumstances, it is doubtful that he assumed the risk and the event should not be treated as a condition barring the activation of the obligor's duty.[148] Notwithstanding some protestation following this analysis that the rule "is not directed at the avoidance of actual forfeiture and unjust enrichment,"[149] the thrust of the RESTATEMENT 2d analysis seems clearly and

---

[143] Logghe v. Jasmer, 686 P.2d 694, 698 (Alaska 1984). *See also* Lockwood v. Wolf Corp., 629 F.2d 603, 610 (9th Cir. 1980).

[144] Rohauer v. Little, 736 P.2d 403, 405 (Colo. 1987).

[145] *See* Mellon Bank, N.A. v. Aetna Bus. Credit, Inc., 619 F.2d 1001, 1006 (3d Cir. 1980).

[146] Southland Corp. v. Emerald Oil Co., 789 F.2d 1441, 1443 (9th Cir. 1986).

[147] Nunez v. Dautel, 86 U.S. (19 Wall.) 560, 22 L. Ed. 161 (1874).

[148] RESTATEMENT 2d § 227 comment b.

[149] *Id.* The explanation is that the intentions of the parties must be viewed as of the time of contract formation, i.e.,

pervasively directed toward that goal.

A promise to pay an engineer for his services "as soon as the plant is in successful operation," was followed by a clause explaining that, because of the expenditures in placing the plant in operation, disbursements had to be delayed until the plant produced income. In determining whether there was a condition of successful operation, the failure of which would have discharged the duty to pay the engineer, the court considered the engineer's original offer that contained a fee for his services that was not conditional. Since he later agreed to a counter offer at the same fee, the court suggested that it was unlikely he would have done so if the parties intended a contingent fee arrangement.[150] This rationale achieved the overriding goal of avoiding a forfeiture.

"Pay-When-Paid." vs. "Pay-if-Paid." A number of cases have dealt with the same issue in contracts between general contractors and subcontractors where the contract indicates that the subcontractor will be paid when, or within a certain time after, the general contractor is paid. Where the contract provided that the subcontractor would be paid, "provided like payment has been made by owner to contractor," the court emphasized guides to interpretation used to determine whether language created a promise or a condition together with a clear abhorrence of forfeitures: (1) a condition precedent is not favored and will, therefore, be given effect only through clear and unequivocal language. (2) In cases of doubt, courts resolve the doubt in favor of construing the engagement as a promise rather than a condition. Since the payment clause in this case was not clear and unequivocal, the court found that it created an unconditional promise to pay the subcontractor.[151] While language of condition such as "if and only if" or "unless and until" is necessary to suggest the parties intended a condition, but even the phrase "condition precedent" is no conclusive of that intention. There is no escape from determining from the whole contract whether the parties intended to transfer the risk of nonpayment from the general to the subcontractor.[152] Absent emphatically clear language to the contrary, the modern courts reason that the subcontractor did not assume the risk that the general contractor would not be paid. Thus, the language in the contract is viewed as merely establishing a convenient time for payment rather than a condition upon which any payment depended.[153] A rare exception appears in an older case where the appellate court was reluctant to disturb a finding of fact by a trial court,[154] or a

---

the test is whether a particular interpretation would have avoided the risk of forfeiture at that time and not whether such an interpretation would avoid actual forfeiture in a dispute arising later.

[150] North Am. Graphite Corp v. Allan, 184 F.2d 387, 87 U.S. App. D.C. 154 (1950). See also Hood v. Gordy Homes, Inc., 267 F.2d 882 (4th Cir. 1959), where the court volunteers the view that a subsequent agreement to pay a pre-existing debt upon the occurrence of an event is payable within a reasonable time if the event does not occur.

[151] Main Elec., Ltd. v. Printz Servs. Corp., 980 P.2d 522 (Colo. 1999).

[152] Sloan Co. v. Liberty Mutual Ins. Co., 2009 U. S. Dist. LEXIS 75955 at *19 (E. D. Pa. 2009). As the court notes, neither is a statement in promissory language ("payment shall be made") sufficient, alone, to conclude that the statement is a promise to pay rather than a condition. The interpretation must occur in context. It is, however, possible to draft a clause that leaves virtually no doubt that the parties intended to shift the risk to the subcontractor. The *Sloan* court quotes the clause from Fixtures Specialists, Inc. v. Global Construction, LLC, 2009 U. S. Dist. LEXIS 27015 (D. N. J. 2009) which repeats the term "condition precedent" and expressly rejects its construction as a time of payment clause.

[153] *See* Koch v. Construction Tech., Inc., 924 S.W.2d 68, 71 n. 1 (Tenn. 1996); Statesville Roofing & Heating Co. v. Duncan, 702 F. Supp. 118, 119–121 (W.D.N.C. 1988); Peacock Constr. Co. v. Modern Air Conditioning, Inc., 353 So. 2d 840 (Fla. 1977), and cases cited therein (payment due five days after owner pays general contractor).

[154] *See* Mascioni v. I. B. Miller, Inc., 261 N.Y. 1, 184 N.E. 473 (1933) (where the trial court found that the parties intended that the subcontractor would assume the risk where the language indicated that the sub would receive

court's adherence to the now disfavored plain meaning rule of interpretation, i.e., discovering "unambiguous" language of condition.[155]

§ 104   CONDITIONS OF SATISFACTION

[A]   The Meaning of "Satisfaction"

The parties may agree that one or both performances under the contract must be "satisfactory," so that "satisfaction" or "approval" becomes a condition to one or both duties under the contract. The essential problem with conditions of satisfaction or approval is the determination of whether the promisor has to be personally (subjectively) satisfied, or whether satisfaction as used by the parties was intended to mean objective satisfaction, i.e., would a reasonable party be satisfied regardless of whether the promisor was subjectively satisfied. As suggested by one court, "[R]easonableness and good faith are distinct concepts. A decision is unreasonable when it is arbitrary, capricious or lacking in evidentiary support. A lack of good faith, on the other hand, suggests a moral quality, such as dishonesty, deceit or untruthfulness"[156] Courts have viewed the problem as one of interpretation with a strong infusion of the avoidance of forfeitures.

A condition of personal satisfaction will not be implied.[157] If the language of the contract clearly and convincingly states that the duty of one of the parties is conditioned on the subjective satisfaction of that party, however, courts will apply the subjective test because that is the announced intention of the parties.[158] When a promisor's duty is so conditioned, the promisee assumes a substantial risk. An artist who creates a painting under a contract subject to such a condition is assuming the risk that the prospective buyer will like the painting. If the buyer does not like the painting though the painting is heralded by connoisseurs as a magnificent work of art, the condition has not occurred and the buyer's duty is not activated. This result may be viewed as a forfeiture of the artist's expectation interest. Yet, by assuming the risk that the buyer would like the painting, the reasonable expectation of the artist includes that risk. The artist did not agree merely to produce a painting that would meet workmanlike standards. Rather, the artist agreed to produce a painting that would meet the subjective satisfaction of the buyer. When that satisfaction standard is not met, the buyer's duty under the contract is not activated.[159]

---

payments after the general received payments, and the appellate court deferred to this finding).

[155] See A.A. Conte v. Campbell-Lowrie-Lautermilch Corp., 132 Ill. App. 3d 325, 327, 87 Ill. Dec. 429, 431, 477 N.E.2d 30, 32 (1st Dist. 1985), where the phrases included, "if payment for invoiced material has been received by" the general contractor, and "if payment for such labor and material so invoiced has been received" by the general contractor. A spirited dissent points out that the first illustration under RESTATEMENT 2d § 227 clearly suggests the prevailing view. 477 N.E.2d at 34. See also Brown & Kerr, Inc. v. St. Paul Fire & Marine Ins. Co., 940 F. Supp.1245, 1249 (N. D. Ill. 1996).

[156] Storek & Storek, Inc. v. Citicorp Real Estate, Inc., 100 Cal. App. 4th 44, 59, 122 Cal. Rptr. 2d 267, 281 (2002); see also, Kennedy Assocs. v. Fischer, 667 P.2d 174 (Alaska 1983).

[157] Incomm, Inc. v. Thermo Spas, Inc., 1991 Conn. Super. LEXIS 549, at *10 (Conn. Super. Ct. Mar. 12, 1991) ("[I]n the absence of such an express condition . . . a condition of personal satisfaction will not be implied by the courts.").

[158] "If the agreement leaves no doubt that it is only honest satisfaction that is meant and no more, it will be so interpreted, and the condition does not occur if the obligor is honestly, even though unreasonably, dissatisfied." RESTATEMENT 2d § 228 comment a.

[159] In Gibson v. Cranage, 39 Mich. 49, 33 Am. Rep. 351 (1878), the plaintiff was to make an enlarged picture of

Where the subject matter of the contract is art or another performance that necessarily involves personal taste or judgment, the inclusion of a condition of personal satisfaction, notwithstanding the possibility of forfeiture, is more than plausible. Whether a particular artistic performance is "satisfactory" does not lend itself to an objective test. Hence, the RESTATEMENT 2d permits the application of a subjective standard since an objective test is not practicable.[160] Where a painting was consigned to Christie's for auction sale allowing Christie's" to rescind any subsequent sale if in its "sole judgment" it determined that the sale may subject Christie's and/or the consignor to any liability, Christie's rescinded a sale of the consignor's painting to an art gallery which refused to pay when trade talk indicated that the painting was not attributable to artist Carl Wimar. In an action by the consignor, the court construed "sole judgment" as akin to a condition of personal satisfaction that only required Christie's to exercise the judgment in good faith.[161]

If the subject matter is normally viewed in terms of commercial value, mechanical utility, or operative fitness, rather than aesthetic qualities, courts are not inclined to apply the subjective standard simply because the language of the contract speaks in terms of "satisfaction." The strong policy against forfeitures compels courts to interpret such general "satisfaction" language as requiring the application of an objective (reasonable person) standard.[162] Yet, apt and convincing language may lead a court to conclude that the subjective standard must be applied even in a case that may be said to involve a performance that is normally subject to a reasonableness standard.[163] Absent clear language to the contrary, except where the subject matter involves aesthetic qualities, it is assumed that "satisfaction" or "approval" means satisfaction of a reasonable person in the position of the obligor, rather than the subjective

---

defendant's deceased daughter that the defendant "would like" and would be "perfectly satisfactory" to the defendant. The defendant did not like the picture and refused to take it or pay for it. The court suggested that, although the picture may have been excellent and the defendant ought to have been satisfied, under the agreement the defendant, alone, had the right to decide this question.

[160] *See* RESTATEMENT 2d § 228 ill. 5.

[161] Mickle v. Christie's, Inc., 207 F. Supp. 2d 237 (S. D. N. Y. 2002).

[162] See Employee Benefits Plus, Inc. v. Des Moines Gen. Hosp., 535 N.W.2d 149, 154 (Iowa Ct. App. 1995): "When a contract conditions one party's performance on the 'satisfaction' of another, there are two standards which can be applied to determine satisfaction: the objective reasonable satisfaction standard and the subjective personal satisfaction standard. Absent express contractual language indicating which standard to apply, the objective reasonable satisfaction standard is applied when the contract involves commercial quality, operative fitness or mechanical utility which knowledgeable persons are capable of judging; the subjective personal satisfaction standard is applied when the contract involves personal aesthetics, taste or fancy. When the express language or nature of the contract do not make it clear that personal satisfaction is required, the law prefers the objective (reasonable person) standard." (Citations omitted.) In *Kennedy, supra* note 156, a clause permitted termination according to the approval of the lender's representatives and the court applied the objective test because the matter was one of commercial value. *See also* Hall v. W.L. Brady Invs. Inc., 684 S.W.2d 379 (Mo. Ct. App. 1984) (economic value of structure as security for a loan involved commercial value and objective test applies). The RESTATEMENT 2d § 228 prefers the objective test where it is "practicable to determine whether a person in the position of the obligor would be satisfied."

n The FIRST RESTATEMENT § 265 suggested the same preference as noted in Aztec Film Prods. v. Prescott Valley, 128 Ariz. 402, 626 P.2d 132 (1981). See, however, Mattei v. Hopper, 51 Cal. 2d 119, 330 P.2d 625 (1958), involving an executory contract for the sale of land for a shopping center, providing that the buyer's obligation to consummate the deal was subject to the procurement of leases satisfactory to the purchaser. The court applied the subjective (honest satisfaction) test because of the multiplicity of factors which must be considered in evaluating a lease. *See also* Aster v. BP Oil Corp., 412 F. Supp. 179 (M.D. Pa. 1976), *aff'd per curiam*, 549 F.2d 794 (3d Cir. 1977) (satisfaction clause applied to sewage system held to require subjective (good faith) approval).

[163] See Ard Dr. Pepper Bottling Co. v. Dr. Pepper Co., 202 F.2d 372 (5th Cir. 1953), where the language indicated that the licensor's judgment (in good faith) would be sole, exclusive, and final.

satisfaction of the actual obligor.[164] Again, this preference is predicated upon the avoidance of forfeiture to the obligee and the consequent unjust enrichment of the obligor. It is, however, conceivable that a contract to perform an ordinary task, such as house painting, cement work, or carpentry, could produce a performance that an honest obligor would find unsatisfactory. While the ordinary individual may see little or no difference in how a door is hung or a wall painted, the trained eye of a carpenter or painter who had promised to pay for such services only if he were satisfied with them could discern defects in the performance leading to his honest dissatisfaction. If the language of personal satisfaction in the contract is emphatically clear, courts should not avoid an interpretation of subjective (actual) satisfaction in such a case, though protection of the performer's restitution interest in an appropriate case may be in order.

[B]   Subjective Satisfaction — Consideration — The Good Faith Standard

Where the condition of satisfaction is interpreted as requiring the personal satisfaction of the obligor, a question may arise as to whether there is any consideration moving from the obligor. After all, if the obligor may simply state his dissatisfaction and thereby escape the bargain, was he ever bound to any duty? While it is possible to discover case law finding promises conditioned on the personal satisfaction of the promisor illusory,[165] there is ample case law holding such promises to be supported by consideration on the footing that the promisor is committing himself to perform if he is, in fact, honestly satisfied with the performance.[166] Thus, in cases of the subjective satisfaction of the obligor, the question will often be whether the obligor was, in fact, honestly satisfied with the performance, i.e., did the obligor operate in good faith in stating his dissatisfaction.

If a defendant announces that he is not satisfied with the performance and will not pay for it, how does a plaintiff prove that the defendant is operating in bad faith?[167] While it is possible to discover statements of the defendant that he is, in fact, satisfied with the performance but will lie about his satisfaction because he is not satisfied with the bargain he made,[168] such evidence is rarely available. If the defendant has simply failed to examine the work, the condition of personal satisfaction should be excused because the defendant prevented its occurrence.[169] If the obligor has made statements to others that he is, in fact, satisfied with the performance, this evidence is admissible concerning his state of mind to

---

[164] RESTATEMENT 2d § 228. While the RESTATEMENT 2d prefers this objective standard, in matters of personal taste or aesthetic qualities such as art, it would apply the subjective test because it is not practicable to apply an objective test.

[165] See E. I. Du Pont de Nemours & Co. v. Claiborne-Reno Co., 64 F.2d 224 (8th Cir.), cert. denied, 290 U.S. 646, 54 S. Ct. 64, 78 L. Ed. 561 (1933). See also Gibson v. Cranage, supra note 159, where the court expresses some doubt as to whether a contract exists because of the satisfaction clause, but proceeds to hold that it did exist.

[166] See, e.g., Kennedy, supra note 156; Black Lake Pipe Line Co. v. Union Constr. Co., 538 S.W.2d 80 (Tex. 1976); Mattei v. Hopper, 51 Cal. 2d 119, 330 P.2d 625 (1958).

[167] The plaintiff has the burden of establishing the defendant's dissatisfaction. See Hortis v. Madison Golf Club, Inc., 92 A.D.2d 713, 461 N.Y.S.2d 116 (4th Dep't 1983) (a condition of personal satisfaction in an employment contract is generally interpreted to vest discretion in the honest, good faith judgment of the employer).

[168] See the statement of Judge Learned Hand in Thompson-Starrett Co. v. La Belle Iron Works, 17 F.2d 536, 541 (2d Cir.), cert. denied, 274 U.S. 748, 47 S. Ct. 763, 71 L. Ed. 1330 (1927), "The promisor may in fact be satisfied with the performance, but not with the bargain." See also RESTATEMENT 2d § 228 comment.

[169] See Hartford Elec. Applicators of Thermalux, Inc. v. Alden, 169 Conn. 177, 363 A.2d 135 (1975), where the

establish bad faith.[170] Bad faith may also be established if the obligor states dissatisfaction for reasons that were known at the time of contract formation.[171] Some courts will permit evidence of unreasonableness as an inference of bad faith.[172] If such evidence is admitted, however, there may be a tendency by the finder of fact to find bad faith simply because the decision of the obligor appears unreasonable. Though the mere statement of the obligor that he is dissatisfied will not be conclusive,[173] absent evidence of the kind suggested, it will be particularly difficult for a party to prove bad faith where the subject matter is aesthetic and the other party, after examining the work, simply announces that it does not satisfy him.

[C]   Third Party Satisfaction — Architects, Engineers and Others

Many construction contracts require the satisfaction of a third party expert, such as an architect or engineer, rather than the owner. Where a particular individual is named as the third party to be satisfied, the condition can only be met if that named individual is honestly satisfied, i.e., the court may not substitute its judgment for the good faith judgment of the third party expert.[174] Though there is a risk of forfeiture to the obligee where a third party must be satisfied with the obligor's performance, the preference for an interpretation to avoid the risk of forfeiture does not apply.[175] If, for example, a named architect refuses to grant a certificate because of honest dissatisfaction with the contractor's performance, the contractor cannot recover on the contract, even though he can produce testimony from other architects that the work has been substantially performed.[176] If, however, the architect's refusal is based on the fraud or bad faith of the architect,[177] or gross mistake amounting to bad faith,[178] the condition would be excused.[179] The failure of the architect or other third party expert to examine the work would amount to bad faith and the condition would be excused.[180]

Even if the third party expert is operating in good faith but either grants approval of the work or refuses to issue a certificate for reasons *beyond the scope* of his expertise, the condition will be excused. Thus, where an engineer granted his approval of defective work in a school building because he was motivated to permit the children to get to school on time,[181]

---

condition of personal satisfaction rested with a third party (architect) who refused to examine repaired work and the condition was excused.

[170] *See* First Restatement § 265 ill. 1.

[171] *See* Western Hills, Oregon, Ltd. v. Pfau, 265 Or. 137, 508 P.2d 201 (1973).

[172] *See, e.g.*, Volos, Ltd. v. Sotera, 264 Md. 155, 286 A.2d 101 (1972) (dissatisfaction with employee where contract required performance to be subject to employer's satisfaction).

[173] *See* Restatement 2d § 228 comment a.

[174] This view is widely accepted. *See, e.g.*, James Julian, Inc. v. State Hwy. Admin., 63 Md. App. 74, 492 A.2d 308 (1985); Elec-Trol, Inc. v. C. J. Kern Contractors, Inc., 54 N.C. App. 626, 284 S.E.2d 119 (1981); Brezina Constr. Co. v. South Dakota Dep't of Transp., 297 N.W.2d 168 (S.D. 1980).

[175] *See* Restatement 2d § 227 comment c and ill. 5.

[176] Moreover, an architect is not liable for directing an owner to terminate a contract unless the architect operates in bad faith. *See* Dehnert v. Arrow Sprinklers, 705 P.2d 846 (Wyo. 1985).

[177] *See* Austin Bridge Co. v. State of Texas, 550 S.W.2d 135 (Tex. Civ. App. Waco 1977).

[178] *See* City of Mound Bayou v. Roy Collins Constr. Co., 499 So. 2d 1354 (Miss. 1986); Arena Constr. Co. v. Town of Harrison, 71 A.D.2d 647, 418 N.Y.S.2d 3 (2d Dep't 1979).

[179] *See* First Restatement § 303.

[180] *See Hartford Electric, supra* note 169.

[181] *See* James I. Barnes Constr. Co. v. Washington Township, 134 Ind. App. 461, 184 N.E.2d 763 (1962).

the condition was excused. Similarly, where an architect refused to grant a certificate because he did not want to appear to be issuing it as a prelude to litigation, the condition was excused.[182] Unfortunately, the courts in these cases felt compelled to resort to traditional categories in holding the condition excused. Thus, in the school case, the court stated that the engineer had either failed to make an honest judgment or his judgment was based on a gross mistake. Neither rationale is correct. The engineer decided to operate as a school authority, which was clearly beyond his engineering expertise. Similarly, where the architect refused to issue the certificate because he did not want to appear to be issuing it "for a case," the court resorted to a finding of "constructive fraud."[183] This is another analytical failure since, again, the third party was basing his judgment on the desirability of avoiding litigation, which was beyond the scope of his expertise.

If the architect or other expert dies or becomes incapacitated to such an extent that he or she cannot make an honest judgment about the performance, the condition will be excused and a standard of reasonableness will be substituted.[184] If, however, the named third party is supposed to make a judgment of value concerning a work of art or other aesthetic quality for which there is no market price, the death or other unavailability of that trusted person may justify a court in finding both parties excused since their bargain was based on the judgment of that particular expert and no other expert will do.[185] Absent abundantly clear language in a construction contract, a court should not find both parties excused where an architect or other expert becomes unavailable. This is particularly true where the performance has conferred a benefit upon the owner or where the contractor can be said to have justifiably relied upon a performance that may not have conferred such a benefit. Again, the strong policy against forfeiture should continue to influence courts in their determination of when a condition is properly excused.

[D] Uniform Commercial Code — "Sale on Approval" — "Sale or Return"

The UCC recognizes contracts that permit a proposed buyer to receive goods and examine or test them before committing to accept the goods.[186] A buyer may not be willing to commit to a purchase of goods before testing or examining them to determine whether they meet satisfaction or approval. Typically, all of the terms of the contract have been agreed to, but the buyer's duty is conditioned on his or her approval. Even though the goods meet all warranty standards, the buyer has the power to return them if they do not meet his or her approval, i.e., it is a contract of *sale on approval*.[187] Where the subject matter of the contract is an "industrial machine," a Comment to § 2-326 states that the section takes no position as to

---

[182] *See* Rizzolo v. Poysher, 89 N.J.L. 618, 99 A. 390 (1916).

[183] See Anthony P. Miller, Inc. v. Wilmington Hous. Auth., 179 F. Supp. 199 (D. Del. 1959), which expressly regrets the using of "constructive fraud" on this ground.

[184] *See* Grenier v. Compratt Constr. Co., 189 Conn. 144, 454 A.2d 1289 (1983).

[185] See UCC § 2-205 comment 4, which distinguishes the trusted expert valuing a work of art and a named expert with respect to a commodity with a market price. The unavailability of the latter expert may not destroy the contract, while the unavailability of the former may destroy the contract.

[186] *See* UCC §§ 2-326(1)(a) and 2-327(1).

[187] American Natl. Bank & Trust. v. Matrix IV, Inc., 319 B. R. 553, 565 (N. D. Ill. 2005): "A transaction qualifies as a contract for sale on approval when the buyer has an unfettered or absolute right to return the goods irrespective of whether they conform to the contract." *See* UCC § 2-326 comment 1: "The present section is not concerned with

whether "satisfaction" should be construed as "reasonable satisfaction."[188] Similarly, once it is determined that the parties have agreed to a contract of sale on approval, whether the parties have agreed to a subjective or objective standard is, again, a question of interpretation for which the UCC provides no guidance. As suggested earlier, where the parties merely use the term "satisfaction," courts will be inclined to apply an objective test, rather than a subjective test, to avoid forfeiture. As in other matters where the Code does not expressly displace prior law, general principles of law apply.[189] Thus, the interpretation of "satisfaction" would presumably be "reasonable satisfaction," i.e., the objective test.[190] While the UCC recognition of the condition of personal satisfaction is reasonably clear in its "sale on approval" analysis, it is also clear that no sale of goods has occurred until the buyer accepts the goods, i.e., receipt and examination or testing of the goods does not complete the sale. "Acceptance" of the goods must be distinguished from mere "receipt" of goods.[191] The buyer's approval, however, may be inferred from conduct inconsistent with nonapproval, and if the contract states a time for approval, failure to notify the seller of nonapproval prior to the expiration of that period constitutes approval.[192] Even though the goods are in the possession of the buyer under a contract for sale on approval, until the buyer accepts the goods, the risk of loss remains on the seller.[193]

Sale or Return. It is important to distinguish a "sale on approval" from a "sale or return" contract. The difference is essentially in the intended purpose of the buyer. If the buyer intends to *use* the goods but contracts with the understanding that he has the power to return them if he disapproves of them, the contract is a "sale on approval" contract.[194] If, however, the buyer intends to *resell* the goods and contracts on the basis that he has the power to return any unsold goods, the contract is viewed as a "sale or return" contract.[195] A "sale or return" contract is often characterized as a sale on consignment. It is to be distinguished from a temporary entrustment of possession of goods to a bailee who has no intention of reselling them.[196] Among the more common issues relating to "sale or return" contracts is whether unsuspecting third party creditors may rely upon such goods in possession of a buyer under

---

remedies for breach of contract. It deals instead with a power given by the contract to turn back the goods even though they are as warranted."

[188] Comment 2 to UCC § 2-326. See Empire South, Inc. v. Repp, 51 Wash. App. 868, 875, 756 P.2d 745, 748 (1988). *See also* U.S. Nemrod, Inc. v. Wheel House Dive Shop, Inc., 120 Misc. 2d 156, 465 N.Y.S.2d 674 (Civ. Ct. 1983); *In re* Prior Bros., 29 Wash. App. 905, 632 P.2d 522 (1981) (whether the contract was intended to be a sale on approval was a question of fact for the trial court).

[189] UCC § 1-103.

[190] *See* Empire South, Inc. v. Repp, 51 Wash. App. 868, 756 P.2d 745 (1988).

[191] UCC § 2-606 deals with the three methods of accepting goods. These methods will be discussed later in this Chapter at § 109 D.

[192] Mahler v. Allied Marine, 513 So. 2d 677 (Fla. Dist. Ct. App. 1987).

[193] UCC § 2-327(1)(b). Normally, the risk of loss will pass to the buyer no later than the time the buyer receives the goods and, if the contract term so specifies, even earlier, *e.g.*, at the time of delivery of the goods to the carrier under an FOB "shipment" contract.

[194] UCC § 2-326(1)(a).

[195] UCC § 2-326(1)(b). *See* Summer Communs., Inc. v. Three A's Holding, LLC, 1999 U.S. App. LEXIS 3174, at *6 (2d Cir. Feb. 26, 1999). See also Charles Bloom & Co. v. Echo Jewelers, 279 N.J. Super. 372, 652 A.2d 1238 (App. Div. 1995), where the court makes this distinction in a difficult determination of whether the transaction before it was a sale on approval or sale or return.

[196] *See* Glenshaw Glass Co. v. Ontario Grape Growers' Mktg. Bd., 67 F.3d 470, 476 (3d Cir. 1995).

such a contract as collateral for the creditors' loans.[197]

§ 105 NONPERFORMANCE AND CONSTRUCTIVE CONDITIONS

[A] Nature of the Problem

Where parties exchange promises of performances, they typically focus upon the extent of the promised performances and fail to consider the effects of nonperformance. In particular, there are three situations which the parties may not consciously consider: (1) the order in which their respective promises must be performed; (2) what effect a partial failure to perform a promise in the required order, or a delay in the performance, will have upon the rights and duties of the other party; and (3) what effect the prospective inability or unwillingness of one party to perform his promise, in whole or in part, shall have on the rights and duties of the other party. A simple illustration helps to clarify these questions.

Suppose A contracts to work for B for one year at a salary of $50,000, nothing being said as to when, or in what amounts, the salary should be paid to A. In what order must A and B respectively perform, i.e., should A perform the work before receiving payment, should B pay in advance for A's labor, and, in either event, should A work for the entire year before being paid, should B pay the entire $50,000 in advance of any work by A or should some other arrangement be legally effectuated? If A fails to work, may he nevertheless recover the agreed salary? If A should be ill for a month and unable to work, what effect should this nonperformance have upon the rights and duties of the parties? If B should become insolvent, would A be excused from further performance? These and other questions are not to be answered through an interpretation of the manifested intention of the parties because the parties, in their words or conduct, have expressed nothing about them. The parties have not stated, either expressly or impliedly, what relationship was intended between their promised performances. This relationship, however, must be determined before any satisfactory analysis of the parties' rights and duties can be made where a dispute arises concerning performances under their contract.

Since the parties have not provided an express or implied basis to guide courts in determining the relationship that should exist between their performances, it is necessary for courts to *construct* such a basis. In constructing such a process, courts are "making a contract for the parties" and thereby departing from the principle that courts are only supposed to effectuate the manifested intention of the parties. If courts refrained from such construction, there would be no effective method to determine the rights and duties of the parties.

The process of construction used by courts is typically one of common sense. Thus, in a contract to install a guardrail in connection with a highway project, the guardrail installer agreed to a price based on a price quoted by a supplier with a time limitation similar to the time the highway was to be completed. When the highway contractor delayed completion by some nine months, the installer insisted upon a higher price since it could no longer procure the guardrail at the earlier quoted price. When the contractor rejected the higher price, the installer refused to perform. In an action by the contractor, the court held for the installer. Because it was obvious that the guardrail could not be installed until the site was ready for

---

[197] Such issues are discussed in sales, secured transactions and commercial law books and courses. For an illustration of the issues, see *In re* Flo-Lizer, Inc., 946 F.2d 1237 (6th Cir. 1991).

such installation, the court constructed a condition that such site would be available at the time for installation contemplated by the parties.[198] The condition was "constructed" rather than implied from the parties' expression of agreement through their words or conduct. Though the court refers to the condition as "implied," it must be taken to mean "implied-in-law" or created by law as contrasted with an implied-in-fact condition from the parties' manifested intention.[199] It is desirable to characterize such judicially created conditions as "constructed" since it avoids confusion with implied-in-fact conditions that are just as real as conditions expressed in words.[200]

In the sections that follow, we will see how courts have used constructive conditions to resolve numerous questions that are otherwise unanswerable through the manifested intention of the parties to the contract.[201] Before we explore how modern courts have constructed solutions to the kinds of nonperformance issues that parties typically fail to consider at the time they made the contract, however, it is important to consider how earlier courts dealt with these matters. After all, the kinds of questions to which these constructed solutions apply are fundamental to a determination of the rights and duties of the parties and must have occurred in the earliest contract cases. Moreover, as suggested with respect to numerous contract concepts already explored, a historical perspective is essential for reasons other than an understanding of antiquity. Unless the student of contract law understands this perspective, he will find it impossible to understand the modern solutions afforded by contemporary courts because he will not understand the purpose of such doctrines as constructive conditions of exchange.

[B]   The Origins of Constructive Conditions — Independent Covenants

The early law had a very simple solution for the problems suggested above. It took the view that the performances were *independent* unless the parties in express terms indicated that performance by one was in some specified way *dependent* upon performance by the other. This meant that each party to a contract of exchanged promises was under a duty to perform his or her own undertaking, regardless of whether the other performed or offered to perform, unless performance on one side was expressly made dependent or conditional upon performance on the other side. Thus where *A* promised to work for *B* for one year and, in return, *B* promised to pay him 20 pounds, it was said that *A* could sue for and recover the stipulated salary, even though he never did any work.[202] Similarly, where *A* promised to sell a cow to *B*, and *B* promised to pay fifty shillings therefor, both promises being absolute in

---

[198] R. G. Pope Constr. Co. v. Guard Rail of Roanoke, Inc., 219 Va. 111, 244 S.E.2d 744 (1978).

[199] *See* Holloway v. Jackson, 412 So. 2d 774 (Ala. 1982) (quoting First Restatement § 253 — the effect that a constructive condition is not based upon an interpretation of the agreement).

[200] *See* Restatement 2d § 226 comment c.

[201] See Onderdonk v. Presbyterian Homes of N.J., 85 N.J. 171, 425 A.2d 1057 (1981), suggesting that constructive conditions may be imposed where fairness and justice so require. See, however, United Cal. Bank v. Prudential Ins. Co., 140 Ariz. 238, 681 P.2d 390 (Ct. App. 1983), suggesting that courts should not read a term into a contract which would materially alter the obligations of the parties.

[202] Anonymous [1500], Y.B. 15 Henry VII, folio 10b, placitum 7; Langdell, Selected Cases on Contracts 461 (1879). Actually, this case, which dealt with an exchange of sealed promises, antedates the problems of nonperformance which became evident with the enforcement of executory bilateral contracts toward the end of the sixteenth century through the development of the writ of assumpsit. For an historical sketch of this development, see *supra* Chapter 1, § 4.

terms, it was held that *A* could sue for and recover the fifty shillings without showing that she had even so much as offered to deliver the cow.[203] *B* could also sue for and recover the value of the cow without paying or offering to pay the fifty shillings. Thus, for the purpose of enforcement, the law treated the two exchanged promises like two separate and distinct contracts. They were *independent* promises (covenants) bearing no relationship (dependency) to each other.

Such a solution is absurd. It exemplifies the primitive notion that the language of a transaction must be enforced literally in all cases. The absurdity of this literalism becomes evident on the slightest reflection. In the first place, the solution may result in two lawsuits, when one ought to be sufficient to settle almost any controversy that is likely to arise in connection with such a transaction. In the second place, it takes no account of the essential nature and purpose of a contract of exchanged promises which are obviously dependent on each other.

When two people exchange promises, these promises are the consideration for each other and comprise the contract. It is not, however, in the exchange of the promises that the parties are primarily interested. Their main interest in making the contract is to assure the performances of the exchanged promises. It is perfectly evident that the purpose of the usual "bilateral" contract is to bring about the future exchange of promised performances which are the agreed equivalent for each other, i.e., the performance promised by the one party is the agreed equivalent or exchange for the performance or performances promised by the other. The purpose of the legal concepts that deal with this problem should be to bring about the contemplated exchange, and to do it in such a way as to reduce to a minimum the possibility that either party will receive an unfair advantage. When this purpose cannot be achieved through an interpretation of the parties' expressions of agreement, an equitable adjustment must be discovered under rules which prevent unnecessary litigation. The early law wholly ignored these objectives and proceeded entirely on the basis of the literal language of the contract. It overlooked the pertinent fact that the language in which the contract was expressed was not always, or even usually, chosen advisedly with reference to the contingencies that might arise during the course of contract performance.

Courts began to realize that their simple solution of the problem was not a sensible one. Not being willing, at first, to overrule the old cases outright, they nevertheless took steps to discover some word or phrase linking the two promises in the contract, which could, with some show of plausibility, be said to make the one performance expressly *dependent* upon the other.[204] The language most commonly seized upon for this purpose was the word "for" and

---

[203] Nichols v. Raynbred, Hobert 88 [1615]. *See also* Pordage v. Cole, 1 Williams' Saunders 319 [1669].

[204] "But I expressed my dislike of those cases, though they are too many to be now overruled, where it is determined that the breach of one covenant, though plainly relative to the other, cannot be pleaded in bar to an action brought for the breach of the other; as where there are two covenants in a deed, the one for repairing and the other for finding timber for reparations; this notion plainly tending to make two actions instead of one, and to a circuity of action and multiplying actions, both which the law so much abhors. If therefore this were a new point, I should be inclined to be of opinion that, though where there are mutual covenants relative to one another in the same deed a plaintiff is not obliged in an action brought for the breach of them to aver the performance of the covenant which is to be performed on his part, yet that the defendant in such action may in his plea insist on the nonperformance of the covenant to be performed on the part of the plaintiff; but this has been so often determined otherwise, that it is too late now to alter the law in this respect. But where the words make a condition precedent or a qualification of a covenant, as the present case plainly is, all the cases agree that the plaintiff in his declaration must aver the performance of such condition or qualification." Willes, C.J., in Thomas v. Cadwallader, Willes 469, 499 (1744).

the phrase "in consideration of." If the performance was, by the express terms of the contract, said to be "for" or "in consideration of" the other, the court might hold that the one was an express condition of the other. Elaborate rules with many fine distinctions were developed for determining just when, in a given case, this language had the effect indicated.[205]

It remained, however, for Lord Mansfield to take the first major step in the direction of putting the whole matter on a reasonably satisfactory basis. The 1773 case of *Kingston v. Preston*[206] seems to be the first reported case in which a court held that performance of one promise in a bilateral contract might be *dependent* upon the performance of the other promise, even though there were no words in the contract that could be said to justify that result. Lord Mansfield apparently justified his decision on the ground that it accorded with the manifested intention of the parties. The case departed from prior holdings only in its admission that an apparent intention, though not expressed in words, to have one performance depend upon the other, might be given effect. Once this step was taken, it was but a short additional step to the view that such a condition might be read into the contract in the interests of justice,[207] though it might be clear that the parties themselves had no actual intention whatsoever in regard to the matter, and consequently had manifested none. This was in fact the ultimate development. *The modern view treats performances in a bilateral contract as dependent,*[208] except in certain special cases which do not concern us now. It is necessary to understand the nature of that dependency.

Courts frequently hesitate to admit that conditions are being read into the contract. The tendency is to conceal the true nature of the process under the cloak of a spurious interpretation — a tendency which unfortunately obscures the real nature of the problem and its solution.[209] This reluctance undoubtedly grows out of the historic view that a court must

---

[205] *See* Thorp v. Thorp, 12 Mod. 455 [1702].

[206] 2 Doug. 689.

[207] See the concurring opinion by Beatty, J., in Homa-Goff Interiors, Inc. v. Cowden, 350 So. 2d 1035 (Ala. 1977), suggesting that the doctrine of Kingston v. Preston is designed to avoid unjust results otherwise reached through literalism.

[208] *See, e.g.,* National Union Fire Ins. Co. v. Robert Christopher Assocs., 257 A.D.2d 1, 8, 691 N.Y.S.2d 35, 40 (1st Dep't 1999): "As a matter of long established law, the covenants of an agreement are dependent" (citing Kingston v. Preston).

[209] Thus, in Corn Exch. Nat'l Bank & Trust Co. v. Taubel, 113 N.J.L. 605, 616, 175 A. 55 (1934), it is said, "The tendency of modern decisions is to hold promises mutually dependent. The order in which the things are to be done, it would seem, is now a significant, if not the controlling, factor. While the 'older cases lean to construe covenants of this sort to be independent, contrary to the real sense of the parties and the true justice of the case,' the interpretation of such promises now rests upon 'the good sense of the case and the order in which the things are to be done.' The underlying test is the intention of the parties." (Citations omitted.) So also in R. C. A. Photophone, Inc. v. Sinnott, 146 Or. 456, 459, 30 P.2d 761 (1934), the court, in holding that a promise that was in terms absolute was nevertheless dependent, said, "Plaintiff relied upon the theory of independent covenant to pay. In determining whether covenants in a contract are dependent or independent, the intention of the parties must govern and this intention must be ascertained from the contract itself where the language is plain and unambiguous." *Compare* Lion Brewery v. Loughran, 131 Misc. 331, 226 N.Y.S. 656 (Sup. Ct.), *rev'd,* 223 A.D. 623, 229 N.Y.S. 216 (1928), where Justice Cotillo said:

> As I understand it, the doctrine of implied conditions in contract law is a creation of the courts, by way of judicial fiction, in order to give the defendant an advantage which logically and equitably should be given to him by way of defense. The doctrine of conditions implied in law dates back to the decision of Lord Mansfield in 1773, sitting on the King's Bench, in the case of *Kingston v. Preston,* cited in 2 Doug. 689. It is a creation of the courts in order to overcome the hardships of the strict enforcement of the letter of contract law. An express condition is, of course, a real condition actually created by the parties and intended by them, whereas the condition implied in law is an invention of the courts, created by the law in an endeavor to do justice by the parties. In other words, where an unforeseeable and unforeseen contingency arises

not "make a contract" for the parties in any respect — a view which cannot be supported on any rational basis if we are to have a workable law of contracts. As an original matter, it would probably have been wiser had the courts, instead of dealing with the problem through the medium of so-called implied condition,[210] frankly admitted that they were confronting a situation calling for an equitable adjustment of the rights and duties of the parties under circumstances they had not addressed.[211] Such a realistic approach would have facilitated the desired result and avoided the fictions and confusion which are all too evident in many of the cases dealing with these questions.

The way having been paved by Lord Mansfield's decision in *Kingston v. Preston*, modern courts developed various rules and principles of more or less general application for determining the relationship of the performances in bilateral contracts. These rules and principles will now be set forth. As suggested earlier,[212] there are three major questions involved in determining the relationship of performances where the parties have exchanged promises, i.e., the required order of performance, the effect of a failure or delay of performance upon the rights and duties of the other party, and the effect of a prospective failure or unwillingness to perform on the rights and duties of the other party. Very often in the solution of a given case, however, only one of these questions needs to be answered. Which of these questions is involved in the decision of a particular case will depend largely upon the point in the life of the contract at which the dispute arose. We will first consider those rules and principles by which the legally required order of performance in a bilateral transaction is to be determined followed by a discussion of the rules and principles by which we can ascertain the effect of a partial failure of performance, or of a delay in the performance, by one of the parties. We will then consider the effect of a prospective inability or unwillingness of one party to perform, either in whole or in part on the rights and duties of the other party.

A word of caution in regard to these rules and principles seems appropriate. First, the three sets of rules and principles mentioned are not mutually exclusive. They deal with different aspects of what is essentially one problem and may frequently be employed interchangeably. Second, it must not be forgotten that the problem involved is one of bringing about an equitable adjustment between conflicting interests after a dispute has arisen regarding a matter not provided for in the contract. This being so, all the surrounding circumstances of the particular case must be taken into account. It is, of course, evident that no generalized principle can take into account all of the circumstances of every possible case. From this fact it would seem to follow that the rules and principles laid down should be regarded as controlling only if the result they produce is equitable. It is more important that the result be just than a particular rule be applied. A careful study of the decided cases suggests that this is the attitude and practice of the courts.

---

which the parties, naturally enough, failed to provide for or to contemplate, the law in such an event will think for them along equitable lines, and will imply such conditions as would have been in the minds of the parties, had they thought of them." *See* Jacob & Youngs, Inc. v. Kent, 230 N.Y. 239, 129 N.E. 889 (1921).

[210] *See In re* Excalibur Auto. Corp., 859 F.2d 454 (7th Cir. 1988) (quoting 3 CORBIN § 632 to the effect that constructive conditions are neither express nor implied conditions).

[211] For a candid recognition of this process, see Computer Assocs. Int'l, Inc. v. State Street Bank & Trust Co., 789 F. Supp. 470, 476 (D. Mass. 1992), where the court recognizes the "omitted case" is not solved through "implication" or "inference." Rather, "A clearer and more candid explanation is to describe the process as 'extrapolating' from the contract." Such extrapolation, however, is not unlimited. Quoting from Lord Mansfield, the court states that "the answer must be consistent with 'the essence of the contract.' "

[212] *See supra* subsection A.

§ 106 DETERMINING WHEN PERFORMANCES ARE EXCHANGED UNDER AN EXCHANGE OF PROMISES — LEASE, ALEATORY, AND DIVISIBLE CONTRACTS

[A] The Essential Test

The rules and principles which we will explore are applicable to all bargains in which promises are exchanged for an exchange of performances, i.e., each promise and each performance is at least part of the consideration for the other.[213] It does not matter whether the particular bargain is expressed formally or informally, or whether it is expressed in one writing or in a number of separate writings. If the promises are exchanged as part of a single contract, the rules and principles apply. It is not always clear whether there is one contract or separate contracts when each party gives more than one promise or gives some performance in addition to a promise as part of the bargain. However, if every promise by one party is at least part of the consideration for every promise by the other party, there is only one, single exchange in which all of the promises on each side are exchanged for all of the promises on the other side. To determine whether there is a single contract or separate contracts, the court must consider the actual bargain of the parties rather than the form of the agreement.[214] There are cases involving two writings in which the courts have decided that there are two contracts notwithstanding the fact that the transaction was essentially a unit and bilateral in nature.[215] This view has been clearly abandoned. Currently, whether there is one writing or several, whether separate performances are the subject of only one promise or separate promises, or whether the agreement of the parties is entirely or partially written or oral, the form itself will not be conclusive. The test is whether the parties exchanged promises contemplating an exchange of performances in which each promise and each performance was contemplated as at least part of the consideration for the other.

Consider a fact situation in which X owns a viable business but is considering its sale. X is healthy and active and does not wish to retire, notwithstanding the sale of his business. He agrees to sell the business to Y for a consideration equal to the value of the business, which sale is evidenced by a writing. Moments later, X and Y execute a separate writing in which X agrees to work for Y for a specific term at a specific salary. When Y unjustifiably discharges X within one month, may X refuse to complete the transfer of the business to Y?[216] The determination of whether there is one contract or two contracts is highly significant. If there are two contracts, Y has breached the employment contract and X has breached the sales contract. However, if there is only one contract, Y has breached the single contract and X has not breached since X was excused from any further performance of his duties to complete the transfer of the business upon the breach of duty by Y. To determine whether the bargain of the parties manifests two contracts or only a single contract, the test suggested above is applied: was each promise and each performance contemplated as at least part of the

---

[213] *See* Crowley v. TVSM Inc., 1991 U.S. Dist. LEXIS 17558, at *9 (S.D.N.Y. Dec. 4, 1991). *See also* RESTATEMENT 2d § 231.

[214] RESTATEMENT 2d § 231 comment d.

[215] *See, e.g.,* Przyblyski v. Pellowski, 141 Minn. 193, 169 N.W. 707 (1918).

[216] *See* Rudman v. Cowles Communications, Inc., 30 N.Y.2d 1, 280 N.E.2d 867 (1972). *See also* Star Credit Corp. v. Molina, 59 Misc. 2d 290, 298 N.Y.S.2d 570 (1969); Continental Supermarket Food Serv., Inc. v. Soboski, 210 Pa. Super. 304, 232 A.2d 216 (1967).

consideration for the other? If the parties understood that X would not have sold his business to Y (notwithstanding receipt of fair market value for that business as evidenced in the separate writing) unless Y also agreed to employ X in the business for a certain term at a certain salary, the parties then contemplated each promise and each performance as at least part of the consideration for the other and there is one contract. However, if the promise of X to work for Y was no part of the consideration for Y's promise to purchase the business, and the promise of Y to employ X was no part of the consideration for X's promise to sell the business, there are two contracts since this is the bargain contemplated by the parties.[217] There are situations in which there is an exchange of promises where the parties do not contemplate an exchange of performances in the ordinary sense. It is important to consider these exceptions to the general rule that promises are exchanged for an exchange of performances. We will now consider three exceptional situations where the old concept of independent covenants reappears. The first situation, covenants or promises in leases, is predicated on historic accident. The second situation, "aleatory" promises, is an analytical exception to the general rule. The third situation, divisible contracts, is based upon the manifested intention of the parties to divide their respective performances into agreed equivalents.

[B]   Leases of Real Property — Constructive Eviction — Warranty of Habitability

A lease of real property may appear to be an ordinary contract where the lessor promises to provide such property for a certain term in exchange for the lessee's promise to pay a certain rent. If leases were viewed in this fashion, they would be viewed as other contracts and the promise to pay rent would be dependent upon the performance of the lessor's promise to provide the property. Historically, however, leases were viewed as conveyances rather than contracts, i.e., a lease created an estate or interest in land in the lessee rather than a mere personal right to enforce the lessor's promises. The payment of the rent was regarded as the exchange for the transfer of this interest in land. The lessee, therefore, received the material, agreed equivalent, or exchange for his promise as soon as the lease was executed. If the landlord rented a dwelling place and promised to keep it in good repair and to supply heat, light, and other normal incidents of such property, these promises or covenants, no matter how material, were viewed as mere collateral incidents to the conveyance. They were construed as *independent* covenants or promises. A failure of the lessor to provide heat or light, or other failures to perform his covenants were actionable. While the lessee could sue the lessor for nonperformance of these promises, the lessee was still required to pay the rent because the promise to pay the rent was an independent covenant which bore no relation to any nonperformance by the lessor. The rent was viewed as consideration for a past performance by the lessor (the conveyance of the premises) and not for the performance of any of the lessor's collateral promises. If the lessee stopped paying the rent, he could be evicted from the premises even though he could prove that the lessor failed to perform his promise to keep the premises in good repair[218] or otherwise failed to perform one or more

---

[217] *See* RESTATEMENT 2d § 231 ill. 5.

[218] *See, e.g.,* Duncan Dev. Co. v. Duncan Hardware, Inc., 34 N.J. Super. 293, 112 A.2d 274 (1975); Arnold v. Krigbaum, 169 Cal. 143, 146 P. 423 (1915).

promises set forth in the lease.[219] Unless the lease expressly made such covenants or promises dependent, they were construed as independent.

A typical lessee who rents an apartment or office space where heat and light are not provided, where the roof leaks, or where the failure to otherwise keep the premises in sufficient repair so that the apartment or office becomes uninhabitable may view the law as unjust when he is told that he must continue to pay the rent and his only recourse is to sue the lessor. He will take little solace in the historical explanation that rules in relation to performances in leases became definitely settled at a time when it was also the rule in other types of contract that mutual performances were independent, unless made dependent in express terms, or that leases were always viewed as part of the law of conveyancing dealing with a thing apart from the law of contracts.[220]

Where a problem in society is clearly exposed and the traditional legal reaction is flawed, courts almost invariably find ways to break the historical shackles which have bound them to untenable positions. The most dramatic and conclusive change would have been to treat covenants in leases the same as promises in any type of contract, i.e., to presume their dependency. Stability and predictability, however, are high values in any legal system and, absent any legislative change, courts are reluctant to overturn long vested concepts. Rather, they resort to covert tools to achieve just results. The first major fiction used by courts to accomplish this end in lease cases was the concept of "constructive eviction." The single warranty implied in leases at common law was the warranty of "quiet enjoyment." Courts used this concept to develop the principle that, where the continued enjoyment of the premises was so severely impaired as to make them untenable, the lessee could rightfully abandon the premises and stop paying the rent even though no actual eviction had occurred. Thus, where a landlord violates his express covenant to repair or to furnish other necessary services, courts are willing to consider whether such nonperformance is a material failure by the lessor to perform his covenants and, assuming sufficient materiality, the lessee may abandon the premises without liability for rent. The expressed rubric is "constructive eviction."[221] It is clear that the doctrine of "constructive eviction" is merely a device used by courts to achieve fair results. It is often accompanied by a statement that the covenant of "quiet enjoyment" has been breached leading to constructive eviction:

> There was an ameliorative exception to this otherwise harsh general rule which was known as 'constructive eviction': If the tenant's possession of the rented premises was so disturbed by unprivileged acts of the landlord that the tenant was deprived of their use, occupation, and enjoyment and was forced to abandon them, the tenant was viewed as effectively 'evicted' and his or her obligation to pay rent was discharged.[222]

---

[219] *See, e.g.*, P. J. W. Moodie Lumber Corp. v. A. W. Banister Co., 286 Mass. 424, 190 N.E. 727 (1934) (failure to pay taxes on the premises).

[220] For a judicial statement of this history, see Davidow v. Inwood North Professional Group-Phase I, 747 S.W.2d 373 (Tex. 1988).

[221] See, e.g., Charlotte Theatres, Inc. v. Gateway Co., 191 F. Supp. 834 (D. Mass. 1961), *rev'd*, 297 F.2d 483 (1st Cir. 1961), where the court viewed the inexcusable failure to provide air conditioning as such a serious or material failure of the lessor to perform that a constructive eviction had occurred.

[222] Napolski v. Champney, 295 Or. 408, 414 n.10, 667 P.2d 1013, 1018 n.10 (1983). "Constructive eviction" has traditionally suggested an act of a permanent character which the landlord intends (subjective intention is not necessary) to have the effect of depriving the tenant of the premises or part thereof leading to the tenant's abandonment of such premises. Wesson v. Leone Enterprises, 437 Mass. 708, 713, 774 N. E. 2d 611, 616 (Mass. 2002).

Another device reacted to the common law rule that, absent an express promise by the lessor, the lessor was not obligated to keep the premises in good repair. Recognizing this antiquarian rule as the product of an agrarian society which does not reflect contemporary housing patterns, courts have implied a *warranty of habitability* in residential leases.[223] The standards of this implied warranty of habitability may be analogized to the UCC implied warranty of merchantability,[224] or to extant housing codes which landlords are not free to ignore.[225] The warranty of habitability may also be created by statute.[226] Protection of lessees through the "constructive eviction" or implied warranty of habitability devices was facilitated where the lessee was a consumer rather than a commercial tenant. The consumer was often faced with a "take-it-or-leave-it" lease and the obvious inequality of bargaining power raised the specter of unconscionability. A number of courts, however, have been willing to use these devices to protect even commercial tenants.[227] The extension of these devices and other statutory and judicial protection of tenants is simply a manifestation of the basic issue recognized by an increasing number of courts, i.e., that leases should be treated as contracts and the mutual performances under the lease should be viewed as dependent or, in the more modern usage, constructive conditions of exchange.[228] While many courts cling to the antiquarian independent covenant analysis of leases,[229] with the continuous development of mitigating doctrines there is growing doubt whether the old analysis will continue to prevail. While the trend is clear, the current situation is fluid:

> Some courts interpret commercial leases as they would any other commercial contract; while others have taken a step in that direction by abolishing the independent covenants rule in favor of a rule of mutually dependent covenants. Still other courts have acted at the extremes, either by continuing strictly to apply the independent covenants rule, or by moving to the other end of the spectrum and recognizing an implied warranty of suitability in commercial leases. While we conclude that there is a need to move away from the rule of independent covenants, we continue to recognize that there are significant differences between commercial and residential tenancies and the policy considerations appropriate to each.[230]

---

[223] *See* Javins v. First Nat'l Realty Corp., 428 F.2d 1071, 138 U.S. App. D.C. 369, *cert. denied*, 400 U.S. 925, 91 S. Ct. 186, 27 L. Ed. 2d 185 (1970). *See also* Lemle v. Breeden, 51 Haw. 426, 462 P.2d 470 (1969); Pines v. Perssion, 14 Wis. 2d 590, 111 N.W.2d 409 (1961).

[224] UCC § 2-314. For a discussion of this UCC warranty, see *supra* § 101[C].

[225] *See Javins, supra* note 223.

[226] For a discussion of the Oregon statutes requiring landlords to maintain rental properties in habitable condition, see *Napolski, supra* note 222. *See also* MINN. STAT. § 504.18.

[227] See Richard Barton Enters. v. Tsern, 928 P.2d 368, 376 (Utah 1996). See also *Davidow, supra* note 220, where the implied warranty of habitability was extended to non-residential leases. See also Reste Realty Corp. v. Cooper, 53 N.J. 444, 251 A.2d 268 (1969), where a lessee of office space was said to have been constructively evicted when the premises were repeatedly flooded with several inches of water.

[228] *See Javins, supra* note 223, at 1075. See also Old Town Dev. Co. v. Langford, 349 N.E.2d 744 (Ind. Ct. App. 1976), *superseded*, 267 Ind. 176, 369 N.E.3d 404 (1977), suggesting that reevaluation of the lessor-lessee relationship was inevitable for numerous reasons, the most important of which was that leases were essentially contractual in nature. The RESTATEMENT 2d does not deal with leases in its treatment of constructive conditions of exchange. Rather, it refers the user to RESTATEMENT 2D OF PROPERTY § 5.1 comment a, § 7.1 comments a and c, and § 13.1 comment a. The FIRST RESTATEMENT § 290 contains a statement of the traditional rule of independent covenants.

[229] *See, e.g.*, South Forks Shopping Ctr. v. Dastmalchi, 446 N.W.2d 440 (N.D. 1989).

[230] Wesson v. Leone Enterprises, 437 Mass. 708, 718–19, 774 N. E. 2d 611, 619–20 (Mass. 2002) (citing cases). The court also provides a cogent summary of the erosion of the independent covenant concept.

Strong evidence that the antiquarian citadel of independent covenants in leases is crumbling is found in commercial leases that seek to retain them by expressly stating that the intention of the landlord and tenant is that, regardless of any damage or destruction of the building from whatever cause, the condemnation of the property, the prohibition or limitation of the tenant's use of the property any default of the landlord under the lease, or any other cause, similar or dissimilar to the foregoing, "the obligations of the tenant under this lease shall be separate and independent covenants and agreements, that the basic rent . . . and all sums payable by tenant under this lease shall continue unaffected. . . ."[231]

[C]   Performance in Spite of Nonoccurrence of Condition — "Aleatory" Promises

To this point, we have seen that, except for the historical aberration of covenants in leases, mutually promised performances are the contemplated equivalent and exchange for each other. Thus, to return to a simple example, where *A* agrees to work for *B* in exchange for *B*'s promise to pay *A* a certain sum at the completion of the work, the mutual promises are *dependent* in that *B*'s performance of payment is dependent upon *A*'s performance of the work. In more modern usage, *A*'s performance is a constructive condition (precedent) to *B*'s duty of payment. If *A* does not perform, *B*'s duty is not activated. In the sections which follow, we will explore specific rules designed to implement the basic concept of dependent promises or constructive conditions of exchange. Before exploring those rules, however, it is important to consider another exception to this general concept, an exception which, unlike the exception for exchanged promises in leases, is not the product of historic accident.

Where *B* promises to pay *A* for work performed by *A*, *B*'s promise is clearly conditioned on *A*'s performance. *B* may be said to have assumed a risk that *A* will not perform. Yet, if *A* fails to perform, *B* knows that he will be discharged from his duty to pay because he did not assume the risk of paying the amount promised unless *A* performed. Remember that *A*'s performance was a constructive condition of *B*'s duty to pay. There are, however, two situations where mutual performances are not the contemplated exchange for each other, i.e., where a promisor assumes the greater risk that he will perform even though a condition does not occur: (1) where the performance on only one side of the contract is made to depend upon some fortuitous event; and (2) where each of the performances is made to depend upon different fortuitous events. The promises made in such cases are often characterized as "aleatory."[232]

The typical illustration of the first situation is the insurance contract where the insured promises to pay a definite premium in exchange for the insurer's promise to pay a stipulated amount only in the event a specified loss is suffered, such as loss of life or casualty to property. Thus, the performance of the insurer's contract is made to depend upon the fortuitous event of

---

[231] Reasco v. Resource Support Assoc., Inc., 208 Fed. Appx. 632, 637–38 (10th Cir. 2006). Notwithstanding such a "hell or high water" provision as the "catch-all" clause ("any other cause"), the court held that Colorado courts would not enforce such a provision where a party engaged in wrongful conduct preventing the other party from performing the contract. Such conduct violates the public policy of Colorado.

[232] The FIRST RESTATEMENT § 291 defines an aleatory promise as one that is "conditional on the happening of a fortuitous event, or an event supposed by the parties to be fortuitous." The RESTATEMENT 2d § 239(2) describes this situation but mentions the term "aleatory" only in the accompanying comment b, without defining that term. "Aleatory" is derived from the Latin, *alea*, meaning dice, and aleatory contracts are often characterized as "betting" contracts. See Romanski v. Detroit Entertainment, LLC, 428 F 3d 629 (6th Cir. 2005).

the death of the insured or the loss of his house due to fire. Clearly, the insurer is not promising to compensate the insured for an actual, expensive loss in exchange for the relatively small, individual premium paid by the insured.[233] Rather, the insurer is *assuming the risk* that death or property loss may occur in exchange for the premium payment. Moreover, the parties contemplate that the insured will perform his promise to pay premiums even though the condition to the duty of the insured never occurs. A life insurance contract in the amount of a million dollars must be performed though the insured is struck by lightning and dies after paying only one relatively small premium. Similarly, a homeowner who has paid fire insurance premiums for a lifetime cannot reclaim those premiums because no fire occurred.[234] In fact, both parties hope that the condition will never occur.[235] This "aleatory" contract "wager" is not an illegal bargain since the insured has an interest, an insurable interest, in his property.[236]

The second situation is illustrated by an exchange of guaranty promises. *A* promises *X* to guarantee the payment of the debt of *B* in exchange for *X*'s promise to *A* to guarantee the payment of the debt of *Y*. Each of the performances is made to depend upon different fortuitous events. Neither *B* nor *Y* may default on his obligation as principal debtor, i.e., neither fortuitous event may occur and neither *A* nor *X* will be required to perform. Both *B* and *Y* may default, thereby activating the duties of *A* and *X* to perform. If, however, only one of the principal debtors, *B* or *Y*, defaults and the other does not default, the guarantor of that debt (*A* or *X*) must perform while the other guarantor has no duty to perform. It is clear that *A* and *X* each assumed the unusual risk of performing even though the other party to the contract may not have to perform. *X* was not promising to pay *Y*'s debt in exchange for *A*'s agreeing to pay *B*'s debt, since each party contemplated the possibility that one would have to pay while the other would have no duty to pay. Rather, it was the risk assumed by one party — that the stipulated fortuitous event may occur — that is the agreed exchange for the assumption of a similar risk by the other. Thus, the mutually promised *performances* were not the contemplated equivalent and exchange for each other.

With respect to both situations,[237] courts have long ago settled on the rule that, unless the promised performances are expressly made dependent, i.e., constructive conditions of the

---

[233] Jackson Nat'l Life Ins. Co. v. Receconi, 113 N.M. 403, 410, 827 P.2d 118, 125 (1992): "Unlike most bilateral contracts, the promise of each party to an aleatory contract is not given in exchange for the prospect of performance of the other party's promise."

[234] *See* Nationwide Mut. Ins. Co. v. Voland, 103 Md. App. 225, 653 A.2d 484, 489 (1995) (A promise by an insurer to pay $5000 to settle a claim without knowledge that the insured had already settled with the insurer of the other party involved in a collision for $25,000. There is no mistake in such an agreement and, absent fraud, misrepresentation or the like, all risks are assumed in such settlements).

[235] This analysis is quoted in In re Texas Assn. of School Boards, Inc., 169 S. W. 3d 653, 658–59 (Tex. 2005).

[236] An "aleatory" promise is often characterized as a betting promise. See, e.g., Davidson & Jones, Inc. v. North Carolina Dep't of Admin., 60 N.C. App. 563, 317 S.E.2d 718 (1984), *aff'd, in part, rev'd, in part,* 315 N.C. 144, 337 S.E.2d 463 (1985), where the court quotes from Professor Corbin's treatise: a "When a contractual promise is aleatory in character, the performance being expressly conditioned upon an uncertain and hazardous event, the promisee bets that it will happen and the promisor bets that it will not. The consideration exchanged for such a promise varies in proportion to their opinion as to probability. They consciously assume the risk. If the event occurs sooner than the promisor expects, he is the loser; if it fails to occur or occurs later than the promisee expects, it is he who is the loser. The opinion of one of them as to probability is thus shown to have been erroneous; but his mistake is not ground for rescission because he consciously assumed the risk." See also Harlan v. Aetna Life Ins. Co., 6 Wash. App. 837, 496 P.2d 532 (1972), where the court characterizes an insurance contract as an aleatory or betting contract.

[237] In Craig Corp. v. Albano, 55 B.R. 363 (N.D. Ill. 1985), the court suggests that insurance and guaranty contracts

other, they are independent promises and each party may sue the other for a breach without regard to whether or not he himself is in default.[238] This is a fair solution in light of the great disparity between the values of the ultimate performances promised. If they were held to be dependent or constructively conditional, the party with the less burdensome performance, were he in default, would forfeit an amount wholly out of proportion to the loss suffered by the other party to the contract. Since the performances are not the agreed exchange for each other, there is no reason to regard them as dependent or conditional. In this situation, it is not inappropriate to adjust the rights of the parties through cross actions.

[D]   "Divisible" ("Severable") Versus "Entire" Contracts

A single bilateral contract may require several performances on one or both sides. If the failure to perform one of these promised performances is material, the entire contract is breached and the aggrieved party is discharged.[239] The parties, however, may have divided their respective performances in a single contract into units on both sides with the intention that a given unit on one side was the agreed equivalent for a given unit on the other side. When this is the manifested intention of the parties, their contract is said to be *divisible* ("severable").[240] As contrasted with an *entire* ("indivisible") contract, if the contract is divisible, a breach of a divisible part does not discharge the other party from its duty to perform other divisible parts of the contract.[241] The popular labels, "divisible" and "entire" have not escaped considerable criticism as conclusions depicting "results already reached."[242] Where the parties intend their part performances in a single contract to be treated as agreed equivalents, the Restatement 2d recognizes the captions "divisible" and "severable" as only "loosely" describing such contracts since the performances are not separate contracts. Thus, the section is captioned, "Part Performances as Agreed Equivalents."[243] A statement that,

---

are aleatory, as is a contract to sell something a person does not yet and may never own (*e.g.*, an inheritance). While these types of contracts are the typical illustrations of aleatory contracts, the concept can be applied much more generally. Thus, in Davidson v. Jones, *id.*, the issue was whether the contractor could recover for the excavation of a large amount of rock beyond the 800 cubic yards of rock the parties had included in the contract. The court found that the parties were aware of the fact that the amount of rock to be excavated could be greater or lesser than 800 cubic yards and established a unit price on that basis. In this aleatory contract, the contractor "bet" that the amount of rock would be lesser than 800 cubic yards, while the promisee "bet" that the amount of rock would exceed the stated estimate. Both parties were aware of and assumed this risk. While affirming the Court of Appeals on this holding, the North Carolina Supreme Court reversed the refusal of the Court of Appeals to allow extra "duration-related" costs. 315 N.C. 144, 337 S.E.2d 463 (1985). See NLRB v. Columbus Printing Pressmen & Assistants' Union No. 252, 543 F.2d 1161 (5th Cir. 1976), where the court distinguishes arbitrable provisions of a labor contract from cost-of-living clauses by, *inter alia*, suggesting that a cost-of-living clause is in the nature of an aleatory contract.

[238] *See Jackson v. Rececconi, supra* note 233; *Harlan v. Aetna, supra* note 236; Panizzi v. State Farm Mut. Auto. Ins. Co., 386 F.2d 600 (3d Cir. 1967), *cert. denied*, 392 U.S. 937, 88 S. Ct. 2308, 20 L. Ed. 2d 1395 (1968) (auto insurance). Older cases include Massachusetts Bonding & Ins. Co. v. State *ex rel.* Black, 76 Ind. App. 16, 127 N.E. 223 (1920) (contractor's surety bond); Cushing v. Williamsburg City Fire Ins. Co., 4 Wash. 538, 30 P. 736 (1892) (fire insurance contract); Dwelling-House Ins. Co. v. Hardie, 37 Kan. 674, 16 P. 92 (1887) (fire insurance contract); Trade Ins. Co. v. Barracliff, 45 N.J.L. 543, 46 Am. Rep. 792 (N.J. Ct. Err. & App. 1883) (fire insurance contract). *See also* FIRST RESTATEMENT § 293.

[239] Whether a breach is "material" will be explored in §§ 108–109 *infra.*

[240] See Kimco Corp. v. Murdoch, Coll and Lillibridge, Inc., 313 Ill. App. 2d 768, 246 Ill. Dec. 678, 730 N.E.2d 1143, 1148 (1st Dist. 2000).

[241] *See* National Consultants, Inc. v. Burt, 186 Ga. App. 27, 366 S.E.2d 344 (1988).

[242] Corbin on Contracts § 35.8.

[243] RESTATEMENT 2d § 240. Comment b. See also § 183, "When Agreement Is Enforceable as to Agreed Equivalents."

whether a contract is "divisible" or "entire" is a matter of intention, is a truism. The dominant analytical concept in the case law to conclude that a contract is "divisible" is evidence that the parties have dealt with a part of the performance on one side as the contemplated agreed equivalent or agreed exchange for a corresponding part of the performance on the other side. Again however, whether the parties have manifested that intention is a question of interpretation.[244] To determine whether the parties intended their respective part performances as "agreed equivalents," courts will typically consider whether the parties assented to all promises as a single whole, whether there was a single consideration rather than consideration for each part, and whether the performances were divided into parts.[245] In a classic case involving a single contract for the purchase and sale of dressed hogs at a stated price per pound to be delivered immediately, and live hogs at a different price per pound to be delivered later, the court held the contract to be divisible.[246] Not only was it possible to apportion the parties' performances into corresponding pairs of performance; it was also possible to regard each pair as the agreed equivalent of the corresponding pair.[247]

The "agreed equivalents" concept, however, has also been criticized on the footing that it is fruitful only where the parties have specified a part of the contract price for a specific part of the other party's performance which, the court opined, is not frequent. While recognizing the initial importance of ascertaining whether the parties have divided their respective performances into parts or installments, the court deemed the ultimate test as whether they would have been willing to exchange their part performances regardless of what transpired, or whether they viewed the divisions were made simply to allow for periodic payments as the work progressed.[248] In construction contracts, it is common for the parties to agree upon a schedule of progress payments to be paid at intervals as the work progresses. Though the owner makes such payments at stated intervals for each part of the work completed, the parties typically are not treating separate payments for each part of the construction performance as the agreed equivalents of each other. A progress payment may be due when the contractor completes the initial excavation of the building site. The parties are not treating that progress payment as the agreed equivalent for the hole in the ground.[249] While the form

---

Comment a, refers to § 240 in situations where a material breach of one "agreed equivalent" does not preclude the breaching party from insisting on performance of another "agreed equivalent" part of the contract. Here the comment concludes that the terminology "divisible" or "severable" is avoided because it wrongly suggests "that an agreement itself can be characterized as 'divisible' or 'severable' for all purposes and in any circumstances. A court may conclude that an agreement that is 'divisible' or 'severable' for one purpose or in some circumstances is no 'divisible' or 'severable' for another purpose or in other circumstances. The concept is a flexible one, to be applied only on a case by case basis."

[244] Though the question is one of interpretation as to the manifested intention of the parties, "the divisibility of a contract is a matter of law" which allows a court to grant summary judgment. Harris v. Dial Corp., 954 F.2d 990, 993 n.2 (4th Cir. 1992).

[245] *See* Ellison v. Tubb, 295 Ark. 312, 749 S.W.2d 650 (1988); Big River Hills Ass'n v. Altmann, 747 S.W.2d 738 (Mo. Ct. App. 1988); Stratemeyer v. West, 136 Ill. App. 3d 1095, 484 N.E.2d 389, 91 Ill. Dec. 840 (5th Dist. 1985); Cahn v. Antioch Univ., 482 A.2d 120 (D.C. App. 1984); Wilderness Country Club Partnership, Ltd. v. Groves, 458 So. 2d 769 (Fla. Dist. Ct. App. 1984); Woodger v. AMR Corp., 106 Idaho 199, 677 P.2d 512 (Ct. App. 1984).

[246] *See* Tipton v. Feitner, 20 N.Y. 423 (1859).

[247] These are the two elements suggested by the RESTATEMENT 2d at § 240.

[248] Fidelity & Deposit Co. of Maryland v. Rotec Industries, Inc.,392 F.3d 944 (7th Cir. 2004). See also, Management Servs. Corp. v. Development Assocs., 617 P.2d 406, 408 (Utah 1980) suggesting that the basic test may be viewed as whether the parties would have agreed on less than the whole performance promised or would have insisted upon the entire consideration exchanged.

[249] *See, e.g.*, Lagrange Constr. v. Kent Corp., 83 Nev. 277, 429 P.2d 58 (1967).

of the agreement is not controlling, it is influential.[250] The intention of the parties is dominant, however. Though a contract may be severable by its terms, it will be construed as entire if that appears as the overriding intention of the parties.[251] Where a corporation entered into an industrial preparedness contract with the Army Signal Corps, the corporation was to receive payments at the completion of four "steps" under the contract. Each of the first three steps was designed to develop a level of preparedness enabling supply volume production of certain devices in the event of war. Except for a small payment, the corporation was paid for steps I, II and III. When it could not perform step IV, it sought to recover the balance due for the three steps it had completed on the footing that the contract was divisible and it should be paid for each of the agreed equivalents it had performed even though it could not perform the last step. The court held the contract to be entire rather than divisible since the Signal Corps had agreed to make payments *to achieve the purpose of step IV,* i.e., it had not agreed to pay for each of the first three steps as agreed equivalents.[252]

While courts will generally presume a contract is entire rather than divisible,[253] they may demonstrate a proclivity toward finding a contract divisible in certain cases.[254] For example, monthly employment contracts are said to "fit neatly into the usual definition of a divisible contract."[255] Where an employee completes a month's work and then breaches the contract, treating the completed work as a divisible part of a contract allows the employee to recover the contract price for the work done. Otherwise, the employee would suffer a forfeiture for the work performed.[256] This distinction emphasize the *effect* flowing from the characterization of a contract as divisible versus entire. It is important to elaborate that effect.

[1]   The Effect of Nonperformance in a Divisible vs. Entire Contract

The defendant had agreed to supply seven outdoor display signs for the plaintiff in exchange for a total payment of $95 per month for three years and the contract specified the payment for each of the signs. The defendant failed to perform with respect to two of the seven signs, even though the plaintiff had made payments for all of the signs. When the plaintiff sought to recover for defendant's breach, the court found the contract to be divisible so that the defendant was entitled to retain the payments for the five signs he had installed properly and had to return only that portion of the payments for the two signs that had not been properly installed.[257] Had the court found the contract to have been entire rather than divisible, the plaintiff could have recovered the total payment because the *effect* of breaching an entire

---

[250] Ginett v. Computer Task Group, 962 F.2d 1085, 1098 (2d Cir. 1992).

[251] Stika v. Albion, 150 Ariz. 521, 724 P.2d 607 (Ct. App. 1986).

[252] Pennsylvania Exch. Bank v. United States, 170 F. Supp. 629, 145 Ct. Cl. 216 (1959).

[253] *See* Monarch Photo, Inc. v. Qualex, Inc., 935 F. Supp. 1028, 1032 (D.N.D. 1996) (presumption against divisibility).

[254] *See* RESTATEMENT 2d § 240 comment e.

[255] Kimco Corp. v. Murdoch, Coll and Lillibridge, Inc., 313 Ill. App. 3d 768, 774, 246 Ill. Dec. 678, 683, 730 N.E.2d 1143, 1148 (1st Dist. 2000).

[256] Courts were inclined to discover a divisible contract for employment even where the terms of the contract were not clear to avoid forfeitures. The problem has been largely overcome by state legislation mandating the payment of wages on a reasonable periodic basis.

[257] John v. United Advertising, Inc., 165 Colo. 193, 439 P.2d 53 (1968).

contract (assuming a *material* breach)[258] is to discharge the innocent party from his duty to perform. If, however, the contract is divisible, the failure to perform a distinct part does not discharge the other party from paying for the severable or divisible parts performed by the breaching party.[259] In this sense, therefore, each divisible agreed exchange of a contract is viewed as independent of other divisible parts of the contract, i.e., the performance of one divisible part is not a constructive condition of the performance of different divisible parts, though the performance of one divisible part by one party is a constructive condition of the corresponding divisible part to be performed by the other party.[260] If the nonperformance of a divisible part is not a constructive condition to the performance of other divisible parts of the contract, can such nonperformance have *any* effect on the other divisible parts, i.e., can each divisible part of a single contract always be treated as if it were a separate contract, or, are there circumstances where the failure to perform an earlier divisible part justifies the other party in refusing to perform the remainder of the contract?

[2]   Material Nonperformance in a Divisible Contract — Installment Contracts — Uniform Commercial Code

Even though a divisible contract is one contract, a single unit of performance on one side with its corresponding equivalent on the other side may be viewed as if it were a separate and distinct contract since each portion of the performance on one side is treated as the full, agreed exchange for the corresponding portion on the other side. If divisible parts were always viewed as separate contracts, nonperformance of a divisible part would never have an effect on duties to perform other divisible parts. This may appear highly desirable since the parties apportion the consideration in divisible contracts and there is no apparent unfairness in making a party pay for what he has received when he has promised to pay that amount for a divisible portion of the contract. Again, if that party were permitted to refuse payment, the party who had performed the divisible portion would suffer a forfeiture. Yet, a divisible contract is not a series of separate contracts; it is one contract. Since all of its divisions are part of one contract, it is possible that the parties would not have contracted with regard to one or more portions of the

---

[258] The concept of material breach and related doctrines, such as substantial performance, are explored *infra* §§ 108–109.

[259] *See National Consultants, supra,* note 241.

[260] It should be noted that the respective performances for each divisible part are viewed as dependent or constructively conditional on the performance of *that* divisible part. Any material failure or performance by one party of his side of a given division of a divisible contract excuses the other party from performing his side of that division, regardless of what may be the rights and duties of the parties with respect to the other divisions of the contract. Thus, in the case involving the signs, the parties had agreed that proper installation and maintenance of the largest sign was the agreed equivalent for the plaintiff's promise to pay $35 per month. Had that sign not been properly installed and maintained, the plaintiff's duty to pay $35 per month would not have been activated because the constructive condition of exchange (proper installation and maintenance of the sign) had not occurred. This would, however, have no effect on other divisible parts of the contract fully performed by the defendant. See also Gill v. Johnstown Lumber Co., 151 Pa. 534, 25 A. 120 (1892), where the parties agreed that Gill would drive certain logs of different types and cross ties down a river to particular locations. The contract specified different prices for different types of logs and cross ties to different locations. While Gill succeeded in driving some of the logs and ties to the specified locations, the Johnstown flood swept other logs and ties beyond the locations. The court held the contract to be divisible and permitted the plaintiff to recover for each of the logs and ties transported to the prescribed locations at the prices specified in the contract. However, plaintiff could not recover for logs or ties transported only part of the way since the court treated each of the severable parts of the contract as a contract for transportation of each described good all the way to the prescribed location. *See also* Sherrill-Russell Lumber Co. v. Krug Lumber Co., 216 Mo. App. 1, 267 S.W. 14 (1924); Portfolio v. Rubin, 233 N.Y. 439, 135 N.E. 843 (1922); Jackson v. Rotax Motor & Cycle Co., 2 K.B. 937 [1910].

agreed performances without the others. Each portion is, after all, but a part of a larger whole. Nonperformance of one divisible part may not appear to be significant, but it could be a part which the other party views as a critical part.

Suppose there is nonperformance of more than one divisible part. Does the other party have to await performance of the remaining parts even after repeated failures of performance as to earlier installments? If there is nonperformance of one part and good reason to believe that other divisible parts will not be performed, should the other party be able to treat the whole contract as breached? Earlier courts confronted these questions with some difficulty traceable to nineteenth century English cases that were not entirely clear and were subject to misinterpretation in later cases.[261] With respect to contracts for the sale of goods, however, the matter was effectively dealt with under the old Uniform Sales Act[262] and is currently governed by similar concepts under the UCC.[263]

The UCC does not present an analysis in terms of divisible versus entire contracts. Where a contract either requires or authorizes goods to be delivered in separate lots to be separately accepted, under the Code such a contract is an "installment contract."[264] Even if the writing evidencing the transaction contains a phrase, such as "each delivery is a separate contract," the contract is still one installment contract.[265] It is clear that a contract will be an installment contract where installment deliveries are tacitly authorized by the circumstances or by the option of either party.[266] Unlike the situation where only one shipment of goods is contem-

---

[261] In Withers v. Reynolds, 2 B. & Ad. 882 [1831], a buyer failed to pay for a delivered installment of goods and said that he would not pay for any further installments at the time of delivery, but would always keep one installment in arrears. The court engaged in dictum suggesting that the refusal to pay for one installment would not have excused the seller, but the buyer's repudiation of the whole contract excused the seller. In the subsequent case of Hoare v. Rennie, 5 H. & N.19 [1859], where the nonperformance was the seller's failure to deliver the correct quantity of goods on time, the court held the buyer excused from taking later deliveries. Later cases, however, suggested that the failure to perform one installment of a divisible contract excuses the other party only when that failure evinces an intention to repudiate the remainder of the contract. Freeth v. Burr, 9 L R.C.P. 208 [1874]. This view was apparently adopted by the House of Lords in Mersey Steel & Iron Co. v. Naylor, 9 App. Cas. 434 [1884], and was written into the English Sale of Goods Act, St. 56 and 57 Vict. C. 71, § 31, subd. 2. See, however, Maple Flock Co. v. Universal Furn. Prods., Ltd., 1 K.B. 148 [1934], where Lord Hewart suggested that the test should be objective concerning the whole purpose of the contract and should include the ratio quantitatively, which the breach bears to the contract as a whole, and the degree of probability or improbability that the breach will be repeated. The confusion of the English cases found its way into American cases. *See* 2 WILLISTON, SALES § 467(c) and (d) (rev. ed. 1948).

[262] USA § 45(2).

[263] UCC § 2-612.

[264] UCC § 2-612(1). It should be noted that both UCC § 2-307 and RESTATEMENT 2d § 233 set forth the rule that where a complete performance can be provided at one time, the complete performance, rather than divisible portions or installments over a period of time, is expected. This general rule, however, is almost swallowed by its exceptions. The parties may, of course, expressly agree upon installment deliveries. Installment deliveries may also be inferred from the circumstances such as trade usage (UCC § 1-205(2), RESTATEMENT 2d § 221) or course of dealing (UCC § 1-205(1), RESTATEMENT 2d § 223). Other circumstances may suggest that one delivery is absurd. Thus, if all of the brick necessary for the construction of a large building was delivered at once, construction of the building may be seriously impeded. If installment deliveries are appropriate, the price, if it can be apportioned, must be paid upon the completion of each delivery. RESTATEMENT 2d § 233(2).

[265] *Id.*

[266] UCC § 2-612 comment 1. *See* Extrusion Painting, Inc. v. Awnings Unlimited, Inc., 37 F. Supp. 2d 985, 997 (E.D. Mich. 1999). Where, however, separate purchase orders with separate prices, quantities, styles and delivery terms evidence the transactions, there are single delivery contracts rather than an installment contract. Knic Knac Agencies v. Masterpiece Apparel, 1999 U.S. Dist. LEXIS 3267, at *38 (S.D.N.Y. Mar. 17, 1999).

plated by the parties and the buyer may reject the goods for *any* defect,[267] the buyer may reject an installment of goods only where the nonconformity in such installment *substantially impairs* its value and cannot be cured.[268] "Substantial impairment of value" is best understood as the UCC version of "material breach."[269] If the nonconformity in one or more installments substantially impairs the whole contract, there is a breach of the whole contract.[270] The determination of when the buyer may have the right to treat the whole contract as discharged because of a nonconformity in one or more installments can be difficult because it is a question of fact,[271] though an undisputed failure to perform on successive occasions may constitute substantial impairment of the value of the contract as a matter of law.[272] The Code policy is clear in urging a continuation of the installment contract. The test is not whether a nonconformity in a given installment indicates an intent or likelihood that future deliveries will also be defective. Rather, the test is whether the non-conformity substantially impairs the value of the whole contract.[273]

---

[267] *See* UCC § 2-601. This Code section is explored subsequently in the section dealing with the "perfect tender" rule, *infra* § 109.

[268] UCC § 2-612(2).

[269] Neptune Research & Development, Inc. v. Teknics Industrial Systems, Inc., 235 N. J. 522, 532, 563 A. 2d 465, 470 (1989). The concept of material breach is fully explored *infra* § 108. "The common law concept of 'material breach' is at least a first cousin to the concept of 'substantial nonconformity,' and it offers a fruitful analogy to one who seeks to determine whether the seller's performance substantially nonconforms." J. White & R. Summers, Uniform Commercial Code § 8-3, at 315 (2000).

[270] UCC § 2-612(3). See ASI Industries GmbH v. MEMC Electronic Materials, Inc., 2008 U. S. Dist. LEXIS 10732 (D. Mo. 2008) (when did "substantial impairment of the value of the value of the whole contract" occur?).

[271] Neufer v. Video Greetings, Inc., 931 F.2d 56 (6th Cir. 1991) (court instructed district court on remand to consider whether the cumulative effect of VGI's performance based on the totality of the circumstances including several shipments of nonconforming goods and the limited steps taken by VGI to fulfill its warranty obligations substantially impaired the value of the whole contract to the plaintiff). In Cherwell-Ralli, Inc. v. Rytman Grain Co., 180 Conn. 714, 433 A.2d 984 (1980), the buyer was behind in its payments for shipments almost from the inception of the installment contract. The seller repeatedly called for payment while continuing to ship the goods. The buyer sent a check but stopped payment on the check, alleging concern that the seller may not continue in business (the court found no valid reason for the buyer's stoppage of payment). The court found the continuous default in payment and the stop payment order to be sufficiently egregious to constitute substantial impairment of the value of the whole contract. In Continental Forest Prods., Inc. v. White Lumber Sales, Inc., 256 Or. 466, 474 P.2d 1 (1970), a 9% variance below grade of one of 20 carloads of lumber provided by contract where a 5% variance was acceptable was held not to be such a substantial nonconformity as to be a breach of the whole contract. *See also* Trunkline LNG Co. v. Trane Thermal Co., 722 S.W.2d 722 (Tex. App. Houston 1986) (the buyer's rejection of only one installment does not establish that the contract was breached); Bodine Sewer, Inc. v. Eastern Ill. Precast, Inc., 143 Ill. App. 3d 920, 97 Ill. Dec. 898, 493 N.E.2d 705 (4th Dist. 1986) (occasional deliveries of defective pipe which were always cured on demand did not constitute nonconformities which substantially impaired the value of the entire contract).

[272] *See* L & M Enters. v. BEI Sensors & Sys. Co., 231 F.3d 1284, 1287 (10th Cir. 2000) (undisputed failure to pay for shipments establishes, as a matter of law, substantial impairment justifying cancellation as to the future undelivered balance of the contract).

[273] UCC § 2-612 comment 6.

§ 107   THE ORDER OF PERFORMANCES IN EXCHANGED PROMISES

[A]   The General Principle

We have criticized the early common law view that treated the performances in a bilateral contract as independent covenants unless they were expressly made dependent by the stated terms of the contract.[274] To avoid the unacceptable consequences of that view and to determine whether a given party is under a present duty of performance, it is necessary to determine the required order of performances in such an exchange of promises.

If the parties have expressed their intention concerning the order of their performances, either in words[275] or through conduct,[276] that intention will control. It is only in those cases where there is no evidence of their intention that a problem arises. It should not be forgotten that the purpose of determining the required order of performances in bilateral contracts is to assure the exchange of mutual performances in a fashion that precludes the possibility that one party will, at any stage of the performance, have an unfair advantage over the other party. To appreciate the common sense guidelines that have been adopted by our courts to avoid any unfair advantage, it is necessary to consider various possibilities of ordering performance and the judicial reaction to them.

[B]   Promises Capable of Simultaneous Performances When They Are Agreed Equivalents — Concurrent Conditions — "Tender" and "Offer to Perform"

If the exchanged promises, by their nature and consistency with the terms of the contract, can be performed simultaneously (concurrently), and if the two promised performances are the agreed equivalents for each other, it is uniformly held that the two performances must be exchanged simultaneously, i.e., the two performances are viewed as constructive *concurrent* conditions.[277] Where the performances are concurrent conditions and the question arises, which party should perform before the other, the curious answer is "neither" or "either." Consider, for example, a contract for the sale of land where the terms of the contract do not require either party to perform before the other. If *A* simply agrees to sell and *B* to buy *A's* land for a price of $50,000, the delivery of the deed and payment of the purchase price are concurrent conditions.[278] If *neither* party made an offer to perform or tender, neither party can be in default since neither was required to perform before the other.[279] If neither party

---

[274] *See supra* § 105.

[275] *See, e.g.*, Industrial Mercantile Factors Co. v. Daisy Sportswear, Inc., 56 Misc. 2d 104, 288 N.Y.S.2d 209 (1967).

[276] *See, e.g.*, Siple v. Logan, 232 Pa. Super. 322, 335 A.2d 758 (1975) (prior course of dealing can create a constructive condition precedent).

[277] *See* El Dorado Hotel Props., Ltd. v. Mortensen, 136 Ariz. 292, 665 P.2d 1014 (Ct. App. 1983); Herring v. Prestwood, 379 So. 2d 548 (Ala. 1979). *See also* RESTATEMENT 2d § 238. The RESTATEMENT 2d avoids the use of the phrase "concurrent condition" which had been used in the FIRST RESTATEMENT § 251 but even there considered an "elliptical expression."

[278] *See* Fogarty v. Saathoff, 128 Cal. App. 3d 780, 180 Cal. Rptr. 484 (4th Dist. 1982) (stating the general principle but finding that the obligation to provide a termite clearance and title insurance were not concurrent conditions).

[279] *See* Bell v. Elder, 782 P.2d 545 (Utah Ct. App. 1989): "During the executory period of a . . . contract whose time of performance is uncertain but which contemplates simultaneous performance by both parties, . . . neither party can

offers to perform and the time stated in the contract for performance has expired, or where no time is stated, a reasonable time for either party to offer performance has expired, both parties are discharged since the constructive concurrent conditions to their respective performances can no longer occur.[280] Similarly, if *either* party seeks to activate the duty of the other to perform, that party must offer to perform first.[281] If such an offer occurs and the other party fails to perform, the latter is in default because the constructive concurrent condition has occurred, thereby activating the latter's duty, and there has been a breach of that duty by failure to perform. The underlying rationale is simple and clear: neither party is required to risk his own performance without receiving the bargained-for-exchange.

"Offer to Perform" vs. "Tender." It is important to clarify the difference between an "offer to perform" and "tender" which is not always clear in the case law. An "offer of performance" is less exacting than a "tender" of performance. In our example of the sale of land, a tender would require the buyer to actually present the $50,000 to the seller to place the seller in default. To place the buyer in default, the seller would have to present the deed to the property. If such a tender were made, it would more than meet the requirement of an "offer to perform." A technical tender, however, is not necessary to place the other party in default. Proof of an "offer to perform" is demonstrated by notice to the other party of a present readiness and willingness to perform.[282] Thus, in our example, the buyer would simply have to offer to pay the $50,000 with manifested present ability to make the payment.

Concurrent conditions are constructed typically in contracts for the conveyance of land and contracts for the sale of goods.[283] Certain acts may be necessary in preparation for an offer to perform or tender. If *A* agrees to sell and deliver goods to *B* at *B*'s residence for which *B* promises to pay a certain amount, and nothing is said as to the time for performance, the transaction involves concurrent conditions though *A* will have to bring the goods to *B*'s house

---

be said to be in default until the other party has tendered his own performance" (quoting Century 21 All W. Real Estate & Inv. v. Webb, 645 P.2d 52, 55–56 (Utah 1982)).

[280] Pitman v. Canham, 2 Cal. App. 4th 556, 559, 3 Cal. Rptr. 2d 340 (2d Dist. 1992).

[281] Aviation Dev. Co. PLC v. C&S Acquisition Corp., 1999 U.S. Dist. LEXIS 3627, at *35 (S.D.N.Y. Feb. 1, 1999) (unless a party demands performance, he has no claim for breach of contract).

[282] See Bavarian Pastry Shop v. Bavarian Bakeries, 1995 Tex. App. LEXIS 2973, at *5 (Tex. App. Dallas Nov. 22, 1995), where the court states that, in a contract with concurrent conditions, a party need not tender performance, but only be ready and willing to perform and notify the other party to that effect. *See also* Stoner v. Humphrey, 1994 Ark. App. LEXIS 421, at *7 (Ark. Ct. App. Sept. 14, 1994). RESTATEMENT 2d § 238 comment b. Sections 45 and 62 of the RESTATEMENT 2d illustrate the more exacting requirement of a tender of performance. In a contract for the sale of goods, the UCC requires "tender" of delivery as a condition to the buyer's duty to accept the goods and pay for them (UCC § 2-507(1)), or tender of payment as a constructive condition to the seller's duty to tender and complete delivery of the goods (UCC § 2-511(1)). "Tender of delivery" under the Code requires the seller to "put and hold conforming goods at the buyer's disposition and give the buyer any notification reasonably necessary to enable him to take delivery." § 2-503(1). Comment 1 to this section suggests that "due tender" only contemplates an offer coupled with a present ability to fulfill all the conditions resting on the tendering party . . . ," which appears to be an "offer to perform" rather than a technical tender. The Comment explains that the use of "due" is only for "clarification and emphasis." It does, however, suggest another possible meaning of "tender," i.e., "an offer of goods or documents under a contract as if in fulfillment of its conditions," — a technical tender — and concludes that, "Used in either sense . . . , 'tender' connotes such performance by the tendering party as puts the other party in default if he fails to proceed in some manner."

[283] *See, e.g.*, Willener v. Sweeting, 107 Wash. 2d 388, 730 P.2d 45 (1986) (land); Fletcher v. Jones, 314 N.C. 389, 333 S.E.2d 731 (1985) (land); Aurora Aviation, Inc. v. AAR Western Skyways, Inc., 75 Or. App. 598, 707 P.2d 631 (1985) (sale of aircraft).

to tender performance.[284] The transport of the goods is not part of the promised performance. It is an action which *A* must perform in preparation for an offer to perform. The law is not concerned with such preparation. Rather, it correctly concerns itself only with the performances which have been expressly undertaken.[285] Performances under an exchange of promises may be performed concurrently in four situations: (a) the same time is set for performance by either party;[286] (b) the same period of time is fixed for both performances;[287] (c) a time is fixed for the performance of one promise and no time is set for the performance of the other;[288] (d) no time is fixed for the performance of either promise.[289]

[C]   Promises Capable of Simultaneous Performances Where They Are Not Agreed Equivalents

Where the performance of one or both parties is divided into parts so that one part is not the agreed equivalent of all or a part of the performance of the other party, can some of the performances still be due simultaneously, i.e., may they be concurrently conditional? Suppose that *A* agrees to convey land to *B*, who agrees to pay a total price of $50,000 in five installments of $10,000, the contract specifying that the land will be conveyed at the same time that the last installment payment is due. It is uniformly held that the conveyance and the last installment payment are concurrently conditional.[290] Since the vendor has already received four installments and will receive the remainder of the entire agreed exchange for his conveyance when he receives the last payment, there is no reason for any further credit to be extended by the purchaser before he receives the conveyance. If the parties had agreed that the conveyance would be made at the time of an earlier installment, the payment and that installment would be concurrently conditional.[291]

---

[284] The classic case is Morton v. Lamb, 7 Term. Rep. 125 [1797].

[285] *See Fogarty v. Saathoff, supra* note 278.

[286] *See* School Dist. No. 2 v. Rogers, 8 Iowa (8 Clarke) 316 (1859). First Restatement § 267(a); Restatement 2d § 234(1) and comment b.

[287] Beach v. First Fed. Sav. & Loan Ass'n, 140 Ga. App. 882, 232 S.E.2d 158 (1977); Goodison v. Nunn, 4 Term. Rep. 761 [1792]. *See* First Restatement § 267 (d); Restatement 2d § 234(1) and comment b.

[288] *See* Palmer v. Fox, 274 Mich. 252, 264 N.W. 361 (1936); Morton v. Lamb, 7 Term. Rep. 125 [1797]. First Restatement § 267(b); Restatement 2d § 234(1) comment b.

[289] *See Fletcher v. Jones, supra* note 283; George W. Merrill Furniture Co. v. Hill, 87 Me. 17, 32 A. 712 (1894); First Restatement § 267(s) and Restatement 2d § 234(1) and comment b.

[290] *See* Kane v. Hood, 30 Mass. (13 Pick.) 281 (1832) (payment in three installments meant that the third payment and conveyance were concurrent conditions). *See* Restatement 2d § 234(1) and ill. 6 thereto. See also E. E. E., Inc. v. Hanson, 318 N.W.2d 101 (N.D. 1982), where the contract required two installment payments to be made before the delivery of the abstract. Originally, the abstract had to be delivered concurrently with the third installment. That portion of the contract was, however, deleted. Held: the first two installments were required without delivery of the abstract, i.e., they were not concurrently conditional. Citing Professor Corbin's treatise at § 664, the court emphasized that the purchaser had agreed to extend credit to the seller through the first two installment payments. In Ideal Family & Youth Ranch v. Whetstine, 655 P.2d 429 (Colo. Ct. App. 1982), the contract required delivery of a deed in escrow prior to any payments. Such delivery was not concurrently conditional with payments; rather, it was a constructive condition precedent to the buyer's obligation to pay. The language of the contract may specify that the buyer shall first make the payments before the conveyance will be made. Some courts manifest a strong preference for finding simultaneous performance by holding that the last payment is still concurrently conditional with the conveyance. *See, e.g.,* Zintsmaster v. Werner, 41 F.2d 634 (3d Cir. 1930), *aff'd,* 61 F.2d 298 (3d Cir. 1932).

[291] Egbert v. Chew, 14 N.J.L. 446 (N.J. 1834); Green v. Reynolds, 2 Johns. 207 (N.Y. 1807).

A situation may be supposed where each of the mutual performances in a bilateral contract are to be continuous and will require a period of time for completion during which both performances are to occur. If, for example, A agrees to remodel B's property, for which B promises to perform masonry work for A and no time is set for performance, each party must perform within a reasonable time. In such a case, there is no basis for requiring either performance to occur before the other. Neither party, to preserve his rights, should be forced to part with any more of his performance than absolutely necessary without receiving some assurance that he will receive the agreed exchange. The fairest solution is to require the performances to occur concurrently.[292]

[D]   Performances Requiring Time Exchanged for Instant Performance[293]

Where a material part of the promised performance on one side of a bilateral contract is of a kind that will necessarily extend over a period of time and the performance on the other side can be rendered in an instant, it is uniformly held that the performance that takes time is a constructive condition precedent absent contrary manifestations of contract language or the circumstances.[294] If A contracts to construct a building for B for which B promises to pay a certain price, nothing being said about the time of payment, the building must be completed, at least substantially, before B's duty to pay is activated.[295]

This principle appears to have originated in employment contracts.[296] Since employers, as a class, were considered more financially responsible than employees, courts elected to adopt a rule compelling the employee to extend credit to the employer, rather than the reverse. The rule seemed particularly appropriate at the time it was established when it was common for the employer to furnish board and lodging to the employee in addition to the stipulated wage. The principle, however, remains and is currently applied to virtually any kind of contract for services which require time for performance as contrasted with a single payment for services which occurs instantaneously.[297] The classic example is the building contracts requiring the builder to extend credit to the owner. The builder's risk, however, has been mitigated by the allowance of statutory liens to the extent of the work performed by the builder.

It must be emphasized that the principle requiring the party whose performance takes time to perform first must always be consistent with the purpose of the contract. If, for example, an owner for whom a building was to be erected agreed to furnish a bond to secure the

---

[292] *See* Sutton v. Meyering Land Co., 248 Mich. 601, 227 N.W. 783 (1929); Rosenthal Paper Co. v. National Folding Box & Paper Co., 226 N.Y. 313, 123 N.E. 766 (1919). Ihrke v. Continental Life Ins. & Inv. Co., 91 Wash. 342, 157 P. 866 (1916).

[293] This section is cited in RESTATEMENT 2d § 234, Reporter's Note to comment e.

[294] RESTATEMENT 2d § 234(2) and comment e.

[295] Stewart v. Newbury, 220 N.Y. 379, 115 N.E. 984 (1917). *See* Royal McBee Corp. v. Bryant, 217 A.2d 603 (D.C. App. 1966) (duty to pay rental was constructively conditioned on lessor's duty to keep equipment in good repair). Also, in a divisible contract, if an agreed equivalent on one side requires time for its performance and the corresponding agreed equivalent can be performed instantaneously, the same rule applies. *See* Walsh v. New York & Ky. Co., 88 A.D. 477, 85 N.Y.S. 83 (1903) (contract of employment divisible by months — no recovery for part of a month).

[296] *See* Skagway City Sch. Bd. v. Davis, 543 P.2d 218 (Alaska 1975) (employee's substantial performance is a constructive condition precedent to employer's duty to pay wages).

[297] Beeland Interests, Inc. v. Armstrong, 1999 U.S. Dist. LEXIS 15744, at *41 (S.D.N.Y. Sept. 30, 1999): "[T]he presumption is that the performance of the service is a condition precedent to the payment for it."

performance of his payment obligation, and no time was set for furnishing the bond, the owner must furnish the bond as a condition precedent to any duty of performance by the builder.[298] The purpose of a payment bond is to assure the builder of payment for any work performed. The builder should not be required to perform any work until the payment bond is furnished.[299]

[E] Performances at Different Times — Condition Precedent — Progress Payments

Parties often form bilateral contracts where the exchanged performances are expressly due at different times.[300] Under such a contract, the performance due first is a constructive condition precedent to the performance due later, provided that the first performance is a *material* part of the agreed exchange for the later performance.[301] The requirement that the first performance be a material part of the agreed exchange to constitute a constructive condition precedent requires a preview of the concept of materiality of breach. As will be seen in the next section,[302] it is not every failure of performance that excuses the counter performance. A failure of performance may be so insubstantial that the other party must still perform, though there has been a technical failure of performance (breach) for which the first party is liable. If performance that fails is not material, that performance will not be viewed as a constructive condition precedent since the failure of a condition to occur after it can no longer occur has the effect of discharging the duty of the other party.[303] To permit the other party to be discharged from his duty to perform because of an insubstantial failure of performance (immaterial breach) by the first party would result in a forfeiture. Where a party agreed to make two $25,000 payments at specified times to settle an alleged claim, a three day delay in the payment of the second installment was not a material breach that discharged the duty of the other party.[304] Only a material breach will constitute a failure of a constructive condition.[305] It is important to remember that we are discussing "constructive" conditions, i.e., conditions created by the law rather than the parties that are designed to order the performances in bilateral contracts in a fair manner. Where the performance that fails is immaterial, courts will not create such a condition because, again, to view such immaterial

---

[298] *See* Clark v. Gulesian, 197 Mass. 492, 84 N.E. 94 (1908).

[299] Where a seller of whiskey had agreed to furnish advertising, the court held that the furnishing of advertising within a reasonable time was a condition precedent to the duty of the buyer to pay any installments that matured after the lapse of a reasonable time. Rochester Distilling Co. v. Geloso, 92 Conn. 43, 101 A. 500 (1917). *See also* Lake Dorr Land Co. v. Parker, 104 Fla. 378, 140 So. 635 (1932) (furnishing of abstract within a reasonable time held a condition precedent to duty to pay installments of purchase price maturing thereafter).

[300] The fact that the performances are due at different times has no effect on the enforceability of such a contract. *See* Owens v. Miller, 1992 U.S. Dist. LEXIS 8987, at *3 (E.D. Pa. June 22, 1992) (citing this section).

[301] Bernard v. Las Americas Communs., 84 F.3d 103, 108 (2d Cir. 1996); Conley v. Pitney Bowes, 34 F.3d 714, 717 (8th Cir. 1994), *cert. denied*, 528 U.S. 1136, 120 S. Ct. 979, 145 L. Ed. 2d 930 (2000); RESTATEMENT 2d § 237. The exception to this rule occurs in divisible contracts. Where there are pairs of agreed equivalents, the performance of one part of such a pair is viewed in the same fashion as if that pair of performances were the only pair of performances promised. *See* RESTATEMENT 2d § 240.

[302] *See infra* §§ 107–108.

[303] *See* RESTATEMENT 2d § 225(2). The determination of whether a failure of performance is material or immaterial will be explored *infra* § 107. In general, see RESTATEMENT 2d § 241.

[304] Associated Builders, Inc. v. Coggins, 722 A.2d 1278 (Me. 1999).

[305] Resolution Trust Corp. v. Federal Sav. & Loan Ins. Corp., 25 F.3d 1493, 1500 (10th Cir. 1994).

performance as a condition precedent will result in a forfeiture.

Constructive conditions will be created not only where the two performances in question are the entire performances mutually promised, but also in cases where the contract is performable in installments on either or both sides. Thus, in a construction contract, it is common to divide the performances into installments to provide the builder with sufficient monies to continue performance.[306] Upon completion of one part of the building, the builder will receive what is typically called a "progress payment." If *A* promises to construct a building for *B* in exchange for progress payments at stated intervals during the course of the work, a series of alternate conditions precedent will be constructed. Again, assuming that each part of the respective performances constitutes a material part of the whole, the first stage of the work is a condition precedent to the first progress payment, and the first progress payment, in turn, is a condition precedent to the second part of the work. Each successive part of the work and progress payment constitutes a condition precedent to the counter performance that is to follow.[307]

The rule that a material part of the exchange due first is a constructive condition precedent to the duty of the other party is based upon simple fairness to that party. Unless the party whose performance is due later receives substantially what he bargained for as the exchange for his own performance without material delay, he should not have to perform his own promise.[308] By treating the first due material part of the performance as a condition precedent, our law assures this result.

[F] Performances at Different Times — Becoming Concurrent Conditions

We have just seen that the performance due first, if material, will be viewed as a condition precedent to the later performance. We have also seen that a material failure of performance due first will discharge the duty of the other party who may bring an action for damages against the breaching party. Suppose, however, the failure of the performance first due is an immaterial delay and the time for the counter performance is now due. Thus, in a contract for the sale of *A*'s auto to *B* for $10,000, assume that *A* is supposed to deliver the car on May 1 and *B* is to pay on May 3. *A*'s failure to deliver the car on May 1 is a failure of performance but it is an immaterial failure. Thus, *B* is not discharged from his duty. If *B* waits until May 3 to seek *A*'s performance, the performances due under the contract are now simultaneously due so that each performance becomes a concurrent condition of the other. As seen earlier,[309] to place either party in default, the other will have to tender performance. The same analysis applies even to a material failure of the first due performance if the other party chooses to ignore that failure and wait until his own performance is due.[310]

---

[306] Such a contract is not a divisible contract because the pairs of installments are typically not agreed equivalents.

[307] *See* K & G Constr. Co. v. Harris, 223 Md. 305, 164 A.2d 451 (1960); Ringelberg v. Kawka, 242 Mich. 665, 219 N.W. 593 (1928); Guerini Stone Co. v. P. J. Carlin Constr. Co., 248 U.S. 334, 39 S. Ct. 102, 63 L. Ed. 275 (1919). Again, if the part of the performance that is due first is not a material part of the agreed exchange, it will not be a condition precedent. *See, e.g.*, Leiston Gas Co. v. Leiston-Cum-Sizewell Urban Dist. Council, 2 K.B. 428 [1916].

[308] *See* RESTATEMENT 2d § 237 comment b.

[309] *See supra* subsection B.

[310] *See* RESTATEMENT 2d § 234 comment d.

Where the parties to an entire contract divide their performances into installments on one or both sides, a similar analysis applies. Assume that *A* contracts to convey land to *B*, no time being set for conveyance, for which *B* promises to pay a total of $100,000 in four equal installments. Assume that *B* pays the first two installments, but fails to pay the third until the fourth and final installment is due. If *B'* s failure to pay the third installment on time is a material failure of performance (constructive condition precedent which has not occurred), *A* is discharged. If, however, that failure is immaterial and, therefore, not a constructive condition precedent, or it is a material breach but ignored by *A*, the conveyance and the payment of the third and fourth installments are due simultaneously, i.e., they are concurrent conditions.[311]

§ 108   FAILURE OF PERFORMANCE — MATERIAL BREACH

[A]   General Principles

Where the parties have a bilateral contract and one party fails to perform, our law could have assumed either of the following polar positions:

(1) A party in default should never have the right to insist upon performance by the other. This solution fails to consider the injustice that would often result. The defaulting party, for example, may have performed a substantial part of his promised performance. If that party is not permitted to recover notwithstanding his default, he would suffer a serious forfeiture while the loss sustained by the other party would be relatively insignificant.[312] Even where the defaulting party has not begun to perform, the defects in his tender of performance may be so slight that, as a matter of fairness, he should not be deprived of the benefit of his bargain.

(2) The opposite position which our law could have adopted is that a defect in performance, no matter how substantial, should never prevent an action on the contract by the defaulting plaintiff. Rather, it should only furnish the basis for the defendant's recoupment of the loss suffered by the plaintiff's failure to perform. This position suggests the archaic view that all covenants in contracts are independent and multiplicity of litigation is a desirable solution.

Neither of these polar positions has been adopted. While any breach of contract is actionable, our legal system has developed a principle for distinguishing between cases where the failure to perform discharges the duty of the other party and those where the failure to perform does not discharge that duty. The principle is stated succinctly by one court: "Not every breach of duty by one party to a contract discharges the duty of performance of the other; only breach that is sufficiently material and important to justify ending the whole

---

[311] RESTATEMENT 2d § 234 comment d and ill. 8. *See also* Henderson v. Morton, 109 Fla. 300, 147 So. 456 (1933); Walsh v. Coghlan, 33 Idaho 115, 190 P. 252 (1920); Underwood v. Tew, 7 Wash. 297, 34 P. 1100 (1893); Beecher v. Conradt, 13 N.Y. (3 Kernan) 108, 64 Am. Dec. 535 (1855). *Cf.* Littlefield v. Brown, 394 A.2d 794 (Me. 1978) (after exercise of option, the arrangement becomes an executory land contract where delivery of payment and conveyance of land become concurrent conditions).

[312] It may be argued that the solution to this problem should be found in permitting the defaulting plaintiff to bring an action in quasi contract, i.e., a restitutionary action to prevent unjust enrichment. *See* Dodge v. Kimball, 203 Mass. 364, 89 N.E. 542 (1909). This solution, however, would deprive the promisee of the benefits of a profitable bargain when, in many cases, there is little reason for so doing. Moreover, where the performance of the defaulting plaintiff has not conferred any measurable benefit on the other party, no restitutionary remedy would be possible.

transaction is a total breach that discharges injured party's duties."[313]

Having concluded that some failures of performance or breaches of contract may be substantial or material while others will be insubstantial or immaterial, the essential question is, how does a court determine whether a particular failure of performance (breach) is material (substantial) or immaterial (insubstantial)?

[B]　Failure of Performance (Material Breach) — RESTATEMENTS Compared

In determining whether a breach is material, many cases rely upon the analyses in both the FIRST AND SECOND RESTATEMENTS OF CONTRACTS. A comparison of the different approaches in the two Restatements enhances the understanding of the concept.[314] Under the FIRST RESTATEMENT, if the failure to perform or delay in performance is so material that it will or may result in the other party not receiving the substantial benefit of his bargain, the duty of the injured party is discharged and he is wholly excused from his undertaking.[315] On the other hand, if the failure to perform or delay in performance is not sufficiently material, the injured party is not discharged or excused, but retains his duty to perform, i.e., there is still a breach of contract but the innocent party must recoup his loss for the immaterial breach while he is still bound to perform.[316] Numerous courts have stated similar generalities.[317] While there is no question that the application of the principle is designed to prevent unreasonable forfeitures to defaulting parties and to assure fairness to innocent parties, the application requires further guidance.

[1]　FIRST RESTATEMENT — Guidelines

The standard of materiality is not susceptible to mechanical rules.[318] There was never any doubt in the minds of drafters of either RESTATEMENT that it would be impossible to suggest anything more than guidelines to assist courts in making this distinction. Thus, the FIRST RESTATEMENT listed six "influential circumstances" to assist courts in this effort.[319] These

---

[313] Fitz v. Coutinho, 622 A.2d 1220, 1223 (N.H. 1993). In Ott v. Buehler Lumber Co., 541 A.2d 1143 (Pa. Super. 1988), the second edition of this book is cited for the proposition that a party may not insist upon performance if that party has committed a material breach. Where the default is so serious that the defaulter is precluded from recovering on the contract, he may seek a remedy in quasi contract (restitution) to recover the value of any benefits conferred on the other party, even though the performance was defective as measured by the contract.

[314] The comparative analysis that follows is extensively quoted in Frazier v. Mellowitz, 804 N. E. 2d 796 (Ind. App. 2004), from an earlier edition of this treatise.

[315] *See* FIRST RESTATEMENT §§ 274, 397.

[316] FIRST RESTATEMENT § 274(1). *See* Millis Constr. Co. v. Fairfield Sapphire Valley, Inc., 86 N.C. App. 506, 358 S.E.2d 566 (1987); Aldape v. Lubcke, 107 Idaho 316, 688 P.2d 1221 (Ct. App. 1984); Jacob & Youngs, Inc. v. Kent, 230 N.Y. 239, 129 N.E. 889 (1921); Tichnor Bros. v. Evans, 92 Vt. 278, 102 A. 1031 (1918); Manthey v. Stock, 133 Wis. 107, 113 N.W. 443 (1907).

[317] A more recent example is Sokol v. Bruno's, Inc., 527 So. 2d 1245 (Ala. 1988), where the court suggests that a material breach touches the fundamental purpose of the contract and defeats the object of the parties.

[318] *See* McDuffy, Edwards & Assocs., Inc. v. Peripheral Sys., Inc., 93 Or. App. 226, 762 P.2d 299 (1988).

[319] FIRST RESTATEMENT § 275 provides: Rules for determining materiality of a failure to perform.

In determining the materiality of a failure fully to perform a promise the following circumstances are influential:

(a) The extent to which the injured party will obtain the substantial benefit which he could have reasonably anticipated;

guidelines were designed to expose "the inherent justice of the matter" in answering the basic question, "Will it be more conformable to justice in the particular case to free the injured party, or, on the other hand, to require her to perform her promise, in both cases giving her a right of action if the failure to perform was wrongful?"[320] The First Restatement recognized the tendency to treat questions of *delay* in performance as different from other types of failure of performance. It devoted a separate section to this question where it listed five "rules" to guide courts in determining whether a delay in performance constituted a material breach.[321]

[2]   Restatement 2d — Constructive Condition, Cure, Suspension, Termination

The Restatement 2d lists guidelines similar to its predecessor but approaches the problem in a significantly different fashion. It begins by characterizing a party's duties under a contract as *constructively conditioned* on the lack of any *uncured material* failure by the other party to render any performance due earlier.[322] When a breach is material, the Restatement 2d views the breaching party's performance as the non-occurrence of a constructive condition that prevents the activation of the innocent party's duty, temporarily, or permanently when the constructive condition can no longer occur.[323] While continuing the guidelines to distinguish material and immaterial breaches[324] and treating a material breach as the nonoccurrence of a

---

(b) The extent to which the injured party may be adequately compensated in damages for lack of complete performance;

(c) the extent to which the party failing to perform has already partly performed or made preparations for performance;

(d) The greater or less hardship on the party failing to perform in terminating the contract;

(e) The wilful, negligent or innocent behavior of the party failing to perform;

(f) The greater or less uncertainty that the party failing to perform will perform the remainder of the contract.

Two well-known cases applying these criteria, both concluding that the breach was immaterial, are Walker & Co. v. Harrison, 347 Mich. 630, 81 N.W.2d 352 (1957) (failure to clean sign by lessor of sign was immaterial though annoying), and Continental Grain Co. v. Simpson Feed Co., 102 F. Supp. 354 (D. Ark. 1951), which also applies § 276 (immaterial delay in performance).

[320] First Restatement § 275 comment a.

[321] First Restatement § 276 begins with the "rule" that, absent an agreement of the parties to make performance on the exact day of "vital importance," failure to perform on that day does not discharge the duty of the other party (§ 276(a)). In mercantile contracts, timely performance is important but a material breach will not be found unless the delay is "considerable" in light of the nature of the transaction and seriousness of the consequences (§ 276(b)). If a party delays before rendering *any* performance, less delay is necessary to constitute a material breach than if the delaying party had begun to perform (§ 276(c)). More delay is necessary in contracts for the sale of land than in mercantile contracts to constitute a material breach (§ 276(d)). Where the suit is for specific performance in a contract for the sale of land, "considerable delay in tendering performance does not preclude enforcement of the contract" where the delay can be compensated unless the contract states that timely performance is essential or the circumstances indicate that enforcement will be unjust (§ 276(e)).

[322] Restatement 2d § 237.

[323] Restatement 2d § 237 comment a.

[324] Restatement 2d § 241 provides:

"In determining whether a failure to perform or to make an offer to perform is material, the following circumstances are significant:

(a) the extent to which the injured party will be deprived of the benefit which he reasonably expected;

(b) the extent to which the injured party can be adequately compensated for the part of that benefit of which he will be deprived;

condition,[325] the RESTATEMENT 2d makes a further important distinction between *material* breaches which may or may not be "cured." The concept of cure is borrowed from the Uniform Commercial Code. Where a buyer rejects goods because they do not conform to the contract description, the seller may notify the buyer of the seller's intention to cure, i.e., to remedy the nonconformity make a conforming tender of the goods if time for performance remains under the contract.[326]

The RESTATEMENT 2d suggests a number of inquiries with respect to the application of "cure" which are more than reminiscent of the general guidelines for determining whether a breach is material: (1) To what extent has the reasonable expectation of the injured party already been secured? (2) Does the injured party have security to assure performance by the defaulting party? (3) Did the breaching party submit any reasonable assurances that the breach would be cured? (4) Has the market changed for the goods or services in question so as to make the contract more favorable to the defaulting party? (5) Has the defaulting party breached other contracts or other installments of the contract in question? (6) What is the financial or other condition of the breaching party in relation to his ability to cure? *See* RESTATEMENT 2d § 241 comment c. Thus, the RESTATEMENT 2d suggests that where there is a material breach, there is a constructive condition to the innocent party's duty to perform that has not occurred. If, however, time remains for that condition to occur, i.e., if the breaching party could still perform in a relatively timely fashion, the innocent party may *not* treat the failure of performance

---

(c) the extent to which the party failing to perform or to offer to perform will suffer forfeiture;

(d) the likelihood that the party failing to perform or to offer to perform will cure his failure, taking account of all the circumstances including any reasonable assurances;

(e) the extent to which the behavior of the party failing to perform or to offer to perform comports with standards of good faith and fair dealing."

Illustrative cases relying on the § 241 RESTATEMENT 2d guidelines are Rubloff CB Machesney v. World Novelties, Inc., 363 Ill. App. 3d 558, 844 N. E. 2d 462 (2006); Widmer Engineering, Inc. v. Dufalla, 837 A. 2d 459 (Pa. Super. 2003); Nov Associated Builders, Inc. v. Coggins, 722 A.2d 1278 (Me. 1999); Grace v. Insurance Co. of N. Am., 944 P.2d 460 (Alaska 1997); Mirco Indus. v. Dan Clark Leasing, 1997 U.S. App. LEXIS 32298 (6th Cir. Nov. 13, 1997); Conley v. Pitney Bowes, 34 F.3d 714 (8th Cir. 1994); Bernstein v. Nemeyer, 213 Conn. 665, 570 A. 2d 164 (1990); Bailie Communications, Ltd. v. Trend Bus. Sys., 53 Wash. App. 77, 765 P.2d 339 (1988); Miles v. CEC Homes, 753 P.2d 1021 (Wyo. 1988); Kersh v. Montgomery Developmental Ctr., Ohio Dep't of Mental Retardation etc., 35 Ohio App. 3d 61, 519 N.E.2d 665 (1987); Rohauer v. Little, 736 P.2d 403 (Colo. 1987); Rose v. Davis, 474 So. 2d 1058 (Ala. 1985); Prudential Ins. Co. v. Stratton, 14 Ark. App. 145, 685 S.W.2d 818 (1985).

[325] An immaterial breach is not treated as the nonoccurrence of a condition because the injured party may not even suspend, much less terminate, his performance in response to such a breach.

[326] UCC § 2-508(1). A simple illustration suggests the reasonableness of this provision. If X has agreed to supply certain goods to Y by the 30th day of the month and delivers nonconforming goods on the 15th of the month which Y rejects, if X notifies Y that he will deliver conforming goods between the 15th and the 30th and does so, Y has received timely delivery of precisely what he ordered. As to whether the repair of goods is a sufficient cure, *see* Zabriskie Chevrolet, Inc. v. Smith, 99 N.J. Super. 441, 240 A.2d 195 (1968) (substitute transmission in automobile), and Wilson v. Scampopli, 228 A.2d 848 (D.C. App. 1967) (new television set required to be returned to shop). Cure is stated in § 2-508 of the Code as available only after the buyer has *rejected* the goods. If the buyer has already accepted the goods and then revokes his acceptance as permitted under UCC § 2-608, the question arises whether cure is still available to the seller if contract time remains. Courts are split on this question. *Cf.* Fitzner Pontiac-Buick-Cadillac, Inc. v. Smith, 523 So. 2d 324, 328 n. 1 (Miss. 1988), *with* Gappelberg v. Landrum, 666 S.W.2d 88 (Tex. 1984). It should also be noted that while the typical application of cure under the UCC is one in which contract time remains at the time the goods are rejected, § 2-508(2) suggests the possibility of cure even where no time remains under the contract but the seller has "reasonable grounds to believe" that the goods which were tendered would be acceptable with or without a money allowance. In such a situation, the seller would then have "a further reasonable time to substitute a conforming tender." *See* Schroder v. Plus Mark, 1995 Tenn. App. LEXIS 214, at *12 (Tenn. Ct. App. Mar. 31, 1995).

(nonoccurrence of the condition) as a termination of his duties.[327] Rather, the duties of the innocent party are merely *suspended* because the breaching party may perform or offer to perform in time to *cure* the material breach.[328] Consider, for example, a building contract requiring progress payments as the construction proceeds. The owner may fail to make a progress payment at some stage during the construction. Traditionally, such a failure has been regarded as a material breach by the owner. Absent a progress payment, the builder may not be able to continue the construction because he will be unable to pay subcontractors, material suppliers and the like.[329] If, however, the delay in making the progress payment was very short, the contractor should not be justified in *abandoning* the work.[330] The contractor would be justified in *suspending* performance until sufficient time expired to permit the owner to cure the material breach. Once that time expires, however, the duties of the contract are discharged, i.e., he may treat the contract as terminated.[331] As to the length of time that must expire before the injured party may treat his duties as not simply suspended but discharged, again, the answer depends upon the circumstances. The Restatement 2d lists certain "significant" circumstances to aid courts in arriving at a satisfactory analysis.[332]

The first guideline suggests that courts consider all of the circumstances set forth in the section designed to determine whether a breach is material.[333] The second guideline considers the extent to which the delay may prevent or hinder the injured party in making reasonable substitute arrangements,[334] and the third guideline considers the extent to which the agreement provided for performance without delay.[335] The Restatement 2d emphasizes that a material failure to perform on a stated day does not, in itself, discharge the other party's duties unless the circumstances indicate that performance or an offer to perform by that day is important. The underlying concept, however, remains: forfeitures are to be avoided. Thus, even a materially breaching party is to be treated fairly. If a breach is immaterial, neither suspension nor termination of the innocent party's duties is permitted. He must continue to perform though he retains a cause of action for any losses he may have sustained.[336] Even

---

[327] In UCC § 2-106(4), "cancellation" is defined as either party putting an end to the contract for breach by the other. This is distinguished from "termination," which is defined in UCC § 2-106(3) as either party putting an end to the contract pursuant to a power conferred by the agreement. "Termination," however, is often used in a fashion synonymous with the concept of "cancellation" under the UCC.

[328] Restatement 2d § 237 comment b.

[329] *See* Aiello Constr. v. Nationwide Tractor Trailer Training & Placement Corp., 122 R.I. 861, 413 A.2d 85 (1980); Zulla Steel, Inc. v. A & M Gregos, Inc., 174 N.J. Super. 124, 415 A.2d 1183 (1980).

[330] See Turner Concrete Steel Co. v. Chester Constr. & Contracting Co., 271 Pa. 205, 211, 114 A. 780, 782 (1921), where the court states: "[I]t cannot be said that the abandonment of a contract of the magnitude here shown, within a few hours of a large payment, was justifiable." *See also* Underground Constr. Co. v. Sanitary Dist. of Chicago, 367 Ill. 360, 11 N.E.2d 361 (1937).

[331] *See* John Kubinski & Sons, Inc. v. Dockside Dev. Corp., 33 Ill. App. 3d 1015, 339 N.E.2d 529 (1st Dist. 1975).

[332] Restatement 2d § 242.

[333] Restatement 2d § 242(a), referring to the five criteria set forth in § 241 which are quoted *supra* note 324.

[334] Restatement 2d § 242(b).

[335] Restatement 2d § 242(c). *See also* June G. Ashton Interiors v. Stark Carpet Corp., 142 Ill. App. 3d 100, 96 Ill. Dec. 306, 491 N.E.2d 120 (1st Dist. 1986) (delay of two to three weeks in delivery of carpeting was a material breach where timely delivery was understood).

[336] UCC § 2-717 permits a party to deduct damages for "partial" breach by deducting the amount of damages from the contract price. It is important to distinguish "partial" breach from "total" breach. An injured party may not suspend or terminate the contract where the breach is immaterial. He may, however, sue for a partial breach that is immaterial even though he is still obligated to perform the contract. Even where the breach is material and the injured

where the breach is material, the RESTATEMENT 2d insists upon an allowance for cure of that breach so as to prevent what may amount to a technical claim by the injured party that he has a right to treat his duties as discharged at the moment the material breach occurred. Thus, if a material breach can be cured shortly after it occurs, it is highly preferable to view the contract as a continuing obligation. To achieve that goal, the analysis permits the injured party only to suspend his performance to allow for cure and a continuation of the contract. This is the basis for characterizing the situation as one involving constructive conditions. If the material breach is cured, it may be said that the constructive condition has occurred, thereby activating the duty of the formerly injured party.

[C]   Factors Determining Materiality — In Limine, Wilful, Delay

As suggested earlier, the determination of materiality is a question of fact which depends upon the particular circumstances surrounding the contract. This is not at all remarkable since contract law is filled with such questions. The guidelines or "circumstances" provided by the FIRST RESTATEMENT and RESTATEMENT 2d to assist courts in determining questions of materiality have already been mentioned.[337] Here we will consider three circumstances that require further emphasis.

[1]   Breach at Outset — In Limine

It is often suggested that a relatively small breach occurring at the outset of the contract is likely to be viewed as material.[338] The rationale is clear: if a party has breached prior to rendering anything other than an insignificant part of his promised performance, he will suffer no substantial forfeiture if the other party is discharged because of the breach. Moreover, when the breach occurs at the earliest stages of the contract, it is difficult to determine the ultimate effect of the breach on the other party were he required to take the performance that is offered or is yet to come. It is fair to resolve the matter in favor of the innocent party. Like other guidelines, the so-called "breach in limine" (at the outset) guideline is not absolute.[339] Although the breach occurs at the outset, it may be so clearly harmless to the defendant that a court would not be justified in denying the plaintiff an action though he would lose nothing more than the value of his bargain if it were denied.

---

party is entitled to suspend his performance, he may choose to continue his performance and sue for partial breach which the RESTATEMENT 2d defines in § 236(2) as "A claim for damages based on only part of the injured party's remaining rights to performance." It is only where the injured party is entitled to terminate the contract, i.e., the breach is material and the time for any cure has expired, that he treats the breach as a "total" breach. "Total" breach is defined in the RESTATEMENT 2d (§ 236(1)) as, "A claim for damages . . . based on all of the injured party's remaining rights to performance."

[337] See supra § 108[B] (quoting or discussing §§ 275 and 276 of the FIRST RESTATEMENT and §§ 241 and 242 of the RESTATEMENT 2d).

[338] See Leazzo v. Dunham, 95 Ill. App. 3d 847, 51 Ill. Dec. 437, 420 N.E.2d 851 (1st Dist. 1981); Hong v. Independent Sch. Dist. No. 245, 181 Minn. 309, 232 N.W. 329 (1930); Hoare v. Rennie, 5 H. & N. 19 [1859]. FIRST RESTATEMENT § 275(c).

[339] See Lutz v. Currence, 91 W. Va. 225, 112 S.E. 506 (1922) (promise to cut and sell logs to be sawed and scaled by a named person held not excused merely because the named person could not be procured by the purchaser to do the work).

[2]   Wilful Breach — "Good Faith and Fair Dealing"

Another guideline found in many decisions is the suggestion that a wilful failure to perform is more likely to be regarded as material than a non-wilful breach.[340] Courts typically do not define "wilful" though they appear to be concerned with the motive of the defaulting party. There is judicial support for the view that one whose motive is good should be entitled to greater consideration than one who acts from improper motives.[341] There is, however, considerable difficulty in determining the motivation of a defaulting party in many cases. The principal vice in the use of the "wilful" element is found in cases which hold that a wilful breach is always material in discharging the other party from his duties under the contract even though the breach may be quantitatively and qualitatively slight.[342] The "wilful" element should never be considered anything more than a guideline to aid in the determination of materiality, rather than a conclusive test to impose a forfeiture upon the defaulting party. There are preferable decisions supporting this view[343] and the RESTATEMENT 2d substitutes a standard of "good faith and fair dealing" for the "less precise" term "wilful," while emphasizing the inconclusive effect of the new standard.[344]

[3]   Delay in Performance — "Time of Essence"

Courts have not always dealt effectively with the question of delay in performance. As seen earlier, both RESTATEMENTS deal with delay in sections separate from those setting forth guidelines to determine the question of materiality,[345] and the RESTATEMENT 2d considers delay a significant factor in determining whether an uncured material breach results in the suspension or the discharge of the other party's duty.[346] It is important to consider certain types of cases which have dealt with the problem of delay in performance.

There are cases suggesting that delay in a duty to pay money is usually less material than delay for a similar period in the performance of some other duty.[347] A rationale for this view may be that the promisee can borrow money and then claim easily calculated damages for breach, rather than subjecting the delaying party to forfeiture. As usual, however, there may be cases where the failure to pay even a small sum for a relatively short time could be viewed

---

[340] FIRST RESTATEMENT § 275(e) considers whether the conduct of the party failing to perform was wilful, negligent, or innocent. The "wilful" element is stronger than the "negligent" element.

[341] See, e.g., Golwitzer v. Hummel, 201 Iowa 751, 206 N.W. 254 (1925); Rischard v. Miller, 182 Cal. 351, 188 P. 50 (1920); Farmer v. First Trust Co., 246 F. 671 (7th Cir. 1917).

[342] See, e.g., McCormick v. Proprietors of Cemetery of Mt. Auburn, 285 Mass. 548, 189 N.E. 585 (1934). See also Bright v. Ganas, 171 Md. 493, 189 A. 427 (1937), and Comment, 50 HARV. L. REV. 1315 (1937) (action by employee against employer to recover for his services where court held it was a complete defense that the employee had, unknown to employer, made improper advances to employer's wife).

[343] See, e.g., Hadden v. Consolidated Edison Co., 34 N.Y.2d 88, 356 N.Y.S.2d 249, 312 N.E.2d 445 (1974) ("wilful" element is not dispositive of materiality — it is only one factor and does not compel a finding of material breach where the value of the performance has not been substantially impaired). See also Mathis v. Thunderbird Village, Inc., 236 Or. 425, 389 P.2d 343 (1964); McNeal-Edwards Co. v. Frank L. Young Co., 51 F.2d 699 (1st Cir. 1931).

[344] RESTATEMENT 2d § 241(e) and comment f. See Shay v. Gallagher, 1995 Conn. Super. LEXIS 192, at *15 (Conn. Super. Ct. Jan. 18, 1995).

[345] See supra note 337 and text at notes 348, 349, and 350.

[346] RESTATEMENT 2d § 242.

[347] See Farris v. Ferguson, 146 Tenn. 498, 242 S.W. 873 (1922); Vulcan Trading Corp. v. Kokomo Steel & Wire Co., 268 F. 913, 916 (7th Cir. 1920).

as a material breach. This would be true, for example, where a debtor's solvency is doubtful and there is a justifiable suspicion that he will be unable to make later payments.[348] A delay in the construction of a large building that was estimated to take more than a year to build may not be material, while a delay of three months to build a simple house may very well be a material, uncured breach.[349] It should be recalled that the failure of an owner to make a progress payment to a contractor is considered material in terms of permitting the builder to suspend rather than abandon performance until it is determined whether the breach can be cured.[350]

Delay in the performance of a contract for the sale of goods is treated differently from delay in the performance of a contract for the sale of land. Typically, market prices for goods are subject to much greater fluctuation than contracts for the sale of land, and goods are often purchased for resale so that the buyer is more concerned about time. For many years, therefore, courts have been willing to state that time is of the essence in contracts for the sale of goods.[351] In land contracts, however, most of our courts have refused to imply any understanding that time is of the essence.[352] The RESTATEMENT 2d suggests that considerable delay will not preclude enforcement of a land contract, absent special circumstances, and assuming the availability of adequate compensatory damages.[353]

The treatment of delay in performance as a unique form of breach is traceable to the statement in older cases that time is of the essence at law. It is highly questionable whether this view was literally accepted even in those nineteenth century cases in which it appeared.[354] It is clear that delay in performance is now considered like any other circumstance in determining the severity of the breach, i.e., it is only one factor to be considered under all of the circumstances.[355]

The parties may include an express provision in the contract that the time for performance is important. Questions of interpretation arise, however, with respect to the language and circumstances of such a provision. If, for example, the contract merely provides for performance on a stated date, failure to perform on that date does not discharge the duty of the injured party. Under an older analysis, the delay would be treated as immaterial and would

---

[348] *See* Wolverine Packing Co. v. Hawley, 251 Mich. 215, 231 N.W. 617 (1930) (specific performance refused where plaintiff was one day late in providing payment for cherries); National Mach. & Tool Co. v. Standard Shoe Mach. Co., 181 Mass. 275, 63 N.E. 900 (1902) (delay of ten days in the payment of a small sum). *Cf.* RESTATEMENT 2d § 241(d).

[349] Where the buyers of a house allowed the builder three additional months to perform or cure and the house was not completed, the breach was material since the original estimate for the construction of the house was only three months. Richmond v. Rone, 1991 Tenn. App. LEXIS 130 (Tenn. Ct. App. Feb. 27, 1991).

[350] *See supra* text prior to note 341.

[351] *See* Norrington v. Wright, 115 U.S. 188, 6 S. Ct. 12, 29 L. Ed. 366 (1885). Buyers, however, often receive more tolerant treatment than sellers. Moreover, a court will not treat a buyer's delay as material if there is some suspicion that the seller was eager to discover a breach by the purchaser. *See* Continental Grain v. Simpson Feed Co., 102 F. Supp. 354 (D. Ark. 1951).

[352] *See* Twin Towers Dev., Inc. v. Butternut Apts., L.P., 257 Neb. 511, 515, 599 N.W.2d 839, 844 (1999) ("While in an ordinary contract for the sale of real estate, time is not of the essence, time may be made of the essence when provided for in the agreement itself or clearly manifested by the agreement construed in light of surrounding circumstances."). *See also* String v. Steven Dev. Corp., 269 Md. 569, 307 A.2d 713 (1973); MacFadden v. Walker, 5 Cal. 3d 811, 488 P.2d 1353, 97 Cal. Rptr. 537 (1971) (even wilful delay was not sufficient to create material breach).

[353] RESTATEMENT 2d § 242 comment c.

[354] *See* CORBIN § 37.1.

[355] In some states, statutes provide that time shall not be of the essence unless the terms of the contract expressly so provide. *See, e.g.*, S.D. CODIFIED LAWS § 53-10-3.

have to continue for some time to become material when it would discharge the injured party from any further duty. Under the RESTATEMENT 2d, the delay may be viewed as an uncured material breach permitting the other party to suspend performance to determine whether the breach could be cured. If further delay occurred, no cure would be possible and the injured party would be discharged.[356] If the provision in the contract is one that either states or amounts to an agreement that time for performance is of the essence of the contract and there is little or no question that this was the intention of the parties, failure to perform on time will be a material breach discharging the duty of the other party.[357] In this situation, there is no suspension stage. There is no possibility of curing the breach. As usual, the problem is to determine whether the parties genuinely intended time to be of the essence. If the writing is a printed form containing the stock "time is of the essence" clause, it should not necessarily be interpreted as manifesting the intention of the parties.[358] As in other questions of interpretation, all of the surrounding circumstances must be considered.[359]

[D]   Erroneous Judgment Concerning Materiality

In light of the fact that the determination of materiality is a question of fact and even courts can be disconcerted in applying the various guidelines that have been suggested over the years, an innocent party may find it difficult to determine whether a failure of performance by his counterpart constitutes a material breach discharging the innocent party from further duties under the contract. If the innocent party treats his duties as discharged because he has decided that the other party has materially breached and, as a matter of judicial hindsight, his judgment is wrong, the innocent party is no longer innocent. In a well-known case,[360] the defendant leased a sign which the lessor promised to repair and clean when necessary. On several occasions, the defendant requested that the sign be cleaned but the requests went unheeded. The irritated defendant treated his duties under the contract as discharged. The lessor brought an action under an acceleration clause of the lease contract and the issue was whether the defendant properly treated his duties as discharged. If the lessor's breach in not cleaning the sign was material, the duties of the defendant were discharged. In deciding that the lessor's breach was immaterial, the court cautioned, "[T]he injured party's determination that there has been a material breach, justifying his own repudiation, is fraught with peril, for should such determination, as viewed by a later court in the calm of its contemplation, be unwarranted, the repudiator himself will have been guilty of material breach and himself have become the aggressor, not an innocent victim."[361]

This position appears harsh with respect to an innocent party who is not attempting to escape from his contractual duty. The judgment of the innocent party hinges on his determination of materiality. To permit the other party who has repeatedly refused to perform

---

[356] RESTATEMENT 2d § 237 comment b.

[357] RESTATEMENT 2d § 242(c) and comment d.

[358] See Pederson v. McGuire, 333 N.W.2d 823 (S.D. 1983), where the court suggests that whether time is of the essence depends upon the intention of the parties and the purpose of the contract rather than a printed clause in the contract. *See also* RESTATEMENT 2d § 242(c) comment d and ill. 9.

[359] *See* Chariot Holdings, Ltd. v. Eastmet Corp., 153 Ill. App. 3d 50, 106 Ill. Dec. 285, 505 N.E.2d 1076 (1st Dist. 1987) (even where the contract contains a time-of-essence clause, courts will inquire as to whether the delay constitutes a material breach).

[360] Walker & Co. v. Harrison, 347 Mich. 630, 81 N.W.2d 352 (1957).

[361] *Id.*, 347 Mich. at 635, 81 N.W.2d at 355.

certain duties, albeit immaterial duties, to treat an innocent though erroneous judgment and action thereon as a material breach, which has the effect of discharging the party who first breached, borders on sanctioning a forfeiture. While another case would not permit such an erroneous judgment by an innocent party to discharge the duties of the party who first breached immaterially,[362] there is a dearth of case law in this area. Where an apparently good faith but erroneous interpretation of a contract led a party to commit an anticipatory repudiation (*see* § 110 *infra*), the court relied on RESTATEMENT 2d § 250 in holding that a party acts at his peril if, insisting on what he mistakenly believes his rights, he refused to perform. The court, however, distinguished the situation where a party, still manifesting a willingness to perform, asserts an innocent but erroneous interpretation of the contract.[363] The holding and rationale in the sign cleaning case suggests a mechanical application of the concept of material breach that should be avoided to preclude the possibility of forfeiture. If, however, a party operates in bad faith in judging a breach to be material so as to bring about a discharge of his duties in a bargain he no longer views as beneficial, there should be no judicial concern over his fate.

§ 109 SUBSTANTIAL PERFORMANCE — MATERIAL BREACH COMPARED — "PERFECT TENDER" RULE

[A] Material Breach — "Failure of Consideration" — Failure of Performance

We have seen the traditional view that whether a breach permits the innocent party to treat her duties as discharged depends upon whether the breach was material. Under the RESTATEMENT 2d, the innocent party would have to show not only a material breach, but the fact that the time for cure of that breach had passed, thereby discharging her duty rather than merely suspending it. Under the traditional view, there was some confusion through the use of the anomalous phrase, "failure of consideration," i.e., the nonperformance of the plaintiff amounted to a "failure of consideration" discharging the defendant. The term "consideration" is used in this context to suggest a failure of performance that is a material failure, but a failure of performance may be either material or immaterial. Moreover, "consideration" should be relegated to the formation stage of the contract. To avoid needless confusion, the RESTATEMENT 2d properly rejects the phrase "failure of consideration" and substitutes "failure of performance."[364]

[B] Immaterial Failure of Performance — The Doctrine of Substantial Performance — "Wilful" Default

Courts may treat certain failures of performance by a plaintiff under the doctrine of "substantial performance." For many years, there was a tendency to treat the doctrine of substantial performance as related to but separate from the question of materiality of breach. As will be seen, the doctrine of substantial performance is a dimension of the materiality of

---

[362] *See* Riess v. Murchison, 503 F.2d 999 (9th Cir. 1974), *cert. denied*, 420 U.S. 993, 95 S. Ct. 1430, 43 L. Ed. 2d 674 (1975).

[363] Chamberlin v. Puckett Constr., 277 Mont. 198, 921 P.2d 1237 (1996).

[364] RESTATEMENT 2d § 237 comment a. *See* Converse v. Zinke, 635 P.2d 882, 886 (Colo. 1981).

breach analysis. The substantive identity of the two doctrines, however, becomes clear only upon an understanding of the origins of the doctrine of substantial performance.

The story begins with the creation of the doctrine of constructive conditions which was considered earlier in this chapter.[365] In creating the concept of dependent covenants which allowed for the constructive condition analysis,[366] Lord Mansfield made one of his significant contributions to the common law of contracts.[367] The sensible concept of constructive conditions could, however, lead to unjust results in certain cases. Thus, where performance by *A* is a constructive condition to the duty of *B*, a strict application of that concept suggests that *any* failure of performance by *A* is a failure of a constructive condition to *B*'s duty, and *B*'s duty would never be activated. Yet, where a failure of performance is slight and could be easily compensated in damages, *A* should not suffer a forfeiture simply because the last scintilla of his performance has not occurred. Under a materiality of breach rubric, such a failure of performance would be viewed as an immaterial breach and *B*'s duty would not be discharged. Again, under a strict application of the doctrine of constructive conditions, however, *B*'s duty would never be activated and *B*, in effect, would be discharged from his duty because of an immaterial breach by *A*.

Just four years after he created the doctrine of constructive conditions, Lord Mansfield remedied this defect. In *Boone v. Eyre*,[368] he made it clear that a defendant could not escape his contractual duty by pleading failure of a constructive condition precedent to his duty when the failure was slight. The doctrine of substantial performance was, therefore, designed to mitigate the injustice that could result from a literal or strict application of the doctrine of constructive conditions. The landmark case in the twentieth century elaborating the doctrine is *Jacob & Youngs, Inc. v. Kent*,[369] in an opinion written by another judicial giant, Benjamin Nathan Cardozo.

A building contract included a specification which required all wrought-iron pipe used in the building to be "of Reading manufacture." Through oversight, physically identical pipe manufactured by Cohoes was used in the building. The contractor was instructed to replace all of the pipe which was, for the most part, encased in the walls of the building. Replacement of the pipe would have required demolition of large portions of the completed structure resulting in considerable economic waste. When the contractor refused to replace the pipe under these circumstances, the architect refused to issue his certificate, which was a condition to the last progress payment due the builder. The builder brought an action to recover this payment. The court recognized that, while a party to a contract has a duty of full performance as a general rule, a failure of performance, "both trivial and innocent, will sometimes be atoned for by allowance of the resulting damage, and will not always be the breach of a [constructive] condition to be followed by a forfeiture. . . ."[370] The question in such a case is whether the constructive condition precedent to the owner's duty to make the last progress payment

---

[365] *See* § 105 *supra*.

[366] Even modern courts sometimes mention the independent/dependent covenant distinction which is generally articulated in the language of constructive conditions. *See* Hunt v. Salon De Coiffures, 3 Ohio Misc. 2d 5, 444 N.E.2d 488 (Mun. Ct. 1982).

[367] *See* Kingston v. Preston, 2 Doug. 689 [1773].

[368] 1 H. Bl. 273 [1777].

[369] 230 N.Y. 239, 129 N.E. 889, 23 A.L.R. 1429 (1921).

[370] *Id.*, 129 N.E. at 890.

should be excused because the plaintiff has, notwithstanding his default, substantially performed his duties under the contract. Judge Cardozo suggested criteria, virtually indistinguishable from the circumstances courts traditionally consider in determining whether a breach is material, to assist courts in determining whether a particular plaintiff has substantially performed.[371] The essential question is whether the builder's failure to perform was a material or immaterial breach.[372] A finding of immaterial breach would have allowed the builder to recover the contract price minus any provable loss caused of the breach. Here, the court determined that the builder had "substantially performed" and should recover the contract price minus any diminution in value to the owner caused by the builder's insubstantial (immaterial) failure of performance.

It is now abundantly clear that a finding of substantial performance is necessarily a finding that the breach is immaterial. As one court suggests, "[S]ubstantial performance is performance without a material breach, and a material breach results in performance that is not substantial."[373] Courts have begun to slide easily between the "doctrine" of substantial performance and the criteria for determining materiality of breach by using the "circumstances" of materiality as the guidelines for substantial performance.[374] Just as questions of materiality of breach are not reducible to mechanical rules, neither are questions of substantial performance.[375]

"Wilful" Default. Earlier we explored the "wilful" element in determining whether a breach was material.[376] In *Jacob & Youngs*, Judge Cardozo insisted that the doctrine of substantial performance would not be available to a "wilful" defaulter.[377] This view continues to be announced in modern cases.[378] Yet, just as the RESTATEMENT 2d has modified the "wilful" criterion of material breach to a standard of "good faith and fair dealing" and insisted that neither this criterion of materiality nor others be viewed as conclusive,[379] an identical analysis of this criterion in relation to substantial performance is now more likely in modern cases.[380]

---

[371] "We must weigh the purpose to be served, the desire to be gratified, the excuse for deviation from the letter, the cruelty of enforced adherence." *Id.*, 129 N.E. at 893.

[372] The RESTATEMENT 2d recognizes that "[I]t is common to state the issue, not in terms of whether there has been an uncured material failure by the contractor, but in terms of whether there has been substantial performance by him. The manner of stating the issue does not change the substance, however, and the rule [concerning material versus immaterial failures of performance] also applies to such cases."

[373] United States v. Castaneda, 162 F.3d 832, 838 n.31 (5th Cir. 1998).

[374] See International Food Concepts, Inc. v. Eastern U.S. Agric. & Food Export Council Corp., 2000 U.S. App. LEXIS 28095, at *6 (9th Cir. Nov. 3, 2000); Henry v. Bitar, 1998 Wash. App. LEXIS 125 (Wash. Ct. App. Jan. 30, 1998); Prudential Ins. Co. v. Stratton, 14 Ark. App. 145, 685 S.W.2d 818 (1985); Vincenzi v. Cerro, 186 Conn. 612, 442 A.2d 1352 (1982); Della Ratta, Inc. v. American Better Community Developers, Inc., 38 Md. App. 119, 380 A.2d 627 (1977).

[375] Roberts & Co. v. Sergio, 22 Ark. App. 58, 733 S.W.2d 420 (1987).

[376] *See* § 108[C][2], *supra.*

[377] "The wilful transgressor must accept the penalty of his transgression. For him there is no occasion to mitigate the rigor of implied [constructive] conditions. The transgressor whose default is unintentional and trivial may hope for mercy if he will offer atonement for his wrong." *Jacob & Youngs*, 129 N.E. at 893.

[378] *See, e.g., International Food Concepts, supra* note 374; Huntsville & Madison County R. Auth. v. Alabama Indus. R. Inc., 505 So. 2d 341 (Ala. 1987).

[379] RESTATEMENT 2d § 241(e).

[380] *See* Vincenzi v. Cerro, 186 Conn. 612, 442 A.2d 1352 (1982).

[C]   Substantial Performance and Express Conditions

In the *Jacob & Youngs* opinion, Judge Cardozo took pains to distinguish the situation before the court involving a constructive condition from one involving an express condition: "This is not to say that the parties are not free by apt and certain words to effectuate a purpose that performance of every term shall be a condition of recovery. That question is not here."[381] If, therefore, the parties have made an event an express condition, no mitigating standard of materiality or substantiality is available to relieve against a forfeiture.[382] If, however, the express condition was not a material part of the agreed exchange and its non-occurrence would cause disproportionate forfeiture, the condition may be excused.[383] Since the doctrine of substantial performance was designed to avoid forfeitures where a constructive condition did not occur,[384] where the parties have included an express condition of little significance or value, such a condition may be excused if it would cause an extreme forfeiture.[385] The RESTATEMENT 2d includes an illustration of this concept based on facts similar to those in *Jacob & Youngs*. The facts of the case are changed to make the specification for the proper brand of pipe an express condition rather than a constructive condition, and the unpaid balance of the contract price is greater. The illustration concludes that a court may excuse even this *express* condition if it determines that the nonoccurrence of the condition was so relatively unimportant to the owner that the resulting forfeiture to the builder would be extreme.[386] Even an extreme forfeiture resulting from the non-occurrence of an express condition will be enforced, however, where the risk has been assumed by one of the parties.

Where a contract provided for additional compensation to one of the parties amounting to $25 million or more, expressly conditioned on a published government regulation, proposed regulation or ruling by a certain date, the non-occurrence of that condition precluded the payment of the additional compensation, notwithstanding the occurrence of the publication less than eight months after the date set forth in the contract.[387] Answering the plaintiff's claim that the condition in this case was not a material part of the agreed exchange and should, therefore, be excused because of the extreme forfeiture, the court stated that both the doctrine of substantial performance and the RESTATEMENT 2d concept of excuse to avoid forfeitures are based on a denial of compensation after a party has relied substantially by preparation or performance on the expectation of receiving compensation.[388] In this case, there was no performance or preparation for performance. The payment of additional

---

[381] 129 N.E. at 891.

[382] Oppenheimer & Co., Inc. v. Oppenheim, Appel, Dixon & Co., 86 N.Y.2d 685, 636 N.Y.S.2d 734, 660 N.E.2d 415, 419 (1995) (relying on RESTATEMENT 2d § 237, comment d).

[383] *Id.* RESTATEMENT 2d § 229.

[384] Brown-Marx Assocs., Ltd. v. Emigrant Sav. Bank, 703 F.2d 1361, 1367 (11th Cir. 1983) ("The intent of the doctrine is equitable: to prevent unjust enrichment or the inequity of one party's getting the benefit of performance albeit not strictly in accord with the contract's terms, with no obligation in return. The courts will allow recovery under the contract, less allowance for deviations, where a party in good faith has substantially performed its obligation.").

[385] RESTATEMENT 2d § 229.

[386] RESTATEMENT 2d § 229 ill. 1.

[387] Hoosier Energy Rural Elec. Coop. v. Amoco Tax Leasing IV Corp., 34 F.3d 1310 (7th Cir. 1994). *See* Oppenheimer & Co., Inc. v. Oppenheim, Appel, Dixon & Co., 205 A.D.2d 412, 613 N.Y.S.2d 622 (1st Dep't 1994) (applying the doctrine of substantial performance where conditions had been met orally, but written consents were not delivered by the deadline in a sublease transaction).

[388] *Id.* at 1320.

compensation depended upon the occurrence of an event controlled exclusively by a third party (the government) by a certain date. That event did not occur and the duty to pay the additional compensation was not activated. If this results in a forfeiture, " 'the law permits a man to make a contract which will result in a forfeiture; and when it is clear from the terms of the contract that the parties have so agreed, the forfeiture will be enforced.' "[389]

The RESTATEMENT 2d effort to overcome extreme forfeitures even in the face of express conditions is commendable. Yet, the difficulties in determining whether a particular forfeiture is "extreme" and whether the nonoccurrence of an express condition is relatively unimportant should not be underestimated.[390]

[D] Scope of Substantial Performance and Related Concepts

[1] Application to Non-Construction Contracts

While the classic example of substantial performance is the building illustration where the builder has virtually completed the building and would suffer a forfeiture if the constructive condition of absolutely complete performance is not excused, it is clear that the doctrine of substantial performance will be applicable to virtually any other type of contract.[391] Since the analysis is really a materiality of breach analysis and courts are currently using the terms "substantial performance" and "immaterial breach" interchangeably, other than tradition, there is no basis for suggesting that the "doctrine" of substantial performance does not apply to a particular type of contract, except one type.[392] The major exception to the use of the doctrine of substantial performance is found in contracts for the sale of goods.

If the doctrine of substantial performance applied to contracts for the sale of goods and a seller delivered substantially conforming goods (goods with immaterial defects) to the buyer, the seller could recover the contract price minus any loss to the buyer caused by such defects. Prior to the UCC, which now governs contracts for the sale of goods throughout the country, courts refused to apply the doctrine of substantial performance to such contracts,[393] and modern courts continue to reflect the view that "[s]trict performance is generally required in the case of a commercial contract."[394] The failure of the seller to deliver the exact quantity or

---

[389] *Id.* (quoting Winston Personnel Agency, Inc., v. Abcon Industries, Inc., 108 Misc. 2d 695, 438 N.Y.S.2d 669, 670 (Civ. Ct. 1980)).

[390] A similar suggestion in the second edition of this book is mentioned approvingly in *Jackson v. Richards 5 & 10, Inc.*, 289 Pa. Super. 445, 433 A.2d 888 (1981), which deals with the question of excusing an express condition in the light of substantial performance. Another possibility is the application of the substantial performance doctrine to permit the substantially performing party to recover the contract price minus whatever may be required to comply with the express condition. *See* Della Ratta, Inc. v. American Better Community Developers, Inc., 38 Md. App. 119, 380 A.2d 627 (1977).

[391] *See* Russell v. Salve Regina College, 938 F.2d 315 (1st Cir. 1991) (contract between student and college); Prudential Ins. Co. v. Stratton, 14 Ark. App. 145, 685 S.W.2d 818 (1985).

[392] See Hadden v. Consolidated Edison Co., 34 N.Y.2d 88, 356 N.Y.S.2d 249, 312 N.E.2d 445 (1974), where the court applies the doctrine of substantial performance to an employment contract and suggests criteria such as those used for determining materiality of breach.

[393] "There is no room in commercial contracts for the doctrine of substantial performance." L. Hand in Mitsubishi Goshi Kaisha v. J. Aron & Co., 16 F.2d 185, 186 (2d Cir. 1926). For an historical analysis, see Ramirez v. Autosport, 88 N.J. 277, 440 A.2d 1345 (1982).

[394] Tolzman v. Town of Wyoming, 1999 Minn. App. LEXIS 188, at *7 (Minn. Ct. App. Mar. 2, 1999).

quality of goods in conformity with the contract description of such goods excused the buyer from performing, even where the buyer could have been adequately compensated in damages for any loss he may have suffered.[395] It is important to consider how the current governing statute, the UCC, deals with this issue.

[2]   UCC — The "Perfect Tender Rule" — Rejection — Revocation of Acceptance

At first glance, the UCC suggests compliance with prior law in contracts for the sale of goods by stating a "perfect tender rule," i.e., a buyer's absolute right of rejection. "[I]f the goods or the tender of delivery fail *in any respect* to conform to the contract, the buyer may (a) reject the whole or (b) accept the whole [notwithstanding any nonconformity]; or (c) accept any commercial unit or units and reject the rest."[396]

If a contract requires delivery of 500 expensive wooden cabinets and the seller delivered 498 in perfect condition while two were very slightly scratched, the literal application of the foregoing UCC language would permit the buyer to reject the goods notwithstanding the possibility of easy removal of the scratches in inexpensive fashion. The negative "absolute right to reject" is often seen as the positive requirement that the seller make a perfect tender of perfect goods, the so-called "perfect tender" rule. A literal application of this rule could easily lead to forfeitures. The UCC, however, does not mitigate the potential harshness of this rule through doctrines of immaterial breach or substantial performance. Rather, it surrounds this apparently absolute rule with express and implied qualifications that substantially diminish its thrust.

There are six identifiable qualifications to the buyer's "absolute" right to reject or the correlative duty of the seller to make a "perfect tender:"

(1) As in many other sections of Article 2 of the UCC, the buyer's so-called absolute right to reject is qualified by the phrase, "unless otherwise agreed."[397] The parties, therefore, may agree to limit the buyer's apparent absolute right to reject.[398]

(2) The right to reject does not apply to breaches of installment contracts as they are defined in the Code.[399] If the contract is an installment contract, the buyer may reject any nonconforming installment only if the defect "substantially impairs the value of the whole contract and cannot be cured."[400] The "substantial impairment of the value" test is the equivalent of the materiality test.[401] Thus, when the contract is an installment contract, the

---

[395] For a collection and discussion of the cases, see Note, *Application of the Doctrine of Substantial Performance in the Law of Sales*, 33 COLUM. L. REV. 1021 (1933).

[396] UCC § 2-601 (emphasis added).

[397] UCC § 2-601. *See* BellSouth Telesensor v. Information Sys. & Networks Corp., 1995 U.S. App. LEXIS 24802 (4th Cir. Sept. 5, 1995).

[398] The broad definition of "agreement" under the UCC must be emphasized in this regard: " 'Agreement' means the bargain of the parties in fact as found in their language or by implication from other circumstances including course of dealing or usage of trade or course of performance. . . ." UCC § 1-201(3). Thus, an agreement based on prior course of dealing, trade usage or course of performance could limit the absolute right to reject.

[399] "An 'installment contract' is one which requires or authorizes the delivery of goods in separate lots to be separately accepted. . . ."

[400] UCC § 2-612(2).

[401] The "substantial impairment of value" standard is also set forth in UCC § 2-610, dealing with anticipatory

buyer may not reject for *any* defect; the defect must be material.[402]

(3) Where the contract is an F.O.B. "shipment" contract, i.e., F.O.B. seller's plant,[403] the seller must place the goods in the possession of a reasonable (independent) carrier for transport, obtain and promptly deliver or tender any necessary documents to the buyer, and promptly notify the buyer of the shipment.[404] Since the rejection section of the UCC permits the buyer to reject not only because of *any* defect in the goods, but also for *any* defect in the *tender* of the goods,[405] it may appear that a failure by a seller either to make a proper contract with a carrier or to notify the buyer of the shipment would create a right of rejection in the buyer. Certainly, either failure would constitute a defective tender. Yet, the UCC section setting forth the seller's duties to make an effective tender indicates that a failure of either of these tender duties "is a ground for rejection only if *material* delay or loss ensues."[406] This is sensible since a failure to notify the buyer or to contract with a proper carrier should not cause a forfeiture to the seller unless there is a substantial loss to the buyer. Thus, the buyer may not reject because of *any* defect in the tender.

(4) If slightly defective goods are shipped to the buyer and the buyer rejects, there may be evidence that the buyer rejected only because he sought to escape his bargain and used the absolute right to reject as a technical excuse to do so. Such a rejection would not have been made in "good faith," a standard that permeates the entire UCC and particularly Article 2 of the Code dealing with contracts for the sale of goods.[407]

(5) The buyer has only a reasonable time to *reject* the goods.[408] If the buyer fails to reject the goods within a reasonable time, he will be said to have accepted the goods.[409] Once the acceptance stage occurs, the right of rejection is lost. The buyer, however, may still be able to

---

repudiation. A comment to that section states, "The most useful test of substantial value is to determine whether *material* inconvenience or injustice will result. . . ." UCC § 2-610, comment 3 (emphasis supplied). In this section of the UCC (2-612(2)), the statute refers only to substantial impairment of the value of that installment. Comment 3 indicates that it "must be judged in terms of the normal or specifically known purposes of the contract." In UCC § 2-608(1), a buyer may revoke acceptance of goods "whose non-conformity substantially impairs the value *to him.*" (Emphasis supplied.) This adds a subjective element to be considered later in this section.

[402] *See* Bodine Sewer, Inc. v. Eastern Ill. Precast, Inc., 143 Ill. App. 3d 920, 97 Ill. Dec. 898, 493 N.E.2d 705 (4th Dist. 1986).

[403] UCC § 2-319(1)(a).

[404] UCC § 2-504.

[405] UCC § 2-601. For a discussion of "tender of delivery" under UCC § 2-503(1), see Washington Freightliner, Inc. v. Shantytown Pier, Inc., 351 Md. 616, 719 A.2d 541 (1998).

[406] UCC § 2-504 (emphasis added). See also comment 6 to this section.

[407] *See* Neumiller Farms, Inc. v. Cornett, 368 So. 2d 272 (Ala. 1979) (rejection based on a claim of dissatisfaction not made in good faith constitutes a breach of contract). See also Printing Center of Texas v. Supermind Publishing Co., 669 S. W. 2d 779 (Tex. App. 1984).

[408] UCC § 2-602(1) indicates that the rejection of goods must occur within a reasonable time after their delivery or tender. What is a reasonable time is ordinarily a question of fact and will depend upon such factors as whether the goods were perishable, highly fluctuating in price, the nature of the goods, trade usage, the difficulty of determining defects, and any other relevant circumstances. *See* Sherkate Sahami Khass Rapol (Rapol Constr. Co.) v. Henry R. Jahn & Son, Inc., 701 F.2d 1049 (2d Cir. 1983).

[409] UCC § 606(1)(b). The other methods of "acceptance" of the goods in this section of the Code are found in § 2-606(1)(a), where the buyer signifies to the seller that he will accept the goods, and § 2-606(1)(c), where the buyer performs an act inconsistent with the seller's ownership. *See* Intervale Steel Corp. v. Borg & Beck Div., Borg-Warner Corp., 578 F. Supp. 1081 (E.D. Mich. 1984), *aff'd per curiam*, 762 F.2d 1008 (6th Cir. 1985).

"revoke his acceptance" of the goods.[410] Unlike the right of rejection, the right to *revoke acceptance* is expressly qualified under the UCC as requiring substantial impairment of the value of the goods *to the buyer*.[411] On its face, this section may be read as requiring a showing of subjective materiality, i.e., if the value of the goods is substantially impaired to the particular buyer even though the value to a reasonable (objective) buyer would not be substantially impaired, the particular buyer may revoke his acceptance.[412] A comment to this UCC section clearly confirms the *subjective* nature of the revocation of acceptance test.[413] Courts are uncomfortable with any subjective test in contract law and they have, therefore, sought to limit the subjective nature of the inquiry. While the test for substantial impairment "to the buyer" is subjective in focusing upon the actual rather than a reasonable buyer, it is also objective in determining whether the value of the goods to that particular buyer may be said to be impaired.[414] The so-called perfect tender rule or corollary absolute right to reject is, therefore, limited when the goods are accepted since the buyer must prove substantial impairment of the value of the goods to him (the buyer) before he can properly exercise the right to revoke acceptance.

(6) The most significant limitation on the "absolute" right to reject is the UCC concept of *cure* which was discussed earlier.[415] Under this section, the seller has the right to cure (repair or replace) any nonconforming good within "contract time," i.e., the normal time for performing one's contractual duty.[416] Unless the time for performance is clearly bargained not to extend beyond a certain time, it is likely that a court would permit a seller some commercially reasonable time to cure in most cases. Moreover, the UCC, itself, expressly permits cure beyond "contract time" where the seller had reason to believe that the nonconforming goods would be accepted with or without some money allowance.[417] Where the goods have been accepted and the buyer rightfully revokes acceptance, courts are split on whether to permit the seller to cure since the cure section of the Code speaks only in terms of the buyer's rejection of goods.[418]

---

[410] UCC § 2-608. *See* Jensen v. Seigel Mobile Homes Group, 105 Idaho 189, 668 P.2d 65 (1983).

[411] UCC § 2-608(1).

[412] Similarly, if the value to the particular buyer is not substantially impaired, though it would have been impaired to a reasonable buyer, the subjective analysis would preclude the exercise of the right to revoke acceptance.

[413] "For this purpose the test is not what the seller had reason to know at the time of contracting; the question is whether the non-conformity is such as will in fact cause a substantial impairment to the buyer though the seller had no advance knowledge as to the buyer's particular circumstances." UCC § 2-608 comment 2.

[414] GMC v. Dohmann, 247 Conn. 274, 722 A.2d 1205, 1213 (1998). In Jensen v. Seigel Mobile Homes Group, 105 Idaho 189, 668 P.2d 65 (1983), the court suggests that the test is subjective in that it addresses whether the nonconformities substantially impaired the value of the home to the actual buyer, rather than the reasonable buyer. However, the actual buyer is to be considered in light of objective evidence of that buyer's purposes and proclivities. *See* Asciolla v. Manter Oldsmobile-Pontiac, 117 N.H. 85, 370 A.2d 270 (1977) (particularly prudent and painstaking car buyer). Note the use of "substantial impairment of value" in installment contracts (UCC § 2-612(2)) at note 416 *supra*.

[415] UCC § 2-508. *See supra* § 108[B][1]. at note 326.

[416] UCC § 2-508(1). *See* Leitchfield Dev. Corp. v. Clark, 757 S.W.2d 207 (Ky. Ct. App. 1988); Schiavi Mobile Homes, Inc. v. Gagne, 510 A.2d 236 (Me. 1986).

[417] UCC § 2-508(2) and comment 2.

[418] *See* the discussion in note 326, § 108[B][2][c], *supra*.

[3]   CISG — "Fundamental Breach" — UNIDROIT Principles

International contracts for the sale of goods governed by CISG are not subject to a perfect tender rule. CISG applies a concept called "fundamental breach": "A breach of contract by one of the parties is fundamental if it results in such detriment to the other party as substantially to deprive him of what he is entitled to expect under the contract, unless the party in breach did not foresee and a reasonable person of the same kind in the same circumstances would not have foreseen such a result."[419] A party may *avoid* a contract, i.e., be discharged from duties under the contract, only if the breach is *fundamental.*[420] The UNIDROIT Principles replicate CISG in permitting a party to terminate a contract only "where the failure of the other party to perform an obligation under the contract amounts to a fundamental non-performance."[421] Principles proceeds to list guidelines to determine whether a failure of performance is "fundamental" that are quite similar to the guidelines to determine material breach under the RESTATEMENT 2d.[422]

§ 110   PROSPECTIVE FAILURE OF PERFORMANCE — ANTICIPATORY REPUDIATION

[A]   Nature of the Problem

Our discussion of failure of performance to this point assumed that the time for performance had arrived and one of the parties failed to perform, i.e., the constructive condition to the performance of the innocent party had not occurred. There are myriad situations, however, where the time for performance has not arrived and there is very good reason to believe that performance will not occur when it is due. Prior to the time for performance, for example, one party may announce that he will not perform when performance is due. Even without such an announcement, the circumstances may be abundantly clear that one party will be incapable of performance when it is due. In other

---

[419] CISG, Art. 25. Whether the language of "substantial deprivation" in this definition of fundamental breach should be equated to material breach or the absence of substantial performance is discussed in Flechtner, *Remedies Under the New International Sales convention: the Perspective from Article 2 of the U.C.C.,* 8 J. L. & COM. 53, 75 (1988).

[420] CISG Art. 49(1)(a) (buyer's avoidance); Art. 64(1)(a) (seller's avoidance). Absent a fundamental breach or a *Nachfrist* exception (where a party fixes a reasonable additional time for performance by the other party — Articles 47 & 63), an aggrieved party will follow the "nonavoidance" procedure that will require the party to continue to perform the contract and seek damages for provable losses.

[421] Principles, Art. 7.3.1(1).

[422] Principles Art. 7.3.1 (2) and RESTATEMENT 2d § 241. Thus, in subsection (a), Principles replicates CISG Art. 25 in considering whether the non-performance substantially deprives the aggrieved party of what it was entitled to expect as the result was reasonably foreseeable by the other party. RESTATEMENT 2d § 241(a) considers the extent to which the injured party will be deprived of the benefit which he reasonably expected. RESTATEMENT 2d subsection (c) seeks to avoid forfeiture for the party who has failed, in some respect, to perform while Principles (e) worries about disproportionate loss by the non-performing party. In (c), Principles considers whether the non-performance is intentional or reckless, while the RESTATEMENT 2d (e) suggests that compliance with standards of good faith and fair dealing are significant factors. RESTATEMENT 2d (d) considers the likelihood that the non-performing party will cure his failure, while Principles (d) asks whether the aggrieved party has reason to believe that it cannot rely on the other party's future performance. The only substantial difference in the guides suggested is the respective subsections (b). RESTATEMENT 2d (b) is concerned about the extent to which the injured party can be adequately compensated for the benefit of which he will be deprived, while Principles (b) focuses upon whether strict compliance with the obligation that has not been performed is of the essence under the contract.

situations, the circumstances prior to the time for performance may suggest reasonable doubt, rather than certainty, that one of the parties may not perform when performance is due. These situations give rise to fundamental questions: Should a cause of action *ever* be recognized before the duty of immediate performance is due? If such a cause of action should be recognized, should the recovery be limited to actual rather than prospective losses? Are there situations where a cause of action prior to the time for performance should not be recognized, but one of the parties should, nonetheless, be entitled to suspend performance? These and related questions will now be addressed.

[B]   Anticipatory Repudiation — Origin of the Doctrine — *Hochster v. De La Tour*

The earlier law did not, in general, recognize the possibility that an action for breach of contract could be brought before the time for performance had arrived.[423] Beyond the cold logic that a contract cannot be breached before the duty of the other party is due, providing a promisee relief at an earlier date is granting more than he was promised. Damages are measured as of the date of performance.[424] The further in advance of that date they are computed, the more difficult it becomes to approximate the amount to which the promisee would ultimately have been entitled. In 1853, Queen's Bench decided the famous case of *Hochster v. De La Tour*.[425] In April of 1852, Hochster was a courier who contracted with De La Tour to accompany him on a tour commencing on June 1. On May 11, however, De La Tour informed Hochster that he was discharged. Hochster brought an action on May 22 and the court was confronted with deciding whether such an action would lie before the time for performance under the contract.[426] Defense counsel argued that, since there could be no breach until June 1, Hochster had to remain ready and willing to perform until the date of performance, i.e., he could not accept another position prior to that date and continue to have a cause of action against the defendant. The court was not persuaded by these arguments. Reviewing precedent, the court first pointed to a case where a man promised to marry on a future day, but married another prior to that day and was "instantly liable" for breach of promise. A promise to lease property for a certain term is breached immediately if, before the lease is to commence, the lessor enters into a lease with another. Similarly, a promise to sell goods is breached immediately if the goods are sold to another before the time of their delivery under the first contract. Recognizing the theoretical possibility that, in each of these cases, the promisor might be free to perform the repudiated contract by the time for its performance (the first wife could die and the lease or goods could be repurchased), the court chose a more realistic rationale. A relationship is created between the parties to a contract prior to the date of performance as in the case of a man and woman engaged to each other prior to marriage. Indeed, such a relationship may amount to an "implied contract" that they will not renounce their promises prior to the date of performance. The critical rationale, however, is that a party such as Hochster should not be forced to remain willing and ready to perform a contract which he knows will not be performed by the other party. To require him to remain idle, to make useless preparations for such performance, and to preclude him from seeking other employment immediately that could mitigate damages, is senseless.

---

[423] *See* Daniels v. Newton, 114 Mass. 530, 19 Am. Rep. 384 (1874).

[424] *See* First Restatement § 338 comment a (1932).

[425] 2 El. & Bl. 678 [1853].

[426] Sometime after June 1, Hochster obtained an engagement with Lord Ashburton.

The court concluded that a renunciation of the contract prior to the time for performance "dispenses with a condition to be performed in the meantime by the other." If the decision of the court were limited to this pristine holding, an innocent party would be discharged of all duties under the contract prior to the time for performance, thereby meeting the court's concerns. He could then bring the action at the time for performance. The court, however, curiously decided that, because the plaintiff was no longer bound to the contract, there was no reason to await the time for performance to seek a remedy.[427] Thus, what has come to be known as the *doctrine of anticipatory repudiation* or, inaccurately, "anticipatory breach," was born.

It is sometimes suggested that the court arrived at its conclusion because it saw only three possibilities: (1) renounce the contract, with the consequence that the innocent would thereafter be devoid of any remedy or limited to the remedy of an action for restitution for any benefits conferred; (2) ignore the repudiation entirely and stand ready to perform; or (3) treat the repudiation as an immediate breach of the contract with all the consequences that ensue from that situation.[428] The opinion, however, clearly recognizes a fourth alternative, namely, treating the repudiation as excusing constructive conditions precedent to the innocent party's duty without surrendering the right to sue for breach of contract when the time for performance arrives. Having not only discovered this alternative but insisting on its logic and fairness, there was no reason to allow an action to be brought prior to the time for performance. The doctrine of anticipatory repudiation, therefore, has been subject to controversy for over a hundred years.[429] With the exception of Massachusetts which does not recognize the doctrine outside of the commercial law context,[430] the *Hochster* doctrine has been generally accepted both in England and in this country. Its curious rationale, however, has led courts to view it with varying degrees of favor or frowns. Some courts have accepted it wholeheartedly; others, while paying lip service to it, have surrounded it with distinctions and qualifications.

[C]   What Is an Anticipatory Repudiation? — Degree of Definiteness — Restatement 2d, Uniform Commercial Code, Good Faith Denial of Liability

In view of the foundation on which the anticipatory repudiation doctrine rests, if it is to have a rational justification, it would seem that it should apply in all cases where it has become reasonably certain that a promisor does not intend to perform his promise substantially. Unfortunately, a few cases arose at a time when the doctrine had not yet become fully

---

[427] The court was not impressed with the argument that damages are difficult to assess in advance of the time for performance since an early breach after the date of performance would still require an assessment of future damages.

[428] This view is expressed in Frost v. Knight, L.R. 7 Ex. 111 [1872].

[429] For opposing views as to the merits of the anticipatory breach doctrine and the theoretical bases for it, see Williston, *Repudiation of Contracts*, 14 Harv. L. Rev. 317, 421 (1900), Selected Readings On Contracts 1044 (1931); Ballantine, *Anticipatory Breach and the Enforcement of Contractual Duties*, 22 Mich. L. Rev. 329 (1923), Selected Readings On Contracts 1072 (1931); Vold, *The Tort Aspect of Anticipatory Repudiation of Contracts*, 41 Harv. L. Rev. 340 (1928), Selected Readings On Contracts 1127 (1931); Limburg, *Anticipatory Repudiation of Contracts*, 10 Cornell L.Q. 135 (1925), Selected Readings On Contracts 1090 (1931).

[430] The doctrine was rejected in Daniels v. Newton, 114 Mass. 530, 19 Am. Rep. 384 (1874). Most recently see Pedersen v. Klare, 910 N.E.2d 382, 386-87 (Mass. App. 2009). Contracts within the UCC adopted in Massachusetts are subject to the anticipatory repudiation doctrine in UCC § 2-610. Moreover, equitable relief allows for the application of the doctrine. *See* Cavanagh v. Cavanagh, 33 Mass. App. Ct. 240, 598 N.E.2d 677, 679 (1992).

established where the promisor, though making it reasonably clear that he would not perform, did not repudiate his promise in absolute terms. It was held that an action for anticipatory repudiation would not lie under these circumstances. Thus, in *Dingley v. Oler*[431] the promisor said that he would not perform unless a specified event should happen when it was reasonably certain the event would not happen. The Supreme Court of the United States held there had been no such repudiation as to justify the application of the doctrine since the promisor's statement was "very far from being a positive, unconditional, and unequivocal declaration of fixed purpose not to perform in any event or at any time."

It is quite clear from an examination of this case[432] and similar cases that the decisions were motivated at the time[433] either by the desire to put off the day of having to decide whether to accept the doctrine at all, or by a dislike of the doctrine and a desire to limit its application. Largely as a result of these cases, there are a number of subsequent judicial utterances to the effect that nothing short of an absolute and unequivocal renunciation of the contract will suffice for an anticipatory repudiation.[434] The UCC suggests a less stringent test.[435] The RESTATEMENT 2d expressly rejects the holding of *Dingley v. Oler*.[436] It only requires an expression to be "sufficiently positive to be reasonably interpreted to mean that the party will not or cannot perform."[437] In accordance with the Code, it treats an expression of intention not to perform except on conditions going beyond the contract as a repudiation. Notwithstanding these less stringent articulations, numerous courts cling to the traditional "definite, unequivocal and absolute" or similar standard.[438] It is not rare to find a court mentioning the classic "definite and unequivocal" language, while adopting the RESTATEMENT 2d and UCC statements.[439] A positive statement reasonably interpreted to mean that the

---

[431] 117 U.S. 490 (1886).

[432] *Id.* at 550. The court said: "The construction we place upon what passed between the parties renders it unnecessary for us to discuss or decide whether the doctrine of these authorities can be maintained as applicable to the class of cases to which the present belongs; for, upon that construction, this case does not come within the operation of the rule invoked." In the later case of Roehm v. Horst, 178 U.S. 1 (1900), the general doctrine was accepted and applied in the case of an executory contract to sell goods.

[433] *See* Vittum v. Estey, 67 Vt. 158, 31 A. 144 (1894) (vendor said he would not convey unless his father, who refused to do so, should concur); Johnstone v. Milling, 16 Q.B.D. 460 [1886] (landlord stated that he would not be able to perform his promise to rebuild the leased premises).

[434] See Dow Chem. Co. v. United States, 226 F.3d 1334, 1344 (Fed. Cir. 2000); J. M. Clayton Co. v. Martin, 177 Ga. App. 228, 339 S.E.2d 280 (1985) (absolute refusal to perform and unqualified repudiation of the entire contract is required); Stonecipher v. Pillatsch, 30 Ill. App. 3d 140, 332 N.E.2d 151 (2d Dist. 1975) (definite and unequivocal statement of repudiation required). *See also* Diamos v. Hirsch, 91 Ariz. 304, 372 P.2d 76 (1962); McCloskey & Co. v. Minweld Steel Co., 220 F.2d 101 (3d Cir. 1955).

[435] UCC § 2-610 does not attempt to define "repudiation." Though the section is captioned "Anticipatory Repudiation," the section only sets forth the choices available to an "aggrieved party" (defined in § 1-201(2) as a party entitled to a remedy) where the other party has repudiated in advance of the time for performance. Comment 2, however, suggests: "Repudiation can result from action which reasonably indicates a rejection of the continuing obligation." Later, the same comment indicates that "a statement of intention not to perform except on conditions which go beyond the contract" is an anticipatory repudiation. As the Reporter's Note to § 250 of the RESTATEMENT 2d indicates, this comment statement is opposed to the holding in *Dingley v. Oler, supra* note 431. It should be remembered, however, that the "Official" comments are not part of the enacted law.

[436] RESTATEMENT 2d § 250.

[437] RESTATEMENT 2d § 250 comment b. *See* Minidoka Irrigation Dist. v. DOI, 154 F.3d 924, 927 (9th Cir. 1998).

[438] Crosspoint Seven v. Mfrs. Life. Ins. Co.,148 Fed. Appx. 535, 537 (7th Cir. 2005) (Indiana law); Roger Edwards, LLC v. Fiddes & Sons, Ltd., 387 F.3d 90, 85 (1st Cir. 2004) (Maine law).

[439] *See* Truman L. Flatt & Sons Co. v. Schupf, 271 Ill. App. 3d 983, 208 Ill. Dec. 630, 649 N.E.2d 990 (4th Dist. 1995).

promisor will not or cannot perform his contractual duty constitutes a repudiation in modern courts.[440] Statements of doubt by the obligor as to his ability or willingness to perform are insufficient, though such statements may suggest reasonable grounds for insecurity and ultimately constitute a repudiation.[441] Language which, alone, would not be sufficient to constitute a repudiation, may constitute a repudiation when accompanied by some nonperformance.[442]

Conduct. A positive manifestation that the obligor cannot or will not perform need not be expressed in language. It may be inferred from *conduct* that is wholly inconsistent with an intention to perform.[443] Any voluntary affirmative act which actually or apparently precludes the obligor from performing amounts to a repudiation.[444] Thus, in accordance with precedent that even preceded *Hochster v. De La Tour*, a sale or lease of goods or lands which are necessary to perform a contract, or a contract for their sale or lease prior to the time for performance, has been held to furnish a basis for an action for total breach of the contract.[445] Such conduct must meet the usual requirement that they were voluntary and affirmative to constitute repudiations.[446] Thus, neither insolvency, bankruptcy or other financial difficulties, in themselves, constitute an anticipatory repudiation.[447]

Good Faith Denial. Where a statement of future nonperformance is sufficiently positive, or a voluntary and affirmative act will make performance impossible, there can be no question that a repudiation has occurred. Suppose, however, the statement is made or action is taken in a good faith denial of liability. If a party simply does not believe that he has certain duties under a contract,[448] should that party who acts in good faith, albeit mistakenly, be charged with anticipatory repudiation? If the belief of the mistaken party is not only honest but reasonable, there is a plausible argument for not subjecting that party to the consequences of an anticipatory repudiation. Notwithstanding such good faith, if a party not only announces his different interpretation but also states that he will not perform the contract according to any other interpretation, he assumes the risk that his interpretation will later be declared to be correct. If it is not correct, it will constitute a repudiation that will have the effect of a

---

[440] Borough of Landsdale v. PP&L, Inc., 2006 U. S. Dist. LEXIS 14972 at *16 (E. D. Pa. 2006).

[441] UCC § 2-609; RESTATEMENT 2d § 251. See the discussion of prospective inability to perform *infra*, subsection G. of this section.

[442] RESTATEMENT 2d § 250 comment b, referring to RESTATEMENT 2d § 243(2), which states that a partial breach and a repudiation will constitute a total breach. *See* ill. 3 to § 243.

[443] *See* RESTATEMENT 2d § 250 (b). *See* Wholesale Sand & Gravel v. Decker, 630 A.2d 710 (Me. 1993); Aero Consulting Corp. v. Cessna Aircraft Co., 867 F. Supp. 1480 (D. Kan. 1994).

[444] Olyaie v. GE Capital Bus. Asset Funding Corp., 217 Fed. Appx. 606, 610 (9th Cir. 2007) (where a promisor's conduct precludes its power to perform so as to make substantial performance impossible, such conduct constitute an "implied repudiation").

[445] Pappas v. Crist, 223 N.C. 265, 25 S.E.2d 850 (1943); Crane v. East Side Canal & Irrigation Co., 6 Cal. App. 2d 361, 44 P.2d 455 (1935); Suburban Improv. Co. v. Scott Lumber Co., 67 F.2d 335, 90 A.L.R. 330 (4th Cir. 1933) (dictum); Engelbrecht v. Herrington, 101 Kan. 720, 172 P. 715 (1917); Synge v. Synge, 1 Q.B. 466 [1894].

[446] *See* RESTATEMENT 2d § 250 (b). *See also* Ringel & Meyer, Inc. v. Falstaff Brewing Corp., 511 F.2d 659 (5th Cir. 1975).

[447] *See* Beeche Sys. Corp. v. D.A. Elia Constr. Corp. (*In re* Beeche Sys. Corp.), 164 B.R. 12 (N.D.N.Y. 1994) (discussing Bankruptcy Code, 11 U. S. C. § 365).

[448] For example, a party may interpret the contract in such a fashion that he honestly does not believe that he must perform certain duties under the contract. Another party may honestly believe that he is discharged because his counterpart has repudiated the contract.

material breach, discharging the duties of the other party and placing the honestly mistaken party in the position of a repudiator before the time for performance has arrived.[449] It is, however, important to distinguish the situation in which a party's erroneous interpretation of its contractual rights is not accompanied by his refusal to perform. Such an erroneous interpretation is not, in itself, an anticipatory repudiation.[450] Where parties have a good faith but major disagreement concerning the proper interpretation of their contract, rather than risk an anticipatory repudiation or material breach of contract, they may seek a declaratory judgment that allows courts to "declare the rights and other legal relations of any interested party seeking such declaration, whether or not further relief is or could be sought."[451]

[D]   Effects of Anticipatory Repudiation — Time of Breach — Statute of Limitations — "Acceptance" and "Election"

The effects of an anticipatory repudiation may be catalogued as follows: (1) it discharges the duties of the obligee;[452] (2) it permits but does not require the obligee to bring an immediate action for total breach of contract;[453] (3) it excuses the nonoccurrence of a condition to the duty of the obligee;[454] (4) if it accompanies nonperformance which would otherwise constitute only a partial breach, the combination of that nonperformance and repudiation will give rise to a total breach.[455] If the repudiation is subsequently nullified as it may be,[456] these consequences are similarly nullified.[457] As we will see in some detail,[458] an innocent obligee may respond to an anticipatory repudiation in different ways. His two basic choices are to treat the contract as immediately breached prior to the time for performance or to await performance by the repudiating obligor.[459] Since the obligee may choose to do nothing in

---

[449] *See* Chamberlin v. Puckett Constr., 277 Mont. 198, 921 P.2d 1237 (1996) (demand for performance of terms not contained in the contract and refusal to perform if the demands were not met).

[450] United Cal. Bank v. Prudential Ins. Co., 140 Ariz. 238, 681 P.2d 390, 431 (Ct. App. 1983).

[451] See the Federal Declaratory Judgment Act, 28 U.S.C.A. § 2201.

[452] RESTATEMENT 2d § 253(2). *See* Thermo Electron Corp. v. Schiavone Constr. Co., 958 F.2d 1158, 1164 (1st Cir. 1992).

[453] RESTATEMENT 2d § 253(1). *See* Far West Fed. Bank, FSB v. Office of Thrift Supervision, 119 F.3d 1358, 1365 (9th Cir. 1997); Acme Inv. v. Southwest Tracor, 105 F.3d 412 (8th Cir. 1997).

[454] RESTATEMENT 2d § 255. The repudiation, however, must contribute substantially to the nonoccurrence of the condition. Thus, illustration 1 to this section suggests that a condition to a casualty insurance policy requiring written notice of loss would be excused if the insurance company repudiated its obligation following the loss because a useless act need not be performed. Illustration 2, however, involves a condition of obtaining mortgage financing attached to the obligor's duty to purchase property. If the seller anticipatorily repudiated that contract and the bank refused to grant the mortgage loan, the condition would not be excused because the repudiation did not substantially contribute to the nonoccurrence of the condition. A party must be able to demonstrate that he would have been able to perform had the anticipatory repudiation not occurred. *See* Yale Dev. Co. v. Aurora Pizza Hut, Inc., 95 Ill. App. 3d 523, 51 Ill. Dec. 409, 420 N.E.2d 823 (2d Dist. 1981). See also RESTATEMENT 2d § 254(1), which discharges the repudiator's duty if it appears that the obligee would not have been able to perform his return promise.

[455] RESTATEMENT 2d § 243. For a similar listing of possible responses to an anticipatory repudiation, see Kinesoft Dev. Corp. v. Softbank Holdings, Inc., 2001 U.S. Dist. LEXIS 1888, at *72 (N.D. Ill. Feb. 16, 2001).

[456] *See infra* subsection E.

[457] RESTATEMENT 2d § 256.

[458] *See* § 110[E], *infra.*

[459] There may be circumstances where the injured party may not be reasonable in awaiting performance though that response is typically permissible. See Oloffson v. Coomer, 11 Ill. App. 3d 918, 296 N.E.2d 871 (3d Dist. 1973), where the court held that buyer of corn was unreasonable in awaiting performance until the time for performance some

response to the repudiation and the obligor may decide to perform when the time for performance arrives, the repudiation is not, in itself, a breach. It may or may not become a breach. The distinction can be important in a given situation.

Where an action would be time barred if the statute of limitations began to run from the time of the repudiation, rather than from the time of the breach, since the repudiation is not a breach, the statute does not begin to run until the repudiation is treated as a breach.[460] Beyond the pristine logic of this view, the opposite view would unwittingly allow a repudiator to shorten the statute of limitations by a wrongful act. If it is appropriate to permit the innocent obligee to ignore the repudiation, the statute would begin to run as of the time for performance.[461]

Another illustration of the distinction occurred where a seller committed an anticipatory repudiation of a contract for the purchase and sale of a vessel at $2.65 million with the intention of selling the vessel to the defendant for $2.95 million. The plaintiffs were the original buyers, who brought an action for tortious interference with a contract against the defendant. The defendant claimed that the seller's anticipatory repudiation of the $2.65 million contract was a breach and, therefore, no cause of action for tortious interference would lie since defendant had no role in purchasing the vessel until after the repudiation/breach. The court, however, found that an anticipatory repudiation is not a breach.[462] English law applied to this transaction, which necessitated a discussion of whether an anticipatory repudiation must be "accepted" by the obligee. An early English case where the court was less than enthusiastic about the doctrine of anticipatory repudiation may be responsible for this view,[463] which is supported by some cases under United States law.[464] There is, however, no requirement of notice amounting to an "acceptance" by the innocent party to convert an anticipatory repudiation into a present breach.[465] In the vessel case, the court uses the terms "acceptance" and "election" to describe the choices available to an obligee in response to an anticipatory repudiation. If the analysis just suggested is kept in mind, there may be no great harm in using the term "election." Since, however, "election" is used in other contexts, it seems preferable to characterize the choices available to the innocent obligee as *permissible responses.*

---

months later where he knew or should have known that the performance would not be possible after the farmer stated that he was not going to plant corn. The buyer also knew that the farmer would not supply the corn from another source.

[460] Cary Oil Co., Inc. v. MG Ref. & Mktg., Inc., 90 F. Supp. 2d 401 (S.D.N.Y. 2000).

[461] Under UCC § 2-610(a), the aggrieved party may await performance by the repudiating party only for a commercially reasonable time. See the discussion in the text at note 467, *infra.*

[462] International Minerals & Resources S. A. v. American Gen. Resources, Inc., 1999 U.S. Dist. LEXIS 13234 (S.D.N.Y. Aug. 26, 1999).

[463] Johnstone v. Milling, 16 Q.B.D. 460 [1860].

[464] In Lumbermens Mut. Casualty Co. v. Klotz, 251 F.2d 499 (5th Cir. 1958), the court treats an anticipatory repudiation as a "tender of a breach of the entire contract which, on acceptance, permits the other party to obtain damages for a breach." *See also* City of Algona v. City of Pacific, 35 Wash. App. 517, 667 P.2d 1124 (1983).

[465] The aggrieved party may, for example, rely on the repudiation without notifying the repudiator. *See* Truman L. Flatt & Sons Co. v. Schupf, 271 Ill. App. 3d 983, 208 Ill. Dec. 630, 649 N.E.2d 990 (4th Dist. 1995).

[E] Permissible Responses to Anticipatory Repudiation

A number of questions arise concerning the obligee's response to an anticipatory repudiation which will now be considered.

[1] May an Anticipatory Repudiation Be Ignored?

Since an anticipatory repudiation must occur prior to the time for performance, the obligee may simply ignore it and await the time for performance. If the obligor then refuses to perform, there is a present breach upon which the obligee may bring an action. In making this choice, the obligee may not recover for any losses that could have been avoided if he had not awaited the time for performance. This is a *mitigation* principle discussed in detail in a later chapter dealing with contract remedies.[466] Unlike the common law that allowed the obligee to await performance until it was due, the UCC permits the obligee to await performance only for a commercially reasonable time.[467] While that "reasonable time" may, in most situations, permit the obligee to await performance until the time for performance specified in the contract, there are situations where he should not be permitted to wait that long. Where, for example, a farmer agreed to deliver his navy bean crop at the time of the future October harvest, but, in May, committed an anticipatory repudiation, the buyer waited until September to effect a substitute purchase ("cover"). The court held that the buyer had awaited performance well beyond a reasonable time and its damages would be measured, not by the market price at the time for performance or when he covered, but at the time of the repudiation when the market price was less than half of the September price.[468]

[2] Must the Obligee Give Notice That He Treats the Anticipatory Repudiation as a Breach?

If the obligee may not ignore the repudiation, must he notify the repudiator that the repudiation will be treated as a breach? The obligee need not "accept" the repudiation by notification to the repudiator. The obligee may simply commence his action for total breach of the contract.[469]

[3] Must the Obligee Commence an Action if He Chooses to Treat the Anticipatory Repudiation as a Breach?

The obligee need not bring an action to treat the anticipatory repudiation as a breach. If the obligee relies on the repudiation, the reliance is sufficient evidence of his choice to treat the repudiation as a breach, even though he does not bring his action until later.[470] Moreover, it is not necessary that the obligee notify the repudiator of the obligee's change of position.[471]

---

[466] *See infra* Chapter 9.

[467] UCC § 2-610(a).

[468] Trinidad Bean & Elev. Co. v. Frosh, 1 Neb. Ct. App. 281, 494 N.W.2d 347 (1992).

[469] *See* Strategis Asset Valuation & Mgmt., Inc. v. Pacific Mut. Life Ins. Co., 805 F. Supp. 1544, 1550 ((D. Colo. 1992). RESTATEMENT 2d § 253(1).

[470] Guerrieri v. Severini, 51 Cal. 2d 12, 330 P.2d 635 (1958) (obligee changed his position by purchasing winery to procure necessary wine); Bu-Vi-Bar Petroleum Corp. v. Krow, 40 F.2d 488 (10th Cir. 1930) (promisee permitted a lease to lapse, the assignment of which was a condition precedent to the promisor's duty).

[471] Cf. UCC § 2-611(1), which suggests that the repudiator may retract the repudiation unless the aggrieved party

[4]　If the Obligee Does Not Commence an Action or Rely on the Repudiation, May He Still Treat the Repudiation as a Present Breach?

Again, while notice is not essential to treat an anticipatory repudiation as a breach, where the obligee has neither relied nor brought an action for present breach, he may treat the anticipatory repudiation as a breach by simply notifying the repudiator to that effect.[472] An exercise of the obligee's remedial rights under the contract also signifies that he treats the repudiation as a breach.[473]

[5]　May the Obligor Retract the Repudiation?

The obligor may retract the repudiation if he does so before the obligee has indicated that he treats the repudiation as a breach or, without any notification, materially changes his position in reliance on the repudiation.[474] No particular method of retraction is required, i.e., it may occur through words or conduct.[475] A retraction must be unconditional and unambiguous.[476] An effective retraction reinstates the contractual rights and duties of the parties, i.e., the anticipatory repudiation is nullified.[477] The effect of the obligee's reliance or other indication that he treats the repudiation as a breach renders any attempted retraction by the obligor impossible.

[6]　Obligee Provides a Time for Retraction (*Locus Poenitentiae)*

An obligee may provide the obligor with a time for retraction, i.e., a *locus poenitentiae.* If the obligee places a time limitation on a *locus poenitentiae,* the repudiation is final at the conclusion of that period, regardless of any reliance by the obligee. Where, for example, the plaintiff notified the defendant that the repudiation would be treated as a breach unless the defendant retracted within three days, defendant failed to retract within three days but attempted to retract later on the basis that the plaintiff had yet to rely on the repudiation. The court held the repudiation became a breach, regardless of reliance, at the end of the three day period.[478] Moreover, even where the obligee has urged the obligor to retract the repudiation and indicated that he would await the obligor's performance, he may change his mind and bring

---

has materially changed his position "or otherwise indicated that he considers the repudiation final."

[472] Truman L. Flatt & Sons Co. v. Schupf, 271 Ill. App. 3d 983, 208 Ill. Dec. 630, 649 N.E.2d 990 (4th Dist. 1995).

[473] In Gateway Aviation, Inc. v. Cessna Aircraft Co., 577 S.W.2d 860 (Mo. Ct. App. 1978), when the obligor failed to make payments on an airplane, the obligee repossessed pursuant to a security agreement with the obligor. This act signified the obligee's treatment of the repudiation as a breach and since a repudiation is a material breach, the obligee's duties under the contract were discharged.

[474] UCC § 2-611(1); RESTATEMENT 2d § 256(1). *See* Taylor v. Johnston, 15 Cal. 3d 130, 123 Cal. Rptr. 641, 539 P.2d 425 (1975).

[475] UCC § 2-611(2); RESTATEMENT 2d § 256(2). It may, however, be necessary for the repudiator to provide adequate assurances of performance.

[476] Argonaut Partnership, L.P. v. Grupo Sidek, S.A. de C.V., 1996 U.S. Dist. LEXIS 15925, at *18 (S.D.N.Y. Oct. 24, 1996), *aff'd,* 1998 U.S. App. LEXIS 3232 (2d Cir. Feb. 27, 1998).

[477] UCC § 2-611(3); RESTATEMENT 2d § 256 comment a.

[478] United States v. Seacoast Gas Co., 204 F.2d 709 (5th Cir. 1953), *cert. denied,* 346 U.S. 866, 74 S. Ct. 106, 98 L. Ed. 377 (1953). See also UCC § 2-611(1), which suggests that an anticipatory repudiation can become a breach simply through the obligee's indication that "he considers the repudiation final."

an action or, in good faith, rely on the repudiation.[479] Thus, if the repudiator is informed that he has a *locus poenitentiae* of three days, the obligee could change his mind and either commence an action or rely before the end of the three days and either action would treat the repudiation as final. If this is thought to be misleading to the obligor, it must be remembered that the obligor is a repudiator who created the situation.[480]

[F] Anticipatory Repudiation Inapplicable to Unilateral Obligations — Disability Insurance

It is important to remember that one of the bases for the doctrine of anticipatory repudiation was the necessity to relieve the obligee of maintaining a state of readiness to perform when the time for performance arrived. To avoid that necessity, the obligee was permitted to commence an action before the time for performance which discharged his duties under the contract.[481] In a unilateral contract or a bilateral contract that has been fully performed on the side of the obligee, the problem of remaining in a state of readiness to perform does not exist. In a unilateral contract, the obligor has received the full exchange promised by the obligee at the time of contract formation. If the contract was originally a bilateral contract but the obligee has fully performed, the effect is the same. In such a case, an early court suggested that the reason for the anticipatory repudiation doctrine no longer existed and it was inapplicable.[482] Since then, it has generally been held that no action will lie for the anticipatory repudiation of an unconditional, unilateral obligation to pay money or to perform some other act.[483] Professor Corbin however, found the "readiness" justification weak and concluded that it would be "strange" to prohibit an immediate action based on anticipatory repudiation.[484] Corbin's "partial justification" for allowing an immediate action

---

[479] *See* UCC § 2-610(b) and comment 4.

[480] UCC Section 2-610(b) supports this analysis. Comment 4 suggests that the repudiator should not be considered misled. The same comment, however, also suggests the possibility of some action by the aggrieved party (obligee) which, in good faith, requires notification to the repudiator. It would seem, however, that the only situation where such notification would be required would occur when the obligee has provided a *locus poenitentiae* and knows or reasonably should know that the obligor will take action in reliance in such a fashion as to exceed his contractual obligation and suffer losses beyond that obligation. While this situation is conceivable, there is no recorded case suggesting this possibility.

[481] *See supra* subsection B.

[482] This was the view expressed in one of the earliest English cases on the subject where the plaintiff sued for anticipatory repudiation of a covenant to rebuild contained in a lease. Johnstone v. Milling, 16 Q.B.D. 460 [1886]. The opinions were predicated upon the traditional view that covenants in a lease were independent (unless expressly made dependent) so that the covenant to repair appeared to be an independent obligation that was not constructively conditioned upon the performance of the lessee. Consequently, the lessee need not be in a state of readiness to perform since the lessor's performance did not depend upon the lessee's performance. Modern courts, however, recognize that leases should be viewed as contractual obligations which are dependent or constructively conditional. Therefore, the doctrine of anticipatory repudiation would apply to leases at the present time. *See* Schneiker v. Gordon, 732 P.2d 603 (Colo. 1987).

[483] *See* Parker v. Moitzfield, 733 F. Supp. 1023, 1025 (E.D. Va. 1990) (citing cases). *See also* Cornett v. Roth, 233 Kan. 936, 666 P.2d 1182 (1983); Kozasa v. Guardian Elec. Mfg. Co., 99 Ill. App. 3d 669, 54 Ill. Dec. 920, 425 N.E.2d 1137 (1st Dist. 1981); Davis v. First Nat'l Bank of Ariz., 124 Ariz. 458, 605 P.2d 37 (Ct. App. 1979). Contrary views typically lack an effective rationale. In Pitts v. Wetzel, 498 S.W.2d 27, 28 n. 1 (Tex. Civ. App. Austin 1973), the court recognizes a view contrary to that of Professor Williston based an older Texas case, Pollack v. Pollack, 46 S.W.2d 292, 295 (Tex. Comm'n App. 1932), that simply announces the application of the doctrine to unilateral obligations to pay money.

[484] In agreement with Corbin, see Combs v. International Ins. Co., 354 F.3d 568, 599 *et seq.* (6th Cir. 2004) (precluding anticipatory repudiation from unilateral contracts "makes little sense").

based on anticipatory repudiation of a unilateral obligation is the value of the existing contract right before the time for that right to be fulfilled. Such a contract right has a market value prior to the time for performance that could be assigned. A repudiation by the other party causes the value of such a contract right to depreciate.[485] Nonetheless, the clearly prevailing view is such an action is not immediately available upon an anticipatory repudiation. A particular type of case has caused consternation.

Disability Insurance — Future Payments. Disability insurance contracts require the insurance company to make periodic payments to the insured as long as the disability continues in accordance with the contract description. If the company decides that the disability no longer continues, it will cease making payments inducing an action by the insured claiming not only the payments due to the time of the lawsuit, but damages for total breach. If the payments were scheduled to continue for life, the calculation of damages could be based on actuarial tables and then reduced to present value since the payments are being made in advance. The insurer, however, will resist such a lump sum payment as exceeding its present obligation. The insurer will claim that an obligation to pay money is a unilateral obligation to which the doctrine of anticipatory repudiation does not apply. Therefore, the company should be liable only for disability payments presently due and not for future payments.[486] The insured will counter that he should not be burdened with the necessity of continuous litigation to receive his future disability payments. He may also claim that the obligation of the insurer is not unilateral since the insured is typically required to submit to future medical examinations to determine continued disability and, therefore, the doctrine of anticipatory repudiation should apply.[487] The confusion in such cases is caused by a failure to recognize that they involve a partial breach (failure to make certain installment payments) coupled with a repudiation (manifested intention that future payments will not be made). A present breach by nonperformance accompanied by a repudiation gives rise to a claim for total breach.[488] Earlier, we saw that a "good faith" repudiation is still a repudiation.[489] Thus, the fact that an insurer refuses in good faith to make future payments should be irrelevant.[490] The essential challenge is one of calculating uncertain future damages. One possible solution is to adhere to the traditional view that restricts recovery to payments already due,[491] with a decree that future payments be made when due.[492] In a leading case, the court was not satisfied to limit payments to those already due, but it was also not convinced that the remedy of a calculated

---

[485] Corbin on Contracts, § 961.

[486] *See* Greguhn v. Mutual of Omaha Ins. Co., 23 Utah 2d 214, 461 P.2d 285 (1969).

[487] This argument was rejected in Cobb v. Pacific Mut. Life Ins. Co., 4 Cal. 2d 565, 51 P.2d 84 (1935), on the footing that such a requirement is so inconsequential that it should not be regarded as an unperformed obligation.

[488] RESTATEMENT 2d § 243(2). See, however, *Greguhn v. Mutual of Omaha, supra* note 486, where the majority opinion mischaracterizes the situation as one involving anticipatory repudiation as the dissenting opinion observes.

[489] *See* § 110[C], *supra.*

[490] In New York Life Ins. Co. v. Viglas, 297 U.S. 672, 676, 56 S. Ct. 615, 616, 80 L. Ed. 2d 971, 974 (1936), however, Justice Cardozo writes, "There is nothing to show that the insurer was not acting in good faith in giving notice of its contention that the disability was over. If it made a mistake, there was a breach of a provision of the policy with liability for any damages appropriate thereto." (Citations omitted.) Finding no renunciation or abandonment of the contract as a whole, the court limited recovery to payments already due.

[491] *See* RESTATEMENT 2d § 243(3).

[492] *See* John Hancock Mut. Life Ins. Co. v. Cohen, 254 F.2d 417 (9th Cir. 1958). But, the court does suggest that if the insurance company fails to make future payments requiring the insured to file another action, the court should then fashion relief to compel future performance.

lump sum payment was appropriate. It chose a middle ground by granting a judgment for amounts already due and for all future installments when they became due.[493] A subsequent case refined this analysis by holding that an insurer who in bad faith refused to make payments should be liable for a lump sum payment.[494] While a declaratory judgment is another desirable alternative since it avoids the risk of repudiation, if a court follows the traditional view that the plaintiff may recover only amounts already due, the amount in controversy may fall short of the jurisdictional amount required for such a judgment.[495]

[G]   Prospective Failure of Performance That Is Not a Repudiation — Demanding Adequate Assurances

[1]   Demanding Adequate Assurances — Effect — Scope

We have seen that words or conduct must be sufficiently positive to constitute a repudiation. Situations often arise which cause reasonable doubt in the obligee that the obligor will be able to perform when the time for performance arrives, but the obligor's statements or conduct are not sufficiently clear ("unequivocal") to constitute an anticipatory repudiation. If the obligee treats the manifestation as a repudiation and, therefore, refuses to perform, he may discover that he has become the repudiator when the obligor's manifested intention is determined by judicial hindsight to have been insufficient to constitute an anticipatory repudiation.[496] What is the obligee to do under these circumstances?

The UCC and the RESTATEMENT 2d provide a relief mechanism in this situation called a *demand for adequate assurances*. It asserts a principle that the parties are entitled to "a continuing sense of reliance and security that the promised performance will be forthcoming when due. . . ."[497] It permits the obligee to *suspend* performance where he has "reasonable grounds for insecurity" with respect to the obligor's future performance.[498] At this point, the obligee's duties are not discharged but, again, merely suspended. If, however, the obligor fails to provide adequate assurances within a reasonable time not exceeding 30 days under the

---

[493] Caporali v. Washington Nat'l Ins. Co., 102 Wis. 2d 669, 682, 307 N.W.2d 218, 224 (1981): "We adopt a middle ground." The insured is ordered to make payments as they fall due. *See also* Equitable Life Assur. Soc'y v. Goble, 254 Ky. 614, 72 S.W.2d 35 (1934). The most satisfactory solution to the problem which insures a minimum of litigation and expense without imposing undue hardship upon an insurance company that denies liability in good faith is to limit the immediate recovery to payments matured at the time, while entering an order providing for the continuance of the case on the court docket and directing the insurance company to pay future installments, if and when they mature.

[494] DeChant v. Monarch Life Ins. Co., 204 Wis. 2d 137, 554 N.W.2d 225 (Ct. App. 1996).

[495] See Berlly v. United States Life Ins. Co., 2001 U.S. Dist. LEXIS 269 (S.D.N.Y. Jan. 16, 2001), where the monthly payments of $4000 per month due plaintiff totaled $16,000 when the declaratory judgment was sought. The court held that the jurisdictional amount required for such a judgment ($75,000) would not include anticipated future payments. Under such a holding, the plaintiff would be required to wait for one year and seven months before it would be eligible for a declaratory judgment.

[496] In Drake v. Wickwire, 795 P.2d 195, 198 (Alaska 1990), a court found that an attorney was guilty of negligence "in advising precipitate conduct in the face of an ambiguous statement which was insufficient to indicate that the buyers would breach the contract."

[497] RESTATEMENT 2d § 251, cmt. a (quoting UCC § 2-609, cmt. 1, *as quoted in* Danzig v. AEC Corp., 224 F.3d 1333 (Fed. Cir. 2000)).

[498] UCC § 2-609(1); RESTATEMENT 2d § 251(1). *See also* Julian v. Montana State Univ., 229 Mont. 362, 747 P.2d 196 (1987) (and cases cited therein); Conference Center, Ltd. v. TRC — The Research Company, 189 Conn. 212, 455 A.2d 857 (1983).

UCC,[499] or simply within a reasonable time under the RESTATEMENT 2d,[500] such a failure will be treated as a repudiation. Where there is doubt as to whether there has been an anticipatory repudiation, this mechanism allows an innocent obligee to avoid the pitfall of committing an anticipatory repudiation by treating his own duties as discharged only to discover later that his judgment concerning the obligor's "repudiation" was mistaken.[501]

The demand for adequate assurances is a creature of statute, Article 2 of the UCC, that applies only to contracts for the sale of goods, though courts manifest a willingness to extend it analogously beyond its technical ambit. The concept has been "generalized" for application to any type of contract under the RESTATEMENT 2D OF CONTRACTS,[502] but "[t]he Restatement of course is not law."[503] Either by analogy to the UCC section or by adopting the RESTATEMENT 2d version, however, courts have extended the mechanism to other types of contracts.[504]

Questions concerning the basis for the demand of adequate assurances, the nature of the demand, the form of the demand, and the effect of insolvency have arisen. We now address these questions.

[2]   Basis for the Demand of Adequate Assurances

An obligee may not demand adequate assurances just because he has certain subjective concerns about the future performance of the obligor.[505] He must have *reasonable* grounds for insecurity. Moreover, such reasonable grounds for insecurity must occur *after* the contract was formed.[506] Under the UCC standard, "reasonable grounds" will be measured by commercial, not legal, standards. The grounds need not arise from the contract in question. Repeated

---

[499] UCC § 2-609(4).

[500] RESTATEMENT 2d § 251(2).

[501] For a thorough analysis of the origins and desirability of the "demand for adequate assurances" mechanism, see Norcon Power Partners, L.P. v. Niagara Mohawk Power Corp., 92 N.Y.2d 458, 682 N.Y.S.2d 664, 705 N.E.2d 656 (1998). *See also* Ross Cattle Co. v. Lewis, 415 So. 2d 1029 (Miss. 1982).

[502] See McNeal v. Lebel, 2008 N. H. LEXIS 86 (July 11, 2008) where the Supreme Court of New Hampshire noted the quandary of a party to a construction contract with reasonable grounds for insecurity who could not otherwise take effective action absent an anticipatory repudiation. To assist such parties, the court extended the concept of the demand for adequate assurances to contracts beyond the UCC pursuant to Restatement 2d § 251.

[503] C.L. Maddox, Inc. v. Coalfield Servs., 51 F.3d 76, 81 (7th Cir. 1995) (federal court adopts the concept for application to a construction contract on the footing that the principle is sound "and we have no reason to doubt that it would be so regarded by the courts of Illinois").

[504] When a federal district court would not recognize the mechanism as applied to a contract for electricity, which is not a contract for the sale of goods under New York law, the question was certified to the New York Court of Appeals. Norcon Power Partners, L.P. v. Niagara Mohawk Power Corp., 110 F.3d 6 (2d Cir. 1997). By analogy to contracts for the sale of goods, the New York Court of Appeals held that it would apply to other types of contracts but limited it to such long-term commercial contracts between the entities such as those in the case. The court explained that it chose its traditional, careful and prudent "incremental, common law developmental process basis" rather than a sweeping change *See Norcon Power Partners*, note 501, *supra*. In the application of the mechanism, the United States Court of Appeals for the Second Circuit noted the extension of the concept to other types of contracts, e. g., construction and real estate contracts. Norcon Power Partners, L.P. v. Niagara Mohawk Power Corp., 163 F.3d 153, 155 (2d Cir. 1998). More recently, the concept has been applied to government contracts. Danzig v. AEC Corp., 224 F.3d 1333 (Fed. Cir. 2000), *cert. denied sub. nom.* AEC Corp. v. Pirie, 149 L. Ed. 2d 638 (2001). *See also* Lakeview Mgt. v. Care Realty, LLC, 2009 U. S. Dist. LEXIS 28171 at *52, n. 7 (D. N. H. 2009) (lease of facilities).

[505] Cole v. Melvin, 441 F. Supp. 193, 203 (D.S.D. 1977).

[506] UCC § 2-609 comment 1; RESTATEMENT 2d § 251 comment c.

delinquencies will be treated as cumulative.[507] If the obligee was aware of certain risks at the time of contract formation, he has assumed those risks and may not later invoke them as reasonable grounds for insecurity.[508] Whether an obligee has reasonable grounds for insecurity to support a demand of adequate assurances is a question of fact.[509] Where he has reason to believe that the obligor's performance has become uncertain or where there have been repeated breaches of the contract, a demand for adequate assurances is justified.[510] If an obligor continuously refuses to sign a contract after substantial work has been performed, the obligee has a clear right to demand adequate assurances.[511] If an obligor goes out of business, reasonable grounds for insecurity exist.[512]

Where a construction company (Shore) sold its asphalt plant to a manufacturer of asphalt and road materials (Koch), as part of the sale Shore agreed to purchase all of its asphalt requirements from Koch for seven years with minimum purchases of at least two million gallons of asphalt per year. Moreover, Shore agreed to utilize at least 2.5 million yards of a Koch product (Novathip) annually, either in its own business or through sublicenses. Three years later, Shore announced its sale to another contractor, except for the sublicense agreement that would "continue to exist." Koch demanded adequate assurances, but Shore refused to provide them. Koch, therefore, claimed that Shore had repudiated the contract. The court held that Koch had reasonable grounds of insecurity with respect to the exclusive supply contract, not simply with respect to the two million gallon minimum, but from potential requirements above the minimum. Moreover, Shore had successfully pursued sublicensing agreements concerning Novachip in the past. The court recognized the insecurity in Koch wondering how Shore intended to ascertain that sublicenses would continue to be sold without a business-no telephones, computers or even office furniture. By not responding to Koch's demand for reasonable assurances, Shore had repudiated the contract.[513]

It is impossible to provide an exhaustive litany of circumstances that may amount to reasonable grounds for insecurity. It is, possible, however, to state a workable test: Under all of the circumstances, "Would a reasonable merchant feel threatened that his expectation of receiving full performance was threatened?"[514]

[3]   Nature of the Demand of Adequate Assurances

A demand of adequate assurances must be made in good faith. Where the plaintiff had a distributorship contract with the defendant and the plaintiff's owner requested a letter agreement from the defendant so that it could be presented to the plaintiff's banker for

---

[507] Brisbin v. Superior Valve Co., 398 F.3d 279, 286 (3d Cir. 2004).

[508] Moreover, even as to events arising after the time of contract formation, if such events arose because of risks assumed by the obligee at the time of formation, they may not be used as reasonable grounds for insecurity. RESTATEMENT 2d § 251 comment c.

[509] *See* SPS Indus., Inc. v. Atlantic Steel Co., 186 Ga. App. 94, 366 S.E.2d 410 (1988); AMF v. McDonald's Corp., 536 F.2d 1167 (7th Cir. 1976).

[510] USX Corp. v. Union Pac. Resources Co., 753 S.W.2d 845 (Tex. App. Fort Worth 1988).

[511] C.L. Maddox, Inc. v. Coalfield Servs., 51 F.3d 76 (7th Cir. 1995).

[512] Smith-Scharff Paper Co. v. P.N. Hirsch & Co. Stores, Inc., 754 S.W.2d 928 (Mo. Ct. App. 1988).

[513] Koch Materials Co. v. Shore Slurry Seal, Inc., 205 F. Supp. 2d 324 (D. N. J. 2002).

[514] By-Lo Oil Co. v. Par-Tech, Inc., 11 Fed. Appx. 538, 544 (6th Cir. 2001) quoting the test from commercial law expert Professor William Hawkland in HAWKLAND UNIFORM COMMERCIAL LAW SERIES 2-609:2 (2000).

inventory financing, the "banker" was the owner, himself. The court held that the plaintiff had not requested assurances for himself. His request for an imaginary banker was not made in good faith and did not constitute an effective demand for adequate assurances.[515] Unjustified or repeated demands that harass the obligor are not good faith demands. In an earlier exploration, it was not unusual to find a court stating that a demand for performance beyond the terms of the contract, coupled with a clear manifestation of intention not to perform unless the demand was met, would constitute an anticipatory repudiation.[516] Where, however, a party has reasonable grounds for insecurity, it is almost inevitable that a demand that will satisfy such insecurity will require some performance beyond the terms of the contract.[517] Requiring some prepayment or other security not authorized by the terms of the contract is not unusual. It is certainly possible for a demand to be so excessive that it amounts to an anticipatory repudiation, such as a demand for assurances that has the effect of forcing a modification of the contract.[518] Again, however, if a demand for adequate assurances were relegated to the literal terms of the original contract, it would have preciously little significance in a commercial context.

The demand must seek adequate assurance of *performance*. Thus, a mere request for a meeting is not a demand for adequate assurance of performance.[519] Neither is a request for information.[520] As to the kind of assurance that will be deemed "adequate," this is a question of fact requiring a consideration of all of the surrounding circumstances including prior course of dealing, trade usage, the general reputation of the obligor, the reason for the initial insecurity, and the time for performance.[521]

[4] Form of Demand for Adequate Assurances

The UCC requires the demand for assurances to be evidenced by a writing,[522] whereas the RESTATEMENT 2d recognizes the possible effectiveness of an oral demand in certain circumstances though it states a preference for a written demand.[523] While the case law indicates that a written demand is normally required,[524] courts have been willing to give effect to oral demands where a pattern of interaction exists demonstrating a clear understanding between the parties that suspension would occur absent assurances.[525]

---

[515] Roger Edwards, LLC v. Fiddes & Sons, Ltd. 387 F.3d 90 (1st Cir. 2004) citing RESTATEMENT 2d § 251 comment d.

[516] *See, e.g.*, Chamberlin v. Puckett Constr., 277 Mont. 198, 921 P.2d 1237 (1996).

[517] *See* Top of Iowa Coop. v. Sime Farms, Inc, 608 N.W.2d 454, 469 (Iowa 2000).

[518] Scott v. Crown, 765 P.2d 1043 (Colo. Ct. App. 1988); Louisiana Power & Light Co. v. Allegheny Ludlum Indus., Inc., 517 F. Supp. 1319 (E.D. La. 1981); Pittsburgh-Des Moines Steel Co. v. Brookhaven Manor Water Co., 532 F.2d 572 (7th Cir. 1976).

[519] Penberthy Electromelt Int'l, Inc. v. United States Gypsum Co., 38 Wash. App. 514, 686 P.2d 1138 (1984).

[520] SPS Indus., Inc. v. Atlantic Steel Co., 186 Ga. App. 94, 366 S.E.2d 410 (1988).

[521] UCC § 2-609(2) and comment 4; RESTATEMENT 2d § 251 and comment d.

[522] UCC § 2-609(1).

[523] RESTATEMENT 2d § 251 comment d, which allows for an oral demand if time is of particular importance because "the additional time required for a written demand might necessitate an oral one."

[524] *See* Automated Energy Sys., Inc. v. Fibers & Fabrics, 164 Ga. App. 772, 298 S.E.2d 328 (1982).

[525] In Chronister Oil Co. v. Unocal Ref. & Mktg., 34 F.3d 462, 464 (7th Cir. 1994), the court recognizes cases where courts have been willing to waive the requirement of a writing where the party on whom the demand is made knows that it has been made. *See* AMF v. McDonald's Corp. 536 F.2d 1167, 1170–71 (7th Cir. 1976). See also Scott v. Crown,

[5]   Insolvency as Prospective Failure of Performance

While courts did not recognize a demand for adequate assurances at common law, insolvency was an exception.[526] An obligor who cannot pay his debts in the ordinary course of business or as they mature is insolvent.[527] Insolvency is not a repudiation because the act is not voluntary and affirmative.[528] Moreover, it may not even provide reasonable grounds to believe that the obligor will not perform in a given situation. For example, in a personal service contract, an employee may become insolvent, but such insolvency may not affect his ability to perform the services for which he has contracted.[529] If, however, the contract is one for sale of goods, the insolvency of the buyer provides reasonable grounds to believe that the buyer will not be able to pay for the goods at the time of performance. Under these circumstances, the UCC permits a seller to refuse delivery except for cash.[530] Unlike the Code, the RESTATEMENT 2d pursues the common law approach in permitting the buyer to either make payment, tender payment, or provide reasonable security to assure his performance.[531] Where insolvency provides reasonable grounds to believe that the obligor will be unable to perform, the obligee has the unqualified power to suspend his own performance.[532] If the obligee wishes to be discharged of his duties, however, he must pursue the process of demanding adequate assurances and await those assurances for a reasonable time.[533] If the obligee merely doubts the solvency of the obligor, again, he must pursue the process of demanding adequate assurances.[534]

[H]   Leases — CISG — UNIDROIT Principles

The UCC Article on leases includes sections on a demand for adequate assurance of performance[535] and anticipatory repudiation[536] that replicate the Article 2 sections dealing with contracts for the sale of goods.[537]

---

765 P.2d 1043 (Colo. Ct. App. 1988), indicating the same analysis but finding no pattern of interaction in the facts of this case to justify an oral demand. There is no authority under the UCC or elsewhere indicating that the policies underlying the parol evidence rule are applicable to a written demand for adequate assurances.

[526] Norcon Power Partners, L.P. v. Niagara Mohawk Power Corp., 110 F.3d 6, 8 (2d Cir. 1997).

[527] Both the RESTATEMENT 2d (§ 252(2)) and the UCC (§ 1-201(23)) define "insolvency" very broadly: "A person is insolvent who either has ceased to pay his debts in the ordinary course of business or cannot pay his debts as they become due or is insolvent within the meaning of the federal bankruptcy law." The Bankruptcy Code definition of "insolvent" is found in 11 U.S.C. § 101(26).

[528] If an obligor is adjudicated a bankrupt, his contract may be rejected by the trustee representing the estate. Such a rejection has the effect of a repudiation. 11 U.S.C. § 365(g)(1).

[529] See RESTATEMENT 2d § 252 ill. 2.

[530] UCC § 2-702(1), which also requires cash payment for all unpaid goods delivered prior to the insolvency as well as permitting the seller to stop delivery under § 2-705.

[531] RESTATEMENT 2d § 252(1). See Leopold v. Rock-Ola Mfg. Corp., 109 F.2d 611 (5th Cir. 1940); Diem v. Koblitz, 49 Ohio St. 41, 29 N.E. 1124 (1892); Ex parte Chalmers, In re Edwards, L. R. 8 Ch. 289 [1873].

[532] RESTATEMENT 2d § 252 comment a.

[533] RESTATEMENT 2d § 251.

[534] Doubts as to solvency may give rise to reasonable grounds to believe that the obligor will breach, and a demand for adequate assurances under § 251 of the RESTATEMENT 2d would be appropriate. Section 252 of the RESTATEMENT 2d applies only to situations where the obligor is, in fact, insolvent.

[535] UCC § 2A-401.

[536] UCC § 2A-402.

[537] The only changes are due to leasing terminology.

Under CISG, a party may suspend performance of an international contract for the sale of goods where, after the contract is formed, "it becomes apparent that the other party will not perform a substantial part of his obligations."[538] Evidence of inability to perform can be any deficiency in his ability to perform, creditworthiness, or conduct in preparing to perform or performing the contract.[539] The suspending party must give immediate notice of the suspension and must resume performance if the other party provides "adequate assurance of his performance."[540] If it is not merely *apparent* that the other party will not perform a *substantial* part of his obligations, but *clear* that he will commit a *fundamental* breach,[541] the innocent party may declare the contract avoided.[542] If, however, "time allows," he "must give reasonable notice to the other party to permit him to provide adequate assurance of his performance,"[543] unless that "party has *declared* that he will not perform his obligations."[544]

The UNIDROIT Principles section is captioned "Anticipatory non-performance," which is virtually identical with the CISG section called "Anticipatory breach," i.e., where it is "clear" that there will be "fundamental non-performance", the innocent obligee may "terminate the contract."[545] Where, however, a party only "reasonably believes" that there will be a fundamental breach, i.e., it is not "clear" that such a breach will occur, the obligee may only demand adequate assurance of due performance and suspend his performance until such assurance is provided. If the assurance is not provided, the obligee "may terminate the contract."[546]

§ 111   EXCUSE OF CONDITION

[A]   Nature of the Problem

Where a contractual duty will not be activated until a condition occurs, circumstances may permit that condition to be excused. The occurrence of a condition may be prevented or hindered through the bad faith of a party to the contract. There may be a subsequent promise to perform notwithstanding the nonoccurrence of the condition, or performance may be accepted even though a condition failed to occur. The conditional duty may be repudiated or the performance of the condition may be impossible or impracticable. In the subsections that follow, we will explore these and related circumstances relating to the excuse of conditions. It should be noted that the problem is analyzed in essentially the same fashion regardless of whether the condition is an express condition or a constructive condition.[547]

---

[538] CISG Art. 71(1).

[539] CISG Art. 71(1)(a) & (b).

[540] CISG Art. 71 (3).

[541] CISG Art. 25 defines "fundamental" breach as one that "results in such detriment to the other party as substantially to deprive him of what he is entitled to expect under the contract. . . ."

[542] CISG Art. 72(1).

[543] CISG Art. 72(2).

[544] CISG Art. 72(3).

[545] Principles Art. 7.3.3.

[546] Principles Art. 7.3.4.

[547] There is, however, one distinction that is important. An express condition may be waived unless it is a material part of the agreed exchange. RESTATEMENT 2d § 84(1)(a). A constructive condition, however, may be waived even if it is

[B]   Prevention or Hindrance of Condition — Good Faith

Where a contractual duty is conditional, there is a generally recognized duty of good faith and fair dealing placed on the promisor[548] to demonstrate reasonable cooperation by either refraining from conduct that would prevent or hinder the occurrence of a condition, or by taking positive steps to cause its performance. A classic example of the *negative* obligation is found in a well-know case where a prenuptial agreement promised a large payment to the wife if she survived her husband. The condition of survival was prevented in the most direct way by the husband. He shot and killed his wife before committing suicide, which may be described euphemistically as a failure to cooperate. The nonoccurrence of the condition was, obviously, excused.[549] After completing most of the engineering services required by a contract, the plaintiff was terminated. When he sought payment for his services, the defendant relied on contract language stating that such payments were made on the basis of "actual construction costs" which did not exist because the defendant had abandoned the project. The court held that the defendant could not escape its liability by relying on the non-occurrence of a condition which he had caused by abandoning the project.[550] A typical example of the *positive* obligation is found in contracts for the purchase and sale of real property where the buyer's duty is conditioned on his ability to obtain adequate financing, i.e., a mortgage loan. A buyer has no duty to obtain the loan under such a contract. He does, however, have a duty to use his best efforts to obtain the loan in accordance with the general principle of good faith and fair dealing, and the specific principle that he should, in such a situation, take positive steps in attempting to secure such a loan. His failure to do so excuses the condition.[551] Similarly, a failure to present an accurate financial position to auditors prevents an auditor from performing its contract.[552] The justification for the rule making prevention or hindrance a violation of the duty of good faith and fair dealing, as well as an excuse of the condition, is the fundamental assumption by the parties to the contract that the promisor would not interfere with the occurrence of the condition, or that he would take reasonable steps to ascertain its occurrence.[553]

While there are occasional statements in the case law suggesting that it is necessary to show that the condition would have occurred except for the lack of the promisor's cooperation,[554] most courts find it sufficient to show that the failure to cooperate has *contributed materially* to the nonoccurrence of the condition.[555] In the prenuptial agreement

---

a material part of the agreed exchange. RESTATEMENT 2d § 246. The concept of waiver of conditions will be explored later in this section.

[548] Both the UCC and the RESTATEMENT 2d impose these duties on all contractual parties with respect to the performance and enforcement of contracts. UCC § 1-203; RESTATEMENT 2d § 205.

[549] Foreman State Trust & Sav. Bank v. Tauber, 348 Ill. 280, 180 N.E. 827 (1932). *See also* Zady Natey, Inc. v. United Food & Commercial Workers Int'l Union, Local No. 27, 826 F. Supp. 142, 146 (D. Md. 1992), *aff'd*, 995 F.2d 496 (4th Cir. 1993) (firing employees made assignment clause of contract impossible).

[550] Perkins v. Cedar Mt. Sewer Improvement Dist., 2004 Ark. LEXIS 770 (2004).

[551] *See* Bellevue College v. Greater Omaha Realty Co., 217 Neb. 183, 348 S.W.2d 837 (1984). *See also* Lach v. Cahill, 138 Conn. 418, 85 A.2d 481 (1951).

[552] Begier v. Price Waterhouse, 1992 U.S. Dist. LEXIS 14020 (E.D. Pa. Sept. 14, 1992).

[553] This concept, as found in the second edition of this book, was relied upon in Barnes v. Atlantic & Pac. Life Ins. Co., 295 Ala. 149, 325 So. 2d 143 (1975). *See also* Smith v. Morgan Drive Away, Inc., 613 S.W.2d 469 (Mo. Ct. App. 1981).

[554] *See* Eager Beaver Buick, Inc. v. Burt, 503 So. 2d 819 (Ala. 1987).

[555] In Moore Bros. Co. v. Brown & Root, Inc., 207 F.3d 717, 725 (4th Cir. 2000), the court states, "The prevention

case, it would have been impossible to prove that the wife would have survived her husband had he not killed her. Since he destroyed any opportunity for her to meet the condition of survival, it is eminently fair to conclude that the husband's failure to cooperate contributed substantially to the prevention of the condition, which should be excused. Where a party failed to perform a constructive condition to recommend approval of a settlement to a bankruptcy court, the court found that it contributed materially to the rejection of the settlement.[556] Where a local union failed to obtain the necessary approval of the international union, the failure was a material contribution to the failure of the contract to be approved.[557] If, however, the *promisor* can show that his lack of cooperation has not materially affected the occurrence of the condition, the condition is not excused.[558]

[C]   Condition Excused by Repudiation or Other Inability to Perform — Impossibility, Impracticability

If it appears that a promise will not be performed at the time for performance, a condition attached to that promise will generally be excused.[559] Just as the obligor's nonperformance will excuse a condition to his duty, his repudiation will have the same effect since the obligee is entitled to take the obligor at his word.[560] Like excuse of condition for nonperformance,[561] excuse of condition for repudiation depends upon whether the repudiation contributed materially to the nonoccurrence of the condition.[562] If the condition would not occur regardless of the repudiation, both parties are discharged from their duties.[563] If the condition, however, would occur, failing to excuse it in light of the promisor's repudiation would appear to insist upon a useless requirement. Whether a condition would have occurred absent the repudiation is sometimes a matter of speculation. Thus, where a buyer of a condominium with a boat slip repudiated a contract because he was dissatisfied with the seller's reasonable assurances that the slip would be effective, the buyer sought to be discharged because the seller had failed to arrange proper financing in accordance with the contract. The court held that the financing condition was excused because the seller may have arranged proper financing by the time for performance and the burden of proof was on the buyer to show that the seller would not have arranged such financing.[564] Courts have also

---

doctrine does not require proof that the condition would have occurred 'but for' the wrongful conduct of the promisor; instead, it only requires that the conduct have 'contributed materially' to the non-occurrence of the condition." *See also* Casino Res. Corp. v. Harrah's Entertainment, Inc., 2002 U. S. Dist. LEXIS 5110, *26 (D. Minn., Mar. 22, 2002); RESTATEMENT 2d § 245.

[556] Cummings v. Beaton & Assocs., 249 Ill. App. 3d 287, 187 Ill. Dec. 701, 618 N.E.2d 292 (1st Dist. 1992).

[557] NLRB v. Local 554, Graphic Communications Int'l Union, 991 F.2d 1302, 1308 (7th Cir. 1993).

[558] It should be emphasized that the burden is on the party in breach to show that the condition would not have occurred notwithstanding his lack of cooperation. RESTATEMENT 2d § 245 comment b.

[559] *See* Champion v. Whaley, 280 S.C. 116, 311 S.E.2d 404 (Ct. App. 1984) (condition to brokerage commission that house be sold excused when seller sold house to another); Craddock v. Greenhut Constr. Co., 423 F.2d 111 (5th Cir. 1970) (condition of supplying performance bond excused through repudiation). *See also* Chadd v. Midwest Franchise Corp., 226 Neb. 502, 412 N.W.2d 453 (1987). RESTATEMENT 2d § 255.

[560] RESTATEMENT 2d § 255 comment a.

[561] RESTATEMENT 2d § 245.

[562] Kiewit Tex. Mining Co. v. Inglish, 865 S.W.2d 240, 245 (Tex. App. Waco 1993). RESTATEMENT 2d § 255.

[563] Stanwood v. Welch, 922 F. Supp. 635, 642 (D.D.C. 1995). RESTATEMENT 2d § 255 comment a.

[564] Puget Sound Serv. Corp. v. Bush, 45 Wash. App. 312, 724 P.2d 1127 (1986). *See* RESTATEMENT 2d § 245 comment b.

demonstrated unwillingness to permit the repudiating party to use the possibility of the nonoccurrence of a condition as a defense to repudiation. A broker brought an action for his commission on the sale of a house. The contract was conditional on the buyer obtaining certain financing. Before the closing date, the seller repudiated by selling the house to a third party. The seller presented evidence that the buyer would not have been able to obtain the required financing in time for the closing. The court held for the broker on the footing that whether the condition would have been met in time was a matter of speculation and the seller should not be discharged from its duty through its own wrongdoing.[565]

Beyond repudiation, the condition may also be excused because performance of the promise may be impossible or impracticable. The concepts of impossibility and impracticability require separate discussion later in this volume.[566] At this point, it is appropriate to recognize that, if the occurrence of a condition becomes impossible or impracticable[567] and the condition is not a material part of the agreed exchange, the condition is excused.[568] A classic example is the condition found in building contracts that the architect must be satisfied with each portion of the work before the owner's duty to make each progress payment is activated. If the architect dies or becomes so incapacitated that he or she is incapable of making the judgment of approval, that condition will be excused.[569] While impossibility or impracticability is normally considered in relation to the performance of the contract, just as performance can be excused on these bases, a condition may also be excused.

[D]   Acceptance of Benefits After Nonoccurrence of Condition

If a condition does not occur but the promisor nevertheless accepts benefits under the contract which are part of the contemplated exchange for his own conditionally promised performance, it is generally held that the condition is excused.[570] Thus, when a promise to do certain excavating work was conditioned on the work being performed by a specified date, it was held that when the promisor permitted the work to continue after the expiration of that

---

[565] Champion v. Whaley, 280 S.C. 116, 311 S.E.2d 404 (Ct. App. 1984).

[566] *See infra* Chapter 8.

[567] RESTATEMENT 2d § 261, following § 2-615(a) of the UCC, states that where a party's performance is made impracticable without his fault by the occurrence of an event the nonoccurrence of which was a basic assumption on which the contract was made, his duty to render that performance is discharged, unless the contract language or circumstances indicated the contrary.

[568] RESTATEMENT 2d § 271.

[569] *See* Grenier v. Compratt Constr. Co., 189 Conn. 144, 454 A.2d 1289 (1983). *See* RESTATEMENT 2d § 271 ill. 1. In general, see Multi-Serv. Contractors, Inc. v. Town of Vernon, 193 Conn. 446, 477 A.2d 653 (1984). Earlier, we saw that parties may enter into a "sale of approval" contract which is sometimes referred to as a sale "on trial" or a sale "on satisfaction." In such a transaction, "the seller undertakes a particular business risk to satisfy his prospective buyer with the appearance or performance of the goods in question." UCC § 2-326(1)(a) and comment 1. Presumably, a condition naming a party to be satisfied in such an agreement could be excused if that party was unavailable or incapable of making a good faith judgment. Another UCC section, § 2-305, deals with a missing price term that will be supplied by a named third party upon whose judgment the parties to the contract have agreed to rely. Comment 4 to that section, however, mentions the special situation where a particular party's judgment is not chosen by the parties merely as a barometer or index of a fair price, but as an essential condition to the parties' intention to make any contract at all. In that situation (*e.g.*, a trusted expert is to "value" a particular painting), the unavailability of such a third party will prevent the formation of the contract.

[570] Accusoft Corp v. Palo, 237 F.3d 31, 55 (1st Cir. 2001) (continued acceptance of benefits under a settlement agreement with knowledge that conditions had not been performed).

date, the condition was excused.[571] The nonoccurrence of the condition where the promisor knows or has reason to know of such nonoccurrence operates as a promise to perform despite that nonoccurrence.[572] Any other rule could result in a serious forfeiture to the promisee without any equivalent loss to the promisor. Where, however, the defective performance is so attached to the promisor's real or personal property that he cannot avoid availing himself of its use if he is to make any beneficial use of his property, the mere use of the property without knowledge of the nonoccurrence of the condition will not excuse the condition.[573] On the other hand, if the promisor knew or had reason to know of the nonoccurrence of the condition and indicated acceptance of the performance notwithstanding such nonoccurrence, he may not rely upon that nonoccurrence to be discharged from his duty.[574]

Under the UCC, acceptance of goods with knowledge of a nonconformity will preclude the buyer from later rejecting the goods or revoking acceptance unless the acceptance was based on the assumption that the nonconformity would be cured.[575] Even the acceptance of nonconforming goods, however, does not preclude the buyer from recovering damages for such accepted goods. The seller remains liable for breach of warranty.[576] A promisor sometimes only accepts and retains part of the performance. A number of cases have held that a promisor may not decide to accept part of the entire performance and reject another part[577] even though these cases often dealt with contracts for the sale of goods. Under the UCC, that concept has been modified with respect to such contracts. While the buyer may reject goods under the Code, he also may choose either to accept the whole shipment or accept any "commercial unit or units and reject the rest."[578] In contracts other than those for the sale of goods, the general rule remains that a promisor may not decide to reject part and accept another part of an entire performance.[579] Even under the UCC, if the performance is

---

[571] Dunn v. Steubing, 120 N.Y. 232, 24 N.E. 315 (1890). *See also* Longenecker v. Brommer, 59 Wash. 2d 552, 368 P.2d 900 (1962) (acceptance of timber though not felled and bucked in accordance with regulations required by the contract); Venz v. State Auto Ins. Ass'n, 217 Iowa 662, 251 N.W. 27 (1933) (acceptance of premium by insurer with knowledge of nonoccurrence of condition); Neil v. Kennedy, 319 Ill. 75, 149 N.E. 775 (1925) (vendor's acceptance of overdue installments of price on land contract precludes a termination of the contract to sell though time of payment was of the essence). *See also* RESTATEMENT 2d § 246(1).

[572] *See* SEC v. Vision Communs., Inc., 1994 U.S. Dist. LEXIS 8708, at *9 (D.D.C. June 28, 1994). RESTATEMENT 2d § 246(1).

[573] Becker Roofing Co. v. Little, 229 Ala. 317, 156 So. 842 (1934); Fitzgerald v. La Porte, 64 Ark. 34, 40 S.W. 261 (1897); Hanley v. Walker, 79 Mich. 607, 45 N.W. 57 (1890). *See also* RESTATEMENT 2d § 246(2) and comment d.

[574] *See* RESTATEMENT 2d § 246 ill. 7.

[575] *See* Courtesy Enters., Inc. v. Richards Labs., 37 U.C.C. Rep. Serv. (CBC) 765, 768 (Ind. Ct. App. 1983). "Even if one were to assume that the [nonconformity existed, the] acceptance of the shipment with knowledge of that tendency precluded its revocation of acceptance." The court cited UCC § 2-607(2) as support for this statement. On revocation of acceptance, see UCC § 2-608(1)(b).

[576] UCC § 2-714(1). *See In re* Precise Tool & Gauge Co., 39 U.C.C. Rep. Serv. (CBC) 474 (Bankr. E.D. Tenn. 1984). *See also* RESTATEMENT 2d § 246 comment b.

[577] *See* Loveland v. Aymett's Auto Arcade, Inc., 121 Conn. 231, 184 A. 376 (1936) (buyer of oil burner and tank accepted tank but attempted to return defective burner); Shohfi v. Rice, 241 Mass. 211, 135 N.E. 141 (1922) (buyer of goods under an entire contract who accepted some that conformed to the contract specifications could not reject others that were defective); Pacific Timber Co. v. Iowa Windmill & Pump Co., 135 Iowa 308, 112 N.W. 771 (1907) (buyer of car of lumber could not accept part and reject part that was defective).

[578] UCC § 2-601. "Commercial unit" is defined in § 2-105(6) as "such a unit of goods as by commercial usage is a single whole for purposes of sale and division of which materially impairs its character or value on the market or in use."

[579] RESTATEMENT 2d § 246 comment c.

promised in installments and the nonconformity of one or more past installments gives the buyer the right to treat the whole contract as materially breached, the buyer's subsequent acceptance of another nonconforming installment reinstates the contract absent notification of cancellation because it signals the buyer's intention to continue the contract.[580]

[E]   Unjustifiable Basis for Nonperformance as Excuse of Condition

If a condition fails to occur and the promisor refuses to perform but states a wholly unjustifiable reason for his refusal rather than the nonoccurrence of the condition, should the condition be excused? Some older cases took the position that the condition must be excused because the promisee has the right to assume that the promisor was relying exclusively on the unjustifiable reason and it would be unjust to permit him to discover the justifiable reason at a later time, i.e., the nonoccurrence of the condition.[581] The corresponding assumption was that, by stating a particular reason for his refusal to perform, the promisor is necessarily indicating satisfaction with all other aspects of the promisee's performance and a willingness to forego all other possible defenses.[582] Neither of these assumptions is warranted. Where a party rejects a performance, he need not state any reasons for his rejection. A problem may occur, however, if a party decides to particularize the reasons for his rejection and his reasons are not justifiable.

Under the UCC, where the buyer of goods could have stated the justifiable reason for his rejection but, instead, stated an unjustifiable reason, the seller may be misled. If the seller can show that he would have cured the defect if the justifiable reason had been stated within a reasonable time,[583] the nonoccurrence of the condition is excused.[584] The seller has a right to cure under the UCC and, where the Code does not apply, we have seen that even a material breach is subject to cure under the RESTATEMENT 2d. Material interference with the right to cure can, therefore, operate to excuse the condition to the promisor's duty.[585] The RESTATEMENT 2d conforms to the Code in this situation.[586]

---

[580] Similarly, if the buyer brings an action only with respect to past installments or demands future installments, he is indicating his intention that the contract be continued. UCC § 2-612(3). *See* Traynor v. Walters, 342 F. Supp. 455 (M.D. Pa. 1972) (though buyer had the right to treat the whole contract as breached, when the buyer demanded delivery of portion of undelivered goods, the buyer reinstated the contract).

[581] *See* Ginn v. W. C. Clark Coal Co., 143 Mich. 84, 106 N.W. 867 (1906). *Accord* Cummings v. Connecticut Gen. Life Ins. Co., 102 Vt. 351, 148 A. 484 (1930), *noted*, 39 YALE L.J. 906 (denial of liability under life insurance policy on one ground held to prevent reliance on any other defense); Powers v. Bohuslav, 84 Neb. 179, 120 N.W. 942 (1909) (action for real estate broker's commission); Chevrolet Motor Co. v. Gladding, 42 F.2d 440 (4th Cir.), *cert. denied*, 282 U.S. 872, 51 S. Ct. 78, 75 L. Ed. 770 (1930), *noted*, 44 HARV. L. REV. 646 (1930) (unjustified attempt to cancel a contract under one clause prevented treating contract as cancelled under another clause where there was reason to activate that clause).

[582] *See* Oelbermann v. Toyo Kisen Kabushiki Kaisha, 3 F.2d 5 (9th Cir.), *cert. denied*, 268 U.S. 693, 45 S. Ct. 511, 69 L. Ed. 1161 (1925) (carrier who answers written claim for loss on merits loses right to object to delay in presenting claim).

[583] See UCC § 2-508 and the discussion of "cure" at § 108[B][2], *supra*.

[584] *See* UCC § 2-605. *See also* Uchitel v. F. R. Tripler & Co., 107 Misc. 2d 310, 434 N.Y.S.2d 77 (1980).

[585] *See* RESTATEMENT 2d § 245 comment b; *see also* All EMS, Inc. v. 7-Eleven, Inc., 181 Fed. Appx. 551,555 (7th Cir. 2006) (a breaching party is not liable where the other party to the contract unjustifiably caused the breach by preventing the breaching party from performing).

[586] RESTATEMENT 2d § 248. The UCC, of course, preempts with respect to contracts for the sale of goods so that the RESTATEMENT 2d may not differ from the UCC in such cases. In other types of contracts, however, the RESTATEMENT 2d clearly follows the Code with rare exception.

§ 112 "WAIVER" OF CONDITION — ESTOPPEL AND ELECTION

One of the difficulties encountered in attempts to analyze the case law excusing conditions is the use of the nebulous term "waiver." For many years, writers have criticized the use of the term as one of imprecise and indefinite connotation.[587] It is almost invariably though inexactly defined as the voluntary or intentional relinquishment of a known right,[588] though it is also equated with excuse of conditions.[589] There is additional confusion as to whether a "waiver" must be supported by consideration or detrimental reliance (promissory estoppel). Thus, one court may suggest that "[t]he essence of waiver is estoppel. Where there is no estoppel, there is no waiver."[590] Another court insists that "While waiver is a member of the family of estoppel, . . . estoppel in pais has connections in nowise akin to waiver."[591] Still another court may state that "A waiver, to be operative, must be supported by an agreement founded upon a valuable consideration,"[592] while another tells us that waiver "does not require or depend upon a new contract or a new consideration. Nor does it depend upon estoppel. . . ."[593] Though noting that waiver and estoppel are often used interchangeably, a more recent opinion suggests "*waiver* describes the act, or the consequences of the act, while estoppel involves some element of reliance by or prejudice to the other party."[594] An especially candid statement of this curious term by Judge Posner suggests the dangers of self-serving testimony, i.e., "You can always say that the other party to your contract had orally waived the enforcement of a provision favorable to him."[595] Yet, the efficacy of a waiver generally does not require evidence of reliability, such as a writing, consideration, reliance or a higher standard of proof.[596] Notwithstanding the pervasive confusion in the use of the term, courts continue its use. It also appears in statutes, including the UCC, without definition.[597] Earlier in this volume, the concept of waiver was explored in relation to contract modifications under the UCC,[598] where we recognized that the characterization of waiver is much more pliable than the concept of modification. Notwith-

---

[587] *See* Ewart, *Professor Williston's Review of Waiver*, 11 MINN. L. REV. 415 (1926). *See also* Wachovia Bank & Trust Co., N.A. v. Rubish, 306 N.C. 417, 293 S.E.2d 749 (1982) (meaning of "waiver" is at best elusive).

[588] *See* Burger King v. E-Z Eating, 572 F.3d 1306, 1315 (11th Cir. 2009); Cole Taylor Bank v. Truck Ins. Exch., 51 F.3d 736, 739 (7th Cir. 1995); Penmanta Corp. v. Hollis, 520 N.E.2d 120 (Ind. Ct. App. 1988); East Larimer County Water Dist. v. Centric Corp., 693 P.2d 1019 (Colo. Ct. App. 1984); Hauenstein & Bermeister, Inc. v. Met-Fab Indus., Inc., 320 N.W.2d 886 (Minn. 1982). One of the problems with this definition is the inference that the promisor must be aware of his legal rights and intend the legal consequences of his "waiver." Most courts hold that it is enough that he has full knowledge of all the material facts or reason to know such facts. *See* Garrard v. Lang, 514 So. 2d 933 (Ala. 1987), and RESTATEMENT 2d § 84 comment b.

[589] *See* RESTATEMENT 2d § 84 and comment b.

[590] Williams v. Neely, 134 F. 1, 10 (8th Cir. 1904).

[591] Quoted with approval in Hayes v. Manning, 263 Mo. 1, 172 S.W. 897, 907 (1914).

[592] Smith v. Minneapolis Threshing Mach. Co., 89 Okla. 156, 158, 214 P. 178, 180 (1923).

[593] Champion Spark Plug Co. v. Automobile Sundries Co., 273 F. 74, 79 (2d Cir. 1921).

[594] Pitts v. Amer. Sec. Life Ins. Co., 931 F.2d 351, 357 (5th Cir. 1991).

[595] *See Cole Taylor Bank*, *supra* note 588.

[596] *Id.*

[597] *See, e.g.*, UCC §§ 2-209(4) and 2-605. UCC § 1-107 uses the term "waiver" or "renunciation" in relation to discharging a debt without consideration. RESTATEMENT 2d § 277(1) more properly limits the surrender of a claim to a written "renunciation" which discharges the claim.

[598] *See* § 65[E], *supra*. There, UCC §§ 2-209(4) and (5) dealt with the possible "waiver" of the statute of frauds (§ 2-209(3) incorporating § 2-201 for modifications of contracts) or a so-called "private" statute of frauds in § 2-209(2) as manifested in a no-oral-modification (NOM) clause.

standing the lack of precision in the use of "waiver," we will now explore those situations where the word is used in relation to the excuse of conditions.

By language or conduct,[599] a promisor may manifest his intention[600] to forego the benefit of ("waive") a condition.[601] This manifestation may occur (1) prior to or at the time of contract formation, (2) after formation but prior to the time for occurrence of the condition, or (3) after formation *and* after the time for occurrence of the condition.

[A]   "Waiver" at or Prior to Contract Formation

If a promisor manifests her intention to forego the benefit of a condition prior to the formation of a contract that will be evidenced by a writing containing that condition, there is an obvious parol evidence problem. As suggested earlier in this volume, the parol evidence rule precludes the admissibility of evidence of prior or contemporaneous agreements that will, *inter alia*, contradict or vary the terms of a subsequently formed contract evidenced by a writing. Thus, it would seem that such evidence would not be admissible and the condition would not be excused.[602] In typical cases involving insurance contracts,[603] most of our courts have admitted the evidence and excused the condition, usually on the footing that the promisee has changed her position in reliance upon the promisor's manifestation of intention to forego the benefit of the condition (estoppel).[604] Modern courts may not, however, insist upon a showing of estoppel. Thus, where an insurer was constructively aware of the nonoccupancy of a building before issuing a policy containing a condition of occupancy, the court found that a constructive waiver of that condition could be shown without insisting upon a showing of estoppel.[605] This is in keeping with the modern view discussed below that certain conditions may be excused absent any validation device.[606]

---

[599] Nortel Networks, Inc. v. Gold & Appel Transfer, S. A., 298 F. Supp. 2d 81, (D. D. C. 2004); Pipe Indus. Ins. Fund Trust of Local 41 v. Consolidated Pipe Trades Trust of Mont., 233 Mont. 162, 760 P.2d 711 (1988).

[600] Whether a waiver has occurred is a question of intention, i.e., a question of fact. *See* East Larimer County Water Dist. v. Centric Corp., 693 P.2d 1019 (Colo. Ct. App. 1984).

[601] The burden of proof is on the party asserting the waiver, i.e., the promisee. *Pipe Indus. Ins. Fund Trust of Local 41, supra* note 599.

[602] *See* Lumber Underwriters of New York v. Rife, 237 U.S. 605 (1915); Franklin Fire Ins. Co. v. Martin, 40 N.J.L. (11 Vroom) 568, 29 Am. Rep. 271 (N.J. Ct. Err. & App. 1878).

[603] For a case involving franchising, see Ehret Co. v. Eaton, Yale & Towne, Inc., 523 F.2d 280 (7th Cir. 1975), *cert. denied*, 425 U.S. 943, 96 S. Ct. 1683, 48 L. Ed. 2d 186 (1976).

[604] *See* Roberts v. Maine Bonding & Casualty Co., 404 A.2d 238 (Me. 1979); Kimball Ice Co. v. Springfield Fire & Marine Ins. Co., 100 W. Va. 728, 132 S.E. 714 (1926); Gordon v. St. Paul Fire & Marine Ins. Co., 197 Mich. 226, 163 N.W. 956 (1917); Big Creek Drug Co. v. Stuyvesant Ins. Co., 115 Miss. 561, 76 So. 548 (1917). *See also* Satz v. Massachusetts Bonding & Ins. Co., 243 N.Y. 385, 153 N.E. 844 (1926) (insurance company estopped to show nonperformance of a "condition" where it acquiesced in such nonperformance at the time of issuing the policy, but it was not estopped to rely upon breach of "warranty"). *See* Note, 75 U. Pa. L. Rev. 477 (1926).

[605] The court suggested that the line between waiver and estoppel is often blurred, and where an insurer, with knowledge of the facts, performs in a fashion inconsistent with its intention to insist upon a strict compliance with conditions in the contract, the insurer will be treated as having waived their occurrence. Standard Supply Co. v. Reliance Ins. Co., 49 N.C. App. 616, 272 S.E.2d 394 (1980).

[606] *See* Restatement 2d § 84(1) and comment d.

[B]   "Waiver" After Formation and Before Time for Occurrence of Condition

A post-formation manifestation of intention to forego the benefit of a condition is not affected by the parol evidence rule which applies only to promises made before or at the time of formation. Any promise which is supported by consideration to forego the benefit of a condition is a modification of the contract and is clearly enforceable, assuming that any statute of frauds requirement is met. The parties have discharged the old contract and entered the new conditionless contract. Often, however, a promise made after formation, but before the time for occurrence of the condition to forego the benefit of a condition, is not supported by consideration. Courts have readily moved to enforcement of such promises on the basis of detrimental reliance whether the time for the condition has or has not arrived.[607] The problem arises where there is no consideration, promissory estoppel, or any other validation device.

Where a party manifests an intention to perform his promise notwithstanding the nonoccurrence of a condition to his duty before the time for the condition has arrived, the condition will be excused if it was not a material part of the agreed exchange.[608] Certain conditions are not a material part of the agreed exchange. They are merely technical or procedural, such as those requiring proof of loss or notice within a certain time. A promise to forego the benefit of this type of condition is enforceable without any validation device though it subjects the promisor to a new duty. The new duty, however, does not differ significantly from the original duty.[609] If, however, the condition is a material part of the agreed exchange, it will not be "waived."[610] An agreement for the purchase and sale of property contained a condition requiring clear and marketable title. The condition for clear and marketable title was not merely technical or procedural; it was a material part of the agreed exchange and the condition was not excused.[611] An absurd example makes the point even more clearly. An insurance policy will be paid up to $200,000 on condition that the insured suffers a casualty. If

---

[607] *See* Fehl-Haber v. Nordhagen, 59 Wash. 2d 7, 365 P.2d 607 (1961) (by accepting four late monthly payments, conditional vendor "waived" its right to forfeiture which could be reinstated only by giving vendee reasonable opportunity to comply with contract); General Motors Acceptance Corp. v. Hicks, 189 Ark. 62, 70 S.W.2d 509 (1934) (vendor's right to forfeit a conditional sale for default in payments was lost by accepting many other payments late); Hartford Fire Ins. Co. v. Aaron, 226 Ala. 430, 147 So. 628 (1933) (benefit of condition in fire policy stipulating against change in insured's interest in the property lost by failing, after receiving notice of the change of interest, to declare a forfeiture of the policy before a fire after receiving notice of the change of interest). Contracts often contain "anti-waiver" or "nonwaiver" clauses which seek to preserve conditions previously waived. In effect, these clauses are designed to automatically reinstate conditions to future performance even though there have been one or more waivers of such conditions in the earlier performance of the contract. The existence of a nonwaiver clause does not preclude excuse of conditions by manifestation of intention to forego the benefit of one or more conditions. TSS-Seedman's, Inc. v. Elota Realty Co., 72 N.Y.2d 1024, 531 N.E.2d 646 (1988); Carver v. Preferred Acci. Ins. Co., 218 Iowa 873, 256 N.W. 274 (1934); Green v. Minnesota Farmers' Mut. Ins. Co., 190 Minn. 109, 251 N.W. 14 (1933); Ley v. Home Ins. Co., 64 N.D. 200, 251 N.W. 137 (1934). A party may be estopped to assert a nonwaiver clause. *See* Dorn v. Robinson, 762 P.2d 566 (Ariz. Ct. App. 1988). If the intention to forego the benefit of the condition is pervasive over a long period, even the nonwaiver clause may be waived. *See* Westinghouse Credit Corp. v. Shelton, 645 F.2d 869, 873–74 (10th Cir. 1981); Dillingham Commercial Co. v. Spears, 641 P.2d 1, 7–8 (Alaska 1982).

[608] See Zetter v. Griffith Aviation, Inc., 2006 U. S. Dist. LEXIS 23192 (E. D. Ky. 2006); Nebraska Pub. Power Dist. v. MidAmerican Energy Co., 234 F.3d 1032, 1045 (8th Cir. 2000). See also RESTATEMENT 2d § 84(1).

[609] *See* RESTATEMENT 2d § 84 comment d.

[610] "Unless the right waived is a minor one, why would someone give it up in exchange for nothing?" *Cole Taylor Bank, supra* note 588.

[611] *See* Rose v. Mitsubishi Int'l Corp., 423 F. Supp. 1162 (E.D. Pa. 1976).

the insurer promises to pay $200,000 to the insured even though no casualty has been suffered, the condition is not excused ("waived") because it was a material part of the agreed exchange.

Where the "waiver" occurs prior to the time for the occurrence of the condition, it may be possible to reinstate the condition. If, for example, an insurance company promised not to insist upon a condition in the casualty policy requiring notice of loss within 60 days from the time of loss, but, before any loss occurred, the insurer notified the insured that it would insist upon such notice should a casualty occur, the insurer's duty would again be subject to the condition, i.e., the excused condition would be reinstated.[612] The condition of notice was within the control of the promisee (insured)[613] and the notification was received while there was still time to cause the condition to occur.[614] Reinstatement of the condition under these circumstances, therefore, is not unjust.[615]

[C] "Waiver" After Formation and After Time for Occurrence of Condition — Election

Where the condition has not occurred after the time for its occurrence, it is impossible to reinstate it. A manifestation of intention to forego the benefit of the condition will certainly excuse the condition if there is reliance upon that manifestation. In the case of a language or conduct promise after the time for occurrence of the condition, that the condition will not be required, reliance is unlikely and some cases have held that the condition is not excused in the absence of reliance (estoppel).[616] More cases, however, hold the condition excused though no reliance has been shown.[617] Both the First Restatement[618] and Restatement 2d[619] arrive at the same conclusion through a different rationale, i.e., as long as the condition was not a material part of the agreed exchange, it may be excused absent reliance or other validation device. The cases supporting the conclusion of the Restatements often characterize the language or (more typically) conduct manifesting an intention to forego the condition as an "election" or "election to waive." For those courts that do not require reliance, the election is absolute. Those requiring reliance, however, permit the promisor to change his mind in the absence of reliance. It cannot be gainsaid that the addition of the less than precise term "election" to the muddled notion of "waiver" may be emotionally satisfying but otherwise of little assistance. The fundamental issue is whether a promise by language or conduct to forego the benefit of a condition will be enforced absent any showing of reliance. The Restatements

---

[612] *See* Restatement 2d § 84(2).

[613] It would be sufficient if it were within the control of a beneficiary to the insurance contract. Restatement 2d § 84(2).

[614] Restatement 2d § 84(2)(a).

[615] Restatement 2d § 84(2)(b).

[616] *See* Coleman Furniture Corp. v. Home Ins. Co., 67 F.2d 347 (4th Cir. 1933), *cert. denied*, 291 U.S. 669, 54 S. Ct. 453, 78 L. Ed. 1059 (1934); Joyce v. South Carolina Mut. Ins. Co., 54 S.C. 371, 32 S.E. 446 (1899).

[617] Whether or not the time for the occurrence of the condition had arrived, in addition to the requirement that the condition not be a material part of the agreed exchange, if the condition is to be excused, the risk of uncertainty that the condition would occur must not have induced the formation of the contract. Thus, a fire insurance policy places the risk of the condition of fire on the insurer. A promise to pay regardless of that condition, therefore, materially affects the value received by the promisor. *See* Restatement 2d § 84(1)(b) and comment c.

[618] First Restatement § 88.

[619] Restatement 2d § 84(1).

suggest the preferable compromise: If the condition is not a material part of the agreed exchange, no reliance is necessary; otherwise, there is no waiver without reliance. If there is a promise to surrender a technical or procedural condition, there is little reason to insist upon some validation device to support that promise. This is not to underestimate the difficulty that can be found in determining whether a condition is a material part of the agreed exchange. The question in that context can be as difficult as any question concerning materiality. Yet, materiality is a standard that has proven generally workable, notwithstanding its pliable character. If the terms "waiver" and "election" would fall into disuse, much of the mystery surrounding excuse of conditions would disappear. Unfortunately, the tenacity of those terms, particularly "waiver," suggests their continuation in the third millennium.

Chapter 8

RISK ALLOCATION — IMPOSSIBILITY, IMPRACTICABILITY, AND FRUSTRATION PURPOSE

§ 113   IMPOSSIBILITY AND IMPRACTICABILITY OF PERFORMANCE

[A]   History — The Rigid Common Law Rule

At the time a contract is formed, the parties are or should reasonably be aware of the circumstances and attendant risks associated with their agreement. After the contract is formed, however, the surrounding circumstances may change to such an extent as to make performance of the contract, according to its terms, either impossible or something quite different from what was expected by the parties when the contract was made. Death, war, changes in the law or its administration, fires, floods, etc., intervene and give rise to the question of whether the promisor should be required to perform, or to pay damages for nonperformance, in spite of the changed conditions. If the parties had sufficient imagination to foresee the particular contingency that has subsequently arisen, they may not have made the kind of contract which they did make. Typical optimism or limited foresight at the time of contract formation, however, may result in general contract language that appears to make the promisor liable though it may be evident that the language was not used advisedly with reference to the situation that has arisen by the time for performance. What is to be done under these circumstances?

It is generally said that the early law of England, which was inclined to enforce a contract in accordance with its literal terms in all cases, took the uncompromising stand that neither impossibility, nor any change of circumstances, however extreme, would excuse performance of a promise. This view is set forth in the case of *Paradine v. Jane*,[1] where it was said that

---

[1] Aleyn 26, 82 Eng. Rep. 897 [1647]. The court held that the fact that a lessee had been deprived of the use of leased premises by the king's enemies did not excuse him from paying the rent reserved in the lease. So far as the actual decision is concerned, the case would probably be followed today. It should be noted that the promisor's performance, i.e., paying the rent, was not made impossible at all by the supervening event. If he were to be excused from

". . . when the party by his own contract creates a duty or charge upon himself, he is bound to make it good, if he may, notwithstanding any accident by inevitable necessity, because he might have provided against it by his contract."

While such a view promotes certainty and ease of application, it ignores the fact that human beings are of limited foresight. To hold a promisor to the literal terms of his bargain is frequently to impose a burden upon him which neither he nor the promisee had considered as a possibility. It may enlarge the risk assumed at the time of formation by outrageous proportions. Even the old English courts at the time of this case recognized obvious exceptions to the rigid rule. If a personal service contract could not be performed because the promisor died, his performance was excused.[2] If performance was prevented by operation of law,[3] or by the destruction of the goods without the fault of the promisor,[4] the performance was held excused. There was, however, an understandable fear to suggest any general principle of excusable nonperformance where these exceptions could be recognized as illustrations.

Whenever a promisor is relieved from an obligation which he has apparently assumed, there is always the possibility that he is being relieved of an obligation which he did in fact assume, or which he would have assumed, had the contingency in question been consciously considered at the time of contracting. At best, the tribunal that must decide the case can only speculate as to whether the parties had a certain risk in mind, or, if not, what they would have done had they considered the possibility. For fear of opening the door too widely to one seeking to escape an obligation which he may have assumed, the tendency was to view the door closed, regardless of the hardship resulting to the promisor, with only the most compelling, isolated exceptions. The challenge was to determine the limited exceptions to the otherwise firm general rule that performance is not excused, and the scope of these exceptions.

[1]   Origins of The Modern Doctrine — Implied Condition — *Taylor v. Caldwell*

The modern doctrine of impossibility of performance emerged from the case of *Taylor v. Caldwell* in 1863.[5] The use of a music hall had been promised to the plaintiff to enable him to give a series of concerts. It was destroyed by an accidental fire before the date set for the first concert. In a suit for breach of the contract, it was held that the owner was excused from performing on the basis of a new "principle":

---

performing, the only basis for such excuse would be frustration of purpose. For a more recent case which applies the language of Paradine v. Jane literally, see Wills v. Shockley, 52 Del. (2 Storey) 295, 157 A.2d 252 (1960). See also Blackburn Bobbin Co. v. Allen & Sons, 1 K.B. 540, 543 [1918], in which McCardie, J., wrote: "The original rule of the English law was clear in its insistence that where a party by his own contract creates a duty or charge upon himself he is bound to make it good notwithstanding any accident by inevitable necessity, because he might have provided against it by his contract." But cf. Page, *The Development of the Doctrine of Impossibility of Performance*, 18 MICH. L. REV. 589 (1919), in which he suggests that the early English law frequently did, in effect, excuse performance under circumstances which today would be dealt with on a theory of excuse because of impossibility of performance.

[2] *See* Hyde v. Dean of Windsor, 78 Eng. Rep. 798 (Q.B. 1597).

[3] Abbot of Westminster v. Clerke, 73 Eng. Rep. 59 (K.B. 1536).

[4] Williams v. Lloyd, 82 Eng. Rep. 95 (K.B. 1629).

[5] 3B. & S. 826, 32 L.J., Q.B. 164 [1863].

[W]here, from the nature of the contract, it appears that the parties must from the beginning have known that it could not be fulfilled unless when the time for the fulfillment of the contract arrived some particular specified thing continued to exist, so that, when entering into the contract, they must have contemplated such continuing existence as the foundation of what was to be done; there, in the absence of any express or implied warranty that the thing shall exist, the contract is not to be construed as a positive contract, but as subject to an *implied condition* that the parties shall be excused in case, before breach, performance becomes impossible from the perishing of the thing without default of the contractor.[6]

By the statement that the parties "must have contemplated" the continuing existence of the music hall as the "foundation" of their contract, the court was not suggesting that the parties consciously adverted to its continuing existence. Rather, "in the course of affairs, men in making such contracts *in general would, if it were brought to their minds,* say that there should be such a condition."[7] The court's analysis augured the modern formulation for the impossibility doctrine. Such a concept appeared radical in 1863. It is not remarkable that the court resorted to the fiction of an *implied condition.* A so-called implied-in-fact condition would suggest that the contract contains an unstated condition intended by the parties. As the last quoted statement from the opinion reveals, however, the court constructed a condition, a so-called "implied-in-law" condition, to arrive at a result it deemed desirable on policy grounds.[8]

It is an open secret that a constructed condition does not involve interpretation of the contract to effect the parties' intentions. When an unforeseen, supervening event changes the circumstances surrounding the contract to such an extent that a greatly increased burden will be imposed upon the promisor, a court must decide whether the promisor must still be liable to perform. Every contract involves the assumption of new risks by the parties. When, without the fault of either party, the normal risks at the time of formation are more than substantially changed by unexpected supervening events over which neither party had any control, courts must determine how the new risks should be allocated between the parties.[9] The early common law exceptions of death in personal service contracts, destruction of the subject matter without the fault of the promisor and discharge of a duty by operation of law continued after 1863, but they were now supported by the implied condition analysis. Moreover, the possibility of new exceptions loomed.

---

[6] *Id.* at 833 (emphasis supplied).

[7] *Id.,* (emphasis supplied).

[8] Justice Holmes tells us that, "You can always imply a condition in a contract. But why imply it? It is because of some belief as to the practice of the community or of a class, or because of some opinion as to policy, or, in short because of some attitude of [the court] upon a matter not capable of . . . founding exact logical conclusions." Holmes, *The Path of the Law,* 10 HARV. L. REV. 457, 466 (1897).

[9] "It is implicit in the doctrine of impossibility . . . that certain risks are so unusual and have such severe consequences that they must have been beyond the scope of the assignment of risks inherent in the contract, that is, beyond the agreement made by the parties." Mishara Constr. Co. v. Transit-Mixed Concrete Corp., 365 Mass. 122, 128, 310 N.E.2d 363, 367 (1974).

[2]   Early Notions of Impracticability

Where supervening events made performance excessively costly, the abhorrence of *forfeiture* induced courts to consider whether performance should be excused even though it was still literally possible to perform. Where performance had become so excessively burdensome that a party should not be reasonably expected to perform, there were instances where performance was excused on the ground that it had become impracticable. From its inception, however, the concept of impracticability was treated with extreme judicial caution. To permit a promisor to be excused from performance because the cost of performance has risen even to extreme levels appeared to threaten the fundamental concept of the social institution of contract. The essential principle remained that any promisor must be said to have anticipated that the contract might prove to be unprofitable, even extremely unprofitable. He should, therefore, be viewed as having assumed that risk.[10] Occasionally, however, extreme losses result from factors abnormal and unexpected, and under circumstances that make it unreasonable to suppose that the promisor would have been expected to assume such a risk had the possibility been contemplated. In such a case, essential fairness could induce a court to hold that the promisor was excused. Several courts reached this conclusion though the rationales have been less than pristine.

A 1916 case became the classic example. A contractor promised to extract all the gravel that he would need to perform a certain project. After taking half of what he needed, he discovered that the rest was below water level and could be removed only at a cost twelve times as great as would otherwise have been the case. The court excused the performance by resorting to one of the three recognized exceptions to the rigid common law rule: (1) the death or incapacity of a promisor in a personal service contract, (2) destruction or unavailability of the subject matter, or (3) a supervening act of state where performance became impossible by operation of law.[11] The rationale, however, bordered on the metaphysical.[12] The court suggested that, in legal contemplation, the specific gravel contracted for did not exist, thereby placing the facts within the second exception that was recognized more than a half century earlier in the famous music hall case where the hall was destroyed by fire. The court insisted that the special circumstances made it impracticable for the promisor to remove the gravel. Thus, like the music hall, the gravel could be deemed not to exist. This rationale allowed the court to convert the case into one that paid homage to the general rule disallowing excuse for impossibility while utilizing a recognized exception. Though the opinion is often viewed as the modern foundation of the

---

[10] *See* Megan v. Updike Grain Corp., 94 F.2d 551 (8th Cir.), *cert. dismissed*, 305 U.S. 663 (1938) (promise to pay rent for grain elevator not excused when unexpected change in rail tariffs caused diversion of so much grain from a certain market as to render leased elevator practically worthless. The court, however, emphasized that the lessee must have been aware of the possibility of the change in tariffs when he took the lease since the I.C.C. had already indicated that it might put such a change into effect); Straus v. Kazemekas, 100 Conn. 581, 124 A. 234 (1924), commented on in 34 Yale L.J. 91 (1924) (contract to purchase Russian rubles to be delivered as soon as possible after the lifting of an existing embargo on their importation not excused when the embargo was continued for about two years, although the price of rubles had dropped very materially).

[11] Common law courts insisted on retaining the general principle that performance is not excusable subject to these three exceptions now found in modern form in the Restatement 2d §§ 261–263.

[12] Mineral Park Land Co. v. Howard, 172 Cal. 289, 156 P. 458 (1916). *See also* Fisher v. United States Fidelity & Guaranty Co., 313 Ill. App. 66, 39 N.E.2d 67 (1942). In Powers v. Siats, 244 Minn. 515, 521, 70 N.W.2d 344, 349 (1955), the court states: "A mere difficulty of performance does not ordinarily excuse the promisor, but where a great increase in expense or difficulty is caused by a circumstance not only unanticipated but inconsistent with the facts which the parties obviously assumed as likely to continue, the basic reason for excusing the promisor from liability may be present." *See* First Restatement § 454 (1932).

doctrine of impracticability, it retains the original common law concept. An analysis comparable to the modern view in 1916 would have been contrary to the strict position of the era in other courts.[13] Again, the essential question is one of risk allocation. It was inevitable that the modern doctrine of impracticability would recognize this fundamental principle.

[B]   The Modern Impracticability Concept — Uniform Commercial Code and RESTATEMENT 2d

[1]   The New Diction

The UCC contains a broad concept of excusable nonperformance:

> Except so far as a seller may have assumed a greater obligation . . . (a) delay in delivery or non-delivery in whole or in part by a seller . . . is not a breach of his duty under a contract for sale if performance as agreed has been made impracticable by the occurrence of a contingency the non-occurrence of which was a basic assumption on which the contract was made. . . ."[14]

Virtually identical language in the RESTATEMENT 2d expands the application of this principle to contracts beyond the sale-of-goods category to which Article 2 of the UCC applies.[15] The UCC and Restatement 2d versions of the impossibility/impracticability concept is often viewed as major enhancement by establishing a positive principal in place of a negative rule with its exceptions.[16] The new iteration was characterized as freeing the doctrine from the earlier fictional and unrealistic strictures of the "implied condition"term.[17] Yet, under the new diction, the doctrine will excuse performance when such performance has been made impracticable *by the occurrence of a contingency* that is inconsistent with the basic assumption of the parties at the time the contract was made. The phrase, "occurrence of a contingency," has the sound and the appearance of "condition." While the statutory language avoids the phrase "implied condition" (since that would be anathema), there is a negative implied (in-fact or in-law) condition in the "basic assumption" of the parties. Within that "basic assumption," a court must determine whether the parties' assumed or should be said to have assumed the *non-occurrence* of a particular supervening event-a "contingency" (dare we say a "condition"). Thus, the much heralded new diction may suggest much less of a major change than has been asserted. It is, quite literally, a "restatement" of the principle. Indeed, the new phraseology was viewed by some as angular. Since the basic assumption must reveal a certain event or contingency that will *not* occur, one court suggested, "The latter part of the test seems a somewhat complicated way of putting Professor Corbin's question of how much risk the promisor assumed."[18]

---

[13] *See infra* § 114.

[14] UCC § 2-615(a).

[15] "Where, after a contract is made, a party's performance is made impracticable without his fault by the occurrence of an event the non-occurrence of which was a basic assumption on which the contract was made, his duty to render that performance is discharged, unless the language or the circumstances indicated the contrary." RESTATEMENT 2d § 261.

[16] *See* The Opera House of Boston v. The Wolf Trap Foundation for the Performing Arts, 817 F. 2d 1094, 1098–99(4th Cir. 1987).

[17] *See* Transatlantic Fin. Corp. v. United States, 363 F.2d 312, 124 U.S. App. D.C. 183 (1966).

[18] United States v. Wegematic Corp., 360 F.2d 674, 676 (2d Cir. 1966).

Both the Code and RESTATEMENT 2d make it clear that the principle is subject to the assumption of greater liability through the agreement of the parties.[19] Courts have also assimilated the change from the narrow defense of impossibility to the broader principle of impracticability.[20] The modern formula, repeated by many courts, consists of three elements: (1) a contingency has occurred which (2) has made performance impracticable, where (3) nonoccurrence of that contingency was a basic assumption upon which the contract was made.[21]

[2] Application to Buyers as Well as Sellers

By its literal terms, the Code section excuses only *sellers* whose performance becomes commercially impracticable, on the assumption that a buyer only has an obligation to pay under a contract for the sale of goods and sellers do not assume the risk that buyers will not pay.[22] A comment, however, suggests the possible application of the section to buyers,[23] and the UCC principle is clearly applicable by analogy beyond its technical scope.[24] The RESTATEMENT 2d section version avoids the problem by referring to "a party."[25] Several courts have concluded that the UCC section should apply to buyers as well as sellers.[26] The remaining conceptual problems are inherent in the fundamental question, what elements must be shown to allow for the excuse of impracticability?

[C] Elements of the Impracticability Principle

There are four discernible elements in the judicial application of this principle. (1) An event must have occurred making performance excessively burdensome (impracticable); (2) the *nonoccurrence* of that event must have been a basic assumption on which the contract was formed, i.e., the event must not have been clearly foreseeable, anticipated or expected, (3) the

---

[19] UCC § 2-615: "Except so far as a seller may have assumed a greater obligation. . . ." *See also* comment 8 to § 2-615. RESTATEMENT 2d § 261: "[U]nless the language or the circumstances indicate the contrary." See also comment c to this section. The RESTATEMENT 2d's expression of "language or circumstances" suggests the broad definition of "agreement" in § 1-201(3) of the UCC which insists that, in addition to language, the "agreement" contains the implication of the parties' intention from all of the relevant circumstances, including prior course of dealing, trade usage, and course of performance.

[20] *See, e.g.*, Harper & Assocs. v. Printers, Inc., 46 Wash. App. 417, 730 P.2d 733 (1986) (narrow defense of impossibility has been subsumed in the more commercially oriented and broader categories of impracticability); Burlington N. & Santa Fe Ry. Co. v. Kansas City S. Ry., 45 F. Supp. 2d 847, 852 (D. Kan. 1999) ("[A]lthough the rule stated in this Section is sometimes phrased in terms of 'impossibility,' it has long been recognized that it may operate to discharge a party's duty even though the event has not made performance absolutely impossible.").

[21] Waldinger v. CRS Groups Engineers, Inc., 775 F. 2d 781, 786 (7th Cir. 1985) (citing cases).

[22] Northern Indiana Pub. Serv. Co. v. Carbon County Coal Co., 799 F. 2d 265, 276 (7th Cir. 1986).

[23] *See* UCC § 2-615 comment 9. The omission of buyers in the section is said to have occurred because the concept of excuse by frustration of purpose (to be discussed later in this section) had been generally accepted as to sellers, but the law with respect to buyers in this area was in a state of development. Thus, the Code drafters decided to leave the matter unsettled but "open-ended." 2 G. GILMORE, SECURITY INTERESTS IN PERSONAL PROPERTY § 41.7, at 1105 (1965).

[24] *See* Thrifty Rent-A-Car systems, Inc. v. South Florida Transport, Inc., 2005 U. S. Dist. LEXIS 38489, *17 (N. D. Okla. 2005).

[25] RESTATEMENT 2d § 261.

[26] *See, e.g.*, Power Eng'g & Mfg., Ltd. v. Krug Int'l, 501 N.W.2d 490, 494 (Iowa 1993); Lawrance v. Elmore Bean Warehouse, 108 Idaho 892, 702 P.2d 930 (Ct. App. 1985); Northern Ill. Gas Co. v. Energy Coop., Inc., 122 Ill. App. 3d 940, 78 Ill. Dec. 215, 461 N.E.2d 1049 (3d Dist. 1984).

event must not have been caused by the promisor seeking to be excused from nonperformance, and (4) the greater risk caused by the event must not have been allocated to the promisor under the contract.

[1]   Event Making Performance Impracticable — Extent of Cost Increase

In determining the meaning of "impracticable," several courts have relied on the commentary in the RESTATEMENT 2d:

> Performance may be impracticable because extreme and unreasonable difficulty, expense, injury or loss to one of the parties will be involved. A severe shortage of raw materials or of supplies due to war, embargo, local crop failure, unforeseen shutdown of major sources of supply, or the like, which either causes a marked increase in cost or prevents performance altogether may bring the case within the rule. . . . However, . . . [a] mere change in the degree of difficulty or expense due to such causes as increased wages, prices of raw materials or costs of construction, unless well beyond the normal range, does not amount to impracticability since it is this sort of risk that a fixed-price contract is intended to cover.[27]

A comment to the UCC section provides similar guidance. Beginning with the stark warning that "[i]ncreased cost *alone* does not excuse performance *unless the rise in cost is due to some unforeseen contingency which alters the essential nature of the contract*," it proceeds to exclude a rise or collapse in the market as a sufficient excuse since such a risk is precisely the kind contracting parties assume.[28] Thus, an unforeseen or unexpected supervening event over which the promisor had no control must cause "increased cost" or loss. The next question is, how extensive must a loss be to create a successful impracticability defense?

Both the UCC and the RESTATEMENT 2d insist that the increased cost of performance must amount to considerably more than a change in the degree of difficulty of performance to constitute impracticability. Just because performance is made "impractical" does not mean that it is "impracticable." A promisor is expected to use reasonable efforts to surmount obstacles to performance. A performance is impracticable only if it cannot be overcome by such reasonable efforts.[29] The fact that costs have risen, even substantially, is not impracticable since, absent a contrary manifestation of agreement, this is a risk allocated by the typical contract.[30] The

---

[27] RESTATEMENT 2d § 261, comment d, *as quoted in* Contempo Design, Inc. v. Chicago & Northeast Ill. Dist. Council of Carpenters, 1998 U.S. Dist. LEXIS 8357, at *15 (N.D. Ill. May 20, 1998).

[28] UCC § 2-615 comment 4 (emphasis supplied). *See* Lawrance v. Elmore Bean Warehouse, 108 Idaho 892, 702 P.2d 930 (Ct. App. 1985); Northern Ill. Gas Co. v. Energy Coop., 461, N.E.2d 1049 (Ill. App. Ct. 1984); Resources Inv. Corp. v. Enron Corp., 669 F. Supp. 1038 (D. Colo. 1987). *See also* American Trading & Production Corp. v. Shell Int'l Marine, Ltd., 453 F.2d 939, 944 (2d Cir. 1972) (citing the first edition of this book).

[29] Waddy v. Riggleman, 216 W. Va., 250, 259, 606 S. E. 2d 202, 231 (2004) quoting RESTATEMENT 2d § 261 comment d.

[30] RESTATEMENT 2d § 261 comment d; UCC § 2-615 comment 4: "Neither is a rise or a collapse in the market in itself a justification, for that is exactly the type of business risk which business contracts made at fixed prices are intended to cover." *See* Lawrance v. Elmore Bean Warehouse, 108 Idaho 892, 702 P.2d 930 (Ct. App. 1985) (market shifts or financial instability do not change one's performance); Maple Farms, Inc. v. City Sch. Dist., 76 Misc. 2d 1080, 1805, 352 N.Y.S.2d 784, 790 (Sup. Ct. 1974) ("There is no precise point, though such could conceivably be reached, at which an increase in price of raw goods above the norm would be so disproportionate to the risk assumed as to amount to [impracticability] in a commercial sense."). *See also In re* M & M Transp. Co., 13 B.R. 861, 869 (Bankr. S.D.N.Y. 1981)

First RESTATEMENT suggested that the loss must be "extreme and unreasonable" and, through its illustrations, indicated that tenfold increases or costs multiplied fifty times would constitute such "extreme and unreasonable" burdens.[31] Cases have held that increases of fourteen percent,[32] thirty one and one-half percent,[33] fifty percent,[34] or even a doubling of the cost of performance[35] would be insufficient to meet the requirement of a sufficient increase in cost even if that increase were caused by an unforeseen or unexpected contingency. On the other hand, a ninety-three percent increase[36] and a $75 million dollar out-of-pocket loss,[37] have been held sufficient. Where the promisor contemplated a profit of $18 million to $20 million on a contract, but the cost of performing a promise to dispose of waste fuel would not only eliminate any profit but cost well over $80 million, the court held the promise excused.[38] The case, however, included significant factors beyond excessive costs that appeared to influence the court's decision. The method of disposal had not been conceived at the time the contract was formed and, as of the date of the case, it was not available. A less than firm estimate suggested its availability within twenty-three years.[39] Thus, an acceptable method to perform the promise and the excessive cost of pursuing such a method were clearly unforeseeable and unexpected at the time of formation.

It is abundantly clear that a significant increase in cost, even if unforeseeable and caused exclusively by factors beyond the control of the promisor, is unlikely to convince a court to excuse the promisor unless the increase is not only material, but grossly disproportionate to any conceivable loss.

[a]   "Objective" vs. "Subjective" — Burden of Proof

Related to the size of the loss is the question of the ability or capacity of the promisor to perform as contrasted with the impracticability of performance itself. The ability of a particular promisor to perform would focus upon the individual promisor, sometimes called a "subjective" test, whereas a concern for whether performance, itself, was impracticable would be an "objective" inquiry, regardless of the particular promisor's capacity or resources. There is a difference between objective impossibility — "the thing cannot be done" — and subjective impossibility — "I cannot do it."[40] It is clear that courts will not excuse a promisor who simply

---

(citing § 202 of the third edition of this book to this effect).

[31] FIRST RESTATEMENT §§ 454 and 460, ills. 2 and 3. RESTATEMENT 2d § 261 comment d suggests, "Performance may be impracticable because extreme and unreasonable difficulty, expense, injury or loss to one of the parties will be involved."

[32] Transatlantic Fin. Corp. v. United States, 363 F.2d 312, 124 U.S. App. D.C. 183 (1966).

[33] American Trading & Production Corp. v. Shell Int'l Marine, Ltd., 453 F.2d 939 (2d Cir. 1972).

[34] Ocean Tramp Tankers Corp. v. V/O Sovfracht, (The Eugenia), 2 Q.B. 226 [1964].

[35] Tsakiroglou & Co. v. Noblee Thorl G.m.b.H., 2 Q.B. 348 [1960].

[36] Northern Corp. v. Chugach Elec. Ass'n, 518 P.2d 76, *modified on other grounds*, 523 P.2d 1243 (Alaska 1974). *See, however*, Publicker Indus., Inc. v. Union Carbide Corp., 17 U.C.C. Rep. Serv. (CBC) 989 (E.D. Pa. 1975) (not aware of any cases where something less than 100% cost increase has been held to make a seller's performance impracticable).

[37] Aluminum Co. of Am. v. Essex Group, Inc., 499 F. Supp. 53 (W.D. Pa. 1980).

[38] Florida Power & Light Co. v. Westinghouse Elec. Corp., 826 F.2d 239, 277 (4th Cir. 1987), *cert. denied*, 485 U.S. 1021, 108 S. Ct. 1574, 99 L. Ed. 2d 890 (1988).

[39] *Id.*

[40] Goldstein v. Fidelity & Guar. Ins. Underwriters, 1995 U.S. Dist. LEXIS 9923, at *18 (N.D. Ill. July 14, 1995) (only objective impossibility will excuse performance), *aff'd*, 86 F.3d 749 (7th Cir. 1996).

cannot perform even though the performance is objectively practicable.[41] Thus, a promisor who becomes insolvent or even bankrupt will not be excused because his subjective ability to perform has become impracticable. There is an implied duty on the party of the promisor to not permit himself to become so financially disabled that he is unable to perform the contract.[42] A related issue is whether courts should focus on the isolated transaction or consider the overall resources of the promisor. If the isolated transaction would meet the requirement of an egregious loss, should a promisor's overall ability to absorb loss be considered in determining the impracticability of the performance? If the total capacity of the promisor to sustain a huge loss were relevant, the standard would be "subjective" in the sense of considering the particular promisor and its resources, rather than the transaction itself. The better reasoned opinions maintain the consistent standard of refusing to consider such ability, just as courts have refused to excuse nonperformance because of subjective inability. Instead, they focus on the reasonableness of the expenditure at issue.[43]

It is clear that courts will place the burden of proving impossibility of performance[44] or impracticability of performance[45] on the party claiming excuse.

[2]   "Basic Assumption" — "Unforeseen" or "Unexpected"

The contract must evidence the parties' basic assumption that a supervening event that was not anticipated by the parties at the time of contract formation would *not* occur, but it did occur and *caused* impracticability of performance. Impracticability is typically associated with an event that occurs after contract formation — during the performance stage of the contract. We will later see that the analysis of existing impracticability at the time of contract formation is quite similar to that applied to supervening impracticability. At this point, however, it is important to concentrate on supervening or post-formation impracticability.

An *unanticipated* event may be one that is simply *unexpected*, or it may be one that is *unforeseen*. Comments to the UCC section suggest that the supervening event must be *unforeseen*[46] and many courts cling to that characterization.[47] The RESTATEMENT 2d, however,

---

[41]   See Transatlantic Fin. Corp. v. United States, 363 F.2d 312, 319, 124 U.S. App. D.C. 183 n.13 (1966) ("The issue of impracticability should no doubt be 'an objective determination of whether the promise can reasonably be performed rather than a subjective inquiry into the promisor's capability of performing as agreed.' "). Symposium, *The Uniform Commercial Code and Contract Law: Some Selected Problems*, 105 U. PA. L. REV. 880, 887 (1957). "Dealers should not be excused because of less than normal capabilities. But if both parties are aware of a dealer's limited capabilities, no objective determination would be completed without taking into account this fact." Accord RESTATEMENT 2d § 261 comment e, which prefers not to use the terms "subjective" and "objective." Jennie-O-Foods, Inc. v. United States, 580 F.2d 400, 217 Ct. Cl. 314 (1978), relies upon this RESTATEMENT 2d section and comment.

[42]   East Capitol View Community Development v. Denean, 941 A. 2d 1036, 1041(D. C. App. 2008).

[43]   *See* Alimenta (U.S.A.), Inc. v. Cargill, Inc., 861 F.2d 650 (11th Cir. 1988); Asphalt Int'l, Inc. v. Enterprise Shipping Corp., S.A, 667 F.2d 261 (2d Cir. 1981). *See, however,* Missouri Pub. Serv. Co. v. Peabody Coal Co., 583 S.W.2d 721 (Mo. Ct. App.), *cert. denied,* 444 U.S. 865, 100 S. Ct. 135, 62 L. Ed. 2d 88 (1979).

[44]   Mattvidi Assocs. Ltd. Partnership v. NationsBank of Virginia, N.A., 100 Md. App. 71, 639 A.2d 228 (1994); Nan Ya Plastics Corp. v. DeSantis, 237 Va. 255, 377 S.E.2d 388, *cert. denied,* 492 U.S. 921, 109 S. Ct. 3248, 106 L. Ed. 2d 594 (1989); Ocean Air Tradeways, Inc. v. Arkay Realty Corp., 480 F.2d 1112 (9th Cir. 1973).

[45]   Iowa Elec. Light & Power Co. v. Atlas Corp., 467 F. Supp. 129 (N.D. Iowa 1978), rev'd on other grounds, 603 F.2d 1301 (8th Cir. 1979), *cert. denied,* 445 U.S. 911, 100 S. Ct. 1090, 63 L. Ed. 2d 327 (1980).

[46]   *See* UCC § 2-615 comment 1: "Unforeseen supervening circumstances not within the contemplation of the parties." See also comment 4, referring to an "unforeseen shutdown of major sources of supply or the like."

[47]   *See* Specialty Beverages, LLC v. Pabst Brewing Co., 537 F. 3d 1165, 1176 (10th Cir. 2008) (Under Oklahoma law,

emphasizes the requirement that the nonoccurrence of the supervening event must be a "basic assumption" of the parties to the contract and concludes, "The fact that the event was foreseeable, or even foreseen, does not necessarily compel a conclusion that its nonoccurrence was not a basic assumption."[48] Perhaps the best known case dealing with the new concept of impracticability substitutes "unexpected" for "unforeseen" and other authorities are in accord. As suggested in a leading case,

> Foreseeability or even recognition of a risk does not necessarily prove its alloca-
> tion. . . . Parties to a contract are not always able to provide for all the possibilities
> of which they are aware, sometimes because they cannot agree, often simply because
> they are too busy. Moreover, that some abnormal risk was contemplated is probative
> but does not necessarily establish an allocation of the risk of the contingency which
> actually occurs.[49]

If "foreseeable" is equated with "conceivable," nothing is unforeseeable.[50] An application of the tort standard of foreseeability would be more than confusing.[51] The foreseeability standard in contract remedies, explored in the next chapter, does not augur success. There is simply no escape from the hard question of risk allocation.[52] If a risk was anticipated or expected, it would be prohibitively difficult to find a basis for excusable nonperformance. If a risk was foreseeable, it is reasonable to assume that the parties contracted on that basis. That assumption, however, may not be warranted if the foreseeable event was an improbable contingency that reasonable parties may not have expressly or impliedly addressed in their agreement.

[3]   Causation — Beyond the Control of the Promisor

Regardless of the extent of the loss, if that loss was not *caused* by an unforeseeable or unexpected supervening event which changed the basic assumption or foundation of the contract, nonperformance will not be excused. The excusing event must not be within the "reasonable control" of the party asserting the excuse, i.e., a party may not affirmatively cause the event that prevents his performance, nor may a party rely on an excusing event if he could have taken reasonable steps to avoid it. In a contract for the sale of land, the seller's lawyer mistakenly assumed that it would not be difficult to secure certain releases of liens and encumbrances in time to meet the closing date. When the delay in securing the releases

---

the impracticability defense is available only if the occurrence making performance impracticable was unforeseeable). See also, Waldinger Corp. v. CRS Group Eng'rs, Inc., Clark Dietz Div., 775 F.2d 781, 786 (7th Cir. 1985); Barbarossa & Sons, Inc. v. Iten Chevrolet, Inc., 265 N.W.2d 655, 658–61 (Minn. 1978). *See also* Eastern Air Lines, Inc. v. Gulf Oil Corp., 415 F. Supp. 429 (S.D. Fla. 1975).

[48] RESTATEMENT 2d § 261 comment b. *See also* § 265 comment a.

[49] Transatlantic Fin. Corp. v. United States, 363 F.2d 312, 318, 124 U.S. App. D.C. 183 (1966). This view is expressly adopted in Opera Co. of Boston, Inc. v. Wolf Trap Found. for Performing Arts, 817 F.2d 1094 (4th Cir. 1987), and another well-known impracticability case, Aluminum Co. of Am. v. Essex Group, Inc., 499 F. Supp. 53 (W.D. Pa. 1980) as noted in Specialty Tires of Am., Inc. v. CIT Group/Equipment Fin., Inc., 82 F. Supp. 2d 434, 438 (W.D. Pa.), *aff'd*, 2000 U.S. App. LEXIS 31822 (3d Cir. Nov. 20, 2000). The same view is adopted in the RESTATEMENT 2d at § 261 and comments b and c thereto.

[50] *Quoted in* Hoosier Energy Rural Elec. Coop., Inc. v. John Hancock Life Ins. Co., 588 F. Supp. 2d 919, 932 (S. D. Ind. 2008) citing the same quote in Speciality Tires of America, *id.*

[51] *See* Eastern Air Lines, Inc. v. McDonnell Douglas Corp. 532 F.2d 957, 992 n.97 (5th Cir. 1976).

[52] See Posner & Rosenfeld, *Impossibility and Related Doctrines in Contract Law: An Economic Analysis*, 6 J. LEGAL STUD. 83, 98–100 (1977).

precluded closing on the prescribed date, the seller claimed excuse under the impossibility doctrine. The court held that where a supervening event that the promisor could have avoided by reasonable diligence prevents his performance, the promisor's performance is not excused.[53] Clearly, a party may not rely upon the excuse of impossibility created by its own failure to perform another duty.[54] Even if an unforeseen event had occurred and the promisor had suffered a loss great enough to suggest commercial impracticability, the inability of the promisor to prove that the loss resulted from the supervening event as contrasted with the promisor's actions would prevent a successful use of the defense.

Where, for example, the party seeking to be excused could not overcome evidence that a major share of the loss was caused by its own actions, the court would not excuse performance.[55] Moreover, the failure to pursue affirmative efforts to overcome the effects of a supervening effect will preclude the excuse of impossibility. Where a promisor breached its promise to lease space at its convention for the presentation of a controversial subject on the footing that the presentation would be disruptive and potentially dangerous, the court held that the promisor failed to show that it had taken reasonable steps to obviate the danger by providing for sufficient security to guard against groups that opposed the presentation. Relying on the RESTATEMENT 2d,[56] the court held that a party invoking the impossibility defense must show affirmatively that performance was impossible or impracticable despite the exercise of skill, diligence and good faith. The defendant failed to provide adequate evidence of such efforts and therefore was not excused from performing.[57]

[4]   Risk Allocation by Agreement — *Force Majeure* Clause

In approaching the question of impracticability, courts typically consider whether the parties have allocated the risk either expressly or impliedly by their agreement.[58] As suggested by one court, "Since impossibility and related doctrines are devices for shifting risk in accordance with the parties presumed intentions, . . . they have no place when the contract explicitly assigns a particular risk to one party or the other."[59] Both the UCC and the RESTATEMENT 2d expressly recognize the right of the parties to allocate risks by their contract in a fashion that differs from the risk allocation formulas that would apply absent such

---

[53] Waddy v. Riggleman, 606 S. E. 2d 222 (W. Va. 2004). *See also* Nissho-Iwai Co. v. Occidental Crude Sales, Inc., 729 F.2d 1530 (5th Cir. 1984).

[54] *See, e.g,* Louis Dreyfus Corp. v. 27,946 Long Tons of Corn, 830 F. 2d 1321 (5th Cir. 1987) (where the Coast Guard orders the promisor's ship to remain in its berth because the ship is not seaworthy, promisor could not rely upon the excuse of impossibility in not performing its promise to vacate the berth since the promisor caused the impossibility by failing to maintain the seaworthiness of the vessel).

[55] See Iowa Elec. Light & Power Co. v. Atlas Corp., 467 F. Supp. 129 (N.D. Iowa 1978), *rev'd on other grounds,* 603 F.2d 1301 (8th Cir. 1979), *cert. denied,* 445 U.S. 911, 100 S. Ct. 1090, 63 L. Ed. 2d 327 (1980) (while the loss suffered was insufficient to excuse the defendant's performance, even it had been sufficient, the defendant failed to prove what share of the cost increase was attributable to unforeseen conditions and what share was attributable to its own corporate decisions). *See also* Eastern Air Lines v. Gulf Oil Corp., 415 F. Supp. 429, 441 (S.D. Fla. 1975).

[56] RESTATEMENT 2d § 261 comment d.

[57] McCalden v. California Library Ass'n, 955 F.2d 1214, 1219 (9th Cir.), *cert. denied sub nom.* Simon Wiesenthal Ctr. for Holocaust Studies v. McCalden, 504 U.S. 957, 112 S. Ct. 2306, 119 L. Ed. 2d 227 (1992) (presentation designed to question the history of the holocaust).

[58] *See* Martin v. Vector Co., 498 F.2d 16 (1st Cir. 1974).

[59] Northern Indiana Public Serv. Co. v. Carbon County Coal Co., 799 F.2d 265, 278 (7th Cir. 1986).

agreement.[60] Parties may, for example, include a price formula which a court will accept as the allocation of the risk by agreement.[61] Where a contract expressly limited a contractor's risk to excavating "existing rock now exposed," the contractor did not assume the risk of an unexposed ledge that could only be removed at great expense which he otherwise would have been said to have assumed.[62]

The parties may include a *force majeure* (superior or irresistible force) clause, in their contract. The traditional clause listed a series of events that the parties have agreed upon as excuses for "Act of God" events such as earthquakes, storms, floods, and other natural disasters. Such natural occurrences, however, may be quite foreseeable and expected in certain regions. Thus, hurricanes in Florida would not constitute a sufficient *implied* cause for impracticability of performance in Florida, though they may be sufficient in Nebraska.[63] If, however, the parties expressly state that the non-occurrence of even a clearly foreseeable event as an express condition the duties of both parties or even one party, such a condition should have the same effect as any other express condition. The typical *force majeure* clause would also list events caused by humans such as wars and civil strife, strikes or other labor disputes that the parties have agreed upon as excuses for nonperformance.[64] No matter how complete such clauses may appear, an unlisted event may occur on which the promisor may base her claim for excusable nonperformance. After the tragic events of September 11, 2001, major issues arose concerning the effectiveness of war exemption and other insurance clauses in the absence of an officially declared war and the necessity for new terrorism exemption clauses in insurance policies.[65] Care must also be taken in the drafting of such clauses to assure that implied legal protection is not lost. For example, the *ejusdem generis* guide to interpretation

---

[60] UCC § 2-615 begins with, "Except so far as a seller may have assumed a greater obligation. . . ." As suggested earlier in this section, courts are willing to apply the section to buyers as well as sellers. The RESTATEMENT 2d (§ 261) conditions its risk allocation formula as follows: "[U]nless the language or the circumstances indicate the contrary." While the UCC language may be seen to suggest that the agreement may permit a party to assume a "greater obligation" but not a lesser obligation than that suggested by the Code formula (*see* Hawkland, *The Energy Crisis and Section 2-615 of the Uniform Commercial Code* , 79 COM. L.J. 75 (1974)), there is language in the UCC at § 2-615 comment 8, suggesting the possibility of "express agreements as to exemptions designed to enlarge upon *or supplant* the provision of this section. . . ." Moreover, courts have sanctioned agreements enlarging the exemptions, i.e., permitting a lesser obligation than expressed in the Code formula. *See* Interpetrol Bermuda Ltd. v. Kaiser Aluminum Int'l Corp., 719 F.2d 992 (9th Cir. 1983); Eastern Air Lines, Inc. v. McDonnell Douglas Corp., 532 F.2d 957 (5th Cir. 1976). The *Interpetrol* case, however, stresses the fact that general language in such clauses ought not to be interpreted as expanding excuses not provided for by the UCC.

[61] Publicker Indus., Inc. v. Union Carbide Corp., 17 U.C.C. Rep. Serv. (CBC) 989 (E.D. Pa. 1975) (ceiling provision in price formula was an intentional allocation of risk). *See, however*, Aluminum Co. of Am. v. Essex Group, Inc., 499 F. Supp. 53 (W.D. Pa. 1980) (mistaken price formula did not allocate the risk).

[62] Iannuccillo v. Material Sand & Stone Corp., 713 A.2d 1234, 1239 (R.I. 1998) (absent the express limitation of liability in the contract, the ledge was foreseeable; with that limitation, it became unforeseeable and the doctrine of commercial impracticability applied).

[63] See Thrifty Rent-A-Car Sys. v. South Florida Transport, Inc., 2005 U. S. Dist. LEXIS 38489 at *13–14 (N. D. Okla. 2005).

[64] Facto v. Pantagis, 380 N. J. Super. 227, 232, 915 A. 2d 59, 62 (App. Div. 2007). The RESTATEMENT 2d does not address the effect of a strike on the duty of performance as did the FIRST RESTATEMENT § 461 ill. 7. The RESTATEMENT 2d expressly omits that treatment "because the parties often provide for this eventuality and, where they do not, it is particularly difficult to suggest a proper result without a detailed statement of all of the circumstances." RESTATEMENT 2d Reporter's Note, final paragraph of comment d. *See also* Mishara Constr. Co. v. Transit-Mixed Concrete Corp., 365 Mass. 122, 310 N.E.2d 363 (1974) (issue of impossibility due to labor dispute was properly submitted to jury).

[65] See Jane Kendall, *The Incalculable Risk: How the World Trade Center Disaster Accelerated the Evolution of Insurance Terrorism Exemptions*, 36 U. Rich. L. Rev. 569 (2002).

suggests that where general language follows the enumeration of specific items, the general words are to be construed to refer only to items of the same kind or class as those enumerated. It is, therefore, wise to follow the listing of specific items with a phrase such as "including but not limited to" so as to preserve the general protection that would be automatically afforded under a UCC or RESTATEMENT 2d formulation of impracticability without such a clause.[66] Similarly, since contracts for the sale of goods are subject to the automatic protection of the UCC principle of impracticability, drafters should avoid the unwitting effect of diminishing that protection through less than careful drafting.[67]

It is important to understand that if an event is listed in the most carefully drafted *force majeure* clause, the event must not be within the reasonable control of the party asserting the excuse.[68] Prior course of dealing, trade usage, or course of performance can also provide a manifestation of the parties' intention to allocate the risk. Absent any manifestation of intention, however, the court is forced to pursue the more difficult process of judicially imposed risk allocation. It must proceed to examine whether there was an unanticipated supervening event that caused the impracticability.

[D]   Implementation of the Impracticability Standard — Illustrative Cases — Energy Cost and "Suez" Cases — Long Term Supply Contracts and Gross Inequity Clauses

Having examined the essential elements for the establishment of the impracticability excuse, we will see that it has proven extremely difficult to discover these necessary ingredients in attempted applications. Consider, for example, the prototype impracticability case involving a rise in energy prices caused by the OPEC cartel.

In the 1960s, the Westinghouse Corporation entered into a number of uranium supply contracts in conjunction with its desire to sell nuclear power plants. While the uranium supply contracts differed from customer to customer, they were typically requirements contracts under which Westinghouse agreed to have uranium supplied to its nuclear power plant customers for a fixed period. At that time, utility companies were wary of converting to nuclear power for a number of reasons, including, but not limited to, their lack of understanding of all of the risks associated with such conversions.[69] When uranium and other energy costs skyrocketed, Westinghouse informed its customers that it was excused in whole or in part from performing the energy supply contracts. The costs to Westinghouse and other energy suppliers in settling these lawsuits were more than substantial.[70] Efforts by energy

---

[66] *See* Eastern Air Lines, Inc. v. McDonnell Douglas Corp., 532 F.2d 957 (5th Cir. 1976).

[67] To the extent that courts are influenced by the virtually identical formulation in § 261 of the RESTATEMENT 2d, the same may be said of contracts that are not within the scope of Article 2 of the UCC. *See* Indiana-Kentucky Elec. Corp. v. Green, 476 N.E.2d 141 (Ind. Ct. App. 1985) (considering whether the phrase "impossible or not impracticable" incorporates the impracticability standard of UCC § 2-615).

[68] *See* Nissho-Iwai Co. v. Occidental Crude Sales, Inc., 729 F.2d 1530 (5th Cir. 1984) (suggesting the elements of "reasonable control" (text at note 48 *supra*) and holding that a party may not rely on a *force majeure* event if that event could have been avoided by the party asserting the excuse).

[69] See this attitude reflected in *In re* Westinghouse Elec. Corp. Uranium Contracts Litig., 517 F. Supp. 440 (E.D. Va. 1981).

[70] The October 21, 1976 issue of the Wall Street Journal (page 2, cols. 3 & 4) reports that the Westinghouse Annual Report disclosed settlements of 14 lawsuits exceeding $700 million. A number of other energy supply cases were brought against other suppliers.

suppliers to defend their refusal to perform these contracts through the use of the impracticability defense have been notoriously unsuccessful for one or more of the following reasons: (a) the contingency that occurred (OPEC action) was considered "foreseeable," i.e., not unexpected; (b) even if the contingency had been unforeseen or unexpected, the loss suffered was not sufficient to constitute impracticable performance; (c) the party asserting impracticability failed to show that impracticability was the sole or substantial cause of the increased cost of performance.[71] Similarly, in a series of cases involving the closing of the Suez Canal by the Egyptian government, resulting in numerous actions involving the impracticability excuse,[72] neither the unforeseeability nor sufficient loss factor could be established to demonstrate impracticability.

A number of cases, including many of the energy cases, involved long-term supply contracts. In what has become a singular exception to the general refusal of courts to recognize the impracticability defense in such a contract, a court discovered the elements of impracticability where a converter of alumina complained that it would lose in excess of $60 million over the life of the contract because a price formula was based on an assumption that was incorrect.[73] The case is a dubious precedent, however, since it is essentially a mutual mistake case and there is a serious question as to whether the appellate court would have agreed with findings of a lack of foreseeability and sufficient loss to constitute impracticability.[74] Courts are reluctant to apply the UCC formula in cases where contracts have been carefully negotiated, thereby suggesting that all risks are likely to have been assumed. Any suggestion that courts should adjust such a contract creates seemingly insuperable difficulties because courts feel that they lack the information and expertise to make such adjustments.[75] Considerable scholarly effort has been expended on various suggestions for using the impracticability concept in such contracts.[76]

---

[71] *In re* Westinghouse Elec. Corp. Uranium Contracts Litig., 517 F. Supp. 440 (E.D. Va. 1981) (not shown that Westinghouse lost money on entire undertaking). *See also* Missouri Pub. Serv. Co. v. Peabody Coal Co., 583 S.W.2d 721 (Mo. Ct. App.), *cert. denied*, 444 U.S. 865, 100 S. Ct. 135, 62 L. Ed. 2d 88 (1979) (imposition of the Arab oil embargo was foreseeable and may have contributed to the appreciation in value of promisor's coal reserves); Iowa Elec. Light & Power Co. v. Atlas Corp., 467 F. Supp. 129 (N.D. Iowa 1978), *rev'd on other grounds*, 603 F.2d 1301 (8th Cir. 1979), *cert. denied*, 445 U.S. 911, 100 S. Ct. 1090, 63 L. Ed. 2d 327 (1980) (some unforeseen factors, but others were foreseeable, and some of the increase in cost to Atlas resulted from internal decisions).

[72] *See* American Trading & Prod. Corp. v. Shell Int'l Marine Ltd., 453 F.2d 939 (2d Cir. 1972); Transatlantic Fin. Corp. v. United States, 363 F.2d 312, 124 U.S. App. D.C. 183 (1966); Glidden Co. v. Hellenic Lines, Ltd., 275 F.2d 253 (2d Cir. 1960); Ocean Tramp Tankers Corp. v. V/O Sovfracht (The Eugenia), 2 Q.B. 226 [1964]; Tsakiroglou & Co. v. Noblee Thorl G.m.b.H., 2 Q.B. 348 [1960].

[73] Aluminum Co. of Am. v. Essex Group, Inc., 499 F. Supp. 53 (W.D. Pa. 1980).

[74] Compared to other cases, the court applied an extremely liberal concept of "commercial" foreseeability and found that the $60 million loss over 16 years would be sufficient to meet the requirement of a sufficient loss. The opinion must be read in the context of mutual mistake, which does not require the same level of loss to permit avoidance of the contract, i.e., mutual mistake only requires a material effect upon performance. *See* Farnsworth, Brickell & Chawaga, *Relief for Mutual Mistake and Impracticability*, 1 J.L. & Com. 1, 26–29 (1981). Settlement of this case occurred after the somewhat unusual request by the United States Court of Appeals for the Third Circuit that the parties negotiate.

[75] See Hillman, *Court Adjustment of Long-Term Contracts: An Analysis Under Modern Contract Law*, 1987 Duke L.J. 1.

[76] See Hillman, *id.*; Scott, *Conflict and Cooperation in Long-Term Contracts*, 75 Cal. L. Rev. 2005 (1987); Gillette, *Commercial Rationality and the Duty to Adjust Long-Term Contracts*, 69 Minn. L. Rev. 521 (1985); Speidel, *Court-Imposed Price Adjustments Under Long-Term Supply Contracts*, 76 Nw. U. L. Rev. 369 (1981); Macneil, *Contracts: Adjustment of Long-Term Economic Relations Under Classical, Neo-Classical and Relational Contract Law*, 72 Nw. U. L. Rev. 854 (1978).

The general refusal of courts to sanction the impracticability defense in long-term supply contracts led to the inclusion of "gross inequity" clauses, sometimes called "good faith adjustment" clauses.[77] The clauses are designed to prevent hardship to one of the parties due to economic conditions not contemplated by the parties.[78] It is possible to insert a clause that would require renegotiation of the contract where economic conditions cause only a material change in the original agreement, i.e., a change that would not amount to excuse for impracticability but one that would meet the necessary extent of change under a mutual mistake analysis.[79] It is, however, one thing to conceive of such a clause; it may be quite another to convince the other party to the contract to agree to it. At the time of this writing, the use of the impracticability defense in long term supply contracts where a supervening event has changed the risks more than substantially is, at least, impracticable.

[E] Existing (Antecedent) Impracticability — Mistake Analysis Compared — Effect

To this point, we have been considering situations where an event which the parties assumed would not occur has occurred *after* the formation of the contract, causing performance to become impracticable. The event or contingency making performance impracticable, however, may exist at the time of contract formation, i.e., it may be a situation of *existing* impracticability rather than supervening impracticability. The most obvious illustration of existing impracticability occurs in situations where parties are unaware at the time of formation that the subject matter of the contract is unavailable. In the famous case of the destruction of the music hall explored earlier in this chapter,[80] the hall was destroyed after the parties had formed their contract and was, therefore, a case of supervening impossibility. If, however, the hall had been destroyed prior to the formation of the contract without the knowledge of the parties, the case would have involved existing impossibility of performance.

We will explore how the UCC treats the destruction of the subject matter either before or after contract formation in a subsequent section.[81] There are only two differences in the analyses of existing and supervening impracticability. Unlike the requirement that a party must not have foreseen or expected a *supervening* event to occur, a party asserting *existing* impracticability must have had *no reason to know* of the fact causing impracticability at the time of contract formation.[82] The other difference is the legal effect of the type of

---

[77] *See* Consumers Power Co. v. Nuclear Fuel Servs., Inc., 509 F. Supp. 201 (W.D.N.Y. 1981).

[78] In Georgia Power Co. v. Cimarron Coal Corp., 526 F.2d 101, 103 (6th Cir. 1975), *cert. denied*, 425 U.S. 952, 96 S. Ct. 1727, 48 L. Ed. 2d 195 (1976), the clause read: "Any gross proven inequity that may result in unusual economic conditions not contemplated by the parties at the time of the execution of this Agreement may be corrected by mutual consent. Each party shall in the case of a claim of gross inequity furnish the other with whatever documentary evidence may be necessary to assist in effecting a settlement."

[79] For an example of such a clause, see J. E. Murray, Jr., *Long-Term Supply Contracts: Foreseeing the Unforeseeable*, 2 Eastern Mineral Law Found. (1981).

[80] *See* § 113[A], *supra.*

[81] *See* § 114[C], *infra.*

[82] *See* Restatement 2d § 266(1). Patterson v. Methodist Healthcare-Memphis Hosps., 2010 Tenn App. LEXIS 78 (2010) (physicians had reason to know of insurance market when they agreed to become bound to bylaws); Twombly v. Association of Farmworker Opportunity Programs, 212 F.3d 80, 85 (1st Cir. 2000) (reason to know of existing definition of "participant"); McMahon v. New London County Mut. Ins. Co., 1999 Conn. Super. LEXIS 2338 (Conn. Super. Ct. Aug. 23, 1999) (reason to know of provision in insurance contract); Roy v. Stephen Pontiac-Cadillac, Inc., 15 Conn. App. 101, 543 A.2d 775 (1988) (reason to know at time contract was made that truck would not be manufactured

impracticability. If supervening impracticability is established, existing duties of performance are excused. Where existing impracticability is discovered, however, no duty arises under the contract.[83] For example, where the parties contract to purchase and sell a specific item, such as a used automobile which, at the time of formation without the knowledge or fault of either party, has been destroyed, no duty arises under the contract.[84]

A difficult problem involving existing impracticability occurs where a party undertakes a performance requiring a technological breakthrough. If such a party has reason to know the state of the art at the time of contract formation, he is assuming the risk of such breakthrough and his failure to achieve it will not be excused through impracticability.[85] If, however, a party simply agrees to build a device according to assumptions or plans made by the other party and the builder has no reason to know that it is impossible to comply with such assumptions or plans, existing impracticability will be shown.[86]

The concept of existing impracticability overlaps the mutual mistake analysis. Where, at the time of formation, the parties make a mistake as to a basic assumption on which the contract was made, the contract is voidable by the adversely affected party if he can demonstrate a *material effect on the agreed exchange*.[87] To demonstrate existing impracticability, however, he must meet the more onerous standard of establishing impracticability which, as we have seen, courts are not willing to find simply on the basis of a materially more onerous burden on the party seeking to be excused from performance.[88]

§ 114 TRADITIONAL CATEGORIES OF IMPOSSIBILITY — IMPRACTICABILITY

[A]   The Traditional Categories and the Modern Doctrine

We have seen that, while earlier courts were more than reluctant to grant excuse for nonperformance of a contractual duty, they recognized certain obvious exceptions to this general rule. We have also seen that the general rule of the common law was subsumed under the modern concept of impracticability. This evolution, however, did not emasculate the common law exceptions which retain their vitality. Such exceptions as the death or incapacity

---

without heavy duty package); Vollmar v. CSX Transp., Inc., 705 F. Supp. 1154 (E.D. Va. 1989) (reason to know of foreign exclusion at time of contract formation), *aff'd*, 898 F.2d 413 (4th Cir. 1990); *In re* Estate of Zellmer, 1 Wis. 2d 46, 82 N.W.2d 891 (1957) (reason to know that policy had lapsed at time of contract formation).

[83] RESTATEMENT 2d § 266(1), comment a.

[84] *See* ill. 1 to RESTATEMENT 2d § 266.

[85] *See* Aerosonic Instrument Corp., 1959-1 Cont. App. Dec. (CCH) ¶ 2115, at 9093 (Mar. 12, 1959) (contract to provide three tachometer testers, each tester to weigh no more than thirty pounds, a specification which had not been met to that time; when contractor delivered tachometers, each weighing 51 pounds, the Board stated that where the parties are conscious of existing facts and make their agreement on that assumption, the nonexistence of such facts does not affect the validity of the agreement).

[86] *See* Waldinger Corp. v. Ashbrook-Simon-Hartley, Inc., 564 F. Supp. 970 (C.D. Ill. 1983) (relying on ill. 10 to RESTATEMENT 2d § 266), *aff'd, in part, remanded, in part*, 775 F.2d 781 (7th Cir. 1985).

[87] RESTATEMENT 2d § 152(1). See the analysis of mistake *supra* Chapter 5, § 92.

[88] For a discussion of existing impracticability and mutual mistake, see Petroworks SA v. Rollings, 2009 U. S. Dist. LEXIS 21372 (S. D. Tex. 2009); (Clayton X-Ray Co. v. Evenson, 826 S.W.2d 45 (Mo. Ct. App. 1992). *See also* Aluminum Co. of Am. v. Essex Group, Inc., 499 F. Supp. 53 (W.D. Pa. 1980); National Presto Indus. v. United States, 338 F.2d 99, 167 Ct. Cl. 749 (1964), *cert. denied*, 380 U.S. 962, 85 S. Ct. 1105, 14 L. Ed. 2d 153 (1965).

of the promisor in a personal service contract, the destruction or other unavailability of specific property necessary to carry out performance, or the prevention of performance by operation of law are now seen as specific applications of the general principle that a supervening event may excuse performance which has become impracticable.[89] The transition from a general rule precluding excuse, unless the facts fell within a particular exception, to a general rule of impracticability permitting excusable nonperformance with the former exceptions becoming *applications* of the new general rule, may suggest a radical change. Yet, we have also seen that successful illustrations of the new impracticability standard are notoriously few. The change to this point, therefore, may be more apparent than real. The former exceptions which are now applications of the new standard remain intact. It is important to explore these categories which became valid at common law and retain their vitality.

[B] Death, Incapacity, or Threatened Incapacity of a Person

The typical contract does not require the continued existence of a particular person. Consequently, the typical contractual obligation survives the death of a party to that contract.[90] Where, however, the existence of a particular person, whether a party to the contract or a third party, is essential to the performance of a contractual duty, the basic assumption of that contract is that death or such incapacity to that person making performance impossible or impracticable would not occur. If the death or incapacity occurred without the fault of the promisor, the promisor is excused from performance unless the language or the circumstances indicate that the risk of such death or incapacity was assumed by the promisor.[91] If the parties have not expressly indicated whether the continued existence of a particular person is essential under the contract, a court must consider all of the surrounding circumstances to make that determination.[92]

Where the parties have named a particular person to establish a price for an item to be sold, they may have named that person as one of a number of reasonable experts who could establish a fair price. In that event, the death of the named person would not excuse the duty

---

[89] See, e.g., RESTATEMENT 2d § 262, concerning the traditional exception of death or incapacity of a person necessary for performance, which states, in comment a: "This Section states a common specific instance for the application of the rule stated in § 261 [the general principle]." Comment a of § 263 concerning the destruction or deterioration of property necessary for performance and comment a of § 264 concerning prevention by governmental regulation or order state identical rationales.

[90] *See* Burka v. Patrick, 34 Md. App. 181, 366 A.2d 1070 (1976).

[91] Firebaugh v. Whitehead, 263 Va. 398, 405, 559 S. E. 2d 611, 616 (2002) (contracts requiring artistic or mechanical skill, ability or training are personal contracts where the death of the promisor discharges the obligation). See RESTATEMENT 2d §§ 262 and 261. *See* Dow v. State Bank of Sleepy Eye, 88 Minn. 355, 93 N.W. 121 (1903) (promise to become a member of a partnership excused by death of the promisor); Lacy v. Getman, 119 N.Y. 109, 23 N.E. 452 (1890) (promise to employ a workman who was to work under the immediate direction of his employer was excused by the employer's death); Yerrington v. Greene, 7 R.I. 589, 84 Am. Dec. 578 (1863) (promise by employer to employ a clerk and salesman excused by death of employer); Wolfe v. Howes, 20 N.Y. 197, 75 Am. Dec. 388 (1859) (promise to render personal services excused by death of promisor). If the death or incapacity of an essential person was a fact at the time of contract formation and there was no reason to know of that fact, the same analysis applies under § 266(1).

[92] *See* Ames v. Sayler, 267 Ill. App. 3d 672, 205 Ill. Dec. 223, 642 N.E.2d 1340 (4th Dist. 1994) (refusal of owner to allow a party to farm land after original party died); Cazares v. Saenz, 208 Cal. App. 3d 279, 256 Cal. Rptr. 209 (4th Dist. 1989) (law partner refusal to accept substitute on a case where original partner became a judge); Kelley v. Thompson Land Co., 112 W. Va. 454, 164 S.E. 667 (1932) (duty to form corporation where the skill and judgment of the promoter were essential).

of either promisor. If, however, the parties manifest their intention to rely exclusively upon a trusted expert to place a value on an item, such as a famous painting, a court may find that the parties did not intend to be contractually bound where such a person is unavailable through death or incapacity.[93]

Incapacity of a particular person may take a variety of forms. Where, for example, a faculty member's visa expired, the college was excused from performing its contract because it could no longer legally employ the professor.[94] A reasonable apprehension that performance will result in incapacity or serious injury to the promisor or third persons will also excuse performance. Where, for example, a famous actor took reasonable measures to ascertain that his throat condition would not worsen, his failure to perform was excused.[95] In another well-known case, the court excused a duty to pay for conducting a baby show where an epidemic of infantile paralysis threatened the children.[96] Clearly, such cases increase risk of performance well beyond a material increase because the risk threatens the life or well-being of a promisor or third parties.

[C]   Destruction or Unavailability of Essential Subject Matter — Uniform Commercial Code — "Identification"

Ever since the lessor of a music hall was excused from performance upon the destruction of the hall in *Taylor v. Caldwell*,[97] there has been no doubt that the destruction or unavailability of a specific thing essential to the performance of the contract excuses that performance, absent fault or assumption of the risk by the promisor.[98] This was one of the generally recognized common law "exceptions" to the general principle that one must perform his promise regardless of the circumstances. The modern doctrine would suggest that, where the existence of a specific thing is necessary for performance, its failure to come into existence or its destruction or unavailability is an event the nonoccurrence of which was a basic assumption on which the contract was made.[99] It is simply an application of the general principle of impracticability.[100] Regardless of the characterization, the elements necessary for excusable nonperformance under this "exception" or "application" are unchanged. A modern illustration of the music hall case is found in a promise to provide space on a radio tower for the radio station of a seminary for a period of 99 years. When the tower was destroyed by a windstorm,

---

[93] UCC § 2-305 comment 4.

[94] Ling v. Doane College Bd. of Trustees, 1999 Neb. App. LEXIS 210 (Neb. Ct. App. July 27, 1999) (court based its decision on frustration of purpose rather than impossibility or impracticability. *See* RESTATEMENT 2d §§ 265 and 114 *infra.*

[95] Wasserman Theatrical Enter., Inc. v. Harris, 137 Conn. 371, 77 A.2d 329 (1950).

[96] Hanford v. Connecticut Fair Ass'n, 92 Conn. 621, 103 A. 838 (1918).

[97] *See* § 113[A], *supra.*

[98] *See* Robb v. Parten, 178 Minn. 188, 220 N.W. 610 (1928), *rev'd*, 178 Minn. 191, 226 N.W. 515 (1929) (contract to install plumbing in a building excused by destruction of building); Jones-Gray Constr. Co. v. Stephens, 167 Ky. 765, 181 S.W. 659 (1916) (promise to move barn excused by accidental destruction of barn); Angus v. Scully, 176 Mass. 357, 57 N.E. 674 (1900) (contract to move and repair a building excused by destruction of the building); Stewart v. Stone, 127 N.Y. 500, 28 N.E. 595 (1891) (contract to manufacture butter and cheese at a certain factory excused when factory was destroyed).

[99] RESTATEMENT 2d § 263.

[100] *See* RESTATEMENT 2d § 263 comment a. *See also* Olbum v. Old Home Manor, Inc., 313 Pa. Super. 99, 459 A.2d 757 (1983); Sunflower Elec. Coop. v. Tomlinson Oil Co., 7 Kan. App. 2d 131, 638 P.2d 963 (1981).

the court excused the defendant's performance under the authority of the common law rationale as well as the modern rationale.[101]

While the principle finds its most frequent application in cases of contracts to sell or to hire specific property,[102] it is not limited to that type of case. Even though the specific property may be available, its use may be prevented by the nonexistence of a necessary condition. Where lightning caused a severe power outage that could not be remedied in time for a performance in an outdoor concert area, the lack of lighting caused a hazardous condition to thousands of patrons both at the site and on pathways to parking areas. Recognizing the evolution of the doctrine of impossibility of performance to impracticability, the court reversed a holding that the doctrine would not apply and remanded the case for findings concerning foreseeability.[103]

[1]   Failure of Source of Supply

Where a grower contracted to sell and deliver a definite quantity of potatoes to be grown on a *specified tract of land*, the Court of Queen's Bench long ago held that the failure of the crop, through no fault of the grower, excused him from performing.[104] The holding has been replicated in many subsequent cases[105] and in modern applications of the impracticability standard.[106] The critical finding in such cases is that both parties made a basic assumption that the sole source of supply of the goods was the identified tract of land upon which they were to be grown. Where that basic assumption is not evident, i.e., where the parties did not assume that the supply would emanate from a particular tract of land, a crop failure due to weather or other conditions on certain land will not excuse the supplier who assumed the risk of supplying the goods regardless of a particular source.[107]

With respect to the supply of any kind of goods, it is not enough that the seller, alone, anticipates a particular source of supply. Unless both parties have contemplated that source as the single source from which the goods would be procured, there is no mutually contemplated basic assumption as to the source of supply. Where a defendant claimed commercial impracticability excused its contractual duty to supply school buses because its source of supply failed, the court noted that, unless the contract makes the seller's duty expressly contingent on adequate supply, courts are reluctant to excuse a seller who could have insisted

---

[101] Central Baptist Theological Seminary v. Entertainment Communications, Inc., 356 N.W.2d 785 (Minn. Ct. App. 1984).

[102] In addition to the cases already discussed, see, e.g., Texas Co. v. Hogarth Shipping Co., 256 U.S. 619, 41 S. Ct. 612, 65 L. Ed. 1123 (1921) (promise to furnish a specified ship for a voyage excused when the ship was requisitioned for use by the British government); Martin Emerich Outfitting Co. v. Siegel, Cooper & Co., 237 Ill. 610, 86 N.E. 1104 (1908) (promise to permit a party to carry on a business in a specified building excused by accidental destruction of the building).

[103] Opera Co. of Boston v. Trap Found. for Performing Arts, 817 F.2d 1094 (4th Cir. 1987).

[104] Howell v. Coupland, 1 Q.B.D. 258, 46 L.J., Q.B. 147 [1876]. *See also* International Paper Co. v. Rockefeller, 161 A.D. 180, 146 N.Y.S. 371 (1914) (contract for the sale of spruce to be cut from a certain tract of land was prevented when a fire destroyed the trees on that tract; performance was excused).

[105] *See, e.g.,* Ranney-Davis Mercantile Co. v. Shwano Canning Co., 111 Kan. 68, 206 P. 337 (1922).

[106] *See* Olbum v. Old Home Manor, Inc., 313 Pa. Super. 99, 459 A.2d 757 (1983) (parties contemplated coal coming from two specific veins of coal); Sunflower Elec. Coop. v. Tomlinson Oil Co., 7 Kan. App. 2d 131, 638 P.2d 963 (1981) (sale of natural gas limited to a particular well and well was exhausted).

[107] *See* Clark v. Wallace County Coop. Equity Exch., 267 Kan. 754, 986 P.2d 391, 394 (1999) (parties did not assume a particular tract of land was the sole source of supply).

on such a clause.[108] Moreover, even where *both* parties contemplate a sole source of supply, the failure of that source must not have been *foreseeable* at the time the contract was made. Where, therefore, the seller can foresee the possible failure of a sole source of supply, "he tacitly assumes the risk" of that failure.[109]

While the UCC includes a comment suggesting that the failure of an agreed source for causes beyond the seller's control should, if possible, be excused,[110] another comment elaborates the analysis:

> The provisions of this section are made subject to assumption of greater liability by agreement and such agreement is to be found *not only in the expressed terms of the contract* but in the circumstances surrounding the contracting. . . . Thus, the exemptions of this section do not apply when the contingency in question is *sufficiently foreshadowed* at the time of contracting to be included among the business risks which are fairly to be regarded as part of the dickered terms, either consciously or as a matter of reasonable commercial interpretation from the circumstances.[111]

[2]   UCC Casualty to "Identified" Goods

The UCC devotes a separate section to deal with "casualty to identified goods" as a species of impracticability which is essentially identical to the common law "exception":

> Where the contract requires for its performance goods identified when the contract is made, and the goods suffer casualty without fault of either party before the risk of loss passes to the buyer . . .
>
> (a) if the loss is total the contract is avoided. . . .[112]

An understanding of this Code section requires a basic familiarity with the concepts of "identification" and risk of loss. The Code distinguishes "existing" from "identified" goods.[113] A simple illustration illuminates the distinction. A seller of refrigerators has hundreds of refrigerators in its inventory. These refrigerators are "existing" goods because they have already been manufactured. They are not, however, "identified" since no particular refrigerator has been specifically referred to a contract with a particular buyer. A consumer who agrees to buy a refrigerator from the seller is typically not agreeing to purchase an "identified" refrigerator. The consumer only expects to receive a refrigerator as described in the contract of sale and that expectation will be fulfilled if any one of many refrigerators of that model and

---

[108] Tomlinson v. Wander Seed & Bulb Co., 177 Cal. App. 2d 462, 2 Cal. Rptr. 310, 314 (2d Dist. 1960). *See also* Gulf Oil Corp. v. Federal Power Comm'n, 563 F.2d 588 (3d Cir. 1977), *cert. denied*, 434 U.S. 1062, 98 S. Ct. 1235, 55 L. Ed. 2d 762 (1978).

[109] Rockland Indus., Inc. v. E+E (US), Inc., Manley-Regan Chems. Div., 991 F. Supp. 468, 472 (D. Md. 1998). *See also* Alamance County Bd. of Educ. v. Bobby Murray Chevrolet, Inc., 121 N.C. App. 222, 465 S.E.2d 306 (1996) (seller of school buses not excused because he could have made the contract expressly contingent on an adequate supply).

[110] UCC § 2-615, comment 5.

[111] UCC § 2-615, comment 8 (emphasis supplied).

[112] UCC § 2-613. Subsection (b) indicates that, if the loss is partial either in quantity or quality, the buyer may treat the contract as avoided or accept the goods with due allowance for the difference in quantity or quality without further rights against the seller.

[113] UCC § 2-105. A contract to sell goods that are not both existing and identified is a contract to sell "future" goods. For a helpful case analyzing "existing and identified" goods, see Martin Marietta Corp. v. New Jersey Nat'l Bank, 612 F.2d 745, 749 (3d Cir. 1979), *aff'd, in part, rev'd, in part*, 653 F.2d 779 (3d Cir. 1981).

description is delivered. Thus, the refrigerator was not identified at the time the contract was made. If, however, the seller had a floor model which he displayed to the consumer and the parties agreed that they would buy and sell *that particular refrigerator and no other*, the refrigerator would be identified at the time the contract was made. As in the analysis of cases involving crops from a *specified* tract of land, where the item to be bought and sold is a specified item, *e.g.*, the display model refrigerator, the seller's one and only used car, or any unique item such as a famous painting, the parties have contracted for goods identified at the time the contract is made.[114] This is a critical determination because the parties are making a basic assumption that this particular good exists and will be delivered to the buyer. If casualty to such identified goods occurs before the risk of their loss passes to the buyer and without the fault of the seller, the contract is avoided.

Risk of loss will be explored more thoroughly later in this chapter. For now, it is appropriate to suggest the general principle that risk of loss will not pass to the buyer until the seller has delivered the goods to a carrier or tendered or delivered the goods to the buyer.[115] The goods, therefore, remain in the possession and control of the seller. If they are destroyed or damaged without the seller's fault and, again, if they were identified at the time of contract formation, the seller cannot hold the buyer liable because the risk of loss has not yet passed to the buyer. Because those goods no longer exist, the seller cannot deliver them. Again, where the parties agreed to purchase and sell only the particular, identified refrigerator, car, etc. that was destroyed without the fault of the seller, the seller has no duty to deliver similar or identical good. If the parties had agreed to purchase and sell any one of hundreds of identical refrigerators and one of those refrigerators was destroyed without the fault of the seller, the seller would not be excused since the parties had not agreed to buy and sell that specific refrigerator or, in the language of the Code, the refrigerator was not identified at the time the contract was made.[116] While the Code section may appear different from the common law analysis because the Code is structured properly in the form of a statute and uses concepts such as "identification" and risk of loss, it does not differ from the common law analysis in any significant fashion.

The application of these concepts to construction contracts achieves the same result though not without some analytical difficulty. Where a building is partially constructed under a contract and, before completion, it is destroyed without the fault of either party, absent any manifestation of intention as to how the risk should be allocated, the risk of loss will fall on the contractor if he was in complete control of the premises. In such a case, some courts suggest that no specific building was contracted for; rather, the builder was to supply a particular type of building that was not existing, much less identified, at the time the contract was formed.[117] Not only is the duty of the builder not discharged, he is also liable for breach of contract.[118] A preferable rationale would simply allocate the risk to the builder on the footing that the builder

---

[114] *See* Specialty Tires of Am., Inc. v. CIT Group/Equipment Fin., Inc., 82 F. Supp. 2d 434, 439 (W.D. Pa.) (citing this section), *aff'd*, 2000 U.S. App. LEXIS 31822 (3d Cir. Nov. 20, 2000).

[115] *See* UCC § 2-509(1) and (3).

[116] *See* Bunge Corp. v. Recker, 519 F.2d 449 (8th Cir. 1975).

[117] Stees v. Leonard, 20 Minn. 494 (1874); School Dist. No. 1. v. Dauchy, 25 Conn. 530, 68 Am. Dec. 371 (1857).

[118] *See* United States Fidelity & Guar. Co. v. Parsons, 147 Miss. 335, 112 So. 469 (1927). *See also* RESTATEMENT 2d § 263, ill. 4. The same result will follow even where the owner is to furnish the materials from which the building is to be constructed. Albus v. Ford, 296 S.W. 981 (Tex. Civ. App. 1927); Vogt v. Hecker, 118 Wis. 306, 95 N.W. 90 (1903). A few cases have held that, where the builder and owner are cooperating in the construction, the contract is essentially one for a future, specific building, presumably to be made of the first combination of assembled materials. Thus, if the

would normally assume that risk had the parties considered that risk at the time of contract formation. Where the contract is one for repair of an existing building, such a contract assumes the continuing existence of a specific ("identified") building, and when it is destroyed without the fault of either party, the repair contractor is excused.[119]

Where the contractor promised to construct a building according to certain plans and specifications which proved to be inadequate, a few older cases suggested that the builder assumed the risk that the owner's plans may be defective.[120] The better decided cases, however, have applied a theory of implied warranty. Thus, if the owner rather than the contractor prepared the plans and specifications and they prove to be inadequate, the builder is excused because the party providing them warrants their sufficiency.[121]

[D]   Performance Prevented by Operation of Law — Delays — Temporary Impracticability

We have seen that a bargain that is contrary to public policy cannot be recognized as a contract.[122] An agreement, however, may be perfectly lawful at the time of formation, but a supervening change in the law may make its performance unlawful. The classical "exception" of a "supervening act of state" excused the performance which had become unlawful as impossible because the contract was subject to the "implied condition" that the law would continue to permit performance.[123] In accordance with the modern treatment of the classical exceptions, a performance prevented by operation of law is now regarded as an application of the generic principle that parties should not be bound where an event has occurred, the nonoccurrence of which was a basic assumption of their contract.[124] As in the other traditional categories, the analysis is unchanged though the characterizations are different. Thus, older cases clung to the implied condition notion,[125] while the modern cases arrive at the same

---

structure is destroyed, the contract becomes impossible of performance since no house can be built of that original combination of labor and materials. Helms & Willis v. Unicoi County, 166 Tenn. 639, 64 S.W.2d 200 (1933); Butterfield v. Byron, 153 Mass. 517, 27 N.E. 667 (1891).

[119] See RESTATEMENT 2d § 263, ill. 3, which is based on FIRST RESTATEMENT § 460, ill. 10. (Destruction of a house discharges the duties of the parties under a contract to shingle the roof on the house.) This example is distinguished in Aaland v. Lake Region Grain Coop., 511 N.W.2d 244, 247 (N.D. 1994), where the specific "employer" continued to exist.

[120] See N.J. Magnam Co. v. Fuller, 222 Mass. 530, 111 N.E. 399 (1916); Board of Educ. v. Empire State Surety Co., 83 N.J.L. 293, 85 A. 223 (Super. Ct. 1912).

[121] See Chantilly Constr. Corp. v. Commonwealth, Department of Highways & Transp., 6 Va. App. 282, 369 S.E.2d 438 (1988); Chaney Bldg. Co. v. City of Tucson, 148 Ariz. 571, 716 P.2d 28 (1986); Gilbert Eng'g Co. v. City of Asheville, 74 N.C. App. 350, 328 S.E.2d 849 (1985); Marine Colloids, Inc. v. M. D. Hardy, Inc. 433 A.2d 402 (Me. 1981); United States v. Spearin, 248 U.S. 132, 39 S. Ct. 59, 63 L. Ed. 166 (1918).

[122] Thus, in RESTATEMENT 2d § 266(1), the effect of existing impracticability differs from supervening impracticability in that existing impracticability results in no duty arising rather than excuse of duty.

[123] Baily v. De Crespigny, L.R. 4 Q.B. 180 [1869] (covenant of landlord to prevent the erection of any buildings on adjoining land excused when the land was taken by a railroad under authority granted by act of Parliament).

[124] RESTATEMENT 2d § 264. See Twombly v. Association of Farmworker Opportunity Programs, 212 F.3d 80, 85 (1st Cir. 2000) (law preceded contract-no excusable nonperformance).

[125] See, e.g., Wischhusen v. American Medicinal Spirits Co., 163 Md. 565, 163 A. 685 (1933) (contract to employ manager of distillery excused when government refused to issue permit to operate distillery unless a different manager was employed); Moore & Tierney, Inc. v. Roxford Knitting Co., 250 F. 278 (D.N.Y. 1918), aff'd, 265 F. 177 (2d Cir.), cert. denied, 253 U.S. 498, 40 S. Ct. 588, 64 L. Ed. 1031 (1920) (contract to manufacture goods excused when the government requisitioned the factory's output); Metropolitan Water Bd. v. Dick, Kerr & Co., A.C. 119 [1918] (contract

result on the footing that the change in the law is an event which the parties assumed would not occur.[126]

The change in the law need not be statutory or judicial; a regulation or administrative order will be sufficient. After the plaintiff was awarded the contract on a highway project that included the cleaning and repainting of twelve bridges, the Occupational Safety and Health Administration (OSHA) issued revised regulations concerning the repainting of bridges containing lead-based paint which significantly enhanced the cost of cleaning and repainting. The court held that the plaintiff's duty under the contract concerning these items was excused by the change in the OSHA regulations which was contrary to the basic assumption of the parties at the time the contract formed.[127] The governmental action, however, must be mandatory, i.e., a mere recommendation will not suffice.[128] The governmental regulation or order, including a municipal ordinance, need not be valid, but a party seeking to be excused because of such governmental intervention must exercise good faith in attempting to avoid its application.[129]

Failure of performance caused by a party's own fault will not excuse performance. Thus, where a party fails to meet the filing requirements of a government planning commission, a court will not excuse the performance of such a party because of his own nonfeasance.[130] Where a municipal ordinance prevents the performance of a contract previously made with the same municipality, the municipality is not excused.[131] Where an injunction is issued due to the fault of the promisor, he is not excused.[132]

---

to build a reservoir excused when the Ministry of Munitions ordered work stopped for an indefinite period).

[126] See Centex Corp. v. Dalton, 840 S.W.2d 952, 954 (Tex. 1992) (government regulation or order that makes impracticable the performance of a duty is an event the non-occurrence of which was a basic assumption on which the contract was made). *See also* Landis v. Hodgson, 109 Idaho 252, 706 P.2d 1363 (Ct. App. 1985) (assumption that state would continue a lease). See also Moncrief v. Williston Basin Interstate Pipeline Co., 880 F. Supp. 1495, 1508 (D. Wyo. 1995), where the court found that the "basic assumption" requirement was absent because changing governmental regulations of the gas industry was the rule, rather than the exception, and must, therefore, have been expected.

[127] M.J. Paquet, Inc. v. New Jersey DOT, 171 N. J. 378, 794 A. 2d 141 (2002). See also UNCC Properties v. Green, 111 N.C. App. 391, 432 S.E.2d 699, 702 (1993) (notice of condemnation made conveyance of easement impossible); *Centex, supra* note 126 (regulation of Federal Home Bank Board); McDonnell Douglas Corp. v. Islamic Republic of Iran, 591 F. Supp. 293 (E.D. Mo. 1984) (seller could not ship parts under Iranian Assets Control Regulations), *aff'd*, 758 F.2d 341 (8th Cir.), *cert. denied*, 474 U.S. 948, 106 S. Ct. 347, 88 L. Ed. 2d 294 (1985). RESTATEMENT 2d § 264 comment b suggests that the regulation or order may emanate from any level of government, including municipalities or administrative agencies, i.e., "governmental action" is the generic concept which disregards distinctions between laws, regulations, orders, and the like.

[128] Allen v. City of Yonkers, 803 F. Supp. 679, 709 (S.D.N.Y. 1992); Wien Air Alaska v. Bubbel, 723 P.2d 627 (Alaska 1986).

[129] G. W. Andersen Constr. Co. v. Mars Sales, 164 Cal. App. 3d 326, 210 Cal. Rptr. 409 (2d Dist. 1985) (relying on RESTATEMENT 2d § 264 comment b).

[130] Gorzelsky v. Leckey, 402 Pa. Super. 246, 586 A.2d 952, 956 (1991).

[131] See West Haven Sound Dev. Corp. v. City of West Haven, 201 Conn. 305, 514 A.2d 734 (1986) (city entered into contract which later became impossible when ordinance of same city made the performance illegal). *See also* Elsemore v. Hancock, 137 Me. 243, 18 A.2d 692 (1941).

[132] See Peckham v. Industrial Sec. Co., 31 Del. (1 W.W. Harr.) 200, 113 A. 799 (1921) (defendant pleaded injunction secured by third person as an excuse for not performing but did not explain reason for injunction; held: where the impossibility is due to a judicial order secured by a private litigant, the burden is on defendant to show that the order did not result from his fault). Where, however, performance is prevented by an injunction through no fault of the promisor, he is excused from performing. Kuhl v. School Dist. No. 76, 155 Neb. 357, 51 N.W.2d 746 (1952).

The question of whether performance prevented by *foreign* governmental regulation is sufficient caused some difficulty in earlier cases which were inclined to seek other traditional "exceptions" to excuse impossibility, rather than the "prevention by law" exception.[133] Both the UCC[134] and the RESTATEMENT 2d[135] expressly permit excuse for nonperformance because of either foreign or domestic governmental intervention.

As in all other applications of the modern principle, the fundamental requirements remain, i.e., the parties must not have allocated the risk by their agreement, the supervening event must be unforeseen or unexpected, it must not be caused by the fault of the party seeking to be excused, and the event must cause the performance to become impracticable as that term is defined.

[1]   Temporary Impracticability

Where the performance is merely *delayed* because of governmental action, the question is whether the delay caused performance to become impracticable. If the delay is merely *temporary*, the promisor's performance is merely suspended until the impossibility ceases, followed by an appropriate extension of time for performance.[136] The delay, however, must be directly and proximately caused by events beyond the control of the promisor.[137] Where the parties entered into a two-year option contract for the purchase of land conditioned on the approval of a governmental authority, the refusal of the authority to grant approval only suspended the performance of the seller. When the authority's interest in the property was no longer present, the court held that the exercise of the option within the option period created a contract for which the remedy of specific performance would be granted.[138]

If the supervening event prevents performance for a sufficiently long time with the effect of reallocating the risks in the original contract, however, performance may be excused entirely. Where, for example, war prevents the building of a plant in another country because of a shortage of materials, or prevents the export of goods to another country for the duration of the war, the promise to ship the goods may be excused because of a substantial reallocation of the original risks assumed by the parties.[139] Similarly, a personal service contract interrupted by military service may be excused because of the duration of the war and the consequent change in the rights and duties of the parties that has become so materially burdensome as to

---

[133] See, e.g., Texas Co. v. Hogarth Shipping Co., 256 U.S. 619, 41 S. Ct. 612, 65 L. Ed. 1123 (1921) (act of British Government made performance impossible and court held performance excused on the ground of unavailability of subject matter).

[134] UCC § 2-615(a).

[135] RESTATEMENT 2d § 264.

[136] Glen Hollow Partnership *ex rel.* Big Hollow Land Trust v. Wal-Mart Stores, 1998 U.S. App. LEXIS 3214, at *9 (7th Cir. Feb. 26, 1998). RESTATEMENT 2d § 269.

[137] *Id.* Evidence did not show that the delay was due to such events (zoning regulations). A significant reason for the delay was the absence of construction financing. "Zoning regulations" were within the force majeure clause allowing performance to be excused under "government regulations." Whether the supervening event is one that would be recognized absent such a clause or because of such a clause, however, it must be the direct and proximate cause of the delay.

[138] Sutheimer v. Stoltenberg, 127 Idaho 81, 896 P.2d 989 (Ct. App. 1995).

[139] *See* Minnesota v. Fairbanks, Morse & Co., 226 Minn. 1, 31 N.W.2d 920 (1948); Heidner v. St. Paul & Tacoma Lumber Co., 124 Wash. 652, 215 P. 1 (1923), *cert. denied*, 263 U.S. 721, 44 S. Ct. 230, 68 L. Ed. 524 (1924).

reallocate the risks of the original contract.[140] If the contract expressly allocates the risk of a prolonged delay, however, the party assuming that risk will not be excused from performing, regardless of the excessive burden imposed by that risk. Thus, where the parties agreed on the purchase and sale of a number of building lots conditioned on sewage connections, the decision of the governmental authority not to grant such connections for an indefinite time would have normally suspended performance for a commercially reasonable time, beyond which performance would have been excused. An express allocation of that risk in the contract, however, extended the time for performance up to twenty-one years, the maximum time permitted under the rule against perpetuities.[141]

[E]   Failure of Contemplated Mode of Performance — Partial Impracticability

Where the performance of the promisor is impracticable only in part, it is possible that such partial impracticability may create such an onerous burden in performing the remainder of her promise that she should be excused entirely from her duty.[142] In the more likely case, however, the partial impracticability is either so insubstantial as to provide no excuse for nonperformance, or the impracticability is substantial but the promisor can render a reasonable substitute performance. Where, for example, a foreseeable conflict closed the Suez Canal, it was possible to deliver the goods to the stated destination by a longer voyage. Even though this route was necessarily more costly, a number of courts refused to excuse the promisors since this alternate mode of performance was a reasonable substitute.[143] Similarly, where a payment was to be made to a governmental authority that later ceased to exist, the lease could be reformed to allow payment to the lessor.[144] Wherever a commercially reasonable alternative performance exists, the impracticability does not excuse substantial performance.[145]

The UCC requires a commercially reasonable substitute method of delivery, transportation, or payment to be tendered and accepted,[146] and the RESTATEMENT 2d requires the promisor to render such a reasonable substitute performance in order to meet his general obligation of good faith under the contract.[147]

---

[140] *See* Autry v. Republic Productions, Inc., 30 Cal. 2d 144, 180 P.2d 888 (1947) (plaintiff's artistic career and the quality of artistic performance might be affected by the passage of time).

[141] Long Signature Homes v. Fairfield Woods, 248 Va. 95, 445 S.E.2d 489 (1994).

[142] RESTATEMENT 2d § 270 comment a.

[143] *See* American Trading & Prod. Corp. v. Shell Int'l Marine, Ltd., 453 F.2d 939 (2d Cir. 1972); Transatlantic Fin. Corp. v. United States, 363 F.2d 312, 124 U.S. App. D.C. 183 (1966); Glidden Co. v. Hellenic Lines, Ltd., 275 F.2d 253 (2d Cir. 1960); Ocean Tramp Tankers Corp. v. V/O Sovfracht (The Eugenia), 2 Q.B. 226 [1964]; Tsakiroglou & Co. v. Noblee Thorl G.m.b.H., 2 Q.B. 348 [1960].

[144] *See* Barnacle Bill's Seafood Galley v. Ford, 453 So. 2d 165 (Fla. Dist. Ct. App. 1984).

[145] *See* United Equities Co. v. First Nat'l City Bank, 52 A.D.2d 154, 383 N.Y.S.2d 6 (1st Dep't 1976) (commercially reasonable alternative in yen transaction) (relying on UCC § 2-614), *aff'd*, 41 N.Y.2d 1032, 363 N.E.2d 1385 (1977).

[146] UCC § 2-614.

[147] RESTATEMENT 2d § 270 comment b, referring to the good faith requirement in § 205. The UCC also contains a general obligation of good faith in § 1-203.

[1]   Partial Impossibility — Allocation of Production

Where only a part of the seller's capacity to perform is affected by the impracticability, the seller must allocate production and deliveries among his contract customers, but may also include regular customers not then under contract as well as his own requirements for further manufacture in that allocation which must always be fair and reasonable.[148] In effect, the promisor is required to perform if substantial performance can be rendered.[149] Moreover, where substantial performance cannot be rendered, if the obligee promises to perform in full, the obligor must continue to render performance.[150]

Where a substituted performance will necessarily delay performance, the party who, in good faith, is tendering such substitute performance should not be liable for any reasonable delay. Such a delay may, in fact, be required in order to meet the good faith obligation to render a substitute performance.[151] Where the buyer receives a seller's notice of a material or indefinite delay or an allocation justified under § 2-615, the buyer's agreement to the seller's modification will be enforceable without consideration. The buyer may, however, terminate any delivery concerned or, where the prospective deficiency constitutes a substantial impairment of value of the whole contract, terminate any unexecuted portion of the contract.[152] If the buyer is silent in response to a seller's notice, the silence will be interpreted as a termination.[153] A clause in the original contract that requires the buyer to stand ready to perform whenever the seller is excused by unforeseen circumstances is unenforceable.[154]

[F]   "Impediments" — CISG and UNIDROIT Principles

Under the heading "exemptions," CISG excuses a party from performing his contractual obligations by proof that an "impediment" beyond his control that he could not reasonably have taken into account when the contract was formed caused the failure of his performance.[155] In the absence of precedent interpreting and constructing this Article of CISG (79), an American court applied the analysis under UCC § 2-615 to determine where an

---

[148] UCC § 2-615(b). *See* Cliffstar Corp. v. Riverbend Products, Inc., 750 F. Supp. 81 (W.D.N.Y. 1990) (The "fair and reasonable" standard does not necessarily suggest equal allocation. Past relationship with customers, customer loyalty, past performance and needs may not result in equal allocations.). *See also* Alimenta (U.S.A.), Inc. v. Cargill, Inc., 861 F.2d 650 (11th Cir. 1988) (allocation rule applies absent a provision in the contract that seller will perform even though the contingencies that permit allocation might occur).

[149] Yost v. Council Bluffs, 471 N.W.2d 836, 840 (Iowa 1991). Lower court held that the remaining performance was not "substantial" because it was not unique. The decision was reversed on appeal. Relying on RESTATEMENT 2d § 270, the court states, "Substantial in this context is something that is worthwhile, or value to the other contracting party, that requires a reasonable amount of effort, labor or expense to complete, as contrasted to an act of de minimis effect or of no real importance to the contractual purpose of accomplishment. It is clear that the performance remaining under Yost's contract was substantial since it cost the city $75,000 to complete the work." The total contract price was $135,000.

[150] See RESTATEMENT 2d § 270(b), comment c and ill. 4, based on the facts of Van Dusen Aircraft Supplies, Inc. v. Massachusetts Port Auth., 361 Mass. 131, 279 N.E.2d 717 (1972).

[151] *See* UCC § 2-615 comment 7: "However, good faith and the reason of the present section and of the preceding one may properly be held to justify and even to require any needed delay involved in a good faith inquiry seeking a readjustment of the contract terms to meet the new conditions."

[152] UCC § 2-616.

[153] See the Comment to § 2-616.

[154] § 2-616(3).

[155] CISG Art. 79(1).

"impediment" excused performance when a port was frozen over: (1) a contingency has occurred which (2) made performance impracticable where (3) the nonoccurrence of the contingency was a basic assumption on which the contract was made.[156] The party seeking to be excused is required to provide notice of the impediment and its effects to the other party within a reasonable time after he knew or ought to have known of the impediment.[157] The UNIDROIT Principles replicate this exemption under the heading, *Force Majeure*.[158] Both CISG and the Principles allow for "temporary" impediments where the excuse for nonperformance is effective only for the time during which the impediment exists.[159]

§ 115 FRUSTRATION OF PURPOSE

[A] History and Nature of Concept

One of the parties to the contract may wish to receive the literal performance of the other party, not because that performance itself is desired, but because it will enable the first party to accomplish a more remote, specific purpose. A difficult question of contract adjudication is presented when the literal performance is quite capable of being rendered, but the more remote purpose, which is the fundamental desire of the promisor, becomes meaningless due to supervening events. This question was presented to the English courts in the celebrated "Coronation" cases which arose because the coronation procession of Edward VII was cancelled due to his illness. In one of these cases, a party residing on the proposed line of march made a contract to let his apartment to the defendant to enable him to view the procession. When an action was brought to recover the amount of the rental, the court held that the cancellation of the procession excused the defendant from paying the balance of the agreed price for the use of the apartment.[160] There was no literal impossibility or impracticability of performance since both promises could have been performed without difficulty. The court extended the doctrine of impossibility of performance to include situations where the ultimate purpose of the contract was frustrated because the specific state of affairs "foundational" to the contract did not exist.[161] Other courts have reached the same conclusion on similar facts.[162]

---

[156] Raw Materials, Inc. v. Manfred Forberich GmbH & Co., 2004 U. S. Dist. LEXIS 12510 at *13–14 (N. D. Ill. 2004). See also Hilaturas Miel, S. L. v. Republic of Iraq, 573 F. Supp. 2d 781,797–98 (S. D. N. Y. 2008) (delivery precluded by withdrawal of inspectors due to war).

[157] CISG Art. 79(4).

[158] Principles Art 7.1.7.

[159] CISG Art. 79(3); Principles, Art. 7.1.7(2).

[160] Krell v. Henry, 2 K.B. 740 [1903]. The defendant had made a down payment which he did not seek to recover. This is discussed subsequently in the text of this section.

[161] The court has been criticized for holding that performance of the contract was prevented. *See* 6 Corbin § 1355 (1962). While such criticism is correct, the court's opinion can be read as suggesting that performance became impossible *in effect*, though not literally impossible. It is not strange to find a court taking such a route to a particular result in a case of first impression.

[162] La Cumbre Golf & Country Club v. Santa Barbara Hotel Co., 205 Cal. 422, 271 P. 476 (1928) (contract to pay a monthly fee for the privilege of having hotel guests given membership privileges at a golf club excused when hotel burned); Gulf & S. I. R. Co. v. Horn, 135 Miss. 804, 100 So. 381 (1924) (contract to employ one as a claim agent to be trained under a chief about to retire excused when the chief retired immediately); The Stratford, Inc. v. Seattle Brewing & Malting Co., 94 Wash. 125, 162 P. 31 (1916) (lease of premises for saloon purposes only held annulled when prohibition law prevented operation of a saloon); Alfred Marks Realty Co. v. Hotel Hermitage Co., 170 A.D. 484, 156

The essential judicial challenge in this area is the danger involved in excusing the promisor. After all, the promisee is not concerned with the ultimate purpose of the promisor in making the contract. His sole interest is in obtaining the price for his performance. A purchaser of stock may wish to buy it only because it is reasonably foreseeable that the price of the stock may go up. If that "state of affairs" fails to materialize, the buyer would not be excused from paying the purchase price. This is the usual rule, i.e., supervening disappointments do not excuse the promisor. When, if ever, should such a rule change?

The first criterion suggested by the cases is the extent of the frustration. In the coronation case, the promisor was entitled to view an empty Pall Mall during the period stipulated in the contract, but there could be no real benefit to him in so doing. The cancellation of the procession was a total frustration of the purpose of the rental, a fact that was well-known to both parties as attested by the inflated price for the flat and the fact that the period of tenancy was relegated to the approximate time during which the procession was scheduled. In the stock-purchasing case, the fact that there is no rise in the price of the stock may have been disappointing to the purchaser, but he retains a substantial benefit unless the shares have become worthless. Even assuming the stock has become worthless, there is another difference between the two cases which illustrates the second criterion found in the decided cases. In the coronation case, had the parties thought about it, would the promisor have agreed to pay an inflated rental for a brief period whether or not the procession occurred? Or would the parties have agreed on some alternative in the event the procession cancelled? Once again, the question of risk allocation must be faced. In the stock-purchase case, the very nature of the subject matter suggests that the purchaser is assuming all risks in relation to the decline in the stock's value, even to the extent of it becoming worthless. To allocate risks in these cases, the courts must consider the customs and mores of society in relation to the particular circumstances involved. If the circumstances surrounding the making of the contract have been such that there is a probability that the promisor would have been expected to assume the risk of what has occurred, he is not excused even though the parties did not anticipate the contingency which has supervened.[163] On the other hand, if the circumstances indicate that the promisor would not have been expected to assume the risk, the courts must decide upon whom the risk must fall as between two innocent parties.

N.Y.S. 179 (1915) (contract to pay for an advertisement to be published in a "souvenir and program" of a yacht race excused when race was cancelled). Cf. Retail Merchants' Business Expansion Co. v. Randall, 103 Vt. 268, 153 A. 357 (1931), in which it was held that a storekeeper who had contracted for assistance in carrying on an advertising campaign was not excused by the accidental destruction of his store and stock of goods.

[163] Bunting v. Orendorf, 152 Miss. 327, 120 So. 182 (1929) (duty of lessee to pay rent not discharged by the fact that an unprecedented flood prevented the use of the land); Burgett v. Loeb, 43 Ind. App. 657, 88 N.E. 346 (1909) (duty to pay rent for premises leased for saloon purposes was not discharged when the lessee was denied a license to operate a saloon); London & Northern Estates Co. v. Schlesinger, 1 K.B. 20 [1916] (obligation to pay rent for a flat leased for personal occupancy with right to sub-let on lessor's assent not excused by fact that a later order in council prohibited the lessee, an alien enemy, from residing in the flat); Herne Bay Steam Boat Co. v. Huttone, 2 K.B. 683 [1903] (promise to pay a stipulated sum for the privilege of having a steamer at the promisor's disposal to take passengers to see a naval review not excused when the review was cancelled). It is on this basis that the cases are justified which hold a school board bound to continue a teacher's salary notwithstanding an epidemic which closes the school. See Phelps v. School Dist. No. 109, 302 Ill. 193, 134 N.E. 312 (1922) (teacher); Montgomery v. Board of Educ., 102 Ohio St. 189, 131 N.E. 497, 15 A.L.R. 715 (1921) (bus driver); Crane v. School Dist. No. 14, 95 Or. 644, 188 P. 712 (1920) (bus driver). Contra Gregg School Township, Morgan County v. Hinshaw, 76 Ind. App. 503, 132 N.E. 586, 17 A.L.R. 1222 (1921) (teacher); Sandry v. Brooklyn Sch. Dist. No. 78, 47 N.D. 444, 182 N.W. 689, 15 A.L.R. 719 (1921) (bus driver).

[B]   The Modern Doctrine

Frustration of purpose may be obvious in a given situation. For example, Land O' Lakes (LOL) agreed to purchase weaned piglets from Pieper with the intention of selling them to third-party finishers who would raise them to market weight. Farmland Industries, a pork processor, would then purchase the pigs under its agreement with Pieper. A recital clause stated that LOL would purchase the piglets only while Farmland purchased pigs of market weight from third-party finishers. Pieper's president confirmed this understanding in his deposition testimony. When Farmland stopped purchasing pigs from the finishers, LOL terminated the agreement with Pieper and defended Pieper's lawsuit on the footing that there was no longer any purpose in purchasing the piglets since the purpose of the contract had been frustrated. Since the court viewed the recital clause as creating no duties beyond the obligations set forth in the contract, it was necessary to admit extrinsic evidence of the purpose of the contract. On the basis of the analysis in the classic coronation case of *Krell v. Henry*, the court held that the purpose of the contract between LOL and Pieper had been frustrated by Farmland's refusal to purchase any more pigs from the third-party finishers.[164] A much less obvious situation occurred in the best-known American case dealing with frustration of purpose. In *Lloyd v. Murphy*,[165] a lease stated that the purpose was solely for conducting the business of displaying and selling new automobiles. The court rejected the common law notion that lessees could never be excused because of impossibility or frustration.[166] Here, however, it refused to excuse the duty of the lessee on two fundamental grounds: (1) the restriction on the manufacture of new automobiles due to the war effort was commonly known at the time the lease was executed. Therefore, the lessee certainly should have foreseen the lack of supply. (2) The lack of new automobiles did not prevent the lessee from selling used automobiles, which constituted the essential domestic automobile market during World War II. Moreover, since the lessor waived its rights to insist that the premises be used only for the purposes stated in the lease, the defendant could also repair automobiles or even sublease the premises to any responsible tenant. Consequently, the value of the lease was not totally destroyed. The opinion of the court, written by Justice Roger Traynor, set a tone for future frustration cases that not only required the particular purpose of the contract to be the dominant or sole purpose, but also required that purpose to be totally frustrated.

The RESTATEMENT 2d suggests four elements to establish frustration of purpose which are virtually identical to its test for impracticability. While the first element for supervening impracticability is that performance must have become impracticable,[167] the first element for discharge by supervening frustration requires a party's principal purpose to be substantially frustrated.[168] Otherwise, the elements are identical: the frustration must occur without the fault of the party claiming frustration, the frustration must be caused by an event, the non-occurrence of which was a basic assumption on which the contract was made, and the party seeking to be excused must not have assumed a greater obligation under the contract to

---

[164]   Pieper v. Land O' Lakes Farmland Feed LLC, 390 F. 3d 1062 (8th Cir. 2004).

[165]   25 Cal. 2d 48, 153 P.2d 47 (1944).

[166]   The common law concept treated a lease as a contract to sell land where the risk of loss passes to the buyer at the time of contract formation since the buyer is then the equitable owner of the land. The modern view, however, recognizes the lease as different from the sale of land, i.e., it is essentially a lease of the buildings on the land, rather than any transfer of the land itself. *See* RESTATEMENT 2D PROPERTY § 5.4.

[167]   RESTATEMENT 2d § 261.

[168]   RESTATEMENT 2d § 265.

perform in spite of an event that would have allowed for excuse by frustration. National Cart Company agreed that Viking would be the exclusive distributor of National's shopping corrals to the Target Company. When Target decided to deal with manufacturers of products instead of distributors, National properly notified Viking that the distributorship was terminated. When Viking sued, National raised the frustration of purpose defense as set forth in § 265 of the Restatement 2d. The court held that, unless Target was willing to purchase the corrals through Viking, the contract made little sense. Absent evidence that National was at fault in Target's decision, National's performance under its contract with Viking was excused.[169] The doctrines differ, therefore, only in the effect of the fortuitous event. Thus, courts are comfortable in seeking guidance from cases dealing with impossibility or impracticability of performance.[170]

Like the doctrine of commercial impracticability, courts apply frustration of purpose "sparingly."[171] Many cases reflect the immense difficulty of discovering the necessary combination of elements essential to establish frustration as an excuse. All or some of the elements suggested by the RESTATEMENT 2d are typically not met.[172] While the fact that the event causing frustration was foreseeable should not, alone, preclude a finding of frustration,[173] foreseeability will still be emphasized where the risk is one that should have been fairly regarded as assumed by the party seeking to be excused.[174] Though other elements are met, the fault of the party seeking to be excused may have contributed to the occurrence of the frustrating event,[175] the purpose of the contract may not have been "substantially frustrated,"[176] the counterperformance may retain value notwithstanding the frustration,[177] or the purpose that has been frustrated may not have been the sole purpose of the contract.[178] Because courts are reluctant to excuse parties from the performances they have promised, like its impracticability counterpart, the number of successful uses of the frustration of purpose doctrine are quite small compared to the number of times it has been raised in the case law.[179]

---

[169] Viking Supply Co. v. National Cart Co., 310 F. 3d 1092 (8th Cir. 2002). See also Mel Frank Tool & Supply Co. v. Di-Chem Co., 580 N.W.2d 802 (Iowa 1998).

[170] See Chase Precast Corp. v. John J. Paonessa Co., 409 Mass. 371, 566 N.E.2d 603 (1991).

[171] Dorn v. Stanhope Steel, Inc., 368 Pa. Super. 557, 534 A.2d 798 (1987).

[172] See National Recruiters, Inc. v. Toro Co., 343 N.W.2d 704 (Minn. Ct. App. 1984).

[173] See West Los Angeles Inst. for Cancer Research v. Mayer, 366 F.2d 220, 225 (9th Cir. 1966), cert. denied, 385 U.S. 1010, 87 S. Ct. 718, 17 L. Ed. 2d 548 (1967). See also RESTATEMENT 2d § 265 comment a. Contra Gold v. Salem Lutheran Home Ass'n, 53 Cal. 2d 289, 1 Cal. Rptr. 343, 347 P.2d 687 (1959).

[174] Scullin Steel Co. v. PACCAR, Inc., 708 S.W.2d 756 (Mo. Ct. App. 1986); United States Smelting, Ref. & Mining Co. v. Wigger, 684 P.2d 850 (Alaska 1984).

[175] Groseth Int'l, Inc. v. Teneco, Inc., 410 N.W.2d 159 (S.D. 1987).

[176] See Mel Frank Tool, note 169supra.

[177] See Bitzes v. Sunset Oaks, 649 P.2d 66 (Utah 1982).

[178] See Beals v. Tri-B Assocs., 644 P.2d 78 (Colo. Ct. App. 1982).

[179] Beyond successful uses already discussed, see, e. g., Unihealth v. U.S. Healthcare, 14 F. Supp. 2d 623 (D.N.J. 1998), finding the elements of RESTATEMENT 2d § 265 to have been met. See also Cleasby v. Leo A. Daly Co., 221 Neb. 254, 376 N.W.2d 312 (1985) (termination of two-year employment contract where employee's illness caused absences and employer proved that a knowledgeable manager was required in Saudi Arabia and employee was barred from returning to Saudi Arabia without the consent of a party whose consent could not be obtained before a certain date).

[C]   Existing or Temporary Frustration of Purpose

Just as existing as contrasted with supervening impracticability will prevent a duty of performance from arising,[180] existing frustration of purpose has the same effect.[181] Thus, where an existing ordinance prohibited the use of certain premises as a health resort or milk farm, the lessee's duty never arose.[182] Similarly, in one of the coronation cases, it was discovered that the licensing of a room to view the procession occurred shortly after the decision to perform surgery on the king precluded the procession. Since neither party was aware of the existing frustration at the time the contract was made, no duty of the lessee arose under the contract.[183] As in the case of existing impracticability, existing frustration of purpose must be distinguished from the mutual mistake analysis.[184]

Where frustration of purpose is only temporary, the effect is identical to temporary impracticability, i.e., the duty of performance is, at least, suspended, and if the existing or supervening event is of sufficient duration as to increase the burden of performance so materially that the original risks assumed by the parties are reallocated, the duty of performance either never arises or it is discharged.[185]

§ 116   EFFECTS OF IMPRACTICABILITY AND FRUSTRATION OF PURPOSE

[A]   Effect on Excused Party

In prior discussion, we have mentioned that the effect of a failure to perform on a party whose performance is excused because of impracticability or frustration of purpose will depend upon whether the excused performance is due to a supervening event or whether the event giving rise to the excuse existed at the time of contract formation. Thus, if the impracticability or frustration occurred because of a supervening event, the existing duty of the excused party is discharged.[186] If, however, the excused party's performance is impracticable or frustrated at the time the contract is made, no duty to render performance for which that party could be held liable ever arose.[187]

While the effect of excusable nonperformance on the excused party is relatively simple, it is essential to consider the effect of that party's excused performance on the other party to the contract.

---

[180] *See supra* § 112[D].

[181] RESTATEMENT 2d § 266(2).

[182] *See* Mariani v. Gold, 13 N.Y.S.2d 365 (Sup. Ct. 1939).

[183] Griffith v. Brymer, 19 T.L.R. 434 (K.B. 1903).

[184] *See supra* § 112[D].

[185] RESTATEMENT 2d § 269. *See also supra* § 113[D]. In the case of existing frustration, the duty would never arise, while supervening frustration would discharge the duty.

[186] RESTATEMENT 2d § 261.

[187] RESTATEMENT 2d § 266. Prior discussion of these concepts is found at § 112 D.

[B]   Effect of Excused Party's Nonperformance on Other Party's Prospective Failure

In the earlier discussion of breach of contract, we saw that there is a constructive condition that there be no uncured material breach to any duty to render performance.[188] Where a party's performance has been excused through impracticability or frustration of purpose, he is not liable for breach of contract. Yet, he has not fulfilled the constructive condition to the other party's performance. Thus, the failure of the excused party to render performance is treated in the same fashion as a breach of contract even though, again, he is not liable for that breach because his performance has been excused.[189] If, for example, the excused party brings an action against the other party, the other party may defend as if the excused party has breached the contract.[190] Certainly, a party should not be required to perform his duty if it is clear that he will not receive what he bargained for even though the counter-performance is legally excused. The legally excused failure to perform, however, must have the same effect as an uncured material breach to discharge the other party.[191] If the legally excused failure to perform does not amount to an uncured material breach, the other party is not discharged.[192]

The same analysis occurs where the failure to perform is prospective rather than a present failure. It should be recalled that an anticipatory repudiation may be treated as a total breach of contract,[193] and reasonable grounds to believe that the obligor will commit a breach allows the obligee to demand adequate assurances of performance and to suspend his own performance until such assurances are received.[194] Though the prospective failure of performance may be excused, the other party's performance may be discharged or he may be permitted to suspend performance.[195] As in other cases of prospective failure of performance, however, there is the danger that the other party may mistakenly view his performance as justifiably terminated where only suspension of performance was justifiable. For example, where an artist promised to attend rehearsals for six days prior to a fifteen-week performance contract and, because of illness, could not arrive until two days prior to the first scheduled performance, the termination of the artist's contract was not justified because the artist's delay would not have amounted to a material failure of performance had it not been legally excusable.[196] Suspension of performance would have been justified though termination was not justified. On the other hand, where another artist engaged to perform for three months became ill during rehearsals and could not perform by opening night, the termination of that

---

[188] See Restatement 2d §§ 237 and 238.

[189] Restatement 2d § 267.

[190] See, e.g., In re Roy's Estate, 278 Mich. 6, 270 N.W. 196 (1936) (payment of note given for promise to marry which was to occur before note was due excused when marriage became impossible due to death of maker); Prescott & Co. v. J. B. Powles & Co., 113 Wash. 177, 193 P. 680 (1920) (buyer of goods excused when seller failed to deliver full quantity under contract though failure was legally excusable).

[191] See, e.g., Hong v. Independent Sch. Dist. No. 245, 181 Minn. 309, 232 N.W. 329 (1930) (school teacher absent because of illness during first five weeks of school year); American Mercantile Exch. v. Blunt, 102 Me. 128, 66 A. 212 (1906) (collection agency prevented from performing part of its contract by a supervening statute).

[192] See, e.g., Leiston Gas Co. v. Leiston-Cum-Sizewell Urban Dist. Council, 2 K.B. 428 [1916] (gas company was prohibited from lighting street lights for nine months during war time on a six-year contract).

[193] Restatement 2d § 253(1). UCC § 2-610.

[194] Restatement 2d § 251; UCC § 2-609.

[195] Restatement 2d § 268. See also Juarez v. Hamner, 674 S.W.2d 856 (Tex. App. Tyler 1984).

[196] Bettini v. Gye, 1 Q.B.D. 183 [1876].

artist's contract was justified because the artist's inability to perform was of uncertain duration and would have amounted to an uncured material failure of performance had it not been legally excusable.[197]

[C]   Relief — Restitution — Divisibility — CISG — Reliance — RESTATEMENT 2d

Where performance is excused due to impracticability or frustration but one party has received a benefit from the part performance by the other, the party receiving the benefit is considered unjustly enriched and, notwithstanding his discharge from contractual duties, he must pay the other party who is entitled to restitution for the value of the benefit conferred. Where a plaintiff made a $50,000 earnest money payment to lease, with an option to purchase, a Sunoco fuel center as a going concern, he was not approved as a Sunoco franchisee. Absent such approval, the lease was essentially worthless. The court held that he was entitled to restitution of his $50,000 earnest money payment.[198] Where a carpenter agrees to perform certain work for a homeowner but dies before he completes the work, his duties are discharged under the contract. The value of the benefit conferred upon the homeowner, however, may be recovered by the carpenter's representative to avoid the unjust enrichment of the homeowner. The benefit is usually measured by its reasonable value, i.e., what it would have cost the homeowner to obtain the benefit from a party in the position of the carpenter.[199] Even if the benefit has been destroyed because of the supervening event making performance impracticable, the restitution interest is still protected. Thus, if the carpenter managed part performance before the house was destroyed without the fault of either party, he would still be entitled to his restitution interest,[200] though the measure of recovery should be the increased value of the house as contrasted with the reasonable cost of performing the carpentry work.[201] The determination of appropriate compensation may be complex, however, where the parties relied upon a government regulation that has been repealed. In such a case, the parties did not intend to be bound by a reasonable value measurement.[202]

If the part performance rendered prior to impracticability or frustration was a *divisible* portion of the contract,[203] recovery can be had only for that severable portion. Where a vessel ran aground on a coral reef in Florida, the ship's owner hired Hudson to do the repairs. After

---

[197] Poussard v. Spiers, 1 A.B.D. 410 [1876].

[198] Jabero v. Harajli, 2004 Mich. App. LEXIS 1507 (2004). *See also* Unihealth v. U.S. Healthcare, 14 F. Supp. 2d 623 (D.N.J. 1998); Frigillana v. Frigillana, 266 Ark. 296, 584 S.W.2d 30 (1979); Quagliana v. Exquisite Home Builders, Inc., 538 P.2d 301 (Utah 1975). *See also* RESTATEMENT 2d §§ 272 and 377.

[199] *See* Carroll v. Bowersock, 100 Kan. 270, 164 P. 143 (1917); Young v. City of Chicopee, 186 Mass. 518, 72 N.E. 63 (1904). *See also* RESTATEMENT 2d § 371(a).

[200] See cases cited *supra* note 198.

[201] See RESTATEMENT 2d § 377 comment b and RESTATEMENT 2d § 371(b), which is the restitutionary measure of the increase in value of wealth to the recipient of the benefit as compared to the reasonable cost measure in § 371(a). The two measures are often different. Thus, the cost of a benefit could be greater or less than the value of that benefit to the owner. These matters will be discussed in the next chapter dealing with contract remedies.

[202] See *Unihealth, supra* note 198, where the court recognized that the restitutionary measure of recovery would normally govern cases where benefits have been conferred, but frustration of purpose has excused performance. Where the parties have failed to foresee that the government regulation of hospital payments to health maintenance organizations would be repealed, however, the court felt compelled to appoint a special master to facilitate a resolution of the dispute.

[203] The concept of divisible (or severable) versus entire contracts is explored *supra* § 106[D].

they were partly performed, hurricanes further damaged the reef. The repair contract contemplated the possibility of severe weather and provided for renegotiation. When the renegotiation was unsuccessful, Hudson sought payment for the part of the work performed under the original contract since the performance of that contract was impracticable. The court noted that restitution damages are unavailable where the parties are governed by a lump sum contract that contemplated the event making the performance impracticable (citing Restatement 2d § 377). The court then supplied a term to the original contract pursuant to Restatement 2d § 204 to allow Hudson to be compensated for a divisible percentage of the work done.[204] In a contract for the international sale of goods, CISG includes a remedy that allows a buyer to reduce the price in the same proportion as the value of goods delivered at the time of delivery and the value that conforming goods would have at the time of delivery.[205]

The issue of an appropriate remedy arose in the coronation cases, well-known as the creators of the doctrine of frustration of purpose. In the principal coronation case,[206] the defendant had agreed to pay £75 to license the flat near the upcoming coronation procession. He paid £25 in advance and refused to pay the balance. The plaintiff brought an action for the remaining £50 for which the defendant was not held liable due to the creation of the frustration of purpose excuse. The defendant did not seek recovery of the £25 paid in advance. In another coronation case, however, the defendant agreed to pay £141 for a desirable vantage point. This contract required the entire amount to be paid immediately after the contract was formed. The defendant paid only £100 and, when the procession was cancelled, he refused to pay the balance and brought an action to recover the £100 payment. The court not only refused to grant restitution of the amount paid; it also held the defendant liable for the £41 not paid on the footing that the defendant's performance was due before the procession was scheduled to occur and, since everything done before the frustrating event was assumed to be validly done, the defendant was liable for the entire contract price.[207] The absurdity of allocating risks on the sheer accident of when the parties had agreed to perform their promises is clear if one assumes a hypothetical contract where the parties had agreed that the amount would be paid only after the procession. In that case, the defendant would owe nothing. To the court's credit, it recognized this arbitrary analysis but, confronted by a dilemma, it chose what it considered the more desirable horn to adjudicate disputes between two innocent parties. The case was eventually overruled where an advance payment on a contract for machinery was recovered when war prevented performance of the contract.[208]

While overcoming the nonsensical precedent, this case found its own dilemma. The seller contended that it had performed considerable work on the machines prior to the supervening event causing impracticability and argued that it should recover the cost of the work performed. Here, the court was confronted with an argument for the *reliance* interest, i.e., the minus quantity or loss suffered by the seller as contrasted with the restitution interest, the benefit retained by the seller (the advance payment) at the expense of the buyer. While the restitution interest generally displays a greater claim to protection because it is not only a loss to one party but a corresponding gain to the unjustly enriched party, there is no apparent reason why both interests cannot be considered in such a case. The court, however, felt that it

---

[204] Sea Byte, Inc. v. Hudson Marine Mgt. Services, Inc., 2009 U. S. App. LEXIS 8429 (11th Cir. 2009).

[205] CISG Art. 50.

[206] Krell v. Henry, 2 K.B. 740 [1903].

[207] Chandler v. Webster, 1 K.B. 493 [1904].

[208] Fibrosa Spolka Akcyjna v. Faribarne Lawson Combe Barbour, Ltd., A.C. 32 [1943].

had achieved all that it could by granting the buyer restitution of his advance payment, and, if other relief were in order, only the legislature could achieve that goal. Parliament had been hard at work since the 1930s studying the question of relief for part performance in such cases. In 1943, it enacted the Frustrated Contract Act,[209] which encompassed all contract duties discharged by impracticability or frustration. That act permits a party such as the machinery buyer to recover his advance payment (restitution), but it also permits a court to decide that the seller can retain all or part of that payment because of expenses incurred by the seller (reliance). The curiosity is that the legislation did not deal with the situation where no benefit was conferred but expenses were incurred, i.e., where there was no restitution interest but there was a reliance interest. Thus, in the machinery case, had the buyer made no advance payment but the seller had incurred the same expenses, the seller would recover nothing because of the accident that no advance payment was made. Protection of the reliance interest was, therefore, made to depend upon whether there was a restitution interest to protect in the other party.

Extant authority in American case law would prevent protection of the reliance interest.[210] Moreover, there is no authority permitting recovery of the reliance interest even where the other party is entitled to recover the restitution interest. Indeed, the RESTATEMENT 2d insists that one's reliance interest may not be deducted from the amount of benefit he has received.[211] The illustration supporting this view, however, suggests that the reliance loss may be "taken into consideration in deciding whether to allow" restitution in the form of the cost of performance or the increase in value when the former is higher.[212] This is particularly confusing and may reflect the total absence of case law to achieve a result desired by the drafters of the RESTATEMENT 2d — a result that is augured by a general section on relief found in the chapter dealing with impracticability and frustration.[213] Part of that section suggests that a court may grant relief to avoid injustice and such relief may include protection of the reliance interest.[214] Having set the stage in that section, the RESTATEMENT 2d proceeds to deny that recovery in the subsequent section, though its illustration appears particularly confusing in this regard.[215]

---

[209] 6 & 7 Geo. 6, c. 40.

[210] See the cases cited *supra* note 198.

[211] RESTATEMENT 2d § 377 comment b.

[212] RESTATEMENT 2d § 377 ill. 5.

[213] RESTATEMENT 2d Ch. 11.

[214] RESTATEMENT 2d § 272(2).

[215] Illustration 5 to § 377 of the RESTATEMENT 2d suggests a contract to shingle a roof at a price of $5000. A, the contractor, has spent $2000 doing part of the work and has received a progress payment of $1800 from B. The house is destroyed by fire without the fault of either party. Moreover, $500 worth of shingles placed near the house were also destroyed. The illustration suggests that A cannot recover the $500, nor can he deduct it from the $1800 received from B which A must repay. The prior illustration indicates that A is not entitled to restitution in the amount of $2000 because the increase in the value of the house due to the partly completed shingle job was only $1500. When, however, the fact of the $500 loss in shingles is added, the illustration suggests that the court may decide to grant A restitution in the amount of $2000 rather than the $1500, i.e., the court may, presumably, consider reliance, not by protecting the reliance interest, but by choosing the higher possible restitution interest. If that choice is made *because* of reliance, however, why should the reliance interest be protected in this awkward fashion, i.e., choosing a higher restitution interest which is necessarily only an accident? This circumvention is apparently due to the lack of any case law support for the protection of the reliance interest. It is a particularly harmful way to restate the law.

§ 117   RISK OF LOSS — UNIFORM COMMERCIAL CODE

[A]   From Property to Contract

Among the changes wrought by Article 2 of the UCC, the sections dealing with risk of loss are notable as a prime illustration of the conceptual change in the Code to a contracts orientation from the property orientation of the law the Code replaced. The legal consequences are stated as following directly from the contract and action taken under it without resorting to the idea of when property or title passed or was to pass as being the determining factor.[216] Risk of loss would not, therefore, be determined on the basis of the "title" or ownership of the goods.[217] Rather, it would be determined by the contract between the parties.[218] Where the goods are to be delivered through an independent carrier, normally the risk of loss will remain on the seller until the seller delivers the goods to an independent carrier or to the buyer.[219] These normal rules would change where there has been a breach by the seller in not shipping conforming goods or by the purchaser in not paying for the goods or otherwise repudiating. A comprehensive treatment of risk of loss must be left to treatises on commercial transactions. A summary of the UCC treatment of risk of loss follows.

[B]   Risk of Loss in the Absence of Breach

Some of the confusion that students develop in dealing with the basic risk of loss section in the UCC, § 2-509, is that the section begins with "shipment" or "destination" contracts, i.e., contracts where the goods will be shipped by an independent carrier rather than the seller's

---

[216] UCC § 2-101 comment. *See also* UCC § 2-509 comment 1: "The underlying theory of these sections on risk of loss is adoption of the contractual approach rather than an arbitrary shifting of the risk with the 'property' in the goods." *See also* Martin v. Melland's, Inc., 283 N.W.2d 76 (N.D. 1979); Taylor & Martin, Inc. v. Hiland Dairy, Inc., 676 S.W.2d 859 (Mo. Ct. App. 1984); Hughes v. Al Green, Inc., 65 Ohio St. 2d 110, 418 N.E.2d 1355 (1981).

[217] *See* Burnett v. Purtell, 1992 Ohio App. LEXIS 3467, at *4 (Ohio Ct. App., Lake County June 30, 1992). Section 2-401 of the UCC deals with the concept of "title" and the time title passes. It is, however, important to recognize the principal purpose of this section. There are criminal statutes, tax statutes, and governmental regulations beyond the UCC that required the determination of "title." There are also "title" questions in insurance policies concerning the ownership of the property. It is, therefore, essential to have a "title" concept for these extra-code purposes. See Ben & Jerry's Homemade v. Coronet Priscilla Ice Cream Corp., 921 F. Supp. 1206, 1210 (D. Vt. 1996), where the court relies upon UCC § 2-401(2)(a), stating that title passes in an FOB shipment contract at the time and place of shipment. *See Martin v. Melland's, Inc., supra* note 216, at n.3. Even though the term "title" is found in other UCC sections, *e.g.*, §§ 2-327(1)(a) (sale on approval), 2-312 (warranty of title) and even in the definition of "sale," 2-106(1), *supra*, these uses are traditional and do not require a separate section devoted to the question of when title passes.

[218] *See* Russell v. Transamerica Ins. Co., 116 Mich. App. 93, 322 N.W.2d 178 (1982) (plaintiffs maintained possession of the boat after title passed to buyer and risk of loss was on plaintiffs).

[219] The party in possession should normally bear the risk because that party is in a better position to control and protect the goods. The curiosity is that this was the view of the early law. By the time of Tarling v. Baxter, 6 Barn. & C. 360, 108 Eng. Rep. 484 [1827], however, risk of loss became an incident of title and the question was who had title at the time of loss. The party not in possession may have been "vested" with title and would bear the risk of loss. The "title" approach, however, was an attempt to solve too many problems with a single rule. When faced with criticism of his refusal to adhere to the title concept, Karl Llewellyn provided a classic response: "May I say one other thing in that connection, and say it without any hesitancy for the record? The number of lawyers who have an accurate knowledge of sales law is extremely small in these United States. My brother Bacon has taught sales law for 28 years. When he says it isn't too difficult to determine where the courts will decide the title is or isn't or is going to be or should be, he is speaking a truth within limits for people who have taught sales law for 28 years. I submit to you sir, that there are not many of them." (Statement of K. Llewellyn, 1 HEARINGS BEFORE THE NEW YORK LAW REVISION COMMISSION ON THE UCC 96 [160] (1954).).

own truck, and where the contract places the risk of loss on the buyer either at the time the goods are delivered to the carrier ("shipment")[220] or at the time they are tendered to the buyer ("destination").[221] The elaboration of "shipment" and "destination" contracts is found in definitions of those terms and the attendant duties of the seller in each.[222] A "shipment" contract is normally identified by the term "FOB shipment" (or "FOB seller's plant"), which requires the seller to bear the risk and expense of putting the goods in the possession of an independent carrier at the seller's location.[223] The seller must choose a reasonable carrier, make a proper contract for the transportation of the goods in relation to the nature of the goods, obtain and promptly deliver any appropriate documents such as bills of lading that the buyer requires to obtain the goods, and promptly notify the buyer of shipment.[224]

A "destination" contract is normally identified by the term, "FOB the place of destination" (or "FOB buyer's plant"), and requires the seller to transport the goods to that destination at his own expense and risk and tender delivery of the goods to the buyer at that destination.[225] The tender requires the seller to make the goods available at the buyer's disposition at a reasonable hour with proper notice to the buyer to enable him to take delivery.[226]

Once a contract is deemed to be a "shipment" contract, the risk of loss passes to the buyer when the goods are duly delivered to an independent carrier, while in a "destination" contract, the risk passes to the buyer when the goods are duly delivered to the buyer at the buyer's destination.[227] If the contract is silent as to whether the contract is a "shipment" or "destination" contract, the presumption is that the parties intended a "shipment" contract since that is the "normal" one and the destination contract is viewed as a "variant."[228] In addition to identifying a contract as a "shipment" or "destination" contract, the FOB term may add "vessel car or other vehicle."[229] This obligates the seller to load the goods on board at the seller's expense and risk. Where the contract also contains a "C.I.F." term (cost, insurance and freight) or "C. & F." term (cost and freight), it is a "shipment" contract and has no effect on the normal allocation of risk. Just because the cost of transportation and/or insurance is included in the price, there is no change in the risk of loss rules.[230]

---

[220] UCC § 2-509(1)(a).

[221] UCC § 2-509(1)(b).

[222] UCC §§ 2-319 and 2-320 define shipment terms such as F.O.B., F.A.S., C.I.F. and C. & F. terms. There is, however, a growing consensus that such terms are outdated in commercial practice and should, therefore, be interpreted in light of applicable trade usage, course of dealing and course of performance. In light of the growth of international commerce, the use of *Incoterms of the International Chamber of Commerce* (2000) (a set of international rules for the interpretation of the most commonly used terms in foreign trade) are viewed as preferable.

[223] UCC § 2-319(1)(a).

[224] UCC § 2-504. It should be noted that failure to make a proper contract or to notify the buyer of shipment is a ground for buyer's rejection of the goods only if material delay or loss ensues from such failures.

[225] UCC § 2-319(1)(b).

[226] UCC § 2-503.

[227] UCC §§ 2-509(1)(a) and (1)(b). Thus, where the goods are destroyed prior to shipment, the risk of loss remains on the seller. See Silver v. Wycombe, Meyer & Co., 124 Misc. 2d 717, 477 N.Y.S.2d 288 (Civ. Ct. 1984), *aff'd*, 130 Misc. 2d 227, 498 N.Y.S.2d 334 (App. Term 1985).

[228] UCC § 2-503 comment 5. *See* Windows, Inc. v. Jordan Panel Sys. Corp., 177 F.3d 114 (2d Cir. 1999).

[229] UCC § 2-319(1)(c).

[230] UCC § 2-320 and comment 1. The FOB term will not be construed as a price term; it is a delivery term. *See* A.M. Knitwear Corp. v. All Am. Export-Import Corp., 41 N.Y.2d 14, 390 N.Y.S.2d 832, 359 N.E.2d 342 (1976). See, however, Clark v. Messer Indus., 222 Ga. App. 606, 475 S.E.2d 653 (1996), where the customer shipping order stated that the

Myriad kinds of goods are stored in warehouses in the possession of a bailee (warehouseman). The owners of such goods often contract to sell them and the buyer takes delivery even though the goods remain where they are, i.e., they simply belong to the buyer. The transaction, therefore, contemplates *delivery of the goods without moving them.* The UCC contains a risk of loss rule under which the risk passes to the buyer in such a case upon his receipt of a negotiable document of title (a warehouse receipt), or his receipt of a non-negotiable document or other written direction, or, finally, upon the bailee's acknowledgment of the buyer's right to the goods.[231]

The residual subsection deals with cases not involving shipment through independent carriers or delivery of goods without moving them. It governs a large number of transactions in goods where, for example, the seller will deliver in his own truck, the buyer will go to the seller's plant to take the goods in the buyer's truck, the consumer takes delivery of a new or used car, and millions of other transactions. This residual section can, therefore, be considered the general rule of risk of loss: the risk passes to the buyer on his receipt of the goods if the seller is a merchant, and it passes on tender of delivery of the goods if the seller is not a merchant.[232] For the purposes of this Code section, a "merchant" would be very broadly defined as anyone in business.[233] While the difference between the buyer's receipt and the seller's tender may be insignificant, it could be controlling in a given case and the Code drafters apparently intended to favor the non-merchant seller at least to the extent of removing the risk from such a seller sooner than it would be removed from a merchant seller. Questions of whether the buyer has "received" the goods[234] or delivery was tendered[235] still arise, though not very often. Where a buyer went to a lumber yard to purchase a 12 foot, 100 pound beam, the beam was lifted by the seller's fork lift truck onto the six foot open truck bed of the defendant's truck. At the buyer's request, the seller placed a flag on the end of the beam extending four feet from the truck bed. The buyer did not otherwise secure the beam on the truck. The buyer drove the truck until the beam fell into a public street. The beam was hit by another motorist and a shattered piece struck the buyer causing a serious injury. The court held that the seller's duty ended when the beam was received by the purchaser under UCC § 2-509(3). Receipt occurred when the beam was placed in the buyer's truck. At that point, risk of loss passed and the seller was not liable for any losses sustained by the buyer.[236]

---

shipment was "F. O. B. shipping point," but the court found that since the parties agreed the seller bore the expense of transporting the goods, the contract was a "destination" contract. This view is diametrically opposed to Comment 5 to UCC § 2-503, which expressly rejects pre-Code rules that a term requiring the seller to pay the cost of transportation converts the contract into a "destination" contract.

[231] UCC § 2-509(2). *See* Whately v. Tetrault, 29 Mass. App. Dec. 112, 5 U.C.C. Rep. Serv. (CBC) 838 (1964) (risk of loss passed on acknowledgment). *See also* Jason's Foods, Inc. v. Peter Eckrich & Sons, Inc., 774 F.2d 214 (7th Cir. 1985) (title is separated from risk of loss under § 2-509(2) and the acknowledgment must be *to the buyer* rather than the seller; acknowledgment need not be written but the question of whether acknowledgment means receipt or mailing not decided).

[232] UCC § 2-509(3).

[233] *See* UCC § 2-104, comment 2.

[234] *See* Ron Mead T.V. & Appliance v. Legendary Homes, Inc., 746 P.2d 1163 (Okla. Ct. App. 1987).

[235] *See* Merchants Acceptance, Inc. v. Jamison, 752 So. 2d 422, 425 (Miss. Ct. App. 1999) (goods delivered to post office box instead of street address constituted an ineffective tender). *See also* St. Paul Fire & Marine Ins. Co. v. Toman, 351 N.W.2d 146 (S.D. 1984).

[236] Ganno v. Lanoga Corp., 119 Wn. App. 310, 80 P. 3d 180 (2003). While a sign in the lumberyard stated that it was not the seller's policy to secure loads for customers, the court did not rely upon the sign for its conclusion as to when the risk of loss passed to the buyer.

In keeping with the freedom of contract philosophy of the UCC in permitting the parties to vary the effect of its provisions,[237] the last subsection expressly permits such variation,[238] i.e., the parties may vary the affect of risk of loss rules by their agreement.[239] This section presents uncertainty because it requires interpretation of myriad statements in the agreement which may or may not constitute a § 2-509(4) variation by agreement.[240] Because the use of such language to shift the risk of loss is unusual, a court may require the language to be "clear and unequivocal" to be effective.[241]

[C]   Risk of Loss Where There Is a Breach

If the seller ships goods which are nonconforming, or if the goods are perfect but the *tender* of delivery is nonconforming,[242] the buyer has a *right* of rejection.[243] That right of rejection will reallocate the normal risk of loss rules, i.e., the rules that would apply in the absence of breach. In an FOB shipment contract, the risk would normally pass to the buyer upon delivery of the goods to the carrier. In a destination contract, the risk would normally pass when the goods were tendered to the buyer. When, however, it is discovered that the tender or goods delivered were nonconforming, giving rise to a right of rejection in the buyer, those normal risk of loss rules no longer apply. Instead, the risk of loss remains on the seller until the buyer has accepted the goods,[244] or until the nonconformity is cured.[245]

If the buyer has accepted the goods, she can no longer reject them. She may, however, be able to revoke her acceptance of the goods which will place her in the same position as if she had rejected.[246] If a buyer rightfully revokes her acceptance of the goods, she may treat the risk of loss as remaining on the seller (though, again, normally the risk would be on the buyer)

---

[237] UCC § 1-102 comment 2.

[238] UCC § 2-509(4). It also suggests that the provisions of § 2-509 are subject to § 2-327 (sale on approval contracts where the risk of loss does not pass until the buyer accepts the goods (§ 2-327(1)(a)), whereas in a "sale or return" contract, the risk remains on the seller throughout the contract. *See* comment 3 to § 2-317. The very concept of "approval" suggests that the buyer is in possession of the goods to determine if he wants to purchase them. In a "sale or return" contract, however, a sale has been made though the buyer may choose to return the goods if he does so seasonably. UCC § 2-327(2)(a). Section 2-509(4) proceeds to suggest that the provisions of § 2-509 are also subject to § 2-510, which deals with risk of loss where there has been a breach of contract and will be discussed in the next subsection.

[239] *See* Forest Nursery Co. v. I.W.S., Inc., 141 Misc. 2d 661, 534 N.Y.S.2d 86 (Dist. Ct. 1988).

[240] *See, e.g.,* Consolidated Bottling Co. v. Jaco Equip. Corp., 442 F.2d 660 (2d Cir. 1971) (holding the "f. o. b. purchaser's truck" was a contrary agreement).

[241] Hawkins v. Federated Mut. Ins. Co., 1996 U.S. Dist LEXIS 21436, at *11 (N.D. Miss. Aug. 14, 1996).

[242] *See* William F. Wilke, Inc. v. Cummins Diesel Engines, Inc., 252 Md. 611, 250 A.2d 886 (1969).

[243] *See* UCC § 2-601.

[244] Acceptance of the goods may occur in any of three ways: (a) the buyer signifies his acceptance, whether or not the goods are conforming, (b) the buyer fails to make an effective rejection under UCC § 2-602 and, thereby, is deemed to have accepted the goods, or (c) the buyer does any act inconsistent with the seller's ownership of the goods, such as using the goods, unless such use is essential and operates to mitigate damages. UCC § 2-606.

[245] UCC § 2-510(1). *See* Graaff v. Bakker Bros., 85 Wash. App. 814, 934 P.2d 1228 (1997); Moses v. Newman, 658 S.W.2d 119 (Tenn. Ct. App. 1983); Jakowski v. Carole Chevrolet, Inc., 180 N.J. Super. 122, 433 A.2d 841 (1981). Cure (repairing or replacing the good to overcome the nonconformity), is described in UCC § 2-508.

[246] Revocation of acceptance is found in UCC § 2-608 and requires a substantial impairment of the value of the goods, which is a much higher standard than the rejection standard of UCC § 2-601 since rejection can occur for any defect including an insubstantial defect. Beyond the "substantial impairment" requirement, the buyer must also show either (1) he accepted the goods on the reasonable assumption that the nonconformity would be cured and it was not

but only to the extent of any deficiency in her insurance coverage.[247] If the buyer has complete coverage, the risk of loss is entirely hers. If she has no coverage, it is entirely on the seller, and if the buyer has incomplete coverage, the risk is on the seller as to the "deficiency" in the buyer's coverage. A moment's thought about this risk of loss rule clearly indicates its anti-subrogation quality, i.e., if the buyer's insurance company must pay for the casualty to the goods, there is no claim to which the insurance company can be subrogated because the insured buyer would have such a claim against the seller only if the buyer's insurance were deficient.

Where the buyer breaches the contract, a similar analysis applies. The situation is fascinating but unlikely as the following example suggests. Buyer and seller form a contract for the sale of equipment. The seller takes conforming equipment from its inventory and marks or otherwise designates it as referring to the buyer, i.e., this particular machine will be sent to the buyer. In so designating this specific machine for the buyer, the seller has *identified* the goods to the contract.[248] The contract is an FOB shipment contract. Before the machine is delivered to the carrier, however, the buyer repudiates the contract. Under normal risk of loss rules, the risk of loss has not yet passed to the buyer because, again, the machine has yet to be delivered to the carrier. Shortly after the repudiation, the machine is destroyed without the fault of the seller. If all of these elements are met, i.e., where the goods are conforming and already identified to the contract when the buyer repudiates and before the risk of loss would normally pass to the buyer, the seller may, to the extent of any deficiency in its insurance coverage, treat the risk of loss as resting on the buyer for a commercially reasonable time.[249] Again, the provision is clearly an anti-subrogation provision because it precludes recovery by a subrogee insurance company by limiting the seller's claim against the buyer only to that for which the seller is not insured.[250]

The extant case law concerning the UCC risk of loss mechanism suggests no major problems in its operation.

---

cured, or (2) he did not discover the substantial impairment either because (i) it was too difficult to discover, or (ii) he did not discover it because of the seller's assurances.

[247] UCC § 2-510(2). *See* Beal v. Griffin, 123 Idaho 445, 849 P.2d 118, 119 (Ct. App. 1993).

[248] See UCC § 2-501 and the discussion of "identification," *supra* at § 114[C].

[249] UCC § 2-510(3). For a rare application of this section, see Multiplastics, Inc. v. Arch Indus., Inc., 166 Conn. 280, 348 A.2d 618 (1974). In Mercanti v. Persson, 160 Conn. 468, 280 A.2d 137 (1971), the court could discover no breach by the buyer. In Portal Galleries, Inc. v. Tomar Prods., Inc., 60 Misc. 2d 523, 302 N.Y.S.2d 871 (Sup. Ct. 1969), more than a "commercially reasonable time" had passed so that the risk no longer rested on the buyer.

[250] Comment 3 to § 2-510 removes the last fig leaf of doubt about the anti-subrogation nature of this section. The father of the UCC, Karl Llewellyn, thought insurance companies ought to pay without being subrogated since they receive premiums to assume such risks.

Chapter 9

REMEDIES FOR BREACH OF CONTRACT

§ 118 SURVEY — CONTRACT INTERESTS, COMPENSATION, ECONOMICS, AND REMEDIES

[A] The Three Interests

The purpose of contract law is often stated as the fulfillment of those expectations that have been induced by the making of a promise.[1] If the promise is breached, the goal is to protect expectations by placing the injured promisee in the position he would have been in had the promise been performed.[2] This remedy assures the promisee the "benefit of the bargain."[3] While the expectation interest is paramount in contract remedies, there are two other interests with strong claims to protection.[4]

---

[1] MCA TV, Ltd. v. Public Interest Corp., 171 F.3d 1265, 1270 (11th Cir. 1999) (quoting this treatise).

[2] RESTATEMENT 2d § 344(a); UCC § 1-305 (formerly§ 1-106(1). Cipala v. Lincoln Technical Institute, 179 N. J. 45, 53, 843 A. 2d 1069, 1074 (2004). *See also* Wells v. Minor, 219 Ill. App. 3d 32, 578 N.E.2d 1337, 1344 (4th Dist. 1991) ("the well-accepted general rule that damages for breach of contract should place the party in the position he would have been [in] had the contract been performed"); Pelletier v. Pelletier Dev. Co., 1996 Conn. Super. LEXIS 748, at *13 (Conn. Super. Ct. May 14, 1996) ("The general rule in breach of contract cases is that the award of damages is designed to place the injured party, so far as can be done by money, in the same position as that which he would have been in had the contract been performed").

[3] *Id.* The RESTATEMENT 2d § 344(a) suggests that the expectation interest may be described as whatever the promisee would have gained but has lost by the breach.

[4] The expectation, reliance, and restitution interests are fully explored in the classic two-part article by Fuller and

A promisee may rely to his detriment and suffer a loss (a minus quantity) because of a promise which has been made to him. The same promise may have induced reasonable expectations. In a given situation, the expectation interest may not be protected because it cannot be accurately measured. Yet, the promisee has reasonably relied upon the promise and changed her position, thereby incurring a loss. In this situation, the legal system may protect the measurable reliance interest of the promisee.[5] Instead of protecting expectations by placing the promisee in the future position she would have been in had the contract been performed, the object of the reliance interest is to place the promisee in the same position she was in before the promise was made. It restores her to her original position by enforcing her claim against the promisor in the amount of loss suffered. Unlike the reliance interest, the expectation interest does not require any showing of out-of-pocket loss.

A third interest protected by the legal system is even more compelling since it involves both a loss to the injured promisee and a corresponding gain or benefit to the defaulting promisor. The injured promisee has not only relied on the promise and suffered a loss; the promisee has also conferred a benefit of some value on the defaulting promisor. When the promisor fails to perform, the promisor must surrender the value of the benefit she has unjustly received from the promisee. The promisor has been *unjustly enriched* at the expense of the promisee. Thus, the object of the restitution interest is to compel the defaulting promisor to surrender the unjust enrichment (gain) and to restore the injured promisee to her position prior to the making of a promise. By compelling the promisor to return the plus quantity or enrichment to the promisee, the minus quantity in the promisee is cancelled and she is restored to *status quo ante*. The restitution interest is based upon the foundational concept that *no one should be enriched at the expense of another.*[6]

It is essential to understand each of the three interests — the expectation, reliance, and restitution interests.[7] We will explore them in detail. It is also, however, essential to understand certain fundamental concepts in order to avoid needless confusion in the sections which follow.

[B] Compensation

The term "compensation" is often used in discussions of contract remedies. Compensation, however, is a generic term and must always be followed with the question: compensation for what?[8] While remedies are designed to compensate for injuries, this is not a sufficient answer. Whether the legal system is attempting to compensate for injury to disappointed expectations, detrimental reliance, or unjust enrichment caused by a breach of contract, it is attempting to provide redress to the injured promisee for the loss caused by that breach. Our legal system does not *compel* the fulfillment of promises. It does not punish contract breakers except in

---

Perdue, *The Reliance Interest in Contract Damages*, 46 YALE L.J. 52, 373 (1936), upon which the discussion in this section is largely based.

[5] RESTATEMENT 2d § 344(b). See Westfield Holdings, Inc. v. United States, 407 F.3d 1352 (Fed Cir. 2005).

[6] RESTATEMENT 2d § 344(c). See MC Baldwin Financial Co. v. TB Institutional Services, Inc., 845 N. E. 2d 22 (Ill. App. 2006).

[7] See Touloumes v. E. S. C., Inc., 587 Pa. 287, 294, 899 A. 2d 343, 347 (2006) citing this treatise). For a discussion of the three interests, see Bentley v. LCM Corp., 2009 U.S. Dist. LEXIS 29284 (W. D. La. 2009) applying Virginia law. *See also* Potter v. Oster, 426 N.W.2d 148 (Iowa 1988).

[8] *See* Cooter & Eisenberg, *Damages for Breach of Contract*, 73 CAL. L. REV. 1432 (1985).

egregious situations with a tort dimension.[9] Rather, it focuses on overcoming the loss to the aggrieved promisee.[10] It is conceivable that a legal system could compel the enforcement of promises through its criminal law or at least allow recoveries to injured promisees which go beyond mere compensation. But the Anglo-American legal system has not chosen this route.[11] It has chosen to develop remedies with the purpose of placing the injured promisee in the position she would have occupied had the promise been performed (expectation interest) or to restore her to the position she was in before the promise was made (reliance and restitution interests).

[C] Economic Theory — "Efficient Breach"

In general, it may be said that economic theory supports the protection of the expectation interest through substitutional relief in the form of money damages.[12] At the beginning of this volume, we summarized the economic theory of the social institution of contract-the allocation of the resources of society through voluntary agreements facilitating future exchanges.[13] Value maximization is effectuated where goods worth \$1000 to X are worth \$1500 to Y, who has \$1500 to spend so that the total value is \$2500. If the parties agree to an exchange of the goods for \$1500, the result is that X now has \$1500 and Y has goods worth \$1500 for a total of \$3000.[14] After making a contract to sell the goods for \$1500, X may discover another buyer (Z) who is willing to pay \$2200 for them. If X breaches the contract but fully compensates Y to the extent of \$500, he is better off because his net return is \$1700 after the sale to Z for \$2200. Z is pleased because he has received goods worth \$2200 to him. This results in economic efficiency but it involves a breach of contract. The protection of the expectation interest through a substitutional money damages remedy induces *efficient breach*.[15]

It is important, however, to recognize the limitations of this approach. Even from an economics perspective, it does not consider transaction costs, i.e., those costs associated with the bargaining process and dispute resolution. Nor does it consider non-economic

---

[9] See Allapattah Servs. v. Exxon Corp., 61 F. Supp. 2d 1326 (S.D. Fla. 1999), and cases cited therein.

[10] Norman's Heritage Real Estate Co. v. Aetna Cas. & Sur. Co., 727 F.2d 911 (10th Cir. 1984); Quigley v. Pet, Inc., 162 Cal. App. 3d 223, 208 Cal. Rptr. 394 (5th Dist. 1984), *cert. denied sub nom.* Comora v. Radell, 495 U.S. 941, 110 S. Ct. 2196, 109 L. Ed. 2d 523 (1990).

[11] Windsor Securities, Inc. v. Hartford Life Ins. Co., 986 F.2d 655, 664 (3d Cir. 1993) (quoting this treatise).

[12] *See* Cooter & Eisenberg, *supra* note 8.

[13] *See* Chapter 1, § 7 *supra*.

[14] "Value" is measured by the value to the individual and the parties' willingness and ability to transfer the goods and to pay. Economic theory does not suggest a preferable measure of value.

[15] "The key result is that the expectation remedy is the only remedy that creates efficient incentives with respect to breaches of contracts. This is because the expectation remedy forces the breaching party to pay in damages the value of the good to the breached-against party. If another buyer values the good more than this, then it is efficient for that buyer to have the good. Given the expectation measure of damages, the seller will have an incentive to breach in order to obtain the higher offer. . . . [I]f damages are below expectation damages an inefficient breach might occur. This is the problem with the reliance remedy, because it leads to a level of damages below the expectation level. The restitution remedy is even worse because it provides less than the reliance measure of damages." A. M. POLINSKY, AN INTRODUCTION TO LAW AND ECONOMICS 33–34 (2d ed. 1989). See, however, Chapter 8 of the same volume which reinforces an earlier conclusion that a breach of contract remedy that is efficient with respect to every consideration does not exist, i.e., while the expectation remedy is preferable with respect to a decision to breach the contract, the restitution remedy is preferable with respect to a reliance decision and a liquidated damage remedy is preferable with respect to risk allocation.

perspectives, such as any moral obligation to keep one's promises.[16] Yet, viewing contract remedies from the economic perspective is important in dealing with numerous questions, including such questions of whether the remedy of specific performance should be expanded[17] or whether liquidated damage clauses to which parties agree at contract formation should be made more available.[18] In general, however, the impact of law and economics scholarship on the law of contracts to this time has been illuminating primarily in providing economic theory in support of existing structure.[19]

[D] Contract Remedies

Before exploring contract remedies in detail, it is beneficial to consider certain fundamental concepts that will provide necessary background for that exploration.

[1] Right to Damages — Nominal Damages

Any breach of contract, total or partial, provides the aggrieved party with a right to bring an action for damages unless the claim for damages has been suspended or discharged.[20] If the breach of contract causes no loss or where a purported loss cannot be adequately proven, the breach remains and the aggrieved party has a damage claim to a nominal amount as a manifestation of breach without any provable damage.[21] There may be relatively rare situations where an action for nominal damages will serve, in effect, as a declaratory judgment of the rights and duties of the parties to the contract. Where a party's proof of damages fails for uncertainty, his failure to claim nominal damages may affect his opportunity to claim reasonable attorney's fees.[22]

---

[16] *See* Restatement 2d, Introductory Note to Chapter 16. See also Mark P. Gergen, *A Theory of Self-Help Remedies in Contract*, 89 B.U. L. Rev. 1397, 1433 (2009), "But economic theories of contract are not wedded to the theory of efficient breach. The theory of efficient breach is no more than a normatively-tinged description of one type of behavioral response to the expectation damage measure."

[17] Specific performance, however, would preclude efficient breach if it were available in the example suggested in the text. For differing views of the expanded availability of specific performance, see Schwartz, *The Case for Specific Performance*, 89 Yale L.J. 271 (1979), as contrasted with Kronman, *Specific Performance*, 45 U. Chi. L. Rev. 351 (1978).

[18] *See* Goetz & Scott, *Liquidated Damages, Penalties, and the Just Compensation Principle: Some Notes on an Enforcement Model and Theory of Efficient Breach*, 77 Colum. L. Rev. 554 (1977).

[19] One writer remarked, "At most, the results suggest that 'law and economics' is a source of sometimes useful information for working within already established rules. It does not alter rules nor does it alter the weighing of various judicial interests." Harrison, *Trends and Traces: A Preliminary Evaluation of Economic Analysis in Contract Law*, 1988 Annual Survey of American Law [New York Univ.] 73, 98–99 (1989). Other literature on the economics of contract law includes The Economics of Contract Law (Kronman & Posner eds. 1979); Posner, Economic Analysis of Law ch. 4 (7th ed. 2007); Birmingham, *Breach of Contract, Damage Measures and Economic Efficiency*, 24 Rutgers L. Rev. 273 (1970).

[20] Restatement 2d § 346(1). The duty to pay damages can be suspended or discharged through the agreement of the parties or otherwise. If the damage claim is discharged, the right to damages is extinguished. If the duty of performance, as contrasted with the duty to pay damages, is suspended or discharged as, for example, when the performance becomes impracticable or the purpose of the performance is frustrated, no breach has occurred. Therefore, there is no right to a damage remedy. For a study of the history of the development of the modern law relating to the recovery of damages in contract actions, see Washington, *Damages in Contract at Common Law*, 47 Law Q. Rev. 345 (1931), and 48 Law Q. Rev. 90 (1932).

[21] Restatement 2d § 346(2). *See* Freund v. Washington Square Press, Inc., 34 N.Y.2d 379, 314 N.E.2d 419 (1974) (inability to prove royalties on unpublished book resulted in nominal damages of six cents).

[22] MindGames, Inc. v. Western Publ'g Co., 218 F.3d 652, 654 (7th Cir. 2000), *cert. denied*, 121 S. Ct. 882, 148 L. Ed.

[2]   Money Damages — Expectation Interest — Reliance Interest

The usual remedy available to an aggrieved party when a breach of contract has occurred is an action for the recovery of compensation in the form of money damages to protect the expectation interest, i.e, an award that will place the injured promisee in the same position he would have been in had the contract been performed. Where, for example, a buyer agrees to purchase an automobile for $25,000 and the seller breaches that contract, the typical buyer will purchase the car elsewhere. Assuming a reasonable substitute or "cover" purchase price of $27,000, the buyer has been damaged to the extent of the difference between the contract and cover prices and should be awarded $2000 in damages.[23] The court may also award money damages to protect the reliance interest, i.e., the loss caused by the reliance of the promisee to place him in the position he would have occupied had no promise been made to him.[24] Where, for example, a party expends certain sums to start a new business venture relying on a promise that is breached, the promisee's profit expectation may not be provable, but his out-of-pocket loss can be shown. The court should award damages to protect the reliance interest in such a case.

The foregoing illustrations suggest the normal operation of the legal system in protecting the expectation interest or reliance interest of an injured promisee. The party seeking relief brings his action "at law," rather than as a "suit in equity," because the relief he seeks is a damage award.

[3]   Specific Performance or Injunction — Expectation Interest — Election of Remedy

What is generally considered an exceptional remedy may also protect the expectation interest. Where the normal remedy of money damages is inadequate to protect the expectation interest, the court may seek to protect that interest by decreeing *specific performance* of the contract, i.e., ordering the promisor to perform or by issuing an injunction to enjoin the performance of the contract.[25] The remedy of specific performance does not provide substitutional relief as does the damage remedy. The court simply orders the promisor to perform so as to provide the promisee with the specific or literal performance promised. The most common example of this remedy occurs in contracts for the sale of land where the damage remedy is obviously inadequate since any tract of land is unique, at least in terms of its location. Since the buyer cannot purchase that particular land elsewhere as he could purchase an ordinary automobile or other ordinary chattel, the buyer may justifiably claim that the damage remedy would be inadequate. The same analysis would apply to any unique chattel.[26]

2d 791 (2001). Arkansas law permits a prevailing party to recover attorney's fees in a breach of contract case. *See* Dawson v. Temps Plus, Inc., 337 Ark. 247, 987 S.W.2d 722 (1999).

[23] The "cover" remedy is found in UCC § 2-712. It is the counterpart of the seller's "resale" remedy in UCC § 2-706. Where the buyer breaches and the seller finds another buyer, if the reasonable resale price is lower than the contract price, the seller is entitled to the difference between the higher contract price and the lower resale price.

[24] RESTATEMENT 2d § 345(a) and comment b.

[25] *See* RESTATEMENT 2d § 345(b). "[W]e do not grant specific relief ordinarily, but only exceptionally where substituted relief (money damages) is held inadequate." R. POUND, INTRODUCTION TO THE PHILOSOPHY OF LAW 135 (rev. ed. 1954).

[26] The UCC extends this concept to goods that, in effect, are unique because of scarcity. See § 2-716(1), where the remedy of specific performance will be granted where the buyer cannot effect a cover or in other reasonable circumstances.

The buyer is not compelled to seek specific performance, i.e., he may choose his damage remedy. The election of the specific performance remedy will not waive a later choice to seek damages instead unless the defendant has materially changed its position in reliance on the original choice of remedy.[27] Where the remedy of specific performance will not fulfill the total expectation interest of the plaintiff, a court may enforce the promise to the extent possible and also grant damages for that part of the performance that cannot occur.[28]

[4] Restoration or Damages — Restitution Interest

A court can protect the restitution interest (prevention of the enrichment of one party at the expense of another party) either by awarding damages, or, in an appropriate case, by requiring the enriched party to restore a specific thing to the other party (specific restitution).[29] If, for example, a seller is induced to convey land through the misrepresentation of the buyer, the buyer has been enriched at the seller's expense and the seller may have the land restored to him through specific restitution.[30] The seller is then placed in the same position as if the misrepresentation had not occurred.

[5] Declaratory Judgment and Arbitration Award

In addition to the foregoing judicial remedies, courts are also empowered to grant declaratory judgments which determine the legal relations between the parties to a contract without granting damages or other relief. A clarification of the rights and duties of the parties may occur even prior to any breach of contract and can be an effective means to resolve disputes as well as preventing litigation.[31]

The parties to a contract may choose *alternative dispute resolution* methods to resolve their disputes. The premier alternative method is *arbitration.* As part of their contract, the parties agree that any dispute concerning the contract will be submitted to arbitration. Even if the parties have not made that agreement at the time of formation, when a dispute arises, they may agree to submit it to arbitration. As noted earlier, the Federal Arbitration Act has been interpreted to provide a strong federal policy in support of the enforcement of arbitration agreements.[32] While the dollar amount of disputes submitted to arbitration were originally small, multi-million dollar commercial disputes are currently submitted to the arbitration process, rather than the judicial process. The award rendered by the panel of non-judges will

---

[27] In Homeland Training Center, LLC v. Summit Point Automotive Research Ctr., 2010 U.S. App. LEXIS 2309 (4th Cir. 2010), the plaintiff sought specific performance, but as the litigation progressed, it became apparent that there was no hope of salvaging the contract. When the plaintiff then sought damages, the trial court held that the original decision to seek specific performance constituted a waiver of its right to a remedy in damages. On appeal, the instant court held the lower court was in error under either the modern state rules of civil procedure or substantive contract law. The court cited § 378, comment a, of the Restatement 2d in holding that a party would be precluded from seeking damages instead of its original choice of specific performance only if the other party had materially changed its position in reliance on the original choice.

[28] The other relief may take the form of damages or restitution, as well as indemnity against future harm. *See* RESTATEMENT 2d § 358(3) and comment c.

[29] RESTATEMENT 2d § 345(d) (damages) and (c) (specific restitution).

[30] *See* RESTATEMENT 2d § 372(1) and ill. 1.

[31] RESTATEMENT 2d § 345(e).

[32] *See* Chapter 6, *supra*, § 97[B][2][f].

typically be transformed into a judgment by a court through summary procedures.[33] Arbitration awards are normally upheld on appeal in the absence of abuse of the arbitrator's discretion.

[6]   Uniform Commercial Code Remedies — CISG Remedies

Where the parties form a contract for the sale of goods, the UCC applies. The Code provides remedies protecting the expectation interest for breaches of such contracts. These remedies are a combination of traditional contract remedies and the creativity of the chief architect of the Code, Professor Karl Llewellyn.[34] It is important to recognize the symmetry between UCC remedies and traditional contract law remedies. Discussion of UCC remedies and their effect on traditional contract remedies, therefore, appear throughout this Chapter. Since international contracts for the sale of goods are now governed in some fifty-eight nations by the Vienna Convention (the United Nations Convention on Contract for the International Sale of Goods or CISG), CISG remedies are also considered throughout this Chapter. Finally, a summary of UCC and CISG remedies appears at the end of this Chapter for convenient reference to those remedies.

§ 119   THE EXPECTATION INTEREST — BREACH BY BUILDER — COST OF COMPLETION VERSUS DIMINUTION IN VALUE

[A]   The General Concept

If the expectation interest normally envisions protecting an aggrieved party by placing him in the position he would have occupied had the contract been performed,[35] how is that interested protected? The aggrieved party should recover any loss in value under his particular circumstances,[36] as well as any other loss caused by the breach, including incidental

---

[33] RESTATEMENT 2d § 345(f).

[34] See Peters, *Remedies for Breach of Contracts Relation to the Sale of Goods Under the Uniform Commercial Code*, 73 YALE L.J. 199 (1963).

[35] See Crest, Inc. v. Costco Wholesale Corp., 128 Wn. App. 760, 770, 115 P. 3d 349, 354 (2005); Vanderpool v. Higgs, 10 Kan. App. 2d 1, 690 P.2d 391 (1984); Thorp Sales Corp. v. Gyuro Grading Co., 111 Wis. 2d 431, 331 N.W.2d 342 (1983). See also RESTATEMENT 2d § 344 and comment b. See also UCC § 1-305(a) (formerly § 1-106(1)): "The remedies provided by [the Uniform Commercial Code] shall be liberally administered to the end that the aggrieved party may be put in as good a position as if the other party had fully performed. . . ." Professors Cooter and Eisenberg in their article, *Damages for Breach of Contract*, 73 CAL. L. REV. 1432, 1468 (1985), summarize three meanings of "expectation": (1) "expectation principle," which is the usual understanding of placing the injured promisee in the position he would have been in if the contract had been performed, (2) "expectation theory," which bases damages on the measure that parties situated like the contracting parties probably would have agreed to if they had bargained under ideal conditions and addressed the damage issue, and (3) "statistical expectation," where a party makes a number of comparable contracts with a known probable rate of breach in which case he should enjoy the overall profit level he expected to achieve, rather that the profit level he would have achieved if the rate of breach were zero. The authors conclude that where the expectation principle and expectation theory diverge, as where a seller has a statistical expectation, the theory rather than the principle should govern. Consequently, where damages would be measured by the seller's lost volume (to be discussed later in this chapter in the exploration of UCC § 2-708(2)), the parties would probably have agreed (expectation theory) to a much smaller measure of damages, such as the forfeit of a deposit rather than the seller's profit on the contract of sale which has been breached, had the parties consciously adverted to the damages question.

[36] See RESTATEMENT 2d § 347(a) and comment b.

and consequential damages.[37] This is sometimes stated as allowing compensation for gains prevented as well as losses incurred, i.e., the injured promisee is entitled to recover the economic equivalent of the performance promised at the time and place specified in the contract, plus any losses incurred or gains prevented through failure of performance. To accomplish this end, the aggrieved party receives substitutional relief, i.e., compensation in money for defeated expectations in place of the breaching promisor's performance.[38] If, however, a breach occurs prior to the completion of the promisee's performance, he is saved from the time, effort, and expense of completion because of the promisor's breach. Any saved costs or other loss that the promisee has avoided by not having to perform must be deducted from the money damages to which he is otherwise entitled.[39] This is in accordance with the general principle that an aggrieved party may not recover damages that could have been avoided without undue risk, burden or humiliation.[40]

[B]   Cost of Completion Versus Diminution in Value — Builder's Breach

The principle that the aggrieved party is entitled to the economic equivalent of the promised performance as well as damages for attendant losses can be easily applied in the garden variety case. If, for example, a builder promises to construct a building and he fails to complete performance in accordance with the contract, it would appear obvious that any additional cost to the owner in having another builder complete the structure would be the measure of damages. The normal remedy in such cases is to award damages for *cost of completion*.[41]

Assume a contractor has agreed to construct a building for $400,000 and, after completing a portion of the building for which he has received $200,000, he refuses or is unable to complete the building. If the reasonable cost of completing the building by another contractor is $300,000, the total cost of the building is $500,000. To fulfill the owner's expectation of receiving the completed building for the contract price of $400,000, the court will award the owner $100,000 in damages.[42] This straightforward analysis becomes complicated, however,

---

[37] P.C. Data Ctrs. of Pa., Inc. v. Federal Express Corp., 113 F. Supp. 2d 709, 715 (M.D. Pa. 2000). See also RESTATEMENT 2d § 347(b) and comment c, describing incidental damages as any reasonable effort to avoid loss, and consequential damages as losses such as injury to person or property resulting from the breach.

[38] The object is accomplished "so far as can be done by money" in the position the aggrieved party would have occupied had there been no breach. Pelletier v. Pelletier Dev. Co., 1996 Conn. Super. LEXIS 748, at *13 (Conn. Super. Ct. Mar. 14, 1996).

[39] See In re Kellett Aircraft Corp., 191 F.2d 231, 236 (3d Cir. 1951); Bucholz v. Green Bros. Co., 272 Mass. 49, 172 N.E. 101 (1930). RESTATEMENT 2d § 347(c). If, for example, a builder is not permitted to complete a construction contract through the repudiation of the owner, the saved cost of completion is normally deducted from the contract price to arrive at the builder's measure of expectation damage recovery. This and other formulas will be explored in the next section.

[40] RESTATEMENT 2d § 350. This is often referred to as the mitigation principle or principle of avoidable consequences. It will be explored later in this chapter.

[41] See, e.g., *Pelletier*, note 38*supra*.

[42] This example is set forth in Wells v. Minor, 578 N.E.2d 1337, 1344 (Ill. App. Ct. 4th Dist. 1991). Another case in the same jurisdiction provides a realistic example. In a contract for the construction of a house at a price of $89,000, the builder's performance was defective. The buyer had paid $76,400 to the dismissed builder, and then paid $27,407 to repair the structure. Thus, the buyer had paid $103,807 for the house it expected to receive for $89,000. The trial court awarded plaintiff the cost of repair $27,407. This calculation would have provided the buyer with the completed

where the cost of completing performance substantially exceeds the increased value the promisee would have enjoyed had the contract been performed.

In the classic case of *Jacob & Youngs, Inc. v. Kent*,[43] the builder used the wrong brand of galvanized pipe that was physically identical to the specified brand in the construction of a house. The normal measure of damages would have been the cost of replacing all of the pipe encased in the walls throughout the house which would have involved considerable deconstruction and reconstruction of the house at great expense. The defect in the builder's performance was not a structural defect. Had the defect been structural, exposing the owner to a dangerous condition, the cost of replacement (sometimes known as cost of repair) would have been appropriate.[44] Absent any idiosyncratic reason why the specified brand had to be used,[45] the use of a substitute brand that was physically identical should permit the owner to recover only the diminution in the value of the property caused by the breach where the cost of completion would be grossly disproportionate to the loss in value. In an opinion by Judge Cardozo, the court refused to permit recovery of the cost of replacement and relegated the owner to the difference in value which, it suggested, would be either nominal or nothing in this case. It is fashionable to suggest this result as an avoidance of "economic waste."[46] This is, however, misleading since, if damages were awarded for cost of completion, the typical plaintiff would not destroy the property to replace the existing pipe with identical pipe simply to replace the brand name.[47] Where a subcontractor's concrete slab was defective, the owner insisted that it be replaced instead of repaired. The subcontractor's claim that the replacement involved economic waste was rejected by the court since the contract provided that it had to be replaced. There was no evidence of waste to support the subcontractor's claim.[48]

The cost of repair or replacement (cost of completion) is the normal remedy since it clearly provides the aggrieved party with his expectation recovery[49] and the cost of completion is

---

house for a total price of $76,593-less than the buyer expected to pay. The appellate court reversed. To place the buyer in the position it would have occupied had the contract been performed required the buyer to receive the house it expected to receive, without defects, for a total price of $89,000. Having spent $103,807 to achieve this result, the buyer was entitled to the difference between the cost to complete the house and the original contract price, i.e. a recovery of $14,807. The trial court's calculation would have placed the buyer in a *better* position than he would have occupied had the contract been performed. Castricone v. Michaud, 223 Ill. App. 3d 138, 164 Ill. Dec. 862, 583 N.E.2d 1184 (3d Dist. 1991).

[43] 230 N.Y. 239, 129 N.E. 889 (1921).

[44] *See* Rivers v. Deane, 619 N.Y.S.2d 419 (App. Div. 4th Dep't 1994); Kenney v. Medlin Constr. & Realty Co., 68 N.C. App. 339, 315 S.E.2d 311 (1984). *See also* RESTATEMENT 2d § 348 ill. 3.

[45] If the house was to be owned by the president of the company whose brand was specified in the contract, a reason for the use of that brand and no other, including a physically identical product, would be shown. Even in that situation, however, Judge Cardozo apparently would have required that specification to be an express condition precedent to the duty of the owner before deciding that the pipe had to be replaced with all of the attendant costs of that replacement.

[46] *See* FIRST RESTATEMENT § 346 comment b.

[47] *See* RESTATEMENT 2d § 348 comment c.

[48] *Crest, Inc., supra* note 35.

[49] *See* Gilbert v. Caldwell, 112 Idaho 386, 732 P.2d 355 (Ct. App. 1987) (comparing § 346(1)(a) of the FIRST RESTATEMENT with § 348(2) of the RESTATEMENT 2d). Under the UCC, § 2-714(2), the measure of damages is the difference at the time and place of acceptance between the value of the goods accepted and the value they would have had if they had been as warranted. Many courts have concluded that a useful application of this measure is found in the cost of repair or replacement. *See, e.g.*, Vista St. Clair, Inc. v. Landry's Commercial Furnishings, Inc., 57 Or. App. 254, 643 P.2d 1378 (1982); Winchester v. McCulloch Bros. Garage, Inc., 388 So. 2d 927 (Ala. 1980); S. H. Nevers Corp. v. Husky Hydraulics, Inc., 408 A.2d 676 (Me. 1979); Morrow v. New Moon Homes, 548 P.2d 279 (Alaska 1976).

typically less than the loss in value.[50] The cost of completion measure, therefore, would be mandated by the principle of avoidable damages, i.e., any losses that can be reasonably avoided should be avoided.[51] The same principle, however, should restrict recovery to the diminished value of the property where awarding cost of completion damages would result in a substantial windfall to the aggrieved party. Where, for example, repairs were not completed according to specifications, diminution in value cause by the failure to meet all of the specifications would have been very minor. The court upheld a diminution in value measure of damages.[52] Where the cost of repairing defects that were not structural in a $7000 pool amounted to $11,381, the court remanded the case for a determination of diminution in value.[53] Similarly, where a contract for the sale of a sixteen-year-old building included an express warranty of its condition at that age, the court found a breach of warranty. Replacing sixteen-year-old windows and siding of the building with new windows and siding, however, would enhance its value far in excess of its warranted condition. Instead of the cost of repair damages, the court awarded the plaintiff the difference in the value of the building as warranted and the value of the building received.[54] But where the cost of completion is not clearly disproportionate to the value expected, or where structural defects are discovered, courts agree that cost of completion should be the measure.[55]

In a well-known case,[56] the owner operated a gravel excavation plant on certain land which he leased to the defendant for a term of seven years. The lease contained a clause requiring the lessee to leave the property at a uniform grade at the completion of the term. The defendant failed to perform that promise and the plaintiff sought to recover the cost of completion, which was found to be approximately $60,000. The diminished value of the premises, however, was only $12,000, i.e., if the $60,000 had been expended to provide the uniform grade required by the lease, the increase in value to this industrial tract would have been only one-fifth the cost of the improvement. Yet, the court held that plaintiff was entitled to the cost of completion. The court emphasized the "wilful" nature of the defendant's breach, which is a dubious requirement.[57] It also attempted to distinguish cases involving "economic waste." As suggested earlier,[58] "economic waste" can be misleading in any event because it is more than unlikely that the aggrieved party will spend five times the value of the improvement to complete the contract in accordance with its literal terms.[59] The court failed to inquire into

---

[50] RESTATEMENT 2d § 348 comment c.

[51] RESTATEMENT 2d § 350. *See also* Smart v. Tidwell Indus., Inc., 668 S.W.2d 605 (Mo. Ct. App. 1984) (wherever evidence shows cost of repair to be less than diminution in value, cost of repair should be the measure whether applied to warranty or other contracts cases).

[52] Toth v. Spitzer, 1998 Ohio App. LEXIS 6063 (Ohio Ct. App., Montgomery County Dec. 18, 1998).

[53] Mayfield v. Swafford, 106 Ill. App. 3d 610, 435 N.E.2d 953 (5th Dist. 1982).

[54] Tapestry Village Place Indep. Living, L.L.C. v. Village Place at Marion, L. P., 2009 Iowa App. LEXIS 331 (2009). See UCC § 2-714(2) measuring damages for breach of warranty of nonconforming goods accepted by the buyer as the difference between the value of the goods accepted and the value they would have had if they had been as warranted.

[55] *See* Eastlake Constr. Co. v. Hess, 102 Wash. 2d 30, 686 P.2d 465 (1984).

[56] Groves v. John Wunder Co., 205 Minn. 163, 286 N.W. 235 (1939).

[57] Many courts insist that the diminution in value concept should not apply if the breach is "wilful." Yet, a good faith albeit wilful deviation from construction plans should not be a precluding factor. See Kangas v. Trust, 110 Ill. App. 3d 876, 441 N.E.2d 1271 (2d Dist. 1982), and cases cited therein.

[58] *See supra* text at note 44.

[59] In this case, in fact, the plaintiff did not expend the settlement which approximated the damage award for this purpose. *See* J. DAWSON & W. HARVEY, CASES ON CONTRACTS AND CONTRACT REMEDIES 28 (1959).

the purpose of the contract, i.e., if the promisee seeks a specific result, even if that result would diminish rather than enhance the value of the property, he is entitled to that result.

Assume the extreme hypothetical of a party who desires the erection of a structure on his property that will actually diminish its objective market value. The contract price is $100,000 and the promisor fails to perform. A reasonable substitute contractor requires $200,000. Should the promisor succeed in his defense that the valuation of the property would have diminished had he performed and, therefore, the plaintiff has suffered no damage? The classic retort is found in an old case: "A man may do what he will with his own, . . . and if he chooses to erect a monument to his caprice or folly on his premises, and employs and pays another to do it, it does not lie with the defendant who has been so employed and paid for building it, to say that his own performance would not be beneficial to the plaintiff."[60] Where, however, the promisee seeks no particular result but is interested exclusively in net economic gain, as where the property is held strictly for investment purposes, a court may properly conclude that the diminution in value standard ought to be applied.[61]

Another manifestation of the purpose of the promisee is found in a well-known case where the defendant agreed to restore the farm on which the plaintiffs lived to approximate its original condition after completing a strip mining operation. The cost of the restorative work was estimated at $29,000, which would have enhanced the value of the land by only $300 and the total value of the farm was only $5000. It was clear that the plaintiffs were insistent upon the original contractual commitment of the defendant to restore the land. The court overturned a $5000 jury verdict because it believed that the plaintiffs were entitled only to diminution in value of $300.[62] The case, however, is similar to the construction of a grotesque structure on the land. The plaintiffs were, apparently, untutored and unwise concerning the cost of restoration. They clearly required a result under the contract, i.e., the restoration of their land. Where the property is the dwelling place of a party who insists upon a particular result on that property, the cost of completion appears to be the appropriate measure to protect the expectation interest.[63] Moreover, the result in this case is particularly difficult to accept since it actively encourages nonperformance.[64]

If the diminution in value is difficult to prove with reasonable certainty, the cost of completion measure should apply, even if it appears that the result is something of a windfall for the plaintiff.[65]

---

[60] Chamberlain v. Parker, 45 N.Y. 569, 572 (1871).

[61] *See* Advanced, Inc. v. Wilks, 711 P.2d 524 (Alaska 1985).

[62] Peevyhouse v. Garland Coal & Mining Co., 382 P.2d 109 (Okla. 1962), *cert. denied*, 375 U.S. 906, 84 S. Ct. 196, 11 L. Ed. 2d 145 (1963). The jury award of $5000 (the value of the farm) appeared to have no basis except sympathy for the plaintiff. In another case, there was testimony that $56,350 would be required to cure defects in an otherwise structurally sound house with a market value of $93,000. Another witness testified that the cost of curing the defects would be $800. Diminution in value estimates ranged from $83,000 to $800. The jury awarded $9000, which the court upheld because the amount was within the outside limits of the testimony. Rands v. Forest Lake Lumber Mart, Inc., 402 N.W.2d 565 (Minn. Ct. App. 1987).

[63] *See* Kangas v. Trust, 110 Ill. App. 3d 876, 441 N.E.2d 1271 (2d Dist. 1982).

[64] *See* Vernon, *Expectancy Damages for Breach of Contract: A Primer and Critique*, 1976 Wash. U. L.Q. 179, 228.

[65] *See* Restatement 2d § 348 comment c.

§ 120 EXPECTATION, RELIANCE, AND RESTITUTION INTERESTS — BREACH BY OWNER

Where a builder breaches a construction contract with an owner, we have already seen an example of how courts protect the owner's expectation interest by providing the owner with the cost of completion unless that remedy would foster unreasonable economic waste.[66] We now consider the converse situation where the owner breaches the contract.

[A] Expectation Interest of Builder

Assume an owner breaches a construction contract with a builder where the contract price is $100,000 and the cost of the builder's performance is $90,000. If the builder has not yet begun performance at the time of the owner's breach, the builder expects to receive $10,000 as the benefit of his bargain. A simple formula yields this result: Contract price, or any unpaid portion thereof, ($100,000) minus cost of completion ($90,000) provides the builder with his expectation interest of $10,000. If the builder had constructed a portion of the building at the time of breach and the cost of the work already done is $50,000, leaving $40,000 as the cost of completion, the simple formula of contract price minus cost of completion results in a recovery of $60,000, i.e., $100,000 minus $40,000. Here, the builder has been compensated for his loss of bargain (or profit), amounting to $10,000, and he has also been compensated for his cost of performance to the point where the owner breached, i.e., his out-of-pocket or reliance expenditure of $50,000, which he has expended in performing prior to the breach. The critical element in this formula is the *cost of completion* which may create difficulties of proof. In the absence of contrary evidence, the builder may succeed in proving this amount ($40,000) by simply subtracting the cost of reliance (the amount already expended, i.e., $50,000) from the total cost of complete performance ($90,000).[67]

[B] Reliance Interest — Cost of Completion Cannot Be Shown

An alternate formula for recovery by the builder may be stated as follows: The profit upon the contract (contract price less builder's cost of construction — both expended and to be expended) plus the cost of work actually performed.[68] Under our illustration, the builder's recovery will be identical to that of the first formula: The contract price of $100,000 minus the builder's cost of construction expended and to be expended of $90,000 plus the cost of the works actually performed, $50,000 = $60,000. Why use this formula instead of the first formula of contract price minus the cost of completing which yields the same result and is more simple in application? Where the cost of completion is easily shown, this formula is unnecessary. If, however, the critical element of cost of completion is impossible to prove because the builder cannot demonstrate that he would have made a profit, the first, simple formula (contract price minus cost of completion) is useless. While the second formula cannot be used in its entirety under these circumstances, it does express the element of the reliance interest, i.e., the cost of work already performed ($50,000), and recovery of that portion of the

---

[66] See text at note 40 *supra.*

[67] Since the burden of proof is on the builder, mere speculation as to the cost of completion will not be sufficient to sustain a recovery. *See* Patterson, *Builder's Measure of Recovery for Breach of Contract,* 31 COLUM. L. REV. 1286, 1292–93 (1931).

[68] Warner v. McLay, 92 Conn. 427, 103 A. 113 (1918). *See also* Frank Horton & Co. v. Cook Elec. Co., 356 F.2d 485 (7th Cir. 1966), *cert. denied,* 384 U.S. 952, 86 S. Ct. 1572, 16 L. Ed. 2d 548 (1966).

second formula may be permitted. While the contractor would not recover its profit, it would, at least, recover the amount expended-the reliance interest. Thus, where a contractor agreed to perform construction work that was experimental in nature and the owner breached, the evidence did not allow the builder to prove whether it would have made any profit or whether a loss would have occurred since the cost of completion could not be proved with reasonable certainty. In rejecting the argument of the breaching party that no recovery should be permitted, the court said: It does not lie, however, in the mouth of the party, who has voluntarily and wrongfully put an end to the contract, to say that the party injured has not been damaged at least to the amount of what he has been induced fairly and in good faith to lay out and expend, including his own services, after making allowance for the value of materials on hand; at least it does not lie in the mouth of the party in fault to say this, unless he can show that the expenses of the party injured have been extravagant, and unnecessary for the purpose of carrying out the contract.[69]

Where the cost of completion can be proved, a builder may still desire to recover his reliance interest where his expectation interest would result in a loss because the builder has entered into a losing contract. Thus, where the contract price is $100,000, the cost of work already performed is $50,000 (reliance), and the cost of completion is $60,000, the simple expectation formula of contract price minus cost of completion would provide a recovery of $40,000 — $10,000 less than the cost of the work done. An injured party such as the builder has a right to pursue reliance damages as an alternative to expectation damages.[70] If, however, the breaching party can prove with reasonable certainty that the builder would have sustained a loss on the completed project, that loss is deducted from the builder's recovery. Thus, where the builder seeks his reliance interest of $50,000, the owner will prove the cost of completion of $60,000, thereby precluding a full reliance recovery.[71] The net effect is as follows: if the builder seeks to recover an amount beyond his reliance interest, the burden of persuasion is upon him to show such profit, which he would normally show by evidence of the cost of completion. If he cannot show such profit, he is relegated to his reliance interest. He may, however, recover even less than his reliance interest if the owner can show a cost of completion resulting in a loss to the builder. The burden of persuasion as to such loss is upon the owner.

As we will see in a subsequent exploration, courts will recognize the protection of the reliance interest in any type of contract that is breached.[72]

[C]   Restitution Interest — Contract Damages

For the builder who has entered into a losing contract, we have seen that his expectation interest and his reliance interest will reflect the loss he would have incurred had the contract been completed. There is, however, another alternative for such a builder. Assume the contract price is $100,000 and the builder has substantially underbid. When he completes one-half of the performance, the cost of the work completed is already $150,000 and the cost of completion is another $150,000. If he completes the contract, he will receive the contract price

---

[69] United States v. Behan, 110 U.S. 338, 28 L. Ed. 168 (1884). *See also* RESTATEMENT 2d § 349 ill. 3.

[70] RESTATEMENT 2d § 349.

[71] *See* L. Albert & Son v. Armstrong Rubber Co., 178 F.2d 182 (2d Cir. 1949). *See also* Fuller & Perdue, *The Reliance Interest in Contract Damages*, 46 YALE L.J. 52, 75–80 (1936), and RESTATEMENT 2d § 349, ill. 4.

[72] *See* § 122[D][1], *infra*.

of $100,000, even though it will have cost $300,000 to perform this losing contract. If the owner materially breaches the contract when the project is half completed, assume the reasonable value of the benefit which the builder has conferred upon the owner at that point is $150,000. If the builder seeks his expectation interest, he will recover nothing: $100,000 minus $150,000 (cost of completion) equals a minus quantity. As suggested earlier, the builder may not recover his reliance interest since the owner can prove with reasonable certainty that the project would have been completed at a loss. If, however, the builder elects to recover his restitution interest, the value of the benefit conferred at the time of the breach is $150,000. The builder may recover that amount and neither the contract price of $100,000 nor proof that the contract was a losing contract will limit the recovery.[73]

[D]   Limitation on Restitution Recovery — Complete Performance

There is one significant limitation on an aggrieved party's recovery of the restitution interest. If the plaintiff has completely or substantially performed, case law precludes the protection of the restitution interest and relegates the plaintiff to the expectation interest.[74] Thus, in our example, if the builder had completely performed and conferred a benefit of $300,000, he would be relegated to his recovery of the contract price (his expectation interest) of $100,000 since he had completed performance. On the other hand, as suggested earlier, if he had completed only half of his performance, he would recover $150,000. The rule precluding the protection of the restitution interest when the plaintiff has completed performance had its origins in the common-law forms of action.[75] The modern explanation precludes such relief for the fully performing party when the only remaining performance is the payment of money to avoid involving courts in the monetary measurement of the benefit conferred, since the parties, themselves, have already made that measurement by their contract.[76] Further discussion of the restitution interest is found in a subsequent section.[77]

§ 121   THE FORESEEABILITY LIMITATION

[A]   History and Rationale — *Hadley v. Baxendale*

If all of the risks of a breach of contract were placed on a defaulting promisor, regardless of the unusual nature of the risks, a crushing burden may be imposed upon him. In the typical case, the promise is made in a time of optimism on the assumption that it will be performed. If the promisor later discovers that he cannot perform the promise or, at least, that it has become highly inexpedient for him to do so, fairness demands that some equitable division of

---

[73] "Because the doctrine of restitution looks to the reasonable value of any benefit conferred upon the defendant by the plaintiff, and is not governed by the terms of the parties' Agreement, restitution is available even if the plaintiff would have lost money on the contract if it had been fully performed." Bausch & Lomb v. Bressler, 977 F.2d 720, 730 (2d Cir. 1992).

[74] *See* Oliver v. Campbell, 43 Cal. 2d 298, 273 P.2d 15 (1954); RESTATEMENT 2d § 373(2).

[75] See 5 CORBIN § 1110, where the author suggests that it may seem strange that one who has fully performed can recover only the contract price, while another who has not fully performed can sue either on the express contract or in restitution. In the latter case, however, there was no common law action of debt permitted on the contract, whereas the plaintiff who had fully performed had an action in debt. Thus, the party who performed only part of the contract was permitted to bring an action in quantum meruit (restitution).

[76] John T. Brady & Co. v. Stamford, 599 A.2d 370, 377 (Conn. 1991). *See also* RESTATEMENT 2d § 373, comment b.

[77] *See* § 127, *infra*.

the risks of loss flowing from nonperformance occur so that the reasonable expectations of the promisee may be fulfilled without simultaneously placing an undue burden upon the defaulting promisor. After considerable groping,[78] a principle for the accomplishment of this aim was finally evolved and set forth in the leading case of *Hadley v. Baxendale*,[79] decided by the English Court of Exchequer in 1854. The owner of a mill, which was shut down because of a broken shaft, made a contract with the defendant to transport the shaft to another city, where it was to be used as a model for making a new one. When making the contract, the miller notified the carrier that haste in the delivery of the shaft was essential, but did not inform him that the operation of the mill was dependent upon the prompt delivery of the shaft.[80] In an action by the miller for negligent delay in the delivery, a claim was made for damages for loss of profits from the nonoperation of the mill. On appeal from a verdict for the plaintiff, the court held that the miller should not recover for loss of such profits, since the carrier could not have been expected to anticipate that the operation of the mill would be suspended by the delay in the delivery of the shaft, as no notice to that effect had been given him. The court elaborated the rule to be applied in measuring the damages:

> Where two parties have made a contract which one of them has broken, the damages which the other party ought to receive in respect of such breach of contract should be such as may fairly and reasonably be considered either arising naturally, i.e., according to the usual course of things, from such breach of contract itself, or such as may reasonably be supposed to have been in the contemplation of both parties, at the time they made the contract, as the probable result of the breach of it. Now, if the special circumstances under which the contract was actually made were communicated by the plaintiffs to the defendants, and thus made known to both parties, the damages resulting from the breach of such a contract, which they would reasonably contemplate, would be the amount of the injury which would ordinarily follow from a breach of contract under these special circumstances so known and communicated. But, on the other hand, if these special circumstances were wholly unknown to the party breaking the contract, he, at the most, could only be supposed to have had in contemplation the amount of injury which would arise generally, and in the great multitude of cases not affected by any special circumstances, from such a breach of contract. For, had the special circumstances been known, the parties might have specially provided for the breach of contract by special terms as to the damages in that case; and of this advantage it would be very unjust to deprive them.

This principle, known popularly as the rule of *Hadley v. Baxendale*, has demonstrated a remarkable record of consistent application since it was first announced in 1854. It has been universally accepted by our courts as a correct statement of the principle in accordance with which the extent of the recovery is to be determined in an action for breach of contract.[81] It has

---

[78] *See* Washington, *Damages in Contract at Common Law*, 47 LAW Q. REV. 345 (1931), and 48 LAW Q. REV. 90 (1932).

[79] 9 Ex. 341, 156 Eng. Rep. 145 [1854].

[80] In the reporter's summation of the facts in this case (9 Ex. at 344), the statement is made that the carrier *was* informed that the mill was stopped because of the broken shaft. This statement is inconsistent with the court's understanding of the fact situation. The reporter's summation was declared erroneous in Victoria Laundry (Windsor), Ltd. v. Newman Indus., 2 K.B. 528, 537, 1 All E.R. 997, 1001 [1949].

[81] *See, e.g.*, Leister v. Dovetail, Inc., 546 F.3d 865, 883 (7th Cir. 2008); Citgo Petroleum Corp. v. Ranger Enterprises, Inc., 632 F. Supp. 2d 878, 901 (W. D. Wis. 2009); MLK, Inc. v. University of Kansas, 23 Kan. App. 2d 876, 886, 940 P.2d 1158, 1164 (1997); Florida E. C.R. Co. v. Beaver St. Fisheries, Inc., 537 So. 2d 1065 (Fla. Dist. Ct. App. 1989); Kenford Co. v. County of Erie, 73 N.Y.2d 312 (1989); Midland Hotel Corp. v. Reuben H. Donnelley Corp., 188 Ill. 2d 306, 515

been codified in the UCC.[82]

More than ninety years after it was first announced, another English court explained the two rules in *Hadley v. Baxendale*:[83]

> Everyone, as a reasonable person, is taken to know the "ordinary course of things" and consequently what loss is liable to result from a breach of contract in that ordinary course. This is the subject matter of the "first rule" in *Hadley v. Baxendale*. But to this knowledge, which a contract-breaker is assumed to possess whether he actually possesses it or not, there may have to be added in a particular case knowledge which he actually possesses, of special circumstances outside the "ordinary course of things," of such a kind that a breach in those special circumstances would be liable to cause more loss. Such a case attracts the operation of the "second rule" so as to make additional loss also recoverable.

Still another way of stating the test is to look upon the "first rule" of *Hadley v. Baxendale* as *imputed* foreseeability or contemplation — that which any reasonable person should have foreseen — and the "second rule" as actual foreseeability or contemplation — what the reasonable person with particular knowledge should have foreseen. The test is objective. The extent of the recovery is to be measured, not by what the defendant actually foresaw when he made the contract, but by what a hypothetical, reasonable person in the position of the defendant, with the defendant's knowledge of the circumstances surrounding the transaction, could reasonably have been expected to foresee, had he directed his attention to the effect of a breach. If the losses suffered or the gains prevented by the breach are unusual, it becomes necessary to ascertain whether the defendant was made aware of the special circumstances out of which they grew,[84] but, if they are no more than the usual consequence of such a breach as has occurred, no inquiry as to the state of the defendant's knowledge is necessary.

In summary, it is important to note the following elements of the foreseeability concept: (1) It is a *limitation* on the recovery of plaintiffs. Liability will *not* attach for damages which were not within the contemplation of the parties or brought within such contemplation through special knowledge at the time the contract was made.[85] (2) Though the opinion of Baron Alderson speaks of "the contemplation of both parties," the modern versions of the rule suggest that only the foreseeability of the breaching party is relevant.[86] (3) The foreseeability of *probable* consequences must be determined as of the time of contract formation. If additional

---

N.E.2d 61, 113 Ill. Dec. 252 (1987); Spang Indus. Inc., Ft. Pitt Bridge Div. v. Aetna Cas. & Sur. Co., 512 F.2d 365 (2d Cir. 1975). *See also* RESTATEMENT 2d § 351.

[82] *See* UCC § 2-715(2)(a): "Consequential damages resulting from the seller's breach include: (a) any loss resulting from general or particular requirements and needs of which the seller at the time of contracting had reason to know and which could not reasonably be prevented by cover or otherwise. . . ." *See* Cricket Alley Corp. v. Data Terminal Sys., Inc., 240 Kan. 661, 732 P.2d 719 (1987) (Section 2-715 of the Code simply codifies *Hadley v. Baxendale*). *See also* Troxler Elecs. Labs., Inc. v. Solitron Devices, Inc., 722 F.2d 81 (4th Cir. 1983); Sun-Maid Raisin Growers v. Victor Packing Co., 146 Cal. App. 3d 787, 194 Cal. Rptr. 612 (5th Dist. 1983).

[83] Victoria Laundry (Windsor), Ltd. v. Newman Indus., 2 K.B. 528, 1 All E.R. 997 [1949].

[84] See Cardozo, C.J., in Kerr S.S. Co. v. Radio Corp. of Am., 245 N.Y. 284, 157 N.E. 140, 142, *cert. denied*, 275 U.S. 57, 48 S. Ct. 118, 72 L. Ed. 424 (1927), in regard to what constitutes knowledge of special circumstances.

[85] It is a default rule. Absent the rule, the parties could limit damages by their agreement. See Melvin A Eisenberg, *The Principle of Hadley v. Baxendale*, 80 Calif. L. Rev. 563, 566 (1992).

[86] "[T]he promisor is not required to compensate the injured party for injuries that *he had no reason to foresee* as the probable result of his breach when he made the contract" (emphasis added). Traynor, J., in Coughlin v. Blair, 41 Cal. 2d 587, 603, 262 P.2d 305, 314 (1953). *See also* UCC § 2-715(2)(a); RESTATEMENT 2d § 351.

knowledge comes to the promisor subsequent to that time, it is irrelevant.[87] (4) The objective test is used — the defaulting promisor is liable not only for those consequences which he actually thought were *probable* but also those which a reasonable person *should* have considered *probable*.[88]

[1] CISG and Foreseeability

The Vienna Convention on Contracts for the International Sale of Goods allows damages consisting of a "sum equal to the loss, including loss of profit, suffered by the other party as a consequence of the breach."[89] The foreseeability principle in CISG has been viewed as a reiteration of the *Hadley v. Baxendale* rule.[90] The CISG version, however, is not identical. CISG damages are limited to the losses that the breaching party "foresaw or ought to have foreseen" at the time the contract was formed "as a *possible* consequence of the breach."[91] The *Hadley* rule is invariably stated as limiting damages to the *probable* consequences of the breach.[92] By its terms, the CISG test is broader than the *Hadley* rule. The failure to observe this difference may be attributable to the tendency of courts to interpret CISG through a domestic law lens, notwithstanding the expressed CISG aspiration that "regard is to be had" to its international character.[93]

[B]   Nomenclature — "General," "Special," "Consequential" and "Incidental" Damages

"General" damages are said to arise naturally from a breach of contract in the sense that they are within "the common experience of ordinary persons"[94] and are, therefore, implied or presumed by the law. Because they arise in the ordinary course of events, they manifest the "first rule" of *Hadley v. Baxendale*.[95] General damages measure the market value of the very

---

[87] *See* Hale v. Stoughton Hosp. Ass'n, 126 Wis. 2d 267, 376 N.W.2d 89 (Ct. App. 1985) (like tort damages, contract damages compensate the aggrieved party but are limited by foreseeability at the time of contract formation). *See also* Eastern Advertising Co. v. Shapiro, 263 Mass. 228, 234, 161 N.E. 240, 242 (1928) ("The defendant was liable for the consequences of the breach, which were reasonably foreseeable at the time the contract was entered into as probable if the contract were broken."). *See also* Holmes, J., in Globe Ref. Co. v. Landa Cotton Oil Co., 190 U.S. 540, 544, 23 S. Ct. 754, 756, 47 L. Ed. 1171 (1903) ("The suggestion thrown out by Bramwell, B., in Gee v. Lancashire & Yorkshire Ry. Co., 6 H. & N. 211, 218, that perhaps notice after the contract was made and before breach would be enough, is not accepted by the later decisions. . . . The consequences must be contemplated at the time of the making of the contract."). For a comparison of *foreseeable* damages under *Hadley v. Baxendale* with the limitation of *foreseeable liability* in tort law, see Evra Corp. v. Swiss Bank Corp., 673 F.2d 951 (7th Cir.), *cert. denied*, 459 U.S. 1017, 103 S. Ct. 377, 74 L. Ed. 2d 511 (1982).

[88] "The assumption cannot be less than this, that whatever a carrier could ascertain by diligent inquiry as to the nature of the undisclosed transaction, this he should be deemed to have ascertained, and charged with damages accordingly." Cardozo, C.J., in Kerr S.S. Co. v. Radio Corp. of Am., 245 N.Y. 284, 290, 157 N.E. 140, 142, *cert. denied*, 275 U.S. 557, 48 S. Ct. 118, 72 L. Ed. 424 (1927).

[89] CISG Art. 74.

[90] Delchi Carrier SpA v. Rotorex Corp., 71 F.3d 1024, 1030 (2d Cir. 1995).

[91] CISG Art. 74.

[92] RESTATEMENT 2d § 351(1).

[93] CISG Art. 7. See Murray, *Ten Years of the United Nations Sales Convention: The Neglect of CISG: A Workable Solution*, 17 J. L. & COM. 365 (1998).

[94] RESTATEMENT 2d § 351, comment b.

[95] See text at note 85 *supra*.

performance promised.[96] If a seller fails to deliver promised goods or services, it is within the common experience of ordinary persons that the buyer will purchase substitute goods or services elsewhere. If the buyer must pay more for the substitute goods or services, the buyer's additional cost is an ordinary loss that reasonable parties are presumed to foresee. Damages in the amount of the difference between the original contract price and the higher substitute purchase price, however, may not adequately compensate the injured party, i.e., such damages may not place that party in the full position she reasonably expected to be in as a result of the contract.

The failure to deliver goods or services (or the failure to deliver them in accordance with the contract) may have caused other losses within the "second rule" of *Hadley v. Baxendale* — losses that were not within the common experience of ordinary persons at the time the contract was formed. The buyer may have been precluded from operating her business because the goods or services were not delivered at all or on time. As in *Hadley v. Baxendale* itself, the failure to deliver the repaired shaft on time precluded the operation of the mill during the period of delay. If such a loss is unforeseeable to the ordinary party in the position of the seller of goods or services, there is no recovery of damages for this kind of loss. If at the time of contract formation, however, the seller is made aware of the "special" circumstances that could give rise to such unusual losses, the seller is liable for these additional "special" damages.[97] "Special" damages "are measured, not by the value of the promised performance alone [the goods or services themselves] but by the gains such performance could produce for collateral reasons, or the loss that is produced by the absence of such performance."[98]

"Special" damages are often called "consequential" damages,[99] but the term "consequential" is unclear.[100] It is, for example, common to refer to lost profits as "consequential" damages.[101] The term, however, can be misleading. Where, for example, a wholesaler fails to deliver a product to a retailer, the ordinary profit that the retailer would earn on the resale of the product is certainly within the ordinary experience of the typical wholesaler. It is only where the retailer made an arrangement with a customer to resell the product at an extraordinary profit that the wholesaler would not naturally or ordinarily be aware of such "special" circumstances unless it had been so informed at the time the contract was made.[102]

---

[96] MRO Communs., Inc. v. AT&T, 1999 U.S. App. LEXIS 32522, at *14 (9th Cir. Dec. 13, 1999).

[97] RESTATEMENT 2d § 351, comment b.

[98] *MRO Communs.*, *supra* note 96.

[99] "Special" and "consequential" are terms applied to damages which result other than in the ordinary course of events. Mitsui O.S.K. Lines, Ltd. v. CONRAIL, 327 N.J. Super. 343, 743 A.2d 362, 364 (App. Div. 2000).

[100] "There has been substantial confusion in the courts and among litigants about what consequential damages actually are. . . ." AM/PM Franchise Assn. v. Atlantic Richfield Co., 526 Pa. 110, 118 584 A. 2d 915, 919 (1990).

[101] *See, e.g.*, Sullivan Indus., Inc. v. Double Seal Glass Co., 192 Mich. App. 333, 480 N.W.2d 623 (1991).

[102] UCC § 2-715(2)(a) defines "consequential damages" as "any loss resulting from the *general* or *particular* requirements and needs of which the seller at the time of contracting had reason to know. . . ." (emphasis supplied). Thus, "consequential" damages emanating from the general needs of a buyer which a seller is presumed to know at the time the contract is made would be recoverable under the "first rule" of Hadley v. Baxendale, and "consequential" damages emanating from a buyer's particular needs (the "second rule" of Hadley v. Baxendale) would also be recoverable. UCC § 2-715(2)(b) includes injury to person or property proximately resulting from any breach of warranty. Under the Code, where a seller fails to deliver conforming goods and cannot "cure" the breach, the buyer may, *inter alia*, choose the "cover" remedy (a substitute purchase from another supplier-§ 2-712) and recover the difference between the contract price and the cover price together with any consequential damages.

Other damages may be "incidental," i.e., additional expenses incurred as a result of the breach. Where, for example, a seller delivers nonconforming goods to a buyer, the buyer may incur expenses in receiving, inspecting, transporting and caring for the defective goods. The buyer may incur additional expenses in purchasing substitute goods ("cover").[103] Like other damages,"incidental" expenses must be foreseeable at the time the contract is formed.

Because the terms, "general," "special," "consequential" and even "incidental" may be misleading in how they are used, the RESTATEMENT 2d does not deem it necessary to distinguish among them to apply properly the foreseeability rule of *Hadley v. Baxendale* as restated.[104]

[C]   The "Tacit Agreement" Concept

Early in the twentieth century, an attempt was made to modify the principles of *Hadley v. Baxendale*. The question was whether a defaulting promisor should be made liable for "unusual" or "special" damages[105] simply because the promisor was made aware of special circumstances at the time the contract was formed, thus bringing the knowledge of such special circumstances within the circle of foreseeability. Writing for the Supreme Court of the United States, Justice Holmes stated, "It may be said with safety that mere notice to a seller of some interest or probable action of the buyer is not enough necessarily and as [a] matter of law to charge the seller with special damage on that account if he fails to deliver the goods."[106] Earlier, the Supreme Court of Massachusetts suggested that a defendant could not be held liable for such damages "unless at the time of the sale he, in substance, assented that he would be so held."[107] The suggestion in both cases was that some form of agreement had to be found to make the defaulting promisor liable for special damages, i.e., foreseeability alone would not place the risk of such damages on the promisor. The agreement or assent, however, could be implied. There was no need to prove that an actual agreement existed. Thus, Justice Holmes stated, "the extent of liability in such cases is likely to be within his [the defendant's] contemplation, and whether it is or not, should be worked out on terms which it fairly may be presumed he would have assented to if they had been presented to mind."[108] This variation of the *Hadley v. Baxendale* concept, which attracted a limited following,[109] appears to be founded upon a mistaken notion of the purpose of the rule. The cases following the Holmes

---

[103] UCC § 2-715(1).

[104] RESTATEMENT 2d § 351, comment b.

[105] The term "unusual" herein is sometimes used synonymously with the term "consequential" or "special."

[106] Globe Ref. Co. v. Landa Cotton Oil Co., 190 U.S. 540, 545, 23 S. Ct. 754, 756, 47 L. Ed. 1171 (1903). For critical analyses of this case, see 11 WILLISTON § 1357 (3d ed. 1968); 5 CORBIN § 1010 (1951).

[107] Lonergan v. Waldo, 179 Mass. 135, 140, 60 N.E. 479, 481 (1901). *But cf. Eastern Advertising Co. v. Shapiro, supra* note 87.

[108] Globe Ref. Co. v. Landa Cotton Oil Co., 190 U.S. 540, 543, 23 S. Ct. 754, 47 L. Ed. 1171 (1903). The Massachusetts Court in *Lonergan v. Waldo, supra* note 107, states, "If knowing all the circumstances, the defendant sold the pipe without any protest or statement that he would in no event be liable for a caving of the ditch, he might be found by the jury to have assented to pay damages for its caving if that should be caused by breach of his contract to deliver the pipe."

[109] This rule is sometimes referred to as the requirement of a tacit agreement to assume the particular risk. C. MCCORMICK, LAW OF DAMAGES § 141 (1935). Prior to the decision in Erie R.R. v. Tompkins, 304 U.S. 64, 58 S. Ct. 817, 82 L. Ed. 1188 (1938), it was generally followed in lower federal courts. Since then, however, there has been a gradual erosion of its popularity. *See, e.g.*, Krauss v. Greenbarg, 137 F.2d 569 (3d Cir.), *cert. denied*, 320 U.S. 791, 64 S. Ct. 207, 88 L. Ed. 477 (1943).

suggestion seem to assume that the purpose of the rule was to afford a basis for the recovery of consequential damages. As suggested earlier, the rule is designed to exclude liability for such damages where it would be unjust to impose such liability. Some courts adopted the variation or qualification of *Hadley v. Baxendale* because the variation appeared to furnish a means of making the application of the original rule even more flexible than it would otherwise be.[110] Through it, unusual damages could readily be ruled out as too remote, even though they were clearly within the terms of the rule as originally formulated, if a court concluded that it was unjust to permit their recovery under the particular circumstances. As one opinion put it:

> [W]here the damages arise from special circumstances, and are so large as to be out of proportion to the consideration agreed to be paid for the services to be rendered under the contract, it raises a doubt at once as to whether the party would have assented to such liability, had it been called to his attention. . . . To make him liable for the special damages in such a case, there must not only be knowledge of the special circumstances, but such knowledge 'must be brought home to the party sought to be charged under such circumstances that he must know that the person he contracts with reasonably believes that he accepts the contract with the special condition attached to it.'[111]

Notwithstanding some early support, the "tacit agreement" variation of the basic rule has been expressly rejected by numerous courts,[112] the UCC,[113] and the RESTATEMENT 2d.[114] Though the literal "tacit agreement" test has been thoroughly repudiated, a court may be troubled by awards of clearly foreseeable damages in certain cases. Where, for example, a seller breached a contract to sell land at a price of $1.3 million, and there was evidence that the buyers expected to earn a twenty percent profit of $260,000 on the transaction, the buyers instead brought an action for the difference between the contract and the market price of the land — the usual damages rule — that would have resulted in a recovery of $575,000. Recognizing the "usual rule," the court stated that it "is not a rigid rule" since "[p]rinciples of contract damages do not have it as their design to put a plaintiff in a *better* position than if the defendant had performed the contract." The plaintiffs were limited to their expectation as supported by the evidence.[115] The court relied, in part, on a qualification of the *Hadley v. Baxendale* concept as found in the RESTATEMENT 2d that would allow a court to limit foreseeable damages if the court concludes that justice requires the avoidance of disproportionate compensation.[116] Relevant factors include gross disproportion between the foreseeable damages and the price charged, and informality of dealing as evidenced by the absence of a detailed record of the contract, and the consequent lack of attention to the risks involved which would

---

[110] See Bauer, *Consequential Damages in Contract*, 80 U. PA. L. REV. 687 (1931), which approves this qualification of the rule because of its added flexibility. The fact of the matter is that the rule, as it is usually stated, has been made very flexible in application by omitting to define too carefully the requirement of "notice." *See* McCormick, *supra* note 109, at 507.

[111] Hooks Smelting Co. v. Planters' Compress Co., 72 Ark. 275, 287, 79 S.W. 1052, 1056 (1904). The test continues in Arkansas. See Bank of America, N. A. v. C. D. Smith Motor Co., Inc., 353 Ark. 228, 106 S. W. 3d 425 (2003).

[112] *See* Native Alaskan Reclamation & Pest Control, Inc. v. United Bank of Alaska, 685 P.2d 1211 (Alaska 1984); Krauss v. Greenbarg, 137 F.2d 569 (3d Cir.), *cert. denied*, 320 U.S. 791, 64 S. Ct. 207, 88 L. Ed. 477 (1943).

[113] UCC § 2-715 comment 2, states, "The 'tacit agreement' test for the recovery of consequential damages is rejected."

[114] RESTATEMENT 2d § 351 comment a.

[115] Foster v. Bartolomeo, 31 Mass. App. Ct. 592, 596, 581 N.E.2d 1033, 1035 (1991) (emphasis supplied).

[116] RESTATEMENT 2d § 351(3).

typically occur in a non-commercial setting.[117] The absence of successful applications of this RESTATEMENT 2d provision, however, reflects the reluctance of courts to disturb the allocation of risks as set forth in the contract.[118]

§ 122   THE CERTAINTY LIMITATION

[A]   The Second Limitation

In addition to the foreseeability limitation on the recovery of contract damages created in the doctrine of *Hadley v. Baxendale*, American courts are often credited with devising another limitation, i.e., the requirement that the proof of contract damages be certain both in terms of the fact of loss and the amount of loss.[119] It is not difficult to find American cases adhering to the view that contract damages must not be speculative or a matter of conjecture or surmise.[120] If this requirement merely required two elements to be shown, i.e., (1) that the damage was caused by the breach, and (2) that the amount of damage claimed was actually suffered, there is no doubt as to its soundness.[121] The concept, however, was designed for a different purpose. It suggested a special requirement as to the quantum and character of proof necessary to establish these two elements.

A plaintiff must normally establish his civil case by a *preponderance* of the evidence, i.e., that it is more likely than not that a particular event occurred.[122] The certainty requirement was designed to impose a greater burden on the party claiming damages. Modern cases, however, typically require no more than a preponderance of the evidence because the original certainty limitation has been modified to a requirement of only "reasonable certainty."[123] The cases are legion in which the requirement of "reasonable certainty" is stated as the

---

[117] RESTATEMENT 2d § 351, comment f.

[118] M. M. Silta, Inc. v. Cleveland Cliffs, Inc., 572 F.3d 532 (8th Cir. 2009) (where the risks should have been anticipated, courts generally will not interfere simply because damages are disproportionate to the contract price. The defendant was a sophisticated commercial entity that had entered into many contracts like the one at issue); Perini Corp. v. Greate Bay Hotel & Casino, Inc., 129 N.J. 479, 610 A.2d 364 (1992) (damage award of $14 million where the compensation was $600,000 The court recognized the argument of gross disproportion under RESTATEMENT 2d § 351(3), but concluded that it should not apply where the transaction was in a commercial setting and the written evidence of the contract was clearly not an informal deal). *See also* All Points Towing v. City of Glendale, 153 Ariz. 115, 735 P.2d 145 (Ct. App. 1987).

[119] Professor McCormick believed that this was a distinctive contribution of American courts. *See* McCormick, *supra* note 109, at 124 (1935). See, however, *Washington, supra* note 78, 47 LAW Q. REV. at 363–66, suggesting a similar limitation in English cases. *See* Griffin v. Colver, 16 N.Y. 489, 69 Am. Dec. 718 (1858) (damages must be certain and not speculative or conjectural in either respect); Winston Cigarette Mach. Co. v. Wells-Whitehead Tobacco Co., 141 N.C. 284, 53 S.E. 885 (1906) (damages must be certain in their nature and in respect to their causes). A recent case suggests that the fact of loss as well as the amount of loss must be reasonably certain. Merion Spring Co. v. Muelles Hnos. Garcia Torres, S.A., 315 Pa. Super. 469, 462 A.2d 686 (1983).

[120] *See* Matson Plastering Co. v. Plasterers & Shophands Local No. 66, etc., 852 F.2d 1200 (9th Cir. 1988); Schon-Klingstein Meat & Grocery Co. v. Snow, 43 Colo. 538, 96 P. 182 (1908). *See also Griffin v. Colver, supra* note 119.

[121] *See* Indiana Bell Tel. Co. v. O'Bryan, 408 N.E.2d 178 (Ind. Ct. App. 1980).

[122] *See In re* Appeal in Maricopa County Juvenile Court, 138 Ariz. 282, 674 P.2d 836 (1983) (preponderance means more probable than not); *In re* Rogers, 297 N.C. 48, 253 S.E.2d 912 (1979) (preponderance is greater weight of evidence).

[123] *See, e.g.*, Hein v. M & N Feed Yards, Inc., 205 Neb. 691, 289 N.W.2d 756 (1980) (although plaintiff does not have to prove damages to a mathematical certainty, he does have the burden to prove by a preponderance of the evidence the amount of his damages with reasonable certainty).

standard.[124] Courts sometimes list "exceptions" to the certainty requirement.[125] In some cases, it is abundantly clear that it will be impossible to determine the amount of damage suffered as a result of the breach. Thus, where a publisher breached its contract to publish a book authored by the plaintiff, the amount of royalties to be earned on the unpublished book were impossible of determination.[126] In other cases involving lost profits, the determination of such profits may appear too uncertain to allow a recovery. Courts are loathe, however, to permit a breaching party to escape the consequences of his breach because damages are uncertain. It is generally agreed that doubts will be resolved against the party in breach.[127] It is important to consider how courts have reacted to the antinomies of the requirement of reasonable certainty and the policy of precluding the breaching party from avoidance of his responsibility.

[B]   Reasonable Certainty and Lost Profits — "New Business" Rule

Where a business has been established and earning profits for some time, there is little difficulty in establishing lost profits for such a business assuming that the prior and subsequent experiences are comparable.[128] Courts have also stretched to admit credible

---

[124] *See, e.g.*, Spang & Co. v. United States Steel Corp., 519 Pa. 14, 545 A.2d 861 (1988) (citing the second edition of this treatise for this proposition). *See also* Nebula Glass International, Inc. v. Reichhold, Inc., 454 F.3d 1203, 1213 (11th Cir. 2006) ("damages must be reasonably certain, not absolutely certain"); Clarke v. Bank of New York, 687 F. Supp. 863 (S.D.N.Y. 1988) (plaintiff never availed himself of the use of a law library where he would have discovered that only those damages proven with reasonable certainty are recoverable); Native Alaskan Reclamation & Pest Control, Inc. v. United Bank of Alaska, 685 P.2d 1211 (Alaska 1984) (mathematical certainty is unnecessary — only reasonable certainty required); Midwest Sheet Metal Works v. Frank Sullivan Co., 215 F. Supp. 607, 611 (D. Minn. 1963), *aff'd*, 335 F.2d 33 (8th Cir. 1964) ("Both parties agree that the measure of damages is loss of anticipated profits, and that such loss must be proved 'with a reasonable degree of certainty and exactness.'. . . But 'This rule does not call for absolute certainty.' "); Perfecting Serv. Co. v. Product Dev. & Sales Co., 259 N.C. 400, 417, 131 S.E.2d 9, 22 (1963) (" 'Absolute certainty is not required but evidence of damages must be sufficiently specific and complete to permit the jury to arrive at a reasonable conclusion.' "); Tobin v. Union News Co., 18 A.D.2d 243, 245, 239 N.Y.S.2d 22, 26 (4th Dep't 1963), *aff'd*, 13 N.Y.2d 1155, 196 N.E.2d 735 (1964) ("Mathematical certitude is unnecessary. A reasonable basis for the computation of approximate result is the only requisite."). *See also* RESTATEMENT 2d § 352 and UCC § 1-106 comment 1 ("reject any doctrine that damages must be calculable with mathematical accuracy") and § 2-715 comment 4 (as to consequential damages, like the section on the liberal administration of remedies (§ 1-106), this section "rejects any doctrine of certainty which requires almost mathematical precision in the proof of loss").

[125] In Miller v. Allstate Ins. Co., 573 So. 2d 24, 28 (Fla. Dist. Ct. App. 1990), the court lists six exceptions: (a) if the fact of damage is proved with certainty, the extent or amount may be left to reasonable inference; (b) where the defendant's wrong has caused the difficulty of proof of damage, he cannot complain of the resulting uncertainty; (c) mere difficulty in ascertaining the amount of damage is not fatal; (d) mathematical precision is not required; (e) if the best evidence of the damage of which the situation admits is furnished, this is sufficient; (f) the plaintiff may recover the value of his contract, and this may be measured by the value of the expected profits.

[126] Freund v. Washington Square Press, Inc., 34 N.Y.2d 379, 314 N.E.2d 419 (1974). In this case, the court awarded nominal damages (six cents) in the absence of reasonably certain proof of royalty damages. In such a case, the author would be well-advised to insist upon a liquidated damages clause, which is designed for situations where actual damages are necessarily fatally uncertain.

[127] See "exception" (b) in note 126 *supra*. *See also* Locke v. United States, 283 F.2d 521, 151 Ct. Cl. 262 (1960) (contract breaker should not profit from his own wrong by insisting on unobtainable proof of damages); Bead Chain Mfg. Co. v. Saxton Prods., Inc., 183 Conn. 266, 439 A.2d 314 (1981) (breach made it impossible to go forward with production that would have made historically accurate figures available; therefore, theoretical cost and price estimates were acceptable). *See also* A-S Dev., Inc. v. W.R. Grace Land Corp., 537 F. Supp. 549 (D.N.J. 1982), *aff'd per curiam*, 707 F.2d 1388 (3d Cir. 1983); Vitex Mfg. Corp. v. Caribtex Corp., 377 F.2d 795 (3d Cir. 1967); RESTATEMENT 2d § 352 comment a.

[128] *See* Tull v. Gundersons, Inc., 709 P.2d 940 (Colo. 1985).

evidence of such profits rather than permit the breaching party to avoid liability on the basis of lack of sufficient certainty.[129] A number of older cases found an insuperable obstacle in permitting a "new business" to recover anticipated profits on the footing that such damages were necessarily too speculative,[130] and there are recent cases that cling to that position.[131] The rule, however, has undergone erosion, at least in terms of its absolute, *per se* character. In many jurisdictions, the modern "new business rule" applies the same requirement future lost profits in such a business must be capable of reasonably accurate measurements which will necessarily be more difficult to establish in a new business.[132] While a new business venture necessarily labors under a greater burden than a going concern to prove anticipated profits, simply because a business is new should not justify a *per se* rule precluding such proof so long as reasonably certain data are provided as the basis for recovery.[133] Notwithstanding the difficulty of proof, expert testimony, market analyses and surveys, as well as economic and financial data, including the records of similar businesses, may provide sufficient certainty to

---

[129] *See, e.g.,* Thorp Sales Corp. v. Gyuro Grading Co., 107 Wis. 2d 141, 319 N.W.2d 879 (Ct. App. 1982), *aff'd,* 111 Wis. 2d 431, 331 N.W.2d 342 (1983) (15 pieces of equipment had an auction value ranging between $89,600 to $131,000, which court determined was a reasonable range for estimating lost profits with reasonable certainty); Buxbaum v. G. H. P. Cigar Co., 188 Wis. 389, 206 N.W. 59 (1925) (profits allowed on exclusive right to sell a product even though plaintiff had made no profits for a number of years; evidence was admissible that the new selling agent had made a profit so as to permit a basis for computing profits plaintiff would have made had he been permitted to continue); Randall v. Peerless Motor Car Co., 212 Mass. 352, 99 N.E. 221 (1912) (profits recoverable for breach of auto sales agency contract even though breached during the first month of plaintiff's operation of agency; evidence was admissible to show the number of cars sold by defendant and others in territory as basis for computing anticipated profits); Lewiston Iron Works v. Vulcan Process Co., 139 Minn. 180, 165 N.W. 1071 (1918) (evidence of profits made by others similarly situated held to furnish basis for allowing recovery of profits).

[130] *See, e.g.,* Evergreen Amusement Corp. v. Milstead, 206 Md. 610, 112 A.2d 901 (1955). Delay by contractor in completing work on new outdoor theater prevented opening until the middle of August, rather than June. Expert evidence of profits of drive-in theaters in the same territory, including evidence of population, weather, and other elements of market survey, were excluded. Court stated that it was not laying down a "flat rule" that such profits could never be recovered under such circumstances, but no case had permitted profits under such circumstances.

[131] Blair-Naughton L.L.C. v. Diner Concepts, Inc., 2010 U.S. App. LEXIS 5458 at *26 (10th Cir. 2010) ("Georgia's new business rule generally precludes a claim for lost profits arising from the operation of a new business because such damages are considered too speculative, remote and uncertain."

[132] Specialty Beverages, L.L.C. v. Pabst Brewing Co.,537 F.3d 1165, 1178 (10th Cir. 2008) (Oklahoma law). *See also* Iron Steamer, Ltd. v. Trinity Restaurant, Inc., 110 N.C. App. 843, 847–48, 431 S.E.2d 767, 770 (1993) (refusing to apply " 'New Business Rule' which categorically precludes an award of damages for lost profits where the party seeking damages is a new business with no record of profitability. . . . Instead, we have chosen to evaluate the quality of evidence of lost profits on an individual case-by-case basis in light of certain criteria to determine whether damages have been proven with 'reasonable certainty.' "). *See also* Drews Co. v. Ledwith-Wolfe Assocs., Inc., 296 S.C. 207, 371 S.E.2d 532 (1988); Pauline's Chicken Villa, Inc. v. KFC Corp., 701 S.W.2d 399 (Ky. 1985); Merion Spring Co. v. Muelles Hnos. Garcia Torres, S.A., 315 Pa. Super. 469, 462 A.2d 686 (1983). See ill. 6 to RESTATEMENT 2d § 352, which rejects the holding and rationale in the *Evergreen Amusement* case (note 130, *supra*). *See* UCC § 2-708 comment 2: "It is not necessary to a recovery of 'profit' to show a history of earnings, especially if a new venture is involved." Quoted with approval in Bead Chain Mfg. Co. v. Saxton Prods., Inc., 183 Conn. 266, 439 A.2d 314 (1981) (plaintiff's president testified concerning lost profits by setting forth the elements considered in pricing the job; it was not fatal that his cost and price estimates were theoretical).

[133] Handi Caddy, Inc. v. American Home Prods. Corp., 557 F.2d 136 (8th Cir. 1977) (cornerstone of plaintiff's proof was expert opinion testimony). For a case suggesting lack of certainty, see Kenford Co. v. County of Erie, 67 N.Y.2d 257, 502 N.Y.S.2d 131, 493 N.E.2d 234 (1986) (plaintiff not entitled to recover anticipated appreciation in the value of peripheral land when domed stadium contract was breached). The New York Court of Appeals upheld this decision, emphasizing lack of foreseeability (*see* Kenford Co. v. County of Erie, 73 N.Y.2d 312, 540 N.Y.S.2d 1, 537 N.E.2d 176 (1989)). *See also* Matson Plastering Co. v. Plasterers & Shophands Local No. 66, etc., 852 F.2d 1200 (9th Cir.), *cert. denied,* 488 U.S. 994, 109 S. Ct. 561, 102 L. Ed. 2d 586 (1988) (lost opportunity to bid on subsequent contracts was too speculative and uncertain).

permit the recovery of anticipated profits.[134] Even where courts appear to insist on the continued existence of the rule, it hardly continues as an absolute rule. The most fundamental criticism of an absolute rule is the encouragement of tortious behavior that would not allow proof of estimated profits of a new business against one guilty of interfering with contractual relationships.[135] Thus, where courts insist that the rule continues, it will not preclude evidence of lost profits in such a case.[136] Where a state court felt compelled to correct previous federal court holdings that interpreted the state law as having abandoned the "new business rule," the court recognized that arguments for abandonment of the rule were persuasive and proceeded to analyze the facts in the event the rule did not apply.[137] As one court suggests, "Damages must be proved and just not dreamed [but] some degree of speculation is permissible in computing damages."[138] An expert's opinion, however, will not substitute for factual evidence that supports that opinion.[139]

[C]   Recovery of Conjectural Value — Aleatory Contracts

In certain types of cases, courts have been willing to stretch the reasonable certainty requirement beyond its limits to permit a recovery. In cases involving aleatory contracts, i.e., contracts where at least one of the parties is under a duty that is conditional on the occurrence of an event that is a matter of chance (a fortuitous event),[140] a breach prior to the occurrence of the fortuitous event will prevent sufficient proof of what would have occurred had there been no breach. Thus, where fifty women were chosen by popular vote in a beauty contest and twelve were to receive prizes based on interviews, the wrongful deprivation of plaintiff's interview was held to permit the recovery of the value of her chance as determined by a jury.[141] There can be no question that the value of a chance or opportunity is highly conjectural and the chance of winning may be so remote that a court will not recognize its value.[142] Yet, other cases have permitted recovery of the value of a chance. A joint venture agreement required a developer to secure anchor tenants for a contemplated mall on the plaintiff's land. The developer breached its promise to secure the tenants. The plaintiff

---

[134] International Telepassport Corp. v. USFI, Inc., 89 F.3d 82, 86 (2d Cir. 1996) ("new business rule is not a per se rule forbidding the award of lost profits damages to new businesses, but rather an evidentiary rule that creates a higher 'level of proof needed to achieve reasonable certainty as to the amount of damages' ") (quoting Travellers Int'l, A.G. v. Trans World Airlines, 41 F.3d 1570, 1579 (2d Cir. 1994)). See RESTATEMENT 2d § 352 comment b.

[135] TK-7 Corp. v. Estate of Barbouti, 993 F.2d 722 (10th Cir. 1993).

[136] See, e.g., Lockheed Info. Mgmt. Sys. Co. v. Maximus, Inc., 259 Va. 92, 524 S.E.2d 420, 429–30 (2000), where the court allows that evidence of lost profits may be considered in a case involving tortious interference with contract, while insisting that the "new business" rule lives in its jurisdiction.

[137] Bell Atlantic Network Servs. v. P.M. Video Corp., 322 N.J. Super. 74, 730 A.2d 406, 420 (App. Div. 1999) (holding that previous statements by the United States Court of Appeals for the Third Circuit stating that New Jersey had abandoned the "new business rule" were not supported by holdings of the State Supreme Court).

[138] MindGames, Inc. v. Western Publ'g Co., 218 F.3d 652, 658 (7th Cir. 2000), cert. denied, 121 S. Ct. 882, 148 L. Ed. 2d 791 (2001) (applying Arkansas law and predicting that a strict "new business rule" would not apply).

[139] Upper Deck Co., LLC v. BreaKey International, BV, 390 F. Supp. 2d 355 (S. D. N. Y. 2005) (insufficient track record).

[140] See RESTATEMENT 2d § 379 comment a.

[141] Chaplin v. Hicks, 2 K.B. 786 [1911].

[142] DeNardo v. GCI Communications Corp., 983 P.2d 1288 (Alaska 1999) (chance of 9 out of 50,000); Phillips v. Pantages Theatre Co., 163 Wash. 303, 300 P. 1048 (1931) (damage for breach of prize contest held too speculative on the ground that there was no evidence that plaintiff had a real chance to win).

landowner sued the developer for damages measured by the difference in the value of the undeveloped land and the value of the land with the mall. While the district court found that the defendant had breached its duty to secure tenants, it also found that had the defendant not breached, there was a one in four chance that the mall would have been constructed. The court concluded that the value of that one-in-four chance was worth $350,000 to the plaintiff. The judgment was affirmed on appeal.[143] Where the defendant failed to prosecute certain causes of action after promising one-half of the recoveries to the plaintiff, the plaintiff was permitted to go to the jury on the question of the amount that the lawsuits probably would have produced.[144] These departures from the reasonable certainty requirement are explicable only on the basis that courts are simply unwilling to permit a breaching party to avoid liability solely on the basis of the plaintiff's difficulty of proving loss where it was clear at the time of formation that such loss would be impossible to prove with reasonable certainty.

While the RESTATEMENT 2d limits recovery of a value of a chance or opportunity to cases where the promise is aleatory,[145] a court may ignore this limitation. Where, for example, an insurer breached a promise to its insured to redeliver an automobile that was severely damaged in an accident, the insured was permitted to bring an action to recover damages for the lost opportunity to bring a products liability action against the manufacturer of the car.[146]

[D]   Alternate Bases of Recovery — Reliance and Rental Value

If courts cannot overcome the barrier of reasonable certainty, they may permit relief for less than the optimal, measurable damages where possible. This alternative relief typically takes two forms: (i) protection of the reliance interest and (ii) recovery of the rental value of the premises.

[1]   Reliance Interest Alternative

We have already considered how courts may permit the recovery of the reliance interest where the expectation interest (lost profits) is precluded due to a lack of sufficient certainty in the proof of damages in a construction contract.[147] The reliance interest is generally recognized as an alternative remedy for breach of contract regardless of its subject matter. Where lost profits cannot be proven with reasonable certainty, courts are quite willing to allow recovery of out-of-pocket expenditures to place the injured party in the position he would have been in if

---

[143] University City, Inc. v. Price Development Co., 1991 U.S. App. LEXIS 14111 (9th Cir. 1991). *See also,* Van Gulik v. Resource Dev. Council, 695 P.2d 1071 (Alaska 1985); Mange v. Unicorn Press, Inc., 129 F. Supp. 727 (D.N.Y. 1955); Wachtel v. National Alfalfa Journal Co., 190 Iowa 1293, 176 N.W. 801 (1921). See, however, Collatz v. Fox Wisconsin Amusement Corp., 239 Wis. 156, 300 N.W. 162 (1941), where the court found no value in a contest where plaintiff's chances were no worse than 1 out of nine.

[144] Jaffe v. Alliance Metal Co., 337 Pa. 449, 12 A.2d 13 (1940). *Cf.* Herbert Clayton & Jack Waller, Ltd. v. Oliver, A.C. 209 [1930] ($1000 damages allowed for injury to reputation where a theatrical producer breached contract with an actor to give him a leading part in a forthcoming play).

[145] RESTATEMENT 2d § 348(3), which limits recovery to such contest cases or other fortuitous event cases such as those involving wrongful cancellation of insurance contracts by an insurer. Commissioner of Ins. v. Massachusetts Acc. Co., 314 Mass. 558, 50 N.E.2d 801 (1943).

[146] Miller v. Allstate Ins. Co., 573 So. 2d 24 (Fla. Dist. Ct. App. 1990) (spoilation of evidence).

[147] *See supra* § 120[B].

no contract had been formed.[148] The RESTATEMENT 2d recognizes this alternate remedy which includes expenditures made in preparation for performance. When the defendant refused to close on a contract to sell 12 acres of property to the plaintiff on which the plaintiff intended to construct a shopping center, the plaintiff's action for lost profits was dismissed because such damages would be speculative. A count for the difference between the contract price and market price failed because the market price at closing was found to be higher than the contract price. A lower court held that, reliance damages would be limited to "those ordinarily incurred regarding such a contract such as title search, survey and attorney's closing fees." The New York Court of Appeals found this statement to be "incorrect." Quoting § 349 of the Restatement 2d of Contracts, the court noted that, as an alternative to expectation based damages, the plaintiff was entitled to recover "damages based on his reliance interest, including expenditures made in preparation for performance or in performance, less any loss that the party in breach can prove with reasonable certainty the injured party would have suffered had the contract been performed." Thus, the plaintiff was entitled to recover money spent in preparing for performance including efforts to arrange financing and obtain tenants for the shopping center.[149] Where a Hollywood celebrity cancelled an appearance, the court found the plaintiff's attempt to prove lost profits to be speculative, but did allow reliance expenditures.[150] In a well-known case,[151] a manufacturer of a furnace containing a new type of oil and gas burner wished to exhibit the device at a trade convention. The manufacturer contracted with a carrier which agreed to deliver all of the parts of the furnace to the convention. The carrier failed to deliver a critical part, thereby preventing display of the device. The manufacturer could show no loss of direct profit. It had, however, incurred expenses for the shipping charges, the expenses of employees, and the cost of renting a booth at the convention. The court protected the reliance interest of the manufacturer in allowing a recovery for all of these expenses.[152] While the reliance recovery alternative is available for any type of contract, if the breaching party can prove with reasonable certainty that the completion of the contract would have resulted in a loss to the plaintiff, reliance damages will be reduced by the amount of such a provable loss.[153]

The RESTATEMENT 2d insists that the recovery or reliance damages cannot exceed the contract price. "If the injured party's expenditures exceed the contract price, it is clear that, at least to the extent of the excess, there would have been a loss."[154] In a construction contract with a price of $100,000, the builder's reliance expenditures exceeding that price clearly indicate a losing contract. Since a party should never be placed in a better position than he

---

[148] Lord's & Lady's Enters. v. John Paul Mitchell Sys., 46 Mass. App. Ct. 262, 267, 705 N.E.2d 302, 305 (1999) ("as good a position as if no contract had existed").

[149] St. Lawrence Factory Stores v. Ogdensburg Bridge & Port Auth., 13 N.Y. 3d 204 (Ct. App. N.Y. 2009). *See also* Silva v. Crossman, 1996 Tenn. App. LEXIS 708 (Tenn. Ct. App. Nov. 1, 1996) (preparation and renovation expenditures in lease of a nightclub); Brennan v. Carvel Corp., 929 F.2d 801, 810 (1st Cir. 1991) (expenditures in performance).

[150] Hollywood Fantasy Corp. v. Gabor, 151 F.3d 203, 212 (5th Cir. 1998).

[151] Security Store & Mfg. Co. v. American R. E. Co., 227 Mo. App. 175, 51 S.W.2d 572 (1932).

[152] *See also* Reimer v. Badger Wholesale Co., 147 Wis. 2d 389, 433 N.W.2d 592 (Ct. App. 1988) (reliance interest protected in at-will employment contract).

[153] Chooseco LLC v. Lean Forward Media LLC, 2009 U.S. Dist. LEXIS 2522 at *13–14 (D. Vt. 2009) (emphasizing that the burden is on the defendant to prove that a plaintiff seeking the reliance interest was in a losing contract, quoting Bausch & Lomb v. Bressler, 977 F.2d 720, 729 (2d Cir. 1992)); Restatement 2d of Contracts § 349, comment a.

[154] RESTATEMENT 2d § 349 comment a.

would have occupied had the contract been performed, a contract price ceiling on reliance recovery in such a case may be justified.[155] It must, however, be remembered that the burden of proving any loss on the part of the relying party had the contract been performed is clearly on the defendant. If he cannot prove that the completed contract would result in a loss to the plaintiff, reliance expenditures exceeding the contract price should be recovered. For example, where an actor failed to perform his contract for a leading role in a film for which he would have received &1050, the court permitted a reliance recovery of &2750 for wasted expenditures when the film could not be produced.[156] The profit on the film could not be proven since it was never produced. In such a case, there is little justification for limiting the reliance damages to the contract price since the completion and distribution of the film may well have resulted in an amount that would not only have defrayed the cost of the actor's contract and all reliance expenditures, but also resulted in a profit to the producer.[157]

[2]   The Rental Value Alternative

Beyond the reliance alternative, courts may discover a reasonably certain basis for affording a remedy by permitting recovery of the rental value of the property where lost profits would be conjectural. Where, for example, a complete crop failure resulted due to unmerchantable seed wheat, the court permitted recovery of the rental value of the land.[158] It should also be noted that the court also permitted recovery of the expenses of planting the worthless seed. Thus, it permitted both a rental value and reliance recovery. The court did not overcompensate the plaintiff, however, since his gross profit would have enabled him to pay for the cost of planting and would still have permitted a net profit which is simulated by the rental value.[159] Where the construction of a new outdoor theater was delayed during crucial summer months and the court applied what would now be viewed as an outmoded requirement of proving damages with certainty, thereby denying lost profits, the court still permitted a recovery of the rental value of the theater property during the delay plus out-of-pocket (reliance) costs for that time.[160] Again, the strong judicial policy in favor of compensating the aggrieved party with damages based on some reasonably certain basis and denying the breaching party a technical basis for avoiding liability is revealed.

---

[155] *See* L. Albert & Son v. Armstrong Rubber Co., 178 F.2d 182 (2d Cir. 1949). *See also* H.M.O. Sys., Inc. v. Choicecare Health Servs., Inc., 665 P.2d 635 (Colo. Ct. App. 1983).

[156] Anglia Television Ltd. v. Reed, [1971] 3 All E. R. The court permitted recovery of reliance expenditures before the contract with the actor was made, as well as reasonable expenditures incurred after the contract was made, since the expenditures prior to contract formation were within the reasonable contemplation of the parties as likely to be wasted if the contract was broken.

[157] *See also* Security Store & Mfg. Co. v. American R. E. Co., 227 Mo. App. 175, 51 S.W.2d 572 (1932) (contract price of $147 (express charges) and total reliance damages of $801.50 plus interest (total amount of $1000); the $801.50 included the $147 transportation charge which was a wasted expenditure). *See also* Wartzman v. Hightower Prods., Ltd., 53 Md. App. 656, 456 A.2d 82 (1983) (failure of law firm to properly incorporate entity created to promote a flagpole sitting stunt where court awarded reliance expenditures presumably much greater than reasonable legal fee).

[158] Moorhead v. Minneapolis Seed Co., 139 Minn. 11, 165 N.W. 484 (1917).

[159] *Accord* Paola Gas Co. v. Paola Glass Co., 56 Kan. 614, 44 P. 621 (1896) (recovery of wasted expenditure in attempting to operate plant without gas plus rental value or interest on the value of property). RESTATEMENT 2d § 348(1) permits damages based on rental value of the property or on interest on the value of the property as an alternative to proof of loss of value to the injured party where a breach delays the use of the property. The interest on the value property alternative is viewed as "a last resort" where damages based on a fair rental value cannot be shown with reasonable certainty. *See* RESTATEMENT 2d § 348 comment a.

[160] Evergreen Amusement Corp. v. Milstead, 206 Md. 610, 112 A.2d 901 (1955).

§ 123   THE MITIGATION LIMITATION

[A]   The Third Limitation

In addition to the foreseeability limitation and the certainty limitation already explored, there is a third limitation which may be called the mitigation limitation or the limitation of avoidable losses or avoidable consequences.[161] In the interest of fairness to the defaulting promisor, it is a universally accepted rule that the promisee cannot recover those damages for breach of contract which he could have avoided through the exercise of reasonable diligence if he can do so without incurring undue risk, expense, or humiliation.[162] An aggrieved party should not be placed in a *better* position that it would have occupied had the contract been performed.[163] This rule has both negative and positive dimensions. On the negative side, if an innocent promisee is to be made whole, he is required to refrain from the performance of his own undertakings under the contract, or from any other act which would increase the loss to be paid by the defaulting promisor, unless such refraining would unreasonably prejudice some other interest of the promisee. Thus, where a bridge builder had started to perform and was notified by the county that the contract had been cancelled, the builder could not recover for that portion of the bridge he completed after the notice of cancellation because he could have avoided the cost of completion.[164]

On the positive side, the rule requires the injured promisee, *if he is to be made whole*, to take such affirmative steps as may be appropriate and reasonable, in view of the circumstances, to avert losses which would result were he to remain inactive. If he does not take such steps he will, nevertheless, be limited in his recovery to the amount to which his loss would have been reduced had he done so. The injured party, however, is only required to use reasonable diligence. Thus, where a contractor's performance was deficient and the injured party chose to attempt to remedy the defects instead of beginning anew, the fact that the remedial efforts were not wholly successful did not mean that the decision was unreasonable when made.[165] The burden of proving that the injured party has acted in an unreasonable

---

[161] "Mitigation of damages in contract law . . . corresponds to avoidable consequences in tort law." Outboard Marine Corp. v. Babcock Indus., 106 F.3d 182, 184 (7th Cir. 1997), referring to the exploration of the relationship between the concept of avoidable consequences (mitigation principle) in contract or tort law and the foreseeability rule of *Hadley v. Baxendale* in Evra Corp. v. Swiss Bank Corp., 673 F.2d 951, 957–58 (7th Cir.), *cert. denied*, 459 U.S. 1017, 103 S. Ct. 377, 74 L. Ed. 2d 511 (1982).

[162] *See, e.g.*, National Communs. Ass'n v. AT&T, 2001 U.S. Dist. LEXIS 951, at *20 (S.D.N.Y. Feb. 5, 2001). Grill v. Adams, 123 Ill. App. 3d 913, 79 Ill. Dec. 342, 463 N.E.2d 896 (1st Dist. 1984); Lincoln Nat'l Life Ins. Co. v. NCR Corp., 603 F. Supp. 1393 (N.D. Ind. 1984), *aff'd*, 772 F.2d 315 (7th Cir. 1985); Soules v. Independent Sch. Dist. No. 518, 258 N.W.2d 103 (Minn. 1977). *See also* RESTATEMENT 2d § 350(1). It should be noted that historically, a commercial landlord had no duty to mitigate damages when a tenant defaulted and left the premises vacant. Landlord-tenant relationships have been based on property rather than contract law. For a recent case rejecting the common law view and holding that a landlord has a duty to mitigate damages, see Austin Hill Country Realty v. Palisades Plaza, 948 S.W.2d 293 (Tex. 1997). Other jurisdictions are unclear concerning the application of the mitigation concept to landlords. *See, e.g.*, Federal Realty Inv. Trust v. Kids Wear Blvd., Inc., 1996 U.S. Dist. LEXIS 2378, at *24 (E.D. Pa. Feb. 28, 1996) (referring to Pennsylvania law on this issue as "murky"). Other courts, however, perceive a clear trend to adopt the mitigation principle in such cases. Roy, Gene & Ron Kahn v. Taco Bell Corp., 1993 U.S. Dist. LEXIS 11089, at *10 (S.D.N.Y. Aug. 3, 1993) (while recognizing New York law as "unclear" on the subject, the court suggests a trend view where twelve other jurisdictions have rejected the traditional rule in favor of a duty to mitigate).

[163] Cooney Indus. Trucks, Inc. v. Toyota Motor Sales, U.S.A., Inc., 168 F.3d 545, 546 (1st Cir. 1999).

[164] Rockingham County v. Luten Bridge Co., 35 F.2d 301, 66 A.L.R. 735 (4th Cir. 1929).

[165] Marchesseault v. Jackson, 611 A.2d 95, 99 (Me. 1992).

fashion is on the breaching party.[166] Where a bank had sustained serious economic damage through the defendant's breach and chose not to pursue a significant risk of further damage, the court held that the bank's action was not unreasonable.[167]

[B]   Expenses or Losses Incurred in Attempts to Mitigate

An aggrieved party may incur expenses or losses in his reasonable and good faith efforts to mitigate damages. Since such expenses or losses are occasioned by the breach, it is fair to allocate them to the breaching party. Thus, it is a generally accepted corollary to the mitigation principle that the innocent promisee may also recover expenses and losses resulting from good-faith attempts to lessen the injury suffered or anticipated from a breach.[168] If the effort to lessen the injury was reasonably warranted by and proportioned to the injury, and if it was conducted with reasonable skill and efficiency, recovery for such expenses and losses may be had although the effort proved futile.[169]

Where a contract for specially manufactured goods is partially completed by the manufacturer when the buyer breaches, the seller may decide that he should recover the contract price minus any costs saved, including any scrap or salvage value the uncompleted goods may bring. If, however, the seller makes a good faith judgment that completion of the manufacture may permit a resale at the contract price or an approximation of the contract price, he may follow this reasonable course of action and complete the manufacture even after the breach. If that reasonable and good faith effort, through no fault of the seller, results in even greater loss than the negative course of stopping manufacture and procuring the salvage value, the seller's reasonable mitigation efforts should be compensated.[170]

---

[166] Young v. Frank's Nursery & Crafts, Inc., 58 Ohio St. 3d 242, 569 N.E.2d 1034, 1036 (1991).

[167] Citizens Federal Bank, A Federal Savings Bank v. United States, 2005 U.S. Claims LEXIS 191 (2005).

[168] Aircraft Gear Corp. v. Kaman Aerospace Corp., 875 F. Supp. 485, 499 (N.D. Ill. 1995) (citing this section); West Haven Sound Dev. Corp. v. City of West Haven, 201 Conn. 305, 514 A.2d 734 (1986) (bank loans, corporate and individual loans, accounts payable to suppliers, and related costs incurred to remain in business after the breach may be recovered if reasonable); Nunnally Co. v. Bromberg & Co., 217 Ala. 180, 115 So. 230 (1928) (lessee who was given possession of only part of demised premises entitled to recover the extra cost involved in making that part usable); Hoehne Ditch Co. v. John Flood Ditch Co., 76 Colo. 500, 233 P. 167 (1925) (one who had breached contract to carry water in an irrigation ditch held liable for the cost of procuring substitute carrier); Elias v. Wright, 276 F. 908 (2d Cir. 1921) (contractor who broke contract to install glass in building held liable for cost of putting muslin on the windows to protect interior until glass could be installed). *See also* RESTATEMENT 2d § 350 comment h and UCC §§ 2-704(2) and 2-706.

[169] *See* Automated Donut Sys., Inc. v. Consolidated Rail Corp., 12 Mass. App. Ct. 326, 424 N.E.2d 265 (1981) (even if the costs enhanced the damages, if reasonable they may be recovered); Ninth Ave. & Forty-Second St. Corp. v. Zimmerman, 217 A.D. 498, 217 N.Y.S. 123 (1st Dep't 1926) (where attorney negligently recommended purchase of an unmarketable leasehold, client recovered expense of an unsuccessful suit to clear title). *See also* Casey v. Nampa & Meridian Irrig. Dist., 85 Idaho 299, 379 P.2d 409 (1963) (whether plaintiff's method of minimizing damages due to flooding of his land caused by defendant's negligence was reasonable is a question for the jury under the evidence presented).

[170] See UCC § 2-704(2), which permits the seller to cease manufacture or complete manufacture of the goods if either of these actions is an exercise of reasonable commercial judgment. See also UNIDROIT Principles, Art. 7.4.8(2), allowing reasonable expenses in efforts to reduce harm.

[C]   "Duty" to Mitigate — UCC and CISG

It is important to emphasize that the negative and positive dimensions of the mitigation principle were stated as "requirements" *if the promisee is to be made whole.* While courts often characterize the principle of avoidable consequences as a "duty," it is not a duty. Breach of a duty makes one liable to another party with a correlative right. A breaching party has no enforceable right against an injured party who fails to mitigate damages. The effect of such a failure is "merely to reduce the damages otherwise recoverable."[171] For example, in the earlier example of a breach of the contract for the construction of the bridge, there was no *duty* on the builder of the bridge to cease his performance. By continuing his performance after being notified that the completed bridge would be valueless, however, he exacerbated losses to the promisor which could have been avoided through reasonable diligence. The mitigation principle simply precludes his recovery of such avoidable losses. The breaching promisor, however, has no cause of action against the builder for continuing the performance and enhancing damages since, again, the builder had no duty to cease performance. While the Convention on Contracts for the International Sales of Goods (CISG) states that a party "must take such measures as are reasonable in the circumstances to mitigate loss," failure to do so merely allows the breaching party to "claim a reduction in the damage in the amount by which the loss should have been mitigated."[172] Under the UCC, consequential damages which could have been avoided are not recoverable.[173] Typically, such damages can be avoided by making substitute arrangements. Thus, where a seller fails to deliver certain goods under a contract with a buyer, the buyer will purchase identical or similar goods elsewhere, i.e., the buyer will resort to his remedy of *cover.*[174] This remedy will avoid unnecessary losses for the buyer. Where a particular device is necessary to conduct the buyer's business and the seller fails to deliver the device as promised, the buyer may not simply allow lost profits to accumulate if he could avoid such losses by purchasing a substitute device from another source. The buyer's damages in such a situation would include the difference between the contract price and any reasonably higher (cover) price for the substitute purchase.[175] They would not, however, include any consequential losses that could have been prevented by cover or otherwise. Similarly, if a party who uses a truck in his business loses the use of the truck because of a breach of warranty, he may not recover consequential damages (lost profits) that could have been avoided if he had leased a truck while awaiting the repair of the unmerchantable truck.[176]

---

[171] St. George Chicago v. George J. Murges & Assocs., 296 Ill. App. 3d 285, 293, 230 Ill. Dec. 1013, 1019, 695 N.E.2d 503, 509 (1st Dist. 1998). See also Mason v. Artwork Pictures, L.L.C., 2008 U.S. Dist. LEXIS 46267 (D. Nev. 2008).

[172] CISG Art. 77. *See also* UNIDROIT Principles, Art. 7.4.8(1).

[173] UCC § 2-715(2)(a).

[174] UCC § 2-712.

[175] UCC 2-712(2). *See also* Huntington Beach Union High Sch. Dist. v. Continental Info. Sys. Corp., 621 F.2d 353 (9th Cir. 1980) (difference between higher cost of substitute computer and contract price).

[176] UCC § 2-714(2) measures damages for breach of warranty as the difference at the time and place of acceptance between the value of the goods as accepted and the value they would have had if they had been as warranted, and § 2-714(3) also permits the recovery of both incidental and consequential damages in a proper case. The typical direct damage will be the repair cost of the accepted goods. Consequential damages, however, may be permitted if lost profits are shown because the goods are not available. Such damages are not recoverable, however, if they could have been avoided by cover or otherwise under UCC § 2-715(2)(a).

The UCC, however, does contain a provision that creates a duty of mitigation concerning rejected goods. If a merchant buyer rejects goods because they are nonconforming, and the breaching seller has no agent or place of business at the market where the goods have been rejected, the buyer is under a duty to follow reasonable instructions from the seller with respect to such rejected goods.[177] Moreover, if the goods are either perishable or threaten to decline speedily in value, the buyer must make reasonable efforts to resell them if no reasonable instructions from the seller have been received.[178] The buyer is entitled to be reimbursed for any expenses associated with his selling efforts, as well as any expenses incurred in caring for the rejected goods.[179] If the goods are neither perishable nor threaten to decline speedily in value, the absence of reasonable instructions from the seller permits the buyer to store the goods for the seller's account, to reship them to the seller or to resell them for the seller's account.[180] In summary, the UCC requires merchants to operate in a commercially reasonable manner which is, essentially, the Code definition of good faith as applied to a merchant.[181]

[D]   Personal Service (Employment) Contracts

In personal service contracts, an employee who is wrongfully discharged cannot sit idly by and recover the promised wages or salary, if it is possible to secure other employment of the same general character and without undue hardship. In such a case, the defaulting employer is entitled to deduct from the promised salary whatever the injured employee could have earned in such other employment.[182] If an employee recovered the salary from the breached contract even though he earned a second salary which he could not have earned had the contract not been breached, he would have received a windfall, i.e., he would be placed in a much better position than he would have been in had the contract been performed. His recovery, therefore, should not exceed his expectation interest.[183] An employee, however, need not accept employment that is substantially different from the original employment to mitigate damages. "If a general counsel of a large corporation is wrongfully discharged, he is not required, in order to mitigate his damages, to take a job as a dishwasher."[184] Neither must

---

[177] UCC § 2-603(1) states that "a merchant buyer is under a duty after rejection of goods in his possession or control to follow any reasonable instructions received from the seller. . . ."

[178] *Id.*

[179] UCC § 2-603(2).

[180] UCC § 2-604.

[181] UCC § 2-103(1)(b).

[182] Soules v. Independent Sch. Dist. No. 518, 258 N.W.2d 103 (Minn. 1977) (teacher failed to exert reasonable efforts to pursue or accept other suitable employment despite reduced salary offer). *See also* Hollwedel v. Duffy-Mott Co., 263 N.Y. 95, 188 N.E. 266 (1933); Harrington v. Empire Cream Separator Co., 120 Me. 388, 115 A. 89 (1921); Ogden-Howard Co. v. Brand, 30 Del. (7 Boyce) 482, 108 A. 277 (1919).

[183] As to whether the employee's recovery should be diminished by amounts received from other sources, such as unemployment compensation, there is a split of authority, though the prevailing view appears to indicate that they should not be deducted. *See, e.g.,* Sporn v. Celebrity, Inc., 129 N.J. Super. 449, 324 A.2d 71 (1974); Pennington v. Whiting Tubular Prods., Inc., 370 Mich. 590, 122 N.W.2d 692 (1963). *Contra* Dehnart v. Waukesha Brewing Co., 21 Wis. 2d 583, 124 N.W.2d 664 (1963).

[184] S.A. Healy Co. v. Milwaukee Metro. Sewerage Dist., 50 F.3d 476, 481 (7th Cir.), *cert. denied*, 516 U.S. 1010, 116 S. Ct. 566, 133 L. Ed. 2d 491 (1995).

he seek employment in another locality.[185] The burden of proof is on the employer to prove both the employee's opportunity to secure comparable employment and the employee's failure to mitigate damages.[186] Whether the substitute employment is "comparable," "substantially similar," or "substantially equivalent" to the original employment can be a difficult issue.[187] Where, for example, an actress agreed to star in a musical to be filmed in California that would display certain singing and dancing talents, defendant breached the contract and offered the plaintiff a starring role in a western to be filmed in Australia that would not display her musical talents. The original contract also provided the plaintiff with certain approval rights concerning the director of the film that would not be part of the substitute arrangement. A divided court held that plaintiff's refusal to accept the substitute employment was justified and could not be used in mitigation of $750,000 in damages owed to the plaintiff.[188] Where, however, the famous basketball player Michael Jordan sued to recover for a breach of contract which required him to make television commercials, the defendant claimed that Jordan failed to make reasonable efforts to mitigate damages. Jordan relied on the holding and rationale of the case involving the actress, but the court noted that at the time the defendant breached, Jordan had already begun a business strategy of not accepting endorsement opportunities because they may have interfered with his overriding goal of owning a National Basketball Association franchise. Neither was the court persuaded by Jordan's claim that another endorsement contract would dilute his impact as an endorser and damage his business interests. Another endorsement contract would only require him to do what he had done for other clients over a number of years.[189]

While a school superintendent need not accept a position as a teacher,[190] even where the employer offers the wrongfully discharged employee similar compensation and responsibilities, the surrounding circumstances may allow a trier of fact to conclude that the substitute employment need not have been pursued in mitigation of damages.[191]

---

[185] *See* American Trading Co. v. Steele, 274 F. 774 (9th Cir. 1921); James v. Board of Comm'rs, 44 Ohio St. 226, 6 N.E. 246 (1886).

[186] See Morris v. Clawson Tank Co., 459 Mich. 256, 587 N.W.2d 253 (1998), where the court insists that defendant prove an unreasonable failure by the discharged employee to seek employment. See also Gulf Consol. Int'l, Inc. v. Murphy, 658 S.W.2d 565 (Tex. 1983). In Stewart v. Board of Educ. of Ritenour Consolidated Sch. Dist., 630 S.W.2d 130 (Mo. Ct. App. 1982), the court adopted the following statement from Ryan v. Superintendent of Schools of Quincy, 374 Mass. 670, 373 N.E.2d 1178, 1181 (1978): "A former employer meets its burden of 'mitigation of damages' if the employer proves that (a) one or more discoverable opportunities for comparable employment were available in a location as, or more convenient than, the place of former employment, (b) the improperly discharged employee unreasonably made no attempt to apply for any such job, and (c) it was reasonably likely that the former employee would obtain one of those comparable jobs." See also Sayre v. Musicland Group, Inc., subsidiary of American Can. Co., 850 F.2d 350 (8th Cir. 1988), holding that the employer must establish such factors as an affirmative defense.

[187] The quoted terminology is often found in cases involving mitigation in employment situations. *See, e.g.*, Kern v. Levolor Lorentzen, Inc., 899 F.2d 772, 778 (9th Cir. 1990).

[188] Parker v. Twentieth Century-Fox Film Corp., 3 Cal. 3d 176, 89 Cal. Rptr. 737, 474 P.2d 689 (1970). (Parker is better known as Shirley MacLaine.)

[189] In re Worldcom, Inc., 2007 Bankr. LEXIS 383 (S. D. N. Y. 2007).

[190] Salem Community Sch. Corp. v. Richman, 406 N.E.2d 269 (Ind. Ct. App. 1980). *See also* Williams v. Robinson, 158 Ark. 327, 250 S.W. 14 (1923) (woman employed to take charge of kitchen need not accept a more menial position); Cooper v. Stronge & Warner Co., 111 Minn. 177, 126 N.W. 541 (1910) (one employed as manager of the millinery department need not accept position as sales clerk).

[191] See Voorhees v. Guyan Mach. Co., 191 W. Va. 450, 446 S.E.2d 672 (1994), where an employer's threat to pursue an unenforceable noncompetition clause caused the employee to lose his job with another employer and resulted in a tort action by the employee. Because of the enmity between the parties, the court did not view an offer by the original

[E]   The "Lost Volume" Concept

We have just seen that an employee will not recover damages if he could have secured comparable employment in a convenient location. If the employment is not "substantially similar," the employee need not take the job. If, however, he does accept the new employment, the wages earned in the new employment will be deducted from the damages recovered from the first employer if it was not possible to perform both jobs simultaneously.[192] An employee, however, may be able to perform two jobs. "Moonlighting" is a common practice. If the second employment would be performable without interfering with the breached employment, the value of the second employment is not deducted from the employee's recovery since he would have earned the wages from the second employment whether or not the original contract was breached.[193] While this common sense principle is clear, it can become difficult in cases where there is doubt as to whether the second opportunity could have been pursued along with the breached opportunity.

A supplier of services may be able to convince a court that he would have been able to perform a second opportunity that became available after the original contract was breached. Consider, for example, an individual plumber who never subcontracts his work and who has contracted to perform services that will require a full day's effort. If the owner repudiates that contract and the plumber proceeds to work elsewhere on the day scheduled to perform the original contract, must he deduct his earnings from the second job in mitigation of damages recovered from the breached contract? It is certainly possible that the plumber could have performed the second contract as well as the first if he could have delayed the second job. In the case of enterprises that provide services, courts are inclined to view them as "lost volume" enterprises,[194] i.e., they are entitled to the profits on both contracts because, presumably, they could have performed both contracts and received both profits absent strong evidence to the contrary.[195] To qualify as a "lost volume" seller and recover lost profits, the seller must

---

employer to rehire the employee as a basis for mitigation. In Boehm v. American Broadcasting Co., 929 F.2d 482 (9th Cir. 1991), the employer offered a position at the same base compensation and same responsibilities as the former position, though the discharged employee would report to his successor in the original position. The court upheld a jury finding that the new position, which the employee described as "phony," was not substantially similar to the old position.

[192] *See* Erler v. Five Points Motors, Inc., 249 Cal. App. 2d 560, 57 Cal. Rptr. 516 (4th Dist. 1967).

[193] Soules v. Independent Sch. Dist. No. 518, 258 N.W.2d 103 (Minn. 1977) (only earnings from employment which are incompatible with the employee's contractual obligations may be offset as mitigated damages); Dixon v. Volunteer Co-op. Bank, 213 Mass. 345, 100 N.E. 655 (1913) (attorney employed to examine land titles for a bank on a fee basis); Nuckolls v. College of Physicians & Surgeons, 7 Cal. App. 233, 94 P. 81 (1907) (dentist employed part-time as teacher).

[194] In Teradyne, Inc. v. Teledyne Indus., Inc., 676 F.2d 865, n.2 (1st Cir. 1982), the court attributes the coinage, "lost volume seller" to Professor Robert J. Harris in his article, *A Radical Restatement of the Law of Seller's Damages: Sales Act and Commercial Code Results Compared*, 18 STAN. L. REV. 66 (1965), and notes that the phrase has been widely adopted in such cases as Famous Knitwear Corp. v. Drug Fair, Inc., 493 F.2d 251, 254, n.5 (4th Cir. 1974); Snyder v. Herbert Greenbaum & Assocs., Inc., 38 Md. App. 144, 157, 380 A.2d 618, 624 (1977); Publicker Indus., Inc. v. Roman Ceramics Corp., 652 F.2d 340, 346 (3d Cir. 1981). As seen in the quote above, it has also been adopted by the RESTATEMENT 2d §§ 347, comment f: "Whether a subsequent transaction is a substitute for the broken contract sometimes raises difficult questions of fact. If the injured party could and would have entered into the subsequent contract, even if the contract had not been broken, and could have had the benefit of both, he can be said to have a 'lost volume' and the subsequent transaction is not a substitute for the broken contract. . . . It is sometimes assumed that [the contractor would have taken the subsequent contract regardless of the breach], but the question is one of fact to be resolved according to the circumstances of each case." *See* Vinmar, Overseas LED v. E-Biofuels, LLC, 2009 U.S. Dist. LEXIS 110036 at *14 (S. D. Tex. 2009) quoting comment f. *See also* RESTATEMENT 2d § 350 comment d.

[195] Quoted in Bitterroot Int'l Sys. v. Western Star Trucks, Inc., 153 P.3d 627, 641 (Mont. 2007). Also quoted in Jetz

establish three factors: (1) it must demonstrate that it had the capacity to make the additional sale; (2) the additional sale would have been profitable; (3) if the original buyer had not breached, the additional sale would still have been made.[196]

[1]   "Lost Volume" Seller Under the Uniform Commercial Code

In contracts for the sale of goods, if a party contracts to sell a unique item and the buyer breaches that contract, the seller's resale to another buyer will produce profit that should be deducted from her damages against the first buyer in mitigation because she could not possibly have made two profits on the only item of its kind, i.e., she can only sell that item once. If, however, the seller has a virtually inexhaustible supply of goods for sale, the fact that she resells an item to a second buyer after the first buyer breaches the contract should not deprive the seller of profits on both sales.[197] Consider, for example, the seller of automobiles who contracts to sell a typical car to X. X refuses to accept delivery of the auto and the seller resells the car to Y. One of the seller's remedies under the UCC is the remedy of resale, which permits the seller to recover the difference between the contract price and the resale price as the measure of damages.[198] In a standard-priced item such as a new automobile, that differential will typically be zero since the contract price and the resale price will be identical. Yet, presumably the seller would have made the sale to Y regardless of X's breach, i.e., the seller did not search for buyer Y because X breached, he sought Y and as many other customers as he could discover regardless of X's breach. Thus, to characterize the transaction with Y exclusively as a resale of the car X was supposed to purchase is misleading. In fact, the seller has lost the profit he would have earned on the sale to X and the profit earned on the sale to Y should not be deducted in mitigation since the seller would have made that profit from the Y contract in any event.[199]

The UCC recognizes the inadequacy of the remedy of resale or its counterpart, the difference between the contract price and market price at the time and place for tender.[200] Either of these remedies would provide the "lost volume" seller with either no recovery or a

---

Serv. Co. v. Salina Props., 19 Kan. App. 2d 144, 865 P.2d 1051, 1055 (1993). *See* Kearsarge Computer v. Acme Staple Co., 116 N.H. 705, 366 A.2d 467, 86 A.L.R.3d 1081 (1976) (these businesses are expandable and the law presumes that they can accept a virtually unlimited amount of business so that income generated from accounts acquired after breach does not mitigate the plaintiff's damages); Gollaher v. Midwood Constr. Co., 194 Cal. App. 2d 640, 15 Cal. Rptr. 292 (2d Dist. 1961) (personal services are not involved in this kind of contract since the contractor is required only to accomplish a specific result which could be achieved by having hired servants perform it and to take as many other contracts elsewhere as the contractor chooses to take).

[196] Rodriguez v. Learjet, Inc., 24 Kan. App. 2d 461, 946 P.2d 1010, 1015 (1997). See also Collins Entertainment Corp. v. Coats and Coats Rental Amusement, 629 S. E. 2d 635 (S. C. 2006).

[197] Advanced Medical, Inc. v. Arden Med. Sys., Inc., 955 F.2d 188, 201 (3d Cir. 1992) (citing this section). While the paradigm case is the seller with a virtually inexhaustible supply of good, the same dilemma confronts a "jobber" who sells goods without ever coming into possession of them. When a buyer breaches the contract, the jobber need not arrange for the goods to be acquired, but he loses the profit on that sale. A seller of highly specialized goods may not have a market to resell them. That seller has lost the profit on the sale. See Kenco Homes, Inc. v. Williams, 94 Wash. App. 219, 972 P. 2d 125 (1999).

[198] UCC § 2-706(1).

[199] This example is essentially that found in Neri v. Retail Marine Corp., 30 N.Y.2d 393, 334 N.Y.S.2d 165, 285 N.E.2d 311 (1972), taken from W. Hawkland, Sales and Bulk Sales 153–54 (1958).

[200] UCC § 2-708(1) allows the contract price/market price differential, which would be available to a seller who chooses not to resell or who has resold but has not complied with all of the requirements of the resale section, § 2-706, in making the resale in a commercially reasonable manner.

recovery that would be substantially lower than the damages necessary to place him in the position he would have occupied had the contract been performed — the standard generally required by the Code.[201] To overcome this inadequacy, the Code includes a provision permitting the seller to recoup his lost profit on the broken contract notwithstanding subsequent sales that would have occurred in any event:

> If the measure of damages provided in subsection (1) is inadequate to put the seller in as good a position as performance would have done then the measure of damages is the profit (including reasonable overhead) which the seller would have made from full performance by the buyer, together with any incidental damages provided in this Article (Section 2-710), due allowance for costs reasonably incurred and due credit for payments or proceeds of resale.[202]

Two major problems have arisen in the interpretation of this section due to infelicitous drafting. The last phrase ("due credit for payments or proceeds of resale") may literally suggest that the proceeds of resale are to be deducted from the seller's recovery. If the literal interpretation is accepted, it would destroy the concept of permitting the lost profit on the broken contract. Courts have uniformly rejected this literal interpretation because it would undermine the purpose of the statute.[203] The phrase has been interpreted as referring to the privilege of the seller to realize salvage value when he has not completed manufacture of a product and it would be useless to complete the manufacture.[204]

The second major problem in the statutory language is the parenthetical phrase "including reasonable overhead," which is part of the profit the seller has earned. The only inkling of the meaning of "profit" is found in a comment suggesting that profit means "list price less cost to the dealer or list price less manufacturing cost to the manufacturer."[205] When dealing with standard priced goods, the "list price" or "standard price" minus dealer or manufacturer cost can easily be envisioned. If the contract is formed at a price other than "list" or "standard," we may simply use the unpaid contract price from which the cost will be deducted. If we assume a typical transaction involving an automobile with a price of $25,000 and subtract from that the amount the dealer had to pay the manufacturer, e.g., $21,000, plus any expenses including transportation costs, dealer preparation costs and the like which, we will assume, increases the total dealer's cost to $23,000, the seller should recover $2000, i.e., price minus costs. The costs we have considered to this point, however, are *variable* costs, i.e., costs directly related to the

---

[201] UCC § 1-106(1).

[202] UCC § 2-708(2).

[203] *See, e.g.*, Snyder v. Herbert Greenbaum & Assocs., Inc., 38 Md. App. 144, 380 A.2d 618, 625 (1977): "Practically, if the 'due credit' clause is applied to the lost volume seller, his measure of damages is no different from his recovery under § 2-708(1). Under § 2-708(1) he recovers the contract/market differential and the profit he makes on resale. If the 'due credit' provision is applied, the seller recovers only the profit he makes on resale plus the difference between the resale price and the contract price, an almost identical measure to § 2-708(1). If the 'due credit' clause is applied to the lost volume seller, the damage measure of 'lost profits' is rendered nugatory, and he is not put in as good a position as if there had been performance." *Accord* National Controls, Inc. v. Commodore Bus. Machs., Inc., 163 Cal. App. 3d 688, 689, 209 Cal. Rptr. 636, 637 (1st Dist. 1985); Famous Knitwear Corp. v. Drug Fair, Inc., 493 F.2d 251, 254 n.7 (4th Cir. 1974); *Neri v. Retail Marine Corp.*, *supra* note 199.

[204] *See Neri v. Retail Marine Corp.*, *supra* note 199, at 314, n.2, which relies upon the 1952 Official Draft of Text and Comments of the UCC [1954] and to commentators who have concluded that the reference in § 2-708(2) is to resale as scrap under § 2-704. The note also finds support in the analysis of the language by Professor Harris in his article cited *supra* note 194, at 104.

[205] UCC § 2-708 comment 2.

sale of this particular automobile. There are, however, other costs which sellers must defray which are *overhead* or *fixed* costs which will remain stable regardless of the number of cars sold.[206] "Profit" may be viewed as "gross profit," i.e., the difference between revenues (price) and variable costs, or "net profit" which is the difference between revenues and a sum representing both variable and fixed costs.[207] Fixed or overhead costs would include such constant costs as utilities, property taxes, rent, and administrative salaries. These costs are defrayed by spreading them over the total number of sales of automobiles or other products being sold. Each sale must carry its share of the fixed costs which will remain the same regardless of the number of units sold.[208] The total number of sales will not be determined until the end of the fiscal year, at which time an accurate measure of overhead or fixed cost per unit of sale may be ascribed. The allocation of overhead cost per unit of sale is, therefore, an accounting construct. Thus, in our automobile example where the price was $25,000 and the variable costs were $23,000, the fixed or overhead allocated cost to that particular sale was $500. One interpretation of the Code language would suggest that it is necessary to subtract from the contract price ($25,000) not only the $23,000 variable costs, but also the accountant's construct of fixed or overhead cost ($500) which would reveal the *net profit* on one sale to the seller of $1500. The Code, however, expressly permits the recovery of *overhead* ("including reasonable overhead"). Following this circular route, therefore, after having deducted the $500 overhead cost, it would then be added back in to allow a recovery to the seller of $2000. The courts are in agreement that "profit (including reasonable overhead)" means net profit plus overhead, or gross profit including overhead.[209] Since the determination of reasonable overhead to a particular contract is an accounting construct, it is superfluous to follow the complicated, circuitous route to the proper result. The simple formula of subtracting variable costs from list price (or unpaid contract price) will necessarily include the reasonable overhead which the Code permits the seller to recover.

[F]   Anticipatory Repudiation and Mitigation — UCC — "Learned of the Breach"

Anticipatory repudiation of a contract was explored earlier in this treatise.[210] Since an anticipatory repudiation is not, in itself, a breach, should a party recover damages that could have been avoided after the repudiation but before it became a breach? Older cases eschewed the concept of mitigation in response to an anticipatory repudiation on the footing that the repudiation could be ignored by the innocent party.[211] Prior to the UCC, there was authority

---

[206] *See* David Sloane, Inc. v. Stanley G. House & Assocs., Inc., 311 Md. 36, 532 A.2d 694 (1987).

[207] *See* Bead Chain Mfg. Co. v. Saxton Prods., Inc., 183 Conn. 266, 439 A.2d 314, n.4 (1981) (citing Childres & Burgess, *Seller's Remedies: The Primacy of UCC § 2-708(2)*, 48 NYU L. Rev. 833, 846–47 (1973)).

[208] *See* Vitex Mfg. Corp. v. Caribtex Corp., 377 F.2d 795, 799 (3d Cir. 1967).

[209] *See Bead Chain Mfg. Co. v. Saxton Prods.*, *supra* note 207 (citing Unique Sys., Inc. v. Zotos Int'l, Inc., 622 F.2d 373, 378 (8th Cir. 1980), and Jericho Sash & Door Co. v. Building Erectors, Inc., 362 Mass. 871, 872, 286 N.E.2d 343 (1972), in support). See the criticism of Restatement 2d § 347 comment f (*Lost Volume*) for its suggestion that, "The injured party's damages are then based on the net profit that he has lost as a result of the broken contract," as not recognizing the inclusion of overhead cost, in Teradyne, Inc. v. Teledyne Indus., Inc., 676 F.2d 865, 868 (1st Cir. 1982).

[210] See § 110, *supra*.

[211] *See, e.g.*, Barber Milling Co. v. Leichthammer Baking Co., 273 Pa. 90, 116 A. 677 (1922); John A. Roebling's Sons' Co. v. Lock-Stitch Fence Co., 130 Ill. 660, 22 N.E. 518 (1889).

supporting the same proposition in contracts for the sale of goods.[212] This view was always difficult to justify. While the innocent promisee may choose to treat the repudiation as an immediate breach or await performance for a commercially reasonable time, the promisee should not be permitted to recover unnecessary damages where the promisor clearly manifests his intention not to perform the contract. Since it is generally agreed that an anticipatory repudiation excuses the promisee from performing conditions precedent[213] and allows him generally to suspend his performance,[214] requiring reasonable action to avoid unnecessary losses is more than justified.

The UCC has reacted to pre-Code cases that would permit the aggrieved party to ignore the repudiation by allowing him to await the repudiating party's performance only for a commercially reasonable time.[215] Later in this Chapter we will survey UCC remedies. For now, it is important to recognize that the basic remedy permitting damages measured by the difference between the contract price and market price for buyers measures the market price at the time the buyer *learned of the breach* and for sellers, at the time of tender[216] rather than the time of the repudiation. Another UCC section, however, states that where the action involving market price damages comes to trial before the time for performance, damages based on market price will be measured when the aggrieved party learned of the repudiation.[217] The likelihood of a typical case *coming to trial* before the time for performance, however, is small. It should, therefore, be recalled that the UCC section on anticipatory repudiation permits an aggrieved party to await performance only *for a commercially reasonable time* after the repudiation.[218] Where it is clear that a repudiating party will not perform at the time set forth in the contract, a court may find that the aggrieved party is unreasonable in failing to take appropriate steps to effectuate a substitute purchase (cover). Instead of measuring market price damages by the time of tender or the time the buyer learned of the breach, a court may choose a commercially reasonable time after the repudiation as the time for measuring a rising contract price,[219] or the court may use the time of repudiation as the market price measure, thereby avoiding unreasonable losses.[220]

---

[212] Reliance Cooperage Corp. v. Treat, 195 F.2d 977 (8th Cir. 1952) (the well-known case involving anticipatory repudiation of a contract to deliver barrel staves).

[213] RESTATEMENT 2d § 255.

[214] UCC § 2-610(c).

[215] UCC § 2-610(a). The aggrieved party also has the choice of resorting to any remedy for breach immediately upon the repudiation. § 2-610(b).

[216] UCC §§ 2-713 (buyers); 2-708(1) (sellers).

[217] UCC § 2-723.

[218] UCC § 2-610(a).

[219] Oloffson v. Coomer, 11 Ill. App. 3d 918, 296 N.E.2d 871 (3d Dist. 1973). Farmer informed grain dealer that he would not plant corn because the season had been too wet. The dealer knew or should have known that the farmer would not be able to supply the corn at the time of the farmer's announcement that he would not plant. The court held that it was unreasonable for the dealer to await performance under these circumstances. *See also* First Nat'l Bank v. Jefferson Mortg. Co., 576 F.2d 479 (3d Cir. 1978).

[220] Trinidad Bean & Elev. Co. v. Frosh, 1 Neb. Ct. App. 281, 494 N.W.2d 347 (1992).

§ 124 EMOTIONAL DISTRESS LIMITATION

In addition to the economic losses caused by a breach of contract, any breach may cause the aggrieved party to suffer mental or emotional distress. It is foreseeable that the aggrieved party will often be unhappy after a breach and the breach may even cause some mental pain and suffering. Notwithstanding such foreseeable results, courts have been particularly reluctant to allow damages for emotional distress in contract actions.[221] Thus, another limitation on contract damages may be seen in the refusal of courts to permit the recovery of such damages. Some courts simply hold that contract actions for mental anguish are not available, others recognize the possibility of such actions in cases of serious emotional disturbance, while other courts follow an approach suggested by the RESTATEMENT 2d.[222] Another perspective is suggested in a recent opinion:

> Although the general rule is that emotional damages for breach of contract will not lie [citing the Restatement 2d § 353], this rule is simply a shorthand way of saying that emotional distress is usually not a foreseeable consequence of breach. But when the nature of the contract is such that emotional distress is foreseeable, emotional damages will lie.[223]

Thus, where serious emotional disturbance is not only foreseeable but a particularly likely result of a breach, damages for such emotional distress may be recoverable.[224] Contracts for the burial of a spouse or other family member are particularly sensitive. Any funeral director should be aware of the emotional nature of such contracts and that a breach may very well cause emotional distress.[225] Where a messenger service is made aware of the meaning or import of a death message, it should be aware of the likelihood of emotional distress if it breaches its contract by not delivering the message or delivering it so late that a relative is precluded from attending the funeral.[226] Where persons agree to be filmed for a television broadcast on the condition that their faces not be revealed, the breach of that promise may give rise to emotional distress damages.[227] The public humiliation attending the mistreatment or expulsion of guests of hotels,[228] or passengers from public carriers,[229] or ticketholders in places of entertainment or amusement[230] are traditional categories which courts have regarded as

---

[221] *See* Picogna v. Board of Educ. of Township of Cherry Hill, 143 N.J. Super. 391, 396–97, 671 A.2d 1035, 1037 (1996) ("potential for fabricated claims justifies a requirement of enhanced proof to support an award of such damages"). *See also* RESTATEMENT 2d § 353.

[222] See Munday v. Waste Mgmt. of N. Am., Inc., 997 F. Supp. 681, 686 (D. Md. 1998) (citing cases for each of the views).

[223] Sheely v. MRI Radiology Network, P. A., 505 F.3d 1173, 1200 (11th Cir. 2007).

[224] RESTATEMENT 2d § 353: ". . . [T]he contract or the breach is of such a kind that serious emotional disturbance was a particularly likely result."

[225] *See* Lamm v. Shingleton, 231 N.C. 10, 55 S.E.2d 810 (1949); Fitzsimmons v. Olinger Mortuary Ass'n, 91 Colo. 544, 17 P.2d 535 (1932); Renihan v. Wright, 125 Ind. 536, 25 N.E. 822 (1890).

[226] *See* Wadsworth v. Western Union Tel. Co., 86 Tenn. 695, 8 S.W. 574 (1888).

[227] Huskey v. National Broadcasting Co., 632 F. Supp. 1282, 1292–93 (N.D. Ill. 1986).

[228] *See* Frewen v. Page, 238 Mass. 499, 131 N.E. 475 (1921).

[229] *See* Gillespie v. Brooklyn H. R. Co., 178 N.Y. 347, 70 N.E. 857 (1904). While cases involving a public carrier evicting a person from a train or bus are within an exception, emotional distress claims allegedly caused by the delay of a shipper in transporting household goods were not recognized in Richter v. North Am. Van Lines, Inc., 110 F. Supp. 2d 406 (D. Md. 2000).

[230] *See* Aaron v. Ward, 203 N.Y. 351, 96 N.E. 736 (1911).

exceptional situations giving rise to recoverable damages for emotional distress.[231] However, damages for alleged mental distress due to a refusal to pay a fire insurance claim,[232] the refusal to pay employee equal wages, allegedly for gender reasons,[233] or breach of a house construction contract[234] were denied.[235]

Another exception includes breaches of contract that also involve bodily harm. Breach of promise to perform a Caesarean operation to avoid another stillbirth[236] or breach of a cosmetic surgery contract to beautify a nose[237] permitted the recovery of emotional distress damages, while a failure to respond to the call of a patient did not.[238] This exception is troublesome because it is not clear whether an independent tort must accompany the breach of contract. The RESTATEMENT 2d limits this exception to cases in which the breach also caused "bodily harm"[239] and explains that "the action may nearly always be regarded as one in tort."[240] It then suggests, however, that courts generally do not require the plaintiff to specify the nature of the action, i.e., they permit the recovery of emotional distress damages without classifying the wrong.[241] While some cases require conduct amounting to a tort to accompany the breach of contract to allow emotional distress damages,[242] other courts insist that it is not necessary to prove a tort to fall within this exception.[243] Rather, wilful, wanton, or insulting conduct, albeit not amounting to a tort, will be sufficient.[244] At least one reason for this confusion may arise from the clear requirement that *punitive* damages, as contrasted with damages for emotional distress, are recoverable only where the conduct constituting the breach amounts to a tort.[245] Emotional distress damages are generally regarded as sharing the normal purpose of contract

---

[231] See FIRST RESTATEMENT § 341 and the elaboration thereof in the concurring opinion of Mr. Justice Musmanno in Gefter v. Rosenthal, 384 Pa. 123, 119 A.2d 250, 251 (1956).

[232] Moorehead v. State Farm Fire & Cas. Co., 123 F. Supp. 2d 1004 (W.D. Va. 2000) (alleged misrepresentation of claim).

[233] Jean Anderson Hierarchy of Agents v. Allstate Life Ins. Co., 2 F. Supp. 2d 688 (E.D. Pa. 1998).

[234] Hancock v. Northcutt, 808 P.2d 251 (Alaska 1991).

[235] See, however, Kishmarton v. William Bailey Constr. Co., 754 N. E. 2d 785, 788 (Ohio 2001) ("Today we join the minority of courts that allow emotional distress damages in contracts cases involving transactions between vendees and builder-vendors. . . .")

[236] Stewart v. Rudner, 349 Mich. 459, 84 N.W.2d 816 (1957).

[237] Sullivan v. O'Connor, 363 Mass. 579, 296 N.E.2d 183 (1973).

[238] St. Charles v. Kender, 38 Mass. App. Ct. 155, 646 N.E.2d 411 (1995) (question whether the failure to return the patient's calls caused a miscarriage and emotional distress resulting therefrom).

[239] RESTATEMENT 2d § 353.

[240] RESTATEMENT 2d § 353 comment a.

[241] *Id.*

[242] *See* Deli v. University of Minnesota, 578 N.W.2d 779 (Minn. Ct. App. 1998); Chung v. Kaonohi Ctr. Co., 62 Haw. 594, 618 P.2d 283 (1980).

[243] *See* Trimble v. Denver, 697 P.2d 716 (Colo. 1985).

[244] *Id.* It should be noted, however, that third parties may not be entitled to such damages though their emotional distress was clearly foreseeable at the time of contract formation. Thus, where a newborn was kidnaped from a hospital and held for more than four months, the parents were not entitled to recover because they had no cause of action due to a lack of duty on the part of the hospital to the parents. Johnson v. Jamaica Hosp., 62 N.Y.2d 523, 478 N.Y.S.2d 838, 467 N.E.2d 502 (1984). Similarly, where a parent suffering from Alzheimer's disease was not properly cared for in a nursing home, the children of the parents had no cause of action. Oresky v. Scharf, 126 A.D.2d 614, 510 N.Y.S.2d 897 (2d Dep't 1987).

[245] RESTATEMENT 2d § 355.

damages, i.e., they are designed to have a *compensatory* effect, as contrasted with punitive damages which are designed to have a *deterrent* effect.[246]

§ 125   DAMAGES WITH PURPOSES OTHER THAN COMPENSATION — PUNITIVE AND NOMINAL DAMAGES

As we have seen, the normal purpose of contract damages is to *compensate* the aggrieved party, typically by placing that party in the position he would have occupied had the contract been performed, thereby protecting his expectation interest.[247] There are, however, two other types of damages which clearly have no *compensatory* purpose: *punitive* damages and *nominal* damages.

[A]   Punitive Damages — "Efficient Breach"

Since the purpose of contract law is to compensate the aggrieved party, the traditional view is that damages should not be awarded for the purpose of punishing the contract breaker in an effort to deter similar conduct. On the other hand, in tort actions, particularly outrageous conduct by the tortfeasor will often give rise to punitive damages in addition to compensatory damages for the actual harm suffered. Myriad cases support the general rule that punitive or exemplary damages are not recoverable in a contract action unless the breach of contract is also a tort for which punitive damages would be recoverable.[248] An underlying justification for this rule is the recognition of an "efficient breach" discussed earlier.[249] If a party will be better off by breaching a contract and still assure the expectation interest of the other party through compensation, such an "efficient breach" is encouraged.[250] Awarding punitive damages may, therefore, operate to deter such breaches.[251] There is, however, a view that punitive damages should be allowed, at least for wilful breaches involving opportunistic behavior, because they do not enhance societal wealth. Moreover, since the efficient breach theory does not account for transaction costs, including such costs as assessment of damages at trial, allowing punitive

---

[246] *See* Mortgage Fin., Inc. v. Podleski, 742 P.2d 900 (Colo. 1987) (pointing out the confusion in Denver Pub. Co. v. Kirk, 729 P.2d 1004 (Colo. Ct. App. 1986), in which the court labeled damages for emotional distress as "exemplary" (punitive)). *See also* Aaron v. Ward, 203 N.Y. 351, 355, 96 N.E. 736, 737 (1911) ("And it must be borne in mind that a recovery for indignity and wounded feelings is compensatory and does not constitute exemplary damages."). Punitive damages are explored in § 125, *infra*.

[247] We also considered the protection of the reliance and restitution interests which restore the aggrieved party to *status quo ante*, i.e., they place the party in the position it would have occupied had no contract been formed.

[248] Ford v. Trendwest Resorts, 43 P.3d 1223, 1227 (Wn. 2002) ("The central objective behind the system of contract remedies is compensatory, not punitive. Punishment of a promisor for having broken his promise has no justification on economic or other grounds" [citing Restatement 2d §§ 356 & 355]. *See also*, Vanwyk Textile Sys., B.V. v. Zimmer Mach. Am., 994 F. Supp. 350, 362 (W.D.N.C. 1997) ("To state a claim in tort, a plaintiff must allege a duty owed him by the defendant separate and distinct from any duty owed under a contract."). *See also* Palmer v. Ted Stevens Honda, Inc., 193 Cal. App. 3d 530, 238 Cal. Rptr. 363 (6th Dist. 1987); Wien Air Alaska v. Bubbel, 723 P.2d 627 (Alaska 1986); Morrow v. L.A. Goldschmidt Assocs., Inc., 112 Ill. 2d 87, 96 Ill. Dec. 939, 492 N.E.2d 181 (1986); Ellmex Constr. Co. v. Republic Ins. Co., 202 N.J. Super. 195, 494 A.2d 339 (1985); Kamlar Corp. v. Haley, 224 Va. 699, 299 S.E.2d 514 (1983); Z. D. Howard Co. v. Cartwright, 537 P.2d 345 (Okla. 1975). Restatement 2d § 355.

[249] *See* § 118[C], *supra.*

[250] *See* Thyssen, Inc. v. S.S. Fortune Star, 777 F.2d 57, 63 (2d Cir. 1985) (efficient breaches that are wealth-enhancing should be encouraged since the breaching party will still profit after compensating the other party for its expectation interest).

[251] *See* E.I. DuPont de Nemours & Co. v. Pressman, 679 A.2d 436, 446 (Del. 1996).

damages to induce the negotiation of a release may be more efficient.[252]

A few courts have awarded punitive damages in the absence of a tort where, for example, the conduct is fraudulent though not tortious.[253] More recently, a number of courts have been willing to award punitive damages where there has been a wilful breach of a fiduciary duty, such as that owed by a real estate broker to a client[254] or by an insurance company to a client. Where an insurance company wilfully withholds payment of a claim, i.e., where it has no reasonable basis for denying the claim and it knows that it has no basis for denial or recklessly disregards its lack of a reasonable basis for denial, the insurer has not only breached the contract, it has acted in extreme bad faith which, according to a number of courts, amounts to a tort.[255] Other courts have rejected this view.[256] As we saw earlier,[257] there is an *implied covenant of good faith* in every contract and it is possible to construe a wilful violation of that covenant as tortious as well as a breach of contract. The application of the concept beyond insurance or other special relationship contracts to ordinary commercial contracts provoked considerable controversy[258] and was severely weakened when a case restricted the "bad faith breach" concept to contracts involving special relationships.[259] Seven years later, it was definitively dispatched.[260] Bad faith breach cases were, again, relegated to cases involving fiduciary or special relationships between the parties. In the meantime, an amendment to a comment in the UCC section on good faith made it abundantly clear that the Code does not support an independent cause of action for failure to perform or enforce a contract in good faith:

> Rather, this section means that a failure to perform or enforce, in good faith, a specific duty or obligation under the contract, constitutes a breach of that contract or makes unavailable, under the particular circumstances, a remedial right or power.[261]

---

[252] William S. Dodge, *The Case for Punitive Damages in Contracts*, 48 DUKE L.J. 629 (1999).

[253] In South Carolina, this view was enunciated many years ago in Welborn v. Dixon, 70 S.C. 108, 49 S.E. 232 (1904). *See also* Boise Dodge, Inc. v. Clark, 92 Idaho 902, 453 P.2d 551 (1969).

[254] *See* Phillips v. Lynch, 101 Nev. 311, 704 P.2d 1083 (1985); Robison v. Katz, 94 N.M. 314, 610 P.2d 201 (Ct. App. 1980); Security Aluminum Window Mfg. Corp. v. Lehman Assocs., Inc., 108 N.J. Super. 137, 260 A.2d 248 (1970).

[255] *See* White v. Unigard Mut. Ins. Co., 112 Idaho 94, 730 P.2d 1014 (1986); Rawlings v. Apodaca, 151 Ariz. 180, 726 P.2d 596 (Ct. App. 1985), *aff'd in part, vacated in part, en banc*, 151 Ariz. 149, 726 P.2d 565 (1986). Statutes may allow punitive damages against insurance companies. E. g., N. D.Cent Code § 32-03.2-11.1 (insurer that violates duty of good faith is liable for punitive damages if it is guilty by clear and convincing evidenece of oppressions, fraud or actual malice.") See Moore v. Am. Family Mut. Ins. Co., 576 F.3d 781 (8th Cir. 2009); Pa. C. S. § 8371 (court may award punitive damages to insurer who acts in bad faith toward the insured). See Smith v. Continental Cas. Co., 2009 U.S. App. LEXIS 22240 (3d Cir. 2009).

[256] *See* Pillsbury Co. v. National Union Fire Ins. Co., 425 N.W.2d 244 (Minn. Ct. App. 1988); Garden State Community Hosp. v. Watson, 191 N.J. Super. 225, 465 A.2d 1225 (1982); Kewin v. Massachusetts Mut. Life Ins. Co., 409 Mich. 401, 295 N.W.2d 50 (1980).

[257] *See* § 97[C], *supra*.

[258] Seaman's Direct Buying Serv., Inc. v. Standard Oil Co., 36 Cal. 3d 752, 206 Cal. Rptr. 354, 686 P.2d 1158 (1984) (egregious breach of the implied covenant of good faith by denial of existence of contract), *overruled by* Della Penna v. Toyota Motor Sales, U.S.A., Inc., 11 Cal. 4th 376, 45 Cal. Rptr. 2d 436, 902 P.2d 740 (1995).

[259] Foley v. Interactive Data Corp., 47 Cal. 3d 654, 254 Cal. Rptr. 211, 765 P.2d 373 (1988) (refusal to extend concept to employment contract).

[260] Freeman & Mills, Inc. v. Belcher Oil Co., 11 Cal. 4th 85, 44 Cal. Rptr. 2d 420, 900 P.2d 669 (1995).

[261] UCC § 1-304, comment 1 (formerly § 1-203).

[B]   Nominal Damages

Unlike the commission of a tort, whenever a breach of contract has occurred that was not legally excusable, a cause of action exists regardless of the lack of compensable loss.[262] If the aggrieved party has suffered no compensable loss and is not entitled to exemplary (punitive) damages, she may recover nominal damages.[263] If the aggrieved party cannot establish damages because of a fatal lack of certainty in the proof, the court will award nominal damages.[264] The typical recovery will be a token, such as six cents or one dollar.[265] Where the plaintiff has made a good faith but unsuccessful effort to prove damages, the court may award her court costs.[266] A failure to claim nominal damages may affect an opportunity to recovery reasonable attorney's fees.[267]

An action for nominal damages may be pursued simply to establish certain contractual rights that may be more effectively pursued in a declaratory judgment action. Where issues of material fact exist, even in the absence of any evidence of actual damages, a court should deny a motion for summary judgment because the plaintiff has a claim for nominal damages.[268] Another court, however, may not bother reversing an erroneous grant of summary judgment where the only reason for remanding the case would be to allow the plaintiff to recover nominal damages.[269]

§ 126   AGREED DAMAGES — LIQUIDATED DAMAGES, PENALTIES, AND LIMITATIONS ON LIABILITY

[A]   Purposes of Agreed Damages Provisions

It is not uncommon for parties who make a contract to agree that a specified amount will be paid to the aggrieved party in the event of a breach, instead of having damages assessed in the usual way. The question is whether such a stipulation will be enforced by the courts.

An agreed damages provision may be designed to accomplish any one of at least three distinct purposes. (1) It may be intended to coerce the promisor into performing his contract by fixing a sum to be paid, in case of breach, that far exceeds the probable, actual loss that

---

[262] This is a matter of puzzlement for one of America's most distinguished jurists. In Chronister Oil Co. v. Unocal Ref. & Mktg., 34 F.3d 462, 466 (7th Cir. 1994), Chief Judge Richard Posner remanded a case with directions to enter judgment for nominal damages "to which for reasons we do not understand every victim of a breach of contract, unlike a tort victim, is entitled."

[263] Harper v. Consolidated Bus Lines, 117 W. Va. 228, 185 S.E. 225 (1936); W. H. Kiblinger Co. v. Sauk Bank, 131 Wis. 595, 111 N.W. 709 (1907). RESTATEMENT 2d § 346(2).

[264] *See* Freund v. Washington Square Press, Inc., 34 N.Y.2d 379, 357 N.Y.S.2d 857, 314 N.E.2d 419 (1974) (publisher breached contract to publish book and plaintiff could not establish royalty loss with reasonable certainty so court awarded nominal damages of six cents).

[265] Georgia, however, will award much more significant "nominal" damages, *e.g.*, $1000 or $1500 would not be uncommon. *See* First Fed. S & L Ass'n of Atlanta v. White, 168 Ga. App. 516, 309 S.E.2d 858 (1983).

[266] *See* Freund v. Washington Square Press, Inc., supra note 264.

[267] MindGames, Inc. v. Western Publ'g Co., 218 F.3d 652, 654 (7th Cir. 2000), *cert. denied*, 121 S. Ct. 882, 148 L. Ed. 2d 791 (2001).

[268] Scallon v. United States AG Ctr., Inc., 42 F. Supp. 2d 867 (N.D. Iowa 1999).

[269] Sattell v. Continental Casualty Co., 157 Wis. 2d 503, 460 N.W.2d 446 (Ct. App. 1990).

would result from a breach of the contract. The fear of having to pay an excessive amount could operate *in terrorem* to induce the promisor to carry out his performance, regardless of the circumstances confronting him.[270] (2) The stipulation may be intended merely as a convenient method of determining the amount to be paid in case of breach, i.e., it may be an honest pre-estimate of the probable loss which will be caused by the breach. (3) Such a stipulation may be designed to put a limit on the amount of the loss to be borne by the promisor in case of breach, as where parties fix a sum to be paid which is obviously less than the probable, actual loss that would be suffered by the promisee if a breach should occur.

[1] History — Conditioned Penal Bonds — Penalties vs. Liquidated Damages

It is clear from the decided cases that if the stipulation calls for the payment of what amounts to a penalty for nonperformance designed to coerce performance, it is unenforceable. This has not always been so. A typical debt of the early common law was evidenced by a conditional bond, originally a sealed instrument. It was a conditional promise by the obligor to pay a much larger sum, perhaps twice the amount of the debt, conditioned, however, on the obligor's payment of the original amount of the debt on time. By fulfilling the condition, the penalty was discharged.[271] The Court of Chancery, however, was called upon to relieve defaulting obligors from the forfeitures they were suffering under conditional penal bonds. They did so on the ground that it is unconscionable for a private person to exact a penalty or to insist upon a forfeiture because of another's nonperformance of duty, even though the penalty or forfeiture is agreed upon by the parties. They also wished to prevent the collection of usury. By the seventeenth century, common law courts began to assimilate equitable concepts in allowing relief for certain kinds of penal bonds with the attendant emphasis upon the principle of compensation as a genuine pre-estimate of damages, rather than an *in terrorem* penalty to induce performance.[272] This was the origin of the modern distinction between "penalty" clauses, which became unenforceable, and "liquidated damages" clauses that are enforceable because they are an honest forecast of actual damages.[273] Where the stipulation exacts a penalty, it will be disregarded and the damages will be assessed as if the contract were silent on the question of the amount to be paid in case of breach.[274] It is, however, perfectly proper for the parties to a contract to pre-estimate the probable loss in case of breach and to stipulate for the payment of the amount so determined to avoid the necessity for the assessment of damages in the usual way. If this is the apparent purpose of the stipulation, the amount agreed to be paid will be called liquidated damages, as distinguished from a penalty, and the promisee will recover the stipulated amount, and only that amount, regardless of whether the actual loss suffered from a breach is greater or less than the stipulated amount.[275]

---

[270] See River Road Assocs. v. Chesapeake Display & Packaging Co., Inc., 104 F. Supp. 2d 418, 424–25 (D. N. J. 2000).

[271] *See* A. W. B. SIMPSON, A HISTORY OF THE COMMON LAW OF CONTRACT 90 (1987).

[272] *Id.* at 118–25. The author (at 123) insists that the "compensatory principle" as a theory long antedated the modern recognition that a party should recover only the loss actually suffered. There was, however, a "divorce between contractual theory and practice" for many centuries.

[273] *See* 5 HOLDSWORTH, HISTORY OF ENGLISH LAW 293 (1924). *See also* Sun Printing & Pub'g Ass'n v. Moore, 183 U.S. 642, 22 S. Ct. 240, 46 L. Ed. 366 (1902); Burnside v. Wand, 170 Mo. 531, 71 S.W. 337 (1902).

[274] See RESTATEMENT 2d § 356 comment a, referring to § 184(1), which permits a court to enforce the remainder of the agreement where part of the agreement is unenforceable on grounds of public policy.

[275] *See* Monsen Eng'g Co. v. Tami-Gaithens, Inc., 219 N.J. Super. 241, 530 A.2d 313 (1987); Owen v. Christopher,

The only question of difficulty encountered in the application of these principles comes in determining whether an agreed damages provision in a given case is to be dealt with as a liquidated damages clause or as a penalty that will not be enforced. It is important to consider the judicial tests used to make this distinction.

[B]   Traditional Tests to Distinguish Liquidated Damage Clauses From Penalties

[1]   Traditional (Common Law) Test

The common law courts developed a test to determine the enforceability of an agreed damages provision that contained three requirements: (1) the parties must have intended to agree on damages in advance of any breach; (2) the anticipated damages had to be difficult of ascertainment, i.e., they were uncertain; (3) the amount stipulated was a reasonable forecast of losses that would ensue in the event of a breach, i.e., the amount is not greatly disproportionate to an honest estimate of probable damages.[276]

The first element is of dubious importance. While the parties must objectively manifest their intention to agree on a damages clause, their actual intention as to the validity of the clause is irrelevant.[277] The only question of intention is whether the parties made an honest pre-estimate of the probable loss,[278] though questions may also arise as to whether a given clause should be interpreted as an agreed damages clause at all.[279] The name given to the clause by the parties, i.e., either "liquidated damages" or "penalty," will not control[280] though it is hardly advisable to draft a clause intended to allow for liquidated damages by characterizing the clause as a "penalty."[281]

---

144 Kan. 765, 62 P.2d 860 (1936); Robbins v. Plant, 174 Ark. 639, 297 S.W. 1027 (1927); Wise v. United States, 249 U.S. 361, 39 S. Ct. 303, 63 L. Ed. 647 (1919); Learned v. Holbrook, 87 Or. 576, 170 P. 530 (1918), *adhered to*, 87 Or. 589, 171 P. 222 (1918).

[276] *See* Grossinger Motorcorp, Inc. v. American Nat'l Bank & Trust Co., 240 Ill. App. 3d 737, 180 Ill. Dec. 824, 607 N.E.2d 1337, 1345 (1st Dist. 1992); Yerton v. Bowden, 762 P.2d 786 (Colo. Ct. App. 1988); *Monsen Eng'g Co. v. Tami-Gaithens, Inc.*, *supra* note 275; Berger v. Shanahan, 142 Conn. 726, 118 A.2d 311 (1955).

[277] Demczyk v. Mutual Life Ins. Co. (*In re* Graham Square), 126 F.3d 823, 829 (6th Cir. 1997).

[278] That their intention as to how the stipulation shall be regarded is immaterial is evidenced from the results reached. It is clear from those results that their intention is important, if at all, only insofar as it relates to the basis on which the sum fixed is determined. It is only the intention to make an honest pre-estimate of the probable loss that counts. Thus, it has been said, "[b]ut agreements to pay fixed sums plainly without reasonable relation to any probable damage which may follow a breach will not be enforced. This circumstance tends to negative any notion that the parties really meant to provide a measure of compensation — 'to treat the sum named as estimated and ascertained damages.'" Kothe v. R. C. Taylor Trust, 280 U.S. 224, 226, 50 S. Ct. 142, 74 L. Ed. 382 (1930). Another court suggests that "[t]he question is not what the parties intended but 'whether the sum fixed is, in fact, in the nature of a penalty.'" Central Trust Co. v. Wolf, 255 Mich. 8, 14, 237 N.W. 29, 31 (1931).

[279] The clause may be quite different, *e.g.*, it could be an exculpatory clause, or it could be a manifestation of the parties to allow for alternative performances. These issues are discussed later in this section.

[280] *See In re* Lammers, 211 F. Supp. 448 (E.D. Ark. 1962); Independent Sch. Dist. v. Dudley, 195 Iowa 398, 192 N.W. 261 (1923); Horn v. Poindexter, 176 N.C. 620, 97 S.E. 653 (1918); United States v. Bethlehem Steel Co., 205 U.S. 105, 27 S. Ct. 450, 51 L. Ed. 731 (1907).

[281] Such a characterization presents an obstacle, albeit not an insuperable one, to a court in deciding that the clause is an enforceable agreed damages (liquidated damages) clause. There is no point in creating any obstacle to that determination if the intention is to have an enforceable clause.

The second element requiring damages to be uncertain is designed to corroborate the parties' assumed intention to honestly forecast damages in the event of a breach. If damages are easily ascertainable, the need for such a clause is dubious and there is some suspicion that the clause was designed for purposes other than the legitimate purpose of honestly forecasting damages. There are situations which are particularly appropriate for agreed damages clauses because actual damages are so uncertain. A contract containing a restrictive covenant not to compete, for example, is an example of precisely the kind of promise which, if breached, does not lend itself to easy or accurate measurement of actual loss.[282] A severance clause, where an employee is to receive a salary for some period of time, recognizes the uncertainty as to when and at what compensation the employee will find new employment.[283] One of the most common uses of such a clause is found in highway construction or similar projects where government departments will include a clause for a certain amount of damages for each day of delay.[284] These clauses are typically set forth in prefabricated terms, i.e., there will be a stated amount of liquidated damages per day and that amount may vary with the contract price — the higher the contract price, the larger the amount of daily liquidated damages since delays on larger contracts are typically more costly to the state than delays on smaller projects. The damages are always quite difficult to ascertain. Measurement of harm to the public where performance is delayed is extremely difficult to calculate with reasonable certainty.[285] Courts, therefore, concentrate on the amount in the clause as the paramount question.[286] Whether a provision is an enforceable damages clause or a penalty is a question of law.[287] The party challenging the clause has the burden of proving that it is unenforceable.[288]

Where damages resulting from a breach will be readily ascertainable, such as a contract for the sale of ordinary goods with a prevailing market price, it is particularly difficult to justify an agreed damages clause. While there is criticism of the uncertainty requirement and suggestions that the question of enforceability is typically not decided on that basis, the judicial test invariably contains this element. Numerous cases repeat the guideline stated in the RESTATE-

---

[282] *See* Raymundo v. Hammond Clinic Ass'n, 449 N.E.2d 276 (Ind. 1983). Physician worked in a clinic which grossed over $8 million dollars annually. His division produced over $384,000 each year, of which he provided over $100,000 in a little more than six months. A liquidated damages provision for breach of a covenant not to compete, which required his payment of $25,000, was upheld as clearly not disproportionate to the probable loss of his leaving the clinic.

[283] Boone v. Platinum Tech., Inc., 2000 U.S. Dist. LEXIS 19315, at *14 (E.D. Pa. Dec. 20, 2000) (employee worked in computer software and the clause allowed a full year's salary at $130,000 plus a bonus; employee did find new employment two months after leaving, but at a salary $20,000 less than the former salary). A grossly disproportionate amount, however, will not be enforced. *See* AFLAC, Inc. v. Williams, 264 Ga. 351, 444 S.E.2d 314 (1994) (clause in a contract between an attorney and a corporation required company to pay an unreasonably high sum with no consideration of mitigation of damages or the possibility that the attorney could be discharged for cause).

[284] *See* Ledbetter Bros., Inc. v. North Carolina Dep't of Transp., 68 N.C. App. 97, 314 S.E.2d 761 (1984); Dave Gustafson & Co. v. State, 83 S.D. 160, 156 N.W.2d 185 (1968). Current practice suggests that it is not uncommon for contractors to agree to such clauses if a corresponding clause granting the contractor a bonus for early completion of projects is included.

[285] Space Master Int'l, Inc. v. Worcester, 940 F.2d 16, 18 (1st Cir. 1991) (delay of more than 200 days in providing classrooms).

[286] Rohlin Constr. Co. v. Hinton, 476 N.W.2d 78, 81 (Iowa 1991). Where a county engineer deviated from traditional liquidated damage amounts for a city-county road resurfacing project, his reason for increasing the amount was due to the desire for a completion date prior to the start of the school year with its attendant increased traffic. The engineer stated, "[W]e wanted the liquidated damage amount to be sufficient to make the contractor aware that we need that project completed." The court found no evidence that the amount was justified and refused to enforce the clause.

[287] *See Boone v. Platinum Technology, supra* note 283, at 11.

[288] DJ Mfg. Corp. v. United States, 86 F.3d 1130, 1134 (Fed. Cir. 1996).

MENT 2d, "The greater the difficulty either of proving that loss has occurred or of establishing its amount with the requisite certainty, the easier it is to show that the amount fixed is reasonable."[289] While the uncertainty element is important, it is clear that the third element is unquestionably of paramount concern to courts, i.e., whether the amount fixed in the clause was highly disproportionate to the amount of probable loss in the event of a breach.

[C]   The Revised Liquidated Damages Test — Relevance of Actual Loss — UCC and RESTATEMENT 2d

It is important to emphasize that the traditional test is applied at the time of contract formation:[290] did the parties agreed upon an amount at the time they formed the contract which, in light of *anticipated harm*, was an honest and reasonable forecast of actual damages?[291] If the forecast was reasonable at the time of formation, actual damages should be irrelevant.[292] The parties, after all, are substituting their private agreement on damages for the usual judicial assessment process. If they have made an honest forecast of such damages, why should that forecast not control, regardless of the actual losses that may have become ascertainable after the breach but were unascertainable at the time of formation? If actual damages are to be measured, the need for an agreed damages clause is questionable. This logic, however, encounters two significant challenges. First, the Uniform Commercial Code modified the traditional test to include a comparison of the amount in the clause with either anticipated or actual loss and this change was later absorbed in the RESTATEMENT 2D OF CONTRACTS. Second, under either the traditional or modified test, what should a court do if a clause appears reasonable in light of anticipated harm but events prove that no actual harm of any significance occurred? We will now explore each of these challenges.

[1]   Uniform Commercial Code and RESTATEMENT 2d Modification — "Single Look" vs. "Second Look"

The UCC made an important change in the test to be applied to agreed damages provisions[293] and the RESTATEMENT 2d replicates the Code provision.[294] While retaining the uncertainty requirement,[295] the Code and RESTATEMENT 2d provisions state that the amount in

---

[289] RESTATEMENT 2d § 356, comment b. *See Space Master International, supra* note 285, at 17. *See also* DJ Mfg. Corp. v. United States, 86 F.3d 1130, 1134 (Fed. Cir. 1996); Miller v. Nissan Motor Acceptance Corp., 2000 U.S. Dist. LEXIS 15645, at *101 (E.D. Pa. Oct. 27, 2000).

[290] *See* AFLAC, Inc. v. Williams, 264 Ga. 351, 444 S.E.2d 314, 317 n.5 (1994). *See also Yerton v. Bowden, supra* note 276, and *Monsen Eng'g Co. v. Tami-Gaithens, Inc., supra* note 275.

[291] Barrie School v. Patch, 401 Md. 497, 508–09, 932 A. 2d 382, 388–89 (Ct. App.2007).

[292] See Frick Co. v. Rubel Corp., 62 F.2d 765 (2d Cir. 1933), where Judge Learned Hand suggests that his brothers on the court think that actual losses are irrelevant where there is an enforceable agreed damages clause because only losses in *contemplation* of breach are relevant to test the validity of such a clause. Learned Hand disagreed. He was not entirely alone in his view. In fact, a few courts had previously held that it was necessary to determine whether the amount stipulated was reasonable in light of the *actual* loss sustained by the aggrieved party. *See* Ian Macneil, *Power of Contract and Agreed Remedies*, 47 CORNELL L.Q. 495, 504 (1962).

[293] UCC § 2-718(1).

[294] RESTATEMENT 2d § 356(1). *See* Lind Bldg. Corp. v. Pacific Bellevue Dev., 55 Wash. App. 70, 776 P.2d 977 (1989); Illingworth v. Bushong, 297 Or. 675, 688 P.2d 379 (1984).

[295] UCC § 2-718(1) suggests that damages may be liquidated "in the light of . . . the difficulties of proof of loss and the inconvenience and nonfeasibility of otherwise obtaining an adequate remedy." Notwithstanding this language, it is

the clause must be reasonable "in the light of the anticipated *or* actual harm caused by the breach. . . ."[296] The provision is designed to extend the enforceability of agreed damages clauses by permitting the amount in the clause to be compared with anticipated or actual harm. Where the UCC governs, decisions that had previously restricted their analyses of validity of agreed damages provisions exclusively to anticipated harm were, to this extent, abrogated by the Code.[297] The change, however, has not escaped criticism. Where, for example, a clause appearing clearly disproportionate to anticipated harm is designed as a penalty at the time of formation, if it turns out not to be unreasonably disproportionate to actual damages as later measured, the clause could be enforced under the modified test even though such enforcement may be said to violate two fundamental policies of the common law. First, the court would be enforcing a clause that was intended as a penalty, which is antithetical to the compensation concept. Second, since the large actual damages were not anticipated at the time of formation, they were not foreseeable. The enforcement of the clause, therefore, would violate the foreseeability limitation to which the Code and RESTATEMENT 2d adhere and our courts have insisted upon since *Hadley v. Baxendale* in 1854.[298]

[2]   The "No Harm" Problem — "First Look" vs. "Second Look"

Another vexing issue occurs where there is no actual loss, but the liquidated damages clause is reasonable with respect to anticipated harm. Where the plaintiffs agreed to purchase residential real estate for $355,000, they paid a total deposit of $17,750. A clause in the contract stated that if the buyers failed to fulfill their obligations under the contract, all deposits would be retained by the seller as liquidated damages. The closing date was September 1. The buyers repudiated on August 9 and the defendant sold the property to another purchaser for $360,000 on August 24. The plaintiffs sought the return of their deposits. The trial court held for the defendants. The Court of Appeals relied upon illustration 4 in § 356 of the Restatement 2d of Contracts in which there was no actual loss in reversing the trial court. The Supreme Judicial Court of Massachusetts, however, reversed the Court of Appeals.[299] The Supreme Court

---

doubtful that courts will insist upon great uncertainty under this Code provision. For example, with respect to a contract for the purchase of an automobile breached by the buyer, the court suggested that a clause allowing the seller twenty percent of the price as liquidated damages may be reasonable in light of the UCC allowance of lost profit to lost volume sellers under § 2-708(1). The fact that such profits may have been ascertainable at the time of contract formation was not mentioned. *See* Kaiserman v. Martin J. Ain, Ltd., 112 Misc. 2d 768, 450 N.Y.S.2d 135 (App. Term 1981). Neither the UCC nor the RESTATEMENT 2d bother stating that the parties must have intended to liquidate damages. In light of many years of doubt concerning this "requirement," the absence is not remarkable.

[296] UCC § 2-718(1) (emphasis added). The only change in the RESTATEMENT 2d language is the use of the term "loss" instead of "harm." RESTATEMENT 2d § 356(1).

[297] Equitable Lumber Corp. v. IPA Land Dev. Corp., 38 N.Y.2d 516, 381 N.Y.S.2d 459, 344 N.E.2d 391 (1976).

[298] "It is true that the Code is unusually generous in its appraisal of the amount set by the contracting parties. Even if this amount was entirely unreasonable, as of the time of contract, it can apparently be recovered so long as it turns out, purely as a matter of accident, to approximate the harm actually caused by the buyer's breach." Peters, *Remedies for Breach of Contract Relating to the Sale of Goods Under the Uniform Commercial Code: A Roadmap for Article Two*, 73 YALE L.J. 199, 278 (1963). Prior to the approval of what now appears as RESTATEMENT 2d § 356(1), the author, at the request of the Reporter for the RESTATEMENT 2d, met with the Reporter to suggest changes in certain draft provisions of the RESTATEMENT 2d relating to damages. The Reporter accepted six of seven recommendations. The seventh recommendation had suggested that the RESTATEMENT 2d should not follow the UCC section on liquidated damages for the reasons stated in the text. The Reporter conveyed the clear impression that, since the American Law Institute was half responsible for the UCC (i.e., along with the National Conference of Commissioners on Uniform State Laws), it was necessary to follow the Code.

[299] Kelly v. Marx, 428 Mass. 877, 705 N. E. 2d 1114 (1999).

emphasized the importance of viewing liquidated damages clauses as of the time of formation since this "first look" approach promotes efficiency and certainty while it prevents costly litigation. The Court viewed the "second look" at actual damages approach as undermining peace of mind and certainty of result that the parties sought through the inclusion of their liquidated damages clause. Where the parties have created a fair and reasonable damages clause at the time of formation, allowing the party to raise a comparison between the anticipated amount and actual damages induces the very litigation the clause was designed to avoid. The Court, therefore, agreed with "the decisions of many other States, that a judge in determining the enforceability of a liquidated damages clause, should examine only the circumstances at contract formation."[300]

The "second look" approach emphasizes the underlying policy of contract remedies to place a party in the same position, but not a better position, she would have occupied had the contract been performed. Where parties contracted for the purchase and sale of property at a price exceeding $4 million, the agreement required the buyer to make an initial down payment of $20,000 and additional deposits prior to the time for closing. After these deposits were made, the parties agreed on successive extensions of time for the closing requiring additional deposits. When the buyer could not close by the final extended closing date, the amount of deposits paid to that time amounted to $250,000. A clause in the contract allowed the seller to retain "the deposit" as liquidated damages. One month after the purchaser defaulted, the property was sold to another buyer for $1 million more than the original purchase price. The court held that, where the damage envisioned by the parties in framing their liquidated damage clause never occurs, neither justice nor the intent of the parties is served by its enforcement.[301]

Another case suggests the challenges courts may confront in similar circumstances. A contractor agreed to perform by a certain date under a contract containing an agreed damages provision for $750 per day for each day of delay, which was a reasonable amount in the light of anticipated harm. The contractor insisted that his subcontractor agree to a similar clause. The subcontractor failed to complete its work on time as did the contractor. The trial court, however, found that the sub's delay did not cause the contractor's delay. The court struggled to what it deemed a just result, i.e., limit the subcontractor's liability to an amount not greater than the number of days of delay for which the contractor was liable.[302] It is important to consider the "no harm" issue in other parts of the world.

---

[300] *Id.*, 705 N. E. 2d at 1116. The court noted the appendix to the court of appeals decision (which it had reversed) listing twenty-two courts applying the "single look" approach, and twenty courts applying the "second look" approach. Kelly v. Marx, 44 Mass. App. Ct. 825, 832 (1998). See a more recent discussion of this split of authority in Hutton Contracting Co., Inc. v. City of Coffeyville, 487 F.3d 772, 781 (10th Cir.2007).

[301] Lind Bldg. Corp. v. Pacific Bellvue Dev., 55 Wash. App. 70, 776 P.2d 977 (1989). *See also* RESTATEMENT 2d § 356 comment b: "If to take an extreme case, it is clear that no loss at all has occurred, a provision fixing a substantial sum as damages is unenforceable." Other well-known cases espousing the "second look" approach include Wasserman's, Inc. v. Middletown, 137 N J.238, 251, 645 A. 2d 100, 107 (1994); Yockey v. Horn, 880 F.2d 945, 952–53 (7th Cir. 1989).

[302] Mattingly Bridge Co. v. Holloway & Son Constr. Co., 694 S.W.2d 702 (Ky. 1985). The court discovered this solution through a clause in the subcontract indicating that liquidated damages should cease when the work was accepted by the owner.

[3]   International Contracts for the Sale of Goods — CISG and UNIDROIT Principles

There is considerable variation in national laws concerning the validity of stipulated damages provisions. As explained in a comment to the UNIDROIT Principles, civil law countries generally enforce penalty clauses as a deterrent, while common law systems reject them.[303] Presumably because a consensus could not be achieved on this issue, CISG is silent concerning stipulated damages. Principles, however, includes a provision that enforces clauses "to pay a specified sum to the aggrieved party for . . . non-performance."[304] The illustration to this section suggests an employment contract at a monthly salary of 10,000 Australian dollars with a severance allowance of 200,000 dollars. When the employee is dismissed without justification, he is entitled to the severance allowance, though he was immediately hired to perform identical work elsewhere at double the original salary. A statement in the comment is clearly opposed to a "no harm" limitation.[305] In the "grossly excessive" cases, however, even Principles allows the specified sum to be reduced to a reasonable amount.[306]

[D]   Blunderbuss Clauses

Where a liquidated damages clause will, by the terms of the contract, be activated for any one of several possible breaches of that contract including minor breaches, it cannot be an honest forecast of actual loss in the event of a breach of a minor covenant. For example, a technology agreement included a clause requiring a breaching buyer to pay 120 times the fee charged by the plaintiff on genetically modified soybeans protected by the plaintiff's patents for a total of $780,000. The 120 multiplier applied to minor as well as major breaches. Applying what the Federal Circuit calls an "anti-one-size-rule," the court held that the clause was a penalty and unenforceable.[307] Other courts have been willing to assume that the parties intended such a clause to apply only to major breaches though the parties failed to specify such a restrictive application of the clause.[308] The view espoused by a number of scholars suggests that the clause should be enforceable if it otherwise would be enforceable with respect to the breach that actually occurred.[309] This certainly appears to be the preferable view. Thus, a court modified its precedent in holding that, in a commercial agreement between sophisticated parties that contains a liquidated damages provision applicable to multiple covenants, it may be presumed that a liquidated damages provision is applicable only to

---

[303] UNIDROIT Principles, Art. 7.4.13, comment 2.

[304] Principles, Art. 7.4.13(1).

[305] "The non-performing party may not allege that the aggrieved party sustained less harm or none at all." Principles, Art 7.4.13, comment 2.

[306] Principles, Art. 7.4.13(2). The illustration accompanying this subsection suggests a contract for machinery requiring 48 monthly payments of 30,000 French francs. The failure to pay one installment terminates the contract, authorizes the seller to retain sums already paid and to recover all future installments as damages as well as the return of the machinery. The buyer makes 10 payments on time and fails to make the eleventh installment payment. The seller retains the 300,000 francs already received and claims the return of the machinery and the 1,140,000 francs representing the 38 outstanding installments. The illustration suggests that a court will reduce the amount because the benefit to the seller would be "grossly excessive."

[307] Monsanto Co. v. McFarling, 363 F.3d 1336 (Fed. Cir. 2004).

[308] *See* Hackenheimer v. Kurtzmann, 235 N.Y. 57, 138 N.E. 735 (1923).

[309] *See* CORBIN ON CONTRACTS § 58.14; C. MCCORMICK, MCCORMICK ON DAMAGES § 151; Macneil, *Power of Contract and Agreed Remedies*, 47 CORNELL L.Q. 495 (1962).

material breaches for which the provision may properly be enforced.[310] In terms of drafting such a contract, however, one should not rely upon the possibility of a favorable judicial construction since the entire problem can be avoided by expressly limiting the operation of a liquidated damages clause to specific breaches.

[E]   Liquidated Damages or Alternative Performances

Where a contract states that the promisor must either perform a particular act or pay a stipulated amount, two possible interpretations arise: (1) the parties intended that the promisor have a real choice between two alternative performances,[311] or (2) they intended that only the specified act would constitute performance and the stipulated amount is an agreed damages provision.[312] Parties should not be permitted to disguise a penalty clause as an alternative performance.[313] If the parties intended genuine alternative performances, either performance of the act *or* payment of the amount would constitute full performance and would discharge the promisor's duty.[314] Absent an indication in the contract, the promisor may elect between the alternative performances. If she manifests a choice and fails to perform that alternative, she should be liable for failure to perform the alternative she has selected. The promisee may not sue for breach of the other alternative.[315] If, however, the parties intended that payment of the amount in the clause should occur only after the promisor failed to perform the act, the failure to perform should be treated as a breach and the agreed damages clause should become activated only after the breach. In that situation, the promisor's duty would not be discharged by proffering payment of the stipulated amount. It could only be discharged by performing the act. Difficult interpretation issues are often raised by these cases and the issues are not resolved by phrases in the contract referring to "liquidated damages" or "alternative performances."[316] There must be a reasonable relationship between the alternatives to be determined essentially by their relative values at the time of contracting.[317]

A related situation occurs with respect to deposits which the contract indicates shall be forfeited in the event of a breach. The clause allowing for such forfeiture should not be enforced if the amount retained is not a reasonable forecast of actual loss in the event of a breach, i.e., it should not become an enforceable penalty simply because it is captioned

---

[310] In Cummings Properties, LLC v. National Communications Corp., 449 Mass. 490, 869 N. E. 2d 617 (2007).

[311] *See* Western Camps, Inc. v. Riverway Ranch Enters., 70 Cal. App. 3d 714, 138 Cal. Rptr. 918 (2d Dist. 1977); Chandler v. Doran Co., 44 Wash. 2d 396, 267 P.2d 907 (1954).

[312] *See* Maybury v. Spinney-Maybury Co., 122 Me. 422, 120 A. 611 (1923) (promise to pay a fixed sum by a certain date or half that amount at an earlier date); Pennsylvania Re-Treading Tire Co. v. Goldberg, 305 Ill. 54, 137 N.E. 81 (1922) (promise to deliver stock with a market value of $120,000 or to pay $50,000 in cash); Goodyear Shoe-Mach. Co. v. Selz, Schwab & Co., 157 Ill. 186, 41 N.E. 625 (1894) (promise to pay a certain amount as royalties if paid by the 15th of the month or twice that amount if paid thereafter).

[313] Carlyle Apts. Joint Venture v. AIG Life Ins. Co., 333 Md. 265, 635 A.2d 366, 371 (1994).

[314] American Soil Processing v. Iowa Comp. Petrol. Underground Storage Tank Fund Bd., 586 N. W. 2d 325, 334 (Iowa 1998) ("[I]n a true alternative contract, the alternatives are not damages provisions but rather performance alternatives.").

[315] Comrie v. Enterasys Networks, Inc., 837 A. 2d 1, 19 (Del. Ch. 2003).

[316] *See Chandler v. Doran Co.*, *supra* note 311, at 910: "It must be solved as a question of factual interpretation, and the form of words used by the parties is not controlling."

[317] *See also* RESTATEMENT 2d § 356 comment c. See Comrie v. Enterasys, *supra* note 315, at 18.

"retention of deposit" or similar phrase.[318] Unfortunately, where the contract is one for the sale of land with payments to be made in installments, there has been a tendency to permit the retention of installment payments which are disproportionately greater than the loss suffered by the aggrieved party. There is authority, however, that would require the repayment of any disproportionate sum to avoid the unjust enrichment of the aggrieved party.[319]

UCC 2-718(2). Retention of Deposit. As to the retention of deposits in a contract for the sale of goods contracts, the UCC permits restitution to the buyer of any amount by which his payments exceed the amount to which the seller is entitled by virtue of an enforceable agreed damages clause, or, absent such a clause, twenty percent of the value of the total performance for which the buyer is obligated or $500, whichever is smaller.[320]

[1]   Alternative Remedies: Specific Performance and Liquidated Damages

Where specific performance or an injunction would otherwise be available to an aggrieved party, the prevailing view is that the presence of a liquidated damages clause will not preclude either equitable remedy unless that remedy is expressly excluded by the contract.[321] The RESTATEMENT 2d suggests that a liquidated damages clause should not be viewed as the price for failure to perform. Such a clause necessarily suggests that damages are uncertain, thereby justifying specific performance since the remedy at law is inadequate.[322]

Where a buyer failed to timely close on a real estate transaction, the seller nonetheless urged the court to grant specific performance. The contract contained a provision allowing the seller to retain the $150,000 deposit as liquidated damages. The court held that awarding the seller liquidated damages while simultaneously granting specific performance would provide the seller with a windfall greatly exceeding the seller's right to be placed in the position it would have occupied had the contract been performed.[323] If a plaintiff successfully enjoins the defendant from competing in a certain profession within a certain geographic area pursuant to a restrictive covenant in the contract, the plaintiff may not enjoy that relief and still expect enforcement of an otherwise valid liquidated damages clause. The plaintiff will be relegated to

---

[318] *See* Spivack v. Connecticut Smiles, Inc., 128 Conn. 146, 20 A.2d 731 (1941); Jaeger v. O'Donoghue, 57 U.S. App. D.C. 191, 18 F.2d 1013 (1927).

[319] *See* Schwartz v. Syver, 264 Wis. 526, 59 N.W.2d 489 (1953).

[320] UCC § 2-718(2). *See also* Feinberg v. J. Bongiovi Contracting, 110 Misc. 2d 379, 442 N.Y.S.2d 399 (Dist. Ct. 1981).

[321] Bradley v. Health Coalition, 687 So. 2d 329, 332 (Fla. Dist. Ct. App. 1997). RESTATEMENT 2d § 361. *See also* Allegheny Energy, Inc. v. DQE, Inc., 171 F.3d 153, 165 (3d Cir. 1999), *aff'd*, 216 F.3d 1075 (3d Cir. 2000). For an illustration of a contrary agreement, see Blankenau v. Kern, 1999 Neb. App. LEXIS 264 (Neb. Ct. App. Sept. 28, 1999), where a restrictive covenant provided that if the purchaser elected to recover liquidated damages, such damages would constitute the sole and exclusive remedy. The contract also provided for the remedy of specific performance. The lower court granted both liquidated damages and specific performance. The appellate court reversed since the covenant stating that the choice of liquidated damages would be the sole and exclusive remedy implied that the choice of specific performance would also be an exclusive remedy.

[322] RESTATEMENT 2d § 361, comment a. The remedies of specific performance and injunctions is explored in § 128, *infra*.

[323] Perroncello v. Donahue, 448 Mass.199, 859 N. E. 2d 827 (2007).

any actual damages which can be proved for violating the restrictive covenant before the injunction issued.[324]

While specific performance is not precluded because of the presence of a liquidated damages clause, if payment of the amount in the clause was intended as a true alternative performance and the obligor chooses to pay that price, equitable relief will not be available.[325]

[F]   "Underliquidated Damages" — Exculpatory Clauses

The typical liquidated damages issue is directed toward determining whether the amount in the clause is disproportionately large in comparison to the amount of anticipated loss. There are situations, however, where the amount appears disproportionately low to the anticipated loss. If the clause appears to be an honest forecast of harm, courts are not nearly as sympathetic to the argument that the amount is unreasonably low.[326] In a contract for security services, the buyer of the services suffered a significant loss and the "liquidated damages" clause provided a nominal amount that was not a reasonable forecast of actual damages.[327] These clauses are, in fact, attempts to disclaim liability disguised as liquidated damages clauses.[328] As such, they are to be tested by the enforceability of exculpatory clauses. Such clauses may be unconscionable and, therefore, unenforceable.[329]

---

[324] See Karpinski v. Ingrasci, 28 N.Y.2d 45, 320 N.Y.S.2d 1, 268 N.E.2d 751 (1971), where the court held that it would be grossly unfair to grant the injunction and simultaneously enforce a $40,000 liquidated damages clause which the parties intended to apply to a total breach of the covenant since the injunction would hold further violation of the covenant. The liquidated damages provision will not be enforced in these circumstances. Instead, plaintiff will be relegated to showing its actual damages. To the same effect, see Gismondi v. Franco, 104 F. Supp. 2d 223, 236 (S.D.N.Y. 2000).

[325] *See* RESTATEMENT 2d § 361 comment b and ill. 2.

[326] See Roscoe-Gill v. Newman, 1997 Ariz. App. LEXIS 32 (Ariz. Ct. App. Mar. 6, 1997), relying on Mahoney v. Tingley, 85 Wash. 2d 95, 529 P.2d 1068 (1975), holding that a seller in a real estate transaction cannot seek to avoid a contractual liquidated damages clause on grounds that it constitutes a penalty because it is too low.

[327] *See, e.g.*, Better Food Mkts., Inc. v. American Dist. Tel. Co., 40 Cal. 2d 179, 253 P.2d 10 (1953) (the clause allowed for the payment of $50 in liquidated damages in a contract for security services where the buyer of the services was a supermarket).

[328] See Tessler & Son, Inc. v. Sonitrol Sec. Sys., Inc., 203 N.J. Super. 477, 497 A.2d 530 (1985), where the court stated that the "real effect" of such clauses is exculpation from liability because they deny liability for all but a nominal amount of damages. Here, the amount was $250, which was not an attempt to fairly estimate the plaintiff's likely damage from a break-in since defendant had paid an $800 service cost at the outset of the contract and $600 per year plus telephone charges to the defendant. The clause also contained a statement limiting damages to $250 for the failures of Sonitrol in any respect, even Sonitrol's negligence. While suggesting the possibility that a promise not to sue for simple negligence would be effective, such a promise would not be enforced with respect to an intentional tort or wilful act or gross negligence since the enforcement of such a clause would be contrary to public policy.

[329] *See* UCC § 2-718 comment 1: "An unreasonably small amount . . . might be stricken under the section on unconscionable contracts of clauses" [§ 2-302]. Similarly, see RESTATEMENT 2d § 356 comment a, referring to the RESTATEMENT 2d section on unconscionability, § 208.

[1]   Limitation of Remedies Under the Uniform Commercial Code — "Failure of Essential Purpose"

Just as implied warranties under the UCC can be disclaimed,[330] the parties to a contract may agree to supplement, substitute or limit the damages otherwise recoverable under the Code.[331] The great majority of contracts, evidenced by clauses in printed forms, contain a major substitution and alteration of UCC remedies that are expressly permitted under the Code where the contract states that the seller will repair/replace nonconforming goods, or the seller will repay the purchase price upon the buyer's return of the nonconforming goods.[332] Such a substitute remedy may operate as an exclusive remedy if it is "expressly agreed to be exclusive."[333] In construing this provision, some courts have insisted on clear and unambiguous language,[334] while others have suggested a more liberal construction.[335] There is no possibility of eliminating remedies entirely under the UCC since, "it is of the very essence of a sales contract that at least minimum adequate remedies be available."[336]

If an allowable limited remedy in substitution for normal UCC remedies "fails of its essential purpose," normal Code remedies are restored.[337] Suppose, for example, a seller of equipment provides an exclusive repair or replacement warranty in place of the normal, more extensive warranty protection provided by the Code, but the equipment fails and cannot be repaired. What appeared to be a minimum adequate remedy when the contract was formed is a nullity. The remedy has "failed of its essential purpose" and the buyer has the phalanx of UCC remedies available to him.[338]

A typical repair or replacement remedy may also contain an exclusion of consequential damages. While consequential damages may be limited or excluded under the UCC, such a limitation is unenforceable if it is unconscionable.[339] In our earlier exploration of whether the failure of an exclusive remedy leaves the exclusion of consequential damages provision intact,

---

[330] UCC § 2-316(2) and (3).

[331] UCC § 2-719(1)(a).

[332] UCC § 2-719(1)(a).

[333] UCC § 2-719(1)(b).

[334] Where the contract stated that the seller's liability "shall not exceed the cost of correcting defects in the goods," the court held that these words did not create an exclusive remedy. Gaynor Elec. Co. v. Hollander, 29 Conn. App. 865, 618 A.2d 532 (1993).

[335] Figgie Int'l, Inc. v. Destileria Serralles, Inc., 190 F.3d 252, 256 (4th Cir. 1999) (while UCC § 2-719(1)(b) requires an exclusive remedy to be "explicit," the UCC definition of "agreement" (§ 1-201(3)) includes trade usage which may evidence the parties' intention to treat the remedy as exclusive); Cognitest Corp. v. Riverside Publishing Co., 107 F.3d 493, 498 (7th Cir. 1997) (such a provision need not contain the term "exclusive"; rather, the court will look to whether a reasonable construction indicated the parties' intention to make the remedy exclusive).

[336] UCC § 2-719, comment 1.

[337] UCC § 2-719(2). See Ford Motor Co. v. Mayes, 575 S.W.2d 480 (Ky. Ct. App. 1978); Clark v. International Harvester Co., 99 Idaho 326, 581 P.2d 784 (1978). See also Eddy, On the "Essential" Purposes of Limited Remedies: The Metaphysics of U. C. C. Section 2-719(2), 65 Cal. L. Rev. 28 (1977), and Anderson, Essential Purpose and Essential Failure of Purpose: A Look at Section 2-719 of the Uniform Commercial Code, 31 Sw. L.J. 759 (1977).

[338] UCC § 2-719(2). See Rose v. Colorado Factory Homes, 10 P.3d 680 (Colo. Ct. App. 2000); Bishop Logging Co. v. John Deere Indus. Equip., Inc., 317 S.C. 520, 455 S.E.2d 183 (Ct. App. 1995).

[339] UCC § 2-719(3). Limitation of consequential damages for injury to the person in the case of consumer goods (good for family or household purposes) is prima facie unconscionable, but limitation where the loss is commercial is not.

we concluded that, absent clear language to the contrary, where the exclusive remedy fails but the exclusion of consequential damages is not unconscionable, most courts adopt the view that UCC §§ 2-719(2) and (3) are independent and will enforce the exclusion.[340]

[G]   Attorney's Fees and Bonds

Unlike its English counterpart, the American common law system, with certain exceptions, does not permit recovery of attorney's fees by the party who wins the lawsuit.[341] While the Convention on Contracts for the International Sale of Goods does not deal with attorney's fees, our courts have applied the American rule in such cases.[342] Numerous statutory exceptions allow recovery of such fees.[343] Absent an exception, the winner will not be awarded attorney's fees and those fees can be substantial. It is, therefore, not uncommon to discover a clause in a contract requiring the payment of reasonable attorney's fees to the winning party.[344] Such a clause will be enforced. By limiting fees to reasonable levels, there is no violation of policies governing liquidated damages.[345] Where, however, the clause awarding attorney's fees contains a specified amount, that clause is subject to the same judicial scrutiny as any other agreed damages clause.[346]

Various types of bonds contain clauses for the payment of a specified amount unless a conditioning event occurs. When the condition occurs, the obligation under the bond is discharged. For example, if a distributor of a manufacturer's goods is supposed to account for all monies due the manufacturer, a bond may have been issued to secure that commitment. When the distributor performs properly, the bond obligation is discharged. If the condition does not occur, i.e., the distributor does not account for all of the monies collected for the manufacturer, the stated amount in the bond will not be enforced beyond the loss caused by the failure of the condition.[347] This result is consistent with the underlying concept of the enforcement of agreed damages provisions in providing compensation rather than penalties.

---

[340] See this discussion at § 97[B][2][e], *supra.*

[341] Alyeska Pipeline Serv. Co. v. Wilderness Soc'y, 421 U.S. 240, 247, 95 S. Ct. 1612, 44 L. Ed. 2d 141 (1975). Even the common law rule is not absolute. For example, where a court determines that an unsuccessful party has pursued a lawsuit in bad faith-vexatiously, wantonly or for oppressive reasons-a court may allow reasonable attorney's fees to the oppressed party who prevailed. Wells v. Bowen, 855 F.2d 37, 46 (2d Cir. 1988).

[342] See Zappata Hermanos Sucesores, S. A. v. Hearthside Baking Co., 313 F.3d 385 (7th Cir.2002).

[343] For an interesting interpretation of the difference between "costs" and "attorney's fees" and numerous statutes including such terms, see West Virginia Univ. Hosps. v. Casey, 499 U.S. 83, 111 S. Ct. 1138, 113 L. Ed. 68 (1991).

[344] Printed form contracts often contain clauses for attorney's fees for collection and related purposes.

[345] *See* Puget Sound Mut. Sav. Bank v. Lillions, 50 Wash. 2d 799, 314 P.2d 935 (1957), *cert. denied*, 357 U.S. 926, 78 S. Ct. 1373, 2 L. Ed. 2d 1371 (1958).

[346] See Equitable Lumber Corp. v. IPA Land Dev. Corp., 38 N.Y.2d 516, 381 N.Y.S.2d 459, 344 N.E.2d 391 (1976), where the court tested a clause awarding attorney's fees of 30 percent under the UCC test of liquidated damages in UCC § 2-718(1).

[347] *See* State v. Alpha Oil & Gas, Inc., 747 S.W.2d 378 (Tex. 1988). Restatement 2d § 356 comment e.

§ 127   MEASURE OF RECOVERY FOR RESTITUTION INTEREST

[A]   The Restitution Concept

The exploration of contract remedies began by distinguishing the three interests that are protected by contract law,[348] the expectation, reliance, and restitution interests. We have discussed the three interests in terms of builder's contracts[349] and other types of contracts. Throughout this volume, we have dealt with the protection of each of the interests in varying contexts. Our principal concern in this section is to consider the measure of recovery when the restitution interest is protected. At the outset, it is important to recall briefly the concept of restitution, i.e., what is protected by a court when it grants a restitution recovery.

The restitution interest is the most deserving of the three interests protected in contract law because it involves the unjust enrichment of one party at the expense of another. The aggrieved party has conferred a benefit upon the unjustly enriched party, who is retaining that benefit at the expense of the aggrieved party. Unlike the reliance interest where a party has suffered an out-of-pocket loss and seeks to recover that minus quantity from the party who induced the reliance, the restitution interest represents an exacerbated situation of a minus to the aggrieved party and a plus (benefit or enrichment) to the other party. The purpose of restitution is to restore the aggrieved party to *status quo ante*, i.e., to place him in the position he would have been in had he not conferred a benefit upon the enriched party.[350] It may be said that the reliance interest has the same purpose. In restitution, however, the plus quantity or benefit is subtracted from the enriched party and the aggrieved party is restored, whereas in reliance, there is no benefit or enrichment to the inducing party. Rather, the relying party simply receives the reasonable value of his detrimental reliance.[351] Since restitution is designed to prevent unjust enrichment,[352] in this section we focus on how the benefit or enrichment is measured so as to restore the aggrieved party to status quo. Before we proceed with that exploration, however, it is important to consider circumstances that would lead a reasonable party to choose the protection of the restitution interest rather than the expectation or reliance interest.

[B]   Choosing the Restitution Interest as the Interest to Be Protected

An aggrieved party who has an action for breach of contract will normally choose to protect her expectation interest because that interest will typically provide the maximum recovery by placing the party in the position she would have occupied had the contract been performed.[353] There are, however, numerous situations in which it would be prudent to choose the restitution interest for protection over the other interests.

---

[348] *See supra* § 118.

[349] *See supra* § 120.

[350] *See* Potter v. Oster, 426 N.W.2d 148 (Iowa 1988) (restoring the status quo is the goal of restitution).

[351] The three interests have been explored *supra* § 118.

[352] *See* J. Dawson, Unjust Enrichment (1951).

[353] It should be recalled that the expectation interest requires neither a minus (reliance) nor minus and plus (restitution) situation. Rather, this normal contract remedy simply protects the expectation of the aggrieved party.

[1]　The Absence of Contract — Quasi Contract

The concept of *quasi contract* was introduced earlier in this volume.[354] It developed from the common law forms of action to allow an action under the writ of assumpsit where there was no contract, but one party had been enriched at the expense of another. It appears in myriad fact situations. Where, for example, the parties thought they had a contract but there was no mutual assent, the plaintiff was still entitled to recover the reasonable value of services and materials that benefitted the defendant as measured by the reasonable value of the benefit conferred.[355] Where a school district refused to perform its statutory duty in providing transportation for certain children and their father transported them to school during the school year, the district was unjustly enriched at the expense of the father. He was entitled to recover the value of the transportation services since he was an appropriate person to perform the legal duty of another at his expense.[356] Where a surgeon performed emergency services for an unconscious patient, no contract could be found but the surgeon was entitled to recover the reasonable value of his services since the patient has been unjustly enriched to that extent.[357] In any number of situations where benefits have been conferred under circumstances that suggest unjust enrichment to the recipient of the benefit, the restitution interest is protected though there is no contract. It will be recalled that such actions are characterized as "quasi contract" actions or the unfortunate phrase, "contracts implied-in-law," which is a contradiction since there never was any contract in these situations.[358]

[2]　Unenforceable Contracts — Fatal Uncertainty

Where there has been an uncured material breach, the aggrieved party may seek protection of the restitution interest rather than the expectation interest because he has no other choice. Where, for example, the contract is unenforceable because it fails to meet the requirements of the Statute of Frauds, but the plaintiff has partly performed the contract by conferring a benefit upon the defendant, such as a down payment under a contract for the sale of land or contract for the sale of goods, the restitution interest will be protected. It would be particularly egregious to permit a party to retain money to which he is not entitled simply because he can raise the defense of the Statute of Frauds. Courts, therefore, grant restitution of the benefit conferred in such cases[359] unless the statute, itself, provides otherwise or the purpose of the statute would be frustrated by allowing restitution.[360] Similarly, courts grant restitution of

---

[354] *See* § 21 *supra.*

[355] Anderson v. Schwegel, 118 Idaho 362, 796 P.2d 1035 (Ct. App. 1990).

[356] Sommers v. Putnam County Bd. of Educ., 113 Ohio St. 177, 148 N.E. 682 (1925). The duty must be performed by a "proper person" since an officious party will not receive restitution. *See* Greenspan v. Slate, 12 N.J. 426, 97 A.2d 390 (1953) (payment to a doctor by friend of minor).

[357] Mathieson v. Smiley, 2 D.L.R. 787 [1932]. Performance of emergency services by a non-professional, however, will not allow for a restitutionary recovery since such services are presumed to have been performed gratuitously.

[358] *See Anderson v. Schwegel,* note 355 *supra.*

[359] *See* Montanaro Bros. Bldrs., Inc. v. Snow, 190 Conn. 481, 460 A.2d 1297 (1983); Wolf v. Malevani, 343 So. 2d 949 (Fla. Dist. Ct. App. 1977); Gilton v. Chapman, 217 Ark. 390, 230 S.W.2d 37 (1950).

[360] *See* Phillippe v. Shapell Indus., 43 Cal. 3d 1247, 241 Cal. Rptr. 22, 743 P.2d 1279 (1987), *cert. denied,* 486 U.S. 1011, 108 S. Ct. 1742, 100 L. Ed. 2d 205 (1988) (statute required broker's contracts to be evidenced by a writing and a restitutionary (quantum meruit) recovery in such a case would frustrate the purpose of the statute). *See also* Restatement 2d § 375 ill. 3.

benefits conferred under voidable contracts,[361] as well as contracts discharged because of non-occurrence of a condition, impracticability, or frustration of purpose.[362]

Where the value of the expectation interest is in doubt because damages cannot be shown with reasonable certainty, the aggrieved party may have no adequate expectation remedy but may be able to demonstrate reasonable certainty with respect to the restitution interest.[363] Even if lost profits cannot be shown, the aggrieved party is certainly entitled to recover amounts paid before the breach.[364] This is the most rudimentary form of restitution, i.e., money paid under a contract which has been breached clearly enriches the defendant unjustly.

[3]   Alternative Remedy — Losing Contracts

Where the aggrieved party has a cause of action for total breach by the other party who had received a benefit prior to the breach through the performance of the aggrieved party, the aggrieved party may choose to pursue his restitution interest even though he could have chosen either the expectation or reliance interest. Restitution is often called an alternative remedy for breach of contract and it is available to the extent of the benefit conferred on the other party.[365] Why, however, should the aggrieved party choose the restitution interest when the expectation or reliance interest is available? As explored earlier in relation to a builder's losing contract,[366] where a party has entered into a contract that would produce a loss if performed, breach by the other party before performance is completed may produce a considerably larger recovery under the restitution interest than the expectation or reliance interests.[367] If a seller of land materially breached the contract by losing marketable title to the land which has depreciated

---

[361] *See* Bowling v. Sperry, 133 Ind. App. 692, 184 N.E.2d 901 (1962). *See also* RESTATEMENT 2d § 376.

[362] RESTATEMENT 2d § 377.

[363] *Id.* Courts will apply a requirement of reasonable certainty to the recovery of restitution interest damages. *See* Lewiston Pre-Mix Concrete v. Rohde, 110 Idaho 640, 718 P.2d 551 (Ct. App. 1985).

[364] *See* CBS, Inc. v. Merrick, 716 F.2d 1292 (9th Cir. 1983) (recovery of pre-payments made to David Merrick who breached contract under which he was supposed to allow CBS the use of a book to which he had the rights and he was also supposed to perform as the producer of the film).

[365] *See, e.g.*, McEnroe v. Morgan, 106 Idaho 326, 678 P.2d 595 (Ct. App. 1984). RESTATEMENT 2d §§ 344(c), 370, and 373, particularly comment b thereto.

[366] *See* § 120 *supra*.

[367] *See* Harris v. Metropolitan Mall, 112 Wis. 2d 487, 334 N.W.2d 519 (1983) (where profits are uncertain or a losing contract is breached, the plaintiff may have his restitution interest protected). *See also* Murdock-Bryant Constr. Co. v. Pearson, 146 Ariz. 57, 703 P.2d 1206, 1217 (Ct. App. 1984) (contract price is not a limitation on restitutionary recover); Boomer v. Muir, 24 P.2d 570 (Cal. App. 1933) (recovery of $230,000 in excess of contract price). In Johnson v. Star Bucket Pump Co., 274 Mo. 414, 202 S.W. 1143, 1153 (1918), the opinion states, "The defendant cannot undertake to limit the recovery by the terms of the contract, because he has breached the contract. To permit him to use his breached contract to limit a recovery against him would be to pay to him a premium for his own wrong. The law does not contemplate such." See, however, Johnson v. Bovee, 40 Colo. App. 317, 574 P.2d 513 (1978), and Wuchter v. Fitzgerald, 83 Or. 672, 163 P. 819 (1917), which preclude restitutionary recovery in excess of the contract price. See G. PALMER, LAW OF RESTITUTION § 4.4 (1978), which supports the concept of recovery in excess of the contract price. RESTATEMENT 2d § 373 comment d suggests, "In the case of a contract on which [the injured party] would have sustained a loss instead of having made a profit, however, his restitution interest may give him a larger recovery than would damages on either [expectation or reliance] basis. The right of the injured party under a losing contract to a greater amount in restitution than he could have recovered in damages has engendered much controversy. *The rules stated in this section give him that right.*" (Emphasis added.) The only limitations are (1) the usual limitation that the recovery be limited to the benefit conferred pursuant to § 370, and (2) if the aggrieved party has completed performance and the other party has only the duty to pay the price, the aggrieved party is limited to the contract price (comment b to § 373).

in value, the recovery of the restitutionary interest will be greater than the expectation interest.[368]

[4]   Recovery by a Defaulting Plaintiff to Avoid Forfeitures

Where a party materially breaches a contract after he has partly performed the duties under that contract, he obviously has no cause of action on the contract he breached. Yet, he may have conferred a benefit on the innocent party who would be unjustly enriched if she were allowed to retain that benefit at no cost. Claims that a contract breaker should recover the value of the benefit conferred produced early reactions of incredulity.[369] In 1834, however, the opinion in *Britton v. Turner*[370] presented a different view.

The plaintiff agreed to work for one year in exchange for $120 to be paid at the end of the year. He worked for more than nine months and then breached the contract by leaving the employment. He brought an action in quasi contract[371] for the value of his services that conferred a benefit upon the employer. The court permitted a recovery on the logical footing that the longer the plaintiff performed, the more he lost. Had he not commenced working at all under the contract, his damages would have been insignificant. Unless a recovery was granted, the law would be countenancing a forfeiture which it abhors.[372] This logic has prevailed since that decision. Before considering certain limitations on the defaulting plaintiff's recovery, it important to recognize that the logic of *Britton v. Turner* was soon extended to independent contractors providing services,[373] and there has been no doubt of its viability as applied to any service contract since that time.[374] In contracts for the sale of goods, defaulting sellers were eventually permitted to recover for goods retained by the purchaser under the Uniform Sales Act.[375] Where buyers made down payments that exceeded actual damages suffered by sellers, however, the sellers could retain the excess and be unjustly enriched.[376] The contract would sometimes provide that the deposit would be retained as liquidated

---

[368] *See Potter v. Oster, supra* note 350.

[369] For example, in Stark v. Parker, 19 Mass. (2 Pick.) 267, 13 Am. Dec. 425 (1824), the court wondered why anyone would have any doubt whatsoever about denying relief to a party who breached the contract since, *inter alia*, the ancient maxim should apply, i.e., no man should profit from his own wrong.

[370] 6 N.H. 481, 26 Am. Dec. 713 (1834).

[371] The method of pleading such actions was under the common counts. Thus, in a personal services case, the action would be brought under the common count *quantum meruit* (work and labor done). If the quasi contract action were one to recover money belonging to the plaintiff, the common count used was *money had and received.* If the quasi contract action were for the value of goods delivered to the recipient, the action was often called *quantum valebat* or *quantum valebant* (goods sold and delivered).

[372] For a modern recognition of this analysis, see Lancellotti v. Thomas, 341 Pa. Super. 1, 491 A.2d 117 (1985).

[373] *See* Pinches v. Swedish Evangelical Lutheran Church, 55 Conn. 183, 10 A. 264 (1887) (building contract).

[374] *See* Maxton Builders, Inc. v. Lo Galbo, 68 N.Y.2d 373, 509 N.Y.S.2d 507, 502 N.E.2d 184 (1986) (in most areas of the law, legislatures and courts have adopted a rule permitting the party in default to recover for part performance of the contract to the extent of the net benefit conferred; however, this is not true with respect to restitution in contracts for the sale of land (discussed in text *infra* note 399 *et seq.*)); *Lancellotti v. Thomas, supra* note 372 (adopting the "modern rule" of RESTATEMENT 2d § 374 and setting forth numerous cases under First RESTATEMENT § 357 and RESTATEMENT 2d § 374 to support the view that restitutionary recovery is now allowed generally).

[375] U.S.A. § 44. The UCC permits a buyer to accept all or any commercial unit of the goods delivered by the seller even though the goods are non-conforming. UCC § 2-601. The buyer is liable for the price of any goods accepted, UCC § 2-709(1)(a), though he has a cause of action for any breach of warranty as to accepted goods, UCC § 2-714.

[376] *See, e.g.,* Atlantic City Tire & Rubber Corp. v. Southwark Foundry & Mach. Co., 289 Pa. 569, 137 A. 807 (1927).

damages which courts would enforce, though the amounts may have exceeded reasonable forecasts of actual damages. There was considerable creativity which produced judicial devices that were, at least, semi-covert in attempts to reach the logic of *Britton v. Turner* in non-employment cases.[377] The UCC confronted the problem in sale-of-goods cases by simply directing that buyers are entitled to restitution of any amount of their down payment exceeding a valid agreed damages clause.[378] In the absence of such a clause, the Code places a ceiling on the amount the seller may retain.[379] In contracts for the sale of land, there has been a great reluctance on the part of courts to permit a defaulting buyer to recover a down payment ("earnest money") even though it exceeds the actual damages of the vendor.[380] There is, however, a clear trend toward the avoidance of unjust enrichment in such cases by permitting a recovery of an amount exceeding the loss,[381] particularly in cases where the amount retained grossly exceeds the actual damages of the seller.[382] The influence of the UCC has been felt in such cases[383] and, since the Restatement 2d adopts this view,[384] it is reasonable to conclude that it will become the prevailing view in contracts for the sale of land as it has with respect to other types of contracts.

---

[377] See, e.g., the description of money advanced by a buyer or lessee as mere security rather than a down payment that could be retained upon breach in Amtorg Trading Corp. v. Miehle Printing Press & Mfg. Co., 206 F.2d 103 (2d Cir. 1953).

[378] UCC § 2-718(2)(a).

[379] Twenty percent of the value of the total performance for which the buyer is obligated or $500, whichever is smaller. UCC § 2-718(2). *See* the earlier discussion of this concept *supra* § 126.

[380] *See* Annot., 4 A.L.R.4th 993 (1981). See also *Maxton Builders, Inc. v. Lo Galbo, supra* note 374, which recognizes the modern view in other types of contracts but adheres to the doctrine of Lawrence v. Miller, 86 N.Y. 131 (1881) (precluding restitutionary recovery for a defaulting vendee because allowing such a recovery would be "ill doctrine"), particularly if the down payment does not exceed 10 percent of the contract price. The First Restatement § 357(2) also excepted the payment of "earnest money" from the general rule allowing restitution for defaulting plaintiffs. The Restatement 2d § 374 comment c, subjects "earnest money" payments to the same reasonableness test applied to liquidated damages. See also *Lancellotti v. Thomas*, supra note 372, which adopts Restatement 2d § 374 as Pennsylvania law and sets forth an excellent detailed analysis of why the "modern" view should be adopted, suggesting that the modern view is now the prevailing view. As to restitution by a defaulting purchaser in contracts for the sale of land, however, the court was constrained by precedent, i.e., Kaufman Hotel & Restaurant Co. v. Thomas, 411 Pa. 87, 190 A.2d 434 (1963), and Luria v. Robbins, 223 Pa. Super. 456, 302 A.2d 361 (1973), which denied restitution. The court suggests that *Luria* is distinguishable because, in land contracts, the seller has several remedies against the buyer, including specific performance, and as long as the seller remains ready, willing, and able to perform, there should be no right to restitution. Other case law certainly supports this qualification — see, e.g., Washington v. Claassen, 218 Kan. 577, 545 P.2d 387 (1976), as does the Restatement 2d in § 374 comment a: "If the injured party has a right to specific performance, he may keep what he has received and sue for specific performance of the balance."

[381] For an early case discussing the traditional concept and suggesting the modern trend, see Schwartz v. Syver, 264 Wis. 526, 59 N.W.2d 489 (1953).

[382] *See* Lind Bldg. Corp. v. Pacific Bellevue Dev., 55 Wash. App. 70, 776 P.2d 977 (1989) (deposits of $250,000 could not be retained by seller who, one month after buyer's breach, sold the property for a million dollars more than the contract price). *See also* McLendon v. Safe Realty Corp., 401 N.E.2d 80 (Ind. Ct. App. 1980); De Leon v. Aldrete, 398 S.W.2d 160 (Tex. Civ. App. San Antonio 1965); Honey v. Henry's Franchise Leasing Corp., 64 Cal. 2d 801, 415 P.2d 833 (1966); Newcomb v. Ray, 99 N.H. 463, 114 A.2d 882 (1955).

[383] *See* Maxey v. Glindmeyer, 379 So. 2d 297 (Miss. 1980) (suggesting that seller should not retain an amount beyond actual damages, analogizing to UCC § 2-718(2)). It should also be noted that the dominant scholarly influence in the entire movement toward permitting defaulting plaintiffs to recover is generally regarded as the giant of twentieth century contract law, Professor Corbin. See his treatise at §§ 1122–1135.

[384] Restatement 2d § 374(2). The comment to this section adds, however, "If the injured party has a right to specific performance and remains willing and able to perform, he may keep what he has received and sue for specific performance."

[5]　Limitations on Recovery by Defaulting Plaintiff

[a]　Wilful Breaches

While adopting the view that a defaulting plaintiff should be able to recover the amount of the benefit in excess of the harm that he caused the defendant, the First RESTATEMENT insisted upon an exception for a "wilful and deliberate" breach.[385] The notion that a court will aid a party who wilfully breached a contract to protect that party against the unjust enrichment of the innocent party suggests a contradiction of the equitable influence surrounding actions in restitution. The "wilful" breacher does not have clean hands. If he is the agent of the defendant with all of the fiduciary responsibilities attached to that status, courts will find it particularly difficult to protect his restitution interest.[386] Notwithstanding the arguments that can be made against a party who is not a mere contract breaker but a "wilful" contract breaker, very few cases can be found denying restitutionary relief to such a party,[387] while a number can be found stating that a wilful breach is not a bar to such recovery.[388] Certainly, courts adopting "the more enlightened approach" of the RESTATEMENT 2d are aware that it does not include the "wilful" exception of the First Restatement.[389] The only notion of a "wilful" breach in the RESTATEMENT 2d is found in a comment suggesting that restitution should not be granted where a party *intentionally*[390] furnishes services or builds a building that is materially different from his promised performance on the ground that he has acted officiously, i.e., he has provided services that were not requested by the innocent party who should not have to pay for them any more than he should have to pay for any other unsolicited benefit.[391] If the deviations were not intentional, the unintentional defaulter could recover for the value of benefits conferred, though he would still be liable for his innocent breach. Since the UCC is not affected by the wilful character of the breach,[392] it is not remarkable that the RESTATEMENT 2d would adopt a similar view which coincides with its fundamental approach to contract remedies.[393]

---

[385] First RESTATEMENT § 357(1)(a). Comment e to this section distinguishes a "wilful" from a "knowing" breach, i.e., the latter type of breach may occur as a result of negligence or error of judgment or mistake of fact or law; it may be due to hardship, insolvency, or circumstances that tend appreciably toward moral justification. Such a breach is not "wilful."

[386] See, e.g., Fidelity Fund, Inc. v. Di Santo, 347 Pa. Super. 112, 500 A.2d 431 (1985), where the court denied restitution guided, in part, by RESTATEMENT 2d Agency § 469 (no compensation has been apportioned if the conduct is wilful).

[387] *See, e.g.*, Harris v. The Cecil N. Bean, 197 F.2d 919 (2d Cir. 1952).

[388] *See, e.g.*, Gardner v. Olson, 1997 Wash. App. LEXIS 1245 (Wash. Ct. App. Aug. 4, 1997); Kitchin v. Mori, 84 Nev. 181, 437 P.2d 865 (1968); Caplan v. Schroeder, 56 Cal. 2d 515, 15 Cal. Rptr. 145, 364 P.2d 321 (1961).

[389] *See* Lancellotti v. Thomas, 341 Pa. Super. 1, 491 A.2d 117 (1985).

[390] The use of the term "intentional," as meaning "wilful," can create confusion. *See* Dodge v. Kimball, 203 Mass. 364, 89 N.E. 542 (1909). An intentional breach may simply be a "knowing" breach which is not "wilful." The RESTATEMENT 2d apparently intends to use "intentional" here to mean "wilful," as contrasted with merely "knowing."

[391] *See* RESTATEMENT 2d § 374, comment b. *See also* RESTATEMENT OF RESTITUTION § 112. In § 113 comment a, the following rationale is presented: "The principle underlying the rule stated in § 112 is that one who officiously intervenes to perform the duty of another is not entitled to compensation. . . ." It should be recalled, however, that one may not avoid the restitutionary duty that will attach if he watches services being performed that will benefit him where the party performing those services apparently assumes he will be compensated. *See* Day v. Caton, 119 Mass. 513, 20 Am. Rep. 347 (1876).

[392] UCC § 2-718(2).

[393] In the Introductory Note to Chapter 16, Remedies, which precedes § 344, the RESTATEMENT 2d emphasizes the

[b]   Contract Price Limitation, Liquidated Damages, and Specific Performance — Divisible Contracts

It must be emphasized that a defaulting plaintiff is still a contract breaker and, like any other contract breaker, is liable for any damages that can be established by the aggrieved party. The aggrieved party is entitled to prove whatever damages it has sustained resulting from the breach and deduct that amount from whatever restitution benefit the defaulting plaintiff can prove.[394] While the contract price is not conclusive evidence of the benefit, it operates as an absolute limit on the defaulting plaintiff's recovery. It is not necessary for the defaulting party to render substantial performance to recover for benefits conferred, but he may not recover for benefits conferred in excess of the contract price or ratable portion thereof.[395] If the cost of completing the performance is greater than the value of the benefits conferred by the defaulting plaintiff, no restitution will be granted.[396] Thus, the defaulting plaintiff can recover only for the *net* benefit conferred.[397] The burden of proving the excess of benefits over the loss to the innocent defendant must be borne by the defaulting plaintiff,[398] and if there is any doubt about the measurement of the benefit, the doubt will be resolved against him and he will receive the less generous measure.[399] In a sale of land contract, if the vendor remains ready, willing, and able to perform and has a right to specific performance, restitution of a down payment for the defaulting vendee will be denied.[400] No restitutionary recovery will be permitted if the amount of the down payment is in an enforceable agreed damages clause even if that clause is in the form of an "earnest money" payment or some other characterization, but would have been sustained as a valid clause.[401] Finally, it should be recalled that where the contract is "divisible" or "severable," i.e., where the parties have contracted for performances on each side as *agreed equivalents*, a defaulting party may recover for the full performance of any divisible portion of the contract and this recovery is one for his expectation interest according to the expressed intentions of the parties, rather than his restitution interest.[402]

---

underlying theory of compensation to the aggrieved party as contrasted with compulsion of the promisor. *Inter alia*, it suggests that, " 'Willful' breaches have not been distinguished from other breaches. . . ."

[394] Denver Ventures, Inc. v. Arlington Lane Corp., 754 P.2d 785 (Colo. Ct. App. 1988) (the cost of remedying breach far exceeded the value of any benefit conferred; there was no restitutionary recovery).

[395] RESTATEMENT 2d § 374, comment b. *See* Boyce Constr. Corp. v. District Bd. of Trustees of Valencia County, 414 So. 2d 634 (Fla. Dist. Ct. App. 1982).

[396] See *Denver Ventures, supra* note 394. A party should recover only the reasonable value of benefits conferred which exceed the loss created by his own breach. Survey Eng'rs, Inc. v. Zoline Found., 190 Colo. 352, 546 P.2d 1257 (1976), *cert. denied*, 434 U.S. 1071, 98 S. Ct. 1253, 55 L. Ed. 2d 773 (1978).

[397] *See* RESTATEMENT 2d § 374.

[398] J. David Conti, Inc. v. Stokes Equip. Co., 1995 U.S. App. LEXIS 36350, at *15 (4th Cir. Dec. 22, 1995); Ben Lomond, Inc. v. Allen, 758 P.2d 92 (Alaska 1988).

[399] See RESTATEMENT 2d § 374, comment b, referring to the two measures of benefit set forth in § 371, (a) the reasonable value of the benefit to the other party in terms of what it would have cost him to obtain that benefit from a person in his position, or (b) the extent to which his property has been increased in value or his other interests advanced via the benefit conferred.

[400] *See* discussion of *Lancellotti v. Thomas, supra* note 372.

[401] RESTATEMENT 2d § 374 comment c.

[402] See RESTATEMENT 2d § 240 and the discussion of divisible contracts *supra* § 106[D].

[C]   Measuring the Restitution Interest (Benefit Conferred) — Specific Restitution — Duty to Return Benefit

The restitution interest should be measured by the benefit conferred on the unjustly enriched party. Where the plaintiff is merely seeking a return of money paid to that party, the measurement is quite simple.[403] This is a form of specific restitution. Similarly, if the benefit conferred is in a form other than money, the return of that specific benefit will be preferred since there is no question about the measurement of the value of the benefit.[404] In many cases, however, the benefit conferred can be measured in two different ways: (a) by the reasonable value to the enriched party of what it would have cost him to obtain that benefit from someone in the position of the plaintiff, or (b) the extent to which the other party's wealth or property has been increased in value.[405]

In a simple case involving the performance of carpentry services, the court remanded the case for a determination of which of these two forms of measurement should control, i.e., what it would have cost the defendant to obtain these services from another carpenter in the position of the plaintiff, or the enhanced value to defendant's property.[406] Where a city contracted with a utility to provide street lighting services but the contract term expired and the utility continued to supply the services, the court held that the continued service should be measured by the cost to the city of having such services rendered rather than the benefit received in terms of furthering the interests of the city because the latter interest was speculative.[407] Indeed, this measure (cost to enriched party in obtaining the value of the services elsewhere) is the preferred measure of benefit unless it is unduly difficult to measure because it is speculative.[408] Moreover, a party entitled to restitution should normally receive that measure of benefit because it is typically more generous than the other measure.[409] In situations where the increase in value to the recipient is greater than what it would have cost him to receive the benefit from another party, the latter remains the preferred measure where it would be absurd to grant the increase in value measure. Thus, where emergency surgery is performed which saves the life of the recipient, it is conceivable that the increase in the value of his continued existence could be measured in astronomical sums. He should not be liable for anything more than the reasonable value of the services rendered in terms of what another

---

[403] *See* Far West Fed. Bank, S.B. v. Office of Thrift Supervision, 119 F.3d 1358, 1367 (9th Cir. 1997) (investment of $26.6 million returned); Harris v. Metropolitan Mall, 112 Wis. 2d 487, 334 N.W.2d 519 (1983) (recovery of amount of investment, $238,100). *See also* CBS, Inc. v. Merrick, 716 F.2d 1292 (9th Cir. 1983) (recovery of $833,333.33 prepaid to defendant who failed to perform).

[404] *See* Lewiston Pre-Mix Concrete v. Rohde, 110 Idaho 640, 718 P.2d 551 (Ct. App. 1985). Where the benefit is land conveyed to the unjustly enriched party, specific restitution will be granted unless it would unduly interfere with title to land or otherwise cause injustice. RESTATEMENT 2d § 372(1)(a). Specific restitution will not be granted to a defaulting plaintiff. RESTATEMENT 2d § 372(1)(b). If a plaintiff has a claim for restitution, the defendant may discharge his duty by tendering specific restitution before suit is brought. RESTATEMENT 2d § 372(3).

[405] Yeong Gil Kim v. Magnotta, 49 Conn. App. 203, 714 A.2d 38, 43 (1998), *rev'd, remanded on procedural grounds*, 249 Conn. 94, 733 A.2d 809 (1999). RESTATEMENT 2d § 371.

[406] Lee v. Foote, 481 A.2d 484 (D.C. App. 1984).

[407] Lanphier v. Omaha Pub. Power Dist., 227 Neb. 241, 417 N.W.2d 17 (1987).

[408] Resolution Trust Corp. v. Federal Sav. & Loan Ins. Corp., 25 F.3d 1493, 1505 (10th Cir. 1994); Noel v. Cole, 98 Wash. 2d 375, 655 P.2d 245 (1982).

[409] *See* RESTATEMENT 2d § 371 comment b.

surgeon in the plaintiff's position would have charged.[410]

[1]   Duty to Return Benefit

Since the purpose of restitution is to restore the parties to status quo, if the party seeking restitution has received a benefit, the general rule requires the plaintiff to return the benefit received or offer to return it, conditional on any restitution to himself.[411] If the benefit cannot be returned, as where the buyer of real property seeks restitution of his down payment but has had the benefit of the property, the buyer will be required to account for reasonable rental value.[412] If the plaintiff seeking restitution has received services which cannot be restored in specie, he should offer to compensate the defendant for these services.[413] If, however, property received by the plaintiff is worthless because of defects or if its destruction or loss was caused by the other party, no return or offer to return such property is necessary.[414]

[D]   Inconsistent Remedies — Election Among Different Interests

Where a breach of contract is total, i.e., an uncurable material breach, the aggrieved party may choose among different remedies to protect different interests. A plaintiff may not, however, recover expectation, reliance and restitutionary damages for the same injury.

In a contract for the purchase and sale of land, if a buyer is granted specific performance of the contract, he must pay for the land, i.e., he may not have the land as well as restitution of the purchase price or whatever portion thereof he has paid. Similarly, if a builder completes a structure and the owner refuses to pay the contract price, it would be absurd to permit the builder to recover the contract price as well as restitution for benefits conferred (the reasonable value of the structure) or his reliance interest (the cost of the labor and materials). The reliance interest is incorporated in the expectation interest if the builder seeks to protect the expectation interest and the owner is not unjustly enriched if he pays the amount of the contract price in damages. As we have seen, the builder may choose to protect a different interest — either the reliance or restitution interest. If either of these remedies is granted, he is precluded from an expectation interest recovery.[415]

---

[410] *See* Cotnam v. Wisdom, 83 Ark. 601, 104 S.W. 164 (1907).

[411] The actual return is not necessary. An offer to return is sufficient. King-Roberts v. United States Postal Serv., 1999 U.S. App. LEXIS 18783, at *5 (Fed. Cir. Aug. 13, 1999). *See also* Puskar v. Hughes, 179 Ill. App. 3d 522, 127 Ill. Dec. 880, 533 N.E.2d 962 (2d Dist. 1989); Restatement 2d § 384, comments a and b.

[412] Williams v. Dunas, 40 Ill. App. 3d 782, 352 N.E.2d 266 (1st Dist. 1976); Mahurin v. Schmeck, 95 Ariz. 333, 390 P.2d 576 (1964).

[413] Briggs v. Clinton County Bank & Trust Co., 452 N.E.2d 989 (Ind. Ct. App. 1983) (no necessity to tender such compensation here since there was a $9000 C.D. in litigation).

[414] *See* Rivera v. Wyeth-Ayerst Lab., 121 F. Supp. 2d 614, 620 (S.D. Tex. 2000) (class action to recover amounts paid for drug that was withdrawn from market). *See also* Kunkle Water & Elec., Inc. v. Prescott, 347 N.W.2d 648 (Iowa 1984). Restatement 2d § 384(2)(b) comment c.

[415] *See* Restatement 2d § 378. In Slattery v. United States, 583 F.3d 800 (Fed. Cir. 2009), while noting that restitution is not recoverable in addition to reliance damages for the same injury (citing American Capital Corp. v. FDIC, 472 F.3d 859, 870 (Fed. Cir. 2006)), the court held that an award of restitution damages was incompatible with an award of expectation damages for the same injury.

UCC remedies are also cumulative. Article 2 of the UCC "rejects any doctrine of election of remedies."[416] Whether one remedy is inconsistent with another "depends entirely on the facts of the individual case."[417]

[1]   Different Remedies for Different Injuries — Expectation, Reliance and Restitution

While an award of restitution and reliance or expectation damages for the *same injury* would be inconsistent, protection of different interests for different injuries would not be inconsistent. In *CBS, Inc. v. Merrick*,[418] for example, David Merrick, controlled the rights to a best selling book and agreed to produce a screenplay for CBS based on the book. CBS paid Merrick over $916,000. In reliance on his promises, CBS also paid sizeable amounts to a director and screenwriter chosen by Merrick under contracts that required them to be paid even if the play was never produced. Merrick breached the contract and the screen play was never produced. Expectation damages for CBS were necessarily speculative and unrecoverable. The trial court allowed restitution of the $916,000 paid to Merrick, but refused to allow CBS any damages for its reliance interest in its payments to the director and screenwriter.

The court of appeals reversed since it saw no inconsistency in permitting the reliance remedy along with a restitution remedy for different injuries. CBS could not recover its out-of-pocket reliance damages for payments to the director and screenwriter in restitution since Merrick was not unjustly enriched by that benefit. It could not recover on reliance or restitution theories from the director and screenwriter since they did not breach. CBS, however, had suffered a reliance injury in its out-of-pocket payments. If it could not recover its reliance interest from Merrick simply because it was entitled to recover its restitution interest to prevent Merrick's own unjust enrichment, CBS could not have been restored to *status quo ante*, i.e., the position it was in *before* the contract was made.[419]

[2]   Alternative Remedies — Damages — Specific Performance

If a party seeks to protect its expectation interest, the typical remedy would be damages to place that party in the position he would have occupied had the contract been performed. A plaintiff may *pursue* such a remedy for damages and alternatively seek specific performance. If specific performance is granted, however, the plaintiff may not recover damages for breach since the remedy of specific performance has affirmed the contract and fulfilled the plaintiff's expectation.[420] The remedies are inconsistent and if both were granted, the plaintiff would have a double recovery, placing him in a much better position that he would have occupied had the

---

[416] UCC § 2-703, Comment 1.

[417] *Id.* UCC § 2-703 lists seller's remedies, while § 2-711 lists buyer's remedies.

[418] 716 F.2d 1292 (9th Cir. 1983). See, in particular, the concurring opinion by Nelson, J.

[419] *See* RESTATEMENT 2d § 370 comment a, which insists that restitution is available only for benefits conferred upon the other party. It then suggests, "The injured party may, however, have an action for damages, including one for recovery based on his reliance interest." In § 378 comment d, the RESTATEMENT 2d suggests that "a party who seeks restitution may, for example, be entitled to damages to compensate him for costs of transportation of goods that he has incurred." Such damages are reliance damages.

[420] Douglas Theater Corp. v. Chicago Title & Trust Co., 288 Ill. App. 3d 880, 224 Ill. Dec. 249, 681 N.E.2d 564, 569 (1st Dist. 1997).

contract been performed.[421]

Simply because a plaintiff commences a lawsuit for remedies that are inconsistent or amends his complaint to seek a different remedy does not, however, preclude pursuit of either remedy unless the other party has materially changed his position in reliance on the plaintiff's manifestation to seek a particular remedy.[422] Where, for example, a seller brings an action in damages for the buyer's alleged breach of a land contract and the buyer, relying on that cause of action, makes valuable improvements to the land, the seller's later pursuit of the remedy of specific performance would normally be precluded.[423] Again, however, where the remedy is *granted*, the plaintiff may not have the advantage of inconsistent remedies that would provide a windfall recovery.[424]

§ 128 SPECIFIC PERFORMANCE AND INJUNCTIONS

[A] Equitable Remedies and the Common Law

The damage remedy for breach of contract which has been explored to this point provides substitutional relief to the aggrieved party rather than the very performance promised. There are situations, however, where a court should provide the specific performance promised.[425] Since the aggrieved party receives exactly what he was promised when he receives specific relief, such a remedy may be preferable.[426] Unlike the civil law system where specific performance is ordered wherever possible, however, the common law system from its inception was based on the notion of substitutional relief. To this day, substitutional relief in money damages is the normal common law remedy for breach of contract whereas specific performance, injunctions, and other equitable remedies are extraordinary remedies.

It is important to consider some salient background of the development of equitable remedies. In general terms, common law courts were *property* oriented, i.e., any notion of specific relief came through proprietary actions, such as replevin to recover specific property

---

[421] *See* MCA TV, Ltd. v. Public Interest Corp., 171 F.3d 1265 (11th Cir. 1999) (once plaintiff was guaranteed the full contract price, any further recovery would exceed plaintiff's expectation interest).

[422] Dunn v. EAO Switch Corp., 1997 Conn. Super. LEXIS 3055 (Conn. Super. Ct. Nov. 10, 1997) (material change of position not shown). RESTATEMENT 2d § 378.

[423] RESTATEMENT 2d § 378, ill. 1. There are exceptions to this rule, however. Where the plaintiff's choice of remedy was based on ignorance of facts due to, e.g., mistake or misrepresentation, an amendment cause of action would not be precluded, regardless of the defendant's reliance. Where, for example, a party mistakenly pursues a remedy that does not exist, he is not precluded from seeking other remedies. Far West Fed. Bank, S.B. v. Office of Thrift Supervision, 119 F.3d 1358, 1365 (9th Cir. 1997). Similarly, if after the plaintiff chooses a particular remedy, the defendant commits a later breach, the choice of remedy may be changed regardless of the defendant's reliance. *See* RESTATEMENT 2d § 378, comment b.

[424] In this sense, the remedies of specific performance or an injunction is inconsistent with a remedy of damages for total breach. Similarly, the remedy of specific performance or an injunction and restitution are also inconsistent. RESTATEMENT 2d § 378, comment d. A court may, however, award damages in addition to specific performance or restitution where such damages are appropriate, as where a delay in performance caused damages for which the defendant would be liable notwithstanding a decree of specific performance. RESTATEMENT 2d § 358, comment c.

[425] Specific Performance and Injunctions are explored in §§ 357–369 of the RESTATEMENT 2d.

[426] In terms of economic analysis, it may be argued that specific performance neither overcompensates nor undercompensates the aggrieved party's expectation interest and is, therefore, more precise than substitutional damages. *See* Schwartz, *The Case for Specific Performance*, 89 YALE L.J. 271 (1979). But see Kronman, *Specific Performance*, 45 U. CHI. L. REV. 351 (1978), suggesting that specific performance may overcompensate the claimant.

owned by the plaintiff. An action for contract damages was often in the form of the old common law action (writ) of debt based on the half-completed exchange idea, e.g., failure to pay for goods delivered. If the plaintiff prevailed in his debt action, he would be awarded a judgment for the price of the goods. In effect, this provided the seller with specific performance since the seller was receiving exactly what he had bargained for. Early courts, however, did not think in those terms but, rather, in terms of substitutional relief for breach of contract. Equity jurisprudence and courts of equity came from another source.

Common law writs such as debt and covenant were quite narrow. Until the sixteenth century, there was no writ to enforce what we would now view as the typical modern contract, an exchange of informal promises. Where a party had an otherwise meritorious claim but could find no procrustean common law writ to pursue that claim in a common law court, he may have sought assistance from the Chancellor, who was the keeper of the King's conscience, a high official who was supposed to operate *ex aequo et bono*, i.e., in equity and good conscience. Since chancellors were typically clerics, it is not remarkable that canon law influenced their thinking. The Chancellor would not provide relief to someone who acted unreasonably or unconscionably. The classic equitable maxims include the requirement that a party seeking equity must come to the equity court "with clean hands." An equitable remedy is subject to the *discretion* of the court because it developed from the discretion of the chancellor. A party would seek relief from the Chancellor because there was *no adequate remedy at law* (typically, no proper writ), and when the Chancellor granted a remedy, it was based, in part, on that fact. Thus, the normal remedy was the remedy at law, but if no law remedy was available, one could appeal to the King's conscience through the keeper of that conscience for an extraordinary remedy.

The Chancellor granted relief in the form of a decree, i.e., an order to a person to perform an act or refrain from performing an act. The common law courts were not concerned with ordering anyone to do anything. They were typically concerned with awarding judgments for money and those judgments could be satisfied by having the sheriff seize and sell the defendant's property. Thus, the Chancellor (equity) operated *in personam* — ordering the person — while courts of law operated *in rem* — against the property of the defendant. Again, however, the *in personam* equitable remedy had been designed to overcome the inadequacies of common law remedies. By the sixteenth century, after the development of the writ of assumpsit, equity "followed the law" in requiring the same elements to be shown for an enforceable contract as did courts of law. The question then began to turn on the nature of the remedy. The remedy, however, had clearly become the extraordinary remedy. The claimant was supposed to pursue his remedy at law and only if that remedy proved inadequate would the court of equity entertain jurisdiction. If equity granted jurisdiction, again, it would "follow the law" in requiring all other elements of an enforceable contract to be shown. It might, however, withhold equitable relief because, in its discretion, it might conclude that such relief would be too great a hardship on the defendant or that the plaintiff had operated less than fairly or, again, had come to the court of conscience, the court of equity, with unclean hands. The plaintiff may not have been diligent and may, therefore, have lost favor in the eyes of the court of equity because "equity aids the vigilant."

[1]   Flexible Equitable Relief

There are no longer any separate courts of equity. Law courts now sit as courts of equity where the relief sought in a given case is specific performance, an injunction, or other form of equitable relief. The court is being asked for discretionary relief which is filled with historic notions of equity and good conscience. The discretion is not unbridled because it must be exercised on the basis of much of the history of the development of equity. The judge in an equity case may still be called "chancellor" for that case.[427] Whatever the judge is called, where equitable relief is sought, the ambience changes. There are no jurors because it is the judge, the successor to the chancellor, who will make the *ex aequo et bono* judgment as to whether the plaintiff is entitled to the extraordinary relief sought.[428] If the court decides to grant relief, it can mold a decree to fit the case precisely, i.e., it need not be concerned with all-or-nothing remedies. Specific performance or an injunction may not be completely effective relief.[429] The court may, therefore, order performance that is not identical to the promised performance.[430] It may also attach money damages to its decree to provide complete relief,[431] or it may condition its order on certain performance by the party seeking equitable relief.[432] We have already seen that specific performance or an injunction may be granted notwithstanding a provision for liquidated damages.[433] "The objective of the court in granting equitable relief is to do complete justice to the extent that this is feasible."[434]

We have seen that the normal substitutional remedy of damages is subject to limitations, such as foreseeability, certainty, and mitigation. Since the ordinary remedy is so circumscribed, it is not remarkable that extraordinary equitable remedies contain special limitations. It is important to explore those limitations.

[B]   The Inadequacy Limitation

Scores of cases state that specific performance or an injunction will not be granted where there is an adequate remedy at law, i.e., where the normal remedy of substitutional damages is adequate to protect the expectation interest of the aggrieved party.[435] The inadequacy limitation may be seen in various situations.

---

[427] *See, e.g.*, McIllwain v. Bank of Harrisburg, 18 Ark. App. 213, 713 S.W.2d 469 (1986).

[428] Equitable matters are triable *de novo* on appeal, i.e., factual issues are tried *de novo* on the record and reach a conclusion independent of the trial court except that where credible evidence is in conflict on a material issue of fact, the appellate court considers and may give weight to the fact that the trial court heard and observed the witnesses and accepted one version of the facts rather than another. Pallas v. Black, 226 Neb. 728, 414 N.W.2d 805 (1987).

[429] Norwich Community Dev. Corp. v. Arbucci, 1993 Conn. Super. LEXIS 112 (Conn. Super. Ct. Jan. 5, 1993).

[430] *See* Chastain v. Schomburg, 258 Ga. 218, 367 S.E.2d 230 (1988) (court cannot decree specific performance of a contract where vendor purports to sell land of another, but it can order specific performance of vendor's own interest in the land).

[431] *See* Tamarind Lithography Workshop, Inc. v. Sanders, 143 Cal. App. 3d 571, 193 Cal. Rptr. 409 (2d Dist. 1983) (injunction to prevent continued distribution of film without screen credits for writer-director-producer — $25,000 damages to time of trial). *See also Chastain v. Schomburg, id.*, where the court could only order specific performance in part and suggested that damages could be attached for remaining compensation.

[432] *See* Ruth v. Crane, 392 F. Supp. 724, 734 (E.D. Pa. 1975), *aff'd per curiam*, 564 F.2d 90 (3d Cir. 1977). *See also* Restatement 2d § 363.

[433] See Restatement 2d § 361 and the earlier discussion of this concept, § 127[B][5][b], *supra*. See also Fabian v. Sather, 316 N.W.2d 10 (Minn. 1982), suggesting that, when vendors resell land to a third party, they can recover only liquidated damages under their contract with the original breaching buyer rather than actual damages.

[434] Restatement 2d § 358, comment a.

[435] *See, e.g.*, Abrams v. Rapoport, 163 Ill. App. 3d 748, 114 Ill. Dec. 788, 516 N.E.2d 943 (1st Dist. 1987) (remedy at law adequate and specific performance would require continuous judicial supervision); Levista v. Ranbaxy Pharms, Inc., 2010 U.S. Dist. LEXIS 11136 at *16–17 (E. D. N. Y. 2010). *See also* Restatement 2d § 359(1).

[1]   The Uncertainty Limitation

The terms of any contract must be sufficiently certain to allow a court to grant an appropriate remedy.[436] The terms may be sufficiently certain to allow a court to calculate damages, but they may not be certain enough to permit a court to create an order for specific performance or an injunction. In that situation, no equitable remedy is possible.[437] On the other hand, the terms of the contract may be sufficiently certain but the calculation of damages is too speculative. This situation provides one of the illustrations of the inadequacy limitation, i.e., the uncertainty of damages limitation.

It will be recalled that the normal damage remedy is available only if proof of such damage is reasonably certain.[438] Conversely, one of the ways a plaintiff may secure equitable jurisdiction by showing inadequacy of the damage remedy is by establishing that the damages would necessarily be *uncertain*.[439] Though modern courts have liberalized the certainty requirement, situations remain where the proof is fatally uncertain. Consider, for example, a contract for the sale of an heirloom with dubious market value but great sentimental value to the buyer. There is no possibility of providing sufficiently certain proof of such sentimental value measured in money. Absent specific performance, the aggrieved party would have no remedy. Such a case, therefore, constitutes a classic application of the equitable remedy.[440] A breach of a covenant not to complete, threatening the loss of customers, presents another immeasurable loss.[441] In a commercial context, though courts have become much more willing to find ways to allow sufficient proof of lost profits of a new business and, therefore, award damages for breach in such cases,[442] situations remain where such evidence is considered too speculative. In such cases, specific performance may be the only available remedy.[443] Similarly, damages for repudiated output or requirements contracts may be too uncertain and specific performance may be granted.[444]

---

[436] *See* RESTATEMENT 2d § 33.

[437] *See* Miller v. Ogden, 134 Or. App. 589, 896 P.2d 596 (1995), *aff'd*, 325 Or. 248, 935 P.2d 1205 (1997) (uncertainty in terms of memorandum to purchase real property). See also the concurring opinion by Webber, J., in J.R. Sinnott Carpentry, Inc. v. Phillips, 110 Ill. App. 3d 632, 66 Ill. Dec. 671, 443 N.E.2d 597 (4th Dist. 1982) (contract stated that plans for addition to house would be attached and no plans were attached — terms insufficient to grant specific performance). RESTATEMENT 2d § 362.

[438] *See supra* § 122.

[439] *See* Cabot Corp. v. Ashland Oil, Inc., 597 F. Supp. 436 (D. Mass. 1984) (damages impossible to calculate); Link v. State of Montana, 180 Mont. 469, 591 P.2d 214 (1979) (refusal to maintain transportation to park made damages to park concessionaire too uncertain).

[440] *See* RESTATEMENT 2d § 360 comment b.

[441] See Ferrofluidics Corp. v. Advanced Vacuum Components, Inc., 789 F. Supp. 1201, 1211 (D.N.H. 1992), *aff'd*, 968 F.2d 1463 (1st Cir. 1992) (injunction against violating restrictive covenant in employment contract).

[442] *See supra* § 122 B.

[443] *See* Hogan v. Norfleet, 113 So. 2d 437 (Fla. Dist. Ct. App. 1959).

[444] *See* Laclede Gas Co. v. Amoco Oil Co., 522 F.2d 33 (8th Cir. 1975) (requirements contract); Eastern Air Lines, Inc. v. Gulf Oil Corp., 415 F. Supp. 429 (S.D. Fla. 1975) (requirements contract); Eastern Rolling Mill Co. v. Michlovitz, 157 Md. 51, 145 A. 378 (1929) (output contract — steel scraps). It should be noted, however, that prior to the UCC, cases such as *Eastern Rolling Mill* were uncommon. *See also* UCC § 2-716 comment 2: "Output and requirements contracts involving a particular or peculiarly available source or market present today the typical commercial specific performance situation. . . ."

[2] Inadequate Substitute Limitation

[a] Unique Goods — Inability to Cover — Uniform Commercial Code — Insolvency

Where a promise to deliver an heirloom is breached, not only is proof of damage with reasonable certainty impossible, no damage award will adequately compensate the aggrieved party since he cannot purchase that unique chattel elsewhere. Thus, even if the value of the chattel can be measured with reasonable certainty, such as a famous painting or sculpture, the buyer is entitled to specific performance of the contract on the footing that it will be impossible to purchase an adequate substitute.[445] The UCC has extended the availability of specific performance beyond the classical categories of heirlooms, priceless paintings, and custom-made goods.[446] It continues to authorize specific performance where the goods are unique. The remedy is now available, however, "in other proper circumstances."[447] Such "circumstances" include output and requirements contracts, typically on the footing that damages are uncertain though the lack of any reliable substitute supplier may constitute an independent rationale.[448] "Other proper circumstances" should not include the bankruptcy of the defendant since granting specific performance in such a case would constitute a preferential transfer that is contrary to federal bankruptcy policy.[449] Insolvency, however, is viewed as a factor, if not an exclusive ground, for granting specific performance.[450] Thus, if the contract is fair and remains executory on both sides, specific performance will not cause a preferential transfer because other creditors will be benefitted by the consideration received by the party ordered to perform.[451] The fact that damages can be measured with reasonable certainty should not, therefore, preclude specific performance in such cases whether or not they involve the sale of goods.[452] The ground for specific performance in such cases is the prospective inability to collect damages which, alone, is a basis for fulfilling the requirement of inadequacy.

Though the UCC manifests a clear intention to expand the availability of the remedy of specific performance in contracts for the sale of goods, the meaning of "other proper circumstances" is anything but clear, and courts tend to cling to pre-Code analyses of the

---

[445] *See* Fast v. Southern Offshore Yachts, 587 F. Supp. 1354 (D. Conn. 1984) (specific performance of contract to sell custom yacht); Sedmak v. Charlie's Chevrolet, Inc., 622 S.W.2d 694 (Mo. Ct. App. 1981) (contract to purchase Corvette automobile, which was one of a limited number manufactured to commemorate the selection of the Corvette as the pace car for the Indianapolis 500 auto race).

[446] *See* UCC § 2-716 comment 2.

[447] UCC § 2-716(1).

[448] *See supra* note 420.

[449] See, however, Proyectos Electronicos, S. A. v. Alper, 37 B.R. 931 (E.D. Pa. 1983), criticized in J. White & R. Summers, Uniform Commercial Code § 6-6, at 274 (3d ed. 1988).

[450] *See* Milan Steam Mills v. Hickey, 59 N.H. 241 (1879) (no adequate remedy at law because of insolvency); Heilman v. Union Canal Co., 37 Pa. 100 (1860) (insolvency alone is not a ground for equitable remedy); but Estate of Brown, 446 Pa. 401, 289 A.2d 77 (1972), suggests that insolvency supports the granting of specific performance. See also Restatement 2d § 360, where ill. 9 suggests that insolvency is a factor tending to show that damages are inadequate.

[451] *See* Restatement 2d § 360 comment d. *See also* Restatement 2d § 365, ill. 4.

[452] See, however, White & Summers, *supra* note 449, suggesting at page 274 that specific performance should not be granted in such cases because damages can be easily measured.

remedy's availability.[453] Thus, the use of specific performance in a UCC context remains relatively traditional. The UCC also permits the separate remedy of replevin of goods when they have been "identified"[454] to the contract and the seller refuses to deliver.[455]

[b]   Land — Specific Performance for Buyer

Courts have always regarded land as unique because any tract of land is necessarily unique in terms of its location. A buyer who desires a particular tract of land should not have to be satisfied with any substitute. If the buyer intends to resell the land and is, therefore, motivated exclusively by the profit he will earn on the resale, it may be argued that he should not be entitled to specific performance because he can be adequately compensated in damages. After all, he had only money in mind and was not concerned with living on the land or using for any other special purpose.[456] Yet, the strong policy favoring specific performance for the buyer of land has led to a virtual[457] per se view, and the buyer will still be granted specific performance if he so desires.[458]

---

[453] In their well-known book on the UCC, Professors White & Summers (*supra* note 449) arrive at this conclusion, though they mention an occasional case that evidences the expansion of the remedy, *e.g.*, Stephan's Mach. & Tool, Inc. v. D. & H. Mach. Consultants, Inc., 65 Ohio App. 2d 197, 417 N.E.2d 579 (Ohio Ct. App., Lucas County 1979) (equipment failed to function and, though damages were clearly measurable and the equipment was not unique since it was available elsewhere, plaintiff could not afford to purchase a replacement; the court granted specific performance).

[454] The concept of identification found in UCC § 2-501 has been explored at § 114 C *supra*.

[455] Under UCC § 2-502(1), where a buyer has paid all or part of the price for unshipped goods which have been identified in the contract and the seller has become insolvent within ten days after receipt of the first installment payment, the buyer may recover the goods if he makes and keeps good a tender of any unpaid portion of the price. This section is so filled with conditions that its utility is suspect. Failure to meet any of these conditions may relegate the buyer to § 2-716(3), which does not contain all of these conditions but does condition the right of replevin on the identification of the goods, the inability of the buyer to effect cover, *or* a showing that a cover effort would be unavailing, *or* a showing that the goods have been shipped under reservation, and that satisfaction of the security interest in the goods has been made or tendered. Except for the showing that the goods have been shipped under reservation, the buyer may find considerable overlap between specific performance in § 2-716(1) and replevin in § 2-716(3) since both are predicated, essentially, on the inability to cover.

[456] *See* Watkins v. Paul, 95 Idaho 499, 511 P.2d 781 (1973) (buyers had no unique purpose in obtaining the land but simply wanted to resell it for a profit).

[457] Occasionally, a court will insist that the presumption that damages are inadequate for a buyer of land and specific performance, therefore, is required, is only a rebuttable presumption. *See* Hancock v. Dusenberry, 110 Idaho 147, 715 P.2d 360 (Ct. App. 1986); Converse v. Fong, 159 Cal. App. 3d 86, 205 Cal. Rptr. 242 (1st Dist. 1984). This is, however, contrary to the great weight of authority.

[458] Courts have applied the same view to contracts for the purchase and sale of a condominium. *See* Kalinowski v. An-Chi Yeh, 9 Haw. App. 473, 847 P.2d 673 (1993). It is sometimes suggested that where the buyer is forced to breach his resale contract because the seller refused to convey the land, the buyer's damages will not be sufficiently certain absent litigation. The notion that uncertainty of damages is a reason for permitting such a buyer to obtain specific performance is a makeweight rationale in many cases. Since courts favor the avoidance of litigation, however, specific performance will accomplish this objective with respect to the resale contract. Again, however, the strong policy in favor of granting specific performance to buyers in land contracts simply does not admit of exceptions in the overwhelming number of jurisdictions. *See* RESTATEMENT 2d § 360 comment e.

[c]   Land — Specific Performance for Seller — "Mutuality of Remedy" — Adequate Security of Performance

Where a buyer breaches a contract for the sale of land, the seller is usually entitled to specific performance though there is nothing unique about the performance of the buyer, i.e., the seller receives the contract price.[459] The rationale for this curious result was sometimes based on "mutuality of remedy," i.e., the notion that one party would not be entitled to a remedy if the same remedy would not be available to the other party.[460] The "broken-down requirement" of mutuality of remedy is often traced to a nineteenth century treatise,[461] but has been steadily proceeding toward oblivion in the second half of the twentieth.[462] The concept underlying "mutuality of remedy" is to assure the party in breach that he will receive the performance due from the aggrieved party after the breaching party performs pursuant to the equity decree. If, for example, a breaching seller of land is ordered to convey the land, he should have reasonable assurance that he will receive the purchase price. This result can be achieved without resorting to the doctrine of mutuality of remedy. The court can, for example, order specific performance conditioned upon the buyer providing adequate security through a mortgage or otherwise.[463] It is not necessary to provide exactly the same remedies for both parties.[464] Mutuality of remedy has been discarded even in jurisdictions which had codified it.[465] If the court cannot order adequate security for the specifically performing party, it will refuse to grant an equitable remedy.[466]

[d]   Essential Equitable Relief

Situations may occur where it is patently clear that the only effective remedy is an equitable remedy. A cogent example occurs where one's religion may require certain acts on the part of a spouse to obtain a religious divorce. Thus, under traditional Jewish law, a written

---

[459] Deans v. Layton, 89 N.C. App. 358, 366 S.E.2d 560 (1988); Kunzman v. Thorsen, 303 Or. 600, 740 P.2d 754 (1987); Pallas v. Black, 226 Neb. 728, 414 N.W.2d 805 (1987); Perron v. Hale, 108 Idaho 578, 701 P.2d 198 (1985); Tombari v. Griepp, 55 Wash. 2d 771, 350 P.2d 452 (1960). RESTATEMENT 2d § 360 comment e.

[460] *See* Ames, *Mutuality in Specific Performances*, 3 COLUM. L. REV. 1 (1903); Stone, *The Mutuality Rule in New York*, 16 COLUM. L. REV. 443 (1916). Modern authorities, however, suggest another reason for affording the vendor the remedy of specific performance in a land contract, i.e., the difficulty of locating a willing buyer with acceptable credit, particularly if the value of the property is declining. *See* Deans v. Layton, 89 N.C. App. 358, 366 S.E.2d 560 (1988).

[461] FRY, SPECIFIC PERFORMANCE § 460 (1858).

[462] For an exploration of "mutuality of remedy," including Professor Corbin's characterization of "the broken down requirement of mutuality of remedy" (5A CORBIN ON CONTRACTS § 1183), see Northcom, Ltd. v. James, 694 So. 2d 1329, 1336 (Ala. 1997).

[463] *See* RESTATEMENT 2d § 363.

[464] *See* Heritage Nat'l Assocs., Ltd. Pshp. v. 21st Inv. Group L.L.C., 2000 Tex. App. LEXIS 2553, at *20 (Tex. App. Dallas. Apr. 19, 2000); Lackey v. Green Tree Fin. Corp., 330 S.C. 388, 402, 498 S.E.2d 898, 905 (Ct. App. 1998) ("the fact that one party is not allowed specific performance or an injunction is not a sufficient reason to refuse it to the other party"). In Cohoon v. Wilcoxen, 1993 Neb. App. LEXIS 401, at *10 (Neb. Ct. App. Oct. 12, 1993), the court states that instead of the remedy of specific performance and the possibility of a contempt order to compel the payment of the balance of the purchase price, damages provided a more practical and efficient remedy under the circumstances.

[465] For example, California amended CAL. CIV. CODE § 3386 in 1969 to dispense with the requirement of mutuality and to replace it with a flexible concept similar to what now appears in RESTATEMENT 2d § 363. *See Converse v. Fong*, *supra* note 457. *See also* Sablosky v. Edward S. Gordon Co., 73 N.Y.2d 133, 538 N.Y.S.2d 513, 535 N.E.2d 643 (1989) (mutuality of remedy has been generally discarded and is not required in arbitration contracts).

[466] See RESTATEMENT 2d § 363, indicating that neither specific performance nor an injunction will issue unless the court is satisfied that there is adequate security for the reciprocal performance.

document of severance of all marital bonds (a "get") is an essential condition to a remarriage by a wife. A "get" can be obtained exclusively by the husband's assertion that it is being sought of his own free will. The parties may have made an agreement that the husband would cooperate in this effort. While courts may feel constrained in such cases because of implied or expressed preclusions of judicial intervention in religious matters, some courts have been willing to grant equitable relief since, in this type of case, any substitute relief is woefully inadequate.[467] Damages in such a case are obviously uncertain. Yet, even if damages were more than reasonably certain, they would be clearly inadequate to provide the aggrieved party with anything resembling effective relief.

[C]   The Fairness Limitation

It is important to emphasize the discretionary nature of equitable relief. Notwithstanding the fact that an agreement may contain all of the necessary common law elements for enforcement, a court may deny such relief because it concludes that it would be unfair to grant it. "Fairness" includes any number of factors that a court may consider. Specific performance will be refused where the contract was induced by mistake or unfair practices.[468] It will also be refused where it would cause unreasonable hardship or loss to the breaching party or third persons,[469] or where the exchange is grossly inadequate.[470] A cogent example of the last situation is the case of *McKinnon v. Benedict*,[471] where prospective buyers of property were in need of financial assistance and agreed to major restrictions on the commercial property they intended to buy in exchange for a loan of $5000 and assistance from the lender in promoting the use of the property. Facing failure in their new venture, the buyers pursued an expansion of the property that violated their contract. The lender sought to enjoin the buyers from further violations. In denying the plaintiff the equitable remedy of injunction, the court considered the following factors: (1) the gross inadequacy of consideration,[472] (2) the hardship to the defendant as compared with the benefit to the plaintiff,[473] (3) whether the defendant's promise was induced by some sharp practice, misrepresentation or mistake,[474] and (4) the

---

[467] *See* Avitzur v. Avitzur, 58 N.Y.2d 108, 459 N.Y.S.2d 572, 446 N.E.2d 136 (1983), *cert. denied*, 464 U.S. 817, 104 S. Ct. 76, 78 L. Ed. 2d 88 (1983); Minkin v. Minkin, 180 N.J. Super. 260, 434 A.2d 665 (1981). These cases and others are discussed in Annot., 29 A.L.R.4th 746 (1988).

[468] RESTATEMENT 2d § 364(1)(a).

[469] *See* Umbra Cuscinetti v. Beaver Precision Prods., 1998 U.S. App. LEXIS 10335 (9th Cir. 1998). *See also* Star Enter. v. Thomas, 783 F. Supp. 1564 (D.R.I. 1992) (defendant relied on statement that option would never be exercised). RESTATEMENT 2d § 364(1)(b).

[470] RESTATEMENT 2d § 364(1)(c).

[471] 38 Wis. 2d 607, 157 N.W.2d 665 (1968).

[472] The court computed the value of the loan to the defendants at $145, which was not even an unsecured loan since plaintiffs took a mortgage on other property owned by defendants. Plaintiff had also made general promises to assist the defendants in their enterprise. The plaintiff's performance of those promises was nominal. In exchange for this value, the defendants had surrendered valuable rights in the operation of a recreation facility. Where equitable relief is sought, courts do inquire into the "adequacy of consideration" (relative values exchanged), while the general rule is that they will not so inquire where the relief sought is the normal remedy of damages. *See* RESTATEMENT 2d § 364(1)(c).

[473] *See* Van Wagner Advertising Corp. v. S & M Enters., 67 N.Y.2d 186, 501 N.Y.S.2d 628, 492 N.E.2d 756 (1986) (disproportionate harm to defendant and benefit to plaintiff).

[474] *See* Concert Radio, Inc. v. GAF Corp., 108 A.D.2d 273, 488 N.Y.S.2d 696 (1st Dep't 1985), *aff'd*, 73 N.Y.2d 766, 536 N.Y.S.2d 52, 532 N.E.2d 1280 (1988) (defendant mistakenly triggered an option agreement which plaintiff then sought to specifically enforce; court denied equitable relief because plaintiff took no risks, invested no money, and

disparity of business background between the parties.[475] The historical concept of unconscionability is also a significant factor in the exercise of judicial discretion to determine whether equitable relief should be granted.[476] A court will balance all of these factors in any case where equitable relief is sought.[477]

Where the contract expressly precludes specific performance or an injunction, a court may grant the equitable relief sought if denial of the relief would be unfair to the party seeking relief or to third persons.[478]

[D]   "Public Policy Limitation"[479]

Even where an agreement is enforceable at law with respect to money damages, public policy elements may prevent the granting of equitable relief.[480] Where, for example, the granting of specific performance would result in reversing a valid conviction of the defendant for securities fraud and the dismissal of indictments, a court may refuse to grant the relief sought.[481] Specific performance of an alimony agreement was denied where the paramour cohabited with the wife and such activity was considered contrary to public policy.[482] Where a public utility commission approved the construction of a transmission line essential for the public welfare, a court refused to enjoin the breach of an agreement that would have prevented that construction and harmed the public welfare.[483] There is no end to such illustrations since they run the gamut of per se actions that are bundled beneath the nebulous caption, "public policy." Nonetheless, it is important to recognize this additional limitation on the granting of equitable relief. Where a decree of specific performance would violate public policy, e.g., a federal statute, a court may still award compensatory damages.[484]

---

suffered no losses, while defendant would lose large sums simply because of his misinterpretation of contract language).

[475] In questions of equitable relief, courts are particularly conscious of unconscionable conduct. While the court could discover no sharp practice, dishonesty, or overreaching by the plaintiff, it took note that the plaintiff was an attorney and experienced business man, while the defendant was a person of limited financial ability and business background.

[476] *See* the exploration of unconscionability at § 97 *supra.*

[477] *See* RESTATEMENT 2d § 364.

[478] "Regardless of the existence of a remedy at law or the clarity of the contract, specific performance may be granted 'if denial of such relief would be unfair because it would cause unreasonable hardship or loss to the party seeking relief or to third persons.'" Greyhound Fin. Corp. v. TSM Fin. Group, 1993 U.S. Dist. LEXIS 10873, at *8–9 (N.D. Ill. Aug. 4, 1993) (quoting RESTATEMENT 2d § 364(2)).

[479] *See* Chapter 8 of RESTATEMENT 2d.

[480] RESTATEMENT 2d § 365.

[481] United States v. McGovern, 822 F.2d 739 (8th Cir. 1987), *cert. denied*, 484 U.S. 956, 108 S. Ct. 352, 98 L. Ed. 2d 377 (1987).

[482] Garlinger v. Garlinger, 129 N.J. Super. 37, 322 A.2d 1190 (1974).

[483] Stellwagon v. Pyle, 390 Pa. 17, 133 A.2d 819 (1957).

[484] W. R. Grace & Co. v. Local Union 759, International Union of United Rubber, etc., 461 U.S. 757, 769, 103 S. Ct. 2177, 76 L. Ed. 2d 298 (1983). *See also* Van Waters & Rogers, Inc. v. International Brotherhood of Teamsters, Local Union 70, 913 F.2d 736 743 (9th Cir. 1990).

[E]   The Judicial Supervision Limitation — Personal Service Contracts

[1]   General Problems in Judicial Supervision

If there is no other limitation on the granting of an equitable remedy, a court may still refuse to grant that remedy if the difficulties of supervision are disproportionate to the benefits of that remedy. If courts are thrust into making judgments about the quality of the performance and/or the supervision of performance will occur over a long period, courts shirk from granting equitable relief.[485] One of the classic examples of these supervisory problems occurs in construction contracts. Typically, breaches of construction contracts can be adequately compensated through the normal remedy of money damages. When asked to specifically enforce the contract of a builder, courts will generally refuse that remedy, partly because damages at law may be adequate, but also because of the difficulty courts would face in attempting to supervise that performance.[486] This is not to suggest that courts will invariably refuse equitable relief in such a contract where such relief was otherwise indicated and supervisory problems are not insuperable.[487] Moreover, what may appear to create almost insuperable supervisory problems may turn out to be a situation which the court can easily supervise.[488] A certain type of contract, however, is particularly troublesome to courts in terms of supervision and other policy constraints. We will now explore the problems in granting equitable relief in personal service contracts.

[2]   Personal Service Contracts — Injunction — Reinstatement

Notwithstanding some very early lip service paid to the view that "a bird that will not sing will be made to sing," our legal system insists on liberty even at the expense of broken promises.[489] It is clear that personal service promises will not be specifically enforced.[490] While the original resistance to specific enforcement of such promises was based on the difficulties of judicial supervision, the prohibition of involuntary servitude under the Thirteenth Amendment to the Constitution of the United States may also be violated by such an equitable decree.[491]

---

[485] *See* RESTATEMENT 2d § 366 comment a.

[486] Yonan v. Oak Park Fed. Sav. & Loan Ass'n, 27 Ill. App. 3d 967, 326 N.E.2d 773 (1st Dist. 1975).

[487] *See* Walgreen Company v. Sara Creek Property Co., 966 F.2d 273 (7th Cir. 1992) (A shopping center breached exclusivity clause in a lease with Walgreen. While recognizing that a permanent injunction requires supervision that is costly, the trial court did not exceed the bounds of reasonable judgment in concluding that the costs of the damages remedy would exceed the costs of an injunction.).

[488] *See* Egbert v. Way, 15 Wash. App. 76, 546 P.2d 1246 (1976) (trial court had based its refusal to grant specific performance on mistaken assumptions of supervision and appellate court concluded that it could supervise the clearing of tax liens and inheritance tax on contract for the sale of real property).

[489] *See* De Rivafinoli v. Corsetti, 4 Paige Ch. 264 (N.Y. Ch. 1833), and A. CORBIN, CONTRACTS at § 1204, *as quoted in In re* Robert A. Noonan, 17 B.R. 793 (Bankr. S.D.N.Y. 1982).

[490] Bear, Sterns & Co. v. Sharon, 550 F. Supp. 2d 174 (D. Mass. 2008); Motown Record Corp. v. Brockert, 160 Cal. App. 3d 123, 137, 207 Cal. Rptr. 574 (2d Dist. 1984), and RESTATEMENT 2d § 367(1). See, however, the enforcement of a contract resulting in compelling the president of a company who acted outrageously to read in person a bargaining order to assembled employees. Conair Corp. v. NLRB, 721 F.2d 1355, 232 U.S. App. D.C. 194 (D.C. Cir. 1983), *cert. denied sub nom.* Local 222, International Ladies' Garment Workers' Union v. NLRB, 467 U.S. 1241, 104 S. Ct. 3511, 82 L. Ed. 2d 819 (1984).

[491] *See* Beverly Glen Music, Inc. v. Warner Communs., Inc., 178 Cal. App. 3d 1142, 1144, 224 Cal. Rptr. 260 (2d Dist.

Other statutory prohibitions on servitude may also preclude specific performance.[492] Since specific performance is not available, aggrieved parties may seek injunctions against the defendant's performance elsewhere. Enjoining the defendant from performing for another is sometimes referred to as "negative enforcement" of the defendant's obligation.[493]

In the famous case of *Lumley v. Wagner*,[494] a Prussian opera singer (Wagner) had agreed to sing exclusively for three months for the plaintiff, who was the proprietor of Her Majesty's Theatre in London. Wagner also stipulated that she would not compete with the employer for the term of the engagement. When she broke her agreement and agreed to sing at another theatre,[495] Lumley sought an injunction to restrain her from performing elsewhere. The injunction was granted with the Chancellor noting that the effect of the injunction may cause her to perform her original promise.[496] Later courts were willing to grant an injunction absent an express stipulation that the employee would not compete during the term of the employment.[497] There are numerous instances of courts granting injunctions against the defendant performing elsewhere if the services of the defendant are unique.[498] Yet, whether the remedy sought is specific performance or an injunction, courts will be loathe to grant it if it will compel the continuance of personal association or will preclude the employee from making a living.[499]

Where an employee seeks a mandatory injunction ordering reinstatement, courts recognize the impracticability of ordering a relationship of trust and confidence, as well as the obstacles of judicial supervision of such an arrangement. They will, therefore, typically deny such a remedy.[500] Neither will other extraordinary remedies, such as mandamus[501] or a temporary restraining order,[502] be granted to compel the maintenance of the employer-employee relationship in such cases.[503] Courts may also call upon traditional obstacles to the granting of equitable relief, such as the requirement that damages must be inadequate and, when applied to personal services contracts, the court may be willing to discover adequate damages more

---

1986); American Broadcasting Cos. v. Wolf, 52 N.Y.2d 394, 438 N.Y.S.2d 482, 420 N.E.2d 363 (1981).

[492] See, e.g., § 541(a)(6) of the federal Bankruptcy Code, which prohibits creditors from forcing debtors into future servitude for payment of debts. *In re* James Taylor, 91 B.R. 302 (Bankr. D.N.J. 1988), *aff'd*, 103 B.R. 511 (D.N.J. 1989), *aff'd*, 913 F.2d 102 (3d Cir. 1990).

[493] *See American Broadcasting Cos. v. Wolf, supra* note 491.

[494] 1 DeG. M. & G. 604, 42 Eng. Rep. 687 [Ch. 1852].

[495] She was induced to do so by Frederick Gye, who headed the Royal Italian Opera in Covent Garden.

[496] *See Lumley v. Wagner, supra* note 494, 42 Eng. Rep. at 693.

[497] Implied covenant recognized in Montague v. Flockton, L.R. 16 Eq. 189 [1873].

[498] *See* Dallas Cowboys Football Club, Inc. v. Harris, 348 S.W.2d 37 (Tex. Civ. App. Dallas 1961) (football player); Philadelphia Ball Club, Ltd. v. Lajoie, 202 Pa. 210, 51 A. 973 (1902) (baseball player).

[499] *See American Broadcasting Cos. v. Wolf, supra* note 491. *See also* RESTATEMENT 2d § 367(2).

[500] See Nicholas v. Pennsylvania State Univ., 227 F.3d 133, 146 (3d Cir. 2000). *See also* Jetborne Int'l, Inc. v. Cohan, 584 So. 2d 176 (Fla. Dist. Ct. App. 1991).

[501] State *ex rel.* Cleary v. Board of Sch. Comm'rs of Indianapolis, 438 N.E.2d 12 (Ind. Ct. App. 1982) (mandamus, like injunctions, will not issue when the result will be specific performance of personal service contracts).

[502] Miller v. Foley, 317 N.W.2d 710 (Minn. 1982).

[503] Though employer's promises generally will not be specifically enforced, it is not uncommon for courts to order reinstatement of discharged employees where the employer has violated anti-discrimination statutes or collective bargaining agreements. *See* RESTATEMENT 2d § 367 comment b.

easily.[504] A court may, however, conclude that irreparable harm may overcome other obstacles of equitable relief in a given situation. Thus, a defendant may be ordered to reinstate a physician in a residency program since the plaintiff's opportunity for board certification may be unreasonably hampered.[505]

Beyond the obstacles of judicial supervision and involuntary servitude, the plaintiff seeking equitable enforcement of a personal service contract must show that the services are unique. While the services of professional athletes or other performers may be presumptively unique,[506] other personal services may be so perfunctory or ministerial that specific enforcement of such contracts would avoid the obstacles normally precluding such relief.[507] Thus, where a realtor sought a writ of mandamus ("We command") ordering respondent to perform her duties as official court reporter by delivering a free statement of facts in a given case, the court granted the relief.[508]

[F]   Power of Termination Limitation

A contract may expressly provide a party with a power of termination or such a power of avoidance may be provided by law, e.g., to protect an infant from imprudent acts.[509] Courts will properly consider such powers when asked to grant equitable relief against such a party because he may exercise that power and nullify the decree.[510] This is particularly true where the termination would take effect almost immediately. If notice of exercise of the power of termination had to be given some time before the party's performance was discharged, however, a court may grant equitable relief for that period.

Where the party with the power of termination is the party *seeking* equitable relief, there is a problem of assuring the security of the contract for the defendant.[511] If, for example, a court would decree specific performance in such a case and, after the defendant adhered to that order by performing, the plaintiff would exercise his power of termination, the defendant would be irreparably harmed. To avoid that possibility, a court can mold its decree to assure the plaintiff's performance by, for example, extinguishing the power in the plaintiff. There is

---

[504] *See* Radiac Abrasives, Inc. v. Diamond Tech., Inc., 177 Ill. App. 3d 628, 532 N.E.2d 428 (2d Dist. 1988).

[505] Bali v. Christiana Care Health Servs., Inc., 1999 Del. Ch. LEXIS 128 (Del. Ch. June 16, 1999) (the court distinguished typical employment contracts where the employee can find substitute employment, whereas the discharged resident physician can anticipate great difficulty in securing another residency and has little or no prospect for board certification).

[506] *See* Nassau Sports v. Peters, 352 F. Supp. 870 (E.D.N.Y. 1972).

[507] See Restatement 2d § 367 comment a, suggesting a distinction between personal services for which specific performance or injunctions would not be granted, and other non-delegable duties for which such relief would be granted, such as the writing of an autograph or signing of a diploma.

[508] *See* Perez v. McGar, 630 S.W.2d 320 (Tex. App. Houston 1982). It should be noted that the defendant had a statutory duty as a court official to perform this service.

[509] On the power of avoidance by infants and others, *see* §§ 25–28 *supra*.

[510] *See* Ecri v. McGraw-Hill, Inc., 809 F.2d 223 (3d Cir. 1987) (requirements of preliminary injunctions are more stringent than those for specific performance and court must consider power of termination). *See also* State *ex rel.* Schoblom v. Anacortes Veneer, Inc., 42 Wash. 2d 338, 255 P.2d 379 (1953), and Restatement 2d § 368(1).

[511] Restatement 2d § 363 suggests another limitation on the granting of equitable relief, i.e., such relief will be denied if a substantial part of the agreed exchange of the performance to be compelled is unperformed, i.e., the performance of the party seeking relief, and that performance is not secured to the satisfaction of the court.

no preclusion of equitable relief in such cases unless the security of the defendant cannot be assured.[512]

[G]   Equitable Relief for Defaulting Plaintiff

Where a party seeking specific performance, an injunction, or other equitable relief is, himself, in breach of the contract, whether the court may grant the relief sought may depend upon the nature of the breach. It should be recalled that an uncured material breach will discharge the duties of the other party to the contract. A court could not, therefore, order specific performance (or negative enforcement) of duties that were already discharged.[513] On the other hand, if the defaulting plaintiff's breach was immaterial so that the duties were not discharged, specific performance or an injunction should not be precluded.[514] In a contract for the sale of land, for example, the buyer's delay in making a payment according to the terms of the contract may be a minor breach that should not permit the seller to avoid his or her obligation to convey the property.[515] The First RESTATEMENT permitted specific performance by a defaulting plaintiff, even in the case of a serious breach, if that was necessary to avoid an unjust penalty or forfeiture.[516] The RESTATEMENT 2d omits that exception "as unnecessary in the light of the merger of law and equity and the greater flexibility of legal rules that deal with penalties and forfeitures."[517]

§ 129   UNIFORM COMMERCIAL CODE AND CISG REMEDIES — SURVEY

Throughout this Chapter on contract remedies, numerous references to the UCC and CISG have appeared. On occasion, aspects of both the Code and the Convention have been explored in some detail. These explorations will not be repeated in this section. It is, however, important to survey UCC and CISG remedies in an holistic fashion so that these remedies will not be viewed as different from contract remedies in general. Both the UCC and CISG deal with contracts for the sale of goods. Remedies for breach of contract for the sale of goods protect the normal expectation interest of the parties by placing the aggrieved party in the position he or she would have occupied had the contract been performed.[518] It is important to view these remedies as facets of a prism protecting that interest. The survey that follows is not intended to be an exhaustive treatment of UCC or CISG remedies for breach of contract. Such remedies are explored in sales law or international transactions courses or both. The following survey begins with an exploration of UCC remedies.

---

[512] *See* Stamatiades v. Merit Music Serv., Inc., 210 Md. 597, 124 A.2d 829 (1956). *See also* RESTATEMENT 2d § 368(2).

[513] Ballantyne House Assocs. v. City of Newark, 269 N.J. Super. 322, 635 A.2d 551 (App. Div. 1993).

[514] Regan v. Garfield Ridge Trust & Sav. Bank, 220 Ill. App. 3d 1078, 163 Ill. Dec. 605, 581 N.E.2d 759, 765 (2d Dist. 1991).

[515] *See* Fleenor v. Church, 681 P.2d 1351 (Alaska 1984). *See also* RESTATEMENT 2d § 369.

[516] First RESTATEMENT § 375(1).

[517] RESTATEMENT 2d § 369 (Reporter's Note).

[518] *See* UCC § 1-305(a).

[A]   UCC Prerequisites — Repudiation, Failure of Performance, Rejection, Revocation of Acceptance, Inspection

Before a buyer or seller is entitled to a UCC remedy in a contract for the sale of goods, one of four basic events must occur: (1) one of the parties must repudiate the contract[519] (the concept of repudiation was explored earlier);[520] (2) one of the parties must fail to perform, *e.g.*, the seller fails to deliver the goods or the buyer fails to pay for the goods;[521] (3) the buyer must rightfully reject the goods because they are nonconforming (*e.g.*, defective)[522] which provides a cause of action against the seller,[523] or the buyer must wrongfully reject the goods which provides the seller with a cause of action against the buyer;[524] (4) the buyer must revoke his acceptance of the goods upon discovery of a substantial nonconformity,[525] which provides him with a cause of action against the seller,[526] or the buyer wrongfully revokes acceptance, which provides the seller with a cause of action against the buyer.[527] We have earlier explored the concept of revocation of acceptance.[528]

It should be noted that before a buyer is normally bound to accept or make payment for goods delivered, he has the right to inspect the goods.[529] As is typical throughout Article 2 of the Code, the parties may modify this statutory provision by their contract. If, for example, the parties agree that the shipment is C.O.D. (cash on delivery), they have obviously agreed that payment shall be made at the time of delivery, i.e., prior to inspection.[530] Any similar agreement can eliminate the buyer's prior right to inspection.[531] If such an agreement is made, a nonconformity of the goods does not excuse the duty of payment unless the nonconformity appears without inspection, or unless a justifiable injunction would issue against honor of the documents against which payment is to be made.[532] Payment — even a payment which the buyer has agreed to make prior to inspection — does not constitute acceptance of the goods.[533]

---

[519] *See* UCC § 2-610.

[520] *See* Chapter 7 *supra.*

[521] *See* UCC § 2-301.

[522] *See* UCC § 2-601. As to the requirements of a rightful rejection, see UCC § 2-602.

[523] *See* UCC § 2-711.

[524] UCC § 2-703.

[525] UCC § 2-608.

[526] UCC § 2-711.

[527] UCC § 2-703.

[528] *See* Chapter 7 *supra.*

[529] UCC § 2-513.

[530] UCC § 2-514(3)(a).

[531] If, for example, the parties agree that payment is to be made against documents (*e.g.*, bill of lading), such payment is then due prior to inspection. UCC § 2-513(3)(b).

[532] UCC § 2-512(1).

[533] UCC § 2-512(2).

[B]   Comparison of Seller and Buyer Remedies Under the UCC

Two sections of the UCC list the remedies of the seller and the buyer. Section 2-703 lists the seller's remedies, and § 2-711 lists the buyer's remedies. It is useful to compare the counterpart remedies of each of the parties.

[1]   Resale and Cover — "Lost Volume" Seller

When the buyer fails to perform, the seller may resell the goods intended for the buyer to a second buyer.[534] The operation of this remedy in the normal case is quite simple. *S* agrees to sell goods to *B* for $1000 and *B* repudiates. Assuming no additional selling or transportation expense, *S* resells the same goods to *B* for $900. To fulfill *S*'s reasonable expectations, he should be awarded damages in the amount of $100 against *B*, i.e., the difference between the contract price and the resale price. The resale must be in good faith and it must be commercially reasonable.[535] It may be either "public," which requires notice of the time and place of resale, or "private," which requires notice to the buyer.[536] The seller must also be able to show that the particular goods delivered to the second buyer were the goods that would have been shipped to the first buyer.[537] While the resale remedy will protect the expectation interest of a seller of a single or unique item, it will not protect that seller if he would have made the second sale in any event, i.e., if he is a "lost volume" seller. We have already explored the remedy for such a seller — the profit he would have made on the breached contract.[538] Since many sellers are "lost volume" sellers, the resale remedy will not provide them with sufficient protection of their expectation interest. The resale remedy, therefore, is only effective where the seller has only one item to sell and can only make one profit thereon.

The buyer's counterpart to the seller's resale remedy is the buyer's remedy of *cover*.[539] The cover remedy allows the buyer to make a reasonable and good faith substitute purchase where the seller fails to supply conforming goods under the contract. Where the buyer makes such a substitute purchase, he may recover the difference between the contract price and the cover price.[540] The substitute goods purchased need not be identical to those under the broken contract. It is sufficient if the cover was reasonable and without unreasonable delay ("seasonable").[541] Unlike the seller's resale remedy, which we have seen operates effectively only if the seller would not have made the second sale in any event, the buyer's cover remedy

---

[534] *See* UCC § 2-706.

[535] *See* Servbest Foods, Inc. v. Emessee Indus., Inc., 82 Ill. App. 3d 662, 37 Ill. Dec. 945, 403 N.E.2d 1 (1st Dist. 1980).

[536] *See* Mobil Oil Corp. v. Earhart Petroleum, Inc., 2000 U.S. App. LEXIS 8674 (4th Cir. 2000). In Sprague v. Sumitomo Forestry Co., 104 Wash. 2d 751, 709 P.2d 1200 (1985), the court found that failure to notify the buyer precluded the use of the resale remedy and seller was relegated to damages for buyer's nonacceptance or repudiation under § 2-708(1) (discussed *infra*). The trial court had awarded resale damages, which happened to be the same amount that should have been awarded under § 2-708(1). The court, therefore, affirmed.

[537] *See* Hunt-Wesson Foods, Inc. v. Marubeni Alaska Seafoods, Inc., 23 Wash. App. 193, 596 P.2d 666 (1979) (failure to show that the goods delivered to second buyer was caused by first buyer's breach precluded the use of the resale remedy).

[538] *See supra* § 123[E].

[539] UCC § 2-712. For an analysis of this remedy, see Kanzmeier v. McCoppin, 398 N.W.2d 826 (Iowa 1987).

[540] UCC § 2-712(2).

[541] *See* Meshinsky v. Nichols Yacht Sales, Inc., 110 N.J. 464, 541 A.2d 1063 (1988).

is the normal remedy of the buyer who presumably requires the goods the seller failed to supply.

[2]   Buyer and Seller Remedies for Difference Between Contract Price and Market Price

The seller need not pursue his resale remedy, and the buyer need not pursue his cover remedy. Absent certain limitations that will be considered, either party is free to pursue a traditional remedy for the difference between the contract price and market price of the goods. The comparison here, however, is more complicated than the earlier comparison between resale and cover.

[a]   Cover — Preferred Remedy

It is important to understand that the buyer's cover remedy is different from remedies available to him under pre-Code law. If the buyer uses the cover remedy properly, he is entitled to recover the difference between the contract price and his actual cover price, i.e., the price he actually pays for substitute goods. Pre-Code law generally measured the difference between the contract price and the market price, regardless of the buyer's cover purchase.[542]

If the buyer paid more than the market price for the substitute goods, he would be relegated to the difference between the contract and market price regardless of his cover price. Cover, therefore, is a more precise measure of the actual damage suffered by the buyer and is clearly the most important remedy for an aggrieved buyer. Notwithstanding the availability of cover, the Code permits the buyer to ignore that remedy.

[b]   "Hypothetical Cover" — Contract/Market Price Difference

The buyer may choose not to cover and still may recover the difference between the contract price and the market price at the time the buyer "learned of the breach."[543] We have already considered a number of problems surrounding the phrase "learned of the breach," particularly with respect to anticipatory repudiation.[544] At this point, it is important to note that, just as the resale remedy for the typical (lost volume) seller is anything but useful, the contract price/market price remedy for the buyer has lost much of its utility in light of the cover remedy.[545] The only significant use of that remedy occurs where the buyer has not covered at all because he changed his mind about the purchase, cannot buy substitute goods, or where he attempted to cover and failed to meet the necessary conditions of a good faith, reasonable cover.[546]

---

[542] *See* McGinnis v. Wentworth Chevrolet Co., 295 Or. 494, 668 P.2d 365 (1983).

[543] UCC § 2-713(1).

[544] *See supra* § 123[F].

[545] Where a buyer has only "partially covered," he may pursue his additional economic loss under the contract/market price differential, § 2-713. Savage Indus. v. American Pulverizer Co., 1996 U.S. App. LEXIS 33157 (10th Cir. Dec. 18, 1996).

[546] Where the buyer elects not to cover, his damages are governed by UCC § 2-713. Moridge Mfg. Co. v. Butler, 451 N.E.2d 677 (Ind. Ct. App. 1983). *See also* Dickson v. Delhi Seed Co., 26 Ark. App. 83, 760 S.W.2d 382 (1988) (§§ 2-712 and 2-713 are alternative remedies and § 2-712 is, therefore, available to the buyer unless he did not cover). To the same effect, see State *ex rel.* Concrete Sales & Equip. Rental Co. v. Kent Nowlin Constr., 106 N.M. 539, 746 P.2d 645 (1987).

Where a buyer chooses not to make a readily available substitute purchase, he may have done so because he has discovered no need for the goods or because he was purchasing the goods for resale and decided that the resale prospects were dim. In either case, the seller has done the buyer a favor by breaching the contract. Should the buyer recover damages even though he chose not to cover? How has the buyer been damaged? The buyer was entitled to certain goods at a certain time at a certain price. Had he received those goods, he would have had goods worth the market price for which he would have paid the contract price. If the contract price is lower than the market price, the buyer has been damaged to the extent of the difference. Though he did not receive the goods and chose not to cover, he has lost the benefit of his bargain to the extent of the contract price/market price differential.[547] The remedy is sometimes referred to as "hypothetical cover,"[548] i.e., if the buyer had covered, presumably he would have paid the market price for substitute goods at the time and place of tender, although this may be unrealistic because cover need not and often does not occur at the time and place of tender.[549] Although "hypothetical cover" is obviously less precise than actual cover, it remains a decent approximation of damages in the absence of actual cover. It has been called a "statutory liquidated damages clause,"[550] which is a sensible characterization since it suggests a reasonable forecast of direct damages in the event of seller's failure to deliver.[551]

The mechanical use of a § 2-713 formula may conflict with the overriding principle that a party should not be placed in a *better* position that he would have occupied had the contract been performed. In *Allied Canners & Packers, Inc. v. Victor Packing Co.*,[552] the seller agreed to sell raisins to the buyer, who had made resale contracts which would net a profit of just under $4,500. The California raisin crop was severely damaged by rain and, because the raisin market is regulated in California, cover could not occur until much later. The diminished supply of raisins resulted in a huge increase in the market price. The buyer did not cover but avoided any liability to its customers. Since the market price had increased more than substantially, the § 2-713 measure of recovery was over $150,000, which the buyer sought to recover though it expected to earn a profit of less than $4500 if the contract had been performed. The court was faced with choosing between the "statutory liquidated damages" concept of § 2-713, and the general directive of the Code under § 1-106 that an aggrieved party should be placed in no better position than he would have occupied had the contract been performed. The court chose the latter view, thereby adhering to the basic principle of contract damages.

---

[547] See Panhandle Agri-Service, Inc. v. Becker, 231 Kan. 291, 644 P.2d 413 (1982), where counsel on either side and the trial court demonstrated a remarkable lack of understanding about this remedy under the UCC. Fortunately, the Supreme Court of Kansas manifested a much better understanding.

[548] Allied Canners & Packers, Inc. v. Victor Packing Co., 162 Cal. App. 3d 905, 209 Cal. Rptr. 60 (1st Dist. 1984).

[549] *See* Dangerfield v. Markel, 278 N.W.2d 364 (N.D. 1979) (reasonable time for cover may go beyond time and place for tender).

[550] See *Allied Canners & Packing, Inc. v. Victor Packing Co.*, *supra* note 548, which mentions this characterization suggested by Judge (formerly Professor) Peters in her article, *Remedies for Breach of Contract Relating to the Sale of Goods Under the Uniform Commercial Code: A Roadmap for Article Two*, 73 Yale L.J. 199 (1963).

[551] For an analysis and criticism of § 2-713, see J. WHITE & R. SUMMERS, UNIFORM COMMERCIAL CODE 212 (2000).

[552] *See supra* note 548.

[c]   Seller's Damages for Nonacceptance or Repudiation — "Hypothetical Resale"

Just as the buyer need not cover and may resort to damages for nondelivery under UCC § 2-713, the seller need not resell, and may resort to damages for the buyer's nonacceptance or repudiation under § 2-708.[553] This counterpart to § 2-713 (the buyer's measure of damages) differs in one significant respect. The market is measured under § 2-708(1) at the time and place of tender[554] whereas the buyer's remedy in § 2-713 is measured at the time the buyer "learns of the breach" and it also fixes the market as the market at the place of tender, except, where the goods have been rejected or the buyer revokes acceptance of the goods, at the place of arrival.[555] The determination of the market under § 2-713, therefore, is consistent with the concept of "hypothetical cover" since it uses the market where the buyer would probably have covered. If § 2-708(1) may be viewed as the seller's "hypothetical resale" remedy, the determination of the market at the place of tender may be unrealistic with respect to goods that have been delivered to the buyer. In the typical "FOB shipment" contract, the place of tender will be the seller's location where the goods were delivered to a carrier. If, however, the goods have been delivered to the buyer, who refuses to accept them even though they are conforming goods, the seller is likely to resell in that market.

Why would a seller choose damages for nonacceptance or repudiation over the resale remedy? Again, the resale remedy is appropriate only if the seller has only one item for sale. If he is a "lost volume" seller,[556] the resale remedy will typically provide nominal damages since he will receive only the difference between the contract price and resale price. These prices will often be identical or virtually identical. Where the seller chooses his § 2-708(1) remedy, he will be in the same unfortunate position since that remedy is, in effect, a "hypothetical resale" remedy providing the difference between the contract price and market price, which will often be the same.[557] To overcome that injustice to a seller who would have earned profit on the broken contract and all subsequent contracts, § 2-708(2) provides the seller with his lost profit, including reasonable overhead.[558]

---

[553] UCC 2-708(1): Subject to subsection (2) and to the provisions of this Article with respect to proof of market price (§ 2-723), the measure of damages for nonacceptance or repudiation by the buyer is the difference between the market price at the time and place for tender and the unpaid contract price, together with any incidental damages provided in this Article (2-710), but less expenses saved in consequence of buyer's breach. *See* Allsopp Sand & Gravel, Inc. v. Lincoln Sand & Gravel Co., 171 Ill. App. 3d 532, 121 Ill. Dec. 878, 525 N.E.2d 1185 (4th Dist. 1988).

[554] *See* Northwest Airlines v. Flight Trails, 3 F.3d 292 (8th Cir. 1993); Wendling v. Puls, 227 Kan. 780, 610 P.2d 580 (1980) (determination of date of tender).

[555] UCC § 2-713(2). Where the current market price under this section is difficult to prove, a comparable market price may be used. See § 2-713, comment 3. See also Robert Egerer v. CSR West, L.L.C., 116 Wash. App. 645, 67 P. 3d 1128 (2003).

[556] See *supra* text preceding and subsequent to note 518.

[557] For a discussion of why § 2-708(1) is manifestly unjust as applied to the "lost volume" seller, see Snyder v. Herbert Greenbaum & Assocs., Inc., 38 Md. App. 144, 380 A.2d 618 (1977).

[558] The analysis of lost profits for the "lost volume" seller appears *supra* § 123[E].

[C] Restricting Uniform Commercial Code Remedies to Expectation Interest

Throughout the discussion of contract remedies in this entire Chapter, we have emphasized the purpose of contract law as the realization of those expectations induced by the making of a promise, which means that the aggrieved party should be placed in the position he would have been in had the contract been performed — no better and no worse.[559] We have also emphasized the adherence of the UCC to this purpose. In § 1-106 of the Code, that purpose is clearly codified: "The remedies provided by this Act shall be liberally administered to the end that the aggrieved party may be put in as good a position as if the other party had fully performed. . . ."[560] There is language in the Code and its comments, however, that can be interpreted to suggest a contradiction of that purpose. For example, in the section listing the seller's remedies, a comment rejects any notion of election of the various remedies of the seller, i.e., such remedies are cumulative.[561] A section of the buyer's cover remedy indicates that the buyer's failure to effect cover "does not bar him from any other remedy."[562] Countervailing comment language is found in the buyer's remedy for nondelivery or repudiation,[563] and, of course, there is the general statement of the purpose of remedies under the Code quoted above.

Treating Code remedies as totally available to buyers or sellers under any and all circumstances will necessarily contradict the basic philosophy of Code remedies. Consider, for example, a buyer who decides to cover at a reasonable cover price of $10,000 where the contract price is $7000. The cover measure of damages is $3000. If, however, the relevant market price is $12,000 and the buyer is free to choose his damage for nondelivery or repudiation remedy, he will choose that remedy since it will provide a recovery of $5000. That recovery will, however, overcompensate him to the extent that he is placed in a better position than he would have been in had the contract been performed. Where actual cover has occurred, the buyer should not be able to choose the § 2-713 remedy for the purpose of recovering additional damages.[564] Similarly, where a seller who is not a "lost volume" seller has made a reasonable resale of an item, he should be relegated to his resale remedy and recover the difference between the contract and resale price, rather than taking advantage of an unanticipated decline in the market price that would produce greater damages under his remedy for nonacceptance or repudiation. We have already seen a court deny the contract price/market price differential to a seller who contemplated profits amounting to less than five percent of that amount,[565] thus effectuating the purpose of UCC remedies. In furtherance of

---

[559] We have also examined the protection of the reliance and restitution interests which place the aggrieved party in the position he had been in prior to the contract or prior to the unjust enrichment.

[560] UCC § 1-106(1).

[561] UCC § 2-703 comment 1.

[562] UCC § 2-712(3).

[563] UCC § 2-713, comment 5: "The present section provides a remedy which is completely alternative to cover under the preceding section [2-712 — cover] and applies only when and to the extent that the buyer has not covered."

[564] See Sun-Maid Raisin Growers v. Victor Packing Co., 146 Cal. App. 3d 787, 792, 194 Cal. Rptr. 612 (5th Dist. 1983), which limits damages to an amount that would place the plaintiff in as good a position as if the defendant had performed, consistent with UCC § 1-106. See also Chronister Oil Co. v. Unocal Ref. & Mktg., 34 F.3d 462 (7th Cir. 1994) (buyer replaced undelivered goods from its inventory and attempted to claim "cover" damages; the court rejected this effort at "self cover").

[565] See Allied Canners & Packers, Inc. v. Victor Packing Co., supra note 548.

that same purpose, another court denied the seller the use of his "lost volume" measure of damages[566] and awarded damages for the difference between the contract price and market price[567] to protect the seller's reasonable expectation of profits, rather than permitting the seller to recover more than three times that amount simply by choosing a different remedy.[568] The statement of the purpose of remedies under the UCC should be given the overriding effect that it has been accorded by the courts to this time.

[D]   Damages for Accepted Goods

Much earlier, we explored the buyer's rights of rejection and revocation of acceptance in our discussion of the "perfect tender" rule.[569] If a buyer receives nonconforming goods, he may reject them[570] if he does so within a reasonable time.[571] If he fails to reject within a reasonable time, he has, in effect, accepted the goods, as he may no longer reject them.[572] Even if the goods are accepted, however, the buyer will be able to revoke his acceptance and return to the status of rejection if the nonconformity in the goods substantially impairs the value of the goods to the buyer, and the nonconformity was not discoverable upon a reasonable inspection or it was discovered and the buyer accepted because the seller gave assurances that he would cure the nonconformity and failed to do so.[573] If the buyer has neither rejected nor revoked his acceptance and the time has passed for the revocation so that he can no longer thrust the goods back on the seller, does he have any claim for nonconformity in the goods which he has accepted? The buyer may have a cause of action for breach of warranty.[574] Section 2-714(1) of the Code permits the buyer to recover the loss resulting from any nonconformity and § 2-714(2) measures that loss as the difference at the time and place of acceptance between the value of the goods accepted and the value they would have had if they had been as warranted.[575] The cost of repairing a defect or other nonconformity in the goods may constitute evidence of the difference in value.[576] If, for example, the buyer of accepted equipment discovers a defect and the seller refuses to perform its warranty obligation, the buyer may have the equipment repaired by another. The buyer had received equipment that

---

[566] UCC § 2-708(2).

[567] UCC § 2-708(1).

[568] *See* Nobs Chem., U.S.A., Inc. v. Koppers Co., 616 F.2d 212 (5th Cir. 1980). *See also* Madsen v. Murrey & Sons Co., 743 P.2d 1212 (Utah 1987) (failure to mitigate damages requires damages to be measured by § 2-708(1) rather than by § 2-708(2)).

[569] *See* § 109[D][2], *supra.*

[570] Unless the parties otherwise agree or the contract is an installment contract, the buyer has a right of rejection under UCC § 2-601.

[571] UCC § 2-602 specifies the manner of a rightful rejection.

[572] UCC § 2-606(1)(b) indicates that one instance of accepting goods occurs where the buyer fails to make an effective rejection. The buyer may also accept by signifying to the seller that the goods are conforming (§ 2-606(1)(a)) or doing anything with the goods that is inconsistent with the seller's ownership, i.e., acting as if he accepted the goods (§ 2-606(1)(b)).

[573] UCC § 2-608.

[574] See the discussion of warranties at § 101 *supra.*

[575] *See* Michiana Mack, Inc. v. Allendale Rural Fire Protection Dist., 428 N.E.2d 1367 (Ind. Ct. App. 1981) (§ 2-714 applies to accepted goods where revocation of acceptance is not possible). *See* UCC § 2-714 comment 1.

[576] *See* Holden Machinery v. Sundance Tractor & Mower, 218 B. R. 247 (M. D. Ga. 1998); Continental Sand & Gravel, Inc. v. K & K Sand & Gravel, Inc., 755 F.2d 87 (7th Cir. 1985); Midland Supply Co. v. Ehret Plumbing & Heating Co., 108 Ill. App. 3d 1120, 64 Ill. Dec. 601, 440 N.E.2d 153 (5th Dist. 1982).

was less valuable than it should have been. The repair, however, restored the equipment to the value it should have had if it had been as warranted. The cost of repair, therefore, is a convenient measure of the difference in value, but it only evidence of the difference in value. In a contract for the purchase and sale of steel, for example, after receiving the steel from the seller, the buyer expended $2000 in processing before delivering it to its buyer. The steel as originally delivered by the seller had been too soft and could not be used after processing. In addition to recovering the contract price, the buyer also recovered the cost of processing, though this recovery protected the reliance rather than the expectation interest.[577] Though the difference in value is the measure of damages set forth in § 2-714(2), the general directive should not be overlooked, i.e., recovery of "the loss resulting . . . from the seller's breach as determined in any manner which is reasonable."[578]

[E]   Consequential and Incidental Damages — Seller's Consequences

In addition to direct or "general" damages recoverable under the UCC remedies already discussed, the UCC permits buyers to recover consequential damages and it also permits buyers or sellers to recover incidental damages.[579] We have seen that consequential damages are defined in terms of the basic foreseeability concept, i.e., "any loss resulting from general or particular requirements and needs of which the seller at the time of contracting had reason to know. . . ."[580] We have also examined the use of the ambiguous term "consequential," which is often equated with "special" damages, though "consequential" damages may be those which any ordinary promisor would foresee at the time the contract is formed.[581] The buyer's incidental damages include a variety of expenses including the cost of inspecting the goods, to caring for goods which the buyer has rejected, expenses connected with reasonable efforts to cover, or other reasonable expenses caused by the seller's breach.[582] Where the buyer breaches, the seller may encounter various expenses stopping delivery and transportation, as well as care and custody of any conforming goods the buyer has refused to accept.[583] It may be necessary for a seller to modify goods in order to take advantage of the seller's resale remedy. Where a seller had to spend more than $10,000 in modification costs to resell equipment upon the buyer's breach, the court permitted these costs to be recovered as incidental damages.[584] A garden variety case illustrates the differences among general (direct), consequential (special), and incidental damages.

---

[577] Toyomenka (Am.), Inc. v. Combined Metals Corp., 139 Ill. App. 3d 654, 94 Ill. Dec. 295, 487 N.E.2d 1172 (1st Dist. 1985).

[578] UCC § 2-714(1).

[579] See Wright Schuchart, Inc. v. Cooper Indus., 1994 U.S. App. LEXIS 31520 (9th Cir. Nov. 8, 1994). In UCC § 2-712(2) (cover), the buyer is expressly permitted to recover incidental and consequential damages. *See also* § 2-713(1) and § 2-714(3). The seller is expressly permitted to recover incidental damages in § 2-706(1) (resale). *See also* § 2-708(1) and § 2-708(2).

[580] UCC § 2-715(2)(a). *See supra* § 121.

[581] *See supra* § 121, note 99.

[582] UCC § 2-715(1).

[583] UCC § 2-710.

[584] Florida Recycling Servs. v. Peterson Industries, Inc., 858 So. 2d 1114 (Ct. App. Fla. 2003).

In *Carbo Industries, Inc. v. Becker Chevrolet, Inc.*,[585] the defendant car dealer sold an auto to the plaintiff, a car leasing firm. The firm leased the car to a commercial client. Mechanical problems required the car to be returned to the dealer on several occasions and the defendant refused to make necessary repairs after the engine seized. The court permitted recovery of the cost of replacing the defective engine, i.e., general or direct damages, to bring the car to the value it would have had without a breach of warranty. Similarly, the damages in the amount of the monthly lease payments were allowed for the period during which the car was unusable since these payments represented "the difference between the car's value if it had functioned as warranted . . . and its actual value."[586] Towing charges and other expenses incurred in diagnosing the problem with the car were viewed as incidental damages. The plaintiff also presented evidence that, because of the difficulty with this car, its customer had cancelled an order for an additional vehicle. The court characterized these damages as consequential, i.e., they represented lost profit to the plaintiff. Another court permitted the recovery of car insurance expenses as well as the cost of license plates, lost wages, and interest on the purchase price of a defective automobile as incidental damages.[587] Like other courts, however, it would not permit the recovery of attorney's fees as incidental damages.[588]

The UCC sections on seller's remedies include no provision for consequential damages. It is certainly conceivable that a seller would incur consequential damages after a breach by the purchaser in a given situation.[589] Courts, however, have declined to award "consequential" damages to sellers though it has been suggested that courts can be imaginative in characterizing certain recoverable damages as "incidental" which could have been easily called "consequential."[590] In the usual situation, however, the seller is entitled only to the contract price or any unpaid portion thereof plus incidental damages. This is viewed as complete protection of his expectation interest.

[F]　Action for the Price — Specific Performance

We have already examined the somewhat expanded availability of specific performance for buyers under the UCC.[591] Specific performance for the seller of goods is the buyer's payment of the contract price. The Code expressly permits the seller to bring an action for the price plus any incidental damages under certain circumstances.[592] It may sound like a truism to suggest that where the buyer *accepts* goods delivered by the seller, the buyer should pay for the goods. In prior discussions, we have seen that acceptance of goods under the Code can occur in any one of three essential ways:[593] (1) the buyer's signification that he accepts the

---

[585] 112 A.D.2d 336, 491 N.Y.S.2d 786 (2d Dep't 1985).

[586] 112 A.D.2d at 340, 491 N.Y.S.2d at 790.

[587] *See* Devore v. Bostrom, 632 P.2d 832 (Utah 1981).

[588] See Nick's Auto Sales, Inc. v. Radcliff Auto Sales, Inc., 591 S.W.2d 709 (Ky. Ct. App. 1979) (though the UCC definition of incidental damages, like other UCC remedies provisions, is to be liberally administered in accordance with § 1-106, § 2-715(1) does not include attorney's fees). *See also* Murray v. Holiday Rambler, Inc., 83 Wis. 2d 406, 265 N.W.2d 513 (1978).

[589] The buyer may know at the moment of formation that his breach would cause lost profits to the seller well beyond the lost profits on the particular contract with the buyer.

[590] White & Summers, *supra* note 551, at 300–03.

[591] *See* § 128[B][2], *supra*.

[592] UCC § 2-709.

[593] UCC § 2-606.

goods;[594] (2) the buyer's failure to make an effective rejection of the goods;[595] and (3) the buyer's use of the goods inconsistent with the ownership of the seller.[596] Of these, only (2) causes any analytical difficulty in terms of buyer's acceptance giving rise to the seller's action for the price. A buyer may effectively reject goods though the rejection is substantively wrongful, i.e., a buyer may comply with all of the necessary requirements for an effective rejection,[597] but may have no substantive basis for that rejection. For example, a buyer may mistakenly believe that the goods are nonconforming and reject them. Even though the rejection is substantively wrongful, the rejection is effective to deny the seller his price remedy since the buyer did not "accept" the goods.[598] Whether a buyer who has accepted but wrongfully revokes his acceptance has still "accepted" so as to allow the seller his action for the price is unclear. The better view is that such a wrongful revocation does not affect the former acceptance so that the action for the price should lie.[599]

Where conforming goods have not been accepted but have been lost or damaged within a commercially reasonable time after their risk of loss has passed to the buyer, the seller may bring his action for the price.[600] For example, risk of loss will pass to the buyer in an FOB "shipment" contract upon delivery of the goods to an independent carrier. If the goods are damaged or destroyed in transit, or misdelivered, the buyer must pay the contract price since the risk of loss was on the buyer.[601]

The last situation which allows the seller to have an action for the price occurs where the goods have been identified[602] to the contract for shipment to the buyer and the seller is, after a reasonable effort, unable to resell them at a reasonable price or it is clear that such a resale effort would be fruitless.[603] The typical example involves specially manufactured goods that are not resalable to others. The underlying philosophy of the seller's action for the price is that only the foregoing situations make that remedy necessary. Typically, the seller can resell goods which the buyer refuses to accept and the seller is in a better position than the buyer to resell. To force the sale on the buyer so that he can resell them makes no economic sense since the buyer typically has no experience in selling such goods. The seller's expectation interest can be protected through other UCC remedies. If, however, the buyer has accepted the goods,

[594] *See* Lupofresh, Inc. v. Pabst Brewing Co., 505 A.2d 37 (Del. Super. Ct. 1985), *aff'd*, 510 A.2d 487 (Del. 1986) (buyer wrote sellers that it had accepted the goods, thereby giving rise to seller's action for the price under § 2-709).

[595] *See* Parkwood Lumber, Inc. v. Rivisco, Inc. 2000 U.S. App. LEXIS 661 (2d Cir. Jan. 14, 2000) (failure to make effective rejection constituted acceptance permitting seller to recover price). *See also* Akron Brick & Block Co. v. Moniz Eng'g Co., 365 Mass. 92, 310 N.E.2d 128 (1974) (failure to reject within a reasonable time or to revoke acceptance constituted acceptance permitting seller to recover unpaid portion of contract price).

[596] *See* Dehahn v. Innes, 356 A.2d 711 (Me. 1976) (whether there is an acceptance through acts of the buyer inconsistent with seller's ownership is a question of fact).

[597] UCC § 2-602.

[598] *See* Knic Knac Agencies v. Masterpiece Apparel, Ltd., 1999 U.S. Dist. LEXIS 3267 (S. D. N. Y. 1999.

[599] *See Lupofresh, Inc. v. Pabst Brewing Co.*, *supra* note 594, where, in note 3, the court opines that goods are no longer accepted where there is a "justified" revocation of acceptance.

[600] UCC § 2-709(2)(b).

[601] *See* Montana Seeds v. Holliday, 178 Mont. 119, 582 P.2d 1223 (1978).

[602] *See* UCC § 2-501. *See also* Great Western Sugar Co. v. Pennant Prods., Inc., 748 P.2d 1359 (Colo. Ct. App. 1987) (identification where the goods are fungible).

[603] UCC § 2-709(1)(b). *See* Ultralite Container Corp. v. American President Lines, Ltd., 170 F.3d 784 (7th Cir. 1999); Colonel's Inc. v. Cincinnati Milacron Mktg. Co., 1998 U.S. App. LEXIS 11756 (6th Cir. June 1, 1998) (difference between UCC §§ 2-708(2) and 2-709).

there is no justification for the buyer's refusal to pay the contract price. Nor is there any justification for refusal to pay the price where the goods were destroyed when the risk was on the buyer because the seller has no goods to resell. If the goods were damaged when the risk was on the buyer, the seller should not be placed in the business of selling damaged goods. If the goods were custom-made for the buyer, the seller should not be asked to resell such goods if other buyers do not want them.

[G]   The CISG Remedial Structure

[1]   Overview[604]

American lawyers use the term "avoidance" to characterize the end of a contractual obligation without liability. Thus, for example, where the parties agree to buy and sell identified goods and the goods are destroyed, without the fault of the seller, before the risk of their loss passes to the buyer, the contractual obligation is avoided.[605] At common law, an infant or a mentally ill person may have a power of avoidance based upon his or her incapacity. Under CISG, *avoidance* has a different meaning. Where a breach occurs under CISG, the aggrieved party may *avoid* the contract if a substantial breach, called a *fundamental breach*, has occurred. A fundamental breach is one which causes substantial deprivation to the aggrieved party in terms of *reasonable expectations* where the breaching party or a reasonable person in his or her position would have foreseen the result.[606] If a fundamental breach occurs, thereby permitting the aggrieved party to avoid the contract, the contractual obligation is at an end but the aggrieved party is entitled to recover damages much like the damages recoverable by buyers and sellers under the UCC.[607] The common law concept of foreseeability, codified in the UCC,[608] is also an overriding limitation under CISG,[609] though earlier we considered the difference between foreseeable damages as *probable* versus *possible* consequences of the breach.[610] With only one exception,[611] where the breach is not a fundamental breach, the aggrieved party cannot avoid the contract. In this *nonavoidance* posture, the contract will be performed but damages will be awarded much like UCC damages.[612] It is important to note that the aggrieved party may choose the nonavoidance route even where the other party has committed a fundamental breach.[613] By choosing the *nonavoidance* route, the

---

[604] For a helpful exploration of remedies under CISG, see H. Flechtner, *Remedies Under the New International Sales Convention: The Perspective From Article 2 of the U. C. C.,* 8 J.L. & Com. 53 (1988).

[605] UCC § 2-613(a).

[606] A breach is *fundamental* "if it results in such detriment to the other party as substantially to deprive him of what he is entitled to expect under the contract, unless the party in breach did not foresee, and a reasonable person of the same kind in the same circumstances would not have foreseen, such a result." CISG Art. 25.

[607] CISG Art. 75 combines the buyer's remedy of replacement purchase (UCC "cover") and the seller's resale remedy. CISG Art. 76 permits an aggrieved buyer or seller to recover the difference between the contract and market prices.

[608] UCC § 2-715(2).

[609] CISG Art. 74.

[610] *See* § 121[A][1], *supra.*

[611] The exception is known as *Nachfrist* and will be discussed *infra* § 129[G][3].

[612] For example, the seller has an action for the price of the accepted goods under CISG Art. 62 and Art. 74 provides damages for losses including lost profit.

[613] CISG Articles 49(1)(a) and 64(1)(a) insist that the aggrieved party *may* avoid the contract where the other party

aggrieved party activates the set of remedies available where there is no fundamental breach, some of which go beyond anything available to an American buyer under the UCC. For example, CISG permits a buyer choosing nonavoidance to demand substitute goods if the lack of conformity of the goods constitutes a fundamental breach.[614] If not unreasonable under the circumstances, a buyer may demand that the seller repair any nonconformity in the goods even though the nonconformity did not amount to a fundamental breach.[615] Neither of these remedies is available to an American buyer under the UCC. The UCC permits the *seller* to cure any defects if he can do so within contract time,[616] but it does not permit the buyer to demand replacement goods or repair. The nonavoiding buyer is also entitled to "reduce the price in the same proportion as the value that the goods actually delivered had at the time of delivery bears to the value that conforming goods would have had at that time."[617]

By far, the most significant difference between the remedial structures of the UCC (or common law) and CISG is the *availability of the specific performance remedy*. In furtherance of the civil law tradition, that remedy is generally available under CISG[618] though, as we will see, it is subject to limitations.

[2] Fundamental Breach

Before considering particular CISG remedies in more detail, it is important to consider the CISG concept known as fundamental breach which, as we have just seen, with only one exception to be discussed below, is a necessary condition to activate the avoidance path for an aggrieved party. The definition of fundamental breach,[619] which requires the aggrieved party to be *substantially deprived of what he is entitled to expect*, sounds very much like the UCC standard of substantial impairment of value,[620] which, in turn, is typically regarded as a material breach standard.[621] Should the standard of fundamental breach be equated with the familiar standard of material breach in the contract law of the United States?

Language in two other sections of the Convention is sometimes used to suggest that the standards are different, i.e., that a fundamental breach requires more than a material breach. Article 71 permits a party to suspend performance if it becomes apparent that the other party

---

commits a fundamental breach. *See* Medical Mktg. Int'l, Inc. v. Internazionale Medico Scientifica, S.R.L., 1999 U.S. Dist. LEXIS 7380, at *5 (E.D. La. May 17, 1999).

[614] CISG Art. 46(2). *See* Hilaturus Miel, S.L. v. Republic of Iraq, 573 F. Supp. 2d 781, 799 (S.D.N.Y. 2008).

[615] CISG Art. 46(3).

[616] UCC § 2-508(1). Section 2-508(2) will provide the seller with additional time to cure if he had reason to believe such time would be available.

[617] CISG Art. 50. This concept differs from the UCC § 2-717 deduction of damages resulting from *any* breach from the price. The measure in Article 50, however, is very similar to the measure found in UCC § 2-714(2) ("The measure of damages for breach of warranty is the difference at the time and place of acceptance between the value of the goods accepted and the value they would have had if they had been as warranted. . . ."), though the latter is a measure of damages rather than a price reduction measure and the time of "delivery" (CISG) differs from the time of "acceptance" (UCC).

[618] CISG Articles 46(1) and 62.

[619] CISG Art. 25. *See* Delchi Carrier SpA v. Rotorex Corp., 71 F.3d 1024, 1028 (2d Cir. 1995).

[620] See this standard in §§ 2-608(1) and 2-612(2) and (3) of the UCC.

[621] It should be noted, however, that the UCC § 2-608(1) phraseology is substantial impairment of the value "to him," i.e., the buyer, a subjective standard. *See* comment 2 to UCC § 2-608.

will not perform a *substantial part* of his or her obligations.[622] Article 72 permits the aggrieved party to declare the contract avoided if it is clear that the other party will commit a fundamental breach.[623] This distinction suggests that "[A] breach may be 'substantial' without being 'fundamental'."[624] The Article 71 standard, however, is more than reminiscent of the familiar right to suspend performance upon reasonable grounds for insecurity and the attendant right to demand adequate assurances[625] because, under the CISG language, it is only apparent that the other party will not perform a substantial part of his contractual obligation — the evidence is insufficient to find what American lawyers would call an anticipatory repudiation.[626] The Article 72 standard, on the other hand, is invoked only when "it is *clear* that one of the parties will commit a fundamental breach," i.e., it is *clear* that at the time for performance he will not perform. American lawyers will remember the requirement that a repudiation must be clear and unequivocal.[627] Since the argument based on Articles 71 and 72 can be overcome in this fashion or in other ways,[628] it seems appropriate to avoid unnecessary confusion in the comparison of fundamental breach with material breach. Moreover, the definition of fundamental breach in CISG suggests no such distinction.

Another aspect of the definition of fundamental breach is more challenging. The definition requires that the substantial deprivation of the aggrieved party must have been foreseeable.[629] It does not, however, suggest whether the substantial deprivation had to be foreseeable at the time of contract formation or only later, at the time of breach. The question has produced scholarly debate.[630] The first CISG Article in the section on damages directs that foreseeability must be measured at the time of contract formation.[631] It is difficult to quarrel with this familiar common law standard and its express inclusion in CISG may appear to resolve the dispute. That would, however, be an unfortunate analysis since foreseeability as to damages (which should be measured as of the time of contracting) has nothing to do with foreseeability of substantial deprivation. Though it may be difficult for a lawyer from the common law tradition to think of foreseeability in these terms, CISG does not view a breach as fundamental with its consequences of avoidance unless the breaching party knew or should have known that

---

[622] CISG Art. 71(1).

[623] CISG Art. 72(1).

[624] *See* Flechtner, *supra* note 604, at 75.

[625] UCC § 2-609. This is not to suggest, however, that Article 71 of CISG and § 2-609 of the UCC are identical. They are quite similar.

[626] Article 71 also suggests two situations which sound very much like reasonable grounds for insecurity, "[a] serious deficiency in his ability to perform or in his creditworthiness" (71(a)), or "[h]is conduct in preparing to perform or in performing the contract" (71(b)).

[627] While there are parallels between CISG Art. 72 and UCC § 2-610 (anticipatory repudiation), there are differences. For example, Article 72(2) permits the aggrieved party to avoid the contract only if (time permitting) he provides reasonable notice to permit the other party to provide adequate assurance of performance. There is no similar provision in UCC § 2-610.

[628] *See, e.g.*, Flechtner, *supra* note 604, at n.101.

[629] CISG Art. 25.

[630] *See* Ziegel, *The Remedial Provisions in the Vienna Sales Convention: Some Common Law Perspectives*, International Sales: The United Nations Convention on Contracts for the International Sale of Goods § 9.03, at 9–19 (1984) (suggesting that foreseeability should be measured at the time of contracting) and Flechtner, *supra* note 604, at 75–78 (suggesting that, for the purposes of avoidance as contrasted with damage liability, foreseeability should be measured at the time of the breach).

[631] CISG Art. 74.

the breach would cause substantial deprivation, i.e., substantial deprivation, per se, is insufficient to constitute a fundamental breach. Absent that kind of foreseeability, CISG prefers the contract to be continued though some compensable loss may be suffered. While the UCC modified certain technical or draconian common law views with an eye to fostering performance of the contract, CISG is even more committed to the view of completion of the exchange as evidenced, *inter alia*, by the civil law tradition of the relatively liberal allowance of the remedy of specific performance, which will be discussed below.

[3]   *Nachfrist* Procedure

There is just one exception to the requirement of fundamental breach if a party chooses to avoid the completion of the contract. CISG permits an aggrieved party to avoid the contract, absent a fundamental breach, only if the *Nachfrist* procedure is followed. The concept of *Nachfrist* is taken from German law and permits an aggrieved party to fix an additional reasonable period for performance by the other party.[632] If, for example, a seller has failed to deliver goods on time, the buyer may be uncertain as to whether the seller's delay amounts to a fundamental breach which would permit the buyer to choose avoidance of the contract. To eliminate that uncertainty, the buyer may fix the additional reasonable time for performance by the seller.[633] If the seller does not deliver the goods within this time frame, or declares that he will not perform within that period, the buyer may declare the contract avoided.[634] The seller may pursue the same procedure with respect to a buyer who fails to perform an obligation to pay the price or take delivery of the goods[635] with the same avoidance result if the buyer does not perform within the additional period or declares that he will not perform within that period.[636] While the *Nachfrist* concept is not devoid of all ambiguity,[637] it is a workable and desirable concept.

[4]   Nonavoidance Procedure — Specific Performance

To foster completion of the contract, notwithstanding the possibility of compensable losses, CISG evidences the civil law tradition in providing a liberal remedy of specific performance. The buyer may *require* performance by the seller.[638] Thus, the buyer may require the seller to cure the defect by, for example, delivering substitute goods if the lack of conformity constitutes a fundamental breach. This possibility is in stark contrast to the UCC which would not require a seller to cure the breach. The buyer may also require the seller to repair defects in the goods,

---

[632] CISG Articles 47 and 63.

[633] CISG Art. 47(1). During the additional time, the buyer is not permitted to pursue any other remedy including avoidance or a price reduction. See Valero Mktg. Supply Co. v. Greeni Oy, 2007 U.S. App. LEXIS 17282 (3d Cir. 2007).

[634] CISG Art. 49(1)(b).

[635] CISG Art. 63(1).

[636] CISG Art. 64(1)(b).

[637] Professor Flechtner points to the failure of the drafters to distinguish material from immaterial failures of performance during the *Nachfrist* period. Assuming, for example, a party completes all but a trivial portion of his performance during that period, should such a failure amount to a fundamental breach leading to avoidance? Professor Flechtner suggests that Articles 49(1)(b) and 64(1)(b) should be construed to permit avoidance only where there has been a *material* failure of performance during the *Nachfrist* period. He bases this suggestion on Article 7(2), which directs questions to be settled in accordance with general principles of CISG and one of those principles is that avoidance should be permitted only upon a serious breach. He also suggests the policy in Article 7(1), i.e., that the Convention be interpreted to promote good faith in international trade. Flechtner, *supra* note 604, at 71–73.

[638] CISG Art. 46(1).

unless it would be unreasonable to insist upon such performance.[639] Under the UCC or domestic contract law in general, the breaching party would not be required to perform. The seller may *require* the buyer to pay the price of the goods, take delivery of them or perform other obligations.[640] While the UCC permits the seller to bring an action for the price under certain circumstances,[641] the UCC does not require a buyer to take delivery or perform other obligations.

If the civil-law oriented specific performance remedy applied to the United States, it would be opposed not only to traditional common law contracts principles, but it could constitute a violation of the United States Constitution under the Thirteenth Amendment. To meet this challenge, CISG provides that a court is not bound to enter a judgment for specific performance unless it would do so under its own law with respect to similar contracts of sale not governed by CISG.[642] While this provision does not compel a court to be governed by its own law of specific performance, it permits the court to disavow the liberality of the CISG remedy. A United States court could, therefore, apply a UCC standard of specific performance without violating CISG.

Other limitations may raise different challenges. Since CISG does not deal with rights of third parties,[643] domestic law may permit such parties to have rights in the goods that would frustrate the nonavoidance/specific performance choice. The duties of a seller to take reasonable steps to preserve goods where the buyer delays in taking them or paying for them may interfere with the specific performance remedy.[644] Similarly, where the goods are of such a nature as to deteriorate, they may have to be sold to another.[645] Notwithstanding these limitations, the CISG remedy of specific performance is generally available and is not subject to the inherent limitations found in the UCC or common law remedy of specific performance.[646]

[5]   Securing the Nonavoidance Route

We have seen that a fundamental breach or the use of the *Nachfrist* procedure allows a party to avoid the contract. We have also seen that such a party may choose to pursue the completion of the contract and still recover damages for any losses. To secure this nonavoidance path, the aggrieved party must follow a certain procedure. Where the seller breaches by shipping nonconforming goods, the aggrieved buyer must provide notice to the seller specifying the nature of the nonconformity[647] and this notice must be given within a reasonable time after the buyer discovered or should have discovered the defect, or two years from the

---

[639] CISG Art. 46(3).

[640] CISG Art. 62.

[641] UCC § 2-709(1)(a).

[642] CISG Art. 28.

[643] CISG Art. 4.

[644] CISG Art. 85.

[645] CISG Art. 88(2).

[646] UCC § 2-716(1) restricts the right to specific performance where the goods are unique (the common law restriction dealing with an inadequate remedy at law) "or in other proper circumstances." The latter situation, though originally touted to expand the remedy significantly, has been limited essentially to situations where the buyer was unable to cover, i.e., make a substitute purchase. In effect, where cover is not available, the goods have taken on a "unique" quality, i.e., their immediate scarcity makes them, in effect, unique.

[647] CISG Art. 39.

date of delivery to the buyer, whichever is shorter.[648]

If a seller chooses the nonavoidance route, the seller must take reasonable steps to preserve the goods in her control, though she can be reimbursed for any expenses in performing that duty.[649] Where the seller is performing that duty and the buyer delays unreasonably in taking the goods, the seller is *permitted* to resell them after notifying the buyer of that intention.[650] If the goods are subject to rapid deterioration, the seller *must* make a reasonable effort to resell them after providing notice to the buyer to the extent possible under the circumstances.[651]

While the basic remedy of the nonavoiding plaintiff is the right to specific performance that we have just explored, CISG includes additional remedies, such as the right of the buyer to demand substitute goods where the breach was fundamental (though the buyer chose the nonavoidance route),[652] and the buyer's right to demand repair of the nonconformity if that is not unreasonable under the circumstances.[653] The buyer may also reduce the price in proportion to the loss in value of the delivered goods.[654] All of these remedies may not, however, fully protect the reasonable expectations of an aggrieved party. CISG, therefore, provides further relief to compensate for losses, including lost profit, suffered as a consequence of the breach.[655]

[6]   Securing the Avoidance Route

The commission of a fundamental breach allows the aggrieved party to avoid the contract. It is important to emphasize the effect of avoidance: both the aggrieved party and the breaching party are relieved from their obligations under the contract, but the breaching party remains subject to any damages caused by the breach.[656] Notice of avoidance must be given by the aggrieved party[657] and if that party attempted to communicate the notice by appropriate means, the notice will be effective if it contains errors, if it is delayed, or even if it is not received

---

[648] CISG Art. 39(2). Both Articles 39 and 43 of CISG insist that a notice specifying the breach be given as a condition to an aggrieved buyer pursuing either the avoidance or nonavoidance routes. UCC § 2-607(3)(a) is a general notice provision requiring a buyer who has accepted the goods to give notice of the breach within a reasonable time after the buyer discovered or should have discovered the breach. While there has been some controversy concerning the content of the notice based upon different interpretations of the second paragraph of comment 4 to § 2-607 (*see, e.g.*, Eastern Air Lines, Inc. v. McDonnell Douglas Corp., 532 F.2d 957 (5th Cir. 1976)), there is no UCC requirement that the notice be particularized. Where, however, the buyer fails to state a particular defect in the notice which defect was ascertainable by reasonable inspection, and this failure interferes with the seller's right to cure the defect under § 2-508, the buyer may not rely on the unstated defect to justify rejection or establish breach. UCC § 2-605.

[649] CISG Art. 85.

[650] CISG Art. 88(1).

[651] CISG Art. 88(2). If the proceeds exceed the reasonable expense of preserving and reselling, the seller must account to the buyer for such excess proceeds under Art. 88(3).

[652] CISG Art. 46(2).

[653] CISG Art. 46(3).

[654] CISG Art. 50.

[655] CISG Art. 74. See Sky Cast, Inc. v. Global Direct Distribution, LLC, 2008 U.S. Dist. LEXIS 21121 (E. D. Ky. 2008).

[656] CISG Art. 81(1). The parties' rights and obligations "consequent upon the avoidance of the contract" are also preserved under this Article.

[657] CISG Art. 26.

by the other party.[658] There is a curiosity in CISG, however, regarding the *time* for notice. Where the goods have arrived late, the buyer must exercise the right to avoid within a reasonable time after the delivery was made.[659] Where the goods have arrived on time but are nonconforming, avoidance must occur within a reasonable time after the buyer knew or ought to have known of the breach.[660] Where there has been no delivery of goods to the buyer, CISG does not suggest any time for notice of avoidance. Where the buyer breaches through lateness in taking delivery or paying the price, the seller must avoid the contract before becoming aware that performance has been rendered.[661] If the buyer's breach is other than lateness, such as refusal to accept conforming goods, the seller must avoid within a reasonable time after it knew or should have known of the breach.[662] Where the buyer has not paid the price, there is no CISG indication of the time in which notice of avoidance must be given. Thus, with respect to unpaid sellers or buyers who have not received delivery, CISG does not indicate when notice of avoidance must be given. The absence of such a provision is said to relieve an aggrieved party from the often difficult task of estimating when a delay in performance amounts to a fundamental breach.[663]

CISG permits a buyer to *partially avoid* the contract by treating any nonconforming or missing goods as if they were the subject matter of a severable contract. Partial avoidance, however, is possible only if the breach as to part of the goods was a fundamental breach or if the seller has not delivered within the time fixed in a *Nachfrist* notice.[664] If the breach is fundamental, the buyer may reject the nonconforming goods or withhold payment for them, though the buyer will also be able to exercise nonavoidance rights with respect to such goods.[665] CISG also provides that an aggrieved party can avoid an installment of an installment contract if the other party has committed a fundamental breach with respect to that installment.[666] Moreover, where a breach as to any installment permits the aggrieved party to conclude (with "good grounds") that a fundamental breach may occur with respect to future installments, he may declare the contract avoided for the future.[667]

---

[658] CISG Art. 27.

[659] CISG Art. 49(2)(a).

[660] CISG Art. 49 (2)(b)(i). *Cf.* UCC § 2-607(3)(a).

[661] CISG Art. 64(2).

[662] CISG Art. 64(2)(b)(i).

[663] *See* J. Honnold, Uniform Law for International Sales Under the 1980 Sales Convention at 320, 363–64 (1982).

[664] CISG Art. 51(1).

[665] For example, the buyer can require the seller to repair (Art. 46(3)) or the buyer can pursue its claim for damages (Art. 45(1)(b)).

[666] CISG Art. 73(1). While this provision may appear to be a replication of UCC § 2-612(2), the purposes of these two provisions are different. Generally, the UCC permits rejection for any defect (the "perfect tender" rule). With respect to installment contracts, however, the UCC applies a material breach standard, i.e., substantial impairment of the value. To avoid the interruption of an installment contract through a defect in one installment, UCC § 2-612(2) insists that an installment can be rejected only if the nonconformity substantially impairs the value of that installment and cannot be cured. The purpose of Article 73(1), however, is to permit each installment to be treated as if it were a severable contract.

[667] CISG Art. 73(2). See Dingxi Longhi Dairy, Ltd. v. Becwood Tech. Group, L.L.C., 2008 U.S. Dist. LEXIS 51066 (D. Minn. 2008). The similarity between this CISG Article and UCC § 2-612(3) should not obscure the major difference in the purposes of these provisions. The UCC provision is designed to avoid the "perfect tender" rule by requiring a material breach (substantial impairment of value). Since CISG requires a fundamental breach for any avoidance, there is no need for CISG to emulate the UCC in this regard. Article 73(2) essentially permits the aggrieved party to utilize what American lawyers would call anticipatory repudiation for future deliveries under the installment contract.

Where the contract is avoided, CISG requires restitution from both parties. If the seller has supplied goods or if the buyer has made payments under the contract, each party has a duty to make restitution of whatever has been supplied or paid.[668]

The aggrieved party who avoids the contract may claim damages that are generally measured in a fashion familiar to American lawyers, i.e., the difference between the contract price and the price in a reasonable substitute contract.[669] Moreover, an aggrieved party may also recover consequential and incidental damages.[670] For an aggrieved seller who has not resold or an aggrieved buyer who has not entered into a substitute transaction (i.e., the buyer has not "covered"), CISG measures damages by the difference between the contract price and the current market price,[671] which are familiar standards for the UCC lawyer.[672] Both CISG and the UCC follow the same general standard as to which market should control for measuring market price, i.e., the market price at the place of tender.[673] Where the goods have arrived and the buyer rejects or revokes acceptance pursuant to the UCC, however, the market for measurement is the place of arrival under the Code.[674] The UCC provision that deals with a "lost volume" seller[675] is reflected very simply in CISG in an article allowing the recovery of lost profits where supplementary damages are required.[676]

[7]   Summary

Notwithstanding differences between the remedial structures of CISG and the UCC, the Convention and the Code are designed, essentially, to protect the expectation interests of the parties.[677] The frugal language of the remedial structure of CISG will require considerable interpretation and construction. The American lawyer, however, is not placed in a position of being forced to become conversant with a system that is totally unfamiliar.

---

[668] CISG Art. 81(2). Problems may arise where the buyer has received goods and made payment, the seller commits a fundamental breach, and the buyer seeks restitution of his part payment but the seller refuses. The buyer may then retain the goods and eventually sell the goods for the account of the seller under Article 88(1).

[669] CISG Art. 75. See UCC §§ 2-706 (seller's resale damages) and 2-712 (buyer's cover damages), which are very similar though CISG imposes no duty upon the seller concerning notice of resale.

[670] CISG Art. 74.

[671] CISG Art. 76(1).

[672] UCC §§ 2-708(1) and 2-713 use the contract price/market price differential. CISG Art. 76, however, measures market price at the time of avoidance or, if avoidance occurs after the buyer has taken over the goods, at the time the goods are taken over. The UCC seller's damages are measured by the market price at the time of tender and the buyer's damages are measured by the market price at the time the buyer learned of the breach. In anticipatory repudiation situations, where the case comes to trial prior to the time for performance, the measure is the market price at the time of repudiation under UCC § 2-723.

[673] CISG Art. 76(2). UCC §§ 2-708(1) and 2-713(2).

[674] UCC § 2-713(2).

[675] For a lost volume seller, i.e., one who sells standardized goods and has a theoretically inexhaustible supply, the resale remedy or contract price/market price differential will theoretically yield no damages. The lost volume seller would have made the additional sale in any event and has, therefore, lost the profit (plus reasonable overhead) on the contract that the buyer has breached. UCC § 2-708(2) permits such a seller to recover lost profit on that sale plus reasonable overhead.

[676] CISG Art. 74.

[677] See United Nations Conference on Contracts for the International Sale of Goods-Official Records, U. N. Doc. A/Conf. 97/59 (1981), indicating the basic philosophy of placing the aggrieved party in the same economic position he or she would have been in had the contract been performed.

Chapter 10

CONTRACT BENEFICIARIES

§ 130   THIRD PARTY BENEFICIARY CONTRACTS

[A]   Nature and History

This chapter focuses on an essential question: where *A* makes a promise induced by *B* that *A* will render a stated performance to *C*, may *C* enforce *A*'s promise? What rights, if any, accrue to a third person who will receive a benefit if the contract is performed, when that person is neither a promisor nor promisee of the contract? Until a repeal by Parliament in 1999, English courts, by an almost unbroken line of decisions, adhered to the view that such a person has no enforceable rights.[1] The reasons which led the English courts to reach the conclusion that such a person has no enforceable rights have been stated in a leading English case:

My Lords, in the law of England certain principles are fundamental. One is that only a person who is a party to a contract can sue on it. Our law knows nothing of a

---

[1] *See* Vandepitte v. Preferred Acc. Ins. Corp., A.C. 70 [1933]; Tweedle v. Atkinson, 1. B. & S. 393 [1861]; Bourne v. Mason, 1 Ventirs 6 [1669].

jus quaesitum tertio arising by way of contract. Such a right may be conferred by way of property, as, for example, under a trust, but it cannot be conferred on a stranger to a contract as a right to enforce the contract in personam. A second principle is that if a person with whom a contract not under seal has been made is to be able to enforce it consideration must have been given by him to the promisor or to some other person at the promisor's request. These two principles are not recognized in the same fashion by the jurisprudence of certain Continental countries or of Scotland, but here they are well established. A third proposition is that a principal not named in the contract may sue upon it if the promisee really contracted as his agent. But again, in order to entitle him to sue, he must have given consideration either personally or through the promisee, acting as his agent giving it.[2]

Thus, there is no consideration moving from the third person who is a stranger to the contract. Such a person cannot be a "party" to the contract. The same thought was often expressed by the statement that the third person was not in "privity" and, therefore, could not have an action on the contract. The term "privity," at least as used in this sense (and probably in any other sense), is meaningless.[3] It suggests that the third person is not one of the parties who "made" the contract, i.e., that such a person is neither promisor nor promisee. Why a person who is neither promisor nor promisee may not be a party to the contract (in "privity") is never explained. As typically used, the lack of privity in a third person is a conclusion though it is stated as the reason for refusing to allow the third person to bring an action on the contract. Since they are analytically unsound, it may well be doubted whether the fundamental assumptions of the English common law in this area adequately protect and secure the legitimate interests involved in the transactions whose legal effect is controlled by them. While there are challenges in determining when one should have rights and how they should be sanctioned under a contract to which he is neither promisor nor promisee and for which he has provided no consideration, a mature legal system should be able to overcome those obstacles and create a design to react effectively to these issues. Such a design would not only avoid unnecessary litigation, it would be consistent with the manifest intention of the parties who made the contract with the intention to benefit the third party.

As developed in the United States, there were two classic categories of third party beneficiaries: (1) For a consideration, A promises B to render a performance to C which is intended to discharge a legal obligation then owing by B to C; (2) for a consideration, A promises B to render a performance to C as a gift to C or which, at any rate, will not operate to discharge any legal obligation then owing by B to C. In the first type of case, C is traditionally called a "creditor" beneficiary because he had a prior legal relationship with B, e.g., B was C's debtor and the debt is satisfied if A performs his promise for the benefit of C.[4] In the second type of case, he is traditionally called a "donee beneficiary" because the performance by A will confer a gift on C.[5] Unless such beneficiaries have rights under the contract, the intentions of the parties will be defeated. This is particularly true in the case of

---

[2] Lord Haldane in Dunlop Pneumatic Tyre Co. v. Selfridge & Co., A.C. 847, 853 [1915].

[3] One of the better judicial statements concerning "privity" is that of Justice Stone in La Mourea v. Rhude, 209 Minn. 53, 295 N.W. 304, 307 (1940): "Privity in the law of contracts, is merely the name for a legal relation arising from right and obligation. . . . To affirm one's right under a contract is therefore to affirm his privity with the party liable to him."

[4] *See* FIRST RESTATEMENT § 133(1)(b).

[5] *See* FIRST RESTATEMENT § 133(1)(a).

a donee beneficiary. Unlike the creditor beneficiary, the donee beneficiary has a claim only against the promisor since he has no enforceable right against the promisee. If, however, a creditor beneficiary could not recover against the promisor, his original claim against the promisee remains.

Unless enforceable rights are recognized for intended beneficiaries, unnecessary litigation will frequently be the inevitable result. In view of these facts, and taking into account the conclusory rationale for the rule of the English courts, it is not strange that inroads should have been made upon that rule. The rule has been almost universally abandoned in this country. While there were judicial inroads on the effects of the rule in England, the opposition to its abandonment required an Act of Parliament, the "Contract (Rights of Third Parties) Act of 1999." These matters will be discussed in the sections which follow.

[1]   Distinguishing Property Rights in Third Persons

Before we consider these and related questions, however, we should distinguish cases where a contract between the parties gives rise to what the law views as a "property right" in a third person, as distinguished from a contract right. It is generally agreed that a third person may become the legal or equitable owner of property as the result of a contract to which he is not a party and for which he furnished no consideration. This occurs when one person, by agreement with another, holds specific property either as bailee or as trustee for a third person. In these cases the right of the third person springs out of the fact that he has acquired rights in the property in question. Such a right is capable of being vindicated in appropriate proceedings regardless of the law relating to contract beneficiaries. It is only in the cases in which no property right in the third person results from the transaction that the problem becomes acute. In such a case, unless a third party beneficiary has a right *in personam* on the promise made for his benefit, he may be without redress. It is also well settled that if a contracting party is in fact acting as agent for a principal when he makes an informal contract with another, the principal may enforce the promise just as if it had been made directly with him as the promisee. In that situation, the fact of agency must be established before the third person can establish a claim as principal.

[B]   English Law

While the English courts consistently held that a mere contract beneficiary had no enforceable rights, they occasionally mitigated the effects of this rule by the use of a fiction. In some cases where A had made a promise to B to render a performance to C, they assumed that what the parties had in mind was that A should render the performance to B as trustee for C.[6] On this view of the facts, C becomes the beneficiary of a trust, and, as such, does have rights that are indirectly enforceable. B, who is a party to the contract, and who furnished the consideration, can enforce the contract to the full extent, but, as a mere trustee of the right, he holds the proceeds of any recovery in trust for C. Moreover, if B should fail to enforce the obligation, C, as the beneficiary of a trust, is entitled to bring a suit to which B will be made a party, to compel A to perform his undertaking. Such an approach to the problem requires a perversion of the facts. As might be expected, the English courts were not always consistent

---

[6] *See, e.g.,* Les Affreuteurs Reunia Societe v. Walford, 2 K.B. 498 [1918], X. 801 [1919].

in the application of this theory, It was applied only in a few of the more urgent cases.[7] A nineteenth century English statute, the Married Women's Property Act,[8] protected a wife, husband, or child named as beneficiary in a policy of life insurance as the party entitled to the proceeds of the policy. Yet, such a beneficiary could not sue for them directly.

The English Law Revision Commission recommended recognition of third party contract rights in 1937 and again in 1965. The Law Revision Report of 1996 led to the introduction of a bill in the House of Lords on December 3, 1998. Almost a year later, it passed the House of Commons and then, in modified form, passed the House of Lords on November 10, 1999. Upon Royal Assent the following day, the "Contract (Rights of Third Parties Act of 1999") became the law of the land.

[C]   American Law

Although there were some early cases in Massachusetts[9] based upon dicta found in early English cases which held that a third person might have a direct right of action at law on a contract to which he was not a party and for which he had not furnished any part of the consideration, these cases were overruled when it became clear that English law did not countenance such a view.[10] It remained for New York, in the leading case of *Lawrence v. Fox*,[11] finally to break the tradition and to start a movement, which has since spread throughout the country, that a beneficiary does have rights, in a proper case, which he can enforce directly, just as if he were a promisee.

In what was to become a famous case though it was not celebrated when it was first decided, Holly (*A*) loaned $300 to Fox (*B*) and told Fox that Holly owed that amount to Lawrence (*C*). In repayment of the loan, Fox agreed to pay the $300 to Lawrence. Fox did not perform his promise and Lawrence brought an action on the contract against Fox. Thus, the court was squarely confronted with the question, where *A* provides consideration to induce *B* to promise to perform for the benefit of *C*, may *C*, though neither promisor nor promisee, recover on the contract? Fox argued that no consideration had moved from Lawrence to Fox and there was no "privity" between Lawrence and Fox, i.e., Lawrence was not a party to the contract. The jury found for Lawrence and Fox appealed to the superior court, which affirmed the judgment. An appeal was then taken to the New York Court of Appeals, which found a basic principle announced as early as 1806: *where one person makes a promise to another for the benefit of a third person, the third person may maintain an action to enforce that promise.*

The court recognized that much of the precedent announcing this principle had involved trusts where the trustee has a duty to pay the beneficiary of a trust. Two concurring judges[12] insisted the promise to Fox was really the promise of Holly made through the medium of an agent, and the decision could be justified by perverting the facts so that they fit within a

---

[7] The English cases decided prior to 1930 are collected and discussed in Corbin, *Contracts for the Benefit of Third Persons*, 46 LAW Q. REV. 12 (1930).

[8] 45 & 46 Vict., ch. 75 § 11 [1882]. There are other statutory exceptions in England.

[9] *See* Brewer v. Dyer, 61 Mass. (7 Cush.) 337 (1851).

[10] *See* Marston v. Bigelow, 150 Mass. 45, 22 N.E. 71 (1889); Exchange Bank of St. Louis v. Rice, 107 Mass. 37 (1871).

[11] 20 N.Y. 268 (1859).

[12] Johnson, C. J., and Denio, J.

familiar doctrinal category.[13] The court, however, insisted that the principle had been applied to trust and other cases not because it was relegated to such cases. Rather, it was a basic principle that could be applied to trust cases and other cases, including a case such as the one before the court, i.e., a third party beneficiary contract. It was the court's insistence in recognizing the basic principle to be applied regardless of the form in which it arises that made *Lawrence v. Fox* a landmark opinion.

While the holding of *Lawrence v. Fox* is necessarily limited to the recognition of *creditor* beneficiaries, there is nothing in the opinion suggesting that its rationale should be so limited. Moreover, a subsequent opinion recognized the application of the principle with respect to non-creditor beneficiaries.[14] Five years later, however, in the case of *Vrooman v. Turner*,[15] the court held that the rule of *Lawrence v. Fox* must be limited to its holding. Consequently, a beneficiary could have no right of action unless the promise was made for his benefit which would discharge a legal duty of the promisee owed to the beneficiary. Such a relationship supplied the "privity" deemed necessary to give the beneficiary a right under the contract. So stated, the rule was limited in its application to the protection of creditor beneficiaries exclusively. For more than a century, New York courts struggled to free themselves from this limitation. The first inroad was made by a court taking the position that a moral obligation owed by the promisee to the beneficiary, such as the moral duty owed by a husband-promisee to make provision for his wife, is a substitute for the legal obligation and supplied the connecting link demanded by the holding in *Vrooman v. Turner*.[16] Opinions sometimes reflected a recognition that the principle of *Lawrence v. Fox* should not be limited.[17] A particularly candid recognition of the evolution occurred in a 1935 case: "The requirement of some obligation or duty running from the promisee to the third party beneficiary has been progressively relaxed until a mere shadow of the relationship suffices, if indeed it has not reached the vanishing point."[18] Another half century would pass, however, before the highest court of New York expressly rejected any necessity of such a duty or obligation from the promisee to the beneficiary, insisting that the modern rule manifests the "essence" of prior holdings, which the court characterized as merely suggesting "unnecessary differentiations

---

[13] As to the law of trusts and agency as they apply to the protection of third parties, see RESTATEMENT 2d § 302 comment f.

[14] Thorp v. Keokuk Coal Co., 48 N. Y.253 (1872).

[15] 69 N.Y. 280 (1877).

[16] Buchanan v. Tilden, 158 N.Y. 109, 52 N.E. 724 (1899). Here, the court relied heavily upon a seventeenth century English case, Dutton v. Poole, 2 Lev. 210 [1677], where the defendant promised his father for a consideration paid by the father to pay the plaintiff, his sister, a sum of money. The court held the sister was entitled to enforce the promise on the ground that her close relationship to the parties to the contract satisfied the requirement of privity to the promise and the consideration. The case, however, was later disapproved in *Tweedle v. Atkinson, supra* note 1.

[17] Seaver v. Ransom, 224 N.Y. 233, 240, 120 N.E. 639, 641 (1918): "The doctrine of Lawrence v. Fox is progressive, not retrograde. The course of the late decisions is to enlarge, not to limit the effect of that case."

[18] McClare v. Massachusetts Bonding and Ins. Co., 266 N.Y. 371, 195 N.E. 15 (1935). The same thought is expressed in Lait v. Leon, 40 Misc. 2d 60, 242 N.Y.S.2d 776 (1963), suggesting that, if there is any requirement of duty from the promisee to the third party (i.e., if there is any requirement that only third party *creditor* beneficiaries may recover), the requirement is nebulous. See, however, Scheidl v. Universal Aviation Equip., Inc., 159 N.Y.S.2d 278 (Sup. Ct. 1957), where the court held that a third party beneficiary could not recover because (1) he had not parted with any consideration in exchange for defendant's promise, and (2) no obligation existed between the promisee and the third party. See also Walker v. Phinney, 120 Misc. 2d 513, 466 N.Y.S.2d 227 (Sup. Ct. 1983), suggesting the continued viability of *Vrooman v. Turner*.

and circuitous language."[19]

This vacillation in New York, however, reflected decisions in other jurisdictions that limited the right of recovery to a creditor beneficiary or one deemed to be in an analogous position.[20] Paradoxically, courts in Pennsylvania had allowed only donee beneficiaries to recover.[21] By 1957, however, it was clear that creditor beneficiaries could recover in Pennsylvania.[22] There is no longer any doubt that courts in every jurisdiction now recognize a cause of action in an intended third party beneficiary, regardless of whether there was any prior obligation owed by the promisee to the beneficiary.

Massachusetts had the distinction of refusing to recognize a right in either creditor or donee beneficiaries. Finally, in 1979, Massachusetts overcame more than 125 years of precedent in recognizing the right of a third party beneficiary.[23]

[1] Statutory Recognition of Third Party Beneficiaries

Statutes in several jurisdictions recognize the rights of a third party beneficiary as part of the codifications in the substantive law urged by David Dudley Field in the 19th century. Such statutes may well contain a broad recognition of the right of a third party beneficiary: "A contract, made expressly for the benefit of a third person, may be enforced by him at any time

---

[19] Fourth Ocean Putnam Corp. v. Interstate Wrecking Co., 66 N.Y.2d 38, 495 N.Y.S.2d 1, 485 N.E.2d 208, 212 (1985) (adopting the RESTATEMENT 2d formulation discussed *infra*). Currently, the court applies a modern analysis as if the checkered history never occurred. See Cal. Pub. Employees Retirement Sys. v. Sherman & Sterling, 95 N. Y. 2d 427, 741 N. E. 2d 101 (2000); Colavito v. New York Organ Donor Network, 438 F.3d 214, 228 n. 14 (2d Cir. 2006).

[20] *See, e.g.*, West v. Norcross, 190 Ark. 667, 80 S.W.2d 67 (1935) (sharecropper held to be without remedy on a contract made for his benefit between his landlord and the United States). Arkansas, however, has rejected that concept. *See* Coley v. English, 235 Ark. 215, 357 S.W.2d 529 (1962). Minnesota long adhered to the view that only creditor beneficiaries could recover. It repudiated that view, however, in La Mourea v. Rhude, 209 Minn. 53, 295 N.W. 304 (1940). Courts of equity arrived at a similar conclusion through the equitable doctrine of subrogation, i.e., where a surety discharges the obligation for which the principal debtor is primarily liable, he has a right to be substituted for the creditor with respect to securities or other obligations that were available to the creditor for collection of his claim. By analogy, this doctrine was extended to give an unpaid creditor a claim against any securities the principal debtor had given his surety for the surety's indemnification. *See* Jennings, *A Creditor's Rights in Securities Held by His Surety*, 22 MINN. L. REV. 316 (1938). Following this analogy to its logical conclusion, equity courts have said that the creditor beneficiary is in the position of such a creditor, i.e., by promising to pay the promisee's debt, the promisor has become the principal debtor and the promisee has become a surety. Thus, the argument goes, the doctrine of subrogation gives the creditor beneficiary the right to be substituted for the promisee-surety and he can enforce the promise pursuant to the right of the promisee. *See* Keller v. Ashford, 133 U.S. 610, 10 S. Ct. 494, 33 L. Ed. 667 (1890). If this is the foundation of the beneficiary's right, it obviously provides no support for a donee beneficiary. Professor Corbin was critical of the view that the doctrine of subrogation is properly applicable to the case of a creditor beneficiary. Corbin, *Contracts for the Benefit of Third Persons*, 27 YALE L.J. 1008, 1015–16 (1918). *See also* Langmaid, *Contracts for the Benefit of Third Persons in California*, 27 CAL. L. REV. 497, 499 (1939).

[21] *See* Greene County use of Crescent-Portland Cement Co. v. Southern Surety Co., 292 Pa. 304, 141 A. 27 (1927). The Pennsylvania situation was confused for a long time. *See* Corbin, *The Law of Third Party Beneficiaries in Pennsylvania*, 77 U. PA. L. REV. 594 (1928).

[22] *See* Burke v. North Huntingdon Township Mun. Auth., 390 Pa. 588, 595, 136 A.2d 310, 314 (1957): "That a third party, not in privity to the original contract, may sue as a creditor beneficiary is now the rule in Pennsylvania. . . ." (citations omitted).

[23] Choate, Hall & Stewart v. SCA Servs., Inc., 378 Mass. 535, 392 N.E.2d 1045 (1979), *on remand*, 22 Mass. App. Ct. 522, 495 N.E.2d 562 (1986).

before the parties thereto rescind it."[24] Such broad statutes are not designed to deal specifically with many issues that arise concerning third party contracts. Thus, even with a broad statutory principle as a base, the analyses of third party beneficiary issues in these jurisdictions is typically not materially different from analyses in jurisdictions recognizing third party beneficiaries as a matter of common law. Both the First and Second Restatements of Contracts are viewed as desirable aids in such jurisdictions.

In addition to statutes broadly recognizing such rights, a number of jurisdictions enacted statutes recognizing specific types of third party beneficiaries in life insurance policies, as well as protecting others such as laborers and materialmen, mortgagees whom grantees of mortgagors promised to pay, and third party tort victims caused by a party carrying liability insurance. The Uniform Commercial Code incorporated a third party beneficiary concept to recognize that parties other than the buyer of goods may suffer injury in a contract for the sale of goods. That analysis appears later in this chapter.[25]

§ 131 PROTECTED VERSUS INCIDENTAL BENEFICIARIES — RESTATEMENTS

[A] Separating Protected From Unprotected Beneficiaries — Intention of the Parties

One of the most troublesome problems courts have encountered is deciding who shall be considered a protected beneficiary. Contracts often benefit third parties who were not consciously considered, much less intended, beneficiaries of those contracts. If parties agree to construct a new shopping mall, nearby business establishments may benefit from that contract. Consumers would benefit at least in terms of the convenience of not having to travel to more distant shopping centers. Should all of these "beneficiaries" and numerous others who might benefit from this contract be viewed as "protected" beneficiaries, i.e., parties who have a cause of action if the contract to build the new mall is breached? It is clear that not everyone who would receive a benefit, were the promise performed, should enjoy rights as intended parties to the contract. Where Ames and Barnes agree to construct an expensive residence on Ames' land, Carr, who owns adjoining land, may benefit from such an improvement to area, but neither Ames nor Barnes may be aware of who owns the adjoining land, much less intend to benefit such a third party.[26]

For more than twenty years, FB, a national distributor of Boar's Head deli products, had a terminable at will contract with Coastal which resold the products to retailers. When FB terminated the contract, Coastal claimed that its separate entity, Coastal Real Estate (CRE), had a claim as a third party beneficiary under the deli contract because CRE had constructed a facility in reliance on that agreement. The court disagreed, noting that Coastal's argument would create limitless third party beneficiaries in commercial situations since any party standing to profit from the performance of another contract could claim intended beneficiary

---

[24] *See, e.g.,* CAL. CIV. CODE § 1559; Idaho Code § 29-102; North Dakota Century Code § 9-02-04;S. D. Codified Laws, 53-2-6.

[25] § 135, *infra.*

[26] See RESTATEMENT 2d § 302 ill. 13.

status.[27] Having agreed to sell two manufactured modules to Technip, Express Metal contracted with a freight broker, Translink, to arrange for the transportation of the modules. Translink contracted with Robbins to haul the modules. To recover freight costs exceeding the estimate, Robbins claimed that it was a third party beneficiary of the contract between Express Metal and Technip. The court noted that any contract to manufacture and sell goods that requires transportation of those goods will create incidental beneficiaries in the form of transportation companies. Such a contract, however, does not transform such parties into third party beneficiaries with enforceable rights against the promisor in the manufacturing contract.[28] To allow any third party to sue a promisor simply because she could demonstrate a potential benefit from a breached contract between other parties would subject a promisor to a liability that would not only exceed any risk contemplated by a contracting party, but even the limitations of remote liability in tort.[29] It was imperative to devise appropriate tests to draw the line between "protected" beneficiaries, who would have a cause of action under a contract made by others, and "incidental" beneficiaries, who would benefit to some extent from the performance of the contract, but should not be viewed as parties who had a right to enforce that contract. It is important to consider these tests.

[B]   The RESTATEMENTS Compared

[1]   FIRST RESTATEMENT — Procrustean Categories — Interdependent Contractors

It is often suggested that the first Restatement of Contracts provides three categories of beneficiaries, two categories of protected beneficiaries, i.e., those who had rights under the contract between the promisor and promisee, and one category of unprotected beneficiaries, i.e., those who had no such rights. In fact, the first Restatement recognizes four categories of beneficiaries The first protected category is the "donee" beneficiary that includes two separate types. Either the promisee desires to make a gift to the beneficiary *or* desires to confer upon the beneficiary a right against the promisor to some performance neither due nor supposed to be due from the promisee to the beneficiary.[30] Where the promisee does not intend to make a gift, but does intend to confer a right to enforce the contract to a third party to whom the promisee neither actually nor supposedly owes anything, to characterize such a beneficiary as a "donee" is inaccurate. Thus, under the "donee" beneficiary rubric, there are two types-the true donee (gift) beneficiary and the beneficiary on whom the promisee wishes to confer an enforceable right. Because of the "donee" characterization, however, the second type of beneficiary under this category who was not a true "donee" could easily be ignored by courts who would limit this compartment to third parties who could demonstrate a promisee's donative intent. The second protected category is the "creditor" beneficiary,[31] where the purpose of the promisee was to satisfy an actual, supposed, or asserted duty of the promisee to the beneficiary. The third and unprotected category, called "incidental" beneficiaries,[32]

---

[27] Frank Brunckhorst Co., L. L. C v. Coastal Atlantic, Inc., 2008 U.S. Dist. LEXIS 6748 (E. D. Va. 2008).

[28] Robbins Motor Transportation, Inc. v. Translink, Inc., 2009 U.S. Dist. LEXIS 25189 (E. D. Pa. 2009).

[29] See the opinion by Judge Posner in Vidimos v. Laser Lab, 99 F.3d 217, 219 (7th Cir. 1996).

[30] FIRST RESTATEMENT § 133(1)(a).

[31] FIRST RESTATEMENT § 133(1)(b).

[32] FIRST RESTATEMENT § 133(1)(c) and ills. 11 and 12.

includes all other beneficiaries who simply do not fit within either of the protected categories. Under the First Restatement rubric, therefore, courts only had to consider the purpose of the promisee. If the purpose of the promisee in making the contract was to benefit the third party, either in terms of satisfying an actual or supposed obligation to that party, the third party had a right under the contract as a creditor beneficiary. If the purpose of the promisee was to confer a gift upon the third party, the third party was a protected donee beneficiary. If courts construed the "donee" category as also including third parties who were neither donees nor actual or supposed creditors of the promisee, but simply third parties upon whom the promisee intended to confer a right to enforce the contract, such an expansive construction may have left little room for criticism. Unfortunately, courts often saw only two types of third party beneficiaries under the First Restatement, donee or creditor beneficiaries whose procrustean nature did not allow for cases involving intended beneficiaries who could not be squeezed into either compartment. Consider, for example, a construction project where the owner makes contracts with two prime contractors, each responsible for separate portions of the work. The delay of one contractor causes delays by the second contractor who suffers losses because of these delays. The second contractor brings an action as a third party beneficiary of the contract between the first contractor and the owner under circumstances where all of the parties were aware of the interdependent nature of the work, and the second contractor's agreement to perform at a certain contract price was based on the assumption that the first contractor's work would be completed on time. In such a case, a court held that the second contractor could recover as a third party beneficiary, but not through an application of the First Restatement analysis where the second contractor would not fit easily within either of the protected categories.[33]

Other situations created similar concerns over the limited First Restatement compartments. The promisor, A, may be induced to make a promise to B, who desires a particular performance to third party C, not because B intends to make a gift to C (B may dislike C intensely),[34] nor because B has any actual or supposed obligation to C, but because A's performance to C will benefit B with respect to another transaction. Unless a court would recognize the second type of beneficiary described earlier under the "donee" banner, C is neither a gift nor creditor beneficiary, though B made the contract with A for the express benefit of C. B intended to confer a right upon C against A. Even though B's *motive or purpose* was not to satisfy an actual or supposed obligation to C or to make a gift to C, B *intended C* to be a third party beneficiary of the contract.[35]

[33] See Moore Constr. Co. v. Clarksville Dep't of Electricity, 707 S.W.2d 1 (Tenn. Ct. App. 1985), where the court suggests that the FIRST RESTATEMENT categories were too procrustean (citing cases). For another case holding that a second prime contractor can recover as a third party beneficiary, *see* Broadway Maintenance Corp. v. Rutgers State Univ., 90 N.J. 253, 447 A.2d 906, 910 (1982). The *Moore* opinion recognizes a split of authority on this question and cites cases *contra*.

[34] The promisee need not have an altruistic motivation. *See* Vikingstad v. Baggott, 46 Wash. 2d 494, 282 P.2d 824 (1955).

[35] The distinction between motive or purpose and intention in a third party beneficiary context is set forth in Hamill v. Maryland Cas. Co., 209 F.2d 338 (10th Cir. 1954) (party agrees with contractor to advance portions of contract price to contractor to stabilize contractor's financial condition; issuer of payment bond recovers as third party beneficiary). *See also* Vikingstad v. Baggott, 46 Wash. 2d 494, 282 P.2d 824, 826 (1955) (intent of promisee to confer a benefit upon third party is relevant; promisee's motive is immaterial).

[2]   RESTATEMENT 2d Test — "Intended Beneficiary."

The Restatement 2d approach is a reaction against the "donee" and "creditor" labels. The heart of the new approach is found in § 302:

§ 302 Intended and Incidental Beneficiaries

(1) Unless otherwise agreed between promisor and promisee, a beneficiary of a promise is an intended beneficiary if recognition of a right to performance in the beneficiary is appropriate to effectuate the intention of the parties and either

(a) the performance of the promise will satisfy an obligation of the promisee to pay money to the beneficiary; or

(b) the circumstances indicate that the promisee intends to give the beneficiary the benefit of the promised performance.

(2) An incidental beneficiary is a beneficiary who is not an intended beneficiary.

The first section begins with the important qualification, "Unless otherwise agreed," that allows the parties to resolve the question of their intention to benefit or not benefit a particular third party.[36] The familiar First Restatement "donee" and "creditor" beneficiary categories are eliminated because "they carry overtones of obsolete doctrinal difficulties." In particular, it was a reaction to including the second type of beneficiary who was not a donee under the "donee" label. The Reporter's notes to § 302 indicate that the use of "donee" with respect to the intention of a promisee to confer a right but not a gift was not entirely appropriate.[37] The new version claims to recognize only two categories, "intended" and "incidental" beneficiaries. Indeed, in one sense, it identifies only one category — "intended" — since an "incidental" beneficiary is defined simply as a party who is not an "intended" beneficiary. To determine whether a party is an "intended" beneficiary under the Second Restatement is a two step process. The first step is a threshold requirement that "recognition of a right to performance in the beneficiary is *appropriate* to effectuate the intention of the parties."[38] By itself, this broad, discretionary requirement could hardly be called a test. The second step requires the third party to fall within either of two additional categories: (1) performance by the promisor will satisfy an obligation of the promisee to *pay money* to the beneficiary-the "duty owed" category *or* (2) under the circumstances, the promisee intended to give the beneficiary the benefit of the promised performance-the "intention to benefit" category.[39]

Category (1) is a very narrow version of First Restatement"creditor" category and category (2) is very similar to the old RESTATEMENT "donee" category. Yet, the RESTATEMENT 2d insists that the terms "donee" and "creditor" not be used. Some wondered whether the "new diction" was beneficial.[40]

---

[36] See, e.g., Amerifirst Bank v. TJX Co., 564 F.3d 489 (1st Cir. 2009) expressly relying upon the "unless otherwise agreed" statement in § 302(1) where the contract expressly stated that it was not for the benefit of any third party.

[37] Restatement 2d, Introductory Note to Chapter 14.

[38] RESTATEMENT 2d § 302(1) (emphasis supplied).

[39] A comparison of the two RESTATEMENTS in relation to third party beneficiaries is found in *In re* Edward M. Johnson & Assocs., Inc., 845 F.2d 1395 (6th Cir. 1988).

[40] In a casebook co-authored by the Chief Reporter of the RESTATEMENT 2d after the appearance of the tentative draft on third party beneficiaries, the following statement appears: "It is not altogether clear what is gained by the new diction." E. FARNSWORTH, W. YOUNG & H. JONES, CASES AND MATERIALS ON CONTRACTS 882 (2d ed. 1972).

As to the "creditor" category, the First Restatement would include beneficiaries to whom the promisee owed an actual, supposed, or asserted duty-the "duty owed" category.[41] Not just any "duty owed," however, will place the beneficiary in that category in the Restatement 2d which requires the promisor to satisfy "an obligation of the promisee *to pay money* to the beneficiary."[42] A comment explains that, if the promisee's obligation is easily liquidated, it falls within this category, but less liquid obligations would be dealt with under the "gift" ("intention to benefit") category.[43] This is a curious change since a promisee who seeks to benefit a third party as well as himself by discharging an unliquidated obligation to that third party certainly does not intend to make a gift. Apparently, the Restatement 2d was concerned that only third parties to whom the promisee was under a duty would be included, and, to effectuate that purpose, chose to limit it to situations where manifestations of that duty were clear and certain.[44] Where the duty is actual though unliquidated, the third party will now be classified in the "gift" category which has come to be viewed more broadly as the "intention to benefit" category. *A fortiori*, where the duty is only supposed or asserted, or where there is no actual, supposed, or asserted duty, the intended beneficiary will be placed in the "intention to benefit" category. The expansion of this category avoids precise delineation as to where a particular third party should be categorized because the overriding concern is to recognize the right to performance in the third party where that would be *appropriate* to effectuate the intention of the parties.[45]

The Section 302 analysis appears cumbersome. A judicial determination that recognition of a right in a third party is "appropriate to effectuate the intention" of both the promisor and promisee can only be made by an engagement with all of the relevant evidence to determine the parties' intention. Having decided that it is appropriate to conclude that both parties intended to benefit the third party, the court must then find either an obligation by the promisee to pay money to the third party (a determination of fact apart from any additional evidence of intention), *or* evidence of the intention of the *promisee*, alone, to confer a right on the third party. Thus, it would appear that, at least in relation to the promisee, except where he had an obligation to pay money to the third party, a court must pursue a second look to determine whether the promisee intended to benefit the third party. The Reporter for the Second Restatement, Professor Alan Farnsworth, noted that the additional requirement that the promisee had an intention to benefit the third party "seems curious at first." Noting that the implication of such liability is not simple, however, he justified such a second look as a safeguard that "the promisee would have been willing to pay the fair value for the promisor's undertaking a duty to the beneficiary."[46]

---

[41] FIRST RESTATEMENT § 133(1)(b).

[42] RESTATEMENT 2d § 302(1)(b) (emphasis supplied).

[43] RESTATEMENT 2d § 302 comment b. An example of an easily convertible obligation would be an obligation to deliver commodities or securities actively traded in organized market. A "less liquid" obligation would be a duty that would have to be litigated to determine its value. The beneficiary of a promise to discharge a lien on the promisee's property would also be included in the "gift" category.

[44] RESTATEMENT 2d § 302 comment b suggests that, "there is no suretyship if the promisee has never been under any duty to the beneficiary." Hence, such cases are not covered by the "duty owed" category, § (1)(a).

[45] RESTATEMENT 2d § 302(1).

[46] Alan Farnsworth, CONTRACTS, § 10.3 at 662 (4th ed. 2004).

In *Hickman v. Safeco Ins. Co. of America*,[47] Hickman's failure to provide proof of casualty insurance coverage on his home induced the mortgagee to purchase the coverage as permitted under the mortgage agreement. When a casualty occurred, the insurer (Safeco) refused to recognize Hickman as a third party beneficiary of the policy because he was not named in the policy. The court of appeals agreed that Hickman was only an incidental beneficiary of the insurance contract between Safeco and the mortgagee. Though barely mentioning the "appropriate" test of § 302 of the Restatement 2d, and finding no obligation by the mortgagee (promisee) to "pay money" to Hickman (purported third party), the Supreme Court of Minnesota emphasized that only the intention of the promisee was relevant under § 302(1)(b) and found such an intention to benefit Hickman. Recognizing that a third party need not be identified by name at the time the contract is formed, the court focused on the express obligations in the policy to "borrower" including the commitment by the insurer to pay the borrower amounts in excess of the mortgagee's interest in the property as well as coverage of personal property in which the mortgagee had no interest. Moreover, the policy stated that "Safeco will adjust all losses with borrower." Thus, the promisee (mortgagee) manifested an intention to benefit "borrowers" which included Hickman as the third party beneficiary.

[a]   Reliance Test Under the RESTATEMENT 2d

Though nothing in the "black letter" statement of § 302 mentions another test to determine third party beneficiary status, a comment suggests that a promise to pay a debt or make a gift to the beneficiary makes "reliance by the beneficiary both reasonable and probable." Such reliance would be reasonable *per se*. Actual reliance is unnecessary in either of these situations.[48] "Other cases" such as "a promise to perform a supposed or asserted duty of the promisee, a promise to discharge a lien on the promisee's property, or a promise to satisfy the duty of a third person" would include the third party within the "protected" category (apparently the "gift" category) because the third party would be reasonable in *relying* on the promise.[49] Again, a showing of actual reliance in these "other cases" would be unnecessary, but neither would they carry the presumption of reasonable reliance *per se*. They would require a determination that the third party would have been reasonable in relying on the promise as intending an enforceable third party right under the contract.[50] Where there is doubt as to whether such reliance would be reasonable, courts may consider other policy factors in determining whether recognition of the right in the third party would be "appropriate."[51]

To determine whether a third party is reasonable in relying upon a promise is a desirable test. It is consistent with the extension of promissory estoppel in the RESTATEMENT 2d to

---

[47] 695 N. W. 2d 365 (Minn. 2005).

[48] *See* RESTATEMENT 2d § 302 comment d.

[49] *Id.*

[50] For recognition of hypothetical reliance as a test to determine third party beneficiary status, see Riggsbee v. A & S Property Mgt., 1996 Conn. Super. LEXIS 2350; Beverly v. Macy, 702 F.2d 931, 941–42 (11th Cir. 1983); Rae v. Air-Speed, Inc., 435 N. E. 2d 628, 633, n. 3 (Mass. 1982). The "empty hypothetical reliance test" of this section is criticized by Professor Melvin Eisenberg, *Third Party Beneficiaries*, 92 Colum. L. Rev. 1358, 1384 (1992).

[51] RESTATEMENT 2d § 302 comment d. For example, there may be an overriding public policy consideration in a statute that would urge a court to recognize or not recognize the right in the third party. Such a policy could also suggest a third party beneficiary right regardless of the intention of the parties.

enforce promises to relying third parties which we explored much earlier in this volume.[52] It is predicated on the view that "reasonable and probable" reliance by a classical donee or creditor beneficiary is obvious, and such reliance by a third party who would not otherwise fit within the classical categories should also be protected.[53] While this test appears only as a comment and may ideally deserve more conspicuous treatment, the purpose of the American Law Institute was to *restate* the extant law on the subject. It would have been prohibitively difficult to support the new concept with preciously little case law to restate.[54] As we will see, however, the lack of a conspicuous statement has not deterred several courts from recognizing the test.

[3]   Reliance by the Promisee as a Basis for Third Party Enforcement

In the earlier discussion of promissory estoppel, we recognized the modern view that even parties who were not third party beneficiaries could enforce promises made to a promisee if it was reasonable for the promisor to expect the third party to rely on the promise.[55] A related issue is whether reliance by a promisee that a third party will receive a benefit is sufficient to allow enforcement by the third party. The plaintiff was the named beneficiary of a life insurance policy on the life of her husband. When the parties were estranged, the husband changed the beneficiary as permitted by the insurance contract. Upon a resumption of an amicable relationship, however, the husband clearly relied on a confirmation from the insurer that the wife had been renamed as the beneficiary. In fact, however, she had not been renamed and, upon the death of the husband, brought an action against the insurer on the basis of promissory estoppel pursuant to the reliance of her husband. The court held that the promisor should be held liable for the reliance of either the promisee or third party. The court found a strong basis for this holding since a promisee's reliance is even more foreseeable than reliance by a third party.[56]

[4]   "Intention to Benefit" — Interpretation — Parol Evidence — Intention of Promisee or Both Parties

[a]   Interpretation

Before we explore the application of various tests to distinguish protected from unprotected beneficiaries, it is important to recognize certain fundamental issues. The emphasis upon "intention to benefit" necessarily requires interpretation of the contract between the promisor and promisee. Essentially, the same guides to interpretation that were explored much earlier in this volume are employed by courts to determine the intention of the

---

[52] See § 67[B][2], *supra*, concerning RESTATEMENT 2d § 90.

[53] RESTATEMENT 2d § 302 comment d.

[54] The Reporter's note mentions Commercial Ins. Co. v. Pacific-Peru Constr. Corp., 558 F.2d 948 (9th Cir. 1977), concerning reliance, but recognizes that this case was relying upon a tentative draft of the new concept. Other cases are mentioned as including an actual or probable reliance element though "this factor was not discussed." As we will see, however, other courts have begun to recognize the major importance of the reliance test.

[55] See § 67, *supra*.

[56] Green v. Jackson National Life Ins. Co., 2006 U.S. App. LEXIS 21239 (6th Cir. 2006).

parties.[57] If the contract expressly states that it is designed for the benefit of a third party, that manifested intention will be enforced. As in other expressions of agreement, however, the terms of the contract may not clearly express the intention of the parties. In such a case, the preferable view would follow modern guides to interpretation by allowing evidence of surrounding circumstances to determine the intention of the parties. Where Janet Shaver rented her mother Betty's house, a fire occurred. Allstate Insurance paid Janet $80,000 under her renter's insurance policy. Allstate then claimed that it was subrogated to Janet's rights as a third party beneficiary under a furnace maintenance contract between her mother and Sears that Sears had allegedly breached. The trial court held that Janet was not a third party beneficiary of that contract, but the appellate court applied the Restatement 2d analysis in finding that Betty intended to benefit Janet by paying the premiums for the maintenance contract. Moreover, Sears had serviced the furnace at Janet's request which was course of performance evidence assisting the court to determine Janet's third party beneficiary status.[58]

[b]   Parol Evidence Rule

While third party beneficiary contracts should not be exempt from the parol evidence rule, neither should the application of the rule distort the parties' intention. Where a manufacturer and retailer of a product sought to invoke the parol evidence rule to preclude evidence that they were not intended as third party beneficiaries under a release between the injured party and the homeowner's insurer, the court allowed the introduction of the evidence on the footing that "strangers" to the contract could not invoke the parol evidence rule.[59] In another case, the plaintiffs sought to recover as third party beneficiaries under an insurance policy issued to the county which, by its terms, covered the sheriff's department. The insurer and the county sought to introduce evidence that they had no intention of covering the sheriff's department. Plaintiffs sought to invoke the parol evidence rule to preclude such evidence. The court admitted the evidence because plaintiffs were strangers to the contract.[60] Where, however, the plaintiffs agreed to purchase a business and assume the indebtedness of the seller to a third party beneficiary, the parol evidence rule barred admission of evidence of an alleged prior agreement between the plaintiffs and the third party that the indebtedness would be settled for a smaller sum. In this situation, the third party was certainly not a "stranger" to the contract.[61]

---

[57] *See* Chapter 5, §§ 89–91, *supra.*

[58] Allstate Ins. Co. v. Sears Roebuck & Co., 2007 Ohio App. LEXIS 4408 (2007). Trans-Orient Marine Corp. v. Star Trading & Marine, Inc., 925 F.2d 566, 573 (2d Cir. 1991) followed the RESTATEMENT 2d § 302 in the application of New York law: "In determining third party beneficiary status it is permissible for the court to look at the surrounding circumstances as well as the agreement." See, however, Georgia R.R. Bank & Trust Co. v. Federal Deposit Ins. Corp., 758 F.2d 1548, 1553 (11th Cir. 1985): "Under Georgia law, a person cannot be deemed a third-party beneficiary unless it clearly appears from the contract that the contract was intended for the benefit of the third person."

[59] Lemke v. Sears, Roebuck & Co., 853 F.2d 253 (4th Cir. 1988).

[60] Pitman v. Providence Washington Ins. Co., 394 So. 2d 223 (Fla. Dist. Ct. App. 1981).

[61] Cate v. Irvin, 44 Ark. App. 39, 866 S.W.2d 423 (1993).

[c]   Intention — Promisor *and* Promisee, or Intention of Promisee

One of the basic issues in determining intention to benefit is whether the intention must be that of both the promisor and promisee or the promisee, alone. The traditional viewed focused on the promisee since the motivating cause of the promisor is to receive the consideration for performing a promise induced by the promisee's motive or purpose to benefit the third party. A number of courts were persuaded by this view.[62] Other courts insisted that *both* the promisor and promisee must intend to benefit to the third party.[63] As noted earlier, the threshold requirement to establish a sufficient intention to benefit a third party under the Second Restatement is whether recognition of a third party's beneficiary right would be "appropriate to effectuate the intention of the *parties*," both promisor and promisee.[64] If the performance of the promise will satisfy an obligation of the promisee to pay money to the third party, no further evidence of either the promisor or promisee's intention is necessary.[65] If, however, there is an intention to benefit the third party beneficiary that will not satisfy the promisee's obligation to pay money to the beneficiary, only the promisee's intention is relevant.[66] Thus, except for the obligation to pay money to the beneficiary, all other third party beneficiary claims must manifest the promisee's intention to benefit the third party. The confusion in this test is illustrated by Grigerik v. Sharp[67] where the trial court found that the intention of both the promisor and promisee were necessary while the intermediate court found a "serious" flaw in that instruction by the trial court and focused on the intention of the promisee under § 302 of the Restatement 2d. The Supreme Court of Connecticut, however, concluded, "Thus, the language of the Restatement (Second) suggests that the right to performance is determined both by the intention of the contracting parties *and* by the intention of one of the parties [the promisee] to benefit the third party."[68] Though the quoted statement is confusing on its face, it is a correct statement of the § 2-302 requirements.[69]

---

[62] *See, e.g.,* Hamill v. Maryland Cas. Co., *supra* note 35; Hill v. Sonitrol of Southwestern Ohio, Inc., 521 N. E. 2d 780, 784 (1988).

[63] *See* Silverman v. Food Fair Stores, Inc., 407 Pa. 507, 180 A.2d 894 (1962); Colonial Discount Co. v. Avon Motors, Inc., 137 Conn. 196, 75 A.2d 507 (1950); Ridder v. Blethen, 24 Wash. 2d 552, 166 P.2d 834 (1946).

[64] RESTATEMENT 2d § 302.

[65] § 302(1)(a).

[66] § 302(1)(b).

[67] 247 Conn. 293, 721 A.2d 526 (1998).

[68] 721 A. 2d at 539.

[69] Pennsylvania decisions also manifest confusion. A Pennsylvania court concluded that § 302(1) requires the intention of both parties "unless the circumstances are so compelling that recognition of the beneficiary's right is appropriate to effectuate the intention of the parties, and the performance satisfies an obligation of the promisee to pay money to the beneficiary or circumstances indicate that the promisee intends to give the beneficiary the benefit of the promised performance." Scarpitti v. Weborg, 530 Pa. 366, 372–73, 609 A. 2d 147, 150–51 (1992). The court's quoted "unless" clause is a paraphrase of § 302 which raises the question, does Pennsylvania law require both parties to intend to benefit the third party "unless" § 302 applies? The court's "unless" quote is based on phraseology in Guy v. Liederbach, 501 Pa. 47, 459 A. 2d 744 (1983) which first adopted § 302.by carving out an exception to a 1950 case, Spires v. Hanover Ins. Co., 364 Pa. 52, 70 A. 2d 828 (1950) which had insisted that the intention of both the promisor and promisee rather than only the promisee's intention was critical. The confusion in Pennsylvania case law in this area has led another court applying Pennsylvania law to conclude that *Spires* is the law of Pennsylvania and § 302 is recognized in only narrow situations. Flex Homes v. Ritz-Craft Corp. of Michigan, 2008 U.S. Dist. LEXIS 21339 (N. D. Ohio 2008).

[5]   Tests Applied — RESTATEMENT 2d, "Direct Obligation," "Direct Benefit," "Main Purpose" and Reliance

The RESTATEMENT 2d "test" is often cited by courts as a basis for finding that a third party was either protected or unprotected. The application of the test, however, may vary. Where an accounting firm allegedly breached a contract by issuing a qualified opinion concerning a debtor's financial status that resulted in a trade creditor losing a large sum, the creditor claimed third party beneficiary status under the contract between the firm and the debtor. The court recognized that the contract was not designed to pay money to the creditor. The plaintiff, therefore, could only establish its rights as a protected beneficiary if the promisee (debtor) intended to give the beneficiary the benefit of the promised performance.[70] Having placed the case in that RESTATEMENT 2d category, the court analyzed the relevant facts concerning intent. Both the debtor and firm testified that there was no intent under this auditing contract to benefit the creditor. The promisor (accounting firm) was unaware that the debtor intended to provide copies of the audit to Dun and Bradstreet where the plaintiff (creditor) discovered the financial status of the debtor and, relying thereon, extended further credit which it presumably would not have done if the report had been accurate. The court noted that there was no express statement in the contract designating the plaintiff as an intended beneficiary. While this omission was not dispositive, the court viewed it as supporting its holding that the evidence was insufficient to meet the RESTATEMENT 2d directive that it would be appropriate to recognize a right to performance in the plaintiff.[71] The court, therefore, ultimately considered the specific facts to apply the broad RESTATEMENT 2d principle of intention to benefit. While the RESTATEMENT 2d analysis has been applied consistently with its purpose in other cases,[72] even while citing the RESTATEMENT 2d, courts often feel compelled to impose qualifying language to assure that the intention to benefit is emphatically "clear."[73]

A number of courts distinguish protected from unprotected beneficiaries by determining whether the parties intended that the promisor assume a *direct obligation* to the third party. The utility of such a test may well be doubted since *direct obligation* is uncertain. The parties rarely consider the fact that they are creating legal rights and duties. They simply expect their respective promises to be performed. Where a court insists upon the *direct obligation* test, it departs from a simple "intention to benefit" test[74] and insists that both parties must intend to

---

[70] RESTATEMENT 2d § 302(1)(b).

[71] Raritan River Steel Co. v. Cherry, Bekaert & Holland, 329 N.C. 646, 407 S.E.2d 178 (1991).

[72] *See, e.g.*, Leamington Co. v. Nonprofits' Ins. Ass'n, 615 N.W.2d 349 (Minn. 2000) (owner of building who was mistakenly omitted from insurance contract between the insurer and insured may have standing as a third party beneficiary); Vogan v. Hayes Appraisal Assocs., 588 N.W.2d 420 (Iowa 1999) (contract between bank and appraisal company which allegedly misinformed bank of progress on the construction of a new home inducing bank to make progress payments to the injury of the homeowner who was a third party beneficiary of the contract). *See also* Fourth Ocean Putnam Corp. v. Interstate Wrecking Co., Inc., 66 N.Y.2d 38, 485 N.E.2d 208, 495 N.Y.S.2d 1 (1985) (adopting RESTATEMENT 2d analysis).

[73] See, e. g., Gambill v. Packard, 2007 Mass, App. Div. LEXIS 52 at *5 (2007) ("clear and definite"); Owner-Operators Indep. Drivers Assn. v. Concord EFS, Inc., 59 S. W. 2d 63, 68–69 (Tenn. 2001) ("clear intent"); Perry v. Baptist Health, 358 Ark.238, 248, 189 S. W. 2d 54, 58 (2004) ("substantial evidence of clear intention").

[74] Grigerik v. Sharpe, 247 Conn. 293, 312, 721 A.2d 526, 536 (1998). For a case manifesting the "direct obligation" test in this jurisdiction, see Colonial Discount Co. v. Avon Motors, Inc., 137 Conn. 196, 75 A.2d 507 (1950). *See also* Robins Dry Dock & Repair Co. v. Flint, 275 U.S. 303, 48 S. Ct. 134, 72 L. Ed. 290 (1927); Montgomery v. Spencer, 15 Utah 495, 50 P. 623 (1897).

create a direct obligation from the promisor to the promisee.[75]

Another test found in some cases[76] may be called the *direct benefit* test: if the promisor has promised to render a performance directly to or for the third party, it is for his benefit and he may enforce it. If, however, the benefit is indirect, springing from a performance rendered to the promisee, the third party is a mere incidental beneficiary with no rights. This test is very narrow since it excludes third parties who are intended to be the ultimate beneficiaries of the promisor's performance, although that performance will be rendered directly to or for the promisee.

Consider, a case where third parties were damaged by the negligence of an attorney in drafting a will. The promisee (testator) intended to benefit certain legatees by entering a contract with his attorney to achieve that goal. The promisor (attorney) failed to perform his duty so as to effectuate that intention at all or in part. The attorney's performance, however, ran directly to or for the promisee though the *main purpose* of the promisee was to benefit the third parties. Under a test that requires the performance to be rendered directly to third parties, these parties would be incidental beneficiaries. In *Lucas v. Hamm*,[77] the court stated, "It is true that under a contract for the benefit of a third person performance is usually to be rendered directly to the beneficiary, but this is not necessary." Rather, where the main purpose of the promisee is to exact the performance from the promisor for the benefit of the third party, the third party has the right to enforce the promisor's duty regardless of whether that performance was to run directly to the third party.[78] Though broad, this test allows courts to effect the intention of the promisee if it is clear that the promisee's main intention was to benefit the third party, unhampered by the categorization of the beneficiary or by the fact that, in order to effectuate that intention, the promisor's performance may be rendered directly to the promisee. The promisee's "main intention" need not be his sole and exclusive motivation. In a creditor beneficiary situation, for example, it is clear that the promisee intends to benefit himself as well as the third party creditor beneficiary. When the promisor performs, the creditor beneficiary's claim against the promisee will be satisfied, thereby benefitting the promisee.[79]

---

[75] The Connecticut Supreme Court reaffirmed its adherence to the "direct obligation" test in Gazo v. City of Stamford, 255 Conn. 245, 765 A.2d 505 (2001).

[76] *See* Grossman v. Murray, 144 N.H. 345, 741 A.2d 1218, 1220 (1999), where the court quotes the RESTATEMENT 2d before quoting from an earlier case applying New Hampshire law, "Unless the performance required by the contract will directly benefit the would-be intended beneficiary, he is at best an incidental beneficiary." See Cooper Power Sys. v. Union Carbide, Chems. & Plastic Co., 123 F.3d 675, 680 (7th Cir. 1997), where the court states that Ohio law requires an intention to directly benefit the third party. *See also* Fidelity & Deposit Co. v. Rainer, 220 Ala. 262, 125 So. 55 (1929); Carson Pirie Scott & Co. v. Parrett, 346 Ill. 252, 178 N.E. 498 (1931). This test was prescribed in MICH. COMP. LAWS § 600.1405.

[77] 56 Cal. 2d 583, 15 Cal. Rptr. 821, 364 P.2d 685, 688 (1961), *cert. denied*, 368 U.S. 987, 82 S. Ct. 603, 7 L. Ed. 2d 525 (1962). Reaffirmed by the California Supreme Court in Heyer v. Flaig, 70 Cal. 2d 223, 74 Cal. Rptr. 225, 449 P.2d 161 (1969).

[78] A number of courts have recognized third party rights with respect to intended beneficiaries of wills. *See, e.g.,* Bishop v. Ing, 93 Haw. 223, 998 P.2d 1114 (2000); Noble v. Bruce, 349 Md. 730, 709 A.2d 1264 (1998); Ogle v. Fuiten, 102 Ill. 2d 356, 80 Ill. Dec. 772, 466 N.E.2d 224, 227 (1984); Auric v. Continental Cas. Co., 111 Wis. 2d 507, 331 N.W.2d 325, 329 (1983); Needham v. Hamilton, 459 A.2d 1060, 1062 (D.C. 1983); Stowe v. Smith, 184 Conn. 194, 441 A.2d 81, 83 (1981); Jaramillo v. Hood, 93 N.M. 433, 601 P.2d 66, 67 (1979); McAbee v. Edwards, 340 So. 2d 1167, 1170 (Fla. Dist. Ct. App. 1976).

[79] *See* Visintine & Co. v. New York, C. & S. L. R. Co., 169 Ohio St. 505, 160 N.E.2d 311 (1959). The beneficiaries' motives may be mixed. See, however, *Grossman v. Murray, supra* note 76, where the court suggests a "motivating

The reliance test discussed earlier[80] of determining whether a third party has enforceable rights because he reasonably relied upon a contract has already been recognized as a major factor under the RESTATEMENT 2d analysis.[81]

It is important to recognize the underlying concern manifested by various phrases emphasizing the importance of discovering a clear intent to benefit test. The concern is whether there is an intention to confer upon the third party a right to sue the promisor — a concern that is rarely expressed by the promisee and promisor.[82] Yet, if there is an "ultimate" test of the parties' intention, it is found in the statement, Did the contract clearly evidence an intent to permit enforcement by the third party?[83]

[6]   Incidental Beneficiaries

The RESTATEMENT 2d follows the traditional view that an incidental beneficiary is a party who will benefit from the performance of a contract where he is neither promisor nor promisee, but was not intended by the parties as a beneficiary of that contract.[84] The label, "incidental beneficiary," however, is a conclusion. We have seen different tests applied to determine whether a third party is a protected or unprotected beneficiary. The critical issue is *why* a court decided that a third party has no enforceable rights. There are many obvious situations, such as a contract between a department of prisons with a supplier of cable television service allowing inmates to purchase the service where an inmate claimed third party beneficiary status to contest a rate change.[85] A contract to improve certain land that will benefit a nearby landowner was not designed to benefit the landowner.[86] Other situations are not obvious. Where a physician treated an injured employee and was not fully paid for the treatments, he claimed that he was a third party beneficiary under the contract between the insurer and employer. The court held that the employee was an intended beneficiary of the employer's

---

cause" test. Such a test may not be harmful if it is qualified to suggest that a promisee may have more than one motive.

[80] See text at note 40 *supra*.

[81] *See* Leary v. Minichiello, 1999 Mass. Super. LEXIS 97, 9 Mass. L. Rep. 629 (Super. Ct. 1999) (gratuitous promised not relied upon by third party, applying an analysis identical to RESTATEMENT 2d § 90); Weninegar v. S.S. Steele & Co., 477 So. 2d 949 (Ala. 1985); Beverly v. Macy, 702 F.2d 931 (11th Cir. 1983).

[82] "To be a third party beneficiary is to have the rights of a party, which is to say the power to enforce the contract. . . . Parties to a contract are naturally reluctant to empower a third party to enforce their contract, so third party beneficiary status is not inferred from the circumstances but must be express." Johnson Bank v. George Korbakes & Co., LLP, 2006 U.S. App. LEXIS 31058 (7th Cir. 2006, Posner, J.). In SEC v. Prudential Secs., 136 F.3d 153, 159 (D.C. Cir. 1998), the court suggests that the test is not only whether the contracting parties intend to confer a benefit directly on third parties, but also whether the parties intended the third party to be able to sue to protect the benefit. The court, however, was discussing the appropriate test to be applied in determining whether a third party had a right under a consent decree. With respect to government consent decrees, third parties are denied such rights unless they are explicitly recognized in the decree.

[83] Consolidated Edison, Inc. v. Northeast Utilities, 426 F.3d 524, 528 (2d Cir. 2005), citing *Fourth Ocean*, 66 N.Y. 2d at 45.

[84] See RESTATEMENT 2d § 302 comment e and § 315, which simply indicates that the incidental beneficiary acquires no right against the promisor or promisee.

[85] Clifton v. Suburban Cable TV Co., Inc., 434 Pa. Super. 139, 642 A.2d 512 (1994), *cert. denied*, 513 U.S. 1173, 115 S. Ct. 1152, 130 L. Ed. 2d 1110 (1995) (plaintiff was an incidental beneficiary).

[86] Under a lease of lands from the state,, Parker Ranch had a duty to control a noxious weed (gorse) which it failed to perform. A lessee of adjacent land claimed it was a third party beneficiary of the lease contract between Parker Ranch and the state. The court held that he was, at best, an incidental beneficiary with no enforceable claim. Freddy Norbriga Enterprises, Inc. v. State of Hawaii, 2008 Haw. App. LEXIS 64 (2008).

contract with the insurer, but the physician was an incidental beneficiary who receives payment for the medical services he provides but has no enforceable right under the insurance contract.[87] A contract between an owner and an architect did not confer third party beneficiary rights on a commercial lender.[88] Where a bank makes a loan commitment to a home buyer, rights are not created in the home seller though he would benefit from the performance of the contract.[89] An agreement to extend credit to a failing business does not necessarily create rights in creditors of that business even if the creditors are aware of the agreement and prepare to continue to supply the debtor.[90] In a contract for the sale of goods, where the parties know and even name a third party buyer to whom the goods will be resold and delivered, the third party may not be a protected beneficiary.[91] Mere knowledge of resale to a third party is insufficient to create third party beneficiary rights in that party.[92] There is a vast difference between knowing that something will occur and intending to cause that result. These cases illustrate that, even though a third party may be identified as having a relationship with the contract, he may be a mere incidental beneficiary.[93] Guides discussed earlier that may prove useful include the determination of the main purpose of the promisee, i.e., not necessarily his sole purpose, but his dominant purpose in exacting the commitment from the promisor, and the ultimate test of whether the promisor and promisee intended to confer an enforceable right on the third party.

§ 132 IDENTIFICATION OF BENEFICIARY — "VESTING"

[A] Identification of Beneficiary

For some time it has been clear that a beneficiary may have rights under a contract although he is not specifically named in the contract.[94] It is sufficient if he is a member of an identifiable class or group of persons.[95] Nor must the beneficiary be identified when the contract is made, though the lack of identification at that time could bear on whether such a beneficiary was intended as a protected beneficiary as well as the question of whether the right created in such a beneficiary is revocable.[96] While the failure to name a third party in the

---

[87] Jou v. National Interstate Ins. Co. of Hawaii, 157 P.3d 561 (Ct. App. Haw. 2007).

[88] Mears Park Holding Corp. v. Morse/Diesel, Inc., 427 N.W.2d 281 (Minn. Ct. App. 1988).

[89] Khabbaz v. Schwartz, 319 N.W.2d 279, 284–86 (Iowa 1982).

[90] Braten v. Bankers Trust Co., 60 N.Y.2d 155, 468 N.Y.S.2d 861, 456 N.E.2d 802, 806 (1983).

[91] See Corrugated Paper Prods., Inc. v. Longview Fibre Co., 868 F.2d 908 (7th Cir. 1989), and cases cited therein.

[92] Spiegel v. Sharp Elecs. Corp., 125 Ill. App. 3d 897, 903, 446 N.E.2d 1040, 1045, 81 Ill. Dec. 238 (1st Dist. 1984).

[93] See Colonial Discount Co. v. Avon Motors, Inc., 137 Conn. 196, 75 A.2d 507 (1950) (commercial lender named in contract was not an intended beneficiary, but was named simply to assure promisee that financing arrangements in promisee's business would be conducted through an established commercial lender).

[94] See, e.g., Newman & Schwartz v. Asplundh Tree Expert Co., 102 F.3d 660, 662 (2d Cir. 1996); Ables v. United States, 2 Cl. Ct. 494 (1983), aff'd, per curiam, 732 F.2d 166 (Fed. Cir. 1984); Spector v. National Pictures Corp., 201 Cal. App. 2d 217, 224, 20 Cal. Rptr. 307, 311 (2d Dist. 1962).

[95] See Hickman v. Safeco Co., supra note 47 (casualty insurance policy that was issued to mortgagee when mortgagor did not carry that insurance referred to "borrower" which included Hickman, the mortgagor); Perry v. Baptist Health, 189 S. W. 3d 54, 58 (2004) (unnamed physician qualified as third party beneficiary under an agreement between a hospital and an association of physicians of which he was a member).

[96] Vencor Hosps. v. Blue Cross Blue Shield, 169 F.3d 677, 680, n. 5 (11th Cir. 1999) (though a particular hospital is not identified or identifiable at the time the contract is made, a contract between the insurer and patient for "Medigap"

contract is not dispositive, it is a factor in the determination of the intent to benefit a third party.[97] Again, however, if the third party is identifiable at the time for performance and is an intended beneficiary, he is entitled to enforce the contract.

[B]   When Beneficiary Rights Become Irrevocable — "Vesting"

A contract between A and B designed to benefit a particular third party, C, may be formed without the knowledge of the third party. For example, A promises \$25,000 to B in exchange for B's promise to deliver B's automobile to C (A's daughter) on her twenty-first birthday. A wants the gift to be a surprise and C is unaware of the contract. Absent knowledge of the contract, does C have any rights under it? The analysis may begin by assuming that, prior to the time for delivery of the auto, A becomes disenchanted with C and decides that he does not wish her to have the automobile. If A had promised to give an auto directly to C, absent C's reliance or other validation device, A would not be obligated to perform a gratuitous promise. Should it make any difference that A's gift promise involves another party in a third party beneficiary context? This requires us to consider whether A and B may modify or rescind the contract without the consent of C who has yet to learn of the contract for her benefit. Another way of putting the question is, when do the rights of a third party beneficiary "vest"?

[1]   Immediate Vesting

Over the years, courts have suggested three different responses to determine when a third party's rights vest, thereby precluding any modification of the contract without the consent of the third party. A number of older cases took the position that the right vests immediately, i.e., at the moment the contract is formed, though the third party is unaware of the contract.[98] This was the almost universal rule in the case of ordinary life insurance beneficiaries, although it was not generally followed with respect to insurance certificates issued by mutual benefit associations.[99] The FIRST RESTATEMENT was heavily influenced by the insurance cases in suggesting that the rights of *any* donee beneficiary vested immediately unless the power to discharge or modify the contract was reserved in the contract.[100] The courts refused to adopt this position except for ordinary life insurance policies.[101] Since insurance companies began inserting standard clauses in such policies to allow for modification or rescission, it is difficult to discover an illustration of immediate and irrevocable vesting.[102] In an insurance contract or

---

coverage manifests an intention to benefit the hospital identified only when performance is due as a third party beneficiary). *See* RESTATEMENT 2d § 308. On the question of revocability, see RESTATEMENT 2d § 311 and the discussion of "vesting" of third parties' rights, *infra*.

[97] Restatement 2d § 308, comment a.

[98] *See* Tweeddale v. Tweeddale, 116 Wis. 517, 93 N.W. 440 (1903) (gift beneficiary); Starbird v. Cranston, 24 Colo. 20, 48 P. 652 (1897) (creditor beneficiary); Bay v. Williams, 112 Ill. 91, 1 N.E. 340 (1884) (creditor beneficiary).

[99] For a history of the rule applied in life insurance cases, see Page, *The Power of the Contracting Parties to Alter a Contract for Rendering Performance to a Third Person*, 12 WIS. L. REV. 141, 167–81 (1936). The rule was not applied to fraternal benefit association life insurance contracts because of statutes, as well as charter and by-law provisions. RESTATEMENT 2d § 311 comment c.

[100] FIRST RESTATEMENT § 142. The special rule relating to life insurance policies may be based on the assumption that a third party, such as a wife, may have sacrificed to pay premiums on such a policy and should, therefore, have an irrevocable right. *See* W. VANCE, LAW OF INSURANCE §§ 107 and 108 (3d ed. 1951).

[101] *See* Comment, *The Third Party Beneficiary Concept: A Proposal*, 57 COLUM. L. REV. 406 (1957).

[102] *See, however*, Biggins v. Shore, 523 Pa. 148, 565 A.2d 737 (1989) (majority insisted on retaining the immediate vesting rule suggesting that parties could otherwise agree).

any other context, the parties may, of course, agree that the rights of the third party may not be modified without consent.[103] Absent such an agreement, the question remains, at what point will the rights of the third party become irrevocable?

[2]   Vesting Upon Reliance

A second view espoused by other cases was that the rights do not vest until the third party relies on the contract made for his benefit.[104] This view is not without justification. If a beneficiary is unaware of the contract, he can have no expectations. Where is the injustice in permitting the promisor and promisee to modify or rescind their agreement at this point? It may even be suggested that *after* the beneficiary becomes aware of the contract, absent reliance, there is still no reason to deny the promisor and promisee the power of rescission or modification. This, however, is not the position that has been adopted by our courts.

[3]   Prevailing View — RESTATEMENT 2d

The RESTATEMENT 2d precludes any modification or rescission of the contract without the third party's consent where (1) the parties have so contracted,[105] or (2) where the third party materially changes his position on the promise, or (3) brings suit thereon, or (4) otherwise manifests assent to it.[106] An agreement named a third party as released from liability but was later modified to exclude that party. The court recognized his status as a third party beneficiary in the original contract but applied the Restatement 2d in holding that the promisor and promisee were free to modify the contract until the third party materially changed his position in reliance on the contract, brought suit, or otherwise manifested assent invited by the promisor or promisee. Since the third party was unaware of the contract until after it was modified, he had no enforceable third party beneficiary rights under the contract.[107]

---

[103] RESTATEMENT 2d § 311(1).

[104] *See, e.g.*, Sears Roebuck & Co. v. Jardel Co., 421 F.2d 1048 (3d Cir. 1970) (creditor beneficiary); Morstain v. Kircher, 190 Minn. 78, 250 N.W. 727 (1933) (creditor beneficiary); John F. Clark & Co. v. Nelson, 216 Ala. 199, 112 So. 819 (1927) (creditor beneficiary). The FIRST RESTATEMENT § 143(b) took the position that the rights of the creditor beneficiary vested if he brought suit or otherwise changed his position before he became aware of any modification or rescission of the contract. It also recognized vesting without reliance if the promisee's action would amount to a fraud on creditors.

[105] RESTATEMENT 2d § 311(1).

[106] RESTATEMENT 2d § 311. *See* Supplies for Indus., Inc. v. Christensen, 135 Ariz. 107, 659 P.2d 660 (Ct. App. 1983), where a contract between an employer and employee contained a covenant not to compete and the employer attempted to release the employee of his covenant. The court held such a release would have been valid except that it was executed after the employee's contract was assigned to the successor company which was a third party beneficiary of the contract between the company and employee and had vested rights in that contract. Detroit Inst. of Arts Founders Soc'y v. Rose, 127 F. Supp. 2d 117 (D. Conn. 2001) (plaintiff was a third party beneficiary of contract to deliver Howdy Doody puppet; rights vested in accordance with § 311); Olson v. Etheridge, 117 Ill. 2d 396, 686 N.E.2d 563, 226 Ill. Dec. 780 (1997) (adopting § 311); Genentech, Inc. v. Regents of the Univ. of Cal., 939 F. Supp. 639 (S.D. Ind. 1996) (applying § 311 and discussing the reliance concept); Burns v. GMC, Pontiac Div., 950 F. Supp. 137 (D. Md. 1996) (discussing vesting through filing an action). See, however, Biggins v. Shore, 523 Pa. 148, 565 A.2d 737 (1989), where the Pennsylvania Supreme Court, over a vigorous dissent, clings to the FIRST RESTATEMENT position and expressly rejects the adoption of the RESTATEMENT 2d position "merely to align ourselves with the 'weight of authority'." The holding was followed in Wareham by Trout v. Wareham, 716 A.2d 674 (Pa. Super. Ct. 1998).

[107] Rowan Cos. v. Acadian Ambulance Servs., 2008 U.S. Dist. LEXIS 36573 (S. D. Tex. 2008). *See also* Fleet Dev. Ventures LLC v. Brisker, 2008 U.S. Dist. LEXIS 66045 at *25 (D. Conn. 2008).

[a]   "Assent"

Unless the "assent" of the beneficiary is "in a manner invited by the promisee or promisor," the third party's rights may not be modified or discharged without his consent.[108] This view is predicated on making the third person a "party" to the contract to satisfy the old "privity" requirement. To make the beneficiary a "party" to the contract, it was necessary that he *assent* to the contract made for his benefit.[109] The *assent* rule is expressly based essentially on an offer and acceptance analogy.[110] In effect, the contract "offers" the benefit to the third party, who may "accept" it and thereby terminate the power of the promisor and promisee to modify or rescind it. Having "accepted" the "offer," the third person becomes a "party" to the contract who is, therefore, necessarily in "privity" — satisfying the classical requirements.[111]

The rationale is unconvincing. The ghost of "privity" haunts us from its grave. The notion of making the beneficiary a "party" to the contract inheres in the requirement that the beneficiary's assent must be invited by the promisee or promisor. If the third party learns of the contract for her benefit indirectly and manifests assent, why is that not sufficient?[112]

[b]   Bringing Suit

The justification for bringing suit to preclude the promisor and promisee from modifying or discharging the obligation to the third party is simple. It is viewed as nothing more than a "sufficient manifestation of assent."[113] Yet, such a lawsuit is hardly invited by either the promisor or promisee. There is no redeeming virtue in the perhaps unwitting result. Where a third party becomes aware of a contract which names him as an intended beneficiary, absent an invitation from the promisor or promisee, any attempt to *assent* other than by bringing suit will be ineffective. The method of bringing suit to "vest" the third party's rights may also result in unintended consequences. Where the driver of a Kawasaki motorcycle collided with a BFI truck, his settlement with BFI was evidenced by a release discharging BFI and all other persons, corporations and firms that might be liable. At the time of the release, Kawasaki was defending a products liability action brought by the driver. Kawaski amended its answer and moved for summary judgment claiming third party beneficiary status under the release. The court found that Kawasaki was a third party beneficiary under the release and its amended answer constituted "bringing suit" which precluded the promisor and promisee from modifying or discharging the obligation.[114]

---

[108] Restatement 2d § 311, comment h.

[109] "[U]ntil the third person brings himself into privity with the one who has promised to be his debtor by at least assenting thereto, he has no legal right to the benefit of the promise." *Tweeddale v. Tweeddale, supra* note 98, 93 N.W. at 441.

[110] Restatement 2d § 311, comment h.

[111] *See* Copeland v. Beard, 217 Ala. 216, 218, 115 So. 389, 391 (1928). Illustration 10 to Restatement 2d § 311 is expressly based on this case.

[112] Without elaboration, James v. Zurich-American Ins. Co., 203 F.3d 250, 257 (3d Cir.2000) held that assent would not be effective because it was not requested by the promisee or promisor Except in the case of an infant as discussed in the next section, assent will not be presumed. Detroit Bank & Trust Co. v. Chicago Flame Hardening Co., Inc., 541 F. Supp. 1278 (N.D. Ind. 1989) (mere knowledge is insufficient and court will not presume assent as it will in the case of an infant beneficiary).

[113] Restatement 2d § 311, comment h.

[114] Auer v. Kawasaki Motors Corp., 830 F.2d 535 (4th Cir. 1987), *cert. den.*, 485 U.S. 905 (1988).

[c]   Reliance

Without any invitation from the promisor or promisee, a material change of position in justifiable reliance on the contract by the beneficiary should certainly prevent any variation or discharge of the contract without the third party beneficiary's consent.[115] There is an argument that actual reliance by a third party should be the exclusive method of preventing any modification or discharge of her rights.[116] While the argument has superficial appeal, it would eliminate third party beneficiary rights. Since reliance on the part of a third person is now recognized as a protectable right under the promissory estoppel doctrine,[117] the third party beneficiary analysis would become superfluous. A contract between two parties could not create a "right" in a third party since no right would exist in a third party to enforce the contract absent reliance. If only reliance would create the obligation, enforcement would be limited to the extent of the reliance. The Supreme Court of Indiana recently found that logic persuasive in holding that, where reliance by a third party precludes modification of the contract, the reliance outweighs the rights of the contracting parties to modify the contract only to the extent of the reliance.[118] If, in addition to reliance, Indiana continues to recognize "assent" and "bringing suit" as alternate methods of precluding modification or discharge under the Restatement 2d, how would the remedy of a third party who merely assents to the contract in a manner invited by the promisor or promisee be treated? If such a third party would have his expectation interest protected by mere assent without any reliance, the inevitable question is why should such an assenting party be favored over a party who has suffered a detriment through reliance?

The Restatement 2d partially supports the "assent" theory through an argument for hypothetical reliance. In addition to the offer and acceptance analogy, the Second Restatement recognizes that the third party's reliance may be difficult to prove. Rather than place that burden on the beneficiary, his manifestation of assent is said to indicate a willingness to accept the benefits of the contract. Because he may begin to rely immediately upon the contract, his rights vest upon his assent.[119] This *possibility of reasonable reliance* concept is consistent with the RESTATEMENT 2d view that a test to determine whether a third party is a protected beneficiary is whether such a party would be reasonable in relying on the contract.[120]

Finally, if the promisor and promisee attempt to modify or rescind the contract after the beneficiary's rights have vested, the beneficiary is not subject to any defenses the promisor may assert against the promisee which affect the rights of the third party.[121]

---

[115] See Restatement 2d § 311, comment g. *See also,* Toll Bros. v. Century Surety Co., 2009 U.S. App. LEXIS 6243 (3d Cir. 2009).

[116] See Eisenberg, *supra* note 50, at 1418–19 suggesting a reliance test.

[117] *See* § 67[B][2], *supra.*

[118] City of East Chicago, Ind. v. East Chicago Second Century, Inc., 908 N. E. 2d 611, 625 (2009), pursuing suggestions by Professor Eisenberg, *id.*

[119] RESTATEMENT 2d § 311 comment h. *See also* Bridgman v. Curry, 398 N.W.2d 167 (Iowa 1986); Detroit Bank & Trust Co. v. Chicago Flame Hardening Co., 541 F. Supp. 1278 (N.D. Ind. 1982).

[120] *See* § 131[B][2][a], *supra.*

[121] *See* RESTATEMENT 2d § 309(3).

[C] Disclaimer of Benefit — Infant Beneficiaries

While assent will be sufficient to vest the ordinary third party's interest, the third party need not assent. He is like an offeree who may reject an offer, i.e., the third party may disclaim the benefit within a reasonable time after learning of it.[122] If he first assents and then disclaims, the disclaimer is effective only if it meets the requirements for discharge of a contractual duty.[123] While neither knowledge nor assent is necessary to give the beneficiary a right under the contract, if assent is not given after he learns of the contract, his right would appear to be revoked since he has chosen not to assent. In the case of an infant who lacks capacity, however, this inference is not justified. Some courts have concluded that the assent of an infant is *presumed.*[124] Where, however, a husband and wife orally contracted with an uncle to help the uncle with his farm in exchange for "good wages" and a promise to give the couple's six-year-old son a quarter section of land when the son became twenty-one years old, the promisor and promisees were allowed to modify the contract three years later without concern for the rights of the son. The court recognized that the rights of an infant beneficiary are sometimes presumed, but since the rights under the contract remained executory and the parties apparently did not intend that the son receive a vested interest for performing services for the uncle that any child would perform for a family member, the child's right did not vest when the oral contract was formed.[125]

§ 133 GOVERNMENT CONTRACTS — SURETYSHIP — MORTGAGE ASSUMPTION — WILLS

Whatever test a court chooses to apply in third party beneficiary cases, it is important to consider how courts decide upon third party beneficiary status in clusters of cases that manifest unusual issues.

[A] Government Contracts

Where government at the federal, state, or local level makes a contract, the contract is typically made for the benefit of the public.[126] The question arises, should any member of the public or a class of citizens have a cause of action against a promisor who fails to perform where the main or even exclusive purpose of the promisee-government in exacting the promise was to benefit its citizens? Justice Cardozo wrote, "In a broad sense it is true that every city contract, not improvident or wasteful, is for the benefit of the public. More than this, however, must be shown to give a right of action to a member of the public, not formally a party."[127] While government contracts benefit the public, individual members of the public are treated as incidental beneficiaries unless a different intention is manifested.[128]

---

[122] RESTATEMENT 2d § 306.

[123] RESTATEMENT 2d § 306 comment b referring to RESTATEMENT 2d § 37.

[124] *See* Plunkett v. Atkins, 371 P.2d 727 (Okla. 1962); Rhodes v. Rhodes, 266 S.W.2d 790 (Ky. 1953).

[125] Lehman v. Stout, 261 Minn. 384, 112 N.W.2d 640 (1961). *See also* RESTATEMENT 2d § 311 comment d.

[126] *See* Berberich v. United States, 5 Cl. Ct. 652 (1984), *aff'd, per curiam,* 770 F.2d 179 (Fed. Cir. 1985).

[127] H. R. Moch v. Rensselaer Water Co., 247 N. Y. 160, 164, 159 N. E. 2d 896, 897 (1928).

[128] Harris v. Aero Testing Alliance, 2008 U.S. Dist. LEXIS 1185 (E. D. Tenn. 2008). See also Mantie v. Inn at Manchester, 1997 Conn. Super. LEXIS 98 (Conn. Super. Ct. Jan. 9, 1997) (member of the "traveling public" alleged

The famous Cardozo opinion in *H.R. Moch Co. v. Rensselaer Water Co.*,[129] denied recovery to a property owner who brought an action as a third party beneficiary under a contract between the city and the water company for the latter's failure to maintain sufficient hydrant pressure which allegedly caused the citizen's house to burn down. There are a number of "water company" cases like *Moch* which have reached identical results.[130] The citizen in such cases is called an incidental beneficiary, which is a conclusion reached after deciding that the water company should not be held liable for other reasons. The same water company can be liable to a citizen beneficiary, however, with respect to the company's promise to provide household water at stated rates.[131] The distinction is said to be based on the fact that water rates are charged directly to citizens and where performance runs directly to a party, he should be a protected beneficiary.[132] This rationale, however, is not sufficient. The risk of the water company with respect to its promise to maintain rates no higher than stated levels is a risk that does not threaten the water company's existence so as to leave the city with no water.[133] If a water company or other public utility were subject to damages caused by its failure to maintain hydrant pressure, it may not be able to survive.[134] Insufficient water pressure could cause whole neighborhoods to burn. A policy judgment is made in such cases that it is preferable to have the water company survive and continue to serve the public, even in its defective fashion, than to treat a particular citizen as a third party beneficiary, particularly where that citizen can obtain fire insurance. The RESTATEMENT 2d suggests the same thought when it calls a direct action by a third party citizen "inappropriate" where there is a "likelihood of impairment of service" among other factors.[135] In case after case, members of the public are denied third party status under such contracts.[136] When an underground

---

that she was a third party beneficiary of a contract between defendant and the municipality concerning roadway improvements). *See* RESTATEMENT 2d § 313, comment a.

[129] 247 N.Y. 160, 159 N.E. 896 (1928).

[130] *See, e.g.*, Luis v. Orcutt Town Water Co., 204 Cal. App. 2d 433, 22 Cal. Rptr. 389 (2d Dist. 1962); Earl E. Roher Transfer & Storage Co. v. Hutchinson Water Co., 182 Kan. 546, 322 P.2d 810 (1958). *Contra* Potter v. Carolina Water Co., 253 N.C. 112, 116 S.E.2d 374 (1960).

[131] Pond v. New Rochelle Water Co., 183 N.Y. 330, 76 N.E. 211 (1906). Similarly, a cable TV subscriber may be viewed as a protected beneficiary of the contract between the municipality and the cable company with respect to announced rates. Bush v. Upper Valley Telecable Co., 96 Idaho 83, 524 P.2d 1055 (1974).

[132] *See* Touchberry v. Florence, 295 S.C. 47, 367 S.E.2d 149 (1988) (homeowner was protected beneficiary of contract between county and city to provide owner with water and sewer service since contract was made directly for his benefit).

[133] The current view of *Moch* is reflected in a New York lower court opinion: "The *Moch* court held that the failure to supply water constituted the denial of a benefit, but did not constitute an actionable wrong, essentially for public policy reasons of limiting utilities' tort liability." Hughes v. City of New York, 799 N. Y. S. 2d 161 (2002).

[134] *See* RESTATEMENT 2d § 313(2), stating that a promisor who contracts with a government or governmental agency is not subject to contractual liability to a member of the public for consequential damages, subject to exceptions that will be discussed *infra*.

[135] RESTATEMENT 2d § 313 comment a.

[136] *See, e.g.*, Angleton v. Pierce, 574 F. Supp. 719 (D.N.J. 1983), *aff'd, per curiam*, 734 F.2d 3 (3d Cir. 1984), *cert. denied*, 469 U.S. 880 (1984) (agreement between Department of Housing and Urban Development (HUD) and owner to create condos from rental units did not make tenants of those units third party beneficiaries, though the whole purpose of this governmental effort was to benefit parties such as these tenants); Schell v. National Flood Insurers Ass'n, 520 F. Supp. 150, 157–58 (D. Colo. 1981) (contract between Federal Government and NFIA did not create duty to inform public at large about flood insurance though existing policyholders may qualify as third party beneficiaries because of reliance — in this connection, see Beverly v. Macy, 702 F.2d 931 (11th Cir. 1983)); Gallagher v. Continental Ins. Co., 502 F.2d 827, 833 (10th Cir. 1974) (no third party beneficiary status for member of the public to enforce contract between state and contractor); Martinez v. Socoma Cos., 11 Cal. 3d 394, 521 P.2d 841 (1974) (failure of

water main burst flooded a utility power company's substation causing disrupting electrical service to the Manhattan garment industry during "Buyer's Week" when merchandisers from all of the world were visiting to place orders, more than fifty lawsuits against the utility were brought by plaintiffs who claimed third party beneficiary status. The court held that they are mere incidental beneficiaries.[137] The RESTATEMENT 2d, therefore, suggests that, the likelihood of impaired service, government control over litigation, the settlement of claims, and excessive financial burden are factors that must be considered in determining whether a third party should have a direct action against the promisor.[138]

Where there is language in the contract on which the courts might fasten an intention to benefit directly a member of the public, however, courts may declare the citizen a protected beneficiary.[139] A number of cases involve government consent decrees where third parties will necessarily have only incidental beneficiary status unless the decree itself stipulates that it can be enforced by a third party.[140] The RESTATEMENT 2d suggests that a citizen can become a protected beneficiary where the government has a duty to the citizen, the promisor undertakes that duty, and nothing in the contract precludes a direct action by the citizen. Thus, if a city owes a duty to keep streets in repair and contracts with another who promises to maintain the streets but fails to do so, a citizen whose injury occurs because of an unrepaired street will be a protected beneficiary, i.e., he will have a direct action against the promisor.[141] The breadth of such potential contractual liability, however, is not acceptable to all courts. Thus, where a citizen sustained a "slip and fall" and claimed rights as a third party

---

defendants (companies) to perform contracts with U.S. government to provide jobs for hard-core unemployed residents did not confer protected beneficiary status on those who the promisee (U.S.) sought to benefit). *Martinez* was distinguished, however, in Zigas v. Superior Court of the City and County of San Francisco, 120 Cal. App. 3d 827, 174 Cal. Rptr. 806 (1st Dist. 1981), *cert. denied*, 455 U.S. 943, 102 S. Ct. 1438, 71 L. Ed. 2d 655 (1982), where tenants claimed third party status under a contract between their landlords and the Department of Housing & Urban Development (HUD), claiming their landlords had not adhered to maximum rental schedules. The court distinguished *Martinez* (1) because that contract required a refund to the government whereas the landlord case involved a loss to the tenants; (2) the *Martinez* case involved bargained-for limited liability which did not exist in this case; (3) the purpose in *Martinez* was to provide training, not only for individuals, but for local enterprises and the government itself. Here, however, the contract was expressly designed to provide moderate rental housing for families with children.

[137] Milliken & Co. v. Consolidated Edison Co., 84 N. Y. 2d 69, 644 N. E. 2d 268 (1994). The same conclusion greeted plaintiffs who third party status for injuries suffered during another power failure. Shubitz v. Consolidated Edison Co., 59 Misc. 2d 732, 301 N.Y.S.2d 926 (1969).

[138] RESTATEMENT 2d § 313 comment a.

[139] See, e.g., Plantation Pipe Line Co. v. 3-D Excavators, Inc., 160 Ga. App. 756, 287 S.E.2d 102 (1981), where the court found language that it viewed sufficiently similar to the language of RESTATEMENT 2d § 313 ill. 3 to confer protected beneficiary status. The contract language in the illustration has a contractor promising to pay damages directly to any person who may be injured in the construction project. The language which the court felt sufficiently similar was, "Any damage to existing structures . . . shall be repaired or made good by the contractor at no expense to the owner." This language could be viewed as mere indemnity of the owner from any liability the owner would suffer. The court, however, provided a more liberal interpretation, thus creating protected beneficiary status. *See also* La Mourea v. Rhude, 209 Minn. 53, 295 N.W. 304 (1940) (plaintiff's property was injured by contractor's blasting and the contract contained a clause making the contractor liable for damage to public or private property). *See* RESTATEMENT 2d § 313(2)(a).

[140] Securities & Exchange Comm'n v. Prudential Secs., Inc., 136 F.3d 153 (D.C. Cir. 1998).

[141] *See* RESTATEMENT 2d § 313, illustration 5. See Fowler v. Chicago R. Co., 285 Ill. 196, 120 N.E. 635 (1918); Cleveland R. Co. v. Heller, 15 Ohio App. 346 (Cuyahoga County 1921); Phinney v. Boston E. R. Co., 201 Mass. 286, 87 N.E. 490 (1909). See also Matternes v. City of Winston-Salem, 286 N.C. 1, 209 S.E.2d 481 (1974), distinguishing these cases from its facts where the city contracted with the State Highway System to assist in maintaining certain roads. Plaintiffs alleged the failure of the city to perform its contract and argued as protected beneficiaries. The court held

beneficiary under a contract to remove snow and ice, the court was unpersuaded by the RESTATEMENT 2d or its illustration.[142]

[B]   Construction Contracts — Owners — Contractors — Subcontractors

To perform a construction contract, a general contractor enters into a contract with the owner and enters into separate contracts with subcontractors to provide labor and materials for various part of the project. Two third party beneficiary issues are raised by these contracts: (1) Is a subcontractor an intended third party beneficiary of the contract between the general contractor and the owner? (2) Is the owner a third party beneficiary of the contract between the general contractor and subcontractors?

The Halifax Corporation contracted with the City of Richmond to provide a computerized records management system. Halifax entered into a contract with BIS to meet certain requirements under the contract. Testing on the work partially completed revealed defects. The City terminated the remainder of the contract with no objection from Halifax. BIS claimed that, as a subcontractor, it had the status of a third party beneficiary under the contract between Halifax and the City. BIS received a judgment of $1.6 million at trial. On appeal, the court stated that the contract was analogous to the typical construction contract. Unless otherwise agreed, the sole intended beneficiaries of such a contract are the general contractor and the owner. Any third party such as subcontractors who benefit from such contracts are mere incidental beneficiaries with no enforceable right against a promisor such as the City in this case.[143]

While there have been a few cases recognizing the owner as a third party beneficiary of contracts between the general contractor and subcontractors, the better and apparently prevailing view is that owners are not intended beneficiaries of such contracts unless the parties have otherwise agreed. A subcontractor's performance does not discharge the duty of the general contractor. If the subcontractor's work is completed but the building is destroyed by fire before it is delivered to the owner, the general contractor must pay the subcontractor and replace the building for the owner. The owner, therefore, is not an intended beneficiary of the contract between the general contractor and subcontractor.[144]

[C]   Suretyship — Payment and Performance Bonds

Contractors understand that they must provide assurances of performance on any significant project with the government or a private party. It is common practice for owners to require contractors to obtain surety bonds to provide such assurance to the owner. The owner, therefore, has an additional promisor. The contractor as the principal obligor has promised to perform all of the duties under the contract and the bonding company is providing assurances

---

that the road was still a state road, notwithstanding the contract with the city, and, unlike the earlier cases cited, the city had no duty to the citizens to maintain a state road.

[142] Gazo v. City of Stamford, 255 Conn. 245, 765 A.2d 505, 517 (2001).

[143] BIS Computer Solutions, Inc. v. City of Richmond, 2005 U.S. App. LEXIS 651 (4th Cir. 2005).

[144] Nelson v. Anderson Lumber Co., 140 Idaho 709, 99 P.3d 1099 (2004). See also Outlaw v. Airtech Air Conditioning & Heating Inc., 412 F.3d 156 (D.C. Cir. 2005) (action by owner against subcontractor resulted in summary judgment for the subcontractor on the traditional view that, absent a different indication in the contract, property owners are not intended third party beneficiaries of contracts between general contractors and subcontractors).

if the contractor defaults. When he does default, he usually has no money and laborers and materialmen on the job are justifiably eager to discover someone to pay them. They would like to be viewed as third party beneficiaries. The bonding company has made a suretyship promise that it will ascertain *performance* of the contract if the contractor defaults. Such *performance* bonds are designed to benefit the owner. Labor and materialmen will not be protected beneficiaries of such contracts.[145]

In addition to performance bonds, however, owners require *payment* bonds. The question is whether payment bonds are designed simply to indemnify the owner against any loss he might suffer, or should be interpreted to create rights in third party labor and material suppliers against the bonding company. The situation has been made clear in government contracts which are exempt from mechanics' liens. Since laborers and materialmen cannot obtain such liens against the government, any payment bond can have only one purpose, i.e., the payment of these third parties, since the lien-immune government would have no other reason for insisting upon a payment bond. There are statutes requiring payment bonds in government contracts and some of the statutes make the protected beneficiary status of suppliers of labor and materials clear.[146]

In private contracts, the owner can be saddled with mechanic's liens if the contractor fails to pay its labor and material suppliers. In procuring a payment bond, the owner appears to be interested in protecting himself, rather than intending any benefit for third parties. If payment bonds are interpreted as only providing indemnity to the owner against such liens, thus saving him harmless for his liability, the laborers and materialmen become incidental beneficiaries.[147] While the language of a bond is critical, if a reasonable interpretation of the language allows, payment bonds will be interpreted as providing protected third party beneficiary status to labor and material suppliers even though they may also have the protection of mechanic's liens.[148]

---

[145] The distinction between performance and payment bonds and third party recovery under either is discussed in Stahlhut v. Sirloin Stockade, Inc., 568 S.W.2d 269 (Mo. Ct. App. 1978).

[146] See the Miller Act, 40 U.S.C. §§ 270a-270e, particularly subsection b. *See also* Carolina Builders Corp. v. AAA Dry Wall, Inc., 43 N.C. App. 444, 259 S.E.2d 364 (1979); H. H. Robertson Co. v. Globe Indem. Co., 268 Pa. 309, 112 A. 50 (1920).

[147] See Fidelity & Deposit Co. v. Rainer, 220 Ala. 262, 125 So. 55, 77 A.L.R. 13 (1929), where the language conditioned the obligation of the bond on the principal's payment of all persons who had contracts directly with the principal for labor and materials and third party beneficiary recoveries were allowed. In Ross v. Imperial Constr. Co., 572 F.2d 518 (5th Cir. 1978), the court distinguished *Fidelity* where the "completion guarantee" did not expressly commit the defendant to pay materialmen or suppliers and held them to be mere incidental beneficiaries.

[148] *See* Ceco Corp. v. Plaza Point, Inc., 573 S.W.2d 92, 94 (Mo. Ct. App. 1978), (intention to benefit third party subcontractors exists more frequently in payment bonds than performance bonds, citing the second edition of this treatise.) *See also* Board of Educ. of Community H.S. Dist. 99 v. Hartford Acc. & Indem. Co., 152 Ill. App. 3d 745, 504 N.E.2d 1000, 105 Ill. Dec. 715 (2d Dist. 1987); Autocon Indus., Inc. v. Western States Constr. Co., 728 P.2d 374 (Colo. Ct. App. 1986); Barbero v. Equitable Gen. Ins. Co., 607 P.2d 670 (Okla. 1980); Pennsylvania Supply Co. v. National Casualty Co., 152 Pa. Super. 217, 31 A.2d 453 (1943). In Hoiness-La Bar Ins. v. Julien Constr. Co., 743 P.2d 1262 (Wyo. 1987), the insurer mistakenly failed to issue a payment bond along with the performance bond which was issued, and court allowed recovery by third party beneficiary.

[D] The Mortgage Assumption Situation — "Subject to" — "Assuming," "Break in the Chain"

To understand the particular problem of third party beneficiaries in mortgage assumption situations, it is necessary to provide a sketch of the mechanics of assuming a mortgage indebtedness. A mortgage is a security interest in real property which is granted by the owner (mortgagor) to secure a loan made by a lender (mortgagee), such as a bank or other commercial lender. A prospective buyer of real estate will often seek to finance that purchase through a loan.[149] The lender will typically agree to lend the money only if the owner agrees to repay the loan with interest and to secure the loan by executing a mortgage on the property. Normally, the debt secured by the mortgage is significantly less than the value of the property. If the debt is not paid, the lender will attempt to collect from the owner. If the owner cannot pay, the lender (mortgagee) will initiate foreclosure proceedings by having the property sold to satisfy the debt.

Mortgaged real estate is common throughout the United States and it is quite common for an owner of mortgaged property to agree to sell that property. He cannot, however, sell it free of the mortgage which is publicly recorded.[150] When he sells his mortgaged property, what the owner is really selling is his "equity of redemption," i.e., that portion of the value of the property that he owns free of any encumbrance. Thus, e.g., if the mortgagor owns property worth $100,000 which is encumbered by a debt of $50,000, the mortgagor's "equity" in the property is $50,000. With this background sketch, it is possible to understand the operation of the third party beneficiary concept in this context.

First, assume that the owner-mortgagor (R) conveys the property to a grantee (X). There is nothing in the contract concerning the mortgage. The mortgage, however, does not disappear — it is still "attached to the land." If the outstanding mortgage debt is not paid, the mortgagee-bank (E) will foreclose, regardless of the conveyance from R to X. If the foreclosure sale produces sufficient funds to cover the debt and attendant costs of foreclosure, R has no liability. If, however, the land is sold at foreclosure for less than the outstanding debt owed to E,[151] E may recover a deficiency judgment against its debtor, R. X, the grantee, has lost the land. If, however, he did not promise to become liable on the mortgage indebtedness which his grantor (R) owed to the bank-mortgagee (E), X is not personally liable to E. In this situation, we say that X took "subject to" the mortgage between R and E. There was no mention of the mortgage debt in the contract between R and X. Again, however, X could not purchase the property free of that mortgage unless the debt had been satisfied. Since it was not satisfied, X took a conveyance of the property "subject to" the mortgage. Another way of stating the situation is that E was not a third party beneficiary of the contract between R and X, again, because X did not promise to become liable on that debt to E.

---

[149] The traditional transaction involved an indebtedness evidenced by a promissory note or bond payable to the lender in the amount of the mortgage loan plus interest.

[150] Where mortgaged property is sold, the typical mortgage agreement will contain a "due on sale" clause (acceleration clause) whereby the entire outstanding amount of the mortgage debt will become due under this clause when the mortgaged property is sold. As to the enforceability of such clauses, see Annot., 61 A.L.R.4th 1070 (1988).

[151] Land values may depreciate and the depreciation may be rapid and substantial as evidenced by the value of farm land in parts of the United States. The farm foreclosures that have occurred in recent years are a strong, albeit sad, illustration of this possibility.

If we now assume that the conveyance from R to X recited that X "assumes and agrees to pay" the mortgage debt to E which is not uncommon in land transactions, and we further assume that the mortgage debt was not paid in full, E may sue X, who has become personally liable for the payment of that debt. E is a third party ("creditor") beneficiary of the contract between R and X because X has agreed to pay R's debt to E. The promisee (R) has induced X to promise a performance to E and R intends E to be a third party beneficiary of the contract.[152] If X does not perform by satisfying the debt, E *may still bring an action against R* who has not been released from his indebtedness to E.[153] R, however, is no longer the principal debtor. X became the principal debtor when he "assumed" the mortgage debt and R became a surety for the payment of that debt. If X does not satisfy the indebtedness to E, E may foreclose on his security, the mortgage, and the property will be sold. If the selling price at the foreclosure sale is sufficient to cover the outstanding debt and attendant foreclosure costs, the debt will be satisfied and neither R nor X would be liable though X, of course, would have lost the property. If the selling price were not sufficient, however, *e.g.*, land values had declined, E would then be entitled to recover the amount of any deficiency from X. If X failed to pay the deficiency, R, the surety, would be liable thereon. If R paid the deficiency, he would be paying an amount that X should have paid and R would stand in the shoes of E as the creditor of X. We say that R, in that situation, is *subrogated* to the rights of E who has been satisfied.[154] If X were incapable of paying E, it is unlikely that R will have much luck in collecting any judgment from X. R, however, is entitled to recover from X the amount R paid to E.

[1]   "Break in the Chain of Assumption"

A problem that has caused significant difficulty occurs where R conveys to X who "assumes" the mortgage debt, X conveys to Y who takes "subject to" the mortgage, and Y conveys to Z who "assumes" the debt. There has been a "break in the chain of assumption." E was a creditor beneficiary of the contract between R and X, but he was not a creditor beneficiary of the contract between X and Y since Y failed to assume the indebtedness and was not personally liable to E. When Y sold to Z and Z assumed the indebtedness, is Z liable to E notwithstanding the break in the chain of assumption that occurred when Y took the property only "subject to" the mortgage, instead of assuming the debt?

There is considerable difficulty in understanding the motivation of Y, who was not personally liable, in asking Z to become personally liable on the mortgage debt to E. Unless Y *sought to make a gift to the mortgagee*, E, Y's intention to benefit E is questionable. It is unlikely that a

---

[152] See Joyner v. Vitale, 926 P.2d 1154, 1157 (Alaska 1996), where the court states that a mortgagee may recover, as a third party beneficiary, from a purchaser who assumed the mortgage. *See also* Bridgman v. Curry, 398 N.W.2d 167 (Iowa 1986).

[153] *If E* had agreed to accept X in substitution for R as E's exclusive debtor, R would have been released at the time the contract was formed. At that moment, the only debtor and creditor relationship would have been one between X and E. The consideration to E would be the new duty created in X and the consideration to X would be the property which he owns through the conveyance from R. R would receive consideration in the release from E. Where such a tri-partite contract is formed — where the creditor releases one debtor and takes another in substitution-the contract is called a *novation*, which is not a third-party beneficiary contract since, at the moment of formation, only two parties have a legal relationship. Novation is one of several methods of discharging a contractual obligation.

[154] Subrogation allows the restitution interest to be protected. R has paid a debt to E that X should have paid to E. X has, therefore, been unjustly enriched at R's expense. By allowing R to be "subrogated" to E, i.e., standing in the shoes of E, R may recover the amount paid to E from X who has been unjustly enriched at R's expense.

private party would be interested in making a gift to a bank. If the mortgagee is a party other than a stranger, it is possible to discover a gratuitous intention.[155] The recorded case law in this area is in conflict. Some courts have allowed the mortgagee to enforce the agreement as written on the footing that the mortgagee is a gift beneficiary.[156] Courts denying recovery have not agreed on the rationale. Some have viewed the right of a beneficiary as necessarily growing out of the doctrine of subrogation which would be applicable only where the beneficiary is a creditor of the promisee.[157] Others have apparently treated the contract as though it had been reformed to call merely for the indemnification of the grantor, and have accordingly reached the conclusion that the mortgagee is a mere incidental beneficiary.[158] Where the language of the contract expresses the intention of the parties, of course, there is every reason for permitting the beneficiary to enforce the promise.[159]

The RESTATEMENT 2d suggests two possibilities to deal with the "break in the chain of assumption" situation. If the last assuming grantee had agreed to pay the mortgage debt with knowledge of all of the facts, i.e., knowledge of the break in the chain, that grantee is liable to the mortgagee — the mortgagee is a protected beneficiary.[160] If, however, the assuming grantee can show by clear and convincing evidence that the scrivener of the deed inserted the grantee's promise to pay the debt by mistake contrary to the true intention of the grantor and grantee, the equitable remedy of reformation would lie so as to reform the writing to state the true intentions of the parties and the mortgagee would not be a protected beneficiary.[161] The last illustration, however, is conditioned on the absence of any change in the circumstances making reformation inequitable. It should be recalled that, under the RESTATEMENT 2d, as contrasted with the FIRST RESTATEMENT, unless there is an *actual* money obligation owed by the promisee to the third party, the third party cannot be a "creditor" beneficiary. On the other hand, the second category of protected beneficiaries under the RESTATEMENT 2d, albeit labeled "gift" beneficiaries, is much broader than the FIRST RESTATEMENT's donee category.[162] That category would include a third party who "would be reasonable in relying on the promise as manifesting an intention to confer a right on him."[163] As suggested in the earlier analysis of this

---

[155] *See* Schneider v. Ferrigno, 110 Conn. 86, 147 A. 303 (1929) (promisee intended to benefit brother-in-law).

[156] *See* Corkrell v. Poe, 100 Wash. 625, 171 P. 522, 12 A.L.R. 1524 (1918). Additional cases are collected in Annot., 12 A.L.R. 1537 (1921). See also *Schneider v. Ferrigno, supra* note 155, where at 147 A. at 304, the opinion reads, "If the grantor of the equity of redemption who has not assumed the mortgage has no object to protect himself, an intent to confer a right to sue upon the holder of the mortgage would be the most natural motive to assign to him in requiring his grantee to agree to pay it."

[157] *See* Vrooman v. Turner, 69 N.Y. 280 (1877). It should be recalled that this case limited the landmark case of *Lawrence v. Fox* to its facts, i.e., to creditor beneficiaries. *See supra* § 130[C]. Other cases are collected in Annot., 12 A.L.R. 1531 (1921).

[158] *See, e.g.,* Fry v. Ausman, 29 S.D. 30, 135 N.W. 708 (1912).

[159] See Federal Bond & Mortg. Co. v. Shapiro, 219 Mich. 13, 188 N.W. 465 (1922), where a grantor was not liable on the first mortgage but had granted a second mortgage on the land for which he was liable. Thus, he had a real interest in having the first mortgage satisfied since its payment would minimize the possibility of his having to pay any deficiency on the second mortgage. In such a case, the contract should be given effect according to its terms and the beneficiary allowed to enforce it as held by the Michigan court. *See also* FIRST RESTATEMENT § 144 ill. 2.

[160] RESTATEMENT 2d § 312 ill. 3.

[161] RESTATEMENT 2d § 312 ill. 4.

[162] *See supra* § 131[B][1].

[163] *See* RESTATEMENT 2d § 312 comment a, referring to §§ 302 and 304 and comments to those sections. In § 304 comment e, the reliance factor is separated from others: "In cases of doubt, the question whether such an intention [to benefit the third party] is to be attributed to the promisee may be influenced by the likelihood that recognition of

concept, actual reliance is not necessary, i.e., the test is whether a third party would be reasonable in relying on the promise. If a deed evidenced an assumption of the debt by the grantee notwithstanding a break in the chain, a mortgagee might be reasonable in relying thereon even in the mistake situation. Absent actual reliance, however, reformation may be granted to deprive the mortgagee of protected beneficiary status.

[E]   Beneficiaries and Statute of Wills

Where a contract conditions the right of a beneficiary upon his surviving the promisee, some courts found insuperable difficulty in protecting such a beneficiary. They were concerned that the contract was an attempt to make a testamentary disposition of the property without complying with the Statute of Wills and was, therefore, nugatory. There never was any justification for such a holding which involved a confusion of thought concerning property rights and contract rights. A contract does not purport to dispose of existing rights; rather, it creates a right to performance that did not previously exist. The Statute of Wills, therefore, is not applicable. The fact that a contract right may be contingent on the death of the promisee is immaterial. Moreover, when the testamentary policy behind typical statutes of wills is considered, the matter is even more clear. Cases which had discovered such problems are now viewed as something of an embarrassment.[164]

§ 134   CUMULATIVE RIGHTS — DEFENSES

[A]   Cumulative Rights of Beneficiary

A third party "gift" or "donee" beneficiary typically has a cause of action only against the promisor for his failure of performance.[165] Since the promisee owes nothing to a gift beneficiary, the donee beneficiary has no claim against the promisee. A creditor beneficiary, on the other hand, has two sources of satisfaction. The question arises, if the beneficiary chooses to bring an action against the promisor, has he "elected" to surrender any rights he had against the promisee, his original debtor? A few older cases proceeded on the footing that the creditor beneficiary's election to bring an action against the promisor was, in effect, the acceptance of an offer of novation which released the promisee. If he chose to pursue the promisee on the original obligation, he was viewed as rejecting the offer of novation and

---

the right will further the legitimate expectations of the promisee, make available a simple and convenient procedure for enforcement, or *protect the beneficiary in his reasonable reliance on the promise.*" (Emphasis added.).

[164] See, e.g., McCarthy v. Pieret, 281 N.Y. 407, 24 N.E.2d 102 (1939), which was strictly limited to its facts in *In re* Estate of Hillowitz, 22 N.Y.2d 107, 291 N.Y.S.2d 325, 238 N.E.2d 723 (1968) (in the event of the death of a partner, his share will be transferred to his wife — wife considered protected beneficiary). Decker v. Fowler, 199 Wash. 549, 92 P.2d 254 (1939), was also confused about third party beneficiary contracts and the Wills Statute. In Toulouse v. New York Life Ins. Co., 40 Wash. 2d 538, 245 P.2d 205 (1952), the court announced that the *Decker* view was changed by statute and went on to admit that the overwhelming weight of authority was opposed to *Decker*. There was authority for what has clearly become the prevailing view at the time of *McCarthy* and *Decker*. See, e.g., Franklin Washington Trust Co. v. Beltram, 133 N.J. Eq. 11, 29 A.2d 854 (Super. Ct. 1943); *In re* Di Santo's Estate, 142 Ohio St. 223, 51 N.E.2d 639 (1943); Warren v. United States, 68 Ct. Cl. 634 (1929), *cert. denied*, 281 U.S. 739, 50 S. Ct. 346, 74 L. Ed. 1154 (1930).

[165] It should be recalled that the promisor and promisee may vary or even rescind the contract without the consent of the beneficiary until the rights of the beneficiary "vest." If the variation or rescission is wrongful and the promisee received consideration for such variation or rescission, the beneficiary may be entitled to that consideration or part thereof to avoid the unjust enrichment of the promisee. See RESTATEMENT 2d § 311(4) and comment j thereto.

surrendering his right to enforce the contract made for his benefit.[166]

There never was any basis for this approach which apparently arose in still another attempt to find that the third party was in privity which, as we have seen, is a term used as a conclusory label after a court decides that a third party is a protected beneficiary. In the normal third party (creditor) beneficiary situation, there is no thought that the third party is surrendering the promisee as the original obligor. The promisee does become a surety as the promisor becomes the principal debtor.[167] Surety status, however, does not relieve the promisor of his obligation.[168] The third party is not even required to bring an action first against the promisor.[169] If the creditor decides to recover from the promisee and the promisee satisfies the debt, the promisee may then recover from the promisor who, as principal debtor, was supposed to pay the third party. If, however, the beneficiary brings an action against either promisor or promisee and does not achieve satisfaction of the outstanding debt, he may then bring an action against the other party for the balance of the debt.[170] The beneficiary may join the promisor and promisee in the same action and obtain a judgment against both though he is entitled to only one satisfaction.[171]

[B] Promisee's Right to Enforce the Promise

Third party beneficiaries are usually quite willing to enforce promises made on their behalf. On occasion, a promisee will attempt to enforce the promise. Since the promisee must intend to benefit the third party to enable that party to have an actionable right against the promisor, should the promisee be permitted to sue the promisor?

Where the beneficiary is a "gift" beneficiary, the promisee expects no measurable benefit to himself. He does, however, have a significant interest in ascertaining that the promise for which he has parted with consideration is performed. Where the third party does not attempt to enforce the promise, the promisee may secure a decree of specific performance of the promise for the third party's benefit since it is clear that the promisee has no adequate remedy at law.[172] Where a promisee does not pursue specific performance, but pays the third

---

[166] Wood v. Moriarity, 15 R.I. 518, 9 A. 427 (1887); Bohanan v. Pope, 42 Me. 93 (1856).

[167] This situation was explored with respect to the mortgagee (creditor) beneficiary, *supra* § 133[D].

[168] Once the beneficiary is aware of the suretyship, he cannot avoid it since, without his consent, a contract of suretyship has occurred. If, therefore, the beneficiary would simply release the promisor, on the face of it, it would appear that he has also released the promisee-surety. Unless, therefore, the surety has consented to remain liable on the original obligation, or the beneficiary has expressly reserved rights against the promisee, the promisee's duty would be discharged. If the beneficiary decides to modify the duty of the promisor, such a modification could result in augmenting the risk of the promisee. Courts will not impose greater risks upon promisees under these circumstances, i.e., they will enforce the promisee's (surety's) duties only to the extent that they have not been enhanced by modifications of the promisor's duty over which the promisee-surety had no control. *See* RESTATEMENT 2d § 314.

[169] RESTATEMENT OF SECURITY § 130. Section 131, however, suggests the possibility of great hardship to the promisor, which may require the creditor beneficiary to use the promisor's available assets before seeking relief from the surety-promisee.

[170] *See* Erickson v. Grand Ronde Lumber Co., 162 Or. 556, 94 P.2d 139 (1939). *See also* Albert Steinfeld & Co. v. Wing Wong, 14 Ariz. 336, 128 P. 354 (1912); Webster v. Fleming, 178 Ill. 140, 52 N.E. 975 (1899); Davis v. National Bank of Commerce, 45 Neb. 589, 63 N.W. 852 (1895).

[171] *See* Kraus v. Willow Park Pub. Golf Course, 73 Cal. App. 3d 354, 140 Cal. Rptr. 744 (1st Dist. 1977) (filing claims in bankruptcy proceeding did not preclude creditor beneficiaries from pursuing their rights against promisor). *See also* RESTATEMENT 2d § 310.

[172] *See In re* Marriage of Smith & Maescher, 21 Cal. App. 4th 100, 26 Cal. Rptr. 2d 133, 137 (4th Dist. 1993); Stevens

party donee beneficiary's expenses, she may be relegated to nominal damages if she had no obligation to pay such expenses since she may not recover damages suffered by the third party.[173]

Where the third party is a creditor beneficiary, the promisee's pecuniary interest in the performance of the promise is clear since that performance will satisfy his obligation to the third party. Beyond these obvious damages, the promisee may suffer additional damages because the promisor has failed to perform.[174] The modern view is that the promisee has a cause of action against the promisor.[175] Older cases taking a contrary view were concerned about "privity" and indulged the fallacy that the contract created an offer of novation to the beneficiary. When he "accepted" this offer, he was deemed to be substituted for the promisee so that only an action against the promisor would lie.[176] A more serious concern was the risk of double liability to the promisor. Since the promisee may recover the amount of the debt from the defaulting promisor before the promisee pays the creditor beneficiary (which he may never do),[177] the promisor would still be liable to the creditor beneficiary. There are various solutions to the problem. An action by the promisee could simply be barred.[178] There is, however, no justifiable basis for barring the promisee's action. Another solution is to bar the promisee from recovering the amount of the debt from the promisor unless and until he first pays the beneficiary. There is some case law support for this view, though courts refusing to permit recovery prior to payment often suggest that the promisee has no right to recover for the promisor's breach, i.e., the promisee may seek reimbursement of payments made since he has become a mere surety for the payment of the debt and is liable on an implied promise to indemnify.[179] This is an unfortunate analysis since, as we have already seen, the promisee may

---

v. Stevens, 798 S.W.2d 136, 139 (Ky. 1990) (father breached agreement to pay for daughter's education and mother (promisee) had standing to sue); Drewen v. Bank of Manhattan Co., 31 N.J. 110, 155 A.2d 529 (1959). Parents executed divorce agreement which required father to leave a certain portion of his estate to the son. After executing that will in satisfaction of the contract, the father changed the will leaving a much smaller portion of his estate to the son, but including an *in terrorem* clause which would have deprived the son of the smaller legacy should he contest the will. Court granted decedent promisee's representative specific performance of the contract. *See also* Croker v. New York Trust Co., 245 N.Y. 17, 156 N.E. 81 (1927) (promisee permitted to sue for specific performance in a gift-beneficiary case since promisee's remedy at law was inadequate having suffered no damages as a result of the breach). *See* RESTATEMENT 2d § 307.

[173] Hawkins v. Gilbo, 663 A. 2d 9 (Me. 1995) (promisee who could have sued for specific performance cannot collect expenses which she voluntarily paid for the third party).

[174] *See* Miholevich v. Mid-West Mut. Auto Ins. Co., 261 Mich. 495, 246 N.W. 202 (1933) (where insurance company wilfully delayed payment of a judgment against the insured and the insured was imprisoned under a body execution which was permitted at the time of this case).

[175] *See* Petit v. Country Life Homes, Inc., 2009 Del. Super. LEXIS 139; Hikita v. Nichiro Gyogyo Kaisha, Ltd., 713 P.2d 1197, 1200 (Alaska 1986) (individual shareholder may sue for breach of a shareholders agreement intended to benefit corporation). *See also* Buschmann v. Professional Men's Ass'n, 405 F.2d 659 (7th Cir. 1969); Dann v. Studebaker-Packard Corp., 288 F.2d 201 (6th Cir. 1961); Eden v. Miller, 37 F.2d 8 (2d Cir. 1930); RESTATEMENT 2d § 305.

[176] *See* North Ala. Dev. Co. v. Short, 101 Ala. 333, 13 So. 385 (1893) (dictum).

[177] *See* Heins v. Byers, 174 Minn. 350, 219 N.W. 287 (1928). *See also* Jones v. Bates, 241 S.C. 189, 127 S.E.2d 618 (1962).

[178] Some courts have held that the promisee may not bring an action against the promisor. They do consider the promisee to be a surety, however, and, if he has paid the creditor-beneficiary, the promisee may be reimbursed by the principal debtor-promisor. *See* John Deere Plow Co. v. Tuinstra, 47 S.D. 555, 200 N.W. 61 (1924); Poe v. Dixon, 60 Ohio St. 124, 54 N.E. 86 (1899).

[179] *See, e.g.,* White v. Upton, 255 Ky. 562, 74 S.W.2d 924 (1934); Thomsen v. Kopp, 204 Iowa 1176, 216 N.W. 725 (1927); Lowry v. Hensal's Heirs, 281 Pa. 572, 127 A. 219 (1924).

suffer consequential damages resulting from the promisor's failure to perform which should always be recoverable regardless of any prior payment to the beneficiary by the "surety"-promisee. More effective and just solutions are available to modern courts, which can infuse equitable notions into the relief granted to avoid double liability to the promisor and simultaneously insure that the promisee has a cause of action where that is necessary. Thus, in an action by the promisee, a court could insist that the judgment awarded, at least in terms of the debt owed, must be paid to the creditor beneficiary.[180] When sued by either the third party or the promisee, the promisor could interplead the other party to whom it may also be liable, or simply pay the amount owed into the court and permit the court to determine who should receive it. While a single payment will ordinarily discharge the promisor's duties to both the third party and promisee,[181] again, the possibility of consequential damages to the promisee through the promisor's failure of performance allows a separate, as contrasted with double, recovery.

[C]   Promisor's Defenses Against Beneficiary

[1]   Defenses on the Contract

The right of a third party beneficiary can exist only when a contract has been made by the promisor and promisee. The rights of a third party, therefore, rise no higher than that of a promisee. Contractual terms define and limit the rights a third party beneficiary may have.[182] With certain exceptions discussed below, all defenses that the promisor would have against the promisee on the original contract are available to the promisor against the third party beneficiary.[183] If there is a lack of mutual assent,[184] consideration, or capacity, the beneficiary is subject to such defenses.[185] Defenses of fraud,[186] breach of express[187] or constructive[188] conditions, mistake,[189] or failure of performance[190] are also included. If the promisor was

---

[180] *See Heins v. Byers, supra* note 177.

[181] RESTATEMENT 2d § 305 comment b.

[182] Cathay, Inc. v. Vindalu, 962 A. 2d 740, 746 (R. I. 2009) (third party rights are limited by the terms of the contract). *See also* Haas v. DaimlerChrysler Corp., 611 N.W.2d 382, 395 (Minn. Ct. App. 2000), *cert. denied*, 121 S. Ct. 781, 148 L. Ed. 2d 678 (2001).

[183] *See, e.g.*, General Ins. Co. of Am. v. Interstate Serv. Co., Inc., 118 Md. App. 126, 701 A.2d 1213, 1218 (1997); Seaboard Sur. Co. v. Garrison, Webb & Stanaland, P.A., 823 F.2d 434 (11th Cir. 1987); District Moving & Storage Co. v. Gardiner & Gardiner, Inc., 63 Md. App. 96, 492 A.2d 319 (1985); Martin v. John Hancock Mut. Life Ins. Co., 120 Misc. 2d 776, 466 N.Y.2d 596 (Sup. Ct. 1983); United States v. Industrial Crane & Mfg. Corp., 492 F.2d 772 (5th Cir. 1974). *See also* RESTATEMENT 2d § 309.

[184] Culbro Land Resources, Inc. v. Casle Corp., 1997 Conn. Super. LEXIS 3540, at *4 (Conn. Super. Ct. Dec. 29, 1997).

[185] *See* Lawhead v. Booth, 115 W. Va. 490, 177 S.E. 283 (1934); Barlow Grain & Stock Exch. v. Nilson, 57 N.D. 624, 223 N.W. 700 (1929); Kuske v. Jevne, 174 Minn. 484, 219 N.W. 766 (1928); Wainwright Trust Co. v. Prudential Life Ins. Co., 80 Ind. App. 37, 134 N.E. 913 (1922).

[186] *See* Ashmore v. Herbie Morewitz, Inc., 225 Va. 141, 475 S.E.2d 271 (1996), *cert. denied*, 520 U.S. 1120, 117 S. Ct. 1254, 137 L. Ed. 2d 335 (1997).

[187] J. C. B. Dev., Inc. v. TCC Ctr. Cos., 1992 Minn. App. LEXIS 40 (Minn. Ct. App. Jan. 14, 1992).

[188] Guscott v. City of Boston, 1992 U.S. App. LEXIS 28959 (1st Cir. Mar. 25, 1992).

[189] Broadbent v. Hutter, 163 Wis. 380, 157 N.W. 1095 (1916); Rogers v. Castle, 51 Minn. 428, 53 N.W. 651 (1892).

[190] Connors v. Mulvehill, 679 F. Supp. 1071 (N.D. Ala. 1988); Conrad v. Thompson, 137 Cal. App. 2d 73, 290 P.2d 36 (4th Dist. 1955); Duncan v. Nowell, 27 Ariz. 451, 233 P. 582 (1925).

entitled to arbitration in any dispute with the promisee, she is entitled to arbitration in any dispute on the same contract with the third party.[191] It is important to emphasize that the right of a protected beneficiary is direct and not merely derivative, i.e., while any defenses arising out of the contract which will benefit the third party are available to the promisor, claims and defenses of the promisee arising out of separate transactions between the promisor and promisee have no effect on the third party.[192] Since the right of the third party is direct, it is subject to any claim or defense arising out of the beneficiary's own conduct or agreement.[193]

[2]   Breach by Promisee — Setoffs

Among the defenses available to the promisor, we have included failure of performance by the promisee. Whether the promisor may avail himself of setoffs that would have been available against the promisee is a different question. If the promisee's breach is one that does not discharge the promisor's duty, should he be allowed to reduce the beneficiary's recovery through a setoff? The prevailing view is that the setoff will be permitted if it arises from the same transaction, but not from separate transactions between the promisor and promisee.[194]

[3]   Exceptions

[a]   Contract Precludes Defenses — Statute of Limitations

There are exceptions to the rule that the beneficiary is subject to the defenses the promisor would have been able to assert against the promisee. The obvious exception occurs where the contract expressly provides that the promisor's duty will not be subject to certain defenses. A hospital third party beneficiary was not subject to certain defenses where the contract so stated.[195] In a fire insurance contract, the loss payable clause usually recites that the mortgagee may recover the insured amount of the loss even though the mortgagor has failed to perform certain conditions.[196] Where the contract provided that the warranty was extended only to the first purchaser of a vehicle, but could be extended to a second purchaser who met certain conditions, the third party had no enforceable rights under that warranty if the conditions were not met.[197] If the contract reduces the statute of limitations for the promisee, it is reduced for the beneficiary.[198] If the contract is silent with respect to the statute of

---

[191] See Johnson v. Pennsylvania Nat'l Ins. Cos., 527 Pa. 504, 594 A.2d 296, 299 (1991). See also Benton v. Vanderbilt University, 137 S. W. 3d 614 (Tenn. 2004). The contract language, however, may be interpreted to limit arbitration to the original parties, the promisor and promisee. In City of Peru v. Illinois Power Co., 258 Ill. App. 3d 309, 630 N. E. 2d 454 (1994) (the contract stated required arbitration between "parties" and the court found that the definition of "party" in the agreement did not include the beneficiary).

[192] See RESTATEMENT 2d § 309 comment c.

[193] See Swiss Reinsurance Am. Co. v. Airport Indus. Park, Inc., 2009 U.S. App. LEXIS 9701 (3d Cir. 2009).

[194] See *United States v. Industrial Crane & Mfg. Corp.*, *supra* note 183, where the court permitted an offset of damages based on the promisee's breach of a covenant not to compete which was not an independent transaction. See also Fulmer v. Goldfarb, 171 Tenn. 218, 101 S.W.2d 1108 (1937). The RESTATEMENT 2d supports this view. See § 309 comment c.

[195] Sisters of St. Joseph of Peace, Health, & Hosp. Servs. v. Russell, 318 Or. 370, 867 P.2d 1377, 1383 (1994).

[196] See Goldstein v. National Liberty Ins. Co. of Am., 256 N.Y. 26, 175 N.E. 359 (1931).

[197] See *DaimlerChrysler*, *supra* note 182 (second purchaser can procure remaining warranty coverage by having the Chrysler dealer submit a "transfer of coverage" application at a cost of $150 to the second purchaser).

[198] See Barr v. McGraw-Hill, Inc., 710 F. Supp. 95 (S.D.N.Y. 1989); Hercules, Inc. v. Stevens Shipping Co., 629 F.2d

limitations, however, the better view is that the statute does not begin to run until the third party is aware of the breach.[199]

[b] Promisee's Liability vs. Absolute Promise

A situation that appears quite similar occurs where the contract requires the promisor to perform a certain duty and there is a question as to whether the promisor must *discharge the liability* of the promisee, or make a certain payment to the third party *regardless of the promisee's liability*. What has become a well-known case illustrates the distinction. The promisor assumed payment of $850 for a heating plant as part of the contract to purchase a house. When payment was demanded, the promisor asserted a defense of incorrect installation of the heating plant. The court refused to permit this defense because it interpreted the assumption of the indebtedness in the contract as an absolute obligation regardless of the liability of the promisee. If the contract language had committed the promisor to discharge any liability of the promisee for the heating plant, the defense would have been available to the promisor.[200] Other courts agree, in conformity with Professor Corbin's analysis: "There is nothing to prevent a promisor from undertaking a larger duty than the duty owed by the promisee to the beneficiary. . . . If he promises to pay a third party a sum claimed by him against the promisee, irrespective of defenses that the promisee may have, he is bound by his promise in the teeth of those defenses."[201]

[c] Employee Benefit Plans — National Labor Policy

The most significant policy exception involves collective bargaining agreements which require employers to make payments to certain funds for the benefit of employees who are the union members. The members may be in no position to prevent actionable wrongs committed by their union. If the employer was able to raise such defenses, the employee-beneficiaries could be deprived of the fund created for their benefit. As one court observed, early in the history of pension and welfare plans, the Supreme Court established that breach by the union would not relieve the employer of its obligation to make pension contributions.[202]

---

418 (5th Cir. 1980). See also UCC § 2-725(1), permitting parties to agree to reduce statute of limitations period to no less than one year, but precluding them from extending it beyond the four-year term.

[199] See Sodora v. Sodora, 2000 N.J. Super. LEXIS 476 (N.J. Super. Ct. Ch. Div. Dec. 18, 2000), which adopts "discovery" view though recognizing that it is not uniformly followed. *See, e.g.,* Skylawn v. Superior Court of Solano County, 88 Cal. App. 3d 316, 151 Cal Rptr. 793 (1st Dist. 1979).

[200] *See* Rouse v. United States, 215 F.2d 872, 94 U.S. App. D.C. 386 (1954). *See also* XL Disposal Corp. v. John Sexton Contractors Co., 168 Ill. 2d 355, 213 Ill. Dec. 665, 659 N.E.2d 1312 (1995).

[201] CORBIN, CONTRACTS § 46.8, quoted from an earlier edition in Nu-Way Plumbing, Inc. v. Superior Mech., Inc., 315 So. 2d 556, 557 (Fla. Dist. Ct. App. 1975). The RESTATEMENT 2d suggests that "a promise to render a performance whether or not there is a pre-existing duty is effective according to its terms. *Prima facie* an unqualified promise to render the performance has the same effect, but mistake as to the existence of the duty may make the contract voidable." RESTATEMENT 2d § 312 comment b. This is, essentially, the same analysis of the mortgage assumption situation where there has been a break in the chain of assumption. *See supra* § 133[D].

[202] Central States, SE & SW Areas Pension Fund v. Gerber Truck Serv., Inc., 870 F.2d 1148 (7th Cir. 1989) (referring to Lewis v. Benedict Coal Corp., 361 U.S. 459, 80 S. Ct. 489, 4 L. Ed. 2d 442 (1960)). *See also* Cement & Concrete Workers Dist. Council Welfare Fund v. Frascone, 68 F. Supp. 2d 166, 177 (E.D.N.Y. 1999); Goldies, Inc. v. Alaska Hotel & Restaurant Employees Health & Welfare Fund, 622 P.2d 979 (Alaska 1981), and cases cited therein.

§ 135 "THIRD PARTY BENEFICIARIES" UNDER THE UNIFORM COMMERCIAL CODE — PRODUCTS LIABILITY — HORIZONTAL AND VERTICAL PRIVITY

The typical remedy for bodily injury caused by a defective product is the tort products liability remedy under Section 402A of the Restatement 2d of Torts. Prior to the wide adoption of that concept by courts throughout the country, the injured party could bring a tort action against the manufacturer of the product without any concern for the notion of "privity of contract." As every first-year law student learns, Judge Cardozo provided the "quiet revolution" of allowing any injured party who was presumably intended user of the product to sue the remote manufacturer with whom it had not dealt.[203] This possibility, however, was qualified by the requirement that negligence against the remote seller had to be proven. While theoretically fair, to prove that the defect in the product was caused by the remote seller's negligence could be a major obstacle. To avoid that burden, an alternative was pursued.

In a contract for the sale of goods, the buyer and the seller are the only contracting parties and, under the old terminology, they are in "privity" with each other. The seller may have made certain promises or factual representations about the quality of the goods, or he may have shown the buyer a sample or model of the goods. Even without promises, representations, samples, or models, goods are described and the description constitutes statements of fact about them. If the goods do not meet the quality standards established by such descriptions, representations, promises, samples, or models, there is a breach of an express warranty.[204] If a seller is a merchant who normally sells the product that turned out to be defective, he makes an implied warranty of merchantability that the goods will be of fair, average quality, fit for their ordinary purposes and properly contained and labeled.[205] If the seller was aware of the buyer's purpose and the buyer relied on the seller's skill and judgment in choosing the product, the buyer has the additional implied warranty of fitness for a particular purpose.[206] When a breach of warranty occurs, there has never been any question about the buyer's right to sue his immediate seller with whom the buyer made the contract. Two other questions, however, have created almost interminable litigation over the years: (1) Does the buyer have the right to sue not only his immediate seller but, also, the remote manufacturer of the goods with whom he has not dealt and with whom he made no contract? The buyer's immediate seller made a contract with either the manufacturer or a middleman in the distributive chain. May the buyer qualify as a third party beneficiary of that contract? (2) Does anyone other than the buyer, *e.g.*, a member of the buyer's family or household or guest in the home or buyer's employee, have any right to sue either the buyer's immediate seller or other suppliers up to the remote manufacturer, even though the non-buyer has made no contract with any of them? Should such a party be viewed as a protected beneficiary of the contract between the actual buyer and the seller?

The first question has been popularly characterized as a question of "vertical privity," i.e., may the buyer proceed *up* the channel of distribution not only against his immediate seller but all the way to the remote manufacturer of the goods? Another way of putting this question simply is, *Who may be sued?* The second question is popularly characterized as involving

[203] McPherson v. Buick Motor Company, 217 N. Y. 382, 393, 11 N. E. 1050, 1054 (1916).
[204] UCC § 2-313.
[205] UCC § 2-314.
[206] UCC § 2-315.

"horizontal privity," i.e., *across* the horizontal line of the buyer, who may claim the status of a third party beneficiary of the contract between the buyer and the buyer's immediate seller? The "horizontal privity" question is, *Who may sue*? For a number of years, the courts have been moving in the direction of abolishing both horizontal and vertical privity as bars to actions by buyers and other contemplated users of goods against immediate and remote sellers. It was a poorly kept secret that the use of a warranty theory was a device to permit buyers to recover for personal injuries, property damage or both without proving negligence in tort simply by changing the caption atop the complaint to "breach of warranty."

When the UCC was in the drafting stages, the courts had already begun to recognize warranty theory for personal injuries due to defective products. The chief architect of the UCC, Professor Karl Llewellyn, had precociously suggested an enterprise liability formula as early as 1941 to be included in the Code. Though the formula was the essence of what became part of the Restatement (Second) of Torts more than three decades later, the comprehensive Llewellyn concept was vetoed by the Commissioners on Uniform State Laws as "tort" law that would be an unacceptable inclusion in a "sales" statute.[207] Notwithstanding the rejection of still another Llewellyn idea whose time had not come, the drafters felt compelled to include a provision reflecting the case law development to that time. Since they rejected a comprehensive approach, they included scattered pieces of product liability development[208] which has created some confusion in the courts. For example, they addressed themselves exclusively to the question of horizontal privity, i.e., who can sue.[209] They did not deal with vertical privity in the section language, though an interesting comment can be read as manifesting neutrality with respect to judicial extensions of the horizontal privity concepts in the section.[210] The most widely enacted version of § 2-318 permits a buyer or any member of his family or household, or household guest, to sue for personal injuries sustained because a product was not as warranted.[211] The second alternative of the same section extends to any "natural user" of the product to sue for breach of warranty when he sustains bodily injury, thereby extending the horizontal line well beyond members of the family, household or guests in the home to such obvious users as employees who use the equipment purchased by the companies for which they work.[212] The third and most liberal alternative continues the extension to any contemplated user but also includes artificial "persons" such as partnerships or corporations to sue not only for bodily injuries but for property damage caused by the defective product.

---

[207] *See* Note, *Karl Llewellyn and the Intellectual Foundations of Enterprise Liability Theory*, 97 YALE L.J. 1131 (1988) (suggesting that Llewellyn has not received anything like the credit he deserved for the foundational ideas of enterprise liability which many judges and tort scholars wittingly or unwittingly used in their development of the concept). Llewellyn had included § 16-B in the Uniform Revised Sales Act (later to become the basis for Article 2 of the UCC) as the central products liability section. At a meeting in Indianapolis, the Commissioners on Uniform State Laws rejected this suggestion.

[208] In addition to § 2-318 providing third party beneficiary rights to an injured party, the Code expressly permits recovery of consequential damages for "injury to person or property proximately resulting from any breach of warranty" in § 2-715(2)(b).

[209] UCC § 2-318.

[210] UCC § 2-318 comment 3. The comment is interesting since it suggests that courts should not regard the categories established in the enacted language as frozen. It has been seen by some as an open invitation to judicial extension of the statute.

[211] UCC § 2-318 Alternative A.

[212] Alternative B of § 2-318 extends protection "to any natural person" which would clearly include a highly foreseeable user of a product such as an employee.

There is, however, considerable confusion concerning the meaning of UCC § 2-318 from one jurisdiction to another. For example, what is known as Alternative A was the original statute before the alternatives were added. While it remains the dominant, enacted alternative, the interpretation and construction of Alternative A will vary among the jurisdictions as will the interpretation and construction of the other alternatives. Though the statute is unchanged, the highest court of the state may have eliminated horizontal privity, thereby allowing parties other than members of the family, household or guests in the home who have been injured by a product to sue as a third party beneficiary. Some courts have also eliminated vertical privity that would allow a warranty action against a remote manufacturer, but other jurisdictions have retained the vertical privity requirement. Some legislatures have also enacted statutes such as "anti privity" statutes that will affect the rights of an aggrieved party. A relatively recent decision by the Supreme Court of Indiana which eliminated vertical privity provides a helpful review of the development in Indiana and other jurisdictions.[213]

A comprehensive discussion of products liability is beyond the scope of this book. Our discussion is limited to a brief review of essential differences between § 402A theory and warranty theory. Section 402A currently dominates products liability cases involving injury to the person or to property, i.e., injuries that manifest tortious conduct. While warranty theory continues to be available for such injuries, it may be attended by the privity limitations suggested earlier that do not apply to § 402A actions. Moreover, implied warranties may also be disclaimed by the manufacturer under the UCC.[214] Warranty theory has been utilized by plaintiffs who have failed to bring their § 402A tort action within the personal injury statute of limitations. In some jurisdictions, warranty theory would be available to such a plaintiff solely because of the UCC four-year statute of limitations.[215]

Tort theory is not available for purely economic injury to the defective product itself.[216] Where, for example, a product simply fails to function and does not cause bodily harm or injury to other property, relief is relegated to warranty theory, though warranty theory may be used in actions involving personal injury, damage to other property or to a malfunctioning product. A later challenge was to determine whether a jury could find that a product causing injury was not defective under § 402A, but, nevertheless, was unmerchantable under the UCC. While the theories may appear symmetrical, a court may find that a distinction can be made on the footing that the tort (§ 402A) theory pursues a "risk-utility" analysis, while the warranty

---

[213] Hyundai Motor America, Inc. v. Sandra Goodin, 822 N. E. 2d 947 (Ind. 2005).

[214] UCC § 2-316. The implied warranty of merchantability, however, may not be disclaimed in the sale of a consumer product if the product contains a "full" or "limited" express warranty that meets the definition of such a warranty under the Magnuson-Moss Warranty-Federal Trade Commission Improvement Act, 15 U.S. C. §§ 2301–2312. See Crickenberger v. Hyundai Motor America, 404 Md. 37, 944 A. 2d 1136 (2008). An implied warranty of merchantability, however, may be limited in duration under the "limited" Magnuson-Moss warranty that is typically provided by the manufacturer."Full" warranties for consumer products are extremely rare species.

[215] See Williams v. West Penn Power Co., 502 Pa. 557, 467 A.2d 811 (1983). The UCC statute of limitations (§ 2-725) is four years from the time the cause of action accrues which occurs when the breach occurs, regardless of the aggrieved party's knowledge of the breach. A breach of warranty is occurs when tender of delivery is made. Thus, the buyer has four years to discover the nonconformity. If a third party in horizontal privity sued within four years from the time of delivery, the action would like under the UCC though the tort statute of limitations had expired.

[216] Using a tort products liability theory for defects in carpeting was permitted in the Santor v. A & M Karagheusian, Inc., 44 N. J. 52, 207 A. 2d 305 (1965) (Justice Francis), while the use of a tort theory for pure economic injury to the product itself was rejected in Seely v. White Motor Co., 63 Cal. 2d 9, 45 Cal. Rptr. 17, 403 P.2d 145 (1965) (Justice Traynor). The *Seely* analysis prevailed. See East River Steamship corp. v. Transamerica Delaval, Inc., 476 U.S. 858 (1986).

theory is predicated on a "consumer-expectation" analysis. Where, for example, a Ford Bronco swerved on a normal road and rolled over, a court held that the jury could find that the Bronco was not defective under tort theory, but was unmerchantable because it failed to meet consumer expectations for ordinary driving on city streets.[217] Similarly, handles on a roasting pan may not have been defective under 402A, but could still be unmerchantable under warranty theory.[218]

While § 402A will continue to be the dominant theory in bodily injury cases, warranty theory continues to be necessary for pure loss of bargain with respect to nonconforming goods. It is also important to recognize that even where there is no breach of the implied warranty of merchantability, there may be a breach of an express warranty or implied warranty of fitness for a particular purpose which may be pursued only under a contract action for breach of warranty.

---

[217] Denny v. Ford Motor Co., 87 N.Y.2d 248, 639 N.Y.S.2d 250, 662 N.E.2d 730 (1995).

[218] Castro v. QVC Network, Inc., 139 F.3d 114 (2d Cir. 1998) (adopting the *Denny* analysis).

Chapter 11

THE ASSIGNMENT OF RIGHTS AND DELEGATION OF DUTIES

§ 136 NATURE OF ASSIGNMENTS

[A]   Concept and Terminology

This chapter explores the extent to which and in what manner the law permits the *transfer* of contractual rights and duties to a third person by one party to the contract without the consent of the other party. The conventional term used to describe the transfer of a contractual right is *assignment*, while the transfer of a contractual duty is called a *delegation.* In either case, the essential concept is the *transfer* of a right or duty to a third party and the legal significance of that transfer or attempted transfer. The effect will differ depending upon whether it is a right or duty that is being transferred. We will see that when a right is effectively assigned, the right is extinguished in the transferor (assignor) and recreated in the transferee (assignee). Where, however, a duty is transferred (delegated), the duty is not extinguished in the transferor but it is recreated in the transferee. We will also see that not every right can be assigned nor can every duty be delegated. A party may be able to assign a right under the contract but unable to delegate his correlative duty under that contract. Thus, a famous portrait painter has the power to assign the right to her fee for her service since the other party to the contract should not care to whom the fee is paid. The painter, however, is not empowered to unilaterally delegate the duty of painting the portrait to another because the other party to the contract has typically chosen this painter because of her particular skill and artistry and, therefore, clearly cares who paints the portrait. It is important to consider the nature of the contractual right that is the subject of transfer.

[1]   Contract Right — "Property"

Where a party assigns his contract right to a third person, it is common to say that he is assigning a property right, although the assigned right is to property that is *intangible* or what the common law courts called a "chose in action." A contract right, however, is not property in the usual sense of that term. It is an abstract right against a particular party who has a correlative duty. An owner of land or chattels has rights in such tangible property against any other party, i.e., others may not trespass on his land or take possession of his chattels absent his consent. A portrait painter who is owed the contract price for her work does not have a property right in this sense. Rather, her contract right is the subject matter of property rights. By calling it a "chose in action," the common law courts distinguished it from a "chose in possession."[1] The distinction is seen in a case involving a life insurance policy naming a wife as

---

[1] Professor Corbin explains that the term "chose" is French expressing the same concept as the Latin "res" or the

beneficiary. A decree of divorce was granted under which the former wife was to become the owner of all personal property on the premises. The insurance policy was on the premises. The insured sought to change the beneficiary as permitted by the policy to name his second wife as the policy expressly permitted. The first wife refused to surrender the policy and the insured notified the insurer of the change. The insured died and the first wife sought the proceeds of the policy. The court recognized that the policy — the document — was not property in the typical sense of a tangible chattel. Rather, it represented the contract rights of the insured that were the subject of property rights. The court held that such rights do not depend upon the situs of the document. The rights were personal rights that only the insured could enforce. The first wife had no rights under the policy.[2] While courts may refer to a contract right as a "property right," it is important to remember the special connotation of that phrase as applied to contract rights.

[2]   Mechanics and Terminology of Assignment and Delegation — Beneficiary Contracts Distinguished

Prior to this chapter, we spoke essentially in terms of promisors and promisees, adding third party beneficiaries in the last chapter. Where a contract right has been assigned or a contract duty delegated, the contract still involves promisors and promisees, but our focus will be on the transfer of those rights and duties. A party to a contract, who has not yet performed his duty, owes an obligation to the other party and, in that sense, he is an *obligor*. The party to whom the obligation is owed is called an *obligee*, who has a contract right against the obligor. By transferring that contract right, the obligee becomes an *assignor*. The third party to whom that right is assigned is an *assignee*, who now has the right against the obligor that the assignor had before the assignment. An obligor may transfer his duty to a third party by delegating it to that party. It is possible to refer to the parties in such a transfer as a delegator and delegatee, though the transferee of such a duty is typically called a *delegate*. A party may assign his rights *and* delegate his duties to a third party which is often called a "transfer of the contract" to the third party. Since an assignment or delegation involves a third party assignee or delegate, it is important to distinguish these arrangements from third party beneficiary contracts.

As we saw in the preceding chapter, where a promisee induces another (promisor) to make a promise for the benefit of a third party, a traditional third party beneficiary contract is formed and the third party has rights even before he is aware of the contract made for his benefit.[3] A third party assignee or delegate, on the other hand, becomes a party through the

---

English, "thing." A chattel, such as a book or an automobile, is a "chose in possession." If I agree to sell my automobile to another, I have a chose in possession until I deliver the car to the buyer. As soon as the contract is formed, however, I have a "chose in action" against the buyer which is the price he has agreed to pay for the car. Where there is no tangible property involved, as in a contract to paint a house, the painter has a chose in action against the owner. This terminology is no longer used. *See* CORBIN ON CONTRACTS § 47.2.

[2] *See* Olinger v. Northwestern Mut. Life Ins. Co., 153 Ind. App. 376, 287 N.E.2d 580 (1972). It should be noted, however, that stock certificates, bonds, and other "commercial specialties" are treated as "property" since the transfer of such a document is considered to be a transfer of property much like the transfer of any chattel. See Wolf v. Wolf, 147 Ind. App. 251, 259 N.E.2d 89 (1970), holding that bonds are personal property. The transfer of a negotiable instrument (draft, check, promissory note, or certificate of deposit) is subject to the rules and principles set forth in Articles 3 and 4 of the UCC. It is briefly explored later in this chapter, though full discussion is found in treatments of commercial paper.

[3] The rights, however, become "vested" only upon assent or reliance, including the bringing of an action.

unilateral act of one of the parties to an *existing* contract, i.e., such a third party becomes involved in the contract *after formation.* Where, however, a duty is delegated under an existing contract, a new third party beneficiary contract is created. Consider, for example, a contract where S agrees to supply goods or services to B at a price of $5,000. In exchange for consideration, X agrees to assume B's duty to S, i.e., B delegates his duty to X to pay the $5,000 to S. S is a third party (creditor) beneficiary of this contract delegating B's duty to X. B is a promisee, S is a promisor and X is a third party beneficiary. B is also an obligor, X is a delegate who has become an obligor and S is an obligee. If S had assigned his $5,000 right to Y, S is an assignor and Y is an assignee. S is no longer an obligee because his right has been extinguished and recreated in Y, the new obligee. A mere assignment of a right is not a third party beneficiary contract because, after the assignment, only two parties remain. Y has become the sole obligee to whom the duty to pay the $5,000 is owed. Where, however, there has been a delegation of a duty, X, the delegate of the correlative duty to pay the $5,000, must now pay Y instead of S. If X fails to pay Y, however, Y may still recover from B since B's duty was not extinguished through his delegation of the duty to X.[4] This is a third party beneficiary contract since, after the delegation, three parties remain as parties to the contract which was intended to benefit S. As an assignee of S's right, Y now "stands in the shoes" of S as the new and sole third party beneficiary.

[B]   Evolution of Assignment and Delegation

[1]   Opposition at Early Common Law

The early common law developed a general rule, subject to a few exceptions which are not important for our present purpose,[5] that an attempted assignment of a contract right was of no legal effect whatever.[6] This result was apparently reached because of a belief that such a right was too personal to be capable of being placed in hands other than those selected by the obligor. When one considers the severity of the penalties that could be invoked against a defaulting debtor in the early days of the common law, one can understand why the courts were inclined to take the view that he could be made liable only to the person whom he had selected

---

[4] As we will see, a party may extinguish a right in himself and recreate the right in an assignee without the consent of the other party to the contract, but a party may not rid himself of a duty by delegating it to a third party without the consent of the other party to the contract.

[5] The following exceptions to this rule were recognized from very early times:

(a) Assignments made to or by the Crown were effective and in such cases the assignee could sue at law in his own name. *See* Holdsworth, *The History of the Treatment of Choses in Action by the Common Law*, 33 Harv. L. Rev. 997 (1920), Selected Readings on Contracts 706, 714 (1931).

(b) Negotiable instruments were assignable by the law merchant, which in time became a part of the common law. The law relating to such instruments has been codified both in England and in the United States. In England, it was codified in the Bills Of Exchange Act which was passed in 1882. In the United States, it was codified in what is known as the Uniform Negotiable Instruments Law and more recently in Articles 3 and 4 of UCC, which is now the prevailing law. For a good discussion of the difference between negotiable instruments and non-negotiable choses in action, see Gilmore, *The Commercial Doctrine of Good Faith Purchase*, 63 Yale L.J. 1057, 1063–68 (1954).

(c) Certain covenants in conveyances are said to run with the land; that is, transfer of ownership of the land, in relation to which the covenant was made, carries with it the right or duty, as the case may be, growing out of the covenant. *See* 3 Holdsworth, History of English Law 130–35 (1923).

[6] *See* Mowse v. Edney, Rolle's Abr., 20 Pl. 12 [1600]; Penson & Higbed's Case, 4 Leon. 99. *See generally* Bailey, *Assignments of Debts in England from the Twelfth to the Twentieth Century*, 47 Law Q. Rev. 516 (1931), 48 Law Q. Rev. 248, 547 (1932).

as obligee.[7] It has sometimes been supposed that it was the law against maintenance — encouraging or "stirring up litigation" — that invalidated the assignment of contract rights.[8] This explanation is dubious, however, since it is clear that the rule prohibiting assignments antedates the law relating to maintenance.[9] Though the historical explanation remains controversial, there is no question that the medieval common law precluded the assignment of a right.[10]

[2]   Circumvention — Agency — Power of Attorney

Although contract rights were not assignable, a way of accomplishing much the same result was soon found. It was permissible, even in the early law, for one man to appoint another his agent to receive, in his name and stead, a performance that was due him. If he gave the other person permission to retain what was received by way of performance of the obligation, the essential objective of an assignment was attained. Consequently, it became customary for a creditor who wished to transfer his claim to appoint the transferee his agent to collect, with a proviso that the agent should retain the proceeds when collected. So common did this practice become, that, in the course of time, the rule emerged that any attempted assignment, even without an express grant of a power of attorney, by implication conferred upon the assignee such a power to collect in the name of the assignor and to retain the proceeds for his own use.[11] This mode of giving effect to an assignment, however, had distinct disadvantages. Since an assignee acquired merely a power of attorney to enforce the claim in the right of the assignor, if it became necessary to bring an action, that action had to be prosecuted in the name of the assignor. Moreover, this power of attorney was subject to the usual infirmities inherent in such a power, i.e., it was revocable by the assignor and it did not survive either his death or his bankruptcy.[12]

[3]   The Intervention of Equity

In view of the difficulties which beset the assignee under the common law, it is not strange that he should have appealed to the chancellor. The equity courts seemingly took a different view of the matter from a very early day and soon began to hold that the assignee might bring a suit on the assigned claim in that court in his own name.[13] Moreover, they concluded that the assignee's right was not revocable by the assignor.[14] In fact, they treated the assignee as having a claim in his own right. As a consequence, it came to be said that contract rights were

---

[7] *Id.*, 48 Law Q. Rev. 547, at 547.

[8] *See* Lampet's Case, 10 Coke Rep. 46b at 48a.

[9] The objection of maintenance did, however, retard the development of the idea of assignability for a long time. *See* 7 HOLDSWORTH, HISTORY OF ENGLISH LAW 534 (1925); Ames, *Disseisin Of Chattels*, 3 SELECT ESSAYS IN ANGLO-AMERICAN LEGAL HISTORY 580 (1909).

[10] *See* A. W. B. SIMPSON, A HISTORY OF THE COMMON LAW OF CONTRACT 80–81 (1987).

[11] Apparently, at first, a power of attorney expressed in terms was essential. *See* Mallory v. Lane, Cro. Jac. 342.

[12] *See* Blackwell v. Litcott, 2 Keble 331 [1669]. The same infirmities attach at the present time. A power of attorney is revocable and expires at the death of the grantor. It cannot qualify as an assignment. *See* Kelly Health Care, Inc. v. Prudential Ins. Co., 226 Va. 376, 309 S.E.2d 305 (1983).

[13] *See* Cook, *The Alienability of Choses in Action*, 29 HARV. L. REV. 816 (1916), SELECTED READINGS ON CONTRACTS 738, at 742 (1931).

[14] Peters v. Soame, 2 Vern. 428 [1701]; Fashion v. Atwood, 2 Ch. Cas. 7 [1688].

assignable in equity but not at law.[15] Spurred on by this development in equity, the common law courts later re-examined the question and, in the latter part of the 18th century, began to hold that the power of attorney created by an attempted assignment was irrevocable,[16] and that it was not affected by the death or bankruptcy of the assignor.[17] They stopped short, however, of permitting the assignee to sue in his own name in the absence of a statute permitting it, as did the courts of equity.

[4] Real Party in Interest Statutes

Today, there are statutes throughout the country — "real party in interest statutes" — which require an assignee to bring an action in his own name in a court of law.[18] Since an assignment extinguishes the right in the assignor, only the assignee can enforce that right.[19] Because of the changed attitude on the part of the law courts, equity courts renounced the jurisdiction which they once exercised in assignment cases, culminating in a rule that an assignee must seek redress in a law court, in the absence of special circumstances making the remedy in that court inadequate.[20] As a result of these fundamental changes in the law relating to the assignment of contract rights, the nature of the assignee's right had become a prolific source of controversy. The essential dispute was whether the assignee was to be viewed as the legal as well as the equitable owner of the assigned right, or whether he merely held an irrevocable power of attorney to enforce the right with the equitable ownership of the right remaining in the assignor.[21] This dispute is now a matter of antiquarian interest. With the development of "real party in interest" statutes, it is clear that the assignee is the exclusive holder of the contract right without distinguishing between legal and equitable ownership. It is also abundantly clear that, "The force of human convenience and business practice was too strong for the common-law doctrine that choses in action are not assignable."[22]

---

[15] "That a debt may be assigned in equity there is no doubt, and I should rejoice if the scandal did not exist of there being one rule at law and another in equity." Martin B., in Liversidge v. Broadbent, 4 H. & N. 603 [1859].

[16] Welch v. Mandeville, 14 U.S. (1 Wheat.) 233, 4 L. Ed. 79 (1816) (a dismissal of the suit by the assignor in collusion with the defendant does not bar a later suit by the assignee in the assignor's name); Legh v. Legh, 1 B. & P. 447 [1799] (a release of the debtor by the assignor, when the former had knowledge of the assignment, did not bar a suit by the assignee in the assignor's name).

[17] Winch v. Keeley, 1 Term Rep. 619 [1787] (bankruptcy). If the assignor dies, suit may be brought by the assignee in the name of the assignor's executor or administrator. Foss v. Lowell Five Cents Sav. Bank, 111 Mass. 285 (1873).

[18] See FED. R. CIV. P. 17(a). See also Clark & Hutchins, The Real Party in Interest, 34 YALE L.J. 259 (1925). For a compilation of such enactments, see RESTATEMENT 2d, Statutory Note to ch. 15.

[19] E & L Rental Equip. v. Gifford, 2001 Ind. App. LEXIS 415 (Ind. Ct. App. Mar. 12, 2001), effective assignment of wage claim precluded employee from bringing action in his own name because he was not a "real party in interest").

[20] Hayward v. Andrews, 106 U.S. (16 Otto) 672, 1 S. Ct. 544, 27 L. Ed. 271 (1883); Walker v. Brooks, 125 Mass. 241 (1878); Cator v. Burke, 1 Bro. C.C. 434. But cf. Farmers Exch. v. Walter M. Lowney Co., 95 Vt. 445, 115 A. 507 (1921), in which it was held that the rights of an assignee, where the assignment is inferred from the assignor's conduct and was not expressed in language, are cognizable only in equity. The soundness of such a holding is open to question.

[21] See Cook, The Alienability of Choses in Action, 29 HARV. L. REV. 816 (1916), SELECTED READINGS ON CONTRACTS 738 (1931), 30 HARV. L. REV. 449 (1917), SELECTED READINGS ON CONTRACTS 763 (1931); Williston, Is the Right of an Assignee of a Chose in Action Legal or Equitable?, 30 HARV. L. REV. 97 (1916), SELECTED READINGS ON CONTRACTS 754 (1931), 31 HARV. L. REV. 822 (1918), SELECTED READINGS ON CONTRACTS 790 (1931).

[22] Gurski v. Rosenblum, 276 Conn. 257, 267, 885 A.2d 163, 168 (2005) (quoting this treatise which quoted the statement from Union Life Ins. Co. v. Priest, 694 F.2d 1252 (10th Cir. 1982) which, in turn was quoting CORBIN ON CONTRACTS § 47.3). For a recent review of the history of assignment, see Sprint Communications, L. P. v. APCC Services, Inc., 128 S. Ct. 2531, 171 L. Ed. 2d 424 (2008) (citing J. Murray, 9 CORBIN ON CONTRACTS, § 47.3.)

§ 137   THE UNIFORM COMMERCIAL CODE — ASSIGNMENTS

One of the most significant uses of assignments in modern commerce occurs in the context of commercial financing. Where a retail business sells goods to consumers, more often than not, the sale is on credit, i.e., the buyer promises to pay the price plus interest at some time in the future. The retailer receives a promise from the buyer that can take different forms. Whatever the form, the retailer is interested in converting that promise into money, which he may do by assigning his right to a commercial lender, such as a bank or other financing institution. The retailer's seller, who may be a manufacturer or wholesaler, pursues the same process with respect to the retailer's promise to pay for goods sold to the retailer on credit. This is sometimes known as "accounts receivable financing," i.e., the buyer is treated as an "account." The UCC deals with assignment of rights and delegation of duties in Article 2 (concerned only with the sale of goods)[23] and in Article 9, which deals with security interests in personal property.[24] A security interest secures payment or performance of an obligation.[25] Thus, a debtor[26] enters into a security agreement[27] with a creditor which transfers a security interest in certain property (collateral)[28] of the debtor to assure the creditor of payment of any outstanding obligation. Once he has such assurance of payment, the creditor is a secured party, i.e., he has a security interest in the property specified in the security agreement.[29] To have an *attached and enforceable* security interest, there must be (a) either a security agreement signed by the debtor or the collateral must be in the possession or under the control of the secured party pursuant to agreement, (b) the secured party must have given value[30] in exchange for the grant of the security interest, and (c) the debtor must have rights in the collateral.[31] An attached and enforceable security interest will protect the secured party as to his debtor, certain purchasers of the collateral, and unsecured creditors.[32] The secured party, however, needs protection against other secured creditors of the debtor as well as lien creditors.[33] This protection can be obtained through the perfection of the security interest in the collateral,[34] which occurs typically through filing a financing statement in one or more appropriate state offices,[35] or through possession of the collateral which perfects the security interest without filing.[36] Thus, Article 9 of the UCC establishes a comprehensive structure for

---

[23] *See* UCC § 2-210.

[24] UCC §§ 9-404, 405 and 406 (formerly § 9-318). All references to Article 9 of the UCC are to the 1999 version which, at the time of this writing has been adopted in thirty-two jurisdictions and introduced in 2001 in 20 additional jurisdictions.

[25] UCC § 1-201(37).

[26] UCC § 9-102(a)(28).

[27] UCC § 9-102(a)(73).

[28] UCC § 9-102(a)(12).

[29] UCC § 9-102(a)(72).

[30] UCC § 1-201(35) (definition of security interest).

[31] UCC § 9-203(a) & (b).

[32] UCC § 9-201.

[33] UCC § 9-317.

[34] UCC § 9-308.

[35] UCC § 9-501.

[36] UCC § 9-313. While possessory security interests are pragmatic in isolated situations, commercial financing often requires the debtor to retain possession of the collateral which is to be sold or used so as to pay the outstanding indebtedness. Thus, a secured party may take a security interest in a retailer's inventory, i.e., goods held for resale or

security interests in personal property and fixtures[37] which secure payment or performance of obligations. Article 9 is one of the most significant contributions of the Code since it brings uniformity to an aspect of commercial law which had been subjected to highly variable state statutes dealing with such pre-Code security devices as chattel mortgages, conditional sales, trust receipts and factor's liens. All of these devices are simply facets of the unitary security interest under Article 9 of the Code. While a comprehensive exploration of Article 9 is beyond the scope of this volume, it is important to be aware of the Article 9 influence on assignments.

Article 9 may appear to have little to do with assignments since it deals with the transfer of security interests which, again, are property interests designed to assure the repayment of outstanding obligations. The debtor retains rights in the collateral, i.e., he still own the collateral, though he has pledged the collateral as security for the loan, just as a mortgagor still owns his real property even though he has granted the bank (mortgagee) a security interest in that property. Granting a security interest in collateral, therefore, is not an assignment of the debtor's rights in the collateral. How, then, does Article 9 affect the law of assignments?

Since commercial financing is filled with the transfer of accounts for the reasons suggested at the beginning of this section,[38] the drafters of Article 9 had to consider whether they were real assignments or whether the debtor was simply granting a security interest in the accounts. Theoretically, Article 9 should apply only to the latter situation since, again, it deals with the creation of security interests in collateral. The reality of commercial financing, however, makes it very difficult to determine precisely whether the debtor has sold (assigned) the accounts or merely granted a security interest in them. Because this distinction is often "blurred,"[39] the drafters decided to include within the coverage of Article 9 the *sale* or assignment of accounts as well as security interests in accounts.[40] If Article 9 applies to the assignment of accounts, the requirements of that Article must be met with respect to any such assignment, i.e., the elements of attachment and enforceability as well as the requirements for perfection must be met.

Essentially, Article 9 will apply to the assignment of accounts in a commercial financing context. A transaction involving the sale of accounts will not be included if it is not designed to finance the business. Thus, for example, the sale of accounts as part of a sale of the business out of which they arose, the assignment of accounts for collection purposes, a transfer of a right to payment under a contract to an assignee who is also to perform under the contract, or the assignment of an account to an assignee in whole or partial satisfaction of a pre-existing debt

---

for lease (§ 9-102(48)). The debtor must have possession of such inventory if he is to earn income so as to, *inter alia*, repay the outstanding debt plus interest which is the secured party's primary goal. When the retailer sells off the inventory, the secured party's security interest is automatically continued in the substitutes for that inventory, such as cash, checks, or accounts receivable, i.e., the secured party's interest continues in the *proceeds* received by his debtor (§ 9-315). Another example of the collateral remaining in the possession of the debtor would be the common situation of a security interest in the debtor's equipment (§ 9-102(33)) which the debtor must retain to remain in business and, again, to achieve the primary goal of the secured creditor, i.e., the repayment of the outstanding loan with interest. Thus, possessory security interests are relegated to jewelry, certificates of stock, documents of title (*e.g.*, bills or lading or warehouse receipts), or other valuables which the debtor can do without during the term of the loan.

[37] UCC § 9-334.

[38] An "account" is any right to payment of a monetary obligation, whether or not yet earned by performance, for goods sold, leased, licensed or assigned, for services rendered or to be rendered and other specific obligations listed in § 9-102(2). Exceptions include rights to payment evidenced by chattel paper or an instrument.

[39] UCC § 9-109(a)(3) and comment 4.

[40] UCC § 9-109(a)(3).

are not typical commercial financing assignments of accounts. Therefore, Article 9 does not apply to such assignments which means that the requirements of Article 9 need not be met with respect to such assignments.[41] While Article 9 does apply to commercial financing assignments of accounts, if a particular assignment does not transfer a significant part of the outstanding accounts of the assignor (alone or in conjunction with other assignments), there is no need to meet the filing requirements of Article 9 to perfect that assignment and thus provide protection from other secured creditors or lien creditors under Article 9. That type of commercial financing assignment is perfected without filing.[42]

The foregoing sketch of Article 9 as it relates to assignments does not deal with myriad complications that arise in related Article 9 questions. Those questions must be left for the study of commercial law. It is, however, important for the student of contract law to recognize the critical intersection between the common law of assignments and Article 9 of the UCC since, again, innumerable assignments of this type occur daily.

§ 138   THE FORM AND REVOCABILITY OF ASSIGNMENTS

[A]   Manifestation of Intention

[1]   Oral — Written — Statute of Frauds — Uniform Commercial Code

Because the law generally favors assignments,[43] in the absence of a statute or a contract provision to the contrary, there are no prescribed formalities which must be observed to make an effective assignment. It suffices that the assignor has in some way manifested an intention to make a present transfer of his rights to the assignee.[44] This intention may be manifested by words, by conduct, or both.[45] Unless required by statute or the contract itself, the manifested intention to assign need not be evidenced by a writing.[46] Statutes of Frauds, however, apply to assignments. Thus, an assignment of an estate or interest in real property for more than one year requires a writing.[47] An assignment of personal property may require a writing under the UCC. Unrevised Article 1 includes a statute of frauds for "kinds of personal property not

---

[41] UCC § 9-109(d).

[42] UCC § 9-309(2).

[43] Lone Mountain Production Co. v. Natural Gas Pipeline Co., 984 F.2d 1551, 1556 (10th Cir. 1992) ("Generally, the law favors the assignability of contractual rights, unless the assignment would add to or materially alter the obligator's duty or risk").

[44] Zimmerman v. Kyte, 53 Wash. App. 11, 765 P.2d 905 (1988). *See also* Penny Lane Owners Corp. v. Conthur Dev. Co., 2000 U.S. Dist. LEXIS 1503, at 43 (S.D.N.Y. Feb. 15, 2000).

[45] Miller v. Wells Fargo Bank Int'l Corp., 406 F. Supp. 452 (S.D.N.Y. 1975) (may be manifested by conduct, writing, or parol), *aff'd*, 540 F.2d 548 (2d Cir. 1976).

[46] *See, e.g., In re* Estate of Bryan, 513 Pa. 554, 522 A.2d 40 (1987) (oral assignments are permissible); Kershner v. Hilt Truck Line, Inc., 637 S.W.2d 769 (Mo. Ct. App. 1982) (oral assignment effective when made and not postponed because of later formal assignment). *See also* Anaconda Aluminum Co. v. Sharp, 243 Miss. 9, 136 So. 2d 585 (1962); General Excavator Co. v. Judkins, 128 Ohio St. 160, 190 N.E. 389 (1934); Jewett Lumber Co. v. Anderson Coal Co., 181 Iowa 950, 165 N.W. 211 (1917). RESTATEMENT 2d § 324.

[47] *See, e.g.,* Rosefan Constr. Corp. v. Salazar, 114 Misc. 2d 956, 452 N.Y.S.2d 1016 (Civ. Ct. 1982).

otherwise covered" under other UCC Articles,[48] but revised Article 1 (already be enacted in more than thirty jurisdictions) repeals that section on the footing that it is inappropriate for such a requirement to be included within the UCC.[49] As suggested in the prior section, an assignment of accounts requires compliance with Article 9 of the Code so that an oral assignment of accounts would not only be unenforceable; it would not even attach.[50] Where, however, an assignor testifies that the assignment occurred, as in other cases of admitting the existence of an oral agreement, the statute of frauds should be satisfied so as to make the oral assignment effective.[51]

[2]   Present Transfer

An assignment is not a contract since it is not a promise. It is a manifestation of intention to immediately extinguish a right in the assignor and recreate the same right in the assignee.[52] It is abundantly clear that anything other than a manifestation of an intention to make a *present transfer* of a right will not amount to an assignment, whatever else the legal significance of such a manifestation.[53] The right may arise from an executory contract, i.e., a house painter may assign his right under a contract to paint the obligor's house before he paints the house.[54] To be effective, an assignment must be a completed transaction between the parties which is intended to vest in the assignee a present right,[55] since, again, an assignment extinguishes the right in the assignor and passes all of the assignor's interest to the assignee.[56] A promise to give a party any proceeds recovered from a claim is not an assignment.[57] Neither is a promise to make an assignment to a creditor in the future or to collect a sum of money owed

---

[48] UCC § 1-206.

[49] See the "Legislative Note" following the new § 1-206 in the revised Article 1. Other sections of the Code deal with the statute of frauds requirements for the sale of goods, and security agreements. These provisions prevent enforcement against the assignor, but they do not prevent enforcement against the obligor. RESTATEMENT 2d § 324 comment b (referring to § 144). See also § 140.

[50] First Nat'l Bank v. Autrey, 9 Kan. App. 2d 96, 673 P.2d 448 (1983) (also holding that the assignment of accounts was not excluded under UCC § 9-104(f) (§ 9-109(d) in the 1999 version) as a transfer of a right to payment to an assignee who is also to do the performance under the contract since that exception applies only to situations where the assignor both delegates a duty to perform and assigns the right to payment to the same person).

[51] *See Zimmerman, supra* note 44.

[52] Restatement 2d § 317(1). See Stillwell v. American Gen. Life Ins. Co., 555 F. 3d 572, 577 (7th Cir. 2009), quoting this section of the Restatement 2d and adding, "The existence of an assignment is determined according to the intention of the parties, and that intention is a question of fact to be derived not only from the instruments executed by them but from the surrounding circumstances." See also Kroeplin Farms Gen. Partnership v. Heartland Crop Insurance, 430 F. 3d 906, 911 (8th Cir. 2005) ("when a contract right is assigned, the assignor's right to performance by the obligor is extinguished and the assignee acquires the right.")

[53] See DC 3 Entertainment, LLC v. John Galt Entertainment, Inc., 412 F. Supp. 2d 1125, 1141 (W. D. Wash. 2006) noting the importance of not confusing an assignment that is a present transfer with a contract which promises future performance). *See also* Western United Assurance Co. v. Hayden, 64 F.3d 833, 838 (3d Cir. 1995) (distinguishing promise to assign from a present transfer (citing RESTATEMENT 2d § 330)); ESR Invs., Ltd. v. Fontana, 1993 U.S. App. LEXIS 16220 (9th Cir. June 25, 1993); Emmons v. Lake States Ins. Co., 193 Mich. App. 460, 484 N.W.2d 712, 714 (1992).

[54] *See* RESTATEMENT 2d § 320.

[55] Weston v. Dowty, 163 Mich. App. 238, 414 N.W.2d 165 (1987).

[56] *In re* Musser, 24 B.R. 913 (W.D. Va. 1982). *See also* Patrons State Bank & Trust Co. v. Shapiro, 215 Kan. 856, 528 P.2d 1198 (1974) (right of assignor is divested).

[57] *See Weston v. Dowty, supra* note 55.

the promisor and pay it to the promisee an assignment.[58] Where a document stated that a party agreed with another that the latter was "entitled" to one half the commission to be earned on the sale of property, the court held that it represented a mere agreement to assign, rather than an assignment.[59] Since the question is one of intention, different interpretations and constructions of language are inevitable. Where hospital patients signed a form stating, "I assign and hereby authorize claims by the hospital of all insurance and health plan benefits otherwise payable to or on behalf of me for this hospitalization or outpatient or emergency services rendered," one court found that it manifested an intention to assign,[60] while another court construed similar language as simply allowing the hospital to receive direct payments from the insurer. It was not an "unequivocal assignment" and did not, therefore, provide a right in the hospital to pursue litigation when the defendant insurer refused to pay.[61]

[3]   Order Assignments — Checks

Where money is owed by an obligor to an obligee, the obligee may deliver a written instrument to an assignee which orders the obligor to pay the assignee with the intention that the assignee retain that payment. Such an order constitutes an assignment since the apparent intention of the obligee is to make a present transfer to the assignee.[62] If, however, the obligee simply directs that order to the obligor, the third party is not an assignee since the intention to transfer to the assignee is absent.[63] Where a checking account customer (drawer) draws a check on his bank (drawee) which orders the bank to pay to the order of a named party (payee), the payee is not an assignee because the order is directed to the general credit of the bank.[64] If, however, an order is made payable from a particular fund, it is normally held to be an assignment since, by making it payable from a specified fund, there is a manifestation of intention to transfer to the payee presently the drawer's (obligee's) right to the fund or to so much of it as is directed to be paid to the payee.[65]

---

[58] *See* State Cent. Sav. Bank v. Hemmy, 77 F.2d 458 (8th Cir. 1935); Lauerman Bros. Co. v. Komp, 156 Wis. 12, 145 N.W. 174 (1914).

[59] Donovan v. Middlebrook, 95 A.D. 365, 88 N.Y.S. 607 (1st Dep't 1904).

[60] Dallas County Hosp. Dist. v. Blue Cross Blue Shield of Texas, 2006 U.S. Dist. LEXIS 10443 (N.D. Tex. 2006).

[61] Cooper Hosp. Univ. Med. Ctr. v. Seafarers Health & Benefit Plan, 2007 U.S. Dist. LEXIS 71358 (D.N.J. 2007). In Touro Infirmary v. American Maritime Officer, 2007 U.S. Dist. LEXIS 86574 (E.D. La. 2007), the court stated that it was more persuaded by the *Cooper* rationale with respect to such language since the so-called "assignment of benefits" simply authorized direct payment to the hospital.

[62] RESTATEMENT 2d § 325(1).

[63] Miller v. Wells Fargo Bank Int'l Corp., 406 F. Supp. 452 (S.D.N.Y. 1975), *aff'd*, 540 F.2d 548 (2d Cir. 1976); Associated Metals & Minerals Corp. v. Isletmeleri, 6 Ill. App. 2d 548, 128 N.E.2d 595 (1st Dist. 1955). If the obligor pays the third party, however, obligor's debt is discharged to that extent. Again, the third party is not an assignee and has no right against the obligor.

[64] UCC § 3-408. *See* Smith v. Cash Store Mgmt., Inc., 195 F.3d 325, 330 (7th Cir. 1999).

[65] Andrews Elec. Co. v. St. Alphonse Catholic Total Abstinence Soc'y, 233 Mass. 20, 123 N.E. 103 (1919); Fourth Street Nat'l Bank v. Yardley, 165 U.S. 634, 17 S. Ct. 439, 41 L. Ed. 855 (1897); Brill v. Tuttle, 81 N.Y. 454, 37 Am. Rep. 515 (1880). Under a prior version of Article 3 of the UCC, § 3-105(g) precluded such an instrument from being a negotiable instrument under the UCC. The current version, however, states that a promise or order is not made conditional because payment is limited to resort to a particular fund or source. § 3-106(b)(ii).

[B]   Consideration — Gratuitous Assignments

[1]   Gift Assignments — Revocability — History

There should no longer be any question as to the effectiveness of a gratuitous assignment. The obligor may not defend on the ground that the assignee gave no consideration or that there was no substitute validation device.[66] The problem, however, is that gratuitous assignments are generally said to be revocable. To understand how courts decided that certain gratuitous assignments became irrevocable, it is important to begin with some history.

As we have already seen, an assignment was effective only on the theory that it created in the assignee a power of attorney to enforce the claim in the right of the assignor.[67] Such a power, in the course of time, was held to be irrevocable when consideration was paid for it. If it was conferred upon the assignee gratuitously, it continued to be revocable by the assignor and terminable on his death or bankruptcy like any other agency similarly conferred. Moreover, even the court of equity, which seemed to treat the assignee who paid value for his assignment as owner of the claim, was hesitant to take this view in the case of one who had paid no consideration. The oft repeated maxim that "equity will not aid a volunteer" was apparently thought to stand in the way.[68] As time went on, however, courts of law, assisted by legislation, adopted a more favorable attitude toward the assignment of contract rights. They began to deal with the matter by analogizing to the law governing the transfer of tangible chattels.

[2]   Gift Analogy — Seal — Symbolic Documents — the Contract

[a]   Seal

A gift of a chattel normally occurred through delivery of the chattel with donative intent. Delivery of a deed of gift under seal, however, was also effective.[69] Courts, therefore, were pleased to treat delivered,[70] gratuitous assignments under seal as completed (irrevocable) gifts.[71]

---

[66] *See* Union Life Ins. Co. v. Priest, 694 F.2d 1252 (10th Cir. 1982) (quoting Professor Corbin at the predecessor section to § 48.1 to the effect that it is no longer necessary to review the learned arguments made for and against the theory that an assignment was ineffective unless it was for value). The cases holding a gift assignment effective are legion. *See* Restatement 2d § 332.

[67] *See supra* § 136[B].

[68] The early authorities are collected and discussed in Anson, *Assignment of Choses in Action*, 17 Law Q. Rev. 90 (1901); Costigan, *Gifts Inter Vivos of Choses in Action*, 27 Law Q. Rev. 326 (1911); Jenks, *Consideration and the Assignment of Choses in Action*, 16 Law Q. Rev. 241 (1900). It has, of course, always been true that so long as the power of attorney which is implied from the fact of assignment is unrevoked and has not been legally terminated, the assignee has authority to collect the assigned claim. Therefore, want of consideration for the assignment is not, by itself, a defense to the debtor when he is sued by the assignee. Perkes v. Utah Idaho Milk Co., 85 Utah 217, 39 P.2d 308 (1934); Morrison v. Ross, 113 Ind. 186, 14 N.E. 479 (1887); Briscoe v. Eckley, 35 Mich. 112 (1876).

[69] *See* Restatement 2d § 332 comment b.

[70] The concept of "delivery" is treated the same way for gratuitous assignments as it is for gifts of chattels. For an analysis, see Brown, Personal Property §§ 7.2–7.9 (3d ed. 1975).

[71] Abrain v. Pereira, 336 Mass. 460, 146 N.E.2d 360 (1957); Chase Nat'l Bank v. Sayles, 11 F.2d 948 (1st Cir.), *cert. denied*, 273 U.S. 708, 47 S. Ct. 99, 71 L. Ed. 851 (1976); Meyers v. Meyers, 99 N.J. Eq. 560, 134 A. 95 (N.J. Ch. 1926). Restatement 2d § 332(1)(b).

[b] Symbolic Documents

Certain types of documents are treated as more than mere evidence of a contract right, i.e., the right inheres in the document. They are documents that have to be at least presented or even surrendered to activate the right to performance.[72] The classic example is the savings bank passbook. Delivery of such a passbook with the requisite donative intent creates an irrevocable gratuitous assignment or simply a valid *inter vivos* gift of a chose in action.[73] An *inter vivos* gift (from one living person to another) is a completed gift upon delivery and acceptance by the donee. A *causa mortis* gift (in contemplation of death) is revoked upon the survival of the donor. A gratuitous assignment, *causa mortis*, is subject to the same rule as if it were the gift of a tangible chattel.[74] The same analysis applies to insurance policies[75] and shares of stock.[76] A gratuitous assignment of a mortgage, promissory notes and subordination agreement is effective.[77] The form of an assignment of patent rights is governed by statute[78] and, if properly executed, requires no consideration to be effective.[79]

[c] Unsealed, Nonsymbolic Writings

With the abolition or substantial weakening of the seal, it is now generally agreed that an assignment in writing, signed and delivered by the assignor to the assignee, or to one on his behalf with an intention to vest the right in the assignee, would constitute an irrevocable gratuitous assignment.[80] The interesting question is whether delivery of such a writing will be effective to transfer rights represented by symbolic documents, i.e., if there are shares of stock or an insurance policy, will the courts insist that the symbolic document be delivered rather than a writing evidencing an intention of the present transfer of that right to the assignee? The cases that have dealt with this question do not require delivery of the symbolic document to effectuate an irrevocable gratuitous assignment.[81]

---

[72] Several commercial documents fall into this classification, *e.g.*, a document of title (bill of lading or warehouse receipt), UCC § 1-201(15), or a certificated security, UCC § 8-102.

[73] Hileman v. Hulver, 243 Md. 527, 221 A.2d 693 (1966).

[74] RESTATEMENT 2d § 332 comment e.

[75] *See* Neenan v. ITT Hartford, 256 A.D.2d 1247, 682 N.Y.S.2d 783 (4th Dep't 1998) (an insurance policy is a chose in action, and delivery to the assignee or donee with intent to vest title is essential to a valid gift and accomplishes a valid assignment not impaired by the Statute of Frauds); Bimestefer v. Bimestefer, 205 Md. 541, 544, 109 A.2d 768, 770 (1954) (insurance policy certificate under a group life plan could be assigned by insured handing the certificate to his son and saying," 'I want you to have it. It will be a nest egg for you and will help with David's education.' . . . 'This is yours.' ").

[76] Herbert v. Simson, 220 Mass. 480, 108 N.E. 65 (1915). *See* RESTATEMENT 2d § 332(1)(b).

[77] Nebco & Assoc. v. United States, 23 Cl. Ct. 635, 645 (1991).

[78] 35 U S.C. § 261.

[79] Keller v. Bass Pro Shops, 15 F.3d 122 (8th Cir. 1994).

[80] Speelman v. Pascal, 10 N.Y.2d 313, 178 N.E.2d 723 (1961) (applying New York statute); Berl v. Rosenberg, 169 Cal. App. 2d 125, 336 P.2d 975 (1st Dist. 1959); Thatcher v. Merriam, 121 Utah 191, 240 P.2d 266 (1952); Petty v. Mutual Ben. Life Ins. Co., 235 Iowa 455, 15 N.W.2d 613 (1944); Steffen v. Davis, 52 S.D. 283, 217 N.W. 221 (1927). RESTATEMENT 2d § 332(1)(a).

[81] *See* Leedham v. Leedham, 218 Iowa 767, 254 N.W. 61 (1934) (rights in shares of stock were effectively assigned by written assignment); Petty v. Mutual Ben. Life Ins. Co., 235 Iowa 455, 15 N.W.2d 613 (1944) (rights under insurance policy effectively assigned by written assignment).

[d]   Evidentiary Writings — Restatement 2d Extension

If there is no symbolic document and no written assignment, may a party assign a contract right by delivery of the "contract" itself, i.e., by delivery of the written evidence of the contract? The case law is scant and divided.[82] The Restatement 2d suggests that some kinds of writings, albeit not the traditional symbolic document that must be exhibited or surrendered to enforce the right contained therein, are still more than mere written evidence of the contract. The Restatement 2d calls these writings "evidentiary writings" and describes them as the type where the right is "so integrated in the writing" that the parol evidence rule would apply and its delivery is an "appropriate formality" though, again, it is not required.[83] Illustrations include a writing evidencing a contract for the sale of land[84] and a bank receipt[85] -the type of writing that would make its delivery "an appropriate formality to validate a gift of that right."[86] Presumably, the drafters of this extension felt that they had gone as far as possible in a *restatement* of the law. The final extension would have recognized an effective gratuitous assignment without delivery of any writing, i.e., an oral assignment where the evidence of donative intent is clear and convincing.[87] The conventional wisdom, however, does not extend this far.[88]

[C]   Revocation of Gratuitous Assignments — Disclaimer

Where there is no completed gift, i.e., where there is no delivery of any of the effective writings described above, a gratuitous assignment, like a gift promise, is revocable. If an assignment is supported by consideration, it is not a gratuitous assignment any more than a promise supported by consideration is a gratuitous promise.[89] Again, however, it is important to remember that an assignment is not a promise — it is a *present* transfer of a right, i.e., there is nothing *in futuro* about it. An assignment that is not supported by consideration may still have been given for value. The value may have been in total or partial satisfaction of a pre-existing debt or it may have been given as security for such a debt. Value is defined more broadly than consideration[90] and an assignment for value is not a gratuitous assignment, i.e., it is irrevocable.

Absent consideration, security for or total or partial satisfaction of a pre-existing obligation,[91] delivery of a symbolic or "evidentiary" writing, or a lesser writing evidencing the assignment, the gratuitous assignment is revocable upon the death or incapacity of the assignor, by his assignment of the right to a subsequent assignee (evidencing his intention to

---

[82] *See, e.g.*, Cook v. Lum, 55 N.J.L. 373, 26 A. 803 (1893) (ineffective assignment); *In re* Huggins' Estate, 204 Pa. 167, 53 A. 746 (1902) (effective assignment).

[83] Restatement 2d § 332 comment d.

[84] Restatement 2d § 332 ill. 5, based on *In re Huggins' Estate, supra* note 82.

[85] Restatement 2d § 332 ill. 6, based on Cronin v. Chelsea Sav. Bank, 201 Mass. 146, 87 N.E. 484 (1909).

[86] Restatement 2d § 332 comment d.

[87] *See* Guardian State Bank & Trust Co. v. Jacobson, 220 Neb. 235, 369 N.W.2d 80 (1985) (following Dinslage v. Stratman, 105 Neb. 274, 180 N.W. 81 (1920)).

[88] Gartin v. Taylor, 577 N.W.2d 410 (Iowa 1998) (oral release of daughter's debt to parents was not an effective gratuitous assignment). A rare exception is Brown v. Fore, 12 S. W. 2d 114 (Tex. Ct. App. 1929).

[89] *See* Restatement 2d § 332(5)(a).

[90] See the definition of "value" in UCC § 1-204.

[91] *See* Restatement 2d § 332, comment h.

revoke the original assignment), or by a straightforward notice received by the assignee or obligor from the assignor that the assignment is revoked.[92] The power of revocation, however, can be thwarted before its exercise if the assignee obtains payment or satisfaction of the obligation from the obligor,[93] is awarded a judgment against the obligor on the assigned right,[94] or effects a novation with the obligor,[95] i.e., the assignee agrees to accept a new obligor in substitution for the original obligor who is discharged. Moreover, since consideration or value exchanged for the assigned right will make the assignment irrevocable as a non-gratuitous assignment, it is not remarkable that a gratuitous assignment inducing detrimental reliance by the assignee will be irrevocable to the extent necessary to avoid injustice.[96] Finally, it should be noted that an assignee may disclaim an assignment made for his benefit,[97] though acceptance of a gratuitous assignment beneficial to the assignee is often said to be presumed.[98]

§ 139 ASSIGNABLE RIGHTS — LIMITATIONS

Modern courts recognize the general principle that contract rights are freely assignable,[99] but, like other general principles in our law, this principle is subject to limitations. Assuming an effective assignment, the right that was extinguished in the promisor and recreated in the assignee differs only in the sense that the obligor's duty under the contract is now owed to the assignee who has the right to receive the performance from the obligor. Whether the law will permit such a change to be made in the obligation of the promisor without his consent will depend upon the circumstances of the particular case.[100] It is important to explore the limitations on the assignability of contract rights.

[A] Limitation — Material Change in Duty of Obligor

[1] The Principle

The fundamental limitation on the assignment of a contract right has been stated in numerous cases, codified in the UCC and repeated in the RESTATEMENT 2d: a contract right can be assigned unless such assignment would materially change the duty of the obligor, or materially increase the burden of risk imposed on him by his contract, or materially impair his

---

[92] RESTATEMENT 2d § 332(3). Under federal bankruptcy law, the bankrupt's trustee may exercise the power of revocation of a gratuitous assignment, 11 U.S.C. § 541. If the gratuitous assignment has been irrevocable, the trustee may still be able to set it aside under certain circumstances. 11 U.S.C. § 548.

[93] RESTATEMENT 2d § 332(3)(a).

[94] RESTATEMENT 2d § 332(3)(b).

[95] RESTATEMENT 2d § 332(3)(c).

[96] *See In re* Hazelwood, 43 B.R. 208 (Bankr. E.D. Va. 1984) (citing the second edition of this book at 601 for this proposition). *See also* RESTATEMENT 2d § 332(4).

[97] RESTATEMENT 2d § 327(2).

[98] Exeter Exploration Co. v. Fitzpatrick, 202 Mont. 209, 661 P.2d 1255 (1983). RESTATEMENT 2d § 327(1) suggests that acceptance is essential to make an assignment effective unless a third party gives consideration for it, or the assignment was irrevocable by delivery of a writing to a third person.

[99] Gurski v. Rosenblum Financial, LLC, 276 Conn.257, 266, 885 A.2d 163, 167–68 (2005).

[100] Munchak Corp. v. Cunningham, 457 F.2d 721 (4th Cir. 1972).

chance of obtaining performance.[101] The essential concern is that a materially greater risk should not be imposed upon an obligor beyond the risk he voluntarily assumed at the time the contract was formed simply because the obligee decided to assign his right. The challenge is to determine whether a change or increase in that risk is material. Where, for example, a union attempted to assign its right to arbitrate to an individual member of the union, the court found that the recognition of such an assignment would potentially increase materially the burden on the employer by significantly increasing the number of arbitrations — a risk the employer had not assumed under the original contract.[102] It is important to recognize this essential limitation in myriad situations.

[2]   Payment — Land — Goods — Output and Requirements — Express Warranty

At one extreme, a simple right to be paid money clearly appears to be an assignable right because it has no material effect on the obligor's duty. It should make little difference to the obligor that he must pay a certain sum to the assignee rather than the obligee.[103] The obligee may have been more lenient in permitting the obligor additional time to pay, but this is not a sufficient reason for denying effect to the general rule that money claims are freely assignable.[104] The fact that the assignee can be shown to be *persona non grata* to the obligor, i.e., the obligor would not have contracted with the assignee, is also irrelevant.[105] While the right to purchase land[106] or goods[107] may suggest no material change in the risk of the obligor and, therefore, appear freely assignable, the terms of the contract may leave such discretion in the buyer that a change in buyers could materially increase that risk. Where, for example, a small ice cream company agreed to purchase all of its requirements of ice from a particular supplier and the buyer assigned its rights to a larger ice cream company operating in an

---

[101] UCC § 2-210(2); RESTATEMENT 2d § 317(2)(a). See Highland Village Partners, L. L. C. v. Bradbury & Stamm Construction Co., Inc., 219 Ariz. 147,150, 195 P. 3d 184, 187 (Ariz. App. 2008). *See also* Bobbitt v. Safeco, 1999 Conn. Super. LEXIS 2347, at *3 (Conn. Super. Ct. 1999); Financial Servs. of Puget Sound, Inc. v. Phenneger & Morgan, Inc., 1999 Wash. App. LEXIS 2010, at *11 (Wash. Ct. App. Nov. 29, 1999); Herzog v. Irace, 594 A.2d 1106, 1109 (Me. 1991).

[102] Padovano v. Borough of E. Newark, 329 N.J. Super. 204, 747 A.2d 303 (App. Div. 2000).

[103] In Talmadge v. United States Shipping Bd. Emergency Fleet Corp., 54 F.2d 240, 243 (2d Cir. 1931), Judge Hand writes the opinion for the court which includes the following: "Had the Shipbuilding Company assigned their right in toto, nobody can dispute that the plaintiffs might have sued at law, though the assignment would strictly have varied the defendant's obligation, compelling it to draw cheques to the plaintiff's order, and not as stipulated. So much change in performance is, however, permissible."

[104] Cf. UCC § 9-406(d) (1999) (formerly § 9-318(4)), making an anti-assignment clause ineffective with respect to accounts in commercial financing transactions, discussed later in this chapter.

[105] *See* C. H. Little Co. v. Caldwell Transit Co., 197 Mich. 481, 163 N.W. 952 (1917); Fitzroy v. Cave, 2 K.B. 364 [1905].

[106] *See* Lockhart Co. v. B.F.K., Ltd., 107 Idaho 633, 691 P.2d 1248 (Ct. App. 1984) (sellers obliged under land sale contract to convey title upon payment of all installments and to provide notice of default; though the assignment added another party to be notified of default, the increased burden was not material). *See also* Moore v. Gariglietti, 228 Ill. 143, 81 N.E. 826 (1907). *See also* Smithfield Oil Co. v. Furlonge, 257 N.C. 388, 126 S.E.2d 167 (1962) (assignment of lease and option to purchase).

[107] Beachler v. Amoco Oil Co., 112 F.3d 902, 907 (7th Cir. 1997) ("a contract for the sale of goods is generally assignable. . . ."); US Golf Sys. v. WPI Acquisition Corp., 1992 U.S. Dist. LEXIS 2676, at *8–9 (N.D. Ill. Mar. 6, 1992) (There is no difference from a seller's perspective in having to deliver goods to an undisclosed principal or having to deliver the same goods to an assignee).

additional geographic market, the court held the right not assignable.[108] The court's rationale manifested the pre-UCC view which held that rights under requirement and output contracts were generally held not assignable because of the wide personal discretion that buyers and sellers had under such contracts. The UCC, however, substitutes a standard of good faith in such contracts,[109] which includes commercial reasonableness.[110] This objective standard should allow more effective assignments of rights under output and requirements contracts.[111] Under the modern view, the only basis for finding that such a right is nonassignable is a showing of a material change in the duty and risk originally assumed by the obligor. A modern argument for the ice supplier might suggest that the assignee's requirements could be reduced substantially if not entirely where costs made it more advantageous to produce ice cream in the assignee's other market, a risk not assumed by the supplier at the time the contract was made.

Unless precluded by the terms of the contract, an express warranty is a creature of contract and can, therefore, be assigned. Since an assignment places the assignee in the shoes of the assignor, the assignee who holds that right is in privity of contract with the obligor just as the assignor had been in privity.[112] While an implied warranty of workmanship and habitability does not run automatically to a subsequent purchaser of commercial property, there is no reason why the original buyer cannot expressly assign that warranty to a purchaser.[113]

[3]   Personal Services

Where the obligor has contracted to perform personal services, the question of assignability of the right to those services can be more difficult. In an employment contract, if no direction or supervision by the assignee is contemplated, the assignment will be effective.[114] A television station's right to the performance of its news anchorperson was held assignable since the performance of the anchor was not based upon a personal relationship or special confidence and was not changed in any material way by the assignment.[115] Similarly, a professional basketball player's contract was assignable when the franchise was sold. While a personal service contract requiring special skill and based on the personal relationship between the parties may be nonassignable, like the television anchor case, there was no personal relationship between the player and the stockholder owners of the team. There was no material difference in the player's required performance under new ownership.[116] An employee's covenant not to compete with his employer is a right that may appear assignable as part of the

---

[108] Crane Ice Cream Co. v. Terminal Freezing & Heating Co., 147 Md. 588, 128 A. 280 (1925). *See also* Kemp v. Baerselman, 2 K.B. 604 [1906]. *Contra* C. H. Little Co. v. Caldwell Transit Co., 197 Mich. 481, 163 N.W. 952 (1917); Tolhurst v. Associated Portland Cement Co., A.C. 414 [1903].

[109] UCC § 2-306(1).

[110] See UCC § 2-103(1)(b), defining good faith in the case of a merchant as honesty in fact plus commercial reasonableness.

[111] UCC § 2-210 comment 4.

[112] Collins Co., Ltd. v. Carboline Co., 125 Ill. 2d 498, 127 Ill. Dec. 5, 532 N.E.2d 834 (1988). *See also* Independence Apts. Assocs. v. Louisiana-Pacific Corp., 44 F. Supp. 2d 1120 (D. Or. 1999).

[113] Highland Village Partners, L. L. C. v. Bradbury & Stamm Construction Co., Inc., 219 Ariz. 147, 150, 195 P. 3d 184, 187 (Ariz. App. 2008).

[114] *C. H. Little Co., supra* note 108.

[115] Evening News Ass'n v. Peterson, 477 F. Supp. 77 (D.D.C. 1979).

[116] Munchak Corporation v. Cunningham, 457 F. 2d 721 (4th Cir. 1972).

sale of a business since it requires no personal contact with the successor employer.[117] There is, however, a split of authority on this issue. Courts refusing to enforce such covenants refer to the "personal" nature of such a commitment by an employee based upon the employee's confidence in the character and personality of the original employer which necessarily does not exist with the new employer who is a "stranger."[118] Other courts conclude that the trust and confidence rationale is quaint but unpersuasive. They assume that the new employer will agree to honor the employment contracts and the employees will also honor their commitments.[119]

Where, however, there is a personal relationship or special confidence factor in a personal service contract, an effective assignment without the employee's consent may be precluded. A client may not assign his right to be represented by a lawyer who may have chosen not to represent the assignee.[120] A right of a distributor of a product who had an obligation to use "best efforts" to market the product within a designated territory could not be assigned to a competitor of the obligor.[121]

[4]   Fire Insurance Policy

An assignment of the insured's rights under a fire insurance policy has been held ineffective because it may increase the risks of the obligor insurance company.[122] Theoretically, the insurer has issued the policy at least in part on the basis of an evaluation of the character of the insured. After the loss has occurred, however, an assignment of the proceeds of the policy will be valid, regardless of conditions in the policy concerning assignments. Prior to the fire, the insured had only an inchoate or contingent right, but after the loss, the right becomes absolute and transferable without the consent of the obligor-insurer.[123]

---

[117] *See* Torrington Creamery, Inc. v. Davenport, 126 Conn. 515, 12 A.2d 780 (1940) (employee's covenant not to compete with employer is assignable, even by implication, with sale of business). *See also* Sickles v. Lauman, 185 Iowa 37, 169 N.W. 670 (1918).

[118] See Smith, Bell & Hauck, Inc. v. Cullins, 123 Vt. 96, 101, 183 A.2d 528, 532 (1962). *See also* Hess v. Gebhard & Co., 580 Pa. 148, 808 A.2d 912 (2002).

[119] See J. H. Renarde v. Sims, 312 N. J. Super. 195, 711 A.2d 410, 412–14 (Super. Ct. Ch. Div., 1998); Auto-Med Technologies v. Eller, 160 F. Supp. 2d 915, 924 (N. D. Ill. 2001). *See also* Atromick International, Inc. v. Koch, 143 Ohio App. 3d 805, 759 N. E. 2d 385, 387–88 (Ohio Ct. App. 2001); Alexander & Alexander, Inc. v. Koelz, 722 S. W. 2d 311, 312–13 (Mo. Ct. App. 1986). These cases are discussed in Sogeti USA LLC v. Scariano, 606 F. Supp. 2d 1080 (D. Ariz. 2009) which emphasized the reasonableness of the restriction rather than any personal relationship in holding the right to a restrictive covenant can be assigned.

[120] *See* One Nat'l Bank v. Antonellis, 80 F.3d 606, 614 (1st Cir. 1996) ("[W]e refuse to allow a third party, of whom the attorney does not know, to assume the rights of a client through assignment."). The same analysis would apply to any doctor/patient relationship.

[121] Berliner Foods Corp. v. Pillsbury Co., 633 F. Supp. 557 (D. Md. 1986).

[122] Batsford v. Farm Family Mut. Ins. Co., 1996 Mass. Super. LEXIS 608, at *10 (Mass. Super. Ct. Mar. 26, 1996). The mortgagee of insured property can, however, effectively assign its rights under a fire insurance policy issued to the mortgagor which contains a loss-payee clause for the protection of the mortgagee. Central Union Bank v. New York Underwriters' Ins. Co., 52 F.2d 823 (4th Cir. 1931).

[123] Antal's Restaurant v. Lumbermen's Mut. Cas. Co., 680 A.2d 1386, 1389 (D.C. App. 1996).

[5]   Assigning Executory Rights — UCC

If a house painter assigns his right to payment before the house is painted,[124] he may have lost some incentive for performing since he has already transferred his right under that contract to another. An assignment will not be ineffective, however, simply because of this possible loss of incentive.[125] Otherwise, only rights that have already been earned by performance could be assigned. There are situations, however, where the executory duties of the assignor are such that it will be difficult to evaluate the sufficiency of their performance. For example, where a patentee licensed another to exercise his patent on a royalty basis and promised to cooperate with the licensee in furthering the exploitation of the patent, an assignment of the right to future royalties was ineffective.[126] Similarly, if a party attempts not only to assign his rights under an executory contract, but to delegate a substantial part of his duties which are nondelegable, the obligor is entitled to disregard the assignment of the rights as well as the delegation of the duties.[127] The same result follows where the assignor repudiates his liability under the contract.[128] If, however, the assignor substantially performs the duty in spite of the purported assignment, the assignment will be effective if the assignor had a sufficient incentive to perform.

If a party assigns his right and delegates his duty under a contract calling for the other party to perform before he receives performance from the assignor, there is old authority holding the assignment to be ineffective. For example, it has been said that a right to purchase goods on credit cannot be effectively assigned because the seller is entitled to the credit of the buyer with whom he contracted.[129] The erroneous assumption is that the delegate succeeds in ridding himself of his duty by way of the assignment and delegation. As will be seen later, this is impossible absent the consent of the obligor. There is no sound reason for denying effect to such an assignment and numerous courts have so held.[130]

The UCC, however, recognizes that the obligor may be legitimately concerned about the reliability of the new party who is to perform the duty.[131] Thus, in *any* assignment coupled with a delegation of duty within its scope, the Code views the obligor as a party with reasonable grounds for insecurity,[132] giving rise to a right in the obligor to demand adequate assurances of performance by the delegate.[133]

---

[124] As suggested earlier, rights under an executory contract may be assigned.

[125] *See* Somont Oil Co. v. Nutter, 228 Mont. 467, 743 P.2d 1016 (1987).

[126] Paper Prods. Mach. Co. v. Safepack Mills, 239 Mass. 114, 131 N.E. 288 (1921).

[127] "Where a person contracts with another to do work or perform service, and it can be inferred that the person employed has been selected with reference to his individual skill, competency or other personal qualification, the inability or unwillingness of the party so employed to execute the work or perform the service is a sufficient answer to any demand by a stranger to the original contract of the performance of it by the other party, and entitles the latter to treat the contract as at an end, notwithstanding that the person tendered to take the place of the contracting party may be equally well qualified to do the service." British Waggon Co. v. Lea, 5 Q.B.D. 149 [1880].

[128] Western Oil Sales Corp. v. Bliss & Wetherbee, 299 S.W. 637 (Tex. Comm'n App. 1927).

[129] *See* Arkansas Valley Smelting Co. v. Belden Mining Co., 127 U.S. 379, 8 S. Ct. 1308, 32 L. Ed. 246 (1888).

[130] *See, e.g.,* Voigt v. Murphy Heating Co., 164 Mich. 539, 129 N.W. 701 (1911); Minnetonka Oil Co. v. Cleveland Vitrified Brick Co., 27 Okla. 180, 111 P. 326 (1910).

[131] UCC § 2-210, comment 5.

[132] UCC § 2-609(1) permits a party to demand adequate assurance of performance where reasonable grounds for insecurity arise.

[133] UCC § 2-210(5). *See* Arkla Energy Resources v. Roye Realty & Dev., 9 F.3d 855, 864 (10th Cir. 1993).

[6]   Assignability of Options

As every contracts student knows, an offer creates a power of acceptance that may be exercised only by the party to whom it is addressed.[134] An option contract is designed to make the power of acceptance irrevocable.[135] Should the right to the irrevocable power of acceptance under an option contract be assignable even though that would result in a party other than the original offeree exercising that power? While the general rule requiring that only the offeree may exercise the power of acceptance is sound, when the power of acceptance is also a contractual right under an option contract, there is no reason why it should not be assignable like any other contract right, i.e., subject to the same limitations of any other assignment. There is, therefore, no prohibition on the assignment of rights simply because they exist under an option contract.[136]

[7]   Partial Assignments

If an obligor owes the obligee $10,000, we have seen that there is no obstacle to effectively assigning the right to the payment of money. If, however, the obligee decides to assign $5,000 of that right to an assignee, is the burden on the obligor materially increased so as to make such a partial assignment ineffective?

Historically, the assignment of part of a single claim or cause of action under a contract was not recognized over the objection of the obligor.[137] Common law courts consistently refused to entertain a suit involving more than two parties having adverse interests. If such an assignment were held to be effective, contrary to the will of the debtor, in a law action, the result would be that a creditor could "split" his cause of action by making partial assignments, thus subjecting the debtor to a multiplicity of suits.[138] In a court of equity, on the other hand, any number of parties with adverse interests could be brought into a single suit, either as plaintiffs or defendants. As has been well said:

> In equity the interests of all parties can be determined in a single suit. The debtor can bring the entire fund into court, and run no risks as to its proper distribution. If he be in no fault no costs need be imposed upon him, or they may be awarded in his favor. If he be put to extra trouble in keeping separate accounts he can, if it is reasonable, be compensated for it. In many ways a court of equity can, while a court of law, with its present modes cannot, protect the rights and interests of all parties concerned.[139]

---

[134]   RESTATEMENT 2d § 29(1).

[135]   RESTATEMENT 2d § 25.

[136]   *See, e.g.*, Van Kirk & Riles Interest, Inc. v. Forest Oil Corp., 206 F. Supp. 2d 856, 858–59 (S. D. Tex. 2002) (option to purchase an oil platform was assignable). *See also* DiPietro v. Boynton, 628 A.2d 1019, 1023 (Me. 1993) and Melrose Enters. v. Pawtucket Form Constr. Co., 550 A.2d 300 (R.I. 1988), where the court held the assignment of an option to purchase real estate effective since there was no evidence that the option was dependent upon any trust, confidence or qualification reposed in the original holder of the option. *See also* RESTATEMENT 2d § 320.

[137]   *See* Mandeville v. Welch, 18 U.S. (5 Wheat.) 277, 5 L. Ed. 87 (1820).

[138]   See Angeles Real Estate Co. v. Kerxton, 737 F.2d 416, 419 (4th Cir. 1984), discussing the rationale for the old rule. That rule may be stated as follows: The assignment of the whole of what amounts to a separate and distinct cause of action under a contract, though it is not the whole of what will eventually become due, is not a partial assignment within the rule and is effective at law. Timmons v. Citizens Bank of Waynesboro, 11 Ga. App. 69, 74 S.E. 798 (1912) (assignment of a progress payment under a construction contract).

[139]   National Exch. Bank v. McLoon, 73 Me. 498, 505, 40 Am. Rep. 388, 389 (1882).

This has become the modern view in actions at law. An assignment of part of a right is effective in the same manner as if the party had been assigned a separate right.[140] If, however, the obligor has not agreed to perform as to the separate part of the right, the obligor may resist any legal proceeding to enforce that separate part unless all parties entitled to the entire promised performance are joined in the proceeding.[141] Modern procedural codes make such joinder possible. If joinder in a given case is not feasible, the action may proceed against the obligor to enforce the separate right only if it is equitable to proceed absent joinder of all the parties.[142]

[B]   Limitation — Public Policy

A major limitation on the assignability of rights is the refusal of courts to recognize assignments which are contrary to public policy. Either by statute or judicial decision, certain assignments are considered contrary to public policy for a variety of reasons. The most conspicuous statutory prohibition occurs in relation to attempted assignments of wages.[143] Different types of statutes restricting the assignment of wages were enacted throughout the country to protect the wage earner against his own improvidence as well as against unscrupulous parties who might otherwise take advantage of him. Statutes regulated retail installment sales containing provisions affecting assignment by the seller of his rights under a regulated contract. Pursuant to a survey of such statutes, the Federal Trade Commission found no harm to consumers that allowed installment payments to be made through payroll deductions or preauthorized electronic funds transfers. The Commission, however, found harm to consumers in wage garnishments leading to a 1984 regulation that made an assignment of wages or other earnings an unfair trade practice unless the assignment was revocable at will by the debtor, or was an authorized payroll deduction or preauthorized payment plan where the consumer authorized the deductions as a means of payment, or the assignment applied to wages already earned at the time of the assignment.[144] In a subsequent section,[145] we will see how such statutes and regulations make certain defenses available to a consumer buyer of goods against an assignee.

Apart from statutory regulation, other assignments are held to be void under the rules of the common law because they are deemed to be contrary to public policy.[146] Since the rules applying to the enforceability of contracts generally are applicable to assignments, the

---

[140] *See* Advanced Testing Techs, Inc. v. Desmond, 337 F. 3d 38, 46 (1st Cir. 2003)); J & B Slurry Seal Co. v. Mid-South Aviation, Inc., 88 N.C. App. 1, 362 S.E.2d 812 (1987) (plaintiff assigned to insurer to the extent of insurer's compensation for plaintiff's loss). *See also* RESTATEMENT 2d § 326(1).

[141] *See* Dill v. Blakeney, 568 So. 2d 774 (Ala. 1990); Space Coast Credit Union v. Walt Disney World Co., 483 So. 2d 35 (Fla. Dist. Ct. App. 1986). *See also* RESTATEMENT 2d § 326(2).

[142] See RESTATEMENT 2d § 326, comment c, stating criteria: the probability of material prejudice to the obligor, the extent to which relief can be shaped to avoid prejudice, the adequacy of relief that can be afforded to parties before the court and the availability of alternate remedies. FED. R. CIV. P. 19. See also Phoenix Ins. Co. v. Woosley, 287 F.2d 531 (10th Cir. 1961), where nine partial assignees totaled their respective interests so as to equal the jurisdictional amount.

[143] A useful collection of these statutes and commentary thereon is found in the Statutory Note to Chapter 15 of the RESTATEMENT 2d (prior to § 316) under the caption, "Wage Assignments."

[144] 16 C. F. R. § 444.2 Many state statutes allowing wage assignments were affected by this regulation.

[145] *See* § 142[F], *infra.*

[146] *See* Federal Deposit Ins. Corp. v. Barness, 484 F. Supp. 1134, 1151–53 (E.D. Pa. 1980). *See also* RESTATEMENT 2d § 317(2)(b).

determination of whether an assignment is against public policy requires courts to balance public policy interests against the policy of free assignability.[147] If, for example, an assignee took an assignment knowing that it was contrary to a court order, the assignment would be ineffective.[148] It is generally held that the assignment of salary not yet due by a public officer is void because it tends to impair the efficiency of the public service.[149] Likewise, the assignment of a life insurance policy to one who has no insurable interest in the life of the insured is invalid when the assignment is part of a preconceived plan to evade the rule of law which prohibits the making of wagering contracts.[150] Tort claims, such as malpractice,[151] defamation, abuse of process, malicious prosecution or conspiracy to commit fraud or unfair practices, are not assignable.[152] There is a strong policy against the assignability of unliquidated personal injury claims to preclude champerty and particularly to prevent the unscrupulous from purchasing causes of action dealing in pain and suffering.[153]

[1]   Structured Settlements

To resolve tort claims, a plaintiff may enter into a settlement agreement to receive periodic payments, typically in the form of an annuity contract issued by an insurance company. A multi-billion dollar business has developed under which "factoring" companies offer lump-sum payments to the tort victim in exchange for an assignment of the victim's future annuity payments. Extensive and effective advertising may induce a necessitous victim to assign her right in exchange for a discounted payment that could further threaten the victim's financial stability. Many states have enacted Structured Settlement Protection Acts designed to protect the victim by imposing disclosure requirements as well as judicial supervision of such transactions to ascertain that they are fair and reasonable.[154]

There is no end to illustrations of public policy questions. Suffice to say that the public policy concepts discussed earlier in this volume in relation to the enforceability of contracts are applicable to assignments.[155]

---

[147] McKnight v. Rice, Hoppner, Brown & Brunner, 678 P.2d 1330 (Alaska 1984).

[148] *Id.*

[149] Byers v. Comer, 50 Ariz. 8, 68 P.2d 671, *modified,* 50 Ariz. 134, 70 P.2d 330 (1937). As to who is a public officer within the meaning of the rule, cf. Kimball v. Ledford, 13 Cal. App. 2d 602, 57 P.2d 163 (1936) (holding that a school teacher is not a public officer), and Schmitt v. Dooling, 145 Ky. 240, 140 S.W. 197 (1911) (holding that a fireman is a public officer).

[150] The cases are collected in Annot., 30 A.L.R.2d 1310 (1953). A few jurisdictions make the assignment of a life insurance policy to one who has no insurable interest illegal *per* se. The majority of courts hold otherwise.

[151] Weston v. Dowty, 163 Mich. App. 238, 414 N.W.2d 165 (1987).

[152] Investors Title Ins. Co. v. Herzig, 330 N.C. 681, 413 S.E.2d 268, 271 (1992).

[153] Chiropractic Nutritional Assocs. v. Empire Blue Cross and Blue Shield, 447, Pa. Super. 436. 452–53, 669 A.2d 975, 983 (1995) (citing this treatise). *See also* Picadilly, Inc. v. Raikos, 582 N. E. 2d 338, 340 (Ind. 1991).

[154] See, e. g., N. J. Stat. 2A-15-63 *et. seq.* ; Conn. Gen Stat., § 52-225f; Fla. Stat. § 626. 99296; Kt. Stat. Ann.§ 454.430 *et. seq.*; NYCLS Gen. Oblig. § 5-1701 *et. seq.*; Cal. Ins. Code, § 10234 *et. seq.*

[155] *See supra* Chapter 6, § 99. *See also* RESTATEMENT 2d Chapter 9.

[C]   Limitation — Prohibition of Assignment — UCC — "Structured Settlements"

[1]   Antiassignment Clauses — Promise Not to Assign — Surrendering Power to Assign

To what extent the parties to a contract can, by agreement, effectively prohibit or restrict the assignment of rights or duties created by the contract that would otherwise be assignable is a question upon which the courts, over the years, have demonstrated some confusion. On the one hand, some older cases suggested that the assignment of money claims,[156] and of rights under contracts for the purchase of land,[157] cannot be prohibited by agreement of the parties, on the ground that such a prohibition is an unlawful restraint on alienation. The theory is that a money claim or a contract right to land is sufficiently like ownership of a tangible chattel or land and should be free from restraints on alienation. On the other hand, cases of the same vintage sometimes asserted categorically that a prohibition or restriction of assignment of any kind of a claim is effective, and may render ineffective the attempt to assign a right or a duty that would otherwise be assignable.[158] The conflict between the policy of freedom of contract and the policy precluding restraints upon alienation was painfully obvious.

Older case law revealed that a prohibition of assignment provision in a contract may take any one of at least three distinct forms,[159] and the form of the provision could very well condition its legal effect: (1) The contract may contain a promise by one or both parties to refrain from assigning. Unless this promise were specifically enforceable, an assignment that violates it would remain effective. The promise creates a duty in the promisor not to assign. It does not deprive the assignor of the *power* to assign and its breach, therefore, would simply subject the promisor to an action for damages while the assignment would be effective.[160] (2) If the contract provides that an assignment will make the *contract* void, the assignment is effective but the obligor may, at his or her election, avoid the contract for breach of condition.[161] (3) The contract may provide that any attempted *assignment* shall be void. Such a stipulation obviously contemplates that the assignment itself shall be deemed ineffective, unless the obligor consents to it.[162] The court concluded that when such clear language stating that any attempted assignment is "void," one would have to do violence to the language to conclude that it constituted a mere promise not to assign. The modern approach emphasizes the difference

---

[156] State St. Furniture Co. v. Armour & Co., 345 Ill. 160, 177 N.E. 702 (1931). See also the statements of Justice Holmes in Portuguese-American Bank v. Welles, 242 U.S. 7, 37 S. Ct. 3, 61 L. Ed. 116 (1916).

[157] *See* Goddard, *Non-Assignment Provisions in Land Contracts*, 31 Mich. L. Rev. 1 (1932).

[158] "Without discussion, it is settled law that parties to a contract can agree that the contract in all its terms shall be nonassignable both at law and in equity, and that the Commonwealth in the pending case could refuse to recognize any assignment not within the strict provisions of it." Federal Nat'l Bank v. Commonwealth, 282 Mass. 442, 450, 185 N.E. 9, 12 (1933). *See also* Concrete Form Co. v. W. T. Grange Constr. Co., 320 Pa. 205, 181 A. 589 (1935).

[159] This analysis as it appeared in the second edition of this book was cited with approval in Cedar Point Apts., Ltd. v. Cedar Point Inv. Corp., 693 F.2d 748 (8th Cir. 1982), *cert. denied*, 461 U.S. 914, 103 S. Ct. 1893, 77 L. Ed. 2d 283 (1983).

[160] *See* Reuben H. Donnelley Corp. v. McKinnon, 688 S.W.2d 612 (Tex. App. Corpus Christi 1985); Hull v. Hostettler, 224 Mich. 365, 194 N.W. 996 (1923); Randol v. Totum, 98 Cal. 390, 33 P. 433 (1893). *See also* Restatement 2d § 322(2)(b).

[161] *See* Merrill v. New England Mut. Life Ins. Co., 103 Mass. 245, 4 Am. Rep. 548 (1869).

[162] Allhusen v. Caristo Constr. Corp., 303 N.Y. 446, 103 N.E.2d 891, 37 A.L.R.2d 1245 (1952).

between a promise not to assign and the surrender of the power to assign.[163] Many other courts have adopted this analysis. Thus, if the language is sufficiently clear to manifest an intention to surrender the *power* to assign, an attempted assignment would be ineffective. A mere promise not to assign, however, makes the assignor liable in damages for breaching the promise without affecting the assignment.[164] Many courts insist on language such as "void," "null" or "of no effect." Others, while agreeing with the concept, may be put off by the requirement of such "magic words" and would subject the language to the usual interpretative process to ascertain the parties intention to either promise not to assign or to surrender the power to assign.[165]

The UCC and the RESTATEMENT 2d manifest the modern trend toward limiting the validity of restraints on alienation.[166] Following the UCC,[167] unless the language or circumstances indicate the contrary, prohibition of an assignment of "the contract" is construed to bar only the delegation of duties and not the assignment of rights.[168] Like the UCC,[169] the RESTATEMENT 2d indicates that where a whole contract has been breached or fully performed on one side, a term prohibiting assignment to the assignment of damages or payment for the performance is ineffective.[170] Unless the parties manifest a different intention, the RESTATEMENT 2d prefers an interpretation that an antiassignment clause is the breach of a duty not to assign, allowing the obligor to sue the obligee for provable damages, but does not render the assignment ineffective, i.e., it does not preclude the *power* to assign.[171]

[2] UCC Limitations on Antiassignment Provisions — The Article 9 Qualification

The significant UCC changes are not without confusion. In Article 2 of the Code (sales and contracts for the sale of goods), there is a presumption of free assignability of rights.[172] The language directing such free assignability, however, begins with a familiar Code phrase, "Unless otherwise agreed," thereby indicating that the parties may agree that all or some of the rights under the contract are not assignable. This provision must be compared with certain provisions of Article 9 of the UCC.

---

[163] In Rumbin v. Utica Mutual Ins. Co., the court stated, "The contract may contain a promise by one or both parties to refrain from assigning. . . . The promise creates a duty in the promisor not to assign. It does not deprive the assignor of the power to assign and its breach, therefore, would simply subject to the promise to an action in damages while the assignment would be effective." 254 Conn.259, 272–72, 757 A.2d 526, 533 (2000) quoting an earlier edition of this treatise.

[164] See, e.g., Sourcecorp, Inc. v. Villandry Holdings, 2007 U.S. Dist. LEXIS 78069 (E. D. Pa. 2007); Traicoff v. Digital Media, Inc., 439 F. Supp. 2d 872 (S. D. Ind. 2006).

[165] Bank of America, N. A. v. Moglia, 330 F. 3d 942 (7th Cir. 2003) albeit Judge Posner notes that many states require the "magic words."

[166] RESTATEMENT 2d § 322, comment a.

[167] UCC § 2-210(3).

[168] RESTATEMENT 2d § 322(1).

[169] UCC § 2-210(2).

[170] RESTATEMENT 2d § 322(2)(a). Indeed, comment b indicates that where a right to the payment of money is fully earned by performance, a provision that would cause such payment to be forfeited upon an attempt to assign such payment would be a violation of the rule against contractual penalties (citing § 356).

[171] RESTATEMENT 2d § 322(2)(b). See Bel-Ray Co. v. Chemrite Ltd., 181 F.3d 435, 442 (3d Cir. 1999) (New Jersey law).

[172] UCC § 2-210(2).

As suggested earlier,[173] Article 9 applies to the sale (assignment) of "accounts" which, under the current version of Article 9 of the Code, includes executory contract rights.[174] This is true, though Article 9 is centrally concerned with the transfer of security interests in tangible and intangible collateral. The earlier discussion explained that in modern commercial financing transactions, the line between a security transfer and outright sale of accounts is often blurred. Therefore, the Article 9 draftsmen decided to include such outright sales (assignments). Another provision of Article 9 literally makes anti-assignment provisions totally ineffective when applied to the assignment of accounts,[175] suggesting a possible contradiction with Article 2. There is, however, a reconciliation. As we saw earlier, Article 9 exempts from its coverage certain assignments of accounts that have nothing to do with commercial financing.[176] Thus, Article 9 does not apply to such sales when they form part of a sale of the business out of which they arose, when they are exclusively for the purpose of collection, when the assignee is obligated to perform under the contract, where the assignment is a single account in full or partial satisfaction of a pre-existing indebtedness or where the assignment is a claim under a policy of insurance.[177] If Article 9 does not apply, its provision invalidating anti-assignment clauses does not apply.

As noted earlier, Insurance companies enter into contracts to settle claims against the insured by creating "structured settlements" that will provide periodic payments to the injured party. These agreements will typically contain an anti-assignment provision because of negative tax consequences that may otherwise ensue.[178] Claims that such clauses are rendered ineffective under Article 9[179] have been consistently rejected.[180] Article 9 expressly exempts an assignment of a claim under a policy of insurance from its coverage.[181]

---

[173] *See supra* § 137.

[174] An earlier (1968) version of Article 9 included a separate category of "contract rights" to deal with executory contract rights, i.e., rights not yet earned by performance. "Accounts" had been previously relegated to rights earned by performance, i.e., where the contract for the sale or lease of goods or for services had been performed. Under the 1972 version of Article 9, "account" includes rights to payment for goods or services whether earned or unearned, thus encompassing the former separate classification of "contract rights." The current (1999) version (§ 9-109(a)(2)) further expands the definition of "account" to include certain "general intangibles" as they were defined in the previous version.

[175] UCC § 9-406(d) (formerly § 9-318(4)).

[176] See § 137, text preceding note 42.

[177] UCC § 9-109(d)(4)–(8).

[178] *See* CGU Life Ins. Co. of Am. v. Metropolitan Mortg. & Secs. Co., Inc., 2001 U.S. Dist. LEXIS 1138, at *23 (E.D. Pa. Feb. 2, 2001).

[179] The claims are based on the earlier version of Article 9, § 9-318(4), which is found in § 9-109(d) of the 1999 version.

[180] In addition to *CGU Life, supra* note 178, see Liberty Life Assurance Co. of Boston v. Stone St. Capital, Inc., 93 F. Supp. 2d 630 (D. Md. 2000); Bobbitt v. Safeco, 1999 Conn. Super. LEXIS 2347 (Conn. Super. Ct. 1999); Henderson v. Roadway Express, 308 Ill. App. 3d 546, 242 Ill. Dec. 153, 720 N.E.2d 1108, 1113 (4th Dist. 1999); Wonsy v. Life Ins. Co. of N. Am., 32 F. Supp. 2d 939 (E.D. Mich. 1998).

[181] The earlier version to which cases refer is § 9-104(g). The current (1999) version replicates this provision in § 9-109(d)(8), though it narrows it by covering assignments by or to "health care insurance receivables" as defined in § 9-102(46).

§ 140   THE ASSIGNMENT OF "FUTURE RIGHTS"

[A]   Meaning of "Future Right"

There is no question that one can make an effective assignment of an executory right and even a right subject to an express condition under an existing contract. If A agrees to paint B's house for $10,000, B's duty to pay the $10,000 is constructive conditioned on A's painting the house. Nonetheless, once the contract is made but before he performs, A may assign his executory right to $10,000 to C or any other assignee. Similarly, the fact that a contract right is subject to an express condition does not impair its assignability though the condition may never occur.[182] Where a plumber assigned his right to future payment, the court recognized that "properly speaking," no assignment could be made of a nonexistent subject. The right, however, had "potential existence" and when it became a reality, equity would regard the earlier agreement as an "assignment *pro tanto* of the payment.[183] In *Field v. Mayor of New York*,[184] no contracted existed, but a course of dealing provided a basis for a realistic expectation that a right to payments for printing services would exist, allowing the court to find a retroactive equitable assignment of that right.

A "future right" may generally be regarded as one which the assignor does not then have but which he expects to acquire. There are, however, two types of "future rights" which must be distinguished: (1) If the assignor is operating under an *existing contract* and expects to acquire rights in the future under that contract, the rights do not exist. However, they are more than mere hopes since the probabilities are great that they will exist. Thus, if X is employed at a rate of $1000 per week under a contract terminable at will, he has no right to future wages since he could be terminated at any time. Yet, absent statutory prohibitions, he may assign his wages for a future period to Y because he is operating under an employment relationship, though it is indefinite in duration.[185] (2) Another type of purported assignment of a future right occurs when X has a hope of *entering into a contract* of employment and attempts to assign a right to his first month's wages to Y. Here, there is not only no presently existing right; there is no realistic assumption that the right will exist. There is simply a hope that one will exist. Thus, where Gabriel Pascal had the exclusive right to convert the famous George Bernard Shaw play, Pygmalion into a musical and film version, and assigned a portion of the royalties from musical productions of the play for which contracts, much less the productions, did not exist, a court held such an assignment effective.[186] Here the "future right" assigned was more than a mere hope.[187] It is important to make this basic distinction at the outset of any discussion of the assignment of "future rights."

---

[182] *See* Advanced Testing Techs, Inc. v. Desmond, 337 F. 3d 38, 47 n.13 (1st Cir. 2003); Bonanza Motors v. Webb, 104 Idaho 234, 657 P.2d 1102 (Ct. App. 1983); Rockmore v. Lehman, 129 F.2d 892 (2d Cir. 1942). *See also* RESTATEMENT 2d § 320, particularly illustration 5.

[183] Seymour v. Finance & Guaranty Co., 155 Md. 514, 142 A. 710 (1928).

[184] 6 N.l Y. 179 (1852).

[185] Citizens' Loan Ass'n v. Boston & M. R.R., 196 Mass. 528, 82 N.E. 696 (1907).

[186] Speelman v. Pascal, 10 N.Y.2d 313, 222 N.Y.S.2d 324, 178 N.E.2d 723 (1961). The musical (stage and screen) productions followed under the now famous title, "My Fair Lady."

[187] See Leon v. Martinez, 84 N.Y.2d 83, 614 N.Y.S.2d 972, 638 N.E.2d 511, 513 (1994), where a writing stated that the defendant "gives" five percent of any recovery that he may receive in existing litigation to each of the plaintiffs who cared for defendant after an accident.

[B]   Earlier Case Law

Older decisions generally took the position that an attempted assignment of any future right, i.e., whether emanating from an existing contract or a mere expectancy, must necessarily fail for the same reason that attempted transfers of after-acquired tangible property were frequently held to fail — simply because one could not transfer a right that did not exist.[188] If it were true that an assignment could operate, if at all, only as a transfer of an existing right, the conclusion stated necessarily followed. The analogy to transfer of tangible property, however, was defective. We know that, historically, an assignment of a chose in action did not operate in the same way in any case. On the contrary, such an attempted transfer was held to vest in the assignee, at most, an irrevocable power of attorney to require performance of the assigned claim and to retain the proceeds thereof.[189] If an assignment be deemed to operate in this way, there is obviously no logical objection to the effectiveness of the assignment of a future right, since it is perfectly possible presently to confer upon another an irrevocable power to require performance of a future obligation. Even on a transfer theory, it would be perfectly consistent to say what has sometimes been held in the case of attempted transfers of after-acquired tangible property, namely, that the assignment at least amounts to a contract to assign when the right is acquired, and that equity, which regards that as done which ought to be done, will look upon the assignee as acquiring, the moment the right comes into existence, an equitable title to the claim, or an equitable lien on it, which is good against everyone but a bona fide purchaser for value.

[C]   The Modern View — "Equitable" Assignments

The semantic difficulties suggested at the beginning of this section must be kept in mind in attempting to understand the modern law in this area. There are many decisions dealing with "future" rights and those decisions do not always distinguish rights arising out of an existing contract (though not presently enforceable) and rights which are mere expectancies where no contract exists. The former are now treated as if they were present, existing rights and are as assignable as any other present right.[190] As to rights expected to arise where no contract yet exists, modern courts treat purported assignments of such rights as they have always been treated in the past, i.e., only as promises to assign such rights when they arise, providing the purported assignee with a power to enforce them. They are often referred to as "equitable assignments," again on the footing that equity will treat such an assignment as a promise to assign and will normally decree specific performance of that promise when the right comes into existence because "equity looks upon that as done which ought to have been done."[191]

---

188 *See, e.g.,* O'Niel v. Helmke, 124 Wis. 234, 102 N.W. 573 (1905). *See also* Williston, *Transfers of After-Acquired Personal Property*, 19 Harv. L. Rev. 557 (1906).

189 *See supra* § 136[B].

190 *See Bonanza Motors, supra* note 182. *See also* Chicorp Fin. Servs. v. University of State, 1994 Mass. Super. LEXIS 718 (Mass. Super. Ct. Aug. 4, 1994); Loyola Univ. Med. Ctr. v. Med Care HMO, 180 Ill. App. 3d 471, 129 Ill. Dec. 360, 535 N.E.2d 1125 (1st Dist. 1989); Bank of Cave Spring v. Gold Kist, Inc., 173 Ga. App. 679, 327 S.E.2d 800, 802 (1985). Restatement 2d § 321(1).

191 *See* Western United Assurance Co. v. Hayden, 64 F.3d 833, 838 (3d Cir. 1995). See also Restatement 2d § 330 comment c, which also suggests that they may be called "equitable liens." If a party grants a mortgage on real property or a security interest in personalty (a "chattel mortgage") even though he does not own the property, he grants no property interest in his actions. Yet, on the footing that the promise should be enforceable when he acquired rights in the property, the mortgagee acquires an equitable lien.

Thus, under the modern view, the characterization "future rights" refers only to those rights which arise from a continuing business or employment relationship and are reasonable expectancies though they are not based upon an existing contract and do not exist at the time of assignment.[192]

If the assignment is characterized as an "equitable assignment," there will normally be little significance to the characterization as between the purported assignor and assignee since, again, when the right comes into existence, specific performance will usually be decreed. Such rights, however, are susceptible to being defeated. Thus, the right of an equitable assignee may be subordinate to an attaching creditor,[193] or an assignee in insolvency or bankruptcy,[194] or the assignor himself and his personal representatives.[195] So long as the assignor of such a future right has not revoked the assignee's power to require performance or it has not been terminated by the death or bankruptcy of the assignor or by the intervention of an attaching creditor, the right (when it comes into existence) may be enforced. In effect, the equitable assignee has a revocable power to enforce the future right, at least to the extent that contractual remedies are available.[196] It is more than likely that such an assignment, while ineffective to transfer the right to the assignee, will be interpreted as a contract to account to the assignee for the proceeds, when they have been obtained by the assignor from a subsequent obligor.[197]

From a commercial financing perspective, the principle that the assignment of non-existent rights would be viewed as an equitable assignment that could be defeated by attaching creditors and good faith purchasers did not provide the necessary security. The only reliable collateral was existing collateral. Long term financing relationships could not exist under these circumstances. The UCC provided a comprehensive solution to this problem.

[D] Uniform Commercial Code — After-Acquired Property

The most significant example of the assignment or transfer of "future rights" occurs in commercial financing situations, which are governed by Article 9 of the UCC. In a previous section, the implications of Article 9 in the law of assignments were surveyed.[198] The most significant manifestation of the transfer of "future rights" occurs in modern commercial financing. A simple example of how "future rights" can be secured in this context will assist comprehension of the application of Article 9.

Joseph Adams operates the Adams hardware store. To purchase his new inventory, Adams must borrow money from the local bank. The bank and Adams have agreed that from time to time the bank will lend Adams amounts to permit the replenishing of the Adams inventory. Adams will correspondingly repay the outstanding indebtedness on a continuous basis, i.e., as he resells the inventory at a profit, he will repay the amounts to the bank. It is contemplated,

---

[192] See RESTATEMENT 2d § 321, captioned "Assignment of Future Rights," and comment a.

[193] O'Niel v. Helmke, 124 Wis. 234, 102 N.W. 573 (1905). Mulhall v. Quinn, 67 Mass. (1 Gray) 105, 61 Am. Dec. 414 (1854).

[194] Taylor v. Barton-Child Co., 228 Mass. 126, 117 N.E. 43 (1917) (book accounts). *Contra In re* United Fuel & Supply Co., 250 Mich. 325, 230 N.W. 164 (1930).

[195] *In re* Nelson's Estate, 211 Iowa 168, 233 N.W. 115, 72 A.L.R. 850 (1930).

[196] *See* RESTATEMENT 2d § 330 comment d.

[197] RESTATEMENT 2d § 330(2).

[198] *See supra* § 137.

therefore, that Adams and the bank will be in a continuous debtor-creditor relationship. The bank, however, will not lend these amounts to Adams on a pure credit basis. The bank, like most creditors, will insist on some security to assure the repayment of the loans. The best security for the bank is the inventory of Adams' store, for that is probably Adams' most valuable asset.[199] When the continuous loan agreement was formed, the bank insisted that Adams sign a security agreement granting the bank as secured creditor a security interest in all of Adams' present inventory,[200] but the bank was also interested in Adams' future inventory, i.e., his "after-acquired" inventory.[201] In addition, the bank was interested in the *proceeds* which Adams would receive, i.e., cash, checks, accounts, and the like, when he sold the inventory to his customers.[202] The bank wants Adams to sell his inventory and make a profit to repay the loan. If, however, the bank has a security interest exclusively in the inventory and not the proceeds, the bank's security disappears as the inventory is sold off. The bank wants a security interest in that which is received by Adams when the inventory is sold (proceeds), and it also wants a way of ascertaining that it will have an automatic, attached, and perfected security interest in the new inventory purchased by Adams as soon as Adams has rights in that inventory. So, the bank takes a security interest not only in the *present* inventory and proceeds but in all *after-acquired inventory and proceeds*. Adams granted that security interest (the property right) in such after-acquired inventory and proceeds (future rights) at the time the arrangement was initially consummated.

Conceptually, it is difficult to think of the transfer of nonexistent, future rights in this context and, prior to the Code, it was either impossible or extremely difficult and cumbersome to do so. Article 9 of the Code has removed the obstacles to this transfer of rights in after-acquired property and, today, commercial financing of innumerable establishments occurs on this basis. It is sometimes popularly referred to as a "floating lien" or "floor planning" method of commercial financing.

The question arises: when does the transfer of rights in the after-acquired inventory and proceeds occur? Suppose that Adams must restock certain screwdrivers in its hardware store and orders $5,000 worth of these goods from a supplier. When is the property interest (the security interest) in these particular goods transferred to the bank to partially secure the repayment of Adams' debt to the bank? Assume that Adams ordered the screwdrivers on February 1, 1998 and they were delivered on February 7, 1998. The security agreement granting an interest in such after-acquired property was signed by Adams and the bank on June 1, 1996. On June 2, 1996, the bank filed a financing statement (signed by Adams) in the

---

[199] The following definitions appeared in the 1972 version of Article 9 in § 9-109. They now appear in the 1999 version in § 9-102. "Inventory" is goods that are held for sale or lease or to be furnished under contracts of service, or raw materials, work in process or materials used or consumed in a business (§ 9-102(48)). Anything held for sale (e.g., appliances, furniture, food, clothing, hardware, raw materials, etc.) or lease (the autos of a car leasing company) are inventory. The office or production machinery used to operate the business is not inventory — it is "equipment" (§ 9-102(33)). Goods purchased primarily for personal, family, or household purposes are consumer goods (§ 9-102(23)). Crops (growing or to be grown), livestock (born or unborn), and their products as well as supplies used in farming operations are "farm products" (§ 9-102(35)).

[200] UCC § 9-203(a).

[201] *See* UCC § 9-204(a).

[202] UCC § 9-315(c). "Proceeds" includes whatever is received when collateral is sold, leased exchanged, collected, or otherwise disposed of. Money, checks, and the like are "cash" proceeds. Other proceeds, including accounts, are non-cash proceeds. Proceeds also includes whatever is received from the sale or exchange of proceeds, i.e., the original proceeds may be converted into different proceeds. § 9-102(64).

appropriate public offices.[203] This public notice of the security interest in Adams' inventory and after-acquired property placed all of Adams' creditors on notice that the bank, the Article 9 secured creditor, had a prior claim to the specific collateral described in the publicly filed statement. Should Adams become insolvent and perhaps bankrupt, the bank would have priority over all of the inventory as against all of Adams' other creditors and, if he went bankrupt, even against the trustee in bankruptcy. The public recording of the financing statement (perfecting the security interest) is critical to a secured creditor engaged in long term financing arrangements with businesses such as the Adams' hardware store. The UCC does not pretend that a security interest attaches until the debtor (Adams) has rights in the collateral.[204] Adams cannot grant a security interest in property that he does not yet own. The screwdrivers may not have existed — they were not yet manufactured — at the time the security agreement was signed or the financing statement was signed or filed. Yet, there is a recognition of the fact that a security interest in that *future* property — after-acquired property — will exist as soon as the debtor obtains rights in that collateral, which will occur as soon as the goods are *identified* for shipment to Adams[205] since the other elements of "attachment" have occurred, i.e., the signed security agreement and the giving of value by the bank.[206] From the moment the financing statement was filed, however, the *priority* security interest, publicly recorded so as not to defraud other potential creditors, was held by the bank. By providing certainty and stability to the financing of after-acquired property, the UCC system was and continues to be a particularly important factor in economic development.

§ 141 DELEGATION OF DUTIES

[A]   Distinguished From Assignment

While an effective assignment extinguishes the right in the assignor and creates a similar right in the assignee, a party cannot "assign a duty" in the sense that he can extinguish the duty in himself and create a similar duty in the assignee.[207] "Many a debtor wishes that by such an expression he could get rid of his debts. Any debtor can express such an intention, but it is not operative to produce such a hoped-for-result."[208] Where a party assigns his right and delegates his duty without the consent of the other party to the contract, he no longer has any right, but he remains liable as a surety for the performance of the duty.[209] If the delegate performs the duty, the duty is discharged, both as to the delegate and the obligor who

---

[203] The place of filing will depend upon the kind of collateral in which the security interest was taken. *See* UCC § 9-501.

[204] UCC § 9-203(b)(2).

[205] UCC § 2-501.

[206] UCC § 9-203(b).

[207] Rosenberger v. Son, Inc., 491 N.W.2d 71 (N.D. 1992); Smith v. Wrehe, 199 Neb. 753, 261 N.W.2d 620 (1978); McAlpine v. AAMCO Automatic Transmissions, Inc., 461 F. Supp. 1232 (E.D. Mich. 1978); Contemporary Mission, Inc. v. Famous Music Corp., 557 F.2d 918 (2d Cir. 1977) (also suggesting that lawyers often inartfully use the term "assignment" to encompass delegation which has a different effect). UCC § 2-210(1). RESTATEMENT 2d § 318(3).

[208] See *Rosenberger, id.* at 74 (quoting the predecessor section to CORBIN ON CONTRACTS § 49.6).

[209] Headrick v. Rockwell Int'l Corp., 24 F.3d 1272, 1278 (10th Cir. 1994). *See* Martinesi v. Tidmore, 760 P.2d 1102, 1103 (Ariz. Ct. App. 1988) (where an owner coveys property to a third party notwithstanding an option contract, the grantee takes subject to the option if he has either actual or constructive knowledge of the option; in any event, the owner is liable for the breach of the option contract).

delegated the duty.[210] If the obligee had agreed to release the obligor and accept a delegate in his place, the obligor is discharged since the parties would have effected a novation.[211] Before further exploration of these effects, it is important to distinguish delegable from nondelegable duties.

[B]   Delegable vs. Nondelegable Duties

Just as certain rights are not assignable notwithstanding the policy of free assignability, certain duties are not delegable even though delegability of duties is favored. Unless the duty is a personal one which must be performed by the obligor, or if it is a duty involving personal skill or discretion, the duty may be delegated to another, provided the obligor stands ready to perform in the event the delegate does not perform.[212] Unless the parties otherwise agree, delegation of a duty is considered a normal incident of a contract unless a substantial reason can be shown why the delegated performance would not be as satisfactory as the performance by the delegator.[213] The fact that the contract is one for personal services, alone, does not make the duties nondelegable. As suggested in a famous passage,

> All painters do not paint portraits like Sir Joshua Reynolds, nor landscapes like Claude Lorraine, nor do all writers write dramas like Shakespeare or fiction like Dickens. Rare genius and extraordinary skill are not transferable, and contracts for their employment are therefore personal, and cannot be assigned. But rare genius and extraordinary skill are not indispensable to the workmanlike digging down of a sand hill or the filling up of a depression to a given level, or the construction of brick sewers with manholes and covers, and contracts [duties] for such work are not personal and may be assigned.[214]

The obligor may, however, have a substantial interest in having a particular person perform. Duties involving artistic skill or unique abilities are not delegable since there is no objective method to determine whether performance by a delegate would be substantially identical with the delegator's performance.[215] The duty to produce entertainment[216] or to create advertis-

---

[210] *Id.*

[211] *See Rosenberger, supra* note 207, at 75. *See also* Barton v. Perryman, 265 Ark. 228, 577 S.W.2d 596 (1979). RESTATEMENT 2d § 318 comment d.

[212] *See* UCC § 2-210(1): "A party may perform his duty through a delegate unless otherwise agreed or unless the other party has a substantial interest in having his original promisor perform or control the acts required by the contract. . . ." *See, e.g.,* Rogers v. HSN Direct Joint Venture, 1998 U.S. Dist. LEXIS 13932, at *6 (S.D.N.Y. Sept. 3, 1998) (duty to pay royalties is not one for personal service and is thus delegable). RESTATEMENT 2d § 318(2).

[213] Contemporary Mission, Inc. v. Famous Music Corp., 557 F.2d 918 (2d Cir. 1977) (most obligations can be delegated as long as performance by the delegate will not vary materially from performance by the delegant).

[214] Taylor v. Palmer, 31 Cal. 240, 247–48 (1866).

[215] *In re* Compass Van & Storage Corp., 65 B.R. 1007 (E.D.N.Y. 1986). Trustee in bankruptcy may not assume personal service contract under 11 U. S. C. § 365(c)(1)(A) of the federal Bankruptcy Code. The issue was whether a franchise agreement for moving services was such a contract. The court stated that there is a plethora of case authority dealing with delegable duties under personal service contracts. For example, a contract to paint a picture; a contract between an author and his publisher; an agreement to sing; and an agreement to render service as a physician. Just because the contract is one for personal services, however, does not preclude the delegability of duties. Duties involving judgment, skill, taste, or special ability may not be delegated. Duties that are not so properly characterized, however, should be delegable. The court held that there was no special personal relationship, special knowledge, or unique skill or talent in a distributorship agreement involving the moving and storage business.

ing[217] typically involves artistic judgment, creativity, or special skill so as to make the duty nondelegable. Duties involving unique abilities, such as those of an attorney[218] or a physician,[219] are, for the same reasons, nondelegable. Duties of corporations may be thought to be clearly delegable since the delegator-corporation itself would not have performed the duties. They would have been performed by individuals within the corporation. The obligor, however, may have contracted with the corporation on the basis that certain individuals, with unique abilities and supervisory skills, would perform the duty. Under these circumstances, delegation to another entity is ineffective unless the same individuals will perform the duty.[220] The delegate may be an agent or franchisee of the obligor and the same principles apply. If there is nothing in the agency that requires particular skill or judgment, the duty should be delegable.[221] If, however, the agent's duty involves cooperation in good faith or the use of "best efforts,"[222] the obligee may have "a substantial interest in having that person perform or control the acts promised."[223]

The delegation of a duty involving ordinary mechanical repairs or any other duty which can be objectively measured is normally delegable.[224] Where a duty to install and maintain vending machines was transferred as part of the sale of the business, the court held the duty delegable notwithstanding the fact that the obligee had dealt with the delegate in the past and had chosen the obligor. The duty was delegable because there was not such a material difference in the performance of the duty as to justify the obligee in refusing to recognize the delegation.[225] Again, the test is whether the obligee has a substantial interest in having the promisor perform or control the duties promised.[226] In the absence of contrary agreement, courts will determine that question on the basis of whether a reasonable party in the position of the obligee has any

---

[216] *See* Standard Chautauqua Sys. v. Gift, 120 Kan. 101, 242 P. 145 (1926) (duty to select entertainers, musicians, and other personnel was nondelegable).

[217] Eastern Advertising Co. v. McGaw, 89 Md. 72, 42 A. 923 (1899).

[218] *See* Fund of Funds, Ltd. v. Arthur Andersen & Co., 567 F.2d 225, 234 (2d Cir. 1977).

[219] *See* Deaton v. Lawson, 40 Wash. 486, 82 P. 879 (1905).

[220] *See* Milton L. Ehrlich, Inc. v. Unit Frame & Floor Corp., 5 N.Y.2d 275, 157 N.E.2d 495 (1959). See also Rossetti v. New Britain, 163 Conn. 283, 303 A.2d 714 (1972), where the court indicated that a duty to perform architectural services is normally nondelegable, but where the delegate was a new partnership consisting of two of the three original partners, the duty was delegable since the obligee was receiving the performance for which it had bargained.

[221] *See* Quality Healthcare Equip., Inc. v. Lumex, Inc., 1996 U.S. Dist. LEXIS 15485, at *8 (N.D. Ill. Oct. 15, 1996) ("The mere fact, however, that a contract calls for the performance of labor or service is not sufficient to render it nonassignable, if, from a consideration of the entire contract, it appears that personality is not an essential consideration, and that only a certain object or result is contracted for and not the personal labor or services of the promisor.").

[222] Sally Beauty Co. v. Nexxus Prods. Co., 801 F.2d 1001, 1007 (7th Cir. 1986) (*a fortiori* where the delegate is in competition with the obligee). *See also* Berliner Foods Corp. v. Pillsbury Co., 633 F. Supp. 557 (D. Md. 1986).

[223] This is the language of RESTATEMENT 2d § 318(2). The same test is found in UCC § 2-210(1). The test is amorphous. There is no escape from a critical analysis of each situation.

[224] British Waggon Co. v. Lea, 5 Q.B.D. 149 [1880] (ordinary repair of wagons).

[225] Macke Co. v. Pizza of Gaithersburg, Inc., 259 Md. 479, 270 A.2d 645 (1970).

[226] RESTATEMENT 2d § 318(2); UCC § 2-210(1). A performance by the delegate may be an express or constructive condition to the duty of the obligee. The delegability of the performance of that condition (whether or not it is a duty of the delegate) is subject to the same RESTATEMENT 2d test as the delegation of duty, i.e., whether the obligor has a substantial interest in having the delegate perform or control the required performance. RESTATEMENT 2d § 319(2). In the delegation of duties or performance of conditions, the delegation would not be effective if contrary to public policy. RESTATEMENT 2d §§ 318(1) and 319(1). *Cf. supra* § 139[B].

substantial basis for objecting to the performance of the duty by a delegate.

[C]   Contractual Prohibition of Delegation

If the performance does not require artistic skill, unique abilities, or the like, the obligor is still entitled to receive performance from the delegator if the parties clearly understood that this was the basis of the bargain. Thus, the performance of an ordinary mechanical repair or the mowing of grass which would normally be delegable becomes nondelegable if the parties clearly understood that only the original promisor would perform such duty, i.e., the parties may agree that an otherwise delegable duty will be nondelegable, just as they may agree that an otherwise nondelegable duty will be delegable.[227]

The parties may include in their contract an ambiguous statement such as, "Assignment of the contract is prohibited." To promote the policy of free transferability of rights, as well as the policy of permitting the parties to restrict delegation of duties, both the UCC and the RESTATEMENT 2d construe such clauses as barring only the delegation of duties, rather than the assignment of otherwise assignable rights.[228] The rationale for this narrow construction is that the obligor would normally not suffer any harm by the mere assignment of otherwise assignable rights, such as the right to receive payment.[229]

[D]   Repudiation — Novation — Reservation of Rights — Nondelegable Duty

[1]   Repudiation

As we have seen, unlike the assignment of a right which extinguishes the right in the assignor and creates a similar right in the assignee, an effective delegation of a contractual duty does not discharge the delegator.[230] If the obligor repudiates his duty, the obligee is at liberty to refuse performance tendered by the delegate which he would otherwise be obliged to accept, and may treat the repudiation as a breach of contract, with its attendant consequences. Where, for example, a party assigned its rights and delegated its duties, it then informed the other party that it was no longer liable under the contract. This constituted a repudiation of the contract discharging the obligee from performance thereunder.[231]

---

[227] *See* Snellman v. A.B. Dick Co., 1987 U.S. Dist. LEXIS 2306 (N.D. Ill. 1987), relying on RESTATEMENT 2d § 318(2) that begins with the phrase, "Unless otherwise agreed. . . ." See also comment c to this section. Similarly, UCC § 2-210(1) includes "unless otherwise agreed" in its subsection dealing with delegability of duties.

[228] UCC § 2-210(5) and RESTATEMENT 2d § 322(2).

[229] Wonsey v. Life Ins. Co. of N. Am., 32 F. Supp. 2d 939, 943 (E.D. Mich. 1998). *See also* Aldana v. Colonial Palms Plaza, Ltd. 591 So. 2d 953, 955 (Fla. Dist. Ct. App. 1991); Cedar Point Apts., Ltd. v. Cedar Point Inv. Corp., 693 F.2d 748, 753 (8th Cir. 1982), *cert. denied*, 461 U.S. 914, 103 S. Ct. 1893, 77 L. Ed. 2d 283 (1983).

[230] *See supra* subsection [A].

[231] Western Oil Sales Corp. v. Bliss & Wetherbee, 299 S.W. 637 (Tex. Comm'n App. 1927). See RESTATEMENT 2d § 329(1), which states that the legal effect of a repudiation is not affected by the fact that the delegate is a competent party who has promised to perform the duty. See, however, Meyer v. Washington Times Co., 64 U.S. App. D.C. 218, 76 F.2d 988, *cert. denied*, 295 U.S. 734, 55 S. Ct. 646, 79 L. Ed. 1682 (1935), holding that an obligee is not excused from accepting performance from a purchaser at a receiver's sale.

[2]   Novation — Reservation of Rights

We have seen that the obligee may expressly accept the delegate in substitution for the delegator and discharge the delegator, i.e., the parties may agree upon an express novation.[232] The fact that a duty has been delegated or that the obligee has accepted performance from the delegate, however, does not constitute a novation.[233] If, however, the obligee is aware of a repudiation by the delegator, he is presumed to know that the performance of the delegate is offered as a novation and, if the obligee silently accepts the performance under these circumstances, he has accepted an offer of novation.[234] The obligee, however, is not forced into what may be an oppressive choice between accepting repudiation by the delegator and substitute performance by the delegate. As just noted, his silence will indicate such assent to accept the delegate in substitution, thereby effecting a novation. But if the obligee notifies either the obligor, delegate, or both that he is receiving the performance "without prejudice" or "under protest," or similar language manifesting an intention to reserve his rights against the delegator, the delegator is not discharged.[235]

[3]   Delegation of Nondelegable Duty

Where the performance of the delegator is personal and not capable of being delegated, an attempted delegation of such a duty is not a repudiation. Nor is it an implied offer of novation.[236] As we have seen, the obligee need not accept the performance of such a duty from a delegate. If the obligee knows that the work is being performed by the delegate and assents to the substituted performance by failing to object, there is still no novation. The obligor, however, has probably waived his right to demand performance by the obligor, though the obligor remains liable in the event of a breach by the delegate.[237]

[E]   Liability of Delegate for Nonperformance — Interpretation of General Language of Delegation and Assignment — Can a "Contract" Be Assigned?

As we have seen, in the absence of a showing that a novation has been agreed upon by the parties, the obligor remains liable to the obligee for nonperformance of delegated duties. It should not be assumed that simply because the duties have been delegated, the delegate becomes liable to the obligee. The obligee must accept performance of a delegable duty from a delegate. If, however, the delegate fails to perform, the obligor remains liable but there is no cause of action in the obligee against the delegate unless the delegate has made a binding

---

[232] *See Rosenberger, supra* note 207, at 75.

[233] *See* § 141[A], *supra*, at notes 207–209. *See also* Pandya v. Doshi, 1993 U.S. Dist. LEXIS 11962 (N.D. Ill. Aug. 24, 1993); Heffelfinger v. Gibson, 290 A.2d 390 (D.C. App. 1972); National Dairy Prods. Corp. v. Lawrence Am. Field Warehousing, 22 A.D.2d 420, 255 N.Y.2d 788 (1st Dep't 1965).

[234] Restatement 2d § 329(2).

[235] *See* UCC § 1-207 in the unrevised Article 1. This section does not appear in the revised Article 1. See also Restatement 2d § 329(2) and comment c.

[236] *See* Clark v. General Cleaning Co., 345 Mass. 62, 185 N.E.2d 749 (1962).

[237] Seale v. Bates, 145 Colo. 430, 359 P.2d 356 (1961) (attempted delegation of duty to provide dance lessons and obligee took lessons from delegate; though obligee was bound to continue to take lessons from delegate, the delegator remained liable in the event of a breach by the delegate, i.e., there was no novation).

promise to perform, i.e., unless he assumed the duty.[238] If a delegate does assume the duty, the obligee becomes a third party beneficiary of the contract between the delegator and delegate.[239] The student should recall the example of a sale of real property with a mortgage indebtedness. Where the grantee (delegate) assumes the mortgage indebtedness, the mortgagee (obligee) becomes a third party beneficiary. The grantor becomes a surety and the grantee is the principal debtor. The mortgagee now has two debtors instead of one. If the grantee fails to pay and the surety (grantor) must pay, the surety has a cause of action against the grantee, i.e., he is subrogated to the rights of the mortgagee against the grantee.[240]

The delegation of duties is often accompanied by an assignment of rights, i.e., a party assigns his rights *and* delegates his duties to the assignee. A question of interpretation arises when an "assignment" (delegation) of duties, or an assignment of both rights and duties, is made in general terms to one who accepts the assignment but does not make a promise to the assignor to perform the delegated duties. In such a case, will a promise to the assignor to perform these duties be inferred, which the other party to the contract may enforce as a third party beneficiary? In the absence of special circumstances showing a contrary intention, such an implication would seem to be justified in the usual case.[241] Nor is there any valid reason why the right of a beneficiary should not be predicated upon a tacit promise as well as upon an orally expressed promise. This is the position adopted by the UCC[242] and the RESTATEMENT 2d.[243]

A number of cases involving contracts for the sale of land, however, have held that the delegate is not liable in the absence of an expressed-in-language assumption of such a duty.[244] The results in these cases may have been influenced in part by the generally accepted rule that one who takes a conveyance of land subject to a mortgage does not, without more, become obligated to pay off the mortgage. Yet, it is doubtful whether the mortgage cases should be viewed analogously since the grantor in such cases does not purport to transfer to the grantee

---

[238] Rochester Lantern Co. v. Stiles & Parker Press Co., 135 N.Y. 209, 31 N.E. 1018 (1892).

[239] *Rosenberger, supra* note 232, at 74.

[240] *See* § 133[D], [C], *supra.*

[241] In support of this view, see Grismore, *Is the Assignee of a Contract Liable for Non-Performance of Delegated Duties?*, 18 MICH. L. REV. 284 (1920).

[242] UCC § 2-210(4): "An assignment of 'the contract' or of 'all my rights under the contract' or an assignment in similar terms is an assignment of rights and unless the language or the circumstances (as in an assignment for security) indicate the contrary, it is a delegation of performance of the duties of the assignor and its acceptance by the assignee constitutes a promise by him to perform those duties. This promise is enforceable by either the assignor or the other party to the original contract."

[243] RESTATEMENT 2d § 328. *See Rosenberger*, note 207 *supra* , at n. 1. *See also* Newton v. Merchants & Farmers Bank, 11 Ark. App. 167, 668 S.W.2d 51 (1984).

[244] The leading case is Langel v. Betz, 250 N.Y. 159, 164 N.E. 890 (1928), which expressly repudiates FIRST RESTATEMENT § 164. Among numerous other cases recognizing this principle, see Cedar Point Apts., Ltd. v. Cedar Point Inv. Corp., 693 F.2d 748, 753 (8th Cir. 1982), *cert. denied*, 461 U.S. 914, 103 S. Ct. 1893, 77 L. Ed. 2d 283 (1983); Hahn v. Earth City Corp., 625 S.W.2d 640 (Mo. Ct. App. 1981); Henock v. Yeamans, 340 F.2d 503, 505 (5th Cir. 1965). See also National Real Estate Development Partners, LLC v. Manes, 2009 Bankr. LEXIS 1292 (D. Ariz. 2009) where numerous investors were assignees of fractional interest in loans in exchange for their investments in Mortgages, Ltd. which made more loans than it could fund. The plaintiffs claimed the investors were not only assignees of rights but delegates of duties under the usual presumption of Restatement 2d § 328. While recognizing that presumption and the fact that Arizona courts look to the Restatement in the absence of contrary authority, the court found contrary Arizona precedent stating that the assignment of rights does not have the effect of delegating duties. Thus, the assignments, alone, in this case did not imply an assumption of duties.

of the equity of redemption the duties which he owes the mortgagee. The result reached by the majority of the courts in the land contract cases may also be due, in part, to the traditional reluctance of our courts to extend the area of enforceability of promises by beneficiaries. It should also be noted that in a number of cases it has been held that the assignee is under an obligation to reimburse the assignor for damages sustained by the assignor because of the assignee's failure to perform delegated duties, although the assignee had made no expressed-in-words promise to perform those duties.[245]

The RESTATEMENT 2d has taken cognizance of this line of cases by including an explanation of the land contract situation in terms of the mortgage assumption heritage and the doctrinal difficulties that early courts faced with respect to the rights of assignees and third party beneficiaries. Though such doctrinal problems have now been overcome, the RESTATEMENT 2d concludes that "the shift in doctrine has not yet produced any definite change in the body of decisions," thereby causing the Institute to express "no opinion on the application of [the general principle] to an assignment by a purchaser under a land contract."[246] There is, however, willingness of some courts to permit an inference of the assumption of duties in a land contract by clear and convincing evidence that the parties so intended, though they would not regard the mere acceptance of benefits by the obligee as sufficient to establish the assumption of duties.[247] Another case suggests that the mere acceptance of benefits alone is sufficient, though the facts allow an assumption of the duties by the assignee to be implied.[248]

Notwithstanding the preferred interpretation that an assignment in general terms is both an assignment of rights and a delegation of duties, such an interpretation may be rebutted by evidence of a contrary intention. If the assignment of "all of the rights" under a contract is made to a financial institution as security for an indebtedness, the parties generally do not envision an assumption of duties by the assignee.[249]

[F]   Authorization of Assignment and Delegation

As suggested earlier,[250] rights and duties that are otherwise nonassignable and nondelegable may be made assignable and delegable by the terms of the contract. If the contract contains a provision permitting assignment, such a provision will be given effect according to the apparent intention of the parties.[251] Yet, the mere fact that the contract specifies that it shall bind or benefit "assigns" will not necessarily be held to accomplish this result, in the absence of some additional evidence that the language was used advisedly for the

---

[245] Imperial Ref. Co. v. Kanotex Ref. Co., 29 F.2d 193 (8th Cir. 1928); Corvallis & A.R. R. Co. v. Portland, E. & E. R. Co., 84 Or. 524, 163 P. 1173 (1917); Atlantic & N.C. R. Co. v. Atlantic & N.C. Co., 147 N.C. 368, 61 S.E. 185 (1908).

[246] RESTATEMENT 2d § 328 comment c.

[247] Pelz v. Streator Nat'l Bank, 145 Ill. App. 3d 946, 496 N.E.2d 315 (3d Dist. 1986); Haarmann v. Davis, 651 S.W.2d 134 (Mo. 1983).

[248] *See* Kunzman v. Thorsen, 303 Or. 600, 740 P.2d 754 (1987).

[249] UCC §§ 210(4) and 9-402 (formerly § 9-317); RESTATEMENT 2d § 328 comment b. *See* Phil Greer & Assocs., Inc. v. Continental Bank, 614 F. Supp. 423, 426 (E.D. Pa. 1985).

[250] *See* § 141[C], *supra.*

[251] Saliterman v. Finney, 361 N.W.2d 175 (Minn. Ct. App. 1985). Mail-Well Envelope Co. v. Saley, 262 Or. 143, 497 P.2d 364, 367–68 (1972). D. L. Stern Agency, Inc. v. Mutual Ben. Health & Acc. Ass'n, 43 F. Supp. 167, 169 (D.N.Y. 1941). RESTATEMENT 2d § 323(1).

purpose of conveying that meaning.[252] It is not uncommon, in the final clause of a written contract, to use the following or an equivalent expression: "This contract shall bind and benefit the parties, their heirs and assigns." Such a clause is usually a mere formality, and, in the normal case, the probabilities are that the parties in using it did not have in mind the question of assignment at all. Consequently, if this language, standing alone, were always construed to authorize the assignment of what would otherwise be nonassignable, violence would be done too often to the real understanding of the parties.

As we have seen, if a party accepts performance of nondelegable duties from the assignee without objection, he will not thereafter be permitted to say that those duties were nondelegable.[253] If the contract expressly prohibits assignment and delegation, these prohibitions can be waived by the subsequent assent of the parties.[254] Absent consideration, however, the waiver of such a provision may be withdrawn until there is reliance on the waiver.[255]

§ 142   DEFENSES, SETOFFS, COUNTERCLAIMS, AND EQUITIES AVAILABLE AGAINST THE ASSIGNEE — UNIFORM COMMERCIAL CODE CHANGES

[A]   General Rule

One of the rules of contract law which has been repeated so often that it has become axiomatic is that the assignee "stands in the shoes of the assignor,"[256] i.e., he takes rights of the assignor which can be no greater in the assignee than they were in the assignor.[257] This suggests that the assignee takes subject to all defenses, setoffs, counterclaims, and other equities which the obligor could have asserted against the assignor.[258] With certain qualifications, this is true. As with many applications of seemingly clear and relatively simple rules, however, certain qualifications and complex issues must be confronted.

At the inception, it must be emphasized that the assignment of a right does not enlarge the duty of the obligor, i.e., the unilateral action of the other party to the contract should not subject the obligor to any greater risk than she originally assumed. To protect the obligor, the assignee is subject to all of the terms of the *contract* between the obligor and assignor, and

---

[252] Banke Assoc., Inc. v. New England Fin. Resources, Inc., 1989 U.S. Dist. LEXIS 18313, at *7 (D.N.H. Aug. 22, 1989); Standard Chautauqua Sys. v. Gift, 120 Kan. 101, 242 P. 145 (1926); Paige v. Faure, 229 N.Y. 114, 127 N.E. 898 (1920); Swarts v. Narragansett Elec. Lighting Co., 26 R.I. 436, 59 A. 111 (1904). RESTATEMENT 2d § 323 comment b.

[253] *See supra* text at note 216.

[254] Giles v. Sun Bank, N.A., 450 So. 2d 258 (Fla. Dist. Ct. App. 1984).

[255] RESTATEMENT 2d § 323 comment c.

[256] *See, e.g.*, National Enters. v. Smith, 114 F.3d 561, 564 (6th Cir. 1997); FDIC v. Bledsoe, 989 F.2d 805, 810 (5th Cir. 1993).

[257] "[T]he common law puts the assignee in the shoes of t he assignor, whatever the shoe size." Olivera v. Blitt & Gaines, P. C., 431 F. 3d 285, 289 (7th Cir. 2005) (Posner, J.). *See also*, Commerce Bank, N.A. v. Chrysler Realty Corp., 2001 U.S. App. LEXIS 4297, at *20 (10th Cir. Mar. 22, 2001).

[258] *See* Enterprises, Inc. v. Becker, 36 Conn. Supp. 213, 416 A.2d 183 (Super. Ct. 1980) (citing the second edition of this book for this statement). *See also* Business Fin. Servs. v. Butler & Booth Dev. Co., 147 Ariz. 510, 711 P.2d 649 (Ct. App. 1985); Olsen-Frankman Livestock Mktg. Serv., Inc. v. Citizens Nat'l Bank, 605 F.2d 1082 (8th Cir. 1979). RESTATEMENT 2d § 336(1) and (2).

any defense or claim arising from the contract itself is available against the assignee.[259] If the assignor's right is voidable or otherwise unenforceable against the obligor, it is similarly voidable or unenforceable against the obligor when asserted by the assignee.[260] If the statute of limitations is available against the assignor, it is available against the assignee.[261] If the duty of the obligor is subject to the occurrence of a condition, the duty is not activated if the condition does not occur, notwithstanding the assignment of the conditional right.[262]

[B]   Notification of Assignment

The reason for emphasizing the fact that the assignee takes subject to all defenses *arising from the contract itself* is to avoid the misconception that notification of the assignment to the obligor cuts off all defenses. Notification of the assignment has no effect on the defenses which the obligor can assert if, again, those defenses arise from the terms of the contract itself.[263] Notification, however, is important in relation to the freedom of the obligor to render performance to the assignor or, as we will see below, to claims or defenses accruing after notification of the assignment.

If the obligor renders performance to the assignor, or secures a discharge of his obligation for consideration, or, for value, acquires any other defense good against the assignor, before he has knowledge or notice of the assignment, the assignee's right is subject to such defense.[264] The inherent justice in such a rule is obvious. The obligor is entitled to assume that the right continues in the assignor until he is aware of the assignment. It is, however, important to emphasize that the obligor does become liable to the assignee after receiving notice of the assignment. Where an obligor had received notice of the assignment but paid the obligee, the obligor remained liable to the assignee.[265] As to whether an obligor has received notification or otherwise become aware of the fact of assignment, the definition of the receipt of notice in the UCC is the preferred, modern view.[266] Where rights under a contract to sell

---

[259] UCC § 9-404(a), comment 2 (1999) (formerly § 9-318(1)(a)). "[I]f the account debtor's defenses on an assigned claim arise from the transaction that gave rise to the contract with the assignor, it makes no difference whether the defense or claim accrues before or after the account debtor is notified of the assignment." See also RESTATEMENT 2d § 336(1).

[260] RESTATEMENT 2d § 336(1).

[261] Twenty First Century Recovery v. Mase, 279 Ill. App. 3d 660, 216 Ill. Dec. 513, 665 N.E.2d 573, 576 (5th Dist. 1996).

[262] RESTATEMENT 2d § 320, comment b. See also Lech v. State Farm Ins. Co., 335 N. J. Super.254, 258, 762 A.2d 269, 271 (2000) "While an assignee's rights can be no greater than those of the assignor, neither can they be any less."

[263] James Talcott, Inc. v. H. Corenzwit & Co., 76 N.J. 305, 387 A.2d 350 (1978).

[264] Kaw Valley State Bank & Trust v. Commercial Bank of Liberty, N.A., 567 S.W.2d 710 (Mo. Ct. App. 1978); Farmers Acceptance Corp. v. De Lozier, 178 Colo. 291, 496 P.2d 1016 (1972); Ornbaun v. First Nat'l Bank, 215 Cal. 72, 8 P.2d 470 (1932); Erlandson v. Erskine, 76 Mont. 537, 248 P. 209 (1926); Le Porin v. State Exch. Bank, 113 Kan. 76, 213 P. 650 (1923). UCC § 9-404(a)(2) and comment 2 (2000) (formerly § 9-318(1)(b)); RESTATEMENT 2d § 336(2). Failure of performance by the assignor may be shown by way of recoupment though it occurred subsequently to notice of the assignment, since the right to claim damages for breach existed from the time of making the contract. Apple v. Edwards, 92 Mont. 524, 16 P.2d 700, 87 A.L.R. 179 (1932); Annot., 87 A.L.R. 187 (1933).

[265] Van Waters & Rogers, Inc. v. Interchange Resources, 14 Ariz. App. 414, 484 P.2d 26 (1971).

[266] UCC § 1-201(27) provides: "Notice, knowledge or a notice or notification received by an organization is effective for a particular transaction from the time when it is brought to the attention of the individual conducting that transactions, and in any event from the time when it would have been brought to his attention if the organization had exercised due diligence. An organization exercises due diligence if it maintains reasonable routines for communicating

furniture were assigned to a bank and notice of the assignment was provided to a clerk, who had not issued the purchase orders and stated he had no authority to sign such notices of assignment, the court held the notice of assignment was ineffective.[267] A general contractor's field supervisor on a construction project signed a subcontractor's notice of assignment to a bank without authority. The issue was whether the general contractor exercised due diligence in maintaining reasonable routines for communicating significant information under the UCC definition.[268] The Code also sets forth what the notice must contain, i.e., it must reasonably identify the rights assigned[269] and the obligor may request that the assignee furnish reasonable proof that the assignment has been made.[270]

[C]   Uniform Commercial Code — Modification or Substitution

Under the common law, an assignee could acquire no rights under a modified or substituted contract between the obligor and assignor. This rule was changed by versions of UCC Article 9 prior to the current version. If the assigned right *had not yet been earned by performance*, the obligor and assignor, in good faith and in accordance with reasonable commercial standards, could effect a modification or substitution of their contract notwithstanding notification of the assignment.[271] The latest version of Article 9 provides that good faith modifications of assigned contracts bind the assignee to the extent that (1) the right to payment has not been fully earned, or (2) the right to payment has been fully earned but notification of the assignment has not been given to the obligor.[272] The modification or substitution is effective against the assignee, but the assignee acquires rights under the good faith modification or substitution.

[D]   Claims and Defenses — Setoffs and Counterclaims

[1]   Rationale for Setoffs and Counterclaims

Students often become confused concerning the availability of setoffs or counterclaims to an obligor against an assignee. Where transactions giving rise to setoffs or counterclaims arose from collateral transactions between the assignor and obligor as contrasted with the contract which provided the assignee with rights, the assignee had nothing to do with such transactions. Yet, it is generally held that the obligor may use them against the assignee. To understand why this is so, consider the house painter who has completed his work and is to be paid within thirty days the contract price of $20,000. The obligor sells new and used cars and agrees to sell a used car to the painter for $10,000 on credit. The obligor is not at all concerned about extending

---

significant information to the person conducting the transaction and there is reasonable compliance with the routines. Due diligence does not require an individual acting for the organization to communicate information unless such communication is part of his regular duties or unless he has reason to know of the transaction and that the transaction would be materially affected by the information."

[267] Bank of Salt Lake v. Corporation of President of Church of Jesus Christ of Latter-Day Saints, 534 P.2d 887 (Utah 1975) (relying on UCC definition of receiving notice, *id.*).

[268] Millikin Nat'l Bank v. Peter Schwabe Corp., 177 Ill. App. 3d 66, 126 Ill. Dec. 447, 531 N.E.2d 1074 (4th Dist. 1988).

[269] UCC § 9-406(b)(1) (formerly § 9-318(3)).

[270] UCC § 9-406(c) (formerly found in § 9-318(3)).

[271] UCC § 9-318(2) (1972 version).

[272] UCC §§ 9-405(a) and (b)(1) and (2).

$10,000 in credit to a party to whom he owes $20,000. If the painter assigned his right to the $20,000 payment and the obligor was unaware of that fact when he extended the $10,000 credit to the painter, the obligor should not be penalized for making a basic assumption concerning the security for the credit extended to the painter. He should be able to offset the $10,000 owed by the painter against the assignee's right to collect $20,000.[273] If, however, the obligor had been notified of the assignment prior to the extension of credit to the painter, the obligor has assumed the risk of providing $10,000 of unsecured credit knowing that he must pay $20,000 to the assignee and it is, therefore, fair to preclude the use of the setoff against the assignee. Thus, as to setoffs and counterclaims good against the assignor, i.e., arising from collateral transactions between the obligor and assignor before the obligor is notified of the assignment, it is commonly stated that the obligor may avail himself of such claims.[274]

[2] Determining Which Setoffs and Counterclaims Are Available — "Matured" — "Accrued"

The right to setoff and counterclaim is largely statutory. Older state statutes were not uniform, resulting in variations in different jurisdictions as to the circumstances under which the obligor could avail itself, as against the assignee, of such claims good against the assignor. There were holdings in some jurisdictions requiring only that the claim have matured at the time of suit, regardless of whether the counterclaim or the assigned claim had matured at the date of the assignment or notice thereof.[275] In other jurisdictions, both the assigned claim and the counterclaim must have matured at the date of the assignment before any counterclaim would be permitted against the assignee.[276] The lack of uniformity in these statutes was cured by the UCC, and the RESTATEMENT 2d has followed its normal course in adhering to the Code position.[277] Unfortunately, the otherwise desirable, uniform change is not entirely clear.

Under the RESTATEMENT 2d and the UCC, the rights of an assignee are subject to "any other defense or claim of the account debtor against the assignor which *accrues* before the account debtor receives notification of the assignment authenticated by the assignor or assignee."[278] The term "accrues" is unclear. It probably means the point in time when a cause of action exists since it is typically used in relation to statutes of limitation.[279] "Accrued" does not mean

---

[273] *See* Maryland Cooperative Milk Producers, Inc. v. Bell, 206 Md. 168, 110 A.2d 661 (1955).

[274] *See* FED. R. CIV. P. 13. Unless the assignee has assumed the liabilities of the assignor, however, such claims may only be used defensively. The assignee is not liable for any excess. Shepard v. Commercial Credit Corp., 123 Vt. 106, 183 A.2d 525 (1962).

[275] *See* St. Louis Nat'l Bank v. Gay, 101 Cal. 286, 35 P. 876 (1894); First Nat'l Bank v. Bynum & Daniel, 84 N.C. 24, 37 Am. Rep. 604 (1881).

[276] *See* Koegel v. Michigan Trust Co., 117 Mich. 542, 76 N.W. 74 (1898) (assigned claim not matured at date of the assignment); Fuller v. Steiglitz, 27 Ohio St. 355, 22 Am. Rep. 312 (1875) (both assigned claim and counterclaim unmatured at the date of assignment).

[277] UCC § 9-404(a) (formerly § 9-318(1)(b)); RESTATEMENT 2d § 336(2).

[278] UCC § 9-404(a)(2) (emphasis added). Farmers Acceptance Corp. v. De Lozier, 178 Colo. 291, 496 P.2d 1016 (1972), holds that a "setoff" is the type of claim contemplated by this section of the UCC.

[279] See, e.g., UCC § 2-725(1), which states that an action for breach of contract (contract for the sale of goods) must be commenced within four years after the cause of action accrues. Subsection (2) then states that, "A cause of action accrues when the breach occurs. . . ." *See* Bank of Kansas v. Hutchinson Health Servs., Inc., 13 Kan. App. 2d 421, 428, 773 P.2d 660, 665 (1989), *aff'd*, 246 Kan. 83, 785 P.2d 1349 (1990) ("A claim could 'accrue:' (1) when the obligation to pay is incurred; or (2) when the obligation is actually due and payable. The first definition reflects a fiscal view, appropriate to accounting or tax law. The second definition reflects the more usual sense of accrue, that is, that 'a claim or setoff

"matured" since an "account" under the Code may refer to what used to be called a "contract right," i.e., a right not yet earned by performance or not yet mature.[280] The choice between "mature" and "accrued" has been described as "arbitrary" line drawing to allow some setoffs and counterclaims against the assignee without destabilizing the critically important commercial financing practice of assigning accounts.[281] The result is that the obligor must be able to establish that a setoff or counterclaim accrued before he received notification of the assignment if he wishes to assert such defenses or claims against the assignee.[282]

[E]   The Effect of Latent Equities

An assignee may innocently take an assignment for value without knowledge that the right of a third party may be involved. Where, for example, the holder of a contract right is induced to assign it through the fraud of the assignee, and that assignee assigns the right to an innocent purchaser for value, should the innocent assignee be able to assert the right regardless of the first assignor's claim of fraud? The issue is often phrased in terms of whether the assignee takes subject to latent equities in favor of third persons. It is a question on which the decided cases have not been in agreement. This lack of agreement has apparently resulted from a difference of opinion in regard to the nature of an assignee's ownership. The older cases, which proceeded on the theory that the assignee's ownership is equitable rather than legal, reached the conclusion that the assignee takes subject to the prior equity of a third person.[283] On the other hand, as we have already seen, the present tendency is to deal with transfers of contractual rights according to the same rules that control transfers of tangible property. A court proceeding on this theory is likely to take the view that an assignee for value, without notice of the equity of a third person, takes free from it.[284] This rule has the merit of facilitating the transfer of contract rights, since it is practically impossible for an

---

accrues when a cause of action exists' [citing Seattle-First Nat'l Bank v. Oregon Pac. Indus., Inc., 262 Or. 578, 500 P.2d 1033 (1972)]. On balance, we believe that the policies of simplicity and commercial certainty underlying the UCC favor the second definition."). In comparing the FIRST RESTATEMENT analysis which required setoffs and presumably counterclaims to be "based on facts existing at the time of the assignment" with the requirement that such claims have "accrued" before notification to the obligor of the assignment, Professor Gilmore suggests, "It may be admitted that it is no easier to tell when a 'claim' 'accrues' than it is to tell when a 'fact' 'arises.'" Gilmore, *The Assignee of Contract Rights and His Precarious Security*, 74 YALE L.J. 217, 230 (1964).

[280]   Under the current Article 9, "account" is now defined in § 9-102(2) (formerly § 9-106) and includes a right to payment, whether or not earned by performance. "Contract right" appeared in an earlier version of Article 9 to deal with accounts not yet earned by performance and later replaced by the broader and more inclusive definition of "account."

[281]   *See Seattle-First Nat'l Bank, supra* note 279.

[282]   *See* UCC § 9-404, comment 2: "Under subsection (a)(2), the assignee takes subject to *other* defenses or claims only if they accrue before the account debtor has been notified of the assignment." (Emphasis supplied.) *See also* Ertel v. Radio Corp. of Am., 261 Ind. 573, 307 N.E.2d 471 (1974); Fall River Trust Co. v. B. G. Browdy, Inc., 346 Mass. 614, 195 N.E.2d 63 (1964).

[283]   Levenbaum v. Hanover Trust Co., 253 Mass. 19, 148 N.E. 227 (1925) (trustee in bankruptcy sought to recover funds paid by the bankrupt in unlawful preference of creditor who deposited the funds in a bank and then assigned his claim against the bank; trustee prevailed over assignee who paid value and had no notice); Downer v. South Royalton Bank, 39 Vt. 25 (1866) (deputy sheriff deposited money which he had collected on an execution in a bank and then wrongfully assigned a judgment recovered by him against the bank to a third person; held: the execution creditor had a better right to the judgment than the assignee).

[284]   *See* McKnight v. Rice, Hoppner, Brown & Brunner, 678 P.2d 1330 (Alaska 1984) (assignee's service after court order but before notice of the order were in good faith and he is entitled to enforce the right to the extent of the value of services performed before notice was received). *See also* Akin v. Security Sav. & Trust Co., 157 Or. 172, 68 P.2d 1047,

assignee to learn of the existence of the latent equities of third persons.

[F]   Assignor's Duties to Assignee — Transfer Warranties

Where an obligor has not been notified of the assignment, he reasonably believes that his only duty is to the party with whom he contracted. Thus, his payment of the obligation or an accord and satisfaction or the other party's voluntary release of the obligation upon which the obligor relies would constitute a discharge of the obligation. The other party, however, knows that he has made an assignment of the discharged right, a right the assignor no longer possessed. By discharging the innocent obligor, the assignor has interfered with the assignee's right.

The assignor makes implied warranties to the assignee, analogous to the transfer warranties made by the transferor of a negotiable instrument for consideration but without endorsement to the transferee.[285] The Restatement 2d of Contracts recognizes such transfer warranties in assignments under seal (where the seal is valid) or those made for value. The assignor warrants to the assignee that he will do nothing to impair the value of the assignment and is unaware of facts that would result in such impairment.[286] The assignor warrants that the assigned right exists and is not subject to any limitations or defenses good against the assignor other than those stated or apparent at the time of the assignment. He also warrants that any writing evidencing the assigned right which induced the assignee to accept the assignment is genuine.[287] These implied warranties may be disclaimed in the same fashion as implied warranties of merchantability or fitness for a particular purpose are disclaimed in contracts for the sale of goods.[288] An issue has arisen where an assignment of accounts receivable is "without recourse" which means that the assignor is excluding liability for the failure of underlying obligors to pay the amounts due on the assigned receivables. Courts have rejected the claim that such a "without recourse" assignment constitutes a disclaimer of the implied warranties made by the assignor.[289] The assignor does not impliedly warrant that the obligor is solvent or that he will perform his obligation.[290]

In addition to implied warranties, the assignor can make affirmations and promises to the assignee that are treated like express warranties made in the sale of goods.[291] Where an

---

71 P.2d 321 (1937); Lasser v. Philadelphia Nat'l Bank, 321 Pa. 189, 183 A. 791 (1936); Williams v. Donnelly, 54 Neb. 193, 74 N.W. 601 (1898). *Accord* RESTATEMENT 2d § 343.

[285] UCC § 3-416 recognizes that a transferor of a negotiable instrument for consideration but without endorsement impliedly warrants that the transferee is entitled to enforce the instrument, all signatures are authorized and authentic, the instrument has not been altered, it is not subject to a defense or claim in recoupment against the warrantor, the warrantor is unaware of any insolvency proceedings with respect to the maker of the note or drawer of the draft, and with respect to remotely-created consumer items, the person on whose account it was drawn authorized its issuance. See First Amer. Title Ins. Co. v. Cumberland County Bank, 633 F. Supp. 2d 566. 585 (M. D. Tenn. 2009) dealing with assignor's transfer warranties and citing Tenn. Code Ann. § 47-3-416.

[286] SMS Demag Aktiengesellschaft v. Material Sciences Corp., 2005 U.S. Dist. LEXIS 22643 at *6–7 (S. D. Ill. 2005) (though licensing of technology was not an assignment, the transaction was sufficiently analogous to imply such a transfer warranty).

[287] Restatement 2d § 333(1).

[288] UCC § 2-316. Restatement 2d § 333, comment b.

[289] Lifewise Master Funding v. Telebank, 374 F. 3d 917, 925 (10th Cir. 2004) (citing Restatement 2d § 333).

[290] Restatement 2d § 333(2).

[291] Restatement 2d § 333(3) and comment b.

assignment is made to an intermediate assignee who then assigns the right to a sub-assignee, absent evidence of a contrary intention, the assignor's warranties do not extend to the sub-assignee.[292] The remedy for breach of an assignor's warranty is the usual remedy for breach of contract that allows protection of the expectation interest, to place the assignee in the position she would have occupied had the assigned right been as warranted.[293] If the assignor has been unjustly enriched by a wrongful collection from the obligor, the assignee can maintain a quasi contract action in restitution for the amount of that injury.[294]

[G]   Waiver of Defenses Against the Assignee — Holder in Due Course

Another question involving defenses against the assignee is whether the obligor and assignor may, at the time their contract is formed, agree that the obligor will not assert defenses against the assignee. To grasp the problem in its most realistic setting requires the student of contract law to become aware of some of the basic elements of the law of negotiable instruments, or, in more archaic terms, "bills and notes."[295] Any extensive inquiry into the law of commercial paper is beyond the scope of this volume.[296] As in some other sections of this work, however, it is necessary to provide some of the basic framework of that branch of law to facilitate comprehension of the problem at hand.

[1]   A Commercial Paper Primer — Holder in Due Course

The modern law of commercial paper involving promissory notes and drafts (including checks) is found in Articles 3 and 4 of the UCC. If certain formalities are found in a writing, the writing takes on the unique status of a negotiable instrument.[297] The most popular and easily recognized negotiable instrument is the typical personal or business check. A glance at a typical check reveals that if it is signed by the proper party (drawer) and made payable to a party or to his order (payee) and drawn against a bank which is ordered to pay the "sum certain" set forth in the writing, it meets the basic requirements to attain the status of a negotiable instrument. Such an instrument is often called an "order" instrument or "three-party paper" because it is drawn by the customer of the bank (drawer) against the bank (drawee) and made payable to the party whom the drawer wishes to pay or to his order (payee).

---

[292] Restatement 2d § 333(4) and comment c.

[293] Restatement 2d § 333, comment d.

[294] Doenges Motors, Inc. v. Bankers Invest. Co., 369 P. 2d 611 (Okla. 1962).

[295] Traditionally, negotiable instruments were classified into two types: (1) promissory notes and (2) bills of exchange. A promissory note represented a promise by the maker or issuer of the instrument to pay a sum of money to another, i.e., the payee. Thus, the transaction involved only two parties (*see* Title III of the Uniform Negotiable Instruments Act). A bill of exchange represented an order by the issuer (drawer) of the instrument to a third party, i.e., the drawee, to pay a sum of money to the payee. Thus, three parties were involved (*see* Title II of the Uniform Negotiable Instruments Act). This terminology is changed under the UCC.

[296] *See generally* J. WHITE & R. SUMMERS, UNIFORM COMMERCIAL CODE Chs. 13–18 (2000).

[297] UCC § 3-104(a) sets forth the definition of a "negotiable instrument" as an unconditional promise or order in a signed writing to pay a fixed amount of money, with or without interest or other charges described in the promise or order that is payable to bearer or to order either on demand or at a definite time. The instrument must not state any other instruction by the person promising or order payment to perform any act in addition to the payment of money, but it may contain an undertaking or power to give, maintain or protect collateral to secure payment, an authorization or power to the holder to confess judgment or realize or dispose of the collateral, or a waiver of the benefit of any law intended for the advantage or protection of the obligor.

The payee is a "holder" of the instrument,[298] and only he can properly transfer that instrument to another. The payee transfers the instrument by "negotiating" it and "negotiates" it by indorsing it, usually by signing his name on the reverse side.[299] He may indorse it to another person, to a bank, or any other entity. Like the payee, the party to whom the payee has "negotiated" the instrument (check) becomes a holder. Moreover, if the transferee (holder) takes the instrument for value, in good faith, and without notice that the instrument is overdue, or has been dishonored or that there is any defense against or claim to it on the part of any person, the transferee is much more than a mere holder — he is a *holder in due course.*[300]

The holder in due course has a unique status as a transferee as compared with a mere assignee of a contract right. He takes the instrument free from all defenses of any party to the instrument with the exception of certain very basic defenses, such as incapacity, duress, "real" or "essential" fraud, and discharge in insolvency proceedings.[301] Except for these so-called "real" defenses, the holder in due course need not worry over more likely defenses (often called "personal" defenses), such as the failure on the part of his transferor (the payee-holder) to perform his promise for the benefit of the drawer. Thus, the holder in due course has better rights than his transferor. *He does not merely stand in the shoes of the transferor — the shoes have become much larger.* The basic reason for this unique status is to permit the holder in due course to negotiate this instrument without fear that it will prove to be a worthless piece of paper. This assures the free transferability of such instruments which are so important to the commercial life of a complex industrialized society.

[2]   Waiver of Defenses

This simplistic sketch of the transfer of a negotiable instrument is necessary if one is to understand a device known as *waiver of defenses* by an obligor against an assignee. Another method of accomplishing the same goal of permitting a transferee of a contract right to stand in a *better* position than his transferor is to insert a provision in the original contract between the obligor and assignor whereby the obligor agrees not to assert defenses (which the obligor could have asserted against the assignor) against the assignee, should an assignment occur. Prior to the Code, there was considerable debate about the enforceability of such clauses and, in a number of jurisdictions, they were either unenforceable or enforceable only under certain modified circumstances.[302] The Code includes a provision[303] making such agreements enforceable, but subject to any statute or judicial decision of the particular jurisdiction involved which established a different rule for buyers or lessees of *consumer* goods.[304] Absent such a different rule, the Code provides that such a clause, waiving the defenses of the obligor against the

---

[298] UCC § 1-201(20) defines "holder" as a "person who is in possession of a document of title or an instrument or an investment security drawn, issued or indorsed to him or to his order or to bearer or in blank."

[299] UCC § 3-204.

[300] UCC § 3-302. The court notes the distinction in Fine v. Sovereign Bank, 2009 U.S. Dist. LEXIS 111063 (D. Mass. 2009).

[301] UCC § 3-305.

[302] The cases are collected in Annots., 31 A.L.R. 876 (1924); 110 A.L.R. 774 (1937).

[303] UCC § 9-403(b) (formerly § 9-206). For a discussion of § 9-206 and its relationship to the usual rule that defenses and claims are available against the assignee pursuant to former § 9-318 (now § 9-404), see First New England Fin. Corp. v. Woffard, 421 So. 2d 590 (Fla. Dist. Ct. App. 1982).

[304] "Consumer goods" are goods "used or bought for use primarily for personal, family or household purposes." UCC § 9-102(23) (formerly § 9-109).

assignee, is enforceable.[305] To invoke the benefits of this clause, the assignee must have taken the assignment in good faith, for value, and without notice of the same kind of claim or defense which would be effective against a holder of a negotiable instrument who seeks to become a holder in due course. The same "real" defenses available against a holder in due course of a negotiable instrument are available against such an assignee. Therefore, the Code treats the assignee of a contract right under such waiver of defenses clause as identical to a holder in due course.[306]

[3]   Holder in Due Course, Waiver of Defenses, and the Consumer

While real holder in due course status or an effective simulation of that status through the use of a waiver of defenses clause has certainly promoted the desirable policy of free transferability of commercial paper, its effect on consumers could be oppressive in given cases. Consider the example of a simple purchase of a product for which the consumer buyer makes a down payment and then signs a negotiable promissory note for the balance. The note is transferred (negotiated) to a bank or other commercial lender who buys such "paper" from retailers. If there is no negotiable instrument involved, there is the effective substitute, i.e., a clause waiving defenses, to provide the assignee with the same protection he would have had as a holder in due course of a negotiable instrument. After a few weeks, the product develops defects making it inoperable. The retailer is no longer in business and nowhere to be found. The consumer is notified by the bank that she must continue to make her monthly payments for the defunct product since the bank has nothing to do with the operative fitness of such goods, i.e., warranties of merchantability or other warranties. Defenses such as breach of warranty are not available against either a holder in due course or a transferee of non-negotiable paper that contains the waiver of defenses clause. The consumer has nowhere to turn.

Courts began recognizing this problem by considering the connection between the retailer and the bank or other lender with whom the retailer often dealt on a continuous basis. Often the lender would even supply the printed forms to the retailer for the consumer's signature. Where a commercial lender is so *closely connected* with the retail seller that the lender should not be heard to say that it was an innocent purchaser for value in good faith when it purchased the commercial paper from the retailer, the lender could not be a holder in due course and the normal defenses by an obligor (consumer) against an assignee (lender) are available.[307] Fearing the loss of holder in due course status, a number of lenders began using the waiver of defenses clause in their printed forms to achieve the same protection against the normal defenses of the obligor against the assignee. The waiver of defenses clause is even less obvious in a printed form than the effects of a negotiable instrument about which some consumer may have a myopic but real apprehension in signing. Judicial vigilance in an age of consumer protection penetrated this device and the "close connectedness" analysis was applied to waiver

---

[305] *See* RESTATEMENT 2d § 336 comment f.

[306] UCC § 9-403, comment 3 (1999): "Like former Section 9-206, this section is designed to put the assignee in a position that is no better and no worse than that of a holder in due course of a negotiable instrument."

[307] One of the requirements for holder in due course status is that the holder take the instrument in good faith. If there is a close or intimate connection between the transferor and transferee, the latter may have difficulty showing that he took the instrument in good faith, thus destroying holder in due course status and making the transferee subject to defenses. The seminal case is Mutual Fin. Co. v. Martin, 63 So. 2d 649, 44 A.L.R.2d 1 (Fla. 1953). See also Rehurek v. Chrysler Credit Corp., 262 So. 2d 452 (Fla. Dist. Ct. App. 1972), suggesting the close connection theory which may occur where the financial institution has a close working relationship with the retail seller in a consumer credit transaction.

of defenses clauses as it had been applied to holder in due course status.[308] Beyond consumer transactions, however, the doctrine has seen no success as applied to a holder in due course or a waiver of defenses.[309]

Statutory and regulatory efforts to protect consumers throughout the country included restrictions on holder in due course status that might deprive the consumer of the benefit of her bargain. The most significant effort was a new regulation from the Federal Trade Commission issued on November 14, 1975, requiring consumer credit contracts to contain conspicuous notices of the fact that any holder of the contract would be subject to all claims and defenses which the debtor could assert against the seller of goods or services.[310] The same concept is found in state legislation throughout the country.[311] The effect is to negate holder in due course status for purchasers of contract rights in consumer transactions.[312]

§ 143 PRIORITIES — SUCCESSIVE ASSIGNEES — ATTACHING CREDITORS

[A] Common Law Priorities — Successive Assignees — "Four Horsemen"

An assignee who takes an assignment of a claim with notice or knowledge of a prior assignment of the same claim takes subject to the rights of the earlier assignee. Where, however, an assignor has made successive assignments of the same claim to each of two or more assignees, each assignment having been made for a valuable consideration, and the later assignee has no notice or knowledge of the earlier assignment, a difficult question of priority arises, causing conflict in the decisions. One line of decisions took the view that a party receiving his assignment first has the better right in the absence of a superior equity existing in the second assignee.[313] Those courts taking this so-called "New York" or "American" view

---

[308] The seminal case is Unico v. Owen, 50 N.J. 101, 232 A.2d 405 (1967). For a recent discussion of the *Unico* analysis, see First National Acceptance Co. v. Bishop, 187 S. W. 3d 710, 715–16 (Tex. App. 2006).

[309] *See, e.g.*, A. I. Trade Fin. v. Laminaciones de Lesaca, S.A., 41 F.3d 830, 840 (2d Cir. 1994) ("close connectedness" doctrine, not recognized in New York, failed to deprive party of holder in due course status); Vitols v. Citizens Banking Co., 10 F.3d 1227, 1234 (6th Cir. 1993) (setting forth five factors to determine whether the transferee of a negotiable instrument is so closely connected to the original payee and the underlying transaction that the transferee cannot be found to have taken the instrument in good faith, but holding that the transferee was a holder in due course); Leasing Serv. Corp. v. River City Constr., Inc., 743 F.2d 871, 876 (11th Cir. 1984) (waiver of defense clause upheld: "We have not been able to locate any case in which the court has invalidated a waiver of defense clause in a commercial transaction based on close connections alone.").

[310] 16 C.F.R. § 433.2.

[311] *See, e.g.*, Uniform Consumer Credit Code § 3-307 and Iowa Code § 537.3307.

[312] The 1999 version of Article 9 includes a section that is consonant with the Federal Trade Commission rule, § 9-403(d), which "effectively renders waiver-of defense clauses ineffective in the transactions with consumers to which it applies." Comment 5.

[313] In State *ex rel.* Crane Co. v. Stokke, 65 S.D. 207, 272 N.W. 811 (1937), the court held that, as between a contractor's surety who took an assignment from the principal debtor and a creditor-assignee of the principal debtor who took an assignment to secure the same claim which the surety undertook to secure, the creditor has the stronger equity and is entitled to priority, though he was the second assignee in point of time. See also Coon River Co-op. Sand Ass'n v. McDougall Constr. Co., 215 Iowa 861, 244 N.W. 847 (1932), holding that a second unconditional assignment to a creditor of a contractor takes priority over an earlier conditional assignment to the contractor's surety.

The United States Supreme Court formerly treated the question as one of general law and applied its own rule

regarded an assignee as having legal ownership of the claim, i.e., when the assignor makes the first assignment he parts with all his ownership in the assigned right and so has nothing to transfer to the second assignee.[314] Other courts reached the same conclusion proceeding on the theory that an assignee acquires at most an equitable title, but applied the equitable maxim, where the equities are equal, the first in point of time prevails.[315] A second line of decisions, based on an early English case,[316] held that the assignee who first notifies the obligor of his assignment is entitled to priority, on the theory that the ownership of the assignee is not complete until he has notified the obligor of his claim.[317] This view was no doubt motivated by the belief that it is good policy to require the assignee to give notice to the obligor for the protection of third persons who may be induced to deal with the claim in reliance upon information as to its ownership obtained from the obligor.[318]

A third position, sometimes referred to as the "four horsemen" rule, supported by both RESTATEMENTS,[319] permits the first assignee (in time) to prevail unless the first assignment is ineffective, revocable, or voidable by the assignor or subsequent assignee, or the subsequent assignee, in good faith, gives value and obtains any of the following: (1) payment or satisfaction of the obligation;[320] (2) judgment against the obligor;[321] (3) a new contract with the obligor (novation);[322] or (4) possession of a symbolic writing.[323] There is judicial support for this compromise between the "American" and "English" views. The cases favoring the subsequent assignee in the exceptional situations have usually been justified either on the ground that the subsequent assignee has drawn a "legal title" to his equity and so has the better right,[324] or on the ground of estoppel.[325] We will now explore the quite different approach of the UCC in

---

holding that "mere priority of notice to the debtor by a second assignee, who lent his money to the assignor without making any inquiry of the debtor, is not sufficient to subordinate the first assignment to the second," regardless of the rule adopted in the state in which the case arose. Salem Trust Co. v. Manufacturers' Fin. Co., 264 U.S. 182, 199–200, 44 S. Ct. 266, 271, 68 L. Ed. 628, 635–36 (1924). However, since the decision in Erie R.R. v. Tompkins, 304 U.S. 64, 58 S. Ct. 817, 82 L. Ed. 1188 (1938), the state rule must be applied in federal courts.

[314] Perhaps the best known illustration of this position is found in Superior Brassiere Co. v. Zimetbaum, 214 A.D. 525, 212 N.Y.S. 473 (1925), where the plaintiff had manufactured goods for a dealer and took assignments for moneys due from the dealer's customers as payment for the manufactured goods. The dealer made a second assignment to the defendant, who proceeded to collect from most of the dealer's customers. The court held that "[a] subsequent assignee takes nothing by his assignment because the assignor has nothing to give."

[315] See Salem Trust Co., supra note 313.

[316] Dearle v. Hall, 3 Russ. 1, 48 [1828].

[317] The cases are collected in Annots., 31 A.L.R. 876–79 (1924); 110 A.L.R. 774–75 (1937).

[318] See Jenkinson v. New York Fin. Co., 79 N.J. Eq. 247, 82 A. 36 (N.J. Super. Ct. Ch. Div. 1911). See also Note, 24 COLUM. L. REV. 501 (1924). For a comparative analysis of the American (New York) and English views, see Evans v. Joyner, 195 Va. 85, 77 S.E.2d 420 (1953).

[319] See FIRST RESTATEMENT § 173; RESTATEMENT 2d § 342. See McKnight v. Rice, Hoppner, Brown & Brunner, 678 P.2d 1330 (Alaska 1984).

[320] See Aetna Cas. & Sur. Co. v. Harvard Trust Co., 344 Mass. 160, 181 N.E.2d 673 (1962). Rabinowitz v. Peoples Nat'l Bank, 235 Mass. 102, 126 N.E. 289 (1920); Bridge v. Wheeler, 152 Mass. 343, 25 N.E. 612 (1890).

[321] See Judson v. Corcoran, 58 U.S. (17 How.) 612, 15 L. Ed. 231 (1855).

[322] See Strange v. Houston & T. Co. R.R. Co., 53 Tex. 162 (1880); New York & N.H. R. Co. v. Schuyler, 34 N.Y. 30 (1865).

[323] See Herman v. Connecticut Mut. Life Ins. Co., 218 Mass. 181, 105 N.E. 450 (1914); Washington Tp. v. First Nat'l Bank, 147 Mich. 571, 111 N.W. 349 (1907).

[324] See Coffman v. Liggett's Adm'r, 107 Va. 418, 59 S.E. 392 (1907).

[325] See the cases cited supra note 313.

dealing with successive assignments of the same right in modern commercial financing transactions.

[B]   Modern Commercial Financing — Successive Assignees

What has been set forth to this point is the prevailing law of priority between successive assignees in relation to wage claims, rights under insurance policies, bank accounts, and certain other types of transactions. However, priority problems involving these types of rights are relatively rare. The most significant issues of priority among successive assignees occurs in relation to the assignment of accounts now governed by Article 9 of the UCC.[326] Prior to the Code, the assignment of accounts was dealt with in accordance with the common law positions discussed above. It could make a great deal of difference, therefore, whether the particular jurisdiction involved applied the New York (first in time) view, the English (first to notify) view, or the "four horsemen" (sometimes called "Massachusetts") view. The situation was made much more complex because of the federal Bankruptcy Code.[327] The two basic purposes of the Bankruptcy Act are (1) to permit an insolvent debtor to gain a fresh start by discharging him from his debts (with exceptions), and (2) to assure that the creditors of the bankrupt receive an equitable distribution of the insolvent debtor's assets.[328] In pursuance of the second purpose of equitable distribution among the creditors, the Bankruptcy Act makes certain preferences voidable by the trustee in bankruptcy. For example, if within a certain period prior to bankruptcy,[329] the bankrupt should pay all or virtually all of his remaining assets to one of his many creditors to satisfy antecedent debts, the trustee in bankruptcy could recover this amount from the preferred creditor for the benefit of all the creditors.[330] As to the assignment of accounts receivable, however, such transfers were normally not made on account of an antecedent debt, i.e., they were usually not made to pay an existing (prior) indebtedness. Since only transfers made on account of an antecedent debt were capable of being voidable preferences under the Act, it did not affect the typical accounts receivable transfer which was normally made for a contemporaneous advance ("new value"). However, a 1938 amendment to the Bankruptcy Act provided that a transfer was "deemed" to take effect

---

[326] We have discussed the importance of the assignments of accounts (defined in § 9-102(2), formerly § 9-106) of the UCC.

[327] Article 1, section 8, clause 4 of the United States Constitution empowers Congress to "establish uniform laws on the subject of Bankruptcies throughout the United States." Congress used this power to pass four different Bankruptcy Acts during the nineteenth century. The first three had brief lives. The Act of 1800 was repealed in 1803; the Act of 1841 was repealed after only 18 months; the Act of 1867 was repealed in 1878. The fourth, the Bankruptcy Act of 1898, lasted for 81 years. During this period, it was substantially amended and subjected to a great deal of judicial interpretation. It was replaced by our current Bankruptcy Code (Title 11 of the United States Code), most of which became effective on October 1, 1979, and was amended in 1984.

[328] The majority of bankruptcies are liquidation bankruptcies (Chapter 7 of the Bankruptcy Code). The assets of the bankrupt (debtor) are collected by a trustee in bankruptcy and then liquidated. The proceeds are used to pay the expenses of bankruptcy and to provide equitable distribution of the remainder to creditors. Where the bankrupt is an individual, his debts are discharged and he is provided with a "fresh start." If the debtor is a corporation, it will typically be dissolved. Chapter 11 bankruptcies are rehabilitation bankruptcies (reorganization), though Chapter 13 bankruptcies also have rehabilitation as a goal (adjustment of debts of an individual with regular income). Here, the debtor's obligations are either reduced in amount, deferred in time, or both. By allowing the debtor to continue under these circumstances, creditors will receive more than they would have received had the assets been liquidated and the proceeds therefrom distributed.

[329] The 1950 version of the Bankruptcy Act contained a four month rule. It was later limited to ninety days.

[330] 11 U.S.C. § 547(b).

(in relation to preferences) only when it was "so far perfected" (sufficiently perfected) that it would prevail against bona fide purchasers for value and creditors under the appropriate state law.[331] Under the English view, absent notice to the obligor, an assignment would never become perfected. A practice of "nonnotification" assignments of accounts was prevalent in commercial financing at the time. Under this practice, the assignee would not notify the obligor of the assignment because the assignor did not wish the fact of assignment to be known for pragmatic and good will reasons. If nonnotification assignments were combined with the English (first to notify) rule, no notice to the obligor would ever be given. Therefore, for the purposes of the Bankruptcy Act, the transfer (which was deemed to take effect only when it was secure against creditors and bona fide purchasers) would not be effective when it actually occurred — it would be effective only upon notification to the obligor. Since there was no notification, the transfer was said to take effect immediately prior to bankruptcy which brought the transfer within the four month rule,[332] "for an antecedent debt," at a time when the debtor was insolvent. These innumerable assignments of accounts were, therefore, considered voidable preferences by the United States Supreme Court in the famous *Klauder* case.[333] To avoid the problems created by this interpretation, various state statutes were enacted, including "validation" statutes and notice filing statutes.[334] Pennsylvania, the jurisdiction involved in *Klauder*, and two other states passed "book-marking" statutes,[335] which were subsequently highly criticized. In 1950, Congress amended the Bankruptcy Act again and removed the "bona fide purchaser test" from the critical subsection. The Bankruptcy Reform Act of 1978 produced a new Code which was amended in 1984.[336]

The various state statutes were superseded by the public filing provisions of the UCC, which reacts effectively to these problems. Under the Code, an assignee of an account obtains priority over other assignees, regardless of which assignee was first in time or first notified the obligor, by perfecting a security interest in the account through filing.[337] The first-to-file rule prevails.[338] It is necessary to file a financing statement in the appropriate office. As suggested earlier, however, certain types of accounts are excluded from Article 9,[339] and other

---

[331] This was § 60(a)(2) of that version of the Act.

[332] Now the ninety day rule.

[333] Corn Exch. Nat'l Bank & Trust Co. v. Klauder, 318 U.S. 434 (1943).

[334] *See, e.g.,* CAL. STAT. ch. 766, § 1 (1943).

[335] 1941 PA. LAWS No. 255. *See also* 1943 GA. LAWS No. 178; 1949 N.D. LAWS ch. 113, § 1.

[336] 11 U.S.C. § 101 *et. seq.*

[337] *See* Perkins v. Local 32, United Ass'n of Plumbers & Pipefitters, 2000 Wash. App. LEXIS 578, at *14 (Wash. Ct. App. Apr. 10, 2000) (an attempt to use the common law "successive assignee" analysis was rejected because the security interest had been perfected). UCC § 9-501 deals with the place of filing, which will differ depending upon the type of collateral described in the financing statement, i.e., the statement that is filed. Section 9-502 deals with formal requisites of a financing statement, i.e., what it must contain and the fact that it must be signed by the debtor. The typical financing statement is a prescribed form used throughout the country, though filing must occur in respective state offices since the UCC is a state statute. Section 9-516(a) deals with the effective moment of filing (presentation to the filing officer coupled with the fee) and 9-515 deals with the duration of the filing statement (with certain exceptions, five years unless a continuation statement is filed no more than six months prior to the end of that period).

[338] UCC § 9-322(a)(1) (formerly § 9-312(5)) states that the priority is in time of filing, or perfection, whichever is earlier. Perfection as to certain types of collateral can occur through possession or filing. If neither security interest is perfected, the first to attach (§ 9-203) has priority.

[339] UCC § 9-109(d).

types of accounts do not have to be filed in order to be "perfected" for the purposes of priority over other assignees.[340]

[C]   Priorities — Assignees vs. Attaching Creditors

Almost everyone has creditors who are general (unsecured) creditors, i.e., they have no interest in any particular asset or right of the obligor. A general creditor can, however, procure a specific interest in his debtor's property. He can, for example, become a lien creditor[341] by securing a judgment and having the sheriff "levy" on certain property of the obligor or by securing a writ of attachment and becoming an attaching creditor as to certain accounts of his debtor. If a priority dispute arises between an assignee and a general creditor, the assignee will prevail since he owns the right assigned and the general creditor has no specific interest in that right. When the dispute is between an assignee and an attaching creditor of the assignor, each party has a right in the same chose in action and it is quite generally held that the one first in point of time has the better right. Since the assignee gave value to the assignor in reliance on the particular claim, whereas the attaching creditor relied upon the general credit of the assignor, it is thought that the assignee has the greater equity, and so should prevail, regardless of whether or not he gave notice to the obligor.[342] This is the rule even in those jurisdictions which, in the case of successive assignees, prefer the one who gives notice to the obligor first. However, if the obligor has paid the attaching creditor before he receives notice of the assignment, he will be protected against further liability.[343] Moreover, a number of courts have held that unless the obligor receives notice of the assignment before the attaching creditor obtains a judgment against him, so that he can defend the action and prevent the entry of judgment, the attaching creditor will prevail.[344] Others have held that the assignee will be entitled to priority, even though he gives no notice until after the entry of judgment in the garnishment proceedings, provided such notice be given before the debtor has satisfied the judgment.[345]

As in the discussion of priorities among successive assignees in the previous section, if the assignment is encompassed by Article 9 of the Code, the priority between the assignee and an attaching creditor is easily resolved in the normal case. The Code treats an attaching creditor as a "lien creditor."[346] An Article 9 assignee who has not "perfected" his assigned right is subordinate to such an attaching (lien) creditor.[347] The assignment of many types of collateral

---

[340]   UCC § 9-309(2).

[341]   UCC § 9-102(52) defines a "lien creditor" as a creditor who has acquired a lien on the property involved by attachment, levy, or the like and includes an assignee for benefit of creditors from the time of assignment and a trustee in bankruptcy from the date of the filing of the petition or a receiver in equity from the time of appointment.

[342]   RESTATEMENT 2d § 341 comment a. *See In re* Anchorage Nautical Tours, Inc., 102 B.R. 741, 744 (B.A.P. 9th Cir. 1989).

[343]   Houtz v. Daniels, 36 Idaho 544, 211 P. 1088 (1922).

[344]   Peterson v. Kingman, 59 Neb. 667, 81 N.W. 847 (1900).

[345]   McDowell, Pyle & Co. v. Hopfield, 148 Md. 84, 128 A. 742 (1925), followed in RESTATEMENT 2d § 341(2), ill. 1 (obligor who does not receive notification of the assignment until after losing the opportunity to assert assignment as a defense in the proceeding in which the judicial lien was obtained is discharged from his duty to the assignee to the extent of his satisfaction of the lien).

[346]   *See supra* note 317.

[347]   *See* UCC § 9-317(a)(2). *See also* Sun Bank, N.A. v. Parkland Design & Dev. Corp., 466 So. 2d 1089 (Fla. Dist. Ct. App. 1985) (under Article 9's priority rules, an unperfected assignee of an account is subordinate to a lien creditor;

under Article 9 may be "perfected" either by filing a financing statement in the appropriate public offices or by taking possession of the collateral. In relation to accounts, however, the only method allowing for "perfection" is filing.[348] There is only one exception in relation to assignment of accounts. When such an assignment does not transfer a significant part of the outstanding accounts of the assignor, the assignment is perfected without filing,[349] i.e., the assignment would be perfected upon "attachment."[350] If the assignment is perfected either by filing or by attachment because it is the kind of assignment that comes within the exception, the perfected assignment takes priority over the attaching creditor because the interest of a lien creditor is subordinate to the interest of a prior perfected security interest in the same collateral, regardless of how perfection occurred.[351]

---

a garnishing judgment creditor qualifies as a lien creditor).

[348] UCC § 9-313 comment 2.

[349] UCC § 9-309(2).

[350] UCC § 9-203. The concept of attachment was discussed in § 137.

[351] UCC § 9-317(a)(2).

Chapter 12

THE DISCHARGE OF CONTRACTS

§ 144   METHODS OF DISCHARGING A CONTRACTUAL DUTY

[A]   A Survey of Methods

The normal method of discharging a contractual duty is by performing it. There are, however, numerous other ways to discharge an obligation, many of which we have seen throughout this volume. If a party commits an uncured material breach, the duty of the other party is discharged. If a duty is subject to a condition, the nonoccurrence of the conditioning event will discharge the duty if the condition can no longer occur. If a performance becomes impossible or impracticable, or if its purpose is frustrated, the performance will be excused and, thereby, discharged. A party lacking capacity or defrauded can exercise a power of avoidance and effectively discharge his duty in that fashion. A party may be discharged in bankruptcy or an action to enforce his duty may be barred by the statute of limitations, thereby effecting a discharge.

This is certainly not an exhaustive list of methods of discharge. In this chapter we will consider methods of discharge that we have not explored in detail earlier in this volume, though some have been discussed at appropriate points. We begin by considering three methods of discharge that are fundamental: discharge by informal agreement, gift, and rejection of tender.

[B]   Discharge by Informal Agreement, Gift, Rejection of Tender or Waiver of Breach

Gifts. If it is supported by consideration, an agreement to discharge a contractual obligation is as enforceable as any other contract. Absent consideration, or the requisites for an executed gift, however, our law has generally proceeded on the theory that an informal agreement for the divestment of a right, in the absence of a statute providing otherwise, is not effective.[1] The traditional elements of an effective inter vivos gift are donative intent, delivery and acceptance.[2] Since contract rights are intangible, there is often nothing to deliver or accept.[3] Where the right is evidenced by a written instrument which, by the terms of the contract or by law or usage, is surrendered to the obligor when he performs the duty, it is generally held that such a surrender operates as a discharge by gift.[4] Absent such an instrument, however, the delivery of a receipt or other substitute document with donative intent is essential.[5]

Much earlier, we explored the considerable criticism and modifications of the pre-existing duty rule where we discussed the doctrine of *Foakes v. Beer*,[6] based on precedent almost three centuries older to the effect that payment of a lesser sum cannot be satisfaction for the full amount of the debt owed.[7] If a debtor owes $1000 and the creditor is willing to accept $500 and forgive the remainder of the debt, the refusal to recognize the entire debt as discharged has

---

[1] *See* RESTATEMENT 2d § 273. A promise under seal at common law also met the requirements and would do so today where the seal is still effective. Similarly, where a promise of discharge has induced reasonable reliance, the promise is effective. Contrary to the general rule, some very early English cases held that a voluntary exoneration of the obligor by the obligee, *if made before breach of the primary obligation*, was effective to bar the later enforcement of the contract, even though it was not supported by consideration. *See* Conier's v. Holland, 2 Leon 214 [1588]; Langden v. Stokes, 3 Cro. Car. 383, 79 Eng. Rep. 935 [1634]; Edwards v. Weeks, 2 Mod. 260, 86 Eng. Rep. 930 (dictum). While such holdings would protect the obligor who changed his position in reliance upon the obligee's affirmation that performance would not be required, the rule was not limited to that type of case but was applied generally without any reference to consideration. Once the debt had arisen of the promise that was breached, a promise to forgive the debt or claim (mere words) was insufficient. Before the breach, however, there were only promises that could be discharged by mere words. *See* A. W. B. SIMPSON, A HISTORY OF THE COMMON LAW OF CONTRACT 470–71 (1987).

[2] Ross v. Fierro, 659 A.2d 234, 238 (D. C. App. 1995).

[3] *Id.*

[4] *See* the discussion of gratuitous assignments *supra* Chapter 11, § 138[B][1].

[5] *Ross v. Fierro, supra* note 2. See also Gartin v. Taylor, 577 N. W. 2d 410 (Iowa 1998) (oral release of obligation without consideration is ineffective).

[6] 9 App. Cas. 605 [1884], discussed at § 65[B], *supra.*

[7] Pinnel's Case, 5 Coke Rep. 117a, 77 Eng. Rep. 237 [1600]. This, however, was dictum. *See* A. W. B. SIMPSON, A HISTORY OF THE COMMON LAW OF CONTRACT 106 (1987).

been called "one of the relics of antique law which should have been discarded long ago."[8] Courts have departed from the strictures of the rule when an obligee who is entitled to money payable in installments, as in the case of rent reserved under a lease,[9] or money payable under a separation agreement,[10] agrees to accept less than the amount stipulated in full satisfaction of his claim. Such an agreement has been held to be effective to discharge the obligor's duty *to the extent to which it has been performed* before the obligee insists on recovering past deficiencies, although no consideration can be found to support the original promise to accept less. The underlying theory is that of an executed gift or waiver (renunciation) of past amounts owed. A statute may provide that a written discharge of a debt is effective absent consideration.[11]

Waiver of Breach. An aggrieved party may waive a breach of contract. A party had ceased performance of a construction contract but resumed work for another eight months pursuant to a clarification and modification of the contract, completing 90 percent of the work before being terminated. The court held since the clarification and modification had not been induced by a misrepresentation even assuming the earlier cessation of performance was a material breach, the breach had been waived.[12] The UCC provides that a written waiver or renunciation signed and delivered by the aggrieved party discharges any claim or right arising out of an alleged breach.[13] The UCC also contains clear directives concerning the discharge of a negotiable instrument without consideration.[14]

While there is little doubt that our courts would enforce a promise to discharge a debt when the elements of a promissory estoppel are present,[15] the traditional requirement of consideration to effectuate a discharge of an obligation remains.[16] A rejection of an effective tender of performance will operate to discharge the obligation if the performance promised is of such a kind that it can only be rendered at the time fixed.[17] If, however, a promisee agrees to accept, and does accept, a defective performance of a promise as full satisfaction of the

---

[8] Rye v. Phillips, 203 Minn. 567, 569, 282 N.W. 459, 460 (1938). Relying upon this dictum, twenty-three years later, the same court held that the doctrine should be discarded. Winter Wolff & Co. v. Co-op. Lead & Chem. Co., 261 Minn. 199, 111 N.W.2d 461 (1961).

[9] Taylor v. Taylor, 39 Cal. App. 2d 518, 103 P.2d 575 (1940); C. S. Brackett & Co. v. Lofgren, 140 Minn. 52, 167 N.W. 274 (1918).

[10] Vigelius v. Vigelius, 169 Wash. 190, 13 P.2d 425 (1932).

[11] *See* N.Y. Gen. Oblig. Law § 5-1103 (2000).

[12] Madden-Phillips Constr. v. GGAT Dev. Corp., 2009 Tenn. App. LEXIS 645 (2009).

[13] UCC § 1-107, which is replicated in Restatement 2d § 277(1). *See* Philbin v. Matanuska-Susitna Borough, 991 P.2d 1263, 1269 (Alaska 1999). See also UCC § 3-605, which permits the holder of a negotiable instrument without consider to discharge any party to the instrument, *inter alia*, by renouncing his rights by a signed and delivered writing or by delivery of the instrument to the party to be discharged.

[14] UCC § 3-604 (formerly § 3-605). See First Dakota Nat'l Bank v. Maxon, 534 N.W.2d 37, 43 (S.D. 1995), discussing various ways under UCC Article 3 for discharging liability on an instrument.

[15] Jazlowiecki v. Nicoletti, 34 Conn. Supp. 670, 387 A.2d 1081 (Super. Ct. 1977); Fried v. Fisher, 328 Pa. 497, 196 A. 39 (1938); Maryland Steel Co. v. United States, 235 U.S. 451, 35 S. Ct. 190, 59 L. Ed. 312 (1915). *See* Restatement 2d § 273(c).

[16] Restatement 2d § 273 comment a. See Law Co. v. Mohawk Constr. & Supply Co., 2010 U.S. Dist. LEXIS 24302 at *77 (D. Kan. 2010) (waiver operates to disclaim a duty only if the requirements for discharge of contract are met (Restatement 2d § 306, comment b) and such requirements appear to include consideration (citing § 273)).

[17] Under the UCC, a rejection of nonconforming goods (§§ 2-601 and 602) will be final unless "contract time" remains and the seller exercises his right to cure (§ 2-508).

promisor's obligation, he cannot thereafter maintain an action for breach of promise because of the defective performance.[18] If, in such a case, the promisor tenders a different (substitute) performance, its acceptance will involve the receipt of a consideration by the promisee, which furnishes ample support for the discharge of the original obligation. When the promisor offering the defective performance purports to do only what his contract requires him to do, there is no consideration for the purported discharge, and yet it is frequently held to be effective. The discharge is said to be accomplished by "waiver."[19]

[C]   Rescission

The parties to an executory bilateral contract may decide that they are mutually dissatisfied with their agreement and desire simply to call it off. Just as parties can form a contract by the exchange of mutual promises, they can abandon the contract in the same fashion.[20] To accomplish this result, they may form a new contract which has only one purpose, i.e., the discharge of the original contract. This is known as a contract of *rescission*, where each party agrees to discharge the other party's remaining duties of performance under an existing contract.[21] The mutual release of the parties' rights constitutes consideration for such an agreement.[22] A contract of rescission has only one purpose, i.e., to discharge the existing contract and, in performing that sole purpose, it discharges itself. Thus, a contract of rescission is formed, performed and thereby discharged simultaneously. Like other contracts, a contract of rescission may be inferred from conduct.[23]

It is important to distinguish an *agreement* of rescission, which is a contract to discharge an executory bilateral contract as just described, from the use of the term "rescission" to refer to discharge of a party's obligation where the other party has breached the contract. A repudiation of a contract was followed by the repudiator's return of the other party's funds that were used to institute the project. The repudiator argued that this constituted a rescission of the contract. The court held that there was no evidence that the other party had agreed to discharge the other's duties under the contract. Where a party repudiates a contract and the other party demands his money back, such a demand is not an offer to rescind the

---

[18] Weisser v. Grand Forks Fed. Sav. & Loan Ass'n, 406 N.W.2d 696 (N.D. 1987); Kangas v. Trust, 110 Ill. App. 3d 876, 65 Ill. Dec. 757, 441 N.E.2d 1271 (2d Dist. 1982). RESTATEMENT 2d § 277(2). *See also* Lawson & Nelson Sash & Door Co. v. Kraus-Anderson of St. Paul Co., 279 Minn. 218, 156 N.W.2d 208 (1968) (whether acceptance of defective performance occurred is a question of fact).

[19] Frank Japes Co. v. Pagel, 246 Mich. 700, 225 N.W. 521 (1926) (owner who makes payments to contractor without objection for work done after contract time expired cannot recover damages for delay). *See also* Pressy v. McCornack, 235 Pa. 443, 84 A. 427 (1912).

[20] Smith v. Deluca, 36 Conn. App. 839, 654 A.2d 368, 369 (1995).

[21] *Eodem modo quo oritur, eodem modo dissolvitur* (In the manner in which a thing is created, in that manner it may be dissolved).

[22] Seaquest Diving L. P. v. S & J Diving, Inc., 579 F.3d 411 (5th Cir. 2009). See also Billings v. Gardner, 88 Or. App. 370, 372, 745 P.2d 792, 793 (1987) ("the deal's off" — "everybody acquiesced in that"); Kallenbach v. Lake Publications, Inc., 30 Wis. 2d 647, 652, 142 N.W.2d 212, 215 (1966) (where parties decide to call off a contract or declare a contract at an end there is a rescission). *See also* Lemlich v. Board of Trustees, 282 Md. 495, 385 A.2d 1185 (1978) (since a rescission is a contract, there must be an offer and acceptance and the offer may be revoked prior to acceptance). RESTATEMENT 2d § 283.

[23] Braith v. Hagerty, 1999 Minn. App. LEXIS 788, at *5, 39 U.C.C. Rep. Serv. 2d (CBC) 251 (Minn. Ct. App. 1999) (question of fact); Doss v. Epic Healthcare Mgmt. Co., 901 S.W.2d 216, 220 (Mo. Ct. App. 1995) (unanswered offer of rescission may manifest acceptance by conduct). *See also* Peppler v. Chipman, 142 Wis. 2d 945, 419 N.W.2d 574 (Ct. App. 1987).

contract or a waiver of other remedial rights.[24] Recognizing the misuse of "rescission" and "cancellation," the UCC provides a safeguard against unintentional loss of rights through their use by directing that such terms, in the absence of a contrary intention, are not to be construed as a discharge of a claim for damages.[25] Where an executory bilateral contract has been partially performed by one or both parties who form a contract to rescind their original contract, courts disagree as to whether there is a right to recover for the partial performance. If the contract of rescission itself either expressly or impliedly manifests the parties' intention, their intention should be enforced. Often, however, the contract of rescission does evidence the intention of the parties. Some courts take the unfortunate position that the very nature of a rescission requires a return to status quo and, therefore, any partial performance by one party must be compensated by the other to preclude the latter from becoming unjustly enriched.[26] This position ignores the fact that a rescission is a contract by which one of the parties who has not performed at all may have agreed to enter into the rescission only if the other party, who has partly performed, agreed to surrender all of his rights against the first party in exchange for the surrender by the first party of his remaining rights. The better view rejects any presumption that a right to recover for part performance rendered prior to the rescission is intended to be reserved to either party in the absence of affirmative evidence of such intention. Like any other contract, it is a question of the apparent intention of the parties at the time the agreement of rescission was formed.[27]

[D]   Renunciation

If the contract was originally unilateral, or if it was bilateral and one party had lost all rights under it through the other party's performance or otherwise, a rescission would not be enforceable because that party has nothing to exchange in consideration of the other party's promise to rescind. Yet, when one of the parties has lost all of his rights under a bilateral contract because he has committed an uncured material breach of the contract and the nondefaulting party elects to *renounce* the contract, it has been held that the defaulter's obligation to pay damages or to perform specifically is discharged. He can be held only to make restitution of the performance already rendered by the nondefaulting party in a quasi-contract action.[28] It is frequently suggested that a nondefaulting party has a right to choose between alternative remedies which are inconsistent.[29] Once he has elected to renounce the

---

[24] American Heritage, Inc. v. Nevada Gold & Casino, 259 S. W. 3d 816 (Tex. App. 2008). *See also* Hudson v. McClaskey, 597 N.E.2d 308 (Ind. 1992), where the court disagreed with the court of appeals in holding that the election to seek rescission as a remedy abandoned any claim for damages.

[25] UCC § 2-106(4); Restatement 2d § 720. See further discussion at § 146[E], *infra*.

[26] In Dilts v. Lynch, 655 S.W.2d 118, 121 (Mo. Ct. App. 1983), the court recognizes that some courts recognize the question as one of interpretation, but Missouri courts "appear to hold that restitution is required unless the rescission agreement makes some other provision therefor, or the parties agree to some other arrangement." In Anderson v. Copeland, 378 P.2d 1006, 1007 (Okla. 1963), the court suggests that the parties rescinded a contract which had the effect of allowing defendant to use plaintiff's tractor without paying for it. Thus, the law implies a contract for defendant to pay the reasonable rental value of the tractor so as to avoid unjust enrichment of the defendant.

[27] Billings v. Gardner, 88 Or. App. 370, 745 P.2d 792, 793 (1987); McBee Binder Co. v. Fred J. Robinson Lumber Co., 267 Mich. 637, 255 N.W. 329 (1934); Coletti v. Knox Hat Co., 252 N.Y. 468, 169 N.E. 648 (1930); Aderholt v. Wood, 66 Cal. App. 666, 226 P. 950 (1924). Restatement 2d § 283(2).

[28] The quasi-contract action would protect the renouncing party's restitution interest.

[29] Walter-Wallingford Coal Co. v. A. Himes Coal Co., 223 Mich. 576, 194 N.W. 493 (1923); Thackeray v. Knight, 57 Utah 21, 192 P. 263 (1920).

contract and to seek restitution, he is not permitted to change his mind to sue on the contract itself. A renouncing party should no longer be allowed the remedy of specific performance if the promisor, relying upon the promisee's renunciation, has changed his position in such a way that performance has become more difficult or impossible. It is, however, difficult to understand why an election is irrevocable if the promisor has not been in any way misled by what had previously been done by the promisee. Discharge of the contract by renunciation under these circumstances is frequently spoken of as "rescission" which only adds to the confusion. While renunciation may preclude the obligee's right to sue for damages or specific performance, it does not preclude an action for restitution. A mutual agreement to rescind the contract, however, must be determined wholly from the terms of the agreement itself that may indicate no intention to provide any restitution of prior benefits conferred.

The Uniform Commercial Code allows any claim or right arising from an alleged breach of contract to be discharged in whole or in part without consideration by a written waiver or renunciation of the contract that is signed and delivered by the aggrieved party.[30] The RESTATEMENT 2d replicates this principle for contracts not governed by the Code.[31] The usual UCC and RESTATEMENT 2d requirement of "good faith" must accompany any such renunciation.[32]

§ 145   ACCORD AND SATISFACTION AND SUBSTITUTE CONTRACT

[A]   Distinguishing Accord and Satisfaction From Substitute Contract

Much earlier, we introduced the contract of discharge known as *accord and satisfaction* in the context of a check marked "payment in full" to satisfy a disputed claim.[33] It is not uncommon for parties to an existing contract, which may or may not have been breached at the time, to make a subsequent agreement, which, or the performance of which, they contemplate as a substitution for the obligations under the original contract. The question is, does an unperformed (executory) subsequent agreement alone or only the *performance* of that agreement operate to discharge the obligations under the original contract? It would seem simple enough to answer the question by referring to the intention of the parties. If the parties intended to discharge their prior contract at the moment they form a substitute contract, their intention should be effected. If, however, they did not intend the rights and duties under the original contract to be discharged until the subsequent contract was performed, that intention should be respected. Unfortunately, the issue became complicated by historic accident that caused courts to separate cases involving this question into two distinct categories which differ from each other only superficially.

---

[30] UCC § 1-107. *See* Philbin v. Matanuska-Susitna Borough, 991 P.2d 1263, 1269 (Alaska 1999). In Billings Leasing Co. v. Payne, 176 Mont. 217, 577 P.2d 386, 389 (1978), the court emphasizes the fact that UCC § 1-107 does not exclude an oral waiver, i.e., "It simply allows a written waiver to be enforced even though it is not supported by consideration."

[31] RESTATEMENT 2d § 277(1). Section 277(2) allows the obligee to renounce a claim for partial breach orally and without consideration if he has accepted some performance from the obligor under the contract.

[32] UCC § 1-107, comment. *See* Allapattah Servs. v. Exxon Corp., 188 F.R.D. 667, 682 (S.D. Fla. 1999).

[33] *See* § 65[B][3], *supra.* There we explored the 1990 amendment which added UCC § 1-207(2) to eliminate confusion over whether that section was intended to qualify a common law accord and satisfaction. UCC § 3-311 is a modern statement of this methodology. For a recent illustration, see Valley Asphalt, Inc. v. Stimpel-Wiebelhaus Assocs., 2001 U.S. App. LEXIS 1707 (10th Cir. 2001).

If the new agreement was not made until after the maturity or breach of the original contract, the new agreement is called an *accord* and its performance in discharge of the original contract is designated a *satisfaction.*[34] If, however, the new agreement is made before the maturity or breach of the original obligation, older cases spoke of the agreement as a *substitute contract.*[35] While it is not uncommon for modern cases to use the terms interchangeably[36] and both types of agreements seem to involve essentially the same issues that should be dealt with in the same way, we will later explore differences in result that may follow from this distinction. To understand the distinction, it is important to consider its evolution.

That an accord or a substitute contract which is fully performed will operate to discharge the obligations under the original contract, if it is supported by consideration and if that was the intention of the parties, has never been doubted from the earliest times.[37] It appears that the question of the discharge of matured obligations by substitute agreement came before the courts a great many times in the days before informal contracts were known to our law.[38] Since an informal promise, even though it was supported by what we now know as consideration, was not legally enforceable at that time, it is easy to understand why the courts would have held that an accord which is an informal promise could not be enforced to discharge a prior obligation so long as it was unperformed ("unsatisfied"). Once informal promises supported by consideration became obligatory, there was no longer any reason why an accord (sometimes called a "concord" in the early common law) should not have been held to be binding and to discharge prior obligations if that was the intention of the parties. Nevertheless, the courts were slow to take this step because of the many cases in which it had been said, under the old law, that an unperformed accord not only was not a bar, but was not an enforceable contract.[39] Many courts apparently forgot that the reason why an accord could never operate as a bar in the old law was because it could not be an enforceable contract; and they apparently assumed that the reverse was true, namely, that such a transaction did not result in an enforceable obligation because it was not a bar. Consequently, we find that for a

---

[34] "Accord and Satisfaction is the purchase of a release from an obligation whether arising under a contract or tort by means of any valuable consideration, not being the actual performance of the obligation itself." Scrutton, L.J., in British-Russian Gazette, Ltd. v. Associated Newspapers, Ltd., 2 K.B. 616, 643 [1933]. RESTATEMENT 2d § 281(1) defines an accord as a contract under which an obligee promises to accept a stated performance in satisfaction of the existing duty of the obligor, and performance of the accord discharges the original duty.

[35] *See* Bandman v. Finn, 185 N.Y. 508, 78 N.E. 175 (1906); Taylor v. Hillary, 1 Cromp. M. & R. 741 [1835]. This distinction was undoubtedly made, in the first instance, in order that the so-called substitute contract could be given effect in accordance with the intentions of the parties without going counter to the established precedents. The rule in relation to the technical accord was well-settled to the effect that such an agreement not only could not be pleaded in bar to the original obligation but was not even an enforceable contract, even though it may have had the usual requisites of an informal contract. Since this rule had very little to commend it other than its antiquity, it is not strange that later courts should have found ways of refusing to apply it further than was required by the facts of earlier decisions.

[36] In Paramount Aviation Corp. v. Agusta, 178 F.3d 132, 147 (3d Cir.), *cert. denied*, 528 U.S. 878, 120 S. Ct. 188, 145 L. Ed. 2d 158 (1999), the court states, "An accord and satisfaction is a substitute contract for settlement of a debt. . . ."

[37] *See* A. W. B. SIMPSON, A HISTORY OF THE COMMON LAW OF CONTRACT 470–75 (1987).

[38] "From time immemorial the acceptance of anything in satisfaction of the damages caused by a tort would bar a subsequent action against the wrong-doer. Accord and satisfaction was, likewise, a bar to an action for damages arising from a breach of covenant." Ames, *Specialty Contracts and Equitable Defenses*, 9 HARV. L. REV. 49, 55 (1895).

[39] Thus, in Allen v. Harris, 1 Ld. Raym. 122 [1701], in sustaining a demurrer to a plea of accord, the court said, "But upon an accord no remedy lies. And the books are so numerous that an accord ought to be executed that it is not impossible to overthrow all the books." *See* Gold, *Executory Accords*, 21 B.U. L. REV. 465 (1941).

long time, even after informal contracts came into our law, it was held that if a transaction, although it had all the earmarks of a valid, informal contract, was intended as an accord, it could not be given effect as an enforceable obligation, to say nothing of making it a bar to suit on a prior obligation.[40] It is now clear that an executory accord, like any other contract, is legally enforceable.[41]

Again, it is important to consider the surrounding confusion in the use of language that permeates discussions of the discharge of contracts. We have already noted the confusion in the unwieldy use of the term, "rescission," that should be relegated to a contract of discharge. Courts have complained about this confusion[42] and it exists in relation to accord and satisfaction and substitute contracts. An accord can be viewed as a substitute contract in the sense that the parties have agreed upon a contract to substitute for their original obligations. If the parties intend their new executory agreement to discharge their prior obligations the moment it is made and before it is performed, that intention should be effectuated and courts have given such agreements that effect.[43] It is possible to characterize this kind of agreement as one type of accord, i.e., an accord which the parties intend to immediately discharge their prior obligations. It is also quite logical to refer to this type of new agreement as a substitute contract. Where the intention of the parties is to discharge the prior duty only after the new contract is performed, the old obligation continues to exist along with the new contract.[44] It is possible to characterize this new agreement as a substitute contract though it appears more reasonable to view it as an accord which will have to be satisfied (performed) to discharge the original obligation simultaneously with the accord.[45] Since it is unlikely that an obligee would ordinarily wish merely to exchange one cause of action for another, it is generally presumed that the parties intended the old obligation to be discharged only upon the performance of the new contract, in the absence of affirmative evidence of a contrary intention.[46] However one

---

[40] See Hall v. Knapp, 552 S.W.2d 299 (Mo. Ct. App. 1977) (citing the second edition of this book for this proposition).

[41] The formation and enforceability of an accord is governed by the same rules as those applicable to other contracts. See Anderson v. Rosebrook, 737 P.2d 417 (Colo. 1987); McKibben v. Mohawk Oil Co., 667 P.2d 1223 (Alaska 1983). See also Flagel v. Southwest Clinical Physiatrists, P.C., 157 Ariz. 196, 755 P.2d 1184 (Ct. App. 1988) (there is consideration if only part of the claim is unliquidated). See RESTATEMENT 2d § 281 comment a.

[42] See, e.g., Bargale Indus., Inc. v. Robert Realty Co., 275 Md. 638, 343 A.2d 529 (1975), where the court suggests confusion between "novation" and other forms of discharge, such as accord, substitute contract, and other methods. Some jurisdictions still insist that there are two forms of novation, i.e., two party and three party novation. See Dere v. Montgomery Ward & Co., 224 Va. 277, 295 S.E.2d 794 (1982).

[43] Ohlson v. Steinhauser, 218 Or. 532, 346 P.2d 87 (1959); In re Kellett Aircraft Corp., 173 F.2d 689, 692 (3d Cir. 1949), aff'g 77 F. Supp. 959 (D. Pa. 1948).

[44] Sherman v. Sidman, 300 Mass. 102, 14 N.E.2d 145 (1938); Reilly v. Barrett, 220 N.Y. 170, 115 N.E. 453 (1917). Professor Corbin suggests that there is "unlimited authority" for this proposition. 6 CORBIN § 1269.

[45] In Pan Am. World Airlines, Inc. v. Midlantic Nat'l Bank/North, 1990 U.S. Dist. LEXIS 5722, at *13 (D.N.J. May 7, 1990), the court distinguishes the two types of agreement as follows: An accord and satisfaction involves "two analytically distinct steps." Until substitute performance is completed, the agreement is an "executory accord" and the obligee may sue on the underlying obligation (the original contract) if the accord is not performed. If it is performed, the obligee must accept the substituted performance. The court likens accord and satisfaction to a "unilateral" contract. On the other hand, a "substitute contract" is likened to a "bilateral" contract since it involves the "single step" of an exchange of mutual promises that extinguishes prior claims. The court suggests that the RESTATEMENT 2d § 281 adopts this distinction. The RESTATEMENT 2d, however, does not analogize the two types of agreements under the rubrics, "unilateral" and "bilateral." Such labels in this context may be more confusing that helpful.

[46] Poggi v. Kates, 115 Ariz. 157, 564 P.2d 380 (1977); In re Kellett Aircraft Corp., supra note 43 (federal district court opinion); Fricke v. Forbes, 294 Mich. 375, 293 N.W. 686 (1940); Wyatt v. New York, O. & W. R. Co., 45 F.2d 705 (2d Cir. 1930), cert. denied, 283 U.S. 829, 51 S. Ct. 353, 75 L. Ed. 1442 (1931). RESTATEMENT 2d § 279 comment c is in accord with

characterizes the new agreement, it is the intention of the parties that should be effected. The RESTATEMENT 2d chooses the logical path of calling those agreements which are intended by the parties to discharge the original duty as soon as the new agreement is formed, "substitute contracts," and those agreements which are intended to discharge the original obligation only upon performance (satisfaction) of the new agreement, "accords."[47] This distinction removes some of the confusion in this area.[48] Whether the parties intended an accord and satisfaction or a substituted contract is a question of interpretation in accordance with the usual guidelines to interpretation.[49] Doubtful cases are resolved in favor of an intention to create an accord since an obligee is less likely to accept a mere promise in satisfaction of the original duty.[50]

[B]   Obligee's Repudiation of Accord or Substitute Contract

Whether an obligee may repudiate an accord and enforce the original duty, even though the obligor is not in default under the accord, is a question that caused considerable difficulty for common law courts. When an obligee enters into an accord with an obligor, although he has no intention of discharging the prior duty immediately, it is certainly a fair assumption that he has, by implication, promised to refrain from enforcing the original duty unless and until there has been a breach of the new contract. Moreover, it is perfectly consistent with generally accepted principles to take the view that this tacit promise should be specifically enforced, if for no other reason than to prevent unnecessary litigation. This result could have been accomplished either by permitting the obligor to plead the new agreement in abatement of a suit founded on the original obligation, thus preventing a suit on it in the absence of a default by the obligor on the new contract, or by permitting a suit in equity for an injunction against enforcement of the original duty, pending performance of the new contract. Unfortunately, the first of these remedies was at war with the common law notion that a cause of action once suspended is necessarily barred forever. Paying deference to this mistaken premise,[51] the common law courts logically inferred that an agreement to suspend a cause of action

---

this view and adds, "It will therefore be less likely to find a substituted contract and more likely to find an accord if the original duty was one to pay money, if it was undisputed, if it was liquidated and if it was matured."

[47] *See* RESTATEMENT 2d § 279 comment c. Substitute contracts are covered in § 279, while accord and satisfaction are dealt with in § 281.

[48] Todd v. Antonio, 1999 Mass Super. LEXIS 31, at *5 n.2, 9 Mass. L. Rep. 510 (Mass. Super. Ct. 1999), quotes the RESTATEMENT 2d definition of accord and satisfaction in § 281: (1) An accord is a contract under which an obligee promises to accept a stated performance in satisfaction of the obligor's existing duty. Performance of the accord discharges the original duty. (2) Until performance of the accord, the original duty is suspended unless there is such a breach of the accord by the obligor as discharges the new duty of the obligee to accept the performance in satisfaction. If there is such a breach, the obligee may enforce either the original duty or any duty under the accord. (3) Breach of the accord by the obligee does not discharge the original duty, but the obligor may maintain a suit for specific performance of the accord, in addition to any claim for damages for partial breach. A "substituted contract" is defined in § 279(1) as "a contract that is itself accepted by the obligee in satisfaction of the obligor's existing duty."

[49] Michael J. Benenson Assocs. v. Orthopedic Network of New Jersey, 54 Fed. Appx. 33, 36–37, 2002 U.S. App. LEXIS 23559 (3d Cir. 2002).

[50] RESTATEMENT 2d § 279, comment e. *See* Community Builders v. Indian Motorcycle Assocs., 44 Mass. App. Ct. 537, 692 N.E.2d 964, 972 (1998); K-Line Builders v. First Fed. Sav. & Loan Ass'n, 139 Ariz. 209, 677 P.2d 1317 (Ct. App. 1984); Sergeant v. Leonard, 312 N.W.2d 541 (Iowa 1981). *See also* Robison v. Hansen, 594 P.2d 867 (Utah 1979) (substituted agreement may be implied from conduct); Johnson v. Utile, 86 Nev. 593, 472 P.2d 335 (1970) (whether it is an accord or substitute agreement turns on the intention of the parties).

[51] *See* 5 CORBIN § 1251 (1951), and 6 CORBIN § 1274 (1963 ed.).

temporarily could have no effect on the original obligation,[52] but merely furnished a basis for a cross-action when the new agreement was violated.[53] At least one definite exception to this rule was found where a negotiable instrument is executed to cover a pre-existing debt.[54] Yet, the antiquated notion had the character of tenacity in many of our older cases[55] and even later some courts adhered to the rule by holding that the obligee may enforce the original duty at law though the obligor had tendered performance of the substitute agreement in due time, and even rendered part performance that was accepted by the obligee.[56]

Under the modern view, if the obligor has not breached the accord, the original obligation is suspended to provide the obligor an opportunity to complete the performance of the accord.[57] Once he performs the accord, both his original duty and the duty under the accord are discharged.[58] If the obligee breaches the accord and seeks to recover on the original obligation, the obligor may raise the accord as an affirmative defense[59] and be granted specific performance of the accord and injunctive relief to prevent any action on the accord while the obligor continues to perform the accord in accordance with its terms.[60] The obligor may also recover damages for partial breach.[61]

The failure of an obligee to perform a *substitute contract* has no effect on the discharge of the original obligation which the parties intended to be discharged at the moment they formed the substitute contract. Any attempt by the obligor to enforce the original obligation under these circumstances would be met with the affirmative defense that such obligation had been

---

[52] To hold otherwise would have done violence to the intention of the parties since the antiquated rule transformed any effort to suspend a cause of action into a completed discharge of the original obligation. It was not the parties' intention to discharge the obligation by the creation of an executory substituted agreement.

[53] Ford v. Beech, 11 Q.B. 852, 116 Eng. Rep. 693 [1848]. See, however, Beech v. Ford, 7 Hare 208 [1848], where the appropriate relief was procured in equity.

[54] Walter H. Goodrich & Co. v. Friedman, 92 Conn. 262, 102 A. 607 (1917).

[55] But see Morgan v. Butterfield, 3 Mich. 615 (1855), and Robinson v. Godfrey, 2 Mich. 408 (1852), which hold that an agreement not to sue on a contract for a limited time effects a modification of the original contract and may be pleaded in bar of a suit on it. See generally Shepard, *The Executory Accord*, 26 Ill. L. Rev. 22 (1931), where the cases are collected and discussed.

[56] Taylor v. Central of Ga. R. Co., 99 Ga. App. 224, 108 S.E.2d 103 (1959); Reilly v. Barrett, 220 N.Y. 170, 115 N.E. 453 (1917).

[57] *See* Spaulding v. Cahill, 146 Vt. 386, 505 A.2d 1186 (1985). *See also* Restatement 2d § 281(2) and comment b.

[58] Restatement 2d § 281 comment b.

[59] *See* Bestor v. American Nat'l Stores, Inc., 691 S.W.2d 384 (Mo. Ct. App. 1985).

[60] *See* Dobias v. White, 239 N.C. 409, 80 S.E.2d 23 (1954) (specific performance); Union Cent. Life Ins. Co. v. Imsland, 91 F.2d 365 (8th Cir. 1937) (accord enforced against attempt to foreclose mortgage); Boston & Me. R.R. v. Union Mut. Fire Ins. Co., 92 Vt. 137, 101 A. 1012 (1917) (accord specifically enforced and action on original claim enjoined); Chicora Fertilizer Co. v. Dunan, 91 Md. 144, 46 A. 347 (1900) (specific enforcement); Cook v. Richardson, 178 Mass. 125, 59 N.E. 675 (1901) (accord specifically enforced and action on original claim enjoined); Very v. Levy, 54 U.S. (13 How.) 345, 14 L. Ed. 173 (1852). *Accord* Restatement 2d § 281(3) (obligor may specifically enforce accord and also claim any damages for partial breach by obligee). *See also* Bestor v. American Nat'l Stores, Inc., *id.*, which holds that an accord and satisfaction is an affirmative defense and the defendants did not have to seek specific performance since the breach of the accord was sufficient to release defendants from all claims asserted by the plaintiff.

[61] Restatement 2d § 281(3), comment c. *See* Berryhill v. Hatt, 428 N.W.2d 647, 658 (Iowa 1988). See also Penobscot Indian Nation v. Key Bank, 112 F.3d 538, 559 n.28 (1st Cir.), *cert. denied*, 522 U.S. 913, 118 S. Ct. 297, 139 L. Ed. 2d 229 (1997), indicating a difference of opinion and some confusion concerning the recovery of damages for partial breach together with specific performance.

discharged.[62]

[C]   Obligor's Failure to Perform Accord or Substitute Contract

Where the obligor fails to perform an accord, it is clear that the obligee may elect to enforce either the original duty or the accord.[63] On the other hand, if the parties intended to form a substitute contract to discharge the original duty upon consummation of that contract, and if the obligor failed to perform it, the common law courts found determination of the remedy more difficult. It has frequently been said in such cases that the only redress available to the obligee is to sue on the substitute contract.[64]

[D]   Accord and Satisfaction With a Third Person

The question of whether an obligation is discharged if the obligee accepts something in satisfaction of his claim from a person other than the obligor is one that has been disputed in the cases. While it is undoubtedly true that the obligor may refuse to recognize the discharge of his obligation when it is sought to be accomplished without his consent, there seems to be no good reason why it should not be regarded as effective since it was unfair that the creditor should receive two satisfactions for his claim.[65] However, some cases took the view that it was not effective unless it was obtained by the third person as agent for, and on behalf of, the obligor, and with his prior authorization or later ratification.[66] It is probable that the objection to giving the obligor the benefit of such a transaction, when it was not pursued by one who could be said to be his agent, grew out of the rule of the later common law that one who has furnished no part of the consideration for a contract can have no rights under it.[67] Today, it is a generally accepted rule that such a discharge is effective unless it is disclaimed by the obligor.[68] The obligor is an intended beneficiary of the contract between the obligee and the

---

[62] RESTATEMENT 2d § 279(2). In T & N, PLC v. Pennsylvania Ins. Guar. Ass'n, 44 F.3d 174, 187 (3d Cir. 1994), the court states, "[T]he old contract is dead. The subsequent agreement extinguished the old one and the remedy for any breach thereof is under the superseding agreement."

[63] Paramount Aviation Corp. v. Agusta, 178 F.3d 132, 147 (3d Cir.), *cert. denied*, 528 U.S. 878, 120 S. Ct. 188, 145 L. Ed. 2d 158 (1999); International Regulatory Consultants, L. C. v. Optis, S. A., 2005 U.S. Dist. LEXIS 37045 (D. Utah 2005)); Estate of Knapp v. Newhouse, 894 S.W.2d 204, 207 (Mo. Ct. App. 1995); Heritage Life Ins. Co. v. Fox Enters., 1992 R.I. Super. LEXIS 16, at *9 (R.I. Super. Ct. Jan. 14, 1992); Hauswald Bakery v. Pantry Pride Enters., Inc., 78 Md. App. 495, 553 A.2d 1308 (1989); Zenith Drilling Corp. v. Internorth, Inc., 869 F.2d 560, 562 (10th Cir. 1989); RESTATEMENT 2d § 281(2).

[64] Jefferson Island Salt Mining Co. v. Empire Box Corp., 41 Del. (2 Terry) 386, 23 A.2d 106 (1941), *aff'd*, 42 Del. (3 Terry) 432, 36 A.2d 40 (1944); Taft v. Valley Oil Co., 126 Conn. 154, 9 A.2d 822 (1939); City of Trinidad v. Trinidad Waterworks Co., 67 Colo. 344, 184 P. 368 (1919); Sioux City Stock Yards Co. v. Sioux City Pkg. Co., 110 Iowa 396, 81 N.W. 712 (1900); Babcock & Russell v. Hawkins, 23 Vt. 561 (1851).

[65] *See* Fitzherbert's Abridgement, title Barre, pl. 166. The case is cited with approval in Belshaw v. Bush, 11 C.B. 191 [1851].

[66] *See* Simpson v. Eggington, 10 Ex. 844 [1855].

[67] *See, e.g.*, Dunlap Pneumatic Tire Co. v. Selfridge & Co., A.C. 847 [1855]; Cottage Street Methodist Episcopal Church v. Kendall, 121 Mass. 528, 23 Am. Rep. 286 (1877).

[68] Stone v. Parenteau, 1991 Kan App. LEXIS 815, at *3 (Kan. Ct. App. Oct. 11, 1991). "A contractual duty may be performed by a third party even in the absence of a delegation. If an obligee accepts, in satisfaction of the obligor's duty, a performance offered by a third person, the duty is discharged." (Citing RESTATEMENT 2d § 278(2).) *See also* Jackson v. Pennsylvania R. Co., 66 N.J.L. 319, 49 A. 730 (1901); Gray v. Herman, 75 Wis. 453, 44 N.W. 248 (1890); Hirchand Punamchand v. Temple, 2 K.B. 330 [1911]. *Accord* RESTATEMENT 2d § 278 comment b.

third person and, like any intended beneficiary, the obligor may disclaim the benefit.[69] While it was not uncommon for a court to assert that the discharge was not effective unless accomplished on the obligor's behalf and with his prior authorization or later ratification, the existence of these supposed requirements is usually presumed or found on such slight evidence as to make it clear that they are dealt with as mere fictions.[70] In view of the fact that our courts have abandoned the requirement that one must furnish some part of the consideration to have rights under a contract, there is no reason to refuse to recognize the effectiveness of a discharge obtained through the performance of a third person regardless of the absence of evidence of any agency. Whether a discharge so brought about can be rescinded by the parties to it, without the consent of the obligor, involves the same question that arises in any case in which the parties to a contract, entered into for the benefit of a third person, seek to rescind that contract. That question was explored in the chapter dealing with third party beneficiaries.[71]

§ 146 OTHER METHODS OF DISCHARGE

[A] Account Stated

At a very early day, there existed a unique device that allowed an obligation to be discharged by an executory agreement. Where parties who had transactions of a monetary character creating the relationship of debtor and creditor struck a balance of account which the debtor promised to pay, a court would enforce that agreement. Such an agreement was called an *account stated* and it was binding even though there was no consideration to support the promise.[72] The device seems to have been regarded as within the early rule of the common law that a precedent debt was consideration to support a later promise to pay that debt. It was said in an early case that an account stated operated by way of merger to discharge the original obligation.[73] This was later denied, however, apparently because of its supposed inconsistency with the rule relating to executory accords.[74]

It is important to note that an account stated does not of itself discharge any duty. Rather, it is an admission by each party that the statement is correct implying the debtor's promise to pay in accordance with its terms.[75] While it is generally said that to furnish a basis for an

---

[69] RESTATEMENT 2d § 278, comment b. It is important to distinguish this situation from a novation to be explored in § 146[B], *infra.*

[70] *See* F.I. Somers & Sons v. Le Clerc, 110 Vt. 408, 8 A.2d 663, 124 A.L.R. 1494 (1939); Danziger v. Hoyt, 120 N.Y. 190, 24 N.E. 294 (1890); Snyder v. Pharo, 25 F. 398 (C.C.D. Del. 1885); Leavitt v. Morrow, 6 Ohio St. 71, 67 Am. Dec. 334 (1856).

[71] *See supra* Chapter 10, at § 132.

[72] United States v. Gastech Eng'g Corp., 2001 U.S. Dist. LEXIS 2285, at *9 (N.D. Okla. Jan. 25, 2001) ("An account stated occurs when there is a manifestation of agreement among two parties as to the correct amount one owes to the other."); De Mentas v. Estate of Tallas, 764 P.2d 628 (Utah Ct. App. 1988) (elements of account stated: previous transactions creating indebtedness which the parties agree is the correct and due balance plus an express or implied promise to pay the amount owing). RESTATEMENT 2d § 282(1): "a manifestation of assent by debtor and creditor to a stated sum as an accurate *computation* of an amount due the creditor."

[73] Milward v. Ingram, 2 Mod. 43 [1678].

[74] Atherly v. Evans, Sayre 269 [1756]; May v. King, 12 Mod. 537 [1701].

[75] Restatement 2d § 282(2). See Diamond v. R&R Elecs., Inc., 2005 Bankr. LEXIS 1465 (C.D. Cal. 2005).

account stated, there must be a manifestation of assent to the account submitted,[76] the necessary assent will be inferred when one party submits an account to the other, who makes no objection to the account for an unreasonable period of time, or in some other way recognizes its correctness.[77] Ashton sent an email to Swanton listing in detail amounts he had paid and the amount still owing as well as his assurance that the balance would be paid. Swanton replied by email seeking Ashton's final payment of the amount still owing as stated in Ashton's email. Ashton died and Swanton sought to recover the amount on the footing that the emails constitute an account stated. The trial court granted Swanton's motion for summary judgment. On appeal, the court rejected the argument that admitting the emails would violate the Deadman's statute precluding testimony by a party-in-interest about transactions with the deceased since emails are "writings" and when printed, they are "original" writings. The court held that the emails constituted an account stated in which Ashton had promised to pay the balance due.[78]

It must be emphasized that an account stated can arise only out of previous transactions of a monetary character which create the relationship of debtor and creditor.[79] The items of the account need not be unliquidated, since the essential requisite is the fixing of the stated sum by way of *computation*, rather than by way of compromise.[80] As already indicated, consideration is not essential to make the promise to pay the amount agreed upon as owed binding.[81] Such a promise must be supported by a pre-existing liability, and it "cannot be made to create a liability per se where none before existed."[82] Moreover, "[a]n account stated may have items on one side only and two items may be sufficient for the purposes of the agreement."[83] An account stated is subject to attack on the grounds of fraud or mistake. The burden of impeaching the account rests with the party seeking impeachment, but the failure to promptly to contest an account to correct an error may preclude the opening of the account on the basis of mistake. This is particularly true where the party seeking a correction has the exclusive knowledge of the mistake.[84] Courts are also quite willing to set an account stated aside if there is any evidence of error or overreaching, for the obvious reasons that such an agreement is not designed to create a new liability, but rather to fix the net amount owed

---

[76] *See* Modern Mills v. Havens, 112 Idaho 1101, 739 P.2d 400 (Ct. App. 1987).

[77] Diamond v. Top Communication, Inc., 2005 Bankr. LEXIS 1242 (C. D. Cal. 2005) (confirmation signed by another was effective because agent knew of it and did not object); Sunnyside Valley Irrigation Dist. v. Roza Irrigation Dist., 124 Wash. 2d 312, 877 P.2d 1283, 1285–86 (1994) ("The notion that an account stated can only be premised on an express mutual agreement to settle the account by payment of a stated sum misapprehends one of the functions of the doctrine, to permit the court to impute agreement to a party in the absence of explicit agreement about that sum. * * * An account stated can result from delivery of a bank statement to which a depositor tacitly assents by holding it for a period of time without objection.").

[78] Swanton v. Brigeois-Ashton, 2006 Wash. App. LEXIS 2067.

[79] Stan's Lumber v. Fleming, 196 Wis. 2d 554, 538 N.W.2d 849, 855 (Ct. App. 1995); Gordon Stores Co. v. Rubin, 39 N.M. 100, 41 P.2d 276 (1935); Chase v. Chase, 191 Mass. 556, 78 N.E. 115 (1906).

[80] *See* Gerstner v. Lithocraft Studios, Inc., 258 S.W.2d 250 (Mo. Ct. App. 1953).

[81] Chrysler Corp. v. Airtemp Corp., 426 A.2d 845, 849 (Del. Super. Ct. 1980) (consideration for account stated rests solely on pre-existing debt or "past consideration" concept). It is, however, possible to discover a consideration rationale, i.e., the forbearance of the debtor to insist on paying a lesser sum and the discharge of the items in the account.

[82] Pope County State Bank v. U. G. I. Contracting Co., 265 Ill. App. 420 (1932). *See also Chrysler Corp. id.*

[83] *In re* Black's Estate, 125 Neb. 75, 249 N.W. 84 (1933).

[84] York Hunter Services, Inc. v. Brooklyn Historical Society, 836 N. Y. S. 2d 491 (2007) (plaintiff had exclusive control of insurance bills and its excuse of a reduced staff was insufficient).

under existing obligations.[85] Therefore, the most significant effect of the account stated may be that it constitutes *prima facie* evidence of the correctness of the balance to be paid, casting upon the adverse party the burden of disproving its correctness.[86]

[B]   Novation

Where the parties make a substituted contract involving a third person who was not a party to the original contract, the new contract is called a novation.[87] Earlier[88] we recognized that where a duty is properly delegated by an obligor to a delegate, the obligor's duty is not discharged. The obligor remains bound in the capacity of a surety who will be obligated to perform if the delegate does not perform. If, however, an obligee not only accepts the delegate as a new debtor but, in agreement with the obligor and delegate, accepts the delegate in total substitution for the obligor who is immediately discharged from any duty, the parties have consummated a novation.[89] The purpose of a novation is to substitute a new (third) party, typically for the obligor, who is discharged at the moment the contract of novation is formed.[90]

The word "novation" originated in the Roman law where it was used to refer to the substitution of a new contract, whether between the same or different parties, for an earlier contract which was thereby discharged. While the common law has borrowed the term, the tendency has been to restrict its use and to apply it only in the type of case described in the text. When the new contract is entered into between the original parties only, the transaction is usually, although not universally, referred to as an accord and satisfaction, a substitute contract, an account stated, a merger, a release, or a rescission, depending upon the particular fact situation. If it is entered into between only one of the parties to the original contract and some third person, it is called an accord and satisfaction with a third person, an assignment, or a beneficiary contract, depending upon the facts of the particular case. We have already discussed these different types of discharge and some judicial tendency to use misnomers.

---

[85] "Neither party, in the absence of fraud or mistake, can question the correctness of the stated sum." Hinkle, Cox, Eaton, Coffield & Hensley v. Cadle Co., 115 N.M. 152, 157, 848 P.2d 1079, 1084 (1993). In Shell Oil Co. v. Livingston Fertilizer & Chem. Co., 9 Wash. App. 596, 513 P.2d 861 (1973), the court suggests that an account stated is a new obligation, taking the place of previous obligations, and previous defenses on the account are lost. In Perry v. Schwartz, 219 Cal. App. 2d 825, 33 Cal. Rptr. 511, 513 (2d Dist. 1963), the court states, "An account stated, by its very nature, normally assumes the consideration of all objections, is usually a compromise, and is a final, conclusive acknowledgment of an exact amount due having in contemplation all credits and offsets. An account stated is an agreed balance of accounts, an account which has been examined and accepted by the parties. It implies an admission that the account is correct, and that the balance struck is due and owing from one party to the other. Its effect is to establish prima facie the accuracy of the items without further proof, and to constitute a new contract on which an action will lie."

[86] "An account stated, once established, 'operates as a promise to pay.' " Industrial Acoustics Co. v. Energy Servs., 1994 U.S. Dist LEXIS 18540, at *12 (S.D.N.Y. Dec. 28, 1994). "Once an account stated is established, it operates as an admission by each party that a certain sum of money is due." Hinkle v. Cadle, *id.*

[87] RESTATEMENT 2d § 280. See Refuse Mgmt. Sys. v. Consolidated Recycling & Transfer Sys., 448 Pa. Super. 402, 671 A.2d 1140, 1145 (1996).

[88] *See* § 141[D], *supra.*

[89] See *In re* Liquidation of Integrated Resources Life Ins. Co., 562 N.W.2d 179, 182 (Iowa 1997), and Fusco v. City of Union City, 261 N.J. Super. 332, 618 A.2d 914, 916 (1993), where both courts make this distinction between a mere assignment and delegation and a novation.

[90] *See* Buttonwood Farms, Inc. v. Carson, 329 Pa. Super. 312, 478 A.2d 484 (1984); Metropolitan Trust Co. v. Wolf, 8 Ark. App. 1, 648 S.W.2d 494 (1983). A novation may substitute a new obligee rather than an obligor. See Fanucci & Limi Farms v. United Agri Products, 414 F. 3d 1075 (9th Cir. 2005) (a novation is the substitution of either a debtor or creditor).

The early law found difficulty in reaching the conclusion that a novation was effective, apparently for two reasons. First, to give it effect as a discharge of the original contract seemed to run counter to the rule that an executory agreement could not discharge a prior obligation.[91] Second, in many of these transactions, the person who was intended to receive the new right or be discharged from the old obligation furnished no part of the consideration for the right or discharge and, therefore, was not in a position to avail himself of it because of the old notion that one could not benefit from a contract in which he had parted with no consideration. This was particularly true in the case of what is called a "simple novation" in which A, who is obligated to B, enters into an agreement with B and C, who, in consideration of the discharge of A by B, promises to do what A was originally obligated to do. While the discharge of A is ample consideration to support the promise of C in such a case, A has furnished no part of it.[92] During the latter part of the nineteenth century, however, these objections were largely ignored. There is no longer any doubt that a contract of novation is effective to discharge the prior contract, regardless of whether the party who was discharged from his old duty or is receiving a right under the new contract furnished any part of the consideration for the new contract.[93]

Among the elements necessary to prove a novation, the first and most obvious is the existence of a previous valid obligation. Absent such an obligation, there is nothing to discharge.[94] Second, it is commonly asserted that discharge by novation can take place only upon agreement of all the parties affected by the new contract.[95] This assertion, however, requires qualification. Where an obligee accept a delegate without intending to discharge the obligor, there is an effective delegation of a duty, but it is not a novation. If, however, only the obligee and the new obligor form a contract intending to immediately discharge the original obligor, that obligor becomes a third party intended beneficiary. If he does not disclaim the benefit, a novation has occurred without his earlier assent. There is no need for the three parties to manifest their mutual assent simultaneously.[96] Third, the formation of the novation contract must manifest the intention of discharging the previous contract. A mere promise by a third party to assume the duty of the obligor with no intention to become the sole obligor does not create a novation.[97] Fourth, a novation is a contract and, like any other contract, it

---

[91] *See* Cuxon v. Chadley, 3 B. & C. 591 [1824]. *See also* Ames, *Novation*, SELECTED READINGS ON CONTRACTS 1213 (1931).

[92] What is called a compound novation occurs where, in one transaction, two prior obligations are discharged by novation of both obligor and obligee, and another obligation or obligations are substituted therefor. Such a transaction is illustrated by the case in which B, who is both a creditor of A and a debtor of C, discharges A and is discharged by C upon the making of a promise by A to pay B's obligation to C. In this type of transaction, consideration is furnished by each of the parties and no difficulty is encountered on that score.

[93] *See, e.g.*, Greenwood Leflore Hosp. Comm. v. Turner, 213 Miss. 200, 56 So. 2d 496, 498 (1952).

[94] Trostel v. American Life & Cas. Ins. Co., 92 F.3d 736, 740 (8th Cir. 1996), *aff'd on remand*, 133 F.3d 679 (8th Cir. 1998).

[95] *Id.* See also *Refuse Mgmt. Systems*, *supra* note 87. We have seen analogous kinds of transactions that may accomplish a similar result, but do not require the consent or agreement of all the parties, e.g., accord and satisfaction with a third person, assignment, and a beneficiary contract. The assent of the creditor to discharge the original obligor may be inferred from facts, circumstances, and conduct attending the transaction. *See* Trustees of First Presbyterian Church of Pittsburgh v. Oliver-Tyrone Corp., 248 Pa. Super. 470, 375 A.2d 193 (1977).

[96] RESTATEMENT 2d § 280, comment c.

[97] Security Ben. Life Ins. Co. v. Federal Deposit Ins. Corp., 804 F. Supp. 217, 225 (D. Kan. 1992) (the obligee may have third party beneficiary rights against the assuming obligor, but the original obligor remains bound).

must meet the requirements for a valid contract such as mutual assent and consideration.[98] The obvious consideration for a novation is the obligee's surrender of its right against the original obligor and the third party's assumption of a duty to the obligee. The burden of proving a novation is on the party asserting it, i.e., it is an affirmative defense.[99] Fifth, to constitute a novation, it is not necessary that an agreement explicitly state that it is a novation. The burden of proof that a novation was intended is satisfied by clear and definite evidence. It need not be "clear and convincing."[100]

[C] Release

It has been a rule of the common law from a very early day that a purported discharge of a contractual obligation by a sealed and delivered writing is effective for the purpose intended, whether or not it is supported by consideration.[101] It was the single generally effective method to terminate any kind of obligation, however the obligation was created at common law.[102] This method of termination is called a *release*.[103] It can still take its traditional form where the seal remains effective. While the UCC treats the seal as inoperative, it allows a claim or right to be discharged by a signed and delivered waiver.[104] This provision has the same effect as the release under seal where the seal is still generally effective and may be viewed as one of many statutory substitutes for the seal. Absent the seal or a statute making an unsealed writing evidencing a release effective,[105] a release is effective if it is supported by consideration or detrimental reliance.[106] While the word "release," in current usage, is frequently employed in the broad sense of discharge from liability by any method whatsoever, the earlier law used it exclusively in the narrower and technical sense indicated.[107] A release must have the effect of discharging a duty immediately or upon the occurrence of a condition.[108] It must be distinguished from a promise to release since such a promise merely creates a duty that can itself be discharged by the parties.[109] An immediate release is not promissory, and a release subject to a condition will take effect upon the occurrence of the condition.[110] While awaiting the occurrence of the condition, the underlying obligation is temporarily suspended.[111]

---

[98] See *Trostel, supra* note 94.

[99] *See Refuse Mgmt., supra* note 87.

[100] Utica Mut. Ins. Co. v. Vigo Coal Co., 393 F. 3d 707 (7th Cir. 2004).

[101] *See* Cairo, T. & S. R. Co. v. United States, 267 U.S. 350, 45 S. Ct. 247, 69 L. Ed. 651 (1925); Ingersoll v. Martin, 58 Md. 67, 42 Am. Rep. 322 (1882).

[102] It should be noted that the discharge of an obligation created by a sealed instrument at common law could only occur through the destruction or mutilation of the instrument, or by the delivery of an instrument of "equal sanctity."

[103] RESTATEMENT 2d § 284.

[104] *See* UCC § 1-306.

[105] *See supra* Chapter 3, § 54.

[106] RESTATEMENT 2d § 284 comment b. *See* Glugover v. Coca-Cola Bottling Co., 1992 U.S. Dist. LEXIS 21688, at *20 (S.D.N.Y. Nov. 13, 1992) (release requires consideration).

[107] The term "release" is sometimes used interchangeably and inaccurately with "covenant not to sue" and "settlement agreement." *See* Bunnett v. Smallwood, 793 P. 2d 157, 159 n.2 (Colo. 1990).

[108] RESTATEMENT 2d § 284(1).

[109] Ismert & Assocs., Inc. v. New England Mut. Life Ins. Co., 801 F.2d 536, 542 (1st Cir. 1986).

[110] RESTATEMENT 2d § 284(2).

[111] Starr v. Nationwide Mut. Ins. Co., 548 A.2d 22, 26 (Del. Ch. 1988), *aff'd*, 575 A.2d 1083 (Del. 1990).

While a written release, signed by the obligee, is presumed to be valid,[112] it remains subject to the rules of interpretation governing contracts generally.[113] It may be voidable because of duress,[114] mistake,[115] or other equitable grounds, such as misrepresentation, overreaching or incapacity.[116] Moreover, a court may refuse to recognize a purported release where the obligor manifests bad faith.[117]

[D]   Contract ("Covenant") Not to Sue

The term "covenant not to sue" is the historic term associated with a formal contract under seal. To avoid the impression that only a promise under seal will be effective, the broader characterization "contract not to sue" is currently employed.[118] The usual release, rescission or accord and satisfaction constitutes an executed discharge of the obligor. It is not promissory in character. Historically, such a discharge of one promisor released co-promisors because of the unitary character of the obligee's right and the possibility that a different rule might allow more than appropriate compensation for the obligee-neither of which justifies the rule.[119] To avoid such an unjust rule, an obligee may simply promise not to sue an individual obligor. Instead of purporting to discharge the obligor immediately, however, an obligee may promise never to sue him on the obligation in question.[120] Assuming such a promise is accompanied by the essential requirements for the formation of either a formal or an informal contract, it is universally given effect as a discharge to prevent circuity of action.[121] Even where an obligee has contracted not to sue a particular obligor but joins that obligor in an action to obtain a judgment against other co-obligors, this is not a breach of the contract if none of the assets of the particular obligor are seized in satisfaction of the judgment.[122] While a release extinguishes the cause of action against all joint obligors, a contract not to sue does not extinguish the cause of action and does not release other joint obligors even if it does not

---

[112] Cooper v. Borough of Wenonah, 977 F. Supp. 305, 311 (D.N.J. 1997).

[113] RESTATEMENT 2d § 284, comment c. See the earlier discussion of the interpretation of releases concerning known and unknown injuries, § 92[K], *supra*.

[114] Joseph v. Chase Manhattan Bank, N.A., 751 F. Supp. 31, 34 (E.D.N.Y. 1990). *But see* Weinberg v. Interep Corp., 2006 U.S. Dist. LEXIS 23746 (D. N. J. 2006) (The failure to include a New Jersey anti-discrimination statute by name in a release, however, was not fatal in light of the all-encompassing language of releasing "all claims arising from his employment including anti-discrimination claims.").

[115] Parrish v. United Bank, 164 Ariz. 18, 790 P.2d 304, 306 (Ct. App. 1990).

[116] *See Cooper, supra* note 112, at 313.

[117] See Pinto v. Allstate Ins. Co., 221 F.3d 394 (2d Cir. 2000), where the court concluded that the defendant had operated in bad faith, which caused the court to convert a general release of the insured's assignment of a bad faith claim into a covenant not to sue to avoid an unjust result.

[118] *See* RESTATEMENT 2d § 285, comment a. *See* New York State Energy Research & Dev. Auth. v. Nuclear Fuel Servs., Inc., 561 F. Supp. 954, 965 (W.D.N.Y. 1983).

[119] RESTATEMENT 2d § 294, comment a.

[120] RESTATEMENT 2d § 285(1).

[121] RESTATEMENT 2d § 285(2). The historic rule insisting that a release of one joint obligor releases all obligors, itself, has undergone an evolution from a conclusive presumption to a rule of presumptive intention so that a manifested intention to release only one obligor will be given the effect of a contract not to sue. Thus, in Truong v. Smith, 28 F. Supp. 2d 626, 630 (D. Colo. 1998), the court held that a "release" that clearly excepted one obligor may discharge others, but not the excepted obligor.

[122] RESTATEMENT 2d § 285(3) and comment b.

specifically reserve the obligee's rights against them.[123] As suggested by one court,

> A covenant not to sue is not a release, but it is to be distinguished from a release, and the distinction, although technical or artificial, is clear. The difference is one of intent and grows out of the construction placed on the terms of the instrument, since a covenant not to sue is not a present abandonment or relinquishment of a right or claim but merely an agreement not to enforce an existing cause of action, and, although it may operate as a release between the parties to the agreements, it will not release a claim against joint obligors or joint tortfeasors.[124]

There can be no doubt that the movement toward removing artificial distinctions between releases and contracts not to sue in order to recognize the intention of the parties proceeds apace.[125]

[E] Cancellation and Termination

In the early law, one of the normal methods of discharging a contract under seal was by the physical destruction or mutilation of the instrument. The obligation created by the formal contract under seal was in legal contemplation so closely identified with the instrument itself that the mutilation or destruction of the instrument was regarded as necessarily destroying the obligation, regardless of the intention of the parties.[126] The old rule has changed so that, at the present time, intention has become dominant. With such intention, a contract under seal or any other written obligation which by its terms, by law, or by usage is unenforceable without delivery of the writing, can be discharged by destruction or mutilation of the instrument by the obligee or by someone authorized by the obligee.[127] Discharge by this method is known as cancellation.[128] Such a written obligation can also be cancelled by its *surrender* to the obligor if the obligee intends to discharge the duty by such surrender.[129] Any

---

[123] McCurry v. School Dist. of Valley, 242 Neb. 504, 496 N.W.2d 433, 441 (1993).

[124] Georgia R. Bank & Trust Co. v. Griffith, 176 Ga. App. 198, 335 S.E.2d 417, 418 (1985).

[125] See *McCurry, supra* note 123, at 442 (quoting PROSSER AND KEETON ON THE LAW OF TORTS § 49, at 335 (5th ed. 1984): "The only desirable rule would seem to be that a plaintiff should never be deprived of a cause of action against any wrongdoer when the plaintiff has neither intentionally surrendered the cause of action nor received substantially full compensation. . . . Where there has been such full satisfaction, or where it is agreed that the amount paid under the release is so received, no claim should remain as to any other tortfeasor; but these are questions of fact, and normally to be determined by the jury, where the amount of the claim is unliquidated. The release, however, may very well be taken as a prima facie acknowledgment of satisfaction, and the burden placed upon the plaintiff to prove that it is not.").

[126] *See* 4 WIGMORE, EVIDENCE § 1177 (3d ed. 1940); Ames, *Specialty Contracts and Equitable Defenses*, 9 HARV. L. REV. 49 (1895).

[127] Wilkins v. Skoglund, 127 Neb. 589, 256 N.W. 31 (1934); McDonald v. Loomis, 233 Mich. 174, 206 N.W. 348 (1925) (note); Rees v. Rees, 11 Rich. Eq. 86 (S.C. 1859); Licey v. Licey, 7 Pa. 251, 47 Am. Dec. 513 (1847) (bond).

[128] RESTATEMENT 2d § 274.

[129] Almond v. Rhyne, 108 N.C. App. 605, 424 S.E.2d 231, 233 (1993) (a debtor's obligation under a non-negotiable promissory note can be discharged when the note is surrendered to the debtor if there is ample evidence of the obligee's intention to discharge the debtor; such evidence was not presented herein). *See also* Connelly v. Bank of Am. Nat'l Trust & Sav. Ass'n, 138 Cal. App. 2d 303, 291 P.2d 501 (4th Dist. 1956); Funston v. Twining, 202 Pa. 88, 51 A. 736 (1902) (creditor delivered bond and mortgage to debtor saying, "Here I give this to you; all you need is to pay the interest at four per cent during my life and then the mortgage is yours"; court held that this was an effective discharge notwithstanding condition of interest payment). *See* RESTATEMENT 2d § 274 and UCC § 3-605(1)(b).

other result would be inconsistent with the view taken by the courts in relation to gratuitous assignments.[130]

It is important to recognize that parties may use the term "cancellation" without intending to discharge all past obligations. Where, for example, an exclusive-right-to-sell real estate listing agreement contained an addendum stating, "all obligations agreed to are hereby canceled," the real estate agency sued to recover a commission allegedly earned before the addendum was signed. The trial court granted summary judgment for the defendant. On appeal, the court relied upon an analysis by Professor Corbin, who noted that the term "cancellation" is not used so uniformly as to be decisive in interpretation, i.e., generally, it is not intended to discharge the right to an agreed price of a performance already rendered.[131] The court held the phrase to be ambiguous and reversed the summary judgment.[132]

The UCC distinguishes "cancellation"[133] from "termination."[134] "Cancellation" occurs when a party puts an end to a contract because of breach by the other party while the cancelling party retains any remedy for breach.[135] "Termination" occurs when a party puts an end to a contract pursuant to a power created by the agreement or by law, i.e., where there is no uncured material breach by the other party. All executory obligations are thereby discharged, but any right based upon prior breach or performance survives.[136] Courts do not, however, always clearly distinguish "termination" from "cancellation."[137]

[F]   Alteration

As just suggested in relation to "cancellation," in the early law "the contract contained in a sealed instrument was bound so indissolubly to the substance of the document that the soul perished with the body when the latter was destroyed or changed in its identity for any cause."[138] In pursuit of this view, the common law courts, with one exception, held that any unauthorized alteration made in a sealed contract, whether by the obligee himself or by any third person, with or without the obligee's knowledge or consent, destroyed the obligation.[139] The single exception was an immaterial alteration made by a stranger without the knowledge

---

[130] *See supra* Chapter 11, at § 138[B]. It should be emphasized that the Restatement 2d allows for the surrender of an *evidentiary* as well as *symbolic* writing to effectuate cancellation to maintain consistency with its analysis of the surrender of such documents as gratuitous assignments. Restatement 2d § 332(1)(b) and comment d. This extension of the usual view was explored in the Chapter 11 section dealing with gratuitous assignments.

[131] Citing the predecessor section to Corbin on Contracts § 67.8.

[132] Mark V, Inc. v. Mellekas, 114 N.M. 778, 845 P.2d 1232, 1237 (1993).

[133] *See* UCC § 2-106(4).

[134] *See* UCC § 2-106(3).

[135] *See* UCC § 2-720.

[136] Sid Richardson Carbon & Gasoline Co. v. Interenergy Resources, 99 F.3d 746, 754 (5th Cir. 1996) (powers of termination operate prospectively but do not discharge obligations that already exist). See Restatement 2d § 283, comment a, distinguishing contracts of rescission from "termination" and "cancellation."

[137] In Century 21 Associated Realty v. Hoffman, 503 N.W.2d 861, 865–66 (S.D. 1993), the court states, "A release requires a writing of some sort. Cancellation requires either physical destruction of the document evidencing an intent to cancel the same, or conduct or words clearly indicating a mutual assent to terminate the contract."

[138] Holmes, J., in Bacon v. Hooker, 177 Mass. 335, 337, 58 N.E. 1078, 1079 (1901).

[139] *Id.*

or consent of the obligee.[140] As time went on there also developed the so-called best evidence rule which, as usually applied, prevented proof of the transaction by secondary evidence only when the best evidence had been destroyed with fraudulent intent.[141] As a result, the basis of the rule that the obligation was destroyed by alteration of the instrument became obscured. As a consequence, it has come to be the generally accepted view in this country that the alteration of a written contract, made without the authority of the obligor, discharges the contract only if the alteration is material *and* if it is made with fraudulent intent, either by the obligee himself, or by someone else, with the obligee's knowledge or consent. Where a presumably unauthorized party completed the space for a lease date and entered an authorized party's initials on a delivery certificate under an equipment lease, the court held that these alterations were not material.[142] Where, however, a party guaranteed a promissory note that was later increased by $18,000, the court held that the change was material and his obligation would be discharged unless he agreed to the changes.[143] The essential determinant of whether a change is material is whether it purports to change the legal relationships under the contract.[144] If the alteration is made by a stranger, the obligation is not discharged even if the alteration is material and fraudulent.[145] The rule applies to any writing that is completely or partially integrated under the parol evidence rule and to memoranda necessary to satisfy the statute of frauds.[146] Before discharge by material alteration can take place, there must have been a contract in existence at the time of the unauthorized alteration. When a writing is altered without proper authority prior to the consummation of the contemplated contract, no obligation is created, and the supposed obligor is not liable whether the alteration be fraudulent or nonfraudulent.[147] This necessarily follows since, in the case of a proposed informal contract, mutual assent is lacking; in the case of a formal contract, the writing as

---

[140] Pigot's Case, 11 Coke 26-b [1615].

[141] 4 WIGMORE, EVIDENCE § 1198 (Chadbourn rev. 1972).

[142] M & I Equip. Fin. Co. v. Lewis county Dairy Corp., 2007 U.S. Dist. LEXIS 3053 (N. D. N. Y. 2007) *See* RESTATEMENT 2d § 286.

[143] United States v. Krehbiel, 1993 U.S. Dist. LEXIS 10927, at *6 (D. Kan. July 20, 1993).

[144] Walker v. Independence Fed. Sav. & Loan Ass'n, 555 A.2d 1019 (D.C. App. 1989) (modern rules of property law permit one party to a deed to correct it unilaterally where the legal effect remains unchanged; the modern rule condemns "material" changes, i.e., changes that alter the conveyance to contravene the parties' wishes). "A material change in a note is one that causes it to speak a language different in legal effect from that which it originally spoke." Bank of Cedar Bluffs v. Beck, 128 Neb. 244, 247, 258 N.W. 528, 529, 96 A.L.R. 1099 (1935) (memorandum on note showing due date which did not affect the liability of the maker was not material). *See also* Hannah v. State Bank of Wood Lake, 195 Minn. 54, 261 N.W. 583 (1935) (alteration made in good faith to correct mistake in writing); Blenkiron Bros. v. Rogers, 87 Neb. 716, 127 N.W. 1062 (1910) (correction of obligee's name not material).

[145] If the alteration, though material and fraudulent, is made by a stranger without the knowledge or consent, directly or indirectly, of the obligee, the obligation is enforceable according to its original terms. *See* RESTATEMENT 2d § 286 comment a. *See also* Drum v. Drum, 133 Mass. 566 (1882). *See also* Owosso Sugar Co. v. Arntz, 244 Mich. 351, 221 N.W. 179 (1928); Clyde S. S. Co. v. Whaley, 231 F. 76 (4th Cir. 1916). Under § 124 of the Uniform Negotiable Instruments Act, a material alteration of a negotiable instrument ("material" was defined in § 125), even though by a stranger, destroyed the obligation. This is changed by the UCC. *See* UCC § 3-407(b) (1990). Former § 3-407(2) defined a "material" alteration as any alteration that changes the contract of the parties in any respect. The revised section (§ 3-407(b)) refers to any such changes simply as an "alteration." Like its predecessor, it retains the requirement that discharge of an instrument occurs only where the alteration is fraudulently made. See comment 1.

[146] RESTATEMENT 2d § 286 comment a.

[147] Mayer v. First Nat'l Co., 99 Fla. 173, 125 So. 909 (1930); Wood v. Steele, 73 U.S. (6 Wall.) 80, 18 L. Ed. 725 (1867); Waterman v. Vose, 43 Me. 504 (1857). *See also* Annotation, 44 A.L.R. 1244 (1926).

altered has never been delivered by the obligor or by someone having the necessary authority.

[G]   Merger

A discharge by what is called merger occurs whenever an existing obligation in one form is recreated in a different form-regarded as a higher form — between the same parties and without any change in the nature or the extent of the obligation.[148] This recreation may occur through the voluntary act of the parties in executing a different form of contract to cover an existing obligation, by a judgment of a court, or an award of arbitrators which fixes the rights and liabilities of the parties to a contract. The subject of discharge of contract by judgment is outside the scope of this book[149] and the subject of arbitration and award deserves separate treatment.[150] We content ourselves with a brief discussion of the execution of a contract in a different and "higher" form.

As a result of the operation of the parol evidence rule, when parties reduce their agreement to writing under such circumstances as to make it evident that they have intended the writing to be the complete and final expression of their agreement, all prior negotiations are merged in the writing which may be called "partially integrated" or "completely integrated." Thereafter the writing alone is the basis of any obligation that exists because all prior agreements are said to be "merged" in the writing.[151] Any obligation that may have previously existed has been superseded and discharged by the writing ultimately agreed upon. So also when the parties to an informal contract, either oral or written, or to a negotiable instrument, later execute a contract under seal covering the same subject matter, the prior obligation is discharged by the sealed contract, which is deemed to be a contract of a higher nature.[152] It

---

[148] First Restatement § 443. The Restatement 2d omits discharge by merger. *See* Reporter's Note to Chapter 12, at 363. It is to be observed that the liquidating of a previously unliquidated obligation is not deemed a change in the nature or extent of the obligation for this purpose.

[149] *See* Corbin § 73.3; First Restatement § 449.

[150] Arbitration is now the prevailing form of alternative dispute resolution. Arbitration awards are freely enforced, though early courts were often said to resist being ousted of their jurisdiction when parties decided to submit their dispute to non-judicial persons called arbitrators. Federal and state statutes have been enacted to ascertain the enforcement of arbitration awards. *See, e.g.*, United States Arbitration Act, 9 U.S.C. § 1 *et seq.* Arbitration has been the dispute resolution model in employer-employee relations for many years. Commercial arbitration, where parties dispute what are typically contracts questions, has been common for many years. The parties may include an arbitration clause in their contracts that courts will enforce, or they may agree to submit their cause to arbitration only after the dispute has arisen. Courts are quite willing to transform these awards into judgments and to resist any review of awards absent an abuse of discretion by arbitrators. The alternative dispute resolution era involves extra-judicial processes that are often viewed as desirable alternatives to the often prolonged and expensive litigation process.

One of the manifestations of the judicial acceptance of arbitration awards is the contrast in the availability of specific performance of such awards at common law and today. Common law courts simply refused to grant specific performance of such awards. Today, if arbitrators grant specific performance, the Restatement 2d suggests that "a court will be less hesitant in confirming such an award [by the arbitrators] than it would in granting specific performance itself" because of the limited scope of judicial review of arbitration awards. Restatement 2d § 366 comment a.

[151] For an exploration of the parol evidence process, see *supra* Chapter 5.

[152] "A simple contract and a contract under seal between the same parties cannot both subsist for the same subject matter or obligation. The contract under seal, being of superior dignity and solemnity in the contemplation of the law, will merge the simple contract. . . . There will be a merger of the simple contract, whether the parties wish it or not, for the two are incompatible, and except where one is intended to be simply collateral to the other, they cannot subsist together for the same thing and the higher must prevail." Magruder v. Belt, 7 App. D.C. 303, 311 (1895), *cert. denied*, 169 U.S. 737, 18 S. Ct. 944, 42 L. Ed. 1216 (1898). Costner v. Fisher, 104 N.C. 392, 10 S.E. 526 (1889); Baker v. Baker,

has been said that the reason for the rule that a duty is discharged by merger when a contract under seal is substituted for some other form of obligation is that "to allow a debt to be, at the same time, of different degrees, and recoverable by a multiplicity of inconsistent remedies, would increase litigation, unsettle distinctions and lead to embarrassment in the limitation of actions and the distribution of assets."[153] These reasons obviously had more weight in the days before the abolition of the distinctions between forms of action, although some of them are not without force even today.

When a negotiable instrument such as a check is taken for an obligation, it might be supposed that it should discharge the obligation. Since such an instrument is capable of being transferred to a holder for value without notice, free from the equities existing between the debtor and prior holders of the instrument, it is arguable that it should be held to merge and discharge the prior duty in order to protect the debtor from the possibility of liability for double payment. As older cases attest, our law has not adopted this view.[154] Yet, much the same result has been accomplished by the rule that the issuance of a negotiable instrument to pay an existing debt *suspends* the obligation until the instrument is dishonored or until it is paid or, in the case of a check, certified. When the instrument is paid or certified, the underlying obligation is discharged. If the instrument is dishonored, the obligation is no longer suspended.[155] The latest version of UCC Article 3 clarifies the use of a certified check, cashier's check or teller's check in payment of an obligation.[156] These instruments are designed to be taken as a cash equivalents by creditors on the assumption that the bank will pay the check.[157] Because of their "higher" status, where such an instrument is taken for an obligation, the obligation is not merely suspended, it is discharged to the same extent discharge would result if the same amount of money had been taken in payment of the obligation.[158]

---

28 N.J.L. 13, 75 Am. Dec. 243 (1859); Howell v. Webb, 2 Ark. 360 (1840). *Accord* First Restatement § 446. The concept, however, takes on an antiquarian perspective in light of the abolition or substantial erosion of the seal.

[153] Jones v. Johnson, 3 Watts & Serg. 276, 277, 38 Am. Dec. 760 (Pa. 1842).

[154] McRae Grocery Co. v. Independence Indem. Co., 33 F.2d 494 (4th Cir. 1929); Segrist v. Crabtree, 131 U.S. 287, 95 S. Ct. 687, 33 L. Ed. 125 (1889). Moreover, the execution of a renewal note will not *ipso facto* discharge or merge a prior note. First Nat'l Bank v. Yowell, 155 Tenn. 430, 294 S.W. 1101, 52 A.L.R. 1411 (1927); State Bank of Isanti v. Mutual Tel. Co., 123 Minn. 314, 143 N.W. 912 (1913).

[155] *See* UCC § 3-310(b) (1990) (formerly § 3-802). *See also* UCC § 2-511(3).

[156] UCC § 3-310(a) (1990).

[157] UCC § 3-411, Comment 1.

[158] UCC § 3-310(a).

Appendix A

UNIFORM COMMERCIAL CODE ARTICLES 1 AND 2[*]

REVISED ARTICLE 1 — GENERAL PROVISIONS

TABLE OF CONTENTS

SECTION 1-308.   **PERFORMANCE OR ACCEPTANCE UNDER RESERVA-
TION OF RIGHTS**
SECTION 1-309.   **OPTION TO ACCELERATE AT WILL**
SECTION 1-310.   **SUBORDINATED OBLIGATIONS**

PART 1 GENERAL PROVISIONS
SECTION 1-101. SHORT TITLES

(a) This [Act] may be cited as the Uniform Commercial Code.

(b) This article may be cited as Uniform Commercial Code–General Provisions.
Official Comments
Source: Former Section 1-101.

Changes from former law: Subsection (b) is new. It is added in order to make the structure of Article 1 parallel with that of the other articles of the Uniform Commercial Code.

1. Each other article of the Uniform Commercial Code (except Articles 10 and 11) may also be cited by its own short title. See Sections 2-101, 2A-101, 3-101, 4-101, 4A-101, 5-101, 6-101, 7-101, 8-101, and 9-101.

SECTION 1-102. SCOPE OF ARTICLE

This article applies to a transaction to the extent that it is governed by another article of [the Uniform Commercial Code].
Preliminary Comments
Source: New.
1. This section is intended to resolve confusion that has occasionally arisen as to the applicability of the substantive rules in this article. This section makes clear what has always been the case–the rules in Article 1 apply to transactions to the extent that those transactions are governed by one of the other articles of the Uniform Commercial Code. See also Comment 1 to Section 1-301.

SECTION 1-103. CONSTRUCTION OF [UNIFORM COMMERCIAL CODE] TO PROMOTE ITS PURPOSES AND POLICIES; APPLICABILITY OF SUPPLEMENTAL PRINCIPLES OF LAW

(a) [The Uniform Commercial Code] must be liberally construed and applied to promote its underlying purposes and policies, which are:

(1) to simplify, clarify, and modernize the law governing commercial transactions;

(2) to permit the continued expansion of commercial practices through custom, usage, and agreement of the parties; and

(3) to make uniform the law among the various jurisdictions.

(b) Unless displaced by the particular provisions of [the Uniform Commercial Code], the principles of law and equity, including the law merchant and the law relative to capacity to contract, principal and agent, estoppel, fraud, misrepresentation, duress, coercion, mistake, bankruptcy, and other validating or invalidating cause supplement its provisions.
Official Comments
Source: Former Section 1-102 (1)-(2); Former Section 1-103.

Changes from former law: This section is derived from subsections (1) and (2) of former Section 1-102 and from former Section 1-103. Subsection (a) of this section combines subsections (1) and (2) of former Section 1-102. Except for changing the form of reference to the Uniform Commercial Code and minor stylistic changes, its language is the same as subsections (1) and (2) of former Section 1-102. Except for changing the form of reference to the Uniform Commercial Code and minor stylistic changes, subsection (b) of this section is identical to former Section 1-103. The provisions have been combined in this section to reflect the interrelationship between them.

1. The Uniform Commercial Code is drawn to provide flexibility so that, since it is intended to be a semi-permanent and infrequently-amended piece of legislation, it will provide its own machinery for expansion of commercial practices. It is intended to make it possible for the law embodied in the Uniform Commercial Code to be applied by the courts in the light of unforeseen and new circumstances and practices. The proper construction of the Uniform Commercial Code requires, of course, that its interpretation and application be limited to its reason.

Even prior to the enactment of the Uniform Commercial Code, courts were careful to keep broad acts from being hampered in their effects by later acts of limited scope. See Pacific Wool Growers v. Draper & Co., 158 Or. 1, 73 P.2d 1391 (1937), and compare Section 1-104. The courts have often recognized that the policies embodied in an act are applicable in reason to subject-matter that was not expressly included in the language of the act, Commercial Nat. Bank of New Orleans v. Canal-Louisiana Bank & Trust Co., 239 U.S. 520, 36 S.Ct. 194, 60 L.Ed. 417 (1916) (bona fide purchase policy of Uniform Warehouse Receipts Act extended to case not covered but of equivalent nature), and did the same where reason and policy so required, even where the subject-matter had been intentionally excluded from the act in general. Agar v. Orda, 264 N.Y. 248, 190 N.E. 479 (1934) (Uniform Sales Act change in seller's remedies applied to contract for sale of choses in action even though the general coverage of that Act was intentionally limited to goods "other than things in action.") They implemented a statutory policy with liberal and useful remedies not provided in the statutory text. They disregarded a statutory limitation of remedy where the reason of the limitation did not apply. Fiterman v. J. N. Johnson & Co., 156 Minn. 201, 194 N.W. 399 (1923) (requirement of return of the goods as a condition to rescission for breach of warranty; also, partial rescission allowed). Nothing in the Uniform Commercial Code stands in the way of the continuance of such action by the courts.

The Uniform Commercial Code should be construed in accordance with its underlying purposes and policies. The text of each section should be read in the light of the purpose and policy of the rule or principle in question, as also of the Uniform Commercial Code as a whole, and the application of the language should be construed narrowly or broadly, as the case may be, in conformity with the purposes and policies involved.

2. **Applicability of supplemental principles of law.** Subsection (b) states the basic relationship of the Uniform Commercial Code to supplemental bodies of law. The Uniform Commercial Code was drafted against the backdrop of existing bodies of law, including the common law and equity, and relies on those bodies of law to supplement it provisions in many important ways. At the same time, the Uniform Commercial Code is the primary source of commercial law rules in areas that it governs, and its rules represent choices made by its drafters and the enacting legislatures about the appropriate policies to be furthered in the transactions it covers. Therefore, while principles of common law and equity may *supplement* provisions of the Uniform Commercial Code, they may not be used to *supplant* its provisions, or the purposes and policies those provisions reflect, unless a specific provision of the Uniform Commercial Code provides otherwise. In the absence of such a provision, the Uniform Commercial Code preempts principles of common law and equity that are inconsistent with

either its provisions or its purposes and policies.

The language of subsection (b) is intended to reflect both the concept of supplementation and the concept of preemption. Some courts, however, had difficulty in applying the identical language of former Section 1-103 to determine when other law appropriately may be applied to supplement the Uniform Commercial Code, and when that law has been displaced by the Code. Some decisions applied other law in situations in which that application, while not inconsistent with the text of any particular provision of the Uniform Commercial Code, clearly was inconsistent with the underlying purposes and policies reflected in the relevant provisions of the Code. *See, e.g.,* Sheerbonnet, Ltd. v. American Express Bank, Ltd., 951 F. Supp. 403 (S.D.N.Y. 1995). In part, this difficulty arose from Comment 1 to former Section 1-103, which stated that "this section indicates the continued applicability to commercial contracts of all supplemental bodies of law except insofar as they are explicitly displaced by this Act." The "explicitly displaced" language of that Comment did not accurately reflect the proper scope of Uniform Commercial Code preemption, which extends to displacement of other law that is inconsistent with the purposes and policies of the Uniform Commercial Code, as well as with its text.

3. **Application of subsection (b) to statutes.** The primary focus of Section 1-103 is on the relationship between the Uniform Commercial Code and principles of common law and equity as developed by the courts. State law, however, increasingly is statutory. Not only are there a growing number of state statutes addressing specific issues that come within the scope of the Uniform Commercial Code, but in some States many general principles of common law and equity have been codified. When the other law relating to a matter within the scope of the Uniform Commercial Code is a statute, the principles of subsection (b) remain relevant to the court's analysis of the relationship between that statute and the Uniform Commercial Code, but other principles of statutory interpretation that specifically address the interrelationship between statutes will be relevant as well. In some situations, the principles of subsection (b) still will be determinative. For example, the mere fact that an equitable principle is stated in statutory form rather than in judicial decisions should not change the court's analysis of whether the principle can be used to supplement the Uniform Commercial Code–under subsection (b), equitable principles may supplement provisions of the Uniform Commercial Code only if they are consistent with the purposes and policies of the Uniform Commercial Code as well as its text. In other situations, however, other interpretive principles addressing the interrelationship between statutes may lead the court to conclude that the other statute is controlling, even though it conflicts with the Uniform Commercial Code. This, for example, would be the result in a situation where the other statute was specifically intended to provide additional protection to a class of individuals engaging in transactions covered by the Uniform Commercial Code.

4. **Listing not exclusive.** The list of sources of supplemental law in subsection (b) is intended to be merely illustrative of the other law that may supplement the Uniform Commercial Code, and is not exclusive. No listing could be exhaustive. Further, the fact that a particular section of the Uniform Commercial Code makes express reference to other law is not intended to suggest the negation of the general application of the principles of subsection (b). Note also that the word "bankruptcy" in subsection (b), continuing the use of that word from former Section 1-103, should be understood not as a specific reference to federal bankruptcy law but, rather as a reference to general principles of insolvency, whether under federal or state law.

SECTION 1-104. CONSTRUCTION AGAINST IMPLIED REPEAL

[The Uniform Commercial Code] being a general act intended as a unified coverage of its

subject matter, no part of it shall be deemed to be impliedly repealed by subsequent legislation if such construction can reasonably be avoided.
Official Comments
Source: Former Section 1-104.

Changes from former law: Except for changing the form of reference to the Uniform Commercial Code, this section is identical to former Section 1-104.

1. This section embodies the policy that an act that bears evidence of carefully considered permanent regulative intention should not lightly be regarded as impliedly repealed by subsequent legislation. The Uniform Commercial Code, carefully integrated and intended as a uniform codification of permanent character covering an entire "field" of law, is to be regarded as particularly resistant to implied repeal.

SECTION 1-105.   SEVERABILITY

If any provision or clause of [the Uniform Commercial Code] or its application to any person or circumstance is held invalid, the invalidity does not affect other provisions or applications of [the Uniform Commercial Code] which can be given effect without the invalid provision or application, and to this end the provisions of [the Uniform Commercial Code] are severable.
Official Comments
Source: Former Section 1-108.

Changes from former law: Except for changing the form of reference to the Uniform Commercial Code, this section is identical to former Section 1-108.

1. This is the model severability section recommended by the National Conference of Commissioners on Uniform State Laws for inclusion in all acts of extensive scope.

SECTION 1-106.   USE OF SINGULAR AND PLURAL; GENDER

In [the Uniform Commercial Code], unless the statutory context otherwise requires:

(1) words in the singular number include the plural, and those in the plural include the singular; and

(2) words of any gender also refer to any other gender.
Official Comments
Source: Former Section 1-102(5). See also 1 U.S.C. Section 1.

Changes from former law: Other than minor stylistic changes, this section is identical to former Section 1-102(5).

1. This section makes it clear that the use of singular or plural in the text of the Uniform Commercial Code is generally only a matter of drafting style–singular words may be applied in the plural, and plural words may be applied in the singular. Only when it is clear from the statutory context that the use of the singular or plural does not include the other is this rule inapplicable. *See, e.g.*, Section 9-322.

SECTION 1-107.   SECTION CAPTIONS

Section captions are part of [the Uniform Commercial Code].
Official Comments
Source: Former Section 1-109.

Changes from former law: None.

1. Section captions are a part of the text of the Uniform Commercial Code, and not mere surplusage. This is not the case, however, with respect to subsection headings appearing in

Article 9. See Comment 3 to Section 9-101 ("subsection headings are not a part of the official text itself and have not been approved by the sponsors.").

SECTION 1-108. RELATION TO ELECTRONIC SIGNATURES IN GLOBAL AND NATIONAL COMMERCE ACT

This Article modifies, limits, and supersedes the Federal Electronic Signatures in Global and National Commerce Act, 15 U.S.C. § 7001 *et. seq.*, except that nothing in this Article modifies, limits, or supersedes section 7001(c) of that act or authorizes electronic delivery of any of the notices described in section 7003(b) of that Act.

Official Comments

Source: New

1. The federal Electronic Signatures in Global and National Commerce Act, 15 U.S.C. Section 7001 *et seq* became effective in 2000. Section 102(a) of that Act provides that a State statute may modify, limit, or supersede the provisions of section 101 of that Act with respect to state law if such statute, *inter alia*, specifies the alternative procedures or requirements for the use or acceptance (or both) of electronic records or electronic signatures to establish the legal effect, validity, or enforceability of contracts or other records, and (i) such alternative procedures or requirements are consistent with Titles I and II of that Act, (ii) such alternative procedures or requirements do not require, or accord greater legal status or effect to, the implementation or application of a specific technology or technical specification for performing the functions of creating, storing, generating, receiving, communicating, or authenticating electronic records or electronic signatures; and (iii) if enacted or adopted after the date of the enactment of that Act, makes specific reference to that Act. Article 1 fulfills the first two of those three criteria; this Section fulfills the third criterion listed above.

2. As stated in this section, however, Article 1 does not modify, limit, or supersede Section 101(c) of the Electronic Signatures in Global and National Commerce Act (requiring affirmative consent from a consumer to electronic delivery of transactional disclosures that are required by state law to be in writing); nor does it authorize electronic delivery of any of the notices described in Section 103(b) of that Act.

PART 2 GENERAL DEFINITIONS AND PRINCIPLES OF INTERPRETATION
SECTION 1-201. GENERAL DEFINITIONS

(a) Unless the context otherwise requires, words or phrases defined in this section, or in the additional definitions contained in other articles of [the Uniform Commercial Code] that apply to particular articles or parts thereof, have the meanings stated.

(b) Subject to definitions contained in other articles of [the Uniform Commercial Code] that apply to particular articles or parts thereof:

(1) "Action", in the sense of a judicial proceeding, includes recoupment, counterclaim, set-off, suit in equity, and any other proceeding in which rights are determined.

(2) "Aggrieved party" means a party entitled to pursue a remedy.

(3) "Agreement", as distinguished from "contract", means the bargain of the parties in fact, as found in their language or inferred from other circumstances, including course of performance, course of dealing, or usage of trade as provided in Section 1-303.

(4) "Bank" means a person engaged in the business of banking and includes a savings bank, savings and loan association, credit union, and trust company.

(5) "Bearer" means a person in possession of a negotiable instrument, document of title, or certificated security that is payable to bearer or indorsed in blank.

(6) "Bill of lading" means a document evidencing the receipt of goods for shipment issued by a person engaged in the business of transporting or forwarding goods.

(7) "Branch" includes a separately incorporated foreign branch of a bank.

(8) "Burden of establishing" a fact means the burden of persuading the trier of fact that the existence of the fact is more probable than its nonexistence.

(9) "Buyer in ordinary course of business" means a person that buys goods in good faith, without knowledge that the sale violates the rights of another person in the goods, and in the ordinary course from a person, other than a pawnbroker, in the business of selling goods of that kind. A person buys goods in the ordinary course if the sale to the person comports with the usual or customary practices in the kind of business in which the seller is engaged or with the seller's own usual or customary practices. A person that sells oil, gas, or other minerals at the wellhead or minehead is a person in the business of selling goods of that kind. A buyer in ordinary course of business may buy for cash, by exchange of other property, or on secured or unsecured credit, and may acquire goods or documents of title under a preexisting contract for sale. Only a buyer that takes possession of the goods or has a right to recover the goods from the seller under Article 2 may be a buyer in ordinary course of business. "Buyer in ordinary course of business" does not include a person that acquires goods in a transfer in bulk or as security for or in total or partial satisfaction of a money debt.

(10) "Conspicuous", with reference to a term, means so written, displayed, or presented that a reasonable person against which it is to operate ought to have noticed it. Whether a term is "conspicuous" or not is a decision for the court. Conspicuous terms include the following:

(A) a heading in capitals equal to or greater in size than the surrounding text, or in contrasting type, font, or color to the surrounding text of the same or lesser size; and

(B) language in the body of a record or display in larger type than the surrounding text, or in contrasting type, font, or color to the surrounding text of the same size, or set off from surrounding text of the same size by symbols or other marks that call attention to the language.

(11) "Consumer" means an individual who enters into a transaction primarily for personal, family, or household purposes.

(12) "Contract", as distinguished from "agreement", means the total legal obligation that results from the parties' agreement as determined by [the Uniform Commercial Code] as supplemented by any other applicable laws.

(13) "Creditor" includes a general creditor, a secured creditor, a lien creditor, and any representative of creditors, including an assignee for the benefit of creditors, a trustee in bankruptcy, a receiver in equity, and an executor or administrator of an insolvent debtor's or assignor's estate.

(14) "Defendant" includes a person in the position of defendant in a counterclaim, cross-claim, or third-party claim.

(15) "Delivery", with respect to an instrument, document of title, or chattel paper, means

voluntary transfer of possession.

(16) "Document of title" includes bill of lading, dock warrant, dock receipt, warehouse receipt or order for the delivery of goods, and also any other document which in the regular course of business or financing is treated as adequately evidencing that the person in possession of it is entitled to receive, hold, and dispose of the document and the goods it covers. To be a document of title, a document must purport to be issued by or addressed to a bailee and purport to cover goods in the bailee's possession which are either identified or are fungible portions of an identified mass.

(17) "Fault" means a default, breach, or wrongful act or omission.

(18) "Fungible goods" means:

(A) goods of which any unit, by nature or usage of trade, is the equivalent of any other like unit; or

(B) goods that by agreement are treated as equivalent.

(19) "Genuine" means free of forgery or counterfeiting.

(20) "Good faith," except as otherwise provided in Article 5, means honesty in fact and the observance of reasonable commercial standards of fair dealing.

(21) "Holder" means:

(A) the person in possession of a negotiable instrument that is payable either to bearer or to an identified person that is the person in possession; or

(B) the person in possession of a document of title if the goods are deliverable either to bearer or to the order of the person in possession.

(22) "Insolvency proceeding" includes an assignment for the benefit of creditors or other proceeding intended to liquidate or rehabilitate the estate of the person involved.

(23) "Insolvent" means:

(A) having generally ceased to pay debts in the ordinary course of business other than as a result of bona fide dispute;

(B) being unable to pay debts as they become due; or

(C) being insolvent within the meaning of federal bankruptcy law.

(24) "Money" means a medium of exchange currently authorized or adopted by a domestic or foreign government. The term includes a monetary unit of account established by an intergovernmental organization or by agreement between two or more countries.

(25) "Organization" means a person other than an individual.

(26) "Party", as distinguished from "third party", means a person that has engaged in a transaction or made an agreement subject to [the Uniform Commercial Code].

(27) "Person" means an individual, corporation, business trust, estate, trust, partnership, limited liability company, association, joint venture, government, governmental subdivision, agency, or instrumentality, public corporation, or any other legal or commercial entity.

(28) "Present value" means the amount as of a date certain of one or more sums payable

in the future, discounted to the date certain by use of either an interest rate specified by the parties if that rate is not manifestly unreasonable at the time the transaction is entered into or, if an interest rate is not so specified, a commercially reasonable rate that takes into account the facts and circumstances at the time the transaction is entered into.

(29) "Purchase" means taking by sale, lease, discount, negotiation, mortgage, pledge, lien, security interest, issue or reissue, gift, or any other voluntary transaction creating an interest in property.

(30) "Purchaser" means a person that takes by purchase.

(31) "Record" means information that is inscribed on a tangible medium or that is stored in an electronic or other medium and is retrievable in perceivable form.

(32) "Remedy" means any remedial right to which an aggrieved party is entitled with or without resort to a tribunal.

(33) "Representative" means a person empowered to act for another, including an agent, an officer of a corporation or association, and a trustee, executor, or administrator of an estate.

(34) "Right" includes remedy.

(35) "Security interest" means an interest in personal property or fixtures which secures payment or performance of an obligation. "Security interest" includes any interest of a consignor and a buyer of accounts, chattel paper, a payment intangible, or a promissory note in a transaction that is subject to Article 9. "Security interest" does not include the special property interest of a buyer of goods on identification of those goods to a contract for sale under Section 2- 401, but a buyer may also acquire a "security interest" by complying with Article 9. Except as otherwise provided in Section 2-505, the right of a seller or lessor of goods under Article 2 or 2A to retain or acquire possession of the goods is not a "security interest", but a seller or lessor may also acquire a "security interest" by complying with Article 9. The retention or reservation of title by a seller of goods notwithstanding shipment or delivery to the buyer under Section 2-401 is limited in effect to a reservation of a "security interest." Whether a transaction in the form of a lease creates a "security interest" is determined pursuant to Section 1-203.

(36) "Send" in connection with a writing, record, or notice means:

(A) to deposit in the mail or deliver for transmission by any other usual means of communication with postage or cost of transmission provided for and properly addressed and, in the case of an instrument, to an address specified thereon or otherwise agreed, or if there be none to any address reasonable under the circumstances; or

(B) in any other way to cause to be received any record or notice within the time it would have arrived if properly sent.

(37) "Signed" includes using any symbol executed or adopted with present intention to adopt or accept a writing.

(38) "State" means a State of the United States, the District of Columbia, Puerto Rico, the United States Virgin Islands, or any territory or insular possession subject to the jurisdiction of the United States.

(39) "Surety" includes a guarantor or other secondary obligor.

(40) "Term" means a portion of an agreement that relates to a particular matter.

(41) "Unauthorized signature" means a signature made without actual, implied, or apparent authority. The term includes a forgery.

(42) "Warehouse receipt" means a receipt issued by a person engaged in the business of storing goods for hire.

(43) "Writing" includes printing, typewriting, or any other intentional reduction to tangible form. "Written" has a corresponding meaning.

Official Comments

Source: Former Section 1-201.

Changes from former law: In order to make it clear that all definitions in the Uniform Commercial Code (not just those appearing in Article 1, as stated in former Section 1-201, but also those appearing in other Articles) do not apply if the context otherwise requires, a new subsection (a) to that effect has been added, and the definitions now appear in subsection (b). The reference in subsection (a) to the "context" is intended to refer to the context in which the defined term is used in the Uniform Commercial Code. In other words, the definition applies whenever the defined term is used unless the context in which the defined term is used in the statute indicates that the term was not used in its defined sense. Consider, for example, Sections 3-103(a)(9) (defining "promise," in relevant part, as "a written undertaking to pay money signed by the person undertaking to pay") and 3-303(a)(1) (indicating that an instrument is issued or transferred for value if "the instrument is issued or transferred for a promise of performance, to the extent that the promise has been performed." It is clear from the statutory context of the use of the word "promise" in Section 3-303(a)(1) that the term was not used in the sense of its definition in Section 3-103(a)(9). Thus, the Section 3-103(a)(9) definition should not be used to give meaning to the word "promise" in Section 3-303(a).

Some definitions in former Section 1-201 have been reformulated as substantive provisions and have been moved to other sections. See Sections 1-202 (explicating concepts of notice and knowledge formerly addressed in Sections 1-201(25)-(27)), 1-204 (determining when a person gives value for rights, replacing the definition of "value" in former Section 1-201(44)), and 1-206 (addressing the meaning of presumptions, replacing the definitions of "presumption" and "presumed" in former Section 1-201(31)). Similarly, the portion of the definition of "security interest" in former Section 1-201(37) which explained the difference between a security interest and a lease has been relocated to Section 1-203.

Two definitions in former Section 1-201 have been deleted. The definition of "honor" in former Section 1-201(21) has been moved to Section 2-103(1)(b), inasmuch as the definition only applies to the use of the word in Article 2. The definition of "telegram" in former Section 1-201(41) has been deleted because that word no longer appears in the definition of "conspicuous."

Other than minor stylistic changes and renumbering, the remaining definitions in this section are as in former Article 1 except as noted below.

1. "Action." Unchanged from former Section 1-201, which was derived from similar definitions in Section 191, Uniform Negotiable Instruments Law; Section 76, Uniform Sales Act; Section 58, Uniform Warehouse Receipts Act; Section 53, Uniform Bills of Lading Act.

2. "Aggrieved party." Unchanged from former Section 1-201.

3. "Agreement." Derived from former Section 1-201. As used in the Uniform Commercial

Code the word is intended to include full recognition of usage of trade, course of dealing, course of performance and the surrounding circumstances as effective parts thereof, and of any agreement permitted under the provisions of the Uniform Commercial Code to displace a stated rule of law. Whether an agreement has legal consequences is determined by applicable provisions of the Uniform Commercial Code and, to the extent provided in Section 1-103, by the law of contracts.

4. "Bank." Derived from Section 4A-104.

5. "Bearer." Unchanged from former Section 1-201, which was derived from Section 191, Uniform Negotiable Instruments Law.

6. "Bill of Lading." Derived from former Section 1-201. The reference to, and definition of, an "airbill" has been deleted as no longer necessary.

7. "Branch." Unchanged from former Section 1-201.

8. "Burden of establishing a fact." Unchanged from former Section 1-201.

9. "Buyer in ordinary course of business." Except for minor stylistic changes, identical to former Section 1-201 (as amended in conjunction with the 1999 revisions to Article 9). The major significance of the phrase lies in Section 2-403 and in the Article on Secured Transactions (Article 9).

The first sentence of paragraph (9) makes clear that a buyer from a pawnbroker cannot be a buyer in ordinary course of business. The second sentence explains what it means to buy "in the ordinary course." The penultimate sentence prevents a buyer that does not have the right to possession as against the seller from being a buyer in ordinary course of business. Concerning when a buyer obtains possessory rights, see Sections 2-502 and 2-716. However, the penultimate sentence is not intended to affect a buyer's status as a buyer in ordinary course of business in cases (such as a "drop shipment") involving delivery by the seller to a person buying from the buyer or a donee from the buyer. The requirement relates to whether *as against the seller* the buyer or one taking through the buyer has possessory rights.

10. "Conspicuous." Derived from former Section 1-201(10). This definition states the general standard that to be conspicuous a term ought to be noticed by a reasonable person. Whether a term is conspicuous is an issue for the court. Subparagraphs (A) and (B) set out several methods for making a term conspicuous. Requiring that a term be conspicuous blends a notice function (the term ought to be noticed) and a planning function (giving guidance to the party relying on the term regarding how that result can be achieved). Although these paragraphs indicate some of the methods for making a term attention-calling, the test is whether attention can reasonably be expected to be called to it. The statutory language should not be construed to permit a result that is inconsistent with that test.

11. "Consumer." Derived from Section 9-102(a)(25).

12. "Contract." Except for minor stylistic changes, identical to former Section 1-201.

13. "Creditor." Unchanged from former Section 1-201.

14. "Defendant." Except for minor stylistic changes, identical to former Section 1-201, which was derived from Section 76, Uniform Sales Act.

15. "Delivery." Derived from former Section 1-201. The reference to certificated securities has been deleted in light of the more specific treatment of the matter in Section 8-301.

16. "Document of title." Unchanged from former Section 1-201, which was derived from Section 76, Uniform Sales Act. By making it explicit that the obligation or designation of a third

party as "bailee" is essential to a document of title, this definition clearly rejects any such result as obtained in Hixson v. Ward, 254 Ill.App. 505 (1929), which treated a conditional sales contract as a document of title. Also the definition is left open so that new types of documents may be included. It is unforeseeable what documents may one day serve the essential purpose now filled by warehouse receipts and bills of lading. Truck transport has already opened up problems which do not fit the patterns of practice resting upon the assumption that a draft can move through banking channels faster than the goods themselves can reach their destination. There lie ahead air transport and such probabilities as teletype transmission of what may some day be regarded commercially as "Documents of Title." The definition is stated in terms of the function of the documents with the intention that any document which gains commercial recognition as accomplishing the desired result shall be included within its scope. Fungible goods are adequately identified within the language of the definition by identification of the mass of which they are a part.

Dock warrants were within the Sales Act definition of document of title apparently for the purpose of recognizing a valid tender by means of such paper. In current commercial practice a dock warrant or receipt is a kind of interim certificate issued by steamship companies upon delivery of the goods at the dock, entitling a designated person to have issued to him at the company's office a bill of lading. The receipt itself is invariably nonnegotiable in form although it may indicate that a negotiable bill is to be forthcoming. Such a document is not within the general compass of the definition, although trade usage may in some cases entitle such paper to be treated as a document of title. If the dock receipt actually represents a storage obligation undertaken by the shipping company, then it is a warehouse receipt within this section regardless of the name given to the instrument.

The goods must be "described," but the description may be by marks or labels and may be qualified in such a way as to disclaim personal knowledge of the issuer regarding contents or condition. However, baggage and parcel checks and similar "tokens" of storage which identify stored goods only as those received in exchange for the token are not covered by this Article.

The definition is broad enough to include an airway bill.

17. "Fault." Derived from former Section 1-201. "Default" has been added to the list of events constituting fault.

18. "Fungible goods." Derived from former Section 1-201. References to securities have been deleted because Article 8 no longer uses the term "fungible" to describe securities. Accordingly, this provision now defines the concept only in the context of goods.

19. "Genuine." Unchanged from former Section 1-201.

20. "Good faith." Former Section 1-201(19) defined "good faith" simply as honesty in fact; the definition contained no element of commercial reasonableness. Initially, that definition applied throughout the Code with only one exception. Former Section 2-103(1)(b) provided that *"in this Article . . . good faith in the case of a merchant means honesty in fact and the observance of reasonable commercial standards of fair dealing in the trade."* This alternative definition was limited in applicability in three ways. First, it applied only to transactions within the scope of Article 2. Second, it applied only to merchants. Third, strictly construed it applied only to uses of the phrase "good faith" *in Article 2;* thus, so construed it would not define "good faith" for its most important use–the obligation of good faith imposed by former Section 1-203.

Over time, however, amendments to the Uniform Commercial Code brought the Article 2 merchant concept of good faith (subjective honesty and objective commercial reasonableness) into other Articles. First, Article 2A explicitly incorporated the Article 2 standard. See Section

2A-103(7). Then, other Articles broadened the applicability of that standard by adopting it for all parties rather than just for merchants. *See, e.g.,* Sections 3-103(a)(4), 4A-105(a)(6), 8-102(a)(10), and 9-102(a)(43). All of these definitions are comprised of two elements–honesty in fact *and* the observance of reasonable commercial standards of fair dealing. Only revised Article 5 defines "good faith" solely in terms of subjective honesty, and only Article 6 and Article 7 are without definitions of good faith. (It should be noted that, while revised Article 6 did not define good faith, Comment 2 to revised Section 6-102 states that "this Article adopts the definition of 'good faith' in Article 1 in all cases, even when the buyer is a merchant.") Given these developments, it is appropriate to move the broader definition of "good faith" to Article 1. Of course, this definition is subject to the applicability of the narrower definition in revised Article 5.

21. "Holder." Derived from former Section 1-201. The definition has been reorganized for clarity.

22. "Insolvency proceedings." Unchanged from former Section 1-201.

23. "Insolvent." Derived from former Section 1-201. The three tests of insolvency–"generally ceased to pay debts in the ordinary course of business other than as a result of a bona fide dispute as to them," "unable to pay debts as they become due," and "insolvent within the meaning of the federal bankruptcy law"–are expressly set up as alternative tests and must be approached from a commercial standpoint.

24. "Money." Substantively identical to former Section 1-201. The test is that of sanction of government, whether by authorization before issue or adoption afterward, which recognizes the circulating medium as a part of the official currency of that government. The narrow view that money is limited to legal tender is rejected.

25. "Organization." The former definition of this word has been replaced with the standard definition used in acts prepared by the National Conference of Commissioners on Uniform State Laws.

26. "Party." Substantively identical to former Section 1-201. Mention of a party includes, of course, a person acting through an agent. However, where an agent comes into opposition or contrast to the principal, particular account is taken of that situation.

27. "Person." The former definition of this word has been replaced with the standard definition used in acts prepared by the National Conference of Commissioners on Uniform State Laws.

28. "Present value." This definition was formerly contained within the definition of "security interest" in former Section 1-201(37).

29. "Purchase." Derived from former Section 1-201. The form of definition has been changed from "includes" to "means."

30. "Purchaser." Unchanged from former Section 1-201.

31. "Record." Derived from Section 9-102(a)(69).

32. "Remedy." Unchanged from former Section 1-201. The purpose is to make it clear that both remedy and right (as defined) include those remedial rights of "self help" which are among the most important bodies of rights under the Uniform Commercial Code, remedial rights being those to which an aggrieved party may resort on its own.

33. "Representative." Derived from former Section 1-201. Reorganized, and form changed from "includes" to "means."

34. "Right." Except for minor stylistic changes, identical to former Section 1-201.

35. "Security Interest." The definition is the first paragraph of the definition of "security interest" in former Section 1-201, with minor stylistic changes. The remaining portion of that definition has been moved to Section 1-203. Note that, because of the scope of Article 9, the term includes the interest of certain outright buyers of certain kinds of property.

36. "Send." Derived from former Section 1-201. Compare "notifies".

37. "Signed." Derived from former Section 1-201. Former Section 1-201 referred to "intention to authenticate"; because other articles now use the term "authenticate," the language has been changed to "intention to adopt or accept." The latter formulation is derived from the definition of "authenticate" in Section 9-102(a)(7). This provision refers only to writings, because the term "signed," as used in some articles, refers only to writings. This provision also makes it clear that, as the term "signed" is used in the Uniform Commercial Code, a complete signature is not necessary. The symbol may be printed, stamped or written; it may be by initials or by thumbprint. It may be on any part of the document and in appropriate cases may be found in a billhead or letterhead. No catalog of possible situations can be complete and the court must use common sense and commercial experience in passing upon these matters. The question always is whether the symbol was executed or adopted by the party with present intention to adopt or accept the writing.

38. "State." This is the standard definition of the term used in acts prepared by the National Conference of Commissioners on Uniform State Laws.

39. "Surety." This definition makes it clear that "surety" includes all secondary obligors, not just those whose obligation refers to the person obligated as a surety. As to the nature of secondary obligations generally, see Restatement (Third), Suretyship and Guaranty Section 1 (1996).

40. "Term." Unchanged from former Section 1-201.

41. "Unauthorized signature." Unchanged from former Section 1-201.

42. "Warehouse receipt." Unchanged from former Section 1-201, which was derived from Section 76(1), Uniform Sales Act; Section 1, Uniform Warehouse Receipts Act. Receipts issued by a field warehouse are included, provided the warehouseman and the depositor of the goods are different persons.

43. "Written" or "writing." Unchanged from former Section 1-201.

SECTION 1-202. NOTICE; KNOWLEDGE

(a) Subject to subsection (f), a person has "notice" of a fact if the person:

(1) has actual knowledge of it;

(2) has received a notice or notification of it; or

(3) from all the facts and circumstances known to the person at the time in question, has reason to know that it exists.

(b) "Knowledge" means actual knowledge. "Knows" has a corresponding meaning.

(c) "Discover", "learn", or words of similar import refer to knowledge rather than to reason to know.

(d) A person "notifies" or "gives" a notice or notification to another person by taking such steps as may be reasonably required to inform the other person in ordinary course, whether or not the other person actually comes to know of it.

(e) Subject to subsection (f), a person "receives" a notice or notification when:

(1) it comes to that person's attention; or

(2) it is duly delivered in a form reasonable under the circumstances at the place of business through which the contract was made or at another location held out by that person as the place for receipt of such communications.

(f) Notice, knowledge, or a notice or notification received by an organization is effective for a particular transaction from the time it is brought to the attention of the individual conducting that transaction and, in any event, from the time it would have been brought to the individual's attention if the organization had exercised due diligence. An organization exercises due diligence if it maintains reasonable routines for communicating significant information to the person conducting the transaction and there is reasonable compliance with the routines. Due diligence does not require an individual acting for the organization to communicate information unless the communication is part of the individual's regular duties or the individual has reason to know of the transaction and that the transaction would be materially affected by the information.

Official Comments

Source: Derived from former Section 1-201(25)–(27).

Changes from former law: These provisions are substantive rather than purely definitional. Accordingly, they have been relocated from Section 1-201 to this section. The reference to the "forgotten notice" doctrine has been deleted.

1. Under subsection (a), a person has notice of a fact when, *inter alia*, the person has received a notification of the fact in question.

2. As provided in subsection (d), the word "notifies" is used when the essential fact is the proper dispatch of the notice, not its receipt. Compare "Send." When the essential fact is the other party's receipt of the notice, that is stated. Subsection (e) states when a notification is received.

3. Subsection (f) makes clear that notice, knowledge, or a notification, although "received," for instance, by a clerk in Department A of an organization, is effective for a transaction conducted in Department B only from the time when it was or should have been communicated to the individual conducting that transaction.

SECTION 1-203. LEASE DISTINGUISHED FROM SECURITY INTEREST

(a) Whether a transaction in the form of a lease creates a lease or security interest is determined by the facts of each case.

(b) A transaction in the form of a lease creates a security interest if the consideration that the lessee is to pay the lessor for the right to possession and use of the goods is an obligation for the term of the lease and is not subject to termination by the lessee, and:

(1) the original term of the lease is equal to or greater than the remaining economic life of the goods;

(2) the lessee is bound to renew the lease for the remaining economic life of the goods or is bound to become the owner of the goods;

(3) the lessee has an option to renew the lease for the remaining economic life of the goods for no additional consideration or for nominal additional consideration upon compliance with the lease agreement; or

(4) the lessee has an option to become the owner of the goods for no additional consideration or for nominal additional consideration upon compliance with the lease agreement.

(c) A transaction in the form of a lease does not create a security interest merely because:

(1) the present value of the consideration the lessee is obligated to pay the lessor for the right to possession and use of the goods is substantially equal to or is greater than the fair market value of the goods at the time the lease is entered into;

(2) the lessee assumes risk of loss of the goods;

(3) the lessee agrees to pay, with respect to the goods, taxes, insurance, filing, recording, or registration fees, or service or maintenance costs;

(4) the lessee has an option to renew the lease or to become the owner of the goods;

(5) the lessee has an option to renew the lease for a fixed rent that is equal to or greater than the reasonably predictable fair market rent for the use of the goods for the term of the renewal at the time the option is to be performed; or

(6) the lessee has an option to become the owner of the goods for a fixed price that is equal to or greater than the reasonably predictable fair market value of the goods at the time the option is to be performed.

(d) Additional consideration is nominal if it is less than the lessee's reasonably predictable cost of performing under the lease agreement if the option is not exercised. Additional consideration is not nominal if:

(1) when the option to renew the lease is granted to the lessee, the rent is stated to be the fair market rent for the use of the goods for the term of the renewal determined at the time the option is to be performed; or

(2) when the option to become the owner of the goods is granted to the lessee, the price is stated to be the fair market value of the goods determined at the time the option is to be performed.

(e) The "remaining economic life of the goods" and "reasonably predictable" fair market rent, fair market value, or cost of performing under the lease agreement must be determined with reference to the facts and circumstances at the time the transaction is entered into.
Official Comments
Source: Former Section 1-201(37).

Changes from former law: This section is substantively identical to those portions of former Section 1-201(37) that distinguished "true" leases from security interests, except that the definition of "present value" formerly embedded in Section 1-201(37) has been placed in Section 1-201(28).

1. An interest in personal property or fixtures which secures payment or performance of an obligation is a "security interest." See Section 1-201(37). Security interests are sometimes created by transactions in the form of leases. Because it can be difficult to distinguish leases that create security interests from those that do not, this section provides rules that govern the

determination of whether a transaction in the form of a lease creates a security interest.

2. One of the reasons it was decided to codify the law with respect to leases was to resolve an issue that created considerable confusion in the courts: what is a lease? The confusion existed, in part, due to the last two sentences of the definition of security interest in the 1978 Official Text of the Act, Section 1-201(37). The confusion was compounded by the rather considerable change in the federal, state and local tax laws and accounting rules as they relate to leases of goods. The answer is important because the definition of lease determines not only the rights and remedies of the parties to the lease but also those of third parties. If a transaction creates a lease and not a security interest, the lessee's interest in the goods is limited to its leasehold estate; the residual interest in the goods belongs to the lessor. This has significant implications to the lessee's creditors. "On common law theory, the lessor, since he has not parted with title, is entitled to full protection against the lessee's creditors and trustee in bankruptcy. . . ." 1 G. Gilmore, *Security Interests in Personal Property* Section 3.6, at 76 (1965).

Under pre-UCC chattel security law there was generally no requirement that the lessor file the lease, a financing statement, or the like, to enforce the lease agreement against the lessee or any third party; the Article on Secured Transactions (Article 9) did not change the common law in that respect. Coogan, Leasing and the Uniform Commercial Code, in *Equipment Leasing — Leveraged Leasing* 681, 700 n.25, 729 n.80 (2d ed.1980). The Article on Leases (Article 2A) did not change the law in that respect, except for leases of fixtures. Section 2A-309. An examination of the common law will not provide an adequate answer to the question of what is a lease. The definition of security interest in Section 1-201(37) of the 1978 Official Text of the Act provided that the Article on Secured Transactions (Article 9) governs security interests disguised as leases, *i.e.*, leases intended as security; however, the definition became vague and outmoded.

Lease is defined in Article 2A as a transfer of the right to possession and use of goods for a term, in return for consideration. Section 2A-103(1)(j). The definition continues by stating that the retention or creation of a security interest is not a lease. Thus, the task of sharpening the line between true leases and security interests disguised as leases continues to be a function of this Article.

This section begins where Section 1-201(35) leaves off. It draws a sharper line between leases and security interests disguised as leases to create greater certainty in commercial transactions.

Prior to enactment of the rules now codified in this section, the 1978 Official Text of Section 1-201(37) provided that whether a lease was intended as security (*i.e.*, a security interest disguised as a lease) was to be determined from the facts of each case; however, (a) the inclusion of an option to purchase did not itself make the lease one intended for security, and (b) an agreement that upon compliance with the terms of the lease the lessee would become, or had the option to become, the owner of the property for no additional consideration, or for a nominal consideration, did make the lease one intended for security.

Reference to the intent of the parties to create a lease or security interest led to unfortunate results. In discovering intent, courts relied upon factors that were thought to be more consistent with sales or loans than leases. Most of these criteria, however, were as applicable to true leases as to security interests. Examples include the typical net lease provisions, a purported lessor's lack of storage facilities or its character as a financing party rather than a dealer in goods. Accordingly, this section contains no reference to the parties' intent.

Subsections (a) and (b) were originally taken from Section 1(2) of the Uniform Conditional Sales Act (act withdrawn 1943), modified to reflect current leasing practice. Thus, reference to the case law prior to the incorporation of those concepts in this article will provide a useful source of precedent. Gilmore, *Security Law, Formalism and Article 9*, 47 Neb.L.Rev. 659, 671 (1968). Whether a transaction creates a lease or a security interest continues to be determined by the facts of each case. Subsection (b) further provides that a transaction creates a security interest if the lessee has an obligation to continue paying consideration for the term of the lease, if the obligation is not terminable by the lessee (thus correcting early statutory gloss, *e.g., In re Royer's Bakery, Inc.*, 1 U.C.C. Rep.Serv. (Callaghan) 342 (Bankr.E.D.Pa.1963)) and if one of four additional tests is met. The first of these four tests, subparagraph (1), is that the original lease term is equal to or greater than the remaining economic life of the goods. The second of these tests, subparagraph (2), is that the lessee is either bound to renew the lease for the remaining economic life of the goods or to become the owner of the goods. In re Gehrke Enters., 1 Bankr. 647, 651–52 (Bankr.W.D.Wis.1979). The third of these tests, subparagraph (3), is whether the lessee has an option to renew the lease for the remaining economic life of the goods for no additional consideration or for nominal additional consideration, which is defined later in this section. In re Celeryvale Transp., 44 Bankr. 1007, 1014-15 (Bankr.E.D.Tenn.1984). The fourth of these tests, subparagraph (4), is whether the lessee has an option to become the owner of the goods for no additional consideration or for nominal additional consideration. All of these tests focus on economics, not the intent of the parties. In re Berge, 32 Bankr. 370, 371-73 (Bankr.W.D.Wis.1983).

The focus on economics is reinforced by subsection (c). It states that a transaction does not create a security interest merely because the transaction has certain characteristics listed therein. Subparagraph (1) has no statutory derivative; it states that a full payout lease does not *per se* create a security interest. Rushton v. Shea, 419 F.Supp. 1349, 1365 (D.Del.1976). Subparagraphs (2) and (3) provide the same regarding the provisions of the typical net lease. *Compare* All-States Leasing Co. v. Ochs, 42 Or.App. 319, 600 P.2d 899 (Ct.App.1979), *with* In re Tillery, 571 F.2d 1361 (5th Cir.1978). Subparagraph (4) restates and expands the provisions of the 1978 Official Text of Section 1-201(37) to make clear that the option can be to buy or renew. Subparagraphs (5) and (6) treat fixed price options and provide that fair market value must be determined at the time the transaction is entered into. *Compare* Arnold Mach. Co. v. Balls, 624 P.2d 678 (Utah 1981), *with* Aoki v. Shepherd Mach. Co., 665 F.2d 941 (9th Cir.1982).

The relationship of subsection (b) to subsection (c) deserves to be explored. The fixed price purchase option provides a useful example. A fixed price purchase option in a lease does not of itself create a security interest. This is particularly true if the fixed price is equal to or greater than the reasonably predictable fair market value of the goods at the time the option is to be performed. A security interest is created only if the option price is nominal and the conditions stated in the introduction to the second paragraph of this subsection are met. There is a set of purchase options whose fixed price is less than fair market value but greater than nominal that must be determined on the facts of each case to ascertain whether the transaction in which the option is included creates a lease or a security interest.

It was possible to provide for various other permutations and combinations with respect to options to purchase and renew. For example, this section could have stated a rule to govern the facts of In re Marhoefer Packing Co., 674 F.2d 1139 (7th Cir.1982). This was not done because it would unnecessarily complicate the definition. Further development of this rule is left to the courts.

Subsections (d) and (e) provide definitions and rules of construction.

SECTION 1-204. VALUE

Except as otherwise provided in Articles 3, 4, [and] 5, [and 6], a person gives value for rights if the person acquires them:

(1) in return for a binding commitment to extend credit or for the extension of immediately available credit, whether or not drawn upon and whether or not a charge-back is provided for in the event of difficulties in collection;

(2) as security for, or in total or partial satisfaction of, a preexisting claim;

(3) by accepting delivery under a preexisting contract for purchase; or

(4) in return for any consideration sufficient to support a simple contract.

Official Comments

Source: Former Section 1-201(44).

Changes from former law: Unchanged from former Section 1-201, which was derived from Sections 25, 26, 27, 191, Uniform Negotiable Instruments Law; Section 76, Uniform Sales Act; Section 53, Uniform Bills of Lading Act; Section 58, Uniform Warehouse Receipts Act; Section 22(1), Uniform Stock Transfer Act; Section 1, Uniform Trust Receipts Act. These provisions are substantive rather than purely definitional. Accordingly, they have been relocated from former Section 1-201 to this section.

1. All the Uniform Acts in the commercial law field (except the Uniform Conditional Sales Act) have carried definitions of "value." All those definitions provided that value was any consideration sufficient to support a simple contract, including the taking of property in satisfaction of or as security for a pre-existing claim. Subsections (1), (2), and (4) in substance continue the definitions of "value" in the earlier acts. Subsection (3) makes explicit that "value" is also given in a third situation: where a buyer by taking delivery under a pre-existing contract converts a contingent into a fixed obligation.

This definition is not applicable to Articles 3 and 4, but the express inclusion of immediately available credit as value follows the separate definitions in those Articles. See Sections 4-208, 4-209, 3-303. A bank or other financing agency which in good faith makes advances against property held as collateral becomes a bona fide purchaser of that property even though provision may be made for charge-back in case of trouble. Checking credit is "immediately available" within the meaning of this section if the bank would be subject to an action for slander of credit in case checks drawn against the credit were dishonored, and when a charge-back is not discretionary with the bank, but may only be made when difficulties in collection arise in connection with the specific transaction involved.

SECTION 1-205. REASONABLE TIME; SEASONABLENESS

(a) Whether a time for taking an action required by [the Uniform Commercial Code] is reasonable depends on the nature, purpose, and circumstances of the action.

(b) An action is taken seasonably if it is taken at or within the time agreed or, if no time is agreed, at or within a reasonable time.

Official Comments

Source: Former Section 1-204(2)-(3).

Changes from former law: This section is derived from subsections (2) and (3) of former Section 1-204. Subsection (1) of that section is now incorporated in Section 1-302(b).

1. Subsection (a) makes it clear that requirements that actions be taken within a

"reasonable" time are to be applied in the transactional context of the particular action.

2. Under subsection (b), the agreement that fixes the time need not be part of the main agreement, but may occur separately. Notice also that under the definition of "agreement" (Section 1-201) the circumstances of the transaction, including course of dealing or usages of trade or course of performance may be material. On the question what is a reasonable time these matters will often be important.

SECTION 1-206. PRESUMPTIONS

Whenever [the Uniform Commercial Code] creates a "presumption" with respect to a fact, or provides that a fact is "presumed," the trier of fact must find the existence of the fact unless and until evidence is introduced that supports a finding of its nonexistence.

Legislative Note:

Former Section 1-206, a Statute of Frauds for sales of "kinds of personal property not otherwise covered," has been deleted. The other articles of the Uniform Commercial Code make individual determinations as to requirements for memorializing transactions within their scope, so that the primary effect of former Section 1-206 was to impose a writing requirement on sales transactions not otherwise governed by the UCC. Deletion of former Section 1-206 does not constitute a recommendation to legislatures as to whether such sales transactions should be covered by a Statute of Frauds; rather, it reflects a determination that there is no need for uniform commercial law to resolve that issue.

Official Comments

Source: Former Section 1-201(31).

Changes from former law. None, other than stylistic changes.

1. Several sections of the Uniform Commercial Code state that there is a "presumption" as to a certain fact, or that the fact is "presumed." This section, derived from the definition appearing in former Section 1-201(31), indicates the effect of those provisions on the proof process.

PART 3 TERRITORIAL APPLICABILITY AND GENERAL RULES

SECTION 1-301. TERRITORIAL APPLICABILITY; PARTIES' POWER TO CHOOSE APPLICABLE LAW

(a) In this section:

(1) "Domestic transaction" means a transaction other than an international transaction.

(2) "International transaction" means a transaction that bears a reasonable relation to a country other than the United States.

(b) This section applies to a transaction to the extent that it is governed by another article of the [Uniform Commercial Code].

(c) Except as otherwise provided in this section:

(1) an agreement by parties to a domestic transaction that any or all of their rights and obligations are to be determined by the law of this State or of another State is effective, whether or not the transaction bears a relation to the State designated; and

(2) an agreement by parties to an international transaction that any or all of their rights and obligations are to be determined by the law of this State or of another State or country is effective, whether or not the transaction bears a relation to the State or country

designated.

(d) In the absence of an agreement effective under subsection (c), and except as provided in subsections (e) and (g), the rights and obligations of the parties are determined by the law that would be selected by application of this State's conflict of laws principles.

(e) If one of the parties to a transaction is a consumer, the following rules apply:

(1) An agreement referred to in subsection (c) is not effective unless the transaction bears a reasonable relation to the State or country designated.

(2) Application of the law of the State or country determined pursuant to subsection (c) or (d) may not deprive the consumer of the protection of any rule of law governing a matter within the scope of this section, which both is protective of consumers and may not be varied by agreement:

(A) of the State or country in which the consumer principally resides, unless subparagraph (B) applies; or

(B) if the transaction is a sale of goods, of the State or country in which the consumer both makes the contract and takes delivery of those goods, if such State or country is not the State or country in which the consumer principally resides.

(f) An agreement otherwise effective under subsection (c) is not effective to the extent that application of the law of the State or country designated would be contrary to a fundamental policy of the State or country whose law would govern in the absence of agreement under subsection (d).

(g) To the extent that [the Uniform Commercial Code] governs a transaction, if one of the following provisions of [the Uniform Commercial Code] specifies the applicable law, that provision governs and a contrary agreement is effective only to the extent permitted by the law so specified:

(1) Section 2-402;

(2) Sections 2A-105 and 2A-106;

(3) Section 4-102;

(4) Section 4A-507;

(5) Section 5-116;

(6) Section 6-103;

(7) Section 8-110;

(8) Sections 9-301 through 9-307.

Official Comments

Source: Former Section 1-105.

Summary of changes from former law: Section 1-301, which replaces former Section 1-105, represents a significant rethinking of choice of law issues addressed in that section. The new section reexamines both the power of parties to select the jurisdiction whose law will govern their transaction and the determination of the governing law in the absence of such selection by the parties. With respect to the power to select governing law, the draft affords greater party autonomy than former Section 1-105, but with important safeguards protecting consumer interests and fundamental policies.

Section 1-301 addresses contractual designation of governing law somewhat differently than does former Section 1-105. Former law allowed the parties to any transaction to designate a jurisdiction whose law governs if the transaction bears a "reasonable relation" to that jurisdiction. Section 1-301 deviates from this approach by providing different rules for transactions involving a consumer than for non-consumer transactions, such as "business to business" transactions.

In the context of consumer transactions, the language of Section 1-301, unlike that of former Section 1-105, protects consumers against the possibility of losing the protection of consumer protection rules applicable to the aspects of the transaction governed by the Uniform Commercial Code. In most situations, the relevant consumer protection rules will be those of the consumer's home jurisdiction. A special rule, however, is provided for certain face-to-face sales transactions. (See Comment 3.)

In the context of business-to-business transactions, Section 1-301 generally provides the parties with greater autonomy to designate a jurisdiction whose law will govern than did former Section 1-105, but also provides safeguards against abuse that did not appear in former Section 1-105. In the non-consumer context, following emerging international norms, greater autonomy is provided in subsections (c)(1) and (c)(2) by deleting the former requirement that the transaction bear a "reasonable relation" to the jurisdiction. In the case of wholly domestic transactions, however, the jurisdiction designated must be a State. (See Comment 4.)

An important safeguard not present in former Section 1-105 is found in subsection (f). Subsection (f) provides that the designation of a jurisdiction's law is not effective (even if the transaction bears a reasonable relation to that jurisdiction) to the extent that application of that law would be contrary to a fundamental policy of the jurisdiction whose law would govern in the absence of contractual designation. Application of the law designated may be contrary to a fundamental policy of the State or country whose law would otherwise govern either because of the nature of the law designated or because of the "mandatory" nature of the law that would otherwise apply. (See Comment 6.)

In the absence of an effective contractual designation of governing law, former Section 1-105(1) directed the forum to apply its own law if the transaction bore "an appropriate relation to this state." This direction, however, was frequently ignored by courts. Section 1-301(d) provides that, in the absence of an effective contractual designation, the forum should apply the forum's general choice of law principles, subject to certain special rules in consumer transactions. (See Comments 3 and 7).

1. *Applicability of section.* This section is neither a complete restatement of choice of law principles nor a free-standing choice of law statute. Rather, it is a provision of Article 1 of the Uniform Commercial Code. As such, the scope of its application is limited in two significant ways.

First, this section is subject to Section 1-102, which states the scope of Article 1. As that section indicates, Article 1, and the rules contained therein, apply to transactions to the extent that they are governed by one of the other Articles of the Uniform Commercial Code. Thus, this section does not apply to matters outside the scope of the Uniform Commercial Code, such as a services contract, a credit card agreement, or a contract for the sale of real estate. This limitation was implicit in former Section 1-105, and is made explicit in Section 1-301(b).

Second, subsection (g) provides that this section is subject to the specific choice of law provisions contained in other Articles of the Uniform Commercial Code. Thus, to the extent that a transaction otherwise within the scope of this section also is within the scope of one of those provisions, the rules of that specific provision, rather than of this section, apply.

The following cases illustrate these two limitations on the scope of Section 1-301:

Example 1: A, a resident of Indiana, enters into an agreement with Credit Card Company, a Delaware corporation with its chief executive office located in New York, pursuant to which A agrees to pay Credit Card Company for purchases charged to A's credit card. The agreement contains a provision stating that it is governed by the law of South Dakota. The choice of law rules in Section 1-301 do not apply to this agreement because the agreement is not governed by any of the other Articles of the Uniform Commercial Code.

Example 2: A, a resident of Indiana, maintains a checking account with Bank B, an Ohio banking corporation located in Ohio. At the time that the account was established, Bank B and A entered into a "Bank-Customer Agreement" governing their relationship with respect to the account. The Bank-Customer Agreement contains some provisions that purport to limit the liability of Bank B with respect to its decisions whether to honor or dishonor checks purporting to be drawn on A's account. The Bank-Customer Agreement also contains a provision stating that it is governed by the law of Ohio. The provisions purporting to limit the liability of Bank B deal with issues governed by Article 4. Therefore, determination of the law applicable to those issues (including determination of the effectiveness of the choice of law clause as it applies to those issues) is within the scope of Section 1-301 as provided in subsection (b). Nonetheless, the rules of Section 1-301 would not apply to that determination because of subsection (g), which states that the choice of law rules in Section 4-102 govern instead.

2. *Contractual choice of law.* This section allows parties broad autonomy, subject to several important limitations, to select the law governing their transaction, even if the transaction does not bear a relation to the State or country whose law is selected. This recognition of party autonomy with respect to governing law has already been established in several Articles of the Uniform Commercial Code (see Sections 4A-507, 5-116, and 8-110) and is consistent with international norms. See, e.g., Inter-American Convention on the Law Applicable to International Contracts, Article 7 (Mexico City 1994); Convention on the Law Applicable to Contracts for the International Sale of Goods, Article 7(1) (The Hague 1986); EC Convention on the Law Applicable to Contractual Obligations, Article 3(1) (Rome 1980).

There are three important limitations on this party autonomy to select governing law. First, a different, and more protective, rule applies in the context of consumer transactions. (See Comment 3). Second, in an entirely domestic transaction, this section does not validate the selection of foreign law. (See Comment 4.) Third, contractual choice of law will not be given effect to the extent that application of the law designated would be contrary to a fundamental policy of the State or country whose law would be applied in the absence of such contractual designation. (See Comment 6).

This Section does not address the ability of parties to designate non-legal codes such as trade codes as the set of rules governing their transaction. The power of parties to make such a designation as part of their agreement is found in the principles of Section 1-302. That Section, allowing parties broad freedom of contract to structure their relations, is adequate for this purpose. This is also the case with respect to the ability of the parties to designate recognized bodies of rules or principles applicable to commercial transactions that are promulgated by intergovernmental organizations such as UNCITRAL or Unidroit. See, e.g., Unidroit Principles of International Commercial Contracts.

3. *Consumer transactions.* If one of the parties is a consumer (as defined in Section 1-201(b)(11)), subsection (e) provides the parties less autonomy to designate the State or country whose law will govern.

First, in the case of a consumer transaction, subsection (e)(1) provides that the transaction must bear a reasonable relation to the State or country designated. Thus, the rules of subsection (c) allowing the parties to choose the law of a jurisdiction to which the transaction bears no relation do not apply to consumer transactions.

Second, subsection (e)(2) provides that application of the law of the State or country determined by the rules of this section (whether or not that State or country was designated by the parties) cannot deprive the consumer of the protection of rules of law which govern matters within the scope of Section 1-301, are protective of consumers, and are not variable by agreement. The phrase "rule of law" is intended to refer to case law as well as statutes and administrative regulations. The requirement that the rule of law be one "governing a matter within the scope of this section" means that, consistent with the scope of Section 1-301, which governs choice of law only with regard to the aspects of a transaction governed by the Uniform Commercial Code, the relevant consumer rules are those that govern those aspects of the transaction. Such rules may be found in the Uniform Commercial Code itself, as are the consumer-protective rules in Part 6 of Article 9, or in other law if that other law governs the UCC aspects of the transaction. See, for example, the rule in Section 2.403 of the Uniform Consumer Credit Code which prohibits certain sellers and lessors from taking negotiable instruments other than checks and provides that a holder is not in good faith if the holder takes a negotiable instrument with notice that it is issued in violation of that section.

With one exception (explained in the next paragraph), the rules of law the protection of which the consumer may not be deprived are those of the jurisdiction in which the consumer principally resides. The jurisdiction in which the consumer principally resides is determined at the time relevant to the particular issue involved. Thus, for example, if the issue is one related to formation of a contract, the relevant consumer protective rules are rules of the jurisdiction in which the consumer principally resided at the time the facts relevant to contract formation occurred, even if the consumer no longer principally resides in that jurisdiction at the time the dispute arises or is litigated. If, on the other hand, the issue is one relating to enforcement of obligations, then the relevant consumer protective rules are those of the jurisdiction in which the consumer principally resides at the time enforcement is sought, even if the consumer did not principally reside in that jurisdiction at the time the transaction was entered into.

In the case of a sale of goods to a consumer, in which the consumer both makes the contract and takes possession of the goods in the same jurisdiction and that jurisdiction is not the consumer's principal residence, the rule in subsection (e)(2)(B) applies. In that situation, the relevant consumer protective rules, the protection of which the consumer may not be deprived by the choice of law rules of subsections (c) and (d), are those of the State or country in which both the contract is made and the consumer takes delivery of the goods. This rule, adapted from Section 2A-106 and Article 5 of the EC Convention on the Law Applicable to Contractual Obligations, enables a seller of goods engaging in face-to-face transactions to ascertain the consumer protection rules to which those sales are subject, without the necessity of determining the principal residence of each buyer. The reference in subsection (e)(2)(B) to the State or country in which the consumer makes the contract should not be read to incorporate formalistic concepts of where the last event necessary to conclude the contract took place; rather, the intent is to identify the state in which all material steps necessary to enter into the contract were taken by the consumer.

The following examples illustrate the application of Section 1-301(e)(2) in the context of a contractual choice of law provision:

Example 3: Seller, located in State A, agrees to sell goods to Consumer, whose principal residence is in State B. The parties agree that the law of State A would govern this transaction. Seller ships the goods to Consumer in State B. An issue related to contract formation subsequently arises. Under the law of State A, that issue is governed by State A's uniform version of Article 2. Under the law of State B, that issue is governed by a non-uniform rule, protective of consumers and not variable by agreement, that brings about a different result than would occur under the uniform version of Article 2. Under Section 1-301(e)(2)(A), the parties' agreement that the law of State A would govern their transaction cannot deprive Consumer of the protection of State B's consumer protective rule. This is the case whether State B's rule is codified in Article 2 of its Uniform Commercial Code or is found elsewhere in the law of State B.

Example 4: Same facts as Example 3, except that (i) Consumer takes all material steps necessary to enter into the agreement to purchase the goods from Seller, and takes delivery of those goods, while on vacation in State A and (ii) the parties agree that the law of State C (in which Seller's chief executive office is located) would govern their transaction. Under subsections (c)(1) and (e)(1), the designation of the law of State C as governing will be effective so long as the transaction is found to bear a reasonable relation to State C (assuming that the relevant law of State C is not contrary to a fundamental policy of the State whose law would govern in the absence of agreement), but that designation cannot deprive Consumer of the protection of any rule of State A that is within the scope of this section and is both protective of consumers and not variable by agreement. State B's consumer protective rule is not relevant because, under Section 1-301(e)(2)(B), the relevant consumer protective rules are those of the jurisdiction in which the consumer both made the contract and took delivery of the goods–here, State A–rather than those of the jurisdiction in which the consumer principally resides.

It is important to note that subsection (e)(2) applies to all determinations of applicable law in transactions in which one party is a consumer, whether that determination is made under subsection (c) (in cases in which the parties have designated the governing law in their agreement) or subsection (d) (in cases in which the parties have not made such a designation). In the latter situation, application of the otherwise-applicable conflict of laws principles of the forum might lead to application of the laws of a State or country other than that of the consumer's principal residence. In such a case, however, subsection (e)(2) applies to preserve the applicability of consumer protection rules for the benefit of the consumer as described above.

4. *Wholly domestic transactions.* While this Section provides parties broad autonomy to select governing law, that autonomy is limited in the case of wholly domestic transactions. In a "domestic transaction," subsection (c)(1) validates only the designation of the law of a State. A "domestic transaction" is a transaction that does not bear a reasonable relation to a country other than the United States. (See subsection (a)). Thus, in a wholly domestic non-consumer

transaction, parties may (subject to the limitations set out in subsections (f) and (g)) designate the law of any State but not the law of a foreign country.

5. *International transactions.* This section provides greater autonomy in the context of international transactions. As defined in subsection (a)(2), a transaction is an "international transaction" if it bears a reasonable relation to a country other than the United States. In a non-consumer international transaction, subsection (c)(2) provides that a designation of the law of any State or country is effective (subject, of course, to the limitations set out in subsections (f) and (g)). It is important to note that the transaction need not bear a relation to the State or country designated if the transaction is international. Thus, for example, in a non-consumer lease of goods in which the lessor is located in Mexico and the lessee is located in Louisiana, a designation of the law of Ireland to govern the transaction would be given effect under this section even though the transaction bears no relation to Ireland. The ability to designate the law of any country in non-consumer international transactions is important in light of the common practice in many commercial contexts of designating the law of a "neutral" jurisdiction or of a jurisdiction whose law is well-developed. If a country has two or more territorial units in which different systems of law relating to matters within the scope of this section are applicable (as is the case, for example, in Canada and the United Kingdom), subsection (c)(2) should be applied to designation by the parties of the law of one of those territorial units. Thus, for example, subsection (c)(2) should be applied if the parties to a non-consumer international transaction designate the laws of Ontario or Scotland as governing their transaction.

6. *Fundamental policy.* Subsection (f) provides that an agreement designating the governing law will not be given effect to the extent that application of the designated law would be contrary to a fundamental policy of the State or country whose law would otherwise govern. This rule provides a narrow exception to the broad autonomy afforded to parties in subsection (c). One of the prime objectives of contract law is to protect the justified expectations of the parties and to make it possible for them to foretell with accuracy what will be their rights and liabilities under the contract. In this way, certainty and predictability of result are most likely to be secured. See Restatement (Second) Conflict of Laws, Section 187, comment *e.*

Under the fundamental policy doctrine, a court should not refrain from applying the designated law merely because application of that law would lead to a result different than would be obtained under the local law of the State or country whose law would otherwise govern. Rather, the difference must be contrary to a public policy of that jurisdiction that is so substantial that it justifies overriding the concerns for certainty and predictability underlying modern commercial law as well as concerns for judicial economy generally. Thus, application of the designated law will rarely be found to be contrary to a fundamental policy of the State or country whose law would otherwise govern when the difference between the two concerns a requirement, such as a statute of frauds, that relates to formalities, or general rules of contract law, such as those concerned with the need for consideration.

The opinion of Judge Cardozo in Loucks v. Standard Oil Co. of New York, 120 N.E. 198 (1918), regarding the related issue of when a state court may decline to apply the law of another state, is a helpful touchstone here:

> Our own scheme of legislation may be different. We may even have no legislation on the subject. That is not enough to show that public policy forbids us to enforce the foreign right. A right of action is property. If a foreign statute gives the right, the mere fact that we do not give a like right is no reason for refusing to help the plaintiff in getting what belongs to him. We are not so provincial as to say that every solution of

a problem is wrong because we deal with it otherwise at home. Similarity of legislation has indeed this importance; its presence shows beyond question that the foreign statute does not offend the local policy. But its absence does not prove the contrary. It is not to be exalted into an indispensable condition. The misleading word 'comity' has been responsible for much of the trouble. It has been fertile in suggesting a discretion unregulated by general principles.

* * *

The courts are not free to refuse to enforce a foreign right at the pleasure of the judges, to suit the individual notion of expediency or fairness. They do not close their doors, unless help would violate some fundamental principle of justice, some prevalent conception of good morals, some deep-rooted tradition of the common weal.

120 N.E. at 201–02 (citations to authorities omitted).

Application of the designated law may be contrary to a fundamental policy of the State or country whose law would otherwise govern either (i) because the substance of the designated law violates a fundamental principle of justice of that State or country or (ii) because it differs from a rule of that State or country that is "mandatory" in that it *must* be applied in the courts of that State or country without regard to otherwise-applicable choice of law rules of that State or country and without regard to whether the designated law is otherwise offensive. The mandatory rules concept appears in international conventions in this field, *e.g.*, EC Convention on the Law Applicable to Contractual Obligations, although in some cases the concept is applied to authorize the *forum* state to apply *its* mandatory rules, rather than those of the State or country whose law would otherwise govern. The latter situation is not addressed by this section. (See Comment 9.)

It is obvious that a rule that is freely changeable by agreement of the parties under the law of the State or country whose law would otherwise govern cannot be construed as a mandatory rule of that State or country. This does not mean, however, that rules that cannot be changed by agreement under that law are, for that reason alone, mandatory rules. Otherwise, contractual choice of law in the context of the Uniform Commercial Code would be illusory and redundant; the parties would be able to accomplish by choice of law no more than can be accomplished under Section 1-302, which allows variation of otherwise applicable rules by agreement. (Under Section 1-302, the parties could agree to vary the rules that would otherwise govern their transaction by substituting for those rules the rules that would apply if the transaction were governed by the law of the designated State or country without designation of governing law.) Indeed, other than cases in which a mandatory choice of law rule is established by statute (see, *e.g.*, Sections 9-301 through 9-307, explicitly preserved in subsection (g)), cases in which courts have declined to follow the designated law solely because a rule of the State or country whose law would otherwise govern is mandatory are rare.

7. *Choice of law in the absence of contractual designation.* Subsection (d), which replaces the second sentence of former Section 1-105(1), determines which jurisdiction's law governs a transaction in the absence of an effective contractual choice by the parties. Former Section 1-105(1) provided that the law of the forum (*i.e.*, the Uniform Commercial Code) applied if the transaction bore "an appropriate relation to this state." By using an "appropriate relation" test, rather than, for example, a "most significant relationship" test, Section 1-105(1) expressed a bias in favor of applying the forum's law. This bias, while not universally respected by the courts, was justifiable in light of the uncertainty that existed at the time of drafting as to whether the Uniform Commercial Code would be adopted by all the states; the pro-forum bias

would assure that the Uniform Commercial Code would be applied so long as the transaction bore an "appropriate" relation to the forum. Inasmuch as the Uniform Commercial Code has been adopted, at least in part, in all U.S. jurisdictions, the vitality of this point is minimal in the domestic context, and international comity concerns militate against continuing the pro-forum, pro-UCC bias in transnational transactions. Whether the choice is between the law of two jurisdictions that have adopted the Uniform Commercial Code, but whose law differs (because of differences in enacted language or differing judicial interpretations), or between the Uniform Commercial Code and the law of another country, there is no strong justification for directing a court to apply different choice of law principles to that determination than it would apply if the matter were not governed by the Uniform Commercial Code. Similarly, given the variety of choice of law principles applied by the states, it would not be prudent to designate only one such principle as the proper one for transactions governed by the Uniform Commercial Code. Accordingly, in cases in which the parties have not made an effective choice of law, Section 1-301(d) simply directs the forum to apply its ordinary choice of law principles to determine which jurisdiction's law governs, subject to the special rules of Section 1-301(e)(2) with regard to consumer transactions.

8. *Primacy of other Uniform Commercial Code choice of law rules.* Subsection (g), which is essentially identical to former Section 1-105(2), indicates that choice of law rules provided in the other Articles govern when applicable.

9. *Matters not addressed by this section.* As noted in Comment 1, this section is not a complete statement of conflict of laws doctrines applicable in commercial cases. Among the issues this section does not address, and leaves to other law, three in particular deserve mention. First, a forum will occasionally decline to apply the law of a different jurisdiction selected by the parties when application of that law would be contrary to a fundamental policy of the forum jurisdiction, even if it would not be contrary to a fundamental policy of the State or country whose law would govern in the absence of contractual designation. Standards for application of this doctrine relate primarily to concepts of sovereignty rather than commercial law and are thus left to the courts. Second, in determining whether to give effect to the parties' agreement that the law of a particular State or country will govern their relationship, courts must, of necessity, address some issues as to the basic validity of that agreement. These issues might relate, for example, to capacity to contract and absence of duress. This section does not address these issues. Third, this section leaves to other choice of law principles of the forum the issues of whether, and to what extent, the forum will apply the same law to the non-UCC aspects of a transaction that it applies to the aspects of the transaction governed by the Uniform Commercial Code.

SECTION 1-302. VARIATION BY AGREEMENT

(a) Except as otherwise provided in subsection (b) or elsewhere in [the Uniform Commercial Code], the effect of provisions of [the Uniform Commercial Code] may be varied by agreement.

(b) The obligations of good faith, diligence, reasonableness, and care prescribed by [the Uniform Commercial Code] may not be disclaimed by agreement. The parties, by agreement, may determine the standards by which the performance of those obligations is to be measured if those standards are not manifestly unreasonable. Whenever [the Uniform Commercial Code] requires an action to be taken within a reasonable time, a time that is not manifestly unreasonable may be fixed by agreement.

(c) The presence in certain provisions of [the Uniform Commercial Code] of the phrase "unless otherwise agreed", or words of similar import, does not imply that the effect of other provisions may not be varied by agreement under this section.

Official Comments

Source: Former Sections 1-102(3)-(4) and 1-204(1).

Changes: This section combines the rules from subsections (3) and (4) of former Section 1-102 and subsection (1) of former Section 1-204. No substantive changes are made.

1. Subsection (a) states affirmatively at the outset that freedom of contract is a principle of the Uniform Commercial Code: "the effect" of its provisions may be varied by "agreement." The meaning of the statute itself must be found in its text, including its definitions, and in appropriate extrinsic aids; it cannot be varied by agreement. But the Uniform Commercial Code seeks to avoid the type of interference with evolutionary growth found in pre-Code cases such as Manhattan Co. v. Morgan, 242 N.Y. 38, 150 N.E. 594 (1926). Thus, private parties cannot make an instrument negotiable within the meaning of Article 3 except as provided in Section 3-104; nor can they change the meaning of such terms as "bona fide purchaser," "holder in due course," or "due negotiation," as used in the Uniform Commercial Code. But an agreement can change the legal consequences that would otherwise flow from the provisions of the Uniform Commercial Code. "Agreement" here includes the effect given to course of dealing, usage of trade and course of performance by Sections 1-201 and 1-303; the effect of an agreement on the rights of third parties is left to specific provisions of the Uniform Commercial Code and to supplementary principles applicable under Section 1-103. The rights of third parties under Section 9-317 when a security interest is unperfected, for example, cannot be destroyed by a clause in the security agreement.

This principle of freedom of contract is subject to specific exceptions found elsewhere in the Uniform Commercial Code and to the general exception stated here. The specific exceptions vary in explicitness: the statute of frauds found in Section 2-201, for example, does not explicitly preclude oral waiver of the requirement of a writing, but a fair reading denies enforcement to such a waiver as part of the "contract" made unenforceable; Section 9-602, on the other hand, is a quite explicit limitation on freedom of contract. Under the exception for "the obligations of good faith, diligence, reasonableness and care prescribed by [the Uniform Commercial Code]," provisions of the Uniform Commercial Code prescribing such obligations are not to be disclaimed. However, the section also recognizes the prevailing practice of having agreements set forth standards by which due diligence is measured and explicitly provides that, in the absence of a showing that the standards manifestly are unreasonable, the agreement controls. In this connection, Section 1-303 incorporating into the agreement prior course of dealing and usages of trade is of particular importance.

Subsection (b) also recognizes that nothing is stronger evidence of a reasonable time than the fixing of such time by a fair agreement between the parties. However, provision is made for disregarding a clause which whether by inadvertence or overreaching fixes a time so unreasonable that it amounts to eliminating all remedy under the contract. The parties are not required to fix the most reasonable time but may fix any time which is not obviously unfair as judged by the time of contracting.

2. An agreement that varies the effect of provisions of the Uniform Commercial Code may do so by stating the rules that will govern in lieu of the provisions varied. Alternatively, the parties may vary the effect of such provisions by stating that their relationship will be governed by recognized bodies of rules or principles applicable to commercial transactions. Such bodies of rules or principles may include, for example, those that are promulgated by intergovernmental authorities such as UNCITRAL or Unidroit (*see, e.g.,* Unidroit Principles of International Commercial Contracts), or non-legal codes such as trade codes.

3. Subsection (c) is intended to make it clear that, as a matter of drafting, phrases such as "unless otherwise agreed" have been used to avoid controversy as to whether the subject matter of a particular section does or does not fall within the exceptions to subsection (b), but absence of such words contains no negative implication since under subsection (b) the general and residual rule is that the effect of all provisions of the Uniform Commercial Code may be varied by agreement.

SECTION 1-303. COURSE OF PERFORMANCE, COURSE OF DEALING, AND USAGE OF TRADE

(a) A "course of performance" is a sequence of conduct between the parties to a particular transaction that exists if:

(1) the agreement of the parties with respect to the transaction involves repeated occasions for performance by a party; and

(2) the other party, with knowledge of the nature of the performance and opportunity for objection to it, accepts the performance or acquiesces in it without objection.

(b) A "course of dealing" is a sequence of conduct concerning previous transactions between the parties to a particular transaction that is fairly to be regarded as establishing a common basis of understanding for interpreting their expressions and other conduct.

(c) A "usage of trade" is any practice or method of dealing having such regularity of observance in a place, vocation, or trade as to justify an expectation that it will be observed with respect to the transaction in question. The existence and scope of such a usage must be proved as facts. If it is established that such a usage is embodied in a trade code or similar record, the interpretation of the record is a question of law.

(d) A course of performance or course of dealing between the parties or usage of trade in the vocation or trade in which they are engaged or of which they are or should be aware is relevant in ascertaining the meaning of the parties' agreement, may give particular meaning to specific terms of the agreement, and may supplement or qualify the terms of the agreement. A usage of trade applicable in the place in which part of the performance under the agreement is to occur may be so utilized as to that part of the performance.

(e) Except as otherwise provided in subsection (f), the express terms of an agreement and any applicable course of performance, course of dealing, or usage of trade must be construed whenever reasonable as consistent with each other. If such a construction is unreasonable:

(1) express terms prevail over course of performance, course of dealing, and usage of trade;

(2) course of performance prevails over course of dealing and usage of trade; and

(3) course of dealing prevails over usage of trade.

(f) Subject to Section 2-209, a course of performance is relevant to show a waiver or modification of any term inconsistent with the course of performance.

(g) Evidence of a relevant usage of trade offered by one party is not admissible unless that party has given the other party notice that the court finds sufficient to prevent unfair surprise to the other party.

Official Comments

Source: Former Sections 1-205, 2-208, and Section 2A-207.

Changes from former law: This section integrates the "course of performance" concept from Articles 2 and 2A into the principles of former Section 1-205, which deals with course of dealing and usage of trade. In so doing, the section slightly modifies the articulation of the course of performance rules to fit more comfortably with the approach and structure of former Section 1-205. There are also slight modifications to be more consistent with the definition of "agreement" in former Section 1-201(3). It should be noted that a course of performance that might otherwise establish a defense to the obligation of a party to a negotiable instrument is not available as a defense against a holder in due course who took the instrument without notice of that course of performance.

1. The Uniform Commercial Code rejects both the "lay-dictionary" and the "conveyancer's" reading of a commercial agreement. Instead the meaning of the agreement of the parties is to be determined by the language used by them and by their action, read and interpreted in the light of commercial practices and other surrounding circumstances. The measure and background for interpretation are set by the commercial context, which may explain and supplement even the language of a formal or final writing.

2. "Course of dealing," as defined in subsection (b), is restricted, literally, to a sequence of conduct between the parties previous to the agreement. A sequence of conduct after or under the agreement, however, is a "course of performance." "Course of dealing" may enter the agreement either by explicit provisions of the agreement or by tacit recognition.

3. The Uniform Commercial Code deals with "usage of trade" as a factor in reaching the commercial meaning of the agreement that the parties have made. The language used is to be interpreted as meaning what it may fairly be expected to mean to parties involved in the particular commercial transaction in a given locality or in a given vocation or trade. By adopting in this context the term "usage of trade," the Uniform Commercial Code expresses its intent to reject those cases which see evidence of "custom" as representing an effort to displace or negate "established rules of law." A distinction is to be drawn between mandatory rules of law such as the Statute of Frauds provisions of Article 2 on Sales whose very office is to control and restrict the actions of the parties, and which cannot be abrogated by agreement, or by a usage of trade, and those rules of law (such as those in Part 3 of Article 2 on Sales) which fill in points which the parties have not considered and in fact agreed upon. The latter rules hold "unless otherwise agreed" but yield to the contrary agreement of the parties. Part of the agreement of the parties to which such rules yield is to be sought for in the usages of trade which furnish the background and give particular meaning to the language used, and are the framework of common understanding controlling any general rules of law which hold only when there is no such understanding.

4. A usage of trade under subsection (c) must have the "regularity of observance" specified. The ancient English tests for "custom" are abandoned in this connection. Therefore, it is not required that a usage of trade be "ancient or immemorial," "universal," or the like. Under the requirement of subsection (c) full recognition is thus available for new usages and for usages currently observed by the great majority of decent dealers, even though dissidents ready to cut corners do not agree. There is room also for proper recognition of usage agreed upon by merchants in trade codes.

5. The policies of the Uniform Commercial Code controlling explicit unconscionable contracts and clauses (Sections 1-304, 2-302) apply to implicit clauses that rest on usage of trade and carry forward the policy underlying the ancient requirement that a custom or usage must be "reasonable." However, the emphasis is shifted. The very fact of commercial acceptance makes out a *prima facie* case that the usage is reasonable, and the burden is no

longer on the usage to establish itself as being reasonable. But the anciently established policing of usage by the courts is continued to the extent necessary to cope with the situation arising if an unconscionable or dishonest practice should become standard.

6. Subsection (d), giving the prescribed effect to usages of which the parties "are or should be aware," reinforces the provision of subsection (c) requiring not universality but only the described "regularity of observance" of the practice or method. This subsection also reinforces the point of subsection (c) that such usages may be either general to trade or particular to a special branch of trade.

7. Although the definition of "agreement" in Section 1-201 includes the elements of course of performance, course of dealing, and usage of trade, the fact that express reference is made in some sections to those elements is not to be construed as carrying a contrary intent or implication elsewhere. Compare Section 1-302(c).

8. In cases of a well established line of usage varying from the general rules of the Uniform Commercial Code where the precise amount of the variation has not been worked out into a single standard, the party relying on the usage is entitled, in any event, to the minimum variation demonstrated. The whole is not to be disregarded because no particular line of detail has been established. In case a dominant pattern has been fairly evidenced, the party relying on the usage is entitled under this section to go to the trier of fact on the question of whether such dominant pattern has been incorporated into the agreement.

9. Subsection (g) is intended to insure that this Act's liberal recognition of the needs of commerce in regard to usage of trade shall not be made into an instrument of abuse.

SECTION 1-304. OBLIGATION OF GOOD FAITH

Every contract or duty within [the Uniform Commercial Code] imposes an obligation of good faith in its performance and enforcement.

Official Comments

Source: Former Section 1-203.

Changes from former law: Except for changing the form of reference to the Uniform Commercial Code, this section is identical to former Section 1-203.

1. This section sets forth a basic principle running throughout the Uniform Commercial Code. The principle is that in commercial transactions good faith is required in the performance and enforcement of all agreements or duties. While this duty is explicitly stated in some provisions of the Uniform Commercial Code, the applicability of the duty is broader than merely these situations and applies generally, as stated in this section, to the performance or enforcement of every contract or duty within this Act. It is further implemented by Section 1-303 on course of dealing, course of performance, and usage of trade. This section does not support an independent cause of action for failure to perform or enforce in good faith. Rather, this section means that a failure to perform or enforce, in good faith, a specific duty or obligation under the contract, constitutes a breach of that contract or makes unavailable, under the particular circumstances, a remedial right or power. This distinction makes it clear that the doctrine of good faith merely directs a court towards interpreting contracts within the commercial context in which they are created, performed, and enforced, and does not create a separate duty of fairness and reasonableness which can be independently breached.

2. "Performance and enforcement" of contracts and duties within the Uniform Commercial Code include the exercise of rights created by the Uniform Commercial Code.

SECTION 1-305. REMEDIES TO BE LIBERALLY ADMINISTERED

(a) The remedies provided by [the Uniform Commercial Code] must be liberally adminis-tered to the end that the aggrieved party may be put in as good a position as if the other party had fully performed but neither consequential or special damages nor penal damages may be had except as specifically provided in [the Uniform Commercial Code] or by other rule of law.

(b) Any right or obligation declared by [the Uniform Commercial Code] is enforceable by action unless the provision declaring it specifies a different and limited effect.
Official Comments
Source: Former Section 1-106.

Changes from former law: Other than changes in the form of reference to the Uniform Commercial Code, this section is identical to former Section 1-106.

1. Subsection (a) is intended to effect three propositions. The first is to negate the possibility of unduly narrow or technical interpretation of remedial provisions by providing that the remedies in the Uniform Commercial Code are to be liberally administered to the end stated in this section. The second is to make it clear that compensatory damages are limited to compensation. They do not include consequential or special damages, or penal damages; and the Uniform Commercial Code elsewhere makes it clear that damages must be minimized. Cf. Sections 1-304, 2-706(1), and 2-712(2). The third purpose of subsection (a) is to reject any doctrine that damages must be calculable with mathematical accuracy. Compensatory damages are often at best approximate: they have to be proved with whatever definiteness and accuracy the facts permit, but no more. Cf. Section 2-204(3).

2. Under subsection (b), any right or obligation described in the Uniform Commercial Code is enforceable by action, even though no remedy may be expressly provided, unless a particular provision specifies a different and limited effect. Whether specific performance or other equitable relief is available is determined not by this section but by specific provisions and by supplementary principles. Cf. Sections 1-103, 2-716.

3. "Consequential" or "special" damages and "penal" damages are not defined in the Uniform Commercial Code; rather, these terms are used in the sense in which they are used outside the Uniform Commercial Code.

SECTION 1-306. WAIVER OR RENUNCIATION OF CLAIM OR RIGHT AFTER BREACH

A claim or right arising out of an alleged breach may be discharged in whole or in part without consideration by agreement of the aggrieved party in an authenticated record.
Official Comments
Source: Former Section 1-107.

Changes from former law: This section changes former law in two respects. First, former Section 1-107, requiring the "delivery" of a "written waiver or renunciation" merges the separate concepts of the aggrieved party's agreement to forego rights and the manifestation of that agreement. This section separates those concepts, and explicitly requires *agreement* of the aggrieved party. Second, the revised section reflects developments in electronic commerce by providing for memorialization in an authenticated record. In this context, a party may "authenticate" a record by (i) signing a record that is a writing or (ii) attaching to or logically associating with a record that is not a writing an electronic sound, symbol or process with the present intent to adopt or accept the record. See Sections 1-201(b)(37) and 9-102(a)(7).

1. This section makes consideration unnecessary to the effective renunciation or waiver of rights or claims arising out of an alleged breach of a commercial contract where the agreement

effecting such renunciation is memorialized in a record authenticated by the aggrieved party. Its provisions, however, must be read in conjunction with the section imposing an obligation of good faith. (Section 1-304).

SECTION 1-307. PRIMA FACIE EVIDENCE BY THIRD-PARTY DOCUMENTS

A document in due form purporting to be a bill of lading, policy or certificate of insurance, official weigher's or inspector's certificate, consular invoice, or any other document authorized or required by the contract to be issued by a third party is prima facie evidence of its own authenticity and genuineness and of the facts stated in the document by the third party.

Official Comments

Source: Former Section 1-202.

Changes from former law: Except for minor stylistic changes, this Section is identical to former Section 1-202.

1. This section supplies judicial recognition for documents that are relied upon as trustworthy by commercial parties.

2. This section is concerned only with documents that have been given a preferred status by the parties themselves who have required their procurement in the agreement, and for this reason the applicability of the section is limited to actions arising out of the contract that authorized or required the document. The list of documents is intended to be illustrative and not exclusive.

3. The provisions of this section go no further than establishing the documents in question as prima facie evidence and leave to the court the ultimate determination of the facts where the accuracy or authenticity of the documents is questioned. In this connection the section calls for a commercially reasonable interpretation.

4. Documents governed by this section need not be writings if records in another medium are generally relied upon in the context.

SECTION 1-308. PERFORMANCE OR ACCEPTANCE UNDER RESERVATION OF RIGHTS

(a) A party that with explicit reservation of rights performs or promises performance or assents to performance in a manner demanded or offered by the other party does not thereby prejudice the rights reserved. Such words as "without prejudice," "under protest," or the like are sufficient.

(b) Subsection (a) does not apply to an accord and satisfaction.

Official Comments

Source: Former Section 1-207.

Changes from former law: This section is identical to former Section 1-207.

1. This section provides machinery for the continuation of performance along the lines contemplated by the contract despite a pending dispute, by adopting the mercantile device of going ahead with delivery, acceptance, or payment "without prejudice," "under protest," "under reserve," "with reservation of all our rights," and the like. All of these phrases completely reserve all rights within the meaning of this section. The section therefore contemplates that limited as well as general reservations and acceptance by a party may be made "subject to satisfaction of our purchaser," "subject to acceptance by our customers," or the like.

2. This section does not add any new requirement of language of reservation where not already required by law, but merely provides a specific measure on which a party can rely as

that party makes or concurs in any interim adjustment in the course of performance. It does not affect or impair the provisions of this Act such as those under which the buyer's remedies for defect survive acceptance without being expressly claimed if notice of the defects is given within a reasonable time. Nor does it disturb the policy of those cases which restrict the effect of a waiver of a defect to reasonable limits under the circumstances, even though no such reservation is expressed.

The section is not addressed to the creation or loss of remedies in the ordinary course of performance but rather to a method of procedure where one party is claiming as of right something which the other believes to be unwarranted.

3. Subsection (b) states that this section does not apply to an accord and satisfaction. Section 3-311 governs if an accord and satisfaction is attempted by tender of a negotiable instrument as stated in that section. If Section 3-311 does not apply, the issue of whether an accord and satisfaction has been effected is determined by the law of contract. Whether or not Section 3-311 applies, this section has no application to an accord and satisfaction.

SECTION 1-309. OPTION TO ACCELERATE AT WILL

A term providing that one party or that party's successor in interest may accelerate payment or performance or require collateral or additional collateral "at will" or when the party "deems itself insecure," or words of similar import, means that the party has power to do so only if that party in good faith believes that the prospect of payment or performance is impaired. The burden of establishing lack of good faith is on the party against which the power has been exercised.

Official Comments

Source: Former Section 1-208.

Changes from former law: Except for minor stylistic changes, this section is identical to former Section 1-208.

1. The common use of acceleration clauses in many transactions governed by the Uniform Commercial Code, including sales of goods on credit, notes payable at a definite time, and secured transactions, raises an issue as to the effect to be given to a clause that seemingly grants the power to accelerate at the whim and caprice of one party. This section is intended to make clear that despite language that might be so construed and which further might be held to make the agreement void as against public policy or to make the contract illusory or too indefinite for enforcement, the option is to be exercised only in the good faith belief that the prospect of payment or performance is impaired.

Obviously this section has no application to demand instruments or obligations whose very nature permits call at any time with or without reason. This section applies only to an obligation of payment or performance which in the first instance is due at a future date.

SECTION 1-310. SUBORDINATED OBLIGATIONS

An obligation may be issued as subordinated to performance of another obligation of the person obligated, or a creditor may subordinate its right to performance of an obligation by agreement with either the person obligated or another creditor of the person obligated. Subordination does not create a security interest as against either the common debtor or a subordinated creditor.

Official Comments

Source: Former Section 1-209.

Changes from former law: This section is substantively identical to former Section 1-209.

The language in that section stating that it "shall be construed as declaring the law as it existed prior to the enactment of this section and not as modifying it" has been deleted.

1. Billions of dollars of subordinated debt are held by the public and by institutional investors. Commonly, the subordinated debt is subordinated on issue or acquisition and is evidenced by an investment security or by a negotiable or non-negotiable note. Debt is also sometimes subordinated after it arises, either by agreement between the subordinating creditor and the debtor, by agreement between two creditors of the same debtor, or by agreement of all three parties. The subordinated creditor may be a stockholder or other "insider" interested in the common debtor; the subordinated debt may consist of accounts or other rights to payment not evidenced by any instrument. All such cases are included in the terms "subordinated obligation," "subordination," and "subordinated creditor."

2. Subordination agreements are enforceable between the parties as contracts; and in the bankruptcy of the common debtor dividends otherwise payable to the subordinated creditor are turned over to the superior creditor. This "turn-over" practice has on occasion been explained in terms of "equitable lien," "equitable assignment," or "constructive trust," but whatever the label the practice is essentially an equitable remedy and does not mean that there is a transaction "that creates a security interest in personal property . . . by contract" or a "sale of accounts, chattel paper, payment intangibles, or promissory notes" within the meaning of Section 9-109. On the other hand, nothing in this section prevents one creditor from assigning his rights to another creditor of the same debtor in such a way as to create a security interest within Article 9, where the parties so intend.

3. The enforcement of subordination agreements is largely left to supplementary principles under Section 1-103. If the subordinated debt is evidenced by a certificated security, Section 8-202(a) authorizes enforcement against purchasers on terms stated or referred to on the security certificate. If the fact of subordination is noted on a negotiable instrument, a holder under Sections 3-302 and 3-306 is subject to the term because notice precludes him from taking free of the subordination. Sections 3-302(3)(a), 3-306, and 8-317 severely limit the rights of levying creditors of a subordinated creditor in such cases.

ARTICLE 2 — SALES

TABLE OF CONTENTS

PART 1   SHORT TITLE, GENERAL CONSTRUCTION AND SUBJECT MATTER

SECTION 2-101.   SHORT TITLE

This Article shall be known and may be cited as Uniform Commercial Code — Sales.

SECTION 2-102.   SCOPE; CERTAIN SECURITY AND OTHER TRANSACTIONS EXCLUDED FROM THIS ARTICLE

Unless the context otherwise requires, this Article applies to transactions in goods; it does not apply to any transaction which although in the form of an unconditional contract to sell or present sale is intended to operate only as a security transaction nor does this Article impair or repeal any statute regulating sales to consumers, farmers or other specified classes of buyers.

SECTION 2-103.   DEFINITIONS AND INDEX OF DEFINITIONS

(1) In this Article unless the context otherwise requires

(a) "Buyer" means a person who buys or contracts to buy goods.

(b) "Good faith" in the case of a merchant means honesty in fact and the observance of reasonable commercial standards of fair dealing in the trade.

(c) "Receipt" of goods means taking physical possession of them.

(d) "Seller" means a person who sells or contracts to sell goods.

(2) Other definitions applying to this Article or to specified Parts thereof, and the sections in which they appear are:

"Acceptance". Section 2–606.

"Banker's credit". Section 2–325.

"Between merchants". Section 2–104.

"Cancellation". Section 2–106(4).

"Commercial unit". Section 2–105.

"Confirmed credit". Section 2–325.

"Conforming to contract". Section 2–106.

"Contract for sale". Section 2–106.

"Cover". Section 2–712.

"Entrusting". Section 2–403.

"Financing agency". Section 2–104.

"Future goods". Section 2–105.

"Goods". Section 2–105.

"Identification". Section 2–501.

"Installment contract". Section 2–612.

"Letter of Credit". Section 2–325.

"Lot". Section 2–105.

"Merchant". Section 2–104.

"Overseas". Section 2–323.

"Person in position of seller". Section 2–707.

"Present sale". Section 2–106.

"Sale". Section 2–106.

"Sale on approval". Section 2–326.

"Sale or return". Section 2–326.

"Termination". Section 2–106.

(3) The following definitions in other Articles apply to this Article:

"Check". Section 3–104.

"Consignee". Section 7–102.

"Consignor". Section 7–102.

"Consumer goods". Section 9–109.

"Dishonor". Section 3–502.

"Draft". Section 3–104.

(4) In addition Article 1 contains general definitions and principles of construction and interpretation applicable throughout this Article.

As amended in 1994.

SECTION 2-104. DEFINITIONS: "MERCHANT"; "BETWEEN MERCHANTS"; "FINANCING AGENCY"

(1) "Merchant" means a person who deals in goods of the kind or otherwise by his occupation holds himself out as having knowledge or skill peculiar to the practices or goods involved in the transaction or to whom such knowledge or skill may be attributed by his employment of an agent or broker or other intermediary who by his occupation holds himself out as having such knowledge or skill.

(2) "Financing agency" means a bank, finance company or other person who in the ordinary course of business makes advances against goods or documents of title or who by arrangement with either the seller or the buyer intervenes in ordinary course to make or collect payment due or claimed under the contract for sale, as by purchasing or paying the seller's draft or making advances against it or by merely taking it for collection whether or not documents of title accompany the draft. "Financing agency" includes also a bank or other person who similarly intervenes between persons who are in the position of seller and buyer in respect to the goods (Section 2–707).

(3) "Between merchants" means in any transaction with respect to which both parties are chargeable with the knowledge or skill of merchants.

SECTION 2-105. DEFINITIONS: TRANSFERABILITY; "GOODS"; "FUTURE" GOODS; "LOT"; "COMMERCIAL UNIT"

(1) "Goods" means all things (including specially manufactured goods) which are movable at the time of identification to the contract for sale other than the money in which the price is to be paid, investment securities (Article 8) and things in action. "Goods" also includes the unborn young of animals and growing crops and other identified things attached to realty as described in the section on goods to be severed from realty (Section 2–107).

(2) Goods must be both existing and identified before any interest in them can pass. Goods which are not both existing and identified are "future" goods. A purported present sale of future goods or of any interest therein operates as a contract to sell.

(3) There may be a sale of a part interest in existing identified goods.

(4) An undivided share in an identified bulk of fungible goods is sufficiently identified to be sold although the quantity of the bulk is not determined. Any agreed proportion of such a bulk or any quantity thereof agreed upon by number, weight or other measure may to the extent of the seller's interest in the bulk be sold to the buyer who then becomes an owner in common.

(5) "Lot" means a parcel or a single article which is the subject matter of a separate sale or delivery, whether or not it is sufficient to perform the contract.

(6) "Commercial unit" means such a unit of goods as by commercial usage is a single whole for purposes of sale and division of which materially impairs its character or value on the market or in use. A commercial unit may be a single article (as a machine) or a set of articles (as a suite of furniture or an assortment of sizes) or a quantity (as a bale, gross, or carload) or any other unit treated in use or in the relevant market as a single whole.

SECTION 2-106.   DEFINITIONS: "CONTRACT"; "AGREEMENT"; "CONTRACT FOR SALE"; "SALE"; "PRESENT SALE"; "CONFORMING" TO CONTRACT; "TERMINATION"; "CANCELLATION"

(1) In this Article unless the context otherwise requires "contract" and "agreement" are limited to those relating to the present or future sale of goods. "Contract for sale" includes both a present sale of goods and a contract to sell goods at a future time. A "sale" consists in the passing of title from the seller to the buyer for a price (Section 2–401). A "present sale" means a sale which is accomplished by the making of the contract.

(2) Goods or conduct including any part of a performance are "conforming" or conform to the contract when they are in accordance with the obligations under the contract.

(3) "Termination" occurs when either party pursuant to a power created by agreement or law puts an end to the contract otherwise than for its breach. On "termination" all obligations which are still executory on both sides are discharged but any right based on prior breach or performance survives.

(4) "Cancellation" occurs when either party puts an end to the contract for breach by the other and its effect is the same as that of "termination" except that the cancelling party also retains any remedy for breach of the whole contract or any unperformed balance.

SECTION 2-107.   GOODS TO BE SEVERED FROM REALTY: RECORDING

(1) A contract for the sale of minerals or the like (including oil and gas) or a structure or its materials to be removed from realty is a contract for the sale of goods within this Article if they are to be severed by the seller but until severance a purported present sale thereof which is not effective as a transfer of an interest in land is effective only as a contract to sell.

(2) A contract for the sale apart from the land of growing crops or other things attached to realty and capable of severance without material harm thereto but not described in subsection (1) or of timber to be cut is a contract for the sale of goods within this Article whether the subject matter is to be severed by the buyer or by the seller even though it forms part of the realty at the time of contracting, and the parties can by identification effect a present sale before severance.

(3) The provisions of this section are subject to any third party rights provided by the law relating to realty records, and the contract for sale may be executed and recorded as a document transferring an interest in land and shall then constitute notice to third parties of the buyer's rights under the contract for sale.

As amended in 1972.

PART 2.   FORM, FORMATION AND READJUSTMENT OF CONTRACT

SECTION 2-201.   FORMAL REQUIREMENTS; STATUTE OF FRAUDS

(1) Except as otherwise provided in this section a contract for the sale of goods for the price of $500 or more is not enforceable by way of action or defense unless there is some writing

sufficient to indicate that a contract for sale has been made between the parties and signed by the party against whom enforcement is sought or by his authorized agent or broker. A writing is not insufficient because it omits or incorrectly states a term agreed upon but the contract is not enforceable under this paragraph beyond the quantity of goods shown in such writing.

(2) Between merchants if within a reasonable time a writing in confirmation of the contract and sufficient against the sender is received and the party receiving it has reason to know its contents, it satisfies the requirements of subsection (1) against such party unless written notice of objection to its contents is given within 10 days after it is received.

(3) A contract which does not satisfy the requirements of subsection (1) but which is valid in other respects is enforceable

(a) if the goods are to be specially manufactured for the buyer and are not suitable for sale to others in the ordinary course of the seller's business and the seller, before notice of repudiation is received and under circumstances which reasonably indicate that the goods are for the buyer, has made either a substantial beginning of their manufacture or commitments for their procurement; or

(b) if the party against whom enforcement is sought admits in his pleading, testimony or otherwise in court that a contract for sale was made, but the contract is not enforceable under this provision beyond the quantity of goods admitted; or

(c) with respect to goods for which payment has been made and accepted or which have been received and accepted (Sec. 2–606).

SECTION 2-202. FINAL WRITTEN EXPRESSION: PAROL OR EXTRINSIC EVIDENCE

Terms with respect to which the confirmatory memoranda of the parties agree or which are otherwise set forth in a writing intended by the parties as a final expression of their agreement with respect to such terms as are included therein may not be contradicted by evidence of any prior agreement or of a contemporaneous oral agreement but may be explained or supplemented

(a) by course of dealing or usage of trade (Section 1–205) or by course of performance (Section 2–208); and

(b) by evidence of consistent additional terms unless the court finds the writing to have been intended also as a complete and exclusive statement of the terms of the agreement.

SECTION 2-203. SEALS INOPERATIVE

The affixing of a seal to a writing evidencing a contract for sale or an offer to buy or sell goods does not constitute the writing a sealed instrument and the law with respect to sealed instruments does not apply to such a contract or offer.

SECTION 2-204. FORMATION IN GENERAL

(1) A contract for sale of goods may be made in any manner sufficient to show agreement, including conduct by both parties which recognizes the existence of such a contract.

(2) An agreement sufficient to constitute a contract for sale may be found even though the moment of its making is undetermined.

(3) Even though one or more terms are left open a contract for sale does not fail for

indefiniteness if the parties have intended to make a contract and there is a reasonably certain basis for giving an appropriate remedy.

SECTION 2-205. FIRM OFFERS

An offer by a merchant to buy or sell goods in a signed writing which by its terms gives assurance that it will be held open is not revocable, for lack of consideration, during the time stated or if no time is stated for a reasonable time, but in no event may such period of irrevocability exceed three months; but any such term of assurance on a form supplied by the offeree must be separately signed by the offeror.

SECTION 2-206. OFFER AND ACCEPTANCE IN FORMATION OF CONTRACT

(1) Unless otherwise unambiguously indicated by the language or circumstances

(a) an offer to make a contract shall be construed as inviting acceptance in any manner and by any medium reasonable in the circumstances;

(b) an order or other offer to buy goods for prompt or current shipment shall be construed as inviting acceptance either by a prompt promise to ship or by the prompt or current shipment of conforming or non-conforming goods, but such a shipment of non-conforming goods does not constitute an acceptance if the seller seasonably notifies the buyer that the shipment is offered only as an accommodation of the buyer.

(2) Where the beginning of a requested performance is a reasonable mode of acceptance an offeror who is not notified of acceptance within a reasonable time may treat the offer as having lapsed before acceptance.

SECTION 2-207. ADDITIONAL TERMS IN ACCEPTANCE OR CONFIRMATION

(1) A definite and seasonable expression of acceptance or a written confirmation which is sent within a reasonable time operates as an acceptance even though it states terms additional to or different from those offered or agreed upon, unless acceptance is expressly made conditional on assent to the additional or different terms.

(2) The additional terms are to be construed as proposals for addition to the contract. Between merchants such terms become part of the contract unless:

(a) the offer expressly limits acceptance to the terms of the offer;

(b) they materially alter it; or

(c) notification of objection to them has already been given or is given within a reasonable time after notice of them is received.

(3) Conduct by both parties which recognizes the existence of a contract is sufficient to establish a contract for sale although the writings of the parties do not otherwise establish a contract. In such case the terms of the particular contract consist of those terms on which the writings of the parties agree, together with any supplementary terms incorporated under any other provisions of this Act.

SECTION 2-208. COURSE OF PERFORMANCE OR PRACTICAL CONSTRUCTION

(1) Where the contract for sale involves repeated occasions for performance by either party with knowledge of the nature of the performance and opportunity for objection to it by the other, any course of performance accepted or acquiesced in without objection shall be relevant to determine the meaning of the agreement.

(2) The express terms of the agreement and any such course of performance, as well as any course of dealing and usage of trade, shall be construed whenever reasonable as consistent with each other; but when such construction is unreasonable, express terms shall control course of performance and course of performance shall control both course of dealing and usage of trade (Section 1–205).

(3) Subject to the provisions of the next section on modification and waiver, such course of performance shall be relevant to show a waiver or modification of any term inconsistent with such course of performance.

SECTION 2-209. MODIFICATION, RESCISSION AND WAIVER

(1) An agreement modifying a contract within this Article needs no consideration to be binding.

(2) A signed agreement which excludes modification or rescission except by a signed writing cannot be otherwise modified or rescinded, but except as between merchants such a requirement on a form supplied by the merchant must be separately signed by the other party.

(3) The requirements of the statute of frauds section of this Article (Section 2–201) must be satisfied if the contract as modified is within its provisions.

(4) Although an attempt at modification or rescission does not satisfy the requirements of subsection (2) or (3) it can operate as a waiver.

(5) A party who has made a waiver affecting an executory portion of the contract may retract the waiver by reasonable notification received by the other party that strict performance will be required of any term waived, unless the retraction would be unjust in view of a material change of position in reliance on the waiver.

SECTION 2-210. DELEGATION OF PERFORMANCE; ASSIGNMENT OF RIGHTS

(1) A party may perform his duty through a delegate unless otherwise agreed or unless the other party has a substantial interest in having his original promisor perform or control the acts required by the contract. No delegation of performance relieves the party delegating of any duty to perform or any liability for breach.

(2) Unless otherwise agreed all rights of either seller or buyer can be assigned except where the assignment would materially change the duty of the other party, or increase materially the burden or risk imposed on him by his contract, or impair materially his chance of obtaining return performance. A right to damages for breach of the whole contract or a right arising out of the assignor's due performance of his entire obligation can be assigned despite agreement otherwise.

(3) Unless the circumstances indicate the contrary a prohibition of assignment of "the contract" is to be construed as barring only the delegation to the assignee of the assignor's performance.

(4) An assignment of "the contract" or of "all my rights under the contract" or an assignment in similar general terms is an assignment of rights and unless the language or the circumstances (as in an assignment for security) indicate the contrary, it is a delegation of performance of the duties of the assignor and its acceptance by the assignee constitutes a promise by him to perform those duties. This promise is enforceable by either the assignor or the other party to the original contract.

(5) The other party may treat any assignment which delegates performance as creating reasonable grounds for insecurity and may without prejudice to his rights against the assignor demand assurances from the assignee (Section 2–609).

PART 3. GENERAL OBLIGATION AND CONSTRUCTION OF CONTRACT

SECTION 2-301. GENERAL OBLIGATIONS OF PARTIES

The obligation of the seller is to transfer and deliver and that of the buyer is to accept and pay in accordance with the contract.

SECTION 2-302. UNCONSCIONABLE CONTRACT OR CLAUSE

(1) If the court as a matter of law finds the contract or any clause of the contract to have been unconscionable at the time it was made the court may refuse to enforce the contract, or it may enforce the remainder of the contract without the unconscionable clause, or it may so limit the application of any unconscionable clause as to avoid any unconscionable result.

(2) When it is claimed or appears to the court that the contract or any clause thereof may be unconscionable the parties shall be afforded a reasonable opportunity to present evidence as to its commercial setting, purpose and effect to aid the court in making the determination.

SECTION 2-303. ALLOCATION OR DIVISION OF RISKS

Where this Article allocates a risk or a burden as between the parties "unless otherwise agreed", the agreement may not only shift the allocation but may also divide the risk or burden.

SECTION 2-304. PRICE PAYABLE IN MONEY, GOODS, REALTY, OR OTHERWISE

(1) The price can be made payable in money or otherwise. If it is payable in whole or in part in goods each party is a seller of the goods which he is to transfer.

(2) Even though all or part of the price is payable in an interest in realty the transfer of the goods and the seller's obligations with reference to them are subject to this Article, but not the transfer of the interest in realty or the transferor's obligations in connection therewith.

SECTION 2-305. OPEN PRICE TERM

(1) The parties if they so intend can conclude a contract for sale even though the price is not settled. In such a case the price is a reasonable price at the time for delivery if

(a) nothing is said as to price; or

(b) the price is left to be agreed by the parties and they fail to agree; or

(c) the price is to be fixed in terms of some agreed market or other standard as set or recorded by a third person or agency and it is not so set or recorded.

(2) A price to be fixed by the seller or by the buyer means a price for him to fix in good faith.

(3) When a price left to be fixed otherwise than by agreement of the parties fails to be fixed through fault of one party the other may at his option treat the contract as cancelled or himself fix a reasonable price.

(4) Where, however, the parties intend not to be bound unless the price be fixed or agreed and it is not fixed or agreed there is no contract. In such a case the buyer must return any goods already received or if unable so to do must pay their reasonable value at the time of delivery and the seller must return any portion of the price paid on account.

SECTION 2-306.   OUTPUT, REQUIREMENTS AND EXCLUSIVE DEALINGS

(1) A term which measures the quantity by the output of the seller or the requirements of the buyer means such actual output or requirements as may occur in good faith, except that no quantity unreasonably disproportionate to any stated estimate or in the absence of a stated estimate to any normal or otherwise comparable prior output or requirements may be tendered or demanded.

(2) A lawful agreement by either the seller or the buyer for exclusive dealing in the kind of goods concerned imposes unless otherwise agreed an obligation by the seller to use best efforts to supply the goods and by the buyer to use best efforts to promote their sale.

SECTION 2-307.   DELIVERY IN SINGLE LOT OR SEVERAL LOTS

Unless otherwise agreed all goods called for by a contract for sale must be tendered in a single delivery and payment is due only on such tender but where the circumstances give either party the right to make or demand delivery in lots the price if it can be apportioned may be demanded for each lot.

SECTION 2-308.   ABSENCE OF SPECIFIED PLACE FOR DELIVERY

Unless otherwise agreed

(a) the place for delivery of goods is the seller's place of business or if he has none his residence; but

(b) in a contract for sale of identified goods which to the knowledge of the parties at the time of contracting are in some other place, that place is the place for their delivery; and

(c) documents of title may be delivered through customary banking channels.

SECTION 2-309.   ABSENCE OF SPECIFIC TIME PROVISIONS; NOTICE OF TERMINATION

(1) The time for shipment or delivery or any other action under a contract if not provided in this Article or agreed upon shall be a reasonable time.

(2) Where the contract provides for successive performances but is indefinite in duration it is valid for a reasonable time but unless otherwise agreed may be terminated at any time by either party.

(3) Termination of a contract by one party except on the happening of an agreed event requires that reasonable notification be received by the other party and an agreement dispensing with notification is invalid if its operation would be unconscionable.

SECTION 2-310.   OPEN TIME FOR PAYMENT OR RUNNING OF CREDIT; AUTHORITY TO SHIP UNDER RESERVATION

Unless otherwise agreed

(a) payment is due at the time and place at which the buyer is to receive the goods even though the place of shipment is the place of delivery; and

(b) if the seller is authorized to send the goods he may ship them under reservation, and may tender the documents of title, but the buyer may inspect the goods after their arrival before payment is due unless such inspection is inconsistent with the terms of the contract (Section 2–513); and

(c) if delivery is authorized and made by way of documents of title otherwise than by subsection (b) then payment is due at the time and place at which the buyer is to receive the documents regardless of where the goods are to be received; and

(d) where the seller is required or authorized to ship the goods on credit the credit period runs from the time of shipment but post-dating the invoice or delaying its dispatch will correspondingly delay the starting of the credit period.

SECTION 2-311. OPTIONS AND COOPERATION RESPECTING PERFORMANCE

(1) An agreement for sale which is otherwise sufficiently definite (subsection (3) of Section 2–204) to be a contract is not made invalid by the fact that it leaves particulars of performance to be specified by one of the parties. Any such specification must be made in good faith and within limits set by commercial reasonableness.

(2) Unless otherwise agreed specifications relating to assortment of the goods are at the buyer's option and except as otherwise provided in subsections (1)(c) and (3) of Section 2–319 specifications or arrangements relating to shipment are at the seller's option.

(3) Where such specification would materially affect the other party's performance but is not seasonably made or where one party's cooperation is necessary to the agreed performance of the other but is not seasonably forthcoming, the other party in addition to all other remedies

(a) is excused for any resulting delay in his own performance; and

(b) may also either proceed to perform in any reasonable manner or after the time for a material part of his own performance treat the failure to specify or to cooperate as a breach by failure to deliver or accept the goods.

SECTION 2-312. WARRANTY OF TITLE AND AGAINST INFRINGEMENT; BUYER'S OBLIGATION AGAINST INFRINGEMENT

(1) Subject to subsection (2) there is in a contract for sale a warranty by the seller that

(a) the title conveyed shall be good, and its transfer rightful; and

(b) the goods shall be delivered free from any security interest or other lien or encumbrance of which the buyer at the time of contracting has no knowledge.

(2) A warranty under subsection (1) will be excluded or modified only by specific language or by circumstances which give the buyer reason to know that the person selling does not claim title in himself or that he is purporting to sell only such right or title as he or a third person may have.

(3) Unless otherwise agreed a seller who is a merchant regularly dealing in goods of the kind warrants that the goods shall be delivered free of the rightful claim of any third person by way of infringement or the like but a buyer who furnishes specifications to the seller must hold the seller harmless against any such claim which arises out of compliance with the specifications.

SECTION 2-313. EXPRESS WARRANTIES BY AFFIRMATION, PROMISE, DESCRIPTION, SAMPLE

(1) Express warranties by the seller are created as follows:

(a) Any affirmation of fact or promise made by the seller to the buyer which relates to the goods and becomes part of the basis of the bargain creates an express warranty that the goods shall conform to the affirmation or promise.

(b) Any description of the goods which is made part of the basis of the bargain creates an express warranty that the goods shall conform to the description.

(c) Any sample or model which is made part of the basis of the bargain creates an express warranty that the whole of the goods shall conform to the sample or model.

(2) It is not necessary to the creation of an express warranty that the seller use formal words such as "warrant" or "guarantee" or that he have a specific intention to make a warranty, but an affirmation merely of the value of the goods or a statement purporting to be merely the seller's opinion or commendation of the goods does not create a warranty.

SECTION 2-314.　IMPLIED WARRANTY: MERCHANTABILITY; USAGE OF TRADE

(1) Unless excluded or modified (Section 2–316), a warranty that the goods shall be merchantable is implied in a contract for their sale if the seller is a merchant with respect to goods of that kind. Under this section the serving for value of food or drink to be consumed either on the premises or elsewhere is a sale.

(2) Goods to be merchantable must be at least such as

(a) pass without objection in the trade under the contract description; and

(b) in the case of fungible goods, are of fair average quality within the description; and

(c) are fit for the ordinary purposes for which such goods are used; and

(d) run, within the variations permitted by the agreement, of even kind, quality and quantity within each unit and among all units involved; and

(e) are adequately contained, packaged, and labeled as the agreement may require; and

(f) conform to the promises or affirmations of fact made on the container or label if any.

(3) Unless excluded or modified (Section 2–316) other implied warranties may arise from course of dealing or usage of trade.

SECTION 2-315.　IMPLIED WARRANTY: FITNESS FOR PARTICULAR PURPOSE

Where the seller at the time of contracting has reason to know any particular purpose for which the goods are required and that the buyer is relying on the seller's skill or judgment to select or furnish suitable goods, there is unless excluded or modified under the next section an implied warranty that the goods shall be fit for such purpose.

SECTION 2-316.　EXCLUSION OR MODIFICATION OF WARRANTIES

(1) Words or conduct relevant to the creation of an express warranty and words or conduct tending to negate or limit warranty shall be construed wherever reasonable as consistent with each other; but subject to the provisions of this Article on parol or extrinsic evidence (Section 2–202) negation or limitation is inoperative to the extent that such construction is unreasonable.

(2) Subject to subsection (3), to exclude or modify the implied warranty of merchantability or any part of it the language must mention merchantability and in case of a writing must be conspicuous, and to exclude or modify any implied warranty of fitness the exclusion must be by a writing and conspicuous. Language to exclude all implied warranties of fitness is sufficient if it states, for example, that "There are no warranties which extend beyond the description on the face hereof."

(3) Notwithstanding subsection (2)

(a) unless the circumstances indicate otherwise, all implied warranties are excluded by expressions like "as is", "with all faults" or other language which in common understanding calls the buyer's attention to the exclusion of warranties and makes plain that there is no implied warranty; and

(b) when the buyer before entering into the contract has examined the goods or the sample or model as fully as he desired or has refused to examine the goods there is no implied warranty with regard to defects which an examination ought in the circumstances to have revealed to him; and

(c) an implied warranty can also be excluded or modified by course of dealing or course of performance or usage of trade.

(4) Remedies for breach of warranty can be limited in accordance with the provisions of this Article on liquidation or limitation of damages and on contractual modification of remedy (Section 2–718 and 2–719).

SECTION 2-317.   CUMULATION AND CONFLICT OF WARRANTIES EXPRESS OR IMPLIED

Warranties whether express or implied shall be construed as consistent with each other and as cumulative, but if such construction is unreasonable the intention of the parties shall determine which warranty is dominant. In ascertaining that intention the following rules apply:

(a) Exact or technical specifications displace an inconsistent sample or model or general language of description.

(b) A sample from an existing bulk displaces inconsistent general language of description.

(c) Express warranties displace inconsistent implied warranties other than an implied warranty of fitness for a particular purpose.

SECTION 2-318.   THIRD PARTY BENEFICIARIES OF WARRANTIES EXPRESS OR IMPLIED

Note:

If this Act is introduced in the Congress of the United States this section should be omitted. (States to select one alternative.)

Alternative A

A seller's warranty whether express or implied extends to any natural person who is in the family or household of his buyer or who is a guest in his home if it is reasonable to expect that such person may use, consume or be affected by the goods and who is injured in person by breach of the warranty. A seller may not exclude or limit the operation of this section.

Alternative B

A seller's warranty whether express or implied extends to any natural person who may reasonably be expected to use, consume or be affected by the goods and who is injured in person by breach of the warranty. A seller may not exclude or limit the operation of this section.

Alternative C

A seller's warranty whether express or implied extends to any person who may reasonably be expected to use, consume or be affected by the goods and who is injured by breach of the warranty. A seller may not exclude or limit the operation of this section with respect to injury to the person of an individual to whom the warranty extends.

As amended in 1966.

SECTION 2-319.   F.O.B. AND F.A.S. TERMS

(1) Unless otherwise agreed the term F.O.B. (which means "free on board") at a named place, even though used only in connection with the stated price, is a delivery term under which

(a) when the term is F.O.B. the place of shipment, the seller must at that place ship the goods in the manner provided in this Article (Section 2–504) and bear the expense and risk of putting them into the possession of the carrier; or

(b) when the term is F.O.B. the place of destination, the seller must at his own expense and risk transport the goods to that place and there tender delivery of them in the manner provided in this Article (Section 2–503);

(c) when under either (a) or (b) the term is also F.O.B. vessel, car or other vehicle, the seller must in addition at his own expense and risk load the goods on board. If the term is F.O.B. vessel the buyer must name the vessel and in an appropriate case the seller must comply with the provisions of this Article on the form of bill of lading (Section 2–323).

(2) Unless otherwise agreed the term F.A.S. vessel (which means "free alongside") at a named port, even though used only in connection with the stated price, is a delivery term under which the seller must

(a) at his own expense and risk deliver the goods alongside the vessel in the manner usual in that port or on a dock designated and provided by the buyer; and

(b) obtain and tender a receipt for the goods in exchange for which the carrier is under a duty to issue a bill of lading.

(3) Unless otherwise agreed in any case falling within subsection (1)(a) or (c) or subsection (2) the buyer must seasonably give any needed instructions for making delivery, including when the term is F.A.S. or F.O.B. the loading berth of the vessel and in an appropriate case its name and sailing date. The seller may treat the failure of needed instructions as a failure of cooperation under this Article (Section 2–311). He may also at his option move the goods in any reasonable manner preparatory to delivery or shipment.

(4) Under the term F.O.B. vessel or F.A.S. unless otherwise agreed the buyer must make payment against tender of the required documents and the seller may not tender nor the buyer demand delivery of the goods in substitution for the documents.

SECTION 2-320.   C.I.F. AND C. & F. TERMS

(1) The term C.I.F. means that the price includes in a lump sum the cost of the goods and the insurance and freight to the named destination. The term C. & F. or C.F. means that the price so includes cost and freight to the named destination.

(2) Unless otherwise agreed and even though used only in connection with the stated price and destination, the term C.I.F. destination or its equivalent requires the seller at his own

expense and risk to

    (a) put the goods into the possession of a carrier at the port for shipment and obtain a negotiable bill or bills of lading covering the entire transportation to the named destination; and

    (b) load the goods and obtain a receipt from the carrier (which may be contained in the bill of lading) showing that the freight has been paid or provided for; and

    (c) obtain a policy or certificate of insurance, including any war risk insurance, of a kind and on terms then current at the port of shipment in the usual amount, in the currency of the contract, shown to cover the same goods covered by the bill of lading and providing for payment of loss to the order of the buyer or for the account of whom it may concern; but the seller may add to the price the amount of the premium for any such war risk insurance; and

    (d) prepare an invoice of the goods and procure any other documents required to effect shipment or to comply with the contract; and

    (e) forward and tender with commercial promptness all the documents in due form and with any indorsement necessary to perfect the buyer's rights.

(3) Unless otherwise agreed the term C. & F. or its equivalent has the same effect and imposes upon the seller the same obligations and risks as a C.I.F. term except the obligation as to insurance.

(4) Under the term C.I.F. or C. & F. unless otherwise agreed the buyer must make payment against tender of the required documents and the seller may not tender nor the buyer demand delivery of the goods in substitution for the documents.

SECTION 2-321.   C.I.F. OR C. & F.: "NET LANDED WEIGHTS"; "PAYMENT ON ARRIVAL"; WARRANTY OF CONDITION ON ARRIVAL

Under a contract containing a term C.I.F. or C. & F.

    (1) Where the price is based on or is to be adjusted according to "net landed weights", "delivered weights", "out turn" quantity or quality or the like, unless otherwise agreed the seller must reasonably estimate the price. The payment due on tender of the documents called for by the contract is the amount so estimated, but after final adjustment of the price a settlement must be made with commercial promptness.

    (2) An agreement described in subsection (1) or any warranty of quality or condition of the goods on arrival places upon the seller the risk of ordinary deterioration, shrinkage and the like in transportation but has no effect on the place or time of identification to the contract for sale or delivery or on the passing of the risk of loss.

    (3) Unless otherwise agreed where the contract provides for payment on or after arrival of the goods the seller must before payment allow such preliminary inspection as is feasible; but if the goods are lost delivery of the documents and payment are due when the goods should have arrived.

SECTION 2-322.   DELIVERY "EX-SHIP"

(1) Unless otherwise agreed a term for delivery of goods "ex-ship" (which means from the carrying vessel) or in equivalent language is not restricted to a particular ship and requires delivery from a ship which has reached a place at the named port of destination where goods of the kind are usually discharged.

(2) Under such a term unless otherwise agreed

(a) the seller must discharge all liens arising out of the carriage and furnish the buyer with a direction which puts the carrier under a duty to deliver the goods; and

(b) the risk of loss does not pass to the buyer until the goods leave the ship's tackle or are otherwise properly unloaded.

SECTION 2-323. FORM OF BILL OF LADING REQUIRED IN OVERSEAS SHIPMENT; "OVERSEAS"

(1) Where the contract contemplates overseas shipment and contains a term C.I.F. or C. & F. or F.O.B. vessel, the seller unless otherwise agreed must obtain a negotiable bill of lading stating that the goods have been loaded on board or, in the case of a term C.I.F. or C. & F., received for shipment.

(2) Where in a case within subsection (1) a bill of lading has been issued in a set of parts, unless otherwise agreed if the documents are not to be sent from abroad the buyer may demand tender of the full set; otherwise only one part of the bill of lading need be tendered. Even if the agreement expressly requires a full set

(a) due tender of a single part is acceptable within the provisions of this Article on cure of improper delivery (subsection (1) of Section 2-508); and

(b) even though the full set is demanded, if the documents are sent from abroad the person tendering an incomplete set may nevertheless require payment upon furnishing an indemnity which the buyer in good faith deems adequate.

(3) A shipment by water or by air or a contract contemplating such shipment is "overseas" insofar as by usage of trade or agreement it is subject to the commercial, financing or shipping practices characteristic of international deep water commerce.

SECTION 2-324. "NO ARRIVAL, NO SALE" TERM

Under a term "no arrival, no sale" or terms of like meaning, unless otherwise agreed,

(a) the seller must properly ship conforming goods and if they arrive by any means he must tender them on arrival but he assumes no obligation that the goods will arrive unless he has caused the non-arrival; and

(b) where without fault of the seller the goods are in part lost or have so deteriorated as no longer to conform to the contract or arrive after the contract time, the buyer may proceed as if there had been casualty to identified goods (Section 2–613).

SECTION 2-325. "LETTER OF CREDIT" TERM; "CONFIRMED CREDIT"

(1) Failure of the buyer seasonably to furnish an agreed letter of credit is a breach of the contract for sale.

(2) The delivery to seller of a proper letter of credit suspends the buyer's obligation to pay. If the letter of credit is dishonored, the seller may on seasonable notification to the buyer require payment directly from him.

(3) Unless otherwise agreed the term "letter of credit" or "banker's credit" in a contract for sale means an irrevocable credit issued by a financing agency of good repute and, where the shipment is overseas, of good international repute. The term "confirmed credit" means that the

credit must also carry the direct obligation of such an agency which does business in the seller's financial market.

SECTION 2-326. SALE ON APPROVAL AND SALE OR RETURN; CONSIGNMENT SALES AND RIGHTS OF CREDITORS

(1) Unless otherwise agreed, if delivered goods may be returned by the buyer even though they conform to the contract, the transaction is

(a) a "sale on approval" if the goods are delivered primarily for use, and

(b) a "sale or return" if the goods are delivered primarily for resale.

(2) Except as provided in subsection (3), goods held on approval are not subject to the claims of the buyer's creditors until acceptance; goods held on sale or return are subject to such claims while in the buyer's possession.

(3) Where goods are delivered to a person for sale and such person maintains a place of business at which he deals in goods of the kind involved, under a name other than the name of the person making delivery, then with respect to claims of creditors of the person conducting the business the goods are deemed to be on sale or return. The provisions of this subsection are applicable even though an agreement purports to reserve title to the person making delivery until payment or resale or uses such words as "on consignment" or "on memorandum." However, this subsection is not applicable if the person making delivery

(a) complies with an applicable law providing for a consignor's interest or the like to be evidenced by a sign, or

(b) establishes that the person conducting the business is generally known by his creditors to be substantially engaged in selling the goods of others, or

(c) complies with the filing provisions of the Article on Secured Transactions (Article 9).

(4) Any "or return" term of a contract for sale is to be treated as a separate contract for sale within the statute of frauds section of this Article (Section 2–201) and as contradicting the sale aspect of the contract within the provisions of this Article on parol or extrinsic evidence (Section 2–202).

SECTION 2-327. SPECIAL INCIDENTS OF SALE ON APPROVAL AND SALE OR RETURN

(1) Under a sale on approval unless otherwise agreed

(a) although the goods are identified to the contract the risk of loss and the title do not pass to the buyer until acceptance; and

(b) use of the goods consistent with the purpose of trial is not acceptance but failure seasonably to notify the seller of election to return the goods is acceptance, and if the goods conform to the contract acceptance of any part is acceptance of the whole; and

(c) after due notification of election to return, the return is at the seller's risk and expense but a merchant buyer must follow any reasonable instructions.

(2) Under a sale or return unless otherwise agreed

(a) the option to return extends to the whole or any commercial unit of the goods while in substantially their original condition, but must be exercised seasonably; and

(b) the return is at the buyer's risk and expense.

SECTION 2-328. SALE BY AUCTION

(1) In a sale by auction if goods are put up in lots each lot is the subject of a separate sale.

(2) A sale by auction is complete when the auctioneer so announces by the fall of the hammer or in other customary manner. Where a bid is made while the hammer is falling in acceptance of a prior bid the auctioneer may in his discretion reopen the bidding or declare the goods sold under the bid on which the hammer was falling.

(3) Such a sale is with reserve unless the goods are in explicit terms put up without reserve. In an auction with reserve the auctioneer may withdraw the goods at any time until he announces completion of the sale. In an auction without reserve, after the auctioneer calls for bids on an article or lot, that article or lot cannot be withdrawn unless no bid is made within a reasonable time. In either case a bidder may retract his bid until the auctioneer's announcement of completion of the sale, but a bidder's retraction does not revive any previous bid.

(4) If the auctioneer knowingly receives a bid on the seller's behalf or the seller makes or procures such a bid, and notice has not been given that liberty for such bidding is reserved, the buyer may at his option avoid the sale or take the goods at the price of the last good faith bid prior to the completion of the sale. This subsection shall not apply to any bid at a forced sale.

PART 4. TITLE, CREDITORS AND GOOD FAITH PURCHASERS

SECTION 2-401. PASSING OF TITLE; RESERVATION FOR SECURITY; LIMITED APPLICATION OF THIS SECTION

Each provision of this Article with regard to the rights, obligations and remedies of the seller, the buyer, purchasers or other third parties applies irrespective of title to the goods except where the provision refers to such title. Insofar as situations are not covered by the other provisions of this Article and matters concerning title become material the following rules apply:

(1) Title to goods cannot pass under a contract for sale prior to their identification to the contract (Section 2–501), and unless otherwise explicitly agreed the buyer acquires by their identification a special property as limited by this Act. Any retention or reservation by the seller of the title (property) in goods shipped or delivered to the buyer is limited in effect to a reservation of a security interest. Subject to these provisions and to the provisions of the Article on Secured Transactions (Article 9), title to goods passes from the seller to the buyer in any manner and on any conditions explicitly agreed on by the parties.

(2) Unless otherwise explicitly agreed title passes to the buyer at the time and place at which the seller completes his performance with reference to the physical delivery of the goods, despite any reservation of a security interest and even though a document of title is to be delivered at a different time or place; and in particular and despite any reservation of a security interest by the bill of lading

(a) if the contract requires or authorizes the seller to send the goods to the buyer but does not require him to deliver them at destination, title passes to the buyer at the time and place of shipment; but

(b) if the contract requires delivery at destination, title passes on tender there.

(3) Unless otherwise explicitly agreed where delivery is to be made without moving the goods,

(a) if the seller is to deliver a document of title, title passes at the time when and the place where he delivers such documents; or

(b) if the goods are at the time of contracting already identified and no documents are to be delivered, title passes at the time and place of contracting.

(4) A rejection or other refusal by the buyer to receive or retain the goods, whether or not justified, or a justified revocation of acceptance revests title to the goods in the seller. Such revesting occurs by operation of law and is not a "sale".

SECTION 2-402. RIGHTS OF SELLER'S CREDITORS AGAINST SOLD GOODS

(1) Except as provided in subsections (2) and (3), rights of unsecured creditors of the seller with respect to goods which have been identified to a contract for sale are subject to the buyer's rights to recover the goods under this Article (Sections 2–502 and 2–716).

(2) A creditor of the seller may treat a sale or an identification of goods to a contract for sale as void if as against him a retention of possession by the seller is fraudulent under any rule of law of the state where the goods are situated, except that retention of possession in good faith and current course of trade by a merchant-seller for a commercially reasonable time after a sale or identification is not fraudulent.

(3) Nothing in this Article shall be deemed to impair the rights of creditors of the seller

(a) under the provisions of the Article on Secured Transactions (Article 9); or

(b) where identification to the contract or delivery is made not in current course of trade but in satisfaction of or as security for a pre-existing claim for money, security or the like and is made under circumstances which under any rule of law of the state where the goods are situated would apart from this Article constitute the transaction a fraudulent transfer or voidable preference.

SECTION 2-403. POWER TO TRANSFER; GOOD FAITH PURCHASE OF GOODS; "ENTRUSTING"

(1) A purchaser of goods acquires all title which his transferor had or had power to transfer except that a purchaser of a limited interest acquires rights only to the extent of the interest purchased. A person with voidable title has power to transfer a good title to a good faith purchaser for value. When goods have been delivered under a transaction of purchase the purchaser has such power even though

(a) the transferor was deceived as to the identity of the purchaser, or

(b) the delivery was in exchange for a check which is later dishonored, or

(c) it was agreed that the transaction was to be a "cash sale", or

(d) the delivery was procured through fraud punishable as larcenous under the criminal law.

(2) Any entrusting of possession of goods to a merchant who deals in goods of that kind gives him power to transfer all rights of the entruster to a buyer in ordinary course of business.

(3) "Entrusting" includes any delivery and any acquiescence in retention of possession

regardless of any condition expressed between the parties to the delivery or acquiescence and regardless of whether the procurement of the entrusting or the possessor's disposition of the goods have been such as to be larcenous under the criminal law.

1988 Conforming Amendments for States Enacting Repealer
of Article 6 — Bulk Transfers
(Alternative A)

(4) The rights of other purchasers of goods and of lien creditors are governed by the Articles on Secured Transactions (Article 9) and Documents of Title (Article 7).

1988 Conforming Amendments for States Enacting Revised Article 6 — Bulk Sales
(Alternative B)

(4) The rights of other purchasers of goods and of lien creditors are governed by the Articles on Secured Transactions (Article 9), Bulk Sales (Article 6) and Documents of Title (Article 7).

As amended in 1988.

PART 5. PERFORMANCE

SECTION 2-501. INSURABLE INTEREST IN GOODS; MANNER OF IDENTIFICATION OF GOODS

(1) The buyer obtains a special property and an insurable interest in goods by identification of existing goods as goods to which the contract refers even though the goods so identified are non-conforming and he has an option to return or reject them. Such identification can be made at any time and in any manner explicitly agreed to by the parties. In the absence of explicit agreement identification occurs

(a) when the contract is made if it is for the sale of goods already existing and identified;

(b) if the contract is for the sale of future goods other than those described in paragraph (c), when goods are shipped, marked or otherwise designated by the seller as goods to which the contract refers;

(c) when the crops are planted or otherwise become growing crops or the young are conceived if the contract is for the sale of unborn young to be born within twelve months after contracting or for the sale of crops to be harvested within twelve months or the next normal harvest season after contracting whichever is longer.

(2) The seller retains an insurable interest in goods so long as title to or any security interest in the goods remains in him and where the identification is by the seller alone he may until default or insolvency or notification to the buyer that the identification is final substitute other goods for those identified.

(3) Nothing in this section impairs any insurable interest recognized under any other statute or rule of law.

SECTION 2-502. BUYER'S RIGHT TO GOODS ON SELLER'S INSOLVENCY

(1) Subject to subsection (2) and even though the goods have not been shipped a buyer who has paid a part or all of the price of goods in which he has a special property under the provisions of the immediately preceding section may on making and keeping good a tender of any unpaid portion of their price recover them from the seller if the seller becomes insolvent

within ten days after receipt of the first installment on their price.

(2) If the identification creating his special property has been made by the buyer he acquires the right to recover the goods only if they conform to the contract for sale.

SECTION 2-503.   MANNER OF SELLER'S TENDER OF DELIVERY

(1) Tender of delivery requires that the seller put and hold conforming goods at the buyer's disposition and give the buyer any notification reasonably necessary to enable him to take delivery. The manner, time and place for tender are determined by the agreement and this Article, and in particular

(a) tender must be at a reasonable hour, and if it is of goods they must be kept available for the period reasonably necessary to enable the buyer to take possession; but

(b) unless otherwise agreed the buyer must furnish facilities reasonably suited to the receipt of the goods.

(2) Where the case is within the next section respecting shipment tender requires that the seller comply with its provisions.

(3) Where the seller is required to deliver at a particular destination tender requires that he comply with subsection (1) and also in any appropriate case tender documents as described in subsections (4) and (5) of this section.

(4) Where goods are in the possession of a bailee and are to be delivered without being moved

(a) tender requires that the seller either tender a negotiable document of title covering such goods or procure acknowledgment by the bailee of the buyer's right to possession of the goods; but

(b) tender to the buyer of a non-negotiable document of title or of a written direction to the bailee to deliver is sufficient tender unless the buyer seasonably objects, and receipt by the bailee of notification of the buyer's rights fixes those rights as against the bailee and all third persons; but risk of loss of the goods and of any failure by the bailee to honor the non-negotiable document of title or to obey the direction remains on the seller until the buyer has had a reasonable time to present the document or direction, and a refusal by the bailee to honor the document or to obey the direction defeats the tender.

(5) Where the contract requires the seller to deliver documents

(a) he must tender all such documents in correct form, except as provided in this Article with respect to bills of lading in a set (subsection (2) of Section 2–323); and

(b) tender through customary banking channels is sufficient and dishonor of a draft accompanying the documents constitutes non-acceptance or rejection.

SECTION 2-504.   SHIPMENT BY SELLER

Where the seller is required or authorized to send the goods to the buyer and the contract does not require him to deliver them at a particular destination, then unless otherwise agreed he must

(a) put the goods in the possession of such a carrier and make such a contract for their transportation as may be reasonable having regard to the nature of the goods and other circumstances of the case; and

(b) obtain and promptly deliver or tender in due form any document necessary to enable the buyer to obtain possession of the goods or otherwise required by the agreement or by usage of trade; and

(c) promptly notify the buyer of the shipment.

Failure to notify the buyer under paragraph (c) or to make a proper contract under paragraph (a) is a ground for rejection only if material delay or loss ensues.

SECTION 2-505. SELLER'S SHIPMENT UNDER RESERVATION

(1) Where the seller has identified goods to the contract by or before shipment:

(a) his procurement of a negotiable bill of lading to his own order or otherwise reserves in him a security interest in the goods. His procurement of the bill to the order of a financing agency or of the buyer indicates in addition only the seller's expectation of transferring that interest to the person named.

(b) a non-negotiable bill of lading to himself or his nominee reserves possession of the goods as security but except in a case of conditional delivery (subsection (2) of Section 2–507) a non-negotiable bill of lading naming the buyer as consignee reserves no security interest even though the seller retains possession of the bill of lading.

(2) When shipment by the seller with reservation of a security interest is in violation of the contract for sale it constitutes an improper contract for transportation within the preceding section but impairs neither the rights given to the buyer by shipment and identification of the goods to the contract nor the seller's powers as a holder of a negotiable document.

SECTION 2-506. RIGHTS OF FINANCING AGENCY

(1) A financing agency by paying or purchasing for value a draft which relates to a shipment of goods acquires to the extent of the payment or purchase and in addition to its own rights under the draft and any document of title securing it any rights of the shipper in the goods including the right to stop delivery and the shipper's right to have the draft honored by the buyer.

(2) The right to reimbursement of a financing agency which has in good faith honored or purchased the draft under commitment to or authority from the buyer is not impaired by subsequent discovery of defects with reference to any relevant document which was apparently regular on its face.

SECTION 2-507. EFFECT OF SELLER'S TENDER; DELIVERY ON CONDITION

(1) Tender of delivery is a condition to the buyer's duty to accept the goods and, unless otherwise agreed, to his duty to pay for them. Tender entitles the seller to acceptance of the goods and to payment according to the contract.

(2) Where payment is due and demanded on the delivery to the buyer of goods or documents of title, his right as against the seller to retain or dispose of them is conditional upon his making the payment due.

SECTION 2-508. CURE BY SELLER OF IMPROPER TENDER OR DELIVERY; REPLACEMENT

(1) Where any tender or delivery by the seller is rejected because non-conforming and the time for performance has not yet expired, the seller may seasonably notify the buyer of his intention to cure and may then within the contract time make a conforming delivery.

(2) Where the buyer rejects a non-conforming tender which the seller had reasonable grounds to believe would be acceptable with or without money allowance the seller may if he seasonably notifies the buyer have a further reasonable time to substitute a conforming tender.

SECTION 2-509. RISK OF LOSS IN THE ABSENCE OF BREACH

(1) Where the contract requires or authorizes the seller to ship the goods by carrier

(a) if it does not require him to deliver them at a particular destination, the risk of loss passes to the buyer when the goods are duly delivered to the carrier even though the shipment is under reservation (Section 2–505); but

(b) if it does require him to deliver them at a particular destination and the goods are there duly tendered while in the possession of the carrier, the risk of loss passes to the buyer when the goods are there duly so tendered as to enable the buyer to take delivery.

(2) Where the goods are held by a bailee to be delivered without being moved, the risk of loss passes to the buyer

(a) on his receipt of a negotiable document to title covering the goods; or

(b) on acknowledgment by the bailee of the buyer's right to possession of the goods; or

(c) after his receipt of a non-negotiable document of title or other written direction to deliver, as provided in subsection (4)(b) of Section 2–503.

(3) In any case not within subsection (1) or (2), the risk of loss passes to the buyer on his receipt of the goods if the seller is a merchant; otherwise the risk passes to the buyer on tender of delivery.

(4) The provisions of this section are subject to contrary agreement of the parties and to the provisions of this Article on sale on approval (Section 2–327) and on effect of breach on risk of loss (Section 2–510).

SECTION 2-510. EFFECT OF BREACH ON RISK OF LOSS

(1) Where a tender or delivery of goods so fails to conform to the contract as to give a right of rejection the risk of their loss remains on the seller until cure or acceptance.

(2) Where the buyer rightfully revokes acceptance he may to the extent of any deficiency in his effective insurance coverage treat the risk of loss as having rested on the seller from the beginning.

(3) Where the buyer as to conforming goods already identified to the contract for sale repudiates or is otherwise in breach before risk of their loss has passed to him, the seller may to the extent of any deficiency in his effective insurance coverage treat the risk of loss as resting on the buyer for a commercially reasonable time.

SECTION 2-511. TENDER OF PAYMENT BY BUYER; PAYMENT BY CHECK

(1) Unless otherwise agreed tender of payment is a condition to the seller's duty to tender and complete any delivery.

(2) Tender of payment is sufficient when made by any means or in any manner current in the ordinary course of business unless the seller demands payment in legal tender and gives any extension of time reasonably necessary to procure it.

(3) Subject to the provisions of this Act on the effect of an instrument on an obligation

(Section 3–310), payment by check is conditional and is defeated as between the parties by dishonor of the check on due presentment.

As amended in 1994.

SECTION 2-512.   PAYMENT BY BUYER BEFORE INSPECTION

(1) Where the contract requires payment before inspection non-conformity of the goods does not excuse the buyer from so making payment unless

(a) the non-conformity appears without inspection; or

(b) despite tender of the required documents the circumstances would justify injunction against honor under this Act (Section 5–109(b)).

(2) Payment pursuant to subsection (1) does not constitute an acceptance of goods or impair the buyer's right to inspect or any of his remedies.

As amended in 1995.

SECTION 2-513.   BUYER'S RIGHT TO INSPECTION OF GOODS

(1) Unless otherwise agreed and subject to subsection (3), where goods are tendered or delivered or identified to the contract for sale, the buyer has a right before payment or acceptance to inspect them at any reasonable place and time and in any reasonable manner. When the seller is required or authorized to send the goods to the buyer, the inspection may be after their arrival.

(2) Expenses of inspection must be borne by the buyer but may be recovered from the seller if the goods do not conform and are rejected.

(3) Unless otherwise agreed and subject to the provisions of this Article on C.I.F. contracts (subsection (3) of Section 2–321), the buyer is not entitled to inspect the goods before payment of the price when the contract provides

(a) for delivery "C.O.D." or on other like terms; or

(b) for payment against documents of title, except where such payment is due only after the goods are to become available for inspection.

(4) A place or method of inspection fixed by the parties is presumed to be exclusive but unless otherwise expressly agreed it does not postpone identification or shift the place for delivery or for passing the risk of loss. If compliance becomes impossible, inspection shall be as provided in this section unless the place or method fixed was clearly intended as an indispensable condition failure of which avoids the contract.

SECTION 2-514.   WHEN DOCUMENTS DELIVERABLE ON ACCEPTANCE; WHEN ON PAYMENT

Unless otherwise agreed documents against which a draft is drawn are to be delivered to the drawee on acceptance of the draft if it is payable more than three days after presentment; otherwise, only on payment.

SECTION 2-515.   PRESERVING EVIDENCE OF GOODS IN DISPUTE

In furtherance of the adjustment of any claim or dispute

(a) either party on reasonable notification to the other and for the purpose of ascertaining the facts and preserving evidence has the right to inspect, test and sample the goods including such of them as may be in the possession or control of the other; and

(b) the parties may agree to a third party inspection or survey to determine the conformity or condition of the goods and may agree that the findings shall be binding upon them in any subsequent litigation or adjustment.

PART 6. BREACH, REPUDIATION AND EXCUSE
SECTION 2-601. BUYER'S RIGHTS ON IMPROPER DELIVERY

Subject to the provisions of this Article on breach in installment contracts (Section 2–612) and unless otherwise agreed under the sections on contractual limitations of remedy (Sections 2–718 and 2–719), if the goods or the tender of delivery fail in any respect to conform to the contract, the buyer may

(a) reject the whole; or

(b) accept the whole; or

(c) accept any commercial unit or units and reject the rest.

SECTION 2-602. MANNER AND EFFECT OF RIGHTFUL REJECTION

(1) Rejection of goods must be within a reasonable time after their delivery or tender. It is ineffective unless the buyer seasonably notifies the seller.

(2) Subject to the provisions of the two following sections on rejected goods (Sections 2–603 and 2–604),

(a) after rejection any exercise of ownership by the buyer with respect to any commercial unit is wrongful as against the seller; and

(b) if the buyer has before rejection taken physical possession of goods in which he does not have a security interest under the provisions of this Article (subsection (3) of Section 2–711), he is under a duty after rejection to hold them with reasonable care at the seller's disposition for a time sufficient to permit the seller to remove them; but

(c) the buyer has no further obligations with regard to goods rightfully rejected.

(3) The seller's rights with respect to goods wrongfully rejected are governed by the provisions of this Article on Seller's remedies in general (Section 2–703).

SECTION 2-603. MERCHANT BUYER'S DUTIES AS TO RIGHTFULLY REJECTED GOODS

(1) Subject to any security interest in the buyer (subsection (3) of Section 2–711), when the seller has no agent or place of business at the market of rejection a merchant buyer is under a duty after rejection of goods in his possession or control to follow any reasonable instructions received from the seller with respect to the goods and in the absence of such instructions to make reasonable efforts to sell them for the seller's account if they are perishable or threaten to decline in value speedily. Instructions are not reasonable if on demand indemnity for expenses is not forthcoming.

(2) When the buyer sells goods under subsection (1), he is entitled to reimbursement from the seller or out of the proceeds for reasonable expenses of caring for and selling them, and if the expenses include no selling commission then to such commission as is usual in the trade or if there is none to a reasonable sum not exceeding ten per cent on the gross proceeds.

(3) In complying with this section the buyer is held only to good faith and good faith conduct hereunder is neither acceptance nor conversion nor the basis of an action for damages.

SECTION 2-604. BUYER'S OPTIONS AS TO SALVAGE OF RIGHTFULLY REJECTED GOODS

Subject to the provisions of the immediately preceding section on perishables if the seller gives no instructions within a reasonable time after notification of rejection the buyer may store the rejected goods for the seller's account or reship them to him or resell them for the seller's account with reimbursement as provided in the preceding section. Such action is not acceptance or conversion.

SECTION 2-605. WAIVER OF BUYER'S OBJECTIONS BY FAILURE TO PARTICULARIZE

(1) The buyer's failure to state in connection with rejection a particular defect which is ascertainable by reasonable inspection precludes him from relying on the unstated defect to justify rejection or to establish breach

(a) where the seller could have cured it if stated seasonably; or

(b) between merchants when the seller has after rejection made a request in writing for a full and final written statement of all defects on which the buyer proposes to rely.

(2) Payment against documents made without reservation of rights precludes recovery of the payment for defects apparent on the face of the documents.

SECTION 2-606. WHAT CONSTITUTES ACCEPTANCE OF GOODS

(1) Acceptance of goods occurs when the buyer

(a) after a reasonable opportunity to inspect the goods signifies to the seller that the goods are conforming or that he will take or retain them in spite of their non-conformity; or

(b) fails to make an effective rejection (subsection (1) of Section 2–602), but such acceptance does not occur until the buyer has had a reasonable opportunity to inspect them; or

(c) does any act inconsistent with the seller's ownership; but if such act is wrongful as against the seller it is an acceptance only if ratified by him.

(2) Acceptance of a part of any commercial unit is acceptance of that entire unit.

SECTION 2-607. EFFECT OF ACCEPTANCE; NOTICE OF BREACH; BURDEN OF ESTABLISHING BREACH AFTER ACCEPTANCE; NOTICE OF CLAIM OR LITIGATION TO PERSON ANSWERABLE OVER

(1) The buyer must pay at the contract rate for any goods accepted.

(2) Acceptance of goods by the buyer precludes rejection of the goods accepted and if made with knowledge of a non-conformity cannot be revoked because of it unless the acceptance was on the reasonable assumption that the non-conformity would be seasonably cured but acceptance does not of itself impair any other remedy provided by this Article for non-conformity.

(3) Where a tender has been accepted

(a) the buyer must within a reasonable time after he discovers or should have discovered any breach notify the seller of breach or be barred from any remedy; and

(b) if the claim is one for infringement or the like (subsection (3) of Section 2-312) and the buyer is sued as a result of such a breach he must so notify the seller within a reasonable time after he receives notice of the litigation or be barred from any remedy over for liability established by the litigation.

(4) The burden is on the buyer to establish any breach with respect to the goods accepted.

(5) Where the buyer is sued for breach of a warranty or other obligation for which his seller is answerable over

(a) he may give his seller written notice of the litigation. If the notice states that the seller may come in and defend and that if the seller does not do so he will be bound in any action against him by his buyer by any determination of fact common to the two litigations, then unless the seller after seasonable receipt of the notice does come in and defend he is so bound.

(b) if the claim is one for infringement or the like (subsection (3) of Section 2-312) the original seller may demand in writing that his buyer turn over to him control of the litigation including settlement or else be barred from any remedy over and if he also agrees to bear all expense and to satisfy any adverse judgment, then unless the buyer after seasonable receipt of the demand does turn over control the buyer is so barred.

(6) The provisions of subsections (3), (4) and (5) apply to any obligation of a buyer to hold the seller harmless against infringement or the like (subsection (3) of Section 2-312).

SECTION 2-608. REVOCATION OF ACCEPTANCE IN WHOLE OR IN PART

(1) The buyer may revoke his acceptance of a lot or commercial unit whose non-conformity substantially impairs its value to him if he has accepted it

(a) on the reasonable assumption that its non-conformity would be cured and it has not been seasonably cured; or

(b) without discovery of such non-conformity if his acceptance was reasonably induced either by the difficulty of discovery before acceptance or by the seller's assurances.

(2) Revocation of acceptance must occur within a reasonable time after the buyer discovers or should have discovered the ground for it and before any substantial change in condition of the goods which is not caused by their own defects. It is not effective until the buyer notifies the seller of it.

(3) A buyer who so revokes has the same rights and duties with regard to the goods involved as if he had rejected them.

SECTION 2-609. RIGHT TO ADEQUATE ASSURANCE OF PERFORMANCE

(1) A contract for sale imposes an obligation on each party that the other's expectation of receiving due performance will not be impaired. When reasonable grounds for insecurity arise with respect to the performance of either party the other may in writing demand adequate assurance of due performance and until he receives such assurance may if commercially reasonable suspend any performance for which he has not already received the agreed return.

(2) Between merchants the reasonableness of grounds for insecurity and the adequacy of any assurance offered shall be determined according to commercial standards.

(3) Acceptance of any improper delivery or payment does not prejudice the aggrieved party's right to demand adequate assurance of future performance.

(4) After receipt of a justified demand failure to provide within a reasonable time not exceeding thirty days such assurance of due performance as is adequate under the circumstances of the particular case is a repudiation of the contract.

SECTION 2-610. ANTICIPATORY REPUDIATION

When either party repudiates the contract with respect to a performance not yet due the loss of which will substantially impair the value of the contract to the other, the aggrieved party may

(a) for a commercially reasonable time await performance by the repudiating party; or

(b) resort to any remedy for breach (Section 2–703 or Section 2–711), even though he has notified the repudiating party that he would await the latter's performance and has urged retraction; and

(c) in either case suspend his own performance or proceed in accordance with the provisions of this Article on the seller's right to identify goods to the contract notwithstanding breach or to salvage unfinished goods (Section 2–704).

SECTION 2-611. RETRACTION OF ANTICIPATORY REPUDIATION

(1) Until the repudiating party's next performance is due he can retract his repudiation unless the aggrieved party has since the repudiation cancelled or materially changed his position or otherwise indicated that he considers the repudiation final.

(2) Retraction may be by any method which clearly indicates to the aggrieved party that the repudiating party intends to perform, but must include any assurance justifiably demanded under the provisions of this Article (Section 2–609).

(3) Retraction reinstates the repudiating party's rights under the contract with due excuse and allowance to the aggrieved party for any delay occasioned by the repudiation.

SECTION 2-612. "INSTALLMENT CONTRACT"; BREACH

(1) An "installment contract" is one which requires or authorizes the delivery of goods in separate lots to be separately accepted, even though the contract contains a clause "each delivery is a separate contract" or its equivalent.

(2) The buyer may reject any installment which is non-conforming if the non-conformity substantially impairs the value of that installment and cannot be cured or if the non-conformity is a defect in the required documents; but if the non-conformity does not fall within subsection (3) and the seller gives adequate assurance of its cure the buyer must accept that installment.

(3) Whenever non-conformity or default with respect to one or more installments substantially impairs the value of the whole contract there is a breach of the whole. But the aggrieved party reinstates the contract if he accepts a non-conforming installment without seasonably notifying of cancellation or if he brings an action with respect only to past installments or demands performance as to future installments.

SECTION 2-613. CASUALTY TO IDENTIFIED GOODS

Where the contract requires for its performance goods identified when the contract is made, and the goods suffer casualty without fault of either party before the risk of loss passes to the buyer, or in a proper case under a "no arrival, no sale" term (Section 2–324) then

(a) if the loss is total the contract is avoided; and

(b) if the loss is partial or the goods have so deteriorated as no longer to conform to the contract the buyer may nevertheless demand inspection and at his option either treat the contract as avoided or accept the goods with due allowance from the contract price for the deterioration or the deficiency in quantity but without further right against the seller.

SECTION 2-614. SUBSTITUTED PERFORMANCE

(1) Where without fault of either party the agreed berthing, loading, or unloading facilities fail or an agreed type of carrier becomes unavailable or the agreed manner of delivery otherwise becomes commercially impracticable but a commercially reasonable substitute is available, such substitute performance must be tendered and accepted.

(2) If the agreed means or manner of payment fails because of domestic or foreign governmental regulation, the seller may withhold or stop delivery unless the buyer provides a means or manner of payment which is commercially a substantial equivalent. If delivery has already been taken, payment by the means or in the manner provided by the regulation discharges the buyer's obligation unless the regulation is discriminatory, oppressive or predatory.

SECTION 2-615. EXCUSE BY FAILURE OF PRESUPPOSED CONDITIONS

Except so far as a seller may have assumed a greater obligation and subject to the preceding section on substituted performance:

(a) Delay in delivery or non-delivery in whole or in part by a seller who complies with paragraph (b) and (c) is not a breach of his duty under a contract for sale if performance as agreed has been made impracticable by the occurrence of a contingency the non-occurrence of which was a basic assumption on which the contract was made or by compliance in good faith with any applicable foreign or domestic governmental regulation or order whether or not it later proves to be invalid.

(b) Where the causes mentioned in paragraph (a) affect only a part of the seller's capacity to perform, he must allocate production and deliveries among his customers but may at his option include regular customers not then under contract as well as his own requirements for further manufacture. He may so allocate in any manner which is fair and reasonable.

(c) The seller must notify the buyer seasonably that there will be delay or non-delivery and, when allocation is required under paragraph (b), of the estimated quota thus made available for the buyer.

SECTION 2-616. PROCEDURE ON NOTICE CLAIMING EXCUSE

(1) Where the buyer receives notification of a material or indefinite delay or an allocation justified under the preceding section he may by written notification to the seller as to any delivery concerned, and where the prospective deficiency substantially impairs the value of the whole contract under the provisions of this Article relating to breach of installment contracts (Section 2–612), then also as to the whole,

(a) terminate and thereby discharge any unexecuted portion of the contract; or

(b) modify the contract by agreeing to take his available quota in substitution.

(2) If after receipt of such notification from the seller the buyer fails so to modify the contract within a reasonable time not exceeding thirty days the contract lapses with respect to any deliveries affected.

(3) The provisions of this section may not be negated by agreement except in so far as the seller has assumed a greater obligation under the preceding section.

PART 7. REMEDIES

SECTION 2-701. REMEDIES FOR BREACH OF COLLATERAL CONTRACTS NOT IMPAIRED

Remedies for breach of any obligation or promise collateral or ancillary to a contract for sale are not impaired by the provisions of this Article.

SECTION 2-702. SELLER'S REMEDIES ON DISCOVERY OF BUYER'S INSOLVENCY

(1) Where the seller discovers the buyer to be insolvent he may refuse delivery except for cash including payment for all goods theretofore delivered under the contract, and stop delivery under this Article (Section 2–705).

(2) Where the seller discovers that the buyer has received goods on credit while insolvent he may reclaim the goods upon demand made within ten days after the receipt, but if misrepresentation of solvency has been made to the particular seller in writing within three months before delivery the ten day limitation does not apply. Except as provided in this subsection the seller may not base a right to reclaim goods on the buyer's fraudulent or innocent misrepresentation of solvency or of intent to pay.

(3) The seller's right to reclaim under subsection (2) is subject to the rights of a buyer in ordinary course or other good faith purchaser under this Article (Section 2–403). Successful reclamation of goods excludes all other remedies with respect to them.

As amended in 1966.

SECTION 2-703. SELLER'S REMEDIES IN GENERAL

Where the buyer wrongfully rejects or revokes acceptance of goods or fails to make a payment due on or before delivery or repudiates with respect to a part or the whole, then with respect to any goods directly affected and, if the breach is of the whole contract (Section 2–612), then also with respect to the whole undelivered balance, the aggrieved seller may

(a) withhold delivery of such goods;

(b) stop delivery by any bailee as hereafter provided (Section 2–705);

(c) proceed under the next section respecting goods still unidentified to the contract;

(d) resell and recover damages as hereafter provided (Section 2–706);

(e) recover damages for non-acceptance (Section 2–708) or in a proper case the price (Section 2–709);

(f) cancel.

SECTION 2-704. SELLER'S RIGHT TO IDENTIFY GOODS TO THE CONTRACT NOTWITHSTANDING BREACH OR TO SALVAGE UNFINISHED GOODS

(1) An aggrieved seller under the preceding section may

(a) identify to the contract conforming goods not already identified if at the time he learned of the breach they are in his possession or control;

(b) treat as the subject of resale goods which have demonstrably been intended for the particular contract even though those goods are unfinished.

(2) Where the goods are unfinished an aggrieved seller may in the exercise of reasonable commercial judgment for the purposes of avoiding loss and of effective realization either complete the manufacture and wholly identify the goods to the contract or cease manufacture and resell for scrap or salvage value or proceed in any other reasonable manner.

SECTION 2-705. SELLER'S STOPPAGE OF DELIVERY IN TRANSIT OR OTHERWISE

(1) The seller may stop delivery of goods in the possession of a carrier or other bailee when he discovers the buyer to be insolvent (Section 2–702) and may stop delivery of carload, truckload, planeload or larger shipments of express or freight when the buyer repudiates or fails to make a payment due before delivery or if for any other reason the seller has a right to withhold or reclaim the goods.

(2) As against such buyer the seller may stop delivery until

(a) receipt of the goods by the buyer; or

(b) acknowledgment to the buyer by any bailee of the goods except a carrier that the bailee holds the goods for the buyer; or

(c) such acknowledgment to the buyer by a carrier by reshipment or as warehouseman; or

(d) negotiation to the buyer of any negotiable document of title covering the goods.

(3) (a) To stop delivery the seller must so notify as to enable the bailee by reasonable diligence to prevent delivery of the goods.

(b) After such notification the bailee must hold and deliver the goods according to the directions of the seller but the seller is liable to the bailee for any ensuing charges or damages.

(c) If a negotiable document of title has been issued for goods the bailee is not obliged to obey a notification to stop until surrender of the document.

(d) A carrier who has issued a non-negotiable bill of lading is not obliged to obey a notification to stop received from a person other than the consignor.

SECTION 2-706. SELLER'S RESALE INCLUDING CONTRACT FOR RESALE

(1) Under the conditions stated in Section 2–703 on seller's remedies, the seller may resell the goods concerned or the undelivered balance thereof. Where the resale is made in good faith and in a commercially reasonable manner the seller may recover the difference between the resale price and the contract price together with any incidental damages allowed under the provisions of this Article (Section 2–710), but less expenses saved in consequence of the buyer's breach.

(2) Except as otherwise provided in subsection (3) or unless otherwise agreed resale may be at public or private sale including sale by way of one or more contracts to sell or of identification

to an existing contract of the seller. Sale may be as a unit or in parcels and at any time and place and on any terms but every aspect of the sale including the method, manner, time, place and terms must be commercially reasonable. The resale must be reasonably identified as referring to the broken contract, but it is not necessary that the goods be in existence or that any or all of them have been identified to the contract before the breach.

(3) Where the resale is at private sale the seller must give the buyer reasonable notification of his intention to resell.

(4) Where the resale is at public sale

(a) only identified goods can be sold except where there is a recognized market for a public sale of futures in goods of the kind; and

(b) it must be made at a usual place or market for public sale if one is reasonably available and except in the case of goods which are perishable or threaten to decline in value speedily the seller must give the buyer reasonable notice of the time and place of the resale; and

(c) if the goods are not to be within the view of those attending the sale the notification of sale must state the place where the goods are located and provide for their reasonable inspection by prospective bidders; and

(d) the seller may buy.

(5) A purchaser who buys in good faith at a resale takes the goods free of any rights of the original buyer even though the seller fails to comply with one or more of the requirements of this section.

(6) The seller is not accountable to the buyer for any profit made on any resale. A person in the position of a seller (Section 2–707) or a buyer who has rightfully rejected or justifiably revoked acceptance must account for any excess over the amount of his security interest, as hereinafter defined (subsection (3) of Section 2–711).

SECTION 2-707. "PERSON IN THE POSITION OF A SELLER"

(1) A "person in the position of a seller" includes as against a principal an agent who has paid or become responsible for the price of goods on behalf of his principal or anyone who otherwise holds a security interest or other right in goods similar to that of a seller.

(2) A person in the position of a seller may as provided in this Article withhold or stop delivery (Section 2–705) and resell (Section 2–706) and recover incidental damages (Section 2–710).

SECTION 2-708. SELLER'S DAMAGES FOR NON-ACCEPTANCE OR REPUDIATION

(1) Subject to subsection (2) and to the provisions of this Article with respect to proof of market price (Section 2–723), the measure of damages for non-acceptance or repudiation by the buyer is the difference between the market price at the time and place for tender and the unpaid contract price together with any incidental damages provided in this Article (Section 2–710), but less expenses saved in consequence of the buyer's breach.

(2) If the measure of damages provided in subsection (1) is inadequate to put the seller in as good a position as performance would have done then the measure of damages is the profit (including reasonable overhead) which the seller would have made from full performance by the buyer, together with any incidental damages provided in this Article (Section 2–710), due

allowance for costs reasonably incurred and due credit for payments or proceeds of resale.

SECTION 2-709. ACTION FOR THE PRICE

(1) When the buyer fails to pay the price as it becomes due the seller may recover, together with any incidental damages under the next section, the price

(a) of goods accepted or of conforming goods lost or damaged within a commercially reasonable time after risk of their loss has passed to the buyer; and

(b) of goods identified to the contract if the seller is unable after reasonable effort to resell them at a reasonable price or the circumstances reasonably indicate that such effort will be unavailing.

(2) Where the seller sues for the price he must hold for the buyer any goods which have been identified to the contract and are still in his control except that if resale becomes possible he may resell them at any time prior to the collection of the judgment. The net proceeds of any such resale must be credited to the buyer and payment of the judgment entitles him to any goods not resold.

(3) After the buyer has wrongfully rejected or revoked acceptance of the goods or has failed to make a payment due or has repudiated (Section 2–610), a seller who is held not entitled to the price under this section shall nevertheless be awarded damages for non-acceptance under the preceding section.

SECTION 2-710. SELLER'S INCIDENTAL DAMAGES

Incidental damages to an aggrieved seller include any commercially reasonable charges, expenses or commissions incurred in stopping delivery, in the transportation, care and custody of goods after the buyer's breach, in connection with return or resale of the goods or otherwise resulting from the breach.

SECTION 2-711. BUYER'S REMEDIES IN GENERAL; BUYER'S SECURITY INTEREST IN REJECTED GOODS

(1) Where the seller fails to make delivery or repudiates or the buyer rightfully rejects or justifiably revokes acceptance then with respect to any goods involved, and with respect to the whole if the breach goes to the whole contract (Section 2–612), the buyer may cancel and whether or not he has done so may in addition to recovering so much of the price as has been paid

(a) "cover" and have damages under the next section as to all the goods affected whether or not they have been identified to the contract; or

(b) recover damages for non-delivery as provided in this Article (Section 2–713).

(2) Where the seller fails to deliver or repudiates the buyer may also

(a) if the goods have been identified recover them as provided in this Article (Section 2–502); or

(b) in a proper case obtain specific performance or replevy the goods as provided in this Article (Section 2–716).

(3) On rightful rejection or justifiable revocation of acceptance a buyer has a security interest in goods in his possession or control for any payments made on their price and any expenses reasonably incurred in their inspection, receipt, transportation, care and custody and may hold

such goods and resell them in like manner as an aggrieved seller (Section 2–706).

SECTION 2-712. "COVER"; BUYER'S PROCUREMENT OF SUBSTITUTE GOODS

(1) After a breach within the preceding section the buyer may "cover" by making in good faith and without unreasonable delay any reasonable purchase of or contract to purchase goods in substitution for those due from the seller.

(2) The buyer may recover from the seller as damages the difference between the cost of cover and the contract price together with any incidental or consequential damages as hereinafter defined (Section 2–715), but less expenses saved in consequence of the seller's breach.

(3) Failure of the buyer to effect cover within this section does not bar him from any other remedy.

SECTION 2-713. BUYER'S DAMAGES FOR NON-DELIVERY OR REPUDIATION

(1) Subject to the provisions of this Article with respect to proof of market price (Section 2–723), the measure of damages for non-delivery or repudiation by the seller is the difference between the market price at the time when the buyer learned of the breach and the contract price together with any incidental and consequential damages provided in this Article (Section 2–715), but less expenses saved in consequence of the seller's breach.

(2) Market price is to be determined as of the place for tender or, in cases of rejection after arrival or revocation of acceptance, as of the place of arrival.

SECTION 2-714. BUYER'S DAMAGES FOR BREACH IN REGARD TO ACCEPTED GOODS

(1) Where the buyer has accepted goods and given notification (subsection (3) of Section 2–607) he may recover as damages for any non-conformity of tender the loss resulting in the ordinary course of events from the seller's breach as determined in any manner which is reasonable.

(2) The measure of damages for breach of warranty is the difference at the time and place of acceptance between the value of the goods accepted and the value they would have had if they had been as warranted, unless special circumstances show proximate damages of a different amount.

(3) In a proper case any incidental and consequential damages under the next section may also be recovered.

SECTION 2-715. BUYER'S INCIDENTAL AND CONSEQUENTIAL DAMAGES

(1) Incidental damages resulting from the seller's breach include expenses reasonably incurred in inspection, receipt, transportation and care and custody of goods rightfully rejected, any commercially reasonable charges, expenses or commissions in connection with effecting cover and any other reasonable expense incident to the delay or other breach.

(2) Consequential damages resulting from the seller's breach include

(a) any loss resulting from general or particular requirements and needs of which the seller at the time of contracting had reason to know and which could not reasonably be prevented by cover or otherwise; and

(b) injury to person or property proximately resulting from any breach of warranty.

SECTION 2-716. BUYER'S RIGHT TO SPECIFIC PERFORMANCE OR REPLEVIN

(1) Specific performance may be decreed where the goods are unique or in other proper circumstances.

(2) The decree for specific performance may include such terms and conditions as to payment of the price, damages, or other relief as the court may deem just.

(3) The buyer has a right of replevin for goods identified to the contract if after reasonable effort he is unable to effect cover for such goods or the circumstances reasonably indicate that such effort will be unavailing or if the goods have been shipped under reservation and satisfaction of the security interest in them has been made or tendered.

SECTION 2-717. DEDUCTION OF DAMAGES FROM THE PRICE

The buyer on notifying the seller of his intention to do so may deduct all or any part of the damages resulting from any breach of the contract from any part of the price still due under the same contract.

SECTION 2-718. LIQUIDATION OR LIMITATION OF DAMAGES; DEPOSITS

(1) Damages for breach by either party may be liquidated in the agreement but only at an amount which is reasonable in the light of the anticipated or actual harm caused by the breach, the difficulties of proof of loss, and the inconvenience or non-feasibility of otherwise obtaining an adequate remedy. A term fixing unreasonably large liquidated damages is void as a penalty.

(2) Where the seller justifiably withholds delivery of goods because of the buyer's breach, the buyer is entitled to restitution of any amount by which the sum of his payments exceeds

(a) the amount to which the seller is entitled by virtue of terms liquidating the seller's damages in accordance with subsection (1), or

(b) in the absence of such terms, twenty per cent of the value of the total performance for which the buyer is obligated under the contract or $500, whichever is smaller.

(3) The buyer's right to restitution under subsection (2) is subject to offset to the extent that the seller establishes

(a) a right to recover damages under the provisions of this Article other than subsection (1), and

(b) the amount or value of any benefits received by the buyer directly or indirectly by reason of the contract.

(4) Where a seller has received payment in goods their reasonable value or the proceeds of their resale shall be treated as payments for the purposes of subsection (2); but if the seller has notice of the buyer's breach before reselling goods received in part performance, his resale is subject to the conditions laid down in this Article on resale by an aggrieved seller (Section 2–706).

SECTION 2-719. CONTRACTUAL MODIFICATION OR LIMITATION OF REMEDY

(1) Subject to the provisions of subsections (2) and (3) of this section and of the preceding section on liquidation and limitation of damages,

(a) the agreement may provide for remedies in addition to or in substitution for those provided in this Article and may limit or alter the measure of damages recoverable under this Article, as by limiting the buyer's remedies to return of the goods and repayment of the price or to repair and replacement of non-conforming goods or parts; and

(b) resort to a remedy as provided is optional unless the remedy is expressly agreed to be exclusive, in which case it is the sole remedy.

(2) Where circumstances cause an exclusive or limited remedy to fail of its essential purpose, remedy may be had as provided in this Act.

(3) Consequential damages may be limited or excluded unless the limitation or exclusion is unconscionable. Limitation of consequential damages for injury to the person in the case of consumer goods is prima facie unconscionable but limitation of damages where the loss is commercial is not.

SECTION 2-720. EFFECT OF "CANCELLATION" OR "RESCISSION" ON CLAIMS FOR ANTECEDENT BREACH

Unless the contrary intention clearly appears, expressions of "cancellation" or "rescission" of the contract or the like shall not be construed as a renunciation or discharge of any claim in damages for an antecedent breach.

SECTION 2-721. REMEDIES FOR FRAUD

Remedies for material misrepresentation or fraud include all remedies available under this Article for non-fraudulent breach. Neither rescission or a claim for rescission of the contract for sale nor rejection or return of the goods shall bar or be deemed inconsistent with a claim for damages or other remedy.

SECTION 2-722. WHO CAN SUE THIRD PARTIES FOR INJURY TO GOODS

Where a third party so deals with goods which have been identified to a contract for sale as to cause actionable injury to a party to that contract

(a) a right of action against the third party is in either party to the contract for sale who has title to or a security interest or a special property or an insurable interest in the goods; and if the goods have been destroyed or converted a right of action is also in the party who either bore the risk of loss under the contract for sale or has since the injury assumed that risk as against the other;

(b) if at the time of the injury the party plaintiff did not bear the risk of loss as against the other party to the contract for sale and there is no arrangement between them for disposition of the recovery, his suit or settlement is, subject to his own interest, as a fiduciary for the other party to the contract;

(c) either party may with the consent of the other sue for the benefit of whom it may concern.

SECTION 2-723. PROOF OF MARKET PRICE: TIME AND PLACE

(1) If an action based on anticipatory repudiation comes to trial before the time for performance with respect to some or all of the goods, any damages based on market price (Section 2–708 or Section 2–713) shall be determined according to the price of such goods prevailing at the time when the aggrieved party learned of the repudiation.

(2) If evidence of a price prevailing at the times or places described in this Article is not readily available the price prevailing within any reasonable time before or after the time described or at any other place which in commercial judgment or under usage of trade would

serve as a reasonable substitute for the one described may be used, making any proper allowance for the cost of transporting the goods to or from such other place.

(3) Evidence of a relevant price prevailing at a time or place other than the one described in this Article offered by one party is not admissible unless and until he has given the other party such notice as the court finds sufficient to prevent unfair surprise.

SECTION 2-724. ADMISSIBILITY OF MARKET QUOTATIONS

Whenever the prevailing price or value of any goods regularly bought and sold in any established commodity market is in issue, reports in official publications or trade journals or in newspapers or periodicals of general circulation published as the reports of such market shall be admissible in evidence. The circumstances of the preparation of such a report may be shown to affect its weight but not its admissibility.

SECTION 2-725. STATUTE OF LIMITATIONS IN CONTRACTS FOR SALE

(1) An action for breach of any contract for sale must be commenced within four years after the cause of action has accrued. By the original agreement the parties may reduce the period of limitation to not less than one year but may not extend it.

(2) A cause of action accrues when the breach occurs, regardless of the aggrieved party's lack of knowledge of the breach. A breach of warranty occurs when tender of delivery is made, except that where a warranty explicitly extends to future performance of the goods and discovery of the breach must await the time of such performance the cause of action accrues when the breach is or should have been discovered.

(3) Where an action commenced within the time limited by subsection (1) is so terminated as to leave available a remedy by another action for the same breach such other action may be commenced after the expiration of the time limited and within six months after the termination of the first action unless the termination resulted from voluntary discontinuance or from dismissal for failure or neglect to prosecute.

(4) This section does not alter the law on tolling of the statute of limitations nor does it apply to causes of action which have accrued before this Act becomes effective.

Appendix B

UNITED NATIONS CONVENTION ON CONTRACTS FOR THE INTERNATIONAL SALE OF GOODS
(Vienna, Jan. 1, 1988) ("CISG")

Items

Public Notice 1004

Text of Convention

Parties to Convention

Message Accompanying Transmittal

Letter of Transmittal

Letter of Submittal

Legal Analysis of Convention

[Public Notice 1004]

U.S. Ratification of 1980 United Nations Convention on Contracts for the International Sale of Goods: Official English Text

On December 11, 1986 the United States deposited at United Nations Headquarters in New York its instrument of ratification of the 1980 U.N. Convention on Contracts for the International Sale of Goods. The United States did so jointly with China and Italy. The Convention will enter into force on January 1, 1988 between the United States and the following countries: Argentina, China, Egypt, France, Hungary, Lesotho, Syria, Yugoslavia and Zambia.

The Convention sets out substantive provisions of law to govern the formation of international sales contracts and the rights and obligations of the buyer and seller. It will apply to sales contracts between parties with their places of business in different countries bound by Convention provided the parties have left their contracts silent as to applicable law. Parties are free to specify applicable law and to derogate from or vary the effect of provisions of the Convention. Certain types of sales and sales of certain types of goods are excluded from the Convention's scope, and the Convention is not concerned with the validity of the contract. Part I of the Convention sets out its sphere of application and general provisions. For the Convention to be applicable the contract of sale need not be concluded in or evidenced by writing unless one of the parties has its place of business in a country that has made a reservation in this regard. The United States did not make this reservation. Article 100 deals with the Convention's applicability to sales contract formation and sales contracts themselves in relation to its entry into force.

United States ratification was coupled with a declaration that the United States would not be bound by Article 1(1)(b), which will have a narrowing effect on the sphere of application of the Convention.

Traders and their counsel are advised to study the Convention carefully in light of international sales and purchases involving parties in the above-mentioned countries and additional countries for which the Convention will eventually be entering into force.

The legal analysis that accompanied the Convention to the Senate and that relates its provisions to the corresponding provisions of the Sales Article of the Uniform Commercial Code may be found in 22 *International Legal Materials* 1368-80 (1984) (a bi-monthly publication of the American Society of International Law). A complete bibliography with citations to publications that reproduce the Convention text and legislative materials concerning the Convention, as well as secondary literature including books, symposia and law review articles, is to be published by Professor Peter Winship, Southern Methodist University School of Law, in the Spring 1987 issue of *The International Lawyer*, the law review published by the Section of International Law and Practice of the American Bar Association.

For the most current information about countries that have ratified or acceded to the Convention, write or phone the United Nations, which was designated as the depository for the Convention: United Nations, Treaty Section, New York, N.Y. 10017 (212) 754-7958/5048).

The Office of Treaty Affairs, Department of State, maintains re cords on multilateral treaties such as the 1980 Sales Convention that are based, in part, on information provided it by the United Nations. It updates that information and, on a monthly basis, publishes information in the *State Department Bulletin* about developments concerning treaties and conventions to which the United States is a party. The Department of State publication "Treaties in Force" annually lists all states parties to treaties and conventions to which the United States is a party, with the status as of January 1 of any given year, noting also whether a state may have made reservations when becoming a party.

The Department understands that a number of legal publications will be printing the text of the Convention and materials that accompanied it to the Senate, some listing countries becoming parties and any reservations or declarations to which their ratification may have been subject. These include: United States Code Annotated, 1987 pocket part to 15 U.S.C.A. Appendix; Uniform Laws Annotated, Appendix to Uniform Commercial Code, with a reference to the Convention in connection with Article 2; United States Code Service in an Appendix at the end of Title 15; Martindale-Hubbell Law Directory in Volume VIII, Part VII: Selected International Conventions to which the United States is a party.

There is reproduced below a photocopy of the United Nations-certified English text of the Convention which traders and their counsel are encouraged to use, as typographical errors may be contained in any other published version of the text. It should be noted that the Arabie, Chinese, French, Russian and Spanish Convention texts have equal authenticity with the English text.

Peter H. Pfund, Assistant Legal Adviser for Private International Law

UNITED NATIONS CONVENTION ON CONTRACTS FOR THE INTERNATIONAL SALE OF GOODS

The states parties to this Convention:

Bearing in mind the broad objectives in the resolutions adopted by the sixth special session of the General Assembly of the United Nations on the establishment of a New International Economic Order,

Considering that the development of international trade on the basis of equality and mutual benefit is an important element in promoting friendly relations among States,

Being of the Opinion that the adoption of uniform rules which govern contracts for the international sale of goods and take into account the different social, economic and legal systems would contribute to the removal of legal barriers in international trade and promote the development of international trade,

Have agreed as follows:

PART I — SPHERE OF APPLICATION AND GENERAL PROVISIONS

CHAPTER I — SPHERE OF APPLICATION

Article 1

(1) This Convention applies to contracts of sale of goods between parties whose places of business are in different States:

(a) When the States are Contracting States; or

(b) When the rules of private international law lead to the application of the law of a Contracting State.

(2) The fact that the parties have their places of business in different States is to be disregarded whenever this fact does not appear either from the contract or from any dealings between, or from information disclosed by, the parties at any time before or at the conclusion of the contract.

(3) Neither the nationality of the parties nor the civil or commercial character of the parties or of the contract is to be taken into consideration in determining the application of this Convention.

Article 2

This Convention does not apply to sales

(a) Of goods bought for personal, family or household use, un less the seller, at any time before or at the conclusion of the contract, neither knew nor ought to have known that the goods were bought for any such use;

(b) By auction;

(c) On execution or otherwise by authority of law;

(d) Of stocks, shares, investment securities, negotiable instruments or money;

(e) Of ships, vessels, hovercraft or aircraft;

(f) Of electricity.

Article 3

(1) Contracts for the supply of goods to be manufactured or produced are to be considered sales unless the party who orders the goods undertakes to supply a substantial part of the materials necessary for such manufacture or production.

(2) This Convention does not apply to contracts in which the preponderant part of the obligations of the party who furnishes the goods consists in the supply of labour or other services.

Article 4

This Convention governs only the formation of the contract of sale and the rights and obligations of the seller and the buyer arising from such a contract. In particular, except as otherwise expressly provided in this Convention, it is not concerned with:

(a) the validity of the contract or of any of its provisions or of any usage;

(b) the effect which the contract may have on the property in the goods sold.

Article 5

This Convention does not apply to the liability of the seller for death or personal injury caused by the goods to any person.

Article 6

The parties may exclude the application of this Convention or, subject to article 12, derogate from or vary the effect of any of its provisions.

CHAPTER II — GENERAL PROVISIONS

Article 7

(1) In the interpretation of this Convention, regard is to be had to its international character and to the need to promote uniformity in its application and the observance of good faith in international trade.

(2) Questions concerning matters governed by this Convention which are not expressly settled in it are to be settled in conformity with the general principles on which it is based or, in the absence of such principles, in conformity with the law applicable by virtue of the rules of private international law.

Article 8

(1) For the purpose of this Convention statements made by and other conduct of a party are to be interpreted according to his intent where the other party knew or could not have been unaware what that intent was.

(2) If the preceding paragraph is not applicable, statements made by and other conduct of a party are to be interpreted according to the understanding that a reasonable person of the same kind as the other party would have had in the same circumstances.

(3) In determining the intent of a party or the understanding a reasonable person would have had, due consideration is to be given to all relevant circumstances of the case including the negotiations, any practices which the parties have established between themselves, usages and any subsequent conduct of the parties.

Article 9

(1) The parties are bound by any usage to which they have agreed and by any practices which they have established between themselves.

(2) The parties are considered, unless otherwise agreed, to have impliedly made applicable

to their contract or its formation a usage of which the parties knew or ought to have known and which in international trade is widely known to, and regularly observed by, parties to contracts of the type involved in the particular trade concerned.

Article 10

For the purposes of this Convention:

(a) If a party has more than one place of business, the place of business is that which has the closest relationship to the contract and its performance, having regard to the circumstances known to or comtemplated by the parties at any time before or at the conclusion of the contract;

(b) If a party does not have a place of business, references are to be made to his habitual residence.

Article 11

A contract of sale need not be concluded in or evidenced by writing and is not subject to any other requirement as to form. It may be proved by any means, including witnesses.

Article 12

Any provision of article 11, article 29 or Part II of this Convention that allows a contract of sale or its modification or termination by agreement or any offer, acceptances or other indication of intention to be made in any form other than in writing does not apply where any party has his place of business in a Contracting State which has made a declaration under article 96 of this Convention. The parties may not derogate from or vary the effect of this article.

Article 13

For the purpose of this Convention "writing" includes telegram and telex.

PART II — FORMATION OF THE CONTRACT

Article 14

(1) A proposal for concluding a contract addressed to one or more specific persons constitutes an offer if it is sufficiently definite and indicates the intention of the offeror to be bound in case of acceptance. A proposal is sufficiently definite if it indicates the goods and expressly or implicitly fixes or makes provision for determining the quantity and the price.

(2) A proposal other than one addressed to one or more specific persons is to be considered merely as an invitation to make offers, unless the contrary is clearly indicated by the person making the proposal.

Article 15

(1) An offer becomes effective when it reaches the offeree.

(2) An offer, even if it is irrevocable, may be withdrawn if the withdrawal reaches the offeree before or at the same time as the offer.

Article 16

(1) Until a contract is concluded an offer may be revoked if the revocation reaches the offeree before he has dispatched an acceptance.

(2) However, an offer cannot be revoked:

   (a) If it indicates, whether by stating a fixed time for acceptance or otherwise, that it is irrevocable; or

   (b) If it was reasonable for the offeree to rely on the offer as being irrevocable and the offeree has acted in reliance on the offer.

An offer, even if it is irrevocable, is terminated when a rejection reaches the offeror.

Article 18

(1) A statement made by or other conduct of the offeree indicating assent to an offer is an acceptance. Silence or inactivity does not in itself amount to acceptance.

(2) An acceptance of an offer becomes effective at the moment the indication of assent reaches the offeror. An acceptance is not effective if the indication of assent does not reach the offeror within the time he has fixed or, if no time is fixed, within a reasonable time, due account being taken of the circumstances of the transaction, including the rapidity of the means of communication employed by the offeror. An oral offer must be accepted immediately unless the circumstances indicate otherwise.

(3) However, if by virtue of the offer or as a result of practices which the parties have established between themselves or of usage, the offeree may indicate assent by performing an act, such as one relating to the dispatch of the goods or payment of the price, without notice to the offeror, the acceptance is effective at the moment the act is performed, provided that the act is performed within the period of time laid down in the preceding paragraph.

Article 19

(1) A reply to an offer which purports to be an acceptance but contains additions, limitations or other modifications is a rejection of the offer and constitutes a counter-offer.

(2) However, a reply to an offer which purports to be an acceptance but contains additional or different terms which do not materially alter the terms of the offer constitutes an acceptance, unless the offeror, without undue delay, objects orally to the discrepancy or dispatches a notice to that effect. If he does not so object, the terms of the contract are the terms of the offer with the modifications contained in the acceptance.

(3) Additional or different terms relating, among other things, to the price, payment, quality and quantity of the goods, place and time of delivery, extent of one party's liability to the other or the settlement of disputes are considered to alter the terms of the offer materially.

Article 20

(1) A period of time for acceptance fixed by the offeror in a telegram or a letter begins to run from the moment the telegram is handed in for dispatch or from the date shown on the letter or, if no such date is shown, from the date shown on the envelope. A period of time for

acceptance fixed by the offeror by telephone, telex or other means of instanteous communication, begins to run from the moment that the offer reaches the offeree.

(2) Official holidays or non-business days occuring during the period for acceptance are included in calculating the period. However, if a notice of acceptance cannot be delivered at the address of the offeror on the last day of the period because that day falls on an official holiday or a non-business day at the place of business of the offeror, the period is extended until the first business day which follows.

Article 21

(1) A late acceptance is nevertheless effective as an acceptance if without delay the offeror orally so informs the offeree or dispatches a notice to that effect.

(2) If a letter or other writing containing a late acceptance shows that it has been sent in such circumstances that if its transmission had been normal it would have reached the offeror in due time, the late acceptance is effective as an acceptance unless, without delay, the offeror orally informs the offeree that he considers his offer as having lapsed or dispatches a notice to that effect.

Article 22

An acceptance may be withdrawn if the withdrawal reaches the offeror before or at the same time as the acceptance would have become effective.

Article 23

A contract is concluded at the moment when a acceptance of an offer becomes effective in accordance with the provisions of this Convention.

Article 24

For the purposes of this Part of the Convention, an offer, declaration of acceptance or any other indication of intention "reaches" the addressee when it is made orally to him or delivered by any other means to him personally, to his place of business or mailing address or, if he does not have a place of business or mailing address, to his habitual residence.

PART III — SALE OF GOODS
CHAPTER I — GENERAL PROVISIONS

Article 25

A breach of contract committed by one of the parties is fundamental if it results in such detriment to the other party as substantially to deprive him of what he is entitled to expect under the contract, unless the party in breach did not foresee and a reasonable person of the same kind in the same circumstances would not have foreseen such a result.

Article 26

A declaration of avoidance of the contract is effective only if made by notice to the other party.

Article 27

Unless otherwise expressly provided in this Part of the Convention, if any notice, request or other communication is given or made by a party in accordance with this Part and by means appropriate in the circumstances, a delay or error in the transmission of the communication or its failure to arrive does not deprive that party of the right to rely on the communication.

Article 28

If, in accordance with the provisions of this Convention, one party is entitled to require performance of any obligation by the other party, a court is not bound to enter a judgment for specific performance unless the court would do so under its own law in respect of similar contracts of sale not governed by this Convention.

Article 29

(1) A contract may be modified, or terminated by the mere agreement of the parties.

(2) A contract in writing which contains a provision requiring any modification or termination by agreement to be in writing may not be otherwise modified or terminated by agreement. However, a party may be precluded by his conduct from asserting such a provision to the extent that the other party has relied on that conduct.

CHAPTER II — OBLIGATIONS OF THE SELLER

Article 30

The seller must deliver the goods, hand over any documents relating to them and transfer the property in the goods, as required by the contract and his Convention.

SECTION I. Delivery of the Goods and Handing Over of Documents

Article 31

If the seller is not bound to deliver the goods at any other particular place, his obligation to deliver consists:

(a) If the contract of sale involves carriage of the goods — in handing the goods over to the first carrier for transmission to the buyer;

(b) If, in cases not within the preceding subparagraph, the contract relates to specific goods, or unidentified goods to be drawn from a specific stock or to be manufactured or produced, and at the time of the conclusion of the contract the parties knew that the goods were at, or were to be manufactured or produced at, a particular place — in placing the goods at the buyer's disposal at that place;

(c) In other cases — in placing the goods at the buyer's disposal at the place where the seller had his place of business at the time of the conclusion of the contract.

Article 32

(1) If the seller, in accordance with the contract or his Convention, hands the goods over to a carrier and if the goods are not clearly identified to the contract by markings on the goods, by shipping documents or otherwise, the seller must give the buyer notice of the consignment specifying the goods.

(2) If the seller is bound to arrange for carriage of the goods, he must make such contracts

as are necessary for carriage to the place fixed by means of transportation appropriate in the circumstances and according to the usual terms for such transportation.

(3) If the seller is not bound to effect insurance in respect of the carriage of the goods, he must, at the buyer's request, provide him with all available information necessary to enable him to effect such insurance.

Article 33

The seller must deliver the goods:

(a) If a date is fixed by or determinable from the contract, on that date;

(b) If a period of time is fixed by or determinable from the contract, at any time within that period unless circumstances indicate that the buyer is to choose a date; or

(c) In any other case, within a reasonable time after the conclusion of the contract.

Article 34

If the seller is bound to hand over documents relating to the goods, he must hand them over at the time and place and in the form required by the contract. If the seller has handed over documents before that time, he may, up to that time, cure any lack of conformity in the documents, if the exercise of this right does not cause the buyer unreasonable inconvenience or unreasonable expense. However, the buyer retains any right to claim damages as provided for in this Convention.

SECTION II.   Conformity of the Goods and Third Party Claims

Article 35

(1) The seller must deliver goods which are of the quantity, quality and description required by the contract and which are contained or packaged in the manner required by the contract.

(2) Except where the parties have agreed otherwise, the goods do not conform with the contract unless they:

(a) Are fit for the purposes for which goods of the same description would ordinarily be used;

(b) Are fit for any particular purpose expressly or impliedly made known to the seller at the time of the conclusion of the contract, except where the circumstances show that the buyer did not rely, or that it was unreasonable for him to rely, on the seller's skill and judgment;

(c) Possess the qualities of goods which the seller has held out to the buyer as a sample or model;

(d) Are contained or packaged in the manner usual for such goods or, where there is no such manner, in a manner adequate to preserve and protect the goods.

(3) The seller is not liable under subparagraphs (a) to (d) of the preceding paragraph for any lack of conformity of the goods if at the time of the conclusion of the contract the buyer knew or could not have been unaware of such lack of conformity.

Article 36

(1) The seller is liable in accordance with the contract and this Convention for any lack of conformity which exists at the time when the risk passes to the buyer, even though the lack of conformity becomes apparent only after that time.

(2) The seller is also liable for any lack of conformity which occurs after the time indicated in the preceding paragraph and which is due to a breach of any of his obligations, including a breach of any guarantee that for a period of time the goods will remain fit for their ordinary purpose or for some particular purpose or will retain specified qualities or characteristics.

Article 37

If the seller has delivered goods before the date for delivery, he may, up to that date, deliver any missing part or make up any deficiency in the quantity of the goods delivered, or deliver goods in replacement of any non-conforming goods delivered or remedy any lack of conformity in the goods delivered, provided that the exercise of this right does not cause the buyer unreasonable inconvenience or unreasonable expense. However, the buyer retains any right to claim damages as provided for in this Convention.

Article 38

(1) The buyer must examine the goods, or cause them to be examined, within as short a period as is practicable in the circumstances.

(2) If the contract involves carriage of the goods, examination may be deferred until after the goods have arrived at their destination.

(3) If the goods are redirected in transit or redispatched by the buyer without a reasonable opportunity for examination by him and at the time of the conclusion of the contract the seller knew or ought to have known of the possibility of such redirection or redispatch, examination may be deferred until after the goods have arrived at the new destination.

Article 39

(1) The buyer loses the right to rely on a lack of conformity of the goods if he does not give notice to the seller specifying the nature of the lack of conformity within a reasonable time after he has discovered it or ought to have discovered it.

(2) In any event, the buyer loses the right to rely on a lack of conformity of the goods if he does not give the seller notice thereof at the latest within a period of two years from the date on which the goods were actually handed over to the buyer, unless this time-limit is inconsistent with a contractual period of guarantee.

Article 40

The seller is not entitled to rely on the provisions of articles 38 and 39 if the lack of conformity relates to facts of which he knew or could not have been unaware and which he did not disclose to the buyer.

Article 41

The seller must deliver goods which are free from any right or claim of a third party, unless the buyer agreed to take the goods subject to that right or claim. However, if such right or claim is based on industrial property or other intellectual property, the seller's obligation is governed by article 42.

Article 42

(1) The seller must deliver goods which are free from any right or claim of a third party based on industrial property or other intellectual property, of which at the time of the conclusion of the contract the seller knew or could not have been unaware, provided that the right or claim is based on industrial property or other intellectual property:

(a) Under the law of the State where the goods will be resold or otherwise used, if it was contemplated by the parties at the time of the conclusion of the contract that the goods would be resold or otherwise used in that State; or

(b) In any other case, under the law of the State where the buyer has his place of business.

(2) The obligation of the seller under the preceding paragraph does not extend to cases where:

(a) At the time of the conclusion of the contract the buyer knew or could not have been unaware of the right or claim; or

(b) The right or claim results from the seller's compliance with technical drawings, designs, formulae or other such specifications furnished by the buyer.

Article 43

(1) The buyer loses the right to rely on the provisions of article 41 or article 42 if he does not give notice to the seller specifying the nature of the right or claim of the third party within a reasonable time after he has become aware or ought to have become aware of the right or claim.

(2) The seller is not entitled to rely on the provisions of the preceding paragraph if he knew of the right or claim of the third party and the nature of it.

Article 44

Notwithstanding the provisions of paragraph (1) of article 39 and paragraph (1) of article 43, the buyer may reduce the price in accordance with article 50 or claim damages, except for loss of profit, if he has a reasonable excuse for his failure to give the required notice.

Section III.   Remedies for Breach of Contract by the Seller

Article 45

(1) If the seller fails to perform any of his obligations under the contract or this Convention, the buyer may:

(a) Exercise the rights provided in articles 46 to 52;

(b) Claim damages as provided in articles 74 to 77.

(2) The buyer is not deprived of any right he may have to claim damages by exercising his right to other remedies.

(3) No period of grace may be granted to the seller by a court or arbitral tribunal when the buyer resorts to a remedy for breach of contract.

Article 46

(1) The buyer may require performance by the seller of his obligations unless the buyer has resorted to a remedy which is inconsistent with this requirement.

(2) If the goods do not conform with the contract, the buyer may require delivery of substitute goods only if the lack of conformity constitutes a fundamental breach of contract and a request for substitute goods is made either in conjunction with notice given under article 39 or within a reasonable time thereafter.

(3) If the goods do not conform with the contract, the buyer may require the seller to remedy the lack of conformity by repair, unless this is unreasonable having regard to all the circumstances. A request for repair must be made either in conjunction with notice given under article 39 or within a reasonable time thereafter.

Article 47

(1) The buyer may fix an additional period of time of reasonable length for performance by the seller of his obligations.

(2) Unless the buyer has received notice from the seller that he will not perform within the period so fixed, the buyer may not, during that period, resort to any remedy for breach of contract. However, the buyer is not deprived thereby of any right he may have to claim damages for delay in performance.

(3) A notice by the seller that he will perform within a specified period of time is assumed to include a request, under the preceding paragraph, that the buyer make known his decision.

(4) A request or notice by the seller under paragraph (2) or (3) of this article is not effective unless received by the buyer.

Article 49

(1) The buyer may declare the contract avoided:

(a) If the failure by the seller to perform any of his obligations under the contract or this Convention amounts to a fundamental breach of contract; or

(b) In case of non-delivery, if the seller does not deliver the goods within the additional period of time fixed by the buyer in accordance with paragraph (1) of article 47 or declares that he will not deliver within the period so fixed.

(2) However, in cases where the seller has delivered the goods, the buyer loses the right to declare the contract avoided unless he does so:

(a) In respect of late delivery, within a reasonable time after he has become aware that delivery has been made;

(b) In respect of any breach other than late delivery, within a reasonable time:

(i) After he knew or ought to have known of the breach;

(ii) After the expiration of any additional period of time fixed by the buyer in accordance with paragraph (1) of article 47, or after the seller has declared that he will not perform his obligations within such an additional period; or

(iii) After the expiration of any additional period of time indicated by the seller in accordance with paragraph (2) of article 48, or after the buyer had declared that he will not accept performance.

Article 50

If the goods do not conform with the contract and whether or not the price has already been paid, the buyer may reduce the price in the same proportion as the value that the goods actually delivered had at the time of the delivery bears to the value that conforming goods would have had at that time. However, if the seller remedies any failure to perform his obligations in accordance with article 37 or 48 or if the buyer refuses to accept performance by the seller in accordance with those articles, the buyer may not reduce the price.

Article 51

(1) If the seller delivers only a part of the goods or if only a part of the goods delivered is in conformity with the contract, articles 46 to 50 apply in respect of the part which is missing or which does not conform.

(2) The buyer may declare the contract avoided in its entirety only if the failure to make delivery completely or in conformity with the contract amounts to a fundamental breach of the contract.

Article 52

(1) If the seller delivers the goods before the date fixed, the buyer may take delivery or refuse to take delivery.

(2) If the seller delivers a quantity of goods greater than that provided for in the contract, the buyer may take delivery or refuse to take delivery of the excess quantity. If the buyer takes delivery of all or part of the excess quantity, he must pay for it at the contract rate.

CHAPTER III   — OBLIGATIONS OF THE BUYER

Article 53

The buyer must pay the price for the goods and take delivery of them as required by the contract and this Convention.

SECTION I.   Payment of the Price

Article 54

The buyer's obligation to pay the price includes taking such steps and complying with such formalities as may be required under the contract or any laws and regulations to enable payment to be made.

Article 55

Where a contract has been validly concluded but does not expressly or implicitly fix or make provision for determining the price, the parties are considered, in the absence of any indication to the contrary, to have impliedly made reference to the price generally charged at the time of the conclusion of the contract for such goods sold under comparable circumstances in the trade concerned.

Article 56

If the price is fixed according to the weight of the goods, in case of doubt it is to be determined by the net weight.

Article 57

(1) If the buyer is not bound to pay the price at any other particular place, he must pay it to the seller:

(a) At the seller's place of business; or

(b) If the payment is to be made against the handing over of the goods or of documents, at the place where the handing over takes place.

(2) The seller must bear any increase in the expenses incidental to payment which is caused by a change in his place of business subsequent to the conclusion of the contract.

Article 58

(1) If the buyer is not bound to pay the price at any other specific time, he must pay it when the seller places either the goods or documents controlling their disposition at the buyer's disposal in accordance with the contract and this Convention. The seller may make such payment a condition for handing over the goods or documents.

(2) If the contract involves carriage of the goods, the seller may dispatch the goods on terms whereby the goods, or documents controlling their disposition, will not be handed over to the buyer except against payment of the price.

(3) The buyer is not bound to pay the price until he has had an opportunity to examine the goods, unless the procedures for delivery or payment agreed upon by the parties are inconsistent with his having such an opportunity.

Article 59

The buyer must pay the price on the date fixed by or determinable from the contract and this Convention without the need for any request or compliance with any formality on the part of the seller.

SECTION II.   Taking Delivery

Article 60

The buyer's obligation to take delivery consists:

(a) In doing all the acts which could reasonably be expected of him in order to enable the seller to make delivery; and

(b) In taking over the goods.

SECTION III.   Remedies for Breach of Contract by the Buyer

Article 61

(1) If the buyer fails to perform any of his obligations under the contract or this Convention, the seller may:

(a) Exercise the rights provided in articles 62 to 65;

(b) Claim damages as provided in articles 74 to 77.

(2) The seller is not deprived of any right he may have to claim damages by exercising his right to other remedies.

(3) No period of grace may be granted to the buyer by a court or arbitral tribunal when the seller resorts to a remedy for breach of contract.

Article 62

The seller may require the buyer to pay the price, take delivery or perform his other obligations, unless the seller has resorted to a remedy which is inconsistent with this requirement."

Article 63

(1) The seller may fix an additional period of time of reasonable length for performance by the buyer of his obligations.

(2) Unless the seller has received notice from the buyer that he will not perform within the period so fixed, the seller may not, during that period, resort to any remedy for breach of contract. However, the seller is not deprived thereby of any right he may have to claim damages for delay in performance.

Article 64

(1) The seller may declare the contract avoided:

(a) If the failure by the buyer to perform any of his obligations under the contract or this Convention amounts to a fundamental breach of contract; or

(b) If the buyer does not, within the additional period of time fixed by the seller in accordance with paragraph (1) of article 63, perform his obligation to pay the price or take delivery of the goods, or if he declares that he will not do so within the period so fixed.

(2) However, in cases where the buyer has paid the price, the seller loses the right to declare the contract avoided unless he does so:

(a) In respect of late performance by the buyer, before the seller has become aware that performance has been rendered; or

(b) In respect of any breach other than late performance by the buyer, within a reasonable time:

(i) After the seller knew or ought to have known of the breach; or

(ii) After the expiration of any additional period of time fixed by the seller in accordance with paragraph (1) of article 63; or after the buyer has declared that he will not perform his obligations within such an additional period.

Article 65

(1) If under the contract the buyer is to specify the form, measurement or other features of the goods and he fails to make such specification either on the date agreed upon or within a reasonable time after receipt of a request from the seller, the seller may, without prejudice to any other rights he may have, make the specification himself in accordance with the requirements of the buyer that may be known to him.

(2) If the seller makes the specification himself, he must inform the buyer of the details thereof and must fix a reasonable time within which the buyer may make a different specification. If, after receipt of such a communication, the buyer fails to do so within the time so fixed, the specification made by the seller is binding.

Article 66

Loss of or damage to the goods after the risk has passed to the buyer does not discharge him from his obligation to pay the price, unless the loss or damage is due to an act or omission of the seller.

Article 67

(1) If the contract of sale involves carriage of the goods and the seller is not bound to hand them over at a particular place, the risk passes to the buyer when the goods are handed over to the first carrier for transmission to the buyer in accordance with the contract of sale. If the seller is bound to hand the goods over to a carrier at a particular place, the risk does not pass to the buyer until the goods are handed over to the carrier at that place. The fact that the seller is authorized to retain documents controlling the disposition of the goods does not affect the passage of the risk.

(2) Nevertheless, the risk does not pass to the buyer until the goods are clearly identified to the contract, whether by markings on the goods, by shipping documents, by notice given to the buyer or otherwise.

Article 68

The risk in respect of goods sold in transit passes to the buyer from the time of the conclusion of the contract. However, if the circumstances so indicate, the risk is assumed by the buyer from the time the goods were handed over to the carrier who issued the documents embodying the contract of carriage. Nevertheless, if at the time of the conclusion of the contract of sale the seller knew or ought to have known that the goods had been lost or damaged and did not disclose this to the buyer, the loss or damage is at the risk of the seller.

Article 69

(1) In cases not within articles 67 and 68, the risk passes to the buyer when he takes over the goods or, if he does not do so in due time, from the time when the goods are placed at his disposal and he commits a breach of contract by failing to take delivery.

(2) However, if the buyer is bound to take over the goods at a place other than a place of business of the seller, the risk passes when delivery is due and the buyer is aware of the fact

that the goods are placed at his disposal at that place.

(3) If the contract relates to goods not then identified, the goods are considered not to be placed at the disposal of the buyer until they are clearly identified to the contract.

Article 70

If the seller has committed a fundamental breach of contract, articles 67, 68 and 69 do not impair the remedies available to the buyer on account of the breach.

CHAPTER V — PROVISIONS COMMON TO THE OBLIGATIONS OF THE SELLER AND OF THE BUYER

SECTION I.   Anticipatory Breach and Instalment Contracts

Article 71

(1) A party may suspend the performance of his obligations if, after the conclusion of the contract, it becomes apparent that the other party will not perform a substantial part of his obligations as a result of:

(a) A serious deficiency in his ability to perform or in his creditworthiness; or

(b) His conduct in preparing to perform or in performing the contract.

(2) If the seller has already dispatched the goods before the grounds described in the preceding paragraph become evident, he may prevent the handing over of the goods to the buyer even though the buyer holds a document which entitles him to obtain them. The present paragraph relates only to the rights in the goods as between the buyer and the seller.

(3) A party suspending performance, whether before or after dispatch of the goods, must immediately give notice of the suspension to the other party and must continue with performance if the other party provides adequate assurance of his performance.

Article 72

(1) If prior to the date for performance of the contract it is clear that one of the parties will commit a fundamental breach of contract, the other party may declare the contract avoided.

(2) If time allows, the party intending to declare the contract avoided must give reasonable notice to the other party in order to permit him to provide adequate assurance of his performance.

(3) The requirements of the preceding paragraph do not apply if the other party has declared that he will not perform his obligations.

Article 73

(1) In the case of a contract for delivery of goods by instalments, if the failure of one party to perform any of his obligations in respect of any installment constitutes a fundamental breach of contract with respect to that instalment, the other party may declare the contract avoided with respect to that instalment.

(2) If one party's failure to perform any of his obligations in respect of any instalment gives the other party good grounds to conclude that a fundamental breach of contract will occur with

respect to future instalments, he may declare the contract avoided for the future, provided that he does so within a reasonable time.

(3) A buyer who declares the contract avoided in respect of any delivery may, at the same time, declare it avoided in respect of deliveries already made or of future deliveries if, by reason of their interdependence, those deliveries could not be used for the purpose contemplated by the parties at the time of the conclusion of the contract.

SECTION II. Damages

Article 74

Damages for breach of contract by one party consist of a sum equal to the loss, including loss of profit, suffered by the other party as a consequence of the breach. Such damages may not exceed the loss which the party in breach foresaw or ought to have foreseen at the time of the conclusion of the contract, in the light of the facts and the matters of which he then knew or ought to have known, as a possible consequence of the breach of contract.

Article 75

If the contract is avoided and if, in a reasonable manner and within a reasonable time after avoidance, the buyer has bought goods in replacement or the seller has resold the goods, the party claiming damages may recover the difference between the contract price and the price in the substitute transaction as well as any further damages recoverable under article 74.

Article 76

(1) If the contract is avoided and there is a current price for the goods, the party claiming damages may, if he has not made a purchase or resale under article 75, recover the difference between the price fixed by the contract and the current price at the time of avoidance as well as any further damages recoverable under article 74. If however, the party claiming damages has avoided the contract after taking over the goods, the current price at the time of such taking over shall be applied instead of the current price at the time of avoidance.

(2) For the purposes of the preceding paragraph, the current price is the price prevailing at the place where delivery of the goods should have been made or, if there is no current price at that place, the price at such other place as serves as a reasonable substitute, making due allowance for differences in the cost of transporting the goods.

Article 77

A party who relies on a breach of contract must take such measures as are reasonable in the circumstances to mitigate the loss, including loss of profit, resulting from the breach. If he fails to take such measures, the party in beach may claim a reduction in the damages in the amount by which the loss should have been mitigated.

SECTION III. Interest

Article 78

If a party fails to pay the price or any other sum that is in arrears, the other party is entitled to interest on it, without prejudice to any claim for damages recoverable under article 74.

SECTION IV. Exemptions

Article 79

(1) A party is not liable for a failure to perform any of his obligations if he proves that the failure was due to an impediment beyond his control and that he could not reasonably be expected to have taken the impediment into account at the time of the conclusion of the contract or to have avoided or overcome it, or its consequences.

(2) If the party's failure is due to the failure by a third person whom he has engaged to perform the whole or a part of the contract, that party is exempt from liability only if:

(a) He is exempt under the preceding paragraph; and

(b) The person whom he has so engaged would be so exempt if the provisions of that paragraph were applied to him.

(3) The exemption provided by this article has effect for the period during which the impediment exists.

(4) The party who fails to perform must give notice to the other party of the impediment and its effect on his ability to perform. If the notice is not received by the other party within a reasonable time after the party who fails to perform knew or ought to have known of the impediment, he is liable for damages resulting from such non-receipt.

(5) Nothing in this article prevents either party from exercising any right other than to claim damages under this Convention.

Article 80

A party may not rely on a failure of the other party to perform, to the extent that such failure was caused by the first party's act or omission.

SECTION V. Effects of Avoidance

Article 81

(1) Avoidance of the contract releases both parties from their obligations under it, subject to any damages which may be due. Avoidance does not affect any provision of the contract for the settlement of disputes or any other provision of the contract governing the rights and obligations of the parties consequent upon the avoidance of the contract.

(2) A party who has performed the contract either wholly or in party may claim restitution from the other party of whatever the first party has supplied or paid under the contract. If both parties are bound to make restitution, they must do so concurrently.

Article 82

(1) The buyer loses the right to declare the contract avoided or to require the seller to deliver substitute goods if it is impossible for him to make restitution of the goods substantially in the condition in which he received them.

(2) The preceding paragraph does not apply:

(a) If the impossibility of making restitution of the goods or of making restitution of the goods substantially in the condition in which the buyer received them is not due to his act or omission;

(b) If the goods or part of the goods have perished or deteriorated as a result of the examination provided for in article 38; or

(c) If the goods or part of the goods have been sold in the normal course of business or have been consumed or transformed by the buyer in the course of normal use before he discovered or ought to have discovered the lack of conformity.

Article 83

A buyer who has lost the right to declare the contract avoided or to require the seller to deliver substitute goods in accordance with article 82 retains all other remedies under the contract and this Convention.

Article 84

(1) If the seller is bound to refund the price, he must also pay interest on it, from the date on which the price was paid.

(2) The buyer must account to the seller for all benefits which he has derived from the goods or part of them:

(a) If he must make restitution of the goods or part of them; or

(b) If it is impossible for him to make restitution of all or part of the goods or to make restitution of all or part of the goods substantially in the condition in which he received them, but he has nevertheless declared the contract avoided or required the seller to deliver substitute goods.

SECTION VI. Preservation of the Goods

Article 85

If the buyer is in delay in taking delivery of the goods or, where payment of the price and delivery of the goods are to be made concurrently, if he fails to pay the price, and the seller is either in possession of the goods or otherwise able to control their disposition, the seller must take such steps as are reasonable in the circumstances to preserve them. He is entitled to retain them until he has been reimbursed his reasonable expenses by the buyer.

Article 86

(1) If the buyer has received the goods and intends to exercise any right under the contract or this Convention to reject them, he must take such steps to preserve them as are reasonable in the circumstances. He is entitled to retain them until he has been reimbursed his reasonable expenses by the seller.

(2) If goods dispatched to the buyer have been placed at his disposal at their destination and he exercises the right to reject them, he must take possession of them on behalf of the seller, provided that this can be done without payment of the price and without unreasonable inconvenience or unreasonable expense. This provision does not apply if the seller or a person authorized to take charge of the goods on his behalf is present at the destination. If the buyer takes possession of the goods under this paragraph, his rights and obligations are governed by

the preceding paragraph.

Article 87

A party who is bound to take steps to preserve the goods may deposit them in a warehouse of a third person at the expense of the other party provided that the expense incurred is not unreasonable.

Article 88

(1) A party who is bound to preserve the goods in accordance with article 85 or 86 may sell them by any appropriate means if there has been an unreasonable delay by the other party in taking possession of the goods or in taking them back or in paying the price or the cost of preservation, provided that reasonable notice of the intention to sell has been given to the other party.

(2) If the goods are subject to rapid deterioration or their preservation would involve unreasonable expense, a party who is bound to preserve the goods in accordance with article 85 or 86 must take reasonable measures to sell them. To the extent possible he must give notice to the other party of his intention to sell.

(3) A party selling the goods has the right to retain out of the proceeds of sale an amount equal to the reasonable expenses of preserving the goods and of selling them. He must account to the other party for the balance.

PART IV — FINAL PROVISIONS

Article 89

The Secretary-General of the United Nations is hereby designated as the depositary for this Convention.

Article 90

This Convention does not prevail over any international agreement which has already been or may be entered into and which contains provisions concerning the matters goverend by this Convention, provided that the parties have their places of business in States parties to such agreement.

Article 91

(1) This Convention is open for signature at the concluding meeting of the United Nations Conference on Contracts for the International Sale of Goods and will remain open for signature by all State at the Headquarters of the United Nations, New York until 30 September 1981.

(2) This Convention is subject to ratification, acceptance or approval by the signatory States.

(3) This Convention is open for accession by all States which are not signatory States as from the date it is open for signature.

(4) Instruments of ratification, acceptance, approval and accession are to be deposited with the Secretary-General of the United Nations.

Article 92

(1) A Contracting State may declare at the time signature, ratification, acceptance, approval or accession that it will not be bound by Part II of this Convention or that it will not be bound by Part III of this Convention.

(2) A Contracting State which makes a declaration in accordance with the preceding paragraph in respect of Part II or Part III of this Convention is not to be considered a Contracting State within paragraph (1) of article 1 of this Convention in respect of matters governed by the Part to which the declaration applies.

Article 93

(1) If a Contracting State has two or more territorial units in which, according to its constitution, different systems of law are applicable in relation to the matters dealt with in this Convention, it may, at the time of signature, ratification, acceptance, approval or accession, declare that this Convention is to extend to all its territorial units or only to one or more of them, and may amend its declaration by submitting another declaration at any time.

(2) These declarations are to be notified to the depositary and are to state expressly the territorial units to which the Convention extends.

(3) If, by virtue of a declaration under this article, this Convention extends to one or more but not all of the territorial units of a Contracting State, and if the place of business of a party is located in that State, this place of business, for the purposes of this Convention, is considered not to be in a Contracting State, unless it is in a territorial unit to which the Convention extends.

(4) If a Contracting State makes no declaration under paragraph (1) of this article, the Convention is to extend to all territorial units of that State.

Article 94

(1) Two or more Contracting States which may have the same or closely related legal rules on matters governed by this Convention may at any time declare that the Convention is not to apply to contracts of sale or to their formation where the parties have their places of business in those States. Such declarations may be made jointly or by reciprocal unilateral declarations.

(2) A Contracting State which has the same or closely related legal rules on matters governed by this Convention as one or more non-Contracting States may at any time declare that the Convention is not to apply to contracts of sale or to their formation where the parties have their places of business in those States.

(3) If a State which is the object of a declaration under the preceding paragraph subsequently becomes a Contracting State, the declaration made will, as from the date on which the Convention enters into force in respect of the new Contracting State, have the effect of a declaration made under paragraph (1), provided that the new Contracting State joins in such declaration or makes a reciprocal unilateral declaration.

Article 95

Any State may declare at the time of the deposit of its instrument of ratification, acceptance, approval or accession that it will not be bound by subparagraph (1)(b) of article 1 of this Convention.

Article 96

A Contracting State whose legislation requires contracts of sale to be concluded in or evidenced by writing may at any time make a declaration in accordance with article 12 that any provision of article 11, article 29, or Part II of this Convention, that allows a contract of sale or its modification or termination by agreement or any offer, acceptance, or other indication of intention to be made in any form other than in writing, does not apply where any party has his place of business in that State.

Article 97

(1) Declarations made under this Convention at the time of signature are subject to confirmation upon ratification, acceptance or approval.

(2) Declarations and confirmations of declarations are to be in writing and be formally notified to the depositary.

(3) A declaration takes effect simultaneously with the entry into force of this Convention in respect of the State concerned. However, a declaration of which the depositary receives formal notification after such entry into force takes effect on the first day of the month following the expiration of six months after the date of its receipt by the depositary. Reciprocal unilateral declarations under article 94 take effect on the first day of the month following the expiration of six months after the receipt of the latest declaration by the depositary.

(4) Any State which makes a declaration under this Convention may withdraw it at any time by a formal notification in writing addressed to the depositary. Such withdrawal is to take effect on the first day of the month following the expiration of six months after the date of the receipt of the notification by the depositary.

(5) A withdrawal of a declaration made under article 94 renders inoperative, as from the date on which the withdrawal takes effect, any reciprocal declaration made by another State under that article.

Article 98

No reservations are permitted except those expressly authorized in this Convention.

Article 99

(1) This Convention enters into force, subject to the provisions of paragraph (6) of this article, on the first day of the month following the expiration of twelve months after the date of deposit of the tenth instrument of ratification, acceptance, approval or accession, including an instrument which contains a declaration made under article 92.

(2) When a State ratifies, accepts, approves or accedes to this Convention after the deposit of the tenth instrument of ratification, acceptance, approval or accession, this Convention, with the exception of the Part excluded, enters into force in respect of that State, subject to the provisions of paragraph (6) of this article, on the first day of the month following the expiration of twelve months after the date of the deposit of its instrument of ratification, acceptance, approval or accession.

(3) A State which ratifies, accepts, approves or accedes to this Convention and is a party to either or both the Convention relating to a Uniform Law on the Formation of Contracts for the

International Sale of Goods done at The Hague on 1 July 1964 (1964 Hague Formation Convention) and the Convention relating to a Uniform Law on the International Sale of Goods done at The Hague on 1 July 1964 (1964 Hague Sales Convention) shall at the same time denounce, as the case may be, either or both the 1964 Hague Sales Convention and the 1964 Hague Formation Convention by notifying the Government of the Netherlands to that effect.

(4) A State party to the 1964 Hague Sales Convention which ratifies, accepts, approves or accedes to the present Convention and declares or has declared under article 92 that it will not be bound by Part II of this Convention shall at the time of ratification, acceptance, approval or accession denounce the 1964 Hague Sales Convention by notifying the Government of the Netherlands to that effect.

(5) A State party to the 1964 Hague Formation Convention which ratifies, accepts, approves or accedes to the present Convention and declares or has declared under article 92 that it will not be bound by Part III of this Convention shall at the time of ratification, acceptance, approval or accession denounce the 1964 Hague Formation Convention by notifying the Government of the Netherlands to that effect.

(6) For the purpose of this article, ratifications, acceptances, approvals and accessions in respect of this Convention by States parties to the 1964 Hague Formation Convention or to the 1964 Hague Sales Convention shall not be effective until such denunciations as may be required on the part of those States in respect of the latter two Conventions have themselves become effective. The depositary of this Convention shall consult with the Government of the Netherlands, as the depositary of the 1964 Conventions, so as to ensure necessary co-ordination in this respect.

Article 100

(1) This Convention applies to the formation of a contarct only when the proposal for concluding the contract is made on or after the due date when the Convention enters into force in respect of the Contracting States referred to in subparagraph (1)(a) or the Contracting State referred to in subparagraph (1)(b) of article 1.

(2) This Convention applies only to contracts concluded on or after the date when the Convention enters into force in respect of the Contracting States referred to in subparagraph (1)(a) or the Contracting State referred to in subparagraph (1)(b) of article 1.

Article 101

(1) A Contracting State may denounce this Convention, or Part II or Part III of the Convention, by a formal notification in writing addressed to the depositary.

(2) The denunciation takes effect on the first day of the month following the expiration of twelve months after the notification is received by the depositary. Where a longer period for the denunciation to take effect is specified in the notification, the denunciation takes effect upon the expiration of such longer period after the notification is received by the depositary.

Done at Vienna, this eleventh day of April, one thousand nine hundred and eighty, in a single original, of which the Arabic, Chinese, French, Russian and Spanish texts are equally authentic.

In witness whereof the undersigned plenipotentiaries, being duly authorized by their respective Governments, have signed this Convention.

PARTIES TO THE CONVENTION

As of January 1, 1987, the folowing states are parties to the Convention:

Argentina[1]

China[2]

Egypt

France

Hungary[3]

Italy

Lesotho

Syria

United States[4]

Yugoslavia

Zambia

MESSAGE ACCOMPANYING TRANSMITTAL

When the Convention was transmitted to the Senate by the President on September 21, 1983, the following message accompanied it (Treaty Document No. 98-9):

LETTER OF TRANSMITTAL

THE WHITE HOUSE, *September 21, 1983*

To the Senate of the United States:

With a view to receiving the advice and consent of the Senate to ratification, I transmit herewith the United Nations Convention on Contracts for the International Sale of Goods. This Convention was adopted on April 11, 1980, by the United Nations Conference on Contracts for the International Sale of Goods and was signed on behalf of the United States at United Nations Headquarters on August 31, 1981.

The Convention would unify the law for international sales, as our Uniform Commercial Code in Article 2 unifies the law for domestic sales.

---

[1] In accordance with articles 96 and 12 of the United Nations Convention on Contracts for the International Sale of Goods, any provisions of article 11, article 29 or Part II of the Convention that allows a contract of sale or its modification or termi nation by agreement or any offer, acceptance or other indication of intention to be made in any form other than in writing does not apply where any party has his place of business in the Argentina Republic.

[2] The People's Republic of China does not consider itself to be bound by subparagraph (b) of paragraph 1 of Article 1 and Article 11 as well as the provisions in the Convention relating to the content of Article 11.

[3] "[The Hungarian People's Republic] it considers the General Conditions of Delivery of Goods between Organizations of the Member Countries of the Council for Mutual Economic Assistance/GCDCMEA, 1968/19795, verison of 1979/to be subject to the provisions of article 90 of the Convention;

[The Hungarian People's Republic] states, in accordance with articles 12 and 96 of the Convention, that any provision of article 11, article 29 or Part II of the Convention that allows a contract of sale or its modification or termination by agreement or any offer, acceptance or other indication of intention to be made in any form other than in writing, does not apply where any party has his place of business in the Hungarian People's Republic."

[4] "Pursuant to article 95 the United States will not be bound by subparagraph (1)(b) of Article 1."

The Convention was prepared, with the active participation of representatives of the United States, by the United Nations Commission on International Trade Law (UNCITRAL) and received the unanimous approval of this worldwide body; the Convention was then adopted, without dissent, by the United Nations Conference of sixty-two States. This unanimity attests to the broadly perceived need for the Convention and the value of its provisions.

The House of Delegates of the American Bar Association recommended in 1981 that the United States ratify the Convention subject to a declaration permitted under Article 95 as to the grounds for applicability. I concur fully in this recommendation for the reasons set forth in the enclosed report of the Department of State.

The report of the Department of State provides a summary of the Convention and describes its approach. Worthy of emphasis is the international deference that the Convention accords to the contract made by the parties to an international sale. The parties may agree that domestic law rather than the Convention will apply, and their contract may modify or supplant the Convention's rules. The uniform international rules play their significant role when, as often occurs, a problem arises that the parties did not anticipate and solve by contract.

International trade now is subject to serious legal uncertainties. Questions often arise as to whether our law or foreign law governs the transaction, and our traders and their counsel find it difficult to evaluate and answer claims based on one or another of the many unfamiliar foreign legal systems. The Convention's uniform rules offer effective answers to these problems.

Enhancing legal certainty for international sales contracts will serve the interests of all parties engaged in commerce by facilitating international trade. I recommend that the Senate of the United States promptly give its advice and consent to the ratification of this Convention.

Ronald Reagan

LETTER OF SUBMITTAL

Department of State, Washington, August 30, 1983

The PRESIDENT,

The White House.

The PRESIDENT: I have the honor to submit to you the United Nations Convention on Contracts for the International Sale of Goods with the recommendation that it be transmitted to the Senate for its advice and consent to ratification. This Convention, adopted without dissent on April 11, 1980, by a United Nations conference of sixty-two States, culminated a half-century of work to prepare uniform law for the international sale of goods.

Sales transactions that cross international boundaries are subject to legal uncertainty — doubt as to which legal system will apply and the difficulty of coping with unfamiliar foreign law. The sales contract may specify which law will apply, out our sellers and buyers cannot expect that foreign trading partners will always agree on the applicability of United States law. Insistence by both parties on this sensitive point can prolong and jeopardize the making of the contract.

The Convention's approach provides an effective solution for this difficult problem. When a contract for an international sale of goods does not make clear what rule of law applies, the Convention provides uniform rules to govern the questions that arise in the making and performance of the contract.

The Convention does not restrict the parties' freedom to settle by contract, the full range of their rights and obligations. Instead it provides that its rules yield to the terms of the international sales contract. A major need for the Convention's uniform law arises from the fact that the buyer and the seller do not anticipate every question that might arise or consider it essential to deal with every problem, and it is often inexpedient to hold up the transaction until the parties find a solution for all foreseeable contingencies. In short, the Convention (like modern national systems of commercial law) serves the significant function of providing solutions for problems that the parties have failed to resolve by contract.

The usefulness of the Convention is enhanced by the fact that its rules were specially fashioned to meet the problems and needs of international trade. Our sellers and buyers now must cope with foreign statutes and code that were prepared a century or more ago, and were designed for domestic sales that bear little resemblance to current international transactions. Even when these problems have been ameliorated by case-law, such developments are often unknown or inaccessible to our lawyers.

The present Convention was adopted in six languages; English of course, is one. The legislative history of the Convention is readily available in English, andmost of the explanatory writing about the Convention is in English. Under the Convention our traders will not be forced to rely on foreign advice concerning the implications of the rules of a wide variety of foreign systems and often inadequate translations of such advice or rules.

This Convention replaces the Hague Sales Convention of 1964 which, because of defects, have not been widely accepted. (The United States has neither signed nor become a party to these Conventions.) These defects were discussed and resolved during a decade of preparatory work by the United Nations Commission on International Trade Law (UNCITRAL). The thirty-six member States of UNCITRAL provided representation for all major legal systems and regions of the world. United States representatives played an active and influential part in this preparatory work and in the 1980 Conference. UNCITRAL unanimously approved the draft Convention, and the 1980 Plenipotentiary Conference of sixty-two States, again without dissent, adopted the final text.

During the eighteen-month period for signing the Convention after the 1980 Conference the following became Signatory States; Austria; Chile; Czechoslovakia; Denmark; Finland; France; German Democratic Republic; Germany, Federal Republic of; Ghana; Hungary, Italy; Lesotho; Netherlands; Norway; People's Republic of China; Poland; Singapore; Sweden; United States of America; Venezuela and Yugoslavia. Steps for both Signatory and non-Signatory States to become parties to the Convention are now under way. Argentina, Egypt, France, Hungary, Lesotho and Syria have already ratified or acceded to the Convention, which will come into force approximately one year after four more countries have submitted their ratifications or accessions (Article 99(1)). Signature and ratification by the United States were recommended by the House of Delegates of the American Bar Association in 1981.

For reasons set forth in Appendix B of the Legal Analysis, I recommend that United States ratification by made subject to the declaration permitted under Article 95 that the United States will not be bound by Article (1)(b) of the Convention. As a result of this reservation, the Convention will be applicable only when the seller and the buyer have their places of business in different Contracting States.

This limitation, also approved by the American Bar Association, provides a clear, fair and adequate basis for the applicability of the Convention.

Enclosed is a Legal Analysis comparing the Convention's provisions with those of the Sales

Article of the Uniform Commercial Code (UCC), which has been enacted by every State of the United States except Louisiana. It will be noted that the Convention embodies the substance of many of the important provisions of the UCC and is generally consistent with its approach and outlook.

The Convention is subject to ratification by signatory states (Article 91(2)), but is self-executing and thus requires no federal implementing legislation to come into force throughout the United States. As already indicated, the Convention's effect is limited to foreign commerce of the United States and it will not affect purely domestic contracts of sale.

The Convention is a notable example of world-wide legal cooperation. It provides practical help for sellers and buyers, in our country and abroad, and by adding certainty to law it will facilitate international trade.

The Department of Commerce supports this recommendation and the Department of Justice has no objection to it.

It is hoped that the Senate will promptly give favorable consideration to this Convention and approve ratification by the United States.

Respectfully submitted.

GEORGE P. SHULTZ

LEGAL ANALYSIS OF THE UNITED NATIONS CONVENTION ON CONTRACTS FOR THE INTERNATIONAL SALE OF GOODS (1980)

The Convention provides uniform rules to resolve questions that have not been answered by the contracts made by the seller and the buyer in an international sale. The salient features of the Convention were summarized in the letter of Submittal to the President. To assist in a closer study of these rules, the present statement provides a brief synopsis of the 101 articles of the Convention.

It is not feasible in this brief analysis to provide a thorough commentary on the Convention's uniform rules of law for the sale of goods. Such a commentary calls for substantial book; detailed studies are provided by books and articles that are listed in Appendix A.

The present document is designed to spot-light the most significant provisions of the Convention, and to indicate the relationship between these provisions and United States law as set forth in Article 2 on Sale of Goods of the Uniform Commercial Code, which has been enacted by virtually all States of the United States.

STRUCTURE OF THE CONVENTION

The uniform rules for sales transactions appear in Parts I-III of the convention. Part I (Arts. 1-13) defines the Convention's field of application and includes other general provisions. Part II (Arts. 14-24) governs formation of the contract. Part III (Arts. 25-88) governs the rights and obligations of the parties to the contract of sale. Part IV ("Final Provisions": Arts 89-101) establishes procedures for im plementing the Convention and sets out the reservations that a State may make.

PART I: SPHERE OF APPLICATION AND GENERAL PROVISIONS

(Articles 1-13)

INTRODUCTION TO PART I OF THE CONVENTION

Part I sets forth rules that apply throughout the Convention. Chapter I defines the Convention's field of application. Chapter II addresses other general questions, notably interpretation of the Convention and the sales contract.

A. The Convention's Field of Application: Chapter I

Article 1 addresses two issues that control the applicability of the Convention: (1) When is a sale "international"? and (2) What contact between the sales transaction and Contracting State will invoke the Convention? (A "Contracting State" is a country that has become a party to the Convention.) Articles 2 and 3 exclude specified types of commodities and transactions. Articles 4 and 5 draw the line between issues that are regulated and those that are excluded; the excluded issues include the validity of the contract, the effect of the contract on the ownership rights of third persons (Art. 4) and liability for death or personal injury (Art. 5). The chapter closes with a brief but important provision (Art. 6) yielding overriding effect to the contract made by the parties.

CHAPTER I.   SPHERE OF APPLICATION (Articles 1-6)

Article 1.   Basic rules on Applicability

Under Article 1 the Convention will apply only if two requirements are met: (1) the seller and the buyer have their "places of business in different States," and (2) both of these States are Contracting States (i.e. States that have adopted the Convention). This simplified basis for applicability reflects a recommendation that the United States ratify subject to a declaration authorized by Article 95; the reasons for making this declaration and its effect are set forth in Appendix B. Thus, an American court would apply the Convention only to sales with an international character between parties in whose countries the Convention is in force.

Article 2.   Exclusions from the Convention

Article 2 provides for six exclusions from the Convention. Three (paragraphs (a)-(c)) are based on the nature of the transaction and three (paragraphs (d)-(f)) are based on the nature of the goods.

Paragraph (a) excludes substantially all consumer purchases by language based on the Uniform Commercial Code (UCC 9-109(1)). The principal impact of the Convention is thus on commercial sales between persons in business.

The remaining five exclusions do not call for discussion in this analysis.

Article 3.   Goods to Be Manufactured: Services

Paragraph (1) makes it clear that a sale is not excluded from the scope of the Convention merely because it calls for the manufacture or production of goods. On the other hand, it also makes it clear that the Convention does not extend to transactions in which the party receiving a finished product supplies "a substantial part" of the necessary materials.

Paragraph (2) excludes "service" contracts, in which the "supply of labour or other services" comprises the preponderant part of the transaction.

Article 4. Issues Covered and Excluded; Validity; Effect on Property Interests of Third Persons

While Articles 1-3 identify the contracts that are subject to the Convention, Article 4 defines the issues to which the Convention applies. Article 4 states that the Convention "governs only" the following: (1) "the formation of the contract" (Part II of the Convention) and (2) "the rights and obligations of the seller and the buyer arising from such a contract" (Part III of the Convention). In addition it ex cludes from the Convention issues with respect to "the validity of the contract or of any of its provisions or of any usage." One example is a rule of national law that prohibits the sale of specified products, such as heroin, and invalidates contracts relating to such illegal sales.

Article 4 also provides that the Convention "is not concerned with . the effect which the contract may have on the property in the goods sold". Whether the sale to the buyer cuts off outstanding property interests of third persons is not dealt with by the Conversion. This specific provision illustrates the general rule of Article 4 that the Convention is concerned only with the "rights and obligations of the seller and the buyer" arising from the sales contract. For the buyer's right, as against the seller, to receive good title, see Articles 41-43, infra.

Article 5. Exclusion of Liability for Death or Personal Injury; "Product Liability"

Article 5 makes the Convention inapplicable to the liability of the seller for death or personal injury caused by the goods. This was done lest the Convention collide with rules of national law on product liability.

Article 6. The Contract and the Convention

The dominant theme of the Convention is the primacy of the contract. See, e.g., Arts. 4 and 35. Of the many provisions that develop this theme, Article 6 is the most important. Thus, the parties may exclude the Convention or "vary the effect" of any of its provisions. The breadth of the parties' freedom to contract is emphasized by the one exception stated in Article 6 — the privilege of an adhering State under Articles 12 and 96 to preserve its domestic rules that require a writing. (See Art. 12, infra).

CHAPTER II. GENERAL PROVISIONS

Article 7. Interpretation of the Convention

A. International Character; Uniformity; Good Faith

Paragraph (1) provides that in interpreting the Convention there shall be regard for two closely-related principles — (a) the Convention's "international character" and (b) "the need to promote uniformity in its application." The latter provision is usual in uniform legislation in the United States. See UCC 1-102(2)(c). Paragraph (1) also provides that in interpreting the Convention there shall be regard for promoting "the observance of good faith in international trade." The Uniform Commercial Code states a "good faith" requirement that is broader than the principle of interpretation stated in the Convention. See UCC 1-203: "Every contract or duty within this Act impose a duty of good faith in its performance or enforcement." See also: UCC 2-103(1)(b).

B. "General Principles" Paragraph (2) provides that, where possible, questions "are to be settled in conformity with the general principles on which [the Convention] is based" — an approach that was designed to strengthen uniform international interpretation of the Convention. A somewhat similar principle is expressed in the Uniform Commercial Code.

For example, section 1-1-2(1) states that the UCC is to be "liberally construed and applied to promote its underlying purposes and policies".

Article 8. Interpretation of Statements or Other Conduct of a Party

While Article 7 deals with interpretation of the Convention, the present Article deals with the interpretation of the statements and conduct of the parties, including the provisions of the contract of sale. When there is no common "intent" of the parties, Article 8(2) applies the objective standard familiar to the common law.

Article 8(3) authorizes "due consideration" of conduct subsequent to the agreement as this may shed light on the intentions and expectations of the parties. Similarly, the Uniform Commercial Code states that in some circumstances a "course of performance accepted or acquiesced in without objection shall be relevant to determine the meaning of the agreement" (UCC 2-208). See also UCC 2-207(3) under which "conduct by both parties which recognize the existence of a contract is sufficient to establish a contract for sale . . ."

Article 9. Practices of the Parties; Trade Usages

One of the important features of the Convention is the legal effect it gives to practices of the parties and to commercial usages.

(1) Practices Established Between the Two Parties

Expectations that have the force of contract can be established by the parties' patterns of behavior. Under Article 9(1) the parties are bound by the "practices which they have established between themselves." The Uniform Commercial Code also gives contractual effect to the "course of dealing between parties" — defined as "a sequence of previous conduct between the parties to a particular transaction which is fairly to be regarded as establishing a common basis of understanding for interpreting their expressions and other conduct." (UCC 1-205)

(2) Usages of Trade

Article 9(2) provides that the agreement embraces a party's expectation that the other party will observe the usages of their trade. Unless the parties have agreed otherwise, effect is given to a trade usage "of which the parties knew or ought to have known" and which "in international trade is widely known to, and regularly observed by, parties to contracts of the type involved in the particular trade concerned." The Uniform Commercial Code also gives contractual effect to a "usage of trade" — defined as "any practice or method of dealing having such regularity of observance in a place, vocation or trade as to justify an expectation that it will be observed with respect to the transaction in question." (UCC 1-205)

Under Article 6, "The parties . . . derogate from or vary the effect" of the provisions of the Convention, and applicable usage has the same effect as provision of a sales contract. In short, the provisions of the Convention yield to the expectations of the parties, whether derived from express contract terms, from their established practices or from applicable trade usage.

Article 10. Definition of "Place of Business"

The Convention refers to a party's "place of business'in several articles: 1, 12, 20(2), 24, 31(c), 42(1)(b), 57(1)(a), 69(2) and 96. If a commercial enterprise maintains a central office and one or more branch offices, Article 10 makes applicable the place of business "which has the closest relationship to the contract and its performance . . ."

Article 11.   Inapplicability of Domestic Requirement that Contract Be in Writing

A. Domestic Rules: "Statutes of Frauds"

In 1677 the English Parliament (29 Car. II, c.3) enacted a Statute of Frauds which required a signed writing for the enforcement of a wide variety of transactions, including the sale of goods. This requirement was embodied in the United Kingdom's Sale of Goods Act (1893), was closely followed in the (U.S.A.) Uniform Sales Act (1896), and formed the basis for an elaborate statute of frauds included in the Uniform Commercial Code (§ 2-201). In recent decades, however, the tide has been running against such formal requirements. In 1954, Britain repealed this part of the Sale of Goods Act — a step that has been followed by many of the other countries that had adopted this Act. Most civil law countries do not impose such formal requirements for the making of commercial contracts. Formal requirements have generated litigation and uncertainty, are generally regarded to be of doubtful value for international trade.

B. The Convention

The 1980 Convention rejects such formal requirements (Article 11). This does not, however, bar the parties from imposing formal requirements. An offeror may require that an acceptance be in writing; an oral "acceptance" is not an "assent" to the offer. (See Arts. 18 and 19 infra.) In addition, pursuant to Article 29, infra, the parties by a contract in writing may require "any modification or termination by agreement" to be in writing.

A Contracting State may protect its formal requirements from Article 11 by making a reservation under Article 96. See Article 12, infra.

Article 12.   Declaration by Contracting State Preserving Its Domestic Requirements as to Form

Laws of the U.S.S.R. impose strict formal requirements for the making of foreign trade contracts. In the UNCITRAL proceedings, delegates of the U.S.S.R. indicated that preserving these requirements was of great importance to protect its established patterns for the making of foreign trade contracts. Most delegates, however, including the United States, concluded that formal requirements were inconsistent with modern commercial practice — particularly in view of the speed and informality that characterized many transactions in a market economy.

The result was a compromise. In Part IV (Final Provisions), Article 96 authorizes a Contracting State "whose legislation requires contracts of sale to be concluded in or evidenced by writing" to make a "declaration" that Article 11 (and certain other provisions of the Convention affecting formal requirements) "does not apply where any party has his place of business in that State." Article 12 articulates the effect of a declaration under Article 96. A declaration (reservation) under Article 96 would not ensure that the formal requirements of the declaring State would apply to transactions involving its buyers and sellers. Such applicability would result only when conflicts rules point to the formal requirements of the declaring State. However, conflicts rules may point to foreign law, which may have no formal requirements or may impose formal requirements that are unfamiliar to traders in the declaring State. These considerations explain why it is not recommended that the United States make a declaration pursuant to Article 96.

Article 13.   Telegram and Telex as a "Writing"

This provision does not call for discussion.

PART II: FORMATION OF THE CONTRACT

(Articles 14–24)

INTRODUCTION TO PART II OF THE CONVENTION

A. Relation Between Part II and Other Parts of the Convention

Part II of the Convention, Formation of the Contract, is subject to the rules of Part I (Arts. 1-18) on the scope and interpretation of the Convention, but is independent of Part III (Arts. 25–88) which deals with the obligations of the parties to the contract. Article 92 (Part IV) permits a Contracting State to declare that it will not be bound either by Part II or by Part III.

B. Structure of Part II

The first four articles (14–17) deal with the offer — the minimum criteria for an offer (Art. 14), and the withdrawn (Art. 15), revocation (Art. 16) or termination (Art. 17) of an offer. The next five articles (18–22) deal with acceptance — "acceptances" that do not match the offer (Art. 19), the period allowed for acceptance (Arts. 20 and 21), and withdrawal of an acceptance (Art. 22). The two final articles (Arts. 23 and 24) relate to the time when a contract is concluded.

Article 14.   Criteria for an Offer

(1) "Public Offers"

Article 14 incorporates the generally accepted premise that a person may make an offer to as large a group as he wishes. However, a communication addressed to a large group, if construed as an offer, can involve practical difficulties and hazards. These practical considerations are reflected in Article 14(2): If a proposal is not "addressed to one or more specific persons," it is not an offer "unless the contrary is clearly indicated by the person making the proposal." See Restatement Second of Contracts § 29.

(2) Definiteness: Unstated Price

Difficult problems arise when the parties neither fix the price, expressly or implicitly, nor agree on a method for fixing the price. The Convention's solution calls for construing Article 14(1) in the light of Article 55, which states that in the above circumstances the parties are considered, in the absence of any indication to the contrary, to have impliedly made reference to the price generally charged for the contrary, to have impliedly made reference to the price generally charged for such goods at the time of the conclusion of the contract. The Uniform Commercial Code (§ 2-305) similarly provides that the parties "if they so intend can conclude a contract for sale even though the price is not settled."

Article 15.   When Offer Becomes Effective; Prior Withdrawal

Under Article 15 an offeror may withdraw an offer by a communication that reaches the offeree ahead of the offer. The reason supporting Article 15 is that the enforcement of contracts is designed to protect expectations; none can arise until the offer reaches the offeree. Cf. Article 18(2), infra.

Article 16.   Revocability of Offer

Article 16 limits the powers of an offeror to revoke an offer which the offeror has stated or indicated will be "firm" or irrevocable, or on which the offeree has reasonably relied. Compare the provisions giving effect to "firm" offers in the Uniform Commercial Code (UCC 2-205). See Restatement Second of Contracts § 87 and Illustration 6.

Article 17.   Rejection of Offer Followed by Acceptance

Under Article 17, an offeree may not accept an offer which he has rejected. The same rule is applied in the United States. See Restatement Second of Contracts § 38.

Article 18.   Acceptance: Time and Manner for Indicating Assent

Article 18 states how an offer may be accepted. Its most significant provision is in paragraph (3): under some circumstances, an offeree may accept an offer by performing an act requested by the offeror, such as dispatch of the goods. For a similar rule see Section 2-206(1)(b) of the Uniform Commercial Code.

Article 19.   "Acceptance" With Modifications

Article 19 faces the situation in which a reply to an offer purports to be an acceptance but contains modifications of the offer. This situation most commonly results from the routine exchange of the buyer's printed purchase order and the seller's printed acknowledgement of sale form. Under the Convention, no contract results from such an exchange if the purported acceptance contains additional or different terms that materially alter the offer. A list of examples of material alterations makes it clear that most alterations are material. However, an acceptance with an immaterial modification will be effective unless the offeror objects.

The Convention's approach to this difficult problem differs from that of the Uniform Commercial Code, under which even a material alteration may not prevent the purported acceptance from creating a contract (UCC 2-207). The Convention would thus avoid many of the problems that have risen under and resulted in criticism of the Code provision.

Articles 20–24

The following articles dealing with various aspects of acceptance do not call for discussion:

Article 20.   Interpretation of Offeror's Time Limits for Acceptance

Article 21.   Late Acceptances: Response by Offeror

Article 22.   Withdrawal of Acceptance

Article 23.   Effect of Acceptance; Time of Conclusion of Contracts

Article 24.   When Communication "Reaches" the Addressee

These articles complete Part II: Formation of Contract.

PART III: SALE OF GOODS

(Articles 25-88)

INTRODUCTION TO PART III OF THE CONVENTION

When an enforceable international sales contract has been formed, Part III governs the rights and obligations of the seller and buyer.

Part III has five chapters. Chapter I (Arts. 25-29) contains general provisions that are applicable throughout Part III of the Convention. Chapter II (Arts. 30-52) deals with the obligations of the seller (secs. I & II) and remedies for the seller's breach (Sec. III). Chapter III (Arts. 53-65), paralleling the structure of Chapter II, states the obligations of the buyer (Secs. I and II) and remedies for the buyer's breach (Sec. III). Chapter IV (Arts. 66-70) is devoted to risk of loss. Chapter V (Arts. 71-88) addresses anticipatory breach (Sec. I), damage measurement had interest (Secs. II & III), excuses ("exemptions") based on serious impediments (Sec. IV), effects of avoidance (Sec. V), and duties to preserve goods that face loss or deterioration (Sec. VI).

CHAPTER I. GENERAL PROVISIONS

Article 25. Definition of "Fundamental Breach"

A. Introduction

The breach of sales contract by one party gives the other party a right to recover damages, but Article 25 relates to other remedies — the buyer's right to reject goods and the seller's right to refuse to deliver. In domestic law these remedies may be called "rejection," "revocation of acceptance," "avoidance," "termination" or "cancellation." In the Convention (Arts. 49 & 64) a party's privilege not to perform the contract because of the other party's breach is called "avoidance of the contract."

In the Convention, as in our legal system, "avoidance" is not available for every breach. Under Articles 49(1)(a) and 64(1)(a), infra, a party may avoid the contract when the other party commits a "fundamental breach" — a term that is defined in Article 25.

The role played by "fundamental breach" under the Convention is similar to that played by Section 2-608 of the Uniform Commercial Code, under which a buyer who has accepted goods that turn out to be defective may revoke his acceptance if the non-conformity "substantially impairs" the value of the goods to him (UCC 2-612, but cf. 2-601).

The UCC does not attempt to define "substantial" impairment. The Convention's definition of "fundamental breach" also allows leeway to consider whether avoidance is needed to assure full protection for the aggrieved party.

Article 26. Notice of Avoidance

Article 26 provides that a "declaration of avoidance of the contract is effective only if made by notice to the other party." This is one of the significant advances of the 1980 Convention over the 1968 hague Convention on Sales (ULIS).

At various points ULIS gave an injured party a remedy called "ipso facto avoidance." This type of avoidance occured automatically with no need to notify the other party (ULIS 25, 26(1)). Consequently, the other party might be led to perform in ignorance of the injured party's decision to refuse performance. At the 1964 Hague Conference the delegations of the United States and other states attempted unsuccessfully to eliminate ipso facto avoidance.

In the UNCITRAL proceedings, the delegations of the United States and other countries were able to remove the doctrine of ipso facto avoidance, resulting in the simple rule of Article 26. Requiring the notice be given of a remedy as drastic as avoidance is consistent with the Uniform Commercial Code. See UCC 2-602(1) (notice of rejection), 2-608(2) (notice of revocation of acceptance).

Article 27. Delay or Error in Communications

Under Article 26, supra, avoidance of a contract is effected "by notice" and in other settings communications have important consequences. E.G. Arts. 39(1) (notice of lack of conformity) and 43 (notice of right or claim of third party). Article 27 addresses the problems that arise when a notice is sent but, because of a mishap in transmission, is delayed, garbled or lost. Article 27 lays down the general rule that a party satisfies his duty to notify if he dispatches the communication "by means appropriate in the circumstances."

This general rule is subject to exceptions in Articles 47(2), 48(4), 63(2), 65(1) & (2) and 79(4). Nearly all of these exceptions involve a communication by a party who is in breach of contract; the "receipt" principle was used so that a mishap in transmission would not add to the burdens of the aggrieved party.

The Uniform Commercial Code similarly requires the buyer to "notify" the seller of breach of "be barred from any remedy," and provides that one "notifies" another "by taking such steps as may be reasonably required to inform the other in ordinary course whether or not such other actually comes to know of it" (UCC 2-607(3) and 1-201(26). The UCC, like the Convention, states exceptions from this general rule (e.g. § 2-616).

Article 28. Specific Performance and the Rules of the Forum

The Convention's system of remedies for breach of contract is based on the promise that a party in breach may be compelled to perform his obligations. On the other hand, restrictions on the right to specific performance appear in Articles 46(2) and 46(3).

Even with the restrictions just mentioned, the Convention grants specific performance on a wider scale than does the common law. As a concession to the common law, Article 28 provides that rules of national law withholding specific performance will prevail over the rules of the Convention. Thus, courts in the United States would still be subject to the limits on such remedies provided in Section 2-716 of the Uniform Commercial Code. Cf. UCC 2-709.

Article 29. Modification of Contract; Requirement of a Writing

Sales contracts sometimes provide that they may be modified only in writing. Article 29 gives effect to these private "statutes of frauds." The Uniform Commercial Code is similar (UCC 2-209(2)).

CHAPTER II. OBLIGATIONS OF THE SELLER

(Articles 30–52)

Introduction to Chapter II

Chapter II opens with a brief statement giving the essence of the seller's obligations (Art. 30). The remaining articles of the Chapter are grouped in three sections. Two sections define the seller's most important duties: The time and place for delivering the goods (Sec. I, Arts. 31-34); the quality of the goods and their freedom from third party claims (Sec. II, Arts. 35-44). The final section sets forth the basic remedies that are given to the buyer when the seller fails to perform his duties under the contract (Sec. III, Arts. 45-52).

The brief summary of Chapter II in Article 30 does not call for further discussion.

SECTION I: DELIVERY OF THE GOODS AND HANDING OVER THE DOCUMENTS

Article 31.   Place for Delivery

When the contract, interpreted in the light of practices and usages, does not state where the seller should deliver the goods, the place of delivery is determined by Article 31. See also the Convention's rules on risk of loss in Article 67 and 69, infra.

Article 32.   Shipping Arrangement

In international sales, the seller usually completes his obligation to deliver by "handing over the goods to the first-carrier for transmission to the buyer." Art. 31, supra, and Article 67, infra. However, the seller also normally makes various arrangements with respect to carriage. Any provision of the sales contract (including usage and any practice between the parties) is decisive as to the seller's obligations in this regard; to the extent that there is no agreement with respect to shipping arrangements. Article 32 fills the gap.

Paragraph (1), requiring the seller to notify the buyer of the ship ment, is similar to Section 2-504(c) of the Uniform Commercial Code. Paragraph (2), dealing with transportation arrangements, is similar to UCC 2-504. Paragraph (3) calls for cooperation between the parties with respect to supplying needed information concerning insurance. Similar rules on co-operation are set forth in the Uniform Commercial Code (2-311, 2-319(1)(c) and 2-319(3)).

Article 33.   Time for Delivery

This article does not call for discussion.

Article 34.   Documents relating to the Goods

Article 34 responds to commercial practice in international sales that permits, and often requires, delivery of the goods to be effected by handing over documents (such as a bill of lading) that control the goods. Accord: UCC 2-310(b). Cf. UCC 2-505 and 2-507(2).

Article 34 also provides that the seller's right to "cure" a defective delivery of goods (Art. 37, infra) extend to the delivery of documents. The Uniform Commercial Code provides that a seller may cure a "tender or delivery," which may include the tender of documents (2-508(1); 2-504(b)).

SECTION II.   CONFORMITY OF THE GOODS AND THE THIRD PARTY CLAIMS

(Articles 35–44)

Introduction to Section II

Articles 35 and 36 define the seller's obligations with respect to the quality of the goods. Articles 37-40 describe procedures that apply when goods are defective — the seller's privilege to cure defects in the goods (Art. 37) and the buyer's obligation to examine the goods and notify the seller of nonconformity (Arts. 38-40). Articles 41 and 42 define the rights of the buyer when the goods are subject to third party claims of ownership (Art. 41) and of rights based on patents, trademarks or other types of intellectual property (Art. 42).

Article 43 requires the buyer to notify the seller of these claims; the concluding article (Art. 44) gives grounds for excusing a failure to notify the seller.

Article 35. Conformity of the Goods

Paragraph (1) of Article 35 emphasizes that the seller must supply goods of the quality provided in the contract. As mentioned earlier (Art. 9, supra) under the Convention the practices established by the parties and applicable trade usages help to determine the contractual obligations of the parties. Accord: UCC 1-205. The Uniform Commercial Code also emphasizes the importance of the contract. (UCC 2-313).

Paragraph (2) of Article 35, like Sections 2-314 and 2-315 of the Uniform Commercial Code, gives effect to the buyer's basic expectations of quality. Paragraph 2(a), on fitness of goods for "the purposes for which goods of the same description would ordinarily be use," is similar to UCC 2-314(2)(c). Paragraph 2(b), on fitness for a particular purpose, is similar to UCC 2-315. Paragraph (2)(c), on conformity with a sample or model, is similar to UCC 2-313(1)(c). Paragraph (2)(d), on packaging, is similar to UCC 2-314(2)(e). Paragraph (3), on the effect of the buyer's knowledge of a lack of conformity, is comparable to UCC 2-316(3)(b).

Article 36. Damage to Goods: Effect on Conformity

Goods often arrive in poor condition because of damage that occurred after the risk of loss passed to the buyer. Paragraph (1) of Article 36 makes it clear that the seller is not responsible for defects that result from transit casualties which the buyer has assumed under the contract or under the Convention's rules on risk of loss (Arts. 66-70, infra). Paragraph (2) deals with the effect of contractual guarantees that goods will retain a specified quality for a prescribed period of time.

Article 37. Right to Cure Up to the Date for Delivery

Under Article 37 the seller, up to the agreed date for delivery, may remedy defects in the goods and thereby prevent destruction of the contract by "avoidance" — the remedy that in U.S. law is termed "rejection" (UCC 2-601) or "revocation of acceptance" (UCC 2-608). The "cure" provisions of Article 37 closely resemble those of UCC 2-508(1). Cf. Art. 48, infra, and UCC 2-508(2).

Article 38. Time for Examining the Goods

Article 38 provides rules on how soon the buyer "must examine" the goods. These rules are given legal effect by Article 39(1), which cuts off the buyer's rights if he fails to notify the seller of a nonconformity within a reasonable time after he "ought to have discovered" it. The rules on inspection and notice in Articles 38 and 39(1) are similar to the notice requirement in UCC 2-607(3)).

Article 39. Notice of Lack of Conformity

Article 40. Seller's Knowledge of Non-Conformity

Article 41. Third-Party Ownership Claims to Goods

Article 42. Third-Party claims Based on Patent or Other Intellectual Property

Article 43. Notice of Claim

One of the limits on the scope of the Convention is set by Article 4: "the Convention . . . is not concerned with . . . (b) the effect which the contract may have on the property in the goods sold." Thus, if a third person claims the goods because of a defect in the seller's title, the question whether the buyer is protected, as a good faith purchaser, against that third-party claim is not governed by the Convention but is left to applicable domestic law.

Article 41 addresses this question. When the seller supplies goods that are subject to a third-party claim, what are the rights of the buyer against the seller? Third-party claims "based on industrial property of other intellectual property" (e.g., a patent or copyright) are dealt with in Article 42.

The protection afforded the buyer under Article 41 is similar to the implied warranty of title provided by the Uniform Commercial Code (UCC 2-312(1)). The Code gives the buyer rights against the seller when a third person establishes a claim "by way of infringement or the like" (UCC 2-312(3)), but does not deal with the problems that arise when the buyer encounters an infringement claim in a country where the seller could not have anticipated that the goods would be used or resold. These problems are addressed in Article 42.

The notice provisions of Article 43 do not call for discussion here. Cf. Articles 39, 40 and 44, supra. (Article 43 does not set a fixed cut-off period for notice comparable to the two-year period in Article 39(2)).

Article 44. Excuse for Failure to Notify

As was mentioned under Article 38, the notice requirement of Article 39(1) is similar to that of UCC 2-607(3). However, Article 39(2) sets an outer limit for notice of two years unless the parties agree otherwise; the UCC states no fixed outer limit for notification. Cf. UCC 2-735 (limitation period for actions of four years after delivery). On the other hand, the Uniform Commercial Code extends to claims, including those for personal injury arising out of consumer purchases, where substantial delays in notification may be justified. As we have already seen, the Convention excludes substantially all consumer transactions (Art. 2(a)) and excludes all claims for death or personal injury (Art. 5).

Article 44 of the Convention relaxes the notice requirement of Articles 39(1) and 43(1) to the extent of allowing the buyer to reduce the price (Art. 50) "or claim damages, except for loss of profit" when the buyer "has a reasonable excuse for his failure to give the required notice." This provision, however, does not remove the two-year outer limit for notification set by Article 39(2) or authorize a buyer, who has failed to give notice within a reasonable time, to exercise other remedies such as avoidance of the contract (Art. 49, cf. Art. 46).

SECTION III. REMEDIES FOR BREACH OF CONTRACT BY THE SELLER

(Articles 45–52)

Introduction to Section III

A. A Bird's-Eye View of the Section

The first two sections of Chapter II define the seller's duties; Section III defines the buyers remedies when the seller is in breach.

Section III opens (Art. 45) with a general overview of the remedial system and indicates the relationship of different remedies to each other. Cf. UCC 2-711, 2-720. Article 46 states the buyer's right to compel performance by the seller. See Art. 28, supra, and UCC 2-716.

Three articles (Arts. 47-49) address the buyer's right to "avoid" the contract, a concept that includes the rejection of goods. Cf. UCC 2-601, 2-608. Article 47 empowers the buyer to fix an additional final periood for the seller's delivery of the goods — a step that clarifies the buyer's right to avoid the contract for delay in delivery. Article 48 empowers the seller to "cure" defects in performance and thus forestall avoidance of the contract. Cf. UCC 2-508. Article 49 states the grounds on which the buyer may avoid the contract. Cf. UCC 2-608.

The section closes with three articles dealing with special situations — the buyer's right to reduce the price (Art. 50), the applicability of remedies to only part of the goods (Art. 51; cf. UCC 2-601(c), 2-608(1)) and deliveries that are to early or excessive in quantity (Art. 52; cf. UCC 2-601(c)). Although the remedy in Article 50 (reduction of price) has its origin in civil law concepts, its formula has been amended so as to approximate the common law right to deduct damages from the price (Cf. UCC 2-717).

B. Relationship to Other Parts of the Convention

Section III of the present chapter provides remedies that apply only to breach by the seller; Section III of Chapter III provides comparable remedies for breach by the buyer.

These two sections are supplemented by remedial provisions in Chapter V that apply to both parties — e.g., anticipatory breach (Sec. I), the measurement of damages, and interest (Secs. II and III), "exemption" from damages (Sec. IV) and the effects of avoidance of the contract (Sec. V).

C. General Comment

It is not feasible for this legal analysis to analyze in detail the remedial provisions of Articles 45-52. It must suffice to note that, with the encouragement of the United States delegation, UNCITRAL reviewed the 1964 Hague Convention (ULIS), unified and simplified its complex provisions, and thereby met the serious objections of the United States delegation to the 1964 Hague Conference

CHAPTER III: OBLIGATIONS OF THE BUYER

(Articles 53–65)

Introduction to Chapter III

The structure of Chapter III is similar to that of the preceding chapter on Obligations of the Seller. Two sections state the buyer's duties: to pay the price (Sec. I, Arts. 53-59; cf. UCC 2-310(a), 2-507(1)) and to take delivery (Sec. II, Art. 60). The final section defines the remedies that are available to the seller when the buyer fails to perform these duties (Sec. III, Arts. 61-65; cf. UCC 2-703). These remedial provisions (like those in Chapter II) are supplemented by general rules on remedies in Chapter V (Arts. 71-88).

Many of the provisions of this chapter on the obligations of the buyer are mirror-images of provisions in the preceding chapter on the obligations of the seller.

CHAPTER IV: PASSING OF RISK

(Articles 66–70)

Introduction to Chapter IV

Casualty to the goods (e.g. by theft or fire) may occur in various setting — while the seller holds the goods before delivering them to a carrier or to the buyer, while the goods are in transit, while the buyer is examining the goods, or while the buyer holds the goods after rejecting them. Usually the loss will be covered by insurance. Allocating the risk of loss between seller and buyer should reflect considerations such as these: Which party is in a better position to evaluate the loss and press a claim against the insurer and to salvage or dispose of damaged goods? Who can insure the goods at the least cost? Who is more likely to carry insurance under standard commercial practice? What rules on risk will minimize litigation over negligence in the care and custody of the goods?

The United States delegates to the 1964 Hague Conference on Sales reporter their disappointment that risk of loss was governed by concepts that were so abstract that results were unpredictable and unresponsive to commercial needs. In UNCITRAL, on the initiative of the United States and other delegations, these objections were met by a thorough overhaul of these rules. As a result, the 1980 Convention speaks of physical acts of transfers of possession — the "handing over" of the goods to a carrier or to the buyer.

Article 67 deals with the important issue of risk of less in transit. When the contract (including the parties' established practices — Art. 9) does not solve this problem, the Convention, like the Uniform Commercial Code, provides the general rule that risk passes to the buyer when the goods are handed over to the carrier. Article 67 also echoes the Code in providing that the seller's retention of "documents controlling the disposition of the goods does not effect the passage of the risk." (See UCC 2-509(1)(a)).

Article 68 deals with contracts for the sale of goods that are already in transit when the contract is made, and provides that risk passes at the making of the contract unless the parties otherwise agree or the circumstances indicate an earlier time. The Uniform Commercial Code does not address this problem.

Article 69 deals, among other matters, with non-transit situations, and makes risk pass to the buyer "when he takes over the goods" — an approach that is similar to UCC 2-509(3). Finally, Articles 69(1) and 70 deal with the effect of breach of contract on risk; in both approach and result these articles are similar to the Uniform Commercial Code (UCC 2-510).

CHAPTER V.   PROVISIONS COMMON TO THE OBLIGATIONS OF THE SELLER AND OF THE BUYER

(Articles 71–88)

This concluding chapter addresses special problems with respect to remedies for breach of contract. Section I, Anticipatory Breach and Installment Contracts (Arts. 71-73), is concerned primarily with protection against impending failure of counter-performance; a party who faces this problem may, in some circumstances, suspend performance (Art. 71; cf. UCC 2-609, 2-705) or avoid the contract (Art. 72; cf. UCC 2-610). Article 73 deals with similar problems that arise in contracts for the delivery of goods by installments (Cf. UCC 2-612). Section II (Arts. 74-77) provides rules for measuring damages. (Cf. UCC 2-706 — 2-710, 2-712 to 2-715, 2-723). Section III consists of a brief provision (Art. 78) allowing the recovery of interest on sums in arrears. Section IV, exemptions (Arts. 79-80), confronts the difficult question of excuse from liability when performance is prevented by an impediment (e.g., force majeure). (Cf. UCC 2-613, 2-615). Section V, Effects of Avoidance (Arts. 81-84), includes provisions on the restitution of benefits received of benefits received under a contract that has been avoided. (Cf. UCC 2-711 (1) & (3)). Section VI, Preservation of the Goods (Arts. 85-88), is designed to prevent the waste or deterioration of goods that have been rejected. (Cf. UCC 2-602(2)(b), 2-603, 2-604).

PART IV. FINAL PROVISIONS

(Articles 89–101)

A. Introduction

Many of these provisions are minsterial. Articles 89 and 91 are administrative provisions commonly included in United Nations conventions. Article 90 deals with the relationship between the 1980 Convention and any other convention that "contains provisions concerning the matters governed by" the 1980 Convention. The most significant provisions in this part deal with permitted reservations and the Convention's entry into force.

(1) "Declarations" (Reservations)

Articles 92–96 specify those "declarations" (reservations) that may be made by Contracting States to modify their obligations under the Convention.

Article 92 permits a Contracting State to declare that it will not be bound by Part II (Formation of the Contract) or by Part III (Obligations of the Parties under a Contract of Sale). At the 1964 Hague Conference, contrary to the position urged by the United States, separate conventions were adopted on formation of the sales contract and on obligations under the contract. In UNCITRAL, the United States position was accepted. Because of the relationship between Parts II and III, it seems advisable for the United States to ratify the entire Convention without a declaration under Article 92.

Article 93 is designed to permit a declaration (reservation) by a Contracting State with a constitutional system different from the United States (e.g. Canada) that embraces territorial units in which "different systems of law are applicable in relation to the matters dealt with" in the Convention. As already indicated, the Convention applies only to international sales. In view of the Constitutional power of the United States federal government over foreign commerce (Constitution Art. I § 8) and the treaty power (Constitution Art. II § 2; Art. VI), a declaration by the United States pursuant to Article 93 would be unnecessary and inappropriate. In the absence of a United States declaration, the Convention will extend to all territories under the jurisdiction of the United States.

Article 94 seeks to meet the needs of States joined in economic communities (e.g. Benelux) by providing for reservations by two or more Contracting States "which have the same or closely related legal rules on matters governed by" the Convention. If two or more States make declarations under Article 94, the Convention will not apply to transactions among parties in these States but will, of course, apply to transactions that run between parties in these States and parties in other States.

See Article 1, supra. There is no need for the United States to make use of such a reservation.

Article 95 permits a Contracting State to declare that it will not be bound by Article 1(1)(b) which would make the Convention also apply "when the rules of private international law lead to the application of the law of a Contracting State." States that make this declaration would apply the Convention only when the seller and buyer have their places of business in different Contracting States (Art. 1(1)(a)). As noted under Article 1, supra, it is recommended that the United States ratify subject to this reservation; the reasons are set forth in Appendix 9 to this analysis.

Article 96 permits a declaration by a State that wishes to protect its domestic legislation that "requires contracts of sale to be concluded in or evidenced by writing", i.e., a "statute of frauds". For the reasons given in the discussion of Articles 11 and 12 of the Convention, it is considered inadvisable for the United States to make use of the reservation permitted by this Article.

(2) Entry Into Force

Article 99(1) provides that the Convention enters into force on the first day of the month following the expiration of twelve months after the tenth State has consented to be bound by the Convention. Article 99(2) governs the time when the Convention enters into force with respect to States whose consent to be bound follows that of the ten initial States.

APPENDIX A

1980 U.N. CONVENTION ON CONTRACTS FOR THE INTERNATIONAL SALE OF GOODS

Bibliography, August 1983

The following bibliography lists most English-language commentaries on the 1980 U.N. Convention on Contracts for the International Sale of Goods.

Convention text

U. N. Conference on Contracts for the International Sale of Goods — Official Records 178–190 (U.N. Doc. A/Conf. 97/19; Sales No. E.82.V.5 (1981)).

19 Int'l Legal Materials 668–699 (1980)

Book

J. Honnold, Uniform Law for International Sales Under the 1980 United Nations Convention (Boston: Kluwer, 1982).

Symposia

International Sales of Goods, 27 Am. J. Comp. L. 223–352 (1979).

Problems of Unification of International Sales Law, in 7 Digest of Commercial Laws (March 1980).

Articles

Bonell, Some Critical Reflections on the New UNCITRAL Draft Convention on International Sales, 1978-II Revenue de Droit Uniforme/Uniform L.Rev. 2–12.

Burke [Student Note], International Trade: Uniform Law of Sales, 22 Harv. Int'l L.J. 473–479 (1981).

Date-Bah, The United Nations Convention on Contracts for the International Sales of Goods, 1980: Overview and Selective Commentary, 11 Rev. Ghansian L. 50–67 (1979).

Date-Bah, Problems of the Unification of International Sales Law from the Standpoint of Developing Countries, 7 Digest of Commercial Laws 39–52 (March 1980).

Dore & DeFranco, A Comparison of the Non-Substantive Provisions of the UNCITRAL Convention on the International Sale of Goods and the Uniform Commercial Code, 23 Harv. Int'l L.J. 49–67 (1982).

Enderlein, Problems of the Unification of Sales Law from the Standpoint of the Socialist Countries, 7 Digest of Commercial Laws 26–38 (March 1980).

Eorsi, Problems of Unifying Law on the Formation of Contracts for the International Sale of Goods, 27 Am.J.Comp.L. 311–323 (1979).

Eorsi, A Propros The 1980 Vienna Convention on Contracts for the International Sale of Goods, 31 Am.J.Comp.L. 333–356 (1983).

Farnsworth, Developing International Trade Law, 9 Cal.W.Int'l L.J. 461–471 (1979).

Farnsworth, Problems of the Unification of Sales Law from the Standpoint of the Common Law Countries, 7 Digest of Commercial Laws 3–25 (March 1980).

Feltham, The United Nations Convention on Contracts for the International Sale of Goods, [1981] J.Bus.L. 346–361.

Herber, The Rules of the Convention Relating to the Buyer's Remedies in Cases of Breach of Contract, 7 Digest of Commercial Laws 104–129 (March 1980).

Honnold, UN Convention on Contracts for the International Sale of Goods, 1980, 15 J.World Tr.L. 265–267 (1981).

Honnold, The Draft Convention on Contracts for the International Sale of Goods: An Overview, 27 Am.J.Comp.L. 223–230 (1979).

Kelso [Student Note], The United Nations Convention on Contracts for the International Sale of Goods: Contract Formation and the Battle of the Forms, 21 Colum.J.Transnat'l L. 529–556 (1983).

Khoo, Formation of International Sales Contracts, 7 Digest of Commercial Laws 130–143 (March 1980).

Lansing, The Change in American Attitude to the International Unification of Sales Law Movement and UNCITRAL, 18 Am.Bus.L.J. 269–280 (1980).

Lansing & Hauserman, A Comparison of the Uniform Commercial Code to UNCITRAL's Convention on Contracts for the International Sale of Goods, 6 N.C.J.Int'l L. & Com.Reg. 63–80 (1980).

Perrott, The Vienna Convention 1980 on Contracts for the International Sale of Goods, 1980 The Int'l Contract — L. & Fin.Rev. 577–584.

Reczei, Area of Operation of the International Sales Conventions, 29 Am.J. Comp.L. 513–522 (1981).

Reczei, The Rules of the Convention Relating to its Field of Application and to its Interpretation, 7 Digest of Commercial Laws 53–103 (March 1980).

Shishkevish [Student Note], The Convention on Contracts for the International Sale of Goods nad the General Conditions for the Sale of Goods, 12 Ga.J.Int'l & Comp.L. 451–458 (1982).

Winship, Formation of International Sales Contracts Under the 1980 Vienna Convention, 17 Int'l Law 1–18 (1983).

Winship, New Rules for International Sales, 69 A.B.A.J. 1230–1234 (1982).

Ziegel, The Vienna International Sales Convention in New Dimensions in International Trade Law: Canadian Perspectives 38–57 (1982).

Ziontz [Student Comment]. A New Uniform Law for the International Sale of Goods: Is It Compatible with American Interests?, 2 Nw.J.Int.L. & Bus. 129–178 (1980).

Miscellania

UN Chronicle 52 (June 1980).

APPENDIX B

PROPOSED UNITED STATES DECLARATION UNDER ARTICLE 95 EXCLUDING APPLICABILITY OF THE CONVENTION BASED ON ARTICLE 1(1)(b)

Under Article 1 the Convention will apply only if two basic requirements are met:

(1) The sale must be international — i.e., the seller and the buyer must have their "places of business in different states," and (2) the sale must have a prescribed relationship with one or more States that have adhered to the Convention. This statement is concerned with the second requirement — the relationship between the Convention and one or more Contracting States.

The Convention, in subparagraphs (1)(a) and (1)(b) of Article 1, states two such relationships, either of which will suffice.

(a) First, under subparagraph (1)(a) the Convention applies when the places of business of the seller and the buyer are in different Contracting States.

(b) Second, under paragraph (1)(b) the Convention would also apply:

(b) when the rules of private international law lead to the application of the law of a Contracting State.

At the 1980 Diplomatic Conference, delegates of the United States and several other countries proposed the deletion of the second of these grounds for applicability — subparagraphs (1)(b) of Article 1. This proposal was defeated; as a compromise, the Convention's Final Provisions (Part IV) provide in Article 95 that a Contracting State may, by reservation, declare "that it will not be bound by subparagraph (1)(b) or Article 1."

The United States, in signing the Convention, stated that ratification subject to the Article 95 reservation was contemplated. This position, recommended by the American Bar Association, will promote maximum clarity in the rules governing the applicability of the Convention. The rules of private international law, on which applicability under subparagraph (1)(b) depends, are subject to uncertainty and international disharmony. On the other hand, applicability based on subparagraph (12)(a) is determined by a clear-cut test: whether the seller and buyer have their places of business in different Contracting States.

A further reason for excluding applicability based on subparagraph (1)(b) is that this provision would displace our own domestic law more frequently than foreign law. By its terms, subparagraph (1)(b) would be relevant only in sales between parties in the United States (a Contracting State) and non-Contracting State. (Transactions that run between the United States and another Contracting State are subject to the Convention by virtue of subparagraph (1)(a).) Under subparagraph (1)(b), when private international law points to the law of a foreign non-Contracting State the Convention will not displace that foreign law, since subparagraph (1)(b) makes the Convention applicable only when "the rules of private international law lead to the application of the law of a Contracting State." Consequently, when those rules point to United States law, subparagraph (1)(b) would normally operate to displace United States law (the Uniform Commercial Code) and would not displace the law of foreign non-Contracting States.

If United States law were seriously unsuited to international transactions, there might be an advantage in displacing our law in favor of the uniform international rules provided by the Convention. However, the sales law provided by the Uniform Commercial Code is relatively modern and includes provisions that address the special problems that arise in international trade.

For these reasons it seems advisable for the United States to exclude applicability of the Convention under sub-paragraph (1)(b) by the declaration (reservation) permited by Article 95. Fortunately, this position will not interfere with broad application of the Convention to international sales. Widespread adoption of the Convention can be anticipated; hence it is expected that eventually a substantial portion of United States international trade will involve other Contracting States and will receive the benefits of the Convention by virtue of subparagraph (1)(a) of Article 1. Moreover, parties who wish to apply the Convention to international sales contracts not covered by Article 1(1)(a) may provide by their contract that the Convention will apply.

TABLE OF CASES

[References are to pages.]

[References are to pages.]

[References are to pages.]

[References are to pages.]

[References are to pages.]

[References are to pages.]

[References are to pages.]

[References are to pages.]

[References are to pages.]

[References are to pages.]

D

[References are to pages.]

[References are to pages.]

[References are to pages.]

[References are to pages.]

[References are to pages.]

[References are to pages.]

[References are to pages.]

I

[References are to pages.]

[References are to pages.]

[References are to pages.]

[References are to pages.]

[References are to pages.]

[References are to pages.]

[References are to pages.]

[References are to pages.]

N

[References are to pages.]

[References are to pages.]

[References are to pages.]

P

[References are to pages.]

[References are to pages.]

Q

R

[References are to pages.]

[References are to pages.]

S

[References are to pages.]

[References are to pages.]

[References are to pages.]

[References are to pages.]

T

[References are to pages.]

U

[References are to pages.]

[References are to pages.]

W

[References are to pages.]

[References are to pages.]

[References are to pages.]

TABLE OF STATUTES

[References are to pages and pages/note numbers.]

[References are to pages and pages/note numbers.]

[References are to pages and pages/note numbers.]

[References are to pages and pages/note numbers.]

[References are to pages and pages/note numbers.]

[References are to pages and pages/note numbers.]

[References are to pages and pages/note numbers.]

[References are to pages and pages/note numbers.]

[References are to pages and pages/note numbers.]

[References are to pages and pages/note numbers.]

Restatement of Contracts

[References are to pages and pages/note numbers.]

[References are to pages and pages/note numbers.]

[References are to pages and pages/note numbers.]

[References are to pages and pages/note numbers.]

[References are to pages and pages/note numbers.]

[References are to pages and pages/note numbers.]

[References are to pages and pages/note numbers.]

[References are to pages and pages/note numbers.]

[References are to pages and pages/note numbers.]

[References are to pages and pages/note numbers.]

[References are to pages and pages/note numbers.]

INDEX

[References are to sections.]

A

ACCEPTANCE (See OFFER AND ACCEPTANCE)

ACCORD AND SATISFACTION
Conditions (See CONDITIONS, subhead: Satisfaction)
Debt, payment of . . . 65[B][3]
Obligee's repudiation of . . . 145[B]
Obligor's failure to perform . . . 145[C]
Statute of frauds (See STATUTE OF FRAUDS, subhead: Satisfaction)
Substitute contract distinguished . . . 145[A]
Third party arrangements . . . 145[D]

ADMINISTRATION OF JUSTICE
Generally . . . 99[H]

ADMINISTRATORS AND EXECUTORS
Suretyship promises . . . 70[A][1]

ADMISSIONS (See UNIFORM COMMERCIAL CODE (UCC), subhead: Admissions)

ADVERTISEMENTS
Offer and acceptance . . . 35[A]

AFFIRMATIVE DEFENSE
Unconscionability . . . 97[B][2][e]

AGENTS
Assignment of rights . . . 136[B][2]
Authority . . . 54[B][9]
Del credere agents . . . 70[A][2][g]
Delegation of duties . . . 136[B][2]
Gratuitous agency . . . 67[A][3]
Purchases by . . . 72[C]
Sales by . . . 72[C]

AGREED DAMAGES PROVISION
Attorneys' fees . . . 126[G]
Bonds . . . 126[G]
Conditioned penal bonds . . . 126[A][1]
History . . . 126[A][1]
Liquidated damages (See LIQUIDATED DAMAGES)
Penalties and liquidated damages distinguished (See LIQUIDATED DAMAGES)
Purposes of . . . 126[A]

AGREEMENTS
Generally . . . 30
Agreements to agree
    Generally . . . 33; 39[B]
    Employment contracts terminable-at-will (See TERMINABLE-AT-WILL EMPLOYMENT CONTRACTS)
    Final writing contemplated . . . 33
    Missing terms (See MISSING TERMS)
    Rental payments . . . 39[B][3]
    Uniform Commercial Code (See UNIFORM COMMERCIAL CODE (UCC), subhead: Agreements to agree)

AGREEMENTS—Cont.
Auction sales . . . 37[A]
Bargain . . . 30
Battle of the forms (See BATTLE OF THE FORMS)
Captions and headings, effect of . . . 36
Cohabitation agreements . . . 99[J]
Collateral agreement test . . . 85[C][4][b]
Consideration of marriage . . . 71
Contemporaneous agreements . . . 85[A]
Contract formation, essential elements of . . . 29
Definiteness requirement . . . 39[A]
Discharge by informal agreement . . . 144[B]
Headings and captions, effect of . . . 36
Indefiniteness and agreements to agree (See subhead: Agreements to agree)
Informal agreement, discharge by . . . 144[B]
Intention of legal consequences (See INTENT)
Marriage, consideration of . . . 71
Married persons, agreements between . . . 32[D]
"Meeting of the minds" . . . 31
Mutual assent . . . 30
Objective versus subjective assent . . . 31
Offer and acceptance (See OFFER AND ACCEPTANCE)
Parties, of . . . 82
Prior agreements . . . 85[A]
Promises . . . 30
Public policy, contravention of . . . 99[M]
Purchase orders . . . 36
Quotations . . . 36
Risk allocation by . . . 113[C][4]
Self-service
    Transactions . . . 37[B]
    Without reserve contracts and . . . 37[C]
Social agreements . . . 32[D]
Standardized agreements (See STANDARDIZED AGREEMENTS)
Subjective versus objective assent . . . 31
Subsequent agreements . . . 83[A]; 85[A]
Tacit agreement . . . 121[C]
Unmarried cohabitants, agreements between . . . 32[D]
Without reserve and self-service contracts . . . 37[C]

ALEATORY CONTRACTS
Certainty limitation . . . 122[C]
Public policy . . . 99[G]

ALEATORY PROMISES
Generally . . . 106[C]

ALTERATION (See MODIFICATIONS)

ALTERNATIVE PERFORMANCE
Contracts not performable within one year of formation . . . 73[C]
Liquidated damages . . . 126[E]

ANTICIPATORY REPUDIATION
Acceptance . . . 110[D]
Convention on Contracts for the International Sale of Goods . . . 110[H]
Defined . . . 110[C]

I-1

[References are to sections.]

[References are to sections.]

[References are to sections.]

[References are to sections.]

[References are to sections.]

[References are to sections.]

[References are to sections.]

[References are to sections.]

[References are to sections.]

I

[References are to sections.]

[References are to sections.]

MIRROR IMAGE RULE—Cont.
Rejection . . . 51[C][2]

MISREPRESENTATION
Concealment and non-disclosure distinguished . . . 96[A]
Defined . . . 96[A]
Effects of . . . 96[E]
Fact versus knowledge . . . 96[D][2]
Fraudulent misrepresentation
    Generally . . . 96[B]
    Execution . . . 96[C]
    Factum . . . 96[C]
    Inducement . . . 96[C]
Knowledge versus fact . . . 96[D][2]
Material misrepresentation . . . 96[B]
Matters of law . . . 96[D][2]
Mistaken . . . 92[C]
Non-disclosure and concealment distinguished . . . 96[A]
Opinion
    Generally . . . 96[D][2]
    Reliance on . . . 96[D][2]
Price . . . 96[D][2]
Quality . . . 96[D][2]
Quantity . . . 96[D][2]
Reliance
    Disclaimer of . . . 96[D]
    Induced party, by . . . 96[D]
    Opinion, on . . . 96[D][2]
Remedies for . . . 96[E]
Value . . . 96[D][2]
Victim's failure to investigate or read . . . 96[D][1]

MISSING TERMS
Generally . . . 33
Immaterial terms . . . 39[B][1]
Material terms . . . 39[B][2]
Performance terms . . . 39[B][5]

MISTAKE
Anatomy of . . . 92[D]
Basic assumption on which contract was made . . . 92[D], 92[D][1]
Computation mistakes . . . 92[H]
Defined . . . 92[A]
Erroneous bids . . . 92[H]
Fact versus law . . . 92[A]
Failure to read . . . 92[C]
Formation . . . 92[D]
Identity, of . . . 92[F]
Impracticability and impossibility of performance compared . . . 113[E]
Integration . . . 92[D]
Intermediary, by . . . 92[J]
Interpretation standards . . . 88[D]
Law versus fact . . . 92[A]
Material effect on agreed exchange . . . 92[D], 92[D][2]
Misrepresentation . . . 92[C]
Mutual mistake . . . 92[E]
Offeree's knowledge of mistake . . . 92[C]
Parol evidence rule (See PAROL EVIDENCE RULE, subhead: Mistake in expression)
Performance . . . 92[D]
Poor judgment and prediction distinguished . . . 92[A]
Prediction and poor judgment distinguished . . . 92[A]

MISTAKE—Cont.
Releases . . . 92[K]
Remedies . . . 92[E]
Risk allocation . . . 92[D], 92[D][3]
Rose 2d of Aberlone . . . 92[I]
Subject matter, of . . . 92[G]
Types of . . . 92[B]
Unilateral mistake . . . 92[E]
Unknown injury rule . . . 92[L]
Value, of . . . 92[I]

MISUNDERSTANDING
Mutual assent, on . . . 88[B][3]

MITIGATION
Generally . . . 123[A]
Anticipatory repudiation . . . 123[F]
Convention on Contracts for the International Sale of Goods . . . 123[C]
Duty to mitigate . . . 123[C]
Employment contracts . . . 123[D]
Expenses or losses incurred for . . . 123[B]
Justifiable ignorance of facts . . . 99[P]
Learned of the breach . . . 123[F]
Locus poenitentiae . . . 99[O]
Lost volume
    Generally . . . 123[E]
    Uniform Commercial Code . . . 123[E][1]
Pari delicto . . . 99[O]
Personal service contracts . . . 123[D]
Restitution . . . 99[O]
Uniform Commercial Code
    Generally . . . 123[C]; 123[F]
    Lost volume seller . . . 123[E][1]

MODIFICATIONS
Assignment of rights . . . 142[C]
Consideration, without (See PRE-EXISTING DUTY RULE, subhead: Modifications without consideration)
Contracts under seal . . . 54[B][11]
Course of performance . . . 90[B]
Discharge . . . 146[F]
Mirror image rule, of . . . 51[C][2]
No oral modification clauses . . . 65[E][3]
Sale of goods . . . 74[B]
Threats . . . 94[G]

MORAL OBLIGATION
Generally . . . 53[B][4]; 68[A][3]
Consideration
    Contracts without (See subhead: Contracts without consideration or detrimental reliance)
    Past acts as . . . 68[A]; 68[A][1]
    Precedent debt as . . . 68[A]; 68[A][2]
Contracts without consideration or detrimental reliance
    Generally . . . 68[B]
    Benefit, promise to pay for . . . 68[B][2]
    Material benefit rule . . . 68[B][3]
    Promise to pay for benefit . . . 68[B][2]
    Promise to perform
        Bankruptcy Reform Act . . . 68[B][1][b]
        Debts discharged in bankruptcy . . . 68[B][1][b]
        Defenses, subject to . . . 68[B][2]
        Statute of limitations . . . 68[B][1][a]

· [References are to sections.]

MORAL OBLIGATION—Cont.
Material benefit rule . . . 68[B][3]

MORTGAGE ASSUMPTION
Generally . . . 133[D]
Break in the chain . . . 133[D][1]
Subject to . . . 133[D]

MUTUAL ASSENT
Generally . . . 30
Misunderstanding . . . 88[B][3]

MUTUALITY OF OBLIGATION
Generally . . . 66
Mutuality of remedy and other doctrines distinguished
    . . . 66[A]

N

NEGLIGENCE
Parol evidence rule . . . 86[B][1]

NEGOTIATIONS
Good faith . . . 97[C][2]
Preliminary negotiations . . . 35[A]

NO ORAL MODIFICATION (NOM) CLAUSES
Generally . . . 65[E][3]

NOTICE
Anticipatory repudiation as breach . . . 110[E][2]
Assignment of rights . . . 142[B]
Bilateral contracts . . . 47[A]
Offeror dispense with necessity . . . 47[B]
Performance, offer requires acceptance by . . . 47[C]
Restatement 2d . . . 47[C]
Shipment contracts . . . 47[D]
Termination, of (See ILLUSORY PROMISES, subhead:
    Notice of termination)
Uniform Commercial Code . . . 47[C]
Unilateral contracts . . . 47[A]

NOVATION
Delegation of duties . . . 141[D][2]
Discharge of contract . . . 146[B]
Suretyship promises . . . 70[A][2][d]

O

OFFER AND ACCEPTANCE
Generally . . . 30
Anticipatory repudiation . . . 110[D]
Conditional acceptance . . . 49[B]
Confirmation as . . . 51[G]
Counter offer (See COUNTER OFFER)
Cross-offers . . . 42[C][1]
Definite expression . . . 51[B]
Effect of offers . . . 34
Equivocal acceptance . . . 49[C]
Firm offers (See FIRM OFFERS)
Form contract
    Essence of acceptance . . . 45[A]
    Intention to exercise power of acceptance . . . 45[C]
    Motivation . . . 45[C]
    No knowledge of offer, acceptance under . . . 45[B]

OFFER AND ACCEPTANCE—Cont.
Form contract—Cont.
    Who accept offer . . . 45[D]
Goods, of . . . 77[C][1]
Grumbling acceptance . . . 49[E]
Implied-in-fact . . . 52[B]
Implied-in-law . . . 52[B]
Mailbox or dispatch rule (See DISPATCH RULE)
Manner and medium
    Generally . . . 46[A]
    Bilateral contracts . . . 46[B]; 46[C][2]
    Counter offer . . . 46[D]; 46[D][1]
    First Restatement . . . 46[B]
    Fundamental change . . . 46[C][1]
    Indifferent offers . . . 46[C]
    Nonconforming goods, shipment of . . . 46[D];
        46[D][1]
    Restatement 2d . . . 46[C]
    Uniform Commercial Code . . . 46[C]
    Unilateral contracts . . . 46[B]
Mirror image rule . . . 49[A]
Notice of acceptance (See NOTICE)
Offeree, identification of . . . 40
Payment, of . . . 77[C][2]
Performance, to . . . 107[B]
Power of acceptance (See POWER OF ACCEPTANCE)
Qualified acceptance . . . 49[B]
Retention of benefits . . . 52[B]
Revocation of acceptance (See REVOCATION)
Seasonable expression . . . 51[B]
Silence . . . 52[A]
Single versus series of contracts . . . 41
Tests to determine whether offer has been made
    Generally . . . 35
    Advertisements . . . 35[A]
    Application . . . 35[C]
    Definiteness . . . 35[A]
    Express warranties . . . 35[B]
    Harvey v. Facey . . . 35[C]
    Identifiable offerees . . . 35[A]
    Opinions . . . 35[B]
    Predictions . . . 35[B]
    Preliminary negotiations . . . 35[A]
    Present intention and promises . . . 35[A]
    Promises and present intention . . . 35[A]
    Summary of guidelines . . . 35[C]
Unordered merchandise . . . 52[C]
Unsolicited goods . . . 52[C]
Variant terms (See BATTLE OF THE FORMS, subhead:
    Variant terms)
Whom offer addressed . . . 40

OMITTED TERMS
Generally . . . 91
Good faith
    Generally . . . 91[A]
    Convention on Contracts for the International Sale of
        Goods . . . 91[A][1]
    UNIDROIT Principles of International Commercial
        Contracts . . . 91[A][1]

OPINIONS
Generally . . . 35[B]

[References are to sections.]

[References are to sections.]

[References are to sections.]

[References are to sections.]

[References are to sections.]

[References are to sections.]

[References are to sections.]